POOLE'S INDEX

TO

PERIODICAL LITERATURE

BY

WILLIAM FREDERICK POOLE, LL.D.

LIBRARIAN OF THE NEWBERRY LIBRARY, CHICAGO

WITH THE ASSISTANCE AS ASSOCIATE EDITOR OF

WILLIAM I. FLETCHER, A.M.

LIBRARIAN OF AMHERST COLLEGE

AND THE COÖPERATION OF THE AMERICAN LIBRARY ASSOCIATION AND THE LIBRARY ASSOCIATION OF THE UNITED KINGDOM

Qui scit ubi sit scientia habenti est proximus

Revised Edition

VOL. I.—PART I. A—J

1802–1881

GLOUCESTER, MASS.
PETER SMITH
1963

Copyright, *1882*,
BY WILLIAM F. POOLE.

REPRINTED 1938; 1958; 1963

72731
016 POO

PRINTED IN THE UNITED STATES OF AMERICA

PREFATORY NOTE.

THE 1882 edition of this Index being out of print, I have assigned the rights of publication to Messrs. Houghton, Mifflin & Co., who are already the publishers of the "First Supplement" of 1888. All the typographical and other errors which have come to my knowledge have been corrected; and hence, for convenience of designation, this issue is called the "Revised Edition."

In order to bring the size and weight of the volume into a form convenient for handling, a lighter paper was used in the earlier issue than has been found advisable. It is the concurrent testimony of librarians that this Index is more used by readers than any other reference book in their libraries; and where the statement does not apply, it is because the volume is not made accessible to readers, or the library has few of the serial publications which are indexed. With such constant use the leaves rapidly wear out. Applications are frequent for signatures and sheets to replace those which are too dilapidated to be repaired, and it has been impossible to supply them. The British Museum requested and was granted leave to reprint pages which were worn out in all the four copies in its reading-room. A heavier and more durable paper has therefore been used in this "Revised Edition," which necessarily increases the bulk of the work. Hence the volume, for convenience in handling, is bound in two parts, each of which corresponds in size with that of the "First Supplement." It is also issued in a single volume for buyers who prefer it in that form.

W. F. Poole

CHICAGO, *February 2*, 1891.

PREFACE.

THIRTY-FIVE years ago, when a student in Yale College and connected with the library of one of the literary societies, I indexed such reviews and magazines as were accessible, and arranged the references under topics for the purpose of helping the students in the preparation of their written exercises and society discussions. I had noticed that the sets of standard periodicals with which the library was well supplied were not used, although they were rich in the treatment of subjects about which inquiries were made in vain every day. My work, though crude and feeble on its bibliographical side, answered its purpose, and brought to me the whole body of students for a kind of help they could not get from the library catalogues, nor from any other source. My manuscript was in great demand, and as it was rapidly wearing out, and printing seemed to be the only expedient for saving the work, it was put to press, and appeared with the title, "Index to Subjects treated in the Reviews and other Periodicals," New York, 1848, 8vo, 154 pp. The edition of five hundred copies was chiefly taken by other colleges, and soon disappeared. The little book is now a curiosity in more senses than one. For twenty years I had not seen a copy, when, in 1877, I saw it in the reading-room of the British Museum, with its leaves discolored and nearly worn through by constant handling.

My first experiment in making a general index to periodicals proved to be so useful, and, notwithstanding its shortcomings, was so kindly received, that I immediately set about the preparation of a larger work on a similar plan, and with such improvements in the arrangement and methods of work as my brief experience suggested. The list of periodicals was much enlarged, and the references were brought down to January, 1852. The second edition, with six times the amount of matter contained in the first, appeared with the title, "Index to Periodical Literature," New York, 1853, 8vo, x + 521 pp. The edition of one thousand copies was soon exhausted, and whenever within the past twenty-five years a second-hand copy has been offered for sale, it has brought the price of a rare book.

With the publication of the edition of 1853 I had supposed that my connection with the work was ended; for my professional duties as a librarian left me no time during the usual working hours to continue it, and the bulk of periodical literature had so enormously increased, that no one person, even if he gave it his whole time, could grapple with it alone. I had hoped that some one with the zeal, experience, and staying qualities needed would appear, to take up the work where I left it, and, with the aid he could readily command, carry it on. Such a person I have diligently sought for, and have patiently instructed and tested several candidates who promised well at first; but, to my sincere regret during these many years, the man I was looking for did not come in sight. In the mean while the libraries of the country and literary men have been clamoring for a new edition of "Poole's Index" brought down to the latest date. Scarcely a day has passed for the past quarter of a century that my mail did not bring some inquiry on the subject. For the want of a new edition, various toilsome and expensive expedients have been devised for keeping up an index to the current periodicals as they appeared. In some libraries the references have been made on cards and inserted in the card catalogue; and in others they have been made on slips and arranged in a separate collection. None of these schemes have proved to be practicable, and after a brief trial have been abandoned, or so modified as to include only the more important articles. Periodical literature was never so rich as during the past thirty years. The best writers and the great statesmen of the world, where they formerly wrote a book or pamphlet, now contribute an article to a leading review or magazine, and it is read before the month is ended in every country in Europe, in America, in India, Australia, and New Zealand. Every question in literature, religion, politics, social science, political economy, and in many other lines of human progress, finds its latest and freshest interpretation in the current periodicals. No one can thoroughly investigate any of these questions without knowing what the periodicals have said and are saying concerning them.

At the first meeting of the AMERICAN LIBRARY ASSOCIATION, held at Philadelphia in October, 1876, the demand was renewed for a new edition of my Index. In response to the call, I stated that if we waited for one person to make it, it would never be made, and proposed to the librarians present a co-operative plan by which the result they so much desired could be reached. The plan, in brief, was this: I would print and send to all the principal libraries a list of periodicals which it was desirable to index, on which such complete sets as the library had would be checked and the lists returned to me. Having received these lists, I would make an equitable distribution of the work, taking a full share of it myself, and giving to the larger libraries more, and to the smaller libraries less. Each library would engage to index according to a code of rules which would be furnished the set or sets of periodicals allotted to it, and send the references to me, who would revise, arrange, and incorporate the same with the matter of the edition of 1853 and with the work of all the other contributors. I would assume all the pecuniary responsibilities incurred, employ such assistance as was needed, print the work, and furnish a copy to each contributing library.

The plan proposed was adopted by acclamation; and I am able to say, with a feeling of pride in the character and zeal of my American associates in the library profession, that every promise of co-operation then made has been faithfully performed. There was no complaint in the allotment of the work, and every contributor's quota was promptly and cheerfully furnished. The "List of Contributors" is given on a succeeding page, and the work done by each is indicated in the last column of the list of "Abbreviations, Titles, and Imprints" which follows.

At the same meeting, and at my suggestion, Mr. JUSTIN WINSOR, Librarian of Harvard University, Mr. CHARLES A. CUTTER, Librarian of the Boston Athenæum, and myself, were constituted a committee for consultation on bibliographical questions relating to the new edition. All the details of the plan were considered and unanimously concurred in by this committee, and circulars were issued to the contributors giving rules for indexing and other directions. My sincere thanks are due to Mr. WINSOR and Mr. CUTTER for their counsel and cordial co-operation during the progress of the work.

In seeking for an Associate Editor to share with me the great task I had undertaken, my first choice was Mr. WILLIAM I. FLETCHER, Assistant Librarian of the Watkinson Library, Hartford, Conn., whose rare executive ability, experience, and perseverance were the special qualities needed. Mr. FLETCHER had been my assistant in the Boston Athenæum Library, and I knew his mettle. His services, with the cordial consent of his chief, Dr. J. HAMMOND TRUMBULL, were fortunately secured; and no praise I can here render will fully express my admiration of the zeal and efficiency with which he has aided me, and my appreciation of his accurate work. Without such assistance as his, the consummation of my plans would have been simply impossible.

In October, 1877, when the co-operative scheme was well in progress in the United States, I visited England with a delegation of American Librarians to attend the first International Conference of Librarians, in London. At this Conference the scheme was explained, and an invitation extended to the Library Association of the United Kingdom, which was then formed, to unite with the American Library Association in carrying it out. The proposal was courteously received, and a committee was appointed to consider and report upon it. The first opinion expressed in the Conference, after the project had been presented, was that the co-operative feature would be a failure; for it was not likely that the librarians of that country would work, as the Americans were doing, without pay. The failure of the Philological Society's Dictionary conducted on the co-operative plan was mentioned in support of this opinion. On further consideration the committee reported in favor of joining in the American scheme, and made an allotment to English librarians of work to be done.

Some of the work allotted was promptly finished and sent in; but much of it was not done in season to be included in this edition. This statement will explain why the *Academy*, *Athenæum*, *Saturday Review*, *Economist*, *Literary Gazette*, *Spectator*, and some other English serials, do not appear in the list of periodicals indexed. The *Academy*, *Athenæum*, and *Saturday Review* were assigned to a warm supporter of the co-operative scheme, Dr. H. O. Coxe, Librarian of the Bodleian Library, Oxford, and were accepted by him. Several letters expressing his interest in the work, and some of his manuscript, were received; and then his illness and death intervened. This incident will be to many English scholars, as it is to the American librarians who made the acquaintance of Dr. Coxe in the Conference at London and were entertained by him at Oxford, a painful reminder of the lamented decease of that genial and eminent scholar.

Of the twenty-five serials allotted by the English committee to the English librarians, eight are included in this edition. There was a genuine and growing interest felt in the work by the English librarians, and an intention to take a larger part in it than appears in the above statement; but it must be said in explanation that their attention was directed to it, and the allotments made, a year later than in America. If the publication had been delayed for a year, doubtless more of the work would have been done. It was a sudden call upon the English librarian to give up for several weeks or months his hours of rest and recreation. Perhaps the climate and social customs of England are not so favorable as they are in America for night work. With the editors it has been wholly a matter of night work, or, as Dr. Bushnell — who defined by another word than *work* that effort which is not a burden, which we do for the love of it, and cannot help doing — would say, night play. A professional pride, and a feeling that what they were doing would be a benefit to others, have doubtless with all the contributors changed toil into a pleasurable recreation.

For several reasons it has seemed advisable not to wait for further contributions, but to go to press with the matter which was ready. The call for immediate publication was urgent; the work of the American contributors was all in; and the material in hand was again six times as large as in the previous edition. The publication of so extended a work in this almost untried field of bibliography was an experiment; and it became a serious question with the publishers whether it was prudent at this time to make it larger. If the experiment, as a business enterprise, failed, it would discourage the publication of other helpful works in bibliography; and if it were a success, many similar works would follow. In any event, whether a success or not, supplements to this edition, bringing the references down to the latest date, and enlarging the list of periodicals, will be issued at stated intervals; and the first supplement will include as much of the work of the English librarians as shall be ready. Supplements in a style uniform with this edition will be issued every five years, which will include not only the periodicals which have appeared during that period, but older serials which are worthy of being indexed, and are not included in this edition. A scheme is also under consideration of issuing, in some form, annual indexes, which will be condensed in the five-year supplements; but the scheme is not sufficiently matured to make at this time a positive announcement.

The plan of the work will best be understood by an inspection of its pages. It will be seen that it is essentially the plan of the edition of 1853; that all the serials indexed are in the English language; and only such of these as are likely to be found in libraries and private collections. Medical, legal, botanical, microscopical, and other purely professional and scientific serials have generally been omitted, as they do not fall within the limits which it was necessary to prescribe for this undertaking. Several of a scientific and semi-professional character have been indexed so far as their articles of general interest are concerned. The main purpose in the work has been to meet the average wants of students, literary men, and writers for the press, — in other words, to help general scholars, who are many, in preference to the few who give their whole attention to a single topic. The specialist will find much in these pages which meets his needs; but he has wants which special indexes only can supply. What Dr. J. S. Billings, in charge of the Medical Library of the Surgeon-General's office in Washington, is so admirably and exhaustively doing for medical bibliography, ought to be done by other specialists for law, botany, geology, astronomy, and every other profession and science.

The work is an index to subjects and not to writers, except when writers are treated as subjects. The contributions of Lord Macaulay to the *Edinburgh Review* do not appear under his name, but under the subjects upon which he wrote, as Bacon, Church and State, Clive, Machiavelli, etc. His name, however, appears with many references; but they are all subject-references, which treat of him as a man, a writer, a historian, and statesman. Critical articles on poetry, the drama, and prose fiction appear under the name of the writer whose work or works are criticised. A review of "Enoch Arden" will be found under Tennyson, and of "Ivanhoe" under Scott; but a review of Froude's History of England will appear only under England, as England is the subject. A poem, a play, a story, or a sketch which can be said to have no subject, appears under its own title. The name of writer when known is given within parentheses. Hawthorne's "Celestial Railroad" first appeared in a periodical, and is indexed "Celestial Railroad (N. Hawthorne)." A review of the same, by a writer who is known, would be indexed, "Hawthorne, Nathaniel. Celestial Railroad (J. Smith)." By this method all criticisms of Hawthorne's imaginative writings are brought together under his name; but the review of a biographical work of his is placed under the subject of the biography.

The following extracts from the printed rules for indexing which were furnished to the contributors will further explain the methods adopted: —

"All references must be made from the inspection and, if necessary, the perusal of each article. Hence no use will be made of the index which is printed with each volume, or of any other index. These indexes are usually made without method or intelligence, and are full of all sorts of errors. . . . No person should be assigned to the work of indexing who is not competent to catalogue books on Mr. Cutter's or the British Museum system. The work of an inexperienced person will be worse than useless. . . . Abundant cross-references will be given, and especially in cases where they will not be obvious to the editors in the final arrangement. . . . A single reference to an article will, in most cases, be sufficient; but if several subjects of importance are treated in the same paper, or it is likely to be looked for under more than one heading, two or more references will be made. The references will be as brief and comprehensive as possible. In most instances the author's own title best expresses the subject of his paper; but if the author has given it an obscure or fanciful title, the indexer will give it a better one, and will place it under the heading where it naturally belongs. References to trivial and inconsequential matters must be avoided. . . . In no case index English reviews and magazines in American editions, unless the paging of the originals and reprints are identical."

The abbreviations used in the references are more concise and systematic than in the previous editions. Proper names do not easily admit of abbreviations, but the words *Review*, *Magazine*, *Journal*, and *Quarterly*, which occur frequently, are indicated intelligibly by the letters *R.*, *M.*, *J.*, and *Q.* *Atlan.* (Atlantic), *Bentley*, *Blackw.* (Blackwood), *Cornh.* (Cornhill), *Fraser*, *Harper*, *Macmil.* (Macmillan), will be understood without the abbreviation for *Monthly*, *Miscellany*, *Magazine*, etc., which make up their full titles. They are usually spoken of by their abbreviated titles, as *Atlantic*, *Bentley*, etc. The titles of the reviews are, in common parlance, abbreviated in the same manner, as *North American*, *North British*, *British Quarterly*, *Quarterly*, and *London Quarterly;* and hence the abbreviations used, *No. Am.*, *No. Brit.*, *Brit. Q.*, *Quar.*, and *Lond. Q.*, will be readily intelligible. It must be noticed that the *Quarterly Review* and *London Quarterly Review* are different serials. The title of the latter, which is the organ of the Methodist denomination in England, is often erroneously given to the former, which is the political organ of the Tory party.[1]

It has not been possible in the references to indicate the minor changes which have been made from time to time in the title of the same serial. That title has been assumed by which the serial is best known. The *American Whig Review* started as the *American Review*, and later took the title which properly describes it. The *Democratic Review* in its later stages had a medley of titles, which if used no one would now recognize. The *Dublin University Magazine*, which stopped in 1880, dropped in 1878 *Dublin* from its title. The whole series of ninety-six volumes are nevertheless referred to as *Dub. Univ.* With a still greater latitude, *Colburn's New Monthly Magazine*, through its whole series of 169 volumes, is referred to as *Colburn*, even when the name did not appear on the titlepage, and the serial had passed out of the hands of the original publisher. The organ of the Presbyterian Church in New York appeared from 1853 to 1871 in three series, each with a different title. The twenty volumes have been brought together and numbered consecutively as *American Presbyterian Review*, — the last of the titles used. The series from 1872, when it united with the *Princeton Review*, to 1877, appears as *Presbyterian Quarterly Review*. The "Chronological Conspectus," Nos. 123 and 231, will enable the owner of the series to number the volumes to correspond with the references in these pages. These instances will serve to explain the manner in which changes in titles, often capricious and unnecessary, have been treated. Strict bibliographical accuracy in representing these changes in the references was out of the question, as it would have introduced a bewildering complication of titles and abbreviations.

[1] See "Chronological Conspectus," Nos. 9 and 120. Allibone's "Dictionary of Authors" uniformly quotes the *Quarterly Review* as *London Quarterly Review*, and Scott's New York reprint gives it the same erroneous title. The lapse is common in other American publications, and is found in the work of some of our best bibliographers. See "Harvard Bulletins," No. 11, Feb. and March, 1879, p. 280; and No. 12, June, 1879, p. 326.

Another difficulty which required heroic treatment has grown out of the absurd practice in many periodicals of breaking the continuity in the numbering of volumes by starting *new series*. The *Eclectic Review* has seven *new series*, and these series are not numbered. The *St. James's Magazine* began with numbering consecutively twenty-one volumes; then occurred a *new series* of fourteen volumes; then a second *new series* of four volumes; then consecutive numbering from the beginning was adopted, and the next volume was numbered thirty-one when it should have been forty, — leaving out nine volumes. In cases like these, what appears on the titlepages has been wholly ignored, and the volumes have been numbered consecutively from the beginning. As a general rule, series have not been regarded, and sets have been numbered consecutively; although in a few instances, and for special reasons, the rule has been varied from. In some periodicals a difficulty of another kind has appeared, where a continuous numbering of volumes has been kept up after both the title and character of the serial has been changed, As an organ of the Methodist Church in the United States, the *Methodist Magazine* was issued from 1818 to 1840, in two series, twenty-two volumes. In 1841 the *Methodist Quarterly Review*, a work of a different character, took its place, and was called *third series*, which has been followed by a *fourth series*, — in all forty-one volumes. They were numbered continuously from the beginning of the *Methodist Magazine*, as well as by the serial number. In this Index these serials have been regarded, as they should have been by the publishers, as two separate periodicals. The former has been referred to by the abbreviation *Am. Meth. M.*, to distinguish it from the *Methodist Magazine*, which was issued contemporaneously in London, and also indexed in this work; and the latter has been referred to as *Meth. Q.*, each with a consecutive numbering of its own, and no regard has been paid to series, or to the numbering on the titlepages of the latter. The "Chronological Conspectus," Nos. 15 and 78, shows the numbering which has been used.

In the previous edition an attempt was made to give with the reference the name of the writer of the article, as far as the writers could be identified. In periodicals which do not give the names of their contributors, the identification is very difficult; yet in several serials, as the *North American Review* and *Christian Examiner*, the writer of nearly every article was given. The identification has been carried still further in this edition, and perhaps more labor has been spent upon it than its importance demanded. No avenue of search or inquiry has been neglected. Every accessible collection of essays and miscellaneous writings which contributors have issued has been gleaned, and volumes of biographies and literary correspondence, without number, have been examined. There was a fascination in the search which made it a recreation. Correspondence to the same end has been carried on with several friends in the great libraries of England and Scotland, who offered me their assistance; but they have been able to give little or no information which was not already in my possession. It is a singular fact that less is there known of the anonymous contributors to the British periodicals than can be ascertained in this country. My friend, Mr. JAMES T. CLARK, Librarian of the Advocates' Library, Edinburgh, took the trouble to examine all the sets of Edinburgh serials in his library for the inserted names of contributors, and failed to find a single one. He sent me, however, a list of contributions to the *North British Review* by an eminent writer, which he expressed some scruples in giving up without the consent of the contributor. Every one of them I had already, and had found them, with many others, carefully penciled in the set of the *North British* in the Chicago Public Library; and with such evidence of accuracy and contemporary authenticity that I had given implicit confidence to the whole record. The scruples which my friend Mr. Clark expressed in giving up, or inquiring into the authorship of, anonymous contributions, I found to be a common feeling with English librarians, and perhaps explains why so little is known on the subject in that country. On this side of the water we have no scruples of that kind, and rather take pleasure in printing the name of a contributor who would like to have it suppressed. The public have literary rights as well as contributors, and are entitled to know whose statements and opinions they are reading. The leading reviews of our day — as the *Nineteenth Century*, *Fortnightly*, *Contemporary*, *North American*, *International*, and nearly all the magazines — recognize this fact, and print the names of their contributors. The old-line serials — as the *Edinburgh*, *Quarterly*, and *Blackwood* — will soon come into this new and better arrangement. There was never any secrecy in these serials as to the authorship of articles written by Macaulay, Carlyle, and other great contributors. The cue was often given to the public in advance of the publication, and served as an advertisement for selling the issue.

Of the introductory tables, perhaps the only one which requires explanation is the "Chronological Conspectus." The serials are here arranged in the order of their seniority, and are numbered consecutively. These numbers are attached to each title in the alphabetical list of "Abbreviations, Titles, and Imprints." The titles of the serials are placed at the top of the table, and the years in the left-hand column. The volume or volumes issued during any year appear at the intersection of these lines. A glance will therefore show when a periodical began; if discontinued, when it ended; and the date when any volume was published. That the tables might not be too much incumbered with figures, only the last volume issued in the year, after the first year, is given, as the others can readily be inferred. The volumes 94, 96, and 98 are given as the issues of the *Edinburgh Review* for 1851, 1852, and 1853. The earlier volumes for these years, which are not expressed, are 93, 95, 97. In these tables the imprint of the volume — which is not made until after the volume is finished — determines bibliographically its date. Considered simply as numbers, a periodical may have a date a year earlier than if treated as a completed volume. Many cataloguers give to periodicals dates, not from imprints, but from the issue of the first numbers. It is therefore proper to state the method which has been followed in these tables, as the dates in many instances will not correspond with those given by the other method. The heavy line across the table at the close of each decennial period will aid the eye in its search. The "Chronological Conspectus" will serve several useful purposes: —

1. It will enable the reader readily to ascertain the date when any article appeared. He has, for instance, the reference "Fortn. 29: 816," and would like to ascertain the date of the article. He turns to *Fortnightly* in the alphabetical list, and finds its number to be 161 in the chronological order of the "Conspectus." He there finds that volume 30 was the last volume of 1878, and hence volume 29 was the first volume of that year. If he knows anything of the size and paging of the *Fortnightly*, he infers that page 816 will be in the number for June, 1878.

2. It will give the volumes of the same date in other serials. Each period has its own topics of interest which gradually give place to others. It is interesting to trace the discussion of a question through contemporary serials, and through earlier and later periods.

3. It will enable librarians and others whose sets are broken up into series or numbered erroneously to re-number the volumes to correspond with the numbering of the Index. This can readily be done by attaching to each volume an adhesive tag with the proper number upon it.

The co-operative feature of this work will attract the attention of persons interested in this special phase of social science. That fifty libraries different in organization and objects, — National, State, stock, subscription, college, and free public institutions, — scattered over this broad country from San Francisco to Boston, and across the ocean in England and Scotland, should have joined hands and worked in harmony for a common object, each receiving the full benefit of the work of all the others, is an incident in bibliography and literature which has no parallel. The American Library Association and the Library Association of the United Kingdom have given the project their sanction and moral support; but these Associations have had no responsibility, direction, or control through committees or otherwise of its management. All the work has been done voluntarily and without pay. No money subscription has been asked of any one, and not a farthing has been contributed from any source; for no money was needed. There has been, however, no gratuitous or charitable feature in it. Every contributing library will receive back the money value — some thirtyfold, some sixty, some a hundred — of the labor which its librarian has put into it. This labor, which has been credited to his library, has been done usually in hours of his own, taken from rest and recreation. The librarian will have his pay in the consciousness that what he has done will benefit his library and his readers, and may help his professional reputation. Persons who look only to pecuniary reward should never engage in this kind of work. Up to this time all the pecuniary reward I have had for indexing during these many years can be represented by the American copper coin which will cover one's thumb nail; and yet I have been well paid. As the person who has had the sole management of all the details of this enterprise, I desire to put on record this testimony in behalf of the co-operative principle. It is simple, effective, and attended with no embarrassments or difficulties of any kind. I have doubt whether a society organization, with its officers, committees, and ample funds for the payment of workers, could bring about more effective results.

When we begin to pay for service the knights leave the line, and their places are filled with retainers and camp followers. When the knights are few and these sulk in their tents, perhaps there is no better substitute for co-operation than an organization with the motto, *Quid pro quo in pecunia.* The acceptable and unexpected services of a contributor, whose name does not appear in the list, must not be overlooked. It was necessary in the progress of the work to make constant use of the express companies in transmitting copy to and fro between Chicago and Hartford. When the manager of the Adams Express Company heard of the character of the work and its co-operative feature, he claimed the privileges of a contributor, and directed that all parcels relating to the work should be transmitted without pay.

Besides continuing the supplements of this Index, is there not other bibliographical work which can be carried on by the same method? At the meeting of the American Library Association in Cincinnati, in May last, I suggested that a General Index to books other than periodicals was much needed by students and literary men.

In writing this closing paragraph, which completes my allotted task, I desire to tender my warmest thanks to my Associate Editor, the contributors, the careful proof-readers of the University Press, and all who have aided in the production of this volume; and to express the hope that when it comes into the hands of my fifty co-workers and personal friends, whose names appear on the opposite page, it will meet their reasonable expectations.

W. F. Poole.

CHICAGO, Nov. 29, 1882.

LIST OF CO-OPERATING LIBRARIES.

No.	Location.	LIBRARIES.	Librarian or Cataloguer.	No. Vols.
1	Albany, N. Y.	New York State Library	Henry A. Homes	84
2	Amherst, Mass.	Amherst College	William S. Biscoe	140
3	Baltimore, Md.	Mercantile Library	John W. M. Lee	38
4	Baltimore, Md.	Peabody Institute	P. R. Uhler	117
5	Berkeley, Cal.	California University	Joseph C. Rowell	71
6	Boston, Mass.	Athenæum Library	Charles A. Cutter	166
7	Boston, Mass.	New Eng. Historic, Genealogical Society	John Ward Dean	33
8	Boston, Mass.	Public Library	Mellen Chamberlain	406
9	Brookline, Mass.	Public Library	Mary A. Bean	75
10	Brooklyn, N. Y.	Brooklyn Library	Stephen B. Noyes	127
11	Burlington, Vt.	Fletcher Library	Thomas P. W. Rogers	94
12	Burlington, Vt.	Vermont University	John E. Goodrich	51
13	Cambridge, Mass.	Harvard University	Justin Winsor	208
14	Chicago, Ill.	Public Library	William F. Poole	634
15	Concord, Mass.	Public Library	Ellen F. Whitney	52
16	Edinburgh, Scot.	Advocates' Library	James T. Clark	56
17	Geneseo, N. Y.	Wadsworth Library	Cornelia B. Olmsted	30
18	Gettysburg, Pa.	Theological Seminary	Charles A. Hay	21
19	Hartford, Conn.	Library Association	Caroline M. Hewins	111
20	Hartford, Conn.	Trinity College	John H. Barbour	31
21	Hartford, Conn.	Watkinson Library	William I. Fletcher	516
22	Ithaca, N. Y.	Cornell University	Willard Fiske	80
23	Lawrence, Mass.	Public Library	Frederick H. Hedge	23
24	Liverpool, Eng.	Free Library	Peter Cowell	14
25	London, Eng.	———	William Brace	6
26	London, Eng.	London Library	Robert Harrison	2
27	London, Eng.	———	Talbot B. Reed	23
28	London, Eng.	Williams's Library	Thomas Hunter	4
29	London, Eng.	———	Alpheus Smith	3
30	Madison, Wis.	Wisconsin State Historical Society	Daniel S. Durrie	104
31	Middletown, Conn.	Russell Library	George F. Winchester	13
32	Middletown, Conn.	Wesleyan University	Charles T. Winchester	61
33	New Bedford, Mass.	Public Library	Robert C. Ingraham	36
34	New Haven, Conn.	Yale College	Addison Van Name	75
35	New York City	Apprentices' Library	J. Schwartz	74
36	New York City	Astor Library	Frederick Saunders	199
37	New York City	Mercantile Library	William T. Peoples	24
38	New York City	Young Men's Christian Association	Reuben B. Pool	53
39	Oxford, Eng.	Radcliffe Library	James B. Bailey	45
40	Peabody, Mass.	Peabody Institute	Thomas M. Osborne	34
41	Philadelphia, Pa.	Library Company	Lloyd P. Smith	10
42	Philadelphia, Pa.	Mercantile Library	John Edmands	34
43	Princeton, N. J.	College of New Jersey	Frederic Vinton	115
44	Rochester, N. Y.	Rochester University	William P. Goodrich	21
45	Salem, Mass.	Essex Institute	William P. Upham	35
46	St. Louis, Mo.	Mercantile Library	John N. Dyer	97
47	St. Louis, Mo.	Public School Library	Frederick M. Crunden	8
48	San Francisco, Cal.	Mercantile Library	Alfred E. Whitaker	157
49	Washington, D. C.	Library of Congress	Ainsworth R. Spofford	162
50	Waterbury, Conn.	Bronson Library	Homer F. Bassett	56
51	Worcester, Mass.	Public Library	Samuel S. Green	108
+	Work in the previous Editions		William F. Poole	1468
	Total number of volumes			6205

ABBREVIATIONS, TITLES, AND IMPRINTS.

The numbers in the last column are those given to the Libraries in the preceding list; and the sign (+) means work by Wm. F. Poole in earlier editions.

Abbreviations.	Numbers in Chronological Conspectus.	TITLES OF PERIODICALS.	Places of Publication.	Dates.	Number of Volumes.	Indexed by
All the Year	133	All the Year Round	London	1859–81	47	14
Am. Alma.	44	American Almanac	Boston	1830–61	32	+, 14
Am. Arch.	217	American Architect	Boston	1876–81	10	14
Am. Bib. Repos.	46	American Biblical Repository	New York	1831–50	30	+
Am. Bibliop.	189	American Bibliopolist	New York	1869–76	8	30
Am. Cath. Q.	218	American Catholic Quarterly	Philadelphia	1876–81	6	8, 14
Am. Church Mo.	129	American Church Monthly	New York	1857–58	3	1
Am. Church R.	111	American Church Review	New Haven and New York	1849–81	36	+, 20, 14
Am. Ecl.	75	American Eclectic	New York	1841–42	4	+
Am. Hist. Rec.	203	American Historical Record	Philadelphia	1872–74	3	13
Am. Inst. of Instruc.	47	American Institute of Instruction	Boston	1831–48	18	+
Am. J. Educ.	127	American Journal of Education, Barnard's	Hartford	1856–80	30	2
Am. J. Sci.	17	American Journal of Science	New Haven	1819–81	122	+, 4, 14
Am. Law R.	171	American Law Review	Boston	1867–81	15	8, 14
Am. Lit. M.	103	American Literary Magazine	Albany	1847–48	2	+
Am. Meth. M.	15	[American] Methodist Magazine	New York	1818–40	22	32
Am. Mo. M.	53	American Monthly Magazine	New York	1833–38	12	30
Am. Mo. R.	50	American Monthly Review	Boston	1832–33	4	+
Am. Natural.	172	American Naturalist	Salem	1867–81	15	4, 14
Am. Presb. R.	123	American Presbyterian Review	New York	1853–71	20	2
Am. Q.	35	American Quarterly Review	Philadelphia	1827–37	22	+
Am. Q. Obs.	54	American Quarterly Observer	Boston	1833–34	3	+
Am. Q. Reg.	41	American Quarterly Register	Andover	1829–43	15	+
Am. Soc. Sci. J.	188	[American] Journal of Social Science	New York	1869–80	11	13, 14
Am. Whig R.	96	American Whig Review	New York	1845–52	16	+
Anal. M.	9	Analectic Magazine	Philadelphia	1813–20	16	+
Ann. Reg.	29	American Annual Register	New York	1825–33	8	+
Anthrop. J.	202	Journal of the Anthropological Institute	London	1872–80	9	4
Anthrop. R.	154	Anthropological Review	London	1863–69	7	4
Antiquary	208	Antiquary, Jewitt's	London	1873–74	4	8
Appleton	190	Appleton's Journal	New York	1869–81	26	21, 14
Arch.	–	Archæologia	London	1770–1879	45	39
Argosy	165	Argosy	London	1866–81	32	10, 14
Art J.	112	Art Journal	London	1849–81	33	36, 21, 14
Atlan.	131	Atlantic Monthly	Boston	1858–81	48	21
Bank. M. (L.)	85	Bankers' Magazine (London)	London	1844–81	41	21

Bank. M. (N. Y.)	104	BANKERS' MAGAZINE (NEW YORK)	New York	1847–81	35	+, 42, 14
Bapt. Q.	173	BAPTIST QUARTERLY REVIEW	Philadelphia	1867–77	11	38
Belgra.	174	BELGRAVIA	London	1867–81	45	14
Bentley	67	BENTLEY'S MISCELLANY	London	1837–68	64	36
Bent. Q.	134	BENTLEY'S QUARTERLY REVIEW	London	1859	2	26
Bib. R.	98	BIBLICAL REVIEW	London	1846–50	6	8
Bib. Sac.	86	BIBLIOTHECA SACRA	Andover	1844–81	38	+, 12, 21
Blackw.	13	BLACKWOOD'S MAGAZINE	Edinburgh	1817–81	130	+, 19, 14
Bost. Mo.	30	BOSTON MONTHLY MAGAZINE	Boston	1825–26	2	6
Bost. Q.	69	BOSTON QUARTERLY REVIEW	Boston	1838–42	5	2
Bost. R.	144	BOSTON REVIEW	Boston	1861–66	6	2
Brit. & For. R.	60	BRITISH AND FOREIGN REVIEW	London	1835–44	18	+
Brit. Q.	87	BRITISH QUARTERLY REVIEW	London	1844–81	74	+, 49, 14
Broadw.	182	BROADWAY	London	1868–72	10	37
Brownson	88	BROWNSON'S QUARTERLY REVIEW	Boston and New York	1844–75	24	+, 36
Canad. J.	128	CANADIAN JOURNAL OF INDUSTRY	Toronto	1856–70	12	4
Canad. Mo.	204	CANADIAN MONTHLY	Toronto	1872–81	20	22, 14
Carey's Mus.	–	CAREY'S AMERICAN MUSEUM	Philadelphia	1787–92	10	+
Cath. World	160	CATHOLIC WORLD	New York	1865–81	33	40, 14
Chamb. J.	89	CHAMBERS'S EDINBURGH JOURNAL	Edinburgh	1844–81	58	14
Chr. Disc.	18	CHRISTIAN DISCIPLE	Boston	1819–23	5	+
Chr. Exam.	27	CHRISTIAN EXAMINER	Boston	1824–69	87	+, 33
Chr. Mo. Spec.	19	CHRISTIAN MONTHLY SPECTATOR	New Haven	1819–28	10	+
Chr. Obs.	3	CHRISTIAN OBSERVER	London	1802–77	77	6
Chr. Q.	191	CHRISTIAN QUARTERLY	Cincinnati	1869–76	8	8
Chr. Q. Spec.	42	CHRISTIAN QUARTERLY SPECTATOR	New Haven	1829–38	10	+
Chr. Rem.	76	CHRISTIAN REMEMBRANCER	London	1841–68	56	16
Chr. R.	63	CHRISTIAN REVIEW	Boston	1836–63	28	+, 14
Colburn	25	COLBURN'S NEW MONTHLY MAGAZINE	London	1821–81	169	8, 14
Cong.	205	CONGREGATIONALIST	London	1872–77	6	25
Cong. M.	16	CONGREGATIONAL MAGAZINE	London	1818–45	28	8
Cong. Q.	135	CONGREGATIONAL QUARTERLY	Boston	1859–78	20	2
Cong. R.	175	CONGREGATIONAL REVIEW	Boston	1867–71	5	2
Contemp.	166	CONTEMPORARY REVIEW	London	1866–81	40	21
Contin. Mo.	149	CONTINENTAL MONTHLY	New York	1862–64	6	45
Cornh.	138	CORNHILL MAGAZINE	London	1860–81	44	46
Danv. Q.	145	DANVILLE QUARTERLY REVIEW	Danville, Ky.	1861–64	4	2
Dark Blue	199	DARK BLUE	London	1871–73	4	37
De Bow	99	DE BOW'S COMMERCIAL REVIEW	New Orleans	1846–60	29	+, 36
Dem. R.	70	DEMOCRATIC REVIEW	New York	1838–59	43	+, 30
Dial	77	DIAL	Boston	1841–44	4	14
Dial (Ch.)	230	DIAL (CHICAGO)	Chicago	1880–81	2	14

Abbreviations.	Numbers in Chronological Conspectus.	TITLES OF PERIODICALS.	Places of Publication.	Dates.	Number of Volumes.	Indexed by
Dub. R.	64	Dublin Review	Dublin	1836–81	89	21
Dub. Univ.	55	Dublin University Magazine	Dublin and London	1833–80	96	+, 22, 14
Ecl. Engin.	192	Eclectic Engineering Magazine (Van Nostrand's)	New York	1869–81	25	14
Ecl. M.	90	Eclectic Magazine	New York	1844–81	97	+, 17, 14
Ecl. Mus.	81	Eclectic Museum	New York	1843	3	+
Ecl. R.	4	Eclectic Review	London	1805–67	125	+, 13
Ed. Mo.	20	Edinburgh Monthly Review	Edinburgh	1819–21	5	+
Ed. Philos. J.	21	Edinburgh Philosophical Journal	Edinburgh	1819–26	14	1
Ed. New Philos. J.	32	Edinburgh New Philosophical Journal	Edinburgh	1826–64	76	1, 14
Ed. R.	1	Edinburgh Review	Edinburgh	1802–81	154	+, 50, 14
Education	232	Education	Boston	1881	1	21
Eng. Dom. M.	167	Englishwoman's Domestic Magazine	London	1866–79	26	8
Evang. R.	115	Evangelical Review	Gettysburg, Pa.	1850–70	21	18
Ev. Sat.	168	Every Saturday	Boston	1866–74	17	13
Ex. H. Lec.	100	Exeter Hall Lectures	London	1846–65	20	14
F. Arts Q.	155	Fine Arts Quarterly	London	1863–67	5	13
For. Q.	36	Foreign Quarterly Review	London	1827–45	37	+
For. R.	37	Foreign Review	London	1828–30	5	+
Fortn.	161	Fortnightly Review	London	1865–81	36	14, 21
Fraser	45	Fraser's Magazine	London	1830–81	104	+, 9, 14
Galaxy	169	Galaxy	New York	1866–77	24	14
Gen. Repos.	10	General Repository	Boston	1812–13	4	+
Gent. M. n. s.	183	Gentleman's Magazine, new series	London	1868–81	27	34, 14
Geog. M.	212	Geographical Magazine	London	1874–78	5	8
Godey	74	Godey's Lady's Book	Philadelphia	1840–76	74	36
Good Words	139	Good Words	London	1860–81	22	48, 14
Harper	116	Harper's Magazine	New York	1850–81	63	21
Hesp.	71	Hesperian	Columbus, Ohio	1838–39	3	30
Hist. M.	130	Historical Magazine (Dawson's)	Boston and Morrisania, N. Y.	1857–75	23	45
Hogg	107	Hogg's Instructor	London	1848–56	16	48
Ho. & For. R.	150	Home and Foreign Review	London	1862–64	4	28
Hours at Home	162	Hours at Home	New York	1865–70	11	10
House. Words	117	Household Words	London	1850–59	19	19
Howitt	105	Howitt's Journal	London	1847–48	3	6
Hunt	72	Hunt's Merchants' Magazine	New York	1839–70	63	+, 35
Ill. Mo.	48	Illinois Monthly Magazine	Vandalia, Ill.	1831–32	2	30
Intel. Obs.	151	Intellectual Observer	London	1862–67	12	35
Internat. M.	118	International Magazine	New York	1850–52	5	40
Internat. R.	213	International Review	New York	1874–81	11	14, 21
Irish Mo.	209	Irish Monthly	Dublin	1873–81	9	14

Irish Q.	119	Irish Quarterly Review	Dublin	1851–60	9	1
J. Frankl. Inst.	33	Journal of the Franklin Institute	Philadelphia	1826–81	112	51, 14
J. Spec. Philos.	176	Journal of Speculative Philosophy	St. Louis	1867–81	15	14
J. Statis. Soc.	73	Journal of the Statistical Society	London	1839–81	44	21
Kitto	108	Kitto's Journal of Sacred Literature	London	1848–68	40	+, 21
Knick.	56	Knickerbocker Magazine	New York	1833–64	64	+, 21
Lakeside	193	Lakeside Monthly	Chicago	1869–74	11	14
Land We Love	177	Land We Love	Charlotte, N. C.	1867–69	6	3
Lib. J.	226	Library Journal	New York	1876–81	6	14
Lippinc.	184	Lippincott's Magazine	Philadelphia	1868–81	28	35, 14
Lit. & Theo. R.	59	Literary and Theological Review	New York	1834–39	6	+
Liv. Age	91	Littell's Living Age	Boston	1844–81	151	+, 11, 15, 21
Lond. M.	22	London Magazine	London	1820–29	23	27
Lond. Q.	120	London Quarterly Review	London	1853–81	57	34, 14
Lond. Soc.	152	London Society	London	1862–81	40	19, 14
Luth. Q.	200	Quar. Rev. of Lutheran Church, and Lutheran Quar.,	Gettysburg, Pa.	1871–81	11	38, 14
Macmil.	140	Macmillan's Magazine	London	1860–81	44	10, 21
M. Am. Hist.	220	Magazine of American History	New York	1877–81	7	14
Mass. Q.	109	Massachusetts Quarterly Review	Boston	1848–50	3	+
Math. Mo.	136	Mathematical Monthly	Cambridge, Mass.	1859–61	3	2
Mercersb.	113	Mercersburg Review	Mercersburg	1849–78	25	38
Meth. M.	2	Methodist Magazine	London	1798–1836	39	32
Meth. Q.	78	Methodist Quarterly	New York	1841–81	41	+, 2, 14
Mind	219	Mind	London	1876–81	6	10
Mo. Rel. M.	92	Monthly Religious Magazine	Boston	1844–74	51	6
Mo. R.	14	Monthly Review	London	1817–44	82	+, 6
Mod. R.	229	Modern Review	London	1880–81	2	14
Month	157	Month	London	1864–81	43	8, 14
Mus.	26	Museum of Foreign Literature, Littell's	Philadelphia	1822–42	45	+, 30
Nation	163	Nation	New York	1865–81	33	13, 21
Nat. M.	121	National Magazine	New York	1852–58	13	31
Nat. Q.	141	National Quarterly Review	New York	1860–80	41	14
Nat. R.	126	National Review	London	1855–64	19	9
Nature	194	Nature	London	1870–81	24	4, 14
Nav. M.	65	Naval Magazine	New York	1836–37	2	1
New Dom.	178	New Dominion Monthly	Montreal	1867–79	21	44
N. Ecl.	185	New Eclectic	Baltimore	1868–71	7	3
N. E. Reg.	106	New England Historical and Genealogical Register,	Boston	1847–81	35	7, 14
New Eng.	82	New Englander	New Haven	1843–81	40	+, 21
New Eng. M.	49	New England Magazine	Boston	1831–35	9	+
New Q	122	New Quarterly Review	London	1853–61	10	37
New York R.	68	New York Review	New York	1837–42	10	+

Abbreviations.	Numbers in Chronological Conspectus.	TITLES OF PERIODICALS.	Places of Publication.	Dates.	Number of Volumes.	Indexed by
Niles's Reg.	7	Niles's Register	Baltimore	1811–35	50	+
19th Cent.	222	Nineteenth Century	London	1877–81	10	14, 21
No. Am.	12	North American Review	Boston and New York	1815–81	133	+, 43, 21
No. Brit.	93	North British Review	Edinburgh	1844–71	53	+, 49
Norton	132	Norton's Literary Letter	New York	1858–60	6	13
O. & N.	195	Old and New	Boston	1870–75	11	23
Olden Time	–	Olden Time (Craig's Reprint)	Cincinnati	1876	2	14
Once a Week	137	Once a Week	London	1859–74	30	48
Overland	186	Overland Monthly	San Francisco	1868–75	15	5
Ox. Prize Ess.	–	Oxford Prize Essays	London	1836	5	+
Pamph.	11	Pamphleteer	London	1813–28	29	+
Penn Mo.	196	Penn Monthly	Philadelphia	1870–81	12	41, 14
Pennsyl. M.	223	Pennsylvania Magazine of History and Biography	Philadelphia	1877–81	5	14
Penny M.	51	Penny Magazine	London	1832–45	14	24
Peop. J.	101	People's Journal	London	1846–51	11	14
Pioneer	126	Pioneer	San Francisco	1854–55	4	48
Pop. Sci. Mo.	206	Popular Science Monthly	New York	1872–81	19	11, 21
Pop. Sci. R.	153	Popular Science Review	London	1862–81	20	10, 14
Portfo.	197	Portfolio	London	1870–79	10	10
Portfo. (Den.)	5	Portfolio (Dennie's)	Philadelphia	1809–25	34	21
Potter Am. Mo.	215	Potter's American Monthly	Philadelphia	1875–81	14	30, 14
Pract. M.	210	Practical Magazine	London	1873–76	7	48
Presb. Q.	207	Presbyterian Quarterly Review	New York	1872–77	6	38
Presb. R.	231	Presbyterian Review	New York	1880–81	2	14
Princ.	43	Princeton Review	Princeton	1829–71	43	+, 2
Princ. n. s.	227	Princeton Review, new series	New York	1878–81	8	14, 21
Prosp. R.	97	Prospective Review	London	1845–54	10	49
Putnam	124	Putnam's Monthly Magazine	New York	1853–70	16	12
Quar.	6	Quarterly Review	London	1809–81	152	+, 43, 14
Radical	170	Radical	Boston	1866–72	10	13
Radical R.	224	Radical Review	New Bedford	1877	1	14
Recr. Sci.	142	Recreative Science	London	1860–62	3	29
Ref. Q.	228	Reformed Quarterly Review	Philadelphia	1879–81	3	38
Rel. Cab.	79	Religious Cabinet	Baltimore	1842–43	2	3
Reliquary	146	Reliquary	London	1861–79	19	49
Republic	211	Republic	Washington	1873–76	7	8
Retros.	23	Retrospective Review	London	1820–54	18	+, 30
St. James	147	St. James's Magazine	London	1861–81	49	48, 14
St. Paul's	180	St. Paul's Magazine	London	1868–74	14	10
Scrib.	198	Scribner's Monthly	New York	1870–81	23	11, 21

Selec. Ed. R.	–	Selections from Edinburgh Review	Paris	1835–36	6	+
Select J.	57	Select Journal	Boston	1833–34	4	+
Sharpe	102	Sharpe's London Magazine	London	1846–70	52	8
So. Hist. Pap.	220	Southern Historical Society's Papers	Richmond	1876–81	9	3, 14
So. Lit. J.	61	Southern Literary Journal	Charleston, S. C.	1835–37	4	+
So. Lit. Mess.	62	Southern Literary Messenger	Richmond	1835–59	29	+, 48
So. M.	201	Southern Magazine	Baltimore	1871–75	10	3
So. Q.	80	Southern Quarterly Review	Charleston, S. C.	1842–56	28	+, 42
So. R.	38	Southern Review	Charleston, S. C.	1828–32	8	+
So. R. n. s.	179	Southern Review, new series	Baltimore	1867–78	24	48
Sparks's Am. Biog.	–	Sparks's Library of American Biography	Boston	1839–48	25	+
Spirit Pilg.	39	Spirit of the Pilgrims	Boston	1828–33	6	+
Stud. & Intel. Obs.	187	Student and Intellectual Observer	London	1868–71	5	21
Sup. Pop. Sci. Mo.	225	Supplement to Popular Science Monthly	New York	1877–78	4	14
Tait	52	Tait's Edinburgh Magazine	Edinburgh	1832–61	32	49
Temp. Bar	148	Temple Bar	London	1861–81	63	46, 14
Theo. & Lit. J.	114	Theological and Literary Journal	New York	1849–61	13	+, 49
Theo. Ecl.	164	Theological Eclectic	Cincinnati	1864–70	7	12
Theo. R.	158	Theological Review	London	1864–79	16	8
Theo. Repos.	–	Theological Repository	London	1769–88	6	45
Tinsley	181	Tinsley's Magazine	London	1868–81	29	8, 14
U. S. Cath. M.	83	United States Catholic Magazine	Baltimore	1843–48	6	3
U. S. Lit. Gaz.	31	United States Literary Gazette	Boston	1825–27	5	+
U. S. Serv. M.	159	United States Service Magazine	New York	1864–66	5	30
Unita. R.	214	Unitarian Review	Boston	1874–81	16	23, 14
Univ. Q.	94	Universalist Quarterly Review	Boston	1844–81	38	+, 13, 14
University Q.	143	University Quarterly	New Haven	1860–61	4	22
Victoria	156	Victoria Magazine	London	1863–80	36	8, 14
Walsh's R.	8	[Walsh's] American Review	Philadelphia	1811–12	4	+
West. J.	110	Western Journal and Civilian	St. Louis	1848–55	14	30
West. Law J.	95	Western Law Journal	Cincinnati	1844–53	10	14
West. Lit. J.	66	Western Literary Journal	Cincinnati	1836	1	30
West. M.	58	Western Monthly Magazine	Cincinnati	1833–36	5	30
West. Mo. R.	40	Western Monthly Review	Cincinnati	1828–30	3	30
West. R.	24	Western Review	Lexington, Ky.	1820–21	4	30
Western	216	Western	St. Louis	1875–80	6	47
Westm.	28	Westminster Review	London	1824–81	116	+, 5, 14
Worc. M.	34	Worcester Magazine	Worcester, Mass.	1826	2	+
Zoist	84	Zoist	London	1843–56	13	30

CHRONOLOGICAL CONSPECTUS OF THE SERIALS INDEXED.

	1 Edinburgh Review.	2 Methodist Magazine.	3 Christian Observer.	4 Eclectic Review.	5 Portfolio (Dennie's).	6 Quarterly Review.	7 Niles's Register.	8 Walsh's American Review.	9 Analectic Magazine.	10 General Repository.	11 Pamphleteer.	12 North American Review.	13 Blackwood's Magazine.	14 Monthly Review.	15 [Am.] Methodist Magazine.	16 Congregational Magazine.	17 Am. Journal of Science.	18 Christian Disciple.	19 Christian Mo. Spectator.	20 Edinburgh Mo. Review.
1802 . .	1	25	1																	
1803 . .	2	26	2																	
1804 . .	4	27	3																	
1805 . .	6	28	4	1.2																
1806 . .	8	29	5	4																
1807 . .	10	30	6	6																
1808 . .	12	31	7	8																
1809 . .	14	32	8	10	1.2	1.2														
1810 . .	16	33	9	12	4	4														
1811 . .	19	34	10	14	6	6														
1812 . .	21	35	11	16	8	8	1.2	1.2												
1813 . .	23	36	12	18	10	9	4	4	1.2	1.2	1									
1814 . .	25	37	13	20	12	11	6		4	4	2									
1815 . .	27	38	14	22	14	13	8		6		4	1								
1816 . .	29	39	15	24	16	15	10		8		6	3								
1817 . .	30	40	16	26	18	17	12		10		8	5	1	84						
1818 . .	31	41	17	28	20	19	14		12		10	7	3	87	1	1				
1819 . .	32	42	18	30	22	21	16		14		12	9	5	90	2	2	1	1	1	1
1820 . .	34	43	19	32	24	23	18		16		14	11	7	93	3	3	2	2	2	3
1821 . .	35	44	20	34	26	25	20				16	13	10	96	4	4	3	3	3	5
1822 . .	37	45	22	36	28	27	22				18	15	12	99	5	5	5	4	4	
1823 . .	38	46	23	38	30	29	24				20	17	14	102	6	6	6	5	5	
1824 . .	40	47	24	40	32	30	26				22	19	16	105	7	7	8		6	
1825 . .	42	48	25	42	34	32	28				24	21	18	108	8	8	9		7	
1826 . .	44	49	26	44		34	30				26	23	20	111	9	9	11		8	
1827 . .	46	50	27	46		36	32				28	25	22	114	10	10	13		9	
1828 . .	48	51	28	48		38	34				29	27	24	117	11	11	15		10	
1829 . .	49	52	29	50		41	36					29	26	120		12	17			
1830 . .	51	53	30	52		43	38					31	28	123	12	13	19			
1831 . .	54	54	31	54		45	40					33	30	126	13	14	21			
1832 . .	56	55	32	56		47	42					35	32	129	14	15	23			
1833 . .	57	56	33	58		49	44					37	34	132	15	16	25			
1834 . .	59	57	34	60		52	46					39	36	135	16	17	27			
1835 . .	61	58	35	62		54	48					41	38	138	17	18	29			

	21 Edinburgh Philos. Journal.	22 London Magazine.	23 Retrospective Review.	24 Western Review.	25 Colburn's New Monthly.	26 Museum of For. Literature.	27 Christian Examiner.	28 Westminster Review.	29 Am. Annual Register.	30 Boston Monthly Magazine.	31 U. S. Literary Gazette.	32 Edinburgh New Philos. Jour.	33 Journal of Franklin Institute.	34 Worcester Magazine.	35 Am. Quarterly Review.	36 Foreign Quar. Review.	37 Foreign Review.	38 Southern Review.	39 Spirit of the Pilgrims.	40 Western Monthly Review.
1802 . .																				
1803 . .																				
1804 . .																				
1805 . .																				
1806 . .																				
1807 . .																				
1808 . .																				
1809 . .																				
1810 . .																				
1811 . .																				
1812 . .																				
1813 . .																				
1814 . .																				
1815 . .																				
1816 . .																				
1817 . .																				
1818 . .																				
1819 . .	1																			
1820 . .	3	1.2	1	1.2																
1821 . .	5	4	3	4	1.2.3															
1822 . .	7	6	5		6	1														
1823 . .	9	8	7		9	3														
1824 . .	11	10	9		12	5	1	1.2												
1825 . .	13	13	11		15	7	2	4	1	1	1									
1826 . .	14	16	13		18	9	3	6	2	2	3	1	1.2	1						
1827 . .		19	14		21	11	4	8	3		4	3	4	2	1.2	1.2				
1828 . .		22	15		24	13	5	10	4			5	6		4	4	1	1.2	1	1
1829 . .		23	16		27	15	7	12	5			7	8		6	6	3	4	2	2
1830 . .					30	17	9	13	6			9	10		8	8	5	6	3	3
1831 . .					33	19	11	15	7			11	12		10	10		7	4	
1832 . .					36	21	13	17				13	14		12	12		8	5	
1833 . .					39	23	15	19	8			15	16		14	14			6	
1834 . .					42	25	17	21				17	18		16	16				
1835 . .					45	27	19	23				19	20		18	18				

1836 . .	63	59	36	64		57	50					43	40	141	18	19	31								48	30	21	25				21	22		20	20				
1837 . .	65		37	66		59						45	42	144	19	20	33								51	31	23	27				23	24		22	22				
1838 . .	67		38	68		62						47	44	147	20	21	35								54	34	25	29				25	26			24				
1839 . .	69		39	70		64						49	46	150	21	22	37								57	37	27	32				27	28			26				
1840 . .	71		40	72		66						51	48	153	22	23	39								60	40	29	34				29	30			28				
1841 . .	73		41	74		68						53	50	156		24	41								63	43	31	36				31	32			30				
1842 . .	75		42	76		70						55	52	159		25	43								66	45	33	38				33	34			32				
1843 . .	78		43	78		72						57	54	162		26	45								69		35	40				35	36			34				
1844 . .	80		44	80		74						59	56	165		27	47								72		37	42				37	38			36				
1845 . .	82		45	82		76						61	58			28	49								75		39	44				39	40			37				
1846 . .	84		46	84		78						63	60				52								78		41	46				41	42							
1847 . .	86		47	86		81						65	62				54								81		43	48				43	44							
1848 . .	88		48	88		83						67	64				56								84		45	50				45	46							
1849 . .	90		49	90		85						69	66				58								87		47	52				47	48							
1850 . .	92		50	92		87						71	68				60								90		49	54				49	50							
1851 . .	94		51	94		89						73	70				62								93		51	56				51	52							
1852 . .	96		52	96		91						75	72				64								96		53	58				53	54							
1853 . .	98		53	98		93						77	74				66						17		99		55	60				55	56							
1854 . .	100		54	100		95						79	76				68						18		102		57	62				57	58							
1855 . .	102		55	102		97						81	78				70								105		59	64				59	60							
1856 . .	104		56	104		99						83	80				72								108		61	66				61	62							
1857 . .	106		57	106		102						85	82				74								111		63	68				63	64							
1858 . .	108		58	108		104						87	84				76								114		65	70				65	66							
1859 . .	110		59	110		106						89	86				78								117		67	72				67	68							
1860 . .	112		60	112		108						91	88				80								120		69	74				69	70							
1861 . .	114		61	114		110						93	90				82								123		71	76				71	72							
1862 . .	116		62	116		112						95	92				84								126		73	78				73	74							
1863 . .	118		63	118		114						97	94				86								129		75	80				75	76							
1864 . .	120		64	120		116						99	96				88								132		77	82				76	78							
1865 . .	122		65	122		118						101	98				90								135		79	84					80							
1866 . .	124		66	124		120						103	100				92								138		81	86					82							
1867 . .	126		67	125		123						105	102				94								141		83	88					84							
1868 . .	128		68			125						107	104				96								143		85	90					86							
1869 . .	130		69			127						109	106				98								145		87	92					88							
1870 . .	132		70			129						111	108				100								147			94					90							
1871 . .	134		71			131						113	110				102								149			96					92							
1872 . .	136		72			133						115	112				104								151			98					94							
1873 . .	138		73			135						117	114				106								153			100					96							
1874 . .	140		74			137						119	116				108								155			102					98							
1875 . .	142		75			139						121	118				110								157			104					100							
1876 . .	144		76			142						123	120				112								159			106					102							
1877 . .	146		77			144						125	122				114								161			108					104							
1878 . .	148					146						127	124				116								163			110					106							
1879 . .	150					148						129	126				118								165			112					108							
1880 . .	152					150						131	128				120								167			114					110							
1881 . .	154					152						133	130				122								169			116					112							

Chronological Conspectus.—*Continued.*

	41 Am. Quarterly Register.	42 Christian Quar. Spectator.	43 Princeton Review.	44 American Almanac.	45 Fraser's Magazine.	46 Am. Biblical Repository.	47 Am. Institute of Instruction.	48 Illinois Monthly Magazine.	49 New England Magazine.	50 American Monthly Review.	51 Penny Magazine.	52 Tait's Edinburgh Magazine.	53 American Monthly Magazine.	54 Am. Quarterly Observer.	55 Dublin University Magazine.	56 Knickerbocker.	57 Select Journal.	58 Western Monthly Magazine.	59 Literary & Theological Rev.	60 British & Foreign Review.
1829 . .	1	1	1																	
1830 . .	2	2	2	1	1															
1831 . .	3	3	3	2	3	1	1	1	1											
1832 . .	4	4	4	3	6	2	2	2	3	1.2	1	1								
1833 . .	5	5	5	4	8	3	3		5	4	2	3	1.2	1.2	1.2	1.2	1.2	1		
1834 . .	6	6	6	5	10	4	4		7		3	4.1	4	3	4	4	4	2	1	
1835 . .	7	7	7	6	12	6	5		9		4	2	6		6	6		4	2	1.2
1836 . .	8	8	8	7	14	8	6				5	3	8		8	8		5	3	3
1837 . .	9	9	9	8	16	10	7				6	4	10		10	10			4	5
1838 . .	10	10	10	9	18	12	8				7	5	12		12	12			5	7
1839 . .	11		11	10	20	2	9				8	6			14	14			6	9
1840 . .	12		12	11	22	4	10				9	7			16	16				11
1841 . .	13		13	12	24	6	11				10	8			18	18				12
1842 . .	14		14	13	26	8	12				11	9			20	20				13
1843 . .	15		15	14	28	10	13				12	10			22	22				15
1844 . .			16	15	30	12	14				13	11			24	24				16
1845 . .			17	16	32	1	15				14	12			26	26				
1846 . .			18	17	34	2	16					13			28	28				
1847 . .			19	18	36	3	17					14			30	30				
1848 . .			20	19	38	4	18					15			32	32				
1849 . .			21	20	40	5						16			34	34				
1850 . .			22	21	42	6						17			36	36				
1851 . .			23	22	·44							18			38	38				
1852 . .			24	23	46							19			40	40				
1853 . .			25	24	48							20			42	42				
1854 . .			26	25	50							21			44	44				
1855 . .			27	26	52							22			46	46				
1856 . .			28	27	54							23			48	48				
1857 . .			29	28	56							24			50	50				
1858 . .			30	29	58							25			52	52				
1859 . .			31	30	60							26			54	54				
1860 . .			32	31	62							27			56	56				

	61 Southern Literary Journal.	62 Southern Literary Messenger.	63 Christian Review.	64 Dublin Review.	65 Naval Magazine.	66 Western Literary Journal.	67 Bentley's Miscellany.	68 New York Review.	69 Boston Quarterly Review.	70 Democratic Review.	71 Hesperian.	72 Hunt's Merchants' Magazine.	73 Journal of Statistical Society.	74 Godey's Lady's Book.	75 American Eclectic.	76 Christian Remembrancer.	77 Dial.	78 Methodist Quarterly Review.	79 Religious Cabinet.	80 Southern Quarterly Review.
1829 . .																				
1830 . .																				
1831 . .																				
1832 . .																				
1833 . .																				
1834 . .																				
1835 . .	1.2	1																		
1836 . .	3	2	1	1	1	1														
1837 . .	4	3	2	3	2		1.2	1												
1838 . .		4	3	5			4	3	1	1.2	1									
1839 . .		5	4	7			6	5	2	4	3	1.2	1							
1840 . .		6	5	9			8	7	3	6		4	3	21						
1841 . .		7	6	11			10	9	4	8		6	4	23	1.2	1.2	1	1		
1842 . .		8	7	13			12	10	5	10		8	5	25	4	4	2	2	1	1
1843 . .		9	8	15			14			12		10	6	27		6	3	3	2	3
1844 . .		10	9	17			16			14		12	7	29		8	4	4		5
1845 . .		11	10	19			18			16		14	8	31		10		5		7
1846 . .		12	11	21			20			18		16	9	33		12		6		9
1847 . .		13	12	23			22			20		18	10	35		14		7		11
1848 . .		14	13	25			24			22		20	11	37		16		8		13
1849 . .		15	14	27			26			24		22	12	39		18		9		15
1850 . .		16	15	29			28			26		24	13	41		20		10		17
1851 . .		17	16	31			30			28		26	14	43		22		11		19
1852 . .		18	17	33			32			30		28	15	45		24		12		21
1853 . .		19	18	35			34			32		30	16	47		26		13		23
1854 . .		20	19	37			36			34		32	17	49		28		14		25
1855 . .		21	20	39			38			36		34	18	51		30		15		27
1856 . .		23	21	41			40			38		36	19	53		32		16		28
1857 . .		25	22	43			42			40		38	20	55		34		17		
1858 . .		27	23	45			44			42		39	21	57		36		18		
1859 . .		29	24	46			·46			43		41	22	59		38		19		
1860 . .			25	48			48					43	23	61		40		20		

1861 . .			33	32	64							28			58	58							26	50			50				45	24	63		42		21		
1862 . .			34		66										60	60							27	52			52				47	25	65		44		22		
1863 . .			35		68										62	62							28	54			54				49	26	67		46		23		
1864 . .			36		70										64	64								56			56				51	27	69		48		24		
1865 . .			37		72										66									58			58				53	28	71		50		25		
1866 . .			38		74										68									60			60				55	29	73		52		26		
1867 . .			39		76										70									62			62				57	30	75		54		27		
1868 . .			40		78										72									64			64				59	31	77		56		28		
1869 . .			41		80										74									66							61	32	79				29		
1870 . .			42		82										76									68							63	33	81				30		
1871 . .			43		84										78									70								34	83				31		
1872 . .					86										80									72								35	85				32		
1873 . .					88										82									74								36	87				33		
1874 . .					90										84									76								37	89				34		
1875 . .					92										86									77								38	91				35		
1876 . .					94										88									79								39	93				36		
1877 . .					96										90									81								40					37		
1878 . .					98										92									83								41					38		
1879 . .					100										94									85								42					39		
1880 . .					102										96									87								43					40		
1881 . .					104																			89								44					41		

Chronological Conspectus.—*Continued.*

	81 Eclectic Museum.	82 New Englander.	83 U. S. Catholic Magazine.	84 Zoist.	85 Bankers' Magazine (London).	86 Bibliotheca Sacra.	87 British Quarterly Review.	88 Brownson's Quarterly Review.	89 Chambers's Edinb. Journal.	90 Eclectic Magazine.	91 Living Age, Littell's.	92 Monthly Religious Magazine.	93 North British Review.	94 Universalist Quarterly.	95 Western Law Journal.	96 American Whig Review.	97 Prospective Review.	98 Biblical Review.	99 De Bow's Review.	100 Exeter Hall Lectures.
1843 . .	1.2.3	1	1.2																	
1844 . .		2	3	1	1	1	1	1	1.2	1.2.3	1.2.3	1	1	1	1					
1845 . .		3	4	2	3	2	3	2	4	6	7	2	3	2	2	1.2	1			
1846 . .		4	5	3	5	3	5	3	6	9	11	3	5	3	3	4	2	1.2	1.2	1
1847 . .		5	6	4	7	4	7	4	8	12	15	4	7	4	4	6	3	3	4	2
1848 . .		6	7	5	8	5	9	5	10	15	19	5	9	5	5	8	4	4	6	3
1849 . .		7		6	9	6	11	6	12	18	23	6	11	6	6	10	5	5	8	4
1850 . .		8		7	10	7	13	7	14	21	27	7	13	7	7	12	6	6	10	5
1851 . .		9		8	11	8	15	8	16	24	31	8	15	8	8	14	7		12	6
1852 . .		10		9	12	9	16	9	18	27	35	9	17	9	9	16	8		14	7
1853 . .		11		10	13	10	18	10	20	30	39	10	19	10	10		9		16	8
1854 . .		12		11	14	11	20	11	22	33	43	12	21	11			10		18	9
1855 . .		13		12	15	12	22	12	24	36	47	14	23	12					20	10
1856 . .		14		13	16	13	24	13	26	39	51	16	25	13					22	11
1857 . .		15			17	14	26	14	28	42	55	18	27	14					24	12
1858 . .		16			18	15	28	15	30	45	59	20	29	15					26	13
1859 . .		17			19	16	30	16	32	48	63	22	31	16					28	14
1860 . .		18			20	17	32	17	34	51	67	24	33	17					29	15
1861 . .		19			21	18	34	18	36	54	71	26	35	18						16
1862 . .		21			22	19	36	19	38	57	75	28	37	19						17
1863 . .		22			23	20	38	20	40	60	79	30	39	20						18
1864 . .		23			24	21	40	21	41	63	83	32	41	21						19
1865 . .		24			25	22	42		42	65	87	34	43	22						20
1866 . .		25			26	23	44		43	67	91	36	45	23						
1867 . .		26			27	24	46		44	69	95	38	47	24						
1868 . .		27			28	25	48		45	71	99	40	49	25						
1869 . .		28			29	26	50		46	73	103	42	50	26						
1870 . .		29			30	27	52		47	75	107	44	52	27						
1871 . .		30			31	28	54		48	77	111	46	53	28						
1872 . .		31			32	29	56		49	79	115	48		29						
1873 . .		32			33	30	58	22	50	81	119	50		30						
1874 . .		33			34	31	60	23	51	83	123	51		31						
1875 . .		34			35	32	62	24	52	85	127			32						
1876 . .		35			36	33	64		53	87	131			33						
1877 . .		36			37	34	66		54	89	135			34						
1878 . .		37			38	35	68		55	91	139			35						
1879 . .		38			39	36	70		56	93	143			36						
1880 . .		39			40	37	72		57	95	147			37						
1881 . .		40			41	38	74		58	97	151			38						

	101 People's Journal.	102 Sharpe's London Magazine.	103 American Literary Magazine.	104 Bankers' Mag. (New York).	105 Howitt's Journal.	106 New England Historical and Genealogical Register.	107 Hogg's Instructor.	108 Kitto's Journal of Sac. Lit.	109 Mass. Quarterly Review.	110 Western Journal.	111 American Church Review.	112 Art Journal.	113 Mercersburg Review	114 Theological and Lit. Journal.	115 Evangelical Review.	116 Harper's Magazine.	117 Household Words.	118 International Magazine.	119 Irish Quarterly Review.	120 London Quarterly Review.
1843 . .																				
1844 . .																				
1845 . .																				
1846 . .	1.2	1.2																		
1847 . .	4	4	1	1	1.2	1														
1848 . .	6	7	2	2	3	2	1	1	1	1										
1849 . .	8	10		3		3	3	3	2	2	1	1	1	1						
1850 . .	10	12		4		4	5	5	3	4	2	2	2	2	1	1	1	1		
1851 . .	11	14		5		5	7	7		6	3	3	3	3	2	3	3	3	1	
1852 . .		16		6		6	9	9		8	4	4	4	4	3	5	5	5	2	
1853 . .		18		7		7	10	11		10	5	5	5	5	4	7	7		3	1
1854 . .		20		8		8	13	13		12	6	6	6	6	5	9	9		4	2
1855 . .		22		9		9	14	15		14	7	7	7	7	6	11	11		5	4
1856 . .		24		10		10	15	17			8	8	8	8	7	13	14		6	6
1857 . .		26		11		11		19			9	9	9	9	8	15	16			8
1858 . .		28		12		12		21			10	10	10	10	9	17	18		7	10
1859 . .		30		13		13		23			11	11	11	11	10	19	19		8	12
1860 . .		32		14		14		25			12	12	12	12	11	21			9	14
1861 . .		34		15		15		27			13	13	13	13	12	23				16
1862 . .		36		16		16		29			14	14			13	25				18
1863 . .		38		17		17		31				15			14	27				20
1864 . .		40		18		18		33			15	16			15	29				22
1865 . .		42		19		19		35			16	17			16	31				24
1866 . .		44		20		20		37			17	18			17	33				26
1867 . .		46		21		21		39			18	19	14		18	35				28
1868 . .		48		22		22		40			19	20	15		19	37				30
1869 . .		50		23		23					20	21	16		20	39				32
1870 . .		52		24		24					21	22	17		21	41				34
1871 . .				25		25					23	23	18			43				36
1872 . .				26		26					24	24	19			45				38
1873 . .				27		27					25	25	20			47				40
1874 . .				28		28					26	26	21			49				42
1875 . .				29		29					27	27	22			51				44
1876 . .				30		30					28	28	23			53				46
1877 . .				31		31					29	29	24			55				48
1878 . .				32		32					30	30	25			57				50
1879 . .				33		33					31	31				59				52
1880 . .				34		34					32	32				61				54
1881 . .				35		35					36	33				63				57

CHRONOLOGICAL CONSPECTUS. — *Continued.*

Year	121 National Magazine.	122 New Quarterly Review.	123 Am. Presbyterian Review.	124 Putnam's Monthly Magazine.	125 Pioneer.	126 National Review.	127 Am. Journal of Education.	128 Canadian Jour. of Industry.	129 American Church Monthly.	130 Historical Magazine.	131 Atlantic Monthly.	132 Norton's Literary Letter.	133 All the Year Round.
1852 . .	1	1											
1853 . .	3	2	1	1.2									
1854 . .	5	3	2	4	1.2								
1855 . .	7	4	3	6	4	1							
1856 . .	9	5	4	8		3	1.2	1					
1857 . .	11	6	5	10		5	3	2	1	1			
1858 . .	13	7	6			7	5	3	3	2	1.2	1.2	
1859 . .		8	7			9	7	4		3	4	4	1
1860 . .		9	8			11	9	5		4	6	6	3
1861 . .		10	9			13	11	6		5	8		5
1862 . .			11			15	12	7		6	10		7
1863 . .			12			17	13	8		7	12		9
1864 . .			13			19	14	9		8	14		11
1865 . .			14				15			9	16		13
1866 . .			15				16			10	18		16
1867 . .			16							12	20		18
1868 . .			17	12			17	11		14	22		20
1869 . .			18	14			18			16	24		22
1870 . .			19	16			21	12		18	26		24
1871 . .			20				22			19	28		26
1872 . .							23			20	30		28
1873 . .							24			21	32		30
1874 . .										22	34		32
1875 . .							25			23	36		34
1876 . .							26				38		36
1877 . .							27				40		38
1878 . .							28				42		41
1879 . .							29				44		43
1880 . .							30				46		45
1881 . .											48		47

Year	134 Bentley's Quarterly.	135 Congregational Quarterly.	136 Mathematical Monthly.	137 Once a Week.	138 Cornhill Magazine.	139 Good Words.	140 Macmillan's Magazine.	141 National Quarterly Review.	142 Recreative Science.	143 University Quarterly.	144 Boston Review.	145 Danville Quarterly Review.	146 Reliquary.	147 Saint James.
1852 . .														
1853 . .														
1854 . .														
1855 . .														
1856 . .														
1857 . .														
1858 . .														
1859 . .	1.2	1	1	1										
1860 . .		2	2	3	1.2	1	1.2	1	1	1.2				
1861 . .		3	3	5	4	2	4	3	2	4	1	1		1.2
1862 . .		4		7	6	3	6	5	3		2	2	2	5
1863 . .		5		9	8	4	8	7			3	3	3	8
1864 . .		6		11	10	5	10	9			4	4	4	11
1865 . .		7		13	12	6	12	11			5		5	14
1866 . .		8		15	14	7	14	13			6		6	17
1867 . .		9		17	16	8	16	15					7	20
1868 . .		10		19	18	9	18	17					8	22
1869 . .		11		21	20	10	20	19					9	24
1870 . .		12		23	22	11	22	21					10	26
1871 . .		13		25	24	12	24	23			Continued as Congregational Review.		11	28
1872 . .		14		27	26	13	26	25					12	30
1873 . .		15		29	28	14	28	27					13	32
1874 . .		16		30	30	15	30	29					14	34
1875 . .		17			32	16	32	31					15	36
1876 . .		18			34	17	34	33					16	39
1877 . .		19			36	18	36	35					17	41
1878 . .		20			38	19	38	37					18	43
1879 . .					40	20	40	39					19	45
1880 . .					42	21	42	41						47
1881 . .					44	22	44							49

Year	148 Temple Bar.	149 Continental Monthly.	150 Home and Foreign Review.	151 Intellectual Observer.	152 London Society.	153 Popular Science Review.	154 Anthropological Review.	155 Fine Arts Quarterly.	156 Victoria Magazine.	157 Month.	158 Theological Review.	159 U. S Service Magazine.	160 Catholic World.
1852 . .													
1853 . .													
1854 . .													
1855 . .													
1856 . .													
1857 . .													
1858 . .													
1859 . .													
1860 . .													
1861 . .	1.2.3												
1862 . .	6	1.2	1	1	1.2	1							
1863 . .	9	4	3	3	4	2	1	1	1				
1864 . .	12	6	4	5	6	3	2	2	3	1	1	1.2	
1865 . .	15			7	8	4	3	3	5	3	2	4	1
1866 . .	18			9	10	5	4	4	7	5	3	5	3
1867 . .	21			11	12	6	5	5	9	7	4		5
1868 . .	24			12	14	7	6		11	9	5		7
1869 . .	27				16	8	7		13	11	6		9
1870 . .	30				18	9			15	13	7		11
1871 . .	33				20	10			17	15	8		13
1872 . .	36				22	11			19	17	9		15
1873 . .	39				24	12			21	19	10		17
1874 . .	42				26	13			23	22	11		19
1875 . .	45				28	14			25	25	12		21
1876 . .	48				30	15			27	28	13		23
1877 . .	51				32	16			29	31	14		25
1878 . .	54				34	17			31	34	15		27
1879 . .	57				36	18			33	37	16		29
1880 . .	60				38	19			35	40			31
1881 . .	63				40	20			36	43			33

Chronological Conspectus. — *Continued.*

	161 Fortnightly Review.	162 Hours at Home.	163 Nation.	164 Theological Eclectic.	165 Argosy.	166 Contemporary Review.	167 Englishwoman's Domestic Magazine.	168 Every Saturday.	169 Galaxy.	170 Radical.	171 American Law Review.	172 American Naturalist.	173 Baptist Quarterly Review.	174 Belgravia.
1865 . .	1.2	1	1	1.2										
1866 . .	6	3	3	3	1.2	1.2.3	1.2	1.2	1.2	1				
1867 . .	8	5	5	4	4	6	3	4	4	2	1	1	1	1.2.3
1868 . .	10	7	7	5	6	9	5	6	6	4	2	2	2	6
1869 . .	12	9	9	6	8	12	7	8	8	6	3	3	3	9
1870 . .	14	11	11	7	10	15	9	9	10	7	4	4	4	12
1871 . .	16		13		12	18	11	11	12	9	5	5	5	15
1872 . .	18		15		14	20	13	13	14	10	6	6	6	18
1873 . .	20		17		16	22	15	15	16		7	7	7	21
1874 . .	22		19		18	24	17	17	18		8	8	8	24
1875 . .	24		21		20	26	19		20		9	9	9	27
1876 . .	26		23		22	28	21		22		10	10	10	30
1877 . .	28		25		24	30	23		24		11	11	11	33
1878 . .	30		27		26	33	25				12	12		36
1879 . .	32		29		28	36	26				13	13		39
1880 . .	34		31		30	38					14	14		42
1881 . .	36		33		32	40					15	15		45

	175 Congregational Review.	176 Journal of Spec. Philosophy.	177 Land We Love.	178 New Dominion Monthly.	179 South. Review, new series.	180 Saint Paul's Magazine.	181 Tinsley's Magazine.	182 Broadway.	183 Gentleman's Mag., new ser.	184 Lippincott's Magazine.	185 New Eclectic.	186 Overland Monthly.	187 Student & Intellectual Obs.	188 American Social Science Association Journal.
1865 . .														
1866 . .														
1867 . .	7	1	1.2	1	1.2									
1868 . .	8	2	4	2	4	1.2	1.2	1.2	1	1.2	1.2	1	1	
1869 . .	9	3	6	3	6	4	4	4	3	4	4	3	3	1
1870 . .	10	4		5	8	6	6	6	5	6	6	5	4	2
1871 . .	11	5		7	10	9	8	8	7	8	7	7	5	3
1872 . .	Continued from Boston Review.	6		9	12	11	10	10	9	10	Continued as Southern Magazine.	9		4
1873 . .		7		11	14	13	13		11	12		11		5
1874 . .		8		13	16	14	15		13	14		13		6
1875 . .		9		15	18		17		15	16		15		7
1876 . .		10		17	20		19		17	18				8
1877 . .		11		19	22		21		19	20				
1878 . .		12		21	24		23		21	22				9
1879 . .		13					25		23	24				10
1880 . .		14					27		25	26				11
1881 . .		15					29		27	28				

	189 American Bibliopolist.	190 Appleton's Journal.	191 Christian Quarterly.	192 Eclectic Engineering Mag.	193 Lakeside Monthly.	194 Nature.	195 Old and New.	196 Penn Monthly.	197 Portfolio.	198 Scribner's Monthly.	199 Dark Blue.	200 Lutheran Quarterly.	201 Southern Magazine.	202 Anthropological Journal.
1865 . .														
1866 . .														
1867 . .														
1868 . .														
1869 . .	1	1.2	1	1	1.2									
1870 . .	2	4	2	3	4	1.2	1.2	1	1					
1871 . .	3	6	3	5	6	4	4	2	2	2	1	1	8.9	
1872 . .	4	8	4	7	8	6	6	3	3	4	3	2	11	1
1873 . .	5	10	5	9	9	8	8	4	4	6	4	3	13	2
1874 . .	6	12	6	11	11	10	10	5	5	9		4	15	3
1875 . .	7	14	7	13		12	11	6	6	11		5	17	4
1876 . .	8	16	8	15		14		7	7	13		6		5
1877 . .		18		17		16		8	8	15		7		6
1878 . .		20		19		18		9	9	17		8		7
1879 . .		22		21		20		10	10	19		9		8
1880 . .		24		23		22		11		21		10		9
1881 . .		26		25		24		12		23		11		

Chronological Conspectus. — *Concluded.*

	203 American Historical Record.	204 Canadian Monthly.	205 Congregationalist.	206 Popular Science Monthly.	207 Presbyterian Quarterly.	208 Antiquary, Jewitt's.	209 Irish Monthly.	210 Practical Magazine.	211 Republic.	212 Geographical Magazine.	213 International Review.	214 Unitarian Review.	215 Potter's American Monthly.	216 Western.	217 American Architect.
1872	1	1.2	1	1	1										
1873	2	4	2	3	2	1.2	1	1.2	1.2						
1874	3	6	3	5	3	4	2	4	4	1	1	1.2			
1875	Continued as Potter's Am. Monthly.	8	4	7	4		3	5	6	2	2	4	4.5	1	
1876		10	5	9	5		4	6	7	3	3	6	7	2	1
1877		12	6	11	6		5	7		4	4	8	9	3	2
1878		14		13			6			5	5	10	11	4	4
1879		16		15			7				7	12	13	5	6
1880		18		17			8				9	14	15	6	8
1881		20		19			9				11	16	17		10

	218 Am. Catholic Quarterly Rev.	219 Mind.	220 Southern Hist. Soc. Papers.	221 Mag. of American History.	222 Nineteenth Century.	223 Pennsylvania Magazine.	224 Radical Review.	225 Sup. to Pop. Science Monthly.	226 Library Journal.	227 Princeton Review, new ser.	228 Reformed Quarterly Review.	229 Modern Review.	230 Dial (Chicago).	231 Presbyterian Review.	232 Education.
1872											Continued from Mercersburg Review.				
1873															
1874															
1875															
1876	1	1	1.2												
1877	2	2	4	1	1.2	1	1	1	1.2						
1878	3	3	6	2	4	2		2	3	1.2					
1879	4	4	7	3	6	3		4	4	4	26				
1880	5	5	8	5	8	4			5	6	27	1	1	1	
1881	6	6	9	7	10	5			6	8	28	2	2	2	1

INDEX

TO

PERIODICAL LITERATURE.

Aard-Vark, or Earth Hog. (E. Oustalet) Pop. Sci. Mo. 14: 572.
Aaron and Esther; or, Three Days in Rabbi Clausener's Life. Chamb. J. 39: 53.
Aaron's Rod in Politics. (A. W. Tourgee) No. Am. 132: 139.
Abailard, Pierre. Ecl. M. 26: 466. Same art. Liv. Age, 34: 39. — Am. Presb. R. 6: 529. 7: 33.
— and Bernard. (S. Sweetser) Bib. Sac. 17: 43.
— and Heloisa. Ed. R. 30: 352. — Westm. 32: 146. — Fraser, 28: 86. — Anal. M. 14: 329. 15: 33. — So. Lit. Mess. 9: 17. — For. Q. 36: 257. — (C. H. Brigham) No. Am. 88: 132. — (O. Delepierre) St. James, 14: 304. — (K. F. A. Kahnis) Mercersb. 25: 56. — (F. W. Roswell) St. James, 11: 361. — Ecl. R. 110: 329.
— Life of. Westm. 96: 91. Same art. Liv. Age, 110: 387.
— Sketch of. (Dr. Wolff) Mercersb. 8: 124.
Abandoned at Sea. (Lieut. Marneford) St. James, 10: 85.
Abattoir, Old Bull's Head. (C. C. Buel) Scrib. 17: 421.
Abattoir Management in Chicago. Pract. M. 5: 255.
Abbandonata; a Poem. Temp. Bar, 2: 141.
Abbas Pacha of Egypt. (E. De Leon) Harper, 38: 264.
Abbaye aux Hommes at Caen. Chr. Obs. 69: 836.
Abbess of Ischia. (R. A. McLeod) Lippinc. 19: 547.
Abbess of Marlow; a Poem. Once a Week, 22: 100.
Abbeville, France, Day at. (B. R. Parkes) Once a Week, 14: 566. Same art. Cath. World, 3: 590.
Abbey of Nuns in the Minories, London. (H. Fly) Arch. 15: 92.
Abbey Farm; a Tale. Month, 2: 69.
Abbey Pieces. (J. Symons) Antiquary, 2: 165.
Abbey Tokens. Antiquary, 4: 309.
Abbey View. Liv. Age, 63: 356.
Abbeys and Cathedrals, Scottish. Quar. 85: 103.
Abbo, Abbot of Fleury. Month, 20: 163. 21: 28.
Abbot, Abiel. Statement of Coventry Church Controversy. Gen. Repos. 1: 145.
— Obituary of. Mo. Rel. M. 21: 195.
Abbot, Benjamin. (J. G. Hoyt) No. Am. 87: 119.
Abbot, E. A. Sermons. Dub. Univ. 86: 500.
Abbot, John E. Life and Character. Chr. Disc. 2: 32.
Abbot Family in New England. (H. H. Barber) Unita. R. 12: 552.
Abbot, The; or, The Hermit of Niagara Falls. So. Lit. Mess. 6: 687.
Abbot of Pinner, Story of; a Poem. (W. Jones) Bentley, 64: 134.

Abbot's Grange, The. (J. Gillies) Colburn, 150: 68-201.
Abbot's Pool; a Tale. All the Year, 20: 545, 570, 589.
Abbotsbury, Abbey Church at. (E. H. W. Dunkin) Antiquary, 2: 285.
Abbotsford. Ev. Sat. 11: 224. — O. & N. 4: 235.
— and Newstead Abbey. (W. Irving) Tait, n. s. 2: 414.
— — Irving on. Mo. R. 137: 225.
— Notanda from. Gent. M. n. s. 2: 586, 680.
— Visits to. (S. E. Ferrier) Temp. Bar, 40: 329. Same art. Liv. Age, 120: 689.
Abbott, Jacob. Writings. (C. D. Pigeon) Lit. & Theo. R. 3: 83. — Chr. Exam. 18: 133. — (E. B. Hall) Chr. Exam. 21: 306.
— Young Christian Series. Meth. Q. 12: 608. — Am. Mo. R. 4: 370.
Abbott, John S. C. (H. O. Ladd) Cong. Q. 20: 1.
Abbott, Joseph. Cong. Q. 12: 333.
Abbreviations, Errata Recepta. (H. Scadding) Canad. J. n. s. 9: 137.
— for Feminine Names. (C. A. Cutter) Lib. J. 5: 176.
— for Male Names. (C. A. Cutter) Lib. J. 1: 405.
Abdallah and Saida. Fraser, 55: 718.
Abdallah's Conversion to Christianity. (G. Axford) O. & N. 3: 45.
Abdel-Hassan; a Poem. (B. R. Plumly) Atlan. 5: 70.
Abd-el-Kader. Blackw. 50: 183. 65: 20. — Dub. Univ. 21: 704. — (E. Clive) Bentley, 20: 83. — Hogg, 1: 397. Same art. Ecl. M. 16: 267.
— at Ambois. Bentley, 31: 259.
— Last Struggle of. Fraser, 37: 658.
Abd-er-Rahman I. Dub. Univ. 23: 730.
Abduction, A once Famous. All the Year, 24: 53.
— of the O'Banagner. Once a Week, 30: 15-101.
Abdul-Aziz and his Successors. Internat. R. 3: 674.
Abdul-Medjid, Sultan of Turkey. Bentley, 35: 91.
Abednego the Money-Lender. (Mrs. Gore) Tait, n. s. 9: 143-762.
Abel Rees. (L. Wood) Tinsley, 18: 665.
Abelard. *See* Abailard.
Abencerage, Adventures of the last. (F. Chateaubriand) West. J. 13: 220-434.
Abeokuta and Dahome, Burton's. Lond. Q. 23: 452.
Abercorn, James, Duke of, with portrait. Dub. Univ. 84: 280.
Abercrombie, John, with portrait. Hogg, 3: 145. Same art. Ecl. M. 23: 426.
— Intellectual Powers. Quar. 45: 341. — (W. Silsbee) Chr. Exam. 14: 43. — Am. Mo. R. 2: 403.

Abercrombie, John. Man of Faith. (A. Alexander) Princ. **8**: 51.
— on Moral Feelings. (H. Hooker) Lit. & Theo. R. **1**: 256. — Am. Mo. R. **4**: 330.
Abercromby, David. Treatise of Wit, 1686. Cong. M. **8**: 487.
Aberdare, Henry A. Bruce, Lord, with portrait. Colburn, **167**: 523.
Aberdare Panic in London. Bank. M. (N. Y.) **30**: 198.
Aberdeen, City of. All the Year, **14**: 304. — Sharpe, **22**: 159.
— Bruce's Eminent Men of. Mo. R. **155**: 579.
— Fish-People of. Penny M. **9**: 369.
— Philosophers of, one hundred Years ago. (J. Valentine) Macmil. **8**: 436.
— Schools of Industry. Chamb. J. **4**: 305, 345.
— Slain's Castle. (B. Murphy) Lippinc. **11**: 646.
— till thirty Years ago. (D. Masson) Macmil. **9**: 52.
— Universities of. (D. C. Macdonald) Appleton, **20**: 312. — Tait, **3**: 182.
Aberdeen, G. H. G., Lord. Ev. Sat. **11**: 79.
— and Palmerston. Tait, n. s. **22**: 65.
— Ministry of, 1854. Dub. Univ. **44**: 131.
Abernethy, John. Colburn, **123**: 403. — Ecl. M. **30**: 557. — Ecl. R. **121**: 409.
— and Sir A. Cooper. Lond. Q. **4**: 44.
— and the Lancet. Lond. M. **11**: 260.
— Macilvain's Life of. Liv. Age, **39**: 662.
— Memoir of. Chr. Obs. **57**: 460.
— Sketch of. Ill. M. **2**: 78.
Aberystwith. Lond. Soc. **14**: 349.
Abigail. Fraser, **72**: 341. Same art. Liv. Age, **88**: 457.
Abigail Ray's Vision. (J. F. Bowman) Overland, **8**: 358, 436.
Ability, Doctrine of. Am. Presb. R. **4**: 578. **8**: 177.
— and Inability, Natural and moral. (E. Pond) New Eng. **13**: 387.
— and Obligation. Cong. M. **15**: 135, 211, 285.
— Natural. Bost. R. **3**: 458.
Abingdon. Penny M. **14**: 388.
— Churchwarden's Accompts of St. Helen's Parish. (J. Ward) Arch. **1**: 11.
— Chronicles of Monastery of. Chr. Rem. **40**: 1.
Abinger, James Scarlett, Lord. Blackw. **122**: 91. — (C. H. Haill) Am. Law R. **12**: 39.
— and the Bar. Quar. **144**: 1. Same art. Liv. Age, **134**: 387.
Abington, Fanny Barton, as Lady Teazle. (D. Cook) Gent. M. n. s. **16**: 198.
— Recollections of. Colburn, **52**: 217.
Abington, Mass., Churches and Ministers of. Am. Q. Reg. **8**: 149.
Abipones, Dobrizhoffer's Account of. (R. Southey) Quar. **26**: 277. — Ecl. R. **35**: 455.
Abkhaasian Insurrection. (W. G. Palgrave) Cornh. **16**: 501.
Abnormales, L'; a Story. (V. Lapoukhyn) Lippinc. **25**: 492.
Aboard the "Constellation." All the Year, **7**: 185.
Aboard the "Promised Land;" a Tale. All the Year, **15**: 16.
Aboard the "Sea Mew." Chamb. J. **46**: 209–265.
Abolition and Sectarian Mobs. Dem. R. **34**: 97.
Abolition Martyrs of United States. (H. Martineau) Westm. **32**: 1.
Abolition Proceedings. Bost. Q. **1**: 473.
Abolition Rebellion in Ohio. (W. G. Day) So. M. **13**: 208.
Abolition Society of Maryland, 1787. Carey's Mus. **7**: App. 6.
Abolition Troubles. Niles's Reg. **49**: 145.
Abolitionism and Puritanism. Dem. R. **36**: 79.
— Conspiracy of. Dem. R. **26**: 385.
Abolitionism, Political. (Tayler Lewis) Am. Whig R. **2**: 3.
— Present Aspect of. So. Lit. Mess. **13**: 429.
— Reflection for. Liv. Age, **31**: 90.
— *vs.* Christianity and the Union. Dem. R. **27**: 1.
— *vs.* the Union. Dem. R. **33**: 289.
Abolitionists. Dem. R. **16**: 3.
— American. Ecl. R. **72**: 154.
— and Anti-Abolitionists. (M. L. Hurlbut) Chr. Exam. **24**: 396.
See also Anti-Slavery ; Emancipation ; Slavery.
Aborigines of America. *See* Indians.
— of British Settlements. Chr. Obs. **37**: 710.
— Treatment of. Mo. R. **165**: 16.
Aborigines Protection Society, 1838. Ecl. R. **68**: 319.
Abou Hassan ; an Allegory. So. Lit. Mess. **7**: 754.
Aboukir, Battle of. Nat. Mag. **2**: 297.
About, E., with portrait. Appleton, **3**: 664. — Bentley, **42**: 588. — Nat. R. **11**: 1. Same art. Liv. Age, **66**: 357. — (K. Cook) Lond. Soc. **27**: 533. — Once a Week, **23**: 122.
— at Home. (A. Rhodes) Galaxy, **18**: 254.
— Etienne. So. M. **12**: 63–340.
— Germaine. Putnam, **10**: 724.
— King of the Mountains. (Comtesse de Bury) No. Am. **92**: 283. — Blackw. **81**: 449.
— Madon. Colburn, **129**: 210.
— Notary's Nose. Dub. Univ. **64**: 334.
— Romance of the Landes. Liv. Age, **57**: 894.
— Trente et Quarante. Bentley, **45**: 472.
— La Vieille Roche. Bentley, **58**: 391. **59**: 47. Same art. Ecl. M. **66**: 428.
— Writings of. Fraser, **72**: 58. — No. Brit. **44**: 411. Same art. Liv. Age, **90**: 67. — Dub. Univ. **64**: 102.
About Nothing. (W. E. Norris) Gent. M. n. s. **25**: 619.
About Sister Jane. (Mrs. S. C. Hall) St. James, **4**: 129.
About to be married. St. James, **18**: 379.
Above Suspicion. (Mrs. J. H. Riddell) Lond. Soc. **26**: 95–471. **27**: 2–481. **28**: 28–519. **29**: 29.
Abraham. (J. F. Mackarness) Good Words, **10**: 337.
— and his Day. (J. W. Thompson) Mo. Rel. M. **8**: 114.
— Covenant with. (T. R. Palmer) Bapt. Q. **5**: 314. — (J. Priestley) Theo. Repos. **2**: 396.
— — and the New Testament Church. Am. Presb. R. **3**: 529.
— Historical Epoch of. (J. C. Moffat) Princ. **29**: 391.
— Life of. (J. H. Kurtz) Mercersb. **8**: 131.
— Position of, in Sacred History. Danv. Q. **4**: 611.
— Promise to. (J. Priestley) Theo. Repos. **4**: 361. **5**: 108. — (A. G. Gaines) Univ. Q. **13**: 375. — (W. R. French) Univ. Q. **18**: 363. — (S. Harris) Bib. Sac. **22**: 79.
— Religion of. (S. S. Hebbard) Univ. Q. **36**: 341.
— Traditions and Legends of. (W. F. Ainsworth) Colburn, **167**: 449.
— Trial of. Chr. Mo. Spec. **5**: 397.
Abraham, — Abron, — Auburn ; a Shaksperian Excursus. (G. Lunt) Cath. World, **17**: 234.
Abraham's Sacrifice ; a Tale. (MM. Erckmann-Chatrian) Temp. Bar, **31**: 322.
Abraham Scrimble's Will ; a Tale. Dub. Univ. **45**: 1.
Abrantes, Duchess d'. Memoirs. *See* Napoleon I.
Abroad without Languages. Hogg, **1**: 257.
Abruzzi, Craven's Excursions in. Mo. R. **145**: 111.
— Shepherds of. Penny M. **2**: 106.
Absalom, Revolt of. Good Words, **5**: 265, 345.
Absence ; a Poem. (L. Bushnell) Scrib. **5**: 543.
Absence of Mind. Chamb. J. **13**: 61.
Absent, To the ; a Song. Dub. Univ. **2**: 8.
Absent-minded Men. Ev. Sat. **11**: 354.
Absentee, To an. (T. Hood) Lond. M. **5**: 375.
Absenteeism. Ed. R. **43**: 54. — Westm. **8**: 70. — (T. P. Thompson) Westm. **10**: 237. **19**: 516. **23**: 411.

Absenteeism, Effects of, on Ireland. Dub. Univ. **35**: 277.
— McCulloch on. Lond. M. **14**: 530.
Absenteeism in Churches. (J. S. Sewall) Cong. Q. **4**: 163.
Absolute, The, Cousin upon Kant's Doctrine of. (F. A. Henry) J. Spec. Philos. **2**: 82.
— and the Infinite. (E. V. Gerhart) Mercersb. **12**: 265, 294.
— Philosophy of. (C. W. Shields) Princ. **34**: 215. — (A. Russell) Contemp. **17**: 338.
Absolute Princes, Manners and Morals of. Ed. R. **41**: 287.
Absolution. (M. Kieffer) Mercersb. **22**: 212. — (A. P. Stanley) 19th Cent. **3**: 183. — Chr. Rem. **17**: 430.
— and Confession. (A. C. Coxe) Am. Church R. **2**: 573. — Lond. Q. **41**: 370.
— Pusey on. Dub. R. **20**: 224.
— Sacerdotal. (C. Hodge and A. Alexander) Princ. **17**: 43.
— Two Forms of. (D. A. Wasson) Chr. Exam. **85**: 1.
Abstinence from Food. Penny M. **10**: 63.
— Place and Power of. (J. Muller) Ex. H. Lec. **12**: 291. *See also* Fasting.
Absurdity, Philosophy of. (W. E. McCann) Lippinc. **4**: 81.
Absynth. St. James, **47**: 156.
Abu Hamood's Mule: and the Cedars of Lebanon. Putnam, **7**: 264.
Abu Taleb Khan, Travels of, 1799–1803. (J. Foster) Ecl. R. **13**: 72.
Abul Hassan, Mirza. Penny M. **3**: 407, 413.
Abulfeda, Adventures of. New Eng. M. **8**: 359.
Abutments, Uniform Cross-Section and T. (W. Cain) Ecl. Engin. **7**: 453.
Abyssinia. (C. Russ) Geog. M. **5**: 228. — Brit. Q. **47**: 179. — Chamb. J. **44**: 660, 731. **45**: 614. — Ev. Sat. **6**: 508. — Lond. Q. **29**: 463. Same art. Ecl. M. **70**: 397, 598. — Sharpe, **46**: 281. — Mo. R. **126**: 13.
— Adule; Gate of Civilization to. Colburn, **142**: 127.
— and the Blue Nile. Westm. **108**: 189.
— and its Border-Lands. (E. P. Evans) Hours at Home, **5**: 246.
— and its People. Chr. Rem. **8**: 227.
— and Kordofan, Travels in. Westm. **42**: 407. Same art. Liv. Age, **4**: 195.
— Artistic Jottings in. (W. Simpson) Good Words, **9**: 605.
— Christian Empire in. (E. De Leon) Internat. R. **7**: 671.
— Christians of. Dub. R. **17**: 105.
— Church of. (J. A. Reubelt) Mercersb. **11**: 594. — Dub. R. **53**: 33. — Nat. Q. **21**: 337. — Chr. Mo. Spec. **1**: 277, 325.
— — Creed of. (A. Clarke) Meth. M. **49**: 605.
— — Holy Orders in. (E. E. Estcourt) Month, **20**: 97, 384. — (J. Jones) Month, **19**: 451. **20**: 229.
— — Hymns and Prayers of. (J. M. Rodwell) Kitto, **38**: 388.
— Dufton and Baker on. (H. Kingsley) Fortn. **8**: 547.
— Dufton's Journey through. Bentley, **62**: 487.
— Egyptian Campaign in. Blackw. **122**: 26. Same art. Liv. Age, **134**: 278.
— Empire and Church of. Chr. Obs. **11**: 621.
— English in. (H. M. Alden) Harper, **37**: 333.
— English Expedition to, 1867. Colburn, **141**: 127. — (D. T. Ansted) Intel. Obs. **12**: 227. — (T. C. De Leon) Land We Love, **4**: 333. — (C. R. Markham) Macmil. **17**: 435. **18**: 87, 193, 289. — Blackw. **103**: 349–728. — Quar. **123**: 510. — Westm. **89**: 169. — Once a Week, **17**: 536. — Tinsley, **1**: 356. — Cornh. **17**: 696. — Lond. Q. **32**: 393.
— — Rassam's Account of. Quar. **126**: 299. Same art. Liv. Age, **101**: 451.
— French in. Colburn, **118**: 127.
— From Tor to Massowah. Once a Week, **28**: 192, 207.
— Gobat's Residence in. New Eng. **8**: 515. — Theo. and Lit. J. **4**: 134.
Abyssinia. Harris on Highlands of Ethiopia. Mo. R. **163**: 216.
— in 1834. Ecl. R. **63**: 123.
— Irenberg and Krapf's Travels in. Chr. Obs. **43**: 751. Same art. Ecl. M. **1**: 236.
— Johnston's Southern. Ecl. R. **81**: 400. — Mo. R. **165**: 254.
— Kassala. Ev. Sat. **5**: 88.
— King Theodore. Chamb. J. **43**: 726. Same art. Ecl. M. **68**: 169. — (A. d'Abbadie) Cath. World, **7**: 265. — (W. L. Gage) Putnam, **12**: 85. — (G. Reynolds) Atlantic, **21**: 701. — All the Year, **18**: 392.
— Last Four Years in, 1863–66. Argosy, **5**: 182.
— Magdala. Ev. Sat. **6**: 188.
— Mythical and Historical. St. James, **20**: 422. **21**: 73.
— Natural History of. Nature, **2**: 29.
— Nile Tributaries of. Macmil. **17**: 145.
— — Baker's. Colburn, **142**: 1.
— Notes from. (H. A. Buretk) Lond. Soc. **13**: 289, 453.
— Parkyns's Life in. Blackw. **75**: 128. — Dub. Univ. **43**: 297. — Fraser, **51**: 26.
— Pearce's Adventures in. Mus. **19**: 615.
— Religion of. Lond. Q. **30**: 317.
— Religious State of, 1812. Chr. Obs. **11**: 197.
— Royal Lady in. Bentley, **55**: 540.
— Rüppell's Travels in. Ed. R. **74**: 307. — For. Q. **28**: 64. — Ecl. R. **73**: 306.
— Salt's Travels in, 1809–10. (J. Foster) Ecl. R. **21**: 217, 404.
— Shoa, New Christian Kingdom of. Penny M. **7**: 367.
— — Mission to. Dub. Univ. **24**: 253.
— Sport in. Dub. Univ. **88**: 119.
— Travels in. Lond. Q. **3**: 42.
Acacia, or Locust Tree. Penny M. **11**: 145.
Academic Culture, Schelling's Idea of. (T. Apple) Mercersb. **15**: 290.
Academical Education, Defects of. (C. Colton) Chr. Mo. Spec. **9**: 578.
— in England. (H. Brougham) Ed. R. **43**: 315.
Academical Errors. Mo. R. **85**: 33.
Academical History of Mr. Chicken. Belgra. **24**: 305.
Academical Organization, M. Pattison's Suggestions on. Fraser, **80**: 407.
Academical Questions, Drummond's. (F. Jeffrey) Ed. R. **7**: 163.
Academical Study in England, Organization of. Nature, **7**: 72.
Academical Test Articles. Ed. R. **88**: 163.
Académie Française. Colburn, **114**: 39. — (M. Arnold) Cornh. **10**: 154. — House. Words, **6**: 300.
Academies and Classical Schools of New England. (C. Hammond) Am. J. Educ. **16**: 403.
— and Universities. (C. W. Hackley) Putnam, **2**: 169.
— in New England, 1830. Am. Q. Reg. **2**: 231. **3**: 288.
— Italian. St. Paul, **2**: 79.
— Literary Influence of. (M. Arnold) Cornh. **10**: 154.
— of Sciences. (E. D. Cope) Penn Mo. **7**: 173, 640.
— Relations of, to Colleges. (H. R. Edson) Cong. R. **11**: 50.
— Royal. Tait, **4**: 454.
Academy, Life at an. Mo. Rel. M. **45**: 603.
— of Design, New York, 1863. Contin. Mo. **3**: 715.
— of Language and Belles Lettres. (E. Everett) No. Am. **14**: 350.
— Utopian. St. James, **24**: 521.
Acadia, Early Missions in. (J. G. Shea) Cath. World, **12**: 628, 826.
— Land of the Mayflower. (Mrs. M. L. Rayne) Lakeside, **1**: 87.
— Settlement of. M. Am. Hist. **2**: 49.
See Nova Scotia.

Acadians, Banishment of. Chamb. J. **22**: 342. Same art. Liv. Age, **44**: 51. — (R. L. Daniels) Scrib. **19**: 383. — (A. Harvey) Canad. Mo. **18**: 337.
— Papers relating to. N. E. Reg. **30**: 17.
— Winslow's Expedition against, 1755. N. E Reg. **33**: 383.
Acadian Governor, An. *See* Vetch, Samuel.
Acapulco. (F. F. Victor) Overland, **6**: 214.
Acari, Mites, Ticks, and other. (E. R. Leland) Pop. Sci. Mo. **14**: 502.
Accents and Prosody, Odell on. Ecl. R. **6**: 994.
Acceptance with God, Grounds of. Chr. Disc. **1**: 90.
Accepted Play; a Story. (B. Webber) Tinsley, **26**: 446.
Accidents caused by runaway Horses, Prevention of. Pract. M. **6**: 307.
— Fatal, how far Preventible. Ed. R. **94**: 98. Same art. Liv. Age, **31**: 49. Same art. Ecl. M. **24**: 1.
— Happy. Chamb. J. **51**: 251. **53**: 345.
— in relation to Providence. (J. C. Kimball) Unita. R. **7**: 41.
— Law of. (G. A. Leakin) Hours at Home, **10**: 215.
— of Sublunary Immortality. Nat. Q. **28**: 252.
— or Providences. Bost. R. **1**: 63.
— Steamboat and Railroad, compared, 1853. J. Frankl. Inst. **57**: 299.
— with Firearms. Chamb. J. **41**: 756.
See also Railroad Accidents.
Accidents will happen; a Tale. (E. Stoddard) Putnam, **11**: 487.
Accident Insurance. Am. Law R. **7**: 585.
Accidentally overheard. (H. E. Scudder) Atlan. **45**: 301.
Acclimatization. All the Year, **5**: 492. — Colburn, **124**: 208. **125**: 253.
— and Preservation of Animals. Nat. R. **17**: 152.
— Report of French Society, 1874. Pract. M. **5**: 333.
Accolade, The; a Poem. (B. Taylor) Galaxy, **13**: 323.
Accommodation. All the Year, **13**: 260.
Accoramboni, Vittoria. All the Year, **2**: 296-394. — Cornh. **19**: 244.
According to Cocker. Chamb. J. **33**: 403.
Accountants, Questions for. Hunt, **11**: 192-446.
Accounts, New Method of keeping. Bank. M. (N. Y.) **15**: 261. — (J. H. Alexander) Bank. M. (N. Y.) **15**: 337.
Accumulation, Passion for. (A. Lamson) Chr. Exam. **22**: 218.
— Property, Capital, Credit. (E. Everett) Hunt, **1**: 20.
Accuracy, Martyrdom of. Once a Week, **20**: 53.
Accused Persons, Testimony of. Am. Law R. **1**: 443.
Ace of Spades; a Sketch. Dub. Univ. **60**: 618.
Aceldama Sparks. (R. T. Cooke) Harper, **19**: 190.
Acerbi, J. Travels in Sweden and Lapland. (H. Brougham) Ed. R. **1**: 163.
Acheen. All the Year, **32**: 151.
Achievements for Wagers. Chamb. J. **51**: 381.
Achill Island, How we saw. Colburn, **154**: 263.
Achilles and Lancelot. (H. M. Moule) Macmil. **24**: 344.
— over the Trench; a Poem. (A. Tennyson) 19th Cent. **2**: 1.
— Shield of. (W. E. Gladstone) Canad. Mo. **5**: 249. — (R. A. Proctor) Stud. & Intel. Obs. **1**: 357. — Penny M. **1**: 241.
Achilles Tatius. Clitophon and Leucippe. Blackw. **55**: 33.
Achilli, Dr. G., Case of, *vs.* Father Newman. Dub. R. **34**: 244. — Chr. Rem. **24**: 401. — Liv. Age, **34**: 277.
— Life of. Dub. R. **28**: 470.
Achsah's Possibilities. (I. G. Meredith) O. & N. **9**: 448.
Acids, Complex inorganic. (W. Gibbs) Am. J. Sci. **114**: 61.
Ackermann, L. Poésies philosophiques. Dub. R. **81**: 340.
Ackworth School, Visit to. Chamb. J. **8**: 151.
Acland, Lady Christiana Harriet. Once a Week, **18**: 520. — (Mrs. C. Halsey) Potter Am. Mo. **7**: 191. — (W. L. Stone) Lippinc. **24**: 452.
— and Major Sir Thomas Acland. (W. L. Stone) M. Am. Hist. **4**: 49.
— and Lady Sale. Liv. Age, **28**: 241.
Acoma and the Acoma Indians. (G. Butler) Cath. World, **16**: 703.
Acominatus, Michael, Archbishop of Athens. Fraser, **104**: 526.
Aconite, Indian. Hogg, **4**: 304.
Acoustic Improvement of Large Halls. Ecl. Engin. **22**: 153. — Am. Arch. **7**: 78.
Acoustic Mechanism. (D. Brewster) J. Frankl. Inst. **15**: 354.
Acoustic Properties of Buildings. Ecl. Engin. **22**: 369.
— Effect of Motion of Air in Auditorium on. (W. W. Jacques) J. Frankl. Inst. **106**: 390.
Acoustic Repulsion. (V. Dvorák) Am. J. Sci. **116**: 22.
Acoustic Transparency and Opacity of the Atmosphere. (J. Tyndall) Nature, **9**: 251, 267. **13**: 72.
Acoustic Unit of Dimensions of Rooms. (F. J. Day) Ecl. Engin. **21**: 405.
Acoustics. So. Lit. J. **3**: 184.
— and Ventilation. (Gen. Scammon) Cath. World, **15**: 118.
— Donkin's. (C. Foster) Nature, **2**: 253.
— Experiments in. (A. M. Mayer) Nature, **6**: 37. Same art. Am. J. Sci. **103**: 267.
— Galileo's Work in. (S. Taylor) Nature, **9**: 169.
— Helmholtz's Sensations of Tone. (S. Taylor) Nature, **3**: 465.
— in Architecture. (A. F. Oakey) Ecl. Engin. **25**: 228.
— Mayer's Discoveries in. (T. Hill) Unita. R. **7**: 371.
— Peirce on. New York R. **4**: 164.
— Phenomena of. (Lord Rayleigh) Nature, **18**: 319.
— Researches in. (A. M. Mayer) Nature, **14**: 318. — (A. M. Mayer) Am. J. Sci. **108**: 81-362. **112**: 329.
See also Sound.
Acropolis of Athens. *See* Athens.
Across the Channel. Lond. Soc. **6**: 150.
Across the Continent. Penn Mo. **1**: 130.
Across the Gulf; a Story. (R. H. Davis) Lippinc. **28**: 59.
Across the Peat-Fields. Cornh. **34**: 489, 570.
Across the Sands; a Tale. Chamb. J. **51**: 371, 397.
Across the Sea. (I. R. Eckart) Canad. Mo. **20**: 199, 381, 531.
Act II. Scene III. Lond. Soc. **19**: 528.
Act and Testimony. Chr. Q. Spec. **7**: 152. — (C. Hodge) Princ. **7**: 110.
Actæon, Fate of. Dub. Univ. **16**: 620.
Acting; Between Tragedy and Comedy. (D. Cook) Once a Week, **11**: 692.
— Natural and acquired. Temp. Bar, **59**: 400.
— Suit the Action to the Word. (D. Cook) Belgra. **45**: 334. Same art. Ecl. M. **97**: 624. Same art. Appleton, **26**: 430.
Actinic Balance. (S. P. Langley) Am. J. Sci. **121**: 187.
Actinium; New Metal. (T. L. Phipson) J. Frankl. Inst. **112**: 464.
Action at a Distance. (J. Clerk Maxwell) Nature, **7**: 323, 341.
Actium, Battle of. Knick. **20**: 35.
Acton, H. Sermons. (G. B. Emerson) Chr. Exam. **42**: 378.
Acton, John Adams. *See* Adams-Acton, John.
Acton, Mass., Churches and Ministers of. Am. Q. Reg. **11**: 392.
Actor, Alloquy of an. Knick. **6**: 216 541.
— London, Forty Years' Recollections of. Bentley, **27**: 481. **28**: 156.

Actor's Conquest; a Tale. (P. Fitzgerald) Belgra. **37**: supp. 54.
Actor's Memories. (W. E. McCann) Lippinc. **3**: 262.
Actor's Story. Lond. Soc. **5**: 209.
Actors. Am. Whig R. **6**: 519. — Blackw. **8**: 508. — Knick. **18**: 207. — So. Lit. Mess. **5**: 17.
— Amateur, Notes on. Once a Week, **13**: 202, 232.
— American, on the Stage. (J. B. Matthews) Scrib. **18**: 321.
— — in England. Dem. R. **19**: 186.
— and Acting. St. James, **19**: 375.
— and Actresses, English. Temp. Bar, **11**: 135.
— — of New York. (J. B. Matthews) Scrib. **17**: 769.
— and Theatricals. Colburn, **6**: 32. Same art. Mus. **3**: 257.
— Anecdotes of. Fraser, **24**: 179.
— at Drury Lane. Temp. Bar, **16**: 540.
— English, in Paris. Colburn, **5**: 259.
— Foreign, in America. (J. B. Matthews) Scrib. **21**: 521.
— — in England. Cornh. **8**: 172.
— French, Notes on Early. Colburn, **53**: 15.
— — A Company of. (J. B. Matthews) Scrib. **16**: 837.
— — Comic. Colburn, **6**: 341. **8**: 341.
— — in the Green Room. Colburn, **4**: 309.
— Galt's Lives of. Mo. R. **125**: 491.
— Great, of 1775. Victoria, **1**: 83–245.
— Instructions to. Dub. Univ. **74**: 452.
— Irish, of 18th Century. Dub. Univ. **62**: 3.
— Life of J. Bernard. Mo. R. **123**: 266.
— Managers, and Dramatists. (Lady Pollock) Temp. Bar, **44**: 331.
— of Queen Anne's Days. Temp. Bar, **53**: 407.
— of Time of Charles II. Temp. Bar, **53**: 554.
— of Time of Garrick. Temp. Bar, **54**: 86.
— Old. (T. P. Grinsted) Bentley, **40**: 95. **46**: 508. — (C. Lamb) Lond. M. **5**: 174, 305. **6**: 349.
— Old and New. (L. C. Davis) Galaxy, **15**: 660.
— — Studies of. Dub. Univ. **62**: 450.
— Religion of. (C. Lamb) Colburn, **16**: 405.
— Sanctity among. Cornh. **15**: 429.
— Social Position of. (E. Yates) Temp. Bar, **8**: 183.
— Some of our. (O. B. Bunce) Galaxy, **5**: 165.
— Strange. (D. Cook) Belgra. **45**: 51. Same art. Appleton, **26**: 267.
— Thespians out of the Cart. Tinsley, **1**: 36.
Actors' Holiday. (M. Lemon) Ev. Sat. **4**: 747.
Actress, Experiences of a strolling. Chamb. J. **56**: 473.
Actresses, Early English. Fraser, **31**: 673.
— Ennobled. (Mrs. Mathews) Bentley, **17**: 594. **18**: 54–601.
— French. Ev. Sat. **15**: 485.
— — Line of. Temp. Bar, **39**: 369.
— Sketches of Famous. Appleton, **20**: 158.
Actress Wife; a Tale. Contin. Mo. **1**: 64, 139.
Actuary's Story. (J. R. Gilmore) Lippinc. **4**: 675.
Acupuncturation, Experiments on, in Paris. Lond. M. **11**: 145.
Ad Meipsum; a Poem. (S. W. Duffield) Putnam, **15**: 49.
Adair, Robert, Career of. Dub. Univ. **75**: 98.
Adalia, in Anatolia, Notes in. (I. Werry) Victoria, **36**: 117.
Adam. (J. W. Thompson) Mo. Rel. M. **7**: 385. — (Dean Buchrucher) Luth. Q. **8**: 244.
— and Eve, and Christ, Biblical Analogy between. Chr. R. **13**: 565.
— and his Sons. (W. Hoffman) Mercersb. **8**: 141.
— Death in, — Life in Christ. (L. J. Fletcher) Univ. Q. **23**: 400.
— Fall of. *See* Fall, The.
— The Historical. (S. H. Giesy) Mercersb. **17**: 325.
— Relation to his Posterity. (S. N. Callender) Mercersb. **5**: 255. — Chr. R. **26**: 438. — (D. F. Fiske) Bib. Sac. **27**: 701.
Adam, Was he the First Man? (E. L. Fancher) Scrib. **2**: 578.
Adam and Eve; a Tale. (L. Parr) Temp. Bar, **58**: 1–433. **59**: 1–433. **60**: 1–433. Same art. Liv. Age, **143**: 731, 804. **144**: 230–755. **145**: 150, 398, 720. **146**: 157, 468, 725. **147**: 150, 301. Same art. Lippinc. **25**: 77–677. **26**: 42–666.
Adam and Eve; a Tale. (R. S. Clarke) Galaxy, **6**: 197.
Adam and Eve at the Agricultural Fair. (B. Auerbach) Scrib. **14**: 481.
Adam and Eve, The New. (N. Hawthorne) Dem. R. **12**: 146.
Adam and Mally; a Story of Scottish Farm-Life. Fraser, **81**: 749. Same art. Liv. Age, **106**: 39. Same art. Ecl. M. **75**: 340. Same art. N. Ecl. **7**: 219.
Adam's Peak, Ceylon. Penny M. **2**: 217.
Adam Cameron's Visit to London. Cornh. **34**: 88, 104, 227.
Adam, Jean. Good Words, **10**: supp. 51.
Adam, R. and J., and their Style. Am. Arch. **9**: 307.
Adam, William, Governor of Madras. (A. G. Sellar) Fraser, **104**: 113. Same art. Liv. Age, **150**: 292.
Adamites. (C. S. Wake) Anthrop. J. **1**: 363.
Adamnán's Vision. Fraser, **83**: 184.
Adams, Charles Francis. Lippinc. **7**: 357. — with portrait, Ecl. M. **68**: 384. — with portrait, Appleton, **8**: 589.
— and Reverdy Johnson. Once a Week, **19**: 348.
— his Struggle for Neutrality. (H. B. Dawson) Hist. M. **19**: 129.
Adams, Miss Hannah. Letters on the Gospels. (J. Sparks) No. Am. **20**: 366. — U. S. Lit. Gaz. **1**: 273.
— Memoirs of. Chr. Exam. **13**: 129. — Am. Mo. R. **1**: 418.
— View of Religions. (S. Willard) No. Am. **7**: 86.
Adams, John, with portrait. (S. G. Drake) N. E. Reg. **11**: 97. — (Geo. D. Budd) Penn Mo. **2**: 325. — Nation, **12**: 293. — Lakeside, **3**: 76. — New York R. **10**: 1.
— at Court of St. James. (E. E. Beardsley) M. Am. Hist. **1**: 649.
— Dr. Bancroft's Funeral Discourse. Worc. M. **2**: 244.
— Correspondence of. Am. Ecl. **3**: 38. — Chr. Exam. **31**: 263. — Quar. **69**: 130. — Niles's Reg. **14**: 364. **15**: 100. — Chr. R. **6**: 557.
— Death of. Ann. Reg. **1**: [225.
— Diary and Autobiography. (A. P. Marvin) New Eng. **11**: 222.
— Eulogies on. (H. Humphrey) Chr. Mo. Spec. **9**: 210, 259. — (E. Wigglesworth) U. S. Lit. Gaz. **5**: 31. — Am. Q. Reg. **1**: 54. — Niles's Reg. **21**: 11.
— Glance at. (H. Flanders) Lippinc. **2**: 261.
— Imaginary Conversation with Jona. Sewall. (E. G. Scott) Penn Mo. **7**: 543.
— Letters of. Hist. M. **4**: 193. — Mus. **44**: 332. — Portfo. (Den.) **33**: 503. — Quar. **69**: 245.
— Services of. (E. Quincy) No. Am. **113**: 187.
— Works of. (E. Everett) No. Am. **71**: 407. — Liv. Age, **31**: 31.
Adams, Mrs. John. Letter to Abbé de Mably. No. Am. **4**: 48.
— Letters of. Chr. Exam. **29**: 245. — (J. G. Palfrey) No. Am. **51**: 362. — Quar. **68**: 469. — Mus. **43**: 484.
— Sketch of. So. R. n. s. **23**: 312.
Adams, John and J. Q., Birthplace of. Appleton, **11**: 527.
Adams, John Quincy. (C. W. Upham) with portrait, Am. Whig R. **1**: 543. — with portrait, Am. Lit. M. **2**: 137. — Mass. Q. **1**: 331. — (A. B. Crane) So. Lit. Mess. **14**: 293. — (J. Floy) Meth. Q. **10**: 197. — West. Law J. **5**: 377. — (M. W. Fuller) Dial (Ch.), **2**: 282.
— Address, July 4, 1821. Niles's Reg. **20**: 326.
— Administration of. Ann. Reg. **3**: 1.

Adams, John Quincy, and Madame de Staël. Lippinc. 8: 95.
— Cincinnati Astronomical Address. Liv. Age, 4: 273.
— declines Chairman of Committee on Manufactures. Niles's Reg. 42: 86.
— Diary of. (G. W. Greene) Nation, 25: 398. — (J. T. Morse, jr.) Internat. R. 10: 97.
— Genealogical Letter of. N. E. Reg. 34: 66.
— Illness and Death of. Liv. Age, 16: 57.
— Inauguration of. Ann. Reg. 1: 29. — Niles's Reg. 28: 8, 19.
— Letter on Politics of 1808. Niles's Reg. 35: 413.
— Letter on Scriptures. Am. Q. Reg. 12: 86.
— Letter to Franklin Association, Baltimore. So. Lit. Mess. 5: 81.
— Life of. Portfo. (Den.) 21: 305.
— — C. F. Adams's. (W. Everett) Atlan. 36: 196. — (E. Quincy) No. Am. 119: 190.
— Memoirs of. Internat. R. 2: 852. — (L. Sabine) No. Am. 85: 1. — (G. W. Greene) Nation, 18: 383. 19: 107. 20: 315. 21: 310. 22: 197, 383. 23: 288. — (C. C. Smith) Unita. R. 2: 152. 3: 457. 4: 267. 5: 390. 6: 599. 8: 666. — O. & N. 10: 508.
— Message, Dec. 5, 1825. Ann. Reg. 1: [9. — Niles's Reg. 29: 233.
— Message, Dec. 5, 1826. Ann. Reg. 2: [1. — Niles's Reg. 31: 233.
— Message, Dec. 4, 1827. Ann. Reg. 4: [1. — Niles's Reg. 33: 235.
— Message, Dec. 2, 1828. Niles's Reg. 35: 234. — Ann. Reg. 4: [15.
— Obituary of. Am. Alma. 1848: 330.
— Poem, Mac Morough. Am. Mo. R. 3: 142. — (F. W. P. Greenwood) Chr. Exam. 14: 22.
— Reception at Cincinnati, 1844. West. Law J. 1: 145.
— Religious Views of. (E. S. Gannett) Chr. Exam. 44: 471.
— Report on Manufactures. Niles's Reg. 44: 204.
— Report on Weights and Measures. No. Am. 14: 190.
— Tariff Report, 1832. Niles's Reg. 42: 231, 244.
— Tariff Speech, Feb. 4, 1832. Niles's Reg. 43: 438.
— Was he a Unitarian? (G. E. Baker) Unita. R. 16: 135.
Adams, Joseph, Memoir of. (C. W. Tuttle) N. E. Reg. 22: 20.
Adams, Nehemiah. Sermon on Injuries done to Christ. (E. B. Hall) Chr. Exam. 30: 345.
Adams, Robert. Narrative of Shipwreck, etc. (J. Foster) Ecl. R. 24: 251.
— Residence in Timbuctoo. (J. Sparks) No. Am. 5: 11, 204. — Ed. R. 26: 383. — Quar. 14: 453. — Mo. R. 82: 26.
— Will of, 1680. N. E. Reg. 9: 126.
Adams, Samuel. (E. H. Gillett) Hours at Home, 2: 389. — (G. A. Simmons) Pennsyl. M. 1: 439. — (G. E. Ellis) Nation, 2: 84. — (G. W. Greene) No. Am. 102: 614. — Anal. M. 3: 231. — (J. B. Moore) Am. Q. Reg. 13: 269.
— Family Record of, 1689 to 1764. N. E. Reg. 8: 283.
— Father of the Revolution. (E. Gray) Harper, 53: 185.
— Last of the Puritans. (S. Burnham) Cong. Q. 11: 1.
— Memoir of, with portrait. (I. N. Tarbox) N. E. Reg. 30: 279.
Adams, Sarah Flower, Poetry of. Ecl. R. 74: 166.
Adams, Thomas. Ecl. R. 115: 533.
— Works of. (E. A. Duyckinck) Putnam, 11: 363.
Adams, W. Adventures in Japan. (C. H. Redhead) Canad. Mo. 8: 477.
Adams Academy. *See* Quincy, Mass.
Adams Family, Genealogy of. (S. G. Drake) N. E. Reg. 7: 39. — (J. A. Vinton) N. E. Reg. 7: 351. — (T. Farrar) N. E. Reg. 10: 89. — (J. Coffin) N. E. Reg. 11: 53. — (A. Sargent) N. E. Reg. 14: 360,
Adams-Acton, John, with portrait. Colburn, 165: 945 1039.
Adamson, Nathan, Narrative of. Lond. M. 6: 152.
Addi, Acts of. (B. H. Cowper) Kitto, 21: 423.
Addington, H. Viscount Sidmouth. *See* Sidmouth.
Addington Genealogy. (T. W. Harris) N. E. Reg. 4: 117.
Addington, Kent, Brasses at. (E. H. W. Dunkin) Antiquary, 1: 100.
Addison, C. G. Knights Templars. Dub. Univ. 20: 197.
Addison, H. R. Dub. Univ. 18: 505.
Addison, Joseph. Fraser, 28: 143, 304. — (C. C. Clarke) Gent. M. n. s. 7: 324. — Lond. Q. 4: 99. — (W. Lyall) Canad. Mo. 15: 411. — Temp. Bar, 41: 319. Same art. Ecl. M. 83: 362.
— Aikin's Life of. (T. B. Macaulay) Ed. R. 78: 193. — Ecl. R. 78: 264. — Mo. R. 161: 261.
— and Steele, Writings of. West. M. 3: 232.
— and his Writings. (H. T. Tuckerman) No. Am. 79: 90.
— Cato, on the Boards. (D. Cook) Once a Week, 5: 72.
— Inedited Letters of. Bentley, 1: 356.
— Life of. (W. B. O. Peabody) No. Am. 64: 314. — Ecl. Mus. 3: 216.
— Man and Writer. Temp. Bar, 55: 33.
Addison County, Vt., History of. Am. Q. Reg. 12: 53.
Adelaide of France. (E. G. Halsey) Potter Am. Mo. 9: 38.
Adelaide, Queen of Sardinia. (E. C. Kinney) Scrib. 1: 524.
— Visit to Court of. Bentley, 31: 639. Same art. Ecl. M. 26: 384.
Adelaide Gallery. London. Penny M. 4: 417.
Adele St. Maur. Land We Love, 1: 52–419.
Adelgitha; a Poem. (T. Campbell) Colburn, 5: 199.
Adeliza, Sister of William the Conqueror. (T. Stapleton) Arch. 26: 349.
Adelsberg, Hungary, Day at. (F. P. Cobbe) Victoria, 2: 202.
— Grotto at. Colburn, 29: 22. — Penny M. 6: 11.
Aden, Ancient Reservoirs of. Chamb. J. 30: 126. Same art. Liv. Age, 59: 190.
— the Gibraltar of the East. Temp. Bar, 60: 389.
— Occupation of. Blackw. 53: 484.
— Three Years in. Once a Week, 14: 263.
— Twelve Hours at. St. James, 13: 449.
Adhesion, Laws of. J. Frankl. Inst. 100: 121.
Adina. (H. James, jr.) Scrib. 8: 33, 181.
Adirondacks, Camping in. (J. Burroughs) Scrib. 15: 68.
— Camp Lou. (M. Cook) Harper, 62: 865.
— Days in. (H. Vane) Harper, 63: 678.
— Glen of. (J. Bonsall) Potter Am. Mo. 10: 401.
— Glimpse of. (L. Rosecrans) Cath. World, 24: 261.
— Headley on. Hogg, 4: 382.
— in August. (A. D. Mayo) O. & N. 2: 343.
— John Brown's Tract. (T. B. Thorpe) Harper, 19: 160. — Knick. 47: 179.
— Journey to. (A. D. Mayo) Unita. R. 4: 511.
— Lakes of. (G. M. Hoppin) Broadw. 2: 263.
— Life in. (Lucy Fountain) Putnam, 14: 669.
— Night-Hunt in. Broadw. 4: 431.
— Raquette Club. (C. Hallock) Harper, 41: 321.
— Saranac Lakes. (T. A. Richards) Harper, 19: 310.
— Shooting in. All the Year, 3: 585.
— Verified. (C. D. Warner) Atlan. 41: 63–755.
— Woods and Waters of. (T. A. Richards) Harper, 19: 454.
— Woods of. (M. H. Merwin) Putnam, 4: 263.
Adjuration, Christ's Teaching on. Bib. R. 6: 226. *See* Oaths; Swearing.
Admeasurement of Shipping. (W. W. Bates) Hunt, 38: 551, 665. 39: 49. 41: 275. *See* Measurement.
Administration, Specialized. (H. Spencer) Fortn. 16: 627.
Administration of Justice; Local Courts. Westm. 36: 58.
Administrations of England and United States compared. Westm. 63: 492.

Administrative Reform in England, 1854. Ecl. R. **102**: 351.
Admiral's Daughter. Sharpe, **24**: 1, 81, 129.
Admiral's Daughters, The. (A. S. Harrison) Once a Week, **6**: 1, 29, 57.
Admiral's Second Wife; a Tale. Chamb. J. **54**: 633–724.
Admirals, English. Cornh. **38**: 36. Same art. Liv. Age, **138**: 241.
Admiralty, English. (S. Osborn) Fortn. **7**: 146.
Admiralty Jurisdiction. (T. H. McCaleb) De Bow, **1**: 179.
Admiralty Law. (A. Benedict) Hunt, **23**: 284.
Admiralty Reform. Macmil. **21**: 193.
Admiralty Islands, Inhabitants of. (H. N. Moseley) Anthrop. J. **6**: 379.
Admiration, Sham, in Literature. (J. Payn) 19th Cent. **7**: 422. Same art. Pop. Sci. Mo. **17**: 48. Same art. Liv. Age, **145**: 165.
Admission Prices, Word on. Chamb. J. **19**: 327.
Admit to Two Boxes. (D. Cook) Belgra. **37**: 341.
Adolphus of Nassau. Dub. Univ. **44**: 613.
Adolphus, John. (J. L. Adolphus) Fraser, **66**: 49.
Adonis, Festival of. (W. M. Nevin) Mercersb. **12**: 86.
Adopted Daughter. (M. H. Parsons) Godey, **21**: 74.
Adorna, Catharine. (F. D. Huntington) Hours at Home, **1**: 293.
Adosinda. (Mrs. H. Smith) Godey, **20**: 174.
Adrain, Robert, with portrait. Dem. R. **14**: 646.
Adrian IV., English Pope. (W. Russell) St. James, **10**: 104.
— and Henry II. U. S. Cath. M. **4**: 657.
— Memoir of. (E. Trollope) Arch. **37**: 39.
Adrian VI., Pope. (C. W. Robinson) Month, **31**: 350.
Adrian; a Tale. Fraser, **66**: 221–761. **67**: 81.
Adriana. (J. Boncœur) Once a Week, **14**: 352–606
Adriatic, Night in. (Mrs. Romer) Bentley, **12**: 582.
Adrien Roux. (D. Costello) Colburn, **79**: 92–484. **80**: 49–321. **81**: 88–466. **82**: 88.
Adrienne's Augusts. Knick. **59**: 68, 136.
Adrift on the World. (K. Cornwallis) Knick. **60**: 285, 381, 484. **61**: 46–542. **62**: 72–554.
Adult Schools. Cong. M. **1**: 15, 76.
Adulteration Acts, History of the. Colburn, **166**: 672. **167**: 99–486.
— of 1872 and 1875. Victoria, **32**: 454.
— Operation of. Once a Week, **27**: 416.
Adulterations, Accum on. Blackw. **6**: 542, 621.
— and their Remedy. Cornh. **2**: 86.
— Detection of. (E. D. Faust) Am. J. Sci. **19**: 70.
— Domestic Chemistry. (A. G. Penn) Lippinc. **10**: 113.
— Hassall on. Colburn, **104**: 167.
— of Food. No. Am. **94**: 1. — Chamb. J. **23**: 273. — Fraser, **52**: 191. — Westm. **91**: 185. — Dub. R. **31**: 589. **39**: 60. — Hunt, **54**: 340. — Dub. Univ. **47**: 78. — Ed. R. **33**: 131. — Knick. **53**: 515. — New Q. **2**: 24. — Once a Week, **2**: 396. — Chr. Rem. **30**: 329. — Ecl. R. **102**: 576. — (A. Wynter) Quar. **96**: 460. Same art. Liv. Age, **46**: 67. Same art. Ecl. M. **35**: 487. — (A. Wynter) Once a Week, **17**: 322. — Penny M. **14**: 71.
— — and Drugs. Fraser, **81**: 718. — Hogg, **15**: 57.
— — — in Germany. (H. von Holst) Nation, **26**: 129.
— of Groceries in England. Hunt, **41**: 652.
— of Wine and Spirits. Lond. M. **19**: 450.
— Science of. Chamb. J. **8**: 76.
See also Food.
Adulteress in the Temple. Kitto, **17**: 65.
Adulterine Bastardy, Law of. Quar. **59**: 62.
Adultery, Speech of Mr. Phillips in a Case of. Pamph. **7**: 87.
— Tebb's Prize Essay on. Quar. **28**: 179.
Advantages of being a cantankerous Fool. (A. K. H. Boyd) Fraser, **74**: 347 Same art. Ecl. M. **67**: 616.
Advent and Christmas in the Breviary. Dub. R. **21**: 273.
Advent, Meditations in. Liv. Age, **76**: 373, 387.
Adventism. *See* Jesus Christ, Second Advent of.
Adventure and Beagle, Voyages of. (Sir J. Barrow) Quar. **65**: 194.
Adventure, The; a Tale. Cath. World, **2**: 843.
— in the Fifteen Acres. Bentley, **9**: 647.
— in a Forest. (J. Payn) Belgra. **37**: 447.
— in Old Ireland. (R. Cunningham) Dub. Univ. **93**: 78.
— in the Snow. (F. Lockley) Lippinc. **4**: 177.
— in Texas. Sharpe, **11**: 282.
— near the Lake of Gers. Sharpe, **12**: 2.
— of Goodwife Egleston. Sharpe, **14**: 148.
— of Rob Roy, 1745; a Poem. (W. Thornbury) Gent. M. n. s. **15**: 159.
— Records of Early English. Ed. R. **152**: 379. Same art. Liv. Age, **147**: 579.
Adventurer, The. (J. Tierney) Sharpe, **20**: 44–257.
— History of an. So. Lit. Mess. **6**: 135, 249, 341.
Adventurers of 18th Century. Appleton, **24**: 52.
— Remarkable. All the Year, **34**: 228–423. **35**: 80–534.
Adventures at Southborne Grange. Dub. Univ. **81**: 226, 336.
— in the Moon. Tait, n. s. **4**: 193.
— in the Wrong House. (R. M. Bird) Godey, **25**: 265.
— of Benjamin Bobbin. (C. Wilson) Bentley, **35**: 525, 619. **36**: 50–495. **38**: 199–618. **39**: 76–199.
— of the Doctor. (K. J. Stewart) So. M. **8**: 407–727.
— of Dr. Brady. (W. H. Russell) Tinsley, **1**: 1–670. **2**: 1–702.
— of a Farce. Colburn, **148**: 15–693. **149**: 111–701.
— of Harry Richmond. (G. Meredith) Cornh. **22**: 257–641. **23**: 99–641.
— of Khodadad. (C. S. Savile) Colburn, **58**: 180, 373.
— of a Lady in search of a Horse. Lond. Soc. **6**: 1–220.
— of a Lady Help. Chamb. J. **56**: 73–103.
— of a Lone Woman. (J. G. Austin) Atlan. **15**: 385.
— of Philip. (W. M. Thackeray) Cornh. **3**: 1–641. **4**: 1–641. **5**: 1–641. **6**: 121, 217. Same art. Harper, **22**: 381–815. **23**: 90–819. **24**: 90–823. **25**: 99–533.
— of a Tale. (Mrs. E. Norton) Bentley, **2**: 511.
— of Three Englishmen and Three Russians in South Africa. (J. Verne) St. James, **30**: 281–645. **31**: 15–662.
— on a Drift Log. (J. Banvard) Putnam, **2**: 187.
Adventurous Investigation. Belgra. **1**: 55.
Adversity and a Gleam; a Poem. Dub. Univ. **13**: 609.
Advertisers and Advertisements. All the Year, **41**: 34.
— and their Disappointments. Temp. Bar, **11**: 551.
— Among the. All the Year, **34**: 485.
— Hints to. Chamb. J. **36**: 161.
Advertising. (G. Wakeman) Galaxy, **3**: 202.
— Age of Veneer. Fraser, **45**: 87.
— and Art. (G. P. Lathrop) Nation, **20**: 342.
— Art of. Ev. Sat. **5**: 732. — Lond. M. **11**: 246.
— as an Art. Chamb. J. **2**: 401. — Tait, n. s. **2**: 575.
— Curiosities of. (W. H. Rideing) Scrib. **20**: 601. — Chamb. J. **15**: 55. — Canad. Mo. **10**: 214.
— Drolleries in. Chamb. J. **55**: 551.
— for a Wife. (D. Costello) Colburn, **82**: 289–442.
— the Grand Force. Fraser, **79**: 380.
— History of. Chamb. J. **52**: 131.
— in New York. All the Year, **32**: 425.
— in Scotland, 1836. Tait, n. s. **3**: 190.
— Modern. Dub. Univ. **49**: 456.
— Philosophy of. Once a Week, **9**: 163.
— Picture, in South America. House. Words, **4**: 494. Same art. Liv. Age, **33**: 82.
See also Puffing.
Advertising System. (A. Hayward) Ed. R. **77**: 1. Same art. Ecl. Mus. **1**: 2.
Advertising Traps. All the Year, **1**: 5, 251.
Advertisements. (A. Wynter) Quar. **97**: 183. Same art. Liv. Age, **46**: 579. Same art. Ecl. M. **36**: 735.

Advertisements, Curious. Chamb. J. **56**: 678.
— Deceptive. Chamb. J. **54**: 70.
— Early. Chamb. J. **40**: 355.
— Early Newspaper. Chamb. J. **9**: 158.
— Extraordinary. Lond. M. **9**: 285. Same art. Portfo. (Den.) **32**: 161.
— Financial. (J. B. Hodgskin) Nation, **9**: 186.
— German. Chamb. J. **48**: 219. — House. Words, **2**: 33.
— Metropolitan. Hogg, **1**: 276.
— Modern. Victoria, **6**: 313.
— Newspaper. (J. J. Belcher) Harper, **33**: 781.
— of the "Times." Chamb. J. **3**: 199. Same art. Liv. Age, **5**: 486.
— Plea for Truth in. Fraser, **62**: 108.
— Queer. Chamb. J. **43**: 210. **44**: 488.
— Some Old. Chamb. J. **43**: 506.
Advertisement Duties. Liv. Age, **31**: 27.
Advertisement Literature of the Age. Colburn, **67**: 111.
Advice. Mo. Rel. M. **8**: 492.
— from a Lady of Distinction. Blackw. **5**: 416.
— to Order. Once a Week, **20**: 163.
Advocacy, Profession of. Cornh. **12**: 105.
Advocates, Moral Responsibility of. Ev. Sat. **10**: 146.
— Practice of. Phillips's Defense of Courvoisier. Liv. Age, **25**: 289.
— Rights and Duties of. Ed. R. **64**: 155. — Brit. & For. R. **2**: 603. — New York R. **8**: 375. — (J. F. Jackson) Knick. **28**: 377. — Ecl. Mus. **1**: 501.
See Law; Legal Profession.
Ægina. Penny M. **2**: 283. — (A. L. Koeppen) Mercersb. **5**: 367.
— Marbles of. (W. H. Pater) Fortn. **33**: 540.
Æneas and Dido. Temp. Bar, **22**: 88.
Æneas Sylvius. *See* Pius II., Pope.
Ænone; a Tale of Slave Life in Rome. Contin. Mo. **5**: 287–619. **6**: 10–610.
Æolic Digamma, History of. (Ugo Foscolo) Quar. **27**: 39.
Aerated Waters. Chamb. J. **9**: 359. — Once a Week, **17**: 80. — Pract. M. **7**: 311.
Aerial Exploration of Arctic Regions. (W. M. Williams) Appleton, **24**: 235.
Aerial Navigation. (W. Pole) Fortn. **35**: 75. Same art. Ecl. M. **96**: 310. — (E. C. Stedman) Scrib. **17**: 566. — Harper, **2**: 168, 323. — (H. Strait) Am. J. Sci. **25**: 15. — (Sir G. Cayley) J. Frankl. Inst. **36**: 132, 202. — Portfo. (Den.) **24**: 324. — West. M. **3**: 354. — Ecl. R. **78**: 51. — Tinsley, **1**: 238. — Lippinc. **10**: 21, 146. — Westm. **48**: 314. Same art. Liv. Age, **16**: 433.
— applied to Scientific Research. (J. Glaisher) Good Words, **4**: 219.
— in France. Cornh. **27**: 336. Same art. Ev. Sat. **14**: 353.
See also Aeronautics; Balloons; Flying-Machines.
Aerial Specters. Nature, **8**: 227.
Aerial Steam Carriage. Colburn, **67**: 544. Same art. Ecl. Mus. **2**: 186, 307.
Aerial Tides. (P. E. Chase) Am. J. Sci. **88**: 226.
See also Air.
Aerial Voyages. Brit. Q. **54**: 302. Same art. Liv. Age, **111**: 387.
Aerolites. (T. M. Hall) Pop. Sci. R. **5**: 407. Same art. Cath. World, **4**: 536. Same art. Ecl. M. **68**: 96. — (J. C. Cremony) Overland, **7**: 32.
— and Meteorolites. Hogg, **8**: 8.
— and Shooting-Stars. (J. Jamin) Canad. J. n. s. **9**: 351.
— and Stars. (W. L. Brown) So. M. **9**: 18.
— Fossil Thunder and Lightning. (G. P. Bevan) Once a Week, **10**: 652.
See also Meteors; Shooting-Stars.
Aerolitics. (N. S. Maskelyne) Am. J. Sci. **86**: 64.
Aerometry. *See* Air-Meters.
Aeronautical Science. (W. Clare) Ecl. Engin. **3**: 113.
Aeronautics. (C. P. Leavitt) Ecl. Engin. **12**: 540. — (R. Gerner) Ecl. Engin. **19**: 439. — (B. W. Ball) Galaxy, **2**: 52. — All the Year, **19**: 281, 300. — Hogg, **6**: 152, 163. — Nat. M. **3**: 160. — Stud. & Intel. Obs. **2**: 205.
— Early. (J. Abbott) Harper, **39**: 145.
— Progress of. (F. W. Brearey) Pop. Sci. R. **15**: 364.
— Real and Fabulous. (Leigh Hunt) Colburn, **48**: 49.
See Aerial Navigation; Balloons; Flying-Machines.
Aeronauts, American. (W. O. Bates) Lippinc. **26**: 137.
Aerostatics. *See* Aerial Navigation.
Aerostation. *See* Aerial Navigation.
Aero-Steam Engine. (R. Eaton) Ecl. Engin. **1**: 1109.
Æschines. Penny M. **2**: 117.
— Ancestry and Education of. (J. R. Boise) Bib. Sac. **23**: 565.
— and Demosthenes. Hesp. **3**: 59.
— and Eloquence. (D. Steele) Meth. Q. **23**: 268.
— Champlin's. (T. D. Woolsey) Bib. Sac. **7**: 426.
Æschylus. (A. De Vere) Cath. World, **22**: 209. — Cornh. **33**: 27. — Dub. Univ. **36**: 155. — Nat. Q. **7**: 1.
— Agamemnon. Blackw. **30**: 350. — (Trans. by T. Medwin) Fraser, **18**: 505.
— — Acting of, at Oxford, 1880. (B. L. Gildersleeve) Nation, **30**: 472.
— — Blackie and Swanwick's Translation. Westm. **84**: 361.
— — Boyd's and Symmons's Translations. Ecl. R. **41**: 31. — Mo. R. **106**: 113.
— — Carnarvon's Translation. Quar. **147**: 533.
— — Felton's. (C. A. Bristed) Knick. **29**: 543. **30**: 260, 325, 374. — (F. Bowen) No. Am. **65**: 239. — (T. Lewis) Knick. **30**: 246. — Am. Lit. M. **1**: 37, 124. — Chr. Exam. **43**: 140.
— — Fitzgerald's. (T. W. Higginson) Nation, **24**: 310.
— — Notes on. (G. T. Adler) Mercersb. **13**: 252, 418, 551.
— — translated. Chr. Rem. **15**: 433.
— — Translation from. Lond. M. **8**: 262.
— and his Tragedies. Penny M. **2**: 18.
— as a Religious Teacher. (B. F. Westcott) Contemp. **3**: 351.
— Blackie's. Dub. Univ. **36**: 672. — Ed. R. **92**: 173.
— Blomfield's. Quar. **25**: 505.
— Butler's. Ed. R. **19**: 477. — Mo. R. **9**: 265. — Ecl. R. **10**: 997.
— Cambridge Edition. Ed. R. **15**: 152, 315.
— Choephoræ. Blackw. **1**: 147. — Westm. **68**: 440. — (Trans. by T. Medwin) Fraser, **6**: 511.
— Dante, and Milton. Tait, n. s. **20**: 513, 577, 641.
— Eumenides; poetical translation. (M. J. Chapman) Blackw. **41**: 386. **45**: 695. — (T. Medwin) Fraser, **9**: 553.
— Herbert's Translations of. (C. C. Felton) No. Am. **69**: 407.
— Hermann's. Ed. R. **100**: 80.
— Lyrical Dramas, Blackie's Translation of. Ecl. R. **92**: 436. Same art. Ecl. M. **22**: 50.
— Meters of, Burney's. Ecl. R. **18**: 152.
— Modern Criticism on. (R. Scott) Quar. **64**: 370.
— Müller's. For. Q. **22**: 407.
— Orestea. (R. Scott) Quar. **70**: 315.
— Persians. (Trans. by T. Medwin) Fraser, **7**: 17.
— Potter's Edition of. Am. Mo. M. **4**: 109.
— Prometheus Bound. Blackw. **7**: 679. — Cornh. **32**: 298. — Penny M. **2**: 2.
— — and Hamlet. Chr. Rem. **17**: 157.
— — poetical translation. Blackw. **7**: 679. — (M. J. Chapman) Blackw. **40**: 721. — (T. Medwin) Fraser, **16**: 209.
— — — Blomfield's. Quar. **5**: 203. — (P. Elmsley) Ed. R. **17**: 211.

Æschylus. Prometheus Bound, Translation of. Dial, **3**: 363.
— Seven against Thebes, poetical translation. (T. Medwin) Fraser, **7**: 437.
— Shakspere, and Schiller. Blackw. **69**: 641.
— Stanley's. Quar. **3**: 389.
— Theology of. (W. S. Tyler) Bib. Sac. **16**: 354.
— Translations of. No. Brit. **16**: 259.
Æsop. Fables illustrated. (J. Hewlett) Colburn, **73**: 13-563. **74**: 70-642. **75**: 68-345.
— — in Chinese. Mo. R. **156**: 413.
Aestel, Observations on. (J. Milles) Arch. **2**: 75.
Æsthetic Culture. (H. N. Day) Am. Bib. Repos. 3d s. **3**: 524. — (C. A. Alexander) Knick. **24**: 103. — (C. Z. Weiser) Mercersb. **18**: 365.
— of Athens. (W. S. Tyler) Bib. Sac. **20**: 152.
Æsthetic Evolution in Man. (Grant Allen) Pop. Sci. Mo. **18**: 339.
Æsthetic Faculty, Topffer on. N. Ecl. **1**: 355.
Æsthetic Influence of Nature. (S. Tyler) Chr. R. **21**: 1.
Æsthetical Criticism applied to Works of Art. Ecl. Mus. **3**: 113.
Æsthetical Study of Art. Brit. & For. R. **14**: 512.
Æsthetics. Chr. R. **26**: 585. — Am. Church Mo. **3**: 442. — Am. Presb. R. **10**: 26.
— Comparative. (V. Lee) Contemp. **38**: 300.
— Fechner's. (J. Sully) Mind, **2**: 102.
— French. (E. Dowden) Contemp. **1**: 279.
— Greek Philosophy of Taste. (Sir D. K. Sandford) Ed. R. **54**: 39.
— Hegel's. Brit. & For. R. **13**: 1.
See also Art, Philosophy of.
— in Common Life. (H. Pearce) Dub. Univ. **84**: 579.
— Moral. (J. Atkinson) Princ. **24**: 38.
— Notes on. (P. G. Hamerton) Portfo. **10**: 120-194.
— of Human Character. (J. Sully) Fortn. **15**: 505.
— Physiological, Grant Allen's. (J. Sully and Grant Allen) Mind, **2**: 387. — (W. James) Nation, **25**: 185.
— Plea for. Art. J. **16**: 74.
— Practical. Brit. Q. **71**: 82.
— Science of, Is there a? (G. S. Hall) Nation, **29**: 380.
— Vischer's. (B. Sears) Bib. Sac. **16**: 469.
Æstheticism, Modern. Mr. Cimabue Brown on the Defensive. Belgra. **45**: 284.
— — Gospel of. Nation, **33**: 357.
Æstivation and its Terminology. (A. Gray) Am. J. Sci. **110**: 339.
— Variation in. (W. J. Beal) Am. Natural. **11**: 257.
Æthelwold's Benedictional; MS. of 10th Century. (J. Gage) Arch. **24**: 1.
Æther. *See* Ether.
Æthiopia. *See* Ethiopia.
Ætna, Mt. *See* Etna, Mt.
Ætna, Classical Poem, Munro's Edition of. (J. Davies) Contemp. **8**: 535.
Affair of the Red Portefeuille. Lond. Soc. **16**: 481.
Affair of the Villa. (W. J. Stillman) Overland, **3**: 230.
Affair Simpson; a Story. Fraser, **102**: 743.
Affectation. So. Lit. Mess. **1**: 365.
— Male and Female. Fraser, **14**: 440.
— Thoughts on. (J. Foster) Ecl. R. **5**: 142.
Affectations, Feminine. Ev. Sat. **6**: 59.
Affections, Doctrine of. Am. Bib. Repos. 3d s. **2**: 445.
— Edwards on. Chr. R. **6**: 492.
— Immortality of. (C. Follen) Chr. Exam. **8**: 115.
— Religious. Chr. Obs. **2**: 337, 596.
Affirmations. Cath. World. **15**: 77, 225.
Affirmative, The. (L. Knatchbull-Hugessen) Macmil. **22**: 47. Same art. Liv. Age, **105**: 784.
Affixes. (W. H. Browne) So. M. **8**: 501.
— to English Words. (E. Schuyler) Nation, **1**: 283.
Afflicted, Manual for. (F. W. P. Greenwood) Chr. Exam. **15**: 153.
Afflicting Providences, Merciful Design in. Chr. Obs. **45**: 265.
Affliction. Chr. Obs. **11**: 203. **52**: 727.
— Sanctifying Efficacy of. Chr. Obs. **38**: 145, 209.
Afghanistan. (H. W. Bellew) Cornh. **6**: 708. — Blackw. **49**: 281. **56**: 133. **126**: 601. — Dub. Univ. **19**: 645. — Quar. **78**: 249. — Fraser, **26**: 493, 505. — Ed. R. **150**: 587. — Geog. M. **1**: 1. **5**: 256. — Nature, **19**: 40. — Penny M. **11**: 324, 361. — Mo. R. **159**: 164.
— Ancient Buddhist Remains in. Fraser, **101**: 189.
— and the Afghans. (W. F. Butler) Good Words, **20**: 39.
— and Herat. Blackw. **95**: 462.
— and India, 1843. Blackw. **52**: 100.
— and Scinde, 1845. Westm. **41**: 521.
— Blunder in, 1850. Chamb. J. **17**: 118.
— Bolan Pass. Geog. M. **5**: 301.
— Border of. Blackw. **118**: 60. Same art. Liv. Age, **126**: 283.
— British, Mischievous Activity in, 1871. (J. W. S. Wyllie) Fortn. **13**: 278.
— Captivity of English in. Tait, n. s. **10**: 512.
— Coins and Antiquities of. For. Q. **29**: 275.
— English in, 1841. Dem. R. **12**: 629.
— Ethnology of. (A. H. Keane) Nature, **21**: 276.
— Expedition to, 1840. Blackw. **47**: 241.
— Ferrier's Travels in. Ed. R. **105**: 266.
— in 1872. Ed. R. **138**: 245.
— in 1881. Westm. **115**: 172.
— Mohan Lal in, 1847. Blackw. **60**: 539.
— Native Gentleman of. All the Year, **43**: 487.
— Notes on. (E. Clarke) Macmil. **39**: 171.
— Passes of. Geog. M. **5**: 277.
— Poetry of. Westm. **78**: 278.
— Races and Rulers of. Fraser, **100**: 534.
— Refugees from, Two. (H. S. Edwards) Macmil. **29**: 232.
— Russian Advance on, 1870. (J. W. S. Wyllie) Fortn. **12**: 585.
— Lady Sale's Journey in. Ecl. M. **2**: 225.
— Succession in, 1879. (E. Bell) Fortn. **21**: 824.
— Through. All the Year, **43**: 469.
— Tribes of. Westm. **92**: 438.
— War in, 1838-39. Dub. Univ. **57**: 530. — Dub. R. **12**: 386. — Mus. **38**: 287. **40**: 119.
— — Havelock on. Mo. R. **153**: 195.
— — Outram on. Mo. R. **152**: 587.
— War in, 1841-43. Dub. Univ. **19**: 645. **20**: 327, 459. **21**: 125. — Tait, n. s. **10**: 370-521. — Chr. Rem. **5**: 606.
— — British Overthrow in. Mus. **45**: 619.
— — Causes of. Mo. R. **159**: 413.
— — Disasters in. Brit. & For. R. **14**: 384. — Westm. **39**: 475. — Mo. R. **161**: 109.
— — Evacuation of Afghanistan. Blackw. **53**: 266. — Ecl. Mus. **2**: 195.
— — Greenwood's Campaign in. Mo. R. **164**: 143.
— — Gen. Nott's Service in. Quar. **78**: 463.
— — Results of. Blackw. **50**: 161.
— War in, 1852. Dub. Univ. **44**: 297. — Fraser, **44**: 537. — Brit. Q. **15**: 220.
— — Kaye's History of. Quar. **91**: 11. — New Q. **1**: 18.
— War in, 1879-80. (M. Williams) Contemp. **34**: 261. — (R. D. Osborn) Contemp. **36**: 193. **38**: 434. — (H. James, jr.) Nation, **27**: 298. — (E. L. Godkin) Nation, **28**: 44, 64. **31**: 152. — (S. W. Williams) New Eng. **38**: 95. — Brit. Q. **69**: 157. — Dub. R. **84**: 95. (W. Minto) 19th Cent. **5**: 132.
— — and Sir Stafford Northcote. (M. E. G. Duff) Fortn. **31**: 131.

Afghanistan, War in, Candahar Campaign, 1880. Ed. R. **152**: 578. — Nation, **31**: 89.
— — Crisis of 1878. (H. E. Rawlinson) 19th Cent. **4**: 969. — Macmil. **39**: 369.
— — Imbroglio of 1878. (M. Maccoll) Gent. M. n. s. **21**: 653.
— — Martial Law at Cabul. (F. Harrison) Fortn. **32**: 767. **33**: 435.
— — Ministerial Misstatements on. (Duke of Argyll) Contemp. **37**: 492.
— — Note-Book of a Staff Officer. Blackw. **127**: 364, 464.
— — Rawlinson on. (A. C. J. Gustafson) Internat. R. **6**: 443.
— — Reflections on, Sept. 1880. (Sir A. Hobhouse) Fortn. **34**: 381.
— — Relations with England preceding. Westm. **111**: 111.
— — Results of. (Sir H. C. Rawlinson) 19th Cent. **6**: 377. — (R. D. Osborn) Nation, **29**: 23, 55, 222.
— — Situation in 1879. (R. D. Osborn) Nation, **29**: 343. — Nation, **30**: 24.
— — Situation in February, 1880. (Sir H. C. Rawlinson) 19th Cent. **7**: 197.
— — Stewart's March from Candahar to Cabul. Macmil. **44**: 53.
— — Viceroy and the Amir in 1879. Brit. Q. **69**: 157.
Afoot. Blackw. **81**: 434-711.
Africa. Blackw. **49**: 109. — (Mrs. Petherick) Blackw. **91**: 673. — Sharpe, **13**: 221. — Mus. **41**: 370. — Meth. Q. **36**: 5.
— Adams's Voyages to. (Sir J. Barrow) Quar. **29**: 508.
— Address on. (D. Livingstone) Ecl. M. **63**: 373.
— Ali Bey in. Colburn, **3**: 1.
— Amu Darya River, Cause of its Change of Course. (H. Wood) Nature, **11**: 229.
— — Expedition to. Nature, **11**: 29.
— — Region of. (N. P. Barbot de Marny) Geog. M. **2**: 362. — (H. Wood) Geog. M. **3**: 22.
— and the Africans. (E. W. Blyden) Fraser, **98**: 178. Same art. Sup. Pop. Sci. Mo. **3**: 385.
— and Arabia, Boteler's Voyage to. Ed. R. **61**: 342. — Mo. R. **137**: 153.
— Andersson's Explorations in. (B. J. Wallace) Am. Presb. R. **10**: 493. — Harper, **14**: 289.
— — Lake Ngami. Bentley, **39**: 611.
— — Okovango River. (A. H. Guernsey) Harper, **24**: 28.
— Antiquities of, Ortholithic. (A. H. Rhind) Arch. **38**: 252.
— — Ruined Cities in. Liv. Age, **76**: 280.
—, Arabia, and Madagascar, Surveys of. Quar. **50**: 121.
— Back Window in. (G. A. Sala) Belgra. **12**: 293.
— Baldwin's Travels in. (A. H. Guernsey) Harper, **26**: 577.
— Beechey's Expedition to Coast of, 1821-22. Ecl. R. **47**: 329.
— Blameless Ethiopian. (J. Hutton) Belgra. **4**: 225.
— Blockade of Coast of. Westm. **52**: 500.
— Books on. Ecl. R. **121**: 128.
— Browne's Travels in, 1792-98. Ecl. R. **5**: 385, 483.
— Burckhardt's Travels in. (E. Wigglesworth) No. Am. **40**: 477.
— Caillie's Travels in. For. Q. **6**: 97.
— Cameron's Journey across. (A. H. Guernsey) Harper, **54**: 866. — (H. James, jr.) Nation, **24**: 209. — Brit. Q. **65**: 426. Same art. Liv. Age, **133**: 259. Same art. Ecl. M. **88**: 654. — Chamb. J. **54**: 214. — Nature, **13**: 202. **15**: 277. — Canad. Mo. **12**: 31. — Geog. M. **1**: 177.
— Cameron, Vernon, and Livingstone in. (A. J. H. Crespi) Colburn, **159**: 57.
Africa, Central. (J. H. Speke) Blackw. **86**: 339, 674. — Blackw. **89**: 440. — (Sir J. Barrow) Quar. **31**: 445. — Ed. R. **141**: 209. — Chamb. J. **19**: 13. **53**: 365, 374. — Quar. **42**: 450. — (E. de Laveleye) Sup. Pop. Sci. Mo. **1**: 146. — Mo. R. **144**: 39.
— — Adventures in. Chamb. J. **26**: 157. Same art. Liv. Age, **51**: 145.
— — Alexander's Discoveries in. Tait, n. s. **5**: 727.
— — Sir S. Baker's Explorations in. (S. S. Conant) Harper, **50**: 233. — Ed. R. **124**: 151. — No. Brit. **44**: 368. — (J. T. L. Preston) So. R. n. s. **2**: 330. — Penn Mo. **6**: 436.
— — Barth and Livingstone on. (D. C. Gilman) New Eng. **16**: 347.
— — Barth's Travels in. *See* Africa, Northern and Central.
— — Bowditch's Mission to Ashantee. Portfo. (Den.) **22** 216.
— — Burton's Gorilla-Land. Appleton, **15**: 225, 258.
— — Burton's Lake Regions of. (C. Nordhoff) Harper, **21**: 622. — Brit. Q. **32**: 389. — Liv. Age, **66**: 489. — Theo. & Lit. J. **13**: 642.
— — Douville's Travels in. For. Q. **10**: 163, 541.
— — Du Chaillu's Travels in. Ed. R. **114**: 212. — Quar. **122**: 406. Same art. Liv. Age, **93**: 675. — (Sir D. Brewster) No. Brit. **35**: 219. — (C. H. Brigham) No. Am. **93**: 574. — Harper, **38**: 164. — (A. H. Guernsey) Harper, **40**: 201. — (B. J. Wallace) Am. Presb. R. **10**: 146. — Colburn, **122**: 186. — Liv. Age, **70**: 3, 306. — Lond. Q. **17**: 73. — New Q. **10**: 451.
— — Early History of. Mus. **42**: 334.
— — Geography of, with map. Blackw. **19**: 687.
— — Geology of East. (J. Thomson) Nature, **23**: 103.
— — Col. Gordon in. Ed. R. **154**: 546. — Nation, **33**: 97.
— — Gorilla Country of. Ecl. R. **113**: 578.
— — Heroes of. Dub. Univ. **78**: 694.
— — illustrated. (L. P. Brockett) Appleton, **5**: 121, 164.
— — laid open, 1864. Colburn, **130**: 127.
— — Lake Region of. (D. C. Gilman) New Eng. **21**: 14. — Colburn, **130**: 253.
— — Latest Travels in, 1881. Month, **42**: 183, 447.
— — Letters from. (G. Schweinfurth) Nature, **3**: 215.
— — Livingstone's Travels in. Quar. **138**: 498. — Harper, **16**: 304. — Ecl. R. **106**: 505. — (W. M. Reynolds) Evang. R. **10**: 130. — Am. J. Sci. **99**: 14. — Geog. M. **2**: 14. — Liv. Age, **52**: 769. — Irish Q. **7**: 1165. — So. Lit. Mess. **26**: 134. — Tinsley, **11**: 59. — Theo. & Lit. J. **10**: 637. — Brit. Q. **27**: 105.
— — Livingstone's Last Expedition. (A. H. Guernsey) Harper, **32**: 709.
— — Livingstone's Last Journals. (S. S. Conant) Harper, **50**: 544. — Nature, **11**: 142, 182.
— — Livingstone's Second Expedition. Chr. Obs. **66**: 520.
— — Livingstone's Work in. Nature, **1**: 72, 240. **9**: 444.
— — Long's Naked Truths. Nature, **14**: 521.
— — Missions in. *See* Africa, Missions in.
— — Mungo Park's Mission to, 1805. (J. Foster) Ecl. R. **22**: 205. — Quar. **13**: 120.
— — Nyassa Lake, Country round. (A. Bellville) Geog. M. **5**: 76.
— — Progress of Discovery in, 1877. Colburn, **160**: 503.
— — Recent Researches in, 1857. Nat. R. **5**: 21.
— — Recent Travels in, 1862. Dub. R. **51**: 428.
— — Recent Travels in, 1881. (G. C. Noyes) Dial (Ch.) **2**: 94.
— — Richardson's Mission to. (G. E. Ellis) Chr. Exam. **54**: 469. — Ecl. R. **98**: 163.
— — Richardson's and Barth's Expeditions, 1850. Westm. **62**: 280.

Africa, Central, Schweinfurth's Travels in. (E. L. Godkin) Nation, 19: 184. — (H. S. Conant) Harper, 48: 772. 49: 16. — Internat. R. 2: 112. — Nature, 9: 340. — Month, 21: 257. — Canad. Mo. 6: 439.
— — South. (A. G. Knight) Month, 34: 14.
— — Stanley in Lake Region of. Geog. M. 5: 145. — (E. King) Scrib. 5: 105.
— — Stanley's Through the Dark Continent. Ed. R. 147: 166. — (J. R. Young) Harper, 57: 667. — Nature, 14: 373. 18: 175. — Lond. Q. 51: 313. — Lond. Soc. 34: 449. — Geog. M. 3: 245.
— — Stanley's Voyage down the Congo. (A. H. Guernsey) Appleton, 19: 130.
— — Thomson's Travels in. (F. A. Edwards) Gent. M. n. s. 26: 347. — Nature, 24: 353. — Nation, 33: 156.
— — To Usambara and back. (J. Thomson) Good Words, 22: 36.
— Civilization of. Ed. R. 72: 241. — (J. McQueen) Blackw. 20: 872. — Blackw. 21: 596. — Westm. 15: 507. — Mus. 42: 53.
— — and the Cotton Trade. (J. P. Thompson) New Eng. 19: 829.
— Clapperton's Second Expedition to. (Sir J. Barrow) Quar. 39: 143. — Westm. 11: 69. — Ecl. R. 49: 161. — Mo. R. 118: 215. 121: 286. — Mus. 14: 506. — U. S. Lit. Gaz. 4: 214.
— Coast of, Life on. Chamb. J. 43: 801.
— Colonization in. (W. G. T. Shedd) Bib. Sac. 14: 622. — For. Q. 9: 145. — Internat. M. 3: 397.
— — by the "Friends of the African." Quar. 82: 153. *See* Colonization; Liberia; Sierra Leone.
— Commerce with. Fraser, 43: 30. Same art. Liv. Age, 28: 410.
— Condition of. De Bow, 24: 300.
— Corry's Account of. Chr. Obs. 6: 806.
— Cumming's Hunter's Life in. *See* Africa, South, Cumming's.
— Debt to; the Hope of Liberia. (A. N. Bell) Am. Church R. 36: 85.
— Denham's Travels in. Colburn, 16: 497. — Ecl. R. 43: 404.
— Denham and Clapperton's Travels in. Westm. 5: 331. — Lond. M. 15: 217. — Meth. M. 49: 380.
— Discoveries in. Quar. 109: 496. Same art. Liv. Age, 69: 541. — Quar. 17: 299. — (Sir J. Barrow) Quar. 33: 518. — (D. Ansted) Macmil. 4: 63. — Ecl. R. 27: 297. — Irish Q. 7: 504. — Mo. R. 85: 126. 110: 18. — Am. Meth. M. 9: 339.
— — History of. House. Words, 2: 400.
— — Old and New. (J. Gerard) Month, 34: 454.
— — Progress of. Penny M. 8: 41, 54.
— — Recent, 1826. Ed. R. 44: 173.
— — —, 1858. (C. H. Brigham) No. Am. 86: 530. — Dub. R. 44: 158. 45: 168.
— — —, 1863. (J. K. Wight) Princ. 35: 238.
— — —, 1878. (J. Gerard) Month, 32: 385. — Geog. M. 5: 188.
— — Results of. (Sir R. Alcock) Macmil. 37: 85. — Temp. Bar, 9: 108.
— Du Chaillu's Travels in. *See above* Africa, Central.
— Early Expeditions to. Meth. M. 58: 116.
— East, Burton's First Footsteps in. Blackw. 80: 489. — Dub. R. 41: 27. — New Q. 5: 442.
— — Equatorial. Lond. Q. 40: 311.
— — Isaac's Travels in, 1836. Mo. R. 140: 416.
— — Krapf's Travels in. No. Brit. 33: 268. Same art. Ecl. M. 51: 224.
— — Krapf and McLeod's Travels. Colburn, 19: 344.
— — Lake Regions of. Colburn, 120: 100.
— — Livingstone's Travels. Westm. 85: 178.
— — McLeod's. Brit. Q. 31: 328. Same art. Ecl. M. 50: 459.

Africa, East, Recent Discoveries in. Lond. Q. 15: 30.
— — Travels in. (C. H. Brigham) No. Am. 92: 326. — (Sir J. Barrow) Quar. 58: 1. — Ecl. M. 2: 534. — For. Q. 33: 43.
— Eastern Coast of, Commerce with. Hunt's, 16: 29.
— Echoes from. (E. W. Blyden) Meth. Q. 40: 88.
— Equatorial. (E. B. Boggs) Am. Church R. 31: 60. — (E. Wentworth) Meth. Q. 40: 232.
— Exploration and Mission Work in. (F. Arnold) Brit. Q. 72: 389.
— Explorers and Organizers of. Lond. Q. 57: 104.
— Explorers of. (W. W. Reade) Nation, 4: 377. — (L. Oliphant) No. Am. 124: 383.
— Future of, Civilization in. (G. Rawlinson) Princ. n. s. 8: 171.
— — Stanley's Discoveries and. Ed. R. 147: 166. Same art. Sup. Pop. Sci. Mo. 2: 488.
— Geographical Researches in. (G. Smith) Ex. H. Lec. 13: 107.
— Geographical Discovery and Research in, 1863. No. Brit. 39: 357. Same art. Liv. Age, 79: 553.
— Geography of. Blackw. 31: 201.
— German Explorations in. (W. Wells) Meth. Q. 32: 77.
— Gold Coast of. *See* Gold Coast.
— Hareem of. Cornh. 23: 726.
— Himadu, or Snowy Mountains of. Colburn, 127: 127.
— Holub's Travels in. Nature, 24: 35, 58.
— Interior of. (Sir J. Barrow) Quar. 31: 445. — Ed. R. 49: 127.
— — Robert Adams's Account of. *See* Adams, Robert.
— Journal in. (J. C. Brent) Knick. 32: 412. 33: 116, 206, 334. 34: 127, 227, 300. 35: 105, 377.
— Journey across. (V. L. Cameron) Good Words, 17: 417–626. Same art. Liv. Age, 130: 176–629. Same art. Ecl. M. 87: 223–588. — (V. L. Cameron) Geog. M. 3: 141.
— Ladies and Slaves in. Victoria, 19: 447.
— Laird and Oldfield's Expedition into. Ed. R. 66: 326.
— Lander's Travels in. Meth. M. 55: 415. — Am. Meth. M. 15: 39.
— Languages of. Month, 43: 1.
— Livingstone's Travels in. *See* Africa, Central.
— M'Queen's Geographical Survey of. Mo. R. 153: 487.
— Matabele Tribes of. (A. Campbell) Canad. Mo. 9: 18.
— Missionary Enterprise in Equatorial. (A. Bushnell) Good Words, 2: 623.
— Missionary Explorations in Central. (R. Babcock) Chr. R. 22: 422.
— Missionary Labors in South. (R. Moffat) Tait, n. s. 9: 528, 597. — Ecl. R. 74: 269.
— — Moffat's. Brit. Q. 14: 106. — Lond. Q. 41: 40. — Mo. R. 158: 343.
— Missionary Travels in South. Quar. 13: 309. 27: 364.
— — Livingstone's. Colburn, 111: 432.
— Missions in. Mo. Rel. M. 28: 83. — Chr. Rem. 4: 636.
— — Episcopal. (H. R. Scott) Am. Church R. 30: 304.
— — in Central, Catholic. Dub. R. 84: 182. 88: 394. 89: 144.
— — — Openings for. (S. J. Douglass) New Eng. 26: 425.
— — — Oxford, Cambridge, and Dublin. Macmil. 4: 163. Same art. Liv. Age, 70: 182.
— — in South. Ecl. R. 94: 591. — Brit. Q. 14: 106. — Lond. Q. 41: 332.
— — — Catholic. Dub. R. 11: 1. — (A. Wilmot) Month, 33: 76. 36: 379.
— — in West. (E. W. Blyden) Fraser, 94: 504. Same art. Liv. Age, 131: 423. — (J. L. Wilson) Princ. 30: 436.
— — on East Coast. (C. G. Hodson) Cath. World, 26: 411.
— — Prospects of. Mercersb. 12: 626. — (A. Caswell) Bap. Q. 9: 364.
— Mollier's Travels. Mo. R. 95: 269.
— Moral Discoveries in. N. Ecl. 6: 162.

Africa, Moral Discoveries in, Notes on. (L. C. Johnson) N. Ecl. 7: 590.
— Mtesa, King, and his Country. (W. F. Ainsworth) Colburn, 158: 167.
— Nachtigall's Travels in. Geog. M. 2: 178. — (E. G. Ravenstein) Geog. M. 1: 277.
— Negro and White Man in. Nat. Q. 9: 135.
— Night of Terror in. Temp. Bar, 43: 68. Same art. Liv. Age, 124: 36. Same art. Ecl. M. 84: 194.
— North. Mo. R. 97: 487. 115: 478.—Colburn, 120: 127.
— — and France. (Earl De la Warr) 19th Cent. 10: 448.
— — and the Niger, Lyons's. (Sir J. Barrow) Quar. 25: 25. — Ecl. R. 34: 23.
— — Sir S. Baker's Travels in. Appleton, 12: 737, 769, 803.
— — Barth's Travels in. Ed. R. 109: 337. — Brit. Q. 26: 382. — Ecl. R. 108: 207. — (D. Curry) Meth. Q. 21: 287. — Colburn, 110: 127-348. 114: 107. — Liv. Age, 59: 368. — Ecl. M. 43: 101, 206. — Lond. Q. 13: 354. — Putnam, 10: 296. — New Q. 7: 253. — Theo. & Lit. J. 11: 294. 13: 390.
— — Day in. (T. B. Aldrich) Harper, 63: 241, 346.
— — French in. Nation, 32: 363. 33: 228.
— — Languages of. Prosp. R. 3: 461.
— — M'Queen on. Colburn, 4: 476.
— — Military Life in. Blackw. 68: 415.
— — Sketches in. Peop. J. 4: 143, 191. 5: 41.
— Northeast, Tribes and Languages in. (C. T. Beke) Ed. New Philos. J. 47: 265.
— Old Maps of. Nature, 18: 149. Same art. Liv. Age, 138: 56.
— Owen's Voyages to. Ecl. R. 58: 181.
— Physical, Historical, and Ethnological. (R. Williams) Univ. Q. 25: 164, 439. 27: 5. 28: 412. 29: 334. 30: 25.
— Pinto's Journey across, 1881. Nature, 24: 215. — Nation, 33: 53.
— Portuguese Discovery in. Colburn, 137: 490.
— Portuguese in. Cornh. 25: 408. Same art. Ecl. M. 78: 651. — Westm. 16: 243.
— Prince Pückler Muskau in. (R. Ford) Quar. 59: 133.
— Races of. (V. L. Cameron) Anthrop. J. 6: 167. — (E. W. Blyden) Fraser, 88: 178. — (E. H. Sears) Chr. Exam. 41: 33. — Ecl. R. 58: 480. — Irish Mo. 9: 299.
— — Ancient. (C. Morris) Nat. Q. 23: 296.
— — — Heeren on. Ecl. R. 55: 225.
— — and their Religions. Chr. Rem. 47: 261.
— — of Equatorial. Westm. 76: 137.
— — of South. Penny M. 7: 73, 84. — (A. Wilmot) Month, 27: 66.
— — — Ethnological Curiosities from. Once a Week, 21: 201.
— — — Fritsch's. (E. B. Tylor) Nature, 9: 479.
— — of West. (J. L. Wilson) Princ. 27: 193.
— — — Natives of old Calabar. (W. F. Daniell) Ed. New Philos. J. 40: 313.
— — — People of the Gold Coast, Characteristics of. (W. F. Daniell) Ed. New Philos. J. 52: 289. 53: 120, 333.
— — Sons of Ham. Cornh. 27: 581. Same art. Liv. Age, 117: 748.
— Reade's Travels in. (C. Nordhoff) Harper, 29: 281. — Anthrop. R. 2: 123.
— Romer in; Mayo's Kaloolah. Blackw. 66: 172.
— Savage Life in. Ho. & For. R. 1: 129.
— Sketches in, Pringle's. Mo. R. 134: 520.
— South. Ed. R. 149: 534. Same art. Liv. Age, 141: 515.—Quar. 55: 39. 108: 120. 147: 552.—Westm. 23: 415.—Tait, n. s. 24: 178. — Meth. M. 59: 517. — Am. Q. Reg. 5: 46.—Mus. 16: 424. Ecl. M. 9: 225.
— — Along the Coast of. (A. W. Drayson) St. James, 12: 80.
Africa, South, and Wm. Shaw. Lond. Q. 44: 266.
— — Barrow's Travels in. Ed. R. 4: 443. 8: 432.
— — Basuto Parliament. (F. B. Glanville) Gent. M. n. s. 17: 428.
— — Boers at Home. (J. J. Muskett) Contemp. 39: 506.
— — British. (J. A. Froude) Fortn. 32: 449. — Ecl. R. 97: 49.
— — — and England. (E. D. J. Wilson) 19th Cent. 2: 230.
— — — Colonial Life in. All the Year, 26: 48.
— — — Government Policy in. (Lord Blachford) 19th Cent. 6: 264. — Quar. 143: 105. — (Earl Grey) 19th Cent. 5: 583.
— — — History of. Westm. 91: 307.
— — — in 1876. Ed. R. 145: 447.
See also Cape Town; Good Hope, Cape of.
— — British Power in. (J. J. Talbot) Penn Mo. 10: 605.
— — Burchell's Travels in. Ecl. R. 35: 505. 39: 493. — Lond. M. 10: 277. — Mo. R. 99: 1, 143. 105: 113.
— — Campbell's Travels in, 1812. (J. Foster) Ecl. R. 22: 135, 305.
— — Colonists and Savages in. (A. G. Knight) Month, 40: 60.
— — Confederation of. Lond. Q. 56: 1.
— — Cumming's Hunter's Life in. Quar. 88: 1. — (F. Bowen) No. Am. 71: 359. — Blackw. 68: 231. — Ecl. R. 92: 476. Same art. Ecl. M. 22: 25.—Chamb. J. 14: 72. — So. Lit. Mess. 17: 199. — Hogg, 5: 412. — Internat. M. 1: 218.
— — Diamond Fields of. *See* Diamonds.
— — Dutch in, Cruelty of. Meth. M. 44: 127.
— — Explorations in. (D. Curry) Meth. Q. 22: 62.
— — Few Months in. (E. Napier) Colburn, 82: 21-456. 83: 51-497. 84: 69-430.
— — Four Years in. Westm. 12: 232.
— — Galton's Explorations in. Liv. Age, 38: 225.
— — Gold Fields of. Colburn, 143: 489. *See also* Gold.
— — Holub's Travels in. Nation, 32: 428.
— — How to get out of Difficulties in. (F. R. Statham) Fortn. 35: 285.
— — in 1880. (Earl Grey) 19th Cent. 8: 933.
— — Irrigation in. Chamb. J. 55: 141.
— — Latrobe's Visit to, 1815-16. Chr. Obs. 19: 243. — Ecl. R. 28: 401.
— — Letters from. (Lady Barker) Lippinc. 17: 226-755. 18: 96-728. 19: 109. — Ecl. M. 86: 411, 542. 87: 621.
— — Letters from. Colburn, 17: 481. 19: 69.
— — Lichtenstein's Travels in. (Sir J. Barrow) Quar. 8: 374. — Ed. R. 21: 50. — Ecl. R. 17: 369.
— — Life and Scenes in. Westm. 69: 1.
— — Livingstone's Travels in. Chr. Rem. 35: 130. — Fraser, 57: 118. — Tait, n. s. 24: 721. 25: 40. — Liv. Age, 55: 802. 56: 1. — Lond. Q. 9: 431. Same art. Ecl. M. 43: 317. *See also* Africa, Central.
— — Management of Native Tribes of. (B. Key) Contemp. 39: 516.
— — Men and Brutes of. (J. H. Perkins) No. Am. 68: 265
— — Methuen's Wanderings in. Liv. Age, 11: 153.
— — Moodie's Ten Years in. Mo. R. 137: 66.
— — Past and Present. (W. F. Butler) Good Words, 17: 52-231.
— — Phillips's Researches in. Ecl. R. 47: 385, 527. — Mo. R. 116: 506.
— — Physical Features of. Brit. Q. 12: 338.
— — Pringle and Moodie on. (Sir J. Barrow) Quar. 55: 74.
— — Progress of Discovery in, 1849. Colburn, 90: 336.
— — — 1852. Tait, n. s. 19: 419. Same art. Liv. Age, 34: 359.
— — — 1853. Hogg, 10: 426.
— — Recent Affairs in Pondoland. (F. A. Edwards) Gent. M. n. s. 22: 490.

Africa, South, Resources and Natives of. Westm. **111**: 386.
— — Rose's Four Years in. Ecl. R. **51**: 31. — Mo. R. **121**: 206.
— — Sketches of. (M. D. Parker) Knick. **36**: 65, 338. **38**: 147, 571.
— — Thompson's Travels in. Colburn, **19**: 385. — Ecl. R. **46**: 129. — Lond. M. **18**: 487. — Westm. **9**: 21.
— — Trollope's Tour in. Lond. Soc. **33**: 369.
— — Tromp on. (E. Lecky) Brit. Q. **72**: 343.
— — Unspoken Speech on. (M. E. G. Duff) Fortn. **36**: 299.
See also Damara; Kaffirs; Zulus; etc.
— Southeast, Lake and Mountain District of. (W. F. Ainsworth) Colburn, **88**: 391.
— — Watering-Place in. Cornh. **16**: 629. Same art. N. Ecl. **1**: 390.
— Southwest, Baines's Explorations in. Colburn, **133**: 74. — Anthrop. R. **4**: 243.
— Sporting in South. Quar. **64**: 188. — Chamb. J. **52**: 503. — For. Q. **34**: 421. Same art. Liv. Age, **4**: 529. — Mus. **36**: 335. *See* Africa, South, Cumming's.
— Statistics of, 1869. Am. J. Educ. **18**: 598.
— Through the Dark Continent in 1720. (W. Minto) Macmil. **38**: 459. Same art. Liv. Age, **139**: 313.
— Timbuctoo Anthology. Colburn, **11**: 22, 121.
— Tracts on. Mo. R. **97**: 412.
— Trade with Colored Races of. (A. Hamilton) J. Statis. Soc. **31**: 25.
— Travel in. (A. R. Wallace) Nature, **8**: 429.
— — Heroes of. Ev. Sat. **12**: 29.
— — Twenty Years of. Blackw. **121**: 682. Same art. Liv. Age, **134**: 27. Same art. Ecl. M. **89**: 137.
— — 300 Years Ago. (P. H. Waddell) Good Words, **9**: 538.
— Travels in. (C. H. Brigham) No. Am. **94**: 174.
— — 1832–34. Mo. R. **143**: 561.
— Travelers in, and their Books. St. James, **33**: 529.
— — Four Great. (H. M. Stanley) Scrib. **6**: 62.
— — Tuckey on. Quar. **18**: 335.
— Weather and Scenery in. (Lady Barker) Ecl. M. **87**: 281.
— West Coast of. (J. Samuelson) Pop. Sci. R. **1**: 100.
— — Bibliography of Languages of. (R. G. Latham) Ed. New Philos. J. **40**: 327.
— — Cruise on. Sharpe, **16**: 275.
— — Dangers of. Portfo.(Den.) **29**: 1.
— Western. Westm. **56**: 1. Same art. Liv. Age, **31**: 449. — Harper, **13**: 161.
— — and Central. (C. Hamlin) Lit. & Theo. R. **4**: 125.
— — British Settlements in. Blackw. **26**: 341. — Mus. **15**: 464.
— — Commerce of. De Bow, **11**: 390. — West. J. **5**: 171.
— — Duncan's Travels in. Ecl. R. **87**: 11.
— — Foulah Tribes of. Meth. M. **57**: 29.
— — Gold Coast of. *See* Gold Coast.
— — Gorilla Country of. (C. Nordhoff) Harper, **23**: 16.
— — Hydrography of. Nature, **15**: 517.
— — Lenz's Sketches from. Nature, **20**: 119.
— — More Palaver about. (N. D. Davis) St. James, **35**: 346.
— — Products of. (W. Robinson) Geog. M. **1**: 22.
— — Slavery, Christianity, and Cotton in. Chr. Obs. **61**: 389.
— — Soolimas in. Meth. M. **48**: 311.
— — Travels in. Mus. **8**: 216. — Mo. R. **108**: 11.
— — Wanderings in. Fraser, **67**: 135, 273, 407.
— Zoölogy and Geography of. Mo. R. **147**: 149.
See also names of countries and localities in Africa, as Abeokuta; Bush; Cape Town; Congo Land; Good Hope, Cape of; Nile; Transvaal; Zulu Land.
African Confessors, A. D. 484. Liv. Age, **61**: 756.
African Cruiser, Journal of. (N. Hawthorne) Dem. R. **16**: 482, 533.
African Handiwork, Schweinfurth's. Nature, **13**: 142.
African Institution. Ed. R. **15**: 485. **16**: 430. **18**: 305. **20**: 58. **21**: 462. — Anal. M. **1**: 1. — Mo. R. **97**: 47
— Reports of, 1810, 11. (J. Foster) Ecl. R. **12**: 641, 721. **14**: 986. — Chr. Obs. **10**: 428. **11**: 729.
— — 1814. (J. Foster) Ecl. R. **21**: 309.
African Kings at Home. Chamb. J. **19**: 379.
African Martyrology. (W. W. Reade) Belgra. **1**: 45.
African Squadron. Ed. R. **92**: 126.
African Treaty with United States, 1822. Niles's Reg. **23**: 109.
African Wanderers, Mrs. Lee's. Dub. Univ. **31**: 252.
After the Accident; a Poem. (Bret Harte) Scrib. **5**: 316.
After the Battle. (F. M. Doherty) Good Words, **14**: 852.
After the Battle of the Wilderness. (R. Rollins) Atlan. **37**: 575.
After the Darkness, Light. (A. Trafton) Scrib. **4**: 562.
After Death; a Poem. Broadw. **5**: 428.
After Dinner. Cornh. **5**: 365.
After the Geographical; a Tale of Borneo. Temp. Bar, **23**: 497.
After long Years; a Tale. Chamb. J. **36**: 377, 395.
After many Days; a Poem. (P. B. Marston) Cornh. **21**: 343.
After the Opera. Lond. Soc. **3**: 39.
After the Pioneer; a Poem. (C. H. Miller) Lakeside, **9**: 343.
After the Season. Lond. Soc. **18**: 334.
After the Storm; a Story. (Mrs. Sale Barker) Victoria, **16**: 37.
After ten Years. (G. Shirley) Sharpe, **32**: 204.
After ten Years; a Poem. Cornh. **22**: 712.
After three Days; a Poem. Temp. Bar, **2**: 566.
After three thousand Years; a Tale. (Jane G. Austin) Putnam, **12**: 38. Same art. Broadw. **8**: 34.
After three Years; a Tale. (V. F. Townsend) Sharpe, **37**: 195.
After two hundred Years. (R. A. Redman) Overland, **15**: 363.
Aga of the Janissaries. Blackw. **31**: 239.
Against all Odds. (F. W. Currey) Dub. Univ. **87**: 1–551.
Against Time. (E. Papendick) O. & N. **10**: 734.
Against Time; a Tale. (A. I. Shand) Cornh. **20**: 471, 621, 734. **21**: 105–731. **22**: 99, 319. Same art. Liv. Age, **103**: 432, 590. **104**: 89–728. **105**: 144–658. **106**: 151–650. **107**: 15.
Agamemnon, Fate of the Family of, on a Fictile Vase. (S. Birch) Arch. **32**: 150.
Agamenticus, Georgiana, or York, Maine. (R. M. Sawyer) Cong. Q. **8**: 141, 267.
Agamist's Holiday. Belgra. **36**: 465.
Agamogenesis. Liv. Age, **58**: 798.
Agassiz, L., with portrait. Ecl. M. **41**: 569. — With portrait. Ecl. M. **61**: 125.—With portrait. Ev. Sat. **11**: 573–594. — Pop. Sci. Mo. **4**: 495. — (R. Bliss, jr.) Pop. Sci. Mo. **4**: 608. — (A. Gray) Nation, **17**: 404. — With portrait. Appleton, **3**: 492. —With portrait. Pract. M. **2**: 321. — Nature, **19**: 573. — All the Year, **43**: 256. — Ecl. M. **23**: 13. — Liv. Age, **62**: 67.
— and Darwinism. (J. Fiske) Pop. Sci. Mo. **3**: 692.
— and J. S. Mill. (A. P. Sprague) Nat. Q. **28**: 234.
— as a Teacher. (G. B. Emerson) Am. J. Educ. **28**: 831.
— at San Francisco. Nature, **6**: 509.
— In the Laboratory with. Ev. Sat. **16**: 369.
— Life and Writings of. Ed. New Philos. J. **46**: 1.
— Natural History of the U. S. (T. Hill) Chr. Exam. **64**: 56.
— on Fossil Fish. Quar. **55**: 234.
— Poem on. (J. R. Lowell) Atlan. **33**: 586.
— Recollections of. (T. Lyman) Atlan. **33**: 221. — (E. P. Whipple) Harper, **59**: 97.
— Tour to Lake Superior. (G. B. Emerson) Chr. Exam. **49**: 9.

Agassiz, L., Works of. Mass. Q. **1**: 96.
Agate, Frederick S. Knick. **24**: 157.
Agates and Agate-Working. (F. W. Rudler) Pop. Sci. R. **16**: 23. Same art. Liv. Age, **132**: 434.
Agatha; a Poem. (Geo. Eliot) Atlan. **24**: 199.
Agatha, St., of Catania, History of. Ecl. R. **121**: 113.
Agathe Marron, a New Caledonian Deportée. Cornh. **30**: 556. Same art. Liv. Age, **123**: 628, 736.
Agathocles; a Novel, translated by Prof. Zander. Dub. Univ. **1**: 483.
Agathon. Blackw. **116**: 760.
Age, Approach of; a Poem. (J. H. Bryant) Putnam, **15**: 560.
— Some Thoughts on. (J. S. Holt) So. M. **8**: 82.
See Growing Old.
Age, The. St. Paul's, **4**: 609.
— a Dramatic Sketch. Lond. M. **16**: 471.
— and Christianity, Vaughan's. Brit. Q. **10**: 525.
— Character of the Present. (E. Fisk) Princ. **2**: 372. **4**: 115. — Am. Bib. Repos. 2d s. **3**: 147.
— Folly of Decrying. Chr. R. **2**: 1. — U. S. Lit. Gaz. **1**: 28, 42.
— Intellectual Aspect of. (A. P. Peabody) No. Am. **64**: 273.
— of Gold; Reading for Children. (D. M. Craik) Macmil. **1**: 293.
— of Honesty. Dub. R. **31**: 589.
— of Veneer. Fraser, **42**: 437. **43**: 147, 472.
— Our Fast. (C. Montague) Potter Am. Mo. **13**: 114.
— Signs and Prospects of. (O. Dewey) Chr. Exam. **36**: 1.
— Spirit of. Knick. **8**: 187.
— that is coming. Peop. J. **5**: 311.
— we live in. Fraser, **24**: 1. — (J. Cumming) Ex. H. Lec. **3**: 357. — (H. Stowell) Ex. H. Lec. **6**: 43.
Ages, Four. Blackw. **114**: 75. Same art. Liv. Age, **118**: 683.
Ages of Faith. Dub. R. **8**: 289.
Aged, Health of the. (H. Martineau) Once a Week, **4**: 119.
Aged Forty; a Poem. (E. Yates) Temp. Bar, **2**: 472.
Agency, Law of. (S. Albee) Hunt, **34**: 706.
— — Principles of. (D. Lord) Hunt, **1**: 325.
Agency System. Lit. & Theo. R. **4**: 280.
Agents, Rights and Duties of. (L. Levi) Bank. M. (N. Y.) **33**: 866.
Agg's Ocean Harp, and other Poems. Anal. M. **13**: 360.
Aggrandizement, Policy of. (Goldwin Smith) Fortn. **28**: 303. Same art. Sup. Pop. Sci. Mo. **1**: 541.
Agincourt, Battle of, Nicolas on. Lond. M. **19**: 299.
— Visit to the Field of. (H. L. Long) Colburn, **83**: 334–478. **84**: 97–466.
Agitation and its Results. (V. Lincoln) Univ. Q. **33**: 348.
Agnas, G. F. Savage Life and Scenes. Ecl. R. **85**: 79.
Agnes Beaufort. Godey, **26**: 169.
Agnes Lee. House. Words, **16**: 36. Same art. Liv. Age, **55**: 23.
Agnes of Sorrento. (H. B. Stowe) Atlan. **7**: 513, 641. **8**: 2–682. **9**: 14–474. Same art. Cornh. **3**: 584, 738. **4**: 106–735. **5**: 107–610.
Agnesi, Maria Gaetana. Argosy, **7**: 374.
— Analytical Institutions. (J. Playfair) Ed. R. **3**: 401.
Agnew, Sir Andrew, Memoir of. Ecl. R. **93**: 145.
Agnewinos. (Latin and English) Fraser, **13**: 639.
Agnostic, Autobiography of an. (B. Thomas) Fraser, **103**: 650. Same art. Liv. Age, **149**: 719.
— Confession of an. No. Am. **129**: 274.
— To an; a Poem. (A. Matheson) Mod. R. **1**: 436.
Agnostic's Apology. (L. Stephen) Fortn. **25**: 840.
Agnostics, Assumptions of. (St.G. Mivart) Fortn. **19**: 718.
— in Parliament and the Press. Month, **40**: 139.
Agnosticism. Canad. Mo. **16**: 665.
— and Atheism. Lond. Q. **54**: 1.
— and the Chinese. (C. A. Stork) Luth. Q. **9**: 371.
Agnosticism and Women. (Mrs. Lathbury) 19th Cent. **7**: 619. Same art. Liv. Age, **145**: 302. (Reply by Miss J. H. Clapperton) 19th Cent. **7**: 840.
— as developed in Huxley's Life of Hume. (J. M'Cosh) Pop. Sci. Mo. **15**: 478.
— in Kant. (A. T. Ormond) Princ. n. s. **6**: 353.
— Poetry *versus*. (J. C. Shairp) Princ. n. s. **5**: 286.
— Science, and Faith. (J. Martineau) Nat. R. **15**: 394.
— Some Difficulties of. (C. P. Mulvaney) Canad. Mo. **17**: 578.
— Thoughts on the Basis of. (W. T. Harris) J. Spec. Philos. **15**: 113.
See Know-Nothing.
Agoult, Countess d', Souvenirs of. Ed. R. **146**: 339.
Agra and its Palaces. Potter Am. Mo. **4**: 295.
— Restoration of Moghul Buildings at. Fraser, **89**: 112. Same art. Ecl. M. **82**: 368.
Agram to Zara. (A. J. Patterson) Fortn. **17**: 359, 509.
Agrarian and Education Systems. So. R. **6**: 1.
Agrarian Contests in Ancient Rome. (R. Beauclerk) Month, **41**: 240.
Agrarianism. (C. C. Hazewell) Atlan. **3**: 393. — (C. S. Roundell) Fortn. **15**: 580.
See Ireland, Land Troubles in; Land.
Agricultural Bank of Ireland. Bank. M. (L.) **3**: 65–301.
Agricultural Chemistry. Westm. **41**: 463. — No. Brit. **3**: 257. — (S. W. Johnson) Am. J. Sci. **82**: 233. — (A. S. Piggott) So. R. n. s. **1**: 430. — (W. H. Browne) So. R. n. s. **3**: 139. — Mo. R. **103**: 493. — Bost. Q. **5**: 371.
— Davy's. Ed. R. **22**: 251. — (T. Young) Quar. **11**: 318. — Ecl. R. **19**: 237.
— Hayward's. Mo. R. **107**: 38.
— in France, Ville's. Nature, **1**: 353.
— Johnson's. Nature, **1**: 426.
— Liebig on. (W. Gregory) Quar. **69**: 329. Same art. Am. Ecl. **4**: 108. — Ecl. M. **6**: 257.
— Squarey on. Mo. R. **157**: 232.
Agricultural Children's Act. (W. C. Taylor) Fraser, **93**: 573.
Agricultural Classes, Condition of. Blackw. **27**: 343.
Agricultural College in 1651. (S. Hartlib) Am. J. Educ. **11**: 191. **22**: 191.
Agricultural Colleges. De Bow, **22**: 495.
— Appropriations for. (D. C. Gilman) No. Am. **105**: 495.
— at Home and Abroad. De Bow, **26**: 250.
— Why so few Students attend. Nation, **30**: 132.
Agricultural Colonies for Young Paupers. Am. J. Educ. **3**: 567.
Agricultural Commerce of United States. (J. H. Lanman) Hunt, **5**: 201.
Agricultural Complaints. Ed. R. **91**: 558.
Agricultural Crisis, 1851. (C. Kingsley) No. Brit. **14**: 85.
Agricultural Development in Old and New World. De Bow, **27**: 495.
Agricultural Education. (T. Baldwin) Nature, **11**: 104. — (M. Tarver) West. J. **10**: 303. — St. James, **26**: 1.
— in Bavaria. Am. J. Educ. **21**: 127.
— in Belgium. Am. J. Educ. **21**: 629.
— in France. Am. J. Educ. **8**: 545. **21**: 545.
— in Ireland. Am. J. Educ. **8**: 567. **22**: 161.
— in Prussia. Am. J. Educ. **21**: 205.
— in Würtemberg. Am. J. Educ. **21**: 339.
— Madison on Professorship of Agriculture. Niles's Reg. **23**: 202.
— Plan of a School for. (J. A. Porter) Am. J. Educ. **1**: 329.
— Schools for, in Saxony. Am. J. Educ. **21**: 307.
Agricultural Encampments. All the Year, **6**: 229.
Agricultural Engineering. Pract. M. **1**: 66.
Agricultural Experiments at Woburn, Eng. Nature, **16**: 129.

Agricultural Experiment Stations. (C. Barnard) Scrib. **21**: 624. — (J. Cheesman) Canad. Mo. **19**: 62.
Agricultural Geology. (W. H. Browne) So. R. n. s. **3**: 139. — No. Brit. **16**: 390.
Agricultural Holdings Bill. (E. Bear) Fortn. **23**: 633.
Agricultural Improvements in the West. (D. Chase) Overland, **4**: 147.
Agricultural Interest and the Ministry, 1851. Blackw. **69**: 368.
Agricultural Labor, Barton on. Ecl. R. **32**: 46.
— Gang System of. Penny M. **12**: 309.
— Market for. Dub. Univ. **1**: 252.
— Question of. Brit. Q. **59**: 421.
Agricultural Laborers. (E. Girdlestone) Macmil. **26**: 256. — Ed. R. **141**: 126. — Fraser, **81**: 427. — Cornh. **9**: 178. **27**: 215, 307. **29**: 686. — Cong. **5**: 400. — St. Paul's, **6**: 31.
— Condition of. Hogg, **10**: 355.
— Congress of, at Leamington, 1872. Cong. **1**: 419.
— Exodus of, from Great Britain. (E. A. Curley) Fortn. **21**: 517.
— Few Words to. Peop. J. **6**: 39, 51, 80.
— Food of. Good Words, **8**: 387.
— in Northumberland, State of. J. Statis. Soc. **1**: 397.
— of Scotland. Fraser, **83**: 641.
— Wages of, in Europe. (T. E. C. Leslie) Fortn. **21**: 705.
— What can be done for? (H. Fawcett) Macmil. **18**: 515.
Agricultural Laborers' Union. (E. Girdlestone) Macmil. **28**: 436. **31**: 160. — (A. J. Wilson) Macmil. **30**: 449. — Brit. Q. **56**: 145. — Lond. Q. **40**: 327.
Agricultural Literature, Ancient. Quar. **87**: 141.
Agricultural Machinery. Pract. M. **4**: 180. **6**: 41.
Agricultural Manufactures. (S. Copland) Canad. J. n. s. **6**: 463.
Agricultural Productions of United States. De Bow, **13**: 295.
Agricultural Prosperity. Dem. R. **28**: 481.
Agricultural Reform, Necessity of. (M. Gross) De Bow, **25**: 144.
— Public Interest in. (W. Bear) 19th Cent. **5**: 1079.
Agricultural School for Girls. Victoria, **34**: 57.
Agricultural Science. (S. W. Johnson) Am. J. Sci. **78**: 71. — (J. P. Benjamin) De Bow, **5**: 41.
Agricultural Shows in England, 1875. Pract. M. **5**: 205, 250.
Agricultural Society, Essex, Mass.; Pickering's Address. Niles's Reg. **15**: 181.
— Royal, of England. Pract. M. **6**: 194.
— — Journal of, 1839. Mo. R. **149**: 27.
— — Meeting of, 1878. (G. E. Waring, jr.) Harper, **58**: 217.
Agricultural Societies. Chr. Rem. **45**: 263.
— and Universities. De Bow, **22**: 495.
— of Virginia. Niles's Reg. **15**: 177. **23**: 260.
Agricultural Statistics. (R. A. Arnold) Fortn. **2**: 431.
— of United States, 1869. Bank. M. (N. Y.) **25**: 705.
Agricultural Strike in England, 1872. Fraser, **85**: 651.
Agricultural Tour in United States and Upper Canada. Barclay's, 1841. Mo. R. **157**: 303.
Agriculture. Quar. **73**: 477. — (J. Sparks) No. Am. **19**: 325. — Blackw. **19**: 287. **46**: 733. — Ox. Prize Ess. **2**: 1. — Dem. R. **40**: 38. — Am. Q. **21**: 1. — (J. R. Burwell) Land We Love, **1**: 24, 146.
— Addresses on. (E. Bates) West. J. **14**: 388. — (G. C. Dixon) West. J. **13**: 393. — (E. Everett, 1857) Ecl. M. **42**: 553. — (J. H. Lathrop) West. J. **11**: 17. — (J. Madison) Niles's Reg. **14**: 345. — (L. J. Minor) West. J. **13**: 166. — (U. Wright) West. J. **11**: 106, 173.
— American. (D. M. Balfour) Hunt, **19**: 477. — Dub. Univ. **56**: 482. — Lond. Q. **7**: 431. — Niles's Reg. **32**: 49. — Irish Q. **9**: 525.
Agriculture and Commerce. Blackw. **23**: 632. — Ed. R. **14**: 50.
— and Draining. Quar. **86**: 79.
— and Education. Dem. R. **37**: 411, 448.
— and the Exhibition of 1851. (H. B. Hall) Colburn, **89**: 78.
— and the French Exhibition of 1856. Canad J. n. s. **1**: 140.
— and Industry. Penn Mo. **7**: 61.
— and Legislation. Ed. R. **14**: 20.
— and Manufactures. Penn Mo. **3**: 512.
— and Prices in England, Rogers on. Brit. Q. **46**: 125. Same art. Ecl. M. **69**: 411.
— and Protection. (J. Western) Lakeside, **3**: 103.
— and Rent. Quar. **37**: 391.
— Application of Chemistry and Geology to. (W. H. Browne) So. R. n. s. **3**: 139.
— Artificial Fertility. All the Year, **13**: 157.
— Beef, Mutton, and Bread. Liv. Age, **43**: 225.
— Chemistry, and Physiology. Brit. Q. **8**: 75.
— Commerce, and Manufactures. Hunt, **3**: 160. — (A. Bradford) Hunt, **1**: 480. — Blackw. **67**: 347.
— — Policy of U. S. Government on. Niles's Reg. **18**: 3.
— Co-operative. O. & N. **3**: 600.
— — Three Experiments in. Fraser, **91**: 529.
— Costaz on. Mo. R. **86**: 469.
— Cultivation of Waste Lands. Quar. **38**: 410.
— Decline of, in Ancient Italy. So. Lit. Mess. **13**: 474.
— Dignity of. Hesp. **3**: 70.
— English. (J. E. T. Rogers) Contemp. **35**: 303. — Ed. R. **123**: 185. — Blackw. **51**: 406. — Penny M. **9**: 33–501.
— — and English Peasants. (G. M. Towle) Harper, **49**: 430.
— — and Foreign. No. Brit. **5**: 157.
— — and Foreign Competition. Fraser, **43**: 236. — Blackw. **67**: 94, 222, 447.
— — and French. Lond. Q. **6**: 289.
— — from 1259 to 1793. Ed. R. **126**: 43.
— — Improving of. Westm. **48**: 1.
— — in 1819, Report on State of. Quar. **25**: 467.
— — in 1821, Distress of. Ed. R. **36**: 452. — Mo. R. **95**: 279, 371. **99**: 79. **121**: 455. — Blackw. **12**: 436, 482, 624. — Westm. **13**: 218. — Pamph. **10**: 395. **17**: 417. **21**: 481.
— — in 1834. Tait, **4**: 132–515.
— — in 1836. Ed. R. **62**: 319.
— — in 1846. Ed. R. **84**: 416.
— — in 1852. Ed. R. **96**: 142.
— — in 1879, Depression of. (W. E. Bear) Fortn. **31**: 253, 435. — (P. T. Quinn) Scrib. **19**: 61. — (Earl of Airlie) Fortn. **32**: 98. — Ed. R. **151**: 1. — (F. Peek) Contemp. **37**: 218.
— — Progress of. Quar. **103**: 390. Same art. Liv. Age, **58**: 163.
— European, Colman's. Chr. Exam. **46**: 281.
— for Southern States, Improved. De Bow, **25**: 395.
— High Farming, Caird's. Blackw. **67**: 447.
— High-Pressure. (R. Jefferies) Fraser, **94**: 193.
— Hints to a Country Gentleman. Blackw. **12**: 482, 624.
— in Connecticut, Humphreys on. Portfo. (Den.) **16**: 385.
— in France. Ed. R. **114**: 348. — Quar. **79**: 202. — Ho. & For. R. **4**: 379. — Penny M. **7**: 105.
— — Progress of. Dub. Univ. **55**: 745.
— in Ireland. Dub. Univ. **83**: 641.
— in Italy. (E. Everett) No. Am. **10**: 49. — (G. P. Marsh) Nation, **2**: 183.
— in Massachusetts. Dial, **3**: 123.
— in Prussia, 1816 to 1875. (A. Delmar) Internat. R. **2**: 339.
— in Reign of Richard II. (W. Bray) Arch. **18**: 281.

Agriculture in Scotland. Ed. R. **24**: 72. — (G. B. Davidson) West. J. **2**: 254, 302. **3**: 29.
— — Progress of. Chamb. J. **24**: 146.
— Influence of, on Manufactures. (E. H. Derby) Hunt, **17**: 547. — (E. H. Derby) West. J. **1**: 73. — Niles's Reg. **17**: 353. **20**: 332.
— Iron Age of. All the Year, **6**: 307.
— Low's Elements of Practical. Mo. R. **135**: 495.
— Moral Lessons of. Mo. Rel. M. **1**: 181.
— Necessities, Competency, and Profits of. Niles's Reg. **15**: 177.
— New and Important Theories in. De Bow, **18**: 195.
— New York Board of. U. S. Lit. Gaz. **4**: 401.
— Outlook of, 1880. Nation, **31**: 127.
— Physical and Social Experiments in. (J. M. Ludlow) Good Words, **16**: 674, 745.
— Practical. Blackw. **57**: 298.
— Practice of. Blackw. **53**: 415.
— Primitive. (A. W. Buckland) Anthrop. J. **7**: 2.
— Principles of. (T. G. Clemson) Land We Love, **2**: 245. — So. R. **1**: 49.
— Profits and Waste of. (G. S. Boutwell) Hunt, **31**: 692.
— Progress of. (N. C. Meeker) Am. J. Educ. **18**: 623.
— Reform in. *See* Agricultural Reform.
— Revolution in, Approaching. Chamb. J. **20**: 291.
— Richardson's Essay on. Mo. R. **86**: 306.
— Scientific. (T. Baldwin) Nature, **13**: 101. — (J. G. Hoyt) No. Am. **89**: 358. — Ed. R. **90**: 357. Same art. Liv. Age, **23**: 417. — Blackw. **51**: 738. — Dub. R. **15**: 52. — Lond. Q. **27**: 285. — Nature, **10**: 199. **20**: 189. — (A. J. Cook) Am. Natural. **15**: 195.
— — and Practical. (D. Lee) West. J. **3**: 318. — Blackw. **65**: 255.
— — Plea for. Macmil. **44**: 70.
— — Progress of. Ed. R. **81**: 89. — Liv. Age, **4**: 675.
— Small Farming. Lond. Q. **13**: 222.
— Steam. Lond. Q. **12**: 55.
— Tropical. De Bow, **20**: 325, 415, 694.
— Unequal. (R. Jefferies) Fraser, **95**: 622.
— U. S. Department of, 1869. Am. J. Educ. **18**: 183.
— — What it should be. Nation, **31**: 373.
— Walker's Report on. (C. Colton) Am. Whig R. **4**: 410.
Agrippa's Reply. (F. Brown) Cong. Q. **19**: 273.
Agrippa, H. C., Magician and Alchemist. Chamb. J. **20**: 340. — Ecl. R. **105**: 467. — Putnam, **9**: 70. — Ecl. M. **40**: 232. — New Q. **6**: 26.
— and the Alchemists. Fraser, **55**: 45.
— on Vanity of the Arts and Sciences. Retros. **14**: 181. — Mus. **10**: 521.
Ague and its Cause. All the Year, **19**: 606.
Aguesseau, H. F. d'. Bentley, **47**: 520.
— and French Jurisprudence. Nat. R. **8**: 441.
— Works of. (H. S. Legaré) So. R. **8**: 399.
Aguilar, Grace, and Modern Judaism. Ecl. R. **107**: 134.
— Grave of. Internat. M. **3**: 513.
Ahasuerus and Kai-Khosru. Kitto, **25**: 385.
— and Artaxerxes of Ezra iv. 6, 7. (E. Biley) Kitto, **37**: 410.
Ahasuerus, the Ever-Living Jew. (F. Paludan-Muller) Liv. Age, **44**: 774. *See* Wandering Jew.
Ahasuerus, the Shoemaker of Jerusalem. Chamb. J. **22**: 390.
Ahmed Agha, the Janissary. (J. A. Johnson) Hours at Home, **9**: 293.
Ahmed Effendi, Resmi, Turkish Historian of War with Russia, 1768–74. (E. Schuyler) Macmil. **42**: 357, 428.
Ahrthal, The, and Mayen. (G. C. Swayne) Once a Week, **12**: 185.
Aht Tribes. Sproat's Studies of Savage Life. (K. R. H. Mackenzie) Anthrop. R. **6**: 366.
Aidé, Hamilton, with portrait. Victoria, **34**: 164.
Aide-de-Camp, Journal of an. Bentley, **60**: 394, 522, 646. **61**: 73.
Aids to Faith. (S. Wilberforce) Quar. **112**: 445. — No. Brit. **36**: 273.
— and Replies to Essays and Reviews. Fraser, **66**: 200.
Aiken, B. Annie Sherwood. Dub. R. **46**: 93.
Aiken, Silas. (J. D. Kingsbury) Cong. Q. **12**: 179.
Aikenhead, Mary, Life of. (H. J. Coleridge) Month, **37**: 48. — Irish Mo. **7**: 422.
Aikin, Dr. John. (Mrs. H. Martin) Fraser, **99**: 615. Same art. Liv. Age, **141**: 562. — (J. L. Taylor) Cong. Q. **9**: 219. — Mus. **4**: 313. — U. S. Lit. Gaz. **1**: 40. — Mo. R. **103**: 30.
Aikin, Lucy, Joanna Baillie, and C. F. Cornwallis. No. Brit. **42**: 327. Same art. Liv. Age, **85**: 598. Same art. Ecl. M. **65**: 270.
— Correspondence with Dr. Channing. (Mrs. C. H. Dall) Unita. R. **2**: 377.
— Letters of. (A. V. Dicey) Nation, **19**: 220. — Theo. R. **2**: 92.
Ailanthine and Ailanthus Silk-Moth. J. Frankl. Inst. **77**: 378.
Aimée; a Tale. (G. H. Peirce) Lippinc. **24**: 557, 707.
Aimée's Sacrifice. (Miss Lutz) Cath. World, **6**: 156.
Aimée's Story. (Ita A. Prokop) Lippinc. **10**: 563, 655.
Aino Cloth, Fabrication of. (D. P. Penhallow) Am. Natural. **14**: 553.
Ainos, or Hairy Men. (H. C. St. John) Anthrop. J. **2**: 248. — (S. C. Holland) Anthrop. J. **3**: 233. — (A. S. Bickmore) Am. J. Sci. **95**: 353, 361.
Ainslie, H. Pilgrim and the Shrine. Westm. **89**: 327.
Ainsworth, Henry. Theo. Ecl. **7**: 225.
Ainsworth, Wm. Harrison, with portrait. Appleton, **8**: 152. — With portrait. Fraser, **10**: 48. — With portrait. Once a Week, **27**: 472.
— Chetwynd Calverley. Colburn, **159**: 93.
— Crichton. Fraser, **14**: 733. — Mo. R. **142**: 53. — Am. Q. **22**: 250.
— Jack Sheppard. Fraser, **21**: 227. — Brit. & For. R. **10**: 223.
— Preston Fight. Colburn, **157**: 65.
Αἰών and Αἰώνιος, Meaning of. (E. S. Goodwin) Chr. Exam. **9**: 20. **10**: 34, 166. **12**: 97, 169. — (M. Stuart) Spirit Pilg. **2**: 405. — (D. M. Knappen) Univ. Q. **4**: 16.
— — as used by Philo Judæus. (H. Ballou, 2d) Univ. Q. **2**: 133.
— and the Resurrection. (T. Abbott) Univ. Q. **26**: 276.
Air, The. All the Year, **12**: 399, 422. — Dub. Univ. **34**: 497.
— Action of, on Alkalic Arsenites. (H. Croft) Canad. J. n. s. **3**: 126.
— and its Component Parts. (C. Bender) Pract. M. **6**: 336.
— and Rain, Smith's. (T. E. Thorpe) Nature, **6**: 325.
— as a Means of Motion. (W. D. Scott-Moncrieff) Good Words, **18**: 401.
— Atmospheric, Ellis on. Ecl. R. **18**: 479, 622.
— Atmospheric Tides. (T. Wise) Scrib. **6**: 186.
— Change of. Lond. Soc. **37**: 435.
— Compressed, Living Force of. Ecl. Engin. **6**: 274.
— — Use of. (D. M. Stanley) J. Frankl. Inst. **94**: 320.
— Compression of. Pract. M. **6**: 137.
— — Method of. (J. P. Frizell) J. Frankl. Inst. **104**: 193. **110**: 145.
— Cooling, Various Systems of. (A. Jonglet) Pract. M. **1**: 450.
— Dense by Day, and Light by Night. So. Lit. Mess. **19**: 727.
— Disease in. (D. A. Gorton) Nat. Q. **30**: 55.
— Filtering. Ecl. Engin. **2**: 374.
— Foul, and Heart Disease. (C. Black) Pop. Sci. Mo. **2**: 183.

Air, Foul, in Mines, and how to live in it. (J. C. Gibbs). Nature, 5: 365.
— Fresh. (E. Lankester) Pop. Sci. R. 3: 6.
— — Give us. (D. M. Craik) Good Words, 2: 38. Same art. Ecl. M. 60: 455.
— — Necessity of, during Sleep. Cornh. 7: 412.
See Air, Pure.
— Friction of, in Mines. (J. J. Atkinson) Ecl. Engin. 12: 209.
— Ground, in its Hygienic Relations. (M. von Pettenkoffer) Pop. Sci. Mo. 11: 280.
— Heated, as Motive Power. (B. Cheverton) J. Frankl. Inst. 55: 365.
— — Elastic Force of. (F. A. P. Barnard) Am. J. Sci. 67: 153.
— in Breathing. Hogg, 8: 353, 377.
— — Amount required. J. Frankl. Inst. 106: 421. — Penny M. 6: 390.
— Life as dependent upon. (W. B. Carpenter) Howitt, 1: 276–355. — (O. Reynolds) Nature, 13: 243. — (M. von Pettenkoffer) Pop. Sci. Mo. 11: 196.
— Liquefaction of. (M. L. Cailletet) J. Frankl. Inst. 105: 128.
— — and Solidification of. (W. N. Hartley) Pop. Sci. R. 17: 155.
— Mechanical Properties of. (J. Bennett) J. Frankl. Inst. 69: 124. *See below*, Air-Engine.
— Moist, Diathermacy of. (J. L. Hoorveg) J. Frankl. Inst. 101: 44.
— — Relation to Health and Comfort. (R. Briggs) J. Frankl. Inst. 105: 10–251.
— Mudie on. Mo. R. 138: 470.
— of Large Towns, Injurious Effects of. (W. Thomson) Ecl. Engin. 20: 488.
— Oxygen in. (E. W. Morley) Am. J. Sci. 118: 168.
— Poisoned. (J. C. Draper) Galaxy, 9: 113.
— Pressure of, and the Human Body. Penny M. 11: 50.
— — and Life. (P. Bert) Pop. Sci. Mo. 11: 316.
— Pure. (R. A. Arnold) Once a Week, 15: 149.
— — in Dwellings. Ecl. Engin. 25: 314. — (T. S. Sozinsky) Potter Am. Mo. 14: 194.
— Supposed Nature of, before Discovery of Oxygen. (G. F. Rodwell) J. Frankl. Inst. 78: 25–404. 79: 194–404. 80: 138–341. 82: 324. 83: 193.
— Temperature of, at Different Heights. Nature, 16: 369.
— Thermal and Mechanical Properties of. (R. H. Thurston) J. Frankl. Inst. 97: 267.
— Transmission of, through Pipes. (R. Sabine) Ecl. Engin. 3: 582. — (W. S. Henson) Ecl. Engin. 4: 205. — (E. Stockalper) Ecl. Engin. 24: 96. — (A. Morin) J. Frankl. Inst. 74: 1.
— Variations of Oxygen in. (E. W. Morley) Am. J. Sci. 122: 417.
— Ventilation and. (W. N. Hartley) Ecl. Engin. 13: 109. — Ecl. Engin. 15: 421.
Air-Bags for raising Vessels. Ecl. Engin. 14: 122.
Air-Brake, Westinghouse. Pract. M. 1: 301, 353.
Air-Compressors. Pract. M. 6: 10.
Air-Engines. J. Frankl. Inst. 5: 314.
— Advantages of. (W. J. M. Rankine) J. Frankl. Inst. 60: 246, 330.
— and Steam Engines, Theory of. (W. J. M. Rankine) Ecl. Engin. 8: 182.
— Compressed. Ecl. Engin. 6: 496, 573. 7: 597. 8: 28.
— — Locomotive for St. Gothard Tunnel. Pop. Sci. Mo. 10: 473.
Air-Meters, Experiments on Cassella's. (C. B. Richards) J. Frankl. Inst. 99: 412.
— Aerometry. (J. Bennett) J. Frankl. Inst. 69: 124–313.
Air-Mothers, The. (C. Kingsley) Ev. Sat. 9: 51.
Air-Pump, Improvement in the Sprengel. (O. N. Rood) Am. J. Sci. 120: 57.
Aird, Thomas. Othuriel and other Poems. Tait, n. s. 7: 318.
— Poems. (G. Gilfillan) Tait, n. s. 16: 101. Same art. Ecl. M. 16: 497. — Ecl. R. 103: 607. Same art. Ecl. M. 38: 499. — Hogg, 2: 257. 15: 449.
— Religious Characteristics of. Blackw. 21: 677.
Airedale College. Am. Q. Reg. 12: 177.
— Historical Sketch of. Cong. M. 14: 581.
Airy, G. B., with portrait. Pract. M. 7: 97. — (A. Winnecker) Nature, 18: 689. — Pop. Sci. Mo. 3: 101.
Airy Lilian; a Story. (F. Tryon) Scrib. 9: 545.
Aïssa, the Fair Circassian, Letters of. Temp. Bar, 54: 563.
— Story of. (W. Besant) Temp. Bar, 32: 41.
Aix and the Falls of Grezy. Irish Mo. 4: 691.
— and its Neighborhood. (Mrs. F. Trollope) Colburn, 70: 554.
— Baths of. Once a Week, 4: 147.
Aix-la-Chapelle. (A. B. Storrs) Cath. World, 15: 795. — Once a Week, 11: 228, 484, 643. — Penny M. 2: 105.
— Legends of. Once a Week, 9: 405, 445, 573.
Ajaccio, Description and History of. Cornh. 18: 496. Same art. Ecl. M. 71: 1513.
Ajunta, Temple Caves of. Fraser, 55: 236.
Akenside, M. (J. Cowen) Colburn, 166: 68.
— Poetry of. (H. T. Tuckerman) So. Lit. Mess. 14: 402.
Akers, Paul. (H. T. Tuckerman) Hours at Home, 2: 525.
Akin by Marriage. (C. W. Philleo) Atlan. 1: 94, 229, 279.
Akin Forever. Liv. Age, 56: 666.
Al Lyn Sahib; a Tale. (F. Percival) Gent. M. n. s. 14: 108–738.
Alabama. De Bow, 12: 56, 148. 18: 21, 154.
— Constitution of. Niles's Reg. 17: 45.
— De Soto in. De Bow, 9: 19.
— Derivation of Name. (A. J. Pickett) Hist. M. 2: 135.
— Geology of. (Prof. Brumby) De Bow, 3: 316.
— — of South. (C. S. Hale) Am. J. Sci. 56: 354.
— — Tertiary Formation of. (E. W. Hilgard) Am. J. Sci. 93: 29.
— Governor's Message, 1818. Niles's Reg. 17: 44.
— Governor's Message, 1825. Niles's Reg. 29: 387.
— Governor's Message, 1828. Niles's Reg. 35: 275.
— Life on a Plantation in. Once a Week, 4: 287.
— Mineral Resources of. De Bow, 18: 677.
— Prairies of. (W. W. M'Guire) Am. Meth. M. 16: 461.
— Statistics of, 1869. Am. J. Educ. 18: 275.
— Travels in. (E. King) Scrib. 8: 385, 513.
— Trip to Northern, 1865. (R. J. Hinton) Nation, 1: 207.
Alabama, Steamer, Cruise of the. All the Year, 11: 138.
— Launch of: a Confederate Poem. (Sir A. Power) Colburn, 168: 498.
Alabama Claims. (E. L. Godkin) Nation, 6: 126. 8: 65, 330. 9: 580. 14: 181, 317. — (C. C. Beaman, jr.) No. Am. 101: 474. — (J. Moncrieff) Ed. R. 135: 549. — (E. E. Hale) O. & N. 5: 121, 377. — (Lord Hobart) Macmil. 23: 224. Same art. Liv. Age, 108: 377. — (T. Lyman) Nation, 8: 209, 373. — (W. F. Rae) Westm. 93: 211. — (G. F. Magoun) Cong. R. 11: 317. — (Goldwin Smith) Macmil. 13: 162. Same art. Liv. Age, 88: 100. — (T. D. Woolsey) New Eng. 28: 575. — Nation, 14: 400. 22: 223. — Ev. Sat. 10: 147. — Am. Law R. 4: 31.
— American Feeling on. (E. Dicey) Fortn. 11: 704. Same art. Ev. Sat. 8: 33.
— and the Canadians. (E. L. Godkin) Nation, 11: 308.
— and Lord Hobart. Ev. Sat. 10: 51.
— Difficulties of Arbitration on. (E. L. Godkin) Nation, 14: 84.
— Distribution of the Damages. (U. H. Crocker) Nation, 17: 271. — (E. L. Godkin) Nation, 16: 36, 70. 18: 390. — (C. C. Nott) Nation, 18: 310. — (A. G. Sedgwick) Nation, 23: 9. 15: 420. 16: 40. 17: 271.

Alabama Claims, England and America. Fraser, **77**: 369.
— German View of. Nation, **8**: 374.
— Gist of the Controversy. (J. N. Pomeroy) Nation, **1**: 549.
— Hobart on. (S. E. Hughes) So. M. **9**: 236.
— Neutral Opinion on. (E. L. Godkin) Nation, **11**: 218.
— Sentiment of. (E. L. Godkin) Nation, **8**: 205.
— Statement of. (G. E. Patten) Lakeside, **7**: 322.
— Sumner on. Nation, **8**: 308.
— — Influence of his Speech in England. (E. L. Godkin) Nation, **8**: 408.
— Unforeseen Results of. (A. G. Sedgwick) Atlan. **41**: 771.
— Unsettlement of. Fraser, **85**: 768.
See Geneva Conference; Treaty of Washington.
Alabamas of the Future. Gent. M. n. s. **4**: 181. Same art. Liv. Age, **104**: 323.
Alabama River, Delta of. (C. S. Hale) De Bow, **3**: 469.
Alabama Slave, The; a Poem. Dub. Univ. **54**: 32.
Alabaster, Cleaning of. J. Frankl. Inst. **2**: 58.
Alabaster Ornaments, Manufacture of. Penny M. **7**: 443.
Alacoque, Marie. (A. Reville) Theo. R. **11**: 138.
Aladdin's Lamp. All the Year, **45**: 326.
Alamo, Fall of. (R. M. Potter) M. Am. Hist. **2**: 1.
Aland Islands. (C. U. C. Burton) Nat. M. **10**: 57.
— Capture of Forts in, 1854. Blackw. **77**: 644.
Alarcon, Garci-Ruiz de. (J. Mew) Gent. M. n. s. **19**: 319.
Alarms, History of. Ed. R. **28**: 59.
— Recent. Ed. R. **33**: 187.
Alarm-Bell of Atri; a Poem. (H. W. Longfellow) Atlan. **26**: 1.
Alarum, The. (G. J. W. Melville) Fraser, **45**: 595.
Alarums and Excursions. All the Year, **27**: 354.
Alasco, and the Play-Licenser. Colburn, **10**: 422.
Alaska. (W. P. Snow) Hours at Home, **5**: 254. — (D. Wise) Meth. Q. **41**: 405. — All the Year, **21**: 177. — Hunt, **58**: 16.
— and its Resources, Dall's. (C. W. Raymond) Nation, **11**: 11. — Ev. Sat. **9**: 381. — (D. Wilson) Canad. J. n. s. **12**: 490. — O. & N. **2**: 360.
— Artist in. (A. H. Guernsey) Harper, **38**: 589.
— Deserted Hearths in. (W. H. Dall) Overland, **13**: 25.
— Ethnography of. (R. G. Latham) Ed. New Philos. J. **40**: 35.
— Glaciers of. (W. P. Blake) Am. J. Sci. **94**: 96.
— illustrated. (R. W. Meade) Appleton, **6**: 91, 123, 366.
— Kodiak and Southern. (W. T. Wythe) Overland, **8**: 505.
— Notes on. (W. H. Dall) Am. J. Sci. **121**: 104.
— Purchase of. Colburn, **140**: 242.
— Resources of. (W. H. Dall) Harper, **44**: 252.
— Russian Church in. (C. R. Hale) Am. Church R. **29**: 402.
— Scientific Expedition to. (G. Davidson) Lippinc. **2**: 467.
— Seal Fisheries in. (O. Howes, jr.) O. & N. **1**: 487.
— Seal Islands of. (C. M. Scammon) Overland, **5**: 297.
— Stikine River. (J. H. Gray) New Dom. **21**: 193, 289.
— Ten Years in. (H. W. Elliott) Harper, **55**: 801.
— What is it worth? (L. Blodget) Lippinc. **1**: 185.
— Whymper's. (R. Giffen) Fortn. **11**: 249. — Chamb. J. **46**: 154.
— Yukon River. (W. H. Dall) O. & N. **1**: 44.
See Sitka; Russian America.
Alaskan Mummies. (W. H. Dall) Am. Natural. **9**: 433.
Alaskans at Home. (W. N. Slocum) Lakeside, **6**: 16.
Alass; a Satire on the Times. So. R. n. s. **9**: 942.
Alastor; a Story. Colburn, **153**: 361–655.
Alastor and Eola; a Sketch. Dub. Univ. **62**: 439.
Alba's Dream; a Tale. (K. O'Meara) Cath. World, **25**: 443, 621, 735.
Albania. Ho. & For. R. **3**: 52.
— and the Albanians. (A. H. Keane) Nature, **22**: 243.
— and its People. (W. H. Green) Princ. **29**: 699.
— and Scanderbeg. Ed. R. **154**: 325.
— Best's Excursions in, 1841. Mo. R. **157**: 371.
— Costumes of. Penny M. **5**: 179, 187, 220.
— Hobhouse's Journey in. Quar. **10**: 175. — (J. Foster) Ecl. R. **22**: 525.
— Holland's Travels in. Ed. R. **25**: 455.
— Hughes on. Ecl. R. **32**: 526.
— Question of, 1880. (C. L. Fitzgerald) Macmil. **42**: 201.
— Shooting in. (R. B. Mansfield) Fraser, **56**: 443.
— With the Ghegs in. (A. Mayhew) Scrib. **21**: 377.
Albanians of South Epirus. Blackw. **129**: 304.
— of Turkey. (H. Skene) Ed. New Philos. J. **46**: 307.
— Turbulence of. (J. H. Skene) Colburn, **88**: 468.
Albano, Plague in. Blackw. **102**: 456.
Albany, Louise M. C., Countess of. Bentley, **51**: 67. — St. James, **12**: 329. Same art. Ecl. M. **64**: 448. — Sharpe, **34**: 137.
— and Alfieri. (A. Hayward) Ed. R. **114**: 145. Same art. Liv. Age, **70**: 451.
Albany, City of. (M. Schuyler) Scrib. **19**: 161. — Harper, **62**: 524. — Hunt, **21**: 50. — Penny M. **6**: 169.
— Capitol at, New. Am. Arch. **1**: 98, 111, 125. **4**: 196. **6**: 206.
— — Designs for. Am. Arch. **1**: 98, 111, 125.
— — Foundations of. (W. J. McAlpin) Ecl. Engin. **21**: 388.
— in 1807. (B. J. Lossing) Harper, **14**: 451.
— Journal of a Voyage to, in 1774. (A. Lott) Hist. M. **18**: 65.
— New Architecture at. Am. Arch. **5**: 19, 28.
— Van Rensselaer Mansion at. (S. B. Clover) Scrib. **6**: 651.
Albany and Susquehanna Railroad War. (C. F. Adams, jr.) No. Am. **112**: 241. — (A. Stickney) No. Am. **112**: 392.
Albany Convention of Congregationalists. (B. J. Wallace) Am. Presb. R. **1**: 630.
Albatross, The. (W. J. Broderip) Fraser, **57**: 713. — Chamb. J. **12**: 277. **55**: 143. — Once a Week, **26**: 234.
Albemarle, Geo. Thomas, Earl. So. R. n. s. **24**: 49. — With portrait. Ecl. M. **70**: 641.
— Memoirs of. Quar. **141**: 466. Same art. Liv. Age, **129**: 771.
— Reminiscences of. Ed. R. **143**: 455.
Albemarle Street, Mornings in. Lond. M. **11**: 618.
Alberico Porro; a Tale. Dub. Univ. **46**: 98, 182, 360, 469, 566.
Alberoni, Giulio, Cardinal. Colburn, **122**: 169.
Albert, Prince, with portrait. Ecl. M. **56**: 283. — Appleton, **13**: 174, 207. — Bentley, **51**: 26. — Blackw. **117**: 114. **120**: 611. **123**: 201. — Ed. R. **147**: 144. — Eng. Dom. M. **3**: 453. — Fraser, **76**: 269. **91**: 209. — Lond. Soc. **12**: 261. — Quar. **111**: 176. — So. Lit. Mess. **18**: 240. — Westm. **34**: 166.
— and Napoleon III. Month, **36**: 453.
— and the Queen. Appleton, **17**: 106.
— as a Composer. Belgra. **8**: 469.
— Character of. (A. H. Japp) Good Words, **16**: 197.
— Death of. Dub. Univ. **59**: 1. — Ecl. M. **55**: 273.
— Early Life of, by Queen Victoria. (A. H. Guernsey) Harper, **35**: 649. — (S. Wilberforce) Quar. **123**: 279. — Blackw. **102**: 375. — Chamb. J. **44**: 628. — Chr. Obs. **67**: 665. — Chr. Rem. **54**: 326. — Ecl. M. **69**: 582. — Lond. Q. **29**: 199. — No. Brit. 47: 189. — Tinsley, **2**: 156.
— Early Years of. Victoria, **9**: 385.
— Eulogy on. Westm. **77**: 225.
— In Memoriam; a Poem. (M. E. Braddon) Temp. Bar, **4**: 180.
— Influence of, on Art. Dark Blue, **1**: 36.

Albert, Prince, Last Years of. Fraser, **101**: 755.
— Life of. Month, **39**: 309.
— — Martin's. Quar. **138**: 107. **145**: 277. **148**: 1.— Ed. R. **141**: 272. **152**: 97.—(W. E. Gladstone) Contemp. **26**: 1. Same art. Ecl. M. **85**: 152.— Westm. **107**: 59. **109**: 430. **112**: 147. Same art. Liv. Age, **143**: 131.—Westm. **114**: 109.—(H. James, jr.) Nation, **20**: 154. **24**: 269.—Temp. Bar, **52**: 596.—Blackw. **127**: 500.—Canad. Mo. **7**: 366. —Cong. **7**: 163.
— Memoir of. Colburn, **57**: 1.
— Memorial of. Temp. Bar, **4**: 570.
— — Story of. All the Year, **36**: 56.
— Music and Poetry of. Colburn, **58**: 425.
— Savings of. Liv. Age, **136**: 55.
Albert Edward, Prince of Wales, with portrait. Ecl. M. **50**: 568.—Galaxy, **9**: 360.
at Oxford. St. James, **13**: 493.
in India. Appleton, **18**: 1.—(A. H. Guernsey) Lond. Soc. **31**: 417.
Marriage of. All the Year, **9**: 107, 180.—Ecl. M. **59**: 75.—Lond. Soc. **3**: 300–338.
— Visit to Canada, 1860. Liv. Age, **66**: 438.
Albert, Charles, Last Days of. Bentley, **57**: 256.
Albert, M., "Ouvrier," Letter to. Westm. **49**: 120.
Albert the Artizan. (G. Barmby) Howitt, **3**: 235.
Albert's Tomb; a Poem. (G. Massey) Good Words, **3**: 479.
Albert Nyanza, Lake, Baker's Explorations of. Dub. Univ. **68**: 101. Same art. Cath. World, **3**: 828.— Quar. **120**: 155.—Chamb. J. **43**: 532.—Colburn, **137**: 369.
— Discovery of. (H. Kingsley) Fortn. **5**: 654.
— Opening of. Colburn, **144**: 719. Same art. Ecl. M. **73**: 199.—Ev. Sat. **8**: 85.
Albertus Magnus vindicated. (A. F. Hewit) Cath. World, **13**: 712.
Albery, James. (P. Wrey) Lond. Soc. **26**: 327.
Albigenses. (H. Ballou, 2d) Univ. Q **7**: 363.—Dub. Univ. **74**: 38.—Lond. Q. **4**: 1.
— and the Troubadours. (W. C. Taylor) Bentley, **19**: 603. **20**: 68, 229.
— and Waldenses, Early Annals of. Chr. Obs. **36**: 403.
— Crusade against. Temp. Bar, **4**: 537.
— Portal Family. Lond. Q. **18**: 390.
— Schmidt's History of. (R. Wheaton) No. Am. **70**: 443.
— Sismondi's History of. Ecl. R. **44**: 399.—Cong. M. **9**: 645.
Albino, On the. Penny M. **9**: 234.
Albion and Rosamond; a Poem. (F. N. Broome) Sharpe, **47**: 15.
Albret, Jeanne d', Q. of Navarre. Chr. Obs. **56**: 173, 269.
Album, An Old-Time. (S. A. Stern) Penn Mo **9**: 104.
— of the Regiment. (E. About) Galaxy, **10**: 335.
Albums. Chamb. J. **50**: 553.
Alcaide, The, of Zalamea. (Calderon, transl. by J. Oxenford) Colburn, **80**: 269.
Alcantara. Penny M. **4**: 336.
Alcesta; or, Reward of Disobedience. (Mrs. M. St. Leon Loud) Godey, **25**: 169.
Alcestis, Fate of. (Mrs. E. F. Ellet) So. Lit. J. **3**: 212.
— Monk's. Quar. **15**: 112.
— Story of. (H. M. Moule) Fraser, **84**: 575.
— Woolsey's. (C. C. Felton) No. Am. **42**: 369.
Alchemist, The; or, The Haunted Tower. Bentley, **64**: 281, 361, 521.
Alchemist's Daughter. (E. W. Contessa) Colburn, **106**: 17–206.
Alchemist's Recipe. (E. Souvestre) So. Lit. Mess. **21**: 689.
Alchemists, The. Cornh. **19**: 713. Same art. Ecl. M. **74**: 580.—Ev. Sat. **8**: 65.—Nat. M. **1**: 308, 402, 496.
— and Paracelsus. Dub. Univ. **51**: 354, 419.
— Cornelius Agrippa and. Fraser, **55**: 45.
Alchemists, The, Last of. Lond. Q. **11**: 156.
— Specimens of. House. Words, **11**: 457–540.
Alchemy. Retros. **14**: 98.—Fraser, **19**: 446.—Tinsley, **23**: 139.
— Ancient and Modern. Colburn, **85**: 425. Same art. Ecl. M. **17**: 206.
— and the Alchemists. Meth. Q. **16**: 468.—Westm. **66**: 279. Same art. Liv. Age, **51**: 385.—(B. A. Brooks) Nat. Q. **27**: 90.—Fraser, **3**: 321.
— — Figuier on. Ecl. R. **105**: 201.
— and Astrology. Quar. **26**: 180.
— and Gunpowder. House. Words, **1**: 135.
— Future of. (C. Froebeck) Pop. Sci. Mo. **4**: 602.
— History of. Chr. Rem. **2**: 249.
— Modern. (A. Walker) Bank. M. (N. Y.) **16**: 407.— *See* Paligenesia.
Alcibiades; a Poem. (T. H. Gibson) Dark Blue, **1**: 226.
Alcibiades, the Boy and Man. (Sir D. K. Sandford) Blackw. **39**: 384, 619. **40**: 33, 309, 470. **41**: 51.
— Dog of. Blackw. **62**: 102.
Alcohol. (L. Mason) Cong. R. **8**: 169.—(T. Wright) Macmil. **11**: 478.
— Action of. (T. L. Brunton) Contemp. **33**: 691. **34**: 157.—Dub. R. **84**: 447.
— Advantages and Disadvantages of. (W. W. Gull) Contemp. **34**: 131.
— and the Vital Principle. (I. Ryder) Canad. Mo. **19**: 625.
— as Food. (B. Carter) Contemp. **34**: 358.—(E. R. Peaslee) No. Am. **82**: 512.—Pop. Sci. Mo. **8**: 103.
— — Medicine or Poison? Cornh. **5**: 707. **6**: 319.
— as Medicine. Dub. Univ. **85**: 230, 324, 467.—(S. A. Abbott) Canad. Mo. **8**: 27.
— Controversy on. Fraser, **78**: 277.
— Conversation on. (C. B. Radcliffe) Contemp. **34**: 345.
— Effects of, on warm-blooded Animals. Nature, **9**: 132.
— Improvements in Manufacture of. Pract. M. **7**: 306.
— Moderate Use of. (Sir J. Paget and J. Bernays) Contemp. **33**: 683. Same art. Sup. Pop. Sci. Mo. **4**: 138.—(J. R. Bennett) Contemp. **34**: 341.
— Natural Production of. (G. Tissandier) Pop. Sci. Mo. **19**: 238.
— Oxidation of, by Ozone. (A. W. Wright) Am. J. Sci. **107**: 184.
— Physiological Influence of. Ed. R. **142**: 145. Same art. Liv. Age, **127**: 259.—(B. W. Richardson) Pop. Sci. R. **11**: 154. Same art. Liv. Age, **113**: 367.—Pop. Sci. Mo. **1**: 219.
— Question of. Month, **35**: 289.—(D. K. Brown) Canad. Mo. **18**: 606.—Canad. Mo. **20**: 488.
— Results of Experience in Use of. (A. B. Garrod) Contemp. **34**: 372.
— Richardson's Lectures on. Cong. **4**: 468.
— Use and Abuse of. Broadw. **7**: 264.
— Use and Effects in the living Body. Westm. **75**: 33. Same art. Liv. Age, **68**: 471.
— Use of, in Diet. (R. T. Edes) Penn Mo. **8**: 582.
— Uses of, in the Animal Economy. Westm. **64**: 104.
— Utility of. (C. Murchison) Contemp. **34**: 136.
Alcoholic Brain-Disorders. (R. Lawson) Sup. Pop. Sci. Mo. **3**: 426.
Alcoholic Drinks. Chamb. J. **58**: 433.—All the Year, **28**: 88.—Once a Week, **23**: 253.
— Does the Bible prohibit? (A. B. Rich) Bib. Sac. **37**: 305, 401.
See Liquors.
Alcoholic Excess, Effects of, on Character. (G. M. Fothergill) Pop. Sci. Mo. **14**: 379.
Alcoholic Intoxication and Ether Drinking. (B. W. Richardson) Sup. Pop. Sci. Mo. **4**: 31.
Alcoholometer. Pract. M. **6**: 324.
Alcott, A. Bronson. Am. J. Educ. **27**: 225.

Alcott, A. Bronson. Conversations on the Gospels. Chr. Exam. **23**: 252.
— on Human Culture. Bost. Q. **1**: 417.
— Record of a School. Knick. **7**: 113.
— Works. Dial, **3**: 417.
Alcott, Louisa M. Victoria, **36**: 4.
— Moods. (H. James, jr.) No. Am. **101**: 276.
— Work. Lakeside, **10**: 246. — (M. Thacher) O. & N. **8**: 104.
Alcott, Wm. A. Am. J. Educ. **4**: 629.
Alcuin, Life of. Chr. R. **6**: 357.
— Teacher of Charlemagne. Am. Presb. R. **11**: 237.
Alcyone; a Poem. So. R. n. s. **5**: 462.
Aldborough Church. (S. Pegge) Arch. **7**: 86.
Aldburgh Coach, The. Chamb. J. **28**: 8.
Aldegonde. *See* Marnix van Sint Aldegonde.
Alden's Rock. (W. Cutter) Godey, **39**: 379.
Alderman Jones in Switzerland. (D. Costello) Bentley, **52**: 331, 441, 637.
Alderman of York. Knick. **59**: 411, 556. **60**: 54, 128, 216.
Alderney, Island of, and its Defenses. Temp. Bar, **4**: 427.
— Season in. St. James, **23**: 314.—(H. J. Stephens) Sharpe, **47**: 63.
— Trip to. Lond. Soc. **40**: 193.
Alderney, Waifs and Strays from. Sharpe, **44**: 236.
Alderney Cows. *See* Cows, Alderney.
Aldershot and Chalons. Fraser, **68**: 190.
Aldershot, Military Training at. St. James, **28**: 639.
— Revisited. All the Year, **43**: 224.
— Sabbath at. (J. R. Macduff) Good Words, **2**: 339.
— Town and Camp at. All the Year, **1**: 401.
Alderson, Edward H. Lond. Q. **12**: 236.
Aldine Press, Prince-Printers of Italy. (C. M. Phillimore) Macmil. **29**: 355, 454. *See* Manutius, Aldus.
Aldona of Kamienez; a Galician Story. Victoria, **35**: 126.
Aldrich, Thomas Bailey. Scrib. **8**: 201. — So. Lit. Mess. **25**: 215.
— Fiction of Atlan. **46**: 695.
— Marjorie Daw. Ev. Sat. **15**: 640.
— Poems. (E. Fawcett) Atlan. **34**: 671. — So. Lit. Mess. **28**: 388.
Ale. All the Year, **20**: 343.
— and Brewing, History of. Temp. Bar, **4**: 467.
— Burton. Ev. Sat. **13**: 697.
— Church, or Holy. St. James, **28**: 129.
— England's National Drink. Ev. Sat. **1**: 409.
Alemanni, Graves of the, at Oberflacht. (W. M. Wylie) Arch. **36**: 129.
Alembert, J. le R., d', Life of. Dub. R. **22**: 190.
Aleppo. Penny M. **10**: 141.
— Evening Party at. Tait, n. s. **25**: 659.
— Picnic at. Chamb. J. **34**: 404.
Alessandro Stradella; a Tale. (E. Polko) Argosy, **17**: 347.
Aleutian Islands. (C. M. Scammon) Overland, **5**: 438.
— and the adjacent Main. Colburn, **140**: 379.
Alewife and the Shad. (J. W. Milner) Harper, **60**: 845.
Alexander the Great. Ed. R. **9**: 40. — (E. A. Freeman) Ed. R. **105**: 305. — (E. S. Creasy) Bentley, **33**: 22, 148, 391. Same art. Ecl. M. **28**: 306, 477. **29**: 162. — Penny M. **8**: 133, 141, 158.
— Character of. Hogg, **10**: 337.
— Expedition to Egypt. Tait, n. s. **16**: 228. Same art. Ecl. M. **17**: 277.
— Expedition to India. (H. T. Prinsep) Ecl. M. **1**: 44.
— Grote's. Nat. R. **3**: 50.
— Moral Estimate of. (F. W. Newman) Fraser, **91**: 667. Same art. Liv. Age, **126**: 3.
— Prize Poem on. Blackw. **7**: 617.
— Successors of, and Greek Civilization in the East. Quar. **149**: 125.
— Tomb of. Ecl. R. **2**: 581.
Alexander I., Czar of Russia, with portrait. Ecl. M. **49**: 414. — Mo. R. **109**: 337. **120**: 375.
— and the Policy of Russia. Brit. Q. **57**: 125.
— and Prince Czartoryski. (M. Heilprin) Nation, **1**: 150.
— Death of. House. Words, **11**: 573. Same art. Liv. Age, **46**: 546.
— Domestic Life of. Sharpe, **12**: 305. Same art. Ecl. M. **22**: 86. Same art. Liv. Age, **28**: 120.
— Last Days of. Sharpe, **14**: 1. Same art. Ecl. M. **6**: 345. Same art. Internat. M. **4**: 233.
— Meeting with Frederick William III. and Francis II. (J. Clifford) Overland, **6**: 446.
— Memoir of, Lloyd's. Ecl. R. **34**: 385.
— Religious Character of. Chr. Obs. **30**: 197, 302.
Alexander II., Czar of Russia. Bentley, **38**: 7. Same art. Ecl. M. **36**: 593. Same art. Liv. Age, **46**: 501. — Lippinc. **6**: 149. — New Q. **4**: 370. — With portrait. Ecl. M. **72**: 752. — No. Brit. **41**: 134.
— Attempted Assassination of. (W. Edgerton) O. & N. **5**: 71.
— Assassination of. (I. Panin) Internat. R. **10**: 594.
— — and its Effect. Am. Cath. Q. **6**: 279.
— Coronation of, with plate. Ecl. M. **68**: 128.
— on the Throne of Poland. Once a Week, **8**: 415, 428, 469.
Alexander VI., Pope. (J. J. Barry) Nat. Q. **26**: 105.
— and his Original Traducers. (J. J. Barry) Am. Cath. Q. **3**: 321.
Alexander Farnese, Sketch of. Blackw. **37**: 957.
Alexander of Abonotichus, a Cagliostro of the 2d Century. (J. A. Froude) 19th Cent. **6**: 551.
Alexander, Archibald. (W. T. Brantley) Chr. R. **21**: 220. — (J. T. Crane) Meth. Q. **22**: 250.
— Death of. Liv. Age, **31**: 551.
— Life of. Theo. & Lit. J. **7**: 684.
— Memoir of. (C. Hodge) Princ. **27**: 133.
— Moral Science of. (E. A. Park) Bib. Sac. **10**: 390.
Alexander, C., Conspiracy against. Am. Law R. **9**: 351.
Alexander, C. F., Poems of. Dub. Univ. **54**: 366. Same art. Ecl. M. **48**: 409.
Alexander, Joseph Addison. Knick. **36**: 421.
— Childhood of. (H. C. Alexander) Hours at Home, **10**: 181.
— Life of. (T. Dwight) New Eng. **29**: 73.—Princ. **42**: 103.
— Reminiscences of, in Travel. (S. H. Cox) Am. Presb. R. **10**: 253.
Alexander, Sir James Edward, with portrait. Colburn, **166**: 513.
Alexander, James W., with portrait. Ecl. M. **48**: 579.
— Letters of. New Eng. **18**: 930.
— Memoir of. (E. Emerson) Mercersb. **12**: 555.
Alexander, L. Congregational Lectures. Ecl. R. **74**: 152.
Alexander, Wm. Waters of Babylon. Ecl. M. **52**: 138.
— and C. F., Poems of. Dub. Univ. **52**: 476.
Alexander, Wm., Bp. of Derry, with portrait. Dub. Univ. **86**: 534.
Alexander the Corrector. Retros. **10**: 25.
Alexandra, Princess of Wales, with portrait. Ev. Sat. **9**: 292.
— England's Welcome to. Once a Week, **7**: 342. — Cornh. **7**: 546.
Alexandra Palace. (J. E. Ritchie) Belgra. **26**: 479.
Alexandra Vase. Art J. **16**: 77.
Alexandria. (W. S. Tyler) Hours at Home, **5**: 481. — Colburn, **13**: 40. — Penny M. **9**: 460. — Colburn, **10**: 348.
— and the Alexandrians. (W. Sewell) Quar. **66**: 64.
— and Cairo. Sharpe, **49**: 101.
— and her Schools, Kingsley on. Ecl. R. **100**: 176.
— and the Overland Route. (G. M. Steele) Meth. Q. **23**: 557.

Alexandria, Christian Schools of. (R. Emerson) Am. Bib. Repos. **4**: 1, 189.—(J. F. Garrison) Am. Church R. **30**: 185.—(J. Tulloch) Good Words, **2**: 613.—No. Brit. **23**: 393.—Dub. R. **55**: 278. Same art. Cath. World, **1**: 33, 721. **3**: 354, 484.—Quar. **2**: 266.
— — Kingsley on. Prosp. R. **10**: 443.
— Damascus, and Jerusalem, Hogg's Visit to. Mo. R. **138**: 369.
— Greek Schools of. (H. J. Warner) Chr. Exam. **80**: 14.
— in the Fifth Century. (Mrs. S. B. Herrick) So. R. n. s. **15**: 186.
— Libraries of. (C. W. Super) Nat. Q. **32**: 37.
— Library of. Ecl. M. **2**: 214. **72**: 496.—(O. Delepierre) St. James, **12**: 432.
— — Burning of. Fraser, **29**: 465.
— Museum of. (C. W. Super) Nat. Q. **36**: 264.
— Old and New. All the Year, **8**: 228.
— Visit to. Hogg, **9**: 313.
— Voyage to. No. Brit. **39**: 429.
Alexandria, Va., Christ Church at. (B. J. Lossing) Potter Am. Mo. **4**: 162.
— Early History of. (L. G. Olmstead) Hist. M. **7**: 213, 244.
— in Colonial Times. (F. H. Lungren) Scrib. **21**: 489.
Alexandrian Christianity. No. Brit. **23**: 393.
Alexandrian Theosophy, The. Prosp. R. **4**: 435.
Alexandrine d' Alopeus, Story of. Month, **5**: 473. **6**: 48.
Alexandrine's Story. St. James, **28**: 508.
Alexis, Grand Duke of Russia, with portrait. Ev. Sat. **11**: 415.
Alfadhel Alderamy; an Arabian Tale. Colburn, **22**: 430.
Alfieri, V. (W. D. Howells) Atlan. **35**: 533.—(F. E. Trollope) Belgra. **40**: 157.—Cornh. **14**: 726. Same art. Ecl. M. **68**: 202.—Penny M. **9**: 434.
— and the Countess of Albany. (M. A. E. Wagner) Galaxy, **20**: 203.—Ed. R. **114**: 145. Same art. Liv. Age, **70**: 451.
— and Schiller. (Mrs. E. F. Ellet) So. Lit. Mess. **2**: 702.
— Filippo. Colburn, **4**: 56.
— Life and Writings of. (E. I. Sears) Nat. Q. **14**: 209.—(R. Southey) Quar. **14**: 333.—(F. Jeffrey) Ed. R. **15**: 274.—(J. T. Headley) Dem. R. **15**: 513.—(F. Jeffrey) Selec. Ed. R. **2**: 143.—Fraser, **43**: 338. Same art. Ecl. M. **22**: 497. Same art. Internat. M. **3**: 229.
— Memoir of. Ecl. R. **11**: 518.
— Political Comedies. Colburn, **5**: 265–334.
— Writings of. Am. Mo. M. **1**: 355.
Alfonso the Wise, King of Castile. (M. Ward) Macmil. **26**: 126. Same art. Liv. Age, **114**: 51.—Fraser, **92**: 627.
Alfonso X. of Spain, and Code of 1256. Am. J. Educ. **27**: 157.
Alford, H. E., Dean. (E. T. Vaughan) Contemp. **16**: 486.—Cong. **2**: 346.
— Life of. Chr. Obs. **73**: 337.
— Poems of. Ecl. R. **123**: 114.—Ed. R. **62**: 297.—Blackw. **39**: 577.—Mus. **28**: 497.
— Sketch of. (R. G. Moses) Bapt. Q. **9**: 235.
Alfred the Great. (W. W. Champneys) Ex. H. Lec. **7**: 327.—(A. G. Knight) Month, **30**: 394. **31**: 12, 201, 316. **32**: 63, 420. **33**: 86, 168.—(Goldwin Smith) Canad. Mo. **2**: 157.—Bentley, **32**: 99.—Fraser, **45**: 74. Same art. Ecl. M. **25**: 308.—Ecl. M. **56**: 24.—No. Brit. **17**: 145.
— and his Times. Nat. Q. **21**: 201.
— as Poet and Man. (J. A. Heraud) Belgra. **7**: 277.
— Ballad from English History. (J. Payn) Colburn, **106**: 304.
— his Tomb at Hyde Abbey. (H. Howard) Arch. **13**: 309.
— Presents to the Cathedrals. (S. Pegge) Arch. **2**: 68.
Alfred the Great, Pauli's Life of. (H. Davis) No. Am. **75**: 208.—Fraser, **45**: 74.
Alfred, Prince, Romance of. Once a Week, **8**: 120.
Alfred Ernest Albert, Prince, Duke of Edinburgh, Marriage of. (W. Senior) Victoria, **22**: 385.
Alfred Deligne's Vindication. Chamb. J. **47**: 625, 645. Same art. Ev. Sat. **9**: 662, 678, 698.
Alfred Walters; a Tale. Fraser, **26**: 245.
Alfric, Earl of Mercia, Seal of. Penny M. **2**: 111.
Algæ, Fossil calcareous. (E. P. Wright) Nature, **19**: 485.
— from a Californian Hot-Spring. (H. C. Wood, jr.) Am. J. Sci. **96**: 31.
— Marine, of North America, Harvey's. (A. Gray) Am. J. Sci. **64**: 1.
— Mode of Growth of some. (J. B. Hicks) Pop. Sci. R. **6**: 1.
— Reproduction in Fresh-Water. (B. D. Halsted) Am. Natural. **11**: 513.
— Structure and Reproduction of. (A. W. Bennett) Pop. Sci. R. **13**: 25.
Algazzali's Confessions. Ed. R. **85**: 340.
Algebra and Arithmetic of the Hindus. Ed. R. **21**: 364. **29**: 141.
— Bonnycastle's Treatise on, 1813. Ecl. R. **19**: 265.
— Bourdon's. Am. Mo. R. **1**: 159.
— Colburn's. U. S. Lit. Gaz. **3**: 241.
— Elements of, Dr. Cumming's. Meth. Q. **5**: 25.
— Euler's Elements of, 1810. Ecl. R. **12**: 864.
— Hackley's. (Dr. Tappan) Meth. Q. **7**: 257.
— Practical System of. Westm. **3**: 275.
— Sherwin's. Bost. Q. **5**: 220.
Algebraic Equations. (G. P. Young) Canad. J. n. s. **5**: 20, 127.
Algebraic Results, Interpretation of. (W. H. Parker) Math. Mo. **1**: 160.
Algebras, Spaces, Logics. (G. B. Halsted) Pop. Sci. Mo. **17**: 516.
Alger Family. N. E. Reg. **29**: 270.
Algeria. Fraser, **52**: 223. Same art. Ecl. M. **36**: 801.—Penny M. **9**: 29, 65.
— Account of. J. Statis. Soc. **2**: 115.
— Adventures in. (W. Russell) St. James, **11**: 24.
— Among the Kabyles. (E. H. Vizetelly) Gent. M. n. s. **11**: 554.
— and Tunis in 1845. Dub. Univ. **28**: 285.
— Arab Christian Villages in. (Lady Herbert) Month, **28**: 297. Same art. Liv. Age, **131**: 500.
— Army of. Bentley, **55**: 150.
— Campaign in. Fraser, **37**: 525.
— Civilization of. Knick. **54**: 191.
— Colonization in. (E. T. Bridges) St. James, **36**: 255, 488.
— — Progress of. (M. B. Edwards) Fraser, **96**: 422.
— French. Quar. **99**: 332. Same art. Liv. Age, **51**: 641.
— French Army in. (C. I. Barnard) Nation, **12**: 28.
— French Commission to, 1833. Westm. **22**: 212.—Mus. **26**: 353.
— French Expedition to. For. Q. **9**: 145.
— French in. Blackw. **50**: 183.—For. Q. **13**: 74.—Mus **24**: 656.—Colburn, **120**: 237, 495. **134**: 253.—Dub. R. **4**: 179.—Hogg, **2**: 335.
— Interiors of. (B. R. Parkes) Once a Week, **4**: 356.
— Invalid's Winter in. (G. MacDonald) Good Words, **5**: 793.
— Jardin d'Essai. Nature, **4**: 447.
— Letters from the South. (T. Campbell) Colburn, **45**: 137. **47**: 159.
— Life in. Ecl. M. **8**: 364.
— Lion Hunters of. Fraser, **69**: 246.
— Past and Present of. For. Q. **37**: 159. Same art. Liv. Age, **11**: 219. Same art. Ecl. M. **8**: 187.
— Past, Present, and Future of. Fraser **52**: 223.

Algeria, Pirates of, Lady's Captivity among. Sharpe, **16**: 65, 139, 215.
— Political State of. Portfo.(Den.) **20**: 384, 416. **21**: 40.
— Proposed Inland Sea in. (J. D. Champlin, jr.) Pop. Sci. Mo. **8**: 665. — Nature, **16**: 353. Same art. Liv. Age, **134**: 764. — (F. H. Smith) So. M. **15**: 410.
— Quivières's Deux Ans en Afrique. Colburn, **111**: 108.
— Regency of. Westm. **20**: 132.
— Rough Ride on Classic Ground. Fraser, **68**: 470.
— Roumi in Kabylia. Lippinc. **11**: 249, 389, 489, 621.
— Rozet's. For. Q. **19**: 1.
— Saint in. Month, **29**: 225, 286.
— Salamé's Expedition to. Blackw. **5**: 81.
— Shaler's Sketches. No. Am. **22**: 409. — U. S. Lit. Gaz. **4**: 74. — Chr. Mo. Spec. **8**: 350.
— Sport in. Colburn, **133**: 240.
— Tunis, and Morocco. No. Brit. **49**: 141.
— Walmsley's Sketches of, during the Kabyle War. New Q. **7**: 325.
— War in, 1853. Liv. Age, **37**: 237.
Algerine Literature of France. No. Brit. **30**: 1. Same art. Ecl. M. **47**: 1. Same art. Liv. Age, **61**: 263.
Algernon Darcy. Colburn, **156**: 1–603. **157**: 1.
Algiers. Blackw. **47**: 217. **60**: 334. — Ecl. R. **111**: 45. — Penny M. **3**: 489. — Ill. M. **1**: 35.
— Algers'Amuse. (E H. Vizetelly) Gent. M. n. s. **11**: 391.
— as it is. (E. H. Vizetelly) Gent. M. n. s. **9**: 258.
— Barber who reigned for a Day. Lond. Soc. **40**: 88.
— Battle of; a Poem. Blackw. **7**: 291.
— Bombardment of. All the Year, **17**: 125. Same art. Ecl. M. **68**: 580.
— Mrs. Broughton's Six Years' Residence in. Tait, n. s. **6**: 399.
— Capture of, 1830. Niles's Reg. **39**: 21, 47.
— Cockpit Royal. All the Year, **15**: 469.
— Com. Decatur's Operations against. Anal. M. **7**: 113.
— Description and Statistics of. Dub. R. **13**: 1.
— Embassy to, 1793. Hist. M. **4**: 262, 296, 359.
— English Slave in. Dub. Univ. **27**: 76.
— Forenoon Call in. Chamb. J. **28**: 39.
— Home Life in. St. James, **7**: 299. Same art. Liv. Age, **78**: 195.
— Hydraulic Works at, 1840. (M. Poirel) J. Frankl. Inst. **29**: 177.
— in the Spring of 1837. Colburn, **54**: 166.
— in 1857. Bentley, **44**: 355.
— in 1865. Cornh. **11**: 426.
— Life in. Once a Week, **12**: 653.
— Lord on. Mo. R. **137**: 311.
— Pananti's Residence in, 1818. Ecl. R. **28**: 472.
— Rambles near. (E. H. Vizetelly) St. James, **32**: 600.
— Sewerage of. (Piarron de Mondesir) J. Frankl. Inst. **69**: 145, 217, 289.
— Six Years' Residence in, 1806–12. Mo. R. **149**: 210.
— The Street of Bab-Azzoun. (G. A. Sala) Temp. Bar, **16**: 188.
— Two Arab Markets. (E. H. Vizetelly) Gent. M. n. s. **11**: 281.
— under the French. Dub. R. **47**: 273.
Algic Languages. (E. Jacker) Am. Cath. Q. **2**: 304.
Algol, The Star. Chamb. J. **47**: 537.
Algonquins, Historical and Mythological Traditions of. (E. G. Squier) Am. Whig R. **9**: 173.
Alhambra, The. House. Words, **19**: 62, 484. — Penny M. **4**: 355.
— and Granada. (S. P. Scott) Lippinc. **27**: 425.
— Glimpse of. (H. Coppée) Appleton, **6**: 683.
— Recollections of. (W. Irving) Knick. **13**: 405. — (W. Irving) Bentley, **6**: 185.
— Reminiscences of. (W. H. Bidwell) Ecl. M. **46**: 434, 581
Al Hariri, Assemblies of. Chamb. J. **45**: 233.

Ali Bey, Travels of. (R. Southey) Quar. **15**: 299. — Mo. R. **82**: 337. **83**: 28. — Anal. M. **8**: 306. — (J. Foster) Ecl. R. **23**: 521.
Ali Pacha, Life of. (E. Everett) No. Am. **18**: 106. — Mo. R. **100**: 281.
— Sketch of. Blackw. **20**: 716.
— Visit to, 1809. Blackw. **13**: 437, 527.
— — 1819. No. Am. **10**: 429.
Alias. (C. Reade) Dark Blue, **4**: 169.
Alice, Princess, Poem on her Death. (Byron Webber) Tinsley, **24**: 130.
— Poem to. (A. Tennyson) 19th Cent. **5**: 575.
Alice; a Poem. Temp. Bar, **4**: 576.
Alice; a Story of Cotton Mather's Time. Dem. R. **25**: 249, 338.
Alice and the Angel. House. Words, **3**: 1.
Alice Blakelock; a Tale. (J. C. Heaviside) Sharpe, **39**: 91.
Alice Gilbert's Confession; a Tale. Temp. Bar, **5**: 253.
Alice Lorraine. (R. D. Blackmore) Blackw. **115**: 269–655. **116**: 42–676. **117**: 44–407. Same art. Liv. Age, **121**: 591–789. **122**: 86–755. **123**: 203–492. **124**: 83–748. **125**: 12–344.
Alice May. (E. Jesse) Bentley, **25**: 469.
Alice Sherwin, and the English Schism. Brownson, **15**: 491.
Alida; or, Town and Country. (O. W. B. Peabody) No. Am. **59**: 434.
Alien Laws. Niles's Reg. **43**: supp. 1. — Am. Alma. **1836**: 85. — Blackw. **116**: 450. Same art. Liv. Age, **123**: 280.
— of England. Ed. R. **42**: 99.
Aliens. Chamb. J. **44**: 598.
Alienation. (A. K. H. Boyd) Fraser, **87**: 67.
Alim; a Story. Irish Mo. **5**: 559, 603, 675.
Alimentation, Economical. Nature, **5**: 45. *See* Food.
Alison, Rev. Archibald, Sketch of. (G. Gilfillan) Hogg, **2**: 193. Same art. Ecl. M. **16**: 568.
— Sermons. Quar. **14**: 429. — (F. Jeffrey) Ed. R. **23**: 424. — Anal. M. **5**: 16. **8**: 424. — Blackw. **2**: 318. — Chr. Obs. **14**: 109.
Alison, Sir Archibald, with portrait. Ecl. M. **28**: 433. — Bentley, **32**: 1. Same art. Liv. Age, **34**: 450. — Blackw. **102**: 125.
— History and Essays. Dub. Univ. **36**: 631. Same art. Ecl. M. **22**: 223.
— History of Europe. *See* Europe; France, Revolution.
— Light Readings in. Colburn, **102**: 406. Same art. Liv. Age, **44**: 155.
— Political Essays. Blackw. **67**: 605.
Alive, and yet Dead: Passages in the Life of a French Convict. Blackw. **130**: 646.
Alive or Dead? (Mrs. A. Fraser) Tinsley, **20**: 446.
Alizarin and allied Coloring Matters, History of. (W. H. Perkin) J. Frankl. Inst. **108**: 88.
Alkali Act, 1863. Ecl. Engin. **14**: 316.
Alkali Trade. (M. M. P. Muir) Nature, **16**: 180.
Alkalies in Minerals. (J. L. Smith) Am. J. Sci. **65**: 234. **16**: 53.
Alkaline and Boracic Lakes of California. (J. A. Phillips) Pop. Sci. R. **16**: 153.
Alkamah's Cave; a Story of Nejd. (W. G. Palgrave) Macmil. **31**: 443, 535. **32**: 73.
Alken, Henry. Blackw. **15**: 219.
All about it; a Tale. (E. W. Thompson) Lippinc. **10**: 458.
All Alone; a Story. (A. Theuriet) Appleton, **24**: 289, 396.
All the Difference. (A. E. T. Watson) Lond. Soc. **28**: 126.
All Fool's Day. (C. Dickens, jr.) Ev. Sat. **7**: 558. — (C. Lamb) Lond. M. **3**: 361.
All Fool's Day; or, The Rival Robbers. Blackw. **81**: 393.
All for the Faith; a Tale. (A. Young) Cath. World, **9**: 684.

All for Greed. (B. de Bury) St. Paul's, **1**: 23–641. **2**: 1–129. Same art. Liv. Age, **95**: 303, 720. **96**: 414, 744. **97**: 85–619.
All for Love. Tinsley, **3**: 327–441
All a Green Willow. Tinsley, **16**: 566.
All a Green Willow; a Tale. (C. Gibbon) Belgra. **39**: supp. 1. Same art. Canad. Mo. **16**: 37.
All-Hallow Eve, Calendars of. (E. Walford) Once a Week, **14**: 570, 595.
— Customs of. Ev. Sat. **11**: 535.
— in Ireland. Colburn, **4**: 254.
All-Hallow Eve; a Tale. (R. Curtis) Cath. World, **1**: 500–785. **2**: 71–813. **3**: 97, 241.
All Hallow's Priory, History of. (O. J. Burke) Dub. Univ. **81**: 547, 661.
All in the Dark. (J. S. Le Fanu) Dub. Univ. **67**: 198–617.
All in the Wrong; or, The Tamer tamed. Blackw. **92**: 671. Same art. Liv. Age, **76**: 3.
All 's well that ends well. (E. Phelps) Knick. **61**: 326. — Bentley, **3**: 72. — Lond. Soc. **12**: 274.
All a Mistake. Tinsley, **12**: 291.
All or Nothing; a Tale. (C. Hoey) All the Year, **41**: 25–563. **42**: 19–282.
All Potterton's Fault; a Tale. (S. Gerard) Sharpe, **47**: 31.
All Saints' Day. (C. Kingsley) Good Words, **16**: 194. — Mo. Rel. M. **30**: 301. **46**: 548. — (C. Palfrey) Unita. R. **4**: 504.
Allan, Col. John, Memoir of. (G. H. Allen) N. E. Reg. **30**: 353.
— Narrative of. N. E. Reg. **12**: 254.
— Operations in Maine and Nova Scotia. Hist. M. **14**: 263.
Allan, Samuel, of Windsor, Conn., Memoir of. N. E. Reg. **30**: 444.
Allan, William, with portrait. Hogg, **5**: 81. — (W. C. Smith) Good Words, **14**: 196.
Allan, Sir William. Blackw. **11**: 439. **21**: 401.
Allan; a Poem. Mo. R. **152**: 562.
Alleghany Co. Bonds, Decision on. Bank. M. (N. Y.) **13**: 467.
Alleghany Mountains, Among the. (J. Harwood) Once a Week, **6**: 156.
— By-Paths in: illustrated. (R. H. Davis) Harper, **61**: 167, 353, 532.
— Crossing the; a Poem. Dial, **1**: 159.
— Fauna of. (E. D. Cope) Am. Natural. **4**: 392.
— Rencontre in. New Eng. M. **7**: 359.
— Travels in. (D. H. Strother) Harper, **44**: 659, 801. **45**: 21–801. **46**: 669. **47**: 821. **49**: 156. **51**: 475.
Alleghany Travels. So. Lit. Mess. **1**: 97.
Allegiance and Naturalization. St. Paul's, **4**: 431.
Allegorical Interpretation. Brit. Q. **2**: 175. — Mo. R. **165**: 350.
Allegorical Painting and Sculpture. Penny M. **7**: 305.
Allegorical Representation, Origin of. (E. Wigglesworth) Chr. Exam. **21**: 158.
Allegorical Sketch. Knick. **23**: 361.
Allegorical Works. Irish Q. **6**: 673.
Allegory, An. Chr. Mo. Spec. **3**: 19.
— at Covent Garden. Once a Week, **27**: 323.
Allegories of the Months. (M. Davies) Colburn, **151**: 131–445.
Allegro; a Tale. (L. T. Cragin) O. & N. **7**: 147.
Alleine, Joseph. Ecl. R. **114**: 611. — Meth. M. **34**: 402.
Allen, Ann. (Mrs. E. F. Ellet) Godey, **44**: 317.
Allen, Cary. Am. Presb. R. **4**: 55.
Allen, Ethan. (B. J. Lossing) Harper, **17**: 721. — New Eng. M. **6**: 302.
— Essay on Being, Human Soul, etc. Hist. M. **21**: 193, 274, 330. **22**: 29, 76.
— Life of. (J. Sparks) Sparks's Am. Biog. **1**: 227.
Allen, George. (R. E. Thompson) Penn Mo. **7**: 56[illegible] 648.
Allen, Henry W. (D. B. Ewing) Land We Love, **3**: 43.
Allen, Gen. Ira. Hist. M. **7**: 105.
Allen, Isaac. (A. Hill) Chr. Exam. **37**: 217.
Allen, John. (J. Macdonald) Meth. M. **35**: 3.
Allen, Joseph. 25th Anniversary Sermon. (H. Ware, jr.) Chr. Exam. **32**: 51.
Allen, Mrs. Lucy Clark, Address at Funeral of. (A. Hill) Mo. Rel. M. **35**: 250.
Allen, Mary Frances, Memorial of. Mo. Rel. M. **18**: 193.
Allen, Gov. Samuel, Memoir of. (J. B. Moore) Am. Q. Reg. **13**: 272.
Allen, Thomas. (S. Burnham) Cong. Q. **11**: 475.
Allen, Thomas, Life of, with portrait. West. J. **9**: 421.
Allen, William. Chamb. J. **10**: 233. Same art. Liv. Age, **20**: 17. — (J. Sherman) Ex. H. Lec. **5**: 433. — Peop. J. **6**: 314. — Am. J. Educ. **10**: 365.
— Life and Labors of. Ecl. R. **87**: 449.
— Memoir of. Chr. Obs. **52**: 89.
— Sermon. Am. Mo. R. **2**: 129.
— Sherman's Memoir of. Ecl. R. **94**: 436.
Allen, William, Cardinal. (J. Thompson) Month, **33**: 369.
Allen, William, Chief Justice. (E. F. De Lancey) Pennsyl. M. **1**: 202.
Allen, William H., Capt. U. S. N., with portrait. Portfo. (Den.) **11**: 1.
Allen, Z., Practical Tourist. Am. Mo. R. **2**: 315.
Allen Family of New Jersey. N. E. Reg. **25**: 144.
Allen Genealogy. (S. M. Allen) N. E. Reg. **10**: 225.
Allentown Church Case, Master's Report. Luth. Q. **8**: 1.
Allerheiligen, Baden and. (T. A. Trollope) Lippinc. **20**: 535.
Allerton, Isaac. (H. W. Cushman) N. E. Reg. **8**: 265.
Alleyn, Edward. House. Words, **13**: 300. — Mo. R. 154, 504.
Allie Fletcher; a Tale. Temp. Bar, **20**: 278, 417.
Allied Powers and Naples. Ed. Mo. R. **5**: 717.
Allies, T. W. Autobiography. (T. S. Preston) Cath. World, **32**: 633.
— Writings. Dub. R. **87**: 243.
Alligator, Adventure with an. Temp. Bar, **24**: 110.
— Habits of. (T. B. Thorpe) Harper, **10**: 37.
— Natural History of. (J. J. Audubon) Ed. New Philos. J. **2**: 270. Same art. Mus. **11**: 272.
Alligators, Day with. Bentley, **51**: 491, 650.
— in England. (C. H. Williams) Once a Week, **15**: 134.
Allingham, Wm. Poem, Laurence Bloomfield. Chamb. J. **41**: 523. — Dub. R. **56**: 320. Same art. Cath. World, **1**: 466. — Irish Q. **7**: 1127. — Putnam, **8**: 19.
— Recollections of. (J. Reade) New Dom. **10**: 1.
Alliott, Rev. R., Memoir of. Cong. M. **23**: 425.
Allison, William B., with portrait. Lakeside, **2**: 373.
Alliteration. Appleton, **6**: 186.
— and Assonance. Liv. Age, **79**: 42.
Allondale Priory. (J. F. Otis) Godey, **40**: 37, 97.
Allotment System. Penny M. **14**: 87.
Allotments *versus* Pauperism. St. James, **11**: 336.
Allotropism. Recr. Sci. **3**: 242.
Alloys, On. J. Frankl. Inst. **1**: 316.
— and Metals, Recent Researches in. (F. C. Calvert) J. Frankl. Inst. **82**: 186.
— Manufacture of. J. Frankl. Inst. **62**: 191.
— of Copper and Tin, Thurston's. (W. C. Roberts) Nature, **21**: 273.
— of Nickel and Iron, Strength of. (W. Fairbairn) J. Frankl. Inst. **66**: 280.
Allspice-Tree. Penny M. **3**: 281.
Allston, Mrs. Joseph, with portrait. Potter Am. Mo. **4**: 257.

Allston, Robert F. W., with portrait. De Bow, **12**: 574. — Godey, **35**: 180.
Allston, Washington. (Mrs. Lee) Howitt, **2**: 395. — (O. W. Holmes) No. Am. **50**: 358. — with portrait, Dem. R. **13**: 431. — Am. Mo. M. **7**: 435.
— Belshazzar's Feast. (W. P. Lunt) Chr. Exam. **37**: 49. — (H. A. S. Dearborn) Knick. **24**: 205.
— Exhibition of his Pictures, 1839. Dial, **1**: 73. — (J. Huntington) Knick. **14**: 163.
— Lectures on Art and Poems. Am. Whig R. **12**: 17. — New Eng. **8**: 445.
— Monaldi. (C. C. Felton) No. Am. **54**: 397. — New York R. **10**: 203. — (S. J. Hale) Chr. Exam. **31**: 374. — So. Lit. Mess. **8**: 281.
— Our first great Painter. (Sarah Clarke) Atlan. **15**: 129.
— Paintings by. O. & N. **4**: 735.
— Poems, and Lectures on Art. (C. C. Felton) No. Am. **71**: 149.
— Sylphs of the Season. (R. H. Dana) No. Am. **5**: 365. — Anal. M. **6**: 151.
Alma, Wreck of the. Once a Week, **1**: 185.
Alma Mater's Roll; a Poem. (E. E. Hale) Scrib. **10**: 623.
Alma-Tadema, Lawrence, Works of. Art J. **27**: 9.
Almachilde; a Dramatic Sketch. Am. Mo. M. **4**: 313, 369.
Almack's. Bentley, **10**: 640. — Lond. M. **17**: 103.
— Recollections of. Lond. Soc. **4**: 145.
— Twelfth-night at. Lond. M. **17**: 205.
Almack's Down East. Knick. **39**: 151.
Almanac, The. Chamb. J. **50**: 99.
— An Old, 1662. Eng. Dom. M. **10**: 59.
— The Old. Chamb. J. **9**: 337.
— Oldest. Dub. Univ. **28**: 187.
— U. S., for 1843. (S. C. Walker) J. Frankl. Inst. **34**: 165.
Almanacs. All the Year, **6**: 318. — Am. Alma. **1830**: 50. — Mo. R. **115**: 160. **118**: 121.
— and Calendars, Old. Brit. Q. **28**: 333.
— Chinese. House. Words, **10**: 203.
— Clog. *See* Clog Almanacs.
— English, under James I. Retros. **18**: 365.
— for 1830. Mo. R. **120**: 583.
— for 1831. Mo. R. **123**: 591.
— for 1841. Fraser, **23**: 101.
— French. All the Year, **40**: 63. — Colburn, **81**: 456. — Knick. **54**: 521.
— — for 1853. (P. Godwin) Putnam, **1**: 49.
— — for 1870. Colburn, **146**: 102.
— History of. (T. Wright) Macmil. **7**: 173. — Chr. Rem. **3**: 108.
— Italian. All the Year, **36**: 150.
— Literature of. (J. Pierce, jr.) Putnam, **4**: 270.
— Oldest of all. Dub. Univ. **28**: 187. Same art. Ecl. M. **9**: 203.
— Some old. (C. W. Elliott) Galaxy, **23**: 24.
See Calendars.
Almost a Catastrophe; a Love Story. (S. Foster) Lippinc. **28**: 508.
Almost a Ghost. (W. A. Thompson) Lippinc. **7**: 175.
Almost a Quixote. Eng. Dom. M. **24**: 293. **25**: 47–323. **26**: 15–68.
Almost a Romance. (J. B. Runnion) Lakeside, **4**: 345.
Almost Wrecked; a Tale. (E. S. Drewry) Victoria, **24**: 209–476. **25**: 569–761.
Alms and Prayers, Memorials before God. (W. M. Reily) Mercersb. **14**: 457.
Alms-giving. Chamb. J. **12**: 113. — (B. Lambert) Good Words, **22**: 625.
— Christian Idea of. (H. Harbaugh) Mercersb. **14**: 165.
— Christ's Rule for, better than our Methods. (I. N. Tarbox) New Eng. **13**: 242.
Almshouse, The; a Poem. Mo. Rel. M. **30**: 249.
Almshouse in Shropshire. Chamb. J. **22**: 193. Same art. Liv. Age, **43**: 243.
Almshouses, County Jails and. (C. L. Brace) Nation, **22**: 199.
Alnwick Castle. (E. Bradley) Once a Week, **4**: 571. — Antiquary, **3**: 285. — Penny M. **5**: 37. — Sharpe, **2**: 209.
— and its Decorations. Art J. **9**: 30.
— Renaissance at. Colburn, **109**: 282.
Aloe, Great American. Sharpe, **15**: 187.
Alone; a Poem in *facsimile*. (E. A. Poe) Scrib. **10**: 608.
Alone in College, and what came of it. Fraser, **103**: 211.
Alone in London; a Poem. (H. B. Baildon) Cornh. **33**: 88.
Along the Links of Alnmouth; a Story. All the Year, **43**: 93, 117, 141.
Along the Route. (M. M. Cole) Lakeside, **5**: 150.
Aloysius Gonzaga, St., Life of. Dub. R. **61**: 301.
Alpaca, Discovery of. Lond. Soc. **36**: 103.
— Naturalization of, Walton on. Mo. R. **155**: 259.
Alpenglow; a Poem. (M. J. Preston) Scrib. **7**: 62.
Alphabet, The, Anecdotes of. All the Year, **28**: 418.
— for Lower Animals. All the Year, **24**: 136.
— Hebrew, Supposed Mosaic Origin of. Chr. Obs. **39**: 169.
— Invention of. (G. Brückner) Kitto, **40**: 178.
— Liberties taken with. All the Year, **27**: 514.
— New Appropriation of the Roman. Meth. Q. **10**: 396.
— Origin of. Once a Week, **26**: 493.
— Poetry of. Broadw. **5**: 223.
— Roman, applied to Eastern Languages. Lond. Q. **11**: 143.
— Significancy of. (Mrs. M. L. Putnam) No. Am. **68**: 160.
— Tormenting. (G. Wakeman) Galaxy, **1**: 437.
— Universal, Lepsius's. (J. S. Ropes) Bib. Sac. **13**: 681.
Alphabet Studies and Chinese Imitations. Lond. M. **4**: 47.
Alphabetic Writing, Origin of. Dub. Univ. **8**: 623. — Nat. Q. **15**: 61.
— Wall on. Dub. Univ. **16**: 130.
Alphabeticals. Blackw. **96**: 325.
Alphabets. Ed. R. **31**: 368.
— History in. (J. C. C. Clarke) Bib. Sac. **31**: 333.
— Manual. Penny M. **2**: 499.
Alphonsus de Liguori, St. Dub. R. **37**: 326.
Alpine Club. Blackw. **86**: 456. Same art. Ecl. M. **48**: 530. Same art. Liv. Age, **62**: 98. — Chamb. J. **32**: 59.
— German-Austrian. (G. G. Ramsay) Good Words, **17**: 402, 532.
— Map of Switzerland. Nature, **11**: 8.
— Peaks and Passes. Brit. Q. **36**: 71.
Alpnach, Slide of. Cong. M. **3**: 111.
Alps, The. (J. Bigelow) No. Am. **38**: 405. — (A. Nicholson) Univ. Q. **5**: 197. — (G. Macdonald) Argosy, **1**: 53, 127. — Blackw. **102**: 418, 540. — Brit. Q. **40**: 28. — Broadw. **6**: 529. **7**: 315. — Ed. R. **130**: 118. — Nature, **16**: 542. — Once a Week, **25**: 437. — Putnam, **5**: 468. — (H. S. Wilson) Tinsley, **16**: 301.
— Æsthetics among. Blackw. **81**: 265. Same art. Ecl. M. **41**: 98.
— Art in the Higher: Loppé's Alpine Paintings. (M. C. O'Morris) St. Paul's, **13**: 25.
— Ascent of. (J. Tyndall) Fortn. **13**: 7. Same art. Liv. Age, **104**: 437. — Blackw. **1**: 59. **2**: 255. **4**: 180. — Anal. M. **15**: 375. — Mus. **9**: 73, 115, 512. **10**: 259, 306, 400. — Dub. Univ. **54**: 231.
— — of the Aletschhorn. (J. Tyndall) Ev. Sat. **9**: 74.
— — of the Buet. Chamb. J. **8**: 94.
— — of the Oldenhorn. Cornh. **9**: 702.
— Austrian, Short Tour in. (L. M. Hoskins) Victoria, **20**: 129.

Alps, The, Avalanches in. Ecl. M. **49**: 133.
— Bad Five Minutes in. Fraser, **96**: 545.
— Berchtesgarden and the Ziller-Thal. Cornh. **15**: 572.
— Berlepsch's. Liv. Age, **71**: 639.
— Beyond the Snow Line. (P. Gussfeldt) Penn Mo. **12**: 665, 721.
— Botany of. No. Brit. **37**: 69. — (H. Coultas) Sharpe, **46**: 144. *See below,* — Flowers of.
— Brute Life in. Blackw. **74**: 539.
— Bye-Day in. Cornh. **29**: 675.
— Châlets and Pasturages of. Penny M. **13**: 474.
— Climbing of. Liv. Age, **68**: 110. — Quar. **123**: 118. — St. Paul's, **1**: 470. Same art. Liv. Age, **96**: 404.
— — The Peak of Terror. (H. S. Wilson) Gent. M. n. s. **15**: 585.
— Col du Géant. (H. Greenfield) Knick. **45**: 503.
— Dangers of Mountaineering in. Temp. Bar, **52**: 213.
— Dent-du-Midi, Mt., Lady's Ascent of. (A. B. Le Geyt) Victoria, **8**: 306.
— Diary of a Traveler in. Fraser, **19**: 221, 329.
— Engineering among. Penny M. **13**: 407, 410.
— Excursions in. Blackw. **86**: 456.
— Exploration of. Dub. Univ. **78**: 302.
— Floods and Avalanches of. Penny M. **13**: 18.
— Flowers of. (A. W. Bennett) Am. Natural. **4**: 521. — (F. Darwin) Nature, **23**: 332.
— — and Birds of. Chamb. J. **56**: 664. Same art. Ecl. M. **94**: 454.
— Forbes's Travels among. Am. J. Sci. **46**: 172. — Quar. **74**: 39. Same art. Liv. Age, **2**: 13.
— Forests of. Penny M. **9**: 273.
— Geology of. (T. S. Hunt) Am. J. Sci. **103**: 1.
— — Former Changes of. (R. I. Murchison) Am. J. Sci. **62**: 245.
— Glaciers of. Dub. R. **49**: 40.
— — Living on. Penny M. **12**: 450.
— — Marvels of. Brit. Q. **32**: 341. Same art. Ecl. M. **52**: 41, 161.
— — Tyndall's. Liv. Age, **67**: 280.
— Grass Farms of. Bentley, **49**: 615.
— Hannibal's Passage of. Ed. R. **43**: 163. — Quar. **123**: 191.
— — Law on. (H. Jackson) Fortn. **7**: 507.
— High. Colburn, **108**: 285.
— — Day and Night among. Liv. Age, **27**: 37.
— — Idle Days in. (J. F. Hardy) Fraser, **99**: 245.
— Ice-Cavern Temples of. Ecl. M. **55**: 44.
— in the last Century. (L. Stephen) Fraser, **82**: 167.
— in Winter. Cornh. **35**: 352. Same art. Liv. Age, **133**: 47.
— Into the Schaflock. Temp. Bar, **3**: 393.
— Journeyings in, Kohl's. Westm. **51**: 497. **52**: 545.
— Jungfrau, Ascent of. (E. Desor) Ed. New Philos. J. **32**: 291. — Sharpe, **3**: 33, 71.
— Jura, Ascent of. Cornh. **8**: 317.
— Life in. Once a Week, **13**: 249. — Brit. Q. **30**: 79.
— — Odds and Ends of. (J. Tyndall) Macmil. **19**: 369, 465. Same art. Liv. Age, **101**: 3, 467. Same art. Ev. Sat. **7**: 402, 425, 522, 554.
— Literature of. Fraser, **60**: 232.
— Lombardy; Monte Generoso. Cornh. **21**: 605.
— Love of. Cornh. **16**: 24, 539. Same art. Liv. Age, **94**: 361.
— Maps of. (E. Whymper) Nature, **6**: 203.
— Matterhorn, Fatal Adventure on. Bentley, **58**: 253. Same art. Ecl. M. **65**: 672.
— — Scaling. (J. Tyndall) Appleton, **1**: 149.
— Midnight on. Ecl. M. **46**: 126.
— Moretti's Campanula. Cornh. **20**: 687.
— Mountaineering in. Cornh. **16**: 539. — Fraser, **67**: 317. — Westm. **82**: 276.
— Notes from, in 1863. Liv. Age, **79**: 39.
Alps, The, of Savoy, Day in. Dub. Univ. **42**: 416. Same art. Liv. Age, **39**: 683.
— — Forbes's Travels through. Ed. R. **80**: 135. — No. Brit. **1**: 527. — Mo. R. **162**: 11.
— On the Skirt of. (G. E. Waring, jr.) Harper, **59**: 641.
— Opening of the Pass. Colburn, **100**: 192–323.
— Origin of. (E. Suess) Am. J. Sci. **110**: 446.
— Over the Moro. Fraser, **75**: 758.
— Peaks and Passes of. Brit. Q. **36**: 71. Same art. Ecl. M. **57**: 133, 158.
— Peasants of. Penny M. **5**: 201.
— Pennine, Italian Valleys of. Chr. Obs. **59**: 590, 659.
— Pedestrianizing among. (H. D. Jenkins) Lakeside, **5**: 215.
— Physical Geography of. (H. and A. Schlagintweit) Am. Jour. Sci. **64**: 359.
— Polish. Cornh. **39**: 213. Same art. Liv. Age, **140**: 602.
— Quiet Day in. (H. S. Wilson) Belgra. **39**: 60.
— Roads in. Tinsley, **12**: 93.
— Ruitor. (T. G. Bonney) Once a Week, **13**: 314.
— St. Bernard, Visit to. (Fanny Tyndall) Victoria, **11**: 311.
— Scrambles amongst. (E. Whymper) Lippinc. **8**: 217–529. **9**: 129–609.
— Sexagenarian Mountaineering. (F. B. Zincke) Fraser, **96**: 152.
— Scenes in. (J. T. Headley) So. Lit. Mess. **10**: 521.
— Simplon, Ascent of. Temp. Bar, **21**: 245.
— Sketches in. St. James, **46**: 419. — (J. Foster) Ecl. R. **21**: 530.
— Sketches of Pontresina. Cornh. **15**: 47.
— Storm in. Fraser, **73**: 257. Same art. Ev. Sat. **1**: 288. Same art. Ecl. M. **66**: 550.
— Summer Retreats in. Lond. Soc. **40**: 81.
— Torrents of. (H. Blerzy) Penn Mo. **3**: 509.
— Tours in. Dub. Univ. **54**: 475.
— Tracing of. Chamb. J. **10**: 321.
— Travel in, Art of. Cornh. **6**: 206.
— Traveler in, Journal of. Blackw. **39**: 131–638. **40**: 239.
— Travelers in. Bent. Q. **2**: 214. — Ed. R. **104**: 433.
— Tyndall's Hours of Exercise in. (T. G. Bonney) Nature, **4**: 198.
— Wanderings in. Appleton, **15**: 65, 161, 193.
— Wengern, Over the. St. James, **14**: 188.
— Whymper's Scrambles among. (L. Stephen) Macmil. **24**: 304.
— Wilson's Ascents and Adventures in. Lond. Soc. **34**: 280.
— Zermatt, Early Stroll to. (G. C. Swayne) Fraser, **82**: 243.
See also names of particular mountains and localities, as Blanc; Cenis; Chamounix; *also* Glaciers.
Alred; a Poem. (E. W. Carey) Internat. M. **4**: 27.
Alsace and Lorraine. Good Words, **11**: 810. — (M. Heilprin) Nation, **11**: 232.
— — French Conquest of. (H. M. Baird) Scrib. **1**: 367.
— — in 1870. (J. N. Pomeroy) Nation, **11**: 253. — Colburn, **148**: 489.
— — since 1871. (L. Montefiore) 19th Cent. **6**: 819.
— — Sketch of. Colburn, **148**: 611.
Alsace, Exiles of. Chamb. J. **51**: 212.
— Sketches of. (G. C. Swayne) Once a Week, **14**: 35, 82, 259.
See Legend of Alsace.
Alsop, John. (J. A. Stevens) M. Am. Hist. **1**: 226.
Alsop, V. Melius inquirendum, etc. Cong. M. **5**: 154.
Alston, E. R., Obituary of. Nature, **23**: 485.
Alt Breisach. Once a Week, **13**: 482.
Altai Mts. and Chinese Frontier. Brit. Q. **8**: 344.
Altar, Christian. (G. L. Staley) Mercersb. **18**: 125.
— and Priest. (W. E. Krebs) Mercersb. **15**: 467.

Altar with Greek Inscription at Corbridge. (J. Pettingal and S. Adee) Arch. **2**: 92, 98.
Altars at Corbridge, Observations on. (D. Barrington and T. Morell) Arch. **3**: 324.
Altbach, Sketch at. Month, **15**: 336.
Altenstein, Life and Sport at. (A. G. C. Liddell) Macmil. **44**: 473.
Alter Ego; a Tale. (K. Hillard) Victoria, **22**: 148.
Altered Man, The. Bentley, **17**: 626.
Altham and his Wife. Blackw. **3**: 542.
Althorp, Viscount, and Reform Act of 1832. (W. Bageshot) Fortn. **26**: 573. Same art. Liv. Age, **131**: 707. — Westm. **106**: 410.
— Memoir of. Ed. R. **144**: 251.
— Sketch of. Tait, n. s. **1**: 60.
Althorp Gallery. (P. G. Hamerton) Portfo. **8**: 1–181. **9**: 1.
Altitudinarian and Latitudinarian Divines. Chr. Obs. **39**: 77.
Altruism, Failure of. Fraser, **100**: 494.
Alum-Works at Hurlet, Day at. Penny M. **12**: 421. Same art. Liv. Age, **19**: 415.
Alumayû, Prince, Who was? (A. H. Keane) Nature, **21**: 61.
Aluminium. (J. W. M'Gauley) Intel. Obs. **1**: 176. — Chamb. J. **22**: 278. — Dub. Univ. **93**: 214. — House. Words, **14**: 507. Same art. Ecl. M. **40**: 362. Same art. Liv. Age, **52**: 229. — J. Frankl. Inst. **61**: 27, 65.
— and its Future in the Arts. Pract. M. **6**: 167.
— in Steel and Iron. (A. A. Blair) Am. J. Sci. **113**: 421.
Aluminium Bronze. (R. Bithell) Recr. Sci. **2**: 100.
Alumni Poem. (I. Lawrence) Dem. R. **43**: 349.
Alured; an Allegory. (F. P. Cobbe) Temp. Bar, **18**: 35. Same art. Ecl. M. **67**: 479.
Alva's Reign of Terror. (W. C. Robinson) Month, **37**: 515.
Alvaston, Derbyshire, Parish Register, etc. of. (E. Poole) Reliquary, **3**: 134.
Always with us; a Poem. (J. D. Finlay) Temp. Bar, **1**: 133.
Alwyn's First Wife. (G. M. Craik) Fraser, **51**: 47, 181. Same art. Liv. Age, **44**: 623.
Amadeus, King of Spain, Abdication of. (A. Laugel) Nation, **16**: 162.
— Fall of. (W. H. Dixon) Gent. M. n. s. **16**: 553.
Amadis de Gaul. St. James, **15**: 47.
— Southey's. (Sir W. Scott) Ed. R. **3**: 109.
Amalek Dagon. House. Words, **18**: 444.
Amalfi, Pæstum, Capri. Cornh. **36**: 151. Same art. Ecl. M. **89**: 454.
— a Poem. (H. W. Longfellow) Atlan. **35**: 513.
Amalgamation. (W. W. Wright) De Bow, **29**: 1.
— of Metals. (P. Casamajor) Ecl. Engin. **15**: 305.
Amaranth's Mystery; a Novel. (A. Gray) Tinsley, **27**: 401–525. **28**: 65.
Amari Aliquid; a Poem. (F. C. Wilson) Temp. Bar, **5**: 430.
Amateur, Pleasure of the. (G. A. Simcox) Portfo. **4**: 25.
Amateur Theatricals. Colburn, **83**: 340.
Amateur's Boudoir. (C. van Vinkbooms) Lond. M. **4**: 655.
Amateurs and Translations. (C. A. Bristed) Galaxy, **16**: 58.
— at Mopetown. All the Year, **26**: 53.
Amateurship; a Dialogue. (P. G. Hamerton) Macmil. **14**: 426.
Amazon River. Brit. Q. **38**: 169. Same art. Ecl. M. **60**: 39. — Chamb. J. **8**: 166. **54**: 501. — Lond. Q. **33**: 70.
— American Home on. (H. H. Smith) Scrib. **18**: 692.
— and the Gulf States. De Bow, **18**: 364.
— At the Mouth of. (M. Mauris) Harper, **58**: 365.
Amazon River, Expedition from Lima to Para, Smyth's. Ed. R. **63**: 395. — West. J. **9**: 166. — (M. Butler) West. J. **11**: 342.
— Expeditions on. (R. Southey) Quar. **57**: 1.
— Geology of. (C. F. Hartt) Am. Natural. **8**: 673.
— — of the Lower. (R. Rathbun) Am. J. Sci. **117**: 464.
— Herndon's Exploration of. Dem. R. **35**: 460. — (W. A. Larned) New Eng. **12**: 362. — Liv. Age, **41**: 429.
— Mediterranean of America. Scrib. **18**: 192.
— Naturalist on. All the Year, **11**: 592.
— — Bates's. Lond. Q. **22**: 48. — Liv. Age, **77**: 523. — Ecl. R. **119**: 20. — Ecl. M. **61**: 348.
— New Survey of, 1878. Geog. M. **5**: 230.
— On the Banks of. St. James, **9**: 439.
— Peruvian and its Tributaries. (N. B. Noland) Appleton, **14**: 545–780.
— Physical Observations on. (J. Orton) Am. J. Sci. **96**: 203.
— Sketches of Life and Nature on. Westm. **80**: 137.
— Wanderings on. (J. E. Warren) Am. Whig R. **6**: 567.
Amazon Valley. (G. P. Disosway) Nat. M. **13**: 297. — (E. Hale, jr.) Hunt, **31**: 39. — (M. F. Maury) De Bow, **14**: 449. **15**: 36. — (C. C. Smith) Chr. Exam. **56**: 353. — Chamb. J. **21**: 375. — De Bow, **14**: 556. **16**: 231. — Lond. Q. **3**: 483.
— Commerce with. West. J. **9**: 321. **12**: 96.
— in Bolivia and Brazil. (G. E. Church) Fortn. **14**: 564. Same art. Ecl. M. **76**: 155.
— Physical History of. (L. Agassiz) Atlan. **18**: 49, 159.
— Primeval Forests of, Bates's. Colburn, **128**: 127. Same art. Liv. Age, **78**: 99.
— Wallace on. (P. Godwin) Putnam, **3**: 272.
Amazonian Drift. (C. F. Hartt) Am. J. Sci. **101**: 294.
Amazons, British. All the Year, **27**: 448.
— Modern. Chamb. J. **39**: 348.
— of Mexico; a Tale. Potter Am. Mo. **9**: 109, 186, 265.
— of South America. Putnam, **6**: 252.
Ambassador, The, in Spite of Himself. (G. W. Bethune) Putnam, **1**: 437.
Ambassadors, Privileges of. Blackw. **116**: 346. Same art. Liv. Age, **123**: 159.
— Extraordinary. Chamb. J. **45**: 585.
— in Bonds. (Caroline Chesebro) Atlan. **13**: 281.
Amber. (M. Reboux) Pract. M. **6**: 314. — (E. A. Smith) Am. Natural. **14**: 179. — Appleton, **8**: 599. — Ecl. Engin. **24**: 206. — Argosy, **12**: 113. — Chamb. J. **15**: 46. **50**: 757. — Ev. Sat. **16**: 45.
— and Ambergris. All the Year, **28**: 607. Same art. Ev. Sat. **13**: 689.
— Diving for. Ev. Sat. **11**: 486.
— of East Prussia. (M. Merivale) St. Paul's, **9**: 75. Same art. Ecl. M. **77**: 729.
— Origin, Nature, and Uses of. Penny M. **8**: 10.
Amber Trade. Pract. M. **6**: 351.
Amber Gods. (Harriet E. Prescott) Atlan. **5**: 7, 170.
Amber Mouthpiece; a Tale. Dub. Univ. **47**: 309.
Amber Witch, Meinhold's. Brit. Q. **3**: 133. — Liv. Age, **2**: 102. — Quar. **74**: 107. — Fraser, **38**: 363. — Ecl. R. **80**: 299.
Amber Witchery. House. Words, **9**: 123.
Amberley, Viscount, Analysis of Religious Belief. (C. B. Upton) Theo. R. **13**: 509. — Radical R. **1**: 357.
Ambidextry. *See* Right and Left.
Ambitieuse, The. (J. T. Lomax) So. Lit. Mess. **7**: 625.
Ambition. (E. A. Sandford) Godey, **56**: 514. — Colburn, **61**: 30. — So. Lit. Mess. **7**: 49.
Ambition; a Farce. Blackw. **50**: 432.
Ambitious Brooklet, The. (A. O. Hall) Internat. M. **2**: 477.
Ambitious Guest; a Story. New Eng. M. **8**: 425.
Amblève, Valley of. (K. S. Macquoid) Belgra. **42**: 152.

Amboise, Georges d', Cardinal and Minister. Temp. Bar, 50: 224. Same art. Liv. Age, 134: 152.
Amboise, Château d'. (A. Laugel) Nation, 25: 346.
Ambrose, St. (J. Gerard) Month, 16: 345. — (S. Osgood) No. Am. 81: 414.
— and his Time. (S. L. Caldwell) Bapt. Q. 7: 257.
— and Milan. (W. O. White) Unita. R. 12: 69.
— Life and Times of. (M. L. Stoever) Evang. R. 21: 234.
Ambrosia; a Legend of Ausgburg. (B. Murphy) Cath. World, 15: 803.
Ambrosian Manuscripts. Quar. 16: 321.
Ambrosian Sepulchres. (G. Lambert) Month, 20: 274.
Ambulance System. Macmil. 19: 87.
Ambulances, Experience of. (J. W. Mario) Fraser, 95: 768. 96: 54, 247.
— Prussian, in the War of 1870–71. Month, 21: 202, 289, 402.
— War of 1870 and. (H. Sandwith) Macmil. 23: 38.
Amelia, Princess, Dramas of. (C. C. Felton) No. Am. 52: 487.
Amelia; or, A Young Lady's Vicissitudes. (Miss Leslie) Godey, 36: 25–357. 37: 37–165.
Amelia Island. Niles's Reg. 14: 169.
Amélie-les-Bains. All the Year, 22: 513. — Good Words, 21: 229.
Amen! (M. Oliphant) Blackw. 94: 497.
Amen-Corner, Legend of. Chamb. J. 17: 227.
America. (Syd. Smith) Ed. R. 33: 69. 49: 473. — Blackw. 34: 285, 548. — Mus. 23: 563. — U. S. Lit. Gaz. 6: 348.
— Abdy's Journal in. Westm. 24: 244.
— Adventure in. Blackw. 67: 34.
— Anburey on. So. Lit. Mess. 6: 710.
— Ancient. No. Brit. 39: 29. Same art. Ecl. M. 60: 273, 427, 495.
— — Civilization in. (M. J. B. Browne) Scrib. 5: 724. — (T. A. Harcourt) Overland, 14: 468.
— — Extinct Races of. (C. Morris) Nat. Q. 25: 121.
— — How originally peopled. (C. H. Smith) Ed. New Philos. J. 38: 1.
— — Legends of. Cornh. 26: 452. Same art. Liv. Age, 119: 761. Same art. Ev. Sat. 13: 469.
— — Mythology of; Myths of Manibozho and Ioskeha. (D. G. Brinton) Hist. M. 12: 3.
— — Notes on a lost Race of. (A. W. Vogeles) Am. Natural. 13: 9.
— — Prehistoric Man in. (J. L. Onderdonck) Nat. Q. 36: 227.
— — Province of Tusayan. (J. W. Powell) Scrib. 11: 193. *See* American Antiquities; Indians.
— and the Americans. (J. Tulloch) Good Words, 16: 641–817.
— and England. (F. Jeffrey) Ed. R. 33: 395. — Blackw. 16: 474. — Am. Q. 15: 240. — Mus. 6: 13. 13: 738. — Am. Mo. M. 1: 34.
— — and France. (M. D. Conway) Fortn. 3: 442. Same art. Liv. Age, 88: 545.
— — Future of. (J. Foster) Ecl. R. 5: 461.
— — in 1865. Dub. Univ. 66: 709.
— — Resemblances between. (J. L. Swift) Overland, 1: 55.
— — Social Relations of. Quar. 142: 251. Same art. Liv. Age, 130: 707.
— and Europe. Am. Whig R. 13: 251. — Mo. R. 117: 192. — Dem. R. 32: 211.
— — Gurowski's, 1861. (J. H. Allen) Chr. Exam. 63: 231.
— and Great Britain, Common Interests of. (W. J. Fox) Peop. J. 1: 172.
— and her Detractors. Ed. R. 55: 479.
— and its Realities. Dub. Univ. 30: 193.
America, Aristocracy in. Mo. R. 150: 392. — Mus. 37: 349.
— — How manufactured. (E. I. Sears) Nat. Q. 23: 277.
— Art in. (L. G. Ware) Chr. Exam. 71: 67. — (J. J. Jarves) Chr. Exam. 73: 63.—(K. Field) Chr. Exam. 75: 97. — Chr. Exam. 77: 175. — Blackw. 16: 129.
— — Future of. Art J. 22: 6.
— Art Museums in. Art J. 22: 129.
— as it is. Mo. R. 130: 298.
— as it is and will be. (C. E. Havens) Pioneer, 2: 16.
— as seen from Europe. (J. P. Thompson) Ev. Sat. 17: 201.
— Ashe's Travels in. Ed. R. 15: 442.
— Backwoods Life in. Brit. Q. 21: 60.
— before the Revolution. (J. Foster) Ecl. R. 9: 165.
— Birkbeck's Journey in, 1818. Ecl. R. 28: 33, 169. — Ed. R. 30: 120. — Quar. 19: 54. — Mo. R. 85: 146.
— Birkbeck and Palmer on. Mo. R. 87: 278.
— Books relating to. (W. Tudor) No. Am. 1: 1, 145, 269. 3: 1, 145, 305. 4: 1, 145, 289. 5: 1, 175. 6: 225.
— — Recent, 1847. Dub. Univ. 29: 224.
— Bradbury's Travels in. Anal. M. 11: 10.
— British. *See* British America.
— Buckingham's. Quar. 68: 250. — Westm. 40: 21. — Ecl. R. 74: 388. 77: 377.
— Mrs. Butler's Journal in. Ed. R. 61: 379.
— Byam's Western Republics of. Ecl. R. 92: 341.
— Chevalier's Letters from. (J. W. Croker) Quar. 55: 497.
— Christianity in. (P. Schaff) Mercersb. 9: 493.
— Church of. (A. A. Livermore) Chr. Exam. 60: 49. — (C. J. Ingersoll) No. Am. 18: 172.
— — and Ministry of. (A. P. Peabody) Chr. Exam. 38: 353.
— — National. O. & N. 2: 327.
— — Schmucker's Appeal to. (Z. Paddock) Meth. Q. 5: 625.
— Church Establishments of. Fraser, 12: 464, 575.
— Church History of. Dem. R. 24: 151. — Worc. M. 1: 16. — Quar. 2: 309. — Am. Church R. 2: 391.
— — Materials for. (J. Sparks) No. Am. 23: 275.
— Churches of. (J. A. James and Dr. Cunningham) Cong. M. 27: 502.
— — Historical Aspect of. (A. P. Stanley) Macmil. 40: 97. — Same art. Liv. Age, 142: 3.
— — Planting of. Princ. 41: 194.
— — Reed and Matheson's Visit to. Ecl. R. 61: 421.
— — State of Religion in. (H. B. Smith) Am. Presb. R. 16: 555.
— Civilization in. (W. T. Moore) Chr. Q. 4: 433. — (E. Phelps) Contin. Mo. 6: 102, 121. — Dem. R. 42: 50.
— Climate and Character in. (E. C. Towne) Pop. Sci. Mo. 20: 109.
— Combe on. Quar. 68: 158.
— Commerce of. (F. Gilbert) Lakeside, 5: 125.
— — and Statistics of, Macgregor's. Ed. R. 86: 367.
— Consolation for. (B. Franklin) Carey's Mus. 1: 1.
— Cooper and Capt. Hall on. Mus. 15: 510.
— Davies's American Scenes and Christian Slavery. Ecl. R. 89: 438.
— Davis's Travels in. (H. Brougham) Ed. R. 2: 443.
— Defense of. (Syd. Smith) Ed. R. 40: 427.
— Destiny of. (J. S. Patterson) Contin. Mo. 3: 79, 160.
— — Manifest. (J. B. Austin) Lippinc. 4: 183.
— — Moral. Quar. 3: 108.
— — Political. Mass. Q. 2: 1.
— Dickens's Notes on. (T. Hood) Colburn, 66: 396. — Mo. R. 159: 392. — Ed. R. 76: 497.
— — Change for. (J. G. Lockhart) Quar. 73: 129.
— — Reply to. Mo. R. 161: 483.

America, Directions to such Persons as are inclined to, 1682. Pennsyl. M. **4**: 329.

— Discovery of. Putnam, **4**: 457. — (J. Fiske) Harper, **64**: 111. — (J. W. Foster) Hesp. **1**: 23. — (J. T. Short) Galaxy, **20**: 509.

— — and Naming of. (R. H. Major) Am. Bibliop. **2**: 329. **3**: 9.

— Discovery and Records of. Mo. R. **147**: 483.

— — by Chinese. (C. G. Leland) Contin. Mo. **1**: 389, 500. — (W. Speer) Princ. **25**: 83. — Penn Mo. **6**: 603.

— — by Northmen. (J. L. Diman) No. Am. **109**: 264. — (H. C. Lodge) No. Am. **119**: 166. — (B. F. De Costa) Am. Church R. **24**: 418. — (S. G. Drake) N. E. Reg. **7**: 13. — Nat. M. **8**: 243. — Dem. R. **2**: 85 143. — (E. Everett) No. Am. **46**: 161. — Mass. Q. **2**: 189. — New York R. **2**: 352. — For. Q. **21**: 89. — Anal. M. **16**: 267. — Hist. M. **15**: 170. — Nat. Q. **28**: 75. — Penny M. **12**: 342. — (M. R. Pilon) Potter Am. Mo. **5**: 903. — Mo. R. **155**: 337.

— — by the Welsh. Antiquary, **4**: 65.

— — Effects of. Blackw. **60**: 261.

— — English, Date of. (R. H. Major) Arch. **43**: 17

— — Pre-Columbian. (E. S. Riley, jr.) So. M. **13**: 700. — Am. Ecl. **3**: 241. — (J. L. Onderdonk) Nat. Q. **33**: 1. — Dub. R. **11**: 277.

— — — Bibliography of. (P. B. Watson) Lib. J. **6**: 227.

— Discoveries in, Earliest. (H. Stevens) Am. J. Sci. **98**: 299.

— — Fictitious. Hist. M. **4**: 196.

— — on North Coast. Ecl. Mus. **3**: 276.

— Dixon on. Meth. Q. **9**: 653.

— Dixon's New. Chamb. J. **44**: 229. — Ecl. R. 125, 221.—Chr. Rem. **53**: 429.

— Domestic Manners in. Blackw. **31**: 829.

— Duncan on. Mo. R. **105**: 142.

— Duncan, Flint, and Faux on. Westm. **1**: 101.

— Early English Poets on. Dem. R. **5**: 469.

— Early French Settlements in. (J. Langton) Canad. Mo. **5**: 502.

— Early Voyages to. (J. C. Brevoort) Hist. M. **13**: 45, 129. — (W. Willis) N. E. Reg. **23**: 192. — So. Lit. Mess. **14**: 705.

— — Fictitious, of M. Sagean. Hist. M. **10**: 65.

— Ecclesiastical Affairs in, 1839. Ecl. R. **70**: 121.

— Edinburgh Review on. U. S. Lit. Gaz. **1**: 251.

— Education and Religion in, Lang on, 1840. Mo. R. **153**: 307.

— English and French Travelers in. New York R. **6**: 142.

— English Swell-Mobsman in. All the Year, **43**: 204, 228.

— English Tourists in. Dub. Univ. **44**: 721.

— English Travelers in. (E. L. Chandler) No. Am. **74**: 197.

— English Views of. Am. Q. **14**: 520.

— English Writers on. (W. Irving) Ecl. M. **58**: 106. — Tait, **1**: 229.

— — Calumnies of. Mo. R. **131**: 317.

— — Hostility of. (E. Everett) No. Am. **10**: 334. **13**: 20. — (P. Cruise) No. Am. **24**: 464.

— Englishwoman in. (D. Wilson) Canad. J. n. s. **3**: 129.

— Equality of Condition in. (E. Everett) No. Am. **43**: 183.

— Faux on. (E. Everett) No. Am. **19**: 92. — U. S. Lit. Gaz. **1**: 121. — Blackw. **14**: 561. **16**: 474.

— Fearon on. Ed. Mo. R. **1**: 203. — Quar. **21**: 124. — Mo. R. **87**: 392. — Ecl. R. **29**: 153. — Chr. Obs. **18**: 95.

— Ferrall on. Mo. R. **129**: 57.

— Fidler on. Am. Mo. R. **4**: 216. — (A. H. Everett) No. Am. **37**: 273. — Mo. R. **131**: 317.

— Finch on. Mo. R. **132**: 72.

America, First Impressions of. Fraser, **76**: 534. — (J. J. Ampere) Ecl. M. **29**: 84. — (Duke of Argyll) Fraser, **100**: 748. **101**: 40. Same art. Liv. Age, **144**: 33, 279. Same art. Ecl. M. **94**: 151, 274. Same art. Appleton, **23**: 170, 209.

— First Notice of, in English State Papers, 1578. (H. Kirke) Reliquary, **13**: 70.

— First Sermon in, printed. (H. W. Cushman) N. E. Reg. **25**: 169.

— Foster on. Quar. **68**: 12.

— French Criticism on. Month, **5**: 463.

— from the Cosmopolitical Point of View. Brit. Q. **17**: 565. Same art. Liv. Age, **38**: 3.

— Future of. (C. H. Bell) N. E. Reg. **25**: 317.

— German View of. Putnam, **16**: 101.

— Germans in. Bentley, **53**: 244.

— Godley's Letters from. Ecl. R. **79**: 698. — Mo. R. **164**: 93.

— Gold-Worship in. (H. Sedley) St. James, **12**: 434.

— Grandeur of. (A. B. Muzzey) Mo. Rel. M. **6**: 289.

— Grassi on. (E. Brooks) No. Am. **16**: 229.

— Hall, Basil, on. Westm. **11**: 416. — Mus. **16**: 233. — Quar. **39**: 345. **41**: 417. — Mo. R. **117**: 503. — So. R. **4**: 321.

— — Answer to. Colburn, **32**: 297.

— Hall, Lieut. F., on. (J. Gallison) No. Am. **9**: 135. — Mo. R. **87**: 382.

— Hamilton on. (S. Eliot) Chr. Exam. **15**: 219. — Am. Q. **14**: 520. — (A. H. Everett) No. Am. **38**: 210. — Dub. Univ. **2**: 444, 558. — Fraser, **9**: 42. — Blackw. **34**: 285, 548. **35**: 342. — (A. Norton) Select J. **3**: 81. — Mus. **23**: 468, 563, 648. **24**: 81.

— Hennepin's Early Travels in. Dem. R. **5**: 190, 381. — (J. H. Perkins) No. Am. **49**: 258.

— Historical Footprints in. (D. Wilson) Canad. J. n. s. **9**: 288.

— History of, Early, Materials for. (E. E. Hale) Chr. Exam. **70**: 399.

— — — Notes on. (E. D. Niell) N. E. Reg. **28**: 314. **29**: 295.

— — God in. Chr. Exam. **81**: 1.

— — Materials for. (G. H. Moore) Hist. M. **11**: 297, 321. **12**: 9. **13**: 26–286. **15**: 35. **16**: 300.

— — Munoz's. Am. Bibliop. **8**: 21.

— — Notable Places in. Hist. M. **10**: supp. 5, 45.

— — Notes on. N. E. Reg. **31**: 21, 147, 393.

— — Sources of. (J. G. Shea) Cath. World, **12**: 560.

— Histories of, Recent. Chr. R. **15**: 182.

— Hodson on. (J. Sparks) No. Am. **18**: 222. — Westm. **2**: 170. — Mo. R. **104**: 245.

— Holmes's Annals of. (R. Southey) Quar. **2**: 309.

— Holmes on. Mo. R. **101**: 304.

— Home-Life in, Haliburton's, 1854. Brit. Q. **21**: 60. Same art. Liv. Age, **44**: 361.

— Hotels and Food in. Temp. Bar, **2**: 345.

— How they manage Things in. Blackw. **59**: 439. **61**: 492. Same art. So. Lit. Mess. **13**: 360.

— Humboldt's View of, and its Native Tribes. Colburn, **2**: 127, 403.

— Impressions of. (R. W. Dale) 19th Cent. **3**: 457, 757, 943. **4**: 98, 713. Same art. Ecl. M. **90**: 665. Same art. Sup. Pop. Sci. Mo. **3**: 138, 206, 339. — (W. Forsyth) Good Words, **10**: 213.

— in 1818. Ecl. R. **31**: 401.

— in 1846. Dem. R. **18**: 57.

— Influence of Trading on. (H. W. Bellows) Am. Whig R. **1**: 94.

— Janson's Stranger in, 1805. (J. Foster) Ecl. R. **5**: 461.

— Jerome Napoleon in. All the Year, **8**: 174.

— John Bull in. U. S. Lit. Gaz. **2**: 15.

— Jottings in. (W. Chambers) Chamb. J. **23**: 42-319. **24**: 24, 188.

America, Journal of Travels in. Westm. 24: 244.
— Lakes and Indians of. Mo. R. 132: 505.
— Land of Wealth. (J. A. Church) Galaxy, 2: 622.
— Latest Notes on. Colburn, 96: 229.
— Latin Races in. So. R. n. s. 9: 320.
— Latrobe, Abdy, etc. on. Quar. 54: 392.
— Learned Professions in. Chamb. J. 41: 6.
— Lessons from. Chamb. J. 19: 337.
— Letters from. (P. Godwin) Peop. J. 4: 83–305.— Mus. 14: 289.
— Letters in, Murray's. Canad. J. n. s. 1: 160.
— Liefer's Stranger in. Quar. 53: 310.
— Life in. (H. B. Hall) St. James, 7: 369.—Chr. Obs. 64: 432.—Colburn, 31: 42.
— Aspects of. (C. D. Warner) Atlan. 43: 1.
— — before the Revolution. (H. W. Frost) Galaxy, 18: 200.
— — Dangerous Tendencies in. Atlan. 42: 385.—(A. G. Sedgwick) Nation, 31: 31.
— Life and Scenery in, Sketches of. (L. D. Pychouska) Contin. Mo. 5: 9–643. 6: 544.
— Lyell's Travels in. (H. Merivale) Ed. R. 83: 129.— (Sir D. Brewster) No. Brit. 14: 541.
— Mackay's Travels in. (W. J. Grayson) De Bow, 28: 48.
— Mackenzie on. Mo. R. 131: 411.
— Manners in. (W. C. Brownell) Nation, 30: 343.
— — British Abuse of. Portfo.(Den.) 15: 397.
— — Morals and. (O. Dewey) Chr. Exam. 36: 250.
— Marmier's Notes on. Blackw. 69: 545.
— Marryatt's Diary in. (W. Empson) Ed. R. 70: 66.— Mus. 36: 354.—Blackw. 15: 424.—Ecl. R. 70: 422. 71: 271.—Quar. 64: 308.—Dub. Univ. 14: 513.—Mo. R. 149: 497. 151: 214.
— Miss Martineau on. (E. Everett) No. Am. 14: 15.— (C. Stetson) Chr. Exam. 23: 226.—(J. G. Palfrey) No. Am. 45: 418.—Am. Q. 22: 21.—Fraser, 19: 557.—Meth. Q. 2: 584.—Lit. & Theo. R. 4: 455. —Westm. 28: 470. 30: 365.—Ed. R. 67: 180.
— Michaux on. Ed. R. 7: 155.
— Mission of. (H. W. Bellows) Chr. Exam. 86: 56.— (B. F. Porter) De Bow, 4: 108.—Brownson, 13: 409.
— Murat on. So. R. 7: 102.—For. Q. 11: 1.—Mus. 22: 671.
— Murray's Travels in. New Q. 4: 408.—New York R. 5: 490.—So. Lit. Mess. 6: 72.—Quar. 64: 308.— Ed. R. 73: 77.
— Muskau and Mrs. Trollope on. (E. Everett) No. Am. 36: 1.
— Name of. (R. H. Major) Am. Bibliop. 2: 329. 3: 9.
— — New, suggested. Dem. R. 16: 492.
— — Origin of. (J. Marcou) Atlan. 35: 291.—Scrib. 12: 222.
— North and South, Statistics of, 1869. Am. J. Educ. 18: 523.
— Northern Coasts of. Am. Mo. 3: 437.
— — Simpson on Discoveries on, 1836–39. Mo. R. 162: 76.
— Northwest Coast, Topographical Features of. (T. A. Blake) Am. J. Sci. 95: 242.
— Notions of the Americans. Colburn, 23: 164.
— Obligations to France. (J. G. Shea) Cath. World, 13: 836.
— Ousley on. Quar. 48: 507.
— Parkinson on. (M. Napier) Ed. R. 7: 29.—Ecl. R. 3: 165.
— Past and Present of, 1850. (E. S. Ely) Hogg, 4: 135.
— Peopling of. (A. R. Grote) Am. Natural. 11: 221.
— — Original. Portfo.(Den.) 13: 231, 519. 14: 7.
— Peter Schlemihl in. (M. I. Motte) Chr. Exam. 45: 84.
— Plants of, Derivation of. (A. Gray) Pop. Sci. Mo. 1: 724.
America, Popular Religion in. (J. C. Hutcheson) Belgra. 16: 422.
— Population of. (A. von Humboldt) Niles's Reg. 30: 190.
— Power's Impression of, 1833–35. Mo. R. 139: 297.
— Pre-Columbian History of. (H. R. Schoolcraft) Am. Bib. Repos. 2d s. 1: 430.—(A. B. Chapin) Am. Bib. Repos. 2d s. 1: 191.
— Present State of, 1837. Dub. Univ. 9: 507.
— Progress of. Liv. Age, 14: 191.
— — Comparative View of. (R. P. Porter) Princ. n. s. 4: 493.
— — Indications of Philosophic. For. Q. 24: 279.
— — Macgregor on. Liv. Age, 15: 385.
— Prophecies concerning. (C. Sumner) Atlan. 20: 275. —Hist. M. 15: 140.
— Prospects of. Mus. 13: 704.
— — and her Resources. Ed. Mo. R. 1: 435.
— — — Bristed on, 1818. Ecl. R. 32: 23.
— Pulpit of, Sprague's Annals of. (G. E. Ellis) Chr. Exam. 62: 110.— (E. Everett) Liv. Age, 52: 238.
— Race and Color Antagonisms in. Liv. Age, 105: 131.
— Religion in. (R. W. Dale) Sup. Pop. Sci. Mo. 4: 44.—(E. Dicey) Macmil. 15: 440. Same art. Ecl. M. 69: 19.
— — Liberality and Devotedness in. Cong. M. 21: 405.
— Republics in. (W. H. Dixon) Peop. J. 4: 248. 5: 95.
— Resources of, Sir M. Peto on. Chamb. J. 43: 438.
— Rural Scenes and Natural History of. Chr. Rem. 20: 105.
— Saxe Weimar on. Quar. 41: 417.—Mo. R. 117: 91. (G. Bancroft) No. Am. 28: 226.—So. R. 3: 192. —Am. Q. 4: 244.—For. Q. 3: 630.
— Scenery in. (H. Merivale) Ev. Sat. 6: 721.—Sharpe, 15: 251.
— Schaff on. (B. H. Nadal) Meth. Q. 16: 122.
— Schmidt and Gall on. (E. Everett) No. Am. 17: 91.
— Scotch-Irish in. (G. H. Smyth) M. Am. Hist. 4: 161.
— seen with foreign Eyes. Appleton, 13: 584–815. 14: 17.
— Settlement of, First. Bost. Mo. 1: 169–337.
— — First English Colony on Roanoke Island. (F. Kidder) Contin. Mo. 1: 541.
— Settlements in before Columbus. (T. Ewbank) Hist. M. 12: 75.
— Short Cut to. Chamb. J. 16: 203.
— Social Elevation in. So. Lit. Mess. 2: 381.
— Social Life in. (Mrs. A. L. Phelps) Nat. Q. 1: 350.
— Society in. (J. S. Mill) Westm. 31: 365.—(H. T. Tuckerman) No. Am. 81: 26.—Knick. 9: 163.— Dem. R. 28: 86.—So. Q. 26: 355.
— — Peculiarities of. Cornh. 26: 704. Same art. Liv. Age, 116: 294.
— — Pulszky's Sketches of. Liv. Age, 37: 97.
— — Sketches of. (C. A. Bristed) Fraser, 41: 261, 523. 42: 255, 373, 562. Same art. Ecl. M. 20: 76, 419.
— — Traits of. Fraser, 85: 632. Same art. Ecl. M. 79: 53. Same art. Ev. Sat. 12: 600.
— — Mrs. Trollope on. (J. G. Lockhart) Quar. 47: 39.
— — Young Ladyism in. (J. G. Kohl) Bentley, 50: 273.
— Spanish Conquest of, Helps's. Ed. R. 109: 1.—Brit. Q. 26: 235. Same art. Ecl. M. 42: 283.—Brit. Q. 34: 155. Same art. Ecl. M. 54: 145.—Fraser, 52: 241. 56: 331. 65: 135.—Dub. R. 41: 294.— Dub. Univ. 46: 577.—Sharpe, 22: 221.
— Sporting in. Bentley, 27: 493.
— Statistics of. U. S. Cath. M. 6: 129.
— Stranger in, 1880. (G. J. Holyoake) 19th Cent. 8: 67. Same art. Liv. Age, 146: 354. Same art. Ecl. M. 95: 298.
— Stuart's Three Years in. Am. Q. 13: 469.—Ed. R. 56: 460.—(T. P. Thompson) Westm. 18: 317.— Select J. 2: [19.—Am. Mo. R. 4: 140.
— Sturge's Visit to. Ecl. R. 75: 414.

America, Subaltern in. (G. R. Gleig) Blackw. **21**: 243–709. **22**: 74, 316.
— Sullivan's Rambles in. Blackw. **72**: 680.
— Summary View of. Blackw. **16**: 617. — Westm. **3**: 283. — (J. Sparks) No. Am. **21**: 453. — Mo. R. **107**: 34.
— Summer in. Bentley, **51**: 501, 661. **52**: 57–620. **53**: 35–392.
— Sutcliff on. Mo. R. **84**: 56.
— Taylor's Notes on. Blackw. **69**: 545.
— Things as they are in. (W. Chambers) Chamb. J. **21**: 81–390. **22**: 6–242.
— Three Books about, 1838. Mo. R. **147**: 1.
— Three British Views of, 1879. (W. C. Brownell) Nation, **29**: 181.
— Tracts on. Mo. R. **97**: 200.
— Transatlantic Sketches. (W. Brodie) Bentley, **53**: 469–613. **54**: 185–278.
— Travelers in. (Syd. Smith) Ed. R. **31**: 133.
— Travelers and Traveling in. Penny M. **7**: 23.
— Traveling in. Blackw. **18**: 422. — Knick. **2**: 283. — Mus. **8**: 30. — Cornh. **19**: 321.
— Travels of a Scottish Craftsman in. Ecl. M. **6**: 321.
— Trollope on. Dub. Univ. **60**: 75. — Am Q. **12**: 109. — Am. Mo. R. **2**: 158. — Quar. **47**: 39. — Mo. R. **127**: 540.
— Trollope and Paulding on. Fraser, **5**: 336.
— Vigne on. Mo. R. **128**: 117.
— Visits, Views, and Tours in. Quar. **27**: 71.
— Von Raumer on. (J. T. Crane) Meth. Q. **7**: 211.
— Warden on. (E. Everett) No. Am. **13**: 47.
— Was it known to the Ancients? (G. R. Howell) Potter Am. Mo. **17**: 17.
— Western Territories of, Pike's Travels in, 1805–7. (J. Foster) Ecl. R. **3**: 296.
— What should be the Example of? Knick. **32**: 347.
— White, Red, and Black in, Pulszky's. Chamb. J. **19**: 265, 277.
— Woman in. Dub. Univ. **69**: 279. Same art. Ecl. M. **68**: 678.
— Wonders of. (J. A. Dobson) Potter Am. Mo. **11**: 321.
— Wright, Fanny, on. Mo. R. **97**: 247.
— Wyse's Travels in. Dub. Univ. **30**. 193.
See also names of subdivisions, as North; South; Central; *also*, New World.
American, The. (H. James, jr.) Atlan. **37**: 651. **38**: 15–641. **39**: 1–530.
— in England, 1836. Mo. R. **139**: 330.
— in London. Knick. **16**: 279.
— of Culture, The Self-Made. (W. C. Brownell) Nation, **32**: 385.
American's Tale. Lond. Soc. **38**: supp. 44.
Americans abroad. (A. Gore) Lippinc. **26**: 466. — (H. James, jr.) Nation, **27**: 208, 239.
— and their Detractors. (W. Empson) Ed. R. **55**: 479.
— in England. Liv. Age, **29**: 568.
— in Moral, Social, and Political Relations, Grund on, 1836. Mo. R. **142**: 207. — Bost. Q. **1**: 161.
— in Paris. Nation, **26**: 257.
— Traveling, Character of. (H. W. Jenkins) Overland, **3**: 534.
— Typical. (M. Walsh) Cath. World, **23**: 479.
See American People.
American Academy of Arts and Sciences. (W. Tudor) No. Am. **1**: 370.
American Almanac. Am. Mo. R. **1**: 157.
— 1833. Am. Mo. R. **2**: 478.
— 1834. Am. Mo. R. **4**: 453.
— 1837. No. Am. **44**: 267.
— 1838. No. Am. **46**: 311.
— General Index, 1830–39. Am. Alma. **1839**: 315.
— — 1840–49. Am. Alma. **1849**: 358.
American Almanac, General Index, 1850–59. Am. Alma. **1859**: 372.
American Ambition and Europe's Dilemma, 1854. Dub. Univ. **44**: 111. Same art. Liv. Age, **42**: 243.
American Annual Register, 1825–26. Lond. M. **19**: 1.
American Antiquarian Society, Transactions of. West. R. **3**: 89.
American Antiquities. (T. W. Harris) No. Am. **12**: 225. — Chr. R. **4**: 555. — New York R. **10**: 68. — Knick. **2**: 371. — With drawings, Knick. **10**: 1–457. — (C. L. Brace) Atlan. **1**: 769. — (S. G. Drake) N. E. Reg. **9**: 263. — (A. D. Chandler) Penn Mo. **3**: 385. — (C. Morris) Lippinc. **7**: 514. — Am. Mo. M. **7**: 67. — Broadw. **8**: 538. — Colburn, **90**: 127. — Hesp. **3**: 120. — Dem. R. **28**: 512. — Ed. R. **125**: 332. Same art. Liv. Age, **93**: 547. — Penny M. **14**: 239, 242. — Portfo.(Den.) **15**: 458. **16**: 1. — West. Mo. R. **1**: 656. — West. R. **1**: 96–346. **2**: 29, 112, 153. **3**: 89. — (C. C. Jones, jr.) No. Am. **118**: 70. — (B. F. Porter) Hunt, **15**: 480. — (R. C. Taylor) Am. J. Sci. **34**: 88. — (J. L. Taylor) Bib. Sac. **12**: 433. — (F. Parkman) Chr. Exam. **50**: 417. — Liv. Age, **58**: 20.
— Aboriginal Structures. (L. Cass) No. Am. **51**: 396.
— America the Old World. (L. Agassiz) Atlan. **11**: 373.
— Bradford on. Mo. R. **158**: 141.
— in Pacific States. (H. L. Oak) Overland, **15**: 305.
— in St. Louis Co., Mo. (F. E. Roesler) Western, **1**: 739.
— in United States. (E. G. Squier) Harper, **20**: 737. **21**: 20, 165.
— of Kentucky. (C. S. Rafinesque) West. R. **3**: 53.
— of New York. (E. G. Squier) Am. J. Sci. **61**: 305.
— Origin of. (W. H. C. Hosmer) Overland, **9**: 530.
— Prehistoric Ruins, in Southern Colorado. (H. Gannett) Pop. Sci. Mo. **16**: 666.
— Priest's. Am. Mo. M. **7**: 310.
— Researches in. (A. de Bellacombe) Anthrop. R. **2**: 191.
— Study of. (J. P. McLean) Univ. Q. **36**: 288. **37**: 33, 281.
— Western. Ill. M. **1**: 241.
See America, Ancient; Indians; Mound-Builders.
American Association for Advancement of Education. Am. J. Educ. **1**: 3.
American Association for the Advancement of Science. (E. B. Hunt) Putnam, **2**: 319. — Am. J. Educ. **3**: 147. — Canad. J. n. s. **2**: 63. — Nature, **10**: 441. **12**: 424, 443.
American Authors. Bentley, **33**: 633. — Blackw. **16**: 304, 415, 560. **17**: 48, 186.
— abroad. (T. L. Cuyler) Godey, **32**: 59.
— Alphabetical List of. Am. Q. Reg. **5**: 186. **6**: 23.
— — of 766. Am. Alma. **1840**: 67.
American Authorship. Colburn, **97**: 424. **98**: 77–476. **99**: 77–425. **100**: 73–173. **101**: 105–222. **102**: 283. — So. Q. **23**: 486.
American Autocrats. (F. L. Oswald) Internat. R. **6**: 567.
American Avatar: Sage, Poet, and Hero. Am. Whig R. **13**: 149.
American Bankers' Association. Bank. M. (N. Y.) **31**: 394.
American Bar, The. Dem. R. **28**: 195.
— and Bench. (J. Bryce) Macmil. **25**: 422. Same art. Liv. Age, **113**: 109, 163. — Hist. M. **10**: 4.
American Bards; a Satire. Anal. M. **16**: 188.
American Baron. (J. De Mille) Harper, **42**: 321–862. **43**: 65–862.
American Baronets. Hist. M. **10**: 4.
American Bench. (J. Macdonell) Contemp. **28**: 682.
— Drolleries of. Chamb. J. **54**: 382.
American Bible Society and the English Version. (C. Hodge) Princ. **29**: 507.
— History of. Am. Meth. M. **17**: 459.

American Bible Society, Letter on. (S. H. Turner) Am. Church R. **9**: 547.
— Presidents of. (G. P. Disosway) Nat. M. **5**: 289, 385.
American Biographical Dictionary, Allen's. Am. Mo. R. **2**: 429.
American Biographical Sketches. No. Am. **1**: 328.
American Biography. Penn Mo. **2**: 167.
— Baldwin's Party Leaders. So. Q. **27**: 235.
— Drake's Dictionary of. (W. A. Wheeler) No. Am. **115**: 453.
— Sparks's Library of. (O. W. B. Peabody) No. Am. **38**: 466.—(J. G. Palfrey) No. Am. **43**: 267, 516.—(O. W. B. Peabody) No. Am. **59**: 96.—Meth. Q. **8**: 503.
American Board, and its Reviewers. Bost. R. **2**: 258.
— Secretaries of, with engraving. Ecl. M. **58**: 259.
American Boarding Houses. Dub. Univ. **75**: 468.
American Chesterfield, The. Fraser, **5**: 515.
American Church Missionary Society. (N. S. Richardson) Am. Church R. **13**: 390. **18**: 597.
American Citizen, Responsibilities of. (G. C. Maund) Evang. R. **15**: 570.
American Colleges. (A. Suydam) University Q. **4**: 196.
— Porter on. Lakeside, **4**: 316.
— Recollections of. (T. Hughes and W. D. Rawlins) Dark Blue, **1**: 59–316.
See Colleges; Universities.
American Colonies, Bancroft's Account of the. Prosp. R. **4**: 217.
— History of. (L. Sabine) No. Am. **60**: 368.
— — Chalmers's. (L. Sabine) No. Am. **60**: 539.
— — Grahame on. Mo. R. **112**: 407.—(C. F. Adams) No. Am. **32**: 174.
— How they lived in. (H. W. Frost) Galaxy, **18**: 200.
— Controversy with Great Britain. Ann. Reg. **2**: 43. **2**: [22. **5**: 52. **7**: 263.—(E. Everett) Ann. Reg. **5**: 35.—Niles's Reg. **32**: 49.
— Development of Constitutional Government in. (H. O. Taylor) M. Am. Hist. **2**: 705.
— Independence of. N. E. Reg. **30**: 326.
— Journey to, 1679–80. (C. E. Norton) No. Am. **105**: 653.
— Lodge's History of. (H. B. Adams) Nation, **32**: 373.—(W. F. Poole) Dial (Ch.), **2**: 32.
— Middle, in 1755. (D. Dulany) Pennsyl. M. **3**: 11.
— Paper Money of. (J. Q. Howard) Nat. Q. **32**: 96.
— Relics of Early Times in. Hist. M. **8**: 333. **9**: 85.
— Republican Views of. (M. Storey) No. Am. **116**: 425.
American Colonization Society, 1819. West. R. **1**: 142.
American Colony in a Normandy Manor-House, An. (M. B. Wright) Scrib. **15**: 640.
American Common School Society. Am. J. Educ. **15**: 247.
American Competition. Chamb. J. **58**: 289.
— American View of. (E. Atkinson) Fortn. **31**: 383.
— Truth about. (G. B. Powell) Fraser, **103**: 310.
American Congregational Association, 11th Annual Report. Cong. Q. **6**: 313. 12th, **7**: 447. 13th, **8**: 321. 14th, **9**: 300. 15th, **10**: 310. 16th, **11**: 451. 17th, **12**: 446. 18th, **13**: 466. 19th, **14**: 461. 20th, **15**: 460. 21st, **16**: 494. 22d, **17**: 452. 23d, **18**: 466. 24th, **19**: 460. 25th, **20**: 489.
American Congregational Union. (E. W. Gilman) Cong. Q. **1**: 59.—(I. P. Langworthy) Cong. Q. **1**: 321.
— 10th Annual Report. Cong. Q. **5**: 273. 11th, **6**: 306. 12th, **7**: 441. 13th, **8**: 315. 14th, **9**: 308. 15th, **10**: 300. 16th, **11**: 462. 17th, **12**: 461. 18th, **13**: 480. 19th, **14**: 471. 20th, **15**: 473. 21st, **16**: 504. 22d, **17**: 467. 23d, **18**: 479. 24th, **19**: 472.
American Conservatism, English View of. (A. V. Dicey) Nation, **30**: 228, 282.
American Criticism. Mus. **15**: 10.
American Despotisms. (P. Godwin) Putnam, **4**: 528.
American Diplomacy. Fraser, **48**: 299.
American Education Society. Am. J. Educ. **14**: 367.
American Encroachments on British Rights. Pamph. **6**: 33, 361.
American Episcopate before the Revolution. (N. S. Richardson) Am. Church R. **4**: 548.
American Facts. Ecl. M. **5**: 410.
— and Gladstone Fallacies. Sup. Pop. Sci. Mo. **4**: 181.
American Farmer, The, Hints to. Contin. Mo. **5**: 584.
American Female Seminary, School-Days in an. St. James, **31**: 110, 231, 436.
American Forests. Penny M. **6**: 454.
— Fires in. Penny M. **6**: 466.
— Scenes in. Mus. **16**: 323.
American Genius in England. (J. R. Remington) Hunt, **19**: 496. Same art. Bank. M. (N. Y.) **3**: 363.
American Girl, and her Lovers; a Story. (M. E. Blair) Lippinc. **15**: 160.
American Girl, The. (W. C. Brownell) Nation, **30**: 265, 417.
— Shall she be chaperoned? (A. Rhodes) Galaxy, **24**: 451.
American Heraldry, Plea for. (W. H. Whitmore) Hist. M. **14**: 126.
American Heroine in Fiction. (A. Macdonell) Macmil. **32**: 544.
American Home Missionary Society. (J. S. Clark) Cong. Q. **1**: 359. **4**: 38.
— New Rule of. Am. Presb. R. **9**: 286.
American Humor. Brit. Q. **52**: 324.—Cornh. **13**: 28.—No. Brit. **33**: 461.—Ecl. M. **33**: 137. **35**: 267.—All the Year, **6**: 190.
— Slicks, Downings, and Crocketts. Westm. **32**: 137.
American Influence on the Democratic Movement in France. (J. McCarthy) Am. Cath. Q. **5**: 636.
American Institute. Hunt, **3**: 418.
— 1829. Niles's Reg. **37**: 140, 154.
— 1830. Niles's Reg. **39**: 162.
— Fair of. Hunt, **11**: 444.—Am. Whig R. **2**: 538.
American Institute of Instruction. Am. J. Educ. **2**: 19.
— Index to Lectures of. Am. J. Educ. **2**: 241.
— Presidents of. Am. J. Educ. **15**: 211.
American Institutions, 1835. Ecl. R. **62**: 89 257.
— Permanence of. (A. Payne) Chr. R. **17**: 86.
— Perpetuity of. Blackw. **18**: 355.
American Journal of Education, Barnard's, 1856–65. (S. Watson) New Eng. **24**: 513.
— Classified Index. Am. J. Educ. **17**: 17. **26**: 49.
American Journals in France and Germany. (J. Sparks) No. Am. **24**: 226.
American Jurisprudence. Portfo.(Den.) **14**: 590.
American Kitchen-Garden. (A. B. Storey) Good Words, **22**: 167.
American Legislation. (J. D. B. De Bow) De Bow, **2**: 76.
American Letters. (E. W. Johnson) Am. Whig R. **1**: 575.
American Liberties, Past Dangers to. Lippinc. **25**: 60.
American Library. Blackw. **62**: 574.
— of Useful Knowledge. Am. Mo. R. **1**: 53.
American Literature. Ed. R. **50**: 125.—Blackw. **18**: 306. **110**: 422. Same art. Ecl. M. **77**: 671.—Westm. **49**: 333. Same art. Liv. Age, **18**: 361.—For. Q. **21**: 316.—Retros. **9**: 304.—(J. C. Gray) No. Am. **13**: 478.—(T. Flint) Knick. **2**: 161.—So. Lit. Mess. **1**: 1.—(G. Tucker) So. Lit. Mess. **4**: 81. **6**: 707. **11**: 393.—Brownson, **4**: 384.—Ecl. M. **14**: 532.—Dub. Univ. **35**: 461. Same art. Ecl. M. **20**: 325.—(E. S. Gould) Lit. & Theo. R. **3**: 33.—Mo. R. **93**: 297.—Mus. **5**: 87.—So. R. **7**: 436.—(W. Channing) No. Am. **1**: 307.—(A. P. Peabody) No. Am. **92**: 146.—(G. E. Woodberry) Fortn. **35**: 606.—(J. W. Simmons) So. Lit. J. **3**: 65.—(H. T. Tuckerman) No. Am. **82**: 319.—(J. A. Spencer) Am. Church R. **9**: 84.—Am. Presb. R. **6**: 106.—Blackw. **62**: 574.—Westm. **57**: 288. Same art. Ecl. M. **25**: 289.—Portfo.(Den.) **12**: 44.—Temp. Bar, **37**: 396.

American Literature. De Bow, **24**: 173. — Bost. Q. **2**: 1. **3**: 57. — So. Q. **11**: 117. — West. M. **1**: 5, 184.
— and Criticism. (E. S. Gould) Lit. & Theo. R. **3**: 33.
— and English compared. (T. T. Stone) Lit. & Theo. R. **2**: 36. — Am. Q. Obs. **2**: 36. — Dem. R. **22**: 207.
— Bibliography of. Hist. M. **4**: 38.
— Characteristics of. No. Brit. **46**: 456. Same art. Ecl. M. **69**: 186.
— — 1861–68. Westm. **94**: 263. Same art. Liv. Age, **108**: 67.
— Classical Works of. Ecl. Mus. **2**: 179.
— Colonial. Nat. Q. **23**: 315.
— — Bibliography of. (J. D. Butler) Bib. Sac. **36**: 72. — Hist. M. **4**: 73, 235, 328.
— Delinquency of. (W. Channing) No. Am. **2**: 33
— Dramatists of. Lond. M. **16**: 466.
— Duyckinck's Cyclopædia of. Putnam, **7**: 170.
— Future of. Bost. Q. **1**: 106.
— History of. Harper, **52**: 401, 514.
— — Tyler's. (C. C. Smith) Unita. R. **11**: 165. — (T. W. Higginson) Nation, **28**: 16. — Penn Mo. **10**: 624.
— Imaginative. (J. Pollock) Contemp. **22**: 347.
— Impediments of. West. Mo. R. **2**: 481. **3**: 21.
— Prognostics of. (N. Porter) Am. Bib. Repos. 3d s. **3**: 504.
— Prose Writers. Dem. R. **20**: 384.
— — Griswold's. So. Lit. Mess. **13**: 209, 381. **16**: 230.
— Quackery in. (S. S. Haldeman) So. R. n. s. **3**: 210.
— Retrospective Survey of, 1852. Westm. **57**: 288, 633.
— Schools in. (A. C. Coxe) Am. Church R. **3**: 329.
— Southern. (G. W. Curtis) Putnam, **9**: 207.
— Studies of. (P. Chasles) Internat. M. **4**: 165.
— Style of Writers in. (B. J. Wallace) Am. Presb. R. **4**: 135.
— Thoughts on. West. J. **6**: 336.
— to-day, to-morrow. (J. S. Hawks) Dem. R. **29**: 209.
— Transitions in. (J. V. O'Conor) Cath. World, **32**: 363.
— Truly American. (J. R. Dennett) Nation, **6**: 7.
— Turning-Point in. (M. F. Taylor) So. M. **11**: 323.
— Who reads? (J. G. Palfrey) No. Am. **55**: 372.
See New England; Literature.
American Loyalists, Sabine's Sketches of. (G. E. Ellis) No. Am. **65**: 138.
— in Nova Scotia. (L. W. Champney) Lippinc. **27**: 391.
American Marvels. All the Year, **39**: 112.
American Mind, Practical Character of. (D. Peabody) Am. Bib. Repos. **7**: 407.
American Mines and Mining Companies. Blackw. **17**: 592, 741.
American Ministers abroad. (E. L. Godkin) Nation, **4**: 132.
— Dress of. (E. L. Godkin) Nation, **6**: 267.
American Names. Ecl. M. **40**: 271.
American Nationality. (P. Schaff) Mercersb. **8**: 501.
American Newspapers. *See* Newspapers.
American Novels. No. Brit. **20**: 81. — Liv. Age, **2**: 643. — (Mrs. M. F. Sullivan) Cath. World, **28**: 325.
American Novelists, Early. (G. P. Lathrop) Atlan. **37**: 404.
American Orators and Statesmen. (A. Hayward) Quar. **67**: 1. Same art. Mus. **41**: 374.
American People, 1837. Ecl. R. **66**: 51.
— and the Aborigines. Blackw. **59**: 554, 677. **60**: 45.
— and Mrs. Trollope. Colburn, **35**: 446.
— Are they less healthy than Europeans? (S. G. Young) Galaxy, **14**: 630.
— as they are. Mo. R. **115**: 448.
— Beaumont on. Quar. **53**: 289.
— Beauty of. (J. H. Browne) Galaxy, **11**: 108.
— Character of. (T. M. Anderson) Galaxy, **21**: 733. — (J. G. Swisshelm) Galaxy, **22**: 618. — Blackw. **15**: 690. **16**: 91. — Mus. **22**: 611. — Portfo. (Den.) **14**: 18.
— — Defense of. Portfo. (Den.) **21**: 412.
American People, Characteristics of. (T. M. Coan) Putnam, **15**: 351. — Dem. R. **32**: 433. **35**: 99. — Knick. **21**: 245.
— — Grund's. Ecl. R. **66**: 51.
— How to treat. N. Ecl. **4**: 331.
— Looks and Fashions of. (R. Tomes) Putnam, **1**: 308.
— Notes on. Mo. R. **116**: 465.
— Past and Present of. (L. Sabine) No. Am. **66**: 426.
— Physical Future of. (G. M. Beard) Atlan. **43**: 718.
— Physique of. (G. M. Beard) No. Am. **129**: 588.
— Transatlantic Britons. St. James, **30**: 193.
— Who and what are they? Dem. R. **43**: 270.
American Periodical Literature. Ecl. R. **67**: 215. — Blackw. **63**: 106. — (J. G. Palfrey) No. Am. **39**: 277.
American Peripatetics, Winter with. (G. A. Townsend) Galaxy, **1**: 57.
American Philosophical Society. Penn Mo. **11**: 815.
American Philosophical Transactions. (H. Brougham) Ed. R. **2**: 348.
American Philosophy. Westm. **33**: 345. — Brit. Q. **5**: 88.
American Poetry. Ed. R. **61**: 21. — Blackw. **11**: 684. **31**: 646. — Knick. **8**: 637. **12**: 383. — For. Q. **32**: 391. — No. Brit. **17**: 394. Same art. Ecl. M. **27**: 152. — Fraser, **1**: 8. **42**: 9. Same art. Ecl. M. **20**: 561. — Dub. Univ. **5**: 93. — (W. C. Bryant) No. Am. **7**: 198. — (E. Peabody) No. Am. **29**: 220. — (S. A. Eliot) No. Am. **29**: 487. — (A. P. Peabody) No. Am. **82**: 236. — Am. Q. **6**: 240. — (F. W. P. Greenwood) Chr. Exam. **12**: 91. — (E. C. Stedman) Scrib. **22**: 540. — No. Brit. **46**: 456. Same art. Liv. Age, **94**: 167. — (W. B. Weeden) O. & N. **5**: 474. — Liv. Age, **17**: 435. — Ecl. M. **21**: 425. — Mo. R. **123**: 114. **127**: 490. — Anal. M. **14**: 211. — So. Lit. Mess. **5**: 573. — Am. Church R. **22**: 161. — Peop. J. **10**: 101.
— Early. Dub. Univ. **84**: 178.
— Fugitive. So. Q. **14**: 101.
— Humorous. (F. G. Stephens) Macmil. **1**: 203.
— Lake. Am. Q. **11**: 154.
— Landscape in. Art J. **31**: 1–333.
— Lyric. Am. Q. **19**: 101.
— Old and New. (J. Ferguson) Am. Church R. **17**: 199.
— Recent, 1856. Putnam, **6**: 48. — So. Lit. Mess. **5**: 573.
— Vers de Société of. Tinsley, **18**: 705.
American Poets. Dub. R. **74**: 302. **75**: 64. — Lond. Q. **17**: 36. — (J. V. Cheney) Appleton, **15**: 81, 208, 523. — Ecl. R. **98**: 307. Same art. Liv. Age, **93**: 178. — Knick. **30**: 106. — So. Lit. Mess. **8**: 150, 528, 567. — Blackw. **69**: 513. Same art. Ecl. M. **23**: 202.
— and their Critics. Knick. **4**: 11.
— and Poetry. Chr. Rem. **15**: 300. — No. Brit. **46**: 456. — Dub. Univ. **22**: 229. — (A. H. Everett) No. Am. **33**: 297. — (E. P. Whipple) No. Am. **58**: 1. — (J. S. Dwight) Chr. Exam. **33**: 25. — So. Lit. Mess. **8**: 359. — For. Q. **32**: 291. — Am. Q. **6**: 240. — Dub. Univ. M. **22**: 229. — So. Q. **11**: 117. **16**: 224.
— — Griswold's. Internat. M. **1**: 165. — Bib. R. **1**: 317.
— Emerson, Halleck, Bryant, and Longfellow. For. Q. **32**: 159. — Liv. Age, **1**: 41.
— Nine New. (F. Bowen) No. Am. **64**: 402. — So. Lit. Mess. **13**: 292.
— Recent: Lowell, Longfellow, Poe. Lond. Q. **2**: 440.
— Satire on. So. Lit. J. **4**: 300.
— Specimens of. Mo. R. **100**: 28.
American Press. (J. C. Hutcheson) Belgra. **17**: 101.
American Principles and American Catholics. (J. R. G. Hazzard) Cath. World, **31**: 94.
American Prosperity, Clibborn on. Mo. R. **144**: 127.
American Radicals and English Censors. (M. D. Conway) Fortn. **3**: 705.
American Reviews, The Three. Mus. **14**: 149.

American Revolution. (J. G. Palfrey) No. Am. **75**: 125. — So. Lit. Mess. **8**: 257. — U. S. Lit. Gaz. **1**: 49. — Niles's Reg. **14**: 17. — (L. W. Peck) Nat. M. **8**: 1.
— Adams's (Sam.) Regiments at Boston. (R. Frothingham) Atlan. **9**: 701. **10**: 179. **12**: 595.
— Allied Armies before New York, 1781. (J. A. Stevens) M. Am. Hist. **4**: 1.
— American Troops near Boston in 1775, List of. N. E. Reg. **28**: 259.
— and Civil War. (W. Adams) Am. Presb. R. **15**: 78.
— Anecdotes of. (J. C. Gray) No. Am. **15**: 455.
— — English. Olden Time, **2**: 360.
— Attack on Fort Mifflin. Hist. M. **21**: 77.
— Attempt to burn British Frigates in the Hudson. Hist. M. **10**: supp. 84.
— Badge of Military Merit. Hist. M. **3**: 1.
— Ballads of. N. E. Reg. **11**: 337. — Liv. Age, **129**: 766.
— Battle of Golden Hill. (H. B. Dawson) Hist. M. **15**: 1.
— Battles of Brandywine and Germantown. Hist. M. **10**: 202.
— Bancroft's History of. (E. E. Hale) Chr. Exam. **65**: 125. — Ecl. R. **95**: 709. — Internat. M. **5**: 461. — Liv. Age, **33**: 53. **47**: 567. — Anal. M. **5**: 385.
— Beginning of. (F. C. Gray) No. Am. **9**: 376.
— a Blessing to Mankind. Fraser, **3**: 495. — Mus. **42**: 207.
— Border Wars of. (J. H. Perkins) No. Am. **49**: 277.
— Boston Tea Party. (B. J. Lossing) Harper, **4**: 1.
— Botta's History of. Ecl. R. **81**: 444.
— British Officer in Boston in 1775. Atlan. **39**: 389, 544.
— Burgoyne's Surrender: Ralph Cross's Journal. Hist. M. **17**: 8.
— Burning of Falmouth, Me. Hist. M. **15**: 202.
— Campaign against Quebec, 1775. Portfo. (Den.) **9**: 133.
— Causes of. (J. Fiske) Fortn. **34**: 147.
— Colleges in. (J. T. Headley) Knick. **57**: 353.
— Concord Fight. (F. Hudson) Harper, **50**: 777. *See* Concord; Lexington.
— Cornwallis in America. (E. E. Hale) Chr. Exam. **67**: 31. *See* Yorktown.
— Correspondence of. (E. Everett) No. Am. **33**: 449. — (J. G. Palfrey) No. Am. **77**: 80. — Hist. M. **1**: 73, 354. **2**: 6–321. **3**: 7, 169. **10**: 172, 216. **15**: 199, 203.
— Day (May 30, 1781) in the House of Commons. (J. C. Stockbridge) Harper, **64**: 62.
— Diplomacy of. (F. Bowen) No. Am. **75**: 270. — (G. W. Greene) Atlan. **15**: 576.
— Documentary History of. (G. Bancroft) No. Am. **46**: 475. — (G. W. Greene) No. Am. **92**: 364.
— Early Methodists and. Hist. M. **10**: 361. **11**: 291, 338. **12**: 147.
— Early Records of. Hist. M. **7**: 20.
— Early Stages of. (G. E. Ellis) No. Am. **87**: 449.
— English Officer's Account. Hist. M. **9**: 241–329.
— Episode of. (C. Dimitry) Lippinc. **18**: 115.
— Eutaw Flag. (R. Wilson) Lippinc. **17**: 311.
— Events leading to. (W. O. Johnson) No. Am. **80**: 389.
— Evils of. (C. K. Whipple) Liv. Age, **6**: 358.
— Exhortations previous to. (T. Bland, jr.) Hist. M. **2**: 199.
— Finances of. (G. W. Greene) Atlan. **14**: 591. Bank. M. (N. Y.) **18**: 356.
— — Loan Office Certificates. (H. Hall) Am. Hist. Rec. **3**: 356.
— First Blood of. (Seba Smith) Godey, **22**: 257.
— First Trophy of. Hist. M. **4**: 202, 233.
— Fort Motte, 1780. Land We Love, **3**: 136.
— French Allies in. (B. J. Lossing) Harper, **42**: 753.
— — in Rhode Island, 1777. M. Am. Hist. **3**: 385.
— — Officers, List of. M. Am. Hist. **3**: 364.
— — Return of, 1782–83. (J. A. Stevens) M. Am. Hist. **7**: 1.
— Generals of. (J. E. Cooke) Harper, **17**: 500.
American Revolution, George III.'s Letters on. (C. C. Hazewell) No. Am. **105**: 357.
— Glimpse of '76. (C. D. Deshler) Harper, **49**: 230.
— D. Gookin's Diary, in 1779. N. E. Reg. **16**: 27.
— Gordon's History of. Hist. M. **6**: 41, 78.
— Heroes of. Pioneer, **4**: 321.
— Hessians in. (G. W. Greene) Atlan. **35**: 131. — Hist. M. **8**: 54.
— Invasion of Canada in 1775. Hist. M. **12**: 97.
— Journal of a Soldier in 1776. Hist. M. **7**: 367.
— Leaves from History of. (J. J. Hardin) Am. Whig R. **8**: 577.
— Legend of Ball's Lake. (R. Wilson) Lippinc. **2**: 45.
— Letters on. (J. V. Cheney) Scrib. **11**: 424, 862. **12**: 94. — N. E. Reg. **30**: 303, 331. — Hist. M. **6**: 73, 239, 277. — So. Lit. Mess. **28**: 296.
— Letters of British Officers. Hist. M. **5**: 68.
— Letters of De Fersen, 1780. M. Am. Hist. **3**: 300, 369, 437.
— Mahon's History of. Internat. M. **5**: 164.
— Marquis of Hastings in America. (B. J. Lossing) Harper, **47**: 15.
— Martial Law during. (A. B. Gardner) M. Am. Hist. **1**: 705. (G. N. Lieber) M. Am. Hist. **1**: 538.
— Massachusetts Field Officers in. N. E. Reg. **25**: 187.
— Massacre at the Cedars, 1776. (S. E. Dawson) Canad. Mo. **5**: 305.
— Meade's Letters in. So. Lit. Mess. **25**: 22.
— Memorials of. (S. H. Riddel) N. E. Reg. **4**: 67.
— Minority in England, 1774. (T. H. Pattison) New Eng. **40**: 571.
— Mohawk Valley during. (H. Frederic) Harper, **55**: 171.
— Monument to, Projected. Hist. M. **3**: 234.
— Moore's Diary of. Liv. Age, **65**: 190.
— Naval Campaign on Lake Champlain in 1776. (W. C. Watson) Am. Hist. Rec. **3**: 438, 501.
— Naval Fight of, First. (F. A. Parker) M. Am. Hist. **1**: 209.
— Navy in, Memorials of. Hist. M. **3**: 201.
— Negroes as Soldiers in. Contin. Mo. **2**: 324.
— New York in. (E. Lawrence) Harper, **37**: 180. — (A. R. Macdonough) Nation, **28**: 420. — Hist. M. **5**: 269.
— — Military Occupation of, by British. Hist. M. **13**: 33.
— — — Lieut. Mathew's Narrative of. Hist. M. **1**: 102.
— New York Continental Line in. (A. B. Gardner) M. Am. Hist. **7**: 401.
— Officers of. N. E. Reg. **20**: 37.
— Opening Scenes of. Godey, **30**: 90.
— Order Book of, Extracts from. Hist. M. **2**: 353.
— Pamphlets on, in John Carter Brown Library. (J. C. Stockbridge) M. Am. Hist. **6**: 310.
— Papers of. Worc. M. **1**: 134, 165, 198, 232, 267.
— Partisan Warfare in South Carolina, 1776. Potter Am. Mo. **4**: 2.
— Peace Negotiation at Ghent. (C. F. Adams) No. Am. **120**: 231.
— Prison-Ships of, Martyrs of. Nat. M. **4**: 205.
— Prisoners in, Exchange of. Hist. M. **6**: 96. **8**: 200.
— Prisoners in England, 1777–79. N. E. Reg. **33**: 36.
— Quaker Testimonies respecting. Hist. M. **9**: 277.
— Relic of. N. Ecl. **5**: 688.
— Reminiscences of. Dem. R. **5**: 203. **6**: 66. **34**: 508. **38**: 304. — Am. Whig R. **6**: 68.
— Reminiscences of Mary (Morey) Turell, 1821. N. E. Reg. **14**: 149.
— Rochambeau's Quarters in Westchester Co., 1781. (C. A. Campbell) M. Am. Hist. **4**: 46.
— Route of the Allies to Yorktown, 1781. (J. A. Stevens) M. Am. Hist. **5**: 1.
— Smithers; a Bit of History. (E. Spencer) Lippinc. **16**: 368.
— Songs of Moore. Dem. R. **37**: 207.

American Revolution. Southern Campaign, 1781. (C. W. Coleman) M. Am. Hist. **7**: 36, 201.
— Stamp-Act Congress. (B. J. Lossing) Harper, **26**: 34.
— Stedman's History of. Mo. R. **162**: 256.
— Stone's (Enos) Diary in, 1776–77. N. E. Reg. **15**: 299.
— Tea Burning, Annapolis, 1774. (E. S. Riley, jr.) So. M. **14**: 537.
— Ticonderoga, Evacuation of, 1777. (H. Hall) Hist. M. **16**: 84.
— Tilden's Poems during. Hist. M. **3**: 328, 359. **4**: 7.
— Tory Contingent in British Army, 1781. Hist. M. **8**: 321, 355, 389.
— Tory Movements in New Jersey. Hist. M. **5**: 7.
— Tories, Conquered, and the Revolutionary Fathers. Nation, **1**: 358.
— Tracts of. (J. C. Stockbridge) M. Am. Hist. **5**: 427.
— Traditions of. Mus. **26**: 91, 164, 562.
— Traitors of. Hist. M. **9**: 89.
— Trial of J. Hett Smith. Hist. M. **10**: supp. 1–129.
— Uniforms of. Hist. M. **4**: 353.
— — and Flags of. (I. J. Greenwood) Potter Am. Mo. **6**: 31.
— Unpopularity of, in England. (W. Sargent) No. Am. **80**: 236.
— Virginia Navy in. So. Lit. Mess. **24**: 1–273.
— Virginia Soldier in. (R. Beale) So. M. **17**: 602.
— Virginia Regiment, Ninth. Hist. M. **7**: 172.
— H. D. Von Bulow on. Hist. M. **9**: 105, 141.
— Washington at Morristown, 1779–80. (J. E. Tuttle) Harper, **18**: 289.
— Watson's Men and Times of. Dem. R. **37**: 306.
— Women of. (Mrs. E. F. Ellet) Godey, **36**: 77–323. **37**: 6–373. **38**: 106–383. **39**: 28–444. **40**: 183, 257. **41**: 201. **42**: 293. — Hist. M. **15**: 105. — So. R. n. s. **21**: 31.
— — Ellet's. (Mrs. C. M. Kirkland) No. Am. **68**: 362.
— Wright, Aaron, Journal of, 1775. Hist. M. **6**: 208.
American Scenery, Essay on. (T. Cole) Am. Mo. M. **7**: 1.
— Some Features of. Fortn. **10**: 469. Same art. Liv. Age, **99**: 643.
American Scenes and Portraits. Dub. Univ. **63**: 112.
American Scholarship. U. S. Lit. Gaz. **1**: 234. — (J. F. Jackson) Knick. **28**: 1.
American School Society. Am. J. Educ. **15**: 118.
American Schools seen by English Eyes. (D. C. Gilman) Nation, **5**: 205.
American Seasons. (A. B. Street) Ecl. M. **21**: 280.
American Securities Abroad, Market for. Bank. M. (N. Y.) **30**: 841.
American Senator, The; a Novel. (A. Trollope) Temp. Bar, **47**: 1–433. **48**: 1–433. **49**: 117–546. **50**: 113–401.
American Sensations. All the Year, **5**: 131. — Chamb. J. **40**: 353.
American Shipping, Future of. (H. Hall) Atlan. **47**: 166. — (J. Codman) Internat. R. **10**: 184. — (J. Roach) No. Am. **132**: 467. — (W. G. Sumner) No. Am. **132**: 559.
American Social Science Association. Am. J. Educ. **16**: 391.
— and Finance. Bank. M. (N. Y.) **31**: 267.
— Constitution, Officers, and Members, 1878. Am. Soc. Sci. J. **9**: 165.
— Health Department. O. & N. **8**: 228.
American Society, Caste in. (K. G. Wells) Atlan. **48**: 823.
— Patrician Element in. (G. B. Loring) No. Am. **132**: 533.
— Recollections of. (S. W. Oakey) Scrib. **21**: 416.
— Sketches of. (C. A. Bristed) Fraser, **43**: 91–650.
American Society for the Diffusion of Useful Knowledge. Am. J. Educ. **15**: 239.
American Sportsmen. All the Year, **5**: 564.
American Stage, Anecdotes of. Chamb. J. **58**: 612.
American Statesmen, 1853. Fraser, **47**: 31. Same art. Liv. Age, **36**: 341.
— English Notices of, 1854. Liv. Age, **43**: 592.
— Late. (F. Wharton) Princ. n. s. **6**: 166. **8**: 95.
— Works of. (P. Godwin) Putnam, **1**: 642.
American Sunday School Union. Am. J. Educ. **15**: 705.
American Timidity. (T. M. Coan) Galaxy, **10**: 176.
American Titles. Penny M. **8**: 428.
American Tract Society. (S. W. S. Dutton) New Eng. **3**: 272. — Am. Q. **10**: 68.
— and Slavery. (H. C. Kingsley) New Eng. **16**: 612. **17**: 618.
American Trade, Crisis of, 1837. Ed. R. **65**: 263.
American Traditions. (J. Galt) Fraser, **2**: 321. **4**: 96. **5**: 275.
American Unitarian Association. (H. H. Barber) Unita. R. **3**: 511.
American Vessels in British Navy. N. E. Reg. **20**: 322.
American Woman of Business, An. (Mrs. A. Smith) Tinsley, **29**: 490.
American Women. (Mrs. V. Sherwood) Contin. Mo. **6**: 416.
— abroad. (L. H. Hooper) Galaxy, **21**: 818.
— Defense of. Portfo.(Den.) **20**: 276.
See American Girl.
Americanisms. (J. Challen) Nat. Q. **2**: 230. — (W. Channing) No. Am. **1**: 307. — (W. W. Crane) Putnam, **16**: 519. — (H. Reeves) Lippinc. **3**: 310. — (R. G. White) Atlan. **41**: 495, 656. **42**: 97, 342, 619. **43**: 88, 379, 656. **44**: 654. — Galaxy, **24**: 376, 681. — (J. F. Lounsbury) Internat. R. **8**: 472, 596. — (S. Willard) No. Am. **3**: 355. — Anal. M. **3**: 404. — So. Lit. Mess. **14**: 623. — Blackw. **89**: 421. — Hours at Home, **5**: 361. — So. R. n. s. **9**: 529. — Lond. Q. **57**: 392.
— American Nicknames. Chamb. J. **52**: 171.
— Bartlett's Dictionary of. (S. G. Brown) No. Am. **69**: 94. — Liv. Age, **20**: 79. — (W. P. Garrison) Nation, **26**: 171.
— British. (R. G. White) Atlan. **45**: 669. **47**: 697.
— De Vere's. (Goldwin Smith) Canad. Mo. **1**: 87.
— Pickering's Vocabulary of. Ecl. R. **31**: 356.
— Popular. All the Year, **25**: 270.
— Thoughts on. Lakeside, **3**: 154.
Americanists, International Congress of. Nature, **14**: 355.
Americus Vespucius. (C. Cushing) No. Am. **12**: 318.
Ames, Edward B. (A. Stevens) Nat. M. **7**: 385.
Ames, Fisher, with portrait. Portfo.(Den.) **9**: 1. — (E. H. Gillett) Hours at Home, **1**: 315. — (E. Quincy) Nation, **14**: 75.
— Biography of. Anal. M. **3**: 309.
— Character of. Walsh's R. **1**: 104.
— Essays of. Quar. **53**: 548.
— Life of, with portrait. Portfo.(Den.) **34**: 89. — With portrait. Bost. Mo. **1**: 409.
— Speech on Biennial Elections, 1788. Carey's Mus. **3**: 358.
— Works. (S. G. Brown) No. Am. **80**: 208. — (A. Lamson) Chr. Exam. **57**: 78. — Brownson, **11**: 502.
Ames, Nathaniel, Almanac-Maker. (W. B. Trask) N. E. Reg. **16**: 255.
Amherst, Voyage of the. Westm. **20**: 22.
Amherst College. (R. W. Marsh) Potter Am. Mo. **9**: 410.
— Reports of the Faculty. (N. Hale) No. Am. **24**: 485.
— Revivals of Religion in. (H. Humphrey) Am. Q. Reg. **11**: 317.
— Services of Austin Dickinson to. (O. Eastman) Cong. Q. **14**: 282.
Amianthus, Cloth and Paper made from. J. Frankl. Inst. **8**: 78.
Amicis, Edmondo de. Lippinc. **19**: 685.

Amicus Redivivus. (C. Lamb) Lond. M. **8**: 613.
Amiens, City of. (F. Hunt) Hunt, **19**: 617.
— Cathedral of. Penny M. **3**: 52.
— Visit to. Tinsley, **1**: 429.
Amiens Gravel. (A. Tylor) Am. J. Sci. **96**: 302.
Amina and the Mill-Wheel. All the Year, **5**: 320.
Ammalát Bek; a Tale of the Caucasus, transl. from the Russian. (T. B. Shaw) Blackw. **53**: 281, 464, 568, 746.
Ammer, Pilgrimage on the. (M. D. Conway) Fraser, **84**: 618.
Ammergau; an Idyll. Macmil. **22**: 271. *See* Ober-Ammergau; Passion Plays.
Ammonia and Ammoniacal Salts. (M. Seidel) J. Frankl. Inst. **105**: 27.
— Distribution of. (R. A. Smith) Ecl. Engin. **19**: 374.
— New Method of Manufacturing, 1859. (A. Williams) J. Frankl. Inst. **68**: 402.
Ammoniacal Gas as a Motive Power. (E. Lamm) Ecl. Engin. **5**: 290.
Ammonias, Compound. (T. S. Hunt) Am. J. Sci. **63**: 206.
Amnesty Measures. (J. N. Pomeroy) Nation, **12**: 52.
Amœba: its Structure, Development, and Habits. (W C. Williamson) Pop. Sci. R. **5**: 188.
Among the Black Boys. (L. A. Edgar) Victoria, **3**: 442–501. **4**: 45–547.
Among the Fir-Trees. Fraser, **82**: 765.
Among the Heather; a Story. Lond. Soc. **38**: 289, 385, 481. **39**: 92–398.
Among the Hop Gardens. Lond. Soc. **8**: 314.
Among the Pines. (J. R. Gilmore) Contin. Mo. **1**: 35–710. **2**: 28, 127.
Among Relations. (Ruth Harper) Harper, **33**: 731.
Among the Shades; a Tale. Broadway, **3**: 27.
Among Thieves. (N. S. Dodge) Putnam, **14**: 234.
Among the Trees; a Poem. (W. C. Bryant) Putnam, **13**: 15.
Amoor River. (B. Hart) New Eng. **19**: 352. — Colburn, **120**: 111.
— Another Chapter on. Fraser, **63**: 318.
— Atkinson's Travels in the Region of. Liv. Age, **66**: 631. — (A. H. Guernsey) Harper, **21**: 610.
— Explorations of. (J. G. Swan) Hunt, **39**: 176. — (P. D. McCollins) Harper, **17**: 221.
— India, and China, Atkinson's Travels in. Brit. Q. **32**: 304. Same art. Ecl. M. **52**: 240, 326.
— Russians on. (E. G. Ravenstein) Bentley, **41**: 551. — Colburn, **124**: 96.
— Russian Conquests on. Quar. **110**: 179.
— the latest Acquisition of Russia. Fraser, **51**: 10. Same art. Liv. Age, **44**: 408.
— To and upon. (T. W. Knox) Harper, **37**: 289.
Amor in Extremis. Fraser, **84**: 650.
Amory, T. Memoirs of several Ladies of Great Britain. Retros. **6**: 100.
Amory Genealogy. (T. C. Amory) N. E. Reg. **10**: 59.
Amos, Prophet, and River of the Wilderness. (E. Wilton) Kitto, **33**: 175. *See* Bible; Amos.
Amour (L') ou la Mort; a Tale. Galaxy, **10**: 522.
Amours de Voyage; a Poem. (A. H. Clough) Atlan. **1**: 419, 536, 667, 784.
Amoy. Penny M. **12**: 137.
— Colloquial Dialect of. (W. H. Cumming) Canad. J. n. s. **11**: 81.
Ampère, André M. (H. M. Douglass) Penn Mo. **8**: 854. — Blackw. **115**: 451. Same art. Ecl. M. **82**: 733. — O. & N. **6**: 740.
— and Jean-Jacques. (A. Laugel) Nation, **20**: 373. — (T. S. Perry) No. Am. **121**: 315. — Ed. R. **143**: 74. Same art. Liv. Age, **128**: 771. — (H. James, jr.) Galaxy, **20**: 662.
Ampersand Mountain, N. Y., Ascent of. (W. Read) O. & N. **10**: 342.
Amphictyonic Confederacy. For. Q. **6**: 141.
Amphion, Loss of the Ship. Meth. M. **23**: 367.
Amphioxus Lanceolatus, Observations on. (H. J. Rice) Am. Natural. **14**: 1, 73.
Amphlett Love-Match. House. Words, **16**: 173.
Amputation of Limbs. Ev. Sat. **10**: 575.
Amsden Genealogy. (A. H. Ward) N. E. Reg. **15**: 21.
Amsterdam. Penny M. **3**: 317.
— and its Suburbs. (C. A. White) Peop. J. **8**: 141, 162, 177.
— Legend of. Once a Week, **15**: 380.
— Sketch of. Colburn, **62**: 265.
Amsterdam, Isle of. (H. Copinger) Colburn, **156**: 398, 623. **159**: 48, 182. — (E. P. Wright) Nature, **17**: 326. — Geog. M. **2**: 47.
Amuck-Running in the East. (A. Locher) Scrib. **8**: 538.
Amulet, The; a Tale. Fraser, **71**: 210–754. **72**: 92.
Amulets. Penny M. **14**: 333.
— Cranial. (J. Bertillon) Pop. Sci. Mo. **7**: 607.
— Talismans, and Charms. Chamb. J. **36**: 57.
Amusement. (F. Brown) Peop. J. **10**: 301.
— and Recreation. (S. Smiles) Peop. J. **2**: 13.
Amusements. (E. Peabody) Chr. Exam. **45**: 157. — (O. Dewey) Chr. Exam. **8**: 201. — Chr. R. **45**: 157. — (E. Pond) New Eng. **9**: 345. — (R. W. Dale) Good Words, **8**: 329. — (G. H. Emerson) Univ. Q. **17**: 378. — (H. Irving) All the Year, **36**: 133. — (J. H. Seelye) Bost. R. **6**: 400. — Blackw. **100**: 698. — De Bow, **29**: 330. — Mo. Rel. M. **21**: 26. — New Eng. **26**: 399.
— Ancient and Modern. Meth. M. **54**: 550.
— Ancient English. Antiquary, **2**: 16.
— and the Church. (W. W. Patton) Hours at Home, **7**: 417.
— and Education of the Sensibilities. (W. De L. Love) Cong. R. **10**: 237.
— and Religion. (D. Walk) Chr. Q. **5**: 52.
— at Home. Godey, **59**: 47. — (E. F. Mosby) Potter Am. Mo. **15**: 285.
— at Sea. Chamb. J. **53**: 654. **56**: 235.
— Burder's Sermon on. Chr. Obs. **4**: 232, 306.
— Casuistry of. (E. R. Russell) Theo. R. **16**: 181.
— Cheap. (A. Ogilvy) Once a Week, **15**: 638.
— Diversions and Holidays. Portfo.(Den.) **31**: 218.
— Drawing-Room. Lond. Soc. **31**: 71–364.
— Duty of Christians as to. (A. Keene) Unita. R. **16**: 21.
— Fashionable. (E. Beecher) Chr. Mo. Spec. **8**: 32.
— Fireside Frolics. Lond. Soc. **7**: 7.
— for the Holidays. Godey, **75**: 525.
— for the Poor. O. & N. **10**: 258.
— in Cities. (H. D. Evans) Am. Ch. Mo. **2**: 127.
— Indoor, of the Ladies of the Middle Ages. Art J. **11**: 113.
— Ladies'. (F. P. Cobbe) Ev. Sat. **9**: 101.
— London. St. Paul's, **8**: 559. **9**: 45.
— Music Halls, Our. Tinsley, **4**: 216.
— of Clergymen and Christians. Portfo.(Den.) **29**: 377.
— of the English People. (G. Turner) 19th Cent. **2**: 820. — St. James, **26**: 504.
— of the Learned. Chamb. J. **56**: 555.
— of the Mob. Chamb. J. **26**: 225, 281, 371.
— of the Moneyless. Chamb. J. **23**: 305.
— Out-of-Door. (T. Wright) Art J. **11**: 217.
— Philosophy of Pastime. Godey, **57**: 238.
— Popular. (J. Clark) Mercersb. **6**: 399. — (E. Corderoy) Ex. H. Lec. **12**: 329. — (W. S. Jevons) Contemp. **33**: 499. — (A. H. Forrester) Bentley, **27**: 514, 624. **28**: 101, 186, 430. — Brownson, **16**: 129. — Dub. Univ. **84**: 233. — Hogg, **11**: 362. — Am. Church R. **24**: 538.

Amusements, Popular, Ancient and Modern. Westm. **66**: 163. Same art. Ecl. M. **39**: 285.
— Public. (H. Bentley) Cong. M. **2**: 334. — (T. E. Hook) Colburn, **56**: 289. — Ed. R. **54**: 100. — Chr. Exam. **63**: 47.
— — Places of. (C. F. Briggs) Putnam, **3**: 141.
— Rational, Need of. Blackw. **100**: 698. Same art. Liv. Age, **92**: 88.
— Sawyer's Plea for. U. S. Cath. M. **7**: 467.
— Social, under the Restoration. (R. Bell) Fortn. **2**: 193, 299, 460.
— Winter, for Children. Eng. Dom. M. **26**: 216–298.
— Worldly. Chr. Obs. **40**: 129, 193.
See also Recreations; Sports.
Amusing Trifles. Chamb. J. **58**: 203.
Amy; a Poem. (M. Collins) Temp. Bar, **2**: 330.
Amy Carlton; a Story. (R. Rendle) St. James, **46**: 235.
Amy, the Child. House. Words, **8**: 431.
Amy's Lover; a Tale. (Florence Marryat) Temp. Bar, **33**: 179. Same art. Lippinc. **6**: 128.
Amyot, Jacques. Colburn, **123**: 422.
Anabaptist Revival of the 16th Century. (H. S. Fagan) Good Words, **17**: 337.
Anabaptists; an Historical Inquiry. (H. S. Burrage) Bapt. Q. **9**: 350.
— Bigotry of. Chr. Obs. **39**: 107.
— in Switzerland. (L. Mayer) Mercersb. **2**: 213.
Anachronism, An. Dub. Univ. **11**: 701.
Anachronisms, Artistic. Chamb. J. **53**: 476.
Anacreon. Dub. Univ. **14**: 148. — Lond. Soc. **19**: 140.
— and his Dog, Figures of, on Vases. (S. Birch) Arch. **31**: 257.
— Life and Songs of. Bentley, **11**: 479, 644. **12**: 254, 466.
— Memoirs of. Portfo.(Den.) **23**: 401. **24**: 1, 265. **25**: 62, 249. **26**: 232, 249. **27**: 395, 501. **28**: 37, 89.
— Moore's. (G. Ticknor) Gen. Repos. **1**: 102. — Ed. R. **2**: 462. — Dub. Univ. **19**: 355.
— Richardson's Translation of. Mo. R. **105**: 265.
— Six Odes from. Dub. Univ. **22**: 399.
Anacreontic; a Poem. (J. Ashby-Sterry) Dark Blue, **1**: 509.
Anacreontic Song. Dub. Univ. **2**: 248.
Anacreontics. Blackw. **8**: 171.
Anæsthesia. (S. W. Barker) Harper, **31**: 453. — (A. S. Piggott) So. R. n. s. **3**: 452.
Anæsthetic, Carbonic Acid as an. Cornh. **6**: 546.
— Nitrous Oxide as an. (C. W. Eliot) Nation, **2**: 811.
Anæsthetics. (T. L. Phipson) Pop. Sci. R. **2**: 15. — Westm. **71**: 99. **96**: 198. Same art. Liv. Age, **110**: 498.
— and Pain. Nat. Q. **12**: 338.
— Discovery of. (Sir J. Paget) 19th Cent. **6**: 1119. Same art. Ecl. M. **94**: 219.
See also Chloroform; Ether.
Anagrams. Cornh. **27**: 424. Same art. Liv. Age, **117**: 376. — Macmil. **7**: 13. — Ev. Sat. **14**: 484.
— Wheatley on. Dub. Univ. **60**: 387.
Anaïk Timor, the Sorceress. (E. Souvestre) Sharpe, **27**: 126.
Anak; a Story. (Mrs. H. Davy) Colburn, **168**: 116–658. **169**: 92, 188.
Analogies, Natural. Penny M. **5**: 199, 207.
Analogy. (R. F. Clarke) Month, **20**: 178. — Knick. **60**: 477.
— of Religion, Old and New. Month, **43**: 457. *See* Religion.
— Philosophical. (J. D. Whelpley) Am. J. Sci. **55**: 33, 328.
Analysis, Organic, by Illuminating Gas. (C. M. Wetherill) J. Frankl. Inst. **58**: 107, 184, 274.
— — Liquid Diffusion applied to. (T. Graham) J. Frankl. Inst. **72**: 273.
Analysis, Organic, Process for. (Alexander and Morfit) J. Frankl. Inst. **57**: 102, 173, 267.
— Indeterminate. (A. D. Wheeler) Math. Mo. **2**: 21, 55, 193, 398.
— Synthesis and. (L. Withington) Bib. Sac. **23**: 603.
Analytical Statics, Todhunter's. Canad. J. n. s. **1**: 63.
Anarchist, Proudhon's Confessions of an. Ecl. R. **91**: 157.
Anarchy and Authority. (M. Arnold) Cornh. **17**: 30, 239, 745. **18**: 91, 239. Same art. Ev. Sat. **5**: 131, 262, 801. **6**: 139, 257. Same art. N. Ecl. **1**: 297.
Anastasius, Hope's. Quar. **24**: 511. — Ed. Mo. R. **4**: 423. — Mo. R. **91**: 1, 131. — (Syd. Smith) Ed. R. **35**: 92. — (E. Everett) No. Am. **11**: 271.
— Authorship of. Blackw. **10**: 200.
Anastatic Printing. So. Lit. Mess. **11**: 383. — Liv. Age, **5**: 56, 534. **6**: 144.
Anatole, Monsieur. (G. Turner) Belgra. **13**: 183.
Anatole de Salis. Colburn, **89**: 4–482. **90**: 90–468.
Anatolia, Northeastern, Tour of. (W. G. Palgrave) Cornh. **25**: 662. Same art. Liv. Age, **117**: 421. Same art. Ev. Sat. **13**: 33.
Anatolian Specter-Stories. Cornh. **27**: 89. Same art. Ev. Sat. **14**: 160.
Anatomist, Difficulties of. Chamb. J. **30**: 218.
Anatomy. Lond. M. **22**: 265.
— and Art. (R. Knox) Art J. **11**: 69.
— and Modern Art. (E. Von de Warker) Penn Mo. **7**: 607.
— and Physiology, Parsons's Lecture on. U. S. Lit. Gaz. **5**: 88.
— — Todd's. Nature, **4**: 343.
— Comparative, and Physiology, Owen's. Anthrop. R. **6**: 301. — No. Brit. **28**: 313.
— — Generalization of. Quar. **93**: 46.
— — Huxley's. (W. James) No. Am. **100**: 290.
— — of Domesticated Animals, Chauveau's. Nature, **8**: 158.
— — Ord's Notes on. (P. H. Pye-Smith) Nature, **5**: 79.
— — Philosophical. (St. G. Mivart) Contemp. **26**: 938.
— — Progress of. Quar. **90**: 362.
— — Schmidt's. (P. H. Pye-Smith) Nature, **5**: 298.
— — Two Discoveries in. Cornh. **6**: 403.
— Dissection in, Importance of. Westm. **10**: 116.
— Elementary, Mivart's. Nature, **8**: 221.
— Human, as a Part of the Biological Curriculum. Nature, **13**: 151.
— Human Foot and Leg. Blackw. **5**: 532.
— Microscopic. (T. Rowney) Recr. Sci. **2**: 325.
— Nomenclature of, Barclay's. Ed. R. **3**: 101.
— of Invertebrated Animals, Huxley's. Canad. Mo. **13**: 554.
— Poetry of. (J. B. Brown) No. Am. **82**: 443.
— Quain's. Nature, **14**: 129.
— Regulation of. Westm. **16**: 482.
— Reviews and Abstracts in. (W. I. Burnett) Am. J. Sci. **66**: 251, 393. **67**: 89. **68**: 104.
— Science of: its History and Progress. Lond. Q. **2**: 412.
— — Obstructions to. Mo. R. **127**: 91.
— — Study of. (J. Ware) Chr. Exam. **8**: 160.
— Subjects for, Supply of. Lond. M. **23**: 121.
— Use of the Dead to the Living. (Southworth Smith) Westm. **2**: 59.
See Bones.
Anatomy in Long Clothes, Vesalius's. Fraser, **48**: 539.
Anaxagoras as a Scientist and Educator. Nat. Q. **27**: 203.
Ancestor Worship. (H. Spencer and E. B. Tylor) Mind, **2**: 415.
— in the Black Mountains. (A. J. Evans) Macmil. **43**: 219, 295, 357.
Ancestors, A Day with our. Chamb. J. **37**: 218.
— Who are our? (C. Wright) Nation, **20**: 405.

Ancestral Enormities. Lond. M. 1: 23.
Ancestry, Question of. All the Year, 21: 318.
Anchises; a Poem. St. James, 48: 469.
Anchor, At. Fraser, 104: 624.
— Uses and Manufacture of an. Penny M. 9: 319, 322.
Anchors and Chain Cables. Chamb. J. 42: 439.
— and Chains of Vessels, Weight, etc., of. (C. H. Haswell) J. Frankl. Inst. 82: 11.
— Porter & Co.'s Patent. J. Frankl. Inst. 34: 66.
Anchorites. *See* Hermits.
Ancient Books and Writings, Transmission of. Mo. R. 114: 53. — New York R. 3: 273.
Ancient Commerce of Western Asia. (A. Barnes) Am. Bib. Repos. 5: 48. 2d s. 3: 310.
Ancient Dandy; a Tale. Blackw. 52: 590.
Ancient Days. (M. J. Quin) Colburn, 53: 82–181.
Ancient Fragments, Cory's. Blackw. 44: 105. — (J. C. Moffat) Princ. 11: 479.
Ancient Graves and their Contents. Nat. Q. 22: 315.
Ancient Learning, Lost Elements of. (F. R. Conder) Dub. Univ. 90: 321.
Ancient Manners, Blunt's Vestiges of. Blackw. 14: 254. — Ecl. R. 38: 505.
Ancient Mariner, Original. Liv. Age, 39: 433.
Ancient Money Transactions. (J. H. Gibbon) Chr. Exam. 51: 266.
Ancient Saints of God; a Tale. (Cardinal Wiseman) Cath. World. 1: 19.
Ancient Times and Ancient Men. (Max Müller) Macmil. 37: 510. Same art. Ecl. M. 90: 734.
Ancient Vegetation of the Earth. (A. Brongniart) Am. J. Sci. 34: 315.
Ancient Wagoner. Blackw. 4: 571.
Ancient Writings, Genuineness of. (J. Brazer) No. Am. 42: 1.
Ancillon. Essays of Politics and Philosophy. Mo. R. 103: 476.
Ancona. (H. D. Jenkins) Overland, 1: 393.
— Siege of. Month, 5: 362.
Ancor-Viat, the Giant City. Month, 6: 171. Same art. Cath. World, 5: 135.
— — Ruins of. (T. Yelverton) Overland, 10: 30.
Ancre, Marshal d'. (Miss Pardoe) Sharpe, 8: 37.
Ancren Riwle, The. Fraser, 51: 307.
Andalusia, Chit-chat from. Lippinc. 6: 620.
— Cities and Wilds of. (R. D. Murray) Bentley, 14: 59. — Brit. Q. 11: 315.
— Robber Adventure in. Once a Week, 13: 345.
— Scott's Travels in. (R. Ford) Quar. 63: 279.
— Sketches from. Month, 2: 186.
— Stoppage in the Mountains of. Colburn, 135: 473. 136: 55.
— Summer in, 1836. Mo. R. 149: 416.
Andalusian Tales. All the Year, 5: 401.
Andaman Islands. (F. A. de Roëpstorff) Geog. M. 3: 182. — Good Words, 7: 305. — Ecl. M. 52: 278.
— and Andamanese. (G. E. Dobson) Anthrop. J. 4: 457.
— Objects from. (A. L. Fox) Anthrop. J. 7: 434.
Anderport Records. Am. Whig R. 10: 235, 345, 459.
Andersen, H. C., with portrait. (H. W. Dodge) Appleton, 6: 45. — (W. Hurton) Liv. Age, 61: 67. — (C. Hope) St. James, 45: 505. — (T. Johnson) Putnam, 13: 92. — (R. H. Stoddard) Nat. M. 7: 428. — Chamb. J. 24: 236. Same art. Liv. Age, 47: 437. — Bentley, 20: 311. — Sharpe, 5: 216. — Potter Am. Mo. 5: 835. — (L. Katscher) Internat. R. 10: 153. — Temp. Bar, 43: 387. Same art. Ecl. M. 84: 418. — with portrait, Hogg, 6: 225. — Victoria, 25: 1022. — with portrait, (Mary Howitt) Howitt, 1: 352.
— and Thorwaldsen. Temp. Bar, 45: 171. Same art. Liv. Age, 127: 431. Same art. Ecl. M. 86: 73.
Andersen, H. C., Autobiography of. Ecl. R. 86: 342.
— Correspondence. Temp. Bar, 59: 503. Same art. Liv. Age, 147: 92. Same art. Ecl. M. 95: 408.
— Fairy Legends of. (H. E. Scudder) Nat. Q. 3: 235.
— Friendships of. (A. Wood) Temp. Bar, 51: 493. Same art. Liv. Age, 135: 807.
— German Stories. Dub. R. 42: 1.
— Improvisatore. Quar. 75: 497. — Tait, n. s. 12: 252.
— Last Days of. (D. G. Hubbard) Potter Am. Mo. 11: 194.
— Last Song of. Temp. Bar, 45: 184.
— Life of. Dem. R. 21: 525. — Ecl. M. 12: 224.
— Life and Writings of. Dub. Univ. 45: 605. Same art. Ecl. M. 35: 390. Same art. Liv. Age, 45: 707.
— New Tales. Liv. Age, 75: 376.
— Only a Fiddler. Fraser, 76: 199.
— Pictures of Sweden. Internat. M. 3: 450.
— Sand Hills of Jutland. Liv. Age, 67: 28.
— Short Stories. (H. E. Scudder) Atlan. 36: 598.
— Works of. Blackw. 62: 387. Same art. Liv. Age, 16: 1.
Anderson, Alexander, Biography of. Art J. 10: 271.
— Memorial of. Chr. Obs. 59: 202.
— Two Angels. Dub. Univ. 86: 747.
Anderson, Christopher, Life and Letters of. Ecl. R. 101: 187.
Anderson, Mrs. Garrett, and Lady Doctors. Once a Week, 26: 299.
Anderson, George B. (S. Gales) Land We Love, 3: 93.
Anderson, Isaac. Am. Presb. R. 6: 194.
Anderson, John, Sketch of. (D. O. Madden) Hogg, 1: 364.
Anderson, Robert, Memorial of. Chr. Obs. 45: 481.
Anderson, Rufus, with portrait. Ecl. M. 67: 755.
— Tour in Greece. (F. W. P. Greenwood) Chr. Exam. 49: 376.
Anderson, Thomas G., with portrait. New Dom. 14: 273.
Anderson, William. (G. Gilfillan) Hogg, 2: 280.
Anderson School of Natural History, Penikese, 1873. (B. G. Wilder) Nation, 17: 174. — Nature, 11: 167.
Andersonville Prison. (R. B. Richardson) New Eng. 39: 729. — (J. Jones) N. Ecl. 6: 176. — (J. W. Jones) So. Hist. Pap. 1: 161. — (L. M. Park) So. M. 14: 528. — Republic, 6: 235, 299, 359. 7: 33.
— Diary of a Prisoner at. Hist. M. 19: 1.
— Prison Experience at. Atlan. 15: 285.
— Southern View of. (F. W. Palfrey) Nation, 23: 385.
— Visit to. (M. A. Shearman) Hours at Home, 5: 409.
Andes, The. (G. P. Disosway) Nat. M. 12: 198, 385. 13: 114. — (W. G. Dix) Contin. Mo. 5: 229.
— Across. St. James, 33: 513.
— and the Amazon, Orton's. Nature, 15: 154.
— Barometric Anomalies about. (M. F. Maury) Am. J. Sci. 69: 385.
— Holton's Twenty Months in. So. Lit. Mess. 24: 373.
— Journey in. So. Lit. Mess. 5: 513.
— of Ecuador, Geological Notes on. (J. Orton) Am. J. Sci. 97: 242.
— of Peru and Bolivia. (E. G. Squier) Harper, 36: 545. 37: 16, 145, 307.
— Peaks and Valleys of. Chamb. J. 39: 313. Same art. Ecl. M. 59: 363.
— Physical Observations on. (J. Orton) Am. J. Sci. 96: 203.
— Strain's Ride over. (J. T. Headley) Harper, 17: 577.
— Up and down among. (A. H. Guernsey) Harper, 13: 739.
Andorra, Empress of. (J. A. Wilson) Belgra. 36: 335.
— Republic of. Cath. World, 4: 561. — Ed. R. 113: 345.
— State Dinner in. (P. W. S. Menteath) Macmil. 40: 319. Same art. Liv. Age, 142: 569.
— Tale of. Chamb. J. 25: 209, 234, 245.

Andover, Mass., Town Records. N. E. Reg. **2**: 377. **3**: 65.
— Phillips Academy. (H. E. Scudder) Harper, **55**: 562.
— Theological Seminary, Alumni of. Am. Q. Reg. **12**: 198.
— — and Princeton, Theologies of. (R. P. Stebbins) Chr. Exam. **52**: 309.
— — Catalogue, 1810–21. Cong. Q. **11**: 375. **12**: 48. **13**: 16–417. **14**: 398, 529.
— — Heresy in. (C. T. Thayer) Chr. Exam. **55**: 80.
— — Plan of Exercises at. Am. Q. Reg. **1**: 17.
— — Sacred Music in. (E. W. Hooker) Cong. Q. **6**: 268.
— — Sketches and Statistics of. (O. A. Taylor) Am. Q. Reg. **11**: 63.
— — Students in, Memoranda concerning. Cong. Q. **15**: 305.
— — Tabular View of. Am. Q. Reg. **9**: 375.
Andover, England, Nonconformity in. Cong. M. **14**: 197, 670.
André, Major John, with portrait. Am. Bibliop. **1**: 331. — (C. B. Carlisle) Potter Am. Mo. **6**: 292. — (L. G. Clark) Lippinc. 8: 518. — (A. W. Kercheval) N. Ecl. **6**: 227. — (D. D. Willbea) Potter Am. Mo. **14**: 174. — (C. C. Smith) No. Am. **93**: 83. — Hist. M. **7**: 250. — Niles's Reg. **20**: 386.
— and Benedict Arnold. (J. K. Medbery) Nat. Q. **6**: 98.
— — Meeting of. Dem. R. **41**: 300.
— and Gen. Washington. (C. J. Biddle) Hist. M. 1: 193.
— Capture of. (C. C. Campbell) Potter Am. Mo. **7**: 167. — (H. Lee) Pennsyl. M. **4**: 61. — Hist. M. **1**: 293. **9**: 177. — (J. Paulding) Hist. M. **1**: 331.
— Case of. (J. C. Stockbridge) M. Am. Hist. **3**: 739.
— Execution of. (T. B. Bradley) So. Lit. Mess. **19**: 429. — Am. Whig R. **5**: 381. — (J. Thacher) New Eng. M. **6**: 353.
— Fate and Character of. (J. C. Pickett) So. Lit. Mess. **11**: 193.
— Honora Sneyd and. (W. Sargent) Atlan. **6**: 715.
— Life of. Am. Bibliop. **4**: 542.
— Map of the Route of. M. Am. Hist. **3**: 756.
— Monument. Am. Arch. **6**: 127.
— Notes in regard to. Am. Bibliop. **2**: 13–193.
— Col. Tallmadge's Account of. Hist. M. **3**: 229.
— Truth concerning. (F. S. Hoffman) Potter Am. Mo. **7**: 98.
— unjustly executed. (W. Sargent) No. Am. **80**: 236.
— Vindication of the Captors of. Anal. M. **10**: 307.
— Will of. N. E. Reg. **6**: 63.
Andrea, Cardinal d'. (H. Wreford) Macmil. **18**: 209. — Galaxy, **8**: 781.
Andrea, Messer, the Sculptor of Bruges. Chamb. J. **7**: 115.
Andreas Hofer; a Tale. Eng. Dom. M. **16**: 243.
Andreini, G. B. Adam; a Drama. Cath. World, **11**: 602.
Andrew, St., Example of. (J. S. Howson) Good Words, **9**: 547.
Andrew and Matthias in the City of Men-Eaters. Kitto, **10**: 167.
Andrew of Hungary. (B. F. Baer) Potter Am. Mo. **10**: 269.
Andrew, James Osgood, Tribute to Memory of. So. R. n. s. **10**: 216.
Andrew, John A. (A. G. Browne, jr.) No. Am. **106**: 249. — (J. F. Clarke) Nation, **6**: 472. — (F. H. Hedge) Mo. Rel. M. **38**: 435. — Harper, **36**: 324.
— Chandler's Memoir of. (T. W. Higginson) Nation, **33**: 77.
— Memoir of. (S. Burnham) N. E. Reg. **23**: 1.
Andrew Carson's Money; a Story of Gold. Dub. Univ. **36**: 225. Same art. Harper, **1**: 503.
Andrew Cranberry; a Tale. (G. W. Curtis) Putnam, **1**: 18.
Andrew Fletcher. (M. W. Wayne) Appleton, **13**: 484, 517, 548, 579.
Andrew Kent's Temptation. (E. S. Phelps) Harper, **31**: 42.
Andrew Lawrie's Return. Lond. M. **8**: 193.
Andrew Rykman's Prayer; a Poem. (J. G. Whittier) Atlan. **11**: 95.
Andrew's Fortune. (S. O. Jewett) Atlan. **48**: 20.
Andrews, John, Provost of University of Pennsylvania. Portfo. (Den.) **9**: 425.
Andrews, Rev. John. (T. B. Fox) Chr. Exam. **40**: 24.
Andrews, Launcelot, Bp., Account of. Chr. Obs. **15**: 133.
— Russell's Life of. Chr. Obs. **60**: 846.
Androides and Automata. (T. P. Jones) J. Frankl. Inst. **3**: 125, 192, 342.
Andronicus, Fuller's. Retros. **15**: 396.
Andros, Sir Edmund, Government over New England. (J. R. Brodhead) Hist. M. **11**: 1.
— Memoir of. (J. B. Moore) Am. Q. Reg. **13**: 273.
— Taxes under, in 1687. N. E. Reg. **32**: 313. **34**: 269, 371. **35**: 34, 124.
Androscoggin Lakes. (E. Abbott) Harper, **55**: 23.
Andryane, Alexander, Memoir of. So. Lit. Mess. **6**: 473. — Mo. R. **152**: 118.
Anecdotes and Aphorisms. Sharpe, **14**: 272.
— Arvine's Cyclopædia of. (S. F. Smith) Chr. R. **17**: 333.
— Banking and Financial. Bank. M. (L.) **25**: 77–1341. **26**: 16–531.
— King's. Ed. Mo. R. **1**: 460.
— of Antiquaries. Blackw. **1**: 136.
— of Public Men. Galaxy, **14**: 39.
— Percy. Ed. Mo. R. **5**: 116, 180, 278.
— Social and Political. Bentley, **34**: 432.
— Spence's. Ed. R. **33**: 202. — (J. W. Croker) Quar. **23**: 400.
Anecdotical Gatherings. (R. B. Peake) Bentley, **17**: 225.
Anemometers, Whirled. (G. G. Stokes) Nature, **24**: 250. Same art. Ecl. Engin. **25**: 265.
Anemone; a Poem. (E. Goodale) Scrib. **17**: 815.
Anemone; a Tale. Month, **33**: 459. **34**: 82–473. **35**: 104–565. **36**: 124–540. **37**: 105–562.
Anemones, Sargartia. Once a Week, **5**: 46.
— Sea. *See* Sea Anemones.
Aneroid, Goldschmid. Ecl. Engin. **25**: 300.
Anet, Castle of. (W. L. Gane) Bentley, **14**: 233.
Aneurin's Harp; a Poem. (G. Meredith) Fortn. **10**: 255.
Angas, Wm. Henry, Cox's Memoir of. Ecl. R. **61**: 107.
Angel in the House. (G. Brimley) Fraser, **54**: 473.
— of Death, The; a Poem. Dub. Univ. **28**: 665.
— of Florence. (P. T. Horry) So. M. **8**: 616.
— of Jehovah. (C. Goodspeed) Bib. Sac. **36**: 593. — (H. A. Sawtelle) Bib. Sac. **16**: 805. — Chr. R. **24**: 594.
— of Mercy; a Poem. (H. Skidmore) Irish Mo. **9**: 636.
— of Sleep; a Poem. Dub. Univ. **16**: 602.
— of Toil; a Tale. (D. F. McCarthy) Dub. Univ. **32**: 119.
— of the Unfortunate. Howitt, **2**: 186, 195.
Angel-Hunting. Lond. M. **15**: 388.
Angel's Mission; a Poem. (M. T. Wightman) Hogg, **4**: 336.
Angels. (W. Hurlin) Chr. R. **24**: 18. — (M. Kieffer) Mercersb. **16**: 25. — (J. P. Lange) Mercersb. **3**: 93. — (E. Nisbet) Bapt. Q. **10**: 1. — (J. A. Brown) Luth. Q. **3**: 374. — (M. Stuart) Bib. Sac. **1843**: 88.
— and Demonology. (Mrs. A. B. Garrett) Nat. Q. **5**: 25.
— Doctrine respecting. Bib. Sac. **1**: 768. **2**: 108.
— Existence and Character of. Kitto, **12**: 122.
— Fall of. (I. M. Ely) New Eng. **11**: 375. — (Prof. Rudelbach) Evang. R. **8**: 171.
— Fallen. (T. J. Sawyer) Univ. Q. **1**: 294. — (H. L. Dox) Luth. Q. **8**: 555.
— — were only Sons of Seth. Theo. Repos. **5**: 166.
— Good. (H. L. Baugher) Evang. R. **20**: 221.
— Guests of Abraham at Mamre. Am. Meth. M. **16**: 99.
— Intelligence of. Am. Meth. M. **22**: 151.
— Lament over Lost Souls; a Poem. (T. D. Woolsey) New Eng. **1**: 276.
— Men above, in Kingdom of Christ. (J. T. Smith) Bost. R. **5**: 61.

Angels, Ministry of. Kitto, **8**: 283.—Am. Meth. M. **21**: 275.
— of Matt. xviii. 10; Who are they? (J. T. Gray) Kitto, **1**: 365.
— Scripture Doctrine of. (W. R. Smith) Sup. Pop. Sci. Mo. **1**: 514.
— Sketches of Doctrine of. Bib. R. **4**: 289.
— Song of. (E. Bond) Lit. & Theo. R. **1**: 428.
— Spiritual Idea of. (L. Mayer) Am. Bib. Repos. **12**: 356.
— upon Earth. Colburn, **69**: 48.
— Views of the Fathers concerning. Tait, n. s. **9**: 261.
— Visits of. (W. F. Stevenson) Good Words, **6**: 17. Same art. Liv. Age, **84**: 241.
Angel, Benj. F., with portrait. Dem. R. **40**: 330.
Angela; a Tale. Cath. World, **9**: 634, 756. **10**: 38–617.
Angela's Prayer. (L. Wood) Tinsley, **20**: 512.
Angelica's Betrothal. Lond. Soc. **9**: 14. Same art. Ecl. M. **66**: 344.
Angelico, Fra, with portrait. (E. Lafonde) Cath. World, **4**: 671.
— Work of, in St. Mark's, Florence. Good Words, **16**: 848.
Angélique Arnauld; a Poem. Scrib. **1**: 448.
Angélique's Martingale. All the Year, **41**: 516.
Angeln, Description of. (B. S. Blyth) Once a Week, **11**: 6.
Angelo; a Tale from V. Hugo. Blackw. **51**: 799.
Angelo, Michael. *See* Michael Angelo.
Angeloni, Luigi, on Political Force. Lond. M. **15**: 231.
Angelus Silesius, the Cherubic Pilgrim. Hogg, **5**: 99.
Anger. Chr. Obs. **5**: 11, 336. **6**: 232.
— Lawfulness of. Chr. Obs. **5**: 147. **6**: 12.
Angerstein, J. J. Collection of Pictures. Quar. **31**: 210.
Angkor-Wat. *See* Ancor-Viat.
Anglade, L. G. d', Trial of. House. Words, **12**: 298.
Angle, Trisection of an. (J. O'Donoghue) J. Frankl. Inst. **75**: 382.
Angles, Glass Circle for the Measurement of. (L. M. Rutherfurd) Am. J. Sci. **112**: 112.
Angler, Kind of Fish. (J. Couch) Intel. Obs. **1**: 353.
Angler, The. Dub. Univ. **17**: 661.
Angler in May. (E. Jesse) Once a Week, **6**: 611.
Angler's Souvenir, Fisher's. Mo. R. **139**: 157.
Anglers, Fancies of. Chamb. J. **12**: 345.
— of the Dove. (H. Martineau) Once a Week, **7**: 85–197.
— Women. Victoria, **34**: 72.
Anglesea, Marquis of, with portrait. Blackw. **25**: 215. —Bentley, **35**: 531.
— and Ghost of his Leg, Dialogue between. Blackw. **30**: 715.
Anglesey, Ancient Dwellings in. Antiquary, **2**: 106, 118, 185.
Anglican Church. *See* Church of England.
Anglicans and Reunion. Month, **39**: 413.
— of the Day, 1875. Dub. R. **77**: 342.
Anglican Development. (A. Marshall) Cath. World, **27**: 383.—Am. Cath. Q. **5**: 263.
Anglican Ministry. (J. Bickaby) Month, **40**: 281.
Anglican Prisoners for Conscience' Sake. Month, **43**: 134.
Anglican Sisterhood. (W. Gilbert) Good Words, **22**: 833.
Anglicanism in Australia. Dub. R. **79**: 368.
Anglicani, The, and their 39 Medical Formulæ. Fraser, **84**: 695.
Angling. Am. Whig R. **11**: 32.—Blackw. **21**: 815. **49**: 302.—Quar. **67**: 98.—Chamb. J. **57**: 385.
— and Anglers. Dub. Univ. **49**: 657.
— and Fly-Fishing. Bentley, **13**: 257.—Ecl. Mus. **1**: 67. *See also* Fly-Fishing.
— Annals of. (C. Lanman) Galaxy, **6**: 305.
— Art of. (James Wilson) No. Brit. **8**: 297. Same art. Liv. Age, **17**: 1.
— Chapter on. Dub. Univ. **29**: 748.
Angling. Complete Susquehanna Angler. (C. A. Munger) Knick. **45**: 598. **46**: 28, 346. **48**: 260.
— Davy's Angler and his Friend. Colburn, **104**: 232.
— English and Scotch. (A. B. Reach) Sharpe, **18**: 149.
— Fascinations of. (G. Dawson) Galaxy, **23**: 818.
— for Pan-Fish. (M. Thompson) Harper, **55**: 395.
— for Salmon and Trout. Cornh. **19**: 417.
— Hints on. Tait, n. s. **13**: 531.
— in France, Guillemard's La peche à la ligne. Colburn, **109**: 408.
— in the Lake District, Eng., Davy on. Ecl. R. **105**: 604.
— in Wales, Medwin's. Mo. R. **135**: 145.
— Jesse's Angler's Rambles. Tait, n. s. **3**: 625.—Mo. R. **141**: 158.
— Modern. (A. Günther) Nature, **2**: 512.
— Stephen Oliver on. Blackw. **35**: 775.
— Practice of. Dub. Univ. **26**: 153.
— Salmonia. Blackw. **24**: 248.
— Stoddart on. Blackw. **38**: 119. **63**: 673.
— Walton's Complete Angler. Bentley, **16**: 512.—Colburn, **4**: 491.—Lond. M. **7**: 633.—Blackw. **14**: 473.—Knick. **30**: 381.—Retros. **6**: 353.
— with a Trout-Rod. (M. G. Watkins) Fraser, **86**: 524.
— with the Worm. Once a Week, **16**: 239.
See Fishing.
Angling Adventure. Broadw. **2**: 549.
Angling Club, Our. All the Year, **39**: 349.
Angling Literature. Ecl. R. **98**: 15. **99**: 21.
Angling Worthies. (M. G. Watkins) Fraser, **92**: 750.
Anglo-American Type. So. R. n. s. **7**: 311.
Anglo-Catholic Letters to Rev. Charles Fustian. Blackw. **65**: 679.
Anglo-Catholic Movement, Past and Future. (C. J. Ellicott) Princ. n. s. **2**: 612.
Anglo-Catholic Theory. Ed. R. **94**: 527.
Anglo-Catholicism, Progress of. Chr. Rem. **4**: 58.
Anglo-Chinese Kalendar, 1833. Penny M. **2**: 245.
Anglo-Continental Association. (A. C. Coxe) Am. Church R. **10**: 407.
— Objects and Doings of. Chr. Rem. **34**: 334.
Anglo-French Drama. Ed. R. **51**: 225.
Anglo-Indian Life. Mo. R. **145**: 174.
Anglo-Indian Poets. Dub. Univ. **95**: 513.
Anglo-Indian Society of Former Days. Mus. **29**: 224.
Anglo-Indian Tongue. Blackw. **121**: 541.
Anglo-Latin Poets of the Twelfth Century. For. Q. **16**: 386.
Anglo-Norman Building in St. Olave's, Southwark. (G. R. Corner) Arch. **38**: 37.
Anglo-Norman Burial-Places at Bouteilles. (L'Abbé Cochet) Arch. **36**: 258. **37**: 32.
Anglo-Norman Christianity and Anselm. (J. Stoughton) Ex. H. Lec. **17**: 85.
Anglo-Norman Poetry. (Abbé De la Rue) Arch. **13**: 35.—Fraser, **14**: 55.
Anglo-Norman Poets of the 12th Century. (Abbé De la Rue) Arch. **12**: 297.—Brit. Q. **5**: 159.
— of the 13th Century. (Abbé De la Rue) Arch. **13**: 230.
Anglo-Norman Remains found at Bouteilles. (L'Abbé Cochet) Arch. **37**: 399.
Anglo-Norman Trouveres. Blackw. **39**: 806. **40**: 278.
Anglo-Normans. No. Brit. **6**: 431. Same art. Liv. Age, **13**: 16.
Anglophobia. Once a Week, **19**: 173.
Anglo-Russian Difficulty, 1870. (J. N. Pomeroy) Nation, **11**: 399.
Anglo-Saxon Cemetery at Brighthampton. (J. Y. Akerman) Arch. **37**: 391. **38**: 84.
— at Filkins and Broughton Poggs. (J. Y. Akerman) Arch. **37**: 140.
— at Long Wittenham, Berks. (J. Y. Akerman) Arch. **38**: 327. **39**: 135.

Anglo-Saxon Cemetery at Stowting, Kent. (J. Brent) Arch. **41**: 409.
Anglo-Saxon Christianity, and Anglo-Norman. No. Brit. **37**: 35. Same art. Ecl. M. **57**: 289, 511.
— and Augustine of Canterbury. (S. Martin) Ex. H. Lec. **17**: 45.
Anglo-Saxon Chronicle and Anglo-Norman Chroniclers. Chr. Rem. **38**: 144.
Anglo-Saxon Church, Lingard's Antiquities of. (John Allen) Ed. R. **25**: 346. — No. Brit. **6**: 1. — Ecl. R. **86**: 78.
— Soames on the. Chr. Obs. **49**: 345.
Anglo-Saxon Churches. Dub. R. **18**: 128.
Anglo-Saxon Coins discovered at Hexham. (J. Adamson) Arch. **25**: 279. **26**: 346.
Anglo-Saxon Colonies. (J. Stoughton) Ex. H. Lec. **8**: 323.
Anglo-Saxon Home. Ecl. R. **117**: 72.
Anglo-Saxon Kings denominated Bretwaldas. (H. Hallam) Arch. **32**: 245.
Anglo-Saxon Knife found in Kent. (J. Evans) Arch. **44**: 331.
Anglo-Saxon Language. New York R. **3**: 362. — (H. Wheaton) No. Am. **33**: 325. — Am. Bib. Repos. **10**: 386.
— and Literature. Cong. M. **14**: 559.
— Dictionary of, Bosworth's. (H. Rogers) Ed. R. **70**: 221. — Mus. **38**: 9. — Mo. R. **147**: 206.
— Grammar of, Bosworth's. Mo. R. **102**: 148.
— — Rask's. For. R. **3**: 234. Same art. Select J. **2**: 104.
— Hand-Book of, Corson's. (J. Hadley) Nation, **12**: 404.
— Study of. (J. S. Hart) Am. J. Educ. **1**: 33. — (T. W. Hunt) Princ. n. s. **7**: 221. — (S. M. Shute) Bapt. Q. **8**: 17. — (W. W. Skeat) Macmil. **39**: 304.
Anglo-Saxon Laws and Institutes. Brit. & For. R. **12**: 46.
Anglo-Saxon Leechdoms. Dub. Univ. **69**: 519.
Anglo-Saxon Literary Biography. Ecl. R. **78**: 10. — Ed. R. **78**: 365. Same art. Ecl. Mus. **3**: 343.
Anglo-Saxon Literature. (Bro. Azarias) Am. Cath. Q. **2**: 385. — Am. Bib. Repos. 2d s. **6**: 196. — Chr. Rem. **4**: 163. — Dub. R. **15**: 80. — Mus. **37**: 51. — No. Am. **47**: 90. — (J. W. Alexander) Princ. **11**: 527. — So. R. n. s. **7**: 106.
— and Celtic Literature. Dub. Univ. **64**: 298.
Anglo-Saxon MS. in Exeter Cathedral. (J. J. Conybeare) Arch. **17**: 180.
Anglo-Saxon Pennies found at Dorking. (T. Combe) Arch. **19**: 109.
Anglo-Saxon Poetry. Mo. R. **111**: 183. — Fraser, **12**: 76. — Temp. Bar, **38**: 222.
— and Early English. New York R. **9**: 372. — Westm. **7**: 464.
— Characteristics of. Tait, n. s. **27**: 465.
— Illustrations of. Chr. R. **26**: 620.
— Inedited Fragment of. (J. J. Conybeare) Arch. **17**: 173.
— Meter of. (J. J. Conybeare) Arch. **17**: 257.
Anglo-Saxon Pottery. (T. Wright) Intel. Obs. **6**: 119.
Anglo-Saxon Remains at Harnham Hill, near Salisbury. (J. Y. Akerman) Arch. **35**: 259, 475.
— found at Kemble, Wilts. (J. Y. Akerman) Arch. **37**: 113.
— found at Stowting, Kent. (C. R. Smith) Arch. **31**: 398.
Anglo-Saxon Runes. (J. M. Kemble) Arch. **28**: 327.
Anglo-Saxon Song, Lay of the Phœnix. (G. Stephens) Arch. **30**: 256.
Anglo-Saxon Race. (Mrs. J. Ware) No. Am. **73**: 34. (D. J. M. Loop) Am. Whig R. **7**: 28. — (D. A. Hawkins) Meth. Q. **36**: 87.
Anglo-Saxons. Am. Ecl. **4**: 161.
— and the Americans. Am. Whig R. **14**: 187.
— British Race. (J. H. Seeley) Education, **1**: 309.
— Empire of. Am. Church R. **23**: 205.
— Fine Arts among Penny M. **13**: 25.
Anglo-Saxons, History of. (Sir F. Palgrave) Quar. **34**: 248.
— — Lappenberg's. Blackw. **61**: 79.
— — Turner's. Ecl. R. **6**: 653, 775.
— Hwiting Treow of. (J. Y. Akerman) Arch. **42**: 124.
— in Corve Dale. (T. Wright) Once a Week, **15**: 524.
— Laws and Usages of. Am. Q. **22**: 350.
— Legal Procedure of. (H. C. Cook) Arch. **41**: 207.
— Municipal Privileges under. (T. Wright) Arch. **32**: 298.
— Trades of. Penny M. **5**: 91.
Anglo-Saxondom, Dream of. (J. P. Chamberlain) Galaxy, **24**: 788.
Anglo-Turkish Convention. Cong. **7**: 497.
Angola, Monteiro's. Nature, **13**: 161.
— Quissama Tribe of. (J. J. Monteiro) Anthrop. J. **5**: 198.
Angoulême, Marguerite, Duchess of, Journal of. Blackw. **1**: 172.
— Life and Letters of. Chr. Obs. **55**: 757, 819. Same art. Liv. Age, **49**: 385.
Angström, Anders Jonas. Nature, **10**: 376.
Anguisciola, Sofonisba, Italian Paintress, b. 1530. Victoria, **19**: 412.
Anguish in Print. Once a Week, **30**: 259–671.
Angularities and Cantankerousness. Lond. Soc. **38**: 537.
Anhalt, Public Instruction in. Am. J. Educ. **15**: 344.
Anhalt-Dessau, Leopold, Prince of, "The Old Dessauer." (H. S. Wilson) Lond. Soc. **29**: 358.
Aniello, T., called Masaniello, the Fisherman of Naples. Portfo.(Den.) **16**: 425.
Anien Rhaa. (Mary Howitt) Howitt, **2**: 415.
Aniline Dyes. (T. L. Phipson) Pop. Sci. R. **3**: 429.
— and Coal-Tar. Art J. **17**: 25, 102, 301.
— Manufacture of. Pract. M. **2**: 34.
Animal Chemistry. (H. N. Draper) Recr. Sci. **3**: 303. — Am. Ecl. **4**: 459.
— Berzelius on. Ecl. R. **18**: 243. — So. Q. **27**: 207.
— Kingzett's. Nature, **19**: 358.
— Liebig on. Quar. **70**: 98. Same art. Am. Ecl. **4**: 460.
Animal Creation, Burnett's. Ecl. R. **69**: 185.
— Power of God in. (R. Owen) Ex. H. Lec. **19**: 1.
Animal Depravity. Sup. Pop. Sci. Mo. **2**: 184.
Animal Design and Landscape. (W. M. Rossetti) Macmil. **8**: 116.
Animal Electricity. (L. Hermann) Nature, **19**: 561. — Chamb. J. **3**: 68.
Animal Existences, A Vision of. Cornh. **5**: 311.
Animal Food. Ed. R. **2**: 128. — (J. C. Draper) Galaxy, **7**: 550, 837. — Colburn, **5**: 563.
— Abstinence from. (H. Brougham) Ed. R. **2**: 128.
— in Early Times. (J. R. Wilde) Dub. Univ. **43**: 317.
— Pythagorean Objections to. Lond. M. **13**: 380.
— Uses of. (J. Broughton) Intel. Obs. **9**: 452. *See* Food.
Animal Heat. Blackw. **84**: 414.
Animal Kingdom, Cuvier's. Mo. R. **136**: 229. **139**: 119.
— Law of Association in. (E. Perriet) Pop. Sci. R. **19**: 30.
— Swedenborg on. Mo. R. **164**: 167.
Animal Life. (S. E. Shepard) Chr. Q. **8**: 467.
— and Natural Conditions. (E. R. Lankester) Nature, **23**: 405.
— Curiosities of. Cath. World, **3**: 232.
— Dawn of. Westm. **78**: 171.
— Development of, on the Globe. (L. Agassiz) Ed. New Philos. J. **33**: 388.
— Forms of, Rolleston's. (P. H. Pye-Smith) Nature, **2**: 80, 206.
— — Apparition of, and Evolution. (J. W. Dawson) Princ. n. s. **1**: 662.
— — Development of. (A. Thomson) Sup. Pop. Sci. Mo. **1**: 481.
— — Gradations in. Fraser, **87**: 458. Same art. Liv. Age, **117**: 479.

Animal Life, Forms of, Remarkable, Sars's. (T. Hincks) Nature, 8: 189.
— in the Ocean. (G. C. Wallich) J. Frankl. Inst. 72: 237, 321.
— in South Africa. (H. Chichester) Intel. Obs. 10: 42.
— Studies in. Cornh. 1: 61–681.
See Animals and Plants; Biology; Life.
Animal Locomotion. Pract. M. 4: 459.
— Pettigrew's. (A. H. Garrod) Nature, 9: 221.
Animal Magnetism. (Sir B. C. Brodie) Quar. 61: 273.—(Dr. Sam. Brown) No. Brit. 15: 133. Same art. Ecl. M. 23: 271.—(W. B. Carpenter) Pop. Sci. Mo. 11: 12, 161.—(W. Preyer) Sup. Pop. Sci. Mo. 3: 131.—(John Wilson) Internat. M. 4: 27.—Am. Q. 4: 426. 22: 350.—For. Q. 12: 413.—Quar. 61: 151.—Blackw. 1: 563.—So. Lit. Mess. 4: 253. 5: 319.—Fraser, 1: 673.—Ecl. R. 94: 222.—(J. Ware) Chr. Exam. 51: 395.—For. R. 5: 96.—Select J. 3: 133.—Mo. R. 131: 293.—Chr. Q. Spec. 9: 434, 647.—Mus. 23: 361.—(S. Adams) Am. Bib. Repos. 2d s. 1: 362.—Dem. R. 9: 515.—Anal. M. 10: 34.—Am. Mo. M. 10: 424.—Bost. Q. 2: 54.—Dub. R. 4: 202. 5: 407.—Dub. Univ. 38: 383.—Chr. Rem. 13: 366.—Tait, 4: 456.—Nat. M. 2: 56.—Nat. Q. 16: 23.—Portfo. (Den.) 28: 17.—Tait, n. s. 5: 460.—Zoist, 1: 58.
— Address on. (J. Elliotson) Zoist, 1: 227.
— and Ghost-Seeing. Brit. Q. 2: 402. Same art. Ecl. M. 7: 66.—Mo. R. 109: 506.
— and Homœopathy, Lee on. Mo. R. 146: 471.
— and Hypnotism. (L. H. Steiner) Mercersb. 13: 238.
— and Neurhypnotism. Ecl. M. 3: 71.—Fraser, 29: 681. 32: 1.
— Diseases cured by. Zoist, 2: 42–473. 3: 24–512. 4: 68, 517. 5: 1–404. 6: 1–412. 7: 9–437. 8: 12–395. 9: 11–436. 12: 34–415. 13: 27–417.
— Experiments in. Mo. R. 131: 291. Same art. Select J. 2: 259.
— Gregory on. Chamb. J. 15: 327.—(W. C. Engledue) Zoist, 9: 215.
— in Germany. Blackw. 2: 36, 437.
— in London. Blackw. 42: 384.
See Animal Electricity; Magnetism; Mesmerism.
Animal Mechanics, Haughton's. Nature, 9: 239.
— Marey's. Nature, 10: 498, 516.
— Source of Muscular Power. (A. Flint) Pop. Sci. Mo. 12: 729.
Animal Motion, Relation of, to Animal Evolution. (E. D. Cope) Am. Natural. 12: 40.—(E. S. Morse) New Dom. 8: 160.
— Apparatus for Registering. (Prof. Marey) Nature, 14: 214.
Animal Nature, Studies of. (B. Taylor) Atlan. 39: 135.
See Animals, Chapters on.
Animal Parasites and Messmates. Pop. Sci. Mo. 8: 670.
Animal Psychology, Schneider on. (J. Sully) Mind, 5: 424.
Animal Remains at Cissbury. (G. Rolleston) Anthrop. J. 6: 20.
Animal Strength. J. Frankl. Inst. 5: 109.
Animal Substances, Preparations of. (H. Goadby) Am. J. Sci. 63: 15, 227.
Animal Teaching. Ev. Sat. 11: 182.
Animal Volunteers. Chamb. J. 52: 257.
Animal Worship among the old Scandinavians. (Jón A. Hjaltalín) Fraser, 84: 13.
— Totem; or, Prospects of. (M. Browne) St. Paul's, 14: 313.
Animalcule, A newly discovered. (J. W. Bailey) Am. J. Sci. 65: 341.
Animalcules. (R. O. Mason) Lippinc. 25: 483.
— Aquaria Studies. (A. S. Ritchie) Am. Natural. 5: 653.
Animalcules, Hairy-backed. (P. H. Gosse) Intel. Obs. 5: 387.
— in Croton Water. (W. C. Prime) Harper, 18: 451.
— Life in a Drop of Water. (D. Brewster) Good Words, 5: 169.
— Mantell on. Chamb. J. 5: 296. Same art. Liv. Age, 10: 157.
— Rotifera, or Wheel. (P. H. Gosse) Pop. Sci. R. 1: 26, 158, 474. 2: 475.
See Microscope; Infusoria.
Animals, Acclimatization of. Chamb. J. 55: 423.—Colburn, 124: 208. 125: 253.—Ed. R. 111: 161. Same art. Liv. Age, 64: 719.—Nat. R. 17: 152.
— Æsthetic Sense in. (L. Viardot) Pop. Sci. Mo. 4: 729.
— Affections of. Chamb. J. 1: 267.
— Alarming Depravity among. Blackw. 2: 82.
— and Elements in which they live. (L. Agassiz) Am. J. Sci. 59: 369.
— and their Environments. (A. Wilson) Gent. M. n. s. 20: 734. Same art. Sup. Pop. Sci. Mo. 3: 231.
— and Plants. Quar. 126: 248.
— — Analogies between. Chamb. J. 55: 40.
— — Can we separate? Cornh. 37: 336. Same art. Ecl. M. 90: 608.
— — how related? Evang. R. 11: 256.
— Anecdotes of. (E. Jesse) Once a Week, 16: 211.—Lond. M. 18: 531. 19: 121.—Chamb. J. 50: 693.
— Antipathies of. All the Year, 41: 8.
— Aquatic. No. Brit. 29: 396.
— Architecture of. (A. Wilson) Belgra. 34: 163.—(J. L. Cabell) So. R. n. s. 3: 45.
— Artistic Feeling of. Ecl. M. 76: 630.
— as Automata. (T. H. Huxley) Nature, 10: 362–520. Same art. Liv. Age, 123: 67. Same art. Pop. Sci. Mo. 5: 724.—(T. H. Huxley) Fortn. 22: 555. Same art. Liv. Age, 124: 67. Same art. Ecl. M. 84: 49.—(R. G. Hazard) Pop. Sci. Mo. 6: 405.
— as Man's Friends. (B. P. Avery) Overland, 1: 234.
— Chapters on. (P. G. Hamerton) Portfo. 2: 42–187. 3: 11–190.
— Claims of, Styles on. Chr. Obs. 45: 670.
— — and the Rights of Man. (F. P. Cobbe) Fraser, 68: 586.—Victoria, 25: 1083. 26: 60.—Tait, 2: 14, 833.
— Classification of. (J. D. Dana) Am. J. Sci. 86: 321. 87: 10, 157.—(W. Hincks) Canad. J. n. s. 10: 19.—(T. H. Huxley) Nature, 11: 101.—Am. Natural. 9: 65.—Intel. Obs. 6: 362.
— Colonial, and their Origin. (A. Wilson) Gent. M. n. s. 26: 680.
— Colored so as to escape Notice. (A. Murray) Ed. New Philos. J. 68: 66.—Ev. Sat. 9: 510.
— Colors of. (A. R. Wallace) Am. Natural. 11: 641, 713.—Ev. Sat. 17: 9.
— Combats of. All the Year, 44: 401.
— Cruelty to. *See* Cruelty.
— Curative Powers of. (W. E. Hall) Belgra. 9: 116.
— Declaration of Independence by. (J. Bonner) Harper, 14: 145.
— Development of, and what it teaches. (A. Wilson) Gent. M. n. s. 24: 34.
— Diabolical. All the Year, 33: 519.
— Diseases of Wild. (J. Vilain) Pop. Sci. Mo. 16: 11.
— Domesticated. (L. Agassiz) Am. Natural. 7: 641.
— — Effects of Reversion to a Wild State. (J. D. Caton) Am. Natural. 15: 955.
— — History of. No. Brit. 5: 1.
— — Intellectuality of. Dub. Univ. 15: 495.
— — Origin of. (G. de Martillet) Am. Natural. 13: 747.
— Domestication of. (F. Cuvier) Ed. New Philos. J. 3: 303. 4: 45, 292.
— — in the Middle Ages. (T. Wright) Intel. Obs. 6: 318.
— — Wild. Lond. M. 13: 98.—Penny M. 1: 44.

Animals, Enemies of Man among. Chamb. J. **55**: 311.
— Excommunication and Punishment of. (H. White) Stud. & Intel. Obs. **3**: 210.
— Experimentation on. *See* Vivisection.
— Extinct Genera of. Mus. **38**: 68.
— — in the Historic Period. (E. Blanchard) Pop. Sci. Mo. **5**: 331.
— — of the Colonies of Great Britain. (R. Owen) Pop. Sci. R. **18**: 253.
— Fabulous. (F. P. Cobbe) Liv. Age, **123**: 354.
— Fetichism in. Liv. Age, **136**: 254.
— Friendships of. Chamb. J. **55**: 654. Same art. Pop. Sci. Mo. **14**: 182.
— Geographical Distribution of. (L. Agassiz) Chr. Exam. **48**: 181. — Ed. R. **53**: 328. — (S. S. Conant) Harper, **54**: 519. — (W. F. Kirby) Pop. Sci. R. **16**: 261. Same art. Ecl. M. **89**: 321. Same art. Liv. Age, **134**: 308. — (S. I. Smith) Am. Natural. **2**: 14. — (A. R. Wallace) 19th Cent. **5**: 247. — (A. R. Wallace) Am. Natural. **11**: 157. — Chamb. J. **53**: 711. — Hogg, **3**: 149. — Westm. **97**: 28. Same art. Liv. Age, **112**: 387.
— — Difficulties in. (P. L. Sclater) 19th Cent. **4**: 1037.
— — of Marine Species of. (J. D. Dana) Am. J. Sci. **65**: 204. **66**: 153, 314.
— — of Marine, on the Coast of New England. (A. E. Verrill) Am. J. Sci. **102**: 357.
— — Range of North American Animals. (W. J. Hays) Am. Natural. **5**: 387.
— — Sclater on. Nature, **13**: 482.
— — Wallace on. Nature, **14**: 165, 186. — (T. Gill) Nation, **25**: 27, 42.
— Gigantic, discovered in Ice. Cornh. **7**: 416.
— Growth of lower Vertebrates. (A. S. Packard, jr.) Am. Natural. **9**: 632.
— Habitat of, Effects of. Chamb. J. **5**: 401.
— Habitations of. Quar. **120**: 355.
— Have Animals Souls? (J. F. Clarke) Atlan. **34**: 412. — (J. R. G. Hassard) Cath. World, **5**: 510. — Nat. Q. **15**: 242. — Putnam, **7**: 361.
— Higher and Lower. Quar. **127**: 381. Same art. Liv. Age, **103**: 579.
— Humanity in. Chamb. J. **5**: 177. Same art. Liv. Age, **10**: 90.
— Humor in. (S. Lockwood) Am. Natural. **10**: 257.
— Hypnotism in. (J. Czermak) Pop. Sci. Mo. **3**: 618. **4**: 75.
— Immortality of. Chr. Exam. **74**: 199.
— in Captivity. Liv. Age, **122**: 673.
— in Fable and Art. (F. P. Cobbe) Liv. Age, **121**: 451.
— in Geological Times, Primitive Diversity of. (L. Agassiz) Am. J. Sci. **67**: 309.
— I have known and loved. Chamb. J. **57**: 45-272.
— Instincts of. *See* Instinct.
— Intellect of. (A. Weld) Month, **19**: 67. — Lond. Soc. **15**: 43. Same art. Ecl. M. **72**: 318.
— Intelligence of. (G. J. Romanes) 19th Cent. **4**: 653. Same art. Pop. Sci. Mo. **14**: 214. — (A. R. Wallace) Nature, **3**: 182. — Westm. **113**: 448. Same art. Liv. Age, **115**: 643. — Chr. Rem. **14**: 436. — All the Year, **20**: 113. — Chamb. J. **40**: 380. Same art. Ecl. M. **61**: 377. — Month, **35**: 1.
— — Flourens on. Ecl. R. **98**: 649.
— Journeyings and Dispersals of. Pop. Sci. Mo. **10**: 576.
— Language of. (F. R. Goulding) Appleton, **10**: 332. — (E. Howland) Penn Mo. **10**: 509. — (L. A. Jones) O. & N. **4**: 531, 650. — All the Year, **19**: 152. — Chamb. J. **1**: 99. **5**: 276. Same art. Liv. Age, **10**: 137. — Putnam, **6**: 130.
— Legal Prosecutions of. (W. Jones) Pop. Sci. Mo. **17**: 619.
— Legends of. Fraser, **38**: 392.
Animals, Life Histories of, Packard's. (E. R. Lankester) Nature, **15**: 271.
— Links of the World of. (W. B. Dawkins) Nature, **18**: 537.
— Living and Extinct. Temp. Bar, **1**: 533. **3**: 363.
— — in Solid Bodies. Chamb. J. **48**: 650.
— Lost Tribes of. All the Year, **41**: 174.
— Love for. Cath. World, **13**: 545.
— Mental Faculties of. (G. L. Cary) No. Am. **108**: 37.
— Migration of. (A. Wilson) Gent. M. n. s. **21**: 549. Same art. Sup. Pop. Sci. Mo. **4**: 103.
— Mimicry and other Protective Resemblances among. Westm. **88**: 1. Same art. Liv. Age, **94**: 259.
— Mind in the Lower. (W. L. Lindsay) Nature, **8**: 91. — Liv. Age, **146**: 707. — House. Words, **7**: 504.
— — Lindsay on. (W. James) Nation, **30**: 270.
— Mind in Man and. (F. Bowen) Princ. n. s. **5**: 32.
— Moral Faculties of. Intel. Obs. **4**: 211.
— Moral Sense in the Lower. (W. L. Lindsay) Pop. Sci. Mo. **16**: 346.
— Music of. (J. Sully) Cornh. **40**: 605.
— My four-footed Friends. (M. G. Watkins) Belgra. **35**: 216.
— Natural History of. (L. Agassiz) Overland, **9**: 461.
— New and rare, in the Zoölogical Garden. Nature, **23**: 35-487.
— Nutrition in. (J. R. Blake) Land We Love, **1**: 314. **2**: 45.
— of America, Audubon's. (C. W. Webber) Am. Whig R. **4**: 625.
— — Harlan's. (J. Ware) No. Am. **22**: 120.
— of Antiquity as depicted on Monuments. (M. de Serres) Ed. New Philos. J. **16**: 160, 285. **17**: 268. **18**: 59.
— of Argentine Republic, Burmeister's. (W. H. Flower) Nature, **3**: 282.
— of the New England Coast. Nature, **7**: 365.
— Protection of. (G. T. Angell) Am. Soc. Sci. J. **6**: 164.
— Psychology of. (D. F. Weinland) Am. J. Sci. **77**: 1. — Brit. Q. **7**: 347. Same art. Liv. Age, **17**: 595.
— Powers of Offense and Defense of. Chamb. J. **53**: 247. Same art. Pop. Sci. Mo. **9**: 355.
— Reason in. (E. I. Sears) Nat. Q. **9**: 286. — (J. F. James) Am. Natural. **15**: 604. — Once a Week, **18**: 491.
— Resuscitating. All the Year, **2**: 387.
— Sacred. Belgra. **20**: 89.
— Shy Friends. (M. B. Benton) Putnam, **14**: 85.
— Social Life of. (P. J. Van Beneden) Am. Natural. **8**: 521.
— Strange Affections and Habits of. (E. Jesse) Once a Week, **15**: 35.
— Strange Wanderers. Hours at Home, **10**: 426.
— Superstitions concerning. Dub. Univ. **46**: 281.
— Torpidity of. Chamb. J. **10**: 38.
— Transformations of. (A. Wilson) Good Words, **19**: 335, 409.
— — New Views of. (E. Perrier) Pop. Sci. Mo. **16**: 625.
— Treatment of. (W. Chambers) Chamb. J. **54**: 545. Same art. Sup. Pop. Sci. Mo. **1**: 569.
— Unity of Type among. Cath. World. **1**: 71.
— Vertebrated. Lond. Q. **42**: 343.
— — and invertebrated, Missing Link between, Dohrn's. (G. T. Bettamy) Nature, **14**: 195.
— — Huxley's Anatomy of. (A. Thomson) Nature, **5**: 245.
— — in the Liverpool Museum. (H. H. Higgins) Nature, **3**: 481.
— — Origin of. (T. H. Huxley) Nature, **13**: 388-514 **14**: 33.
— — — Dohrn on. Nature, **12**: 479.

Animation, Suspended. (B. W. Richardson) Nature, 20: 107. — Chamb. J. 53: 158.
Animism, Tyler and Spencer on. (A. C. Oughter-Lonie) Mind, 3: 126.
— Primitive Thought and Modern. (J. S. Patterson) Radical, 10: 432.
Anjou. (C. Dempster) Ed. R. 127: 77.
— Monuments at. Ed. R. 127: 77.
Ann Arbor, Michigan, University of. O. & N. 4: 135.
Ann Potter's Lesson. (R. T. Cooke) Atlan. 2: 419.
Anna Hammer; a German Novel. Blackw. 68: 573.
Annabel Brown. Belgra. 22: 382.
Annabel's Dream. St. James, 9: 94.
Annam, China, The French in Tong King. Colburn, 157: 172.
Annapolis Homony Club, 1770. (T. L. Chase) Am. Hist. Rec. 1: 295, 348.
Annapolis Tuesday Club, 1745. Am. Hist. Rec. 2: 149.
Annapolis, Md., U. S. Naval Academy at. (A. D. Brown) Harper, 43: 177.
Anne; a Novel. (C. F. Woolson) Harper, 62: 28–847. 63: 68–735.
Anne Boleyn. (W. H. Dixon) Gent. M. n. s. 16: 289. — Ed. R. 45: 321. — Mo. R. 96: 372.
— and Henry VIII. (J. A. Froude) Fraser, 55: 723.
— and Sir Thomas Wyatt. Bentley, 23: 233.
— Fresh Evidence about. (J. A. Froude) Fraser, 81: 731. 82: 44.
— Letter respecting her Coronation. Arch. 18: 77.
Anne, Queen, and Indian Sachems. Am. Hist. Rec. 3: 462.
— Burton's Reign of. Ed. R. 151: 512. — Blackw. 127: 139. Same art. Liv. Age, 145: 3. Same art. Ecl. M. 94: 385. — Fraser, 101: 337.
— Days of. (E. Lawrence) Harper, 44: 405.
— Farthings of. (F. W. Madden) Once a Week, 6: 273.
— Historians of, Reign of. Blackw. 115: 301. Same art. Liv. Age, 121: 195.
— Stanhope's Reign of. (T. E. Kebbel) Fortn. 13: 603. Same art. Liv. Age, 106: 259. — (G. Smith) Nation, 11: 57. — Ed. R. 132: 519. — Quar. 129: 1. Same art. Ecl. M. 75: 513, 715.
Anne, Czarina of Russia. (J. Forfar) Gent. M. n. s. 25: 215.
Anne d'Auray, Ste. (G. Goldie) Month, 34: 187.
Anne of Austria, Queen Regent. (F. P. Cobbe) Tinsley, 23: 361. — (J. W. Calcraft) Dub. Univ. 44: 674.
— and Voltaire. Dub. Univ. 44: 674. Same art. Liv. Age, 44: 476. Same art. Ecl. M. 34: 193.
Anne of Brittany. Colburn, 108: 414. — Chamb. J. 23: 143. Same art. Ecl. M. 35: 243.
Anne of Cleves, Third Wife of Henry VIII. (B. Murphy) Cath. World, 21: 403. — Once a Week, 21: 293.
Anne of Denmark, Wife of James I. of England. (J. Stevenson) Month, 35: 257.
Anne Furness. (Mrs. T. A. Trollope) Fortn. 14: 74–721. 15: 111–785. 16: 98, 235. Same art. Harper, 41: 572, 747, 881. 42: 123–885. 43: 49–884.
Anne Hereford; a Tale. (Mrs. H. Wood) Argosy, 5: 1–401. 6: 1–481.
Anne Séverin; a Tale. Month, 8: 439, 561. 9: 17–573.
Annecy and St. Francis de Sales. Month, 17: 201.
Anneliddan Worms. (W. Baird) Stud. & Intel. Obs. 3: 91–432. 4: 84.
— Structure of. (E. Claparede) Intel. Obs. 12: 266, 365.
Annesley, James. (W. Chambers) Chamb. J. 52: 273.
— Trial of. Blackw. 88: 565.
Annetta Haverstraw. (E. Leslie) Godey, 26: 38–255.
Annette; a Poem. Fraser, 33: 503.
Annette; a Tale. Chamb. J. 20: 246, 261.
Annette's Love-Story. (J. Kavanagh) Liv. Age, 108: 291.
Annexation. (P. Godwin) Putnam, 3: 183.
Annexation Fever. (E. L. Godkin) Nation, 8: 289.
Annexations, National. Liv. Age, 79: 73.
Annie and her Master. Blackw. 95: 474.
Annie at the Corner; a Tale. Putnam, 7: 629.
Annie, the Emigrant's Daughter. (Prof. Frost) Godey, 26: 109.
Annie with the Madonna Face. (L. Gore) Dub. Univ. 74: 558, 652. 75: 61, 174, 258.
Annie Lee. Liv. Age, 36: 390.
Annie Orme. (Mrs. Oliphant) Sharpe, 16: 129, 199. Same art. Liv. Age, 35: 359.
Annie Seabrook. (E. Pollock) Pioneer, 3: 129.
Annihilation and Immortality. Bost. R. 1: 445.
— and Unconsciousness. (A. K. H. Boyd) Fraser, 80: 380. Same art. Ecl. M. 73: 668.
— of the Wicked, Doctrine of. (S. C. Bartlett) New Eng. 30: 659. — (S. Fuller) Am. Church R. 30: 227. — (W. De L. Love) New Eng. 21: 248. — (J. Murdock) Am. Church R. 8: 565. — (W. L. Parsons) Bib. Sac. 20: 181. — (W. W. Patton) Meth. Q. 21: 31. — (A. C. Thomas) Univ. Q. 29: 90. — Am. Presb. R. 8: 594. — (D. M. Gilbert) Luth. Q. 9: 613.
— — Huntington's Sermons for Doctrine of. (A. S. Chesebrough) New Eng. 38: 201.
— — Refuted. (E. V. Gerhart) Mercersb. 25: 621.
Anning, Mary, the Fossil-Finder. All the Year, 13: 60.
Anniversaries. Sharpe, 1: 151. 2: 414.
— American Religious. Cong. M. 21: 275.
— Fourteenth Day of the Month. Temp. Bar. 16: 395.
— Thoughts on. Tait, n. s. 9: 75.
Anniversary Week in Boston. Ev. Sat. 10: 570.
— of 1846. (F. D. Huntington) Mo. Rel. M. 3: 289.
— of 1847. (E. S. Gannett) Mo. Rel. M. 4: 320.
— of 1872. (F. T. Washburn) Mo. Rel. M. 48: 61.
Announcements and Three Rooms. Blackw. 50: 212.
Annual Biography and Obituary, On the, 1834. Mo. R. 133: 269.
— 1835–36. Mo. R. 136: 196. 139: 273.
Annuals, The. Tait, 2: 524.
— American. Liv. Age, 3: 361.
— Comic, 1840. Mo. R. 151: 109.
— for 1829. Mo. R. 117: 377, 525. 118: 91.
— for 1831. Mo. R. 123: 400. 124: 47.
— for 1832. Mo. R. 126: 370, 523. — Fraser, 6: 653.
— for 1833. Mo. R. 129: 384.
— for 1834. Mo. R. 132: 333, 559. — Fraser, 10: 602.
— for 1835. Mo. R. 135: 423.
— for 1836. Fraser, 15: 33.
— for 1837. Fraser, 16: 757. — Mo. R. 141: 402.
— for 1838. Ecl. R. 66: 657. — Mo. R. 144: 421.
— for 1839. Fraser, 19: 57. — Ecl. R. 68: 599, 715. — Mo. R. 147: 443.
— for 1840. Ecl. R. 70: 692.
— for 1841. Ecl. R. 72: 704.
— for 1842. Ecl. R. 74: 597.
— for 1850. Liv. Age, 24: 226.
Annuaries; a Poem. (Alice Carey) Internat. M. 5: 87.
Annuities, British Government Life, Statistics of. (F. Hendriks) J. Statis. Soc. 19: 325.
— Life Assurance, etc. (J. F. Entz) Hunt, 16: 48, 445. *See* Insurance, Life.
— Poor Men's. All the Year, 13: 225.
Annunciata. (H. H. Boyesen) Scrib. 18: 911.
Anointing with Oil, Revival of. Liv. Age, 37: 401.
Anonymous Admirer; a Story. (S. B. Russ) Appleton, 24: 339.
Anonymous and Pseudonymous Authors and Works. Nat. Q. 23: 41. — Ev. Sat. 11: 127.
Anonymous Criticism. Lond. M. 18: 556.
Anonymous Journalism. (E. L. Godkin) Nation, 5: 112. 12: 234.

Anonymous Letters. Hogg, 6: 56.
Anonymous Literature. (A. Trollope) Fortn. 1: 491.
Anonymous Publications. (J. Galt) Fraser, 11: 549.
Anonymous Writing. (T. Walker) West. Law J. 1: 511.
Anorthoscope, The. (W. B. Carpenter) Stud. & Intel. Obs. 2: 110.
Another Daughter of Eve. (B. Dunphy) Tinsley, 20: 331.
Another Tale of the Tub. Belgra. 16: 210.
Another World, by Hermes; a Review. Macmil. 28: 140.
Another World down here. (W. M. Williams) Ecl. M. 96: 616.
Ansayrii; or, the Assassins, Walpole's. Blackw. 70: 719. — Ecl. R. 95: 43. — New Q. 1: 37.
Anschar, the Apostle of the North. (A. Michelsen) Luth. Q. 8: 501. — (J. H. Allen) Chr. Exam. 54: 188. — Ecl. M. 50: 538. — Ecl. R. 111: 137. — Am. Church R. 23: 226.
Anselm, St., Archbishop of Canterbury. (W. G. Nowell) Chr. Exam. 73: 157. — For. Q. 30: 13. — Meth. Q. 13: 576.
— Life of. Chr. Rem. 5: 362.
— Rémusat on. Chr. Obs. 53: 378.
— Translations from. (J. S. Maginnis) Bib. Sac. 8: 529, 699.
Ansgar, St. *See* Anschar, St.
Anson, George, Lord. (M. Oliphant) Blackw. 104: 676. Same art. Liv. Age, 100: 67.
— Barrow's Life of. Ed. R. 69: 126. — Mo. R. 148: 292.
— South Sea Expedition of. Mus. 44: 134, 367.
— Voyages of, and of Byron. Retros. 10: 285.
Anspach, Elizabeth, Margravine of. Colburn, 16: 90. — Temp. Bar, 2: 241.
— Memoirs of. Lond. M. 14: 243.
Anster, John, with portrait. Dub. Univ. 14: 544.
— Poems of. Blackw. 7: 312.
— Xeniola and other Poems. Dub. Univ. 9: 453.
Anstey, Christopher, Life and Poetry of. Lond. M. 5: 24.
Anstie, Francis Edmund. Nature, 10: 398.
Ant, Natural History of. Hogg, 9: 246.
— Wood. (J. G. Wood) Once a Week, 7: 707.
Ant-Eater. Bentley, 35: 547. Same art. Liv. Age, 42: 133. — Fraser, 49: 157. — Hogg, 11: 26.
Ant-Hill City. (A. McNeill) Belgra. 37: 404.
Ant-Lion, The. (J. H. Emerton) Am. Natural. 4: 705.
Ant-supporting Plants. (J. Britten) Pop. Sci. R. 14: 29.
Ants. (S. B. Herrick) Scrib. 15: 171. — (Ellice Hopkins) Contemp. 37: 941. Same art. Liv. Age, 146: 20. Same art. Ecl. M. 95: 287. — (E. R. Leland) Pop. Sci. Mo. 7: 257. — Ed. R. 145: 67. — Good Words, 13: 674. — Ev. Sat. 13: 491. — So. R. n. s. 18: 360.
— Agricultural. (G. Lincecum) Am. Natural. 8: 513. — Ecl. M. 96: 418.
— — of Texas. (A. R. Wallace) Nature, 20: 501.
— American, Habits of. Chamb. J. 56: 430.
— Bees, and Wasps, Observations on. (Sir J. Lubbock) Nature, 23: 255.
— City of. All the Year, 24: 7.
— Conservatism among, Lubbock on. Liv. Age, 147: 760. Same art. Pop. Sci. Mo. 18: 401.
— Cutting, of Texas. (G. T. Bettany) Nature, 20: 583.
— Driver. (G. A. Perkins) Am. Natural. 3: 360.
— Gossip about. Chamb. J. 27: 299.
— Habits of. (Sir J. Lubbock) Fortn. 27: 287. Same art. Ecl. M. 88: 641. Same art. Pop. Sci. Mo. 11: 39. — (Sir J. Lubbock) Nature, 22: 185.
— Harvesting, and Trap-Door Spiders. (A. R. Wallace) Nature, 7: 337. 11: 245.
— — Florida. (Mary Treat) Lippinc. 22: 555.
— Honey-making. Pop. Sci. Mo. 16: 824. — (H. Edwards) Am. Natural. 7: 722.
Ants, Honey-making, of Texas. Nature, 8: 250.
— Huber on. Ed. Mo. R. 4: 335. — Ed. R. 20: 143. — Ecl. R. 33: 352.
— in Natal. Stud. & Intel. Obs. 3: 336.
— Intelligence of. (G. J. Romanes) 19th Cent. 9: 992. 10: 245. Same art. Pop. Sci. Mo. 19: 495. Same art. Liv. Age, 150: 176. 151: 371.
— Mound-making, of the Alleghanies. (H. C. McCook) Am. Natural. 12: 431.
— New Leaf-cutting. (G. K. Morris) Am. Natural. 15: 100.
— Notes on Mexican. (E. Norton) Am. Natural. 2: 57.
— Observations on. Chamb. J. 53: 5. Same art. Ecl. M. 86: 754.
— of Switzerland, Forel's. Ecl. R. 145: 67. Same art. Liv. Age, 132: 451.
— Parasol, of Texas. (G. T. Bettany) Nature, 21: 17.
— Republics of. So. R. n. s. 16: 391.
— Slave-making. (M. Treat) Lippinc. 28: 79.
— — and War-making. (M. Treat) Harper, 58: 176.
— White, Danger from. (H. A. Hagen) Am. Natural. 10: 401.
See Termites.
Ants' Nest, What I saw in an. (A. Wilson) Belgra. 36: 450. Same art. Sup. Pop. Sci. Mo. 4: 57.
Ants' Nest; a Poem. (H. D. Traill) Fortn. 32: 236.
Antæus; a Poem. (M. Collins) Temp. Bar. 18: 547.
— Lesson of. (D. Swing) Lakeside, 2: 386.
Antagonism and Progression. Chr. Rem. 16: 261.
Antar, The Bedouin Romance of. Blackw. 4: 385. — Kitto, 5: 1. — Penny M. 6: 55.
— Illustrations of Scripture from. Kitto, 5: 1.
Antar and Zara, an Eastern Romance in Songs. (A. de Vere) Cath. World, 19: 226–735. 20: 55.
Antarctic Continent. (Sir W. Thomson) Geog. M. 5: 268.
— Discovery of. Mus. 40: 214.
Antarctic Discoveries. Nav. M. 2: 547.
Antarctic Expedition. Ecl. Mus. 3: 470.
Antarctic Explorations. Liv. Age, 29: 1.
Antarctic Ocean, Adrift in. Temp. Bar. 18: 467. 19: 62, 215.
— Conditions of. (Sir C. W. Thomson) Nature, 15: 104, 120.
Antarctic Regions. Cornh. 27: 293. Same art. Ecl. M. 80: 590. Same art. Ev. Sat. 14: 361, 378.
— Sir J. C. Ross's Voyage to. Quar. 81: 166. — (Sir D. Brewster) No. Brit. 8: 177. — Colburn, 80: 469.
See also Ross, Sir James C.
Antchar, The. (I. Tourguenieff) Galaxy, 15: 330, 461.
Antediluvian Romance, An. Fraser, 43: 470.
Antediluvian Theocracy. Kitto, 12: 382.
Antediluvians, Modern. (J. Western) Lakeside, 2: 123.
Antelope, American. (J. D. Caton) Am. Natural. 10: 193. — (S. W. Williston) Am. Natural. 11: 599.
— Hunting the. (M. L. Meason) Broadw. 2: 234.
Ante-Matrimonial Martyrdom. St. James, 22: 381.
Ante-Nicene Christian Library. (J. A. Brown) Luth. Q. 3: 130.
Ante-Nicene Fathers. Ecl. R. 75: 241. — Chr. Obs. 68: 175.
Ante-Nicene Library. Chr. Rem. 36: 291.
Ante-Nuptial Lie, The. Chamb. J. 35: 291. Same art. Ecl. M. 53: 414. Same art. Liv. Age, 69: 771.
Antepasts of the Future State. Chr. Obs. 46: 513.
Anteros. (G. A. Lawrence) Harper, 40: 274, 381, 754. 41: 125–900. 42: 80–903. 43: 85, 209.
Antes, John. Portfo.(Den.) 9: 329.
Anthem of the Universe; a Poem. (C. A. Munger) Putnam, 12: 536.
Anthesphoria at Athens, The. Fraser, 39: 713. Same art. Liv. Age, 22: 163.

Anthologia Germanica. Dub. Univ. **5**: 393. **6**: 404. **7**: 278, 518. **8**: 142. **9**: 33, 271. **10**: 651. **13**: 44. **14**: 69, 697. **18**: 19. **19**: 201. **21**: 29. **25**: 95. **26**: 283.
— Hibernica. Dub. Univ. **29**: 239, 624. **30**: 66.
Anthology, Conway's Sacred. (J. E. Carpenter) Theo. R. **11**: 191.
— Greek, Chrysanthema. (W. M. Hardinge) Appleton, **21**: 29. *See* Greek Anthology.
— Ionian. Mo. R. **134**: 37.
Anthon, Charles. (R. D. Nesmith) Galaxy, **4**: 610.
— Classical Dictionary. New York R. **8**: 485.—(C. C. Felton) No. Am. **54**: 175.—Dem. R. **9**: 133, 360. —Chr. Exam. **31**: 409.
— Cicero. So. Lit. Mess. **3**: 72.
— Cicero and Tacitus. (J. L. Lincoln) No. Am. **68**: 348.
— Greek Grammar. Knick. **12**: 70.—New York R. **10**: 490.
— Greek and Latin Lessons. New York R. **5**: 237.
— Greek Prosody and Grammar. New York R. **3**: 467.
— Greek Reader. New York R. **7**: 501.—(E. E. Hale) No. Am. **51**: 213, 492. **52**: 238.—Knick. **16**: 166.
— Horace. Am. Q. **8**: 72.
— Sallust. So. Lit. Mess. **2**: 392.—Am. Mo. R. **1**: 181.
— School Classics. Dem. R. **6**: 45.
Anthony, Saint. (M. P. Thompson) Cath. World, **33**: 298. —(A. P. Peabody) No. Am. **93**: 457.—(P. Schaff) Meth. Q. **24**: 29.
— Flaubert's Temptation of. (H. James, jr.) Nation, **18**: 365.
— the Patriarch of Monks. (P. Schaff) Hours at Home, **1**: 334.
Anthony, St., Falls of, Discovery of. Month, **25**: 54.
Anthony; a Poem. (W. B. Scott) Fortn. **10**: 81.
Anthracen. Nature, **15**: 507.
Anthracite Coal. *See* Coal, Anthracite.
Anthracite Iron Manufacture of United States. (H. Fairbairn) J. Frankl. Inst. **47**: 393.
Anthracites and Iron Ores, Analysis of. (W. R. Johnson) J. Frankl. Inst. **28**: 73, 289.
Anthropological Collections from the Holy Land. (R. F. Burton) Anthrop. J. **1**: 300, 320. **2**: 41.
Anthropological Congress at Paris, 1867. Hist. M. **12**: 210.
Anthropological Contributions, Gerland's. Nature, **11**: 384.
Anthropological Explorations, Von Baer on. Anthrop. R. **4**: 238.
Anthropological Review, Origin of. Anthrop. R. **6**: 431.
Anthropological Statistics. (L. H. Steiner) Mercersb. **17**: 78.
Anthropology. (P. Broca) Anthrop. R. **6**: 35.—(I. Kant) J. Spec. Philos. **9**: 16, 239, 406. **10**: 319. **11**: 310, 353. **14**: 154, 299.—Chr. Rem. **7**: 15.
— Address before the British Association. (F. Galton) Am. J. Sci. **114**: 265.
— and Archæology, Congress of. (G. Harley) Nature, **10**: 332.
— — at Brussels, 1872. (M. J. Lalor) Cath. World, **16**: 639, 829.
— Archaic, Gastaldi and Keller on. Anthrop. R. **6**: 114.
— — German. Anthrop. R. **5**: 325.
— — International Congress of. Anthrop. R. **6**: 203.
— Bible. (R. Graham) Chr. Q. **4**: 216.—(J. W. Nevin) Mercersb. **24**: 329.
— Broca on. Anthrop. R. **5**: 193.
— Christian. (J. A. Brown) Am. Presb. R. **18**: 129.
— Comte's. (J. Kaines) Anthrop. J. **1**: 349.
— Continuity applied to. (J. Hunt) Anthrop. R. **5**: 110.
— Dundee Conference on. Anthrop. R. **6**: 71.
— General Pitt Rivers's Collection. Nature, **22**: 489.
— Historic, Baldwin on. Anthrop. R. **7**: 323.
— in America, Progress of, in 1880. (O. T. Mason) Am. Natural. **15**: 616.
— Latham's Works on. Anthrop. R. **4**: 231.
— Microcephali. (C. Vogt) Anthrop. R. **7**: 128.
— Modern. Brit. Q. **38**: 466.
— Müller's Chips on. So. R. n. s. **6**: 70.
— Natural Selection and. (J. Hunt) Anthrop. R. **4**: 320.
— North American, in 1879. (O. T. Mason) Am. Natural. **14**: 348.
— of England and Wales. (D. Mackintosh) Anthrop. R. **4**: 1.
— — Crania Britannica, by Davis and Thurnam. Anthrop. R. **6**: 52.
— of Greece. Anthrop. R. **6**: 154.
— of Holland. Anthrop. R. **3**: 202.
— of Italy. Anthrop. R. **5**: 142.
— — Nicolucci's. Anthrop. R. **2**: 30.
— of Persia. Anthrop. R. **6**: 27.
— of Scotland. (H. MacLean) Anthrop. R. **4**: 209.
— of Western Europe. (C. C. Blake) Anthrop. R. **4**: 158.
— Paris Society of, Proceedings. Anthrop. R. **6**: 104.
— — Transactions, 1865–67. (P. Broca) Anthrop. R. **6**: 225.
— Physio-, at Edinburgh. Anthrop. R. **6**: 64.
— Progress of. (T. H. Huxley) Pop. Sci. Mo. **13**: 668. —(W. James) Nation, **6**: 113.
— — Quatrefages on. Anthrop. R. **7**: 231.
— — Recent. (E. B. Tylor) Pop. Sci. Mo. **16**: 145.—Nature, **21**: 381.
— Science of. Ecl. M. **72**: 314.
— Study of. (J. Hunt) Anthrop. R. **1**: 1.
— Tylor's. (A. Weld) Month, **17**: 78.—(A. R. Wallace) Nature, **24**: 242.—(A. Winchell) Dial (Ch.), **2**: 75.
— Vollgraff's. Anthrop. R. **4**: 226.
— Waitz's. Anthrop. R. **1**: 465.—(R. F. Burton) Anthrop. R. **2**: 233.
See Man.
Anthropologists, Humors of. (W. A. Hammond) Nation, **1**: 141.
Anthropometamorphosis, Bulwer's. Retros. **16**: 205.
Anthropomorphism. (M. S. Phelps) Princ. n. s. **8**: 120.
— Philosophy of. (J. F. Denham) Kitto, **1**: 9.
Anthropotomy. Anthrop. R. **2**: 202.
Anti-Calvinist, Fellowes on the. Chr. Obs. **1**: 172, 233.
Antichrist. Chr. Obs. **66**: 544.—Cong. M. **19**: 538.
— Black on. Theo. & Lit. J. **8**: 168.
— Bonar's Development of. Chr. Obs. **54**: 318.
— Faber on the Little Horn and. Chr. Obs. **6**: 356, 496.
— Meyrick on. Chr. Obs. **64**: 200.
— Renan on. (E. B. Elliott) Chr. Obs. **75**: 275, 373, 463.—(C. K. Paul) Theo. R. **10**: 557.—(A. Laugel) Nation, **17**: 22, 57.—(J. A. Smith) Bapt. Q. **9**: 451.—Lond. Q. **41**: 135.
— Todd's Discourses on. Theo. & Lit. J. **4**: 285.—Quar. **71**: 197.
— 1260 Years of. (F. G. Hibbard) Meth. Q. **26**: 235.
Anti-Coningsby, or the New Generation grown Old. Fraser, **31**: 211.
Anticreed; or, A Code of Unbelief. Lond. M. **21**: 330.
Antietam, Battle of. (D. R. Jones) So. M. **14**: supp. 56. —(D. H. Maury) So. Hist. Pap. **8**: 261.
— — My Hunt after the Captain. (O. W. Holmes) Atlan. **10**: 738.
— — Reminiscence of. (J. S. Johnston) So. Hist. Pap. **8**: 526.
— Trip to. (C. W. Loring) Contin. Mo. **3**: 145.
Antigua, A Hurricane in. (Capt. Mackinnon) Colburn, **85**: 277.
— and the Antiguans. Tait, n. s. **11**: 197.
— Geology of. (S. Hovey) Am. J. Sci. **35**: 75.

Anti-Jacobin and George Canning. Cornh. **15**: 63. Same art. Ecl. M. **68**: 413.
— Literary Partnership of Canning and Frere. Fraser, **90**: 714.
— Poetry of. Westm. **58**: 459. Same art. Liv. Age, **35**: 455.
— Remarks on. Meth. M. **43**: 513.
— Review of. Chr. Obs. **1**: 176, 254, 388. **2**: 256.
Antilles, Lesser. Macmil. **35**: 361. Same art. Liv. Age, **133**: 90.
— Stone-Age in. (J. B. Holden) Scrib. **10**: 427.
Anti-Mason Address. Niles's Reg. **41**: 166.
— Convention. Niles's Reg. **41**: 83, 108.
Anti-Masonic Party, Morgan Excitement and. Hist. M. **16**: 82.
Anti-Masonry. Niles's Reg. **41**: 85, 345.
Antimony, Atomic Weight of. (J. P. Cooke, jr.) Am. J. Sci. **115**: 41, 107. **119**: 382.
— Discovery of, in Sonora, Mexico. (E. T. Cox) Am. J. Sci. **120**: 421.
Antinomian Controversy in New England. (B. F. Bronson) Bapt. Q. **6**: 280.
Antinomianism. Chr. Obs. **17**: 296, 382. **18**: 31.— Cong. M. **8**: 569.— Ecl. R. **27**: 401, 528.
— Cottle's Strictures on. Chr. Obs. **23**: 709.
— Fletcher's Checks to. Am. Meth. M. **11**: 413.
— Modern, 1824. Ecl. R. **40**: 508.
— Short History of, Authorship of. Hist. M. **1**: 321. **2**: 22, 170.
— unmasked. Meth. M. **43**: 21.
— — Chase on. Chr. Obs. **18**: 530.
— What is? Chr. Obs. **47**: 1.
Antinous. (J. A. Symonds) Cornh. **39**: 200, 343.
— Intaglio of, in Strozzi Collection. (W. Bowman) Arch. **1**: 112.
Antioch during the Crusades. (F. Damiani) Arch. **15**: 234.
— Siege of. (J. H. Clinch) Knick. **8**: 173, 257.
Antioch in Syria. (J. S. Lee) Univ. Q. **32**: 60.
Antioch College. O. & N. **4**: 510.
— Co-education at. Nation, **11**: 24.
— and Horace Mann. (H. C. Badger) Chr. Exam. **79**: 252.
Antiparos. Sharpe, **48**: 84.
Antipathies. (C. Waddy) St. James, **29**: 619.— Chamb. J. **51**: 504.— Colburn, **4**: 68. **79**: 310.
— Curious. Chamb. J. **58**: 53.
— Physical. Once a Week, **2**: 113. Same art. Liv. Age, **65**: 252.
Antipodes and Periœci. (H. Butterworth) Pop. Sci. Mo. **2**: 489.
— Navigation of. Blackw. **62**: 515.
Antiquarian Club Books. Quar. **82**: 309.
Antiquarian Delusions. Chamb. J. **20**: 56.
Antiquarian Excavations in the Middle Ages. (T. Wright) Arch. **30**: 438.
Antiquarian Logic. Chamb. J. **46**: 529.
Antiquarian Researches in 1854. (J. Y. Akerman) Arch. **36**: 175.
Antiquarianism in England. Ed. R. **86**: 307.
Antiquarians. Knick. **20**: 305.
Antiquaries, Society of. Ed. R. **154**: 101.
Antique Dream; a Poem. (T. Irwin) Dub. Univ. **45**: 90.
Antiquities, Brande's Popular. Quar. **11**: 259.
— A few Antiques. Scrib. **16**: 316.
— of Christian Church and Colonies. (R. Emerson) Am. Bib. Repos. 2d s. **6**: 212.
— from the Island of Sacrificios. (E. Nepeau) Arch. **30**: 138, 339.
— W. Linton's Colossal Vestiges. Colburn, **126**: 169.
— Novel. Good Words, **7**: 830.
— Smith's Dictionary of Greek and Roman. Mo R. **158**: 509.
See Archæology.
Antiquity. Lond. M. **3**: 527.
— Echoes from. (D. M. Moir) Blackw. **40**: 781.
— Moral Culture of. Liv. Age, **55**: 609.
— Polity and Commerce of the Great Nations of. For. Q. **5**: 141.
Anti-Rent Disturbance in New York. (S. D. Law) New Eng. **4**: 92.—(D. D. Barnard) Am. Whig R. **2**: 577.
Anti-Rentism. West. Law J. **3**: 193.
Anti-Slavery Cause, 1838. Ecl. R. **67**: 54, 458.
— 1843. Ecl. R. **77**: 673.
Anti-Slavery Convention at London, 1840. Ecl. R. **72**: 227. **75**: 37.
Anti-Slavery Men of the South. (E. A. Pollard) Galaxy, **16**: 329.
Anti-Slavery Movement in America, Garrison and the Churches. (D. Dorchester) Meth. Q. **41**: 270, 474. *See* Abolition; Emancipation; Slavery.
Anti-Slavery Principles and Proceedings. (C. Francis) Chr. Exam. **25**: 228.
Anti-Slavery Society. Fraser, **1**: 610. **2**: 334.
Antithetic Fallacies. (F. H. Hill) Fortn. **28**: 395.
Antoine, the Blacksmith; a Story. (F. E. M. Notley) Argosy, **29**: 233.
Antonelli, Cardinal. (E. Ransford) Canad. Mo. **10**: 533. —(F. Gregorovius) Dub. Univ. **77**: 307.— Dub. R. **80**: 74.— Ecl. M. **88**: 102.— Liv. Age, **67**: 55.— Temp. Bar, **3**: 533.
Antonias; a Story of the South. Blackw. **18**: 601.
Antonina; or, The Fall of Rome. Bentley, **27**: 375.
Antonine Itinerary, Discrepancies in. (C. Warne) Arch. **39**: 85.
Antonine Pillars at Rome. (M. Folkes) Arch. **1**: 117.
Antoninus, Marcus Aurelius. (M. Arnold) Victoria, **2**: 1. —(E. Renan) 19th Cent. **7**: 742.— Colburn, **125**: 423.— So. Q. **22**: 360.
— and the Stoic Philosophy. (F. Pollock) Mind, **4**: 47.
— and the Talmud. (E. H. Plumptre) Contemp. **10**: 81. — Ev. Sat. **7**: 236.
— as a Philosopher. (C. Vaux) Pop. Sci. Mo. **11**: 461.
— Life of. (J. W. Stearns) Bapt. Q. **6**: 187.
— Meditations of. Month, **9**: 429.—(A. S. Colton) Princ. **36**: 297.
— a Persecutor. (W. Moyle) Kitto, **30**: 114, 318.—(W. Moyle) Theo. Repos. **1**: 77, 147.
— Statue of, in the Capitol. (M. Folkes) Arch. **1**: 122.
— Thoughts of. (R. B. Richardson) New Eng. **40**: 415.
Antoninus of Placentia, Pilgrimage of, A.D. 570. Kitto, **36**: 404.
Antonio di Carara; a Paduan Tale. Blackw. **32**: 525.
Antonio da Pelago; an Italian Innkeeper and Carrier. Temp. Bar, **40**: 499. **45**: 243.
Antonio Salvini; a Tale. (Mrs. E. F. Ellet) Godey, **22**: 15.
Antony, St., of Padua, Chronicle of. (H. J. Coleridge) Month, **25**: 248.
Antony, Mark. Fraser, **35**: 64.
— and Cicero. Fraser, **32**: 314.
— Fall of. Am. Mo. M. **4**: 208.
Antrim, Round the Coast of. (P. Q. Keegan) Colburn, **159**: 342.
— Iron Mines of. (R. A. Watson) Dub. Univ. **83**: 1.
Antrim Castle. Dub. Univ. **56**: 628. **57**: 163, 303.
Antwerp. (J. H. Pettingell) Appleton, **22**: 385.— Penny M. **1**: 369. **9**: 281.
— and Holland, A Peep into. (E. E. Chase) Scrib. **18**: 519.
— Commerce of. Penny M. **7**: 345.
— Day at. Blackw. **90**: 365.
— Legend from. Blackw. **64**: 444.
Anviti, Count, Assassination of. Month, **6**: 381.
Apache Race. (J. C. Cremony) Overland, **1**: 201.
Apaches, Adventure among the. (M. S. Severance) O. & N. **8**: 702.

Apaches, Ride with. (J. Mendivil) Overland, **6**: 341.
Apamean Medal, Observations upon. Arch. **4**: 315, 331, 347.
Apartment-Houses. (T. Richardson) Scrib. **8**: 63.
— in Philadelphia. (C. Barnard) Scrib. **11**: 477.
Apartment to let; a Story. Galaxy, **14**: 672.
Apartment to let, by an Old Maid. Victoria, **34**: 102.
Apartments to let. All the Year, **30**: 515, 560. — Lond. Soc. **3**: 27.
Apatites containing Manganese. (S. L. Penfield) Am. J. Sci. **119**: 367.
Ape and the Serpent. (A. E. Brown) Am. Natural. **12**: 225.
Apes and Man. (St. G. Mivart) Pop. Sci. R. **12**: 113, 243. Same art. Ecl. M. **80**: 698. **81**: 422.
— — Resemblances of. (St. G. Mivart) Nature, **3**: 481. *See* Man.
— Anthropoid. Chamb. J. **39**: 308.
— Nest-Building. (J. Hollingshead) Once a Week, **7**: 111. *See* Monkeys.
Apennines. Tait, n. s. **16**: 661.
— Adventure in. Fraser, **35**: 483. Same art. Liv. Age, **13**: 362.
— Geology of. Ed. R. **26**: 156.
— Month in. Hogg, **11**: 132.
— Ride across. Temp. Bar, **45**: 243.
— Village Life in. (E. M. Clerke) Cornh. **39**: 723. Same art. Liv. Age, **142**: 162.
Aphasia, or Privation of Voice by Paralysis. Chamb. J. **44**: 83. Same art. Ev. Sat. **2**: 44.
— in regard to Language and Thought. Cath. World, **24**: 411.
Aphides. Chamb. J. **8**: 183. **53**: 303.
— Development of Viviparous. (W. I. Burnett) Am. J. Sci. **67**: 62, 261.
Aphorisms. (A. Colton) Contin. Mo. **5**: 413–689. **6**: 78–609. — (J. S. Mill) Westm. **26**: 348.
— and Anecdotes. Sharpe, **14**: 272.
— Books of. Fraser, **6**: 712.
— Utility and Futility of. (W. R. Alger) Atlan. **11**: 178.
Aphrodité; a Poem. (G. C. Davies) Dark Blue, **3**: 449.
Aphroessa Island and George I. Once a Week, **15**: 38.
Apion and Josephus. (E. Pond) Meth. Q. **30**: 274.
Apocalypse of the Old and New Testaments. Kitto, **34**: 76, 462. *See* Bible, Revelation.
Apocalypse of Sister Nativité. (R. Southey) Quar. **33**: 375. **36**: 305.
Apocrypha, Analytical Account of. Chr. Rem. **51**: 255.
— Book of Enoch and. (A. G. Laurie) Univ. Q. **35**: 339.
— Character of. Chr. Obs. **25**: 480, 558.
— Controversy on, in Bible Society. Cong. M. **9**: 193. — Ecl. R. **42**: 185, 377. **43**: 352. **44**: 86, 193, 567.
— of Old Testament. (M. S. Terry) Meth. Q. **41**: 77.
— — Eschatology of. (E. C. Bissell) Bib. Sac. **36**: 320.
— — History in, as related to Christ. (A. S. Twombly) New Eng. **36**: 329.
— Thornwall on. (C. Hodge) Princ. **17**: 268.
See names of several books, as Enoch, Judith, Tobit.
Apocryphal New Testament. (A. Lamson) Chr. Exam. **14**: 1. — (H. J. Rose) Quar. **25**: 348. — Quar. **30**: 472. — Chr. Obs. **22**: 1, 65, 129.
Apocryphal Gospels. Ed. R. **128**: 81. — (J. J. Taylor) Theo. R. **4**: 149. — Lond. Q. **31**: 427. — Liv. Age, **52**: 449.
— Christ of. (O. B. Frothingham) Chr. Exam. **53**: 21.
— Inferiority of. Ed. R. **128**: 81. — Same art. Liv. Age, **98**: 707.
Apollo, Hymn to. (A. Pike) Blackw. **45**: 820.
— Representations of. Lond. Soc. **9**: 200.
Apollo Belvedere, Statue of. Lippinc. **18**: 131. — Liv. Age, **137**: 496.
Apollonius Tyanæus. (S. G. Bulfinch) Chr. Exam. **84**: 159. — (W. M. W. Call) Fortn. **2**: 488. — 19th Cent. **6**: 551. Same art. Liv. Age, **143**: 81. — Lond. Q. **27**: 362.
— Bewick's Life of. Quar. **3**: 417.
— Life of. Ecl. R. **13**: 215.
— Life and Miracles of. Kitto, **30**: 88.
— Reville's Essay on. (J. S. Watson) Contemp. **4**: 199.
— Sketch of. (B. L. Gildersleeve) So. R. n. s. **4**: 94.
Apologetics, Christian. (T. G. Apple) Mercersb. **25**: 165. — (J. A. Reubelt) Chr. Q. **2**: 35.
— and Jurisprudence, Recent Changes in. (F. Wharton) Princ. n. s. **2**: 149.
— and Philosophy. (C. W. Shields) Princ. n. s. **4**: 196.
— Condition and Importance of. (O. Zöckler) Theo. Ecl. **5**: 165.
— Evangelical, Plea for. (J. M. Gibson) Presb. R. **1**: 321.
— Literature of. No. Brit. **15**: 331.
Apologetical Literature, Recent, Survey of. (O. Zöckler) Theo. Ecl. **6**: 97.
Apologies. Liv. Age, **139**: 186.
Apologists, Christian. (J. Carroll) Month, **26**: 436.
— and Martyrs, Pressensé's. (W. H. Withrow) Meth. Q. **32**: 533.
Apologue, An. (J. L. Patterson) Month, **33**: 67.
Apology, An; a Poem. (A. J. Begbie) Dark Blue, **1**: 96.
— for Harmony. Dub. Univ. **17**: 571.
Apophthegms. *See* Apothegms.
Apoplexy. (J. R. Black) Pop. Sci. Mo. **6**: 705.
— Cheyne on. Ecl. R. **18**: 342.
Apostasy, The, and the Man of Sin, 2 Thess. ii. 1–12. Theo. & Lit. J. **12**: 86.
— Warning against. (N. M. Williams) Bapt. Q. **6**: 359.
Apostle of Matrimony; a Sketch. (H. Gullifer) Tinsley, **27**: 552.
Apostles, Diversities of. (N. M. Williams) Bapt. Q. **8**: 399.
— Doctrine of. (H. Messner) Bib. Sac. **26**: 713. **27**: 135, 430.
— Inspiration of. (J. Priestley) Theo. Repos. **4**: 189. — (Dr. Steudel) Chr. R. **26**: 69, 215. **27**: 67.
— Language of. Liv. Age, **76**: 155.
— Lives of. Meth. Q. **1**: 9. — Chr. Exam. **5**: 371.
— Ministry of. Am. Meth. M. **11**: 105.
— Relations of Paul with. (T. Hill) Unita. R. **11**: 650.
— Renan on. (D. Bowen) Radical, **2**: 156. — (J. L. Davies) Contemp. **2**: 177. — (G. P. Fisher) New Eng. **25**: 542. — (O. B. Frothingham) Nation, **3**: 45. — (C. K. Paul) Theo. R. **3**: 389. — (H. Rogers) Fortn. **5**: 513. — (S. Stead) Contemp. **3**: 199. — Brit. Q. **44**: 474. — Lond. Q. **26**: 491.
— The Three, and Three Christian Ages. (S. S. Hebberd) Univ. Q. **33**: 133.
— Vindication of Conduct of. Theo. Repos. **1**: 59–454. **2**: 59–134, 183.
Apostles' Creed. (J. E. Carpenter) Theo. R. **7**: 145. — (A. P. Stanley) 19th Cent. **8**: 207. — (J. W. Proudfit) Princ. **24**: 602. — (G. P. Disosway) Meth. Q. **20**: 478.
— and Evangelicalism. (J. W. Nevin) Mercersb. **10**: 383.
— Defense of. (J. W. Nevin) Mercersb. **4**: 606.
— History of. (J. W. Nevin) Mercersb. **1**: 105, 201, 313. — Westm. **88**: 367.
— Importance of. (J. W. Nevin) Mercersb. **14**: 33.
— Origin and Structure of. (J. W. Nevin) Mercersb. **16**: 148.
— Unity of. (J. W. Nevin) Mercersb. **16**: 313.
"Apostles" Society, Cambridge University. (W. D. Christie) Macmil. **11**: 18.
Apostleship, a Temporary Office. (J. A. Alexander) Princ. **21**: 355, 542.
Apostolic Age. Nat. R. **9**: 117.

Apostolic Christianity, Godkin's. Ecl. R. **77**: 414.
— James Martineau on, and the British Quarterly. Brit. Q. **14**: 473.
Apostolic Church. Tait, n. s. **26**: 701.
— Barnes on. (J. A. Alexander) Princ. **15**: 386.
— Colman on. (E. Pond) New Eng. **4**: 182.
— Dissensions in. (E. Harwood) Am. Church R. **9**: 481. **10**: 259.
— Doctrine of. Lond. Q. **19**: 445. **24**: 207.
— Government of. (C. Elliott) Am. Meth. M. **19**: 1.
— — and Discipline of. (P. Schaff) Meth. Q. **11**: 429.
— History of, Baur on. (G. P. Fisher) New Eng. **23**: 401.
— — Schaff's. (L. Bacon) New Eng. **12**: 237. — Am. Church Mo. **3**: 304. — Chr. R. **20**: 1. — (C. Hodge) Princ. **26**: 148.
— King's Exposition of. Bib. Sac. **8**: 378.
— Origin of Persecution of. (B. Smith) Univ. Q. **32**: 343.
Apostolic Churches, Congregational. Cong. Q. **9**: 148.
— State of Opinion in. (H. Ballou, 2d) Univ. Q. **1**: 84, 329.
Apostolic Commission. (S. N. Callender) Mercersb. **14**: 325. — (J. Harkness) Theo. & Lit. J. **7**: 266. — (D. Y. Heisler) Mercersb. **11**: 337. — (E. E. Higbee) Mercersb. **21**: 231.
— Scope of. Theo. & Lit. J. **10**: 389.
Apostolic Constitutions. (A. Lamson) Chr. Exam. **44**: 223. — (J. Forsyth) Princ. **21**: 42. — Chr. R. **13**: 201. — Chr. Rem. **27**: 253.
— Chase's. (A. B. Chapin) Am. Church R. **1**: 536.
— 46th Chapter of. Am. Church R. **24**: 489.
— Object in forging. Chr. R. **15**: 505.
Apostolic Fathers. (J. A. Brown) Evang. R. **4**: 356. — Brit. Q. **4**: 378. — Lond. Q. **28**: 201. Same art. Theo. Ecl. **5**: 82.
Apostolic Office, Permanency of. (C. Hodge) Princ. **28**: 1. — (N. S. Richardson) Am. Church R. **8**: 406.
Apostolic Salutations and Benedictions. (J. J. Owen) Bib. Sac. **19**: 707.
Apostolic Succession. (C. S. Gerhard) Mercersb. **22**: 408. — (J. A. Alexander) Princ. **14**: 129. **19**: 539. — (S. E. Shepard) Chr. Q. **1**: 403. — (J. Whitby) Am. Meth. M. **22**: 51. — Cong. M. **21**: 705. **22**: 189, 629. — Ecl. R. **68**: 547. — So. R. n. s. **11**: 1, 249. **12**: 249.
— Anglican Claim for. Dub. R. **7**: 139.
— Controverted. (G. Anderson) Bapt. Q. **5**: 167.
— Episcopal Recorder on. (N. S. Richardson) Am. Church R. **15**: 284.
Apostolic Tradition. (M. Loy) Evang. R. **3**: 537.
— Strictures upon. (C. P. Krauth) Evang. R. **4**: 57.
Apothecaries. House. Words, **14**: 108.
Apothecary's Wife; a Russian Story. Dub. Univ. **31**: 75, 179.
Apothegms. (W. A. Kendall) Overland, **8**: 462.
— in Verse. (L. Withington) Bib. Sac. **24**: 263.
— Pensée Writers, — the Hares, Novalis, Joubert. (J. M. Ludlow) Macmil. **1**: 280.
Apotheosis of Dulness; a Poem. Dem. R. **32**: 115.
Appalachian Language, Specimen of. Hist. M. **4**: 40.
Appalachian Mountains. (A. H. Guyot) Am. J. Sci. **81**: 157.
— as Time-Boundaries in Geological History. (J. D. Dana) Am. J. Sci. **86**: 227.
— Geognosy of. (T. S. Hunt) Nature, **5**: 15, 32, 50, 451.
— Southern Silurian Age of. (F. H. Bradley) Am. J. Sci. **109**: 279, 370.
Apparatus for the One-Handed, with cuts. Pamph. **22**: 431.
Apparition, True Account of an. House. Words. **5**: 27.
— of Jo. Murch. (N. Brooks) Scrib. **17**: 76.
— of Monsieur Bodry. House. Words, **17**: 277.
Apparitions. (G. Bradford) Chr. Exam. **12**: 106. — Fraser, **34**: 231. — Anal. M. **2**: 388. — All the Year, **10**: 224.
— Alderson and Hibbert on. Mo. R. **106**: 360. — Mus. **7**: 157.
— and Hallucinations. (A. G. Knight) Month, **39**: 210.
— Ferriar's Theory of. Chr. Obs. **12**: 803.
— Philosophy of. Quar. **48**: 287. — Fraser, **2**: 33. — Westm. **1**: 471. — Quar. **9**: 304. — Mus. **4**: 458. **22**: 517. — Brit. Q. **12**: 382. — Irish Q. **9**: 337.
See Ghosts; Magic; Mesmerism; Spiritualism; Witchcraft.
Appeal in Criminal Cases. Dub. R. **45**: 188.
Appellant Courts of British Empire. Brit. & For. R. **12**: 287
Appenzell, Little Land of, Switzerland. (B. Taylor) Atlan. **20**: 213.
— Folk-Life in. (W. Wells) Scrib. **4**: 50.
— Linen and Cotton Manufactures of. Penny M. **11**: 6.
— My Days in. (G. C. Swayne) Once a Week, **16**: 488.
Apperley, Charles J., Life and Times of. Mus. **44**: 466.
Appetite. (A. H. Forrester) Bentley, **25**: 511.
— Good. (E. E. Hale) O. & N. **7**: 667.
Apple, as a Criterion of Taste. (W. M. Nevin) Mercersb. **1**: 68.
— Produce of. Penny M. **13**: 142.
Apple Frolics in America. (F. Morton) Once a Week, **1**: 377.
Apple Leaf-Folder. (W. Lebaron) Am. Natural. **5**: 209.
Apple Paring, The. Penny M. **6**: 426.
Apple Tree, Life of. (H. Coultas) Sharpe, **36**: 65.
Apple Tree Table, The. Putnam, **7**: 465.
Apple of the Dead Sea; a Story. Galaxy, **16**: 540.
Apple of Life; a Poem. (R. Lytton) Fortn. **2**: 184.
Apples, History and Dignity of. (E. Spencer) Hours at Home, **3**: 505.
— Wild. (H. D. Thoreau) Atlan. **10**: 513. — Sharpe, **38**: 294.
Apples; a Comedy. (J. Sturgis) Blackw. **124**: 23. Same art. Liv. Age, **138**: 502.
Appleton, C. E. Nature, **19**: 386.
Appleton, Jesse, Life and Writings of. (B. Tappan) Lit. & Theo. R. **4**: 351. — (T. T. Stone) Am. Bib. Repos. **6**: 19.
— Sermons of. Chr. Mo. Spec. **5**: 434.
Appleton, Nathan, with portrait. (J. H. Sheppard) N. E. Reg. **16**: 1.
Appleton, Nathaniel W. Am. Q. Reg. **13**: 76.
Appleton, Samuel, with portrait. (E. Peabody) N. E. Reg. **8**: 9. — (E. Peabody) Hunt, **30**: 291. — with portrait, Am. Q. Reg. **11**: 1. — Am. J. Educ. **12**: 403.
— Life of. West. J. **11**: 426.
Appleton, Thomas, Will of, 1504. N. E. Reg. **7**: 37.
Appleton, William, with portrait. (J. H. Sheppard) N. E. Reg. **17**: 293.
Appleton Family of Ipswich, Mass. N. E. Reg. **27**: 36.
Appleton, Wisconsin, Lawrence University. O. & N. **4**: 140.
Application to Study. Colburn, **6**: 533.
Applied Science; a Story. (C. Barnard) Galaxy, **23**: 79, 160.
Appointing Power. (G. F. Hoar) No. Am. **133**: 464.
Appomattox Court-House, Recollections of. (E. A. Pollard) O. & N. **4**: 166.
— Lee and Gordon at. So. Hist. Pap. **8**: 37.
— Surrender of Lee at. (E. P. Alexander) So. M. **12**: 747
— — True Story of. (J. W. Jones) Hist. M. **22**: 235.
Apportionment Bill, 1832. Ann. Reg. **7**: 94.
Apprentice Laws. Pamph. **3**: 217.
Apprentices. (G. Howell) Contemp. **30**: 833.
— London. Colburn, **5**: 172.

Apprenticeship. (J. S. Whitney) Penn Mo. **3**: 189.
— Indenture of, 1747. N. E. Reg. **34**: 311.
— in France. (J. G. Rosengarten) Nation, **27**: 180.
— of the Future. (S. P. Thompson) Contemp. **38**: 472. Same art. abridged, Pop. Sci. Mo. **18**: 26, 202.
Apprenticeship Schools in France. (B. Murphy) Cath. World, **30**: 400.
Apprenticeship System, Negro. Ed. R. **66**: 250.
Appropriation Act, 1835. Westm. **23**: 448.
April. (A. H. Baldwin) Fraser, **67**: 515.—(J. Burroughs) Scrib. **13**: 799, 803.—(W. Howitt) Howitt, **1**: 191.—Fraser, **49**: 522.
— a Poem. (W. G. Simms) So. Lit. Mess. **3**: 194.
April Days. (T. W. Higginson) Atlan. **7**: 385.—(H. D. Thoreau) Atlan. **41**: 445.
April Fancies. (D. F. M'Carthy) Dub. Univ. **41**: 395.
April 1 at Netherby Place. (E. F. Mosby) Potter Am. Mo. **16**: 350.
April Fool, An. Lond. Soc. **5**: 310.
April Fools. Belgra. **17**: 182.—Lond. M. **23**: 397.—St. James, **24**: 82.
— and other Fools. (H. St. John) Belgra. **29**: 207.
— May Day, and other Sentimentals. Fraser, **17**: 553.
— or, A hundred Matrimonial Letters. Fraser, **11**: 369.
April Reverie. (J. F. Waller) Dub. Univ. **39**: 403.
April Shadows; a Poem. Temp. Bar, **9**: 544.
Apsley House. Quar. **92**: 446. Same art. Ecl. M. **29**: 241.
— Story of. (N. S. Dodge) Overland, **6**: 255.
Apteryx of New Zealand, Bird or Reptile? (H. O. Forbes) Belgra. **36**: 317.
— at Dinner. (O. S. Round) Recr. Sci. **1**: 178.
Apuleius. (C. G. Prowett) Fraser, **88**: 464.
— and the 2d Century. Ecl. R. **94**: 67.
— Golden Ass; or, Metamorphoses. (W. H. Mallock) Fraser, **94**: 363.—Ed. R. **94**: 472. Same art. Ecl. M. **25**: 75.—Ecl. R. **112**: 269.—House. Words, **13**: 285.
Aquarium, The. (Mrs. I. James) No. Am. **87**: 143.—Chamb. J. **22**: 35. Same art. Liv. Age, **42**: 414.—Chamb. J. **53**: 357, 391.
— at Crystal Palace. (W. A. Lloyd) Nature, **4**: 469.
— Brighton. (W. S. Kent) Nature, **8**: 531.—Chamb. J. **50**: 529.
— Fresh-Water. (C. B. Brigham) Am. Natural. **3**: 131, 207, 373, 486. **4**: 23.
— Gosse's. Fraser, **50**: 190.—Colburn, **102**: 117.
— in Miniature. Recr. Sci. **2**: 345.
— Management of. (D. W. Cheever) Atlan. **8**: 322.
— Marine. (S. C. Hall) Art J. **8**: 145.—(C. Kingsley) Am. Natural. **2**: 262.
— — for Inland Students. Nature, **19**: 260.
— — Management of. (A. W. Wills) Nature, **13**: 189.
— — Sea Anemones in. Lond. Q. **8**: 76.
— Modern. (A. Wilson) Colburn, **160**: 295.
— New York. (W. S. Ward) Scrib. **13**: 577.
— Preparation of Artificial Sea-Water for. (G. Wilson) Ed. New Philos. J. **58**: 129.
— Royal, at Westminster. Pract. M. **6**: 65.
— Southport. (C. E. de Rance) Nature, **11**: 393.
— Uses of. (W. E. Simmons, jr.) Pop. Sci. Mo. **5**: 687.
— with Tidal Arrangements. Intel. Obs. **3**: 245.
Aquaria. (W. A. Lloyd) Am. Natural. **10**: 611.—Eng. Dom. M. **24**: 102, 213, 301.—Godey, **54**: 525. **55**: 45.—House. Words, **9**: 506.—No. Brit. **22**: 55.
— Great. (J. G. Bertram) St. James, **35**: 623.
— Management of. (S. Hibberd) Recr. Sci. **1**: 73.
— Marine. Dub. Univ. **48**: 353.—Recr. Sci. **2**: 58.
— — and Fresh-Water. Godey, **56**: 51.
— Present, Past, and Future of. (W. A. Lloyd) Pop. Sci. R. **15**: 253. Same art. Ecl. M. **87**: 592.
Aquarium Car, First California. (L. Stone) Overland, **13**: 228, 311.
Aquatic Architects. Recr. Sci. **1**: 106.
Aqueduct of Segovia. Am. Arch. **6**: 93.
— Wooden, across Alleghany River. (J. C. Trautwine) J. Frankl. Inst. **34**: 1.
Aqueducts. Pop. Sci. Mo. **11**: 26.
— and Canals. Quar. **73**: 281. Same art. Ecl. M. **2**: 190.
— of Ancient Rome. (G. P. Marsh) Nation, **32**. **147**.
— of the Ancients. Chamb. J. **1**: 34.
Aqueous Vapor, Influence of, on Meteorology. (W. H. S. Monck) Nature, **3**: 495.
Aquinas, Thomas. *See* Thomas Aquinas, St.
Arab, The; a Poem. So. Lit. J. **4**: 256.
Arab's Revenge; a Story. (E. H. Vizetelly) Belgra. **25**: 405.
Arab Chief; a Ballad. Fraser, **38**: 167.
Arab Seaport in War Time. All the Year, **28**: 487.
Arab Story-Teller, Tale of an. Fraser, **39**: 112.
Arab Village. Bentley, **51**: 292.
Arab Wife; a Tale. Chamb. J. **53**: 707-835.
Arabs, The. (B. J. Wallace) Am. Presb. R. **9**: 177.
— Among. All the Year, **5**: 516.
— and Persians. (T. P. Thompson) Westm. **5**: 202.
— — Trade of. Blackw. **4**: 135, 292, 460.
— at Amboise. Bentley, **31**: 258. Same art. Liv. Age, **33**: 177.
— at Hor . (A. Rhodes) Galaxy, **13**: 605.
— before Mahomet. Chr. Rem. **29**: 83.
— Civilization of, and what we owe it. Nat. Q. **13**: 258.
— De France's Captivity among. Mo. R. **151**: 524.
— Derby Day among. Fraser, **68**: 77.
— Geography of. For. Q. **27**: 265.
— Hospitality of. Belgra. **12**: 39.
— Humor of. Temp. Bar. **62**: 65, 194. **63**: 36. Same art. Appleton, **26**: 21, 144, 423.
— in Italy, Sicily, etc. For. Q. **22**: 374.
— in Palestine. (C. Clermont-Ganneau) Macmil. **32**: 361. Same art. Ecl. M. **85**: 538.
— Invasion of Spain by. For. Q. **1**: 19.
— in Spain. Dub. Univ. **37**: 771. **45**: 657. Same art. Ecl. M. **35**: 551. *See* Moors; Spain.
— Manners and Ceremonies of. Sharpe, **23**: 109.
— Metaphysical Schools among. Kitto, **34**: 354.
— of the Desert. (J. Hall) Princ. **3**: 215.
— Pagan and Moslem. (R. S. Poole) Fortn. **2**: 549.
— Politeness of. Nat. M. **9**: 58.—All the Year, **24**: 41.
— Pre-Islamic. (W. H. Thomson) New Eng. **21**: 385.
— Travels among. Westm. **4**: 495.
— Women of. So. R. n. s. **14**: 363.—(C. S. Robinson) Scrib. **7**: 559.
Arabella, Lady. So. Lit. Mess. **3**: 601.
Arabia. (J. Forsyth) Princ. **37**: 350.
— and Africa, Boteler's Voyage of Discovery to. Mo. R. **137**: 153.
— and Palestine, Early and Recent Travels in. No. Brit **27**: 513. Same art. Ecl. M. **43**: 145.
— and Persia, Trade with Russia. Blackw. **4**: 135, 292, 460.
— Biblical Geography of. Bib. R. **5**: 165.
— Burckhardt's Travels in. Colburn, **25**: 379.—Ed. R. **50**: 164.—Mo. R. **119**: 1.
— Burton's El-Medinah and Mecca. Bentley, **39**: 366.—Dub. R. **39**: 76. **41**: 27.—Fraser, **52**: 318. **53**: 320.—Liv. Age, **46**: 553.—New Q. **5**: 138.
— Central and Eastern, and the People. Chr. Rem. **50**: 357.
— Commerce and Products of. Hunt, **3**: 61.
— Forster on. Quar. **74**: 325.—Liv. Age, **3**: 113.
— Further Discoveries in. (L. P. Brockett) Hours at Home, **4**: 52.
— Heart of. (B. Taylor) Scrib. **3**: 545.—Broadw. **10**: 538.
— Historical Geography of, Forster on. Quar. **74**: 325.
— History of. For. Q. **20**: 137.—Mo. R. **132**: 362.
— — Crichton's. Am. Mo. M. **3**: 217.—Ecl. R. **50**: 484.
— — Price's. Ecl. R. **42**: 440.

Arabia, History of, Recent Page of. (W. S. Blunt) Fortn. **33**: 707. Same art. Liv. Age, **145**: 538.
— Palgrave's Travels in. (J. D. Baldwin) No. Am. **103**: 276. — (R. S. Poole) Fortn. **1**: 459. — (E. C. Towne) Chr. Exam. **79**: 327. — Blackw. **98**: 723. — Brit. Q. **42**: 297. — Ecl. R. **122**: 139. — Ed. R. **122**: 482. — Lond. Q. **25**: 136. Same art. Liv. Age, **87**: 529. — Macmil. **13**: 518. Same art. Ecl. M. **65**: 737. — No. Brit. **44**: 1. — Quar. **119**: 182. — Westm. **84**: 381.
— Pretended Patriarchal Inscriptions of. Dub. Univ. **24**: 724.
— Wellsted's Travels in. Quar. **61**: 301. — Mo. R. **145**: 255.
— Wilds of. Chamb. J. **42**: 563.
See Khartum.
Arabia Felix, Military Expedition into. Liv. Age, **34**: 375.
Arabia Petræa, Antiquities discovered in. Anal. M. **14**: 264.
— In a Caravan with Gérome the Painter. Lippinc. **13**: 532.
— Laborde's Journey through. (Sir J. Barrow) Quar. **59**: 87. — Mo. R. **140**: 338. — Dub. R. **1**: 174. — Mus. **31**: 267. — Am. Bib. Repos. **9**: 431. — (E. Robinson) No. Am. **44**: 382. — Chr. Obs. **36**: 688, 746.
— Lowth's Travels in. New Q. **5**: 230.
— Stephens's Travels in. (L. Cass) No. Am. **48**: 181. — (H. Ware, jr.) Chr. Exam. **24**: 31. — Princ. **10**: 55. — New York R. **1**: 351. — Am. Q. **21**: 439. — Hesp. **1**: 174.
Arabian Desert, The. (W. T. Savage) Cong. R. **8**: 274, 371, 555.
Arabian Design and Art. Ecl. Engin. **2**: 491.
Arabian Empire. Blackw. **43**: 661.
Arabian Nights. (G. W. Peck) Am. Whig R. **6**: 601. — For. Q. **24**: 139. — Cornh. **32**: 711. — Dub. R. **8**: 105.
— in London. St. James, **9**: 367.
— Lane's Translation of. Ecl. R. **72**: 641.
— New Series of. Colburn, **16**: 336.
— New Translations. Westm. **33**: 101. — Mo. R. **109**: 362.
— People of. Nat. R. **9**: 44. Same art. Liv. Age, **62**: 327.
Arabian Tales, New. For. Q. **14**: 350.
Arabic and Persian Lexicography. (J. A. Alexander) Princ. **4**: 190.
Arabic Fables. (J. Mew) Gent. M. n. s. **27**: 217.
Arabic Grammar, De Sacy's. (J. A. Alexander) Princ. **4**: 543.
Arabic Language and Lexicography, Gesenius on. Mo. R. **158**: 192.
— and Literature. (J. Packard) Am. Bib. Repos. **8**: 429. — (E. I. Sears) Nat. Q. **7**: 59.
— and the Turkish. (H. S. Osborn) Bib. Sac. **38**: 646.
— Lexicon, Freytag's. (H. P. Goodrich) No. Am. **48**: 461.
— — Wilkins's. Ecl. R. **4**: 581, 801.
— Something about Modern. Fraser, **64**: 504.
— Study of. Meth. M. **47**: 102.
Arabic Literature. So. Lit. Mess. **6**: 457, 563. **7**: 113. **8**: 47, 448. — Meth. Q. **2**: 540. — For. R. **3**: 377. — For. Q. **3**: 1. — Colburn, **4**: 262.
— and Love-Lore. (N. S. Dodge) Overland, **9**: 522.
Arabic MSS. in Spain. Westm. **21**: 378.
Arabic Masters, My. Chamb. J. **22**: 172.
Arabic Numerals, Early Use of. (S. Denne) Arch. **13**: 107, 141.
— Introduction into England. (G. North) Arch. **10**: 360.
Arabic, Persian, and Turkish Poetry. Dub. Univ. **15**: 377.
Arabic Philosophy. Ed. R. **85**: 340.
— History of. Ecl. M. **46**: 153.
— Influence of, in Mediæval Europe. (Earl Stanhope) Fraser, **75**: 114. Same art. Ecl. M. **68**: 369.
Arabic Poetry. Retros. **5**: 332.
— in Spain and Sicily. Ecl. M. **68**: 742.
Arabic Prize Poem, An Ancient. (E. H. Palmer) Internat. R. **2**: 651.
Arabic Proverbs. Lond. Soc. **9**: 325.
Arabic Stories and Traditions. (N. S. Dodge) Overland, **10**: 443.
Arabic Verses in 13th Century. Cornh. **26**: 213.
Aracan, North, Hill Tribes of. (R. F. St. A. St. John) Anthrop. J. **2**: 233.
Arachne in Sloane Street. Cornh. **29**: 571.
Arago, F. (D. Lardner) Am. Whig R. **4**: 162. — Ecl. M. **9**: 322. — Liv. Age, **11**: 140. — Dub. Univ. **28**: 253. — Fraser, **26**: 737. — (Dr. Janssen) Nature, **21**: 418.
— and Brougham on Black, Cavendish, Priestley, and Watt. Quar. **77**: 105.
— Incident in Life of. (H. Christmas) Internat. M. **4**: 41.
— Life and Discoveries of. (Sir D. Brewster) No. Brit. **20**: 459. Same art. Ecl. M. **32**: 145.
— Life and Labors of. Ecl. R. **102**: 743.
— Life and Works of. Ed. R. **104**: 301.
— Notes on the Life of. Ed. New Philos. J. **56**: 57.
— on Comets. (J. Farrar) No. Am. **42**: 196.
— on Lunar Influences. For. Q. **11**: 503.
— Sketch of. Hogg, **2**: 189.
— Voyage round the World. Lond. M. **7**: 310. — Quar. **28**: 332.
— Youth of. Chamb. J. **25**: 11. Same art. Liv. Age, **48**: 533. — So. Lit. Mess. **21**: 97, 162.
Aragon, Sketch from Portugal and. Fraser, **84**: 356.
Aral, Lake, Shores of. Wood's Nature, **14**: 66.
— and Caspian, Basins of. (H. H. Howorth) Geog. M. **3**: 106.
— — Separation of. (H. Wood) Nature, **12**: 313.
Arama, the Seeker of Oblivion. So. Lit. Mess. **5**: 734.
Arapahoes, Among the. (H. R. Lemly) Harper, **60**: 494.
Ararat. (A. Geikie) Nature, **17**: 205. — (B. B. Thatcher) Am. Bib. Repos. **7**: 390. — Nat. M. **1**: 26.
— and Armenian Highlands. Blackw. **65**: 577. — Westm. **51**: 199.
— and Eden. (F. Lenormant) Contemp. **40**: 453.
— and the Three Churches. So. Lit. Mess. **10**: 131.
— Ascent of. (B. Botcherby) Liv. Age, **94**: 282. — Chamb. J. **55**: 364.
— — Mr. Bryce's. Liv. Age, **135**: 443.
— Parrot's Journey to. Am. Meth. M. **18**: 201. — For. Q. **15**: 288. — Ecl. R. **82**: 710.
— Tale of. Blackw. **28**: 24.
— Visit to. Fraser, **60**: 111.
— Wagner's Journey to. Westm. **51**: 107. Same art. Liv. Age, **29**: 313.
Aratus. Phenomena and Diosemeia translated. Chr. Rem. **17**: 63.
Araucanians, The. Bost. Mo. **1**: 346.
Arbela, Battle of. (E. S. Creasy) Bentley, **24**: 390.
Arber's Reprints of old Writers. Dub. Univ. **75**: 43.
Arbitrary Governments, Present Policy and Future Fate of. Ed. R. **39**: 281. — Selec. Ed. R. **4**: 342. — Mus. **4**: 385.
Arbitration, Boards of Conciliation and. (Eckley B. Coxe) Penn Mo. **2**: 109.
— International. (C. C. Beaman, jr.) No. Am. **102**: 473. — (A. J. H. Crespi) Colburn, **156**: 144. — (T. D. Woolsey) Internat. R. **1**: 104. — Tait, n. s. **22**: 293.
— — Fate of. (E. L. Godkin) Nation, **18**: 390.
— — *versus* War. Ecl. R. **90**: 236.
Arblay, Frances Burney, Madame d'. Blackw. **51**: 784. — Quar. **11**: 123. — Ecl. M. **9**: 549. — Argosy, **19**: 441. — Eng. Dom. M. **25**: 154, 178. — House. Words, **5**: 392. Same art. Liv. Age, **34**: 412. — Liv. Age, **11**: 484. — Am. Whig R. **13**: 267, 305. — (Mrs. M. C. Nute) Lakeside, **2**: 85. — Mus. **45**: 565. — Victoria, **32**: 370.

Arblay, Frances Burney, Madame d', Diary and Letters. (T. B. Macaulay) Ed. R. **76**: 523. Same art. Ecl. Mus. **1**: 449. — (J. W. Croker) Quar. **70**: 243. — Ecl. R. **75**: 451. **76**: 319. **85**: 57. — Tait, n. s. **9**: 183, 246, 385. — Colburn, **64**: 271. **66**: 526.
— The Wanderer. (W. Hazlitt) Ed. R. **25**: 320. — Portfo.(Den.) **12**: 457.
Arbouville, Madame d', Poems and Novels of. Dub. R. **41**: 411.
Arbues, Peter, and the Spanish Inquisition. Dub. Univ. **84**: 335.
Arbuthnot, George, Life and Writings of. Retros. **8**: 285. — Mus. **4**: 44.
Arbuthnot, Dr. John. Cornh. **39**: 91.
Arbuthnot, Sir William. Blackw. **26**: 844.
Arbuthnot and Ambrister, Trial of. Niles's Reg. **15**: 270, 394.
Arbutin, Constitution of. Nature, **3**: 137.
Arc of the Meridian, measured in India. Ed. R. **21**: 300.
Arcachon, France. Colburn, **7**: 66.
— as a Health Resort. Chamb. J. **57**: 139.
— Bay of. Chamb. J. **47**: 529.
Arcadi, Academy of the. (V. Lee) Fraser, **97**: 779. **98**: 33.
Arcadia. Cornh. **20**: 588. *See* Sanazzaro, J.; Sidney, P.
Arcadian Revenge; a Story. (J. Payn) Cornh. **41**: 164. Same art. Ecl. M. **94**: 437.
Arcadian Scene. Dub. Univ. **64**: 699.
Arch, Joseph, and the new Emancipation. (J. McCarthy) Galaxy, **15**: 452.
Arch, Graphic Method applied to. (A. J. Du Bois) Ecl. Engin. **13**: 341.
— known by the Ancients. Ed. R. **7**: 441.
— New Constructions in Graphical Statics. (H. T. Eddy) Ecl. Engin. **16**: 1-481. **17**: 1, 97.
— of Ctesiphon. Colburn, **165**: 1074.
— Skew. (E. W. Hyde) Ecl. Engin. **12**: 97, 193, 289.
— — at Harrisburg. (T. M. Cleemann) Ecl. Engin. **14**: 361.
— — Bonding in. Ecl. Engin. **8**: 23.
— St. Louis. (H. T. Eddy) Ecl. Engin. **17**: 204. — (C. S. Smith) Ecl. Engin. **17**: 105.
— Trussed. (D. Wood) J. Frankl. Inst. **77**: 223.
Arches and Suspension Chains, Strain on. J. Frankl. Inst. **74**: 240, 300.
— Conical, at South St. Bridge, Philadelphia. (D. McN. Stauffer) J. Frankl. Inst. **107**: 191.
— Equilibration of. Am. Arch. **10**: 8.
— for Bridges, Formula for proportioning. (J. C. Trautwine) J. Frankl. Inst. **68**: 301.
— Iron. (W. Airy) Ecl. Engin. **3**: 449, 641.
— Metal and Timber. (J. Gaudard) Ecl. Engin. **4**: 359.
— Ovals and Three-Centre. (J. B. Henck) Math. Mo. **1**: 25, 41.
— Pointed, Origin of. (S. Smirke) Arch. **21**: 521.
— Stability of. Ecl. Engin. **2**: 636. **6**: 565. — (E. S. Gould) Ecl. Engin. **13**: 226. — (L. S. Ware) Ecl. Engin. **15**: 33. — (G. F. Swain) Ecl. Engin. **23**: 265.
— Stresses of Rigid. (W. Bell) Ecl. Engin. **6**: 307.
— Theory of. (W. Allan) Ecl. Engin. **10**: 97-385. — (G. Rennie) J. Frankl. Inst. **38**: 226.
— — of Solid and Braced Elastic. (W. Cain) Ecl. Engin. **21**: 265, 353, 443.
— Voussoir, Practical Theory of. (W. Cain) Ecl. Engin. **11**: 289, 385. **13**: 514. **20**: 52, 97, 201.
— Ware's Treatise on, 1809. Ecl. R. **10**: 593.
Archæan Rocks of Wahsatch Mountains. (A. Geikie) Am. J. Sci. **119**: 363.
Archæologia. Retros. **16**: 217. — Westm. **7**: 375. **11**: 401. **20**: 47.
Archæological Collection at Yale College. (D. C. Gilman) University Q. **4**: 277.
Archæological Collections in North America. (F. W. Putnam) Am. Natural. **7**: 29.
Archæological Discovery near Saratoga. (W. L. Stone) M. Am. Hist. **5**: 34.
Archæological Discoveries. Am. Ecl. **3**: 393.
Archæological Institute of Boston. Am. Arch. **5**: 137, 153, 162.
Archæological Maps, Symbols on. (J. Evans) Anthrop. J. **5**: 427.
Archæological Science in America. So. Lit. Mess. **11**: 420.
Archæology. (L. C. Boistiniere) U. S. Cath. M. **4**: 44, 172.
— Age of Bronze. Ed. R. **147**: 437.
— American Institute of, Proposed. (T. Davidson) Nation, **32**: 403.
— and Anthropology, Brussels Congress of, 1872. (M. J. Lalor) Cath. World, **16**: 639, 829.
— Classical, Relation of, to Literature and History. (P. Gardner) Macmil. **43**: 465.
— English School of, at Athens and Rome. (R. C. Jebb) Contemp. **33**: 776.
— General Views on. (A. Morlot) Am. J. Sci. **79**: 25.
— Lubbock on. Kitto, **38**: 217.
— Modern Excavations. (J. P. Mahaffy) Contemp. **29**: 888.
— Newton's Essays on. (C. E. Norton) Nation, **31**: 449.
— of the Earth and its Inhabitants. (M. Sanford) Univ. Q. **4**: 289.
— Rossi, John Baptist de, Works of. Cath. World, **17**: 272.
— A Scottish Crannog. (R. Munro) Nature, **22**: 13, 34.
— Stone Annals of the Past. (C. Morris) Lippinc. **6**: 506.
— Teaching, in Schools. (O. Browning) Fortn. **22**: 495.
See Antiquities; Prehistoric; *also names of various countries.*
Archaic Ages; a Geological Sketch. (W. Downes) Ecl. M. **95**: 722.
Archangel. Penny M. **8**: 393.
— Recollections of. Bentley, **29**: 203.
Archbishop, The, and Gil Blas. (O. W. Holmes) Atlan. **46**: 205.
Archbishops of Canterbury, Hook's Lives of. Chr. Obs. **61**: 100. — Dub. R. **53**: 275. — Bentley, **49**: 205. — Ecl. R. **125**: 391.
Archduke Charles, Wreck of the. Bentley, **23**: 392.
Archer, James. Art J. **23**: 97.
Archer and Prince. (F. Whittaker) Galaxy, **22**: 117.
Archer-Fishes. (E. Sauvage) Pop. Sci. Mo. **12**: 302.
Archery. (M. Thompson) Appleton, **9**: 525. — (M. Thompson) Scrib. **14**: 273. — All the Year, **39**: 185. — Chamb. J. **33**: 169. — Godey, **45**: 253. — Lond. Soc. **6**: 208.
— Anecdotes of. (J. M. Gutch) Reliquary, **19**: 157.
— Ascham's Toxophilus. Am. J. Educ. **3**: 41. — Retros. **4**: 76.
— in England. Once a Week, **11**: 64.
— in Scotland. (R. Macgregor) Belgra. **43**: 338.
— Merry Days with Bow and Quiver. (M. Thompson) Scrib. **16**: 1.
— Our modern Archers. Gent. M. n. s. **13**: 160, 348.
— Practice of. (D. Barrington) Arch. **7**: 46.
— Silver Arrow. Once a Week, **11**: 107.
— *versus* Love. Lond. Soc. **10**: 354.
Archetypes. Chr. R. **26**: 177.
Archie Lovell; a Novel. (A. Edwards) Temp. Bar, **16**: 155-455. **17**: 65-498. **18**: 77-491. Same art. Galaxy, **1**: 36-661. **2**: 60-677.
Archimedes, Burning-Specula of. Chamb. J. **25**: 220.
— Works of. Quar. **3**: 89.
Archipelago, Turkish Rule in, with Map. Geog. M. **5**: 165, 198.
See Indian Archipelago.

Architect an Artist, The. (W. H. Furness) Penn Mo. **2**: 295.
— Practice of. (T. R. Smith) Brit. Q. **72**: 420. Same art. Am. Arch. **8**: 258.
— Profession of. Brit. Q. **71**: 335.
Architect's Wife ; a Story. Argosy, **29**: 393.
Architects, American Institute of. Penn Mo. **4**: 499.
— — Tenth Annual Convention. Am. Arch. **2**: supp. 1.
— — Eleventh Annual Convention. Am. Arch. **3**: 50, 66.
— — Annual Convention, 1879. Am. Arch. **5**: 91, 106, 122. **6**: 171.
— and Architecture. (T. C. Clarke) Chr. Exam. **49**: 278.
— and Clients. Am. Arch. **2**: 222, 350–366.
— — Duties of. Am. Arch. **5**: 141, 146, 162.
— and Engineers. Am. Arch. **4**: 54, 62, 89. — Ecl. Engin. **2**: 1.
— — Studies of. Ecl. Engin. **19**: 419.
— and Organization. Am. Arch. **4**: 154.
— A Batch of. Fraser, **15**: 324.
— Becket on the Frailties of. Am. Arch. **3**: 107.
— Compensation of. Am. Arch. **2**: 230, 239.
— Competitions of. Am. Arch. **4**: 202. **5**: 2, 18. — Westm. **35**: 52.
— English Government. Am. Arch. **10**: 257.
— Gothic and Renaissance. (B. Champneys) Portfo. **4**: 8.
— Legal Responsibilities of. Am. Arch. **4**: 190, 194.
— Lives of Celebrated. Mus. **10**: 181. — Mo. R. **111**: 125.
— on Probation. Am. Arch. **2**: 174.
— Professional Trials of. Am. Arch. **5**: 101.
— Qualifying of. Am. Arch. **3**: 134, 142.
— Responsibility of. Am. Arch. **3**: 26.
— Royal Institute of British. (H. Carr) Ecl. Engin. **6**: 249.
— Transactions of. (R. Ford) Quar. **58**: 524.
— True School for. Fraser, **86**: 743.
— Young, Professional Study for. Am. Arch. **5**: 58.
Architects' Contracts. Am. Arch. **6**: 12, 18.
— Drawings, Custody of. Am. Arch. **3**: 206.
— — Ownership of. Am. Arch. **6**: 7, 17.
Architectural Designs, American, Causes of Failure in. (W. A. Potter) Am. Arch. **7**: 27, 35.
Architectural Education in England and Germany. Am. Arch. **7**: 180.
Architectural Fashions. (H. A. Sims) Penn Mo. **7**: 700.
Architectural Holdings Act. (Duke of Argyll) Contemp. **27**: 497.
Architectural Madness. Fraser, **4**: 727.
Architectural Metal-Work. (T. W. Tonks) Ecl. Engin. **22**: 392.
Architectural Revivalism and Puginism. Fraser, **28**: 593.
Architectural Sketches, Freeman's. (J. T. Clarke) Nation, **26**: 137.
Architectural Talkers and Doers. All the Year, **24**: 180.
Architectural Tours, Knight's. Ed. R. **69**: 74.
Architecture. Ox. Prize Ess. **1**: 35. — New Eng. **8**: 418. — (D. Wadsworth) Am. J. Sci. **24**: 257. — (W. N. Lockington) Overland, **15**: 281. — (R. C. Long) U. S. Cath. M. **2**: 297. — Blackw. **108**: 531. — Tinsley, **14**: 145.
— Acoustics in. (A. F. Oakey) Am. Arch. **1**: 139.
— Adornment of St. Paul's. Brit. Q. **61**: 69.
— Æsthetic Principles of. (C. A. Evans) Ecl. Engin. **11**: 443.
— Ancient. (C. Follen) No. Am. **88**: 341.
— — Rawlinson on. (J. Fergusson) Fortn. **9**: 31.
— and Archæology of Middle Ages, Britton on. Mo. R. **138**: 444.
— and Underwriting. Am. Arch. **5**: 170, 179, 189.
— and Modern Life. Fraser, **88**: 762.
— and Music. (J. M. Capes) Fortn. **8**: 703. Same art. N. Ecl. **1**: 129.
Architecture and Utility. (E. M. Barry) Am. Arch. **7**: 92.
— Antiquities of. Quar. **4**: 474. — Mo. R. **111**: 375.
— Art in. (J. Fergusson) Am. J. Educ. **22**: 85. — Art J. **7**: 272.
— Art of spoiling Public Buildings. Ecl. Engin. **6**: 66.
— as a Decorative Art. (J. B. Atkinson) F. Arts Q. **1**: 349.
— at the French Exposition. Am. Arch. **5**: 10, 21, 27.
— at the Royal Academy. Am. Arch. **5**: 174, 197.
— Audsley's Dictionary of. Am. Arch. **10**: 110.
— Basilica Style of. Westm. **41**: 109.
— Bill for Bureau of. Am. Arch. **1**: 65–142.
— Byzantine. Art J. **17**: 55. — Ed. R. **121**: 456.
— Cathedral Restorations. Brit. Q. **69**: 135.
— Character in. No. Brit. **15**: 461.
— Christian. (W. A. Dod) Mercersb. **9**: 358, 561. — (T. E. Giraud) U. S. Cath. A. **4**: 627.
— — and Pagan. Brit. & For. R. **7**: 1.
— — of Europe. No. Brit. **34**: 513.
— Chromatics as pertaining to. (T. U. Walter) J. Frankl. Inst. **32**: 32.
— Church. (N. G. Batt) Dub. Univ. **83**: 48. — Quar. **6**: 62. **75**: 179. — **99**: 371. — (J. Fergusson) Am. Church R. **18**: 375. (E. F. Brown) Am. Church R. **31**: 265. — (G. F. Magoun) Cong. Q. **1**: 375. — (W. A. Dod) Princ. **27**: 625. — (R. M. Hunt) Am. Arch. **2**: 374, 384. — (Franz Kugler) Art J. **9**: 323. — (E. T. Littell) Am. Arch. **3**: 10. — (T. Worthington) Theo. R. **9**: 105. — Brit. Q. **23**: 325. — Dub. Univ. **21**: 614. — Chr. Exam. **44**: 316. — (W. E. Coale) Am. Church R. **3**: 372. — Chr. Rem. **3**: 353. — Dub. R. **74**: 210.
— — and the Masses. (G. F. Magoun) Cong. Q. **4**: 25.
— — and the Plastic Arts. (B. Murphy) Cath. World, **30**: 368.
— — and Preaching. (J. Q. Bittenger) Cong. R. **11**: 136.
— — and Ritual, "Oratorianism." Chr. Rem. **20**: 141.
— — and Worship. (R. G. Greene) Cong. Q. **11**: 502. — (J. Edwards) Cong. Q. **11**: 511.
— — Catholic, and the Church of England. Chr. Rem. **2**: 105.
— — Examples of. Chr. Rem. **1**: 113.
— — Grecian. (W. A. Dod) Am. Church R. **16**: 57.
— — in England. Sharpe, **1**: 186, 276, 308.
— — — Early. (W. Blackwood) Potter Am. Mo. **9**: 16.
— — in the Middle Ages. (J. T. Clarke) Nation, **31**: 345.
— — in New York. Dem. R. **20**: 139. — (N. S. Richardson) Am. Church R. **18**: 501. — (C. Cook) Putnam, **2**: 233.
— — in Russia. For. Q. **26**: 37.
— — Jesuit Style of. (H. W. Brewer) Month, **35**: 322.
— — Knight and Bunson on. Quar. **75**: 334.
— — Modern and Ancient. Dub. R. **3**: 360.
— — Modern English Cathedral. Chr. Rem. **42**: 466.
— — Norman. (W. Blackwood) Potter Am. Mo. **8**: 416.
— — of England and France. (T. Rickman) Arch. **25**: 159. **26**: 27.
— — of Ireland. Quar. **76**: 193.
— — Petit on. Mo. R. **157**: 289.
— — Present State of, in England. Dub. R. **10**: 301. **12**: 80.
— — Romanesque, Advantages of. Chr. Rem. **3**: 576.
— — Relation to the Plastic Arts. (B. Murphy) Cath. World, **30**: 368.
— — Sharpe on. Am. Arch. **2**: 255.
— — Styles of. Chr. Rem. **4**: 257. **5**: 81.
See also Churches; Cathedrals.
— College of. (D. B. Reid) Am. J. Educ. **2**: 629.
— Common-Sense in. (C. A. Adams) Ecl. Engin. **22**: 95.
— Cottage, Garden and Villa. Art. J. **20**: 50–192.
— Cyclopean, in the Ionian Islands. (D. T. Ansted) Art J. **16**: 33.

Architecture, Dallaway on. Ecl. R. **4**: 508.
— Decorative, Origin of. (S. Ware) Arch. **18**: 336.
— Design in. (F. T. Palgrave) F. Arts Q. **1**: 114.
— — and Decoration in. Fraser, **1**: 63.
— Domestic. (J. E. Cabot) Atlan. **1**: 257. — New Eng. M. **2**: 30. — New Eng. **9**: 57. — Bent. Q. **2**: 474. — Penny M. **2**: 339. **8**: 356.
— — and Decoration in England. (C. C. Townshend) Portfo. **8**: 169.
— — and Secular. Art J. **10**: 17.
— — House-Building. (J. E. Cabot) Atlan. **10**: 423.
— — in England. Dub. R. **36**: 20.
— — Modern. Dub. Univ. **94**: 736.
— — — Examples of. (H. C. Boyes) Portfo. **10**: 51.
— — of the 14th Century. Art J. **6**: 229.
— — Old English. Quar. **45**: 471.
— Effect of Altitude on Vertical Dimensions. Am. Arch. **5**: 135, 167.
— Egyptian. Am. Q. **5**: 1.
— Etruscan, in Rome. (D. T. Ansted) Art J. **18**: 201.
— Expression in. (H. Davids) Lippinc. **3**: 617. — Ecl. Engin. **14**: 162.
— — Sources of. Ed. R. **94**: 365.
— Fergusson's Handbook of. Ed. R. **105**: 112. — Ecl. R. **103**: 402. — Quar. **106**: 285.
— Fire-Proof. (P. B. Wight) Am. Arch. **1**: 195, 203, 211. **3**: 75. — (R. G. Hatfield) Am. Arch. **2**: 399.
— — Slow-Burning Construction. Am. Arch. **5**: 182, 199. **6**: 14–127.
— Flemish, Specimens of. Ev. Sat. **11**: 508, 511.
— Future of. Ecl. Engin. **13**: 134.
— Gothic. (Renel Gabriel) Western, **4**: 733. — (R. S. Peabody) No. Am. **118**: 204. — (G. W. Samson) So. R. n. s. **3**: 378. — (J. J. Stevenson) Good Words, **17**: 64. — Harper, **52**: 234. — (T. E. Van Bibber) Putnam, **2**: 191. — No. Brit. **28**: 346. — Quar. **2**: 118. **69**: 57. — Ed. R. **49**: 420. — Retros. **10**: 1. — (T. Kenrick) Arch. **16**: 292.
— — Æsthetics of. Brit. Q. **10**: 46.
— — and Saxon. Dub. Univ. **78**: 428.
— — Eastlake's Revival of, in England. (B. Murphy) Cath. World, **15**: 443.
— — English. New Q. **10**: 48. — Mo. R. **153**: 223.
— — — Bane of. Brit. Q. **73**: 382.
— — — Old English Houses and Households. Brit. Q. **14**: 369.
— — English Origin of. (J. H. Parker) Arch. **43**: 73.
— — Grecian, and Egyptian. Westm. **8**: 31.
— — in Italy and Sicily. Arch. **15**: 363.
— — in Spain. Ed. R. **122**: 143. — F. Arts Q. **5**: 251.
— — Literature of. Ecl. R. **89**: 33.
— — Mediæval. (F. P. Johnson) Ecl. Engin. **8**: 250.
— — Millner and Whittington on. (J. Foster) Ecl. R. **16**: 1166.
— — Modern, Shortcomings of. (H. Bedford) Month, **21**: 1.
— — Origin of. (T. Pownall) Arch. **9**: 110. — (G. Saunders) Arch. **17**: 1.
— — Plea for. Ecl. Engin. **7**: 129.
— — Pugin on. Mo. R. **155**: 552.
— — Principles of. (W. Sewell) Quar. **69**: 111.
— — Religious Aspect of. (A. P. Stanley) Good Words, **19**: 394.
— — Spirit of. (D. H. Caverno) University Q. **2**: 273.
— Hamilton and others on. Quar. **58**: 61.
— History and Styles of. Chr. Rem. **18**: 182.
— — Early Christian and Roman. (W. Blackwood) Potter Am. Mo. **8**: 336.
— — Early Christian and Byzantine. Prosp. R. **3**: 157.
— — Fergusson's. Anthrop. R. **1**: 216. — New Q. **5**: 273. — Quar. **120**: 425.
— — Hope's. Quar. **53**: 338.
Architecture, History of, of Anglo-Saxons and Normans. (W. Wilkins) Arch. **12**: 132.
— — of the 11th Century. (A. H. Parker) Ecl. Engin. **10**: 338.
— — of Middle Ages. Quar. **25**: 112. — (E. B. Lamb) J. Frankl. Inst. **22**: 135, 208.
— — — Ramée's. Prosp. R. **5**: 184.
— How to build a House and live in it. Blackw. **59**: 758. **60**: 349. **61**: 727.
— Illustrated Handbook of. Art J. **8**: 86.
— in Africa. Art J. **19**: 126.
— in America. (Austin Bierbower) Penn Mo. **8**: 936. — (H. R. Cleveland) No. Am. **43**: 356. — (W. Minot, jr.) No. Am. **52**: 317. — (A. D. Gilman) No. Am. **58**: 436. — (H. Greenough) Dem. R. **13**: 206. — Am. J. Sci. **17**: 249. **18**: 11, 212. — (H. Greenough) So. Lit. Mess. **19**: 513. — Am. Arch. **4**: 138.
— — Colonial. Am. Arch. **10**: 71–102.
— — Development of. (A. W. Colgate) Contin. Mo. **5**: 466.
— in Ancient Assyria and Persia. Theo. & Lit. J. **4**: 313.
— in Athens. Ed. R. **95**: 395.
— in Boston, Recent, 1877. Art J. **29**: 299.
— in Canada. (R. C. Windeyer) Canad. Mo. **16**: 482.
— in China. Ecl. Engin. **10**: 135.
— in the Eastern States, Condition of. (P. B. Wight) Am. Arch. **7**: 107, 118.
— in England. (M. D. Conway) Harper, **49**: 617, 777. **50**: 35. — St. Paul's, **2**: 678.
— — British School of. Blackw. **40**: 227. — Westm. **41**: 113.
— — Domestic. (W. E. Timmins) Belgra. **22**: 429.
— — — Turner's History of. Chr. Obs. **52**: 185.
— — English Country-Houses. Chamb. J. **13**: 1–154.
— — English Timber-Houses. Penny M. **13**: 89.
— — Foreign and Domestic. For. Q. **24**: 288.
— — Hope of. Quar. **137**: 354. Same art. Liv. Age, **123**: 771.
— — in the Hanoverian Age, Picturesque Aspects of. (G. A. Simcox) Portfo. **3**: 55.
— — in the 17th Century. Brit. Q. **55**: 56.
— — Modern. (H. H. Statham) Fortn. **26**: 479.
— — National. Lond. M. **22**: 94–198.
— — Progress of. Blackw. **6**: 660.
— — — in 1838. J. Frankl. Inst. **28**: 57.
— — Promotion of, with illustrations. Westm. **41**: 219.
— — Reaction of Taste in. (J. J. Stevenson) Ecl. Engin. **11**: 231.
— — State of, 1872. Quar. **132**: 295.
— — Tudor, Hunt on. Ecl. R. **51**: 58.
— in France, Châteaux of the Renaissance. (E. F. S. Pattison) Contemp. **30**: 579. Same art. Liv. Age, **135**: 111.
— — in the West. (J. H. Parker) Arch. **34**: 273. **35**: 34, 359.
— — Mediæval, Viollet le Duc's. (R. Sturgis) Nation, **9**: 134, 173.
— — — in Aquitaine. (J. H. Parker) Arch. **36**: 1, 311.
— — Taste in. (F. T. Palgrave) Fraser, **55**: 583.
— in Germany, Present School of. For. Q. **14**: 92.
— — Brick, of North of Germany. (A. Nesbet) Arch. **39**: 93.
— in Greece (W. Blackwood) Potter Am. Mo. **8**: 176. — Blackw. **11**: 705. — For. Q. **15**: 145. **19**: 201. — Westm. **8**: 31. — Canad. Mo. **8**: 433.
— — and Italy, contrasted. For. Q. **19**: 377.
— in India. Art J. **23**: 65.
— in Ireland. Dub. Univ. **29**: 693.
— — Ancient Domestic. (J. H. Parker) Arch. **38**: 149.
— in Italy, Church Dub. R. **72**: 105.
— — Bacini, in Italian Church Architecture. (C. D. E. Fortnum) Arch. **42**: 379.

Architecture in Italy, Ecclesiastical, Knight on. Mo. R. **165**: 585.
— — — to 15th Century. Mo. R. **162**: 399.
— — Palladian. Quar. **32**: 42.
— — Pictures of. Art J. **25**: 49. **26**: 81–250. **27**: 361. **28**: 169.
— in London. Chamb. J. **38**: 186.
— — Foreign Office, Classic or Gothic? (E. A. Freeman) Nat. R. **10**: 24.
— — Future of. (H. Conybeare) Fortn. **8**: 501.
— — Improvements of. Blackw. **27**: 17. — Quar. **34**: 180. — Westm. **21**: 195. **36**: 191.
— — in relation to Climate. (H. Merivale) Fortn. **4**: 407.
— — New Courts-of-Justice Designs. Belgra. **2**: 35.
— — of New House of Commons. Westm. **22**: 163.
— — Strictures on new Houses of Parliament and British Museum. Fraser, **42**: 165.
— — of Shop Fronts. Westm. **36**: 436.
— — of Thames Tunnel. Westm. **19**: 10.
— — Street. Intel. Obs. **10**: 174. — Nat. R. **5**: 42.
— in Palermo. Am. Arch. **4**: 2.
— in Rome. (W. Blackwood) Potter Am. Mo. **8**: 256.
— — Building Materials used in. (C. T. Ramage) Ed. New Philos. J. **3**: 246.
— in Spain. (R. Ford) Quar. **77**: 496.
— in the United States. (W. Fogerty) Pract. M. **6**: 77. — Ecl. Engin. **14**: 61.
— — at the National Capitol, History of. (J. A. Howard) Internat. R. **1**: 736.
— — Development of. (A. W. Colgate) Contin. Mo. **5**: 466.
— — Domestic. (A. J. Bloor) Art J. **31**: 57, 169.
— — Future of. (E. C. Bruce) Lippinc. **16**: 305.
— — Government. (P. B. Wight) Am. Arch. **1**: 75, 83, 91.
— — Hints from American Practice. (W. Fogerty) Ecl. Engin. **15**: 246.
— — Popular. (R. Sturgis, jr.) No. Am. **112**: 160.
— — Taste in. (W. Blackwood) Potter Am. Mo. **4**: 192.
— in Venice. Art J. **3**: 108.
— Influence of Construction on Style. For. Q. **19**: 62.
— Iron Construction. Ecl. Engin. **4**: 279.—Westm. **51**: 104.
— Modern. Art J. **15**: 26. — Ed. R. **141**: 386.
— — Alleged Degeneracy of. (R. C. Long) J. Frankl. Inst. **32**: 246.
— — Half-and-half Style in. Ecl. Engin. **5**: 370.
— — Styles in. Ed. R. **118**: 71.
— — Styles and Examples of. Chr. Rem. **46**: 84.
— Natural History of. Lond. Q. **13**: 31.
— New Style of. Art J. **7**: 145.
— Notes on, Narjoux's. (J. T. Clarke) Nation, **26**: 359.
— of Banks. Bank. M. (N. Y.) **21**: 645, 739, 805.
— — in the Country. Bank. M. (N. Y.) **10**: 761, 917.
— — in New York. Bank. M. (N. Y.) **9**: 582. **10**: 598.
— — Plans by Davis. Bank. M. (N. Y.) **21**: 739, 805.
— of Birds. Mus. **19**: 482.
— of Bridges. Gen. Repos. **2**: 141.
— of Engineering Works. (A. P. Boller) J. Frankl. Inst. **87**: 319. — (J. K. Fisher) West. J. **10**: 106. — (W. C. Kerr) Ecl. Engin. **8**: 513. — (C. H. Rew) Ecl. Engin. **6**: 241.
— of great Cities. (J. Pyne) Nat. Q. **30**: 1.
— of Manufactories. Lond. M. **13**: 471.
— of Music Halls. (H. H. Statham) Ecl. Engin. **8**: 345.
— of Schools. Dem. R. **23**: 391.
— on Technical Principles. Ecl. Engin. **25**: 221.
— Optical Effects in. (W. H. Goodyear) Scrib. **8**: 432.
— Orders of. J. Frankl. Inst. **31**: 194.
— Philosophy of. Chamb. J. **23**: 344.
— Pointed, Symbolism of. Ecl. R. **78**: 1.
— Popular. Chamb. J. **9**: 232.
— Position of. (J. A. Picton) Ecl. Engin. **16**: 424.
— Practice of, British and American. (W. Fogerty) Ecl. Engin. **12**: 132.
Architecture, Practice of, Scope of. Ecl. Engin. **8**: 110.
— Present State of, 1854. Quar. **95**: 338.
— Principles of the Art of. (G. E. Street) Am. Arch. **9**: 185.
— Problems of the Day in. Ecl. Engin. **4**: 507.
— Proportion and Ornamentation in. (E. M. Barry) Am. Arch. **7**: 128.
— Reform in. (H. Van Brunt) Nation, **2**: 438, 469.
— Renaissance in. (T. M. Coan) Galaxy, **8**: 512.
— Requirements of. (R. Sturgis, jr.) No. Am. **112**: 370.
— Restoration. Am. Arch. **3**: 98.
— — and Ante-Restoration. (S. Colvin) 19th Cent. **2**: 446.
— — of the Parthenon. Ed. R. **38**: 126.
— Restorations of Mediæval. Brit. Q. **69**: 135.
— Romanesque, Origin and Growth of. (E. A. Freeman) Fortn. **18**: 373. Same art. Liv. Age, **115**: 451. — (E. A. Freeman) Ecl. Engin. **7**: 599. — (E. A. Freeman) Am. Arch. **7**: 28–66.
— Rural. (W. Flagg) Atlan. **37**: 428. — West. J. **10**: 329.
— — and Church, Popular Taste in. (F. D. Huntington) Chr. Exam. **31**: 60.
See Landscape Gardening.
— Ruskin on. Blackw. **95**: 740. — No. Brit. **21**: 172. — New Q. **3**: 375. (W. A. Dod) Princ. **28**: 461.
— — Seven Lamps of. (Dr. John Brown) No. Brit. **12**: 309.
— — Stones of Venice. No. Brit. **15**: 461. — Westm. **60**: 589. **61**: 315.
— — Works on. So. Q. **27**: 372.
— Russian Church. Quar. **26**: 37.
— Scientific and Æsthetic Aspects of. (E. M. Barry) Ecl. Engin. **11**: 462.
— Sculpture, and Painting. Mo. R. **114**: 472.
— Sheet-Metal in. Am. Arch. **1**: 234, 239, 365.
— Street. (J. H. Pollen) Month, **3**: 521.
— Students of. Am. Arch. **1**: 307–378. **2**: 10–90.
— Study and Practice of. (G. E. Street) Am. Arch. **9**: 137.
— — and Records of. Westm. **46**: 60.
— — Methods of. Am. Arch. **5**: 74.
— — Modern. For. Q. **7**: 432.
— Style in. Ecl. Engin. **5**: 428.
— — Periods of Transition in. (A. Payne) Ecl. Engin. **14**: 412.
— — Possibility of a new. (A. F. Oakey) Am. Arch. **3**: 22.
— Styles of, in various Countries. Chr. Rem. **34**: 43.
— — Appreciation of the various. Quar. **27**: 308.
— Theory and Practice in. (J. C. Bayles) Internat. R. **4**: 172.
— Vitality in. Ecl. Engin. **17**: 201.
— Vitruvius on. Quar. **21**: 25.
— Wightwick's Palace of. Fraser, **22**: 359, 751.
— Work of English Masons. Chamb. J. **49**: 33.
Archives, Public Management of. Brit. & For. R. **4**: 120.
Archon of Demosthenes. (E. Hincks) Kitto, **33**: 409. — (T. Parker) Kitto, **33**: 158. **34**: 171.
Arctic, Steamship, Loss of; a Poem. (C. G. Rosenburg) Dem. R. **34**: 397.
Arctic and Antarctic. All the Year, **5**: 54.
Arctic Archipelago, Fragments of Firwood in. (Sir R. I. Murchison) Am. J. Sci. **71**: 377.
Arctic Continent and Ocean. (J. Chavanne) Geog. M. **1**: 208.
Arctic Contributions to Science, 1852. Chamb. J. **18**: 373. Same art. Liv. Age, **36**: 231.
Arctic Discoveries, with map. Westm. **29**: 373. — Dub. R. **37**: 37.
— Dease and Simpson's Narrative, with map. Westm. **29**: 273.
— Latest, 1867. Month, **7**: 214.
Arctic Expedition, Austrian, 1872–74. (A. H. Guernsey) Appleton, **2**: 289, 385. — Chamb. J. **54**: 55. — Geog. M. **1**: 354, 358. — Nature, **10**: 439, 523. **11**: 366, 396, 415.

Arctic Expedition, Back's. (Sir J. Barrow) Quar. 56: 278. — Ed. R. 63: 287. — Mo. R. 140: 176. 146: 592. — Penny M. 1: 386. 7: 310, 318. — West. M. 5: 494.
— Bennett's. Chamb. J. 55: 396.
— Dutch, 1877. Geog. M. 5: 156, 308.
— English, 1874–76. (C. P. Daly) No. Am. 124: 229. — (C. R. Markham) Contemp. 22: 678. Same art. Liv. Age, 119: 341. — (A. Petermann) Colburn, 160: 97. — Canad. Mo. 7: 360. — Cornh. 29: 359. 31: 222. Same art. Ecl. M. 84: 442. — Geog. M. 2: 65–357. 3: 1, 117. 4: 1, 22. — Nature, 9: 37, 97. 11: 61, 114. 12: 61. 15: 1, 11. 18: 118.
— — Chaplain's Account of. Fraser, 94: 771. Same art. Liv. Age, 132: 94.
— — Government and. Nature, 7: 157.
— — Results of. Geog. M. 5: 137. — Quar. 143: 146. Same art. Ecl. M. 88: 385. Same art. Liv. Age, 132: 643.
— — Scientific Aims of. (R. Browne) Pop. Sci. R. 14: 154. Same art. Liv. Age, 126: 27.
— English, Projected, 1868. Colburn, 142: 631. Same art. Liv. Age, 98: 131.
— First, to the Northwest. (J. B. Brown) Contemp. 21: 529. Same art. Liv. Age, 117: 100. — (J. B. Brown) Ecl. R. 111: 243. Same art. Ecl. M. 50: 95.
— Franklin's, 1819–22. Brit. Q. 11: 102. — (Sir J. Barrow) Quar. 28: 372. — Ecl. R. 37: 521. — Chr. Obs. 24: 107, 163. — Lond. M. 7: 573. — Colburn, 7: 392. — Liv. Age, 24: 275, 279. 62: 618.
— Franklin's Second. (Sir J. Barrow) Quar. 38: 335. — Ecl. R. 48: 385. — Mo. R. 102: 1, 156. 117: 1. — So. R. 3: 261.
— German, 1869. Appleton, 13: 1, 33, 65.
— — Koldewey's. Nature, 11: 63.
— Hall's. Chamb. J. 42: 238. — (H. M. Bannister) Lakeside, 7: 225. — (T. B. Maury) Galaxy, 11: 514. — Hunt, 53: 417. — Overland, 7: 201. — Month, 4: 357. — Potter Am. Mo. 5: 621. — St. James, 15: 515. — Temp. Bar, 16: 144.
— Hall's Second. (E. H. Yarnal) Am. Natural. 14: 332.
— Hartstein Relief Expedition. (E. Merriam) Hunt, 33: 666.
— Hayes's. Liv. Age, 72: 17.
— Hayes's Boat Journey. Liv. Age, 65: 793. 66: 190.
— Howgate's. (H. W. Howgate) No. Am. 128: 86. — (O. T. Sherman) No. Am. 128: 191.
— Kane's. (Sir D. Brewster) No. Brit. 26: 407. Same art. with portrait, Ecl. M. 40: 433. — (J. D. Dana) Am. J. Sci. 74: 235. — Brit. Q. 25: 320. — Chamb. J. 26: 387. Same art. Liv. Age, 52: 481. — Colburn, 108: 379. — Chr. Obs. 57: 471.
— Kane's Grinnell. (A. H. Guernsey) Harper, 4: 11. 8: 433. — (T. Hill) Chr. Exam. 62: 238. — Liv. Age, 40: 516. — Putnam, 7: 449.
— Lyon's, 1824. Meth. M. 48: 167.
— McClintock's. Blackw. 87: 117. Same art. Liv. Age, 64: 375. — Chamb. J. 33: 36. — Cornh. 1: 96. — Dub. Univ. 55: 208.
— Nares's. (A. Petermann) Colburn, 160: 97. — (E. G. Ravenstein) Pop. Sci. R. 16: 64. — All the Year, 35: 301, 323. — Geog. M. 3: 301, 313. — Cornh. 34: 680. — Nature, 15: 24.
— — Results of. Sup. Pop. Sci. Mo. 3: 406.
— Nordenskiöld's. (W. H. Dall) Nation, 29: 441. — Nature, 12: 556. — (G. D. Sars) Nature, 15: 412, 435. 20: 606, 631. — Month, 38: 451. — (S. H. Peabody) Dial (Ch.), 2: 278.
— Pavy's. (D. Walker) Overland, 8: 549.
— Polaris. Nature, 8: 217, 435. 9: 404. 12: 49.
— — Letters from Officers. Geog. M. 1: 125.
— Richardson's. Dub. Univ. 39: 458. — Ecl. R. 95: 177. — (H. A. Proût) West. J. 8: 432. 9: 50.
Arctic Expedition, Swedish, 1868. Am. J. Sci. 98: 227.
— Tegethoff. (E. Bessels) Nation, 25: 45.
Arctic Expeditions. No. Brit. 16: 236. — Liv. Age, 25: 18. 26: 572. — Ecl. M. 20: 60. — Fraser, 38: 603. Same art. Liv. Age, 20: 289. — Colburn, 88: 350. 97: 312.
— in Search of Franklin. (C. F. Dunbar) Chr. Exam. 68: 430. — Colburn, 90: 372. 93: 193–483. 112: 288. — De Bow, 13: 1. — Ecl. M. 29: 307. — Harper, 2: 588. — Liv. Age, 31: 291.
Arctic Exploration. (C. R. Markham) Nature, 5: 77. — (J. Rae) Nature, 5: 110, 165. 7: 117. — Nature, 9: 240. — (A. Petermann) Nature, 11: 37. — (H. Lincoln) Bapt. Q. 1: 341. — (J. Piggot) Fraser, 91: 789. — Chamb. J. 57: 785. — (A. Woodbury) No. Am. 80: 307. — Blackw. 117: 777. Same art. Ecl. M. 85: 235. — Colburn, 155: 682. — Ecl. R. 109: 419. Same art. Ecl. M. 48: 17. — Geog. M. 5: 306. — Liv. Age, 24: 453. 39: 628. 63: 418. — Lond. Q. 14: 226. — New Q. 3: 32.
— Aerial. (W. M. Williams) Gent. M. n. s. 25: 101.
— American. Liv. Age, 26: 45.
— Bellot's Journal of. New Q. 3: 305.
— Benefits from. Quar. 118: 137. Same art. Liv. Age. 86: 529.
— Colonization Plan of. (H. W. Howgate) Am Natural. 11: 226. — Colburn, 133: 379.
— Dutch. (A. H. Markham) Good Words, 20: 90, 172, 244. — (S. R. Van Campen) Geog. M. 3: 23. — Nature, 14: 246.
— German and Swedish. (R. A. Proctor) Nature, 1: 312.
— — Recent. Am. J. Sci. 103: 50.
— German Commission on. Nature, 13: 73.
— History of. (Sir D. Brewster) No. Brit. 16: 445. — (I. I. Hayes) No. Am. 118: 23.
— — and Results of. Nat. M. 16: 24.
— in 1852–54. Colburn, 106: 51.
— in 1860. Hunt, 46: 55.
— in 1872–76. Ed. R. 145: 155.
— Markham on. Month, 20: 102.
— New Scheme of. (R. A. Proctor) Temp. Bar, 21: 536.
— Osborn's. Liv. Age, 34: 59.
— Recent. Liv. Age, 24: 193. 26: 241.
— Results of. (A. Woodbury) No. Am. 84: 95. — Geog. M. 5: 249.
— — Recent. Ed. R. 141: 447. Same art. Liv. Age, 125: 579.
— since 1815. (F. Lushington) Macmil. 1: 268.
— Swedish. Geog. M. 5: 193. — Nature, 13: 116.
— Transits and. (R. A. Proctor) Pop. Sci. R. 14: 264.
— Use of Dogs in. (G. Fleming and R. Brown) Geog. M. 2: 56.
— Weyprecht on. Nature, 12: 539.
— Yachting Cruise to Novaya Zembla. (A. H. Markham) Good Words, 22: 89, 205, 277.
See Polar Exploration.
Arctic Explorers. (T. A. Jenvier) Potter Am. Mo. 8: 169. — Lond. Q. 47: 391. Same art. Liv. Age. 132: 323.
— Lost. Liv. Age, 44: 195, 451.
Arctic Föhn. (G. S. Nares) Geog. M. 4: 317.
Arctic Literature, Recent, 1879. (W. H. Dall) Nation, 29: 296.
Arctic Ocean, Temperatures of. J. Frankl. Inst. 45: 435.
Arctic Regions. Ed. R. 98: 342. Same art. Liv. Age, 39: 603. — Pop. Sci. Mo. 3: 363. — Nature, 13: 146. — Putnam, 7: 138.
— Adventure in. Blackw. 81: 366. — Liv. Age, 52: 321.
— — Day of. (D. Walker) St. James, 3: 267.
— and the Eskimo. Quar. 142: 346. Same art. Ecl. M. 88: 1. Same art. Liv. Age, 131: 515.

Arctic Regions, Animals of. (T. B. Maury) Putnam, **14**: 727.
— Eastern Polar Basin. (A. Petermann) Macmil. **35**: 215. Same art. Liv. Age, **132**: 494.
— Fossil Flora of. Nature, **14**: 336. — (J. S. Gardner) Nature, **19**: 124.
— Geography of. (A. Petermann) Liv. Age, **48**: 205.
— — and Ethnology of. Nature, **12**: 103.
— Geology of. (C. E. de Rance) Nature, **11**: 447–508.
— Ho! for the Pole. Liv. Age, **65**: 615. **66**: 263, 351.
— Ice Travels. (C. R. Markham) Pop. Sci. Mo. **7**: 468.
— — Sledges in, 1876. Geog. M. **4**: 83, 88, 89, 139, 169.
— Life in. (A. H. Markham) Good Words, **18**: 137, 169, 281, 300.
— Manual of, Jones and Adams's. Nature, **12**: 81.
— Marine Vegetation of. (M. P. Merrifield) Nature, **12**: 55.
— Markham's great Frozen Sea. Nature, **18**: 201.
— Markham's Unknown. Nature, **9**: 138.
— Meteorology of. Nature, **16**: 358.
— Natural History of. Ed. New Philos. J. **54**: 72.
— New Lands of, Payer's. Nature, **15**: 62, 81.
— Projected Settlement in. Colburn, **133**: 379.
— Routes to. (S. Osborn) Geog. M. **1**: 221.
— Scene in. (G. W. Archer) N. Ecl. **6**: 55.
— Seas of. (T. B. Maury) Putnam, **14**: 521.
— — and Ice of. (T. Latta) Ed. New Philos. J. **2**: 86.
— Supposed Change of Climate in. (J. Fleming) J. Frankl. Inst. **7**: 382.
— Traveling in, Curiosities of. Colburn, **94**: 431. Same art. Liv. Age, **33**: 593.
— — in Winter. (G. Kennan) Putnam, **16**: 313.
— Vegetation of. Nature, **11**: 433.
— Winter in, Fluctuations of Temperature in. (J. J. Murphy) Canad. J. n. s. **6**: 521.
— — two hundred Years ago. Chamb. J. **35**: 36, 56. Same art. Liv. Age, **68**: 743.
— Wonders of. (W. H. Moore) Potter Am. Mo. **4**: 139.
— Yachting in, Lamont's. Appleton, **15**: 385, 417, 449.
See also North Pole; Northeast Passage; Northwest Passage; etc.
Arctic Robinson Crusoe. Ecl. R. **95**: 117. Same art. Ecl. M. **27**: 250. Same art. Liv. Age, **35**: 226.
Arctic Voyages. Colburn, **88**: 83. — Ecl. R. **34**: 50. — Ecl. M. **19**: 414. — House. Words, **10**: 361–457.
— Barrow's. Blackw. **4**: 157.
— — from 1818. Quar. **78**: 45.
— Beechey's. Colburn, **31**: 373. — Ed. R. **78**: 68.
— Belcher's. Chamb. J. **25**: 229.
— Kotzebue's. Blackw. **11**: 521.
— Last of the, 1856. Brit. Q. **23**: 361.
— Lyon's, 1824. Meth. M. **48**: 167.
— of the Whaler Diana, 1866–67. Cornh. **15**: 748.
— of the Resolute. Liv. Age, **55**: 53.
— Parry's. Meth. M. **51**: 386.
— Parry's Second Voyage. Colburn, **10**: 453.
— — Cochrane's Letter on. Colburn, **10**: 549.
— Recent. Pop. Sci. Mo. **7**: 320.
— Recent and Future, 1880. Quar. **150**: 111. Same art. Liv. Age, **146**: 451.
— Ross's, 1829–33. Mo. R. **137**: 210.
— Ross's Second. (Sir D. Brewster) Ed. R. **61**: 417. *See also* Ross.
— Scoresby's. Blackw. **2**: 363. — Ecl. R. **33**: 219.
— Snow's, in the Prince Albert. Colburn, **91**: 234. — Ecl. R. **93**: 315.
Arcueil, Society of, Memoirs of. Quar. **3**: 462. — (J. Leslie) Ed. R. **15**: 142.
Ardagh, Robert, Fortunes of. Dub. Univ. **11**: 213.
Arden of Feversham. (A. H. Bromilow) Colburn, **164**: 175.
Arden or Ardennes, Castle of. (C. E. Browne) Fraser, **93**: 468. — Bentley, **13**: 177.
— Forest of. Chamb. J. **7**: 6. — Ecl. M. **65**: 731. — Tinsley, **7**: 49. — Good Words, **21**: 589. — (M. P. Thompson) Cath. World, **31**: 506.
— — In the Heart of. (Mrs. R. Church) Belgra. **9**: 494. — (K. S. Macquoid) Belgra. **42**: 280.
— — Through. (F. L. Oswald) Lippinc. **28**: 539.
— Legends from. Once a Week, **13**: 598.
— Old Chateau in. (K. S. Macquoid) Belgra. **41**: 153.
— Sketcher in. Fraser, **68**: 513.
Ardent Spirits. *See* Alcohol; Liquor.
Ardes, Lords of. (E. A. Freeman) Brit. Q. **71**: 1.
Ardmore. Fraser, **32**: 286, 393.
Are you my Wife? a Tale. (K. O'Meara) Cath. World, **20**: 596, 738. **21**: 41–742. **22**: 13–735. **23**: 22–316.
Arenenberg, Visit to. Temp. Bar, **35**: 255.
Arethusa, On Board the. All the Year, **37**: 100.
Aretino, Pietro. Tait, n. s. **13**: 681.
— Career of. Dub. Univ. **77**: 624.
Arezzo, Guittone d', Early Italian Poet. Lond. M. **8**: 501.
Argand Lamp, The. Penny M. **3**: 119.
Argelander, Friedrich W. A. Am. J. Sci. **112**: 113.
Argenis, Queen; a Poem. Blackw. **46**: 767.
Argentine Republic. (A. H. Guernsey) Harper, **18**: 325. — (S. F. Streeter) No. Am. **69**: 43. — Am. Church R. **22**: 218.
— History of. Canad. Mo. **6**: 523.
— in 1810–40. Chr. Exam. **85**: 185.
— in the Days of the Tyrants. New Eng. **27**: 666.
— King's. Ecl. R. **84**: 192. — Ed. R. **87**: 534.
— Life in. (V. Vaughan) Putnam, **12**: 624.
— McCann's Travels in. New Q. **2**: 222.
— Notes on. (C. Oxland) Pop. Sci. R. **19**: 1.
— Pampas of, Leybold's Excursion to. Nature, **9**: 59.
— Science in. (C. G. Wheeler) Pop. Sci. Mo. **9**: 463.
— Sheep-Farming in. (N. M. Clerk) Good Words, **12**: 712.
Argis, Church of. House. Words, **12**: 561.
Argolis, Three Days in. (H. M. Baird) Putnam, **3**: 62.
Argonauts, Voyage of, Pre-Homeric Legends of. Dub. R. **84**: 164.
Argonauts of '49. (J. L. Ver Mehr) Overland, **10**: 434, 546.
Arguelles, Extradition of. (G. W. Lawton) Potter Am. Mo. **14**: 457.
Argument from Analogy. Ecl. R. **119**: 94.
Argus and its surrounding Nebula. (F. Abbott) Nature, **4**: 478.
Argyll, John Campbell, 7th Duke of. (H. Holbeach) St. Paul's, **10**: 149.
Argyll, G. J., 8th Duke of. (G. M. Towle) Putnam, **14**: 569. — with portrait, Ev. Sat. **10**: 371. — with portrait, Ecl. M. **87**: 377. — with portrait, (G. M. Towle) Appleton, **5**: 675. — (J. McCarthy) Galaxy, **17**: 5.
— and Disestablishment in Scotland. Brit. Q. **67**: 462.
— Political Portrait of. St. James, **25**: 113.
Argyll, House of. Chamb. J. **48**: 181
Argyll's Rising in 1685. Hogg, **3**: 227. — (P. Bayne) Contemp. **25**: 683. Same art. Liv. Age, **125**: 643.
Argyllshire Rocks and Caves, Legendary Stories of. (C. Bede) Belgra. **32**: 323.
Argyllshire Vision, An. (A. Bell) Good Words, **16**: 54.
Ariadne; a Poem. (W. C. Bennett) Internat. M. **4**: 316. — (E. W. Ellsworth) Internat. M. **5**: 45. — (W. J. Tate) Once a Week, **15**: 126.
Ariadne at Naxos; a Poem. Cornh. **2**: 674.
Arianism. (C. L. Kitchel) New Eng. **26**: 565. — (J. W. Nevin) Mercersb. **14**: 426. — Am. Church R. **24**: 458. — Theo. Repos. **3**: 259, 434.
— and the Roman Patriarchate. Am. Church R. **26**: 206.
— Arguments for. Theo. Repos. **3**: 452.

Arianism, Athanasius's Controversy with. (H. Wace) Good Words, **19**: 681. — Presb. R. **5**: 353, 529. — Chr. Rem. **4**: 32, 246. — Univ. Q. **9**: 35.
— Controversy on. (A. Lamson) Chr. Exam. **12**: 298. — Spirit Pilg. **4**: 420.
— Defense of. Theo. Repos. **4**: 153.
— Nature and Origin of. (J. Priestley) Theo. Repos. **4**: 307. **6**: 376.
— Objections to. Theo. Repos. **5**: 1.
— Rise of. (J. Priestley) Theo. Repos. **4**: 70. **6**: 484.
— What it is, and how it arose. Chr. Rem. **19**: 331. *See* Arius.
Arians are not Unitarians. Theo. Repos. **4**: 338.
— are Unitarians. Theo. Repos. **5**: 56.
— of 4th Century, History of, Newman's. Ed. R. **63**: 44.
Arica, Peru, Earthquake at, 1868. (E. W. Sturdy) Scrib. **5**: 22.
Ariège, Valley of. (M. P. Thompson) Cath. World, **33**: 260.
Ariel; a Visionary Romance. Dub. Univ. **95**: 9.
Arion, Lay of. Lond. M. **11**: 521.
Ariosto, L. (W. W. Fife) Sharpe, **20**: 77. — (L. Hunt) Lond. M. **3**: 63. — (Alice King) Argosy, **8**: 52. — (E. I. Sears) Nat. Q. **10**: 207. — (W. H. Prescott) No. Am. **19**: 367. — Knick. **18**: 305. — Dub. Univ. **26**: 187, 581. **27**: 90.
— Homes and Haunts of. (T. A. Trollope) Belgra. **34**: 29.
— Orlando Furioso. Retros. **8**: 145. **9**: 263.
— — Rose's translation. Blackw. **14**: 30. **15**: 418. — Lond. M. **9**: 623. — Quar. **30**: 40.
Aristænetus, Love Epistles of. Fraser, **26**: 76, 176, 609. **27**: 578.
Aristides, Apology of. (S. J. Barrows) Unita. R. **11**: 680.
Aristocracy. Westm. **14**: 482. **23**: 156. **31**: 283. — Blackw. **38**: 98. — Carey's Mus. **2**: 235. — Ecl. R. **79**: 1.
— American. Dem. R. **8**: 113. — Mo. R. **150**: 392.
— — as manufactured. (E. I. Sears) Nat. Q. **23**: 277.
— and Democracy, Heeren on. For. Q. **20**: 340.
— Anecdotes of. Chamb. J. **11**: 188.
— Causes of. (J. T. Wiswall) De Bow, **28**: 551.
— Education of. Brit. & For. R. **1**: 298. — Westm. **23**: 303.
— English. (H. Brougham) Ed. R. **61**: 64. — Quar. **72**: 88. — Blackw. **54**: 51. — Fraser, **38**: 516.
— — Tompkins on. Quar. **53**: 540.
— Englishman's Thoughts on. (C. Allerton) Penn Mo. **5**: 658.
— Hints to. Blackw. **35**: 68.
— of Rank; is it the Aristocracy of Talent? Fraser, **34**: 159.
Aristocracies, Influence of. Westm. **42**: 392.
— — on Revolutions of Nations, Macintyre on. Mo. R. **161**: 429.
— of Fashion. Blackw. **53**: 68.
— of London Life. Blackw. **53**: 67. Same art. Ecl. Mus. **1**: 26.
— of Power. Blackw. **53**: 227.
— of Talent. Blackw. **53**: 386.
Aristocrat and the Pauper. Bentley, **57**: 510, 626. **58**: 48, 133.
Aristocratic Annals. Blackw. **65**: 468.
Aristocratic Institutions, American. (R. B. Kimball) Galaxy, **17**: 259.
Aristocratic Revelations. Westm. **22**: 314.
Aristocratic Society, French and English, 1831–47. Chr. Rem. **35**: 191.
Aristocratic Taxation. Westm. **21**: 140.
Aristology; or, Science of Dinners. (M. Collins) Belgra. **15**: 342.
Aristomenes, the Messinian. Knick. **20**: 25.
Ariston; a Tragedy. Internat. R. **1**: 611.
Aristophanes. (E. I. Sears) Nat. Q. **3**: 70. — Fraser, **15**: 285. **40**: 147. — Ecl. R. **77**: 260. — Tait, n. s. **20**: 449.
— Acharnenses, Mitchell's. (D. K. Sandford) Ed. R. **61**: 323.
— and Socrates. (E. Everett) No. Am. **14**: 273.
— Birds of. Fraser, **18**: 127, 317.
— — Cary's translation. Ecl. R. **40**: 217.
— Clouds of. Quar. **21**: 271. — (G. Dunbar) Blackw. **18**: 351. — Poetical translation, Blackw. **38**: 516.
— Comedies of. Quar. **9**: 139. **23**. 474. **24**: 424. — Anal. M. **1**: 413. **3**: 177. — Ecl. R. **17**: 263. — Westm. **95**: 291.
— English Translations of. (J. Davies) Contemp. **6**: 502.
— Frere's Version of. (C. C. Felton) No. Am. **76**: 166.
— Frogs of; poetical translation. Blackw. **4**: 421.
— Knights of. Fraser, **19**: 639. **20**: 379.
— Mitchell's. Ed. R. **34**: 271.
— Peace of. Blackw. **23**: 551.
— Plutus of; poetical translation. (D. K. Sandford) Blackw. **38**: 763.
— Possums of, recently recovered. Fraser, **14**: 285.
— Rooks of; poetical translation. Blackw. **32**: 669.
— Spirit of. Tait, n. s. **11**: 312, 511, 634.
Aristotle. (E. A. Park) Bib. Sac. **1**: 39, 280. — (W. S. Tyler) Am. Bib. Repos. 2d s. **12**: 443. 3d s. **2**: 1. — (E. Everett) No. Am. **17**: 389. — (E. R. Humphreys) Nat. Q. **3**: 316. — Am. Presb. R. **1**: 567.
— and Cuvier. Mo. R. **139**: 119.
— and Plato. (D. McG. Means) Bib. Sac. **34**: 514. — Chr. Rem. **54**: 103. — So. R. n. s. **9**: 664.
— Characteristics of. Westm. **116**: 1.
— Educational Views of. Am. J. Educ. **14**: 131.
— Ethics of. (D. McG. Means) Bib. Sac. **35**: 255. — Dub. Univ. **75**: 361. — Westm. **87**: 24.
— — Grant's. (C. E. Norton) Nation, **3**: 106. — (J. L. Warren) Fortn. **5**: 247.
— Grote's. (J. S. Mill) Fortn. **19**: 27. — Brit. Q. **57**: 463. — Ed. R. **136**: 515.
— History of Animals. (T. Gill) Am. Natural. **7**: 458. — Quar. **117**: 28.
— Life and Philosophy of. Westm. **103**: 84.
— on Free Will. Liv. Age, **146**: 634.
— Opinions and Writings of. (G. Cuvier) Ed. New Philos. J. **9**: 60.
— Philosophy of. (G. W. F. Hegel) J. Spec. Philos. **5**: 61, 180, 251. — Am. Presb. R. **2**: 64. — No. Brit. **45**: 105.
— — Systematic. Westm **116**: 320.
— Poetics, Analysis of. (J. F. de La Harpe) Portfo (Den.) **22**: 361, 441.
— Politics of. Dub Univ. **75**: 361. — Westm. **98**: 98.
— — Macaulay on. Macmil. **32**: 218.
— Scientific Writings of. Westm. **82**: 80. — Chr. Rem. **49**: 290.
— — Lewes on. Brit. Q. **40**: 51. — Blackw. **96**: 147.
— Theology of (D. McG. Means) Bib. Sac. **34**: 228.
— Works of. Ecl. R **69**: 285.
— — and Philosophy of. Dub. Univ. **72**: 3. Same art. Ecl. M. **71**: 1165.
Aristotelian and modern Place of Man in Zoölogy. (C. M. Dewey) Am. Presb. R. **12**. 394.
Aristotelianism, Oxford. No. Brit. **29**: 367.
Aristus and Dinus, Story of. Blackw. **1**: 367.
Arithmetic. (W. Colburn) Am. Inst. of Instruc. **1830**: 277. — (K. von Raumer) Am. J. Educ. **8**: 170. — (J. Wheeler) Meth. Q. **24**: 233.
— Ancient and Modern. Lond. Q. **11**: 415.
— and Metrology, Tonal System of. (J. W. Nystrom) J. Frankl. Inst. **76**: 263, 337, 402.
— Concrete, Orme's. Nature, **6**: 178.
— Curiosities of. Chamb. J. **8**: 207.

Arithmetic, Early Methods in. (E. O. Vaile) Pop. Sci. Mo. **16**: 204.
— Foundation of. (H. Wedgwood) Mind, **3**: 572.
— History of. (Sir J. Leslie) Ed. R. **18**: 185.
— Humors of. Colburn, **64**: 366.
— Intellectual. (F. A. Adams) Am. Inst. of Instruc. **1845**: 165.
— Leslie's Philosophy of. Mo. R. **88**: 401.
— Recent Works on, 1873. Nature, **8**: 159.
— Romance of. Chamb. J. **49**: 449. Same art. Ecl. M. **79**: 369.
— Simplifications of. Penny M. **2**: 26, 54, 71, 91, 190.
— Universal Statements of. (W. K. Clifford) 19th Cent. **5**: 513.
Arithmetical Notations, Decimal and other. (F. Brooks) Ecl. Engin. **18**: 548.
Arithmometer, Colmar's. Bank. M. (N. Y.) **28**: 774. — J. Frankl. Inst. **91**: 372. — Nature, **8**: 325. — Pract. M. **6**: 304.
Arius and Athanasius. (R. Ellis) Chr. Exam. **58**: 275.
— Life of. Chr. Mo. Spec. **4**: 192.
— Dean Stanley on. (A. Lamson) Chr. Exam. **72**: 224.
Arizona Territory. (A. G. Brackett) Lakeside, **1**: 167. — (C. H. Miller) Overland, **13**: 65.
— Adventures in. (S. Powers) Overland, **6**: 82.
— and Silver Mining. (G. R. Gibson) Bank. M. (N. Y.) **32**: 811.
— Camp Life in. (J. Clifford) Overland, **4**: 246.
— Copper Mine in. (J. Gilbert) Canad. J. n. s. **2**: 321.
— Deserts of. (J. Clifford) Overland, **4**: 537.
— Legend of. (S. Hyacinth) Overland, **4**: 278.
— Mining Districts of. (B. Silliman) Am. J. Sci. **91**: 289.
— Tour through. (J. R. Browne) Harper, **29**: 553, 689. **30**: 22-409.
— Vegetation in. (W. J. Hoffman) Am. Natural. **11**: 336.
Ark of the Covenant. (A. Hovey) Chr. R. **17**: 572. — (E. Pond) Am. Bib. Repos. 2d s. **10**: 290.
Arkansas, Bill for prohibiting Slavery in. Niles's Reg. **16**: supp. 173.
— Condition of, 1869-75. (E. L. Godkin) Nation, **20**: 90.
— Governor's Message, 1820. Niles's Reg. **19**: 182.
— Hot Springs of. (A. Van Cleef) Harper, **56**: 193.
— Ice-bound in. All the Year, **16**: 79.
— Letters from, 1835. New Eng. M. **9**: 263.
— Life in. (A. Pike) Am. Mo. M. **7**: 25, 154, 295.
— Minerals and Springs of. De Bow, **25**: 199.
— Northern. De Bow, **5**: 301.
— Nuttall's Journal in. (J. Bigelow) No. Am. **16**: 59.
— Repudiation in, Jefferson Davis and. (R. J. Walker) Contin. Mo. **5**: 479.
— Statistics of, 1869. Am. J. Educ. **18**: 281.
— Travels in. (E. King) Scribner, **8**: 641.
Arkism. (M. Heilprin) Nation, **7**: 35.
Arkite Ceremonies in the Himalayas. (W. Simpson) Good Words, **7**: 601.
Arles, France, Amédée Pichot's. Colburn, **120**: 179.
— The Aliscamps in. (M. P. Thompson) Cath. World, **28**: 43.
Arlincourt, Viscount V. d'. L'Etrangère. Lond. M. **11**: 403.
— Van Arteveld, the Brewer of Ghent, and his Son Philip. For. Q. **14**: 413.
Arlington House, Virginia. (B. J. Lossing) Harper, **7**: 433. — (B. J. Lossing) Potter Am. Mo. **6**: 81.
Arlingtons, The. Colburn, **140**: 489. **141**: 97-416. **142**: 52-678. **143**: 24.
Arlotto, Mainardi. Cornh. **28**: 705. Same art. Ev. Sat. **16**: 6.
Arm-Chair of Tustenuggee. (W. G. Simms) Godey, **20**: 193.
Armada. *See* Spanish Armada.
Armadale; a Novel. (W. Collins) Cornh. **10**: 513, 642. **11**: 1-641. **12**: 60-723. **13**: 81-683. Same art. Harper, **30**: 79-760. **31**: 76-768. **32**: 67-738. **33**: 75, 186.
Armadillos, Gigantic extinct. (J. A. Ryder) Pop. Sci. Mo. **13**: 139.
Armageddon; the last Battle-Field of Nations. So. R. n. s. **12**: 128.
— On the Hebrew Word. (E. B. Elliott) Chr. Obs. **69**: 634, 873.
Armagh, Archbishop of. Dub. Univ. **16**: 86.
— Investigation in. Dub. Univ. **5**: 319.
— Stuart's History of. Ecl. R. **33**: 504.
Armament: Shot and Shields. St. James, **4**: 273.
Armaments, European, 1874. (E. L. Godkin) Nation, **19**: 297. **21**: 5.
— of the five Great Powers. St. Paul's, **1**: 182. Same art. Ecl. M. **70**: 67.
Armand, Gen., Marquis de la Rouerie. (T. Ward) Pennsyl. M. **2**: 1.
Armenia. Chr. Exam. **4**: 519.
— and the Armenians. (T. C. Trowbridge) New Eng. **33**: 1.
— the Cradle of History. Ecl. M. **47**: 248.
— Curzon's. Colburn, **100**: 464. — Dub. Univ. **44**: 79.
— Devil-Worshipers of. Fraser, **51**: 587. Same art. Liv. Age, **46**: 240.
— Excursions in. Fraser, **55**: 602.
— Folk-Songs of. Fraser, **93**: 283.
— History of. Ecl. R. **58**: 118, 277. — (W. Clark) New Eng. **22**: 507, 672.
— How the Turks rule. (H. Sandwith) 19th Cent. **3**: 314. Same art. Liv. Age, **136**: 809.
— Missionary Researches in. Cong. M. **18**: 167. — Mo. R. **135**: 379. — Ecl. R. **58**: 369.
— Modern. Am. Q. Reg. **8**: 249.
— Past and Future of. (G. Smith) Good Words, **19**: 160.
— Question of, 1880. Contemp. **37**: 533.
— Russian Despotism in. (J. J. Ryan) Putnam, **2**: 182.
— Russians in, 1877. (A. A. Wheeler) Fortn. **30**: 852.
— Smith's Researches in. Am. Mo. R. **3**: 349.
— Smith and Dwight on. Spirit Pilg. **6**: 464.
Armenian Church. (J. A. Reubelt) Mercersb. **11**: 605.
— and Mount Ararat. Nat. M. **1**: 26.
— History and Doctrine of. Chr. Rem. **33**: 349.
— in Turkey. Ecl. R. **101**: 532.
— — Evangelical. (G. W. Clark) Chr. R. **24**: 1.
— Protestant Reformation in, Dwight on. Chr. Obs. **55**: 451.
Armenian Family. Liv. Age, **49**: 620.
Armenian Leper; a Tale. Chamb. J. **8**: 6.
Armenian Marriage at Constantinople. Penny M. **2**: 439.
Armenians at Constantinople. Am. Mo. M. **1**: 365.
— Faith and Literature of. Dub. R. **7**: 333.
— Persecution among. (J. P. Thompson) New Eng. **4**: 410.
Armgart; a Tragic Poem. (Geo. Eliot) Macmil. **24**: 161. Same art. Atlan. **28**: 94.
Armin, the Liberator of Germany. (K. Blind) Fraser, **92**: 243.
Arminian Doctrine of Self-Determination. (S. C. Brace) Lit. & Theo. R. **5**: 371.
Arminian View of the Fall and Redemption. (D. D. Whedon) Meth. Q. **21**: 647.
Arminianism. Am. Meth. M. **10**: 336.
— and Calvinism, Controversy of, Pearson's. Chr. Obs. **1**: 787.
— and Grace. (J. C. Rankin) Princ. **28**: 38.
— — Princeton Review on. Meth. Q. **16**: 257.
— Controversy on, in the Low Countries. Meth. Q. **4**: 425, 556.

Arminianism, Difficulties of. (S. Comfort) Am. Meth. M. **21**: 319.
— Historic. Bost. R. **1**: 287.
— Inconsistencies and Errors of. So. R. n. s. **22**: 464.
Arminius, J. (W. F. Warren) Meth. Q. **17**: 345.
— and Arminians in Holland. Meth. M. **36**: 23.
— and Arminianism. (G. M. Steele) Chr. Exam. **68**: 393. — (D. D. Whedon) Meth. Q. **39**: 405.
— Dr. Beecher on. Am. Meth. M. **11**: 160.
— Life and Times of. (M. Stuart) Am. Bib. Repos. **1**: 226.—Lit. & Theo. R. **6**: 337.—Am. Meth. M. **15**: 8.
— Nichols on Works of. Chr. Obs. **27**: 544, 610, 675.
— on Theology. Meth. M. **45**: 222.
— Theological Position of. Mo. Rel. M. **6**: 49.
— Works of. Am. Meth. M. **9**: 95. — Meth. M. **48**: 748. **51**: 755.
Armitage, Edward. (J. B. Atkinson) Portfo. **1**: 49. — (P. G. Hamerton) Portfo. **6**: 62. — Art J. **15**: 177.
Armor, Ancient. Quar. **30**: 335. — (F. Jeffrey) Ed. R. **39**: 346. — Art J. **8**: 45. — Chamb. J. **35**: 129.
— Ancient Mode of putting on. (S. R. Meyrick) Arch. **20**: 496.
— and Arms, Mediæval. (J. Hewitt) Reliquary, **10**: 13–246. **11**: 48, 209.
— Body, recently worn in England. (S. R. Meyrick) Arch. **19**: 120.
— Coat, in the United States. (W. H. Whitmore) N. E. Reg. **22**: 255.
— Engravings on a Suit made for Henry VIII. (S. R. Meyrick) Arch. **22**: 106.
— Horse, in the Tower. Penny M. **9**: 9–489.
— The Man in. All the Year, **28**: 610.
Armor-Plate Experiments at Spezia. J. Frankl. Inst. **103**: 177.
Armor-Plates. (H. E. Brown) Ecl. Engin. **9**: 544.
— Iron and Steel. Ecl. Engin. **21**: 28.
Armorer, Art of the. Art J. **20**: 30.
Armorer of Munster. Fraser, **37**: 312, 441, 549.
Armorers of London, Grant to the Guild of St. George. (W. S. Walford) Arch. **38**: 135.
Armorial Bearings. Chamb. J. **35**: 273.
Armory. *See* Heraldry.
Arms and Ammunition, American. (W. C. Church) Scrib. **19**: 436.
— and Armies, Modern. Dem. R. **19**: 15.
— and Soldiery, British, Ancient and Modern. Dub. Univ. **71**: 629. Same art. Ecl. M. **71**: 1052.
— Breech-Loading, Invention and History of. Hunt, **55**: 336.
— Small, History of Manufacture of. (J. D. Goodman) J. Statis. Soc. **28**: 494.
See Artillery; Cannon; Fire-arms; Ordinance; Rifles.
Armstead, Henry Hugh. (J. L. Tupper) Portfo. **2**: 129.
Armstrong. (P. S. Knight) Overland, **12**: 563.
Armstrong, Edmund J. Ed. R. **148**: 57.
Armstrong, George D. Lecture on Chemistry. So. Lit. Mess. **4**: 367.
Armstrong, George Francis, with portrait. Colburn, **165**: 1058, 1152.
— Ungone; a Tragedy. Dark Blue, **1**: 251.
Armstrong, Com. James, U. S. N. (G. H. Preble) N. E. Reg. **25**: 271.
Armstrong, Gen. John. (W. M. Darlington) Pennsyl. M. **1**: 183.
— Letters of. Hist. M. **8**: 16.
Armstrong, John, Life and Writings of. Lond. M. **6**: 241. Same art. Portfo.(Den.) **30**: 177.
Armstrong, Thomas. (S. Colvin) Portfo. **2**: 65.
Armstrong, Sir W. G., and the Manufacture of Ordnance. Pract. M. **4**: 81.
Armstrong Gun, The. St. James, **5**: 3. — Temp. Bar, **4**: 459. **5**: 183. **12**: 381.
Army, Cooking for an. Chamb. J. **39**: 51.
— Domestic Economy of. Chamb. J. **23**: 253, 265.
— Health of. (H. Martineau) Atlan. **8**: 571, 718. — (H. Martineau) Macmil. **8**: 332.
— Mobilization of. (J. C. Paget) St. James, **38**: 298.
— Model for. Chamb. J. **34**: 291.
— Modern Tactical Organizations. (H. B. Crosby) Gent. M. n. s. **17**: 308 — (W. W. Knollys) Gent. M. n. s. **15**: 574.
— Moral Discipline of. (G. R. Gleig) Quar. **76**: 387.
— Organization of. (G. B. McClellan) Harper, **48**: 670. **49**: 101, 401. — Westm. **87**: 1. — Macmil. **23**: 73.
— — and Movements. (C. W. Tolles) Contin. Mo. **5**: 707. **6**: 1–601.
— Patriotic, *vs.* a Hireling Soldiery. Tait, n. s. **4**: 710.
— Popular *vs.* Professional. (W. R. Greg) Contemp. **16**: 351.
— Punishments in. Blackw. **15**: 399.
— Rapid Transportation of. (J. H. Haynie) Macmil. **37**: 491.
— Regulations for. (J. L. Seton) Colburn, **149**: 75–314.
— Sanitary and Nursing Appliances for. (Dr. Treuenpreuss) Internat. R. **3**: 492.
— Sanitary Improvement in. No. Brit. **36**: 153.
— Standing. All the Year, **38**: 17. — Dem. R. **30**: 131. — Republic, **4**: 209.
— — and Loans. Westm. **52**: 205.
— — in America. Mo. R. **130**: 73.
— — inconsistent with Free Government. Pamph. **10**: 109.
— — Is it unconstitutional? St. Paul's, **6**: 138.
Army Correspondence. (H. Villard) Nation, **1**: 79, 114, 144.
Army Scenes. So. Lit. Mess. **8**: 405, 453, 655. **9**: 109.
Army of the Potomac. (C. S. Weyman) Nation, **2**: 597. *See* Potomac.
Army Physician, Adventures of. Chamb. J. **17**: 37.
Armies and Armaments, European. No. Brit. **47**: 404.
— and Modes of Warfare, Modern. (S. Amos) Internat. R. **4**: 614.
— English and French. All the Year, **17**: 318.
— — Comparative Cost of. (W. H. Sykes) J. Statis. Soc. **27**: 1. — Cornh. **7**: 310.
— European, and their Organization. Temp. Bar, **12**: 77.
— — How Officered. Fraser, **73**: 592.
— — Question of. (H. von Holst) Internat. R. **11**: 1.
— Modern. Lond. Q. **36**: 131.
— National, and Modern Warfare. Fraser, **81**: 543.
— of Asia and Europe, Upton on. (G. Mallery) Nation, **26**: 376.
— of Europe, 1856. Putnam, **6**: 196–569.
— of Russia and Austria. (E. B. Hawley) 19th Cent. **3**: 844.
— Size and Organization of. (J. H. Wilson) Internat. R. **5**: 514.
Arnal, Etienne. (C. Hervey) Belgra. **36**: 60.
— and Madame Doche. Colburn, **86**: 420.
Arnaldo da Brescia. *See* Arnold of Brescia.
Arnaud, H., and the Waldenses. Liv. Age, **37**: 771.
Arnauld Family. (J. W. Alexander) Princ. **21**: 467.
Arnault, A. V. Souvenirs d'un Sexagenaire. (J. W. Croker) Quar. **51**: 1. Same art. Select J. **4**: 145.
Arndt, Ernst Moritz. (W. L. Blackley) Fortn. **14**: 377. Same art. Ecl. M. **75**: 656. — Ed. R. **132**: 414. Same art. Liv. Age, **109**: 3. — All the Year, **24**: 317.
— and his Sacred Poetry. Brit. Q. **36**: 309. Same art. Ecl. M. **58**: 119.
— Life of. (W. P. Garrison) Nation, **29**: 45.
— Reminiscences of. For. Q. **31**: 169.
Arndt, John. (J. G. Merris) Evang. R. **4**: 222. — With portrait. Meth. M. **33**: 129.
Arnell, D. R. Poems. (F. Tuthill) Am. Whig R. **8**: 174.

Arnheim, Marie von. Dub. Univ. **31**: 663.
Arnhem, Storming of. (J. L. Ver Mehr) Overland, **6**: 306.
Arnold of Brescia. (A. Panizzi) No. Brit. **1**: 440. — Colburn, **117**: 432.
Arnold, Benedict, Governor of Rhode Island, 1657–60. (J. B. Moore) Am. Q. Reg. **13**: 276.
Arnold, Benedict, Traitor. (B. J. Lossing) Harper, **23**: 721. — Am. Hist. Rec. **3**: 444.
— and Major John André. M. Am. Hist. **3**: 747. — Nat. Q. **6**: 98.
— — Meeting of. Dem. R. **41**: 300.
— and his Apologist. (J. A. Stevens) M. Am. Hist. **4**: 181.
— and Joseph Surface. (E. Spencer) So. M. **16**: 508.
— Arnold's Life of. Penn Mo. **11**: 235.
— at the Court of George III. (I. N. Arnold) M. Am. Hist. **3**: 676.
— Beman's Account of. (B. F. De Costa) Hist. M. **13**: 273.
— Correspondence of. N. E. Reg. **35**: 153.
— Descendants of. Am. Hist. Rec. **3**: 495. — N. E. Reg. **34**: 196.
— Documents relating to. Hist. M. **18**: 361.
— Letter to Henry Clinton. Hist. M. **3**: 294.
— Life of. (A. R. Macdonough) Nation, **29**: 425. — (J. Sparks) Sparks's Am. Biog. **3**: 1.
— Love Affair of, with letter. N. E. Reg. **11**: 75.
— Mount Pleasant Mansion. Lippinc. **17**: 588.
— Plot of. Portfo.(Den.) **18**: 217.
— Retreat after Battle of Valcour. (W. C. Watson) M. Am. Hist. **6**: 414.
— Sparks's Life of. Am. Mo. M. **5**: 135.
— Treason of. (C. C. Smith) No. Am. **93**: 83. — (B. J. Lossing) Harper, **3**: 451. — Nat. M. **3**: 392.
Arnold, Edwin. Hero and Leander. Belgra. **25**: 534.
— The Light of Asia. (W. C. Brownell) Nation, **29**: 314. — (O. W. Holmes) Internat. R. **7**: 345. — (S. Lane-Poole) Macmil. **41**: 496. — (H. C. Robinson) New Eng. **39**: 198. — (I. N. Tarbox) New Eng. **39**: 709. — Cath. World, **32**: 473. — (F. T. Jones) Canad. Mo. **17**: 584. — (G. T. Flanders) Univ. Q. **37**: 5.
— Poems. (F. F. Browne) Dial (Ch.), **1**: 133. — Blackw. **75**: 303.
Arnold, Matthew. (J. Benton) Appleton, **15**: 341. — (E. C. Stedman) Scrib. **7**: 463. — with portrait, Appleton, **3**: 46. — with portrait, Dub. Univ. **91**: 14. — with portrait, Once a Week, **27**: 320. — with portrait, Ecl. M. **86**: 760. — with portrait, Ev. Sat. **9**: 798. **12**: 351. — Theo. R. **10**: 377. — Tinsley, **3**: 146.
— and the Church of England. (L. Stephen) Fraser, **82**: 414.
— and Clough, A. H. Liv. Age, **137**: 410.
— and the Dissenters. Cong. **2**: 427.
— and D. F. MacCarthy. Dub. Univ. **51**: 331. Same art. Ecl. M. **44**: 59.
— and William Morris. (J. Skelton) Fraser, **79**: 230. — Temp. Bar, **27**: 35. Same art. Ecl. M. **73**: 551.
— and his new Religion. (J. L. Davies) Contemp. **21**: 842. — Cong. **2**: 338.
— and Nonconformists. (R. W. Dale) Contemp. **14**: 540.
— and A. C. Swinburne. (P. Bayne) Contemp. **6**: 337. Same art. Ev. Sat. **4**: 753. Same art. N. Ecl. **1**: 144.
— as a Critic. Westm. **80**: 469.
— as Religious Teacher. (W. Binns) Theo. R. **15**: 88.
— Culture and Anarchy. (W. Kirkus) Fortn. **11**: 371. — No. Brit. **50**: 190. — Lond. Q. **33**: 209. Same art. Theo. Ecl. **6**: 585.
— Essays. (W. C. Brownell) Nation, **29**: 276. — (T. F. Wedmore) Colburn, **133**: 478. — Canad. Mo. **15**: 740. — Internat. R. **6**: 695. — (E. W. Gurney) Nation, **1**: 24.
Arnold, Matthew, Essays on Criticism. (H. T. Tuckerman) Hours at Home, **2**: 5. — Month, **3**: 107. — N. Brit. R. **42**: 158.
— Literature and Dogma. (A. J. Gordon) Bapt. Q. **9**: 412. — (E. E. Hale) O. & N. **8**: 497. — (F. W. Newman) Fraser, **88**: 114. — (J. M. Sturtevant) New Eng. **34**: 92. — Blackw. **113**: 678. Same art. Liv. Age, **118**: 39. Same art. Ecl. M. **81**: 212. — Dub. R. **72**: 357. — Cornh. **24**: 25, 471. Same art. Liv. Age, **110**: 515. — Chr. Obs. **73**: 575. — Penn Mo. **4**: 577. — Luth. Q. **3**: 537. — So. R. n. s. **14**: 245.
— Merope; a Tragedy. Chr. Rem. **55**: 39. — Fraser, **57**: 691. — Nat. R. **6**: 259.
— New Poems. (I. G. Ascher) St. James, **21**: 375. — (A. C. Swinburne) Fortn. **8**: 414. — Victoria, **11**: 375. — Ecl. M. **69**: 631.
— on Bishop Butler. Brit. Q. **66**: 85.
— on Israel. (C. Palfrey) O. & N. **8**: 746.
— Poetry of. (T. Bayne) St. James, **40**: 59. — (H. G. Hewlett) Contemp. **24**: 539. — (W. Le Sueur) Canad. Mo. **1**: 219. — (G. S. Merriam) Scrib. **18**: 281. — (E. S. Nadal) Dark Blue **1**: 711. — (W. Townsend) Canad. Mo. **14**: 335, 546. — (G. E. Woodberry) Nation, **27**: 274. — Blackw. **75**: 303. Same art. Brit. Q. **55**: 313. Same art. Liv. Age, **113**: 482. — Chamb. J. **44**: 682. — Chr. Rem. **27**: 310. — Dub. Univ. **43**: 753. **51**: 331. — Ecl. R. **101**: 276. — Fraser, **49**: 140. — New Q. **3**: 36. — No. Brit. **21**: 493. — Prosp. R. **10**: 99. — Putnam, **6**: 225. — St. James, **29**: 29, 181, 236. — Temp. Bar, **27**: 35, 170. **28**: 33. — Westm. **61**: 146.
— Poet and Essayist. Brit. Q. **42**: 243.
— Poetry of Criticism. (W. D. Adams) Gent. M. n. s. **14**: 467.
— Prophet of Culture. (H. Sidgwick) Macmil. **16**: 271. Same art. Ecl. M. **69**: 490.
— St. Paul and Protestantism. Brit. Q. **52**: 170, 386.
— Speech at Eton. Cornh. **39**: 538.
— Works of. Ed. R. **129**: 486.
Arnold, Stephen, Case of. Hist. M. **18**: 299.
Arnold, Thomas. (G. C. Bibb) Western, **5**: 574. — (F. W. Farrar) Macmil. **37**: 456. Same art. Liv. Age, **137**: 428. — (P. Frank) Ecl. M. **23**: 110. — (Alice King) Argosy, **27**: 346. — (L. Reuben) Nat. Q. **4**: 244. — Peop. J. **11**: 155. — Chamb. J. **3**: 24. — Dub. Univ. **53**: 3. — Ecl. M. **32**: 318. — Ed. R. **76**: 357.
— and Rugby School. (S. Eliot) Am. J. Educ. **28**: 753. — (A. P. Stanley) Macmil. **30**: 279. — No. Brit. **28**: 123.
— and Smyth on Modern History. Fraser, **26**: 631.
— and Socrates, the ancient and modern Teacher. (T. H. Robinson) Luth. Q. **1**: 34.
— as a Teacher. (S. Eliot) Am. J. Educ. **4**: 545.
— Character of. (G. Gilfillan) Hogg, **13**: 349.
— The Christian Life. Theo. & Lit. J. **8**: 525.
— Influence of, on the Church. Bentley, **20**: 190.
— Lectures on Modern History. Fraser, **33**: 596. — Blackw. **53**: 141. — Am. Whig R. **10**: 248. — (W. R. Greg) Ed. R. **76**: 184. Same art. Ecl. Mus. **1**: 435.
— Life of, Stanley's. Chr. Obs. **45**: 152. — (E. Lake) Quar. **74**: 467. — Chr. Rem. **8**: 547. — Ed. R. **81**: 190. — Prosp. R. **1**: 121.
— Life and Writings. (E. Maitland) No. Brit. **2**: 403. — (H. W. Torrey) No. Am. **62**: 165. — Quar. **74**: 467. Same art. Liv. Age, **3**: 224, 353. — (W. R. Greg) Westm. **42**: 363. — (J. M'Clintock) Meth. Q. **6**: 266. — (N. Porter) New Eng. **5**: 364. — (S. F. Smith) Chr. R. **10**: 83. — (J. W. Alexander) Princ. **17**: 283. — Ecl. M. **4**: 145. — (W. R. Greg) Westm. **39**: 1. — Ed. R. **81**: 190. — Am. Ecl. **3**: 161.

Arnold, Thomas, Miscellaneous Works of. Bib. R. 1: 235. — Prosp. R. 1: 416.
— Neander's View of. Bib. R. 2: 39.
— On Church and State. Brit. & For. R. 16: 263.
— Sermons of. (A. Lamson) Chr. Exam. 36: 38. — Select J. 3: [62. — Lond. Q. 51: 109.
— Theological Opinions of. (B. Tappan, jr.) Bib. Sac. 15: 1.
Arnold, Thomas K. (E. D. Mead) Unita. R. 8: 117, 288.
Arnold Family. (E. Hubbard) N. E. Reg. 33: 427, 432.
Arnold; a Poem. (C. Newton) Hogg, 14: 35-455.
Arnold's Creed; a Tale. Galaxy, 1: 730.
Arnot, William, Sketch of. (A. M. Symington) Good Words, 18: 570.
Arnott, Neil. Nature, 9: 364.
— Physics. Mo. R. 121: 86.
Arnould, Sophie. Temp. Bar, 52: 519.
Aroostook, Hermit of. (C. Lanman) Am. Whig R. 6: 263.
Arques, Normandy. Penny M. 8: 453, 481.
Arrah Niel. (G. P. R. James) Dub. Univ. 22: 35-736. 23: 55-681. 24: 52-191.
Arran, Island of. Chamb. J. 12: 253. — (J. L. Cloud) Harper, 62: 506.
— Three Weeks' Loafing in. (C. Simeon) Macmil. 2: 496.
Arrom, C. B. de F. *See* Caballero, F.
Arrow-Heads, Unsymmetric. (S. S. Haldeman) Am. Natural. 13: 292.
Arrow-Headed Inscriptions. (B. J. Wallace) Am. Presb. R. 9: 623.
Arrowsmith, Edmund. Month, 27: 221.
Ars, Le Curé d'. Contemp. 6: 208, 296. — Dub. R. 53: 322.
— Statue of. Cath. World, 8: 200.
Ars in 1877. Month, 30: 319.
— a Pilgrimage to. Cath. World, 1: 24.
Arsenic as an Impurity of metallic Zinc. (C. W. Eliot and F. H. Storer) Am. J. Sci. 82: 380.
— Detection of, in Animal Bodies. (J. L. Smith) Am. J. Sci. 40: 278. 42: 75.
— in Paper-Hangings. Art J. 10: 240. — Ev. Sat. 11: 230.
— Practical Tests of. (T. Cooper) Am. J. Sci. 4: 155. — (D. P. Gardner) Am. J. Sci. 44: 240.
— Separation from Substances. (J. Marsh) J. Frankl. Inst. 22: 338.
Arsenic-Eaters. (F. W. Clarke) Appleton, 7: 158.
— of Austria. Chamb. J. 16: 389.
Arsenic Eating. (F. H. Storer) Am. J. Sci. 80: 209.
— and Poisoning. Chamb. J. 36: 115. Same art. Liv. Age, 71: 31.
Art, Academies of, Haydon on. Mo. R. 150: 414. — Brit. & For. R. 14: 512.
— Ambitious. (G. A. Simcox) Portfo. 3: 24.
— "An artist, sir, should rest in art." (W. Meynell) Art J. 32: 366.
— Ancient. Art J. 11: 267.
— — and Mediæval. Ecl. R. 92: 84.
— — History of. (Grace A. Ellis) O. & N. 5: 633.
— — Plaster-Casting in. (W. W. Story) Internat. R. 7: 508, 642.
— — Sources of. (A. H. Layard) Internat. M. 1: 5.
— — Winckelmann on. (S. G. Brown) No. Am. 71: 99. — Nat. Q. 15: 263. — Am. Arch. 9: 15.
— and Anthropology. Anthrop. R. 5: 28.
— and Antiquarianism. (G. A. Simcox) Portfo. 5: 136.
— and Architecture. Dub. Univ. 33: 151.
— — Notes on. Dial, 4: 107.
— and Artists. (J. H. Ward) Chr. Exam. 67: 208. — Dub. Univ. 70: 92. — (G. I. Cowan) Peop. J. 6: 60.
— — in England, Waagen on. Mo. R. 146: 1.
— and Beauty. (J. H. Pollen) Month, 3: 42, 359. — Brit. Q. 8: 498. — Dem. R. 3: 253.
— and Culture. (R. St. J. Tyrwhitt) Contemp. 13: 362.
Art and Democracy. Cornh. 40: 225.
— and History. Dub. Univ. 62: 210. — Fraser, 56: 498.
— and its Relations. (G. H. Ballou) Univ. Q. 5: 329.
— and its Vehicles. Blackw. 48: 255.
— and Life. (C. C. Shackford) Chr. Exam. 65: 157.
— and Morality. Westm. 91: 148. — Cornh. 32: 91. — (G. A. Simcox) Macmil. 26: 487. Same art. Ecl. M. 79: 718. Same art. Canad. Mo. 2: 466. Same art. Ev. Sat. 13: 483. 14: 386.
— and Nature. (J. E. Cabot) Atlan. 13: 183, 313. — (J. L. Roget) Macmil. 10: 164. — Blackw. 51: 435. — For. Q. 37: 380. — Cornh. 14: 28. — Sharpe, 48: 11, 87.
— and Politics. (T. H. H. Caine) Colburn, 167: 162, 275.
— and Psychology. (J. Sully) Mind, 1: 479.
— and Religion. (C. Cantu) Cath. World, 15: 518. — (E. D. Cheney) Radical, 4: 1. — (W. T. Harris) J. Spec. Philos. 10: 204. — (E. E. Higbee) Mercersb. 21: 341. — (J. S. Lee) Univ. Q. 28: 5. — (H. W. Parker) No. Am. 79: 1. — Nat. R. 4: 30.
— — Influences of Catholicism and Protestantism. (C W. Bennett) Meth. Q. 37: 79.
— and Science, Relations of. Westm. 96: 398. — (G. Holmes) Canad. Mo. 2: 74. — (J. F. Weir) New Eng. 33: 173. — Westm. 96: 398. Same art. Liv. Age, 111: 438. — (P. G. Hamerton) Portfo. 1: 143. — Dub. Univ. 36: 1, 127. — (J. B. Atkinson) F. Arts Q. 1: 125.
— and Society, Chorley's. (W. H. Browne) So. M. 15: 417.
— Apologia of. Cornh. 40: 533.
— Artistic Spirit. (P. G. Hamerton) Fortn. 1: 332.
— as an Aim in Life. Macmil. 23: 417.
— as an Interpreter of History. (H. Coppée) Princ. n. s. 2: 352.
— as a Profession in England. Ev Sat. 10: 474.
— Autographic. (P. G. Hamerton) Portfo. 3: 56.
— Carr's Essays on. (W. J. Stillman) Nation, 28: 437.
— Catholic Church and modern. Cath. World, 5: 546.
— Chemistry in. Ecl. R. 89: 559.
— Christian. (R. St. J. Tyrwhitt) Contemp. 1: 68. 2: 59, 393. 3: 180. 4: 340. 5: 418. 6: 372. 10: 178. — (M. C. Stothart) Cath. World, 30: 220, 530, 768. 31: 316. — Art J. 16: 197. — St. Paul's, 3: 90. Dub. R 22: 486. — Quar. 116: 143. Same art. Ecl. M. 63: 265.
— — and Architecture. Prosp. R. 3: 157.
— — Early. (J. S. Northcote) Month, 32: 273. — (W. H. Withrow) Canad. Mo. 1: 119. — Blackw. 62: 446. — (J. N. Porter) Penn Mo. 12: 774, 801.
— — Garrucci on. Month, 28: 47.
— — History of. Chr. Rem. 16: 261.
— — — Lindsay's. No. Brit. 8: 1. — Quar. 81: 1.
— — Ideal of. Chr. Rem. 1: 284.
— — — Mrs. Jameson on. Dub. R. 55: 402.
— — Influence and Traditions of. Chr. Rem. 20: 175.
— — Museum of. (J. P. Thompson) New Eng. 27: 239.
— — Philosophy of. Dub. R. 1: 435.
— — Poetry of. Blackw. 80: 350.
— — Rio's. Dub. R. 63: 150. 71: 448.
— — Symbolism in. No. Brit. 42: 437. Same art. Ecl. M. 65: 194.
— — Teaching of the Primitive Church. (L. G. Ware) O. & N. 10: 125.
— — Traditions of. (E. L. Cutts) Art J. 27: 120, 169, 297. 28: 53-197. 29: 5, 52.
— — Tyrwhitt on. (L. G. Ware) O. & N. 7: 96.
— Christian Ideal in. Art J. 22: 33.
— Classical. (G. W. F. Hegel) J. Spec. Philos. 12: 145, 277.
— — Study of. (S. Colvin) Fortn. 30: 661.

Art, Classical and Romantic Schools of. (C. C. Everett) No. Am. 84: 379.
— Commercial. Chamb. J. 22: 327.
— Contemporary, Some Aspects of. (M. G. Van Rensselaer) Lippinc. 22: 706.
— Copyright in Works of. Westm. 113: 355.
— Criticism on. *See* Art-Criticism.
— Cultivation or Patronage of. Blackw. 9: 26.
— Curiosities of. Ed. R. 124: 341.
— Decorative. Am. Arch. 5: 4.
— — analytically considered. Art J. 4: 233, 293.
— — and Furniture. Cornh. 9: 337.
— — in the Household. Blackw. 105: 361.
See Decoration; Furniture; Ornament.
— Development in. Nat. Q. 26: 132. — (C. H. Woodman) Nat. Q. 37: 155. 38: 151. 39: 117, 348.
— Diabolic. Art J. 24: 245.
— Dramatic Aspects of. (J. Pollock) Contemp. 23: 363.
— Ethics of. Brit. Q. 10: 441. — (C. Reade) Dub. Univ. 91: 197.
— Exaggeration of. Once a Week, 20: 123.
— Expression in. Internat. M. 4: 401.
— — Anatomy and Philosophy of. Chr. Rem. 8: 130.
— Fact and Truth in. (H. S. Wilson) Mod. R. 1: 324.
— Failure in, Causes of. (G A. Simcox) Portfo. 4: 168.
— Familiar Colloquy on recent. (W. H. Mallock) 19th Cent. 4: 289.
— Gothic, Ruskin on. Lond. Q. 7: 478.
— Greek. Ecl. R. 93: 203.
— — Canon of Beauty in. Ed. R. 140: 168.
— — History of. (E. Everett) No. Am. 12: 178.
— — in the Kimmerian Bosporos. (C. T. Newton) Portfo. 5: 146, 181.
— — in Rome. (R. St. J. Tyrwhitt) Contemp. 30: 981.
— — Inspiration and Ideals of. Westm. 87: 91.
— — Lines in. (H. Van Brunt) Atlan. 7: 654. 8: 76.
— — Plastic. Danv. Q. 1: 479.
— — Remains of. Dub. Univ. 89: 612.
— Hierarchy of. (F. P. Cobbe) Fraser, 71: 97, 334. Same art. Ecl. M. 64. 476, 678.
— Hints to Amateurs. Blackw. 40: 131.
— History of. (C. C. Felton) No. Am. 41: 146.
— — Cleghorn's Ancient and Modern. Blackw. 64: 145.
— — Lübke's. (S. Colvin) Fortn. 10: 697.
— How to observe Works of. Mo. R. 162: 105.
— Imitative, Ideal in. Dub. Univ. 28: 18.
— in America. (S. G. W. Benjamin) Harper, 59: 241–817. — (S. A. Eliot) No. Am. 83: 84. — (H. Greenough) Dem. R. 13: 45. — (H. B. Hall) St. James, 8: 237. — (J. J Jarves) F. Arts Q. 1: 393. — (W. Minot, jr.) No. Am. 52: 301. — (R. Sturgis, jr.) No. Am. 102: 1. — (J. T. Wood) Potter Am. Mo. 14: 100, 273.
— — and Artists. Am. Whig R. 2: 658. — Chr. Exam. 77: 175.
— — and Art-Unions. (R. C. Waterston) Chr. Exam. 48: 205.
— — Chapter of. (G. C. Mason) Galaxy, 22: 789.
— — Museum of, Design for. (T. R. G. Hassard) Scrib. 2: 409.
— — Museums of. (J. J. Jarves) Scrib. 18: 405. — O. & N. 1: 503.
— — Present Tendencies of. (S. G. W. Benjamin) Harper, 58: 481.
— — Progress and Prospects of. (J. F. Weir) Princ. n. s. 1: 815.
— in Belgium. (T. J. Lucas) Portfo. 10: 178.
— in Berlin. Art J. 6: 238.
— — Modern. Fraser, 64: 341.
— in California. (B. P. Avery) Overland, 28: 113.
— — Possibilities of. (J. W. Wilkinson) Overland, 2: 248.

Art in the Charnel-House and Crypt. (L. Jewitt) Art J. 25: 329, 361.
— in China and Japan. (J. Falke) Ecl. Engin. 5: 539.
— in the Community. (J. T. Bunce) Fortn. 28: 340 Same art. Ecl. M. 89: 555.
— in Education. (J. M. Hoppin) New Eng. 25: 601.
— — Importance of. (M. A. Dwight) Am. J. Educ. 2: 409, 587. 4: 191.
— — Phidian. (R. St. J. Tyrwhitt) Contemp. 35: 51.
— in England. (J. B. Payne) Macmil. 20: 156. — Ed. R. 59: 48. — (T. Gautier) Temp. Bar, 5: 320. 6: 258, 420.
— — and Artists. Quar. 62: 131. — (G. F. Waagen) Bentley, 3: 173.
— — and Public Taste. Temp. Bar, 8: 135.
— — Contemporary. (S. G. W. Benjamin) Harper, 54: 161.
— — Dawn of. (J. Aleyne) Canad. Mo. 20: 365.
— — English Character in. Quar. 147: 81.
— — Foreign Criticism of. Art J. 7: 5.
— — French Criticism of. Art J. 7: 5–297. 8: 77.
— — Historical. (F. T. Palgrave) Fraser, 63: 773.
— — in 1871. Lond. Q. 37: 369.
— — in 1875. Lond. Q. 44: 413.
— — in the Gothic Centuries. Brit. Q. 52: 451.
— — in the Provinces. Art J. 10: 189–337. — Dub. R. 78: 374.
— — Modern Sacred. Lond. Q. 18: 51. Same art. Ecl. M. 59: 118.
— — National. Dub. R. 25: 478.
— — Native, and National Advancement. Dub. Univ. 28: 360.
— — Notes on. Lond. M. 20: 18.
— — Parisian Opinion of. Hogg, 14: 370.
— — Prospects of. Blackw. 64: 145.
— — — 1859. Bent. Q. 1: 143. — Colburn, 100: 457.
— — Schools of. Ecl. R. 87: 68.
— — Ugliness of. Temp. Bar, 32: 462.
— — under George III. (S. Colvin) Fortn. 21: 342, 658.
— — Waagen's. Ed. R. 67: 384.
— — Wedmore's Studies in. Portfo. 9: 112.
— — Where are we in? (Lady F. P. Verney) Contemp. 36: 588.
See Art in Great Britain; Art Exhibitions.
— in Europe. (P. G. Hamerton) Internat. R. 3: 283, 426. 4: 134–721. 5: 114.
— — Contemporary. (W J. Hoppin) Atlan. 32: 200, 257.
— in Florence, Designs of the old Masters. (A. C. Swinburne) Fortn. 10: 16.
— in France, Contemporary. (S. G. W. Benjamin) Harper, 54: 481.
— — in 14th Century. Dub. Univ. 74: 243.
— — Modern. (G. B. Brown) 19th Cent. 8: 56. Same art. Appleton, 24: 271.
— — Sympathetic. (M. D. Conway) Harper, 43: 801.
— in Germany. (C. C. Felton) No. Am. 55: 425. 57: 373. — For. Q. 25: 406. 28: 455. — New York R. 10: 448. — Dub. Univ. 30: 50).
— — Contemporary. (J. B. Atkinson) Portfo. 4: 145, 163, 178. — (S. G. W. Benjamin) Harper, 55: 1.
— — Flanders and Holland. Quar. 109: 463.
— — Haakh's History of. Colburn, 134: 97.
— — Modern Schools of. (J. B Atkinson) Portfo. 9: 165.
— — Protestantism of Mediæval. (Mrs. E. E. Ford) New Eng. 33: 533.
— — Revival of. (J. B. Atkinson) Art J. 16: 61.
— in Great Britain, and Art Critics. Temp. Bar, 38: 542.
— — Cultivation and Patronage of. Blackw. 9: 26.
— — Desultory Thoughts on. (C. Redding) Colburn, 122: 70.
— — Galleries of. Colburn, 6: 67–403. 7: 71–568. 8: 67–403. 10: 211–461. — Bentley, 30: 78–344.

Art in Great Britain in 1858. No. Brit. **29**: 103.
— — National Gallery of. Ed. R. **97**: 390. — (R. Redgrave) Am. J. Educ. **22**: 63. — Colburn, **11**: 399.
— — Prospects of, 1850. Art J. **2**: 1. — Brit. Q. **2**: 466.
— in Holland. Liv. Age, **115**: 761. — Ecl. M. **64**: 76.
— in the House. Am. Arch. **5**: 43.
— in the Household. Temp. Bar, **43**: 673.
See Art, Decorative; Furniture.
— in Ireland. Dub. Univ. **52**: 197.
— in Italy. Ed. R. **30**: 524. — Fraser, **52**: 286, 429. — Blackw. **83**: 603.
— — Early. Ed. R. **122**: 74. — Mo. R. **153**: 544.
— — Hemans's ancient Christianity and. Chr. Obs. **74**: 501.
— — in 1840. (C. H. Wilson) Ed. New Philos. J. **30**: 90.
— — Notes on modern. (J. J. Jarves) Fraser, **82**: 626.
— — Records of early. For. Q. **34**: 324.
— — Rise of. Nat. Q. **21**: 1.
— — Schools of. (A. Rye) Canad. Mo. **11**: 486, 683.
— — Taine on. Westm. **85**: 481.
— in Japan. (Sir R. Alcock) Art J. **27**: 101, 201, 333. **28**: 41–141. — Art J. **21**: 182.
— in the Lutheran Church. (W. Strobel) Luth. Q. **9**: 169.
— in Middle Ages. Sharpe, **44**: 19.
— — Relics of. Art J. **4**: 113–305.
— in Munich, Three Phases of. (J. B. Atkinson) Portfo. **1**: 13.
— in the 19th Century, Springer's. (H. J. Warner) Chr. Exam. **76**: 338.
— in Paris, Glimpses of. (H. Bacon and F. H. Allen) Scrib. **21**: 169, 423, 734.
— in Rome. Colburn, **101**: 66.
— in Russia. For. Q. **20**: 328. — (J. B. Atkinson) Portfo. **3**: 87, 105, 124, 130.
— in Scotland, Ireland, and the Provinces. Art J. **11**: 116–243. **13**: 26.
— in Spain. Blackw. **65**: 63.
— — Head and Stirling on. Quar. **83**: 1.
— — National, and English. Dub. R. **25**: 478.
— in United States. *See* Art in America.
— in the Universities. (C. Reade) Belgra. **27**: 32.
— in Washington. Internat. R. **1**: 327.
— Industrial. *See* Industrial Art; Art Manufactures.
— Influence of, in daily Life. (J. B. Atkinson) Good Words, **21**: 356–777. **22**: 571. Same art. Appleton, **24**: 128, 210, 415. **25**: 37.
— — of Character upon. Art J. **21**: 67.
— — of the Greeks on. Westm. **32**: 99.
— Influences of Physical Condition on. Art J. **20**: 172.
— Interpretation in. (H. H. Morgan) Western, **2**: 360. — Chamb. J. **18**: 329.
— Language of. Dub. Univ. **80**: 349. — St. James, **12**: 440. **13**: 71.
— Leslie's Handbook of. (Mrs. E. D. Cheney) No. Am. **83**: 422.
— Literature of. Dub. R. **12**: 38. **13**: 35. — Dub. Univ. **78**: 341.
— — British. Brit. & For. R. **6**: 610.
— — Latest, 1879. (H. Van Brunt) Atlan. **44**: 160.
— — Recent. Chr. Rem. **34**: 267.
— Masters, Old and modern. Irish Q. **4**: 198.
— Materials of, Natural. (P. L. Simmonds) Art J. **26**: 121.
— Mathematics in. (A. P. Peabody) No. Am. **79**: 229.
— Modern. So. Q. **21**: 86.
— — and Greek Beauty. (F. W. Cornish) Fortn. **20**: 326. Same art. Ecl. M. **81**: 612.
— — Free Exhibition of. Peop J. **7**: 208, 223.
— — Prospects and Pioneers of. Dub. Univ. **36**: 544.
— — Teachings of. Am. Church R. **26**: 51.
— Modesty in, Law of. (M. Browne) Contemp. **20**: 584.
— Monstrous in. (S. Kneeland) Pop. Sci. Mo. **14**: 731.
Art, Museums of. (Christopher Dresser) Penn Mo. **8**: 117. — Quar. **150**: 374. — (C. C. Perkins) No. Am. **111**: 1. — (J. J. Jarves) Galaxy, **10**: 50.
— — and Schools. Dub. Univ. **45**: 742.
— — and their Uses. (D. Dorr) Penn Mo. **12**: 561.
— — British National and Provincial. (J. C. Robinson) 19th Cent. **7**: 979. **8**: 249.
— — French. Art J. **5**: 49.
See Art in America, Museum of.
— National, and National Advancement. Dub. Univ. **28**: 360.
— Natural Philosophy of. Art J. **4**: 6, 121.
— Nature in. For. Q. **37**: 380. — Blackw. **51**: 435.
— Nature of. (F. A. Rauch) Mercersb. **12**: 332.
— — and Function of. Putnam, **6**: 267.
— — Eidlitz on. (H. Van Brunt) Nation, **33**: 515.
— Necessity *versus*. (B. Murphy) Cath. World, **17**: 558.
— Notes on. Lakeside, **10**: 77.
— Objects of. Fraser, **81**: 667. Same art. Liv. Age, **105**: 751.
— of the Renaissance, Dualism of. (V. Lee) Contemp. **36**: 44.
— Old and New, Poynter's Lecture on. Once a Week, **28**: 53.
— Origin and Character of. (S. G. Fisher) No. Am. **81**: 212.
— Patronage of. Westm. **13**: 197.
— Philosophy of. (G. W. F. Hegel) J. Spec. Philos. **5**: 368. **6**: 125, 252. **7**: 33. — (G. W. F. Hegel) Western, **5**: 477, 594. — (G. S. Morris) J. Spec. Philos. **10**: 1.
— — Hegel's. (C. Bénard) J. Spec. Philos. **1**: 36–220. **2**: 39, 157. **3**: 281, 317.
— — Hegel's Æsthetics. Brit. & For. R. **13**: 1. Same art. Am. Ecl. **4**: 38.
— — in the Netherlands, Taine on. (J. F. Weir) New Eng. **30**: 45. — Brit. Q. **68**: 1.
— Pictorial, Nomenclature of. (J. B. Pyne) Art J. **7**: 6, 86, 197. **8**: 97, 325.
— Plea for. So. Lit. Mess. **15**: 624.
— Poynter's Lectures on. (H. Quilter) Fraser, **102**: 199. Same art. Ecl. M. **95**: 578. — (P. G. Hamerton) Internat. R. **8**: 619. **9**: 50.
— Practical View of. (J. M. Tracy) Western, **4**: 404.
— Present Conditions of, 1880. (G. F. Watts) 19th Cent. **7**: 235. Same art. Liv. Age, **144**: 670.
— Principles of. (Mrs. M. W. Cook) Contin. Mo. **3**: 562, 698. **4**: 20–567. **5**: 14. — (J. M. Hoppin) New Eng. **24**: 674. — So. Q. **27**: 398.
— — Elementary. Macmil. **16**: 1.
— — True, Fergusson on. Ecl. R. **89**: 420.
— Prospects and Aspirations of. Ecl. R. **101**: 129.
— Progress of. Westm. **41**: 71. — Ecl. M. **2**: 497.
— Psychology in. (H. A. Page) Contemp. **12**: 437.
— Question concerning. (C. E. Prichard) Macmil. **13**: 443.
— Revival of. Once a Week, **28**: 278.
— Romantic. (G. W. F. Hegel) J. Spec. Philos. **12**: 403. **13**: 113.
— Rome as a School of. Lond. M. **1**: 42.
— Ruskin's Lectures on. (S. A. Brooke) Macmil. **22**: 423. Same art. Ecl. M. **75**: 680. Same art. Liv. Age, **107**: 451.
— Ruskin's New Lectures on, 1870. New Eng. **29**: 659.
— Sacred and Legendary. *See* Jameson, Mrs.
— Science and Poetry of. Lond. Q. **4**: 403.
— Sentiment in. (G. A. Simcox) Portfo. **1**: 110.
— Shop-Side of. All the Year, **10**: 374.
— Spiritualism in. (B. Murphy) Penn Mo. **11**: 453.
— State, Influence and Prospects of. Dub. Univ. **23**: 215.
— Supernatural in. (V. Lee) Cornh. **42**: 212.
— Symbolic. (G. W. F. Hegel) J. Spec. Philos. **11**: 337. **12**: 18.

Art, Talk about. (J. F. Bowman) Overland, **9**: 169. — (W. H. Winslow) O. & N. **8**: 240.
— Talkers and Doers in. All the Year, **23**: 271.
— Taste in. (F. T. Palgrave) Cornh. **18**: 170.
— — of Collectors and Artists' Palettes. St. James, **32**: 217.
— Thoughts on. Dial, **1**: 367. — Dub. Univ. **61**: 315.
— Treasures of, Exhibition at Manchester, Eng. Lond. Q. **9**: 78.
— — in Great Britain. Art J. **6**: 193.
— — — Waagen's. Quar. **94**: 467. — Westm. **62**: 304. — New Q. **3**: 370.
— — National, Housing of. (P. G. Hamerton) Fortn. **2**: 90.
— Tricks in the Art Traffic. Chamb. J. **3**: 389.
— Truth in. Temp. Bar, **8**: 358.
— Type of the Renaissance. (E. M. Clerke) Fraser, **101**: 58.
— Tyranny of. All the Year, **20**: 438.
— Undefinable in. Cornh. **38**: 559. Same art. Liv. Age, **139**: 760.
— Whistler's Theories and his Art. (F. Wedmore) 19th Cent. **6**: 334.
— Works of. Brit. & For. R. **9**: 1.
See also Fine Arts; Painting; etc.
Art Amusements for Ladies. (G. Dodd) St. James, **12**: 197.
Art China ceramically considered. (W. de B. Fryer) Penn Mo. **11**: 941.
Art Clubs. (L. Greg) Good Words, **17**: 454.
See Art-Unions.
Art Collections. *See* Art, Museums of.
Art Criticism. (S. Colvin) Fortn. **32**: 210. Same art. Appleton, **22**: 320. — (C. P. Cranch) Galaxy, **4**: 77. — (E. Dowden) Dark Blue, **1**: 475. — (F. Leifchild) F. Arts Q. **5**: 162, 335. — (H. H. Morgan) Western, **1**: 1. — (R. St. J. Tyrwhitt) Contemp. **11**: 101. — Irish Q. **3**: 1.
— and Art Philosophy. Lond. Q. **31**: 116.
— and Art Sales in England, in the 18th Century. Temp. Bar, **42**: 199.
— Limits of. (R. St. J. Tyrwhitt) 19th Cent. **4**: 512.
— Professional and Lay. Temp. Bar, **28**: 170.
— Samson's. (E. P. Evans) No. Am. **104**: 603.
— What is? (R. Sturgis) Nation, **2**: 504.
— What it should be. Cornh. **8**: 334.
Art Education. (M. A. Dwight) Am. J. Educ. **5**: 305. — (L. R. O'Brien) Canad. Mo. **15**: 584. — (C. Reade) Belgra. **29**: 174. — (W. R. Ware) No. Am. **116**: 189. Am. J. Educ. **22**: 93. — Chr. R. **25**: 618.
— for Mechanics. Republic, **4**: 37.
— for the People. (H. Cole and Redgrave) Art J. **5**: 15. — (G. Wallis) Peop. J. **3**: 9–230.
— in America. (C. C. Perkins) Am. Soc. Sci. J. **3**: 37.
— in Boston. (G. P. Lathrop) Harper, **58**: 818.
— in Public Schools. (C. G. Leland) Penn Mo. **11**: 868.
— Industrial, in the United States. (E. S. Drone) Internat. R. **2**: 636.
— Influence on daily Life. Good Words, **22**: 571.
— Is a great School of Art possible? (E. I. Barrington) 19th Cent. **5**: 714.
— National. (M. J. Dyer) Nat. Q. **34**: 341.
— Old and new System of. Art J. **32**: 373.
— Popular. (J. F. Weir) No. Am. **132**: 64.
— Schools for. (C. Dresser) Penn Mo. **8**: 215. — (C. C. Perkins) Am. Soc. Sci. J. **4**: 95. — J. Frankl. Inst. **23**: 206.
— — French and Belgian. (R. Sturgis) Nation, **2**: 121, 152. — Blackw. **50**: 689.
— — in Belgium and Dusseldorf. (J. Sparks) Ecl. Engin. **17**: 538.
Art Schools in England, Early. (D. Cook) Once a Week, **14**: 134.
— — in London. (P. D. Natt) Lippinc. **25**: 629.
— — in Paris. (P. D. Natt) Lippinc. **27**: 269.
— — of New York. (W. C. Brownell) Scrib. **16**: 761.
— — of Philadelphia. (W. C. Brownell) Scrib. **18**: 737.
— Schools of Design. Westm. **27**: 116*. — Blackw. **49**: 583. — Ed. R. **85**: 452. **90**: 473.
— Training-School at South Kensington. Am. J. Educ. **22**: 111.
Art Exhibition at Manchester, 1857. Dub. Univ. **49**: 608.
— at Westminster Hall, 1844. Colburn, **71**: 549.
— Boston, of Contemporary Art, 1878. Am. Arch. **5**: 103–159.
— by Female Artists. Dub. Univ. **53**: 455.
— of Ireland, 1852. Dub. Univ. **40**: 470.
— — 1859. Dub. Univ. **53**: 539.
— Royal Academy, 1862. (W. M. Rossetti) Fraser, **66**: 65.
— — 1864. (W. M. Rossetti) Fraser, **70**: 57.
Art Exhibitions of 1859. Bent. Q. **1**: 582. — Dub. Univ. **53**: 148. **54**: 94, 208, 239.
— of 1860. Dub. Univ. **55**: 477. **56**: 89.
— Strictures on. Fraser, **2**: 93.
See names of places where International Exhibitions have been held, as London, Paris, Vienna, etc.
Art Experience of an Ignoramus. (S. B. Wister) Lippinc. **15**: 712.
Art Hints, Jarves's. (J. Neal) No. Am. **81**: 436.
Art Industries. (G. J. Cayley) Fraser, **66**: 489. — (C. Dresser) Penn Mo. **8**: 12. — (A. H. Markley) Potter Am. Mo. **10**: 45.
— From old Masters. Art J. **22**: 18–349.
Art Knowledge, Wisdom of. Art J. **25**: 77.
Art Manufacture. J. Frankl. Inst. **56**: 274, 333. — Putnam, **2**: 402.
— at the Centennial. (C. W. Elliott) Galaxy, **22**: 489.
— Designs for. Art J. **32**: 5–369.
— in the French Exhibition, 1855. Hogg, **14**: 231.
— in Great Britain, Progress of. Art J. **8**: 132, 184.
— in the Classical Epochs. (E. Braun) Art J. **2**: 4, 69, 144.
— Mediæval. Art. J. **4**: 25–336. **5**: 20, 286, 306. **6**: 12–358. **7**: 28. **8**: 56.
Art Museums. *See* Art, Museums of.
Art Needlework. (M. Alford) Appleton, **25**: 421. — (G. F. Watts) Appleton, **25**: 426.
Art Philosophers, Two. (P. G. Hamerton) Fortn. **5**: 343.
Art Protestantism. (R. St. J. Tyrwhitt) Dark Blue, **1**: 755.
Art Purchases, Recent, 1869. All the Year, **22**: 297.
Art Union, American. Knick. **32**: 442. — Hunt, **16**: 593.
Art Union Critics, Hints to. Am. Whig R. **4**: 599.
Art Unions. Westm. **41**: 515. — (R. C. Waterston) Chr. Exam. **48**: 205. — Internat. M. **2**: 191. — Irish Q. **3**: 990. — No. Brit. **26**: 505. — Dub. Univ. **55**: 364.
— Apology for. Fraser, **30**: 471.
Art Work in Syria and Palestine. (M. E. Rogers) Art J. **26**: 49–369.
Art Workmanship in the Middle Ages. Art J. **3**: 28.
Art, L', and Art Journalism. Portfo. **6**: 137.
Art; a Dramatic Tale. (C. Reade) Bentley, **34**: 633. **35**: 68. — Liv. Age, **40**: 363.
Art of Living. (E. L. Godkin) Nation, **5**: 249.
Art of putting Things. (A. K. H. Boyd) Liv. Age, **67**: 596.
Art Study at Imperial School in Paris; a Story. (E. Shinn) Nation, **8**: 292, 492. **9**: 67.
Artaphernes the Platonist. (Mrs. E. L. Bulwer) Fraser, **17**: 513.
Artemus Ward. *See* Browne, C. F.
Artesian Springs, Temperature of. (R. Paterson) J Frankl. Inst. **29**: 274.

Artesian Well at Grenelle, Paris. Penny M. **10:** 441.
— at Louisville, Ky. (J. L. Smith) Am. J. Sci. **77:** 174.
Artesian Wells. (C. T. Hinckley) Godey, **47:** 295, 389. — (W. Buckland) Ed. New Philos. J. **37:** 318. — (Sir D. Milne) J. Frankl. Inst. **37:** 126. **13:** 213. **27:** 425. — (M. Michal) J. Frankl. Inst. **75:** 411 — Penny M. **4:** 131. — Am. Q. **22:** 330. — Liv. Age, **3:** 68.
— in London. Liv. Age, **10:** 153. — Chamb. J. **21:** 258. Same art. Liv. Age, **41:** 598.
— in the Great Sahara. (S. Schroeder) Pop. Sci. Mo. **16:** 530. — J. Frankl. Inst. **65:** 210.
— Report on Machine for boring. J. Frankl. Inst. **54:** 425.
— New Method of boring for, 1846. J. Frankl. Inst. **42:** 369.
— of Grenoble. J. Frankl. Inst. **33:** 331.
— of Lafayette, Ind. (C. M. Wetherill) Am. J. Sci. **77:** 241.
— Origin of. (F. Arago) Ed. New Philos. J. **18:** 205.
Artevelde, Jacob van. (De Vericour) Dub. Univ. **54:** 579. — Ed. R. **153:** 63. Same art. Liv. Age, **148:** 451.
Artevelde, Philip van. (Miss McFarlane) Hours at Home, **2:** 184. — Bost. R. **3:** 597.
See Arlincourt, V. d'; Taylor, Henry.
Arthur, King. Colburn, **85:** 307.
— and his Times. Chamb. J. **46:** 550.
— Dramatic Opera of, Dryden's. Fraser, **45:** 196.
— In King Arthur's Land. (D. M. Craik) Ev. Sat. **3:** 225.
— Knighting of. (S. Evans) Ev. Sat. **8:** 254.
— Legends of. Univ. Q. **17:** 329.
— — English Versions of. Dub. Univ. **80:** 481, 683.
— — Literature of. (L. G. Ware) Chr. Exam. **67:** 391.
— — Some old. Dub. Univ. **76:** 616.
— — Sources of, Celtic. Dub. Univ. **65:** 292.
— Morte d'. Dub. Univ. **55:** 497.
— of History and Romance. (R. W. Boodle) Canad. Mo. **18:** 582.
— Romances of. (H. W. Preston) Atlan. **38:** 129. — (T. Wright) Arch. **32:** 335.
— — Origin of. Dub. Univ. **78:** 121.
— Round Table of. Blackw. **88:** 311. — (H. R. Hamilton) Antiquary, **4:** 270, 282, 295. — (J. J. Reed) Nat. Q. **19:** 330. — Ecl. R. **110:** 399.
— Scotland of. (J. S. S. Glennie) Macmil. **17:** 161.
Arthurian Romance and Mr. Tennyson. Brit. Q. **51:** 200. *See* Tennyson, A.
Arthur, Prince, Romances of. (A. J. Curtis) Hours at Home, **9:** 64, 205.
Arthurs, The, of Britain. Sharpe, **12:** 65.
Arthur, Prince of Wales, Portraits of. (G. Scharf) Arch. **39:** 457.
Arthur, Prince, 1870. with portrait. Ev. Sat. **9:** 386.
Arthur; a Dramatic Fable. (T. Aird) Blackw. **38:** 84.
Arthur de Boisfleury, a Chronicle of 1407. Fraser, **38:** 261.
Arthur, Archibald. Discourses. Ed. R. **4:** 168.
Arthur Arden, the Medical Student. Bentley, **35:** 24–572. **36:** 59, 353.
Arthur Bonnicastle. (J. G. Holland) Scrib. **5:** 32–688. **6:** 32–704.
Arthur O'Leary. (C. Lever) Dub. Univ. **21:** 1–521. **22:** 1–635.
Artichoke, Jerusalem. (J. H. Trumbull and A. Gray) Am. J. Sci. **113:** 347.
Articles, Thirty-Nine. *See* Thirty-Nine.
Articulata, Aquatic, Plateau's Researches on. Nature, **7:** 469.
Articulate Sounds, Natural Significancy of. (J. W. Gibbs) Am. Bib. Repos. 2d s. **2:** 166.
Articulate Vibrations, Recording, by Photography. (E. W. Blake, jr.) Am. J. Sci. **116:** 54. Same art. abridged, Nature, **18:** 338.
Artifice, Naturalness of. Once a Week, **20:** 325.
Artificer-Soldiers. Chamb. J. **23:** 390. **28:** 46.
Artificial Flower Makers. Victoria, **6:** 106.
Artificial Flower Trade of London and Paris. Ev. Sat. **14:** 315.
Artificial Flowers, Making. (W. H. Rideing) Appleton, **20:** 97. — (C. T. Hinckley) Godey, **48:** 295.
— Trade in. Pract. M. **1:** 262.
Artificial Limbs. Once a Week, **19:** 226.
— Human Wheel. (O. W. Holmes) Atlan. **11:** 567. *See* Wooden Legs.
Artificial Stone. Appleton, **2:** 204.
— Manufacture and Application to Construction. (F. Ransome) Pract. M. **3:** 130.
Artigas, the Rob Roy of La Plata. Tait, n. s. **7:** 302.
Artillery. Quar. **90:** 445.
— Ancient. Ev. Sat. **11:** 80.
— — and modern. Harper, **10:** 458.
— and Fire-arms. Dub. Univ. **39:** 447.
— and Ships of War. Ed. R. **96:** 452.
— English Railway. (W. B. Adams) Once a Week, **1:** 127.
— Experiments with, at Shoeburyness. Temp. Bar, **18:** 522.
— Facts about. (W. F. Barry) U. S. Serv. M. **1:** 12.
— Field. Ecl. Engin. **6:** 169, 604.
— Heavy. Ecl. Engin. **12:** 511.
— — Construction of. (L. Thomas) Ecl. Engin. **2:** 14, 312, 369. — Nature, **3:** 69, 128.
— — Progress of. (F. Lean) Fortn. **32:** 57.
— History of. Irish Q. **9:** 764.
— Mârine. Colburn, **118:** 491.
— Material of, Recent Changes in. (S. P. Oliver) Ecl. Engin. **8:** 142.
— Modern, and Gunpowder. Fraser, **82:** 218. Same art. Ecl. M. **75:** 489.
— — and Tactics. Ecl. Engin. **1:** 970.
— Modern Field-Guns. Belgra. **15:** 378.
— Modern Improvements in. (E. Simpson) Ecl. Engin. **11:** 79.
— past, present, and future. Dub. Univ. **57:** 215.
— Prospects of, 1862. Dub. Univ. **59:** 213. Same art. Ecl. M. **56:** 173.
— System of working. (Capt. Moncrieff) Ecl. Engin. **1:** 870.
Artisan in Europe. Chamb. J. **47:** 433, 454, 474.
— in the United States. Chamb. J. **47:** 584.
Artisan's Saturday Night. (P. Greg) Macmil. **2:** 285.
Artisan's Story: a Poem. (W. Buchanan) Good Words, **2:** 208.
Artisans and Apprentices on the Continent. Penny M. **12:** 62.
— and Machinery. Quar. **31:** 391.
— — Gaskell on, 1836. Mo. R. **139:** 449.
— Education of. Brit. & For. R. **6:** 76.
— Intellectual Tastes in. Penny M. **6:** 483.
Artist and Craftsman; a Tale. Dub. Univ. **54:** 3–695. **55:** 35, 172, 297.
— and Critic. Fraser, **92:** 255.
— and his Purpose. (C. Cobb) Western, **5:** 445.
— The Blind. Dem. R. **21:** 538.
— in Love. St. James, **17:** 245.
— Inspiration of. Dub. Univ. **25:** 538.
— Journal of. Am. Whig R. **10:** 176.
— Merchant, and Statesman, Lester's. Hunt, **14:** 235.
— of the Beautiful. (N. Hawthorne) Dem. R. **14:** 605.
— the Seer and Minister of Beauty. (W. M. Reily) Ref. Q. **28:** 378.
— The Tramping. Dub. Univ. **50:** 667.
— The Young. (J. A. Ingraham) Godey, **20:** 81, 113.
Artist Life, Cervaro of 1871. Lippinc. **8:** 147.
— in the 15th Century. Cornh. **33:** 327.
— in New York. (W. H. Bishop) Scrib. **19:** 355.

Artist Life in Paris, 1848. Dub. Univ. **36**: 137.
— in Rome. Dub. Univ. **52**: 233, 342, 480.
— Romance of. (G. L. Austin) Penn Mo. **5**: 756.
— Scenes of. (F. Gérard) Art J. **3**: 93, 175, 313. **4**: 15–251.
Artist's Despair, The. Fraser, **29**: 212.
Artist's Dream of Death; a Poem. (E. Arnold) Once a Week, **17**: 427.
Artist's Festa. Rome. Art. J. **6**: 271.
Artist's Love, An. (F. Asheton) Lippinc. **16**: 94, 230.
Artist's Married Life. (L. Schefer) Dub. Univ. **31**: 757.
Artist's Model, An. (A. W. Baldwin) Belgra. **14**: 176.
Artist's Ramble from Antwerp to Rome. Art J. **5**: 22–316.
Artist's Story. (P. G. Hamerton) Ev. Sat. **10**: 95. — Colburn, **160**: 23.
Artist's Tragedy. (T. A. Trollope) Ev. Sat. **9**: 422.
Artists, Amateur, Life among some. (M. B. Wright) Scrib. **16**: 121.
— American, with portrait of West. Am. Whig R. **3**: 517.
— — in Rome. (A. Brewster) Lippinc. **3**: 196.
— — Living. (D. O'C. Townley) Scrib. **2**: 40, 401. **3**: 599.
— Anachronisms of. Chamb. J. **47**: 602.
— and Actors, Salaries of. Ecl. M. **22**: 274.
— and Angels. (S. Webber) New Eng. M. **8**: 352.
— and Artisans. (R. St. J. Tyrwhitt) Contemp. **29**: 1043.
— and their Models. (W. Thornbury) Art J. **18**: 77, 229.
— Anecdotes of. Chamb. J. **56**: 321.
— British, Cunningham's Lives of. Ed. R. **59**: 48.
— — their Style and Character. (J. Constable) Art J. **7**: 9–293. **8**: 333. **9**: 5–337. **10**: 9–329. **11**: 13–325. **12**: 41–357. **13**: 9–325. **14**: 9–201.
— Copyright for. (W. H. Hunt) 19th Cent. **5**: 418. — (F. Leighton and H. T. Wells) 19th Cent. **6**: 968. — Westm. **113**: 355.
— The Devil among. Blackw. **11**: 591.
— Education of. New Q. **10**: 343.
— English, Tombs of. Art J. **10**: 44–322. **11**: 16–272. **12**: 44.
— Gould's Dictionary of. Westm. **23**: 103.
— Health of. (H. Martineau) Once a Week, **3**: 370.
— Marks of. Art J. **8**: 1.
— New York, 1856. Knick. **48**: 26.
— of Scotland, Living. Blackw. **2**: 313.
— of Spain, Annals of, Stirling's. Blackw. **65**: 63. — Fraser, **38**: 300. — Quar. **83**: 1.
— — Modern. Art J. **31**: 123.
— Old Age of. Colburn, **6**: 210.
— Personal Recollections of great. (E. V. Rippingille) Art J. **11**: 109–332.
— Physical Science for. (J. N. Lockyer) Nature, **18**: 29–223.
— Rising. (F. Wedmore) Gent. M. n. s. **27**: 91.
— Sillig's Dictionary of Ancient. For. Q. **22**: 72.
— Studios of. (E. J. Tarver) Art J. **32**: 249. **33**: 109.
— Thoughts of. (W. W. Lloyd) Portfo. **1**: 45, 93.
— Tuckerman's Book of. So. R. n. s. **4**: 149.
— Turning-Points in the Lives of great. Art J. **13**: 39.
— Women. Nat. Q. **22**: 1. — So. R. n. s. **5**: 299. — Westm. **70**: 163. Same art. Liv. Age, **58**: 803.
— — Ellet's. Liv. Age, **64**: 245.
— Young, in New York. (W. H. Bishop) Scrib. **19**: 355.
Artists; a Poem. (E. T. Lander) Lakeside, **8**: 120.
Artists in Love and Poison. (W. Stigand) Belgra. **7**: 104.
Arts. Blackw. **40**: 131. — Anal. M. **6**: 363.
— and Artisans at Home and Abroad, 1840. (J. C. Symons) J. Frankl. Inst. **29**: 306, 361. **30**: 1, 73, 145. — Mo. R. **149**: 279.
— and Manufactures. Brit. & For. R. **6**: 76.
— — Aikin's Illustrations of, 1841. Mo. R. **156**: 338.
— — Prince Albert's Industrial College of. No. Brit. **17**: 520.
Arts and Sciences, Vanity and Uncertainty of, Amory's. Retros. **14**: 181.
— Application of Science to. Chr. Exam. **7**: 187.
— as Tidemarks of History. Liv. Age, **128**: 131.
— before the Flood. Hogg, **10**: 29. Same art. Liv. Age, **39**: 50.
— Decline of. (J. Q. Day) Chr. Exam. **29**: 312.
— Dictionary of, Ure's. Nature, **12**: 182.
— Fine. *See* Fine Arts.
— in England. Anal. M. **4**: 489.
— in Portugal. Blackw. **69**: 338.
— of Design, Dunlap's History of. Mo. R. **138**: 88.
— of the Middle Ages. Ecl. R. **103**: 484.
— Royal Academy of. Fraser, **31**: 583.
— School of. (W. Johnson) Am. Inst. of Instruc. **1835**: 271.
See Technical Education.
— Self-Decorative. All the Year, **20**: 182.
— Useful, Origin and Prospects of. (W. B. O. Peabody) No. Am. **33**: 81.
— — Progress and Influence of. Am. Whig R. **5**: 87.
— wherein Ancients excel Moderns. Ox. Prize Ess. **2**: 253.
— wherein Moderns excel Ancients. Ox. Prize Ess. **1**: 207.
Arundel, Lady Alathea. Lond. Soc. **20**: 363.
Arundel, Henry de, Legend of; a Poem. St. James, **28**: 608.
Arundel Castle. Dub. R. **82**: 111.
— Ramble round. (A. Meynell) Good Words, **22**: 528.
Arundel Marbles. (S. Weston) Arch. **14**: 33.
Arundel Society. Blackw. **88**: 458.
Arundines Cami. (J. W. Croker) Quar. **69**: 440. — (F. W. Shelton) Knick. **38**: 95. — Dub. R. **14**: 121.
Arvine's Cyclopædia of Anecdotes. Chr. R. **17**: 333.
Aryan Ancestor. (K. Cook) Dub. Univ. **92**: 1, 177.
Aryan and the Semite. (J. W. Jackson) Anthrop. R. **7**: 333.
Aryan and Semitic Languages. (J. F. McCurdy) Bib. Sac. **33**: 78, 352. **36**: 672. **37**: 528, 752. **38**: 116.
Aryan Faith. (F. R. Conder) Theo. R. **13**: 104.
Aryan Language and Literature. (T. A. Becker) Am. Cath. Q. **3**: 73.
— What we learn from Aryan Words. (J. Fiske) Atlan. **47**: 478.
Aryan Nomades. (H. H. Howorth) Anthrop. J. **6**: 41.
Aryan Race. Anthrop. R. **1**: 232. — (M. C. Ladreyt) Radical, **9**: 285.
— Subdivisions of. (J. H. Wright) New Eng. **40**: 470.
Aryan Races of Peru. (A. Lang) Macmil. **27**: 424. Same art. Ecl. M. **80**: 624.
Aryan Society, Early. (H. W. Lucas) Month, **31**: 406.
— and Civilization. Westm. R. **112**: 62.
Aryans, Myths of. Lond. Q. **35**: 77.
— Who are? (J. Fiske) Atlan. **47**: 224.
As good as engaged; a Story. Lakeside, **6**: 19.
As he comes up the Stair; a Tale. (H. Mathers) Gent. M. n. s. **17**: 257, 386.
As long as she lived; a Tale. (F. W. Robinson) Canad. Mo. **9**: 286, 362, 457. **10**: 1, 93, 185, 328, 418, 538. **11**: 47, 196, 304.
As surly as a Bear. St. James, **23**: 349.
Asathor's Vengeance. (H. H. Boyesen) Atlan. **35**: 345.
Asay, E. G., of Chicago, Library of. (D. Gray) Am. Bibliop. **6**: 165. **7**: 56.
Asbestos Cloth, Fire-Proof. Penny M. **8**: 411.
Asbestos Industry, American. Pract. M. **5**: 262.
Asbury, Francis, the Pioneer Bishop. (E. E. Hale) Chr. Exam. **66**: 382. — Meth. Q. **14**: 407. — Am. Meth. M. **13**: 82. — Harper, **33**: 210. — Knick. **53**: 75.
Asbury College, Baltimore. Am. Meth. M. **1**: 109.
Ascension, The. Chr. Obs. **38**: 337, 357.

Ascension Island. *See* Ponape.
Asceticism. (J. G. Fichte) Western, **3**: 469, 528. — (P. Schaff) Mercersb. **10**: 600. — Cong. M. **23**: 510.
— and Modern Life. (T. Meyrick) Month, **12**: 308.
— Cultus Ventris. (W. C. Conant) New Eng. **30**: 616.
— Early Female. Liv. Age, **41**: 135.
— Practice of. Cong. **1**: 107.
— Principles of. Cong. **1**: 269.
See Monasticism.
Ascetics, Early Christian, Literature and Philosophy of. Fraser, **64**: 283. Same art. Ecl. M. **54**: 347.
Ascham, Roger. Am. J. Educ. **3**: 23. — (J. Baldwin) Western, **7**: 428.
— The Schoolmaster. Am. J. Educ. **4**: 155.
— Toxophilus. Retros. R. **4**: 76.
Ascidians, Hypophysal Gland in. Nature, **24**: 68.
Ascot Races. Lond. Soc. **2**: 97. **4**: 156, 270. — All the Year, **38**: 377.
Asgill, John; and the Cowardliness of Dying. (K. Cook) Fraser, **84**: 150.
Asgrimsson, Eystein. Lilja. (M. Blind) Dark Blue, **1**: 524.
Ash-Tree, The. Penny M. **11**: 484.
— Folk-Lore of. (H. C. Appleby) Victoria, **36**: 400.
— Symbolism of. (C. G. Leland) Contin. Mo. **2**: 682.
— Uses of. Penny M. **12**: 470.
Ashango Land, Du Chaillu's Journey. (W. Forsyth) Quar. **122**: 406. — Chamb. J. **44**: 361. — St. James, **18**: 473.
Ashantee. Blackw. **115**: 518.
Ashantee Country. Belgra. **22**: 60. — Ed. R. **41**: 336.
— and the Ashantees. (G. M. Towle) Harper, **48**: 286. — Cornh. **28**: 679.
— and the Gold Coast, Beecham on. Ecl. R. **74**: 18.
— Bowdich's Mission to. Blackw. **5**: 175, 302. — Quar. **22**: 273. — (Syd. Smith) Ed. R. **32**: 389. — Mo. R. **90**: 286, 363. — Ecl. R. **33**: 231. — Portfo.(Den.) **22**: 216.
— Dupuis's Journal of a Residence in. Colburn, **11**: 378.
— Former Wars. All the Year, **30**: 565. **31**: 13, 31.
— Future of. (G. A. Henty) Geog. M. **1**: 148.
— King of, Visit to. Peop. J. **8**: 23, 36.
— Native Gentleman of. All the Year, **37**: 280.
— Resurrection of. (F. Boyle) Gent. M. n. s. **21**: 605.
— Superstitions. All the Year, **31**: 64.
— War with, 1824–26. Mo. R. **126**: 192.
— — 1873. Canad. Mo. **6**: 309. — Blackw. **116**: 96.
— — unnecessary and unjust. (T. G. Bowles) Fraser, **89**: 124, 268.
Ashburn Rectory. (H. Parr) Liv. Age, **57**: 105.
Ashburnham, Mass., Churches and Ministers of. Am. Q. Reg. **10**: 51.
— Settlement of. N. E. Reg. **16**: 148.
Ashburton, Harriet, Lady. (Lord Houghton) Canad. Mo. **4**: 160.
Ashburton Treaty. (J. Sparks) No. Am. **56**: 452. — Quar. **71**: 306. — Fraser, **26**: 579. **27**: 272. — (C. Buller) Westm. **39**: 160. Same art. Ecl. Mus. **1**: 152. — Westm. **40**: 182.
Ashby, Turner, Avirett's Memoirs of. Land We Love, **5**: 287.
Ashby, Mass., Churches and Ministers of. Am. Q. Reg. **11**: 397.
— Materials for the History of. (F. Kidder) N. E. Reg. **6**: 262.
Ashen Faggot, The. (P. Browne) Dark Blue, **4**: 559.
Ashes, Pot and Pearl. (E. Meriam) Hunt, **13**: 553.
— Wood, Combustibility of. (J. T. Plummer) Am. J. Sci. **42**: 165.
— — Dangerous Properties of. (J. T. Plummer) Am. J. Sci. **43**: 80.
Ashes of Roses. (L. W. Champney) Harper, **33**: 369.
Ashley, Anthony, First Earl of Shaftesbury. *See* Shaftesbury, First Earl of.
Ashley Family Genealogy. (E. Davis) N. E. Reg. **2**: 394.
Ashley Down Orphanages and G. Müller. Liv. Age, **87**: 97.
Ashmolian Meetings. Sharpe, **52**: 257.
Ashmun, Jehudi, Life of. For. Q. **26**: 388. — (B. B. Thatcher) No. Am. **41**: 265. — Chr. Q. Spec. **7**: 330.
— Funeral of. Chr. Mo. Spec. **10**: 535.
Ashmun, John H. Story's Funeral Discourse. Am. Mo. R. **3**: 501.
Ashridge Park. Cornh. **4**: 348.
Ashtabula Bridge Disaster. J. Frankl. Inst. **104**: 135.
Ashton, Peyton, on the Reformation. So. Lit. Mess. **13**: 237.
Ashwell, Johan, Letters of. Retros. **16**: 96.
Asia and the Church. (R. S. Maclay) Meth. Q. **13**: 44.
— Badakshan and Wakhan. Colburn, **152**: 301.
— Buchanan's Christian Researches in. Ecl. R. **13**: 569. **14**: 726.
— Central. (S. Merrill) New Eng. **34**: 1. — Mus. **25**: 114. — For. Q. **14**: 58. — Blackw. **81**: 612. — Quar. **120**: 461. **134**: 516. Same art. Liv. Age, **117**: 771. — Liv. Age, **126**: 707.
— — Ancient Silk-Traders' Route across. Sup. Pop. Sci. Mo. **2**: 377.
— — Atkinson's Travels in. Colburn, **112**: 85.
— — British Ambassadors in, Sacrifice of. For. Q. **34**: 221.
— — British Masterly Inactivity in. (J. W. S. Wyllie) Fortn. **12**: 585.
— — British Mischievous Activity in. (J. W. S. Wyllie) Fortn. **13**: 278.
— — British Policy in. (H. Ottley) Fraser, **88**: 615.
— — Chinese in. Quar. **149**: 463.
— — England and Russia in. (M. E. Grant-Duff) Fortn. **24**: 600. — (E. L. Godkin) Nation, **16**: 109. — Ed. R. **151**: 68. — Macmil. **32**: 54. — Colburn, **138**: 253. — Westm. **115**: 412. — (J. Loewenberg) Victoria, **33**: 340.
— — Ferrier's Travels in, 1845. New Q. **6**: 85.
— — Humboldt's Researches in. (Sir D. Brewster) No. Brit. **5**: 454.
— — Meeting-Place of Empires. Blackw. **128**: 205. — Same art. Liv. Age, **147**: 23. Same art. Ecl. M **95**: 461.
— — Military Sketch of. (J. Adye) Macmil. **27**: 428.
— — Pass of Alexander from, to India. Colburn, **153**: 317.
— — Peshawar, a new Gate to British Commerce. St. James, **13**: 183.
— — Prejevalsky's Explorations in. Geog. M. **5**: 109.
— — Question of. (S. Edwards) Macmil. **33**: 67. — (R. Giffen) Fortn. **10**: 1. — (J. Hatton) Belgra. **8**: 34. — Fraser, **88**: 353.
— — Russians in. Quar. **118**: 529. **136**: 395. — Nat. Q. **23**: 66. — (M. Heilprin) Nation, **32**: 181. — St. Paul's, **4**: 204.
— — Slave-Trade in. (A. Vambéry) Fortn. **7**: 537.
— — Steppes of. (E. Schuyler) Hours at Home, **9**: 318.
— — Travels in. Westm. **55**: 512. Same art. Liv. Age, **30**: 289. Same art. Ecl. M. **24**: 157.
— — Ujfalvy's Travels in. Geog. M. **5**: 288.
— — Vambéry's Travels in. (E. Jonveaux) Cath. World, **3**: 198, 390. — (C. Nordhoff) Harper, **31**: 13. — Blackw. **98**: 723. — Colburn, **133**: 127. — Quar. **117**: 478.
— — Wandering Tribes in. Ecl. R. **93**: 41.
— Civilization in. (J. T. Dickinson) Chr. Exam. **67**: 1.
— Eastern, Future of. (Sir R. Alcock) Macmil. **30**: 435. Same art. Ecl. M. **83**: 703.

Asia, Eastern, Peoples of, Bastian's. Anthrop. R. **5**: 187.
— Embassies to. (J. Brown) No. Am. **47**: 395.
— Geography and History of. Lond. M. **14**: 455.
— — Ancient. (Sir D. K. Sandford) Ed. R. **53**: 306.
— Geology and Climatology of. For. Q. **10**: 45.
— High, Northward to. (F. Vincent, jr.) Lippinc. **15**: 601.
— — Geographical Configuration of. (H. and R. de Schlagintweit) Am. J. Sci. **84**: 101.
— in 1825. Ann. Reg. **1**: 281.
— Malcolm's Travels in. Dub. Univ. **15**: 176.—Mo. R. **149**: 475.
— Missions in, American. (W. Adams) Am. Church R. **17**: 274.
— Murray's History of Discovery in. Ecl. R. **41**: 22.—Mo. R. **94**: 242.—Quar. **24**: 311.
— Omar Pasha's Campaign in. Colburn, **106**: 127.
— Race for Commercial Supremacy in. (R. J. Hinton) Galaxy, **8**: 180.
— Relations of Western Powers with. (Sir R. Alcock) Fortn. **25**: 46.
— Rides through. Blackw. **122**: 592.
— Russians in. *See* Asia, Central, Russians in.
— Russian Campaigns in. Ed. R. **103**: 267.
— Russian Confines of. (R. Michell) Geog. M. **1**: 25, 70, 110, 160.
— Russian Exploration in. Nature, **14**: 534.
— Russian Policy in. (T. W. Knox) Harper, **47**: 214.
— Southern, Duff's Work in. (G. Smith) Good Words, **19**: 307.
— State and Prospects of, 1839. Quar. **63**: 369.
— Statistics of, 1869. Am. J. Educ. **18**: 592.
— Western. Ed. R. **25**: 398.
— — Development of. (A. Arnold) Gent. M. n. s. **22**: 162.
— — Outline Map of the proposed Railway Routes in. Colburn, **150**: 234.
Asia Minor. Chr. Exam. **32**: 218.
— Arundell's Discoveries in. Mo. R. **135**: 41.
— Churches in. (J. B. Lightfoot) Contemp. **5**: 397.—Art J. **15**: 36–250.
— Fellowes's. Dub. Univ. **14**: 480.—Ed. R. **71**: 396.—Mo. R. **149**: 425.
— Forgotten Empire in. (A. H. Sayce) Fraser, **102**: 223.
— Glimpses of. (F. W. Burton) Fortn. **1**: 303.
— Hamilton's Researches in, 1835–37. Mo. R. **159**: 484.
— Kinneir's Journey through, 1813–14. Ecl. R. **28**: 97, 233.
— Recent Works on, 1851. Bib. Sac. **8**: 857.
— Ruins of. F. Arts Q. **4**: 99.
— Russians in, 1876–77. Ed. R. **146**: 256.
— Scenes in. Am. Mo. M. **6**: 89, 174, 263. **8**: 480.
— Travels and Researches in. Hamilton and Fellowes's. Ed. R. **77**: 443.
— Walk in. (A. Bash) Good Words, **8**: 178.
Asiatic and African Nations, Ancient. Ed. R. **59**: 87.
Asiatic Courts, Embassy to. (J. W. Alexander) Princ. **10**: 179.
Asiatic Discoveries of Humboldt and others. Dub. Univ. **1**: 549.
Asiatic Forces in our European Wars. (W. R. Greg) Fortn. **29**: 835.
Asiatic Researches, 1818. Ecl. R. **29**: 282. **48**: 1, 123.—Ed. R. **1**: 26. **9**: 278. **12**: 36. **15**: 175. **16**: 384.
Asiatics, Mobility of. Liv. Age, **136**: 821.
Asinarii Senici. Fraser, **7**: 96. **13**: 362.
Asmar, Maria Theresa. U. S. Cath. M. **5**: 637.
Asmodeus at large. Colburn, **34**: 38–423. **37**: 155.
Asosan, Volcano of, Japan. Liv. Age, **148**: 175.
Asparagus. (W. Collett-Sandars) Gent. M. n. s. **19**: 57.
— of the Cossacks. Hogg, **1**: 352.
Aspasia, Story of. (G. A. Austin) Galaxy, **22**: 748.
Aspasia and Cleomene. (A. E. Porter) Godey, **43**: 38.
Aspen Court. (S. Brooks) Bentley, **33**: 3–611. **34**: 1–457. **35**: 1–425. **36**: 17–561. **37**: 289. **38**: 498.
Asphalt. Am. Arch. **10**: 101.
— and Bitumen in Engineering. (W. H. Delano) Ecl. Engin. **23**: 460.
— Origin and Uses of. (L. Malo) Pop. Sci. Mo. **19**: 539. **24**: 41.
Asphalt Deposit in West Virginia. (W. M. Fontaine) Am. J. Sci. **106**: 409.
Asphalt Mines in Savoy. Ecl. Engin. **2**: 197.
Asphalt Rocks in Foot-Pavements, etc. (A. Ure) J. Frankl. Inst. **29**: 409.
Asphalt Mastic. J. Frankl. Inst. **25**: 411.
Asphalts. (L. Meyn) Ecl. Engin. **8**: 74, 123.—Once a Week, **28**: 215.
Asphaltum, or Bitumen. Penny M. **9**: 485, 494.
Asphodel; a Story. (M. E. Braddon) All the Year, **45**: 265–529. **46**: 1–505.
Aspiration and Achievement. Chamb. J. **21**: 328.
— and Perspiration. (M. Valentine) Luth. Q. **9**: 648.
Aspiro; a Fable. Contin. Mo. **5**: 158.
Aspland, Robert. Sermons. (S. K. Lothrop) Chr. Exam. **19**: 321.—(G. E. Ellis) Chr. Exam. **42**: 378.—Prosp. R. **3**: 290.
Ass, The, in Life and Letters. (H. T. Tuckerman) Putnam, **13**: 129. Same art. Broadw. **6**: 108.
— Feast of; French-Latin Hymn. Cong. M. **5**: 595.
Asses. Cornh. **9**: 69.
— Dogs, Cats. Cath. World, **3**: 688.
— Thoughts on. Blackw. **47**: 57.
— Wild. (D. W. Mitchell) Once a Week, **1**: 454.
Assam, About. Chamb. J. **44**: 468.
— and the Hill Tribes. Colburn, **80**: 308.
— as a Missionary Field. Chr. R. **14**: 423.
Assassin, The Philanthropic. (R. H. Horne) Howitt, **1**: 103, 122.
— A Poetical. All the Year, **28**: 325.
Assassins and Bull-Fights. Blackw. **45**: 656.
— and the Druses. (A. G. Laurie) Univ. Q. **30**: 350, 410.
— and Nihilists. (H. Craig) Harper, **63**: 440.
— British State, and the Plea of Insanity. (J. W. Clarke) Atlan. **48**: 780.
— History of. Ecl. R. **66**: 171.—Mo. R. **137**: 442.
— Von Hammer's History of. (R. P. Gillies) For. Q. **1**: 449.—Mus. **13**: 1.
— Walpole's Ansayrii. Colburn, **94**: 80.—Ecl. R. **95**: 43.
Assassination. (J. F. Watkins) Overland, **4**: 174.
— and Lawlessness in the United States. (E. I. Sears) Nat. Q. **15**: 333.
— and the Spoils System. (D. B. Eaton) Princ. n. s. **8**: 145.
— Discovery of a premeditated. Fraser, **21**: 81.
— *versus* Fraud. Nat. Q. **24**: 314.
Assassinations, Noted. (C. C. Hazewell) Atlan. **16**: 85.—Ecl. M. **97**: 757.
— Socialistic and other. (J. H. Haynie) Atlan. **46**: 466.
Assay Office, United States, at New York. Bank. M. (N. Y.) **9**: 288.
Assaying of Gold and Silver. (W. Abbott) Harper, **23**: 735.
Assent, Grammar of, Newman's. Quar. **129**: 130.
Asser, Historical Doubts relating to. (T. Wright) Arch. **29**: 192.
Assignats, The French. Bank. M. (N. Y.) **29**: 432.
— — History of. Ecl. M. **64**: 441.
Assiniboine Indians. (H. Y. Hind) Canad. J. n. s. **4**: 253.
Assisi, Italy. (M. P. Thompson) Cath. World, **23**: 742.
— and its Memories. Good Words, **6**: 732.
— Mural Paintings at. (C. H. Wilson) Am. Arch. **4**: 141.
Assizes, Tale of the. Blackw. **54**: 275.

Assizes of Jerusalem. (A. Ten Brook) Contin. Mo. **4**: 501.
Assja. (I. Tourguenieff) Galaxy, **23**: 368.
Associated Labor Movement. Ecl. R. **93**: 66.
Associated Press, New York. (W. F. G. Shanks) Harper, **34**: 511.
— Office of. (W. Aplin) Putnam, **16**: 23.
Association. Chamb. J. **40**: 65. — (G. Combe) Peop. J. **4**: 22.
— or Fourierism. (H. N. Hudson) Am. Whig R. **5**: 492. — (J. A. McMaster) Am. Whig R. **7**: 632. — (T. Lewis) Meth. Q. **8**: 29. — (I. N. Tarbox) New Eng. **4**: 56. — (S. Osgood) Chr. Exam. **45**: 194. — (D. W. Clark) Meth. Q. **5**: 545. — Dem. R. **10**: 30, *et seq.* **8**: 451. — (O. A. Brownson) Dem. R. **11**: 481. **12**: 129. **16**: 17. — (A. Brisbane) Dem. R. **18**: 142. — (O. A. Brownson) Brownson, **1**: 450. **5**: 71. — Am. Ecl. **4**: 91. — New York R. **7**: 525. — (J. F. Clarke) Chr. Exam. **37**: 57.
— and Labor. Brownson, **5**: 71.
— French Theory of. Peop. J. **1**: 150–213.
— in Matters of Taste. So. R. **7**: 368.
— of Ideas. (W. James) Pop. Sci. Mo. **16**: 577.
Associations. (W. E. Channing) Chr. Exam. **7**: 105.
— Borrowing Power of. (J. B. Hodgskin) Nation, **12**: 398.
— Channing on. Spirit Pilg. **3**: 129.
— for Benevolent Purposes. (J. Walker) Chr. Exam. **2**: 241.
Associationism and Origin of Moral Ideas. (R. Flint) Mind, **1**: 321.
Assos. (J. T. Clarke) Am. Arch. **10**: 275.
Assuerus. (J. Moresby) Macmil. **8**: 411.
Assunta Howard; a Tale. (Miss Salter) Cath. World, **19**: 765. **20**: 62–474.
Assurance, Christian, Doctrine of. (J. Miley) Meth. Q. **17**: 559. — (J. Swartz) Luth. Q. **10**: 90.
— — as held by Swiss. Cong. M. **9**: 554, 635, 690.
See Insurance.
Assynt, In. Cornh. **40**: 40.
Assyria, Ancient. Westm. **51**: 290.
— — Art in. Art J. **27**: 199.
— and her Monuments. Am. Presb. R. **18**: 146.
— Annals of, B. C. 681–625. No. Brit. **52**: 323.
— Antiquities of. Art J. **12**: 48.
— Buckingham's Travels in. Colburn, **25**: 257.
— Discoveries in, 1849–54. Ecl. R. **105**: 488. — Colburn, **163**: 527.
— — Recent, 1874–75. (W. Chambers) Chamb. J. **52**: 97. — (S. Merrill) Bib. Sac. **32**: 715. — (A. H. Sayce) Fraser, **89**: 702. Same art. Liv. Age, **122**: 177. — (W. H. Ward) Scrib. **10**: 75. — Dub. Univ. **84**: 213. — Lond. Q. **46**: 162.
— — G. Smith's. (W. H. Ward) Nation, **20**: 209. — Nature, **11**: 441.
— Egypt, and the Bible. (W. H. Ryder) Univ. Q. **10**: 329.
— English Studies in. (W. H. Ward) Nation, **32**: 300.
— French Excavations in. Chamb. J. **22**: 197.
— History of. (W. F. Allen) Chr. Exam. **66**: 183.
— — G. Smith's. (H. C. Lea) Nation, **21**: 183.
— Kings of, Ménaut's Annals of. Chr. Obs. **74**: 212.
— Layard's Assyrian Researches. Colburn, **85**: 240.
Assyrian and Babylonian Gods. (J. N. Strassmaier) Month, **36**: 263, 558. **37**: 550.
Assyrian and Babylonian Researches. (R. P. Stebbins) Unita. R. **9**: 610.
Assyrian and Persian Inscriptions. Quar. **79**: 413.
Assyrian Canon. (P. A. Nordell) Bapt. Q. **10**: 141.
Assyrian Chronology of Reigns of Sargon and Sennacherib. Kitto, **13**: 393.
Assyrian Empire. (J. K. Hosmer) No. Am. **90**: 21.
Assyrian Inscriptions. (W. F. Ainsworth) Colburn, **78**: 441. — Kitto, **16**: 414. — Liv. Age, **54**: 509.
— Translation of. Chamb. J. **29**: 101.
See Cuneiform Inscriptions.
Assyrian Language, Sayce's Lectures on. (M. Heilprin) Nation, **27**: 151.
— Verbs in. (E. Hincks) Kitto, **15**: 381. **16**: 141. **17**: 152, 392.
Assyrian Libraries. Am. Bibliop. **7**: 156. — N. Brit. **51**: 305. Same art. Ecl. M. **74**: 589.
Assyrian Monuments in America. (S. Merrill) Bib. Sac. **32**: 320.
Assyrian Sculpture from Khorsabad. (S. Birch) Arch. **32**: 168.
Assyriology. (P. de Lagarde) Bib. Sac. **34**: 563. — (O. D. Miller) Bib. Sac. **35**: 696. — Lond. Q. **49**: 265.
— and the Bible. (S. J. Barrows) Unita. R. **12**: 21. — Month, **36**: 291.
— Studies in. Dub. Univ. **83**: 481.
— — Text-Books for. (W. H. Ward) Bib. Sac. **27**: 184.
Asteroids. Cornh. **37**: 169. Same art. Liv. Age, **136**: 797. Same art. Sup. Pop. Sci. Mo. **2**: 468.
— and the Nebular Hypothesis. (R. A. Proctor) Stud. & Intel. Obs. **4**: 14.
— Discovery of. St. James, **22**: 673. Same art. Liv. Age, **99**: 259.
— Orbits of. (B. A. Gould, jr.) Am. J. Sci. **56**: 28.
— Zone of. (D. Trowbridge) Nat. Q. **31**: 28.
Astley, Philip. (R. B. Baker) Belgra. **38**: 471. — All the Year, **27**: 205.
— Recollections of. Colburn, **51**: 329.
Astley's Theatre. (W. Pinkerton) Once a Week, **8**: 7.
Astor, John J. Harper, **30**: 308. — Hunt, **11**: 153. — Hogg, **1**: 235.
Astor, Wm. B., and Capitalists of New York. (W. Frothingham) Contin. Mo. **2**: 207.
Astor Family in New York. Scrib. **11**: 879.
— Story of. (W. Chambers) Chamb. J. **53**: 81.
Astor Library. (F. H. Norton) Galaxy, **7**: 527. **8**: 528. — Am. Bibliop. **4**: 17. — Internat. M. **2**: 436. — Liv. Age, **40**: 218.
Astorga City. Penny M. **14**: 321.
Astoria. So. Lit. J. **4**: 30.
— Irving's. (E. Everett) No. Am. **44**: 200. — So. Lit. Mess. **3**: 59. — Westm. **26**: 318. — Am. Q. **21**: 60. — Dub. Univ. **9**: 167.
— Scenes about. (C. M. Scammon) Overland, **3**: 495.
Astrakhan. Penny M. **8**: 429.
Astrogony, Ancient Babylonian. (R. A. Proctor) Gent M. n. s. **20**: 319.
Astrolabe, Account of. (C. O. Morgan) Arch. **34**: 259.
Astrolabes of Champlain and Chaucer. (H. Scadding) Canad. Mo. **18**: 589.
Astrologer's Glass; a Tale. Sharpe, **48**: 150, 209.
Astrologers. House. Words, **12**: 141.
Astrology. (R. A. Proctor) Belgra. **31**: 4, 145.
— and Alchemy. Quar. **26**: 180.
— and Magic in Antiquity and the Middle Ages. Westm. **81**: 48.
— Controversial Writers on. Retros. **18**: 255.
— Fossils of. (Mrs. L. H. Stone) Lakeside, **1**: 298.
— Judicial, Exposure of. Penny M. **12**: 366–466.
— Looking into the Future. St. James, **11**: 239.
— Modern. (J. B. Langley) Peop. J. **4**: 13, 67.
— Pleas for. (G. F. Holmes) So. M. **13**: 420.
Astronomers, American. (W. Leitch) Good Words, **2**: 394.
— — Progress by. (D. Trowbridge) Nat. Q. **16**: 332.
— before and at the Time of Galileo. New York R. **9**: 444.
— German, Works of. (N. Bowditch) No. Am. **10**: 260.
Astronomical Almanacs. Nature, **8**: 311, 350, 529. **9**: 69, 123, 210.

Astronomical Annuals. (C. Wright) No. Am. **101**: 134.
Astronomical Calculations for 1869. (S. H. Wright) Am. J. Educ. **18**: 9.
Astronomical Expedition, The Sherman. (C. A. Young) Nature, **7**: 107.
— to Peak of Teneriffe, 1856. J. Frankl. Inst. **63**: 186, 281.
Astronomical Fantasy. (C. Flammarion) N. Ecl. **6**: 677.
Astronomical Forecasts. (P. E. Chase) J. Frankl. Inst. **106**: 314, 353.
Astronomical Improvement in 18th Century. Mo. R. **159**: 135.
Astronomical Observation. Nature, **4**: 30. — Pop. Sci. Mo. **2**: 365.
Astronomical Observations at Greenwich. Cornh. **7**: 381.
— Bond's Clock for registering. Ecl. M. **24**: 384.
— United States Naval. So. Lit. Mess. **13**: 251.
— with the Spectroscope. (L. M. Rutherfurd) Am. J. Sci. **85**: 71.
Astronomical Observatory, in Russia. Ed. New Philos. J. **19**: 71.
— Paper Dome for. (D. Greene) Am. J. Sci. **117**: 55.
Astronomical Observatories. (S. Newcomb) No. Am. **133**: 196.
Astronomical Operations at Pulkova. (J. Nooney) Am. J. Sci. **47**: 88.
Astronomical Refraction, Easy Rules for. (B. S. Lyman) J. Frankl. Inst. **88**: 343.
Astronomical Theories. Nat. Q. **6**: 239.
Astronomical Traditions. Anthrop. R. **3**: 325.
Astronomische Gesellschaft, Meeting of, at Leyden, Aug., 1875. Nature, **12**: 386.
Astronomy. Knick. **37**: 197.
— Airy's Physical. Westm. **7**: 146.
— Ancient. Ed. R. **116**: 80.
— — Lewis on. (Sir D. Brewster) No. Brit. **36**: 485. Same art. Ecl. M. **56**: 433. — Chr. Obs. **63**: 440.
— and Geology. (H. C. Sorby) Nature, **9**: 388.
— and Immortality. (T. B. Thayer) Univ. Q. **10**: 5.
— and Religion. (E. H. Chapin) Univ. Q. **5**: 5. — (E. T. Winkler) Bapt. Q. **5**: 58. — (J. Foster) Ecl. R. **26**: 205, 354, 466.
— — Chalmers on. Chr. Obs. **16**: 588.
— — Milner on. Ecl. R. **79**: 169.
— Application of Photography to. (G. B. Merriman) Meth. Q. **29**: 392.
— Arago's Popular. Chr. Obs. **60**: 9. — Ecl. R. **109**: 354. Same art. Ecl. M. **47**: 415. — Fraser, **53**: 733.
— Aspects of the Heavens. Ecl. M. **57**: 113.
— Babylonian. (A. H. Sayce) Nature, **12**: 489.
— Bailey's History of. (J. Farrar) No. Am. **12**: 150.
— Belgian Contributions to. Nature, **7**: 23.
— Brinkley's. Nature, **11**: 83.
— Chauvenet's Manual of. Am. J. Sci. **86**: 378.
— Chemistry of the Stars. Brit. Q. **10**: 321. Same art. Ecl. M. **19**: 171.
— Colored Suns. (R. A. Proctor) Ev. Sat. **5**: 144.
— Conjectural. Chamb. J. **25**: 100.
— Contemplations of the Heavens. Ecl. M. **56**: 145.
— Cosmical. (P. G. Tait) Good Words, **16**: 19–857.
— Delambre's History of. For. R. **2**: 1. — Ecl. R. **21**: 384.
— Discoveries and Observations on. J. Frankl. Inst. **26**: 109.
— Dunkin's Midnight Sky. Nature, **1**: 215.
— Epitome of. (G. Waterman) Godey, **29**: 274.
— Errors of Modern. (J. Prusol) Colburn, **166**: 476, 626. **167**: 13.
— Essay on. Nav. M. **1**: 474, 528. **2**: 42, 119, 215.
— Ferguson's. (J. Farrar) No. Am. **6**: 205.
- The Heavens in 1864. (A. W. Drayson) St. James, **9**: 241.
Astronomy, Herschel's Outlines of. (B. A. Gould) Chr. Exam. **47**: 268. — Ecl. R. **90**: 576. — Westm. **71**: 284. Same art. Ecl. M. **47**: 33.
— — Survey of Southern Heavens. Quar. **85**: 1. — (Sir D. Brewster) No. Brit. **8**: 491. Same art. Liv. Age, **16**: 577. — Ed. R. **88**: 104.
— Hindu Astronomical Tables. Ed. New Philos. J. **20**: 22.
— Hindu Systems of. (Prof. Hamilton) Ed. R. **10**: 455.
— History of. Mo. R. **131**: 405. — Am. Mo. R. **2**: 106.
— in America. (R. A. Proctor) Pop. Sci. R. **15**: 351. Same art. Pop. Sci. Mo. **10**: 75. Same art. Ecl. M. **87**: 679.
— in 1841. Chr. Rem. **1**: 412.
— Indian, Bentley on. Ed. R. **10**: 455.
— Lockyer's. Pract. M. **5**: 64.
— Mädler's History of. (T. W. Webb) Nature, **6**: 58.
— Magnitudes in. (H. S. Carhart) Pop. Sci. Mo. **14**: 291.
— Mechanism of the Heavens. (Sir J. F. W. Herschel) Quar. **41**: 537.
— Modern. (N. Bowditch) No. Am. **20**: 309. — (E. Loomis) New Eng. **2**: 3. — Lond. Q. **41**: 265. Same art. Liv. Age, **125**: 195.
— — Progress of. (D. Trowbridge) Nat. Q. **36**: 86.
— — Revelations of. Ecl. M. **10**: 79.
— — Theoretical. (S. Newcomb) No. Am. **93**: 367.
— Moral. Chr. Mo. Spec. **6**: 46.
— Music of the Moons. (P. E. Chase) J. Frankl. Inst. **104**: 352, 403.
— — of the Spheres. (P. E. Chase) J. Frankl. Inst. **104**: 161.
— Mysteries of. Colburn, **165**: 1173, 1289.
— Myths of. (R. A. Proctor) Belgra. **33**: 292.
— — Blake's. Nature, **15**: 351.
— Nautical. Quar. **141**: 136. Same art. Ecl. M. **86**: 641.
— New Facts in. Chamb. J. **8**: 244, 347. Same art. Liv. Age, **15**: 555.
— Newcomb's. (J. R. Hind) Nature, **18**: 7.
— Nichol's Architecture of the Heavens. Tait, n. s. **4**: 539.
— Night in July. (A. W. Drayson) St. James, **1**: 387.
— of 18th Century. For. Q. **1**: 631.
— of the Future. (N. Crosland) Fraser, **94**: 593. Same art. Ecl. M. **88**: 97. Same art. Liv. Age, **131**: 667.
— of the Invisible. Cornh. **7**: 544.
— of the Seasons. (D. K. Lee) Univ. Q. **21**: 209.
— Other Worlds and other Universes. (R. A. Proctor) Belgra. **31**: 416. Same art. Ecl. M. **88**: 486.
— Outlines of. Chr. Rem. **19**: 128. **32**: 103.
— Paradoxes of. (R. A. Proctor) Belgra. **33**: 162. Same art. Ecl. M. **89**: 418.
— Perceiving without seeing. (C. Pritchard) Ecl. M. **72**: 530.
— Physical. No. Brit. **18**: 491.
— — Biot's. Quar. **7**: 136.
— — Grant's. (Sir D. Brewster) No. Brit. **18**: 491.
— — Recent Progress in. (J. M. Degni) Am. Cath. Q. **4**: 645. — For. Q. **5**: 231.
— Physical Phenomena of other Worlds. (R. Hunt) Pop. Sci. R. **4**: 311.
— Photography in. (L. M. Rutherfurd) Am. J. Sci. **89**: 304.
— Plurality of Worlds. Westm. **61**: 591. **62**: 242. *See* Worlds.
— Popular. Ecl. R. **79**: 169. — (J. T. Crane) Meth. Q. **39**: 247.
— Practical, André and Rayet's. Nature, **10**: 42.
— Present State of, 1852. (C. W. Hackley) Meth. Q **11**: 32.
— Primitive. (J. Samuelson) Pop. Sci. R. **1**: 426.
— Progress of. (A Hall) Nature, **22**: 570. — So. R n. s. **5**: 148.

Astronomy, Progress and Prospects of. Fraser, 63: 289, 458. Same art. Ecl. M. 53: 66, 455.
— — in 19th Century. So. R. n. s. 8: 161. — No. Am. 125: 363.
— — Recent. (S. Newcomb) No. Am. 123: 86. — (E. S. Holden) No. Am. 131: 375.
— Ptolemaic and Copernican Systems. Ecl. R. 93: 543.
— Recent. Brit. Q. 6: 1.
— — and the Mosaic Record. (S. D. Hillman) Meth. Q. 28: 532.
— — and the Nebular Hypothesis. (H. Spencer) Westm. 70: 185. Same art. Ecl. M. 45: 73, 176.
— Recent Discoveries in. Fraser, 37: 489.
— — in 1834. Tait, 4: 57.
— — in 1852. (J. Lovering) Am. Alma. 1852: 66.
— — in 1853. (J. Lovering) Am. Alma. 1853: 69.
— Recent History of. (Sir D. Brewster) Quar. 38: 1. — Ed. R. 51: 87.
— Revelations of. (Sir D. Brewster) No. Brit. 6: 206.
— Romance of, Miller's. Nature, 8: 140.
— Schiaparelli's Researches. (W. Lassell) Nature, 5: 433.
— Sidereal. (Sir H. Holland) Ed. R. 94: 49.
— Stellar Universe. (D. Trowbridge) Nat. Q. 24: 145.
— Study of. (R. A. Proctor) Fraser, 84: 282. — (R. A. Proctor) Ecl. M. 79: 167.
— Sweep through the Stars. Liv. Age, 58: 32.
— Systems of Uranus and Neptune, Newcomb on. Nature, 12: 515.
— Talks of an Astronomer. (S. Newcomb) Harper, 49: 693, 825.
— Truths of. (A. Winchell) Meth. Q. 33: 181. 34: 70.
— Uses of. (E. Everett) Am. J. Educ. 2: 605.
— Utility of. (L. C. Garland) So. Lit. Mess. 4: 123.
— Utilities of. (E. Everett) Ecl. M. 39: 374.
— Vince's. Ed. R. 14: 64.
— Visible Heavens. Ecl. M. 26: 433.
— Whewell's. Chr. R. 1: 215. — Ed. R. 58: 427.
— Wolf's History of. (J. R. Hind) Nature, 17: 259, 359.
— Woodhouse's. Ed. R. 31: 375. — Quar. 22: 129.
— Worlds in the Sky. Liv. Age, 48: 360.
See names of heavenly bodies, as Sun; Moon; the Planets; etc. *Also* Nebular Hypothesis; Observatories; Stars; etc.
At a little Dinner in Tatter-Street. Lond. Soc. 32: 493.
At Chrighton Abbey; a Tale. Belgra. 14: 353.
At Daggers Drawn; a Tale. (B. White) Belgra. 1: 335.
At her Mercy; a Story. (J. Payn) All the Year, 30: 553, 577, 601. 31: 1-553. 32: 1, 25.
At his Gates. (M. Oliphant) Scrib. 3: 355-713. 4: 34-706. 5: 44, 201.
At Kirkby Cottage. (A. Trollope) Ev. Sat. 10: 22, 46, 59.
At Last. (H. P. Spofford) Scrib. 8: 90.
At One again; a Poem. (J. Ingelow) Harper, 51: 617.
At Rest; a Poem. Cornh. 10: 623.
At Sea; a Poem. (F. N. Broome) Cornh. 20: 90.
At Sea in a Sail-Boat. (C. L. Norton) Lippinc. 8: 293.
At Sea in a Sail-Boat; a Tale. Broadw. 8: 282.
At the Bar; a Tale. (M. Collins) All the Year, 14: 193-553.
At the Bar; a Story. (G. A. Sala) Belgra. 22: 38, 438.
At the Convent Gate; a Poem. (A. Dobson) Cornh. 39: 231.
At the Door; a Story. Mo. Rel. M. 24: 119.
At the Hacienda. Overland, 5: 231.
At the Lattice; a Poem. (A. Austin) Temp. Bar, 3: 376.
At the Morgans'; a Tale. Chamb. J. 48: 44, 59. Same art. Liv. Age, 108: 805. 109: 45. Same art. Ev. Sat. 10: 142, 166.
At the Play. Cornh. 5: 84.
At the Sign of the Savage. (W. D. Howells) Atlan. 40: 36.
Atacama, Desert of, in Peru. Chamb. J. 15: 158.
— Silver Mines of. (J. Schumacher) Scrib. 8: 43.
Atala; a Romance. (F. A. de Chateaubriand) West. J. 7: 51-418.
Atchafalaya River, Battle of. (T. Green) So. Hist. Pap 3: 62.
Athabasca, Missionary in. Colburn, 141: 491.
Athanasian Creed. (J. Jones) Month, 16: 280. — (F. D. Maurice) Contemp. 15: 479. — (J. W. Nevin) Mercersb. 14: 624. — (P. Schaff) Am. Presb. R. 15: 584. — (P. Schaff) Mercersb. 11: 232. — (A. P. Stanley) Contemp. 15: 133, 524. — (J. Wright) Theo. R. 10: 233. — Chr. Obs. 71: 301. 73: 266. — Dub. R. 71: 208. — Lond. Q. 37: 426. — Macmil. 17: 20. 21: 38. — Cong. 2: 177.
— Structure and Origin of. (J. Jones) Month, 22: 192-328. 23: 257. 24: 39-301.
— Swainson on. Chr. Obs. 75: 808.
Athanasian Hypothesis and Transubstantiation. Theo. Repos. 5: 397.
Athanasius, St. Am. Church R. 21: 417. 22: 237.
— and Council of Nicæa. Chr. Rem. 27: 125.
— Contra Mundum. Month, 17: 155.
— Controversy with Arius. (R. Ellis) Chr. Exam. 58: 275. — (C. F. Schaeffer) Bib. Sac. 21: 1. — (H. Wace) Good Words, 19: 681. — Am. Presb. R. 5: 353, 529. — Univ. Q. 9: 35.
— Festal Letters of. Brit. Q. 16: 76. — Ed. R. 105: 433.
— Letters of. Kitto, 14: 255.
— Life of. (J. W. Nevin) Mercersb. 14: 445. — Chr. Mo. Spec. 4: 244.
— Milman on. (M. Mahan) Am. Church R. 14: 565.
— Select Treatises of. Chr. Rem. 4: 32, 246.
Atheism. Cong. M. 20: 577. — Nat. R. 2: 97.
— Ancient. Kitto, 29: 24.
— and Agnosticism. Lond. Q. 54: 1.
— and the Church. (G. H. Curteis) Contemp. 34: 230. Same art. Liv. Age, 140: 415. Same art. Pop. Sci. Mo. 14: 621.
— and its Exponents. (S. Ellis) Univ. Q. 21: 80.
— and Repentance. (W. H. Mallock) 19th Cent. 8: 19. Same art. Liv. Age, 146: 303.
— and the Rights of Man. (W. H. Mallock) 19th Cent. 7: 756.
— and Science. Ecl. M. 67: 746.
— and Theism. (Max Müller) Contemp. 33: 707.
— and the United States. (J. Crawford) Ref. Q. 26: 304.
— as a mental Phenomenon. (T. Finley) Month, 33: 187.
— Evolution, and Theology. Lond. Q. 49: 322.
— Fervent. (C. B. Upton) Mod. R. 1: 98.
— Folly of. (G. P. Fisher) New Eng. 36: 76.
— Godwin on. (A. Alexander) Princ. 9: 576.
— Historical Sketch of. (E. Pond) Am. Bib. Repos. 2d s. 2: 320.
— in England. (Miss Follet) Chr. Exam. 67: 339.
— in New England. New Eng. M. 7: 500. 8: 53.
— in our Colleges. (E. D. Mead) Unita. R. 15: 334.
— in Poetry and Music. (G. D. Haughton) Fraser, 90: 40.
— Last Phase of. (H. J. Warner) Chr. Exam. 78: 78.
— Letter of Hemsterhuys on. Fraser, 91: 696.
— Magnanimous. (F. P. Cobbe) Theo. R. 14: 447.
— Modern. (W. H. Mallock) Contemp. 29: 169. — (L. S. Bevington) 19th Cent. 6: 585, 999. — Dub. R. 70: 135. — So. R. n. s. 10: 120. — Theo. & Lit. J. 9: 672.
— Natural History of. (J. S. Blackie) Good Words, 17: 26, 162, 243.
— The Newest. (N. Porter) Princ. n. s. 5: 359.
— or, the atheistic Statesman and Judge. (I. S. Spencer) Hours at Home, 1: 73.
— Poetry of. (G. W. Gunsaulus) Nat. Q. 38: 275.
— Practical. (C. H. Brigham) O. & N. 3: 204.
— Refutation of. Brownson, 22: 433. 23: 1, 145.
— Steps to. (J. Shea) Am. Cath. Q. 4: 305.

Atheism, Theism and Problem of Evil. (M. D. Conway) Theo. R. 9: 207.
— vs. Pantheism. (J. Bayma) Cath. World, 27: 471. *See* Theism.
Atheisms of Geology. Ecl. R. 107: 61.
Atheistic Controversy. (F. W. Newman) Contemp. 33: 470.
Atheistic Theories. Ecl. R. 73: 85.
Atheistic View of Life. (R. H. Hutton) Fraser, 101: 652.
Atheists in Parliament. (D. C. Lathbury) Fortn. 36: 671.
— Plato against. Chr. Exam. 40: 108.
— What would they have? (J. P. Hopps) Mod. R. 2: 129.
Athelings. (M. Oliphant) Blackw. 79: 625. 80: 26–660. 81: 42–719. Same art. Liv. Age, 50: 167, 488, 778. 51: 395, 460, 721. 52: 348, 487, 727. 53: 226, 403, 723. 54: 84.
Athelstaneford, Sketch of. (J. Purves) Dub. Univ. 86: 479.
Athelstons of Morte d'Athelston; a Tale. Dub. Univ. 85: 25.
Athenaion, Literary Society, Prospectus of. Lond. M. 11: 113, 259.
Athenæum Club House. Fraser, 1: 145.
Athenæus. Cornh. 37: 552.
— Noctes of. Blackw. 36: 431.
— Selections from. Blackw. 3: 650. 4: 23, 413, 666.
— Schweighæuser's Edition of. (P. Elmsley) Ed. R. 3: 131.
Athenian Architecture and Polychrome Embellishments. For. Q. 18: 159.
Athenian Banquets. (J. D. Whelpley) Am. Whig R. 7: 194, 586.
Athenian Democracy. Blackw. 42: 44. — (H. S. Legaré) New York R. 7: 1.
Athenian Letters, The. Retros. 18: 74.
Athenian Navy, Archives of. For. Q. 26: 401.
— Pæans of. Blackw. 62: 736.
Athenian Poets' Creed. Fraser, 18: 443.
Athenian Tale. (J. D. Whelpley) Am. Whig R. 4: 467.
Athenians, Character of. (D. K. Sandford) Ed. R. 61: 323.
— Harbors and Naval Establishments of. (A. L. Koeppen) Mercersb. 7: 163.
— Manners of. Quar. 23: 245. 24: 419.
— Religion of. (B. F. Cocker) Meth. Q. 29: 165.
Athens. (N. Macleod) Good Words, 7: 172. — (M. E. Gates) Harper, 62: 819. — (W. S. Tyler) Hours at Home, 5: 193, 339. — (T. L. Eliot) Unita. R. 15: 225. — Hogg, 2: 133.
— Acropolis of. Ed. R. 110: 35. Same art. Ecl. M. 48: 319. — Nav. M. 1: 137.
— — and the Parthenon. Am. Meth. M. 20: 351.
— — in the Siege of 1821–22. Lond. M. 14: 193.
— Æsthetic Culture of. (W. S. Tyler) Bib. Sac. 20: 152.
— and the Athenians, Bulwer on. Ecl. R. 66: 457. — Mo. R. 143: 185.
— and Attica, Ancient. (A. J. Huntington) Bapt. Q. 11: 215.
— — described. (A. L. Koeppen) Mercersb. 6: 258.
— — Wordsworth's Residence in. Quar. 64: 64. — Dub. Univ. 9: 422.
— and her Enemies; a Poem. (W. Everett) O. & N. 2: 65c.
— and Pentelicus. Fraser, 75: 103.
— Anthesphoria at. Fraser, 39: 713. Same art. Liv. Age, 22: 163.
— Antiquities of. Mo. R. 82: 225.
— Barber's Shop in old. Chamb. J. 21: 177.
— Conversations at, on local Topics. Fraser, 62: 375.
— Damage done to, by Storm of Oct. 26, 1852. (T. Wyse) Arch. 35: 23.
— Day at. (F. P. Cobbe) Fraser, 67: 601.
Athens, École Française at. (W. W. Capes) Fraser, 98: 103. Same art. Liv. Age, 138: 404.
— Egyptian Colony at. (F. S. Schmidt) Arch. 1: 238.
— First Impressions of. Internat. R. 5: 44.
— The Grand Experiment. (W. A. Nichols) Cong. R. 11: 172.
— in the Time of Pericles, and Rome in the Time of Augustus. Ox. Prize Ess. 4: 79.
— in 1853. Blackw. 74: 569.
— in 1863. (H. B. Hall) St. James, 9: 224.
— Letter from. Fraser, 14: 349.
— Modern. (F. Bremer) St. James, 2: 35. — (C. K. Tuckerman) Scrib. 4: 675.
— — and the Acropolis. (A. L. Kœppen) Mercersb. 6: 531. 7: 1.
— Monuments of. Meth. Q. 16: 235.
— Night in. Knick. 30: 189.
— of Thucydides. Brit. Q. 66: 55.
— Owl's City. (W. Thornbury) Good Words, 2: 432.
— Place of, in History. (J. R. Boise) Bapt. Q. 5: 153.
— Political Institutions of. So. Q. 24: 451.
— Public Economy of. (W. W. Goodwin) No. Am. 86: 1.
— Republic of, from Alcibiades to Demosthenes. (A. H. Dana) Nat. Q. 39: 221.
— School Life in. (N. C. Schaeffer) Ref. Q. 26: 217.
— Site and Antiquities of. (J. L. T. Phillips) Lippinc. 11: 147.
— Sketch of. (T. Campbell) Colburn, 13: 217.
— Some Aspects of. (Prof. Colvin) Portfo. 7: 168, 184.
— under King Otho. (W. Thornbury) Gent. M. n. s. 18: 84.
— University Life at. (J. H. Newman) Am. J. Educ. 24: 23.
— Visit to, 1840. (Marchioness of Londonderry) Colburn, 70: 25–539.
— Week in. (G. F. Rodwell) Dub. Univ. 86: 1. — Blackw. 128: 329.
Atherstone, E., Fall of Nineveh. Blackw. 27: 137. — (F. Jeffrey) Ed. R. 48: 47. — Ecl. R. 49: 79.
— Handwriting on the Wall. Dub. Univ. 51: 81. Same art. Ecl. M. 43: 334.
— Last Days of Herculaneum. Lond. M. 3: 379.
Atherton, Charles G., Portrait of. Dem. R. 23: 479.
Atherton Family in England. (J. C. J. Brown) N. E. Reg. 35: 67.
Atherton, John, Bp., Penitent Death of. Chr. Obs. 2: 582, 645.
Athletes at Ease. All the Year, 39: 17.
Athletic Sports at Brompton, England. Ev. Sat. 10: 456.
— Oxford and Cambridge. Dark Blue, 3: 233.
— — and University Studies. (L. Stephen) Fraser, 82: 691.
Athletics. Contemp. 3: 374. Same art. Ev. Sat. 7: 535.
— and Education. (H. H. Almond) Ecl. M. 96: 554.
— Feminine. (J. H. Fletcher) Good Words, 20: 533.
— in Schools. Pop. Sci. Mo. 16: 677.
— Morality of Muscularity. Ev. Sat. 9: 525.
— Risks of. (W. Blaikie) Harper, 58: 923. *See* Gymnastics; Physical Education.
Athleticism, Modern. (W. Turley) Dark Blue, 4: 297.
Athlone. Penny M. 5: 68.
— Siege of, 1691. Dub. Univ. 69: 155.
Athol, Mass., Ministers of. Am. Q. Reg. 10: 51.
Athole Gathering. (E. Courtenay) Belgra. 15: 432.
Athos, Mount. All the Year, 36: 487.
— Monasteries of. Ed. R. 101: 191. — (B. Murphy) Cath. World, 33: 163. — Chr. Rem. 20: 288.
— to Salonica. (W. G. Clark) Macmil. 7: 306.
Atkinson (N. H.) Academy, History of. (W. C. Todd) N. E. Reg. 26: 122.

Atlanta, Ga. (C. W. Hubner) Appleton, **8**: 376. — De Bow, **27**: 462.
Atlanta Campaign, 1864. (C. C. Chesney) Fortn. **24**: 611. — (O. O. Howard) Atlan. **38**: 385, 559. — U. S. Serv. M. **3**: 305. — (T. B. Roy) So. Hist. P. **8**: 337.
Atlantean Race. (J. W. Jackson) Anthrop. J. **2**: 397.
Atlantic, Steamer, Wreck of, 1873; a Poem. St. James, **32**: 606.
Atlantic and Mississippi Railroad. West. Mo. R. **3**: 19, 480.
Atlantic and Pacific Railroad. West. J. **1**: 353. — (Prof. Forshey and J. D. B. De Bow) De Bow, **3**: 474.
Atlantic Telegraph Cable. (G. Mathiot) Am. J. Sci. **77**: 157. — (W. H. Russell) Fortn. **2**: 329. — (W. Thomson) Good Words, **8**: 43. — N. Ecl. **7**: 88. — No. Brit. **29**: 519. **45**: 459.
— and its Lessons. (J. Stephen) Fortn. **5**: 442.
— Atlantic Wedding Ring; a Poem. Blackw. **84**: 458.
— Benefits of. (A. P. Peabody) No. Am. **87**: 532.
— Deep-Sea Soundings for. (W. P. Trowbridge) Am. J. Sci. **78**: 51.
— Electrical Principles of. (G. C. Foster) Pop. Sci. R. **5**: 416.
— Expedition of 1865. (J. C. Deane) Macmil. **12**: 440. — (H. Rogers) Good Words, **6**: 835.
— Field's History of. (J. T. L. Preston) So. R. n. s. **2**: 34.
— Layers of. Temp. Bar, **18**: 424.
— Laying. Victoria, **21**: 452.
— Poem on. (J. A. Boyd) Canad. J. n. s. **4**: 329.
Atlantic City. (M. M. Howard) Potter Am. Mo. **15**: 321. — (A. G. Penn) Lippinc. **6**: 420. — Lippinc. **11**: 609.
Atlantic Coast, Glacial Marks on. (A. S. Packard, jr.) Am. Natural. **11**: 674.
Atlantic Drift, gathered in the Steerage. (C. Brotherton) Cath. World, **16**: 648, 837.
Atlantic Monthly, Theological Animus of. Cong. R. **7**: 244.
Atlantic Ocean. Chamb. J. **31**: 91.
— and Gulf of Mexico, Connection of. De Bow, **20**: 492.
— and Pacific, Junction of. Westm. **53**: 127. Same art. Liv. Age, **27**: 193. Same art. Ecl. M. **20**: 245. — (A. Whitney) De Bow, **4**: 164. **6**: 204. **7**: 1. **22**: 365. — (L. S. O'Connor) Dub. Univ. **35**: 221. Same art. Ecl. M. **20**: 40. — Dub. Univ. **84**: 625, 741. — (M. F. Maury) So. Lit. Mess. **15**: 259. — Am. J. Sci. **41**: 358. — (R. J. Colburn) Lippinc. **1**: 541. — Blackw. **54**: 658. — Colburn, **88**: 172. **89**: 365-444. **90**: 37-314. — Penny M. **12**: 397, 404, 414.
See Interoceanic Canal; Darien; Panama; Tehuantepec.
— Basin of. Chamb. J. **20**: 12.
— Contour of. (J. E. Davis) Geog. M. **1**: 225.
— Crossing. (J. Hatton) Colburn, **168**: 343.
— Deposits of, in Deep Water. (D. T. Ansted) Pop. Sci. R. **9**: 24.
— Fauna of. (F. P. Johnson) Nature, **9**: 15.
— Natural-History Phenomena of. (W. King) Fraser, **68**: 484. Same art. Ecl. M. **61**: 15.
— On the. Good Words, **1**: 457.
— Physical Condition of. Ecl. M. **58**: 390. — (Sir H. S. Holland) Ed. R. **105**: 360. — Westm. **72**: 456. Same art. Ecl. M. **49**: 464.
— Soundings in. (J. J. Wild) Nature, **15**: 377.
— — Examination of. (J. W. Bailey) Am. J. Sci. **67**: 176.
— Survey of the North. Liv. Age, **69**: 75.
— Trip over. (H. Wickoff) Dem. R. **24**: 501.
Atlantic Slope, Mesozoic Sandstone of. (P. Frazer, jr.) Am. Natural. **13**: 284.
— Mesozoic Red Sandstone of. (C. M. Wheatley) Am. J. Sci. **82**: 41.
Atlantic Souvenir. (J. Everett) No. Am. **22**: 444.
Atlantic Souvenir and Memorial. (F. W. P. Greenwood) Chr. Exam. **24**: 228.
Atlantic Steam Navigation. (A. W. Colgate) Galaxy, **20**: 41. — Chamb. J. **15**: 390. — (B. B. Thatcher) Quar. **62**: 186. — Ed. R. **65**: 118.
— First. Hunt, **15**: 610.
See also Steam Navigation.
Atlantic Steamers, American Mail. (J. L. Tellkampf) Hunt, **15**: 51. — St. James, **31**: 177.
Atlantic Voyage. (W. G. Beers) Canad. Mo. **11**: 379.
Atlantic Yacht Race, 1866. All the Year, **22**: 342.
Atlantis, Lost, and the Challenger Soundings. (W. S. Mitchell) Nature, **15**: 553.
Atlantis; the Antediluvian World, Donnelly's. (A. Winchell) Dial (Ch.), **2**: 284.
— Story of. (J. W. Foster) Lakeside, **9**: 411.
Atlas Mountains, Across. Fraser, **65**: 661.
Atlases, American. (J. Sparks) No. Am. **18**: 382.
— Bleaus's Atlas, 17th Century. Chamb. J. **15**: 374.
— K. Johnston's System of. Dub. Univ. **49**: 49.
Atlee, Col. Samuel J. Am. Hist. Rec. **3**: 448, 507. — (S. W. Pennypacker) Pennsyl. M. **2**: 74.
Atmosphere. (J. R. Leifchild) Good Words, **4**: 666. (H. T. Tuckerman) Putnam, **5**: 250. — Liv. Age, **58**: 155. — All the Year, **27**: 510. — Chamb. J. **20**: 244. — So. R. n. s. **16**: 135.
— and the Clouds. (J. Glaisher) Good Words, **8**: 110.
— and Fog-Signaling. (J. Tyndall) Pop. Sci. Mo. **6**: 541, 685.
— Appearances of, Aug. 19, 1825. (C. Meriwether) Am. J. Sci. **11**: 325.
— as an Anvil. (J. P. Cooke, jr.) Pop. Sci. Mo. **5**: 220.
— Changes of aqueous Portion of. J. Frankl. Inst. **42**: 347.
— Chemical Analysis of. (M. Brunner) Am. J. Sci. **23**: 280.
— Chemical and Geological Relations of. (T. S. Hunt) Am. J. Sci. **119**: 349.
— Circulation of. (M. F. Maury) West. J. **6**: 16.
— Components of. Tait, n. s. **23**: 356.
— Condition during Cholera. (R. D. Thomson) J. Frankl. Inst. **61**: 202.
— Constitution of. (J. Johnston) Am. Meth. M. **22**: 110.
— Currents in. (D. Murray) Nature, **15**: 294. — Chamb. J. **33**: 298. Same art. Ecl. M. **51**: 22.
— — and Oceanic Currents. (L. Dubois) Meth. Q. **21**: 206, 374.
— — Hildebrandsson on. Nature, **12**: 123.
— — in West Indies. (W. G. Palgrave) Nature, **10**: 65.
— Distribution of Moisture in. Pop. Sci. Mo. **7**: 483.
— Earth and Air. (S. S. Conant) Harper, **46**: 545.
— Economy of. Dub. R. **9**: 289.
— Etiology of. (D. A. Gorton) Nat. Q. **30**: 55.
— Flammarion on. (W. F. Barrett) Nature, **8**: 22.
— Great Movements of. (A. Buchan) Nature, **3**: 75.
— in its Geological Relations. (E. T. Hardman) Ecl. Engin. **19**: 135.
— Infection in. (J. Tyndall) Pop. Sci. Mo. **10**: 643.
— Influence of, on Health and Diseases. Pamph. **14**: 107.
— Luminous Matter in. (H. Waldner) Nature, **5**: 304.
— of London. Pamph. **15**: 61.
— of Rocky Mountains. (H. Draper) Am. J. Sci. **113**: 89.
— of a World on Fire. (C. Pritchard) Good Words, **8**: 249.
— Optical Phenomena of. (G F. Chambers) Pop. Sci. R. **1**: 216.
— Pressure of. (P. Bert) Pop. Sci. Mo. **11**: 316.
— — as a Source of Power. J. Frankl. Inst. **78**: 271, 343. **79**: 200. **80**: 28, 279.
— — Effect on Level of the Ocean. (Sir J. C. Ross) Am. J. Sci. **69**: 52. Same art. J. Frankl. Inst. **58**: 394.
— — Influence of, on Human Life. Nature, **12**: 472.

Atmosphere, Problems of, Balloon Ascension to solve, 1850. J. Frankl. Inst. **51**: 34.
— Resistance of, to Falling Bodies. (E. Loomis) Am. J. Sci. **68**: 67.
— — to Railroad Trains. (H. Bessemer) J. Frankl. Inst. **44**: 145.
— Spectrum of. (J. P. Maclear) Nature, **5**: 341.
— Transparency of. (C. Abbe) Am. J. Sci. **88**: 28.
— — and Opacity of. Liv. Age, **120**: 692, 815.
— Variations of, Phenomena of. (H. W. Dove) Am. J. Sci. **69**: 31.
— Waves of. (W. R. Birt) J. Frankl. Inst. **46**: 349. — (G. W. Warren) Nation, **15**: 423. — Chamb. J. **16**: 42.
— Weight of, Experiments on, 1648. Lond. Soc. **40**: 260.
— Wonders of. Chamb. J. **50**: 278.
See Air.
Atmospheres and Currents, Thoughts on. (A. K. H. Boyd) Good Words, **3**: 155.
Atmospheric Gas Engines. J. Frankl. Inst. **100**: 262.
Atmospheric Railway. Penny M. **14**: 109, 117.
Atmospheric Telegraph. Nature, **9**: 64, 105.
Atom, Idea of an. (J. D. Whelpley) Am. J. Sci. **48**: 352.
Atoms. (Sir J. W. F. Herschel) Fortn. **1**: 81. — All the Year, **15**: 235. Same art. Ev. Sat. **1**: 387.
— and Equivalents. Nature, **16**: 293.
— and Molecules. (S. D. Tillman) Nature, **6**: 171.
— — Evolution of. (M. M. Pattison) Pop. Sci. R. **18**: 125.
— — spectroscopically considered. (J. N. Lockyer) Nature, **10**: 69, 89.
— Gaudin's World of. Nature, **8**: 81.
— Size of. (Sir W. Thomson) Am. J. Sci. **100**: 38. — Nature, **1**: 551.
Atomic Collision and Non-Collision. (P. Spence) J. Spec. Philos. **14**: 286.
Atomic Constitution in Mineralogy. (E. J. Chapman) Canad. J. n. s. **2**: 435.
Atomic Controversy. Nature, **1**: 44.
Atomic Ratio. (J. P. Cooke, jr.) Am. J. Sci. **97**: 386.
Atomic Theory. Quar. **96**: 43. — (Sir H. Holland) Ed. R. **96**: 43. — (S. T. Preston) Ecl. Engin. **23**: 76. — Dub. Univ. **52**: 463. — (A. Wurtz) Nature, **10**: 345.
— Before Christ and since. Westm. **59**: 167. Same art. Ecl. M. **29**: 1.
— Brown's Lectures on. Brit. Q. **62**: 336. Same art. Ecl. M. **45**: 194. Same art. Liv. Age, **127**: 387.
— of Boscovich. (A. M. Mayer) J. Frankl. Inst. **86**: 253.
Atomic Weights. (C. Marignac) Am. J. Sci. **115**: 89.
— First Table of, Dalton's. (H.E.Roscoe) Nature, **11**: 52.
— Numerical Relation between. (J. P. Cooke, jr.) Am. J. Sci. **67**: 387.
Atomism and Theism. (J. C. Murray) Canad. Mo. **7**: 31.
Atomology. (T. Appel) Mercersb. **23**: 227.
Atonement. (J. Day) Chr. Mo. Spec. **6**: 475, 659. — (M. Stuart) Chr. Mo. Spec. **9**: 268, 308. — (F. G. Hibbard) Meth. Q. **6**: 392. — (A. Wheelock) Am. Bib. Repos. 2d s. **10**: 110. — Chr. Exam. **1**: 367. — Chr. R. **1**: 215. — (D. Holmes, jr.) Meth. Q. **7**: 414. — Spirit Pilg. **2**: 25. — (N. L. Frothingham) Chr. Exam. **34**: 146. — (C. A. Bartol) Chr. Exam. **36**: 331. — (G. E. Ellis) Chr. Exam. **37**: 403. — (J. Butler) Mo. Rel. M. **16**: 113. — (C. W. Clapp) New Eng. **23**: 296. — (S. Comfort) Am. Meth. M. **22**: 443. — (E. L. Frazier) Chr. Q. **5**: 254. — (O. B. Frothingham) Radical, **10**: 401. — (T. E. Hook) Colburn, **55**: 145. — (J. Morgan) Bib. Sac. **34**: 632. — (E. Pond) Bib. Sac. **13**: 130. **19**: 685. — (C. Robbins) Mo. Rel. M. **15**: 401. — (W. G. T. Shedd) Bib. Sac. **16**: 723. — (C. A. Stork) Evang. R. **17**: 372. — Bost. R. **3**: 1. — Chr. Obs. **61**: 160. **62**: 243. — Cong. M. **19**: 769. — Kitto, **18**: 72. **26**: 134. **30**: 47.
Atonement a threefold Satisfaction. (E. B. Webb) Bost. R. **6**: 1.
— and its Repudiators. Chr. Obs. **60**: 729.
— as Basis of Redemption. (L. S. Potwin) New Eng. **24**: 27.
— as a Revelation. (L. S. Potwin) New Eng. **23**: 265.
— Barnes on. (R. Watts) Princ. **31**: 464. — (B. J. Wallace) Am. Presb. R. **8**: 311.
— Beman on. Meth. Q. **7**: 379. — (C. Hodge) Princ. **17**: 84.
— Broad Church Theory of. Ecl. R. **119**: 36.
— Bushnell on. (N. Porter) New Eng. **25**: 228. — (H. James) No. Am. **102**: 556. — (C. Hodge) Princ. **38**: 161. — Am. Presb. R. **15**: 162.
— Bushnell's Forgiveness and Law. (J. T. Tucker) Cong. Q. **17**: 36.
— Bushnell's God in Christ. Prosp. R. **6**: 283.
— Bushnell's Vicarious Sacrifice. Brit. Q. **44**: 410.
— Campbell's Theory. (E. A. Park) Bib. Sac. **30**: 334.
— Carpenter's Remarks on Magee. Chr. Disc. **2**: 198.
— Catholic Doctrine of. Dub. R. **57**: 319.
— Christ's Death a Substitute for Punishment. (A. L. Chapin) Cong. R. **10**: 253.
— Christ's Sacrifice once for all. (J. W. Nevin) Mercersb. **17**: 100.
— Christian Doctrine of. (W. R. Alger) Univ. Q. **5**: 133.
— Coleridge's View of. (L. Grosvenor) Am. Bib. Repos. 2d s. **12**: 177.
— Controversy on. (G. V. Smith) Theo. R. **6**: 441. — Ecl. R. **82**: 249.
— Dale on. (J. Gordon) Theo. R. **13**: 17. — (D. W. Simon) Bib. Sac. **33**: 755. — Brit. Q. **63**: 472.
— Dewar on. Ecl. R. **54**: 306.
— Did Christ suffer as Divine? (L. Curtis) New Eng. **24**: 224.
— Doctrine of. (Dr. Duchal) Theo. Repos. **2**: 328. — (W. K. Pendleton) Chr. Q. **4**: 289. — (C. F. Schaeffer) Evang. R. **2**: 301. — Am. Presb. R. **3**: 630. — Chr. Rem. **27**: 200. — Month, **10**: 253.
— — in Isaiah, chap. lii. and liii. (E. C. Wines) Theo. & Lit. J. **6**: 404.
— Draper on. (E. S. Wilson) Am. Church R. **29**: 175.
— Edwardean Theory of. (W. F. Warren) Meth. Q. **20**: 386.
— Errors of Belief on. Bost. R. **3**: 217.
— Essay on. (T. Merritt) Am. Meth. M. **7**: 201.
— Expiatory Theory of. Brit. Q. **46**: 463. Same art. Theo. Ecl. **5**: 301.
— Extent of. Cong. M. **26**: 745.
— Factors of. (O. S. Taylor) Cong. R. **9**: 247.
— — Rejected. (G. F. Magoun) Cong. R. **9**: 1.
— for Sin, Christ's. (W. F. Gess) Good Words, **4**: 284
— Forensic Imputation. Kitto, **40**: 160.
— Gilbert on. Ecl. R. **64**: 47.
— Griffin on. (E. A. Park) Bib. Sac. **15**: 132. — Chr. Mo. Spec. **2**: 21, 82, 139.
— Grotian Theory of. (F. C. Baur) Bib. Sac. **9**: 259.
— Hargreaves on. Cong. M. **19**: 244.
— Higher Views of. Mo. Rel. M. **35**: 1.
— History of the Doctrine of. (E. Wigglesworth) Chr. Exam. **39**: 1. — Am. Presb. R. **2**: 246.
— in the early Church. (H. C. Sheldon) Meth. Q. **38**: 504.
— in the Light of Conscience. (L. S. Potwin) Bib. Sac. **24**: 141.
— Jenkyn on. Cong. M. **17**: 415. — (J. S. Hart) Princ. **7**: 674.
— Jerram on. Chr. Obs. **4**: 97. **30**: 166.
— Jowett on Doctrine of. Chr. Obs. **55**: 649.
— Justice as satisfied by. Am. Presb. R. **8**: 431.
— Limited, Doctrine of. (T. Dwight) New Eng. **28**: 361.

Atonement, Magee on. (H. Ware, jr.) Chr. Exam. **28:** 63. — Chr. Obs. **2:** 232, 287, 302. **9:** 226. — Ecl. R. **15:** 252, 377. — Meth. M. **34:** 102. — Am. Meth. M. **15:** 258.
— Meaning of. Theo. Repos. **3:** 385.
— — of *Nasa.* (W. H. Cobb) Bib. Sac. **30:** 422.
— — to bear Sin. (W. H. Cobb) Bib. Sac. **32:** 475.
— Means's Scriptural View of. Cong. M. **23:** 691.
— Modern Views of. No. Brit. **46:** 343.
— Moral Principle of. Ecl. R. **79:** 24.
— Moral View of. Brit. Q. **44:** 410. Same art. Theo. Ecl. **4:** 364.
— Nature of. (T. H. Skinner) Am. Bib. Repos. 3d s. **4:** 86.
— Necessity of. (D. T. Fisk) Bib. Sac. **18:** 284. — (E. C. Wines) Theo. & Lit. J. **8:** 134.
— New Englander and Prof. Huntington on, 1856. (W. T. Eustis) New Eng. **14:** 295.
— Objections to Doctrine. (J. Priestley) Theo. Repos. **1:** 17–490.
— — answered. Theo. Repos. **2:** 3.
— Philosophy of. (T. Archer) Ex. H. Lec. **10:** 143.
— Practical View of. Chr. Obs. **9:** 207.
— Present Views of. (Dr. Wing) Am. Presb. R. **3:** 218.
— Question of Authority in. (A. P. Peabody) Chr. Exam. **31:** 387.
— Recent German Discussions on. Theo. Ecl. **3:** 1.
— Relation of, to Holiness. (S. W. S. Dutton) New Eng. **13:** 493. — Mo. Rel. M. **15:** 19, 194.
— — Replies to Mr. Dutton. Mo. Rel. M. **15:** 105–320.
— — to the Moral Universe. (J. H. Dawson) Meth. Q. **37:** 581.
— Sacrifice and Sacrament. (M. Kieffer) Mercersb. **25:** 101.
— Sacrificial. (G. Hill) Univ. Q. **33:** 79.
— Sermons on. Chr. Obs. **56:** 552.
— Solly's Great Atonement. Prosp. R. **4:** 62.
— Steward's Mediatorial Sovereignty. Brit. Q. **39:** 327.
— Suggestions on Doctrine of. Kitto, **27:** 67.
— Symington on. (A. Alexander) Princ. **8:** 201.
— Theories of. (T. G. Apple) Mercersb. **15:** 397. — (J. Morgan) Bib. Sac. **34:** 632. **35:** 114.
— Three Views of. (J. Gilbert) Cong. **7:** 193.
— True Theory of. (L. E. Smith) Bapt. Q. **8:** 379.
— Unitarianism and Orthodoxy on. (G. E. Ellis) Chr. Exam. **61:** 18.
— Vicarious. (H. B. Ridgaway) Meth. Q. **31:** 589.
— — from Orthodox Stand-Point. Mo. Rel. M. **37:** 102.
— Views of. Chr. Exam. **18:** 142. — Prosp. R. **1:** 611.
— Worcester on. Chr. Exam. **11:** 312.
Atonement, Day of, Typical Import of the Ordinances of. (G. J. Walker) Kitto, **3:** 74.
Atonement of Leam Dundas. (E. L. Linton) Cornh. **32:** 129–610. **33:** 97–734. Same art. Lippinc. **16:** 285–731. **17:** 90–723. **18:** 54.
Atrato River, Surveys of. (J. C. Trautwine) J. Frankl. Inst. **74:** 27.
Atrato Ship Canal, Proposed. (E. W. Serrell) J. Frankl. Inst. **60:** 289. — (F. M. Kelley) J. Frankl. Inst. **62:** 83.
Attaché in Difficulties. Tinsley, **9:** 700.
— Recollections of an. (R. M. Walsh) Lippinc. **4:** 565.
Attachment, Law of, in the United States. Bank. M. (N. Y.) **12:** 193.
— — in the States. Bank. M. (N. Y.) **14:** 592.
Attempts upon my Life. Once a Week, **27:** 543, 557.
Atterbom's Island of the Blest. For. R. **2:** 431.
Atterbury, Francis. Cornh. **40:** 277. Same art. Liv. Age, **143:** 98.
Atterley, Joseph. Voyage to the Moon. West. Mo. R. **1:** 674.
Attic Historians and Col. Mure. (E. A. Freeman) Nat. R. **6:** 69.
Attic Orators. Quar. **152:** 526.
— Jebb's. (W. W. Goodwin) Nation, **22:** 324.
Attic Philosopher, Reflections of. (E. Souvestre) Western, **5:** 372.
Attica and Athens, Ancient. (A. J. Huntington) Bapt. Q. **11:** 215.
— — Sketch of. (A. L. Koeppen) Mercersb. **6:** 258.
— Antiquities of. (J. Foster) Ecl. R. **25:** 442.
Attleborough, Mass., Ministers of. Am. Q. **12:** 138.
Attorney, Confessions of an. Chamb. J. **14:** 241, 307. **15:** 118, 178. Same art. Ecl. M. **22:** 121, 207, 533.
— Reminiscences of an. Chamb. J. **17:** 355. Same art. Ecl. M. **23:** 79.
Attorney's Revenge; a Tale. Putnam, **6:** 523.
Attorneys. Brit. & For. R. **2:** 603.
— and Solicitors, Becoming. Chamb. J. **41:** 273.
Attorneyism, The Avatar of. Fraser, **40:** 563.
Attraction and Repulsion resulting from Radiation. Nature, **11:** 494.
— Mathematical Theories of, Todhunter's. (R. Tucker) Nature, **9:** 378, 399.
— of Mountains, Zach on. (J. Playfair) Ed. R. **26:** 36.
Attractions, Molecular. Knick. **4:** 329.
Attacks, Crispus, Who was? Am. Hist. Rec. **1:** 531.
Atwater, Caleb, Writings of. West. M. **2:** 375.
Atwood, David, with portrait. Lakeside, **2:** 213.
Au Sérieux. (E. W. Olney) Atlan. **46:** 329.
Aubanel, T., modern Provençal Poet. (H. W. Preston) Atlan. **34:** 385.
Aubépine, Writings of. (N. Hawthorne) Dem. R. **15:** 545.
Auber, D. F. E. Eng. Dom. M. **11:** 21. — Appleton, **6:** 10. — Ev. Sat. **10:** 527, 551.
Aubigné, the Huguenot Captain. Blackw. **38:** 790. **39:** 17.
Aubigné, C. d'. (A. A. Benton) So. M. **9:** 223.
Aubigné, J. H. Merle d'. *See* Merle d' Aubigné.
Aubigné, T. Agrippa d'. (A. A. Benton) So. M. **9:** 223. — Chr. Obs. **74:** 265.
— and Madame de Maintenon. Blackw. **67:** 174. Same art. Liv. Age, **25:** 49. Same art. Ecl. M. **17:** 97.
Aubrey, John, Antiquary and Gossip. Brit. Q. **24:** 153. Same art. Ecl. M. **39:** 71.
— Miscellanies, Folk-Lore in. (T. T. Wilkinson) Reliquary, **10:** 147.
Aubrey Marston. St. James, **7:** 3–411. **8:** 1–411. **9:** 70.
Auburn, Mt. *See* Mt. Auburn.
Auchmuty, Robert. N. E. Reg. **12:** 69.
Auckland, Lord, Diary and Correspondence of. Ed. R. **113:** 360. — Chr. Obs. **61:** 194.
Auckland to Awamutu. Fraser, **70:** 407.
Auckland Isles. Ev. Sat. **1:** 417.
Auction Duties. Niles's Reg. **21:** 103.
— in New York. Hunt, **14:** 506.
Auction Law. (T. Brinley) Hunt, **2:** 63, 153.
Auction System. Niles's Reg. **27:** 257, 273, 289, 305. **34:** 258, 419. **35:** 380. **36:** 184.
— Baldwin's Speech on. Niles's Reg. **18:** 418.
— of New York. Hunt, **10:** 154.
Auctioneer, A Poetical. Tait, **3:** 722.
Auctions. Chamb. J. **43:** 698. — Sharpe, **14:** 269. **47:** 78.
— and Auctioneers. (N. S. Dodge) Overland, **7:** 113.
— in London. Penny M. **13:** 65, 105, 133.
— Mock. Once a Week, **1:** 490.
Audatype for Printing Phonography. (D. S. Holman) J. Frankl. Inst. **104:** 429.
Aude, Valley of the. Cath. World. **23:** 640.
Audiences at the Play. (H. Louther) Tinsley, **26:** 51.

Audiometer, The. Nature, **20**: 1021.
— Researches with Prof. Hughes's. (B. W. Richardson) J. Frankl. Inst. **108**: 110.
Audiphone, The. (W. Chambers) Chamb. J. **57**: 336, 395.—Nature, **21**: 469.
Audley, Rev. J., Memoir of. Cong. M. **10**: 401.
Audley End. Antiquary, **3**: 109.
Audrey's Christmas Morning. Tinsley, **15**: 424.
Audubon, John James. (J. H. Friswell) Recr. Sci. **1**: 261.—(R. W. Griswold) Internat. M. **2**: 469.—Chamb. J. **46**: 85.—Sharpe, **52**: 237, 299.—Dem. R. **10**: 436.—Ed. R. **132**: 250. Same art. Liv. Age, **106**: 515.
— and Birds. (C. Winterfield) Dem. R. **2**: 279.—(H. T. Tuckerman) Meth. Q. **12**: 415.
— Birds of America. *See* Birds.
— in the New World. Liv. Age, **49**: 695.
— Incidents in the Life of. Godey, **42**: 306.
— Life of. (J. Burroughs) Nation, **9**: 13.
— Quadrupeds of North America. *See* Animals of America.
— Reminiscences of. (Miss Audubon) Scrib. **12**: 333.—(T. M. Brewer) Harper, **61**: 665.
Auerbach, Berthold. (T. S. Perry) Atlan. **34**: 433.—(B. Taylor) N. Ecl. **4**: 569.—(H. J. Warner) Chr. Exam. **82**: 15.—Eng. Dom. M. **10**: 154, 213.
— Freytag, and Heyse. No. Brit. **43**: 323.
— Later Novels. Westm. **110**: 348.
— Little Barefoot. Liv. Age, **54**: 59.
— Tales of the Black Forest. Dub. R. **22**: 354.
— Villa on the Rhine. (E. G. Martin) Nation, **9**: 12
— Waldfried. O. & N. **10**: 134.
— Writings of. (Miss Hale) Chr. Exam. **72**: 422.—Lond. Q. **39**: 344.
Auerstadt and Jena. Bentley, **54**: 616.
Auf Wiedersehen; a Story. (A. Stevens) Harper, **55**: 287.
Augier, E. (J. B. Matthews) Internat. R. **9**: 353.
Augsburg. (Miss Costello) Sharpe, **10**: 265.
— Confessors and Confession of. (F. W. Conrad) Evang. R. **15**: 246.
Augsburg Confession. (C. P. Gregory) Bib. Sac. **32**: 266.
— and Lutheranism. (J. A. Brown) Luth. Q. **1**: 246.
— and the 39 Articles. (J. G. Morris) Luth. Q. **8**: 79.
— Author of. (G. L. Plitt) Luth. Q. **7**: 341.
— Authorship of. (J. H. W. Stuckenberg) Evang. R. **18**: 219.
— Bibliography of. (C. P. Kranth, jr.) Evang. R. **10**: 16
— Civil Affairs and. (L. E. Albert) Luth. Q. **11**: 312.
— Delivery of. (R. Weiser) Evang. R. **18**: 543.
— Holman Lectures on. (J. A. Brown) Evang. R. **17**: 547. **18**: 567. **19**: 489. **20**: 481. **21**: 599.
— Infallibility of, refuted. (J. A. Brown) Luth. Q. **2**: 161.
— Question on. (J. A. Brown) Luth. Q. **8**: 161.
August. (W. Howitt) Howitt, **2**: 89.
— in England. Fraser, **68**: 791.
August Lilies; a Poem. (M. E. Bradley) Scrib. **8**: 423.
August Pastoral; a Poem. (B. Taylor) Atlan. **24**: 470.
Augusta, Queen, and the Red Cross. (Dr. Treuenpreuss) Internat. R. **3**: 492.
Augustine, St. Brit. Q. **6**: 213.—(J. A. Alexander) Princ. **8**: 567.—Chr. R. **5**: 64.—Kitto, **22**: 1.—Lond. Q. **54**: 359.—(E. Pond) Princ. **34**: 406.
— and Adeodatus. (E. H. Plumptre) Good Words, **8**: 107.
— and Calvinism. Brownson, **20**: 289.
— and St. Jerome. Cong. **4**: 227.
— and Pelagius. (A. Neander) Am. Bib. Repos. **3**: 66.
— and Scientific Unbelief. (J. Beckaby) Month, **28**: 195.
— as a Sacred Orator. (O. A. Taylor) Am. Bib. Repos. 2d s. **7**: 375.—Liv. Age, **56**: 385.
— at Hippo. (H. W. Foote) Chr. Exam. **69**: 258.
Augustine, St. City of God. (J. A. Brown) Luth. Q. **2**: 460.—(E. H. Gillett) Am. Presb. R. **14**: 434.—(E. L. Godkin) Nation, **13**: 357.—Chr. Obs. **71**: 745.
— Confessions. (W. Alexander) Contemp. **5**: 133. Same art. Ecl. M. **69**: 433. Same art. Liv. Age, **94**: 67. Same art. Theo. Ecl. **5**: 113.—Chr. R. **15**: 483.—Dub. R. **7**: 430.—Chr. Obs. **77**: 928.
— Early Life and Conversion of. Chr. R. **25**: 415.
— Genius and Theology of. (P. Schaff) Mercersb. **14**: 98.
— Life of. (R. W. Lubienski) Overland, **14**: 24.
— — and Character of. Putnam, **7**: 225.
— — and Labors of. (M. L. Stoever) Evang. R. **19**: 1.—(E. W. Hooker) Princ. **26**: 436.
— Monica, the Mother of. Bost. R. **1**: 363.
— Philosophy of, and Modern Philosophy. (C. Vercellone) Cath. World, **10**: 481.
— Theological System of, and its Sources. Chr. Obs. **61**: 821.
Augustinism and Pelagianism. (H. P. Tappan) Am. Bib. Repos. **5**: 195.
— Mozley on. Dub. R. **40**: 67.—No. Brit. **24**: 217.
— Original Sin. So. R. n. s. **22**: 5.
Augustodunum, Antiquities of. (E. A. Freeman) Brit. Q. **74**: 1.
Auk, Great. (J. Orton) Am. Natural. **3**: 539.
Auld Robin Gray; a Tale. (Mrs. G. W. Godfrey) Temp. Bar. **55**: 263, 405.
Auld Wife's Dream; a Poem. (J. Hogg) Fraser, **7**: 68.
Aulick, Commodore J. H. Am. Hist. Rec. **3**: 291.
Aumale, Duc d', with portrait. (G. M. Towle) Appleton, **7**: 97.
Aunt Anastasia on Society. Tinsley, **1**: 45.
Aunt Ann's Ghost Story. Blackw. **96**: 742.
Aunt Barbara's Present; a Tale. Chamb. J. **56**: 217, 232, 250.
Aunt Bart,—Uncle Bart. Mo. Rel. M. **47**: 137, 265.
Aunt Bessie's Mistake. Tinsley, **10**: 187.
Aunt by Marriage. (J. Payn) Belgra. **31**: 66.
Aunt Cindy's Dinner. (S. W. Kellogg) Lippinc. **16**: 73.
Aunt Dorothy's last Offer; a Tale. (A. Clyde) Sharpe, **43**: 131.
Aunt Dunk; a Tale. (L. K. Knatchbull-Hugessen) Belgra. **20**: 101.
Aunt Edith's Foreign Lover; a Tale. (M. W. Fisher) Lippinc. **22**: 96.
Aunt Eunice's Idea. (N. H. Holdich) Harper, **57**: 357.
Aunt Francisca. (C. Bernhard) Colburn, **115**: 425. **116**: 73, 193.
Aunt Grace's Sweetheart. (M. Lemon) Ev. Sat. **6**: 757.
Aunt Hannah; a Poem. (J. T. Trowbridge) Harper, **52**: 486.
Aunt Janet's Diamonds. Chamb. J. **32**: 88, 100. Same art. Ecl. M. **49**: 60.
Aunt Judy. (J. W. Palmer) Atlan. **18**: 76.
Aunt Justine; a Story. (F. Derrick) Eng. Dom. M. **3**: 18–582.
Aunt Lora's Long Ago. Belgra. **22**: 291.
Aunt Madeline's Cross. (F. L. Curtis) Galaxy, **4**: 550.
Aunt Margaret's Trouble, Tale of. All the Year, **16**: 1–121.
Aunt Margery's Mishaps. (L. Kip) Overland, **2**: 508.
Aunt Mary. (N. Macleod) Good Words, **2**: 137.
Aunt Maxwell's Return; a Dialogue. (Mrs. C. Martin) Irish Mo. **7**: 113.
Aunt May; a Tale. Sharpe, **44**: 73.
Aunt Mercy. (Mrs. C. L. Hentz) Godey, **24**: 47, 127.
Aunt Patty's Pattens; a Sketch. Dub. Univ. **89**: 385.
Aunt Piety Parsons. Knick. **36**: 71.
Aunt Penelope's Girlhood. (A. L. Johnson) Galaxy, **6**: 47.
Aunt Rosy's Chest. (O. A. Wadsworth) Atlan. **30**: 322.
Aunt Sarah's Ghost. Bentley, **11**: 294.
Aunt Tabitha's Railway Adventure. Lond. Soc. **6**: 417. Same art. Ecl. M. **64**: 117.

Aunts, Our. All the Year, **14**: 83.
Auricular Confession. *See* Confession.
Aurignac Cave, Date of Interment in. (W. B. Dawkins) Nature, **4**: 208.
Auriol; or, the Elixir of Life. (W. H. Ainsworth) Colburn, **74**: 421. **76**: 109.
Aurora. Fraser, **68**: 666.
Aurora; a Vision. Blackw. **35**: 992.
Aurora Australis. (J. Meldrum) Nature, **5**: 392.
— Spectrum of. (J. P. Maclear) Nature, **17**: 11.
Aurora Borealis. Am. J. Sci. **16**: 290. — Knick. **4**: 97. — (R. H. Bonnycastle) Am. J. Sci. **30**: 121. — (Lord Lindsay) Nature, **4**: 347. — (E. Loomis) Harper, **39**: 1. — (G. B. Prescott) Atlan. **4**: 740. — (D. Walker) Intel. Obs. **2**: 258. Same art. Ecl. M. **58**: 130. — Chamb. J. **48**: 35. — Ecl. M. **53**: 547. — (R. H. Scott) Nature, **22**: 33. — Penny M. **2**: 489. — St. Paul's, **4**: 598.
— and Aurora Australis. (J. Lovering) Am. Alma. **1860**: 55.
— and Declination of the Needle, Cause of. (G. A. Rowell) J. Frankl. Inst. **44**: 343. — (E. Loomis) Am. J. Sci. **100**: 153. **105**: 245. — (A. D. Bache) J. Frankl. Inst. **16**: 5. **17**: 1.
— and Earth Currents. (W. H. Preece) Nature, **5**: 368.
and a new Form of Declinometer. (J. T. Bottomley) Nature, **5**: 326.
— Arch of March 20, 1865. (A. S. Herschel) Intel. Obs. **7**: 377.
— Arches in. (E. J. Lowe) Recr. Sci. **2**: 244.
— — Height of. (H. A. Newton) Am. J. Sci. **89**: 286.
— Arctic. (G. Kennan) Putnam, **16**: 197.
— at Toronto. (G. T. Kingston) Am. J. Sci. **98**: 65.
— Cause of. (A. De la Rive) Am. J. Sci. **68**: 353. — Am. J. Sci. **19**: 235. — (B. S. Joslin) Am. J. Sci. **35**: 145.
— Character and Spectra of, Capron's. Nature, **21**: 127.
— Early Mention of. (J. Jeremiah) Nature, **3**: 174.
— Explanation of a Phenomenon of. (C. C. Cooper) J. Frankl. Inst. **47**: 120.
— Height of. (J. P. Espy) J. Frankl. Inst. **17**: 294, 363
— — and other Phenomena. (G. A. Rowell) Ed. New Philos. J. **44**: 79.
— in N. Europe. (C. Hansteen) Ed. Philos. J. **12**: 83.
— Observations of. (H. R. Procter) Nature, **18**: 606.
— of Oct. 20, 1827. Am. J. Sci. **14**: 91.
— of Jan. 25, 1837. (D. Olmsted) Am. J. Sci. **32**: 176.
— of July 1, 1837. (C. Dewey) Am. J. Sci. **33**: 143.
— of Nov. 14, 1837. (F. A. P. Barnard) Am. J. Sci. **34**: 267.
— of Sept. 3, 1839. (E. C. Herrick) Am. J. Sci. **38**: 260.
— of 1848–49. (W. Sturgeon) Ed. New Philos. J. **47**: 147, 225.
— of 1850–51. (J. H. Lefroy) Am. J. Sci. **64**: 153.
— of June 11, 1852. (C. S. Lyman) Am. J. Sci. **65**: 55.
— of Aug. 28 to Sept. 4, 1859. (E. Loomis) Am. J. Sci. **78**: 385. **79**: 92, 249, 386. **80**: 79, 339. **82**: 71, 318. — (B. V. Marsh) J. Frankl. Inst. **68**: 352.
— of March 9, 1860. (E. J. Lowe) Recr. Sci. **3**: 63.
— of Sept. 5 and 15, 1868. (W. S. Gilman, jr.) Am. J. Sci. **96**: 390.
— of April 15, 1869, seen in New York. (W. S. Gilman, jr.) Am. J. Sci. **98**: 114.
— of Oct. 14, 1870, Variation of Magnetic Declination during. (A. M. Mayer) J. Frankl. Inst. **90**: 424.
— of Oct. 24, 25, 1870. (A. C. Twining) Am. J. Sci. **101**: 126.
— of Feb. 4, 1872. (J. P. Earwaker) Nature, **5**: 322. — (L. Respighi) Nature, **5**: 511. — (A. C. Twining) Am. J. Sci. **103**: 273. — J. Frankl. Inst. **93**: 356. — (G. F. Barker) Am. J. Sci. **105**: 81.
— Periodicity of. (D. Olmsted) Ed. New Philos. J. **51**: 293.
Aurora Borealis, Relation of, to gravitating Currents. (P. E. Chase) Nature, **4**: 497.
— Spectrum of. (G. F. Barker) Nature, **5**: 172, 324. — (A. J. Angström) Nature, **10**: 210.
— Speculations on. (J. M. Wilson) Nature, **4**: 372.
— Strange Discoveries respecting. (R. A. Proctor) Fraser, **81**: 237. Same art. Ecl. M. **74**: 465.
— viewed as an Electric Discharge. (B. V. Marsh) Am. J. Sci. **81**: 311.
Aurora Polaris. (D. Walker) Overland, **1**: 531. — Ecl. M. **73**: 696.
Auroral and Optical Phenomena. (A. C. Twining) Am. J. Sci. **32**: 217.
Auroras. (F. Morton) Once a Week, **3**: 380. — Good Words, **1**: 753.
— and Sunset. (C. D. Dewey) Am. J. Sci. **38**: 146.
— Capron on. Nature, **21**: 127. Art J. **32**: 91.
— Correspondence of Northern and Southern. (E. Heis) Nature, **4**: 213.
— Daylight. Nature, **4**: 209.
— Geographical Distribution of. Nature, **11**: 14.
Aurora Floyd; a Novel. (M. E. Braddon) Temp. Bar, **4**: 239–505. **5**: 67–481. **6**: 74–512. **7**: 101, 247.
Ausable Chasm, N. Y. (C. P. MacCalla) Scrib. **8**: 192.
Auscultation. Penny M. **3**: 71.
— Latham on. Quar. **57**: 199.
Ausonius, D. M., Poet. (C. T. Brooks) Scrib. **12**: 379. — (J. Mew) Fraser, **99**: 741. — Portfo.(Den.) **13**: 455. **15**: 42.
— Translations from. Blackw. **8**: 678.
Austen, Jane. (S. S. Conant) Harper, **41**: 225. — (T. E. Kebbel) Fortn. **13**: 187. — (Anne Manning) Hours at Home, **11**: 516. — (G. Smith) Nation, **10**: 124. — (A. M. Waterston) Atlan. **11**: 235. Same art. Liv. Age, **76**: 418. **45**: 207. — Blackw. **86**: 99. Same art. Liv. Age, **62**: 424. — Colburn, **95**: 17. Same art. Liv. Age, **33**: 477. — Cornh. **24**: 158. Same art. Liv. Age, **110**: 643. — Ecl. M. **37**: 197. — Eng. Dom. M. **2**: 237, 278. **14**: 187. **24**: 267. — Fraser, **61**: 20. — No. Brit. **52**: 129. — St. Paul's, **5**: 631.
— and Miss Mitford. Blackw. **107**: 290. Same art. Liv. Age, **105**: 38. — (G. F. Chorley) Quar. **128**: 196. Same art. Liv. Age, **104**: 558.
— and her Novels. Dub. R. **67**: 430.
— Early Writings of. (E. Quincy) Nation, **13**: 164.
— Emma. (Sir W. Scott) Quar. **14**: 188.
— Hunting for Snarkes at Lyme Regis. Temp. Bar, **57**: 39. Same art. Liv. Age, **143**: 633.
— Northanger Abbey and Persuasion. (R. Whately) Quar. **24**: 352.
— Novels. (I. M. Luyster) Chr. Exam. **74**: 400. — Chamb J. **47**: 157.
Austerfield, Yorkshire, Extracts from Registers of. N. E. Reg. **4**: 177.
Austerlitz. Bentley, **54**: 519.
— Napoleon's Campaign of, 1805. Temp. Bar, **35**: 506.
Austin, Alfred. Human Tragedy. Dub. R. **79**: 155. — Irish Mo. **4**: 437.
— Madonna's Child. Temp. Bar, **38**: 246.
— Poems. Quar. **144**: 499.
— Rome or Death. Dub. Univ. **83**: 244.—Month, **22**: 102.
Austin, Arthur W., with portrait. Dem. R. **41**: 307.
Austin, Charles. (L. A. Tollemache) Fortn. **23**: 321.
Austin, John. Plea for the Constitution. (J. S. Mill) Fraser, **59**: 489.
Austin, Samuel, Memoir of. Am. Q. Reg. **9**: 201. — Spirit Pilg. **4**: 293.
Austin, S. F., and the Early Times of Texas. De Bow, **24**: 113.
Austin Chasuble's Love Chance; a Story. (T. Gift) Galaxy, **17**: 495.

Austin Canons and Canonesses, at Canonsleigh, Devon. (C. S. Perceval) Arch. **40**: 417.
Austin Friars. Good Words, **19**: 332.
— Remains of the Priory of, at Ludlow. (B. Botfield) Arch. **39**: 173.
Austin Friars; a Story. (Mrs. J. H. Riddell) Tinsley, **4**: 233–536. **5**: 1–665. **6**: 1–701. **7**: 101.
Australasia, The French in. Colburn, **123**: 379.
— Public Affairs in. Fortn. **29**: 494.
— Travels in. Ecl. R. **105**: 426.
— Voyage to, 1800–4. Ecl. R. **10**: 977.
— Wallace's. Nature, **20**: 598.
Australasian Democracy. (Sir D. Wedderburn) Fortn. **26**: 48.
Australia. (A. H. Guernsey) Harper, **6**: 16. — (S. Hyacinth) Overland, **4**: 118. — (G. M. Steele) Meth. Q. **24**: 454. — (J. Ware) Chr. Exam. **6**: 291. — No. Brit. **4**: 281. — Brit. Q. **5**: 29. — Westm. **12**: 166. — Blackw. **62**: 602. — Quar. **68**: 48. — Mus. **10**: 482. — Mo. R. **120**: 513. **121**: 258. **131**: 485. — De Bow, **13**: 584. — Dub. Univ. **52**: 298. — Fraser, **77**: 642. — No. Brit. **4**: 281.
— Aborigines of. (J. Forrest) Anthrop. J. **5**: 316. — (R. Salvado) Anthrop. J. **7**: 280. — (G. Marcel) Pop. Sci. Mo. **19**: 680. — (J. Wisher) Fortn. **32**: 82. — (M. Watson) Irish Mo. **5**: 344. — Chamb. J. **41**: 686. — No. Brit. **32**: 366. — Penny M. **11**: 65.
— — Characteristics of. (G. W. Earl) Ed. New Philos. J. **48**: 219.
— — Condition of, 1852. (W. Westgarth) Ed. New Philos. J. **53**: 225. **54**: 36.
— — Crania of. (S. M. Bradley) Anthrop. J. **2**: 136.
— — Dawson on. (E. B. Tylor) Nature, **24**: 529.
— — Diet of. Bentley, **51**: 544.
— — of South. Dub. Univ. **87**: 84. **88**: 111.
— Adventure on Coast of. (W. P. Snow) Harper, **29**: 417.
— and the East. (Dr. Jobson) Lond. Q. **18**: 201.
— — Hood on, 1841–42. Mo. R. **162**: 115.
— and Europe formerly one Continent. (B. Seeman) Pop. Sci. R. **5**: 18.
— and New Zealand. (R. H. Horne) Contemp. **22**: 699.
— and Van Diemen's Land. Dub. Univ. **13**: 176.
— and its Wealth, 1852. Brit. Q. **16**: 238.
— Anglicanism in. Dub. R. **79**: 368.
— as it is. Once a Week, **25**: 507, 551, 573.
— as it is, 1872. Once a Week, **26**: 64.
— Banking in. Bank. M. (L.) **17**: 850.
— Beagle's Discoveries in. Fraser, **34**: 105.
— Burke's Exploration of. Irish Mo. **4**: 619, 681. — (M. Watson) Irish Mo. **5**: 170. — Temp. Bar, **5**: 43.
— Bush-Life in. (J. Hayes) Overland, **5**: 495. — (W. Chamberlain) Internat. R. **9**: 653. **10**: 87.
— — A Year of. Sharpe, **49**: 202, 262.
See Bush-Life in Queensland.
— Bushranging in. Victoria, **12**: 97.
— Central. Chamb. J. **11**: 13. **35**: 242.
— — Explorations in. Colburn, **129**: 1.
— Charms of an Australian Squatter's Life. Colburn, **91**: 215.
— Chinese in. Liv. Age, **57**: 860.
— Church-Life in. Brit. Q. **32**: 169.
— Climate and Health of. Chamb. J. **19**: 89.
— Colonies of. (Sir J. Barrow) Quar. **68**: 88. — Ecl. R. **60**: 123. — Ed. R. **121**: 349. — Lond. Q. **1**: 517. — Quar. **32**: 311.
— — and Confederation. (H. M. Hyndman) Fraser, **94**: 641.
— — Democratic Government in. Westm. **89**: 480.
— — Federation and Imperial Union. Fraser, **96**: 526.
— — History of. Westm. **110**: 311. — Liv. Age, **139**: 451.
— — Hughes on. Tait, n. s. **19**: 761.
— — or Republics. Fraser, **37**: 566.
Australia, Colonies of, Political and Social Prospects of. Fraser, **57**: 659.
— — Progress of. (J. Douglas) Canad. Mo. **10**: 239.
— Commerce and Finance of. Bank. M. (L.) **15**: 425–791.
— Convict Life and Labor in. Cornh. **4**: 229. **13**: 489.
— Coral Reefs. (Sir H. Holland) Ed. R. **81**: 468.
— Culture in. (A. H. Keane) St. James, **48**: 111, 220.
— Desert of. Chamb. J. **52**: 673.
— Discovery of. Geog. M. **3**: 195.
— — by the Portuguese in 1601. (R. H. Major) Arch **38**: 439.
— — Early. (R. H. Major) Arch. **44**: 233.
— Eastern, Settled Districts in. (J. W. F. Blundell) Colburn, **87**: 84.
— Education in. *See* Education in Australia.
— Election Contest in. Cornh. **5**: 25.
— Emigrant Life in. Sharpe, **33**: 186.
— Emigration to. Chamb. J. **19**: 210. — Mo. R. **132**: 379. — Tait, n. s. **6**: 168.
— — Howitt's Letters on. Tait, n. s. **8**: 270.
— Emigration Company, Letter from the Manager of. Tait, n. s. **6**: 280.
— Emigration Society. Dub. Univ. **14**: 329.
— English in. Sharpe, **12**: 321.
— Entomology of. Colburn, **162**: 195.
— Explorations in. (C. H. Pearson) Nation, **22**: 157. — Ecl. R. **120**: 407.
— — Chapter in History of. Fraser, **66**: 726.
— — in 1838. Ecl. R. **69**: 157.
— — in 1842. Dub. R. **13**: 74.
— — in 1844–46. Ecl. R. **84**: 622.
— — in 1862. Cornh. **5**: 354.
— — Expedition for. Chamb. J. **37**: 108. Same art. Liv. Age, **73**: 37.
— — Forrest's. Nature, **13**: 83.
— — Grey's. Mus. **44**: 361.
— — in Northwestern and Western, 1837–39. Chr. Rem. **3**: 35.
— — in Wilds of. Tinsley, **7**: 33.
— — Leichhardt's. (H. W. Torrey) No. Am. **66**: 482.
— — Mitchell's. Blackw. **44**: 690. **45**: 113. — Ecl. R. **87**: 603.
— — Stoke's. For. Q. **37**: 257.
— — Stuart's, 1857. Once a Week, **4**: 215. Same art. Liv. Age, **69**: 288.
— — Sturt's. Liv. Age, **84**: 250. — Ecl. R. **90**: 599.
— Explorers of. Ed. R. **116**: 1.
— Explorers killing Natives. Ecl. R. **69**: 157.
— Fauna of. Chamb. J. **40**: 219.
— Flinder's Voyage to, 1801–3. (Sir J. Barrow) Quar. **12**: 1. — (J. Foster) Ecl. R. **29**: 359.
— From the Pacific to the Murray. Once a Week, **21**: 61, 83, 93.
— Geological Map of. Nature, **8**: 352.
— — Smyth's. Nature, **13**: 352.
— Glimpse of. (J. H. Perkins) No. Am. **70**: 166.
— Gold in. Colburn, **93**: 353.
— — and the Gold-Supply. Quar. **107**: 1.
— — Discovery of. (C. Stetson) Hunt, **29**: 166. — Ecl. M. **27**: 506.
— — Effects upon the Country. J. Statis. Soc. **24**: 198.
— Gold District of. Dub. Univ. **39**: 607. — Liv. Age, **31**: 406.
— — with Map. Bank. M (L.) **12**: 9.
— Gold-Fields and Gold-Miners of. Ed. R. **117**: 82.
— — Bathurst Diggings. Chamb. J. **16**: 291.
— — Condition and Prospects of, 1862. Bank. M. (L.) **22**: 629.
— — Descent into a Gold-Mine. Gent. M. n. s. **5**: 685.
— — Mining Township in. All the Year, **29**: 352.
— Golden Age of. (R. H. Patterson) Brit. Q. **74**: 332.
— — Highwaymen of. Dub. Univ. **76**: 280.

Australia, History and Resources of. (W. J. A. Bradford) Chr. Exam. **56**: 188.
— Hood on. Tait, n. s. **10**: 586.
— How Llamas got to. Chamb. J. **39**: 340. Same art. Ecl. M. **59**: 507.
— Howitt's. Ecl. R. **82**: 166. Same art. Ecl. M. **36**: 1043.
— in 1830. Ecl. R. **53**: 247.
— Inglis on. (W. H. Bishop) Nation, **31**: 155.
— Kangaroo Drive in. Cornh. **14**: 735.
— Languages of. (A. Mackenzie) Anthrop. J. **3**: 247. — (W. Ridley) Anthrop. J. **2**: 257. — (G. Taplin) Anthrop. J. **1**: 84.
— — and Traditions of. (W. Ridley) Anthrop. J. **2**: 257. **7**: 232.
— — Comparative Table of. (G. Taplin) Anthrop. J. **1**: 84.
— — Position of. (W. H. I. Bleek) Anthrop. J. **1**: 89.
— Letter from. (R. D. Adams) Fraser, **92**: 799.
— Letters from. House. Words, **1**: 475. — Sharpe, **14**: 279.
— Life in. Dub. Univ. **58**: 361. **60**: 349.
— Maritime Discoveries in. Blackw. **1**: 493.
— New Zealand, and Pacific Islands. (J. Vogel) Princ. n. s. **3**: 435.
— Night Passenger in. Chamb. J. **44**: 260.
— Notes on Men and Things in. Colburn, **85**: 58–489. **86**: 152.
— Old and new Squatter in. House. Words, **12**: 433, 471.
— Over the Snowy Mountains. Eng. Dom. M. **9**: 149, 209.
— Population of, Analysis of, 1847. (F. G. P. Neison) J. Statis. Soc. **11**: 38.
— Present and Future of, 1844. Dub. Univ. **24**: 219.
— Prospects for Emigrants, 1848. Howitt, **3**: 384.
— Progress of. Ecl. R. **94**: 158. **96**: 389.
— — and Destiny of. Nat. Q. **12**: 231.
— — Sidney on. Ecl. R. **96**: 565.
— Quadrupeds of. House. Words, **7**: 208.
— Quaker Missions to. Tait, n. s. **10**: 218.
— Residence and Rambles in. Blackw. **72**: 300.
— Rising of. (S. H. Wintle) Nature, **7**: 129.
— Scenes and Adventures in. Lippinc. **15**: 282, 393.
— Sheep-Farming in. (J. Manning) Overland, **5**: 147. — Chamb. J. **15**: 317.
— Sketch in. (M. Watson) Irish Mo. **5**: 511.
— Sketches in. (T. McCombie) Tait, n. s. **10**: 605, 720. **11**: 95, 152, 308. **24**: 104, 626. **25**: 9, 493, 521.
— South. (M. Stapley) Bentley, **44**: 89. — Dub. R. **6**: 449. — Ed. R. **75**: 140. — Westm. **21**: 441. **23**: 213. — Ecl. R. **61**: 167.
— — Colonization of. For. Q. **25**: 374. — Chamb. J. **9**: 395.
— — Eyre's Explorations in. (H. Kingsley) Macmil. **12**: 501. **13**: 55. Same art. Liv. Age, **87**: 481.
— — Fishing in. (G. Hamilton) Colburn, **81**: 160.
— — Hunting in. Colburn, **94**: 362.
— — in 1837, Gouger on. Mo. R. **147**: 507.
— — Leigh's Travels in. Mo. R. **149**: 359.
— — Meteorology of, Todd's. Nature, **21**: 281.
— — Progress and Prosperity of, 1866. Chr. Obs. **66**: 667.
— — Settler in. Chamb. J. **58**: 155.
— Station-Life in, 1860. Knick. **55**: 365.
— Steam Navigation on Rivers of. Hogg, **12**: 519.
— Summer at Port Phillip. Tait, n. s. **11**: 213.
— Summer in. (J. Hussey) Tait. n. s. **28**: 10.
— Superstitions of. (J. Browne) Canad. J. n. s. **1**: 251, 505.
— Survey of, King's Narrative of. Lond. M. **17**: 377.
— Swan River. (J. W. F. Blundell) Colburn, **86**: 475. — Dub. Univ. **14**: 84, 196.
Australia, Swan River, Settlement on, Inland Sea at. Dub. Univ. **9**: 570.
— Sydney in 1869. Temp. Bar, **27**: 504.
— Sydney to Port Phillip. Bentley, **22**: 343.
— Tendencies in. Fraser, **83**: 584.
— Trade and Banking in. Bank. M. (L.) **14**: 117.
— Two Years in, Howitt's. Ecl. R. **82**: 166. Same art. Ecl. M. **36**: 1043.
— United States of. (R. H. Horne) Contemp. **18**: 174.
— Voyage to. (J. B. Mackenzie) Canad. Mo. **10**: 300.
— Western. (J. W. F. Blundell) Colburn, **86**: 166.
— — Benedictines in. Dub. R. **88**: 56.
— — Emigrant in. (J. W. F. Blundell) Colburn, **86**: 359.
— — Irwin's. Dub. Univ. **7**: 149.
— — Sufferings of Capt. Grey's Expedition. Penny M. **11**: 218, 239, 246.
— Working-Man in. Chamb. J. **8**: 44.
See Victoria; Queensland; New South Wales; etc.
Australian, An, in England. Cornh. **13**: 110.
Australian and Tasmanian Races. (A. H. Keane) Nature, **19**: 549.
Australian Capitals, Some. (W. Senior) Gent. M. n. s. **23**: 47.
Australian Fraud; a Tale. Chamb. J. **55**: 731.
Australian Jim Walker. House. Words, **17**: 500.
Australian Museum. Nature, **10**: 81.
Australian Ploughman's Story. House. Words, **1**: 39.
Australian Wife. St. James, **33**: 145.
Australiana. (T. F. Meagher) Putnam, **5**: 598. **6**: 67.
Austria. Brit. & For. R. **11**: 32. **14**: 218. — Ed. R. **40**: 298. — Mo. R. **115**: 102. — (M. Heilprin) Nation, **10**: 298. — All the Year, **1**: 173. — No. Brit. **44**: 51. — Liv. Age, **67**: 182.
— and France, 1859. Colburn, **115**: 366.
— — 1867. Colburn, **141**: 243.
— and Germany, 1849. Quar. **84**: 185.
— — 1863. Ho. & For. R. **3**: 35.
— — Alliance of, 1879. (E. de Laveleye) Fortn. **32**: 785.
— — and British Trade. (A. J. Wilson) Fraser, **95**: 82.
— — and the Eastern Question. Fraser, **96**: 407.
— — Beust *versus* Bismarck. St. Paul's, **5**: 29.
— and House of Lords. Dub. Univ. **58**: 753. Same art. Ecl. M. **55**: 201.
— and Hungary. (B. Price) Fraser, **65**: 384. — (W. J. Stillman) Fortn. **33**: 785. — Ed. R. **90**: 230. Same art. Liv. Age, **22**: 433. — Blackw. **65**: 614, 697. Same art. Liv. Age, **22**: 103. — Prosp. R. **5**: 369. — Fraser, **64**: 517.
— — in 1848. Tait, n. s. **15**: 732.
— — in 1849. Ecl. R. **90**: 364.
— — in 1860. Westm. **73**: 457. Same art. Ecl. M. **50**: 549.
— — in 1861. Dub. R. **50**: 349.
— — Travelers in. (H. H. Milman) Quar. **65**: 234.
— and Italian Liberals. For. Q. **13**: 340.
— and Italy. Ecl. R. **109**: 581. Same art. Ecl. M. **47**: 538.
— — Alliance between, 1881. (R. Stuart) Contemp. **40**: 921.
— — and France. Ed. R. **109**: 558. Same art. Ecl. M. **47**: 326.
— — Question of, 1849. Fraser, **38**: 677. **39**: 201.
— — — 1859. New Q. **8**: 99.
— — War between, 1866. Westm. **87**: 274.
— and Russia. (L. Kossuth) Contemp. **31**: 555.
— and Sardinia, 1859. Bentley, **1**: 629.
— and Turkey. Fraser, **94**: 1.
— Aristocracy of. Cornh. **14**: 629.
— Army of, English Cadet in. Cornh. **15**: 104, 174, 326.
— — in 1855. Colburn, **104**: 1, 127.
— Beust Régime in. Macmil. **18**: 414.
— Concordat with. Dub. R. **39**: 413. — Ecl. R. **103**: 158.
— — Political Aspect of. Ecl. R. **104**: 148.

Austria, Constitutional Development of. No. Brit. 51: 136.
— Constitutionalism in. Westm. **79**: 334.
— Court of, Holy Thursday at. (W. I. Kip) Overland, **2**: 164.
— — in 18th Century. Dub. Univ. **64**: 580. — Ed. R. **98**: 1. Same art. Liv. Age, **38**: 579.
— — Memoirs of. Westm. **63**: 303. Same art. Liv. Age, **45**: 401.
— — Vehse's. Bentley, **39**: 454. — Ecl. R. **104**: 576. — New Q. **5**: 286.
— Coxe's History of the House of. Ed. R. **12**: 181. — Select Ed. R. **4**: 69. — Ecl. R. **8**: 951, 1059.
— Despotism of. Brit. Q. **10**: 548.
— Don John of. Blackw. **63**: 70. Same art. Liv. Age, **16**: 337.
— Education in. *See* Education in Austria.
— Emperors of. Lond. Q. **8**: 107. Same art. Ecl. M. **41**: 169.
— Empire of, and the German Confederation. Quar. **84**: 425.
— Finances of, 1859. Bank. M. (N. Y.) **14**: 537. — For. Q. **32**: 436.
— Financial Progress and Projects of, 1855. Bank. M. (L.) **15**: 666, 785.
— Foreign Policy and Internal Administration. For. Q. **18**: 257.
— Future of. Quar. **114**: 1.
— Government of, Secret History of. Dub. Univ. **55**: 102. Same art. Ecl. M. **49**: 329.
— — and People of. Westm. **30**: 487.
— in the Past. Brit. Q. **30**: 105.
— in 1824. Ed. R. **40**: 298.
— in 1835. Brit. & For. R. **4**: 26.
— in 1848–49, Stiles's. New Q. **2**: 106. — Princ. **24**: 442. — So. Lit. Mess. **18**: 535.
— in 1862. No. Brit. **37**: 285.
— in 1869. St. Paul's, **4**: 411.
— Kohl's Hundred Days in. For. Q. **13**: 92. — Mo. R. **162**: 135.
— Kohl on. Ecl. R. **78**: 502.
— Manners and Customs of. Mus. **2**: 498.
— Military Education in. Am. J. Educ. **13**: 409.
— Modern. (J. S. C. Abbott) Harper, **23**: 776.
— Monetary Question in. (M. Wirth) Bank. M. (N. Y.) **34**: 105, 432. — Internat. R. **3**: 335.
— Nationalities of. (J. G. McLeod) Month, **33**: 346.
— — and Austrian Policy. Fraser, **52**: 163.
— — A Polyglot Empire. (S. Powers) Lippinc. **6**: 480.
— — Question of, 1870. Westm. **94**: 35.
— Navy of, and Admiral Tegetthoff. (J. K. Laughton) Fraser, **97**: 671. Same art. Liv. Age, **138**: 131.
— Odd Corners in. (E. King) Lippinc. **21**: 9.
— past and present. Dub. Univ. **58**: 753.
— Poets of. Fraser, **46**: 213.
— Poets and Peasants of. No. Brit. **36**: 118.
— Political Dualism in. Westm. **88**: 431.
— Politics of, Crisis in, 1865. (M. Heilprin) Nation, **1**: 103. — Fraser, **72**: 457.
— — Constitutional Crisis, 1870. No. Brit. **52**: 493.
— Position and Policy of, 1850. Ecl. R. **92**: 604.
— — 1854. Liv. Age, **41**: 249.
— — 1865. Fortn. **3**: 55.
— Power of. (E. A. Freeman) Fraser, **102**: 29. Same art. Liv. Age, **146**: 387.
— Present Condition of, 1872. (T. P. O'Connor) Dark Blue, **3**: 15.
— Principalities of, 1866. Westm. **85**: 358.
— Protestantism in. Cong. **5**: 617. — Ecl. M. **48**: 491.
— Protestants in, History of Persecution of, Michiels's. No. Brit. **32**: 90.
— **Railroads and Steam Navigation in. Tait, n. s. 7:** 234.
Austria, Reform in. (C. A. Cummings) Chr. Exam. 74: 356.
— Reforms in. Westm. **75**: 503.
— — under Joseph II., 1853. New Eng. **11**: 395.
— Relations of, to the Principalities. Westm. **63**: 186.
— Religious Liberty in. (M. Heilprin) Nation, **6**: 345.
— Religious Policy of, 1859. Westm. **71**: 27.
— Resources, Commerce, and Banking of. (L. Levi) Bank. M. (L.) **38**: 193.
— resurgens. Liv. Age, **29**: 89.
— Revelations of, 1845. Tait, n. s. **13**: 589.
— Revolution in, 1848. Quar. **87**: 190.
— — and its Results. Dub. R. **25**: 40.
— Revolution under Joseph II. Temp. Bar, **51**: 373.
— since Sadowa. Quar. **131**: 90. Same art. Liv. Age, **110**: 771.
— Situation in, 1878. (M. Heilprin) Nation, **27**: 394.
— — 1879. (M. Heilprin) Nation, **29**: 153.
— Southern, Gallop through. (J. Marvel) Bentley, **22**: 381–555.
— State Papers of, 1809. (G. Canning) Quar. **1**: 437.
— Statistics of. Brit. & For. R. **14**: 554. **15**: 529.
— — 1869. Am. J. Educ. **18**: 540.
— Transformation of. (M. Heilprin) Nation, **7**: 126.
— Turnbull on. Mo. R. **151**: 141.
— Two Months in Upper. Once a Week, **5**: 470.
— Two Statesmen of: Lobkowitz and Kaunitz. Chamb. J. **26**: 27.
— *versus* Lord Holland and the Ladies. Colburn, **11**: 261.
— Wanderings in. (B. Murphy) Galaxy, **16**: 379.
— Wilde's. Dub. Univ. **22**: 89. — So. Lit. Mess. **9**: 596. *See* Styria.
Austrian Aide-de-Camp, Campaigns of an. Blackw. **70**: 25.
Austrian Employé, An. Cornh. **1**: 736.
Austrian Hungary. Cath. World, **32**: 33.
Austrian Italy. Bent. Q. **1**: 301.
Austrian Legends. (J. Oxenford) Colburn, **83**: 11.
Austrian Romance, An. (J. C. Young) Canad. Mo. **3**: 339.
Austrian Treaty with England. For. Q. **23**: 143. — Brit. & For. R. **8**: 95.
Austrians. Blackw. **48**: 487. — Mus. **40**: 421.
— at Home. Once a Week, **10**: 72.
— in Bosnia. (A. J. Evans) Macmil. **38**: 495. — (R. H. Lang) Fortn. **32**: 650.
Austro-Prussian War, 1865–66. (C. C. Chesney) Blackw. **101**: 68. — Ed. R. **125**: 363. — (E. Dicey) Macmil. **14**: 386. Same art. Ecl. M. **67**: 528. Same art. Ev. Sat. **2**: 392. — (C. Redding) Colburn, **137**: 494. — Colburn, **139**: 379. — Blackw. **100**: 247. — Chr. Exam. **81**: 233. — So. R. n. s. **5**: 184.
— At Leipzig during. Temp. Bar, **18**: 105.
— Campaign in South Germany. Colburn, **140**: 1.
— Campaigns of 1859, 1866, and 1870–71. Fraser, **84**: 251.
— Diplomacy of. (K. Blind) No. Am. **118**: 152.
— Hozier's. (F. W. Palfrey) Nation, **5**: 106.
— in its Political and Military Bearings. Fraser, **74**: 259.
— Real Significance of. (F. Kapp) Nation, **3**: 130.
— Tale of. (C. Clarke) Temp. Bar, **18**: 316.
Auteuil, Afternoon at. (J. H. Fyfe) Once a Week, **8**: 319.
Author and Actress. St. James, **26**: 17–765. **27**: 76–507. **28**: 66–591. **29**: 283–557.
Author and Editor. Once a Week, **17**: 469, 619. Same art. Ev. Sat. **4**: 625.
Author's Daughter; a Tale. (M. Howitt) Liv. Age, **4**: 491, 555.
Author's Night; a Poem. (J. T. Trowbridge) Atlan. **30**: 144.
Authors, About. (G. Wentz) So. M. **11**: 751.
— Advice to. Sharpe, **43**: 22.
— Allibone's Dictionary of. Liv. Age, **60**: 365.
— **Amateur, and Small Critics. Dem. R. 17:** 62.

Authors, American, Abroad. (T. L. Cuyler) Godey, **32**: 59.
— — Homes of. (P. Godwin) Putnam, **1**: 23. — Liv. Age, **36**: 203.
See American Authors.
— and Actors; a Dramatic Sketch. Bentley, **1**: 132.
— and Books. Sharpe, **10**: 367.
— and Conversation. St. James, **49**: 258.
— and Copyrights. Dem. R. **12**: 294.
— and Matrimony, Woman's View of. St. James, **26**: 535.
— and Publishers. Ecl. M. **15**: 517. — Dem. R. **11**: 396. New Q **3**: 143. — Brit. Q. **59**: 313. Same art. Ecl. M. **83**: 1. Same art. Liv. Age, **122**: 131.
— — Hardwicke's. New Q. **3**: 9.
— and their Ways of Working. (A. B. Harris) Potter Am. Mo. **15**: 217. (H. B. Baker) Argosy, **32**: 378. — Chamb. J. **58**: 437. Same art. Ecl. M. **97**: 423.
— and Writers. U. S. Lit. Gaz. **1**: 346.
— and Works, Anonymous and Pseudonymous. Nat. Q. **23**: 41.
— Anecdotes of. Chamb. J. **56**: 600.
— — of Popular. Hogg, **2**: 37.
— Anonymous Old. Bentley, **4**: 414.
— Apology for. Knick. **19**: 97.
— Calamities of. Chamb. J. **7**: 129.
— Disraeli's. (R. Southey) Portfo. (Den.) **9**: 501. — Quar. **8**: 93.
— Character of, as affecting their Works. Chr. Disc. **3**: 264.
— Contemporary and posthumous Reputation of. Dub. Univ. **45**: 433.
— Conversation of. Lond. M. **2**: 250. — Am. Bibliop. **4**: 455, 535.
— English, Memories of. (M. D. Conway) Harper, **39**: 527.
— — Living. (G. W. Peck) Meth. Q. **10**: 124.
— — Reminiscences of some. (R. H. Horne) Macmil. **22**: 359. Same art. Ecl. M. **75**: 588.
— — Studies of some. (R. H. Stoddard) Scrib. **8**: 336, 451.
— for Hire. Cornh. **43**: 684. Same art. Appleton, **26**: 127.
— Gossip concerning: our Whispering Gallery. (J. T. Fields) Atlan. **27**: 122–763. **28**: 106–750.
— Habits of. Knick. **61**: 438.
— Hints to, on the Biographical. Blackw. **49**: 757.
— — on the Critical. Blackw. **39**: 607.
— — on the Dramatic. Blackw. **49**: 330.
— — on the Epistolary. Blackw. **50**: 711.
— — on the Facetious. Blackw. **39**: 166.
— — on the Genteel. Blackw. **50**: 439.
— — on the Impressive. Blackw. **49**: 56.
— — on the Original. Blackw. **49**: 154.
— — on the Pathetic. Blackw. **50**: 431.
— — on the Philosophical. Blackw. **39**: 357.
— Homes of. Bost. R. **1**: 528.
— in England, Germany, and France, Condition of. Fraser, **35**: 285.
— Justice for. (M. Thomas) St. James, **36**: 64.
— Living, Characters of. Blackw. **10**: 69.
— Moral Influence of. So. Lit. Mess. **6**: 285.
— Noble. Dem. R. **12**: 479.
— of Antiquity. So. Lit. Mess. **9**: 31.
— Originality of. Contin. Mo. **2**: 285.
— Our Young. (F. J. O'Brien) Putnam, **1**: 74.
— Pay of. Liv. Age, **13**: 257.
— Persecuted and Pampered. (E. I. Sears) Nat. Q. **33**: 109.
— Profits of. Appleton, **26**: 186.
— Punishments of. Chamb. J. **8**: 78.
— Recollections of. (C. and M. C. Clarke) Gent. M. n. s. **15**: 162–726. **16**: 85–724. **17**: 89, 223.
Authors, Remarks on my Favorite. (G. F. Deane) Am. Whig R. **9**: 464.
— Rights of. Hesp. **3**: 277. — So. Lit. Mess. **3**: 37. **6**: 69.
— — before Publication. Am. Law R. **9**: 236.
— Royal. Ed. R. **39**: 84. — Dem. R. **12**: 392.
— Royal and Imperial. (S. B. Gould) Once a Week, **12**: 363. Same art. Cath. World, **1**: 323.
— Royal and Noble. Lond. M. **5**: 218, 387, 409. — Quar. **123**: 279.
— — English. Ev. Sat. **5**: 310.
— Vindicated from the Charge of Poverty. Mus. **8**: 363.
Authoresses and Autographs. Colburn, **11**: 217–317.
Authority and Freedom in Faith. (D. Gans) Mercersb. **15**: 157. — (M. Kieffer) Mercersb. **17**: 42.
— in the Church, Protestant Idea of. (J. Martineau) O. & N. **11**: 24.
— in Matters of Faith. Brownson, **23**: 510.
— Influence of, in Matters of Opinion. (W. E. Gladstone) 19th Cent. **1**: 2. Same art. Ecl. M. **88**: 559. Same art. Liv. Age, **133**: 159.
— — Lewis on. Ed. R. **91**: 508.
— Principle of, in Matters of Opinion. (S. Taylor) Macmil. **28**: 19.
— Revival of. (F. Harrison) Fortn. **19**: 1.
Authorship. (T. Binney) Ex. H. Lec. **9**: 319.
— and Literature. (W. E. Smith) Potter Am. Mo. **14**: 465. **15**: 56, 138.
— Disputed, Internal Evidence in a Case of. Brit. Q. **61**: 500.
— Dreams of. So. Lit. Mess. **3**: 468.
— Few Hints to Young Writers. (W. H. Browne) So. M. **14**: 616.
— Furor Scribendi. Victoria, **12**: 385.
— Importance and Rewards of. (J. C. Pattee) Univ. Q. **12**: 394.
— in America. (F. Wharton) No. Am. **52**: 401.
— Intellectual Straining in. Pop. Sci. Mo. **16**: 93.
— Irritable. Hogg, **9**: 137.
— Jacox on Aspects of. Victoria, **20**: 357.
— Miseries of. Tait, **3**: 739. — West. Mo. R. **1**: 523, 648.
— Physiology of. (R. E. Francillon) Gent. Mag. n. s. **14**: 325. Same art. Pop. Sci. Mo. **7**: 93.
— Profession of. Am. Mo. R. **1**: 589.
— Rapid and slow. Penny M. **14**: 410.
Auto da Fe; a Poem. (E. A. Bendall) Dark Blue, **1**: 455.
Autobiographies. No. Brit. **51**: 382.
Autobiography. Blackw. **26**: 737. — Quar. **35**: 149. — Blackw. **66**: 292. — Cornh. **43**: 410. Same art. Appleton, **25**: 499. Same art. Ecl. M. **97**: 44. Same art. Liv. Age, **149**: 283. — Lond. Q. **1**: 494
— An. Mo. Rel. M. **47**: 473, 561. **48**: 152–519.
— of an Agnostic. (B. Thomas) Fraser, **103**: 650. Same Art. Liv. Age, **149**: 719.
— of Bill Money Dollars. Knick. **47**: 361.
— of a Good Joke. Bentley. **2**: 354.
— of an Irreconcilable. St. Paul's, **11**: 54–728.
— of a Joint-Stock Company. Blackw. **120**: 96.
— of a Pair of Top-Boots. Colburn, **85**: 223–454.
— of a Philosopher. (W. M. Fisher) Overland, **14**: 85–568. **15**: 95, 194, 268.
— of a Quack. (S. W. Mitchell) Atlan. **20**: 466, 586.
— of a Small Boy. All the Year, **20**: 217, 241.
— of an Unrecognized Genius. Hogg, **9**: 169–220.
— Sample of some Men's. Mus. **23**: 248, 547.
Autochthones. (B. P. Avery) Overland, **15**: 319.
Autocrat of the Breakfast-Table. (O. W. Holmes) Atlan. **1**: 48–871. **2**: 102–619.
Autograph Collecting. (E. Walford) Once a Week, **12**: 316.
Autograph Collectors, The Father of. Temp. Bar, **47**: 89.
Autograph Hunting. (F. Barrow) Galaxy, **12**: 256.

Autograph Miscellany. Liv. Age, **47**: 129.
Autographomania. (T. F. Dwight) Overland, **3**: 342.
Autographs. Chamb. J. **14**: 155, 204. — Nat. M. **7**: 356.
— and Autograph Collectors. St. James, **37**: 137.
— Curious. Chamb. J. **24**: 31.
— Evening's Conversation about. (Mrs. S. J. Hale) Godey, **22**: 146.
— Historical. (H. Scadding) Canad. J. n. s. **14**: 73, 315, 479, 597. **15**: 145.
— Morning among. (W. Young) Putnam, **11**: 686. **12**: 226, 277.
— National. Liv. Age, **87**: 88.
— of Celebrated Men. Mo. R. **115**: 397. **120**: 212.
— of Distinguished Americans. So. Lit. Mess. **2**: 205, 601.
— Rare, and their Prices. Cornh. **16**: 495.
— Scraps from my Autograph-Book. (G. M. Towle) Hours at Home, **10**: 15.
Autography. Pract. M. **7**: 268.
— Practical Use of. (G. O. Sars) Am. J. Sci. **114**: 277.
Automata. Chamb. J. **53**: 87.
— and Androides. (T. P. Jones) J. Frankl. Inst. **3**: 125, 192, 342.
— Are we? (W. James) Mind, **4**: 1.
— Famous. (J. D. Bell) Appleton, **18**: 254.
Automathes, History of. Retros. **10**: 78.
Automatic Chess-Player. Blackw. **4**: 579. — So. Lit. Mess. **2**: 318. — Penny M. **6**: 28. — Liv. Age, **61**: 585.
— Anatomy of. Fraser, **19**: 717.
— De Kempelen's. Ed. Philos. J. **4**: 393.
— Maelzel's. (T. P. Jones) J. Frankl Inst. **3**: 125.
Automatic Chess and Card-Playing. Cornh. **32**: 584. Same art. Ecl. M. **86**: 46.
Automatic Enigma, An. (J. Hawthorne) Belgra. **35**: 294.
Automatic Representation, Galton on Generic Images and. (G. C. Robertson) Mind, **4**: 551.
Automatism. (A. Main) Mind, **1**: 431. — (H. C. Wood) Lippinc. **26**: 627, 755.
— and Evolution. (C. Elam) Contemp. **28**: 537, 725. **29**: 117. Same art. Ecl. M. **87**: 640. **88**: 166, 342.
— Animal, Lewes on. (G. C. Robertson) Mind, **3**: 24.
— Modern. (F. W. Newman) Fraser, **95**: 665.
Automaton of Dobello. (H. D. Jenkins) Lakeside, **8**: 348.
Automaton-Ear, The. (F. McLandburgh) Scrib. **5**: 711.
Autotype, or Carbon Process in Photography. (C. E. Norton) Nation, **8**: 47. — (T. Taylor) Portfo. **2**: 53. — Pract. M. **6**: 31.
Autotypes. J. Frankl. Inst. **108**: 137.
— On some New Methods of Printing. (G. W. Simpson) Portfo. **2**: 135.
Autotypography, Art of, 1863. (G. Wallis) J. Frankl. Inst. **76**: 53.
Autumn. (C. Lanman) So. Lit. Mess. **6**: 723. — (C. Geikie) Good Words, **12**: 841. — (W. W. Story) Blackw. **114**: 502. — Fraser, **66**: 418.
— a Poem. (R. Noel) Gent. M. n. s. **15**: 432. — (A. Smith) Good Words, **3**: 689.
— in the Country. Fraser, **24**: 269, 455, 524.
— in the Highlands; a Poem. (J. C. Shairp) Good Words, **15**: 713.
— in the North. Fraser, **10**: 488, 573. **11**: 66, 170.
Autumns, English. (C. Boyle) Macmil. **29**: 81.
Autumn Days. (J. Skelton) Fraser, **66**: 715.
Autumn Eclogue. Dub. Univ. **48**: 493.
Autumn Eclogues. (J. F. Waller) Dub. Univ. **50**: 430.
Autumn Foliage. (J. Wharton) Am. J. Sci. **97**: 251.
Tints of. (H. D. Thoreau) Atlan. **10**: 385.
Autumn Leaves Gathered up. Fraser, **30**: 631.
Autumn Love; a Poem. St. James, **2**: 439.
Autumn Maneuvering. (A. à Beckett) Lond. Soc. **20**: 385.
Autumn Pastoral. (W. H. Gibson) Harper, **61**: 857.
Autumn Reverie. (Mrs. E. J. Eames) So. Lit. Mess. **6**: 820.
Autumn Voices; a Poem. (L. Bushnell) Scrib. **4**: 761.
Autumnal Fruits. Dub. Univ. **40**: 383.
Autumnal Meditations; a Poem. (D. M. Moir) Blackw. **13**: 646.
Autumnal Ramble, Hints for an. Blackw. **130**: 393.
Autumnal Sketches; a Poem. (D. M. Moir) Blackw. **38**: 488.
Autun, Christian Inscription found at. Dub. R. **9**: 527.
Auvergne. (T. E. C. Leslie) Fortn. **22**: 737. — Sharpe, **32**: 6.
— April in. (R. W. Baddeley) Belgra. **26**: 253.
— Costello's Pilgrimage to. Mo. R. **157**: 208.
— in 1665. Colburn, **129**: 460.
— — Men and Manners in. For. Q. **35**: 154.
— Month in. (M. Betham-Edwards) Macmil. **42**: 189.
— Volcanoes and Glaciers of. (W. S. Symonds) Pop. Sci. R. **16**: 1.
Ava, Adventure in, 1826. (C. Campbell) Colburn, **55**: 341.
— and England. Cornh. **40**: 213.
— Throne of the Golden Foot. (J. W. Palmer) Atlan. **20**: 453.
— Two Years in, 1824 to 1826. Lond. M. **19**: 128.
— Yule's Mission to the Court of. Liv. Age, **57**: 269.
Availability; or, Politicians *vs.* Statesmen. (E. D. Hudson) Nat. Q. **1**: 485.
Avalanche of the Rossberg. Ecl. M. **54**: 538.
Avalanches. Ecl. R. **110**: 480. Same art. Liv. Age, **63**: 738.
Avaricious Man, Confessions of an. (H. D. Inglis) Colburn, **64**: 554. **65**: 102.
Ave atque Vale; a Poem. (A. C. Swinburne) Fortn. **9**: 71.
Ave Maria; a Breton Legend. (A. Austin) Cornh. **35**: 735.
Ave Maria; a Poem. Cornh. **16**: 208.
Avenger, The; a Tale. (T. De Quincey) Blackw. **44**: 208.
Aventicum, Discovery of. (J. Perry) Antiquary, **2**: 55.
Average, General. (W. Phillips) Hunt, **5**: 67, 157. — (Z. Cook, jr.) Hunt, **5**: 159.
— — York and Antwerp Rules of. (G. Schwab) Nation, **28**: 13. — (A. F. Higgins) Nation, **28**: 48.
Averages, Derivation of, from Observations. (W. A. Guy) J. Statis. Soc. **13**: 30.
Avery, B. P., In Memoriam. (I. D. Coolbrith and S. Williams) Overland, **15**: 585.
Averysboro, N. C., Battle of. So. Hist. Pap. **7**: 31, 125, 195.
Avesta, The. (G. T. Flanders) Univ. Q. **33**: 416. — (J. C. Wightman) Bapt. Q. **9**: 267.
— and the Storm-Myth. (J. Luquiens) New Eng. **39**: 635.
Avezzana, Gen., Italian Minister of War, 1849. (D. Paul) Cath. World, **30**: 854.
Avice Gray. (A. Rothwell) Appleton, **16**: 6–320.
Avignon. Penny M. **9**: 244.
— and the Schism. Brownson, **18**: 324.
Avila, Spain. (M. P. Thompson) Cath. World, **24**: 155.
Avisseau, Charles, the Potter of Tours. Chamb. J. **16**: 318
Avocation: What Life to choose. Colburn, **6**: 284.
Avocations, Some strange. Chamb. J. **57**: 252.
Avon, Towns on the. Temp. Bar, **12**: 192.
— and Stour, By the. Fraser, **77**: 634.
Avonhoe; a Tale. Cornh. **17**: 592, 707. **18**: 73, 199.
Awake and Thinking; a Retrospect. Belgra. **12**: 476.
Awakening, The; a Tale. (K. S. Macquoid) Temp. Bar, **62**: 492.

Awamutu, How we live at. Fraser, **70**: 606.
Away down East; a Poem. (E. J. Hall) Lakeside, **8**: 395.
Awkward Blunder; a Story. (C. Hathway) St. James, **47**: 468.
Awkward Mistake. Belgra. **2**: 443.
Axel; a Tale of the Thirty Years' War. Dub. Univ. **3**: 679.
Axes and Hatchets, Ancient and modern. (A. Rigg) Pop. Sci. Mo. **9**: 186.
Axioms, Philosophical. Dub. R. **65**: 144.
Axis, Uniform Distribution of Points about an. (C. Wright) Math. Mo. **1**: 244.
Axle-Box, Hodge's Self-Lubricating. J. Frankl. Inst. **55**: 154.
Axles and Shafts, Form of, Thorneycroft on. J. Frankl. Inst. **51**: 56.
— Fracture of, Causes of. (W. B. Adams) Ecl. Engin. **4**: 173.
— Hollow Railway. (J. E. M'Connell) J. Frankl. Inst. **56**: 361. **57**: 82.
— Lubrication of Railway. (W. B. Adams) J. Frankl. Inst. **56**: 289.
— Stephenson's Improvement in, 1831. J. Frankl. Inst. **13**: 246.
— Strength of Solid and Hollow. (J. O. York) J. Frankl. Inst. **36**: 332. **38**: 163.
Aye-Aye, The. (W. B. Tegetmeier) Intel. Obs. **1**: 130. — (B G. Wilder) Scrib. **2**: 33. — Penny M. **7**: 425.
Ayen, Duc d', Daughters of. Month, **3**: 68, 163. Same art. Cath. World, **2**: 252.
Ayer and Ayres Genealogies. (W. H. Whitmore) N. E. Reg. **17**: 307.
Aylmer, A. Bentley, **23**: 470, 551.
Aylwin, Lieut. John Cushing. Anal. M. **3**: 54.
Ayr, Auld Clay Biggin in. (I. D. Fenton) Once a Week, **16**: 118.
Ayrshire Curling Song. (N. M'Leod) Blackw. **101**: 148.
Ayrshire Legatees. (J. Galt) Blackw. **7**: 262–589. **8**: 10–501. Same art. Portfo.(Den.) **25**: 410. **26**: 42, 270. **27**: 126, 266, 416.
Aytoun, Sir Robert. Lond. Q. **50**: 337.
Aytoun, William E. Blackw. **103**: 440 Same art. Liv. Age, **97**: 323. — Liv. Age, **68**: 317.
— Bon Gaultier's Ballads. Ecl. M. **32**: 362. — Liv. Age, **5**: 400. — Fraser, **31**: 415. — So. Lit. Mess. **18**: 429.
— Bothwell; a Poem. Blackw. **80**: 222. — Bentley, **40**: 276. Same art. Liv. Age, **50**: 705. — Canad. J. n. s. **1**: 541. — Chr. Rem. **33**: 1. — Fraser, **54**: 347. — Liv. Age, **53**: 216. — Lond. Q. **7**: 201.
— Death of. Blackw. **98**: 384.
— Firmilian. Blackw. **95**: 523. — Dub. Univ. **44**: 488.
— Lays of Scottish Cavaliers. (E. E. Hale) Chr. Exam. **52**: 226. — Dub. R. **27**: 74. — Brit. Q. **11**: 80. — Fraser, **39**: 489. — Dub. Univ. **33**: 215. — No. Brit. **13**: 1. — Liv. Age, **21**: 101, 154.
Aytoun, Wm. E., Martin's Life of. Dub. Univ. **70**: 587.
— Memoir of. Chamb. J. **44**: 648.
— Peacock, and Prout. No. Brit. **45**: 75. Same art. Ecl. M. **67**: 641.
Aytoun; a Tale. Lippinc. **9**: 54–686.
Azalea, a Flycatcher. (W.W.Bailey) Am. Natural. **8**: 517.
Azazel, the Levitical Scape-Goat. (G. Bush) Am. Bib. Repos. 2d s. **8**: 116.
Azeglio, Massimo d'. (A. Gallenga) Fortn. **9**: 629. — (W. D. Howells) Nation, **2**: 202. — (H. J. Warner) Chr. Exam. **83**: 187. — Dub. Univ. **76**: 508. — Galaxy, **1**: 34. — (H. T. Tuckerman) No. Am. **107**: 423.
— and Bunsen. Temp. Bar, **51**: 231.
— Maid of Florence. New Q. **2**: 527.
— Niccolò de' Lapi. Chr. Rem. **16**: 117.
— Recollections of. (T. A. Trollope) Lippinc. **14**: 341.
— Reminiscences of. Quar. **123**: 66. Same art. Liv. Age, **94**: 515.
— Works of. (H. T. Tuckerman) Chr. Exam. **52**: 35.
Azela; a Poem. (A. Carey) Internat M. **1**: 135.
Azimantium, Story of. Blackw. **29**: 224, 446.
Azores, The. Fraser, **97**: 556. Same art. Liv. Age, **137**: 668.
— Among. (L. H. Weeks) Appleton, **20**: 347. — (S. E. Dawes) Potter Am. Mo. **17**: 289.
— and Canary Islands, Summer Cruise among. (Miss Dabney) Harper, **46**: 865.
— Bond's Description of. Mo. R. **136**: 1.
— Cruise among. (S. G. W. Benjamin) Scrib. **6**: 513.
— History of. Quar. **11**: 191.
— Land of Hawks. (C. Wood) St. Paul's, **12**: 82.
— Natural History of, Godman's. Nature, **3**: 303.
— Residence in. Tait, n. s. **8**: 414. — Museum, **43**: 18.
— Summer Cruise among. (A. L. Gihon) Harper, **54**: 546.
— Three Years in. Dark Blue, **4**: 452. Same art. Liv. Age, **116**: 302.
— Winter in, Bullar's. Chr. Exam. **31**: 319. — Dub. Univ. **20**: 227. — Ecl. R. **74**: 534. — Mo. R. **155**: 1.
Azotone. Recr. Sci. **2**: 352.
Aztec Calendar Stone. Am. Hist. Rec. **3**: 456.
Aztecs, Ancient and Modern. (M. McNamara) Canad. Mo. **12**: 258.
— and their Conquerors. (E. Parmer) So. M. **11**: 554.
— and Indians, Arts among. (T. Ewbank) Internat. M. **4**: 307.
— Backgammon among. (E. B. Tylor) Macmil. **39**: 304. Same art. Pop. Sci. Mo. **14**: 491.
— in New York. Internat. M. **5**: 288.
— Mythology of. (T. A. Harcourt) Overland, **15**: 87. — Galaxy, **21**: 633.
— Social Customs of. (L. H. Morgan) No. Am. **122**: 265.
— Society among. Galaxy, **21**: 368.
See Mexico.

B

Baader, Franz, Theosophy of. (J. Hamberger) Am. Presb. R. **18**: 171.
Baalbec. (A. L. Koeppen) Mercersb. **8**: 40. — (F. P. Cobbe) Fraser, **63**: 670. Same art. Ecl. M. **56**: 178.
— Over the Lebanon to. (J. C. M. Bellew) Temp. Bar, **1**: 114, 359.
— Ruins of. Penny M. **3**: 43.
— Temple at. Mo. Rel. M. **26**: 273.
— Visit to. Bentley, **31**: 385.
Bab. *See* Babism.
Bab Lambert; a Story. Cornh. **4**: 421.
Babbage, Charles. (W. Farr) J. Statis. Soc. **34**: 411. — Ecl. Engin. **6**: 275. — Nature, **5**: 28.
— and his Friends. (N. S. Dodge) Lakeside, **9**: 236.
— Calculating Machine of. (C. Nordhoff) Harper, **30**: 34. — Ecl. R. **120**: 487. — Ed. Philos. J. **7**: 274. **8**: 122. — Ed. R. **59**: 263. — J. Frankl. Inst. **11**: 210. — No. Brit. **15**: 553.

Babbage, Charles. Exposition of 1851. No. Brit. **15**: 529.
— on Machinery and Manufactures. Fraser, **8**: 167. — Ed. R. **56**: 313. — Am. Mo. R. **3**: 24.
— Passages from Life of. Brit. Q. **4**: 95. Same art. Liv. Age, **84**: 577. — Chr. Rem. **51**: 1.
— Recollections of. (L. A. Tollemache) Macmil. **27**: 489. Same art. Ev. Sat. **14**: 511.
— Works of. Am. Bibliop. **4**: 18.
Babel. Fraser, **40**: 318.
— Confusion of Tongues at, Kaulen on. Dub. R. **55**: 220.
— Ruins of. Cong. M. **1**: 35.
Baber, Emperor of Hindostan. (F. Jeffrey) Ed. R. **46**: 39. — Mo. R. **112**: 254. — Westm. **8**: 475. — Chr. Rem. **10**: 133. — Ecl. R. **45**: 501. — Retros. **16**: 254.
Babes in the Wood; a Poem. (E. Nugisch) Mo. Rel. M. **21**: 98. **23**: 21, 109, 185.
Babette; a Tale. (K. O'Meara) Cath. World, **28**: 549
Bab-ey-buk, Story of. Blackw **43**: 648.
Babington, Anthony. Reliquary, **2**: 177.
Babington; a Tragedy. Blackw. **18**. 119.
Babinic Republic. Dark Blue, **3**: 103.
Babiroussa, The. Penny M. **10**: 321.
Babism. (R. H. Arbuthnot) Contemp. **11**: 581. **12**: 245. — (J. T. Bixby) Nation, **2**: 793. — (E. P. Evans) Hours at Home, **8**: 210. — All the Year, **22**: 149. — Chamb. J. **29**: 45.
Babrius, Fables of. Fraser, **41**: 529. — Ed. R. **113**: 524.
Babu-English. Chamb. J. **58**: 840.
Babu Nana's Vengeance. Tinsley, **12**: 48.
Baby; a Tale. (A. Young) Cath. World, **6**: 227.
— The. (D. H. Strother) Harper, **52**: 539. — Belgra. **37**: supp. 29.
— The British. Ev. Sat. **9**: 411.
— Day with a. (L. Broughton) St. James, **38**: 481.
— Junior. Chamb. J. **30**: 234.
— or no Baby. Chamb. J. **36**: 405.
— Progressive. (S. F. Hopkins) Galaxy, **23**: 581–727.
— The Second. Chamb. J. **23**: 33.
Baby-Exterminator; a Tale. Putnam, **10**: 50.
Baby-Farm, Month at a. Victoria, **18**: 42.
Baby Grace; a Poem. (R. W. Buchanan) St James, **4**: 315.
Baby Shows. Dem. R. **35**: 315.
Baby-Stealer of the Nundydroog. Chamb. J. **26**: 59.
Baby Suffrage. (E. L. Godkin) Nation, **10**: 236.
Baby-Visiting. (Mrs. A. M. F. Annan) Godey, **29**: 266.
Babies, About. Putnam, **6**: 139.
— and Science. Cornh. **43**: 539. Same art. Appleton, **26**: 27. Same art. Ecl. M. **97**: 26.
— How to take Care of. (J. Chandler) Eng. Dom. M. **23**: 203–291. **24**: 9–280.
— Mental Condition of. Cornh. **7**: 649.
— Poems about. (R. W. Buchanan) St. James, **8**: 441.
— Prize. All the Year, **22**: 249.
— Public Nurseries for. Chamb. J. **46**: 145.
— Wild. Lond. Soc. **35**: 456.
See Babes.
Babylon and Chaldea, Ménant on. Chr. Obs. **75**: 368.
— and Nineveh. Blackw. **76**: 458.
— — and Persepolis. Sharpe, **12**: 39.
— — Layard's. Am. Presb. R. **2**: 603. — Dub. R. **35**: 93. — Liv. Age, **37**: 423. — New Q. **2**: 209.
— and its Priest-Kings. (E. Hincks) Kitto, **22**: 296.
— Brick from the Site of. Arch. **14**: 55, 205.
— Commerce of Ancient. (F. M. Hubbard) Am. Bib. Repos. **7**: 364.
— Cushite Origin of Sacred Writing, Language, and Literature of. (O. D. Miller) Univ. Q. **34**: 452.
— Gems brought from, by A. Lockett. (J. Landseer) Arch. **18**: 371.
— Last Night in. (G. A. Sala) Belgra. **13**: 54.
— Libraries of. No. Brit. **51**: 305. Same art. Ecl. M. **74**: 589.
Babylon, Memoir of. (J. Abbott) Harper, **36**: 162.
— Rich's Memoirs of. Mo. R. **81**: 257. **89**: 41. — Ed. R. **48**: 185. — (B. B. Thatcher) Am. Bib. Repos. **8**: 158. — No. Am. **2**: 183. — West. Mo. R. **2**: 683.
— Ride to. Blackw. **93**: 607.
— Ruins of. Meth. M. **53**: 166. — Portfo.(Den) **19**: 376.
— Topography of. (Major Rennell) Arch. **18**: 243.
See Nineveh and Babylon; Oriental Discovery.
Babylonia, Civilization of. (W. St. C. Boscawen) Anthrop. J. **8**: 21.
— Inscriptions of. (W. F. Ainsworth) Colburn, **78**: 441.
— Literature of, Ancient. (O. D. Miller) Univ. Q. **26**: 159.
— — in Arabic Translations. Chr. Rem. **39**: 417.
Babylonian Monuments in America. (S. Merrill) Bib. Sac. **32**: 320.
Babylonian Princess, Memoir of. Ecl. M. **3**: 177.
Babylonian Researches. (R. P. Stebbins) Unita. R. **9**: 610.
Babylonian Rivers and Cities. (W. F. Ainsworth) Colburn, **74**: 653. **75**: 57
Babylonians, Tammûz and the Worship of Men among. Chr. Rem. **41**: 253.
Bacchanalia Memorabilia. Fraser, **12**: 522. **13**: 225, 727. **14**: 273.
Bacchanalians, Sect of. Westm. **23**: 240.
Bacchants and A B C-Shooters. Am. J. Educ. **5**: 603.
Bacchus, Altar of, at Lord Pembroke's. (S. Pegge) Arch. **1**: 155.
— and Ariadne, Triumph of, a Poem. Cornh. **35**: 458.
— and the Water-Thieves, a Poem. Once a Week, **10**: 657.
Bach, Friedemann. (Mrs. Ellet) Cath. World, **10**: 805.
Bach, John Sebastian. (J. G. Austin) Galaxy, **17**: 375. — A. G. Bowie) St. James, **40**: 386. — (L. T. Cragin) O. & N. **8**: 246. — Bentley, **62**: 74, 177, 317. — Fraser, **34**: 28.
— and Händel, Scores of, Additional Accompaniments to. (W. F. Apthorp) Atlan. **42**: 321.
— Mass in B Minor. Cornh. **33**: 728.
Bache, Alex. Dallas, Account of. (H. Morton) J. Frankl. Inst. **87**: 353.
— Family of. (J. A. Stevens) M. Am. Hist. **1**: 663.
Bachelor, The. U. S. Lit. Gaz. **2**: 139. **3**: 186.
— a Poem. (E. C. Willis) Temp. Bar, **25**: 361.
— Beset; a Tale. So. Lit. Mess. **5**: 751.
— Chapter in Life of. (T. Flint) Knick. **3**: 6.
— Outwitted: a Poem. Colburn, **11**: 104.
Bachelor Bedroom. All the Year, **1**: 355.
Bachelor Ben. (R. V. Chilcott) Belgra. **29**: 87.
Bachelor Invalids and Male Nurses. Once a Week, **25**: 317.
Bachelor's Beat. Blackw. **20**: 755. **22**: 659. **23**: 14. **24**: 335. Same art. Mus. **10**: 168. **12**: 290, 385.
Bachelor's Elysium, The. Portfo.(Den.) **30**: 362.
Bachelor's Hall. (R. Chesterfield) Lakeside, **9**: 29.
Bachelor's Married Life. (A. S. Deas) So. M. **8**: 290.
Bachelor's Protest to the Women of England. Chamb. J. **35**: 385.
Bachelor's Reverie. (D. G. Mitchell) So. Lit. Mess. **16**: 162. — (J. Leitch) St. James, **18**: 508.
Bachelor's Story. Chamb. J. **56**: 391.
Bachelor's Thermometer. Lond. Soc. **4**: 120.
Bachelors, Old. (F. W. Shelton) So. Lit. Mess. **19**: 223.
— of Windsor, Day with. Chamb. J. **22**: 292.
Bachtiari Bandits. (C. S. Savile) Bentley, **21**: 290.
Bacini introduced into Italian Church Architecture. (C. D. Fortnum) Arch. **42**: 379.
Back, Sir George. Geog. M. **5**: 179.
See Arctic Expedition, Back's.
Back to Back; a Story. (E. E. Hale) Harper, **55**: 873.
Back-Log Studies. (C. D. Warner) Scrib. **2**: 261. **3**: 434–693. **4**: 43–348.
Backer, F. Augustine de. Dub. R. **80**: 452.
Backgammon. Penny M. **10**: 100.

Backgammon among the Aztecs. (E. B. Tylor) Macmil. **39**: 304. Same art. Pop. Sci. Mo. **14**: 491.
Backhouse, James. Visit to Mauritius and South Africa. (W. Cubitt) No. Brit. **2**: 105.
Backsheesh, Official, in Turkey. Macmil. **41**: 484. Same art. Liv. Age, **145**: 285. Same art. Ecl. M. **94**: 715.
Backslider, The. Chr. Exam. **20**: 198.
Backus, C., Divinity School of. (J. Vaill) Cong. Q. **6**: 137.
Backus, Isaac, Life and Times of. Chr. R. **14**: 197.
Backwoods, Night in. Chamb. J. **52**: 108.
Backwoods Express. Chamb. J. **41**: 657.
Bacon, David. (L. Bacon) Cong. Q. **18**: 1, 260, 387, 562.
Bacon, Delia, Recollections of. (N. Hawthorne) Atlan. **11**: 43.
Bacon, Francis, Lord. (H. Dixon) Temp. Bar, **1**: 22. — (J. W. Edmonds) Knick. **57**: 271, 378. — (T. B. Macaulay) Ed. R. **65**: 277. Same art. Mus. **31**: 295, 391. — (K. von Raumer) Am. J. Educ. **51**: 663. — (D. A. Wasson) New Eng. **10**: 333. — (E. P. Whipple) Atlan. **22**: 476, 573. — Am. Ch. Mo. **2**: 48. — Bentley, **26**: 84. — Blackw. **93**: 480. — Dub. R. **3**: 305. — Dub. Univ. **48**: 391. — Nat. Q. **2**: 1. — Ecl. R. **100**: 672. Same art. Ecl. M. **34**: 145. — Penny M. **10**: 60. — (J. W. E.) Sharpe, **48**: 181.
— and the Earl of Essex. Westm. **61**: 468. **78**: 263.
— and Friar Bacon. (J. H. Rigg) Meth. Q. **18**: 5, 173.
— and Christianity. (I. D. Van Duzee) Univ. Q. **16**: 248.
— and his Philosophy. (F. Bowen) No. Am. **56**: 69. — Knick. **8**: 560. — (A. B. Bledsoe) Meth. Q. **7**: 22. — (S. Tyler) Princ. **12**: 350. **15**: 481.
— and the Inductive Method. Westm. **68**: 547. — Chr. Rem. **39**: 239.
— and Locke, Philosophical Genius of. (J. Mackintosh) Ed. R. **27**: 180. **36**: 220.
— and Shakspere, Imaginary Dialogue. Blackw. **3**: 270.
— and Shakspere's Plays. Liv. Age, **51**: 481. *See* Shakspere.
— and Sir Thomas More. Ecl. M. **8**: 122.
— Apophthegms of, Selected. Sharpe, **12**: 46.
— as an Essayist. Nat. Q. **6**: 114.
— as a Natural Philosopher. (J. von Liebig) Macmil. **8**: 237, 258.
— as a Politician and Philosopher. (W. R. Claxton) Penn Mo. **12**: 928.
— Character of. (E. Everett) No. Am. **16**: 300. — U. S. Lit. Gaz. **1**: 90. — (H. Giles) No. Am. **93**: 149.
— — and Philosophy of. Fraser, **13**: 143.
— Confession of Faith of. Cong. M. **28**: 428.
— Defense of. Westm. **75**: 579.
— Dixon's Personal History of. (H. Dutton) New Eng. **21**: 37. — Brit. Q. **33**: 391. — Dub. Univ. **57**: 321. **64**: 363. — Ed. R. **113**: 309. Same art. Liv. Age, **69**: 515. — Lond. Q. **16**: 372.
— Essays of. Chr. Obs. **58**: 33. — Cong. **4**: 168. — Dub. Univ. **37**: 14. — Ecl. R. **104**: 257. — Brit. Q. **38**: 67. Same art. Liv. Age, **78**: 579. — Colburn, **108**: 58. — Fraser, **55**: 64. — No. Brit. **27**: 1. — Quar. **99**: 287. Same art. Liv. Age, **51**: 577. Same art. Ecl. M. **40**: 145.
— Influence of, in Religion. (H. M. Whitney) New Eng. **38**: 807.
— — and Genius of. Ecl. R. **67**: 361.
— Latest Facts about. (G. L. Gomme) Colburn, **159**: 86–195.
— Latest Theory about. (J. Spedding) Contemp. **27**: 653, 821. — (E. A. Abbott) Contemp. **28**: 141.
— Letters of. Retros. **6**: 152.
— — and Life of. Chr. Rem. **44**: 388. — Fraser, **66**: 529.
— — to the King of Denmark. (S. R. Gardiner) Arch. **41**: 219.
Bacon, Francis, Lord, Life of. Penny M. **2**: 23. — Ed. R. **150**: 395.
— — and Character of. So. Lit. Mess. **4**: 9, 73, 190.
— Lives of. Westm. **31**: 513.
— Macaulay's Essay on. (J. Spedding) Contemp. **28**: 169, 365, 562. — (W. S. Grayson) So. Lit. Mess. **29**: 177.
— — Grayson on. So. Lit. Mess. **29**: 382.
— — Montague's Answer to. Mo. R. **156**: 206.
— Napier's Essay on. Blackw. **3**: 657.
— Novum Organum. (G. P. Fisher) Hours at Home, **8**: 323. — (B. Montague) Retros. **3**: 141. **4**: 280.
— — edited by T. Fowler. (G. C. Robertson) Mind, **4**: 125.
— Philosophical Works. Fraser, **60**: 387.
— Philosophy of. (W. A. Lawrence) University Q. **4**: 19. — Ecl. R. **108**: 321. — So. R. n. s. **18**: 301.
— — the Cure of Rationalism. Bib. R. **5**: 145.
— — Fischer on. Dub. Univ. **86**: 377.
— — Summary of. Penn Mo. **2**: 546.
— Plato and Bentham. (H. H. Milman) Quar. **61**: 462.
— Prayers by. Cong. M. **28**: 275.
— Public Career and Personal Character of. (J. Rowley) Fraser, **98**: 308. Same art. Liv. Age, **139**: 91. Same art. Sup. Pop. Sci. Mo. **3**: 561.
— Readings from. So. Lit. Mess. **16**: 30, 267.
— Religious Character of. (S. M. Hopkins) Am. Bib. Repos. 3d s. **3**: 127.
— Remusat's Life of. Colburn, **111**: 34.
— Spedding's Life and Letters of. Fraser, **79**: 747. Same art. Ecl. M. **73**: 400. — (M. P. Lowe) Unita. R. **12**: 94.
— Visit to Gorhambury. Once a Week, **7**: 276.
— Was he an Impostor? Fraser, **74**: 718. — (J. von Liebig) Fraser, **75**: 482.
— What has he originated or discovered? (I. H. Weil) Nat. Q. **15**: 316.
— Works of. (A. Barnes) Chr. Q. Spec. **4**: 528. — Liv. Age, **12**: 324. — (H. Giles) Chr. Exam. **72**: 157. — Liv. Age, **52**: 673. — Ed. R. **106**: 287.
— Worldly Wisdom of. Liv. Age, **76**: 562.
Bacon, Rev. Henry. Univ. Q. **14**: 75.
Bacon, Henry D., with portrait. De Bow, **12**: 693.
Bacon, James Munroe. (J. W. Wellman) Cong. Q. **17**: 347.
Bacon, John, Cecil's Life of. Chr. Obs. **1**: 525.
Bacon, Leonard. Nat. M. **3**: 115. — With portrait. Ecl. M. **94**: 633.
— Church Manual. Chr. Q. Spec. **5**: 612.
— Historical Discourses. (F. Parkman) Chr. Exam. **27**: 201. — (N. Porter) Am. Bib. Repos. 2d s. **2**: 217. — (A. Lamson) No. Am. **50**: 161. — New York R. **6**: 48. — Lit. & Theo. R. **6**: 166.
— Plea for Africa. (J. Sparks) No. Am. **21**: 462. — U. S. Lit. Gaz. **3**: 30.
Bacon, Leonard W. Answer to Tract, "Is it Honest?" (A. Young) Cath. World, **7**: 239.
Bacon, Nathaniel, Life of. (W. Ware) Sparks's Am Biog. **13**: 239.
Bacon, Sir Nicolas; with unprinted Papers. (J. P. Collier) Arch. **36**: 339.
Bacon, Richard, jr. So. Lit. Mess. **7**: 785.
Bacon, Roger. (J. Cowen) Colburn, **165**: 864. — (E. H. Plumptre) Contemp. **2**: 364. — (E. W. Reynolds) Univ. Q. **20**: 279. — All the Year, **5**: 318. — Dub. R. **48**: 316.
— and Growth of Christian Thought. (E. E. Butler) Am. Church R. **32**: 287.
— and Lord Bacon. (J. H. Rigg) Meth. Q. **18**: 5, 173.
— in the Light of New Documents. (E. Saisset) Am. Presb. R. **12**: 639.
— Life and Writings of. Westm. **81**: 1.

Bacon, Roger, Minor Works of. Liv. Age, **65**: 337.
— Philosophy of. Westm. **81**: 512.
— Sketch of. St. James, **6**: 28.
— Works of. Liv. Age, **66**: 716.
Bacon, Rev. Thomas, of Maryland, 1745–68. (E. Allen) Am. Church R. **17**: 430.
Bacon, Wm. Thompson. Poems. (F. Bowen) No. Am. **68**: 260. — Knick. **11**: 58, 151. **12**: 20. — Am. Whig R. **4**: 15. — Brownson, **6**: 129. — Bost. Q. **1**: 74.
Bacon's Rebellion. Dem. R. **7**: 243, 453.
Bacon, How we cure our. Chamb. J. **45**: 667.
Bacteria. (J. B. Sanderson) Nature, **17**: 84.
— and their Effects. (L. A. Stimson) Pop. Sci. Mo. **6**: 399.
— as Cause of Disease in Plants. (T. J. Burrill) Am. Natural. **15**: 527.
— Natural Development of, in the Protolamic Parts of various Plants. (A. Bechamp) Pop. Sci. R. **8**: 166.
— Temperature at which they are killed. (H. C. Bastian) Nature, **8**: 273.
Bad Bargain; a Tale. All the Year, **37**: 258.
Bad made Worse. St. James, **25**: 690, 828. **26**: 151, 300.
Badajos, Siege of. All the Year, **30**: 58, 326.
— Storming of. Fraser, **50**: 223. — Mus. **23**: 231, 612.
Badakshan and Wakhan, Frontiers of. Colburn, **152**: 301.
Badcock Genealogy. (W. S. Appleton) N. E. Reg. **19**: 215.
Baddeley, Robert, and his Cake. Temp. Bar, **13**: 443.
Baden and Allerheiligen. (T. A. Trollope) Lippinc. **20**: 535.
— and its Attractions. Dub. Univ. **63**: 702.
— Baths of. Cornh. **35**: 195.
— Castle of. Sharpe, **26**: 178.
— Church and State in. Dub. R. **36**: 269.
— in 1862. Once a Week, **7**: 514.
— Insurrection in. Blackw. **66**: 206.
— Reminiscences of. Colburn, **93**: 145.
Baden-Baden. (C. A. Bristed) Galaxy, **1**: 519. — Bentley, **4**: 353. — Blackw. **48**: 479. — Lond. Soc. **6**: 425. Same art. Ecl. M. **64**: 80.
— and Matlock. Temp. Bar, **10**: 550.
— Day's Hunting at. Colburn, **95**: 412.
— Gambling at. Lond. Soc. **4**: 394.
— in 1853. Sharpe, **52**: 97, 137, 199.
— in 1867. (C. Clarke) Temp. Bar, **21**: 383.
— in a new Light. Tinsley, **3**: 307.
— in Winter. Colburn, **103**: 39.
— Pictures of. (R. M. Richardson) Knick. **41**: 385. **42**: 111–603.
— Rien ne va plus. (C. Hervey) Belgra. **24**: 317.
Badgebury. Godey, **23**: 72.
Badger, Geo. E., Reminiscences. Land We Love, **1**: 283.
— Sketch of. (W. Eaton) Land We Love, **1**: 335.
Badger, Rev. Joseph. Am. Q. Reg. **13**: 317. — (E. H. Sears) Chr. Exam. **57**: 42.
Badger, Milton. (D. B. Coe) Cong. Q. **17**: 1.
Badger, The Penny M. **7**: 245.
— and its Enemies. All the Year, **44**: 200.
Badges. Chamb. J. **19**: 92.
— and Devices, Historic. (Mrs. B. Palliser) Art J. **17**: 313, 325. **18**: 13–325. **19**: 33–261.
— History and Varieties of. Nat. M. **6**: 48.
Badham, David Charles. Fraser, **56**: 162. Same art. Liv. Age, **55**: 62.
Badlam, Ezra, Letter of, 1777. N. E. Reg. **2**: 49.
Baer, Karl Ernst von. Nature, **15**: 138.
— Autobiography of. Quar. **122**: 335. Same art. Liv. Age, **93**: 419.
Baertz, Father Gaspar, at Ormuz. Month, **21**: 435. **22**: 164, 426.
Baffin's Bay, Cruise to. Chamb. J. **52**: 150.
— Sutherland's Voyage in, 1850. Colburn, **96**: 102.
Bagdad. Lond. Soc. **36**: 497. — Penny M. **14**: 9.
— Caravansary of. Good Words, **1**: 425.
— Fall of. Blackw. **48**: 595.
— Plague of. Penny M. **2**: 458.
— Visit to. Ev. Sat. **2**: 530.
Bage, Robert. (H. Kirke) Reliquary, **10**: 33.
— Life and Character of. Mus. **7**: 369.
Bagehot, Walter. (R. H. Hutton) Fortn. **28**: 453. Same art. Liv. Age, **135**: 387. — (G. B. Smith) Fraser, **99**: 298. Same art. Liv. Age, **141**: 131. — (G. Walker) Nation, **28**: 436. — Liv. Age, **133**: 245.
— and the Economist. (G Walker) Nation, **24**: 204.
— as an Economist. (R. Giffen) Fortn. **33**: 549.
— Biographical Studies. (A. V. Dicey) Nation, **32**: 426.
— Journalism as exemplified by. (J. Arbuckle) Scrib. **18**: 846.
— Physics and Politics. Penn Mo. **4**: 558.
— Sketch of. Pop. Sci. Mo. **12**: 489.
Baggage under Difficulties. All the Year, **20**: 233.
Bagged on the First. Lond. Soc. **28**: 247.
Bagh O' Bahar; or, The Garden and the Spring. Colburn, **149**: 676. **150**: 59, 108.
Bagimont's Roll, in Advocate's Library, Edinburgh. (N. Carlisle) Arch. **17**: 231.
Bagleyhole Folk. (H. S. Vince) St. James, **41**: 407.
Bagpipe Music, Highland. (D. Campbell) Tait. n. s. **16**: 369.
Bagpipes. Penny M. **13**: 278.
— of Tottenham Court Road. Lond. M. **1**: 389.
Bahador. *See* Jung-Bahador.
Bahamas. (S. G. W. Benjamin) Harper, **49**: 761.
— Formation of. Hunt, **44**: 45.
Bahia, A Day at. Dub. Univ. **53**: 114.
Baie-Verte Canal. (T. Guerin) Ecl. Engin. **11**: 240. **14**: 54, 359. — (C. Herschel) Ecl. Engin. **14**: 150.
Baïf, Jan Antoine de, Early French Poet. Lond. M. **5**: 335.
Bail. West. R. **1**: 292.
Bailey, Ebenezer. Am. J. Educ. **12**: 429.
Bailey, Gamaliel, a Pioneer Editor. (J. E. Snodgrass) Atlan. **17**: 743. — (I. Washburne) Univ. Q. **25**: 298.
Bailey, Jacob. (L. Sabine) No. Am. **78**: 202.
Bailey, Jacob Whitman, Address in Commemoration of. (A. A. Gould) Am. J. Sci. **75**: 153.
Bailey, Philip James. Ev. Sat. **13**: 498. — Irish Q. **6**: 1.
— Angel World. Prosp. R. **6**: 267. — Westm. **54**: 335.
— Festus. (E. P. Whipple) Am. Whig R. **2**: 55. — (H. N. Hudson) Am. Whig R. **5**: 43, 123. — New Eng. **5**: 175. — (W. H. Channing) Chr. Exam. **39**: 365. — Brit. Q. **3**: 377. — Dem. R. **17**: 454. — De Bow, **10**: 430. — Dub. Univ. **30**: 91. — Blackw. **67**: 415. — (T. S. King) Univ. Q. **2**: 385. — (J. Clark) Mercersb. **3**: 401. — Chr. Rem. **20**: 346. — Dial, **2**: 231. — Ecl. R. **70**: 654. **121**: 540. — Hogg, **11**: 264. — Ecl. M. **29**: 128. — Prosp. R. **3**: 511. — So. Q. **11**: 166.
— The Mystic and other Poems. Bentley, **38**. 609. — Chr. Rem. **31**: 267.
Bailey, W. Sermons. Chr. Disc. **4**: 293.
Baillie, Lady Grisell. Blackw. **80**: 456. — (W. Chambers) Chamb. J. **51**: 529.
Baillie, Joanna, with portrait. Ecl. M. **23**: 128. — (P. Frank) Ecl. M. **23**: 420. — (J. W. Calcraft) Dub. Univ. **37**: 529. — Bentley, **29**: 453. — Blackw. **16**: 162. — Chamb. J. **15**: 257. — Dub. Univ. **37**: 529. — Eng. Dom. M. **14**: 19. **25**: 272, 294. — Peop. J. **11**: 253. — Internat. M. **3**: 140. — Nat. M. **12**. 7. — No. Brit. **42**: 337. Same art. Liv. Age, **85**: 598. Same art. Ecl. M. **65**: 270.
— and Lord Jeffrey. Internat. M. **3**: 312.

Baillie, Joanna, Dramas of. Fraser, **13**: 236.—(A. Norton) Chr. Exam. **4**: 29.—(F. W. P. Greenwood) Chr. Exam. **22**: 1.—(F. Jeffrey) Ed. R. **2**: 269. **5**: 405. **19**: 261.—Quar. **55**: 264.—Am. Q. **14**: 160.—Anal. M. **2**: 108.—Westm. **33**: 401.—Mo. R. **110**: 174.—Blackw. **16**: 162. **39**: 1, 265.—Quar. **55**: 487.—Ed. R. **63**: 73.—Mo. R. **139**: 260.
— Fugitive Verses. Quar. **67**: 437.
— Letters and Journals of. Mo. R. **157**: 25.
— Metrical Legends. Mo. R. **96**: 72.—Ecl. R. **34**: 428.
— Plays of. Ecl. R. **18**: 21, 167.—Portfo.(Den.) **25**: 339.
— — Plan of. (F. Jeffrey) Select Ed. R. **1**: 264.
— Poems of. Mus. **41**: 307.—Ecl. R. **38**: 264. **93**: 407.—Selec. Ed. R. **2**: 149.
Baillie, Matthew, Works, Wardrop's. Colburn, **14**: 364.
Baillie, Neil B. E. Mohammedan Law of Sale. Internat. M. **1**: 275.
Baillie, Robert, the Covenanter. (T. Carlyle) Westm. **37**: 43. Same art. Am. Ecl. **3**: 282.
— Letters and Journals of. Cong. M. **26**: 233.—Ecl. R. **74**: 633. **77**: 449.—Mus. **44**: 454.
Bailly, J. S. Memoirs of French Revolution. (F. Jeffrey) Ed. R. **6**: 137.
— Notes on. Colburn, **109**: 288.
Baily, Edward Hodges, Works of. Ecl. R. **94**: 146.
Baily, Francis, the Banker. Bank. M. (N. Y.) **5**: 96.
Bain, Alexander. Nature, **15**: 218.
— on Free Will. (H. W. Lucas) Month, **21**: 275.
— Sketch of. Pop. Sci. Mo. **9**: 360.
Bainbridge, William, Commodore, with portrait. Portfo. (Den.) **10**: 553.—Am. Q. **21**: 415.—Ann. Reg. **8**: [449.
Baines, Edward. Ecl. M. **24**: 31.
— Life of. Ecl. R. **94**: 203.—Colburn, **92**: 491.—House. Words, **3**: 414.
Baines, William, Imprisonment of. Cong. M. **24**: 415.
Bairam, The, Mohammedan Festival. Colburn, **25**: 352.
Baird, Sir David. Ann. Reg. **5**: [265.—Select J. **1**: [134.
Baird, James, Sketch of. (J. S. Jeans) Pract. M. **1**: 246.
Baireuth in the 18th Century. Dub. Univ. **64**: 91, 216.
Bajazet Gag. (D. Jerrold) Colburn, **62**: 322–369. **63**: 82–489. **64**: 177.
Bakehouse, Work in the. Chamb. J. **39**: 43.
Baker, Augustin. Sancta Sophia. Dub. R. **79**: 337.
Baker, Edward D., Col. (J. Hay) Harper, **24**: 103.
Baker, John, Case of. Niles's Reg. **36**: 29, 193.
Baker, Osmon C., Bishop. (C. Adams) Meth. Q. **38**: 111.
Baker, Sir R. (F. Lawrence) Sharpe, **23**: 341.
Baker, Remember. (P. H. White) Hist. M. **9**: 326.
Baker, Sir Samuel W., and his Explorations of the Nile Sources. Macmil. **14**: 205
— Political Aspects of his Expedition, 1875. (A. J. Wilson) Fraser, **91**: 338. *See* Africa.
Bakers. (W. Chambers) Chamb. J. **6**: 65.
— and their Trade. Dub. Univ. **80**: 473.
— Battle of. St. James, **5**: 201.
— Health of. (H. Martineau) Once a Week, **3**: 540.
— of London. Chamb. J. **10**: 47.
— of Paris. Chamb. J. **41**: 734.
Bakewell, Robert. Travels. Mo. R. **103**: 271.
Baku, Burning Peninsula of. Chamb. J. **38**: 33. Same art. Liv. Age, **74**: 371.—Penny M. **7**: 44.
Bal de l'Opéra; a Poem. Belgra. **7**: 485.
Bal Masqué at Mi-Carême. Lond. Soc. **21**: 249.
Balaam. (R. Martineau) Theo. R. **15**: 327.—(J. T. Smith) Bapt. Q. **3**: 464.
— Character and Prophecies of. (R. C. D. Robbins) Bib. Sac. **3**: 347, 699.
— History of. Chr. Obs. **38**: 295, 350.
Balaam, History and Oracles of. (M. S. Terry) Meth. Q. **28**: 553.
— Prophecies of. (H. C. Lea) Nation, **26**: 245.
Balaams, The; a Tale. Putnam, **10**: 97.
Balacchi Brothers. (R. H. Davis) Lippinc. **10**: 66.
Balaklava, Kind Thoughts for. Chamb. J. **23**: 20.
— Life at, 1854. Liv. Age, **44**: 39.
— Martyr of. (L. Poyntz) Galaxy, **16**: 221.
Balance of Life, The. Cornh. **6**: 545.—Ecl. M. **20**: 137.
Balance of Power. (H. Brougham) Ed. R. **1**: 345.—Dem. R. **18**: 273.—Carey's Mus. **2**: 240.
— in Europe. Ed. R. **1**: 345.—Selec. Ed. R. **5**: 1.
Balance of Trade and Course of Exchange. (C. H. Carroll) Bank. M. (N. Y.) **32**: 949.—(L. Levi) Bank. M. (N. Y.) **32**: 369.
Balances. (F. Peale) J. Frankl. Inst. **44**: 59.
Balancing the Books; a Tale. (J. F. Waller) Dub. Univ. **47**: 1. Same art. Liv. Age, **49**: 148.
Balanus, The. Chamb. J. **24**: 10.
Balasagun. (H. H. Howorth) Geog. M. **2**: 217.
Balaton, Lake of. Sharpe, **19**: 244.
Balboa, V. N. de. (J. T. Headley) Harper, **18**: 467.—Liv. Age, **46**: 492.
— and Pizarro, Lives of. Blackw. **32**: 359.
Balch, Rev. Stephen B. So. Lit. Mess. **7**: 860.
Balche Genealogy. (W. F. Balch) N. E. Reg. **9**: 233.
Balcombe Street Mystery. House. Words, **17**: 486.
Bald Barrys; a Poem. Dub. Univ. **85**: 618.
Balder the Beautiful. (R. Buchanan) Contemp. **29**: 691, 800, 1004.
Baldwin I., Emperor. Irish Q. **7**: 29.
Baldwin, Rev. Abraham. Chr. Mo. Spec. **9**: 449.
Baldwin, James Fowle. (U. Parsons) N. E. Reg. **19**: 97.
Baldwin, John, of Stonington, Conn. N. E. Reg. **27**: 148.
Baldwin, Joseph G., Party Leaders. So. Lit. Mess. **21**: 65.
Baldwin, Roger S., Discourse on. (S. W. S. Dutton) New Eng. **22**: 259.
Baldwin, Simeon. (S. W. S. Dutton) New Eng. **9**: 426.
Baldwin, Theron. (J. M. Sturtevant) Cong. Q. **17**: 213, 395.—Cong. R. **10**: 353.
Baldwin Family. N. E. Reg. **26**: 295.—(B. A. Baldwin) N. E. Reg. **25**: 153.
Bale, John, Bishop of Ossory. (G. G. Perry) Contemp. **10**: 96.
Balearic Islands, Visit to. (B. Taylor) Atlan. **20**: 680. **21**: 73.
Balfe, Michael W., with portrait. Dub. Univ. **38**: 66.—Eng. Dom. M. **10**: 19.
Balfour, Sir James, Collection of Manuscripts. Chamb J. **15**: 406.
Balfour, Walter. (E. G. Brooks) Univ. Q. **32**: 133, 261.
Balkans, The, Counter-Revolution in. (A. J. Evans) Fortn. **33**: 491.
— Over, with Gourko. (F. V. Greene) Scrib. **20**: 721.
Ball, Edward. (L. C. Ball) N. E. Reg. **9**: 158.
Ball, Frances, Nun of Loreto. (H. J. Coleridge) Month, **37**: 59.
Ball, John T., Lord Chancellor of Ireland, with portrait. Dub. Univ. **85**: 402.
Ball, William, Poems of. Ecl. R. **51**: 251.
Ball's Bluff, Battle of, Report of. (W. H. Jenifer) So. R. n. s. **6**: 470.
Ball at Delmonico's. Galaxy, **17**: 513.
Ball-Giving and Ball-Going. (C. Boyle) Macmil. **27**: 458.—Canad. Mo. **3**: 448.
Ball Season in Paris. Temp. Bar, **11**: 90.
Balls. (F. Fitzgerald) Belgra. **1**: 225.—All the Year, **27**: 322.
Balls, Chinese How made. J. Frankl. Inst. **47**: 130.
Ballachulish, from London to, and back. Macmil. **4**: 481.
Ballad, Nature and Lit. Affinities of. (W. S. Dalgleish.) Brit. Q. **59**: 1. Same art. Liv. Age, **120**: 579.

Ballad of Arabella. (J. T. Trowbridge) Harper, **53**: 161.
— of the Boston Tea-Party. (O. W. Holmes) Atlan. **33**: 219.
— of Calden Water. (P. Carey) Scrib. **3**: 488.
— of Carmilhan; a Poem. (H. W. Longfellow) Atlan. **29**: 389.
— of Christopher Aske. (R. T. Cooke) Atlan. **43**: 283.
— of Fair Ladies in Revolt. (G. Meredith) Fortn. **26**: 232.
— of the French Fleet. (H. W. Longfellow) Atlan. **39**: 446.
— of the Gold Country. (H. M. Jackson) Scrib. **4**: 613.
— of Isobel. (J. Payne) Colburn, **165**: 1125.
— of Leonore. (G. A. Bürger) Dub. Univ. **4**: 509.
— of Richard Burnell. (W. Howitt) House. Words, **1**: 372.
— of Sir Ball. (W. D. O'Connor) Galaxy, **5**: 328.
— of Sir John Franklin. (G. H. Boker) Internat. M. **4**: 473.
— of Sir Ronald. Broadw. **3**: 219.
Ballad Books. (F. J. Child) Nation, **7**: 192.
Ballad Land, Into. (M. G. Watkins) Fraser, **88**: 648.
Ballad Literature. Mass. Q. **1**: 240.
— of Ancient Greece. (W. C. Taylor) Bentley, **12**: 494.
— of England in Middle Ages. (Miss E. Wormeley) Putnam, **4**: 378.
Ballad Poetry, Ancient and Modern. Blackw. **61**: 622. — Cornh. **31**: 709. Same art. Ecl. M. **85**: 205.
— of England. (H. W. Herbert) Godey, **29**: 262.
— of Ireland. Dub. Univ. **61**: 442.
— of Scotland. Blackw. **84**: 462. — Ecl. R. **94**: 567. Same art. Liv. Age, **32**: 487.
Ballad Singers, English. Colburn, **5**: 212.
Ballad Singing. Broadw. **3**: 454.
Ballad Subjects. Chamb. J. **39**: 333.
Ballad Writers, Modern. Westm. **55**: 1.
Ballade de la Gueuserie. (E. D. Jerrold) Temp. Bar, **55**: 404.
Ballads, Ancient. So. Lit. Mess. **28**: 195.
Ballads and Ballad Music illustrative of Shakspere. (A. E. Barr) Harper, **63**: 52.
— and Traditions of Northern Europe. Colburn, **130**: 479. **131**: 39.
— Ante-Revolutionary. Hist. M. **2**: 164.
— Art among. (L. Jewitt) Art J. **31**: 6–305.
— Bouquet of. (W. E. Aytoun) Dub. Univ. **33**: 606.
— Breton; translated. Blackw. **86**: 488.
— Cavalier. (W. G. Thornbury) Dub. Univ. **48**: 611.
— Danish, Ancient. Westm. **75**: 1.
— Dissertation on. Fraser, **19**: 407.
— from English History. (J. Payn) Colburn, **106**: 304–485.
— Historical. Brit. Q. **33**: 443.
— Illustrative Designs to Foreign. Chr. Rem. **2**: 395.
— from the German. Dub. Univ. **46**: 496.
— National. So. Lit. Mess. **15**: 10.
— of England, Ancient. Ecl. R. **73**: 169. **85**: 171. — Liv. Age, **54**: 124. — Penny M. **7**: 169–369. — Retros. **17**: 144, 209. — Mo. R. **163**: 390.
— — — Pictures on. (L. Jewitt) Art J. **30**: 74, 118.
— — and of Scotland. (W. M. Nevin) Mercersb. **2**: 155, 345. — Knick. **54**: 497.
— — Historical. Penny M. **8**: 94–278.
— — Modern. (H. G. Hewlett) Contemp. **26**: 958. — Hogg, **9**: 28.
— — Romantic. Penny M. **7**: 404–489. **8**: 17, 44.
— of the English People. Westm. R. **63**: 25. Same art. Liv. Age, **44**: 593.
— of Ireland. Liv. Age, **47**: 798.
— — Street. Cath. World, **9**: 32. — House. Words, **4**: 361. Same art. Liv. Age, **32**: 481.
— — — Modern. (W. Barry) Macmil. **25**: 190. Same art. Liv. Age, **112**: 308. — (A. M. Williams) Nation, **6**: 135.
Ballads of Lower Brittany. Dub. Univ. **81**: 361.
— of Scotland. (A. Smith) Liv. Age, **53**: 129. — Quar. **105**: 305. — Liv. Age, **56**: 65. — So. Lit. Mess. **27**: 374.
— — Aytoun's. (D. Wilson) Canad. J. n. s. **4**: 295, 468. — New Q. **7**: 224.
— of Seven Dials. Quar. **123**: 382.
— of Spain. House. Words, **19**: 408.
— — Lockhart's Ancient. Mo. R. **156**: 421. **158**: 427.
— Our modern Minstrelsy. (W. Leighton) St. James, **27**: 151.
— Percy's Manuscript. (W. L. Blackley) Contemp. **6**: 357.
— Political, of England and Scotland. Ed. R. **113**: 87.
— Provincial. Colburn, **14**: 217.
— Roxburghe. No. Brit. **6**: 25.
— — Collier's Book of. Ecl. R. **85**: 469.
— Street. Nat. R. **13**: 397.
— Traditionary. (Mary Howitt) Tait, n. s. **2**: 27–820.
Ballantyne Controversy with Lockhart. Tait, n. s. **6**: 657.
Ballantyne's Novelists' Library. Blackw. **15**: 406.
Ballerini and Liguori. Month, **20**: 240.
Ballet, The. All the Year, **12**: 94. — (M. E. Haweis) St. Paul's, **12**: 324.
— and Stage Morality. Blackw. **105**: 354. Same art. Ecl. M. **72**: 620.
— English. Ev. Sat. **14**: 429.
— of the Ratcatcher. Temp. Bar, **57**: 399.
Ballet Dancer, The. Chamb. J. **19**: 387.
Ballet Dancing, History of. (J. B. Matthews) Appleton, **19**: 306.
Ballet Girls of Paris. Lond. Soc. **17**: 25, 181. — Ev. Sat. **9**: 55.
Ballets and Ballet Dancers. (D. Cook) Belgra. **25**: 522.
Ballinasloe Fair. Dub. Univ. **42**: 628.
Balliol Scholars, 1840–43. (J. C. Shairp) Macmil. **27**: 376. Same art. Ecl. M. **80**: 572.
Balloon, Descent from, in a Parachute. All the Year, **7**: 501.
— Five Weeks in a. (Sir F. C. L. Wraxall) St. James, **8**: 315.
— for crossing the Atlantic, Wise's. Pract. M. **2**: 219.
— from America to England. Nature, **8**: 364.
— How I left Paris in a. (W. de Fonvielle) Temp. Bar, **31**: 166.
— Nadar's. Chamb. J. **41**: 37.
— Navigable. Ecl. Engin. **6**: 640.
— — Lome's. Pract. M. **1**: 80. — Chamb. J. **32**: 367.
— Royal. Liv. Age, **45**: 228.
— Three Trips in a. Chamb. J. **16**: 302.
— with Power. Ecl. Engin. **14**: 354.
Balloon and Pigeon Posts. Chamb. J. **48**: 129, 154.
Balloon Adventure, Fatal, with drawings. Knick. **10**: 342.
Balloon Ascension, First, in England, 1784. Chamb. J. **28**: 60.
— of MM. Barral and Bixio. Dub. Univ. **36**: 304.
— to solve Atmospheric Problems, 1850. J. Frankl. Inst. **51**: 34.
— Woolwich. (C. O. Browne) Pop. Sci. R. **13**: 404.
Balloon Ascensions. All the Year, **18**: 447.
— Account of. (J. Glaisher) J. Frankl. Inst. **78**: 389.
— Blanchard's. House. Words, **7**: 483.
— History of. Knick. **54**: 380.
— in Paris. Chamb. J. **14**: 234.
— Scientific Importance of. (J. Glaisher) Pop. Sci. R. **4**: 403. Same art. Ecl. M. **66**: 505.
Balloon Traveling. Chamb. J. **55**: 109.
Balloon Voyage in England, First. (J. Glaisher) Good Words, **4**: 719.
— over Illinois. (P. Bowles) Lakeside, **6**: 299.
— over London. Lond. M. **15**: 351.
Balloon Voyaging. (G. T. Ferris) Appleton, **12**: 225.

Ballooning. Chamb. J. **17**: 214. **31**: 157. Same art. Liv. Age, **61**: 312. — Chamb. J. **41**: 150. **53**: 161. —Ecl. M. **58**: 424. **61**: 151. — Ev. Sat. **1**: 403. — House. Words, **4**: 97 — Liv. Age, **31**: 499. — Westm. **48**: 314 Same art. Liv. Age, **16**: 433. — Brit. Q. **54**: 302. Same art. Ecl. M. **77**: 641.
— and Animal Magnetism, Early Notices of. Hist. M. **9**: 208.
— as it is hoped to be. Chamb. J. **43**: 643.
— Glaisher's Travels in the Air. Nature, **4**: 3.
— History of. Knick. **45**: 150.
— in France. Cornh. **27**: 336. — Nature, **5**: 334.
— in its Infancy. Colburn, **96**: 197.
— in later Years. Colburn, **96**: 286.
— Past and present. Once a Week, **9**: 680.
— Scientific. (J. Glaisher) J. Frankl. Inst. **75**: 263. **76**: 49, 319. **82**: 46, 132. — (J. Glaisher) Ex. H. Lec. **18**: 1. — J. Frankl. Inst. **81**: 388. — Nature, **18**: 639. — Belgra. **12**: 204. — So. R. n. s. **7**: 191. Brit. Q. **19**: 61.
— H. Turnor's Astra Castra. Colburn, **135**: 238.
See Aerial Navigation; Aeronautics.
Balloons. (A. Oppenheim) J. Frankl. Inst. **101**: 123, 209. — (W. Pole) Fortn. **35**: 75. Same art. Ecl. M. **96**: 310. — (G. G. Searle) Cath. World, **14**: 757. — All the Year, **44**: 17. — (J. R. Thompson) Scrib. **1**: 385. — Chamb. J. **31**: 157. Same art. Ecl. M. **47**: 129. — Lond. Soc. **4**: 481.
— and Aeronauts. Once a Week, **13**: 386, 526.
— and Voyages in the Air. Quar. **139**: 105. Same art. Ecl. M. **85**: 385. Same art. Liv. Age, **126**: 451. — Nat. M. **2**: 74.
— Chapter on. Fraser, **40**: 33. Same art. Liv. Age, **22**: 313.
— for Military Purposes. (W. de Fonvielle) Nature, **3**: 115, 135, 175. — (H. B. Pritchard) Nature, **18**: 491. — Once a Week, **23**: 393, 411. — All the Year, **21**: 297. — Ev. Sat. **9**: 695. — All the Year, **24**: 536.
— — Day with War Balloons. (H. Elsdale) 19th Cent. **9**: 108. Same art. Liv. Age, **148**: 298. Same art. Ecl. M. **96**: 320.
— in Arctic Exploration. (H. Coxwell) Temp. Bar, **61**: 169.
— in Meteorological Research. (J. Wise) J. Frankl. Inst. **91**: 345.
— Origin of. (G. Cumberland) J. Frankl. Inst. **7**: 20.
— Progress in the Art of. Once a Week, **21**: 96.
— Steering of. (A. Moigno) Pract. M. **4**: 239.
— Three Months with. St. James, **7**: 96.
See Flying-Machines.
Balloon Ball, Game of. (R. Macgregor) Belgra. **44**: 193.
Ballot, The. Fraser, **2**: 717. **3**: 183. **16**: 289. — Ecl. R. **67**: 97. **69**: 401. **72**: 713. — Brit. & For. R. **4**: 585. **9**: 289. — (J. Mill) Westm. **13**: 1. — Macmil. **26**: 417. — Quar. **61**: 507. — Tait, **2**: 647, 660, 683.
— Abuse of, and its Remedy. (G. W. Julian) Internat. R. **8**: 534.
— Advantages of Voting by. Westm. **94**: 437.
— and Bribery at Elections. Westm. **115**: 443.
— Dialogue on. Westm. **30**: 201.
— Last Words on. Brit. Q. **55**: 188.
— Notes on. (F. Taylor) Canad. Mo. **3**: 488.
— Protection of. (C. F. Adams, jr.) Am. Soc. Sci. J. **1**: 91.
— Secret. Westm. **91**: 383.
— — Shall we have? Nation, **28**: 82.
— Sydney Smith on. Tait, n. s. **6**: 219.
— Vote by. Dem. R. **34**: 19. — Ecl. R. **124**: 378.
— Vox Populi. (W. Ambruster) Lippinc. **2**: 408.
Ballot-Box, Forty-one Hours with a. (E. Leigh) Belgra. **29**: 194.
— Responsibility of. Am. Whig R. **4**: 435.
Ballots, Votes, and Blackballs. Chamb. J. **21**: 231.
Ballou, Hosea. (E. G. Brooks) Univ. Q. **27**: 389. **30**: 40. — (A. P. Putnam) Mo. Rel. M. **45**: 397.
— and Universalism. (A. A. Miner) Univ. Q. **19**: 379.
— Parentage and Early Life of. (H. Ballou, 2d) Univ. Q. **11**: 174.
Ballou, Hosea, 2d. (G. H. Emerson) Univ. Q. **18**: 308. — (T. B. Thayer) Univ. Q. **23**: 240. — (E. G. Brooks) Univ. Q. **35**: 389.
Ballowmere; a Tale. Sharpe, **34**: 191, 242.
Ballymurry; a Tale. (N. Robinson) Cath. World, **28**: 207.
Ballysadare and Kilvarnet, O'Rorke's. (J. Healy) Irish Mo. **6**: 603.
Balmes, James, Letters to a Sceptic. Internat. R. **3**: 108.
Balms and Balsams. Penny M. **13**: 119.
Balmoral. Tait, n. s. **16**: 16.
Balquhidder, In the Braes of. Good Words, **20**: 713.
Baltic, The. (T. Milner) Fraser, **51**: 201.
— and the Black Sea. Bentley, **38**: 221.
— Cruise of the Miranda in, 1854. Colburn, **101**: 39.
— English Fleet in, 1855. Blackw. **78**: 135, 427.
— Letters from. (R. M. Milnes) Quar. **68**: 444. — Mus. **44**: 297. — Mo. R. **156**: 576. — Tait, n. s. **9**: 37.
— Recollections of a Cruise in. Fraser, **92**: 508.
Baltic Fleet. Bentley, **35**: 359. Same art. Ecl. M. **32**: 181.
Baltic Shores, Hill's Travels on. Ecl. R. **100**: 207.
Baltic Trade. Penny M. **8**: 321.
Baltimore, Lord. (G. W. Burnap) Sparks's Am. Biog. **9**: 3.
— and Maryland Toleration. (E. D. Neill) Contemp. **28**: 616.
Baltimore, City of. (H. Cooke) Bentley, **17**: 99. — (F. Downing) Land We Love, **6**: 240. Same art. N. Ecl. **4**: 202. — (E. King) Scrib. **9**: 681. — (J. Sparks) No. Am. **20**: 99. — Niles's Reg. **50**: 68. — (H. Stockbridge) Hunt, **23**: 34.
— City of Monuments. (J. W. Palmer) Lippinc. **8**: 259, 368.
— Commercial Progress of. De Bow, **14**: 470.
— Council of, 1866. (A. F. Hewit) Cath. World, **6**: 618. **9**: 497.
— Dedication of Battle Monument. Portfo.(Den.) **15**: 1.
— Democratic Convention, 1844. Dem. R. **14**: 89.
— Exports of, 1842. Hunt, **8**: 382.
— — 1847. Hunt, **19**: 196.
— Johns Hopkins Hospital. Am. Arch. **3**: 165, 209.
— Johns Hopkins University. *See* Johns Hopkins.
— Old, and its Merchants. (F. Mayer) Harper, **60**: 175.
— Old and New. (W. H. Thorne) Potter Am. Mo. **8**: 321.
— Past and Future of. De Bow, **29**: 290.
— Peabody Institute of, Origin of. Am. J. Educ. **3**: 226.
— Private Sewerage in. (P. B. Ghequière) Am. Arch. **6**: 175.
— Regulation of the Port of. Hunt, **6**: 89.
— Reminiscences of. Bank. M. (N. Y.) **3**: 9.
— Something of. (J. W. Hengiston) Colburn, **97**: 358.
Baltimore and Ohio Railroad. (P. Cruise) No. Am. **28**: 166. — J. Frankl. Inst. **33**: 149. **41**: 1. **43**: 1, 73. **45**: 1. **47**: 4. — Niles's Reg. **32**: 282–396. **33**: 137, 162, 273. **34**: 316. **35**: 142, 434. **36**: 41, 92. **37**: 43, 142. **41**: 192, 347, 369. **47**: 123.
— Artists' Excursion over. (D. H. Strother) Harper, **19**: 1.
Baltimore Beauty. (J. W. Palmer) Lippinc. **8**: 11.
Balty. (P. Mulford) Overland, **6**: 268.
Balwidder's Annals of the Parish. Quar. **25**: 147.
Balzac, Honoré de. (H. B. Baker) Gent. M. n. s. **21**: 617. — (R. S. Hunter) Penn Mo. **5**: 595. — (H. James, jr.) Galaxy, **20**: 814. — (V. W. Johnson) Hours at Home, **5**: 249. — (T. S. Perry) No. Am. **124**: 314. — (A. Rhodes) Scrib. **11**: 636. — Ecl. R. **107**: 522. — Bentley, **46**: 148. — Blackw. **121**: 300.

Balzac, Honoré de. Broadw. **8**: 268. — Dem. R. **32**: 325. — Ed. R. **148**: 528. — Ev. Sat. **1**: 708. — Irish Q. **8**: 389. — Lond. Soc. **21**: 308. Same art. Ecl. M. **78**: 738. — Nat. M. **13**: 358. — Temp. Bar, **54**: 535.
— Age of. (W. S. Lilly) Contemp. **37**: 1004.
— and George Sand. For. Q. **33**: 145.
— and his Publisher. All the Year, **1**: 184, 205. Same art. Liv. Age, **62**: 553.
— and his Writings. Westm. R. **60**: 199. Same art. Ecl. M. **30**: 29.
— and Thackeray, Style of. Dub. Univ. **64**: 620. Same art. Ecl. M. **64**: 229. Same art. Liv. Age, **84**: 51.
— Anecdotes of. Temp. Bar, **52**: 381.
— as Artist and Moralist. (K. Hillard) Lippinc. **8**: 592.
— at Home. St. Paul's, **2**: 418.
— Characteristics of. Dub. Univ. **67**: 603.
— Correspondence of. (A. Laugel) Nation, **23**: 339, 366. **24**: 7.
— Dumas, Soulie, etc. Westm. **31**: 73.
— en Pantoufles, Gozlan's. Nat. R. **4**: 63.
— Eugénie Grandet. Ev. Sat. **14**: 148.
— Hugo's Funeral Oration on. Internat. M. **1**: 316.
— Letters of. (H. James, jr.) Galaxy, **23**: 183.
— Life and Career of. Ev. Sat. **4**: 565.
— — and Writings of. Dub. Univ. **70**: 363, 510.
— Novels of. (J. L. Motley) No. Am. **65**: 85. — (L. Stephen) Fortn. **15**: 17. Same art. Liv. Age, **108**: 515.
— Provincial Bachelor's Household. For. Q. **30**: 369.
— Sketches of Provincial Life. Mo. R. **153**: 110.
— Struggles of. (J. F. Molloy) Tinsley, **29**: 395.
— Works of. (H. T. Tuckerman) So. Lit. Mess. **28**: 81.
Balzac, J.-L. G. de. Bentley, **44**: 492.
Bambassi, Father Benvenuto. (M. P. Thompson) Cath. World, **29**: 64.
Bamboo for Paper Making. (R. Thomson) Pract. M. **7**: 333.
Bamboo-Backsheesh Society. Colburn, **160**: 543.
Bamboo Tree. Chamb. J. **42**: 559.
Bamborough Castle. Sharpe, **8**: 129.
Bamburg-Chucklehausen; a Sketch. Dub. Univ. **81**: 161.
Bamford, Samuel, Life of a Radical. Quar. **74**: 358. — Ecl. R. **84**: 1.
— Memoir of. (Dr. Smiles) Howitt, **3**: 328, 345.
Banana, or Plantain Tree. Penny M. **1**: 252.
Banbury, Beesley's History of. Mo. R. **154**: 113.
Banbury Cakes and Banbury Cross. (J. Timbs) Once a Week, **8**: 583.
Bancroft, Aaron. Half-Century Sermon. (J. Brazer) Chr. Exam. **20**: 240.
— Sermons of. Chr. Disc. **4**: 200.
Bancroft, George, with portrait. Appleton, **8**: 208. — Ecl. M. **63**: 248. — (A. Stevens) Nat. M. **6**: 67. — (G. Ripley) Putnam, **1**: 300. — (J. Wynne) Harper, **25**: 52. — Irish Q. **8**: 915.
— and Col. Joseph Reed. Hist. M. **15**: 45.
— — W. B. Reed's Reply. Hist. M. **11**: 249.
— as a Historian. (S. T. Wallis) So. R. n. s. **4**: 202.
— at King's Mountain. So. Lit. Mess. **22**: 161.
— History of United States. *See* United States.
— Mode of Writing History. (J. Pyne) Nat. Q. **30**: 80.
— Poems of. Chr. Disc. **5**: 466.
— Treatment of Gen. N. Greene. Hist. M. **11**: 124.
Bancroft, Hubert H., Library of. (H. P. Johnston) Am. Bibliop. **7**: 44.
Bandel, E. von, with portrait. Pract. M. **6**: 225.
Bandettini, Teresa. Bentley, **36**: 484. Same art. Ecl. M. **34**: 93.
Bandiera, Attilio and Emilio. (J. Mazzini) Peop. J. **1**: 121.
Bandits, Last of the. (Capt. Medwin) Bentley, **2**: 585.
Banditti of Spain. Quar. **61**: 362.
Banditti, Queer Story about. Once a Week, **16**: 50, 78.
Bands, Textile, Effects of Atmospheric Changes upon. (C. J. H. Woodbury) J. Frankl. Inst. **108**: 52.
Bangkok, Siam. (G. B. Bacon) Scrib. **5**: 421.
— Visit to. (A. D. Brown) Harper, **41**: 359.
Bangor, Me., and its Lumber Trade. Hunt, **18**: 517.
— Theological Seminary. (E. Pond) Cong. Q. **12**: 484.
— — History of. (E. Pond) Am. Q. Reg. **14**: 27.
Bangor, Wales. Lond. Soc. **8**: 368.
— Bishops of. (G. Burgess) Am. Church R. **20**: 183.
— Cathedral of. Penny M. **13**: 409.
Bangs Genealogy. (D. Dudley) N. E. Reg. **8**: 368. **10**: 157.
Banians, Traders of the Indian Seas. (B. Frere) Macmil. **32**: 552.
Banim, John. Irish Q. **4**: 270, 527, 825. **5**: 24–823. **6**: 66.
— Murray's Life of. Liv. Age, **56**: 89, 224.
Banim, M. & J., Father Connell. Tait, n. s. **9**: 458.
— Ghost-Hunter. Tait, **2**: 625.
— O'Hara Family. Lond. M. **13**: 134. **17**: 51.
Banim's Canvassing. (T. P. Thompson) Westm. **22**: 472.
Banishment, Practice of, in Time of James II. (G. Roberts) Arch. **34**: 350.
Bank, Cheque. Chamb. J. **51**: 15.
— Internal Management of a Country. Hunt, **24**: 169.
— London and Westminster. Bank. M. (N. Y.) **4**: 35.
— National. Dem. R. **15**: 129. — New York R. **8**: 409.
— — Plan of. (W. S. Wetmore) Hunt, **4**: 528.
— of America, Sketch of. Bank. M. (N. Y.) **7**: 753.
— of California, Failure of, 1875. (E. L. Godkin) Nation, **21**: 144, 160. — Nation, **21**: 149.
— of England. (L. Levi) Bank. M. (L.) **35**: supp. — (W. H. Wills) House. Words, **1**: 337. — Quar. **43**: 342. — Mo. R. **128**: 530. — Ed. R. **56**: 376. — Pamph. **7**: 375. — Ecl. M. **19**: 254. — Liv. Age, **15**: 375. — with cut, Bank. M. (N. Y.) **1**: 231. **2**: 366, 435. **3**: 486. **7**: 357. **8**: 181. **9**: 610. — Hunt, **55**: 117, 258, 332. — Liv. Age, **48**: 125. — Penn Mo. **1**: 257. — Penny M. **3**: 348.
— — and Currency. Brit. & For. R. **5**: 242.
— — and Country Banks. Blackw. **22**: 734. **23**: 197. — Ed. R. **65**: 61.
— — and the Mint. Westm. **100**: 271.
— — and the Money Market, 1872. Quar. **132**: 114.
— — and the Reserves. Bank. M. (N. Y.) **33**: 45.
— — Banking of. Liv. Age, **56**: 246.
— — Charter of. Tait, **1**: 291, 386, 559, 664.
— — — and Commercial Credit. Lond. Q. **10**: 59. *See* Bank Act of 1844.
— — Description of. (F. Hall) Hunt, **17**: 433.
— — Directors of, 1694–1861. Bank. M. (N. Y.) **17**: 446.
— — Downfall of. Dem. R. **20**: 561.
— — Grenfield's Speech, 1817. Blackw. **1**: 406.
— — History of. Chamb. J. **10**: 52. — (J. Francis) Bank. M. (N. Y.) **16**: 753, 849, 929. — (J. W. Gilbart) Bank. M. (N. Y.) **27**: 532–937.
— — — 1797–1822. (H. Adams) No. Am. **105**: 393.
— — — 1844–61. Bank. M. (N. Y.) **17**: 442–673.
— — — Incidents in. Bank. M. (L.) **6**: 14, 147.
— — — Recent. (L. Levi) Bank. M. (L.) **38**: 487.
— — History and Constitution of. Bank. M. (L.) **32**: 922.
— — in 1854. Hunt, **33**: 581.
— — Management of. Bank. M. (N. Y.) **13**: 181.
— — Note of, and Printing it. Bank. M. (N. Y.) **9**: 685.
— — — Characteristics of. Hogg, **9**: 31.
— — — History of. (C. Dickens) Bank. M. (N. Y.) **5**: 251.
— — Operations of, 1845–54. Bank. M. (N. Y.) **9**: 268.
— — — under Sir R. Peel's Act, 1845–54. Bank. M. (L.) **14**: 481.
— — — 1859. Bank. M. (N. Y.) **14**: 854.

Bank of England, Origin of, Macaulay on. Bank. M. (N. Y.) **10**: 881. **17**: 425.
— — Present Constitution of, 1856. (C. Jellicoe) J. Statis. Soc. **19**: 272.
— — Prestige and Position of. Bank. M. (L.) **35**: 1.
— — Rate of Interest of. (G. Walker) Nation, **22**: 158. —(B. Price) Nation, **22**: 260.
— — — Minimum. (G. Walker) Bank. M. (N. Y.) **32**: 241.
— — — Table of, 1694–1852. Bank. M. (L.) **12**: 229.
— — — Variations in, 1844–77. Bank. M. (L.) **38**: 161.
— — Reform of. Blackw. **99**: 322.
— — Renewal of Charter. (T. P. Thompson) Westm. **17**: 193, 421. **18**: 76. — Fraser, **6**: 231. — Tait, **3**: 543.
— — Report on, 1819. Niles's Reg. **16**: 324.
— — Reserve of. Bank. M. (N. Y.) **28**: 339.
— — — and Interest of. (R. H. I. Palgrave) J. Statis. Soc. **36**: 520.
— — Returns for 1853. Bank. M. (N. Y.) **9**: 39.
— — Specie Payments by. (F. Horner) Ed. R. **2**: 402.
— — Suspension of Charter Act. Bank. M. (N.Y.) **12**: 535.
— — Visit to. Bank. M. (N. Y.) **4**: 917. **17**: 435. — Hunt, **54**: 337.
— — Withdrawal of £1 Notes, 1821–22. Bank. M. (L.) **11**: 9.
— of Exchange, Establishment of. Bank. M. (N. Y.) **9**: 113.
— of France. (F. Lloyd) Bentley, **12**: 47. — Hunt, **11**: 167. — Bank. M. (N. Y.) **1**: 276, 576, 615. — Bank. M. (L.) **3**: 266. **16**: 277. — Ed. R. **121**: 223.
— — Crisis of, 1847. Bank. M. (L.) **6**: 340.
— — Issue of small Notes by. Bank. M. (L.) **10**: 639.
— — Operations of, 1848–49. (M. d'Argout) Hunt, **21**: 483.
— — — 1850. Hunt, **25**: 1.
— — — 1863. Bank. M. (N. Y.) **18**: 905.
— — Report of. Bank. M. (N. Y.) **31**: 285.
— — Resumption of Cash Payments, 1850. Bank. M. (L.) **10**: 517, 684.
— — Sketch of. Bank. M. (N. Y.) **12**: 884, 899.
— — Variations in Rate of Interest, 1844–77. Bank. M. (L.) **38**: 285.
— of Hamburgh. Bank. M. (L.) **9**: 635, 689.
— of Issue, Evils of one. Bank. M. (L.) **1**: 61.
— — National, Plan of. (H. Stansfield) Bank. M. (N. Y.) **18**: 375.
— of London. Bank. M. (N. Y.) **2**: 593.
— of Maryland. Niles's Reg. **49**: 205.
— of Mutual Redemption. Bank. M. (N. Y.) **10**: 54.
— of Prussia, Visit to. (C. Winter) Galaxy, **6**: 553.
— of Scotland. Bank. M. (N. Y.) **3**: 316. — Chamb. J. **10**: 121.
— of United States. (T. B. Myers) Hist. M. **19**: 10. — Bank. M. (N. Y.) **2**: 350. — (O. W. B. Peabody) No. Am. **35**: 485. — (A. Gallatin) Am. Q. **9**: 246. — (G. Bancroft) No. Am. **32**: 21. — Am. Q. **11**: app. — So. R. **8**: 1. — Dem. R. **5**: 499. — For. Q. **10**: 214. — Brit. & For. R. **5**: 537. — Ann. Reg. **5**: 147. — (T. F. Gordon) Ann. Reg. **7**: 63. — Chr. Exam. **31**: 1. — Niles's Reg. **14**: 20, 35, 68, 218. **15**: 70, 161, *et seq.* **16**: supp. 105. **17**: 165. **18**: 34, *et seq.* **19**: 244, *et seq.* **20**: 298. **21**: 133. **23**: 87, 121, *et seq.* **24**: 155. **32**: 124. **35**: 72. **38**: 183. **39**: 347. **41**: 30, 112, 363. **42**: 374, 394. **43**: 272. **45**: 248, 277.
— — and Gen. Jackson. Westm. **21**: 273.
— — Crawford's Report. Niles's Reg. **18**: 34, *et seq.* — Pamph. **17**: 229.
— — Jackson's Veto, 1831. Niles's Reg. **42**: 365. — Ann. Reg. **7**: 60.
— — Jefferson's Opinion. Niles's Reg. **37**: 110.
— — Madison's Letter. Niles's Reg. **41**: 82.
— — McDuffie's Report. Niles's Reg. **38**: 183.
Bank of United States, Meeting at Philadelphia, 1832. Niles's Reg. **42**: 374, 394.
— — Political History of. (T. H. Benton) Bank. M. (N. Y.) **8**: 567.
— — Polk's Speech. Niles's Reg. **44**: 108.
— — Removal of Deposits. Niles's Reg. **45**: 258. — (A. H. Everett) Ann. Reg. **8**: 19.
— — Report of Directors, 1833. Niles's Reg. **45**: 248, 277. **46**: 180, 221.
— — Sketch of chartering the late. (F. Wharton) Hunt, **9**: 303.
— of Venice. (S. Colwell) Bank. M. (N. Y.) **33**: 273.
— What is a? and what does it deal in? (B. Price) Fraser, **101**: 668.
— Yorkshire Penny. Chamb. J. **56**: 101.
Bank Act of 1844. (B. Price) Fraser, **71**: 688. — (E. Seyd) J. Statis. Soc. **35**: 458. — Ho. & For. R. **4**: 402. — Prosp. R. **4**: 165. — Bank. M. (L.) **8**: supp. lvii. —(Lord Hobart) Macmil. **12**: 60. —(F. Hincks) Canad. Mo. **3**: 177. — Westm. **47**: 412.
— — Debate in House of Commons on, 1847. Bank. M. (L.) **8**: supp. i.
— of 1866, and the Crisis. (H. Chubb) J. Statis. Soc. **35**: 171.
— of Louisiana of 1844. Bank. M. (N. Y.) **32**: 344.
— of the United States, 1864. Bank. M. (N. Y.) **19**: 87.
Bank Cashiers. *See* Cashiers.
Bank Checks. *See* Checks.
Bank Clerks, Duties of. Bank. M. (N. Y.) **16**: 633.
Bank Clerks' Association of Missouri. Bank. M. (N. Y.) **27**: 128. **29**: 147. **30**: 136.
— of New York. Bank. M. (N. Y.) **25**: 657. **27**: 884. **29**: 625. **30**: 645.
Bank Clerks' Benefit Association. Bank. M. (N. Y.) **33**: 542. **34**: 546.
Bank Clerks' Provident Funds. Bank. M. (N. Y.) **31**: 460. **32**: 48.
Bank Counter, Stories from a. All the Year, **39**: 202.
Bank Currency. (A. Walker) Bank. M. (N. Y.) **16**: 407.
Bank Deposits, Law of. Bank. M. (N. Y.) **14**: 793.
Bank Director, Extract from his Diary. Dem. R. **2**: 418. **3**: 358.
Bank Directors, Duties of. (A. B. Johnson) Hunt, **24**: 431.
— Personal Responsibility of. (A. T. Innes) Contemp. **34**: 322.
Bank Enabling Acts. Bank. M. (N. Y.) **19**: 865.
Bank Examiner, Powers of. Bank. M. (N. Y.) **30**: 420.
Bank Exchange. Bank. M. (N. Y.) **8**: 265.
Bank Failures. (W. Chambers) Chamb. J. **56**: 145. — Bank. M. (N. Y.) **12**: 322.
— Causes of. Bank. M. (N. Y.) **16**: 1.
Bank Financiering in Pennsylvania. Bank. M. (N. Y.) **14**: 286.
Bank Frauds in England. Bank. M. (N. Y.) **10**: 131.
Bank Issue, Evils of unlimited. Tait, n. s. **3**: 412.
Bank Note and Gold Coin, Colloquy between. New Eng. M. **8**: 45.
— Story of a. All the Year, **38**: 180.
Bank-Note Circulation, Influence of, on Banking. Bank. M. (L.) **38**: 10.
Bank-Note Engraving. Bank. M. (N. Y.) **7**: 253.
Bank-Note Forgeries. (C. Dickens) Bank. M. (N. Y.) **5**: 361, 516.
Bank-Note Manufactory an Invention of the Devil. (W. Cobbett) Tait, n. s. **2**: 504.
Bank-Note Paper. Bank. M. (N. Y.) **3**: 577. **4**: 938.
Bank Notes and Forgeries. Peop. J. **9**: 183.
— English. House. Words, **1**: 426.
— French. Chamb. J. **46**: 670.
— Lost, Who is benefited? Bank. M. (N. Y.) **29**: 116.
— Manufacture of. (A. H. Guernsey) Harper, **24**: 306.
— Threatened Abolition of. Blackw. **130**: 502.

Bank Parlor in New York. Chamb. J. **39**: 250.
Bank Redemption. Hunt, **53**: 324. — Bank. M. (N. Y.) **36**: 370.
Bank Reserves. (J. B. Howe) Bank. M. (N. Y.) **29**: 963, 876.
— Economizing of. (G. Marsland) Bank. M. (N. Y.) **31**: 100.
— a Guarantee of Solvency. Bank. M. (N. Y.) **30**: 923.
Bank Restriction Act. Bank. M. (L.) **7**: 65–533.
— and Financial Crisis of, 1847. (H. C. Carey) Hunt, **17**: 131, 227.
Bank Robberies. Bank. M. (N. Y.) **4**: 85.
— and Frauds. Bank. M. (N. Y.) **19**: 490, 576, 817.
Bank Statements, How to read. (G. Walker) Bank. M. (N. Y.) **33**: 10.
Bank Statistics, 1839. Hunt, **1**: 169–548.
— 1840. Hunt, **2**: 83–432. **3**: 88–552.
— 1841. Hunt, **4**: 282, 476. **5**: 186, 278, 483.
— 1842. Hunt, **6**: 465. **7**: 91.
— 1843. Hunt, **8**: 84–478.
— 1844. Hunt, **10**: 131, 472. **11**: 78, 262, 424.
— 1845. Hunt, **12**: 284. **13**: 266, 564.
— 1846. Hunt, **14**: 274, 460. **15**: 100, 202, 312.
— 1847. Hunt, **16**: 208–604. **17**: 115–429.
— 1848. Hunt, **18**: 105–425. **19**: 105–438.
— 1849. Hunt, **20**: 86–566. **21**: 111–561.
— 1850. Hunt, **22**: 92–570. **23**: 117–548.
— 1851. Hunt, **24**: 91–598. **25**: 99–611.
— 1852. Hunt, **26**: 88–600. **27**: 87–737.
— 1854–62. Bank. M. (N. Y.) **17**: 540.
Bank Stock, Depreciation of. (K. N. McFee) Canad. Mo. **15**: 692.
— Fraudulent Transfers of. Bank. M. (N. Y.) **3**: 201.
— in Boston, Stability of. Hunt, **6**: 465.
— Law of Transfer of. Bank. M. (N. Y.) **26**: 428.
— Liens on. Bank. M. (N. Y.) **28**: 359.
Bank Surplus as a Guarantee Fund. Bank. M. (N. Y.) **31**: 666.
— Taxation of, Report on. Bank. M. (N. Y.) **30**: 640.
Bank Suspension in New York. Bank. M. (N. Y.) **12**: 411.
Bank Trial, Maryland *vs.* R. J. Turner. Bank. M. (N. Y.) **1**: 590.
Banks. Am. Q. **11**: 245.
— and Bank Directors. (T. G. Cary) Hunt, **14**: 211.
— and Bankers in London. Bank. M. (N. Y.) **1**: 488.
— and Banking. Niles's Reg. **14**: 107. — (W. J. Lawson) Bentley, **28**: 84. — (B. Price) Fraser, **75**: 187. — So. Q. **26**: 220.
— — History of. (J. Knox) Bank. M. (N. Y.) **36**: 445.
— — in Illinois. (H. Brown) Hunt, **11**: 240.
— and Currency. (C. F. Adams) Hunt, **1**: 214. — (A. Gallatin) Am. Q. **8**: 441. — (T. H. Benton) Bank. M. (N. Y.) **12**: 559. — Republic, **6**: 316.
— — Foreign. Am. Alma. **1835**: 107.
— — in New England. (N. Hale) No. Am. **22**: 467.
— and the Financial Crisis of 1873. (E. L. Godkin) Nation, **17**: 335.
— and Money. (J. L. Tellkampf) Hunt, **55**: 95, 169.
— — Theory of. (C. F. Adams) Hunt, **1**: 50, 119.
— and Money-Making. Mo. R. **158**: 213.
— and Speculators. Bank. M. (N. Y.) **29**: 121.
— Architecture of. Bank. M. (N. Y.) **21**: 645, 739, 805.
— — in London. Bank. M. (L.) **15**: 196.
— as Promoters of Speculation. Bank. M. (N. Y.) **26**: 657.
— Banking, and Paper Currency. (F. Hunt) Hunt, **4**: 245. — Anal. M. **6**: 489.
— Clearing-House System. Bank. M. (N. Y.) **35**: 929.
— Country, Utility of. Ed. R. **1**: 106.
— Currency, and the Usury Laws. Bank. M. (N. Y.) **14**: 833.
Banks, Evils of, and the Remedy. Am. Mo. M. **10**: 379.
— Fixtures and Appliances in. (G. Sharp) Bank. M. (L.) **12**: supp. 1.
— Foreign, and Currency. Bank. M. (N. Y.) **12**: 102.
— Government as a Bank. (E. L. Godkin) Nation, **27**: 188.
— Government Supervision of. (G. Walker) Nation, **27**: 329.
— Joint Stock. Westm. **27**: 226. — Ed. R. **63**: 419.
— — English. (A. J. Wilson) Fortn. **30**: 284.
— Liabilities of. Bank. M. (N. Y.) **5**: 349.
— Liability for Neglect to protest Drafts. Bank. M. (N. Y.) **1**: 13.
— — on Cashier's Endorsement. Bank. M. (N. Y.) **29**: 463.
— National. (R. Morris) Bank. M. (N. Y.) **30**: 450. — Am. Q. **14**: 493. — (F. J. Kingsbury) New Eng. **31**: 621. — (G. Walker) Nation, **27**: 361. — Bank. M. (N. Y.) **27**: 497. — Hunt, **59**: 130.
— — and Congress. (E. L. Godkin) Nation, **32**: 144.
— — and the Currency. (G. Walker) Internat. R. **6**: 248.
— — and the Finances. Bank. M. (N. Y.) **16**: 518.
— — and the Silver Mania, 1878. (E. L. Godkin) Nation, **27**: 344.
— — and State Banks. (E. W. Keyes) Bank. M. (N. Y.) **24**: 122.
— — and their Fiscal Burdens. Bank. M. (N. Y.) **30**: 835.
— — and the United States Treasury. (H. W. Richardson) Internat. R. **11**: 297.
— — Circulation of. Scrib. **17**: 205.
— — Currency of. (J. B. Hodgskin) Nation, **5**: 394, 457.
— — Decisions regarding. Bank. M. (N. Y.) **25**: 198, 289.
— — Government as a Bank. (E. L. Godkin) Nation, **27**: 188.
— — Government Bank, The. Bank. M. (N. Y.) **33**: 373.
— — History of. Bank. M. (L.) **37**: 281.
— — Legislation on. (J. B. Hodgskin) Nation, **8**: 269.
— — Liens upon Shares in, Decision on. Bank. M. (N. Y.) **29**: 130.
— — List of, 1863. Bank. M. (N. Y.) **18**: 510, 746.
— — — 1865–66. Bank. M. (N. Y.) **20**: 209, 529.
— — — 1867. Bank. M. (N. Y.) **22**: 17.
— — — 1868. Bank. M. (N. Y.) **22**: 871. **23**: 97.
— — — 1871. Bank. M. (N. Y.) **26**: 177.
— — or a National Bank. (D. P. Bailey, jr.) Bank. M. (N. Y.) **30**: 297.
— — Redemption of Notes of. Bank. M. (N. Y.) **20**: 193, 401, 461. — (F. W. Lautz) Galaxy, **23**: 647.
— — Remarks on. (J. S. Ropes) Bank. M. (N. Y.) **22**: 345.
— — Right of Suit. Bank. M. (N. Y.) **29**: 304.
— — State Rights over. Bank. M. (N. Y.) **30**: 390.
— — Statistics of, 1867. Bank. M. (N. Y.) **22**: 514.
— — — 1868. Bank. M. (N. Y.) **23**: 513.
— — — 1869. Bank. M. (N. Y.) **24**: 505.
— — — 1870. Bank. M. (N. Y.) **25**: 497.
— — — 1871. Bank. M. (N. Y.) **26**: 497.
— — System of. Bank. M. (N. Y.) **18**: 184. — (F. Bowen) Bank. M. (N. Y.) **20**: 769. — (G. Walker) Bank. M. (N. Y.) **21**: 674. — (H. McCulloch) Bank. M. (N. Y.) **33**: 971. — (J. Knox) Bank. M. (N. Y.) **36**: 189. — Republic, **6**: 118. — Nat. Q. **11**: 51.
— — — Advantages of. (G. Walker) Bank. M. (N. Y.) **22**: 681. — Bank. M. (N. Y.) **30**: 676.
— — — and its Dangers. Bank. M. (N. Y.) **30**: 753.
— — — Argument on. (C. B. Hall) Bank. M. (N. Y.) **24**: 854.
— — — as a Model. Bank. M. (N. Y.) **29**: 744.

Banks, National, System of, Defects of. Scrib. **3**: 419.
— — — Defense of. Bank. M. (N. Y.) **30**: 489.
— — — Italian View of. (G. Walker) Nation, **23**: 215.
— — — Needed Modifications of., (L. H. Atwater) Scrib. **5**: 737.
— — — Origin of. Hist. M. **9**: 253.
— — — Perils of. Bank. M. (N. Y.) **29**: 1.
— — — Report on. Bank. M. (N. Y.) **18**: 964.
— — Taxation of. Bank. M. (N. Y.) **29**: 209. **34**: 4, 595. **35**: 881.
— — — by the States. Bank. M. (N. Y.) **31**: 820, 888.
— of Canada. Bank. M. (N. Y.) **19**: 620, 697. **29**: 664.
— — and the Usury Laws. (J. B. Hodgskin) Nation, **11**: 289.
— of Circulation. Portfo.(Den.) **13**: 417.
— of Connecticut in 1862. Bank. M. (N. Y.) **17**: 222.
— of France. Bank. M. (L.) **17**: 193, 282.
— of Germany. Hunt, **17**: 530.
— of Great Britain. Bank. M. (N. Y.) **1**: 693.
— of Issue, Evidence before Parliamentary Committee on. Bank. M. (L.) **35**: supp.
— of Italy. Bank. M. (N. Y.) **26**: 481.
— of Massachusetts. (I. Chickering) Hunt, **2**: 134.
— — in 1853. Bank. M. (N. Y.) **8**: 713.
— of the City of New York, 1864. Bank. M. (N. Y.) **19**: 530.
— of Ohio. Bank. M. (N. Y.) **2**: 295.
— of Paris. Bank. M. (N. Y.) **20**: 353.
— of Scotland. Bank. M. (N. Y.) **25**: 824.
— or no Banks. (G. Tucker) Hunt, **38**: 149.
— People's, of Germany. (H. Villard) Am. Soc. Sci. J. **1**: 127. — O. & N. **1**: 704.
— Popular, of Europe. Bank. M. (N. Y.) **30**: 7.
— Provident or Parish. Pamph. **7**: 475.
— Responsibility of, for Collaterals. Bank. M. (N. Y.) **30**: 892.
— Savings. *See* Savings Banks.
— State. Niles's Reg. **46**: 157.
— State-Tamperings with Money and. (H. Spencer) Westm. **69**: 210.
— Suffolk System. (F. O. J. Smith) Hunt, **24**: 316, 439. — (J. B. Foster) Hunt, **24**: 577. — (J. S. Ropes) Hunt, **24**: 700.
— Taxation of. (G. Marsland) Bank. M. (N. Y.) **32**: 164, 337. — Bank. M. (N. Y.) **21**: 241. **22**: 1. **30**: 428. **32**: 456, 769. **35**: 489.
— — Burdens of. Bank. M. (N. Y.) **31**: 472.
— — by States. Bank. M. (N. Y.) **31**: 512. **35**: 836.
— — in Congress. Bank. M. (N. Y.) **32**: 935. **33**: 3.
— — Repeal of, in Congress. Bank. M. (N. Y.) **32**: 594, 862. **36**: 114.
— Tucker's Theory of. New York R. **5**: 334.
— War of. (R. H. Patterson) Fortn. **6**: 1.
Banks of Earth, Pressure of, and Dimensions of Revetments, Barlow on. (D. P. Woodbury) J. Frankl. Inst. **40**: 1.
Bánká, Mineralogy of the Island of. (T. Horsfield) Am. J. Sci. **57**: 86.
Banker, Proper Business of. Bank. M. (N. Y.) **30**: 179.
— What is a, in Law? Bank. M. (N. Y.) **32**: 515.
Banker of Ballyfree; a Tale. Dub. Univ. **53**: 730.
— of Broadhurst; a Sketch. Dub. Univ. **79**: 301.
Banker's Daughter. Colburn, **165**: 728, 845.
Banker's Daughter. Dub. Univ. **17**: 289.
Banker's Daughter. St. James, **5**: 51.
Banker's Daughter. Bank. M. (L.) **30**: 955, 1030. **31**: 9–1068. **32**: 22–37. **33**: 8–335.
Banker's Story. (L. Wingfield) Victoria, **34**: 149.
Banker's Strong Box; a Tale. Bentley, **63**: 261, 399.
Banker's Ward. St. James, **18**: 307.
Bankers. (R. B. Kimball) Galaxy, **21**: 110.
— and Banking. Once a Week, **10**: 65.
Bankers considered as Autocrats. Ev. Sat. **10**: 307.
— Convention of, Saratoga, 1879. Bank. M. (N. Y.) **34**: 1, 207.
— — Saratoga, 1880. Bank. M. (N. Y.) **35**: 64–211.
— — Niagara, 1881. Bank. M. (N. Y.) **36**: 1–209.
— Customs of. (L. Levi) Bank. M. (N. Y.) **35**: 113.
— Eminent, Sketches of. Bank. M. (N. Y.) **24**: 612.
— for the Poor. (E. Howland) Galaxy, **3**: 661.
— Liabilities of. Bank. M. (N. Y.) **15**: 505.
— — for Collections. Bank. M. (N. Y.) **15**: 739.
— List of Foreign. Bank. M. (N. Y.) **1**: 88.
— Private, List of, in the U. S., 1855. Bank. M. (N. Y.) **10**: 468.
— — — 1860. Bank. M. (N. Y.) **15**: 49.
— — — 1865. Bank. M. (N. Y.) **19**: 705.
— — — 1868. Bank. M. (N. Y.) **22**: 177.
Banking. (C. H. Carroll) Hunt, **39**: 306, 443. — (R. H. I. Palgrave) Fortn. **21**: 92. — Hunt, **5**: 27. — Dem. R. **10**: 384. — Quar. **42**: 476. — (J. B. Turner) New Eng. **2**: 48. — Westm. **10**: 360. **35**: 45. — U. S. Lit. Gaz. **5**: 190. — Niles's Reg. **14**: 377.
— Allied Banks of New England. U. S. Lit. Gaz. **4**: 1. — Hunt, **5**: 261.
— Anatomy and Philosophy of. Hunt. **22**: 389.
— Ancient Feudal and Modern. Dem. R. **11**: 249.
— and the Bank of the United States. Chr. Exam. **31**: 1.
— and Bankruptcy. Hunt, **22**: 65, 195, 311.
— and Credit, Notions on. (L. F. M. R. Wolowski) Bank. M. (N. Y.) **30**: 17.
— and Currency. (J. N. Cardozo) Bank. M. (N. Y.) **23**: 673. — (W. G. Hunt) Bank. M. (N. Y.) **13**: 1. — (R. Sulley) Hunt, **31**: 188. **33**: 541. — (J. E. Williams) O. & N. **8**: 589. — Bank. M. (N. Y.) **22**: 737. — Blackw. **49**: 550. — Am. Q. **8**: 441. — Dub. Univ. **15**: 1, 128. **16**: 372, 612. — Dem. R. **2**: 3. **9**: 189, 288. — Penn Mo. **5**: 408.
— — and Credit. (J. S. Ropes) New Eng. **16**: 312.
— — in India, 1860. Bank. M. (L.) **20**: 201.
— — Systems of. So. R. n. s. **7**: 355.
— and Finance, Notes on. Bank. M. (N. Y.) **10**: 672.
— and Money. (C. H. Carroll) Hunt, **37**: 307.
— as a Profession. (G. P. Bissell) Bank. M. (N. Y.) **4**: 924.
— as it ought to be. Dem R. **12**: 425.
— Books on, Lists of. Bank. M. (N. Y.) **13**: 321. **20**: 97. — Bank. M. (L.) **11**: 709.
— — New, 1873. Bank. M. (N. Y.) **27**: 724.
— Commercial. (W. M. Gouge) Hunt, **8**: 313.
— — True Principles of. Dem. R. **2**: 113.
— Companies of Europe. Anal. M. **14**: 433.
— Credit and Currency. Am. Whig R. **10**: 513.
— Do Banks increase loanable Capital? (R. Hare) Hunt, **26**: 702.
— Easy Lesson in Money and. (E. Atkinson) Atlan. **34**: 195.
— Elements of. (L. Levi) Bank. M. (N. Y.) **32**: 208.
— English Views of. Bank. M. (N. Y.) **18**: 365.
— False Theories of. Chamb. J. **28**: 385.
— Familiar Talk on. (W. E. Gould) Bank. M. (N. Y.) **35**: 726.
— for the Poorer Classes. Howitt, **2**: 93.
— Foreign Establishments. Bank. M. (N. Y.) **1**: 239, 276.
— Free. (M. Tarver) West. J. **4**: 211. **12**: 153. — De Bow, **12**: 610. **13**: 127. **14**: 28, 151. — Bank. M. (N. Y.) **9**: 449, 745.
— — Act of Iowa on. Bank. M (N. Y.) **13**: 31.
— — and Bonds. Bank. M. (N. Y.) **34**: 849.
— — Controversy on. (B. Price) Fraser, **77**: 102, 455.
— — in New York. Bank. M. (N. Y.) **11**: 286.
— — in the Southwest. De Bow, **16**: 78.
— — in United States. (W. L. M'Knight) Bank. M. (N. Y.) **7**: 300.

Banking, Free, in Wisconsin. Bank. M. (N. Y.) **9**: 833.
— Free Trade in. (W. H. Sykes) J. Statis. Soc. **30**: 58. — Bank. M. (L.) **1**: 67. — Tait, **3**: 84.
— Gilbart's Practical Treatise on. Hunt, **22**: 68. — Bank. M. (N. Y.) **6**: 33. — Mo. R. **134**: 75. **140**: 384.
— History of. (W. J. Lawson) Bank. M. (N. Y.) **6**: 1, 91, 257.
— — and Principles of. (H. D. M'Leod) Bank. M. (N. Y.) **11**: 593.
— — Gilbart's, Supplement to. Bank. M. (N. Y.) **27**: 417.
— — Gouge's. Am. Mo. R. **4**: 192.
— — Lawson's. Hunt, **23**: 641. — Bank. M. (N. Y.) **5**: 184, 456. **7**: 13, 97.
— — Sketches of. Bank. M. (N. Y.) **9**: 697.
— in Alabama. Bank. M. (N. Y.) **4**: 637.
— in America, Historical Sketch of. (R. Sewell) Bank. M. (N. Y.) **15**: 620.
— in Australia. Bank. M. (L.) **17**: 850.
— in Australasia, Statistics of. (N. Cook) J. Statis. Soc. **37**: 48.
— in Belgium. Bank. M. (L.) **17**: 458.
— in California. (G. R. Gibson) Bank. M. (N. Y.) **31**: 761.
— in Canada. Bank. M. (N. Y.) **36**: 227.
— in China. Bank. M. (N. Y.) **29**: 595.
— in Connecticut. Bank. M. (N. Y.) **15**: 97.
— in England. (W. D. Henderson) Macmil. **32**: 141. Same art. Bank. M. (N. Y.) **30**: 107. — Colburn, **37**: 318.
— — and in America, compared. (G. Walker) Bank. M. (N. Y.) **32**: 505.
— — and Scotland. Pamph. **24**: 529.
— — Report of Bank Committee, 1819. (Earl of Liverpool) Pamph. **14**: 267.
— — System of. Bank. M. (N. Y.) **4**: 279. — Ed. R. **43**: 263.
— — — Palgrave on. Bank. M. (N. Y.) **28**: 373.
— in English Colonies. Bank. M. (L.) **28**: 692–1206. **29**: 8, 111, 363.
— in Europe, Modern. Bank. M. (N. Y.) **19**: 183.
— — on the Continent. Bank. M. (L.) **8**: 281.
— — Systems of. Bank. M. (N. Y.) **15**: 713.
— in France. Bank. M. (N. Y.) **23**: 497. — Bank. M. (L.) **16**: 374–677. **17**: 193, 282. **24**: 589.
— — Controversy on. (G. Walker) Bank. M. (N. Y.) **19**: 769.
— in Germany. Bank. M. (L.) **17**: 369, 837.
— in Great Britain. Bank. M. (N. Y.) **12**: 795.
— — Capital employed in. Bank. M. (L.) **37**: 361.
— — Progress of. Bank. M. (N. Y.) **14**: 438.
— — Statistics of. (J. Dun) J. Statis. Soc. **39**: 1.
— — Sweden, Denmark, Hamburg. (R. H. I. Palgrave) J. Statis. Soc. **36**: 27.
— — System of. Bank. M. (N. Y.) **30**: 691.
— in Holland. Bank. M. (L.) **17**: 573.
— in Illinois. Bank. M. (N. Y.) **9**: 102.
— in Indiana. Bank. M. (N. Y.) **9**: 937.
— — History of. (H. F. Baker) Bank. M. (N. Y.) **12**: 161.
— in Ireland, State of, 1844. Bank. M. (L.) **1**: 121, 285, 335. — Bank. M. (N. Y.) **4**: 201.
— in Massachusetts. (G. P. Bissell) Bank. M. (N. Y.) **7**: 673. **8**: 861. **9**: 848. **10**: 769. **12**: 722. **15**: 860. **17**: 754.
— — History of. (D. P. Bailey, jr.) Bank. M. (N. Y.) **31**: 113, 207, 301.
— — — Early. (C. Stetson) Bank. M. (N. Y.) **4**: 1009.
— — in 1864. Bank. M. (N. Y.) **19**: 800.
— — in 1865. Bank. M. (N. Y.) **20**: 790.
— — Policy of. (W. H. Foster) Bank. M. (N. Y.) **4**: 169.
— — System of. (J. B. Congdon) Bank. M. (N. Y.) **5**: 995. — (J. B. Congdon) Hunt, **3**: 411.
Banking in Mississippi, and Repudiation. Bank. M. (N. Y.) **18**: 89.
— in New York. Bank. M. (N. Y.) **7**: 85. **9**: 716, 961. **10**: 858. **12**: 615. **13**: 609. **14**: 639, 673. **15**: 637. **17**: 737. **18**: 809.
— — History of. Bank. M. (N. Y.) **10**: 81. **16**: 665. **31**: 657.
— — System of. (M. Fillmore) Bank. M. (N. Y.) **2**: 513. **3**: 678. **8**: 1, 775, 817. **13**: 753. **19**: 349, 597. **31**: 746.
— in New York City. Bank. M. (N. Y.) **2**: 710. **3**: 137, 325.
— — Clearing-House. Internat. R. **3**: 595.
— in the Olden Time. Bank. M. (N. Y.) **30**: 41.
— in Philadelphia. Dem. R. **6**: 3, 97, 369.
— in Portugal, Crisis in. Bank. M. (N. Y.) **31**: 275.
— in Russia. Bank. M. (N. Y.) **30**: 620.
— — Hints from. Bank. M. (N. Y.) **31**: 103.
— in Scandinavia. Bank. M. (L.) **17**: 637.
— in Scotland. (W. Wood) Atlan. **34**: 85. — Blackw. **56**: 671.
— — History of. Bank. M. (L.) **37**: 24, 292.
— in Switzerland. Bank. M. (N. Y.) **29**: 186. **30**: 97.
— in Tennessee. Bank. M. (N. Y.) **11**: 81.
— in Turkey, 1860. Bank. M. (L.) **20**: 138.
— in United States. (J. H. Lanman) Hunt, **11**: 424. — Bank. M. (N. Y.) **1**: 113. **15**: 81, 169, 359.
— — and in Canada. Bank. M. (L.) **21**: 218–833. **22**: 6–54.
— — Capital employed in. Bank. M. (N. Y.) **8**: 932. **9**: 646. **10**: 791. **12**: 647. **15**: 768.
— — Circulation of. Bank. M. (N. Y.) **15**: 257.
— — Early. Bank. M. (N. Y.) **7**: 1, 753, 849. **32**: 353.
— — History of. Bank. M. (N. Y.) **11**: 161.
— — in the several States. Bank. M. (N. Y.) **8**: 637.
— — — History of. (H. F. Baker) Bank. M. (N. Y.) **9**: 1. **11**: 241–417.
— — National System of. *See* Banks, National.
— — System of, 1839. (F. A. von Gerstner) J. Frankl. Inst. **31**: 3.
— Influence of Note Circulation on. (R. H. I. Palgrave) Bank. M. (L.) **37**: 637, 832.
— International, and Currency. (D. Wilder) Bank. M. (N. Y.) **30**: 550.
— Joint Stock, Philosophy of. (A. B. Johnson) Hunt, **25**: 153.
— Law of, Connecticut Decisions. Bank. M. (N. Y.) **7**: 200, 263.
— — Decisions of the Supreme Court of Maine. Bank. M. (N. Y.) **6**: 454.
— — — in Massachusetts, Digest of. Bank. M. (N. Y.) **7**: 708–976. **8**: 195.
— — — in New York, Digest of. Bank. M. (N. Y.) **7**: 428, 512, 596.
— — General, Frauds on. Bank. M. (N. Y.) **8**: 765.
— — in Germany. Bank. M. (N. Y.) **30**: 304.
— — in Illinois. Bank. M. (N. Y.) **15**: 777.
— — in Massachusetts. Bank. M. (N. Y.) **5**: 601.
— — — 1851. Bank. M. (N. Y.) **6**: 13.
— — in Michigan. Bank. M. (N. Y.) **13**: 241.
— — in Missouri. Bank. M. (N. Y.) **11**: 753. **14**: 811.
— — in New York. Dem. R. **5**: 427.
— — — 1849. Bank. M. **4**: 25.
— — in Switzerland. Bank. M. (N. Y.) **30**: 706.
— — Progress of. Bank. M. (N. Y.) **35**: 496, 690, 849.
— — Recent Decisions in. Bank. M. (N. Y.) **26**: 403.
— Lawson's History of. Bank. M. (L.) **10**: 471.
— Lectures on. (L. Levi) Bank. M. (L.) **35**: supp. **36**: 406–598. **37**: 459–757. **38**: 193, 304, 386, 487.
— Legislation on. (H. R. Grenfell) 19th Cent. **5**: 534.
— — National. (J. B. Hodgskin) Nation, **8**: 269.
— Moral Influence of. Bank. M. (L.) **36**: 809.

Banking, Organization in. (G. Marsland) Bank. M. (N. Y.) **32**: 20.
— — of a New Bank. Bank. M. (N. Y.) **5**: 949.
— Practical Treatise on. (J. W. Gilbart) Bank. M. (N. Y.) **5**: 469–737. **6**: 36–389.
— Principles of. (N. Bonnefoux) Bank. M. (N. Y.) **3**: 103. — (T. Hankey) Bank. M. (N. Y.) **21**: 688.
— — Change in. Bank. M. (N. Y.) **11**: 497.
— — General. (J. R. McCulloch) Bank. M. (N. Y.) **1**: 77, 147.
— — Sound. (H. V. Poor) Bank. M. (N. Y.) **22**: 841. — Bank M. (N. Y.) **22**: 921.
— — True. (W. M. Gouge) Bank. M. (N. Y.) **12**: 460. — Bank. M. (N. Y.) **28**: 329.
— Prize Essay on. (L. Sabine) Bank. M. (N. Y.) **22**: 558.
— Provincial. Pamph. **18**: 51.
— Reform in. Brit. Q. **45**: 356.
— Scotch and English. Bank. M. (N. Y.) **31**: 12.
— — in England. Bank. M. (N. Y.) **29**: 274. **31**: 193.
— Stability of, Safeguards of. Bank. M. (N. Y.) **32**: 417.
— Suffolk System. Hunt, **5**: 261. — Bank. M. (N. Y.) **1**: 65.
— Treatise on. (A. B. Johnson) Bank. M. **3**: 733.
— True Functions of. (G. Walker) Bank. M. (N. Y.) **31**: 753, 829.
— Use and Abuse of. Chr. Exam. **31**: 1.
— Utility and Economy of. (T. Hankey) Bank. M. (N. Y.) **13**: 868.
Banking House; a Tale. Blackw. **54**: 576, 719. **55**: 50.
Banking Institute. Bank. M. (L.) **11**: 453–677.
— in Scotland. Bank. M. (N. Y.) **31**: 65, 134.
Banking Institutes. (L. Levi) Bank. M. (N. Y.) **33**: 946.
Banking Institutions, Foreign. Bank. M. (N. Y.) **3**: 25. **10**: 434, 835.
Banking Securities, Good. Bank. M. (N. Y.) **4**: 215.
Banking System. Hunt, **46**: 113.
— and Rights of Industry. Quar. **47**: 408.
Bankrupt Law. (D. Raymond) West. Law J. **1**: 489. — (R. M. Young) West. Law J. **3**: 315.
— Abuses of. Am. Law R. **7**: 641.
— American. (B. F. Porter) Hunt, **28**: 439. — Am. Mo. M. **10**: 505. Hunt, **5**: 360. — (J. Van Cott) Hunt, **4**: 22. — No. Am. **7**: 25. — Niles's Reg. **19**: 403. **21**: 243. **40**: 157.
— — Act of 1867. Bank. M. (L.) **23**: 65.
— — — Repeal of. (A. G. Sedgwick) Nation, **22**: 124. — Am. Law R. **10**: 393.
— — Necessity of a General. Nat. Q. **4**: 97.
— — Suggestions as to. Nation, **17**: 381.
— — United States Statute of. (J. Lowell) Internat. R. **9**: 697.
— and Mercantile Corruption. Fraser, **99**: 428.
— English. Pamph. **13**: 359. — Westm. **52**: 419.
— — Anomalies of. Bank. M. (L.) **13**: 609.
— — in 1826. Ann. Reg. **2**: 74.
— — New Bill on, 1877–78. Bank. M. (L.) **37**: 445. **38**: 464.
— — Reform in, 1849. Bank. M. (L.) **9**: 322.
Bankrupt Legislation, Urgency of. Fortn. **31**: 469.
— in New York, 1819. Niles's Reg. **16**: supp. 85.
— Mr. Sergeant's Speech on. Niles's Reg. **21**: 382.
— Mr. Stevenson's Speech on. Niles's Reg. **21**: 407.
— of the States. Bank. M. (N. Y.) **33**: 718.
Bankrupts, Rich and Poor. All the Year, **19**: 540.
— What shall we do with? (R. Lowe) 19th Cent. **10**: 308.
Bankruptcy and Banking. Hunt, **21**: 513. **22**: 65, 195, 311.
— and Bankrupt Bill. New York R. **7**: 440.
— and Bargain-Hunting. (H. Silver) Once a Week, **16**: 646.
— and Insolvency. (C. H. Carroll) Hunt, **60**: 193. — Westm. **46**: 500.
Bankruptcy, Glimpse of. (J. W. Brown) Hunt, **7**: 261.
— in 1858. Bank. M. (N. Y.) **13**: 637.
Bankruptcy Court, In the. All the Year, **18**: 92, 105, 136.
Bankruptcy Reform. Bank. M. (L.) **14**: 289.
— Story of. Dem. R. **13**: 286.
See Insolvency.
Banks, Sir Joseph, Memoirs of. Portfo.(Den.) **30**: 92.
— Statue of. Penny M. **2**: 340.
Banks, Nathaniel P., as a Historian. (M. F. Sullivan) Am. Cath. Q. **1**: 353.
Bankside. All the Year. **43**: 276.
Banneker, Benjamin, Negro Astronomer. (M. D. Conway) Atlan. **11**: 79. — Sharpe, **37**: 133. — So. Lit. Mess. **23**: 65.
Banner-Bearer of Olaf the Saint; a Poem. (G. Massey) Dub. Univ. **90**: 91.
Banners used in the English Army. Retros. **15**: 90.
Bannister, Charles. Fraser, **32**: 593.
Bannister, John, the Comedian. Blackw. **45**: 392. — (T. P. Grinsted) Bentley, **42**: 63. — Mo. R. **148**: 309.
— Recollections of. Colburn, **48**: 487. **52**: 530.
Bannockburn, Battle of. Penny M. **2**: 234.
Banquets, Civic. (N. Hawthorne) Atlan. **12**: 195.
— London. Chamb. J. **22**: 385.
— Utopian. Nat. R. **9**: 100.
Ban-Shee, The; an Irish Tale. Portfo.(Den.) **30**: 125.
— of the MacShanes. (E. J. Curtis) Dub. Univ. **86**: 76.
Banting, Doing. Temp. Bar, **19**: 117.
Banton, Michael, Will of, 1674. N. E. Reg. **8**: 169.
Banvard, John, Account of. Howitt, **2**: 145. **3**: 211.
— Life on the Mississippi. Liv. Age, **15**: 511.
— Panorama of the Mississippi. Liv. Age, **14**: 594. **20**: 314. — Peop. J. **7**: 26, 281. — Chamb. J. **7**: 395.
Banwell Caverns, Visit to. Chamb. J. **19**: 74.
Banyan Tree. Penny M. **1**: 184.
Banyar, Goldsbrow, Diary of, 1757. M. Am. Hist. **1**: 25.
Baobab Tree. (J. R. Jackson) Stud. & Intel. Obs. **1**: 321.
Baptism. (A. P. Stanley) 19th Cent. **6**: 685. — (H. T. Anderson) Chr. Q. **4**: 403. — (D. G. Porter) Chr. Q. **4**: 198, 367. — (J. S. Sweeney) Chr. Q. **8**: 513. — (E. Beecher) Am. Bib. Repos. **5**: 24. 2d s. **6**: 28. 2d s. **9**: 59, 424. — (C. P. Krauth, jr.) Evang. R. **17**: 309. — (H. A. Miles) Chr. Exam. **33**: 213. — (J. Porter) Am. Meth. M. **17**: 254. **21**: 304. — Chr. Obs. **2**: 141–521. — (R. P. Smith) Chr. Obs. **75**: 3. — (A. Walæus) Mercersb. **10**: 426. — Chr. Rem. **16**: 191, 406. — Cong. M. **27**: 761. **28**: 743, 897.
— a consecratory Rite. (I. E. Dwinell) Bib. Sac. **15**: 54.
— a positive Law. (S. Dyer) Bapt. Q. **7**: 108.
— a Symbol of Commencement of new Life. (H. L. Wayland) Bib. Sac. **15**: 744.
— Anabaptist, how administered? Chr. R. **26**: 399.
— and the Augsburg Confession. Luth. Q. **11**: 262.
— and the Bridal, The. Dub. Univ. **25**: 609.
— and Christian Discipleship. Bib. R. **2**: 1.
— and Christian Union. (D. G. Porter) Chr. Q. **8**: 433.
— and Church Membership. (T. G. Apple) Mercersb. **23**: 335.
— and the Communion. (G. D. B. Pepper) Bapt. Q. **6**: 167.
— and Lord's Supper, Nonconformist Doctrine on. Cong. M. **27**: 745.
— — Dr. Pusey on. Chr. Rem. **11**: 467.
— and the New Covenant, Taylor's View of. Chr. Obs. **36**: 796.
— and Predestination. (H. Martensen) Mercersb. **5**: 276.
— and Regeneration. *See* Baptismal Regeneration.
— and Remission. (J. W. Willmarth) Bapt. Q. **11**: 296. — (J. E. Farnham) Bapt. Q. **11**: 476. — (W. K. Pendleton) Chr. Q. **1**: 356.
— and Repentance. (S. W. Harkey) Luth. Q. **7**: 493.

Baptism and Union with Christ. (T. G. Apple) Mercersb. **14**: 87.
— as a Heathen Rite, Maurer on. (R. B. Anderson) Nation, **33**: 238.
— as taught by the German Reformed Church. (E. V. Gerhart) Mercersb. **15**: 180.
— Beecher on. (E. B. Hall) Chr. Exam. **45**: 456. — (E. Turney) Chr. R. **14**: 217. — (J. W. Alexander) Princ. **21**: 206.
— Burgess on. Chr. R. **3**: 84, 196.
— Buried with Christ in. (D. Drummond) Kitto, **4**: 394. — (P. Mearns) Kitto, **5**: 231.
— by Water, by Fire, and by the Spirit. Theo. & Lit. J. **11**: 70.
— Carson on. (S. L. Graham) Princ. **19**: 34. — Cong. M. **27**: 357.
— Carson and Cox on. Spirit Pilg. **5**: 539.
— Christian. (H. Martineau) Mercersb. **4**: 305, 475. **5**: 276.
— Classic. (S. E. Shepard) Am. Q. **3**: 54, 358, 466.
— — Dale's. (A. C. Kendrick) Bapt. Q. **3**: 129.
— Controversy on, Mozley's Review of. Chr. Obs. **63**: 104.
— — Present State of, 1875. (A. Hovey) Bapt. Q. **9**: 129.
— Cox on. Cong. M. **7**: 529, 662, 717.
— Dale on. (W. H. Whittsitt) Bapt. Q. **11**: 175. — (J. A. Brown) Luth. Q. **5**: 321.
— Dialogue on. (S. S. Wilson) Cong. M. **21**: 229.
— Doctrine of. So. R. n. s. **13**: 178.
— Ebrard's View of. (G. R. Bliss) Bapt. Q. **3**: 257.
— Eclectic Review on. Chr. Obs. **15**: 443, 570.
— Effects of. Meth. M. **39**: 340.
— Efficacy of. (E. V. Gerhart) Mercersb. **10**: 1.
— Ellison on. Cong. M. **18**: 765.
— for the Dead. (I. Chase) Chr. R. **27**: 412. — (H. D. Ganse) Am. Presb. R. **12**: 83. — (A. C. Kendrick) Chr. R. **27**: 143. — (S. W. Whitney) Chr. R. **17**: 296. — Chr. R. **20**: 587. — Cong. M. **18**: 540, 614, 679. **27**: 103.
— Gotch on. (E. Henderson) Cong. M. **24**: 356.
— Heidelberg Catechism on. (E. V. Gerhart) Mercersb. **20**: 537.
— Henderson on. (F. W. Gotch) Cong. M. **24**: 769.
— Household. (W. R. Powers) Am. Presb. R. **14**: 422.
— Import of. (E. Turney) Chr. R. **13**: 609. **14**: 1.
— in the Greek Church. (A. N. Arnold) Bapt. Q. **4**: 80.
— in the Holy Spirit. (R. Richardson) Chr. Q. **6**: 450.
— Infant. Chr. Mo. Spec. **10**: 340, 590. — (D. Dana) Lit. & Theo. R. **4**: 159. — Am. Bib. Repos. 2d s. **11**: 222. — Spirit Pilg. **5**: 59. — (M. A. Curtis) Am. Church R. **11**: 399. **20**: 343. — (J. Priestley) Theo. Repos. **3**: 231. — (J. S. Sweeney) Chr. Q. **5**: 458. — (S. Tracy) Cong. R. **8**: 53. — Am. Presb. R. **3**: 529. — So. R. n. s. **16**: 171. — Meth. M. **43**: 671.
— — and Baptismal Regeneration. Chr. R. **26**: 33.
— — and Calvinism. (C. P. Krauth) Mercersb. **21**: 103.
— — and Christian Nurture. (G. F. Magoun) Bost. R. **6**: 590.
— — and Church Membership. (G. Haven) Meth. Q. **19**: 5. — (W. H. H. Marsh) Bib. Sac. **29**: 665. — (G. F. Wright) Bib. Sac. **31**: 265, 545. — (L. W. Atwater) Princ. **29**: 1.
— — and Infant Salvation. (C. P. Krauth) Mercersb. **21**: 103.
— — and the Southern Review. So. R. n. s. **15**: 140.
— — Apostolical Origin of. (P. Schaff) Mercersb. **4**: 388.
— — Budd on. Chr. Obs. **28**: 323.
— — Bushnell on. (I. Chase) Chr. R. **28**: 501.
— — Causes of Decline of. (F. Wilson) Chr. R. **22**: 271.
— — defended. Am. Meth. M. **6**: 387.
— — Difficulties of. (A. N. Arnold) Bapt. Q. **3**: 24.
Baptism, Infant, Historical Argument for. (A. B. Koplin) Mercersb. **18**: 588.
— — History of. So. R. n. s. **14**: 331.
— — in Early Church. Bost. R. **1**: 21.
— — an Invention of Man. (A. Hovey) Bapt. Q. **3**: 168.
— — Irenæus and. (W. R. Powers) Am. Presb. R. **16**: 239.
— — Jerram's Conversations on. Chr. Obs. **18**: 601.
— — Justin Martyr's Testimony on. Chr. R. **6**: 302.
— — Miller on. So. R. n. s. **15**: 221.
— — Neglect of. (J. H. Baird) Princ. **29**: 73.
— — of Children of non-professing Parents. (J. Oswald) Evang. R. **10**: 347. — (S. S. Schmucke) Evang. R. **11**: 389. — Cong. M. **19**: 472, 743.
— — Origen on. (I. Chase) Chr. R. **19**: 180.
— — Practical View of. (J. C. Rankin) Princ. **33**: 680.
— — Report on, to General Association of Connecticut. (L. H. Atwater) Princ. **35**: 622.
— — Ritual and Spiritual. (A. Fleming) Cong. R. **9**: 153.
— — Roots of. (W. W. Patton) Cong. R. **10**: 324.
— — Summers on. So. R. n. s. **16**: 227.
— — Unity of the Church on. (J. G. Hale) New Eng. **23**: 482.
— — Wood's Argument on. (H. J. Ripley) Chr. R. **16**: 506.
— — Wood's Letters on. Spirit Pilg. **1**: 295.
See Children, Baptized.
— Internal Evidences of Adult. Chr. R. **1**: 430.
— Interior Facts of. (J. T. Smith) Bapt. Q. **6**: 204.
— Jewish. (S. E. Shepard) Chr. Q. **4**: 317, 454. — (C. H. Toy) Bapt. Q. **6**: 301.
— — and Household. (W. Barrows) Cong. R. **7**: 502.
— Lay. (R. Heber) Quar. **7**: 200.
— — Validity of. (S. H. Giesy) Mercersb. **15**: 506.
— Letters on. (T. Milner) Cong. M. **25**: 469, 535.
— Lutheran Doctrine of. (F. W. Conrad) Luth. Q. **4**: 477.
— Mode of. (M. Stuart) Am. Bib. Repos. **3**: 288. — (J. Tracy) Bib. Sac. **29**: 532. — Cong. M. **24**: 18–845. — (J. C. Rankine) Princ. **33**: 215. — (B. B. Smith) Am. Church R. **14**: 487.
— Nature and Effects of. (S. Totten) Am. Church R. **12**: 606.
— — and Subjects of. (A. N. Arnold) Bib. Sac. **26**: 38. — Cong. M. **25**: 229–845. **26**: 170, 247.
— Noel on. (J. W. Nevin) Mercersb. **2**: 231. — Meth. Q. **10**: 454. — (R. Turnbull) Chr. R. **15**: 1.
— Nonconformists and. Chr. Obs. **46**: 577, 595.
— not Immersion. (J. G. Hale) Cong. R. **8**: 155.
— of Fire. (C. Hole) Kitto, **3**: 162. — (W. Niblock) Kitto, **4**: 135.
— of Heretics in 3d Century. (J. W. Nevin) Mercersb. **4**: 527.
— Old Doctrine of. (J. W. Nevin) Mercersb. **12**: 190.
— Order of. (J. Calvin) Mercersb. **11**: 298.
— Outline History of. (A. S. Hale) Chr. Q. **3**: 515.
— Presbyterian Theory of. (T. G. Apple) Mercersb. **20**: 628.
— Qualifications of Administrator of. (J. M. C. Breaker) Chr. R. **24**: 238.
— Re-Baptism. (T. F. Curtis) Chr. R. **11**: 186. (K. Brooks) Bapt. Q. **1**: 129.
— Scott on. Chr. Obs. **15**: 619.
— Scripture View of. (D. Y. Heisler) Mercersb. **18**: 405
— Spiritual. (M. Goodrich) Univ. Q. **11**: 127.
— Spiritual Law of. (S. Bailey) Chr. R. **12**: 605.
— Subjects of. (J. C. Rankine) Princ. **33**: 446.
— Syriac Word for. (J. Murdock) Bib. Sac. **7**: 733.
— Tertullian on. (A. Hovey) Bapt. Q. **5**: 75.
— Triangular Fight on. So. R. n. s. **20**: 154.
— Wardlaw and Birt on, reviewed. Cong. M. **8**: 530.
— Water. (W. R. French) Univ. Q. **15**: 240.

Baptism, Water, and that of the Spirit. (S. J. Baird) Princ. 36: 484.
— Wolff on. Chr. R. 28: 260.
Baptismal Creed of Early Roman Church. (G. Salmon) Contemp. 33: 51. Same art. Liv. Age, 138: 659.
Baptismal Formula. (T. J. Sawyer) Univ. Q. 21: 93.— Chr. 20: 281.
— in Matthew xxviii. 19, 20. (J. Strong) Meth. Q. 10: 399.
Baptismal Office of the Anglican Church. Cong. 1: 424.
Baptismal Offices. Chr. Obs. 48: 721.
Baptismal Rituals. House. Words, 1: 107.
Baptismal Regeneration. (J. H. A. Bomberger) Mercersb. 5: 147.—(H. Cowles) Bib. Sac. 33: 425.—(J. Davison) Quar. 15: 476.—(E. F. Giese) Luth. Q. 9: 390.—(J. W. Nevin) Mercersb. 4: 373.—(N. S. Richardson) Am. Church R. 6: 184. 14: 686.—(J. W. Santee) Mercersb. 15: 45.—(C. F. Schaeffer) Evang. R. 8: 303.—(B. Tyler) New Eng. 2: 397.—(D. Worley) Evang. R. 18: 46.—Am. Church R. 24: 122.—Cong. M. 26: 555, 641, 903.—Ecl. R. 90: 478.
— and Ritualism in American Episcopal Church. Chr. Obs. 72: 326.
— Boyd on. Chr. Obs. 65: 489.
— Elizabethan Divines on. Chr. Rem. 19: 1.
— Faber on. (Z. Paddock) Meth. Q. 14: 599.
— in the English Church, 1850. Brit. Q. 11: 411.
— Robertson on. (A. J. Gordon) Bapt. Q. 3: 405.
— Spurgeon on. Chr. Obs. 64: 568.
— Watts on. Cong. M. 7, 129, 178.
Baptismal Service. Mercersb. 6: 187.
— of Church of England, Old Key to. Chr. Obs. 70: 641.
Baptist *vs.* Catholic. (A. F. Hewit) Cath. World, 16: 383.
Baptist and Pedobaptist Theories of Church Membership. Chr. R. 12: 529.
Baptist Bible Society. Meth. Q. 1: 535.
Baptist Brethren, German, at Ephrata, Pa. (W. T. Wallace) Potter Am. Mo. 5: 814.
Baptist Church, Close Communion of. (D. L. Ogden) New Eng. 13: 562.
— in Connecticut. (R. C. Learned) New Eng. 18: 595.
Baptist Churches, their Mutual Relation. (W. H. H. Marsh) Bapt. Q. 8: 458.
— of America, Polity of. (T. C. Teasdale) New Eng. 2: 39.
— Principles and Practices of. (J. B. Jeter) Chr. R. 22: 245.
Baptist Church Polity. Chr. R. 11: 64.
Baptist Controversy in Denmark. (S. F. Smith) Chr. R. 11: 278.
Baptist Denomination, Distinctive Features of. (E. B. Underhill) Chr. R. 17: 48.
— Influence of. Chr. R. 3: 333.
Baptist Doctrine and the Pulpit. (G. D. B. Pepper) Bapt. Q. 11: 85.
Baptist Educational Convention. (S. S. Cutting) Bapt. Q. 5: 206.
Baptist General Conference, Division of. Chr. R. 10: 481.
Baptist General Tract Society. Chr. R. 1: 403.
Baptist Historical Society. (H. Malcom) Bapt. Q. 5: 197.
Baptist History, Cramp's. (H. Osgood) Bapt. Q. 3: 329.
— Early. Chr. R. 25: 120.
Baptist Interest in New England States. (R. Babcock) Am. Q. Reg. 13: 57.
— in Middle States. (R. Babcock) Am. Q. Reg. 13: 182.
— in South and West. (J. M. Peck) Am. Q. Reg. 14: 42, 370.
Baptist Ministers in New Hampshire, 1795. Am. Q. Reg. 11: 44.
Baptist Ministry, one hundred Years ago. (J. A. Broadus) Bapt. Q. 9: 1.
Baptist Missionaries in India, 1808. (J. Foster) Ecl. R. 7: 440.
Baptist Missionary Report, 1848. Chr. R. 14: 167.
Baptist Missionary Society. (R. Southey) Quar. 1: 109.—Westm. 39: 407.
Baptist Missions, 1792–1842, Cox's History of. Ecl. R. 76: 637.
— Gammell's History of. (A. P. Peabody) No. Am. 70: 57.
— History of. (O. O. Stearns) Chr. R. 14: 556.
Baptist Principles, Progress of. (J. N. Brown) Chr. R. 21: 132, 194.—Dem. R. 37: 160.
Baptist Psalmist. (J. Floy) Meth. Q. 9: 448.
Baptist Pulpit, Sprague's Annals of. Chr. R. 25: 79.
Baptist Register. Chr. R. 1: 407.
Baptist Southern Convention. Chr. R. 11: 114.
Baptist Succession. (W. W. Everts) Bapt. Q. 11: 409.
Baptist Translation of the Bible. (J. W. Yeomans) Princ. 10: 413.—Chr. R. 2: 21.
Baptists and their Sentiments. (E. B. Cross) Chr. R. 11: 1.
— and Disciples, Union of. (W. T. Moore) Chr. Q. 3: 335.
— Early modern, and Pedobaptists. Chr. R. 27: 1.
— Education among, 1776–1876. (H. M. King) Bapt. Q. 10: 445.
— English, 1871. Westm. 96: 425.
— History of English. (F. Parkman) Chr. Exam. 10: 220.
— in America. (J. M. Peck) Chr. R. 19: 1.
— — 1836. Ecl. R. 63: 480.
— — Cox and Hoby on. Cong. M. 19: 505.
— in American Culture. (W. H. Whittsitt) Bapt. Q. 7: 1.
— in Central New York, Early. Hist. M. 19: 391.
— in Maine, History of. (S. F. Smith) Chr. R. 10: 384.
— in the Middle States. Chr. R. 14: 517.
— in the Mississippi Valley. (J. M. Peck) Chr. R. 17: 481.
— in Pennsylvania. (H. G. Jones) Hist. M. 14: 76.
— Our Mission as. (J. H. Cuthbert) Bapt. Q. 8: 222.
— Progress of a Century, 1776–1876. (A. Hovey) Bapt. Q. 10: 467.
— Puritan Treatment of. (J. Chaplin) Bapt. Q. 7: 277.
— Religious Belief of. Chr. R. 1: 514.
Baptisteries, Ancient. (R. G. Hatfield) Bapt. Q. 3: 349.
Baptized Children. *See* Children, Baptized.
Βαπτίζω, Import and Use of. Chr. R. 18: 194.
— Meaning of. (N. Rounds) Meth. Q. 4: 325.—(H. E. Bindseil) Bib. Sac. 1: 703.—(E. Greenwald) Evang. R. 15: 449.
Bar, American. Dem. R. 28: 195.
— Admission to. (L. L. Delafield) Penn Mo. 7: 960.—(F. L. Wellman) Am. Law R. 15: 295.
— and the Bench. (E. L. Godkin) Nation, 12: 56.—(A. G. Sedgwick) Nation, 9: 529.—T. G. Shearman) Nation, 5: 71.
— and the Courts, 1877. (E. L. Godkin) Nation, 25: 222.
— and the Law Schools. (E. L. Godkin) Nation, 22: 109.
— and its Logic. Colburn, 11: 74.
— as a Trade. (P. Kent) Gent. M. n. s. 22: 593.
— Chances of. Liv. Age, 4: 588.
— Emoluments of, and Judicial Salaries. Liv. Age, 30: 170.
— English. Fraser, 41: 578.
— — and the Inns of Court. Quar. 138: 138.
— — in 1775. Tait, n. s. 11: 574.
— Etiquette of. Tait, n. s. 18: 713.
— History of. West. Law J. 8: 355.
— How to get on at. Fraser, 50: 261.
— in England and France. Brit. Q. 11: 171. Same art. Ecl. M. 20: 145.—Cornh. 10: 672.
— Leaders of. (F. Arnold) Lond. Soc. 21: 218.
— Monopoly of. (J. J. Merriman) St. James, 36: 589.
— New England, Fathers of. (N. S. Dodge) Lakeside, 9: 116.

Bar of Ontario in 1800. (D. B. Read) Canad. Mo. **14**: 65, 489.
— Profession of. Lond. M. **11**: 323.
— Roman. (G. Matile) No. Am. **96**: 289.
See Law; Legal Profession.
Bar Associations. So. Lit. Mess. **4**: 583.
Bar at Mouth of Mississippi River. (D. S. Howard) J. Frankl. Inst. **69**: 1.
Bars in Rivers and Harbors, Formation of. (D. S. Howard) J. Frankl. Inst. **66**: 73.
Barante, A. G. P. B de. Liv. Age, **55**: 199.—Colburn, **110**: 184.—Mo. R. **150**: 402.
Barat, Sophia Magdalen. Irish Mo. **8**: 558.
— Early Days of. (C. M. Caddell) Irish Mo. **4**: 459, 493.
— Life and Work of. (A. F. Hewit) Cath. World, **23**: 592.
Barba Yorghi, The Greek Pilot. Lond. M. **23**: 337.
Barbadoes. (A. Van Cleef) Harper, **54**: 385.—Fraser, **94**: 257.—Penny M. **8**: 329, 347, 354.
— History of. (Sir R. H. Schomburgk) Colburn, **82**: 80.—Retros. **14**: 226.—Mus. **10**: 509.
— How the Wind blows in. Ev. Sat. **9**: 426.
— Ligon's History of. Cong. M. **6**: 544.
— Outrages in. Ed. R. **42**: 479.—Am. Meth. M. **8**: 390.
— Rainfall of. (F. A. R. Russell) Nature, **10**: 241.
— Riots against Methodists in. Meth. M. **47**: 126.
— Temperature of. (R. Lawson) Ed. New Philos. J. **35**: 57.
— Vessels to New England from. N. E. Reg. **8**: 206.
— Voyage to. (Sir R. H. Schomburgk) Bentley, **22**: 30, 286, 443.
Barbara, L. C. Petites Maisons. Dub. Univ. **66**: 206.
Barbara Fleming's Fidelity; a Ballad. (M. Howitt) Cornh. **4**: 482.
Barbara Frietchie. (J. G. Whittier) Liv. Age, **79**: 191.
Barbara S——. (C. Lamb) Lond. M. **11**: 511.
Barbara's Duty. (C. Chesebro) Atlan. **31**: 54.
Barbara's Ghost Story. (Mrs. G. J. Gunthorpe) Colburn, **150**: 42–287.
Barbara's Nuptials. House. Words, **9**: 488.
Barbara's Outing; a Story. (T. Gift) Galaxy, **21**: 641.
Barbarelli, Giorgio, School of. (W. H. Pater) Fortn. **28**: 526. Same art. Liv. Age, **135**: 362.
Barbarian Eye, The. Fraser, **12**: 164.
Barbarian Rambles. Blackw. **67**: 281.
Barbarians, The Rights of; a Dialogue. Month, **35**: 551.
— and Savages. (N. Tripier) N. Ecl. **6**: 394.
Barbarossa. *See* Frederick I., Barbarossa.
Barbary, Western, Hay on, 1844. Mo. R. **164**: 429.
Barbary Pirates. Ed. R. **26**: 449.
Barbary Powers, American Diplomacy with. Am. Whig R. **13**: 27.
Barbary States. Quar. **15**: 139.—Anal. M. **7**: 105.
— Christian Slavery in. Liv. Age, **42**: 51.
— Eaton's Expedition to. (J. T. Headley) Harper, **21**: 496.
— a new Source of Trade. (H. A. Buckingham) Hunt, **6**: 28.
— Notes from. (A. H. Guernsey) Harper, **5**: 451.
— United States and. (F. Sheldon) Atlan. **6**: 641.
— Visit to. Good Words, **3**: 659.
Barbauld, Anna Letitia. (H. B. Baker) Argosy, **31**: 303. Same art. Liv. Age, **149**: 439.—Cornh. **44**: 581. Same art. Liv. Age, **151**: 579.—(E. Quincy) Nation, **18**: 206.—(C. Beard) Theo. R. **11**: 388.
— Works of. (W. O. B. Peabody) Chr. Exam. **3**: 299.—Quar. **7**: 309.—Mo. R. **107**: 294.—Mus. **7**: 391.
Barbecue in Mississippi. (R. Cleland) Canad. Mo. **13**: 500.
Barber, D., Revolutionary Services of. Hist. M. **7**: 83.
Barber of Beaulieu. (G. Soane) Bentley, **12**: 37.
— of Duncow; a Real Ghost Story. (J. Hogg) Fraser, **3**: 174.
— of Northallerton. (D. Meadows) Bentley, **11**: 287.
Barber's Supper. Blackw. **42**: 116.
Barbers. Chamb. J. **26**: 293. **33**: 353.—Victoria, **4**: 193.
Barbers and Surgeons. Penny M. **13**: 87, 91.
Barberini Vase. (J. G. King and C. Marsh) Arch. **8**: 307, 316.
Barberry, The. Once a Week, **9**: 719.
Barberry; a Story. (J. G. Austin) Galaxy, **21**: 246.
Barbets and their Distribution. (P. L. Sclater) Intel. Obs. **12**: 241.
Barbier, Henri Auguste. Ev. Sat. **9**: 407.
Barcelona. Cornh. **20**: 182.
— Exchange of. Penny M. **12**: 172.
— From Scotland to. (J. Hannay) Temp. Bar, **25**: 27.
— Port and City of. Penny M. **5**: 145.
Barckley, R. Felicitie of Man. Retros. **1**: 271.
Barclay, Alexander. The Ship of Fools. (F. Hall) Nation, **21**: 359.
Barclay, Robert, of Ury. (A. Gordon) Theo. R. **11**: 524.
— Marrow of. (A. Gordon) Theo. R. **12**: 387.
Barclay, Perkins & Co's. Brewery. Penny M. **10**: 121.
Barclay Compton; or, the Sailor's Return. (Miss Leslie) Godey, **25**: 212, 294.
Bard of Iveraln; a Story. (J. Monteath) Tinsley, **28**: 166.
Bardello, Tragedy in the Palazzo. N. Ecl. **2**: 385.
Bardic Poetry, Old. (W. Barnes) Macmil. **16**: 306.
Bardic Triad of Wales. Dub. Univ. **65**: 104.
Bardism of the Druidic Period. (A. Vardd) Internat. R. **3**: 161.
Bards, Celtic. House. Words. **17**: 379.
Barefoote, Walter, Governor of New Hampshire, 1685. (J. B. Moore) Am. Q. Reg. **13**: 277.
— Deposition concerning, 1676. N. E. Reg. **5**: 358.
Bareith, Princess de, Memoirs of. (F. Jeffrey) Ed. R. **20**: 255. Same art. Anal. M. **1**: 241.—Ecl. R. **16**: 1012.
Barents, Voyages of. Geog. M. **4**: 70.
Barère's Memoirs. (T. B. Macaulay) Ed. R. **79**: 275. Same art. Liv. Age, **1**: 93.—Ecl. M. **2**: 238.—For. Q. **30**: 191.—Ecl. R. **81**: 151.—Fraser, **47**: 408.
Barfreston Church. Penny M. **14**: 113.
Barga. (L. Villari) Fraser, **97**: 334.
Bargain-Hunters. Chamb. J. **4**: 33.
Bargain-Hunting. Chamb. J. **31**: 163.
Bargaining. Chamb. J. **43**: 401.
Barham, Richard Harris. Bentley, **18**: 198. **21**: 103.—Fraser, **83**: 302.—(J. Hughes) Colburn, **74**: 526. **79**: 273.—Temp. Bar, **31**: 61. Same art. Ecl. M. **76**: 203.
— Blasphemer's Warning; Lay of St. Romwold. Colburn, **73**: 297.
— Brothers of Birchington; a Poem. Colburn, **74**: 145.
— House-Warming. Colburn, **68**: 346.
— Ingoldsby Legends. Liv. Age, **13**: 128.—Brit. Q. **53**: 391. Same art. Liv. Age, **109**: 323.
— Life and Works of. Brit. Q. **53**: 391.
— Lord of Thoulouse. Colburn, **70**: 321.
— Wedding-Day. Colburn, **70**: 465.
Baring, Charles, Bishop of Durham. Cong. **3**: 472.
Baring Family of London. (H. R. F. Bourne) Lond. Soc. **9**: 367. Same art. Ecl. M. **67**: 28.—Bank. M. (N. Y.) **19**: 214.
Baring-Gould, S. *See* Gould, S. Baring.
Barite Crystals. (G. C. Broadhead) Am. J. Sci. **113**: 419.
Bark, Fibrous. (J. R. Jackson) Stud. & Intel. Obs. **2**: 407.
Bark "True Love"; a Poem. (B. F. Taylor) Lakeside, **11**: 31.
Barker, George F. Pop. Sci. Mo. **15**: 693.
Barker, Jacob. Penn Mo. **3**: 639.
Barker, John, & Co. Colburn, **169**: 69.
Barker, Joshua, and Massachusetts Shipbuilding. N. E. Reg. **24**: 297.
Barker, J. T., Memoir of. Cong. M. **16**: 389.
Barker, T. J., and his Paintings. Art J. **30**: 97.
Barking through the Fence. Temp. Bar, **51**: 461.
Barlaam and Josaphat, Indian Saints. Month, **41**: 137.

Barlass, Wm., Sermons. Chr. Mo. Spec. **1**: 189, 259.
Barling, E., Memoir of. Cong. M. **16**: 641.
Barlow, Joel. (A. C. Baldwin) New Eng. **32**: 413.—(C. B. Todd) Lippinc. **26**: 68.
— and his Family. (Mrs. C. H. Dall) Unita. R. **6**: 159.
— Columbiad. (F. Jeffrey) Ed. R. **15**: 24.—Portfo. (Den.) **1**: 59, 432. **2**: 463.—Ecl. R. **11**: 403.
— Life and Writings of, with portrait. Anal. M. **4**: 130.
— Oration, 4th July, 1787. Carey's Mus. **2**: 135.
Barlow, Rebecca. (Mrs. E. F. Ellet) Godey, **37**: 69.
Bar-Maids. St. James, **24**: 539.
Barmecide Dainties. All the Year, **26**: 105.
Barmouth, and its scientific Attractions. (J. Samuelson) Pop. Sci. R. **2**: 28.
— Round about. Argosy, **19**: 120.
Barnabas, The Epistle of. (K. Wieseler) Am. Presb. R. **20**: 625.—Kitto, **32**: 66. **33**: 103.
— — from the Codex Sinaiticus. Am. Presb. R. **13**: 29, 440.
— — Recent Editions of. (J. Donaldson) Theo. R. **16**: 113.
Barnaby Genealogy. (E. W. Peirce) N. E. Reg. **18**: 361.
Barnaby Palms. Blackw. **39**: 35.
Barnaby Pass. (C. F. Woolson) Harper, **55**: 261.
Barnaby Rudge. (C. Dickens) Mus. **42**: 81–541. **43**: 110–539. **44**: 118, 239.
Barnaby Rudge's Raven. Ev. Sat. **9**: 542, 742, 749.
Barnabys, The, in America. (Mrs. F. Trollope) Colburn, **64**: 504. **65**: 17–528. **66**: 17–494. **67**: 33–496.
Barnacles. (J. S. Kingsley) Am. Natural. **11**: 102.
— Facts and Fiction of. (J. C. Galton) Pop. Sci. R. **12**: 384.
Barnard, Daniel D., Life and Services of, with portrait. Am. Whig R. **7**: 521.
Barnard, F. A. P., with portrait. Ecl. M. **86**: 376.—Am. J. Educ. **5**: 753.—Pop. Sci. Mo. **11**: 100.
Barnard, George C., Judge, with portrait. Ev. Sat. **11**: 463.
Barnard, George G., Trial of. Am. Law R. **7**: 181.
Barnard, Henry, Educational Labors in Connecticut and Rhode Island. Am. J. Educ. **1**: 659.
Barnard, John. (S. J. Spaulding) Cong. Q. **4**: 376.
Barnard, Joseph, Death of, 1695. N. E. Reg. **9**: 156.
Barnard Castle, England. Liv. Age, **142**: 701.
Barnes, Albert, with portrait. Ecl. M. **57**: 566.—(J. Dyer) Penn Mo. **2**: 75.—(Z. M. Humphrey) Am. Presb. R. **20**: 446.—Liv. Age, **60**: 626.—Knick. **34**: 189.
— Introduction to Butler's Analogy. Meth. Q. **4**: 325.
— Reminiscences of. (R. W. Dickinson) Am. Presb. R. **20**: 379.
— Trial for Heresy. (C. Hodge) Princ. **8**: 441.—(N. W. Taylor) Chr. Q. Spec. **3**: 292.—(G. W. Burnap) Chr. Exam. **21**: 187.—(C. Hodge) Princ. **9**: 138.
Barnes, Daniel H. (G. C. Verplanck) Am. J. Educ. **14**: 513.
Barnes, William, Dorsetshire Poet. (Chamb. J. **39**: 281.—Macmil. **6**: 154.—No. Brit. **31**: 339.—Chamb. J. **45**: 487. **49**: 730.
Barneveldt, John of, and De Witt. Ed. R. **76**: 443.
— Motley's Life of. (A. V. Dicey) Nation, **18**: 300, 316.—(C. C. Smith) O. & N. **10**: 128.—(R. H. Stoddard) Harper, **48**: 831.—Ed. R. **140**: 107. Same art. Liv. Age, **123**: 3.—Nat. Q. **29**: 168.—Quar. **137**: 131. Same art. Liv. Age, **122**: 643.—So. R. n. s. **19**: 59.
Barnewood Bells; a Poem. (C. Newton) Temp. Bar, **3**: 440.
Barney, Commodore Joshua, Life of. Am. Q. **13**: 1.
Barney Brady's Goose; a Tale. (W. Carleton) Dub. Univ. **11**: 604.
Barney Geoghegan, the Irish Member. Ecl. M. **79**: 362, 457.
Barney Moore. Fraser, **4**: 253.
Barnicott House, Sketch of. Hogg, **7**: 57.
Barnstable, Mass., Church Records. N. E. Reg. **9**: 279. **10**: 37, 345.
— Settlers of. (D. Hamblen) N. E. Reg. **2**: 64–388. **3**: 84, 133, 271. **4**: 192.
Barnstable County, Mass., Ministers of, to 1842. (E. Pratt) Am. Q. Reg. **15**: 58.
Barnum, P. T. Fraser, **51**: 213. Same art. Ecl. M. **34**: 410.—Blackw. **77**: 187.—So. Lit. Mess. **16**: 758.
— and H. Greeley contrasted. (W. H. Hurlbut) Chr. Exam. **58**: 245.
— Autobiography. Knick. **45**: 235.
— the great American Humbug. Tait, n. s. **22**: 73.
— in Congress. (E. L. Godkin) Nation, **4**: 190, 295.
— Lesson of his Life. Liv. Age, **44**: 149.
— Life of. New Q. **4**: 180.
Barnwells, The, of South Carolina. Land We Love, **2**: 53.
Barnwell Priory, Charter of. Arch. **10**: 396.
— Collection of Subsidy. (R. Gough) Arch. **10**: 386.
Barny O'Reirdon, the Navigator. (S. Lover) Dub. Univ. **1**: 17, 127. Same art. Liv. Age, **30**: 385.
Baroda. Once a Week, **25**: 280.
— Government and Maladministration of. Westm. **104**: 126, 391.
Barometer. (J. Lewis) Am. J. Sci. **90**: 233.—Penny M. **10**: 194.
— Action of, during a Hurricane. (J. Chappellsmith) Am. J. Sci. **73**: 18.
— Aneroid. (J. Lovering) Am. J. Sci. **59**: 249.—Ecl. Engin. **18**: 104, 201.
— as an Engineering Instrument. (J. M. Richardson) J. Frankl. Inst. **66**: 307, 366.
— Automatic registering and printing. (G. W. Hough) Am. J. Sci. **91**: 43.
— for the Coast. Recr. Sci. **2**: 98.
— Gas, Heat and Pressure on. (C. Decharme) Ecl. Engin. **25**: 515.
— Glycerine, Construction of. Nature, **21**: 377.
— History of. (Sir J. Leslie) Ed. R. **20**: 169.
— in the Polar Regions. (W. Ferrel) Nature, **4**: 226.
— Lines of Equal Pressure. (H. A. Hazen) Am. J. Sci. **121**: 361.
— Marine. Ed. R. **9**: 419.
— Mirror. Nature, **19**: 586.
— Reading the. (R. Fitzroy) J. Frankl. Inst. **73**: 313.
— Reduction to Sea-Level. (H. A. Hazen) Am. J. Sci. **121**: 453.
— Self-indicating Balance. J. Frankl. Inst. **64**: 104.
Barometric Anomalies about the Andes. (M. F. Maury) Am. J. Sci. **69**: 385.
Barometric Cycles. (B. Stewart) Nature, **23**: 237.
Barometric Fluctuations. (P. E. Chase) Am. J. Sci. **88**: 380.
Barometric Gradient, and Velocity of the Wind. (W Ferrel) Am. J. Sci. **108**: 343.—(W. C. Ley) Nature, **24**: 8.
Barometric Pressure, Diurnal Oscillations of. (J. A. Broun) Nature, **19**: 366.
— — Cause of. (J. P. Espy) J. Frankl. Inst. **5**: 278.
— in the Tropics, Abnormal Variations of. (F. Chambers) Nature, **23**: 88.
— Inequality of. (H. F. Blanford) Nature, **14**: 314.
— Periodic Oscillations of. (J. A. Broun) Nature, **23**: 556.
Barometric Variations. (J. A. Broun) Nature, **14**: 572.—(W. H. S. Monck) Nature, **5**: 407.
Baron, Michel, French Actor. All the Year, **39**: 160.
Baron Fritz; a Tale. Temp. Bar, **45**: 104.
Baron Jauïoz; a Poem. (T. Taylor) Once a Week, **1**: 109.
Baron of Courtstown, The. Fraser, **12**: 629.
Baron of St. Castine; a Poem. (H. W. Longfellow) Atlan. **29**: 332.

Baron von Dullbrainz; a Tale. (W. Jerdan) Bentley, **6**: 316.
Baron von Pfaffenberg; a Tale. Bentley, **16**: 299.
Baron's Coffin; a Tale. (A. Buisson) Belgra. **9**: 351.
Baron's Revenge; a Tale. Colburn, **95**: 77–183.
Barons' War, in the 13th Century. Mo. R. **163**: 491.
Baronial and Monastic Remains, Parkyns on. Ecl. R. **24**: 553.
Baronial Housekeeping in the olden Times. Hogg, **6**: 68.
Baronies in Abeyance. Antiquary, **3**: 231, 304. — (W. D. Pink) Antiquary, **4**: 116, 212.
Barrack, Life in a. Cornh. **7**: 441.
Barracks, Living in. Chamb. J. **30**: 124.
Barrack-Yard, The. Fraser, **36**: 588.
Barré, Colonel, and his Times. (H. F. Elliot) Macmil. **35**: 109. Same art. Liv. Age, **132**: 22.
Barrel-making Machinery, Holmes's. Pract. M. **5**: 284.
Barren Honor. (G. A. Lawrence) Fraser, **64**: 265–732. **65**: 75–751.
Barrett, George C., with portrait. Ev. Sat. **11**: 449.
Barrett, Dr. John. Dub. Univ. **18**: 350.
— Anecdotes of. Lond. M. **5**: 53.
— Eccentricities of. Mus. **43**: 449.
Barrett, Samuel, Sermon on Death of. (C. A. Bartol) Mo. Rel. M. **36**: 69.
Barricades, Results of the Triumph of. Blackw. **36**: 209. Same art. Mus. **25**: 406.
Barrington, Basil, and his Friends. Westm. **14**: 224.
Barrington, D. Antiquities of the Statutes. Retros. **9**: 250.
Barrington, J. S., Viscount, Memoir of. Cong. M. **17**: 65.
Barrington, Sir Jonah. Irish Sketches. Mo. R. **128**: 510. — Dem. R. **33**: 325. — Lond. M. **18**: 241.
Barrington, Rutland, Actor, with portrait. Victoria, **35**: 157.
Barrington, W. W., Viscount, Political Life of. Quar. **14**: 505.
Barrister, Experiences of a. Chamb. J. **11**: 24–403. **12**: 147, 177, 242. Same art. Ecl. M. **21**: 163. Same art. Liv. Age, **21**: 267.
— Tales of a. Quar. **79**: 61.
Barrister's Clerk. Argosy, **31**: 367.
Barrister's Story. Tinsley, **9**: 33.
Barritt, Thomas, of Manchester. (T. Gibbons and others) Reliquary, **9**: 133. **12**: 205. **13**: 43.
Barrossa, Battle of. (S. Moggridge) Blackw. **21**: 695.
Barrow, Isaac. Quar. **127**: 353. Same art. Liv. Age, **104**: 259.
— Works of. (D Curry) Meth. Q. **6**: 165. — (D. A. Wasson) New Eng. **9**: 498. — Sharpe, **14**: 26.
Barrow, Sir John. Chamb. J. **11**: 44.
— Autobiography of. (C. H. Warren) No. Am. **66**: 348.
— Excursions to North of Europe, 1830–33. Mo. R. **133**: 550.
— Voyages. Quar. **3**: 194.
Barrow, John, jr. Tour round Ireland. Dub. Univ. **7**: 693.
Barrows. Penny M. **3**: 494.
— Ancient British. Nature, **1**: 460, 583.
— British. (W. B. Dawkins) Nature, **18**: 429.
— — at Bartlow, Essex. (J. Gage) Arch. **25**: 1.
— — — Further Discoveries at. (J. Gage) Arch. **28**: 1.
— — — Final Excavations at. (J. G. Rokewoode) Arch. **29**: 1.
— — — Roman Remains in. (J. Gage) Arch. **26**: 300.
— — at Iffins Wood, near Canterbury. (J. Y. Akerman) Arch. **30**: 57.
— — at Stoney Littleton, Somerset Co. (Sir R. C. Hoare) Arch. **19**: 43.
— — at West Kennet, Wiltshire, Long chambered. (J. Thurman) Arch. **38**: 405.
— Cornish, Discoveries in. (E. H. W. Dunkin) Antiquary, **2**: 77.
— Folk-Lore of. (R. J. King) Once a Week, **14**: 693.
Barrows in Cambridgeshire. (R. C. Neville) Arch. **32**: 357.
— in South Dorsetshire. (J. Sydenham) Arch. **30**: 327.
— in South Wilts. (J. Y. Akerman) Arch. **35**: 480.
— in Wiltshire, Long. (J. Thomson) Arch. **42**: 161.
— — Round. (J. Thurnam) Arch. **43**: 285.
Barrow-in-Furness, and Sir James Ramsden. Pract. M. **2**: 1.
— Iron and Steel Institute at. Pract. M. **4**: 262.
Barrows, Lieut. William. Anal. M. **2**: 394.
Barry, M. J. G., Duchesse de. (L. H. Hooper) Lippinc. **23**: 122. — Fraser, **6**: 1.
— Adventures of. (D. Costello) Colburn, **83**: 182. **84**: 81.
— and Madame Roland. Dem. R. **43**: 286.
— and Louis XV. Temp. Bar. **39**: 318. Same art. Liv. Age, **119**: 422.
— Capefigue's. Colburn, **115**: 295. Same art. Ecl. M. **47**: 56.
Barry, Edward M. Art J. **32**: 139. — Am. Arch. **7**: 83.
Barry, Gerald. (J. Healy) Irish Mo. **6**: 134.
Barry, James, the Irish Painter. (P. Knight) Ed. R. **16**: 293. — Blackw. **8**: 277. — Dub. Univ. **20**: 274, 443. — Irish Q. **3**: 230. — (S. Colvin) Portfo. **4**: 150. — (E. Townbridge) Sharpe, **47**: 205. — Penny M. **7**: 65–153. — Colburn, **7**: 339. — Ecl. R. **11**: 396.
Barry, John, Commodore. Portfo.(Den.) **10**: 1.
Barry, Spranger, Actor. (E. Townbridge) Sharpe, **48**: 32. — Dub. Univ. **60**: 580.
Barstow, John, with portrait. (A. Caswell) N. E. Reg. **18**: 370.
Barth, Christian Gottlob, Character of. Good Words, **4**: 264.
Barth, H. (W. L. Gage) Harper, **33**: 65. — Liv. Age, **59**: 368.
See Africa.
Barthet, Armand. Nouvelles. New Q. **1**: 427.
Bartholdi, Auguste, and his Works. (C. de Kay) Scrib. **14**: 129.
— Statue of Liberty. Am. Arch. **4**: 77. — (J. G. Shea) Am. Cath. Q. **5**: 586.
Bartholomew, E. S. (H. T. Tuckerman) Hours at Home, **2**: 525.
Bartholomew Fair. (A. Smith) Bentley, **12**: 390. — Blackw. **14**: 259. — Fraser, **2**: 431.
— Memoirs of. Brit. Q. **29**: 463.
— Morley's Memoir of. Colburn, **115**: 181. — Nat. R. **8**: 425.
Bartholomew's Day, Massacre of. *See* St. Bartholomew.
Barthomley, Hinchliffe's. Fraser, **57**: 620.
Bartleby, the Scrivener. (H. Melville) Putnam, **2**: 546, 609.
Bartleman, James, Memoir of. Fraser, **48**: 164.
Bartlett, Rev. John. (C. T. Thayer) Chr. Exam. **46**: 484.
Bartlett, John Russell, Library of. (H. Rogers) Am. Bibliop. **7**: 192.
Bartlett, Josiah, Governor of New Hampshire, 1790. (J. B. Moore) Am. Q. Reg. **13**: 278.
Bartlett, William Francis. (A. G. Sedgwick) Nation, **26**: 406.
Bartol, C. A., Discourses of. (C. Lowe) Unita. R. **1**: 242. — (H. W. Bellows) Chr. Exam. **54**: 103. — New Eng. **8**: 434. — (E. P. Whipple) No. Am. **70**: 199.
— Key of the Kingdom. Mo. Rel. M. **22**: 1.
— Sermons. (A. P. Peabody) Chr. Exam. **48**: 110. — Unita. R. **15**: 451.
Bartolini, Lorenzo, the Sculptor. Colburn, **11**: 231.
Barton, B. S., with portrait. Portfo.(Den.) **15**: 273.
Barton, Bernard, Quaker Poet, with portrait. Hogg, **5**: 353. — Knick. **39**: 514. — Liv. Age, **61**: 195.

Barton, Bernard, Life and Letters of. Liv. Age, 23: 529.
— Napoleon and other Poems. Chr. Obs. 23: 293.
— Poems. (F. Jeffrey) Ed. R. 34: 348. — (J. Wilson) Blackw. 12: 767. — Mo. R. 93: 267. 98: 185. — Ecl. R. 33: 181, 254. 36: 155, 476. 40: 49. 43: 236, 560. 45: 231. 49: 140. — Lond. M. 2: 194.
— — and Letters. Liv. Age, 24: 113.
Barton, Clara H. (L. P. Brockett) Appleton, 7: 204.
Barton, Elizabeth, the Nun of Kent. Chamb. J. 28: 341. Same art. Liv. Age, 56: 107.
Barton, Fanny. *See* Abington, Fanny B.
Bartram, John, and his Garden. (H. Pyle) Harper, 60: 321.
— and H. Marshall, Darlington's Memoirs of. (Mrs. I. James) No. Am. 70: 210. — Am. J. Sci. 59: 85.
— and Peter Collinson. Am. J. Educ. 28: 872.
Baruch, Ethiopic Book of. (G. H. Schrodde) Luth. Q. 8: 333.
Baryta; its manifold Uses in the Arts. (L. Feuchtwanger) J. Frankl. Inst. 97: 356.
Barytone, The great. Chamb. J. 43: 17.
Basalt. (H. P. Malet) Geog. M. 1: 188, 232.
— Origin of the columnar Structure of. (R. Mallet) Am. J. Sci. 109: 206.
Bascom, Henry B. Knick. 34: 308.
Base, The, do call it Convey; a Tale. (R. Thynne) Dub. Univ. 83: 317.
Base-Ball and Cricket. (A. G. Sedgwick) Nation, 9: 167
Base-Ball Business. Lakeside, 4: 325.
Basedow, Johann Bernhard. (K. von Raumer) Am. J. Educ. 5: 487.
Basevi, Capt. James Palladio. Nature, 4: 419.
Bashan. (J. L. Porter) Bib. Sac. 13: 789.
— and the Cities of Moab. Chr. Obs. 61: 10. 66: 302. Same art. Liv. Age, 69: 220.
— and the Cities of Og. Liv. Age, 62: 70.
— Giant Cities of. (L. J. Fletcher) Univ. Q. 33: 67.
— Historico-Geographical Sketch of. (J. L. Porter) Kitto, 13: 281.
Bashful Gentleman. (M. M. Noah) So. Lit. Mess. 1: 429.
Bashfulness, Miseries of. So. Lit. Mess. 2: 465.
Bashi-Bashi-Bazouks. Fraser, 54: 375.
— on the Drina Frontier of Bosnia. (J. S. Stuart-Glennie) Gent. M. n. s. 18: 362.
Basil the Great, St. Chr. R. 20: 263.
— and Baptism. (I. Chase) Chr. R. 23: 568. 24: 102.
— Life and Letters of. No. Am. 90: 356.
— Some Letters of. (J. H. Egar) Am. Church R. 30: 391, 567. 31: 25, 118, 401.
Basil's Faith; a Tale. (A. W. Dubourg) Temp. Bar, 45: 143, 285. Same art. Appleton, 14: 488, 521, 552.
Basilia; a Tale of Modern Athens. Colburn, 25: 432.
Basilica of Santa Petronilla. (S. Wood) Good Words, 15: 732.
— of St. Saturnin. (M. P. Thompson) Cath. World, 8: 101.
Basilicas of Rome, Bunsen on. Ed. R. 85: 143.
Basilides, De Groot's. (O. Cone) Univ. Q. 26: 17.
Basilis, A Coin of. (T. Combe) Arch. 18: 344.
Basilisk, The. Belgra. 1: 479.
— The modern. Chamb. J. 33: 91.
Basilisks, physical and moral. (W. W. Newton) Penn Mo. 7: 788.
Basing House, Hampshire. Penny M. 9: 257. — Sharpe, 11: 222.
Basire, Dr. Isaac, Correspondence of. Mo. R. 125: 326.
Baskets and their Materials. Penny M. 11: 445.
Basle to Domo d' Ossola. Galaxy, 12: 848.
Basque Blood. House. Words, 9: 364.
Basque Country, The. Ed. R. 119: 369. Same art. Ecl. M. 62: 409. — Penny M. 11: 146.
— and People. (C. H. Brigham) No. Am. 87: 211.
Basque Country, Glimpse into. Month, 20: 29.
— Language of. Liv. Age, 87: 128.
— Ramble in. Chamb. J. 56: 449.
— Ramble through, 1836–37. Blackw. 52: 200, 379, 498.
— Stephens on. Mo. R. 144: 1.
Basque Customs. Fraser, 97: 632. Same art. Liv. Age, 137: 749.
Basque Legends. (T. F. Crane) Internat. R. 6: 386. — (D. Fitzgerald) Gent. M. n. s. 19: 286.
Basque Literature, Specimens of. Dub. Univ. 86: 732.
Basque Posada, Snow-bound in a. (K. N. Blodgett) Lakeside, 3: 383.
Basques, The. (M. P. Thompson) Cath. World, 22: 646. — (A. H. Sayce) Nature, 15: 394. — All the Year, 23: 534. — Chamb. J. 1: 277, 294.
— and the Kelts. (W. Webster) Anthrop. J. 5: 5.
— Northern Range of. (W. B. Dawkins) Fortn. 22: 323.
— of Spain. Ecl. M. 37: 337.
— Origin of. (W. Webster) Anthrop. J. 2: 150.
— Social Customs of. (H. C. Lea) No. Am. 107: 644.
Bas-Relief, An ancient. (J. Millingen and S. Weston) Arch. 19: 70, 99.
Bass, The Fish. (A. H. Baldwin) Once a Week, 12: 261.
— Black, Habits of. (S. T. Tisdale) Am. Natural. 5: 361.
— in the Potomac. (W. M. Laffan) Lippinc. 20: 454.
— Striped. (F. Endicott) Scrib. 21: 698.
Bass Rock, The. Hogg, 1: 19. — Penny M. 2: 265. — Sharpe, 23: 53. Same art. Ecl. M. 37: 347.
— and its Tenants. Chamb. J. 30: 107.
— History of. Ecl. R. 90: 226.
— Sketch of. Colburn, 83: 13*.
— Trip to. Month, 11: 386.
Bass and Burton Breweries. Lond. Soc. 39: 39.
Bassano, Italy. Fraser, 96: 17. Same art. Liv. Age, 134: 491.
Basselin, Oliver, Poetry of. Fraser, 21: 47.
Bassi, Laura M. C., Female Doctor of Philosophy. Chamb. J. 12: 31.
Bassi, Ugo. (E. Carrington) Brit. Q. 73: 12.
Bassompierre's Embassy to England, 1626. Blackw. 5: 275. — Retros. 13: 316. 14: 69. — Mo. R. 91: 28.
Bassos, The; a Tale. (F. S. Cozzens) Putnam, 14: 288.
Bastardy, Adulterine, Law of. Quar. 59: 48.
Bastian, H. C. Pop. Sci. Mo. 8: 108.
— Brain as an Organ of Mind. Nature, 22: 381.
Bastiat, F. (J. E. Cairnes) Fortn. 14: 411. — Liv. Age, 65: 554.
— Popular Fallacies. Dub. Univ. 34: 640.
— Works of. Ed. R. 149: 355.
Bastille, The. (G. Masson) Once a Week, 17: 688. — Chamb. J. 46: 167, 185.
— Anecdotes of. Ev. Sat. 5: 711.
— Appointment of Sir John Fastolfe as Keeper, 1421. (J. G. Nichols) Arch. 44: 112.
— Archives of. Lond. Q. 28: 45. Same art. Ecl. M. 69: 57.
— Fall of, Contemporary Narrative of. Fortn. 34: 359. Same art. Liv. Age, 147: 160.
— Truth about. Fraser, 93: 162. Same art. Ecl. M. 86: 429.
— Women of. Colburn, 130: 433.
Bastnäsite and Tysonite from Colorado. (O. D. Allen and W. J. Comstock) Am. J. Sci. 119: 390.
Basutos and the Cape Colony. 19th Cent. 9: 177.
— and Sir Bartle Frere. (W. Fowler) 19th Cent. 9: 547.
Bat, The. Chamb. J. 48: 457.
— Kalong. Penny M. 3: 305.
Bats. Ev. Sat. 10: 151.
— and their Young. (B. G. Wilder) Pop. Sci. Mo. 7: 641.
— Dobson's Catalogue of. Nature, 14: 472. 18: 585.

Bats, Something about. (B. G. Wilder) Hours at Home, 10: 321.
— What are? (St. G. Mivart) Pop. Sci. R. 15: 225. Same art. Pop. Sci. Mo. 9: 523.
— Winged Quadrupeds. (E. Coues) Penn Mo. 6: 341.
Bataks, Journey to the. Ecl. R. 44: 421.
Batalha and Alcobaca, Beckford on Monasteries of. Mo. R. 138: 39.
Batavia, Gillan's Account of. Portfo.(Den.) 23: 46.
— Two Days at. Bentley, 57: 57. Same art. Ecl. M. 65: 109.
Batcheller, Tyler. (C. Cushing) Cong. Q. 6: 125.
Bateman, Laura, and Edith Heraud, Comparative Criticism of. Victoria, 13: 167.
Bateman, T., with portrait. Reliquary, 2: 87. — Chr. Obs. 20: 665. — Ecl. R. 44: 310.
Bateman, Thomas O. (L. Jewitt) Reliquary, 15: 97.
Bateman Household; a Tale. (J. Payn) Chamb. J. 33: 1–233.
Bates, Edward, with portrait. De Bow, 12: 106.
Bates, Isaac C., Memoir of. Am. Whig R. 3: 186. — with portrait, (H. A. Hill) N. E. Reg. 31: 141.
Bates, Joshua. (G. Ticknor) Am. J. Educ. 7: 270.
Bates's Tour, personally conducted. Blackw. 119: 164.
Bath, Eng. (L. S. Costello) Bentley, 17: 168. — Once a Week, 13: 122. — Macmil. 10: 477.
— and Cheltenham, Society in. Lond. Soc. 18: 116.
— Cathedral of. All the Year, 34: 222. — Penny M. 2: 268.
— Literary Ramblings about. Cornh. 27: 543, 688. 28: 27.
— Mineral Waters of. (Sir C. Lyell) Am. J. Sci. 89: 13.
Bath, Va., Historical Sketch of. So. Lit. Mess. 20: 721.
Bath, Order of the. Retros. 15: 439.
Bath-Chair Man's Story. (Mrs. R. Church) Temp. Bar, 22: 507. Same art. Ev. Sat. 5: 432.
Bath, Fashionable, of the Olden Time. Cornh. 35: 195.
— Implements for the, found at Urdingen. (G. Witt) Arch. 43: 250.
— The Social. Once a Week, 13: 352.
Baths, Ancient. Chamb. J. 5: 195.
— — in the Island of Lipari. (W. H. Smythe) Arch. 23: 98.
— — Thermal. Dub. Univ. 57: 29.
— — Turkish, etc. Cornh. 3: 375.
— and Bathing-Places, Ancient and modern. Quar. 129: 151. Same art. Ecl. M. 75: 385.
— and Wash-Houses. Lond. Q. 7: 182.
— Free, at East Smithfield. Chamb. J. 8: 102.
— — in Cities. (A. W. Ely) De Bow, 2: 228. — (J. Wharton) Penn Mo. 5: 452.
— German. Blackw. 120: 670. Same art. Liv. Age, 132: 224.
— of Broussa. (Mrs. Walker) Good Words, 8: 524.
— of Lenk. Penny M. 7: 217.
— of Mont Dor. Blackw. 61: 448.
— of Santa Catarina. Fraser, 80: 635.
— of Silesia. Dub. Univ. 38: 223, 283.
— on the Seine. Hogg, 6: 230.
— Tale of a Tub. Liv. Age, 70: 613.
— Turkish. *See* Turkish Baths.
See Spas.
Bather's Ideal. (E. Myers) Fraser, 102: 276.
Bathing. Penny M. 4: 354.
— abroad and at Home. Liv. Age, 79: 67.
— and Bodies. (B. Taylor) Putnam, 4: 532.
— Hot-Air Baths. Dub. Univ. 82: 224.
— How, when, and where to bathe. (W. Strange) Gent. M. n. s. 1: 296.
— in Winter. Lond. M. 1: 63.
— its Use and Abuse. (Sir A. Clarke) Nat. M. 3: 152.
— Luxurious. Chamb. J. 57: 391.
Bathing, Obstructions to. (W. Howitt) Peop. J. 2: 221.
— Russian Vapor Bath. (T. S. Traill) Ed. New Philos. J. 13: 14.
Bathing Dresses, Ladies'. Godey, 83: 43.
Bathometer. J. Frankl. Inst. 101: 314.
— The Morse. Ecl. Engin. 3: 37.
Bathurst, Sir Benjamin; a mysterious Crime. Liv. Age, 56: 21. 75: 231.
Bathurst, Henry, Life of. Ecl. R. 67: 555.
Bathybius and the Moners. (E. Haeckel) Pop. Sci. Mo. 11: 641.
— What is? (W. C. Williamson) Pop. Sci. R. 8: 350. Same art. Am. Natural. 3: 651.
Batley and its Shoddy Manufactures. All the Year, 25: 440.
Baton Rouge, Up the Mississippi to. Broadw. 7: 372. — (R. Keeler and A. R. Waud) Ev. Sat. 11: 140.
Batrachians, Carboniferous, in Nova Scotia. (J. W. Dawson) Am. J. Sci. 112: 440.
— Development without Metamorphosis. Nature, 15: 491.
Battersea Bridge, Old. (K. S. Macquoid) Art J. 33: 33.
Battery, Ericsson's. (I. Newton) J. Frankl. Inst. 73: 73.
— Stevens Iron-clad. (R. H. Thurston) J. Frankl. Inst. 98: 165.
Battery, Air-tight Galvanic. (C. T. Chester) J. Frankl. Inst. 85: 257.
— Bunsen, Manufacture of Carbon Elements for. (J. (Young) J. Frankl. Inst. 70: 37.
— Ground. (A. G. Ballantyne) J. Frankl. Inst. 83: 329.
— Moncrieff. Once a Week, 20: 120.
— Platinized Graphite. (C. V. Walker) J. Frankl. Inst. 69: 110.
— Thermo-electric, Clamond's. Pract. M. 4: 314.
— Voltaic, Chemical Theory of. (J. P. Cooke) J. Frankl. Inst. 92: 329, 406. 93: 131. 94: 60.
Batticaloa, India. (J. George) Meth. M. 54: 170.
Battle, and who won it; a Tale. (C. F. Browne) Temp. Bar, 31: 525.
— and Triumph of Dr. Susan. (F. H. Ludlow) Harper, 27: 338, 467.
— at Sea. All the Year, 23: 565.
— of the Bees; a Poem. Putnam, 8: 164.
— of Bennington; a Poem. (T. D. English) Harper, 21: 325.
— of the Boyne; a Ballad. Dub. Univ. 13: 302.
— of Bunkerloo, The. (W. H. Bishop) Scrib. 14: 351.
— of the Churches. (J. Martineau) Westm. 54: 441.
— of Dorking. (G. Chesney) Blackw. 109: 539. Same art. Liv. Age, 109: 725.
— — London at the Time of. Victoria, 19: 1.
— — made impossible. Macmil. 28: 375.
— — Review of. Ev. Sat. 11: 26, 75.
— of the Eyes. Dub. Univ. 20: 659.
— of Gilboa; a Poem. Good Words, 3: 88.
— of the Kegs; a Ballad of 1778. (F. Hopkinson) Hist. M. 3: 233.
— of Lansdowne; a Poem. Temp. Bar, 11: 98.
— of Life. (H. S. Brown) Ex. H. Lec. 12: 221. — Sharpe, 17: 129.
— of Life and Death; a Story. (B. Auerbach) Howitt, 3: 82, 103, 121. Same art. Am. Whig R. 9: 265.
— of the Seas; a Poem. (W. Jones) Bentley, 62: 30.
— of the Standard; a Poem. (W. A. Gibbs) St. James, 36: 225–616. 37: 99, 217, 317.
— of Talavera; a Poem. Chr. Obs. 9: 152.
— of the Twins. Tinsley, 10: 471.
— of von Blannase. (F. A. Parker) Knick. 51: 229.
— of Wilo-Wilo, with Chinese Pirates. Putnam, 8: 302.
— with Time; a Poem. Cornh. 6: 270.
See names of particular battles, as Gettysburg; Waterloo; etc.

Battles, Decisive, of the World. (E. S. Creasy) Ecl. M. **14**: 227, 380, 524. **15**: 511.
— Creasy's Fifteen decisive. (T. D. Woolsey) New Eng. **10**: 56. — Westm. **56**: 125.
— Great, in History. (H. Vethake) U. S. Serv. M. **2**: 138, 340, 551. **3**: 330. — Ecl. M. **26**: 471.
— of the Bible. (E. Bayley) Ex. H. Lec. **19**: 469.
— Prose of. Chamb. J. **39**: 129.
Battle Abbey. (B. R. Parkes) Once a Week, **15**: 414. — Penny M. **2**: 211.
— Chronicle of. Dub. R. **49**: 1.
— Roll of. N. E. Reg. **2**: 25.
Battle Array, Ancient and modern. All the Year, **1**: 84.
Battle-Field; a Poem. (W. C. Bryant) Dem. R. **1**: 15.
Battle-Fields of 1859. Fraser, **61**: 168.
Batuta, Ibn, Travels of. Ecl. R. **49**: 524. — Blackw. **49**: 597.
Baubie Wishart; a Story. Lippinc. **26**: 719.
Baudelaire, Charles. (L. Fountain) Lippinc. **8**: 383. — (J. A. Harrison) So. M. **12**: 54. — (H. James, jr.) Nation, **22**: 279. — (G. Saintsbury) Fortn. **24**: 500. — (W. Stigand) Belgra. **15**: 438. — Ev. Sat. **4**: 528.
— Translation of Poe's Poems. Ev. Sat. **11**: 503.
Baudoyn, Book of. Blackw. **41**: 106.
Bauer, Bruno, and the Universities of Prussia. Prosp. R. **2**: 174.
Bauer, Marie-Bernard; a Jewish Convert. (B. Murphy) Cath. World, **15**: 211.
Bauer, William, Trials of. Once a Week, **7**: 221, 247.
Baugniet, Charles. Art J. **19**: 42.
Baum the Cornet-Player. (A. Webster, jr.) Scrib. **6**: 596.
Baur, F. C. (O. B. Frothingham) Chr. Exam. **64**: 1.
— and the Tubingen School of Criticism. Brit. Q. **45**: 297. Same art. Theo. Ecl. **5**: 1.
— and others, Theories on the Fourth Gospel. Nat. R. **5**: 82.
— Writings of. Mo. Rel. M. **35**: 43, 83, 301.
Baurmeister's Narrative of Capture of New York, 1776. M. Am. Hist. **1**: 33.
Bausset, M. de. Memoirs. Fraser, **47**: 413.
Bautain, Abbé. Irish Q. **9**: 555.
Bavaria, Catholicism in. Contemp. **14**: 495. **17**: 261.
— Church Crisis in. Contemp. **19**: 120.
— Court of, Vehse's History of. Ed. R. **104**: 399.
— Customs of the Haberfeld Treiben. Cornh. **16**: 667.
— Headquarters of Beer-Drinking. (A. Ten Broeck) Atlan. **14**: 185.
— Highlands of. Appleton, **13**: 449, 481, 513, 545.
— — Week in. (A. A. Buckland) Victoria, **36**: 60.
— King of. *See* Louis I.
— Lakes of. Bentley, **34**: 17.
— Prisons of. Irish Q. **9**: 764.
— Productive Forces of. (A. Delmar) Internat. R. **3**: 615.
— Summer in. (E. Phipps) Colburn, **55**: 380–453. **56**: 81–526.
Bawr, Madame, Sketch of. Once a Week, **6**: 426.
Baxter, Charles. Art J. **16**: 145.
Baxter, Joseph, Journal of, in 1717. N. E. Reg. **21**: 45.
— Memoir of. (J. Langdon Sibley) N. E. Reg. **20**: 157.
Baxter, Richard. (A. P. Stanley) Macmil. **32**: 385. Same art. Liv. Age, **127**: 46. — (A. Woodbury) Chr Exam. **66**: 157. — (Sir J. Stephen) Ed. R. **70**: 181. — Ecl. R. **114**: 257. — Meth. M. **30**: 481. — Am. Q. Reg. **4**: 1. — Spirit Pilg. **2**: 243. **5**: 151, 215. — (F. Parkman) No. Am. **35**: 36. — Chr. R. **8**: 1.
— and Owen. Nat. R. **15**: 95.
— and his Times. (J. C. Ryle) Ex. H. Lec. **8**: 363.
— End of Controversy. (E. A. Park) Bib. Sac. **12**: 348.
— Home of, at Kidderminster. (W. W. Campbell) Harper, **52**: 43.
— Orme's Life of. Am. Meth. M. **15**: 121. — Ecl. R. **52**: 381.
Baxter, Richard. Posing Question. Cong. M. **6**: 715.
— Review of religious Opinions of. Chr. Obs. **9**: 65, 129.
— Saints' Rest. (J. Woodbridge) Lit. & Theo. R. **2**: 461.
— Theology of. (G. P. Fisher) Bib. Sac. **9**: 135, 300.
Baxter, W. Philological Letters. (G. Sharpe) Arch. **1**: 205.
Baxter, Wm. E., with portrait. Dub. Univ. **88**: 652.
— Impressions of Europe. Quar. **86**: 265.
Bay-Tree, The. Penny M. **3**: 313.
Bayard, James A., Biography of. Anal. M. **7**: 333.
Bayard, P. du T., Chevalier. (J. G. Wilson) Harper, **48**: 478. — (J. G. Wilson) U. S. Serv. M. **5**: 333. — Lond. Soc. **6**: 238. — Penny M. **14**: 31, 45.
— Memoir of. (R. Southey) Quar. **32**: 355. — Mo. R. **118**: 175. — Mus. **7**: 72. **14**: 465. — Ecl. R. **88**: 213.
— Sketches of. Am. Mo. M. **5**: 81, 161
Bayadères, The. Fraser, **18**: 729.
Bayeux Tapestry. (J. Piggot) Antiquary, **4**: 15. — Chamb. J. **45**: 366. — Hogg, **7**: 159. — Liv. Age, **48**: 341. — Sharpe, **28**: 150.
— Memoir on. (Abbé de la Rue) Arch. **17**: 85.
— Observations on. (T. Amyot) Arch. **19**: 88, 192. — (H. Gurney) Arch. **18**: 359. — (C. Stothard) Arch. **19**: 184.
Bayle, Pierre. (F. Sheldon) No. Am. **111**: 377.
Bayley, Solomon, Account of pious Negro. Chr. Obs. **33**: 275, 328.
Baylies, William, Biography of. Am. Q. Reg. **13**: 77.
Bayly, Thomas Haynes, West-End Poet. Fraser, **99**: 352. — with portrait, Colburn, **31**: 550. — Mo. R. **164**: 438.
— Life and Poetry of. Chamb. J. **1**: 251. Same art. Liv. Age, **1**: 442.
— Seasonable Ditties. Colburn, **39**: 64–403.
Bayne, Peter. Christian Life. (J. A. Macaulay) Meth. Q. **16**: 549. — So. Lit. Mess. **23**: 321.
— Lessons from my Masters. (W. C. Brownell) Nation, **29**: 351.
Bayonet, Origin and History of. (J. Y. Akerman) Arch. **38**: 422.
Bayonne, Remains of an ancient Camp near. (S. Baring-Gould) Arch. **34**: 399.
— to St. Sebastian. Sharpe, **38**: 24.
Bayou Tèche. (E. de Leon) Fraser, **91**: 27.
Bayreuth Performances. (A. A. Wheeler) Nation, **23**: 148–325. — All the Year, **37**: 39.
Bayreuth, Wagner at. Scrib. **12**: 361.
See Wagner.
Bazaine, Gen. François Achille. (A. Forbes) Gent. M. n. s. **12**: 76.
— Condemnation of. (E. L. Godkin) Nation, **17**: 401.
— Trial of. (A. Laugel) Nation, **17**: 287.
Bazalgette, Sir Joseph, with portrait. Colburn, **165**: 1040.
Bazar, The deserted. Fraser, **36**: 88.
Bazaars. Chamb. J. **38**: 49.
Bazas, France. (M. P. Thompson) Cath. World, **30**: 159.
Beach, E. T. P. Pelayo; an Epic Poem. Ecl. M. **62**: 371.
Beach, Sir Michael E. H. B., with portrait. Dub. Univ. **85**: 654.
Beach, S. B. Escalala. (J. Sparks) No. Am. **20**: 210. — U. S. Lit. Gaz. **1**: 279.
Beaches, Motions of Shingle. (H. R. Palmer) J. Frankl. Inst. **21**: 135.
— Raised, and their Origin. (E. Hull) Pop. Sci. R. **5**: 169. Same art. Ecl. M. **67**: 90.
— — of Barnstaple Bay. Stud. & Intel. Obs. **4**: 338.
Beach-Combers. (J. J. Roche) Galaxy, **21**: 648. — Chamb. J. **58**: 83.
Beach Men, Stories of. All the Year, **6**: 234.
Beachy Head. (W. W. Fenn) St. James, **35**: 633.
Beacon, Black Rock, L. I., Description of. (W. H. Swift) J. Frankl. Inst. **36**: 385.

Beacons, Antiquity and Use of. (J. Ward) Arch. **1**: 1.
— Origin of. Penny M. **11**: 281.
Beaconsfield, B. Disraeli, Earl of. (E. S. Nadal) Scrib. **14**: 190. — (M. Sullivan) Lippinc. **23**: 197. — Blackw. **104**: 129, 491. — Lond. Soc. **19**: 427. — (A. G. Sedgwick) Nation, **33**: 278. — (B. Murphy) Cath. World, **31**: 410, 491. — (P. M. Potter) Scrib. **22**: 262. — ("Shirley," M. Maccoll, and A. Austin) Contemp. **39**: 971. Same art. Ecl. M. **94**: 129. — (G. C. Noyes) Dial (Ch.), **2**: 1.
— as a Novelist. Appleton, **25**: 354.
— Brandes's Study of. (A. G. Sedgwick) Nation, **30**: 420. — Internat. R. **9**: 42.
— Death of. (J. Bryce) Nation, **32**: 331. — Blackw. **129**: 674. — Same art. Ecl. M. **97**: 1.
— Endymion. Ed. R. **153**: 103. — Quar. **151**: 115. — Dub. R. **88**: 145. — (R. M. Milnes) Fortn. **35**: 66. Same art. Liv. Age, **148**: 617. Same art. Canad. Mo. **19**: 205. — (A. G. Sedgwick) Nation, **31**: 413. (J. MacCarthy) Am. Cath. Q. **6**: 112. — Appleton, **25**: 70. — Fraser, **102**: 705. — (M. W. Fuller) Dial (Ch.), **1**: 188.
— Florin; a Story. Lond. Soc. **40**: 313.
— French Estimate of. (A. Laugel) Nation, **27**: 209.
— French Popularity of. (A. Laugel) Nation, **30**: 345.
— Ministry of. (H. W. Lucy) Gent. M. n. s. **22**: 423.
— — Policy of. Fraser, **97**: 135.
— Political Adventures of. Fortn. **29**: 477, 691, 867. **30**: 250. Same art. Liv. Age, **137**: 276, 657. **138**: 14, 615.
— Political Career of. Brit. Q. **64**: 147.
— Two Papers on, by a Whig and a Tory. Contemp. **36**: 665.
— Wit and Humor of. (W. S. Sichel) Macmil. **44**: 139. Same art. Liv. Age, **150**: 55. Same art. Appleton, **26**: 164: 375.
— Worldly Wisdom of. Ecl. M. **96**: 329.
See Disraeli, B.
Beaconsfield, England, A Day at, 1857. Fraser, **56**: 33. Same art. Liv. Age, **54**: 429.
Beads, Ancient Drawings of. (J. Y. Akerman) Arch. **34**: 46.
Bead Manufactory at Venice. Am. J. Sci. **27**: 78.
Bead Medicine's Mystery; a Story. (L. W. Champney) Lippinc. **25**: 473.
Beadles. Lond. Soc. **2**: 71.
Beadon, Sir Cecil, Defense of. (J. M. Capes) Fortn. **8**: 180.
Beagle, Voyage of the. (Sir J. Barrow) Quar. **65**: 194.
— Voyages of, King and Fitzroy's. Ed. R. **69**: 467.
Beale, Anne. Gladys the Reaper. Liv. Age, **68**: 100.
Beale, Robert. So. M. **17**: 602.
Beale, Thurley, Singer, with portrait. Colburn, **167**: 425.
Beams and Joists, Wrought-Iron. (W. Fairbairn) J. Frankl. Inst. **64**: 53.
— Bars, etc., Cohesive Strength of. J. Frankl. Inst. **7**: 43, 49.
— Cast-Iron, Experiments on Strength of. (T. J. Cram) J. Frankl. Inst. **22**: 153.
— Deflection of, under transverse Strains. (W. A. Norton) Ecl. Engin. **3**: 70.
— Formula for normal Stress of. (G. F. Swain) Ecl. Engin. **23**: 63.
— Iron, Experiments on Wrought. (T. Davies) J. Frankl. Inst. **63**: 271.
— — Strength and best Forms of. J. Frankl. Inst. **13**: 202, 261, 325, 378. **14**: 26.
— Lattice, Strain upon Diagonals of. (W. T. Doyne) J. Frankl. Inst. **55**: 224, 294.
— of uniform Resistance. (S. W. Robinson) Ecl. Engin. **16**: 199.
— of uniform Strength. J. Frankl. Inst. **73**: 109.
Beams, Problems on. J. Frankl. Inst. **75**: 256.
— — on open built. (D. Wood) J. Frankl. Inst. **74**: 385.
— Strength of. (W. H. Barlow) J. Frankl. Inst. **62**: 4, 73. **65**: 296. — (B. Baker) Ecl. Engin. **23**: 444.
— Theory of continuous. (J. P. Frizell) J. Frankl. Inst. **94**: 39, 122, 171, 249.
Beam Trusses, Economical Construction of. (G. S. Morrison) J. Frankl. Inst. **86**: 99-394. **87**: 34.
Beaminster, England, Dissenting Church at. Cong. M. **18**: 713. **19**: 269.
Bean, Col. Ellis P. De Bow, **14**: 46.
Bear, The. (W. E. Simmons, jr.) Pop. Sci. Mo. **6**: 281.
— Encounter with a. Chamb. J. **30**: 365.
— Grizzly. J. Frankl. Inst. **2**: 178.
— — Adventure with a. Chamb. J. **22**: 42.
Bears. (D. Piatt) Galaxy, **11**: 363. — All the Year, **4**: 390. — House. Words, **7**: 577. — Liv. Age, **29**: 19.
— and Bear-Hunting. (T. B. Thorpe) Harper, **11**: 591. — (C. Wright) Am. Natural. **2**: 121.
— and Wolves, British. (W. B. Dawkins) Pop. Sci. R. **10**: 241.
— History and Habits of. Harper, **2**: 546.
— Natural History and geographical Distribution of. (A. L. Adams) Pop. Sci. R. **13**: 250.
— Polar. Penny M. **2**: 100.
— Tame, in Sweden. (J. Wager) Sup. Pop. Sci. Mo. **2**: 479.
Bear-Baiting and Mr. Martin's Bill. Blackw. **17**: 600.
Bear-Dancing at Rome. Penny M. **14**: 52, 62.
Bear-Hunt, The; a Poem. (A. Lincoln) Potter Am. Mo. **6**: 190.
— in the Himalayas. Temp. Bar, **19**: 229.
— in Sweden. (A. Gülbrandson) Putnam, **15**: 265.
Bear-Hunting. Blackw. **27**: 807. **28**: 1. — Chamb. J. **39**: 62. **51**: 131.
— in Canada. Blackw. **32**: 260.
— in India. Fraser, **46**: 373.
— in Lithuania. Penny M. **6**: 27.
— Metaphysics of. (C. Winterfeld) Am. Whig, **2**: 171.
— in the South. (J. Gordon) Scrib. **22**: 857.
Bear-Skin, The; a Tale. Chamb. J. **15**. 131.
Bear-Steak; a Gastronomic Adventure. Chamb. J. **16**: 10.
Bear's Grease, Trip in Search of. Chamb. J. **23**: 300.
Bearbrook Archives. (J. P. Quincy) Putnam, **5**: 299.
Bear-Valley Coal Basin, and Bear-Mountain Railroad. (T. E. Nichols) Hunt, **14**: 141.
Beard, C., Sermons by. (F. P. Cobbe) Theo. R. **12**: 292.
Beard, Ithamar W., with portrait. Dem. R. **41**: 242.
Beard, J. R., Sermons. Chr. Exam. **12**: 223.
— Nine Lectures on Owenism. Chr. Exam. **28**: 255.
Beard, W. H., and his Paintings. Art J. **30**: 321.
Beard's Theater of God's Judgment. Blackw. **8**: 496.
Beards. (J. Waters) Knick. **35**: 352, 445, 495. — (W. Collier) Bentley, **11**: 575. — Ev. Sat. **11**: 66, 439. — Chamb. J. **38**: 308. — Irish Q. **8**: 1194. **9**: 282. — Once a Week, **16**: 189. — Penny M. **3**: 367. — Westm. **62**: 48. Same art. Ecl. M. **33**: 377. Same art. Liv. Age, **42**: 304. — (T. Robinson) St. James, **48**: 378.
— and the Hair. Temp. Bar, **3**: 247.
— and Moustaches. All the Year, **23**: 510.
— Concerning. (A. K. H. Boyd) Fraser, **73**: 306.
— of our Fathers. Chamb. J. **27**: 369.
— Thoughts on. Blackw. **34**: 670.
See Hair.
Bearer of Dispatches in London. (T. S. Fay) Lippinc. **14**: 370.
Béarnais Sketch. Once a Week, **15**: 569, 611.
Beast, Name and Number of the. (A. Flemming) Cong. R. **7**: 31.
— Number of. (J. T. Holly) Am. Church R. **31**: 284 — (E. S. Wilson) Am. Church R. **27**: 428.

Beasts of Burden. Chamb. J. **40**: 302.
Beata; or, What's in a Name? Blackw. **126**: 31–657.
Beating the Bounds. Chamb. J. **20**: 49. — Am. Arch. **10**: 64.
Beatitude in Human Nature. (A. F. Hunt) Cath. World, **27**: 533.
Beatitudes, The. (C. Stothard) Cath. World, **30**: 713.
Beatrice; a Verse-Drama. Dub. Univ. **66**: 533, 671. **67**: 110.
Beatrice and Angelo; a Poem. (H. Hogg) Hogg, **11**: 21.
Beatrice Boville; or, Pride *versus* Pride. (L. de la Ramé) Bentley, **49**: 641. Same art. Broadw. **5**: 1, 155.
Beatrice Cenci. (S. M. B. Piatt) Overland, **7**: 68.
Beatrice di Tenda; a Tale. Broadw. **4**: 47.
Beatrice's Dream; a Theological Argument. Temp. Bar, **43**: 539.
Beatrice's Mirror. (Mrs. A. D. Perkins) O. & N. **1**: 493.
Beattie, George. Cornh. **25**: 453. Same art. Liv. Age, **113**: 431. Same art. Ev. Sat. **12**: 514.
Beattie, James. (G. Gilfillan) Ecl. M. **29**: 405. — Blackw. **128**: 17. — (T. S. Perry) Atlan. **46**: 810.
— Bower's Life of. Ecl. R. **1**: 172.
— Forbes's Life of. (J. Foster) Ecl. R. **5**: 1, 112. — (F. Jeffrey) Ed. R. **10**: 171. — Chr. Obs. **6**: 389, 466, 473, 513.
— Life and Poetry of. Lond. M. **5**: 313.
Beatty, Maj. Erkuries, Diary of, 1786–87. M. Am. Hist. **1**: 175–432.
Beatty, Wm., Journal of, 1776–80. Hist. M. **11**: 79, 147.
Beau, The; a Tale. (J. H. D. Zschokke) Ecl. M. **40**: 238.
Beau Brummell. *See* Brummell.
Beaucaire, Fair at. Sharpe, **24**: 264.
Beauchamp; or, the Error. (G. P. R. James) Colburn, **74**: 535. **75**: 94–420. **76**: 69–385. **77**: 63–422. **78**: 44–299.
Beauchamp & Co.; a Story. (Mrs. H. Martin) Fraser, **104**: 84.
Beauchamp's Career. (G. Meredith) Fortn. **22**: 249–676. **23**: 132–739. **24**: 123–869.
Beauchamp Family, of England. Temp. Bar, **17**: 332.
Beauchampe. (W. G. Simms) Sharpe, **1**: 17–105.
Beauclercs, The, Father and Son. (C. Clarke) Fraser, **72**: 565, 692. **73**: 104–781. **74**: 112, 212, 385.
Beauclerk, Topham. Cornh. **31**: 281.
Beaudrot; a Poem. (T. D. English) So. Lit. Mess. **29**: 410.
Beaufort, Cardinal, Jewels pledged to, 17 Henry VI. (J. Caley) Arch. **21**: 34.
Beaufort, Margaret, Mother of Henry VII., Life of. Dub. R. **8**: 130.
Beauharnais, Prince Eugene de, Memoirs of. Liv. Age, **60**: 323.
Beaulieu, Summer Day at. (E. Walford) Once a Week, **17**: 413.
— Tragedy at. (M. B. Williams) Lakeside, **7**: 210.
Beaumanoir, Mareschal de, Monument to. (M. d'Auvergne) Arch. **6**: 144.
Beaumarchais, P. A. C. de. (W. Sargent) No. Am. **84**: 122. — (Lady C. C. Jackson) Temp. Bar, **61**: 176. — Blackw. **105**: 30.
— and his Times. Quar. **135**: 201. Same art. Liv. Age, **119**: 67. — Temp. Bar, **43**: 604. Same art. Ecl. M. **84**: 731. — Bentley, **39**: 171, 293. — Brit. Q. **23**: 519. Same art. Ecl. M. **38**: 394. Same art. Liv. Age, **50**: 193. — New Q. **5**: 381.
— and Sophie Arnould. Westm. **42**: 146. Same art. Ecl. M. **3**: 271.
— Fifteen Louis-d'Or. Ev. Sat. **7**: 129, 181.
— Life of. Am. Bibliop. **7**: 155.
— Loménie's Life of. (J. Bonner) Harper, **14**: 76. — Ed. R. **104**: 453. — Fraser, **49**: 330.
— the Merchant. (J. Bigelow) Hours at Home, **11**: 160.
Beaumarchais, P. A. C. de, Passage in Life of. (G. Hogarth) Bentley, **1**: 233.
— Plan to aid the American Colonies. (G. C. Genet) M. Am. Hist. **2**: 663.
— Sketch of. Am. Mo. M. **8**: 384.
Beaumaris Castle, Anglesey. Penny M. **5**: 51.
Beaumont, Christophe de, Archbishop of Paris. (A. G. Knight) Month, **40**: 198, 370. **41**: 36.
Beaumont, F., and Fletcher, J. (C. C. Clarke) Gent. M. n. s. **7**: 27. — (J. Pyne) Nat. Q. **33**: 302. — (E. P. Whipple) Am. Whig R. **4**: 68, 131. — Liv. Age, **14**: 385. — Fraser, **22**: 189. **41**: 321. — Ecl. M. **12**: 174. — Temp. Bar, **42**: 460.
— — and Cervantes. Fraser, **91**: 592.
— — and their Contemporaries. (W. Spalding) Ed. R. **73**: 209.
— — Dyce's edition. Ed. R. **86**: 42. — Quar. **83**: 377.
Beaumont, Joseph, an overlooked Poet. (F. M. Bird) Hours at Home, **11**: 560.
— Psyche. Retros. **11**: 288. **12**: 229.
Beauregard, Gen. G. T. Service in West Tennessee, 1862. (T. Jordan) So. Hist. Pap. **8**: 404.
Beausoleil, Baroness de, Sketch of. (S. B.-Gould) Once a Week, **16**: 417.
Beauties of Nature Penny M. **1**: 150.
Beauties, Professional. Lond. Soc. **36**: 449.
Beautiful, The. (J. G. Whittier) Hogg, **2**: 326.
— and the Picturesque. Brit. Q. **8**: 498.
— and the Pretty. (F. T. Palgrave) F. Arts Q. **1**: 308.
— Function of. (S. W. McDaniel) Mo. Rel. M. **48**: 310.
— Love of. (H. Giles) Chr. Exam. **84**: 330. — (J. Swett) Pioneer, **1**: 207.
— Natural Philosophy of. Art J. **4**: 215.
— Perception of. (Mrs. L. H. Sigourney) Godey, **20**: 9.
— Plea for. Chamb. J. **16**: 161.
— Tyler's Theory of. So. R. n. s. **15**: 243.
— Witness of Artists to. (J. B. Atkinson) Portfo. **5**: 117, 131.
Beautiful Arts, Claims of. Dem. R. **3**: 253.
Beautiful Lucy Parson. Lond. Soc. **2**: 223.
Beautiful Miss Johnson. Lond. Soc. **12**: 56–355.
Beautiful Miss Roche; a Story. (Mrs. G. W. Godfrey) Temp. Bar, **61**: 344, 501. **62**: 75. Same art. Liv. Age, **149**: 403.
Beautiful Perdita, The. St. James, **5**: 149.
Beautiful Women. (F. G. Fairfield) Appleton, **16**: 328.
Beauty. (F. W. Winthrop) No. Am. **7**: 1. — (M. B. Hope) Princ. **21**: 251. — Blackw. **5**: 564. **14**: 672. — (J. B. Atkinson) Good Words, **21**: 638. — Hesp. **1**: 481. — (T. C. Henley) Peop. J. **11**: 353. — Portfo. (Den.) **13**: 148, 220.
— Aids to. Cornh. **7**: 391, 738.
— Alison on. (F. Jeffrey) Ed. R. **18**: 1.
— Alison explained by Jeffrey. Blackw. **13**: 385.
— and Art. (W. Barnes) Macmil. **4**: 126. — (J. H. Pollen) Month, **3**: 42, 359.
— and the Beast. (W. R. S. Ralston) 19th Cent. **4**: 990. — (B. Taylor) Atlan **17**: 13.
— and the Beast; a Story. (A. I. Thackeray) Cornh. **15**: 676. Same art. Ev. Sat. **3**: 801. **4**: 1.
— and the Beast; a Story. Sharpe, **52**: 180.
— and the Beast; a Story. (F. E. Leupp) Galaxy, **22**: 209.
— and a Bracelet. Colburn, **149**: 367–634.
— and Duty. (H. Holbeach) St. Paul's, **12**: 73.
— and other Conditions of Face. Lond. M. **7**: 526.
— and Realism. (E. J. Poynter) Fortn. **15**: 709.
— and Ugliness of Person. Cornh. **14**: 334.
— and Utility. (W. E. Gladstone) Ecl. M. **86**: 291.
— Art in Aid of. St. James, **10**: 466.
— Art of. (M. E. Haweis) Ecl. M. **78**: 472.
— Art of preserving. (A. H. Everett) No. Am. **32**: 444.

Beauty, Blackie on. Tait, n. s. **25**: 245.
— Divine Love of, in Creation. (D. Olmsted) New Eng. **16**: 770.
— Evolution of. (F. T. Mott) Sup. Pop. Sci. Mo. **3**: 361.
— Female, How to get and keep. (R. Tomes) Harper, **37**: 116.
— — Criticism on. Mus. **7**: 405.
— Few Words on. Art J. **8**: 4.
— Gladstone on Marketable. Liv. Age, **142**: 765.
— Greek and Christian Views of. (R. St. J. Tyrwhitt) Contemp. **37**: 474. Same art. Ecl. M. **94**: 587.
— Hay's new Theory of. Chamb. J. **15**: 266.
— Hay's Geometric Principle of. Mo. R. **162**: 390.
— Human. (W. M. Fernald) Mo. Rel. M. **46**: 264.
— Ideal. Chamb. J. **13**: 257, 294.
— in Common Life. (A. D. Mayo) Univ. Q. **33**: 389.
— in what does it consist? (F. Jeffrey) Ed. R. **7**: 307.
— Jeffrey's Theory of. Westm. **53**: 1.
— Moral Uses of. (M. Tarver) West. J. **14**: 1.
— Nature of. (H. N. Day) Am. Presb. R. **16**: 391.
— New Theory of. Chamb. J. **15**: 266.
— of Sounds and Colors. Blackw. **4**: 178.
— of the Universe; a Poem. So. R. n. s. **9**: 205.
— of Vicq D'Azir. (L. de la Ramé) Bentley, **51**: 440.
— Personal. Dub. Univ. **81**: 301.
— — and Moral. Tait, n. s. **23**: 402.
— — in different Countries. Penny M. **14**: 475.
— Power of; a Syrian Tale. Lond. M. **10**: 165. Same art. Mus. **6**: 210.
— Principle of, in ancient Sculpture. (J. M. Tracy) Western, **4**: 78.
— Real and Ideal. Blackw. **74**: 727.
— Reason and, Relations of. (E. Gurney) Mind, **4**: 482.
— Religion of. Dial, **1**: 17.
— Sense of. (W. M. Reily) Ref. Q. **28**: 395.
— transformed. (Mrs. C. L. Hentz) Godey, **21**: 194.
Beauty Draught; a Tale. Blackw. **48**: 795.
Beauvais. Penny M. **3**: 67.
Beaux, The. (Miss Leslie) Godey, **24**: 19–259.
Beaver, Capt. Philip, Life of. (R. Southey) Quar. **41**: 375. Same art. Liv. Age, **12**: 268. — Mo. R. **119**: 189. — Mus **16**: 127.
Beaver, The. (J. D. Godman) J. Frankl. Inst. **4**: 98, 160, 227. — Chamb. J. **50**: 598. — Penny M. **2**: 129.
— Early Notices of. (D. Wilson) Canad. J. n. s. **4**: 359.
— Fabulous History of. (J. D. Godman) J. Frankl. Inst. **4**: 227.
Beavers. All the Year, **20**: 176. — Liv. Age, **24**: 519.
— and Beaver-Meadows in North America. Penny M. **9**: 103.
— of Bute. Chamb. J. **55**: 95.
Beavis, Richard, Works of. Art J. **29**: 97.
Beche-de-Mer, The. Chamb. J. **54**: 15.
Becher, Lady. Fraser, **97**: 477. — (Miss O'Neill) Eng. Dom. M. **14**: 129.
Bechuana Proverbs, Riddles and Tales. Hogg, **9**: 139.
Beck, J. T. of Tübingen, his Views of the Bible. (J. H. W. Stuckenberg) Luth. Q. **1**: 111.
Becker, W. A. Gallus. Dub. R. **17**: 69.
— Gallus and Charicles. Quar. **79**: 336. — (A. P. Peabody) No. Am. **66**: 401.
Becket, Thomas à, St. Dub. R. **38**: 355. — (H. W. Torrey) No. Am. **64**: 118. — No. Brit. **6**: 456. — Ecl. M. **8**: 229. — (W. G. Read) U. S. Cath. M **2**: 193. — Ecl. R. **111**: 255. Same art. Liv. Age, **65**: 479.
— and his Biographers. (E. A. Freeman) Nat. R. **10**: 321.
— De Vere on. (J. McCarthy) Cath. World, **23**: 848.
— Froude on. (J. Gerard) Month, **32**: 1. — (E. A. Freeman) Contemp. **31**: 821. **32**: 116, 473. **33**: 213. Same art. Liv. Age, **137**: 150, 323. **138**: 108, 139. — Dub. R. **82**: 292.
— Legend of. Fraser, **20**: 389, 560.
Becket, Thomas a, St., Letters relating to. Chr. Rem. **3**: 444. **5**: 559.
— Life of. Dub. R. **3**: 313. **48**: 253. **62**: 60, 458. — Dub. Univ. **56**: 661.
— Life and Times of. (J. A. Froude) 19th Cent. **1**: 547, 843. **2**: 15–669. Same art. Liv. Age, **134**: 3–540. **135**: 32, 723. Same art. Ecl. M. **89**: 168, 294, 480, 610. **90**: 40.
— Literature of. (J. C. Robertson) Contemp. **1**: 270.
— Murder of. (J. A. Froude) 19th Cent. **2**: 669. Same art. Liv. Age, **135**: 410. — Quar. **93**: 349. Same art. Liv. Age, **39**: 515. Same art. Ecl. M. **31**: 28.
Beckett's Troth; a Poem. (R. Buchanan) Once a Week, **10**: 573.
Beckford, William. (O. Tiffany) No. Am. **90**: 297. — Chamb. J. **31**: 93. — Liv. Age, **60**: 406.
— and Fonthill. Chamb. J. **2**: 101.
— and the Literature of Travel. (H. T. Tuckerman) So. Lit. Mess. **16**: 7.
— Conversations with. Colburn, **72**: 18–516.
— Memoirs of. Tait, n. s. **26**: 76.
— Recollections of, with portrait. (C. Redding) Colburn, **71**: 143, 302.
— Travels. Quar. **51**: 426.
— Vathek. (P. Q. Keegan) Colburn, **160**: 674.
Beckwourth, J. P., Indian Scout. (T. B. Thorpe) Harper, **13**: 455.
Becon, Thomas. (A. Alexander) Princ. **5**: 504.
— Memoir of. Cong. M. **10**: 457.
Becquerel, Antoine César. Nature, **17**: 244. Same art. Liv. Age, **136**: 574.
Bed for Invalids, Arnott's Hydrostatic. J. Frankl. Inst. **15**: 61.
— Going to. (M. Browne) Ev. Sat. **13**: 249.
— — Old Customs in. All the Year, **33**: 274.
Beds. All the Year, **17**: 41. — Chamb. J. **36**: 260.
— and Bedsteads. St. James, **17**: 91.
Beddoes, T. L. (K. Hillard) Victoria, **22**: 352. — (K. Hillard) Lippinc. **12**: 550. — (M. Collins) Dub. Univ. **94**: 513. — (T. F. Kelsall) Fortn. **18**: 51. — Ecl. M. **24**: 446.
— Bride's Tragedy. Blackw. **14**: 723. — Lond. M. **7**: 169.
— Poems. Liv. Age, **31**: 312.
— Stock's Life of. Ecl. R. **13**: 491.
Bede, Venerable. Dub. R. **36**: 290. — (G. Allen) Gent. M. n. s. **25**: 84. — Putnam, **10**: 40.
— and his Works. (F. M. Hubbard) No. Am. **93**: 36.
— Ecclesiastical History. Chr. Rem. **11**: 331. — Ecl. R. **94**: 192. — Princ. **42**: 401.
Bedell, William, Bp. of Kildare. Dub. R. **15**: 415.
— Account of. Chr. Obs. **15**: 271, 339, 415.
— Mason's Life of. Ecl. R. **78**: 217.
Bedfellows, Some strange. All the Year, **40**: 485.
Bedford. Penny M. **8**: 181.
Bedford and Bath Springs. (H. H. Hayden) Am. J. Sci. **19**: 97.
Bedford, John, 4th Duke of, Correspondence of. Ecl. R. **77**: 55. **85**: 221. — Dub. Univ. **23**: 354. — Mo. R. **160**: 75. **162**: 33.
Bedford Level, The great. Chamb. J. **10**: 213. — Liv. Age, **20**: 81. — Penny M. **3**: 133.
Bedford, Mass., Ministers of. Am. Q. Reg. **11**: 387.
Bedford Park, London. (M. D. Conway) Harper, **62**: 481. — Chamb. J. **58**: 839.
Bedouin Arabs. (J. A. Johnson) Hours at Home, **10**: 228. — Penny M. **3**: 227.
— and Wahabys. Ed. R. **52**: 72. — Mo. R. **122**: 213.
— Lady Blunt's. (F. W. Holland) Unita. R. **12**: 431.
— Life among. (A. Rhodes) Galaxy, **22**: 43.
— Notes on. (J. L. Burckhardt) Am. Bib. Repos. **4**: 711.
— of the Arabian Desert. (R. D. Upton) Fraser, **95**: 432.

Bee, The. Hogg, 8: 309, 358.
— Endocranium and Maxillary Suspensorium. (G. Macloskie) Am. Natural. 15: 353.
— Honey. (Mrs. Griffiths) No. Am. 27: 338. — Westm. 7: 362. — Mus. 11: 123. — (J. C. V. Heuvel) Am. J. Sci. 3: 79.
— — and Bee Books. (T. James) Quar. 71: 1. Same art. Ecl. Mus. 1: 354.
— — and Hive. (Mrs. S. B. Herrick) So. R. n. s. 14: 163.
— — Bevan's. (A. R. Wallace) Nature, 3: 385.
— — Cells of, Economy and Symmetry of. (C. Wright) Math. Mo. 2: 304.
— — Sting of. Pop. Sci. Mo. 14: 635.
— — Tongue of. (A. J. Cook) Am. Natural. 14: 271.
— — Tongue and Glands of. (J. Spaulding) Am. Natural. 15: 113.
Bee Culture. Land We Love, 6: 390.
— Modern. (M. Howland) Harper, 61: 777.
— Principles of. (F. W. Vogel) Am. Natural. 5: 17.
Bee-Hives. Chamb. J. 43: 456.
— Temperature of, in Winter. Liv. Age, 13: 11.
— Ventilation of. Liv. Age, 42: 366.
Bee-Hunt, The. Knick. 42: 368.
Bee-Hunting. (R. E. Robinson) Scrib. 21: 201.
— and Bee-Keeping in America. Penny M. 7: 146.
— in Australia. Once a Week, 18: 165.
Bee-Keepers, Hints to. Chamb. J. 54: 301.
Bee-Keeping. (J. Hunter) Good Words, 17: 846. — Eng. Dom. M. 18: 178, 241. 21: 71. 26: 187. — (E. Jesse) Once a Week, 15: 442. — Penny M. 3: 11.
Bees. (S. B. Herrick) Scrib. 15: 100. — All the Year, 12: 133, 222. — Chamb. J. 35: 73. 47: 629. — Ev. Sat. 15: 499. — J. Frankl. Inst. 7: 36, 81. — Once a Week, 12: 187. — Putnam, 8: 268.
— Among the Honey-Makers. (H. E. Prescott) Atlan. 16: 129.
— and the Art of Queen-Making. (W. Leitch) Good Words, 2: 443.
— and Bee-Keeping. Lond. Q. 26: 100.
— and Bee-Hives. Good Words, 1: 292.
— and their Counterfeits. (H. N. Humphreys) Intel. Obs. 1: 165.
— and Flowers, Müller on. Nature, 13: 10.
— and Wild Honey. Chamb. J. 36: 408. Same art. Ecl. M. 55: 443.
— and Wasps, Habits of. (Sir J. Lubbock) Nature, 9: 408.
— — and Ants. (Sir J. Lubbock) Nature, 13: 37.
— Beautiful exotic. (H. N. Humphreys) Intel. Obs. 1: 334.
— Brazilian Species of. (H. Müller) Nature, 10: 31.
— Curiosities of. Belgra. 21: 491.
— Economy of Time practiced by. (A. S. Wilson) Good Words, 22: 684.
— Gossip about. Once a Week, 26: 431.
— Home of. (A. S. Packard, jr.) Am. Natural. 1: 364, 596.
— Huber on. Ed. R. 9: 319. 25: 363. — Mo. R. 82: 494. — Ecl. R. 33: 352.
— in Greek Literature. (C. C. Felton) No. Am. 93: 137.
— in the Past and Present. (Lady Verney) Good Words, 14: 600.
— in Russia and Portugal. Penny M. 4: 190.
— Instincts and Habits of. (S. Hibberd) Intel. Obs. 6: 94. — (W. Dunbar) Ed. Philos. J. 3: 143. 4: 133.
— Natural History of, Bevan on. Lond. M. 18: 50.
— Observations on, Lubbock's. (A. S. Packard, jr.) Am. Natural. 10: 148.
— Parasites of. (A. S. Packard, jr.) Am. Natural. 2: 195.
— Pastoral. (J. Burroughs) Scrib. 18: 13.
— visiting Flowers. (F. Darwin) Nature, 9: 189.
— Why they work in the Dark. J. Frankl. Inst. 77: 389.
Bees, Wild. Chamb. J. 55: 735. — (J. Burroughs) Putnam, 16: 41.
— Zierzon's Theory of Sex-Propagation. Once a Week, 19: 373.
Bee and Beatrix. (L. B. Walford) Blackw. 119: 79. Same art. Liv. Age, 128: 717, 786.
Bee Darrell. Tinsley, 7: 690.
Bee in the Bonnet. (D. Cook) Once a Week, 3: 72.
Bee-Eaters, Wrynecks, Creepers, and Nuthatches. (W. J. Broderip) Fraser, 57: 342.
Bee-Flies, Larval Habits of. (C. V. Riley) Am. Natural. 15: 438.
Beech Lodge. Bentley, 42: 306.
Beech-Tree, The. (E. Jesse) Once a Week, 3: 388.
— History of a. (H. Coultas) Pop. Sci. R. 2: 365.
— of Aldershaw. Fraser, 52: 476.
— Uses of. Penny M. 12: 158, 173.
Beechdale. (M. V. Terhune) Galaxy, 5: 581, 729. 6: 69–634.
Beecher, Catherine Esther. Am. J. Educ. 28: 65.
— Letters on Religion. (A. Alexander) Princ. 8: 515.
— Religious Writings of. (E. C. Towne) Chr. Exam. 77: 301.
Beecher, Edward. Conflict of Ages. (G. E. Ellis) Chr. Exam. 55: 394. — (D. N. Lord) Theo. & Lit. J. 6: 580. 7: 50.
Beecher, H. W., with portrait. Appleton, 10: 400. — with portrait, Ecl. M. 74: 755. — (C. Cook) Putnam, 11: 504. — (H. R. Haweis) Contemp. 19: 317, 477. Same art. Liv. Age, 113: 195, 278.
— and H. W. Bellows, Discussion between. O. & N. 2: 87.
— and his Church. (L. C. Redden) Lakeside, 7: 251.
— as a Preacher. Dem. R. 37: 42.
— as a Social Force. (A. McE. Wylie) Scrib. 4: 751.
— Church of, at Brooklyn. (J. Parton) Atlan. 19: 38.
— Norwood. (O. A. Brownson) Cath. World, 10: 393.
— Political Position of, 1866. (T. G. Shearman) Nation, 3: 330.
— Preaching of. (T. Parker) Atlan. 1: 862.
— Sermons of. (J. M. Hoppin) New Eng. 29: 421.
— Theology of. Bost. R. 1: 129, 228.
— Trial of. (E. P. Buffett) Overland, 15: 188.
— — Beechers and the Tiltons. (E. I. Sears) Nat. Q. 29: 299.
Beecher, Lyman. (A. H. Guernsey) Harper, 30: 697. — (D. E. Snow) Cong. Q. 8: 359. — (J. F. Tuttle) Am. Presb. R. 12: 291. — Bost. R. 5: 531. — Ecl. R. 122: 1. — Nat. M. 1: 6.
— and Martin Luther. Hours at Home, 1: 59.
— Autobiography. (N. Porter) New Eng. 23: 354. — Chr. Exam. 79: 175.
— Letter to Dr. Woods. Spirit Pilg. 5: 493.
— Occasional Sermons. Chr. Mo. Spec. 10: 481. — Spirit Pilg. 1: 266.
— Recollections of. (C. E. Stowe) Cong. Q. 6: 221.
— Sermon at Litchfield. Chr. Mo. Spec. 2: 360.
— — at Salem. Chr. Mo. Spec. 1: 625. 2: 77, 193.
— — at Worcester. (J. Walker) Chr. Exam. 1: 48.
— Trial for Heresy. Chr. Exam. 19: 116. — Spirit Pilg 3: 17, 72, 181. — Chr. Mo. Spec. 7: 94–300.
— Views of Theology. Princ. 9: 216, 364.
Beecher Family. Fraser, 46: 518. Same art. Liv. Age, 35: 591.
Beecherism and its Tendencies. (O. A. Brownson) Cath. World, 12: 433.
— and Legalism. (T. Munnell) Chr. Q. 4: 21.
Beechey, F. W. Voyage to Pacific and Behring's Straits. (Sir J. Barrow) Quar. 45: 57. — Am. Q. 12: 87. — Ed. R. 53: 210. 78: 36. — Blackw. 30: 34. — Mo. R. 124: 601. — Nav. M. 2: 153.
Beechgrove Family. House. Words, 12: 289.

Beef, Exportation of, from the United States. (A. B. Allen) Harper, **61**: 93.
— Where it comes from. Lippinc. **24**: 573.
Beefsteaks. Once a Week, **13**: 461.
Beefsteak Club, of London. Temp. Bar, **38**: 399.
Beefsteak Clubs. Ev. Sat. **3**: 360.
— Sublime Society of Beefsteaks. Chamb. J. **46**: 353.
Beejapòre, Visit to the Ruins of. Bentley, **60**: 381.
Beekman, James W. (E. A. Duyckinck) M. Am. Hist. **1**: 653.
Beer. (S. G. Young) Galaxy, **23**: 62. — Chamb. J. **40**: 385.
— and Hops. All the Year, **36**: 180.
— and Temperance Problem. (C. Graham) Contemp. **30**: 72. Same art. Sup. Pop. Sci. Mo. **1**: 257.
— — in England. (A. Garfit) Contemp. **23**: 590.
— Antiquity of. Penny M. **1**: 3.
— Bitter, and Beer in general. Chamb. J. **32**: 235.
— Bottled, Who invented? Once a Week, **21**: 20.
— Brewing and Public Houses. Quar. **131**: 392.
— Drop of good. (H. Lake) Belgra. **19**: 62.
— Historical Notes on. Pract. M. **5**: 300.
— in Bavaria. Sharpe, **52**: 78.
— London Stout. Fraser, **50**: 513. Same art. Ecl. M. **35**: 57.
— Pasteur's Manufacture of. Nature, **6**: 418.
See Ale; Lager Beer; Malt Liquors.
Beer Act, 1830. Mo. R. **123**: 180.
Beer Bill, 1859, England. Ecl. R. **110**: 527.
Beer-Drinking, Headquarters of. (A. Ten Broeck) Atlan. **14**: 185.
— in the 16th Century. Penny M. **7**: 230.
Beer, Town of, England, Witches, Ghosts, and Smugglers of. Dark Blue, **4**: 41.
Beet Sugar. (T. P. Kettell) Hunt, **48**: 17. — Ed. R. **65**: 110.
— Crookes on. Nature, **3**: 4.
— in France. (J. Scoffern) Belgra. **8**: 241.
— Manufacture of. (D. L. Childs) No. Am. **48**: 415.
— Purification of. (E. Rousseau) Canad. J. n. s. **6**: 292.
Beethoven, L. van, with portrait. Appleton, **4**: 16. — with portrait, Peop. J. **10**: 35. — with portrait, Ecl. M. **77**: 630. — (H. H. Statham) Fortn. **33**: 375. — (Mrs. Ellet) Cath. World, **9**: 523, 607, 783. — (G. Hogarth) Colburn, **62**: 157. — (R. Lytton) Fortn. **18**: 19. — (T. Ross) Bentley, **23**: 115. — Argosy, **10**: 157. **13**: 431. — Bost. Q. **3**: 332. — Brit. Q. **55**: 27. — Eng. Dom. M. **3**: 530. — New Dom. **15**: 344. — Penny M. **9**: 14. — Tait, n. s. **25**: 205, 264.
— and his Works; a Study. (E. Dannreuther) Macmil. **34**: 193.
— Biographical Sketch of. Tait, n. s. **8**: 34.
— Centennial of. (R. L. Collier) O. & N. **3**: 367.
— Childhood and Youth of. (A. W. Thayer) Atlan. **1**: 847.
— Drama on. (S. Hale) O. & N. **8**: 378.
— Gossip about. Ecl. M. **21**: 274.
— Letters of. (H. R. Haweis) Contemp. **2**: 357. — (H. J. Warner) Nation, **2**: 756.
— Life of. (J. W. Webster) No. Am. **53**: 289. — (R. G. White) Am. Whig R. **3**: 641. — For. Q. **8**: 439. — Westm. **32**: 327.
— Lives and Letters of. Ed. R. **138**: 366. Same art. Liv. Age, **119**: 483.
— Loves of. Once a Week, **12**: 470.
— Moschele's Life of. Mo. R. **154**: 375.
— Music of. (W. T. Harris) Western, **1**: 218.
— Sketch of. St. James, **6**: 366.
— Sonata Appassionata. (C. W. Chapman) J. Spec. Philos. **9**: 61.
— — in F Minor. (A. B. Marx) J. Spec. Philos. **4**: 274.
Beethoven, L. van, Symphony of, Third. (C. L. Bernays) J. Spec. Philos. **2**: 241.
— — Sixth. (W. T. Harris) Western, **1**: 381.
— — Seventh. (C. W. Chapman) J. Spec. Philos. **2**: 37.
— Youth of. Ecl. M. **63**: 89.
Beetles. Chamb. J. **49**: 292. Same art. Ev. Sat. **12**: 575.
— Blister, Transformations and Habits of. (C. V. Riley) Am. Natural. **12**: 213, 282.
— Burying. (H. N. Humphreys) Recr. Sci. **1**: 307.
— Carpet. (J. A. Lintner) Am. Natural. **12**: 536.
— Classification of. (J. L. Leconte) Am. Natural. **8**: 385, 452.
— English and Tropical. (H. N. Humphreys) Intel. Obs. **3**: 1.
— Goldsmith, Habits of. (S. Lockwood) Am. Natural. **2**: 186.
— Hunting Amblychila. (F. H. Snow) Am. Natural. **11**: 731.
— Natural History of. Hogg, **8**: 56.
— Parasitic. (E. C. Rye) Intel. Obs. **10**: 409.
— Stag. Once a Week, **9**: 511.
— — Anatomy of. (A. Hammond) Pop. Sci. R. **20**: 14.
— Water, Dytiscus. (W. F. Cooper) Recr. Sci. **3**: 83.
— Whirligig. (J. Samuelson) Recr. Sci. **2**: 305.
Beetle Family, The. Chamb. J. **12**: 247.
Beetle-Hunting. Ev. Sat. **6**: 526.
Beffroy de Reigny, L. A. Cousin Jacques. All the Year, **45**: 232.
Before the Shrine; a Poem. (K. P. Osgood) Scrib. **4**: 346.
Before Sunrise; a Poem. (C. Thaxter) Atlan. **29**: 47.
Bega, Cornelius. Art J. **5**: 110, 131.
Bega, Sancta. (C. Camden) St. Paul's, **12**: 584.
Begare, Abbey of, Alien Cell of. (N. Carlisle) Arch. **16**: 326.
Beggar of Vernon. (R. Harrison) Belgra. **8**: 490.
Beggar's Legacy. (J. Engles) Blackw. **77**: 251.
Beggar's Soliloquy; a Poem. (G. Meredith) Once a Week, **4**: 378.
Beggar's Wallet. (Mrs. Gore) Tait, n. s. **1**: 233, 531. **2**: 17, 452, 668. **3**: 163, 445, 649. **4**: 221, 629.
Beggars. (C. A. Collins) Macmil. **5**: 210. — (T. Lee) Peop. J. **5**: 61. — Blackw. **77**: 251. — Fraser, **33**: 666.
— Amongst. Once a Week, **30**: 720.
— and Almsgivers. Colburn, **85**: 301.
— and Beggary. (J. C. Learned) Western, **3**: 511, 592.
— and Begging in America. Penny M. **6**: 322.
— Chinese. Once a Week, **29**: 283.
— Complaint of Decay of. (C. Lamb) Lond. M. **5**: 532.
— in Italy. Once a Week, **4**: 23.
— Plague of. Fraser, **37**: 395.
Beggars' Opera, Proposed Reform in. Blackw. **3**: 575.
Beggary, Few Words about. St. James, **12**: 242.
Beggee Jân. Penny M. **4**: 70.
Begging, Social Problem of. Chamb. J. **38**: 216.
— Trade of. Chamb. J. **32**: 333.
See Mendicancy.
Beginning and End. (P. Heyse) Ev. Sat. **7**: 111, 149.
Beginning and End of Mrs. Muggeridge's Wedding-Dinner. (M. Howitt) Howitt, **1**: 25.
Beginning Life; a Phantasy. Dub. Univ. **92**: 351.
Beginning well, Art of. Belgra. **27**: 239.
Beguinage of Ghent. Lippinc. **8**: 310.
Begumbagh; an Episode of the India Mutiny. Chamb. J. **46**: supp. 1.
Behavior in a Crowd. Lond. Soc. **38**: 74.
Behemoth and Leviathan in Job. (T. C. Porter) Mercersb. **5**: 75. — Ed. New Philos. J. **19**: 263.
Behind the Curtains. Chamb. J. **34**: 129.
Behind the Scenes. (T. C. Haliburton) Bentley, **8**: 458.
Behind the Scenes. (G. A. Sala) Belgra. **7**: 197.

Behind the Scenes. Galaxy, 13: 404.
Behind their Fans. (G. Droz) Lippinc. 15: 610.
Behind the Veil; anonymous Novel. Ev. Sat. 11: 246.
Behistun Rock and Inscription. (B. W. Savile) Chr. Obs. 76: 620.
Behmen, Jacob. *See* Boehme, Jacob.
Behn, Mrs. Aphra, and her Novels. Dub. Univ. 47: 536. Same art. Liv. Age, 49: 800.
— Dramatic Writings of. Retros. 17: 1.
— England's first Lady Novelist. St. James, 7: 351.
— Works of. Am. Bibliop. 4: 303.
Behnes, William. Cornh. 9: 688.
Behold, it was a Dream; a Tale. Temp. Bar, 36: 503.
Behring's Strait and Polar Basin. (Sir J. Barrow) Quar. 18: 431.
Being and Nothing. (D. A. Wasson) J. Spec. Philos. 2: 245.
— Principles of real. (F. Bayma) Cath. World, 18: 433, 577, 824. 19: 1, 173, 289.
— Purpose of. (R. Roberts) Ex. H. Lec. 18: 53.
"Being built," Shall we say? (F. E. Hall) Scrib. 3: 700.
Beirût, Journey from, to Aleppo. (W. M. Thomson) Bib. Sac. 5: 1.
— Visit to. Dub. Univ. 62: 222.
— Water-Works at. (J. C. Hurd) Ecl. Engin. 14: 119.
Beke, C. T. Origines Biblicæ. Quar. 52: 496.
Belatucader, Remarks on. (S. Pegge) Arch. 3: 101.
Belcher, Capt. Edward. Voyage round the World. Ecl. M. 1: 145. — Mo. R. 160: 468.
Belcher, Jonathan, Governor of Massachusetts, 1730. (J. B. Moore) Am. Q. Reg. 13: 441.
— Letters of, 1731-40. N. E. Reg. 19: 128.
Belcher, Joseph. N. E. Reg. 11: 335.
Belcher Family. N. E. Reg. 27: 239.
Belchertown, Mass., Historical Sketches of. (M. Doolittle) N. E. Reg. 2: 177.
Belfast, Me, Longevity in. N. E. Reg. 1: 73.
Belfrage, J., Memoir of. Cong. M. 7: 337.
Belfries, English, and Belgian Carillons. (H. R. Haweis) Contemp. 17: 41.
Belfront Castle; a Tale. Blackw. 55: 334.
Belgian Questions. (J. H. Fyfe) Macmil. 26: 70.
Belgiojoso, Princess, on Italy. (H. T. Tuckerman) Putnam, 14: 456.
Belgium. (J. Bowring) Howitt, 1: 174. — Dub. Univ. 20: 403. — Brit. & For. R. 3: 1. — New Eng. M. 4: 480. 7: 460. — Westm. 32: 357. — Fraser, 2: 604. 73: 795. — Dub. Univ. 17: 535. — Broadw. 8: 264. — Quar. 112: 379.
— and France, Home Colonies in. For. Q. 13: 132.
— — Reunion of. (T. P. Thompson) Westm. 11: 494.
— and Holland. Ed. R. 56: 412. — For. Q. 5: 222. — Dub. R. 5: 463.
— — Journey in, 1854. Art J. 6: 338.
— — Religious Condition of. (J. J. Tayler) Theo. R. 5: 91.
— and Holy Alliance. (T. P. Thompson) Westm. 15: 267.
— and the Holy See. Dub. R. 87: 399. — Month, 40: 103.
— and Western Germany, Mrs. Trollope's. Quar. 52: 203. — Mo. R. 134: 467.
— Art-Rambles in. Art J. 17: 209, 253, 277.
— Banking in. Bank. M. (L.) 17: 459.
— Belgians at Home. (H. T. Armfield) Argosy, 4: 230.
— Catholic Church in. *See* Roman Catholic Church.
— Clerical Party in. (E. de Laveleye) Fortn. 18: 503.
— Commerce and Manufactures of. Brit. & For. R. 7: 521.
— Commerce of. Brit. Q. 31: 375.
— Commercial Regulations of. Hunt, 8: 373.
— Commercial and Financial History of. (D. A. Wells) Nation, 14: 213.
— Constitutional Monarchy in. (T. J. Bennett) Brit. Q. 73: 56.
Belgium, Constitution of, and the Catholic Church. Dub. R. 56: 171.
— Days in. (A. Opie) Tait, n. s. 7: 177, 293.
— Education in. *See* Education in Belgium.
— Flemings and the Walloons of. (K. Blind) Fraser, 93: 69.
— Flemish Interiors. Dub. R. 41: 230.
— Fortnight in, June and July, 1863. (A. V. Kirwan) Fraser, 68: 335.
— Husbandry in. Chamb. J. 51: 216. Same art. Liv. Age, 121: 503.
— in 1848 and 1870. Macmil. 22: 435.
— Independence of, Importance of. (T. P. Thompson) Westm. 20: 125.
— Industrial and Moral State of. For. Q. 24: 75.
— Kings and great People of. Chamb. J. 25: 279.
— Leopold I., and the Duke of Brabant. Fraser, 48: 116.
— Les Braves Belges. (S. B. Wister) Lippinc. 8: 200.
— Literature of. Am. Ecl. 3: 146.
— Monetary Documents of. (G. Walker) Bank. M. (N. Y.) 32: 420, 692, 772.
— Notes on, 1841. (G. W. Hughes) J. Frankl. Inst. 32: 73, 154, 224, 298. — Penny M. 8: 322, 336, 351.
— Old Cities of. (J. E. Ritchie) Tinsley, 16: 25.
— Peasantry and Farms of. (T. E. C. Leslie) Fraser, 76: 679.
— Politics of, 1878. (E. de Laveleye) Fortn. 30: 191.
— Question of. Blackw. 31: 448.
— Railroads in, 1845. (J. Anderson) Ed. New Philos. J. 39: 302.
— Religious and Social Condition of, 1845. Dub. R. 19: 332.
— Religious Future of. Cong. 5: 712.
— Religious Processions in. (A. Storrs) Cath. World, 15: 546.
— Remarks on Holland and. Colburn, 29: 412.
— Revolution of 1830. (E. A. Grattan) No. Am. 54: 141. — For. Q. 6: 497. — Westm. 13: 378. 14: 161. 32: 357. — Mus. 18: 131. — Dub. Univ. 6: 570, 593.
— — White on. Mo. R. 137: 196.
— St. George's Saunter in, 1835. Mo. R. 140: 233.
— Seaside Towns of. Lond. Soc. 30: 47.
— since Revolution of 1830, Trollope on. Mo. R. 158: 437.
— Sketches and Studies from. Fraser, 52: 378, 651. 55: 94.
— State and Prospects of, 1834. Westm. 20: 433.
— Tennent's. Quar. 68: 1. — Mo. R. 154: 561.
— Territorial Dismemberment of. Brit. & For. R. 9: 555.
— Tour in. Dub. Univ. 48: 454.
— Trade and Manufactures of. (A. Jones) Hunt, 6: 409. 13: 327.
— Travels in. New Q. 5: 418.
— Treaty with. Hunt, 14: 564.
— under Leopold I. Lond. Q. 15: 346.
— Vagabondizing in. (M. Talbot) Harper, 17: 323.
— Wayside Pictures through. Bentley, 24: 128-568. 25: 57-624. 26: 35-145.
— Weights and Measures of. Hunt, 16: 303.
Belgrade and Stamboul. Month, 28: 321.
— From, to Constantinople overland. (H. Sandwith) Fraser, 94: 230. Same art. Liv. Age, 130: 741.
— From, to Samakov. (H. Sandwith) Fortn. 32: 879.
Belgravia, An Echo from. Victoria, 11: 500.
— out of Doors. Cornh. 5: 218.
— Prose Ballads of. Belgra. 1: 80, 336, 462. 2: 110.
Belief and Evidence. (W. Hincks) Canad. J. n. s. 10: 232.
— and Unbelief. (O. Dewey) Chr. Exam. 7: 345.
— — Barry and Wace on. Quar. 151: 128.
— Conditions of Religious. (J. H. Allen) Chr. Exam. 75: 1.
— Courage in. (D. A. Wasson) Chr. Exam. 74: 383.
— Development of. Westm. 97: 121.

Belief, Ethics of. (W. K. Clifford) Contemp. **29**: 289. — (H. W. Lucas) Month, **31**: 43, 190, 239. — (H. Wace) Contemp. **30**: 42.
— Fixation of. (C. S. Pierce) Pop. Sci. Mo. **12**: 1.
— Fundamental Laws of. (C. F. Thwing) Bib. Sac. **38**: 303.
— Grounds of. (J. E. Cabot) No. Am. **111**: 222. — (C. Hudson) Chr. Exam. **40**: 247. — (M. Hopkins) Princ. n. s. **7**: 19. — (G. P. Fisher) Nation, **30**: 452.
— Knowledge and. (D. G. Thompson) Mind, **2**: 309.
— Newman's Theory of. (L. Stephen) Fortn. **28**: 680, 792.
— Psychology of. (W. B. Carpenter) Contemp. **23**: 123.
— Responsibility of. (N. S. Richardson) Am. Church R. **15**: 392. — So. R. n. s. **9**: 497.
— Steps of, J. F. Clarke's. O. & N. **2**: 355.
— Unity amid Diversities of. (E. A. Park) Bib. Sac. **8**: 594.
See Faith.
Beliefs, Chaos of. Bost. R. **4**: 295.
— extinguished. All the Year, **23**: 558.
— Verification of. (H. Sidgwick) Contemp. **17**: 582.
Believing too much, Safety of. Chr. Disc. **1**: 433.
Belinda's Brother Jack; a Story. (A. de Bubna) Potter Am. Mo. **15**: 251.
Belinda Mason's Romance. (W. Spring) Dub. Univ. **85**: 100.
Belisarius, Life of. (R. M. Johnston) So. R. n. s. **4**: 357. — Mo. R. **119**: 274.
— and Marlborough. (J. W. Calcraft) Dub. Univ. **42**: 135.
— Was he blind ? Blackw. **61**: 606.
Belknap, Jeremy, Life of. (F. Parkman) Chr. Exam. **44**: 78.
— Papers of. (C. C. Smith) Unita. R. **7**: 604. — (G. W. Greene) Nation, **26**: 310.
Belknap, W. W., Secretary of War, Case of, 1876. (E. L. Godkin) Nation, **22**: 154, 172.
Belknap Genealogy. (W. I. Warren) N. E. Reg. **13**: 17.
Bell, Alexander G., and the Telephone. (E. E. Quimby) Nation, **29**: 279. *See* Telephone.
Bell, Andrew, and James Lancaster. Ecl. R. **81**: 249. — (R. Southey) Quar. **6**: 264.
— and Madras System of Instruction. Am. J. Educ. **10**: 467.
— Life of. Liv. Age, **4**: 145.
— Southey's Life of. Mo. R. **165**: 518.
Bell, Sir Charles. Fraser, **91**: 88. — Quar. **72**: 192.
— Bridgewater Treatise. Mo. R. **132**: 424.
— Essays of. Ecl. M. **2**: 289.
— Letters and Discoveries of. Ed. R. **135**: 394. Same art. Liv. Age, **113**: 451.
— Note concerning. (C. Bell) Fraser, **92**: 129.
— Pichot's Life of. Liv. Age, **63**: 255.
— Study of. (E. Taylor) Good Words, **12**: 309.
Bell, Currer. *See* Brontë, Charlotte.
Bell, Garvin M., with portrait. Hunt, **22**: 377.
Bell, Henry, the Engineer. St. James, **47**: 350.
Bell, Adm. Henry H. (E. A. Pollard) Galaxy, **6**: 598.
Bell, I. L., and Metallurgical Progress, with portrait. Pract. M. **5**: 33.
Bell, John, Address of. Niles's Reg. **48**: 229.
— Speech at Nashville, 1835. Niles's Reg. **48**: 331.
Bell, Samuel, Governor of New Hampshire, 1819. (J. B. Moore) Am. Q. Reg. **14**: 15.
Bell, Samuel D., Memoir of. (C. H. Bell) N. E. Reg. **23**: 249.
Bell, Thomas, Obituary of. Nature, **21**: 499.
Bell, Man in the. Portfo.(Den.) **31**: 185.
Bell of the Wanderers. (Miss Sanderson) Cath. World, **12**: 593.
Bells. (H. R. Haweis) Contemp. **13**: 177. Same art. Ecl. M. **76**: 658. Same art. Liv. Age, **104**: 753. Same art. N. Ecl. **6**: 441. — (J. H. Sniveley) Appleton, **11**: 43. — (H. Willis) Bentley, **9**: 90. — Argosy, **18**: 458. — Chamb. J. **24**: 87. Same art. Liv. Age, **46**: 700. — Chamb. J. **28**: 398. — Penny M. **3**: 404.
— and Chimes. (G. B. Griffith) Potter Am. Mo. **11**: 451.
— and Bell-Founders of Nottinghamshire. (W. P. W. Stiff) Reliquary, **13**: 81.
— Archæology of. (E. H. W. Dunkin) Antiquary, **2**: 260, 271. **3**: 13.
— Art in the Belfry. (L. Jewitt) Art J. **25**: 21–171.
— Bell Metal, and Bell Founding. Pract. M. **3**: 84, 207.
— Blessing of. Cong. **6**: 257.
— Change-ringing. Chamb. J. **54**: 731. Same art. Liv. Age, **137**: 247. — Ev. Sat. **9**: 286.
— Chat on. (M. Schele de Vere) Harper, **40**: 450.
— Church. (J. Piggot) Antiquary, **4**: 139. — Chamb. J. **47**: 266. Same art. Ecl. M. **75**: 108. Same art. Ev. Sat. **5**: 316. — Mo. Rel. M. **6**: 312. **7**: 211. – Quar. **95**: 308. Same art. Ecl. M. **34**: 155.
— — of Cornwall. (E. H. W. Dunkin) Reliquary, **14**: 8–203. **15**: 9–209. **16**: 35–220. **17**: 105. **18**: 99, 153.
— — of Derbyshire. (L. Jewitt) Reliquary, **13**: 1, 97, 171. **14**: 33–225. **15**: 53–241. **16**: 113, 193. **17**: 40, 112. **18**: 109.
— Charles Dickens on. (G. D. Cowan) Belgra. **28**: 380.
— Early, of Massachusetts. (E. H. Goss) N. E. Reg. **28**: 176, 279.
— Gossip about. Cath. World, **2**: 32. — Chamb. J. **42**: 414.
— History of. J. Frankl. Inst. **5**: 107.
— Notes on. Once a Week, **3**: 707.
— of Avignon; a Poem. Cath. World, **1**: 783.
— of Botreaux; a Legend. Blackw. **83**: 41. Same art. Liv. Age, **56**: 436.
— of Lynn; a Poem. (H. W. Longfellow) Atlan. **17**: 47.
— of Yarrick. Chamb. J. **57**: 217, 233, 250.
— Origin and History of. So. R. n. s. **22**: 367.
— Traditions of. Sharpe, **30**: 265. Same art. Ecl. M. **49**: 127.
— What can be said about. (H. R. Haweis) Good Words, **20**: 250, 309.
Bell-Animalcule. (J. Samuelson) Pop. Sci. R. **1**: 145.
Bell-Birds of America. (P. L. Sclater) Intel. Obs. **10**: 401.
Bell Founder; a Tale. Dub. Univ. **30**: 279.
Bell Foundry and Clock Factory. Penny M. **11**: 121.
Bell Metal. All the Year, **24**: 197. — Ev. Sat. **9**: 550.
Bell Ringer, The. Chamb. J. **55**: 7–42.
Bell Tower; a Tale. Putnam, **6**: 123.
— at Westminster Palace. (J. Hunter) Arch. **37**: 23.
Bell Voices. Chamb. J. **19**: 42.
Bella Donna; a Tale. (P. Fitzgerald) Dub. Univ. **61**: 273–666. **62**: 101–656.
Bellamar, Cave of, Cuba. (F. F. Cavada) Harper, **41**: 826.
Bellamy, George Anne, the Actress. Dub. Univ. **64**: 447, 559.
— and Peg Woffington. Temp. Bar, **52**: 316.
Bellamy, Dr. Joseph, Works of. (J. Woodbridge) Lit. & Theo. R. **2**: 58.
— True Religion. (L. Hart) Chr. Q. Spec. **2**: 397.
Bellarmine, Cardinal. (W. Dubberley) Month, **37**: 1, 153, 305.
— Birthplace of. (F. Goldie) Month, **22**: 36.
Bellay, Joachim de, Early French Poet. Lond. M. **5**: 231
Belle's Black Coachman; a Tale. Chamb. J. **49**: 744, 761.
Belle's Choice, The. Fraser, **32**: 610.

Belle of Belgravia. (G. W. Garrett) Dub. Univ. 80: 427, 557, 632. 81: 56–583.
Belle of Santa Cruz. Lond. Soc. 36: 30.
Belle Dame sans Merci; a Poem. (R. Bell) St. James, 10: 240.
Belle Prairie, British North America. Temp. Bar, 15: 544.
Belles Demoiselles Plantation. (G. W. Cable) Scrib. 7: 739.
Belles of Beechwood; a Tale. (H. L. Nicholson) St. James, 41: 293.
Belles of the Island, The. (Mrs. Bushby) Colburn, 119: 30–435. 120: 51.
Belleau, Remy, Early French Poet. Lond. M. 5: 331.
Bellefontaine Cemetery; a Poem. (E. Stagg) West. J. 10: 143.
Bellerophon. Blackw. 76: 256. — Overland, 2: 91.
Belles Lettres, Thoughts on. West. M. 2: 310.
Bellew, J. C. M., with portrait. Once a Week, 26: 101.
Belli, Giuseppe. (F. E. Trollope) Belgra. 42: 60.
— Sonnets in the Roman Dialect. Fortn. 21: 209.
Belligerent Claims and Neutral Rights. (Earl Airlie) Fortn. 27: 580.
Belligerent Rights, 1865. (H. W. Torrey) Nation, 1: 69.
Belligerents and Neutrals. Nation, 23: 69.
— Maritime Rights of. (W. T. Thornton) Macmil. 7: 231. — Fraser, 64: 375.
Belling the Cat. Tinsley, 13: 336.
Bellingham, Richard. (J. B. Moore) Am. Q. Reg. 14: 16.
— Letters to, 1668–69. N. E. Reg. 7: 186.
— Will of. N. E. Reg. 14: 237.
Bellingham, Mass., Ministers of. Am. Q. Reg. 8: 47.
Bellini, G. Westm. 31: 467. — Art J. 10: 65, 97.
— Romance of. (Mrs. Ellet) Cath. World, 6: 408.
Bellmanship, The; a Tale. Blackw. 46: 381.
Bellomont, Richard Coote, Earl of. (J. Colburn) N. E. Reg. 19: 235.
Bellot, J. René. Bentley, 38: 236. — Dub. Univ. 46: 712. Same art. Ecl. M 37: 240. — Liv. Age, 47: 176.
Bellows, Henry W., Discussion with H. W. Beecher. O. & N. 2: 87.
— on the Moral Government of God. New Eng. 6: 249.
— Sermons. (C. A. Bartol) Chr. Exam. 68: 221.
Bellows Nozzles, Experiments on Form of. (T. Ewbank) J. Frankl. Inst. 65: 339.
Beloit College. (A. L. Chapin) New Eng. 31: 334.
Beloochistan. Blackw. 82: 474.
— and Scinde, Pottinger's. Quar. 15: 85.
— Travels in. Mo. R. 83: 259.
Belsham, Thomas, Memoir of. (J. Walker) Chr. Exam. 15: 69.
— Philosophy of the Mind. Ed. R. 1: 475.
— Translation of Paul's Epistles. Quar. 30: 79.
Belt, Thomas, Naturalist in Nicaragua. Chamb. J. 51: 120. — Nature, 18: 570.
Belting. J. Frankl. Inst. 76: 34.
Belting Experience, A. Lond. Soc. 36: 435.
Belting Facts and Figures. (J. Spiers) Pract. M. 4: 153. — (J. H. Cooper) J. Frankl. Inst. 86: 173–382. 87: 40–377. 88: 23–382. 89: 26–324. 90: 33–377. 91: 17–317. 92: 36–389. 93: 32, 325. 94: 28–343. 95: 98, 323. 96: 233, 327. 408. 97: 401. 98: 254.
Belting Machinery. (R. Tyler) J. Frankl. Inst. 24: 245.
Belts. (A. Morin) J. Frankl. Inst. 38: 22.
— Adhesion of. (H. R. Towne) J. Frankl. Inst. 85: 89. — (J. H. Cooper) J. Frankl. Inst. 109: 414.
— Driving Power of. (J. H. Cooper) J. Frankl. Inst. 106: 308. 107: 309. — (R. Briggs) J. Frankl. Inst. 107: 374.
— or Straps, Efficiency of. (O. Reynolds) Ecl. Engin. 14: 357.
Belts, Theory of Tension of. (L. G. Franck) J. Frankl. Inst. 99: 321.
See Driving-Bands.
Belt Dynamometer, Siemens's. (R. Briggs) J. Frankl. Inst. 110: 1.
Beltane, the Druid Festival. (R. R. Macgregor) Belgra. 35: 426.
Belton Estate. (A. Trollope) Fortn. 1: 24–641. 2: 11–651. 3: 12–411. Same art. Liv. Age, 86: 1–593. 87: 17–608. 88: 11–112.
Beltrami, J. C., Pilgrimage in Europe and America. Quar. 37: 448.
Belvidere, Countess of. Chamb. J. 6: 324.
Belville, Va., Settlement of, 1785–95. Hesp. 3: 25–431.
Belvoir Castle. Antiquary, 3: 229. — Penny M. 8: 217.
Belzoni, Giovanni. Hogg, 8: 104.
— Discoveries in Egypt. (H. Salt) Quar. 24: 139. — Mo. R. 95: 77.
— Sepulcher of. Lond. M. 12: 609.
— Story of. House. Words, 2: 548. Same art. Liv. Age, 29: 173. Same art. Ecl. M. 23: 104.
Belzoni, Mrs. and Dr. Young Fraser, 9: 629.
Bem, General. Ecl. M. 23: 28.
— First Campaign in Transylvania. Brit. Q. 13: 1.
Bemis's Heights, N. Y., Visit to. Bost. Mo. 1: 505.
Ben; a Tale. (R. H. Davis) Putnam, 15: 163.
Ben's Bear. All the Year, 10: 493.
Ben's Beaver. All the Year, 12: 35.
Ben-na-Groich. Blackw. 45: 409.
Ben Nevis and Ben Muich Dhui. Blackw. 62: 149.
Ben Serraq. House. Words, 13: 4.
Benares. Macmil. 3: 58. — Penny M. 14: 401. — (H. M. Alden) Harper, 38: 750. — (F. Vincent, jr.) Scrib. 10: 182.
Bench, Pleasantries of the. Chamb. J. 7: 138, 167.
— and the Bar. Brit. & For. R. 6: 209.
— — of New York, Proctor's. (A. R. Macdonough) Nation, 12: 91.
See Bar and Bench.
Benchers. Chamb. J. 51: 601.
— of the Inner Temple. (C. Lamb) Lond. M. 4: 279.
Bendemann, Edward. Art J. 17: 229.
Bendish, Bridget. (T. H. Gill) Cong. 4: 594.
Benedetti, Count, Diplomatic Career of. (C. K. Adams) No. Am. 114: 233.
Benedict, St., of Nursia. Kitto, 29: 72, 293.
— and the Benedictines. (S. L. Caldwell) Bapt. Q. 10: 29. — (P. Schaff) Contin. Mo. 5: 451. — Ed. R. 89: 1. Same art. Ecl. M. 16: 433. Same art. Liv. Age, 20: 433. — Am. J. Educ. 24: 525. 26: 264.
— and the Monasteries. Univ. Q. 8: 221.
Benedict, David, his Life and Labors. (H. C. Graves) Bapt. Q. 10: 99.
Benedict, Erastus C. (G. F. Betts) M. Am. Hist. 6: 78.
Benedict, Sir Julius, A Morning with. (K. Field) Scrib. 13: 480.
Benedict Club. (R. Johns) Bentley, 3: 578.
Benedicta, Mary. (K. O'Meara) Cath. World, 13: 207.
Benedictine of Mount Etna. (J. Pardoe) Dub. Univ 22: 469.
Benedictines, The. (M. Kaeder) Cath. World, 31: 243.
— French. (Sir J. Stephen) Ed. R. 89: 1.
— in England. Lond. Q. 16: 313.
— of St. Maur. Dub. R. 21: 217.
— Return of, to Scotland. (R. Seton) Cath. World, 24: 131.
Benedictine Monastery on Monte Casino. Dem. R. 38: 56. *See* Monte Casino.
Benediction, The. (O. E. Daggett) Cong. Q. 11: 388.
— Apostolic. (J. W. Yeomans) Princ. 33: 286.
Benedictional of Athelwold. (J. Gage) Arch. 24: 1.
— of Archbishop Robert. (J. Gage) Arch. 24: 118.

Benedix, R. Ev. Sat. **15**: 501.
Benefactor, The. (B. S. Barclay) Godey, **25**: 34.
Benefactors. (W. Chambers) Chamb. J. **53**: 417.
— Public. (E. P. Peabody) Hunt, **36**: 659.
Beneficence the noblest Aim. (G. B. Ide) Chr. R. **16**: 524.
— Oppressiveness of vulgar. (F. Jacox) Colburn, **142**: 546.
— Systematic. (P. Bergstresser) Luth. Q. **6**: 117. — (J. S. Pendleton) Chr. R. **16**: 200.
Benefit of Clergy. (F. W. Rowsell) Stud. & Intel. Obs. **2**: 331. — All the Year, **43**: 448. — Belgra. **19**: 216. — Chamb. J. **44**: 244.
Benefit Societies. (Dr. Beard) Peop. J. **3**: 250, 327.
— Causes of their Failure. (Dr. Beard) Peop. J. **4**: 41, 97.
Beneke and German Pedagogy. Am. J. Educ. **24**: 49.
— Psychological and Pedagogical Views of. Am. J. Educ. **28**: 50.
Beneventum, Italy, Archiepiscopal Palace at. (M. P. Thompson) Cath. World, **27**: 234.
Benevolence. (J. Brazer) Chr. Exam. **13**: 137. — (A. Stevens) Am. Meth. M. **18**: 287. — Chr. Obs. **23**: 465, 529.
— and Modesty. So. Lit. Mess. **4**: 751.
— and Pauperism. (A. Lewis) Dark Blue, **2**: 205.
— and Selfishness. (J. Day) Am. Bib. Repos. 2d s. **9**: 1.
— as an Act of Worship. (H. S. DeForest) Cong. Q. **18**: 43.
— Christian. Danv. Q. **3**: 483. — Princ. **42**: 279.
— Ground and Nature of. (R. B. Thurston) Am. Presb. R. **19**: 328.
— Church's Philosophy of. Chr. R. **2**: 85.
— Disinterested, Genesis of. (P. Friedmann) Mind, **3**: 404. Same art. Pop. Sci. Mo. **13**: 735.
— Duty of. (L. Withington) Cong. R. **8**: 176.
— Motives to active. Chr. Mo. Spec. **4**: 617.
— of the Church. (A. C. Wedekind) Luth. Q. **5**: 451.
— Sensational. (R. Quiddam) St. James, **38**: 160.
— Systematic. (C. A. Stork) Luth. Q. **1**: 13. — (H. Harbaugh) Mercersb. **3**: 27. — (P. Schaff) Mercersb. **4**: 191, 209 — New Eng. **9**: 14.
— Theory and Practice of. Pamph. **13**: 391. **14**: 65. *See* Almsgiving; Philanthropy.
Benevolent Action, First Principles of. Lit. & Theo. R. **4**: 373.
Benevolent Effort, Hindrances to. Am. Q. Reg. **8**: 241.
Benevolent Efforts of the Age. Chr. Mo. Spec. **4**: 113.
Benevolent Institutions of United States. Am. Alma. **1836**: 154.
Benevolent Objects, Associations for. (J. Walker) Chr. Exam. **2**: 241.
Benevolent Operations of the Church. Chr. Mo. Spec. **4**: 522.
Benevolent Societies and Agents. Cong. Q. **3**: 182. — Chr. Q. Spec. **9**: 255.
— Officers and Table of. Am. Q. Reg. **2**: 51.
— Responsibility in Management of. (L. Bacon) New Eng. **5**: 28.
Benevolent Work of the Churches, Financial Aspects of. (C. Cushing) Cong. Q. **17**: 18.
Benezet, Anthony, Life of. Portfo.(Den.) **18**: 43.
— Memoir of. Ecl. R. **28**: 367.
Bengal, Agricultural Show in. Chamb. J. **41**: 308.
— Annals of. Ed. R. **129**: 200.
— Army of. Colburn, **112**: 1.
— as a Field of Missions. Hogg, **14**: 165.
— Census of, 1872. (H. Beverley) J. Statis. Soc. **37**: 69.
— Colebrooke's Remarks on. Ed. R. **10**: 27.
— Cooks and Cookery in. All the Year, **28**: 348.
— Cyclone Wave in. Nature, **15**: 261.
— Deville's Letters on. For. Q. **1**: 123.
— Domesday-Book of. (F. W. Rowsell) 19th Cent. **6**: 1033.
Bengal, Education in. (J. G. Palfrey) No. Am. **43**: 266. **45**: 254. — (M. B. Hope) Princ. **15**: 333. — (J. Walker) Chr. Exam. **21**: 21.
— — Popular. St. James, **5**: 483.
— Educational Question in. St. James, **29**: 604.
— English Administration in. Lond. Q. **30**: 426.
— Famine in, 1770. St. James, **22**: 281.
— — 1874. (H. Copinger) Colburn, **155**: 93.
— — Sir Cecil Beadon's Defense. (J. M. Capes) Fortn. **8**: 180.
— Hill Tribes of Chittagong. Chamb. J. **46**: 59.
— Large and small Game of, Baldwin's. Dub. Univ. **89**: 408.
— History of, Stewart's. Ecl. R. **19**: 140.
— Indigo-Planting in, and the Breach-of-Contract Bill, Fraser, **65**: 610.
— Magistrate of. All the Year, **22**: 87.
— Mutiny in, 1857. Blackw. **82**: 372. Same art. Liv. Age, **55**: 321.
— Peasant Life in. (J. T. Wheeler) Macmil. **42**: 211. Same art. Liv. Age, **146**: 347. Same art. Ecl. M. **95**: 400.
— Planters and Ryots in. Nat. R. **14**: 114.
— Rail, Road, and River in. Once a Week, **29**: 81.
— Ryot of. Blackw. **113**: 147.
— Soonderbuns of. Chamb. J. **43**: 45.
— Statistics of Civil Justice in. (W. H. Sykes) J. Statis. Soc. **12**: 1.
— Timber Trees of. (Capt. Munro) Ed. New Philos. J. **46**: 84.
— Village Life in. All the Year, **21**: 58.
— Young. Chamb. J. **29**: 199. — (W. Knighton) Contemp. **38**: 888.
Bengalee in Europe. Dub. Univ. **83**: 742.
Bengalese Correspondence. Temp. Bar, **11**: 295.
Bengali Historical Novel. (Prof. Cowell) Macmil. **25**: 455.
Bengali Life, Realities of. Fraser, **99**: 358.
Bengali Play; Nil Darpan. All the Year, **6**: 158.
Bengali Will. Good Words, **8**: 669. Same art. Ev. Sat. **4**: 600.
Bengel, Johann Albrecht. Lond. Q. **11**: 191.
— Life and Writings of. Ecl. R. **67**: 21.
— Memoir of. Chr. Obs. **41**: 724, 780.
— Table-Talk of. Chr. Obs. **41**: 591, 661.
Beniden de Berg. (N. P. Willis) Colburn, **49**: 26.
Benito, the Horse-Tamer. Chamb. J. **8**: 277.
Benito Cereno. Putnam, **6**: 353, 459, 633.
Benjamin of Breslau. Bentley, **15**: 596.
Benjamin of Tudela. Blackw. **52**: 551. — Dub. Univ. **92**: 598.
Benjamin, B., and Sons. Colburn, **169**: 171.
Benjamin, Park, Poems of. Dem. R. **15**: 494. — Am. Mo. R. **3**: 76.
Benlow's Books. (J. Sterling) Blackw. **42**: 483.
Bennett, George, with portrait. Dub. Univ. **34**: 526.
Bennett, J. G., sen. (J. Parton) No. Am. **102**: 373. — (E. I. Sears) Nat. Q. **25**: 169. — with portrait, Dem. R. **31**: 409.
— Character of. Am. Bibliop. **4**: 394.
— Memoirs of. Dem. R. **36**: 106.
— Scintillations of. (P. Peebles) Galaxy, **14**: 258.
Bennett, Sir John, Sketch of, with portrait. Pract. M. **5**: 66.
Bennett, Mrs., afterwards Lady Heneage Finch. Temp. Bar, **35**: 524.
Bennett, Sir Sterndale, Place of, in Music. Fraser, **91**: 299.
— Some Recollections of. Fraser, **92**: 20.
Bennett, Rev. W., Memoir and Letters of. Cong. M. **6**: 1–113.
Bennett, Wm. C., Poems of. Peop. J. **10**: 361. — Ecl. R. **93**: 563. — (R. H. Stoddard) Nat. M. **2**: 137.

Bennett Family of Ipswich, Mass. (J. M. Bradbury) N. E. Reg. **29**: 165.
Bennett Case, Judgment in. Chr. Obs. **72**: 543, 561. — Cong. **1**: 435. — (C. Beard) Theo. R. **9**: 389.
Bennett Murder Case. (N. F. Davin) Canad. Mo. **18**: 300.
Bennington, Battle of. (H. B. Dawson) Hist. M. **17**: 289.
— — Gen. Stark and. (H. W. Herrick) Harper, **55**: 511.
Bennington County, Vt., Ministers of. (J. Anderson) Am. Q. Reg. **15**: 131.
Benson, Christopher. In Memoriam. St. James, **22**: 255.
Benson, Edgworth, Travels and Opinions of. Lond. M. **3**: 9, 173.
Benson, Joseph, Character of, with portrait. (J. Bunting) Meth. M. **45**: 1.
Benson, Mrs. Sarah. Meth. M. **33**: 453.
Benson, Stephen Allen, President of Liberia. (W. Coppinger) Nat. M. **8**: 311.
Bent Family, Recollections of. (W. Waldo) Western, **6**: 247.
Bentham, Jeremy. (J. Bowring) Howitt, **2**: 123. (A. V. Dicey) Nation, **27**: 352. — (W. Empson) Ed. R. **78**: 460. — Selec. Ed. R. **2**: 289. — (J. Neal) Atlan. **16**: 575. — Am. Ecl. **4**: 207. — (J. S. Mill) Westm. **29**: 467. — (J. H. Burton) Westm. **37**: 265. — Dem. R. **8**: 251. — Mus. **21**: 244. — Select J. **1**: 82. — Colburn, **10**: 68. **35**: 42.
— and Benthamese. (J. Plummer) Victoria, **4**: 103.
— and Benthamism in Politics and Ethics. (H. Sidgwick) Fortn. **27**: 627.
— and Theory of Legislation. (G. H. Smith) Nat. Q. **3**: 51.
— and the Utilitarians. (H. S. Legaré) So. R. **7**: 261.
— Bacon and Plato. (H. H. Milman) Quar. **61**: 462.
— Book of Fallacies. (Syd. Smith) Ed. R. **42**: 367.
— Brougham, and Law Reform. Westm. **11**: 447.
— Character and Writings of. (H. Brougham) Tait, n. s. **5**: 483.
— Chrestomathia. Mo. R. **90**: 197.
— Deontology. (T. P. Thompson) Westm. **21**: 1.
— Early Life of. Dem. R. **10**: 545.
— Letter to Count Toreno. Mo. R. **99**: 386.
— Life and Works of. Mo. R. **158**: 73. **160**: 128.
— Memoirs of. (J. Bowring) Tait, n. s. **7**: 21–697. **8**: 26–728. **9**: 443.
— on Church of England. Quar. **21**: 167. — Mo. R. **88**: 52.
— on Codification. (Sir S. Romilly) Ed. R. **29**: 217.
— on Judicature, Dumond's. For. R. **5**: 153.
— on Usury. *See* Usury.
— Principles of Legislation, Dumond's. (F. Jeffrey) Ed. R. **4**: 1.
— Rationale of Evidence. Ed. R. **48**: 457.
— Science of Morality. Ed. R. **61**: 365. — (T. P. Thompson) Westm. **11**: 254. **12**: 246. *See* Utilitarianism.
— Theory of Legislation. (W. Phillips) No. Am. **51**: 384.
— Theory of Punishments, Dumont's. Ed. R. **22**: 1.
— Works of. Tait, **2**: 49. n. s. **3**: 607.
Bentinck, Lord George. Blackw. **71**: 121. — Irish Q. **2**: 75.
— Disraeli's Life of. Colburn, **94**: 104. — Dub. Univ. **39**: 114. — Ecl. R. **95**: 190.
— Life of. Ecl. R. **95**: 190. — Blackw. **71**: 121.
— Obituary Notice of. Tait, n. s. **15**: 715.
Bentley, Richard, and Trinity College. Am. J. Educ. **28**: 407.
— Correspondence of. Mo. R. **157**: 446.
— Life and Works of. (E. Everett) No. Am. **43**: 458. — Ed. R. **51**: 321. — Blackw. **28**: 437, 644. — Mo. R. **122**: 317.
— Monk's Life of. (C. J. Blomfield) Quar. **46**: 118. — Ecl. R. **52**: 189.
Bentley, Rev. William, Letters of. N. E. Reg. **27**: 351.
— Papers of. Hist. M. **18**: 339. **22**: 245, 364.
Bentley, Rev. William. Washington's Birthday Oration, 1793. Hist. M. **17**: 3.
Benton, Thomas H., with portrait. Dem. R. **1**: 83. — with portrait, Dem. R. **42**: 60. — Land We Love, **5**: 119.
— Dinner to, 1835. Niles's Reg. **48**: 462.
— Portrait of. Dem. R. **13**: 1.
— Thirty Years' View. So. Q. **27**: 277.
Benvenuto Cellini; a Tale. Am. Whig R. **14**: 163, 208.
Benvolio; a Story. Galaxy, **20**: 209.
Benyowski, Count de, Death of. Lond. M. **17**: 261.
Benzole. Fraser, **40**: 452. Same art. Liv. Age, **23**: 369.
Beolco, Angelo; and the Commedia dell' Arte. Blackw. **129**: 753.
Beothucs. (T. G. B. Lloyd) Anthrop. J. **4**: 21. **5**: 222.
Beothuc Skulls. (G. Busk) Anthrop. J. **5**: 230.
Beowulf. Canad. Mo. **2**: 83. — House. Words, **17**: 459.
Beppo, the Conscript. (T. A. Trollope) Once a Week, **9**: 421–701. **10**: 21–337.
Beppo's Escape. Chamb. J. **58**: 667.
Bequests. *See* Legacies.
Béranger, P. J. de. (C. A. Sainte-Beuve) Atlan. **1**: 469. — (J. A. Harrison) So. M. **12**: 454. — (J. F. Hurst) Meth. Q. **18**: 418. — (A. Rhodes) Scrib. **7**: 390. — with portrait, Ecl. M. **75**: 629. — with portrait, Peop. J. **5**: 204. — with portrait, Fraser, **11**: 300. **40**: 531. — Dem. R. **24**: 248. — Ecl. M. **14**: 269. — For. Q. **12**: 28. — Blackw. **83**: 102. — Colburn, **6**: 305. **8**: 305. **43**: 471. — Dub. Univ. **51**: 437. — House. Words, **16**: 185. Same art. Liv. Age, **55**: 339. — Internat. M. **1**: 454. — Nat. R. **5**: 411. — N. Ecl. **4**: 604. — No. Brit. **27**: 498. — Temp. Bar, **49**: 463.
— and Burns compared. (C. Mackay) 19th Cent. **7**: 443.
— and his Songs. (W. Dowe) Dub. Univ. **23**: 205, 738. — (J. H. Vosburg) Nat. Q. **18**: 256.
— Autobiography of. Bentley, **43**: 209.
— Character of. Lond. M. **22**: 173.
— Genius and Influence of. Knick. **2**: 171.
— Horace, and Burns: Lyrists. Cornh. **17**: 150. Same art. Liv. Age, **97**: 3.
— Last Songs of. Bentley, **42**: 574.
— Life and Writings of. Lond. Q. **20**: 74.
— Life of. (T. Sedgwick) No. Am. **29**: 123. — Mus. **23**: 490, 524.
— Memoir of. Howitt, **3**: 196.
— Memoirs of. Bentley, **42**: 346.
— Poems of. Lond. M. **10**: 593. — Brit. Q. **26**: 449.
— Posthumous Memoirs and Songs. Ed. R. **108**: 175
— Songs after. Blackw. **33**: 844.
— Songs of. Blackw. **13**: 507. **41**: 703. — (T. P. Thompson) Westm. **10**: 198. — Quar. **46**: 461. — Select J. **2**: 135. — So. R. **7**: 42. — Tait, **3**: 149. — Dub. Univ. **26**: 204.
— Songs and Politics of. (E. Clarke) Fraser, **102**: 175.
— Story of, and his Songs. Irish Mo. **2**: 167.
— Translations from. Dub. Univ. **2**: 255. — New Q. **6**: 174.
Berber Languages. Prosp. R. **3**: 461.
— Hodgson's Memoirs on. (A. H. Everett) No. Am. **35**: 54.
Berchtesgaden and Salzburg, Day at. Once a Week, **15**: 444.
— and the Ziller-Thal. Cornh. **15**: 572.
— Visit to Salt-Mines of. St. James, **23**: 518.
Berck-sur-Mer. All the Year, **24**: 20.
Berdan, D., Memoirs of. Knick. **14**: 471.
Berendeens. (H. H. Howorth) Geog. M. **3**: 310.
Berengar of Tours, Life of. Chr. Rem. **51**: 311.
Berenice; a Tale. (E. A. Poe) So. Lit. Mess. **1**: 333.
Berents and Ubiquity. (J. H. Ebrard) Mercersb. **6**: 321.
Berg, Joseph E., Last Words of. (J. W. Nevin) Mercersb. **4**: 283.

Bergamo, Visit to. (A. Laugel) Nation, 29: 188.
Bergen. (G. T. Temple) Good Words, 21: 767.
— Days at. (Mrs. H. H. Jackson) Atlan. 47: 770.
Bergerac, Savinien Cyrano de. (H. Morley) Fraser, 51: 273. Same art. Liv. Age, 46: 287. — House. Words, 14: 524.
— Satirical Characters. Retros. 1: 270.
Bergh, Henry, and his Work. (C. C. Buel) Scrib. 17: 872.
Berghem, Nicholas. Art J. 3: 306.
Berigonium. All the Year, 32: 31.
Berith, Hebrew Word, Principal Meaning of. Chr. Obs. 73: 96, 199.
Berkeley, Elizabeth, Margravine of Anspach. Internat. M. 3: 303.
Berkeley, George, Bp. (J. Dyer) Penn Mo. 5: 312. — (G. E. Ellis) O. & N. 4: 591. — (E. E. Beardsley) Am. Church R. 36: 241. — (M. Oliphant) Blackw. 105: 1. Same art. Liv. Age, 100: 395.
— and his Philosophy. (F. Bowen) Chr. Exam. 24: 310.
— and his Works. Chr. R. 26: 313.
— and Kant. (R. Noel) Contemp. 20: 72.
— and Positivism. (St.G. Stock) Theo. R. 16: 342, 437.
— and Rationalism. Bentley, 31: 294.
— A. C. Fraser on. (G. C. Robertson) Mind, 6: 421.
— Huxley on. (M. D. Conway) Radical, 9: 176.
— Idealism of. (O. A. Brownson) Brownson, 1: 29. — Blackw. 51: 812. 53: 762. — Dub. Univ. 7: 437, 534. — Evang. R. 21: 200. — No. Brit. 34: 452. 53: 368.
— in America. (D. C. Gilman) Hours at Home, 1: 115.
— Life and Character of. Am. Church R. 6: 407.
— — and Philosophy of. Quar. 132: 85.
— — and Thoughts of. Dub. Univ. 94: 129.
— — and Writings. (J. McClenahan) Nat. Q. 4: 121. (J. S. Mill) Fortn. 16: 505. — (W. G. Sumner) Nation, 13: 59. — Brit. Q. 26: 75. — Dub. R. 69: 180.
— on the Nature of Matter. (T. C. Simon) J. Spec. Philos. 3: 336.
— Philosophy of. (C. S. Peirce) No. Am. 113: 449.
— Principle of Knowledge, Krauth's edition. (T. Appel) Mercersb. 21: 160.
— Real World of. (Prof. Fraser) Macmil. 6: 192.
— Siris. Retros. 11: 239.
— Theory of Vision. (J. S. Mill) Westm. 38: 318. 39: 491.
— Works of. (J. H. Stirling) J. Spec. Philos. 7: 1. — Ed. R. 136: 1. — Lond. Q. 37: 265.
— — Fraser's edition. Brit. Q. 53: 482. Same art. Liv. Age, 55: 257.
Berkeley, Grantley F., and his Novel. Fraser, 14: 242.
— Assault on Mr. Fraser. Fraser, 15: 100.
— Life of. Dub. Univ. 70: 102. — (R. M. Kettle) Colburn, 168: 429.
— Memoirs of. Temp. Bar, 14: 111.
— Sandnon Hall. Fraser, 22: 637.
Berkeleys, The; a political Lesson. Macmil. 11: 467.
Berkeley, Mass., Ministers of. Am. Q. Reg. 12: 139.
Berkeley Castle. Antiquary, 3: 157.
Berkshire Co., Mass., Geology of. (J. D. Dana) Am. J. Sci. 114: 37–257.
— Jubilee of, 1843. Knick. 24: 181. — (F. A. Butler) Colburn, 76: 127.
— — Sequel to. Dem. R. 15: 400.
— Quartzite and Associated Rocks of. (J. D. Dana) Am. J. Sci. 104: 362, 450. 105: 47, 84. 106: 257.
— Road in. (W. H. Gibson) Harper, 63: 643.
— Summer in. (G. Merriman) O. & N. 7: 695.
Berkshire Ministerial Association, Centennial Anniversary. (N. H. Eggleston) Cong. Q. 6: 142.
Berkshire, England. Quar. 106: 205.
— Holidays in. (A. B. Reach) Sharpe, 18: 292.
— Tour through. Temp. Bar, 11: 52.
Berkshire Lady, The. (T. Hughes) Lippinc. 17: 458.
Berlin. (W. Wells) Scrib. 1: 172.
— and Potsdam, Visit to. (H. Bedford) Month, 38: 373.
— and Vienna. (J. M. Hart) Lippinc. 17: 553.
— Bird's-Eye View, with Key, 1871. Ev. Sat. 11: 103.
— Club Life in. (H. Tuttle) Gent. M. n. s. 14: 43.
— Description of. Howitt, 3: 236.
— Ecclesiastical Crisis in. (A. Chalmers) Theo. R. 15: 142.
— Environs of. (J. W. Wall) Galaxy, 2: 694.
— Holiday at. Bentley, 25: 43.
— Lette-House of. Victoria, 26: 334.
— Low Life in. (W. Wells) Scrib. 6: 288.
— Manners and Mode of living in. Penny M. 6: 319.
— Museum of, Frescos in. Art J. 5: 79.
— — Olympia Antiquities in. (E. von Curtius) Internat. R. 4: 1.
— Notes on. Hogg, 8: 126.
— Popular Life in. Westm. 51: 216. Same art. Ecl. M. 17: 262.
— Princeton Graduate at. (J. M. Hart) Am. J. Educ. 27: 641.
— Revolution of 1848 in. (T. S. Fay) Galaxy, 16: 244, 363.
— Salons of. Bentley, 50: 148. Same art. Liv. Age, 71: 59.
— Social Life in. Bentley, 46: 414.
— Three Nights in. Blackw. 50: 466.
— Three old Legends of. All the Year, 26: 10.
— University of. (H. H. Boyesen) Scrib. 18: 205. — Chr. Exam. 21: 213.
— — Programme of Lectures. Am. J. Educ. 28: 921.
— Unter den Linden. (G. A. Sala) Temp. Bar, 11: 34. — Broadw. 8: 570. — Lippinc. 7: 523.
Berlin Academy. Ecl. R. 105: 160.
Berlin Artillery and Engineers' School. Am. J. Educ. 12: 351.
Berlin Chronicles, Leaf from. Dub. Univ. 22. 558.
Berlin Conference of 1857. (W. Nast) Meth. Q. 18: 427, 538.
Berlin Congress, 1878, and its Results. (M. Maccoll) Gent. M. n. s. 21: 236.
— England's Policy at. (E. Dicey) 19th Cent. 3: 779.
— Peace of. Dub. R. 83: 479. — Fraser, 98: 385.
Berlin Theater, Hundred Years of. Ecl. M. 63: 187.
Berlin Treaty, Fulfillment of. (E. A. Freeman) Princ. n. s. 5: 57.
Berlin Workingmen's Club. Nature, 2: 429.
Berlioz, Hector. (E. Schuyler) Nation, 14: 26. — (E. Royall) Harper, 60: 411. — All the Year, 21: 495. — Lond. Soc. 39: 375. — Ecl. M. 15: 535. — Fraser, 38: 421. — (C. Adams) Potter Am. Mo. 16: 132. — Cornh. 44: 69. Same art. Ecl. M. 97: 531. Same art. Liv. Age. 150: 478.
— Correspondence of. (H. T. Finck) Nation, 29: 145.
— Episode in Life of. (W. F. Apthorp) Atlan. 41: 32.
— Life and Passion of. (E. King) Appleton, 24: 444.
— Memoirs. Ed. R. 133: 33.
— Symphony of Romeo and Juliet. Fraser, 45: 527.
Bermondsey, Journal of a Residence in. St. Paul's, 14: 220, 297.
— Leather at. Pract. M. 4: 71.
Bermudas. (A. V. Darrell) Godey, 63 28. — (M. L. Hoffman) Overland, 7: 138. — (W. Irving) Knick. 15: 17. — (C. Rounds) Harper, 48: 484. — Cong. M. 28: 649. — Dub. R. 76: 153. — St. James, 32: 692. 33: 20. 46: 385.
— and the Blockade. Galaxy, 3: 890.
— Challenger Expedition. Nature, 9: 369.
— Commerce of. Hunt, 10: 332.
— Independent Church in. (E. D. Neill) New Eng. 38: 471.

Bermudas, Observations in. (J. M. Jones) Nature, **6:** 262.
— Recollections of. (H. O'Brien) Dub. Univ. **76:** 223.
— Reptiles, Fishes, and Leptocardians of. (G. B. Goode) Am. J. Sci. **114:** 289.
— Sojourn in. Once a Week, **26:** 587.
— Trip to. (S. L. Clemens) Belgra. **34:** 183, 345.
— Visit to. Canad. Mo. **11:** 392.
— Visit to Walsingham Caves. Argosy, **12:** 311.
Bernadotte, King of Sweden. Liv. Age, **2:** 609. — Anal. M. **3:** 168. — Mus. **6:** 41. — Ecl. M. **3:** 299. — Chamb. J. **2:** 380. — Mus. **40:** 277.
— and Charles XIV. For. Q. **25:** 282.
— Anecdotes of. Fraser, **31:** 206.
Bernard, St., of Clairvaux. (J. C. Morison) Fortn. **17:** 77. — (F. Parkman) Chr. Exam. **30:** 1. — (H. W. Thorpe) Evang. R. **6:** 330. — Ecl. R. **117:** 197.
— and Abelard. (S. Sweetser) Bib. Sac. **17:** 43.
— and his Contemporaries. Chr. Rem. **5:** 501.
— and his Letters. (R. Colley) Month, **20:** 337, 433.
— as a Preacher. (A. Brömel) Bib. Sac. **37:** 338.
— Hymn by, A. D. 1150. Cong. Q. **3:** 278.
— Life and Times of, Morison's. Chr. Obs. **63:** 834. — Dub. R. **54:** 211. — (H. Morley) Fortn. **10:** 695. — Chr. Rem. **46:** 1. — Lond. Q. **20:** 351. Same art. Liv. Age, **81:** 195, 243.
— Thoughts from. (C. Petre) Month, **24:** 146.
Bernard of Ventadour, and his Works. Blackw. **39:** 523.
Bernard, Charles de. Blackw. **61:** 589. — (G. Saintsbury) Fortn. **29:** 909. — Dub. Univ. **64:** 330. — Fraser, **72:** 504.
Bernard, Claude. Nature, **17:** 304. — Pop. Sci. Mo. **13:** 742.
Bernard, Francis. (J. B. Moore) Am. Q. Reg. **14:** 24.
Bernard, John. Retrospections of the Stage. Am. Mo. R. **1:** 414.
Bernard Delitiosi and the Inquisition. (T. M. Lindsay) Good Words, **20:** 732.
Bernardin de St. Pierre, J. H. (W. Besant) Belgra. **24:** 411. — (W. D. Le Sueur) Canad. Mo. **5:** 324. — (A. H. Everett) No. Am. **13:** 200.
— Account of. Colburn, **1:** 441.
— Neander on. Mo. R. **161:** 1.
— Paul and Virginia. Liv. Age, **58:** 788.
Bernardine, St., of Siena, Contemporaries of. Month, **27:** 261. **28:** 129.
Bernardo del Carpio, Old Romances concerning. (J. Oxenford) Colburn, **76:** 84.
Bernardston, Mass., Helderberg Formation of. (J. D. Dana) Am. J. Sci. **114:** 379.
Berne in Winter. (S. B. Wister) Lippinc. **7:** 466. Same art. Broadw. **8:** 410.
— Patriotic Celebration. (H. M. Baird) Putnam, **2:** 371.
— Tale of. Fraser, **7:** 268.
Berners, Juliana, and her "Boke of Venerie." (E. Jesse) Once a Week, **17:** 388.
Bernese Jura, Conflict in. (L. M. Hogg) Good Words, **15:** 666.
Bernese Oberland, The. So. Lit. Mess. **25:** 193.
— Botanizing in. Sharpe, **42:** 63.
Bernhardt, Sara. (R. G. White) Atlan. **47:** 95. — (M. G. van Rensselaer) Lippinc. **27:** 180.
— in Hernani. (A. G. Sedgwick) Nation, **31:** 383.
— in Phèdre. (A. G. Sedgwick) Nation, **31:** 399.
Berni, Francisco, Homes and Haunts of. (T. A. Trollope) Belgra. **36:** 179.
— Orlando Innamorato. Rose's translation. Blackw. **13:** 299.
Bernier, F. Travels. Mus. **13:** 340. — Retros. **15:** 245.
Bernis, François Joachim de, Cardinal. (J. W. Tipping) Colburn, **153:** 163.
Berri, Duchess of. For. Q. **19:** 245. — Am. Q. **14:** 442. — Mus. **23:** 625. — Quar. **50:** 189. — Mo. R. **132:** 301. — Select J. **3:** 82.
— Adventures of. (J. S. C. Abbott) Galaxy, **12:** 739.
— Dermoncourt's. Dub. Univ. **2:** 655.
— in the Cachette of Nantes. Chamb. J. **20:** 84. Same art. Liv. Age, **38:** 748.
— in La Vendée. Tait, **4:** 404.
Berrian, Francis, or the Mexican Patriot. (J. C. Gray) No. Am. **24:** 210.
Berridge, John, and his Correspondence. Cong. M. **24:** 597, 867.
— Letters of. Cong. M. **28:** 27, 271, 740.
— Works of. Chr. Obs. **39:** 120, 300.
Berrien, J. M., and Blair Correspondence. Niles's Reg. **40:** 375.
— Dinner to. Niles's Reg. **40:** 260.
Berries, Some new. (E. P. Roe) Scrib. **22:** 267.
Berry, C. F. d'Artois, Duc de. Ev. Sat. **16:** 9.
— Lamartine's History of. Chamb. J. **19:** 238. Same art. Liv. Age, **37:** 673.
Berry, Miss Mary. Ecl. M. **28:** 138. — Ecl. R. **123:** 189. — Liv. Age, **36:** 178.
— her Friends and her Times. Brit. Q. **43:** 60.
— Journals and Correspondence. Chr. Rem. **51:** 128. — Ed. R. **122:** 297. — Colburn, **136:** 174. — Liv. Age, **87:** 437. — Quar. **119:** 154.
Berry, Misses, Sketch of. Hogg, **10:** 112.
Berryer, P. A. de. Blackw. **42:** 126. — Ecl. Mus. **1:** 300, 537. — Fraser, **27:** 99.
— Autobiographical Recollections. Ed. R. **76:** 121.
— Chat with. (F. Johnson) Hours at Home, **8:** 248.
— Hour or two with, 1841. Colburn, **62:** 228.
Berrytown; a Tale. (R. H. Davis) Lippinc. **11:** 400, 579, 697. **12:** 35.
Bertaut, Jean. Early French Poet. Lond. M. **6:** 361.
Bertha's Cross; a Story of the Middle Ages. Dub. Univ. **35:** 287.
Bertha's Home; a Story. Sharpe, **27:** 9. **28:** 282.
Bertha's Love; a Story. Fraser, **48:** 43, 173. Same art. Liv. Age, **38:** 370, 671. Same art. Harper, **7:** 506, 643.
Berthalde Reimer's Voice. House. Words, **6:** 507. Same art. Liv. Age, **36:** 566.
Berthe's Wedding-Day; a Tale. (K. S. Macquoid) Temp. Bar, **40:** 221. Same art. Liv. Age, **120:** 547.
Berthet, Elie. Le Réfractaire. New Q. **1:** 423.
— Novels of. Dub. Univ. **60:** 399.
Berthollet, the Maître d'Armes; a Sketch. (Lady Pollock) Temp. Bar, **49:** 170.
Bertie, Charles, Letters of. Retros. **16:** 177.
Bertie Bray. (P. Cudlip) St. James, **9:** 386, 512. **10:** 116, 250, 378.
Bertie Griffiths. (A. Edwards) Temp. Bar, **19:** 189.
Bertonelli, Lucia. (E. Ellis) Galaxy, **24:** 322.
Bertran de Born, the Troubadour. (F. Hueffer) Gent. M. n. s. **17:** 185.
Bérulle, Pierre de, and the French Carmelites. Chr. Obs. **73:** 299.
Berwick, Letters relating to the Government of. (R. Porrett) Arch. **30:** 160.
Berzelius, Johan J., Account of. J. Frankl. Inst. **46:** 343.
— Biographical Sketch of. (H. Rose) Ed. New Philos. J. **53:** 189. **54:** 1. — (H. Rose) Am. J. Sci. **66:** 1, 173, 305. **67:** 103.
— Life and Writings of. (P. Louyet) Ed. New Philos. J. **47:** 1.
Beside the Rille; a Tale. (K. S. Macquoid) Temp. Bar, **51:** 70.
Beside the Still Waters; a Sermon. (C. Beard) Mo. Rel. M. **46:** 133.

Bessarabia, An English Governess in. Victoria, 28: 206.
Bessemer, Henry. Lond. Soc. 36: 11.
— Address before Iron and Steel Institute. Ecl. Engin. 4: 617.
— and Gun Metal. (W. B. Adams) Once a Week, 1: 85.
— and his Inventions, with portrait. Pract. M. 6: 98.
Bessemer Machinery. (A. L. Holley) J. Frankl. Inst. 94: 252, 391. 95: 233.
Bessemer Process of making Iron and Steel. J. Frankl. Inst. 62: 267–349. 63: 133, 416.
See Iron; Steel.
Bessemer Saloon Steamboat. Ecl. Engin. 8: 211. 13: 78.— Nature, 7: 41. 11: 342.
— Gyroscope Apparatus for. Ecl. Engin. 12: 120.
Bessemer Steel, Manufacture of, in America. (R. W. Hunt) Pract. M. 7: 44.
Bessie and I; a Poem. (E. Coller) Belgra. 20: 53.
Bessie Leigh. Bentley, 54: 1.
Bessie Rane. (Mrs. H. Wood) Argosy, 9: 1–401. 10: 1–401.
Bessie's Beginnings. (Mrs. S. C. Hall) St. James, 1: 249.
Besson, Charles Jean Baptiste, Père. O. & N. 4: 708.
Besson, Hyacinthe. Month, 3: 100.
Bessy Lowry; a Tale of Ulster. Peop. J. 10: 166, 207.
Best, Thomas, Obituary. Chr. Obs. 65: 475.
Best Bat in the School. Lond. M. 23: 113.
Best Fellow in the World. (R. H. Davis) Scrib. 8: 235.
Best of Husbands. (J. Payn) Chamb. J. 51: 81–424.
Best of Three; or, the Officer's Charger. Fraser, 43: 397.
Betel-Nut Chewing. Ev. Sat. 7: 741.
Betel-Nut Tree. Penny M. 5: 25.
Beth Gélert; a Ballad. Putnam, 10: 289.
Bethabara. (C. R. Conder) Good Words, 19: 678.
Betham, Matilda, Letters of Coleridge, Southey, and Lamb to. (M. B. Edwards) Fraser, 98: 73. Same art. Liv. Age, 138: 416.
Betham, Sir W., Letters to Croker. Sharpe, 36: 89.
Bethel. Hours at Home, 6: 327, 430.
Bethel; a Poem. (A. J. H. Duganne) Atlan. 10: 345.
Bethel Flag. New Eng. M. 6: 289.
Bethesda and its Miracle. (J. M. Macdonald) Bib. Sac. 27: 108.
Bethlehem. (J. F. W. Ware) Mo. Rel. M. 29: 95, 121, 190. — Meth. M. 40: 695. — Month, 4: 1.
— and the Bedouins. Colburn, 28: 225.
— and Golgotha; a Poem. (F. Rückert) Mercersb. 9: 246.
— and Mount of Olives. (A. Lamson) Mo. Rel. M. 9: 132.
— Pilgrimage to. Broadw. 7: 542. — Cath. World, 6: 462.
Bethlehem, England, Hospital for the Insane. Westm. 85: 331. — Mo. R. 162: 395. — Liv. Age, 55: 297.
Bethlehem, Pa., as the Seat of Government, 1780. Pennsyl. M. 2: 153.
Bethnal Green, Sight-Seeing in. All the Year, 28: 228.
Bethnal Green Museum. (S. Colvin) Fortn. 18: 458.
Bethune, Alexander, Poems of. Dub. Univ. 12: 455.
— and John. (F. Bowen) No. Am. 67: 486.
— Tales of Scottish Peasantry. Mo. R. 145: 371.
Bethune, George W. Liv. Age, 73: 542.
Bethune, Mrs. George W., Reminiscences of. (Mrs. E. E. Evans) Hours at Home, 10: 492.
Bethune, John, Poems and Life of. Tait, n. s. 8: 603. — Mo. R. 153: 425.
Bethune; a Tale. (J. Scott) St. James, 40: 279.
Beton Building. Ecl. Engin. 1: 824.
Betrothal, An Eastern. (J. P. Brown) Knick. 50: 107.
— by Proxy. (J. P. Quincy) Atlan. 11: 420.
Betsey Clark; a Tale. Putnam, 8: 124.
Betsinda and her Bun. Cornh. 36: 325.
Betsy Brown. Blackw. 87: 327.
Betsy Lee, a Fo'c's'le Yarn. Macmil. 27: 441. 28: 1. Same art. Ev. Sat. 14: 527, 559, 585.
Betterton, Thomas, Actor. Cornh. 6: 412. — Temp. Bar, 53: 564.
Bettina, Few Words for. Blackw. 58: 357.
Betting and Bookmaking, Exposition of. Fraser, 96: 75.
— Legislation on. Fraser, 90: 611.
— — Bill of 1874. Dub. Univ. 83: 636.
— on Races. (R. A. Proctor) Gent. M. n. s. 21: 465. Same art. Sup. Pop. Sci. Mo. 4: 83.
Betting-Offices. Chamb. J. 18: 57.
Bettws-y-coed, At. (W. W. Fenn) Broadw. 1: 124.
Betty, W. H. W., the Young Roscius. (T. P. Grinsted) Bentley, 42: 410. — Chamb. J. 51: 648. — Temp. Bar, 42: 346. Same art. Ecl. M. 83: 734. — Tinsley, 15: 415.
Betty, Our Old. Chamb. J. 24: 19.
Between Heaven and Earth; a Tale. Liv. Age, 61: 277.
Between Moor and Main. (H. S. Wilson) Dark Blue, 4: 432.
Between the Lights. Lond. Soc. 7: 535. Same art. Ecl. M. 65: 206.
Between two Stools. (C. Hervey) Argosy, 29: 296.
Between two Stools; a Story. (M. E. Fairman) Colburn, 161: 459, 557.
Beuggen, Seminary for Orphan and Destitute Children at. Am. J. Educ. 3: 383.
Beugnot, Count Albert, Memoirs of. Ed. R. 125: 303. Same art. Liv. Age, 93: 483.
Beust, F. Ferdinand von, with portrait. Ecl. M. 71: 1535. — (C. I. Barnard) Nation, 14: 139.
— Chat with. Hours at Home, 7: 149.
— Régime of, in Austria. Macmil. 18: 414.
Beverages, Antique Epistle concerning. Am. Mo. M. 10: 539.
Beveridge, William, Bp., Memoir of. Chr. Obs. 24: 201.
Beverley Manor. (M. F. Swann) So. M. 16: 276.
Beverly, Mass., Stone's History of. (S. Willard) Chr. Exam. 34: 248.
Bewick, Thomas. (W. P. Garrison) Harper, 57: 514. — Broadw. 2: 384. — Penny M. 10: 260, 268.
— and Art Culture. Am. J. Educ. 26: 727.
— and John, Works of. (D. C. Thomson) Art J. 33: 245.
— Life and Works. Blackw. 18: 1. 23: 873. 41: 352. — Brit. Q. 2: 554. — Ecl. M. 7: 266.
— Memoir and Portrait of. (W. Howitt) Howitt, 2: 178.
— Sketch of. St. James, 27: 499.
Bewick, William. Chamb. J. 48: 500.
Bewitched Farm, The. Chamb. J. 42: 497, 523.
Bewitched in Mid-Ocean. (J. M. Cobban) Belgra. 45: 39.
Bewley, Anthony, Martyrdom of. (C. Elliott) Meth. Q. 23: 626.
Beyle, Henri. (Mrs. D. Holmes) Dub. Univ. 22: 403. — (H. James, jr.) Nation, 19: 187. — (T. B. Stork) Penn Mo. 12: 691.
— De l'Amour. Colburn, 5: 423.
— Life and Writings of. Ed. R. 103: 203. Same art. Liv. Age, 48: 640. Same art. Ecl. M. 38: 28.
— Literary Life of. (J. H. Browne) Appleton, 16: 415.
Beyond. (M. B. Wyman) Overland, 7: 166.
Beyond; a Poem. (E. A. Stansbury) Putnam, 12: 664.
Beyond the Breakers. (R. D. Owen) Lippinc. 3: 5–577. 4: 61–633. 5: 74, 198.
Beyond the Grave. (J. E. Schadd) Knick. 44: 146.
Beyond the Portals; a Poem. (E. C. Stedman) Scrib. 6: 461.
Beyond Recall; a Story. Belgra. 42: 30.
Beyrout. *See* Beirût.
Beza, Theodore de, as a Translator. (J. A. Corcoran) Am. Cath. Q. 4: 521. 5: 701.
— Character of. Cong. M. 7: 169.

Beza, Theodore de, Life and Character of. (R. D. C. Robbins) Bib. Sac. **7**: 501.
Bézique. (H. Jones) Gent. M. n. s. **4**: 169.
— How to play. Once a Week, **20**: 216.
Bhagavad Gita, Oriental Philosophy and. (W. T. Harris) Western, **1**: 635. — (O. D. Miller) Univ. Q. **26**: 389. — (B. F. Hosford) Bib. Sac. **16**: 788.
Bhats and Charons of Guzrat. Liv. Age, **72**: 347.
Bhau Dajee. Nature, **10**: 270.
Bhurtpore, Siege of. Blackw. **23**: 914. **24**: 94.
Bhutan Frontier, The. (T. D. Beighton) Fraser, **99**: 1.
Bianca. (W. E. Norris) Belgra. **37**: 47. Same art. Liv. Age, **139**: 787.
Bianca Cappello, Fortunes of. (Mrs. E. F. Ellet) Godey, **26**: 65.
Bianconi, Charles. (W. Chambers) Chamb. J. **55**: 337. — with portrait, Dub. Univ. **85**: 16.
— and what he did for Ireland. (S. Smiles) Good Words, **15**: 23, 114.
Biarritz, France. Liv. Age, **52**: 168.
— Story of a Season at. Lond. Soc. **39**: supp. 67.
Bibb, G. M., Speech on Nullification. Niles's Reg. **43**: supp. 62.
Bible, The. (G. Bailey) Univ. Q. **33**: 23. — (E. H. Hall) Unita. R. **14**: 421. — Retros. **11**: 197. — Chr. Exam. **33**: 151. — (G. Livermore) Chr. Exam. **51**: 53. — (W. R. Smith in Encyc. Britannica) Sup. Pop. Sci. Mo. **1**: 289.
— a Book of Facts. (D. Oliphant) Cong. R. **7**: 231.
— a Key to the Natural World. (A. Alexander) Princ. **1**: 101.
— a perfect Book. (C. P. Krauth, jr.) Evang. R. **4**: 110.
— a Revelation. New Eng. **4**: 142.
— a Divine Revelation. (P. Kleinert) Meth. Q. **30**: 45.
— a sufficient Revelation. (W. Spaulding) Univ. Q. **11**: 5.
— Account of. (R. W. Allen) Am. Meth. M. **21**: 199.
— Agricultural Implements of. Hogg, **9**: 172.
— always the same. Chr. Q. Spec. **8**: 519.
— and Assyrian Discoveries. (J. McSwiney) Month, **20**: 11.
— and Assyrian Inscriptions. (T. Laurie) Bib. Sac. **14**: 147.
— and the Catechism. (H. J. Reutenik) Mercersb. **7**: 466.
— and the Church. (C. Loyson) Good Words, **16**: 30. — Dub. R. **41**: 317.
— — Authority of, compared. Dub. R. **37**: 450.
— and the Catholic Church. (G. Deshon) Cath. World, **7**: 657.
— and Church of England. Ed. R. **117**: 498.
— and Civil Government. Am. Whig R. **12**: 511. — (E. C. Wines) Meth. Q. **11**: 633.
— and the Common People. Kitto, **13**: 1.
— and Criticism. (G. L. Cary) Unita. R. **16**: 425.
— and Egyptology. (W. Orton, jr.) Bib. R. **4**: 203. — (R. S. Poole) Liv. Age, **66**: 56. — (P. Schaff) Internat. R. **5**: 333.
— and Geology. (A. Essick) Evang. R. **13**: 173. — Dem. R. **29**: 353. — (D. R. Malone) Chr. Q. **8**: 13. — Mo. R. **154**: 1.
— — Pye Smith on. Mo. R. **153**: 392.
See below, Bible, Old Test., Genesis; *also*, Geology.
— and its Critics. (S. L. Blake) Cong. Q. **11**: 528.
— — Garbett on. Chr. Obs. **61**: 696.
— and its Literature. (E. Robinson) Am. Bib. Repos. **5**: 334.
— and Josephus. Kitto, **6**: 292.
— and the Koran. Chr. Obs. **67**: 429.
— and Man. Dub. Univ. **20**: 109.
— and modern Infidelity. Cong. R. **8**: 524.
— and modern Progress. (J. H. Rigg) Ex. H. Lec. **14**: 247.
Bible, The, and moral Necessities of Man. (H. McNeill) Ex. H. Lec. **5**: 253.
— and Nature, Analogy of. (A. P. Peabody) Chr. Exam. **61**: 321.
— and our Liberties. (J. W. Richard) Luth. Q. **6**: 221.
— and the Reformation. Dub. R. **3**: 428.
— and the School. (E. de Pressensé) New Eng. **29**: 496.
— and Science. (R. Milligan) Chr. Q. **1**: 319. — (W. Rupp) Mercersb. **21**: 42. — (M. de Serres) Ed. New Philos. J. **38**: 239. — (J. E. Smith) Mercersb. **25**: 386. — (J. Stoughton) Ex. H. Lec. **1**: 1. — Am. Church Mo. **3**: 133. — Am. Presb. R. **5**: 642. — Chr. Obs. **70**: 28, 99. — Danv. Q. **4**: 187. — Liv. Age, **5**: 376. — Chr. Obs. **72**: 509.
— — Brunton on. (G. J. Romanes) Nature, **24**: 332.
— and Social Reform. Theo. & Lit. J. **13**: 345.
— and the State. (W. C. Conant) Bapt. Q. **5**: 276.
— and Tradition. (J. A. Reubelt) Chr. Q. **7**: 106.
— and the Working Classes. Hogg, **9**: 247.
— Animals of. Hours at Home, **10**: 139.
— Anthropomorphism of. Ecl. R. **119**: 323.
— Application and Misapplication of. (B. Powell) Kitto, **2**: 253.
— Arabic, Eli Smith's. Princ. **28**: 732.
— M. Arnold's New Religion of. (J. L. Davies) Contemp. **21**: 842.
— M. Arnold's Literature and Dogma. (J. M. Sturtevant) New Eng. **34**: 92. — Blackw. **113**: 678. — Westm. **101**: 309. *See* Arnold, Matthew.
— as the Rule of Faith. Dub. R. **35**: 273.
— as a Text-Book. (C. M. Davis) University Q. **2**: 92.
— Authenticity and Inspiration of. Am. Meth. M. **2**: 320. — (R. S. Candlish) Ex. H. Lec. **6**: 517.
— Authority of. (E. de Pressensé) Cong. **1**: 98, 149.
— Baptist Revision of. Danv. Q. **4**: 57.
— Baptist Translation of. (J. W. Yeomans) Princ. **10**: 413. — Chr. R. **2**: 21.
— Bards of. *See below*, Bible, Poetry of.
— Beke's Origines Biblicæ. Quar. **52**: 496.
— Bellamy's Translation of. Chr. Obs. **17**: 228, 281. — Ecl. R. **28**: 1, 130, 280. — Quar. **19**: 250, 446. **23**: 287.
— Bibliography of. Cong. M. **20**: 166, 373, 437.
— Blasphemy against. Dub. R. **40**: 200.
— Books of, Real Character of. (W. Goodhugh) Quar. **19**: 250, 446. — Chr. Obs. **68**: 415.
— Boothroyd's Translation of. Ecl. R. **31**: 48. **41**: 236. **44**: 446. **64**: 142.
— Botany of. Theo. Ecl. **2**: 81. — Hogg, **8**: 253.
— Bunsen's Biblical Researches. Tait, n. s. **28**: 103. — Brit. Q. **29**: 418.
— Breton Version of. (S. P. Tregelles) Kitto, **39**: 95.
— Canon of Sacred Scripture. (T. W. Coit) Am. Church R. **17**: 583. — Dub. R. **23**: 104. — Gen. Repos. **4**: 1. — Kitto, **7**: 174. **30**: 102.
— — according to St. Cyril. (J. Rickaby) Month, **28**: 39.
— — Alexander on. U. S. Lit. Gaz. **5**: 327.
— — Catholic Doctrine of. (A. F. Hewit) Cath. World, **33**: 323.
— — Gaussen on. Chr. Obs. **62**: 694.
— — History of. (L. W. Heydenrich) Evang. R. **18**: 502.
— — Tridentine. Dub. R. **21**: 131.
— Catholic Versions of. Dub. R. **2**: 475.
— Chalmers's Daily Readings of. Theo. & Lit. J. **1**: 353. — (R. Babcock) Chr. R. **13**: 412.
— Christ's Testimony to. Bost. R. **3**: 274.
— Chronological Arrangement of, Townsend's. Ecl. R. **61**: 371, 460.
— Chronology of. *See* Chronology, Biblical.
— Commentaries on. Kitto, **24**: 284.
— — Hints respecting. (M. Stuart) Am. Bib. Repos. **3**: 130.

Bible, The, Commentaries on, Modern. (R. S. Poole) Macmil. **13**: 143. **14**: 196. — Bib. Sac. **7**: 379.
— — Notes on. (S. C. Bartlett) Cong. R. **11**: 63.
— Commentary on, Hewlett's. Ecl. R. **29**: 345.
— — Lange's. (P. Schaff) Princ. **36**: 653.
— — Livermore's. Chr. Exam. **31**: 127. — (R. P. Stebbins) Chr. Exam. **37**: 252.
— — Olshausen's. Mercersb. **9**: 322.
— — Paige's. (A. Lamson) Chr. Exam. **38**: 417.
— — Speaker's. Quar. **147**: 293. — Chr. Obs. **71**: 498–903. **74**: 698. **75**: 750, 900. — Ed. R. **140**: 32.
— Commentators on. (W. L. Alexander) Kitto, **2**: 222.
— Comprehensive Study of. Chr. Obs. **38**: 224, 282, 344.
— Conciliar Decrees on. (M. P. Thompson) Cath. World, **17**: 195.
— Conquest's edition of. Cong. M. **24**: 576.
— Criticism of. *See* Biblical Criticism.
— Customs illustrative of. (D. G. Wait) Kitto, **3**: 309.
— Daily Use of. Chr. Disc. **2**: 19.
— Destiny of. Hogg, **10**: 87.
— Dictionaries of. (C. H. Brigham) No. Am. **105**: 682. — Quar. **116**: 383.
— Dictionary of, Brown's. Bib. R. **3**: 364.
— — Calmet's. Am. Mo. R. **3**: 87. — Mo. R. **155**: 457.
— — Herzog's Encyclopædia. (C. P. Krauth) Evang. R. **7**: 580.
— — Kitto's Biblical Cyclopædia. Bib. R. **1**: 355. — Ecl. R. **84**: 417. — (J. A. Alexander) Princ. **18**: 554.
— — Robinson's. Am. Mo. R. **3**: 490.
— — Smith's. (C. H. Brigham) Chr. Exam. **76**: 223. — Chr. Obs. **60**: 771. **61**: 23. — Ho. & For. R. **4**: 623. — Nat. R. **18**: 51.
— — — and Kitto's. Ed. R. **121**: 42.
— — Winer's. (C. P. Krauth) Evang. R. **1**: 297. — (W. Carrick) Kitto, **4**: 19. — Bib. R. **6**: 666.
— Difficult Passages of, Notes on. (F. A. Adams) Am. Presb. R. **16**: 103.
— Difficulties in Reception of. Chr. Obs. **68**: 641, 721.
— Discrepancies of, Alleged. (E. Pond) Chr. R. **23**: 390.
— Divine and human Elements in Scripture. Chr. Obs. **63**: 112. — Lond. Q. **22**: 408.
— Divine Authority of. (A. R. Abbott) Univ. Q. **26**: 261. — (H. Carleton) Theo. & Lit. J. **12**: 632. — Chr. Obs. **1**: 420.
— Divine Origin of. Meth. Q. **37**: 667.
— Division of, into Verses. Chr. Rem. **3**: 455. **4**: 418.
— — in early MSS. of Latin. Chr. Rem. **3**: 672.
— Doctrines and Precepts of. (D. Green) Chr. Mo. Spec. **9**: 1.
— Douay or Catholic. (A. B. Rich) Cong. R. **7**: 576.
— Double Sense of Scripture. (W. S. Tyler) Am. Presb. R. **15**: 214.
— Dramatic Element in. (S. Judd) Atlan. **4**: 137.
— Efficacy of. (L. Woods) Lit. & Theo. R. **1**: 400.
— Eloquence of. Chr. Mo. Spec. **2**: 404.
— English. (J. A. Albro) Cong. Q. **12**: 33. — (F. W. Holland) Chr. Exam. **86**: 263. — (J. S. Hart) Princ. **8**: 157. — Chr. R. **3**: 34.
— — and new Versions. (S. Davidson) Theo. R. **3**: 188.
— — Anderson's Annals of. No. Brit. **5**: 132. Same art. Liv. Age, **10**: 18. — Brit. Q. **3**: 438. — Bib. R. **1**: 425. **2**: 173. — Ecl. R. **83**: 82.
— — Authorization of. (R. T. Davidson) Macmil. **44**: 436.
— — Authorized Version of. (W. Walford) Cong. M. **20**: 355. — Dub. Univ. **48**: 345. — Cong. M. **1**: 410, 468.
— — — and the American Bible Society. (C. Hodge) Princ. **29**: 507.
— — — and the Speaker's Commentary thereon. Brit. Q. **55**: 135.
— — — Boothroyd on. Ecl. R. **24**: 590. — Portfo. (Den.) **18**: 112.
Bible, The, English, Authorized Version of, Chapter Headings in. (C. K. Paul) Theo. R. **6**: 99.
— — — Defects and Monopoly of. Cong. M. **24**: 1.
— — — Early Editions of. (E. W. Gilman) Bib. Sac. **16**: 56.
— — — in America. Liv. Age, **64**: 131.
— — — King James folio editions. Hist. M. **5**: app.
— — — State of. Cong. M. **16**: 229.
— — — Text of. Chr. Rem. **52**: 393.
— — Bishop's Version. Cong. M. **1**: 305.
— — Bug Bible, 1551. Ev. Sat. **10**: 235.
— — Critical Study of. (J. A. Alexander) Princ. **11**: 201.
— — Geneva Version. Cong. M. **1**: 129.
— — History of. Dub. Univ. **66**: 363. Same art. Ecl. M. **66**: 52. — Lond. Q. **32**: 265. — Quar. **128**: 301. Same art. Ecl. M. **75**: 1, 197. Same art. Liv. Age, **105**: 451.
— — — Westcott's. Chr. Obs. **69**: 523.
— — Italic Readings of. Chr. Obs. **40**: 752.
— — New Variorum, 1880. (R. S. Poole) Contemp. **39**: 211.
— — Printing, Errors in. Cong. M. **6**: 70, 247. — Tait, n. s. **6**: 483.
— — — Monopoly in. Cong. M. **16**: 334, 411, 665. — Ecl. R. **57**: 509. **58**: 161. **73**: 216. — Kitto, **24**: 211.
— — Revision of. (J. B. Bittenger) Putnam, **15**: 668. Pamph. **13**: 287. — Chr. Q. Spec. **5**: 655. — New Eng. M. **5**: 89. — (J. Cumming) Ex. H. Lec. **12**: 265. — (G. P. Fisher) Internat. R. **1**: 514. — (G. P. Fisher) Nation, **16**: 198. — (J. W. Gibbs) New Eng. **17**: 489. — (E. W. Gilman) New Eng. **17**: 144. — (E. E. Hale) O. & N. **7**: 535. — (C. W. Hodge) Princ. **43**: 36. — (W. G. Humphry) Macmil. **22**: 111. — (J. Hunt) Contemp. **17**: 80. — (A. St. J. Chambré) Univ. Q. **36**: 133. — (J. T. Lewis) Am. Church R. **10**: 15. — (J. Lillie) Chr. Q. **6**: 337. — (G. P. Marsh) Nation, **11**: 238, 261, 281. — (J. H. Means) Cong. Q. **13**: 514. — (M. H. Seymour) Chr. Obs. **75**: 620. — (L. E. Smith) No. Am. **88**: 184. — (G. C. McWhorter) Appleton, **9**: 104, 141. — Am. Presb. R. **6**: 255. — Brit. Q. **51**: 67. Same art. Theo. Ecl. **7**: 137. — Chr. Obs. **58**: 404. **70**: 439. — Chr. Rem. **32**: 451. — Am. Church R. **24**: 522. **26**: 510. — Ecl. R. **108**: 303. **111**: 553. — Ed. R. **122**: 103. Same art. Liv. Age, **86**: 433. — Kitto, **14**: 268. **17**: 52. **18**: 249. **19**: 130, 353. **23**: 326. **29**: 116. **36**: 190, 447. — Lond. Q. **35**: 187. — Penn Mo. **6**: 718. — Quar. **133**: 147. — Westm. **67**: 137. — Cong. M. **13**: 79–526.
— — — and the American Bible Society. (C. S. Robinson) Scrib. **23**: 447.
— — — The Coming. (H. Crosby) No. Am. **131**: 447.
— — — Convocation of Canterbury on, 1870. (H. F. Jenks) Mo. Rel. M. **45**: 409.
— — — Ellicott on. (J. R. Beard) Theo. R. **7**: 526.
— — — of Old Testament. (T. K. Cheyne) Contemp. **2**: 141. — (R. Martineau) Theo. R. **8**: 53. — (R. E. Thompson) Penn Mo. **2**: 44.
— — — of New Testament. (H. Alford) Contemp. **8**: 321. — (L. Campbell) Contemp. **27**: 848. **28**: 93, 462. — (T. Dwight) New Eng. **38**: 385. — (H. F. Jenks) Mo. Rel. M. **46**: 197. — (A. C. Kendrick) Bapt. Q. **5**: 129. — So. R. n. s. **19**: 253.
— — — — Lightfoot on. Chr. Obs. **72**: 786, 829. — Luth. Q. **3**: 294.
— — — — Trench on. Princ. **31**: 257.
For articles on the revised New Testament after its issue, *see below*, Bible, New Testament.
— — — Plea for. Kitto, **39**: 156, 481.
— — — Specimens of amended Version. Cong. M. **14**: 76, 138.

Bible, The, English, Supposed Errors in. Kitto, 19: 130.
— — Wickliffe's. (G. Livermore) Chr. Exam. 51: 53. — Kitto, 8: 116. — Peop. J. 6: 71.
— English Translations of. (J. G. Shea) Cath. World, 12: 149. — (J. G. Wilson) Potter Am. Mo. 11: 197. — Am. Bib. Repos. 6: 451. — Chr. Exam. 14: 328. — Bib. Sac. 15: 261. — Ecl. M. 56: 112. — Mus. 43: 373.
— Enigmatical Passages in. (S. Sharpe) Theo. R. 6: 238.
— Ephraim Rescript. Chr. Rem. 44: 273.
— Ethics of. (T. Lewis) Am. Bib. Repos. 3d s. 4: 554.
— Ethical System of. Theo. & Lit. J. 7: 666.
— Everything or Nothing. (T. Lewis) Am. Bib. Repos. 3d s. 4: 100.
— Exegesis of. (C. P. Krauth) Evang. R. 4: 270.
— — Practical. (C. P. Krauth) Evang. R. 7: 173.
— — Theological. (J. T. Beck) Luth. Q. 2: 31.
— Exploration as verifying. (J. L. Porter) Princ. n. s. 2: 1.
— Exposition of, Aphorisms on. (G. Thomasius) Evang. R. 14: 351.
— — Practical. (G. Thomasius) Luth. Q. 2: 179.
— Facts in Illustration of. (Mrs. Postans) Sharpe, 5: 42–257. 6: 57, 173, 241. 7: 156.
— Facts of, Collyer on. (J. Foster) Ecl. R. 6: 856.
— Fairbairn's Revelation of Law in. Chr. Obs. 69: 599.
— Fallibility of. Westm. 75: 89.
— Familiar Study of. (J. Hall) Princ. 15: 77.
— Familiarity with. Chr. Exam. 5: 168.
— Figurative Language of. (D. N. Lord) Theo. & Lit. J. 1: 353. 7: 352. — (E. Pond) Theo. & Lit. J. 4: 687. — (E. Robie) Bib. Sac. 13: 314. — (W. P. Lunt) Chr. Exam. 48: 390. — Chr. Disc. 5: 178.
— Flowers of. (L. H. Grindon) Dub. Univ. 90: 84.
— for the Last Fifty Years. (J. Hamilton) Ex. H. Lec. 8: 506.
— for Learners. (G. L. Cary) Unita. R. 15: 239.
— for the Pandits. Liv. Age, 68: 236.
— Formal and the Vital in. (I. E. Dwinell) New Eng. 38: 655.
— Foundation of Faith in. Am. Presb. R. 7: 454.
— from God? (B. Grant) Bib. R. 6: 103.
— Genuineness and Authenticity of. Meth. M. 27: 255.
— Geographical Accuracy of. Chr. R. 20: 451.
— Geography of. *See* Biblical Geography.
— German, and M. Luther. Am. Meth. M. 19: 46.
— — Luther's Translation. (C. P. Krauth) Mercersb. 16: 180.
— Gliddon's Criticisms on. (S. Reufs) Chr. Exam. 57: 340.
— Gothic Version by Ulfilas. (D. H. Montgomery) Unita. R. 9: 660. — Danv. Q. 1: 248. — Ecl. R. 87: 315. — (S. Loewe) Kitto, 3: 320. — Lond. Q. 40: 347.
— Harman's Introduction to. (J. Todd) Meth. Q. 40: 72.
— Hebrew. (E. A. Huntington) Am. Presb. R. 20: 541.
— — Airy's Notes on earlier Hebrew Scriptures. Chr. Obs. 76: 263.
— — and its Competitors. (G. W. Henning) Meth. Q. 41: 231.
— — Introduction to the Rabbinic. (C. D. Ginsburg) Kitto, 31: 382.
— — Text of. Dub. Univ. 50: 690.
— — — History of. (W. W. Willett) Am. Meth. M. 21: 164.
— — — Variæ Lectiones of. Kitto, 17: 137. 18: 100.
— Historical and Chronological Trustworthiness of. Chr. Rem. 12: 298.
— Historical Books of, Coincidences in. Chr. Rem. 15: 410.
— Historical Evidence of the Truth of. (H. W. Warren) Meth. Q. 22: 446. — Westm. 74: 33.
Bible, The, Historical Evidence of the Truth of, Rawlinson on. Chr. R. 25: 499. — New Q. 8: 454. — Theo. & Lit. J. 12: 177.
— History of. *See* Biblical History.
— Horne's Introduction to Study of. Bib. R. 3: 305. — Cong. M. 10: 137. — (J. C. Upham) No. Am. 17: 130. — Chr. Obs. 18: 723. — Ecl. R. 29: 21, 182. 35: 75. 36: 557. 60: 478. 84: 183. — Meth. M. 45: 372. — (W. H. Green) Princ. 29: 375.
— How we read. (H. H. Barber) Unita. R. 12: 328.
— How we should use it. Mo. Rel. M. 34: 193.
— Hussey's new Commented Edition. Colburn, 68: 121.
— Illustrations of. Bib. R. 2: 413. 3: 244. — Cong. M. 22: 26–495.
— — from Bible Lands. (T. Laurie) Bib. Sac. 36: 534, 647.
— — Martin's. Westm. 20: 452.
— — Oriental. Ecl. R. 61: 361.
— — Pictorial, Early History of. (W. C. Prime) Harper, 60: 738.
— — Roberts's. Mo. R. 136: 433.
— in American History. (J. G. Shea) Am. Cath. Q. 3: 131.
— in the Counting-House. (L. H. Atwater) Princ. 25: 390.
— in France, Modern Ignorance of. Chr. Obs. 69: 531.
— in its Catholic Aspects. Dub. R. 56: 1.
— in France. Brit. Q. 41: 412. Same art. Liv. Age, 85: 433.
— in the Middle Ages. Lond. Q. 54: 186.
— in Public Schools. (I. Errett) Chr. Q. 2: 187. — (D. Gans) Mercersb. 17: 150. — (E. L. Godkin) Nation, 9: 430. 10: 219. — (H. Humphrey) Am. Inst. Instruc. 1843: 1. — (A. D. Mayo) Univ. Q. 31: 261. — (A. P. Peabody) Mo. Rel. M. 45: 113. — (O. F. Safford) Univ. Q. 34: 194. — (S. T. Spear) Princ. n. s. 1: 361. — (F. T. Washburn) Mo. Rel. M. 48: 261. — So. R. n. s. 11: 371.
— — Binney on. Cong. 1: 562.
— — of Victoria. Victoria, 18: 445. — Cath. World, 11: 91.
— in Spain, Borrow's. *See* Borrow, George.
— Indiscriminate Reading of. Dub. R. 23: 145.
— Infallibility of. (C. K. Whipple) Radical, 2: 359.
— Inferential Reasoning from Silence of. Kitto, 4: 277.
— Influence of. Danv. Q. 4: 201.
— — on Intellectual Character. Chr. Mo. Spec. 9: 169.
— — on the Liberties of our Country. (S. W. Harkey) Luth. Q. 4: 59.
— — on Literature. (D. Cortes) U. S. Cath. M. 7: 393, 456. — (J. A. Seiss) Evang. R. 5: 1.
— — Silent. (J. Few Smith) Evang. R. 2: 353.
— Inspiration of. *See* Inspiration.
— inspired and inspiring. (A. A. Livermore) Chr. Exam. 56: 165.
— Intelligent Study of. (H. Alford) Ex. H. Lec. 10: 203.
— Internal Evidence of. Chr. R. 24: 420.
— Interpretation of. (R. G. Jones) Theo. Ecl. 6: 282. — (C. E. Stowe) Bib. Sac. 10: 34. — (E. Pond) Theo. & Lit. J. 4: 415. — (Prof. Hahn) Am. Bib. Repos 1: 111. — (M. Stuart) Am. Bib. Repos. 1: 139. 2: 124. 7: 241. — (T. C. Upham) No. Am. 14: 391. — (J. Muenscher) Am. Bib. Repos. 5: 92. — No. Brit. 29: 71. — Theo. & Lit. J. 9: 174. 10: 315. Mo. R. 163: 280.
— — and Criticism of, by the Tübingen School. Westm. 80: 510.
— — Authority of the Church in. (T. S. Johnston) Mercersb. 14: 401.
— — Brownson on. Theo. & Lit. J. 11: 4.
— — Conybeare on. Meth. M. 47: 752.
— — Davidson on. Theo. & Lit. J. 10: 315.

Bible, The, Interpretation of, Dobie on Axioms and Laws of. Theo. & Lit. J. **9**: 174.
— — False. (D. Gans) Mercersb. **14**: 633.
— — from Apostolic Age to Origen. (O. Cone) Univ. Q. **30**: 298. **31**: 36.
— — Importance of correct. (S. Sweetser) Bib. Sac. **29**: 91.
— — its own Interpreter. (H. P. Tappan) Am. Bib. Repos. 3d s. **3**: 95. — (T. H. Skinner, jr.) Princ. **32**: 389.
— — Jowett on. (H. A. Du Bois) Am. Church R. **14**: 332. — Kitto, **27**: 98.
— Jewish Doctrine of the Word. (W. G. Nowell) Chr. Exam. **74**: 44.
— Knowledge of, in the Middle Ages. Chr. Rem. **8**: 287.
— Koran, and Talmud. (G. Weil) Bib. R. **1**: 309.
— Lands of. Liv. Age, **15**: 539.
— — Customs and Manners of. Chamb. J. **53**: 651.
— — Wilson on. Chr. Obs. **47**: 482, 546.
See Palestine.
— Language of, Perversion of. (S. Willard) Chr. Exam. **2**: 98.
— Literary Attractions of. (J. Hamilton) Ex. H. Lec. **5**: 89. — (J. Hamilton) So. Lit. Mess. **17**: 673. — Theo. & Lit. J. **11**: 168. — Portfo. (Den.) **34**: 55.
— Literary History of. Hogg, **1**: 107.
— — Townley's Introduction to. Meth. M. **52**: 33.
— Lost Books of. (J. W. Davidson) Am. Church R. **29**: 56.
— — M'Culloh on. (T. E. Bond, jr.) Meth. Q. **13**: 256.
— Manuscripts of, recently discovered. (F. M. Holland) No. Am. **92**: 250.
— Many-Sidedness of. (E. Wilton) Good Words, **4**: 790, 884.
— Misquotation of. (A. C. Thompson) Bib. Sac. **32**: 452. — Bib. R. **3**: 268, 429.
— Modern Correctors of. (W. J. Wiseman) Nat. Q. **11**: 119.
— Modern Depreciation of. Ecl. R. **96**: 49.
— Modern Speculation and. (J. W. M'Lane) Bib. Sac. **18**: 338.
— Money of. (W. H. Green) Princ. **28**: 238.
— Mysteries of. (W. G. Howard) So. Lit. Mess. **6**: 624.
— Names in. Theo. & Lit. J. **4**: 82.
— — Local, Antiquity of. Cong. **5**: 611.
— — Origin and Meaning of. (G. F. Oehler) Theo. Ecl. **4**: 463.
— National Obligation to. (R. Bickersteth) Ex. H. Lec. **6**: 1.
— Natural History of. Chr. Disc. **3**: 49. — (J. W. Alexander) Princ. **7**: 559. — Quar. **114**: 42. — Am. Mo. R. **4**: 80.
— Naturalism *versus* Inspiration. Brit. Q. **14**: 178.
— Neglect of. (R. W. Dickinson) Theo. & Lit. J. **5**: 403.
— New Translation of. (J. A. Bolles) New Eng. M. **5**: 89.
— Night Scenes of, Bell's. Chr. Obs. **68**: 221.
— not of Man. (R. W. Dickinson) Princ. **20**: 206.
— Notes upon. (H. Ware) Chr. Exam. **1**: 5–409.
— of Humanity. (O. B. Frothingham) Radical, **10**: 256.
— Old Testament and New compared. Cong. **2**: 321.
— — — Connection of. (Prof. Twesten) Am. Bib. Repos. **11**: 232. — (S. Osgood) Chr. Exam. **39**: 116.
— — — — Daubeny on. Chr. Obs. **1**: 507.
— — — Dispensations compared. Chr. Obs. **60**: 661.
— — — Harmony of. Cong. M. **24**: 405.
— — — Properties of. Chr. Mo. Spec. **1**: 232.
— — — Relation of. (H. Harbaugh) Am. Presb. R. **15**: 33. — (J. M. Titzel) Mercersb. **16**: 48. — Theo. Ecl. **7**: 285.
See below Bible, Old Testament; Bible, New Testament.
— only Guide of Life. Chr. Obs. **25**: 1, 65.
Bible, The, or Tradition as the Rule of Faith. Chr. Obs. **70**: 401.
— Oriental Features of. (J. S. Lee) Univ. Q. **34**: 39.
— Origin and Authority of. Cong. M. **17**: 97.
— Paragraph. Ed. R. **102**: 418. Same art. Liv. Age, **47**: 513.
— Parallelisms of. Kitto, **6**: 179. **8**: 184.
— People's Dictionary of. Ecl. R. **93**: 423.
— People's Right to. (S. Miller) Princ. **3**: 249.
— Perversions of. Fraser, **20**: 310.
— P'shito Version. (F. A Gast) Ref. Q. **27**: 241.
— Philosophy of. (J. Rowland) Am. Bib. Repos. 3d s. **4**: 510.
— Photographic Illustrations for. Dub. Univ. **51**: 174.
— Pictures for, Modern. Ecl. R. **112**: 180, 261.
— Place of, in a Science of Religion. Brit. Q. **61**: 98.
— Poetry of. (J. A. Brown) Evang. R. **16**: 283. — Knick. **6**: 189. — Am. Bib. Repos. 3d s. **3**: 323. — (G. B. Cheever) No. Am. **31**: 337. — (W. B. O. Peabody) No. Am. **35**: 473. — (A. P. Peabody) No. Am. **63**: 201. — Lond. M. **10**: 513. — (J. Reade) New Dom. **11**: 193, 260. — Brit. Q. **65**: 26. Same art. Liv. Age, **132**: 707. — Nat. R. **9**: 447. Same art. Liv. Age, **64**: 259. — (G. Gilfillan) Hogg, **6**: 345, 358.
— — Gilfillan on. (W. A. Larned) New Eng. **9**: 198. — Kitto, **7**: 419. — New Eng. **9**: 198. — (M. Stuart) No. Am. **73**: 238. — Ecl. R. **93**: 718. — (S. K. Kollock) Princ. **24**: 53.
— — Heilprin's Historical. (J. W. Chadwick) Nation, **29**: 60.
— — Lyrical. (G. H. Hastings) Am. Bib. Repos. 3d s. **3**: 323. — (G. B. Cheever) No. Am. **31**: 337. — (W. B. O. Peabody) No. Am. **35**: 473. — (A. P. Peabody) No. Am. **63**: 201.
— Political Economy of. (T. Chalmers) No. Brit. **2**: 1.
— Polyglott. Kitto, **17**: 327.
— — Complutensian, Critical Sources of. (J. Thomson) Bib. R. **3**: 186.
— Popular Misapplication of. Good Words, **1**: 84.
— Popular Use of. (G. E. Ellis) Chr. Exam. **56**: 321.
— Portraits in, Physiognomy of. Cong. **1**: 23–275.
— Proper Standard of Character. (B. B. Edwards) Bib. Sac. **3**: 23.
— Protestant Attacks upon. (A. F. Hewit) Cath. World, **5**: 789.
— Protestant Versions, Early, and Catholic compared. (J. W. Gibbs) New Eng. **10**: 300.
— Psychology of. (O. D. Miller) Univ. Q. **26**: 297.
— Punctuation of. Chr. Disc. **1**: 113.
— Quotations in. Kitto, **39**: 369.
— Radical's Attitude towards. (O. B. Frothingham) Radical, **1**: 449.
— Reading of. (O. Dewey) Chr. Exam. **12**: 141. — Chr. Mo. Spec. **4**: 404. — Brownson, **18**: 492.
— Realistic Features of. (J. S. Lee) Univ. Q. **36**: 272.
— Relation of, to Human Inquiry. (W. M'Combie) Kitto, **2**: 46.
— Republican Tendencies of. (E. Pond) Am. Bib. Repos. 3d s. **4**: 283. — (J. V. Moore) Meth. Q. **6**: 202.
— Reserved Force in. Bost. R. **6**: 374.
— Rhetorical Figures of. (W. N. Barber) Univ. Q. **13**: 175.
— Right Use of. Chr. R. **9**: 127.
— Saur's German, Germantown, 1743. Hist. M. **3**: 325.
— Scenes in, Croly's and Gilfillan's. Dub. Univ. **39**: 9.
— Science of, Phenomenal. Danv. Q. **4**: 339.
— Self-Evidential. (H. Stowell) Ex. H. Lec. **5**: 1.
— Self-Interpretation of. (T. G. Apple) Ref. Q. **26**: 485.
— Septuagint. (E. W. Grinfield) No. Am. **91**: 1. — Kitto, **16**: 3. **18**: 371.
— — Authority of. Chr. Obs. **9**: 200–738. **10**: 144 401.

Bible, The, Septuagint, Endorsement of, in New Testament. (H. M. Dean) Bib. Sac. 32: 624.
— — Grinfield's Apology for. (J. A. Alexander) Princ. 22: 541.
— — History and Editions of. Chr. Rem. 45: 289.
— — Holmes's Greek. Ecl. R. 3: 85-337. — Chr. Obs. 20: 544-746.
— — Origen's Hexapla. Month, 3: 424.
— — Origin and Structure of. (T. Rubinsohn) Chr. Exam. 54: 165.
— — Text of. Chr. Rem. 38: 292. — Liv. Age, 63: 550.
— Tischendorf's Edition of. (W. M. Reynolds) Evang. R. 5: 120.
— Shaksperian Glossary for. (L. S. Potwin) Bib. Sac. 19: 551.
— Silence of. (G. W. Gardner) Bapt. Q. 2: 303. — No. Brit. 32: 68. Same art. Liv. Age, 64: 677. — (J. C. Miller) Ex. H. Lec. 13: 139.
— Julia Smith's Translation of. (M. P. Lowe) Unita. R. 5: 322.
— Some main Features considered. Chr. Obs. 68: 331.
— Spanish Orientalisms and. (M. P. Lowe) Chr. Exam. 87: 65.
— Spirit of, Higginson on. Prosp. R. 10: 229.
— Spiritual Mind prerequisite to Judgment on. (E. V. Gerhart) Mercersb. 25: 82.
— Spiritual Understanding of. (E. Beecher) Chr. Mo. Spec. 8: 1.
— States Bible of Holland. (T. W. Chambers) Ref. Q. 27: 382.
— Stone on genuine and spurious Scripture. Chr. Obs. 6: 41.
— Stuart on the original Languages of. (C. W. Upham) No. Am. 14: 51.
— Study and Circulation of. (H. Ziegler) Evang. R. 3: 389.
— Study of. Chr. Q. Spec. 3: 116. — Chr. Mo. Spec. 2: 119, 169. — (J. R. Keiser) Evang. R. 11: 461.
— — Coghlan on. Mo. R. 163: 137.
— — Franck's Guide to. Meth. M. 36: 506.
— — Horne on. Ecl. R. 105: 172.
— — in 15th Century. (J. Gairdner) Fortn. 1: 710. 2: 59. Same art. Liv. Age, 86: 556.
— — in the Original. Am. Q. Reg. 15: 52.
— Studies in, Titcomb's. Chr. Obs. 59: 673.
— Style of, Boyle on. Cong. M. 5: 99.
— Superhuman Origin of, Rogers on. Chr. Obs. 74: 458.
— Supposed Errors in. (F. Gardiner) Bib. Sac. 36: 496.
— Swedenborgian Methods of interpreting. (B. Grant) Bib. R. 6: 178.
— Symbols of Prophecy. (D. N. Lord) Theo. & Lit. J. 7: 177, 386, 575. 8: 1.
— Syriac MS. of. Chr. Obs. 9: 273, 348.
— Theology and Nature. Bib. R 2: 416.
— Translation of. (W. Goodhugh) Quar. 23: 287. — Cong. M. 24: 749.
— — into the Languages of Britain. Chr. R. 13: 234.
— — into Eastern Languages. (J. Foster) Ecl. R. 9: 136, 418.
— — Rules for. Theo. Repos. 5: 200.
— Translations of, Marsh's History of. Chr. Obs. 12: 112.
— Truth of the Mosaic Records. (S. A. Lee) Nat. M. 7: 346.
— Turkish Version of. Cong. M. 9: 99.
— Typology of, Fairbairn's. (J. W. Nevin) Mercersb. 4: 76. — Theo. & Lit. J. 4: 353. 12: 529.
— — Principles and Limits of. Bib. R. 2: 431.
— Unitarian Version of. Cong. M. 17: 347.
— Unitarian Views on. (G. E. Ellis) Chr. Exam. 61: 235.
— Unity of. (W. F. Bainbridge) Bapt. Q. 10: 83.
— Use of, in Theology. (A. Duff, jr.) Bib. Sac. 37: 77.
Bible, The, Various Readings and Versions of. Chr. Mo. Spec. 2: 514.
— Vernacular Versions of. (J. A. Corcoran) Am. Cath. Q. 4: 344.
— — and the Reformation. (F. Vinton) Presb. R. 2: 384.
— Versio Itala. (J. Kenrick) Theo. R. 11: 318. — (F. Köckemann) Month, 12: 68.
— Versions of. Dub. R. 1: 367. — (C. T. Brooks) Mo. Rel. M. 8: 385. — Dub. R. 44: 181.
— View of the Divine Influence in. (E. Lyman) Chr. Q. Spec. 7: 591.
— — of Imputation in. (M. Stuart) Am. Bib. Repos. 7: 241.
— Vulgate. (T. Rubinsohn) Chr. R. 18: 237.
— — and Catholic Church. (R. Wahl) Univ. Q. 35: 69.
— — Early History of. (R. F. Clarke) Month, 31: 292.
— — Some Account of. (A. F. Hewit) Cath. World, 33: 590.
— Noah Webster's Edition of. Chr. Q. Spec. 5: 655.
— What is? (T. Edwards) Scrib. 13: 521. — (E. Janes) New Eng. 35: 114. — U. S. Cath. M. 5: 422.
— What we find in. (T. Colani) Mo. Rel. M. 26: 39.
— Whately and Ellicott on. (A. P. Peabody) No. Am. 102: 294.
— Wilbur's Reference. (G. Howe) Chr. Mo. Spec. 9: 161.
— with Emendations. Ecl. R. 74: 665. 75: 221.
— Witness to Christ a Proof of its Authority. (E. P. Miller) Am. Church R. 31: 14.
— Wonders of. (H. Stowell) Ex. H. Lec. 8: 1. — (E. W. Reinecke) Mercersb. 25: 73.
— Word-Pictures of, Interpretation of. (W. J. Beecher) Am. Presb. R. 18: 107.
— the Written Word. (O. Stearns) Chr. Exam. 61: 157.
— — and the Incarnate Word. (P. S. Davis) Mercersb. 16: 325.
Bible, Old Testament. (W. R. Smith in Encyc. Brit.) Sup. Pop. Sci. Mo. 1: 289. — (S. R. Calthrop) Unita. R. 14: 289.
— — and Christianity. Brit. Q. 25: 111. — Am. Church R. 24: 256.
— — and Evidence of History. Ecl. R. 125: 193.
— — and the Heathen World. (C. A. Auberlen) Good Words, 4: 710.
— — and the Jewish Church, Robertson on. (C. H. Toy) Nation, 32: 425.
— — and modern Criticism. Meth. Q. 31: 562.
— — Authority of, as a Rule of Duty. (W. J. Beecher) Am. Presb. R. 20: 550.
— — Authorship and Chronology of. (C. E. Grinnell) No. Am. 115: 437.
— — Barnes and Bush on. (G. R. Noyes) Chr. Exam. 38: 321.
— — Canon of. (T. Edwards) Chr. Q. Spec. 10: 69.
— — Characters of, Baring-Gould on Legends of. Chr. Obs. 72: 587.
— — Christ's Testimony to. (T. Doggett) Am. Presb. R. 17: 215.
— — Chronology of. Chr. Mo. Spec. 1: 339. — (E. Pond) Meth. Q. 27: 389. — (E. Pond) Theo. & Lit. J. 9: 239.
See Chronology.
— — Citations of, in the New Testament. (F. A. G. Tholuck) Bib. Sac. 11: 568. — (J. T. Gray) Kitto, 2: 197. — (J. J. Van Oosterzee) Theo. Ecl. 4: 45.
— — — in Discourses of Jesus. Chr. R. 24: 368, 543.
— — Commentaries on. (M. Heilprin) Nation, 9: 234.
— — Criticism of. (J. H. Allen) Unita. R. 7: 135. — Nat. R. 17: 261.
— — Davidson's Introduction to. Lond. Q. 19: 285. — (W. H. Green) Princ. 36: 53. — Westm. 78: 40, 511. 80: 220.

Bible, Old Testament, De Wette's Introduction to. No. Brit. **7**: 355.
— — De Wette and T. Parker on. Brit. Q. **15**: 453.
— — Difficulties in. Prosp. R. **4**: 281.
— — Distinctive Character of. Theo. Ecl. **7**: 83.
— — Eschatology of. (O. Street) New Eng. **33**: 655.
— — Geography and Biography of. Quar. **106**: 368. Same art. Liv. Age, **63**: 771.
— — Girdlestone's Synonyms of. Chr. Obs. **72**: 449.
— — Gliddon on Inspiration of. (D. R. Goodwin) Am. Church R. **8**: 27.
— — Glory of. (H. Stowell) Ex. H. Lec. **10**: 115.
— — Hävernick's Introduction to. Ecl. R. **79**: 164.
— — Hebrew and Greek Scriptures of. Kitto, **8**: 251.
— — Historical Books, Recent Commentaries on, 1873. Chr. Obs. **73**: 527, 694.
— — Historical Illustrations of. (G. H. Whittemore) Bib. Sac. **31**: 159.
— — History of Research concerning Structure of. (A. Duff) Bib. Sac. **37**: 729.
— — Injudicious Use of. Chr. Exam. **9**: 58.
— — judged by the New. Chr. R. **20**: 409.
— — Kalisch's Commentary on. Westm. **70**: 550.
— — Keil's Introduction to. Chr. Obs. **71**: 185.
— — Kurtz's History of the Old Covenant. Lond. Q. **12**: 447. — (W. H. Green) Princ. **28**: 173.
— — Letter and Spirit of. Kitto, **6**: 156. **7**: 146.
— — Maurice on. Ecl. R. **95**: 168.
— — Moral Difficulties of. (J. H. M'Ilvaine) Bib. Sac. **34**: 672. — Chr. Obs. **77**: 283, 527.
— — Newman and Greg on. No. Brit. **16**: 119.
— — Noeldeke on. (C. H. Brigham) No. Am. **109**: 602.
— — Palfrey on. (J. Walker) Chr. Exam. **25**: 106.
— — Primeval History of. Quar. **52**: 496.
— — Prophecies of, applied in New. (J. Priestley) Theo. Repos. **5**: 111.
— — Recollections of the East illustrative of. (Mrs. Postans) Kitto, **2**: 101. **4**: 46.
— — Religious Ideas of. Cong. Q. **2**: 257.
— — Rhetorical Figures of. (E. C. Bissell) Cong. R. **10**: 28.
— — Sharpe's Translation. Theo. R. **2**: 574.
— — Spirit of. (E. P. Peabody) Chr. Exam. **16**: 174, 305.
— — Structure of. (W. H. Green) Princ. **37**: 161.
— — Stuart on. (G. R. Noyes) Chr. Exam. **40**: 69.
— — Supernaturalism of. (G. T. Flanders) Univ. Q. **22**: 401.
— — Text of. Chr. Obs. **73**: 834. — Kitto, **33**: 172.
— — — and its Emendations. Kitto, **32**: 328.
— — — providentially preserved. Chr. Obs. **71**: 428.
— — Theology of. Brit. Q. **16**: 444. — (W. H. Green) Princ. **25**: 102.
— — Townsend's Arrangement of. Meth. M. **45**: 308.
— — Truth of. (E. V. Gerhart) Ref. Q. **27**: 173.
— Pentateuch, Age and Authorship of. (W. L. Alexander) Theo. Ecl. **6**: 215.
— — Ainsworth's. Cong. M. **2**: 403.
— — and Book of Joshua criticised. Chr. Rem. **45**: 225, 484.
— — and Egypt. (A. Sutherland) Meth. Q. **35**: 221.
— — and its Anatomists, Birks on. Chr. Obs. **70**: 212.
— — and its Assailants, Hamilton on. Chr. Obs. **58**: 908. — Ecl. R. **100**: 544.
— — Authenticity of. (C. E. Stowe) Lit. & Theo. R. **2**: 171. — (E. A. Park) Bib. Sac. **2**: 356, 668. — (J. A. Alexander) Princ. **10**: 542.
— — Authorship of. (S. C. Bartlett) Bib. Sac. **20**: 799. **21**: 495, 725. — Westm. **84**: 498. — (J. Burton) Canad. Mo. **20**: 317.
— — Blunt's Review of. Meth. M. **54**: 255.
Bible, Pentateuch, Brightwell's Notes on. Ecl. R. **73**: 415.
— — Colenso on. (R. Martineau) Theo. R. **16**: 507. — (Presbyter Anglicanus) Theo. R. **9**: 197. — (J. Strong) Meth. Q. **23**: 286. — (D. R. Goodwin) Am. Presb. R. **12**: 308, 444. — (I. Taylor) Theo. Ecl. **2**: 1. — Brit. Q. **37**: 147. Same art. Ecl. M. **58**: 315, 413. — Chr. Obs. **62**: 922. **63**: 184, 586. **72**: 248. — Ecl. M. **58**: 241. — Ecl. R. **116**: 506. Kitto, **30**: 257, 385. — Liv. Age, **76**: 118. — Nat. R. **16**: 1. — Theo. R. **2**: 583. — Westm. **79**: 7, 388, 503. — Brit. Q. **40**: 1. — No. Brit. **38**: 36.
— — Commentaries on. Chr. Rem. **52**: 265.
— — Contents and Inspiration of. Brownson, **5**: 507.
— — Credibility of. Chr. Obs. **64**: 517.
— — Genuineness of. (W. H. Green) Princ. n. s. **1**: 142. — Univ. Q. **22**: 336.
— — Graves on. Chr. Obs. **7**: 25.
— — Greek Version of. (H. B. Hackett) Bib. Sac. **4**: 188.
— — Hävernick's Introduction to. Ecl. R. **92**: 594.
— — Hengstenberg on. (H. M. Harman) Meth. Q. **13**: 75. — Ecl. R. **79**: 267.
— — Historical Character of. (S. C. Bartlett) Bib. Sac. **20**: 381.
— — Historical Value of. (J. M. Macdonald) Princ. **30**: 420.
— — Indian Copy of. (A. Holmes) Am. Q. Reg. **9**: 59.
— — Indian Roll of. Chr. Obs. **9**: 144, 609.
— — Kingsley on. Chr. Obs. **64**: 804.
— — Legislation of. (R. Martineau) Theo. R. **9**: 474.
— — Mosaic Origin of. (E. W. Hengstenberg) Am. Bib. Repos. **11**: 416. — Am. Bib. Repos. **12**: 458.
— — Palfrey on. Bost. Q. **1**: 261.
— — Samaritan. (J. Mills) Kitto, **31**: 131. — (T. Walker) Chr. Exam. **28**: 147. **29**: 63. — (M. Stuart) Am. Bib. Repos. **2**: 681. — (M. Stuart) No. Am. **22**: 274. — Kitto, **11**: 298 — (B. Pick) Bib. Sac. **33**: 265, 533. **34**: 79. **35**: 76, 309.
— — Science in. (S. Hopkins) New Eng. **36**: 58.
— — Smith on. Dub. R. **63**: 1.
— — Study of. (R. P. Stebbins) Unita. R. **11**: 128, 254. **12**: 244, 515.
— — Theory of. Chr. Rem. **31**: 309.
— — Transmission of the Books of Moses. Chr. Obs. **65**: 707.
— Genesis, and Geology. Blackw. **82**: 312. — Chr. Obs. **66**: 535. **67**: 249, 329, 447. Lond. Q. **48**: 52. — No. Brit. **27**: 325. — Kitto, **6**: 261.
— — Antiquity of. (J. C. Moffat) Princ. **33**: 37.
— — Author of. (E. Pond) Meth. Q. **23**: 601.
— — Bush on. (M. W. Jacobus) Princ. **11**: 271.
— — Candlish on. Ecl. R. **77**: 566. — Mo. R. **164**: 349.
— — Christ in. Am. Church R. **24**: 397.
— — Chronology of, Vindication of. Cong. M. **2**: 154, 218.
— — Close on. Chr. Obs. **27**: 227.
— — Complement of. (E. V. Gerhart) Mercersb. **24**: 265.
— — Date of Ethnological Table in. (A. H. Sayce) Theo. R. **11**: 59.
— — Different Computations on the first two Periods in. (E. Bertheau) Kitto, **2**: 115.
— — Early Narratives in. (F. Gardiner) Am. Church R. **30**: 361.
— — Exegesis of. Kitto, **21**: 253.
— — Explanation of some Passages in. (R. D. C. Robbins) Bib. Sac. **8**: 58.
— — First Murder and first City. (F. Lenormant) Contemp. **37**: 263.
— — Genealogies from Adam to the Deluge. (F. Lenormant) Contemp. **37**: 565.
— — Hedge's Primeval World. So. R. n. s. **8**: 459.

Bible, Genesis, Historical Character of. (G. H. Schodde) Luth. Q. **10**: 74.
— — Kalisch on. No. Brit. **29**: 561.
— — Narrative of Creation in. (J. O. Means) Bib. Sac. **12**: 83, 323.
— — Notes on. Chr. Obs. **67**: 447–927.
— — Numbers of, De Bertheau on. (J. E. Kerschner) Ref. Q. **26**: 434.
— — Panoramic Theory of. (J. T. Tucker) Cong. Q. **14**: 502.
— — Turner on. (C. F. Cruse) Meth. Q. **5**: 391.
— — Works on. (J. A. Alexander) Princ. **14**: 199. *See* Cosmogony; Creation; Geology.
— — Chapter i. (T. Hill) Bib. Sac. **32**: 303. — Univ. Q. **12**: 277.
— — — i. and ii., Exposition of. (S. Hopkins) Bib. Sac. **33**: 510, 716. **34**: 51, 422.
— — — i.-iii. Meth. M. **38**: 837.
— — — i.-xi. (H. B. Hackett) Bib. Sac. **22**: 395.
— — — xi. 26, Note on. (F. Gardiner) Bib. Sac. **34**: 755.
— — — xiv., Remarks on. (F. Tuck) Kitto, **2**: 80.
— — — xxv. 1, Observations on. Theo. Repos. **3**: 244.
— — — xlix. 10, a disputed Prophecy. (T. K. Cheyne) Theol. R. **12**: 300.
— — — xlix. 22–26, Exegesis of. (J. G. Hale) Cong. Q. **17**: 506.
— Genesis and Exodus, Alford's Commentary on. Chr. Obs. **73**: 124.
— Exodus, Buddicom on. Chr. Obs. **27**: 227. **28**: 96.
— Leviticus, Bonar on. Princ. **20**: 74.
— — Bush's Notes on. Princ. **15**: 164.
— — Kalisch's Commentary on. Chr. Obs. **75**: 54. — Lond. Q. **38**: 194.
— — Chapter xi. 3–7, and Deuteronomy xiv. 6–8. Kitto, **37**: 383.
— Numbers, Bush's Notes on. Theo. & Lit. J. **11**: 173.
— Deuteronomy as the Production of Moses. Kitto, **20**: 313.
— — Authorship of. Canad. Mo. **13**: 490.
— — Modern Theory of. Chr. Obs. **77**: 859.
— — Chapter xxiv., Poem on. Chr. Obs. **4**: 18.
— Joshua. Chr. Rem. **45**: 225, 484.
— — Colenso on. Bost. R. **3**: 190.
— — Introduction to. (K. F. Keil) Kitto, **4** : 217. **5**: 96.
— — Keil on. (W. H. Green) Princ. **22**: 59.
— — Typical Character of Book of. Chr. Obs. **58**: 457.
— — Chapter x., Miracle of. Am. Meth. M. **11**: 334. — — Chr. R. **15** : 595. — Theo. Repos. **1**: 103. — Chr. Obs. **75**: 780.
— Judges. (E. Pond) Theo. & Lit. J. **12**: 463.
— Ruth: Scripture Poetry. Portfo. (Den.) **30**: 478.
— Chronicles, Date of Books of. (W. H. Green) Princ. **35**: 499.
— Ezra and Nehemiah. Meth. M. **28**: 533.
— — Esdras and Josephus on. Kitto, **31**: 143, 413.
— — Sir I. Newton on. Kitto, **29**: 456. **30**: 143. — (I. W. Bosanquet) Kitto, **30**: 166, 421. **31**: 423.
— — Saulcy's Study of. (M. Heilpronn) No. Am. **109**: 272.
— Esther. (S. F. Smith) Chr. R. **13**: 365.
— — Remarks on. Kitto, **25**: 112.
— Job. (J. Muenscher) Chr. R. **23**: 75. — (G. R. Noyes) Chr. Exam. **23** : 29. — So. Lit. Mess. **6**: 563. — (E. Rénan) Mo. Rel. M. **45**: 350. — (C. F. Schaeffer) Evang. R. **14**: 1. — Brit. Q. **46**: 71. — Ecl. R. **112**: 13. **116**: 29. — (F. Greeves) Ex. H. Lec. **15**: 397. — Kitto, **39** : 338. — Lond. Q. **50** : 368. **51**: 52. — (W. H. Green) Princ. **29**: 281.
— — and its Theory of Life. Westm. **60**: 417.
— — and Plato's Dialogue on Justice. (H. W. Hoare) Fortn. **24**: 625.
Bible, Job, as an Art Composition. (J. G. Herder) J. Spec. Philos. **4**: 284.
— — Authorship of. Theo. Repos. **1**: 70. — Westm. **72**: 567.
— — Barnes on. (G. R. Noyes) Chr. Exam. **38**: 321.
— — Carey's Translation of. (G. C. M'Whorter) Am. Church R **12**: 249.
— — Closing Chapters of. (T. Lewis) Mercersb. **12**: 410.
— — Common Interpretation of. Chr. Obs. **59**: 797.
— — Conant's Translation of. (G. R. Noyes) Chr. Exam. **67**: 254.
— — Date of. (E. Renan) Mo. Rel. M. **45**: 241. — (T. G. Vaihinger) Am. Bib. Repos. 3d s. **3**: 174. — Bib. R. **2**: 93.
— — Difficult Passages in. Kitto, **36**: 374. **37**: 304. **38**: 377.
— — Doctrine of Immortality in. (O. Dewey) Mo. Rel. M. **50**: 385.
— — Essays on. (R. Wardlaw) Cong. M. **23**: 274–660. **24**: 624–838.
— — — Raymond's. (R. L. Gerhart) Ref. Q. **26**: 277.
— — Ewald on. Bib. R. **1**: 23.
— — Exegesis of. Kitto, **22**: 325.
— — Fry's Translation of. Ecl. R. **49**: 240.
— — Good on. Ecl. R. **23**: 132.
— — Good's Translation of. Chr. Obs. **12**: 300.
— — Gospel in. (G. B. Bacon) New Eng. **21**: 746.
— — Introduction of. (L. Hirzel) Bib. Sac. **7**: 144.
— — Introduction to. Kitto, **39**: 338.
— — Kant on Vindication of Job. Bib. R. **6**: 566.
— — Literature of. Kitto, **22**: 25.
— — New Translation of. Kitto, **27**: 361.
— — Noyes's Translation of. New York R. **4**: 457. — (S. Willard) No. Am. **26**: 40. — (S. Barrett) Chr. Exam. **4**: 309. — U. S. Lit. Gaz. **6**: 339.
— — Paraphrase from. Dub. Univ. **2**: 348.
— — Patriarchal Religion of. (A. Barnes) Am. Bib. Repos. 2d s. **3**: 163.
— — Philosophy of. Chr. Rem. **17**: 157.
— — Rénan on. (C. H. Brigham) Chr. Exam. **68**: 201.
— — Rénan's Translation of. Nat. R. **15**: 27.
— — Revised English Version of. Kitto, **23**: 257.
— — Revised Translation of. (J. M. Rodwell) Kitto, **39**: 208, 399. **40**: 129, 352.
— — Miss Smith's Translation of. Ecl. R. **14**: 657, 768.
— — Umbreit's Version. Cong. M. **21**: 644.
— — Chapters xxxii.-xxxvii., Authenticity of. (H. Ferguson) Am. Church R. **29**: 420.
— — Chapter xxxvi. 14, Original Text of. Theo. Repos. **1**: 448.
— — — xxxix. 19–25, Metrical Rendering. Theo. Repos. **1**: 219.
— Psalms. (W. M. L. De Wette) Am. Bib. Repos. **3**: 445. — Chr. Obs. **69**: 721, 801.
— — Alexander's Lectures on. Dub. Univ. **89**: 666.
— — Alternative Versions of. (W. Lee) Kitto, **38**: 1.
— — Burgh's Commentary on. Dub. Univ. **55**: 741.
— — Bush's Commentary on. (J. A. Alexander) Princ. **7**: 73.
— — Characteristics of. Chr. Obs. **55**: 365, 433, 513. **56**: 6, 77, 153.
— — Commentary on, from Old Writers. Chr. Rem. **39**: 264.
— — French and Skinner's Translation. Ecl. R. **54**: 151.
— — Commentaries on. (N. S. Folsom) Unita. R. **7**: 624. Ecl. R. **85**: 533.
— — — 1860–71. Chr. Obs. **72**: 113.
— — Fry's Translation of. Ecl. R. **32**: 342.
— — Hengstenberg and Phillips on. Bib. R. **4**: 145.
— — Hibbard on. (J. M'Clintock) Meth. Q. **17**: 117.
— — Hupfield on. Ecl. R. **103**: 612.

Bible, Psalms, Imprecatory. (J. J. Owen) Bib. Sac. **13**: 551. — Am. Presb. R. **9**: 575. — Chr. Rem. **19**: 110. — Theo. Ecl. **2**: 121.
— — — Authorship of. (T. Bulfinch) Chr. Exam. **52**: 244.
— — — in the Light of the United States Civil War. (E. A. Park) Bib. Sac. **19**: 165.
— — — Interpretation of. Bib. R. **3**: 199.
— — in Worship. New Eng. **4**: 312.
— — Jewish Psalter. (E. W. E. Reuss) Univ. Q. **33**: 292.
— — Mant's Version of. Ecl. R. **41**: 1.
— — Metrical Translations of. Chr. Obs. **17**: 510. — New Eng. **4**: 72.
— — Moll's Commentary on. Chr. Obs. **73**: 170.
— — Neale's Commentary on. (J. H. Hopkins) Am. Church R. **28**: 388.
— — New Readings of. (C. H. Brigham) Chr. Exam. **73**: 227.
— — Noyes's Translation of. (W. B. O. Peabody) No. Am. **35**: 473. — (F. W. P. Greenwood) Chr. Exam. **11**: 99. — (D. Fosdick) Chr. Exam. **43**: 204. — (G. R. Noyes) Chr. Exam. **43**: 289. — Am. Mo. R. **1**: 31.
— — Perowne's Commentary on. Chr. Obs. **64**: 765. — Lond. Q. **24**: 267.
— — Phillips's Commentary on. Chr. Obs. **72**: 894.
— — Position of, in the Plan of the Old Testament. — (W. H. Green) Princ. **39**: 256.
— — Recent Criticism of. (J. F. McCurdy) Bib. Sac. **32**: 637.
— — Reuss on. Lond. Q. **45**: 202.
— — Revision and. (J. DeWitt) Presb. R. **1**: 499.
— — Sandys's Paraphrase of. Cong. M. **20**: 101, 754.
— — Songs of Degrees. Kitto, **14**: 39. **15**: 56.
— — Tholuck on the Messianic. Bib. R. **5**: 25.
— — Tholuck's Introduction to. Bib. R. **4**: 344.
— — Versions of, and Commentary on. Chr. Rem. **33**: 473.
— — Walford's Translation of. Cong. M. **21**: 297.
— Psalm ii., Exposition of. (S. M. Vail) Meth. Q. **19**: 118.
— — — Translation and Exposition of. (C. E. Stowe) Bib. Sac. **7**: 352.
— — viii., Exposition of. (S. M. Vail) Meth. Q. **20**: 640.
— — xvi. (S. M. Vail) Meth. Q. **22**: 615.
— — — Interpretation of. (M. Stuart) Am. Bib. Repos. **1**: 51. — (E. W. Dickinson) Chr. R. **11**: 155.
— — xviii. 6–16, real, not figurative. Theo. & Lit. J. **4**: 91.
— — xix., Paraphrase of. Radical, **4**: 134.
— — xxii. (F. G. Hibbard) Meth. Q. **30**: 98, 366.
— — xxiii., Tholuck on. Cong. M. **25**: 145.
— — xxiv., xlii., cxxiii., Paraphrases of. Chr. Obs. **16**: 91.
— — lxviii. Tait, n. s. **28**: 77.
— — cvii., New Translation, with Notes. Chr. Obs. **9**: 1.
— — cxxvi., illustrated from Livy. Cong. M. **18**: 273.
— — cxxxix., Paraphrase of. Radical, **3**: 402. — Theo. Repos. **3**: 291.
— Proverbs, Pedagogical Value of. (J. A. Bauman) Ref. Q. **28**: 7.
— — Chapter xxiii. 26, Exegesis of. (W. H. Evans) Bapt. Q. **6**: 93.
— — — xxiii. 29–35. Kitto, **36**: 75.
— Ecclesiastes. Nat. R. **14**: 150.
— — Author of. Danv. Q. **3**: 38.
— — Bridges on. Chr. Obs. **60**: 264.
— — Did Solomon write? (E. Riggs) Princ. **24**: 79.
— — Hengstenberg on. Theo. & Lit. J. **13**: 526.
— — Philosophy of. (Prof. Nordheimer) Bib. Repos. **12**: 197. — Bib. R. **1**: 433.
— — Plan and Structure of the Book. Meth. Q. **9**: 173, 417. — Chr. Mo. Spec. **4**: 524.
— — Preaching of. (J. A. Goodhue) Chr. R. **19**: 434.
Bible, Ecclesiastes, Scope and Plan of. (W. H. Green) Princ. **29**: 419.
— — View of Life in. Kitto, **28**: 100.
— Song of Solomon. (W. M. Reynolds) Evang. R. **5**: 578. — (I. Riley) Am. Presb. R. **19**: 614. — Chr. Obs. **74**: 321. — Kitto, **8**: 320.
— — Authorship and Date of. Westm. **101**: 342.
— — Character of. (J. Pye Smith) Cong. M. **21**: 543.
— — Commentaries on. (W. H. Green) Princ. **26**: 1.
— — Divine Authority of. (J. Pye Smith) Cong. M. **20**: 413, 784. — (B. Rice) Cong. M. **21**: 197. — Cong. M. **13**: 232, 294.
— — Exegesis of. Cong. M. **21**: 471.
— — Hengstenberg on. (J. Forsyth) Theo. & Lit. J. **6**: 493.
— — Literature of. Kitto, **21**: 1.
— — Nature and Design of. Am. Q. **22**: 313.
— — New Reading of its Plot. Am. Presb. R. **19**: 145.
— — Sermon on. (Richard of Hampole) Kitto, **39**: 394.
— — Specimen of Targum on. Cong. M. **20**: 494.
— — Spiritual Sense of. (J. Bennett) Cong. M. **20**: 610. **21**: 142.
— — translated and annotated. (I. Horner) Meth. Q. **22**: 391. — Chr. Rem. **47**: 27.
— Prophets. (J. H. Allen) Chr. Exam. **56**: 374. — (J. Priestley) Theo. Repos. **4**: 97.
— — Ewald on. Kitto, **10**: 329.
— — Noyes's Translation of. (S. G. Bulfinch) Chr. Exam. **83**: 15. — (J. G. Palfrey) No. Am. **107**: 301.
— — Transpositions in Books of. Bib. R. **1**: 153.
— — Williams's Version of. (B. H. Cowper) Kitto, **38**: 70. — (G. D. Haughton) Fortn. **5**: 120. — (W. H. Green) Princ. **38**: 646.
— Isaiah. (G. V. Smith) Theo. R. **3**: 1, 541. — (J. E. Carpenter) Modern R. **2**: 1, 225. — Ecl. R. **116**: 148.
— — Alexander on. (A. P. Peabody) Chr. Exam. **46**: 48. — (D. N. Lord) Theo. & Lit. J. **1**: 544. — Ecl. R. **91**: 584. — Bib. R. **2**: 321. **4**: 441.
— — and Enoch, Apocryphal Books of. For. Q. **24**: 351.
— — Authorship of last Portion. (H. Cowles) Bib. Sac. **30**: 521.
— — Exposition of Figures of. (D. N. Lord) Theo. & Lit. J. **2**: 1–633. **3**: 60–595. **4**: 62, 218, 426. **5**: 74, 233, 461. **6**: 321, 479. **7**: 145–625. **8**: 149, 512. **9**: 333, 469. **10**: 501, 661. **12**: 153–663. **13**: 149–558.
— — Genuineness of. (E. W. Hengstenberg) Am. Bib. Repos. **1**: 700. — Princ. **2**: 153.
— — Henderson's Translation. Cong. M. **24**: 123. — Ecl. R. **73**: 285.
— — in Hebrew and English, Stock's. Ecl. R. **2**: 495.
— — Jenour's Translation. Ecl. R. **54**: 407.
— — — and Jones's Translation. Cong. M. **14**: 349.
— — Jewish Commentaries on. Kitto, **6**: 346.
— — Later Prophecies of. (S. H. Turner) Am. Church R. **1**: 29.
— — New Interpretation of. Theo. Repos. **6**: 344.
— — New Translation of Part of. Cong. M. **23**: 433.
— — New Works on. (J. A. Alexander) Princ. **13**: 159.
— — Prophecies of. (J. Kitto) Kitto, **4**: 356.
— — Recent Commentaries on, 1867–71. Chr. Obs. **72**: 607, 674.
— — Reuss and Urwick on. Lond. Q. **48**: 153.
— — Two Isaiahs, or one? (W. H. Cobb) Bib. Sac. **38**: 230, 658.
— — Chapter i. 2, New Translation of. Theo. Repos. **5** 317.
— — — iv., Spiritual Interpretation of. (N. Rounds) Meth. Q. **11**: 262.
— — — vi., Critical Notes on. Cong. M. **20**: 684.
— — — vii. 14–17, Interpretation of. Chr. Obs. **69**: 62

Bible, Isaiah, Chapter vii. 10–23; viii. 5–19, Observations on. Theo. Repos. **5**: 38.
— — — ix. 1, 2, as quoted by Matthew. Theo. Repos. **5**: 123.
— — — ix. 1–8, Interpretation of. Chr. Obs. **69**: 188.
— — — ix. 6, Explanation of. Theo. Repos. **5**: 182.
— — — xviii., New Translation of. Kitto, **31**: 273.
— — — xx. Chr. Obs. **49**: 145–361.
— — — xxxvi.–xxxix., and Assyrian Discoveries. (A. H. Sayce) Theo. R. **10**: 15.
— — — lii. and liii. (J. W. Lindsay) Meth. Q. **20**: 92.
— Jeremiah, Text of. (W. H. Green) Princ. **32**: 69.
— Ezekiel, Commentaries on. Chr. Obs. **76**: 580.
— — Introduction to. (H. A. C. Hävernick) Kitto, **1**: 22.
— — Penn on. Ecl. R. **21**: 91.
— Daniel. (R. Martineau) Theo. R. **2**: 172, 478. — Chr. R. **7**: 1. — Ecl. R. **79**: 53. — (F. E. Abbot) Radical, **7**: 28. — Chr. Rem. **49**: 1.
— — and Revelation. Theo. & Lit. J. **9**: 314, 484. **11**: 53.
— — as viewed by Hippolytus, Porphyry, and others. Kitto, **32**: 257.
— — Cumming's Lectures on. Theo. & Lit. J. **7**: 513.
— — Four Great Empires. Theo. & Lit. J. **13**: 276.
— — Fourth Kingdom. (O. S. Stearns) Bapt. Q. **10**: 331.
— — Genuineness of. (H. M. Harman) Meth. Q. **14**: 553.
— — Hengstenberg's Vindication of. (C. Hodge) Princ. **4**: 48.
— — Introduction to. Am. Presb. R. **1**: 32, 208.
— — Nebuchadnezzar's Golden Image. Theo. & Lit. J. **13**: 475.
— — Newton's Lectures on. Theo. & Lit. J. **12**: 340.
— — Prophecies of. (B. B. Edwards) New Eng. **1**: 231. — Meth. M. **36**: 667.
— — Prophecy of the Weeks in. Kitto, **40**: 210, 438.
— — Pusey on. Ecl. R. **122**: 164. — (J. J. S. Perowne) Contemp. **1**: 96. — (F. Parker) Kitto, **35**: 345. — Chr. Obs. **65**: 128. — Dub. R. **57**: 189.
— — Recent Expositions of. (W. H. Green) Princ. **43**: 397.
— — Seventy Weeks of. (E. Greenwald) Evang. R. **18**: 204.
— — — Stonard on. Ecl. R. **44**: 242.
— — Stuart's Commentary on. (R. P. Stebbins) Chr. Exam. **51**: 368.—(D. N. Lord) Lord's Theo. J. **3**: 352.
— — Times of. Kitto, **13**: 435. **14**: 364. **15**: 157. — Dub. Univ. **25**: 612. **27**: 497.
— — Chapter vii. 25, xii. 7, the 1260 Years. Chr. Obs. **5**: 614, 688. **6**: 17–773. **7**: 1–481. **8**: 541. **9**: 257, 688. **10**: 6–337. **12**: 278. **13**: 163. **14**: 281, 427, 498. **28**: 396. **38**: 287.
— — — viii. 9, Little Horn of He-Goat. Chr. Obs. **6**: 356, 496. **7**: 209, 685. **8**: 68.
— — — viii. 13, 14, the 2300 Days. Chr. Obs. **6**: 151, 701. **9**: 596, 688. **10**: 6, 278, 404. **13**: 486. **26**: 266.
— Minor Prophets, Commentaries on. Chr. Rem. **22**: 143. **43**: 148.
— — Henderson on. Bib. R. **1**: 249.
— Hosea. (W. H. Green) Princ. **31**: 74.
— Obadiah, expounded by Caspari. Princ. **24**: 226.
— Amos, Analysis of. (E. Wilton) Kitto, **33**: 180.
— — Baur's Commentary on. (B. P. Pratten) Kitto, **1**: 353.
— Jonah. (F. H. Hedge) Mo. Rel. M. **45**: 441. — Kitto, **39**: 437.
— — Abbot's Exposition of. Ecl. R. **84**: 217.
— — Commentary on. (E. B. Pusey) Theo. Ecl. **3**: 182.
— — Essay on. (J. B. Kerschner) Mercersb. **18**: 303.
— — Great Fish of, a Shark. Cong. M. **20**: 703.
— — How far Historical? Kitto, **36**: 110.
— — Natural Characteristics of. So. Q. **22**: 505.
Bible, Jonah, Observations on. (J. Foster) Cong. M. **27**: 253.
— — Thoughts on. Kitto, **39**: 437.
— Micah, Prophecy of Christ in. (J. A. Alexander) Princ. **35**: 610.
— Nahum. (B. B. Edwards) Bib. Sac. **5**: 551.
— — Prophecy of, concerning Nineveh. (W. H. Green) Princ. **27**: 102.
— Malachi, Jewish Expositions of. (W. H. Green) Princ. **27**: 308.
— — New Translation and Exposition of. (T. V. Moore) Meth. Q. **15**: 9, 169.
Bible, New Testament. (W. R. Smith in Encyc. Britannica) Sup. Pop. Sci. Mo. **1**: 385. — (C. P. Krauth) Evang. R. **5**: 376. — Quar. **113**: 95.
— — American Commentaries on. (H. Crosby) Am. Presb. R. **12**: 602.
— — Annotations on. (H. Crosby) Am. Presb. R. **16**: 160.
— — Authorship of. (A. Lamson) Chr. Exam. **14**: 1.
— — Authorship, Use, and Preservation of. (G. E. Ellis) Chr. Exam. **34**: 186.
— — Baptist Version of. (G. B. Jewett) Cong. R. **8**: 405. **9**: 66, 123. — Chr. R. **2**: 21.
— — Barnes's Notes on. Bib. R. **4**: 212.
— — Biblical Theology of. Lond. Q. **36**: 155.
— — Bloomfield's Annotations on. Kitto, **7**: 210.
— — Campbell on. Ecl. R. **73**: 683.
— — Canon of, in first two Centuries. (O. Cone) Univ. Q. **23**: 133.
— — — Muratorian. (W. G. T. Shedd) Am. Presb. R. **18**: 100. — Lond. Q. **41**: 434.
— — Christology of. Mo. Rel. M. **24**: 403.
— — Chronological, Townsend's. Cong. M. **10**: 84.
— — Citations of, by Apostolic Fathers. (W. Calkins) Bib. Sac. **23**: 593.
— — Commentary on. Chr. Rem. **22**: 143.
— — — Cobb's. (J. O. Skinner) Univ. Q. **24**: 277.
— — Cook on. Ecl. R. **35**: 310.
— — Criticism on, British. No. Brit. **25**: 110.
— — Davidson's Introduction to. Bib. R. **6**: 303. — (H. G. Spaulding) Chr. Exam. **85**: 196. — (J. A. Alexander) Princ. **21**: 144. — No. Brit. **16**: 422. — New Eng. **9**: 35. — (J. Kitto) Kitto, **2**: 342. **4**: 343. **8**: 98. — Ecl. R. **89**: 81. **91**: 187. **95**: 537. — Kitto, **8**: 98. — Lond. Q. **32**: 1. — Theo. R. **5**: 373. — Bib. R. **5**: 316.
— — Dickinson's Version of. Am. Mo. R. **3**: 219.
— — Divine Authority of, Bogue on. Chr. Obs. **1**: 112, 320, 733.
— — Dunbar on Interrogative Use of ΜΗ and ΟΥ in. Bib. R. **2**: 310.
— — Ecclesiastical Polity of. Chr. Obs. **71**: 622. — (G. B. Smith) Chr. R. **14**: 53.
— — Ἐγὼ εἰμι in. (J. Kenrick) Theo. R. **12**: 306.
— — English Hexapla. Ecl. R. **74**: 418. — Cong. M. **25**: 179. — Mo. R **156**: 427.
— — English Version. (C. F. Schaeffer) Bib. Sac. **26**: 486.
See Bible, English, Revision of; *also below*, Bible, New Testament, Revised Version.
— — Errors of Lexicons of. (W. E. Manley) Univ. Q. **25**: 59.
— — Ethics of. Bib. R. **5**: 205.
— — Exegetical and critical Account of. Westm. **90**: 36.
— — Forged Fragments of. Chr. Rem. **46**: 175.
— — Genealogies of. Mo. Rel. M. **30**: 314.
— — Geneva Version of. (F. Fry) Kitto, **33**: 279. — Chr. Obs. **36**: 229.
— — Georgian Version of. (S. C. Malan) Kitto, **35**: 360.
— — Gnostic Testimonies to, De Groot on. (H. M. Harman) Meth. Q. **30**: 485.

Bible, New Testament, Grammatical Accuracy of. (J. A. H. Tittmann) Am. Bib. Repos. 1: 160.

— — Greek. Chr. Rem. 22: 61. 26: 125. — Bib. R. 4: 38, 173. — Ecl. R. 70: 539. 79: 542.

— — — Alford's. (W. G. Humphry) Contemp. 13: 211. — Chr. Obs. 51: 39, 201. — Kitto, 9: 91. — Lond. Q. 1: 473.

— — — American Bible Union's. (G. B. Jewett) Cong. R. 9: 301.

— — — Ancient and modern compared. (W. E. Manley) Univ. Q. 26: 91.

— — — and Anglo-Saxon Version. Chr. Rem. 52: 68.

— — — Beza's. Am. Meth. M. 14: 112. — Chr. Rem. 48: 416.

— — — Bloomfield's. (C. Hodge) Princ. 9: 266. — Chr. R. 2: 210. — (G. E. Ellis) Chr. Exam. 22: 170. — Meth. M. 56: 563. — Cong. M. 11: 193.

— — — Codex Alexandrinus. Chr. Rem. 41: 367.

— — — — and Sinaiticus. (W. H. Grun) Princ. 33: 150.

— — — Codex Augiensis, Scrivener's. Kitto, 23: 1.

— — — Codex Sinaiticus. (B. H. Cowper) Kitto, 35: 108, 161. — (C. A. Hay) Luth. Q. 1: 122. 10: 153. — Brit. Q. 33: 353. 38: 343. — Chr. Rem. 51: 377. — Theo. R. 1: 214. — Evang. R. 20: 71. — Kitto, 31: 1. — Liv. Age, 48: 594. — (C. Tischendorf) Theo. Ecl. 3: 193. — Chr. Rem. 45: 374. — Lond. Q. 21: 238. Same art Ecl. M. 60: 477.

— — — Codex Vaticanus. (T. J. Conant) Bib. Sac. 26: 758. — (O. T. Dobbin) Dub. Univ. 54: 614. — Brit. Q. 47: 345. — Chr. Rem. 54: 405. — Ecl. R. 108: 398. — Ed. R. 112: 256.

— — — — Syriac Gospels and Codex Augiensis. Chr. Rem. 37: 467.

— — — — Tischendorf's. (J. J. Tayler) Theo. R. 4: 362.

— — — — Various Editions of. (T. J. Conant) Bib. Sac. 26: 758.

— — — Critical Editions of. Brit. Q. 18: 41.

— — — Editions of Mai, Beza, Tischendorf. Brit. Q. 28: 315.

— — — Erasmus's. (R. B. Drummond) Theo. R. 5: 527.

— — — Grammar of. Chr. Obs. 48: 182.

— — — Greek of. (G. H. Whittemore) Bapt. Q. 8: 58. — Ed. R. 94: 1. — (D. A. Whedon) Meth. Q. 28: 325, 485.

— — — — Definitive Article in, Sharpe on. Chr. Obs. 1: 438. 2: 363, 419.

— — — — Lexicography of. (E. Robinson) No. Am. 23: 80. — (F. A. Tholuck) Am. Bib. Repos. 1: 552.

— — — — Style in. (G. J. Plank) Am. Bib. Repos. 1: 638.

— — — — Use of the Article in. Theo. Repos. 4: 224, 374, 427.

— — — — Vocabulary of. (L. S. Potwin) Bib. Sac. 32: 703. 33: 52. 37: 503, 640.

— — — Hansell's. Brit. Q. 40: 308.

— — — Late Editions of. Brit. Q. 24: 183. — Ecl. R. 56: 465.

— — — Literature of. Lond. Q. 19: 492.

— — — Manuscripts of. (A. N. Arnold) Bapt. Q. 1: 445. — (W. H. Burr) Radical, 6: 391.

— — — — and Editions of. (M. Stuart) Bib. Sac. 1843: 254.

— — — — Griesbach's Classification of. Chr. Obs. 13: 573.

— — — — Most ancient. (C. Tischendorf) Theo. Ecl. 6: 236.

— — — — Scrivener on. Chr. Obs. 66: 94.

— — — Modern. (W. E. Manley) Univ. Q. 26: 287.

— — — Recension of. Chr. Rem. 3: 17.

— — — Revision of. Brit. Q. 59: 131.

Bible, New Testament, Greek, Robinson's Lexicon of. Ecl. R. 67: 269. — (M. Stuart) No. Am. 72: 261. — Chr. R. 16: 461. — So. Q. 19: 263.

— — — Study of. Am. Meth. M. 9: 415. — Chr. Rem. 15: 259.

— — — Text of. (J. D. Green) No. Am. 15: 460. — (W. Sanday) Contemp. 40: 985. — Bost. R. 4: 258. — Chr. Rem. 51: 377. — Ed. R. 94: 1.

— — — — amended. (F. W. P. Greenwood) Chr. Exam. 6: 353.

— — — — History of. Chr. R. 13: 545.

— — — — Sources of. Kitto, 12: 367.

— — — Textual Criticism of. Chr. Rem. 43: 385.

— — — Tischendorf's. (B. Hawley) Meth. Q. 34: 213. — Bib. R. 6: 221. — (S. P. Tregelles) Kitto, 4: 197. 5: 197.

— — — Tischendorf *vs.* Tregelles. (C. Tischendorf) Kitto, 29: 369.

— — — Tregelles's. Brit. Q. 53: 180. — Chr. Obs. 71: 132.

— — — Webster's and Wilkinson's. Chr. Obs. 62: 25.

— — — Winer's Grammar of. Theo. & Lit. J. 12: 339, 397. — Lond. Q. 34: 187.

— — — Wordsworth's. Chr. Obs. 68: 112.

— — Greek Vulgate. Kitto, 10: 116.

— — Griesbach's. Chr. Mo. Spec. 5: 187. — (J. G. Palfrey and J. Sparks) No. Am. 31: 267. — So. R. 6: 513. — Ecl. R. 72: 484. — Chr. Disc. 3: 321. — Gen. Repos. 1: 89.

— — Hebraisms of. (W. E. Manley) Univ. Q. 9: 21.

— — Hebrew. (W. E. Manley) Univ. Q. 28: 26.

— — — Egyptian Words in. Bib. R. 1: 389.

— — — History of. (B. Pick) Luth. Q. 8: 363.

— — Hilgenfeld's Introduction to. (P. H. Wicksteed) Theo. R. 12: 515. 13: 1. — Lond. Q. 44: 308.

— — Historical Books of. (H. Olshausen) Am. Bib. Repos. 9: 207.

— — How it came down to us. (G. P. Fisher) Scrib. 21: 611.

— — Hug's Introduction to. Chr. R. 1: 597. — Cong. M. 10: 657.

— — Immer's Hermeneutics of. (O. Cone) Univ. Q. 33: 436.

— — Improved Version of, 1808. Quar. 1: 276. — Ecl. R. 9: 24, 236, 329. — Chr. Obs. 8: 634.

— — in the Negro Tongue. (R. Southey) Quar. 43: 553.

— — Inspiration of. (S. C. Bartlett) Princ. n. s. 5: 23. — (E. Fisher) Univ. Q. 27: 261. *See* Inspiration.

— — Interpretation of. (F. A. Tholuck) Am. Bib. Repos. 3: 684. — Chr. R. 4: 481.

— — Japanese Translations of. Kitto, 16: 388.

— — Kirchhofer on the History of Canon of. Bib. R. 2: 222.

— — Lange's Commentary on. (P. Schaff) Evang. R. 15: 298.

— — Literary History of. Bib. R. 1: 344. — Brit. Q. 3: 96. — Ecl. R. 83: 39.

— — Literature of. No. Brit. 16: 422.

— — Livermore's Commentary on. (R. P. Stebbins) Chr. Exam. 37: 252.

— — Mahratta Version of. Ecl. R. 51: 266.

— — Marginal Readings of. (C. F. Schaeffer) Bib. Sac. 26: 486.

— — Michaelis's Introduction to. Chr. Obs. 1: 433, 727. 3: 548.

— — Narratives of, Real and ideal. (J. C. Miller) Ex. H. Lec. 17: 483.

— — Noyes's Translation of. (H. G. Spaulding) Chr. Exam. 87: 54.

— — Numismatic Illustrations of, Akerman's. Bib. R. 4: 560.

Bible, New Testament, Observations on some Places in. (W. Linwood) Kitto, **40**: 23.
— — Old Testament in, Citations of. (F. A. G. Tholuck) Bib. Sac. **11**: 568. — Chr. Exam. **5**: 53.
— — — Dogmatic Use of. (O. Cone) Univ. Q. **26**: 133.
— — Olshausen's Commentary on. (C. P. Krauth) Evang. R. **10**: 124. — (E. Strong) New Eng. **15**: 301. — Lit. & Theo. R. **1**: 142.
— — Paige's Commentary on. (H. Ballou, 2d) Univ. Q. **1**: 396.
— — Parallelisms of. Kitto, **37**: 205.
— — Philosophy of. (E. Robinson) Am. Bib. Repos. **4**: 154.
— — Poetry of. Hogg, **6**: 298.
— — Politics of. Tait, n. s. **11**: 749. Same art. Liv. Age, **4**: 185.
— — Proverbial Phrases in. Theo. & Lit. J. **9**: 167.
— — Psychology of. (H. Olshausen) Meth. Q. **19**: 254.
— — Punctuation of, Exegetical. (C. F. Schaeffer) Bib. Sac. **25**: 593.
— — Recent Commentaries on. (A. P. Peabody) No. Am. **87**: 235.
— — Recent Study of, 1855. Fraser, **52**: 696.
— — Recent Translation of. Lond. Q. **45**: 265.
— — Revised Version, 1881. Ed. R. **154**: 157. — (G. P. Fisher) Scrib. **22**: 293. — (T. Walrond) Macmil. **44**: 149. Same art. Liv. Age, **150**: 67. — (G. Vance Smith) 19th Cent. **9**: 917. — Ecl. M. **97**: 223. — (F. Gardiner) Bib. Sac. **38**: 553. — (J. J. S. Perowne) Contemp. **40**: 150. — Dub. R. **89**: 127. — (P. Schaff) No. Am. **132**: 427. — (A. Roberts) Fraser, **103**: 727. — (W. C. Doane) Am. Church R. **36**: 63. — Lond. Q. **56**: 471. — (E. McSweeny) Am. Cath. Q. **6**: 300. — (H. A. Buttz) Meth. Q. **41**: 715. — (J. A. Corcoran) Am. Cath. Q. **6**: 481. — (J. Gibb) Brit. Q. **74**: 128. — (E. M. Geldart) Mod. R. **2**: 603. — (M. R. Vincent) Presb. R. **2**: 633. — (T. A. Becker) Cath. World, **33**: 558. — (O. D. Miller) Univ. Q. **37**: 454.
— — — and the Authorized Version. (T. R. Beck) Ref. Q. **28**: 535.
— — — English of. (R. B. Drummond) Mod. R. **2**: 732.
— — — Greek Text employed in. Quar. **152**: 307.
— — — Plan of. (T. W. Chambers) Presb. R. **2**: 449.
— — — Reception of, in England. (J. Bryce) Nation, **33**: 68.
— — — Some Advantages of. (J. S. Howson) Good Words, **22**: 594. Same art. Ecl. M. **97**: 631.
— — Rhemish. (B. Hawley) Meth. Q. **31**: 107.
— — Sawyer's Version of. Princ. **31**: 50. — (D. R. Goodwin) Am. Church R. **12**: 99.
— — Scientific Criticism of. (O. B. Frothingham) Chr. Exam. **57**: 94.
— — Serampore Mahratta Version of. Cong. M. **13**: 137.
— — Sharpe's Translation of. Prosp. R. **1**: 165.
— — Speaker's Commentary on. Quar. **151**: 352.
— — Stowe's History of. (E. Abbot) No. Am. **107**: 307.
— — Supernatural in. Lond. Q. **44**: 377.
— — Synonyms of. (N. White) Univ. Q. **37**: 213.
— — — Trench on. Lond. Q. **7**: 406. — Theo. & Lit. J. **7**: 514.
— — Syriac. Liv. Age, **32**: 88.
— — — and Syrian Churches. Bib. R. **6**: 196.
— — Studies in, Aid of Talmud in. Bost. R. **4**: 340.
— — Tauchnitz Edition of. Ev. Sat. **8**: 443.
— — Textual Criticism of. Chr. Rem. **48**: 40.
— — — Tregelles on. (W. Skae) Kitto, **8**: 208.
— — Translations of. Chr. Rem. **3**: 17.
— — Transmission of the Books of. So. R. n. s. **19**: 432. — (G. P. Fisher) Scrib. **21**: 611.
— — — Milligan on. Chr. Obs. **74**: 622.
— — Turkish. Ecl. R. **44**: 326.

Bible, New Testament, Two Religions in. (O. B. Frothingham) Radical, **3**: 11–284. **5**: 367.
— — Tyndale's. (J. S. Hart) Princ. **10**: 325. — Chr. R. **3**: 130. — (J. L. Porter) Good Words, **22**: 103.
— — — and Fry's Facsimiles. Kitto, **34**: 295.
— — — and Luther's. Ch. Obs. **36**: 731.
— — — Dabney's Edition of. (J. Walker) Chr. Exam. **23**: 273. — Spirit Pilg. **2**: 658.
— — under a new Aspect. (G. Grove) Macmil. **20**: 428. Same art. Ecl. M. **73**: 618.
— — Unity of, Maurice on. (S. Osgood) Unita. R. **11**: 581.
— — Usage of the Terms translated Spirit, Soul, and Life. (H. Ballou) Univ. Q. **7**: 138.
— — Various Passages illustrated by Transposition. Theo. Repos. **1**: 45.
— — Von Gerlach's Commentary. (G. R. Crooks) Meth. Q. **9**: 268.
— — Wakefield's Translation of. Chr. Disc. **2**: 1.
— — Wycliffe's Version. (H. S. Brown) Good Words, **3**: 467. Same art. Liv. Age, **76**: 579. — Am. Bib Repos. **7**: 226.
— — Words in, Illustrations of. (T. B. Thayer) Univ. Q. **3**: 316.
— — Writers of, Credibility of. Chr. R. **5**: 568.
— Gospels. (C. A. Sainte-Beuve) O. & N. **2**: 662. — Cong. M. **15**: 748. **17**: 726. **18**: 226, 668, 730. **19**: 164–673. **20**: 297, 616. **21**: 343, 413. — So. R. n. s. **21**: 5.
— — Adam's Exposition of. Chr. Obs. **37**: 663, 705.
— — Alcott's Conversation on. Chr. Exam. **23**: 252.
— — and Acts in Hebrew, London Society's Translation of. Chr. Obs. **16**: 161.
— — and modern Criticism. Contemp. **5**: 340.
— — Antiquity of. No. Brit. **4**: 347.
— — 'Απομνημόνευματα of the Apostles. Chr. Obs. **7**: 623.
— — Authenticity of. (B. A. Hinsdale) Chr. Q. **4**: 57.
— — Authors of. (J. Eastwood) Univ. Q. **33**: 171.
— — Barnes on. (J. A. Alexander) Princ. **7**: 149. — (A. P. Peabody) Chr. Exam. **20**: 66.
— — Burgon's Plain Commentary on. (W. A. Dod) Am. Church R. **12**: 465.
— — Chronology of. (H. C. Vedder) Bapt. Q. **11**: 193. — Quar. **130**: 497.
— — H. J. Coleridge on. Dub. R. **77**: 173.
— — Carci's Translation of. (T. A. Trollope) Brit. Q. **72**: 23.
— — Credibility of. Ecl. R. **87**: 24.
— — Criticism on, Beneficial Results of. (O. B. Frothingham) Chr. Exam. **76**: 374.
— — Date of. (O. Cone) Univ. Q. **24**: 5. — (C. Tischendorf) Theo. Ecl. **3**: 208.
— — — Tischendorf on. (A. Hovey) Bapt. Q. **1**: 66.
— — Directions for reading. Chr. R. **3**: 443.
— — Evidence in Favor of. Chr. Obs. **26**: 321.
— — First three, Godet on. (J. Wright) Theo. R. **8**: 512.
— — — Origin of. (G. P. Fisher) New Eng. **23**: 577. — (G. T. Ladd) Bib. Sac. **26**: 1, 209.
— — Folsom's Translation of. (S. G. Bulfinch) Chr. Exam. **87**: 270. — (R. Metcalf) O. & N. **6**: 191.
— — the fourfold Biography. Brit. Q. **35**: 108.
— — Genuineness of. (L. J. Livermore) Unita. R. **12**: 1. — (J. H. Morison) Chr. Exam. **56**: 46. — (H. Ballou, 2d) Univ. Q. **5**: 179.
— — — and Authenticity of. (B. A. Hinsdale) Chr. Q. **3**: 29, 287, 431.
— — — Norton on. (G. E. Ellis) Chr. Exam. **58**: 117. — (A. P. Peabody) No. Am. **42**: 206. — (A. Lamson) Chr. Exam. **22**: 321. **36**: 145. **43**: 148. — (M. Stuart) Am. Bib. Repos. **11**: 265. — Brit. Q. **7**: 431. — Chr. R. **3**: 53. — Mo. R. **144**: 46. — Ecl. R. **87**: 423. — Mo. Rel. M. **5**: 97, 145. — Prosp. **1**: 83.

Bible, Gospels, Genuineness of, Tischendorf's Plea for. (F. H. Hedge) Chr. Exam. **80**: 503.
— — Greek MSS. of, Scrivener's Collation of. Kitto, **11**: 346.
— — Harmonizing. (Duke of Manchester) Kitto, **19**: 56.
— — Harmony of. (H. J. Coleridge) Month, **29**: 102. — (J. Priestley) Theo. Repos. **2**: 38–313. **3**: 462. — Chr. Exam. **10**: 358. — (L. Carpenter) Chr. Exam. **13**: 87. — Cong. M. **14**: 536, 663. **15**: 273. **16**: 463, 601. **17**: 266. — Kitto, **10**: 60. — (J. A. Alexander) Princ. **28**: 393.
— — — Carpenter's. (A. P. Peabody) Chr. Exam. **22**: 43. — Ecl. R. **70**: 505.
— — — Chronological. Kitto, **6**: 75.
— — — Da Costa's. Evang. R. **6**: 563.
— — — Greswell on. Dub. R. **55**: 421. — Ecl. R. **57**: 1, 299.
— — — Robinson's Greek. Ecl. R. **83**: 732.
— — — Strong's. (G. R. Crooks) Meth. Q. **13**: 354.
— — — Stroud's new Greek. Chr. Obs. **54**: 115. — Meth. Q. **14**: 77.
— — — Studies in. (W. H. Settlemyer) Luth. Q. **8**: 538.
— — Hegelian Assaults on. (C. E. Stowe) Bib. Sac. **8**: 503. Same art. Kitto, **36**: 124, 283.
— — Hemmingius on. Cong. M. **15**: 415.
— — Historical Character of. (C. A. Row) Kitto, **35**: 311. **36**: 1, 343. **37**: 58, 275. **38**: 251.
— — Historical Criticism on. Brit. & For. R. **12**: 515.
— — How to use. (H. Alford) Theo. Ecl. **2**: 235.
— — Huidekoper on. (J. H. Morison) Unita. R. **12**: 661.
— — Inspiration of. (G. F. Simmons) Chr. Exam. **54**: 351. — Kitto, **12**: 58. **13**: 50. **23**: 117.
— — Internal Evidences to Truth of. (J. P. Thompson) No. Am. **97**: 74.
— — Jesus Christ and. (W. H. Furness) Mo. Rel. M. **47**: 342, 423.
— — Kenrick on. Brownson, **6**: 409.
— — Literal Truthfulness of. (C. Vince) Ex. H. Lec. **20**: 73.
— — Moral Criticism of. Theo. R. **2**: 608.
— — Narratives of, Logical Order of. (E. E. Hale) Chr. Exam. **65**: 205.
— — Nast's English Commentary on. (W. F. Warren) Meth. Q. **28**: 30.
— — New Version and Vulgate. Brownson, **3**: 472.
— — Norton's Translation of. (G. E. Ellis) Chr. Exam. **59**: 72.
— — Object of the Writers of. Chr. R. **7**: 246.
— — Olshausen's Commentary on. Chr. Obs. **52**: 467.
— — Oneness of. (E. H. Sears) Mo. Rel. M. **39**: 165.
— — Origin of. (W. H. Furness) Chr. Exam. **70**: 49. — (J. I. Mombert) Bib. Sac. **23**: 352, 529. — (James Smith) Kitto, **15**: 135.
— — — and Connection of, James Smith on. Kitto, **12**: 174.
— — Proofs of Christianity in. (G. P. Fisher) Princ. n. s. **7**: 191. **8**: 223.
— — Prophetic Element in. (W. R. Greg) Contemp. **28**: 990.
— — Question of, in 1851. (C. E. Stowe) Kitto, **36**: 124, 283.
— — Rénan on. (A. Laugel) Nation, **25**: 179, 210. — (W. Sanday) Theo. R. **15**: 116.
— — Ripley's Notes on. Chr. R. **2**: 289.
— — Seiss's Lectures on. So. R. n. s. **22**: 115.
— — Synoptical Study of, and recent Literature pertaining to it. (H. B. Hackett) Bib. Sac. **3**: 1.
— — Syriac, Dr. Cureton's. (P. N. Laud) Kitto, **22**: 140. — (S. P. Tregelles) Kitto, **22**: 407. — Ed. R. **110**: 168.
— — Textual Criticism of, Results of. (James Smith) Kitto, **15**: 323.
Bible, Matthew. Dub. Univ. **72**: 363. — Kitto, **28**: 269. — (M. Stuart) Am. Bib. Repos. **12**: 133. — So. R. n. s. **22**: 90.
— — Commentary on. (U. Zwingli) Mercersb. **4**: 55, 453.
— — Conant's Commentary on. Chr. R. **26**: 92, 264.
— — Gospel for the Jew. (D. S. Gregory) Princ. **40**: 481
— — Introductory Chapters interpolated. Theo. Repos **4**: 484.
— — Original Language of. (W. L. Alexander) Kitto, **3**: 499. — (S. P. Tregelles) Kitto, **5**: 151.
— — Quesnel's Commentary on. Chr. Obs. **69**: 261.
— — Revision of authorized Version of. Chr. Obs. **35**: 34–283.
— — Structure of. (H. J. Coleridge) Month, **23**: 17, 296. **25**: 1.
— — Whedon on. (A. C. George) Meth. Q. **29**: 346.
— — Chapters ii. and iii., Commentary on. (H. A. W. Meyer) Bib. Sac. **8**: 85.
— — — ii. 23. (J. H. R. Biesenthal) Bib. Sac. **32**: 161.
— — — iii. 7–12, Illustration of. Theo. Repos. **1**: 396.
— — — v. 29, 30, Explanation of. (H. Ballou, 2d) Univ. Q. **1**: 170.
— — — vi. 7, "Use not vain repetitions." Theo. Repos. **6**: 178.
— — — xi. 2–14. Chr. R. **24**: 606.
— — — xiii. and its Interpreters. Ecl. R. **118**: 500.
— — — xxiv., Annotations on. (C. F. Schaeffer) Evang. R. **13**: 55. — Theo. Repos. **6**: 186.
— — — xxv. 46, Christ's Coming to Judgment. (E. G. Brooks) Univ. Q. **31**: 389.
— — — xxvi. 50, discussed. (T. D. Woolsey) Bib. Sac. **31**: 314.
— — and Mark, Morison's Commentaries on. Chr. Obs. **74**: 115.
— Mark. (S. Davidson) Theo. R. **4**: 494. — Lond. Q. **23**: 514. — Dub. Univ. **73**: 154.
— — Alexander on. (E. D. Yeomans) Mercersb. **11**: 361.
— — Explanation of some Passages. Theo. Repos. **4**: 227.
— — the Gospel for the Romans. (D. S. Gregory) Princ. **43**: 325.
— — Last twelve Verses of. Am. Church R. **24**: 218. **26**: 379.
— — Relation of, to Matthew and Luke. Prosp. R. **6**: 60.
— — Chapter iv. 49, 50, Interpretation of. Meth. Q. **10**: 81.
— Luke. Dub. Univ. **73**: 3. — Am. Church R. **24**: 359, 511. — (Z. S. Barstow) Cong. R. 8: 477.
— — Codex Zacynthius. Chr. Rem. **43**: 128.
— — Godet's Commentary on. Chr. Obs. **75**: 707.
— — Greek Palimpsest of. Dub. Univ. **59**: 303.
— — Origin and Purpose of. (H. Constable) Kitto, **29**: 380.
— — Preface to. Kitto, **4**: 301.
— — Sources of. (A. H. Newman) Bapt. Q. **9**: 306.
— — Thomson's Lectures on. Bib. R. **6**: 598.
— — Chapter iii. 7, and John ii. 20, Dates of. (J. Pratt) Kitto, **38**: 468.
— — — xvii. 20, 21, Exegetical Remarks on. (E. Schaubach) Bib. R. **1**: 202.
— — — xxiii. 39–43, Exegesis of. (P. Church) Bapt. Q. **7**: 88.
— John. (L. Abbott) Internat. R. **5**: 343. — (S. Davidson) Theo. R. **7**: 297. — (W. Milligan) Contemp. **6**: 101. — (J. H. Godwin) Contemp. **19**: 361. Same art. Liv. Age, **112**: 738. — (E. Rénan) Contemp. **30**: 542. — (E. H. Sears) Mo. Rel. M. **42**: 1. — Cong. **4**: 365. — So. R. n. s. **22**: 404. **23**: 65. — Theo. R. **1**: 528.
— — and Apocalypse. (W. Milligan) Contemp. **18**: 87, 212.
— — and Epistles of John, Ewald on. Nat. R. **17**: 125
— — — New Revision of, 1837. Mo. R. **146**: 195.

Bible, John, and Justin Martyr. (J. Drummond) Theo. R. **12**: 471. **14**: 155.
— — and modern Criticism. (W. Beyschlag) Contemp. **30**: 768, 923.
— — Ancient MS. of. (J. Milner) Arch. **16**: 17.
— — Attraction of. (E. V. Gerhart) Mercersb. **3**: 52.
— — Authenticity of. (J. Martineau) O. & N. **10**: 201.
— — Author not John the Apostle. Westm. **83**: 406.
— — Authorship of. Theo. R. **3**: 264, 564. — (J. F. Clarke) Chr. Exam. **84**: 72. — Ed. R. **145**: 1. — (E. Higginson) Theo. R. **5**: 189. — (E. Abbot) Unita. R. **13**: 142, 237, 490. — Brit. Q. **56**: 408. — Dub. Univ. **73**: 243, 483. — Chr. Obs. **76**: 34, 344, 434. **77**: 189. — Mo. Rel. M. **33**: 193. **35**: 83. — (F. R. Conder) Fraser, **92**: 51. — (A. Edersheim) Fraser, **92**: 270.
— — — Abbot on. Penn Mo. **11**: 895.
— — Credibility of Christ's Discourses in. (F. Godet) Bapt. Q. **8**: 307.
— — Design of. (C. E. Luthardt) Bib. Sac. **30**: 1, 237.
— — Eternal Life in. Lond. Q. **49**: 358.
— — Exegetical Studies in. (P. Schaff) Am. Presb. R. **19**: 699.
— — Genuineness of. (G. P. Fisher) Bib. Sac. **21**: 225. — (J. P. Lange and P. Schaff) Princ. **41**: 323.
— — Gilly's Romaic Version of. Ecl. R. **91**: 554.
— — Introduction to. Chr. R. **12**: 192. — Chr. Disc. **3**: 326. — (F. A. Tholuck) Kitto, **2**: 1.
— — Latest Commentaries on, 1880. Lond. Q. **56**: 150.
— — Literary Character of. (F. R. Conder) Fraser, **91**: 373, 802. — (A. Edersheim) Fraser, **91**: 764. — (T. L. Hill) Fraser, **91**: 666.
— — Maurice on. Ecl. R. **106**: 45.
— — Modern Criticism on. Lond. Q. **24**: 504.
— — Olshausen and Lange on. Bib. R. **5**: 184.
— — the Regula Fidei. (T. Lewis) Am. Presb. R. **13**: 46.
— — Revised Version of, 1857. Chr. Obs. **57**: 532.
— — Revision of. Kitto, **20**: 1.
— — E. H. Sears on. (C. C. Everett) O. & N. **6**: 584.
— — — C. C. Everett's Criticism of. (E. H. Sears) O. & N. **7**: 233.
— — — Theology of the Fourth Gospel and Dr. Sears. Mo. Rel. M. **48**: 442.
— — Theories of Baur and others on. Nat. R. **5**: 82.
— — Tholuck's Commentary on. (C. P. Krauth, jr.) Evang. R. **7**: 301. **9**: 301. — Lit. & Theo. R. **3**: 439. — (L. Bacon) Chr. Q. Spec. **8**: 319. — Chr. R. **1**: 276. — Am. Bib. Repos. **7**: 440.
— — Chapter i., Rothe on. Lond. Q. **52**: 166.
— — — i. 1. Theo. Repos. **2**: 186. **5**: 295, 385.
— — — i. 1–18. (M. Stuart) Bib. Sac. **7**: 13, 281.
— — — i. 15, Interpretation of. Theo. Repos. **1**: 295.
— — — i. 16. (J. C. Yule) Bapt. Q. **5**: 79.
— — — i. 18, Syriac Version of. Theo. Repos. **1**: 73.
— — — i. 51, Interpretation of. Theo. Repos. **6**: 424.
— — — ii. 20, Date of. (J. Pratt) Kitto, **38**: 468. **39**: 233.
— — — iii. 1–10, illustrated. Theo. Repos. **6**: 194.
— — — iii. 13, Illustration of. Theo. Repos. **1**: 355.
— — — iv., Interpretation of. Theo. Repos. **6**: 419.
— — — vi., Interpretation of. Theo. Repos. **6**: 415.
— — — vii. 37, Sermon on. (A. Monod) Mo. Rel. M. **16**: 48.
— — — vii. 53–viii., Genuineness of. (A. P. Peabody) Mo. Rel. M. **43**: 521.
— — — ix. (A. G. Pease) Mercersb. **24**: 74.
— — — xiv. 1, 2, 3. Theo. Repos. **5**: 355.
— — — xvi. 23. (Z. S. Barstow) Cong. R. **8**: 133.
— — — xvi. 26, 27; viii. 58. Theo. Repos. **4**: 345.
— — — xviii. (E. P. Gould) Bapt. Q. **8**: 337.
— — — xvii. 9, Observations on. Theo. Repos. **3**: 127.
Bible, Acts of the Apostles. (J. Martineau) O. & N. **10**: 724. — Ecl. R. **85**: 183. — Chr. R. **20**: 161.
— — Aim of. (J. R. Oertel) Theo. Ecl. **6**: 389.
— — Alexander on. Kitto, **20**: 443.
— — Authorship of. Kitto, **7**: 406. **25**: 296. **28**: 166.
— — Baumgarten on. Ecl. R. **99**: 154.
— — Baur on. (G. P. Fisher) New Eng. **23**: 401.
— — Bennett's Lectures on. Bib. R. **3**: 210.
— — Critical Remarks on. Liv. Age, **56**: 563.
— — Hackett's Notes on. (G. W. Samson) Chr. R. **23**: 528. — (T. D. Woolsey) New Eng. **10**: 129. — Chr. R. **24**: 306.
— — Historical Unreliableness of. Westm. **63**: 214.
— — how far historical? Nat. R. **10**: 392.
— — Illustrations of, from recent Discoveries. (J. B. Lightfoot) Contemp. **32**: 288. Same art. Liv. Age, **137**: 685.
— — Origin and Composition of. Chr. Exam **71**: 40.
— — Rénan on. Westm. **86**: 310.
— — Rénan on the Apostles. (G. P. Fisher) New Eng. **25**: 542.
— — why written. (B. Smith) Univ. Q. **14**: 65.
— — Chapter i. 16–22, Illustration of. Theo. Repos. **1**: 63.
— — — xiii.–xxviii., Chronological Arrangement. Am. Presb. R. **7**: 278.
— — — xvii., Observations on. Theo. Repos. **3**: 70.
— — — xx. 28. (E. Abbot) Bib. Sac. **33**: 313.
— — — xxvi. 28, 29, Exegesis of. (H. S. Burrage) Bib. Sac. **31**: 401.
— Epistles of St. Paul, Belsham's Translation of. (W. Goodhugh) Quar. **30**: 79. — Cong. M. **8**: 28.
— — Belsham on. Ecl. R. **37**: 385, 502.
— — Errors in. (A. P. Peabody) No. Am. **77**: 173.
— — Exegesis of difficult Texts. Kitto, **33**: 65, 275.
— — Jowett on. (G. E. Ellis) Chr. Exam. **60**: 431. — Chr. Obs. **56**: 18. — Quar. **98**: 148.
— — Pastoral. Am. Church R. **22**: 263, 399, 553.
— — — Introduction to. (B. B. Edwards) Bib. Sac. **8**: 318.
— — — Peculiarities of. (M. J. Cramer) Meth. Q. **36**: 458.
— — Taylor's Key to. Chr. Obs. **6**: 5–501.
— — to Thessalonians, Galatians, and Romans, with Criticisms. Chr. Rem. **31**: 445.
— Romans. (R. Ellis) Unita. R. **8**: 465. — Chr. R. **5**: 182. — Ecl. R. **72**: 417. **79**: 663.
— — Barnes on. (C. Hodge) Princ. **7**: 285.
— — Bauer's Theory on. (O. Cone) Univ. Q. **27**: 306.
— — Colenso on. Lond. Q. **18**: 1.
— — Corrections in. Theo. Repos. **4**: 211.
— — Notes on. (W. Walford) Bib. R. **1**: 382.
— — Revised Version. Theo. Ecl. **2**: 143.
— — Revision of. Kitto, **21**: 384.
— — Rückert on. (C. Hodge) Princ. **8**: 39.
— — Stuart on. (C. Hodge) Princ. **5**: 381. — Chr. R. **14**: 40. — Am. Mo. R. **2**: 388. — (J. P. Cowles) Chr. Q. **4**: 661. — Am. Meth. M. **15**: 175. — Chr. Obs. **36**: 168. — Ecl. R. **59**: 289, 464.
— — Talmudic Notes on. (F. Delitzsch) Luth. Q. **11**: 477.
— — Whitwell's Translation of. (E. S. Gannett) Chr. Exam. **44**: 458.
— — Chapters i.–iii., Notes on. Kitto, **35**: 408.
— — Chapter i. 1–17, A Study of. (N. S. Folsom) Mo. Rel. M. **49**: 362.
— — — i. 18–23. Chr. R. **25**: 105, 268.
— — — v. 1. Lond. Q. **50**: 78.
— — — v. 12–14. (J. Priestley) Theo. Repos. **2**: 154. — Theo. Repos. **2**: 411.
— — — — Paul's Reasoning on. Theo. Repos. **3**: 115.
— — — v. 12–21, Forbes on. (D. T. Fiske) Bib. Sac. **27**: 697. — (J. Forbes) Bib. Sac. **28**: 739.
— — — vi. 7. (T. J. Sawyer) Univ. Q. **10**: 166.

Bible, Romans, Chapter vii. (H. Ballou, 2d) Univ. Q. **2**: 424.

— — — vii. 7–25. (W. N. Clarke) Bapt. Q. **9**: 385.

— — — vii. 14–25. Chr. Obs. **2**: 265. **3**: 67–264. — (J. Tomlinson) Luth. Q. **11**: 558.

— — — viii. Chr. Mo. Spec. **2**: 399.

— — — viii. 18–25. (M. Stuart) Am. Bib. Repos. **11**: 363.

— — — — New Version of. Bib. R. **1**: 114.

— — — viii. 19–23, Creation or Creature? (A. N. Arnold) Bapt. Q. **1**: 143. — (H. N. Day) Chr. Q. Spec. **10**: 105.

— — — — Exegetical View of. Am. Presb. R. **6**: 451.

— — — ix.–xi., with Notes. (H. Ballou, 2d) Univ. Q. **9**: 270.

— — — ix. 3. (W. M. Smythe) Chr. R. **19**: 383.

— — — ix. 5. (G. V. Smith) Mod. R. **1**: 191.

— — — ix. 22–24. (E. T. Fitch) Chr. Q. Spec. **7**: 382.

— — — xii. 11. (R. Collyer) Radical, **1**: 6.

— I. and II. Corinthians. No. Brit. **29**: 71.

— — Christianity of. (R. Ellis) Unita. R. **5**: 267. **6**: 257.

— — Criticisms on. Chr. Rem. **31**: 445.

— — Stanley on. Ecl. R. **109**: 113.

— I. Corinthians. Ecl. R. **83**: 513.

— — Chapter iv. 20. (W. H. Furness) Radical, **1**: 126.

— — — vi. 1–3, Interpretation of. Bib. R. **3**: 262.

— — — ix. 15–18, Remarks on. Theo. Repos. **2**: 250.

— — — xiii. 9–13. (W. Scott) Meth. Q. **10**: 371.

— — — xiv. 34, 35, Speaking or Babbling? Cong. Q. **16**: 576.

— — — xv. (H. Ballou, 2d) Univ. Q. **2**: 149.

— — — — New Translation of. Theo. Repos. **6**: 79.

— — — xv. 22. (J. A. Brown) Luth. Q. **2**: 448.

— — — xv. 27. Theo. Repos. **3**: 255.

— — — xv. 28, Thoughts on. Bib. R. **3**: 147.

— II. Corinthians, Chapter iii. 13–18, Criticism on. Bib. R. **2**: 214, 306.

— — — v. 1, etc., Illustration of. Theo. Repos. **6**: 428.

— — — v. 10. (M. Goodrich) Univ. Q. **17**: 88.

— — — v. 14. (W. S. C. Otis) Bib. Sac. **27**: 545.

— Galatians. (R. Ellis) Unita. R. **4**: 471. — (G. Bradford) Chr. Exam. **5**: 285. — Ecl. R. **82**: 392. — Lond. Q. **25**: 217.

— — Argument of. (H. B. Hackett) Bib. Sac. **5**: 97.

— — Contents of. Chr. R. **26**: 577.

— — Renderings of common Version. (H. B. Hackett) Bib. Sac. **19**: 211. **22**: 138.

— — Threefold Crucifixion in. Lond. Q. **46**: 26.

— — translated. (P. Schaff) Mercersb. **13**: 5.

— — Chapter iii. 16. (F. Gardiner) Bib. Sac. **36**: 23.

— — — iii. 20, Criticism on. Theo. Repos. **3**: 130.

— — — iv. 21–31. (G. Bush) Princ. **4**: 525.

— Ephesians, Commentary on. (D. Bagot) Chr. Obs. **65**: 1, 93, 172.

— — Eadie's Commentary on Greek Text of. Ecl. R. **99**: 676.

— — Ellicott's Commentary on. Theo. & Lit. J. **10**: 174.

— — Greek and English, with Commentary. (S. H. Turner) Theo. & Lit. J. **9**: 172.

— — Hodge's. (J. W. Nevin) Mercersb. **9**: 46, 192. — Theo. & Lit. J. **9**: 170.

— — Holy Spirit in. Lond. Q. **47**: 31.

— — Revised Version of. Lond. Q. **57**: 1.

— — Stier's Commentary on. (H. I. Schmidt) Evang. R. **1**: 430.

— Philippians. Ecl. R. **81**: 633.

— — Lightfoot on. Lond. Q. **31**: 189. — Chr. Obs. **70**: 363.

— — Chapter ii. 5–11. Bib. R. **2**: 248. — Theo. Repos. **2**: 141, 219. **3**: 257. — (H. L. Baugher) Luth. Q. **8**: 119. — Kitto, **37**: 401.

— — — iii. 7–21, Criticism on. Theo. Repos. **2**: 83.

— Colossians. Ecl. R. **81**: 296.

— — Critical Examination of. (P. Mearns) Kitto, **3**: 349.

Bible, Colossians, Expositions of. Chr. Obs. **45**: 343.

— — Gisborne's Exposition of. Chr. Obs. **15**: 524.

— — Hidden Life in. Lond. Q. **47**: 365.

— Thessalonians, Jowett on. Kitto, **17**: 1.

— I. Thessalonians, Chapter iv. 13–18, Exposition of. (J. O. Skinner) Univ. Q. **11**: 280.

— — II. Timothy. Meth. Q. **13**: 534.

— — Chapter iii. 16. (J. Medway) Cong. M. **21**: 491.

— — — — Translation of. (J. P. Smith) Cong. M. **21**: 208, 425. — (W. Walford) Cong. M. **21**: 356.

— Titus, Chapter ii. 13, Exegesis of. (J. A. Brown) Luth. Q. **3**: 285.

— Hebrews. (C. C. Everett) Mo. Rel. M. **46**: 485.

— — Analysis of. (C. Ayer) Bapt. Q. **4**: 448.

— — Authorship and Canonicity of. (J. H. Thayer) Bib. Sac. **24**: 681.

— — Authorship of. Ecl. R. **78**: 237. — Kitto, **25**: 102, 193. **39**: 236. — Dub. R. **67**: 57. — (R. D. C. Robbins) Bib. Sac. **18**: 469. — (E. Pond) Cong. R. **8**: 29.

— — Canonical Authority of. (J. J. Gurney) Am. Bib. Repos. **2**: 409.

— — Character and Design of. Chr. Disc. **5**: 435.

— — Criticism on. Bib. R. **2**: 54.

— — Dale on. Ecl. R. **121**: 281. — Theo. R. **2**: 305.

— — Delitzsch on. Evang. R. **2**: 184. — Meth. Q. **31**: 379.

— — Doctrine of last Things in. (W. R. Alger) Chr. Exam. **53**: 157.

— — Element of Admonition in. Danv. Q. **3**: 205.

— — Moulton on. Lond. Q. **54**: 446.

— — Paul's Troas Parchment. Cong. R. **8**: 569.

— — Philological Questions on. Bib. R. **4**: 282.

— — Some Expressions in. Bib. R. **4**: 409.

— — Sampson's Commentary on. Theo. & Lit. J. **9**: 340.

— — Steward on. Lond. Q. **39**: 406.

— — Stuart on. (I. Chase) No. Am. **28**: 134. — (Dr. Marsh) Chr. Q. Spec. **1**: 112. — (A. Norton) Chr. Exam. **4**: 495. **5**: 37. **6**: 198, 230. — So. R. **3**: 308. — Spirit Pilg. **1**: 629. **2**: 15, 80, 538. — Cong. M. **11**: 419, 536. **17**: 33.

— — to whom addressed? Kitto, **25**: 269.

— — Chapter i. 2, etc. Theo. Repos. **3**: 316.

— — — i. 2, Criticism on. Theo. Repos. **3**: 112.

— — — ii. 9, Syriac Version of. Theo. Repos. **1**: 73.

— — — ii. 16, Illustration of. Theo. Repos. **5**: 161.

— — — vi. 4–8. (I. Loewenthal) Princ. **27**: 39.

— — — vi. 4–6. (G. Peck) Am. Meth. M. **17**: 221.

— — — — Exposition of. Cong. M. **24**: 315–602.

— — — vii. 2–22. (J. Priestley) Theo. Repos. **2**: 285.

— — — ix. 16, 17. Theo. Repos. **4**: 139.

— — — xii. 18–24. (H. M. King) Bapt. Q. **4**: 339.

— — — xiii. 10. (J. A. Brown) Luth. Q. **5**: 564.

— James, Epistle of. Chr. Obs. **77**: 455.

— — Doctrine of. (E. P. Gould) Bib. Sac. **35**: 681.

— — Stier's Commentary on. (H. I. Schmidt) Evang. R. **1**: 430.

— — Chapter ii. 12. (S. Johnson and J. F. Clarke) Radical, **1**: 49–342.

— — — v. 14, 15, Exegesis of. Cong. R. **8**: 383.

— Peter, Epistles of. Kitto, **26**: 257. **27**: 255.

— I. Peter, Brown on. (N. Porter) New Eng. **9**: 243. — No. Brit. **9**: 334. — Ecl. R. **88**: 278.

— — Chapters iii. 18–20, and iv. 6. (H. Ballou, 2d) Univ. Q. **10**: 221. — Theo. Repos. **3**: 444.

— — — v. 8, Illustration of. Theo. Repos. **3**: 484.

— II. Peter. (J. Jones) Theo. & Lit. J. **8**: 585.

— — Chapter i. 17–19. Theo. Repos. **3**: 247.

— — — iii., Notes on. (M. Goodrich) Univ. Q. **9**: 363.

— — — iii. 13. (T. H. Mudge) Meth. Q. **10**: 252.

— Epistles of John. Ecl. R. **116**: 348.

— I. John: Final Document of Revelation. Lond. Q. **46**: 265.

— — Chapter ii. 22, Antichrist in. Chr. Obs. **6**: 356, 496.

Bible, I. John, Chapter v. 7, Controversy on. Quar. 26: 324. 33: 65.
— — — — Genuineness of. Am. Church R. 26: 625. — (N. E. Cornwall) Am. Church R. 29: 509. — Theo. Repos. 5: 195.
— II. John, Kuria in. (J. C. M. Laurent) Am. Presb. R. 16: 166.
— Jude, and Assumption of Moses. (J. E. Carpenter) Theo. R. 5: 259.
— — and II. Peter compared. (F. Gardiner) Bib. Sac. 11: 114.
— — Authorship of. (E. Arnaud) Chr. R. 23: 329, 484.
— — Introduction to. Chr R. 26: 592.
— — Structure of. Kitto, 29: 310.
— — Verse 9. (T. R. Beck) Ref. Q. 27: 209.
— Revelation. (N. L. Frothingham) Chr. Exam. 8: 146. — (D. N. Lord) Theo. & Lit. J. 1: 11. — Chr. Exam. 37: 192. — Chr. R. 2: 323. — (E. Pond) Cong. R. 8: 345. — (E. Reuss) Luth. Q. 1: 535. Am. Presb. R. 1: 529. — Nat. R. 18: 311.
— — a Dramatic Allegory. (A. C. Rose) Meth. Q. 32: 54.
— — Alford on. Chr. Obs. 62: 517.
— — analyzed and explained. (G. R. Noyes) Chr. Exam. 68: 325.
— — and Daniel. Kitto, 34: 76. — (W. Webster) 34: 462. — Theo. & Lit. J. 9: 314, 484. 11: 53.
— — and Gospel of St. John. (W. Milligan) Contemp. 18: 87, 212.
— — and its Exposition. (H. M. Harman) Meth. Q. 25: 230.
— — Anti-Papal and Anti-Pagan Interpretation of. Chr. Rem. 26: 383.
— — Apocalyptic Literature. (G. H. Schodde) Luth. Q. 9: 346. — Kitto, 19: 249.
— — — Recent. Kitto, 6: 107.
— — Apocalyptic Reveries, Thom's. Ecl. R. 90: 568.
— — Authenticity and Inspiration of. Chr. Obs. 1: 723.
— — Author of. (R. D. C. Robbins) Bib. Sac. 21: 319, 551. — Chr. Obs. 48: 217, 289, 361.
— — Barnes's Notes on. Theo. & Lit. J. 5: 150.
— — Character of. Chr. Q. Spec. 9: 570.
— — Commentaries on. Kitto, 26: 15.
— — Composition of. (J. Albee) Chr Exam. 65: 60.
— — Cumming's Lectures on. Theo. & Lit. J. 7: 527. — Lond. Q. 13: 407.
— — Cuninghame on Prophecies of. Chr. Obs. 13: 163, 752.
— — Date of. (J. M. Macdonald) Bib. Sac. 26: 457. — Bib. R. 1: 169. 2: 206, 347, 446. Kitto, 30: 452.
— — — Neronic. Kitto, 15: 184, 421.
— — Design and Plan of. Bib. R. 3: 173–384. 4: 95 219.
— — Ebrard on. (W. H. Green) Princ. 26: 276.
— — Eichhorn's Illustrations of. Chr. Disc. 4: 65.
— — Elliott on. (A. Alexander) Princ. 19: 141. 28: 113. Cong. M. 27: 872.
— — Emblems of. Kitto, 28: 120.
— — — Analysis of. Kitto, 18: 344. 19: 386. 21: 120. 22: 359. 23: 137, 348. 24: 71, 345. 25: 143, 384.
— — — Generic Application of. Bost. R. 1: 398.
— — explained. (F. G. Hibbard) Meth. Q. 26: 235.
— — Exposition of. Brownson, 15: 514.
— — Future of God's Kingdom revealed in. Theo. & Lit. J. 13: 599.
— — Gascoyne's Theory of Theo. & Lit. J. 13: 352.
— — Greek Text of. (T. J. Conant) Bapt. Q. 4: 129.
— — — Erasmian Codex. (Prof. Herzog) Kitto, 29: 64.
— — Harmony of. Theo. & Lit. J. 2: 159.
— — Hengstenberg on. (J. A. Alexander) Princ. 24: 59. — Theo. & Lit. J. 5: 170.
— — Hooper's Theory of. Ecl. R. 115: 40.
— — Inspiration of. Bib. R. 6: 145.
Bible, Revelation, Interpretation of. Chr. Obs. 45: 11. — Westm. 100: 338.
— — — and Criticism of. Westm. 76: 448.
— — Introduction to Study of. Chr. Obs. 30: 129.
— — Lectures on. Mo. R. 122: 245.
— — Lord's Exposition of. (E. R. Tyler) New Eng. 5: 585.
— — Martyrdom in. (B. F. Hosford) Bib. Sac. 23: 309.
— — Poetry of. Bib. R. 1: 413. 2: 81, 259.
— — Position and Meaning of. Kitto, 28: 387.
— — Prophecies of. Chr. Obs. 6: 430–706. 7: 481, 688, 757.
— — — Nature of. Theo. & Lit. J. 9: 485.
— — Scope of. (T. W. Chambers) Ref. Q. 28: 507.
— — Six Seals of Chapter vi. Chr. Obs. 43: 436, 449, 577. 44: 542, 644.
— — — Scene and Era of. Chr. Obs. 30: 210, 278, 330.
— — Smyth on. (N. L. Frothingham) Chr. Exam. 2: 75.
— — Structure of. Chr. Obs. 46: 65.
— — Stuart on. (E. R. Tyler) New Eng. 4: 139. — (G. W. Burnap) Chr. Exam. 40: 161. — (S. M. Vail) Meth. Q. 7: 5. — (E. Beecher) Am. Bib. Repos. 3d s. 3: 272. — (D. N. Lord) Theo. & Lit. J. 1: 54. — (G. Duffield) Am. Bib, Repos. 3d s. 3: 385. — Ecl. R. 83: 156.
— — Symbols of. Theo. & Lit. J. 5: 312.
— — Tilloch on. Ecl. R. 41: 343.
— — Vaughan's Lectures on. Chr. Obs. 63: 916.
— — Whittemore on. (H. Ballou, 2d) Univ. Q. 5: 304. — (C. T. Brooks) Chr. Exam. 44: 386.
— — Woodhouse's Translation of. Chr. Obs. 5: 553.
— — Wordsworth's Lectures on. Theo. & Lit. J. 5: 423.
— — Chapters ii., iii., Epistles to the Seven Churches in Asia, Trench on. Chr. Obs. 62: 132.
— — — — Seven Angels of Seven Churches. (I. Jennings) Bib. Sac. 12: 339.
— — — vi., Exposition of. (S. D. Church) Chr. Q. 8: 397.
— — — xi. 13, Faber's Interpretation of. Chr. Obs. 9: 133, 196.
— — — xvi., Vials. Chr. Obs. 7: 688, 757. 8: 541.
— — — xxi., Vision of the celestial Jerusalem. Bib. R. 2: 30.
Bible, or Christmas Eve; a Tale. Cath. World, 2: 397.
Bibles, Anecdotes of. Chamb. J. 58: 449.
— Loftie's Century of. Am. Bibliop. 4: 636.
— Old. Am. Bibliop. 4: 460.
— Photographs for our. Liv. Age, 57: 143.
Bible Class, The Minister's. Theo. Ecl. 1: 271.
Bible Classes. Lond. Q. 19: 204.
— Formation and Arrangement of. Cong. M. 12: 20.
— Manual for. (S. Miller) Princ. 11: 31.
Bible Pictures, Modern. Ecl. R. 112: 180, 261.
Bible Society in 1675. Cong. M. 8: 407.
— American. Chr. Disc. 5: 146. — Chr. R. 1: 299.
— — E. D. Griffin's Speech on. Chr. Mo. Spec. 2: 598.
— — Speeches on. Chr. Mo. Spec. 2: 429, 483.
— — Dr. Spring on. Chr. R. 11: 585.
— Baptist. Meth. Q. 1: 535.
— British and Foreign. Quar. 4: 68. — (R. Southey) Quar. 36: 1. — Pamph. 6: 269. — Chr. Obs. 16: 833. 18: 402. — Lond. Q. 1: 353. — Meth. M. 36: 663. 54: 477.
— — Attack of Trinitarian on. Chr. Obs. 39: 474, 518.
— — Cambridge Auxiliary, 1811. Chr. Obs. 10: 805. 11: 173.
— — Controversy on, 1818. Ecl. R. 27: 201.
— — Henderson's Appeal to. Cong. M. 9: 473.
— — History of. Chr. Obs. 60: 162. — Meth. M. 40: 257.
— — in 1810–14. Ecl. R. 13: 59, 255. 16: 1210. 18: 580. 19: 64.
— — Letter to. (H. Lindsay) No. Am. 4: 187.
— — Milner on Marsh's Objections to. Chr. Obs. 12: 376, 451, 782. 13: 93.

Bible Society, British and Foreign, Norris's Tendency and Proceedings of. Chr. Obs. **13**: 37.
— — Owen's History of. Chr. Obs. **15**: 717. 20: 25. — Ecl. R. **25**: 413.
— — Question of, 1832. Chr. Obs. **32**: 141, 206.
— — Recollections of. (R. Halley) Cong. **4**: 428.
— — Review of Pamphlets on, 1810. Chr. Obs. **9**: 441, 764. **11**: 173, 289.
— First Continental. Cong. M. **15**: 329.
— of Paris. Chr. Disc. **4**: 351.
— Roman Catholic, in London. Meth. M. **36**: 898.
Bible Societies. Blackw. **18**: 621. — Am. Q. Reg. **2**: 29.
— and Missionaries. Mo. R. **124**: 1.
— Bishop Hobart's Strictures on. Chr. Mo. Spec. **6**: 36, 62, 140.
— Felice's Essay on. Mo. R. **103**: 499.
— Influence of, Chalmers on. Ecl. R. **20**: 168.
Bible Truth and its Opponents. Ecl. R. **103**: 348.
Bible Union, American. Dem. R. **40**: 41.
Biblical Anthology. So. Lit. Mess. **3**: 594.
Biblical Archæology, Jahn's. Am. Mo. R. **1**: 482.
Biblical Blank. (R. M. Patterson) Presb. R. **2**: 738.
Biblical Cabinet, Edinburgh. Am. Bib. Repos. **9**: 319. — Chr. R. **6**: 576. — Ecl. R. **72**: 472. **74**: 278. **75**: 407.
Biblical Chronology. *See* Chronology, Biblical.
Biblical Criticism. (J. W. Chadwick) Unita. R. **11**: 62. — (J. H. Morison) Unita. R. **10**: 651. — (W. M. Reynolds) Evang. R. **5**: 365. — Ed. R. **72**: 69. — No. Brit. **9**: 182. — (A. Norton) Chr. Exam. **1**: 201. — Chr. R. **6**: 66. — Chr. Mo. Spec. **3**: 169. — Ecl. R. **91**: 25. — (W. M. Willett) Meth. Q. **3**: 34. — Bib. R. **3**: 53. — Ed. R. **72**: 132.
— Colenso and Davidson on. Quar. **113**: 422.
— Davidson on. (G. R. Noyes) Chr. Exam. **54**: 419. — (J. Strong) Meth. Q. **13**: 549. — Ecl. R. **72**: 270. **97**: 320. — Mo. R. **152**: 552. — Kitto, **11**: 146. — No. Brit. **19**: 423.
— First Lessons in. Kitto, **5**: 415 **7**: 174.
— German. New York R. **2**: 133.
— Is it favorable to Piety? (H. Burgess) Kitto, **4**: 111.
— Kenrick's Biblical Essays. Theo. R. **1**: 51.
— Methods of. Kitto, **32**: 1.
— Modern. (E. A. Washburn) Princ. n. s. **4**: 27.
— Nicolas's Etudes de. Theo. R. **2**: 21.
— Principles of Textual. (G. R. Noyes) Chr. Exam. **48**: 26.
— Reformers and Destructives in. Brit. Q. **38**: 186.
— Right, Duty, and Limits of. (C. A. Briggs) Presb. R. **2**: 550.
Biblical Genealogy, Barrett on. Ecl. R. **5**: 207. **6**: 586, 678.
Biblical Geography. (E. Robinson) Bib. Sac. **5**: 79, 770.
— Notes on. (E. Robinson) Bib. Sac. **1843**: 563.
— Works on. Chr. Obs. **72**: 850.
Biblical Hermeneutics. Dub. R. **50**: 312.
Biblical History. (J. A. Alexander) Princ. **26**: 484.
— Illustrations of. (J. Floy) Meth. Q. **3**: 325.
— Mohammedan Version of. Ev. Sat. **5**: 624.
— Neill's Lectures on. (C. Hodge) Princ. **18**: 456.
Biblical Knowledge. (E. P. Barrows) Am. Bib. Repos. **11**: 60. — Meth. Q. **2**: 97.
Biblical Legends, Veil's. Chr. Obs. **46**: 747.
— of the Mussulmans. Chr. Rem. **11**: 435.
Biblical Literature. Brit. Q. **2**: 175. — (S. F. Smith) Chr. R. **9**: 266. — Meth. Q. **2**: 485. — West. M. **2**: 204.
— Essays on. (D. Young) Princ. **2**: 321.
— in France in Middle Ages. (G. Masson) Kitto, **36**: 81.
— in Scotland. No. Brit. **3**: 39.
— Practical Hints for Students of. Meth. Q. **16**: 288.
Biblical Literature, Townley's History of. Ecl. R. **36**: 385. — Meth. M. **45**: 517.
Biblical Monographs. Meth. Q. **29**: 422.
Biblical Repertory. (F. Jenks) Chr. Exam. **2**: 65.
Biblical Science, Comparative Value of English and German. (C. A. Aiken) Bib. Sac. **11**: 67.
— Present State of. (B. B. Edwards) Bib. Sac. **7**: 1.
— Sawyer's Reconstruction of. Bost. R. **2**: 635.
Biblical Sketches. (D. M. Moir) Blackw. **7**: 274. **9**: 149.
Biblical Theology. (A. Norton) Chr. Exam. **4**: 334.
Biblical Truth tested and justified. Kitto, **5**: 215.
Bibliographical Chronology. Am. Bibliop. **7**: 117.
Bibliographical Dictionary, 1804. Ecl. R. **5**: 396.
Bibliographical Table Talk. (W. Bradford) Hist. M. **3**: 8.
Bibliographie Biographico-Romancière, Petite, 1839. Mo. R. **150**: 537.
Bibliography. (S. A. Allibone) Evang. R. **19**: 33. — (T. F. Dibdin) No. Am. **2**: 46. — (C. P. Krauth) Evang. R. **3**: 291.
— American. (J. D. Butler) Bib. Sac. **36**: 72.
— as a Science. (R. A. Guild) Lib. J. **1**: 67.
— Book-Makers as Book-Lovers. (E. Howland) Lippinc. **5**: 673.
— Classical, Moss's Manual of. Ecl. R. **44**: 5.
— Class-Room. (A. S. Packard) Lib. J. **2**: 66.
— Darling's Cyclop. Bibliographica. Lond. Q. **10**: 120.
— of American History. (W. Bradford) Hist. M. **3**: 74.
— of English Books. (E. Arber) Lib. J. **1**: 224.
— of Mathematics. Dub. R. **21**: 1.
— of the U. S. Civil War. Hist. M. **6**: 113–342.
— Photo-Bibliography. (H. Stevens) Lib. J. **2**: 162.
— Universal, Danjou's Scheme. (W. E. A. Axon) Lib. J. **5**: 205.
— What is? Am. Bibliop. **5**: 84
Bibliomania. Appleton, **3**: 350. — Am. Bibliop. **3**: 56, 169. — Chamb. J. **36**: 251. **58**: 85. — Cong M. **4**: 8, 69. — Hist. M. **9**: 40. — No. Brit. **40**: 70. — Sharpe, **35**: 24. — (J. Skelton) Fraser, **100**: 71. — (A. Lang) Internat. R. **7**: 267.
— Poetry of. (W. E. A. Axon) Reliquary, **9**: 151. Same art. Lib. J. **5**: 199.
— Revival of. Am. Bibliop. **6**: 8.
Bibliomaniac; a Tale. Eng. Dom. M. **14**: 298.
Bibliophilist, The. (T. Raikes) Bentley, **3**: 564.
Bibliotheca Sacra. (A. P. Peabody) No. Am. **98**: 87.
Bibliothèque Nationale, Paris, Exhibition of, 1878. (A. Laugel) Nation, **28**: 80.
Bice; a Tale. Temp. Bar, **56**: 110.
Bicêtre and La Salpêtrière. All the Year, **43**: 373.
Bichat, Life of. (H. Ware) No. Am. **15**: 132.
Bichel, Andrew the Buccaneer of Girls. Knick. **2**: 268.
Bickersteth, Edward, with portrait. (G. Gilfillan) Hogg, **3**: 81.
— Birk's Memoir of. Chr. Obs. **51**: 842.
— Last Days of. (C. E. Eardley) Liv. Age, **26**: 570.
Bickersteth, Edward H. Yesterday, To-Day, and Forever. Chr. Obs. **67**: 376. — Nat. Q. **21**: 124.
Bickersteth, Robert, Bishop of Ripon. Cong. **3**: 605.
— Sermons of. Chr. Obs. **66**: 321.
Bicknacre Priory. (J. H. Major) Arch. **11**: 255.
Bicycle, The, and riding it. (J. Wilcox) Lippinc. **24**: 623. — Chamb. J. **46**: 280.
Bicycles. (T. Cradocke) Tinsley, **26**: 589.
— Era of. (E. Howland) Harper, **63**: 281.
— Natural History of. Belgra. **10**: 441.
Bicycling; a Wheel around Boston. (C. E. Pratt) Scrib. **19**: 481.
Biddeford, Me., Second Church of. (J. D. Emerson) Cong. Q. **11**: 241.
Biddle, Edward. (C. Biddle) Pennsyl. M. **1**: 100.
Biddle, James, Capt. U. S. N., with portrait. Portfo. (Den.) **14**: 429. — Anal. M. **6**: 383.

Biddle, Nicholas. So. Lit. Mess. 4: 349. — with portrait, Portfo. (Den.) 2: 279.
— Memoir of. Am. Mo. M. 11: 425.
Biddle, Maj. Thomas, Life of. Ill. M. 1: 549.
Biddy Tibs, who cared for Nobody. (H. Holl) Bentley, 2: 288.
Biddy Whelan's Business. Blackw. 49: 311, 439.
Bidlake, John. Sermons. Chr. Obs. 8: 390. 10: 512.
— The Year; a Poem. Ecl. R. 18: 456.
Bidpai, Fables of. (T. Lewis) Putnam, 12: 74. — Broadw. 8: 425. — Dub. Univ. 78: 601.
— — Transmission of, to Persia. Penny M. 4: 390.
— Story of. (J. Hatton) Gent. M. n. s. 3: 697.
— Wit and Wisdom of. (J. Hatton) Gent. M. n. s. 2: 563, 693. 3: 75-313.
Bidwell, Wm. H., with portrait. Ecl. M. 63: 121.
Bierstadt, Albert. (H. T. Tuckerman) Galaxy, 1: 678.
Big Bear of Arkansas. Bentley, 27: 35.
Big Black River, Confederate Expedition to. All the Year, 24: 245.
Big Buck, The. (C. W. Webber) Putnam, 3: 438.
Big Jack Small. (J. W. Gally) Overland, 14: 446.
Bigelow, A. Travels in Malta, etc. (J. Walker) Chr. Exam. 11: 259. — (A. H. Everett) No. Am. 35: 228.
Bigelow, Erastus B. (N. Cleaveland) Hunt, 30: 162. — (L. Stephen) Macmil. 7: 126.
— Carpeting, Quilt, and Coach-Lace Machines. Hunt, 14: 155.
Bigelow, Dr. Jacob. (A. Gray) Am. J. Sci. 117: 263.
— Inaugural Address. No. Am. 4: 271.
Bigg, J. Stanyan. Night and Soul. Hogg, 11: 489.
Bigg, John, Hermit of Dinton. (J. Wilkins) Once a Week, 14: 111.
Bigg, John, Will of, 1641. N. E. Reg. 29: 260.
Biggs, William, Captivity of. West. M. 5: 213.
Biglow Papers. *See* Lowell, J. R.
Bigotry. (J. C. Miller) Ex. H. Lec. 15: 41.
— in scientific Controversy. Pop. Sci. Mo. 9: 324.
Bigsby, Robert, Poems and Essays of. Mo. R. 159: 545. 160: 551.
Bilderdijk, William. Internat. M. 4: 65. — (W. P. Westervelt) Princ. 34: 104, 286.
Bill of Rights, The. Penny M. 9: 388.
Bill-Posting. Ev. Sat. 11: 191.
Bills and Notes, Law of, Byles on. Bank. M. (N. Y.) 22: 713.
Bills of Credit, Nature and Effects of. So. Q. 23: 455.
Bills of Exchange. Bank. M. (N. Y.) 3: 144, 265, 337.
— and Bill of Lading. (G. Eustis) De Bow, 1: 534.
— Damages on protested. Hunt, 5: 265. — Niles's Reg. 30: 127.
— Grace on Sight. (R. H. Marr) De Bow, 7: 356.
— History of. (J. B. Byles) Bank. M. (N. Y.) 4: 461.
— in Great Britain, 1828-47. (W. Newmarch) J. Statis. Soc. 14: 143.
— in Louisiana. (S. F. Glenn) De Bow, 1: 153.
— Law of. Bank. M. (N. Y.) 25: 593. 27: 1.
— — German. Bank. M. (N. Y.) 35: 791.
— — in the States. Bank. M. (N. Y.) 18: 521, 632, 696.
— — Unification of. Bank. M. (N. Y.) 30: 462.
— Story on. Hunt, 9: 69.
Bills of Lading as collateral Security. Bank. M. (N. Y.) 27: 373, 509, 609.
— Conditions in. (W. Parkin) Am. Law R. 14: 431.
— Law of. Bank. M. (N. Y.) 30: 559, 565.
— Uses of. (P. C. Wright) De Bow, 2: 65.
Bills of Sale. Chamb. J. 58: 673.
Billerica, Mass., History of. (F. Kidder) N. E. Reg. 6: 85.
Billet, Pierre. (R. Ménard) Portfo. 6: 19.
Billet at Carrigahinch; a Tale. (J. F. Fuller) Dark Blue, 3: 397. Same art. Liv. Age, 114: 98.
— at Cloonbawn. (J. F. Fuller) Dark Blue, 2: 387.
Billiards, Game of. Chamb. J. 29: 374. — Temp. Bar, 30: 377.
— and Billiard Players. Lond. Soc. 13: 375. Same art. Ev. Sat. 5: 503.
Billiard Player's Experience. Chamb. J. 31: 312.
Billiard Table Manufacture. Pract. M. 4: 312.
Billings, William, Biographical Notice of. Penny M. 4: 114.
Billingsgate. All the Year, 35: 206. — Chamb. J. 16: 189. — Lond. Soc. 10: 520.
Billingsgate Market. Penny M. 13: 439.
Billingsley, William. (L. Jewitt) Art J. 20: 186.
Billington, Mrs. Elizabeth, Actress. Colburn, 54: 345.
Billion, What is a? Pract. M. 7: 335.
Billopp House, Staten Island. (B. J. Lossing) Potter Am. Mo. 6: 241.
Bill-Sticker, The. Chamb. J. 20: 121.
Bill-Sticking. House. Words, 2: 601. — Ev. Sat. 11: 191.
Billy Buttons. (N. Macleod) Ev. Sat. 5: 11.
Billy Malowney's Taste of Love and Glory. Dub. Univ. 35: 692.
Billy's Wife. (H. W. Baker) Overland, 13: 402.
Bi-Metalism. (W. S. Jevons) Contemp. 39: 750. Same art. Ecl. M. 97: 8. — (W. D. Kelley) Penn Mo. 10: 912. — (H. H. Gibbs) Bank. M. (N. Y.) 34: 452. — (W. G. Sumner) Princ. n. s. 4: 546.
— and Finances of India. (J. B. Robertson) Westm. 115: 200.
— and Free Trade. (E. de Laveleye) Fortn. 36: 108.
— Case against. (R. Giffen) Fortn. 32: 278.
— in Europe. (G. Walker) Bank. M. (N. Y.) 32: 850. — (H. White) Nation, 29: 75.
— in Germany. Bank. M. (N. Y.) 35: 196.
— Practical. (G. M. Weston) Bank. M. (N. Y.) 35: 617.
— Walker on. (W. G. Sumner and F. A. Walker) Nation, 26: 94, 113.
Bi-Metalists. (B. F. Nourse) Nation, 29: 41.
— and the Commercial Crisis, 1879. (E. L. Godkin) Nation, 28: 346.
Bimini; a Poem. (H. Heine) Lakeside, 9: 198.
Binck, Jacob. (G. W. Reid) F. Arts Q. 2: 372.
Binding. *See* Book-Binding.
Bingham, Caleb. (W. B. Fowle) Am. J. Educ. 5: 325.
Binghamton, N. Y., Inebriate Asylum at. (H. T. Tuckerman) No. Am. 94: 387. — (J. W. Palmer) Atlan. 24: 109. — (J. Parton) Atlan. 22: 385.
Binney, Horace. Am. Law R. 10: 176.
Binney, Thomas. (J. B. Brown) Contemp. 23: 884. — Ecl. R. 113: 113. — Hogg, 6: 353.
— Ecclesiastical Portrait of. St. James, 25: 154.
— Memoir of. Cong. 3: 193.
— Sermons. (C. Beard) Theo. R. 6: 401.
Binocular Vision. J. Frankl. Inst. 70: 325.
— Phenomena of. (J. LeConte) Am. J. Sci. 120: 83.
Biogenesis and Gravitation, Thomson on Laws of. (E. R. Lankester) Nature, 4: 368.
Biographer, Duty of a. Dem. R. 28: 254.
Biographers, Hints to. Fraser, 21: 291.
Biographia Dramatica. Blackw. 89: 218.
Biographical Book-Making. Tait, n. s. 18: 164.
Biographical Dictionary, Appleton's. (J. P. Dabney) No. Am. 83: 317.
— of Society of Useful Knowledge. Ed. R. 76: 237. — Mo. R. 158: 481.
— Thomas's. No. Am. 114: 408.
Biographical Literature. (S. Bailey) Chr. R. 21: 552. — Lond. Q. 48: 342.
Biographical Mania, The. Tait, n. s. 21: 16.
Biographical Peculiarities. Lakeside, 2: 138.
Biographical Sketches and Anecdotes. (J. W. Calcraft) Dub. Univ. 44: 397, 674.
— H. Martineau's. Victoria, 12: 472.

Biographical Sketches, Senior's. Liv. Age, **76**: 511.
Biographical Studies. Dub. Univ. **65**: 352.
Biographie Moderne, 1789–1811. (J. Foster) Ecl. R. **16**: 713. — Mo. R. **151**: 201.
Biographies, Batch of. Fraser, **41**: 443. Same art. Ecl. M. **20**: 224.
— Modern: Whittaker, Treacher, Arnott. Colburn, **35**: 556.
— Some recent. (J. F. Hitchman) Belgra. **23**: 181.
— Universal. Lond. M. **23**: 207.
Biography. (T. Carlyle) Fraser, **5**: 253. — (E. A. Duyckinck) No. Am. **84**: 406. — (W. C. Mills) Am. Church R. **18**: 622. — Ox. Prize Ess. **3**: 193. — Am. Mo. M. **1**: 251. — Fraser, **5**: 255. — Blackw. **69**: 40. Same art. Ecl. M. **22**: 293. — Penn Mo. **6**: 274.
— and Biographical Dictionaries. Westm. **76**: 335.
— Art of. So. Lit. Mess. **23**: 282.
— at a Discount. (C. A. Collins) Macmil. **10**: 158.
— Coleridge's Northern Worthies. Colburn, **95**: 177.
— College Rank of distinguished Men. (C. F. Thwing) Scrib. **15**: 467.
— Curiosities of. (F. W. Fairholt) Bentley, **29**: 15, 180.
— Christian, Difficulties of. Chr. Obs. **32**: 693.
— Ecclesiastical, Wordsworth's. Chr. Obs. **10**: 41, 117. — (J. Foster) Ecl. R. **11**: 428.
— gone mad. Blackw. **79**: 285. Same art. Liv. Age, **49**: 65.
— Greybeard's Gossip. Colburn, **80**: 38–431. **81**: 83–415. **82**: 14–329.
— in History. Brit. Q. **18**: 484.
— Limits of. New Eng. **25**: 218.
— Lodge's Illustrated. Quar. **38**: 378.
— Men and Women of the 18th Century, Houssaye's. Dem. R. **30**: 444.
— Military, Chesney's. (D. F. Maury) So. M. **15**: 533.
— Modern. Blackw. **65**: 219.
— New Kind of. (R. Goodbrand) Contemp. **14**: 20.
— New School of. (M. A. Dodge) Atlan. **14**: 579.
— of Aunt Jemima. (F. H. Rankin) Bentley, **1**: 382.
— of a bad Shilling. Internat. M. **3**: 92.
— of great Men. New York R. **10**: 348.
— Political. Quar. **143**: 361. Same art. Liv. Age, **133**: 771.
— — and literary. Blackw. **68**: 199.
— Religious. Dub. Univ. **52**: 259. Same art. Liv. Age, **59**: 193.
— Representative Men. Once a Week, **2**: 26–364. — (I. Scott) Once a Week, **4**: 343. — (H. Martineau) Once a Week, **4**: 455, 575, 652. **5**: 35–693.
— — and Women. Once a Week, **3**: 205–651.
— Scottish Ecclesiastical. Lond. Q. **49**: 75.
— Sincerity in. Temp. Bar, **62**: 329. Same art. Appleton, **26**: 276.
— Studies in. Fraser, **100**: 255.
— Study and Composition of, Stanfield on. (J. Foster) Ecl. R. **19**: 113.
— Universal. Mo. R. **118**: 548. — Mus. **15**: 17.
— Walton's Lives. Cong. M. **9**: 41.
Biological Nomenclature. (E. D. Cope) Am. Natural. **12**: 517.
Biological Research in the United States. (E. D. Cope) Penn Mo. **6**: 202.
Biological Sciences and Medicine. (T. H. Huxley) Nature, **24**: 342. Same art. Pop. Sci. Mo. **19**: 795.
Biology. (T. H. Huxley) Ev. Sat. **17**: 344.
— Address at Glasgow. (A. R. Wallace) Am. J. Sci. **112**: 354.
— Address to the Linnean Society. (G. Bentham) Nature, **4**: 92–192.
— and Woman's Rights. (W. Bagehot) Pop. Sci. Mo. **14**: 201.
Biology, Animal Development. (A. Wilson) Gent. M. n. s. **24**: 34.
— Animals and Plants. (St.G. Mivart) Contemp. **36**: 13.
— as an academical Study. (T. J. Parker) Nature, **24**: 543, 573.
— Borderland between Animals and Vegetables. (T. H. Huxley) Macmil. **33**: 373. Same art. Ecl. M. **86**: 418. Same art. Liv. Age, **128**: 643. Same art. Pop. Sci. Mo. **8**: 641.
— Joseph Cook's Lectures on. (G. M. Beard) Bib. Sac. **35**: 381. — (J. T. Bixby) Unita. R. **9**: 69. — (G. S. Hall) Nation, **25**: 397. — So. R. n. s. **23**: 219.
— for Beginners. (S. H. Stevenson) Pop. Sci. Mo. **6**: 340, 574.
— Forms and Colors of living Creatures. (St.G. Mivart) Contemp. **36**: 313.
— Geometry and. (T. Hill) Unita. R. **9**: 129.
— Huxley and Martin on. Nature, **12**: 530.
— in Schools. (A. Wilson) Fraser, **94**: 756.
— Lecture at Edinburgh University. (W. Thomson) Nature, **4**: 74, 90.
— Lowest Animals. (C. S. Minot) Internat. R. **8**: 646.
— Modern, Some Tendencies of. (A. Wilson) Mod. R. **1**: 574.
— Modern Inquiry in. (J. L. LeConte) Pop. Sci. Mo. **8**: 285.
— Modern Philosophical. (E. Cazelle) Pop. Sci. Mo. **8**: 595, 710.
— Nicholson's Introduction to. Nature, **6**: 258.
— Organic Unity in Animals and Vegetables. (C. Martins) Meth. Q. **23**: 29.
— Principle of Life. (T. Hughes) Am. Cath. Q. **6**: 542.
— Relation of Animal to Vegetable World. (M. Jacobs) Evang. R. **11**: 256.
— Scientific Relation of Sociology to. (J. L. LeConte) Pop. Sci. Mo. **14**: 425.
— Some Animal Biographies. (A. Wilson) Gent. M. n. s. **26**: 87, 176.
— Spencer on. (F. E. Abbot) No. Am. **107**: 377. — (C. Wright) Nation, **2**: 724. — Westm. **84**: 77.
— Study of. (G. J. Allman) Am. Natural. **8**: 34. — (T. H. Huxley) Nature, **15**: 219. — (T. H. Huxley) Am. Natural. **11**: 210. — (T. H. Huxley) Pop. Sci. Mo. **10**: 527.
— — and Teaching of. (H. N. Martin) Pop. Sci. Mo. **10**: 298.
— Superfluous Developments. (T. S. Cobbold) Nature, **6**: 183.
— Teleological Mechanics, Pfluger's. Mind, **3**: 264.
See Animals; Life; Natural History.
Bion and Moschus. (J. Davies) Contemp. **17**: 349.
— Idyls, translated. Blackw. **35**: 871. **41**: 435. — Dub. Univ. **1**: 163, 192.
— — translated by H. King. Blackw. **110**: 577.
— Pastoral Poetry of. Fraser, **12**: 541.
— Threnody on Adonis. (A. C. Brackett) J. Spec. Philos. **5**: 360.
— — translated. Blackw. **38**: 65.
Bioplasm, Influence of Light upon. (A. Downes) Nature, **18**: 398.
Bioscope, or Dial of Life. (J. Foster) Ecl. R. **20**: 373.
Biot, Jean Baptiste. Scientific Gossip. Blackw. **84**: 675 Same art. Liv. Age, **60**: 259. — Ecl. M. **47**: 84.
Biran, Maine de. *See* Maine de Biran.
Birboniana, or Italian Antiquaries and Antichitá Blackw. **59**: 543, 765.
Birch, Charles Bell, with portrait. Colburn, **166**: 14.
Birch, Samuel, with portrait. Dub. Univ. **90**: 53.
Birch Tree, The. Penny M. **11**: 409.
— Uses of. Penny M. **12**: 91, 109.
Birchington, a Health Resort in Kent. Tinsley, **28**: 258.
Bird, Rev. C. S. Chr. Rem. **50**: 87.

Bird, Edward, the Painter. Chamb. J. **14**: 213.
Bird, Henry, Adventures of. Anal. M. **6**: 295.
Bird, Robert M. Broker of Bogota. Am. Mo. M. **3**: 61.
— Calavar. Am. Mo. M. **4**: 172. — (O. W. B. Peabody) No. Am. **40**: 232. — Am. Q. **16**: 375. — West. M. **3**: 41.
— Hawks of Hawk Hollow. So. Lit. Mess. **2**: 43. — Am. Q. **18**: 441.
— Nick of the Woods. So. Lit. Mess. **3**: 254.
— Robin Day. So. Lit. Mess. **5**: 420.
Bird, Thomas, and his Descendants. (W. B. Trask) N. E. Reg. **25**: 21.
Bird, A pet. (R. Ridgeway) Am. Natural. **3**: 309.
Bird Fancies. All the Year, **14**: 153.
Bird Lime in Japan. Pract. M. **7**: 273.
Bird-Mounting. (O. S. Round) Recr. Sci. **2**: 162.
Bird-Nesting Extraordinary. Chamb. J. **44**: 625.
Bird of Passage; a Tale. (J. S. Le Fanu) Temp. Bar, **29**: 59–350. Same art. Ecl. M. **75**: 179, 317, 437.
Bird Ramble on the Lincolnshire Coast. Chamb. J. **51**: 108.
Bird Shops. (E. E. Sterns) Scrib. **5**: 161.
Bird Story. (W. M. F. Round) Lippinc. **22**: 82.
Bird Tracks of Nova Scotia. (C. F. Hartt) Am. Natural. **1**: 169, 234.
Bird World, Moral Sketches from. Chamb. J. **31**: 357, 376.
Birds. (Mrs. Child) Hogg, **2**: 157. — (E. Ingersoll) Scrib. **12**: 689. — (J. Wilson) Blackw. **19**: 105. — — (C. Winterfield) Am. Whig R. **1**: 371. **2**: 279. — Chamb. J. **29**: 175, 407. — Godey, **26**: 5. — Land We Love, **6**: 325, 403. — No. Brit. **30**: 309. — Once a Week, **11**: 347. **18**: 543.
— Æsthetic Feeling in. (Grant Allen) Pop. Sci. Mo. **17**: 650.
— Affection in. Chamb. J. **54**: 268, 368.
— and Audubon. (H. T. Tuckerman) Meth. Q. **12**: 415.
— and Bird-Keeping. Chamb. J. **37**: 401. **55**: 113.
— and Bird Voices. (N. Hawthorne) Dem. R. **12**: 604.
— and Birds. (J. Burroughs) Scrib. **15**: 354.
— and Fruit. Chamb. J. **56**: 715.
— and Insects, Color in. (Lady Verney) Good Words, **18**: 835.
— — Curiosities of. Ecl. M. **44**: 531.
— and Insect Food. Penny M. **2**: 279.
— and Poets, illustrating each other. (C. Winterfield) Am. Whig R. **3**: 129. *See* Birds of the Poets.
— and Reptiles, Animals intermediate between. (T. H. Huxley) Pop. Sci. R. **7**: 237. — (H. O. Forbes) Belgra. **36**: 317. Same art. Pop. Sci. Mo. **13**: 719.
— Architecture of. (E. Jesse) Once a Week, **10**: 47. — (T. M. Brewer) Scrib. **16**: 47, 305. **17**: 161. — Cath. World, **5**: 349. — Chamb. J. **2**: 331. **42**: 455. Same art. Ecl. M. **65**: 475. — Westm. **15**: 195. — Mo. R. **125**: 566.
— at Home. (M. Titcomb) Harper, **32**: 545.
— at Nest-Time. Chamb. J. **26**: 175.
— Australian Love Birds. (A. E. Jamrach) Ecl. M. **96**: 704.
— Battles of. (M. Thompson) Appleton, **19**: 159.
— Beach. (N. C. Brown) Lippinc. **23**: 620.
— Bee-Eaters, Wrynecks, Creepers, and Nuthatches. (W. J. Broderip) Fraser, **57**: 342.
— Bird Lore. All the Year, **40**: 365.
— Bones of, Discovery of, at Christ Church, Hampshire. (G. Brander and S. Pegge) Arch. **4**: 117, 414.
— — of the Head of, Magnus's. Nature, **4**: 364.
— Breeding of. (E. Coues) Am. Natural. **9**: 75.
— Cage. (A. C. Austin) Godey, **39**: 71, 201, 442. **40**: 213, 262, 412. **41**: 229, 274, 361.
— — Winter Management of. (W. Kidd) Recr. Sci. **1**: 93.
Birds, Charm of. (C. Kingsley) Fraser, **75**: 802. Same art. Liv. Age, **94**: 110. Same art. Ev. Sat. **4**: 7.
— Classification of, Garrod's New. Nature, **9**: 290.
— Color and Geographical Distribution in. (R. Ridgway) Am. J. Sci. **104**: 454. **105**: 39.
— Courtship of. (T.W. Wood) Stud. & Intel. Obs. **5**: 113.
— Covering of. (W. Macgillivray) Ed. New Philos. J. **3**: 253. **4**: 123.
— Curious Things about. (F. H. Stauffer) Sharpe, **46**: 158.
— Decrease of, in United States. (J. A. Allen) Penn Mo. **7**: 931.
— Destruction of, by Wire. (E. Coues) Am. Natural. **10**: 734.
— Diseases and Injuries in. (R. W. Shufeldt) Am. Natural. **15**: 283.
— Domestic Life of. (W. Bruce) Good Words, **2**: 335.
— Eastern Snow-Bird. (S. Lockwood) Am. Natural. **15**: 518.
— Edible. Sharpe, **35**: 11, 178.
— Eyes of. (E. Coues) Am. Natural. **2**: 505, 570.
— Families of. (W. Hincks) Canad. J. n. s. **9**: 230.
— Fatio on Plumage of. Intel. Obs. **10**: 377. **11**: 172.
— Feathers of. (H. S. Conant) Harper, **57**: 385.
— — Anatomy of. (W. K. Brooks) Pop. Sci. Mo. **4**: 686.
— Feathered Life. (J. Burroughs) Galaxy, **8**: 168.
— Feathered Minnesingers. Chamb. J. **30**: 81.
— Flight of. (E. J. Marey) Am. Natural. **5**: 29. — (J. T. Wood) Potter Am. Mo. **15**: 265. — All the Year, **13**: 366, 450. — Temp. Bar, **3**: 564.
— — and Principles involved. (A. C. Campbell) J. Frankl. Inst. **111**: 440.
— Fossil. (S. J. Mackie) Pop. Sci. R. **2**: 354.
— — Passerine, from Colorado. (J. A. Allen) Am. J. Sci. **115**: 381.
— Friendship of. (G. L. Austin) Appleton, **18**: 156, 325.
— Game, and Wild Fowl, Knox's. Ecl. R. **93**: 55. — Fraser, **45**: 47.
— — Gallinaceous. Penny M. **10**: 401, 414.
— — Some American. (M. Thompson) Appleton, **16**: 481.
— Garden and Orchard. (W. Flagg) Atlan. **2**: 592.
— Geographical Distribution and Migration of. Hogg, **3**: 231.
— Geographical Variation in. (J. A. Allen) Am. Natural. **8**: 534.
— Golden Oriole and Water Ouzel. Once a Week, **13**: 546.
— Gould's. Westm. **35**: 137.
— Great Crested Flycatcher. (M. Treat) Am. Natural. **15**: 601.
— Habits of. (T. M. Brewer) Am. Natural. **1**: 113.
— How I found the Dotterel's Nest. (D. Bruce) Ecl. M. **97**: 643.
— Hunting with the Long-Bow. (M. Thompson) Harper, **55**: 238.
— Ill-omened. (A. Young) Atlan. **34**: 325.
— in the British Museum. Nature, **10**: 378.
— in Captivity. Sharpe, **16**: 33–330. **17**: 120, 249.
— in the Hemlocks. (J. Burroughs) Atlan. **17**: 672.
— in the Snow; a Story. (L. de la Ramé) Belgra. **40**: 460.
— in Winter. Chamb. J. **23**: 69. Same art. Ev. Sat. **1**: 76.
— Instincts of. (J. Blackwall) Ed. New Philos. J. **14**: 241. — (J. Blackwall) J. Frankl. Inst. **16**: 354. **17**: 68, 139. — (J. Webb) Intel. Obs. **7**: 221.
— — in young. (D. A. Spaulding) Nature, **6**: 485. Same art. Pop. Sci. Mo. **2**: 561.
— Intellectual Powers of. (A. L. Adams) Pop. Sci. R. **12**: 276. — Pop. Sci. Mo. **3**: 614. — (T. M. Brewer) Atlan. **28**: 41. — (C. C. Abbott) Am. Natural. **11**: 276.

Birds, Intelligence of. (M. Treat) Lippinc. 24: 359.
— Key to Heart of. (W. Kidd) Recr. Sci. 1: 31.
— Kings of the Air. (B. G. Wilder) Scrib. 1: 239.
— Language of. Hogg, 4: 334.
— Law among. Chamb. J. 58: 22.
— Life of. (T. W. Higginson) Atlan. 10: 368. — (S. D. Snevets) Potter Am. Mo. 9: 270.
— — Brehm on. Nature, 5: 180.
— Little. (J. G. Wood) Good Words, 21: 557.
— Locomotion of. Nature, 13: 3.
— Man-of-War Birds, Boobies and Noddies. (W. J. Broderip) Fraser, 58: 65.
— Michelet's L'Oiseau. Colburn, 112: 127.
— Migrations of. (H. Gätke) Nature, 20: 97. — (A. Newton) Nature, 10 : 415. 19: 433. — (T. M. Trippe) Am. Natural. 7: 389. 8: 338. — (H. D. Minot) Am. Natural. 15: 870. — (A. Weissmann) Contemp. 34: 531. Same art. Liv. Age, 140: 673. — Chamb. J. 37: 236. — Ev. Sat. 10: 551.
— — and Sojournings of. (S. T. Frost) Harper, 32: 233.
— — of European. (A. L. Adams) Pop. Sci. R. 4: 324. Same art. Cath. World, 2: 57.
— — of inland. (C. C. Abbott) Pop. Sci. Mo. 7: 183.
— — of North American. (J. Bachman) Am. J. Sci. 30: 81.
— — Palmén on. Nature, 15: 465.
— — Strange Wanderers. (M. Schele de Vere) Hours at Home, 10: 111.
— Migratory, Summer. Chamb. J. 52: 627.
— Minstrelsy of. (S. Hibberd) Intel. Obs. 2: 18. 3: 112. 5: 17.
— Mission of. (T. M. Brewer) Atlan. 23: 405.
— Mythological. (A. W. Buckland) Anthrop. J. 4: 277.
— Natural History of. Colburn, 50: 189.
— — Belon's. House. Words, 14: 7.
— Night. (W. Flagg) Atlan. 4: 171.
— Notes of. Chamb. J. 40: 161. — Sharpe, 48: 80.
— Notes on. (J. A. Allen) Am. Natural. 6: 263, 342, 394.
— of Ailsa Craig, Scotland. (R. Gray) Intel. Obs. 4: 114.
— of America. (J. Burroughs) Scrib. 12: 479. — (S. Hyacinth) Overland, 4: 38.
— — Familiar. (M. Treat) Harper, 54: 656, 785.
— — Four. (C. A. Munger) Putnam, 13: 725.
— — occurring in Europe. (H. Gaetke) Canad. J. n. s. 6: 459.
— — Water. (R. Ridgway) Am. Natural. 8: 108. *See below*, Birds of North America.
— of Australia. (J. Wilson) No. Brit. 1: 440. — Chamb. J. 11: 28.
— of the Beach. Once a Week, 13: 488.
— of Borneo. Nature, 11: 407.
— of California. (J. G. Cooper) Am. Natural. 10: 90.
— — Song. (W. Paton) Overland, 14: 562.
— of Canada. Canad. J. n. s 6: 6, 129.
— of the Colorado Valley. (E. Coues) Penn Mo. 10: 234.
— of Connecticut. (J. H. Linsley) Am. J. Sci. 44: 249.
— of Egypt, Shelley's. Nature, 7: 178.
— of Europe, Dresser's. Nature, 11: 485.
— — Sharpe and Dresser's. Nature, 6: 390.
— of Germany, Singing. (A. Ashbury) Lakeside, 2: 272.
— of Gibraltar, Irby's. Nature, 12: 364.
— of Great Britain. Penny M. 8: 265–465. — Westm. 33: 373.
— — and Bird Lovers. Cornh. 32: 35.
— — compared with American. (D. H. Minot) Am. Natural. 14: 561.
— — Harting's. Nature, 7: 101.
— — in the Border Counties. Once a Week, 7: 81.
— — in Norfolk, Stevenson's. Fraser, 76: 608.
— — in Northumberland and Durham, Hancock's. Nature, 11: 281.

Birds of Great Britain, Macgillivray's. No. Brit. 19: 1. — Tait, n. s. 5: 45. — Mo. R. 152: 541.
— — Notes on. Chamb. J. 37: 280.
— — of the Humber. (M. G. Watkins) Fraser, 88: 324.
— — Protection of. Quar. 151: 100.
— — Singing. Sharpe, 34: 176.
— — — and their Nests. Sharpe, 34: 176.
— — Slaney's Outline of. Penny M. 1: 258.
— — Smaller. Mo. R. 129: 85.
— — Yarrell's History of. Ecl. R. 76: 144. 80: 23.
— of Illinois, Catalogue of. (H. Pratten) West. J. 11: 397.
— — Prairie. (R. Ridgway) Am. Natural. 7: 197.
— of India. (H. J. Bruce) Am. Natural. 6: 460.
— of Ireland. Dub. Univ. 39: 307.
— of Jamaica, Gosse's. Westm. 47: 308. Same art. Liv. Age, 14: 433. — Ecl. R. 86: 399. — Tait, n. s. 16: 543.
— of Kerguelen's Land, Coues's. Nature, 14: 317.
— of Killingworth; a Poem. (H. W. Longfellow) Atlan. 12: 680.
— of the Lesser Antilles. (P. L. Sclater) Nature, 4: 473.
— of the Levant. Chamb. J. 44: 587.
— of London. (S. Hibberd) Intel. Obs. 7: 167. — Once a Week, 22: 247.
— of Massachusetts, Rarer. (J. A. Allen) Am. Natural. 3: 505, 568, 631.
— of May. O. & N. 3: 717.
— of the Months and their Associations. (H. G. Adams) Hogg, 4: 1–392. 5: 28–232.
— of the Mountain. Once a Week, 14: 517.
— of New England. (T. M. Brewer) No. Am. 107: 290.
— — Notes on a few. (H. Merrill) Pop. Sci. Mo. 17: 386.
— of New Guinea, Gould's. Nature, 14: 208.
— of New Jersey. (C. C. Abbott) Am. Natural. 4: 537.
— of New Zealand, Giant. (I. C. Russell) Am. Natural. 11: 11.
— of N. E. Africa, Von Heuglin on. Nature, 13: 289.
— of North America. (J. E. Cabot) Atlan. 1: 209. — (R. Ridgway) Am. Natural. 7: 602. — Blackw. 19: 661. 20: 243. — Mo. R. 127: 386. — Mus. 21: 69.
— — Audubon's. Ed. New Philos. J. 10: 317. 18: 131. — Mo. R. 138: 160. *See* Audubon; Ornithology.
— — Coues's. Nature, 8: 22.
— — Distribution of. (S. F. Baird) Am. J. Sci. 91: 78–337. — (A. E. Verrill) Am. J. Sci. 91: 249.
— — Habits of. (J. Burroughs) Atlan. 15: 513.
— — Night. (H. W. Herbert) Putnam, 2: 616.
— of Palestine and Panama. (E. D. Cope) Am. Natural. 2: 351.
— of Paradise. (T. H. Partridge) Pop. Sci. Mo. 5: 556. — (A. R. Wallace) Harper, 39: 183. — Appleton, 1: 239. — Penny M. 2: 82.
— — New. (P. L. Sclater) Nature, 8: 305.
— of the Poets. (J. Burroughs) Scrib. 6: 565.
— of the Polar Region. Chamb. J. 52: 490. Same art. Ecl. M. 86: 100.
— of Shetland. Chamb. J. 12: 181. 51: 668.
— — Saxby's. Nature, 11: 81.
— of Sweden, Game. Westm. 88: 405.
— of the United States. (E. Coues) Am. Natural. 7: 321.
— — Eastern and Western. (T. M. Trippe) Am. Natural. 5: 632.
— — in Cumberland, Pennsylvania. (W. M. and S. F. Baird) Am. J. Sci. 46: 261.
— — of the Mississippi Valley. (J. M. Peck) West. J. 10 : 29.
— — of the North. (P. A. Chadbourne) Putnam, 15: 636.
— — of White Mountains in Summer. (H. D. Minot) Am. Natural. 10: 75.
— — Western. (S. C. Clark) Putnam, 4: 75.

Birds of the United States, Western, Breeding of. (E. Holterhoff, jr.) Am. Natural. 15: 208.
— — Winter. (E. Ingersoll) Appleton, 17: 97.
— of Willamette Valley, Oregon. (O. B. Johnson) Am. Natural. 14: 485, 635.
— Paddle-winged. (McL. Martin) Recr. Sci. 2: 253.
— Pasture and Forest. (W. Flagg) Atlan. 2: 863.
— Petition for. All the Year, 5: 526.
— Phases of Bird-Life. (C. C. Abbott) Pop. Sci. Mo. 9: 343.
— Power of, to remain submerged. (B. R. Morris) Canad. J. n. s. 7: 509.
— Preserving. (O. S. Round) Recr. Sci. 1: 117. — J. Frankl. Inst. 8: 31, 103. *See* Taxidermy.
— Protection of wild. Chamb. J. 50: 820. 52: 321. 53: 65. — All the Year, 29: 509.
— — Act for. Nature, 8: 1.
— Rare. (A. Wilson) Good Words, 17: 427.
— Sea. (O. S. Round) Recr. Sci. 2: 285.
— Sense of Sight in. Putnam, 6: 491.
— Sharp-eyed. (J. Burroughs) Scrib. 16: 460.
— Sharpe's Catalogue of. Nature, 16: 541.
— Singing. (W. Flagg) Atlan. 2: 285. — Colburn, 53: 40. 62: 198–476. — Victoria, 11: 57.
— — of the West. (R. Ridgway) Harper, 56: 857.
— The Skua of Shetland Islands. All the Year, 9: 320.
— Some noteworthy. (S. Lockwood) Am. Natural. 14: 715.
— Songs of; a Poem. (A. Webster) Good Words, 22: 550. Same art. Ecl. M. 97: 514.
— — and Eccentricities of. (W. Flagg) Atlan. 44: 349.
— Structure and Habits of. Ecl. R. 75: 144.
— Talking. Sharpe, 37: 123, 177. — Ecl. M. 96: 704.
— Variations in Habits of. (R. Ridgway) Am. Natural. 8: 197.
— Vassar College Museum of. (J. Orton) Am. Natural. 4: 711.
— Vertebræ of recent. (O. C. Marsh) Am. J. Sci. 117: 266.
— visiting Ships at Sea. Chamb. J. 30: 408. Same art. Liv. Age, 60: 608.
— Voices of. Ecl. M. 42: 389.
— Waders or Stilted. (W. Hincks) Canad. J. n. s. 11: 147.
— Warblers. (T. M. Trippe) Am. Natural. 2: 169.
— — Winter. Once a Week, 14: 126.
— Wild, Capture and Shooting of. (M. G. Watkins) Fraser, 97: 176.
— Wingless. (W. C. L. Martin) Recr. Sci. 1: 41.
— Wings and Tails of. Penny M. 6: 132, 154, 180.
— Winter. (W. Flagg) Atlan. 3: 319.
— Winter Pensioners. Chamb. J. 38: 329.
— with Teeth. (O. C. Marsh) Am. J. Sci. 110: 403. 111: 509. — (O. C. Marsh) Am. Natural. 9: 625. — (H. Woodward) Pop. Sci. R. 14: 337.
— — of Kansas, Marsh on. Nature, 22: 457.
See names of various Species of Birds, as Canaries; Cuckoo; Eagle; Owl; etc.
Birds' Eggs, Collecting and preserving. (H. J. Bellars) Recr. Sci. 2: 28.
— Instructions for preparing. (W. Wood) Nature, 6: 191.
— Preparation of. (W. Wood) Am. Natural. 6: 281.
— Preservation of. (A. D. Bartlett) Recr. Sci. 2: 57.
Birds' Nests. (J. Burroughs) Atlan. 23: 701. — (H. D. Minot) Harper, 55: 90, 256. — Once a Week, 20: 230. — Penny M. 5: 305.
— Do Birds improve in Nest-building? Pop. Sci. Mo. 2: 485.
— Edible. Hogg, 4: 51. — Chamb. J. 52: 527. — Penny M. 10: 367.
— Is Nest-Building an Instinct? (B. T. Lowne) Pop. Sci. R. 18: 274.
— Notes on. Hogg, 3: 140.
Birds' Nests, Philosophy of. (A. R. Wallace) Intel. Obs. 11: 413. — Once a Week, 24: 593.
— Variations in Nests of same Species. (T. M. Brewer) Am. Natural. 12: 35.
Birds of Passage; from the Swedish. Cornh. 32: 346.
Birds of Prey; a Tale. (M. E. Braddon) Belgra. 1: 5–383. 2: 5–383. 3: 5–442.
Birdofredum Sawin, Esq., to Mr. Hosea Biglow; a Poem. (J. R. Lowell) Atlan. 9: 126, 385.
Birdsall of Mapleton. (J. T. McKay) Scrib. 10: 229.
Birkbeck, M., Oration of. Niles's Reg. 23: 73.
— Some Account of. Portfo. (Den.) 34: 445.
Birkenhead, Expedition to the End of. (A. Smith) Bentley, 20: 635.
— Visit to. Chamb. J. 3: 305.
Birkenhead, H. M. S., Wreck of. So. Lit. Mess. 24: 204.
— — Poem on. (G. P. R. James) So. Lit. Mess. 24: 207.
Birmingham, England. Gent. M. n. s. 13: 43. — Penny M. 5: 41, 81.
— Arts and Manufactures in. Art J. 18: 223.
— a Century ago. All the Year, 21: 462.
— Few October Days around. (A. K. H. Boyd) Ev. Sat. 12: 148.
— Newdigates of Arbury. (J. Goodwin) Gent. M. n. s. 2: 289.
— Philanthropic Work in. (H. A. Page) Good Words, 17: 352.
— Town Hall of. Penny M. 3: 239.
See Black Country.
Birmingham and Liverpool Railway, Report on, 1835. (J. Locke) J. Frankl. Inst. 20: 409.
Birmingham Caucus. (E. Schuyler) Nation, 28: 161.
Birmingham College of Science. Nature, 11: 331.
Birmingham Factories, Day at. Penny M. 13: 465, 501.
Birmingham Liberal Association. (W. Crosskey) Macmil. 35: 299.
— and its Assailants. (H. W. Crosskey) Macmil. 39: 151.
Birmingham Library, Burning of. Lib. J. 4: 19, 56.
— The new. Lib. J. 4: 450.
Birmingham Skepticism. Lond. Q. 36: 310.
Birmingham School Board. (W. Harris) Fortn. 23: 422.
Birney, Gen. David B. U. S. Serv. M. 4: 465.
Birnie, Alexander. Editor's Tragedy. Liv. Age, 73: 390.
Birth of a Child. (N. Macleod) Good Words, 14: 842.
— of Fleance Krüger. (C. Chesebro) Knick. 46: 457, 573.
Births and Deaths, European Registers of. Mo. R. 133: 159.
— — in the Prussian States. Penny M. 6: 395.
— Marriages, and Deaths. Peop. J. 6: 194, 208.
— — — in England. Lond. Q. 27: 38. 32: 379.
— — Registration of. Penny M. 8: 298.
— "Mrs. Meek, of a son." (C. Dickens) House. Words, 2: 505.
— Remarkable. All the Year, 34: 329, 354.
Birthday, The. Colburn, 4: 337.
Birthday; a Poem. Cornh. 19: 711.
Birthday Gifts. Dem. R. 6: 122.
Birthday Thoughts. (N. Macleod) Good Words, 14: 420.
Birthday Treat. Belgra. 27: 375.
Birthdays. St. James, 20: 417.
— Anniversaries of. Hogg, 6: 17.
— Historic. (S. Johnson) Radical, 8: 81.
Birting the Strong. (H. H. Boyesen) Galaxy, 21: 25.
Biscay, Province of. Penny M. 13: 69.
— and the Biscayans. Hogg, 8: 247, 262.
— Bacon's Six Years in. Mo. R. 146: 252.
— Shores of. Blackw. 112: 548.
Biscayans, Among the. (G. L. Catlin) Lippinc. 24: 649.
Bisceliais, Le. Sharpe, 13: 364. 14: 33.
Bisclaveret; a Breton Romance. (H. Kingsley) Macmil. 41: 216.
Biscuits, Manufacture of. Penny M. 9: 130.

Biscuits, Manufacture of, at Weovil. Chamb. J. **16**: 12.
Bishop, Matthew, Life of. Retros. **16**: 42.
Bishop, N. H. Voyage in a Sneak-Box. (W. Chambers) Chamb. J. **57**: 241.
Bishop, Robert Hamilton. Am. Presb. R. **4**: 414.
Bishop, A New-Testament. Cong. M. **15**: 411.
— Godly Admonition of. (G. W. Hodge) Am. Church R. **32**: 325.
— in the New Testament a Teacher. (J. B. Bittinger) Evang. R. **10**: 311.
— of a primitive Type. Chamb. J. **23**: 161.
— Office of. (D. Gans) Mercersb. **11**: 107.
— — Rise of. (G. S. Merriam) New Eng. **26**: 466.
— Sermon on the Election of. (E. B. Boggs) Am. Church R. **32**: 62.
— What is a? Fraser, **79**: 269.
Bishop, The, and the Knight; a Poem. Cornh. **6**: 100.
— astray. Blackw. **129**: 59. Same art. Ecl. M. **96**: 492.
— to be. (P. Thompson) Lakeside, **10**: 87.
Bishop's Confessions; a Story. Cornh. **43**: 555.
Bishop's Daughter, The. Chr. Obs. **42**: 361, 453.
Bishops and Clergy of other Days, Ryle on. Chr. Obs. **69**: 52.
— and clerical Subscription. (H. D. Haughton) Fortn. **2**: 452.
— and their Incomes. Tait, n. s. **18**: 505.
— Elect, Archiepiscopal Confirmation of. Chr. Obs. **70**: 50.
— Clergy, and the People. Fraser, **31**: 127.
— Curious Facts about. (J. H. Merrick) Am. Church R. **14**: 221.
— Duties of. Chr. Obs. **43**: 147, 198.
— Election of, in Episcopal Church. (S. C. Thrall) Am. Church R. **27**: 219. — (M. Hoffmann) Am. Church R. **28**: 235.
— in Parliament, Speech on. (Lord Say and Seale) Cong. M. **18**: 281.
— Inherent Rights of. (H. D. Evans) Am. Church Mo. **3**: 33, 161.
— Ladies'. So. Lit. Mess. **8**: 98.
— Lay Vote in Election of. (W. R. Whittingham) Am. Church R. **11**: 88.
— Office and Work of. (E. B. Boggs) Am. Church R. **29**: 618.
— Overseers. (S. E. Shepard) Chr. Q. **1**: 117.
— Persecuting. (Syd. Smith) Ed. R. **37**: 433.
— Pioneer or Missionary. (J. F. Spalding) Am. Church R. **29**: 1.
— Plea for. Am. Bib. Repos. **13**: 1.
— Primitive Mode of electing. Kitto, **25**: 165.
— Right of Dissenting Ministers to name. Cong. M. **10**: 124.
— Successors of the Apostles. (J. Williams) Am. Church R. **11**: 621.
See American Episcopate; Episcopacy; Episcopal Church.
Bishops' Transcripts. (J. Amphlett) Gent. M. n. s. **26**: 106.
Bishopthorpe, Public Day at. Bentley, **28**: 48.
Bismarck, Louisa W., Mother of the Prince. (A. D. Vandam) Tinsley, **31**: 485. Same art. Liv. Age, **135**: 626.
Bismarck, Prince Otto von. (W. H. Browne) N. Ecl. **4**: 446. — (S. S. Conant) Harper, **40**: 648. — (C. W. Elliott) Galaxy, **4**: 159. — (E. P. Evans) Hours at Home, **8**: 485. — (S. Hyacinth) Overland, **3**: 271. — (F. Kapp) Nation, **1**: 711. — (M. Schlesinger) Fortn. **5**: 385, 600. — with portrait, Ecl. M. **67**: 371. — with portrait, Ev. Sat. **9**: 354. — All the Year, **25**: 127. — Blackw. **120**: 448. Same art. Liv. Age, **138**: 553. — Fortn. **30**: 765. Same art. Liv. Age, **140**: 195. — Lond. Soc. **30**: 1. — Penn Mo. **5**: 676.
Bismarck, Prince Otto von, and the Catholic Church. (J. Gibb) Contemp. **20**: 172. — (J. MacCarthy) Cath. World, **31**: 577. — (J. S. Henderson) Good Words, **14**: 283. — Brownson, **22**: 259. — Brit. Q. **61**: 1. — Ed. R. **139**: 360. — Month, **19**: 1.
— and European Politics. (W. G. Todd) Month, **20**: 352.
— and the Franco-Prussian War. (K. Hillebrand) Internat. R. **6**: 425.
— — Peace Negotiations. (C. Kommen) Cath. World, **28**: 817.
— and German Unity. (D. Ker) Nat. Q. **39**: 30.
— and Gortschakoff. Ed. R. **144**: 203. — Blackw. **120**: 450. Same art. Ecl. M. **87**: 667.
— and the Jesuits. (J. McCarthy) Cath. World, **16**: 1.
— and the Pope, 1873. (A. Bierbower) Luth. Q. **3**: 513. — (W. H. Dixon) Gent. M. n. s. **12**: 290.
— and Protection. (J. E. Curran) Internat. R. **7**: 661.
— and the three Emperors. (M. P. Thompson) Cath. World, **16**: 474.
— as a Friend of America, and a Statesman. (M. Busch) No. Am. **131**: 1, 157.
— at Home. Belgra. **13**: 39.
— Busch on. (H. T. Finck) Nation, **28**: 85. — Penn Mo. **10**: 386.
— Character and Career of. Ed. R. **130**: 417. Same art. Liv. Age, **104**: 67.
— Dinner with. Hours at Home, **5**: 548.
— Early Life of. (J. S. Henderson) Good Words, **14**: 755. — Ev. Sat. **15**: 696.
— Every-Day Life of. Ev. Sat. **11**: 283.
— Few Words for. (E. Goadby) Macmil. **23**: 339.
— Hesekiel's Life of. Lakeside, **4**: 68.
— How Things are under. Irish Mo. **2**: 86.
— in 1868. Ed. R. **130**: 417.
— Letters of. Penn Mo. **10**: 60.
— Life and Letters. Quar. **147**: 113.
— Literary Faculty of. (F. Hueffer) Gent. M. n. s. **18**: 55. Same art. Liv. Age, **132**: 305.
— Political Career of. (H. Villard) No. Am. **108**: 165.
— Political Life-Work of. Westm. **112**: 444.
— Prussia, and Pan-Teutonism. Quar. **130**: 71.
— Prussia of. Gent. M. n. s. **5**: 470.
— Public Life of. (J. S. Henderson) Good Words, **15**: 387.
— Some Words of. (C. E. Maurice) Contemp. **16**: 454.
— Speeches of. Dub. R. **77**: 106.
— Statesmanship of. Ev. Sat. **9**: 722.
— Talks with. (F. Kapp) Nation, **11**: 233.
Bismarckism. (F. Harrison) Fortn. **14**: 631.
— in England. (E. Jenkins) Contemp. **22**: 107.
Bismark, Count F. W. von, and his Works. Blackw. **19**: 590.
Bison, The. Penny M. **3**: 273. **4**: 387.
— of North America, and its Extermination. (J. A. Allen) Penn Mo. **7**: 214. *See* Buffalo.
Bison-Hunting in India. Fraser, **47**: 39.
Bison-Shooting. (M. L. Meason) Broadw. **2**: 330.
Bisset, the Animal Trainer. Chamb. J. **10**: 22.
Bisset, J. Meth. M. **22**: 470.
Bisset's Youth. St. James, **22**: 576, 700. **23**: 33-601. **24**: 177-577. **25**: 96, 737.
Bit of Alchemy; a Story of Dr. Dee. Knick. **59**: 275.
Bit of Eastern Experience. (M. H. Breck) Overland, **6**: 373.
Bit of Nature; a Story. (A. Rhodes) Appleton, **21**: 114, 133, 253.
Bit of Preferment. (J. Hewlett) Colburn, **71**: 67.
Bit of Shore Life. (S. O. Jewett) Atlan. **44**: 200.
Bitche and Verdun, France. All the Year, **24**: 389.
Biter bit; a Tale. (J. A. St. J. Blythe) Temp. Bar, **30**: 332.

Bitter Fruit; a Dramatic Tale. (A. W. Dubourg) Temp. Bar, **44**: 484. **45**: 76. Same art. Appleton, **14**: 264–359.
Bitter Words; a Poem. (R. H. Stoddard) Internat. M. **5**: 457.
Bitterns. (W. E. Endicott) Am. Natural. **3**: 169.
Bittle, David F., Life of. (G. Diehl) Luth. Q. **7**: 541.
Bitumen, and its practical Applications. Ecl. Engin. **7**: 550.
— Indurated, in the Trap of the Connecticut Valley. (J. D. Dana) Am. J. Sci. **116**: 130.
Bitumens, Chemical and Geological History of. (T. S. Hunt) Am. J. Sci. **85**: 157.
— Native. (W. O. Crosby) Am. Natural. **13**: 229.
Bituminization of Wood. (W. Carpenter) Am. J. Sci. **36**: 118.
Bitzius, A. (J. Gotthels) Eng. Dom. M. **10**: 274.
Björnson, B. (R. Buchanan) Contemp. **21**: 45. — with portrait, Appleton, **11**: 104. — with portrait, Scrib. **20**: 336.
— Arne. (K. Janson) Dial (Ch.), **2**: 140.
— as a Novelist. Brit. Q. **61**: 364.
— Dramas. (H. H. Boyesen) No. Am. **116**: 109.
Black, Jeremiah S. Letter to Henry Wilson. Galaxy, **11**: 257.
— Portrait of. Galaxy, **13**: 293.
Black, Joseph. (A. C. Brown) Nature, **18**: 346. — Brit. Q. **2**: 233.
— Cavendish, Priestley, and Watt. (J. W. Croker) Quar. **77**: 105.
— Lectures on Chemistry. (H. Brougham) Ed. R. **3**: 1. **6**: 502.
Black, William, with portrait. Appleton, **12**: 257. — with portrait, Dub. Univ. **94**: 295. — with portrait, Ecl. M. **88**: 503. — with portrait, Victoria, **32**: 493.
— Madcap Violet. (A. Lang) Fortn. **27**: 88.
— Novels of. Nat. Q. **41**: 190.
Black, William, Journal of, 1744. Pennsyl. M. **1**: 117, 233, 404. **2**: 40.
Black and Blue. House. Words, **14**: 276. Same art. Liv. Age, **51**: 428.
Black and White House in the Dell. Chamb. J. **39**: 105, 116.
Black Bess. (H. P. Spofford) Galaxy, **5**: 517.
Black Chamber; a Ghost Story. Dub. Univ. **52**: 687.
Black Country of England. Dub. Univ. **58**: 114. — Tinsley, **4**: 423.
— Peep at. (Mrs. C. A. White) Sharpe, **41**: 309.
— Saturday Night in. Dub. Univ. **58**: 114. Same art. Ecl. M. **54**: 135.
Black Cross, The. Macmil. **14**: 61. Same art. Ecl. M. **67**: 235.
Black Death, The. All the Year, **43**: 436. — Cornh. **11**: 594. — Penny M. **8**: 478.
— and its Place in English History. (F. Seebohm) Fortn. **2**: 149, 268.
— England before and after. (J. E. T. Rogers) Fortn. **3**: 191.
— in New England. (H. Butterworth) Pop. Sci. Mo. **3**: 28.
— Population of England before. (F. Seebohm) Fortn. **4**: 87.
Black Dwarf, Original of. Anal. M. **11**: 332.
Black Exchange; an Attorney's Story. Chamb. J. **39**: 213. Same art. Ecl. M. **60**: 87.
Black Fast, The. Good Words, **13**: 371.
Black Forest, The. Month, **13**: 523. — Liv. Age, **67**: 671.
— and Vicinity, Legends of. (Mrs. Bushby) Colburn, **143**: 443, 578. Same art. Ecl. M. **72**: 27, 189.
— Byways of. Bentley, **44**: 307.
— Charities in. Good Words, **4**: 25.
— Day in. Bentley, **7**: 186.
Black Forest, The, Days in. (G. C. Swayne) Once a Week, **10**: 390, 418. **11**: 670.
— Home through the Valley of Hell. (D. Costello) Colburn, **85**: 210.
— Roe-Shooting in. Cornh. **17**: 317.
— Society in. (E. O'Hara) St. James, **9**: 174. — Dub. Univ. **76**: 230.
— Tour through. Bentley, **29**: 523.
Black Friday in New York. (K. Cornwallis) So. M. **17**: 535. — (W. R. Hooper) Galaxy, **12**: 753.
Black Fritz. Sharpe, **3**: 4–68.
Black Hawk, Life of. (W. J. Snelling) No. Am. **40**: 68. — Am. Q. **15**: 426. — New Eng. M. **6**: 420. — Hesp. **2**: 167.
Black-Hawk War. (J. M. Higbee) No. Am. **51**: 107.
— Drake's. Hesp. **1**: 327.
Black Head; a Cornish Story. Lond. Soc. **40**: 105.
Black Hills of Dakota, Trip to. (L. P. Richardson) Scrib. **13**: 748.
— Value of. Potter Am. Mo. **5**: 616.
Black Joke; a Legend of Ulster. (F. Browne) Peop. J. **3**: 360.
Black Knot. (B. D. Halsted) Am. Natural. **10**: 341.
Black-Lead, and Black-Lead Pencils. Penny M. **10**: 394.
Black Marble, The. (E. Bögh) Scrib. **7**: 432.
Black Mare with a white Star; a Tale. Chamb. J. **45**: 417, 441.
Black Mask. Dub. Univ. **7**: 508.
Black Mill. All the Year, **6**: 304.
Black Monday. Colburn, **89**: 160.
— of the Glens. Dub. Univ. **6**: 333.
Black Mountain, Usages, Customs, and Superstitions of. So. Lit. Mess. **6**: 720. *See* Montenegro.
Black Museum, London. Liv. Age, **135**: 501.
Black Panther's Raid. Temp. Bar, **20**: 530.
Black Pearl. (V. Sardon) Lippinc. **10**: 314.
Black Pocket-Book; a Tale. Internat. M. **2**: 89.
Black Point. (C. F. Woolson) Harper, **59**: 84.
Black Pool. Sharpe, **29**: 113.
Black Prophet; a Tale of the Irish Famine. (W. Carleton) Dub. Univ. **27**: 600, 739. **28**: 75–717.
Black Ram. (J. Y. Akerman) Bentley, **11**: 498.
Black Robe; a Novel. (W. Collins) Canad. Mo. **18**: 499, 561. **19**: 15–588.
Black Rock. (A. La Forge) Scrib. **7**: 209.
Black Sea. Bentley, **38**: 221.
— Anatolian Shores of. Bentley, **37**: 235.
— and the Caspian. Ecl. Engin. **15**: 122.
— — Union of. (D. Ker) Geog. M. **3**: 11.
— Commerce of. (J. B. Brown) Hunt, **21**: 1. — De Bow, **17**: 50. — West. J. **14**: 24, 92.
— Eastern Shores of. Blackw. **78**: 521.
— Russian Commerce in. Bank. M. (L.) **15**: 497.
— Russian Shores of, Oliphant's. Liv. Age, **39**: 815. — Hogg, **11**: 58.
— Trade of. (W. Phillips) No. Am. **10**: 168.
Black Sea Fleets; a Poem. Dub. Univ. **44**: 203.
Black Sea Question, The. Colburn, **148**: 1.
Black Sheep; a Tale. (M. V. Terhune) Godey, **62**: 47, 145.
Black Sheep; a Tale. (E. Yates) All the Year, **16**: 145–553. **17**: 1–313. Same art. Ev. Sat. **2**: 277–430.
Black Sheep, A. Fraser, **71**: 183.
Black Tarn; a Tale. All the Year, **3**: 235, 258, 278. — Same art. Liv. Age, **67**: 358. Same art. Harper, **21**: 378.
Black Thursday. House. Words, **13**: 388.
Blackbird, The. Chamb. J. **9**: 56. — (S. Hibberd) Recr. Sci. **2**: 238.
Blackbirds. (E. Ingersoll) Lippinc. **20**: 376.
— Cow. (T. M. Trippe) Am. Natural. **3**: 291.
— Yellow-headed. (E. Coues) Am. Natural. **5**: 195.

Blackbirds, The; a Comedietta. (J. B. Greenough) Atlan. **39**: 31.
Blackburn, Francis, with portrait. Dub. Univ. **24**: 470.
Blackburn, Gideon. (J. W. Hall) Am. Presb. R. **1**: 549.
Blackburn Independent Academy. Am. Q. Reg. **9**: 133.
Blackburn on Strike. All the Year, **40**: 516.
Blackburn Sewing Schools, 1863. Temp. Bar, **7**: 339.
Blacker, William. Dub. Univ. **17**: 628.
Blackfeet Indians. (H. M. Robinson) Appleton, **18**: 37.
— Traditions of. (J. M. Brown) Galaxy, **3**: 157.
Blackfriars. All the Year, **26**: 541.
— Old. (R. Rowe) Good Words, **19**: 115.
Blackfriars Theater. (Miss G. C. Bibb) Western, **1**: 87.
Blackhall, Gilbert, Services by. Liv. Age, **10**: 206.
Blackheath Subsidences. (T. V. Holmes) Pop. Sci. R. **20**: 235.
Blackie, John Stuart, with portrait. Dub. Univ. **87**: 404. — Penn Mo. **11**: 969.
Blacking Factory, Day and Martin's. Penny M. **11**: 509.
Blacklegs, Derivation of Term. Once a Week, **10**: 570.
Blackletter Recreations. Dub. Univ. **26**: 537.
Blacklock, Thomas. Blackw. **2**: 495.
Blacklock Forest. Colburn, **142**: 652. **143**: 56–655. **144**: 182, 523. **145**: 56–548. **146**: 305–671. **147**: 329–705. **148**: 100, 235.
Blackmail. All the Year, **30**: 247.
Blackmere Hollow. (H. B. Baker) Tinsley, **21**: 645.
Blackmore, Richard D., Novels of. Internat. R. **7**: 406. — Dub. Univ. **93**: 541. — Penn Mo. **11**: 619.
Blacksmith's Foundling; a Story. (C. A. White) Peop. J. **8**: 63.
Blacksmiths of Holsby. (L. Crow) Once a Week, **10**: 113, 154. Same art. Harper, **28**: 643.
Blackstone, Sir Wm. (J. Maurice) Knick. **47**: 288.
— Commentaries. Am. Mo. R. **3**: 430. — Chr. R. **13**: 228.
— — Warren's. Blackw. **78**: 199.
Blackstone, William, of Boston. (L. M. Sargent) Hist. M. **18**: 353.
Blackwell, Dr. Elizabeth. Chamb. J. **29**: 350. Same art. Liv. Age, **58**: 231.
— Lectures. Chamb. J. **31**: 255.
— Record of a noble Woman. Tait, n. s. **8**: 539.
— Sketch of. (I. Scott) Once a Week, **2**: 577.
Blackwood, Capt. F. P., Voyage and Survey. Quar. **81**: 468. Same art. Liv. Age, **15**: 577. Same art. Ecl. M. **10**: 151.
Blackwood, Sir Henry. Blackw. **34**: 1.
Blackwood, William. (J. Neal) Atlan. **16**: 660.
— Death of. Blackw. **36**: 571.
Blackwood's Irish Judge. Dub. Univ. **5**: 263.
Blackwood's Magazine. (H. Smith) Liv. Age, **33**: 215.
— answered. Knick. **38**: 205.
— Contributors' Gathering, Aug. 12, 1819. Blackw. **5**: 597, 627.
— in America. Blackw. **62**: 442.
— *versus* Washington. So. Lit. Mess. **8**: 283.
Bladensburg, Md., Dueling Ground at. (F. A. Foster) Harper, **16**: 471.
Bladud, King. (S. P. Day) Victoria, **36**: 311.
Blagdon Controversy. Chr. Obs. **1**: 179.
Blaine, James G., with portrait. Ev. Sat. **10**: 169, 174.
Blainville, H. D. de, and Cuvier. Brit. Q. **24**: 365. Same art. Liv. Age, **51**: 417.
Blair, Adam. Blackw. **11**: 349, 466.
— Life of. Portfo. (Den.) **28**: 320.
— Sketch of. Lond. M. **5**: 485.
Blair, Francis P., with portrait. Dem. R. **17**: 10.
Blair, Hugh. Anal. M. **5**: 188.
— Hill's Life of. (J. Foster) Ecl. R. **6**: 1037.
Blair, Robert, Critical Notice of. (G. Gilfillan) Hogg, **9**: 113. Same art. Ecl. M. **26**: 368.
Blair, Samuel. (A. Alexander) Princ. **9**: 536.
Blake, Michael, Bp. of Dromore. Irish Mo. **9**: 376–613.
Blake, Robert, Admiral. Chamb. J. **17**: 342. — House. Words, **5**: 326. — Ecl. R. **96**: 407. — (J. Hannay) Quar. **104**: 1. Same art. Ecl. M. **45**: 470. Same art. Liv. Age, **58**: 643. — Sharpe, **15**: 319.
Blake, William. (J. C. Carr) Belgra. **29**: 366. — (T. M. Clark) O. & N. **7**: 67. — (W. A. Cram) Radical, **3**: 378. — (E. P. Evans) Hours at Home, **11**: 55. — (H. G. Hewlett) Contemp. **28**: 756. **29**: 207. — Art J. **16**: 25. — Blackw. **97**: 291. — Cornh. **31**: 721. Same art. Liv. Age, **126**: 67. — (C. Hargrove) Mod. R. **2**: 565. — (F. Wedmore) Temp. Bar, **62**: 52. Same art. Liv. Age, **149**: 557. Same art. Ecl. M. **97**: 104. — (H. E. Scudder) Scrib. **20**: 225. — Ecl. R. **119**: 373. — Liv. Age, **59**: 848. — Once a Week, **26**: 438. — Sharpe, **46**: 19. — Westm. **81**: 101.
— and Varley, Sketch-Book. (W. B. Scott) Portfo. **2**: 103.
— Chat about. (W. Allingham) Hogg, **2**: 17.
— Drawings at the Burlington Fine Arts Club. (H. H. Statham) Macmil. **34**: 55.
— Genius of. (H. E. Scudder) No. Am. **99**: 465.
— Gilchrist's Life of. Colburn, **130**: 309. — Liv. Age, **79**: 579. — Lond. Q. **31**: 265. — Quar. **117**: 1.
— Life and Works of. (W. F. Rae) F. Arts Q. **3**: 56.
— Pictor Ignotus. (M. A. Dodge) Atlan. **13**: 433.
— Poems. Ecl. M. **84**: 372. — (C. E. Norton) No. Am. **108**: 641. — Penn Mo. **7**: 843.
— Seer and Painter. Temp. Bar, **17**: 95.
— Swinburne on. (M. D. Conway) Fortn. **9**: 216.
— Works of. (M. G. van Rensselaer) Am. Arch. **8**: 215.
Blakesmoor in H—shire. (C. Lamb) Lond. M. **10**: 225.
Blakhal, Father Gilbert, Episodes in Life of. (T. B. Parkinson) Month, **16**: 374. **17**: 33.
Blanc, Jean Joseph Louis. Once a Week, **24**: 473. — Westm. **49**: 103. — Blackw. **56**: 265. — (G. Barmby) Ecl. M. **14**: 160.
— and national Workshops of 1848. (C. Barrère) Fraser, **90**: 437.
— History of ten Years. For. Q. **32**: 61. — Ecl. R. **80**: 88.
Blanc, Mont. (F. W. P. Greenwood) Chr. Exam. **6**: 52. — (A. Nicholson) Univ. Q. **5**: 197. — (N. Colgan) Irish Mo. **8**: 17–246. — Nat. M. **8**: 168. — Broadw. **7**: 432. — Ed. R. **50**: 221. — (J. van Rensselaer) Am. J. Sci. **2**: 1. — Liv. Age, **31**: 84.
— and the Alps. (A. Hichborn) Univ. Q. **5**: 179.
— and Geneva. So. Lit. Mess. **25**: 309.
— Ascent of. (A. Smith) Blackw. **71**: 35. Same art. Liv. Age, **32**: 289. Same art. Ecl. M. **25**: 391. — (M. Barry) Ed. New Philos. J. **18**: 106. — Bentley, **40**: 441. — Blackw. **4**: 180. — Cornh. **11**: 717. — Fraser, **52**: 1. Same art. Liv. Age, **46**: 387. — Am. Meth. M. **8**: 386. — Good Words, **1**: 521, 529. — (H. H. Jackson) Colburn, **19**: 458.
— — Auldjo's. (H. Brougham) Ed. R. **50**: 221.
— — Beaufoy's. Blackw. **1**: 59.
— — by Clark and Sherwill, 1825. Colburn, **16**: 434, 590. **17**: 289.
— — by Mlle. d'Angeville. (C. Müller) Colburn, **160**: 387.
— — First. Mus. **44**: 273.
— Bad Weather on. Liv. Age, **60**: 810.
— Glaciers of. Colburn, **125**: 308, 476. **126**: 44.
— How we did. Cornh. **11**: 717.
— Monarch of Mountains. (L. Abbott) Harper, **42**: 811.
— Poaching on. Fraser, **80**: 97. Same art. Liv. Age, **102**: 551. Same art. Ecl. M. **73**: 268. Same art. Ev. Sat. **8**: 183.
— Sherwill's Visit to. Colburn, **17**: 533. **19**: 40, 150.
— Sunset on. Cornh. **28**: 457. Same art. Liv. Age, **119**: 432.

Blanc, Mont, Topography of. No. Brit. **42**: 137.
— Up and down. (F. Copcutt) Putnam, **12**: 385. — Chamb J. **43**: supp.
— without a Guide. Chamb. J. **53**: 513.
See Alps; Switzerland.
Blanchard, Claude, Journal of Campaign of. Cath. World, **11**: 787.
Blanchard, Edward L., with portrait. Victoria, **33**: 463.
Blanchard, Joseph, Journal of, 1725. N. E. Reg. **7**: 184.
Blanchard, Laman, and his Writings. Colburn, **76**: 131.
— Life of. Liv. Age, **5**: 191. — (Sir E. L. Bulwer) Liv. Age, **8**: 249. — Dub. Univ. **28**: 509. — (W. M. Thackeray) Fraser, **33**: 332. — Ecl. R. **83**: 692.
— Writings of. Colburn, **73**: 428.
Blanchard, Mrs. Margaret B., Obituary Notice of. (H. H. Barber) Unita. R. **7**: 82.
Blanchard, Thomas, the Inventor. (H. Waters) Harper, **63**: 254.
Blanchard, William. (D. Meadows) Bentley, **11**: 473.
Blanche. (M. B. Edwards) Once a Week, **14**. 290, 316.
Blanche; a Poem. (J. D. Frazer) Dub. Univ. **43**: 90.
Blanche Blake's Choice; a Tale. (N. Robinson) Cath. World, **28**: 790.
Blanche Delamere; a Tale. (Mrs. Johnstone) Tait, n. s. **6**: 40-597.
Blanche of Bourbon, Death of. Blackw. **6**: 485.
Blanche Tréguier; a Story. Macmil. **21**: 534. Same art. Ecl. M. **74**: 691.
Blanchief Abbey, Derbyshire. (H. Kirke) Reliquary, **7**: 193.
Bland, Robert, Poems of. Ecl. R. **10**: 730.
Bland Papers. So. Lit. Mess. **9**: 657.
Blandy, Mary, Trial of. House. Words, **14**: 473.
Blank in the Lottery. Bentley, **57**: 466, 588. **58**: 82.
Blanks and Prizes. (C. G. F. Gore) Tait, n. s. **11**: 1–348.
Blank Verse. Cornh. **15**: 620.
Blankenberghe, the Belgian Trouville. (F. W. Cherson) St. James, **35**: 135.
Blankshire Hounds. House. Words, **8**: 508.
Blanqui, Adolphe. Journey in England and Scotland. Lond. M. **11**: 564.
Blanqui, L. A., Election of. (Mrs. G. M. Crawford) Nation, **28**: 333.
Blarney; a Poem. (J. Tuckey) Temp. Bar, **48**: 515.
Blarney and Hypocrisy; a Sketch. Lond. M. **15**: 536.
Blasphemy against the Bible. Dub. R. **40**: 200.
— against the Holy Ghost. (W. J. Clark) Princ. **18**: 376.
— Law of. Lond. M. **19**: 360.
— Punishment of. (F. Parkman) Chr. Exam. **16**: 93.
Blast, Hot, Application of. (T. Clarke) J. Frankl. Inst. **24**: 46.
— — in Gas Reverberatory Furnaces. Pract. M. **7**: 302.
— — in Manufacture of Cast-Iron. (T. Clarke) J. Frankl. Inst. **22**: 127.
— — Use of, in France, 1836. (A. Guenyveau) J. Frankl. Inst. **21**: 62, 135, 354.
Blast-Blowing by Water. (W. Lewis) J. Frankl. Inst. **5**: 189–378. **6**: 9, 73, 327.
Blast Furnace, Blowing-in a. Pract. M. **1**: 327.
— Chemical Action of. Pract. M. **3**: 248.
— Economy of. (F. Prime, jr.) Pract. M. **4**: 379. Same art. Ecl. Engin. **11**: 271.
— Value of superheated. (Prof. Tunner) Ecl. Engin. **11**: 149.
See Iron.
Blast-Furnace Hearths and Linings. (J. Birkinbine) J. Frankl. Inst. **112**: 429.
Blast-Furnace Slag, Utilization of. Pract. M. **7**: 248.
Blast-Heating Apparatus. (J. E. Mills) Ecl Engin. **15**: 165.
Blasting of Rocks. (A. Kirk) J. Frankl. Inst. **111**: 43. — (A. Kirk) Am. Arch. **9**: 69. — (R. Hare) J. Frankl. Inst. **16**: 221. — J. Frankl. Inst. **10** 62. — Penny M. **12**: 66.
— Dangers and Remedies of. Am. J. Sci. **17**: 132.
— Method of. (G. Thornton) Ecl. Engin. **21**: 77.
— Submarine, 1847. (G. Edwards) J. Frankl. Inst. **43**: 353. — Hunt, **30**: 191. — West. J. **9**: 82.
Blasting-Gelatine. (H. B. Pritchard) Nature, **20**: 32.
Blayney, Lord. Journey through Spain. Quar. **14**: 112.
Blazon, Noble Science of. Chamb. J. **28**: 51.
Bleaching. J. Frankl. Inst. **11**: 63, 131.
— Apparatus for. (J. Rennie) J. Frankl. Inst. **3**: 22, 117.
— Chemical Agents used in. (J. Rennie) J. Frankl. Inst. **3**: 155-394. **4**: 9, 82.
— Chemical and physical Nature of Stuffs. (J. Rennie) J. Frankl. Inst. **4**: 152.
— History of Art of. (J. Rennie) J. Frankl. Inst. **2**: 171-338.
— Processes followed in. (J. Rennie) J. Frankl. Inst. **4**: 157, 231, 293.
— Theory of. (J. Rennie) J. Frankl. Inst. **4**: 381.
Bleaching Powder, Chloride of Lime or. (A. Ure) J. Frankl. Inst. **5**: 318, 375.
Bleak House. (C. Dickens) Harper, **4**: 649, 809. **5**: 87–791. **6**: 93–812. **7**: 93–659.
Bleak Wind of March; a Story. (M. C. Harris) Appleton, **26**: 562.
Bleau's Atlas, 17th Century. Chamb. J. **15**: 374.
Bledsoe, Mary. (Mrs. E. F. Ellet) Godey, **42**: 43.
Bleeding Diamond, The. All the Year, **8**: 256.
Bleeker, P. Nature, **17**: 286.
Blenheim. Penny M. **8**: 317.
— Battle of. (H. W. Warren) Meth. Q. **24**: 419.
Blennerhassett, H. (J. S. C. Abbott) Harper, **54**: 347. — (A. G. Bradley) Macmil. **42**: 99. Same art. Ecl. M. **95**: 208. — (W. Wallace) Am. Whig R. **2**: 133. — (S. P. Hildreth) Am. Whig R. **7**: 368.
— Life of. (M. F. Force) No. Am. **73**: 152.
— Story of. So. Lit. Mess. **27**: 457.
— Visit to his Island. (A. C. Hall) Potter Am. Mo. **16**: 289.
Blennerhassetts, Latter Days of the. (M. P. Woodbridge) Lippinc. **23**: 239.
Blessed Isles, Literature of. Lond. Soc. **1**: 80, 150.
Blessed Life, The. (S. Coley) Ex. H. Lec. **16**: 315.
Blessings in Disguise. (T. S. Arthur) Godey, **21**: 15.
Blessington, Countess of. (C. C. Felton) No. Am. **81**: 257. — with portrait, Fraser, **7**: 267. — (H. B. Baker) Belgra. **42**: 342. — Dub. Univ. **45**: 333. Same art. Ecl. M. **35**: 29. Same art. Liv. Age, **45**: 86. — Irish Q. **2**: 773. — Liv. Age, **4**: 227. — Nat. M. **7**: 258. — Tait, n. s. **1**: 204.
— Book of Beauty for 1838. Mo. R. **145**: 39.
— Confessions of an elderly Gentleman. Mo. R. **141**: 391.
— Life and Correspondence. Fraser, **51**: 467. — New Q. **4**: 169. — Ecl. R. **101**: 513.
— Lionel Deerhurst. Dub. Univ. **29**: 338.
— Lottery of Life. Mo. R. **159**: 127.
— Madden's Life of. Liv. Age, **44**: 795. **45**: 61.
— Memoirs of a Femme-de-chambre. Colburn, **77**: 367.
— Novels. Ed. R. **67**: 349.
— Recollections of. (P. G. Patmore) Bentley, **26**: 162.
— The Repealers. Westm. **19**: 446.
— Sketch of. So. Q. **28**: 149.
— Tomb of. Bentley, **27**: 531. Same art. Internat. M. **1**: 126.
Blight, Natural History of. Chamb. J. **11**: 90.
Blind; a Poem. (C. F. Bates) Scrib. **2**: 400.
Blind, The. (B. B. Bowen) Univ. Q. **23**: 412. — Nat. R **10**: 75. — Quar. **118**: 430.

Blind, The, Alphabets for. Penny M. 7: 111.
— and their Education. (B. B. Bowen) Univ. Q. 11: 399.
— and their Limitations. (B. B. Bowen) Univ. Q. 13: 147.
— Books for. Nat. M. 8: 540.
— by the Roadside, Appeal for. St. James, 24: 193.
— Education of. (W. H. Prescott) No. Am. 31: 66. — (S. G. Howe) No. Am. 37: 20. — (S. G. Howe) Am. Inst. of Instruc. 1836: 1. — New Eng. M. 4: 177. — Mo. R. 132: 275. — Mus. 24: 230. — West. M. 3: 150. — (J. H. Hunter) Canad. Mo. 18: 171.
— Fingers *versus* Eyes. Tinsley, 8: 676.
— Gall on Literature for. Chr. Obs. 35: 175.
— How we treat. Hogg, 15: 131.
— Institutions for. (L. P. Brockett) Nat. M. 10: 33-419.
— — and Instruction for. (L. P. Brockett) Am. J. Educ. 4: 127.
— Instruction of. Penny M. 5: 387.
— Literature for. Mus. 26: 571.
— Massachusetts Asylum for. No. Am. 50: 520. — Chr. Exam. 28: 359.
— Music for. Penny M. 7: 219.
— Musical Instruction to, Campbell's. Cornh. 33: 349.
— Normal Musical School for. (D. M. Craik) Good Words, 14: 634.
— Plea for. Chr. Obs. 74: 375.
— Printing for. (J. R. Dennett) Nation, 12: 431.
— Sketches of. Irish Q. 9: 63.
— Ways and Works of. Good Words, 2: 313. — Chamb. J. 44: 381. — Ed. R. 99: 61. Same art. Liv. Age, 40: 435.
— Writing-Machine for. Chamb. J. 45: 136.
— Writing-Table for. Ev. Sat. 11: 71.
Blind Alick of Stirling. Penny M. 2: 194.
Blind and Deaf Boy, Account of. (Sir J. Mackintosh) Ed. R. 20: 462.
Blind Artist. Dem. R. 25: 538.
Blind Authors. St. James, 17: 111.
Blind Beggars. (C. Camden) Good Words, 13: 205, 284.
Blind Boy; a Poem. (T. G. Hake) Scrib. 3: 189.
Blind Fiddler. (V. DeForest) Godey, 26: 2.
Blind Girl of Sorrento, Mastriani's. Tinsley, 17: 474.
Blind Girl's Love. Ecl. M. 11: 259.
Blind Harpist. Chamb. J. 24: 201.
Blind Jacques. (Mrs. E. F. Ellet) Dem. R. 15: 41.
Blind Kate. All the Year, 31: 548, 568.
Blind Lady and her Neighbors. St. James, 3: 295.
Blind Lovers of Chamouny. (C. Nodier) Ecl. M. 62: 358.
Blind Man, at the Exhibition of 1862. Temp. Bar, 7: 227.
Blind Man's Wreath. House. Words, 9: 51.
Blind Pastor; a Poem. Mo. Rel. M. 9: 216.
Blind Preacher, Rev. J. Waddell, and the British Spy. So. Lit. Mess. 10: 679.
Blind Rosa. (H. Conscience) Sharpe, 15: 257. Same art. Liv. Age, 33: 535.
Blind Student; a Tale. Cath. World, 20: 802.
Blind Tom, the musical Prodigy. All the Year, 8: 126.
Blind Walter; a Story. Chamb. J. 16: 349.
Blind Workers and Blind Helpers. Cornh. 9: 603.
Blind Youths, Paris Institution of. Good Words, 21: 763.
Blindness and Deafness. (B. B. Bowen) Univ. Q. 15: 412.
— and the Blind. So. Lit. Mess. 8: 519. 9: 6. 10: 30.
— and Idiocy. (W. H. Hurlbut) Chr. Exam. 44: 448.
— Dr. Bull's Sense of Vision. Liv. Age, 63: 701.
— Hydrocyanic Acid for. Chamb. J. 1: 3.
Bliss, H. Robespierre; a Tragedy. Colburn, 102: 171.
Blitzius, A. Stories of Peasant Life. (L. P. Hale) Chr. Exam. 71: 264.
Blizzard of 1836, in the West. (A. A. Graham) Potter Am. Mo. 14: 63.
Blobbs of Wadham. House. Words, 12: 513.
Block, Eugene François de. Art J. 18: 73.
Blocks, Ancient Methods of moving and raising. (J. Bennett) J. Frankl. Inst. 70: 303.
Block Books. Once a Week, 9: 481. – Month, 9: 39.
Block Island, R. I. (H. T. Beckwith) Hist. M. 2: 98. — (C. Lanman) Harper, 53: 168.
— Early Settlers of. (J. D. Champlin, jr.) N. E. Reg. 13: 37.
Block Printing, Ancient and Modern. Art J. 14: 153.
Blockade. (J. P. Benjamin) De Bow, 1: 499.
— and maritime Capture. (Lord Hobart) Macmil. 9: 41.
— How we ran the. (L. M. Palmer) Overland, 2: 47.
— Law of maritime Capture and. Nat. R. 16: 116.
— Running the. So. Hist. Pap. 9: 369.
— Through the: All the Year, 11: 497.
Blockade, the; an Episode of the End of the Empire. (MM. Erckmann-Chatrian) Ecl. M. 70: 123-727. 71: 882.
Blockade Run, My first and last St. James, 8: 346.
Blockade Runner in 1864. Bentley, 63: 638. 64: 80.
Blockader, Life on a. Contin. Mo. 6: 46.
Bloemestries of Haarlem. (J. G. Bertram) Once a Week, 17: 634.
Blois, City of. House. Words, 12: 556. Same art. Ecl. M. 37: 547. — Once a Week, 17: 717.
Blomfield, C. J., Bishop of London. Blackw. 93: 731. — Ecl. R. 118: 157. — Liv. Age, 55: 247. 77: 355. — Westm. 42: 160.
— Life and Times of. Dub. R. 54: 1.
— Memoir of. Chr. Rem. 46: 386. — Chr. Obs. 63: 528, 573.
Blonde, Exit the. (D. H. Jacques) Galaxy, 6: 840.
Blondes, Chancel's Book of. Lond. Soc. 16: 522.
— *versus* Brunettes. Temp. Bar, 15: 109.
Blonde Beauty. (L. M. Anderson) Potter Am. Mo. 10: 451.
Blondel Parva; a Tale. (J. Payn) Chamb. J. 45: 273-555.
Blondin, M. Eng. Dom. M. 11: 349.
— and his Rope-Walking. (A. Fonblanque, jr.) Once a Week, 5: 12.
Blondins, Mediæval. Chamb. J. 37: 264.
Blood, Brande on the. Ed. R. 22: 178.
— Circulation of. (J. C. Dalton) Galaxy, 8: 667. — (H. L. Fairchild) Pop. Sci. Mo. 19: 460, 644. — Blackw. 84: 148. Same art. Liv. Age, 58: 243.
— — Buchanan on. Nature, 11: 184.
— — Discovery of. Chamb. J. 6: 39. 30: 56. — Ed. R. 147: 25. — Fraser, 52: 352. Same art. Ecl. M. 36: 910.
— — — Flourens's History of. Quar. 97: 28.
— — — Forerunner of Harvey. All the Year, 43: 533.
— — — History of. (G. J. Fisher) Pop. Sci. Mo. 11: 294.
— Functions of. Chamb. J. 23: 232. — (C. W. Heaton) Intel. Obs. 12: 86.
— Healthy and diseased Properties of. Quar. 48: 375.
— Motive Power of. So. Lit. Mess. 20: 631.
— Objections to eating of. Theo. Repos. 3: 212.
— Organisms in. (H. C. Bastian) Nature, 20: 50.
— Transfusion of. (G. Lemattre) Pop. Sci. Mo. 2: 679.
— Wonders and Curiosities of. Blackw. 84: 148. Same art. Ecl. M. 45: 16.
Blood of the Sundons. House. Words, 17: 608.
Blood will tell. (O. S. Adams) Lippinc. 6: 398.
Blood-Letting, Origin of. (E. R. Lankester) Nature, 1: 76.
— in Fever, Welch on. Mo. R. 95: 244.
Blood-Poisoning, Nature of. Pract. M. 2: 235.
Blood-Prodigies. Chamb. J. 12: 228.
Blood-Relationship. (F. Galton) Nature, 6: 173.
Blood Seedling. (J. Hay) Lippinc. 7: 281.
Bloodless Battle of Brighton. Lond. Soc. 1: 442.
Blood-stained Chapel. (A. M. Birkbeck) Sharpe, 19: 297.
Bloody Brook, Battle of. Knick. 8: 436.

Bloody Parliament of Wilemow. (A. H. Wratislaw) Fraser, **94**: 294.
Bloomer Costume. Chamb. J. **16**: 280. — Bentley, **30**: 640.
Bloomfield, Robert. (R. Donkersley) Nat. M. **12**: 523. — (T. Oper) Sharpe, **28**: 304.
— Banks of the Wye. Ecl. R. **14**: 1103.
— May-Day with the Muses. Blackw. **11**: 722.
— Verses on. (B. Barton) Lond. M. **8**: 346.
Blooming of the Aloe. Lond. Soc. **20**: 132, 345.
Bloomington, Indiana, State University at. (R. Owen) O. & N. **4**: 134.
Bloomsbury, Old House in. Victoria, **36**: 509.
Bloomsbury Lodgings. (C. W. Stoddard) Overland, **14**: 17, 123.
Blore, Thomas. (L. Jewitt) Reliquary, **3**: 1.
Blossoming of an Aloe. (Mrs. C. Hoey) Chamb. J. **51**: 545–821.
Blount, California Pioneer. (W. I. Kip) Overland, **2**: 401.
Blount Family, Pedigree of. Colburn, **1**: 325.
Blow, Duration of a. J. Frankl. Inst. **102**: 403.
Blows and Pressure, Relative Values of. Ecl. Engin. **17**: 268.
Blowing-Machines. (J. Bennett) J. Frankl. Inst. **69**: 234.
Blown off Land; a Sketch. Dub. Univ. **56**: 475.
Blown up; a Poem. (T. D. English) Scrib. **6**: 48.
Blown up for Nothing; a Tale. Chamb. J. **44**: 113.
Blowpipe, The. (T. F. Moss) J. Frankl. Inst. **35**: 284. **36**: 104. — Chamb. J. **9**: 151.
— Hydro-Oxygen, Improvements in, 1846. (R. Hare) J. Frankl. Inst. **43**: 196.
— Hydrostatic. (R. Hare) J. Frankl. Inst. **1**: 160.
— Modes of increasing the Heat of. (H. Wurtz) Am. J. Sci. **77**: 179.
— Self-Acting. J. Frankl. Inst. **1**: 84.
— Use of. (J. Prideaux) J. Frankl. Inst. **24**: 161, 266.
— Works on. Nature, **13**: 164.
Blowpipe Analysis. Ecl. Engin. **11**: 356.
Bloxams and Mayfields. (Miss Leslie) Godey, **30**: 6–243.
Bloxham's New Paradise regained. Dub. Univ. **6**: 398.
Blücher, Marshal, Life of. Quar. **70**: 446. Same art. Am. Ecl. **4**: 552.
— March through France, 1814. All the Year, **24**: 420.
Blue, Color of aerial. (G. Harvey) Good Words, **10**: 620.
Blue and the Gray; a Tale. (S. M. Allcott) Putnam, **11**: 737.
Blue and the Gray; a Poem. (F. M. Finch) Atlan. **20**: 369.
Blue and Yellow. (L. de la Ramé) Bentley, **47**: 300.
Blue-Beard. (E. Vizetelly) Gent. M. n. s. **22**: 368. — (T. C. Woolsey) Lakeside, **5**: 314.
— Origin of Story of. (W. C. Taylor) Bentley, **23**: 136.
— Original. Once a Week, **18**: 15.
— rehabilitated; Verses. (W. H. Harrison) Dub. Univ. **90**: 728.
Blue-Beard's Ghost. (W. M. Thackeray) Fraser, **28**: 413.
Blue-Beard's Keys. Cornh. **23**: 192, 688. Same art. Liv. Age, **108**: 686. **110**: 139.
Blue Blanket, The. Hogg, **7**: 178.
Blue Blood and Red. (J. F. Waller) Dub. Univ. **87**: 641.
Blue Books, Anecdotes from. Ecl. M. **66**: 677.
— Romance and Humor of. St. Paul's, **10**: 402. **11**: 215.
Blue Cabinet; a Christmas Story. (L. H. Hooper) Lippinc. **3**: 47.
Blue Chamber; a Tale. All the Year, **31**: supp.
Blue-Coat Boys at Supper. St. James, **14**: 463.
Blue-Coat Bumbledom. All the Year, **39**: 77.
Blue Distance. Temp. Bar, **9**: 298.
Blue Dragon, The; a Story of circumstantial Evidence. Blackw. **64**: 207. Same art. Liv. Age, **18**: 481.
Blue Dragoon. Ecl. M. **34**: 525.
Blue Eyes, Future Extinction of. Cornh. **7**: 781.
Blue Eyes and Golden Hair. (A. Cudlip) Lond. Soc. **34**: 259–462.
Blue Friar Pleasantries. Fraser, **15**: 223, 382, 571. **16**: 151, 357, 637. **17**: 62–677. **18**: 245. **19**: 319. **20**: 333. **21**: 414. **22**: 177.
Blue-Gum, or Fever Tree. (T. S. Sozinskey) Potter Am. Mo. **13**: 452. — Chamb. J. **51**: 443.
Blue Handkerchief. Contin. Mo. **3**: 276.
Blue Jackets and Marines of the Royal Navy. Fraser, **92**: 131.
Blue-Laws and Witches in Old England. Portfo.(Den.) **18**: 508.
— of Connecticut. (J. G. Shea) Am. Cath. **2**: 475. — Blackw. **107**: 477. — U. S. Cath. M. **4**: 613, 715.
— — Blackwood's Magazine on. (W. L. Kingsley) New Eng. **30**: 248.
— — Forgeries of Rev. Samuel Peters. (W. L. Kingsley) Meth. Q. **38**: 67.
— of New Haven. Portfo.(Den.) **9**: 75.
— of the old States. (J. L. Kingsley) No. Am. **48**: 501. — Anal. M. **4**: 55. — (J. L. Kingsley) Chr. Q. Spec. **2**: 686.
Blue Man, The. Lond. M. **17**: 244.
Blue Ridge Mountains in Virginia, Geology of. (W. M. Fontaine) Am. J. Sci. **109**: 14, 93.
Blue Ridge, Tale of the. So. Lit. Mess. **3**: 173, 227.
Blue River Bank Robbery. (W. G. Woods) Atlan. **25**: 332.
Blue Spinster. (H. R. Addison) Bentley, **16**: 318.
Blue-Stocking; a Tale. (A. Edwardes) Temp. Bar, **50**: 433. **51**: 1, 289.
Blue-Stockings. (D. Cook) Once a Week, **15**: 580. Same art. Ev. Sat. **2**: 763.
Blue-Water. Cornh. **3**: 625.
Blue Wonder. (H. Zschokke) Bentley, **1**: 450.
Bluebird, The. (J. Burroughs) Scrib. **6**: 421.
Bluebottle-Fly; a French Art Student's Story. All the Year, **27**: 61–132.
Bluehill, Me., First Settlers of. (J. Williamson) N. E. Reg. **34**: 385.
Blues, The. Once a Week, **22**: 99.
— a Poem. Am. Mo. M. **9**: 147.
— Cure for. (A. Ogilvy) Once a Week, **17**: 350.
Blues and Buffs; a Sketch of a contested Election. Fraser, **101**: 548, 683, 831. **102**: 1.
Blundell, William, a loyal Catholic Cavalier. (T. E. Gibson) Month, **34**: 164, 273, 412. **35**: 59.
Blunderers. Colburn, **57**: 267.
Blundering by Act of Parliament. All the Year, **43**: 391.
Blunders, Amusing literary. Ev. Sat. **10**: 418.
— Another Book of. Fraser, **21**: 461.
— of the remarkably skillful. Colburn, **45**: 17.
— Philosophy of. Ev. Sat. **9**: 462.
— Professional. Appleton, **14**: 717.
— Queer. Chamb. J. **55**: 617.
Blunt, John James, Works of. Quar. **104**: 151. Same art. Liv. Age, **58**: 723.
Blunt, Joseph. Formation of the Confederacy. (G. Otis) No. Am. **22**: 460.
Blusterings from Barport. Tinsley, **18**: 431.
Blyth, Sir Arthur, with portrait. Colburn, **165**: 1289, 1386.
Boa Constrictor. Penny M. **1**: 289. **3**: 393.
Boar, Wild. Penny M. **7**: 140.
— Hunting. (G. A. Stockwell) Lippinc. **23**: 41. — Penny M. **2**: 397.
Boar Hunt. (J. Manning) Overland, **4**: 446.
— in Burgundy. St. Paul's, **3**: 74.
— in Brittany. Fraser, **34**: 416. **35**: 655.
Board of Green Cloth. All the Year, **12**: 308.
Boards of Management. (E. P. Rowsell) Colburn, **106**: 178.
— of Trade, Origin of. Bank. M. (N. Y.) **13**: 678.

Board-School Babies. All the Year, 39: 494.
Boarding out in New York City. (J. C. Hutcheson) Belgra. 21: 43.
Boarding-Houses. All the Year, 30: 515, 560. 31: 59–419.
— abroad. Lippinc. 18: 378.
— American. St. James, 18: 353.
— Eccentricities of. (H. Holme) Canad. Mo. 18: 398, 461.
Boarding-School. Knick. 45: 134.
Boarding-Schools, French and other. (Mrs. C. M. Kirkland) Putnam, 3: 164.
Boardman, George D., Missionary to Burmah. (J. A. Bolles) No. Am. 40: 376. — Mo. R. 137: 367.
Boasters among us. (J. Eagles) Blackw. 72: 432.
Boats, Metallic. Chamb. J. 26: 254.
— of rude Nations. Penny M. 11: 70.
— Row, and Skating-Boats. Chamb. J. 41: 53.
Boat Clubs, College. (E. F. Blake) University Q. 2: 99.
Boat-Race, Intercollegiate, 1879. Atlan. 44: 333.
Boat-Races, Intercollegiate. (B. W. Dwight) New Eng. 35: 251. — (G. W. Green) New Eng. 35: 548.
— Harvard and Oxford, 1869. (A. G. Sedgwick) Nation, 8: 431. — (E. L. Godkin) 9: 187.
— on the Schuylkill. Penn Mo. 10: 548.
— Oxford and Cambridge. Chamb. J. 37: 305.
— University. Chamb. J. 48: 366. — Lond. Soc. 3: 452. 12: 65. — Once a Week, 6: 442.
— — First, 1829. Lond. Soc. 7: 317.
— — of 1860. (G. O. Trevelyan) Macmil. 2: 19.
— — of 1867. (L. Barrett) Overland, 3: 278.
— — of 1871. (R. C. Marsden) Dark Blue, 1: 234.
— — of 1872. Dark Blue, 3: 227.
— Yale and Harvard, 1881. (G. W. Greene) Nation, 33: 6.
— Yankee. Chamb. J. 44: 750.
Boat-Racing. Gent. M. n. s. 2: 173.
— Hygiene of. Nation, 16: 335.
Boat Song; a Poem. (T. Hood) St. James, 3: 257.
Boat Trip from Toronto to Gulf of Mexico. (R. Tyson) Canad. Mo. 17: 397, 489, 602.
Boat Wreck; a Poem. Dub. Univ. 12: 387.
Boating at Commemoration. Lond. Soc. 12: 345.
— down the Alleghany. (J. M. Mulligan) Knick. 45: 561.
— How I was upset. Cornh. 2: 689.
— Oxford and Cambridge Rowing. (R. A. Proctor) Belgra. 38: 153.
See Canoe.
Boating Life at Oxford. Lond. Soc. 11: 289–541.
Boatman, The. (Lord Lytton) Blackw. 94: 653.
Boatswain's Mate. Nav. M. 1: 517.
Bob, Old, Story of. (W. Chambers) Chamb. J. 53: 7.
Bob Burke's Duel with Ensign Brady. Blackw. 35: 743.
Bob Fletcher; a Poem. (T. Haines) Internat. M. 1: 104.
Bob Kennedy's Canvass. Belgra. 7: 263.
Bob Kennedy's Widow-Hunt. (T. H. S. Escott) Belgra. 12: 104.
Bob Racket's Search for Shoes. (E. Youl) Howitt, 1: 91.
Bob Ruly's Experiences at the Fair; a Poem. So. Lit. Mess. 23: 453.
Bob Spavins's Bridal. St. James, 17: 55.
Bob White, The Bird. (T. B. Thorpe) Harper, 39: 505.
Bobbin-making Machine, Fell's. Pract. M. 6: 176.
Bobbin-Net Manufacture. Penny M. 3: 278.
Bobinette Berlops. (L. E. Furniss) Harper, 35: 545.
Bocage, The, and its Poets. Fraser, 21: 46.
Bocarmé Tragedy. (Mrs. Ward) Sharpe, 18: 41. Same art. Ecl. M. 30: 38.
Bocher, M. de. Chamb. J. 55: 346.
Boccaccio, Giovanni. (W. W. Fyfe) Sharpe, 19: 332.
— and Petrarch, Friendship of. Macmil. 33: 540. Same art. Liv. Age, 129: 372.
Boccaccio, Giovanni. Decameron. (C. Cushing) No. Am. 19: 68.
— — Tales from. Dub. Univ. 89: 526.
— Homes and Haunts of. (T. A. Trollope) Belgra. 33: 31.
— Life of. Dem. R. 42: 290. — (A. Gaye) St. James, 45: 282, 363, 452.
— — and Writings of. Lond. M. 15: 145.
— Writings of. So. Lit. Mess. 15: 154.
Bocking, Congregational Church at, History of. Cong. M. 11: 337, 449, 505.
Boddam Lighthouse, Under. Lond. Soc. 39: supp. 20.
Boddington, Mrs. Poems. Ed. R. 71: 171. — Ecl. R. 72: 334.
Boddlebak, the Bear-Tamer. Knick. 36: 151.
Bode, Law of; Gaps in the Solar System filled up. (Prof. Kelland) Macmil. 4: 364.
Boden See, Capper's Shores and Cities of. (J. M. Hubbard) Nation, 33: 56.
Bodenstedt, Fred. M. Penn Mo. 10: 965.
— Songs of Mirza Schaffy. (A. Forestier) Lippinc. 17: 367.
Bodenton, Another Bode for. Lond. M. 9: 71.
Bodiam Castle. Penny M. 13: 196.
Bodily Illness as a mental Stimulant. Cornh. 39: 412.
Bodily Work and Waste. (F. T. Bond) Pop. Sci. R. 3: 149. Same art. Ecl. M. 61: 303.
Bodin, Jean, and the History of Witchcraft. (H. White) Stud. & Intel. Obs. 4: 327.
Bodleian Letters. (J. Foster) Ecl. R. 19: 158.
Bodleian Library, Oxford. Liv. Age, 75: 173. — Lond. Q. 32: 132. — Month, 9: 136. — Penny M. 10: 228.
— Bodley and. (R. J. King) Fraser, 87: 647. — Ev. Sat. 14: 662.
— Future of. (C. Reade) Belgra. 25: 174.
— A Morning in. Dark Blue, 2: 683. — Ev. Sat. 12: 204.
Bodley, Sir Thomas, Life of. Am. Bibliop. 1: 354.
Body, The, and the Character. (H. Holbeach) Ecl. M. 79: 115.
— and Mind. *See* Mind and Body.
— Discipline of. (R. W. Dale) Good Words, 8: 375.
— Human, and its Connection with Man, Wilkinson on. Ecl. R. 95: 422.
— — in its spiritual Relations. Am. Church R. 24: 439.
— Moral Value of, to the Soul. (J. C. Crane) Meth. Q. 18: 228.
— not Spirit, the Type in Religion. Chr. Rem. 13: 484.
— to be subordinated to the Spirit. (W. C. Conant) New Eng. 30: 616.
Body-Snatchers. Ev. Sat. 9: 166.
Body-Snatching and Burking. Once a Week, 10: 261.
Boehm, Anthony William, Account of. Chr. Obs. 6: 561.
Boehm, Henry, Reminiscences of. (L. W. Peck) Meth. Q. 26: 386.
Boehm, M. Am. Meth. M. 6: 210.
Boehm, J. P., Papers relating to. Mercersb. 23: 528.
Boehme, Jacob. (G. W. F. Hegel) J. Spec. Philos. 13: 179. — (R. E. Thompson) Unita. R. 2: 243, 447. — Chr. R. 19: 440.
— Death-Bed of. Dub. Univ. 33: 90.
Boerne, Louis. Fraser, 97: 617. Same art. Liv. Age, 137: 793.
— and Heine, and ultra-liberal Press of Germany. For. Q. 10: 150. Same art. Select J. 4: 222.
Boers and the Transvaal. (W. F. Butler) Contemp. 39: 220. — (Sir B. Frere) 19th Cent. 9: 211.
— and Zulus. (B. Pine) Contemp. 35: 541.
— at Home. Blackw. 130: 753. — (J. J. Muskett) Ecl. M. 96: 849.
— With the. (Mrs. Hutchinson) Temp. Bar, 57: 319.
Boerland, Birthdays in. All the Year, 46: 437, 538.
Boethius, A. M. T. S. De Consolatione Philosophiæ. Chr. Obs. 67: 708.

Boethius, Hector, Sketch of. Hogg, **7**: 13.
Böttger, Johann, Inventor of Dresden China. Chamb. J. **28**: 257.
Bog, An upland. (E. Lawless) Belgra. **45**: 417.
Bogardus, James, Inventions and Improvements patented by. J. Frankl. Inst. **41**: 337, 403.
Bogatzky, C. H. von. (J. G. Morris) Evang. R. **6**: 453.
Bogeys, New and old. Once a Week, **21**: 500.
— of the Day. (Earl of Pembroke) Contemp. **25**: 789. Same art. Liv. Age, **125**: 490.
Boggleberry's Wooing. Tinsley, **15**: 544.
Bognor and Goodwood. Temp. Bar, **6**: 236.
Bogota in 1836–37, Steuart on. Mo. R. **150**: 282.
Bogue, David, Bennett's Life of. Ecl. R. **48**: 103.
— Memoir of. Cong. M. **9**: 1, 57.
Bohemia and the Slavonic Nations. For. Q. **20**: 21.
— Art-Life in. All the Year, **23**: 601.
— Ballads of, Ancient. Westm. **12**: 304.
— Few Hours in. (I. A. Prokop) Lippinc. **17**: 185.
— Fictions of. Quar. **103**: 328. Same art. Liv. Age, **58**: 93.
— History of the Church in. (J. Anketell) Am. Church R. **30**: 41–601. **31**: 35, 91, 201. .
— How it became Romanist. Chr. Obs. **71**: 91.
— Hungary, and Germany, Gleig's Visit to, 1837. Mo. R. **148**: 203.
— Legends of the Giant Mountains of. Colburn, **154**: 79–525.
— Letters from the Queen of, to Sir Edward Nicholas. (J. Evans) Arch. **37**: 224.
— Literature of. For. Q. **2**: 145. — Westm. **116**: 372.
— — in 14th Century. (A. W. Ward) Macmil. **38**: 40.
— Midsummer-Eve in. Once a Week, **11**: 54.
— Precursors of John Huss in. (A. H. Wratislaw) Contemp. **13**: 196.
— Protestant Clergy in. Kitto, **30**: 282.
— Protestants of. (A. H. Wratislaw) Good Words, **3**: 607.
— Question of, 1869. (M. Heilprin) Nation, **9**: 246.
— reconquered in 1620–28. Cong. **4**: 615.
— Reformation in. (J. M. Sherwood) Am. Presb. R. **13**: 114. — Bib. R. **1**: 123.
— — History of the Counter-. Chr. Rem. **53**: 271.
— Sea-Coast of; a vexed Question. (F. Jacox) Bentley, **61**: 205.
— Vicissitudes and Literature of. (K. Blind) Nat. Q. **24**: 1.
— Walk across. Fraser, **29**: 290.
— Whitty's Friends of. Dub. Univ. **50**: 101.
Bohemian, A, of the 16th Century. Temp. Bar, **16**: 551.
Bohemians; translated from Murger's Scènes de la Bohème. Knick. **41**: 12–419. **42**: 19–596. **43**: 20–485.
— Famous. (A. D. Vandam) Tinsley, **17**: 288. **18**: 33–546.
— New Theory of. (C. A. Bristed) Knick. **57**: 311. Same art. Sharpe, **50**: 289.
— Varieties of. Temp. Bar, **49**: 101.
Bohemian and Moravian Church. (J. Anketell) Am. Church R. **29**: 357, 557.
Bohemian and Slovak Literature, History of. Westm. **112**: 413.
Bohemian Coal Beds, Feistmantel on. Nature, **14**: 268.
Bohemian Glass. Nat. M. **3**: 489.
Bohemian Embassy to England, Spain, etc., in 1466. Quar. **90**: 413.
Bohemian Fortune-Teller. Chamb. J. **30**: 369.
Bohemian Schoolmaster. House. Words, **3**: 496.
Bohemians and Bohemianism. Cornh. **11**: 241. Same art. Ev. Sat. **2**: 535. — Temp. Bar, **8**: 551.
Bohemianism in French Politics. (E. L. Godkin) Nation, **13**: 237.
Bohemianism, Literature of. Westm. **79**: 32.
— What is? (G. F. Parsons) Overland, **1**: 425.
Bohun, Edmund, Autobiography of. Liv. Age, **56**: 193.
Bohun, Joanna de, Opening of Coffin of, at Hereford. (J. Merewether) Arch. **32**: 60.
Boiardo, M. M. (W. H. Prescott) No. Am. **19**: 353. — (J. Mew) Gent. M. n. s. **21**: 69.
— Orlando Innamorato. (J. A. Symonds) Fortn. **20**: 758.
Boileau, N., and Pope. (C. Mackay) 19th Cent. **10**: 830.
Boiler, The Steam. (J. Harrison) J. Frankl. Inst. **83**: 89, 161.
— Benson's High-Pressure. (J. J. Russell) J. Frankl. Inst. **73**: 121.
— Field. (F. Wise) J. Frankl. Inst. **80**: 317.
— for high Pressure with expanded Steam. J. Frankl. Inst. **73**: 241.
— Harrison Cast-Iron, Description of, 1864. J. Frankl. Inst. **78**: 38.
— Lancashire, Construction, Equipment, etc., of. (L. E. Fletcher) J. Frankl. Inst. **103**: 197, 241.
— Mouchot's Solar. J. Frankl. Inst. **101**: 166.
Boiler Flues, Alarm for Steam. (A. D. Bache) J. Frankl. Inst. **14**: 217.
— Strength of. (W. C. Unwin) J. Frankl. Inst. **102**: 171. — Ecl. Engin. **24**: 29.
Boiler Iron, Tests of, and Provisions of Steamboat Law. (J. A. Dumont) J. Frankl. Inst. **106**: 411.
Boiler-Making, Some Points in. (R. Briggs) J. Frankl. Inst. **106**: 129.
Boiler Tubes, Destruction of. (J. H. Kidder) Ecl. Engin. **10**: 71.
Boilers, Steam. (Z. Colburn) J. Frankl. Inst. **78**: 361.
— Action of fatty Matter on. (M. A. Mercier) J. Frankl. Inst. **108**: 259. — (G. Pereyra) J. Frankl. Inst. **107**: 314.
— Analysis of Reports of Belgic Association. (B. F. Isherwood) J. Frankl. Inst. **104**: 310.
— and Chimneys. (R. Briggs) J. Frankl. Inst. **101**: 246.
— and Surface Condensers. (T. Prosser) J. Frankl. Inst. **65**: 94.
— at Centennial, Tests of stationary. J. Frankl. Inst. **104**: 105.
— Causes of Injury to. (C. W. Williams) J. Frankl. Inst. **35**: 311.
— Circulation of Water in. (R. Briggs) J. Frankl. Inst. **102**: 86.
— Construction of. (B. Goodfellow) J. Frankl. Inst. **70**: 308.
— — and proper Proportions of. (A. Murray) J. Frankl. Inst. **40**: 172.
— Corrosion of, by Soot from Smoke. (B. F. Isherwood) J. Frankl. Inst. **104**: 305.
— Cylindrical, Strength of. (B. H. Latrobe) J. Frankl. Inst. **14**: 149. **35**: 396. **36**: 54, 279. — (T. W. Bakewell) J. Frankl. Inst. **36**: 100, 209. **37**: 56.
— Cylindrical Spiral. (J. Elder) J. Frankl. Inst. **70**: 391.
— Dimpfel's Patent, 1850. J. Frankl. Inst. **51**: 390.
— Effect of salt Water in. J. Frankl. Inst. **11**: 289.
— Effects of Surface Condensers on. (J. Jack) J. Frankl. Inst. **77**: 169.
— Experiment on Evaporation of a Corliss. (J. B Francis) J. Frankl. Inst. **89**: 391.
— Experiments on. (B. F. Isherwood) J. Frankl. Inst. **107**: 161, 248.
— — on setting Land. (B. F. Isherwood) J. Frankl. Inst. **58**: 193, 259.
— Explosion of. (M. Arago) J. Frankl. Inst. **99**: 398. **10**: 44. — (Z. Colburn) Ecl. Engin. **9**: 209. — (T. Ewbank) J. Frankl. Inst. **13**: 361. **14**: 1, 80, 226. — (W. Fairbairn) J. Frankl. Inst. **56**: 73. — (W. M. Henderson) J. Frankl. Inst. **93**: 35. — (J. W. Nystrom) J. Frankl. Inst. **108**: 254.

Boilers, Steam, Explosion of. (J. Sewel) J. Frankl. Inst. **59**: 338, 396. — (E. A. Corbin and H. G. Goodrich) J. Frankl. Inst. **108**: 395. — Ecl. Engin. **12**: 340. — J. Frankl. Inst. **10**: 327. **11**: 154, 289. **12**: 234–374. **13**: 12–361. **14**: 1–226. **15**: 15. **21**: 369. **22**: 90. **24**: 33. **25**: 129. **31**: 242. **32**: 8. **33**: 96, 111, 161. **39**: 308, 361. **46**: 140, 268, 335. **47**: 344. **48**: 32, 149, 403. **49**: 43, 204, 282. **50**: 263. **51**: 30, 51, 205. **53**: 322, 413. **56**: 358. **75**: 49. **88**: 94. — Intel. Obs. **7**: 28. — Portfo.(Den.) **19**: 47.
— — and of Gunpowder, Energy in. (G. B. Airy) J. Frankl. Inst. **77**: 244.
— — at Linthorpe Iron Works. (J. Head) Ecl. Engin. **11**: 166.
— — at Philadelphia, 1864. (J. W. Nystrom) J. Frankl. Inst. **77**: 326, 339, 385.
— — at Westfield, Mass., 1871. (R. H. Thurston) J. Frankl. Inst. **92**: 233.
— — Causes of. (W. Fairbairn) J. Frankl. Inst. **52**: 128, 175. — (W. K. Hall) J. Frankl. Inst. **61**: 296. — (E. Strong) J. Frankl. Inst. **66**: 289. — (A. Guthrie) West. J. **8**: 86.
— — — and Effects of. (F. A. Abel) J. Frankl. Inst. **74**: 124.
— — — and Prevention of. (A. L. Hayes) Luth. Q. **2**: 494.
— — — Guthrie on. J. Frankl. Inst. **53**: 423.
— — Experimental. (A. H. Thurston) J. Frankl. Inst. **93**: 89, 180, 268.
— — of Locomotives. (W. Fairbairn) J. Frankl. Inst. **59**: 1, 79. **66**: 361.
— — of a Locomotive, 1845. J. Frankl. Inst. **39**: 298.
— — of Locomotive Neversink, 1847. (W. Hamilton) J. Frankl. Inst. **43**: 331.
— — of Locomotive Richmond, 1844. (W. Hamilton) J. Frankl. Inst. **39**: 16.
— — on the Great Eastern, 1859. J. Frankl. Inst. **68**: 277.
— — on Steamboat Medora, 1842. (B. H. Latrobe) J. Frankl. Inst. **34**: 312. **35**: 101. — (C. Reeder) J. Frankl. Inst. **35**: 280.
— — on Steamboat Mohegan, 1843. (T. Ewbank) J. Frankl. Inst. **35**: 400.
— — on Steamboat New England, 1833. J. Frankl. Inst. **17**: 55, 126, 289.
— — on Steamship Portsmouth, 1844. (W. Hamilton) J. Frankl. Inst. **39**: 31.
— — Preventing. (A. C. Jones) J. Frankl. Inst. **49**: 133. — (J. L. Smith) J. Frankl. Inst. **51**: 407. — J. Frankl. Inst. **63**: 408. **64**: 311. — (W. T. Haycraft) West. J. **5**: 252.
— — — Apparatus for. J. Frankl. Inst. **78**: 55.
— — — Report of Association for, 1863. J. Frankl. Inst. **75**: 36–393. **76**: 23–396. **77**: 176–393. **78**: 49–393.
— — Report of Experiments, 1836. J. Frankl. Inst. **21**: 1–289. **22**: 217, 289, 361. **23**: 73.
— — Report on. Ecl. Engin. **2**: 577, 585.
— — Theories of. (F. Fischer) J. Frankl. Inst. **98**: 311.
— Feed-Water to. (I. Hahn) J. Frankl. Inst. **92**: 404. **93**: 320.
— Giffard Injector for. (J. W. Nystrom) J. Frankl. Inst. **74**: 391. — J. Frankl. Inst. **69**: 325. **86**: 54, 124, 194.
— Horse-Power of. J. Frankl. Inst. **91**: 187. **92**: 91. **94**: 91, 377. **96**: 396. — (W. B. Le Van) J. Frankl. Inst. **95**: 394.
— Improvements in, 1853. (J. Harrison) J. Frankl. Inst. **55**: 85.
— Incrustation of. J. Frankl. Inst. **70**: 297. **81**: 18, 349. — (J. G. Rogers) J. Frankl. Inst. **94**: 161.
— — and Deposits. J. Frankl. Inst. **75**: 51.
Boilers, Steam, Incrustation of, Experiments with American Anti-Incrustator. (C. M. Cresson) J. Frankl. Inst. **85**: 121.
— — of marine. (P. Jensen) J. Frankl. Inst. **82**: 79, 145. — (J. R. Napier) J. Frankl. Inst. **79**: 30.
— — Prevention of. J. Frankl. Inst. **40**: 222, 255.
— — Report on, 1872. J. Frankl. Inst. **95**: 172.
— Locomotive, Principles of. (D. K. Clarke) J. Frankl. Inst. **55**: 361. **56**: 1.
— — Ramsbottom's Improved. J. Frankl. Inst. **51**: 6.
— — Strength of. (W. Fairbairn) J. Frankl. Inst. **56**: 349. **59**: 1, 79.
— Loss of Heat by Radiation from. (J. C. Hoadley) J. Frankl. Inst. **103**: 233.
— Marine, Design and Construction of. (C. H. Haswell) J. Frankl. Inst. **104**: 335.
— — Improved, 1852. (A. Lamb) J. Frankl. Inst. **54**: 116.
— Notes on. (W. M. Henderson) J. Frankl. Inst. **87**: 166–392.
— Perkins's. J. Frankl. Inst. **19**: 379.
— Report on Trial of, American Institute, 1871. J. Frankl. Inst. **93**: 377.
— Strength of. (T. W. Bakewell) J. Frankl. Inst. **8**: 135. — (W. M. Henderson) J. Frankl. Inst. **87**: 316. — (J. M. Gray) J. Frankl. Inst. **71**: 398.
— — of Materials for, Report on, 1837. J. Frankl. Inst. **23**: 73–409. **24**: 1, 73. — (C. Huston) J. Frankl. Inst. **105**: 93.
— Tubular, Facts and Fallacies as to. J. Frankl. Inst. **79**: 377.
— — Vertical. J. Frankl. Inst. **50**: 196.
— Water-Tube and Fire-Tube. (B. F. Isherwood) J. Frankl. Inst. **107**: 14, 97.
— Wear and Tear of. (F. A. Paget) J. Frankl. Inst. **80**: 13–217.
— Zinc in, as preventive of Fresh-Water Scale. (B. de Corbigny) J. Frankl. Inst. **105**: 49.
Boiling to Death as a Punishment. Tait, **2**: 105.
Boiling Water; Boiling Springs of Iceland. Westm. **67**: 198. Same art. Ecl. M. **41**: 114.
Boisguilbert, P. le Pesant de, French Economist. Westm. **100**: 45.
Boissy, Thérese, Marquise de, Reminiscences of. (M. R. D. Smith) Victoria, **22**: 1.
Bokee, David A., with portrait. Am. Whig R. **14**: 171.
Boker, George H. (B. Taylor) Internat. M. **4**: 156.
Bokhara, Burnes's Travels into. (Sir J. Barrow) Quar. **52**: 367. — Brit. & For. R. **1**: 459. — Mo. R. **134**: 450. — Ecl. R. **60**: 204. — Ed. R. **60**: 395.
— Description of. Dub. R. **18**: 485.
— Round of Life in. (A. Vámbéry) Argosy, **1**: 22.
— Russian Mission to. (J. W. Croker) Quar. **36**: 106.
— Wolff's Mission to. Chamb. J. **4**: 146. — Chr. Obs. **46**: 364. — Liv. Age, **6**: 373.
Bokhara Victims, Grover's. Ed. R. **82**: 132. — Colburn, **74**: 130.
Bokhum, H. Stranger's Gift. (G. Putnam) Chr. Exam. **20**: 17.
Bolas Magna, Pilgrimage to. St. James, **29**: 298.
Bolckow, H. W. F., Sketch of, with portrait. (T. Fenwick) Pract. M. **1**: 81.
Bold Dick Donahue. (J. Manning) Overland, **3**: 113.
Bold Stroke; a Tale. Belgra. **32**: supp. 57.
Bolderoe's Widow. All the Year, **37**: 157.
Boleyn, Anne. *See* Anne Boleyn.
Bolingbroke, Lord. Quar. **149**: 1. — Brit. & For. R. **2**: 209. **4**: 611. — Princ. **9**: 349. — Westm. **23**: 362. — So. Lit. Mess. **8**: 783. **9**: 25. — Brit. Q. **29**: 126. — No. Brit. **26**: 185.
— and Pope. (C. Redding) Colburn, **118**: 459.

Bolingbroke, Lord, and the Reign of Queen Anne. No. Brit. **39:** 120. Same art. Ecl. M. **40:** 197.
— as a Statesman. Fraser, **67:** 687. Same art. Liv. Age, **78:** 508. — Nat. R. **16:** 389.
— Cooke's Memoirs of. Ed. R. **62:** 1. — Mo. R. **137:** 557.
— in Exile. Quar. **151:** 67. — West. M. **4:** 8.
— Literary Life of. Quar. **151:** 316.
— Macknight's Life of. Ed. R. **118:** 404.
— Man and Statesman. Temp. Bar, **50:** 73.
— Memoirs of. Quar. **54:** 368.
— Writings of. Fraser, **72:** 475. — Ecl. M. **66:** 92.
Bolingbroke Grinds. (W. Bradwood) Belgra. **27:** 130.
Bolivar, Simon. (C. Cushing) No. Am. **28:** 203. — Anal. M. **6:** 284. — (E. Lawrence) Harper, **40:** 594.
— and Bolivian Constitution. (C. Cushing) No. Am. **30:** 26.
— Political Career of. Colburn, **7:** 4.
— Presents to. Niles's Reg. **24:** 354.
— Resignation of. Niles's Reg. **28:** 221, 280.
Bolivia and Brazil in the Amazon Valley. (G. E. Church) Fortn. **14:** 564.
— in 1827. Ann. Reg. **2:** 263.
— Journey in. (A. J. Duffield) St. James, **41:** 477.
— Northern, Amazon Outlet of. (G. E. Church) Harper, **44:** 499.
Bollandist Acta Sanctorum. (C. Stothart) Cath. World, **27:** 756. **28:** 81.
Bollandists and their Library. Am. Bibliop. **7:** 158.
Bollingbrook, Va., British at. So. Lit. Mess. **6:** 85.
Bollman, Justus E., Life of. Nation, **30:** 421.
Bologna. (N. Colgan) Irish Mo. **6:** 377.
— and its Campo Santo. St. James, **49:** 419.
— Learned Women of. (Mad. Villari) Internat. R. **5:** 185, 353.
— University of, in Middle Ages. (F. C. Savigny) Am. J. Educ. **22:** 275.
Bolsover Forest. Fraser, **78:** 34, 498. **79:** 27.
Bolt-forging Machine, Abbe's. Pract. M. **4:** 431.
Bolts and Nuts, Tools for threading. Pract. M. **6:** 112.
Bolting in Politics. (W. Gladden) Scrib. **20:** 906.
Bolton, James, Life and Sermons of. Chr. Obs. **63:** 771.
Bolton, Monks of. (R. Collyer) Mod. R. **1:** 598.
Bolton Castle, Room in which Mary Queen of Scots was confined. (T. Amyot) Arch. **21:** 160.
Bolton, Mass., Ministers of. Am. Q. Reg. **10:** 52.
Bombardinio in Italy. Fraser, **12:** 356.
— on Manners, Fashions, etc. Fraser, **14:** 441.
— on Things in general. Fraser, **12:** 137.
Bombast in celebrated Writers, Specimens of. (J. W. Calcraft) Dub. Univ. **37:** 652.
Bombay. House. Words, **5:** 181. Same art. Ecl. M. **26:** 460.
— and the Parsees. (A. G. Constable) Harper, **42:** 66.
— Miss Roberts's Overland Journey to. Mo. R. **154:** 305.
— Towers of Silence in. Chamb. J. **56:** 775.
Bombay Society, Transactions of, 1819. Ecl. R. **29:** 423.
Bon-Bon; a Tale. (E. A. Poe) So. Lit. Mess. **1:** 693.
Bon Gualtier. *See* Aytoun, W. E.; Martin, T.
Bon Harbor, Ky. (R. Triplett) West. J. **2:** 86.
Bon Marché. Colburn, **169:** 73.
Bonaparte, Elizabeth Patterson. Blackw. **126:** 543. Same art. Liv. Age, **143:** 735. Liv. Age, **143:** 248.
— Letters from Europe. (E. L. Didier) Scrib. **18:** 289, 381.
Bonaparte, François Charles, Death of. Colburn, **35:** 432.
Bonaparte, Jerome. (P. Girard) Cath. World, **28:** 289. — Liv. Age, **49:** 273. **66:** 259. **70:** 507.
— and Court of Westphalia. Quar. **22:** 481.
— and his American Wife. Liv. Age, **71:** 83.
— the Bonaparte with two Wives. Liv. Age, **68:** 571.
Bonaparte, Joseph. Am. Q. **3:** 543. — Liv. Age, **4:** 285. — Ed. R. **100:** 348. Same art. Liv. Age, **43:** 435.
Bonaparte, Joseph, Du Casse's Memoirs of. Quar. **94:** 212.
— in New Jersey. Appleton, **12:** 360.
— Sketch of. (H. Berkley) Godey, **30:** 184.
Bonaparte, Lucien, and F. von Raumer. Blackw. **41:** 21. — Quar. **57:** 374.
— Letters of. Penn Mo. **10:** 443.
— Life of. Mus. **40:** 366.
— Memoirs of. (J. W. Croker) Quar. **57:** 374. — Mo. R. **141:** 411.
— Poem of Charlemagne. Ecl. R. **22:** 226, 364.
Bonaparte, Napoleon. *See* Napoleon I.
Bonaparte, Pierre, and Victor Noir, with portraits. Ev. Sat. **9:** 99, 117.
— Trial of. Am. Law R. **5:** 14. — Ev. Sat. **9:** 275.
Bonaparte Family. No. Brit. **11:** 158. Same art. Ecl. M. **17:** 289. Same art. Liv. Age, **21:** 598. — Once a Week, **23:** 194.
— at Florence. Bentley, **33:** 469. Same art. Liv. Age, **37:** 469.
— Portraits of. Art J. **5:** 284.
Bonapartes, The. (I. Scott) Once a Week, **2:** 452. — Ev. Sat. **9:** 220.
— American. (J. W. Sheahan) Lakeside, **9:** 139.
— of Baltimore. (E. S. Didier) Scrib. **10:** 1.
— Restoration of, 1871. Ev. Sat. **10:** 554.
— Rise and Fall of. Nat. Q. **40:** 1.
Bonapartism. Dub. R. **49:** 104.
— Downfall of. Brit. Q. **53:** 441. Same art. Ecl. M. **77:** 129.
— in Italy. Westm. **72:** 526. Same art. Ecl. M. **49:** 214, 341.
Bond and Free; a Tale. House. Words, **13:** 364. Same art. Ecl. M. **38:** 471. Same art. Liv. Age, **50:** 42.
Bonds, United States, Description of. Bank. M. (N. Y.) **30:** 810.
— — Ownership of. Bank. M. (N. Y.) **36:** 170.
— — Taxation of. (A. Walker) Hunt, **54:** 409.
Bondholders, Who are? (E. L. Godkin) Nation, **6:** 104.
Bondocani, Il, from Weisser. Fraser, **22:** 17.
Bone, Alimentary Substances from. (M. d'Arcet) J. Frankl. Inst. **9:** 330.
— Composition of. (M. Barrett) Canad. J. n. s. **10:** 194.
— its Uses in the Arts. (A. Aikin) J. Frankl. Inst. **31:** 32.
— Value of. Penny M. **10:** 218.
Bone Caves. (H. P. Malet) Geog. M. **1:** 95.
— of Gibraltar, Malta, and Sicily. (A. L. Adams) Pop. Sci. R. **5:** 429. Same art. Ecl. M. **67:** 720.
— of Gower. Chamb. J. **30:** 314.
Bone-Cave Inscription, The. Chamb. J. **55:** 152.
Bone-Setter's Mystery. (W. Chambers) Chamb. J. **56:** 113.
Bone-Setting, Hood's. (A. Maclaren) Nature, **6:** 22.
Bone Trade. Hunt, **6:** 193.
Bones, Forms of. (W. C. Minor) No. Am. **86:** 153.
— of our Sovereigns. Ecl. M. **44:** 306.
Bones and I. (G. J. Whyte Melville) Lond. Soc. **13:** 3-541. **14:** 160.
Bonfires, Beacons, and Signals. All the Year, **23:** 306.
— Derivation of the Word. (E. L. Hervey) Once a Week, **17:** 501.
Bonheur, Rosa. (R. Ménard) Portfo. **6:** 98. — with portrait, Ecl. M. **72:** 499. — Liv. Age, **58:** 397.
— and her Work. Chamb. J. **39:** 218.
— Morning with. Liv. Age, **63:** 124.
Boniface VIII. Brit. & For. R. **13:** 415. — Dub. R. **11:** 505.
— at Home. All the Year, **33:** 342.
— Jubilee of. (W. Dubberley) Month, **24:** 1.
Boniface of Savoy. (J. W. Cummings) U. S. Cath. M **6:** 645.
Bonifacio, Corsica, Siege of. Tinsley, **24:** 274.
Bonius Islands. Chamb. J. **56:** 444.

Bonn, Church Conference at, 1875. (H. H. Barber) Unita. R. **4**: 402. — (G. M. Raymond) Cath. World, **22**: 502. — (E. C. Smyth) Cong. Q. **18**: 27. — (W. S. Perry) Am. Church R. **28**: 368. — Lond. Q. **46**: 57.
— Jubilee at. All the Year, **20**: 426.
Bonnat, Léon. (R. Ménard) Portfo. **6**: 67.
Bonner, Edmund, Bishop of London. Liv. Age, **47**: 750. Mo. R. **158**: 357.
Bonnet Carré, Great Crevasse at. (R. Keeler and A. R. Waud) Ev. Sat. **10**: 548.
Bonnets, Straw, Manufacture of. (E. W. Carpenter) Harper, **29**: 576.
Bonneval, Count de. All the Year, **35**: 159.
Bonneval, Countess de. Liv. Age, **55**: 126. **58**: 77.
Bonneville, Lake, Outlet of. (G. K. Gilbert) Am. J. Sci. **119**: 341.
Bonnifield Claim. (H. Humphrey) Overland, **15**: 558.
Bonnivard, François, the real Prisoner of Chillon. (L.W. Bacon) Lippinc. **22**: 46. — Fraser, **93**: 582. Same art. Ecl. M. **87**: 26.
Bonpland, Amie. Liv. Age, **58**: 717.
Bonshiel, The. Lond. Soc. **17**: 72. — Chamb. J. **29**: 248.
Bonstetten, Carl Victor von, a Swiss Patrician. (A. Venner) Lippinc. **24**: 88. — (C. Dempster) Ed. R. **119**: 413.
Boobies of West Indies, Night with. Once a Week, **1**: 395.
Boodle Romance, The. Tinsley, **15**: 664.
Book of Common Prayer. *See* Common Prayer.
— of Gold; a Poem. (J. T. Trowbridge) Harper, **54**: 65.
— of Jashar. *See* Jashar, Book of.
— of Kells. (W. Chambers) Chamb. J. **53**: 49.
— of Life. (E. H. Sears) Chr. Exam. **36**: 45.
— of the Season. Fraser, **11**: 414.
Books. (A. McLachlan) Canad. Mo. **1**: 421.
— About. (O. Thorne) Lakeside, **7**: 400. — Irish Mo. **2**: 106.
— Abuse of. (C. W. Hatson) So. M. **9**: 536.
— Among and within. (L. Cross) Colburn, **165**: 989, 1087.
— Ancient, Form and Material of. Penny M. **5**: 310.
— and Authors. Sharpe, **10**: 367.
— and Bookbinding in Syria and Palestine. Art J. **20**: 41, 113.
— and Book-Collectors. Dub. Univ. **68**: 397.
— and Book-Hunting. Lond. Q. **57**: 122.
— and Bookmaking. All the Year, **38**: 135.
— and Critics; a Lecture. (M. Pattison) Fortn. **28**: 659. Same art. Ecl. M. **90**: 93. Same art. Sup. Pop. Sci. Mo. **2**: 159.
— and long Evenings. (I. Taylor) Good Words, **5**: 786.
— and Reading. *See* Reading.
— and the reading Public. Liv. Age, **13**: 5.
— and their Bindings. Lond. Q. **14**: 167.
— and their Buyers. Temp. Bar, **62**: 487.
— and their Uses. (M. K. Cross) Cong. Q. **20**: 26 — Macmil. **1**: 110.
— Anecdotes of. Temp. Bar, **40**: 80.
— Antiquarian Club Books. Quar. **82**: 309.
— before the Invention of Printing. Chamb. J. **24**: 243. Same art. Ecl. M. **36**: 1120.
— Bevy of little. Dub. Univ. **23**: 221.
— Blessedness of. Chamb. J. **41**: 577.
— Block. *See* Block Books.
— Booksellers, and Bookmakers. Lond. M. **21**: 254. — Mus. **13**: 282.
— Bookwriters and Bookworms. Sharpe, **8**: 15. **9**: 72.
— Bundles of. (G. Gilfillan) Hogg, **6**: 173.
— Buying of. Temp. Bar, **62**: 319. Same art. Ecl. M. **97**: 407. Same art. Appleton, **26**: 547.
— Cheap Finery in. Am. Bibliop. **7**: 265.
— Children's. *See* Children, Books for.
— Choice of. (F. Harrison) Fortn. **31**: 491. Same art. Appleton, **21**: 432. Same art. Liv. Age, **141**: 259.
Books, Classification of. (W. T. Harris) J. Spec. Philos. **4**: 114.
— Communion of. Colburn, **167**: 61.
— Companionship of. N. Ecl. **1**: 203.
— Costly and curious. Dem. R. **13**: 473.
— Country, Rambles among. Cornh. **42**: 662. Same art. Ecl. M. **96**: 204.
— Death of. (T. W. Chesebrough) University Q. **2**: 284.
— Decoration of, Butsch on. (C. C. Perkins) Lib. J. **3**: 341.
— Destroyers of, Early. Hogg, **3**: 220.
— Duty on foreign. (C. J. Ingersoll) No. Am. **18**: 163. — (C. C. Jewett) Hunt, **14**: 452. — For. Q. **9**: 212. — (E. L. Godkin) Nation, **10**: 117, 138, 157. — (H. C. Lea) Nation, **4**: 195, 239. — Nation, **4**: 218, 259. — O. & N. **1**: 363.
— Fireside Gossip about. Liv. Age, **38**: 17.
— for Children. *See* Children, Books for.
— for the People. Chr. Exam. **35**: 86.
— Forming Opinions of. (M. Browne) Argosy, **1**: 242. Same art. Ev. Sat. **1**: 261.
— Friendship of, F. D. Maurice on. Penn Mo. **5**: 509.
— Holiday. (E. Jerrold) Tinsley, **19**: 197.
— How to read. (J. Dennis) Good Words, **22**: 393.
— Illustrated. Quar. **74**: 168. Same art. Liv. Age, **2**: 87. Same art. Ecl. M. **3**: 90. — All the Year, **18**: 151. — Chamb. J. **38**: 135.
— in Germany, Purchase of. (A. Stutzer) Fraser, **93**: 569.
— in the Middle Ages. Hogg, **9**: 93. — Penny M. **3**: 87.
— in the running Brooks. Sharpe, **32**: 225. **33**: 24.
— Influence of. Dem. R. **37**: 556.
— — on Manners. Colburn, **22**: 409.
— Insect Enemies to. (H. A. Hagen) Lib. J. **4**: 251. — (W. Flint) Lib. J. **4**: 376. — Scient. Am. supp. **6**: 2200, 2282.
— — Literature concerning. (H. A. Hagen) Lib. J. **4**: 373.
— Little, with large Aims. Fraser, **44**: 26.
— Makers and Readers of. (H. R. Boss) Lakeside, **4**: 304.
— Man among his. Hogg, **2**: 369.
— Mediæval. Dub. Univ. **68**: 481. Same art. Cath. World, **4**: 804.
— Manufacture of. (A. H. Guernsey) Harper, **32**: 1.
— Multiplication of, in ancient Times. Cornh. **9**: 26.
— My. (J. A. Bolles) New Eng. M. **3**: 207. **4**: 114, 391, 454. **5**: 130, 299, 465. **6**: 135. **7**: 309. — So. Lit. Mess. **2**: 652.
— Nisard's Histoire des Livres populaires. Liv. Age, **44**: 505.
— of Devotion. (W. F. Stevenson) Good Words, **2**: 682.
— Old. (H. M. Dexter) Am. Bibliop. **6**: 110. — (G. P. Fisher) Knick. **32**: 31.
— — in New York. (W. C. Prime) Harper, **44**: 385.
— — My Friend's Library. (J. T. Fields) Atlan. **8**: 440.
— — Reading of. Lond. M. **3**: 128.
— Old Bookshops of London and Paris. (E. Howland) Lippinc. **6**: 152.
— on my Table. Fraser, **10**: 505. **14**: 1.
— Our Life in. Land We Love, **5**: 515.
— Papal Index of prohibited. Brit. Q. **14**: 133.
— Personality of. Blackw. **118**: 273. Same art. Liv. Age, **127**: 177.
— Providence of God in. (J. Belcher) Chr. R. **22**: 43.
— Publication of. Am. Alma. **1836**: 69.
— Rambles among. Cornh. **42**: 662. **43**: 410. **44**: 278. Same art. Ecl. M. **96**: 204. **97**: 44, 610. Same art. Appleton, **25**: 112, 499. **26**: 411.
— Rare, and their Prices. Cornh. **16**: 485.
— Rarities at Washington. (F. Vinton) Bib. Sac. **31**: 97.
— Rise and Progress of. Cath. World, **4**: 104.
— Ruskin on. Victoria, **6**: 67, 131.
— Seasoned. (N. R. Waters) Radical, **9**: 371. **10**: 218.

Books, Selections of. (M. Dewey) Lib. J. **1**: 391.
— Sizes of printed. (C. Evans) Lib. J. **1**: 58. — (J. B. Huling) Lib. J. **1**: 168. — (D. Wight) Lib. J. **5**: 177.
— — Designation of. Lib. J. **2**: 37.
— — Discussion on. Lib. J. **1**: 106, 139.
— — English standard. Lib. J. **5**: 13.
— — Reports on. Lib. J. **1**: 178. **3**: 19. **4**: 199.
— Smallest, in the World. Am. Bibliop. **8**: 118.
— Suppressed and censured. Ed. R. **134**: 161. Same art. Liv. Age, **111**: 259.
— Thoughts about. (I. Taylor) Good Words, **5**: 942.
— Titles of. Am. Bibliop. **4**: 530. — Chamb. J. **1**: 221. — Chamb. J. **47**: 833. Same art. Ecl. M. **76**: 332. — Potter Am. Mo. **5**: 715.
— — Lettering of. (H. A. Homes) Lib. J. **5**: 315.
— — Thoughts on making. (B. R. Wheatley) Lib. J. **5**: 133.
— Use of. (I. B. Barker) University Q. **3**: 116.
— Uses and Abuses of. (F. W. P. Greenwood) Chr. Exam. **10**: 240.
— we read. (J. G. Craighead) Hours at Home, **9**: 240.
— which are Books. Am. Whig R. **1**: 521.
— Writing of, Propriety of abolishing. (J. Skelton) Fraser, **63**: 92. Same art. Ecl. M. **52**: 347.
— written in Prison. All the Year, **27**: 30.
Book Auction in Gotham. Knick. **32**: 529.
— Perkins's. Chamb. J. **50**: 709.
Book-Auction Catalogues. (A. R. Spofford) Lib. J. **3**: 53.
Bookbinder, Day with a. Penny M. **11**: 377.
Bookbinding. All the Year, **20**: 564. — Chamb. J. **26**: 33. — (E. G. Allen) Lib. J. **5**: 214. — Art J. **32**: 200. — (L. Robinson) Art J. **33**: 113. — Penny M. **2**: 505.
— Ancient. Art J. **11**: 279.
— — and modern. (J. Cundall) J. Frankl. Inst. **45**: 211.
— — Ornamental. F. Arts Q. **1**: 172.
— and decorative Works in stained Leather. Art J. **13**: 275.
— Buckram as a Material for. (E. B. Nicholson) Lib. J. **2**: 207, 271. **5**: 304.
— Domestic. Chamb. J. **28**: 79.
— Examples of. Art J. **6**: 81, 113.
— for public Libraries. (Sir R. Barry) Lib. J. **2**: 203. — (F. P. Hathaway) Lib. J. **4**: 248. — (C. Walford) Lib. J. **2**: 201.
— History of. Am. Bibliop. **2**: 176, 220, 316. — (M. A. Tooke) Art J. **28**: 5–77.
— in International Exhibition, 1874. (H. T. Wood) Pract. M. **4**: 59.
— Mediæval. Chamb. J. **46**: 237.
— — Decorative. Art J. **30**: 106.
— Ornamental. Art J. **2**: 228.
— — in 16th Century. Pract. M. **1**: 48.
— Wood Carving for Book Covers. Art J. **6**: 296.
Bookbindings and Gas-Light. Lib. J. **3**: 64.
— Deterioration of. (W. Gibbs) Lib. J. **3**: 229.
Bookcase, Rotating. Nature, **18**: 15.
Book-Club, Fuss in a. Fraser, **38**: 629.
Book-Clubs. (J. H. Burton) Blackw. **90**: 440. — O. & N. **6**: 227.
— and Collectors. Temp. Bar, **40**: 80.
— for all Readers. Penny M. **13**: 179.
— in the Country. Colburn, **22**: 216.
Book-Collecting. (W. Sargent) No. Am. **76**: 273.
— Mania of. All the Year, **44**: 544.
Book-Collectors. (E. Howland) Lippinc. **7**: 308.
— and Book Illustrators. St. James, **36**: 101.
— Irish. Dub. Univ. **80**: 1.
Bookcraft. So. R. n. s. **7**: 436.
Booker, Luke. Springs of Plynlimmon; a Poem. Mo. R. **134**: 121.
Book-Haunted. St. James, **14**: 372.
Book-Hawking and popular Literature. Month, **4**: 19.
Book-Hoax, The £1,000. (J. Sabin) Am. Bibliop. **7**: 34, 59.
Book-Hunter. (J. H. Burton) Blackw. **89**: 645. **90**: 55. Same art. Liv. Age, **70**: 67, 387.
— Burton's. Chamb. J. **38**: 121.
Book-Hunting in the Middle Ages. Dub. Univ. **72**: 147.
Booking through, System of. Good Words, **17**: 565.
Bookkeeping, Analysis of. (T. Jones) Hunt, **7**: 513.
— Double Entry. Hunt, **1**: 256.
— Progress of. Dub. R. **19**: 433.
See Accounts.
Book-Love. Fraser, **36**: 199.
Book Makers as Book Lovers. Broadw. **7**: 275. Same art. Ev. Sat. **11**: 342.
Bookmakers for betting at Races. Chamb. J. **45**: 177.
Book Making. Lakeside, **2**: 432.
— as one of the Fine Arts. Bentley, **3**: 465.
— Byways of. (H. S. S. Edwards) Macmil. **34**: 457. Same art. Ecl. M. **87**: 748.
— Mechanics of. (W. Sargent) No. Am. **79**: 344.
Book Notices, Superficial. (J. W. Nevin) Mercersb. **4**: 408.
Book Plates. (M. A. Tooke) Art J. **28**: 267.
Book Rovers. Am. Whig R. **14**: 250.
Booksellers. Chamb. J. **7**: 87. Same art. Liv. Age, **13**: 260.
— Author. Dem. R. **11**: 397.
— Combinations of, and Underselling. Westm. **57**: 530.
Bookselling abroad. Chamb. J. **3**: 169.
— after the Invention of Printing. Chamb. J. **3**: 148. Same art. Liv. Age, **5**: 390, 471.
— before the Printing-Press. Chamb. J. **3**: 140. Same art. Liv. Age, **5**: 313.
— in England. Chamb. J. **3**: 204.
— in the 13th Century. Cornh. **9**: 475.
Bookstall, Romance of a. Chamb. J. **45**: 625.
Bookstalls. House. Words, **7**: 289.
Book Thief, Capture of a. (S. S. Green) Lib. J. **5**: 48.
Book Thieving and Mutilation. (W. B. Clarke) Lib. J. **4**: 249.
— Operations of Dr. Pichler. Ev. Sat. **10**: 439.
Book Trade. Mus. **9**: 282.
— Makers, Sellers, and Buyers of Books. Fraser, **45**: 711.
— German, 1836. Ecl. R. **65**: 614.
— in Edinburgh, 1805–20. Tait, n. s. **4**: 469.
— in England. (G. P. R. James) J. Statis. Soc. **6**: 50.
— in London. Westm. **57**: 511. Same art. Ecl. M. **26**: 188.
— of Germany, History of. (M. H. Meidinger) J. Statis. Soc. **3**: 161. Same art. Hunt, **9**: 399.
— Roman, under the Empire. (Sir G. Lewis) Fraser, **65**: 432. Same art. Liv. Age, **73**: 345.
Bookworm; a Poem. St. Paul's, **10**: 615.
— Gossip of an old. (W. J. Thoms) 19th Cent. **10**: 63, 886. Same art. Liv. Age, **151**: 813. Same art. Ecl. M. **97**: 489.
Bookworm's Dream. Cong. M. **7**: 181.
Bookworms. Hogg, **7**: 344. — Liv. Age, **139**: 381.
Boole, George, with portrait. Pop. Sci. Mo. **17**: 840.
— Mathematical Works. Brit. Q. **44**: 141.
Boomerang. (A. W. Howitt) Nature, **15**: 312. — (J. Lovering) Am. Alma. **1859**: 67.
— and its Vagaries. Dub. Univ. **11**: 168.
Boone, Daniel. (B. J. Lossing) Harper, **19**: 577. — (— Wentworth) Meth. Q. **13**: 364. — with portrait, West. M. **1**: 95. — All the Year, **28**: 127. — Colburn, **6**: 519. **8**: 519. — Hogg, **1**: 56.
— Adventures of. Chamb. J. **5**: 170. Same art. Liv Age, **10**: 93. — Carey's Mus. **2**: 321.
— Birthplace of. Potter Am. Mo. **13**: 470.
— Grave of. (J. M. Peck) Chr. R. **13**: 402.
— Life of. (J. M. Peck) Sparks's Am. Biog. **13**: 3.
— Scene in Life of. West. M. **1**: 385.

Boone, Daniel, Sketch of. Ill. M. 1: 202.
Boorde, Andrew, the original Merry Andrew. Fraser, 83: 629.—Chamb. J. 32: 257.
Boos, Martin. (W. F. Stevenson) Good Words, 3: 132. — Am. Meth. M. 19: 302. — Ch. Obs. 27: 517.
Bootan and the Booteras. Once a Week, 12: 205.
Bootblacks. *See* Shoeblacks.
Booth, Barton, Memoir of. Colburn, 54: 355.
— and the Actors of Queen Anne's Days. Temp. Bar, 53: 407.
Booth, Edwin. (L. C. Calhoun) Galaxy, 7: 77. — with portrait, (W. Winter) Harper, 63: 61. — (E. C. Stedman) Atlan. 17: 585. — with portrait, Colburn, 168: 64.
— Acting of. (O. B. Frothingham) Nation, 2: 395.
— as Hamlet. Appleton, 14: 657, 689. — with portrait, Ev. Sat. 9: 258, 273.
— as Richelieu, with portrait. Ev. Sat. 9: 402, 409. 10: 80, 91.
— in Chicago. Lakeside, 9: 349.
Booth, Junius Brutus. (I. C. Pray) Galaxy, 2: 158. — All the Year, 36: 77.
Booth, David. English Dictionary. Mo. R. 100: 22.
Boothby, Sir B. Fables and Satires. Quar. 3: 43.
Boothby, Mrs. Lætitia, Memoirs of. Colburn, 152: 134.
Boots, Easy. All the Year, 5: 511.
— and Shoes, History of. Chamb. J. 36: 21. — Godey, 45: 70–426. 46: 156.
— — Machinery for sewing. Pract. M. 4: 181.
— Tollemache on. Chamb. J. 39: 302.
Bopeep the Great. (G. A. Sala) Belgra. 21: 501.
Borage Burs. (A. Gray) Am. Natural. 10: 1.
Borax, California. Hunt, 56: 191.
— Deposits of, on the Pacific Coast. (H. G. Hanks) Overland, 11: 71.
Borax Lagoons of Tuscany. Chamb. J. 13: 361. Same art. Liv. Age, 26: 172.
Borcette, September at. (Mrs. S. C. Hall) St. James, 2; 205.
Bordeaux. (M. P. Thompson) Cath. World, 13: 158.— All the Year, 43: 323, 395.—Hunt, 18: 376.— Penny M. 8: 492.
— and Arcachon; Vine and Pine. Temp. Bar, 17: 340.
— Antiquities at. (S. Lethieullier) Arch. 1: 75.
— Vineyards of. Blackw. 71: 617.
— Vintage at. Chamb. J. 9: 93.
— Walk in the Landes of. Colburn, 85: 324.
Bordentown and the Bonapartes. (J. B. Gilder) Scrib. 21: 28.
Border Antiquities of England and Scotland, Scott on. (J. Foster) Ecl. R. 28: 305.
Border Beauty, History of a. (J. Hogg) Fraser, 9: 97.
Border Traditions. U. S. Lit. Gaz. 5: 40.
Border Witch. Lond. Soc. 2: 181.
Bore, Origin of the Term. (D. Cook) Once a Week, 12: 349.
Bores and Prigs. Tinsley, 8: 219.
— of my Acquaintance. Dub. Univ. 3: 285. 6: 185.
Boreen; a Tale. (N. Robinson) Cath. World, 29: 498, 629.
Borgia, Lucretia. (T. F. Crane) Harper, 52: 498.—(Alice King) Argosy, 8: 191. — (H. S. Wilson) 19th Cent. 6: 664. — Ed. R. 142: 233. Same art. Liv. Age, 126: 515. — So. Lit. Mess. 19: 208.
— Gilbert's Life of. Colburn, 144: 689. Same art. Ecl. M. 73: 538.
Borgias, The, Gregorovius's History of. No. Brit. 53: 351. Same art. Liv. Age, 109: 259.
Boring for Artesian Wells, New Method of, 1846. J. Frankl. Inst. 42: 369.
— for Minerals, Water, etc. (J. Thomson) J. Frankl. Inst. 47: 68.
— for Oil. (B. White) Atlan. 35: 671.
Boring for Water. J. Frankl. Inst. 1: 24, 86, 174. 2: 34. 3: 37, 427.
— square Holes, Hancock's Machine for. J. Frankl. Inst. 4: 289.
Borings and Deep Wells. (G. R. Burnell) J. Frankl. Inst. 74: 223, 305.
Boring-Machine. Pract. M. 3: 106.
— Earth. J. Frankl. Inst. 60: 129.
— — for Telegraph Poles. (J. Gavey) J. Frankl. Inst. 98: 430.
— for Mines. Ecl. Engin. 3: 12.
Borlase, William, a Cornish Genius, Old Haunts and Remains of. Lond. Q. 17: 385.
— St. Aubyn, and Pope. Quar. 139: 367. Same art. Liv. Age, 127: 579.
Bormus; a Linus Song. Ecl. M. 97: 648.
Born, Bertran de, the Troubadour. (F. Hueffer) Gent. M. n. s. 17: 185.
Born away from Home. (T. M. Coan) Galaxy, 23: 533.
Born to be a Poet. St. James, 6: 198.
Born to Sorrow. Sharpe, 44: 113–281. 45: 1–281. 46: 1–169.
Borneil, Giraud de. (M. Davies) Colburn, 157: 467.
Borneo. All the Year, 7: 511. — Brit. Q. 7: 261. — Dub. Univ. 27: 387.
— and Celebes. Quar. 83: 340. — Lit. & Theo. R. 2: 333. — Ecl. R. 87: 567.
— and the Dyaks. Chamb. J. 42: 551.
— and the Indian Archipelago. Ed. R. 84: 147. — Quar. 78: 1. — Ecl. R. 83: 552.
— — Marryatt's. Ecl. R. 88: 51. — Liv. Age, 17: 33.
— and its Populations. Chr. Rem. 15: 20.
— and Japan. Liv. Age, 10: 310.
— Brooke's Residence in. (Sir D. Brewster) No. Brit. 9: 432. Same art. Ecl. M. 15: 228. — (G. Reynolds) Atlan. 18: 667. — Chamb. J. 5: 180, 200. — Colburn, 82: 513. *See* Brooke, Sir James.
— Burbidge's Naturalist in. (J. M. Hubbard) Nation, 33: 96.
— English in. For. Q. 37: 63.
— English Adventure in. Dub. Univ. 31: 647.
— Events in, 1848. Dub. R. 24: 295.
— Expedition to. Colburn, 76: 365.
— Life in Forests of. Ed. R. 116: 398.
— Milanows of. (De Crespigny) Anthrop. J. 5: 34.
— Piracy in. (W. E. Gladstone) Contemp. 30: 181.— Dub. Univ. 35: 107.
— St. John's. No. Brit. 37: 198.
— Scenes in. Sharpe, 6: 203, 266.
— Slaughterings in, 1849. Ecl. R. 91: 137.
— Slave-Hunt in. (F. Boyle) Gent. M. n. s. 18: 489. Same art. Liv. Age, 133: 365.
Bornou. (Sir J. Barrow) Quar. 29: 508.
Borough, English, Law of. St. James, 15: 443.
— Some Account of a. Chamb. J. 24: 193.
Boroughs, Disfranchisement of. Blackw. 70: 296.
— Grouping of. (E. A. Freeman) Fortn. 5: 257.
— Merewether's History of. Mo. R. 136: 562.
— Pocket, in England. Cornh. 18: 299.
Borough Road Schools, London. Am. J. Educ. 10: 381.
Borrhomeo the Astrologer; a Tale. Dub. Univ. 59: 55.
Borri, F. G., the Charlatan. (W. E. A. Axon) Colburn, 158: 657. — Cornh. 15: 366.
Borrow, George. Ecl. M. 23: 392. — (A. E. Hake) Macmil. 45: 56. Same art. Liv. Age, 151: 560. Same art. Appleton, 26: 451. — Peop. J. 11: 144.
— Bible in Spain. (F. W. Holland) Chr. Exam. 34: 170. — Ecl. R. 77: 170. — Ecl. Mus. 1: 252, 338. — Chr. R. 11: 516. — So. Lit. Mess. 9: 465. — Dub. Univ. 21: 248. — Mo. R. 160: 104. — (R. Ford) Ed. R. 77: 105. — Quar. 71: 169. — Tait, n. s. 10: 75, 161. — U. S. Cath. M. 2: 321.

Borrow, George. Gypsies of Spain. *See* Gypsies.
— Lavengro. Colburn, **91**: 290. — Dub. Univ. **37**: 711. — Fraser, **43**: 272. — Sharpe, **13**: 184, 229. — Tait, n. s. **18**: 270. — Blackw. **69**: 322. — Ecl. R. **93**: 438.
— Real Adventures of. Internat. M. **3**: 183.
— Recollections of. Liv. Age, **150**: 817. **151**: 174.
— Romany Rye. Quar. **101**: 468.
Borrowed Book. House. Words, **7**: 317.
Borrowing and Lending in old Times. Chamb. J. **22**: 15.
— as a social Science. (J. H. Browne) Scrib. **5**: 476.
— Philosophy of, from Punch. Ecl. Mus. **1**: 202.
Borrowing Trouble. All the Year, **25**: 162.
Borthwick Castle. St. James, **16**: 332. — Penny M. **9**: 477.
Borussia, Wreck of the. (W. S. Lecky) Chamb. J. **57**: 485.
Boruwlaski, Joseph, celebrated Dwarf. (C. Hutton) Bentley, **17**: 240.
Bory de St. Vincent, Voyage of, 1801-2. Ed. R. **6**: 121.
Boscobel. House. Words, **17**: 569. — Once a Week, **27**: 496.
Boscobel; a Tale of the Year 1651. (W. H. Ainsworth) Colburn, **2**: 1-447. **150**: 1-391.
Boscobel House, Charles II. at. Penny M. **9**: 193.
Boscobel Tracts; Escape of Charles II. Blackw. **82**: 727. — Westm. **69**: 428. Same art. Liv. Age, **57**: 420. Same art. Ecl. M. **44**: 459.
Bosnia and Bulgaria, Travels in. Ed. R. **144**: 535.
— Austrians in. (A. J. Evans) Macmil. **38**: 495. — (R. H. Lang) Fortn. **32**: 650.
— Herzegovina and Austria. Brit. Q. **68**: 393.
— in 1875. (A. P. Irby) Victoria, **26**: 69. Same art. Liv. Age, **127**: 643.
— Occupation of. (H. Tuttle) Nation, **27**: 161.
— Peep at. Sharpe, **18**: 334.
— Ride through. Fraser, **92**: 549.
— Short Trip into. House. Words, **3**: 182.
— Trip into. (H. Sandwith) Fraser, **88**: 698.
Bosnian Fugitives, Work among. Good Words, **17**: 638.
Bosom Serpent. (Mrs. C. L. Hentz) Godey, **26**: 141.
Bosphorus, The, Geology of. (G. Washburn) Am. J. Sci. **106**: 186.
— Life on. Bentley, **57**: 478. Same art. Ecl. M. **65**: 82.
— Night on. Chamb. J. **50**: 545.
— Summer on. (J. L. Farley) Belgra. **23**: 312. *See* Kertch.
Bossuet, Jacques Bénigne. (A. Laugel) Nation, **20**: 221. — Liv. Age, **49**: 101. — Bost. R. **1**: 538.
— and Bourdaloue. (J. J. van Osterzee) Am. Presb. R. **17**: 91.
— — and Massillon. Am. Church R. **20**: 438, 572.
— and Fénelon, Butler's Lives of. (R. Southey) Quar. **10**: 409. — Anal. M. **3**: 200.
— and his Contemporaries. Month. **23**: 108.
— and Leibnitz. (A. de Broglie) Cath. World, **2**: 483.
— as a Persecutor. (H. M. Baird) Meth. Q. **26**: 22.
— Early Life of. Kitto, **28**: 291. **31**: 17.
— Memoirs of, Abbé Le Dieu's. Ed. R. **107**: 194. Same art. Ecl. M. **43**: 433. Same art. Liv. Age, **57**: 83. — Lond. Q. **6**: 400. — Chr. Obs. **23**: 69-333. — Chr. Rem. **27**: 88.
Bostaquet, Dumont de, Memoirs of. Ed. R. **121**: 493.
Boston, Mass. (E. H. Derby) Hunt, **23**: 483.
— a Poem. (R. W. Emerson) Atlan. **37**: 195.
— the American Athens. (J. G. Kohl) Bentley, **50**: 620. Same art. Liv. Age, **72**: 131.
— Ancient Names in. (J. Farmer) N. E. Reg. **1**: 193.
— and Boston, Eng. (G. A. Sala) Temp. Bar. **14**: 477.
— and Harvard University. Nature, **21**: 149.
— and Lowell. (W. Chambers) Chamb. J. **21**: 390.
— Application for a City Charter, 1650. (J. B. Felt) N. E. Reg. **11**: 206.
Boston, Mass., Art Museum. (G. P. Lathrop) Harper, **58**: 818. — Am. Arch. **8**: 205. — Ev. Sat. **10**: 426.
— Athenæum. (E. Wigglesworth) Am. Q. Reg. **12**: 149. — (G. Bradford) No. Am. **23**: 206. — U. S. Lit. Gaz. **4**: 310.
— — Catalogue of. (N. Hale) No. Am. **24**: 477.
— Berkeley St. Congregational Church. Cong. Q. **6**: 33.
— Brattle Square Church, Removal of. Ev. Sat. **11**: 187.
— Jeremiah Bumstead's Diary at, 1722 to 1727. N. E. Reg. **15**: 193, 305.
— Charities of. (S. A. Eliot) No. Am. **91**: 149.
— — Public and private. Am. Alma. **1846**: 163. — (S. A. Eliot) No. Am. **61**: 135.
— Charter for, 1876. (G. Bradford) No. Am. **123**: 1.
— Christ Church. (H. W. French) Potter Am. Mo. **17**: 481.
— Church Affairs in, 1720-30. Hist. M. **21**: 196.
— Churches in. Am. Q. Reg. **7**: 53.
— City Missions. Am. Q. Reg. **14**: 429.
— Commerce of. (J. H. Lanman) Hunt, **10**: 421.
— Commercial Fixity of. (C. F. Adams, jr.) No. Am. **106**: 1.
— Commercial Growth of. De Bow, **14**: 251.
— Commercial Projects at, 1868. (C. F. Adams, jr.) No. Am. **106**: 557.
— Commercial Sketch of. (A. Bradford) Hunt, **1**: 124.
— Committee of Correspondence, 1776. N. E. Reg. **34**: 14, 167, 251.
— Congregational Ministers of. Chr. Exam. **1**: 263.
— Diary of Mary Fleet in, 1755-1803. N. E. Reg. **19**: 59.
— during J. Quincy's Mayorship. (F. Bowen) No. Am. **74**: 490.
— East, History of. Dem. R. **43**: 114.
— Educational Benefactions in. Am. J. Educ. **8**: 522. **9**: 606.
— Effects of the Port Bill, 1774. N. E. Reg. **30**: 373.
— Evacuation of, 1776. (E. Taylor) N. E. Reg. **8**: 231.
— Faneuil Hall. (B. J. Lossing) Potter Am. Mo. **7**: 321.
— Fast Day Sermon, 1636. (J. Wheelwright) Hist. M. **11**: 215.
— Fire of 1760. N. E. Reg. **34**: 288.
— — of November, 1872. (J. M. Bugbee) No. Am. **117**: 108. — (E. E. Hale) O. & N. **7**: 2. — (A. G. Sedgwick) Nation, **15**: 311.
— — — Losses to Literature and Art by. N. E. Reg. **27**: 369.
— First Bank in, 1714. (J. W. Thornton) N. E. Reg. **19**: 167.
— First Church, History of. Gen. Repos. **1**: 363.
— First Meeting-House in. N. E. Reg. **14**: 152.
— Grammar Schools. (F. Bowen) No. Am. **61**: 523.
— Green Dragon Tavern. Hist. M. **21**: 28.
— Hanover St. Church. (J. A. Palmer) Cong. Q. **14**: 259.
— High and Latin School Building. Am. Arch. **5**: 107.
— Hollis Street Council, 1842. Dial, **3**: 201.
— in 1687, French Protestant Refugee in. Hist. M. **12**: 294.
— in 1713. Hist. M. **10**: supp. 82, 119.
— in 1782. Hist. M. **6**: 242.
— Items from E. Price's Interleaved Almanac, 1778. N. E. Reg. **19**: 329.
— Jail, Journal of John Leach in, 1775. N. E. Reg. **19**: 255, 313.
— King's Arms Tavern. (J. T. Hassam) N. E. Reg. **34**: 41.
— Latin School. Am. J. Educ. **12**: 529. **27**: 65. — Education, **1**: 499.
— La Tour in. Liv. Age, **25**: 219.
— Lawyers of, in olden Time. (J. T. Morse, jr.) Internat. R. **9**: 542.
— Literary and social. (G. P. Lathrop) Harper, **62**: 381.
— Marriages in, 1701-43. N. E. Reg. **34**: 83-190.

Boston, Mass., Memorial History of. (J. Winsor) Nation, **31**: 378. — (W. F. Poole) Dial (Ch.), **1**: 152. **2**: 239. — (S. Gilbert) Dial (Ch.), **2**: 3.
— Ministers of, 1630–1842. (J. C. Odiorne) N. E. Reg. **1**: 134, 240, 318.
— Mutual Admiration Society of. Knick. **63**: 219.
— Newspapers of, 1704–31, Items from. N. E. Reg. **10**: 33.
— Old Corner Bookstore. (N. B. Shurtleff) Ev. Sat. **10**: 131.
— Parks for, Proposed. Am. Arch. **1**: 194, 215.
— Peace Jubilee, 1869. (A. G. Sedgwick) Nation, **8**: 491.
— — 1872. O. & N. **6**: 207.
— Post-Office. Hunt, **14**: 129.
— Printers, Publishers, and Booksellers in, before 1800. (S. G. Drake) Hist. M. **17**: 216.
— Printing in, Early History of. (W. L. Stone) Contin. Mo. **4**: 257.
— Proceedings of Committee of Safety. N. E. Reg. **30**: 380, 441. **31**: 31, 290. **32**: 44. **33**: 23.
— Progress in Population. (J. Chickering) Hunt, **13**: 555.
— Progressive Wealth and Commerce of. (L. Shattuck) Hunt, **15**: 34.
— Province House. (B. J. Lossing) Potter Am. Mo. **5**: 882.
— Public Library of. (L. C. Davis) Lippinc. **3**: 278. — (G. S. Hillard) Am. J. Educ. **2**: 203. — (C. C. Smith) No. Am. **93**: 567. — (J. Winsor) Scrib. **3**: 150. — Am. J. Educ. **7**: 253.
— — Fiction Lists. Lib. J. **1**: 257, 292.
— — in 1867. (J. R. Dennett) Nation, **4**: 73.
— — Resignation of Mr. Winsor. Lib. J. **1**: 395, 401.
— Public Schools of. (E. Everett) Ecl. M. **60**: 68. — U. S. Lit. Gaz. **1**: 1. — (C. C. Felton) No. Am. **66**: 446.
— — before 1800. (W. B. Fowle) Am. J. Educ. **5**: 325.
— Puritan. (G. E. Ellis) Atlan. **45**: 158.
— Records of, 1630–62. N. E. Reg. **2**: 76–400. **3**: 38, 126, 147. **4**: 55–359. **5**: 97, 243, 333. **6**: 183, 377. **7**: 159, 281. **8**: 37, 345. **9**: 165, 249. **10**: 67, 217. **11**: 199, 330. **12**: 107, 347. **13**: 213. **14**: 133, 347. **16**: 45. **18**: 168, 330. **19**: 29, 168. **20**: 168.
— — of New Brick Church. N. E. Reg. **18**: 237, 337. **19**: 230, 320.
— Religious Denominations in. (L. Shattuck) Chr. Exam. **42**: 460.
— Reminiscences of. (J. S. Boies) N E. Reg. **6**: 255.
— School Teachers and Mr. Mann. (F. Bowen) No. Am. **60**: 224.
— Sewerage of. Am. Arch. **1**: 44. **2**: 265–420.
— Shipping of. Hunt, **14**: 83.
— Shurtleff's Topographical Description of. O. & N. **3**: 603.
— Siege of, 1775–76. (G. Reynolds) Unita. R. **5**: 242. — (H. E. Scudder) Atlan. **37**: 466. — Hist. M. **8**: 326. — Pennsyl. M. **1**: 168. — N. E. Reg. **30**: 369.
— — Frothingham's. (F. Bowen) No. Am. **70**: 405. — (B. F. Tweed) Univ. Q. **8**: 69.
— — Incidents of. Am. Hist. Rec. **1**: 546.
— Sketches of early Life in. Appleton, **1**: 44–275.
— Streets of, in 1708. Hist. M. **14**: 117.
— — in 1732. Hist. M. **17**: 33.
— Summer in. Contin. Mo. **3**: 40.
— Views of. (E. Everett) Hunt, **2**: 180.
— Walk around. Dem. R. **3**: 79.
— Water Celebration. (C. A. Bartol) Chr. Exam. **46**: 40.
— Water Works. Am. Alma. **1850**: 187. Same art. Bank. M. (N. Y.) **4**: 828.
— Wayside Relics in and about. (S. A. Drake) Appleton, **9**: 460, 495, 719.
— Young Men's Christian Union. (F. W. Clarke) O. & N. **5**: 251.
Boston Book. (B. B. Thatcher) Chr. Exam. **19**: 314.
Boston Courier, Biography of. Hist. M. **10**: 45.
Boston Harbor; Fort Independence. Hist. M. **5**: 310.
Boston, Hartford, and Erie Railroad, 1869. (A. G. Sedgwick) Nation, **9**: 6.
Boston Massacre. All the Year, **27**: 349.
Boston Ministers; a Ballad. N. E. Reg. **13**: 131. **26**: 419.
Boston Portraits in French Setting. (E. Duvergier de Hauranne) Ev. Sat. **1**: 85.
Boston Road, The old. (E. S. Nadal) Scrib. **14**: 465.
Boston Tea Party. (F. S. Drake) O. & N. **9**: 97. — (E. E. Hale) O. & N. **9**: 145. — Niles's Reg. **33**: 75.
Boston Teachers' Association. Am. J. Educ. **15**: 527.
Boston, England. (N. Hawthorne) Sharpe, **35**: 148. — (A. P. Peabody) No. Am. **88**: 166.
— Church and Town of. Penny M. **5**: 385.
— and St. Botolph's. Putnam, **14**: 424.
— Old and New. (A. Rimmer) Belgra. **43**: 44.
— Pilgrimage to. (N. Hawthorne) Atlan. **9**: 88.
— St. Botolph's Church. (E. Trollope) Reliquary, **14**: 129, 209. **15**: 17.
Boswell, James. Dub. Univ. **49**: 359. **74**: 313. — (J. Purves) Dub. Univ. **84**: 702. — (F. W. Shelton) Knick. **37**: 153. — Ed. R. **105**: 456. Same art. Liv. Age, **53**: 521. — Quar. **103**: 279. Same art. Liv. Age, **57**: 593. — (A. Clive) Gent. M. n. s. **13**: 68. Same art. Ev. Sat. **17**: 146. Same art. Liv. Age, **105**: 366. — Sharpe, **14**: 48. Temp. Bar, **56**: 314.
— Letters of. Bentley, **41**: 204. — Chr. Obs. **59**: 9. — Chamb. J. **27**: 88. Same art. Ecl. M. **40**: 548. — Fraser, **55**: 282. — Liv. Age, **52**: 631. — Lond. Q. **8**: 501.
— Loves of. (P. Fitzgerald) Belgra. **16**: 220.
Bosworth Field. Blackw. **25**: 421.
— Battle of. Penny M. **10**: 433.
Botanic Gardens. Penny M. **7**: 361.
Botanical Excursion. (H. C. Wood, jr.) Am. Natural. **1**: 517.
— in North Carolina. (A. Gray) Am. J. Sci. **42**: 1.
Botanical Geography. No. Brit. **20**: 501.
— Meyer on. For. Q. **20**: 201.
Botanical Literature, Notices of. (A. Gray) Am. J. Sci. **63**: 42.
Botanical Miscellany, Hooker's. Mo. R. **125**: 317.
Botanical Museums. Nature, **3**: 401. — (W. Carruthers) Nature, **6**: 449.
Botanical Nomenclature, Laws of. (A. L. P. P. de Candolle) Am. J. Sci. **96**: 63.
Botanical Problems, Cohn's. Nature, **11**: 261.
Botanical Professorship, Cambridge. Quar. **19**: 434.
Botanical Researches; a Poem. (F. Parke) Dub. Univ. **83**: 426.
Botanical Writings of Rafinesque. Am. J. Sci. **40**: 221.
Botanist, Rambles of a, in California. (J. Muir) O. & N. **5**: 767.
— in Europe. (W. G. Farlow) Am. Natural. **8**: 1, 112, 295.
Botanizing. (W. Flagg) Atlan. **27**: 657.
— at Oakshott Heath. (S. Hibberd) Intel. Obs. **4**: 266.
Botany. Westm. **51**: 356. — So. Lit. Mess. **7**: 777.
— Address in London, 1866. (A. L. P. P. de Candolle) Am. J. Sci. **92**: 230.
— and Botanists. Westm. **58**: 385.
— — Scottish. No. Brit. **31**: 197.
— and Gardening. Ecl. R. **86**: 167.
— — Pleasures of. Ecl. M. **13**: 117.
— applied to Arts and Art-Manufacture. (C. Dresser) Art J. **9**: 17–340. **10**: 37–362.
— as a Branch of Female Education. Victoria, **24**: 67.
— Bigelow's Medical. (W. Channing) No. Am. **9**: 23.
— British Alpine. No. Brit. **37**: 67.

Botany, Brown's Manual of. Nature, **11**: 345.
— Classic Flora. (M. A. Lloyd) Galaxy, **18**: 115. **19**: 801.
— Classification in. (W. L. Davidson) Mind, **5**: 513.
— Comstock's and Phelps's. Am. Mo. R. **4**: 112.
— Cryptogamic Vegetation. Lond. Q. **1**: 88.
— Decandolle's. (L. Ray) No. Am. **38**: 32.
— Decandolle's Geographical. Ed. R. **104**: 490.
— Do Varieties wear out? (A. Gray) Am. J. Sci. **109**: 109.
— Gray's Text-Books on. (Mrs. I. James) No. Am. **87**: 321. — (G. B. Emerson) No. Am. **56**: 192. **61**: 254. — Am. J. Sci. **55**: 377.
— Henfrey's. (A. W. Bennett) Nature, **18**: 217.
— Hooker's Primer of. (M. A. Lawson) Nature, **14**: 8.
— Hooker's American. Am. J. Sci. **9**: 263.
— in America. (J. D. Hooker) Nature, **18**: 325.
— in Germany. Nature, **17**: 158.
— in North America from 1635–1858. (F. Brendel) Am. Natural. **13**: 754. **14**: 25.
— in the Oxford Natural Science School. Nature, **6**: 77.
— in Queensland. (J. R. Jackson) Nature, **11**: 271.
— in Schools. (M. L. Owen) O. & N. **6**: 245.
— in United States in 1879, 1880. (E. E. Bessey) Am. Natural. **14**: 862. **15**: 947.
— Instruction in. (W. G. Farlow) Am. Natural. **10**: 287.
— Keith's. Mo. R. **82**: 126.
— Lindley *versus* Hooker. Mo. R. **134**: 342.
— Natural Systems of. Westm. **54**: 38.
— Nature's Planting. All the Year, **2**: 508.
— Nuttall's. U. S. Lit. Gaz. **6**: 439. — Am. J. Sci. **13**: 99.
— of Antarctic Regions. (A. Gray) Am. J. Sci. **58**: 161.
— of Canada. (W. Hincks) Canad. J. n. s. **6**: 165, 276. — (J. M. Buchan) Canad. J. n. s. **14**: 281.
— of a Coal Mine. (W. Carruthers) Pop. Sci. R. **6**: 289.
— of Eastern Kansas. (E. Hall) Am. J. Sci. **100**: 29.
— of Great Britain, Hooker's. (A. W. Bennett) Nature, **2**: 292.
— — Native. Hogg, **5**: 302, 318. **6**: 59–405.
— — Origin of local Floras. (H. Coultas) Pop. Sci. R. **4**: 28.
— — Smith's. Ed. R. **6**: 79.
— of Illinois. (E. L. Greene) Am. Natural. **3**: 5.
— of India, Hooker's. Nature, **12**: 3.
— — Oliver's. (M. J. Berkeley) Nature, **1**: 234.
— of Japan. (A. Gray) Am. J. Sci. **78**: 187.
— of North America, Gray's. (J. Carey) No. Am. **67**: 174.
— of North of France. Ed. R. **7**: 101.
— of the Quantocks. (W. Tuckwell) Nature, **7**: 48.
— of United States. (C. Cushing) No. Am. **13**: 100.
— — Gray's. (J. Carey) No. Am. **67**: 174. — Chr. Exam. **45**: 142.
— — Statistics of Northern Flora. (A. Gray) Am. J. Sci. **72**: 204. **73**: 62, 369.
— Physiological, Keith's System of. Ecl. R. **27**: 259, 313.
— Popular. (A. L. Phelps) Nat. Q. **2**: 276. — Hogg, **8**: 27, 171.
— Progress of, during 1869. (G. Bentham) Nature, **2**: 91, 110.
— — and State of. (A. Gray) Am. J. Sci. **109**: 288, 346.
— Ruskin's Proserpina. (A. Gray) Nation, **21**: 103.
— Sachs's Text-Book of. (W. R. M'Nab) Nature, **12**: 62. — So. R. n. s. **24**: 314.
— Smith's Grammar of. Ecl. R. **33**: 535.
— Smith's Introduction to. Ed. R. **15**: 118.
— Study of. Ed. Mo. R. **5**: 631. — Mus. **15**: 247. — Mo. R. **129**: 422. — U. S. Lit. Gaz. **2**: 103.
— Systematic Tendencies of. (M. C. Cooke) Pop. Sci. R. **14**: 254.
Botany, Willdenow's. Ed. R. **11**: 73.
See Flora; Flowers; Plants; Trees; Vegetable Anatomy; *also names of separate genera, species, and plants.*
Botany Bay. (Syd. Smith) Ed. R. **32**: 28. **38**: 85.
— Convict's Recollections of. Portfo.(Den.) **34**: 25.
— Oxley's Tour in. (Syd. Smith) Ed. R. **34**: 422.
Botello, James, Adventure of. (W. S. Mayo) Hogg, **9**: 285. Same art. Internat. M. **3**: 40.
Both her Boys; a Story. All the Year, **38**: 228.
Both Sides of the Shield. (R. H. Davis) Scrib. **10**: 88.
Botheration of Billy Cormack. Dub. Univ. **16**: 539.
Bothie of Toper-na-Fuosick. Fraser, **39**: 103. Same art. Liv. Age, **21**: 197.
Bothwell, J. H., Earl of. Blackw. **2**: 30.
— Latter Years of. (R. S. Ellis) Arch. **38**: 308.
— Life of. (W. F. Allen) Nation, **30**: 389.
— Manuscript of. Colburn, **13**: 521.
Bothmer, Baroness von. Cruel as the Grave. Dub. Univ. **79**: 44.
Botta, Charles, Histories of. For. R. **1**: 490.
Böttger. *See* Boettger.
Botticelli, Sandro. (W. H. Pater) Fortn. **14**: 155. — (C. Monkhouse) Art J. **33**: 120.
— Picture of the Nativity. (S. Colvin) Portfo. **2**: 25.
Bottle Hill. *See* Madison, N. J.
Bottle Imp, The. Knick. **56**: 273.
Bottle of Hay. House. Words, **9**: 69.
Bottle Papers at Sea. Penny M. **13**: 494.
Bottle Tit and its Nest. Penny M. **7**: 481.
Botts, J. Minor, with portrait. Am. Whig R. **6**: 504.
Boucher, François. (S. Colvin) Portfo. **3**: 34.
— Incident in Life of; a Poem. St. Paul's, **3**: 460.
Bouchor, Maurice, and his Poetry. (W. Besant) Temp. Bar, **41**: 533. Same art. Ev. Sat. **17**: 93.
Boucicault, Dion, with portrait. Once a Week, **26**: 430.
— Formosa. Once a Week, **21**: 107.
Boucicaut, Aristide. Lond. Soc. **35**: 378.
Boudinot, Elias, with portrait. Portfo.(Den.) **23**: 265. — (H. B. Stryker) Pennsyl. M. **3**: 191.
Bough, Samuel. (A. Fraser) Portfo. **10**: 114.
Bought and sold; a Poem. (R. A. Benson) Once a Week, **1**: 492.
Bought Bridegroom; a Story of Gold. Dub. Univ. **32**: 684. Same art. Liv. Age, **20**: 84.
Boughton, George H. (S. Colvin) Portfo. **2**: 65.
— Divided Attention; Picture by. Portfo. **8**: 159.
— Works of. Art J. **25**: 41.
Bouguereau, Wm. Adolph. (R. Ménard) Portfo. **6**: 42.
Bouilliet, Louis. (E. Reclus) Putnam, **14**: 588, 693.
Boulak, Longshore Life at. (Lady Duff-Gordon) Macmil **15**: 365.
Boulanger, Gustave. (R. Ménard) Portfo. **6**: 178.
Boulders. *See* Bowlders.
Boulogne. Dub. Univ. **45**: 651. — Sharpe, **42**: 240.
— Belfry and Cathedral of. (C. A. Mute) Peop. J. **8**: 99.
— British Settlement at. Lond. Soc. **17**: 52.
— Bubbles from. Colburn, **42**: 214.
— Day at. All the Year, **39**: 245. — (P. F. Howard) Colburn, **80**: 450.
— Education in. Temp. Bar, **21**: 38.
— en Route to Paris. (W. H. Maxwell) Bentley, **26**: 74.
— Fêtes at. Bentley, **36**: 321.
— Fisher-Folk of. (L. A. Chamerovzow) St. James, **34**: 474.
— in 18th Century. (J. Hutton) Tinsley, **19**: 213.
— Museum at. Penny M. **7**: 452, 468.
— Plea for. (A. Smith) Bentley, **20**: 529.
— Roman Lighthouse at. Penny M. **13**: 12.
— Rue de l'Ecu. (G. A. Sala) Temp. Bar, **12**: 184.
— Works on. Fraser, **16**: 379.
Boulton, Matthew, and J. Watt. Ev. Sat. **1**: 175.

Bounce. (I. A. Prokop) Lippinc. **13**: 733.
Bound to John Company; a Novel. (M. E. Braddon) Belgra. **6**: 5–479. **7**: 69–513. **8**: 117–503. **9**: 132–538.
Bound with Paul; a Tale. (M. A. Tincker) Cath. World, **7**: 389.
Boundaries of Empires, Natural. (J. Fitch) Am. J. Sci. **14**: 18. **16**: 99. — (M. Heilprin) Nation, **11**: 133. *See also* Centurial Stones.
Boundary Lines, Indefinable. (F. Jacox) Bentley, **62**: 63.
Boundary Question, Northeastern. (N. Hale) No. Am. **26**: 421. **33**: 262. — (C. S. Davis) No. Am. **34**: 514. — (N. Hale) No. Am. **43**: 413. — (C. F. Adams) No. Am. **52**: 424. — (J. G. Palfrey) No. Am. **53**: 439. — Westm. **40**: 182. — with map, New York R. **8**: 196. — with map, (C. Buller) Westm. **34**: 202. — with map, (N. Hale) Am. Alma. **1840**: 85. — Dem. R. **5**: 342. — Ann. Reg. **4**: 56. **6**: 94. **7**: 13. — Ecl. Mus. **3**: 331. — Niles's Reg. **34**: 356. **42**: 461. — with map, Fraser, **22**: 346. — Quar. **67**: 501. — Bost. Mo. **1**: 571. *See also* Ashburton Treaty.
— Northwestern. (B. Alvord) Putnam, **16**: 300. — Fraser, **27**: 484. — with map, Dub. Univ. **21**: 377. — Niles's Reg. **22**: 149. — Blackw. **48**: 331. *See also* Oregon Question.
Bounties to Soldiers. Republic, **1**: 88.
Bounty, Mutineers of the. (R. A. Young) Scrib. **22**: 54.
— Mutiny of the. Meth. M. **39**: 846.
See Pitcairn's Island.
Bounty Loan. (J. F. Entz) Bank. M. (N. Y.) **19**: 545.
Bouquet, Gen. Henry. Olden Time, **1**: 200. — (G. H. Fisher) Pennsyl. M. **3**: 121.
— Expedition, 1764. Olden Time, **1**: 217, 241. — (J. T. Headley) Harper, **23**: 577.
Bouquet of Roses; a Tale. Sharpe, **44**: 97.
Bouquets. All the Year, **12**: 9.
Bourbaki, Gen. Leonidas, with portrait. Ev. Sat. **9**: 758.
Bourbon. (W. E. Montague) Fraser, **99**: 135.
Bourbon, Catherine de. Cornh. **13**: 213.
— Love and Marriage of. Cornh. **31**: 79. Same art. Ecl. M. **84**: 310. — Liv. Age, **124**: 555.
Bourbon, Charles, Duke of. (J. G. Wilson) U. S. Serv. M. **5**: 114.
Bourbon, Constable. Colburn, **124**: 164. Same art. Liv. Age, **73**: 67.
Bourbon, Henri de, Prince de Condé. (S. S. Hungerford) Potter Am. Mo. **13**: 336.
Bourbon, Maria Immacolata Aloysia de. (A. Young) Cath. World, **21**: 670.
Bourbon, House of. Once a Week, **23**: 387.
Bourbons, The. Ed. R. **39**: 84.
— and Bonapartes. Month, **22**: 319.
— Bones of. All the Year, **12**: 332.
— Italy and. Chr. Obs. **68**: 431.
— Last fifteen Years of. For Q. **29**: 384. Same art. Am. Ecl. **4**: 488.
— of Spain. Ed. R. **21**: 175.
— Pedigree of. (W. D. Pink) Antiquary, **4**: 286.
— Personal Memoirs of, in Spain. (J. Bonner) Harper, **10**: 484.
— Restoration of. (F. Jeffrey) Ed. R. **23**: 1. — Selec. Ed. R. **4**: 306. — Quar. **73**: 68. — For. Q. **11**: 89.
Bourbon Pretenders. St. James, **4**: 486.
See Williams, Eleazar.
Bourbon, Isle of. Liv. Age, **141**: 213.
— Commerce of. (C. T. Campbell) Hunt, **17**: 63.
Bourbonisms. Tait, **4**: 64.
Bourbonnais Railroad, Report of, 1860. (C. Desnoyers) J. Frankl. Inst. **71**: 1, 73.
Bource, Henri. Art J. **19**: 43.
Bourdaloue, Louis, and Bossuet. (J. J. van Osterzee) Am. Presb. R. **17**: 91.
Bourdaloue, Louis, Bossuet, and Massillon. Am. Church R. **20**: 438, 572.
— and his Contemporaries. Month, **31**: 262, 467.
— and Massillon. Ecl. R. **93**: 277.
— in Court of Louis XIV. (J. P. Reynolds) Chr. R. **18**: 382, 537.
— Life and Sermons. Chr. Rem. **27**: 88.
— Sermons of. Bib. R. **1**: 450.
— Works. (H. W. Thorpe, A. M.) Evang. R. **4**: 204.
Bourdillon, F. W, Poems of. Liv. Age, **138**: 636.
Bourdon, Madame, Works of. Month, **1**: 266.
Bourgeois Wedding; a Story. Chamb. J. **16**: 322.
Bourges, an old French City. (B. R. Parkes) Argosy, **2**: 197.
Bourn, Samuel, Memoir of. Ecl. R. **10**: 1136.
Bourne, Edward E., Memoir of, with portrait. (E. B. Smith) N. E. Reg. **28**: 1.
Bourne, Admiral Nehemiah, Memoir of. (I. J. Greenwood) N. E. Reg. **27**: 26.
Bourne, Vincent, and modern Latinists. (T. C. Clarke) Chr. Exam. **45**: 243.
— Poems of. Ecl. R. **8**: 832.
— Writings of. Knick. **24**: 367.
Bournemouth. Lond. Soc. **40**: 497.
— Eocene Flora of. (J. S. Gardner) Nature, **21**: 181.
Visit to. Tinsley, **6**: 146.
Bourse, Business on the. All the Year, **24**: 484.
Boutiques, Chapter about, Codicil to. Fraser, **23**: 328.
Boutwell, George S., with portrait. Ev. Sat. **10**: 339.
— as Secretary of the Treasury. (J. B. Hodgskin) Nation, **9**: 5.
Bow Bells, Within Sound of. Belgra. **26**: 60.
Bow Churchyard, Ancient Buildings in. (T. Lott) Arch. **31**: 318.
Bow-Street Officer, Episodes in the Life of a. Chamb. J. **56**: 409.
Bow-Street Runner, Experiences of a. Chamb. J. **56**: 123.
Bowditch, Nathaniel. (A. Young) Am. J. Sci. **35**: 1. — (A. Young) Hunt, **1**: 33. — Am. Alma. **1836**: 288. — Chr. R. **3**: 321. — New York R. **4**: 308. — Am. Q. Reg. **11**: 309.
— Translation of Mécanique Céleste. (B. Peirce) No. Am. **48**: 143.
— Writings of, Complete List of. Math. Mo. **2**: 57.
Bowdler, John. Poetry. Quar. **21**: 112. — Ed. R. **28**: 335.
— Select Pieces. Portfo.(Den.) **24**: 437.
Bowdoin, James. (F. Bowen) No. Am. **75**: 331.
— Memoir of. (J. B. Moore) Am. Q. Reg. **14**: 152.
Bowdoin College. (G. F. Packard) Scrib. **12**: 47. — O. & N. **4**: 112.
— History of. (A. S. Packard) Am. Q. Reg. **8**: 105.
— May Training at, 1836. (T. B. Read) University Q. **1**: 264.
— Patriotic Record of. (J. H. Thompson) Hours at Home, **3**: 463.
Bowdoin Genealogy. (W. H. Whitmore) N. E. Reg. **10**: 79.
Bowen, Francis. Lowell Lectures. (G. E. Ellis) Chr. Exam. **48**: 88. — (G. I. Chase) Chr. R. **15**: 78.
— Speculative Philosophy. Ecl. M. **5**: 215.
Bower, A. Sharpe, **9**: 90.
Bower Bird, The Spotted. Internat. M. **1**: 386.
Bowers, Col. T. S., Life of. (S. Cadwallader) U. S. Serv. M. **5**: 360.
Bowery Theater, Accident at, 1851. (F. Copcutt) Knick. **38**: 601.
Bowie, James. (Dr. Kilpatrick) De Bow, **13**: 378.
Bowie, Colonel, and his Knife. Temp. Bar, **2**: 120.
Bowker, Joseph. (H. Hall) Hist. M. **12**: 351.
Bowker's Courtship; a Tale. All the Year, **42**: 395.
Bowl of Punch in the Captain's Room; a Sketch. Dub Univ. **47**: 447.

Bowls, Game of. (R. R. Macgregor) Belgra. 36: 352.
Bowlder and Glacial Scratches at Englewood, N. J. (W. B. Dwight) Am. J. Sci. 91: 10.
— Drift, Western. (E. Andrews) Am. J. Sci. 98: 172.
— in the Drift of Amherst, Mass. (E. Hitchcock) Am. J. Sci. 72: 397.
Bowlders. (B. Struder) Am. J. Sci. 36: 325.
— and rolled Stones. Am. J. Sci. 9: 28.
— Scottish. Nature, 6: 477.
Bowles, Caroline. Cornh. 30: 217.
— Poems of. Liv. Age, 11: 230.
— Widow's Tale. Blackw. 11: 286.
Bowles, Major John. N. E. Reg. 2: 192.
Bowles, John, Reflections on the Peace. (Syd. Smith) Ed. R. 1: 94.
Bowles, Leonard C., Obituary Notice of. (H. W. Foote) Unita. R. 5: 418.
Bowles the Waiter. All the Year, 28: 270.
Bowles, William L. (S. C. Hall and Mrs. S. C. Hall) Art J. 1865: 375. Same art. Ecl. M. 66: 216. — (J. A. Heraud) Temp. Bar, 8: 429. — with portrait, Fraser, 13: 300. — Chamb. J. 13: 308.
— Bromhill Parsonage. Blackw. 24: 226.
— Days departed. Blackw. 27: 279.
— Grave of the last Saxon. Blackw. 12: 71.
— Missionary. Blackw. 6: 13.
— Poems of. Quar. 2: 235. 61: 427.
— Spirit of Discovery. Ed. R. 6: 313.
Bowlin, James B., Portrait of. Dem. R. 18: 323.
Bowman, Samuel, Bishop. (J. C. Passmore) Am. Church R. 14: 499.
Bowood, Inmates and Visitors of. Tait, n. s. 8: 26.
Bowring, Sir John. Knick. 2: 358.
— Ancient Poetry of Spain. Ecl. R. 42: 259.
— Matins and Vespers. Chr. Exam. 4: 524. — U. S. Lit. Gaz. 6: 407. — Mo. R. 101: 249. — Chr. Obs. 23: 697.
— Memoirs of. Westm. 108: 387. Same art. Liv. Age, 135: 515.
— Oratory of. Fraser, 34: 465.
— Poems of. Ecl. R. 38: 162.
— Specimens of Russian Poets. Ecl. R. 39: 59. — Lond. M. 3: 316.
Box and Cox, in the Bay of Bengal. Lond. Soc. 14: 385.
Box on the Ears. (J. E. Hartzenbusch) Victoria, 15: 292.
Box with the Iron Clamps. (F. M. Church) Lond. Soc. 13: 422, 515.
Boxall, Sir Wm. (Lord Coleridge) Fortn. 33: 177. — Art J. 32: 83.
Boxer, The. Blackw. 25: 159.
Boxford, Mass. Items from John Cushing's Almanac, 1746. N. E. Reg. 19: 237.
— Taxes in, in 1687. N. E. Reg. 33: 162.
Boxgrave Priory, Matrix of the Seal of. (Sir F. Madden) Arch. 27: 375.
Boxhill and its Picnics. All the Year, 41: 205.
Boxiana; or, Sketches of Pugilism. Blackw. 5: 439, 593, 663. 6: 66, 279, 609. 7: 294. 8: 60. 9: 460.
Boxing and Prize Fights. Blackw. 17: 603. 19: 505. 36: 839.
Boxing Match at Wimbledon. Blackw. 2: 669.
Boxing Night at the East End. Once a Week, 24: 45.
Boy in Gray. (A. C. Redwood) Scrib. 22: 641.
Boy of the Future. Once a Week, 7: 203.
Boy of the Light-House, The; a Poem. Putnam, 8: 40.
Boy on a Hill-Farm. (M. Dean) Lippinc. 22: 310.
Boy Bishop. (J. Bowle) Arch. 9: 39.
Boy Crime and its Cure. Ecl. R. 103: 252.
Boy Laborers, Experiment with. Liv. Age, 19: 165.
Boy Monsters. All the Year, 19: 103.
Boy Poet of Rome, Monument of. Ev. Sat. 11: 287.
Boy Soldiers. (W. W. Knollys) 19th Cent. 6: 1.
Boy's first Fight. Chamb. J. 43: 65.
Boy's Home. (H. King) Once a Week, 15: 215.
Boys. (A. G. Penn) Lippinc. 7: 98. — (H. E. Spofford) Galaxy, 6: 835. — All the Year, 14: 37. 39: 442. — Macmil. 23: 432. — N. Ecl. 5: 446.
— Against. Chamb. J. 39: 145. Same art. Liv. Age, 77: 85.
— and Girls. (D. H. Strother) Harper, 54: 19.
— British Cubs. Sharpe, 32: 293.
— Clever. House. Words, 18: 514.
— Essay on. Broadw. 8: 189.
— Height and Weight of. (F. Galton) Anthrop. J. 5: 174.
— in Books. Ev. Sat. 11: 330.
— Lesson on. (T. P. Bevan) Once a Week, 10: 705.
— Training of. (S. C. Kendall) Scrib. 3: 723.
— Virtues and Vices of. Portfo.(Den.) 31: 463.
Boys not allowed. (S. Loring) Lakeside, 10: 63.
Boyce, John. (Mrs. E. F. Ellet) Godey, 56: 121.
Boycotted. (W. B. Jones) Contemp. 39: 856. Same art. Liv. Age, 150: 113. Same art. Ecl. M. 97: 209.
Boycotting, Genesis of. (E. L. Godkin) Nation, 31: 437.
Boyd, A. K. H. Leisure Hours in Town. (W. E. Boies) New Eng. 21: 442.
— Recreations of a Country Parson. (W. E. Boies) New Eng. 19: 882. — Bost. R. 2: 162. — Liv. Age, 69: 116.
Boyd, Henry S. Translations from the Fathers. Ed. R. 24: 58.
Boyd, Dea. William. Cong. Q. 4: 351.
Boyd, Captain; a Hero's Obsequies. Dub. Univ. 57: 453.
Boydell; a Sketch. (F. McLandburgh) Lakeside, 6: 270.
Boydell's Shakspere. Art J. 3: 85. — Blackw. 39: 683. 45: 402.
Boyden, Seth. (S. B. Hunt) Hours at Home, 11: 115.
Boyesen, Hjalmar H. (F. E. Heath) Scrib. 14: 776.
Boyhood and Barbarism. Am. Whig R. 14: 278.
— Bit of our. Fraser, 43: 631.
— Happy. Once a Week, 25: 261.
— of a Dreamer; a Poem. Dub. Univ. 8: 33.
Boyle, John, Table-talk of. Fraser, 23: 574.
Boyle, Mary L. Bridal of Melcha. Dub. Univ. 23: 508.
Boyle, Robert. All the Year, 5: 87. — Brit. Q. 9: 200. Same art. Ecl. M. 17: 28. — Dub. Univ. 7: 359.
— his Influence on Science and liberal Ideas. (E. I. Sears) Nat. Q. 14: 60.
Boyle Family. Am. J. Educ. 26: 392.
Boyle, Antiquities of. (J. J. Kelly) Irish Mo. 7: 414, 482, 576. 8: 47, 103.
Boyle Lectures for 1874 and 1875. Cong. 5: 213.
Boylston, Dr. Zabdiel. Hist. M. 1: 140.
— and John. (C. W. Parsons) N. E. Reg. 35: 150.
Boylston Genealogy. (T. B. Wyman) N. E. Reg. 7: 145.
Boyne, The River. Dub. Univ. 29: 341, 764.
— and Blackwater, Wilde on. Dub. Univ. 37: 327.
— Campaign of, 1690. Dub. Univ. 68: 154.
Boyse, Joseph. N. E. Reg. 12: 65.
Boyse, Samuel, Life of. Mus. 38: 209.
Boyton, Charles. Blackw. 34: 171.
Boyton, Capt. Paul, Across the Channel with. St. James, 36: 532.
— An Evening with. (A. McNeill) Gent. M. n. s. 14: 715.
Bozzari, Marco. Colburn, 8: 441.
— Death of. Niles's Reg. 25: 183.
Bozzies. Ecl. M. 29: 382.
Brabant, Duke of, Marriage of. Fraser, 48: 482.
Bracciolini, Poggio, Life of. (H. Brougham) Ed. R. 2: 42.
Bracelets. (M. G. Watkins) Belgra. 6: 40. — Godey, 78: 155.
Bracelets, The. (S. Warren) Blackw. 31: 39.

Brachiopoda; a Division of Annelida. (E. S. Morse) Am. J. Sci. **100**: 100. — (A. Wilson) Colburn, **156**: 543.
— Early Stages of. (E. S. Morse) Am. J. Sci. **99**: 103.
— of the United States Coast Survey, Dall's. (J. G. Jeffreys) Nature, **4**: 238.
Bracken, T., with portrait. Bank. M. (L.) **7**: 536.
Bracken Hollow. Harper, **28**: 531. — Once a Week, **10**: 57, 85.
Brackenridge, Henry H. So. Lit. Mess. **8**: 1.
Brackets and Plummer Blocks. Pract. M. **1**: 34.
Bracoon, The; a Louisiana Incident. St. James, **9**: 471.
Bracton; or, Sub Sigillo. (W. H. Anderdon) Irish Mo. **8**: 1–659. **9**: 31–258.
Bradbury, John M., with portrait. (J. W. Dean) N. E. Reg. **31**: 365.
Bradbury, Capt. Thomas, Descendants of. Hist. M. **14**: 205.
Bradbury's Visitor. Lond. Soc. **9**: 115.
Braddock's Defeat. (Dr. Mayo) Dem. R. **20**: 44. — Niles's Reg. **14**: 179. — Hist. M. **8**: 353.
— Beaujeu Victor at. Hist. M. **7**: 265.
— Dr. Franklin on. Olden Time, **1**: 89.
— Route to the Monongahela. Olden Time, **2**: 465, 539.
— Sparks on. Olden Time, **1**: 126.
— Visit to Field of. Olden Time, **1**: 186.
— Who killed Gen. Braddock? Hist. M. **11**: 141.
Braddon, Miss M. E. (H. James, jr.) Nation, **1**: 593. — Liv. Age, **77**: 99.
— Aurora Floyd, and Lady Audley's Secret. Chr. Rem. **46**: 209.
— Lady Audley's Secret. Cornh. **7**: 135.
— The Lady's Mile. Chr. Rem. **52**: 184.
— Novels of. Dub. Univ. **75**: 436. — No. Brit. **43**: 180. Same art. Ecl. M. **65**: 616.
Braden, Forest of, Ancient Limits of. (J. Y. Akerman) Arch. **37**: 257.
Bradfield Inundation. Chamb. J. **51**: 241.
Bradford, Alden, Sketch of. Chr. Exam. **35**: 375.
Bradford, Moses. (C. Cutler) Cong. Q. **6**: 175.
— Memoir of. (H. Wood) Am. Q. Reg. **12**: 128.
Bradford, Robert B., with portrait. Dem. R. **42**: 324.
Bradford, Gov. William. (W. F. Rae) Good Words, **21**: 337.
— Family Bible and Record. N. E. Reg. **1**: 275.
— History of New Plymouth, Discovery of the MS. N. E. Reg. **9**: 231. **10**: 353. **11**: 44.
— Letter to John Winthrop, 1631. N. E. Reg. **2**: 240.
— Memoir of. (J. B. Moore) Am. Q. Reg. **14**: 155. — Cong. M. **9**: 337, 393.
— Relatives of. (F. Kidder) N. E. Reg. **14**: 195.
Bradford, William, Printer. (J. W. Wallace) Hist. M. **7**: 201.
— Works printed by, 1686–1717. Hist. M. **3**: 171.
Bradford, William, American Artist. Hours at Home, **3**: 515.
Bradford Genealogy. (W. Allen) N. E. Reg. **9**: 127. — (R. H. Walworth) N. E. Reg. **14**: 174. — (G. M. Fessenden) N. E. Reg. **4**: 39, 233. — (N. A. Otis) N. E. Reg. **9**: 218.
Bradford, England, and the Worsted Manufacture. (G. Taylor) Pract. M. **2**: 274.
— Industries of. Lond. Soc. **35**: 69.
— to Brindisi, From. All the Year, **25**: 252, 276.
Bradford, Mass., Records of. N. E. Reg. **8**: 236. **18**: 275, 349. **19**: 22.
— Academy at, History of. (J. Merrill) Am. Q. Reg. **13**: 70.
Bradgate Park, Residence of Lady Jane Grey. Lond. M. **5**: 166.
Bradish, Luther, with portrait. Ecl. M. **60**: 111. — Hist. M. **7**: 297.
Bradlaugh, Charles, and the Constitution. (S. Amos) Contemp. **40**: 424.
— and his Opponents. (L. Stephen) Fortn. **34**: 176. Same art. Appleton, **24**: 361.
— Protest against his Admission to Parliament. (H. E. Manning) 19th Cent. **8**: 177. Same art. Appleton, **24**: 359.
Bradley, Amy M., and her Schools. (C. Lowe) O. & N. **1**: 775.
Bradley, Charles. Sermons. Chr. Obs. **19**: 596. **22**: 172.
Bradley, James, Works and Correspondence of. Ed. R. **65**: 119.
Bradley, Mary, Deaf and Blind Mute. Canad. J. n. s. **11**: 184.
Bradstreet, Anne. Poems. No. Am. **106**: 330. — (G. Ainslee) Potter Am. Mo. **12**: 104.
Bradstreet, Col. John, Expedition, 1764. Olden Time, **1**: 337.
Bradstreet, Simon. N. E. Reg. **1**: 75.
— and Anne, Descendants of. N. E. Reg. **8**: 313. **9**: 113. **13**: 203.
— Journal of, 1664–83. N. E. Reg. **8**: 325; reprint, **9**: 43.
Brady, James T., with portrait. Ecl. M. **74**: 243. — Galaxy, **7**: 716. — Am. Law R. **3**: 779.
Brady's Four Acres of Bog. (F. M'Cabe) Colburn, **147**: 29–674. **148**: 90–672. **149**: 62–684.
Braekeleer, Ferdinand de. Art J. **19**: 41.
Braemar, Last Century in. Good Words, **19**: 834.
Brag, Game of. Chamb. J. **41**: 297.
Bragging. Colburn, **62**: 391.
Braham, John. Liv. Age, **49**: 206.
Brahe, Tycho. Nature, **15**: 405. — Ed. R. **80**: 179.
Brahmanism. (J. F. Clarke) Atlan. **23**: 548. — (C. W. Clapp) New Eng. **39**: 487.
— and Christianity. (H. H. Barber) Unita. R. **12**: 323.
— History and Claims of. (L. P. Brockett) Meth. Q. **21**: 638.
— in India. Chr. Rem. **35**: 81.
— Land of the Veda. (Mrs. S. B. Herrick) So. R. n. s. **13**: 67.
— Origin and History of. (J. Pyne) Nat. Q. **32**: 262. *See* Hindus; Vedas.
Brahmanism of New England. Brownson, **20**: 421.
Brahmans, Character of. (J. W. Palmer) Atlan. **2**: 79.
Brahmo Somaj, The. (F. P. Cobbe) Fraser, **74**: 199. — (G. L. Chaney) O. & N. **5**: 679. — (W. H. Fremantle) Contemp. **15**: 67. — (T. J. Scott) Meth. Q. **27**: 400. — Brit. Q. **49**: 510. — Dub. Univ. **81**: 249.
— New Development of. (W. Knighton) Contemp. **40**: 570.
— *versus* the new Dispensation. (S. D. Collet) Contemp. **40**: 726.
Brahmoism and Electicism. (R. Milman) Good Words, **11**: 792.
Braich of Dinas. (T. Pownall) Arch. **3**: 303.
Brain, The. Portfo. (Den.) **11**: 515.
— and the Mind. (W. James) Nation, **24**: 355. — (J. Martineau) Nat. R. **10**: 500. — Dub. R. **88**: 25. — Lond. Q. **54**: 124. **57**: 82. — Appleton, **24**: 367. — Brit. Q. **40**: 440.
— — Calderwood's. (D. Ferrier) Nature, **20**: 309.
— and its Uses. Cornh. **5**: 409.
— and the Nerves, Recent Works on, 1880. (G. M. Beard) No. Am. **131**: 278. — Dub. R. **86**: 372.
— and the Soul. (T. Dwight) Internat. R. **8**: 493.
— and the Stomach. (U. Parsons) Am. Inst. of Instr. **1840**: 113.
— as an Organ of Mind, Bastian on. (G. C. Robertson) Mind, **6**: 120. — (D. Ferrier) Princ. n. s. **4**: 98.
— Cells of, Education of. (J. M. Granville) Pop. Sci. Mo. **16**: 200.

Brain, The, Cerebral Dynamics. (I. Ray) Atlan. **10**: 272.
— Coinages of. (A. Wilson) Belgra. **43**: 168. Same art. Ecl. M. **96**: 166.
— Convolutions of, Ecker on. Nature, **8**: 526.
— Diseases of. Ecl. R. **112**: 551. — Ed. R. **112**: 526. Same art. Ecl. M. **52**: 29. Same art. Liv. Age, **67**: 532.
— — First Beginnings of. Cornh. **5**: 481.
— Functions of. (J. Althaus) 19th Cent. **6**: 1021. Same art. Liv. Age, **144**: 195. — (C. Bernard) Pop. Sci. Mo. **2**: 64.
— — Ferrier on. (G. H. Lewes) Nature, **15**: 73, 93. — (J. M. Marsters) No. Am. **124**: 310. — (G. C. Robertson) Mind, **2**: 92.
— — Localization of. (J. Hunt) Anthrop. R. **6**: 329. **7**: 100, 201.
— Gall's Theory of. Ed. R. **2**: 147. — So. R. **1**: 134.
— Have we two Brains? Cornh. **31**: 149. Same art. Ecl. M. **84**: 401. Same art. Liv. Age, **125**: 115.
— Human. (H. C. Bastian) Macmil. **13**: 63. Same art. Ecl. M. **66**: 170.
— — Origin and Descent of. (S. V. Clevenger) Am. Natural. **15**: 513.
— in Man and Monkeys, Structure of. (R. Wagner) Am. J. Sci. **84**: 188.
— Nature of the invertebrate. (H. C. Bastian) Pop. Sci. Mo. **10**: 27.
— New Method with. (D. Ferrier) Pop. Sci. Mo. **4**: 183.
— of a Negro of Guinea. Anthrop. R. **6**: 279.
— The overworked. Ev. Sat. **10**: 395.
— Physics of. (B. W. Richardson) Pop. Sci. R. **6**: 415. Same art. Ecl. M. **69**: 751.
— Physiology of. (C. Bray) Anthrop. R. **7**: 268.
— Quality of. St. Paul's, **10**: 644.
— Re-education of the adult. (W. Sharpey) Pop. Sci. Mo. **15**: 455.
— Size of, and Size of Body. (H. W. B.) Pop. Sci. Mo. **16**: 827.
— — in Men and Women. Cornh. **7**: 276.
— Unconscious Action of. (W. B. Carpenter) Pop. Sci. Mo. **1**: 544.
— Vagaries of. Chamb. J. **52**: 593.
— Weight Proportions of. (A. Weisbach) Anthrop. R. **7**: 92.
— — of Chinese and Pelew Islanders. (C. Clapham) Anthrop J. **7**: 89.
Brain-Forcing. (T. C. Allbutt) Pop. Sci. Mo. **13**: 217.
Brain-Workers, Need and Methods of Rest for. Hours at Home, **6**: 543.
Brainard, David, Life of. (W. B. O. Peabody) Sparks's Am. Biog. **8**: 259. — Chr. Mo. Spec. **5**: 135.
— Ministry of. (F. Wayland) Am. Presb. R. **14**: 395.
Brainard, J. G. C., Poems of. (J. Sparks) No. Am. **21**: 217. — (L. Bacon) Chr. Mo. Spec. **7**: 324. — U. S. Lit. Gaz. **2**: 167.
Brainerd, Thomas. (A. Barnes) Am. Presb. R. **16**: 77.
Braintree, Mass., Burial Inscriptions at. N. E. Reg. **11**: 297. **12**: 39.
— Ministers of. Am. Q. Reg. **8**: 47.
Brakes. *See* Railway Brakes.
Bramah, Joseph, Memoir of. Colburn, **3**: 208.
Bramber and Shoreham, Summer Day at. (E. Walford) Once a Week, **11**: 253.
Bramin Secret. N. Ecl. **4**: 592.
Bramins and Swells. Galaxy, **13**: 761.
Bramble, Matthew. Bentley, **57**: 295.
Brambleberries. Fraser, **86**: 741. **87**: 74–358.
Brambletye House. Antiquary, **3**: 97.
Bramleighs of Bishop's Folly; a Novel (C. Lever) Cornh. **15**: 642. **16**: 1–641. **17**: 70–641. **18**: 1–385. Same art. Liv. Age, **96**: 3–785. **97**: 211–721. **98**: 101–663. **99**: 94, 220.
Bramshill House. (W. D.) Antiquary, **3**: 313.
Bramwell, Sir George, and the English Bench. (A. V. Dicey) Nation, **33**: 468.
Branch, Gov. J., Exposition of. Niles's Reg. **41**: 5.
Branch of Lilac. (J. L. de la Ramé) Lippinc. **8**: 440, 602.
Brand from the Burning. (E. Fawcett) Galaxy, **22**: 239.
Brandan, St. *See* Brendan, St.
Brande, W. T. Encyclopædia. So. Lit. Mess. **9**: 180, 313.
— Philosophical Papers. Ed. R. **19**: 198.
Brandebourg, Madame de. Bentley, **54**: 593. Same art. Ecl. M. **61**: 227.
Brandenburg, House of, Ranke's. Quar. **86**: 337. — Ecl. M. **19**: 482.
— White Lady of. Chamb. J. **21**: 266.
Branding and Tattooing. Chamb. J. **51**: 4. Same art. Ev. Sat. **16**: 205.
Brandon, Charles, Duke of Suffolk. *See* Suffolk.
Brandon, Vt., Frozen Well at. (A. Lloyd) Hours at Home, **10**: 376.
Brandon Ghost. (J. McN. Wright) Lippinc. **8**: 388.
Brandt, Count Enevold, Narrative of. Chr. Obs. **40**: 80.
Brandt, Gen. Heinrich von, Memoirs of. Ed. R. **131**: 65. Same art. Liv. Age, **104**: 792.
Brandt, Sebastian. Ship of Fools. Cornh. **42**: 229. Same art. Liv. Age, **146**: 684.
Brandy and Salt — Homœopathy and Hydropathy. (Sir B. C. Brodie) Quar. **71**: 83.
— Cognac, Production of. Pop. Sci. Mo. **10**: 428.
— Duties on, at Geneva. Ed. R. **45**: 169.
— Manufacture of. Pract. M. **1**: 258.
— When and why the Devil invented. Bentley, **2**: 518.
Brandywine, Battle of, 1777. (H. M. Jenkins) Lippinc. **30**: 329.
— Field of. (W. L. Stone) Potter Am. Mo. **7**: 94.
Branford, Ct., Early Records of, with *fac-simile*. (C. M. Taintor) N. E. Reg. **3**: 153.
Branks, Ancient Instrument for Cure of Scolds. (L. Jewitt) Reliquary, **1**: 65. **13**: 193.
Brant, Joseph, or Thayendanega, with portrait. (S. G. Drake) N. E. Reg. **2**: 345. **3**: 59. — Am. Hist. Rec. **2**: 289, 318, 354.
— Letter to. (T. Campbell) Colburn, **4**: 97.
— Passage in History of. (W. L. Stone) Knick. **11**: 363.
— Sketch of the Life of. New Dom. **10**: 198, 276, 349.
— Stone's Life of. (B. B. Thatcher) Chr. Exam. **26**: 137. — New York R. **3**: 195. — Chr. R. **3**: 537. — Am. Bib. Repos. **11**: 1. — Am. Mo. M. **12**: 188, 273. — Mo. R. **147**: 349. — Mus. **38**: 214.
Brantley, William T., Memoir of. Chr. R. **10**: 591.
Brantôme, Abbé Pierre de Bourdeille. Cornh. **27**: 62. Same art. Ecl. M. **80**: 358. Same art. Liv. Age, **116**: 433. — Temp. Bar, **59**: 328. Same art. Liv. Age, **146**: 412.
Brantwood; a Lakeside Home. Art J. **33**: 321.
Brasbridge, Joseph, Memoir of. Blackw. **16**: 428.
Brass. Ecl. Engin. **10**: 415.
Brass Monument of 1323 in Pebmarsh Church, Essex, England. (J. Piggot) Reliquary, **9**: 193.
Brasses, Monumental, How to copy. (E. G. Draper) Reliquary, **15**: 225.
— — in Kent. Antiquary, **1**: 100. **2**: 39–259.
— — of England and Wales, List of. (J. Jeremiah) Antiquary, **3**: 28.
Brasseur de Bourbourg, Abbé E. C., and his Labors. (D. G. Brinton) Lippinc. **1**: 79.
Brassey, Thomas. (H. L. Wayland) Bapt. Q. **7**: 149. — with portrait, Victoria, **33**: 73.
— Life of, Helps's. (Goldwin Smith) Canad. Mo. **2**: 309.
— Sketch of. (H. A. Page) Good Words, **13**: 490.
— Voyage of the Sunbeam. Chamb. J. **55**: 289.
Brassey, Mrs. Thomas, with portrait. Victoria, **31**: 255.

Brassey, Mrs. Thomas. Voyage in the Sunbeam. Canad. Mo. **14**: 385.—(W. Chambers) Chamb. J. **57**: 33.
Brastow Genealogy. (G. W. Messinger) N. E. Reg. **13**: 249.
Bratton, John. Report of Confederate Brigade from May, 1864, to January, 1865. So. Hist. Pap. **8**: 547.
Bratton, Martha. (Mrs. E. F. Ellet) Godey, **36**: 321.
Braun, Alexander. Nature, **15**: 490.
Brave Coucou Driver. House. Words, **16**: 264.
Brave Girl of Glenbarr; a Tale. (C. Bede) Belgra. **37**: supp. 77.
Brave Lady. (D. M. Craik) Macmil. **20**: 1–485. **21**: 8–377. Same art. Harper, **38**: 824. **39**: 64–832. **40**: 68–711.
Brave Mrs. Lyle. (S. B. Cooper) Overland, **10**: 51.
Brave Swiss Boy; a Tale. Chamb. J. **56**: 563–660.
Bray, Anna E., Trelawny of Trelawne. Mo. R. **145**: 104.
Bray, Charles, Writings of. Westm. **111**: 488.
Bray, Thomas. Am. J. Educ. **27**: 239.
Braz Coelho. (W. G. H. Kingston) Colburn, **78**: 159.
Brazen Head; a Poem. So. Lit. Mess. **24**: 327.
Brazer, John. (J. H. Morison) Chr. Exam. **40**: 434.
— Sermons of. (J. Flint) Chr. Exam. **46**: 432.
Brazil. Am. Q. **10**: 126.—(S. Fowler) No. Am. **68**: 314.—Ann. Reg. **1**: 199.—Mo. R. **122**: 83.—(R. M'Murdy) Am. Meth. M. **21**: 185.—Hunt, **53**: 337.
— Aborigines of. Penny M. **11**: 89.
— Agassiz's Expedition. Nature, **6**: 216, 229, 270.—N. Ecl. **1**: 492.
— Amazonian Picnic. (Mrs. L. Agassiz) Atlan. **17**: 313.
— and the Amazon. Lond. Q. **33**: 70.
— and Brazilian Society. Sharpe, **40**: 235. **41**: 86, 194. **42**: 81. Same art. Knick. **63**: 523. **64**: 17–410.
— and the Brazilians. (T. M. Eddy) Meth. Q. **19**: 26.
— — Fletcher and Kidder's. Ecl. R. **107**: 155. Same art. Liv. Age, **63**: 31.—Liv. Age, **66**: 297.—(A. P. Peabody) No. Am. **85**: 533.—U. S. Cath. M. **5**: 293.—(J. W. Alexander) Princ. **17**: 357.—(R. A. West) Meth. Q. **5**: 427.
— and her Emperor. (J. Codman) Galaxy, **21**: 822.
— and her People. (M. Field) Potter Am. Mo. **10**: 309.
— and La Plata, 1827. Ann. Reg. **2**: 285.
— — 1829. Ann. Reg. **3**: 539.
— and United States, State Papers. Niles's Reg. **33**: 428.
— Armitage's History of. Mo. R. **140**: 217.
— Blockade, 1829. Niles's Reg. **36**: 126.
— Burton's Explorations in. Anthrop. R. **7**: 170.
— Burton's Highlands of. Chamb. J. **46**: 313.—Tinsley, **3**: 641.
— Civilization of. New Dom. **7**: 257.
— Commerce of. (J. W. Hawes) Bank. M. (N. Y.) **32**: 524.—Hunt, **12**: 159.
— — and Navigation of. Hunt, **19**: 321.
— Consulate Fees of. Hunt, **14**: 187.
— Crisis in, 1879. (J. C. Rodrigues) Nation, **29**: 53.
— Cruise of the Abrolhos. (C. F. Hartt) Am. Natural. **2**: 85.
— Empire of. (S. Fowler) No. Am. **68**: 314.—(E. I. Sears) Nat. Q. **8**: 257.—De Bow, **24**: 1.—Quar. **108**: 303.
— — Baril on. Colburn, **125**: 85.
— Ewbank's Life in. Colburn, **107**: 215. Same art. Liv. Age, **50**: 412.
— from the Atlantic to the Andes. (H. Eckford) Scrib. **15**: 180.
— Future of. (W. P. Garrison) Nation, **5**: 186.
— Gardner's Travels in. Tait, n. s. **14**: 214.
— Geological Survey of. (C. F. Hartt) Am. J. Sci. **111**: 466.
— German Colony in. Colburn, **89**: 178. Same art. Liv. Age, **26**: 85.
— Gold Mines of. Penny M. **9**: 441.
Brazil, Hartt's. (T. S. Hunt) Nation, **11**: 370.
— Health Trip to. (T. C. Evans) Harper, **39**: 489, 625, 818.
— Henderson's History of. Mo. R. **100**: 256.
— How the Ladies live in. Sharpe, **30**: 137.—Godey, **58**: 493.—Lippinc. **23**: 501.
— Independence of. Niles's Reg. **23**: 124, 142.
— India-Rubber Trees in. Geog. M. **4**: 152, 182, 211.
— Indian Cemetery at Minas. (C. F. Hartt) Am. Natural. **9**: 205.
— Indian Pottery of. (C. F. Hartt) Am. Natural. **5**: 259.
— Koster's Travels in. (R. Southey) Quar. **16**: 344.—Mo. R. **87**: 122.—Anal. M. **9**: 487.—(J. Foster) Ecl. R. **25**: 116.—Portfo.(Den.) **18**: 378.—West. R. **4**: 65.
— Life in. Ecl. R. **103**: 578.—Liv. Age, **79**: 604.
— London to Rio Janeiro. (R. F. Burton) Fraser, **72**: 492. **73**: 79, 496. **74**: 159.
— Luccock's Notes on. Ecl. R. **34**: 193.—Portfo.(Den.) **26**: 406.
— Mansfield's. Fraser, **54**: 591. Same art. Liv. Age, **52**: 1.
— Mawe's Travels in, 1812. Ecl. R. **16**: 940.—Ed. R. **20**: 305.—Quar. **7**: 342.—Anal. M. **4**: 353.
— Prince Maximilian's Travels in. Portfo.(Den.) **28**: 2.
— Monetary System of. Bank. M. (N. Y.) **29**: 538–752.
— Naturalist in. (C. F. Hartt) Am. Natural. **2**: 1.
— Observations in. (W. M. Roberts) J. Frankl. Inst. **110**: 324.
— Organ Mountains in. Bentley, **8**: 24.
— Paraguay and La Plata, Mansfield's Letters from. New Q. **15**: 423.
— Penal Settlement of Fernando Noronha. Scrib. **11**: 534.
— People of. Chamb. J. **40**: 228.
— Physical Geography of. O. & N. **3**: 91.
— Race in. (F. D. Y. Carpenter) Lippinc. **27**: 83.
— Recollections of. Colburn, **26**: 75. **28**: 166.
— Resources of. (J. Heywood) J. Statis. Soc. **27**: 245.
— Royal Family of. Ecl. M. **64**: 124.
— Scenes in. Nat. M. **4**: 289, 457.
— Slave Life in. Chamb. J. **56**: 823.
— Slave Trade of, and Sir J. Hudson. Victoria, **3**: 1.
— Slavery in. Once a Week, **13**: 372.
— — Extinction of. Anthrop. R. **6**: 56.
— Southey's History of. (R. Heber) Quar. **18**: 99.—Ecl. R. **12**: 788.—Quar. **4**: 454. **18**: 99.—Mo. R. **87**: 267.—Anal. M. **1**: 328.
— Tariff of. Hunt, **7**: 292.
— Travels in. Quar. **31**: 1.—Mo. R. **94**: 1. **104**: 337.—Mus. **16**: 535.
— — in 1815–23. Ecl. R. **40**: 385.
— Treaty with, 1829. Niles's Reg. **36**: 109. **39**: 33.
— Vacation Trip to. (C. F. Hartt) Am. Natural. **1**: 642.
— Vegetation in. (C. F. P. von Martius) Ed. New Philos. J. **9**: 35.
— Visit to. (T. Ewbank) Harper, **7**: 721. **10**: 721. **11**: 34.
— — Walsh's Notices of. (S. E. Sewall) Chr. Exam. **11**: 150.—Meth. M. **54**: 103.
— Waterfalls of, Day among. Argosy, **14**: 229.
— Winter in, Recollections of a. (F. W. Longman) Fraser, **85**: 612.
See Amazon; Rio de Janeiro; Selva Desert; etc.
Brazilian Bride. Sharpe, **13**: 20, 27.
Brazilian Corals and Coral Reefs. (R. Rathbun) Am. Natural. **13**: 539.
Brazilian Poetry. Liv. Age, **55**: 705.
Brazilian Sandstone Reefs, Hartt on. (R. Rathbun) Am. Natural. **13**: 347.
Brazilian Sketches. (E. Treherne) Once a Week, **12**: 9, 135, 497. **13**: 439.

Brazilians of the Interior. Once a Week, **9**: 527.
Breac Moedog, or Shrine of St. Moedoc of Ferns. (Miss Stokes) Arch. **43**: 131.
Breach of Promise. Chamb. J. **33**: 257. All the Year, **47**: 297.
— Romantic. House. Words, **16**: 260.
Bread. Quar. **105**: 233.
— Adulteration of. (J. C. Draper) Galaxy, **10**: 184.
— Aerated. (A. H. Church) Nature, **19**: 174.
— — and fermented. (J. Dauglish) Am. J. Sci. **80**: 329.
— Chemical Examination of Bakers'. (C. M. Wetherill) J. Frankl. Inst. **59**: 386.
— Dainty. All the Year, **24**: 344.
— How to eat. 19th Cent. **10**: 341. Same art. Ecl. M. **97**: 688.
— Impurities of. Once a Week, **8**: 551.
— in the East. Penny M. **3**: 2.
— Making. All the Year, **2**: 440.
— — in Spain. Once a Week, **1**: 217.
— — New Method of. (J. Liebig) Ev. Sat. **7**: 618.
— Nutritive Qualities of. Blackw. **61**: 768.
— Real Brown. (A. H. Church) Nature, **18**: 229.
— Stale. Once a Week, **1**: 177.
— Town and Country. All the Year, **46**: 374.
— we eat. (M. Dwight) Potter Am. Mo. **17**: 450.
— Wheaten. Penny M. **5**: 74.
Bread cast on the Waters. House. Words, **11**: 326.
Bread of Life, Sermon by J. W. Nevin. (E. M. Epstein) Ref. Q. **26**: 317.
Breadfinder, The. (E. Youl) Howitt, **2**: 294–408.
Breadstuffs. De Bow, **21**: 428.
— Cost and Demand of. (R. Williams) Hunt, **16**: 557.
— Exports of, from the United States. (R. H. Edmonds) Internat. R. **11**: 450.
— Production and Export of. (J. Smith) Hunt, **15**: 575.
Bread-Fruit Tree. Penny M. **1**: 333.
Breakdown, A; a Tale. (K. S. Macquoid) Temp. Bar, **25**: 250.
Breakfast. Temp. Bar, **46**: 109.
— and Breakfasting. Godey, **46**: 549.
— in Bed. (G. A. Sala) Temp. Bar, **6**: 333, 492. **7**: 69–489. **8**: 70–503. **9**: 56, 209.
— Something about. Ev. Sat. **3**: 219.
Breakfast Table, Chats at. (M. H. Ford) Potter Am. Mo. **15**: 282.
Breaking a Butterfly. (G. A. Lawrence) Tinsley, **3**: 1–592. **4**: 12–569. **5**: 100.
Breaking Hearts. (M. A. Howe) Knick. **63**: 165–507.
Breaking of the Shell; a Tale. Belgra. **16**: 183.
Breakneck, Ballad of. (M. C. Pike) Harper, **50**: 50.
Breakwater, Delaware, Observations at, 1830. J. Frankl. Inst. **33**: 10.
— Parlby's, Description of. J. Frankl. Inst. **37**: 145.
Breakwaters, Artificial. (A. G. Findlay) J. Frankl. Inst. **50**: 8. — Penny M. **5**: 222.
Breath, Phenomena of. Ecl. M. **54**: 546.
— of Life. (J. C. Draper) Galaxy, **8**: 755. — (W. Crookes) Pop. Sci. R. **1**: 91. Same art. Liv. Age, **73**: 142. Same art. Ecl. M. **57**: 180.
Breathing, Lecture on. (C. Kingsley) Good Words, **10**: 498.
— Philosophy of. (J. S. Schanck) Princ. **37**: 135.
— Smoke, etc., Appliances for. (E. M. Shaw) Ecl. Engin. **12**: 426.
— under Water, Fleuss's Method. Chamb. J. **57**: 193, 352. Same art. Ecl. M. **95**: 121.
Breay, J. G., Memoir of. Chr. Obs. **41**: 221.
Brébeuf, Father John de. (R. H. Clarke) Cath. World, **13**: 512, 623.
Brébeuf Family. (M. P. Thompson) Cath. World, **30**: 249.
Breck, Edward. N. E. Reg. **2**: 255.
Breck, Samuel, School Reminiscences of. Am. J. Educ. **28**: 145.
Breckenridge, Rev. John. (C. Hodge) Princ. **18**: 585.
Breckenridge, Robert J., Theology of. (D. P. Noyes) Bib. Sac. **16**: 763.
Breckenridge, John C., with portrait. Dem. R. **38**: 1. — Dem. R. **30**: 202.
— Life of. Dem. R. **38**: 146.
— Military Operations of. So. Hist. Pap. **7**: 257, 317, 385.
Brecon Bridge; a Poem. (F. T. Palgrave) Cornh. **22**: 98.
Bred in the Bone. (A. Andrews) Bentley, **57**: 372, 529, 598. **58**: 60–483.
Bred in the Bone. Chamb. J. **47**: 417–806.
Brederode, Gerbrand, Poems of. Lond. M. **8**: 141.
Breech-Loaders. Cornh. **14**: 342. **16**: 177. **19**: 583.
— and their Inventors. (C. Waddy) Belgra. **17**: 325.
— for the British Army. Temp. Bar, **4**: 459. **5**: 183. **12**: 381.
Breeds of British Cattle, Low on. Mo. R. **151**: 512.
Breezes, Land and Sea, Height of. (O. T. Sherman) Am. J. Sci. **119**: 300.
Brehon Law of Ireland. Dub. R. **68**: 385.
— Commission on. Irish Q. **2**: 659.
Breitmann in Politics. (C. G. Leland) Lippinc. **3**: 275, 373, 498. *See* Leland, C. G.
Bremen. Penny M. **8**: 257.
— Lectures at, 1868. Dub. R. **73**: 102.
— Water-Works of. Ecl. Engin. **17**: 399.
Bremer, Frederika. Liv. Age, **3**: 52. — (L. M. Barker) Univ. Q. **2**: 168. — Art J. **18**: 53. Same art. Ecl. M. **67**: 199. — Eng. Dom. M. **24**: 156, 175. — Sharpe, **50**: 134. — Mo. Rel. M. **35**: 187.
— and her Swedish Sisters. Ecl. R. **124**: 1. Same art. Liv. Age, **90**: 259.
— Easter Offering. Ecl. R. **92**: 46.
— Hawthorne's Visit to. Ev. Sat. **11**: 323.
— The Home. Tait, n. s. **10**: 449. — Mo. R. **161**: 215.
— in Switzerland and Italy. Blackw. **89**: 682.
— in United States and Cuba. Victoria, **7**: 1. Same art. Liv. Age, **89**: 675.
— Novels of. (W. B. O. Peabody) No. Am. **57**: 128. — (J. R. Lowell) No. Am. **58**: 480. — (L. J. Hall) Chr. Exam. **34**: 381. — (H. J. Burton) Chr. Exam. **38**: 169. — Ecl. R. **79**: 553. — Fraser, **28**: 505. — Liv. Age, **20**: 529. — (S. Laing) No. Brit. **1**: 168. — Dub. R. **17**: 351. — Chr. Rem. **8**: 13. **17**: 18.
— President's Daughters. Tait, n. s. **10**: 660. — Mo. R. **162**: 224.
— Sketches of Every-Day Life. Mo. R. **163**: 189.
— Strife and Peace. Tait, n. s. **11**: 141. — Mo. R. **162**: 484.
— Summer Journey. Westm. **52**: 227. Same art. Liv. Age, **23**: 472.
— Theology of. (W. P. Lunt) Chr. Exam. **36**: 98.
— Visit to. (M. S. de Vere) Hours at Home, **6**: 148.
— — to Cooper's Landing. Godey, **40**: 125.
Brendan, Saint. (M. Arnold) Fraser, **62**: 133.
— Voyage of. Dub. Univ. **31**: 89.
— — a Poem. (F. Parke) Dub. Univ. **89**: 471.
Brent, J. F., Portrait of. Dem. R. **22**: 241.
Brenton, Albert, Memoirs of. Tait, n. s. **17**: 208.
Brenton, Sir Jahleel, Memoirs of. Quar. **79**: 273. Same art. Liv. Age, **13**: 289. — Chr. Obs. **47**: 166, 226, 293.
Brenton, William, Memoir of. (J. B. Moore) Am. Q. Reg. **14**: 285.
Brentano, Bettina. For. Q. **34**: 304.
Brentano, Clement. Month, **19**: 183.
Brentano Miniatures. (C. Ruland) F. Arts Q. **4**: 27, 311.
Brereton, History of Family of. (Sir F. Dwarris) Arch. **33**: 55.
Brereton Church, Paintings in Window of. (S. Pegge) Arch. **10**: 50. — (S. Denne) Arch. **10**: 334.
Brescia, Italy; Under the Lemons. Once a Week, **7**: 289.

Breslau, Legends of. (J. Oxenford) Colburn, 86: 21.
Bressant. (J. Hawthorne) Appleton, 9: 241–680.
Bresse, Sidney, Sketch of, with portrait. Lakeside, 3: 1.
Brest, Naval School at. Lond. Soc. 30: 117.
Bretagne. *See* Brittany.
Breton, Jules. (R. Ménard) Portfo. 6: 2.
Breton Ballads, Translations of. Blackw. 86: 488.
Breton Bible. (S. P. Tregelles) Kitto, 39: 95.
Breton, Cape. *See* Cape Breton.
Breton College under Napoleon. U. S. Cath. M. 2: 8, 73. — Mo. R. 158: 541.
Breton Legends. All the Year, 10: 318. 17: 547.
Breton Life, Peculiarities of. Dub. Univ. 73: 540.
Breton Peasant-Play. Cornh. 37: 76.
Breton Poetry. Dub. R. 4: 105.
Breton Story, Modern. Bentley, 64: 250.
Breton Students, Insurrection of. Quar. 70: 73.
Bretons and Britons. (H. Jones) Once a Week, 9: 12.
— Faith and Poetry of. (M. Barker) Cath. World, 7: 567. 8: 123.
— Habits and Superstitions of. For. Q. 31: 347. Same art. Ecl. Mus. 3: 58.
— Minstrelsy of. (J. G. Lockhart) Quar. 68: 57.
Bretschneider, K. G. Autobiography. Bib. Sac. 9: 657. 10: 229.
Brett, Edwin John, with portrait. Colburn, 169: 162.
Breviary and Missal. (J. Hall) Princ. 28: 601.
— Famous, at Venice. (Mrs. J. W. Davis) Harper, 60: 343.
— Roman. Blackw. 127: 80.
Brevity, Brief Observations on. Lond. M. 5: 359.
Brewer, Rev. Jehoiada, Memoir of. Cong. M. 1: 169.
Brewers' Company, London. Antiquary, 1: 185.
Brewery, Barclay, Perkins, & Co.'s. Penny M. 10: 121.
Brewing in Japan. (R. W. Atkinson) Nature, 18: 521.
— of Malt Liquors. Pamph. 2: 477.
— of Soma; a Poem. (J. G. Whittier) Atlan. 29: 473.
Brewster, Abraham, Rt. Hon., with portrait. Dub. Univ. 83: 650.
Brewster, Sir David. Brit. Q. 2: 575. — with portrait, Fraser, 6: 416. — with portrait, Ecl. M. 34: 277. — with portrait, Hogg, 3: 289. — Internat. M. 1: 312. — Liv. Age, 62: 3.
— Life of. (Mrs. S. B. Herrick) So. R. n. s. 14: 53.
Brewster, Elder William. (H. M. Dexter) N. E. Reg. 18: 18. — (E. D. Neill) Hist. M. 16: 70.
Brian O'Linn. Bentley, 18: 479, 576. 19: 1–541. 20: 1–608. 21: 91–413. 22: 42–623.
Briars and Thorns. (B. Marryat) Bentley, 59: 87–583. 60: 33–632. 61: 44, 179.
Bribery and Corruption. (A. Fonblanque, jr.) Once a Week, 2: 170. — Chamb. J. 18: 183. — (S. C. Buxton) 19th Cent. 8: 824.
— — Commercial. Fraser, 86: 1.
— and its Remedies. Fraser, 74: 741.
— Anti-Bribery Society. Ecl. R. 86: 513.
— at Elections. Westm. 25: 485. 48: 331. 51: 145. — Ecl. R. 88: 335.
— — and the Ballot. Westm. 115: 443.
— Legislative. (A. G. Sedgwick) Nation, 9: 105.
Bric-à-Brac. (S. Whiting) Once a Week, 6: 402.
— Age of Knickknacks. (B. Murphy) Lippinc. 18: 197.
— and Lace. Blackw. 119: 59.
— High Prices of. (J. G. Wilson) Art J. 30: 313.
— Hunting. (H. B. Hall) Belgra. 2: 204, 411. 4: 99, 459. 5: 92. 9: 505.
Brice, W., Minister of Henley. Cong. 7: 214.
Brick and Marble of the Middle Ages. Ecl. Engin. 12: 297.
— and Stone, Absorption of Moisture by. (J. C. Draper) Ecl. Engin. 6: 127.
Brick and Stone Buildings, Antiquity of. (J. Essex) Arch. 4: 73.
Bricks, Ancient Persian. (B. Vaughan) No. Am. 4: 328.
— and Brick-Making. Ecl. Engin. 19: 353. — Chamb. J. 57: 428. — Penny M. 12: 262.
— Compressed-Stone. (J. J. Bodmer) Ecl. Engin. 10: 245.
— History of. Ecl. Engin. 24: 77.
— Moulded, Use of. (G. C. Mason) Am. Arch. 1: 131, 141.
— of the Modern Babylon. Lond. M. 13: 69.
— Red, in Architecture. Am. Arch. 8: 245.
— Resistance of, to a crushing Force. (G. S. Green, jr.) Pract. M. 3: 178.
— Roman, compared with modern. (J. Webster) Arch. 2: 184.
— Unburned. (M. Hassenfratz) J. Frankl. Inst. 6: 233.
Brick Architecture. Ecl. Engin. 10: 247.
— of the North of Germany. (A. Nesbitt) Arch. 39: 93.
Brick Buildings, Antiquity of, in England. (C. Lyttelton) Arch. 1: 140.
Brick Fields of England. St. James, 28: 621.
Brick-Kiln, Steam. (H. W. Adams) Pract. M. 6: 157. — (H. W. Adams) J. Frankl. Inst. 101: 161.
Brick Machine. Pract. M. 7: 16.
— Durand's and Marais's. Pract. M. 6: 87.
— Harman's. (H. Howson) J. Frankl. Inst. 62: 345.
Brick-Making. Pract. M. 7: 113.
— in Chicago. (P. B. Wight) Am. Arch. 2: 289.
Brick Masonry made impervious to Water. (W. L. Dearborn) Ecl. Engin. 3: 170.
Brick Moon, The. (E. E. Hale) Atlan. 24: 451, 603, 679. 25: 215.
Brick Walls, Incrustations on. (W. Trautwine) J. Frankl. Inst. 105: 259.
Brickwork, Architectural Treatment of. Ecl. Engin. 4: 57.
— Mediæval. Art J. 7: 101.
— Strength of. Ecl. Engin. 7: 425.
Brickyards, English. Ev. Sat. 10: 599. 11: 23.
Brictric of Bristol; a Poem. (M. Collins) Dub. Univ. 46: 341.
Bridal, The. Fraser, 65: 212.
— of the Adriatic; a Poem. Dub. Univ. 13: 618.
— of Carriogvarah. Dub. Univ. 13: 405.
— of Galtrim; a Poem. (S. Lover) Once a Week, 2: 76.
— of Manstone Court. (H. Curling) Bentley, 18: 394.
— of Melcha. Dub. Univ. 23: 508.
— of Pennacook; a Poem. (J. G. Whittier) Dem. R. 15: 233. 16: 537.
— of Triermain. Quar. 9: 480.
Bridal Customs of the Irish. Colburn, 5: 185.
Bridal Poetry. (R. W. Buchanan) St. James, 9: 55.
Bridal Veil; a Tale. (Mrs. Trail) Canad. Mo. 2: 289.
Bridal Visit, The First. Fraser, 32: 707.
Bride of Bullay; a Tale of the Moselle. Temp. Bar, 54: 103.
— of Eberstein. (H. Thompson) Once a Week, 17: 115. Same art. Cath. World, 5: 847.
— of the Fiord; a Tale. Dub. Univ. 32: 460.
— of Glen Arva; a Tale. Dub. Univ. 53: 474.
— of Lindorf. (L. E. Landon) Colburn, 47: 449.
— of Modern Italy. Lond. M. 9: 357.
— of Monstoirac. Liv. Age, 42: 195.
— of Torrisdell; a Poem. (H. H. Boyesen) Atlan. 31: 159.
Bride-Catching. (J. F. McLennan) Argosy, 2: 31.
Bride's Pass. (H. Keddie) Liv. Age, 140: 42–783. 141: 117–332. 142: 230–788. 143: 30.
Bride's Reverie. (M. E. Hewitt) Internat. M. 1: 37.
Bride's Tragedy. Sharpe, 7: 71, 145.
Brides, A Book for. All the Year, 26: 197.
— for Sale in Egypt. Liv. Age, 46: 676.
— of London Society, B. C. 48–A. D. 1714. Lond. Soc. 24: 28–506. 26: 455. 28: 356.
Bridegroom of Barna. Blackw. 48: 680.

Bridekirk Font. (H. Howard) Arch. **14**: 113.
— Runic Inscription on. (W. Hamper) Arch. **19**: 379.
Bridemaid's Story. (R. S. Willis) Cath. World, **11**: 232.
Bridgate in the 17th Century. Lond. M. **10**: 599.
Bridge across the British Channel. Chamb. J. **29**: 325.
— Albert, Cylinders of. (C. Kingsford) Ecl. Engin. **6**: 237.
— Blackfriars. J. Frankl. Inst. **88**: 19, 385.
— — Report on State of, 1833. J. Frankl. Inst. **16**: 283, 342.
— Bollman's Iron Suspension Railroad. (H. Haupt) J. Frankl. Inst. **59**: 289.
— Boutet. Ecl. Engin. **2**: 494.
— Britannia. Ecl. Engin. **19**: 256. — J. Frankl. Inst. **44**: 300.
— — History and Construction of. (G. Grove) J. Frankl. Inst. **51**: 299.
— Charing Cross. (H. Hayter) J. Frankl. Inst. **76**: 237.
— Chelsea Suspension, Construction of. J. Frankl. Inst. **76**: 73.
— Chester, Failure of, 1847. J. Frankl. Inst. **44**: 149, 217.
— Chestnut St., Philadelphia, Superstructure of. (S. Kneass) J. Frankl. Inst. **89**: 92.
— Composite, Description of. (S. H. Long) J. Frankl. Inst. **45**: 202, 258.
— Delaware, 1870. (H. Orr) J. Frankl. Inst. **91**: 1.
— East River. (W. A. Roebling) Ecl. Engin. **7**: 190. **5**: 381. — Appleton, **19**: 1.
— — Caissons of. (F. Collingwood) Ecl. Engin. **7**: 399.
— — in 1867, Report. (J. A. Roebling) J. Frankl. Inst. **84**: 242, 305.
— Finley's Chain. Portfo. (Den.) **3**: 441
— Floating, of Hooghly River. Ecl. Engin. **18**: 474.
— Girard Avenue, Philadelphia. (R. Hering and T. C. Clarke) J. Frankl. Inst. **97**: 179.
— Hannibal. Ecl. Engin. **5**. 306.
— Howe Truss. (C. L. Crandall) Ecl. Engin. **21**: 475. — (L. M. Prevost) J. Frankl. Inst. **33**: 289.
— — Angle-Block of. (J. M. Richardson) J. Frankl. Inst. **59**: 306.
— — Wooden. (J. W. Hill) Ecl. Engin. **21**: 281.
— Hudson River Suspension. Ecl. Engin. **2**: 623.
— Kansas City. (O. Chanute and G. Morison) Ecl. Engin. **3**: 225. — J. Frankl. Inst. **88**: 177.
— — Destruction of a Pier of. Ecl. Engin. **3**: 404.
— Keokuk and Hamilton, Iowa. J. Frankl. Inst. **92**: 47. — (J. S. Smith) J. Frankl. Inst. **93**: 188, 249. — Ecl. Engin. **5**: 374.
— London, Report on the New, 1832. (C. Davy) J. Frankl. Inst. **14**: 205.
— Louisville. Ecl. Engin. **2**: 484.
— Menai Straits. Chamb. J. **10**: 113.
— — Proposed, 1846. J. Frankl. Inst. **41**: 240. **42**: 24, 85. **43**: 303.
— — Suspension, Effect of Wind on, 1839. J. Frankl. Inst. **33**: 210. **37**: 371.
— Minneapolis Suspension. (T. M. Griffith) Ecl. Engin. **18**: 248.
— Mississippi, 1868. J. Frankl. Inst. **86**: 311. **87**: 27.
— Niagara Suspension. (P. W. Barlow) J. Frankl. Inst. **71**: 76–237. — (S. Keefer) Ecl. Engin. **2**: 318. — Chamb. J. **41**: 758.
— — Condition of, 1860. (J. A. Roebling) J. Frankl. Inst. **70**: 361.
— of Béton or Concrete, Description of. (M. Lebrun) J. Frankl. Inst. **35**: 163.
— over the Alleghany River. J. Frankl. Inst. **85**: 30.
— over Cumberland River, Tenn. (F. W. Vaughan) J. Frankl. Inst. **92**: 51.
— over the Ouse, Hydraulic Swing. (Sir W. Armstrong) J. Frankl. Inst. **88**: 239.
Bridge over the Thames, Railroad. (Mr. Lawford) J. Frankl. Inst. **88**: 99.
— over the Theiss, and Tubular Foundations. (M. Cezanne) J. Frankl. Inst. **72**: 1–217.
— Pennsylvania Railroad. (J. M. Wilson) J. Frankl. Inst. **89**: 198.
— — Iron Arched. (H. Haupt) J. Frankl. Inst. **48**: 181.
— Quincy Railway. (T. C. Clarke) Ecl. Engin. **3**: 49.
— Roche-Bernard Suspension. (J. Bennett) J. Frankl. Inst. **71**: 95, 145, 227.
— St. Charles. Ecl. Engin. **5**: 178.
— St. Louis. Ecl. Engin. **1**: 46, 1050. — (J. B. Eads) Ecl. Engin. **4**: 67.
— Suspension, at Bath. (Lord Western) J. Frankl. Inst. **30**: 201.
— — Patent for. (S. H. Long) J. Frankl. Inst. **28**: 325. **32**: 175.
— Susquehanna. J. Frankl. Inst. **83**: 6, 239.
— Tay. *See* Tay Bridge.
— Thames, Barnett's Scheme for a new. Pract. M. **6**: 139.
— Victoria, at Montreal. Chamb. J. **35**: 114.
— — Report on. (R. Stephenson) Canad. J. n. s. **1**: 467.
Bridge of Life; a Poem. (H. Macmillan) Good Words, **16**: 436.
Bridge of Sighs; a Yachting Story. All the Year, **23**: 115–402.
Bridges. J. Frankl. Inst. **36**: 80.
— Accidents to, in America. (G. L. Vase) Am. Arch. **8**: 196, 221.
— — Means of averting. Ecl. Engin. **13**: 305.
— American *versus* English. Ecl. Engin. **12**: 202.
— and Culverts, Angle of. (E. Morris) J. Frankl. Inst. **29**: 290.
— and Ferries. J. Frankl. Inst. **13**: 412.
— and Roofs, Shreve on. (A. P. Boller) J. Frankl. Inst. **95**: 229.
— and Tunnels, Centers of. (J. B. McMaster) Ecl. Engin. **13**: 385, 481.
— Arch. (W. H. Baker) Ecl. Engin. **22**: 33.
— — Calculations of Strains in. (C. Pfeifer) Ecl. Engin. **14**: 481.
— Arches for, Formula for proportioning. (J. C. Trautwine) J. Frankl. Inst. **68**: 301.
— Camber in. (A. P. Boller) J. Frankl. Inst. **81**: 289. **82**: 15.
— Combination, for Railroads. (J. O. Patterson) Ecl. Engin. **11**: 398.
— Construction of. (W. E. Merrill) J. Frankl. Inst. **89**: 328. — (W. E. Merrill) Ecl. Engin. **3**: 89. — (J. W. Murphy) J. Frankl. Inst. **67**: 145, 241. — Ecl. Engin. **1**: 233. **2**: 268. — J. Frankl. Inst. **89**: 100.
— — considered normally. (J. W. Murphy) J. Frankl. Inst. **96**: 242.
— — Improvement in. Am. J. Sci. **38**: 276.
— — of big. Ecl. Engin. **23**: 324.
— — Open Questions in. (F. H. Smith) Ecl. Engin. **10**: 61.
— — Principles of. Ecl. Engin. **4**: 27.
— Continuous, Theory of. (M. Merriman) Ecl. Engin. **15**: 145, 193.
— Cylinders for. Ecl. Engin. **7**: 631.
— Erroneous Formula for. (E. A. Harris) Ecl. Engin. **11**: 183.
— Floating and Flying. Penny M. **12**: 111, 122.
— Foundations of. (T. Page) J. Frankl. Inst. **77**: 21.
— — Pneumatic. (O. Chanute) J. Frankl. Inst. **85**: 387. **86**: 17, 89.
— Framed, Maximum Stress in. (W. Cain) Ecl. Engin. **19**: 71, 146, 289.
— Historical. Ecl. Engin. **22**: 425.

Bridges, Hydraulic Swing. (Sir W. E. Armstrong) Ecl. Engin. 1: 988.
— in alluvial Districts, Railroad. J. Frankl. Inst. 75: 168, 233.
— Iron. Quar. 104: 75. Same art. Liv. Age, 59: 83. —J. Frankl. Inst. 109: 56.
— — American. (Z. Colburn) J. Frankl. Inst. 76: 240.
— — Construction of. (E. Howland) Lippinc. 11: 9.
— Iron Girder, Railroad. J. Frankl. Inst. 71: 156.
— Iron Truss, Merrill on. (C. F. Johnson) J. Frankl. Inst. 93: 316. — J. Frankl. Inst. 89: 107.
— Long's Wooden or Frame. J. Frankl. Inst. 9: 231, 380. 10: 252.
— Large Span. Ecl. Engin. 2: 20. — J. Frankl. Inst. 76: 235. 89: 234.
— Military. (G. R. Gleig) Ed. R. 98: 448. — (Sir W. Scott) Quar. 18: 423.
— — Our System of. Ecl. Engin. 3: 310.
— Movable. Ecl. Engin. 4: 391.
— of India. Ecl. Engin. 7: 100.
— Proportion of Heads of Eye-Bars. (C. Macdonald) Ecl. Engin. 12: 8.
— Proportions of Pins used in. (C. H. Bender) Ecl. Engin. 10: 28. — (V. Wood) Ecl. Engin. 9: 504. — Ecl. Engin. 9: 289.
— Railway. (J. A. Roebling) Ecl. Engin. 2: 78.
— — Calculations for. (E. S. Gould) Ecl. Engin. 11: 433.
— — Rapid Corrosion of Iron in. (W. Kent) Pract. M. 5: 265.
— — Strength of Materials for. (G. Buchanan) J. Frankl. Inst. 46: 1, 152. 47: 223. 49: 201.
— Road and Railway, Modern Examples of. (T. C. Clarke) Ecl. Engin. 8: 248.
— Rolling and Swing. Ecl. Engin. 4: 514.
— Something about. Sharpe, 39: 121.
— Specifications for. (J. M. Wilson) J. Frankl. Inst. 100: 116.
— Stone, Method of proportioning. (J. C. Trautwine) J. Frankl. Inst. 59: 14.
— Suspension. (C. Bender) Ecl. Engin. 4: 594. — Ecl. Engin. 11: 265. — Mo. R. 129: 516.
— — and Arch Truss. (S. W. Robinson) J. Frankl. Inst. 77: 152, 361.
— — Cable-Making for. (W. Heldenbrand) Ecl. Engin. 17: 171, 193, 289.
— — Construction of. (M. le Blanc) J. Frankl. Inst. 35: 95.
— — — of a rigid. (C. Köpcke) J. Frankl. Inst. 71: 316.
— — Deflection of. (H. Cox) J. Frankl. Inst. 72: 154.
— — Disturbances of. (Lukin and Conder) J. Frankl. Inst. 64: 231.
— — Modern American. (C. Clericetti) Ecl. Engin. 23: 111.
— — Montrose. (J. M. Rendel) J. Frankl. Inst. 33: 116.
— — New System of, 1863. (S. W. Robinson) J. Frankl. Inst. 76: 145.
— Suspension Girder, for Railroads. J. Frankl. Inst. 72: 289, 361.
— Temporary, Art of making. (A. W. Drayson) Art J. 17: 237.
— Town's Improvement. Am. J. Sci. 3: 158.
— Trusses for, Maximum Stresses of. (W. Baldwin) Ecl. Engin. 19: 538.
— Tubular. Liv. Age, 19: 209.
— — Britannia and Conway. (Sir F. B. Head) Quar. 85: 399. Same art. Ecl. M. 19: 193. Same art Liv. Age, 24: 353. — (W. C. Unwin) Pop. Sci. R. 1: 416.
— — Resistance of vertical Plates of. (H. Haupt) J. Frankl. Inst. 56: 217.
— — Stephenson and Fairbairn's. (Sir D. Brewster) No. Brit. 13: 399.
Bridges, Charles, Obituarys of. Chr. Obs. 69: 471.
Bridges Genealogy. (J. W. Dean) N. E. Reg. 8: 232.
Bridget of the Moor. (E. Meteyard) Reliquary, 2: 117.
Bridgeton, Me., Survey of, in 1766. N. E. Reg. 28: 63.
Bridgewater, Duke of. Chamb. J. 1: 407.
— Canal of, and James Brindley. Penny M. 5: 363.
Bridgewater Family. Cornh. 4: 348.
Bridgewater Bequest. Ed. R. 58: 422.
Bridgewater Gallery. Fraser, 44: 210.
Bridgewater, Mass., Ministers of. Am. Q. Reg. 8: 149.
— Records of. N. E. Reg. 19: 200.
— — of Marriages in. N. E. Reg. 21: 225.
Bridgewater Treatises. Quar. 50: 1. — So. Lit. Mess. 5: 211, 548. — Fraser, 8: 65, 258. 12: 415. 16: 719.
— Bell's. Mo. R. 132: 424. — (H. Bronson) Chr. Q. Spec. 6: 54.
— Buckland's. Dub. Univ. 8: 692. — Fraser, 59: 227. Same art. Ecl. M. 46: 518. — Ed. R. 65: 1. — Quar. 56: 31.
— Chalmer's. Mo. R. 131: 387. — (T. P. Thompson) Westm. 20: 1. — Select J. 3: 50. — Mus. 24: 1.
— Kidd's. Mo. R. 131: 499.
— Roget's. (F. W. P. Greenwood) Chr. Exam. 20: 137.
— Whewell's. Mo. R. 131: 561.
See names of each of the authors.
Bridging navigable Waters in United States. (G. K. Warren) Ecl. Engin. 22: 296.
Bridgman, Frederick A. (E. Strahan) Harper, 63: 694.
— and his Paintings. Art J. 30: 225.
Bridgman, Laura. (G. S. Hall) Mind, 4: 149. — (S. G. Howe) Am. J. Educ. 4: 383. — (M. Howitt) Howitt, 2: 226. — (J. G. Palfrey) No. Am. 52: 467. — Chr. Exam. 28: 359. — Penny M. 14: 222, 230.
— Education of. (S. G. Howe) Mind, 1: 263.
— Life and Education of. (G. S. Hall) Nation, 27: 259.
— Vocal Language of. (D. Wilson) Canad. J. n. s. 11: 113.
Bridgnorth, Seal of the Bailiffs of the Liberty of. (F. Townsend) Arch. 15: 380.
Bridlington Priory, Survey of. (J. Caley) Arch. 19: 270.
Brieg, Dorothea Sybilla, Duchess of. House. Words, 2: 581.
Brigadier, The. (I. Tourgeneff) Temp. Bar, 63: 486.
Brigandage, Britons and. Tinsley, 7: 421.
— in Greece, 1869. Cornh. 21: 699.
— in Macedonia. Cornh. 44: 355. Same art. Appleton, 26: 469.
— in Naples. St. James, 5: 266.
— in the Pontifical States. Colburn, 142: 253. Same art. Ecl. M. 70: 584.
— in Sicily. Ed. R. 145: 487.
— Italian. (W. Chambers) Chamb. J. 54: 4-727. — (W. D. Howells) No. Am. 101: 162. — Blackw. 93: 576.
— — Moens on. Westm. 86: 22. Same art. Liv. Age, 90: 340.
— Peep into. Liv. Age, 87: 285.
Brigands. All the Year, 25: 256.
— Brush with. Bentley, 53: 353.
— English. Tinsley, 10: 234.
— Greek. Ev. Sat. 9: 307, 391.
— in Asia Minor, Lady's Encounter with. Cornh. 23: 91. Same art. Ecl. M. 76: 357.
— in Italy. All the Year, 15: 91. — Chamb. J. 43: 131. — Ecl. R. 121: 442.
— — Past and present. Once a Week, 8: 357.
— — Three Months with. (A. H. Guernsey) Harper, 33: 286.
— — Visit to some. Ev. Sat. 6: 626.
— Massacre by, at Marathon, 1870. (C. K. Tuckerman) Harper, 45: 434.
— Mexican. N. Ecl. 5: 282.
— Modern. Penny M. 11: 117, 130, 257.

Brigands of Sicily. (L. Monti) Atlan. **37**: 58.
— Pre-Islamitic of Arabia. (W. G. Palgrave) Macmil. **26**: 157. Same art. Liv. Age, **114**: 131, 416.
— Rencontre with. (A. Smith) Bentley, **9**: 375.
— Roman. Penny M. **11**: 20.
Briggs, George N., Portrait of. Am. Whig R. **10**: 443.
Briggs, George W., Discourses of. (C. Robbins) Chr. Exam. **40**: 233.
Briggs, J. J. (L. Jewitt) Reliquary, **17**: 49, 75.
Brigham, Charles Henry. Unita. R. **11**: 325.
Bright, John. (C. Logan) Galaxy. **6**: 115. — (J. McCarthy) Galaxy, **7**: 36. Same art. N. Ecl. **4**: 257. — with portrait, Scrib. **19**: 576. — with portrait, Ev. Sat. **9**: 322. — (W. F. Mallalieu) Meth. Q. **26**: 407. — (S. F. Page) Macmil. **25**: 344. Same art. Ecl. M. **78**: 479. — (G. M. Towle) Contin. Mo. **1**: 525. — (G. M. Towle) Putnam, **13**: 479. — with portrait, (A. Young) Appleton, **7**: 12. — with portrait, Ecl. M. **61**: 524. — Blackw. **100**: 728.
— as an Orator. (N. C. Tyler) Nation, **4**: 436, 477.
— at Home. (R. J. Hinton) Galaxy, **5**: 288.
— Career of. Once a Week, **24**: 31.
— Early Life of. Cong. **7**: 107.
— English Radicals and. (G. M. Towle) Atlan. **16**: 177.
— painted by himself. Nat. R. **10**: 522.
— Political Portrait of. St. James, **24**: 678.
— Return to the Ministry, 1874. Brit. Q. **59**: 159.
— Speeches. Brit. Q. **48**: 171. — (J. Moncrieff) Ed. R. **127**: 269. — No. Brit. **49**: 484. — Westm. **91**: 107. — New Q. **7**: 353.
Bright, Jonathan B., with portrait. (T. Hill) N. E. Reg. **35**: 117.
Bright Family, Fortunes of. Lond. Soc. **37**: 48.
Bright Genealogy, with portrait of T. Bright. (W. H. Whitmore) N. E. Reg. **13**: 97.
Bright College Days. Once a Week, **16**: 679, 709, 739.
Bright Room of Cranmore. Fraser, **41**: 41. Same art. Liv. Age, **24**: 422.
Brighthelmstone, Battle of. Drawing of. Arch. **24**: 292.
Brighton, England. Blackw. **50**: 461. — Lond. Soc. **2**: 90.
— Aquarium at. (W. S. Kent) Nature, **8**: 531.
— a Century ago. Temp. Bar, **36**: 170.
— Chain Pier at. Penny M. **2**: 454.
— Day with the Brookside Harriers at. Bentley, **43**: 48.
— in the Autumn. Colburn, **84**: 169.
— in November. Belgra. **10**: 176. — Broadw. **5**: 472.
— My Journey to. Chamb. J. **55**: 313.
— On the Beach at. St. James, **23**: 173.
— Pavilion Ball at, 1751. Colburn, **91**: 263.
— Reminiscences of. (J. H. Eyre) Belgra. **26**: 374. **28**: 203.
— Sketch of. Colburn, **61**: 163.
— Sketches at. Once a Week, **5**: 602, 632, 688. **6**: 43.
— Visit to. Lond. M. **16**: 460.
Brighton Convention and its Opponents, 1875. Lond. Q. **45**: 84.
Brighton Delilah. (G. Dixon) Belgra. **40**: supp. 52.
Brighton Ghosts. All the Year, **31**: 320.
Brighton Pier; a Poem. Belgra. **1**: 460.
Brighton, Mass., Ministers of. Am. Q. Reg. **11**: 398.
Brillat-Savarin, Anthelme. Irish Q. **8**: 461, 865. — St. James, **22**: 595.
— Anecdotes of. Cornh. **35**: 56. Same art. Ecl. M. **88**: 287.
Brilliant Affair; a Tale of the War. (W. C. Elam) Putnam, **12**: 483.
Brilliant Being; a Story. All the Year, **38**: 372, 395.
Brilliant Keeper. (Mrs. H. Wood) St. James, **3**: 359.
Brimham Rocks, England, Account of. (H. Rooke) Arch. **8**: 209.
Brinckley, R. C., with portrait. De Bow, **11**: 339.
Brindisi to Athens, From. Temp. Bar, **42**: 236.
Brindley, James. All the Year, **12**: 562. Same art. Cath. World, **1**: 238. — J. Frankl. Inst. **7**: 1.
— and Duke of Bridgewater's Canal. Penny M. **5**: 363.
— and the early Engineers. Lond. Q. **25**: 58.
Brines, Chemistry of. (C. A. Goessmann) Am. J. Sci. **94**: 77.
Brington and the Washington Family. Once a Week, **6**: 446.
Brinley, Francis, Catalogue of his Library, 1713. N. E. Reg. **12**: 75.
Brinsly, J. Ludus Literarius. Am. J. Educ. **24**: 186.
Brinsmead, John, and Sons. Colburn, **169**: 80.
Brion, Fredrika, and Goethe. Once a Week, **11**: 358.
Brisbane, Albert. Dem. R. **11**: 302.
Brisbane, A Night in. Colburn, **146**: 442.
Brisinga. Nature, **16**: 249.
Brissons, The. (C. Home) Macmil. **5**: 60.
Brissot, Memoirs of. (T. Sedgwick) No. Am. **38**: 177. — Mo. R. **148**: 416.
Bristed, Charles Astor. (R. G. White) Galaxy, **17**: 473, 545.
— Five Years in Trinity. Am. J. Educ. **28**: 437.
Bristles. (G. F. Emery) Overland, **10**: 280. — Chamb. J. **19**: 181.
Bristol, J. B., and his Paintings. Art J. **30**: 133.
Bristol, England. (L. S. Costello) Bentley, **20**: 170. — Gent. M. n. s. **13**: 290. — Penny M. **3**: 449, 478. — Sharpe, **22**: 204.
— Academy of. Am. Q. Reg. **12**: 68.
— Bishops of. (G. Burgess) Am. Church R. **19**: 177.
— Cathedral at. All the Year, **33**: 438. — Penny M. **14**: 85.
— Christian Work in. (H. A. Page) Good Words, **18**: 316.
— Church of St. Mary Redcliffe at. (G. Pryce) Arch. **35**: 279.
— Churches of. Fraser, **71**: 203.
— First common Seal of. (J. Dallaway) Arch. **21**: 79.
— in the 15th Century. Retros. **16**: 449.
— Incendiaries of, 1730. Chamb. J. **34**: 378.
— Here and there in. (A. S. Gibbs) Lippinc. **22**: 9.
— Military History of, in the 17th Century. (E. Turnor) Arch. **14**: 119.
— Riots in, 1831. All the Year, **17**: 606. — Blackw. **31**: 465. — Quar. **46**: 552.
— — Trial of Magistrates. Blackw. **32**: 956.
Bristol University College. Nature, 14: 470.
Bristol, Conn., Copper Mine at. (B. Silliman, jr., and J. S. Whitney) Am. J. Sci. **70**: 361.
Bristol, R. I., Census of, 1689. N. E. Reg. **34**: 404.
— Church Record, 1687–1710. N. E. Reg. **34**: 132, 259.
Bristol County, Mass., Ministers of. Am Q. Reg. **12**: 135
Bristow, B. H., and the Whiskey Ring. (H. V. Boynton) No. Am. **123**: 280.
Britain after the Romans. Mo. R. **141**: 18.
— Cæsar's Campaigns in. Ed. R. **154**: 37.
— Centuriation of Roman. (H. C. Coote) Arch. **42**: 127.
— Christianity in. (D. Inglis) Princ. **24**: 190. — Chr. Rem. **42**: 441.
— — Extinction of. Chr. Rem. **1**: 98.
— Condition of, from Cæsar to Claudius. (J. Y. Akerman) Arch. **33**: 177.
— Danes and Northmen in. Lond. Q. **3**: 216.
— Expedition of Augustus into. (W. H. Black) Arch. **44**: 65.
— Geoffrey of Monmouth's History of. (T. Wright) Arch. **32**: 335. — (C. M. Kirkland) Am. Whig R. **5**: 84.
— Greater or Lesser. (J. Vogel) Canad. Mo. **12**: 232.
— in the 1st Century, A. D. Dub. Univ. **66**: 41–698.
— Legends of Pre-Roman. (T. Gilray) Dub. Univ. **87**: 385.

Britain, Primeval Archæology of. (E. A. Freeman) No. Brit. 17: 459.
— Raised Beach of. (A. Geikie) Macmil. 5: 311.
— Roman Carrier in. (J. McCaul) Canad. J. n. s. 13: 136.
— Romans in. Ed. R. 94: 177.
— Wright's Early Inhabitants of. Tait, n. s. 19: 446.
See Britons; Great Britain.
Britain's Propensity; a Song. Blackw. 67: 389.
Britannia Tubular Bridge. *See* Bridge, Britannia; Bridges, Tubular.
British Admirals and their Biographers. Cornh. 15: 538.
British Agriculture. *See* Agriculture in Great Britain.
British Ambassadors and their Salaries. Mus. 16: 280.
— Sacrifice of, in Asia. For. Q. 34: 221. Same art. Liv. Age, 3: 3.
British America. (H. Y. Hind) Hunt, 51: 183, 262. — (Gen. Scammon) Cath. World, 13: 108. — (W. J. Stewart) Macmil. 6: 29. — Mus. 14: 400. 21: 107. — (S. F. Miller) De Bow, 6: 181. — Fraser, 5: 77. — Blackw. 92: 696. 100: 156. 108: 704. 109: 48. — Dub. Univ. 15: 93. — Ed. R. 119: 441. — Liv. Age, 63: 268. — Lond. Q. 23: 23. — Meth. M. 57: 36. — Once a Week, 6: 219.
— Adventures in the Northwest Territory. Colburn, 135: 185.
— Alexander's Explorations in. Hogg, 4: 239.
— and the United States, Boundaries between. Colburn, 124: 1.
— Commerce of. (G. R. Porter) Hunt, 10: 15.
— — with the United States, 1853. Westm. 62: 239.
— Commercial Relations with. (A. W. Ely) De Bow, 12: 225.
— Defenses of. St. James, 3: 217.
— Exploration through. Temp. Bar, 15: 544.
— from Norway to York. (H. M. Robinson) Lippinc. 23: 534.
— Growth of. Blackw. 76: 1.
— Importance of. (H. Y. Hind) Canad. J. n. s. 8: 409.
— in Winter. (W. B. Cheadle) Blackw. 100: 366.
— Indian Population of. (J. H. Lefroy) Am. J. Sci. 66: 189.
— Interior of. Nat. R. 13: 62.
— — Habitable. (J. Hector) Ed. New Philos. J. 71: 263.
— — Physical Features of. (J. Hector) Ed. New Philos. J. 71: 212.
— — New Colony in. Colburn, 121: 100.
— McGregor's. Blackw. 31: 907.
— Politics of. (C. Dunkin) No. Am. 49: 373.
— Progress and Resources of. (H. Y. Hind) J. Statis. Soc. 27: 82.
— Proposed Constitution for. (Goldwin Smith) Macmil. 11: 406.
— Route to the Pacific through. (H. Verney) Fraser, 79: 643.
— Seaboard of. Colburn, 124: 127.
— Telegraph Expedition through. Appleton, 11: 193–334.
— Trade of. Penny M. 7: 46, 50.
— Voyage with Voyageurs in. (H. M. Robinson) Appleton, 20: 246.
— Waddington on Route through. Colburn, 144: 1.
— Wheat-Fields of. Liv. Age, 142: 306.
— Who owns? Dem. R. 31: 113, 225.
See Canada; Hudson's Bay Company.
British and Continental Characteristics. No. Brit. 21: 45.
British and Foreign Bible Society, History of. Chr. Obs. 60: 162.
British and Foreign School Society. Am. J. Educ. 10: 371.
British Anti-State Church Association. Ecl. R. 80: 341. 83: 220. 88: 740. 94: 513.
British Anti-State Church Movement. Ecl. R. 92: 99.
British Archæological Association, Meeting at Winchester, 1845. Colburn, 75: 110.
British Archæological Association, Meeting at Warwick, 1847. Colburn, 80: 494.
British Arms and Soldiery, Ancient and modern. Ecl. M. 71: 1052.
British Army. *See* Great Britain, Army.
British Arrogance. Dem. R. 21: 314.
British Association for the Advancement of Science. Fraser, 14: 582. — Brit. & For. R. 1: 361. — Ecl. Mus. 3: 410, 443. — Am. J. Sci. 38: 93. — Liv. Age, 6: 347, 395, 499. — Brit. Q. 46: 354. — Canad. J. n. s. 2: 50. — Dub. Univ. 50: 271. — Lond. Q. 3: 513. — (J. Henry) Princ. 13: 132.
— Address at. (Sir D. Brewster) Am. J. Sci. 10: 305.
— Meetings at York and Oxford, 1831–32. Ed. R. 60: 263.
— — Manchester, 1842. Fraser, 26: 361.
— — Edinburgh, 1850. (Sir D. Brewster) No. Brit. 14: 235. Same art. Ecl. M. 22: 145.
— — Dublin, 1857. Ecl. M. 43: 50.
— — Oxford, 1860. Chr. Rem. 40: 237.
— — Manchester, 1861. Am. J. Sci. 82: 263. — Fraser, 64: 612. Same art. Ecl. M. 55: 74.
— — Cambridge, 1862. Lond. Q. 19: 362. — Ecl. M. 58: 134.
— — Bath, 1864. Sir C. Lyell's Address. Ecl. M. 63: 348.
— — Edinburgh, 1871. Nature, 4: 261–396.
— — Brighton, 1872. Nature, 6: 305–422.
— — Bradford, 1873. Nature, 8: 405–515.
— — Belfast, 1874. Nature, 10: 308–449.
— — Bristol, 1875. Nature, 12: 335–461.
— — Glasgow, 1876. Nature, 14: 170–476.
— — — Address at. (T. Andrews) Ecl. Engin. 15: 451.
— — Plymouth, 1877. Nature, 16: 301–404.
— — Dublin, 1878. Nature, 18: 403–505.
— — Sheffield, 1879. Nature, 20: 383–404.
— — Swansea, 1880. Nature, 22: 181–480.
— — York, 1881. Lond. Q. 57: 412. — Nature, 24: 401–461.
— Report of the Kew Committee, 1869–70. (J. P. Gassiot) Nature, 3: 55.
— Sketch of. Hogg, 12: 408.
British Churches, Ancient. Dub. R. 18: 128.
— Miall on. Ecl. R. 91: 78.
British Colonies. *See* Great Britain, Colonies.
— in America. *See* American Colonies.
British Colonial Empire. De Bow, 6: 310.
British Colonial Politics, 1848. (L. Sabine) No. Am. 67: 1.
British Colonial Trade. (J. H. Lanman) Hunt, 10: 38. — Am. Whig R. 10: 80.
British Columbia. (Col. Coffin) Canad. Mo. 3: 361. — (T. Evans) Overland, 4: 258. — Colburn, 115: 127. Knick. 52: 331. — Nat. R. 13: 340.
— and Columbia. Quar. 109: 1.
— and the Dominion. Canad. Mo. 10: 369.
— and Vancouver's Island. Fraser, 58: 493. — No. Brit. 35: 61.
— Condition of, 1866. Westm. 86: 429.
— Fishing in. Tinsley, 11: 302.
— From Cariboo to California. (W. F. Butler) Good Words, 19: 136–398.
— Overland Route to, Hind's. (W. Hincks) Canad. J. n. s. 7: 200.
— Recent Progress in. Colburn, 128: 50.
— Victoria to Winnipeg. (D. M. Gordon) Good Words, 21: 116, 158, 305.
British Commercial Policy. (T. P. Kettell) Hunt, 12: 538.
British Critics. (E. P. Whipple) No. Am. 61: 468.
— and Travelers. Dem. R. 14: 335.
— North's Specimens of. (J. Wilson) Blackw. 57: 133–771. 58: 114, 229, 366.
British Criticism. (A. H. Everett) No. Am. 31: 27.
British Empire. *See* Great Britain.

British Essayists, The. Penny M. 1: 31.
British Family Histories. (J. Haunay) Quar. 98: 289.
British Guiana. *See* Guiana, British.
British India. *See* India.
British Institution, The. Dub. Univ. 53: 315.
British Labor and Foreign Reciprocity. Blackw. 69: 112.
British Legion, The. Blackw. 42: 169.
British Literature. Anal. M. 2: 314.
British Manufacturing Industries. Nature, 14: 145. 15: 54.
British Matron. (G. C. Clark) Tinsley, 16: 114. Same art. Ecl. M. 84: 491.
British Merchant in Trouble. All the Year, 2: 345.
British Merchant Seamen. (W. Dawson), Fraser, 92: 736.
British Museum. Ed. R. 38: 379. — (G. M. Towle) Harper, 46: 198. — (J. H. Sheppard) N. E. Reg. 23: 73. — (B. B. Edwards) Bib. Sac. 5: 388. — (F. Lawrence) Sharpe, 9: 233. — All the Year, 22: 252. 26: 155. — Brit. Q. 6: 79. — Brit. & For. R. 4: 213. — Colburn, 89: 197. — Penny M. 8: 2. — (J. Holmes) Quar. 88: 136. — Quar. 92: 157. 104: 201. 124: 147.
— and National Gallery, 1852. Ecl. R. 96: 517.
— and Provincial Culture. (W. E. A. Axon) Lib. J. 2: 125.
— Commission on, 1849. (C. Patmore) Ed. R. 92: 371.
— Description of. Penny M. 1: 13-371. 2: 4.
— Egypt in. Month, 3: 279, 587. 4: 279, 366, 629.
— Egyptian Galleries. Temp. Bar, 4: 227. — Penny M. 4: 57. 7: 436.
— Etruscan Antiquities in. Penny M. 12: 20, 48.
— Farnese Statues at. (H. de Triqueti) F. Arts Q. 3: 203.
— Founders of. Lakeside, 7: 415.
— Greek Inscriptions in. (T. Tyrwhitt) Arch. 3: 230.
— Hidden Treasures of. Chamb. J. 25: 237.
— History of. Penny M. 5: 350-395.
— Late Additions to. Chamb. J. 51: 488.
— Library of. (W. P. Courtney) Fortn. 32: 585. — (J. Holmes) Quar. 88: 136. Same art. Liv. Age, 29: 337. Same art. Ecl. M. 22: 477. — Chamb. J. 26: 382. — (C. Patmore) Ed. R. 92: 371. — Ed. R. 109: 201. — (W. H. Russell) Ed. R. 139: 37. — (J. W. Jones) No. Brit. 15: 171. — Lib. J. 4: 161. — Lond. M. 13: 533. — Nature, 19: 253. 20: 33.
— — in 1851. Sharpe, 14: 77.
— — System of classifying Books in. (R. Garnett) Lib. J. 2: 194.
— Literary Gems of. Nat. M. 3: 54.
— MSS. from Egyptian Monasteries in. Quar. 77: 39.
— New Treasures in. Chamb. J. 52: 537.
— Reading-Room of. Bentley, 32: 527. — (E. L. Blanchard) Peop. J. 6: 43. — Chamb. J. 36: 129. — Penny M. 4: 487.
— — Notes in. Month, 7: 538.
— — Suggestions for improving. (J. Spedding) Fraser, 61: 773.
— — Visit to. Mo. Rel. M. 23: 24.
— Report on, 1836. Mo. R. 140: 46.
— Salaries of Officers in. Nature, 17: 197.
— Sculpture in. Penny M. 2: 337.
— Xanthian Marbles in. Penny M. 13: 412.
British Navy. *See* Great Britain, Navy.
British Officer, Stocqueler's. Dub. Univ. 38: 144.
British Opinions of America. Am. Q. 20: 405.
British or English? (J. Foster) Gent. M. n. s. 22: 195.
British Poetry. No. Brit. 36: 412. — Ecl. M. 8: 339, 499.
— at Close of last Century. (O. W. B. Peabody) No. Am. 42: 52.
— Modern. (W. M. Rossetti) Macmil. 33: 418. — Ecl. M. 86: 567.
— Past and present Condition of. Fraser, 33: 577, 708. Same art. Liv. Age, 10: 164.
British Poets. Ed. Mo. R. 2: 125, 247. — (F. Jeffrey) Ed. R. 20: 315. — (R. Southey) Quar. 11: 480. 12: 60. — Anal. M. 14: 111. — (J. Floy) Meth. Q. 7: 505. — Irish Q. 2: 461.
— Campbell's. (F. Jeffrey) Ed. R. 31: 462. — Fraser, 25: 353.
— Child's Edition of. (A. P. Peabody) No. Am. 84: 240.
— Howitt's Homes and Haunts of. Fraser, 35: 210. — Liv. Age, 13: 152.
— Johnson's Lives of. (M. Arnold) Macmil. 38: 153. — Bentley, 36: 445. — Colburn, 103: 18. — Liv. Age, 66: 240.
— Modern. (Sir E. Brydges) Fraser, 10: 423. — Am. Mo. M. 8: 235, 320.
— Old. (Sir E. Brydges) Fraser, 10: 33.
— Reed's Lectures on. Liv. Age, 55: 153.
— Victorian. (E. C. Stedman) Scrib. 5: 357. 6: 49. 7: 101, 463. 8: 100, 160. 9: 167, 426, 585. 10: 609, 679.
See English Poets; Poetry.
British Politics in 1860. Dub. Univ. 55: 634, 734.
British Politicians. Dem. R. 40: 135, 338.
British Popular Vagaries. Fraser, 26: 213.
British Privateers, Story of. (G. E. Patten) Lakeside, 7: 322.
British Pulpit. (H. Rogers) Ed. R. 72: 66.
British Quarterly Review, 100th Number of. Brit. Q. 50: 520.
British Race. (J. R. Seeley) Education, 1: 309.
British Regiments, Famous. All the Year, 29: 469, 492, 563. 30: 12-348. — Chamb. J. 54: 23.
British Seaman, has he deteriorated? (T. Brassey) Contemp. 28: 393. — (J. Williamson) Contemp. 28: 748.
British Shipping, Privileges and Liabilities of. Penny M. 12: 6.
British Spinsterhood Abroad. Dub. Univ. 43: 267.
British Spy; a Poem. Dem. R. 33: 117.
British Statesmanship and Policy. (W. R. Greg) No. Brit. 17: 1. Same art. Ecl. M. 26: 323.
British Statesmen. West. M. 3: 13, 128, 201.
— Four. (R. G. White) Galaxy, 2: 149.
— Macdiarmod's Lives of. (J. Foster) Ecl. R. 8: 855, 994.
— Political Morality of. No. Brit. 21: 545. Same art. Ecl. M. 33: 253.
British Tourists in the United States. (J. T. Crane) Meth. Q. 6: 508.
Britons, Early. (Dr. Haviland) Arch. 1: 54. — (T. Pownall) Arch. 2: 242.
— and Bretons. (H. Jones) Once a Week, 9: 12.
— Chariots of. (S. Pegge) Arch. 7: 211.
— Conversion of. (T. W. Jenkin) Cong. M. 5: 124.
— J. S. Lysons on. Colburn, 136: 64.
— Ornaments and Weapons of. Once a Week, 7: 556.
— Vestiges of, near Heathersage, Derbyshire. (G. Wilkinson) Reliquary, 1: 159.
— Were they Savages? (W. W. Wilkins) Fortn. 4: 193, 464.
Brittany. Dub. R. 85: 111.
— and the Bretons. (G. M. Towle) Hours at Home, 6: 397, 537. — Temp. Bar, 23: 468.
— and Cornwall, Ancient Affinities of. Brit. Q. 52: 281.
— and the Crown of France. Dark Blue, 4: 577.
— and England. Westm. 29: 352.
— Antiquities and Legends of. Nat. Q. 24: 46.
— Ballads of. Dub. Univ. 81: 361. — Lond. Q. 24: 406.
— Bards of. (W. C. Taylor) Bentley, 22: 193.
— — Celtic. Tait, n. s. 22: 555.
— Byways of. Sharpe, 27: 123. 28: 191. 29: 21, 233. 30: 18, 289.
— Carnival Time in. All the Year, 20: 201.
— Courting in. (L. S. Costello) Bentley, 8: 391.

Brittany, Dolmens and Lines in. (S. P. Oliver) Nature, 6: 9.
— Fair of St. Nicodème in. (K. S. Macquoid) Temp. Bar, 46: 386.
— Gatherings in. Belgra. 9: 331, 525.
— Glimpses of. Dub. Univ. 61: 286.
— History of. For. Q. 27: 142.
— in Song. All the Year, 32: 397.
— Industrial and social Condition of. J. Statis. Soc. 13: 134.
— Its People and Poems. (Mrs. Barker) Cath. World, 8: 398. — (J. Anderdon) Cath. World, 11: 390. — (G. R. Barker) Cath. World, 17: 252, 537. 18: 111.
— Journal in. Blackw. 38: 313.
— Life in. (G. M. Towle) Harper, 41: 853. 42: 30. — Cornh. 40: 667. Same art. Liv. Age, 144: 99. Same art. Appleton, 23: 125.
— Modern. Dub. Univ. 76: 241.
— Monument to the Thirty Knights. (M. d'Auvergne) Arch. 6: 144.
— Pardons in. House. Words, 9: 221. — Lond. Soc. 23: 509.
— Peasant Wedding in. All the Year, 21: 150.
— Peep at. All the Year, 31: 186.
— People in. Chr. Rem. 11: 130.
— Popular Poetry of. Tait, n. s. 20: 86.
— Repeal of the Union in. Dub. Univ. 32: 190.
— Roughing it in. Chamb. J. 45: 545.
— Rude Stone Monuments of. Chamb. J. 53: 121.
— Salt-Marshes of. Chamb. J. 55: 29.
— Scenes and Legends in. So. Lit. Mess. 20: 208.
— Ten Days in. Lond. Soc. 32: 17. — Cong. 2: 226.
— To Paris by. (T. G. Bonney) Once a Week, 17: 130.
— Two Tales of. Colburn, 166: 421.
— Vacation in. St. James, 26: 580.
— Wanderings in. (S. G. W. Benjamin) Harper, 51: 205.
— Weld's Vacation in. Ecl. R. 104: 599.
— Wild Sports of. Chamb. J. 53: 42.
Britton, John, Autobiography of. Sharpe, 12: 214. Same art. Liv. Age, 28: 366.
Britton, Thomas, the musical Small-Coal Man. Penny M. 10: 70.
Brizeux, Auguste, Life and Works of. Chr. Rem. 45: 1.
— Telen Arvor; Harp of Armorica. St. James, 2: 313.
Broad away. (W. Y. Wells) Pioneer, 4: 26.
Broads of East Anglia. Chamb. J. 56: 141.
— Visit to. Colburn, 42: 19.
Broad Church, The. (F. H. Hedge) Chr. Exam. 69: 53. — (L. Stephen) Fraser, 81: 311.
— and Universalism. Univ. Q. 19: 362.
— English, and America. (J. I. Forbes) Nation, 1: 88.
— Jowett and. Westm. 72: 41.
— S. Osgood on. (G. P. Fisher) New Eng. 17: 980.
Broad Church Liberalism. (L. H. Atwater) Princ. 33: 59.
Broad Church Movement. Fraser, 97: 353.
Broad Church Party, Position of. (J. Clark) Mercersb. 7: 199.
Broad Church Theology. Chr. Obs. 60: 375.
Broad Churchism, Historical Views of. (A. Gordon) Theo. R. 10: 277.
Broadsides. Chamb. J. 16: 154.
Broadway. (M. E. Hewitt) So. Lit. Mess. 7: 57, 302.
— bedeviled. Putnam, 9: 282.
— a Poem. (N. G. Shepherd) Harper, 25: 1.
Broca, Paul, with portrait. Pop. Sci. Mo. 20: 261. — Nature, 22: 249. — (H. F. C. ten Kake) Nature, 22: 292.
Brock, Isaac, Death of; a Poem. (W. F. Coffin) Canad. Mo. 9: 182.
Brock, the Swimmer. Chamb. J. 4: 45.
Brockhaus Publishing-House. (J. F. Hurst) Hours at Home, 6: 323.
Broderip, William John. In Memoriam. Fraser, 59: 485
Brodhead, Col. Daniel, Correspondence of. Olden Time, 2: 374.
— Expedition against the Indians, 1779. (O. Edson) M. Am. Hist. 3: 649. — Olden Time, 2: 308.
Brodhead, J. Romeyn. (T. W. Chambers) Scrib. 13: 459.
Brodie, Sir Benjamin C. (A. V. Kirwan) Fraser, 67: 113. Same art. Liv. Age, 76: 348. — Nature, 23: 126.
— Autobiography. Fraser, 72: 116. Same art. Liv. Age, 86: 329. — No. Brit. 43: 127.
— Life and Works of. Liv. Age, 87: 214.
Broek, Village of. Penny M. 3: 55.
Brogden, William. (E. Allen) Am. Church R. 9: 105.
Broglie, Duc de. (F. H. Hill) Fortn. 28: 53.
— Fall of, 1874. Dub. R. 75: 132.
— in America. (J. L. Ferrière) Lippinc. 28: 462.
— Memoir of. Ed. R. 135: 347.
— Narrative of, 1782. M. Am. Hist. 1: 180–374.
— Secret du Roi. (A. Laugel) Nation, 27: 347, 382.
Broke Jail. (D. H. Johnson) Atlan. 36: 12.
Broken Bonds. (J. W. Lee) Lakeside, 3: 438.
Broken Bonds; a Tale for Emigrants. (G. C. Munro) Peop. J. 6: 351.
Broken Bridge; a Story. Chamb. J. 50: 433.
Broken Distaff; a Story. (J. Middlemass) Belgra. 40: supp. 120.
Broken-Hearted; a Poem. (J. Leitch) St. James, 18: 199.
Broken into Fragments. Tinsley, 13: 174.
Broken Lily; a Story. Galaxy, 16: 355.
Broken Memories. Tait, n. s. 24: 17–618.
Broken Mug; a Tale. (H. Zschokke) Temp. Bar, 24: 356.
Broken on the Wheel. (J. Hatton) Gent. M. n. s. 4: 1.
Broken Reed; a Story. (M. Cross) Victoria, 35: 443. 36: 12–467.
Broken to Harness; a Novel. (E. Yates) Temp. Bar, 10: 370, 520. 11: 64–501. 12: 50–502. 13: 45, 271.
Broken Trust. (C. L. Young) Once a Week, 25: 331–441.
Broken Wall. St. James, 12: 177.
Brome, Frederick. (G. Busk) Nature, 1: 509.
Bromfield, John. Am. J. Educ. 5: 521.
Bromfield Family. (D. D. Slade) N. E. Reg. 25: 329. 26: 37, 141.
Bromine. (E. Mylius) J. Frankl. Inst. 102: 427. 103: 64.
Brongniart, M. Alexandre. (M. Elie de Beaumont) Am. J. Sci. 55: 155.
Bronikowski, O., Novels of. For. Q. 14: 457.
Brontë, Charlotte. (G. Cerny) Cath. World, 3: 834. — (R. W. Gilder) Hours at Home, 11: 183. — (A. B. Harris) Galaxy, 24: 41. — (T. W. Reid) Macmil. 34: 385, 481. 35: 1. Same art. Liv. Age, 130: 801. 131: 289, 611. Same art. Ecl. M. 87: 699. 88: 83, 192. — (J. Skelton) Fraser, 55: 569. Same art. Ecl. M. 41: 532. — (L. Stephen) Cornh. 36: 723. Same art. Ecl. M. 90: 178. Same art. Liv. Age, 136: 23. — (W. M. Thackeray) Cornh. 1: 485. — (B. J. Wallace) Am. Presb. R. 6: 285. — Blackw. 82: 77. — Brit. Q. 26: 218. Same art. with portrait, Ecl. M. 42: 145. — Eng. Dom. M. 2: 136, 165. 25: 159, 214. — Liv. Age, 45: 396. — Nat. M. 13: 548. — Nat. R. 5: 127. Same art. Liv. Age, 54: 577. — Putnam, 9: 648. — Ecl. M. 22: 286.
— Birthplace of. (G. M. Craik) Canad. Mo. 9: 264. Same art. Ecl. M. 86: 183.
— Gaskell's Life of. Am. Ch. Mo. 2: 113. — Chr. Obs. 57: 487. — Colburn, 110: 317. — Liv. Age, 53: 385, 777. 55: 385. — Tait, n. s. 24: 292.
— Jane Eyre. (E. P. Whipple) No. Am. 67: 354. — No. Brit. 11: 475. — Westm. 48: 581. — Fraser, 36: 690 — Liv. Age, 17: 481. — Chr. Rem. 15: 396. — Dub. R. 28: 209. — Dub. Univ. 31: 608. — Peop. J. 4: 269. — Tait, n. s. 15: 346.

Brontë, Charlotte. Jane Eyre and Rev. F. W. Robertson. (G. G. Hepburne) Am. Church R. **28**: 252.
— — and Vanity Fair. Quar. **84**: 153. Same art. Liv Age, **20**: 497.
— Life of. Chr. Rem. **34**: 87.—New Q. **6**: 223.—Ecl. R. **105**: 630.—Westm. **109**: 34.
— The Professor. Dub. Univ. **50**: 88.—Liv. Age, **54**: 680.
— Reminiscences of. Scrib. **2**: 18.
— Shirley. Ed. R. **9**: 81. Same art. Liv. Age, **24**: 481. —Liv. Age, **23**: 535.—Westm. **52**: 418.—Ecl. R. **90**: 739.—Dub. Univ. **34**: 680.—Dub. R. **28**: 209. —Ed. R. **91**: 153.
— Unpublished Letters. Hours at Home, **11**: 101.
— Villette. (G. W. Curtis) Putnam, **1**: 535.—(W. W. Kinsley) University Q. **2**: 233.—Ed. R. **97**: 380. —Chr. Rem. **25**: 401.—Ecl. R. **97**: 305.—Westm. **59**: 474.—New Q. **2**: 237.—Liv. Age, **36**: 588.
— Visit to Home of. Mo. Rel. M. **31**: 41.
— — to her School at Brussels. (A. Trafton) Scrib. **3**: 186.
— Writings. (Mrs. M. J. Sweat) No. Am. **85**: 293.—Colburn, **95**: 295. Same art. Liv. Age, **34**: 417.—Hogg, **13**: 425. Same art. Ecl. M. **35**: 407. Same art. Liv. Age, **45**: 723.
Brontë, Emily, Writings of. Galaxy, **15**: 226.
— Wuthering Heights. (G. W. Peck) Am. Whig R. **7**: 572.—Internat. M. **2**: 315.—Tait, n. s. **15**: 138.
— — and Agnes Gray. Ecl. R. **93**: 222.
— — Authors of. Liv. Age, **29**: 128, 180.
Brontë, Patrick. Appleton, **22**: 129.
Brontë Family. Cornh. **28**: 54. Same art. Ecl. M. **81**: 287. Same art. Liv. Age, **118**: 307. Same art Ev. Sat. **15**: 97.
— and their Home. (Mrs. E. P. Evans) Putnam, **16**: 278.
— at their Home, Two Days with. Broadw. **7**: 23.
— Winter's Day at Haworth. (W. H. Cooke) St. James, **21**: 161.
Brontë Sisters. (W. W. Kinsley) Lakeside, **1**: 155.
— and their Writings. Tait, n s. **22**: 416.
Bronwen Fair. St. James, **27**: 132.
Bronze. Pract. M. **7**: 114.
— Aera Dionysiana, Vulgaris, or Christiana. (G. Oppert) Arch. **44**: 335.
— Aluminium, for making Instruments. (A. Strange) J. Frankl. Inst. **75**: 414. **76**: 325.
— as an Art Material. (P. L. Simmonds) Art J. **28**: 181.
— Figure-Casting in. Penny M. **13**: 259.
— Imitation of. (M. H. G. de Claubry) J. Frankl. Inst. **20**: 49.
— Phosphor. (C. J. A. Dick) J. Frankl. Inst. **98**: 139.
— Strongest. (R. H. Thurston) Ecl. Engin. **25**: 126.
Bronze Age. (E. Burnouf) Galaxy, **24**: 628.—(W. M. Blackburn) Dial (Ch.), **2**: 120.—Bank. M. (N. Y.) **15**: 433.
— Nilsson on. Anthrop. R. **4**: 85.
Bronze Bracelet found near Altyre. (H. Ellis) Arch. **22**: 285.
Bronze Figure found at Richborough. (S. Weston) Arch. **17**: 176.
Bronze Foundries in France. Ecl. Engin. **1**: 833.
Bronze Implements. (L. Jewitt) Stud. & Intel. Obs. **5**: 275.
— found at Fulbourn, Cambridge, England. (E. D. Clarke) Arch. **19**: 56.
Bronze Object found at Lucera. (R. Garrucci) Arch. **41**: 275.
Bronze Paper-Knife. (J. Hawthorne) Appleton, **7**: 121.
Bronze Statues, Casting of. Penny M. **8**: 483.
— How to keep them clean. Ev. Sat. **10**: 270.
Bronze Vases, Ancient. Art J. **2**: 328.
— incrusted in Silver, Christofle's Process. Pract. M. **1**: 358.
Bronze Weapons found on Arreton Down. (A. W. Franks) Arch. **36**: 326.
— Wright on. Anthrop. R. **4**: 72.
Bronzes found at Colchester. (C. Newton) Arch. **31**: 443.
— How made. Nat. M. **2**: 44.
— Mechanical Properties of. (M. Tresca) Ecl. Engin. **12**: 12.
Bronzing Brass Goods, Plaster, etc. J. Frankl. Inst. **2**: 123, 154.
Brooches and Dress-Fastenings, Ancient. (F. W. Fairholt) Art J. **18**: 46, 141.
Brook, The; a Poem. Broadw. **1**: 194.
Brook, The; a Poem. Dub. Univ. **87**: 592.
Brook and the Mill; a Poem. (B. F. Taylor) Scrib. **8**: 199.
Brook Farm Community. Dial, **4**: 351.
— Home Life of. Atlan. **42**: 458, 556.
— Plan of. (E. P. Peabody) Dial, **2**: 361.
— Reminiscences of O. & N. **3**: 175, 425. **4**: 347. **5**: 517.
— Visit to. (G. B. Kirby) Overland, **5**: 9.
Brook Street, Holborn. All the Year, **26**: 78.
Brooke, Henry. (A. H. Bromilow) Colburn, **162**: 381. —Dub. Univ. **39**: 200.—Internat. M. **5**: 461.
Brooke, Sir James, Rajah of Sarawak. (J. A. St. John) Bentley, **22**: 580. **25**: 71.—(H. St. John) Sharpe, **17**: 228.—Dub. Univ. **35**: 574.—(J. Balestier) Hunt, **18**: 56.—Blackw. **59**: 356.—Colburn, **81**: 474.—House. Words, **18**: 130.—(W. H. Dixon) Peop. J. **4**: 347.—Temp. Bar, **24**: 204.
— and Borneo. (G. Reynolds) Atlan **18**: 667.
— and the Pirates. (J. A. St. John) Bentley, **25**: 347.
— Defense of. (J. A. St. John) Bentley, **27**: 286.
— the Knight Adventurer. (I. Scott) Once a Week, **2**: 364.
— Last of the Vikings. (S. Evans) Macmil. **36**: 146, 256.
— Last Days of. Good Words, **10**: 572.
— Life and Work in Borneo. Westm. **62**: 382.
— Life of. St. James, **22**: 723.
— St. John's Life of. Blackw. **127**: 193. Same art. Liv. Age, **144**: 609. Same art. Ecl. M. **94**: 477.
— Visit to. (P. McQuhae) Bentley, **23**: 65.
See Borneo.
Brooke, Stopford A., with portrait. Dub. Univ. **92**: 299.
Brookfield, Mass., Early History of. N. E. Reg. **35**: 333.
Brookfield Association. (C. Cushing) Cong. Q. **12**: 274.
Brooklyn, N. Y., Church of the Pilgrims. (H. H. McFarland) Cong. Q. **13**: 54.
— Clinton Avenue Congregational Church. Cong. Q. **2**: 212.
— Compulsory Education in. (F. E. Fryatt) Harper, **60**: 218.
— Council of 1874. (H. H. McFarland) Cong. Q. **16**: 446.
— in 1776. (J. Johnson) Nav. M. **1**: 367, 466, 561.
— Library Association Catalogue. Lib. J. **1**: 330.
— Navy Yard. (W. F. G. Shanks) Harper, **42**: 1.
— Old, Reminiscences of. (T. F. DeVoe) Hist. M. **12**: 257, 340.
— Packer Collegiate Institute. O. & N. **6**: 115.
Brooks, Charles Shirley. (J. Hatton) Lond. Soc. **25**: 343.—Ev. Sat. **16**: 549.—(B. Jerrold) Gent. M. n. s. **12**: 561. Same art. Ev. Sat. **16**: 602.—with portrait, Once a Week, **27**: 56.
Brooks, Charles Timothy. German Lyrics. (N. L. Frothingham) Chr. Exam. **55**: 231.—(C. C. Felton) Chr. Exam. **34**: 232.
Brooks, James G., Poems of. So. Lit. Mess. **5**: 303.
Brooks, John, with portrait. (C. Brooks) N. E. Reg. **19**: 193.
— Biography of. Chr. Exam. **2**: 103.—Am. Q. Reg. **14**: 286.
Brooks, Dr. John, Memoir of. Bost. Mo. **1**: 57.

Brooks, Maria *del Occidente*. (Z. B. Gustafson) Harper, **58**: 249.
— and Southey. Internat. M. **1**: 67.
— Poems of. Museum, **41**: 197. — So. Lit. Mess. **8**: 541.
Brooks, N. C. Poem, History of the Church. So. Lit. Mess. **8**: 76.
Brooks, Peter C. (E. Everett) Hunt, **32**: 659. — with portrait, (E. Everett) N. E. Reg. **8**: 297. **9**: 13.
Brooks, Phillips, as a Preacher. (F. W. Fisk) New Eng. **39**: 316.
— on the Influence of Jesus. (C. A. Stork) Luth. Q. **10**: 101.
Brooks, Thomas. Art J. **24**: 197.
Brooks Family of Woburn, Mass. N. E. Reg. **29**: 153.
Brooks Genealogy. (E. Yale) N. E. Reg. **5**: 355.
Brooks Islands in the Pacific. (C. W. Brooks) O. & N. **1**: 828.
Broomstick, Rhapsody on. (C. Mackay) Peop. J. **1**: 344.
Brorsen's Comet. (R. A. Proctor) Fraser, **79**: 158.
Bross, John A., with portrait. Lakeside, **4**: 81.
Bross, William, with portrait. Lakeside, **1**: 321.
Brother Adam. (H. Parr) Good Words, **13**: 613, 685.
Brother against Brother. (M. Reid) Lond. Soc. **22**: 458.
Brother Jacob; a Story. Cornh. **10**: 1.
Brother of Mercy; a Poem. (J. G. Whittier) Atlan. **13**: 279.
Brother's Sin, and a Sister's Love. Victoria, **9**: 14-113.
Brother's Trust. (J. Ingelow) Liv. Age, **88**: 61.
Brothers, The. (M. M. Duncan) Godey, **23**: 273.
Brothers, The. (L. M. Alcott) Atlan. **12**: 584.
Brothers, The. (M. Graham) Godey, **58**: 209.
Brothers, The. (H. W. Herbert) Am. Mo. M. **4**: 73-361.
Brothers, The; an Allegory. Contin. Mo. **4**: 367.
Brothers and Lovers. Liv. Age, **119**: 784.
— of the Christian Schools. Dub. R. **9**: 331.
Brotherhood of the common Lot. (W. M. Metcalfe) Good Words, **19**: 51.
— of Locomotive Engineers. (C. F. Adams, jr.) Nation, **24**: 158, 173.
— of Man. Evang. R. **14**: 578.
Brotherhoods. Chamb. J. **46**: 261.
— Christian. (C. W. Rankin) Am. Church R. **16**: 390.
— European Remedy against. (G. Pollak) Nation, **24**: 318.
Brotherless; a Poem. (W. Smith) Cornh. **7**: 259.
Brotherton, Discoveries in the Church of. (W. Drake) Arch. **9**: 253.
Brou, Votive Church of. (M. P. Thompson) Cath. World, **30**: 322.
Brough, Lionel, with portrait. Once a Week, **26**: 369.
Brougham, Henry, Lord. With portrait, Fraser, **4**: 609. **18**: 461. — Liv. Age, **14**: 429. **31**: 433. — (A. Alison) So. Lit. Mess. **9**: 522. — (S. P. Chase) No. Am. **33**: 227. — Mus. **13**: 228. **20**: 241, 347. — (A. H. Forrester) Bentley, **28**: 215. — (G. Gilfillan) Ecl. M. **31**: 337. — (E. L. Godkin) Nation, **6**: 386. — (A. R. Macdonough) Harper, **44**: 86. — (A. R. Macdonough) Nation, **13**: 43, 260. **14**: 324. — (C. Redding) Colburn, **143**: 108. — (G. A. Sala) Temp. Bar, **23**: 421. — (E. I. Sears) Am. J. Educ. **6**: 467. — (J. G. Wilson) Hours at Home, **7**: 181. — with portrait, Ecl. M. **33**: 430. — Am. Law R. **3**: 1. — Brit. Q. **32**: 1. — Colburn, **100**: 368. Same art. Ecl. M. **35**: 133. — Dub. Univ. **48**: 113. Same art. Ecl. M. **39**: 101: Same art. Liv. Age, **51**: 303. — with portrait, Colburn, **32**: 507. — Ed. R. **135**: 502. — Ev. Sat. **5**: 741. — Internat. M. **1**: 306. — Nat. R. **5**: 164. Same art. Liv. Age, **54**: 612. — Putnam, **10**: 116. — St. Paul's, **5**: 178. — Once a Week, **24**: 404.
— and his Calumniators. Dub. Univ. **13**: 104.
— and his Contemporaries. Temp. Bar, **34**: 350. Same art. Ecl. M. **78**: 411.
— and the Court of Chancery. Fraser, **4**: 301.
Brougham, Henry, Lord, and Law Reform. Quar. **105**: 504.
— and Leigh Hunt. (S. R. T. Mayer) Temp. Bar, **47**: 221. Same art. Ecl. M. **87**: 164. Same art. Liv. Age, **130**: 239.
— and Lyndhurst, Campbell's Lives of. Quar. **126**: 1. Same art. Liv. Age, **100**: 643.
— and Mary, Queen of Scots. Bentley, **18**: 157.
— and the Press. Fraser, **18**: 1.
— and the Prussian Ambassador. Liv. Age, **26**: 391.
— as a Judge. Hogg, **7**: 341.
— as an Orator. (G. Gilfillan) Hogg, **11**: 41, 216. — Ecl. M. **31**: 337. **32**: 21.
— Autobiography. (Goldwin Smith) Canad. Mo. **1**: 557.
— Bridlegoose. Fraser, **9**: 501.
— Campbell's Life of. Am. Law R. **4**: 253.
— Career and Character of. Fraser, **44**: 458. Same art. Ecl. M. **24**: 388.
— Demosthenes. Fraser, **21**: 620.
— Early Life of. Temp. Bar, **32**: 28. Same art. Liv. Age, **110**: 259.
— Eccentricities of. Temp. Bar, **62**: 183.
— Historical Sketches. Dub. Univ. **23**: 112. — Ecl. R. **79**: 501. — Chr. R. **4**: 450, 509.
— Inaugural Address, Glasgow, 1825. Ed. R. **42**: 241. — Mo. R. **107**: 69.
— Innovations of. Fraser, **4**: 93.
— Installation Address, University of Edinburgh, 1860. Liv. Age, **66**: 67.
— Law Reform. Quar. **38**: 241.
— Letter to Sir S. Romilly. Mo. R. **87**: 302.
— Life of. Dem. R. **43**: 58. — Ed. R. **129**: 556.
— — and Career of, McGilchrist on. Chr. Obs. **68**: 611.
— — and Times of. Dark Blue, **1**: 253.
— Lives of Men of Letters of Time of George III. Brit. Q. **2**: 197. — Fraser, **31**: 647. **34**: 67. — Dub. Univ. **25**: 690. — Liv. Age, **6**: 539. **10**: 9. — (W. B. O. Peabody) No. Am. **61**: 383. **64**: 59. — Tait, n. s. **12**: 341. — (J. W. Croker) Quar. **76**: 62. Same art. Ecl. M. **6**: 23. — Blackw. **59**: 615. Same art. Ecl. M. **8**: 532. — Dub. R. **18**: 518. — Liv. Age, **5**: 504.
— National Education. Quar. **19**: 493.
— Natural Theology. *See* Natural Theology.
— Opinions of. Ecl. R. **66**: 287.
— Pamphlets, 1839. Mo. R. **150**: 299.
— Political Philosophy. Ed. R. **81**: 1. Same art. Liv. Age, **5**: 11.
— Professional and political Life. Westm. **112**: 480.
— Speeches. Dub. R. **5**: 437. — Ed. R. **107**: 443. Same art. Liv. Age, **58**: 3. — Mo. R. **147**: 66. — Tait, n. s. **5**: 475, 588. — (W. Forsyth) Ed. R. **107**: 443. Same art. Ecl. M. **44**: 257. — Brit. & For. R. **8**: 490. — Mus. **34**: 279. — Ecl. R. **68**: 421. Same art. Ecl. M. **71**: 1472.
— Statesmen of Time of George III. Ecl. R. **70**: 104. — Dub. R. **15**: 469.
— Theology. *See* Theology.
— The Times, and Irish Law Courts. Dub. Univ. **33**: 478.
— Works of. Liv. Age, **47**: 193. — No. Brit. **30**: 417.
Brougham, John, Winter's Life of. (G. P. Upton) Dial (Ch.), **1**: 260.
Brought to Light; a Tale. (T. Speight) Chamb. J. **43**: 417-755.
Broughton, Rhoda. Joan. (A. Lang) Fortn. **27**: 96.
— Novels of. Temp. Bar, **41**: 197.
Broughton, Thomas, Letters of, 1690. Hist. M. **14**: 277.
Broughton de Broughton; a Tale. All the Year, **13**: 88.
Broughton Castle. Antiquary, **3**: 257.
Brousdon, Robert, and Descendants. (R. H. Eddy) N. E. Reg. **35**: 361.
Broussa, Baths of. (Mrs. Walker) Good Words, **8**: 524.
Brouwer, Adriaan. Lond. Soc. **29**: 118.

Browler's Defalcation; a Tale. (A. Webster) Putnam, **15**: 286.
Brown, Aaron V., with portrait. Dem. R. **41**: 140.
Brown, Albert G., with portrait. Dem. R. **25**: 457.
Brown, Charles Brockden. (W. H. Prescott) Sparks's Am. Biog. **1**: 117. — (G. C. Verplanck) No. Am. **9**: 58. — Am. Whig R. **7**: 260. — Am. Q. **8**: 312. — Retros. **9**: 317. — Mo. R. **99**: 151. — U. S. Lit. Gaz. **6**: 321. — (G. B. Smith) Fortn. **30**: 399.
— and Washington Irving. Blackw. **6**: 554.
— Novels of. West. Mo. R. **1**: 483.
Brown, David, Account of, 1763–1812. Chr. Obs. **16**: 1, 65.
Brown, Ford Madox. (S. Colvin) Portfo. **1**: 81.
— Manchester Frescos. (W. M. Rossetti) Art J. **33**: 262.
— Pictures by. (W. M. Rossetti) Fraser, **71**: 598.
— Theory of Art by. (W. J. Stillman) Scrib. **4**: 157.
— Works of. Art J. **25**: 105.
Brown, Francis, Life of. (H. Wood) Am. Q. Reg. **7**: 133.
Brown, George L. Art J. **32**: 211. — Godey, **34**: 179.
— and his Paintings. Art J. **29**: 370.
Brown, Henry S., Pioneer of Texas. De Bow, **16**: 155.
Brown, J. Appleton, and his Paintings. Art J. **30**: 198.
Brown, J. Baldwin. Sermons. Brit. Q. **31**: 454.
Brown, Gen. Jacob, with portrait. Anal. M. **5**: 292. — with portrait, Portfo. (Den.) **13**: 105.
Brown, Capt. John. (I. Scott) Once a Week, **2**: 105. — Liv. Age, **71**: 161.
— and Harper's Ferry. (W. E. Forster) Macmil. **1**: 306.
— Friends of. (F. B. Sanborn) Atlan. **30**: 50.
— in Massachusetts. (F. B. Sanborn) Atlan. **29**: 420.
— Invasion of Virginia by. (W. G. Day) So. M. **13**: 433.
— Raid on Harper's Ferry. (J. G. Rosengarten) Atlan. **15**: 711.
— — Moral of. (L. Bacon) New Eng. **17**: 1066.
— Three Interviews with. (W. A. Phillips) Atlan. **44**: 738.
— Virginia Campaign of. (F. B. Sanborn) Atlan. **35**: 16–591. **36**: 704.
— Work of. (S. H. Morse) Radical, **4**: 449.
See Brown, Owen.
Brown, Dr. John. Horæ Subsecivæ. (J. Skelton) Fraser, **59**: 443. — (J. H. Ward) New Eng. **21**: 294. — Chamb. J. **35**: 276. — Ecl. M. **55**: 541. — Ecl. R. **114**: 172. — No. Brit. **34**: 481. Same art. Ecl. M. **53**: 319. Same art. Liv. Age, **69**: 686.
— Rab and his Friends. Liv. Age, **60**: 166.
Brown, Rev. Dr. John. Expository Discourses. No. Brit. **9**: 334.
— Life and Works of. No. Brit. **33**: 21.
— Pulpit Expositions. Ecl. R. **93**: 33.
— Scheme of Divinity. Brit. Q. **13**: 540.
Brown, Sir John, with portrait. Pract. M. **7**: 34.
Brown, John, the religious Carrier. Blackw. **12**: 663.
Brown, John Allan. (B. Stewart) Nature, **21**: 112.
Brown, John Carter. Am. J. Educ. **27**: 237.
— Library of. (H. Rogers) Am. Bibliop. **7**: 91, 228. — (J. C. Stockbridge) Bib. Sac. **33**: 293. — Am. Bibliop. **6**: 77.
Brown, Mary A., Poems of. Mo. R. **116**: 81.
Brown, Nicholas. (W. Gammell) Am. J. Educ. **3**: 291.
— Biography of. Hunt, **5**: 538.
Brown, Oliver Madox. (P. B. Marston) Scrib. **12**: 425.
Brown, Owen. Escape from Harper's Ferry. (R. Keeler) Atlan. **33**: 342.
Brown, Richard, "Stumpy," of Woodbridge. Once a Week, **11**: 611.
Brown, Robert, Obituary Notice of. Am. J. Sci. **78**: 161.
Brown, Samuel. Galileo Galilei; a Tragedy. Hogg, **4**: 377. — Ecl. R. **91**: 269.
Brown, Dr. Samuel. (D. Masson) Macmil. **12**: 74. — No. Brit. **26**: 376.
Brown, Dr. Samuel, and his Theories. Brit. Q. **28**: 121.
— Lectures and Essays of. Ecl. R. **108**: 24. — Chamb. J. **29**: 324.
Brown, Simon. (C. Orcutt) N. E. Reg. **3**: 374.
Brown, Thomas. (S. Gilman) No. Am. **21**: 19. — F. Parkman) Chr. Exam. **29**: 202. — Lond. M. **23**: 229.
— on Cause and Effect. Chr. Mo. Spec. **3**: 583.
— Philosophy of the Mind. (S. Gilman) No. Am. **19**: 1. — (J. Sparks) No. Am. **24**: 480. — So. R. **3**: 125. — Chr. Mo. Spec. **8**: 141. — Mo. R. **100**: 402. — U. S. Lit. Gaz. **6**: 161. — Ecl. R. **84**: 674.
See Browne, Sir Thomas.
Brown, Ulysses M., Field-Marshal Count, Memoir of. Dub. Univ. **44**: 738.
Brown, William L. Prize Essay. Mo. R. **82**: 172.
— Sermons. Ed. R. **4**: 190.
Brown Family, Letters relating to. (J. L. Chester) N. E. Reg. **25**: 352.
— Studies on. (R. Turnbull) Hours at Home, **1**: 469. **2**: 62.
Brown Genealogy. (A. W. Brown) N. E. Reg. **6**: 232. **9**: 219.
Brown Institution, Dublin. Nature, **5**: 138.
Brown University, Charter of. (R. A. Guild) Bapt. Q. **9**: 165.
— Early Graduates of. (W. G. Goddard) Am. Q. Reg. **11**: 356.
— Library of. (R. A. Guild) University Q. **3**: 253. — Lib J. **3**: 117.
— Library Catalogue. Chr. R. **8**: 499. — (F. Bowen) No. Am. **58**: 227.
— Wayland's Report on Collegiate Education in. Chr. R. **15**: 442.
See also Collegiate Education.
Brown of Calaveras. (F. B. Harte) Overland, **4**: 284.
Brown of Hangtown. (S. L. Simpson) Overland, **7**: 575.
Brown's Christmas Bundle. (W. M. Laffan) Lippinc. **9**: 70.
Brown's Lecture Tour. (W. W. Sikes) Contin. Mo. **1**: 118.
Brown's Peccadillo. (H. King) Blackw. **119**: 502.
Brown Lady; a Tale. (Mrs. C. Hoey) Belgra. **8**: 53, 197.
Brown-Paper Parcel. All the Year, **21**: 379, 403, 429.
Brown Study; a Poem. (B. Jerrold) Temp. Bar, **3**: 244.
Brown Study; a Story. Galaxy, **24**: 827.
Browne, Charles F., Artemus Ward. Chamb. J. **42**: 357. — Ev. Sat. **3**: 457. — (E. S. Nadal) Scrib. **21**: 144. — (Don C. Seitz) Scrib. **22**: 46.
— at Cleveland. (C. C. Ruthrauff) Scrib. **16**: 785.
— in London. Ev. Sat. **2**: 765.
Browne, Edmund, Letter of, 1676. N. E. Reg. **7**: 268.
Browne, Frances, Blind Poetess, Life and Works of. Dub. R. **17**: 517. — Mo. R. **165**: 575. — Ecl. M. **33**: 452. — Chamb. J. **35**: 281. Same art. Liv. Age, **69**: 723.
Browne, Harold, Bishop of Winchester. Cong. **2**: 558.
Browne, Sir Thomas. (J. H. Barrett) Am. Whig R **8**: 15. — (H. T. Tuckerman) So. Lit. Mess. **14**: 177. — (B. H. Nadal) Meth. Q. **11**: 280. — (L. W. Peck) Meth. Q. **24**: 294. — (L. Stephen) Cornh. **23**: 596. Same art. Liv. Age, **109**: 579 Same art. Ecl. M. **77**: 14. — Blackw. **6**: 197, 435. — Brit. Q. **25**: 143. — Ecl. R. **124**: 81.
— Letters of. Retros. **1**: 161.
— on Urn Burial. (T. N. Talfourd) Retros. **1**: 83. — Cong. M. **6**: 95.
— Prose of. Am. Mo. M. **7**: 581.
— Works of. (Sir E. B. Lytton) Ed. R. **64**: 1. — (C. C. Smith) No. Am. **94**: 371. — Cong. M. **5**: 151.
— — Wilkin's Edition. Ecl. R. **66**: 368. — Quar. **89**: 364 — Ecl. M. **25**: 1.
Browne, William. Pastorals. Retros. **2**: 149.
Brownell, J. (T. Jackson) Meth. M. **46**: 1.

Brownell, Thomas C., Bishop. (R. A. Hallam) Am. Church R. **17**: 261.
Browning, Mrs. E. B. (C. B. Conant) Meth. Q. **22**: 409. —(M. Couthouy) Lippinc. **21**: 747. —(K. Field) Atlan. **8**: 368. —(G. Gilfillan) Tait, n. s. **14**: 620. (E. C. Stedman) Scrib. **7**: 101. —(Mrs. H. Stevenson) Victoria, **22**: 231. —(O. W. Le Vert) N. Ecl. **4**: 221. —with portrait, Ecl. M. **43**: 127. —with portrait, Ecl. M. **67**: 247. —Brit. Q. **34**: 350. —Cornh. **29**: 469. —Ecl. M. **12**: 249. **32**: 423. **54**: 55. **55**: 303. —Ecl. R. **115**: 189, 419. —Eng. Dom. M. **25**: 74. —Ev. Sat. **16**: 510. —Internat. M. **5**: 310. —Liv. Age, **70**: 489. —So. R. n. s. **23**: 34. —Macmil. **4**: 402.
— and Christian Poetry. Bost. R. **1**: 154.
— and her Contemporaries. (R. H. Horne) St. James, **36**: 138. **37**: 21.
— and Miss Lowe. Ecl. M. **22**: 337.
— and Mrs. Adams. (W. J. Fox) Peop. J. **1**: 130.
— Aurora Leigh. (J. Challen) Nat. Q. **5**: 134. —Blackw. **81**: 23. —Dub. Univ. **49**: 460. —Ecl. M. **56**: 74. —Liv. Age, **52**: 427. —Nat. R. **4**: 239. —Putnam, **9**: 28. —Westm. **67**: 306. **68**: 399. Same art. Ecl. M. **43**: 10.
— — Taine on. Ev. Sat. **11**: 611.
— Casa Guidi Windows. Ecl. R. **94**: 306. —Prosp. R. **7**: 313.
— Early Poems. Ecl. R. **84**: 573.
— Essays on Greek and English Poets. Knick. **62**. 212. —Chr. Exam. **75**: 24.
— Isabel's Child. (D. E. Snow) Mo. Rel. M. **48**: 253.
— Last Poems. (A. Wilson) Macmil. **6**: 79. —D. Wilson) Canad. J. n. s. **7**: 210. —Dub. Univ. **60**: 157. Same art. Ecl. M. **57**: 274. —No. Brit. **36**: 514.
— Letters. (H. James, jr.) Nation, **24**: 105.
— — to Author of Orion. (R. H. Horne) Contemp. **23**: 146–799. Same art. Ecl. M. **82**: 213, 346. Same art. Liv. Age, **120**: 281. **121**: 116, 535. **122**: 24.
— Poems. So. Lit. Mess. **11**: 235. —Brit. Q. **2**: 337. —Quar. **66**: 374. —(C. T. Brooks) Chr. Exam. **38**: 206. —(S. F. Adams) Westm. **42**: 381. —Dem. R. **15**: 72, 142, 370. —(E. A. Duyckinck) Am. Whig R. **1**: 38. —(R. C. Pitman) Meth. Q. **6**: 54. —Blackw. **56**: 621. **60**: 488. —Ecl. R. **84**: 573. —Liv. Age, **28**: 552. —Dub. Univ. **25**: 144. —(C. C. Everett) No. Am. **85**: 415. —(C. B. Conant) No. Am. **94**: 338. —(M. G. Lloyd) Nat. Q. **1**: 173. —(I. M. Luyster) Chr. Exam. **72**: 65. —Am. Whig R. **14**: 462. —Chr. Rem. **20**: 346. —Colburn, **107**: 369. —Dub. Univ. **60**: 157. —Ecl. M. **56**: 351. —Ecl. R. **93**: 295. —Fraser, **43**: 178. —Mus. **41**: 195. —Nat. M. **12**: 357. —No. Brit. **26**: 443. Same art. Ecl. M. **41**: 27. —Blackw. **87**: 490. —Brit. Q. **42**: 359. —Chamb. J. **20**: 361. —Prosp. R. **1**: 445. —Tait, n. s. **11**: 720. **23**: 14. —Mo. R. **165**: 300.
— Recollections of. (R. H. Horne) St. James, **35**: 466.
— Seraphim and other Poems. Mo. R. **147**: 119.
— Works of. Ed. R. **114**: 513.
Browning, Robert. (T. Bayne) St. James, **41**: 153. —(J. H. Browne) Galaxy, **19**: 764. —with portrait, Dub. Univ. **93**: 322, 416. —(M. D. Conway) Victoria, **2**: 298. —(A. N. Macnicoll) Gent. M. n. s. **22**: 54. —(J. Skelton) Fraser, **67**: 240. —(G. B. Smith) Internat. R. **6**: 176. —(E. C. Stedman) Scrib. **9**: 167. —with portrait, (R. H. Stoddard) Appleton, **6**: 533. —Contemp. **4**: 1, 133. Same art. Ecl. M. **68**: 314, 501. —Lond. Q. **6**: 493. **22**: 30. —Sharpe, **8**: 60, 122. **38**: 225.
— Agamemnon. Ed. R. **147**: 409.
— and Mrs. E. B., Day with. (E. C. Kinney) Scrib. **1**: 185.
— — Poems. Quar. **118**: 77.
Browning, Robert, and the Epic of Psychology. Lond. Q. **32**: 325.
— and J. R. Lowell. New Eng. **29**: 125.
— and Tennyson. Ecl. R. **120**: 361.
— Aristophanes's Apology. Lond. Q. **44**: 354.
— as a Preacher. (E. D. West) Dark Blue, **2**: 171, 305. Same art. Liv. Age, **111**: 707.
— Balaustion's Adventure. (M. Browne) Contemp. **18**: 284. —(J. R. Dennett) Nation, **13**: 178. —(E. J. Hasell) St. Paul's, **13**: 49. —(R. E. Thompson) Penn Mo. **6**: 928. —Ed. R. **135**: 221. —(S. Colvin) Fortn. **16**: 478. —Lond. Q. **37**: 346.
— Bells and Pomegranates. Chr. Rem. **11**: 316. —(H. F. Chorley) Peop. J. **2**: 38, 104.
— Christmas Eve and Easter Day. Prosp. R. **6**: 267. —Liv. Age, **25**: 403.
— Dramatic Idyls. (G. Allen) Fortn. **32**: 149. —(Mrs. S. Orr) Contemp. **35**: 289. —Fraser, **100**: 103. —(T. Bayne) St. James, **47**: 108.
— Dramatis Personæ. (R. Bell) St. James, **10**: 477. —(T. F. Wedmore) Colburn, **133**: 186. —Dub. Univ. **64**: 573.
— Fifine at the Fair. (C. C. Everett) O. & N. **6**: 609. —(Goldwin Smith) Canad. Mo. **2**: 285. —Ev. Sat. **14**: 283. —Temp. Bar, **37**: 315.
— First Poem of. St. James, **28**: 485.
— in 1869. Cornh. **19**: 249.
— Inn Album. (A. C. Bradley) Macmil. **33**: 347. —(H. James, jr.) Nation, **22**: 49. —(B. Taylor) Internat. R. **3**: 402.
— Latest Poetry of, 1870. No. Brit. **51**: 97.
— Men and Women. Bentley, **39**: 64. —Brit. Q. **23**: 151. —Chr. Rem. **31**: 267. **34**: 361. —Dub. Univ. **47**: 673. —Fraser, **53**: 105. —Irish Q. **6**: 1. —Westm. **65**: 290.
— Paracelsus. Colburn, **46**: 289. —Chr. Rem. **20**: 346.
— Place of, in Literature. (A. Orr) Contemp. **23**: 934. Same art. Liv. Age, **122**: 67.
— Plays and Poems. (J. R. Lowell) No. Am. **66**: 357.
— Poems. (W. H. Browne) N. Ecl. **5**: 711. —C. C. Everett) Chr. Exam. **77**: 51. —(C. C. Smith) Chr. Exam. **48**: 361. —Brit. Q. **49**: 435. —Ed. R. **120**: 537. —Fraser, **43**: 170. —Mo. Rel. M. **7**: 568. —Nat. R. **17**: 417. —No. Brit. **49**: 353. —Peop. J. **9**: 113. —Putnam, **7**: 372. —St. Paul's, **7**: 257. Same art. Ecl. M. **76**: 267. Same art. Liv. Age, **108**: 155. —No. Brit. **34**: 350. —Brit. Q. **6**: 490. — —Ecl. M. **18**: 453. —Chamb. J. **20**: 39. **39**: 91. Ecl. R. **90**: 203. **117**: 436. **120**: 62. —Temp. Bar, **26**: 316. **27**: 170. **28**: 33.
— Prince Hohenstiel-Schwangau. (J. S. Sewall) New Eng. **33**: 493.
— Red Cotton Nightcap Country. (J. R. Dennett) Nation, **17**: 116. —(A. Orr) Contemp. **22**: 87. —Penn Mo. **4**: 657.
— Ring and the Book. (J. W. Chadwick) Chr. Exam. **86**: 295. —(J. Thomson) Gent. M. n. s. **27**: 682. —(E. J. Cutler) No. Am. **109**: 279. —(J. R. Dennett) Nation, **8**: 135. —(J. Morley) Fortn. **11**: 331. —(J. A. Symonds and J. R. Mozley) Macmil. **19**: 258, 544. —Chamb. J. **46**: 473. —Dub. R. **65**: 48. —Ed. R. **130**: 164. —Ev. Sat. **7**: 24, 570. —St. James, **23**: 460. —St. Paul's, **7**: 377. Same art. Ecl. M. **76**: 400. Same art. Liv. Age, **108**: 771. —Tinsley **3**: 665.
— Sordello. (E. Dowden) Fraser, **76**: 518.
— Strafford; a Tragedy. Ed. R. **65**: 132*.
— Wordsworth, and Tennyson. Nat. R. **19**: 27. Same art. Ecl. M. **64**: 273, 415. Same art. Liv. Age, **84**: 3.
— Works of, with portrait. Once a Week, **26**: 165.
Brownism, and its Founder. Theo. Ecl. **7**: 225.
Brownists, Petition of. (S. G. Drake) N. E. Reg. **13**: 259.

Brownlow, John William Spencer, Earl of; a Poem. (G. Massey) Good Words, **8**: 373.
Brownlow, William G., and Andrew Johnson. (W. F. G. Shanks) Putnam, **13**: 428.
Brownlows, The. (M. Oliphant) Blackw. **101**: 93–649. **102**: 1–738. **103**: 42–125.
Brownson, Orestes A. (A. F. Hewit) Cath. World, **23**: 366. — Am. Cath. Q. **1**: 560.
— Argument for the Romish Church. (J. F. Clarke) Chr. Exam. **48**: 227.
— Articles in Democratic Review. Dem. R. **13**: 353.
— Charles Ellwood. Chr. R. **5**: 419. — (W. D. Wilson) Chr. Exam. **28**: 180.
— Conversion of. Dub. R. **19**: 390.
— Development of himself. (R. Smith) Princ. **30**: 390.
— Essays and Reviews. New Q. **2**: 109.
— Exposition of his Philosophy. (O. A. Brownson) Brownson, **22**: 433. **23**: 1, 145.
— — of himself. (L. H. Atwater) Princ. **30**: 117.
— on the Laboring Classes. Meth. Q. **1**: 92.
— Philosophy of. Dub. R. **78**: 36.
— Quarterly Review. (J. W. Nevin) Mercersb. **2**: 33, 307. — (G. Peck) Meth. Q. **5**: 454.
— — Theological Errors of. Dub. R. **54**: 58.
— Religious Views of. U. S. Cath. M. **4**: 152.
— Views of Christianity, etc. Chr. Exam. **22**: 127.
— Writings of. Dial, **1**: 22.
Bruce, Archibald. Am. J. Sci. **1**: 299.
Bruce, Edgar, Actor, with portrait. Victoria, **35**: 421.
Bruce, Lord Edward, Discovery of his Heart at Culross. (Lord Stowell) Arch. **20**: 515.
Bruce, James, Ramsay, and Channing, Friendship of. Once a Week, **8**: 453.
Bruce, Knight, Lord Justice. Lond. Soc. **11**: 185. Same art. Ecl. M. **68**: 428.
Bruce, Michael. Ode to the Cuckoo. (J. C. Shairp) Good Words, **14**: 791. — Brit. Q. **61**: 500.
— Poems of. Dub. Univ. **88**: 297.
Bruce, Robert. Blackw. **61**: 297. — Penny M. **5**: 62.
— Heart of; a Ballad. Blackw. **56**: 15.
— in St. Andrew's Cathedral. (J. C. Shairp) Good Words, **15**: 593.
Bruce, W. Literary Essays. Mo. R. **92**: 280.
Bruen, Matthias, Life of. Ecl. R. **56**: 33.
Bruges, Louis de. *See* Winchester, Earl of.
Bruges, City of. Penny M. **7**: 265, 276.
— from the Belfry Tower. Fraser, **55**: 94.
— Residence of Charles II. at. (G. S. Steinman) Arch. **35**: 335.
— Weird Story of. (J. Grant) Lond. Soc. **25**: 154.
Brullof, Russian Painter, on the Via San Basilio. Lippinc. **15**: 113.
Brumidi, Constantine, Obituary of. Am. Arch. **7**: 94.
Brummagem Morality. Blackw. **127**: 409.
Brummell, George B., Beau. (J. Bonner) Harper, **11**: 185. — Bentley, **16**: 288. **17**: 514. — All the Year, **46**: 106. — Temp. Bar, **35**: 231. Same art. Ecl. M. **79**: 76. Same art. Liv. Age, **113**: 797.
— Life of. Dub. R. **17**: 92. — Liv. Age, **1**: 195, 333. — Tait, n. s. **11**: 382.
— Personal Reminiscences of. Chamb. J. **43**: 244, 263. Same art. Ev. Sat. **1**: 514.
— Sketch of. Chamb. J. **1**: 379.
Brunanburh, Song of. (H. Tennyson) Contemp. **28**: 920.
Brunel, Isambard Kingdom. Fraser, **60**: 620. **83**: 383. Same art. Liv. Age, **63**: 818.
Brunel, Sir Marc Isambard. Chamb. J. **15**: 38.
— Beamish's Memoir of. Colburn, **125**: 64. Same art. Ecl. M. **56**: 418.
Brunels, The, Father and Son. Quar. **112**: 1. Same art. Liv. Age, **74**: 435.
Brunettes *versus* Blondes. Temp. Bar, **15**: 109.
Bruni, Conversion of. All the Year, **44**: 488.
Bruno, Giordano. (J. H. Browne) Atlan. **38**: 550. — (A. Lang) Macmil. **23**: 303. — Fraser, **83**: 364. — (J. Cowen) Colburn, **167**: 125.
— and Galileo. Quar. **145**: 362. Same art. Liv. Age, **138**: 323. Same art. Sup. Pop. Sci. Mo. **3**: 111.
— Life and Works of. (C. D. B. Mills) Chr. Exam. **78**: 206. — Brit. Q. **9**: 540. Same art. Ecl. M. **17**: 307.
Brunswick and Hanover. For. R. **3**: 466.
— Duchy of, Public Instruction in. Am. J. Educ. **15**: 447.
Brunswick, House of, in Germany and England. Fraser, **48**: 445. Same art. Liv. Age, **39**: 620.
Brunswick Theater, Accident at, 1828. All the Year, **20**: 133. Same art. Ev. Sat. **6**: 216.
Brunton, A. Lectures and Sermons. Mo. R. **90**: 188.
Brunton, Mary. Discipline. Portfo.(Den.) **15**: 411.
— Emmeline. Blackw. **5**: 183. — Mo. R. **91**: 174.
Brusa, Trip to. (S. G. W. Benjamin) Nat. M. **11**: 106.
Brush, George J., with portrait. (T. R. Lounsbury) Pop. Sci. Mo. **20**: 117.
Brushes, Manufacture of. (C. T. Hinckley) Godey, **46**: 389.
Brushfield, Thomas. (L. Jewitt) Reliquary, **16**: 209.
Brussels. (M. P. Thompson) Cath. World, **16**: 766. — Penny M. **1**: 377.
— Bubbles from. Colburn, **42**: 499.
— Glimpses of. (L. H. Hooper) Lippinc. **22**: 127.
— Gossip about. House. Words, **2**: 42.
— Grave and gay. Temp. Bar, **16**: 358.
— Hotel de Ville at. Penny M. **2**: 89.
— International Exhibition, 1876. Pract. M. **6**: 274.
— Life in. Chamb. J. **25**: 314.
— My first Visit to. (T. C. Grattan) Colburn, **52**: 486. **53**: 198.
— Sketch of, in 1829. Colburn, **26**: 217.
— Talk about. Tinsley, **14**: 175.
Brussels Conference, 1874. (H. Ottley) Fraser, **91**: 184.
— and Laws of War. (H. S. Edwards) Macmil. **31**: 410.
Bruté, Rt. Rev. S. G., Memoirs of. (R. McSperry) Cath. World, **17**: 711.
Brute Madness. (O. S. Round) Recr. Sci. **1**: 320.
Brute World. Bentley, **46**: 351. Same art. Liv. Age. **63**: 387.
Brutus, *pseud.* *See* Owen, D.
Brutus, Marcus Junius. Colburn, **130**: 177.
Bruycker, François Antoine de. Art J. **18**: 75.
Bruyas, Father. Papers of, 1689–90. M. Am. Hist. **3**: 250.
Bruyn. Blandnia. (Mrs. E. F. Ellet) Godey, **39**: 28.
Bryan, D. Poetical Address. (J. Sparks) No. Am. **24**: 212.
Bryan, Sir Francis. (J. P. Collier) Arch. **26**: 446.
Bryansfort Specter. Belgra. **25**: 245.
Bryant, John, and his Descendants. (W. B. Lapham) N. E. Reg. **35**: 37.
Bryant, John Howard. (A. F. Bridges) Potter Am. Mo **12**: 132.
Bryant, Stephen, and Descendants. N. E. Reg. **24**: 315.
Bryant, William Cullen. (W. Dowe) Nat. Q. **37**: 354. — (J. L. T. Phillips) New Eng. **39**: 614. — (E. S. Nadal) Macmil. **38**: 369. — (H. N. Powers) Scrib. **16**: 479. — with portrait, (R. H. Stoddard) Appleton, **6**: 477. — (J. G. Wilson) Lakeside, **4**: 241. — with portrait, Ev. Sat. **10**: 49, 70. — with portrait, Dem. R. **10**: 290. — New Eng. M. **1**: 398. — So. Lit. Mess. **6**: 106, 329. — with portrait, Ecl. M. **74**: 371. — with portrait, Hogg, **4**: 81. — with portrait, Internat. M. **4**: 588. — Irish Q. **5**: 193. — Liv. Age, **61**: 387. — Nat. M. **1**: 385. — Nat. Q. **37**: 354. — Sharpe, **46**: 126.
— and his Writings. (R. Palmer) Internat. R. **1**: 433.
— as a Man. (H. N. Powers) Lakeside, **8**: 133.
— Death of. (E. C. Stedman) Atlan. **42**: 747.

Bryant, William Cullen, Home of, at Cummington, Mass. Appleton, 9: 193.
— — at Roslyn, L. I. (M. J. Lamb) Appleton, 15: 1.
— Homer's Iliad. *See* Homer.
— Longfellow and Tennyson. (G. Smith) Bentley, 64: 61.
— Poem. Death of Schiller. Dem. R. 3: 66.
— — Hymn of the Sea. Chr. Exam. 33: 95.
— — Future Life. Dem. R. 5: 49.
— — The Fountain. Dem. R. 5: 405.
— — The Winds. Dem. R. 6: 269.
— Poems. Chr. Rem. 15: 300. — Chr. R. 24: 391. — Colburn, 99: 306. Same art. Ecl. M. 31: 78. Same art. Liv. Age, 39: 658. — West. M. 1: 84. — (W. Phillips) No. Am. 13: 380. — (W. J. Snelling) No. Am. 34: 502. — (G. S. Hillard) No. Am. 55: 500. — (W. P. Lunt) Chr. Exam. 22: 59. — (T. A. Turner) De Bow, 9: 577. — So. Lit. Mess. 3: 41. — Am. Q. 20: 504. — For. Q. 10: 121. — Dem. R. 6: 273. 16: 185. — Mo. R. 127: 490. — U. S. Lit. Gaz. 1: 8. — Mus. 20: 578. 21: 404. — Blackw. 11: 686. 16: 310. 31: 646. — (R. Allyn) Meth. Q. 19: 41.
— Symington's Life of. (H. N. Powers) Dial (Ch.), 1: 186.
— Thirty Poems. Liv. Age, 80: 307.
— Tribute to. Unita. R. 10: 84.
Bryant, Dr. Peter. Fourth of July Ode. Hist. M. 21: 334.
Bryant and May, Matchmakers. Colburn, 169: 276.
Bryant's Station, Ky., Attack on, in 1782. West. Mo. R. 3: 113.
Bryce, James, Sermons of. Chr. Obs. 18: 310.
Brydayne, Jacques, Sermons of. Chr. Obs. 25: 690.
Brydges, Sir Egerton. Quar. 51: 342. — with portrait, Fraser, 9: 146. — Mus. 7: 27. — with portrait, Am. Bibliop. 3: 59.
— Autobiography. (Sir E. B. Lytton) Ed. R. 59: 439.
— Letter on Byron. Blackw. 17: 137.
— Recollections. Blackw. 17: 505.
— Reply to Edinburgh Review. Fraser, 10: 725.
— Res Literariæ. Lond. M. 3: 207, 311.
Bubble Girl. Fraser, 40: 513. Same art. Liv. Age, 24: 29.
Bubbles of Finance. Bank. M. (N. Y.) 20: 465, 558, 625.
Bubbleton Parish. (J. G. Adams) Univ. Q. 11: 365.
Buccaneer, The; a Poem. (R. H. Dana) Harper, 45: 641.
Buccaneer, The; a Tale. Lond. M. 4: 161.
Buccaneer; Henry Morgan. (J. T. Headley) Harper, 19: 20.
— R. de Lussan. (J. T. Headley) Harper, 18: 18. — Cornh. 20: 152.
Buccaneers and Pirates. Am. Hist. Rec. 2: 444.
— First and Last of. (W. L. Stone) Lippinc. 4: 559.
— History of. Retros. 9: 327. — Mus. 31: 1.
— of America. (W. L. Stone) Contin. Mo. 3: 703. 4: 175.
— of the Spanish Main. (J. Bonner) Harper, 11: 514.
Buch, Leopold von, Eulogy on. (B. Cotta) Am. J. Sci. 67: 1.
Buchan, Barons of. (J. Skelton) Fraser, 60: 127.
Buchan, Earl of. Essays. Blackw. 3: 515.
Buchan, Mrs. E., and her Followers. Dub. Univ. 81: 617.
Buchan, Peter, Sketch of. Hogg, 4: 180.
Buchanan, Claudius. Meth. M. 40: 656.
— Christian Researches in Asia. Quar. 6: 448.
— Discourses of. Chr. Obs. 10: 248, 310, 363.
— Pearson's Memoirs of. Chr. Obs. 16: 509, 579.
Buchanan, Francis. Travels on the Mysore. Ed. R. 13: 82.
Buchanan, George. Kitto, 25: 76. — No. Brit. 46: 47.
— as a Scholar. (C. Kingsley) Good Words, 9: 729.
— Franciscan and the Brotherhood. Blackw. 26: 488.
— Irving's Life of. Blackw. 1: 286. — Ecl. R. 7: 383.
— Latin Version of the Psalms. Chr. Rem. 14: 314.
— Life and Works of. Brit. Q. 66: 395.
Buchanan, George, Satires of. Cornh. 16: 625.
— Writings of. Blackw. 3: 251.
Buchanan, James. (H. King) Galaxy, 10: 474. — with portrait, Dem. R. 11: 650. — with portrait, Dem. R. 38: 1.
— Administration of. (P. Godwin) Atlan. 1: 745. — Dem. R. 42: 177.
— First Message of. Dem. R. 41: 26.
— Horton's Life of. Dem. R. 38: 64.
— Washington, Jackson, and. Nat. R. 12: 499.
Buchanan, Robert. (G. H. Lewes) Fortn. 1: 443. — (G. B. Smith) Contemp. 22: 873. — (A. M. Symington) Good Words, 19: 15. — Tinsley, 10: 89.
— Book of Orne. Unita. R. 14: 177.
— Idyls and Legends of Inverburn. Ecl. R. 122: 30.
— Poems. (R. H. Stoddard) Nation, 2: 22. — Land We Love, 6: 196. — (R. Noel) Gent. M. n. s. 15: 556. — St. James, 37: 648.
Buchanan, William. Art J. 16: 131.
Buchanites, The. Chamb. J. 6: 362.
Bucharest. Blackw. 81: 205. — House. Words, 8: 104. — Penny M. 9: 357.
— Life at. Temp. Bar, 51: 54. Same art. Ecl. M. 89: 576.
— Trip from, to Constantinople. Nat. M. 6: 172.
Büchner. *See* Buechner.
Buck, Victor, the Bollandist. (M. Russell) Irish Mo. 5: 228.
Buck-Shooting on New Year's Day. Lond. Soc. 13: 69.
Bucke, Charles. Julio Romano. Mo. R. 122: 66.
Buckhaven and its Inhabitants. Blackw. 2: 626.
Buckhurst, Lord. (J. Bruce) Arch. 37: 350.
Buckingham, George Villiers, Duke of. Dub. Univ. 41: 684. Same art. Liv. Age, 38: 209. Same art. Ecl. M. 29: 517. — Dub. Univ. 54: 77. — Tait, n. s. 27: 277.
— and Cardinal Wolsey. Ecl. M. 78: 119.
— Household Book of. (J. Gage) Arch. 25: 311.
— Papers addressed to James I. Arch. 17: 280.
— Ruin of. Liv. Age, 19: 13.
— Sketch of. Colburn, 146: 389.
Buckingham, Grenville R. P., Duke of. Liv. Age, 73: 195.
Buckingham, James Silk. Liv. Age, 45: 354. — with portrait, Peop. J. 9: 273. — Ecl. M. 35: 278. — So. Lit. Mess. 4: 281.
— Autobiography of. Ecl. R. 101: 717. Same art. Ecl. M. 36: 628.
— National Evils and Remedies. Ecl. R. 91: 338.
— Travels in the East. Quar. 26: 374. — Westm. 4: 495. — Mo. R. 107: 257. 118: 491. — Mus. 15: 119.
Buckingham, Joseph T. Liv. Age, 69: 447.
— Miscellanies. U. S. Lit. Gaz. 1: 99.
— Personal Memoirs of. (N. L. Frothingham) Chr. Exam. 53: 414.
Buckingham, William Alfred. (I. N. Tarbox) Cong. Q. 18: 215.
— Memoir of, with portrait. (N. Porter) N. E. Reg. 30: 1.
Buckingham Palace. (W. Thornbury) Belgra. 5: 192, 323. — Ecl. M. 11: 196. — Fraser, 1: 379. — Sharpe, 3: 354, 375, 388.
Buckingham Papers. Ed. R. 99: 1. — Quar. 92: 421.
Buckinghamshire, Walk through. Temp. Bar, 15: 242.
Buckland, Francis T. Liv. Age, 148: 447. — (S. Walpole) Macmil. 43: 303. Same art. Liv. Age, 148: 634. Same art. Pop. Sci. Mo. 18: 812. Same art. Ecl. M. 96: 535.
— Log Book of a Fisherman. Chamb. J. 52: 801.
Buckland, Wm. Bridgewater Treatise. Fraser, 59: 227. — Quar. 56: 31. — Dub. Univ. 8: 692.
— Reliquiæ Diluvianæ. Chr. Mo. Spec. 6: 415.

Buckle, Henry Thomas. (W. F. Allen) No. Am. 117: 223. — (G. A. Simcox) Fortn. 33: 270. Same art. Appleton, 23: 339. Same art. Ecl. M. 94: 457. — (A. V. Dicey) Nation, 16: 270. — Contin. Mo. 2: 253. — Fraser, 66: 337. Same art. Ecl. M. 57: 347. — Fraser, 101: 361. — Liv. Age, 74: 160.
— and the Aufklärung. (J. H. Stirling) J. Spec. Philos. 9: 337.
— and the Economics of Knowledge. (A. W. Benn) Mind, 6: 231.
— and Sir John Coleridge. (J. D. Coleridge) Fraser, 59: 635.
— and Count Montalembert. Dub. Univ. 58: 187.
— and Scottish Christianity. Theo. Ecl. 5: 501.
— as a Thinker. (D. A. Wasson) Atlan. 11: 27.
— Death of. Liv. Age, 74: 383.
— Doctrine as to the Scotch and their History. (D. Masson) Macmil. 4: 177, 309, 370.
— Draper, and a Science of History. (E. B. Freeland) Contin. Mo. 4: 529, 610. 5: 161.
— Huth's Life of. (A. V. Dicey) Nation, 30: 350.
— in the East. (J. S. Stuart-Glennie) Fraser, 68: 171. Same art. Liv. Age, 78: 387.
— Life and Writings of. (F. Rye) Canad. Mo. 18: 150.
— Personal Reminiscences of. (C. Hale) Atlan. 11: 488.
— Reminiscences of. Sharpe, 48: 254.
— Scientific Errors of. Blackw. 90: 582.
Buckler found in the Thames. (J. Gage) Arch. 27: 298.
Buckley, Frederick. Potter Am. Mo. 14: 23.
Buckley, William, the wild White Man. Chamb. J. 29: 177. Same art. Liv. Age, 57: 292.
Buckminster, Rev. J. and J. S. (F. Bowen) No. Am. 69: 353. — New Eng. 8: 30. — (G. Ticknor and A. Norton) Chr. Exam. 47: 169.
Buckminster, Joseph Stevens. (H. T. Tuckerman) So. Lit. Mess. 24: 50.
— Sale of his Library. Gen. Repos. 2: 392.
— Sermons. Chr. Mo. Spec. 5: 145. — Chr. Exam. 7: 43.
Buckram, as a Material for Bookbinding. (E. B. Nicholson) Lib. J. 2: 207, 271.
Buckstone, John Baldwin, with portrait. Fraser, 14: 720.
— with portrait, Once a Week, 27: 430.
Bucolic and Canine Recollections. St. James, 18: 52.
Budd Variation. (M. T. Masters) Pop. Sci. R. 11: 244.
Budd, Henry, Memoir of. Chr. Obs. 56: 194.
Budd, Thomas, Account of Pennsylvania and New Jersey, 1685. Hist. M. 6: 265, 304.
Buddha. (F. Adler) Atlan. 37: 674. — (E. Markwick) Belgra. 28: 419.
— and Buddhism. (A. M. Machar) Canad. Mo. 13: 35, 165. — (E. V. Neale) Macmil. 1: 439.
— and Lao-tzŭ. (L. W. Pilcher) Meth. Q. 36: 645.
— Bigandet's Life of. (S. Beal) Nation, 30: 352.
— First Sermon of. (T. W. R. Davids) Fortn. 32: 899. Same art. Liv. Age, 144: 208.
— Origin of the Legend of. (T. W. R. Davids) Theo. R. 15: 77.
— Preaching of. Dial, 4: 391.
— Tooth of. (T. Yelverton) Overland, 11: 434.
Buddhism. (D. M. Balfour) Univ. Q. 31: 5. — (F. R. Feudge) Galaxy, 16: 342. — (H. M. Johnson) Meth. Q. 19: 586. 20: 68. — New Eng. 3: 182. — Mo. R. 118: 577. — Kitto, 32: 82. 35: 281. — Lond. Q. 10: 513.
— Account of Nirvāna. (T. W. R. Davids) Contemp. 29: 249.
— and the British Government. Lond. Q. 3: 436.
— and Buddhists. Chr. Rem. 35: 81.
— and Christianity. (R. A. Armstrong) Theo. R. 7: 176. — (E. Hungerford) New Eng. 33: 268. — (W. McDonnell) Canad. Mo. 13: 393. — (A. M. Machar) Canad. Mo. 13: 509.
Buddhism and its Founder. Dub. Univ. 82: 206.
— and its Influence. Nat. Q. 13: 90.
— and its Legends. Intel. Obs. 10: 421.
— and Jainism. (M. Williams) Appleton, 23: 366.
— and the New Testament. (J. E. Carpenter) 19th Cent. 8: 971.
— Brahmanism, and Christianity. (S. H. Kellogg) Presb. R. 1: 352.
— Development of, in India. (J. W. Edgar) Fortn. 33: 801. Same art. Liv. Age, 146: 131.
— Failure of. (S. S. Hebbard) Univ. Q. 30: 330.
— in Burmah. (S. Yoe) Appleton, 25: 129.
— in India and China. (J. K. Wight) Princ. 31: 391.
— in Little Tibet. (E. Paske) Anthrop. J. 8: 195.
— in Tibet. Westm. 81: 229.
— Light of Asia. *See* Arnold, Edwin.
— Monachism of, Hardy's. Prosp. R. 6: 473.
— Mythical and historical. Westm. 66: 296.
— Origin and Progress of. (R. H. Graves) Bapt. Q. 6: 409. — (A. L. Koeppen) Mercersb. 10: 294.
— — and Results of. (L. P. Brockett) Meth. Q. 21: 219.
— — Tenets and Tendencies of. So. Lit. Mess. 25: 380, 417.
— Past, present, and future. (J. Pyne) Nat. Q. 31: 1.
— Popular, according to the Chinese Canon. Westm. 109: 328. Same art. Liv. Age, 137: 387.
— Primitive. (K. Cook) Dub. Univ. 92: 257, 407.
— Protestantism of the East. (J. F. Clarke) Atlan. 23: 713.
— Recent Researches on. Ed. R. 115: 379.
— Recent Works on. (Lord Amberley) Theo. R. 9: 293.
— Resemblance of, to Roman Catholicism. (L. M. Child) Atlan. 26: 660.
— Whole Duty of Buddhist Layman. (R. C. Childers) Contemp. 27: 417. Same art. Liv. Age, 129: 60.
Buddhist, The modern. Nature, 2: 372.
Buddhist ancient Belief concerning God. (T. W. R. Davids) Mod. R. 1: 219.
Buddhist Birth Stories. (S. Beal) Nation, 32: 261. — (R. Morris) Contemp. 39: 728.
Buddhist Devil, Wasanartti. Univ. Q. 31: 476.
Buddhist Folk-Lore. (B. F. Hartshorne) Fortn. 30: 214.
Buddhist Maxims. Cornh. 34: 177.
Buddhist Pilgrims. Brit. Q. 30: 392.
Buddhist Praying-Machine. Good Words, 8: 845.
Buddhist Preaching. (H. Alabaster) Good Words, 13: 830.
Buddhist Schools in Burmah. (P. Hordern) Fraser, 96: 626. Same art. Liv. Age, 135: 692.
Buddhist Scriptures. (J. Alwis) Kitto, 31: 78.
Buddhist Superstition. So. Lit. Mess. 25: 257.
Buddicom, R. P., Sermons of. Chr. Obs. 23: 247.
Bude Haven and the Wreck of the Bencoolen. Once a Week, 8: 161.
Bude Light. Penny M. 13: 173.
Budgett, S. (E. Hale, jr.) Hunt, 28: 184. — Chamb. J. 17: 188.
— Life of. Mo. Rel. M. 29: 1.
Buechner, Georg. (L. Vickers) Nation, 32: 224.
Buechner, Louis. Force and Matter. (A. Bayma) Cath. World, 19: 433, 637, 823. *See* Force.
Buel, Alexander W., with portrait. Dem. R. 27: 545.
Buell, Mary. (Mrs. E. F. Ellet) Godey, 41: 201.
Buelau, F. Secret Histories and mysterious Men. Dem. R. 27: 497.
Buelow, Hans G. von, and Wagner. (A. Asbury) Atlan. 29: 140.
— Recollections of. Scrib. 10: 700.
Buelow, Henry, Baron von, Life of. Colburn, 73: 441.
Buena Vista, Battle of. (E. H. Walworth) M. Am. Hist. 3: 705. — Dem. R. 23: 227. — (C. P. Kingsbury) Am. Whig R. 8: 445. — Fraser, 38: 96. — Liv. Age. 13: 186, 233. 20: 474.

Buenos Ayres. House. Words, **3**: 378, 425. — Penny M. **13**: 177. — Niles's Reg. **28**: 47. — Ann. Reg. **5**: 244.
— and Banda Oriental. (Mrs. S. P. Jenkins) Am. Whig R. **3**: 160.
— and Bolivia, War between. For. Q. **20**: 157.
— and Chili. Quar. **35**: 114.
— and the Pampas. Am. Q. **8**: 249.
— and La Plata, Parish on. Mo. R. **149**: 515.
— English and French Intervention. (C. Cushing) Dem. R. **18**: 163, 480.
— Government in. (J. Sparks) No. Am. **24**: 236.
— Letters from, 1818. Niles's Reg. **14**: 288, 361, 430. **15**: 188, 202.
— Pampas of. Hogg, **5**: 222.
— Shepherd Life in. St. James, **21**: 295.
— Tale of the Masorcha Club. Blackw. **62**: 47.
— Travels in, Beaumont's. Lond. M. **21**: 154.
— Treaty with Great Britain. Niles's Reg. **28**: 334.
See Plate River; Rosas, Gen. J. M. de.
Buerger, Godfried August. (S. S. Conant) Hours at Home, **9**: 141.
— and his Translators. Fraser, **57**: 549. Same art. Liv. Age, **57**: 817.
— Biographical Sketch of. Westm. **102**: 567.
— Life and Songs of. Tait, n. s. **2**: 328, 378.
Buét, Mont, Ascent of. Colburn, **130**: 192.
Buffalo, The, and his Fate. (E. Ingersoll) Pop. Sci. Mo. **17**: 40. — (J. A. Allen) Penn Mo. **7**: 214.
— History of. (W. E. Doyle) Am. Natural. **15**: 119.
— Range of. (J. G. Henderson) Am. Natural. **6**: 79.
See also Bison.
Buffalo Bull, Adventure with. Chamb. J. **20**: 417.
Buffalo Hunt in Northern Mexico. (L. Wallace) Scrib. **17**: 713.
Buffalo Hunting. Broadw. **2**: 513. — Tait, n. s. **5**: 648.
— in India. Tinsley, **12**: 328.
Buffalo Pot-Hunt. (H. M. Robinson) Appleton, **16**: 215.
Buffalo Range. (T. R. Davis) Harper, **38**: 147.
Buffalo, City of. Hunt, **16**: 596. — Penny M. **6**: 85.
— in 1854. De Bow, **16**: 490.
— Origin of the Name. Hist. M. **6**: 350.
Buffon, G. L. L., Comte de. St. Paul's, **5**: 81. Same art. Liv. Age, **103**: 310. Same art. Ev. Sat. **8**: 587.
— Life and Writings of. Brit. Q. **13**: 125. Same art. Ecl. M. **23**: 1.
Bug Bible, 1551. Ev. Sat. **10**: 235.
Bugs, Poisonous, of Miana. Penny M. **6**: 310.
Bugeaud, Robert, Marshal of France. (G. B. McClellan) Galaxy, **9**: 673.
Bugis, Princess; a Sketch. (N. W. Beckwith) Canad. Mo. **11**: 616.
Builders, Primitive. All the Year, **28**: 593.
Builders' Combinations in London and Paris. Nat. R. **11**: 314.
Building, Ancient, in North America. Penny M. **13**: 57.
— Antiquity of, in England. (J. Essex) Arch. **4**: 73.
— in Concrete. (W. C. Homersham) Ecl. Engin. **11**: 437.
— New Materials and Inventions for. (T. R. Smith) Ecl. Engin. **13**: 209.
— of the Bridge; a Chinese Legend. Cornh. **32**: 334.
— of St. Sophia; a Poem. (S. B. Gould) Temp. Bar, **21**: 34.
— Roman, in England and Italy. Ecl. Engin. **24**: 465.
— under Water, Method of. (J. Moffat) J. Frankl. Inst. **79**: 295.
Buildings, Act for Security and Stability in. Am. Arch. **6**: 75.
— Construction of, with reference to Sound. (J. B. Upham) Am. J. Sci. **65**: 215, 348. **66**: 21.
— How to ascertain the Dates of. (J. A. Repton) Arch. **33**: 136.
— Sites of, mysteriously changed. Chamb. J. **58**: 251.
Building Acts, Suggestions for Construction of. (A. Stone) Am. Arch. **9**: 27.
Building Arts in India. (Gen. Maclagan) Ecl. Engin. **25**: 118.
Building Construction. Am. Arch. **5**: 196.
Building Materials at Vienna Exhibition. Ecl. Engin. **13**: 73.
— Decay and Preservation of. (D. T. Ansted) J. Frankl. Inst. **70**: 155, 217.
— in the Northwest. Am. Arch. **5**: 140.
— in the United States. (D. Stevenson) Ed. New Philos. J. **31**: 12.
— Mode of testing. (J. Henry) Am. J. Sci. **72**: 30.
— Permeability of. Am. Arch. **7**: 167.
— Porosity of. Am. Arch. **7**: 91.
— Preservation of. (F. Kuhlman) J. Frankl. Inst. **76**: 383.
— Roman. (C. T. Ramage) J. Frankl. Inst. **8**: 85.
— Some new. Ecl. Engin. **6**: 508.
— Strength of. Ecl. Engin. **7**: 254. **9**: 18.
Building Sites, Selection of. Ecl. Engin. **4**: 365. — Am. Arch. **7**: 214.
Building Societies. (E. Wrigley) Penn Mo. **7**: 497. — Ecl. R. **92**: 324.
— and Loan Associations. So. Q. **22**: 489.
— Co-operative. Westm. **90**: 75.
— in Birmingham. (G. J. Johnson) J. Statis. Soc. **28**: 507.
— of Philadelphia. (C. Barnard) Scrib. **11**: 477. — (J. I. Doran) Penn Mo. **7**: 595. — Bank. M. (N. Y.) **34**: 26. — (A. B. Burk) Bank. M. (N. Y.) **36**: 287.
See Co-operative Land Movement; Friendly Societies.
Building Stones. Ecl. Engin. **13**: 499. — Penny M. **12**: 254. — (H. A. Cutting) Am Arch. **10**: 217–265.
— American, Experiments upon. (Q. A. Gillmore) Ecl. Engin. **11**: 533.
— — and foreign. (W. R. Johnson) Am. J. Sci. **61**: 1.
— Decay of. (C. P. Townsley) Ecl. Engin. **14**: 535.
— Standing-Heat Qualities of. (H. A. Cutting) Ecl. Engin. **24**: 491.
Building Superintendence. Am. Arch. **9**: 3–267. **10**: 3–263.
Building System for Cities. (L. Blodget) Penn Mo. **8**: 285.
Built upon Sand; a Tale. Eng. Dom. M. **9**: 65–328. **10**: 1–326. **11**: 1.
Buirette, Isaac de, and Sons. (L. Harper) Hunt, **4**: 546.
Buitenzorg, Excursion to. Fraser, **50**: 111.
Bukowina, The. (E. Kilian) Fraser, **92**: 757.
Bulbs and Tubers, Flowering. Eng. Dom. M. **26**: 150.
Bulfinch, S. G. Lays of the Gospel. (E. Peabody) Chr. Exam. **38**: 315.
— Poems. Am. Mo. M. **4**: 13.
Bulford Hall. Colburn, **158**: 667. **159**: 41.
Bulgaria. Quar. **142**: 544. — (V. Chirol) Fortn. **36**: 284.
— and the Turkish Border, 1876. Geog. M. **3**: 236.
— Bit of. St. James, **20**: 289.
— Church in. (G. M. Mackenzie and A. P. Irby) Good Words, **6**: 197.
— Industrial Condition of. Pract. M. **5**: 37.
— New, 1879. Contemp. **35**: 503.
— Prospects of, 1880. Month, **39**: 567.
— Rambles in, 1856. (J. O. Noyes) Knick. **48**: 1.
— Travels in. Ed. R. **144**: 535.
— Von Moltke's Russian Campaigns in, 1828–29. Quar. **95**: 250.
Bulgarians. (J. Beddoe) Anthrop. J. **8**: 232. — (E. H. Kilian) Fraser, **94**: 537. — Colburn, **116**: 306. — Knick. **52**: 364.
Bulgarian Horrors and Mr. Gladstone. (E. Gaisford) St. James, **39**: 100.
Bulgarian Literature. Westm. **110**: 374.

Bulgarian Song, Bogies of. (J. Oxenford) Macmil. **34**: 547.
— Brigands of. (J. Oxenford) Macmil. **34**: 362. Same art. Liv. Age, **131**: 51.
— Popular. Cornh. **35**: 221.
— — and Proverbs. (E. Riggs) Am. Presb. R. **12**: 65. **13**: 259.
Bulgarian Rayahs. Chamb. J. **46**: 804.
Bulkeley, Peter, Life of. (A. M. Fay) N. E. Reg. **31**: 153.
— Will of, 1658. N. E. Reg. **10**: 169.
Bulkeley Family, Pedigree of. N. E. Reg. **23**: 299.
Bull, Ole. Cornh. **6**: 514. — Knick. **23**: 80. — (E. S Carr) Putnam, **11**: 586.
— Episode in Life of. (H. C. Andersen) Bentley, **21**: 272.
Bull, William. Chr. Rem. **50**: 87. — Ecl. R. **120**: 571. — Theo. Ecl. **2**: 267.
Bull and the Cow, The, in Mythology. (J. Cowen) Colburn, **165**: 1145.
Bull, The Unam Sanctam. Month, **37**: 428.
Bulls and Bears. (F. H. Underwood) Atlan. **2**: 825. **3**: 70–710. — Chamb. J. **42**: 813.
Bulls, Irish. Ev. Sat. **11**: 318.
Bull-Baiting. Chr. Obs. **1**: 363, 432.
— at Arles. Once a Week, **9**: 273.
Bulldozing in 1844. (W. P. Garrison) Nation, **28**: 146.
Bull-Fight, The. Chamb J. **31**: 137. — So. Lit. J. **4**: 43.
— and After-Thoughts. Macmil. **23**: 249.
— At a. House. Words, **18**: 457.
— at Granada in 1880. (N. Colgan) Irish Mo. **9**: 491.
— at Madrid. Internat. M. **5**: 222. — Lippinc. **25**: 90. — (J. B. Waring) Once a Week, **15**: 566. — (P. Merimée) New Eng. M. **9**: 252.
— at Ronda. Internat. M. **4**: 631.
— in Lisbon. Knick. **39**: 526.
— Mr. Leufkin at a. All the Year, **21**: 595.
Bull-Fights in Spain. Blackw. **71**: 225. — Cornh. **17**: 476.
— — Price on. Fraser, **45**: 533.
Bull-Fighter, Juancho the. Blackw. **62**: 197.
Bull-Fighting. Bentley, **60**: 363.
Bull Run, Battle of. (G. A. Custer) Galaxy, **21**: 624, 800. — (J. A. Early) N. Ecl. **4**: 726. — (J. A. Early) Hist. M. **18**: 103. — (J. E. Johnston) Hist. M. **12**: 232.
— and Battle of Wörth. Ev. Sat. **9**: 578.
— Before and after the Battle. (G. P. Putnam) Knick. **58**: 231.
— Second. (J. W. Ames) Overland, **8**: 399.
Bull-Running at Tutbury. (S. Pegge) Arch. **2**: 86.
Bullard, Artemas. Am. Presb. R. **5**: 20.
Bullard, Henry A. (V. H. Joy) De Bow, **12**: 50.
Buller, Charles. Fraser, **39**: 221.
Bullion, Ricardo on high Price of, 1810. Ecl. R. **11**: 216.
— Value of, determined. Bank. M. (N. Y.) **36**: 181.
Bullion Bank, Advantage and Principle of. Bank. M. (N. Y.) **13**: 440.
— of New York. Bank. M. (N. Y.) **13**: 757.
Bullion Committee. (G. Ellis and G. Channing) Quar. **4**: 518. **5**: 120.
— Report of. Chr. Obs. **9**: 653.
Bullion Product of United States. Bank. M. (N. Y.) **30**: 795.
Bullion Question. Pamph. **14**: 17, 225. — Quar. **3**: 152. — Ed. R. **18**: 448.
Bulliondust's Secretary. Once a Week, **30**: 499–554.
Bulmer, Agnes, Poem of. Ecl. R. **59**: 217.
Bülow. *See* Buelow.
Buloz, François. (A. Laugel) Nation, **24**: 100.
Bulstrode, England, Sketch of. Victoria, **9**: 493.
Bulwer, E. L. *See* Lytton, E. L , Lord.
Bulwer, John, Writings of. Retros. **16**: 205.
Bulwers, The. Lippinc. **10**: 237.
Bulwer-Clayton Treaty. Fraser, **54**: 121.
Bumboats and Bumboatmen. Chamb. J. **37**: 175.
Buns. Chamb. J. **23**: 292.
Bunce, Mrs. Frances Ann. (Mrs. L. H. Sigourney Godey, **21**: 275.
Bunch of Violets; a Tale. Temp. Bar, **36**: 99.
Bunch of Wild Flowers; a Poem. (D. C. Murray) Gent. M. n. s. **17**: 714.
Bundle-Wood Work and Workers. Good Words, **20**: 781.
Bung Estates. . (A. W. Cole) Bentley, **33**: 197.
Bungaree, King of the Blacks. All the Year, **1**: 77.
Bungener, Louis F. Preacher and the King. Liv. Age, **37**: 653. — Theo. & Lit. J. **5**: 695.
— Priest and Huguenot. (D. N. Lord) Theo. & Lit. J. **6**: 640.
Bunglers. (C. Thompson) Galaxy, **4**: 423.
Bunhill Fields, Graveyard of. Mo. Rel. M. **29**: 137.
Bunjaras, The. Internat. M. **2**: 377.
Bunker Hill, Battle of. (H. Dearborn) Hist. M. **8**: 267. — with map, (H. Dearborn) Portfo. (Den.) **19**: 179. — (E. Everett) Ecl. M. **55**: 105. — (L. Poyntz) Galaxy, **20**: 98. — (H. E. Scudder) Atlan. **36**: 79. — (I. N. Tarbox) New Eng. **34**: 302. — (D. Webster) No. Am. **7**: 255. — Anal. M. **11**: 150, 250.
— a Poem. Dem R. **2**: 243.
— Burgoyne's Account of. N. E. Reg. **11**: 125.
— Centennial Anniversary of. N. E. Reg. **29**: 395.
— Documents relating to Hist. M. **13**: 321.
— Doubts concerning. (C. Hudson) Chr. Exam. **40**: 247.
— Echoes of. (S. Osgood) Harper, **51**: 230.
— Gen. Putnam at. (F. J. Parker) N. E. Reg. **31**: 403
— Reminiscences of. (W. H. Sumner) N. E. Reg. **12**: 113, 225.
— Reply to Dearborn on. (D. Putnam) Portfo. (Den.) **20**: 3.
— Swett's Notes on. (J. Sparks) No. Am. **22**: 465.
— Who commanded at? N. E. Reg. **22**: 57.
Bunker Hill Monument. Chr. Exam. **29**: 252. — Niles's Reg. **28**: 301.
— designed by Greenough. (S. Swett) N. E. Reg. **18**: 61.
— Laying of Corner-Stone of. Bost. Mo. **1**: 143.
Bunkett's Letter. Temp. Bar, **57**: 82.
Bunkum Flagstaff. (L. G. Clarke) Knick. **35**: 53, 343, 510. **36**: 175, 360. **37**: 65, 527.
Bunkumville Chronicle. Knick. **35**: 30.
Bunsen, C. C. J., Baron. (C. Cook) Putnam, **12**: 365. — (C. H. Dall) Chr. Exam. **85**: 145. — (J. O. Dykes) Theo. Ecl. **6**: 321. — (M. Heilprin) Nation, **7**: 231. (F. D. Maurice) Macmil. **3**: 372. Same art. Liv. Age, **71**: 5. — (F. D. Maurice) Macmil. **18**: 144. — (C. K. Paul) Theo. R. **5**: 440. — Bentley, **50**: 284. — Blackw. **104**: 285. — Broadw. **8**: 45. — Ed. R. **127**: 469. Same art. Liv. Age, **97**: 515.
— and his Critics. Brit. Q. **17**: 535.
— and his Wife. (Lady Verney) Contemp. **28**: 948 Same art. Ecl. M. **88**: 18. Same art. Liv. Age, **131**: 731.
— Bibelwerk. *See* Bible.
— Chronology of. (E. Burgess) Bib. Sac. **24**: 744.
— Church of the Future. No. Brit. **8**: 130. — Ecl. R **87**: 129. — Brit. Q. **6**: 509. — For. Q. **37**: 50.
— — and universal Liturgy. Prosp. R. **2**: 255.
— Correspondence with W. E. Gladstone. Bib. R. **1**: 61.
— Egypt. *See* Egypt.
— God in History. Brit. Q. **25**: 488.
— Hippolytus and his Age. Brit. Q. **17**: 1. — Dub. R **33**: 365. — No. Brit. **19**: 85.
— Life and last Book. (F. P. Cobbe) Fraser, **77**: 783.
— Memoirs of. Brit. Q. **48**: 465. — Chr. Obs. **68**: 688 766. — Chr. Rem. **56**: 35. — Contemp. **8**: 114. — No. Brit. **48**: 429. — Victoria, **11**: 346.
— Signs of the Times. No. Brit. **24**: 386.

Bunsen, Frances, Baroness, Life and Letters of. (A. G. Sedgwick) Nation, **28**: 391. — (H. A. Page) Good Words, **20**: 261.

Bunsen, Heinrich Christian, and d'Azeglio. Temp. Bar, **51**: 231.

Bunsen, R. W., with portrait. Pop. Sci. Mo. **19**: 550. — with portrait, (H. E. Roscoe) Nature, **23**: 597.

Bunting, Edward, with portrait. Dub. Univ. **29**: 64.

Bunting, Jabez, with portrait. Hogg, **2**: 81. — Lond. Q. **12**: 513. — (R. A. West) Meth. Q. **20**: 20.

Bunting, William, Memorials of. Lond. Q. **36**: 119.

Bunyan, John. (T. B. Macaulay) Harper, **14**: 776. Same art. Liv. Age, **53**: 297. — (W. M. Punshon) Ex. H. Lec. **12**: 447. — (A. P. Stanley) Macmil. **30**: 273. Same art. Ev. Sat. **17**: 158. Same art. Ecl. M. **83**: 322. — Ecl. M. **23**: 318. — (G. B. Cheever) No. Am. **36**: 449. — Cath. World, **6**: 535. — Dub. Univ. **37**: 435. — Liv. Age, **42**: 20. — Nat. M. **6**: 97, 205.

— and Bunhill Fields. Fraser, **31**: 308. Same art. Liv. Age, **5**: 107.

— and Dante. (J. Ferguson) Am. Church R. **16**: 337.

— and his Biographers. Chr. R. **4**: 394.

— and Puritanism. (A. V. Dicey) Nation, **30**: 404.

— and Spenser, the Poet and the Dreamer. Meth. Q. **18**: 209.

— and Vane. Westm. **17**: 103.

— and vernacular English. (N. S. Dodge) Lakeside, **10**: 103.

— Cheever on. Chr. Obs. **46**: 501.

— Conversion of. (J. Brazer) Chr. Exam. **18**: 66.

— Genius and Writings of. Cong. M. **1**: 632. **2**: 96. — Ecl. R. **95**: 263. Same art. Ecl. M. **26**: 1.

— Holy War. Chr. Exam. **7**: 181.

— Ivmey's Reprint of Life of, 1692. Chr. Obs. **32**: 805.

— Philip's Life and Times of. Ecl. R. **70**: 468. — Mo. R. **148**: 183. — Tait, n. s. **6**: 273.

— Pilgrim's Progress. (C. Whitehead) Peop. J. **10**: 281.

— — Cheever's. Meth. Q. **9**: 466.

— — Editions of. (S. D. Alexander) Princ. **31**: 232.

— — First Edition of. Cong. **4**: 107.

— — An Italian Study of. (R. L. Nettleship) Macmil. **39**: 23.

— The Prose Poet. Am. Presb. R. **10**: 434.

— Southey's Life of. (T. B. Macaulay) Ed. R. **54**: 450. — (Sir W. Scott) Quar. **43**: 469. — Chr. Obs. **32**: 596, 668. — Fraser, **3**: 54.

— Traditions of. Macmil. **28**: 238. Same art. Liv. Age. **118**: 245.

— Writings. (V. R. Hotchkiss) Chr. R. **19**: 243. — Ecl. R. **83**: 129. Same art. Liv. Age, **33**: 153.

Buonarroti, M. A. *See* Michael Angelo.

Buoy, Automatic Signal, Courtenay's. Pract. M. **6**: 302.

Buoys. Chamb. J. **47**: 33.

— Beacons, etc., Construction of. (G. Herbert) J. Frankl. Inst. **61**: 79.

Burattini, Cassetta de'. Penny M. **14**: 108, 114, 142.

Burbadge, Richard, Shaksperian Actor. Temp. Bar, **53**: 252.

Burbeck, William. (H. Burbeck) N. E. Reg. **12**: 351.

Burbidge, Thomas. Poems. Dub. Univ. **14**: 51.

Burchard, Jedediah. (L. Withington) Lit. & Theo. R. **3**: 228. — (J. Walker) Chr. Exam. **20**: 393.

Burchell, Thomas, Missionary in Jamaica. Ecl. R. **90**: 159.

Burdell, Dr. Harvey, Murder of. Dub. Univ. **82**: 461.

Burder, George, Life of. (A. Alexander) Princ. **5**: 463. — Cong. M. **16**: 675.

— Obituary of. Chr. Obs. **33**: 758.

Burdett, Sir Francis, 1810. Chr. Obs. **9**: 252, 463.

Burdett Riots. All the Year, **17**: 230.

Burdett-Coutts, Angela G., Baroness, with portrait. Appleton, **6**: 281. — with portrait, Dub. Univ. **88**: 404. — with portrait, Ev. Sat. **11**: 553, 575. — (N. S. Dodge) Lakeside, **7**: 206.

Bureaucracy in Germany and Austria. (F. v. Schulte) Contemp. **37**: 432.

Burgar, John, Memoir of. Meth. M. **43**: 321, 361.

Bürger. *See* Buerger.

Burges, Tristram. Am. Q. **17**: 359.

Burges, William, Architect, Obituary of. (A. Rotch) Am. Arch. **9**: 237.

Burgess, Bishop George. (W. S. Bartlet) Am. Church R. **19**: 269. — Am. Church R. **22**: 96. — O. & N. **2**: 94.

Burgess, John Bagnold, Works of. Art J. **32**: 297.

Burgess, Thomas, Harford's Life of. Mo. R. **152**: 412. — Chr. Obs. **40**: 549. — Ecl. R. **73**: 35.

— Obituary of. Chr. Obs. **38**: 64, 784.

Burgess, Character of a. Penny M. **1**: 34.

Burgh Reform. Ed. R. **30**: 503.

Burgher School in Leipsic. Am. J. Educ. **9**: 210.

Burghley, W. Cecil, Lord, Memoirs of. (T. B. Macaulay) Ed. R. **55**: 271. — Mo. R. **116**: 329. **126**: 566.

— Nares's Life of. Colburn, **23**: 507. **31**: 174.

Burghley House. Antiquary, **3**: 301.

Burghley Papers, Haynes's and Murdin's. Retros. **15**: 204, 419.

Burg-Keeper's Secret; a Tale. Temp. Bar, **2**: 450.

Burglar, Adventure with a. Ev. Sat. **9**: 455.

Burglar-Alarm, Electric. Pop. Sci. Mo. **18**: 56.

Burglary at Faustel Eversleigh. Lond. Soc. **10**: 193.

— Science of. Cornh. **7**: 79.

— Story of a. Chamb. J. **43**: 481.

Burgmann's Conversion of S. Duitsch. Retros. **12**: 96.

Burgomaster; a Poem. Dub. Univ. **47**: 730.

Burgomaster Law in Prussia. Chamb. J. **17**: 284.

Burgomaster's Daughter. (F. E. M. Notley) Argosy, **30**: 188.

Burgomaster's Family. (E. C. W. van Walrée) Fraser, **85**: 169-714. **86**: 47-450. Same art. Liv. Age, **114**: 741, 808. **115**: 42-529.

Burgoyne, Gen. Sir John. (G. R. Gleig) Good Words, **12**: 849. — Blackw. **113**: 427. Same art. Liv. Age, **117**: 543.

— Campaign of 1777. (E. H. Walworth) M. Am. Hist. **1**: 273. — (J. W. De Peyster) M. Am. Hist. **2**: 22. (W. L. Stone) Harper, **55**: 673.

— in a new Light. (W. L. Stone) Galaxy, **5**: 78.

— Memoirs of. (W. F. Allen) Nation, **22**: 250.

— Order Book of. (J. T. Headley) Galaxy, **22**: 604.

— Surrender of. Blackw. **63**: 332. Same art. Liv. Age, **17**: 226.

— — Ralph Cross's Journal. Hist. M. **17**: 8.

Burgoyne House, Albany. (A. B. Street) Hours at Home, **9**: 464.

Burgundian Library at Brussels, Visit to. Fraser, **47**: 83.

Burgundy, Among French Friends in. (M. B. Edwards) Fraser, **101**: 392.

— Boar Hunt in. St. Paul's, **3**: 74.

Burgundy, Duchess of, Ambassadors to, from Henry VI. (W. J. Thoms) Arch. **40**: 451.

— Duke of, Marriage to Princess Margaret. (Sir T. Phillips) Arch. **31**: 326.

— Dukes of, Barante's History of. (R. Southey) For. Q. **28**: 287. — For. R. **1**: 1.

Burial. (R. H. Vickers) Once a Week, **9**: 635. — (J. Brazier) Chr. Exam. **31**: 137, 281.

— Ancient Graves and their Contents. Nat. Q. **22**: 315.

— at Sea; a Poem. (E. A. Blake) Tinsley, **29**: 189.

— Burning and, in the East. (F. R. Feudge) Lippinc. **13**: 593.

— Day with the Dead. (M. A. Dodge) Atlan. **6**: 326.

Burial, Disposal of the Dead. (B. W. Richardson) Pop. Sci. R. **14**: 164. Same art. Pop. Sci. Mo. **4**: 592.
— Epitaphs and. (D. H. Strother) Harper, **17**: 799.
— A few Words on. (G. S. Baker) Fraser, **93**: 81.
— Heathen and Christian. House. Words, **1**: 43.
— the last Homes. (F. Talbot) Belgra. **27**: 100.
— of Edward VI., Accounts for. (C. Ord) Arch. **12**: 334.
— of great Persons, Manner of. Arch. **1**: 346.
— of Moses; a Poem. Dub. Univ. **47**: 462.
— of Père Marquette; a Poem. (E. Cook) Cath. World, **29**: 626.
— of Sir John Moore. (T. Johnson) Putnam, **13**: 495.
— Ownership of the Dead. (S. B. Ruggles) Pop. Sci. Mo. **8**: 322.
— Pagan and Christian Sepulchers. Liv. Age, **86**: 481.
— Premature. (G. E. Mackay) Belgra. **35**: 95. Same art. Pop. Sci. Mo. **16**: 389.—(C. R. Drysdale) Victoria, **9**: 320.
— — Hermbstadt on. Colburn, **3**: 115.
— — Prevention of. Liv. Age, **13**: 357.
— — Rarity of. (W. See) Pop. Sci. Mo. **17**: 526.
— Promiscuous or denominational. Chr. Rem. **4**: 624.
— Searching for a Grave in a strange Land. (L. W. Bacon) Lippinc. **16**: 48.
— Silent Majority. (J. H. Browne) Harper, **49**: 468.
— Simple and sanitary. (S. P Day) Victoria, **32**: 576. **33**: 75–272.
— Unquiet Graves. (M. Howland) Lippinc. **19**: 121.
— with the Head towards the East. Dub. Univ. **78**: 705.
See Cremation.
Burial Customs. (D. W. Cheever) No. Am. **93**: 108.
— and Obitual Lore. (Mrs. A. B. Garrett) Nat. Q. **4**: 63.
— in Scotland. Chamb. J. **25**: 204.
— Sepulchral Caverns of Egypt. (Col. Straton) Ed. Philos. J. **3**: 345.
Burial Eccentricities. Chamb. J. **54**: 593.
Burial Grounds. Worc. M. **1**: 275.
— and Gravestones. All the Year, **15**: 592.
— and Metropolitan Board Act, 1854. Chr. Obs. **54**: 267, 515.
See Cemeteries; Churchyards; Graveyards.
Burial Laws. (H. T. Tuckerman) Chr. Exam. **61**: 335.
— and Sentiment of Death. Kitto, **18**: 329.
— Anglican View of. (G. H. Curteis) Macmil. **37**: 505.
— English. (A. P. Stanley) Macmil. **37**: 411.
See below, Burials Bill.
Burial Orders, Strange. All the Year, **41**: 235.
Burial Places and Burials. (E. C. Bishop) West. Lit. J. **1**: 401.
— Barbarous. Sharpe, **8**: 70. **9**: 33.
— Intramural. Chr. Obs. **54**: 515.
— of London. Blackw. **48**: 829.
Burial Practices. Mo. R. **164**: 299.
Burial Rites, Jewish. Good Words, **11**: 562.
— and Sepulchers. Sharpe, **52**: 205.
Burial Service and the Law. Chr. Rem. **48**: 81.
Burial Societies, Trading Benefit and. (A. J. Wilson) Fraser, **90**: 541.
Burial Vagaries. Chamb. J. **49**: 673. Same art. Ev. Sat. **13**: 564.
Burials. (G. Hill) Sharpe, **34**: 97.
— and Burial-Places. (W. Mitchell) Lippinc. **19**: 590.
— and Wakes. Penny M. **13**: 279, 283.
— in ancient Rome. Am. Arch. **4**: 127.
— in Orkney, Ancient. Chamb. J. **58**: 15.
— in Russia. Penny M. **4**: 243.
Burials Bill of 1850. Ecl. R. **91**: 760.
— of 1877. Cong. **6**: 234.—Chr. Obs. **77**: 388.
— — Last Word on. (M. Arnold) Macmil. **34**: 276.
— of 1880. Colburn, **168**: 631. **169**: 23.
— — Probable Results of. (J. G. Rogers) 19th Cent. **8**: 1018.
Burials Question and Church of England. Cong. **3**: 346.
— in England, 1878. Brit. Q. **68**: 145.
Buriates; a Siberian Tribe. (C. H. Brigham) Unita. R. **4**: 412.
Buried alive. (J. F. Otis) So. Lit. Mess. **3**: 338.
Buried alive. All the Year, **8**: 107.
Buried alive. Blackw. **10**: 262.
Buried alive. Chamb. J. **30**: 134.
Buried alive. Ev. Sat. **1**: 365.
Buried alive. Month, **4**: 606. Same art. Cath. World, **3**: 805.
Buried alive, Nearly. Chamb. J. **56**: 252.
Buried alone. Argosy, **6**: 147–537.
Buried Cities of the Gulf of Lyons. (E. Bowles) Month, **28**: 215.
Buried Flower; a Poem. (W. E. Aytoun) Blackw. **64** 108.
Buried in the Deep; a Tale. Chamb. J. **42**: 65–115.
Buried Treasure. (MM. Erckmann-Chatrian) Temp. Bar, **31**: 486.
Burke, Sir Bernard, with portrait. Dub. Univ. **88**: 16.—Irish Q. **9**: 928.—N. E. Reg. **13**: 3.
Burke, Edmund. (B. S. Fry) Meth. Q. **18**: 100.—(Mrs. S. C. Hall) Nat. M. **4**: 101.—(V. W. Kingsley) Nat. Q. **27**: 298.—(J. Morley) Fortn. **7**: 129, 303, 420. **8**: 47.—(G. Shepard) Bib. Sac. **31**: 507.—(C. C. Smith) No. Am. **88**: 61.—(E. Townbridge) Sharpe, **48**: 144.—(H. T. Tuckerman) So. Lit. Mess. **15**: 273.—(W. Hazlitt) Anal. M. **5**: 330.—(G. Croly) Blackw. **[illegible]3**: 277, 597. **34**: 25, 317. **35**: 27, 273, 508. **3[illegible]**: [illegible]8, 322. **56**: 745.—Dem. R. **27**: 305.—Ecl. M. **4**: 99.—Anal. M. **3**: 31.—Mus. **22**: 637. **23**: 169.—Dub. R. **34**: 68.—Internat. M. **2**: 145.—Nat. M. **3**: 432.—Penny M. **10**: 129.—Portfo.(Den.) **10**: 255.—Temp. Bar, **53**: 97.
— and Dr. F. Laurence, Correspondence of. Ed. R. **46**: 269.—Mo. R. **114**: 1.
— and George Washington. Liv. Age, **71**: 291.
— and the Revolution. Cath. World, **20**: 823.
— Anecdotes of. Dub. Univ. **74**: 456.
— as an Orator. (G. Gilfillan) Hogg, **10**: 1, 143. Same art. Ecl. M. **30**: 201.
— as a Prophet. (A. V. Dicey) Nation, **22**: 48.
— Battle of Minority in House of Commons, March 12, 1771. (R. Palgrave) Macmil. **16**: 138. Same art. Ecl. M. **69**: 227.
— Character of his Eloquence. Chr. Mo. Spec. **2**: 294.
— Classical Scholarship of. Chr. R. **11**: 266.
— Cobden's Criticisms on. Dub. Univ. **41**: 386.
— Conservatism of. (A. V. Dicey) Nation, **19**: 253.
— Correspondence of. Liv. Age, **2**: 587.—Dub. R. **17**: 212.—Mo. R. **164**: 598.—Ecl. R. **80**: 414.—Tait, n. s. **12**: 150.
— — with Grattan and others, Unpublished. Irish Mo. **6**: 181.
— Country-House at Beaconsfield, Day at. Fraser, **56**: 33. Same art. Ecl. M. **25**: 20, 159.
— Domestic Life and personal Character of. (J. G Macleod) Month, **38**: 240.
— Life and Character of. Dem. R. **34**. 70.
— — and Genius of. No. Brit. **35**: 445. Same art. Ecl. M. **55**: 192, 354.
— — and Times of. Chr. Rem. **42**: 297.—New Q. **10**: 38.
— — and Writings of. Ecl. R. **60**: 1.
— Macknight's Life of. Dub. Univ. **55**: 116, 275.—Colburn, **112**: 420.
— Morley on. (A. V. Dicey) Nation, **29**: 244.—(E. L. Godkin) Nation, **5**: 497.—Dub. Univ. **71**: 597.
— Original Letter of. Dub. Univ. **1**: 561.
— Original Letters of. Colburn, **14**: 380, 529. **15**: 153.

Burke, Edmund, Prior's Life of. (J. W. Croker) Quar. **34**: 457.—U. S. Lit. Gaz. **2**: 47.—Blackw. **17**: 1.—Mo. R. **114**: 1.—Quar. **34**: 457.—Mus. **6**: 259, 430. **9**: 541.—Chr. Obs. **26**: 281.—Ecl. R. **40**: 312.—Portfo.(Den.) **33**: 38.
Burke, Edmund, of New Hampshire, with portrait. Dem. R. **20**: 73.
Burke, Glendy, with portrait. De Bow, **11**: 218.
Burke, John. (J. B. Burke) N. E. Reg. **12**: 193.
Burke, John Bernard. *See* Burke, Sir Bernard.
Burke and Wills, Expedition of. Fraser, **66**: 726.
Burking, Philosophy of. Fraser, **5**: 52.
Burkitt, Rev. T., Memoir of. Cong. M. **17**: 253.
Burkitt, William. Meth. M. **28**: 289.
Burleigh. *See* Burghley.
Burleigh House. Penny M. **9**: 237, 242.
Burlesque. (J. C. Brenan) Sharpe, **39**: 86.
— Age of. (R. G. White) Galaxy, **8**: 256.
— The Founder of. Temp. Bar, **29**: 318.
— New and old. St. Paul's, **4**: 698.
Burlesque, The, and the Beautiful. (R. H. Horne) Contemp. **18**: 390.
Burlesque Poetry. No. Brit. **43**: 59.
Burlesque Writers of England. (C. C. Clarke) Gent. M. n. s. **7**: 557.
Burlesques. Cornh. **4**: 167.
Burletta, What is a? (D. Cook) Once a Week, **12**: 233.
Burlingame, Anson, with portrait. Ecl. M. **71**: 1155.
— as an Orator. (J. G. Blaine) Atlan. **26**: 629.
Burlington, Vt., University of Vermont. O. & N. **4**: 115.
Burlington House, Home of the Royal Society. Chamb. J. **28**: 71.
Burmah. (A. Fytche) Fortn. **31**: 627. Same art. Liv. Age, **141**: 432.—Nat. M. **4**: 153.—Hogg, **10**: 17.
— and the Burmese. (C. D. Clifford-Lloyd) Dub. Univ. **86**: 584.—(S. Yoe) Cornh. **42**: 582.—Blackw. **85**: 31.
— British, Trade Routes to. (J. Coryton) Geog. M. **2**: 153.
— Buddhists and Buddhism in. (S. Yoe) Cornh. **42**: 721.
— Christianity in. Prosp. R. **10**: 119.
— Empire of, Cox's. Mo. R. **98**: 49.
— — Crawford's Embassy to Court of. Colburn, **25**: 544.
— Forbes's British. Nature, **20**: 3.
— Heroines of, Three. Cornh. **38**: 723.
— Imprisoned in. Chamb. J. **35**: 105.
— in 1875. (E. Browne) Fraser, **92**: 224.
— Letters from. Blackw. **79**: 536.
— Mission to. (J. H. Morison) No. Am. **78**: 21.
— Missions in, American. Chr. Obs. **59**: 473.—Quar. **33**: 37.
— — — Judson's. Lond. M. **18**: 285.
— — Baptist. (R. Southey) Quar. **33**: 37.—Mo. Rel. M. **29**: 144.
— Past and present. Lond. Q. **50**: 284.
— Petroleum in. (J. W. Palmer) Atlan. **22**: 404.
— Political Situation of. (A. Forbes) 19th Cent. **5**: 740.
— Population of. (H. Burney) J. Statis. Soc. **4**: 335.
— Visit to the King of, 1864. (W. C. Pepys) Colburn, **143**: 526, 643.
— War in, 1824–26. (R. Southey) Quar. **35**: 481.—Colburn, **95**: 360.—Meth. M. **50**: 174.
— — How we talked about. Bentley, **32**: 461.
— — Narrative of. Lond. M. **17**: 232.
— — Reminiscence of. Liv. Age, **33**: 524.
Burmese, Among the. (P. Hordern) Fraser, **98**: 85–758. Same art. Liv. Age, **138**: 354, 372. **139**: 232–734. **140**: 375.
— Varnished Ware of. Penny M. **11**: 28.
Burmese Ilpon; a Tale. (J. Ross) Fraser, **94**: 176.
Burmese Translation of the Bible. Chr. R. **1**: 116.
Burnaby, Edwyn S., with portrait. Colburn, **167**: 421.
Burnap, George W. Lectures. Chr. Exam. **29**: 100.—(A. Lamson) Chr. Exam. **33**: 187.—(E. Peabody) Chr. Exam. **38**: 107.
— Sermon on Death of. (E. S. Gannett) Mo Rel. M. **22**: 313.
Burnes, Sir Alex. (J. W. Kaye) Good Words, **6**: 246.
Burnet, Bishop Gilbert, and the English Revolution. (G. W. Conder) Ex. H. Lec. **18**: 277.
— and Macaulay. (J. Williams) Am. Church R. **13**: 593.
— History of his own Times. Ecl. R. **40**: 481.—(R. Southey) Quar. **29**: 165.—Retros. **5**: 349.—Lond. M. **7**: 291.
— Life, Times, and Works of. Chr. Rem. **47**: 319.
Burnet, John, Autobiography of. Art J. **2**: 275.
Burnet, John, of Camberwell. Cong. **3**: 513.
Burnet, Thomas. Theory of the Earth. (H. Southern) Retros. **6**: 133.
Burnet, William, Gov. (J. P. Bradley) Pennsyl. M. **3**: 308.—Am. Q. Reg. **14**: 290.
Burnett, P. H., first Gov. of California, Recollections of. (W. P. Garrison) Nation, **30**: 389.
Burnett, Waldo Irving, Life and Writings of. (J. Wyman) Am. J. Sci. **68**: 255.
Burney, Charles, Memoirs of. (J. W. Croker) Quar. **49**: 97.—Knick. **32**: 206.—Mo. R. **130**: 19.
Burney, Fanny. *See* Arblay, Madame F. d'.
Burnham, Samuel. (A. H. Quint) Cong. Q. **16**: 1.
Burnham and Dorney, Summer Day at. (E. Walford) Once a Week, **12**: 696.
Burnham Beeches. Chamb. J. **57**: 381.
Burnham Thorpe, the Birthplace of Nelson. (E. Walford) Gent. M. n. s. **23**: 471.
Burnham Yews Chamb. J. **38**: 54.
Burning of the Dead. *See* Cremation.
— of Widows. Blackw. **23**: 161. *See also* Suttee; Widows.
— of St. Rosalie. Chamb. J. **34**: 225. Same art. Ecl. M. **53**: 203.
— of Trucklebury; Story of a Home Campaign. Fraser, **22**: 431.
— of the World. (C. Vitringa) Kitto, **2**: 304.
Burning Forest, The. (L. Schefer) Hogg, **6**: 28–70.
Burns, Robert. (T. Carlyle) Ed. R. **48**: 267.—(H. T. Tuckerman) So. Lit. Mess. **7**: 249.—(J. F. Otis) So. Lit. Mess. **2**: 238.—(O. W. B. Peabody) No. Am. **42**: 66.—So. Lit. Mess. **10**: 543.—Knick. **32**: 206.—(Sir W. Scott) Quar. **1**: 16.—Blackw. **46**: 256.—Dub. Univ. **25**: 66, 289.—Blackw. **111**: 140. Same art. Ecl. M. **78**: 513. Same art. Liv. Age, **113**: 3.—Dub. Univ. **89**: 94.—Meth. M. **33**: 24.—Penny M. **10**: 353, 389.
— and Beranger. (C. Mackay) 19th Cent. **7**: 443.
— and Byron. Portfo.(Den.) **32**: 386.
— and Cowper, Lecture on. (E. Elliott) Tait, n. s. **9**: 357.
— and George Crabbe. Dub. Univ. **3**: 489.
— and Ettrick Shepherd. Blackw. **4**: 521.
— and Robert Ferguson. (D. K. Brown) Canad. Mo. **17**: 63.
— and his Ancestors. Hogg, **6**: 185.
— and his School. (C. Kingsley) No. Brit. **16**: 149. Same art. Ecl. M. **25**: 114. Same art. Liv. Age, **31**: 529.
— and his Works. (J. K. Nixon) St. James, **46**: 128.
— and Scotch Song before him. (J. C. Shairp) Atlan. **44**: 502.
— and Scott. (B. Frere) Macmil. **26**: 168.—Ecl. M. **77**: 626.
— Anniversary Poem on. (S. Whiting) Once a Week, **14**: 92.
— at Work. (C. Pebody) Gent. M. n. s. **6**: 593.
— Birthday and Bowl. Once a Week, **6**: 286.
— Centenary. Chamb. J. **31**: 129, 161.
— Chambers's Life of. Chamb. J. **18**: 230.

Burns, Robert, Character of. Knick. **41**: 25.
— Correspondence with Clarinda. Appleton, **10**: 679. — Mo. R. **163**: 144. — Tait, n. s. **10**: 749. **11**: 29.
— Cunningham's Life of. Fraser, **9**: 400.
— Family of. Dub. Univ. **87**: 727.
— Festival, 1844. Blackw. **56**: 370. — Tait, n. s. **11**: 545. — Liv. Age, **60**: 740.
— — at Sheffield, 1849. Peop. J. **7**: 109.
— Genius and Character of. Mus. **41**: 568. — Mo. R. **154**: 261.
— German Translation of Poems of. Ev. Sat. **9**: 625.
— Haunts of. (N. Hawthorne) Atlan. **6**: 385.
— Heroines of. Mus. **35**: 211. — Ecl. M. **21**: 203.
— Highland Mary, Poem to. Blackw. **67**: 309.
— Highland Mary of. Chamb. J. **14**: 1.
— Home of. (J. G. Wilson) Lippinc. **1**: 657.
— Horace, and Béranger; Lyrists. Cornh. **17**: 150. Same art. Liv. Age, **97**: 3.
— Influence of Scenery on his Poetry. Lond. M. **4**: 250.
— Land o'. (W. H. Rideing) Harper, **59**: 180. — Dub. Univ. **18**: 508, 711.
— Life of. Mus. **13**: 247. **14**: 486. — Blackw. **23**: 667.
— — Lockhart's. Lond. M. **20**: 161.
— — and Poems of. Dub. Univ. **41**: 169. — Mo. R. **135**: 87.
— Loves of. (P. Fitzgerald) Belgra. **12**: 421.
— New Edition of. Blackw. **1**: 261. **2**: 65, 201.
— New York and Dundee Statue of. Art J. **33**: 71.
— Poem on. (H. W. Longfellow) Harper, **61**: 321.
— Poetry of. (T. Bayne) St. James, **45**: 493.
— Recent Facts concerning. Chamb. J. **52**: 193.
— Recollections of. Lond. M. **10**: 117.
— Religion of. (J. Kitto) Nat. M. **5**: 52.
— Reliques of. (F. Jeffrey) Ed. R. **13**: 249. Same art. Selec. Ed. R. **2**: 166, 175. — Ecl. R. **9**: 393.
— Some Aspects of. Cornh. **40**: 408. Same art. Appleton, **22**: 516.
— Songs of. Blackw. **46**: 256.
— Sorrows of. (J. H. Vosburg) Nat. Q. **18**: 46.
— Tam o' Shanter. Lond. M. **23**: 557.
— Tyler's. (M. B. Hope) Princ. **21**: 251.
— Unpublished Commonplace Book. Macmil. **39**: 448, 560. **40**: 32, 124, 250.
— Visit to Birthplace of. Ecl. R. **110**: 182.
— Wordsworth's Letter on. Blackw. **2**: 65, 201.
— Writings and Loves of. (J. H. Barrett) Nat. Q. **6**: 74.
Burns, William, an apostolic Missionary. (H. A. Page) Good Words, **11**: 161.
Burns, William C. Theo. Ecl. **7**: 177.
— Memoir of. Chr. Obs. **70**: 601.
Burns and Scalds, Cure of. Penny M. **2**: 14.
Burnside, Gen. Ambrose E., with portrait. Ev. Sat. **10**: 6.
Burnside Army Bill. (G. Mallery) Nation, **28**: 42.
Burnt Njal, Story of. Ed. R. **114**: 425. — Macmil. **4**: 294.
Burr, Aaron. (W. Dorsheimer) Atlan. **1**: 597. — (R. H. Howard) Meth. Q. **18**: 383. — (J. A. Leach) University Q. **3**: 313. — (C. F. Adams) No. Am. **49**: 155. — Am. Q. **21**: 74. **22**: 350. — Dem. R. **1**: 211. **5**: 333. — New York R. **2**: 175. — Mus. **36**: 218. — Niles's Reg. **23**: 279. — Am. Mo. M. **9**: 172. — New Eng. M. **8**: 294. — Fraser, **57**: 363. — (W. Hague) Appleton, **25**: 525.
— and Blennerhassett. (W. Wallace) Am. Whig R. **2**: 133.
— and Gen. Richard Montgomery. Hist. M. **2**: 264.
— Anecdotes of. Hist. M. **2**: 233.
— as a Soldier. (S. Youngs) Hist. M. **19**: 384.
— Conspiracy of. (B. J. Lossing) Harper, **25**: 69. — (R. T. Ford) No. Am. **79**: 297. — Am. Q. **9**: 215.
— Davis's Life and Journal of. Mo. R. **148**: 570.
— Facts concerning. So. Lit. Mess. **27**: 177.
Burr, Aaron, Life and Character of. (V. W. Kingsley) Nat. Q. **32**: 362.
— Parton's Life of. (F. J. Betts) Am. Church R. **11**: 64. — (D. S. Boardman) Am. Church R. **11**: 564. — (I. N. Tarbox) New Eng. **16**: 291. — Liv. Age, **57**: 302. — So. Lit. Mess. **26**: 321.
— Personal Recollections of. (J. Greenwood) Hist. M. **7**: 331.
— Trial of. Am. Whig R. **12**: 367.
Burr, Rev. Aaron, Sketch of. Cong. M. **8**: 105.
Burr, Alexander H., Style of. Art J. **22**: 309.
Burr, John, Style of. Art J. **21**: 337.
Burr, Theodosia. (J. Parton) Harper, **29**: 293.
Burr Seminary, Vt., History of. Am. Q. Reg. **13**: 37.
Burridge, Joseph, Diary of. Blackw. **14**: 702.
Burritt, Elihu. (R. W. Bailey) So. Lit. Mess. **9**: 234. — So. Lit. Mess. **6**: 201. — Liv. Age, **29**: 403. — with portrait, (M. Howitt) Peop. J. **2**: 239. — (J. Crosfield) Peop. J. **3**: 204. — (G. E. Woodberry) Nation, **30**: 293. — Chamb. J. **15**: 193.
— and Peace Societies. Chr. Obs. **46**: 407.
Burroughs, George. (J. Farmer) N. E. Reg. **1**: 37.
Burroughs, John. (J. Benton) Scrib. **13**: 336.
— Pepacton. (T. W. Higginson) Nation, **33**: 16.
Burrowes, Peter, with portrait. Dub. Univ. **33**: 436.
Burrowes, Thomas H. Am. J. Educ. **6**: 107, 555.
Burrowing Animals, Homes of. (M. Titcomb) Harper, **32**: 421.
Burrows, Wm., Lieut. U. S. N. Portfo.(Den.) **11**: 114.
Burschen Life, Sketches of. Dub. Univ. **28**: 54.
Burschenschaft of Germany, Recollections of. Dub. Univ. **29**: 112.
Bursting of the Bud. (J. F. Waller) Dub. Univ. **39**: 355.
Burton, Rev. Asa, with portrait. Am. Q. Reg. **10**: 321.
— Theological System of. (L. Withington) Am. Presb. R. **18**: 5.
Burton, Rev. Henry, Memoir of. Cong. M. **3**: 409.
Burton, John Hill, Obituary of. Blackw. **130**: 401. Same art. Liv. Age, **151**: 161.
Burton, Robert. Anatomy of Melancholy. (C. C. Smith) Chr. Exam. **68**: 211. — Blackw. **90**: 323. — Cornh. **41**: 475. Same art. Appleton, **23**: 512.
Burton, Thomas, Diary. Cong. M. **12**: 663. — Colburn, **23**: 193.
Burton, Warren. Views of Man and Providence. Chr. Exam. **13**: 394.
Burton's Loan, Story of. Chamb. J. **51**: 99, 122.
Bury, Lady Charlotte, Memoir of, with portrait. Colburn, **49**: 76.
Bury, Richard de. Bost. R **3**: 94.
Bury Fair. Antiquary, **1**: 160.
Bury St. Edmunds, Abbey Church of. (E. King) Arch. **3**: 311.
Busbecq, A. G. de. Penny M. **3**: 485. **4**: 7-62.
— Among the Turks, 1554. All the Year, **33**: 174, 204.
— Life and Letters of. (E. L. Godkin) Nation, **32**: 211.
Busby, Thomas, Mus. Doc. All the Year, **27**: 413.
Bush, George. Biblical Notes. Ecl. R. **72**: 571.
— Commentaries of. (G. R. Noyes) Chr. Exam. **38**: 333.
— Notes on Numbers, 1858. Theo. & Lit. J. **11**: 173.
— on Millerism. Am. Mo. R. **3**: 202.
— on the Resurrection. Chr. R. **10**: 325. — (H. W. Bellows) Chr. Exam. **38**: 178. — (J. W. Yeomans) Princ. **17**: 138. — (S. T. Spear) Am. Bib. Repos. 3d s. **1**: 212. — (A. M. Osborn) Meth. Q. **5**: 165. — Ecl. R. **83**: 404.
— on the Soul. (S. Tyler) Princ. **18**: 219.
Bush and Beach. House. Words, **19**: 364.
Bush-Life in Queensland. Blackw. **126**: 703. **127**: 59-768. **128**: 89. Same art. Liv. Age, **144**: 216-621 **145**: 20-787. **146**: 533, 783. **147**: 78, 330.
See **Australia.**

Bushranging Facts. Bentley, 35: 238.
Bushe, Charles K. Dub. Univ. 18: 80. — Irish Q. 3: 51.
Bushire, Journal of a Voyage to, 1830. Colburn, 110: 193.
Bushman Folk-Lore. Cornh. 34: 443.
Bushnell, Horace. (G. S. Drew) Contemp. 35: 815. — (H. M. Goodwin) New Eng. 39: 803. 40: 1. — (G. P. Fisher) Internat. R. 10: 13. — Appleton, 24: 277. — (L. H. Atwater) Presb. R. 2: 114. — (C. C. Nott) Nation, 31: 136. — (R. Ellis) Unita. R. 5: 313. — (J. Dyer) Penn Mo. 7: 287.
— and the Atonement. (L. E. Smith) Bapt. Q. 8: 387.
— Christian Nurture. (H. M. Goodwin) New Eng. 19: 474. — (N. Porter) New Eng. 5: 613. — (G. W. Burnap) Chr. Exam. 43: 435. — New Eng. 6: 121. — (C. Hodge) Princ. 19: 502. — (J. S. Davenport) Am. Church R. 1: 228. — (D. Forbes) Univ. Q. 5: 144.
— Discourse on. (N. Porter) New Eng. 36: 152.
— Discourses. Brit. Q. 14: 437. — (W. W. Lord) Princ. 18: 1. — (C. Hodge) Princ. 21: 259. — (T. S. King) Univ. Q. 6: 302. — (J. H. Morison) Chr. Exam. 46: 453. 47: 238. — (D. N. Lord) Theo. & Lit. J. 2: 173.
— Dissertation on Language. (D. N. Lord) Theo. & Lit. J. 2: 61.
— Ecclesiastical Conflict about. (L. Bacon) New Eng. 38: 701.
— God in Christ. Kitto, 6: 237. — Prosp. R. 6: 283.
— Nature and the Supernatural. (N. Porter) New Eng. 17: 224. — Brit. Q. 31: 53. — Theo. & Lit. J. 11: 529.
— on Home Missions. (H. P. Tappan) Am. Bib. Repos. 3d s. 4: 252.
— or Orthodoxy and Heresy indicated. Brownson, 6: 495.
— Phi Beta Kappa Oration, 1837. No. Am. 46: 301.
— Reconstructed Theology of. (W. Barrows) Bost. R. 6: 213.
— Sermons for the new Life. (H. M. Goodwin) New Eng. 17: 382. — Am. Presb. R. 9: 94. — Theo. & Lit. J. 11: 171.
— — on living Subjects. (J. M. Hoppin) New Eng. 32: 95.
— Vicarious Sacrifice. (N. Porter) New Eng. 25: 228. *See* Atonement.
— Writings of. Chr. Obs. 61: 908.
Bushrangers, New So. Wales. Chamb. J. 16: 134, 285.
Bushy Run, Battle of. (F. Parkman) Knick. 38: 153.
Business. (L. Cross) Colburn, 164: 515, 639. 165: 764.
— and Religion. Mo. Rel. M. 19: 157.
— at the present Day. St. Paul's, 1: 425.
— Buzz of. Lond. Soc. 38: 531.
— Davies on Evils of late Hours of. Mo. R. 163: 151.
— Depression of, and its Causes. Penn Mo. 7: 297. — Bank. M. (N. Y.) 32: 287.
— — Hewitt's Committee on, 1878. (H. White) Nation, 27: 93.
— Economy and Revival of. (A. S. Bolles) Bank. M. (N. Y.) 31: 874.
— Ethics of. (J. B. Clark) New Eng. 38: 157.
— Fortunes made in. Lond. Soc. 35: 60-400. 36: 11-343.
— Frauds and Failures. Temp. Bar, 17: 381. Same art. Ecl. M. 67: 219.
— Limits to State Control of. (T. M. Cooley) Princ. n. s. 1: 233.
— Man of, Absolute. (L. Cross) Colburn, 166: 591.
— Man of Principle in. (T. B. Thayer) Univ. Q. 12: 5.
— Moral End of. (F. Hunt) Hunt, 1: 390.
— Morality in. (T. Lewis) No. Am. 95: 105.
— Noblemen in. Lond. Soc. 33: 214.
— Success in, Elements of. (M. H. Smith) Hunt, 31: 56.
Business Education. (F. Hunt) Hunt, 15: 381.
Business Facilities of New York and London. (G. Gordon) Hunt, 15: 339.
Business Life, End of a. Chr. Exam. 23: 327.
Business Men and Legislation, Relations of. (H. A. Hill) Am. Soc. Sci. J. 3: 148. — (H. A. Hill) Penn Mo. 1: 440, 449.
— as Legislators. (J. B. Hodgskin) Nation, 11: 290.
— Intellectual Occupations of. Bank. M. (N. Y.) 4: 227.
— Manias of. Ev. Sat. 10: 138.
Buss, R. W. Picture of Hogarth at School. Peop. J. 6: 3
Bussey, Benjamin, Biography of. Hunt, 6: 226.
Bustard, The great. Fraser, 50: 328.
Busy Life and idle Life. Tinsley, 9: 77.
Busybody. So. Lit. Mess. 4: 352, 469.
Busybodies. Tinsley, 5: 452.
But, The universal. Dub. Univ. 83: 58.
Butcher and his Meat. All the Year, 19: 54.
Bute and Norfolk Families. Antiquary, 2: 102.
Butler, Benjamin F., with portrait. Dem. R. 5: 33. — with portrait, Dem. R. 14: 223.
Butler, Gen. Benjamin F., and the Worcester Convention, 1871. — (A. G. Sedgwick) Nation, 13: 225. — Ev. Sat. 11: 362.
— as a Republican. (E. L. Godkin) Nation, 27: 220.
— at New Orleans. (A. F. Puffer) Atlan. 12: 104.
— — Infamous Woman Order. So. Hist. Pap. 6: 228.
— defended. Land We Love, 6: 136.
— Visit to, and the Army of the James. Fraser, 71: 434.
Butler, Charles. Horæ Juridicæ. (J. F. Dickman) Knick. 32: 479. 33: 95.
— Reminiscences of. U. S. Lit. Gaz. 1: 225. — (T. D. Woolsey) Chr. Mo. Spec. 7: 40. — Mo. R. 113: 49. — (J. Sparks) No. Am. 20: 272. — Ecl. R. 36: 239.
Butler, E. G. W. (C. Gayarré) So. M. 10: 541, 764.
Butler, Mrs. Fanny Kemble. Journal in America. Quar. 54: 39. — So. Lit. Mess. 1: 524. — (A. H. Everett) No. Am. 41: 109. — Am. Mo. M. 5: 280. — Ed. R. 61: 379.
— Divorce Case. Liv. Age, 20: 350.
— Poems of. Quar. 75: 325. Same art. Ecl. M. 5: 104. — Liv. Age, 2: 455. — Dem. R. 15: 507.
— Year of Consolation. Westm. 47: 399. — Liv. Age, 13: 470. — Quar. 81: 440. Same art. Liv. Age, 15: 481. — Tait, n. s. 14: 413.
See also Kemble, Fanny.
Butler, Bishop Joseph. (J. Alden) Am. Bib. Repos. 10: 317. — Quar. 64: 331. — (G. R. Crooks) Meth. Q. 11: 247. — (J. T. Champlin) Chr. R. 19: 392. — (H. Rogers) Liv. Age, 53: 257.
— Analogy of Religion. Meth. Q. 1: 556. — (A. Barnes) Chr. Q. Spec. 2: 604.
— — Barnes's Introduction to. Meth. Q. 2: 303.
— — Strength and Weakness of. Westm. 102: 1.
— and his recent Critics. Brit. Q. 38: 97. Same art. Theo. Ecl. 1: 159.
— and his Sermons. (C. A. Stork) Luth. Q. 7: 1.
— and his Teaching. (J. H. Fyfe) Good Words, 15: 233.
— and religious Features of his Time. (A. S. Farrar) Ex. H. Lec. 18: 325.
— and the Zeit-Geist. (M. Arnold) Contemp. 27: 377, 571. Same art. Liv. Age, 129: 67.
— Matthew Arnold on. Brit. Q. 66: 85.
— Bartlett's Life of. Dub. Univ. 13: 471, 619.
— Butleriana. Lond. M. 13: 136, 425. 14: 94. 16: 225, 396.
— Life of. (J. J. Blunt) Quar. 64: 331.
— on Evidences. (J. Hunt) Contemp. 22: 903.
— reviewed in Light of modern Thought. Chr. Obs. 71: 681.
— Rogers's Life of. Prosp. R. 10: 524.
— Works of. (J. J. Blunt) Quar. 43: 182. — Liv. Age, 1: 691. — Meth. Q. 3: 128. — (S. F. Smith) Chr. R. 9: 199.

Butler, Laurence, Letters from Ohio Valley, 1784–93. M. Am. Hist. **1**: 40, 112.
Butler, Gen. Richard, Journal of. Olden Time, **2**: 433, 481, 529.
Butler, Samuel. (C. C. Clarke) Gent. M. n. s. **7**: 176.— No. Brit. **24**: 50. Same art. Ecl. M. **37**: 1. Same art. Liv. Age, **48**: 1.
— Genuine and spurious Remains. (H. Baldwin) Retros. **2**: 256.
— Hudibras. (L. C. Allinson) Canad. Mo. **14**: 68.— West. Mo. R. **1**: 732.
— Poems. Fraser, **53**: 342.
— — Bell's Edition. Colburn. **106**: 29.
— Sketches from unpublished MSS. Lond. M. **14**: 401.
Butler, Col. W., Memoir of. Dub. Univ. **45**: 673.
Butler, Rev. Wm. Archer, with portrait. Dub. Univ. **19**: 588. **32**: 244. **34**: 45.
— Remains of. Ed. R. **104**: 229.
— Sermons of. Chr. Obs. **53**: 613.— Lond. Q. **7**: 461.— Ecl. R. **103**: 55.
Butler, Gen. William O., with portrait. Dem. R. **23**: 329.
Butler Family of Rawcliffe. (T. E. Gibson) Month, **40**: 172.
Butler Genealogy. (J. D. Butler) N. E. Reg. **1**: 167.— (C. Butler) N. E. Reg. **2**: 355. **3**: 73, 353.
Butt, Isaac. Dub. Univ. **93**: 710.
— Introductory Lecture. Dub. Univ. **9**: 597.
Butt, The. (Mrs. F. Trollope) Colburn, **70**: 199–415.
Butter. House. Words, **6**: 344.
— and Cream. Brit. Q. **68**: 379.
— and Honey in Is. vii. 15. (J. C. Knight) Kitto, **40**: 337.
— and Milk. (G. E. Waring, jr.) Nation, **27**: 380.
— chemically considered. Ev. Sat. **7**: 637.
— Heraldic. (J. Dunning) Lond. Soc. **24**: 42.
— Making. Penny M. **4**: 274.
— — Machine for. Pract. M. **4**: 112.
— Sham. Chamb. J. **57**: 319.
Buttercups and Ball Bouquets; a Story. (L. H. Hooper) Galaxy, **14**: 618.
Butterfly, Cosmopolitan. (S. H. Scudder) Am. Natural. **10**: 392, 602.
— Curious History of a. (S. H. Scudder) Am. Natural. **6**: 513.
— The first. Recr. Sci. **1**: 283.
— A polymorphic. (S. H. Scudder) Am. Natural. **8**: 257.
— Trunk of, Structure and Action of. (E. Burgess) Am. Natural. **14**: 313.
Butterflies. (C. Hope-Robertson) Pop. Sci. R. **10**: 52.— All the Year, **5**: 228.
— and Moths. (E A. Samuels) Scrib. **18**: 389.
— Antennæ in. (A. R. Grote) Am. Natural. **8**: 519.
— British, Newman's. (W. S. Dallas) Nature, **4**: 219.
— Colony of. (A. R. Grote) Am. Natural. **10**: 129.
— Gossip on. (S. K. T. Mayer) Victoria, **11**: 494.
— Length of Life of. (W. H. Edwards) Am. Natural. **15**: 868.
— Mimicry in. (A. S. Packard, jr.) Am. Natural. **10**: 534.
— Natural History of. Ecl. R. **87**: 549.
— of the Sea. Chamb. J. **53**: 463. Same art. Sup. Pop. Sci. Mo. **1**: 382.
— Pupation of. (C. V. Riley) Nature, **20**: 594.
— Sex in. (C. V. Riley) Am. Natural. **7**: 513.
— — Control of. (M. Treat) Am. Natural. **7**: 129.
— Sexual Colors of. (C. Darwin) Nature, **21**: 237.
— The Temple of. Lond. M. **14**: 495.
— with dissimilar Sexes. (R. Meldola) Nature, **19**: 586.
— Wings of, Growth of. (C. H. Robertson) Recr. Sci. **2**: 316.
See Moths.
Butterfly Bishop. Bentley, **2**: 17.
Buttons. All the Year, **7**: 378.—House. Words, **5**: 106.
— Coat, Manufacture of. Penny M. **9**: 77.
Button-Rose, The. Atlan. **1**: 196.
Butzbach, John. (H. Zimmern) Dub. Univ. **91**: 337.
Buxton, Mrs. B. H. In Memoriam. Tinsley, **28**: 499.
Buxton, Richard. Hogg, **3**: 222.
Buxton, Sydney Charles, with portrait. Colburn, **168**: 623.
Buxton, Thomas Fowell, with portrait. Hogg, **4**: 209.
— Labors against Slavery. (E. Dwight) No. Am. **71**: 1.
— Memoir of. Westm. **34**: 125.— Quar. **83**: 127.— No. Brit. **9**: 370.— Liv. Age, **17**: 537.— (E. Dwight) No. Am. **70**: 331.— Ecl. M. **15**: 145.— Ecl. R. **88**: 1.— Chr. Obs. **45**: 359, 417. **48**: 680.— (T. Binney) Ex. H. Lec. **4**: 353.— (A. Stevens) Nat. M. **6**: 159, 233, 332.
Buxton, Maine. (C. Coffin) Hist. M. **14**: 202.
Buy a Broom; a Tale. Blackw. **24**: 709.
Buyer of Souls; a Russian Story. Chamb. J. **18**: 200.
Buying a Harmonium. Lond. Soc. **1**: 61.
— a Horse. (W. D. Howells) Atlan. **43**: 741.
— and Selling. All the Year, **28**: 439.
Buzzard, Swainson's. (E. Coues) Am. Natural. **8**: 282.
Buzzard's Bay, Naturalist in. (W. D. Gunning) Lippinc. **14**: 574.
By and By; a Tale. (M. C. Hay) Belgra. **29**: 60.
By Cable; a Tale. (A. Fonblanque) Belgra. **36**: supp. 113.
By the Camp Fire. (E. Yette) Lakeside, **3**: 464.
By the Camp Fire; a Poem. (I. Cambridge) Good Words, **16**: 48.
By Celia's Arbor. (W. Besant and J. Rice) Appleton, **18**: 245–491. **19**: 11–538.
By the Lake. (I. A. Prokop) Lippinc. **15**: 718.
By Night Express. House. Words, **17**: 476.
By the Northland Lakes. (C. H. Miller) Overland, **11**: 75.
By the Old Fountain; a Story. All the Year, **43**: 161, 186.
By Order of the King; a Romance of English History. (V. Hugo) Gent M. n. s. **2**: 633. **3**: 1–641. **4**: 14–668.
By our Hearth. (A. H. Baldwin) Fraser, **70**: 466.
By Proxy. (J. Payn) Belgra. **32**: 257, 482. **33**: 1–473. **34**: 1–356. **35**: 104, 366.
By the River; a Poem. (J. T. Trowbridge) Atlan. **12**: 70.
By the Riverside. All the Year, **39**: 35–349. **40**: 392, 516. **41**: 15, 541.
By Rule of Thumb. Once a Week, **26**: 1–473.
By the Seaside; a Poem. (W. Buchanan) Temp. Bar, **5**: 379.
By the Waters of Babylon; a Poem. (C. G. Rossetti) Macmil. **14**: 424. Same art. Liv. Age, **91**: 258.
By the Well; a Tale. (J. Kavanagh) Temp. Bar, **23**: 76.
Byland Abbey, Yorkshire. Penny M. **5**: 353.
Byrd, William. Am. Hist. Rec. **3**: 107.
— Journal of. (E. Parke) So. M. **12**: 21.
Byrom, John, Poetry of. (J. Dyer) Penn Mo. **2**: 590.
— Remains of. Bentley, **37**: 412. **40**: 470. **43**: 594. — Ecl. M. **40**: 82.
Byron, Ada. Bentley, **33**: 69.
Byron, Lord G. G. N. (W. O. B. Peabody) No. Am. **31**: 167.—(T. Carlyle) Knick. **21**: 199.—(T. B. Macaulay) Ed. R. **53**: 544. Same art. Mus. **19**: 411.—(H. Brougham) Ed. R. **11**: 285.—(F. Jeffrey) Ed. R. **27**: 277.—(W. Phillips) No. Am. **5**: 98.— (A. H. Everett) No. Am. **20**: 1.—(J. Ruskin) 19th Cent. **8**: 394, 748.—(M. Arnold) Macmil. **43**: 367. Same art. Liv. Age, **149**: 131.—(G. Fitzhugh) De Bow, **29**: 430.—Appleton, **25**: 413.—(G. Gilfillan) Ex. H. Lec. **7**: 409.—(G. Gilfillan) Tait, n. s. **14**: 447. Same art. Ecl. M. **11**: 556.—(J. Morley) Fortn. **14**: 650.—(J. Paget) Ev. Sat. **13**: 117.— (T. Sheldrake) Colburn, **29**: 295.—with portrait, Colburn, **3**: 1.—Blackw. **106**: 24. **107**: 123, 267. **112**: 49. Same art. Ecl. M. **79**: 385. Same art. Liv. Age, **114**: 387.—Dub. Univ. **73**: 270.

Byron, Lord G. G. N. So. Lit. Mess. **6**: 34. **7**: 32. — Chr. Mo. Spec. **7**: 450. — Anal. M. **4**: 68. — Mo. R. **121**: 217. — Gen. Repos. **4**: 282. — So. R. **5**: 463. — Dem. R. **10**: 225. — Blackw. **11**: 212. **17**: 131. — Mus. **5**: 187.
— Address to the Ocean. Blackw. **64**: 499.
— and Lady Blessington. (J. W. Simmons) So. Lit. J. **3**: 414.
— and Burns. So. Lit. Mess. **15**: 165. — Portfo.(Den.) **32**: 386.
— and Lady Byron. Fraser, **1**: 484.
— and Byronana, Editions of. Am. Bibliop. **1**: 378.
— and Mr. Chaworth, Duel between. Ev. Sat. **3**: 311.
— and M. Casimir Delavigne. For. Q. **4**: 471.
— and Countess Guiccioli. (W. Stigand) Belgra. **7**: 491.
— and his Contemporaries, Hunt's. (J. W. Croker) Quar. **37**: 402. — Blackw. **23**: 362. — Mo. R. **115**: 300. — Mus. **12**: 569. — Colburn, **22**: 84. — Lond. M. **21**: 211.
— and his Times. (R. Noel) St. Paul's, **13**: 555, 618.
— and his Traducers. Am. Mo. M. **8**: 491.
— and his Worshipers. Am. Bibliop. **5**: 23.
— and Mr. Kennedy. Fraser, **2**: 1.
— and Landor. Blackw. **14**: 99.
— and Moore. (F. Jeffrey) Ed. R. **38**: 27.
— and Pope. *See* Pope and Bowles Controversy.
— and Shelley. (W. A. Coche) So. M. **11**: 496. — (C. Kingsley) Fraser, **48**: 568. — Temp. Bar. **34**: 30. — Westm. **69**: 350. Same art. Liv. Age, **57**: 580.
— — and Wordsworth. Am. Bib. Repos. 2d s. **1**: 206.
— — — Place of, in English Poetry. Temp. Bar, **40**: 478.
— and Southey. Blackw. **16**: 71.
— and Tennyson. Quar. **131**: 354. Same art. Ecl. M. **78**: 1.
— as a dramatic Poet. Selec. Ed. R. **2**: 198.
— at Genoa. Blackw. **15**: 696.
— at Newstead Abbey. Chamb. J. **38**: 220.
— At the Tomb of; a Poem. (C. H. Miller) Lakeside, **9**: 246.
— at Work. Chamb. J. **46**: 645. Same art. Liv. Age, **103**: 464.
— Beppo. (F. Jeffrey) Ed. R. **29**: 302. — Blackw. **3**: 323, 421.
— Lady Blessington's Conversations of. Mo. R. **133**: 97.
— Bride of Abydos. Anal. M. **3**: 334. — Portfo.(Den.) **11**: 319.
— Cain. Ecl. R. **35**: 418. — U. S. Lit. Gaz. **1**: 54. — Fraser, **3**: 285.
— Character of. Blackw. **17**: 131. (A. Norton) No. Am. **21**: 300. — Pamph. **24**: 169, 175.
— — and Influence of his Genius. Lond. M. **1**: 124.
— — and Writings of. Chr. Obs. **25**: 79–281. — Temp. Bar, **25**: 364. Same art. Ecl. M. **72**: 547.
— Characteristics of. (E. P. Whipple) No. Am. **60**: 64.
— Childe Harold. (G. Ellis) Quar. **7**: 180 — (Sir W. Scott) Quar. **16**: 172. **19**: 215. — (Prof. J. Wilson) Ed. R. **30**: 87. — (F. Jeffrey) Ed. R. **19**: 466. — Ed. R. **27**: 277. — Mo. R. **87**: 289. — Chr. Obs. **11**: 376. — Ecl. R. **15**: 630. — Portfo.(Den.) **17**: 490.
— — Canto Third. Chr. Obs. **16**: 246.
— — Hobhouse on. Ecl. R. **28**: 323.
— Combolio. Blackw. **11**: 162.
— Conversations at Weimar upon. Fraser, **22**: 573.
— Conversations of. Lond. M. **10**: 449.
— — Medwin's. Colburn, **11**: 407.
— Conversations of an American with. Colburn, **45**: 193–203.
— Conversations with. (Lady Blessington) Colburn, **35**: 5–489. **37**: 214, 308. **38**: 305. **39**: 33–414. — Blackw. **16**: 530, 590, 712. **18**: 137. — U. S. Lit. Gaz. **1**: 289. — Mus. **6**: 58. **21**: 180, 439. **22**: 109, 679, 741. **23**: 367, 588.
Byron, Lord G. G. N., Conversations with, on Religion. Mo. R. **122**: 475. — (W. B. O. Peabody) No. Am. **36**: 152.
— Correspondence of. Colburn, **13**: 107.
— Corsair, The. Chr. Obs. **13**: 245. — Colburn, **1**: 149. — Ecl. R. **19**: 416. — Portfo.(Den.) **12**: 33, 271.
— — and Bride of Abydos. (F. Jeffrey) Ed. R. **23**: 198.
— — and Lara. (G. Ellis) Quar. **11**: 428.
— The Deformed transformed. Lond. M. **9**: 315.
— Doge of Venice. Blackw. **9**: 93.
— Don Juan. Mo. R. **95**: 418. **101**: 316. — Fraser, **7**: 658. — Blackw. **5**: 512. **10**: 107. **14**: 282. — Ed. Mo. R. **2**: 468. — (F. Parke) Dub. Univ. **85**: 630. — Lond. M. **11**: 82. — Portfo.(Den.) **30**: 157. — West. R. **2**: 1.
— Dramas. (R. Heber) Quar. **27**: 476. — Fraser, **10**: 699.
— Edinburgh Ladies' Petition, with his Reply. Colburn, **44**: 420.
— Elze's. (J. R. Dennett) Nation, **14**: 218.
— Event in Life of. Ecl. M. **30**: 415.
— Fame of; a Poem. Dub. Univ. **95**: 224.
— Faults of. So. Lit. Mess. **4**: 269.
— Finden's Illustrations of. Tait, **2**: 128–681.
— French Criticism on. Lond. M. **1**: 492.
— from a new Point of View. Ev. Sat. **5**: 745.
— Galt's Life of. Mo. R. **123**: 240. — Fraser, **2**: 347, 533. — (H. Brougham) Ed. R. **52**: 228.
— Giaour. (F. Jeffrey) Ed. R. **21**: 299. — Anal. M. **2**: 377. — (G. Ellis) Quar. **10**: 331. — Chr. Obs. **12**: 731.
— Goethe, and M. Arnold. (W. H. White) Contemp. **40**: 179. Same art. Appleton, **26**: 335.
— Countess Guiccioli's Recollections of. Blackw. **106**: 24. Same art. Liv. Age, **102**: 428.
— Heaven and Earth. (F. Jeffrey) Ed. R. **38**: 27. — Blackw. **13**: 72, 264. — Mus. **2**: 410. — Colburn, **7**: 353.
— Hebrew Melodies Anal. M. **6**: 192. — Chr. Obs. **14**: 542.
— Home and Grave of. (P. Skelton) Once a Week, **2**: 539. — Harper, **21**: 606. — (C. Parkhurst) Lakeside, **8**: 68.
— Hours of Idleness. (H. Brougham) Ed. R. **11**: 285. Same art. Anal. M. **3**: 469.
— — 1807. Ecl. R. **6**: 989.
— in Greece. Westm. **2**: 225. — Mo. R. **124**: 92. — Temp. Bar, **62**: 100.
— — J. Millingen's Reminiscences of. (A. V. Millingen) New Eng. **38**: 637.
— in Venice. Once a Week, **19**: 287.
— Incident in the Life of. Argosy, **7**: 273.
— Italian Haunts of. (J. A. Harrison) So. M. **15**: 1.
— Journal of. Lond. M. **1**: 295.
— Juvenile Poems. Fraser, **6**: 183.
— Lament of Tasso. Blackw. **2**: 142.
— Lara. Portfo.(Den.) **14**: 33.
— Last Days of. Blackw. **18**: 137.
— Last Portrait of. Colburn, **16**: 243.
— Last Record of. Chamb. J. **46**: 198.
— Letter on Pope. (W. H. Prescott) No. Am. **13**: 450.
— — to Galt. Blackw. **18**: 400.
— Letters of. Sharpe, **49**: 10–291. **50**: 14, 70. — Mus. **16**: 10. — Westm. **12**: 269.
— Letters to. Pamph. **19**: 347. — Blackw. **9**: 421.
— Life and Poetry of. Selec. Ed. R. **1**: 376
— Lost Chapter of History of. (N. L. Dodge) Lippinc. **3**: 666.
— Manfred. (F. Parke) Dub. Univ. **83**: 502. — (F. Jeffrey) Ed. R. **28**: 418. — Blackw. **1**: 289. **2**: 196. **7**: 239. — Mo. R. **83**: 300. — St. James, **35**: 254.
— Marino Faliero. Ecl. R. **33**: 518. — (F. Jeffrey) Ed. R. **35**: 271. — Mo. R. **95**: 41. — Lond. M. **3**: 550.

Byron, Lord G. G. N., Married Life of. Temp. Bar, **26**: 364. **28**: 61.
— Mazeppa. Blackw. **5**: 429. — Anal. M. **14**: 105. — Mo. R. **89**: 309. — Ecl. R. **30**: 147.
— Memorial of, Proposed. Fraser, **93**: 246.
— Monument to. (F. Parke) Dub. Univ. **86**: 727. — Fraser, **99**: 665.
— Moore's Life of. (W. B. O. Peabody) No. Am. **31**: 167. — Quar. **43**: 168. — So. R. **7**: 1. — Blackw. **27**: 389, 421. — Mo. R. **124**: 217. **121**: 585. — Mus. **19**: 50, 155. — Fraser, **1**; 129. **3**: 228. — Colburn, **31**: 159. — West. Mo. R. **3**: 647.
— Moral Characteristics of. (G. W. Blagden) Am. Q. Obs. **2**: 291. — (F. Jeffrey) Selec. Ed. R. **1**: 289.
— Nichol's Life of. (J. M. Hart) Nation, **31**: 344. — (F. F. Browne) Dial (Ch.), **1**: 112.
— North American Review on. Lond. M. **14**: 224.
— Ode on the Death of. (J. Hogg) Blackw. **21**: 520.
— Ode to. Dub. Univ. **6**: 697.
— Count D'Orsay's Portrait of. Colburn, **74**: 661.
— Papers of. Blackw. **19**: 335.
— Personal Character of. Lond. M. **10**: 336. — Mus. **5**: 522. — Portfo.(Den.) **33**: 155, 198.
— Personal Recollections of. Liv. Age, **100**: 416.
— Poem on. (G. H. Miles) So. R. n. s. **6**: 477.
— — on Rogers. Fraser, **7**: 81.
— Poems of. Ecl. R. **25**: 292.
— Poetical Critique on. Blackw. **11**: 456.
— Poetry of. (F. Jeffrey) Ed. R. **27**: 227. — Anal. M. **8**: 252. — Lond. M. **3**: 50.
— — Critical Illustrations of. Fraser, **7**: 303.
— Prisoner of Chillon; Bonnivard. Fraser, **93**: 582.
— Prophecy of Dante. West. R. **4**: 321.
— Recent Criticism of. (T. S. Perry) Internat. R. **7**: 282.
— Recollections of. Lond. M. **10**: 117. — Westm. **3**: 1.
— Religious Opinions of. New Eng. M. **1**: 63, 112.
— Reminiscences of. Blackw. **15**: 696.
— Sardanapalus. Blackw. **11**: 90. **27**: 141. — Portfo. (Den.) **28**: 487.
— saved from his Friends. Mus. **6**: 325.
— Separation from Lady Byron. Blackw. **17**: 134, 450. **27**: 823.
— Southey's Letter to. U. S. Lit. Gaz. **1**: 349.
Byron, Lord G. G. N. Swim across the Hellespont. Lond. M. **3**: 363.
— Tendency of his Poetry. Broadw. **4**: 54.
— Tragedies of. (W. Hazlitt) Ed. R. **36**: 413. — (J. Everett) No. Am. **13**: 227. — Mo. R. **97**: 83. — Blackw. **11**: 90.
— Two Foscari; Cain. Lond. M. **5**: 66.
— Unpublished Story of, and Mary Chaworth. Lippinc. **18**: 637.
— vindicated. Fraser, **80**: 598.
— Voyage from Leghorn to Greece. (G. H. Browne) Blackw. **35**: 56. **37**: 392.
— Werner. (W. Maginn) Blackw. **12**: 710, 782. — Mo. R. **99**: 394. — Ecl. R. **37**: 136.
Byron, Lady, and Mrs. Stowe. (E. L. Godkin) Nation, **10**: 24. — (E. Quincy) Nation, **9**: 167, 189, 210. — Nation, **9**: 208. — (C. Reading) Colburn, **146**: 352. — Am. Bibliop. **2**: 69. — Argosy, **8**: 274. **9**: 269. — Eng. Dom. M. **7**: 194. — Broadw. **3**: 166. — Liv. Age, **104**: 625. — Quar. **127**: 400. **128**: 218. Same art. Liv. Age, **103**: 486. — St. James, **25**: 58, 133. — (H. Martineau) Atlan. **7**: 185.
— Character of. Temp. Bar, **27**: 334. **28**: 61.
— Letter from. Fraser, **1**: 356.
— Remarks occasioned by Moore's Life of Byron. Colburn, **28**: 374.
— True Story of Life of. (H. B. Stowe) Atlan. **24**: 295. Same art. Macmil. **20**: 377.
Byron's Daughter, Lady Lovelace. Argosy, **8**: 358.
Byrons of Newstead. All the Year, **5**: 282.
Byron, Henry James. (P. Wrey) Lond. Soc. **26**: 121.
Byrne, Garret. Chamb. J. **8**: 187.
Bythinia, Adventure in. Fraser, **29**: 52.
Byzantine Anatolia. Cornh. **27**: 409.
Byzantine Churches, and their Modifications for the Greek Ritual. (E. Freshfield) Arch. **44**: 383.
Byzantine Empire. Nat. Q. **19**: 207. — (W. C. King lake) So. M. **17**: 201.
— and the Great Company. Cornh. **20**: 459.
— Fall of. Chr. Rem. **5**: 721. — Lond. Q. **5**: 70.
— Finlay's History of. Blackw. **73**: 691. — No. Brit. **22**: 343.
Byzantine Historians. For. Q. **10**: 102. — For. R. **1**: 574. — Ed. R. **50**: 85. — Mus. **21**: 509.

C

Cab and Omnibus Nuisance. (T. P. Thompson) Westm. **21**: 395.
Cab I got at Tussaud's. Tinsley, **26**: 168.
Cab Drivers. Chamb. J. **43**: 305.
Cabs. All the Year, **2**: 414.
— and Cabmen. Chamb. J. **38**: 332.
— — and Cabmen's Rests. Cong. **6**: 217.
— London Locomotion; or the Cab-Stand. Colburn, **90**: 264.
— of London. Fraser, **43**: 307. — St. James, **22**: 79, 170, 545. **24**: 282.
Cabby and Cocher. (W. Sikes) Galaxy, **22**: 109.
Cabman against Marchioness. (S. M. Quincy) Overland, **12**: 246.
Cabman's Guide. All the Year, **18**: 63.
Cabman's Story. Dem. R. **16**: 225.
Cabmen. (F. W. Robinson) Belgra. **16**: 286.
— Duty towards our. Chamb. J. **34**: 268.
Caballero, Fernan. (J. H. Ingram) Dub. Univ. **90**: 61. — Chamb. J. **31**: 237. Same art. Liv. Age, **62**: 52.
— Estar de Más; a Spanish Enoch Arden. Temp. Bar, **54**: 553.
— Gaviota. Fraser, **76**: 190. Same art. Liv. Age, **94**: 643.
— Ladrone; a Tale. (H. F. Harrington) Godey, **21**: 38.
— Novels of. Ed. R. **114**: 99. — (M. B. Edwards) Macmil. **43**: 145.
Cabarrus, Therese, Our Lady of Thermidor. St. James, **7**: 192.
Cabbage. So. Lit. Mess. **8**: 201.
Cabbage-Tree, The. Penny M. **5**: 327.
Cabell, Joseph C. (J. H. Pleasants) So. Lit. Mess. **22**: 394.
Cabet, the Apostle of Communism. Tait, n. s. **15**: 763.
Cabet, Etienne, and the Icarians. (H. King) Lakeside, **6**: 288. — Quar. **83**: 165.
Cabin at Pharaoh's Ford. (H. King) Overland, **13**: 507.

Cabinet Officers in Congress. Nation, **16**: 233. — (H. White) Nation, **28**: 243. — (E. L. Godkin) Nation, **32**: 107. — (G. Bradford) No. Am. **111**: 330.
Cabinet-Making. Cornh. **41**: 735. Same art. Ecl. M. **95**: 191.
Cabinet System, English. (G. Bradford) No. Am. **118**: 1.
Cabiri, Faber's Mysteries of the. Chr. Obs. **2**: 668, 751.
Cable, George W. The Grandissimes. (W. C. Brownell) Nation, **31**: 415.
Cable-Making for Suspension Bridges. (W. Hildenbrand) Ecl. Engin. **17**: 171, 193, 289.
Cables of Rope and Chain, On Strength of. J. Frankl. Inst. **12**: 90.
— Submarine Telegraph. (F. Jenkin) Ecl. Engin. **1**: 683. — Chamb. J. **54**: 281, 357, 454.
— — British India. Ecl. Engin. **3**: 61.
— — Haps and Mishaps of. Chamb. J. **55**: 593.
— — Laying and raising. (S. F. B. Morse) Ecl. Engin. **3**: 64.
— — Light. Ecl. Engin. **4**: 484.
— — New. J. Frankl. Inst. **108**: 206.
See Atlantic Telegraph; Telegraph, Submarine.
Cabot, George, Biography of. Hunt, **2**: 408.
— Lodge's Life and Letters of. (H. Adams) Nation, **25**: 12.
Cabot, John. Voyage to America, 1497. (J. C. Brevoort) Hist. M. **13**: 129.
— and Sebastian, Date of their Discovery. (R. H. Major) Arch. **43**: 17.
Cabot, Sebastian, Life of. (C. Hayward) Sparks's Am. Biog. **9**: 91. — (G. S. Hillard) No. Am. **34**: 405. — Westm. **16**: 22. — Mo. R. **125**: 514. — Penny M. **5**: 79.
Cabrera, Miguel, Mexican Artist. Cath. World, **13**: 334.
Cabrera, Ramon. Blackw. **60**: 293.
Cabul and Afghanistan. Blackw. **51**: 676.
— and the Punjab, Barr's. Ecl. R. **80**: 44.
— Candahar, and India. (Sir G. W. Cox) Fraser, **102**: 408.
— City of. Penny M. **12**: 441.
— Elphinstone's Account of. Ecl. R. **23**: 457, 556. — Quar. **14**: 152. — Mo. R. **83**: 1.
— English Captives at. Bentley, **14**: 1, 140. **15**: 19, 187.
— Eyre's. Blackw. **53**: 239.
— Late Ameer of. Temp. Bar, **9**: 338.
— Why not colonize? Blackw. **52**: 155.
See Afghanistan.
Cacklers. All the Year, **25**: 249.
Cactus Family. (J. R. Jackson) Stud. & Intel. Obs. **5**: 126. — Chamb. J. **3**: 252.
Cad, Genesis of the. Tinsley, **4**: 178.
Caddell, Cecilia, Obituary of. Irish Mo. **5**: 772.
Caddis-Flies, European. Nature, **22**: 314.
Caddis-Worms and their Houses. (E. M. Smee) Intel. Obs. **5**: 307.
— and their Metamorphoses. (W. Houghton) Pop. Sci. R. **7**: 287.
Cade, Jack, Rebellion of. All the Year, **23**: 181.
Cadell, Francis, and his Explorations in Australia. Once a Week, **8**: 667.
Cadenabbia. (H. D. Jenkins) Lakeside, **3**: 207.
Cader Idris, Mount. Broadw. **3**: 33.
Cadet of Colobrieres. Liv. Age, **10**: 452.
Cadiz. (Prince Löwenstein) Bentley, **24**: 63. — (A. Griffiths) Art J. **33**: 217. — House. Words, **19**: 205. — New Eng. M. **9**: 313. — Penny M. **8**: 172.
— Boatmen of. Temp. Bar, **48**: 28.
— Booty taken at, 1596. (S. R. Meyrick) Arch. **22**: 172.
— during the Siege. Blackw. **40**: 389, 685.
— New Academy of Painting at. (Mrs. Charlton) Colburn, **85**: 422.
— Statistics of. (W. H. Sykes) J. Statis. Soc. **1**: 337.
Cadmium. (B. Wood) J. Frankl. Inst. **70**: 113.
— Alloys of. (B. Wood) J. Frankl. Inst. **71**: 23. **73**: 167.
Cadmon, Cross of. (C. A. De Kay) Scrib. **10**: 554.
Cadoudal, George. Liv. Age, **49**: 513.
Cæcilians, Early Stages of. Nature, **20**: 593.
Cædmon, Genius and Influence of. (Bro. Azarias) Am. Cath. Q. **4**: 22.
— Observations on the History of. (F. Palgrave) Arch. **24**: 341.
— Paraphrase of Scripture History. (H. Ellis) Arch. **24**: 329.
Caen, St. Etienne Abbey and Church. Penny M. **9**: 313.
Caer-Gwent. Sharpe, **28**: 123.
Caerleon, Wales, Antiquities at. (W. Hincks) Canad. J. n. s. **7**: 463.
Caernarvon Castle. Penny M. **3**: 207.
Caerphilly Castle. (F. D. Fenton) Once a Week, **14**: 376.
Caerwent, Excavations within the Walls of, 1855. (O. Morgan) Arch. **36**: 418.
Cæsar; a Poem. (T. Irwin) Dub. Univ. **48**: 603.
Cæsar, Augustus. (T. De Quincey) Blackw. **32**: 949.
Cæsar, Julius. (F. D. Maurice) Macmil. **12**: 23. — (E. S. Creasy) Bentley, **33**: 22, 148, 391. — Mo. R. **102**: 405. — (Sir H. Holland) Quar. **88**: 385. Same art. Ecl. M. **23**: 168. — (T. De Quincey) Blackw. **32**: 551. — Fraser, **76**: 1. Same art. Liv. Age, **94**: 387. — Lond. Q. **24**: 364.
— and Cicero. Dub. Univ. **94**: 202.
— and Cromwell. (F. M. Holland) University Q. **1**: 295.
— Caligula, Claudius, and Nero. (T. De Quincey) Blackw. **33**: 43.
— Campaigns in Britain. Ed. R. **154**: 37. — (H. Owen) Arch. **2**: 134, 159.
— in Gaul. Westm. **77**: 399.
— Character of. Dub. R. **80**: 127.
— — and Career of. Ecl. R. **92**: 513.
— Fall of. Am. Mo. M. **4**: 347.
— Froude on. (W. F. Allen) Nation, **29**: 161. — (W. Y. Sellar) Fraser, **100**: 315. — Quar. **148**: 453.
— Landing in Britain. (G. B. Airy) Arch. **34**: 231. — Arch. **39**: 277. — (G. B. Airy and T. Lewin) Arch. **39**: 303. — (J. Brent) Antiquary, **3**: 315. — Penny M. **6**: 101.
— — Day of. (Earl Stanhope) Arch. **41**: 270.
— — Place of. (Maj. Rennell) Arch. **21**: 501.
— Napoleon III. on. (E. I. Sears) Nat. Q. **13**: 205. — So. Q. **26**: 1. — (C. Merivale) Contemp. **2**: 457. **3**: 118. — (L. P. Smith) U. S. Serv. M. **4**: 43. — (T. A. Thacher) New Eng. **24**: 559. — Brit. Q. **41**: 495. — Chr. Obs. **65**: 679. — Cornh. **11**: 495. — Dub. R. **59**: 1. — Ed. R. **124**: 399. — (Napoleon III.) Fraser, **71**: 655. — Month, **2**: 474.
— Passage over the Thames. (S. Gale) Arch. **1**: 183.
— Recent Histories of. (G. F. Holmes) So. R. n. s. **1**: 383.
— a Sketch. (J. A. Froude) Ed. R. **150**: 498.
— Struggle with Pompey. Chr. Rem. **20**: 241.
— Warfare and Writing of. Atlan. **44**: 273.
See Rome, Merivale's History of.
Cæsar, Sir Julius, Life of, 1557–1636. Ecl. R. **13**: 359.
Cæsars. (T. De Quincey) Blackw. **32**: 541, 949. **33**: 43. **35**: 961. **36**: 67, 173.
— Deification of. Dub. R. **77**: 375.
— De Quincey's. So. Lit. Mess. **29**: 277.
— Flavian. (E. A. Freeman) Nat. R. **16**: 161.
— Patriot Emperors. (T. De Quincey) Blackw. **35**: 961. **36**: 67, 173.
Cæsar Rowan; a Poem. (T. D. English) Scrib. **2**: 300.
Cæsarea Philippi, Christ at. (B. Weiss) Princ. n. s. **3**: 97.
Cæsarism. (J. Mazzini) Macmil. **12**: 259.
— and Ultramontanism. (J. F. Stephen) Contemp. **23**: 497, 989. — Dub. R. **74**: 402.

Cæsarism, French Acceptance of. (E. L. Godkin) Nation, **29**: 37.
— Romieu's. Fraser, **42**: 495.
Café de la Régence. Fraser, **22**: 669. — Mus. **41**: 360.
— des Exilés. (G. W. Cable) Scrib. **11**: 727.
— d'Italia, Romance of. All the Year, **45**: 353, 373.
Cafés, Representative. (H. S. Edwards) Once a Week, **1**: 223.
Caffraria. Chamb. J. **20**: 59.
— British. Brit. Q. **24**: 381.
— Kay's Researches in. Meth. M. **56**: 789. — (B. B. Thatcher) No. Am. **39**: 371. — Ed. R. **58**: 363. — Am. Meth. M. **16**: 241.
Caffre. *See* Kafir.
Cagliostro, Count, the Magician. (C. W. Elliott) Internat. M. **5**: 452. — (T. Carlyle) Fraser, **8**: 19, 132. — (L. Wraxall) Once a Week, **5**: 302. — All the Year, **34**: 281, 293. — Colburn, **123**: 185. — Dub. Univ. **52**: 431. — Irish Q. **5**: 131. — Putnam, **5**: 497. — (W. R. Hooper) Galaxy, **16**: 497.
— and John Pounds. Sharpe, **10**: 142.
— Career of. (W. Axon) Dub. Univ. **78**: 326–686. **79**: 204–537.
— True History of. Chamb. J. **24**: 156. Same art. Ecl. M. **36**: 981. Same art. Liv. Age, **47**: 143.
— Vision of. So. Lit. Mess. **25**: 449. — Blackw. **62**: 408.
Cagliostro of the 2d Century. (J. A. Froude) 19th Cent. **6**: 551.
Cagots, The. (A. Marks) Once a Week, **12**: 162. — All the Year, **41**: 416. — Chamb. J. **25**: 62. — Colburn, **82**: 418. — Ed. R. **87**: 491. — House. Words, **12**: 73. Same art. Liv. Age, **47**: 90. — Temp. Bar, **5**: 549. — Chamb. J. **55**: 497. Same art. Ecl. M. **38**: 19.
Caillié, Rene. Travels in Africa. (B. B. Thatcher) No. Am. **36**: 48.
Cain. (J. P. Widney) Overland, **13**: 30.
— after his Crime; a Tale. Cath. World, **19**: 698.
— Insanity of. (M. M. Dodge) Scrib. **6**: 104.
Caird, John, Sermons of. Ecl. R. **108**: 347. — Fraser, **58**: 222.
Cairnes, John Elliot. (H. Fawcett) Fortn. **24**: 149.
— on American and Irish Questions. (G. Walker) Internat. R. **3**: 145.
Cairngorm Mountains. Chamb. J. **41**: 710. — House. Words, **4**: 40.
Cairns, H. MacC., Lord Chancellor. Belgra. **29**: 54.
— Political Portrait of. St. James, **24**: 171.
Cairo, Egypt. Broadw. **7**: 226. — House. Words, **3**: 332.
— and Damascus. (F. W. Holland) Lippinc. **7**: 197.
— and Franciscan Missions of the Nile. Month, **4**: 592.
— and the Red Sea. (N. Macleod) Good Words, **6**: 233.
— Brides for Sale in. Ecl. M. **38**: 213.
— City of Victory. Fraser, **65**: 317.
— — of Saladin. (J. O. Noyes) Nat. M. **9**: 264.
— Day in. Colburn, **125**: 96.
— Donkey Boys. All the Year, **9**: 199.
— English Schools in. (W. Gilbert) Good Words, **13**: 750.
— Evening with the Grand Mufti. (H. T. Cook) Overland, **6**: 363.
— Festival of the Prophet at. Chamb. J. **11**: 311.
— Frenchman in. Liv. Age, **28**: 179
— Homeward bound and outward bound at. Once a Week, **9**: 123.
— illustrated. (E. T. and M. E. Rogers) Art J. **32**: 17–357.
— Journey from, to Suez. (G. W. Samson) Chr. R. **14**: 141.
— Life in. (Lady Duff-Gordon) Macmil. **11**: 177. Same art. Liv. Age, **84**: 229.
— Magician of. (Lord Nugent) Penny M. **14**: 198.
Cairo, Egypt, Merry Men of. House. Words, **5**: 602.
— Mosques and Architecture of. Am. Arch. **5**: 158, 165.
— Petrified Forest of. Chamb. J. **11**: 359.
— Pyramids of. Sharpe, **49**: 153.
— Reminiscences of, 1862. Colburn, **126**: 202.
— Suburban. (A. Freeland) St. James, **37**: 248.
— to Athens. (M. B. Edwards) Fraser, **86**: 74. Same art. Ecl. M. **79**: 349.
— to Bagdad. (W. P. Fogg) Scrib. **14**: 600.
— Visit to. (R. W. Dale) Cong. **3**: 265. — (W. Knighton) Dub. Univ. **89**: 371.
Cairo, Ill. (E. C. Bruce) Lippinc. **23**: 102.
Cairoli Family. (E. Carrington) Westm. **111**: 77.
Caissons, Stone. Ecl. Engin. **5**: 408.
Cal Culver and the Devil. (R. T. Cooke) Harper, **57**: 574.
Calabar, View of old. Chamb. J. **51**: 526.
Calabash-Tree. Penny M. **3**: 415.
Calaber, Quintus. *See* Quintus Smyrnæus.
Calabrella, Baroness. Tempter and the Tempted. Mo. R. **159**: 127.
Calabria. Mo. R. **128**: 159.
— and Sicily. Ecl. Mus. **1**: 393.
— — Strutt's Pedestrian Tour in. Mo. R. **160**: 186.
— Greek Songs of. Cornh. **44**: 725.
— Red Shirt in. Cornh. **9**: 666.
Calais. (S. Warren) Blackw. **42**: 621.
— Day in. All the Year, **32**: 416.
— Loss of. No. Brit. **45**: 441.
— My Adventures at. Blackw. **42**: 621.
Calamy, Edmund, Life and Times of. Mo. R. **121**: 241.
— Memoirs of. Colburn, **26**: 561. — Cong. M. **6**: 281.
Calas, Jean. (C. K. Paul) Theo. R. **7**: 378.
— Persecutions of. No. Am. **87**: 263.
— Story of. Temp. Bar, **27**: 187.
— Tragedy of. Westm. **70**: 465. Same art. Ecl. M. **46**: 92. Same art. Liv. Age, **59**: 612.
Calbot's Rival; a Tale. (J. Hawthorne) Gent. M. n. s. **17**: 513.
Calcareous Rock-Formations. (J. D. Dana) Am. J. Sci. **64**: 410.
Calcasieu Prairie, August Day on. (M. B. Williams) Lakeside, **9**: 109.
Calcium Light. Ecl. M. **57**: 302.
Calcraft, a Trooper; a Story. Lond. Soc. **40**: 513.
Calculating by Machinery. J. Frankl. Inst. **14**: 357.
Calculating Boys. (R. A. Proctor) Belgra. **38**: 450.
Calculating Machine. (G. B. Grant) Am. J. Sci. **108**: 277. — J. Frankl. Inst. **60**: 391.
— Babbage's. (C. Nordhoff) Harper, **30**: 34. — Ecl. R. **120**: 487. — Ed. Philos. J. **7**: 274. **8**: 122. — Ed. R. **59**: 263. — J. Frankl. Inst. **11**: 210. — No. Brit. **15**: 553.
— Colman's. J. Frankl. Inst. **91**: 372.
— Nystrom's. J. Frankl. Inst. **51**: 262.
Calculation, Helps to. Dub. R. **22**: 74.
Calculous Disorders. Ed. R. **17**: 155. **32**: 418.
— Marcel on. Ecl. R. **27**: 270.
Calculus, Differential, Browne on. Westm. **3**: 550.
— — La Croix on. Mo. R. **87**: 179.
— — Lardner on. Westm. **5**: 130.
— Differential and Integral. Atlan. **3**: 704.
Calcutta. (H. R. Addison) Bentley, **11**: 56. — (N. Macleod) Good Words, **10**: 689, 766, 855. — House. Words, **16**: 393. — Bentley, **30**: 361. Same art. Internat. M. **4**: 611.
— and its Vicinity. (T. Carbonnelle) Cath. World, **2**: 386.
— Artists and Painters in. Blackw. **11**: 561.
— Cathedral of, Painted Window for, 1845. Chr. Obs. **45**: 96.
— City of Palaces. (W. L. Stuart) Harper, **34**: 299.
— Drainage of. Ecl. Engin. **13**: 180.
— Evening in. Once a Week, **1**: 235.

Calcutta in olden Time. (J. Hutton) Gent. M. n. s. **18**: 229.
— Letters from. Blackw. **11**: 429–565. **12**: 133. **13**: 443. — Anal. M. **13**: 340, 388. **14**: 481.
— Natives of. (J. Allardyce) Good Words, **15**: 201, 371, 444.
— Sanitary Improvement in. Nature, **5**: 150.
— Six Months in. Temp. Bar, **25**: 389, 507. Same art. Ecl. M. **72**: 553.
— Twelvemonth in. Chamb. J. **15**: 11–200.
— Vital Statistics of. (C. Finch) J. Statis. Soc. **13**: 168.
— Voyage to. Portfo.(Den.) **30**: 139.
— Year in. Chamb. J. **14**: 65–381.
— Zoölogical Gardens at. Nature, **16**: 28.
Caldaro, Pilgrimage to. Dub. Univ. **25**: 305.
Caldecott, Randolph. (W. E. Henley) Art J. **33**: 208. — (P. Fitzgerald) Gent. M. n. s. **24**: 629.
Calder, James, Scottish Reformer. Tait, n. s. **14**: 269.
Calderon de la Barca, Pedro. Fraser, **55**: 455. — Blackw. **46**: 715. — (M. F. Egan) Cath. World, **33**: 474. — Lond. Q. **44**: 1. — Month, **9**: 348.
— and the Comedy of Superstition. Temp. Bar, **55**: 175.
— and his Dramas. Dub. Univ. **44**: 353.
— Autos Sacramentales. (M. F. Crane) Cath. World, **21**: 32, 213.
— Comedies of. For. R. **5**: 419.
— Comedy: Courtesy not Love. Blackw. **17**: 641.
— Constant Prince. (D. F. McCarthy) Dub. Univ. **38**: 325.
— Dancing-Master. Blackw. **20**: 559.
— Devotion to the Cross. Temp. Bar, **55**: 175. Same art. Appleton, **21**: 424. — Blackw. **18**: 83.
— Ferdinand. Liv. Age, **117**: 643.
— Goblin Lady. Blackw. **47**: 1. — Tait, **4**: 182.
— McCarthy's Life of. Dub. R. **81**: 94.
— Mistress of Gomez Arias. (Tr. by J. Oxenford) Colburn, **78**: 337.
— Outlines from. Fraser, **40**: 175.
— Plays. Blackw. **119**: 673.
— — McCarthy's Translation. Dub. Univ. **59**: 439. — Colburn, **99**: 487. — Tait, n. s. **20**: 701.
— Purgatory of St. Patrick. (E. J. Hasell) St. Paul's, **13**: 313. Same art. Liv. Age, **119**: 292.
— Scarf and the Flower. (D. F. McCarthy) Dub. Univ. **39**: 33.
— Steadfast Prince. Blackw. **113**: 576.
— Tragedies of Jealousy. Blackw. **120**: 229.
— Writings of. Dub. Univ. **78**: 414.
Calderon, Philip H. Art J. **22**: 9.
— and the St. John's Wood School. (Tom Taylor) Portfo. **1**: 97.
— Technical Note on. (P. G. Hamerton) Portfo. **6**: 12.
Calderwood, D. Altare Damascenum, 1623. Cong. M. **8**: 263.
Calderwood, Mrs. Journey from Scotland into England, 1756. House. Words, **13**: 19.
Caldwell, Charles, Autobiography of. Liv. Age, **47**: 427.
Caldwell, Merritt. (S. M. Vaill) Meth. Q. **12**: 574.
Caldwell Family Papers. Quar. **97**: 378.
Caleb and Othniel, Relation between. Kitto, **36**: 338.
Caleb's Lark. (J. G. Austin) Atlan. **22**: 652.
Caleb Stukely; a Tale. (S. Phillips) Blackw. **51**: 224, 306, 445. **52**: 35, 235, 374. **53**: 33, 213, 314.
Caledonia, Chalmers's. Quar. **4**: 342.
Caledonia County, Vt., Ministers of. (L. Worcester) Am. Q. Reg. **13**: 280.
Caledonian Canal. Blackw. **7**: 427.
Caledonian Sketches, 1807, Carr's. Quar. **1**: 155. — (J. Foster) Ecl. R. **9**: 297.
Caledonians, Picts, and Scots, Ritson's Annals of. Westm. **16**: 145. — (Sir W. Scott) Quar. **41**: 120.
Calendar, Changes of Style in. (S. Bonsall) Pennsyl. M. **2**: 394. **3**: 65.
— Civil and Ecclesiastical. (L. H. Steiner) Mercersb. **10**: 228.
— Japanese and English. J. Frankl. Inst. **73**: 48.
— The Year and the Day. Chamb. J. **47**: 577. Same art. Ecl. M. **75**: 737.
Calendars, Ancient and modern. (E. S. Dixon) Recr. Sci. **2**: 180.
— and Almanacs. Brit. Q. **28**: 333. — For. Q. **32**: 371. — Ecl. M. **1**: 493.
— Notes on sundry. (A. Wilcocks) Pennsyl. M. **3**: 202.
— of State Papers. Month, **3**: 288, 346, 453.
Calhoun, John C. (V. W. Kingsley) Nat. Q. **24**: 233. — (J. Parton) No. Am. **101**: 379. — with portrait, Dem. R. **2**: 65. — with portrait, Dem. R. **12**: 93. — with portrait, Am. Whig R. **12**: 164. — Dem. R. **26**: 401. — So. Q. **18**: 486. — Land We Love, **6**: 397. — So. Lit. Mess. **16**: 301.
— and Baltimore Convention. Brownson, **1**: 257.
— and Democratic Review. Dem. R. **16**: 107.
— and Memphis Memorial. (W. Green) Am. Whig R. **7**: 15.
— and his Nullification Doctrine. (A. E. Carroll) Liv. Age, **70**: 444.
— Charges against, while Secretary of War. Niles's Reg. **31**: 292–387. **32**: 1.
— Death of. So. Lit. Mess. **16**: 377.
— Dinner to, 1825. Niles's Reg. **28**: 265.
— — 1826. Niles's Reg. **31**: 94.
— — 1831. Niles's Reg. **40**: 171.
— Efforts against General Jackson. Niles's Reg. **41**: 141. **43**: 79, 90.
— Hammond's Eulogy on. So. Q. **20**: 107.
— Letter on Seminole Question. Niles's Reg. **39**: 447. **40**: 11, 37, 70.
— Life and Speeches of. Brownson, **1**: 105.
— on Government. (J. H. Walker) So. Q. **26**: 121. — Putnam, **7**: 90.
— on Mexican War. (J. D. Whelpley) Am. Whig R. **7**: 217.
— Parliamentary Eloquence of. Dem. R. **14**: 111.
— Private Life of. (M. Bates) Internat. M. **4**: 173.
— Report on incendiary Publications. Niles's Reg. **49**: 408.
— Speech on Jackson's Protest. Niles's Reg. **46**: 213.
— — on Nullification. Niles's Reg. **43**: supp. 155, 221.
— Statue of, by Hiram Powers. Internat. M. **3**: 8.
— Summer Home of. (E. Ingersoll) Scrib. **21**: 892.
— Works of. So. Lit. Mess. **20**: 321.
Caliban, Rénan's. (A. Laugel) Nation, **26**: 401. — (B. F. De Costa) Nation, **27**: 23.
Caliban; or the Missing Link, Wilson's. Canad. Mo. **2**: 573.
Calico-Printer of Jouy. Sharpe, **34**: 290.
Calico-Printing. (C. T. Hinckley) Godey, **45**: 5, 117, 213. — J. Frankl. Inst. **12**: 50.
— Essay on. J. Frankl. Inst. **6**: 169–381.
— in France. (F. A. Lovering) Atlan. **22**: 591.
— Influence of Science on. (F. C. Calvert) J. Frankl. Inst. **70**: 193.
California. (T. De Quincey) Hogg, **9**: 1. — (T. De Quincey) Ecl. M. **25**: 559. — (C. Nordhoff) Harper, **44**: 865. **45**: 65, 255. — (R. H. Patterson) Fortn. **34**: 325. — (H. J. Raymond) Am. Whig. R. **3**: 82. Same art. Liv. Age, **8**: 208. — (G. Putnam) Chr. Exam. **47**: 130. — Am. Whig R. **9**: 331. — Dem. R. **23**: 169. — (R. H. Dana, jr.) No. Am. **55**: 179. — (J. M. Harris) Bank. M. (N. Y.) **3**: 649. — (J. D. B. De Bow) De Bow, **8**: 538. — (E. G. Meek) Meth. Q. **10**: 629. — New Eng. **8**: 585. — Ecl. M. **19**: 548. — De Bow, **3**: 543.—Blackw. **81**: 480.—Sharpe, **11**: 65.

California, Administration of Justice in. Liv. Age, **25**: 354.
— Admission of, Seward on. So. Lit. Mess. **17**: 130.
— Adventures in, 1849. Blackw. **67**: 34.
— Agricultural Capacity of. (J. R. Browne) Overland, **10**: 297. — De Bow, **18**: 201. — (R. Hale) Hours at Home, **5**: 457.
— Alkaline and Boracic Lakes of. (J. A. Phillips) Pop. Sci. R. **16**: 153. Same art. Sup. Pop. Sci. Mo. **1**: 175. Same art. Liv. Age, **133**: 632.
— Alps of, In the Heart of. Scrib. **20**: 345.
— American Pioneers of. (J. Warner) Pioneer, **4**: 287.
— and the Californians, Fremont's. U. S. Cath. M. **5**: 258.
— and China. (W. Speer) Princ. **25**: 83.
— and Mexico, from Chinese Sources. Knick. **36**: 201.
— and New Mexico. (E. G. Squier) Am. Whig R. **8**: 503. — Am. J. Sci. **56**: 376.
— and Palestine. (S. Powers) Lakeside, **8**: 158.
— and Panama, Notes of a Journey in. Hogg, **7**: 110–173.
— and Siberia. Quar. **87**: 396. Same art. Liv. Age, **27**: 444.
— Annals of. Ed. R. **107**: 295. Same art. Liv. Age, **57**: 657.
— Art Possibilities in. (J. W. Wilkinson) Overland, **2**: 248.
— Bank of, Failure of, 1875. (E. L. Godkin) Nation, **21**: 144, 160. — Nation, **21**: 149.
— Banking Panic in, 1855. Bank. M. (L.) **15**: 272.
— Count de Beauvoir in. (E. Howland) Lippinc. **13**: 405.
— Big Trees of. Blackw. **99**: 196. — Broadw. **10**: 296. — Liv. Age, **52**: 438.
— Blue Lakes of. (T. W. Brotherton) So. M. **12**: 310.
— Borthwick's Three Years in. Colburn, **112**: 439. — New Q. **6**: 185.
— Canter to. Blackw. **71**: 187.
— Catholic Missions in. (W. I. Kip) Overland, **10**: 152. — Dub. R. **58**: 1. — West. J. **4**: 104.
— — Early. (C. H. Robinson) Cath. World, **32**: 111.
— Character and Climate of. Dem. R. **20**: 556.
— Characteristics and Prospects of, 1858. (H. Bushnell) New Eng. **16**: 142.
— Chinese in. *See* Chinese in California.
— City in, 180,000 Years old. (A. Bowman) Overland, **15**: 34.
— Climate of. (A. P. Peabody) Am. Natural. **4**: 708. — (G. M. Willing) West. J. **10**: 20.
— Coast of Lower. (C. M. Scammon) Overland, **4**: 230. — (J. P. Caldwell) Overland, **5**: 44.
— Coast Range of, Formation of. (J. L. LeConte) Am. J. Sci. **111**: 297.
— Coast Rangers. (J. R. Browne) Harper, **23**: 1, 306, 593. **24**: 1, 289.
— Commercial Advantages of. Hunt, **19**: 518.
— Commercial and Monetary Interests of. (A. Walker) Overland, **10**: 558. Same art. Bank. M. (N. Y.) **28**: 193.
— Commercial Importance of. Bank. M. (N. Y.) **3**: 690.
— Commercial Resources of. (T. B. King) Bank M. (N. Y.) **3**: 13.
— Copper Fever in. (P. Mulford) Lippinc. **8**: 197.
— Cotton Experiments in. (J. L. Strong) Overland, **6**: 326.
— Cretaceous Rocks of. (W. M. Gabb) Am. J. Sci. **94**: 226.
— — Gabb on. (T. A. Conrad) Am. J. Sci. **94**: 376.
— Dairies in. (H. De Groot) Overland, **4**: 355.
— Dangerous Journey in. (J. R. Browne) Harper, **24**: 741. **25**: 6.
— Dead Rivers of. (J. S. Hittell) Overland, **1**: 430.
— Desert Basin. (C. J. Fox) Overland, **15**: 9.
— Diluvial Deposits in. (J. Blake) Am. J. Sci. **63**: 385.
California, Discoverers of. (J. D. B. Stillman) Overland, **2**: 256.
— Early. (J. Clifford) Lakeside, **8**: 50.
— Early Spanish Settlement of. Appleton, **15**: 105.
— Earthquakes in, during 1856. (J. B. Trask) Am. J. Sci. **73**: 341.
— Education in. *See* Education.
— Educational Society of. Am. J. Educ. **16**: 785.
— Emigrant in. Chamb. J. **56**: 33.
— Farming in. (J. S. Silver) Overland, **1**: 176.
— Finances of. Bank. M. (N. Y.) **19**: 208.
— First Overland Trip to. (J. T. Headley) Harper, **21**: 80.
— Flush Times in. (J. G. Baldwin) So. Lit. Mess. **19**: 665.
— Forbes on, 1839. Tait, n. s. **6**: 277. — Mo. R. **148**: 476.
— Gambling-Houses of. Chamb. J. **31**: 341.
— Geological Survey of. (J. D. Whitney) Overland, **8**: 79. — (J. D. Whitney) Am. J. Sci. **88**: 256.
— — Whitney's. (W. H. Brewer) Am. J. Sci. **91**: 231, 351. — (W. H. Brewer) No. Am. **110**: 228.
— German Notices of. Hunt, **22**: 483.
— Geysers of. (H. B. Auchincloss) Contin. Mo. **6**: 280. — (B. P. Avery) Scrib. **6**: 641. — (D. K. Tripp) Lakeside, **10**: 228. — Potter Am. Mo. **12**: 60.
— Glaciers of. (J. Muir) Harper, **51**: 769.
— Gold in. (J. D. Whitney) No. Am. **75**: 277. — Dem. R. **24**: 1. — Hunt, **24**: 251. — Liv. Age, **20**: 305.
— — Discovery of. (C. Stetson) Hunt, **29**: 166. **31**: 385.
— — — Effect of. Blackw. **69**: 1.
— — — Influence of, on Value of precious Metals. (G. Tucker) Hunt, **24**: 19.
— Gold Fields of. Dem. R. **40**: 29. — Hogg, **3**: 99. — (W. P. Blake) Am. J. Sci. **70**: 72.
— Gold Finding in. Chamb. J. **11**: 61.
— Gold Hunters in, 1850. Brit. Q. **12**: 56. Same art. Ecl. M. **21**: 289.
— Gold Mines of. (H. King) West. J. **4**: 38.
— — History and Geology of. Pioneer, **3**: 311.
— — Voice from the Diggings. Blackw. **70**: 470.
— Gold Washings of. (E. Bryant) Colburn, **85**: 252.
— Hints on a Journey to. (S. C. Woolsey) Scrib. **6**: 25.
— Historical Review to 1875. (J. R. Browne) Overland, **15**: 343.
— History and Resources of, 1848. Ecl. R. **89**: 465.
— in 1848. West. J. **1**: 548. — (C. Walbey) Peop. J. **7**: 125.
— in the last Months of 1849. Hogg, **5**: 323, 343, 398.
— in 1849–50. (J. D. B. Stillman) Overland, **11**: 226–539. **12**: 40, 156, 250.
— in 1850. Chamb. J. **14**: 11. — Dub. Univ. **37**: 99.
— in 1851. (Mrs. L. A. C. Clapp) Pioneer, **1**: 41–347. **2**: 23–351. **3**: 80–354. **4**: 22–345.
— In a California Eden. (C. H. Miller) Overland, **14**: 549. **15**: 79–355.
— Indians of. (S. Powers) Atlan. **33**: 313. — Penny M. **3**: 55.
— — Gallinoméros. (S. Powers) Lakeside, **7**: 352, 448.
— — Money of. (L. G. Yates) Am. Natural. **11**: 30.
— Irrigation in. (F. Carpenter) Ecl. Engin. **16**: 79.
— Journey from New Orleans to. Chamb. J. **24**: 337–408.
— Land of one Idea. (S. Powers) Lakeside, **7**: 436.
— Land Titles in. West. J. **4**: 104.
— Lawyers and Preachers of. All the Year, **20**: 463.
— Life in, 1845. Ecl. R. **84**: 438.
— — in 1846. Hunt, **14**: 349.
— — in 1850. Tait, n. s. **18**: 643.
— — on a Ranch in. Chamb. J. **56**: 647.
— Literature and Art in, 1850–75. (W. C. Bartlett) Overland, **15**: 533.
— a Lottery. Hogg, **7**: 47.
— Lower. (T. Evans) Overland, **11**: 157. — Pioneer, **2**: 26.

California, Lower, Explorations in. (J. R. Browne) Harper, **37**: 576, 740. **38**: 9.
— — Missions in. (B. Clinch) Month, **17**: 454.
— Manufactures in. (H. Robinson) Overland, **2**: 280.
— Marryat's. (A. H. Guernsey) Harper, **11**: 18.
— Mining Camp in. (M. H. Foote) Scrib. **15**: 480.
— Mining Curiosities in. Broadw. **8**: 419.
— Monetary Regulations of. (A. Walker) No. Am. **105**: 677.
— Mountain Lakes of. (J. Muir) Scrib. **17**: 411.
— Mountain Trails in. (W. L. Fawcette) Lakeside, **5**: 385.
— My first Christmas in. (T. W. Brotherton) So. M. **11**: 716.
— Mysteries of, 1847. (J. S. Bell) Godey, **34**: 92, 129.
— Name of. (E. E. Hale) Hist. M. **6**: 312.
— — Etymology of. (J. Archbald) Overland, **2**: 437.
— — Origin of. (E. E. Hale) Atlan. **13**: 265.
— Naturalist in. (J. G. Cooper) Am. Natural. **3**: 182, 470.
— New El Dorado, 1853. Godey, **47**: 101-406.
— New Kind of State Constitution in, 1879. (A. G. Sedgwick) Nation, **28**: 227, 350.
— The new Nation, 1850. Liv. Age, **28**: 535.
— — 1851. Dub. Univ. **37**: 99.
— Newspapers of. All the Year, **20**: 349.
— Northern. (C. Nordhoff) Harper, **47**: 908. **48**: 35.
— Odd Characters in. (S. Powers) Lakeside, **10**: 161.
— Old River-Beds of. (J. L. LeConte) Am. J. Sci. **119**: 176.
— Orange Culture in. (T. Evans) Overland, **12**: 235. — (J. G. Downey) **12**: 560.
— Our Empire on the Pacific. Hunt, **27**: 275.
— Overland Journey to. (M. Powell) Liv. Age, **23**: 155.
— Overland Route to, Kelly's Excursion. Colburn, **92**: 345.
— Past, Present, and Future of. Hunt, **25**: 168.
— Pioneer Days of. (H. Robinson) Overland, **8**: 457.
— a Poem. (L. H. Sigourney) Pioneer, **3**: 23.
— Poetry of. (F. C. Ewer) Pioneer, **1**: 19.
— Position and Prospects of. Dem. R. **24**: 412.
— Primeval. (C. W. Stoddard) Scrib. **22**: 832.
— Queen Elizabeth's. (J. L. Sanborn) Overland, **9**: 440.
— Rambles in. Dem. R. **24**: 70.
— Ranch in. (L. C. Jones) Lippinc. **27**: 366.
— Resources and Wealth of, 1852-53. De Bow, **15**: 237.
— Revolutions of. (D. de Mofras) Pioneer, **2**: 260.
— Romish Missions in. Am. Church R. **21**: 253.
— Route to. Am. Whig R. **8**: 402.
— San Francisco to Sonora. St. James, **16**: 54, 237, 337.
— Saxon's Five Years within the Golden Gate. Colburn, **144**: 36.
— Scene in. Pioneer, **1**: 287.
— Seasons in. Pioneer, **3**: 96.
— Sequoia Forests of. (J. Muir) Harper, **57**: 813.
— Sheep in. (S. Hyacinth) Overland, **4**: 141.
— Sheep Farming in. (J. Hayes) Overland, **8**: 489.
— Silk Culture in. (H. DeGroot) Overland, **4**: 452.
— Six Months in, 1849. (H. DeGroot) Overland, **14**: 316.
— Society in. Quar. **151**: 40.
— Song-Birds of. (W. Paton) Overland, **14**: 562.
— Southern. (A. G. Brackett) Lakeside, **1**: 103. — (S. Hyacinth) Overland, **2**: 19-361.
— — Botanist in. (J. F. James) Am. Natural. **14**: 492.
— Spas of. Lakeside, **6**: 164.
— Statistics of, 1869. Am. J. Educ. **18**: 285.
— Summer Tour in. (W. B. Farwell) Pioneer, **4**: 352.
— Switzerland of. (S. Powers) Lakeside, **10**: 339.
— Territorial Question, Action of Congress on. (F. Bowen) No. Am. **71**: 221.
— to New Orleans by the Isthmus. Dub. Univ. **55**: 485.
— Trade of, for 1859. Bank. M. (N. Y.) **15**: 117.
— Trees of. (A. Murray) Ed. New Philos. J. **67**: 1. **68**: 205.
California, Trip to the Southern Mines, 1854. Pioneer, **2**: 279.
— Tropical. (J. Clifford) Overland, **7**: 297. **8**: 9, 210.
— Tropical Fruits of. (W. C. Bartlett) Overland, **1**: 263.
— University of. (D. C. Gilman) Overland, **9**: 564.
— Upper. (J. D. Dana) Am. J. Sci. **57**: 247.
— — Commerce and Resources of. Hunt, **16**: 34.
— — Mines of. (L. W. Sloat) Hunt, **16**: 365.
— Vegetable Kingdom in. (R. Hale) Hours at Home, **7**: 522.
— *versus* Free Trade. Quar. **90**: 492.
— Vineyards of. (J. S. Silver) Overland, **1**: 307.
— Volcanic Springs in Southern. (J. L. LeConte) Am. J. Sci. **69**: 1.
— Wagon Road in. (F. Poe) De Bow, **21**: 58.
— Wants and Advantages of. (J. Hayes) Overland, **8**: 338.
— Waysides in. (W. P. Gibbons) Overland, **4**: 467. **5**: 153. **15**: 113.
— What she wants. (Mrs. S. A. Downer) Pioneer, **2**: 80.
— Wind Storm in Forests of the Yuba. (J. Muir) Scrib. **17**: 55.
— Wine-Making in. (A. Haraszthy) Harper, **29**: 22. — (A. Haraszthy) Overland, **7**: 489. **8**: 34, 105, 393.
— Young Man who went West. (C. S. Kirkland) Lippinc. **19**: 83.
See San Francisco.
California, Gulf of, Discolored Waters of. (T. H. Streets) Am. Natural. **12**: 85.
California Conjuring Trick. All the Year, **39**: 253.
California Family Cat. (P. Mulford) Lippinc. **9**: 116.
California Gamblers. All the Year, **20**: 489.
California Garden, Evening in. (H. Rosevelt) Overland, **5**: 469.
California Islands, Antiquities of. (W. H. Dall) Overland, **12**: 522.
California Missions, Story of. (B. Clinch) Month, **17**: 169.
California Ranch. (S. Powers) Atlan. **35**: 684.
California Redwoods, In. (S. Powers) Lakeside, **7**: 129.
California Seaside. (C. W. Stoddard) Lippinc. **8**: 459.
Californian abroad. (S. L. Clemens) Overland, **1**: 120, 209, 316.
Californians, Sketches of eminent. Pioneer, **2**: 332.
Caligula, Vision of; a Poem. (B. Simmons) Blackw. **45**: 449.
Caliphate, The. (J. C. McCoan) Fraser, **96**: 399. Same art. Ecl. M. **89**: 629.
Caliphs, The. (W. Spitta) Western, **5**: 291.
Calixtines and the Taborites. Am. Presb. R. **5**: 1.
Calixtus, George. (C. M. Mead) Bib. Sac. **22**: 315. — Ecl. R. **120**: 347.
— and the Pacification of the Church. Chr. Rem. **29**: 1.
Call, W. M. W., Poems. Westm. **97**: 280.
Calls, Morning, in Paris. Ev. Sat. **9**: 125.
Calladon; a Story. (J. Hawthorne) Fraser, **102**: 383.
Callanish, Standing Stones of. (W. J. Millar) Nature, **20**: 127.
Callao, Bombardment of. Once a Week, **28**: 32.
Called Meeting; a Story. (J. Woodville) Lippinc. **27**: 52.
Callimachus. Hymn to Jupiter, translated. Blackw. **40**: 467.
— Hymn to Apollo, translated. Blackw. **42**: 744.
— Hymn to Ceres, translated. Blackw. **43**: 396.
— Hymn to Diana, translated. Blackw. **44**: 52.
Callistus, St., and Hippolytus, Lives of. (J. Morris) Month, **32**: 214, 321.
— and his Accuser. Dub. R. **35**: 447.
— History of. Month, **8**: 1, 181, 285.
Callot, Jacques. Ev. Sat. **3**: 673. **8**: 376. — St. James, **19**: 192.
Callum, Daniel, the Cricket. (C. Bede) Belgra. **39**: 202.
Calmuck. *See* Kalmuck.

Calonne, Monsieur de. Fraser, **6**: 365.
Caloric. (A. Beatty) West. J. **9**: 303, 376.
— Human. Ecl. R. **110**: 47.
Caloric Engine. (J. Ericsson) J. Frankl. Inst. **17**: 416. **18**: 48. **58**: 352. — J. Frankl. Inst. **55**: 123, 365. — (J. H. Bloodgood) J. Frankl. Inst. **58**: 349. — (T. Ewbank) J. Frankl. Inst. **58**: 178, 282, 330. — J. Frankl. Inst. **71**: 44. — Pract. M. **6**: 339.
— Ericsson's. (W. A. Norton) Am. J. Sci. **65**: 393. — Chamb. J. **36**: 231. — Hunt, **27**: 19. — West. J. **8**: 376.
— — Modification of. (F. A. P. Barnard) Am. J. Sci. **66**: 232.
— Expenditure of Heat in different Forms of. (F. A. P. Barnard) Am. J. Sci. **68**: 161.
Calorimetric Investigations. (R. W. E. Bunsen) Am. J. Sci. **101**: 172, 277, 348.
Calpurnia; a Poem. (H. H. Boyesen) Scrib. **22**: 11.
Calrierre, Charlotte de. (E. H. Lacombe) So. M. **16**: 351.
Calumet Island. House. Words, **15**: 55.
Calumnies against the Dead. Blackw. **2**: 400.
— against the Living. Blackw. **3**: 388.
Calvary of St. Sebastian; a Tale. (K. S. Macquoid) Temp. Bar, **34**: 483.
Calvert, Cecilius, Portrait of. (T. S. Mercer) So. M. **8**: 381.
Calvert, George. (M. C. Jenkins) U. S. Cath. M. **5**: 376. — (J. P. Kennedy) U. S. Cath. M. **5**: 369.
— and the Maryland Charter. (B. U. Campbell) U. S. Cath. M. **5**: 193.
Calvert, George H. Count Julian. New York R. **6**: 448.
Calvert, Leonard, Life of. (G. W. Burnap) Sparks's Am. Biog. **19**: 91.
Calvert Family. (E. L. Didier) Lippinc. **6**: 531.
Calvin, John. (E. Garbett) Ex. H. Lec. **19**: 159. — (G. Reynolds) Chr. Exam. **69**: 73. — (P. Schaff) Bib. Sac. **14**: 125. — (O. W. Wight) Univ. Q. **8**: 255. — Bib. Sac. **2**: 329, 489, 710. — (H. Giles) Chr. Exam. **43**: 161. — (J. Floy) Meth. Q. **10**: 571. — Anal. M. **4**: 153. — Lit. & Theo. R. **6**: 325. — Spirit Pilg. **3**: 559, 615. — (J. W. Alexander) Princ. **9**: 29. **11**: 339. — Chr. Mo. Spec. **10**: 239. — Am. Presb. R. **3**: 391. **4**: 104. — Bost. R. **3**: 153–608. — Cong. M. **2**: 306. — Ecl. R. **116**: 1.
— and Beza, Characters of. Cong. M. **7**: 169.
— and Calvinism. (G. S. Abbott) Bib. Sac. **30**: 401.
— and the Church of England. (J. F. Garrison) Am. Church R. **30**: 530.
— and Froude. (J. Young) Contemp. **21**: 431. Same art. Liv. Age, **116**: 746.
— and the Reformation. Lond. Q. **23**: 45.
— and Servetus. Chr. Mo. Spec. **3**: 408. — Lond. Q. **49**: 100. — Brit. Q. **9**: 443.
— Anecdotes of. Cong. M. **1**: 423, 689.
— as a Commentator. (F. W. Gotch) Kitto, **3**: 222.
— as an Interpreter of Scripture. (F. A. G. Tholuck) Am. Bib. Repos. **2**: 541.
— at Geneva. (S. Osgood) Mo. Rel. M. **3**: 15. — Ecl. R. **91**: 521. — Fraser, **93**: 758. — Westm. **70**: 1. Same art. Liv. Age, **59**: 323.
— Audin's Life of. U. S. Cath. M. **4**: 441.
— Dyer's Life of. Dub. R. **29**: 30.
— Ethics of. (T. P. Lobstein) Bib. Sac. **37**: 1.
— Henry's Life of. (R. W. Dickinson) Theo. & Lit. J. **5**: 529.
— in Church and State. Ed. R. **131**: 122. Same art. Liv. Age, **104**: 515.
— Letters of. Liv. Age, **54**: 542.
— Life of. Princ. R. **20**: 279. — Ecl. R. **91**: 521.
— — and Times of. Kitto, **7**: 162. — No. Brit. **13**: 85. Same art. Liv. Age, **25**: 577.
— — Bungener's. Colburn, **127**: 223.
Calvin, John, Lives of. Quar. **88**: 529.
— Love of Christian Union. (W. M. Blackburn) Am Presb. R. **17**: 223.
— Mackenzie and Allen on. Chr. Obs. **16**: 434.
— Merle d'Aubigne's Life of. Dub. Univ. **64**: 350.
— Opinion of, by first Reformers. Chr. Obs. **2**: 141, 275.
— Wife of. Ecl. M. **41**: 82.
Calvin, the Cat. (C. D. Warner) Scrib. **14**: 248.
Calvinism. (R. B. Drummond) Theo. R. **12**: 191. — (G. E. Ellis) Chr. Exam. **54**: 62. — (H. Heppe) Mercersb. **5**: 182.
— and Arminianism, Influence on Civil Liberty. (J. W. McLane) New Eng. **3**: 509.
— — Nichols on. Cong. M. **8**: 139.
— and the German Reformed Church. (T. G. Apple) Mercersb. **19**: 450.
— and Hopkinsonianism contrasted. Gen. Repos. **3**: 324.
— and St. Augustine. Brownson, **20**: 289.
— and modern Doubt. Chr. Rem. **45**: 25.
— as a Force in History. (J. H. Allen) Unita. R. **14**: 110.
— Bishop of Lincoln's Refutation of. Quar. **6**: 191.
— Confutation of. Ecl. R. **29**: 56.
— Controversy on. Chr. Disc. **5**: 212.
— Ethics of. (O. Dewey) Chr. Exam. **19**: 1.
— Froude on. Chr. Obs. **71**: 407. — So. R. n. s. **9**: 970. — (J. G. Meline) Cath. World, **13**: 541.
— in the English Reformation. (W. M. Blackburn) Am. Presb. R. **20**: 70.
— in New England. (F. P. Tracy) Am. Meth. M. **18**: 408.
— in Scotland. Ed. R. **147**: 386. Same art. Liv. Age, **137**: 771.
— Movement to revive. (G. H. Emerson) Univ. Q. **16**: 171.
— New and old. Am. Meth. M. **13**: 222. — (J. M. Williams) New Eng. **40**: 615.
— of Church of England. Cong. M. **5**: 242.
— Phenomenon of. Bost. R. **3**: 566.
— Popular Objections to. Princ. **17**: 572.
— Position of. (R. Aikman) Meth. Q. **33**: 291.
— Princeton and Andover on. (T. G. Apple) Mercersb. **22**: 161.
— Reasons for. (L. Withington) Bib. Sac. **18**: 324.
— Roman Law and. (J. B. Gregg) New Eng. **39**: 447.
— Seabury's Anti-. Am. Ch. Mo. **3**: 321, 401.
— Tomline's Refutation of. Chr. Obs. **10**: 579. **11**: 358–512. — Ecl. R. **14**: 688.
— Unauthorized, of English Bible. (J. J. Turton) Meth. Q. **24**: 380.
— Williams's Defense of modern. Ecl. R. **15**: 486.
Calvinist, Anti-, Fellowes on the. Chr. Obs. **1**: 172, 233.
Calvinists, French, in America. (L. Sabine) No. Am. **80**: 373.
Calvinistic and Arminian Controversy, Faber on. Chr. Obs. **3**: 357.
— Pearson on. Chr. Obs. **1**: 787.
Calvinistic Church. (J. S. Barry) Univ. Q. **16**: 113.
Calvinistic Controversy, Beresford on. Chr. Obs. **17**: 723.
Calvinistic or Reformed Doctrines. (E. D. Morris) Am. Presb. R. **18**: 241.
Calvinistic Theology. (A. D. Mayo) Univ. Q. **8**: 37.
Calypso; a Poem. (F. Fawcett) Putnam, **14**: 547.
Camargo, Mademoiselle de. (A. Houssaye) Internat. M. **5**: 232.
Camargue, The. Sharpe, **42**: 24.
— Holy Maries of. (M. P. Thompson) Cath. World, **29**: 468.
Cambacères, Prince, Langon's Evenings with. Mo. R. **143**: 196.
— Memoirs of. (J. W. Croker) Quar. **58**: 406.
Camberwell Beauty, The. (T. Hood) Colburn, **67**: 145.
Cambodia. Quar. **30**: 251. **116**: 283.

Cambodia, Strange Scenes in. (G. d'Abain) Scrib. 8: 355. *See* Angkor Wat.
Cambodunum, Site of. (J. Hunter) Arch. 32: 16.
Cambrian and Silurian, History of the Names. (T. S. Hunt) Nature, 6: 15, 34, 53.
Cambrian Superstitions. Westm. 17: 382.
Cambridge, George, 2d Duke of. (J. McCarthy) Galaxy, 11: 676.
Cambridge, R. C., Life and Poetry of. Lond. M. 5: 433.
Cambridge, Eng., Account of. Penny M. 5: 168, 209.
— Castle of, Coffins and Skeletons found in. (R. Masters) Arch. 8: 63.
— Church of Holy Sepulcher at. (J. Essex) Arch. 6: 163.
— Fitzwilliam Gallery. Colburn, 11: 177.
— in the last Century, Gunning's Reminiscences. Fraser, 52: 153.
— in 1820. Chamb. J. 44: 145.
— Marbles at, Clarke on. Ed. R. 15: 453.
— Round Church at. Penny M. 13: 220.
— revisited. Once a Week, 18: 304.
Cambridge University. Fraser, 41: 617. — Am. J. Educ. 28: 97, 369, 482. — Galaxy, 9: 321. — (C. L. Balch) University Q. 3: 31. 4: 1. — Nature, 21: 125. — Tait, 4: 265. — (C. C. Felton) No. Am. 44: 178. — Am. Q. Reg. 12: 292, 371. — Pamph. 20: 301. — (B. B. Edwards) Bib. Sac. 5: 192. — Mo. R. 97: 306, 315. 104: 15.
— and its Colleges. Contin. Mo. 2: 662.
— and Oxford. (R. G. White) Atlan. 46: 385. — Blackw. 100: 446. — Liv. Age, 72: 14.
— — Athletic Sports at. Dark Blue, 3: 233.
— — Boat-Race between. *See* Boat-Race, University.
— — German Views of. (W. C. Perry) Macmil. 37: 406.
— Characteristics of, in 17th Century. Theo. Ecl. 6: 35.
— Classical Tripos, 1866. (T. Markby) Contemp. 2: 574.
— Commission on, 1852. Ecl. R. 97: 257.
— Controversy on, 1834. Quar. 52: 466.
— Discipline of. Chr. Obs. 17: 435-794.
— during the Puritan Controversies. New Q. 4: 59.
— Dyer's History of. (J. Foster) Ecl. R. 20: 518.
— Education in. Lond. M. 14: 229, 289.
— Election of Chancellor, 1847. Chr. Rem. 13: 298.
— Everett's On the Cam. (C. A. Bristed) Nation, 1: 182. — (S. R. Calthorp) Chr. Exam. 79: 373. — (W. P. Atkinson) No. Am. 101: 515.
— Expenses of Education at. (W. Emery) J. Statis. Soc. 26: 296.
— Government and System of. (J. Heywood) J. Statis. Soc. 31: 1.
— Life in. Hogg, 13: 459. Same art. Ecl. M. 35: 481. — Lond. Soc. 19: 33. — Nat. M. 7: 328. — Westm. 35: 456.
— — according to C. A. Bristed. Fraser, 49: 89.
— Literature of, Recent. Dub. Univ. 52: 667.
— Manuscripts at. Ho. & For. R. 1: 471.
— Modern History at. Fraser, 45: 170, 261.
— Moral Philosophy at. Westm. 101: 430.
— Natural Science at. (T. G. Bonney) Nature, 1: 451.
— — in 1875. Nature, 11: 353.
— — in 1876. Nature, 13: 292.
— New Cavendish College. Dub. Univ. 93: 669.
— Philosophical Society, Transactions of. (Sir J. Mackintosh) Ed. R. 37: 225.
— Power of Chancellor's Court at. (R. Richardson) Arch. 7: 25.
— Practical Science at. (G. T. Bettany) Nature, 11: 132.
— Prize Poems. Mo. R. 86: 353.
— Problems for Examination, 1801-10. Ecl. R. 13: 281.
— Professors of, Reminiscences of. (H. Scadding) Canad. Mo. 7: 201.
— Reform at, 1855. Westm. 63: 154. — Brit. Q. 32: 204. — Nat. R. 2: 328.
Cambridge University, Report on, 1855-56. Brit. Q. 24: 492.
— Row at, in 1632. Bentley, 4: 249.
— Seven Years at. Lond. M. 17: 441.
— Sports at. Lond. Soc. 5: 375.
— Struggle of a poor Student through. Lond. M. 11: 491.
— Studies. Fraser, 32: 663. — Liv. Age, 27: 289.
— — Sedgwick on. Brit. Q. 12: 360. — Mo. R. 134: 92.
— — Syndicate's Report on. Nature, 13: 415.
— Tatler in. (W. D. Rawlins) Dark Blue, 1: 628.
— Theological Instruction at. Chr. Rem. 3: 514.
— The Union at. (W. Everett) O. & N. 4: 40.
— Wranglers of. Once a Week, 4: 151.
See Oxford and Cambridge.
Cambridge Essays, England, 1855. Ecl. R. 103: 67.
Cambridge, Mass. (C. F. Richardson) Harper, 52: 191.
— Churches and Ministers of. Am. Q. Reg. 11: 178.
— First Church in. (A. McKenzie) Cong. Q. 15: 384.
— Harvard College. *See* Harvard College.
— Inscriptions in Burial-Ground. N. E. Reg. 2: 213.
— Miscellany of Mathematics, Physics, and Astronomy. Chr. Exam. 32: 273.
— Recollections of. (T. C. Amory) N. E. Reg. 25: 221.
— Thirty Years ago. (J. R. Lowell) Putnam, 3: 379, 473.
Cambuscan Bold, Story of. Chamb. J 29: 309.
Cambuskenneth Abbey. Once a Week, 15: 293.
Camden, Wm. Britannia. Retros. 9: 207.
Camden, S. C., and its Associations. Knick. 35: 333.
— Battle of, 1780. Am. Hist. Rec. 2: 103.
— — Gen. Gates at. (J. A Stevens) M. Am. Hist. 5: 241, 425.
— Second Battle of, 1781. Potter Am. Mo. 4: 99.
Camden Society, Character and Influence of. Chr. Rem. 1: 321.
— Publications of. Ecl. R. 71: 327.
Camdentown Baker. Dub. Univ. 12: 68.
Camel, The. Appleton, 2: 34. — Chamb. J. 36: 187. 54: 451. — Once a Week, 16: 495. — Penny M. 2: 116 10: 29.
— Commercial Value of. (W. G. King) Hunt, 30: 660.
— Haunts and Habits of. Chamb. J. 41: 366. Same art. Ecl. M. 63: 68.
— Ship of the Desert. Gent M. n. s. 6: 59 — (J. W. Palmer) Harper, 15: 577.
Camels, Importation of, to the United States. (G. P. Disosway) Nat. M. 11: 481.
Camelford's Body, What has become of? (C. Reade) Belgra. 29: 316.
Camelon, On the ancient. (J. Walker) Arch. 1: 230.
Cameos. (G. H. Sass) So. M. 13: 449. — Argosy, 11: 109.
— in Barberini Vase. (C. Marsh) Arch. 8: 316.
Cameo-Cutting and Mosaic Work. (C. H. Wilson) J. Frankl. Inst. 33: 250.
Cameo-Engraving. Art J. 6: 20.
Camera, Eye and. (A. Abbott) Harper, 39: 476.
Camera Lucida, New. Nature, 18: 312.
Cameron, Sir Ewen, of Lochiel. Fraser, 26: 671. — Hogg, 4: 52, 68.
Cameron, Col. John, of Fassifern. Dub. Univ. 43: 524.
Cameron, Malcolm, with portrait. New Dom. 19: 93.
Cameronian Ballads. (C. Bowles) Blackw. 7: 482.
Cameronians, The. Blackw. 6: 169, 513, 663. 7: 48-508.
Camille. (Countess de Gasparin) Hours at Home, 6: 422, 506. 7: 49, 172, 268.
Camille Desmoulins. (W. Chambers) Chamb J. 54: 17.
Camirus Vase. (C. T. Newton) F. Arts Q. 2: 1.
Camisards, or French Prophets. (E. Calamy) Cong. M. 14: 737. — Quar. 150: 434. — Ed. R. 104: 123.
— Country of. (S. Smiles) Good Words, 11: 641-845.
— Wars of. Ecl. R. 107: 493.
Camma. (T. A. Harcourt) Overland, 13: 184.

Camoens, Luis de, Adamson's Memoir of. Ecl. R. **32**: 559.
— and his Translators. (E. I. Sears) Nat. Q. **2**: 46.
— Cave of. (Mrs. H. Shuck) So. Lit. Mess. **6**: 822.
— Life and Writings. (R. Southey) Quar. **27**: 1.
— Lusiad. St. James, **17**: 422.
— — Duff's Version, 1880. (J. C. Rodrigues) Nation, **30**: 406.
— Poetry of. Ed. R. **6**: 43.—Mo. R. **97**: 405. **109**: 470.
Camoëns; a dramatic Sketch. (F. Halm) Blackw. **48**: 220.
Camorra, La; an Italian Institution. All the Year, **9**: 93.
Camorristi; a Story of Italy. (Mad. Galletti) Good Words, **22**: 109, 187, 257.
Camp. (P. Mulford) Overland, **6**: 478.
— and Barrack Room. Westm. **46**: 473.
— and the Field; a Tale of the Mexican War. Putnam, **10**: 323.
— at Boulogne. Chamb. J. **22**: 232.
Camps and Bivouacs. (Mrs. Ward) Bentley, **34**: 151.
— and Maneuvers. Bentley, **34**: 359.
— on the River Avon at Clifton. (H. M. Scarth) Arch. **44**: 428.
Camp-Fire Lyrics. (E. Kearsley) Lippinc. **15**: 563, 755. **16**: 304-730.
Camp-Meetings. (M. E. Wright) Meth. Q. **21**: 582.—Chr. Disc. **5**: 170.
— in Prairie Land. Knick. **28**: 302.
— in the West fifty Years ago. (W. C. Howells) Lippinc. **10**: 203.
Camp Notes. Chamb. J. **44**: 177-794. **45**: 110, 364.
Campagna of Rome. Mo. R. **165**: 463.
Campaign, Incidents of. (G. F. Struvé) So. Lit. Mess. **8**: 68.
— of 1799, Dumas's. For. Q. **1**: 98.
— of 1809. Ed. R. **18**: 209.
— of 1813-14. Mo. R. **103**: 47.
— of 1815. Blackw. **4**: 220.—Dub. Univ. **23**: 647.
Campaigns of 1859, 1866, and 1870-71. Fraser, **84**: 251.
— in Europe, from 1796-1870, Adams's Great. (F. W. Palfrey) Nation, **26**: 421.
Campaign Songs. (J. R. Dennett) Nation, **7**: 207.
— of 1880. (W. C. Brownell) Nation, **31**: 284.
Campaigner at Home. Fraser, **69**: 214-705. **70**: 75-725.
Campaigning, Practical. U. S. Serv. M. **1**: 364, 474.
Campaigning Life, Sketches of. Fraser, **50**: 223.
Campan, Mad., Journal anecdotique de. Lond. M. **11**: 77.
Campanella, Tommaso, and his Works. Fraser, **29**: 313.
— and modern Italian Thought. (A. Clerke) Ed. R. **149**: 139.
— Sonnets of. Cornh. **36**: 543. Same art. Liv. Age, **135**: 707.
Campbell, Alexander. (J. F. Rowe) Chr. Q. **1**: 456.
— Memoirs of. New Eng. **29**: 259.
Campbell, Alicia Kelly, and Princess Charlotte. (L. C. Frampton) Gent. M. n. s. **17**: 275.
Campbell, Archibald. Blackw. **4**: 437.—Anal. M. **13**: 498.
— Shipwreck and Adventures. Quar. **16**: 69.
— Voyage round the World. Mo. R. **83**: 307.
Campbell, Charles. (R. A. Brock) Potter Am. Mo. **7**: 425.
Campbell, Colin, Lord Clyde. (A. C. Fraser) Good Words, **18**: 33.—with portrait, Ecl. M. **44**: 424.—Liv. Age, **56**: 757. **79**: 109.
— and the Indian Mutiny. Lond. Q. **56**: 281.—Blackw. **84**: 480.
— Shadwell's Life of. Blackw. **129**: 447.—Ed. R. **154**: 189.—(R. D. Osborn) Nation, **32**: 353, 375.
Campbell, Donald, Sketches from Highland Tradition. Tait, n. s. **16**: 367, 516, 565.
Campbell, G. J., Duke of Argyll. *See* **Argyll, Duke of.**
Campbell, John, Lord, Memoirs of. Westm. **115**: 360.—(A. Hayward) Quar. **151**: 1. Same art. Ecl. M. **96**: 514, 591.—(A. K. H. Boyd) Fraser, **103**: 334. Same art. Liv. Age, **149**: 238.—(A. V. Dicey) Nation, **32**: 222, 244.
— Speeches. Ed. R. **76**: 545.
— Untruthfulness of, as a Historian. Westm. **61**: 446.
Campbell, Rev. John. Ecl. R. **121**: 217.—Chr. Rem. **2**: 313.
— Life and Times of. Tait, n. s. **8**: 654.
— Philip's Life of. Cong. M. **25**: 189.—Mo. R. **156**: 228.—Ecl. R. **74**: 324.
Campbell, John Macleod. Blackw. **122**: 283.
— Memorials of. Ed. R. **147**: 386.
— Sketch of. (N. Macleod) Good Words, **13**: 353.
Campbell, Robert, and his Descendants. (H. F. Douglas) N. E. Reg. **32**: 275.
Campbell, Thomas. (S. C. Hall and Mrs. S. C. Hall) Art J. **18**: 149. Same art. Ecl. M. **67**: 69.—(H. T. Tuckerman) So. Lit. Mess. **17**: 212.—Peop. J. **11**: 77.—with portrait, Ecl. M. **23**: 289.—with portrait, Fraser, **1**: 714.—Dub. Univ. **33**: 245.—Fraser, **1**: 563.—Fraser, **30**: 342. Same art. Ecl. M. **3**: 289. Same art. Liv. Age, **2**: 579.—Anal. M. **5**: 234.—Art J. **10**: 107.—Bentley, **18**: 17.—Sharpe, **8**: 250. **9**: 50.—Tait, n. s. **1**: 393.
— and his Writings. (E. Lester) St. James, **44**: 156.
— and the Literary Union. Colburn, **100**: 6.—(C. Redding) Ecl. M. **31**: 367.
— Crabbe, and Southey. Tait, n. s. **1**: 161, 393, 668.
— Epistle to Horace Smith. Colburn, **45**: 192.
— Gertrude of Wyoming. (Sir C. E. Grey and Sir W. Scott) Quar. **1**: 241.—(F. Jeffrey) Ed. R. **14**: 1.—Ecl. R. **9**: 519.—Portfo. (Den.) **2**: 153.
— Irving on. Internat. M. **1**: 230.
— The Last Man. Colburn, **8**: 272.—Lond. M. **11**: 588.
— Letter to Mohawk Chief, John Brant. Colburn, **4**: 97.
— Letters from the South. Ecl. R. **66**: 409.—Mo. R. **143**: 16.
— Life of. (C. Redding) Colburn, **77**: 332-399. **78**: 81-427. **79**: 51-423. **80**: 66-418. **81**: 46-497. **82**: 173. **83**: 28. **84**: 300-454.
— — and Correspondence of. Am. Whig R. **12**: 405.—No. Brit. **10**: 459. Same art. Ecl. M. **17**: 1. Same art. Liv. Age, **21**: 244.—Quar. **85**: 32. Same art. Liv. Age, **22**: 385.—Blackw. **65**: 219.—Quar. **57**: 349.—Ecl. R. **89**: 295.—Meth. Q. **11**: 64.—New Eng. **9**: 261.—Tait, n. s. **16**: 31. Same art. Ecl. M. **16**: 299.—Colburn, **85**: 234.—(W. A. Larned) New Eng. **9**: 261.
— Memoirs of. No. Brit. **32**: 287.
— Modern Poetry. Brit. Q. **9**: 385.
— Mornings with. Chamb. J. **3**: 81, 98. Same art. Liv. Age, **5**: 49.
— The Parrot. Colburn, **53**: 447.
— Personal Recollections of. Dub. Univ. **25**: 557, 679. Same art. Liv. Age, **6**: 129.
— Pilgrim of Glencoe, and other Poems. Mo. R. **157**: 545.
— Plagiarisms of. Blackw. **22**: 347.
— Pleasures of Hope. Art J. **7**: 256.
— Poems. Chr. Rem. **3**: 655.—Ecl. R. **75**: 712. Quar. **57**: 349.—(W. Lyall) Canad. Mo. **14**: 187.
— Poetical Genius of. Chr. Rem. **8**: 62.
— Recollections of. Sharpe, **11**: 321. Same art. Ecl. M. **20**: 505.
— Redding's Reminiscences of. Colburn, **117**: 420.
— Reminiscences of. Colburn, **74**: 163-559.
— Ritter Bann. Blackw. **15**: 440.—Colburn, **10**: 324.
— Songs. Lond. M. **15**: 58.
— Theodric. Quar. **31**: 342.—(F. Jeffrey) Ed. R. **41**: 271.—U. S. Lit. Gaz. **1**: 343.—Blackw. **17**: 102.
— University Scheme. Lond. M. **12**: 36.

Campbell, Z. Age of Gospel Light. New Eng. 9: 544.
Campbell Clan, History of. (G. A. Ellis) Atlan. 27: 559.
Campbell Town Election. Putnam, 6: 67.
Campbellism. (R. W. Landis) Am. Bib. Repos. 2d s. 1: 94, 295. 3: 203.
— and saving Baptism. (J. E. Farnham) Bapt. Q. 11: 477.
— reviewed. (J. M. Peck) Chr. R. 21: 481.
Campbellites, or Disciples. Penn Mo. 11: 547.
Camping out. (G. Y. Lagden) Belgra. 24: 191. — Gent. M. n. s. 25: 49.
— at Rudder Grange. (F. R. Stockton) Scrib. 16: 104.
Campion, Edmund, Martyr. (J. C. Earle) Cath. World, 7: 289. — Ed. R. 148: 469. — Liv. Age, 140: 77.
— Contemporary Eulogy on. Month. 16: 116.
— Star-Chamber Proceedings. (J. Bruce) Arch. 30: 64.
Campomanes, Count, Life of. Fraser, 3: 614.
Camulodunum, Situation of. (T. Walford) Arch. 16: 145. — (H. Jenkins) Arch. 29: 243.
Camus, Bishop J. P. Irish Q. 7: 1054.
Can a Life hide itself? (B. Taylor) Atlan. 23: 605.
Can wrong be right? a Tale. (Mrs. S. C. Hall) St. James, 1: 11–401. 2: 43–421. 3: 13–417.
Canaan, Wars of. Chr. R. 13: 345.
Canaan, Litchfield Co., Conn., Documents relating to. N. E. Reg. 12: 122.
Canada. (C. Graham) Fraser, 87: 131. — (C. M. Grout) Scrib. 20: 80–553. — (Sir F. B. Head) Quar. 61: 249. — (C. C. Nott) Nation, 17: 88. — Blackw. 77: 438–701. — Brit. & For. R. 8: 286. — Blackw. 43: 215, 228. 50: 642. — Fraser, 5: 635. — Dub. Univ. 20: 735. — Chamb. J. 19: 253. — Dub. Univ. 35: 151. — Hogg, 6: 1–321. 7: 200. 9: 37, 321. — Fraser, 47: 183. — Penny M. 7: 25, 33.
— Affairs of, 1830. Fraser, 1: 389.
— — 1839. Westm. 32: 426.
— — 1850. Chr. R. 15: 161.
— Agriculture and Commerce of. Lond. Q. 8: 430.
— Algoma, the North Land. (S. Reid) Canad. Mo. 19: 622.
— and British Columbia. Quar. 109: 1.
— and Colonization, England's best Policy. St. James, 32: 330. 33: 118.
— and Emigration. Dub. Univ. 1: 287. — Lond. M. 10: 577.
— and the Empire. (T. Cross) Canad. Mo. 20: 294.
— and the Far West. Lond. Q. 6: 143.
— and Great Britain. Canad. Mo. 10: 413. — (R. Fisher) Canad. Mo. 15: 543. — (J. Whitman) Canad. Mo. 15: 319.
— and the Great Lakes. Dub. Univ. 38: 159.
— and Indian Tribes. (W. Leggo) Canad. Mo. 18: 139.
— and Ireland. Blackw. 43: 385.
— and Mexico, 1865. Dub. R. 57: 206.
— and New York, Early Trade Contests between. (J. G. Hodgkins) Hist. M. 7: 299.
— and Goldwin Smith. (Sir F. Hincks) Contemp. 40: 825.
— and the United States. (D. B. Lucas) So. R. n. s. 2: 449. — (Sir F. Hincks) No. Am. 130: 338. — (Goldwin Smith) No. Am. 131: 14.
— — Boundary Commission. Colburn, 90: 41. — Geog. M. 1: 282.
— — Commercial Union of. (A. McGown) Canad. Mo. 18: 1.
— and Washington Treaty. (A. Mills) Contemp. 21: 597. — St. James, 32: 12.
— Annexation of, to United States. Dub. Univ. 35: 151. — (J. A. Turner) De Bow, 9: 397. — Republic, 2: 88, 284.
— — Obstacles to. (F. G. Mather) No. Am. 133: 153.
— Art Exhibition, 1880. Canad. Mo. 17: 545.
Canada, as it now is, 1875. Blackw. 118: 44.
— at the Exhibition of 1865. Canad. J. n. s. 2: 32.
— Autumn in. Lond. Soc. 6: 321.
— Azoic Rocks of. (Sir W. E. Logan) Canad. J. n. s. 2: 439.
— Backwoods Life in. All the Year, 12: 190.
— Bank Service in. Chamb. J. 41: 673.
— Banks and the Usury Laws in. (J. B. Hodgskin) Nation, 11: 289.
— Bonnycastle's. Colburn, 78: 460.
— Bouchette's. Am. Q. 11: 412. — Westm. 15: 367.
— British Diplomacy in. (R. G. Haliburton) St. James, 30: 127.
— British Policy in, 1839. (Sir F. B. Head) Quar. 64: 462.
— Campaign in, 1776, Gen. Irvine's Journal. Hist. M. 6: 115.
— Campaigns in. Quar. 27: 406. — Colburn, 17: 541. 19: 162–248.
— Canals of. (E. J. Chapman) Canad. J. n. s. 10: 261.
— Census of 1861. (J. Langton) Canad. J. n. s. 10: 1.
— — of 1871. (A. Harvey) Canad. Mo. 1: 97.
— Charlevoix's New France. (J. R. G. Hassard) Cath. World, 17: 721.
— Christmas in the Canadian Bush. Gent. M. n. s. 8: 81.
— Church System of. Westm. 89: 442.
— — Catholic. (C. Lindsey) No. Am. 125: 557.
— — — Lindsey on. Canad. Mo. 13: 109.
— Civil Government of. Westm. 11: 140.
— Civil Revolution in, 1849. Blackw. 65: 727. 66: 471. 67: 249.
— Clergy Reserves. Am. Church R. 4: 224, 350.
— Colonial Self-Government in. (W. J. Rattray) Canad. Mo. 17: 539.
— Colonialism in. (W. Norris) Canad. Mo. 20: 166.
— — and Sir F. Hincks. (W. Norris) Canad. Mo. 20: 501.
— Commerce of. Hunt, 6: 538.
— — and Resources of. Hunt, 21: 288.
— — — in 1871–72. (J. Young) Canad. Mo. 3: 221.
— — — in 1870–78. (J. Young) Canad. Mo. 13: 186.
— — Growth of. (J. Young) Canad. Mo. 1: 387.
— Commercial and Financial. (J. Young) Canad. Mo. 8: 123.
— Commercial Intercourse with the United States. (C. Lindsey) Canad. Mo. 1: 132. — Canad. Mo. 1: 214.
— Condition and Prospects of, 1852. (S. Hale) No. Am. 74: 261.
— Confederation of. (G. Smith) Canad. Mo. 2: 173. — (A. Herbert) Fortn. 7: 480. — (A. T. Drummond) Canad. Mo. 7: 406. — Colburn, 139: 1. — Westm. 83: 533. Same art. Ecl. M. 65: 129. — (F. G. Mather) Atlan. 46: 56.
— — and Defenses of. (S. M. Jarvis) Canad. Mo. 17: 449.
— — Desirability of. Westm. 86: 394.
— — History of. Canad. Mo. 18: 185.
— Conquest of. (J. W. De Peyster) Hist. M. 15: 297.
— — Warburton's. Ecl. R. 91: 657. — Ecl. M. 19: 102.
— Corn Trade of. Fraser, 6: 362.
— Cost of Government in. (W. McDonnell) Canad. Mo. 17: 173.
— Courtship in. St. James, 7: 359.
— Crown and the Cabinet in. (Sir F. Hincks) 19th Cent. 4: 423.
— Dark Days and Earthquakes in. Hist. M. 8: 60.
— Days of our Apprenticeship. (M. F. Griffin) St. James, 31: 698.
— Debt of, Public. (A. T. Drummond) Canad. Mo. 10: 461.
— Defense of. Fraser, 84: 135. — Blackw. 91: 228.
— Defenses and Resources of. Liv. Age, 6: 76.

Canada, Difficulties of. (R. Fisher) Canad. Mo. **17**: 521.
— Discontents in, Causes of. Tait, n. s. **5**: 132, 199, 265.
— Dominion of, New. Fraser, **82**: 584.
— — First ten Years of, 1878. (G. Smith) Brit. Q. **67**: 305. Same art. Ecl. M. **90**: 712.
— Drift and Lakes of Western. (E. J. Chapman) Canad. J. n. s. **6**: 221.
— Durham's Administration of. (J. W. Croker) Quar. **63**: 223, 457. — Dem. R. **5**: 542. — Westm. **28**: 502. — (J. S. Mill) Westm. **32**: 241, 426. — Dub. Univ. **13**: 355. — Quar. **64**: 255. — (C. Dunkin) No. Am. **49**: 373. — (J. D. Wallenstein) No. Am. **27**: 1. — Fraser, **17**: 233. — Brit. & For. R. **7**: 193. — Chr. Mo. Spec. **2**: 79, 130.
— Early British Rule in. (F. Taylor) Canad. Mo. **2**: 239.
— Early History of. (J. H. Lanman) No. Am. **46**: 409.
— Early Jesuit Missions in. (M. J. Griffin) Canad Mo. **1**: 344.
— Election in. Once a Week, **30**: 380, 402.
— Emigration to. St. James, **36**: 582. — Quar. **23**: 373.
— England, and the United States. (C. Mackay) St. James, **31**: 723.
— English Captives in. N. E. Reg. **28**: 158.
— Excursion to. (H. D. Thoreau) Putnam, **1**: 54, 179, 321.
— — 1849. (H. Cooke) Colburn, **87**: 358.
— Expedition of 1690. N. E. Reg. **9**: 354.
— Farming in. Hogg, **15**: 41–438.
— Federation, Annexation, or Independence? (G. C. Cunningham) Canad. Mo. **17**: 242.
— Female Servants in the Bush. (Mrs. Traill) Sharpe, **15**: 279.
— Female Trials in the Bush. (Mrs. Traill) Sharpe, **15**: 22.
— Few Notes on Matters in, 1857. (Viscount Bury) Fraser, **55**: 312, 554.
— Financial Situation of, 1880. (J. Hedley) Canad. Mo. **18**: 84.
— Fishes of. (A. Rimmer) Gent. M. n.s. **24**: 724. **25**: 315.
— Following the Halcyon to. (J. Burroughs) Scrib. **15**: 577.
— Forest Life in. Blackw. **71**: 355.
— Forests of. Hogg, **8**: 209.
— Fort Vercheres, Defense of. Hist. M. **4**: 131.
— Four Kings of. (J. R. Bartlett) M. Am. Hist. **2**: 151.
— Free-Grant Lands of. (C. Marshall) Fraser, **83**: 46.
— French. (E. L. Godkin) Nation, **7**: 128, 146.
— — and its People. (A. M. Pope) Cath. World, **33**: 696.
— French Government of. (F. Parkman) No. Am. **118**: 224.
— From Quebec through the St. Lawrence. (J. Burroughs) Scrib. **15**: 577.
— Future of. (R. Fisher) Canad. Mo. **8**: 428. — (J. Hatton) Tinsley, **21**: 29. — (N. F. Davin) Canad. Mo. **19**: 490. — (W. Clarke) Contemp. **38**: 305. — (G. Anderson) Contemp. **38**: 396.
— Garneau's History of. Brownson, **10**: 444.
— Geographical Names of, History in. (J. Reade) New Dom. **11**: 344.
— Geological Areas of. (E. J. Chapman) Canad. J. n. s. **15**: 13, 92.
— Geological Survey of. (S. Fleming) Canad. J. n. s. **1**: 238. — Canad. J. n. s. **3**: 320. **4**: 265. — (A. Geikie) Nature, **10**: 144. — (J. D. Whitney) Am. J. Sci. **73**: 305.
— Geology of. (T. S. Hunt) Am. J. Sci. **59**: 12.
— — Age of the Red Sandrock Formation of. (E. Billings) Am. J. Sci. **83**: 100.
— — Dawson's. Canad. J. n. s. **1**: 39.
— — Rocks of. (Sir W. E. Logan and J. W. Salter) Am. J. Sci. **64**: 224.
— Government of. Dub. R. **3**: 113. — Dub. Univ. **11**: 326.
Canada, Grievances of, 1835. Westm. **23**: 269. — (J. A. Roebuck) Westm. **30**: 444.
— Hall's Travels in, 1816–17. Chr. Obs. **18**: 95. — Westm. **4**: 129.
— Head's Emigrant to. Ed. R. **85**: 358.
— Head's Scenes and Incidents in. Westm. **12**: 103. — Fraser, **35**: 96, 467. — (Sir F. B. Head) Quar. **63**: 457.
— Heriot's Travels in. Ed. R. **12**: 212.
— History of, Chapter of. Macmil. **33**: 215.
— — Condition, and Resources of. (H. Murray) De Bow, **13**: 109.
— — Miles's. Canad. Mo. **5**: 182.
— — Sketches from. (J. Craig) New Dom. **17**: 318.
— Home Life in. Chamb. J. **58**: 9.
— How long can Great Britain hold? Dub. Univ. **34**: 314.
— in the Bodleian. (H. Scadding) Canad. J. n. s. **12**: 370.
— in the last Century. (J. Reade) New Dom. **12**: 84.
— in 1825. Westm. **8**: 1.
— in 1829. Blackw. **26**: 332.
— in 1835. Westm. **23**: 269, 519.
— in 1841, Bonnycastle on. Mo. R. **156**: 309.
— in 1851. Chamb. J. **16**: 402.
— in 1865. Bentley, **58**: 111.
— Independence of. Republic, **1**: 134. — (Sir F. Hincks) Canad. Mo. **20**: 400.
— Industries of. Pract. R. **7**: 165.
— Intellectual Progress of. (J. Douglas) Canad. Mo. **7**: 465. — (J. G. Bourinot) Canad. Mo. **18**: 628. **19**: 2, 108, 219.
— Intrusive Rocks in. (Sir W. E. Logan) Canad. J. n. s. **3**: 107.
— Invasion of, 1775. Hist. M. **12**: 97.
— Mrs. Jameson on. Ecl. R. **69**: 331. — Mo. R. **148**: 65.
— Kingston's Western Wanderings. Colburn, **106**: 163.
— Kohl's Travels in. Liv. Age, **66**: 698. **68**: 632.
— Lake Districts of. Canad. Mo. **16**: 1. — Colburn, **124**: 379.
— Laurentian Rocks of. (Sir W. E. Logan) Canad. J. n. s. **3**: 1.
— Life in. (Mrs. Moodie) Internat. M. **5**: 471. — Chamb. J. **58**: 649.
— — in the Backwoods of. (H. B. King) Atlan. **33**: 283, 430. **39**: 287.
— — in a Canadian Country Town: Kisawlee. Macmil. **33**: 165. Same art. Liv. Age, **128**: 185.
— — fifty Years ago. (C. Haight) Canad. Mo. **17**: 2, 561.
— — Traits of. Tinsley, **27**: 573.
— Literature and Education of. Canad. Mo. **17**: 593.
— Lower. Colburn, **124**: 253.
— — Habitat of. (E. Farrer) Atlan. **48**: 771.
— — Political and historical Retrospect. Tait, n. s. **2**: 439.
— Loyalty in, a Sentiment or a Principle? (A. Todd) Canad. Mo. **20**: 523.
— Mackenzie's Voyages from Montreal. (F. Jeffrey) Ed. R. **1**: 141.
— Magrath's Letters from. Dub. Univ. **1**: 600.
— Map Literature of. (H. Scaddin) Canad. J. n. s. **15**: 23.
— Maritime Industry of. (J. G. Bourinot) Canad. Mo. **3**: 89.
— Maritime Provinces of. (E. Burritt) Canad. Mo. **11**: 590.
— Materials for a Fauna of. (W. Hincks) Canad. J. n. s. **7**: 446, 484.
— — for a Literature of. (J. G. Bourinot) New Dom. **7**: 193.
— Militia of. Canad. Mo. **5**: 185. **17**: 293.
— Minerals of, Popular Exposition of. (E. J. Chapman) Canad. J. n. s. **6**: 500. **7**: 108. **8**: 437.
— Monetary System of. (D. P. Bailey, jr.) Bank. M. (N. Y.) **32**: 41, 118.

Canada, Moose-Hunting in. (Earl of Dunraven) 19th Cent. **6**: 45.
— Murray on, 1839. Mo. R. **151**: 1.
— My Route into. Blackw. **63**: 328, 425.
— Narrative of a Settler in. Colburn, **34**: 335.
— National Development of. (J. G. Bourinot) Canad. Mo. **17**: 225.
— New France and her New England Historians. So. R. n. s. **18**: 337.
— Niagara District of. Penny M. **12**: 17, 52, 85.
— Northwest. St. James, **32**: 581. **33**: 346.
— — Half-Breed Races of. (A. P. Reid) Anthrop. J. **4**: 45.
— Notes on Canadian Matters, 1857. (Viscount Bury) Fraser, **56**: 90.
— Ocean to Ocean, Grant's. Canad. Mo. **4**: 83.
— Old and New in. Canad. Mo. **7**: 1.
— Old Links and new Ties. (S. Robjohns) St. James, **33**: 641.
— On the Vermont Boundary. (F. G. Mather) Harper, **49**: 335.
— Our Trade with. Hunt, **34**: 314.
— Parkman's Old Régime in. (H. Adams) No. Am. **120**: 175. — (H. James, jr.) Nation, **19**: 252. — (C. C. Smith) O. & N. **10**: 625. — Canad. Mo. **6**: 485. — Penn Mo. **6**: 140.
— Pathmasters and Road-Work in. Once a Week, **9**: 402.
— Petroleum Springs of. (C. Robb) Canad. J. n. s. **6**: 313.
— Physical and Social Condition of, 1861. Westm. **75**: 57.
— Physical Geology of. (C. Robb) Canad. J. n. s. **5**: 497.
— Pictures from. (W. G. Beers) Scrib. **2**: 449.
— Picturesque. Canad. Mo. **20**: 653.
— Pioneers of Civilization in. St. James, **29**: 387, 493.
— Plants of. (W. Saunders) Canad. J. n. s. **8**: 219.
— Poem on. (A. W. W. Dale) Cong. **7**: 412. — Canad. Mo. **4**: 471.
— Political Destiny of. (Goldwin Smith) Fortn. **27**: 431. Same art. Ecl. M. **89**: 1. Same art. Sup. Pop. Sci. Mo. **1**: 1. Same art. Canad. Mo. **11**: 596. — (F. Hincks) 19th Cent. **3**: 1074. Same art. Canad. Mo. **12**: 56. **15**: 170. Same art. Sup. Pop. Sci. Mo. **3**: 223.
— — Goldwin Smith on. (W. P. Garrison) Nation, **28**: 271.
— Political Future of. (J. Mathews) Canad. Mo. **8**: 54, 89, 495.
— Political History, 1840–45, Hincks's. Canad. Mo. **12**: 662.
— Political Importance of. Quar. **33**: 410.
— Political Parties in, 1880. (W. Norris) Canad. Mo. **19**: 614.
— Political Revolution in, 1878. Nation, **27**: 256.
— Politics of, 1830. Westm. **13**: 45.
— — 1835. Westm. **23**: 269.
— — 1837. Quar. **61**: 137.
— — 1838. For. Q. **21**: 191. — Westm. **26**: 469. — Mus. **31**: 407.
— — 1845. (L. Sabine) No. Am. **60**: 87.
— — 1848. (L. Sabine) No. Am. **67**: 1.
— — 1872. Canad. Mo. **2**: 270, 366, 544.
— — 1873. Canad. Mo. **3**: 57–419. **4**: 58–528.
— — 1874. Canad. Mo. **5**: 62–526. **6**: 54–545.
— — 1875. Canad. Mo. **7**: 67–533. **8**: 68–533.
— — 1876. Canad. Mo. **9**: 69–544. **10**: 74–551.
— — 1877. Canad. Mo. **11**: 92–662. **12**: 83–648.
— — 1878. Canad. Mo. **13**: 95–665. **14**: 103, 233. — Nation, **27**: 111.
— Position and Outlook, 1880. (G. M. Grant) Canad. Mo. **18**: 196.
— — and Policy. (L. Doyle) Nat. Q. **3**: 103.
— Prerogative of the Crown in. (T. Hodgins) Canad. Mo. **18**: 385.
— Prince of Wales in, 1860. Liv. Age, **66**: 438.
Canada, Prisoners from, 1695. N. E. Reg. **24**: 286.
— Prisoners in. N. E. Reg. **6**: 87.
— Prospects of the Liberal Party, 1880. Canad. Mo. **19**: 429.
— Protest from a Colonist. St. James, **32**: 127.
— Provincial Synod of. (J. Bovel) Am. Church R. **14**: 436.
— Public Service in. (E. A. Meredith) Canad. Mo. **3**: 1.
— Question of. Dem. R. **1**: 205. **5**: 8. — Quar. **63**: 227, 482. — For. Q. **22**: 104. — Dub. Univ. **20**: 735. — Blackw. **37**: 909. — Mus. **32**: 497.
— — — in 1871. Ev. Sat. **10**: 362.
— Raid and Ride in. St. James, **30**: 305.
— Railways in. Canad. Mo. **3**: 265. — Dub. Univ. **46**: 127.
— Reciprocity with. (A. P. Peabody) No. Am. **74**: 168. — (C. W. Upham) No. Am. **79**: 464. — Hunt, **28**: 275. **44**: 160. — Penn Mo. **5**: 529. — Republic, **3**: 104, 158.
— Recollections of. (S. D. Huyghue) Bentley, **26**: 489, 630. **27**: 472.
— Religious Statistics of, 1839. Cong. M. **22**: 876.
— Residence in Lower. Colburn, **142**: 315–716.
— Resources of. (A. P. Peabody) No. Am. **74**: 168.
— Rural Aspects of. Chamb. J. **55**: 776.
— Russell's. (A. G. Sedgwick) Nation, **1**: 86.
— School Histories of. Canad. Mo. **9**: 447.
— School System of. Canad. Mo. **4**: 517.
— Shipbuilding in. (N. W. Beckwith) Canad Mo. **3**: 457.
— Sketches in. Bentley, **32**: 300, 381.
— Society in the Bush. (Mrs. Traill) Sharpe, **12**: 129.
— Stray Glimpses in. (F. G. Mather) Potter Am. Mo. **15**: 81.
— Sydenham's Administration in. Mo. R. **161**: 530.
— Talbot's Five Years in. Westm. **2**: 566.
— Tariff of. (Goldwin Smith) Contemp. **40**: 378.
— Titles in. (J. G. Bourinot) Canad. Mo. **12**: 344.
— Travels in. Chamb. J. **11**: 233.
— Treaties concerning. (W. F. Coffin) Canad. Mo. **9**: 349.
— Troubles in, 1827. Westm. **8**: 1.
— Two Weeks' Sport on the Coulonge River. (G. W. Pierce) Atlan. **32**: 267.
— under Lord Dufferin. (W. J. Rattray) Canad. Mo. **14**: 733.
— United States and Cuba, Letters from. Fraser, **53**: 522.
— Upper, by a Backwoodsman. Blackw. **32**: 238.
— — Lieut.-Governor Gore and. Fraser, **47**: 627.
— — Sir Francis Head's Government of. Ecl. R. **69**: 556.
— — Howison's. Ed. R. **37**: 251. — Mo. R. **99**: 171. — Blackw. **10**: 537.
— — Local History of. (H. Scadding) Canad. J. n. s. **14**: 55–658.
— — Normal Schools of. Am. J. Educ **14**: 483.
— — Politics of, 1835. Tait, n. s. **2**: 663.
— — Six Years in the Bush; Journal of a Settler in. Tait, n. s. **5**: 535.
— War in, 1838. Ecl. R. **67**: 214.
— Warburton's Hochelaga and Head's Emigrant. Quar. **78**: 510.
— Welfare of. (W. Canniff) Canad. Mo. **20**: 89.
— West, Devonian Rocks of. (H. A. Nicholson) Canad. J. n. s. **14**: 38.
— Whittlings from the West. Hogg, **6**: 216–411.
— Wild Fowl of. (A. Rimmer) Gent. M. n. s. **26**: 318.
— Wilkie's Sketches in. Tait, n. s. **4**: 265.
— Winter and Summer in. (F. Tolfrey) Colburn, **61**: 382.
— Winter in. (W. Leitch) Good Words, **3**: 722. — Cornh. **5**: 204. — (Col. Fletcher) Temp. Bar, **20**: 102
— Winter Sports in. (F. G. Mather) Harper, **58**: 391.
— Winter Weather in. Chamb. J. **39**: 68.
— With Jonathan in. (J. Hatton) St. James, **41**: 202.

Canada, Wonders of, 1768. M. Am. Hist. **1**: 243.
— Wood of. (S. D. Huyghue) Bentley, **27**: 152.
— Woods and Waters of. (C. D. Shanly) Atlan. **20**: 311. *See* Ontario; Quebec.
Canada Directory, 1857. Canad. J. n. s. **3**: 34.
Canada Expedition of 1758, Holt's Journal during. N. E. Reg. **10**: 307.
Canada Pacific Railway. (J. Douglas) Canad. Mo. **4**: 457. **6**: 229. — (M. B. Hewson) Canad. Mo. **16**: 359. — (H. Verney) Fraser, **79**: 643. — Canad. Mo. **15**: 319, 543. — Internat. R. **1**: 848.
Canada Thistles. (J. R. G. Hassard) Cath. World, **6**: 721.
Canadian, The French. All the Year, **18**: 232.
Canadians, French, of To-day. Chamb. J. **56**: 465.
Canadian Almanac. Canad. J. n. s. **3**: 509.
Canadian College, Life in a. (J. Nelson) Putnam, **1**: 392.
Canadian Culture. (L. A. Jack) Canad. Mo. **14**: 454.— (J. E. Wells) Canad. Mo. **8**: 459.
Canadian Customs. (J. Smalley) Cath. World, **8**: 246.
Canadian Emigrant. Colburn, **11**: 500. **13**: 160–346.
Canadian Element in the United States. (J. G. Shea) Am. Cath. Q. **4**: 581.
Canadian English. (A. C. Geikie) Canad. J. n. s. **2**: 344.
Canadian Fisheries Award. (C. Almy, jr., and E. L. Godkin) Nation, **26**: 145, 178. — Penn Mo. **11**: 716.
Canadian Forest Scenery. (Mrs. C. Trail) Canad. Mo. **6**: 48.
Canadian historic Names. (J. G. Bourinot) Canad. Mo. **7**: 289.
Canadian Idylls. (W. Kirby) Canad. Mo. **19**: 414, 511.
Canadian Indian Treaty of 1874. (F. L. Hunt) Canad. Mo. **9**: 173.
Canadian Legislatures, Powers of. (S. J. Watson) Canad. Mo. **16**: 519, 561.
Canadian Literature, Curios ties of. (W. J. Anderson) Canad. Mo. **1**: 55.
Canadian Longitudes. (E. D. Ashe) Canad. J. n. s. **4**: 453.
Canadian Nationalism. (G. A. Mackenzie) Canad. Mo. **12**: 594. — (W. Norris) Canad. Mo. **13**: 352.
Canadian Nationality. (W. Norris) Canad. Mo. **8**: 237. **17**: 113. — (B. W. K. Tayler) Canad. Mo. **17**: 394.
Canadian Naturalist and Geologist, 1856. (E. Billings) Canad. J. n. s. **1**: 164.
Canadian Noms-de-Plume. (H. Scadding) Canad. J. n. s. **15**: 259.
— identified. (H. Scadding) Canad. Mo. **9**: 89, 205.
Canadian Outpost, Our Life at. Victoria, **35**: 479.
Canadian Parliament. (Goldwin Smith) Canad. Mo. **2**: 59.
— in 1864. (S. J. Watson) Canad. Mo. **1**: 64.
— in 1872. (J. G. Bourinot) Canad. Mo. **2**: 170.
— in 1873. Canad. Mo. **3**: 520.
— Routine of. (J. G. Bourinot) Canad. Mo. **11**: 279.
Canadian Pioneer, Reminiscences of. (S. Thompson) Canad. Mo. **20**: 179–603.
Canadian Pioneers. (J. C. Smalley) Cath. World, **17**: 687.
Canadian Poetry. (A. McLauchlan) Canad. J. n. s. **3**: 17.
Canadian Politics. Nation, **27**: 111.
Canadian Protection vindicated. (D. McCulloch) Fortn. **31**: 748.
Canadian Review. (J. Sparks) No. Am. **19**: 457.
Canadian Sketch; How I caught my first Salmon. Blackw. **121**: 728. Same art. Liv. Age, **133**: 798.
Canadian Sports. (W. G. Beers) Scrib. **14**: 506.
Canadian Timber-Makers, Visit to. Once a Week, **6**: 47.
Canal, Ancient, the Nile and Red Sea. Blackw. **56**: 182.
— du Midi. Ecl. Engin. **15**: 136.
— English, Journey on. House. Words, **18**: 289–354.
— Helder, or Great North Holland. J. Frankl. Inst. **43**: 371. **44**: 10.
— Lock, of Exeter. (P. C. de la Garde) Arch. **28**: 7.
— Michigan and Illinois. Niles's Reg. **28**: 110.
— Soonkesala. (J. H. Latham) Ecl. Engin. **15**: 385, 481.
Canal, Union, of Pennsylvania. J. Frankl. Inst. **4**: 274.
— Welland. (W. H. Merritt) Am. J. Sci. **14**: 159. *See* Darien; Erie; Suez; etc.
Canals. U. S. Lit. Gaz. **5**: 198. — West. Mo. R. **1**: 73.
— and Aqueducts. Quar. **73**: 281.
— and Canal Conveyance. (W. O'Brien) J. Frankl. Inst. **67**: 17, 73.
— and inland Navigation, Improvement of. (J. Robins) J. Frankl. Inst. **65**: 151.
— and Railroads. Quar. **31**: 349. — Niles's Reg. **28**: 143. **30**: 443.
— — Long on. Portfo. (Den.) **33**: 265, 353.
— — of United States, Tanner on, 1840. J. Frankl. Inst. **30**: 230. — Mo. R. **157**: 182.
— Chicago and other. (R. J. Walker) Contin. Mo. **4**: 92.
— Construction of, 1826. J. Frankl. Inst. **1**: 73.
— Docking and Excavating, Wood's. Pract. M. **1**: 104.
— Grahame on. Fraser, **12**: 155.
— in the United States in 1850. West. J. **4**: 407.
— London. Penny M. **11**: 318, 326, 330.
— Navigation by Steam. (A. D. Bache) J. Frankl. Inst. **16**: 361. — (W. Cossage) J. Frankl. Inst. **39**: 73. — (G. E. Harding) Ecl. Engin. **5**: 84. — (N. Robson) J. Frankl. Inst. **66**: 294. — Ecl. Engin. **1**: 744, 920.
— of Canada. (J. G. Bourinot) Canad. Mo. **1**: 538.
— — Historical Sketch of. Ecl. Engin. **5**: 147.
— of India. (W. B. Adams) J. Frankl. Inst. **60**: 217, 293.
— of New York. (W. Phillips) No. Am. **29**: 500. — (M. C. Paterson) No. Am. **14**: 230. — J. Frankl. Inst. **18**: 66.
— — Commerce of. Hunt, **8**: 523. **9**: 386. **11**: 129. **13**: 52. —(D. O. Kellogg) Hunt, **21**: 298.
— — Rates of Toll on. (A. C. Flagg) Hunt, **24**: 156, 447. — Hunt, **13**: 390.
— — Report of, 1841. J. Frankl. Inst. **32**: 87.
— — Trade and Commerce of. Hunt, **22**: 622.
— — — and Tonnage of. (H. Tracy) Hunt, **14**: 543.
— of Ohio, Commerce of. Hunt, **12**: 456.
— of Pennsylvania, Reports on, 1846, 1847. J. Frankl. Inst. **43**: 145. **45**: 84.
— — 1847, 1849–50. J. Frankl. Inst. **45**: 221, 321. **49**: 82. **51**: 161.
— Progress of Inventions in. J. Frankl. Inst. **6**: 188, 228, 295.
— Ruin of. Ecl. Engin. **21**: 381.
— Statistics of. Hunt, **12**: 580.
— Surveys for. (E. F. Johnson) Am. J. Sci. **24**: 19.
— Traction on. Ecl. Engin. **9**: 13.
Canal-Boat. (Mrs. H. B. Stowe) Godey, **23**: 167.
— The fast. Chamb. J. **35**: 88.
Canal-Boats at high Velocities, Experiments with, 1837. J. Frankl. Inst. **23**: 223.
— Experiments on best Form of. J. Frankl. Inst. **19**: 275.
Canal-Lock, Aubois. (W. Watson) Ecl. Engin. **19**: 85.
Canal-Locks, 1837. (W. A. Provis) J. Frankl. Inst. **23**: 218.
— Renwick's Inclined Plane. J. Frankl. Inst. **2**: 257, 321. **3**: 91.
— Ward's Balance. J. Frankl. Inst. **3**: 91.
Canal-Lock Gates, Strain to which subjected. (P. W. Barlow) J. Frankl. Inst. **23**: 396.
Canal Navigation, Resistance in. So. R. **8**: 114. *See* Fluids.
Canal Population, Our. (G. Smith) Fortn. **23**: 233. — Chamb. J. **55**: 257.
Canal Wheel for raising Water, 1853. J. Frankl. Inst. **55**: 93.
Canaletto, or Canale, Antonio, Venetian painter, in London. Colburn, **63**: 33.
Canary, Talking. Once a Week, **19**: 332.
Canaries, Talk about. (E. Ingersoll) New Dom. **21**: 61.

Canaries, Art and Mystery of managing. (J. Forester) Godey, **53**: 107.
Canary Islands, Ancient Inhabitants of. (T. Hodgkin) Ed. New Philos. J. **39**: 372.
— and Azores, Summer Cruise among. (Miss Dabney) Harper, **46**: 865.
— Climate of. (L. von Buch) Ed. New Philos. J. **1**: 93.
— Natives of. Hogg, **1**: 189.
— Summer Cruise among. (A. L. Gihon) Harper, **54**: 664.
Cancer, Indian Cure for. Chamb. J. **9**: 237.
— Middlesex Hospital Report on. Liv. Age, **56**: 30.
Candace, Queen. (J. C. M. Laurent) Am. Presb. R. **14**: 261.
Candahar Campaign. *See* Afghanistan, War of, 1879–80.
Candia, Island of. So. Lit. Mess. **5**: 707.
— Insurrection in, 1866. Bentley, **61**: 367. — Colburn, **138**: 379.
Candid, The. Blackw. **13**: 108, 263.
Candidate from Bull Flat. (P. Mulford) Overland, **4**: 89.
Candidating; or, Old Times in the Southwest. (H. W. Pierson) Appleton, **26**: 233.
— in the 19th Century. Mo. Rel. M. **19**: 396.
Candidature of Mr. Davlish. Belgra. **41**: 297.
Candle, Philosophy of a. (G. Molloy) Irish Mo. **4**: 529.
Candle Factory, Day at a. Penny M. **11**: 41.
— Price's. Colburn, **169**: 402.
Candle-Making. (A. Wynter) Once a Week, **1**: 78.
— Christianity in. No. Brit. **20**: 161.
Candles. (J. Scoffern) Belgra. **13**: 442. — All the Year, **40**: 497.
— and Enlightenment. Hogg, **10**: 49.
— and Soap, Chemistry of. J. Frankl. Inst. **45**: 122.
— Manufacture of. Chamb. J. **21**: 278.
— Stearic, Manufacture of. Pract. M. **7**: 317.
— why they burn blue in Presence of a Ghost. Lond. M. **6**: 133.
Candlemas Day; a Mystery. Kitto, **38**: 413.
Candler Manuscript, Extracts from. N. E Reg. **4**: 179.
Candlesticks of 12th Century from Goodrich Court. (S. R. Meyrick) Arch. **23**: 317.
Candlish, R. Smith. Fraser, **23**: 509.
Candlish, Robert. (A. M. Symington) Good Words, **22**: 134.
Candolle, A. P. de, Life and Labors of. (C. F. P. von Martius) Am. J. Sci. **44**: 217. — (G. B. Emerson) Am. J. Sci. **42**: 217. — (A. Gray) Am. J. Sci. **85**: 1.
Candolles, Ferdinand de. Bentley, **31**: 414.
Candy Manufacture. (A. Wynter) Once a Week, **10**: 318.
Cane, R. Irish Q. **8**: 1005.
Canes, Essay on. (J. H. Ingraham) Am. Mo. M. **12**: 259. *See* Walking-Sticks.
Canham, Kitty, Strange Story of. (Mrs. A. Tindal) Temp. Bar, **59**: 341.
Canina, Luigi. Art J. **9**: 31.
Canker and the Cure; a Story. Howitt, **1**: 75.
Cannæ, Battle of. (C. R. Kennedy) Temp. Bar, **9**: 270.
Cannes. (R. Davey) Lippinc. **13**: 310.
— A Winter in. Broadw. **5**: 327.
Cannibalism. Liv. Age, **75**: 123.
— and Christianity in Fiji. (E. House) Meth. Q. **19**: 601.
— Driven to. All the Year, **28**: 12.
— in the Cars; a Tale. (S. L. Clemens) Broadw. **1**: 189.
— in Galicia. (L. J. Jennings) Once a Week, **4**: 324.
— Remains in Shellheaps. (J Wyman) Am. Natural. **8**: 403.
Cannibals, Cave, of South Africa. (Bowker, Bleek, and Beddoe) Anthrop. R. **7**: 121.
— Cruise after. (A. H. Guernsey) Harper, **7**: 455.
— Fiji. Ev. Sat. **11**: 110.
— Six Years among. House. Words, **7**: 133. Same art. Liv. Age, **37**: 615.
Cannibals all; or Slaves without Masters. De Bow, **22**: 543.
Canning, Elizabeth, Trial of, 1753. Chamb. J. **18**: 108. — Ecl. M. **27**: 246. — Blackw. **87**: 581.
Canning, George. (A. C. Ewald) Temp. Bar, **49**: 310. — (C. C. Smith) No. Am. **90**: 76. — (Visc. Stratford de Redcliffe) 19th Cent. **7**: 27. — (A. H. Everett) No. Am. **26**: 169. — For. Q. **8**: 391. — Mus. **12**: 458. — (Sir J. Mackintosh) Mus. **14**: 216. — Ann. Reg. **4**: 130. — Mus. **20**: 615. — Tait, n. s. **13**: 276. Same art. Ecl. M. **8**: 332. — Liv. Age, **10**: 355. — Fraser, **60**: 513. Same art. Liv. Age, **64**: 3. — Nat. R. **9**: 273.
— and the Anti-Jacobin. Liv. Age, **92**: 280. Same art. Ecl. M. **68**: 413.
— and J. H. Frere, Literary Partnership of. Fraser, **90**: 174. Same art. Liv. Age, **124**: 358.
— — Month at Seaford in 1825 with. (A. G. Stapleton) Macmil. **26**: 25. Same art. Liv. Age, **113**: 691.
— and his Opponents. Lond. M. **18**: 78.
— and his Times. Chr. Obs. **59**: 816. — No. Brit. **31**: 304.
— — Stapleton's. Liv. Age, **63**: 366.
— and his Writings. Cornh. **15**: 63.
— and Huskisson. Westm. **15**: 282.
— and Pitt. Fraser, **60**: 513.
— and the Poetry of the Anti-Jacobin. Hogg, **7**: 161.
— and Wellington. Month, **7**: 397.
— as a Man of Letters. (A. Hayward) Ed. R. **108**: 104.
— Bell's Life of. Colburn, **77**: 89. — Dub. Univ. **28**: 109. — Tait, n. s. **13**: 277.
— Character of. Colburn, **34**: 367.
— Death of. Colburn, **20**: 269.
— Indian Administration. No. Brit. **37**: 222.
— Letters to Earl Camden. Quar. **2**: 412.
— Life of. Mo. R. **115**: 519.
— Literary Remains of. Ed. R. **108**: 104. Same art. Ecl. M. **45**: 120. Same art. Liv. Age, **58**: 608.
— Dr. Philpott's Letter to. Blackw. **21**: 858.
— Policy of. Am. Q. **16**: 1.
— Political Life of. Mo. R. **124**: 325.
— Speech at Liverpool Dinner. Blackw. **7**: 11. — Mo. R. **108**: 188.
— — at Re-election. Pamph. **16**: 215.
— Speeches of. Mo. R. **116**: 285. — Colburn, **22**: 355.
Canning, William, the elder, and the younger, of Bristol. Lond. Soc. **5**: 332.
Canning River, The, and its Settlers, Western Australia. (J. W. F. Blundell) Colburn, **87**: 195.
Cannon, C. J. Works. Brownson, **14**: 503.
Cannon, History of. (J. T. Headley) Harper, **25**: 593.
— Hotchkiss Revolving. Ecl. Engin. **12**: 224.
— Musket, and Rifle. Quar. **90**: 445.
— Rifled, in England and France. Ed. R. **119**: 480.
— — Modern Tactics and. Ed. R. **109**: 514.
— Treadwell's Improvements in. (A. Gray) Am. J. Sci. **91**: 97.
See Artillery; Ordnance.
Cannon-Balls, and their striking Velocity. (G. W. Royston-Pigott) Pop. Sci. R. **10**: 1.
— Measurement of Velocity of. Ev. Sat. **9**: 667.
Cannon-Powder, Modern. Ecl. Engin. **6**: 289.
Canoe, Construction of. (W. L. Alden) Harper, **56**: 754.
— Cruising, and Outfit. (G. E. Chase) Harper, **61**: 395.
— discovered at North Stoke, in Sussex. (T. Phillips) Arch. **26**: 257.
Canoes. (C. L. Norton) O. & N. **7**: 544.
— How to build and manage. (W. L. Alden) Scrib. **4**: 478.
Canoe Convention on Lake George. (C. L. Norton) Canad. Mo. **20**: 426.
Canoe Cruise in the Coral Sea. (C. W. Stoddard) Overland, **5**: 571.
Canoe Voyage. (P. G. Hamerton) Fortn. **7**: 179.

Canoe Voyage through Maine to Canada. (J. C. Hoyt) Scrib. 14: 488.
Canoe-Voyaging. Macgregor's Rob Roy on the Rivers of Europe. (A. H. Guernsey) Harper, 33: 569.
— — — in the Baltic. (M. Titcomb) Harper, 35: 430.
— — — in the English Channel. (H. M. Alden) Harper, 36: 718.
— — — on the Jordan. (A. H. Guernsey) Harper, 41: 49.
— Modern. (R. Tyson) Canad. Mo. 19: 533.
— on the High Mississippi. (A. H. Siegfried) Lippinc. 26: 171, 279.
Canofieno, or Roman Swing. Penny M. 14: 257.
Canon's Clock. House. Words, 18: 229. Same art. Liv. Age, 59: 65.
Canon's Daughter, The. (E. About) Canad. Mo. 1: 362.
Canon Law, as the Ground of penitential Discipline. Chr. Rem. 8: 339.
Canons, Historical Sketch of the. Chr. Obs. 66: 913.
— of the Apostles. Bib. Sac. 4: 1.
— of 1640. Chr. Obs. 42: 211.
— of Sardica, and Charge of mutilating MS. (E. S. Ffoulkes) Macmil. 31: 139. — Month, 23: 122.
Cañon, Day up the. (J. F. Bowman) Overland, 7: 528.
Cañons. (A. Geikie) Nature, 1: 435.
Cañon City, Oregon, Romance of. (C. Swift) Lakeside, 7: 461.
Canonbury Tower. (J. Timbs) Once a Week, 17: 26. — Chamb. J. 27: 181.
Canonization of St. Michael de Sanctis, 1862. Dub. R. 52: 45.
— of Saints. U. S. Cath. M. 4: 137.
Canonsleigh, Austin, Canons and Canonesses at. (C. S. Perceval) Arch. 40: 417.
Canopus Stone. (E. J. Davis) Scrib. 6: 414. — Theo. R. 4: 289.
Canossa on the Slope of the Apennines. Cornh. 37: 468. Same art. Liv. Age, 137: 504.
Canova, Antonio. (Mrs. E. V. Blake) Nat. Q. 22: 244. — (E. A. Salter) Cath. World, 28: 243. — Dial, 3: 454. — (F. S. John-Brenon) Art J. 32: 105. — Penny M. 9: 364. — Sharpe, 34: 309.
— and British Sculptors. (A. Cunningham) Quar. 34: 110.
— and his Works. Dub. Univ. 23: 469. 24: 162, 289.
— and Napoleon. (G. L. Austin) Galaxy, 19: 310. — Lond. M. 11: 451. — Portfo.(Den.) 33: 406.
— Birthplace of. (George Sand) Howitt, 2: 252.
— Life and Works of. (A. H. Everett) No. Am. 29: 441. — (E. Everett) No. Am. 10: 372. — Am. Q. 19: 68. — So. Lit. Mess. 6: 115. — Anal. M. 15: 506. — Quar. 34: 110. — Dub. Univ. 23: 469. — Mo. R. 109: 449. — Niles's Reg. 23: 276. — Fraser, 20: 370. — Ed. R. 43: 496. — Mus. 2: 223. 9: 97.
— Le Monnier's Memoir of. Cath. World, 1: 598.
— Orpheus and Eurydice of. (H. B. McDonald) Godey, 31: 103.
— Studio of. Colburn, 7: 28.
Canrobert, Francois C., Marshal. Colburn, 119: 244. — Ecl. M. 34: 31.
Cant. Tait, n. s. 20: 175. — Temp. Bar, 18: 410.
— and Counter Cant. Macmil. 14: 75.
— Bygone. All the Year, 23: 320.
— Progress of; an Etching. Lond. M. 14: 45.
Can't and Can, only for Ladies. Chamb. J. 35: 411.
Cantab, Confessions of a. Blackw. 16: 459, 571.
Cantate Domino, Steiner and Schwing's. (E. V. Gerhart) Mercersb. 12: 141, 315.
Cantegrel. Fraser, 52: 469.
Canterbury. (A. F. Marshall) Am. Cath. Q. 6: 288. — Penny M. 2: 460. 3: 73. — (H. W. Preston) Atlan. 48: 813. — (P. Walker) Fraser, 86: 117.
Canterbury, Archbishops of. (S. Wilberforce) Quar. 125: 386. — Bentley, 51: 432. 57: 546. Same art. Ecl. M. 56: 235. — Quar. 112: 82.
— — Hook's Lives of. Bentley, 49: 205. — Chr. Obs. 61: 100. — Ecl. R. 125: 391. — Dub. R. 53: 275. — Dub. Univ. 87: 363.
— — in the Reformation. Quar. 125: 386.
— — Lives of early. Chr. Rem. 42: 73.
— Cathedral of. All the Year, 33: 348. — (J. M. Capes) Contemp. 20: 718. — (S. Denne) Arch. 10: 37.
— — Evidence of a Lavatory in. (S. Denne) Arch. 11: 108.
— — French Church in. (S. Smiles) Good Words, 7: 253.
— — Tomb of Theobald. (H. Boys) Arch. 15: 291.
— Modern Pilgrimage to. (R. G. White) Atlan. 45: 524.
— Pilgrimage to. (J. Hawthorne) Appleton, 20: 435.
Cantillon, R., and Nationality of Political Economy. (W. S. Jevons) Contemp. 39: 61.
Cantire, Land's End at. (E. Bradley) Once a Week, 15: 355.
— Grouse-Shooting in. (W. G. Starbuck) Temp. Bar, 18: 56.
Canton, China. All the Year, 14: 15. Same art. Cath. World, 2: 656. — House. Words, 16: 376. — Hunt, 2: 521.
— Curiosities of. Chamb. J. 47: 441.
— Day in. Chamb. J. 44: 49. — Knick. 44: 356.
— French in. Bentley, 43: 403.
— Hong-Kong, and Macao. (W. G. Palgrave) Cornh. 37: 278. Same art. Liv. Age, 137: 51.
— Inside. Cornh. 1: 412.
— Ophthalmic Hospital at. Penny M. 6: 262.
— Street Scenes in. Good Words, 2: 281.
Canton River, China, Burial Inscriptions on French Island in. N. E. Reg. 11: 255.
Canton, Mass., History of English Church at. N. E. Reg. 29: 73.
— Ministers of. Am. Q. Reg. 8: 48.
— Powder Mill in. N. E. Reg. 31: 272.
Canton, N. Y., St. Lawrence University. (R. Fisk, jr.) O. & N. 4: 129.
Cantor's Daughter; a Tale. (E. Polko) Sharpe, 46: 257.
Cantu, Cesare. (G. P. Marsh) Nation, 2: 564.
— Margherita Pusterla. Chr. Rem. 22: 21.
Canvas-Back and Terrapin. (W. M. Laffin) Scrib. 15: 1.
Canvasser's Tale. (S. L. Clemens) Atlan. 38: 673.
Caoutchouc. Hogg, 7: 263. — House. Words, 19: 403.
— and its Gatherers. Appleton, 14: 1, 33.
— and its industrial Uses. (E. Pavoux) Ecl. Engin. 11: 509.
— History and Properties of. (C. Davis) J. Frankl. Inst. 9: 123.
— in British India. Geog. M. 3: 31.
— Manufacture of. (E. Pavoux) Ecl. Engin. 14: 369.
— — and Uses of. (E. Pavoux) J. Frankl. Inst. 98: 356.
— New Source of, in Burmah. Pract. M. 6: 60.
— Vulcanized. Chamb. J. 8: 5.
See also India-Rubber.
Caoutchouc Tree. Penny M. 7: 337.
Cap-and-Bells. (J. M. Legaré) Harper, 27: 775. 28: 36, 184.
Capacity and Genius. Mo. R. 88: 192.
Cape Ann, Mass. (S. G. W. Benjamin) Harper, 51: 465.
Cape Breton, Coal Measures of. (J. P. Lesley) Am. J. Sci. 86: 179.
— Journal of Expedition to, 1745. N. E. Reg. 27: 153.
Cape Coast Castle. Chamb. J. 50: 676. Same art. Ev. Sat. 15: 585.
Cape Cod. (H. D. Thoreau) Putnam, 5: 632. 6: 59, 157.
— A Dash at. Putnam, 9: 62.
— Discovery of Remains of Ship wrecked in Pilgrim Times. (A. Otis) N. E. Reg. 18: 37.

Cape Cod, Highland Light. (H. D. Thoreau) Atlan. **14**: 649.
— on the old Maps. (B. F. De Costa) N. E. Reg. **35**: 49.
Cape Cod Harbor. Hunt, **1**: 181.
Cape Cod Region and Martha's Vineyard. (O. S. Senter) Potter Am. Mo. **9**: 81.
Cape Colony, Eight Days' Ramble in. (G. E. Bulger) Intel. Obs. **11**: 246.
— Gallop through. (Capt. Butler) Colburn, **77**: 312–457.
— in 1827. Lond. M. **18**: 487.
— or the South African Republic. Tait, n. s. **20**: 275, 342.
Cape Horn in 1704. (W. I. Kip) Overland, **10**: 346.
— Navigation of. (M. F. Maury) Am. J. Sci. **26**: 54.
Cape-Horn Post-Office. (L. Kip) Overland, **12**: 424.
Cape May. (T. A. Richards) Knick. **54**: 113.
— in June. Lippinc. **16**: 9.
Cape of Good Hope. *See* Good Hope.
Cape St. Vincent, Naval Battle off, 1797. Meth. M. **23**: 36.
Cape Verd Islands. Sharpe, **25**: 289. — Liv. Age, **2**: 673.
— Summer Cruise among. (A. L. Gihon) Harper, **54**: 674.
Capel, Monsignore T. J. (F. Barrow) Galaxy, **10**: 677. — with portrait, Colburn, **168**: 169.
Capello, Bianca. Cornh. **22**: 580, 598, 711. Same art. Ecl. M. **76**: 60.
Capen, Nahum, with portrait. Dem. R. **41**: 397.
Capen Family Record. N. E. Reg. **2**: 80.
Capen Genealogy. (E. F. Everett) N. E. Reg. **20**: 246.
Caper, Bishop, and the Methodist Church. De Bow, **26**: 173.
Capercailzie: or, Cock of the Woods. Hogg, **10**: 400. — (M. G. Watkins) Fraser, **104**: 320.
— in Northumberland. (W. Topley) Nature, **15**: 7.
— in Scotland, Harvie-Brown's. Nature, **20**: 550.
Capern, Edward. Poems. (J. A. Froude) Fraser, **53**: 489.
Capernaum. (C. R. Conder) Good Words, **19**: 549.
— Site of. (E. Robinson) Bib. Sac. **12**: 263.
Capes, J. M., Conversion of. (W. G. Todd) Month, **20**: 473.
Capgrave's Chronicle. Chamb. J. **44**: 696.
Capillary Attraction. (A. M. Mayer) J. Frankl. Inst. **86**: 336, 400.
— Laplace on. Quar. **1**: 94.
— Nature of. (J. W. Draper) J. Frankl. Inst. **18**: 147.
— Poisson on. For. Q. **9**. 175.
Capillary Wave not hitherto described. (J. Langton) Canad. J. n. s. **2**: 96.
Capital, Accumulations of. Quar. **82**: 206.
— and Currency. No. Brit. **28**: 191.
— and Labor. (P. Girard) Cath. World, **28**: 230. — (E. L. Godkin) Nation, **8**: 249, 277. — (W. T. Moore) Chr. Q. **7**: 526. — (R. Sulley) Hunt, **26**: 448, 578. **56**: 249. — Bost. Q. **3**: 209. — Brit. Q. **67**: 116. — De Bow, **22**: 249. — Dem. R. **25**: 385. **33**: 193. — Bank. M. (N. Y.) **3**: 151. — Potter Am. Mo. **9**: 229, 313.
— — and Profit. (J. E. T. Rogers) Fraser, **81**: 500.
— — and Wages. Republic, **2**: 114.
— — Arbitration between. Pract. M. **5**: 119.
— — Future of. (G. Potter) Contemp. **16**: 437.
— — Union of. Bank. M. (N. Y.) **27**: 802.
— and its Use. Chamb. J. **36**: 209.
— and Population. (G. R. Rickards) De Bow, **21**: 217.
— Association of. Bank. M. (N. Y.) **10**: 1.
— Depreciation of. Bank. M. (N. Y.) **32**: 89.
— Economy of. (R. H. Patterson) Blackw. **95**: 300.
— Emancipation of. (S. S. Hebbard) Univ. Q. **31**: 133.
— Fixed and floating. Bank. M. (N. Y.) **3**: 115.
— Future of. (E. L. Godkin) Nation, **12**: 429.
— Invisible. Blackw. **98**: 701.
— J. S. Mill on. (A. Musgrave) Contemp. **24**: 728.
— Organization of. (E. L. Godkin) Nation, **18**: 37.
— Origin, Growth, and Uses of. Bank. M. (N. Y.) **4**: 147.
Capital, Poverty, and Crime. (E. Roscoe) Victoria, **21**: 561.
— Protection of. O. & N. **3**: 467.
— Ratio of, to Consumption. (F. B. Hawley) Nat. Q. **39**: 95.
— Rights of. (W. T. Thornton) Fortn. **8**: 592.
— Withdrawal of, from Trade; Failures, 1857–75. (W. M. Grosvenor) Nation, **21**: 81.
— Workingman's View of. (E. L. Godkin) Nation, **8**: 85.
— World's Demand for. Bank. M. (N. Y.) **35**: 51.
Capitals of Europe, Northern. Mo. R. **146**: 539.
Capital Farce for Snoole; a Story. (R. M. Jephson) Temp. Bar, **62**: 527.
Capital Punishment. (J. M. Binckley) Lakeside, **9**: 328. — (A. T. Bledsoe) So. R. n. s. **20**: 395. — (E. L. Godkin) Nation, **8**: 166. — (H. King) St. James, **13**: 47. — (E. S. Nadal) No. Am. **116**: 138. — (C. Redding) Colburn, **136**: 225, 342. **143**: 328. — (F. Rowton) Howitt, **2**: 218–386. **3**: 24–170. — (S. Taylor) Tait, **1**: 546. — (E. B. Hall) No. Am. **62**: 40. — (E. R. Tyler) New Eng. **1**: 28. **3**: 562. — (L. Bacon) New Eng. **4**: 563. — (W. Dwight) Chr. Q. Spec. **2**: 505. — Meth. Q. **6**: 462. — Chr. R. **14**: 365. — (A. B. Dod) Princ. **14**: 307. — (F. Parkman) Chr. Exam. **12**: 1. **14**: 298. — Bib. Sac. **4**: 270. — (F. W. Holland) Chr. Exam. **43**: 355. — Dem. R. **10**: 272. **12**: 227, 409. **19**: 90. **20**: 71, 204, 300. — Ed. R. **35**: 314. — Quar. **7**: 159. — Carey's Mus. **4**: 78, 444, 547. **7**: 7, 69. — So. Lit. J. **1**: 302. — Chr. Mo. Spec. **2**: 71. — Mo. R. **114**: 244. — For. Q. **25**: 394. — Blackw. **27**: 865. **58**: 129. — Westm. **17**: 52. — Pamph. **3**: 115. **8**: 281. **12**: 287. — Fraser, **2**: 666. — N. Ecl. **7**: 504. — (F. Rowton) Peop. J. **7**: 295–372. — (T. Walker) West. Law J. **2**: 267. — (E. Archbold) West. Law J. **5**: 421. — (H. Titus) West. Law J. **5**: 448. — (W. W. Fosdick) West. Law J. **7**: 472. — (G. B. Cheever, S. Hand, and W. Phillips) No. Am. **133**: 534. — Bentley, **56**: 171. — Colburn, **142**: 107. — Cong. M. **1**: 412. — Ecl. R. **27**: 284. **29**: 1. **74**: 554. **87**: 393. **88**: 129. **90**: 98, 460. **91**: 33, 221. **92**: 317. — (J. Simon) Ev. Sat. **8**: 673–801. — (A. P. Peabody) Chr. Exam. **14**: 298. — Fraser, **69**: 753. — Irish Q. **7**: 723. — Tait, n. s. **4**: 438. — Zoist, **2**: 295. **7**: 331.
— Abolition of. Westm. **91**: 429. — So. Lit. Mess. **18**: 650.
— and Gen. ix. 6. Kitto, **33**: 314. **34**: 314.
— and Imprisonment for Life. (E. L. Godkin) Nation, **16**: 193.
— and the Prerogative of Pardon. Westm. **81**: 398.
— and retributive Law. (C. Wiley) Am. Presb. R. **20**: 414.
— Anecdotes from the Blue Book. Temp. Bar, **17**: 47. Same art. Ecl. M. **66**: 677.
— Argument against. (E. L. Godkin) Nation, **16**: 213.
— Biblical Argument for. (H. Ballou, 2d) Univ. Q. **6**: 341. — Dub. Univ. **75**: 414.
— Decrease of. Broadw. **4**: 153.
— Dialogue on. Tait, **3**: 590.
— Divine Law on. Kitto, **18**: 35.
— Dymond on. Temp. Bar, **15**: 144.
— Effects of. Cornh. **9**: 304.
— Expediency of. Victoria, **2**: 481.
— for Forgery. Ed. R. **52**: 398. — Cong. M. **1**: 373.
— History and Results of, in England. (F. Rowton) Howitt, **2**: 345.
— in England. (F. W. Rowsell) Contemp. **28**: 628.
— in its moral Aspect. (F. Rowton) Howitt, **3**: 24–170.
— in London. (Earl Ferrers) Bentley, **2**: 595.
— in the Middle Ages. (J. Y. Akerman) Arch. **38**: 54.
— Lord Nugent on. Mo. R. **153**: 342.
— Report of Royal Commission on. Temp. Bar, **17**: 47. — (J. F. Stephen) Fraser, **73**: 232.

Capital Punishment, Use and Abuse of. Am. Mo. M. **1**: 265.
See Criminal Law; Executions; Hanging; Penal Code; Punishment; Scaffold.
Capitalist in Society. (F. W. Newman) Fraser, **92**: 686.
Capitalists, Trade-Union of. Pract. M. **3**: 50.
Capitol Building at Washington. *See* Washington.
Capon Springs, Va. (E. C. Bruce) Harper, **22**: 600.
Cappe, Catherine, Memoir of. Chr. Disc. **5**: 58. — Mo. R. **100**: 391.
Cappe, N. Explication. Chr. Disc. **1**: 141.
— Sermons. Chr. Disc. **1**: 39.
Capponi, Gino. (M. S. Stillman) Nation, **32**: 321.
Caprera, Visit to. Bentley, **54**: 37.
Capri. Blackw. **97**: 72. — Chamb. J. **47**: 608. Same art. Ecl. M. **75**: 742. — Ev. Sat. **14**: 461. — Penny M. **3**: 276.
— and Capriotes. (W. D. Howells) Nation, **3**: 14, 33.
— and its Roman Remains. Ev. Sat. **14**: 518.
— Artist's Island. (D. Benson) Lippinc. **23**: 17.
— Festa-Day at. Colburn, **103**: 449.
— On a Housetop in. (R. McLeod) Lippinc. **18**: 310.
— Pæstum, Amalfi. Cornh. **36**: 151. Same art. Ecl. M. **89**: 454.
— Rambles of Three in. (M. B. Wright) Lippinc. **24**: 393.
— Week on. (B. Taylor) Atlan. **21**: 740.
Caprice and Destiny. Colburn, **145**: 460-648.
Caprices and Ferns; a Story. Galaxy, **18**: 49.
Capsicum House for young Ladies. Liv. Age, **13**: 477, 504, 571. **14**: 30-478.
"Captain," the Turret-Monitor, Loss of. Ecl. Engin. **3**: 455. — Fraser, **83**: 68. — Gent. M. n. s. **5**: 701. — (J. S. Russell) Macmil. **22**: 473.
— and the "Monarch." (J. S. Mackie) Pop. Sci. R. **9**: 173.
Captain's Drum; a Poem. (B. F. Taylor) Atlan. **41**: 593.
Captain's last Love. (W. Collins) Belgra. **31**: 257.
Captain's Prisoner. House. Words, **6**: 469.
Captain's Room. (W. Besant and J. Rice) All the Year, **47**: supp. 1.
Captain's Story. Dem. R. **18**: 305.
Captain's Story. Galaxy, **2**: 725.
Captain Blazon's Preserves; a Tale. (V. Dayrell) Temp. Bar, **3**: 421.
Captain Bob's Farewell to his Sword. (L. W. M. Lockhart) Lond. Soc. **7**: 379.
Captain Clutterbuck's Champagne. Blackw. **90**: 499-645. **91**: 35-178.
Captain Cole's Passenger. (J. Payn) Belgra. **38**: 169.
Captain Dangerous; a Novel. (G. A. Sala) Temp. Bar, **4**: 153-441. **5**: 9-431. **6**: 5-439. **7**: 30, 202.
Captain Davis; a Californian Ballad. Knick. **45**: 331.
Captain Desmond's Daughter. Chamb. J. **58**: 631-693.
Captain Falconer. (F. Marryat) Colburn, **51**: 347. **52**: 162-306.
Captain Garbas. Knick. **56**: 1, 135, 232.
Captain Gaylord's Will. (R. Harper) Harper, **20**: 341.
Captain Henderson's Escape; a Story. (A. E. C. Maskell) Potter Am. Mo. **16**: 169.
Captain Horsfall's Romance. (J. W. De Forest) Galaxy, **12**: 788.
Captain Jack. Bentley, **6**: 322.
Captain Jonas Smith; a Story. (C. G. Leland) Temp. Bar, **56**: 342.
Captain Kidd's Money. (H. B. Stowe) Atlan. **26**: 522.
Captain Lambswool. (G. A. Sala) Belgra. **22**: 185.
Captain Lloyd's Legacy. (N. S. Dodge) Lakeside, **6**: 330.
Captain Luce's Enemy. (J. T. McKay) Scrib. **6**: 161.
Captain Millicent. (M. A. Dodge) Scrib. **7**: 360.
Captain Musters's Widow; a Tale. Eng. Dom. M. **8**: 151.
Captain Norton's Diary. (Mrs. R. Church) Belgra. **11**: 325, 449. **12**: 119.
Captain Put's Novel; a Story. (S. B. Long) Lippinc. **28**: 163.
Captain Spike. (J. F. Cooper) Bentley, **20**: 429, 533. **21**: 8-596. **22**: 68-564. **23**: 77-375.
Captain Tinderbox; a Poem. Temp. Bar, **24**: 217.
Captain Tom's Fright. Galaxy, **3**: 653.
Captain Tremlet's Duel. Liv. Age, **34**: 496.
Captain Viviane; an Operetta. Canad. Mo. **11**: 183.
Captive; a tragic Scene. (M. G. Lewis) Colburn, **46**: 317.
Capture of British Merchantmen at Cohasset, Mass. Hunt, **6**: 462.
Captures and Prize Money in the United States Civil War, 1861-65. U. S. Serv. M. **3**: 260.
Captured by Confeds. Lond. Soc. **21**: 433.
Captured Leprauchan; a Tale. Dub. Univ. **12**: 67.
Capuchin, The. Liv. Age, **13**: 131.
— of Bruges; a Tale. Cath. World, **2**: 237.
— The old, and the young Carmelite. (Bishop Ferrette) O. & N. **10**: 194.
Capuchins, Convent of, at Rome. (A. Searle) Pop. Sci. Mo. **16**: 673.
Capuchin Convent; a Poem. St. James, **26**: 449.
Car, Self-Adjusting Railroad and Street. (J. Pollock) J. Frankl. Inst. **11**: 17.
Cars and Railways, Improvements in, 1827. J. Frankl. Inst. **4**: 317.
— Palace. (H. W. Holland and E. L. Godkin) Nation **25**: 344.
Car-Coupler, Janney. J. Frankl. Inst. **107**: 46.
Car Nicobar, Inhabitants of. (W. L. Distant) Anthrop. J. **3**: 2.
Caraboo, Princess. Ev. Sat. **1**: 712.
Caracas, City of. (H. E. Sanford) Harper, **17**: 187. — All the Year, **14**: 415. **15**: 55.
— Destruction of, by Earthquake, 1812. (A. von Humboldt) Ed. Philos. J. **1**: 272.
— Dupons's Residence at. Ed. R. **8**: 378.
— Peep at. So. Lit. Mess. **9**: 351.
— Semple's Sketch of, 1812. (J. Foster) Ecl. R. **16**: 682.
— Visit to. Liv. Age, **3**: 305.
Caracci, The. (O. F. Adams) Potter Am. Mo. **14**: 59.
— Caravaggio, and Monachism. Blackw. **49**: 371.
Caraccioli, F., Prince, and Nelson. (W. C. Taylor) Bentley, **21**: 143.
Caraccioli, Galeazzo, and the Italian Reformation, 1556. (A. Roberts) Chr. Obs. **68**: 282.
Caracciolo, Enrichetta. Experience as a Nun. (J. Picciotti) Ecl. M. **74**: 99.
Carafa, Anna, Mrs. H. R. St. John on the Court of. Victoria, **19**: 180.
Caraites. *See* Karaites.
Carat, Meaning of the Term. Penny M **13**: 239, 247.
Caravans, Desert. Penny M. **7**: 197.
— Pilgrim, in the East. (S. Merrill) Internat. R. **5**: 639
Caravansaries. Penny M. **3**: 425.
Carbolic Acid, Antidote to. Pract. M. **1**: 320.
Carbon and Iron, Compounds of. (A. Guelt) J. Frankl. Inst. **62**: 335. 396.
— Crystals and Silicon. Ecl. Engin. **22**: 385.
— Fusion on. Am. J. Sci. **10**: 109.
— of Plants, Source of. Nature, **16**: 210.
— Spectrum of. (W. M. Watts) Nature, **23**: 197.
Carbons in the Electric Lamp. (H. W. Wiley) Am. J. Sci. **118**: 55.
Carbonari, The. Chamb. J. **30**: 363. — St. James, **18**: 251.
— Last of. (L. Mariotti) Colburn, **69**: 106.
— of Italy. Dem. R. **38**: 130.
Carbonic Acid as an Anæsthetic. Cornh. **6**: 546.
— Does Chloropyll decompose? (E. R. Lankester) Nature, **21**: 557.
— Liquefaction and Solidification of. (J. K. Mitchell) J. Frankl. Inst. **26**: 289.

Carbonic Acid, Physical Properties of. (J. W. Nystrom) J. Frankl. Inst. 100: 355.
Carbonic Oxide and Cast-Iron Stoves. (I. Remsen) Am. Arch. 10: 95, 120.
Carboniferous Formation in Massachusetts. (W. O. Crosby and G. H. Barton) Am. J. Sci. 120: 416.
Carboniferous Period, Fern Forests of. (L. Agassiz) Atlan. 11: 615.
Carbonization of Wood by Steam. (M. Violette) J. Frankl. Inst. 47: 279.
Cards, Letter-Envelopes, etc. Liv. Age, 11: 25.
— What is on the? (A. Fonblanque, jr.) Once a Week, 4: 469.
Cards, Playing. Argosy, 27: 306. — Chamb. J. 48: 593.
— Cheating at. All the Year, 5: 331.
— Dice and. (C. Nordhoff) Harper, 26: 163.
— Games at. Macmil. 5: 129.
— — for one Player. (W. Pole) Macmil. 31: 242.
— — played by Machinery. Macmil. 33: 241.
— Introduction into England. (R. Gough) Arch. 8: 152.
— Origin and Nomenclature of. (W. Bell) Art J. 13: 249–369.
— Recent Works on. (J. B. Matthews) Nation, 30: 180.
— Strange Hands at. All the Year, 37: 77.
Card Games, Obsolete. Once a Week, 10: 362.
Card-Playing, Antiquity of. (D. Barrington) Arch. 8: 134.
— Observations on. (J. Bowle) Arch. 8: 147.
Card-Sharping. (L. Wraxall) Once a Week, 4: 597.
Cardan, the Bigamist. Liv. Age, 14: 599.
Cardan, Jerome. Blackw. 75: 633.
— Autobiography. Portfo.(Den.) 33: 460.
— Life of. (H. Southern) Retros. 1: 94.
— — Morley's. Lond. Q. 3: 93.
Cardellac, the Jeweler. Dem. R. 13: 162.
Cardiff Giant and other Frauds. (G. A. Stockwell) Pop. Sci. Mo. 13: 197.
— Biography of. Lakeside, 6: 128.
— History of the Hoax. (W. A. McKinney) New Eng. 34: 759.
Cardinals and Popes. (C. Pebody) Macmil. 36: 326. Same art. Ecl. M. 89: 567.
— English, List of. Dub. R. 76: 258.
— — Lives of. Chr. Rem. 56: 402.
— in Conclave. All the Year, 24: 400.
— New, 1879. (D. Paul) Cath. World, 29: 559.
Cardinalate, The. (Mgr. Seton) Cath. World, 21: 359, 472.
Cardiograph, Modified. Nature, 13: 471.
Cardiograph Trace. (A. H. Garrod) Nature, 12: 275.
Cardross Case and the Free Church. Macmil. 2: 293.
Cardwell, E., Military Policy of. Fraser, 82: 537.
— Political Portrait of. St. James, 25: 521.
Care of a Pipe. (A. Fonblanque) Belgra. 7: 414.
Cares of the World, Hancock's. Canad. Mo. 10: 562.
Career of a Capitalist. Atlan. 43: 129.
— of a Wig; a Story. (H. Louther) Tinsley, 28: 484.
Carême, A. Eng. Dom. M. 9: 214.
Carew, Bampfylde-Moore, King of the Beggars. Nation, 13: 420. — Chamb. J. 38: 197.
Carew, Sir Peter. House. Words, 3: 527.
— Life of. (Sir T. Phillips) Arch. 28: 96.
— — and Times of. Liv. Age, 56: 187.
Carew, R. Godfrey of Boulloigne. (T. Roscoe) Retros. 3: 32.
Carew, T. Poems. (G. Robinson) Retros. 6: 224.
Carey, Arthur, Ordination of. Chr. Obs. 43: 532. — (L. Bacon) New Eng. 1: 586.
Carey, Henry C., with portrait. (R. W. Griswold) Am. Whig R. 13: 79. — (R. E. Thompson) Penn Mo. 10: 817.
— Past, Present, and Future. (T. B. Fox) Chr. Exam. 44: 161. — Ecl. R. 90: 148.
Carey, Henry C., Political Economy of. (R. W. Griswold) Internat. M. 2: 402.
Carey, Matthew, Biography of. (E. Holden) Hunt, 1: 437. — (M. Carey) New Eng. M. 5: 404, 489. 6: 60, 93, 227. 7: 61. — Am. Alma. 1841: 275.
— Compliment to. Niles's Reg. 20: 345.
— Dinner to, at Lexington, 1828. Niles's Reg. 34: 337.
— Ireland vindicated. Anal. M. 13: 417.
Carey, William. (J. P. Chown) Ex. H. Lec. 14: 125.
— Life and Character of. Ecl. R. 61: 29.
— Marshman and Ward, Life and Times of. Chr. Obs. 59: 408. — Ecl. M. 49: 14.
— Memoir of. Chr. R. 1: 531. — Am. Q. Reg. 9: 168. — So. Lit. Mess. 4: 578. — Mo. R. 140: 457. — Cong. M. 18: 1, 73, 161. 20: 251, 320. — Ecl. R. 64: 448.
Carey. *See* Cary.
Caribbean Sea. Nature, 22: 242.
— American Dredgings in. (A. Agassiz) Pop. Sci. R. 18: 352.
Caribbees, Ober's Camps in. Nature, 22: 215.
— of Honduras. (T. Meyrick) Month, 13: 97.
Cariboo. (— Wright) Overland, 3: 524.
— Hunting. (C. C. Ward) Scrib. 17: 234.
— — in Canada. (H. Humber) Canad. Mo. 1: 509.
Caricature. Once a Week, 13: 409.
— and Caricaturists. (R. G. White) Harper, 24: 586. — (C. Whitehead) Bentley, 24: 419.
— and Grotesque in Art. (T. Wright) Art J. 15: 5–242. 16: 20–367.
— — in Literature and Art. Quar. 119: 215. Same art. Liv. Age, 88: 556.
— and Satires of the 18th Century. Blackw. 64: 543.
— Century of. Liv. Age, 19: 126.
— Classic and mediæval. Dub. Univ. 72: 519.
— English, under the Georges. Dub. Univ. 74: 3.
— French. (A. Rhodes) Scrib. 6: 2.
— History illustrated by. (T. Wright) Colburn, 83: 411. — All the Year, 21: 184. Same art. Ev. Sat. 7: 205. — Ecl. M. 15: 549.
— History of. (J. Parton) Harper, 50: 323–806. 51: 35–796. 52: 25.
— in America. All the Year, 41: 298.
— Limits of. (C. T. Congdon) Nation, 3: 55.
— Parisian. Westm. 32: 282.
— Pellegrini's. (J. R. Dennett) Nation, 14: 238.
— Statesmen in. Liv. Age, 140: 443.
Caricatures. Westm. 28: 261.
— Political. Quar. 136: 453.
Caricaturists, English. Once a Week, 26: 558.
Carie of Cambridge. Knick. 48: 365.
Carillons. All the Year, 31: 316. — Ev. Sat. 9: 286.
— Belgian, and English Belfries. (H. R. Haweis) Contemp. 17: 41.
Carillon Machine. J. Frankl. Inst. 100: 193.
Caripe, Cavern of. Penny M. 6: 354, 365.
Carisbrook Castle. Penny M. 1: 356.
Carita; a Tale. (M. Oliphant) Cornh. 33: 641. 34: 1–618. 35: 106–738. 36: 1, 235. Same art. Liv. Age, 130: 34–787. 131: 275–802. 132: 238–589. 133: 14–815. 134: 232–548.
Carl Almendinger's Office; a Story. Knick. 59: 342, 457, 546. 60: 9–517. 61: 65–406.
Carlen, E. S. F. Rose of Tistelon. Tait, n. s. 11: 493.
Carleton, William. Dub. Univ. 17: 66.
— Fardorougha. Mo. R. 149: 550.
— Novels. Dub. Univ. 26: 737.
— Traits and Stories. Dub. Univ. 24: 268.
Carleton, Will. Farm Ballads. Chamb. J. 50: 618.
Carlino. (G. Ruffini) Good Words, 11: 1–225. Same art. Liv. Age, 104: 472, 780. 105: 239, 301.
Carlisle, George W. F. Howard, Earl of, with portrait Peop. J. 10: 104. — Tait, n. s. 15: 786.

Carlisle, George W. F. Howard, Earl of, on Pope. (T. De Quincey) Tait, n. s. **18**: 228, 311.

Carlisle, City of. Penny M. **2**: 303.

— Cathedral of. Penny M. **14**: 41.

— — Horns given to. (W. Cole) Arch. **5**: 340.

— Siege of. All the Year, **25**: 558.

Carlism in Spain. (J. W. Preston) Scrib. **7**: 229.

Carlist Chief, A. All the Year, **39**: 413, 438.

Carlists and Christinos, Stephens's Adventures among. Mo. R. **144**: 1.

— Country of the. Once a Week, **28**: 436.

— in Catalonia. Blackw. **65**: 248.

— of Spain. (T. P. Adams) Galaxy, **16**: 399.

— Scraps from my Sabretasche. Colburn, **69**: 17–295.

Carlo the Absconded. Chamb. J. **32**: 346.

Carlo Borromeo, St., Notes on. Colburn, **109**: 144.

Carlo Sebastiani, the Aide-de-Camp. Blackw. **47**: 497, 650, 739.

Carlos, Don, Son of Philip II. of Spain. Fraser, **84**: 26. — Colburn, **5**: 231–352.

— and Philip II. Liv. Age, **84**: 606. — Ed. R. **127**: 1. Same art. Ecl. M. **70**: 525. Same art. Liv. Age, **96**: 480.

— True Story of. (W. C. Robinson) Month, **41**: 546.

Carlos, Don, Spanish Pretender, 1873. Dub. Univ. **81**: 537.

Carlotta, Daughter of Louise Maria of Belgium. (J. S. C. Abbott) Galaxy, **7**: 395.

Carlovingian Dynasty and the Feudal System. Lond. Q. **25**: 32.

Carlovingian Romances. Ed. R. **115**: 359. — Fraser, **36**: 404.

Carlowitz, Treaty of, 1699. Dub. Univ. **50**: 158.

Carlsbad, Invalids at. (H. A. Wise) Harper, **20**: 206, 353.

Carlsruhe, Our first and last Winter at. Colburn, **103**: 284–441.

Carlyle, Alexander, of Inveresk. Blackw. **88**: 734. Same art. Liv. Age, **68**: 287. — Ecl. R. **113**: 174.

— Autobiography. (A. Geikie) New Eng. **23**: 83. — Brit. Q. **33**: 182. — Chamb. J. **35**: 46. — Dub. Univ. **58**: 95. — Ed. R. **113**: 144. — Nat. R. **12**: 230. — No. Brit. **34**: 239. — Quar. **148**: 255. — Theo. & Lit. J. **13**: 539.

Carlyle, J. D., Poems of. Ecl. R. **4**: 528.

Carlyle, Jane Welsh. Chamb. J. **58**: 135.

Carlyle, Thomas. (J. H. Browne) Galaxy, **19**: 44. — (J. F. Clarke) Chr. Exam. **77**: 206. — (H. James) Nation, **1**: 20. — (J. R. Lowell) No. Am. **102**: 419 — (J. Morley) Fortn. **14**: 1. — (G. S. Phillips) Atlan. **1**: 185. — (G. Smith) Nation, **23**: 184. — (A. G. Sedgwick) Nation, **32**: 109. — (J. G. Wilson) Harper, **48**: 726. — (M. D. Conway) Harper, **62**: 888. — with portrait, (R. H. Hutton) Good Words, **22**: 282. Same art. Ecl. M. **96**: 749. — Dub. R. **78**: 97. — (L. Stephen) Cornh. **43**: 349. Same art. Ecl. M. **96**: 742. — Brit. Q. **10**: 1. Same art. Ecl. M. **18**: 285. — (J. W. Chadwick) Unita. R. **15**: 289. — (R. H. Shepherd) Gent. M. n. s. **26**: 361. — (W. M. Barbour) New Eng. **40**: 396. — (G. Putnam) Potter Am. Mo. **16**: 438. — (M. F. Sullivan) Dial (Ch.), **1**: 225. — (R. E. Thompson) Penn Mo. **12**: 199. — (J. V. O'Conor) Cath. World, **33**: 18. — Peop. J. **10**: 239. — Ecl. M. **96**: 564. — Lond. Q. **56**: 189. — Canad. Mo. **19**: 316. — Liv. Age, **148**: 692. — Chamb. **57**: 663. Same art. Liv. Age, **147**: 438. — with portrait, Appleton, **6**: 465. — with portrait, Ecl. M. **27**: 516. — with portrait, Ecl. M. **84**: 761. — with portrait, Once a Week, **27**: 275. — Bentley, **40**: 538. Same art. Ecl. M. **40**: 184. — Bentley, **48**: 471. — Blackw. **85**: 127. — Cornh. **6**: 107. — Meth. Q. **9**: 119, 217. — with portrait, Fraser, **7**: 706. — Ecl. M. **21**: 141.

Carlyle, Thomas. (P. Frank) Ecl. M. **22**: 199. — Liv. Age, **58**: 323. — Gent. M. n. s. **7**: 159. — Quar. **132**: 335. Same art. Liv. Age, **113**: 666. Same art. Ecl. M. **79**: 129.

— and Père Bonhoms. (A. Young) Cath. World, **13**: 820.

— and Mrs. Carlyle; a ten Years' Reminiscence. (H. Larkin) Brit. Q. **74**: 28. *See* Carlyle, Jane Welsh.

— and T. Chalmers. (D. Macleod) Good Words, **22**: 477. Same art. Liv. Age, **150**: 499.

— and Comte. (W. D. Le Sueur) Canad. Mo. **19**: 639.

— and Disraeli. Colburn, **147**: 118.

— and George Eliot. (G. Sarson) Mod. R. **2**: 399. — (J. Bryce) Nation, **32**: 201.

— and his Critics. Ecl. R. **114**: 25.

— and John Howard. Fraser, **41**: 406.

— and Edward Irving. (L. Murray) Canad. Mo. **20**: 303.

— and Macaulay. So. Lit. Mess. **14**: 476.

— and Whitman. N. Ecl. **1**: 190.

— as a Historian. (G. M. Towle) Penn Mo. **3**: 439.

— as a Nicknamer. St. James, **49**: 99.

— as a practical Guide. Putnam, **13**: 519.

— at Edinburgh. Argosy, **1**: 504.

— Chartism. *See* Chartism.

— Conversations with. (W. Knighton) Contemp. **39**: 904.

— Cromwell. *See* Cromwell.

— Early Life of. (J. A. Froude) 19th Cent. **10**: 1. Same art. Liv. Age, **150**: 259. Same art. Ecl. M. **97**: 289.

— Essays. Brit. Q. **2**: 297.

— Ethics of. (L. Stephen) Cornh. **44**: 664.

— Heroes and Hero-Worship. (J. H. Barrett) Am. Whig R. **9**: 339. — Chr. Rem. **3**: 341. — Bib. R. **3**: 183. — Mo. R. **155**: 1.

— Imitation of. (H. Ballou, 2d) Univ. Q. **2**: 214.

— Impressions of, in 1848. (R. W. Emerson) Scrib. **22**: 89.

— Incident in Life of. (G. S. Bower) Colburn, **169**: 238.

— Influence of. (J. K. Foster) Cong. M. **26**: 262. — (E. L. Godkin) Nation, **5**: 194, 235. — (J. F. Kirk) Nation, **5**: 237.

— — and our present Theology. (J. Martineau) Nat. R. **3**: 449.

— Latter-Day Pamphlets. No. Brit. **14**: 1. — Blackw. **67**: 641. — So. Q **18**: 313. — Chamb. J. **14**: 26. — Chr. Obs. **50**: 488. — Ecl. R. **92**: 385. — Prosp. R. **6**: 212. — So. Lit. Mess. **16**: 330.

— Laugh of. (T. W. Higginson) Atlan. **48**: 463.

— Lectures on Periods of European Culture. (E. Dowden) 19th Cent. **9**: 856. Same art. Liv. Age, **149**: 643.

— Life and Works of. (A. H. Guernsey) Appleton, **15**: 754, 780, 805. — Westm. **115**: 457.

— Notes on. (T. W. Cameron) Colburn, **157**: 201.

— on the Negro Question. Liv. Age, **24**: 248, 465.

— on the Sinking of the "Vengeur." Fraser, **20**: 76.

— Past and Present. (J. T. Smith) Am. Bib. Repos. 2d s. **12**: 317. — (O. A. Brownson) Dem. R. **13**: 17. — (M. Richardson) New Eng. **2**: 25. — Blackw. **54**: 121. — Dial, **4**: 96. — Mo. R. **161**: 190. — Tait, n. s. **10**: 339.

— Philosophy of. (H. O. Newcomb) University Q. **4**: 69.

— Political Doctrine of. (W. L. Courtney) Fortn. **32**: 817. Same art Ecl. M. **94**: 242.

— Political Influence of. (E. L. Godkin) Nation, **32**: 201.

— Recollections of. (M. Oliphant) Macmil. **43**: 482. Same art. Liv. Age, **149**: 307. Same art. Appleton, **25**: 510. Same art. Ecl. M. **96**: 721. — (H. James) Atlan. **47**: 593.

— Religious Opinions of. (M. Richardson) Cong. M. **25**: 801. — (I. E. Dwinell) Cong. R. **11**: 413.

— Religious Sentiments of. (M. Richardson) Am. Bib. Repos. 2d s. **8**: 382.

Carlyle, Thomas, Reminiscences of, edited by Froude. Quar. **151**: 385.—Ed. R. **153**: 469.—(A. Lang) Fraser, **103**: 515.—(W. C. Brownell) Nation, **32**: 186.—(L. Murray) Canad. Mo. **20**: 121.—(J. C. Morison) Fortn. **35**: 456. Same art. Ecl. M. **96**: 735.—(Sir H. Taylor) 19th Cent. **9**: 1009. Same art. Liv. Age, **150**: 85.—Ecl. M. **96**: 708.—Month, **41**: 457.—Am. Cath. Q. **6**: 249.—Temp. Bar, **62**: 23.
— — Controversy about. Temp. Bar, **62**: 516.
— — Froude's Editing of. (J. Wedgwood) Contemp. **39**: 821.
— Sartor Resartus. (J. H. Barrett) Am. Whig R. **9**: 121.—(N. L. Frothingham) Chr. Exam. **21**: 74.—Dem. R. **23**: 139.—Mo. R. **147**: 54.—So. Lit. J. **4**: 1.
— Shooting Niagara. (R. Parsons) Cath. World, **6**: 86.
— Sketch of, with portrait. Hogg, **7**: 81.
— Study of. Contemp. **39**: 584. Same art. Liv. Age, **149**: 361.
— Style of. Sharpe, **28**: 66.
— Theories of Education and Life. (M. J. Spalding) Am. Cath. Q. **4**: 1.
— Visit to Home of. (J. D. Sherwood) Hours at Home, **5**: 113, 238.
— Works of. (J. Sterling) Westm. **33**: 1.—Dub. R. **5**: 349. **29**: 169.—Ecl. R. **81**: 377.—Fraser, **72**: 778. Same art. Liv. Age, **88**: 737.—Quar. **66**: 446.—No. Brit. R. **4**: 505.—(A. H. Everett) No. Am. **41**: 454.—New York R. **4**: 179.—New Eng. **8**: 46.—New Q. **5**: 203.
— Wylie's Life of. (R. Buchanan) Contemp. **39**: 792.
Carlyleism. St. Paul's, **1**: 292.
Carlyon's Vacation. (L. de la Ramé) Bentley, **45**: 555.
Carlyon's Year. (J. Payn) Once a Week, **17**: 1–481.
Carmagnola, Francesco. Bentley, **55**: 423.
Carmel, Mt., and Beirût. Month, **4**: 236.
— and Surroundings. (C. H. Brigham) Mo. Rel. M. **14**: 121.
Carmelite Family. (H. J. Coleridge) Month, **33**: 129.
Carmelites, French, and Pierre de Bérulle. Chr. Obs. **73**: 299.
— of Jesi. Chamb. J. **29**: 228.
— Père Hyacinthe's Brethren. Gent. M. n. s. **15**: 304.
Carmencita's Fortune. (A. Trueba) Dub. Univ. **89**: 568.
Carmilla; a Tale. (S. Le Fanu) Dark Blue, **2**: 434–701. **3**: 59.
Carmina; a Tale. (L. Murray) Canad. Mo. **2**: 385, 481.
Carmina Lusoria. Blackw. **71**: 720.
Carmine, Various Preparations of. J. Frankl. Inst. **1**: 299, 332.
Carnac. *See* Karnak.
Carnarvon, H. H. Molyneux, Earl of, Political Portrait of. St. James, **25**: 676.
— Resignation of. (T. H. E. Escott) Gent. M. n. s. **20**: 357.
Carnavalet, Hôtel, Paris. (A. Laugel) Nation, **27**: 314.
Carnbre Castle, Cornwall. Penny M. **9**: 285.
Carné, Count L. de; his Historical Studies. (Count de Champagny) Cath. World, **4**: 197.
Carnedd Llewelyn, Ascent of. Sharpe, **44**: 37.
Carnelian; Romance of a Sleeping-Car. (E. H. House) Overland, **12**: 501. **13**: 9.
Carnesecchi Family Corner. All the Year, **3**: 15.
Carnival at Brussels. Once a Week, **28**: 298.
— at Knight's Cross. (F. W. Robinson) Belgra. **13**: 295.
— at Nice. Liv. Age, **141**: 61.
— at Rome. (T. R. Macquoid) Once a Week, **2**: 281.
— — in 1860. Liv. Age, **65**: 496.
— at Venice. Appleton, **19**: 278.—(S. B. Wister) Atlan. **35**: 176.
— Curiosities of. Cornh. **25**: 214. Same art. Ev. Sat. **12**: 197.
— of Rome; a Story. Atlan. **37**: 289, 385.
— Some Thoughts on. (W. T. Harris) Western, **1**: 30. *See also* Kermesse.
Carnival Song, Florentine, 16th Century. (J. A. Symonds) Cornh. **37**: 104. Same art. Liv. Age, **136**: 450.
Carnival of Crime in Connecticut. (S. L. Clemens) Temp. Bar, **47**: 189.
Carnivora, Origin of the specialized Teeth of. (E. D. Cope) Am. Natural. **13**: 171.
Carnivorous Plants. *See* Insectivorous Plants.
Carnot, Gen. L. N. M. Dem. R. **28**: 305.
— Arago's Life of. (Sir D. Brewster) No. Brit. **15**: 185.—Ecl. M. **23**: 294.
— Defense of. Ed. R. **25**: 442.
— Memorial to Louis XVIII. Ed. R. **24**: 182.
— Plan for invading England. Fraser, **95**: 201.
Carol of Harvest. (W. Whitman) Galaxy, **4**: 605.
Carolinas during the Revolution. So. Lit. Mess. **11**: 144, 231.
— and Georgia, Catholicity in. (A. G. Knight) Month, **36**: 345.
Carolina Sports, Elliott's. (T. G. Cary) No. Am. **63**: 316.
Caroline Wilhelmina, Queen of George II. (M. Oliphant) Blackw. **103**: 195. Same art. Liv. Age, **96**: 579.—Colburn, **130**: 44.
— Maids of Honor of. Lond. Soc. **6**: 109.
Caroline, Queen of George IV. Ed. R. **67**: 1, 556.
— and George IV. (A. Brougham) Ed. R. **68**: 191.
— Case of. (F. Wharton) Internat. R. **4**: 663.—Quar **50**: 207.
— Trial of. Blackw. **8**: 209.—Niles's Reg. **19**: 87.
Caroline Matilda, Queen of Denmark. (L. Wraxall) Temp. Bar, **12**: 98.—All the Year, **11**: 596.—Blackw. **9**: 142.—Colburn, **131**: 479.—Ecl. M. **63**: 287.—Harper, **29**: 750.—Sharpe, **2**: 274.
— Wraxall's. St. James, **11**: 302.
Caroline von Linsingen and William IV. Westm. **114**: 356.
Caroline, Steamer, Burning of. Canad. Mo. **3**: 289.—(J. G. Palfrey) No. Am. **53**: 412.
— Seizure of. Mus. **42**: 77.
Caroline Islands. Geog. M. **1**: 203.—Once a Week, **6**: 379.
— People of. (W. T. Pritchard) Anthrop. R. **4**: 165.
Carolers; a Poem. (T. Hood) St. James, **3**: 65.
Carouse, The; a Song. Dub. Univ. **2**: 166.
Carp, The. (A. H. Baldwin) Once a Week, **10**: 306.—Penny M. **11**: 269.
— Carpiana. (D. C. Badham) Fraser, **48**: 71.
Carpaccio, Vittore. (W. E. Crothers) Temp. Bar, **61**: 395.
Carpeaux, Jean Baptiste. (O. Logan) Lippinc. **25**: 664.
Carpenter, Lant, Memoirs of. Ecl. R. **77**: 205.—Mo. R. **157**: 245.—Chr. Exam. **32**: 102.
— Sermons of. Ecl. R. **73**: 666.—Prosp. R. **5**: 455.
Carpenter, Mary. (E. Simcox) Fortn. **33**: 662. Same art. Liv. Age, **145**: 561.—Lond. Q. **57**: 49.—Dub. Univ. **95**: 356.—Liv. Age, **134**: 305.—(J. H. Morison) Unita. R. **8**: 173. **13**: 264.
— Personal Recollections of. (F. P. Cobbe) Mod. R. **1**: 279. Same art. Liv. Age, **145**: 414.
— Work of, in India. (H. W. Holland) Chr. Exam. **85**: 179.
Carpenter, Philip P. Nature, **16**: 84.
Carpenter, W. B., with portrait. (D. Duncan) Appleton, **5**: 464.—with portrait, Ecl. M. **85**: 374.
— and Dr. Mayer. (J. Tyndall) Nature, **5**: 143.
— Sketch of. (D. Duncan) Pop. Sci. Mo. **1**: 745.
— Views on Phrenology. (T. S. Prideaux) Zoist. **4**: 480.
Carpenter Genealogy. (A. B. Carpenter) N. E. Reg. **9**: 52.
Carpenter, The; a Tale. (W. D. O'Connor) Putnam, **11**: 55.
Carpenter's Widow, The. Hogg, **5**: 10–84.
Carpenters' Scenes. Belgra. **2**: 455.
Carpentry. (M. Mauris) Pop. Sci. Mo. **17**: 233.

Carpet, History of the. Sharpe, **28**: 269. — Godey, **54**: 231.
Carpets. (R. Sturgis) Nation, **2**: 363.
Carpet-Bag, The. Chamb. J. **22**: 209.
Carpet-Factory, Day at a. Penny M. **12**: 329.
Carpet-Manufactory of Baarn, Holland. J. Frankl. Inst. **14**: 126.
— of Messrs. Requillard, Roussel, and Choqueil. Art J. **2**: 121.
Carpet-Weaving. Peop. J. **7**: 281.
Carr, Caleb, Governor of Rhode Island, 1695. Am. Q. Reg. **15**: 19.
Carr, Dabney, Memoir of. So. Lit. Mess. **4**: 65.
Carr, Sir John. Northern Tour. Ed. R. **6**: 394. **10**: 271.
— Spanish Tour. Quar. **7**: 408.
Carr, Robert. (A. C. Ewald) Gent. M. n. s. **25**: 159.
Carr of Carrbrook. St. James, **27**: 755.
Carrara, Francesco Novello da. Bentley, **46**: 29–392. **47**: 277, 544. **48**: 347.
Carrascon, Writings of, 1633. Retros. **15**: 77.
Carrel, Armand. (J. S. Mill) Westm. **28**: 66. — Fraser, **26**: 730.
Carriages and their Changes. All the Year, **15**: 11.
— Blockade of. Chamb. J. **43**: 659.
— Early Use of, in England. (J. H. Markland) Arch. **20**: 443.
— in various Times and Countries. Chr. Rem. **7**: 198.
— Primitive. Penny M. **6**: 275.
— Roads, and Coaches. Quar. **144**: 413.
Carriage Friends. (A. B. Haven) Godey, **59**: 133–510.
Carriage Horses. Our. All the Year, **15**: 112.
Carriage Manufactory of Messrs. Holmes of Derby. Art J. **2**: 378.
Carriage People; an Outburst of Envy. (G. A. Sala) Belgra. **26**: 469.
Carrick, Mary, remarkable Case of Physical Phenomena. (H. A. Willis) Atlan. **22**: 129.
Carrie Fane. (M. N. Prescott) Lippinc. **23**: 233.
Carrie's Courtship; a Tale. Canad. Mo. **9**: 186.
Carrier, Jean Baptiste. (E. H. Lacombe) So. M. **15**: 507.
Carrier Pigeon; a Poem. (D. Greenwell) Good Words, **3**: 120.
Carriers, Common. Hunt, **21**: 306.
— Discrimination in Fares by. (W. McAllister, jr.) Am. Law R. **15**: 186.
Carrigbeg. (J. F. Bouverie) Dub. Univ. **84**: 540.
Carrington, N. T. Dartmoor; a Poem. Quar. **35**: 165. — Ecl. R. **43**: 431.
— Poems. Ecl. R. **37**: 459. — Ed. R. **60**: 317. — Fraser, **11**: 157.
Carroll, Charles, of Carrollton. Niles's Reg. **33**: 79. — (J. C. Carpenter) M. Am. Hist. **2**: 101. — (J. M. Finotti) Cath. World, **23**: 537. — (S. Jordan) Potter Am. Mo. **7**: 401.
Carroll, John. (J. C. Brent) U. S. Cath. M. **2**: 341. — (B. U. Campbell) U. S. Cath. M. **3**: 32–793. **4**: 249–782. **5**: 595, 676. **6**: 31–592.
Carron, Abbé, Life of. Cath. World, **5**: 259.
Carruthers, William A. Cavaliers of Virginia. Am. Mo. M. **4**: 385.
Carrying-Trade of the World. (M. N. Mulhall) Contemp. **40**: 608. Same art. Ecl. M. **97**: 846.
Carson, Alexander, and the Romish Controversy. Chr. R. **24**: 505.
Carson, Kit. (G. D. Brewerton) Harper, **7**: 306.
Carstens, A. J. (E. F. S. Pattison) Portfo. **1**: 76.
Carte Papers. Dub. R. **71**: 49.
Carter, Elizabeth. (M. Collins) Dub. Univ. **90**: 357. — Ev. Sat. **8**: 609. — All the Year, **22**: 497.
— Life and Poems of. Chr. Obs. **6**: 662, 745.
— Memoir of. Ecl. R. **7**: 301.
Carter, James, Obituary of. Art J. **7**: 283.
Carter, James G. Am. J. Educ. **5**: 407.
Carter, John, the crippled Mouth-Painter. Chamb. J. **54**: 241. — (W. J. Dampier) Liv. Age, **28**: 422.
Carter, John, the African Lion-Tamer. Colburn, **161**: 175.
Carter, Rev. John, Memoir of. Cong. M. **1**: 617.
Carter, T. T., Canon, Letter to Archbishop of Canterbury, 1877. Chr. Obs. **77**: 337, 897.
Carter, William. (J. M. Sturtevant) Cong. Q. **13**: 497.
Carter Genealogy. (A. Sargent) N. E. Reg. **17**: 51.
Carter Notch, A Day in. (T. W. Higginson) Putnam, **2**: 672.
Cartes de Visite. (A. Wynter) Good Words, **10**: supp. 57. — Art J. **13**: 306.
Cartesian Doubt. (O. A. Brownson) Cath. World, **6**: 234.
Carthage. Ed. R. **114**: 65.
— Account of the Ruins of. (J. Jackson) Arch. **15**: 145.
— and the Carthaginians. Nat. Q. **3**: 331.
— and her Remains. (D. A. Whedon) Meth. Q. **22**: 429.
— and Phœnicia. (B. J. Wallace) Am. Presb. R. **10**: 291.
— and Tunis. (A. Woodbury) Chr. Exam. **86**: 279. — Fraser, **70**: 109.
— Excavations at. (A. W. Franks) Arch. **38**: 203.
— Explorations at. (A. H. Guernsey) Harper, **22**: 766.
— History of. Chr. Rem. **19**: 373.
— Punic Inscriptions on the Site of. (H. Gurney) Arch. **30**: 111.
— Recent Discoveries at, 1861. Dub. R. **49**: 383.
— Remains of. Blackw. **89**: 148.
— — Davis on. Chr. Obs. **61**: 544.
Carthagena. (M. J. Kelly) Overland, **1**: 418.
Carthaginians and Phœnicians. For. Q. **14**: 197.
Carthusian Legend; a Poem. St. James, **28**: 410.
Cartier, Jacques. (A. Walker) Fraser, **102**: 775. Same art. Ecl. M. **96**: 234. Same art. Canad. Mo. **19**: 88. Same art. Liv. Age, **148**: 102. — Hist. M. **8**: 297.
— Voyage of, 1541. Hist. M. **6**: 14.
Cartoons, Preston's. (W. H. Browne) So. M. **17**: 759.
Cartouche, L. D., on the Stage. All the Year, **1**: 573. — — Fraser, **20**: 447. — Knick. **55**: 241. — Blackw. **39**: 514.
Cartridges. (J. Scoffern) Belgra. **9**: 62.
Cartwright, Edmund. House. Words, **7**: 440. — Mo. R. **162**: 214.
Cartwright, John, English Reformer, Memoirs of. Tait, n. s. **1**: 735.
Cartwright, Thomas, Bishop, Diary of. Tait, n. s. **11**: 163.
Cartwright, Peter. Nat. M. **1**: 41.—(Cucheval-Clavigny) Meth. Q. **32**: 556. **33**: 69.
— and Methodism in the Far West. Good Words, **1**: 123. — House. Words, **18**: 500.
Cartwright, Thomas, Memoir of. Ecl. R. **84**: 221.
Cartwright, Wm., Life and Correspondence of. Mo. R. **110**: 235.
— Plays and Poems of. Retros. **9**: 160.
Carucci, Jacopo. (R. N. Wornum) Portfo. **8**: 117.
Carvalho, S. J., Marquis of Pombal. Temp. Bar, **57**: 350.
— and the Society of Jesus. Month, **31**: 86.
Carved Work, Wonders in. Chamb. J. **52**: 713.
Carver, John. (N. B. Shurtleff) N. E. Reg. **4**: 105. — Am. Q. Reg. **15**: 20.
Carver's Grant, Report on. Niles's Reg. **27**: 407.
Carver's Lesson; a Poem. Cornh. **1**: 560.
Carver's Story. Victoria, **18**: 26.
Carving a Cocoa-Nut. Cornh. **36**: 461.
— and Paneling Machine. Pract. M. **6**: 297.
— in Long Melford Church. (C. Ord) Arch. **12**: 93.
— Natural. (A. M. Edwards) Am. Natural. **3**: 427.
— Notes on. (G. C. Mason) Potter Am. Mo. **10**: 459.
— over Chimney-Piece at Speke Hall. (H. J. Hinchliffe) Arch. **14**: 20.
— Wood, by machinery. Art J. **8**: 241.
— — Fret-Sawing and. (J. Wilcox) Harper, **56**: 533.

Carvosso, W., Memoir of. Am. Meth. M. **19**: 280.
Cary, Alice. Pictures of Country Life. Liv. Age, **63**: 23.
— and Phœbe. Penn Mo. **5**: 765.
Cary, Henry Francis, Memoir of. Ecl. R. **86**: 710.
Cary, Robert, Earl of Monmouth. Bentley, **35**: 59.
— an Elizabethan Pepys. Ecl. M. **31**: 354.
See also Carey.
Carysfort Lighthouse. Hogg, **8**: 95.
Casa Guidi Windows; Poem. (B. Taylor) Atlan. **21**: 671.
Casa Wappy; a Poem. (D. M. Moir) Fraser, **17**: 535.
Casanova, Jacopo. All the Year, **34**: 323–423.
— Escape from the Prisons of the Piombi. Cornh. **23**: 712. Same art. Ecl. M. **77**: 156.
— Memoirs of. Lond. M. **16**: 254. — Westm. **7**: 400. — Mus. **9**: 518. — Mo. R. **144**: 266.
— Under the Leads. All the Year, **7**: 83.
— Visit to Haller and Voltaire. Colburn, **4**: 171–232.
Casas, B. de las. *See* Las Casas.
Casaubon, Isaac. (G. E. Ellis) Unita. R. **4**: 249. — (J. Kenrick) Theo. R. **12**: 372. — (J. C. Morison) Fortn. **23**: 537. — (R. Trevett) Am. Church R. **6**: 249. — Blackw. **117**: 616. Same art. Liv. Age, **125**: 696. — House. Words, **11**: 76. — Temp. Bar, **44**: 102.
— Diary of. Quar. **93**: 462.
— Life of. Ed. R. **143**: 189.
— — Pattison's. (A. V. Dicey) Nation, **21**: 59. — Chr. Obs. **76**: 489.
Cascade Mountains. (J. L. LeConte) Am. J. Sci. **107**: 167, 259.
Case, William, and his Contemporaries. (E. Barrass) Meth. Q. **38**: 448.
Case, Jerome I., with portrait. Lakeside, **4**: 161.
Case of Conscience. (E. Clive) Bentley, **18**: 455.
— of Conscience; a Story. (E. Williams) Galaxy, **13**: 808.
— of George Dedlow. (S. W. Mitchell) Atlan. **18**: 1.
— of Hugh Maynard; a Story. (D. Cook) Belgra. **42**: 71.
— of Vitrifaction. (J. W. De Forest) Harper, **44**: 561.
Cases in Indo-European Languages. (J. W. Gibbs) Chr. Q. Spec. **9**: 109, 415.
Casentino, Three Sanctuaries of. Month, **3**: 383.
Cash Credit System. Bank. M. (L.) **4**: 348. **6**: 17.
Cash or Pedigree. Blackw. **67**: 431.
Cashiers, Bonds of. Bank. M. (N. Y.) **25**: 81.
— Duties and Liabilities of. Bank. M. (N. Y.) **10**: 161. **24**: 371.
— Law of. Am. Law R. **3**: 612.
— Power of, Opinion on. Bank. M. (N. Y.) **32**: 721.
— Young, Suggestions to. (L. Sabine) Bank. M. (N. Y.) **10**: 417. — Bank. M. (N. Y.) **23**: 417.
Cashmere. Bentley, **64**: 138.
— Brinckman's Travels in. Dub. Univ. **60**: 346.
— Floating Gardens of. Penny M. **1**: 365.
— Hügel's Travels in. For. Q. **28**: 45.
— Ireland's Wall Street to. Knick. **53**: 617.
— Royal Wedding-Feast in. (J. F. Elten) Putnam, **13**: 319.
— Summer in. Dub. Univ. **89**: 117.
— Visit to. Fraser, **88**: 98.
Cashmere Goat, The. Penny M. **2**: 361.
Cashmere Shawl, Story of a, how made, etc. Ev. Sat. **9**: 278. *See* Shawls.
Casino, The. (A. Gallenga) Colburn, **80**: 254.
Casino, Monte, Benedictine Monastery of. Dem. R. **38**: 56. — (W. E. Hall) Fortn. **5**: 352, 462.
Casks, Measurement of. Pract. M. **2**: 463.
Cask Making. Pract. M. **6**: 120.
Casket of Jewels; a Tale. Dub. Univ. **59**: 296.
Caspar Hauser. *See* Hauser, C.
Caspian Sea. (H. Wood) Geog. M. **3**: 8, 34. — (D. Ker) Geog. M. **3**: 11. — Chamb. J. **51**: 149.
Caspian Sea and the Aral, Basins of. (H. H. Howorth) Geog. M. **3**: 106.
— and the Black Sea. Ecl. Engin. **15**: 122.
— Fraser's Adventures on the Shores of. Lond. M. **15**: 258. — Mo. R. **110**: 185.
— Steppes of. Dub. Univ. **30**: 298.
— — Travels in. For. Q. **37**: 185. Same art. Ecl. M. **8**: 116. — Am. Ecl. **3**: 230, 490.
Casque and Plume; a Poem. (A. Munby) Temp. Bar, **13**: 42.
Cass, Lewis, Portrait of. Dem. R. **16**: 315.
— Book on the French. For. Q. **29**: 484.
Cassagnac, A. de Granier de. Colburn, **105**: 104.
Cassandra in Ireland. Dub. Univ. **12**: 375.
— of Lycophron. Dub. Univ. **5**: 425.
Cassiterides, The. (W. L. Alden) Galaxy, **5**: 500.
Cassowary, The. Penny M. **2**: 376. — (P. L. Sclater) Nature, **12**: 516.
Casts from organized Substances. Penny M. **13**: 270.
Cast for a Fortune; a Tale. Temp. Bar, **51**: 469.
Cast in the Net; a Detective Officer's Story. Chamb. J. **54**: 756–803.
Cast in the Wagon. (S. Tytler) Good Words, **3**: 145, 201.
Cast Iron. *See* Iron, Cast.
Castaing, Dr. Trial for Poisoning. Chamb. J. **26**: 379.
Castalia, Tour through. Penny M. **2**: 273.
Castanet, Antiquity of. Once a Week, **8**: 609.
Cast Away. Chamb. J. **43**: 355.
Cast Away. Fraser, **80**: 256.
Cast Away. House. Words, **19**: 222.
Castaway; a Novel. (E. Yates) All the Year, **26**: 121–601. **27**: 1–358.
Castaways, The; a Tale of the Caribbean Sea. Bentley, **61**: 159.
Caste in Ceylon. (B. C. Meigs, D. Poor, and W. W. Holland) Bib. Sac. **11**: 470.
— Influence of, on Western Europe. (D. A. Gorton) Nat. Q. **35**: 256.
— System of Hindu. Chr. Obs. **59**: 550.
— Theory and Practice of. Ecl. R. **106**: 445.
Castes. Chamb. J. **5**: 361.
— in India. (J. D. Whelpley) Am. Whig R. **1**: 394. — Ed. R. **48**: 32.
— — Rise and Development of. (G. T. Dippold) Meth. Q. **37**: 626.
— of ancient Egypt. (J. J. Ampère) Bib. Sac. **9**: 529.
Castellane, I. Le Brun de, the French Impostor. Chamb. J. **49**: 209. Same art. Ecl. M. **79**: 90.
Castellani Collection. (F. W. Burton) Portfo. **4**: 130. — Am. Arch. **4**: 151.
Castelar, Emilio, with portrait. Ecl. M. **81**: 758. — (M. E. G. Duff) Fortn. **29**: 816. **30**: 46.
Castelrovinato. Fraser, **67**: 527.
Castiglione, Baldassare. Tinsley, **26**: 390.
Castiglione, History of the Family of. (G. Bowyer) Arch. **32**: 368.
Castile and Andalusia. Dub. Univ. **43**: 30.
— Vintage of. Penny M. **5**: 266.
Castilian Poetry. For. R. **1**: 44. — Fraser, **3**: 355.
Castine, the younger. (J. E. Godfrey) Hist. M. **22**: 121.
Castine, Me. (E. E. Evans) Harper, **55**: 345.
Castine Debadis, Baron of, Letter of, 1725. N. E. Reg. **14**: 139.
Casting in Plaster among the Ancients. (W. W. Story) Internat. R. **7**: 508, 642.
Castings, Large. Ecl. Engin. **5**: 592.
Castle Combe, Scrope's History of. Quar. **92**: 275.
Castle Daly. (A. Keary) Macmil. **29**: 281–488. **30**: 19–486. **31**: 10–484. **32**: 11, 110, 205.
Castle Elmere. Blackw. **35**: 353.
Castle Goblin, The. Lond M. **2**: 247.
Castle Hill, near Land's End. (W. Cotton) Arch. **22**: 300.

Castle Hill Church, History of. Cong. M. 13: 113, 169.
Castle Howard, Yorkshire. Penny M. 8: 113.
Castle in the Air, A. (E. Foxton) Contin. Mo. 6: 272.
Castle in Spain; a Poem. (M. Collins) Temp. Bar, 4: 295.
Castle Island, Boston Harbor. O. & N. 2: 271.
Castle of Dulness; a Poem in four cantos. Fraser, 21: 517.
Castle of the Isle of Rugen. Blackw. 31: 790.
Castle of Monetier; a Poem. (S. T. Bolton) Once a Week, 10: 14.
Castle of Time; a Poem. (D. M. Moir) Blackw. 24: 362.
Castle Schildheiss. (J. Oxenford) Colburn, 84: 283.
Castle Tavern, Boston. (J. T. Hassam) N. E. Reg. 33: 400.
Castles and Shakspere. So. Lit. Mess. 19: 733.
— in Spain. (G. W. Curtis) Putnam, 2: 657.
— in Spain; a Poem. (H. W. Longfellow) Atlan. 39: 601.
— of England. (E. King) Arch. 4: 364. 6: 231.
— of the Taunus. Once a Week, 7: 332, 390, 471.
— of Wales. (D. Barrington) Arch. 1: 278.
Castleacre Priory, Norfolk. Penny M. 9: 409. — Mo. R. 162: 128.
Castlereagh, Robert Stewart, Lord. No. Brit. 10: 215. Same art. Ecl. M. 16: 215. — Blackw. 64: 610. — Dub. Univ. 34: 433. — (W. Dennehy) Cath. World, 30: 543. — Quar. 111: 201. — Blackw. 91: 332.
— Alison's Life of. Dub. Univ. 59: 283.
— and Sir C. Stewart. Ed. R. 115: 510.
— Foreign Policy of. For. Q. 8: 33.
— Life of. Dub. R. 25: 429.
— Memoirs and Correspondence of. Ecl. R. 89: 686. — Fraser, 38: 615. — Liv. Age, 38: 322. — Dub. Univ. 32: 563*. 34: 433. — Ed. R. 109: 157. — Quar. 84: 264. — Colburn, 84: 358.
Castor-Oil Candles. So. Lit. Mess. 8: 199.
Castor-Oil Plant. Penny M. 5: 65.
Castra of the Littus Saxonicum. (T. Lewin) Arch. 41: 421.
Castriot, George, Prince of Epirus. Dub. Univ. 57: 365.
Casual Acquaintance. Lond. Soc. 3: 73.
Casual Cogitations. (C. A. Bristed) Galaxy, 15: 178, 308, 625. 16: 58, 196, 324.
Casuistry. (H. N. Day) New Eng. 32: 110. — Blackw. 46: 455. 47: 260.
— Basis of. (J. G. Cazenove) Contemp. 24: 75.
— Chapters on. Month, 8: 75.
— Maurice's Lectures on. Victoria, 12: 172.
— of Journalism. Cornh. 28: 198.
— Political. (E. L. Godkin) Nation, 23: 353.
— System of. Chr. Rem. 27: 38.
— Theological and legal. (F. Wharton) Princ. n. s. 1: 216.
Caswell, Alexis, Memoir of, with portrait. (W. Gammell) N. E. Reg. 31: 253.
Cat, The. Month, 43: 439. — Pop. Sci. R. 20: 257.
— Ancient and modern. Chamb. J. 55: 171.
— Mivart on. (B. G. Wilder) Nation, 32: 393.
— with nine Lives. Eng. Dom. M. 12: 281.
Cat-o'-Nine-Tails. All the Year, 17: 394.
Cats. (G. J. A. Coulson) N. Ecl. 5: 172.—(J. W. Moses) N. Ecl. 7: 604. — (M. Schele de Vere) Harper, 40: 481. — Appleton, 5: 613. — Chamb. J. 45: 225. 49: 177. 52: 430. 57: 646. — Colburn, 56: 502. — Ev. Sat. 5: 538. 12: 127. — House. Words, 15: 369. — Lond. Soc. 21: 69. Same art. Ecl. M. 78: 373. — Once a Week, 9: 245.
— Ancient History of. (A. J. C. A. Dureau) Ed. New Philos. J. 7: 309.
— Anecdotes of. O. & N. 7: 462.
— Black. Lond. M. 5: 285.
— Calvin the Cat. (C. D. Warner) Scrib. 14: 248.
— Chapter on. Chamb. J. 17: 27. Same art. Internat. M. 5: 372. — Knick. 3: 348.
Cats, Curiosities of. Once a Week, 10: 16.
— Cursory Cogitations concerning. Blackw. 46: 653.
— Extinct, of America. (E. D. Cope) Am. Natural. 14: 833.
— Few Words about. Temp. Bar. 63: 379.
— Modern. (J. W. De Forest) Atlan. 33: 737.
— of Antiquity. (J. W. De Forest) Atlan. 33: 556. Same art. Canad. Mo. 5: 438.
— Poetry of. Chamb. J. 28: 401.
Cat-Fish, Pursuit of, under Difficulties. Hogg, 8: 243.
Cat Painter, The. Penny M. 3: 86.
Cat Stories. All the Year, 7: 308.
Cat's-Cradle. (D. M. Craik) Once a Week, 21: 433, 494.
Cat's Grease. House. Words, 16: 453.
Cat's Mount. House. Words, 7: 385. Same art. Liv. Age, 38: 331.
Catacazy, Constantine de, with portrait. Ev. Sat. 11: 487, 535.
Catacazy, Mme., with portrait. Ev. Sat. 11: 487.
Catacombs, The. Dub. R. 41: 157. 44: 130. 63: 253.
— Art and Symbolism of. (W. H. Withrow) Canad. Mo. 1: 119.
— Baptismal Inscriptions in. Dub. R. 45: 290.
— Basilica of S. Clemente. Dub. R. 69: 402.
— Children's Graves in. Cath. World, 7: 401.
— Christian Art of. (A. J. Faust) Cath. World, 16: 372. — Am. Arch. 8: 261.
— Christian Evidences from. (W. H. Withrow) Meth. Q. 31: 558.
— Chronology of. (J. S. Northcote) Month, 32: 31.
— Church of. (W. Arthur) Ex. H. Lec. 5: 163. — (C. J. Hemans) Contemp. 3: 153. Same art. Ecl. M. 68: 137. Same art. Liv. Age, 91: 303. — (C. Maitland) Bib. R. 2: 161. — (J. Tulloch) Good Words, 2: 481. — (W. S. Southgate) Am. Church R. 8: 105. — Dub. R. 37: 482. — Nat. M. 1: 344, 449.
— — Maitland's. Dub. R. 21: 427. — Hogg, 3: 156.
— exclusively Christian. (J. S. Northcote) Month, 32: 138.
— in Germany. For. Q. 4: 540.
— Inscriptions in. (J. L. Ferriere) Mercersb. 19: 595.
— Jewish, at Rome. Dub. R. 53: 397.
— Night in. (T. Heaphy) St. James, 1: 196. — Blackw. 4: 19.
— of Chiusi. Dub. Univ. 94: 348.
— of Kief. Penny M. 4: 309.
— of Paris. (C. Landor) Lakeside, 1: 355. — Penny M. 1: 317. — Knick. 12: 443. — Quar. 21: 360. — Chr. Mo. Spec. 1: 539. — Portfo. (Den.) 24: 415. 28: 148. — New Q. 4: 115.
— of Rome. (C. Beard) Theo. R. 7: 248. — (S. L. Caldwell) Bapt. Q. 4: 275. — (W. Knighton) Dub. Univ. 88: 590. — (A. Lamson) Chr. Exam. 43: 276. — (J. De Lanney) Chr. Q. 6: 220. — (T. Mommsen) Contemp. 17: 161. — (C. E. Norton) Atlan. 1: 513, 674, 813. 2: 48, 129. — (A. Stevens) Nat. M. 5: 31, 120, 218. — (J. W. Wall) Sharpe, 49: 258. — (J. W. Wall) Knick. 50: 75. — (S. L. Wolmer) Sharpe, 14: 141. — Ecl. M. 24: 240. — (W. I. Kip) Am. Church R. 1: 434. — Chr. Obs. 62: 508. — Chr. Rem. 50: 1. — Dub. R. 65: 393. 82: 33. — Ed. R. 109: 86. Same art. Ecl. M. 47: 13. Same art. Liv. Age, 60: 588. — (H. H. Milman) Quar. 118: 34. Same art. Liv. Age, 86: 481. — Month, 11: 76. — So. R. n. s. 18: 97. — U. S. Cath. M. 4: 593. — (J. W. Ball) Land We Love, 3: 367. — Univ. Q. 24: 190. — Chr. Obs. 69: 817, 903.
— — and their doctrinal Lessons. Theo. Ecl. 5: 43.
— — and primitive Christianity. Cath. World, 24: 371.
— — Night in. Ecl. M. 54: 190.
— — Recent Researches, 1864. Theo. R. 2: 628.

Catacombs of Rome, Visits to. (G. W. Greene) Harper, 10: 577.
— of San Calisto. Art J. 6: 224.
— of the Upper Nile. Chamb. J. 38: 161.
— Paintings in. Dub. R. 4: 96.
— Recent Discoveries in. Dub. R. 55: 501. Same art. Cath. World, 1: 129.
— Rossi's Roma Sotteranea. (J. S. Northcote) Cath. World, 1: 414.
— Studies of the Inscriptions in. (W. H. Withrow) Canad. Mo. 6: 285.
— Withrow on. (C. W. Bennett) Meth. Q. 34: 596.
Catalan Rover, Roger de Flor. Cornh. 20: 452.
Catalani, Madame Angelica. Liv. Age, 22: 331.
— Recollections of. (Mrs. West) Bentley, 27: 582.
— Sketch of. Hogg, 5: 110.
Catalepsy. So. Lit. Mess. 5: 433, 834.
— Marvels of. Knick. 8: 501.
— Religious. (S. Comfort) Meth. Q. 19: 218.
Catalogue, Brooklyn Library Association. Lib. J. 1: 330.
— The coming. (M. Dewey) Lib. J. 1: 423.
— General, to English Literature. (C. Walford) Lib. J. 2: 188.
— — Report on. Lib. J. 3: 225. 4: 418.
— Model Accession Catalogue. (M. Dewey) Lib. J. 1: 315.
— Universal. (J. G. Barnwell) Lib. J. 1: 54. — (W. E. A. Axon) Lib. J. 3: 175. — (B. Cadawalder) Lib. J. 1: 369.
Catalogues, Educational. (C. F. Adams, jr.) Lib. J. 4: 330.
— Inexpensive. Lib. J. 1: 436.
— of Public Libraries, Garnett on. (C. A. Cutter) Lib. J. 4: 452.
— Printed, Economical Suggestions as to. (C. Welch) Lib. J. 4: 439.
— Slip. (H. W. D. Dunlop) Lib. J. 2: 160.
Cataloguing. (J. M. Anderson) Lib. J. 2: 174.
— Abbreviation of Christian Names. (C. A. Cutter) Lib. J. 1: 405. 5: 176.
— Co-operative. Lib. J. 1: 118, 289. — (M. Dewey) Lib. J. 1: 170. — (J. Schwartz) Lib. J. 1: 328. — (C. Cutter) Lib. J. 1: 403. — (G. Depping) Lib. J. 2: 188.
— — College, New York Committee's Report. Lib. J. 1: 434.
— — Discussion on. Lib. J. 2: 264.
— Discussion on. Lib. J. 2: 259.
— Dr. Hagen's Letter on. (C. A. Cutter) Lib. J. 1: 216.
— How to make Catalogues. Blackw. 101: 606.
— Notes on. (C. Walford) Lib. J. 2: 161.
— of anonymous Books. (H. B. Wheatley) Lib. J. 2: 186.
— Photo-Bibliography. (H. Stevens) Lib. J. 2: 162.
— Rules for alphabetical. (J. A. Hjaltalin) Lib. J. 2: 182.
— — Library Association of United Kingdom. Lib. J. 4: 416.
— Use of Capitals. (C. A. Cutter) Lib. J. 1: 162.
See Libraries.
Catalonia, Carlists in. Blackw. 65: 248.
— Lions of. Cornh. 20: 182, 363. 21: 663. 26: 70.
Catamarans, Besieged by. Chamb. J. 49: 318.
Catamount Tavern at Bennington, Vt. Am. Hist. Rec. 1: 1.
Catania. New Eng. M. 8: 205.
— and Messina. Month, 5: 454.
— Trip to, 1832. Nav. M. 1: 521.
Cataract, Adams on. Quar. 18: 158.
— Causes and Cure of. (Sir D. Brewster) J. Frankl. Inst. 25: 416.
Cataractonium, Roman Station. (J. Cade) Arch. 9: 276.
— Observations on. (J. Cade) Arch. 10: 54.
Catarina in Venice. Fraser, 58: 87, 207, 309.
Catarrh. Liv. Age, 40: 234.
Catastrophe at Versailles. (J. M. Legare) Putnam, 3: 71.
Catastrophism and Evolution. (C. King) Am. Natural. 11: 449.
Catastrophism in Geology, C. King on. Pop. Sci. Mo. 11: 491.
Catawba Indians, Last of. (J. B. O'Neale) Hist. M. 5: 46.
Catching a Butterfly. (C. B. Conant) Overland, 10: 315.
Catching Larks; a Tale. Chamb. J. 50: 161-202.
Catching a Lion; a Tale. Internat. M. 1: 512.
Catechetical Instruction. (F. W. Kremer) Mercersb. 6: 205.
Catechetical Methods of Instruction. (W. Ross) Am. J. Educ. 9: 367.
Catechisation. (J. R. Dimm) Evang. R. 19: 434. — (T. Lape) Evang. R. 15: 555. — (F. Bartholomew) Luth. Q. 10: 511. — Lond. Q. 49: 425.
— and the Work of the Pastor. (E. Miller) Luth. Q. 5: 201.
— in the Reformed Church. (H. Harbaugh) Mercersb. 13: 191.
Catechising. (J. S. Clark) Cong. Q. 1: 393. — (J. G Morris) Evang. R. 1: 221.
— History of. (J. W. Alexander) Princ. 21: 59.
— Parochial. Quar. 71: 184.
— Pearson on Duty of. Chr. Obs. 4: 750.
Catechism, Bishop Burgess's. Ecl. R. 46: 318.
— Burgess's Easter. Chr. Obs. 4: 34.
— Church. Cong. 1: 491.
— Congregational. (J. Murdock) New Eng. 2: 180.
— Crossman's. Chr. Obs. 39: 45.
— Geneva. Ecl. R. 27: 1.
— for Churches in France, 1807. Ecl. R. 5: 151.
— Heidelberg *See* Heidelberg Catechism.
— Noyes's, and its Author. (D. P. Noyes) Cong. Q. 11: 361.
— of Church of England. Cong. M. 23: 473. 27: 215.
— of Dr. Nowell. Chr. Obs. 2: 4-591.
— of King Edward, 1553. Chr. Obs. 1: 10-214.
— on Loyalty, Episcopacy, and Confirmation. Chr. Obs. 4: 76.
— Racovian. (A. Alexander) Princ. 5: 180.
— Roman and Tractarian. Chr. Obs. 59: 129.
— Saying the. Am. J. Educ. 30: 369.
— Schmucker's. (C. P. Krauth) Evang. R. 11: 300.
— Short and easy. Chr. Obs. 43: 502.
— Shorter, Green's Lectures on. (A. Alexander) Princ. 2: 297.
— Westminster. Chr. Exam. 8: 293.
— — History of. Chr. Obs. 46: 385.
Catechisms and Missions. (R. Philip) Cong. M. 27: 189.
— of Luther. (J. G. Morris) Evang. R. 1: 67.
— Origin and Characteristic of. (H. Harbaugh) Mercersb. 13: 579.
Catechumen, What is a? (H. Harbaugh) Mercersb. 12: 269.
Catechuminate, The. (J. M. Taylor) Bapt. Q. 8: 412.
Categories, Arrangement of. Blackw. 11: 308.
Caterpillars; My Summer Pets. (M. Treat) Lippinc. 4: 55.
— Preservation of. (S. H. Scudder) Am. Natural. 8: 321.
— Venomous. (A. Murray) Nature, 8: 7.
Catgut, Manufacture of. J. Frankl. Inst. 73: 408.
— Preparation of. J. Frankl. Inst. 3: 222, 292.
Cathari. *See* Albigenses.
Catharine of Aragon, Queen, Divorce of. Ed. R. 152: 258. — Arch. 18: 77.
— Dixon's History of two Queens. Fraser, 88: 212.
— Facts and Fiction about. Fraser, 79: 40.
— Funeral of. (W. Illingworth) Arch. 16: 22.
Catharine Parr, Queen, Death and Burial-Place of. (T. Nash) Arch. 9: 1.
— Great Seal of. (J. C. Brooke) Arch. 5: 232.
Catherine I., Empress of Russia. Temp. Bar, 11: 589. Same art. Ecl. M. 63: 31.
Catherine II., Empress of Russia. (E. Lawrence) Harper, 38: 624. — (J. Forfar) Gent. M. n. s. 27: 609. — Ecl. M. 64: 641. — Colburn, 120: 431. — Quar. 146: 203. Same art. Liv. Age, 138: 707.

Catherine II., Empress of Russia, and Frederick the Great. Bentley, **64**: 307.
— as a Politician. (P. F. Andre) Victoria, **5**: 213.
— at Home. Chamb. J. **31**: 166.
— Autobiography of. Nat. R. **8**: 32. Same art. Liv. Age, **60**: 467.—Colburn, **115**: 218.
— Court of. Temp. Bar, **23**: 564. **24**: 35.
— Herzen's Memoirs of. So. Lit. Mess. **28**: 223.
— on the Dnieper. (Véra Goetz) Lippinc. **9**: 288.
Catharine, St., of Ricci. (R. Spencer) Cath. World, **18**: 420.
Catharine, St., of Siena. Dub. R. **87**: 128.—Irish Mo. **3**: 1, 67, 127. **8**: 328.—Month, **39**: 98. Same art. Cath. World, **2**: 547.
— at Florence. Month, **3**: 54. Same art. Cath. World, **4**: 129.
— Public Life of. Month, **2**: 398.
Catharine de Bourbon, Sister of Henry IV., Life of. Chr. Rem. **51**: 349.
— Love and Marriage of. Cornh. **31**: 79.
Catharine Cornaro. (C. Adams) Harper, **57**: 617.—Bentley, **56**: 623. **57**: 80, 138, 280. Same art. Ecl. M. **64**: 220, 634, 689.
Catharine de Medici. *See* Medici, Catharine de.
Catharine of Würtemburg. Chamb. J. **28**: 86. Same art. Liv. Age, **55**: 292. Same art. Ecl. M. **42**: 228.
Catharine; a Story. Fraser, **19**: 604, 694. **20**: 98, 224. **21**: 106, 200.
Cathedral, The, in America. Am. Church R. **26**: 101.
— Visit to a. Chr. Obs. **31**: 400–669.
Cathedral, The; a Poem. (J. R. Lowell) Atlan. **25**: 1.
Cathedrals and Abbeys, Scottish. Quar. **85**: 103.
— and Cathedral Reform. Chr. Rem. **29**: 332. **30**: 174.
— and Cathedral Towns. (G. B. Griffith) Potter Am. Mo. **14**: 401. **15**: 33.
— and Parishes. (J. H. Egar) Am. Church R. **29**: 16, 338.
— Cluster of. Lond. Soc. **40**: 296.
— English. (A. K. H. Boyd) Fraser, **85**: 43.—(J. M. Hoppin) New Eng. **23**: 68.—All the Year, **33**: 60–541. **34**: 77–413.—Art J. **16**: 216.—Chr. Obs. **32**: 65.—Quar. **118**: 297. Same art. Ecl. M. **66**: 222, 326.
— — Britton's. (R. Southey) Quar. **34**: 305. Same art. Mus. **10**: 1.—Mo. R. **101**: 272.—(J. Foster) Ecl. R. **23**: 450.
— — Southwestern. (A. K. H. Boyd) Fraser, **75**: 125. Same art. Ecl. M. **68**: 457.
— French, Few Words about. Sharpe, **44**: 195.
— of Europe, Dimensions of. J. Frankl. Inst. **44**: 82.
— — Religious Influence of, on Americans. (W. R. Alger) Chr. Exam. **80**: 377.
— of Great Britain. Ecl. R. **21**: 378.
— of Mayence, Worms, and Spires. Am. Arch. **6**: 180.
— of Metz and Strasburg. Am. Arch. **6**: 108.
— of the South Rhineland. (N. H. Chamberlain) Mo. Rel. M. **16**: 7.
— Primitive. (F. Granger) Am. Church R. **29**: 283.
Cathedral Chapters as adapted to the United States. (S. B. Smith) Am. Cath. Q. **3**: 709.
Cathedral Commission, The. Lond. Q. **6**: 120.—Chr. Obs. **55**: 158, 536.
Cathedral Establishments. (W. Sewell) Quar. **58**: 197. —Blackw. **34**: 677.
Cathedral Life and Reform. Contemp. **2**: 488.
Cathedral Reform. Ed. R. **97**: 152.
Cathedral Restorations. Brit. Q. **69**: 135.—(W. Chambers) Chamb. J. **57**: 81, 209, 417.
Cathedral Work. (Canon Westcott) Macmil. **21**: 246, 308.
Catherine. *See above*, Catharine.
Cathetometer, New Form of. (W. Grunow) Am. J. Sci. **107**: 23
Catholic, The Word, in the New Testament. (G. G. Hepburn) Am. Church R. **31**: 458.
Catholic Apostolic Church. (W. W. Andrews) Bib. Sac. **23**: 108, 159.—Lond. Q. **34**: 67. *See* Irvingism.
Catholics, Old. *See* Old Catholics.
— Three Broad Church,—Döllinger, "Janus," Froschammer. (J. Hunt) Contemp. **14**: 311.
See Roman Catholics.
Catholic Charity, Prospects of. Month, **7**: 1.
Catholic Church in America, Is there a? (J. B. Torricelli) Chr. Exam. **87**: 168.
See Roman Catholic Church.
Catholic Elements in Presbyterianism. (E. D. Morris) Princ. n. s. **1**: 99.
Catholic Unity, Reasons for Return to. Cath. World, **11**: 542.
Catholicism, Anglo-, not Apostolical. Ecl. R. **78**: 385.
— of Christianity. (J. W. Nevin) Mercersb. **3**: 1.
See Roman Catholicism.
Catholicity. (B. Price) Contemp. **12**: 161.
— and Individualism. (W. T. Gibson) Am. Church R. **7**: 207.
— and Unity. (J. Young) Good Words, **9**: 477–766.
Catigern, Monument of, at Addington. (J. Colebrooke) Arch. **2**: 107.
Catiline as a Party Leader. (E. S. Beesly) Fortn. **1**: 167.
— Conspiracy of. Westm. **17**: 145. **21**: 89.—(A. Davezac) Dem. R. **9**: 144.—(J. T. Morse, jr.) Nat. Q. **8**: 272.
Catlin, George. Am. Bibliop. **5**: 16.—Nature, **7**: 222.
— North American Indians, Origin of the Enterprise. Dem. R. **11**: 44. *See also* Indians.
— Residence in Europe. Ecl. R. **88**: 357.
Cato, M. Porcius, the elder, Notes on. Colburn, **112**: 156.
Cato of Utica. Colburn, **120**: 287.
Cato Club. Belgra. **43**: supp. 109.
Cato-Street Conspirators. Niles's Reg **18**: 276, 283, 289.
Caton, Elizabeth, Mary, and Louise, with portraits. (E. L. Didier) Harper, **61**: 480.
Caton, John D., with portrait. Lakeside, **3**: 81.
Catoosa County, Ga., Geology of. (A. W. Vogdez) Am. J. Sci. **118**: 475.
Catskill Mountains. (W. Irving) Liv. Age, **31**: 408.—(T. A. Richards) Harper, **9**: 145.—(E. Ingersoll) Harper, **54**: 816. (H. Brace) Harper, **60**: 818.
Catskill Mountain Region. (A. Guyot) Am. J. Sci. **119**: 429.—Lippinc. **24**: 137, 265.
Cattaneo, Carlo. (J. W. Mario) Contemp. **26**: 465.
Cattle. Penny M. **10**: 273, 281.
— American. (C. L. Flint) Nation, **1**: 620. **2**: 45, 239.
— and Cattle Market. All the Year, **19**: 38, 54.
— Apparatus for supplying with Water, on Railways. Pract. M. **1**: 389.
— Low on Breeds of British. Mo. R. **151**: 512.
— Perfection in. West. J. **10**: 399.
— Slaughtering of, at Smithfield, 1850. House. Words, **1**: 325.
— Wild, of Great Britain. Penny M. **7**: 441.
— — of Scotland. (E. L. Sturtevant) Am. Natural. **8**: 135.
Cattle Drive in British Columbia. Once a Week, **16**: 39.
Cattle Drovers. Penny M. **12**: 65.
Cattle Herding in the Great West. Liv. Age, **133**: 126.
Cattle Plague, The. No. Brit. **43**: 487.—Victoria, **5**: 541.—(L. S. Beale) Pop. Sci. R. **5**: 153.
— in England. Cornh. **13**: 297. Same art. Ecl. M. **66**: 584.
— in Norfolk, England, 1868. (W. Smith) J. Statis. Soc. **31**: 395.
— of the 14th Century. (H. Harrod) Arch. **41**: 1.
— Texas. (J. S. Gould) Am. Soc. Sci. J. **1**: 56.
Cattle Plagues. Once a Week, **13**: 436.—Chamb. J. **29**: 19.

Cattle Raising in South America. (M. Couty) Pop. Sci. Mo. 19: 835.
Cattle Ranches in the Far West. (W. B. Grohman) Fortn. 34: 438.
Cattle Show. All the Year, 6: 277.
— in Baker Street. All the Year, 2: 233.
— Scottish. All the Year, 23: 36.
Cattle Shows. Penny M. 11: 52.
Cattle Station, On a. Gent. M. n. s. 26: 55.
Cattle Trade of Scotland with the English Markets. Broadw. 1: 393.
Catullus. (W. Everett) Internat. R. 7: 612. — (H. Nettleship) Fortn. 29: 741. — (C. W. Watson) So. M. 10: 209. — (T. Irwin) Dub. Univ. 61: 539, 673. 62: 67. — Fraser, 39: 320. 64: 47.
— and his Translators. Brit. Q. 55: 74.
— and Horace. Temp. Bar, 15: 588.
— The Attis. (R. Ellis) Fortn. 13: 430.
— Bristed's Cookesley's. (L. G. Clark) Knick. 34: 165. — (J. Hadley) New Eng. 7: 625.
— Hendecasyllables from. (R. Ellis) Fortn. 11: 79.
— Horæ Catulleanæ. (J. Wilson) Blackw. 61: 374, 501, 695.
— Lamb's Translation of. Blackw. 9: 507. — Mo. R. 97: 1. — Lond. M. 4: 86. — Ecl. R. 35: 522.
— Martin's Translation of. Nat. R. 14: 177. — No. Brit. 36: 204.
— Translations from. (R. Ellis) Fortn. 11: 701.
— Writings of. For. Q. 29: 329. — Blackw. 2: 486.
Caucasian Administration, and the Irish Difficulty. Fraser, 77: 525.
— in Trouble. Fraser, 77: 666.
Caucasus, The. (A. W. Dilke) Fortn. 22: 451. — (F. von Koschkull) Am. J. Sci. 96: 214, 335. — Nat. M. 6: 503. — New Eng. 9: 88.
Abkhaasian Insurrection, 1866. (W. G. Palgrave) Cornh. 16: 501. Same art. Ecl. M. 69: 738.
— and the Black Sea. For. Q. 4: 574.
— and the Land of the Cossacks. Blackw. 65: 129. — Westm. 50: 261.
— and Georgia. Ed. R. 28: 302.
— Captivity of Russian Princesses in. New Q. 7: 27.
— Central. Chamb. J. 46: 715.
— Ditson's Tour to. Dem. R. 26: 164.
— Drinking-Bout in. (F. A. Eaton) Macmil. 28: 80.
— Dumas in. Bentley, 46: 179.
— Egyptian Colony, and Language in. (H. Clarke) Anthrop. J. 3: 178.
— Eternal Fires of Baku. Ecl. M. 57: 169.
— Freshfield's Travels in. Ed. R. 130: 337.
— Inhabitants of. Ecl. R. 99: 347.
— Klaproth's Travels in. (J. Foster) Ecl. R. 23: 328.
— Life in. (J. T. Headley) Scrib. 2: 353.
— People of, Bodenstedt's. Internat. M. 1: 300.
— Prisoners in. Mus. 10: 431. — Colburn, 162: 650.
— Russian Rule in. Victoria, 28: 463.
— Schamyl, the Prophet-Warrior of. Westm. 61: 480.
— — and the Russians, 1835–53. Brit. Q. 18: 420.
— Spencer's Travels in Western. Mo. R. 147: 12.
— Travels in, 1868. Ed. R. 145: 44. Same art. Liv. Age, 103: 771.
— Unwritten Literature of the Mountaineers of. (G. Kennan) Lippinc. 22: 437, 571.
— Visit to Schamyl's Country, 1870. (E. Ransom) Fraser, 87: 27. Same art. Liv. Age, 116: 307.
— War in. (W. C. Williamson) No. Am. 81: 389. — Blackw. 48: 619. — Liv. Age, 16: 360. — Mus. 41: 169.
— Wilbraham's Travels in. Dub. Univ. 14: 228.
Caucus, The. Fortn. 30: 721.
— and its Consequences. (E. D. J. Wilson) 19th Cent. 4: 695.
Caucus, The, in Congress. Ev. Sat. 10: 338.
— in England, 1878. (E. L. Godkin) Nation, 27: 141.
— Substitute for. (H. T. Terry) New Eng. 34: 734.
— Trouble with. (D. M. Means) New Eng. 34: 473.
Caucuses, Legalization of. (A. G. Sedgwick) Nation, 8: 86.
Caucus System in the United States. (W. F. Allen) Chr. Exam. 87: 137.
— and the Republican Party, 1868. (E. L. Godkin) Nation, 7: 4.
Caught. Lond. Soc. 33: 355.
Caught at last. Lond. Soc. 10: 80.
Caught by Kuhlborn; a Story. (R. Terry) Galaxy, 18: 484.
Caught by a Thread. Once a Week, 21: 243–593. 22: 15–205.
Caught, Uncaught; a Tale. (H. F. Harrington) Godey, 21: 131.
Caulfield, James, Earl of Charlemont. *See* Charlemont.
Caulier, Ferdinand, Memoir of. Chr. Obs. 30: 261, 325.
Caulkins, Frances M., Memoir of, with portrait. (H. P. Haven) N. E. Reg. 23: 396.
Cauls, Children's. Dub. Univ. 77: 358.
Caumont, Jacques de. (S. B.-Gould) Once a Week, 6: 612.
Causal Judgment, The. (G. I. Chace) Bapt. Q. 3: 157.
Causality, and the Will, Divine and Human. Chr. Rem. 33: 445.
— in Will and Motion. (R. Noel) Contemp. 23: 380.
— Philosophy of: Hume and Kant. (J. H. Stirling) Princ. n. s. 3: 178.
— Problem of. Brownson, 23: 482.
Causation. (J. E. Cabot) No. Am. 106: 447. — (T. Harper) Month, 13: 663. — (S. H. Hodgson) Mind, 4: 500. — (D. A. Wasson) Unita. R. 9: 11.
— and Development. (J. McCosh) Princ. n. s. 7: 369.
— Mill's Theory of. (F. Bowen) No. Am. 78: 82. — Dub. R. 79: 57.
— Uniformity of. Chr. Rem. 41: 271.
Cause and Design. (H. Lawrenny) Fortn. 18: 692.
— and Effect. (J. Bascom) Bib. Sac. 24: 296. — (S. Gilman) No. Am. 12: 395.
— — Brown on. Blackw. 40: 122. — (A. Alexander) Princ. 1: 326.
— — Hume on. Blackw. 43: 190.
— — in connection with Fatalism and Free Agency. Am. Bib. Repos. 2d s. 2: 381.
— — — Reply to the above. (L. Woods) Am. Bib. Repos. 2d s. 3: 174. 4: 217, 467.
— — — — to Dr. Woods. Am. Bib. Repos. 2d s. 5: 153.
— — in Physics. Mo. R. 92: 78.
— — Relation of, Brown on. Chr. Mo. Spec. 3: 583.
— Final, Janet and Newcomb on. (J. McCosh) Princ. n. s. 3: 367.
— The Idea of. (F. Bowen) Princ. n. s. 3: 615.
— Proximate and Remote. Am. Law R. 4: 201.
Cause worth trying. Blackw. 80: 576.
Causes. (C. E. Grinnell) Mo. Rel. M. 47: 413.
— and Final Causes. (F. B. Palmer) Bapt. Q. 8: 165.
— Final. Fraser, 16: 254.
— Mill on. Dub. R. 79: 57.
— Secondary. (J. M. Kendrick) University Q. 2: 40.
Caux, Marquis de. *See* Patti.
Cavaignac, Gen. Eugéne. Bentley, 24: 609. — Dub. Univ. 32: 659.
— and his Father. Fraser, 38: 563. Same art. Ecl. M. 16: 126.
Cavalcanti, Guido. Colburn, 5: 1.
Cavalier and the Puritan; a Tale. (T. Hood) Dub. Univ. 47: 342.
Cavalier's Escape; a Poem. (W. Thornbury) Once a Week, 4: 686.
Cavaliers in America. (E. W. Evans) New Eng. 23: 651

Cavaliers of England, Herbert's. Dem. R. 31: 133.
— Prince Rupert and. (E. Warburton) Bentley, 26: 100.
Cavallier, Jean, and the Camisards. Ed. R. 104: 123. Same art. Liv. Age, 51: 65.
Cavalry, American, of the Revolution. (A. G. Brackett) Galaxy, 2: 616.
— History of, Denison's. Canad. Mo. 13: 403.
— Nolan on. Colburn, 100: 473.
— Reforms needed in the English. Temp. Bar. 13: 391.
Cavalry Charges at Sedan, Lessons of. (G. T. Denison) Canad. Mo. 1: 47.
Cavalry Tactics. For. R. 3: 147.
— Present System of. Dub. Univ. 43: 20.
Cavan, County of, Excursion to. Dub. Univ. 2: 391.
— Legends of. All the Year, 40: 326.
— Superstitions of. (L. M'Clintock) Belgra. 37: 90.
Cave Ha, Yorkshire, Exploration of. (T. McK. Hughes) Anthrop. J. 3: 383.
— Mammoth. *See* Mammoth Cave.
— of Bellamar. Ecl. M. 60: 398.
— of the Winds; a Story. (M. L. Pool) Galaxy, 13: 693, 817. 14: 71, 221.
— Settle, Exploration of. (W. B. Dawkins) Nature, 1: 628. — Anthrop. J. 1: 60. — Fraser, 93: 197.
Caves and their Occupants. (J. M. Mello) Pop. Sci. R. 16: 369. — Chamb. J. 57: 230.
— Bone, in Bavaria. Nature, 6: 87.
— — of Gibraltar, Malta, and Sicily. (A. L. Adams) Pop. Sci. R. 5: 429.
— in Belgium. Ecl. M. 32: 330.
— in East Indies. (H. Macneil) Arch. 8: 251.
— in Indiana. (H. C. Hovey) Scrib. 19: 875.
— of Adelsberg. Belgra. 21: 449.
— Western. (H. C. Hovey) Am. J. Sci. 116: 465.
See Caverns.
Cave Beetles of Kentucky. (A. S. Packard, jr.) Am. Natural. 10: 282.
Cave-Dwellers, Age of, in America. (E. T. Elliott) Pop. Sci. Mo. 15: 488.
— of Nubia. (F. L. Oswald) Pop. Sci. Mo. 12: 37.
See Troglodytes.
Cave Fauna of Kentucky. (A. S. Packard, jr.) Am. Natural. 9: 274.
Cave-Hunting. (W. B. Dawkins) Macmil. 22: 452. 23: 105. 24: 357.
— Dawkins on. (F. W. Putnam) Nation, 20: 42. — Nature, 11: 302.
Cave-Men of Perigord, Crania and Bones of. (P. Broca) Anthrop. R. 6: 408.
Cavendish, Henry. (J. Scoffern) Canad. Mo. 1: 158. — Brit. Q. 2: 243. 14: 257.
— Black, Priestley, and Watt. (J.W. Croker) Quar. 77: 105.
Cavendish, Margaret, Duchess of Newcastle. *See* Newcastle, Duchess of.
Cavendish, Thomas. Lond. Soc. 4: 311.
Cavendish, William. Lond. Soc. 4: 311.
Cavendish College. (J. L. Brereton) Contemp. 33: 361.
Cavendish Family, of Hardwick. Lond. Soc. 4: 311, 457.
— Manor and. (T. Ruggles) Arch. 11: 50.
Cavern of the Schafloch, Alps. Temp. Bar, 3: 393.
Cavern Exploration in Devonshire, England. (W. Pengelly) Am. J. Sci. 114: 299, 387.
Caverns and their Contents. (D. T. Ansted) Pop. Sci. R. 1: 135, 450. Same art. Ecl. M. 57: 398. — (A. Geikie) Good Words, 9: 58.
— in Bombay. (W. Hunter) Arch. 7: 286.
— in Franconia. Temp. Bar, 3: 492.
Caverswell, The Nuns and Ale of. Lond. M. 8: 260.
Cavery River; Scenery of an Indian Stream. Fraser, 92: 785.
Cavour, Count C. B. di. (E. L. Godkin) Nation, 25: 271. — (E. E. Hale) Chr. Exam. 73: 20. — (H. M. Hyndman) Fortn. 28: 219. — (E. C. Mezzrocchi) Nat. Q. 4: 140. — (E. Spenser) St. James, 37: 145, 308, 432. — Bentley, 50: 88. — Chamb. J. 36: 249. — Cornh. 2: 591. 5: 702. — Ecl. M. 50: 258. — Dub. Univ. 60: 624. — Ecl. R. 110: 408. — Ed. R. 114: 269. — Fraser, 97: 185. Same art. Ecl. M. 90: 421. — Liv. Age, 70: 144. — Nat. R. 13: 228. — Quar. 110: 208. Same art. Liv. Age, 70: 601.
— and Garibaldi, their Characters and Labors. Westm. 75: 172.
— and Lamarmora. Westm. 112: 386.
— Burial of; a Poem. Dub. Univ. 58: 81.
— Last Debate of. (E. Dicey) Macmil. 4: 249.
— Life of. Quar. 148: 99. Same art. Liv. Age, 142: 643. — Brit. Q. 34: 234. Same art. Ecl. M. 54: 20. — Westm. 76: 417. Same art. Ecl. M. 55: 1, 174.
— Poem on. (H. C. Pennell) Once a Week, 4: 712.
— Public Life of. New Dom. 19: 97.
— Reminiscences of. Colburn, 126: 475.
— Statesmanship of. (G. M. Towle) No. Am. 96: 45.
— Unification of Italy under. (O. M. Spencer) Harper, 43: 329.
Caving in. (H. R. Haines) Lakeside, 4: 280.
Cawnpore. Macmil. 12: 267. Same art. Ecl. M. 65: 411.
Caxton, William. (Mrs. S. C. Hall) Nat. M. 10: 14. — (H. Mott) New Dom. 21: 119. — Dub. Univ. 89: 544, 726. — Penny M. 10: 2.
— and modern Printing Machinery. Pract. M. 7: 76.
— Knight's Biography of. Mo. R. 165: 33.
— Polycronicon. (A. T. Freed) Lakeside, 4: 229.
— Printer and Mercer. All the Year, 38: 316–390.
— Sketch of. (Mrs. S. C. Hall) Tait, n. s. 18: 127.
Caxton Celebration, 1877. (J. G. Shea) Cath. World, 27: 359.
— End of. Pract. M. 7: 238.
Caxton Memorial. Art J. 11: 68.
Caxtoniana. (Sir E. L. Bulwer) Blackw. 91: 137–702. 92: 40–658. 93: 30–545. 94: 1–418.
Caxtons; a Novel. (Sir E. L. Bulwer) Blackw. 63: 513, 525, 685. 64: 40–672. 65: 33–637. 66: 48–391.
Cayenne; a penal Colony. Bentley, 48: 65. Same art. Ecl. M. 51: 220.
— Prisons of. (J. Munro) Good Words, 19: 746.
Cayla, Comtesse du, Life of. St. James, 23: 445.
Cayla, Pilgrimage to. (M. P. Thompson) Cath. World, 73: 595.
Cayuga Bridge. Knick. 38: 224.
Cayuga Lake. Knick. 36: 536. 37: 412, 487.
— Head Waters of. (G. Smith) Canad. Mo. 4: 123.
Cazotte, Jacques, Prophecy of. (L. Wraxall) Once a Week, 6: 234.
Cecco del Orso. (W. H. Ainsworth) Colburn, 74: 293.
Cecil, Richard, Life and Works of. Chr. Mo. Spec. 8: 417. — Chr. Obs. 10: 759.
Cecil, Wm. *See* Burghley, Lord.
Cecil; a Story. St. James, 38: 517.
Cecil Danby. (E. E. Hale) No. Am. 55: 283.
Cecil's Mistake. Chamb. J. 57: 600, 613.
Cecil's Tryst. (J. Payn) Chamb. J. 48: 481–791.
Cécile, Princess, "la belle Turque." Lond. Soc. 21: 211.
Cecilia, St. Harper, 61: 809. — Cath. World, 13: 477.
— Day of, in Rome. (B. Murphy) Cath. World, 14: 646.
Cedar and the Palm. (J. Hamilton) Ex. H. Lec. 1: 121.
— White. (C. P. Traill) Canad. Mo. 9: 491.
Cedars of Lebanon. (J. Hamilton) Ex. H. Lec. 1: 153. — Liv. Age, 40: 279. — Penny M. 8: 140. 12: 93. — Putnam, 8: 160.
Cedar Creek, Battle of, Gen. Wright's Report. Hist. M. 16: 279.
— — In the Ranks at. (J. F. Fitts) Galaxy, 1: 534.

Cedar Creek, Battle of, Numbers and Losses at. (W. Allan) So. Hist. Pap. **8**: 178.
Cedar Glades. Dem. R. **26**: 73, 143.
Cedar Heights. Knick. **38**: 20.
Cedar Mountain, Battle of. Cornh. **6**: 758.
Cedar Swamp, Night in a. (R. W. Douglas) Canad. Mo. **11**: 157.
Cedar Trees. (J. Quick) Colburn, **161**: 537.
Cedars, The, Massacre at, 1776. (S. E. Dawson) Canad. Mo. **5**: 305.
Celestial Dynamics. (J. R. Mayer) Am. J. Sci. **86**: 261. **87**: 187. **88**: 239, 397.
Celestial Map, Bartlett's. U. S. Lit. Gaz. **4**: 380.
Celestial Measurings and Weighings. (Sir J. F. W. Herschel) Good Words, **5**: 489.
Celestial Peas. (I. T. Hopkins) Scrib. **13**: 619.
Celestial Railroad. (N. Hawthorne) Dem. R. **12**: 515. Same art. Liv. Age, **66**: 740.
Celia; a Story. Temp. Bar, **57**: 519. **58**: 72, 213. Same art. Liv. Age, **144**: 547, 596, 654.
Celibacy. (J. T. Bixby) Nation, **6**: 190.
— Clerical. Am. Church R. **21**: 537.
— Colloquial. Dem. R. **23**: 533.
— Hygienic Relations of. (W. A. Hammond) Nation, **5**: 357.
— in the ancient Church. (P. Schaff) Mercersb. **10**: 607.
— in the Christian Church. So. R. n. s. **24**: 165.
— Sacerdotal. (E. P. Evans) No. Am. **105**: 645. — (G. P. Fisher) Nation, **4**: 514. — Quar. **127**: 514. Same art. Ecl. M. **74**: 443. — Rel. Cab. **1**: 458, 549. — Dub. Univ. **19**: 280. — Mo. Rel. M. **12**: 24.
— *versus* Marriage. (F. P. Cobbe) Fraser, **65**: 228.
Céline's Story. Dub. Univ. **85**: 293.
Cells, Blood-Corpuscle-holding. (W. I. Burnett) Am. J. Sci. **66**: 375.
— Relations of, to Organization. (W. I. Burnett) Am. J. Sci. **65**: 87.
Cell Theory, and some of its Relations. (F. G. Fairfield) Nat. Q. **30**: 303.
— Development of. Nat. Q. **22**: 135.
Cellerier, J. I. S., Sermons of. Chr. Obs. **19**: 399, 468, 546.
Cellini, Benvenuto. Cornh. **12**: 318. — Sharpe, **36**: 40. — Temp. Bar, **43**: 310. — Peop. J. **8**: 119. — U. S. Cath. M. **5**: 465.
— Autobiography of. Sharpe, **13**: 233. — Brit. Q. **8**: 492. — Blackw. **129**: 1. Same art. Liv. Age, **148**: 323.
— Life of. (G. Robinson) Retros. **4**: 1. — Ecl. M. **23**: 121.
— Sketch of. Colburn, **149**: 452.
— Tale of. Am. Whig R. **14**: 163, 208.
Cellini Cup. (S. J. Arnold) Bentley, **24**: 86–638. **25**: 83, 248.
Cellular Tissue, Raspail on. For. R. **2**: 273.
Celluloid. J. Frankl. Inst. **107**: 334. — (M. M. P. Muir) Nature, **22**: 370.
— What it is and how made. (W. H. Wahl) J. Frankl. Inst. **108**: 405.
Céloron, B. de. Expedition to the Ohio, 1749. (O. H. Marshall) M. Am. Hist. **2**: 129.
— Plate deposited on the Ohio by. Olden Time, **1**: 238, 268, 336.
Celsus. (E. Pond) Cong. R. **9**: 503. — (E. Pond) Lit. & Theo. R. **4**: 219, 584.
— and Origen. (J. A. Froude) Fraser, **97**: 142.
— — Three Letters on. (F. W. Newman and J. A. Froude) Fraser, **97**: 548.
— Attack upon Christianity. (G. D. B. Pepper) Bapt. Q. **2**: 48, 139.
Celt and Saxon. Irish Q. **1**: 153.
— of Wales and the Celt of Ireland. Cornh. **36**: 661. Same art. Liv. Age, **136**: 151.
Celt, The, Physical Characteristics of. (D. Wilson) Anthrop. R. **3**: 52.
— Roman, and Saxon, Wright's. Ecl. R. **96**: 579.
Celts and the Germans. Ed. R. **108**: 166. Same art. Ecl. M. **45**: 203.
— Britons, and Anglo-Saxons. Ecl. R. **89**: 479.
— Eastern Origin of. (J. Campbell) Canad. J. n. s. **15**: 73, 277.
— Economy of. Mo. R. **87**: 477.
— Game of. (R. R. Macgregor) Belgra. **35**: 184.
— of Gaul and Britain. (D. Wilson) Canad. J. n. s. **9**: 369.
— of Northumbria, Footprints of. (J. W. Archer) Once a Week, **7**: 585.
— or Teutons, Are we? (J. Fiske) Appleton, **2**: 243–499. **3**: 42, 129.
— Vindication of. Ed. R. **2**: 355. — (E. I. Sears) Nat. Q. **4**: 203.
Celts and other Implements of Bronze. (L. Jewitt) Stud. & Intel. Obs. **5**: 275.
— Brass, found in Ireland. (S. Pegge) Arch. **9**: 84.
— Conjectures on. (R. P. Knight) Arch. **17**: 220.
— discovered in Cornwall. (M. Hitchins) Arch. **15**: 118.
— Metal. Arch. **5**: 106.
Celtic Anthology and Poetic Remains. Cath. World, **4**: 389.
Celtic Antiquities, Higgins on. Ecl. R. **47**: 132.
— of Orkney. (F. W. L. Thomas) Arch. **34**: 88.
Celtic Art. (T. A. Croal) Art J. **33**: 333.
Celtic College, An early. (H. Macmillan) Fraser, **102**: 578. Same art. Liv. Age, **147**: 548.
Celtic Culture. Lond. Q. **45**: 25.
Celtic Ethnology. Ho. & For. R. **4**: 129.
Celtic Grave-Mounds, Derbyshire. (L. Jewitt) Reliquary, **3**: 159.
Celtic Inheritance, Our. Broadw. **7**: 56.
Celtic Language and Dialects. Dub. R. **57**: 69.
— Maclean's History of. Mo. R. **152**: 336.
Celtic Languages, History of. Blackw. **48**: 249. — New York R. **6**: 418.
— in British Isles. (E. G. Ravenstein) J. Statis. Soc. **42**: 579.
— identified with the Etruscan and Phœnician. Dub. R. **15**: 1.
— Prichard on. Ecl. R. **72**: 26. — Quar. **57**: 80.
Celtic Law. (H. Adams) No. Am. **120**: 432.
Celtic Legend, A. (H. de la Villemarque) Cath. World, **3**: 810.
Celtic Legends and Stories. Dub. Univ. **66**: 388, 603.
— in Ireland. Dub. Univ. **69**: 84.
Celtic Literature. Dub. Univ. **63**: 94.
— and Anglo-Saxon. Dub. Univ. **64**: 298.
— Antiquity of. (L. C. Seelye) Putnam, **16**: 389. — Broadw. **7**: 122.
— Early. Dub. Univ. **58**: 351.
— Study of. (M. Arnold) Cornh. **13**: 282–538. **14**: 110. Same art. Ecl. M. **66**: 728. **67**: 201, 274, 443.
Celtic Manuscripts. Dub. Univ. **70**: 399.
Celtic Monuments, Ancient. Dub. Univ. **68**: 42.
— in the Channel Islands. (F. C. Lukis) Arch. **35**: 232.
— Lambry on. Ecl. R. **2**: 788.
Celtic Music. (J. J. Reed) Nat. Q. **18**: 336.
Celtic Nations, Eastern Origin of. Mo. R. **160**: 431.
— Prichard on. Ecl. R. **55**: 145.
Celtic Race, Knox on. Anthrop. R. **6**: 175.
Celtic Races of Britain. Dub. Univ. **74**: 419, 697.
Celtic Relics and Monuments. Dub. Univ. **75**: 104.
Celtic Remains discovered at Stancliffe, Derbyshire. (L. Jewitt) Reliquary, **4**: 201.
— discovered near Cambridge. (E. D. Clarke) Arch. **18**: 340.
— in Brittany and Cornwall. Brit. Q. **52**: 281.

Celtic Researches, Davies's. Ed. R. **4**: 386.
Celtic Romance. Dub. Univ. **65**: 185.
Celtic Society, Miscellany of. Dub. R. **31**: 53.
Celtic Superstitions. Once a Week, **16**: 179.
Celtic Surnames in England. All the Year, **32**: 412.
Celtic Tenures. Westm. **39**: 69.
Celtic Tumuli near Dover, Kent. (C. H. Woodruff) Arch. **45**: 53.
— of Dorset, Warne's. Anthrop. R. **5**: 85.
Celto-scythic Migrations. Dub. Univ. **39**: 277.
Cement, Conversion of Lime into. (H. Y. D. Scott) Ecl. Engin. **7**: 542.
— Coyle's Resinous. J. Frankl. Inst. **33**: 303.
— Elastic. Penny M. **13**: 6.
— Experiments on, at London Exhibition, 1852. J. Frankl. Inst. **53**: 63.
— for Road-Making. Ecl. Engin. **1**: 721.
— Manufacture of, in India. Ecl. Engin. **6**: 204.
— Portland. (M. Leblanc) J. Frankl. Inst. **82**: 25. — (W. Michaelis) Ecl. Engin. **1**: 746. — Am. Arch. **6**: 142. — (H. Faija) Ecl. Engin. **22**: 463. — J. Frankl. Inst. **87**: 173.
— — Adulteration of. Ecl. Engin. **23**: 27.
— — and how to use it. Ecl. Engin. **10**: 349.
— — Architectural Treatment of. (R. Plumbe) Ecl. Engin. **5**: 166.
— — Future of. Ecl. Engin. **22**: 156.
— — Strength of. Ecl. Engin. **5**: 62.
— — Tests of. (I. J. Mann) Ecl. Engin. **17**: 17.
— Ransome's New Hydraulic. J. Frankl. Inst. **108**: 416.
— Roman. (J. I. Hawkins) J. Frankl. Inst. **1**: 197.
— Use of Coignet-Béton. (C. K. Graham) Ecl. Engin. **13**: 203.
Cements. (C. H. Haswell) J. Frankl. Inst. **79**: 361. **80**: 171, 295. — J. Frankl. Inst. **23**: 203.
— Ancient, and Rosendale. (A. Beckwith) Ecl. Engin. **8**: 205. Same art. J. Frankl. Inst. **95**: 204.
— and artificial Stone. Penny M. **11**: 158.
— and Concretes. Pract. M. **7**: 106.
— and Glues. (J. Phin) Am. Arch. **9**: 237.
— and Metals in Conjunction. Ecl. Engin. **6**: 157.
— and Mortars, Set of. Am. Arch. **2**: 256.
— Architectural. Ecl. Engin. **19**: 498.
— at the Philadelphia Exhibition. (Q. A. Gillmore) Ecl. Engin. **16**: 257.
— Bituminous. J. Frankl. Inst. **33**: 293.
— Calcareous. (J. Frost) J. Frankl. Inst. **20**: 217, 376. **21**: 234. **22**: 17. **23**: 193, 277.
— Cohesion of. (B. Bevan) J. Frankl. Inst. **14**: 409.
— Composition of. Ecl. Engin. **1**: 509.
— General Rules for the Use of. Am. Arch. **10**: 160.
— Strength of. Ecl. Engin. **4**: 310. — (G. F. Chantrell) Ecl. Engin. **6**: 430.
— Use of. Ecl. Engin. **24**: 121.
— Useful Formulæ for. Ecl. Engin. **8**: 264.
— Various. J. Frankl. Inst. **5**: 112.
— Vicat on. J. Frankl. Inst. **2**: 371.
Cement Tester. Pract. M. **1**: 319.
Cementi, Signor, Mender of Crockery, etc. (L. P. Hale) Galaxy, **7**: 668.
Cemetery, Adventures in a. Liv. Age, **21**: 470.
— at Munich. Once a Week, **9**: 442.
— at Stanlake, Oxon. (J. Y. Akerman and S. Stone) Arch. **37**: 363.
— of Envermeu, France. (W. M. Wylie) Arch. **35**: 223.
Cemeteries. (A. D. Gridley) New Eng. **22**: 597. — Penny M. **3**: 173. **8**: 489.
— American. (S. Osgood) Mo. Rel. M. **46**: 494. — All the Year, **6**: 226.
— and Catacombs of Paris. (R. Southey) Quar. **21**: 360.
— and Churchyards. Quar. **73**: 438. — Ecl. M. **2**: 449.
Cemeteries and Health. (S. P. Day) Victoria, **35**: 7. — (M. G. Robinet) Pop. Sci. Mo. **19**: 657. — Ecl. R. **77**: 219.
— and Modes of Burial. Nat. Q. **9**: 71.
— and Monuments. (T. D. Woolsey) New Eng. **7**: 489.
— and Sepulchers of the Departed. (G. Diehl) Evang. R. **6**: 124.
— at Naples. (F. C. Gray) No. Am. **5**: 109.
— Climax of. Fraser, **5**: 144.
— Fashion in. So. R. n. s. **22**: 326.
— in London. Once a Week, **5**: 612.
— in Southern Europe. (E. Johnstone) Once a Week, **7**: 314.
— in Towns: Report from Select Committee. Chr. Rem. **4**: 624.
— National, United States. (J. F. Russling) Harper, **33**: 310. — (C. W. Folsom) Nation, **8**: 237.
— of Paris and London. (T. L. Cuyler) Godey, **30**: 10.
— of Roux-Mesnil and of Etran in Normandy. (L'Abbé Cochet) Arch. **39**: 117.
— Ornamental. Penny M. **5**: 153.
— Public. (J. C. Loudon) J. Frankl. Inst. **36**: 46–265.
— Reformed. (J. Weidenmann) Am. Arch. **10**: 134, 146.
— Rural. (Prof. Johnston) Meth. Q. **4**: 35. — Chr. R. **13**: 9. — So. Q. **19**: 523.
See also Burial-Places; Churchyards; Graveyards.
Cenci, Beatrice. (J. Whittle) Bentley, **22**: 105.
Cenci, The, True Tale of. Ed. R. **149**: 30.
Cenis, Mont, Passage of; Road, Railroad, and Tunnel. (D. T. Ansted) Gent. M. n. s. **5**: 645.
— Passes and Passengers of. Once a Week, **17**: 377.
— Tunnel of. (E. G. Buffum) Fortn. **4**: 338. Same art. Liv. Age, **89**: 111. — (W. Forsyth) Ed. R. **122**: 123. — Broadw. **7**: 471. — (H. de Parville) Ev. Sat. **11**: 382. — Cath. World, **1**: 60. — Chamb. J. **42**: 36, 52. **48**: 710. — Ecl. Engin. **6**: 62. — Lippinc. **7**: 443. — Once a Week, **11**: 415. — Pop. Sci. R. **3**: 157. — J. Frankl. Inst. **74**: 377. — St. James, **13**: 355: Same art. Ecl. M. **65**: 288. — Westm. **81**: 30. Same art. Liv. Age, **80**: 402. Same art. Ecl. M. **61**: 423. — Ev. Sat. **1**: 410. — Liv. Age, **107**: 553. (A. H. Guernsey) Harper, **43**: 161. — (F. Kossuth, Ecl. Engin. **5**: 113–465.
— — Geology of. (D. F. Ansted) Pop. Sci. R. **9**: 357.
— — Opening of. Nature, **4**: 415. — with portraits, Ev. Sat. **11**: 437.
— — Scientific Use of. Nature, **4**: 434.
— — Ventilation of. (C. P. Harris) Ecl. Engin. **11**: 530. — (W. Pole) Ecl. Engin. **19**: 396.
— — Works and Machinery on, 1864. (T. Sopwith) J. Frankl. Inst. **77**: 296.
See Tunnels.
Censorious Speech. (H. Giles) Chr. Exam. **35**: 311.
Censure; a Morning Reverie. Cornh. **32**: 229.
Census, The, and Free Trade. Blackw. **70**: 123.
— Curiosities of. All the Year, **5**: 15. — No. Brit. **22**: 401.
— Educational, of England and Wales, 1851. Chr. Obs. **54**: 687.
— of Great Britain, Method of taking. (E. Wyatt Edgell) J. Statis. Soc. **11**: 71.
— — of 1831. (J. R. McCulloch) Ed. R. **49**: 1.
— — of 1841. Quar. **76**: 11. — Ed. R. **80**: 67. — J. Statis. Soc. **3**: 72. **4**: 277. **6**: 1.
— — — and the Non-sensus. Colburn, **62**: 302.
— — — Results of. Ecl. R. **101**: 257.
— — of 1851. (E. Cheshire) J. Statis. Soc. **17**: 45. — Chr. Rem. **27**: 1. — Hunt, **30**: 757. **31**: 126, 367, 637. **32**: 257. **33**: 120, 232, 375. — Tait, n. s. **21**: 548.
— — — Results of. De Bow, **17**: 415. — Hogg, **10**: 264.
— — of 1861. Fraser, **70**: 443. — J. Statis. Soc. **24**: 247, 402. **28**: 73, 125.

Census of Great Britain, of 1861, Some Results of. J. Frankl. Inst. **72**: 195.
— — of 1871. Chamb. J. **48**: 518. — Cornh. **23**: 415. — St. James, **28**: 500. — Geog. M. **3**: 173, 201, 229.
— — — and the Boundaries Question. (R. H. I. Palgrave) Macmil. **28**: 166.
— — — Results of. Pract. M. **1**: 255.
— — Religious, of 1851. Chr. Obs. **55**: 18.
— of the United States, Laws of. (C. F. Johnson) No. Am. **131**: 135.
— — Methods of. (J. A. Garfield) Am. Soc. Sci. J. **2**: 45. — (C. D. Wright) Internat. R. **9**: 405.
— — of 1820. Niles's Reg. **18**: 120, 319. **21**: 345.
— — of 1830. Niles's Reg. **38**: 145. **43**: 27.
— — of 1840. So. Q. **25**: 521. — Dem. R. **5**: 77. — So. Lit. Mess. **9**: 340. — Hunt, **12**: 125. — De Bow, **11**: 416.
— — of 1850. (G. Tucker) Hunt, **19**: 523. — (W. Kirkland) Hunt, **14**: 115. — Dem. R. **25**: 291. **29**: 198. — De Bow, **14**: 127. **16**: 81. — (W. J. A. Bradford) Chr. Exam. **58**: 233. — (P. Godwin) Putnam, **3**: 16. — Harper, **10**: 334. — Chamb. J. **15**: 100. — J. Statis. Soc. **15**: 64.
— — — Curiosities of. (W. Mitchell) Atlan. **5**: 439.
— — of 1860. Princ. **37**: 226.
— — — Results of. Bank. M. (N. Y.) **17**: 241.
— — of 1870. Ed. R. **139**: 130.
— — — Imbroglio about. (H. Adams) Nation, **10**: 116.
— — — Our National Wealth as revealed by. (J. B. Hodgskin) Nation, **12**: 286.
— — — Some Results of. (F. A. Walker) Am. Soc. Sci. J. **5**: 71.
— — of 1880. (H. Stone) Lippinc. **22**: 108. — (G. Walker) No. Am. **128**: 393.
— — — Alleged Frauds in, at the South. (H. Gannett) Internat. R. **10**: 439.
— — — Notes on. (F. J. Mouat) J. Statis. Soc. **43**: 573.
Census Returns. Bank. M. (N. Y.) **7**: 566.
Census Tables, Lessons from. Chamb. J. **20**: 92.
Census-Taking. Republic, **5**: 145.
Centaurs, The. (S. Colvin) Cornh. **38**: 284, 409.
Centenarians. St. James, **49**: 77.
— Physical Condition of. (Sir G. D. Gibb) Anthrop. J. **2**: 78.
Centenarianism. (E. R. Lancaster) Macmil. **24**: 466. — Ecl. M. **77**: 687. — Chamb. J. **57**: 113.
Centennial of 1876, Fruits and Festivals of. (E. C. Bruce) Lippinc. **17**: 9–649.
— Hundred Years ago. Am. Mo. M. **5**: 17–249.
— in London. (J. Bigelow) Galaxy, **15**: 671.
Centennial Bells; a Poem. (B. F. Taylor) Scrib. **12**: 360.
Centennial Discourses. Chr. R. **5**: 47.
Centennial Exhibition. *See* Philadelphia.
Centennial Gleanings, 1875. (T. Evans) Overland, **15**: 464.
Centennial Memories, 1775–1875. Potter Am. Mo. **4**: 250–887. **6**: 166.
Centennial Posie. (C. H. Dall) Unita. R. **6**: 157.
Centennial Thought; an Hour with the Fathers. (J. G. Butler) Luth. Q. **6**: 510.
Center of Gravity, Formulæ for. (J. W. Davis) Ecl. Engin. **20**: 467.
— — Guldin on. (J. B. Cherriman) Canad. J. n. s. **8**: 33.
— of a Polygon. (J. W. Davis) Ecl. Engin. **21**: 323.
Centlivre, Susanna, and her Plays. Temp. Bar, **51**: 247.
— Bold Stroke for a Wife. (A. H. Bromilow) Colburn, **164**: 414.
Central America. Dub. Univ. **19**: 189. — Am. Q. **11**: 212. — (J. D. B. De Bow) De Bow, **6**: 83. — (W. J. A. Bradford) De Bow, **21**: 1. — Dem. R. **37**: 263. **38**: 298. **42**: 441. — Dub. Univ. **80**: 85.
Central America, Ancient and modern. Dub. Univ. **19**: 189.
— and the Administration. Am. Whig R. **13**. 276.
— and Mexico, Tempsky's Travels in. New Q. **7**: 152.
— and the West Indies, Travels in. Colburn, **118**: 86.
— and Yucatan, Ruins of. (A. W. Ely) De Bow, **9**: 44.
— Annexation to the United States. Liv. Age, **50**: 311.
— Biology of. Nature, **21**: 321.
— British Aggression in. Dem. R. **28**: 1.
— Commercial and other Characteristics. De Bow, **18**: 73.
— Discoveries in. Ecl. M. **2**: 522.
— Dunlop's Travels in. Dub. R. **23**: 78.
— Gold Fields of. (J. D. Whelpley) Harper, **12**: 315.
— Guajiquero Indians. (E. G. Squier) Harper, **19**: 602.
— Hunting a Pass. (E. G. Squier) Atlan. **5**: 447. **6**: 44.
— in 1827. Ann. Reg. **2**: 171.
— Jungle in. Temp. Bar, **22**: 458. **23**: 66.
— Languages of. (D. G. Brinton) Hist. M. **15**: 305.
— — Manuscripts in. (D. G. Brinton) Am. J. Sci. **97**: 222.
— Morelet's Travels in. Nature, **5**: 159.
— Oddities of. Chamb. J. **12**: 13.
— Omoa. (J. V. S. Anthony) Harper, **14**: 22.
— Question of. Ed. R. **104**: 267. — De Bow, **27**: 550. — Fraser, **54**: 121.
— Rambles in. (F. L. Oswald) Lippinc. **24**: 5–659.
— Recent Travelers in. Fraser, **58**: 425.
— Relations with United States, 1852. Dem. R. **31**: 337.
— Reminiscences of. (E. G. Squier) De Bow, **29**: 410.
— Republic of. (C. Cushing) No. Am. **26**: 127.
— Revolutions in. Dem. R. **40**: 315.
— Roberts's Voyages and Excursions in. Lond. M. **21**: 1.
— Ruins of. Knick. **11**: 128. — (D. Charnay) No. Am. **131**: 185–519. **132**: 41–578. **133**: 390.
— — and Antiquities of. Ed. R. **78**: 438.
— Ruined Cities of. Art J. **6**: 102. — (A. T. Rice) No. Am. **131**: 89.
— Secret of the Strait. (G. A. Maack) Harper, **47**: 801.
— Silver Mines of. (J. D. Whelpley) Harper, **12**: 721.
— Sketches of. Knick. **36**: 444. — Canad. Mo. **7**: 233–528. **8**: 61.
— Squier's Notes on. Canad. J. n. s. **1**: 359. — Liv. Age, **31**: 104. **49**: 59.
— States of. Brit. Q. **13**: 173.
— Stephens's Ancient Cities of. Dub. R. **12**: 184.
— Stephens's Travels in. (J. G. Palfrey) No. Am. **53**: 479. — Ed. R. **75**: 397. — Mo. R. **156**: 30. — Mus. **43**: 257. — New York R. **9**: 225. — New Q. **3**: 416. — Quar. **69**: 52. — Chamb. J. **48**: 764.
— Treaty with, 1826. Niles's Reg. **31**: 172.
— Trip to. (E. Westervelt) Scrib. **15**: 609.
— Trollope's Spanish Main. Tait, n. s. **27**: 81.
— Unexplored Regions of. (E. G. Squier) Putnam, **12** 549. — Hist. M. **4**: 65. — Broadw. **8**: 250.
— Volcanoes of. (E. G. Squier) Harper, **19**: 739.
See Costa Rica; Darien; Mosquito Shore; Nicaragua; Panama; Tehuantepec; Interoceanic Canal.
Central Forces, Prize Essay on. (D. Trowbridge) Math. Mo. **2**: 150.
— and disturbing Forces. (D. Trowbridge) Math. Mo. **3**: 245.
Central Park, New York City. (C. Cook) Scrib. **6**: 523, 673. — (H. S. Conant) Harper, **59**: 689.
— Gates of, Designs for, 1865. (R. Sturgis) Nation, **1**: 186, 410. **3**: 255.
Centralization. (J. Austin) Ed. R. **85**: 221. — Dem. R. **26**: 289.
— and Self-Government. Ecl. R. **102**: 87.
— and Socialism. De Bow, **20**: 692.
— in Government. Ed. R. **115**: 323.
— in United States Government. (D. D. Field) No. Am **132**: 407.

Centralization of Power. Dem. R. **40**: 311.
— Real. Ev. Sat. **10**: 506.
— Social Evidences of, 1858. (A. K. Syester) Mercersb. **10**: 533.
Centrepole Bill. (G. F. Emery) Overland, **4**: 83.
Centrifugal Force. (T. W. Bakewell) J. Frankl. Inst. **4**: 111.
— *versus* unbalanced Force. (R. D. Napier) Ecl. Engin. **16**: 296.
Centurial Stones, Test of certain. (H. C. Cook) Arch. **44**: 225.
Century, A, ends when? Hist. M. **2**: 12.
Century Plant; a Tale. (F. H. Ludlow) Harper, **21**: 51.
Century Plants. (I. T. Hopkins) Scrib. **17**: 377.
Century since. Colburn, **160**: 645.
Cephalization. (J. D. Dana) Am. J. Sci. **86**: 1. **91**: 163. **112**: 245. — (J. D. Dana) New Eng. **22**: 495.
Cephalonia. Bentley, **47**: 173.
Cephalopods. Hogg, **13**: 93.
— Gigantic, of the North Atlantic. (A. E. Verrill) Am. J. Sci. **109**: 123, 177. **110**: 213. **119**: 284.
Ceramics. (P. E. Chase) J. Frankl. Inst. **103**: 425. — (W. de B. Fryer) Penn Mo. **11**: 941.
Ceramic Art. (F. A. Griesemer) Potter Am. Mo. **10**: 300. — All the Year, **33**: 421, 443. **34**: 11, 38, 62. — Appleton, **10**: 464, 496, 559. — So. R. n. s. **14**: 305. — St. James, **4**: 352.
— and Art Culture. (J. J. Talbot) Penn Mo. **9**: 251, 455, 536.
— at the Centennial. Am. Arch. **1**: 244–342. — (J. J. Young) Lippinc. **18**: 701.
— at Paris Exposition. (R. Sturgis) Nation, **27**: 269.
— China Mania. (C. Drew) Dub. Univ. **87**: 181. — Chamb. J. **52**: 241.
— Decorative Taste in. (G. B. Griffith) Potter Am. Mo. **13**: 295.
— Greek and Chinese Vases. Lond. Soc. **40**: 354.
— in America. (J. J. Young) Atlan. **44**: 588.
— of Japan. Dub. R. **78**: 374.
— Plates and Dishes. (E. Meteyard) Good Words, **11**: 541. *See* China; Cloisonné; Porcelain; Pottery.
Cereals, Microscopical Fungi infesting. (W. Barbeck) Am. Natural. **13**: 612.
Cerealia, The; a Standing Miracle. (A. Harvey) Good Words, **2**: 479.
Cerebral Development, Researches in. (J. Straton) Zoist. **8**: 396.
Cerebral Functions, Localization of. Nature, **8**: 467. — (H. de Varigny) Pop. Sci. Mo. **18**: 599.
Cerebral Physiology. Anthrop. R. **1**: 337.
Cerebration, Changes of Circulation during. (C. S. Minot) Pop. Sci. Mo. **17**: 303.
— Unconscious. (F. P. Cobbe) Macmil. **23**: 24. Same art. Ecl. M. **76**: 70. Same art. Liv. Age, **107**: 598. — (E. M. Gallaudet) Penn Mo. **8**: 634.
— — Dreams as Illustrations of. (F. P. Cobbe) Macmil. **23**: 512. Same art. Ecl. M. **76**: 726. Same art. Liv. Age, **109**: 363.
— — Phenomena of. New Dom. **7**: 338.
Cerebrum, Functions of, Goltz on. (G. C. Robertson) Mind, **2**: 108, 247. **5**: 254.
Cerecloth, Origin of the Word. (J. Ayloffe) Arch. **3**: 400.
Ceremonial, Codes of. Lond. Soc. **14**: 51. **16**: 216.
— of the Catholic Church. Dub. R. **35**: 362.
Ceremonial Government, Evolution of. (H. Spencer) Fortn. **29**: 1–772. **30**: 139. Same art. Pop. Sci. Mo. **12**: 385–641. **13**: 25–292. **14**: 17.
— — Spencer on. (A. G. Sedgwick) Nation, **31**: 97.
Ceremony, International. Blackw. **114**: 667. Same art. Liv. Age, **120**: 101.
Ceremonies. *See* Rites.
Cereopsis of New Holland. Penny M. **5**: 367.
Cereus giganteus of California. (G. Engelmann) Am. J. Sci. **64**: 335. **67**: 231.
Cerevis. Penn Mo. **1**: 180, 210.
Cerro Gordo, Battle of. So. Q. **21**: 121.
Certainty in Religion. (R. Turnbull) Bapt. Q. **6**: 257.
— — Reasonable Basis of. Dub. R. **83**: 381.
— — Wainwright on. Chr. Obs. **65**: 569.
— Empirical. (J. C. Thompson) J. Spec. Philos. **6**: 142.
— in religious Assent. Dub. R. **68**: 253. — Fraser, **85**: 23.
— Reasonable Basis of. (W. G. Ward) 19th Cent. **3**: 531.
— Rule and Motive of. Dub. R. **69**: 40.
Ceruse, or White Lead, Manufacture of. J. Frankl. Inst. **1**: 339.
Ceruso, Giovanni Leonardo. Mo. Rel. M. **24**: 269.
Cervantes, Miguel de. (Alice King) Argosy, **7**: 117. — Bentley, **24**: 626. — Dub. Univ. **68**: 123. Same art. Cath. World, **4**: 14. — Month, **7**: 50.
— and Beaumont and Fletcher. Fraser, **91**: 592.
— and his Writings. Am. Mo. M. **7**: 342.
— and Lope de Vega. (F. Lawrence) Sharpe, **11**: 228.
— Don Quixote. Blackw. **11**: 657. — Cornh. **30**: 595. — Westm. **89**: 299. Same art. Ecl. M. **71**: 909. — (R. J. De Cordova) Knick. **38**: 189.
— — Duffield's Translation. Blackw. **130**: 469.
— — Episodes of. Lond. M. **16**: 557. **17**: 11.
— — Heine on. Temp. Bar, **48**: 235.
— — Jarvis's Translation. Mo. R. **144**: 230.
— — Library of. Fraser, **7**: 324, 565.
— Drama of. (J. Mew) Gent M. n. s. **23**: 446.
— El Buscapié. Dub. R. **26**: 137.
— Entremeses. (J. Mew) Gent. M. n. s. **26**: 451.
— Galatea. (J. Mew) Gent. M. n. s. **24**: 670.
— Life of. (E. Wigglesworth) No. Am. **38**: 277. — (W. H. Prescott) No. Am. **45**: 1. — U. S. Lit. Gaz. **6**: 415. — Mo. R. **134**: 383.
— Novels of. (J. Mew) Gent. M. n. s. **21**: 358. **29**: 95.
— Voyage to Parnassus. (J. Mew) Gent. M. n. s. **24**: 81.
Cesalpino, Andrea. Discovery of Circulation of the Blood. Ed. R. **147**: 25.
Cesnola, Louis Palma di, Explorations at Cyprus. (H. Hitchcock) Harper, **45**: 188. *See* Cyprus.
— Collection of Antiquities. (W. C. Prince) Harper, **55**: 333. — (G. W. Sheldon) Appleton, **17**: 150. — (C. E. Norton) Nation, **16**: 62. — (W. J. Stillman) Nation, **16**: 273. — (E. Shinn) Nation, **16**: 374, 390, 436. — (W. H. Goodyear) Nation, **17**: 38.
Cesspools, Apparatus for emptying. Pract. M. **3**: 205.
Cetaceans, Relations of. (T. Gill) Am. Natural. **7**: 19.
Cetawayo, Zulu King, on the Zulu War. Macmil. **41**: 273.
— Visit to. (M. Magwaza) Macmil. **37**: 421. — Temp. Bar, **58**: 253.
Cette to Carcassonne, From. Temp. Bar, **4**: 532.
Cevennes, Church in the. Good Words, **9**: 52.
— Revolt in, 1663. Ed. R. **104**: 123. — Quar. **150**: 434. — For. Q. **35**: 335.
Ceylon. (E. Jackson) Overland, **3**: 447. — (L. B. Road) Bentley, **53**: 542. — All the Year, **10**: 402. **11**: 198–418. **12**: 342. — Brit. & For. R. **12**: 385. — (T. De Quincey) Blackw. **54**: 622. — Quar. **14**: 1. Dub. Univ. **24**: 400. — Tait, n. s. **27**: 107. — Meth. M. **38**: 295.
— Adventure in. Blackw. **24**: 43.
— and the Cingalese. (H. S. Sirr) Dub. Univ. **32**: 563, 697. **33**: 36–681. **34**: 61–555. — (J. E. Tennent) Bentley, **29**: 224. — No. Brit. **32**: 188.
— — Sirr on. Dub. Univ. **36**: 241.
— Backwoods of. (A. Gray) Fortn. **33**: 769. Same art. Liv. Age, **146**: 3.
— Baker's Eight Years in. Blackw. **75**: 226. — New Q. **5**: 48.

Ceylon, Campbell's Field Sports in. Mo. R. 162: 243.
— Cashiering the King of. Ed. R. 26: 431.
— Christianity in. Dub. R. 25: 71. — Dub. Univ. 37: 557. — Liv. Age, 28: 414. — Chr. Mo. Spec. 1: 155. — Chr. Obs. 77: 437.
— — Tennent's. Dub. R. 30: 410. — Dub. Univ. 37: 557. — Internat. M. 3: 308. — Sharpe, 13: 315.
— Church in. U. S. Cath. M. 7: 633.
— Coffee-Planting in. House. Words, 3: 109.
— Commerce of. Hunt, 16: 339.
— Commercial Statistics of. (J. Capper) J. Statis. Soc. 2: 424.
— Cordiner's Account of. Ed. R. 12: 82. — (J. Foster) Ecl. R. 8: 636, 692.
— Cosseir and Thebes. (H. Coppinger) Sharpe, 49: 124.
— De Butts's Rambles in. Mo. R. 157: 133.
— Duke of Edinburgh's Visit to. Macmil. 29: 466. — Same art. Ecl. M. 82: 574.
— English in. Dem. R. 28: 409.
— Forbes's Eleven Years in, 1826–37. Mo. R. 152: 1.
— Forests and Pearl Fishery of. Fraser, 62: 753. Same art. Ecl. M. 52: 402.
— Gem-Digging in. Once a Week, 21: 383, 402.
— Gleanings from. Victoria, 13: 481. 15: 109.
— History of. Ecl. R. 26: 219.
— — and Description of. Westm. 73: 66.
— Home-Rule in. (W. Digby) Fortn. 24: 241.
— Idolatry of, Hardy on. Mo. R. 154: 369.
— Implements used in. J. Frankl. Inst. 5: 328. 6: 2.
— Irrigation Works of. (W. Phillpotts) Ecl. Engin. 11: 303.
— — Tank. (R. Abbay) Nature, 16: 509. — (R. Abbay) Ecl. Engin. 18: 52.
— Language of. *See* Cingalese.
— Mission to, 1813. Ecl. R. 39: 435.
— Mysteries of. Nat. Q. 22: 215. — Quar. 88: 100
— Natural History of. (W. Y. Brigham) No. Am. 95: 129. — (W. Hincks) Canad. J. n. s. 7: 347. — Nat. R. 11: 374. — All the Year, 2: 244, 268, 516. — Meth. M. 39: 842.
— — Habits of Animals of. (H. N. Moseley) Nature, 6: 65.
— Note-Book in. Chamb. J. 57: 201.
— People and Resources of. Ecl. R. 90: 183.
— Peraharra, Festival in. House. Words, 3: 252.
— Percival's Account of. (Syd. Smith) Ed. R. 2: 136.
— Pridham's Account of. Dub. R. 26: 273.
— Railways in. Ecl. Engin. 5: 489.
— Rifle and Hound in, S. W. Baker's. Fraser, 51: 16.
— Rodiyas of. (B. F. Hartshorne) Fortn. 26: 671.
— Selkirk's Recollections of. Chr. Obs. 44: 428.
— Sketching in. (A. Nicholl) Dub. Univ. 40: 527, 691.
— South, Wesleyan Mission in. Lond. Q. 20: 113.
— Tambeys of. Chamb. J. 55: 790.
— Tennent's Account of. Brit. Q. 30: 339. Same art. Liv. Age, 65: 25. — Chamb. J. 32: 395. — (T. Harlin) Fraser, 61: 627. — Colburn, 118: 176. — Dub. R. 47: 445. — Dub. Univ. 56: 59. — Ed. R. 110: 343. Same art. Ecl. M. 49: 552. — New Q. 8: 408.
— A Voice from. Colburn, 86: 467.
— Weaving in. Penny M. 2: 325.
— Weddas of. (B. F. Hartshorne) Fortn. 25: 406.
— Week's Shooting in. Bentley, 44: 551.
— Zoölogy of. Chamb. J. 36: 392. Same art. Ecl. M. 55: 265.
Cha'b Arabs. (W. F. Ainsworth) Colburn, 82: 43.
Chacornac, Jean. Nature, 8: 512.
Chadwick, Edwin. No. Brit. 13: 40.
Chaff. Once a Week, 19: 402.
Chain Cables, Testing of. (F. A. Paget) J. Frankl. Inst. 78: 86, 145, 217.
Chain Towing on the Elbe. Ecl. Engin. 18: 171.
Chairs, Ancient and modern. (F. A. Griesemer) Potter Am. Mo. 11: 142.
— History of. Temp. Bar, 31: 108.
Chaja, or Crested Screamer. Penny M. 5: 511.
Chalcahual; a Tale. Dem. R. 22: 49, 149.
Chalcedon, Summer Days at. (Mrs. Walker) Good Words, 7: 455.
Chaldea, Ethnography of early. (A. H. Sayce) Kitto, 32: 165. 33: 187. 34: 171. 37: 180.
— Layard and the last of the Chaldees. Colburn, 87: 337.
— Loftus's Discoveries in. Bentley, 41: 264. Same art. Ecl. M. 41: 75. Same art. Liv. Age, 53: 373. — Kitto, 19: 372.
— Mignan's Travels in. Ecl. R. 50: 496.
Chaldean Account of Genesis. (J. W. Dawson) Internat. R. 3: 392.
Chaldean Legend of the Flood. (M. Bennett) Dub. Univ. 81: 146, 376. — (A. H. Sayce) Theo. R. 10: 364.
Chaldeans, Magic and Sorcery of. Lond. Q. 45: 1.
Chaldee Language of Daniel and Ezra. Kitto, 26: 373.
* Chaldee MS., Translation of an ancient. (J. Hogg, J. Wilson, and J. G. Lockhart) Blackw. 2: 89.
Chaldee Paraphrases or Targumim. Chr. Obs. 1: 85.
Chalgrave Field, Battle of. (W. W. Cooper) Bentley, 24: 111.
Chalgrove Church, Oxford, Mural Paintings at. (W. Burges) Arch. 38: 431.
Chalices, Remarks on Early English. (O. Morgan) Arch. 42: 405.
Chalk. (T. H. Huxley) Ev. Sat. 6: 421.
— and the English Chalk Cliffs. Temp. Bar, 2: 465.
— and Eocens in England. (J. S. Gardner) Pop. Sci. R. 18: 55.
— Continuity of. (W. Thomson) Nature, 3: 225.
— Lecture on. (W. B. Carpenter) Good Words, 13: 698.
— On a Piece of. (T. H. Huxley) Macmil 18: 396. Same art. Ecl. M. 71: 1448. Same art. Liv. Age, 99: 108.
— Story of a Piece of. Chamb. J. 45: 247. Same art. Ecl. M. 71: 1094.
Chalk Church, Description of. (C. Clarke) Arch. 11: 317.
— Figures on Porch of. (S. Denne) Arch. 12: 10.
Chalk Cliffs, and their Uses. Temp. Bar, 9: 178.
Chalk Pits at Grays, Essex. (S. Hibberd) Recr. Sci. 3: 33.
— of Kent. (J. G. Wood) Good Words, 20: 749.
Chalk-Stream Studies. (C. Kingsley) Fraser, 58: 323.
Chalkhill, John. Thealma and Clearchus. (H. Baldwin) Retros. 4: 230.
Chalklen, Charles Wm., Obituary of. Westm. 50: 539.
Challenger, H. M. S., and the Valorous, Work of. Nature, 13: 250.
— Collections of. (C. W. Thomson) Nature, 15: 254. 16: 117.
— Cruise of. (J. E. Davis) Geog. M. 1: 183, 225, 286. 2: 38–358. 3: 66, 179. — (C. W. Thomson) Nature, 7: 385. — Nature, 14: 93. 17: 145, 185. — Pop. Sci. R. 20: 50. — Liv. Age, 130: 131. — Lond. Soc. 32: 134.
— in the South Atlantic. Nature, 10: 142.
— In the Wake of. (J. C. Galton) Pop. Sci. R. 15: 1.
— Letters from. (C. W. Thomson) Good Words, 14: 394, 506, 854. 15: 45–814. 16: 489.
— Naturalist on. Chamb. J. 56: 379.
— Notes from. (C. W. Thomson) Nature, 8: 28–400. 12: 315. 14: 14.

* This notable satire appeared in only two hundred copies of the first impression of that number. It was suppressed, and only a few sets of Blackwood have the article. It is reprinted in "Noctes Ambrosianæ," edited by R. S. Mackenzie, N. Y., 1872, v. 1, and Ferrier's ed., Edinb., 1855, v. 4.

Challenger, H. M. S., Results of the Expedition. (T. H. Huxley) Contemp. **25**: 639. Same art. Ecl. M. **84**: 548. Same art. Liv. Age, **127**: 3. Same art. Pop. Sci. Mo. **3**: 451.
— Scientific Orders of. Nature, **7**: 191, 252.
— Thomson's Cruise of. (A. Agassiz) Nation, **26**: 278.
— Work of. Nature, **13**: 70.
Challoner, Richard, Bishop. (T. Arnold) Month, **38**: 59.
Chalmers, G. Paul. In Memoriam. (A. H. Japp) Good Words, **19**: 285.
Chalmers, James R. Report of Cavalry Operations, October, 1863. So. Hist. Pap. **8**: 222.
Chalmers, Thomas. (T. Brainard) Am. Presb. R. **1**: 175. — (S. G. Brown) No. Am. **75**: 489. — (J. Cairns) Ex. H. Lec. **20**: 41. — (G. R. Gleig) Quar. **91**: 402. — (J. Leaf) Sharpe, **11**: 271. — (A. P. Peabody) Chr. Exam. **54**: 256. — No. Brit. **7**: 560. Same art. Liv. Age, **14**: 481. Same art. Ecl. M. **14**: 314, 466. — Fraser, **23**: 505. — (A. and J. A. Alexander) Princ. **13**: 30. — Liv. Age, **14**: 214, 380. **30**: 325. — (T. Lewis) Am. Bib. Repos. 3d s. **4**: 333. — (T. V. Moore) Meth. Q. **9**: 594. — Blackw. **2**: 131. — with portrait, Ecl. M. **12**: 145. — (P. Frank) Ecl. M. **23**: 256. — Mus. **13**: 732. — (T. V. Moore) Meth. Q. **9**: 594. — Macmil. **10**: 203, 365, 458. — with portrait, Peop. J. **3**: 353. **11**: 231. — Sharpe, **11**: 271. **12**: 311. **14**: 326. — Tait, **2**: 189.
— and Channing. (— Murdock) Am. Presb. R. **2**: 438. — (A. Gordon) Unita. R. **13**: 318.
— and Edward Irving. Mus. **3**: 356. — U. S. Lit. Gaz. **2**: 222, 255.
— and Daniel O'Connell. Dem. R. **21**: 124.
— and the Church Establishment Question. Fraser, **17**: 742. **18**: 396.
— as a Political Economist. Blackw. **73**: 598.
— as a Preacher. (S. G. Brown) Am. Bib. Repos. **10**: 374. — Blackw. **2**: 131.
— Astronomical Discourses. (J. Foster) Ecl. R. **26**: 205, 354, 466.
— at Elberfeld. Good Words, **1**: 5.
— Bridgewater Treatise. (T. P. Thompson) Westm. **20**: 1.—Mus. **24**: 1.—Select J. **3**: [50.—Mo. R. **131**: 378.
— Character and Writings. (W. M. Fernald) Univ. Q. **1**: 178.
— Clerical Life of. Chr. Rem. **22**: 1.
— Commercial Sermons. Blackw. **8**: 178. — Chr. Mo. Spec. **4**: 198.
— Daily Scripture Readings. Chr. R. **13**: 412.
— Discourses of. (J. Brazer) Chr. Disc. **1**: 212.
— Hanna's Life and Writings of. Liv. Age, **24**: 285. **27**: 20. **31**: 165. — Dub. Univ. **35**: 634. **38**: 672. **40**: 67, 350. — Prosp. R. **6**: 411. **7**: 318. — Chr. Obs. **53**: 258. — Ecl. R. **95**: 68. **96**: 293. — Fraser, **46**: 1. Same art. Liv. Age, **34**: 439.
— Inductive Method in Philosophy. New Eng. **8**: 203.
— Lectures on National Churches. Ecl. R. **68**: 1.
— Letter to. Portfo.(Den.) **21**: 446.
— Life of. Ecl. M. **19**: 400. — Tait, n. s. **17**: 7, 127, 490. **18**: 561.
— Memoirs of. No. Brit. **17**: 205. Same art. Ecl. M. **26**: 289. — Ecl. R. **92**: 707. — Quar. **91**: 402. — Univ. Q. **10**: 113.
— on Christian Charity. Ed. Mo. R. **1**: 230.
— on Christian Revelation. Blackw. **1**: 73. — Quar. **17**: 451. — Mo. R. **84**: 68.
— on Ecclesiastical Economy. (J. W. Alexander) Princ. **14**: 562.
— on Economy of large Towns. Blackw. **6**: 18, 177. — Chr. Disc. **4**: 190.
— on Mental and Moral Philosophy. (A. Alexander) Princ. **20**: 529.
— on Natural Theology. *See* Natural Theology.
Chalmers, Thomas, on Political Economy. *See* Political Economy.
— Oratory of. Am. Lit. M. **1**: 300.
— Posthumous Works. (Dr. J. Brown) No. Brit. **8**: 393. Same art. Liv. Age, **17**: 61. — Ecl. R. **87**: 353. **88**: 552. — Bib. R. **4**: 334. **6**: 407. — Tait, n. s. **15**: 707.
— Recollections of. Fraser, **36**: 140.
— Right Moral State of the Community. Fraser, **7**: 603.
— A. J. Scott, and Edward Irving. Nat. R. **15**: 350.
— Sermons. Blackw. **5**: 462. — Anal. M. **16**: 91, 179. — (C. A. Goodrich) Chr. Mo. Spec. **7**: 519, 584. — Chr. Mo. Spec. **1**: 631. — Chr. Obs. **18**: 386, 443. **20**: 372, 441. **24**: 436. — Cong. M. **2**: 359, 494. — Ecl. R. **30**: 501. **33**: 92. 54. — Meth. M. **47**: 110. — Portfo.(Den.) **24**: 465.
— Sketch of. Lond. M. **22**: 376. **23**: 327.
— Theology of. (J. M. Manning) Bib. Sac. **13**: 477.
— Works of. Kitto, **5**: 233. — Dub. Univ. **13**: 241. — Cong. M. **20**: 33. — No. Brit. **26**: 1. Same art. Ecl. M. **40**: 1.
Chalons and Aldershot, Chapter on. Fraser, **68**: 190.
— Battle of. (E. S. Creasy) Bentley, **26**: 24.
— Camp at. Bentley, **55**: 201. — Blackw. **85**: 251.
— — and Fête Napoleon. (F. French) Macmil. **10**: 513.
Cham, *pseud.* *See* Noë, A. Comte de.
Chamber of the Bell; a Tale. Fraser, **33**: 530.
Chamber of Refuge. Ecl. M. **17**: 550.
Chamber over the Gate. (H. W. Longfellow) Atlan. **43**: 368.
Chambers in Charlotte Street. (C. W. Stoddard) Overland, **14**: 241.
Chamberlain, Joseph, Sketch of, with portrait. Pract. M. **6**: 193.
Chamberlayne, H., and the Land-Banks. Bank. M. (N. Y.) **29**: 284.
Chamberlayne, Wm. Love's Victory. (G. Robinson) Retros. **1**: 258.
— Pharonnida. (G. Robinson) Retros. **1**: 21.
Chambers, A. B., Sketch of. West. J. **12**: 150.
Chambers, Robert. (J. G. Wilson) Lippinc. **8**: 17. — with portrait, Ev. Sat. **10**: 443. — Ecl. M. **77**: 38.
— Literary Life of. (J. G. Wilson) Appleton, **7**: 485.
— Writings of. Ecl. R. **85**: 588.
Chambers, William and Robert. (J. R. Dennett) Nation, **14**: 243. — Dub. Univ. **37**: 177. — Ecl. M. **22**: 410. — Liv. Age, **28**: 592. — Lond. Q. **51**: 1. Same art. Liv. Age, **139**: 387.
— Publications. Liv. Age, **5**: 102.
— Soirée of. Chamb. J. **4**: 157. Same art. Liv. Age, **3**: 710.
Chambers, Sir William, 1726–96, Biography of. Am. Arch. **8**: 260.
Chambers's Encyclopædia, Changes in American Edition. Chamb. J. **51**: 782.
Chambers's Journal, History of. Chamb. J. **49**: 65.
Chamblas, Mme. de. (J. D. Osborne) Appleton, **21**: 289.
Chambly, Canada, An Evening in. (J. G. Smalley) Cath World, **17**: 765.
— Recollections of. (M. G Smalley) Cath. World, **28**: 102.
Chambly, Fort, on the Richelieu River. (H. Sandham) Scrib. **17**: 129. — Canad. Mo. **4**: 177.
Chambord, Comte de. Fraser, **88**: 764.—Month, **15**: 120.
— and the Pope's Civil Princedom. Dub. R. **75**: 259.
Chambord, Château de. Bentley, **57**: 397. Same art. Ecl. M. **64**: 755.
Chameleon, The. (J. Couch) Intel. Obs. **10**: 321. — (J. R. Greene) Pop. Sci. R. **19**: 97.
— Change of Color in. (H. M. Edwards) Ed. New Philos. J. **17**: 313. — Chamb. J. **54**: 575. Same art. Ecl. M. **90**: 498. Same art. Liv. Age, **134**: 822. — Once a Week, **1**: 248. — (J. Fitzgerald) Pop. Sci. Mo. **6**: 526.

Chameleon, The Florida. (S. Lockwood) Am. Natural. **10**: 4.
— Observations on. (O. R. Bacheler) Pop. Sci. Mo. **15**: 178.
— Popular Account of. (St. G. Mivart) Nature, **24**: 309.
Chamfort, S. R. N., Neglected French Author. Fraser, **46**: 291. Same art. Liv. Age, **35**: 161. Same art. Ecl. M. **27**: 315.
— and Rivarol. (G. Saintsbury) Fortn. **31**: 96.
Chamier, Capt. Frederic, Memoir of, with portrait. Colburn, **52**: 508.
— The young Muscovite. Am. Mo. M. **3**: 163.
Chamisso, Adalbert von. For. Q. **36**: 412.
— Peter Schlemihl. Tait, n. s. **18**: 356.
Chamois, The. Hogg, **2**: 278. — Penny M. **2**: 449.
— Excursion after. Once a Week, **9**: 469.
Chamois Hunt, My first and last. (J. T. Headley) Am. Whig R. **3**: 181.
Chamois-Hunter. (E. Souvestre) Sharpe, **31**: 21.
Chamois-Hunting. Fraser, **44**: 133. Same art. Internat. M. **4**: 344. Same art. Liv. Age, **30**: 481. — Once a Week, **19**: 546. — St. James, **6**: 188. — Colburn, **28**: 527. **29**: 57.
— in Bavaria, Boner's. Chamb. J. **19**: 300. — Colburn, **98**: 166. — New Q. **2**: 317.
— with the Emperor of Austria. (W. A. B. Grohman) Lippinc. **24**: 459.
Chamounix. (H. Bedford) Month, **26**: 25.
— Day at. (J. Wharton) Penn Mo. **4**: 867.
— in 1852. Sharpe, **17**: 23.
— Travelers' Album at. (A. Smith) Bentley, **10**: 576.
— Up, afoot. (B. H. Nadal) Hours at Home, **11**: 397.
— Valley of. So. Lit. Mess. **18**: 522.
Champ d'Asile. Anal. M. **13**: 58.
Champ de Mars. Fraser, **31**: 639.
Champ des Martyrs. Sharpe, **32**: 80, 133.
Champagne Wine. (J. F. Sanderson) Knick. **48**: 232. — House. Words, **11**: 51. — Hogg, **5**: 143. — Lond. Soc. **32**: 321.
— Manufacture of. (F. C. L. Wraxall) St. James, **10**: 72.
Champagne Wine Districts of France. Penny M. **13**: 399.
Champe, J. (A. W. Kercheval) N. Ecl. **6**: 227.
Champeaux, Wm. de, and his Times. Chr. Obs. **72**: 843.
Champernowne, Capt. Francis, Memoir of. (C. W. Tattle) N. E. Reg. **28**: 75, 318, 403.
Champfleury, J. Faience Violin. (W. H. Bishop) Atlan. **43**: 609.
Champion, E. Nat. M. **2**: 404, 555.
Championship of England. Penny M. **4**: 111.
Champlain, Samuel de. Am. Hist. Rec. **1**: 433.
— Astrolabe of. (O. H. Marshall) M. Am. Hist. **3**: 179.
— — and of Chaucer. (H. Scadding) Canad. Mo. **18**: 589.
— Expedition against the Onondagas, 1615. (O. H. Marshall) M. Am. Hist. **1**: 1. **2**: 470. — M. Am. Hist. **1**: 561. — (J. G. Shea) Pennsyl. M. **2**: 103.
— Manuscript of. Hist. M. **7**: 169.
— Tomb of, Discovery of. (J. G. Shea) Hist. M. **11**: 100.
Champlain Valley, Archæology of. (G. H. Perkins) Am. Natural. **13**: 731.
Champollion's and Young's Method of interpreting Hieroglyphics. (R. S. Poole) Arch. **39**: 471.
Chance. (E. A. Lawrence) Hours at Home, **11**: 522.
— and Average. (T. Hill) Unita. R. **2**: 352.
— Foundations of. (J. Venn) Princ. n. s. **2**: 471.
— Logic of, in religious Aspects. (A. P. Peabody) Princ. n. s. **5**: 303.
Chances. Curious. Chamb. J. **55**: 379.
— of War; a Tale. (A. Whitelock) Irish Mo. **3**: 305–665. **4**: 21–561. **5**: 42, 92.
Chance Acquaintance. (W. D. Howells) Atlan. **31**: 17–693.
Chance Child. Liv. Age, **109**: 373.
Chance World, A. Ecl. R. **111**: 405.
Chancel, English square. Mercersb. **12**: 547.
— Use of Stone Seats in. (S. Denne) Arch. **10**: 298.
Chancellor's Great Seal. Ecl. M. **40**: 192.
Chancellors, Lord, of England, Campbell's. (W. Empson) Ed. R. **83**: 275. — (J. G. Lockhart) Quar. **77**: 1. — Quar. **82**: 39. — Lond. Q. **32**: 177. — Tait, n. s. **13**: 73, 169. **14**: 26, 88. — No. Brit. **5**: 100. — Liv. Age, **12**: 144. — Fraser, **37**: 429. — Ecl. M. **7**: 244. — Am. Whig R. **6**: 415. — (W. B. O. Peabody) No. Am. **65**: 159. — West. Law J. **5**: 312. — Prosp. R. **4**: 168.
— since Campbell. Liv. Age, **135**: 469.
Chancellor, Vice-, Project of creating a. Ed. R. **21**: 103.
Chancellorship, Lord. Brit. & For. R. **2**: 248.
Chancellorsville, Va., Battle of. (R. E. Rodes) So. Hist. Pap. **2**: 161. — (R. E. Lee) So. Hist. Pap. **3**: 230. — (J. E. B. Stuart) So. Hist. Pap. **4**: 9. — (F. Lee) So. Hist. Pap. **7**: 545. — (F. W. Palfrey) Nation, **4**: 410. — (C. W. Russell) So. R. n. s. **2**: 461. — (E. A. Perry) So. Hist. Pap. **4**: 203.
— Campaign of. (W. Allan) So. Hist. Pap. **9**: 462.
— — Dodge's. (F. F. Brown) Dial (Ch.), **2**: 39.
— Operations at. (R. E. Colston) So. M. **11**: 57.
Chancery and Inns of Court, Antiq. of. Ecl. R. **1**: 412.
Chancery Cases. Barbour's Reports. Hunt, **17**: 392.
— English. Hunt, **17**: 595.
— Sandford's. Hunt, **18**: 628.
Chancery, Court of. Ed. R. **39**: 246, 432. **41**: 410. — Quar. **30**: 272. — So. R. **3**: 63. — For. Q. **5**: 598. — Westm. **1**: 141. — Blackw. **14**: 202. — Chamb. J. **42**: 106.
— — and Religion of Minors. (J. Walton) Month, **15**: 48.
— — History of, Parkes's. Lond. M. **21**: 246. — Ecl. M. **61**: 108.
— — Origin and History of. So. Lit. Mess. **16**: 303.
— Martyrs of. House. Words, **2**: 250, 493.
Chancery Funds, in England. Cornh. **16**: 200. Same art. Ecl. M. **69**: 456.
Chancery Jurisdiction. (J. Story) No. Am. **10**: 140.
Chancery Reform, 1852. Ecl. R. **97**: 704.
Chancery Suit of Gotobed *versus* Blithers. Chamb. J. **48**: 705, 731, 745.
Chandeliers, Improvements in. Pract. M. **6**: 218.
Chandler, Charles F., with portrait. Pop. Sci. Mo. **16**: 833.
Chandler, Johanna, Philanthropy of. Good Words, **7**: 537.
Chandler, Rev. Thomas B., Memoir of, with portrait. (A. H. Hoyt) N. E. Reg. **27**: 227.
Chandler, W. A. Thrice; a Novel. Colburn, **160**: 578.
Chandler, Winthrop, Memoir of, with portrait. N. E. Reg. **33**: 381.
Chandos, Sir John, Tomb of, at Civaux. (S. R. Meyrick) Arch. **20**: 484.
Chandos Picture; a Poem. (E. Pollock) Pioneer, **2**: 61.
Chanet; a Tale. (J. W. De Forest) Galaxy, **9**: 632.
Chang-How and Anarky; a Tale. (J. Woodville) Lippinc. **22**: 114.
Changarnier, Gen. Nicolas A. T. Ev. Sat. **9**: 614.
Change, Beauty of; a Sermon. (J. H. Morison) Mo. Rel. M. **45**: 375.
— for American Notes. (J. G. Lockhart) Quar. **73**: 129.
— for Gold; a Tale. Chamb. J. **22**: 18.
— in the Cabinet; a Sketch. Cornh. **20**: 412.
— of Heart; a Drama. (H. James, jr.) Atlan. **29**: 49.
— of Luck; a Tale. (W. Cyples) Chamb. J. **45**: 1–242.
— of Views; a Tale. (J. Payn) Belgra. **36**: 172.
Changes of Sixty Years. All the Year, **14**: 179.
Changeling, A; a Poem. Cornh. **1**: 329.
Changeling, The. (J. G. Whittier) Atlan. **16**: 20.
Changing the Venue. Belgra. **8**: 513.

Changing World and an unchanging Saviour. Chr. Obs. 45: 1.
Channel. *See* English Channel.
Channel-Fillings in Upper Devonian Shales. (H. S. Williams) Am. J. Sci. 121: 318.
Channel Islands. (S. G. W. Benjamin) Harper, 51: 1. — (G. S. Lefevre) Fortn. 32: 474. Same art. Liv. Age, 143: 487. — Colburn, 117: 127. — Dub. R. 81: 284. — Ecl. R. 81: 540. — Sharpe, 37: 20, 78, 137. — Penny M. 6: 329, 377. — Lond. Q. 26: 453. Same art. Liv. Age, 91: 67.
— and Land Tenure. (F. B. Zincke) Fortn. 25: 1.
— and their Legends. Bentley, 53: 322, 430.
— Celtic Monuments in. (F. C. Lukis) Arch. 35: 232.
— Inglis on. Mo. R. 134: 126.
— Letters from. Tait, n. s. 15: 6, 188.
Channing, Walter. (M. P. Lowe) Unita. R. 6: 553.
Channing, William Ellery. (A. H. Everett) No. Am. 41: 366. — New Eng. 8: 345. — Am. Q. 16: 1. — Liv. Age, 19: 78. — Dem. R. 9: 115. — (G. Bancroft) Dem. R. 12: 524. — Mus. 16: 265. — (W. H. Furness) Chr. Exam. 45: 259. — (A. Stevens) Meth. Q. 9: 50. — Mass. Q. 1: 423. — (J. Martineau) Westm. 50: 317. — Ecl. M. 15: 289. — Ed. R. 50: 125. — Chr. Exam. 33: 228. — (H. T Tuckerman) So. Lit. Mess. 15: 25. — (A. B. Muzzey) Unita. R. 1: 151. 3: 475. — (E. P. Peabody) Unita. R. 7: 33, 286, 520. 8: 162, 387, 626. — (C. MacCauley) Unita. R. 8: 349. — (J. H. Morison) Unita. R. 13: 339. — (M. P. Lowe) Unita. R. 13: 372. — (C. Whitehead) Bentley, 25: 88. — Brit. Q. 8: 295. — Chamb. J. 10: 89. — Liv. Age, 55: 378. — Prosp. R. 4: 391.
— the Abolitionist. (T. Hughes) Macmil. 42: 59.
— and Lucy Aikin. (C. H. Dall) Unita. R. 2: 377.
— and Chalmers. (— Murdock) Am. Presb. R. 2: 438. — (A. Gordon) Unita. R. 13: 318.
— and Edinburgh Review. So. Lit. Mess. 6: 1.
— and Paley. Nat. R. 6: 397.
— and the Unitarian Movement. (G. Reynolds) Unita. R. 13: 353.
— as a Philosopher and Theologian. (G. P. Fisher) Internat. R. 7: 73.
— Bunsen on. (F. H. Hedge) Chr. Exam. 66: 433.
— Centennial of, Literature of. Appleton, 24: 90.
— — Outcome of. (I. T. Hecker) Cath. World, 31: 421.
— Christology of. Unita. R. 9: 286, 338.
— Death of. Dem. R. 11: 561.
— Dedication Sermon, New York. (A. Norton) Chr. Exam. 4: 61.
— Discourse on Burning of the Lexington. Chr. Exam. 28: 68.
— False literary Taste of. (H. Brougham) Ed. R. 69: 214. — Mus. 35: 46.
— Letter to Mr. Clay. So. Lit. Mess. 4: 480.
— Life of. Dub. R. 25: 406.
— Literary and Political Essays. Fraser, 17: 627. 18: 286.
— Memoir of. Ecl. R. 88: 432. — Howitt, 3: 374. — Tait, n. s. 15: 432.
— on the Divinity of Humanity. Westm. 10: 98.
— on Milton. Mo. R. 115: 471. — Lond. M. n. s. 20: 607.
— on Napoleon. Mo. R. 115: 442.
— on Revealed Religion. Blackw. 18: 160.
— on Slavery. (E. Pond) Lit. & Theo. R. 3: 121.
— Perfect Life. O. & N. 7: 93.
— Poems. (E. A. Poe) So. Lit. Mess. 16: 610.
— Relation to Charities and Reforms. (G. L. Chaney) Unita. R. 13: 303.
— Writings of. (L. Withington) Lit. & Theo. R. 1: 304. — (O. Dewey) Chr. Exam. 14: 54. — Westm. 12: 472.
Channing, Wm. E., 2d, Poems of. Dem. R. 13: 309.
Channing, William F. Municipal Electric Fire Telegraph. Am. J. Sci. 63: 58.
Channing, William H., on the Christian Church and Social Reform. Brownson, 6: 209, 438.
Chanoinesses, About. St. Paul's, 6: 376.
Chanson d'Antioche. (J. G. Sheppard) Fortn. 4: 700.
Chanson de Roland. *See* Roland.
Chansons de Geste, French and English. For. Q. 16: 113. — (C. F. Keary) Fraser, 104: 777.
Chansons, Popular, of France. Dub. Univ. 36: 294.
Chantal, St. Françoise de, and her Children. (E. Bowles) Month, 13: 184–694. — (C. M. Yonge) Hours at Home, 10: 53.
— History of. Dub. R. 61: 125.
Chantemerle, Expedition to. (L. S. Costello) Bentley, 29: 599.
Chanticleer. Chamb. J. 48: 794.
Chantilly, Château of. Peop. J. 7: 183.
— 200 Years ago. (T. A. Trollope) St. Paul's, 14: 40.
Chanting in Episcopal Church and its Author. Am. Hist. Rec. 3: 18.
— Jebb on. Mo. R. 162: 513.
Chantrey, Sir Francis. Blackw. 7: 1. — Liv. Age, 24: 387. — Art J. 2: 44. — Reliquary, 3: 17.
— and Allan Cunningham. Ecl. Mus. 2: 481. — Fraser, 27: 664.
— Jones's Life of. Internat. M. 1: 413. — Ecl. R 92: 653.
— Sketch of. Hogg, 5: 53.
— Two Woodcocks of All the Year, 26: 442.
Chantry Lands, Purchase of, by London Companies. (H. Ellis) Arch. 31: 385.
Chap-Books, Humorous. Chamb. J. 58: 657.
Chap-Book Literature. Chamb. J. 24: 1. Same art. Liv. Age, 46: 469. — Chamb. J. 37: 72.
See Book-Hawking.
Chap-Pictures. Chamb. J. 24: 113.
Chapel, The Word. Month, 9: 102.
— — Use of. Cong. 1: 294.
— of the Palms. (C. W. Stoddard) Lippinc. 10: 649.
Chapels. Am. Church R. 32: 447.
— Proprietary, and Church of England. Chr. Rem. 4: 498.
Chapel Choristers. (A. B. Neal) Sharpe, 31: 212.
Chapel Trust Deeds. Cong. M. 22: 570–796.
Chapelizod, Ghost Stories of. Dub. Univ. 37: 85, 427.
— Gossip about. Dub. Univ. 37: 427.
Chapelle and Bachaumont. (T. L. Peacock) Fraser, 57: 502.
Chapellier, Père. Ev. Sat. 9: 70.
Chaperons, and an Afternoon Tea; a Story. (E. Wanton) Lippinc. 28: 372.
Chapin, Alonzo Bowen. (N. S. Richardson) Am. Church R. 11: 448.
Chapin, Edwin H., with portrait. Appleton, 10: 400.
— Address before Richmond Lyceum. So. Lit. Mess. 5: 725.
— as an Orator. Dem. R. 36: 332.
— Crown of Thorns. (T. S. King) Univ. Q. 4: 317.
— Lectures. So. Lit. Mess. 6: 388.
Chaplet of Pearls. (C. M. Yonge) Macmil. 17: 39–495. 18: 57–461. 19: 55, 144. Same art. Hours at Home, 6: 162–551. 7: 1–557. 8: 73–336.
Chaplain's Manual. Danv. Q. 3: 568.
Chaplains, Naval, Work of. Chr. Obs. 70: 866, 919. 71: 111.
Chaplaincy in the Army. Danv. Q. 3: 255.
Chaplin, Daniel. Spirit Pilg. 5: 65.
Chapman, Ernest T. (F. Guthrie) Nature, 6: 182.
Chapman, George. Dramatic Works. Cornh. 30: 23. — Lond. Q. 43: 32. — (H. Southern) Retros. 4: 333. 5: 317.

Chapman, George, and others. Eastward Ho! Blackw. **10**: 127.
Chapman, Henry C. Evolution of Life. (J. J. Lalor) Cath. World, **17**: 145.
Chapman, Jonathan. (E. Peabody) Chr. Exam. **45**: 316.
Chapman, Jonathan, "Johnny Appleseed." (W. D. Haley) Harper, **43**: 830.
Chapman, John Gadsby. Godey, **33**: 117.
Chapman, R. A. Am. Law R. **8**: 162.
Chapman, Thomas. Tour in the United States, 1795–96. Hist. M. **15**: 357.
Chapped Hands, Hydrochloric Acid for. Pract. M. **2**: 220.
Chappows, of the Turkomans. Penny M. **3**: 146.
Chapter from the Life of a Secretary. (L. Waldenberg) Victoria, **21**: 141.
Chapter of Accidents. Lond. Soc. **30**: 385.
Char, The. Penny M. **11**: 476.
— and Char-Fishing. Penny M. **9**: 158.
Character. (R. W. Emerson) No. Am. **102**: 356. — Irish Mo. **3**: 594.
— Æsthetics of. (J. Sully) Fortn. **15**: 505. Same art. Liv. Age, **109**: 551.
— American Ideal of. Liv. Age, **141**: 437.
— and Characteristic Men, Writings on. (S. Merrill) New Eng. **22**: 36.
— and Condition. (T. T. Stone) Unita. R. **10**: 316.
— and its Predicates. (A. A. Miner) Univ. Q. **10**: 248.
— as affected by Non-Self-Consciousness. (R. McC. Edgar) Theo. Ecl. **7**: 311.
— Bain's Study of. Liv. Age, **72**: 351.
— Elements of. (E. W. Reynolds) Univ. Q. **12**: 160.
— Elevated Standard of. West. M. **3**: 271.
— essential to Success. West. R. **4**: 216.
— First Impressions of. Cong. **4**: 52.
— Formation of. (B. F. Tweed) Univ. Q. **13**: 349. — Chr. R. **3**: 497. — So. Lit. Mess. **8**: 401. — Hesp. **1**: 167.
— Greatness of. West. J. **7**: 65, 135.
— indicated by Costumes, etc. Mus. **4**: 346.
— Infamy of. West. M. **4**: 101.
— Intellectual. (E. P. Whipple) Atlan. **1**: 791.
— Manliness of. (C. Robinson) Mo. Rel. M. **6**: 540.
— Men of. (A. Mitchell) Putnam, **3**: 267.
— Mercantile, True. (J. H. Allen) Mo. Rel. M. **11**: 22.
— Method of. (C. A. Bartol) Radical, **8**: 206.
— Moral and mental Culture in. (L. A. Eichelberger) Evang. R. **2**: 94.
— National, Chenevix on. Ecl. R. **55**: 324.
— — Influence of local Causes on. Westm. **72**: 67.
— of a young Princess, Mrs. More's Hints towards forming. Chr. Obs. **4**: 487, 758. — Ecl. R. **3**: 14, 114.
— Personal. Lond. M. **3**: 291.
— Physical Influences upon. (J. Scott) Victoria, **27**: 116.
— Polarity in; Sex in Mind. (R. Randolph) J. Spec. Philos. **11**: 320, 417.
— Right and wrong Side of. Cornh. **4**: 58.
— Sketches of. Godey, **20**: 93.
— — of modern. (Mrs. C. G. F. Gore) Colburn, **60**: 49–470. **61**: 16.
— The strong. (J. Clark) Mercersb **5**: 313.
— Symmetrical. (G. H. Emerson) Univ. Q. **14**: 188.
— Weight of. West. J. **9**: 353.
See Human Character.
Characters described: Amanda, Theodosia, Eusebia. Chr. Obs. **2**: 16–730.
— Dramatic and Romantic, Originals of. Ev. Sat. **10**: 114.
— not appreciated. Dub. Univ. **79**: 426.
— of living Authors by themselves. Blackw. **10**: 69.
— reconsidered. Chamb. J. **12**: 59.
Character Doctor; or Homœopathy in Education. Dub. Univ. **93**: 18.
Character-Drawing. Liv. Age, **140**: 253.
Characteristics. (T. Carlyle) Ed. R. **54**: 351.
— of the Age. (D. Brewster) Good Words, **4**: 7.
— of the Nineteenth Century. Fraser, **21**: 147. — (J. Adams) So. Lit. J. **2**: 161.
Charade. Colburn, **58**: 356. **59**: 13, 261. **61**: 248, 466.
— An acting. Temp. Bar, **28**: 223.
— and its Consequences. (J. Payn) Belgra. **40**: supp. 71.
Charades. (T. K. Hervey) Lond. Soc. **1**: 156. **2**: 78. **3**: 116. **6**: 175. — Colburn, **55**: 402.
— and Dumb Crambo. Lond. Soc. **6**: 499.
Charcoal, Animal, Uses of. J. Frankl. Inst. **6**: 80.
Charcoal-Burner of the Creux du Vau. Dub. Univ. **88**: 741.
Charcoal-Burners in Connecticut. (M. Russell) Knick. **40**: 429.
Charcoal Vacua. Nature, **12**: 217.
Chardin, Jean-Baptiste-Simeon. (S. Colvin) Portfo. **3**: 50.
Chardon Street and Bible Conventions. Dial, **3**: 100.
Charge at Balaklava; a Poem. (J. B. Hope) So. Lit. Mess. **21**: 444.
— at Valley Maloy; a Poem. (J. T. McKay) Putnam, **14**: 435.
Charing-Cross. All the Year, **27**: 326. — Hogg, **2**: 69.
Charing-Cross Hotel. (G. A. Sala) St. James, **14**: 313.
Chariots of the ancient Britons. (S. Pegge) Arch. **7**: 211.
— — Fragments of. (Sir R. C. Hoare) Arch. **21**: 39.
Charitable Contributions, Divine Method of. Chr. R. **9**: 583.
Charitable Endowments of England. Lond. Q. **29**: 253.
Charitable Institutions. (H. L. Synnot) Contemp. **26**: 487. — Westm. **2**: 97.
— and the Church. (J. H. A. Bomberger) Mercersb. **12**: 64.
— Essays on Principles of. Mo. R. **142**: 574.
— of Genoa. Dub. R. **14**: 97.
— of Naples. Dub. R. **15**: 29.
Charitable Relief, Clergy and. (C. E. Maurice) Macmil. **36**: 168.
Charitable Trusts. Dub. R. **34**: 407.
— Administration of. Ed. R. **83**: 475.
— Bill in England and Wales on, 1846. Ecl. R. **83**: 618.
Charitable Uses, Law of. Chr. Rem. **12**: 30.
Charitable Work and Women. Cornh. **30**: 417.
Charity, The Word, in English New Testament. Chr. Obs. **36**: 466, 648.
Charity. (J. G. Fitch) Fraser, **80**: 679.
— Abuse of, Case of. (W. Gilbert) Contemp. **31**: 770.
— Aims and Means of. (B. Lambert) Contemp. **23**: 462.
— Almsgiving as taught by Cyprian. (J. W. Nevin) Mercersb. **4**: 552.
— and Decision. (O. Dewey) Chr. Exam. **14**: 200.
— and Misery. Dem. R. **40**: 441.
— and Pauperism. (W. G. Howgrave) St. James, **33**: 78.
— and Philanthropy. (O. A. Brownson) Cath. World, **4**: 434.
— at Home. All the Year, **15**: 286.
— Christian, and Political Economy. Dub. R. **81**: 361. **82**: 89. **83**: 13.
— — Method of. (C. F. Barnard) Chr. Exam. **81**: 62.
— Curiosities of. Chamb. J. **37**: 59.
— J. Edwards on. (T. Edwards) New Eng. **10**: 222.
— Indigence and Benevolence. (W. C. Taylor) Bentley, **6**: 575.
— Medical, Extent and Abuses of. Westm. **101**: 174.
— — in England, Methods of Administration of. Westm. **101**: 464.
— More excellent Way of. (O. Hill) Macmil. **35**: 126.
— Noxious and beneficent. Westm. **59**: 62.
— of Men of the World. (L. F. Tisistro) Godey, **25**: 73.
— Official. (G. Howard) Cath. World, **15**: 407.
— Organization of. (F. P. Cobbe) Theo. R. **4**: 553. — (W. H. Hodge) Penn Mo. **11**: 177.
— Ostentatious. Chr. Mo. Spec. **1**: 569.

Charity, Out-Door Parish, in England. Westm. 101: 323.
— Out-Door Relief. Quar. 79: 463.
— Pauperism, and Self-Help. Westm. 103: 107.
— Posthumous, Curiosities of. Chamb. J. 17: 298. Same art. Liv. Age, 33: 612.
— Private, Liberty of. Once a Week, 8: 397.
— — Osborne on Regulation of. Mo. R. 146: 520.
— Public. Hogg, 1: 369. — (F. B. Sanborn) No. Am. 110: 327.
— — without Humiliation. Cornh. 6: 44.
— Relief of casual Distress. St. James, 23: 415.
— Science of. (C. L. Brace) Nation, 8: 457.
— Systematic. (L. Bacon) Chr Mo. Spec. 7: 645.
— True and false. (J. P. Quincy) O. & N. 9: 181.
— Village Homes for Girls. Victoria, 17: 376.
— What is? (T. S. Arthur) Godey, 23: 98.
— Wisdom in. (C. G. Ames) Penn Mo. 8: 48.
— Works of. Dub. R. 41: 123.
See Almsgiving; Beneficence.
Charities, Abuse of. Ed. R. 33: 109. — (H. Brougham) Pamph. 13: 1. — Chr. Obs. 17: 798.
— Ancient and modern. Penny M. 13: 52.
— Bogus, of New York. (R. J. Hinton) O. & N. 11: 477.
— Catholic View of. Irish Q. 9: 227.
— Christianity and. (S.W. S. Dutton) New Eng. 11: 571.
— Church, and Private Munificence. (W. H. Lewis) Am. Church R. 16: 94.
— City parochial. (A. J. Wilson) Macmil. 41: 469.
— East and West. (Countess Spencer) Fraser, 82: 348, 432.
— Endowed, and Pauperism. (H. G. Robinson) Macmil. 41: 242.
— English. (Sir F. B. Head) Quar. 53: 473. — (S. G. Grady) St. James, 1: 131.
— European. (K. G. Wells) Mo. Rel. M. 44: 467. — Mo. Rel. M. 17: 73.
— in the Black Forest. Good Words, 4: 25.
— in Soho. (E. L. Linton) Good Words, 14: 364.
— Inspection of, State and volunteer. (E. L. Godkin) Nation, 32: 345.
— misapplied. St. Paul's, 8: 222.
— of Boston. (S. A. Eliot) No. Am. 61: 135.
— of Cities a Draw for Beggars. (W. Chambers) Chamb. J. 51: 337. 55: 273.
— of Europe. (E. Smith) Theo. R. 3: 49.
— of France. (O. B. Frothingham) Nation, 4: 270.
— of London in 1861. Ecl. R. 117: 167.
— — Parochial. (W. H. James) Contemp. 33: 67. — (R. H. Hadden) 19th Cent. 9: 324. — Good Words, 20: 602.
— — — Ethics of. Good Words, 20: 573.
— — Unseen. Fraser, 39: 639.
— of Rome. (R. Seton) Cath. World, 22: 266.
— Public. (R. H. Clarke) Cath. World, 17: 1. — (F. Parkman) Chr. Exam. 7: 367.
— — and their Abuses. St. James, 33: 665.
— — Supervision of. (F. B. Sanborn) Am. Soc. Sci. J. 1: 72. — Penn Mo. 11: 649.
— Ragged Homes and Ministering Women. Lond. Q. 14: 416.
— Social. (A. B. Neal) Godey, 58: 433.
— Specimen. (J. McCarthy) Cath. World, 21: 289.
— State Aid to private. (J. R. G. Hassard) Cath. World, 29: 127, 255.
— Work of Volunteers in Organization of. (O. Hill) Macmil. 26: 441.
See Begging; Benevolence.
Charity Bazaar. Cornh. 4: 338.
Charity Boy. Hogg, 1: 49.
Charity Electioneering. (C. Trevelyan) Macmil. 29: 171.
Charity Lecture. (G. L. Chaney) Mo. Rel. M. 51: 64.
Charity Organization Society. Macmil. 40: 24.
Charity Schools. Chr. Obs. 3: 541-737.
Charity Schools in England. Westm. 99: 450.
— in France. Lond. M. 21: 14.
Charity School System. Penny M. 6: 349.
Charlecote Hall. Antiquary, 3: 181.
Charlemagne. (E. S. Creasy) Bentley, 33: 22, 148, 391. — Knick. 32: 219. — Sharpe, 45: 30. — (T. De Quincey) Blackw. 32: 786. — (H. H. Milman) Quar. 48: 421.
— and his Times. Nat. Q. 6: 341.
— Character of. Portfo. (Den.) 15: 251.
— James's History of. Ecl. R. 56: 310.
— Legends of. (Earl Stanhope) Fraser, 74: 72.
— Literary Movement in Time of. (A. Ebert) Western, 5: 155.
— Reign of. (Mrs. T. Robinson) No. Am. 81: 113.
— Scholarship of. Brownson, 16: 437.
— Schools of. (J. H. Newman) Am. J. Educ. 24: 44.
— — Mullinger's. (T. Harper) Month, 31: 164.
— Sketch of, with portrait. Ecl. M. 53: 424.
— Tomb of. (M. S. Snow) Western, 6: 286.
— Vétault on. (J. M. Hart) Nation, 25: 301.
— Wars in Spain. Retros. 3: 294.
Charlemont, James, Earl of, Hardy's Life of. (Lord Dudley) Quar. 6: 124. — (F. Jeffrey) Ed. R. 19: 95. — Dub. Univ. 8: 375, 534, 675. 9: 72. — Ecl. R. 17: 1.
Charles I. Am. Q. 13: 197. — Mus. 13: 438. — Dem. R. 21: 33. — Ed. R. 40: 92. — (T. B. Macaulay) Ed. R. 42: 325. 48: 138. — Mo. R. 116: 427. — Retros. 8: 1.
— Miss Aikin's Court of. Ecl. R. 58: 461. — Ed. R. 58: 398. — Am. Q. 15: 1. — Westm. 22: 8.
— and his Father. (P. Bayne) Contemp. 24: 696, 904. Same art. Liv. Age, 123: 387, 549.
— and Marquis of Worcester. All the Year, 32: 227. — St. Paul's, 3: 202.
— and Scotch Commissioners. (J. Allen) Ed. R. 69: 104.
— and the Parliament in 1648. (J. Bruce) Arch. 42: 258.
— and the 30th of January. (D. Cook) Once a Week, 12: 268.
— Arrest of the Five Members by. Quar. 108: 499. — Liv. Age, 66: 413.
— Ashburnham's Narrative of. Mo. R. 123: 387. — (J. Allen) Ed. R. 52: 26.
— Attempted Escapes of. Liv. Age, 36: 100.
— Bunch of Letters of. Hogg, 13: 303.
— Court and Times of. (T. Birch) Colburn, 83: 508.
— Daughters of. Liv. Age, 38: 183. Same art. Ecl. M. 30: 77.
— Diet and Fare of, when Duke of York. (E. Turnor) Arch. 15: 1.
— Discovery of his Body. Anal. M. 2: 322.
— D'Israeli's Life of. Mo. R. 123: 193. — Westm. 14: 486. — Ecl. R. 48: 97. — Colburn, 23: 437.
— Eikon Basilike. Month, 40: 346.
— — Authorship of. (W. B. Odgers) Mod. R. 1: 617.
— Execution of. Selec. Ed. R. 4: 136.
— Forster on the Reign of. Fraser, 70: 539.
— Gardiner's Personal Government of. (A. V. Dicey) Nation, 21: 88. 27: 12.
— Great Men of the Reign of. (L. Hunt) Colburn, 47: 207. — Ecl. R. 67: 605.
— How his Head was loosened. All the Year, 11: 253.
— in Search of a Wife. Bentley, 53: 139. Same art. Liv. Age, 76: 497.
— in 1646. Liv. Age, 50: 713.
— in Carisbrook Castle. (W. S. Dugdale) Macmil. 33: 116.
— Intended Escape from Carisbrook Castle, 1647-48. All the Year, 32: 12. — Arch. 19: 149
— Intended Spanish Marriage of. (J. Spedding) Fraser, 81: 677.

Charles I., Journey into Spain. Mus. **6**: 255.
— Last Days of. Anal. M. **2**: 430.
— — Herbert's. Chr. Obs. **13**: 365.
— Raumer's Character and Times of. Tait, n. s. **4**: 73.
— Reign of. Westm. **112**: 101.
— taking Leave of his Children. Godey, **30**: 196.
— Trial of. (J. Reade) Canad. Mo. **9**: 21. — Liv. Age, **39**: 67.
— — and Execution of. (J. Reade) New Dom. **17**: 145.
— Unpublished Gold Coin of. (M. Noble) Arch. **13**: 23.
— Warrant to deliver the Fleet to the French. (G. Duckett) Arch. **17**: 110.
— Who was the Executioner of? (D. Cook) Once a Week, **11**: 12.
Charles II. Blackw. **82**: 727. — Selec. Ed. R. **4**: 152. — (C. Barker) Retros. **7**: 183. — Mus. **4**: 193. **5**: 427.
— and Catholics. Cath. World, **2**: 827.
— and his Son, James Stuart. Cath. World, **2**: 577.
— Army Establishment of. Mo. R. **151**: 65.
— Concealment at Boscobel. Retros. **14**: 47. — Mus. **9**: 421.
— Court of. Retros. **13**: 167. — So. Lit. Mess. **1**: 312. — West. M. **3**: 248.
— Death of. (T. B. Macaulay) Liv. Age, **20**: 183.
— Escape from Worcester. Once a Week, **30**: 139. — Westm. **69**: 428. — Ecl. M. **44**: 459.
See Boscobel Tracts.
— Last Moments of. House. Words, **9**: 277.
— Letter to Col. Veel to raise Troops. (W. Veel) Arch. **14**: 75.
— Medal struck at his Birth. (M. Noble) Arch. **13**: 20.
— Morals and Literature of the Restoration. (A. Bisset) Macmil. **6**: 35.
— Personal History of. Tait, n. s. **18**: 353. — Liv. Age, **31**: 183.
— Regalia made for the Coronation of. (R. Cole) Arch. **29**: 262.
— Residence at Bruges. (G. S. Steinman) Arch. **35**: 335.
— Sayings of. Liv. Age, **30**: 39.
— Secret History of. Ho. & For. R. **1**: 146.
— Sidney's Diary of Times of. Mo. R. **161**: 320.
Charles V., Emperor. (J. F. Kirk) No. Am. **76**: 299. — (O. Delapierre) St. James, **13**: 433. — Bentley, **24**: 460. — Blackw. **82**: 40. — Ecl. R. **116**: 432. — Ed. R. **101**: 72. Same art. Ecl. M. **34**: 381. Same art. Liv. Age, **44**: 579. — Nat. M. **3**: 273. — Liv. Age, **19**: 561. — Ecl. M. **16**: 229.
— Abdication of. Dub. Univ. **72**: 207.
— Age of. Dub. Univ. **36**: 429. Same art. Ecl. M. **71**: 1332.
— and Francis I., Mignet's. Fraser, **74**: 489. Same art. Ecl. M. **68**: 22.
— and his Contemporaries. Chr. Obs. **52**: 14.
— and the German Protestants. Ecl. M. **69**: 117.
— and a Monk. Lond. M. **1**: 273.
— Autobiography of. Liv. Age, **75**: 331.
— Chief Victories of. Ed. R. **132**: 67.
— Cloister Life of. Chamb. J. **18**: 359. — Cornh. **19**: 482. — Dub. R. **37**: 503. — Chr. Rem. **26**: 99. — Liv. Age, **35**: 529. — Fraser, **43**: 367, 528. Same art. Liv. Age, **29**: 289, 544. Same art. Ecl. M. **23**: 93, 233. Same art. Internat. M. **3**: 376, 520.
— — Stirling's. Chr. Obs. **53**: 234. — (W. C. Robinson) Month, **29**: 333. — Dub. Univ. **41**: 539. — Cath. World. **5**: 671. — Quar. **92**: 107. Same art. Ecl. M. **29**: 13. Same art. Liv. Age, **36**: 481.
— Correspondence of. (W. Bradford) Bentley, **28**: 180. — Dub. R. **29**: 287.
— Death of. Colburn, **156**: 71.
— Last Days of. Colburn, **101**: 379. Same art. Ecl. M. **33**: 488.
Charles V., Emperor, Last Years of. (F. A. Mignet) Bentley, **33**: 452, 530, 661. **34**: 89, 182, 254.
— Robertson's History of the Reign of. New Q. **6**: 77. — Liv. Age, **52**: 365.
Charles VIII. of France, Character and Reign of. Temp. Bar, **47**: 176. Same art. Liv. Age, **130**: 43.
Charles IX. of France, Chronicle of Times of. Westm. **13**: 495.
Charles X. of France, at Holyrood. (M. H. Toland) Cath. World, **19**: 419.
— Coronation of. Colburn, **14**: 223.
— Demolition of the Throne of. (J. S. C. Abbott) Harper, **43**: 114.
Charles II. of Spain; a bewitched King. (J. Bowring) Macmil. **7**: 487. — Mo. R. **151**: 359.
— Court of. Nat. R. **14**: 461. Same art. Ecl. M. **56**: 453. Same art. Liv. Age, **74**: 51.
Charles XI. of Sweden, Remarkable Vision of. Fraser, **1**: 120. — St. James, **15**: 70.
Charles XII. of Sweden. (A. D. Vandam) Tinsley, **20**: 145. — Colburn, **124**: 431. — Tinsley, **24**: 290.
— and Max Emanuel. Fraser, **22**: 171. — Mus. **39**: 369.
— and Peter the Great. (T. Bulgarin) Colburn, **78**: 17.
— Death of. Dub. Univ. **63**: 564.
Charles XIV. of Sweden, Reminiscences of. Colburn, **72**: 53.
Charles XV. of Sweden, Poems of. Cornh. **21**: 91.
Charles the Bold. (J. S. Barry) Univ. Q. **21**: 329. — (E. A. Freeman) Nat. R. **18**: 424. Same art. Liv. Age, **81**: 435. — Blackw. **95**: 249. — Colburn, **125**: 294.
— Kirk's History of. (E. A. Freeman) Fortn. **10**: 349. — (E. E. Hale) Chr. Exam. **76**: 240. — (C. C. Hazewell) No. Am. **109**: 596. — (M. Heilprin) Nation, **6**: 512. — (W. Stigand) Contemp. **9**: 576. — Chr. Obs. **64**: 249. **70**: 625. — Ed. R. **119**: 530. Same art. Ecl. M. **62**: 345, 441. — Liv. Age, **80**: 252, 423.
Charles Edward, the Pretender. (G. W. Greene) No. Am. **64**: 1. — Blackw. **104**: 259. Same art. Liv. Age, **99**: 3. — Colburn, **130**: 296. Same art. Liv. Age, **81**: 131. — Mus. **41**: 345.
— Adventures of, in the Hebrides. Colburn, **60**: 323.
— Birth of. Mus. **44**: 271.
— Ewald's Life of. (A. V. Dicey) Nation, **21**: 389.
— Later Life of. Irish Mo. **3**: 675.
— Memoirs of. Ecl. R. **82**: 686. — Portfo.(Den.) **27**: 23.
— Traditions concerning. (V. P. Griffith) Dub. Univ. **56**: 271.
Charles the Good, Count of Flanders. (W. C. Robinson) Month, **35**: 86.
Charles of Anjou. Colburn, **120**: 417.
Charles of Bourbon and Coriolanus. (J. W. Calcraft) Dub. Univ. **41**: 418.
Charles of Orleans. Cornh. **34**: 695.
Charles, Mrs. E. Schonberg-Cotta Series. (L. Bacon) New Eng. **27**: 164.
Charles, T., Morgan's Life of. Ecl. R. **48**: 445.
Charles Ashton. Chr. Disc. **4**: 437.
Charles Chesterfield; a Novel. *See* Life of Charles Chesterfield.
Charles Maitland; or the Force of Imagination. (Mrs. M. S. Whitaker) Godey, **56**: 402, 498.
Charles O'Malley. (C. Lever) Dub. Univ. **15**: 345–664. **16**: 55–709. **17**: 118–736. **18**: 37–643. Same art. Mus. **41**: 125–605. **42**: 105–587. **43**: 81–532. **44**: 110, 217.
Charles Vernon; a Transatlantic Tale. Ed. R. **89**: 83.
Charles River, Mass. (J. Trowbridge) Appleton, **18**: 193.
Charles River Bridge *versus* Warren Bridge. New York R. **2**: 385.
Charleston, S. C. Mus. **21**: 139, 220, 351. — (F. Hunt) Hunt, **22**: 499.

Charleston, S. C., and Savannah. De Bow, 8: 243. 11: 140. 18: 516.
— and the West. De Bow, 24: 64.
— Climate and Health of. (T. M. Logan) So. Lit. J. 2: 348.
— College of. Am. Q. Reg. 12: 303. — De Bow, 22: 505.
— Commerce of. Hunt, 13: 571.
— Description of. (W. G. Simms) Harper, 15: 1.
— Geology of. (F. S. Holmes) Am. J. Sci. 57: 187.
— Grain and Provision Trade of. De Bow, 17: 541.
— Harbor of. De Bow, 26: 698.
— — Improvement of, by Jetties. (Q. A. Gillmore) Ecl. Engin. 19: 193.
— in 1774. Hist. M. 9: 341.
— in the Civil War. (J. W. De Forest) Atlan. 7: 488.
— — Bombardment of, 1863. Cornh. 10: 99.
— — Confederate Operations before, 1862. So. Hist. Pap. 8: 541.
— — Defense of, July, 1864. (S. Jones) So. Hist. Pap. 2: 192.
— — Defenses of, Gillmore on. No. Am. 101: 241.
— — Four Years under Fire at. (W. F. G. Peck) Harper, 31: 358.
— — Life in Fort Wagner. Land We Love, 3: 351.
— — Operations against, 1863. Fraser, 74: 101.
— — — in Dec., 1864. (S. Jones) So. Hist. Pap. 3: 261.
— — Siege of. (R. S. Davis) U. S. Serv. M. 1: 169, 273, 462. — Nat. Q. 17: 275.
— — Torpedo Service at. (W. T. Glassel) So. Hist. Pap. 4: 225. — (G. T. Beauregard) So. Hist. Pap. 5: 146.
— Life at. Once a Week, 4: 231.
— Maritime Prosperity of. De Bow, 17: 82.
— Medical History of. So. Lit. J. 4: 493.
— Public Improvements of. (E. Herriott) De Bow, 7: 339, 389.
— Reminiscences of, 1830–32. Mo. Rel. M. 25: 111.
— Resources of. (E. Herriott) De Bow, 3: 516.
— Society of. So. Q. 23: 381.
— Statistics of. De Bow, 9: 307.
— Vendue at, in 1842. (N. S. Dodge) Galaxy, 7: 119.
Charlestown, Mass., Burning of Ursuline Convent at. (A. Norton) Chr. Exam. 17: 131. 33: 391.
— Churches and Ministers of. Am. Q. Reg. 10: 54. 12: 234.
— First Church in. (J. F. Hunnewell) N. E. Reg. 24: 273.
— — Account Books of. (J. F. Hunnewell) N. E. Reg. 34: 97.
— Ministers up to 1840. (S. Sewall) Am. Q. Reg. 13: 37.
— Records of. N. E. Reg. 20: 109. 23: 187, 279, 435. 24: 7, 131, 273. 25: 62, 147, 339. 26: 49, 153, 249. 27: 140, 275. 28: 120, 448. 29: 67, 291. 30: 178. 31: 78, 214, 325. 32: 61, 169, 287. 33: 205, 342.
— Robert Calley's Diary at, 1699–1765. N. E. Reg. 16: 34, 129.
Charlestown, N. H., Petition for its Protection, 1746. N. E. Reg. 13: 7.
Charlestown, Pa., Historic Sketch of. (I. Anderson) Potter Am. Mo. 4: 26.
Charlesworth, Maria L. Ministry of Life. Lond. Q. 11: 395.
Charley's Stores; an Egyptian Sketch. Dub. Univ. 60: 495.
Charlia; a Tale. Cornh. 31: 40. Same art. Ecl. M. 84: 362. Same art. Liv. Age, 124: 596.
Charlie Carew. (A. Cudlip) Lond. Soc. 10: 292–497.
Charlie Norman; a Tale. (E. Courtenay) Belgra. 14: 475. 15: 101.
Charlotte Caroline Augusta, Princess of Wales. (A. Manning) Liv. Age, 66: 269, 369 — (Mrs. C. E. Norton) Macmil. 5: 441. — Temp. Bar, 62: 375. — Potter Am. Mo. 10: 23. — Quar. 111: 41. Same art. Liv. Age, 72: 531.
Charlotte Caroline Augusta, Princess of Wales, and Mrs. Campbell. (L. C. Frampton) Gent. M. n. s. 17: 275.
— and Claremont. Ecl. R. 111: 612. 112: 63.
— Death of. Chr. Obs. 16: 746. 17: 44. — Blackw. 2: 250. 4: 353. 10: 222.
— — Croly's Poem on. Ecl. R. 27: 579.
— — Poem on. Blackw. 3: 5. — Lond. M. 2: 146.
— — Sermons on. Ecl. R. 27: 84, 279.
— Unpublished Letters of. Quar. 134: 1. Same art. Ecl. M. 80: 385. Same art. Liv. Age, 116: 515.
Charlotte Elizabeth of Bavaria. All the Year, 7: 498.
Charlotte Elizabeth (*pseud.*). *See* Tonna, C. E.
Charlotte's Inheritance; a Novel. (M. E. Braddon) Belgra. 5: 244–569. 6: 133–601. 7: 128–569.
Charlotte's System; a Story. (Mrs. F. Rye) Canad. Mo. 17: 24.
Charlton House, Kent. Penny M. 14: 265.
Charlton Hunt, The. All the Year, 42: 88. — (I. Fenton) Once a Week, 7: 641.
Charms. Chamb. J. 50: 542.
— and Exorcisms. (A. Wallis) Reliquary, 17: 141.
— Medical Basis of. (E. T. Blake) Dub. Univ. 90: 499.
Charm-Doctor; an Incident of Wales. St. James, 2: 219.
Charmed Cup of Stratford; a Poem. (M. Collins) Dub. Univ. 59: 308.
Charmed Life; a Sketch. (D. Ker) Canad. Mo. 12: 363.
Charming Fellow; a Tale. (F. E. Trollope) All the Year, 33: 457–553. 34: 1–617. 35: 19–467.
Charnwood, Cistercian Monastery at. House. Words, 15: 390.
Charnwood Forest, Potter's History and Antiquities of. Mo. R. 160: 207.
Charts and Dangers at Sea. (A. W. Stiffe) Geog. M. 2: 104.
Charter, The; a Connecticut Tale. Dem. R. 1: 330.
Charter House, The. (G. Turner) Sharpe, 33: 71. — Chamb. J. 34: 35.
— and its Founder. Bentley, 55: 208.
— Chronicles of. Fraser, 35: 340.
— Poor Brothers of. House. Words, 5: 285. 12: 409.
— Visit to. Chamb. J. 2: 49.
Charter Oak. (S. Bliss) Hist. M. 1: 2. — (W. T. R. Saffell) Potter Am. Mo. 6: 412.
Chartier, Alain, Early French Poet. Lond. M. 7: 552.
Chartism. Fraser, 37: 579. — Am. Ecl. 1: 41. — Ecl. R. 75: 429.
— at Home and abroad, 1839. Mo. R. 151: 21.
— Carlyle's. Brit. & For. R. 11: 1. Same art. Am. Ecl. 3: 205. — Brit. & For. R. 12: 303. — Chr. Exam. 29: 119. — Dem. R. 8: 13. — Tait, n. s. 7: 115. — Mo. R. 151: 243.
— in England, 1841. Ecl. R. 75: 429.
— — and English Credit. Dem. R. 8: 179.
— in Monmouthshire. Dub. R. 8: 271.
— Mazzini on. Tait, n. s. 7: 385.
Chartist's Song. Dub. Univ. 17: 248.
Chartists, The. Tait, n. s. 7: 135–811.
— of Britain. Tait, n. s. 15: 295.
— and English Reform. Ecl. R. 87: 620.
— and universal Suffrage. Blackw. 46: 289.
— How to disarm. Blackw. 63: 653.
— Trial of. Tait, n. s. 6: 532, 619.
Chartist Demonstration, April, 1848. Blackw. 63: 780.
Chartist Riots, 1842. Blackw. 52: 410, 642.
Chartley Castle and the Ferrers Family. (Mrs. A. T. Thomson) Fraser, 36: 415.
Chartres, Robert, Duke of. Ecl. Mus. 3: 380. — with portrait, Ev. Sat. 11: 179.
Chartres, Cathedral of. (E. M. Raymond) Cath. World, 18: 235.
— — Porch of. Penny M. 5: 113.
— Our Lady of. (M. P. Thompson) Cath. World, 17: 834.

Chartres, Fort, 1768–81. Hist. M. **8**: 257.
Chartreuse, Grande, Monastery of. Penny M. **1**: 65.
— and the Waldensian Valleys of Piedmont. (J. L. Davids) Victoria, **2**: 143.
— A Night at. (M. P. Thompson) Cath. World, **22**: 712.
— Visit to. (G. Mansfield) Cath. World, **18**: 118. — Lond. Soc. **36**: 271.
Charwoman, The London. Chamb. J. **22**: 119.
Charwoman's Story. House. Words, **6**: 597.
Chase, Carlton, Bishop of New Hampshire. Am. Church R. **24**: 315.
Chase, Irah. Apostolic Constitutions. Am. Church R. **1**: 536. — (R. Emerson) Bib. Sac. **5**: 296. — (A. Lamson) Chr. Exam. **44**: 223. — (J. Forsyth) Princ. **21**: 42. — Chr. R. **13**: 201.
Chase, Jeremiah T., Sketch of. So. Lit. Mess. **4**: 354.
Chase, Philander, Bishop of Ohio. (G. Burgess) Am. Church R. **6**: 24.
— Notable Corruption of the Bible. (J. L. Kingsley) New Eng. **7**: 470.
— Reminiscences. (S. Totten) Am. Church R. **1**: 395. — Chr. Obs. **41**: 499, 738, 793. **42**: 483. **43**: 133. — Mus. **43**: 253.
Chase, Salmon P. (V. B. Denslow) Putnam, **12**: 111. — (E. S. Hamlin) Internat. R. **2**: 662. — (C. C. Nott) Nation, **16**: 330. — Hunt, **63**: 261. — with portrait, Ecl. M. **81**: 373. — Republic, **1**: 297.
— Character of. (S. J. Field) Overland, **11**: 305.
— Election to Senate, 1849. Republic, **4**: 179.
— First Budget of. Nat. R. **14**: 304.
— First Visit to Washington. (J. T. Trowbridge) Atlan. **13**: 448.
— Home Life of. (D. Lloyd) Atlan. **32**: 526.
— Judicial Record of. (J. S. Benson) Harper, **47**: 760.
— Memoir of. Mo. Rel. M. **49**: 583.
— Official Conduct of. (I. Y. Redcliffe) No. Am. **122**: 337.
Chase Genealogy. (J. Coffin) N. E. Reg. **1**: 68.
Chase, A; a Tale. (S. F. Cooper) Internat. M. **1**: 77.
Chase, The, History and Laws of. (A. E. Cockburn) 19th Cent. **8**: 550, 955.
Chase for Love. Tinsley, **11**: 699.
— of the Siren; a Poem. (W. Thornbury) Once a Week, **6**: 629.
Chased by an Engine; a Conductor's Story. (E. P. Buffett) Lippinc. **21**: 754.
Chasles, Michel. (R. Tucker) Nature, **23**: 174, 225. — with portrait, Pop. Sci. Mo. **18**: 840.
Chasles, Philarète. Colburn, **104**: 453. Same art. Liv. Age, **46**: 662. — Ecl. R. **112**: 615.
Chastelân and Mary Stuart. St. James, **10**: 60, 201.
Chastelard, P. de B. de, Story of. (W. G. Simms) Lippinc. **1**: 263.
Chastellux, Marquis de. Cath. World, **1**: 181.
Chastisement, Divine. (N. Macleod) Good Words, **4**: 202.
— Uses of. Princ. **4**: 342.
Chastity, Development and Maintenance of. Westm. **114**: 419.
Château Courance. (J. V. Sears) Lippinc. **20**: 235.
Château de Beaucour; a Ghost Story. Temp. Bar, **19**: 37.
Château de Vandyk, Le. (C. Lever) Dub. Univ. **7**: 73.
Château en Espagne. Tinsley, **19**: 147.
Château Regnier. Ecl. M. **29**: 417.
— a Tale. (M. E. Brooks) Cath. World **14**: 520.
Château Life in England. Chamb. J. **13**: 1–154. Same art. Liv. Age, **25**: 92.
Chateaubriand, F. A. de. (C. H. Brigham) Chr. Exam. **66**: 333. — (K. Cook) Lond. Soc. **22**: 13. Same art. Ecl. M. **79**: 343. — (H. T. Tuckerman) Meth. Q. **13**: 107. — (A. Laugel) Internat. R. **8**: 253, 632. — (A. H. Everett) No. Am. **27**: 226. — with portrait, Ecl. M. **15**: 271. — Am. Q. **21**: 28. — For. Q. **10**: 297.
Chateaubriand, F. A. de. Blackw. **31**: 553. **32**: 217. **35**: 608. **36**: 240, 802. **37**: 620. — Westm. **50**: 568. — Mus. **21**: 289. **25**: 161. **26**: 121. — Ecl. Mus. **2**: 465. — Select J. **1**: 222. — Liv. Age, **19**: 543. **27**: 577. — Colburn, **83**: 464. — West. Mo. R. **1**: 609. — Bentley, **24**: 169, 597. **25**: 66–533. **26**: 70–504. — Chamb. J. **10**: 201. — Nat. R. **12**: 1. Same art. Liv. Age, **68**: 707. Same art. Ecl. M. **54**: 433.
— and De Genoude. Fraser, **27**: 687.
— and his Times. Colburn, **115**: 88. — Temp. Bar, **40**: 194, 373. Same art. Liv. Age, **120**: 480. **121**: 287.
— Autobiography. Blackw. **68**: 33. Same art. Liv. Age, **23**: 49.
— Beauties of Christianity. Anal. M. **2**: 114. — (J. Foster) Ecl. R. **18**: 55, 191.
— Conversations of. Blackw. **37**: 620.
— Criticism of. (L. E. Landon) Colburn, **48**: 62.
— Early Life of. Ecl. R. **90**: 275.
— Latest Productions of. For. R. **1**: 469.
— Life of. Portfo. (Den.) **24**: 207. — Sharpe, **7**: 235.
— Martyrs. (J. Foster) Ecl. R. **16**: 883. Same art. Anal. M. **1**: 355.
— Memoirs. Blackw. **66**: 292. Same art. Liv. Age, **105**: 283. — Brit. Q. **12**: 501.
— Monarchy. Quar. **15**: 419.
— Moral and political Study of. Hogg, **6**: 198.
— Obituary Notice of. Tait, n. s. **15**: 572.
— on the Spanish War. For. Q. **21**: 375.
— Recollections of Italy, England, America, etc. Portfo. (Den.) **16**: 399.
— Villemain's Life of. Colburn, **112**: 453. — No. Brit. **29**: 1. Same art. Ecl. M. **45**: 243. Same art. Liv. Age, **58**: 853.
— Visit to the Tomb of. (L. Forbes) Once a Week, **17**: 232.
Chateaubriand's Ducks. (J. E. Cooke) Lippinc. **11**: 351.
Châtelaine sans Château. (L. de la Ramé) Bentley, **50**: 221. Same art. Liv. Age, **71**: 365.
Chater, Daniel, and William Galley, Murder of, 1747. House. Words, **18**: 547.
Chatham, Earl. *See* Pitt, William.
Chatham Dockyards. House. Words, **3**: 552.
Chatham, Mass., Records of. N. E. Reg. **7**: 81, 153.
Chatsworth. Lond. Soc. **14**: 521. — Penny M. **8**: 349.
— and Haddon, Day at. (T. L. Cuyler) Godey, **29**: 231.
— Day at. (Mrs. S. C. Hall) Art J. **4**: 28. Same art. Internat. M. **5**: 291.
— Seven Foresters of; an old Ballad. Lond. M. **5**: 129.
Chatsworth; an anonymous Novel. Mo. R. **164**: 104.
Chattanooga, Battle of, with map. U. S. Serv. M. **1**: 5. — (W. F. G. Shanks) Harper, **36**: 137.
— Campaign of. (O. O. Howard) Atlan. **38**: 203.
— Raising the Siege of. (R. L. Kimberley) Lippinc. **18**: 211.
Chatterton, Thomas. (R. Edgcumbe) Gent. M. n. s. **21**: 564. — Blackw. **107**: 453. Same art. Ecl. M. **74**: 671. — Quar. **150**: 78. Same art. Liv. Age, **146**: 515. — Lond. Q. **41**: 402. — Lond. M. **20**: 504. — Hogg, **9**: 108. — Ecl. M. **39**: 351. — Liv. Age, **51**: 38. **52**: 603. — Internat. M. **2**: 289. — Sharpe, **8**: 205.
— and his Works. (A. E. Kroeger) Nat. Q. **14**: 306. — Mo. R. **159**: 1. — New York R. **2**: 214. — (Sir W. Scott) Ed. R. **4**: 214. — Ecl. Mus. **1**: 101.
— Death of; a Poem. Tait, n. s. **25**: 81.
— Dix's Life of. (J. Foster) Ecl. R. **67**: 529.
— Life of. Lond. M. **9**: 631.
— Literary Impostures of. Ecl. M. **16**: 489. — Temp. Bar, **17**: 132.
— Poems of. Ecl. M. **67**: 484. — (H. C. Lodge) No. Am. **121**: 234.

Chatterton, Thomas, Story of. (D. Masson) Dub. Univ. **38**: 1, 178, 420. — Appleton, **4**: 246.
— Works. (Sir W. Scott) Ed. R. **4**: 214.
Chatterton, Lady. (B. Murphy) Cath. World, **28**: 145.
— Home Sketches and Foreign Recollections. Dub. Univ. **18**: 12.
Chatterton; or, the Rowley Romance. Tinsley, **14**: 382.
Chaucer, Geoffrey. (E. Ferrier) Evang. R. **18**: 329. — (Alice King) Argosy, **14**: 192. — (H. H. Morgan) Western, **5**: 107. — (H. D. Thoreau) Dial, **4**: 297. — (J. W. Wall) Knick. **43**: 441. — Dub. Univ. **53**: 272. — Lond. Q. **12**: 285. — Nat. R. **14**: 1. — No. Brit. **10**: 293. Same art. Ecl. M. **17**: 64.
— Age and Writings of. Brit. Q. **3**: 105. Same art. Ecl. M. **8**: 161.
— and his Circle. (M. F. Egan) Cath. World, **31**: 695.
— and his Times. (M. P. Case) Bib. Sac. **11**: 394.
— and Shakspere. Quar. **134**: 225. Same art. Liv. Age, **117**: 195.
— and Spenser. Blackw. **2**: 558.
— Canterbury Tales. Dub. Univ. **74**: 157. — (G. W. Thornbury) Lond. Soc. **24**: 518. — Penny M. **14**: 65–497.
— — Bell's Edition of. Bentley, **39**: 252.
— — Gilman's Edition of. Atlan. **45**: 108.
— Characters of. (M. E. Haweis) Dub. Univ. **93**: 26.
— Chronology of Life of. Antiquary, **1**: 80.
— Descriptive Poetry of. (S. A. Brooke) Macmil. **24**: 268. Same art. Liv. Age, **110**: 738.
— Dryden on. (J.Wilson) Blackw. **57**: 617, 771. **58**: 114.
— Early Latin Stories imitated by. (T. Wright) Arch. **32**: 362.
— England of. Chamb. J. **46**: 282, 294.
— Fictitious Lives of. (T. R. Lounsbury) Atlan. **40**: 269, 592.
— Godwin's Life of. (Sir W. Scott) Ed. R. **3**: 437. — Chr. Obs. **3**: 215.
— His Seal, and a Deed relating to him. (J. Hunter) Arch. **34**: 42.
— House of Fame. Penny M. **1**: 190.
— Knight's Tale; modernized. (R. H. Horne) Temp. Bar, **54**: 196.
— Love Poetry of. Cornh. **35**: 280.
— New Facts in Life of. (E. A. Bond) Fortn. **6**: 28.
— Nicolas's Life of. Mo. R. **163**: 448.
— Poetical Works of. Fraser, **53**: 461. — Westm. **96**: 381. — Temp. Bar, **38**: 308. — Chr. Rem. **32**: 327.
— Position, Life, and Influence of. Westm. R. **86**: 184. Same art. Ecl. M. **67**: 684. Same art. Liv. Age, **111**: 416.
— Portrait Gallery of. Penny M. **10**: 65–495.
— Recent Work at. (F. J. Furnivall) Macmil. **27**: 383.
— Romance of the Rose. Brit. Q. **54**: 359.
— Sources and Genius of. (J. R. Lowell) No. Am. **111**: 155.
— Text of. Ed. R. **132**: 1.
— Times and Poetry of. Knick. **34**: 236.
— To his empty Purse; modernized. (R. H. Horne) Temp. Bar, **52**: 353. **54**: 144.
— Troilus and Cressida. Retros. **12**: 106.
— Works of. Retros. **9**: 172. **14**: 305.
Chaucer-English in the Dales. All the Year, **19**: 305.
Chaucer, Thomas. (A. Hall) Antiquary, **2**: 162.
Chaumette. (A. Regnard) Fortn. **17**: 30.
Chaumonot, Father, Missionary in Canada. Cath. World, **15**: 675.
Chauncey Genealogy. (W. C. Fowler) N. E. Reg. **10**: 251, 323. **11**: 149.
Chauncy, Charles, with portrait. (W. C. Fowler) N. E. Reg. **10**: 105, 251. — Chr. Mo. Spec **5**: 335.
— and President Wheelock. (E. H. Gillett) Am. Presb. R. **20**: 463.
Chauncy, Charles, Latin Oration of. Cong. Q. **4**: 265.
Chaussey Islands. (D. T. Ansted) St. James, **3**: 389.
Chautauqua. (D. H. Post) Harper, **59**: 350.
— Scientific Conference at. (W. Wells) Meth. Q. **37**: 57.
Chauvin, Monsieur. (A. Daudet) Temp. Bar, **41**: 552.
Chavannes, Hill of Sacrifices at. (F. Troyon) Arch. **35**: 396.
Cheadlewood's Money; a Story. Chamb. J. **57**: 771–823.
Cheap Castle. Chamb. J. **38**: 314, 325.
Cheap Holiday Joys. (W. W. Fenn) Lond. Soc. **37**: supp. 16.
Cheap Jack. Chamb. J. **6**: 236.
Cheap Passage Home. All the Year, **8**: 544.
Cheap Rides. Chamb. J. **18**: 376.
Cheap Shops of London. Chamb. J. **56**: 161.
Cheap Transportation, Report on, 1874. Nation, **18**: 294.
Cheating the Nor'-Easter. Belgra. **26**: 139.
Checks, Certified, Law of. Bank. M. (N. Y.) **28**: 49.
— — Tax on. Bank. M. (N. Y.) **20**: 164.
— Crossed, on Banks. Bank. M. (N. Y.) **31**: 132.
— Effect of Death of Drawer on. Bank. M. (N. Y.) **33**: 619.
— Extended Use of. Bank. M. (N. Y.) **30**: 271.
— Fraudulent, Law of. Bank. M. (N. Y.) **23**: 875, 954.
— Law of. Bank. M. (N. Y.) **22**: 943. **25**: 737. **30**: 887. **35**: 203.
— Raised, Certification of, Opinion on. Bank. M. (N. Y.) **28**: 959. **29**: 540.
— Rights of Holder of. Bank. M. (N. Y.) **31**: 937.
— *versus* Bank-Notes. (H. C. Baird) Bank. M. (N. Y.) **28**: 409.
Check Circulation of London. Bank. M. (N. Y.) **29**: 368.
Check to the Queen; a Story. Lippinc. **14**: 112.
Checkley, John, Speech of, on his Trial. Hist. M. **13**: 209.
Checkley Genealogy. (S. G. Drake) N. E. Reg. **2**: 349.
Cheek. (W. G. Beers) Canad. Mo. **2**: 256.
Cheerful People. Chamb. J. **36**: 275.
Cheerfulness. (R. W. Dale) Good Words, **8**: 168.
— and Religion. Cong. M. **26**: 313.
— and Sobriety. (O. Dewey) Mo. Rel. M. **49**: 17.
— in Literature. (C. G. Leland) Knick. **59**: 59–505. **60**: 27–291.
— Inveterate. St. James, **23**: 124.
— of the Old. (A. K. H. Boyd) Fraser, **103**: 247.
Cheese. All the Year, **25**: 488.
— American. Penny M. **11**: 98.
— Cheshire. House. Words, **10**: 52.
— Gloucester. Penny M. **4**: 103.
— of Vif. (Marie Aycard) Am. Whig R. **9**: 408.
— Queen's. Ev. Sat. **10**: 478.
Cheese Districts of Italy. Penny M. **13**: 274.
Cheese Factory at Verona, N. Y. (W. H. Rideing) Appleton, **19**: 297.
Cheese Factories, Scientific Value of. Nature, **4**: 104.
Cheese Trade. Hunt, **13**: 100, 203.
Cheever, Ezekiel, and his Descendants. (J. T. Hassam) N. E. Reg. **33**: 164.
— and the New England Free School. (H. Barnard) Am. J. Educ. **1**: 297.
Cheever, George B. Lectures on Pilgrim's Progress. Meth. Q. **9**: 466.
— Letter to Editor of Christian Examiner. Spirit Pilg. **6**: 703.
— Vituperations of. (E. B. Hall) Chr. Exam. **15**: 171.
— Writings of. Chr. Exam. **41**: 404.
Chef's Beefsteak. (V. W. Johnson) Lippinc. **20**: 596.
Cheke, Sir John, Biography of. (J. G. Nichols) Arch. **38**: 98.
Chelmsford, Sir F. Thesiger, Lord. Lond. Soc. **11**: 87. Same art. Ecl. M. **68**: 287.
Chelmsford, Mass., Ministers of. Am. Q. Reg. **11**: 195
Chelsea Church. Penny M. **1**: 316.

Chelsea Hospital. All the Year, **39**: 249.—Penny M. **2**: 92. **13**: 297.—St. James, **28**: 110.
— and its Traditions. Mo. R. **144**: 486.
— Veterans of. (G. R. Gleig) Bentley, **5**: 614. **6**: 51, 450. **8**: 400, 476.
Cheltenham in 1826. Lond. M. **16**: 60.
— Foolery at. Lond. M. **12**: 247.
Chemical Action. (M. M. P. Muir) Nature, **20**: 530.
— of Plants. (A. Vogel) Internat. R. **3**: 184.
Chemical Affinity. (J. Murray) Ed. R. **5**: 141.
— and Cohesion. (M. Faraday) J. Frankl. Inst. **70**: 169, 253.
Chemical Analysis by Spectrum Observations. Nat. Q. **10**: 143.
— Correction for Vacuum in. (G. F. Becker) Am. J. Sci. **116**: 265.
— Crookes's. (T. E. Thorpe) Nature, **4**: 81.
— Dittmar on. Nature, **13**: 507.
— Fresenius's. Nature, **1**: 553.
Chemical and Geological Essays, Hunt's. (J. D. Dana) Am. J. Sci. **109**: 102.
Chemical and Physical Researches, Graham's. (W. C. Roberts) Nature, **15**: 153.
Chemical Apparatus. (W. P. Dexter) Am. J. Sci. **96**: 51.
Chemical Arts, Development of, 1865–75. (A. W. Hofmann) J. Frankl Inst. **100**: 43–423. **101**: 64–413. **102**: 49–422. **103**: 64–414. **104**: 41–399. **105**: 27, 199, 410. **106**: 121, 165, 239.
— — 1869–79. (A. W. Hofmann) J. Frankl. Inst **107**: 24.
Chemical Changes, Theory of. (T. S. Hunt) Am. J. Sci. **65**: 226.
Chemical Classifications. (T. S. Hunt) Am. J. Sci. **57**: 399.
Chemical Cleanliness. Chamb. J. **45**: 735.
Chemical Compounds, Spectra of. (A. Schuster) Nature, **16**: 193.
Chemical Contributions. (M. C. Lea) Am. J. Sci. **82**: 177, 210.
Chemical Denudation and Geological Time, Reade's. Nature, **20**: 526.
Chemical Dictionary, Fehling's. (M. M. P. Muir) Nature, **11**: 165.
Chemical Discoveries of 1864–65, Lectures on. (F. C. Calvert) J. Frankl. Inst. **81**: 195–406.
Chemical Dynamics. (M. M. P. Muir) Nature, **22**: 285.
Chemical Elements. (J. N. Lockyer) 19th Cent. **5**: 285. Same art. Pop. Sci. Mo. **14**: 600.
— Are they simple Bodies? J. Frankl. Inst. **109**: 197.
— Classification of. (J. P. Cooke, jr.) Am. J. Sci. **67**: 387.
— Discovery of. (W. Odling) Pop. Sci. Mo **1**: 474.
— Evolution of. (L. F. Ward) Pop. Sci. Mo. **18**: 526.
— Nature of. (M. Berthelot) Nature, **9**: 231.
Chemical Equilibrium. (M. M. P. Muir) Nature, **21**: 516.
Chemical Equivalents and Atomic Weights. (C. Marignac) Am. J. Sci. **115**: 89.
— Arithmetical Relations between. (M. C. Lea) Am. J. Sci. **84**: 387.
Chemical Essays, Irvine's. (J. Murray) Ed. R. **8**: 138.
Chemical Examinations. (E. Uricoechea) Am. J. Sci. **69**: 243.
Chemical Final Causes. (G. Wilson) Liv. Age, **55**: 513.
Chemical Force, Distribution of, in the Spectrum. (J. W. Draper) Am. J. Sci. **105**: 25, 91.
Chemical Industry, Hofmann's Report on. (A. Oppenheim) Nature, **12**: 365.
Chemical Laboratories in Prussia. Am. J. Educ. **21**: 277.
Chemical Manufactures, Notes on English. (S. Cabot, jr.) J. Frankl. Inst. **102**: 351.
Chemical Mineralogy, Contributions to. (J. D. Dana) Am. J. Sci. **67**: 210.
Chemical Nomenclature. (R. Hare) Am. J. Sci. **32**: 259.
Chemical Nomenclature, New, 1869. (A. Ott) J. Frankl. Inst. **88**: 129, 329. **89**: 52. **90**: 53–282.
Chemical Notation, Basis of. (W. Odling) Nature, **1**: 600.
— Systems of. (M. Berthelot) Am. J. Sci. **115**: 184.
Chemical Philosophy, Cooke's. Nature, **3**: 144.
— Davy's. (T. Young) Quar. **8**: 65.
Chemical Reactions, On. (E. Mitscherlich) J. Frankl. Inst. **39**: 192, 268.
Chemical Research, Methods of. Nature, **14**: 12.
Chemical Science, History and Present of. Ed. R. **50**: 256.
Chemical Society, Research Fund for. (W. J. Russell) Nature, **13**: 461.
Chemical Sources of Light and Heat. (R. Bithell) Recr. Sci. **2**: 280.
Chemical Statics of Organized Beings. (J. P. Dumas) J. Frankl. Inst. **34**: 23–247.
Chemical Studies. (E. Q. Sewall) Chr. Exam. **22**: 273.
Chemical Tables according to Theories of modern Chemistry. (A. R. Leeds) J. Frankl. Inst. **89**: 421. **90**: 49–415.
Chemical Technology, Wagner's. Nature, **7**: 4.
Chemical Theory, Progress of. Nat. Q. **27**: 319.
— of Interpenetration. (C. S. Peirce) Am. J. Sci. **85**: 78.
Chemical Theories. (B. H. Rand) J. Frankl. Inst. **90**: 84.—Chr. Rem. **2**: 249.
Chemical Works, Newcastle, Day at. Penny M. **13**: 201.
Chemise, Tale of a. Mus. **6**: 134.
Chemist of the Internal Revenue. Chamb. J. **48**: 807. Same art. Ecl. M. **29**: 555.
Chemist's Workshop. (J. Jones) Recr. Sci. **2**: 321.
Chemists of the Eighteenth Century. Fraser, **29**: 354, 425.
— Quack. (F. W. Clark) O. & N. **2**: 584.
Chemistry, Agricultural. *See* Agricultural Chemistry.
— Agriculture, and Physiology. Brit. Q. **8**: 75.
— Analytical, Contributions to. (W. Gibbs) Am. J. Sci. **64**: 204.—(H. Wurtz) Am. J. Sci. **75**: 371. **76**: 49, 81, 188.
— — Pink and Webster's. Nature, **9**: 278.
See Chemical Analysis.
— and Algebra. (J. J. Sylvester) Nature, **17**: 284.
— and its traditional Origin. For. Q. **23**: 14.
— and Life. No. Brit. **17**: 131. Same art. Liv. Age, **33**: 485.
— and Medicine. (I. Remsen) Pop. Sci. Mo. **15**: 214.
— and Natural Theology. Brit. Q. **7**: 204. Same art. Liv. Age, **19**: 289.
— and Religion. (A. P. Peabody) Bib. Sac. **22**: 440.—(J. B. Sewall) Bost. R. **5**: 461.—(T. Hill) Unita. R. **15**: 403.—Ecl. R. **120**: 636.
— Animal. *See* Animal Chemistry.
— Application of. So. Q. **27**: 506.
— applied to the Arts. (F. C. Calvert) J. Frankl. Inst. **79**: 246, 321. **80**: 102–397. **81**: 27, 117.
— applied to Commerce and Manufactures. Hunt, **15**: 171.
— Art. Ecl. R. **89**: 559.
— Attfield's. Nature, **1**: 328.
— Barff's Handbook of. (E. J. Mills) Nature, **1**: 80.
— Birth of. (G. F. Rodwell) Nature, **6**: 463, 503, 545 **7**: 36–492. **8**: 56.
— Brande's. Mo. R. **96**: 290.—(J. W. Webster) No. Am. **14**: 369.
— Cannizzaro's Faraday Lecture. Nature, **6**: 143.
— Celestial. (T. S. Hunt) Pop. Sci. Mo. **6**: 420.—(J. N. Lockyer) Nature, **9**: 411, 429.
— Clements's Organic. Nature, **20**: 237.
— Contradictions of. House. Words, **1**: 591.
— Contributions to. (W. Gibbs) Am. J. Sci. **87**: 346. **89**: 58. **94**: 207. **98**: 215. **99**: 376.

Chemistry, Dana's. (J. Ware) No. Am. **22**: 455.
— Davis's. Quar. **8**: 65.
— Domestic. (A. G. Penn) Lippinc. **10**: 113. — Penny M. **7**: 6–94. **9**: 346–490.
— Effect of Discoveries in, on Civilization. (F. Mohr) Pop. Sci. Mo. **1**: 655.
— Experiments in. (S. Piesse) Recr. Sci. **1**: 172.
— — for the Lecture-Table. (A. R. Leeds) J. Frankl. Inst. **85**: 415. **86**: 65.
— Fownes's Manual of. Nature, **17**: 24.
— Frankland's Researches in. (J. E. Reynolds) Nature, **17**: 218, 318.
— Future of. (F. W. Clarke) Pop. Sci. Mo. **6**: 276.
— Gorham's. (S. L. Dana) No. Am. **9**: 113.
— Hinrichs's Principles of. (G. F. Rodwell) Nature, **12**: 288. — Nature, **6**: 79.
— History of. (T. Thomson) Ed. R. **50**: 256. — (E. I. Sears) Nat. Q. **9**: 213.
— — and Uses of. (C. T. Jackson) Am. Inst. of Instruc. **1834**: 207.
— Hofmann's Faraday Lecture. Nature, **11**: 411.
— in Manufactures. Penny M. **11**: 91.
— Industrial. (Prof. Abel) Ecl. Engin. **17**: 393. — (Prof. Abel) Pract. M. **7**: 199. — (Dr. Odling) Nature, **9**: 370.
— — Payen's. Nature, **18**: 218.
— Liebig's Letters on. Mo. R. **162**: 376.
— Microscopic. (J. W. Draper) J. Frankl. Inst. **22**: 378.
— Mineral (T. E. Thorpe) Nature, **2**: 304.
— Mitscherlich's Compendium of. (J. C. Booth) J. Frankl. Inst. **21**: 393.
— Modern. Lond. Q. **6**: 48. — Nation, **3**: 145, 245. — (Sir H. Holland) Quar. **83**: 37. Same art. Liv. Age, **18**: 459. Same art. Ecl. M. **15**: 77.
— — Progress and Extent of. Ed. R. **94**: 254. Same art. Ecl. M. **24**: 38. Same art. Liv. Age, **30**: 443.
— Murray's System of, 1806. Ecl. R. **10**: 905.
— Nascent State of. (H. St. C. Deville) J. Frankl. Inst. **89**: 140, 214.
— New, developed from the old. (M. M. P. Muir) Pop. Sci. R. **19**: 111. Same art. Pop. Sci. Mo. **17**: 393.
— New Theories in. (F. S. Barff) Stud. & Intel. Obs. **1**: 102–367. **2**: 31.
— of a Candle. House. Words, **1**: 439. Same art. Internat. M. **1**: 292.
— of the Carbon Compounds, Schorlemmer's. Nature, **9**: 458.
— of common Life, Johnston's. Lond. Q. **4**: 425. — West. J. **14**: 196. — Blackw. **78**: 548. — Brit. Q. **21**: 115. Same art. Ecl. M. **34**: 340. — Colburn, **104**: 167. — Ed. R. **101**: 480. Same art. Liv. Age, **46**: 11. — Nature, **20**: 25. — New Q. **5**: 40.
— of common Salt. (C. A. Goessmann) Am. J. Sci. **99**: 78.
— of natural Waters. (T. S. Hunt) Am. J. Sci. **89**: 176. **90**: 43, 193.
— of Plants and Agriculture. Chr. Rem. **5**: 745.
— of Summer. Chamb. J. **9**: 279.
— of Autumn. Chamb. J. **10**: 134.
— of Winter. Chamb. J. **10**: 387.
— of the Stars. Brit. Q. **10**: 321. Same art. Ecl. M. **19**: 171.
— of Vegetation. (A. Gray) No. Am. **60**: 156.
— Old and new. (M. M. P. Muir) Pop. Sci. R. **17**: 24.
— Organic. Chr. Rem. **8**: 299.
— — Armstrong's. Nature, **10**: 333.
— — Liebig's. (H. Colman) No. Am. **53**: 147. — (E. Hale) No. Am. **55**: 462. — (S. Borland) So. Lit. Mess. **9**: 238.
— — Raspail's. Mo. R. **144**: 494.
— Past and present State of, 1855. Dub. R. **38**: 98.
Chemistry, Physiological. (G. F. Barker) Am. J. Sci. **96**: 233, 379. **97**: 20, 258, 393. **98**: 49. — West. J. **6**: 94.
— Pioneers in. No. Brit. **18**: 39.
— Practical. Mo. R. **118**: 189.
— — Clowes's. Nature, **11**: 107.
— — Vernon-Harcourt and Madan's. (H. E. Roscoe) Nature, **1**: 50.
— Profession of. Nature, **14**: 125.
— Progress of. For. Q. **23**: 23. — Ho. & For. R. **4**: 433.
— Renwick's and Damas's. New York R. **8**: 183.
— Report, 1832. Niles's Reg. **42**: supp. 1.
— Science *vs.* Art of. (I. Remsen) Pop. Sci. Mo. **10**: 691.
— Scientific Aims and Achievements of. (A. Kekulé) Nature, **18**: 210.
— Silliman's. (C. U. Shepard) Chr. Q. Spec. **3**: 144. — (W. C. Fowler) No. Am. **34**: 79.
— Solar. *See* Sun.
— State of, 1827. (D. Olmsted) Am. J. Sci. **11**: 349. **12**: 1.
— Synthetic. (J. W. Langley) Pop. Sci. Mo. **5**: 39.
— Thomson's System of, 1804. (H. Duncan) Ed. R. **4**: 120. — Ecl. R. **1**: 401.
— Thomson *versus* Brande. Blackw. **12**: 40.
— Turner's. Mo. R. **117**: 465. — Meth. Q. **1**: 156.
— Types in. (T. S. Hunt) Canad. J. n. s. **6**: 120.
— — Theory of. (T. S. Hunt) Am. J. Sci. **81**: 256.
— Ure's Dictionary of. Ecl. R. **33**: 345.
— Valentin's. Nature, **7**: 160.
— Watts's Dictionary of. Nature, **6**: 42. — (R. Meldola) Nature, **12**: 327.
— Webster's. (E. Hitchcock) No. Am. **23**: 349. — U. S. Lit. Gaz. **4**: 378.
— Wilson's Inorganic. Nature, **7**: 441. *See* Atomic Theory.
Chemnitz and the Council of Trent. (H. E. Jacobs) Evang. R. **21**: 398.
— Redivivus. (H. E. Jacobs) Evang. R. **21**: 553.
Chenango Co., N. Y., Reminiscences of. (S. S. Randall) Hist. M. **22**: 13–333.
Chenevix, Richard, Plays of. (F. Jeffrey) Ed. R. **20**: 203.
Cheney Silk Factory, South Manchester, Conn. (E. Howland) Harper, **45**: 836.
Cheneys and the House of Russell. (J. A. Froude) Fraser, **100**: 360. — Liv. Age, **143**: 347.
Chénier, André. (J. A. Harrison) So. M. **12**: 362. — (A. Laugel) Nation, **19**: 380.
— and his Poetry. Once a Week, **6**: 39.
— Malfilâtre, and Gilbert. Once a Week, **15**: 370.
— Poet and Political Martyr. Westm. **98**: 124.
— Prose Writings of. (C. A. Bristed) Am. Whig R. **7**: 71.
Chenonceaux Chateau. (E. T. Potter) Harper, **43**: 871.
Chepstow Castle. Am. Mo. M. **2**: 21, 169. — Liv. Age, **147**: 379.
Cherbourg. All the Year, **2**: 147, 180, 195. — Bentley, **59**: 237.
— Breakwater of. Ecl. R. **108**: 289. — Penny M. **11**: 163.
— Royal and imperial Visit to, 1858. Blackw. **84**: 253–606. Same art. Ecl. M. **45**: 514.
— Visit to. Temp. Bar, **15**: 449.
Cherbuliez, Victor. (T. S. Perry) Nation, **13**: 7. — (G Saintsbury) Fortn. **29**: 247.
— Meta Holdenis. (H. James, jr.) No. Am. **117**: 461.
Cherokee Indians, Among the. (A. M. Williams) Lippinc. **27**: 195.
— Case of. (A. H. Everett) No. Am. **33**: 136. — Am. Q. **11**: 1. — (J. Evarts) Ann. Reg. **5**: 43. **6**: 26. — (S. C. Sewell) Chr. Exam. **9**: 107. — Ann. Reg. **5**: [123. **7**: [364. — So. Lit. J. **1**: 227. — Spirit Pilg. **3**: 141, 492. **4**: 292. — Niles's Reg. **36**: 40, 370. **37**: 189. **38**: 53. **39**: 68, 81, 197. **40**: 67–286. **41**: 174. **42**: 24, 40. **43**: 105, 227, 419.

Cherokee Indians, Drayton's Talk to, 1775. Hist. M. 11: 280.
— Education among. (W. P. Ross) Am. J. Educ. 1: 120.
— Expeditions against, 1776. (E. F. Rockwell) Hist. M. 12: 212.
— Institutions of. Anal. M. 12: 36.
— Land of. Dem. R. 28: 320.
— Legislature, 1829. Niles's Reg. 37: 189.
— Removal of. Niles's Reg. 27: 363, 404.
Cherokee Mission and Alabama. (P. H. White) Cong. Q. 3: 279.
Cherokee Rose, and Hedging at the South. (T. Affleck) De Bow, 5: 82.
Cherokee Schools. Portfo.(Den.) 26: 58.
Cherry, Produce of the. Penny M. 13: 107.
Cherries. All the Year, 7: 401.
Cherry-Girls of Pierre L'Eveque. Tinsley, 11: 527.
Cherry Ripe; a Novel. (H. B. Mathers) Temp. Bar, 49: 1–433. 50: 1–542. 51: 122–433. 52: 117. Same art. Appleton, 17: 162–522. 18: 59–552. 19: 76, 165.
Chersiphron. (W. W. Story) Blackw. 111: 85.
Chertsey, England. Penny M. 9: 397.
— and its famous Characters. (Mrs. S. C. Hall) Internat. M. 5: 147.
— Autumn Day at. (E. Walford) Once a Week, 17: 625.
Cherub's Face under a Forage-Cap. Lond. Soc. 40: 14.
Cherubic Forms, Origin of. Kitto, 10: 154.
Cherubic Symbol. (J. B. Melson) Ex. H. Lec. 6: 479.
Cherubim of the Scriptures. Chr. Q. Spec. 8: 368. — Chr. R. 14: 592. — (E. Riehm) Cong. R. 10: 1. — (G. T. Ladd) Bib. Sac. 33: 32. — (J. Crawford) Bib. Sac. 36: 225.
— and their symbolical Meaning. (E. W. Hengstenberg) Theo. Ecl. 5: 268.
— Chariot of, Notes on, Ezekiel i. (E. White) Cong. 4: 604.
— Scriptural Account of. Kitto, 23: 88.
Cherubini. (F. Hiller) Macmil. 32: 261. Same art. Liv. Age, 126: 439. — Month, 20: 492.
Cherubinic Wanderer; a Poem. (J. Scheffler) J. Spec. Philos. 4: 31.
Cherubino; a psychological Art Fancy. (V. Lee) Cornh. 44: 218. — Ecl. M. 97: 665.
Cherwell, On the. Chamb. J. 53: 609.
Chesapeake Bay, Early Spanish Explorations in, 1566–73. Hist. M. 3: 268.
— Legend of. (J. P. Kennedy) So. Lit. Mess. 24: 223.
Chesapeake River. (J. H. Hengiston) Colburn, 97: 358.
Chesapeake and Delaware Canal. Niles's Reg. 27: 342. 31: 280.
Chesapeake and Ohio Canal. Niles's Reg. 25: 173. 28: 218, 364. 31: 136. 34: 325. 40: 206, 333, 359 42: 441. — Portfo.(Den.) 33: 226.
Chesapeake and Ohio Railroad, Intermediate Section of. (C. Nordhoff) Ev. Sat. 11: 479.
Chesapeake, U. S. Ship, and the Shannon, 1813, Duel of. All the Year, 6: 310. — Anal. M. 2: 129, 521. — Niles's Reg. 18: 171. — Mus. 4: 562.
Cheshire, Customs of ancient. Antiquary, 4: 248.
— Glossary of Words used in. (R. Wilbraham) Arch. 19: 13.
— Songs and Ballads of. St. James, 19: 236.
— Wilds of. St. Paul's, 2: 292.
Chesil Bank. (D. Pidgeon) Once a Week, 4: 91. — Chamb. J. 45: 537.
Chesney, F. R. Dub. Univ. 18: 574.
Chess. (M. D. Conway) Atlan. 5: 662. — Cath. World, 10: 683. — Cornh. 7: 589. — Dem. R. 36: 496. — Lippinc. 7: 209. — Quar. 85: 82. Same art. Liv. Age, 22: 289. — For. Q. 24: 233. — Anal. M. 4: 273.
Chess and Chess-Players. Lond. M. 12: 97. — (J. White) Canad. Mo. 20: 391. — (S. H. Manchee) Canad. Mo. 20: 645.
— and its Antiquity. (J. Keen) Potter Am. Mo. 12: 215.
— and War. Chamb. J. 24: 289. Same art. Ecl. M. 37: 268. Same art. Liv. Age, 48: 33.
— Blindfold. Chamb. J. 36: 373. Same art. Liv. Age, 72: 283.
— by Telegraph. Liv. Age, 5: 523.
— Chaucer's Game at. (A. Hall) Antiquary, 2: 199.
— Curiosities of. Chamb. J. 17: 186.
— Historical Disquisition on. (D. Barrington) Arch. 9: 14.
— History of. All the Year, 13: 345.
— How Mephisto was caught. Gent. M. n. s. 27: 330.
— in Europe during the 13th Century. Colburn, 4: 316–497. 5: 125–315.
— in our Schools and Colleges. Nat. Q. 17: 47.
— Introduction of, into Europe. (F. Madden) Arch. 24: 203.
— Knights-Errant of. Chamb. J. 23: 98.
— Philidor's Studies of. Lond. M. 12: 566.
— with Napoleon, Game of. Fraser, 31: 143.
— without the Chess-Board. Fraser, 21: 302.
Chess Gossip. Lond. Soc. 8: 521.
Chess King, Deschapelles. Mus. 35: 569.
Chess Knight, Tours of. (W. H. Browne) N. Ecl. 6: 481.
Chess Match, London and Edinburgh. Blackw. 68: 97.
Chessmen, Ancient, discovered in the Isle of Lewis. (F. Madden) Arch. 24: 203.
— European Names of. (F. Douce) Arch. 11: 397.
Chess-Player, The. Museum, 38: 207.
Chess-Players, Mechanical. (R. A. Proctor) Belgra. 39: 71. *See also* Automaton Chess-Player.
Chesshyre, Sir John. Library of, at Halton. (W. E. A. Axon) Lib. J. 4: 35.
Chest, Diseases of, and Auscultation. Quar. 57: 108.
— — Gerhard on. Mo. R. 144: 344.
— Expansion and Development of. (A. Maclaren) Macmil. 3: 35.
— Jeffrey's Statics of the Human. Ecl. Mus. 2: 163. — Mo. R. 162: 294.
Chest Measurement of Recruits. (C. L. Fox) Anthrop. J. 5: 101.
Chest of Drawers; a Tale. Internat. M. 4: 73.
Chest with Silver Bands. Knick. 56: 246.
Chester, Earl of, Seal of. (E. King) Arch. 4: 119.
Chester, Joseph Lemuel. Colburn, 168: 626.
Chester Genealogy. (E. Strong) N. E. Reg. 22: 339.
Chester, England. (L. S. Costello) Bentley, 16: 350. — (H. James, jr.) Nation, 15: 7. — Sharpe, 2: 193.
— and Bangor. Sharpe, 38: 202.
— and the Dee. (B. Murphy) Lippinc. 20: 393, 521.
— and its Norman Earls. Hogg, 4: 174.
— Cathedral of. (J. S. Howson) Art J. 30: 328, 353. — Mo. Rel. M. 15: 79. — Penny M. 13: 365. — Antiquary, 4: 305.
— — Communion Table in. (J. S. Howson) Good Words, 17: 600, 780, 821.
— — Restored and unrestored. (J. S. Howson) Art J. 31: 65, 134.
— Day at. Chamb. J. 6: 73.
— Old Houses in. Penny M. 5: 121.
— Races at. All the Year, 38: 255.
— Roman Architectural Remains in. (W. Tite) Arch. 40: 285.
— Sketches of. (B. Murphy) Canad. Mo. 14: 514.
— Visit to. Mo. Rel. M. 22: 379.
— Walk within the Walls of. Colburn, 147: 53.
Chester, Pa., Shipbuilding at. (C. Barnard) Harper, 56: 641.
Chesterfield, Philip, 2d Earl of. Temp. Bar, 48: 206.

Chesterfield, P. D. Stanhope, 4th Earl of. (A. Clive) Dub. Univ. 86: 52. — (L. Stephen) Cornh. 24: 86. Same art. Liv. Age, 110: 613. — (A. Hayward) Ed. R. 82: 421. — (H. T. Tuckerman) Godey, 44: 7. — (E. T. Channing) No. Am. 50: 404. — (C. F. Adams) No. Am. 63: 166. — Ecl. M. 6: 300. — Dem. R. 27: 434. — Bentley, 34: 222. — Blackw. 103: 511. Same art. Liv. Age, 97: 579. — (H. B. Baker) Gent. M. n. s. 18: 621. — Putnam, 10: 339. — Ev. Sat. 13: 519.

— and his Times. (W. C. Taylor) Bentley, 19: 249.

— Letters to his Son. (M. E. G. Duff) Fortn. 31: 824. Same art. Liv. Age, 142: 282. — (Lord Brougham) Quar. 76: 459. — Brit. Q. 10: 75. Same art. Ecl. M. 18: 212.

— Was he a Gentleman? Sharpe, 41: 236.

Chesterfield Junior, Advice to his Father. All the Year, 15: 45-522.

Chesterfield Letters of 1873. Lond. Soc. 24: 30-497.

Chesterfield, Battle of, 1266. (S. Pegge) Arch. 2: 276.

— Church of, and its crooked Spire. Penny M. 4: 111.

Chesterton, George Laval. Autobiography. Ecl. R. 98: 196.

Chestnut Tree. Penny M. 11: 204.

— of Mount Ætna. Nature, 4: 166. — Penny M. 2: 135.

— Uses of. Penny M. 12: 483.

Chetah, or Hunting Leopard. Penny M. 3: 31.

Chetham, Humphrey, of Manchester. Lond. Soc. 6: 466.

— and the Chetham Family. Reliquary, 9: 107, 220. 10: 17.

— and the Manchester Foundations. Brit. Q. 20: 335.

Chetham Library. Blackw. 9: 299.

Chetwyndes, The. House. Words, 19: 341.

Chevalier, N., and his Paintings. (J. Dafforne) Art J. 31: 221.

Chevallier, Jean Baptiste Alphonse. Nature, 21: 132.

Cheverus, John, Cardinal. (J. H. Morison) Chr. Exam. 26: 88. — Bost. Mo. 1: 2. — U. S. Cath. M. 4: 261.

Cheviot Hills. (J. Geikie) Good Words, 17: 11-550. — Penny M. 5: 141.

— Knapsack and Fishing-Rod on. St. James, 3: 301.

Chevreuse, Marie, Duchesse de. (C. J. Wallis) Dub. Univ. 84: 70. — Knick. 53: 523.

Chevtchenko, Taran, a Russian Poet. All the Year, 38: 220. — (J. A. Stevens) Galaxy, 22: 537.

Chevy Chase, Ballad of. All the Year, 28: 588.

— Latin Translation of. Blackw. 6: 199. 7: 323.

Chew, Benjamin, with portrait. Portfo.(Den.) 5: 89.

Chew Family of Pennsylvania. (E. Read) M. Am. Hist. 4: 192.

— Cliveden, the House of, Germantown. Potter Am. Mo. 7: 81.

Chew Tragedy; a Poem. Blackw. 49: 83.

Cheyenne Indians. (W. H. Gardner) Lippinc. 8: 206.

Cheyne, Dr. John, and his Essays. Dub. Univ. 22: 486.

Cheyne, Lord Roland. Lond. M. 8: 418.

Chic. Temp. Bar, 51: 115.

Chicago. (J. W. Shehan) Scrib. 10: 529. — De Bow, 17: 262. — (A. A. Hayes, jr.) Harper, 61: 711. — Hunt, 18: 164. — Land We Love, 5: 469.

— Amusements, Arts, and Sciences in, 1872. (J. B. Runnion) Lakeside, 8: 317.

— and its intellectual Resources. (J. M. Binckley) Lakeside, 9: 492.

— and its Railways. (D. C. Brooks) Lakeside, 8: 264.

— Architectural Correspondence, 1876. (P. B. Wight) Am. Arch. 1: 14-318.

— Art in. (G. P. Upton) Lakeside, 4: 402.

— — in 1872. Lakeside, 9: 64.

— — and Music, in February, 1873. Lakeside, 9: 161.

— as a Bookmaking Center. Lakeside, 2: 435.

— as a Port of Entry. (W. A. Croffut) Lakeside, 4: 337.

Chicago, Board of Trade. Lakeside, 3: 406.

— Building Materials for the new. (J. W. Foster) Lakeside, 7: 155.

— Central Music Hall. (L. G. Hallberg) Am. Arch. 6: 174, 199.

— City Hall Investigation. Am. Arch. 6: 44, 51, 62.

— Court House and City Hall. Am. Arch. 5: 9, 74, 185.

— Currency and Banking in. (W. L. Fawcette) Lakeside, 9: 132.

— Custom House. (F. Gilbert) Lakeside, 9: 183.

— Custom-House Trial. Am. Arch. 5: 154, 193.

— Dearborn Observatory, and J. Y. Scammon. (T. H. Safford) Lakeside, 1: 129.

— Drama in, 1872. Lakeside, 9: 70.

— — in 1873. Lakeside, 9: 165.

— from 1673 to 1725. (J. G. Shea) Hist. M. 5: 99.

— Great Fire of 1871. (F. L. Olmsted) Nation, 13: 302. — (M. A. Shorey) O. & N. 5: 17. — (R. Keeler and A. R. Waud) Ev. Sat. 11: 452, 476. — Ev. Sat. 11: 401-510.

— — and the Relief Committee. (S. H. Gay) Lakeside, 7: 166.

— — Five Months after. (E. Chamberlin) Lakeside, 7: 314.

— — Libraries lost in. Am. Bibliop. 3: 424.

— — Rebuilding of the City. (F. Gilbert) Lakeside, 8: 281.

— — Relief after. (H. D. Jenkins) Overland, 7: 570.

— — Story of. Lakeside, 7: 1-100:

1. *Before the Fire.*
History, Topography, and Architecture. (J. W. Foster) 1.
Trade and Commerce. (C. Randolph) 11.
Æsthetical Development. (J. B. Runnion) 18.

2. *Burning of the City.*
Description of the Fire. (W. S. Walker) 22.
Flight for Life. (H. R. Hobart) 40.

3. *After the Fire.*
Burnt-out People — what was done with them. (A. Shuman) 43.
Among the Ruins. (F. B. Wilkie) 50.
Reconstruction. (W. A. Croffut) 53.

4. *The Losses.*
Real and Personal Property. (E. Colbert) 58.
Commercial and Public Institutions. (F. Gilbert) 64.
Religious and Educational Institutions. (E. O. Haven) 71.
Institutions of Art, Science, and Literature. (G. P. Upton) 76.

5. *The Future.*
What remains. (W. A. Bartlett) 82.
New Chicago. (J. W. Foster) 83.
Supplementary.
The Fires of History. (E Phelps) 86.
Science of the Northwestern Fires. (E. Colbert) 90.
Political Economy of the Fire. (D. H. Wheeler) 96.

— — Year after. (A. Shuman) Lakeside, 8: 241.

— — — Board of Trade in 1872. (C. Randolph) Lakeside, 8: 249.

— — — Business in 1872. (E. Colbert) Lakeside, 8: 254

— — — Effect of the Fire on Real Estate. Lakeside, 8. 260.

— Historical and Commercial Statistics of. West. J. 12: 47.

— House-Raising in. Chamb. J. 35: 49.

— How Unity Church has fared. (R. Collyer) Lakeside, 8: 325.

— in 1836. West. Lit. J. 1: 246.

— in 1856. Putnam, 7: 606.

— in 1867. (J. Parton) Atlan. 19: 325.

— Kinzie House. (B. J. Lossing) Potter Am. Mo. 6: 321.

— Land Titles in Cook County. (J. B. Adams) Lakeside, 7: 161.

— Music in, 1872. Lakeside, 9: 65.

— Musical Progress of. (G. P. Upton) Lakeside, 3: 122.

— Name of, Origin of. (W. H. Wells) Potter Am. Mo. 13: 230.

Chicago of the Poet; a Poem. (B. F. Taylor) Lakeside, 10: 256.
— of the Thinker. (J. M. Binckley) Lakeside, 10: 258.
— of the Annalist. (A. Shuman) Lakeside, 10: 268.
— of the Visitor. (E. Chamberlin) Lakeside, 10: 272.
— of the Farmer. (F. Gilbert) Lakeside, 10: 278.
— of the Connoisseur. (H. N. Powers) Lakeside, 10: 281.
— of the Educator. (L. Stone) Lakeside, 10: 285.
— of the Carrier. (D. C. Brooks) Lakeside, 10: 291.
— of the Engineer. (G. Pierce) Lakeside, 10: 298.
— of the Business Man. (J. W. Shehan) Lakeside, 10: 303.
— of the Publicist. (C. C. Bonney) Lakeside, 10: 306.
— of the Reader. (S. Gilbert) Lakeside, 10: 312.
— of the Manufacturer. (D. H. Mason) Lakeside, 10: 315.
— of the Traveler. (H R. Hobart) Lakeside, 10: 323.
— of the Societist. Lakeside, 10: 326.
— of the Cynic. Lakeside, 10: 332.
— of the Christian. (D. Swing) Lakeside, 10: 335.
— Oil-bearing Limestone of. (T. S. Hunt) Am. J. Sci. 101: 420.
— Public High School in. (W. H. Wells) Am. J. Educ. 3: 531.
— Record of Progress, 1872. Lakeside, 8: 399.
— — Current Events, Nov., 1872. Lakeside, 8: 480.
— — — Dec., 1872. Lakeside, 9: 74.
— — — Jan., 1873. Lakeside, 9: 171.
— Sewage System of. Am. Arch. 2: 170.
— Sketch of Fort Dearborn. Hist. M. 6: 108.
— Sketches of. (A. D. Field) Nat. M. 12: 407.
Chicago Academy of Design, Sketch of. (C. Knickerbocker) Lakeside, 7: 176.
Chicago Academy of Science after the Fire. (J. S. Jewell) Lakeside, 7: 174.
— Transactions. Lakeside, 3: 160.
Chicago Convention, 1847. Hunt, 17: 217. — Am. Whig R. 6: 111. — (H. Greeley) De Bow 4: 291.
— and Memphis Convention. De Bow, 4: 122.
— Speech at. (D. D. Field) Dem. R. 21: 189.
Chicago River Tunnel. Lakeside, 1: 114.
Chicago Theological Seminary. (A. S. Kedzie) Cong. Q. 3: 357. — New Eng. 17: 335.
Chicago University. (J. W. Larimore) Lakeside, 9: 148.
Chichagoff, Admiral, Memoirs of. For. Q. 27: 38. Same art. Am. Ecl. 2: 70.
Chichester Cathedral. Penny M. 13: 473. — Sharpe, 33: 233.
— Statutes, Constitution, and History of. (M. E. C. Walcott) Arch. 45: 143.
Chichester Market-Cross. Penny M. 5: 369. — (R. L. Dabney) So. M. 10: 1. — So. M. 10: 254.
Chickamauga, Battle of. (P. R. Cleburne) Land We Love, 1: 249. — (J. C. Breckinridge) Land We Love, 1: 305. — (D. H. Hill) Land We Love, 1: 393. — (R. L. Kimberly) Lippinc. 17: 713. — (W. F. Smith) Galaxy, 20: 641. — So. Hist. Pap. 7: 161. — (W. N. Polk) So. Hist. Pap. 10: 1. — (A. Anderson) So. Hist. Pap. 9: 386.
Chickasaw Bayou, Battle of; S. D. Lee's Report. So. Hist. Pap. 6: 49.
Chicken Factories. Chamb. J. 9: 186.
Chickering, Jonas, the Piano-Forte Maker. Liv. Age, 39: 820.
Chicory as a Substitute for Coffee. Tait, n. s. 21: 315.
— Outcry about. Chamb. J. 11: 216.
Chidioc Tichbourne. (G. Eastwick) Godey, 22: 275.
Chief, The; or, the Gael and the Sassenach. (J. Galt) Blackw. 33: 503, 763.
Chief Justices of England, Campbell's Lives of. Ed. R. 93: 97. Same art. Ecl. M. 22: 365. — Ed. R. 106: 432. — Fraser, 41: 677. — Chr. R. 15: 427. — So. Q. 18: 157. — Chr. Obs. 50: 848. — Dub. R. 43: 108. — (W. Dowe) No. Am. 74: 72. — Lond. Q. 9: 136.
Chief Justices of the United States. (C. C. Nott) Nation, 17: 421.
— Flanders's. (W. Sargent) No. Am. 81: 346.
— Van Santvoord's. So. Q. 27: 331.
Chiffonier; a Poem. (W. W. Story) Blackw. 102: 244.
Chiffoniers of Paris. Liv. Age, 40: 577.
Chignons. Ev. Sat. 9: 186.
Chihuahua, Mexico, Geology of. (J. P. Kimball) Am. J. Sci. 98: 378.
Chikagou and Tonika. (R. G. Heyer) Sharpe, 15: 309, 328.
Child, David L. Case of Contempt. Am. Mo. R. 2: 327.
Child, Josiah. Lond. Soc. 7: 256.
Child, Lydia Maria. African Appeal. (L. Bacon) Chr. Q. Spec. 6: 445.
— Biographies. Am. Mo. R. 2: 230, 452.
— Good Wives. Am. Mo. R. 3: 462.
— Letters from New York. Mo. R. 162: 300.
— Letters of. (D. G. Mitchell) Am. Whig R. 1: 60. — Dem. R. 16: 569.
— Philothea. (C. C. Felton) No. Am. 44: 77. — So. Lit. Mess. 2: 659.
— Progress of Religious Ideas. Putnam, 7: 73.
— Rebels. (J. C. Gray) No. Am. 22: 405.
— Works of. (G. Mellen) No. Am. 37: 138.
Child, The, Dr. Ploss on. Sup. Pop. Sci. Mo. 2: 240.
— is Father of the Man. (F. Jacox) Colburn, 133: 289.
— Relation to the Home. (E. D. Cheney) Unita. R. 1: 336.
Child of Bristow; a metrical Legend. Retros. 18: 198.
Child of Fame; a Poem. (M. E. Hewitt) Internat. M. 1: 73.
Child of Nature; a Sketch. Cornh. 9: 487.
Child of the Rhine. Dub. Univ. 28: 572.
Child of the State. (E. Chace) Atlan. 40: 334.
Child's Dream of a Star. (C. Dickens) House. Words, 1: 25.
Child's Play. Cornh. 38: 352. Same art. Liv. Age, 139: 28.
Child's Story. (C. Dickens) House. Words, 6: 577.
Child Angel, The. (C. Lamb) Lond. M. 7: 677.
Child Beggar; a Poem. (E. Cook) Cath. World, 26: 683.
Child Ghost; a Story of the last Loyalist. Dem. R. 10: 451.
Child Life as seen by the Poets. St. Paul's, 10: 480. Same art. Ecl. M. 79: 81.
— for Children. (E. Rossiter) 19th Cent. 10: 567.
Child Murder in China. Westm. 95: 237.
Child Seer. House. Words, 12: 80.
Child Song in Winter. (A. C. Swinburne) Fortn. 7: 19. Same art. Liv. Age, 92: 472.
Child-Stealer; a Tale. (MM. Erckmann-Chatrian) Temp. Bar, 32: 108.
Child-Stealing. Chamb. J. 39: 311.
Childbirth, Etherization in. (E. Warren) No. Am. 68: 300.
— Statistics of Death after. Victoria, 7: 175.
Childe, E. V. Edward Vernon. Am. Whig R. 8: 317.
Childe Roland; a Poem. (J. L. Uhland) Once a Week, 11: 451.
Childhood. (F. B. Perkins) Atlan. 18: 385. — (M. Dean) Putnam, 14: 450. — Blackw. 12: 139. — Knick. 14: 512. — Broadw. 6: 156. — Good Words, 15: 490.
— an Element in modern Romance. So. R. n. s. 18: 92.
— and Ignorance. (W. K. Clifford) 19th Cent. 3: 978.
— and its Reminiscences. Fraser, 37: 261. Same art. Liv. Age, 17: 147.
— Christian. (N. Macleod) Good Words, 15: 490.
— Every-Day Wisdom for. (B. Auerbach) Howitt, 3: 13.
— First three Years of. Pop. Sci. Mo. 14: 591.
— Literature of. Westm. 33: 137.
— Religion of. (F. P. Cobbe) Theo. R. 3: 317.
— Hibbard on. (J. T. Crane) Meth. Q. 25: 81.
— Sacred Poetry of. Prosp. R. 2: 521.

Childhood, Sorrows of. (A. K. H. Boyd) Fraser, **65**: 304. Same art. Ecl. M. **56**: 78. Same art. Liv. Age, **73**: 77.
Childless Mother. (H. F. Harrington) Godey, **26**: 175.
Childless Mother; a Poem. (T. Miller) St. James, **5**: 480.
Children. (P. M. Edmondstone) So. M. **14**: 356.—(T. Hood) St. James, **1**: 189.—(H. T. Tuckerman) Galaxy, **4**: 315.—Chamb. J. **39**: 177.—Fraser, **26**: 543.—St. James, **32**: 658.
— Amusements for poor. (M. B. Carret) Unita. R. **7**: 406.
— and Childhood. (R. Collyer) Lakeside, **3**: 34.
— and Children's Stories. Dub. Univ. **27**: 453.
— and the Church. (H. L. Baugher) Evang. R. **7**: 42. —(L. M. Kuhns) Luth. Q. **1**: 520.—(A. D. Mayo) Mo. Rel. M. **51**: 29.—(R. Collyer) Unita. R. **13**: 60.—(C. A. Stork) Luth. Q. **3**: 576.—(M. Valentine) Luth. Q. **9**: 325.—(G. U. Wenner) Luth. Q. **6**: 424.—Cong. **2**: 513–705. **3**: 67.
— — in the Church of England. Chr. Rem. **7**: 1.
— and how to guide them. (J. Brown) Good Words, **2**: 309.
— and their Sayings. (C. H. Webb) Hours at Home, **8**: 167.
— as Performers, Protection of. (A. G. Sedgwick) Nation, **33**: 507.
— as Prophets. Chamb. J. **16**: 145.
— Asylums, Hospitals, etc., for. Brownson, **22**: 289.
— Attention to, by Ministers (S. Miller) Princ. **10**: 23.
— Baptized, and the Church. (J. Eldridge) New Eng. **9**: 372.—(D. H. Riddle) Mercersb. **1**: 169.—(T. F. R. Mercein) Meth. Q. **15**: 90.—(L. Grout) Bib. Sac. **28**: 262.
— Betrothed. House. Words, **10**: 124.
— Books for. (Miss Rigby) Quar. **71**: 54. **74**: 1. Same art. Liv. Age, **2**: 1.—(T. W. Higginson) No. Am. **102**: 236.—(S. Osgood) Atlan. **16**: 724.—(W. A. Jones) Dem. R. **15**: 525.—(F. W. P. Greenwood) Chr. Exam. **8**: 22. **10**: 213.—Chr. Exam. **2**: 291. **5**: 402.—Liv. Age, **1**: 296.—(W. M. Thackeray) Fraser, **33**: 495.—Dub. Univ. **27**: 453. —Brit. Q. **47**: 128.—(M. B. Carret) Unita. R. **1**: 354.—So. Lit. Mess. **18**: 681. **20**: 214.—Chr. R. **20**: 593.—Lond. Q. **13**: 469.—Chr. Rem. **14**: 231. —(W. H. Barnes) Meth Q. **17**: 381.—(H. A Page) Contemp. **11**: 7.—Tait, **4**: 284.
— — Cheap. Liv. Age, **138**: 296.
— — Cruelty of. (E. W. Winthrop) Radical, **6**: 191.
— — Illustrated. (W. M. Thackeray) Fraser, **33**: 495.
— — Importance of. Ecl. M. **49**: 453. **50**: 38.
— — of the last Century. (C. M. Yonge) Macmil. **20**: 229, 302, 448. Same art. Ev. Sat. **8**: 56, 261, 392. Same art. Liv. Age, **102**: 373, 612. **103**: 96.
— — Pernicious. (O. A. Kingsbury) Nat. Q. **39**: 136.
— — Pleasure. Dub. Univ. **43**: 72.
— carried off by Wolves. Ecl. M. **45**: 370.
— Catechetical Teaching of. (F. W. Kurner) Mercersb. **6**: 205.
— Charities for, in London. Month, **11**: 54.
— Christian Nurture of. (P. S. Davis) Mercersb. **15**: 109.
— — Bushnell's. (H. M. Goodwin) New Eng. **19**: 474. *See* Bushnell, Horace.
— — Neglect of. (T. C. Pitkin) Am. Church R. **7**: 86.
— Clever. Liv. Age, **81**: 579.
— Conversion of. (J. McFarlane) Evang. R. **17**: 581.—Cong. **2**: 730.—Meth. Q. **26**: 531.
— — in Sunday School. Princ. **42**: 22.
— Cottage Homes for Workhouse. (M. B. Edwards) Good Words, **11**: 173.
— Criminal and destitute. Ecl. R. **99**: 385.
— Curious Prayers of. (E. A. Walker) Atlan. **45**: 327.
— Dress of. (Mrs. Merrifield) Sharpe, **17**: 65.
Children, Education of. (R. Milligan) Chr. Q. **2**: 358.—Chamb. J. **58**: 513, 533.—Chr. Obs. **10**: 622–825.
— — Parental. Cong. M. **1**: 586.
— Emigrant. Victoria, **14**: 172.
— Emigration Homes for. Cong. **5**: 168.
— Employments of. (J. A. Holmes) Scrib. **1**: 607.—Chr. Rem. **5**: 675. **49**: 332.
— — Commission on. Quar. **119**: 364.
— — Factory Education Bill, England, 1843. Mo. R. **161**: 120.
— Fancies of. (T. W. Higginson) Scrib. **11**: 357.
— French. Blackw. **110**: 739. Same art. Liv. Age, **112**: 259.
— Good Words for. (N. Macleod) Good Words, **4**: 482, 584, 663.
— Gossip about. (L. G. Clark) Liv. Age, **26**: 34.
— Health and Mortality of. (W. Farr) J. Statis. Soc. **29**: 1.
— — and Recreation for. (B. W. Richardson) Gent. M. n. s. **22**: 687.
— Home Training of. (F. D. Huntington) Mo. Rel. M. **10**: 15.
— Hospitals for sick. All the Year, **6**: 454.—Chamb. J. **31**: 273.
— — at Bremen. Good Words, **1**: 689.
— How to make them happy. Ecl. M. **45**: 401.
— I have met. Chamb. J. **51**: 721, 747, 765.
— in the Coal Mines of England. Ecl. R. **76**: 201.—Quar. **70**: 158. Same art. Am. Ecl. **4**: 316.—Westm. **38**: 86.
— in the Country, Pasturing. (J. G. Holland) Hours at Home, **4**: 83.
— in English Workhouses. Month, **1**: 136.
— in the Factories. Quar. **67**: 171.
— — Laws relating to. (E. d'Eichtal) Penn Mo. **3**: 493, 552.—Mo. R. **161**: 120.
— in Italian and English Design. (S. Colvin) Portfo. **2**: 120–192. **3**: 61.
— in the New Testament. (W. M. Reynolds) Evang. R. **5**: 586.
— in the 19th Century. (H. Martineau) Once a Week, **1**: 195.
— in religious Households. Chr. Obs. **69**: 111.
— Inquisitive Disposition of, a Means of Education. (D. March) New Eng. **10**: 493.
— Institutions for, in New York, 1877. (W. P. Letchworth) Am. J. Educ. **28**: 913.
— Invalid, Strolls with. (D. M. Craik) Once a Week, **16**: 384, 503.
— Kindness toward. (L. G. Clark) Knick. **50**: 392.
— Little Laborers of New York City. (C. L. Brace) Harper, **47**: 321.
— Management of. Hogg, **9**: 317.
— Maxims on. (J. Payn) Chamb. J. **45**: 161.
— Mental Potentiality of, in different Races. (W. L. Lindsay) Nature, **10**: 272.
— Moral Culture of. (Mrs. M. R. Hall) West. J. **14**: 435. —Brit. Q. **27**: 383. Same art. Ecl. M. **44**: 145.
— Mortality of. (J. S. Parry) Penn Mo. **2**: 275.
— — Forty per cent die before a Year old. Temp. Bar, **8**: 513. Same art. Ecl. M. **60**: 119.
— Neglected. All the Year, **20**: 540.
— — Right Beginnings with. Am. J. Educ. **31**: 201.
— — Swiss Treatment of. Am. J. Educ. **30**: 145.
— of all Work. All the Year, **5**: 254.
— of the Black Country. (F. Wagstaff) Good Words, **22**: 614.
— of the New Testament. (W. M. Reynolds) Evang. R. **5**: 589.
— Old-Fashioned Children's Pictures. Liv. Age, **132**: 445.
— Other People's. (T. S. Arthur) Godey, **21**: 157.

Children, Our. Once a Week, **30**: 116.
— Our little People. Victoria, **21**: 134.
— Outcast, in New York. (E. Crapsey) Galaxy, **12**: 355.
— Pauper. All the Year, **22**: 301.
— — and Factory. Mo. R. **154**: 486.
— — Boarding-out of. (H. Fawcett) Fortn. **15**: 255.
— — Care of. (C. L. Brace) Am. J. Soc. Sci. **11**: 93.
— — Education of. Chr. Rem. **55**: 161. — (F. J. Mouat) J. Statis. Soc. **43**: 183.
— — Emigration of. (H. M. Blair) Victoria, **23**: 259.
— — in Scotland. (J. Skelton) Fraser, **102**: 212.
— Plays of. (F. Parke) Dub. Univ. **82**: 731.
— — and Holidays of. (H. Bushnell) Am. J. Educ. **13**: 93.
— Playgrounds for poor. (S. E. DeMorgan) Good Words, **8**: 727.
— Plea for the little Ones. Victoria, **12**: 289.
— Poem on. (M. Howitt) Howitt, **1**: 14.
— Preaching to. (J. G. Merrill) New Eng. **40**: 247.
— Precocious Cleverness in. Chamb. J. **56**: 469.
— Protestant Theology for. (J. V. O'Conor) Cath. World, **28**: 672.
— Puritan Training of. (J. S. Clark) Cong. Q. **2**: 198.
— Religious Development of. Chr. Rem. **5**: 665. **6**: 42.
— Religious Education of. (E. Bowen) Am. Meth. M. **20**: 91. — Westm. **104**: 374. — (F. M. Green) Chr. Q. **7**: 191. — Chr. Obs. **5**: 337. — Cong. M. **2**: 278–475.
— — Duty of. (K. G. Wells) Unita. R. **14**: 42.
— — Forced. (F. Jacox) Temp. Bar, **24**: 137.
— Religious Life of. Cong. **3**: 341.
— Rights of. (Mrs. E. C. Embury) Godey, **28**: 80. — (O. B. Frothingham) Nation, **9**: 503. — (C. Burleigh) Victoria, **23**: 106. — Liv. Age, **122**: 230. — (P. Siogvolk) Knick. **39**: 487.
— Sayings of. Chamb. J. **56**: 460.
— Sermon to. (A. P. Stanley) Good Words, **22**: 107.
— Sick. (A. P. Stanley) Good Words, **19**: 140.
— Sigourney's Letters to Mothers. So. R. n. s. **24**: 476.
— Smart, what becomes of them? (J. D. Sherwood) Hours at Home, **7**: 377.
— Street. Good Words, **14**: 178.
— — Homeless, in London. Lond. Soc. **13**: 496.
— — Woman's Work for. (H. M. Blair) Victoria, **23**: 52.
— Teaching the Bible to. (J. W. Richard) Luth. Q. **6**: 204.
— Toiling. Chamb. J. **36**: 334.
— Training of. (S. J. Baird) Princ. **35**: 76. — (F. B. Lockwood) Penn Mo. **9**: 334. — Meth. M. **59**: 751.
— — Half-and-Half. Once a Week, **9**: 357.
— — Murder of the Innocents. (T. W. Higginson) Atlan. **4**: 345.
— Transportation of pauper. Victoria, **23**: 343.
— Troubles of. Chamb. J. **54**: 13.
— Unbaptized. (H. Harbaugh) Mercersb. **14**: 592.
— Village, Cheap Literature for. Macmil. **38**: 210.
— Village Homes for. (J. Williams) O. & N. **9**: 394.
— Word-Pictures of. Chamb. J. **21**: 209.
— Workhouse. (F. Hill) Contemp. **15**: 240.
See Babies; Infants; Juvenile Delinquency.
Children's Circus in Paris. Temp. Bar, **14**: 242.
Children's Cities. (E. Sheppard) Atlan. **10**: 119.
Children's Creed. (A. P. Stanley) Good Words, **21**: 133.
Children's Crusade. *See* Crusade, Children's.
Children's Establishment at Limehouse. (F. W. Robinson) Belgra. **10**: 61.
Children's Labor; a Problem. (E. E. Brown) Atlan. **46**: 787.
Children's Night; a Poem. (Z. B. Buddington) Harper, **50**: 153.
Children's Parties. All the Year, **19**: 186. — Ev. Sat. **9**: 182.
Childrenite, Chemical Composition of. (S. L. Penfield) Am. J. Sci. **119**: 315.
Childs, George W., with portrait. (J. Parton) Ev. Sat. **9**: 589.
Childs, Gen. Thomas, Correspondence of. Hist. M. **22**: 299, 371.
Chili. Westm. **31**: 129. — (S. G. Arnold) No. Am. **73**: 277. — (E. Everett) No. Am. **18**: 288. — (J. Brigham) Chr. Mo. Spec. **10**: 80. — Niles's Reg. **29**: 104. — Macmil. **13**: 334. — Penny M. **11**: 189. — Putnam, **8**: 225.
— Aborigines of. Penny M. **3**: 318.
— and Jamaica, Journal between. Fraser, **21**: 703. **22**: 193. Same art. Mus. **40**: 73, 237.
— and La Plata, Miers's Travels in. Lond. M. **16**: 119. — Westm. **6**: 202. — Mo. R. **110**: 365.
— and Peru. Quar. **30**: 441. — For. Q. **17**: 1. — Mus. **29**: 17.
— — in 1879. (J. Douglas) Canad. Mo. **16**: 113.
— — Letters from, 1832. New Eng. M. **9**: 210.
— and Spain. (J. H. Butler) Nation, **2**: 568.
— Apostolic Mission to. Cath. World, **22**: 548.
— Araucanians. (A. H. Guernsey) Harper, **11**: 607.
— Astronomical Expedition to. (J. Ferguson) Hunt, **21**: 611. — Canad. J. n. s. **2**: 195.
— Commerce and Progress of. Hunt, **13**: 321.
— Earthquake of April 2, 1851, in. (J. M. Gilliss) Am. J. Sci. **71**: 388.
— Exposition of 1875. Penn Mo. **6**: 137.
— Finances of, and her Foreign Commerce. De Bow, **17**: 511.
— Hall's Journal in. Mo. R. **106**: 51.
— Historical Account of. Geog. M. **4**: 90.
— in 1827. Ann. Reg. **2**: 273.
— Mining System of. Penny M. **13**: 398. — Hunt, **13**: 342.
— Molina's Account of. Ed. R. **14**: 133.
— Mrs. Graham's Residence in. Mo. R. **106**: 189.
— Peru and American Blockades. For. Q. **22**: 359.
— Railway Trip in. St. James, **4**: 213.
— Residence in, 1817–19. Ecl. R. **42**: 406.
— State Papers on. Niles's Reg. **14**: 384.
Chiliasm critically examined. (G. Seyffarth) Evang. R. **12**: 341.
Chilicothe, Ohio. (A. Mathews) Harper, **63**: 855.
Chillingham Cattle. Once a Week, **18**: 98.
Chillingworth, William. (T. Tebbets) Mo. Rel. M. **16**: 378. — (J. Tulloch) Contemp. **6**: 32. **7**: 347. Same art. Liv. Age, **96**: 195. — Chr. Disc. **1**: 237. — Chr. Exam. **30**: 290. — Retros. **7**: 1. — Am. Presb. R. **2**: 281.
— Defense of. Chr. Obs. **39**: 220.
— Hales, and Falkland: the earlier Latitudinarians. Nat. R. **17**: 1.
Chillon, Castle of. Appleton, **7**: 348. — Penny M. **5**: 60. — Bentley, **5**: 30.
— Prisoner of. (Mrs. Raymond) Cath. World, **23**: 857. — All the Year, **24**: 150.
— — The real. (L. W. Bacon) Lippinc. **22**: 46.
See Bonnivard.
Chiltern Hills. (C. Reade) Belgra. **29**: 81.
Chiltern Hundreds, Auld Lang Syne in. Lond. Soc. **32**: 376.
Chilvers, F., History of. Lond. M. **5**: 350.
Chimborazo, Mt., Attempts to ascend, 1802. (J. B. Boussingault) Ed. New Philos. J. **19**: 88. **23**: 291.
— Whymper's Ascent of. Ecl. M. **96**: 541.
Chimenti Pictures. (C. A. Joy) Am. J. Sci. **88**: 199.
Chimes, Change-ringing. Chamb. J. **54**: 731. Same art. Liv. Age, **137**: 247.
— Poetry of Steeples. (E. V. Battey) Harper, **52**: 180.
See Carillons.

Chimmerley Gap; a Tale. (J. T. McKay) Galaxy, 8: 228.

Chimneys. (R. Armstrong) Ecl. Engin. 9: 130. — Ecl. Engin. 1: 146.

— Ancient and modern. Am. Arch. 10: 221.

— and Chimney Sweepers. Penny M. 11: 322.

— and Electric Conductors, Tall. J. Frankl. Inst. 103: 118.

— and Steam-Boilers. (R. Briggs) J. Frankl. Inst. 101: 246.

— and Towers, Stability of. (C. A. Evans) J. Frankl. Inst. 96: 411.

— Dangerous. Am. Arch. 10: 292.

— Draft in. Ecl. Engin. 4: 65. — J. Frankl. Inst. 13: 1.

— — Causes which produce. J. Frankl. Inst. 7: 351.

— Hints on building. (D. Morse) Am. Arch. 4: 173.

— of Steam-Engines, Dimensions of. (H. F. Fairbairn) J. Frankl. Inst. 48: 438.

— out of Perpendicular, Remedy for. Ev. Sat. 11: 107.

— Pathology of. Chamb. J. 6: 318.

Chimney Caps and Ventilators. (T. Ewbank and J. L. Mott) J. Frankl. Inst. 34: 104.

Chimney Corner, The. (H. B. Stowe) Atlan. 15: 109–732. 16: 100–672. 17: 88–737. 18: 85, 197, 338.

Chimney Flues. Am. Arch. 8: 135.

Chimney Pieces and Chimneys. All the Year, 6: 65.

Chimney Pots. Fraser, 48: 95.

Chimney Shafts, Tall. Art J. 14: 57.

Chimney-Sweeps' Boys, Cruelty to. Pamph. 22: 407. — (Syd. Smith) Ed. R. 32: 309.

Chimney Sweepers, Praise of. (C. Lamb) Lond. M. 5: 405.

Chimpanzee, The. Penny M. 5: 57.

— Grief in. (A. E. Brown) Am. Natural. 13: 173.

China. (A. H. Forrester) Bentley, 7: 479. — (T. De Quincey) Ecl. M. 41: 65. — (G. W. Peck) Am. Whig R. 7: 231. — (D. M. Moir) Fraser, 11: 542. — Westm. 40: 123. — Ecl. M. 15: 117, 212, 322. — Chr. R. 4: 118. — (J. Owen) Princ. 11: 147. — So. Lit. Mess. 7: 137. — Chamb. J. 14: 169. — Dub. Univ. 15: 579. — House. Words, 3: 325. — No. Brit. 7: 388. Same art. Liv. Age, 15: 211. — Penny M. 4: 297–486. 5: 50–485. — Quar. 115: 1.

— Abel's Residence in. Quar. 21: 67. — Mo. R. 88: 113, 364. — Mus. 26: 676. — Ecl. R. 61: 304.

— Across. All the Year, 43: 59.

— Affairs of, 1839. (Sir J. Barrow) Quar. 65: 537.

— Agriculture in. Chamb. J. 31: 398.

— Lord Amherst's Embassy to, 1818. Portfo.(Den.) 20: 358.

— Ancient, Religion and Worship in. (V. von Strauss) Dub. Univ. 93: 11, 235, 336.

— and British Burmah, Trade Routes to. (J. Coryton) Geog. M. 2: 153.

— and the Chinese. (R. P. Dana) Nation, 8: 357. — Mo. R. 159: 428. — (J. H. Inness) Nat. Q. 37: 1. — (H. S. Sirr) Dub. Univ. 32: 32, 126, 295. — (W. D. Whitney) New Eng. 17: 111. — Bentley, 24: 287. — Brit. Q. 16: 396. Same art. Ecl. M. 28: 229. — Dub. Univ. 57: 560. — Ecl. M. 19: 278. — Lond. Q. 51: 136. — Westm. 67: 526. Same art. Ecl. M. 41: 307.

— — Sirr's. Dub. Univ. 34: 739.

— and Chinese Peace. (F. Wharton) Hunt, 8: 205.

— and the Church. Meth. Q. 10: 592.

— and Great Britain, Commerce of. Brit. Q. 33: 468. — Mo. R. 133: 297.

— — in 1822. Niles's Reg. 22: 349, 355.

— — in the new Parliament, 1857. Brit. Q. 25: 510.

— — Intercourse of. For. Q. 34: 432. Same art. Ecl. M. 5: 382.

— — Relations of. Ed. R. 98: 98. 105: 517.

China and its foreign Relations. (Sir R. Alcock) Contemp. 38: 1000.

— and its prospective Trade. Dem. R. 18: 382.

— and its Rulers. Nat. M. 3: 481.

— and Japan in 1860. Brit. Q. 31: 466.

— — in 1865. Ecl. R. 122: 175.

— — Bishop Wiley's Visitation of. (J. M. Reid) Meth. Q. 40: 405.

— — Commercial Condition, 1872. Pract. M. 3: 393.

— and Madras, Wathen's Voyage to, 1811–12. (J. Foster) Ecl. R. 21: 447.

— and Mongolia, Sosnovski's Expedition to. Geog. M. 3: 243.

— and Russia, 1880. (D. C. Boulger) Fraser, 102: 164.

— and Siberia. Am. Q. 9: 52.

— and surrounding Countries. Am. Q. Reg. 6: 39.

— and the United States, Commerce of. Hunt, 11: 54. — Bank. M. (N. Y.) 15: 125.

— — Commercial Relations of. Hunt, 11: 365.

— — Diplomatic Relations before 1857. (W. B. Reed) No. Am. 89: 478.

— — Duty of United States to China. (J. N. Pomeroy) Nation, 13: 101.

— — Our "Manifest Destiny" in the East. De Bow, 15: 541.

— — Relations of. (A. A. Hayes, jr.) Internat. R. 6: 355.

— — Treaties between. (S. W. Williams) New Eng. 38: 301.

— — Treaty between, Cushing's. Hunt, 14: 93.

— — — of 1868. (E. L. Godkin) Nation, 7: 205.

— — — of 1881. (G W. Greene) Nation, 32: 70.

— and the West. (W. D. Whitney) New Eng. 19: 1.

— Armand's Travels in. Geog. M. 4: 28.

— Arsenals and Armaments of. Cornh. 26: 693.

— Arts and Industries of. (J. A. Whitney) Ecl. Engin. 23: 343.

— Atlas Sinensis. (H. Yule) Geog. M. 1: 147.

— Autumn on Lower Yang-Tze. Fortn. 25: 830. Same art. Ecl. M. 87: 157. Same art. Liv. Age, 130: 53.

— Barrow's Travels in, 1804. Ecl. R. 1: 241, 334. — (F. Jeffrey) Ed. R. 5: 259.

— British in, 1840. Mo. R. 152: 80.

— Campaigning in, 1859. Cornh. 1: 537.

— Captive in. Chamb. J. 37: 119.

— Captivity in. Penny M. 5: 314.

— Cathay, Travelers in, 13th–15th Centuries. (A. Yule) St. Paul's, 8: 427. Same art. Ecl. M. 77: 527. Same art. Liv. Age, 110: 678.

— Ceremonies in. Chamb. J. 43: 666.

— Christianity in. Quar. 94: 171. — Cong. M. 10: 169–345. — For. Q. 5: 485. — Ecl. Mus. 1: 474. — Liv. Age, 53: 795. — Meth. M. 54: 613. 57: 262.

— — Early. (J. L. Dimon) New Eng. 11: 481.

— — Huc's. Colburn, 110: 1. — Dub. R. 42: 438. 44: 501. — Liv. Age, 59: 157.

— — Kesson's. New Q. 3: 223.

— Chronology of Events, 1831–44. Hunt, 12: 77.

— Civil-Service Examinations in. Cornh. 41: 589.

— Civilization in. (C. K. Adams) Bapt. Q. 4: 412. — All the Year, 3: 319.

— — and Commerce in. Dem. R. 42: 337.

— — and Religion of. Brit. Q. 16: 396.

— Coal Formation of. (J. S. Newberry) Am. J. Sci. 92: 151.

— Commerce of. Chamb. J. 35: 4. — Hunt, 3: 465. 16: 198.

— Commercial Progress in. (J. W. Knox) Putnam, 12: 597. — Dub. Univ. 80: 530.

— Competitive Examinations in. (W. A. P. Martin) No. Am. 111: 62. — All the Year, 12: 445. — Once a Week, 24: 323.

China, Condition of. (A. H. Everett) Dem. R. **21**: 397. — (G. Tucker) Dem. R. **22**: 11.
— Consular or Commercial Cities of. Hunt, **21**: 259, 422.
— Costumes, Arts, etc., of. Anal. M. **1**: 412.
— Court of, in 1773. (W. I. Kip) Overland, **13**: 105, 201.
— Cremation in. (H. A. Giles) Cornh. **39**: 335. Same art. Liv. Age, **141**: 309.
— Crime and Criminals in. Cornh. **12**: 235.
— Cruise on the Yang-Tze. St. James, **14**: 229.
— — up the Yang-Tze in 1858-59. Blackw. **89**: 695.
— Curiosities of. Chamb. J. **23**: 283.
— Currency of. (W. G. Sumner) Nation, **26**: 45. — Bank. M. (L.) **23**: 901. — Hunt, **19**: 319.
— — and Banking of. Bank. M. (L.) **7**: 264. **8**: 151. — Bank. M. (N. Y.) **2**: 601.
— Davis on. Ecl. R. **67**: 146. — Mo. R. **155**: 207. — Liv. Age, **33**: 586.
— De Guignes's Journey to Pekin. Ed. R. **14**: 407. — Quar. **2**: 246.
— Democracy of. (W. Speer) Harper, **37**: 839.
— Destiny of. (O. Tiffany) Chr. Exam. **63**: 200.
— Dining with a Mandarin. Ev. Sat. **11**: 551.
— Dinner à la Chinois. Once a Week, **27**: 103.
— Dinners and Morning Calls in. Once a Week, **6**: 417.
— Dobell's Travels in. Westm. **13**: 114.
— Domestic Life in. Temp. Bar, **41**: 49, 235. Same art. Ecl. M. **82**: 678. Same art. Liv. Age, **121**: 436. **122**: 95.
— Early European Intercourse with. Chr. Rem. **5**: 311.
— Education in. Penny M. **7**: 286.
— — Chinamen in School. (M. Lockwood) Potter Am. Mo. **15**: 443.
— — Philosophy and Letters in, W. A. P. Martin on. (S. W. Williams) Nation, **32**: 245.
— Elgin's Mission to. Bentley, **47**: 136. — Blackw. **87**: 255. — Ed. R. **111**: 96. Same art. Ecl. M. **49**: 439.
— Embassy to. Quar. **17**: 464. — Pamph. **15**: 139. — Mo. R. **85**: 1, 113. **119**: 317. — Ed. R. **29**: 433. — Blackw. **9**: 210.
— — Ellis's. Ecl. R. **27**: 23.
— — of 1869. (N. Brooks) Overland, **3**: 559.
— Emperor of; Gutzlaff's Life of Taou-Kwang. Ecl. R. **96**: 81. Same art. Ecl. M. **27**: 51.
— England's Policy in, 1870. (J. B. Robertson) Westm. **93**: 180.
— English in. Liv. Age, **59**: 383. — (H. Martineau) Tait, **1**: 667.
— English Education in. Liv. Age, **2**: 604.
— English Embassies to. Blackw. **89**: 42.
— English Influence in. (C. W. Dilke) Macmil. **34**: 557.
— Englishman in, Cooper's. Cath. World, **14**: 322.
— Ethical Philosophy of. (W. A. P. Martin) Princ. **34**: 193.
— Execution of an Italian in. (E. Everett) No. Am. **40**: 58.
— Exhibition of the English in. Liv. Age, **1**: 462.
— Extraterritoriality in. (Dr. Macgowan) Contin. Mo. **4**: 556.
— Feng-Shui; or, Science in. Cornh. **29**: 337. Same art. Ecl. M. **82**: 603.
— Feudal. Cornh. **30**: 548. Same art. Ecl. M. **84**: 65.
— First Families of. Ev. Sat. **10**: 110.
— Food and Cookery in. (A. Young) Appleton, **8**: 291.
— Foreign Policy of, 1868. Westm. **90**: 399.
— Fortune and Abbé Huc on. Quar. **102**: 126.
— Fortune's Residence in. Bentley, **42**: 48. — Chr. Obs. **57**: 676. — Liv. Age, **54**: 341. — New Q. **6**: 297.
— Fortune's Wanderings in. Chamb. J. **7**: 299. — Dub. R. **23**: 59. — Ed. R. **88**: 403.
— Fortune's Yeddo and Peking. Liv. Age, **77**: 186.
— Foundling Hospitals in. Chamb. J. **26**: 78. Same art. Liv. Age, **51**: 316.
China, Free Trade to. Quar. **50**: 430. — Mus. **24**: 555.
— From Cambodia to. Chamb. J. **49**: 793, 805.
— Frontier of, and Altai Mountains. Brit. Q. **8**: 344.
— Funeral Ceremonies in. (A. W. Loomis) Overland, **3**: 21. — All the Year, **30**: 162.
— Future of. (Sir R. Alcock) Macmil. **30**: 435. — (Sir W. H. Medhurst) Contemp. **36**: 1. Same art. Liv. Age, **143**: 67. — (D. C. Boulger) 19th Cent. **8**: 266.
— Geological Changes in. (A. S. Bickmore) Am. J. Sci. **95**: 209.
— Geological Explorations in. (F. von Richthofen) Am. J. Sci. **100**: 410.
— Col. Gordon's Exploits in, 1863. Cornh. **10**: 625.
— Mrs. Gray's Canton. (S. W. Williams) Nation, **30**: 197.
— Great Wall of. Once a Week, **6**: 668.
— — Gutzlaff's. Am. Q. **17**: 100. — Quar. **51**: 468. — (E. G. Smith) Chr. Q. Spec. **5**: 591. — (B. B. Edwards) Am. Q. Obs. **1**: 330. — Mo. R. **147**: 276. **184**: 225. — Ecl. R. **59**: 369.
— Hindu Nations of. Ed. R. **43**: 373.
— History of. (J. W. Mann) Mercersb. **1**: 548.
— — and Characteristics of. Ecl. M. **12**: 349.
— — Boulger's. (S. W. Williams) Nation, **33**: 335.
— — Chapter on. (G. G. Alexander) Once a Week, **4**: 607.
— — Early. Westm. **34**: 261.
— — Gutzlaff's Sketch of. Tait, n. s. **2**: 44. — Mo. R. **135**: 238.
— — Romance of. (G. G. Alexander) Once a Week, **6**: 51.
— — Study in. (J. S. Sewall) New Eng. **31**: 57.
— Hong Kong, Canton, and Macao. (W. G. Palgrave) Cornh. **37**: 278.
— Huc's Empire of. Chr. Obs. **56**: 43. — Colburn, **102**: 379. — Dub. R. **38**: 134. — Ecl. R. **101**: 309. — Ed. R. **101**: 415. Same art. Liv. Age, **45**: 663. — Fraser, **51**: 409. — Meth. Q. **15**: 614. — Princ. **27**: 687.
— Humane Societies of. (L. Young) Dark Blue, **3**: 467.
— in the 17th Century. Dub. Univ. **65**: 451.
— in 1703-5. U. S. Cath. M. **4**: 586.
— in 1836-38. Mo. R. **146**: 401.
— in 1842. Mo. R. **160**: 272.
— in 1844. Dub. R. **16**: 444.
— in 1852. Dub. Univ. **40**: 318.
— in 1853. (Dr. Ely) De Bow, **14**: 339. — New Q. **2**: 465.
— in 1857. Liv. Age, **56**: 462.
— Indo-, French in. Ed. R. **147**: 52.
— Infanticide in. (H. J. Coleridge) Month, **36**: 309. — Westm. **95**: 237.
— Institutions of. (S. W. Williams) No. Am. **131**: 205.
— Intercourse with. Quar. **4**: 147. — For. Q. **34**: 432. Same art. Liv. Age, **4**: 634.
— Interior of. No. Brit. **27**: 75. Same art. Ecl. M. **42**: 528.
— Interiors in. (T. Yelverton) Overland, **8**: 415.
— Jesuits in. Hours at Home, **9**: 517.
— Jews in. House. Words, **3**: 452.
— S. Johnson on. (G. F. Flanders) Univ. Q. **35**: 59.
— Journal of three Voyages to. Mus. **25**: 257.
— Journey from Canton to Hankow. (A. S. Bickmore) Am. J. Sci. **96**: 1.
— — in Northern. (R. Pumpelly) Galaxy, **8**: 467.
— Kea-King's Will, and He-Chaou's Inaugural, 1821. Niles's Reg. **20**: 185.
— Kidd on. Ecl. R. **75**: 82.
— Ladies' Feet in. All the Year, **30**: 571.
— Laws of. Quar. **3**: 273.
— Letters from Hong Kong and Macao, 1843. (A. R. Ridgway) Colburn, **70**: 153, 353.
— Libraries of. (W. E. A. Axon) Lib. J. **5**: 6, 37.
— Life in. Ecl. R. **105**: 263. — Lond. Soc. **30**: 490.
— Mandarin's Journey across. (W. F. Mayers) Fraser, **76**: 363.

China, Manners and Customs in. Nat. M. **4**: 395.—Temp. Bar, **41**: 49, 235.—Ev. Sat. **16**: 552.
— — Ancient. St. James, **47**: 49, 136.
— Manufactures in, Some Products of. (J. Itier) J. Frankl. Inst. **42**: 281.
— Margary's Journals and Letters. Nature, **14**: 229.
— Marriage and Infanticide in. (W. H. Cuming) Canad. J. n. s. **11**: 178.
— — of the Emperor. (K. Bismark) Galaxy, **19**: 182. —(R. K. Douglas) Cornh. **27**: 82.
— Married Life in. All the Year, **31**: 42.—Ev. Sat. **15**: 627.
— Meadows on. Ecl. R. **104**: 550.
— Medhurst's State and Prospects of. Am. Meth. M. **21**: 94.
— Mediæval Notices of. Ecl. M. **69**: 449.
— Mesmerism, Planchette, and Spiritualism in. (H. A. Giles) Fraser, **99**: 238.
— Midsummer Ride in South. Cornh. **11**: 307. Same art. Liv. Age, **85**: 64.
— Mining District of. (G. J. Morrison) Ecl. Engin. **20**: 424.
— Missionaries in, 1844. Colburn, **90**: 1.
— — and British Relations with. (J. F. N. Talmadge) Am. Presb. R. **19**: 306.
— — and Mandarins. Macmil. **23**: 171.
— Missionary Conference at Shanghai, 1877. Lond. Q. **52**: 1.
— Missionary Efforts in. (W. Sargent) No. Am. **79**: 158.
— Missionary Voyage to. Mus. **29**: 249.
— Mission Fields in. (W. F. Stevenson) Good Words, **20**: 48–818.—(I. W. Wiley) Meth. Q. **22**: 208.
— Mission Work in. (W. J. Boone) Am. Church R. **31**: 256.
— Missions in, Protestant. (E. R. Barrett) Cong. **7**: 417. **18**: 589.—(S. W. Williams) Presb. R. **2**: 33.—Princ. **42**: 613.—(D. P. Kidder) Meth. Q. **22**: 426. —Meth. Q. **39**: 426.
— Mission of, to Christendom. Blackw. **105**: 194. Same art. Liv. Age, **100**: 746.
— Modern, and the Chinese. Temp. Bar, **29**: 385.
— Mogès's Souvenirs d'une Ambassade en. Bentley, **47**: 483.
— Mohammedanism in. Ed. R. **151**: 359. Same art. Liv. Age, **145**: 515.
— Monastery in. Chamb. J. **31**: 323.
— Morality as the Religion of. (H. J. Warner) Nation, **2**: 820.
— Morrison's Works on. Mo. R. **150**: 1.
— Music of. Lond. M. **1**: 159.
— National Life of. Blackw. **75**: 593.
— New-Year's Day in. House. Words, **19**: 258.—Once a Week, **10**: 151.—Ev. Sat. **9**: 82.
— Night in the Tombs in. Chamb. J. **45**: 113, 132.
— North, Alexander Williamson on. Lond. Q. **35**: 301.
— Notes of Travel in. (J. H. Morris) Canad. J. n. s. **2**: 161.
— Notes on a Voyage to. So. Lit. Mess. **19**: 1–749.
— Notices of, 1834. Meth. M. **57**: 435.
— Nummulitic Formation in. (F. von Richthofen) Am. J. Sci. **101**: 110.
— Occult Science in. (A. W. Loomis) Overland, **3**: 160.
— Officials in. All the Year, **45**: 54.
— On a River in. Once a Week, **14**: 632.
— Opium Smuggling in. Penny M. **9**: 89.
— Opium Trade in. Fraser, **20**: 572.
— Osborne's British Relations with, 1860. Tait, n. s. **27**: 619.
— Overland Route to. Colburn, **143**: 1.—Geog. M. **1**: 144.
— Overland Journey to India from. Chamb. J. **49**: 106.
— Paper-Money and Banking in. Chamb. J. **17**: 347.

China, Past and Present, 1858. Westm. **69**: 370.
— Past and Future of. Blackw. **75**: 54.
— Peking and the Chinese. (C. W. Elliot) Putnam, **12**: 178.
— Penal Code of. (F. Jeffrey) Ed. R. **16**: 476.—Ecl. R. **12**: 942, 1025.—Mo. R. **150**: 236.
— People of. Kitto, **22**: 272.
— Philosophers and Moralists of. (C. H. Dall) Chr. Exam. **84**: 297.
— Physicians in. (J. W. Palmer) Atlan. **21**: 257.
— Police in. Cornh. **3**: 154.
— Political Disturbances in. Ed. R. **102**: 346.
— Polity of. Portfo.(Den.) **6**: 112.
— Population of. (J. Bowring) J. Statis. Soc. **20**: 41. Same art. Ecl. M. **41**: 473.—Am. Q. Reg. **14**: 356.
— Porcelain Rock of. (F. von Richthofen) Am. J. Sci. **101**: 179.
— Posting and Post-Offices in. Cornh. **38**: 95.
— Present Condition of, 1870. Fraser, **82**: 554. Same art. Ecl. M. **76**: 16.
— Printing in. Penny M. **7**: 350.
— Prisons of. (O. Wermuth) Overland, **11**: 314.
— Productions of, Natural and artificial. Ecl. Engin. **3**: 349.
— Progress in. (R. Pumpelly) Nation, **8**: 369.—Blackw. **93**: 44, 133.
— — of Science in. (R. K. Douglas) Pop. Sci. R. **12**: 375. Same art. Ecl. M. **81**: 743.
— Quaint Customs in Kwei-Chow. Cornh. **25**: 92. Same art. Ecl. M. **78**: 322. Same art. Ev. Sat. **12**: 79.
— Railway in. Ecl. Engin. **23**: 36.
— Rates of Commission and Insurance in. Hunt, **12**: 378.
— Relation to Foreign Powers. (Sir R. Alcock) Fortn. **25**: 652.—(R. Pumpelly) No. Am. **106**: 592.—Fraser, **95**: 359.
— — in 1859. Colburn, **117**: 379.
— — in 1870. Ed. R. **133**: 176.
— Religions of. (S. Andrews) Atlan. **25**: 469.—Ecl. R. **112**: 583.—Lond. Q. **30**: 393.—Once a Week, **6**: 125.—Theo. & Lit. J. **11**: 141.
— — Johnson on. (S. Beal) Nation, **29**: 97.
— — Three Systems of. (R. H. Graves) Bapt. Q. **6**: 408. —(W. A. P. Martin) New Eng. **28**: 223.
— Reminiscences of a Lady in. Tinsley, **28**: 230.
— Renaissance in. (W. A. P. Martin) New Eng. **28**: 47.
— Residence in Ningpo. Ecl. M. **2**: 553.
— Richthofen's Travels in. (E. Cunningham) Nation, **16**: 282, 299, 314.—(R. Pumpelly) Nation, **26**: 231, 243.—Nature, **16**: 206.
— Father Ripa's Residence at Pekin. Dub. R. **18**: 112.
— River Scenes in. (H. Martineau) Once a Week, **1**: 146, 176.
— Rivers of. (H. B. Guppy) Nature, **22**: 486. Same art. Ecl. Engin. **24**: 63.
— Roman Catholic Church in. Cath. World, **12**: 208.
— — Literature of. Lond. Q. **47**: 293.
— — Persecution of. Dub. R. **8**: 529.
— Routes to, via Assam. (S. E. Peal) Nature, **20**: 583.
— Royal Asiatic Society. Westm. **14**: 261.
— Royal Marines in. Bentley, **51**: 398.
— Russian Mission to, 1820–21. Ecl. R. **46**: 510.—Mo. R. **113**: 247.—Mus. **11**: 193.
— Science in. (J. Fryer) Nature, **24**: 9, 54.—Liv. Age, **149**: 633.
— Secret Societies of. Month, **41**: 402.
— Service in, 1841–42. Tait, n. s. **11**: 664.
— Shops and Signs in. All the Year, **32**: 196. Same art. Ev. Sat. **17**: 47.
— Six Months with the Expedition to. Mus. **42**: 47.
— Six Weeks in a Tower. Blackw. **91**: 715.
— Sketch-Book in. (E. H. Hall) Dark Blue, **1**: 765.

China, Sketches in. (J. K. Duer) Knick. **55**: 298, 398. — Fraser, **68**: 699. — Penny M. **9**: 245–358.
— Social Life in. (J. Doolittle) Harper, **31**: 429.
— — Doolittle's. (Sir J. Bowring) Fortn. **10**: 343.
— — Romance of. Temp. Bar, **59**: 311. Same art. Liv. Age, **146**: 399. Same art. Ecl. M. **95**: 333.
— Socialism in. Chamb. J. **24**: 93. Same art. Liv. Age, **46**: 691.
— Society and Manners of. New Eng. **8**: 274.
— Southern, Midsummer Ride in. Cornh. **11**: 307.
— Southwestern. (H. Yule) Geog. M. **2**: 97.
— Spirit-Writing in. Blackw. **93**: 499.
— State and Prospects of. Ecl. R. **68**: 271.
— — of Affairs in, 1879. (H. A. Giles) Fortn. **32**: 362.
— State Dinner in. Liv. Age, **56**: 817.
— Statesmen and State Papers of. Fraser, **83**: 328, 503, 613.
— Steam Navigation to. (M. F. Maury) So. Lit. Mess. **14**: 246.
— Street Life in. All the Year, **31**: 498.
— Tai-Ping Rebellion in. (J. E. Johnson) New Eng. **30**: 389. — Blackw. **100**: 604, 683. — Chamb. J. **20**: 163. — Dub. Univ. **61**: 24. — Brit. Q. **18**: 309. Same art. Ecl. M. **31**: 90. — Ecl. M. **63**: 469. — Fraser, **71**: 135. — (W. Sargent) No. Am. **79**: 158. — Hogg, **10**: 479. — Hunt, **52**: 38. — Lond. Q. **20**: 304. — (M. S. Culbertson) Princ. **26**: 321. — Quar. **112**: 500.
— — and England's Policy. Lond. Q. **16**: 222.
— — Callery and Yvan's. Liv. Age, **39**: 180.
— — in 1850. Ecl. R. **99**: 39.
— — in 1851. Colburn, **99**: 180.
— — in 1851–52. Blackw. **74**: 203.
— — in 1853. Fraser, **48**: 596.
— — in 1855. Brit. Q. **22**: 110. Same art. Ecl. M. **36**: 933.
— — in 1857. Tait, n. s. **24**: 193.
— — in 1860. Blackw. **117**: 638. — Tait, n. s. **27**: 499, 562.
— — in 1860–64, Col. Gordon's Chinese Force. Blackw. **101**: 165.
— — in 1861. (L. Oliphant) Good Words, **4**: 186.
— — in 1863. Cornh. **10**: 625.
— — Religious System of. (G. W. Samson) Chr. R. **27**: 305.
— Talk with Mr. Burlingame about. (R. J. Hinton) Galaxy, **6**: 613.
— Tariff of Imports and Exports. Hunt, **14**: 182.
— Tartar Invasion of. Retros. **17**: 313.
— Tea Countries of, Fortune's. Chamb. J. **17**: 395.
— Teas and Tea Country of. Colburn, **95**: 439.
— Theater in. Cornh. **9**: 297.
— — Afternoon at a. Lond. Soc. **31**: 501.
— Tientsin Massacre of Jesuit Missionaries, 1870. Victoria, **17**: 536. — Nation, **11**: 189, 221. — Westm. **95**: 404.
— Time Notation in. (E. W. Jones) Good Words, **16**: 486.
— To and in. (J. R. Browne) Overland, **6**: 155, 233.
— To Pekin and back again. Liv. Age, **64**: 53.
— Trade of. Pamph. **14**: 515. — Mus. **37**: 471. — Hunt, **8**: 249. **12**: 44. — Quar. **4**: 127. — Anal. M. **14**: 359. — Westm. **21**: 221.
— — Thompson on, 1835. Mo. R. **138**: 65.
— — with England. (W. H. Sykes) J. Statis. Soc. **25**: 3. — Quar. **132**: 367. Same art. Liv. Age, **113**: 579.
— — and Tariff of, 1859. Bank. M. (L.) **19**: 305.
— Traveling in. Dub. Univ. **49**: 216.
— Travels in. Meth. M. **43**: 934. — Quar. **102**: 126. Same art. Liv. Age, **55**: 129. — So. R. **4**: 176.
— Voyage to, for opening Intercourse. Mus. **24**: 194. — Mo. R. **132**: 30.
— — Notes on a, 1848. So. Lit. Mess. **18**: 65–705.
China, Voyages to, in olden Time. (W. A. Spear) Pioneer, **1**: 201, 276.
— War of 1840–42 with. (F. Wharton) Hunt, **4**: 9. — (E. W. Stoughton) Hunt, **2**: 386. — For. Q. **24**: 106. **25**: 188. **34**: 432. — Brit. & For. R. **10**: 341. — Quar. **65**: 294. — Westm. **40**: 123. — Fraser, **27**: 108. — Ed. R. **52**: 281. — Am. Ecl. **1**: 111, 288. — Dem. R. **7**: 516. — Blackw. **47**: 368, 717, 847. — Ecl. M. **4**: 382. — Dub. Univ. **21**: 125. — Chr. Exam. **30**: 223. — (W. Adams) Chr. Exam. **32**: 281. — Chr. Exam. **33**: 385. — Fraser, **21**: 365. — Ecl. R. **71**: 699. — Chamb. J. **7**: 155. — Mus. **40**: 221. **41**: 237. — Tait, n. s. **7**: 135. **8**: 66–745. **9**: 820. **10**: 525. — Fraser, **55**: 239.
— War of 1857–59. Quar. **107**: 85. — (W. B. Reed) No. Am. **90**: 125. — Blackw. **87**: 430, 535. **89**: 373.
— — Battle on the Peiho. Blackw. **86**: 647. Same art. Ecl. M. **49**: 375.
— Warlike Power of, Revival of. (C. A. G. Bridge) Fraser, **99**: 778. Same art. Liv. Age, **142**: 114.
— Western. Ed. R. **127**: 357. — Geog. M. **3**: 108, 146. — (W. J. Gill) Geog. M. **5**: 129.
— — Trade Routes to. Ed. R. **137**: 289.
— Williams's Middle Kingdom. Westm. **49**: 241. — (A. P. Peabody) No. Am. **67**: 265. — (S. F. Smith) Chr. R. **13**: 270. — (W. T. Eustis) New Eng. **7**: 215. — Dem. R. **22**: 319.
— Women in, Education and Authorship of. (S. W. Williams) New Eng. **38**: 184.
— Works on, 1839. Chr. Obs. **40**: 225, 303.
— Written Language of. Chamb. J. **40**: 35.
— Yankee in. Potter Am. Mo. **11**: 296.
— Yeng-Ping. (E. Wentworth) Nat. M. **13**: 255.
— Yun-Nan. Cornh. **34**: 193.
See Canton; Pekin; Tea Districts, etc.
China Sea and Japan, United States Expedition to, Perry's. New Q. **5**: 376.
— Notes from. Chamb. J. **45**: 729.
— Tour in. (F. R. Feudge) Lippinc. **14**: 148.
— White's Voyage to. U. S. Lit. Gaz. **4**: 47.
China and Glass Ware, How to take Care of. Pract. M. **5**: 269.
— Bristol. (L. Jewitt) Art J. **15**: 213, 236.
— Chelsea. (L. Jewitt) Art. J. **15**: 21, 61.
— Collectors of, Hints to. (C. Monkhouse) Art J. **33**: 197.
— Dresden. (S. Powers) Nation, **2**: 715. — Colburn, **131**: 185.
— — Manufacture of. Liv. Age, **134**: 372. — Pract. M. **7**: 25.
— Flaws in. All the Year, **4**: 414.
— Lowestoft. (L. Jewitt) Art J. **15**: 129.
— Nantgarw and Swansea. (L. Jewitt) Art J. **20**: 219.
— New Hall. (L. Jewitt) Art J. **16**: 23.
— Old. (R. H. Cave) Fraser, **92**: 501. — (C. Lamb) Lond. M. **7**: 269.
— — and Faience. Gent. M. n. s. **15**: 210.
— Piece of. All the Year, **1**: 16, 37.
— Pinxton. (L. Jewitt) Art J. **20**: 281.
— Plymouth. (L. Jewitt) Art J. **15**: 169.
— Rockingham. (L. Jewitt) Art J. **17**: 348.
— Willow-Pattern Papers. (C. Malcolm) Belgra. **23**: 381. **24**: 89.
See Ceramic Art; Porcelain; Sèvres.
China-Clay Industry of Cornwall and Devon. Pop. Sci. R. **17**: 133. Same art. Liv. Age, **137**: 434. — Pract. M. **7**: 180.
China Fancying; a Reminiscence of Dresden. Temp. Bar, **53**: 545.
China Mania. (C. Drew) Dub. Univ. **87**: 181.
China Plate, Story of a. Liv. Age, **25**: 209.
Chinaman on Western Countries. Lond. Q. **54**: 386.
Chincha Islands. Liv. Age, **40**: 213.

Chincha Islands, New Year's Day at. (S. A. Emery) Sharpe, **46**: 307.
Chinchilla, The. Penny M. **6**: 297.
Chinchon, Countess of, Memoir of. Nature, **11**: 383.
Chinese, The. (J. H. Lanman) Am. Whig R. **4**: 392.— Fraser, **19**: 105. **24**: 612.—Quar. **56**: 489.—Ed. Mo. R. **2**: 533, 550.—(G. B. Bacon) Hours at Home, **8**: 4.—Lakeside, **2**: 203.—(J. Dickinson) Chr. Exam. **65**: 177.—Putnam, **9**: 337.—So. R. n. s. **16**: 288.
— abroad. (G. R. F. Cole) Fraser, **98**: 447.—Ev. Sat. **7**: 460.
— afloat. All the Year, **4**: 116.
— American View of. Nation, **9**: 89.
— and the outer Barbarians. Cornh. **1**: 26.
— Are they a religious People? Lond. Q. **56**: 93.
— as Agriculturists. (A. W. Loomis) Overland, **4**: 526.
— as Colonists. (Sir W. H. Medhurst) 19th Cent. **4**: 517. Same art. Liv. Age, **139**: 50.
— as they are, Lay on, 1841. Mo. R. **154**: 465.
— at Home and abroad. Blackw. **72**: 98.
— Commercial Enterprise of. (T. Knox) Harper, **57**: 427.
— Facts about. Chamb. J. **1**: 339–356.
— in Australia. All the Year, **14**: 471.—Liv. Age, **57**: 860.
— — and the West. (J. A. Langford) Gent. M. n. s. **17**: 320.
— in California. (S. Andrews) Atlan. **25**: 223.—(A. J. Hanson) Meth. Q. **41**: 28.—(J. Hatton) Belgra. **32**: 221.—(H. A. Hill) Penn Mo. **2**: 181.—(A. W. Loomis) Overland, **1**: 360.—(J. A. Palmer, jr.) O. & N. **2**: 692.—(J. S. Silver) Lippinc. **2**: 36.—Lippinc. **11**: 219.—All the Year, **21**: 367.—Blackw. **72**: 98.—Internat. R. **5**: 449.—Chamb. J. **16**: 393.—Liv. Age, **34**: 32.—(W. Speer) Princ. **25**: 83.—Nation, **22**: 241.
— — as Servants. (S. E. Henshaw) Scrib. **12**: 736.
— — Employments of. (A. W. Loomis) Overland, **2**: 231.
— — Women of. (A. W. Loomis) Overland, **2**: 344.
— in Central Asia. Quar. **149**: 463.
— — Boulger on. (E. L. Godkin) Nation, **29**: 113.
— in San Francisco. (A. P. Peabody) Am. Natural. **4**: 660.—(T. J. Vivian) Scrib. **12**: 862.
— — Quarter of. (R. Keeler) Lakeside, **3**: 347.
— — Temples of. (A. W. Loomis) Overland, **1**: 453.
— in the Straits of Malacca. (W. A. Pickering) Fraser, **94**: 438.
— in the United States. (J. D. Edgar) Canad. Mo. **6**: 389.—(V. B. Denslow) Internat. R. **10**: 51.—(E. A. Hart) New Dom. **20**: 501.—(F. D. Y. Carpenter) Lippinc. **27**: 404.—(C. W. Wendte) Unita. R. **5**: 510.—(J. Ellis) Presb. R. **1**: 247.—Chamb. J. **58**: 774.—Republic, **7**: 17.—(G. B. Bacon) Hours at Home, **10**: 276.
— — at Beaver Falls. (A. Rhodes) Lippinc. **19**: 708.
— — Immigration of. (J. T. Bixby) Chr. Exam. **87**: 183.—(A. D. Richardson) Atlan. **24**: 740.—(D. S. Cohen) Penn Mo. **10**: 930.—(H. N. Day) New Eng. **29**: 1.—(M. J. Dee) No. Am. **126**. 506.—(E. Cunningham) Nation, **10**: 9, 139.—(E. L. Godkin) Nation, **9**: 44–309. **11**: 20.—(G. A. Potter) Nat. Q. **41**: 303.—(J. H. Preston) Canad. Mo. **20**: 81.—(G. M. Grant) Canad. Mo. **20**: 207.—(S. W. Williams) Am. J. Soc. Sci. **10**: 90.—Ev. Sat. **9**: 482. (J. Kirkland) Dial (Ch.), **1**: 233.—(D. Ker) Nat. Q. **39**: 250.—(E. S. Todd) Meth. Q. **38**: 268.—(J. A. Kunkleman) Evang. R. **21**: 77.—(D. N. Utter) Unita. R. **12**: 48.—(E. D. Mansfield) Internat. R. **3**: 833.—(R. Pumpelly) Galaxy, **8**: 22.—(F. B. Thurber) Unita. R. **6**: 547.—(R. Webb) Nation, **28**: 316.
Chinese, The, in the United States, Immigration of, and Political Economy. (D. M. Means) New Eng. **36**: 1.
— — — Bills to prevent. (E. L. Godkin) Nation, **28**: 130, 145.
— — — Report of Committee. Cath. World, **26**: 700.
— — — Seward on. (W. G. Sumner) Nation, **32**: 134.
— — — Symposium on. (A. A. Hayes, jr.) Scrib. **17**: 491. *See* Chinese Labor.
— Intellectual Progress of. Penny M. **5**: 285.
— Keen Faun. (P. Mulford) Lippinc. **8**: 405.
— Morality among. Pop. Sci. Mo. **16**: 270.
— picturesquely considered. (R. Keeler) Lakeside, **3**: 347.
— Twenty Years with. (H. Roundy) Lakeside, **3**: 136.
— What they really think of Europeans. Fraser, **83**: 395.
Chinese Amusements. All the Year, **13**: 12.
Chinese and Persian Customs, 450 B.C. St. James, **47**: 377.
Chinese Ball. Liv. Age, **34**: 236.
Chinese Balls, how made. J. Frankl. Inst. **47**: 130.
Chinese Beggars. Once a Week, **29**: 283.
Chinese Boats. Penny M. **11**: 356.
Chinese Boys, My. (F. V. de G. Stevenson) Lippinc. **27**: 261.
Chinese Calculation. Ev. Sat. **10**: 395.
Chinese Case of Breach of Promise. Dub. Univ. **59**: 36.
Chinese Characteristics. (Sir J. Bowring) Fortn. **1**: 561. Same art. Cath. World, **2**: 102.—Brit. Q. **33**: 150.
Chinese Classics. (E. Abbot) No. Am. **103**: 549.—(R. D. Hitchcock) Am. Presb. R. **12**: 631.—(R. H. Maclay) Meth. Q. **37**: 305.—Ed. R. **146**: 317.
— Legge's. (A. Van Name) Nation, **11**: 176.—Brit. Q. **45**: 32.
— Readings from. Cong. **4**: 205. **5**: 477.
Chinese Commissioner's European Tour, 1866. Cornh. **21**: 578.
Chinese Companies of San Francisco. (A. W. Loomis) Overland, **1**: 221.
Chinese Coolie Trade. (W. Ashmore) Chr. R. **27**: 211. *See* Coolies.
Chinese Courtship. For. Q. **22**: 390.
— and Poetry. Colburn, **19**: 350.
Chinese Description of the Earth. Liv. Age, **26**: 426.
Chinese Discovery of America; Leland's Fusang. Penn Mo. **6**: 603. *See* America, Discovery of.
Chinese Drama. Quar. **16**: 396.—All the Year, **13**: 29.—(B. K. Douglas) Contemp. **37**: 123. Same art. Ecl. M. **94**: 349.
Chinese Embassy to Foreign Powers. (T. C. Knox) Harper, **37**: 592.—Nation, **6**: 145.
Chinese Emigration. (E. L. Burlingame) Scrib. **13**: 687.—Chamb. J. **36**: 9.
— and Coolie Trade. Westm. **100**: 75.
— to Peru. (C. R. Markham) Geog. M. **1**: 367.
Chinese English. Penny M. **7**: 189.
Chinese Ethics. (F. Gilbert) Lakeside, **2**: 191.
Chinese Exhibition. Fraser, **27**: 176.
Chinese Fairy Tale. All the Year, **26**: 567.
Chinese Fans. (H. A. Giles) Fraser, **99**: 548. Same art. Liv. Age, **141**: 696.
Chinese Filial Affection. Cath. World, **9**: 416.
Chinese Fishing-Camp, Funeral in. (E. H. Demeritt) Lippinc. **25**: 621.
Chinese Folk-Lore. All the Year, **44**: 204.
Chinese Game, Wei-ch'i. (H. A. Giles) Temp. Bar, **49**: 45.
Chinese Garden of the 11th Century. Chamb. J. **24**: 140.
Chinese Gordon. (C. C. Chesney) Fraser, **79**: 135.
Chinese Historical Dramas and Romances. Dub. Univ. **4**: 548.
Chinese Holidays. (A. W. Loomis) Overland, **2**: 144.
Chinese Horology. (D. J. Macgowan) Am. J. Sci. **63**: 241.
Chinese Jests. Colburn, **16**: 281–572.

Chinese Jugglers. Dub. Univ. **32**: 581.
Chinese Junk, Visit to. Chamb. J. **10**: 40.
Chinese Junks. Penny M. **3**: 9.
Chinese Labor. (C. W. Brooks) Overland, **3**: 407. — (F. H. Norton) Scrib. **2**: 61. — (E. Phelps) Lakeside, **8**: 79.
— Plea for. (A. S. Richardson) Scrib. **2**: 286.
— Skilled. (W. F. G. Shanks) Scrib. **2**: 494.
Chinese Laborers. (R. Pumpelly) Nation, **8**: 449.
Chinese Lacquer, Manufacture of. Pract. M. **3**: 439.
Chinese Language. (S. Powers) Overland, **7**: 353. — (J. E. Johnson) Bib. Sac. **30**: 62. — Am. Bib. Repos. **7**: 219. — Bib. Sac. **5**: 751. — Quar. **5**: 372. — Mo. R. **159**: 371. — Ecl. R. **75**: 673.
— and Akkadian. (S. J. Barrows) Unita. R. **15**: 310.
— and Literature. (E. I. Sears) Nat. Q. **5**: 1.
— Book. (H. A. Giles) 19th Cent. **6**: 804. Same art. Ecl. M. **94**: 108.
— Dictionary of, De Guignes's. Quar. **13**: 56.
— Du Ponceau on Nature and Character of. Mo. R. **153**: 579.
— Future Place in Philology. (W. Simpson) Macmil. **29**: 45. Same art. Ev. Sat. **15**: 593. Same art. Liv. Age, **119**: 757.
— Grammar of. (A. H. Everett) No. Am. **17**: 1.
— Scripture Translation in. (E. C. Lord) Chr. R. **22**: 81.
— spoken at Fuh Chau. (M. C. White) Meth. Q. **16**: 352.
— Word for "God" in. (E. W. Syle) Am. Church R. **7**: 32.
— Words for "God" and "Spirit." Bib. Sac. **35**: 732.
Chinese Letters from California. Pioneer, **3**: 161.
Chinese Literature. Am. Ecl. **2**: 318. **3**: 271, 595. — For. Q. **26**: 127. — (L. Bacon) Chr. Mo. Spec. **9**: 23. — (A. W. Loomis) Overland, **1**: 525. — Chamb. J. **2**: 250, 280, 290. — Am. Church R. **23**: 410. — Ecl. R. **30**: 167. **51**: 318. — Ed. R. **129**: 303. — Portfo.(Den.) **5**: 342, 418, 493. **15**: 464. **16**: 15, 128.
— in Europe. Quar. **11**: 332.
— Juvenile Books in. (S. W. Williams) New Eng. **37**: 297.
— Leih-Tsze. Cornh. **30**: 44.
— Mirror of the Mind. (A.W. Loomis) Overland, **8**: 555.
— Missionary. Quar. **15**: 350.
— A Study in. (H. A. Sawtelle) Bapt. Q. **5**: 294.
— Style of Chinese Prose. (W. A. P. Martin) New Eng. **31**: 234.
— Translations from. Quar. **13**: 408.
— Tsien Ki; a Chinese Novel. Colburn, **143**: 603.
Chinese Loess Puzzle. (J. D. Whitney) Am. Natural. **11**: 705.
Chinese Love Story. Fraser, **90**: 484, 585.
Chinese Mandarins. (E. D. Jones) Good Words, **19**: 190.
Chinese Manners. (A. H. Everett) No. Am. **27**: 524.
Chinese Manufacture, Some Products of. (J. Itier) J. Frankl. Inst. **42**: 281.
Chinese Medicine. (W. Axon) Dub. Univ. **81**: 141. — (A. W. Loomis) Overland, **2**: 496.
Chinese Mohammedans. (J. Anderson) Anthrop. J. **1**: 147.
Chinese Museum in Boston. (J. H. Lanman) Hunt, **14**: 347.
Chinese Mythology. Am. Ecl. **3**: 271.
Chinese New Year's Day in San Francisco. (C. Baldwin) Harper, **62**: 70.
Chinese Novel. Mo. R. **161**: 215.
— A historical. (S. W. Williams) New Eng. **39**: 30.
— Leaf from. (J. T. Doyen) Overland, **1**: 95. — Broadw. **6**: 459.
Chinese Novels and Tales. For. R. **1**: 371.
— and Poetry. Quar. **36**: 496.
— Davis's. Blackw. **13**: 450.
Chinese Officials. Cornh. **3**: 25.
Chinese Official Almanac. (M. Harrington) Am. J. Sci. **116**: 472.
Chinese Pirates. Cornh. **2**: 432.
— Expedition against. Dub. Univ. **35**: 521.
Chinese Play in the Haymarket. (J. A. Wilson) Belgra. **43**: supp. 90.
Chinese Poem. Penny M. **3**: 358.
Chinese Poetry. (J. Fenton) Colburn, **160**: 147, 349. — (W. H. Medhurst) Macmil. **39**: 348. — Fraser, **17**: 259. — Mus. **15**: 366. — Once a Week, **5**: 714.
— and Romance. Quar. **41**: 85.
Chinese Poisons. (D. J. Macgowan) Am. J. Sci. **76**: 225.
Chinese Porcelain Seals found in Ireland. Chamb. J. **16**: 364.
Chinese Primer. (H. A. Sawtelle) Overland, **6**: 177.
Chinese Primers. Chr. Obs. **56**: 626.
Chinese Proper Names. All the Year, **33**: 187.
Chinese Proverbs. (A. W. Loomis) Overland, **10**: 82. — Ecl. M. **94**: 630. — All the Year, **32**: 498. — Chamb. J. **56**: 526.
Chinese Romance. (D. Wedderburn) Fortn. **30**. 493.
Chinese Sacred Edict. Anal. M. **13**: 333.
Chinese Sign-Board Literature. (A. W. Loomis) Overland, **1**: 152.
Chinese Slaves adrift. All the Year, **5**: 249.
Chinese Smuggling-Boats. Hunt, **10**: 161.
Chinese Students in America. (C. F. Thwing) Scrib. **20**: 450.
Chinese Studies. Lond. M. **4**: 47.
Chinese Superstitions. All the Year, **32**: 64. — Once a Week, **29**: 301.
Chinese System of Writing, Du Ponceau's. New York R. **3**: 457. — (J. Pickering) No. Am. **48**: 271. — For. Q. **21**: 316.
Chinese Thoughts. All the Year, **14**: 159.
Chinese Transcendentalism. (J. E. Johnson) O. & N. **2**: 186.
Chinese Transcendentalist. (J. T. Bixby) Mo. Rel. M. **50**: 233.
Chinese Triennial Examinations. (R. H. Graves) Overland, **8**: 259.
Chinese View of the Outer Barbarian. Once a Week, **4**: 440.
Chinese Visiting-Cards. Ev. Sat. **11**: 294.
Chinese Wisdom, Tales of. Mo. Rel. M. **10**: 202, 245.
Chinese Writing and Printing. Chamb. J. **50**: 190. Same art. Ecl. M. **80**: 728.
Chinese Writings on Natural History. (Schott) Ed. New Philos. J. **34**: 153.
Chingford, Old Church and Memorials of. (J. Perry) Antiquary, **3**: 273, 287.
Chinook Indians. (P. Kane) Canad. J. n. s. **2**: 11.
Chiopyle, Falls of. Lond. M. **6**: 48.
Chiozza, War of. (Comte Daru) Am. Whig R. **8**: 399, 470.
Chip Dartmouth. (E. Wright) Atlan. **4**: 40.
Chips from the Library Table. Dub. Univ. **23**: 257, 516.
— from my Studio. (S. H. Morse) Radical, **1**: 184–804.
Chipman, John, Declaration of. N. E. Reg. **4**: 23, 251. **31**: 437.
Chipman Genealogy. (R. M. Chipman) N. E. Reg. **15**: 79.
Chippeway, The, and his Copper Mine; a Sketch. (C. G. Leland) Temp. Bar, **47**: 77.
Chippeway Indians. (J. T. Ducatel) U. S. Cath. M. **5**: 24, 92. — (H. R. Schoolcraft) No. Am. **27**: 89. — (Mrs. Trail) Sharpe, **7**: 114.
Chiriqui, Central America, New Route through. (T. F. Meagher) Harper, **22**: 198.
Chiromancy. (A. Enbule-Evans) St. Paul's, **13**: 332.
Chironomia. (N. H. Eggleston) New Eng. **5**: 546.
Chiselhurst, Residence of Eugénie, 1870, with view. Ev. Sat. **9**: 726, 733.

Chishill, England, Congregational Church at. Cong. M. 15: 457.
Chisholm, Caroline. Chamb. J. 18: 193. Same art. Liv. Age, 35: 445. — Chamb. J. 20: 241. — Liv. Age, 34: 615.
Chisholm, Duncan, Story of. Chamb. J. 16: 93. Same art. Liv. Age, 31: 18.
Chisholm Murder Trial, Moral of. (E. L. Godkin) Nation, 29: 202.
Chiswick, A Day at. (E. Walford) Once a Week, 14: 161.
— May 20, 1864; a Poem. Temp. Bar, 12: 303.
Chiswick Press, The. Am. Bibliop. 8: 87.
Chittagong, Hill-Tribes of. Chamb. J. 46: 679. Same art. Ecl. M. 74: 169.
Chivalric Times, Traits of. Dub. Univ. 72: 313.
Chivalry. (G. W. F. Hegel) J. Spec. Philos. 5: 368. — Ev. Sat. 15: 556. — St. James, 22: 237. — Ox. Prize Ess. 2: 109. — For. Q. 6: 350. — Blackw. 47: 280.
— and the Crusades. Knick. 15: 1.
— and the Laboring Classes. Bost. Q. 4: 183.
— and Romance. For. Q. 6: 349.
— History of. (J. R. Coolidge) No. Am. 89: 383.
— Influence on Literature. So. R. 4: 405.
— Mill's History of. Colburn, 14: 444. — Westm. 5: 59. — Mus. 7: 465. — Mo. R. 107: 383.
— Modern. (H. Blackburn) Victoria, 21: 437.
— Orders of. (J. H. L. Archer) Colburn, 149: 245, 429.
— — Opinions on. (J. H. L. Archer) Colburn, 153: 155.
— Poets of. Am. Mo. M. 5: 434.
— Rise and Decline of, in England. Nat. M. 2: 506.
— Romances of. Sharpe, 5: 11, 45, 119.
— St. Palaye's Memoirs of. Retros. 8: 312.
— Stebbing's History of. Ecl. R. 52: 167.
See Orders.
Chivalries, Customary. Good Words, 5: 385.
Chivers, T. H. Atlanta; a Paul Epic. So. Lit. Mess. 19: 379.
Chlamyphorus truncatus. Penny M. 3: 49.
Chloe. Overland, 6: 188.
Chloride of Silver, Solubility in Water. (J. P. Cooke) Am. J. Sci. 121: 220.
Chloral and other Narcotics. (B. W. Richardson) Contemp. 35: 719. Same art. Pop. Sci. Mo. 15: 491, 646. Same art. Liv. Age, 142: 425.
— Few Words on. Once a Week, 21: 305.
Chloral-Eater, Confessions of an English. (G. Stables) Belgra. 26: 179.
Chloral Hydrate, On. (R. F. Fairthorne) J. Frankl. Inst. 91: 327.
Chloride, Bromide, etc., Effect of Light on. (H. Vogel) J. Frankl. Inst. 77: 122, 182.
— of Calcium for watering Streets, Use of. Pract. M. 6: 348.
— of Lime, or Bleaching Powder. (A. Ure) J. Frankl. Inst. 5: 318, 375.
Chlorine and its Compounds. (E. Mylins) J. Frankl. Inst. 102: 139-422.
— Dissociation of. (H. E. Armstrong) Nature, 20: 357.
— Improvement in Production of, Weldon's. (R. Gersth) Pract. M. 1: 238, 299, 448.
— Process for utilizing dilute. Pract. M. 3: 247.
Chloroform. (C. C. Bourbaugh) U. S. Serv. M. 3: 323. — (C. Richet) Pop. Sci. Mo. 12: 738. — (B. Silliman, jr.) Am. J. Sci. 55: 240. — Bentley, 34: 33. Same art. Ecl. M. 30: 84. Same art. Liv. Age, 38: 412. — Chamb. J. 8: 393. — House. Words, 3: 151.
— and Anæsthetics, their Action and Use. Westm. 71: 99.
— and Ether. Dub. R. 29: 226.
— Consciousness under. (H. Spencer) Mind, 3: 555. Same art. Pop. Sci. Mo. 13: 694.
Chloroform in Surgery. Cornh. 1: 499. Same art. Liv. Age, 66: 720.
— Tests and Purification of. Chamb. J. 13: 280.
— Under. (B. W. Richardson) Pop. Sci. R. 9: 15.
— Use of, in Hanging. (G. W. Peck) Am. Whig R. 8: 283.
Chlorophyll. (S. H. Vines) Nature, 23: 561.
— Function of. (S. H. Vines) Nature, 21: 85.
— Coloring-Matters from, Kraus's. (H. C. Sorby) Nature, 8: 202, 224.
Choate, David. (E. P. Crowell) Cong. Q. 17: 481.
Choate, Rufus. (S. W. McCall) Western, 4: 471. — (C. Brown) No. Am. 96: 194. — (C. A. Stoddard) Hours at Home, 4: 66. — (H. Woodman) Atlan. 6: 79. — (V. W. Kingsley) Nat. Q. 26: 26. — with portrait, (E. P. Whipple) Am. Whig R. 5: 63.
— Anecdotes of. Ev. Sat. 11: 71.
— as an Orator. (E. G. Parker) Putnam, 5: 347.
— Example of professional Power. (W. Lamson) Bapt. Q 1: 6.
— Funeral Obsequies of, with portrait. Ecl. M. 48: 362.
— Orations of. (H. C. Lodge) Nation, 27: 287.
— Recollections of. (E. P. Whipple) Harper, 57: 875.
— Reminiscences of. (G. W. Minns) Am. Law R. 11: 1.
Choate Genealogy. (J. A. Boutelle) N. E. Reg. 15: 293.
Chocolate, Chapter on Theobroma. St. James, 28: 628.
— Chiapa. (S. Baring-Gould) Once a Week, 9: 400.
— Factory of, at Noisiel, Menier's. Pract. M. 5: 365.
Chocolate Manufactory, Visit to. Chamb. J. 18: 280.
Choctaws, Visit to. Chamb. J. 30: 322.
Choice and Chance, Whitworth's. (W. S. Jevons) Nature, 2: 4.
— Power of contrary. (M. P. Squier) New Eng. 18: 307.
Choice Secrets. Internat. M. 5: 546.
Choirs and Chancels, Use of, in South of Europe. (A. Ashpitel and J. H. Parker) Arch. 37: 122, 134.
— and Music, Church. Dub. R. 63: 455. 64: 140.
Choiseul, Duke of. Bentley, 30: 475.
Cholera. (W. A. Hammond) Nation, 1: 306. — (T. Markby) Contemp. 10: 114. — (G. Hayward) No. Am. 35: 92. — (G. Perkins) Chr. Q. Spec. 10: 148. — (G. D. Strong) Knick. 20: 243. — Am. J. Sci. 25: 174. — Am. Q. 10: 334. — For. Q. 8: 462. — Westm. 15: 457. — Fraser, 4: 613. 40: 702. — New Eng. M. 3: 147. — Liv. Age, 27: 24. — Mus. 19: 72. 20: 51, 301. — Am. Mo. R. 2: 473. — Ann. Reg. 7: 21. — Quar. 46: 170, 264. — Niles's Reg. 41: 15. — Mo. R. 125: 504. 126: 450. — So. Lit. J. 4: 48. — (J. Mill) Peop. J. 4: 342. — Once a Week, 19: 33. — Nat. Q. 12: 105.
— and the Board of Health. (S. B. Hunt) Hours at Home, 4: 164.
— and Diarrhœa, Ice Treatment of. West. M. 84: 541. 87: 229.
— and its Oriental Sources. Galaxy, 6: 361.
— and Quarantine. Ed. R. 96: 403.
— and Sun-Spots. Nature, 6: 26.
— and Witchcraft in India. Cornh. 16: 409.
— Appearance of, in England, 1832. Tait, 1: 120, 123, 244.
— Asiatic. (A. S. Pigott) Harper, 13: 359.
— at Bilston, 1832. Chr. Obs. 33: 509.
— at Constantinople, How they treat. Once a Week, 25: 545.
— at Seagley, 1832. Chr. Obs. 34: 1.
— Condition of Atmosphere during. (R. D. Thomson) J. Frankl. Inst. 61: 202.
— Contagious Character of. Fraser, 6: 119.
— Copland on. Ecl. R. 55: 260.
— Facts and Opinions about. (W. P. Garrison) Nation, 2: 520.
— First Blow against. Ev. Sat. 1: 505.

Cholera, Fungoid Origin of, Lewis on. Nature, **3**: 391.
— Gerardin and Gaimard on, 1831-32. Mo. R. **144**: 505.
— How to improve a Visit from. Cong. M. **15**: 219.
— in Asia. (J. C. Peters) Putnam, **13**: 547.
— in Boston. New Eng. M. **4**: 19.
— in England in 1849. Chr. Rem. **19**: 164.
— in India. All the Year, **14**: 423. — Am. Meth. M. **14**: 450.
— in London. Liv. Age, **23**: 373.
— in Malta. Fraser, **73**: 93.
— Influence of Elevation on Fatality of. (W. Farr) J. Statis. Soc. **15**: 155.
— — of impure Water on the Spread of. (H. Whitehead) Macmil. **14**: 182.
— Macnamara on. Nature, **4**: 302.
— March of. Galaxy, **1**: 107.
— Moral Preservatives against. Cong. M. **15**: 153.
— not always an Enemy. (D. K. Whittaker) So. Lit. J. **3**: 269.
— not contagious. Peop. J. **6**: 236.
— Notes on. Lond. Q. **27**: 218.
— Origin and Spread of, in a District in Devonshire, 1849. (A. C. McLaren) J. Statis. Soc. **13**: 103.
— Pathology of Discovery of. Liv. Age, **89**: 422.
— Reese on. Am. Meth. M. **15**: 294.
— Spasmodic. Ill. M. **2**: 265, 321.
— Track of. Ev. Sat. **11**: 278.
— Treatment of. (W. Tempest) Canad. J. n. s. **11**: 163. — (S. S. Alison) Peop. J. **6**: 254, 289.
— — and Remedy of. Ecl. R. **98**: 621.
— True Mission of. (J. Saunders) Peop. J. **6**: 211.
— — What is? Hogg, **2**: 273.
Cholera Camp in India. (Mrs. Charlton) Peop. J. **7**: 257.
Cholera Conference, Constantinople, 1866. Quar. **122**: 29.
— Vienna, 1875. Pract. M. **5**: 128.
Cholera Morbus. (D. Uwins) Colburn, **32**: 13.
— at Saratoff. Cong. M. **15**: 27, 144.
Cholera-Orphan Schools, 1833. Tait, **3**: 688.
Cholera Poison. Chamb. J. **21**: 18. Same art. Liv. Age, **40**: 428.
Cholera Seasons of 1832 and 1834. (C. Dade) Canad. J. n. s. **7**: 17.
Chomley Family, Some Passages from the History of. Fraser, **72**: 387.
Chopin, F. (A. R. Gere) Atlan. **31**: 420. — (F. Hueffer) Fortn. **28**: 377. — Ecl. M. **19**: 543. — Bentley, **27**: 191.
— and Schubert. (H. R. Haweis) Contemp. **2**: 80.
— Life of. So. R. n. s. **15**: 435.
— — and Letters of. (H. T. Finck) Nation, **25**: 11.
Chops. All the Year, **21**: 562.
Choral Service. (W. Staunton) Am. Church R. **19**: 238.
Chorister Boys. Tinsley, **28**: 83.
Chorley, Henry F. Ev. Sat. **15**: 654.
— and his Contemporaries. Temp. Bar, **40**: 93.
Chorpenning Claim. (C. C. Nott) Nation, **15**: 228.
Choruses, Ancient English. All the Year, **30**: 316.
Chota Nagpore, Gospel in. (W. F. Stevenson) Good Words, **2**: 35.
Chota Sahib Charlie. (A. S. Harrison) Once a Week, **17**: 721, 751.
Choteau Avenue M. E. Church, South. So. R. n. s. **21**: 201.
Chouan, Song of. Dub. Univ. **3**: 10.
Chouans of Le Maine. Peop. J. **5**: 9-45.
Chrisna, the Queen of the Danube. (X. B. Saintine) Liv. Age, **61**: 345-593.
Christ. *See* Jesus Christ.
Christ of Ausfeldt; a Legend. Cath. World, **10**: 774.
Christ Church, London. Penny M. **1**: 204, 212.
Christ Church Servitors in 1852. Macmil. **19**: 49.
Christ's Hospital, Blue-Coat Boys at Supper. St. James, **14**: 463.
— Speech-Day at. Hogg, **10**: 390.
— Thirty Years ago. (C. Lamb) Lond. M. **2**: 483.
— Trollope's History of. Mo. R. **137**: 480.
Christen, Raphael, Obituary of. Art J. **32**: 208.
Christendom, Ages of, before the Reformation. Brit. Q. **26**: 144. Same art. Ecl. M. **42**: 466.
— and Heathendom. (E. E. Hale) Unita. R. **2**: 385.
— and Islam, a Turkish Effendi on. Blackw. **127**: 1.
— Creed of, Greg on. No. Brit. **16**: 119.
— Divisions of, Ffoulkes on. Dub. R. **60**: 396. **61**: 221.
— Formation of. (T. W. Allies) Month, **30**: 227. — Chr. Rem. **50**: 266. — Dub. R. **57**: 425. — Cath. World, **2**: 356.
— History of, Sketches from. Month, **2**: 253, 357, 398.
— Iron Age of. (A. F. Hewit) Cath. World, **25**: 459.
— Reunion of. Month, **7**: 139.
— — Manning on. Month, **4**: 379. **5**: 160.
— Separated. Month, **31**: 1.
See Church Union; Church Unity.
Christian, Jonathan. Dub. Univ. **84**: 406.
Christian VII., King of Denmark. (L. Wraxall) Temp. Bar, **12**: 98.
— and his Queen. Lond. M. **2**: 176.
Christian, Active, Hinton's. (N. Porter) Chr. Q. Spec. **5**: 552.
— and Mohammedan, Curious Conference between. Lond. M. **17**: 325.
— Inner Life of, Rauch's. (H. Harbaugh) Mercersb. **9**: 435.
— Triumphant. Chr. Obs. **10**: 733.
— What constitutes a? (T. J. Sawyer) Univ. Q. **26**: 80. — (W. R. French) Univ. Q. **22**: 420.
— What is it to be a? (J. T. Bixby) Mo. Rel. M. **49**: 313.
Christians, Allusion to, in Juvenal's 6th Satire. (Earl Stanhope) Arch. **44**: 1.
— Causes of Lukewarmness in. (H. Ware) Chr. Exam. **1**: 13.
— Duty to the World. (H. Ware) Chr. Exam. **1**: 341.
— Early, Festivals of. (A. Lamson) Chr. Exam. **38**: 35.
— — Persecutions of. (F. Dyer) Cong. R. **9**: 36. — (R. Seton) Cath. World, **22**: 104.
— — Piety of. (C. E. Stowe) Am. Bib. Repos. 2d s. **3**: 91.
— — Traits in the Lives of. Chr. R. **8**: 50.
See Church, Early; Church History.
— Eastern. (T. J. Lamy) Dub. R. **84**: 397. — (W. G. Palgrave) Quar. **127**: 1.
— in what Sense called Sons of God. Chr. Mo. Spec. **1**: 289.
— Madness of the Anti-. Brownson, **4**: 86.
— Mitchell's Guide of young. (J. Mitchell) Chr. Q. Spec. **6**: 140.
— Political Duties of. Am. Q. Obs. **1**: 1. — Ecl. R. **70**: 314.
Christian Aims and Instrumentalities. (J. Whitman) Mo. Rel. M. **4**: 164.
Christian Alliance. (G. Peck) Meth. Q. **7**: 151.
— Address of. Cong. M. **28**: 841.
Christian and Ante-Messianic Dispensations compared. (S. Lee) New Eng. **30**: 231.
Christian Antiquities. Princ. **24**: 1.
— at Rome. (G. E. Ellis) Chr. Exam. **28**: 325.
— Coleman's. Ecl. R. **76**: 283.
— Guericke's Manual of. (W. M. Reynolds) Evang. R. **2**: 576.
— Henry's. (J. A. Alexander and S. Miller) Princ. **10**: 153.
— in the East. Month, **3**: 194.
— Smith's Dictionary of. (M. Valentine) Luth. Q. **6**: 303.
Christian Apologetics. *See* Apologetics.

Christian Belief and National Life. (J. B. Brown) Contemp. 38: 737.
Christian Biography. (D. March) New Eng. 7: 399.
Christian Brethren, Dissensions among. (S. R. Andrew) Chr. Q. Spec. 9: 554.
Christian Bride; a Poem. (T. Aird) Blackw. 37: 179.
Christian Brothers. House. Words, 1: 489.
— and their Lesson-Books. Fraser, 89: 186.
— School for poor Children. Am. J. Educ. 3: 437.
Christian Catholic Church of Switzerland, Prayers and Vespers of. (G. F. Siegmund) Am. Church R. 33: 11.
— Eucharistic Office of. (C. R. Hale) Am. Church R. 33: 35.
See Old Catholics.
Christian Certainty, Wainwright on. Chr. Obs. 65: 569.
Christian Character. Chr. Mo. Spec. 4: 349, 584.
— Adaptation to the Age. Chr. Mo. Spec. 10: 561.
— and religious Feeling. (G. H. Emerson) Univ. Q. 19: 401.
— and secular Pursuits. (G. Fisk) Ex. H. Lec. 7: 365.
— in Redemption of the World. (A. Phelps) Bib. Sac. 11: 490.
— Seven Aspects of. (J. S. Howson) Good Words, 15: 141.
— Symmetry of. (S. R. Andrew) Chr. Q. Spec. 7: 546. — (A. P. Peabody) Unita. R. 7: 68.
— Ware on the Formation of. Spirit Pilg. 5: 277.
Christian Charity in the Campaign of 1866. Month, 6: 358.
— Model of. (J. Winthrop, 1630) Am. Q. Reg. 13: 213.
Christian Circumspection. Chr. R. 6: 213.
Christian Citizen. Chr. Exam. 26: 290.
Christian Civilization, Modern. Ecl. M. 47: 175.
Christian Commission, United States. (L. Moss) Nation, 6: 272. — (M. L. Stoever) Evang. R. 16: 258.
— Moss's History of. (J. R. Dennett) Nation, 6: 214.
Christian Communion. (S. K. Lothrop) Chr. Exam. 44: 296. — Meth. M. 26: 407. — Cong. 2: 278.
Christian Comprehensiveness. (H. Bushnell) New Eng. 6: 81.
Christian Conditions. Fortn. 29: 228.
Christian Consolations. (H. Bacon) Univ. Q. 5: 36.
Christian Controversy. (W. R. Waters) Radical, 9: 181.
Christian Cosmos. (A. T. Bledsoe) So. R. n. s. 23: 103, 253. 24: 5, 253.
Christian Courtesy. (W. C. Richards) Chr. R. 19: 498. — Chr. Mo. Spec. 5: 57.
Christian Covenant, Pott's Considerations on. Chr. Obs. 3: 292.
Christian Crown. (J. Savage) Cath. World, 3: 736.
Christian Denomination. (E. Edmunds) Cong. Q. 2: 305.
— Fifty Years of. (T. Munnell) Chr. Q. 8: 289.
— in the United States. (S. Clough) Chr. Exam. 4: 183. — Cong. M. 15: 217.
— Origin and History of the Sect. (E. H. Sears) Chr. Exam. 57: 42.
Christian Devotion to Others. Cong. M. 28: 791.
Christian Disciples. *See* Disciples.
Christian Doctrine. *See* Theology, Doctrinal.
Christian Duty and Doctrine. Meth. Q. 12: 608.
— Theory of. (J. L. Daveis) Fortn. 12: 1.
Christian Education. Spirit Pilg. 1: 561. — Chr. Disc. 1: 444. — So. Lit. Mess. 1: 432. — (F. Close) Ex. H. Lec. 9: 199.
— Babington on. (H. R. Weed) Princ. 4: 82.
Christian Emperors and Pagan Art. Month, 37: 172.
Christian Enterprise. (W. A. P. Martin) Princ. 34: 668.
— Celebration of. (F. D. Huntington) Mo. Rel. M. 8: 459.
Christian Ethics. (S. Osgood) Chr. Exam. 29: 153. 30: 145.
— and Ethics of Christ. Theo. R. 1: 396.
Christian Ethics and J. S. Mill. Dub. Univ. 54: 387.
— Lange's. Bib. Sac. 36: 373.
— Wardlaw's. (N. Porter, jr.) Chr. Q. Spec. 7: 392. — (O. Dewey) Chr. Exam. 19: 1.
See Christian Morals; Ethics.
Christian Experience. (L. L. Pinkerton) Chr. Q. 2: 332.
— and Ministerial Success. (E. B. Smith) Chr. R. 21: 571.
Christian Faith, Confusion in, 1881. (R. B. Welch) Presb. R. 2: 261.
— Simplicity in, Motte on. Chr. Exam. 4: 348.
— Stability in. (O. Dewey) Chr. Exam. 11: 275.
Christian Family and Manners in 2d Century. (J. Tulloch) Good Words, 2: 180.
Christian Fathers. *See* Fathers.
Christian Fellowship. (I. Errett) Chr. Q. 1: 22. — (L. Woods and W. S. Plummer) Lit. & Theo. R. 2: 194. — Prosp. R. 1: 392.
— Range of. (G. W. Cox) Theo. R. 13: 499.
Christian Festivals and Pagan Rites. Canad. Mo. 10: 525.
Christian first Love. Chr. Mo. Spec. 4: 57, 127.
Christian Fraternity, Sermon on. (A. P. Stanley) Good Words, 16: 50.
Christian Idea of God. (G. Matheson) Brit. Q. 71: 127.
Christian Imperialism. Month, 35: 313.
Christian Influence Society, Prize Essays of. Ecl. R. 69: 125.
Christian Inscriptions in France, Early. Brit. Q. 61: 125.
— in Gaul. (W. G. Humphry) Contemp. 3: 410.
Christian Institutions, Stanley's. Quar. 152: 414. — Ed. R. 154: 295.
Christian Intercourse. Chr. Mo. Spec. 4: 504. — (J. Arnold) Chr. Q. Spec. 8: 292.
— in the Early Ages. (A. Lamson) Chr. Exam. 38: 108.
Christian Knowledge Society, Biblical Labors of. Chr. Obs. 53: 547.
Christian Layman. (H. Ware, jr.) Chr. Exam. 28: 122.
Christian Liberty. (W. M. Reynolds) Evang. R. 12: 161. — (O. A. Skinner) Univ. Q. 6: 371. — (F. T. Washburn) Unita. R. 4: 329. — (J. H. Morison) Mo. Rel. M. 43: 455. — (E. H. Sears) Mo. Rel. M. 43: 529. — So. R. n. s. 23: 320.
— Butler's Sermon on. Chr. Obs. 11: 41.
Christian Life. Chr. Q. 7: 363.
— Bayne's. (R. Ellis) Chr. Exam. 59: 438. — Chr. R. 20: 602. — Ecl. R. 103: 386. — Hogg, 13: 465.
— Boardman's Higher. (J. J. Abbott) Bib. Sac. 17: 508.
— Completeness in. (S. Harris) New Eng. 7: 369.
— Is it feasible in these Days? (W. R. Greg) Contemp. 21: 680.
— Line of. (T. Munnell) Chr. Q. 1: 383.
— Primitive. (J. H. Means) Cong. R. 10: 267.
— Reasonableness of. (H. Alford) Good Words, 10: 108.
— Theories of. (Ray Palmer) New Eng. 3: 373.
Christian Literature, Dr. Beard's Library of. Bib. R. 6: 412.
— Early. (J. J. Reed) Nat. Q. 18: 23. — Theo. R. 2: 543.
— Early History of. (G. E. Ellis) Chr. Exam. 35: 55, 137.
— Importance of. Am. Q. Reg. 7: 4.
Christian Living, Plain Words on. (C. J. Vaughan) Good Words, 5: 72–916.
Christian Ministry. *See* Ministry.
Christian Morals. Westm. 20: 100. — Chr. Mo. Spec. 2: 175.
— Fox on. (O. A. Brownson) Chr. Exam. 17: 283.
— French Society of. Chr. Disc. 5: 469.
— Sewell's. (R. S. Candlish) No. Brit. 1: 183.
— Spaulding's Philosophy of. Ecl. R. 81: 579.
Christian Mother, Influence of. Chr. R. 3: 20.
Christian Myths and Pantheism. Chr. Rem. 15: 353.

Christian Name. (S. Cox) Cong. **2**: 147, 210. — (W. K. Pendleton) Chr. Q. **8**: 61.
— and Christian Liberty, Lothrop on. Chr. Exam. **34**: 110.
— Meaning of. Mo. Rel. **36**: 101. — (P. Schaff) Mercersb. **3**: 593.
— only proper Name for Disciples of Christ. (J. Pierce) Mo. Rel. M. **5**: 361, 543.
Christian Names. *See* Names, Christian.
Christian Nurture. (P. S. Davis) Mercersb. **15**: 109. — (A. N. Littlejohn) Am. Church R. **10**: 421.
— Neglect of. (T. C. Pitkin) Am. Church R. **7**: 86. *See* Bushnell, H.; Children.
Christian Obligation for the Conversion of the World. Princ. **4**: 309.
Christian Observer. Liv. Age, **4**: 339. — Chr. Obs. **71**: 842.
Christian Opinions, Early, in New Testament. (J. J. Tayler) Theo. R. **9**: 1, 161.
Christian Orators, Early, and their Age. Dem. R. **14**: 50.
Christian Oratory, Moule's. Liv. Age, **63**: 298.
Christian Patriarchate. (R. C. Jenkins) Contemp. **24**: 842.
Christian Peace or Christian Union? (J. Walker) Chr. Exam. **39**: 53.
Christian Perfection. *See* Perfection.
Christian Persuasion, Work of. (A. Mackennal) Cong. **1**: 513, 577.
Christian Philosopher. (D. Olmsted) Chr. Mo. Spec. **9**: 149.
Christian Philosophy. (R. Whittingham) Am. Church R. **32**: 245.
— Origen, and the Beginning of. (B. F. Westcott) Contemp. **35**: 324, 489. Same art. Liv. Age, **141**: 643. **142**: 131.
Christian Politics. (E. Stearns) Chr. Q. Spec. **7**: 540. **10**: 421.
— Bates on. Chr. Obs. **5**: 482, 621.
Christian Principle, its Influence upon Government. (E. McPherson) Evang. R. **9**: 564.
Christian Profession, Nature of. (R. L. Breck) Danv. Q. **1**: 230.
Christian Professor, James's. (H. G. Ludlow) Chr. Q. Spec. **10**: 90. — (Z. Paddock) Meth. Q. **7**: 338.
Christian Prospects of the World to come. Liv. Age, **45**: 104.
Christian Prudence. Theo. Repos. **3**: 119.
Christian Purity. (L. R. Dunn) Meth. Q. **33**: 206.
Christian Religion. *See* Christianity.
Christian Researches, Jowett's. Chr. Obs. **23**: 30. **25**: 560.
Christian Rites. (O. Dewey) Chr. Exam. **3**: 8.
Christian Sacraments. *See* Sacraments.
Christian Schools and Scholars. Kitto, **40**: 217.
— — Early. (J. E. McGee) Cath. World, **6**: 44.
— and Worship of 2d Century. (J. Tulloch) Good Words, **2**: 69.
Christian Science, Adams's. Am. Church R. **3**: 512.
Christian Society, Genesis of. (J. H. W. Stuckenberg) Luth. Q. **6**: 344.
Christian Societies, Survey of. Chr. Rem. **36**: 102.
Christian Standpoint. (M. Kieffer) Mercersb. **8**: 478.
Christian State, Birks's. Ecl. R. **86**: 535.
Christian Statesmen. (E. H. Gillett) Hours at Home, **1**: 49, 315. **3**: 161, 239. **4**: 67.
Christian System, T. Robinson on. Chr. Obs. **5**: 161, 227.
— Unity of. (J. F. Rowe) Chr. Q. **7**: 69.
Christian Teacher. (H. Ware) Chr. Exam. **25**: 391.
Christian Tracts. Chr. Disc. **2**: 146.
Christian Truth in false Religious Systems. Bost. R. **4**: 170.
Christian Union. (J. W. McLane) New Eng. **4**: 532. — Chr. Q. Spec. **9**: 65, 289. — Dem. R. **12**: 563. — (J. P. Thompson) New Eng. **4**: 132. — (H. Heugh) No. Brit. **1**: 412. **2**: 565. — (S. Miller) Princ. **8**: 11. **20**: 104. — Chr. R. **3**: 109. **7**: 342. — Ecl. R. **81**: 664. — (J. H. Raymond) Chr. R. **12**: 155, 477. — (B. B. Smith) Lit. & Theo. R. **2**: 507. — (S. S. Schmucker) Am. Bib. Repos. **11**: 86, 363. — (O. Dewey) Chr. Exam. **40**: 56. — (G. Putnam) Chr. Exam. **16**: 24. — (L. Woods, jr.) Lit. & Theo. R. **3**: 140, 311. — (W. T. Moore) Chr. Q. **1**: 100. — (J. W. Nevin) Mercersb. **15**: 73. — Cong. M. **22**: 445. **27**: 829.
— and Liturgical Tendencies, 1859. (L. H. Steiner) Mercersb. **11**: 506.
— Basis of. (J. S. Lamar) Chr. Q. **5**: 182. — (Rev. E. Mannering) Cong. M. **22**: 345. — (W. H. H. Marsh) Bapt. Q. **7**: 293. — Mercersb. **21**: 374. — (J. W. Nevin) Mercersb. **21**: 397.
— Calvin's Love of. (W. M. Blackburn) Am. Presb. R. **17**: 223.
— Conference on, Liverpool, Oct. 1, 1845. Cong. M. **28**: 773.
— Essays on. No. Brit. **2**: 565.
— Letters on. (J. Jordan and T. Biddle) Cong. M. **28**: 852.
— Practical Steps of. (W. W. Patton) Cong. Q. **5**: 25.
— Problem of. (D. Burt) Cong. Q. **5**: 161.
— Suggestions on. (A. S. Thelwall) Cong. M. **28**: 810, 847.
See Church Union.
Christian Unity. (T. Richey) Am. Church R. **16**: 441.
— and Church Architecture. (W. A. Dod) Mercersb. **9**: 561.
— Desire for. (W. Adams) Am. Church R. **17**: 460.
— Law of. (C. Wordsworth) 19th Cent. **3**: 888.
See Church Unity.
Christian Vagabond. (B. Jerrold) Gent. M. n. s. **4**: 50–641. **5**: 205–456.
Christian Vigilance. Chr. Obs. **6**: 643.
Christian Virtue originates in Redemption. (S. Harris) Bib. Sac. **28**: 548.
— Peculiarities of. (S. Harris) Bib. Sac. **28**: 553.
Christian Warfare. (W. E. Channing) Chr. Exam. **1**: 102.
Christian Women and English Women. Month, **8**: 529.
— of the first three Centuries. (A. Hovey) Chr. R. **23**: 1.
Christian Work, Voluntary Societies for. (R. Palmer) Cong. Q. **17**: 369.
Christian Worship. *See* Worship.
Christian Year, and J. Keble. (W. C. Lake) Contemp. **2**: 314.
— and Preaching. (G. L. Staley) Mercersb. **16**: 297.
See Church Year.
Christian Hazell's Married Life. Eng. Dom. M. **22**: 1–286. **23**: 1–287. **24**: 11–238.
Christian Wolf; a true Story, from the German. Portfo. (Den.) **24**: 490.
Christiana. (T. Shairp) Belgra. **24**: 220.
Christiania, Visit to. (R. Chambers) Chamb. J. **12**: 328, 337.
Christianity. (R. W. Emerson) Radical, **1**: 34. — (R. G. Ingersoll and J. S. Black) No. Am. **133**: 109. — (R. G. Ingersoll) No. Am. **133**: 477. — Lond. Q. **48**: 322.
— a civilized Heathenism. (J. H. Morison) Unita. R. **3**: 59.
— a new Influx of Power. (E. H. Sears) Mo. Rel. M. **44**: 193.
— a Study for intelligent Men. (H. Colman) Chr. Exam. **1**: 21.
— a sufficient Renovator in State. (M. Smith) Cong. Q. **9**: 235.

Christianity, a supernatural Revelation. (C. A. Bartol) Chr. Exam. **31**: 348.
— the absolute Religion. (S. N. Callender) Ref. Q. **28**: 430.
— Accordance with Nature of Man. Ecl. M. **43**: 1.
— adapted to Man. Chr. R. **2**: 74. — (M. Hopkins) Am. Bib. Repos. **5**: 403.
— Aggressive Spirit of. (E. W. Reynolds) Univ. Q. **16**: 77. — (S. D. Clark) New Eng. **15**: 221.
— Aim of, for those who accept it. (R. S. Storrs) Princ. **39**: 365.
— Allotropic. Westm. **104**: 41.
— Allusions to, by Greek and Roman Writers. (H. T. Tzschirner) Kitto, **10**: 257. Same art. Am. Bib. Repos. **11**: 203.
— an essential Want of Man. Chr. Q. Spec. **9**: 573.
— an Organ of political Movement. Ecl. M. **8**: 221.
— Ancient. Blackw. **101**: 415.
— — Taylor on. Dub. Univ. **15**: 479. — Ecl. R. **76**: 1.
See Christianity, Early; Church History.
— and the Age, Vaughan's. Brit. Q. **10**: 528. — Prosp. R. **5**: 347.
— and Antichristianism. (W. E. Manning) Contemp. **24**: 149.
— and Art. (E. E. Higbee) Mercersb. **21**: 341.
— and Buddhism. (W. McDonnell) Canad. Mo. **13**: 393.
— and Christ. (W. H. Corning) New. Eng. **14**: 250.
— — Originality of. Bost. Q. **1**: 129.
— and the Church. (T. G. Apple) Mercersb. **19**: 623.
— — identical. Brownson, **14**: 327.
— — Schenkel on. Kitto, **39**: 423.
— and Civilization. (R. Ellis) Mo. Rel. M. **49**: 305. — (L. H. Shuck) Bapt. Q. **8**: 50. — (C. P. Wing) Am. Presb. R. **14**: 88.
— and the Clearing-up. (F. A. Henry) J. Spec. Philos. **12**: 171, 337.
— and Colleges. (T. G. Apple) Mercersb. **24**: 634.
— and Commerce, Chalmers on. Meth. M. **44**: 452.
— and Culture. (E. H. Chapin) Univ. Q. **7**: 156. — Theo. Ecl. **6**: 585. *See* Christianity and Modern Culture.
— and Economical Science. Ecl. R. **107**: 415.
— and Epic Poetry. (J. Very) Chr. Exam. **24**: 201.
— and Fall of the Roman Empire. So. Lit. Mess. **20**: 1.
— and the Formative Arts. Prosp. R. **3**: 157.
— and Free Religion. (C. K. Whipple) Radical, **7**: 122.
— and Free Thought. (G. S. Merriam) Scrib. **14**: 820. — (A. Mahan) Ex. H. Lec. **5**: 119.
— and Gentilism. Brownson, **17**: 1.
— and the Germanic Nations. (A. Michelsen) Luth. Q. **8**: 501.
— and Heathenism. (E. Zeller) Contemp. **29**: 1027. Same art. Sup. Pop. Sci. Mo. **1**: 158.
— — Early Conflicts of. Univ. Q. **18**: 413. — (J. J. Keane) Am. Cath. Q. **5**: 468.
— and Hinduism. Liv. Age, **57**: 359.
— and Humanity. (J. W. Nevin) Mercersb. **20**: 469.
— and Islamism. (G. F. Herrick) Bib Sac. **23**: 406. — (G. P. Marsh) Chr. Exam. **65**: 94. — Dem. R. **36**: 375.
— and its Definitions. (W. J. Potter) Radical, **7**: 81.
— and Judaism. Bost. R. **2**: 175. — Cath. World, **27**: 351, 564. — Theo. Repos. **5**: 289, 366.
— — and Heathenism. No. Brit. **47**: 257.
— — — Döllinger on. Dub. R. **43**: 449.
— and Liberty. (D. R. Goodwin) Am. Church R. **28**: 321.
— and Mankind, Bunsen on. Kitto, **15**: 1.
— and modern Criticism. Bost. R. **1**: 261. **2**: 382.
— and modern Culture. Canad. Mo. **8**: 523.
— and modern Progress. (A. Raleigh) Theo. Ecl. **6**: 53.
— and modern Scepticism. (C. K. Paul) Theo. R. **9**: 259.
— and the modern Spirit. Brit. Q. **69**: 273.
Christianity and modern Thought. (E. A. Horton) Unita. R. **13**: 561. — (F. R. Conder) Dub. Univ. **92**: 129.
— and Moral Philosophy. (C. A. Row) Contemp. **11**: 392.
— and Morality. (F. Guizot) Hours at Home, **7**: 235.
— and Mosaism. (H. Alford) Good Words, **10**: 274.
— and Natural Religion. (F. Guizot) Theo. Ecl. **2**: 165.
— and Nature. (W. H. Furness) Chr. Exam. **43**: 31.
— and other Religions. Brit. Q. **29**: 83.
— and our social Relations. (O. S. Stearns) Chr. R. **13**: 572.
— and Paganism. (S. S. Hebberd) Chr. Exam. **86**: 125.
— and Patriotism. (R. F. Littledale) Contemp. **30**: 100. Same art. Sup. Pop. Sci. Mo. **1**: 222. — So. Lit. Mess. **8**: 600.
— and Philosophy. (T. G. Apple) Mercersb. **19**: 225. — (L. Woods, jr.) Lit. & Theo. R. **1**: 483, 669.
— and Positivism. (B. F. Westcott) Contemp. **8**: 371.
— and Probabilities. Chr. Rem. **14**: 39.
— and Pseudo-Christianity. (E. C. Towne) Chr. Exam. **82**: 133.
— and Religion. (E. V. Gerhart) Mercersb. **11**: 483. **12**: 251.
— and the Roman Empire. Dub. R. **60**: 456.
— and Rome before Constantine. (A. Harnack) Princ. n. s. **2**: 239.
— — under Diocletian. Chr. Obs. **1**: 641.
— and Science. (O. A. Brownson) Cath. World, **6**: 330.
— and the Science of Religion. Lond. Q. **55**: 376.
See Science and Religion.
— and Secularism. (G. E. Ellis) Chr. Exam. **55**: 267.
— and Socialism. (S. Osgood) Chr. Exam. **45**: 194.
— and Speculative Theology. (J. Hunt) Contemp. **16**: 422.
— and the State. (R. Patterson) Cong. R. **10**: 209.
— and Theism. (F. E. Abbot) Chr. Exam. **79**: 157.
— and the two Civilizations. Brit. Q. **34**: 406.
— and Utilitarianism. (J. L. Davies) Victoria, **1**: 142.
— and Ultramontanism. (A. P. Stanley) Contemp. **24**: 494.
— and the World's Progress. (A. Barnes) Am. Presb. R. **14**: 564.
— Anglo-Saxon and Anglo-Norman. No. Brit. **37**: 35. Same art. Ecl. M. **57**: 289.
— the *a priori* Novum Organum of. (L. H. Atwater) Princ. n. s. **4**: 517.
— Apologetic Lectures at Bremen. Lond. Q. **34**: 439.
— Apostolic, James Martineau on. Brit. Q. **14**: 473.
— Application to Individuals. (E. Pond) Lit. & Theo R. **1**: 632.
— applied to commercial Life. Portfo.(Den.) **25**: 193.
— Arnold's Views on. (T. S. Perry) No. Am. **117**: 240.
— as affecting our moral Being. Am. Bib. Repos. **3**: 229.
— as a conserving Power. (W. W. Battershall) Am. Church R. **33**: 157.
— as an Organ of political Movement. (T. De Quincey) Tait, n. s. **13**: 215, 341.
— as an Organization. (G. H. Emerson) Univ. Q. **14**: 353.
— as Science and as Life. (S. W. Sutton) Univ. Q. **36**: 24.
— Assumptions against. (C. A. Stork) Luth. Q. **3**: 321.
— Attacks on, by Oxford Clergymen. (F. Bowen) No. Am. **92**: 177.
— — Recent. (N. S. Richardson) Am. Church R. **8**: 544.
— Attitude of, toward Assaults. (S. C. Bartlett) Bib. Sac. **25**: 152.
— the Basis of the Republic. O. & N. **1**: 657.
— Beauties of, Chateaubriand on. (J. Foster) Ecl. R. **16**: 883. **18**: 55, 191.
— Beginning and Perfection of. (N. L. Frothingham) Chr. Exam. **3**: 17, 104.

Christianity, Beginnings of, George P. Fisher on. (A. F. Hewit) Cath. World, **26**: 434, 653. — (C. J. H. Ropes) New Eng. **37**: 385.
— Bible and Historical. (J. W. Nevin) Mercersb. **2**: 353.
— Blackwell *versus* O'Keefe. So. R. n. s. **18**: 153.
— capable of Self-Defense. (G. N. Boardman) Am. Presb. R. **19**: 279.
— Causes that have impeded. (W. Adams) Chr. Q. Spec. **4**: 401.
— Central Idea of. (W. Kenney) Meth. Q. **17**: 84.
— Central Principle of. (S. N. Callender) Mercersb. **23**: 345.
— Central Truth of. (A. C. Barry) Univ. Q. **36**: 82.
— Character of. (F. Bowen) No. Am. **90**: 395.
— Chinese Attack on. (W. Axon) Dub. Univ. **79**: 661.
— Christ's Testimony to. Bost. R. **4**: 149.
— Comte on. (B. F. Westcott) Contemp. R. **6**: 399.
— Conception of. (J. J. Swander) Mercersb. **13**: 497.
— Conflicts of. (H. Bacon) Univ. Q. **7**: 254.
— — Marcy on. (A. F. Hewit) Cath. World, **5**: 701.
— Conservative Element in. (C. White) Bib. Sac. **9**: 540.
— contrasted with other Systems. (R. P. Ambler) Univ. Q. **27**: 431.
— Coquerel's Philosophical History of. Ecl. R. **40**: 1.
— the Correlate of Humanity. (M. J. Savage) Mo. Rel. M. **51**: 97.
— Corruption of, by Paganism. (N. G. Batt) Contemp. **13**: 346. Same art. Liv. Age, **105**: 195. Same art. Theo. Ecl. **7**: 203.
— Cosmical Scope of. (W. Rupp) Mercersb. **22**: 23.
— Credibility of, and Science. Chr. Rem. **44**: 333.
— Critical. Chr. Rem. **15**: 353.
— Decadence of, an Assumption. (C. A. Stork) Luth. Q. **3**: 332.
— Defense of. Ecl. R. **97**: 168.
— Democracy of. Bost. Q. **1**: 444.
— Diffusion of. For. Q. **37**: 494.
— Distastefulness of. (E. D. Smith) Theo. & Lit. J. **6**: 99.
— Distortions of. All the Year, **24**: 78.
— Divine and Human in. (I. E. Dwinell) Bib. Sac. **16**: 499.
— Divine in. (E. C. Towne) Radical, **2**: 129, 202.
— Durability of. (G. H. Emerson) Univ. Q. **13**: 306.
— Early. (R. Ellis) Unita. R. **4**: 113. **8**: 465. — (W. Milligan) Contemp. **10**: 590. **11**: 513. — (J. W. Nevin) Mercersb. **3**: 461, 513. **4**: 1, 202.
— — and modern, Philosophical Relations of. (E. A. Washburn) Bib. Sac. **8**: 34.
— — and Orientalism. Ho. & For. R. **3**: 118.
— — Creed and Heresies of. Westm. **59**: 535.
See Christians, Early; Church History.
— Early Conflicts of, Kip's. (M. Van Rensselaer) Am. Church R. **3**: 197.
— Early Defenders of. (J. Tulloch) Good Words, **2**: 267.
— Early Heathen Witnesses of. (E. C. Mitchell) Chr. R. **24**: 64.
— Early Progress of. Dub. Univ. **31**: 765.
— Early Victory of. Lond. Q. **54**: 422.
— Early Writers on. Kitto, **16**: 241.
— Earthly Triumphs of. (G. Bush) Lit. & Theo. R. **1**: 343.
— Eastern. (J. Pyne) Nat. Q. **35**: 313.
— — and Western, of 4th Century. Lond. Q. **57**: 24.
— End and Unity of Science. (W. Adams) Am. Bib. Repos. 3d s. **3**: 573.
— Enemies of. (H. W. Everest) Chr. Q. **8**: 170.
— Essence of. (J. F. Clarke) Unita. R. **4**: 590. — (C. Ullmann) Mo. Rel. M. **18**: 21. — Bib. R. **6**: 657.
— — and Form of. (H. Harbaugh) Mercersb. **14**: 383.
— — Feuerbach on. (C. C. Tiffany) Bib. Sac. **14**: 731. — (H. Davis) Chr. Exam. **49**: 223.
— — Guizot on. So. R. n. s. **10**: 301.
Christianity, Essence of, Meditations on. Chr. Rem. **50**: 239.
— Essential. (M. Grew) Radical, **8**: 127.
— Essentials of. Chr. Exam. **17**: 43.
— Ethics of. Ecl. M. **46**: 445.
— — and Influence of. Westm. **57**: 182.
— Every-Day. Chr. Obs. **15**: 804.
— Evidences of. (A. Walker) Chr. Exam. **14**: 181. — (J. Brazer) Chr. Exam. **36**: 359. — (F. Parkman) Chr. Exam. **17**: 155. — (J. W. Alexander) Princ. **18**: 359. — (S. F. Smith) Chr. R. **11**: 229. — (N. Porter) New Eng. **4**: 401. — (G. B. Cheever) Lit. & Theo. R. **2**: 436. — (A. Barnes) Chr. Q. Spec. **5**: 126. — (G. W. Burnap) Chr. Exam. **20**: 307. — (W. B. Sprague) No. Am. **36**: 345. — (A. P. Peabody) No. Am. **58**: 39. — (E. Peabody) Chr. Exam. **41**: 216. — New York R. **4**: 428. — Blackw. **18**: 160. — Am. Mo. R. **2**: 466. — Dub. Univ. **6**: 231. — (J. Williams) Am. Church R. **8**: 497. — (Prof. Lorimer) Theo. Ecl. **3**: 30. — Cong. M. **5**: 17, 71. — (W. Adams) Am. Presb. R. **14**: 77. — Am. Meth. M. **1**: 7. **14**: 191. — Chr. Rem. **56**: 271. — Meth. M. **43**: 897. **44**: 760. — (M. B. Hope) Princ. **24**: 250. — So. Lit. Mess. **18**: 473. — West. Mo. R. **3**: 427.
— — Augustine's. (E. H. Gillett) Am. Presb. R. **14**: 434.
— — Beard's Manual of. (S. G. Bulfinch) Chr. Exam. **86**: 258.
— — Branches of, in true, tactical Order. Chr. Obs. **77**: 606.
— — Can they be resisted? Theo. Repos. **3**: 364.
— — Chalmers on. Mo. R. **141**: 469.
— — Historical. No. Brit. **21**: 101.
— — in the 19th Century. (J. H. Allen) Chr. Exam. **86**: 91.
— — in relation to Scepticism. Westm. **99**: 186.
— — Internal. (G. M. Steele) No. Am. **97**: 508.
— — — Jenyns on. (A. Lamson) Chr. Exam. **3**: 140.
— — Modern. (J. Hunt) Contemp. **18**: 152.
— — Modern Aspects of. Lond. Q. **50**: 265.
— — New Chapter of. (J. F. Clarke) Atlan. **23**: 304.
— — Norton on. Bost. Q. **2**: 86.
— — Popular and critical. (R. H. Hutton) Contemp. **28**: 215.
— — Positive. (S. Leathes) Good Words, **17**: 282.
— — Principles laid down by Christ himself. Chr. Obs. **77**: 264.
— — Study of. Ed. R. **86**: 397. — Chr. Rem. **42**: 149.
— — Sumner, Benson, and Faber on. Chr. Obs. **24**: 640, 690.
— — Wilson on. Chr. Obs. **29**: 613. — Ecl. R. **55**: 48.
— — Works on, 1830. Chr. Obs. **30**: 761.
See Hopkins, Mark; Lowell Lectures; Theology, Natural.
— examined in a Court of Law. (J. P. Thompson) New Eng. **5**: 459.
— Excellence of. (A. Young) Chr. Exam. **1**: 44
— Exclusiveness of. (S. H. Kellogg) Presb. R. **1**: 340.
— First Conflict with Rome. (E. E. Higbee) Mercersb. **22**: 321.
— First Promulgation of. Chr. Obs. **1**: 1.
— Folk Lore of. (F. R. Conder) Dub. Univ. **90**: 641.
— foreshadowed in the Writings of Plato. Dub. Univ. **66**: 243, 423. Same art. Liv. Age, **87**: 70, 241.
— foretold under Judaism. (E. P. Barrows) Am. Bib. Repos. 3d s. **3**: 411.
— Fox's Lectures on. Ecl. R. **30**: 124.
— Graetz on Christ and. Lond. Q. **51**: 178.
— Gregory's Letters on. Chr. Obs. **11**: 577.
— Growth of. Westm. **80**: 1.
— Guizot's Meditations on. Ed. R. **121**: 553. — Chr. Obs. **67**: 46. — Ecl. M. **68**: 214. — Month, **5**: 299. — (J. J. Herzog) Theo. Ecl. **5**: 178.

Christianity, Gurney's Essays on. Chr. Obs. **26**: 538. — Ecl. R. **43**: 289.
— Historical. (F. W. P. Greenwood) Chr. Exam. **28**: 166.
— Historical Construction of. (F. W. J. von Schelling) J. Spec. Philos. **12**: 205.
— Historical Development of. Am. Presb. R. **5**: 596.
— Historical Proofs of. (G. P. Fisher) Princ. n. s. **6**: 399. **7**: 35, 191. **8**: 51.
— History of. Ed. R. **8**: 272.
— — Burnap's Lectures on. (A. Lamson) Chr. Exam. **33**: 187.
— — Comte on Philosophy of. (B. F. Westcott) Contemp. **6**: 399.
— — Early. (G. E. Ellis) Chr. Exam. **34**: 53, 186. *See* Christians, Early; Christianity, Primitive.
— — Hinds's. Ecl. R. **49**: 285.
— — — in first Centuries. (F. Dyer) Chr. Q. **8**: 27.
— — Milman's. Brit. & For. R. **12**: 336. — Fraser, **21**: 632. — (G. E. Ellis) Chr. Exam. **29**: 174. — Dub. Univ. **16**: 252. — Princ. **14**: 237. — Mo. R. **151**: 464. — Ecl. R. **72**: 166. — Museum, **43**: 380.
— — Neander's. (J. Walker) Chr. Exam. **12**: 65.
— — of its Propagation. Mo. R. **84**: 140.
— — Taylor's. Ecl. R. **80**: 706. *See* Church History.
— Humanitary Aspect of. (J. G. Forman) Univ. Q. **24**: 332.
— Impending Conflict of. (A. D. Mayo) Mo. Rel. M. **44**: 118.
— imperishable. (S. Sprecher) Evang. R. **13**: 515.
— Importance of American Freedom to. Chr. R. **1**: 193.
— in America. (P. Schaff) Mercersb. **9**: 493.
— in Asia, Pearson on. Chr. Obs. **7**: 370.
— in Conflict with Politics. (J. W. McLane) Am. Bib. Repos. 3d s. **3**: 111.
— in Egypt. (F. G. Peabody) Unita. R. **12**: 233.
— in the Formation of National Character. (C. F. Le Fevre) Univ. Q. **7**: 337.
— in Germany, Influence of Modern Philosophy on. (O. T. Dobbin) Kitto, **2**: 281.
— in Harmony with our Faculties. (A. Coquerel) Kitto, **4**: 34.
— in the Legal Profession. Chr. R. **23**: 415. — So. Lit. Mess. **27**: 66.
— in the 2d Century. (E. H. Sears) Mo. Rel. M. **43**: 409.
— in the 3d Century, and Cyprian. (J. W. Nevin) Mercersb. **4**: 259–513.
— Influence of, on civil and religious Liberty. (R. Baird) Am. Bib. Repos. 3d s. **4**: 191.
— — Civilizing. (W. Hay) Evang. R. **21**: 535.
— — on Civilization. (Mrs. A. W. Little) No. Am. **87**: 170. — Meth. Q. **1**: 39.
— — on Literature. (L. Bacon) Chr. Mo. Spec. **6**: 185.
— — on political and social Interests. Chr. Mo. Spec. **5**: 409.
— — on public Morals. Chr. R. **2**: 495.
— — on the Roman Colonization. (A. G. Laurie) Univ. Q. **35**: 65.
— Introduction into America. Am. Church R. **21**: 338.
— Is it on the Wane? (E. P. Tenney) Cong. R. **10**: 468. — (R. E. Thompson) Penn Mo. **9**: 45.
— Latin. Lond. Q. **4**: 142.
— — and the Germans. (T. Appel) Mercersb. **19**: 11.
— — History of. (J. C. Moffat) Princ. **36**: 249.
— — — Milman's. (N. E. Frothingham) Chr. Exam. **61**: 288. — Chr. Obs. **54**: 592. **57**: 827. — Ed. R. **107**: 51. — Kitto, **14**: 1. — Dub. Univ. **44**: 492. — No. Brit. **22**: 84. — Quar. **95**: 38. — Prosp. R. **10**: 307.
— Law as to Libels against. Ed. R. **58**: 387.
— — of Progress applied to. (W. Adams) Am. Bib. Repos. 3d s. **3**: 193.
Christianity, Liberal. (W. H. Lord) Princ. **40**: 114.
— — Defense of. (A. Norton) Gen. Repos. **1**: 1.
— — in Europe. (W. S. Adamson) Radical, **5**: 412.
— — Prophecies of the Hour concerning. (A. D. Mayo) Univ. Q. **36**: 409.
— Life and Light of Men, Young's. So. R. n. s. **14**: 223.
— Maltby's Illustrations of. Chr. Obs. **1**: 717.
— Means of promoting. Chr. Disc. **1**: 199. — (E. Lord) Lit. & Theo. R. **2**: 3.
— Milner on Gibbon's Account of. Chr. Obs. **8**: 159.
— Modern, Tendencies in. (J. W. Santee) Mercersb. **21**: 602.
— Modern Assailants of. Ecl. R. **99**: 329.
— Modern Spirit in. (S. Osgood) Mo. Rel. M. **44**: 18.
— Moral Forces of. (R. Turnbull) Chr. R. **9**: 325.
— Muscular. *See* Muscular Christianity.
— Mysteriousness of. (C. Prest) Ex. H. Lec. **3**: 313.
— Narrowness of, Alleged. Chr. Exam. **82**: 92.
— Naturalness of. (J. W. Steinmitz) Mercersb. **20**: 44.
— Nature of. (S. N. Callender) Mercersb. **5**: 245.
— Neo-. Westm. **74**: 293.
— The New. (J. J. Keane) Cath. World, **31**: 39, 257.
— New Protestant Criticism of. (P. Girard) Cath. World, **28**: 88.
— Nicholas's Philosophic Researches on. Dub. R. **32**: 1.
— not an original Revelation. Bost. Q. **1**: 8.
— not promoted by the Existence of different Denominations. Chr. Mo. Spec. **4**: 460.
— Objections to rational. Chr. Disc. **5**: 1.
— Obligations of Literature to. Chr. Mo. Spec. **6**: 79.
— Odd Versions of. Tait, **4**: 52.
— of Christ. Dial, **1**: 196.
— of the Present and Future. (H. Alford) Good Words, **11**: 46.
— Oldest Opposition to, and its Defense. (P. Schaff) Meth. Q. **18**: 605.
— on Trial. (C. A. Bartol) Unita. R. **7**: 182. — (B. Franklin) Am. Church R. **36**: 161.
— Opposition of World to true. Chr. Obs. **8**: 9, 70.
— Organ of political Movement. Ecl. M. **8**: 221.
— Organic. (S. H. Giesy) Mercersb. **18**: 485. — (D. H. Riddle) Mercersb. **1**: 169.
— Origin of, German Theories of. Dub. R. **45**: 404.
— — Gfrörer on. Prosp. R. **4**: 435.
— — Havet on. (C. Beard) Theo. R. **16**: 379.
— — Hennell on. Dial, **4**: 137.
— — Rénan on. Ed. R. **124**: 450. — (A. Laugel) Nation, **30**: 8, 41.
— — Sheppard's Divine. Ecl. R. **50**: 204. *See* Christianity, Beginnings of.
— Original in. (L. B. Mason) Univ. Q. **8**: 350.
— Part of the Common Law of England. (A. B. Chapin) Chr. Q. Spec. **8**: 13.
— Past and Future of. (O. Dewey) Unita. R. **3**: 433. — Nat. R. **3**: 200.
— Permanence of. (W. B. O. Peabody) Chr. Exam. **28**: 317. — (S. P. Peabody) Unita. R. **5**: 662. — (J. P Thompson) Bib. Sac. **22**: 223.
— The Permanent in. Am. Presb. R. **10**: 353.
— Permanent Principle of. (G. V. Smith) Unita. R. **1**: 215.
— Philosophical. Chr. R. **14**: 541.
— Philosophical Studies on. Brownson, **10**: 332.
— Philosophy of. (J. A. Reubelt) Chr. Q. **6**: 391.
— Plea for Disorganization of. Ecl. R. **124**: 439.
— Polytheism, and the first Age of. Chr. Rem. **53**: 459.
— Popular, Foxton's. Prosp. R. **5**: 477.
— Popular Progress depending on. (S. Harris) New Eng. **5**: 433.
— Practical. (T. H. Skinner) Am. Bib. Repos. **9**: 159.
— Practical Character of. (J. W. Santee) Mercersb. **25**: 304.

Christianity, Practical Element in. (C. Clever) Ref. Q. **26**: 102. — (C. White) Bib. Sac. **9**: 355.
— Preparation for. Univ. Q. **29**: 422.
— — before Christ. (A. F. Hewit) Cath. World, **27**: 4.
— — in the History of the World, a Proof of its Divine Origin. Meth. Q. **9**: 429, 542.
— Present State of, 1868. (J. Nilan) Nat. Q. **17**: 32.
— — and Hopes of. (W. Adams) Am. Church R. **11**: 369. **12**: 193.
— Primitive. (J. H. Allen) Chr. Exam. **63**: 313. — Dial, **2**: 292. — Meth. M. **54**: 683.
— — and Paganism. Meth. M. **51**: 22.
— — How shall we find? (A. Young) Cath. World, **6**: 622.
— — Phases of. (E. E. Du Bois) Chr. Exam. **82**: 342.
— — Plea for. Am. Church R. **23**: 72.
— — What was? (F. W. Newman) Fraser, **92**: 210. *See* Christianity, Early; Church, Early; Church History.
— Principle and Development of. Westm. **62**: 195.
— Progress of. (R. Ellis) Unita. R. **1**: 401.
— — in recent Years, 1836. (S. J. Coggeshall) Am. Meth. M. **20**: 65.
— — in United States. (P. Schaff) Princ. n. s. **4**: 209.
— — Law of. Bost. Q. **3**: 397.
— Progressive Relations of. (L. L. Paine) New Eng. **30**: 581.
— Promotion of. (J. H. Rice) Cong. M. **18**: 723.
— Providence in the Establishment of. (E. W. Reynolds) Univ. Q. **12**: 14.
— the Readjuster. (J. J. Smyth) Luth. Q. **2**: 202.
— Readjustment of. Am. Presb. R. **11**: 1.
— Relation of, to the Common Law. (M. B. Anderson) Am. J. Soc. Sci. **10**: 55.
— — to Law and Government. (L. Bacon) New Eng. **14**: 447.
— — to natural Rights. (J. D. Woolsey) New Eng. **15**: 603.
— Responsibility of educated Men to. Bost. R. **4**: 225.
— Earl Russell and Viscount Stratford de Redcliffe on. Chr. Obs. **73**: 938.
— Schenkel on. Kitto, **39**: 423.
— Scott's Discourses on. Prosp. R. **4**: 559.
— Secret of. (G. T. Flanders) Univ. Q. **31**: 345.
— Social Influences of. (C. Cushing) Am. Bib. Repos. 2d s. **1**: 180. — (W. E. Baxter) Ex. H. Lec. **13**: 1. — Cath. World, **5**: 414.
— Spirit of. Dub. R. **9**: 1.
— Spiritual, Taylor's Lectures on. Cong. M. **24**: 873.
— Spiritual Essence of. Am. Church R. **25**: 67, 215. **26**: 19.
— Spread of. (J. De Normandie) Unita. R. **9**: 517.
— standing the Test of Ridicule. Theo. Repos. **2**: 417.
— Strauss and. (S. S. Hebbard) Univ. Q. **30**: 197.
— Strength of. (E. F. Burr) New Eng. **17**: 835.
— supported by Law. Chr. Disc. **2**: 368.
— Sure Triumph of. (E. L. Fancher) Meth. Q. **27**: 532.
— Test of. (J. F. Rowe) Chr. Q. **6**: 232.
— the Thing and the Name. Radical, **2**: 296.
— Transient and permanent in. Bost. Q. **4**: 436.
— — Theodore Parker on. (A. P. Peabody) Chr. Exam. **31**: 98.
— Truth of; a Poem. (L. Withington) Chr. Mo. Spec. **8**: 22.
— — Greenleaf and Strauss on. (F. Bowen) No. Am. **63**: 382.
— Truths peculiar to. (C. Stovel) Ex. H. Lec. **3**: 267.
— Two common Objections to. (W. E. Parson) Luth. Q. **6**: 377.
— Two Forms of. Dub. Univ. **95**: 230.
— Two Systems of. (H. Harbaugh) Mercersb. **14**: 306.
— Twofold Symbol of. (P. Dillingham) Unita. R. **11**: 469.
Christianity, Uncompromising Character of. (D. Green) Chr. Mo. Spec. **8**: 609.
— a universal Religion. (T. D. Woolsey) New Eng. **29**: 272.
— Universality of. (T. S. King) Univ. Q. **7**: 177.
— Vaughan on Corruption of. Cong. M. **18**: 753.
— Vital. (S. F. Smith) Chr. R. **10**: 295. — (T. D. Cuyler) New Eng. **3**: 600.
— D. Webster's Defense of. U. S. Cath. M. **3**: 493.
— What if not true? (N. Macleod) Good Words, **3**: 129.
— What is? (E. S. Gannett) Chr. Exam. **36**: 82. — (C. Hodge) Princ. **32**: 118.
— what every Christian must know. Fraser, **54**: 716.
— Whately's Rise and Progress of. Westm. **61**: 392.
— Wilberforce's View of. Chr. Obs. **31**: 87, 147.
— without Christ. (G. E. Ellis) Chr. Exam. **40**: 77.
— without Judaism, Powell's. Brit. Q. **27**: 414. Same art. Ecl. M. **44**: 356.
— World's Debt to. Good Words, **1**: 204.
— Worth of the undisputed Truths of. Chr. Disc. **5**: 420.
Christie, W. D., Oratory of. Fraser, **34**: 661.
Christie's Auction Room. All the Year, **34**: 125.
Christina, Queen of Sweden. Colburn, **116**: 286, 408. Same art. Liv. Age, **63**: 323. — Ecl. R. **118**: 250. — House. Words, **16**: 132. Same art. Liv. Age, **55**: 285. — Liv. Age, **42**: 3. — Temp. Bar, **52**: 35. — Tinsley, **24**: 482. — Colburn, **127**: 361. Same art. Ecl. M. **59**: 357. — St. James, **7**: 166.
Christina, Leonora, in the Blue Tower. (R. H. Stoddard) Harper, **47**: 514.
Christina North. (E. M. Archer) Macmil. **25**: 81–433. **26**: 1–223. Same art. Liv. Age, **114**: 140–602.
Christine; a Troubadour's Song. (G. H. Miles) Cath. World, **3**: 32, 171, 335.
Christine; or, Commonplace People. (J. Robertson) Colburn, **138**: 143–431. **139**: 53. **140**: 115–454. **141**: 68–438. **142**: 71–733. **143**: 101–705. **144**: 57.
Christine Niedever. (J. T. McKay) Lippinc. **8**: 474.
Christino War, Sketches of. Blackw. **48**: 740. **49**: 89. — (C. F. Fynes-Clinton) Bentley, **12**: 398, 498.
Christmas, Henry, and his Works. Hogg, **15**: 161.
Christmas, Joseph Stibbs, Memoir of. (S. Miller) Princ. **4**: 256.
Christmas. (J. Keen) Potter Am. Mo. **13**: 401. — (A. Lamson) Chr. Exam. **38**: 49. — (A. H. Mills) St. James, **21**: 187. — (F. P. Palmer) Bentley, **14**: 618. — (C. Waddy) Belgra. **16**: 326. — Colburn, **57**: 447. — Ev. Sat. **9**: 858. — Lond. M. **6**: 495.
— a Poem. (M. Collins) Temp. Bar, **1**: 268.
— a Poem. (C. Kingsley) Good Words, **9**: 23.
— a Poem. (R. Quiddam) St. James, **39**: 287.
— a Poem. (A. D. T. Whitney) Scrib. **3**: 304.
— abroad. Sharpe, **40**: 309.
— Ancient Customs at. Nat. M. **9**: 536.
— and how it was kept. (M. E. C. Walcott) Once a Week, **6**: 25.
— and New Year in France and Germany. (F. J. Grund) Godey, **36**: 6.
— and the Saturnalia. (J. P. Thompson) Bib. Sac. **12**: 144.
— at the Baron's. (Author of German Home-Life) Lond. Soc. **33**: 83.
— at Ferncliff. (F. Travers) Canad. Mo. **18**: 640.
— at Home and abroad. Victoria, **22**: 97.
— Chronology of. *See* Jarvis's Chronology.
— Customs of the olden Time. Chamb. J. **47**: 22.
— — and Associations of. Chamb. J. **53**: 806.
— English Hearths and English Hearts. (E. Carrington) Colburn, **60**: 538.
— Gipsies' Christmas Gathering. (W. R. S. Ralston) Good Words, **9**: 96.
— Gossip about. (R. Bell) Bentley, **28**: 567.

Christmas has come. (L. Kip) Overland, 4: 72.
— in Barnakerry. Cath. World, 30: 412, 470.
— in the Black Mountain. (A. J. Evans) Macmil. 43: 219, 295, 327.
— in the Breviary. Dub. R. 21: 273.
— in Canada. Belgra. 10: 361.
— in a Caravan. (C. J. Langston) Argosy, 32: 475.
— in a Cavalry Regiment. St. Paul's, 3: 478.
— in the Company of John Doe. (C. Dickens) House. Words, 4: 275.
— in the Desert. (M. B. Edwards) Liv. Age, 95: 691.
— in a Dispensary. Lond. Soc. 21: 64.
— in England and elsewhere. Cornh. 13: 16.
— in Germany. Once a Week, 12: 82.
— in Hamburg. Harper, 18: 359.
— in Lodgings. House. Words, 2: 295.
— in the Metropolis. Chamb. J. 18: 409.
— in Norway. Colburn, 64: 261.
— in Old England and New. (E. E. Hale) Galaxy, 5: 47.
— in the olden Time. Chamb. J. 10: 413. 16: 407. — Cornh. 21: 28. Same art. Liv. Age, 104: 332.
— in old Puritan Days. All the Year, 25: 101.
— in Prison. Chamb. J. 56: 797.
— in Russia. Fraser, 38: 670.
— in Scotland. (E. S. Roscoe) Belgra. 10: 311.
— in a Signal-Box. (W. Sterne) Sharpe, 44: 315.
— in South America. House. Words, 6: 325.
— in Southern Italy. House. Words, 12: 511.
— in Sweden. (F. Bremer) Peop. J. 1: 219.
— in the 13th Century. (B. Murphy) Cath. World, 20: 502.
— in Wales. (W. Sikes) Appleton, 19: 32.
— Keeping. Chamb. J. 46: 823.
— Merry. Cath. World, 12: 463.
— Observance of. (O. M. Spencer) Harper, 46: 241. — (C. White) Peop. J. 10: 344.
— Origin of the Celebration of. Chr. Mo. Spec. 3: 628.
— Spirit of. Dub. Univ. 40: 635.
— with the Baron. Cath. World, 4: 446.
— with a Curé. St. James, 41: 656.
— with Grampus. Lond. Soc. 5: 25.
— with our own Poets. (J. F. Waller) Dub. Univ. 38: 737.
Christmas Adventure; a Story. St. James, 47: 422.
Christmas Banquet. (N. Hawthorne) Dem. R. 14: 78.
Christmas Bells. Cath. World, 4: 471.
Christmas Books. Dub. Univ. 29: 134. — Fraser, 43: 37.
— and Poems, 1852. Dub. Univ. 41: 112.
— Grumble about. (W. M. Thackeray) Fraser, 35: 111.
Christmas Box. St. James, 6: 51.
Christmas Bride. Liv. Age, 40: 165.
Christmas Cards. All the Year, 44: 108.
Christmas Carillons. (A. C. Ketchum) Harper, 62: 1.
Christmas Carol. (Mrs. Gray) Dub. Univ. 25: 144. — (C. G. Rossetti) Scrib. 3: 278. — (J. F. Waller) Dub. Univ. 36: 708. — (H. Wright) Antiquary, 4: 299.
— for 1862. (G. MacDonald) Cornh. 7: 103.
Christmas Carols. (J. V. Blake) O. & N. 8: 698. — (H. Duvar) Canad. Mo. 10: 494. — (J. F. Mackarness) Good Words, 10: 851. — (J. Haughton) Lakeside, 5: 78. — (E. Sedding) Once a Week, 10: 10. Same art. Cath. World, 2: 349.
Christmas Ceremonies at Rome. Chamb. J. 30: 401.
Christmas Chains. Colburn, 156: 83.
Christmas Charities, Curious. (W. Andrews) Victoria, 36: 443.
Christmas Child; a Poem. (I. Craig) Good Words, 3: 55.
Christmas Club. (E. Eggleston) Scrib. 5: 374.
— Our. (B. Murphy) Cath. World, 30: 505.
Christmas Customs. Nat. M. 7: 485.
— and Superstitions. Ho. & For. R. 2: 129.
Christmas Decorations. Lond. Soc. 6: 567.
Christmas Diversions given by the Lord of Misrule. (W. Bray) Arch. 18: 313, 333.
Christmas Dream in a Chimney Corner. Month, 2: 89.
Christmas Dreams. (J. Wilson) Blackw. 23: 1. Same art. Mus. 12: 672.
Christmas Eve; a Poem. (Z. N. Krasinski) Cornh. 19: 45.
Christmas Eve; a Poem. Broadw. 8: 33.
Christmas Eve; a Tale. Dub. Univ. 76: 688.
Christmas Eve, or the Angel Guest; a Poem from the Swedish. (Mrs. E. Baker) Temp. Bar, 55: 73.
— Chant of the Breton Peasants on. (H. Glyndon) Putnam, 13: 47.
— in a Coal Pit; a Tale. (R. Jocelyn) Dark Blue, 2: 578.
— in Germany. Broadw. 7: 513.
— in the Smuggler's Cave. Dub. Univ. 54: 643.
— in a Vicarage; a Sketch. Dub. Univ. 90: 715.
— Old-Fashioned. (H. S Vince) St. James, 41: 644.
Christmas Eves, Two. Belgra. 4: 327.
Christmas Fires. Sharpe, 17: 15, 84. Same art. Liv. Age, 36: 577.
Christmas Games in the olden Time. Penny M. 7: 492.
Christmas Gift to Rupert. (F. B. Harte) Overland, 6: 88.
Christmas Gifts for Home Manufacture. (M. Ford) Potter Am. Mo. 15: 347.
Christmas Gifts; a Tale. (A. Young) Cath. World, 8: 546.
Christmas Hearth, Around the. (H. N. Powers) Lakeside, 9: 44.
Christmas Holidays. (W. Payne) Am. Church R. 6: 512. — So. Lit. Mess. 7: 219.
Christmas Hymn. (C. E. Brooks) Cath. World, 10: 526.
Christmas Legends, Continental. Colburn, 139: 94.
Christmas Literature. (J. L. Stewart) Canad. Mo. 15: 73. — No. Brit. 8: 378. — All the Year, 44: 82.
Christmas Memory; a Tale. (J. C. Smalley) Cath. World, 16: 502.
Christmas Memories. Good Words, 1: 785.
Christmas Music. Once a Week, 20: 61. 21: 458. 23: 472.
Christmas Party one hundred Years ago. Argosy, 29: 68.
Christmas Peal. (A. H. Baldwin) Belgra. 13: 302.
Christmas Pies. Chamb. J. 48: 825.
Christmas Presents, Origin of. (L. W. Heydenreich) Evang. R. 18: 94.
Christmas Raid. (Miss Ramsey) Victoria, 26: 215.
Christmas Recognition; a Tale. (B. Murphy) Cath. World, 16: 448.
Christmas Rhymes. (J. Anster) Dub. Univ. 17: 139.
Christmas Rose; a Tale. Chamb. J. 56: 812.
Christmas Roses. (E. F. Mosby) Potter Am. Mo. 16: 17.
Christmas Soirée. (F. W. Robinson) Belgra. 7: 380.
Christmas Story. (A. B. Haven) Sharpe, 42: 310.
Christmas Story, English. (B. Murphy) Cath. World, 18: 479.
Christmas Stories. (C. Dickens) Harper, 6: 400.
Christmas Storms and Sunshine. (C. M. Mills) Howitt, 3: 4.
Christmas Symphony. (H. M. Jackson) Scrib. 3: 288.
Christmas Tale. Blackw. 81: 74. Same art. Liv. Age, 52: 501.
Christmas Tide; a Poem. Cath. World, 20: 443.
Christmas Times at the Temple. Colburn, 4: 10.
Christmas Treat, My. Sharpe, 38: 281.
Christmas Tree. (C. Dickens) House. Words, 2: 49. — Chamb. J. 15: 9.
Christmas Vigil; a Poem. (C. Kendal) St. James, 47: 431.
Christmas Vigil; a Tale. Cath. World, 22: 541.
Christmas Vision; a Poem. Belgra. 1: 349.
Christmas Week at Glasgow. Fraser, 55: 204.
Christmases, Historic. Ev. Sat. 6: 810.
— Miserable. (G. A. Sala) Belgra. 16: 341.
— Royal Chamb. J. 44: 822.

Christocentric Redemption. (I. E. Graeff) Mercersb. **24**: 213.
Christocentric Theology. (J. W. Nevin) Mercersb. **14**: 28.
Christological View of Faith. (J. W. Nevin) Mercersb. **15**: 566.
Christology. *See* Jesus Christ; Messiah.
Christoph of Bavaria. (J. Goddard and C. Weber) St. James, **37**: 39.
Christophe, King of Hayti. Blackw. **9**: 267. **10**: 545.
— Last Days of. Liv. Age, **48**: 799.
Christopher, St. (F. Eastwood) Hours at Home, **5**: 231.
— Breton Legend of. (M. Barker) Cath. World, **7**: 710.
— Legend of. (F. M. Doherty) Good Words, **14**: 240. — (M. B. Williams) Lakeside, **9**: 49. — (D. M. Craik) St. James, **1**: 59.
Christopher Grum, Rambles of. Nav. M. **1**: 330, 432, 539.
Christopher Kenrick; his Life and Adventures. (J. Hatton) Gent. M. n. s. **1**: 577, 721. **2**: 1-703. **3**: 92.
Christopher Kroy. (S. J. Prichard) Hours at Home, **8**: 64-554. **9**: 52-561.
Christopher North. *See* Wilson, John.
Christowell; a Dartmoor Tale. (R. D. Blackmore) Good Words, **22**: 1-793.
Christus Sylvæ; a Poem. (F. B. Plimpton) Putnam, **13**: 532.
Chromatic Aberration. Galaxy, **4**: 829.
Chromatics. Ed. R. **150**: 368.
— Modern, Rood's. (S. P. Thompson) Nature, **21**: 78. — (C. S. Peirce and R. Sturgis) Nation, **29**: 260.
Chromatypes, Clockwork. (T. Goodchild) Recr. Sci. **1**: 175.
Chromium and Aluminium in Steel and Iron. (A. A. Blair) Am. J. Sci **113**: 421.
Chromo-Lithography. (R. Sturgis) Nation, **4**: 36. — (L. Prang) Nation, **5**: 437.—Art J. **11**: 367.
Chromosphere and Solar Prominences. (C. A. Young) Pop. Sci. Mo. **4**: 385.
Chronicle of the Cid. For. Q. **4**: 438. — (Sir W. Scott) Quar. **1**: 117.
— of England. (J. Sterling) Blackw. **47**: 253.
— of Ethelfled. Sharpe, **15**: 15-321.
— of Evesham Abbey. Dub. R. **67**: 26.
— of a ragged Rascal. (E. Youl) Howitt, **3**: 266, 277, 299.
Chronicles and Characters, R. Lytton on. Ev. Sat. **5**: 391.
Chronicles of Carlingford; the Doctor's Family. (M. Oliphant) Blackw. **90**: 420-689. **91**: 55. Same art. Liv. Age, **71**: 319, 501. **72**: 91, 483.
— — Salem Chapel. (M. Oliphant) Blackw. **91**: 207-758. **92**: 110-713. **93**: 61. Same art. Liv. Age, **72**: 595. **73**: 115, 313, 524. **74**: 80, 299, 458. **75**: 56, 242, 482. **76**: 51, 243.
— — Perpetual Curate. (M. Oliphant) Blackw. **93**: 764. **94**: 97-715. **95**: 49-685. **96**: 113, 255. Same art. Liv. Age, **77**: 595. **78**: 215, 404. **79**: 17, 316, 438. **80**: 54, 311, 509. **81**: 213, 551.
— of Castle Cornet; a Tale. Dub. Univ. **52**: 733. Same art. Ecl. M. **46**: 276.
— of a Country Town. Colburn, **99**: 111-466. **100**: 107.
— of the Place Vendome. Bentley, **6**: 381.
— Old English. Cornh. **15**: 154.
Chronograms and Chronophons. Chamb. J. **49**: 382.
Chronograph, The. Nature, **23**: 59.
— Hipp, and Measurement of small Intervals of Time. (R. Briggs) J. Frankl. Inst. **102**: 89.
— Printing. (C. A. Young) Am. J. Sci. **92**: 99. — (G. W. Hough) Am. J. Sci. **102**: 436.
Chronological Table of Geographical Discoveries. Am. Q. Reg. **5**: 191.
— of principal Foreign Writers. Am. Q. Reg. **5**: 132.
Chronology. Westm. **16**: 327.
Chronology, Ancient. (A. B. Chapin) Chr. Q. Spec. **10**: 656.
— and its Adjuncts. (A. B. Chapin) Am. Church R. **6**: 378.
— Antediluvian. (Trans. by S. Chase) Am. Bib. Repos. 2d s. **6**: 114.
— Archons of Demosthenes. (F. Parker and E. Hincks) Kitto, **33**: 158, 409. **34**: 149, 402. **35**: 86, 214, 396. **36**: 186.
— Biblical. Kitto, **26**: 174, 446. **27**: 153, 416. — Quar. **105**: 382. — (J. Packard) Bib. Sac. **15**: 289. — Chr. Obs. **28**: 409-813. — Bost. Q. **3**: 578. — (G. W. Samson) Bapt. Q. **4**: 297, 341. — (J. H. Mengert) Luth. Q. **5**: 1, 238.
— — Akers's. (J. Strong) Meth. Q. **16**: 448.
— — and Linguistic Science. (H. N. Day) Am. Presb. R. **17**: 483.
— — of Genesis, Chap. v. (F. Gardiner) Bib. Sac. **30**: 323.
— — of the Old Testament. (E. Pond) Meth. Q. **27**: 389.
— — — of the Kings of Israel and Judah. (W. J. Beecher) Presb. R. **1**: 211.
— — — of the Septuagint. Bost. R. **4**: 142.
— — of the New Testament. Kitto, **16**: 261.
— — Parker's. (F. Parker) Kitto, **25**: 417.
— — Rational View of. Kitto, **34**: 107.
— — Russell on. Ecl. R. **59**: 442.
— — Sayce's. Dub. Univ. **83**: 720.
— — Seyffarth's. Am. Ch. Mo. **3**: 312. — Evang. R. **9**: 436.
— — Table of. (J. Strong) Meth. Q. **16**: 600.
— — Theories of. Kitto, **24**: 310.
— — Times of Daniel. Dub. Univ. **27**: 497.
— Earliest Epochs of. Ho. & For. R. **1**: 420.
— Egyptian. Kitto, **12**: 109.
— — and Sacred. Fraser, **60**: 42. — (A. B. Chapin) Chr. Q. Spec. **9**: 193. — Lond. Q. **53**: 265. — Westm. **75**: 567.
— Egyptian Year. (J. P. Thompson) Bib. Sac. **14**: 644.
— Events in, by Months. Cong. M. **28**: 7-862.
— Hale's Analysis of. Ecl. R. **11**: 1. **15**: 298, 420.
— History of. (E. S. Burns) Pop. Sci. Mo. **18**: 760.
— Improved. Hogg, **1**: 305.
— Metonic Cycle and Calippid Period. (F. Parker) Kitto, **34**: 402. **35**: 86. — (W. Wright) Kitto, **35**: 213.
— New Period in. (J. W. French) Am. J. Sci. **100**: 172.
— of History. Mo. R. **132**: 266.
— of Josephus, Restoration of. Kitto, **5**: 60.
— Sacred and profane. (E. Hincks) Kitto, **22**: 126.
— Verification of Christian Epochs. Kitto, **21**: 369. **22**: 103, 168.
Chronometers. Am. J. Sci. **28**: 297. **32**: 330.
— Compensation Balance. (E. J. Dent) Am. J. Sci. **45**: 83.
— Compensation in. (J. B. James) Am. J. Sci. **113**: 113.
— Hartnup on Rates of. Nature, **8**: 394.
— Magnetic Experiments on. J. Frankl. Inst. **17**: 201, 277.
— Plumbago for Oil in. (L. Herbert) J. Frankl. Inst. **9**: 86.
— Tests of. Nature, **8**: 150.
— — Use of. (J. S. Sleeper) Hunt, **16**: 89.
Chronoscopes, Electro-Ballistic. (T. T. S. Laidley) U. S. Serv. M. **4**: 99.
Chrysalis; a Tale. Chamb. J. **56**: 793, 808.
Chrysanthemum, The. Once a Week, **5**: 529.
Chrysanthema from Greek Anthology. (W. M. Harding) 19th Cent. **4**: 869.
Chrysostom. (J. Eadie) Kitto, **1**: 193. — (Wilder Smith) New Eng. **21**: 1. — Brit. Q. **48**: 377. — Lond. Q. **56**: 105. — Ecl. M. **42**: 201. — Ecl. R. **122**: 395. — Hours at Home, **4**: 348.
— and his Eloquence. (S. Osgood) No. Am. **62**: 23.

Chrysostom and Training for the Pulpit. (C. P. Krauth) Evang. R. **1**: 84.
— Antiochene Works of. (J. Rickaby) Month, **19**: 37.
— Homilies of. Chr. Obs. **25**: 408–603. **26**: 12–397.
— Life of. (J. D. Butler) Bib. Sac. **1**: 669.
— — and Times of. Chr. Obs. **72**: 660.
— — and Writings of. Ecl. R. **107**: 21.
— on Questions of present Day. (J. Gerard) Month, **18**: 56.
— Oration on Eutropius. Meth. M. **38**: 855.
— Sermons of. Chr. R. **12**: 512.
Chub, The. (A. H. Baldwin) Once a Week, **9**: 301.
Chubb, Thomas, Remarks on his "Farewell." Theo. Repos. **3**: 156, 321.
Chubb Jackson. Belgra. **14**: 50.
Chuqunaque Indians of Chacaroun. (J. W. Gairey) Lakeside, **5**: 168.
Church, Fred. Edwin. (H. T. Tuckerman) Galaxy, **1**: 422.
— and his Paintings. Art J. **30**: 65. Same art. Ecl. M. **65**: 688.
— American Landscape Painting. Liv. Age, **62**: 817.
— Heart of the Andes. (E. M. Wheelock) Chr. Exam. **68**: 267. — Liv. Age, **63**: 318.
Church, The. (S. Helffenstein, jr.) Am. Bib. Repos. 2d s. **2**: 308. — So. Lit. J. **4**: 129. — (J. S. Lamar) Chr. Q. **4**: 303. — (C. E. Luthardt) Luth. Q. **3**: 43. — (S. Miller) Mercersb. **20**: 363. — (D. Peck) Meth. Q. **4**: 206. — Fraser, **20**: 431. — Niles's Reg. **23**: 139. — (S. R. Smith) Univ. Q. **1**: 113.
— a Business House. Cong. R. **8**: 576.
— a Christian Mystery. (J.W. Nevin) Mercersb. **15**: 576.
— Accumulation of Wealth by. So. R. n. s. **11**: 417.
— against no Church. Brownson, **2**: 137.
— an historical Fact. Brownson, **3**: 153.
— an Organism. Brownson, **15**: 102.
— and Chapel. (W. H. Woodward) Mod. R. **2**: 846.
— and the Chartists. Fraser, **20**: 619.
— and the Chase. Cornh. **20**: 172.
— and the Churches. (R. A. Hallam) Am. Church R. **6**: 207. — (D. P. Noyes) Bib. Sac. **20**: 349.
— — Döllinger on. Brit. Q. **36**: 153.
— — McNeile on. Chr. Obs. **67**: 824.
— and Civil Law in Scotland and America. (A. T. Innes) Princ. n. s. **1**: 24.
— and Civilization. Brownson, **13**: 462. — (J. W. Nevin) Mercersb. **3**: 175. *See* Christianity and Civilization.
— and Crime. (O. A. Burgess) Chr. Q. **5**: 330.
— and Education. (P. Bayma) Am. Cath. Q. **2**: 1, 241. — So. R. n. s. **15**: 37.
— and Empire in Middle Ages. Brit. & For. R. **3**: 23.
— — in 13th Century. Dub. R. **17**: 487.
— and the Empires. (H. W. Wilberforce) Lond. Q. **43**: 344.
— and its Pretensions. (J. Martineau) O. & N. **9**: 462, 554.
— and the Landlords. (R. Southey) Quar. **49**: 198.
— and the Ministry. (W. M. Reynolds) Evang. R. **4**: 413. — Ecl. R. **80**: 149. — (E. R. Tyler) New Eng. **4**: 173. — Chr. Obs. **58**: 125, 511.
— and Monarchy. (O. A. Brownson) Cath. World, **4**: 627.
— and People. (J. Lowell) Chr. Exam. **4**: 124.
— and the Republic, Brownson on. (G. H. Emerson) Univ. Q. **13**: 400. **14**: 155.
— and the Revolution. Brownson, **16**: 145, 281.
— and the Roman Empire, De Broglie on. Dub. R. **60**: 456. Same art. Cath. World, **5**: 362. — Ed. R. **111**: 422.
— and the Sects. (W. A. Dod) Am. Church R. **14**: 635.
— and social Improvement. Theo. Ecl. **2**: 246.
— and Society. (H. M. Storrs) Cong. Q. **2**: 329. — (H. Willard) Cong. Q. **4**: 342.
Church, The, and State. (J. C. Adams) Univ. Q. **34**: 308. — (O. A. Brownson) Cath. World, **5**: 1. **11**: 145. — (Dr. Braun) Cath. World, **19**: 29. — (B. B. Edwards) Am. Bib. Repos. **6**: 207. — (H. D. Evans) Am. Ch. Mo. **2**: 321. — (S. B. A. Harper) Am. Cath. Q. **2**: 498, 695. — (F. Harrison) Fortn. **27**: 653. — (E. G. Holland) Galaxy, **21**: 333. — (M. Kieffer) Mercersb. **1**: 568. — (T. B. Macaulay) Ed. R. **69**: 231. — (A. D. Mayo) Chr. Q. **4**: 95. — (W. T. Moore) Chr. Q. **7**: 533. — (C. Palfrey) Mo. Rel. M. **36**: 223. — (J. N. Pomeroy) Nation, **9**: 146. — (P. Schaff) Mercersb. **9**: 500. — (J. M. Sturtevant) Cong. Q. **15**: 508 — (A. J. Thebaud) Am. Cath. Q. **2**: 193, 430. — Brit. & For. R. **9**: 433. **13**: 316. **16**: 263. — Am. Whig R. **9**: 551. — Am. Bib. Repos. 2d s. **9**: 177. — Am. Church R. **1**: 246. — Am. Ecl. **4**: 233. — Westm. **5**: 504. **26**: 244. **36**: 308. — Mo. R. **127**: 151. — Brownson, **11**: 514. — Chr. Obs. **72**: 174, 265, 340. — Cong. M. **17**: 603. **18**: 23. **22**: 709. — Danv. Q. **1**: 498. — Dub. R. **70**: 135, 285. **78**: 351. — Ecl. R. **54**: 1. **69**: 365. **75**: 470. **77**: 605. **79**: 345. — Ed. R. **146**: 225. — No. Brit. **4**: 255. **32**: 416. — Prosp. R. **1**: 283.
— — Anti-State Church Movement, 1843–51. Ecl. R. **79**: 345, 724. **80**: 341. **83**: 220. **88**: 740. **92**: 99. **94**: 513.
— — Arnold on. Ecl. R. **77**: 361.
— — Belsham on. Cong. M. **3**: 317.
— — Birks on. Chr. Obs. **69**: 690. — (R. Vaughan) Brit. Q. **7**: 1.
— — Chalmers on. Ecl. R. **68**: 1.
— — Church above the State. Brownson, **22**: 353.
— — Concordia Sacerdoti atque Imperii. (Sir G. Bowyer) Contemp. **37**: 347.
— — Conflict between. Dub. R. **83**: 174. — Am. Church R. **25**: 86.
— — S. T. Coleridge on. Cong. M. **14**: 302.
— — Connection of, defended. Dub. Univ. **1**: 185.
— — Education by. Ed. R. **92**: 94.
— — Gladstone on. Ecl. R. **69**: 365. — Quar. **65**: 97.
— — Hergenröther on. Dub. R. **81**: 308.
— — in 1834. Ecl. R. **59**: 168, 402.
— — in England. Dub. R. **17**: 236. — (O. Shipley) Contemp. **20**: 853. *See* Church of England.
— — in Feudal Times. (H. C. Lea) No. Am. **92**: 56, 415.
— — in France. (D. Charraud) Unita. R. **9**: 214.
— — in Germany. (D. A. Wasson) Unita. R. **5**: 1.
— — in Ireland. (J. Moncrieff) No. Brit. **4**: 255.
— — in Prussia. For. Q. **25**: 138.
— — in the United States. (H. W. Bellows) O. & N. **3**: 445. — (W. Walsh) Cath. World, **20**: 615. — Chr. Obs. **33**: 573, 637.
— — Lamartine on. Dub. Univ. **23**: 367.
— — Montagu's Four Experiments in. Chr. Obs. **65**: 833.
— — Noel on. Meth. Q. **9**: 322. — Theo. & Lit. J. **2**: 153. — (F. L. Hawks) Am. Church R. **2**: 212, 213. — Ecl. R. **89**: 251. **90**: 649. — No. Brit. **10**: 350. — Brit. Q. **9**: 99. — Peop. J. **7**: 137, 165. — Prosp. R. **5**: 236.
— — Papists and Dissenters against. Fraser, **13**: 521.
— — Question of Progress of. Ecl. R. **77**: 605.
— — Readjustment of. (C. J. Ellicott) 19th Cent. **3**: 1098.
— — Relation of. (C. Hodge) Princ. **35**: 679. — Westm. **90**: 151.
— — Romanist View of. (G. D. Wolff) Am. Cath. Q. **2**: 144.
— — Separation of. (C. Beard) Theo. R. **8**: 72. — (A. H. Mackonachie) 19th Cent. **4**: 627. — Brownson, **18**: 65. — Chr. Obs. **69**: 18, 98.
— — Stanley on. Contemp. **15**: 274.
— — Theories of. Cong. **7**: 174.
— — Thorn on. Cong. M. **20**: 789.

Church and State, Three Theories of. (G. H. Curteis) Contemp. **31**: 585.
— — Union of, in the Nicene Age. (P. Schaff) Princ. **36**: 1.
— — Value of Individuality to. (E. D. Cheney) Radical, **8**: 24.
See Ecclesiastical Law; National Establishments of Religion.
— and Theater. (J. Dyer) Penn Mo. **10**: 374.
— and the Workingmen. Kitto, **39**: 1.
— and the World. (N. H. Chamberlin) Am. Church R. **19**: 353. — (B. W. Noel) Ex. H. Lec. **4**: 265.
— — Essays on. Chr. Obs. **66**: 641. **67**: 767.
— — Shipley's. (G. D. Haughton) Fortn. **5**: 754. — Month, **5**: 351.
— and Worship, Beauty and Sublimity in. (J. O. Johnson) Ref. Q. **28**: 102.
— Anglican and American, Bristed on. Ecl. R. **37**: 53. *See* Church of England.
— Annihilation of. Theo. Ecl. **6**: 344.
— Apostolic. (S. W. Field) Bapt. Q. **7**: 228.
— as an Aid to good Conduct. (E. L. Godkin) Nation, **25**: 252, 314, 317.
— as a Center of Charities. (R. Ellis) Unita. R. **6**: 384.
— as defined by the Churches. Bib. R. **1**: 204.
— as distinct from the Parish. (Mrs. L. J. K. Gifford) Mo. Rel. M. **46**: 55.
— as it was and ought to be. Brownson, **5**: 327. — (E. R. Tyler) New Eng. **6**: 418.
— as a Profession. Cornh. **9**: 750.
— as a reformatory Agent. (E. L. Godkin) Nation, **10**: 379.
— Attitude toward critical and scientific Inquiry. (E. A. Walker) New Eng. **19**: 323.
— Bannerman on. Chr. Obs. **70**: 660.
— Beginnings of. (T. Appel) Mercersb. **16**: 375. *See* Christianity, Beginnings of.
— Broad. *See* Broad Church.
— A comprehensive. (R. Ellis) Unita. R. **3**: 329.
— constituted at Pentecost. (W. Rupp) Mercersb. **18**: 457.
— Constitution of. (J. W. Nevin) Mercersb. **4**: 359. — (J. Williams) Am. Church R. **12**: 305. — Brownson, **13**: 1. — Chr. Rem. **3**: 90.
— — and Characteristics of. (L. Eichelberger) Evang. R. **5**: 478.
— Continuity and Discontinuity of. (A. P. Stanley) Good Words, **17**: 458.
— Culture and Discipline in. Bost. R. **2**: 397.
— Dangers and Duties of. Chr. Obs. **41**: 1, 65.
— Definitions of. Month, **10**: 183.
— Destinies of. (F. H. Hedge) Chr. Exam. **82**: 1.
— Development in. (F. B. Hornbrooke) Unita. R. **11**: 382.
— — on Apostolic Principles. (S. S. Schmucker) Evang. R. **2**: 151.
— Dictionary of, Hook's. Chr. Obs. **55**: 401.
— distinguished from the Kingdom. (E. J. Fisk) Bapt. Q. **8**: 270.
— Divine Life in. (T. A. Mills) Am. Presb. R. **10**: 37.
— Double Witness of. (D. Peck) Meth. Q. **4**: 125.
— — Kip's. So. R. n. s. **10**: 226.
— Early, Legacy of. (J. Lord) Cong. R. **7**: 65.
— — Life and Practice in. Meth. Q. **39**: 20.
— — Miraculous Triumphs of. (J. A. Seiss) Evang. R. **14**: 157.
— — Rites and Worship of. (A. Neander) Princ. **4**: 9. *See* Christians, Early.
— Essential Being of. (J. J. McElhinney) Am. Church R. **28**: 31.
— Established. *See* Church Establishment; Church of England; etc.
— Evolution and Symbolization. Chr. Rem. **27**: 492.
— a Fellow-Worker with God. Good Words, **21**: 458.
Church, The, Five Theories of. Cong. Q. **6**: 41.
— Genesis of. Am. Church R. **26**: 353.
— God's Regard for. (S. D. Clark) New Eng. **12**: 408.
— — Growth and Petrifaction in. (E. W. Reynolds) Univ. Q. **22**: 5.
— Harris's Witnessing. Chr. R. **3**: 282.
— Head of. (G. I. Wood) New Eng. **4**: 87. — (W. S. Tyler) Am. Bib. Repos. **11**: 344. **12**: 22.
— — Debate on, at Berne, 1528. Mercersb. **6**: 227.
— Historical Development of. (J. W. Nevin) Mercersb. **1**: 512. **4**: 33. — (P. Schaff) Mercersb. **5**: 137.
— the historical Witness. (C. S. Albert) Luth. Q. **9**: 131.
— History of. *See* Church History.
— Howe's Prospects of. Meth. Q. **3**: 60.
— Human Ordinances in. (S. A. Holman) Luth. Q. **10**: 316.
— Idea of. (C. Hodge) Princ. **25**: 249, 338.
— Ideal. (J. W. Howe) Chr. Exam. **79**: 67. — (C. S. Locke) Mo. Rel. M. **27**: 305.
— — Ward's. Quar. **75**: 149. — Brit. Q. **1**: 37.
— Ideal of a National. Temp. Bar, **40**: 42, 404.
— identified, Wilson's. New Eng. **9**: 564.
— Identity of. Danv. Q. **1**: 673.
— in Danger from Herself, Acaster on. Ecl. R. **50**: 465.
— in her Synodical Capacity. (J. Winecaff) Evang. R. **17**: 42.
— in History. (G. D. Wolff) Mercersb. **16**: 459.
— in Jerusalem, Persecution of. (B. Smith) Univ. Q. **36**: 171.
— in a Laodicean State, Is the? Chr. Obs. **66**: 44, 125, 201.
— Inefficiency of. Mo. Rel. M. **15**: 36, 73.
— Influences, Duties, and Hopes of. (S. Coley) Ex. H. Lec. **13**: 273.
— Invisible. (J. M. Hoppin) Cong. Q. **7**: 231.
— Laity's Part in the Work of. (J. Caird) Good Words, **4**: 526.
— Liberty and. (I. M. Atwood) Univ. Q. **24**: 438.
— Litton on. No. Brit. **18**: 447.
— McIlvaine on. (C. Hodge) Princ. **27**: 350.
— Martyr, First Age of. Dub. R. **62**: 362.
— Meaning of Ἐκκλησια in the New Testament. Theo. & Lit. J. **10**: 560.
— Meeting of Extremes in. (W. E. Krebs) Mercersb. **19**: 247.
— Message of, to Laboring Men. (C. Kingsley) Mo. Rel. M. **9**: 60.
— Millennial. Theo. & Lit. J. **8**: 615.
— Mission of. (P. Felts) Luth. Q. **7**: 100. — (T. J. Barkley) Ref. Q. **27**: 414.
— — of Reconciliation. (J. C. Smith) Am. Church R. **32**: 1.
— Moral Inertia of. (C. E. Norton) No. Am. **106**: 376.
— Motive Power in. (A. D. Mayo) Mo. Rel. M. **48**: 389.
— Nature of. (E. E. Higbee) Mercersb. **4**: 486, 578.
— — and Object of. Radical, **2**: 437.
— — and Office of. Brownson, **1**: 243.
— — and Powers of. (A. P. Peabody) Chr. Exam. **12**: 125.
— New Testament Idea of. (J. D. Griebel) Chr. Q. **3**: 319.
— New Testament Organization of. (J. T. Lewis) Am. Church R. **9**: 198.
— No Church, no Reform. Brownson, **1**: 175.
— Northern. (W. D. Northend) So. R. n. s. **4**: 319.
— of Christ, and of the Apostles. (H. Ballou, 2d) Univ. Q. **7**: 403.
— of England. (M. Arnold) Macmil. **33**: 481. — (E. E. Hale) O. & N. **3**: 328. — (H. G. Liddell) Macmil. **9**: 465. — (B. Price) Contemp. **10**: 161. — (L. Stephen) Nation, **5**: 277. — Blackw. **94**: 116, 225. — Bost. R **3**: 412, 503. — Ed. R. **58**: 498. — Brit. & For. R. **1**: 172. — Quar. **69**: 256. — Westm. **5**: 514.

Church of England. (J. Martineau) Westm. **53**: 165. — Westm. **21**: 362. — Blackw. **4**: 341. **19**: 36. — New York R. **2**: 250. — Ed. R. **44**: 490. — Quar. **5**: 352. — Mo. R. **115**: 353. **129**: 207, 284. — Ecl. R. **72**: 121.
— — Aggressive Nonconformity. Quar. **147**: 48.
— — Allies's Defense of. Chr. Obs. **47**: 741.
— — and the Age. (H. Alford) Contemp. **14**: 287. — Quar. **129**: 39.
— — and America compared. New York R. **8**: 285.
— — and Authority. Dub. R. **73**: 67.
— — and the Bible. Contemp. **10**: 321.
— — and the Burial Question. Cong. **3**: 346.
— — and Calvin. (J. F. Garrison) Am. Church R. **30**: 530.
— — and Christendom, Manning on. Dub. R. **61**: 110.
— — and the Church of the Future. Chr. Rem. **15**: 56.
— — and Church Unity, 1842. Chr. Rem. **3**: 422.
— — and Civil Law. Ed. R. **120**: 268.
— — and Bp. Colenso. (E. E. Hale) Chr. Exam. **75**: 97.
— — and Common Law. (F. Bowen) No. Am. **76**: 124.
— — and Congregationalism. (J. L. Davies) Contemp. **17**: 15.
— — and Decrees of the Apostles. Meth. M. **32**: 243.
— — and Dissenters. (J. B. Brown) Contemp. **16**: 298. — Ed. R. **137**: 196. — Chr. Rem. **17**: 285. — Blackw. **16**: 395, 548. **17**: 20. — Fraser, **9**: 127. — Tait, **2**: 269. — Chr. Obs. **71**: 781, 828.
— — and English Institutions. Chr. Obs. **74**: 126.
— — and English Thought. Brit. Q. **37**: 457.
— — and German Protestantism. Chr. Rem. **7**: 363.
— — and the Greek Church. Cath. World, **2**: 429.
— — — Attempt at Union between. Cath. World, **2**: 65.
— — and her Bishops. (S. Wilberforce) Quar. **114**: 538.
— — and her Curates. (S. Wilberforce) Quar. **123**: 220.
— — and her younger Members. (F. W. Farrar) Fortn. **10**: 572. Same art. N. Ecl. **4**: 67.
— — and Industrial Populations. Quar. **145**: 328.
— — and its Defenders. Brit. Q. **60**: 476.
— — and Liberals. Ed. R. **135**: 250. — Fraser, **6**: 88.
— — and the Liturgy. Rel. Cab. **1**: 1.
— — and Methodism. Meth. M. **33**: 103.
— — and Mr. Noel. (J. P. Thompson) New Eng. **7**: 254.
— — and Nonconformists. Nat. Q. **29**: 268.
— — and the Old Catholics; Conference at Bonn. (G. M. Raymond) Cath. World, **22**: 502.
— — and other Protestant Churches. (G. P. Fisher) New Eng. **33**: 121.
— — and Papacy. (A. C. Coxe) Am. Church R. **13**: 423.
— — and the People. (G. Potter) Fortn. **17**: 176.
— — and Presbyterian Orders. Princ. **26**: 377.
— — and Protestantism. Cong. **4**: 554.
— — and Puritanism. (M. Arnold) Cornh. **21**: 180.
— — and Religious Societies. Chr. Rem. **1**: 256.
— — and the Roman Catholic Church. Brit. Q. **43**: 282. — Chr. Rem. **20**: 200. **54**: 158. — Dub. R. **11**: 167, 240. **22**: 271. — (W. Van Wagenen) Univ. Q. **4**: 216. — (E. S. Ffoulkes) Lond. Q. **32**: 102.
— — and School Trusts. Chr. Rem. **14**: 143.
— — and Schools for all Sects. Selec. Ed. R. **3**: 393.
— — and Scotch Church. (J. Tulloch) Contemp. **19**: 223.
— — and the State. Chr. Rem. **3**: 361. **20**: 445.
— — — Ecclesiastical Jurisdiction of the Crown. Ed. R. **121**: 152.
— — — from 1660–63. Ecl. R. **115**: 523.
— — — present and past, 1867. Chr. Rem. **54**: 353.
— — and the Privy Council. Fraser, **69**: 521.
— — and the Universities. (H. Richards) Fortn. **24**: 437.
— — and Voluntary System. (R. Southey) Quar. **53**: 175.
— — and who should stop in it. (F. P. Cobbe) Theo. R. **5**: 482.
— — and the World. Chr. Rem. **53**: 110.
— — Anglican Catholics. Cong. M. **25**: 49.
Church of England, Anglican Neo-Christianity. Dub. R. **49**: 457.
— — Anglican Paddock. Month, **36**: 143.
— — Anglican Advance and Defection from Patristic Church. Chr. Rem. **1**: 393.
— — Anglican Reunionists. Month, **24**: 359.
— — Anglican Sacerdotalism. Month, **9**: 249, 416. **10**: 41.
— — Anglo-Catholicism, Argyll on. (M. MacColl) Contemp. **20**: 783.
— — Antagonistic Systems in. Dub. R. **31**: 1.
— — Apostolical Succession in, Haddon on. Chr. Obs **70**: 896.
— — Matthew Arnold and. (L. Stephen) Fraser, **82**: 414.
— — as a political and Social Institution. St. James, **23**: 590.
— — as a religious Body. (Lord Amberley) Fortn. **6**: 769. **7**: 197.
— — Attacks on. Blackw. **35**: 371, 954.
— — Authority in. (O. Shipley) Fortn. **34**: 601.
— — Bennett Case. Ed. R. **136**: 270.
— — Bentham on. Quar. **21**: 167.
— — Books for parochial Presentation. Chr. Rem. **17**: 402.
— — Broad-Churchism in. (A. Gordon) Theo. R. **10**: 277.
— — Buttresses of; Declarations and Test Acts. Brit. Q. **45**: 384.
— — Cathedral Life and Work. Quar. **130**: 225.
— — Cathedral Reform. (H. Alford) Contemp. **12**: 38, 360.
— — Catholicism of. Chr. Rem. **6**: 353.
— — Catholicity of, Growing. Chr. Rem. **7**: 163.
— — Christ's Church and Churches. (P. Bayne) Contemp. **11**: 27.
— — Church-Rates and Tithes in. Fraser, **9**: 379.
— — — and Vestries. Ed. R. **100**: 306.
— — Church-Rate Question. Ed. R. **109**: 66.
— — Church Union in. (H. Alford) Contemp. **7**: 161.
— — cleared from the Charge of Schism. Chr. Rem. **12**: 377.
— — Completeness of its objective System. Chr. Rem. **7**: 521.
— — Confessional in. Quar. **124**: 83. — (Mgr. Capel) Cath. World, **26**: 590.
— — Confraternity in. (B. F. Westcott) Contemp. **14**: 101.
— — Congress at Oxford, 1862, Proceedings. Chr. Rem. **44**: 441.
— — — at Manchester, 1863. Lond. Q. **21**: 300.
— — — at York, 1866. Chr. Rem. **53**: 227.
— — — at Southampton, 1870. Lond. Q. **35**: 428.
— — — at Leeds, 1872. Cong. **1**: 745.
— — — at Bath, 1873. Chr. Obs. **74**: 277. — Cong. **2**: 742.
— — — at Brighton, 1874. Cong. **3**: 753.
— — — at Plymouth, 1876. Cong. **5**: 689.
— — — of 1878. Cong. **7**: 687.
— — — on Nonconformity. (J. G. Rogers) 19th Cent. **2**: 632.
— — — Congresses of, Notes on some late. Month, **43**: 417.
— — Continuity of. Am. Ch. Mo. **3**: 49.
— — Convocation of. Ed. R. **105**: 78. — Quar. **75**: 464. — Contemp. **1**: 250. — Chr. Rem. **7**: 466. **24**: 342. — Chr. Obs. **52**: 762. **53**: 8. **57**: 447.
— — — and Ritualism. Cong. **4**: 374.
— — — Comedy of. *See* Comedy of Convocation.
— — — History of. Brit. Q. **16**: 544.
— — — Ingoldsby Letters on. Chr. Obs. **67**: 531.
— — — Lathbury on. Chr. Obs. **42**: 613, 683.
— — — Notes on. Chr. Obs. **66**: 241.
— — — of 1852. Chr. Rem. **25**: 140, 458.
— — — of Province of Canterbury, 1861. Chr. Obs. **61**: 275.

Church of England, Convocation of, Reform in. Chr. Obs. **77**: 737.
— — — What will it do? Chr. Obs. **67**: 229.
— — Father Cooper on. Dub. Univ. **24**: 631.
— — Corruption of. Selec. Ed. R. **5**: 301.
— — Daily Prayers in. Chr. Rem. **17**: 335.
— — Dangers of. Chr. Obs. **14**: 735. — Cong. M. **12**: 481. — Month, **126**: 430. — Ecl. R. **91**: 626.
— — Defection from, and its Grounds. Chr. Rem. **7**: 542.
— — Defects of, and their Remedies. Lond. Q. **19**: 508.
— — Discipline of the Clergy of. Chr. Rem. **42**: 251.
— — Disestablishment of. (Duke of Argyll) Contemp. **31**: 217. — (R. W. Dale) Fortn. **25**: 311. — (J. R. Pretyman) Contemp. **35**: 77. — (J. H. Rigg) Internat. R. **4**: 345. — Ed. R. **135**: 366. — Princ. **41**: 267. — Quar. **147**: 48.
— — — Addresses on, 1876. Brit. Q. **63**: 503.
— — — and Disendowment. (H. W. Croskey) Fortn. **27**: 834. — (W. D. Henderson) Macmil. **19**: 357. — (A. H. Mackonochie) 19th Cent. **1**: 686. — Brit. Q. **64**: 379. — Cong. **1**: 607. — Westm. **101**: 1.
— — — Business Aspects of. (A. Arnold) 19th Cent. **3**: 733.
— — — Can Mr. Gladstone save the Church? Cong. **4**: 449.
— — — Clerical Advocates of. Cong. **6**: 308.
— — — Gradual. (J. Hopgood) Contemp. **23**: 966.
— — — Hughes on. Brit. Q. **68**: 441.
— — — in Scotland. Cong. **7**: 45.
— — — Liberal Statesmen on. Cong. **7**: 65.
— — — Liberalism and. (E. Jenkins) Fortn. **29**: 889.
— — — Liberation Society for, 1877. Brit. Q. **66**: 137.
— — — Present Aspects of, 1877. (R. G. Moses) Bapt. Q. **11**: 166.
— — — Probable Results of. Fraser, **95**: 758.
— — — Prospect of, in 1877. Cong. **6**: 577.
— — — Question of. Tait, n. s. **1**: 44-431.
— — — Social Aspects of. (J. G. Rogers) 19th Cent. **1**: 436.
— — — What is? (A. P. Stanley) Contemp. **17**: 281. — (F. W. Newman) Fraser, **96**: 241.
— — — Dean Stanley's Question. Contemp. **17**: 473.
— — — Why Nonconformists desire. (H. Allon) Contemp. **17**: 365.
— — — with a Proposal for a really National Church. (A. R. Wallace) Macmil. **27**: 498.
— — Divine Guidance of. (W. H. Lyttleton) Contemp. **30**: 437. — (G. W. Moberly) Contemp. **30**: 725.
— — Divines of 17th Century. (W. Sewell) Quar. **69**: 471.
— — Doctrinal Unity of. (J. H. Jellett) Contemp. **6**: 488.
— — Doctrine and Discipline of. Dub. R. **28**: 233.
— — Doctrines of. Ecl. R. **73**: 489.
— — Doubt in, Apology for. (O. Shipley) 19th Cent. **6**: 66.
— — Eastward Position in. Chr. Obs. **76**: 46.
— — Ecclesiastical Commission, 1866. No. Brit. **44**: 180.
— — Ecclesiastical Dilapidations. Chr. Rem. **37**: 422.
— — Ecclesiastical Questions of 1864. Brit. Q. **39**: 1.
— — Education of the Clergy. Chr. Rem. **29**: 192.
— — Emerson on. (S. Eliot) Am. Church R. **10**: 197.
— — Endowments in 1830 and 1880. Quar. **151**: 502.
— — Episode in the History of. Fraser, **68**: 746.
— — Establishment of, Chalmers on. Fraser, **17**: 742. **18**: 396.
— — — Claims of. Ecl. R. **60**: 276.
— — — Letter to Brougham on. Tait, n. s. **1**: 368.
— — — Secularity of. Ecl. R. **81**: 227.
— — Ethics and Religion. Westm. **100**: 424.
— — Evangelical Movement in. Liv. Age, **142**: 387.
— — — Early Leaders in. Westm. **111**: 446.
— — — Present Position of, 1873. Chr. Obs. **73**: 83. — Fraser, **97**: 22.
Church of England, Expansion of. Ed. R. **113**: 1.
— — Extension in. Ecl. R. **72**: 207.
— — — and Church Reform. Fraser, **18**: 612.
— — fifty Years ago. (J. A. Froude) Good Words, **22**: 18.
— — Fiscal Burdens of the Clergy. Chr. Rem. **30**: 48.
— — Formularies of. Dub. R. **36**: 212.
— — Forster's Defense of. (J. G. Rogers) 19th Cent. **3**: 509.
— — Free Anglican Church. (E. Hatch) Macmil. **18**: 450.
— — Free Worship and free Offering. Chr. Rem. **51**: 50.
— — Freedom of Opinion necessary in an Established Church in a free Country. Macmil. **21**: 369.
— — — of Thought in. (H. R. Haweis) Contemp. **39**: 278.
— — Future of. Fraser, **67**: 549. — Temp. Bar, **34**: 248.
— — Gains of, 1865. Fraser, **72**: 738.
— — Gorham Judgment. Dub. R. **28**: 233.
— — Heresy in. (G. E. Ellis) Chr. Exam. **73**: 32.
— — Heterodox Clergy and their Treatment. Westm. **78**: 301.
— — High-Church Party in. (R. E. B—) Fraser, **97**: 240. — Month, **30**: 81.
— — — Claims of, exposed. (J. Foster) Ecl. R. **9**: 354.
— — High-Church Theory. Dub. R. **23**: 497.
— — — of dogmatical Authority. Dub. R. **3**: 43.
— — Historical Sketch of. (G. H. Emerson) Univ. Q. **15**: 113.
— — History of. Lond. Q. **51**: 84.
— — — Anderson's. So. Lit. Mess. **17**: 492.
— — — Fortunes of, 1830-60. Chr. Rem. **39**: 80.
— — — in Saxon and Norman Times. Chr. Rem. **37**: 120.
— — — — Lingard's. Ecl. R. **86**: 78.
— — — in 16th Century, Dodd's. Dub. R. **6**: 395.
— — — Sketches of. (G. Burgess) Am. Church R. **19**: 177, 376, 513. **20**: 68, 183.
— — History of the Episcopacy. Ed. R. **64**: 93.
— — Home Rule in. Dub. Univ. **95**: 145.
— — Homilies and Doctrines of. Ecl. R. **73**: 489. Same art. Am. Ecl. **2**: 454.
— — Hook's Archbishops of Canterbury. Blackw. **90**: 1. *See* Canterbury.
— — in 18th Century. Lond. Q. **53**: 24.
— — in 19th Century. Am. Church R. **26**: 526.
— — — Uhden on. Ecl. R. **79**: 529.
— — in 1811. Chr. Obs. **10**: 708, 778.
— — in 1832. Blackw. **31**: 181.
— — in 1840. Mo. R. **153**: 149.
— — in 1841. Chr. Rem. **2**: 10.
— — in 1845. Fraser, **31**: 116.
— — in 1851, Census of. Chr. Rem. **27**: 378.
— — — Crisis in. (J. W. Nevin) Mercersb. **3**: 359.
— — in 1857, Latest Phenomena of Anglicanism. Dub. R. **41**: 95.
— — in 1859-61. Chr. Rem. **43**: 222.
— — in 1862. Brit. Q. **36**: 418.
— — in 1866. Radical, **2**: 230.
— — in 1867. Brit. Q. **47**: 207.
— — in 1874. Quar. **137**: 246.
— — in 1875. Dub. R. **77**: 342.
— — in 1877, Crisis in. (T. T. Carter) 19th Cent. **1**: 417.
— — in the Army and Navy. Blackw. **103**: 251.
— — in American Colonies. (N. S. Richardson) Am. Church R. **10**: 368.
— — in Canada. Chr. Obs. **70**: 451. — Ecl. R. **68**: 249.
— — in the Colonies. Cong. M. **27**: 770. — (N. S. Richardson) Am. Church R. **10**: 368. — Liv. Age, **4**: 534.
— — — Consecration of Bishops in. Chr. Rem. **14**: 419.
— — — Episcopate in. Ed. R. **118**: 552.
— — — Establishment in. Ecl. R. **80**: 317.
— — — in Southern Hemisphere. Chr. Obs. **70**: 589.
— — — Is it without Law? Chr. Obs. **69**: 362.
— — — Jurisdiction in. Lond. Q. **21**: 189.
— — in 17th Century. Am. Church R. **1**: 9.

Church of England in Ireland. Cong. M. 24: 77, 400, 402.
— — — its Suppression proposed. Westm. 86: 281.
— — in Jamaica. Chr. Obs. 70: 927.
— — in Rural Districts. (E. Girdlestone) Macmil. 26: 470.
— — in Wales. Ed. R. 97: 342. Same art. Liv. Age, 37: 515.
— — in the West Riding. Quar. 145: 328. Same art. Liv. Age, 138: 195.
— — Income of Bishops of. Dub. R. 31: 475.
— — Influence in Society. Blackw. 27: 695. — Theo. R. 2: 277.
— — — of T. Arnold on. Bentley, 20: 190.
— — — of Wm. Law in. (G. G. Perry) Contemp. 6: 133.
— — — on Theology. Theo. R. 2: 522.
— — Innovations in. Quar. 141: 526.
— — Interest of. Pamph. 19: 477.
— — Intolerance of. Ecl. R. 69: 106.
— — Is it Protestant? Quar. 146: 519.
— — Is it worth preserving? (W.E. Gladstone) Contemp. 26: 193. — Ecl. M. 85: 291. — Liv. Age, 126: 387.
— — Laity in, Few Thoughts on. Contemp. 13: 80.
— — Lambeth and Archbishops. Ecl. M. 74: 93, 189, 327.
— — Latitudinarianism in, 1864. Chr. Rem. 49: 376.
— — Law of, and Church Prospects. Quar. 139: 248.
— — — What is? (J. F. Stephen) Fraser, 71: 225.
— — Law of Primates and Metropolitans. Chr. Rem. 38: 428.
— — Lay Work in. (E. H. Plumptre) Contemp. 8: 397.
— — Learning in. Nat. R. 16: 187.
— — Lectionary of, Revision of. (J. A. Hessey) Contemp. 11: 178.
— — Lectures on, 1840. Ecl. R. 72: 121.
— — Leeds Experiment in Anglicanism. Dub. R. 32: 69.
— — Letters from the Vicarage. Blackw. 16: 548. 17: 20, 167.
— — Liberalism in. (G. Smith) No. Am. 110: 151.
— — Liturgy of. Blackw. 18: 573. — Quar. 50: 509.
— — — and ancient Ritual Books. Chr. Rem. 13: 88.
— — — Reform in. No. Brit. 17: 369.
— — — M'Neile's Lectures on. Cong. M. 24: 30–461.
— — Miall's Motion on Disestablishment. Brit. Q. 54: 187.
— — Miall's Title-Deeds of. Ecl. R. 115: 178.
— — Missions of, and Church Extension. Am. Church R. 2: 107.
— — Monopoly of. Westm. 21: 62.
— — Music in. Chr. Rem. 7: 438.
— — — Choral. Chr. Rem. 13: 329.
— — — Ritual. Chr. Rem. 12: 114.
— — the National Church. Ed. R. 128: 251.
— — — How it became. Chr. Obs. 76: 780.
— — Nationalization of. (E. Maitland) Westm. 102: 200.
— — Nonconformist Essays on. (H. Alford) Contemp. 15: 1.
— — Nonconformist View of. (J. B. Mayor) Contemp. 12: 500.
— — Nonconformity and. Quar. 130: 432.
— — — and Liberalism in. Westm. 95: 355.
— — Objections to. Dub. Univ. 3: 208.
— — on the Continent. Chr. Obs. 63: 259.
— — Orders in, Estcourt on. (Dr. Ryder) Cath. World, 19: 467, 610. — Month, 18: 456.
— — — Late Works on. Am. Church R. 22: 481.
— — — Lee on. Dub. R. 67: 110.
— — Ordination in. Dub. R. 76: 191.
— — — and Confession. Quar. 144: 539.
— — Ought we to obey the new Court? (O. Shipley) Contemp. 26: 123.
— — Overton's Poetical Portraiture of. Ed. R. 58: 31.
— — Parties in. (R. F. Littledale) Contemp. 24: 287. — (E. H. Plumptre) Contemp. 7: 321. Same art. Liv. Age, 97: 67. — (C. A. Row) Kitto, 39: 184. — Brit. Q. 53: 352. — Ed. R. 98: 273.
Church of England, Parties in, and Preachers of. (C. Deshler) Harper, 52: 568.
— — Perry's History of. Ed. R. 115: 577.
— — Peterborough Questions. Cong. M. 4: 364.
— — Plan of a new. Month, 130: 371.
— — Policy of, 1868. Fraser, 78: 411.
— — — Essays on. Chr. Rem. 56: 356.
— — Politics and Prospects of, 1864. Chr. Rem. 49: 204.
— — Political Parties and. Quar. 118: 193.
— — Popular Objections against. Chr. Obs. 2: 209, 341.
— — Position and Prospects of, in 1837. Dub. R. 2: 493.
— — — in 1845. Ecl. R. 81: 346.
— — — in 1866. Chr. Obs. 66: 182.
— — — in 1872. Dub. R. 71: 476.
— — — in 1874. (J. L. Davies) Contemp. 25: 224.
— — — in 1876. (T. Hughes) Contemp. 29: 963.
— — Practical Work of. (B. B. Smith) Am. Church R. 10: 534.
— — Present and future. (C. J. Ellicott) 19th Cent. 1: 50.
— — Present Position of, 1863. Fraser, 66: 695.
— — Present State of, 1874. (M. R. Barker) Cath. World, 20: 41.
— — Present Struggles and final Issues. Liv. Age, 1: 401.
— — Principles at Stake. (H. Alford) Contemp. 9: 321, 481.
— — Progress of, 1867. Quar. 124: 225.
— — Property and Government of. Blackw. 28: 794.
— — Propagandism of. Dub. R. 43: 427.
— — Protestantism of. Dub. R. 12: 525.
— — Pulpit of. Kitto, 9: 394.
— — Purchase in. (J. Martineau) 19th Cent. 7: 78.
— — Puritanism and, Arnold's. Ed. R. 133: 399.
— — Pusey on. (A. P. Stanley) Contemp. 1: 534. — Cath. World, 2: 530. — Dub. R. 58: 188. — Month, 3: 534.
— — Questions affecting. Chr. Rem. 56: 439.
— — Rationalism in. Dub. R. 39: 199. — No. Brit. 33: 217.
— — Recent Movements in, 1867. Fraser, 74: 277.
— — Reform in. Ed. R. 56: 203. — Westm. 27: 99. 30: 257. — Mo. R. 125: 79. 141: 325. — Quar. 48: 542. — Meth. Q. 3: 165. — Blackw. 111: 567. — Chr. Obs. 69: 881. — Cong. M. 19: 173. — Dub. Univ. 1: 401. 5: 243. 28: 366. 34: 111. — Fraser, 7: 346, 476. 11: 247. — Macmil. 30: 121, 334. — Nat. R. 17: 203.
— — — and Dr. Arnold. Chr. Rem. 8: 547.
— — — by Comprehension, 1689 and 1873. (T. W. Jex-Blake) Macmil. 27: 417.
— — — Conference on, 1641. Chr. Obs. 73: 259.
— — — Lord Henley on. (A. Brougham) Ed. R. 56: 203. — Ecl. R. 55: 512. 56: 525.
— — — in 1833. Tait, 2: 242, 385.
— — — in 1845. Prosp. R. 1: 537.
— — — in 1858. (F. H. Dickinson) Am. Church R. 11: 1.
— — — Thoughts and Works on. Chr. Obs. 32: 437, 519, 565. 33: 303–689. 34: 47–229.
— — Reunion Movement in. (F. G. Lee) Contemp. 23: 978. — Dub. R. 54: 279.
— — Revelations of, in 1862. Ecl. R. 117: 84.
— — Revenues of. Blackw. 28: 273. — Ecl. R. 90: 257.
— — Revolution in. Brit. Q. 58: 504.
— — Ritual of. Quar. 72: 124. 137: 542.
— — — Report of Commission, 1867. Chr. Rem. 54: 445.
— — Ritual Conformity. Chr. Rem. 7: 183.
— — Ritualism in. *See* Ritualism.
— — Romanism in. Brit. Q. 40: 102.
— — — Existing Tendencies to. Chr. Rem. 6: 538.
— — — Progress of. (G. Poynder) Chr. Obs. 67: 613.
— — Rubric, Amendment of. Ed. R. 126: 499.
— — — *versus* Usage. Quar. 89: 203.
— — Rubrics and Ritual of. (H.H. Milman) Quar. 72: 232.
— — Rubrical Discipline, Irregularity in. Chr. Rem. 5: 525.

Church of England, Rubrical Question in. Chr. Rem. 9: 476.
— — Secession from. Dub. R. 43: 287.
— — — Hurn on. Cong. M. 14: 169.
— — — in 1843. Blackw. 55: 221. — (J. Williams) Am. Church R. 4: 259.
— — Services of. Chr. Obs. 74: 851.
— — — Reform of. (J. M. Capes) Contemp. 16: 519.
— — Statistics of. Chr. Rem. 13: 273.
— — Subscription to Formularies. Chr. Rem. 48: 350. *See* Subscription.
— — Succession of. (C. Elliott) Am. Meth. M. 19: 121.
— — Synods, Clergy, and Laity of. (R. C. Jenkins) Cong. Q. 15: 28.
— — System of. Dub. R. 12: 222.
— — Theology in. Chr. Rem. 6: 241.
— — — Warner on. Lond. M. 4: 516.
— — Thirty-nine Articles a Test of Heresy. Chr. Rem. 16: 456.
— — — The Anglicani and their 39 Medical Formulæ. Fraser, 84: 695.
See Subscription; Thirty-nine Articles.
— — Thoughts on. (H. Price) Tait, n. s. 4: 294.
— — Tithe Impropriation. Ed. R. 117: 361.
— — Toleration within. Fraser, 63: 483.
— — Treason within. Fraser, 18: 187, 751. 19: 367.
— — Tyacke's Congé d'élire. (H. Goodwin) Contemp. 7: 515.
— — under Cromwell. Princ. 39: 629.
— — Unity and Catholicity of. Dub. R. 11: 311.
— — Unreality of its Belief. Dub. R. 21: 461.
— — Vestments of. (S. Cheetham) Contemp. 2: 557.
— — — and the Eastward Position. Chr. Obs. 77: 900.
— — — Law of. Chr. Obs. 66: 698. 67: 304.
— — Voluntary System in. Quar. 53: 94.
— — Mr. Voysey and Mr. Purchas. Fraser, 83: 457.
— — Want of Candidates for Holy Orders. Chr. Rem. 7: 335.
— — Whately's Cautions for the Times, 1854. Fraser, 49: 553.
— — Whately's Petition for Legislation on. Dub. R. 15: 277.
— — Which is? Tinsley, 15: 260, 516.
— — Why does it exist? Tait, 4: 92, 121, 200.
Church-of-Englandism, Scotland taxed for. Tait, 1: 235.
Church of France, of Ireland, etc. *See* France, Ireland, etc.
— of the Future. (H. Alford) Contemp. 9: 161. — (C. H. Bromby) Contemp. 19: 155. — (O. A. Brownson) Cath. World, 8: 145. — (J. M. Leavitt) Am. Church R. 23: 450. — (W. T. Moore) Chr. Q. 1: 433. Bost. Q. 5: 1. — Chr. Rem. 15: 56. — Ecl. R. 87: 129. — Fraser, 99: 626. — Galaxy, 6: 85.
— — Bunsen on. Chr. Obs. 49: 753. — No. Brit. 8: 130. — Prosp. R. 2: 255.
— — Condition of. For. Q. 37: 27.
— — Prosperity of. (L. P. Hickok) Am. Presb. R. 6: 177.
— of God on Earth. Bost. Q. 2: 326.
— of the Holy Sepulcher. (J. Mills) Kitto, 38: 137.
— of the Middle Ages. Dub. Univ. 88: 570.
— of the New Age. (E. H. Sears) Mo. Rel. M. 33: 129. 34: 157.
— of the Spirit. (C. A. Bartol) Radical, 2: 385.
— Officers of, Bible on. (A. B. Ely) Cong. Q. 14: 509.
— Origin and Constitution of. Bost. R. 3: 341.
— Original. (N. Bangs) Meth. Q. 3: 550.
— Palmer on. New York R. 10: 100. — (J. Miller) Princ. 17: 215.
— Paul's Idea of. (J. W. Nevin) Mercersb. 9: 205.
— Periods of. (J. W. Santee) Ref. Q. 26: 513.
— Perpetuity of. (G. B. Bishop) Princ. 8: 362. — (C. Hodge) Princ. 28: 689.
Church, The, Pillar and Ground of the Truth. (D. Y. Heisler) Mercersb. 16: 578.
— Present Position of. (T. M. Clark) Am. Church R. 6: 422. — Cong. M. 21: 33, 241.
— Present Tendencies of. (A. P. Peabody) Chr. Exam. 35: 182.
— Present Work of. (A. H. Quint) Cong. Q. 7: 42.
— Priesthood of. Chr. Rem. 3: 529. — Meth. Q. 3: 485.
— Primitive. (A. Neander) Am. Bib. Repos. 4: 241. — (J. P. Thompson) Cong. Q. 3: 288.
— — Chapin's. (L. Bacon) New Eng. 1: 390.
— — Colman's. (E. Pond) New Eng. 1: 182.
— — Government of. (G. S. Camp) Am. Presb. R. 14: 245, 408.
— — Hopkins's. (W. Mitchell) Chr. Q. Spec. 8: 225.
— — Lord King on. Cong. M. 27: 755.
— Progress in, Fallacies of. Chr. Rem. 49: 108.
— Protestant Theory of Genesis of. (J. O'Connor) Am. Cath. Q. 3: 385.
— Question of. Princ. 41: 546.
— — and German Theology. (P. Schaff) Mercersb. 51: 124.
— — European. (A. T. Innes) Contemp. 26: 809.
— Questions concerning. (H. Rust) Mercersb. 6: 293, 481. 7: 20.
— Relation of, to human Nature. Mo. Rel. M. 28: 240.
— — to Society. (E. J. O'Reilly) Irish Mo. 2: 48–660. 3: 45–713. 4: 41–711. 5: 107. — Dub. R. 78: 73.
— Responsibilities of, in Conversion of the World. (T. H. Skinner) Am. Q. Reg. 6: 205.
— Review of Essays on. Chr. Obs. 38: 640.
— Rock of. (C. F. Cruse) Am. Church R. 1: 75, 218.
— Search for. Chr. R. 20: 422.
— Secession, History of. Ecl. R. 81: 695.
— Secularization of. Nation, 11: 39.
— Sermons by Bishop Blomfield. Cong. M. 25: 691, 773.
— Social Life in. Bost. R. 4: 537. — (J. B. Clark) New Eng. 39: 305.
— Social Power of. (J. H. Allen) Chr. Exam. 60: 398.
— Social Reform and. (G. M. Harmon) Univ. Q. 36: 179.
— Sociological Significance of. (J. Dyer) Penn Mo. 10: 693.
— Spirituality of. (A. Fleming) Bib. Sac. 12: 724.
— Stability of. (J. Brubaker) Luth. Q. 11: 200.
— Strange Doings in, long ago. Chamb. J. 40: 291.
— Theories of. (C. Hodge) Princ. 18: 137.
— Theses upon, by Dr. Harnack. Evang. R. 13: 122.
— Thoughts concerning. Univ. Q. 20: 146. — (J. W. Nevin) Mercersb. 10: 169, 383.
— Triumph of. Brownson, 17: 51.
— A true, and a valid Ministry. (E. S. Janes) Meth. Q. 29: 325.
— True Mission of. Danv. Q. 3: 311.
— Undeveloped Resources of. (W. B. Sprague) Evang. R. 14: 452.
— Utility of Learning in. Retros. 18: 354.
— *vs.* Church-Member. (C. K. Whipple) Radical, 5: 234.
— Visible. (J. M. Hoppin) Cong. Q. 6: 333. — (J. D. Lewis) Fortn. 34: 347.
— — and invisible. (D. Gans) Mercersb. 15: 312. — (H. C. Haithcox) Luth. Q. 11: 503.
— Visibility of. (C. Hodge) Princ. 25: 670.
— Vocation of. Brit. Q. 34: 1.
— Voluntary Principle in. (P. Schaff) Mercersb. 9: 514.
— What is it? (D. W. Faunce) Bapt. Q. 10: 165.
— When organized? Chr. Mo. Spec. 3: 290.
— without a Bishop. Meth. Q. 5: 120.
— Witness of. (A. L. Stone) Cong. Q. 6: 350.
— Work and Responsibility of. (A. L. Stone) Cong. Q. 6: 190.
— The World in. Am. Church R. 4: 123.
Church, The, among the tall Chimneys. Fraser, 50: 272.

Church of the Cup of cold Water; a Tale. (Mrs. R. Barker) Cath. World, 29: 697.
— of the Glass of Water. Sharpe, 25: 22.
— of the Vasa d'Agua; a Tale. Internat. M. 1: 400.
Churches and the Church. (F. H. Hedge) Chr. Exam. 41: 193.
— and Church-Membership. (D. Burt) Cong. Q. 8: 374.
— Battle of. (J. Martineau) Westm. 54: 441.
— Chapter about. (J. B. Varnum) Am. Whig R. 3: 523.
— Dangers and Constitution of. Prosp. R. 5: 431.
— Dead and alive. St. James, 27: 60.
— Decline of. (J. V. Blake) Radical, 1: 625.
— Early, Life and Practice in. (W. H. Withrow) Meth. Q. 31: 20.
— Established. (H. Giles) Chr. Exam. 31: 209.
— — National Aspects of. Brit. Q. 73: 140.
— Evil in. (J. Hall) Princ. n. s. 1: 345.
— Fellowship among, Basis of. (S. B. Goodenow) New Eng. 33: 337.
— — Promotion of. (E. W. Gilman) Cong. Q. 13: 225.
— in New England, Practices of. Cong. Q. 17: 253.
— Independent, their first Formation. (J. L. Dagg) Bapt. Q. 5: 478.
— Independence and Equality of local. (H. M. Dexter) Cong. Q. 6: 147.
— Intercommunion of. (T. W. Aveling) Cong. 6: 437. — Cong. M. 15: 8.
— New; Progress of Dissent. (R. Southey) Quar. 23: 549. 31: 229. — Fraser, 13: 249.
— Numbering of, and their Members. (A. H. Quint) Cong. Q. 1: 135.
— of the three Kingdoms. (W. Empson) Ed. R. 81: 526. — Brit. Q. 12: 217.
— Preservation and thorough Order of. Chr. Rem. 8: 517.
— Right of, to hold Property. Spirit Pilg. 1: 113. 2: 128.
— Primitive and Apostolic. (N. Van Alstine) Luth. Q. 7: 54.
— — Secession of. (J. P. Wilson) Chr. Mo. Spec. 10: 281.
— Schelling on Characteristics of different Christian. Am. Presb. R. 14: 283.
— The Seven. Mus. 18: 142. — Art J. 15: 36–250.
Churches, Ancient, Observations on. (E. Ledwick) Arch. 8: 165.
— — Restoration of. (B. Champneys) Portfo. 3: 8. — (G. Crabbe) Fraser, 97: 449.
— and Cathedrals, Continental. Chr. Rem. 16: 27.
— and Parsonages. (O. E. Day) New Eng. 12: 276.
— Anglican Arrangement of. (W. Patton) Pioneer, 4: 35.
— Anglo-Saxon, Ceremonial of consecrating, etc. (J. Gage) Arch. 25: 235, 275.
— Building of. (I. P. Langworthy) Cong. Q. 2: 20. — New Eng. 6: 1. — (A. D. Gridley) Hours at Home, 10: 549.
— — by Capitalists. Chr. Rem. 5: 733.
— — Eras in. Hours at Home, 7: 385.
— — Extravagance in. Am. Arch. 5: 34.
— — in the Middle Ages. (J. W. Chadwick) Unita. R. 15: 97. — (J. MacAlister) Dial (Ch.), 1: 125.
— — Modern. Am. Arch. 5: 50, 66. — (A. F. Oakey) Am. Arch. 8: 89.
— Chapters on. Sharpe, 11: 288.
— Chat about our. (E. S. Gould) Putnam, 11: 754.
— Consecration of. (F. C. Oakeley) Irish Mo. 2: 65.
— Country, Plan for. (M. J. O'Connor) Cath. World, 7: 135.
— Decoration of recent. (C. Cooke) Scrib. 15: 569.
— Dorset. Antiquary, 4: 273.
— Episcopal Chairs, Stone Seats, etc., in. (C. Clarke) Arch. 11: 317.
— Free and open. (Earl Nelson) St. James, 37: 74.
— Gothic Congregational. (J. A. Clapham) Cong. 7: 202.
— — in New England. (C. D. Warner) Cong. 7: 100.
Churches, How to construct. (J. S. Sewall) New Eng. 21: 24.
— in France and Switzerland in Time of Charlemagne. (J. H. Parker) Arch. 37: 244.
— in London, Against Demolition of. (C. K. Paul) 19th Cent. 7: 486. Same art. Liv. Age, 145: 52.
— Interior Arrangement of. (C. C. Edgerton) Am. Church R. 30: 26.
— Internal Decoration and Arrangement. Quar. 102: 88.
— of Europe. Art J. 22: 22–375. 23: 14–271. 24: 50–235.
— Open. Theo. R. 2: 103. — Chr. Rem. 24: 81.
— Popish Fittings in. Chr. Obs. 48: 104, 251.
— Responsibility attached to Restoration of. Chr. Rem. 8: 138.
— Round, Origin and Antiquity of. (J. Essex) Arch. 6: 163.
— Rural. New York R. 9: 180.
— What they cost. (J. M. Whiton) Scrib. 13: 404.
See Architecture, Church; Meeting-Houses.
Church Administration. (T. W. Aveling) Cong. 6: 168–433.
Church Architecture. *See* Architecture, Church.
Church Attendance. (J. W. Kimball) New Eng. 21: 537.
— Is it worth while? (C. A. Humphreys) Unita. R. 8: 189.
— Regular. (O. Dewey) Chr. Exam. 4: 110.
Church Authority. (E. V. Gerhart) Mercersb. 19: 180.
— and personal Responsibility. (A. De Vere) Cath. World, 20: 577.
— Nature and Extent of. Danv. Q. 4: 1.
— Wilberforce on. Brownson, 12: 339. — Chr. Obs. 55: 255. — Dub. R. 37: 450.
Church Bell at Farum; a Danish Poem. (C. Larsen) Lakeside, 8: 182.
Church Calendars. Chr. Rem. 40: 386.
Church Commission and English Cathedrals. Dub. Univ. 14: 3.
Church Courts, Royal Commission on. Fraser, 103: 530.
— Slavery in. Danv. Q. 4: 516.
Church Covenant, English, 1654. Cong. Q. 4: 21.
Church Development. (J. M. Cramp) Bapt. Q. 4: 455.
Church Discipline. (E. L. Godkin) Nation, 17: 366. — (S. B. Goodenow) Cong. R. 9: 360. — (D. Y. Heisler) Mercersb. 25: 268. — Chr. R. 9: 416. — (G. Diehl) Luth. Q. 10: 362.
— and Business. (T. W. Aveling) Cong. 6: 433.
— Anglican Layman on. Month, 38: 282.
— Imperfect Rights and Obligations as related to. (L. A. Atwater) Princ. 38: 94.
— in Boston, 1646, Case of. (G. E. Ellis) Mo. Rel. M. 3: 75.
— Process of. (H. M. Dexter) Cong. Q. 5: 256.
Church Economics. Ecl. R. 116: 308.
Church Education Society. Dub. Univ. 23: 628.
Church Efforts to reform the World. (E. Lord) Lit. & Theo. R. 1: 443.
Church Endowments, their Origin. Cong. 3: 449.
Church Establishments. Ed. R. 38: 145. — Cong. M. 16: 355. — Westm. 21: 372.
— and Voluntary System. Dub. Univ. 16: 218, 325, 409.
— Dealtry and Wilks on. Chr. Obs. 32: 103.
— National, Works on. Chr. Obs. 38: 653, 763.
— Principles of. Fraser, 14: 131.
— Wardlaw on. Ecl. R. 69: 695.
Church Expansion, Pearson on. Chr. Obs. 54: 391.
Church Extension. (A. J. Kynett) Meth. Q. 32: 268. — Quar. 103: 139.
— Debate on, 1840. Ecl. R. 72: 207.
— Early Methods of. (J. S. Clark) Cong. Q. 1: 53.
— Paul's Method of. (S. McCall) Cong. Q. 3: 249
Church Fellowship, Duty of. Cong. M. 1: 314.
Church Festivals and their Household Names. Chr. Rem. 24: 385.

Church Finance, Apostolic System of. (J. C. Wightman) Bapt. Q. 5: 385.
Church Goods, Instructions for the Survey of. (J. Caley) Arch. 18: 298.
— and Chantries of Derbyshire in the 16th Century. (M. E. C. Walcott) Reliquary, 11: 1, 81.
Church Government. (N. Adams) Bib. Sac. 1: 591. — Chr. Mo. Spec. 3: 462. — (J. Porter) Am. Meth. M. 22: 13.
— First. (W. C. Dawson) Chr. Q. 5: 145, 387.
— Hints on. (I. E. Graeff) Mercersb. 23: 472.
— History of Changes in. (E. Pond) New Eng. 13: 295.
— Self-Government in. (P. Schaff) Mercersb. 9: 522.
— Society, The, and the Church. (A. D. Stowell) New Eng. 36: 487.
— Turnbull on. Ecl. R. 34: 398.
Church Historians, German. No. Brit. 29: 340.
Church History. Chr. R. 1: 417. — Brit. Q. 2: 72. — (A. Lamson) Chr. Exam. 33: 1. — (J. A. Alexander) Princ. 5: 47. — (R. Robbins) Chr. Q. Spec. 3: 433. — (A. Lamson) Chr. Exam. 22: 27. — (D. P. Kidder) Meth. Q. 28: 203. — (C. F. Schaeffer) Evang. R. 10: 586. — (M. J. Spalding) U. S. Cath. M. 3: 205–341. — Cong. M. 28: 437, 511. — Ecl. R. 122: 426. — Univ. Q. 12: 266.
— Alzog's. (W. Dowe) Nat. Q. 38: 177. — Meth. Q. 40: 504.
— and the Baptists. Chr. R. 20: 569.
— Anderson's Colonial. Chr. Obs. 49: 615.
— as a Science. (P. Schaff) Bib. Sac. 7: 54.
— Bede's. Ecl. R. 94: 192.
— before the Reformation, Ages of. Brit. Q. 26: 144.
— Döllinger's. Mo. R. 151: 464. 152: 603.
— Early. (S. Osgood) Chr. Exam. 55: 358. — (L. Withington) Bib. Sac. 14: 770.
— — Mossman's. Chr. Obs. 74: 258.
— Eusebius's. Ecl. R. 68: 369.
— Fry's. Ecl. R. 43: 37.
— Gieseler's. (P. Schaff) Mercersb. 10: 327. — Ecl. R. 80: 402. — Bib. R. 3: 1. — (J. A. Alexander) Princ. 29: 636.
— Growth and Petrifaction in the Early Church. (E. W. Reynolds) Univ. Q. 22: 5.
— Guericke's Manual of. (W. M. Reynolds) Evang. R. 10: 146.
— Hardwick's. Chr. Obs. 56: 741.
— Hase's. (W. D. Godman) Meth. Q. 15: 457.
— in 2d Century. (J. M. Cramp) Bapt. Q. 7: 24.
— in 2d and 3d Centuries, Kaye on. Chr. Obs. 27: 347.
— in 4th–5th Centuries. (A. G. Laurie) Univ. Q. 21: 466.
— in Dark Ages. Brownson, 6: 330.
— in Middle Ages. (G. E. Ellis) Chr. Exam. 46: 345.
— — Janeway's. (G. B. Russell) Mercersb. 5: 50.
— — Trench on. (M. P. Lowe) Unita. R. 11: 208. — Dub. R. 82: 447.
— Killen's Ancient. Chr. Obs. 60: 77.
— Kirkton's. (Sir W. Scott) Quar. 18: 502.
— Kurtz's. (C. P. Krauth) Evang. R. 6: 287.
— Later, Hagenbach's. (J. F. Hurst) Meth. Q. 24: 195.
— Lee's. Dub. Univ. 51: 286.
— Lights and Shadows of. (M. Mahan) Am. Church R. 15: 608.
— Lost Chapter of. Month, 2: 241.
— Manual of. (W. M. Reynolds) Evang. R. 10: 146.
— Mayer's. (E. Heiner) Mercersb. 3: 398.
— Method of. (J. A. Alexander) Princ. 26: 300.
— Milner's. Chr. Disc. 4: 301. — Chr. Obs. 2: 609, 676, 746. 3: 29, 109. 9: 26.
— Modern. (S. Osgood) Chr. Exam. 48: 411.
— Mosheim's. Ecl. R. 19: 217.
— Nature and Worth of the Science. (H. B. Smith) Bib. Sac. 8: 412.
Church History, Neander's. (B. Sears) Bib. Sac. 4: 386. — Am. Church R. 3: 228. — Chr. R. 1: 565. — (E. R. Tyler) New Eng. 5: 472. – Am. Bib. Repos. 3d s. 4: 126. — (J. Walker) Chr. Exam. 12: 65. — (A. Lamson) Chr. Exam. 36: 108. — (G. F. Simmons) Chr. Exam. 43: 427. — (J. W. Alexander) Princ. 16: 155. — (N. L. Frothingham) Chr. Exam. 58: 265. — (A. P. Peabody) No. Am. 80: 199. — Ecl. R. 55: 460. 76: 376. — No. Brit. 21: 101. — Brit. Q. 12: 305.
— Old and new Writers on. Chr. Rem. 43: 26.
— Original Mode of editing. Blackw. 2: 305.
— Philosophy of. (W. Adams) Am. Church R. 12: 193. 13: 193, 361.
— Pictures from early. Good Words, 1: 581, 721, 737.
— Province and Uses of. (J. S. Lee) Univ. Q. 26: 463.
— Relation of Reformed Churches to. (H. B. Smith) Am. Presb. R. 4: 177.
— Schaff's, of the Apostolic Age. (L. Bacon) New Eng. 12: 237. — (H. Harbaugh) Mercersb. 14: 476. — (J. W. Nevin) Mercersb. 3: 296. — (C. P. Krauth) Evang. R. 3: 107. — (D. N. Lord) Theo. & Lit. J. 6: 665. — (N. S. Richardson) Am. Church R. 12: 369. — (C. F. Schaeffer) Evang. R. 10: 586. — Cath. World, 8: 417. — Ecl. R. 100: 399. — (C. A. Aiken) Princ. 39: 392.
— Schmidt's Freedom of Thought and Faith in 1st Century. Prosp. R. 3: 542.
— Scott's, 1530–46. Chr. Obs. 27: 29, 96. 29: 761. — Ecl. R. 45: 536. 49: 331. 51: 433. 56: 512. — Chr. Obs. 31: 753, 800.
— Smith's Tables of. (L. Whiting) No. Am. 92: 318.
— Study of. (S. Martin) Ex. H. Lec. 15: 293.
— — Stanley on. Chr. Obs. 57: 769.
— Theodoret's. Ecl. Mus. 3: 447.
— Transformations in. Tait, n. s. 7: 69.
— Value of. (A. Hovey) Chr. R. 19: 48.
— Waddington's. (D. Welsh) Ed. R. 62: 132.
— Welsh's. No. Brit. 3: 444.
— Wilkinson's Review of Milner on. Chr. Obs. 6: 34.
— Yeate's Indian. Ecl. R. 29: 250.
See Christianity, History of.
Church Independency and the State. (A. M. Fairbairn) Brit. Q. 73: 441.
Church Lands, Secularization of. (J. P. Quincy) O. & N. 7: 580.
Church Lane, St. Giles. Fraser, 37: 257.
Church Law, Administration of. (G. G. Reynolds) Meth. Q. 40: 605.
— Blunt's Book of. Chr. Obs. 77: 299.
Church Life, Requisites of. (J. Gilbert) Cong. 3: 285.
— Type of. (J. Williams) Am. Church R. 5: 63.
Church Manual. (D. Wight, jr.) Cong. Q. 7: 163.
Church-Member, Mitchell's. (S. Miller) Princ. 8: 243.
Church-Members, Absent, and what to do with them. (S. B. Goodenow) Cong. Q. 17: 534.
— Faults of, no Excuse for not making a Profession. (E. Kellogg) Chr. Mo. Spec. 8: 281.
— Litigation among. (S. Tracy) Cong. Q. 12: 211.
Church-Membership, Admission to. Cong. M. 14: 656, 711.
— and Creeds. (C. Cushing) Cong. Q. 19: 261.
— — as Tests. (K. Twining) New Eng. 32: 670.
— and Meetings. (T. W. Aveling) Cong. 6: 345.
— Entrance into. (J. W. Santee) Mercersb. 17: 373.
— — Sermon on. (F. D. Huntington) Mo. Rel. M. 10: 481.
— Hasty Admissions to. (T. Edwards) Princ. 5: 306.
— Qualifications for. Cong. M. 3: 375.
— What constitutes? (T. G. Apple) Mercersb. 23: 325.
See Communion.
Church Missionary Principles. (C. F. Childe) Chr. Obs 76: 401.

Church Missionary Society. Chr. Rem. **5**: 52.
— Reports. Chr. Obs. **63**: **64**: **66**: app.
— Review of Pamphlets on, 1818. Chr. Obs. **17**: 97, 865.
Church Monopoly. Westm. **21**: 62.
Church Music. *See* Music, Church.
Church Observances and religious Life. (J. D. Long) Unita. R. **3**: 257.
Church Officers. Spirit Pilg. **4**: 186. — (S. E. Shepard) Chr. Q. **1**: 251.
Church Organization. Mo. Rel. M. **12**: 301. **19**: 13.
— and Government. (D. G. Porter) Chr. Q. **5**: 64, 201.
— Report on, 1865. (E. H. Sears) Mo. Rel. M. **40**: 85.
Church Order, Rules of. (H. M. Dexter) Cong. Q. **5**: 323.
Church Party, Spirit of. Ecl. R. **71**: 262.
Church Parties. Liv. Age, **39**: 451.
— as Apologists. (F. Wharton) Bib. Sac. **37**: 440.
Church Pastoral-Aid Society, Report, etc., 1849. Chr. Obs. **49**: app.
Church Poetry and Music. (B. J. Wallace) Am. Presb. R. **6**: 488.
Church Policy, Essays on. Chr. Obs. **68**: 517.
Church Politics, Comparative, 1881. (A. M. Fairbairn) Brit. Q. **74**: 399.
Church Polity. (H. D. Evans) Am. Ch. Mo. **1**: 11. — (S. E. Shepard) Chr. Q. **5**: 342. — Am. Meth. M. **14**: 438.
— and Establishments, Dick on. Cong. M. **18**: 561.
— in the first Age. (A. Hovey) Bapt. Q. **4**: 225.
Church Principles and Life. Ecl. R. **112**: 372.
— and Polity: Litton and Barrett. Lond. Q. **2**: 459.
— Gladstone on. Chr. Obs. **41**: 677. — Ecl. R. **73**: 369.
— in Church History. (W. Kirkus) Am. Church R. **32**: 41, 135.
Church Property and Trust Deeds. Brit. Q. **39**: 357.
— Appropriation of. (T. H. Lister) Ed. R. **60**: 483.
— Custody of. (G. W. Hodge) Am. Church R. **31**: 42.
— in Canada. (A. N. Bethune) Am. Church R. **7**: 41.
— E. Miall on. Lond. Q. **20**: 1.
— Questions of, in the South. (E. N. Cobleigh) Meth. Q. **31**: 614.
— Taxation of. (A. W. Pitzer) No. Am. **131**: 362. — (E. E. Hale) No. Am. **133**: 255. — (H. W. Foote) Unita. R. **7**: 349, 465. — (E. McChesney) Meth. Q. **36**: 243. — (E. L. Godkin) Nation, **22**: 23. — (W. T. Moore) Chr. Q. **6**: 175. — (J. P. Quincy) O. & N. **6**: 649. — (H. J. Van Dyke) Cong. **3**: 560. — So. R. n. s. **20**: 169.
Church Psalmody. Am. Q. Reg. **5**: 25. *See also* Hymns and Psalms.
Church Question. (J. A. Seiss) Evang. R. **2**: 58.
Church Questions, Recent Pamphlets on, 1877. Chr. Obs. **77**: 504–825.
Church Rates. Ed. R. **66**: 295. — (J. Allen) Ed. R. **70**: 48. — (J. J. Blunt) Quar. **57**: 363. — Quar. **110**: 544. — Fraser, **15**: 146. — Ecl. R. **65**: 290, 375. **66**: 109.
— Abolition of. Westm. **70**: 30. — Ed. R. **65**: 178*.
— and Disraeli, 1861. Ecl. R. **113**: 218.
— and Ecclesiastical Commission. Fraser, **11**: 457.
— and Scotch Church. Blackw. **41**: 682.
— Sir John Coleridge on, 1860. Ecl. R. **111**: 89
— Imprisonment for not paying. Cong. M. **24**: 415.
— in 1835. Ecl. R. **62**: 519.
— in 1836. Ecl. R. **65**: 290, 375.
— in 1837. Ecl. R. **66**: 109.
— in 1853. Ecl. R. **98**: 80.
— in 1859. Ecl. R. **109**: 56, 325.
— Legislation on, and Vestry Contests, 1855. Ecl. R. **101**: 348.
— Question of, 1859. Ecl. R. **110**: 630.
Church Reform, Riland on. Cong. M. **13**: 369, 488, 545.
Church Revenues and Church Rates. Ed. R. **66**: 295.
Church Robbery. Blackw. **38**: 248.
Church Scandal in Rome in 3d Century. (J. Tulloch) Good Words, **3**: 307.
Church Schools and Colleges. (S. Eliot) Am. Church R. **12**: 66.
Church Service, Forms of. Mercersb. **6**: 355.
Church Services. Once a Week, **21**: 560.
Church Union. (T. G. Apple) Mercersb. **16**: 481. — (J. W. Nevin) Mercersb. **21**: 5. — (J. A. Reubelt) Chr. Q. **2**: 167. — Brit. Q. **47**: 478. — Chr. Rem. **3**: 621. **51**: 156. **52**: 155. — No. Brit. **24**: 140.
— and the Confessions. (T. G. Apple) Mercersb. **25**: 560.
— and the Old Catholic Movement. (J. W. Nevin) Mercersb. **20**: 285.
— Basis for. (T. M. Clark) Am. Church R. **28**: 481.
— Bonn Conference, 1875. Lond. Q. **46**: 57.
— Essays on. Chr. Rem. **55**: 202.
— Movement for. (T. Munnell) Chr. Q. **1**: 111.
— Order of corporate Reunion. (F. G. Lee) 19th Cent. **10**: 744.
— Principles of. Prosp. R. **10**: 483.
— Reunion of entire Church. Brownson, **19**: 1.
— — Döllinger on. Chr. Obs. **73**: 241.
— — Leibnitz on. (S. Stead) Contemp. **5**: 50, 437.
— — Organic. (J. P. Lacroix) Bib. Sac. **35**: 391.
Church Unity. (P. Berry) Mercersb. **4**: 322. — (A. C. Coxe and W. Tatlock) Am. Church R. **31**: 211. — (J. M. Hoppin) New Eng. **33**: 107. — (Earl Nelson) 19th Cent. **10**: 120. — (T. Kliefoth) Am. Presb. R. **2**: 383. — (M. Loy) Evang. R. **8**: 1. — (A. D. Mayo) O. & N. **5**: 363. — (J. H. Merle d'Aubigné) Cong. M. **27**: 576. — (T. F. Scott) Am. Church R. **11**: 288. — (H. Tappan) Am. Bib. Repos. 3d s. **1**: 617. — (J. W. Yeomans) Princ. **20**: 104. — Am. Ch. Mo. **1**: 99. — Chr. Obs. **74**: 801. — Am. Church R. **31**: 304. — Ecl. R. **107**: 512.
— and Conversion of the World. (J. A. Bolles) Am. Church R. **32**: 26.
— and its Doctrines. (J. H. Merle d'Aubigné) Lit. & Theo. R. **2**: 588. — (J. H. Merle d'Aubigné) Am. Bib. Repos. **6**: 332.
— and social Amelioration. Brownson, **1**: 310.
— Cyprian's View of. (J. W. Nevin) Mercersb. **4**: 350.
— English. Chr. Rem. **5**: 1.
— Movements towards. (F. H. Dickinson) Am. Church R. **7**: 59.
— Need of visible. (N. S. Richardson) Am. Church R. **17**: 611.
— The one Body. (C. M. Parkman) Am. Church R. **29**: 102.
— Organic, William E. Knox on. (A. F. Hewit) Cath. World, **24**: 657.
— Spiritual. (L. Mann) Theo. R. **8**: 154.
Church Vestments. (A. P. Stanley) Contemp. **25**: 476.
— Marriott on. Chr. Obs. **70**: 178.
— A. P. Stanley on. (R. F. Littledale) Contemp. **25**: 571.
— Surplice or Gown. Chr. Obs. **71**: 291.
Church Work in large Cities. (W. Welsh) Am. Church R. **17**: 39. — Am. Presb. R. **9**: 551.
— Suggestions about. (G. U. Wennor) Luth. Q. **6**: 440.
Church Year. (H. I. Schmidt) Evang. R. **2**: 16.
— Conception and Claims of. (J. W. Nevin) Mercersb. **8**: 456.
— Lessons of. (E. V. Gerhart) Mercersb. **20**: 422.
— Relation of Sermon to. (Dr. Plètt) Evang. R. **18**: 169. *See* Christian Year.
Churchill, Charles, the Satirist. Temp. Bar, **47**: 493.
— Parson and Poet. (J. F. Hitchman) St. James, **13**: 168.
— Poetical Works of. (J. Forster) Ed. R. **81**: 46. Same art. Ecl. M. **4**: 496. Same art. Liv. Age, **4**: 420.
Churchill Genealogy. (F. F. Starr) N. E. Reg. **34**: 301.
Churchliness, Characteristics of. (T. G. Apple) Mercersb. **12**: 40.

Churchman ascertained, Overton's True. Chr. Obs. **1**: 24–440. **2**: 562. **3**: 421–633. **4**: 689.
— Oxford and Evangelical. Brit. Q. **1**: 436.
Churchmen guiding modern Thought. (J. H. Ward) Am. Church R. **35**: 219.
Churchwarden's Accounts for Minchenhampton, Gloucestershire, Eng. (J. Bruce) Arch. **35**: 409.
— of the Parish of Leverton. (E. Peacock) Arch. **41**: 333.
— — of Wing, Bucks. (F. Ouvry) Arch. **36**: 219.
Churchyard, Seaside. House. Words, **2**: 257.
Churchyards and Epitaphs. Sharpe, **32**: 156. **33**: 157. **34**: 252.
— and Metropolitan Board Act, 1854. Chr. Obs. **54**: 267.
— Chapters on. (C. Bowles) Blackw. **15**: 467. **16**: 317, 468. **17**: 28, 345, 437. **20**: 610. **22**: 33, 206, 341. **23**: 55–309. **25**: 163–601.
— Concerning. (A. K. H. Boyd) Fraser, **58**: 47.
— of London. Chamb. J. **37**: 406. — Westm. **40**: 149.
Churchyard Eclogue. (T. Aird) Blackw. **36**: 615. **50**: 760.
Churchyard Wanderings. Colburn, **5**: 84.
Churton, H. Toinette. (R. S. Rust) Meth. Q. **35**: 473.
Chute Genealogy. N. E. Reg. **13**: 123.
Ciarlatano, Il. Penny M. **14**: 145.
Cibaria Memorabilia. Fraser, **15**: 371, 434.
Cibber, Colley. (H. A. Huntington) Lippinc. **21**: 563. Colburn, **124**: 34. — Cornh. **37**: 187. — Ev. Sat. **13**: 312.
— and his Associates. Temp. Bar, **36**: 32.
— and Caio Gabriel. Once a Week, **26**: 255.
— and his Descendants. Temp. Bar, **53**: 60.
— Apology for his own Life. Blackw. **13**: 294. — (T. N. Talfourd) Retros. **1**: 167.
— Richard the Third. Lond. M. **3**: 433.
— *vs.* Shakspere. (H. B. Baker) Gent. M. n. s. **18**: 343.
Cicadæ, The. (W. M. Nevin) Mercersb. **3**: 426.
— New Species of. (J. K. Lord) Intel. Obs. **8**: 428.
— Song of. (F. C. Clark) Am. Natural. **9**: 70. — (J. C. Galton) Pop. Sci. R. **16**: 353.
Cicada septendecim. Penny M. **6**: 87.
Cicely's Christmas. (C. F. Woolson) Appleton, **6**: 753.
Cicero. (H. R. Cleveland) No. Am. **46**: 20. — (T. De Quincey) Blackw. **52**: 1. **95**: 544. — Quar. **150**: 337. — Penny M. **7**: 261.
— and Clodius. (E. S. Beesly) Fortn. **5**: 421.
— and Demosthenes. Mo. R. **152**: 89.
— and his Contemporaries. Lond. Q. **8**: 355. Same art. Ecl. M. **42**: 191.
— and Julius Cæsar. Dub. Univ. **94**: 202.
— as a Man of Letters. (A. Trollope) Fortn. **28**: 401.
— as an Orator. (G. Shepard) Bib. Sac. **28**: 123. — Mo. R. **149**: 68. — (E. G. Parker) Chr. Exam. **65**: 333.
— as a Politician. (A. Trollope) Fortn. **27**: 495.
— Character of. (R. Ornsby) Dub. R. **87**: 1.
— De Legibus, Critical Notes on. (W. D. Pearman) Canad. J. n. s. **14**: 503.
— De Oratore. (Prof. Billroth) Evang. R. **19**: 574.
— Kelsall's Translations of. Ed. R. **22**: 127.
— Letters to Atticus. Mo. R. **109**: 397.
— Life and Character of. Westm. **64**: 353.
— Life of. (E. F. Stewart) Am. Church R. **34**: 199.
— — Forsyth's. (O. B. Frothingham) Nation, **1**: 49. — (H. J. Warner) Chr. Exam. **79**: 57. — Chr. Obs. **64**: 488. — Lond. Q. **22**: 301. Same art. Ecl. M. **63**: 137. — (H. C. Cameron) Princ. **38**: 577. — Quar. **115**: 68.
— — Passages in. (C. J. Vaughan) Ex. H. Lec. **9**: 275.
— — Trollope's. Blackw. **129**: 211. Same art. Liv. Age, **148**: 643. — (J. V. O'Conor) Cath. World, **33**: 200.
— Lives of, Old and new. (N. Porter) Hours at Home, **1**: 346.
Cicero, Negative Character of. Nat. Q. **11**: 297.
— on the Immortality of the Soul. (J. N. Bellows) Chr. Exam. **33**: 129, 316.
— the Orator, and Antony the Triumvir. Fraser, **32**: 314.
— Philosophy of. (B. F. Clark) Penn Mo. **11**: 522.
— Proconsulate of. (J. G. MacLeod) Month, **32**: 187, 458.
— Republic of. (S. Willard) Chr. Exam. **6**: 370. — (C. Cushing) No Am. **17**: 33. — So. R. **4**: 136. — Mo. R. **103**: 337. — Lond. M. **7**: 437.
— — Featherstonaugh's Translation. (H. S. Legaré) So. R. **4**: 136.
— — Maio's Discovery of. Ecl. R. **38**: 413.
— Thoughts on. So. Lit. Mess. **16**: 495.
Cicesbeo, or Customs of Sicily. (W. D. Potter) So. Lit. Mess. **10**: 601, 681.
Cid, The. (Prof. de Vericour) Dub. Univ. **56**: 596. — St. James, **19**: 288.
— Chronicle of. For. R. **4**: 438. — Quar. **1**: 117.
— — Southey's. Ecl. R. **9**: 201.
— Herder's. House. Words, **5**: 415.
— Poem of. (M. Arnold) Macmil. **24**: 471.
— Sketch of. Am. Mo. M. **7**: 533.
— Song of. (F. Parke) Dub. Univ. **85**: 121.
Cider Cellar. Lond. M. **2**: 384.
Cider-Making. Penny M. **4**: 271.
Cider-Mill, American. Penny M. **6**: 194.
Ci-devants. Once a Week, **25**: 115.
Cigar, Defense of my. Fraser, **17**: 155.
Cigars. All the Year, **13**: 35. — Pract. M. **3**: 129.
— and Tobacco; a Sketch. New Q. **10**: 26.
— from Elsinore; a Romance. St. James, **15**: 226.
— Havana. All the Year, **17**: 108.
— Manufacture of. Hunt, **6**: 193 — Pract. M. **1**: 267.
Cigarettes. Chamb. J. **45**: 617. — Galaxy, **23**: 471.
— Havana. Lond. Soc. **21**: 505.
Cilia, Vibrating, Experiments with. (J. Wyman) Am. Natural. **5**: 611.
Ciliary Motion. Chamb. J. **5**: 382.
Cilicia, Langlois's Travels in. (C. H. Brigham) No. Am. **94**: 309. — Colburn, **122**: 127.
— Researches in. Colburn, **163**: 313.
Cilician Pirates. (W. F. Smith) Cornh. **7**: 530.
Cilley, Jonathan, with portrait. (N. Hawthorne) Dem. R. **3**: 67.
— Duel with Graves. Dem. R. **1**: 493. **10**: 482. — New York R. **3**: 268.
Cimabue, John and Giotto. (W. de B. Fryer) Penn Mo. **12**: 574, 654.
Cimarosa, D. Eng. Dom. M. **10**: 285.
Cimbri, Ethnography of the. (G. Rawlinson) Anthrop. J. **6**: 150.
— Visit to. (W. D. Howells) Nation, **1**: 495.
Cinchona Forests of South America. (H. S. Wellcome) Pop. Sci. Mo. **17**: 507.
Cinchona Plant. Chamb. J. **41**: 696.
— Culture of. (H. B. Brady) Nature, **8**: 555.
— — in India. Ed. R. **118**: 507.
Cincinnati, City of. De Bow, **16**: 615.
— Commerce of. De Bow, **12**: 88.
— Early History of. Ill. M. **2**: 459.
— Faience Pottery of. (A. C. Hall) Potter Am. Mo. **15**: 357.
— 45th Anniversary of Settlement. West. M. **2**: 145.
— in 1826. J. Frankl. Inst. **3**: 262. — West. Mo. R. **1**: 61.
— in 1835. West. M. **5**: 26.
— in 1850–51. Hunt, **25**: 429.
— in 1867. (J. Parton) Atlan. **20**: 229.
— Music Hall. Am. Arch. **1**: 300. **3**: 145.
— Musical Festival, 1873. (G. P. Upton) Lakeside, **9**: 472
— Porkopolis: Busch's Wanderungen. Colburn, **103**: 139.
— Private Picture Collections in. (G. W. Nichols) Galaxy, **10**: 511.

Cincinnati, Queen of the West. Fraser, **73**: 42.
— Sinton Rostrum. Am Arch. **1**: 121, 297.
— Statistics of. (W. Tudor) No. Am. **3**: 219.
— View of, 1816. Portfo.(Den.) **15**: 25.
— Walk in, 1829. Knick. **9**: 259.
— Woodward High School in. Am. J. Educ. **4**: 520.
Cincinnati and Charleston Railroad. West. M. **5**: 538.
Cincinnati, Society of. (W. Sargent) No. Am. **77**: 267.
— List of Pennsylvania Members. Hist. M. **21**: 107.
— New England Society. N. E. Reg. **1**: 106.
— of New Hampshire, Correspondence with Washington. Hist. M. **19**: 116.
Cinderella. Argosy, **22**: 385. Same art. Liv. Age, **131**: 672. — (W. R. S. Ralston) 19th Cent. **6**: 832. — Appleton, **23**: 19.
— Our. Chamb. J. **23**: 145.
Cinderella; a Poem. (R. Buchanan) Good Words, **17**: 750.
Cinderella; a Poem. (F. R. Condor) Dub. Univ. **90**: 667.
Cinderella; a Story. (A. I. Thackeray) Cornh. **13**: 721. Same art. Liv. Age, **95**: 792.
Cingalese, Translations from. (J. Bowring) Fraser, **48**: 349.
Cinnabar City. (J. T. McKay) Scrib. **8**: 465.
Cinnabar, Deposits of, Genesis of. (S. B. Christy) Am. J. Sci. 117: 453.
— Mines of, at New Almaden, Cal. (J. R. Browne) Harper, **31**: 545.
Cinnamon Tree, and its Products. Penny M. **2**: 402.
Cinq-Mars and de Thou, Death of. Blackw. **6**: 494.
Cinque Ports. All the Year, **37**: 35–134.— Sharpe, **2**: 225.
— and the Bredenstone at Dover. (E. Walford) Once a Week, **5**: 320.
— Chronicles of. (H. Curling) Bentley, **20**: 27.
— History and Institutions. St. James, **2**: 387.
Cintio, Giambatista G. L'Arbecche. (R. P. Gillis) Blackw. **21**: 727.
Ciocci, R. (N. Bangs) Meth. Q. **5**: 248.
Cipher; a Novel. (J. G. Austin) Galaxy, **6**: 437, 581, 725. **7**: 5–607.
Cipher deciphered. Chamb. J. **43**: 193.
Ciphers. Chamb. J. **24**: 134. **25**: 175. — Cornh. **29**: 172.
— and Cipher-Writing. All the Year, **35**: 508.
— Art of Cipher-Writing. Macmil. **23**: 328.
— Curiosities of. (S. B.-Gould) Once a Week, **9**: 607.
— deciphered. Chamb. J. **44**: 70.
— Mathematical Holocryptic. (P. E. Chase) Math. Mo. **1**: 194.
— Secrets exposed. Chamb. J. **20**: 161. Same art. Liv. Age, **39**: 342.
See Cryptograms.
Cipher Telegrams, 1876. (E. L. Godkin) Nation, **27**: 234, 250. **28**: 112. — (J. R. G. Hassard) No. Am. **128**: 315. — (E. S. Holden) Internat. R. **6**: 405.
Circassia. Blackw. **42**: 636, 747. — For. Q. **19**: 433. — Blackw. **48**: 84. **51**: 629.—House. Words, **15**: 319.
— and the Caucasus. Dem. R. **31**: 301.
— and the Circassians. Penny M. **7**: 137, 150, 159.
— and Krim Tartary. (J. Barrow) Quar. **59**: 362.
— — Spencer's Travels in. Tait, n. s. **4**: 605. — Mo. R. **143**: 516. **147**: 12.
— and Schamyl. Sharpe, **20**: 96.
— and the Turks. Nat. Q. **25**: 141.
— and the Vixen. Westm. **27**: 196.
— Bell's Residence in, 1837–39. Mo. R. **153**: 356.
— Campaign in, Recollections of. Univ. M. **34**: 516.
— Exodus from, 1864. Once a Week, **11**: 302. — Quar. **116**: 97. Same art. Ecl. M. **63**: 420.
— Marigny's Account of. Mo. R. **143**: 265.
— Travels in. Blackw. **79**: 692. **80**: 45.
— Tribes of. Nat. M. **5**: 547.
See Caucasus.
Circassians, The. Dub. R. **9**: 454. — Dub. Univ. **64**: 705.
— Longworth's Year among. Mo. R. **153**: 289.
Circassian Chief, Visit to. (H. W. D'Arcy) Colburn, **73**: 251–344.
Circassian Lovers; a Story. Peop. J. **4**: 233.
Circe. (B. White) Belgra. **3**: 108, 240, 303.
Circe; a Story of Paris in 18th Century. Putnam, **7**: 284.
Circe; three Acts in the Life of an Artist. (B. White) Belgra. **2**: 113–480.
Circle, Quadrature of. (T. P. Jones) J. Frankl. Inst. **12**: 1. — Chamb. J. **46**: 45. Same art. Ecl. M. **72**: 455.
— Approximate Quadratures of. (P. E. Chase) J. Frankl. Inst. **108**: 45, 105. **109**: 409. **111**: 379.
Circle of the Regicides; a Drama. (R. H. Horne) Dub. Univ. **92**: 50.
Circles, Arcs of, Construction of. (J. K. Whilldin) J. Frankl. Inst. **73**: 56.
Circourt, Comte de, Conversations with. (N. W. Senior) Fortn. **33**: 87.
— Memoirs of. Ed. R. **154**: 466.
Circuit, On. Chamb. J. **26**: 97. **48**: 145.
Circuit Notes in Ireland. Dub. Univ. **1**: 193. **2**: 576.
Circular Parts, Napier's Rules of. Math. Mo. **3**: 99.
Circular Swindle. (E. Crapsey) Galaxy, **11**: 652.
Circulation in Plants. (F. Howlett) Intel. Obs. **9**: 352.
Circulates, Collin's Property of. (J. E. Oliver) Math. Mo. **1**: 345.
Circumcision and Baptism. (W. Hull) Evang. R. **19**: 395.
— Early Spread of. Chr. Obs. **47**: 107.
— of Christ. (W. Rupp) Mercersb. **19**: 124.
Circumstances and their Victims. Knick. **41**: 411.
Circumstantial Evidence. (S. Amos) Westm. **83**: 158. Same art. Ecl. M. **64**: 696. — Appleton, **15**: 143, 587. — (J. C. Fowler) Brit. Q. **71**: 422. — Cornh. **6**: 689. — So. Lit. Mess. **1**: 142. — Temp. Bar, **1**: 91. **2**: 131. **6**: 579.
— Curious Cases of. (J. F. Mayo) Good Words, **19**: 771.
— Dangers of. All the Year, **18**: 66.
— Problem in. (S. Warren) Blackw. **51**: 553.
— Story of. Blackw. **64**: 207. Same art. Liv. Age, **18**: 481. — Dem. R. **11**: 508.
— Value of. (N. S. Dodge) Overland, **5**: 251.
— Wills on. Chr. Obs. **51**: 164.
Circumstantial Evidence; a Story. Eng. Dom. M. **7**: 57, 286.
Circumstantial Evidence; a Tale. (Mrs. Burbury) Sharpe, **13**: 147.
Circumstantial Puzzle. Lond. Soc. **39**: 315.
Circus. Knick. **13**: 67.
— Astley Redivivus. (A. Ogilvy) Once a Week, **17**: 547.
— In a. All the Year, **24**: 540.
— in Scotland. All the Year, **13**: 18.
— Juglini's Champion. All the Year, **16**: 398.
Circus Life, Town and Country. All the Year, **6**: 181.
Cirencester, England. (L. S. Costello) Bentley, **20**: 390.
Cissbury Camp, Sussex, Excavations in. (A. L. Fox) Anthrop. J. **5**: 357.
Cistercians, History of the Order in England. Chr. Rem. **54**: 1.
Cistercian Abbeys of Yorkshire. (J. Piggot) Fraser, **94**: 341.
Cisterns and Tie-Rods, Strength of. J. Frankl. Inst. **53**: 360.
— of Venice. (J. F. Frazer) J. Frankl. Inst. **75**: 361.
Citizen, The Christian. (L. Perrin) New Eng. **13**: 422.
— Duty of. (A. L. Hayes) Luth. Q. **4**: 97.
Citizens, Rights of. (J. N. Pomeroy) Nation, **12**: 335.
Citizen Schneider; a Tale. (MM. Erckmann-Chatrian) Eng. Dom. M. **12**: 201.
Citizen Soldier, The. Bost. Q. **4**: 475.
Citizenship. (O. Dewey) Chr. Exam. **51**: 195.

Citizenship, Duty of. (H. T. Tuckerman) Hours at Home, **4**: 280.
City, The ancient, Coulanges's. Penn Mo. **6**: 354.
— and Country. (E. L. Godkin) Nation, **25**: 327.
— — Life in. (E. L. Godkin) Nation, **5**: 256.
— — Relative Influence on Morality and Health. (J. S. Hough) Penn Mo. **5**: 28.
— — Relative Morals of. (W. S. Peirce) Penn Mo. **6**: 266.
City of Brass. (J. W. De Forest) Atlan. **24**: 389.
City of the Deceived; a Tale. Chamb. J. **15**: 386.
City of Good-Will; a Poem. (J. T. Trowbridge) Scrib. **9**: 48.
City of Rocks, Idaho Territory. (J. Murphy) Appleton, **22**: 367.
City of Temptation; a dramatic Sketch. Fraser, **18**: 694.
Cities, American, Administration of. (S. Sterne) Internat. R. **4**: 631.
— — and Towns, Increase of thirty-six principal. (J. Chickering) Hunt, **10**: 461.
— — — of 5,000 and less than 10,000 Inhabitants, Increase of. (J. Chickering) Hunt, **11**: 38.
— — as Units in our Policy. (W. R. Martin) No. Am. **128**: 21.
— — Atlantic and Interior. (R. W. Scott) Hunt, **19**: 383.
— — Building of. (L. Kip) Hours at Home, **11**: 206.
— — Commerce of. De Bow, **6**: 428.
— — Growth of. (B. C. Magie, jr.) Scrib. **15**: 418. — (M. Tarver) West. J. **5**: 283.
— — — and Decay of. Portfo.(Den.) **16**: 300.
— — Progress of. De Bow, **9**: 639.
— and the Gospel. (G. H. Johnston) Mercersb. **24**: 365.
— Christianity in, Chalmers on. Meth. M. **45**: 105.
— Conversion of. (W. Patton) Cong. M. **11**: 283.
— Debts of. (C. Hale) Atlan. **38**: 661.
— Desolate. Chr. Obs. **64**: 845, 891. **65**: 42.
— Disease in. (E. B. Dalton) No. Am. **106**: 351.
— Duty of the Church in. (E. E. Hale) Unita. R. **10**: 638.
— Government of. (D. B. Eaton) Am. Soc. Sci. J. **5**: 1. — (E. E. Hale) O. & N. **7**: 249.
— — Ideal local Government for London. (J. Hare) Macmil. **7**: 441.
— — in Massachusetts. (W. F. Allen) Nation, **33**: 169.
— — in New York State, Constitutional Amendment on, 1878. (E. L. Godkin) Nation, **26**: 108.
— — Relations of, to State Governments. (S. Bowles) Am. Soc. Sci. J. **9**: 140.
See Municipal Government.
— Great. Putnam, **5**: 254.
— — and their public Influence. Gent. M. n. s. **13**: 43-599.
— — Decline and Fall of. Fraser, **29**: 91, 203.
— — Evils of, and some Remedies. Good Words, **1**: 364.
— — Fate of. (E. Lawrence) Harper, **43**: 903.
— — Mortality of. Cath. World, **5**: 422.
— — Religion in the Age of. Prosp. R. **1**: 102.
— — Vaughan's Age of. Mo. R. **160**: 89.
— Health and Physique in English. (Lord Brabazon) 19th Cent. **10**: 80.
— Management of. (I. Butts) Galaxy, **13**: 173.
— Moral Economy of large Towns. (W. C. Taylor) Bentley, **6**: 476, 575. **7**: 131, 470, 596. **8**: 355, 558.
— Municipal Expenditure of Birmingham. (T. Avery) J. Statis. Soc. **29**: 78.
— Municipal Extravagance. (D. L. Harris) Penn Mo. **7**: 913.
— of Europe. Appleton, **11**: 47-720.
— of Refuge. Bentley, **53**: 525. — Godey, **62**: 229, 319. — Meth. M. **40**: 670.
— of the Zuyder Zee, Living and dead. (A. H. Guernsey) Appleton, **16**: 150, 246.
— Physiognomy of. (G. W. Peck) Am. Whig R. **6**: 233.
Cities. Problem of municipal Nuisances. (R. S. Tracy) Pop. Sci. Mo. **18**: 585.
— Representative. (W. S. Tyler) Hours at Home, **4**: 314, 506. **5**: 25-481. **6**: 275, 437.
— Sanitary Care, and Utilization of Refuse of. (J. J. Storer) J. Frankl. Inst. **97**: 48. — (C. A. Leas) J. Frankl. Inst. **97**: 206.
— Sociological Problems of. (E. Howland) Harper, **62**: 122.
City and Country Spring; a Poem. Putnam, **9**: 620.
City Aspirations; a Poem. Cath. World, **2**: 680.
City Companies, Origin and History of. Brit. Q. **70**: 130.
City Cousins. Knick. **64**: 141-550.
City Dwellings and City Gardens. (C. T. Browne) Once a Week, **9**: 67.
City Life in the United States. Contemp. **40**: 710.
— from a new Standpoint. Hogg, **10**: 149.
— Mysteries of. Hogg, **3**: 357, 391.
City Missions. (W. H. Lewis) Am. Church R. **8**: 392. — (W. Hull) Luth. Q. **6**: 592. — No. Brit. **24**: 165. — Prosp. R. **1**: 102.
City Sonnets. Lond. M. **14**: 392.
City Young Men. (E. L. Godkin) Nation, **2**: 326.
Civil Authority, Natural Grounds of. (W. H. Lowrie) Princ. **33**: 720.
Civil Courts and ecclesiastical Tribunes. (R. H. Dana, jr.) Nation, **12**: 102.
Civil Discipline. (E. L. Godkin) Nation, **5**: 296.
Civil Engineers, Education of. (T. C. Clarke) Ecl. Engin. **11**: 471. — Nature, **3**: 301.
Civil Engineering, Lectures on. (Prof. Millington) So. Lit. Mess. **5**: 592.
— What is ? (S. E. Warren) J. Frankl. Inst. **84**: 418. **85**: 132.
See Engineering.
Civil Government, Ethics of. (D. A. Gorton) Nat. Q. **37**: 209.
Civil Institutes, F. Forti's. For. Q. **30**: 397.
Civil Law. So. Lit. Mess. **8**: 249. — For. Q. **17**: 27.
— and Church Law in America. (H. D. Jenkins) Presb. R. **1**: 549.
— New School of. New York R. **5**: 270.
— Study of. (L. S. Cushing) No. Am. **11**: 407. — For. R. **2**: 41. **5**: 65.
— Triumphs of. Knick. **50**: 448.
Civil Liberty, Progress of. So. Lit. Mess. **7**: 848. — Dem. R. **21**: 419.
Civil List. St. Paul's, **8**: 48.
— and Retrenchment. Ed. R. **33**: 471.
Civil Policy of America, Draper's. (C. E. Norton) Nation, **1**: 407.
Civil Polity of the United States and Christianity. (J. W. Apple) Mercersb. **24**: 585.
Civil Procedure in England, Reform of, advocated, 1868. Westm. **90**: 313.
Civil Rights, Andrew Johnson on. (T. G. Shearman) Nation, **2**: 422.
Civil-Rights Bill, 1874. (A. G. Sedgwick) Nation, **19**: 180.
Civil Servant, A. (E. E. Hale) O. & N. **9**: 58.
Civil Service. (A. Trollope) Fortn. **2**: 613. — Chamb. J. **26**: 103. **27**: 217.
— as a Profession. Cornh. **3**: 214.
— Competitive Examinations for. (E. Chadwick) J. Statis. Soc. **21**: 18. **22**: 44. — Nat. R. **1**: 351.
— Education for. (E. E. Hale) O. & N. **10**: 116.
— in England. (F. W. Roswell) Macmil. **29**: 1. — (W. B. Scoones) Macmil. **31**: 347. — Chamb. J. **55**: 401. — Cornh. **19**: 341. — Dub. Univ. **46**: 409. — Fraser, **91**: 720. — Lond. Q. **36**: 366
— — and in America. (A. W. Jackson) Unita. R. **16**: 197, 331.

Civil Service in England, Cost and Organization of. (H. Mann) J. Statis. Soc. **32**: 38.
— — Eaton on. (A. R. Macdonough) Nation, **30**: 46.
— — Examination Scheme. (A. Bain) Contemp. **30**: 944.
— — Grievances of. Tait, n. s. **22**: 729.
— — History and Constitution of. Westm. **105**: 166, 464.
— — Inside the. Chamb. J. **41**: 209.
— — Language in. (A. Bain) Pop. Sci. Mo. **12**: 152.
— — Playfair Commission, 1875. (A. G. Bowie) St. James, **36**: 284. — (T. H. Farrar) Fortn. **23**: 714. — (G. W. Brown) Atlan. **43**: 580. — (J. Chapman) Westm. **62**: 68. — Westm. **63**: 450. — Ecl. R. **103**: 424.
— — Reform of. No. Brit. **23**: 137.
— — — How it was done. (E. O. Graves) Scrib. **14**: 242.
— — Statistics of. (W. Farr) J. Statis. Soc. **11**: 103. — (H. Mann) J. Statis. Soc. **31**: 407.
— — Writers of. Chamb. J. **56**: 72.
— in France. Colburn, **143**: 404.
— in India. *See* India.
— in Prussia. (H. Tuttle) Nation, **30**: 150, 172.
— in the United States. (J. Bing) Putnam, **12**: 233. — (T. A. Jenckes) No. Am. **105**: 478. — (E. I. Sears) Nat. Q. **15**: 365. — (A. Stickney) Scrib. **22**: 353, 570, 723. — Internat. R. **8**: 546. — (C. W. Storey) Am. Law R. **11**: 197. — Republic, **6**: 282. — All the Year, **24**: 429.
— — Appointing Power. (G. F. Hoar) No. Am. **133**: 464.
— — Aspects of. (W. H. Babcock) Putnam, **15**: 50.
— — Assassination and the Spoils System. (D. B. Eaton) Princ. n. s. **8**: 145.
— — Century of. (L. M. Dorman) Scrib. **15**: 395.
— — Chapter in History of. (E. L. Godkin) Nation, **12**: 412.
— — Experience in P. O. Appointments. Scrib. **14**: 829.
— — Experiment with. Republic, **4**: 329.
— — Power of public Plunder. (J. Parton) No. Am. **133**: 43.
— — Recollections of. (A. Delmar) Appleton, **11**: 781. **12**: 48–714.
— — Reform of. (R. H. Bancroft) Unita. R. **9**: 496. — (J. D. Cox) No. Am. **112**: 81. — (J. Jay) No. Am. **127**: 273. — (A. D. Mayo) Unita. R. **3**: 587. — (G. W. Curtis) Unita. R. **10**: 495. — (S. Eliot) Am. Soc. Sci. J. **1**: 112. — (J. G. Rosengarten) Am. Soc. Sci. J. **4**: 33. — (T. T. Gault) Western, **4**: 187. **6**: 411. — (D. B. Eaton) Lippinc. **27**: 580. — (D. B. Eaton) Penn Mo. **12**: 241, 881. — (T. Leaming) Penn Mo. **12**: 758. — (E. E. Hale) O. & N. **10**: 145. — (A. R. Macdonough) Harper, **40**: 546. — (E. Cary) Harper, **60**: 898. — (H. B. Adams) No. Am. **109**: 443. — (H. W. Bellows) No. Am. **130**: 247. — (J. I. Platt) Galaxy, **24**: 654. — Ev. Sat. **10**: 50. — (J. G. Rosengarten) Penn Mo. **1**: 409. — Republic, **2**: 3.
— — — and the Administration. (E. Cary) Internat. R. **6**: 227.
— — — and Boss-ism. (J. A. Harris) Penn Mo. **12**: 524.
— — — Bill for, 1868. (J. G. Rosengarten) Nation, **6**: 425.
— — — — 1869. (E. L. Godkin) Nation, **9**: 308.
— — — Experiment in. (D. B. Eaton) Am. Soc. Sci. J. **8**: 54.
— — — in Campaign of 1880. (C. C. Nott) Nation, **31**: 56.
— — — Is it constitutional? (J. N. Pomeroy) Nation, **13**: 68.
— — — Objections to. (A. G. Sedgwick) Nation, **8**: 329.
— — — Promise of. Scrib. **6**: 97.
— — — *vs.* Reformation. (A. W. Tourgée) No. Am. **132**: 305.
— — Regulations for, 1872. (E. S. Nadal) Nation, **14**: 269.
— — Rotation in Office. (E. L. Godkin) Nation, **32**: 5.
— — Spoils System. (W. Clarke) Contemp. **40**: 633.
Civil Service in the United States, Uncle Sam's Treatment of his Servants. (J. Parton) Atlan. **24**: 645.
— — Tourgée on. (D. B. Eaton) No. Am. **132**: 546.
— Informer's Relations to. (C. C. Nott) Nation, **18**: 215.
— Tests for public Service. Nat. R. **12**: 129.
— Von Mohl on. (B. Coxe) Am. Soc. Sci. J. **4**: 74.
— Women in. Victoria, **12**: 438.
See Competitive Examinations.
Civil-Service Reform. (G. E. Casey) Canad. Mo. **11**: 83.
— English Objections to. Nation, **16**: 146.
— History and Literature of. Princ. **42**: 1.
— What does it mean? Lakeside, **6**: 219.
Civil-Service Supply Association. Chamb. J. **55**: 81. — Cornh. **28**: 45.
Civil Sovereignty in modern States. Dub. R. **77**: 39.
Civil War. (T. E. Hook) Colburn, **55**: 289.
— in County of Devon. Retros. **12**: 179.
— Some Uses of. (H. M. Thompson) Contin. Mo. **6**: 361.
Civil Wars, Great. Mo. Rel. M. **33**: 65.
Civiletti, Benedetti. (L. Monti) Harper, **63**: 82.
Civility. (S. T. Spear) Hours at Home, **6**: 522.
— is never lost. (N. P. Willis) Godey, **25**: 112.
Civilization. (J. S. Mill) Westm. **25**: 1. — Fraser, **34**: 1. — So. Q. **3**: 1. **4**: 157. — (P. G. Robert) Western, **6**: 93. — Lond. M. **13**: 207.
— Agency of Intellect in. (F. Bowen) No. Am. **93**: 519. — (I. Ray) No. Am. **87**: 388.
— American. (E. Phelps) Contin. Mo. **6**: 102, 121.
— — Ancient. (M. T. B. Browne) Scrib. **5**: 724.
— — and European. (Prof. Goodwin) Am. Whig R. **3**: 611. **4**: 27.
— an organized Brotherhood. (W. C. Gannett) Radical, **10**: 84.
— Ancient and modern. (W. Blair) So. M. **8**: 209. — Dem. R. **24**: 449.
— and the Census. (J. Eagles) Blackw. **77**: 21.
— and Christ. N. Ecl. **4**: 216.
— and Christianity. (L. H. Shuck) Bapt. Q. **8**: 50. — (C. P. Wing) Am. Presb. R. **14**: 88.
— and Equality. (W. H. Mallock) Appleton, **26**: 525.
— and Faith. Nat. R. **6**: 198.
— and its Laws. (C. M. O'Leary) Cath. World, **28**: 605.
— and Morals. (J. N. Larned) Pop. Sci. Mo. **11**: 549.
— and Noise. (J. Sully) Fortn. **30**: 704. Same art. Sup. Pop. Sci. Mo. **4**: 111.
— and Savageism. (H. H. Bancroft) Pop. Sci. Mo. **7**: 195.
— and Science. (E. Du-Bois Reymond) Pop. Sci. Mo **13**: 257–529.
— and the State. (J. H. Oliver) Mercersb. **15**: 485.
— and the Vatican. (R. Caird) Brit. Q. **70**: 372.
— as accumulated Force. (L. Dumont) Pop. Sci. Mo. **1**: 602.
— Asiatic. (J. T. Dickinson) Chr. Exam. **67**: 1.
— Aspects of. (M. Tarver) West. J. **8**: 1.
— Barbarisms of. (F. W. Newman) Contemp. **35**: 471.
— Birthplace of. (J. Campbell) Canad. J. n. s. **13**: 152.
— Buckle's History of. (J. Bascom) New Eng. **21**: 173. — (J. F. Clarke) Chr. Exam. **71**: 374. — (H. Lincoln) Bib. Sac. **20**: 279. — (S. Y. McMasters) Am. Church R. **17**: 103. — New Q. **7**: 313. **10**: 396. — (T. Mayo) Fraser, **60**: 293. — (T. Parker) Chr. Exam. **64**: 233. — (T. C. Sanders) Fraser, **56**: 409. — (E. I. Sears) Nat. Q. **1**: 113. — Lond. Q. **17**: 301. — Blackw. **84**: 515. — Brit. Q. **28**: 1. — Chr. Obs. **58**: 685. **61**: 476. Chr. R. **24**: 113. — Colburn, **113**: 162. Same art. Liv. Age, **58**: 464. — Dem. R. **43**: 267. — Dub. Univ. **51**: 12. — Ecl. R. **107**: 534. — Ed. R. **107**: 465. **114**: 183. — Ecl. M. **54**: 244. **55**: 467. — Nat. R. **6**: 198. — (W. H. Lowrie) Princ. **36**: 411. — Quar. **104**: 38. Same art. Liv. Age, **58**: 668 — So. Lit. Mess. **27**: 269. — Westm. **68**: 375. **76**: 187.

Civilization, Buckle's History of, Fallacies of Theory of. (J. Fiske) Nat. Q. 4: 30.
— by Force. (A. Marshall) Cath. World, 30: 353.
— Christianity the Means of. Meth. Q. 1: 39.
— Cost of. (F. H. Hedge) Mo. Rel. M. 43: 445.
— Course of. Dem. R. 6: 208.
— Curiosities of. Chamb. J. 35: 27.
— Diefenbach's History of. Anthrop. J. 3: 196.
— Early Phases of. Westm. 106: 43.
— English. So. R. 8: 462.
— European. (J. W. Yeomans) Princ. 11: 114.
— Failures of Temp. Bar, 6: 483.
— Guizot's History of. (T. D. Woolsey) New Eng. 19: 409, 871. — Fraser, 21: 582. — Ecl. R. 67: 241. — Chr. R. 8: 535. — Ed. R. 67: 357. — No. Am. 47: 496. — Westm. 31: 306. — Meth. Q. 1: 222. — So. Q. 3: 1. 4: 157. — Mo. R. 143: 115. 144: 139.
— Hellenic Influence in. Sup. Pop. Sci. Mo. 3: 398.
— High. Colburn, 48: 1–299.
— Higher, Phenomena of. (E. B. Tylor) Anthrop. R. 5: 303.
— Hindrances to. Bost. R. 4: 565.
— History of. Chr. Rem. 35: 330.
— in the 5th Century. Month, 1: 293. Same art. Cath. World, 1: 775.
— in Egypt and Greece, Influence of geographical Position on. (J. B. McMaster) Nat. Q. 34: 29.
— in England. So. R. 8: 462. *See above*, Civilization, Buckle's History of.
— in India, John on. Chr. Obs. 12: 306.
— Inductive Theory of. Am. Whig R. 6: 381.
— Influence of Catholic Prayer on. Brownson, 5: 345.
— — of Catholicism on. (J. Cordner) Chr. Exam. 52: 165.
— — of European and Asiatic. Dem. R. 15: 62.
— — of Geography on. Dem. R. 11: 135.
— — of Germany on. For. Q. 24: 56.
— — of intellectual Action on. (H. R. Cleveland) Am. Inst. of Instruc. 1836: 143.
— — on public Health. For. Q. 1: 178.
— MacKinnon's History of. Dub. Univ. 29: 126.
— Modern. (G. Fitzhugh) De Bow, 29: 62. — (J. W. Nevin) Mercersb. 3: 165. — (I. Washburne) Univ. Q. 15: 5. — (J. B. Woodruff) Nat. Q. 8: 95.
— — Roman Element in. (J. L. Diman) New Eng. 31: 1. — No. Brit. 44: 249. Same art. Ecl. M. 67: 257.
— — a Teutonic Product. (J.S.Hittell) Overland, 14: 251.
— — Tendency of. Bost. Q. 1: 200
— Moral Uses of. (W. Warren) Cong. R. 8: 230.
— Moreton on. Mo. R. 140: 541.
— not Regeneration. (G. W. Briggs) Mo. Rel. M. 17: 297.
— of 19th Century. (W. S. Lilly) Month, 27: 165.
— of Tongataboo. (F. Parke) Dub. Univ. 82: 488.
— Origin of. (D. Smith) Univ. Q. 14: 27. — (R.Whately) Ex. H. Lec. 10: 1. — De Bow, 25: 653. — Ecl. M. 75: 750.
— — Lubbock on. (O. A. Brownson) Cath. World, 13: 492. — (S. Evans) Nature, 3: 362. — Nature, 11: 401.
— Our. Cornh. 27: 671. Same art. Ev. Sat. 14: 691.
— Philosophy of. Knick. 16: 1.
— Primitive. (S. B. Harper) Cath. World, 22: 626.
— — Different Centers of. (T. H. McLeod) Am. J. Sci. 70: 201.
— — Records of. (W. J. Stillman) Nation, 16: 273. 17: 150.
— Problems of. (T. Hughes) Macmil. 27: 404. 28: 84. Same art Ecl. M. 80: 607. 81: 98. Same art. Ev. Sat. 14: 370, 578.
— Progress from Barbarism to. Penny M. 5: 411.
— Progress of. Am. Mo. M. 3: 361. — Bost. Q. 1: 389. — West. M. 3: 351.
— Relations to Property and social Life. (W. S. Grayson) De Bow, 26: 161.
Civilization, Savage Views of. Chamb. J. 9: 406.
— Science and the Arts. (D. March) New Eng. 9: 481.
— struggling with Barbarism. Ecl. R. 84: 643.
— Two Theories of. (N. S. Richardson) Am. Church R. 16: 20.
— *versus* Barbarism. Dem. R. 37: 239.
— Vestiges of. Meth. Q. 13: 213.
— What is? (B. Murphy) Cath. World, 17: 486. — (W. M. Blackburn) Dial (Ch.), 2: 7.
See Savage Life.
Civilizing Forces. (J. B. Woodruff) Nat. Q. 10: 33.
Civille, François de. (S. B. Gould) Once a Week, 4: 431.
— Remarkable Escapes of. Lond. Soc. 13: 362.
Claes, M. Art J. 18: 267.
Claghorn Collection of Prints. Art J. 31: 153.
Claiborne, William, Memoir of. N. E. Reg. 27: 125.
Claims of United States on Denmark. (G. Otis) No. Am. 22: 456.
— of United States on France. *See* French Spoliations.
— of United States on Naples and Holland. (E. Everett) No. Am. 21: 269.
— on Government. Am. Law R. 1: 653. 10:81.
Claimant, A 16th-Century. Chamb. J. 52: 616.
— Story of a. (E. S. Roscoe) Belgra. 18: 53.
Claimants, Celebrated, in England. Temp. Bar, 33: 338.
Claimant Imposture, A French. Chamb. J. 49: 209.
Clairon, Hippolyte. Temp. Bar, 53: 233. — Fraser, 48: 353. Same art. Ecl. M. 30: 372.
— Incident in the Life of. House. Words, 1: 15.
Clairvaux, Visit to. Penny M. 6: 226, 238.
Clairvoyance, Case of. Fraser, 20: 17.
— Delusions of. (G. M. Beard) Scrib. 18: 433.
— Facts in. (J. Ashburner) Zoist, 6: 96.
— forbidden in the Bible. (G. Sandby) Zoist, 8: 1.
— Gregory on. Chamb. J. 15: 327. — Liv. Age, 30: 63.
— Imposture of. (W. Chambers) Chamb. J. 19: 25.
— Instances of. Chr. Rem. 3: 55.
— of Alexis. Zoist, 2: 477.
— Reality of. (J. Esdaile) Zoist, 7: 213.
Clairvoyant, The. (C. Chesebrough) Knick. 36: 414.
— from the German of Zschokke. Gent. M. n. s. 6: 570, 696. 7: 53.
Clairvoyant's Revelation. (W. Dixon) Once a Week, 16: 165.
Clairvoyants, Conjurers and. Tait, n. s. 27: 229.
Clairwoods, The; a Tale. So. Lit. Mess. 9: 401.
Clamps-in-the-Wood, Night in. Chamb. J. 42: 419.
Clams. (E. Ingersoll) Appleton, 20: 454. — (E. S. Morse) Am. Natural. 3: 21.
Clan Maclean, History of. Mo. R. 145: 535.
Clans of the Highlands of Scotland. Ecl. R. 92: 458. — Liv. Age, 28: 306. — Mo. R. 138: 358. 140: 94.
— Old English. Cornh. 44: 329. Same art. Liv. Age, 151: 95.
Clan Tartans and Bagpipes. All the Year, 46: 489.
— and Plaids. All the Year, 30: 177.
Clanship and the Highlands. Chamb. J. 48: 140.
— Horrible Instance of Effects of. (J. Hogg) Blackw 28: 680.
Clap, Thomas. Chr. Mo. Spec. 1: 605. — (J. L. Kingsley) Am. Q. Reg. 8: 22.
Clap Genealogy. (E. Clapp and W. B. Trask) N. E. Reg. 15: 225.
Claparède, Edouard René. Nature, 4: 224.
Clapham Sect. (Sir J. Stephen) Ed. R. 80: 251. Same art. Ecl. M. 3: 1. Same art. Liv. Age, 2: 193.
Clapp, Mrs. S. F., Sermon on Death of. (F. H. Hedge) Mo. Rel. M. 22: 108.
Clapp, T. Autobiographical Sketches. Brownson, 15: 413.
Claque, La. Ev. Sat. 9: 331.
— in Parisian Theaters. Once a Week, 20: 251. Same art. Ev. Sat. 5: 102. — Lond. M. 12: 241.

Claqueur System. (G. Hogarth) Bentley, 4: 591.
Clara Corsini. Chamb. J. 16: 210.
Clara's Courtship. (M. Seton) Colburn, 162: 471, 585, 712.
Clare, John, Agricultural Laborer and Poet. Lond. M. 1: 7. — (J. Plummer) Liv. Age, 70: 148. — Chamb. J. 42: 470. — Eng. Dom. M. 2: 39. — Ecl. R. 122: 101.
— Life and Poems of. Liv. Age, 89: 1.
— Martin's Life of. Colburn, 134: 439.
— Literary Career of. (J. Plummer) St. James, 10: 438.
— Poems. (R. Southey) Quar. 23: 166. — Anal. M. 16: 255. — Mo. R. 91: 296. — Ecl. R. 31: 327. 35: 31.
— Relics of. (B. P. Avery) Overland, 10: 134.
— Rural Muse. Blackw. 38: 231. — Lond. M. 1: 323.
— Shepherd's Calendar and Poems of. Ecl. R. 45: 509.
— Village Minstrel. Mo. R. 97: 256.
— Visit to. Lond. M. 4: 540.
Clare, Lord. Dub. Univ. 30: 671.
Clare Market. All the Year, 27: 275.
Clarendon, Edward Hyde, 1st Earl of. (P. Bayne) Contemp. 27: 912. 28: 421. Same art. Liv. Age, 129: 707. 130: 643. — Mo. R. 146: 385.
— and his Contemporaries. Ed. R. 96: 176. Same art. Ecl. M. 27: 37. — Fraser, 45: 341. Same art. Ecl. M. 25: 531.
— Character of. Mo. R. 113: 323.
— — Ellis on. Lond. M. 19: 25.
— Correspondence of. Mo. R. 115: 111.
— Fall of. Ecl. M. 66: 77.
— History of English Rebellion. (E. Brooks) No. Am. 27: 300.
— Lister's Life of. Ed. R. 68: 460. 69: 104. — (J. W. Croker) Quar. 62: 505. — Ecl. R. 68: 345. 76: 241.
Clarendon, G. W. F. Villiers, 4th Earl, Administration of. Ed. R. 93: 208. — Quar. 86: 228.
— In Memoriam. Macmil. 22: 292.
— Policy of, in Ireland, 1847–52. Dub. Univ. 37: 136.
— Political Portrait of. St. James, 25: 676.
Clarendon Correspondence. Colburn, 23: 349.
Clarendon Gallery, Lady Theresa Lewis's. Quar. 91: 196. — Bentley, 31: 377.
Clarendon, Wilts, Survey of the Manor and Forest of. (Sir T. Phillipps) Arch. 25: 151.
Clarian's Picture. (E. Spencer) Atlan. 5: 707. 6: 66.
Clarice; a Tale. (E. Trevor) Canad. Mo. 6: 25.
Clark, Abraham. (E. P. Buffett) Pennsyl. M. 1: 445.
Clark, Alvan G., Double Stars discovered by. (S. W. Burnham) Am. J. Sci. 117: 283.
Clark, Davis W., Life of. (E. O. Haven) Meth. Q. 34: 5.
Clark, George Rogers. (J. Reynolds) Hist. M. 1: 168.
— Expedition of. (W. W. Henry) Potter Am. Mo. 5: 908. 6: 308. 7: 140. — (S. Evans) Potter Am. Mo. 6: 191, 451.
— Life and Times of. West. J. 3: 168, 216.
Clark, H. F., with portrait. Dem. R. 40: 97.
Clark, James G. Song Composer. (G. Birdseye) Potter Am. Mo. 15: 20.
Clark, John A. Glimpses of Old World. Ecl. R. 71: 576.
Clark, Joseph. Art J. 15: 49.
Clark, Joseph S. (E. A. Park) Cong. Q. 4: 1.
Clark, Louis Gaylord. (T. B. Thorpe) Harper, 48: 587.
— Portrait of. Knick. 34: 1.
Clark, Mrs., Pioneer Mother of the West. (Mrs. E. F. Ellet) So. Lit. Mess. 18: 85.
Clark, Sheldon, and his Benefactions. Am. J. Educ. 28: 887.
— Biography of. (B. Silliman) Am. J. Sci. 41: 217.
Clark, Thomas. (J. Farmer) N. E. Reg. 1: 35.
Clark, Wm., born 1788, a Cambridge Professor of the last Generation. (C. K. Watson) Macmil. 21: 267.
Clark, W. George. Summer Months in Spain. Internat. M. 1: 261.
Clark, Willis Gaylord. Knick. 18: 74.
Clark, Willis Gaylord, Poems of. Am. Q. 22: 459.
Clarke, Adam. (J. J. Blunt) Quar. 51: 117. — Am. Meth. M. 16: 174. — Meth. M. 56: 115.
— as a Preacher. (S. Dunn) Meth. Q. 27: 50.
— Discourses. Meth. M. 51: 673.
— Life and Works of. Chr. Obs. 33: 666, 741, 791. — Cong. M. 15: 641, 737. 17: 735.
— Life of. (R. Southey) Quar. 51: 117. — Am. Mo. R. 3: 454.
— Christian Spectator on. Am. Meth. M. 12: 219.
Clarke, Daniel A., Sermons of. Chr. Mo. Spec. 8: 475. — (G. Shepard) Am. Bib. Repos 2d s. 6: 297.
Clarke, Edward D., Life and Remains of. Ed. R. 44: 219. — U. S. Lit. Gaz. 6: 109. — Lond. M. 10: 393. — Colburn, 11: 81.
— on Blowpipes and Volcanoes. Ed. R. 32: 430.
— Travels of. Ed. R. 16: 334. 21: 130. 39: 140. — Anal. M. 1: 144. 8: 405. 9: 32. — Mo. R. 86: 415. 87: 34, 171. — (J. Foster) Ecl. R. 12: 673, 923, 1011. 24: 18, 292. 29: 509. — (R. Southey) Quar. 4: 111. 17: 160. — (R. Heber) Quar. 9: 162.
Clarke, Edward H., M. D. (W. O. White) Unita. R. 9: 62.
Clarke, G. R. American Pioneer. Harper, 22: 784. 23: 52. 28: 302.
Clarke, Henry, Governor of Vienna and Berlin. Dub. Univ. 47: 100.
Clarke, James Freeman. Sermon on the Church. Brownson, 5: 327.
— Steps of Belief. (O. A. Brownson) Cath. World, 12: 289.
Clarke, John, Pioneer Statesman. (C. E. Barrows) Bapt. Q. 6: 483. — (J. C. C. Clarke) Bapt. Q. 10: 180, 257.
Clarke, John S., Comedian. (W. Stuart) Lippinc. 28: 497. — (L. C. Davis) Atlan. 19: 750.
Clarke, Joshua V. H. (H. C. van Schaack) Hist. M. 18: 35.
Clarke, Nathaniel, Elegy on. (S. Wigglesworth) N. E. Reg. 4: 89.
Clarke, Samuel, Sermons of. Chr. Mo. Spec. 9: 638.
Clarke, Thomas Brooke, Account of. Colburn, 1: 51.
Clarke, Wm. H., Tribute to. (B. Herford) Unita. R. 10: 438.
Clarkson, Thomas. Ecl. R. 85: 1. — (S. Osgood) Mo. Rel. M. 5: 289. — with portrait, Howitt, 2: 338.
— and Abolition. Ecl. R. 85: 1.
— Autobiography of. Chr. Obs. 66: 481.
— Obsequies of. (R. Taylor) Peop. J. 2: 219.
Clary, Dexter. (A. L. Chapin) Cong. Q. 18: 357.
Clary's Trial. (R. T. Cooke) Atlan. 45: 465.
Class-Day at Harvard. Appleton, 10: 113. — Ev. Sat. 9: 434. 11: 18.
Class-Meetings. (R. A. West) Meth. Q. 22: 599.
Classical Authority for modern Trifles. Dub. Univ. 11: 730.
Classical Authors, Recent Editions of. Bib. Sac. 5: 171, 771.
Classical Bibliography. So. Lit. Mess. 2: 677. — Mo. R. 109: 147.
Classical Biography and Mythology, Smith's. Bib. R. 6: 385.
Classical Dictionary, Anthon's. Am. Mo. M. 1: 337. 2: 31.
Classical Education. (D. Cole) Am. J. Educ. 1: 67. — (T. Fowler) Fortn. 9: 95. — (R. Lowe) Am. J. Educ. 27: 871. — (J. H. Ward) Nation, 1: 267. — (W. P. Atkinson) No. Am. 101: 515. — Ed. R. 35: 317. 64: 56. — Chr. R. 5: 336. — U. S. Lit. Gaz. 6: 401. — Westm. 53: 393. — (J. Pickering) No. Am. 9: 192, 412. — Month, 8: 217, 321. 35: 589.
— Advantages of. (C. Short) No. Am. 112: 229.
— Against. (R. P. Shipman) Pop. Sci. Mo. 17: 145.
— and English Public Schools. Westm. 82: 1.
— and Scientific Teaching. (E. I. Sears) Nat. Q. 32: 134. — (F. Wayland, jr.) Nation, 4: 174, 196. — (C. K. Adams) Nation, 38: 487. — (G. Rolleston) Nature, 2: 250.

Classical Education, Common-Sense in. (E. R. Humphreys) Education, 1: 294, 444.
— Defense of. Fraser, 36: 276.
— Erasmus on. (K. von Raumer) Am. J. Educ. 4: 729.
— Foster's Objection to. Cong. M. 2: 541.
— in German Gymnasia. (H. Wimmer) Bib. Sac. 7: 108.
— of Boys. Chr. Exam. 17: 302.
— of the Day. (T. A. Becker) Am. Cath. Q. 1: 33.
— Pillans on. (Sir W. Hamilton) Ed. R. 64: 106.
— System of. Dub Univ. 17: 722.
— Temple on. Am. J. Educ. 22: 417.
— Value of. Dub. Univ. 75: 248.
— *versus* Scientific. (J. E. Cabot) No. Am. 101: 578
— *versus* Utilitarian. (J. E. Cabot) No. Am. 104: 610. *See* Classical Studies.
Classical Instruction. (A. H. Weld) Am. Inst. of Instruc. 1844: 163. — (K. von Raumer) Am. J. Educ. 7: 471.
— Elementary. (L. F. Cady) Am. J. Educ. 12: 561.
Classical Learning. (Syd. Smith) Ed. R. 15: 39. — (G. Bancroft) No. Am. 19: 125. — (A. Crosby) Am. Q. Obs. 1: 237. — (C. C. Felton) Am. Inst. of Instruc. 1830: 299. — Am. Q. 17: 1. — (H. S. Legaré) So. R. 1: 1. — Bost. Mo. 1: 584.
— Advantages of. Cong. M. 12: 523.
— in England. (C. C. Felton) No. Am. 54: 269.
— in Subserviency to Theological Studies. Ox. Prize Ess. 2: 139. — Knick. 9: 209.
— Prejudice against. (C. H. Lyon) Am. Meth. M. 20: 209.
— Reasons for Decline of. Land We Love, 1: 328.
— Russell on Advantages of. Mo. R. 139: 319.
— Utility of. Selec. Ed. R. 3: 366.
Classical Literature, Browne's History of. New Q. 1: 24. 2: 500. — Westm. 57: 253.
— Fiske's Eschenburg's Manual. Chr. R. 5: 289. — (S. M. Worcester) Am. Bib. Repos. 9: 358.
— Oration on. (Sir E. B. Lytton) So. Lit. Mess. 20: 278.
Classical Notes. (W. D. Pearman) Canad. J. n. s. 14: 51.
Classical Poets, Translations of. Prosp. R. 7: 370.
Classical Reader. (W. Channing) No. Am 24: 234.
Classical Romances, Recent. Ed. R. 92: 468.
Classical Schools, Group of American. (H. E. Scudder) Harper, 55: 562, 704.
— in New England. (C. Hammond) Am. J. Educ. 16: 403.
Classical School-Books, Arnold's. Fraser, 47: 173.
Classical Study. (J. Mulligan) Am. Inst. of Instruc. 1837: 23. — (A. Crosby) Am. Inst. of Instruc. 1835: 15. — (B. L. Gildersleeve) N. Ecl. 5: 385.
— Aids to. (E. D. Sanborn) Am. Bib. Repos. 3d s. 4: 299.
— Bible with. (C. E. Stowe) Am. Bib. Repos. 2: 724. — (M. Stuart) Am. Q. Reg. 3: 161.
— in America. (W. P. Atkinson) Nation, 1: 205.
— Objects and Methods of. (D. G. Porter) New Eng. 39: 521.
Classical Studies. (T. D. Woolsey) New Eng. 1: 580. — (L. Bacon) Chr. Q. Spec. 8: 389. — (G. S. Hillard) No. Am. 57: 184. — (J. C. Gray) No. Am. 11: 413. — (M. Carey) So. Lit. Mess. 2: 557, 693. 3: 11. 4: 264. 6: 582. — (G. E. Dabney) So. Lit. Mess. 5: 83. — (M. Stuart) Am. Q. Reg. 1: 85. — (E. D. Sanborn) Am. Bib. Repos. 2d s. 6: 56. — (T. Lewis) Lit. & Theo. R. 5: 581. 6: 106. — So. Lit. Mess. 1: 213. — Ed. R. 43: 329. — Am. Q. Reg. 1: 204. — Chr. Exam. 35: 264. — Am. J. Sci. 15: 324. — Carey's Mus. 6: 109, 186. — So. Lit. Mess. 2: 221. — Blackw. 1: 567. — Dub. R. 71: 384.
— Advantages of. (R. G. H. Kean) So. Lit. Mess. 16: 479. — Mo. R. 149: 403.
— and Mathematical. Westm. 4: 147. — Ox. Prize Ess. 3: 171. — (B. B. Edwards) Bib. Sac. 8: 1.
— at Harvard College. (F. Bowen) No. Am. 54: 35.
Classical Studies, St. Basil on Influence of. Chr. Obs. 32: 338.
— Brooks's Ovid and Christian Education. (H.W.Thorpe) Evang. R. 2: 382. — Mo. R. 165: 121.
— Controversy on. (A. Bain) Contemp. 35: 832. Same art. Pop. Sci. Mo. 15: 631. — Dub. R. 59: 200.
— Historical Development of. (C. S. Parker) Am. J. Educ. 24: 39.
— Importance of. (J. R. Boise) Bapt. Q. 2: 8.
— in India. (M. Müller) Contemp. 18: 141.
— in United States. Chr. R. 20: 365.
— Mathematical and. (B. B. Edwards) Bib. Sac. 8: 1.
— Radical Reform in. (J. S. Blackie) Contemp. 34: 795.
— Utility of. (E. S. Gallup) Chr. R. 18: 219.
— Value of. (D. H. Chamberlain) New Eng. 35: 222.
— Worth of. (B. Price) Contemp. 34: 802. *See* Classical Education.
Classics, Ancient. Blackw. 116: 365. Same art. Liv. Age, 124: 104. Same art. Ecl. M. 84: 32.
— and Colleges. (B. L. Gildersleeve) Princ. n. s. 2: 67.
— and Mental Discipline. (L. H. Steiner) Mercersb. 18: 190.
— and Romantics. Colburn, 7: 522. — Mus. 3: 190.
— English against. Pop. Sci. Mo. 1: 707.
— How to teach. (C. Hoole) Am. J. Educ. 17: 267.
— in Translations. Cornh. 16: 109. Same art. Ecl. M. 69: 272.
— Influence on Christianity. Chr. Obs. 31: 652. 32: 338.
— Lowe and Huxley on. (I. G. Smith) Contemp. 9: 37.
— MSS. of, Loss and Recovery of. (W. S. Liscomb) Education, 1: 556.
— Necessity of. So. Q. 26: 145.
— Study of. (C. Elliott) Internat. R. 1: 781. — (G. B. Miller) Evang. R. 9: 401. — (C. Pease) Bib. Sac. 9: 507. — (C. Short) Evang. R. 15: 498. — (A. Tholuck) Am. Bib. Repos. 2: 494. — Temp. Bar, 6: 114.
— — Argument against. (C. Z. Weiser) Mercersb. 24: 232.
— Translations from the less familiar. Blackw. 7: 614. 8: 311, 458, 678. 9: 192, 385.
— Use of Greek and Roman, in Education. Dub R. 33: 321.
Classics, Christian, as School Text-Books. (L. R. Packard) New Eng. 35: 108.
Classification of Organized Beings. (W. Hincks) Canad. J. n. s. 11: 31.
— Zoölogical. Intel. Obs. 6: 362.
— — Agassiz on. (L C. Johnson) So. R. n. s. 4: 465.
— — Principles of. (A. L. Fox) Anthrop. J. 4: 293.
Classification of Knowledge. (S. Adams) Am. Inst. of Instruc. 1843: 31.
Classis of Mercersburg. (J. W. Nevin) Mercersb. 1: 379.
Classmates, My. So. Lit. Mess. 1: 106.
Claude; a Poem. (N. Michell) Colburn, 126: 229–364.
Claude, M., a famous French Policeman. Lond. Soc. 40: 346.
Claude Blouet's Sufferings. (A. Theuriet) O. & N. 1: 185.
Claude Lorraine. Art J. 3: 165.
— The Annunciation. Peop. J. 6: 309.
Claude Radwinter's Mother. Tinsley, 20: 478–600.
Claudia and Pudens, Williams's. Blackw. 65: 487.
Claudian, Translations from. Blackw. 9: 385.
Claudine; a Poem. (N. Michell) Colburn, 124: 422. 125: 80–393.
Claudius and Cynthia, Doom of. (M. Thompson) Scrib. 17: 547.
— Merivale's Account of. (G. M. Lane) No. Am. 101: 228.
Claudius, Matthew, Sketch of. (W. F. Stevenson) Good Words, 3: 425.
— Works of. New York R. 5: 173.

Claver, Peter, Biography of. (A. C. Coxe) Am. Church R. **13**: 266.
— Sketch of. Victoria, **31**: 470.
Claverhouse, John G., Viscount Dundee. *See* Dundee.
Claverhouse of Macaulay and Aytoun. No. Brit. **13**: 1.
Claverings, The; a Novel. (A. Trollope) Cornh. **13**: 129–641. **14**: 85–702. **15**: 1–513. Same art. Galaxy, **1**: 5–708. **2**: 1–741. **3**: 76–517. Same art. Liv. Age, **88**: 658. **89**: 89–540. **90**: 93–657. **91**: 26–514. **92**: 73–515.
Clavier, Etienne. Early History of Greece. Quar. **5**: 1.
Clay, Henry. (A. H. Everett) No. Am. **33**: 351. — (G. H. Colton) Am. Whig R. **2**: 639. — Dem. R. **7**: 99. — (V. W. Kingsley) Nat. Q. **25**: 52. — (J. Parton) No. Am. **102**: 147.
— and Andrew Jackson. So. Lit. Mess. **19**: 521, 585.
— and Anti-Masons. Niles's Reg. **41**: 260.
— and Lexington Resolutions. (C. King) Am. Whig R. **6**: 551.
— and Restrictive System. Dem. R. **12**: 302.
— and Texas Question. (T. Lewis) Am. Whig R. **1**: 75.
— as an Orator. (W. A. Larned) New Eng. **2**: 105. — (E. G. Parker) Putnam, **3**: 493.
— at Cincinnati. Niles's Reg. **35**: 43.
— Charge of Coalition. Ann. Reg. **2**: 27. — Niles's Reg. **28**: 21–203. **32**: 315, 337, 391. **33**: 94, 167, 223. **34**: 306. **35**: 123. **36**: 106, 141, 153. **37**: 125.
— Death of. Dem. R. **31**: 142.
— Dinner to, at Frederick, Md., 1829. Niles's Reg. **36**: 124.
— — at Lexington, 1820. Niles's Reg. **18**: 327.
— — — 1825. Niles's Reg. **28**: 267.
— — at Natchez, 1830. Niles's Reg. **38**: 142.
— — at Philadelphia, 1823. Niles's Reg. **24**: 94.
— — at Pittsburg, 1827. Niles's Reg. **32**: 298.
— — at Washington, D. C., 1829. Niles's Reg. **36**: 38.
— — at Washington, Pa., 1825. Niles's Reg. **28**: 243.
— Duel with John Randolph. Niles's Reg. **30**: 115.
— in the Field again! Dem R. **11**: 205.
— Journey, 1833. Niles's Reg. **45**: 174.
— Last seven Years of. (D. F. Bacon) New Eng. **14**: 543.
— Life and Character of. (C. M. Butler) Am. Church R. **5**: 377.
— — and Times of. Dub. Univ. **27**: 325.
— Portrait of. Am. Whig R. **1**: 1. **13**: 383. — Anal. M. **15**: 1.
— Private Concerns of. Niles's Reg. **34**: 295.
— Private Correspondence of. Liv. Age, **48**: 248.
— Reflections on the Death of. (W. J. Tuck) So. Lit. Mess. **18**: 470.
— Sketch of, with portrait. Ecl. M. **53**: 253.
— Speech at Cincinnati, Aug. 3, 1830. Niles's Reg. **39**: 25.
— — at Lewisburg, Pa., 1826. Niles's Reg. **31**: 60.
— — at Lexington, 1821. Niles's Reg **20**: 301.
— — — 1827. Niles's Reg. **32**: 373.
— — — 1829. Niles's Reg. **36**: 399.
— — on Appointing and Removing Power. Niles's Reg. **48**: 458.
— — on Bank Veto, July 12, 1832. Niles's Reg. **42**: 429.
— — on Me. Boundary, 1832. Niles's Reg. **42**: 399, 459.
— — on Minister to Buenos Ayres. Niles's Reg. **14**: 121.
— — on Public Lands, 1832. Niles's Reg. **43**: 57.
— — — 1834. Niles's Reg. **46**: 268.
— — on Removal of Deposits. Niles's Reg. **45**: 349.
— — on Tariff, Jan. 11, 1832. Niles's Reg. **41**: 385.
— — — Feb. 2, 1832. Niles's Reg. **42**: 2.
— — — Feb. 12, 1832. Niles's Reg. **43**: 411.
— Speeches of. U. S. Lit. Gaz. **6**: 278.
Clay, John, Memoir of. Dub. Univ. **58**: 545.
Clay, Lias. Hogg, **1**: 349.
Clays, and their Uses. (D. T. Ansted) St. James, **2**: 341.
Clayborne, William. Am. Hist. Rec. **3**: 101.
Clayton, John, Hugh Trevor. Victoria, **27**: 532.
Clayton, Rev. John. Answer of the Christian Observer. Cong. M. **20**: 629.
Clayton, John M. Speech on Nullification. Niles's Reg. **43**: supp. 109.
Clayton Family, Memorials of. Ecl. R. **125**: 413.
Clean Sweep, A. Tinsley, **7**: 148.
Cleanliness, Natural Law of. Chamb. J. **10**: 269. Same art. Liv. Age, **20**: 130.
— *versus* Godliness. Chamb. J. **50**: 410.
Cleanthes. Hymn to Zeus. (E. Beecher) O. & N. **5**: 62. — Broadw. **9**: 368. — Cong. M. **26**: 901. — Hours at Home, **6**: 566.
Clear, Cape. (C. Davis) Month, **43**: 476.
Clearing-House of New York. (J. S. Gibbons) Bank. M. (N. Y.) **14**: 41. — Bank. M. (N. Y.) **8**: 344, 445. **9**: 409. **32**: 341. — Internat. R. **3**: 395.
— — in 1857–58. — Bank. M. (N. Y.) **13**: 6.
Clearing-House Associations, Reports of. Bank. M. (N.Y.) **18**: 217.
Clearing-House Methods. Bank. M. (N. Y.) **30**: 10.
Clearing-House System. Bank. M. (N. Y.) **13**: 882. **29**: 929. **35**: 929.
Clearing-Houses of the U. S. Bank. M. (N. Y.) **31**: 332.
Clearing of the Glens; a Poem. Blackw. **67**: 475.
Cleaveland, John; Royalist, Wit, and Poet. (E Goadby) Gent. M. n. s. **10**: 205.
Cleburne, Gen. P. R. (W. F. Douglass) Land We Love, **2**: 460.
Cleena; a Poem. (R. Scott) Dub. Univ. **87**: 669.
Cleland Testimonial, Glasgow. Penny M. **5**: 147.
Clelia. (A. Mils) Liv. Age, **104**: 159–213.
Clemence. (K. S Macquoid) Ecl. M. **79**: 299. Same art. Liv. Age, **114**: 625.
Clemence d'Orville. (C. Detlef) Liv. Age, **103**: 608–783.
Clémence Tourelle; a Reminiscence. Victoria, **4**: 203.
Clemencia; a Tale of Andalusian Life. Victoria, **18**: 97–189.
Clemengis, Nicholas de, Life and Times of. Am. Presb. R. **5**: 437.
— Writings of. Am. Presb. R. **5**: 617.
Clemens Alexandrinus. *See* Clement of Alexandria.
Clemens Romanus. *See* Clement I.
Clemens, S. L., Mark Twain, with portrait. (G. T. Ferris) Appleton, **12**: 15. — with portrait, Once a Week, **27**: 518.
— The Gilded Age. O. & N. **9**: 386.
Clement I., Bishop of Rome. (D. W. Simon) Bib. Sac. **22**: 353. — (S. W. Whitney) Univ. Q. **29**: 24. — Chr. Obs. **1**: 689, 761. **2**: 1. — Dub. Univ. **90**: 245. — Cong. M. **25**: 682. — (J. Donaldson) Theo. R. **14**: 35. — (J. R. G. Hassard) Cath. World, **6**: 93. — Dub. R. **46**: 42.
Clement XIII. and XV., Popes, Ravignan's Times of. Dub. R. **39**: 109.
Clement XIV. and the Jesuits. (H. H. Milman) Quar. **83**: 70. Same art. Liv. Age, **18**: 590.
Clement of Alexandria. (B. H. Cowper) Kitto, **10**: 129. — (A. Lamson) Chr. Exam. **23**: 137. — Chr. R. **17**: 321. — Kitto, **29**: 317.
— Account of. Ecl. R. **62**: 307.
— Hortatory Address. (R. Ornsby) Month, **19**: 231.
— Hymn to Christ. Cong. M. **24**: 458.
— Writings of. Chr. Obs. **69**: 34.
Clement; a Poem. (W. D. Howells) Galaxy, **1**: 210.
Clement's Reward; a Tale. Bentley, **62**: 394.
Clement's Trouble; a Tale. Bentley, **61**: 397.
Clement Crew; a Tale. All the Year, **12**: 522.
Clementina Kinniside; a Tale. (E. L. Linton) Galaxy, **5**: 549.
Clementine Homilies. (G. P. Gould) Theo. R. **15**: 1.
Clemenza, La, di Tito; a Drama. Colburn, **54**: 409.

Cleomenes the Greek. (D. M. Craik) Bentley, **26**: 17.
Cleon. Colburn, **129**: 153.
Cleopatra of Egypt. (H. A. Dick) Dub. Univ. **79**: 229, 317.
— a Poem. (W. W. Story) Blackw. **98**: 254. Same art. Liv. Age, **87**: 86.
— a Poem. (A. Swinburne) Cornh. **14**: 331.
— Ancient encaustic Painting of. Lond. M. **15**: 65.
— Biographical Sketch of. (A. H. Dick) St. James, **19**: 242, 357.
— Character of. Cornh. **24**: 344. Same art. Ecl. M. **77**: 582.
— Death of. Am. Mo. M. **4**: 267.
— in a striking Attitude. Once a Week, **19**: 297.
— Madame Girardin's. Colburn, **82**: 102.
— Shakspere's Character of. Fraser, **40**: 277.
— Stahr's. (H. J. Warner) Nation, **3**: 326. — Liv. Age, **84**: 333.
Cleopatra's Needle. All the Year, **1**: 562. Same art. Liv. Age, **64**: 821. — Am. Arch. **6**: 135. — Chamb. J. **28**: 363. **54**: 225. — Ecl. Engin. **17**: 340. — Internat. M. **4**: 367. — Lond. Soc. **17**: 347.
— and its Workmen. Ecl. Engin. **19**: 263.
— and the Wind Pressure. Nature, **19**: 25.
— Dixon's Plan for removing. Pract. M. **7**: 81.
— Launching of. Pract. M. **7**: 241.
— Proposed Transport to England. Pract. M. **5**: 362.
— Transportation of. (J. Dixon) Ecl. Engin. **16**: 540.
Cleopatra's Needles. Godey, **29**: 129.
Clerc, Alexis. Irish Mo. **8**: 271.
Clerget and his Designs. Art J. **2**: 26.
Clergy and the Courts. (E. L. Godkin) Nation, **9**: 124.
— and Laity. (J. D. Lewis) Fortn. **22**: 782.
— and the People. (O. Dewey) Chr. Exam. **2**: 1. — Ecl. M. **6**: 517.
— and Politics. (R. F. Littledale) Contemp. **23**: 92.
— and World. (J. V. Campbell) Am. Church R. **9**: 244.
— Attitude of, towards Science. (J. Hannah) Contemp. **6**: 1. **9**: 395. Same art. Ecl. M. **69**: 608.
— Benefit of. All the Year, **43**: 448.
— Bishop of Oxford, and the Reverend Cabmen of Paris. Fraser, **71**: 558.
— Business Capacity of, and of the Laity. (R. F. Littledale) Contemp. **40**: 697.
— Duties and Training of. Quar. **111**: 400.
— English. Cornh. **9**: 750.
— — Ineligibility of, to Parliament. (J. E. T. Rogers) Fraser, **75**: 769. Same art. Ecl. M. **69**: 207.
— — Professional Studies of. (R. F. Littledale) Contemp. **35**: 1.
— — Submission of. Quar. **148**: 544.
— Etiquette of the Chancel. (G. Z. Gray) Am. Church R. **27**: 244.
— French, Manners and Miseries of. Fraser, **47**: 590.
— Improvement in Condition of. (T. P. Thompson) Westm. **16**: 394.
— Lawlessness of. Am. Church R. **23**: 291.
— Modern Dogmatism and Modern Thought. (G. R. Wynne) Fortn. **4**: 513.
— Non-Resident. Ed. R. **5**: 301.
— Notions on Church Reform. Westm. **27**: 99.
— of Old, Dr. Doran on. Chamb. J. **45**: 683.
— Patriotism of, in New England. (J. S. Clark) Cong. Q. **3**: 242.
— Political Conduct of. Fraser, **4**: 641.
— Poverty of the English. All the Year, **4**: 177.
— Priests or Ministers? (J. J. S. Perowne) Contemp. **31**: 54.
— Relation of, to People. (H. H. Milman) Quar. **76**: 316.
— Remarks on. (E. Eggleston) Scrib. **17**: 483.
— Rights of. Niles's Reg. **23**: 230, 291.
— Ruskin's Letters to. Lond. Q. **56**: 132.
Clergy, Secular, in the Middle Ages. (E. L. Cutts) Art J. **16**: 308, 331, 349.
— Secular Studies of. (R. F. Littledale) Contemp. **19**: 55. Same art. Liv. Age, **112**: 451.
— Shall they vote? (C. Weber) St. James, **33**: 674.
— Should they study Natural Science? (J. C. Koller) Luth. Q. **4**: 597.
— Should they take Part in Politics? Fraser, **15**: 423.
— Sturges on Residence of. (Syd. Smith) Ed. R. **2**: 202.
— Support of. Ed. R. **19**: 360.
— Temporal Influence of. So. Lit. J. **4**: 162.
— Varieties in the Life of English. Temp. Bar, **32**: 229.
— Wisdom in. (C. B. Hadduck) Am. Q. Reg. **2**: 193.
— Word for. Dem. R. **34**: 241.
See Sacerdotal.
Clergy Discipline Bill. Chr. Obs. **47**: 501, 563.
Clergy Relief Bill. Quar. **86**: 40.
Clergyman, The City. Ev. Sat. **11**: 114.
Clergyman's Confession. (W. Collins) Canad. Mo. **8**: 139, 244.
Clergyman's Tale. Chamb. J. **41**: 279.
Clergymen and the Laws of Health. (G. M. Beard) Hours at Home, **7**: 539.
— and Literature. (S. B. James) St. James, **37**: 542.
— as scientific Men. (E. L. Godkin) Nation, **23**: 252–298.
— Bearing of Arms by. (R. W. Lowrie) Am. Church R. **18**: 585.
— New England. (H. B. Stowe) Atlan. **1**: 485.
— Salaries of. (O. B. Frothingham) Nation, **2**: 362. — (J. T. Lewis) Am. Church R. **10**: 217.
See Ministers.
Clerical Abuses, Durham Case. Ed. R. **37**: 350.
Clerical Changes. (J. H. Nichols) Am. Church R. **2**: 59.
Clerical Characteristics. Chr. Obs. **4**: 468–732.
Clerical Customs. (L. Hart) Chr. Mo. Spec. **7**: 292.
Clerical Discipline. Chr. Disc. **4**: 103.
Clerical Duties. (O. Dewey) Chr. Exam. **5**: 101.
Clerical Eccentricities. (M. Davies) Belgra. **27**: 364.
Clerical Economics. Chr. Exam. **34**: 202. — Quar. **96**: 117.
Clerical Education. *See* Ministry, Education for.
Clerical Habits of Study. Am. Q. Reg. **14**: 71.
Clerical Life in England. Dub. Univ. **56**: 411.
— in Ireland. Dub. Univ. **49**: 300.
— Scottish. Ecl. R. **113**: 392.
Clerical Manners and Habits. (S. Gilman) No. Am. **28**: 503. — Chr. Mo. Spec. **9**: 487. — U. S. Lit. Gaz. **6**: 377.
Clerical Market. Chamb. J. **46**: 737.
Clerical Obligation, Theory of. (R. Williams) Fortn. **9**: 257.
Clerical Obliquities of Mind. (P. Frost) Fortn. **24**: 259.
Clerical Office, Dignity of. Chr. Exam. **12**: 349.
Clerical Pretensions. Ecl. R. **80**: 373.
Clerical Policy of 19th Century, Von Sybel on. Chr. Obs. **75**: 203.
Clerical Profession. (J. Wright) Theo. R. **4**: 22.
Clerical Reminiscences, Cheshire Co., N. H. Mo. Rel. M. **49**: 49.
Clerical Statistics. (S. F. Smith) Chr. R. **13**: 501.
Clericality. Fraser, **96**: 442.
Clerk, Scenes in the Life of a. (J. A. Parker) Hunt, **5**: 530. **6**: 56.
Clerk of the Weather; a Chronicle of Nevelandregenstein. Cornh. **25**: 551.
Clerk's Daughter; a Tale. Belgra. **19**: 341.
Clerks. Chamb. J. **54**: 570.
— at Washington, and their Salaries, 1822. Niles's Reg. **22**: 70.
— Shopmen, and Apprentices, Advice to. Fraser, **12**: 267.
Clerkenwell, Walk round. (E. Walford) Gent. M. n. s. **1**: 769.

Clerkenwell Discovery, 1628. Month, **31**: 220.
Clermont, and Auvergne Mountains. Penny M. **5**: 134.
Clermont Assizes, Fléchier's Chronicle of. Blackw. **63**: 47. Same art. Liv. Age, **16**: 309.
Cleveland, John. Poetical Works. Retros. **12**: 123.
Cleveland, R. J. Voyages. (R. H. Dana, jr.) No. Am. **55**: 144. — Hunt, **8**: 143. — Mo. R. **159**: 290.
Cleveland, England. (R. J. King) Fraser, **91**: 478.
— Nomenclature of. (J. C. Atkinson) Anthrop. J. **3**: 115.
Clevenger, S. Vail, the Sculptor. So. Lit. Mess. **5**: 263. — Dem. R. **14**: 202.
Clever and dull Boys. Ecl. M. **31**: 567.
Clever Men. (T. F. Pearse) St. James, **46**: 159.
Clever Woman of the Family. (M. Oliphant) Liv. Age, **84**: 25-593. **85**: 71, 152.
Cleverness. (Mrs. S. C. Hall) Ecl. Mus. **2**: 386.
Cleybornes, The. (Miss Leslie) Godey, **39**: 187-434.
Client in Person; a Tale. Broadw. **1**: 285.
Client's Story. Liv. Age, **1**: 87.
Clifden Confessors, Acts of. (A. Whitelock) Irish Mo. **7**: 598.
Cliff-Dwellers. (E. C. Hardacre) Scrib. **17**: 266.
Cliff-Dwellers of the Far West. (S. B. J. Skertchly) Good Words, **20**: 486.
Clifford, Anne, Countess of Dorset. Chr. Rem. **10**: 26.
Clifford, Sir Charles, Sketch of, with portrait. Colburn, **165**: 1172, 1256.
Clifford, Nathan, with portrait. Dem. R. **21**: 360.
Clifford, William Kingdon. (F. Pollock) Fortn. **31**: 667. — Liv. Age, **141**: 657. — Fraser, **100**: 685. Same art. Liv. Age, **143**: 665. — Pop. Sci. Mo. **15**: 258. — Nature, **19**: 443. — (J. Fiske) Internat. R. **8**: 80.
— Atheism of. (N. Porter) Princ. n. s. **5**: 359.
— Lectures and Essays. Month, **37**: 292. — Ed. R. **151**: 474. — (W. James) Nation, **29**: 312.
Clifford the Astrologer; a Legend of Craven. Blackw. **25**: 1.
Cliffords of Craven; a Tradition. (A. Picken) Fraser, **11**: 275.
Clifton, William, Biography of. Anal. M. **3**: 479.
Clifton, Camps on the River Avon at. (H. M. Scarth) Arch. **44**: 428.
Clifton College School of Nat. Science. Nature, **4**: 329.
Clifton Pebble, A. Belgra. **2**: 355.
Climate and Complexion. (J. M. Buchan) Pop. Sci. Mo. **17**: 1.
Climate and social Development. (H. Spencer) Pop. Sci. Mo. **5**: 322.
— and Time. (H. W. Lucas) Month, **30**: 448.
— — Croll on. (E. Lewis, jr.) Pop. Sci. Mo. **7**: 719. — (W. T. MacGee) Pop. Sci. Mo. **16**: 810. — (S. Newcomb) Am. J. Sci. **111**: 263. — Nature, **12**: 121, 141.
— — in their geological Relations. (A. Winchell) Internat. R. **3**: 519.
— as influenced by Distribution of Land and Water. (H. Hennessy) Am. J. Sci. **77**: 316.
— Change of. Chamb. J. **20**: 4.
— Changes of. Temp. Bar, **5**: 268. — (C. Dewey) No. Am. **87**: 507. — New Dom. **13**: 214.
— — No Variation during historic Times. (F. Arago) Ed. New Philos. J. **16**: 205.
— Sir James Clark on. Ed. R. **76**: 420. Same art. Ecl. Mus. **1**: 484. — Blackw. **28**: 372.
— Curative Influence of. Ecl. R. **53**: 495.
— Hints for Tourists and Invalids on Italian. (F. Boott) Nation, **2**: 330.
— Influence of, on Agricultural Productions. De Bow, **20**: 715.
— — on Animals and Plants. (J. W. Scott) De Bow, **28**: 648.
— — on Character. (M. Tarver) West. J. **14**: 75.
— — on Disease. Mo. R. **122**: 55.
Climate, Influence of, on human Development. (J. W. Scott) De Bow, **28**: 495.
— — on Longevity. (J. McCune Smith) Hunt, **14**: 319, 403.
— — on Mankind. (S. B. Buckley) Penn Mo. **12**: 32.
— — on Plants and Animals. (E. Emmons) Ed. New Philos. J. **56**: 118.
— Influence of Cultivation upon. J. Frankl. Inst. **25**: 422.
— — of Vegetation on. Pop. Sci. Mo. **11**: 385. — Liv. Age, **29**: 190.
— Investigation of. (T. Stevenson) Nature, **15**: 556.
— of Canada, and the United States. Penny M. **6**: 258.
— of Europe. Chamb. J. **6**: 343.
— of Great Britain. (Lord de Manley) Gent. M. n. s. **18**: 452. — Intel. Obs. **11**: 113.
— of Scotland, Supposed Change of. (A. Buchan) Nature, **11**: 329.
— Secular Changes of. Brit. Q. **64**: 297. Same art. Ecl. M. **88**: 54. Same art. Liv. Age, **131**: 323. — (W. J. McGee) Am. J. Sci. **122**: 437.
Climates for Invalids. (T. M. Coan) Harper, **58**: 583.
— Geological. Quar. **126**: 359.
— of the Northwest. Appleton, **7**: 37.
— Sea and Mountain. (B. Yeo) Fortn. **28**: 195.
Climatic Theory of the Earth. (H. B. Adams) No. Am. **107**: 465.
Climatology. (C. Dewey) No. Am. **91**: 327. — (C. Wright) Chr. Exam. **63**: 384.
— of United States. Dem. R. **11**: 449.
— — Blodget's. Am. J. Sci. **75**: 235. — Canad. J. n. s. **3**: 28.
— — Has it changed? (D. Draper) Pop. Sci. Mo. **1**: 665.
Climbing Boys. (Syd. Smith) Ed. R. **32**: 309.
Climbing Plants. (F. Darwin) Liv. Age, **146**: 560. Same art. Pop. Sci. Mo. **17**: 635. — Chamb. J. **18**: 169.
— and Tendrils. Good Words, **13**: 53.
— Darwin's. (A. Gray) Nation, **22**: 12, 30.
Clingman, Thomas L., Speeches of. (W. P. Garrison) Nation, **25**: 155, 170.
Clinochlore of Achmatowsk. (N. von Kokscharov) Am. J. Sci. **69**: 176.
Clinton, De Witt. (H. T. Tuckerman) No. Am. **79**: 485.
— as a Politician. (J. Bigelow) Harper, **50**: 409, 563.
— Character of. (W. G. Hunt) West. Mo. R. **2**: 56.
— Discourse in New York, 1814. No. Am. **1**: 390.
— Life of. (W. Phillips) No. Am. **29**: 496. — Am. Q. **5** 473. — Chr. R. **6**: 507. — Ann. Reg. **4**: 156.
— Vases presented to. Niles's Reg. **28**: 120.
Clinton, George. (W. L. Stone) M. Am. Hist. **3**: 329. — (W. L. Stone) Potter Am. Mo. **7**: 189. — with portrait, M. Am. Hist. **7**: 401.
Clinton, Sir Henry, Dispatch of, 1777. Am. Hist. Rec. **3**: 8.
Clinton, Henry F., Life and Writings of. Ecl. R. **102**: 277.
Cliona of Munster; a Legend. Dub. Univ. **76**: 481.
Clipped Wings. Liv. Age, **112**: 373.
Cliques and Criticism. Temp. Bar, **20**: 321.
Clisson, Castle-Ruin of. (G. M. Towle) Hours at Home, **9**: 231.
Clive, Mrs. Archer. Fraser, **88**: 348.
— Paul Ferroll. Nat. R. **12**: 489.
— Poems and Novels. (J. Davies) Contemp. **23**: 197.
Clive, Mrs. Catherine, Actress. Dub. Univ. **74**: 541.
Clive, Robert, Lord, Life of. (T. B. Macaulay) Ed. R. **70**: 295. Same art. Mus. **38**: 353. — Fraser, **16**: 433.
Clive Weston's Wedding Anniversary; a Tale. (Mrs. Lephron) Canad. Mo. **2**: 97, 193.
Cloak-Cubby and Blue-Room. (E. A. Walker) Scrib. **2**: 625.
Clock, Astrological, in Society of Antiquaries. (W. H. Smyth) Arch. **33**: 8. **34**: 1, 259.
— Astronomical, A new. Nature, **15**: 227. *See* Strasburg Clock.

Clock, Mysterious, Robert's. (A. Moigno) Pract. M. **4**: 238.
— New Calendar. Nature, **20**: 35.
— of Westminster Palace. Chamb. J. **25**: 5.
Clock and Watch Making, Poppe's History of. J. Frankl. Inst. **5**: 151, 245, 294.
— and Watch Work. All the Year, **32**: 233.
Clock's Romance. Argosy, **31**: 138.
Clocks. Chamb. J. **32**: 361.
— and Clockwork, Electrical. (H. D. Gardner) Nature, **20**: 345.
— and Watches, Curiosities of. Temp. Bar, **20**: 55.
— — Quaint and curious. Once a Week, **17**: 334.
— Conspiracy of. Chamb. J. **16**: 264.
— Earliest Introduction of, into England. (D. Barrington) Arch. **5**: 416.
— Historical Account of. Penny M. **3**: 187, 195, 220.
— How they keep Time. Chamb. J. **18**: 214. Same art. Liv. Age, **35**: 413.
— Pneumatic. Nature, **22**: 227.
— Synchronized. Nature, **19**: 55.
See Horology.
Clock-Dials, Self-Luminous. (H. Morton) J. Frankl. Inst. **107**: 51.
Clock-Factory and Bell-Foundry. Penny M. **11**: 121.
Clockmaker's Salt-Works at Goza. Penny M. **5**: 326.
Clockmaking. Pract. M. **7**: 303.
Clog Almanacs. (J. Harland) Reliquary, **5**: 121, 205. **7**: 173.
— Staffordshire. (J. B. Davis) Arch. **41**: 453.
Cloisonné Enamel. (J. J. Young) Harper, **58**: 211.
Cloister, Art in the. Irish Q. **6**: 707.
Cloncurry, Lord, Fitzpatrick's Life of. New Q. **4**: 283.
— and John O'Connell, Memoirs of. Quar. **86**: 126.
— Memoir of. Dub. Univ. **34**: 475. **38**: 413.
— Recollections of. Fraser, **40**: 591.
Clonmacnoise, Day at. Irish Mo. **2**: 129.
Clonmel Tragedy. Bentley, **48**: 173.
Clontarf, Battle of. Fraser, **82**: 514.
Clootz, Jean Baptiste. Ev. Sat. **3**: 631.
Close, Francis, Dean of Carlisle. Cong. **4**: 562.
Close Colony, Iowa. (P. Bigelow) Harper, **62**: 764. — (R. Benson) Macmil. **44**: 65.
Closer than a Brother; a Story. All the Year, **36**: 84, 109.
Closet and the Pulpit. (R. Bailey) Chr. Mo. Spec. **8**: 441.
Clothes. (E. M. Lynch) St. Paul's, **14**: 309.
— and Fashion. All the Year, **28**: 319.
— Ethics of. (J. P. Lacroix) Chr. Q. **3**: 511.
— Old. All the Year, **11**: 40.
— On the Subject of. (D. M. Craik) Macmil. **1**: 211.
— Some Words on. Once a Week, **12**: 132.
— we wear. Godey, **88**: 65.
Clothing. Am. Alma. **1830**: 131.
Clothing and Dress, Economics of. Godey, **48**: 421.
— and its Materials. Pract. M. **7**: 152.
— Dyeing, and Calico Printing. Dem. R. **19**: 305.
— Medical Aspect of. Lond. M. **1**: 451.
— Office of. (E. P. Evans) No. Am. **104**: 156.
— Proper. (E. Lankester) Pop. Sci. R. **3**: 338.
— Relations of Air to. (M. von Pettenkoffer) Pop. Sci. Mo. **10**: 654.
Clotilda of Kynast; a Silesian Legend. Lond. M. **10**: 531.
Cloud, Col., Passages in Life of. Blackw. **18**: 32.
Cloud, Life of a. (J. J. Fox) Recr. Sci. **2**: 13.
— New Form of. (A. Poëy) Nature, **4**: 489.
— Remarkable. (T. Stevenson) Nature, **12**: 487.
Clouds. Chamb. J. **8**: 149. — Knick. **35**: 125. — Liv Age, **15**: 341. — So. R. n. s. **16**: 449. — Temp. Bar, **2**: 230.
— Air, atmospheric Meteors, etc., in Art. (Prof. Ansted) Art J. **15**: 193.
— and the Atmosphere. (J. Glaisher) Good Words, **8**: 110.
— and their Changes. Dub. Univ. **76**: 676.
Clouds and the Poor. (J. R. Wise) Fortn. **1**: 590. — Cath. World, **2**: 213.
— and Sunshine. (M. M. Duncan) Godey, **30**: 68, 109.
— Classification of. Nature, **9**: 163. — (W. C. Ley) Nature, **21**: 207.
— Columnar, Northeast Storms, etc. (J. P. Espy) J. Frankl. Inst. **22**: 239.
— Highway of. Liv. Age, **108**: 305.
— New Classification of. (Prof. Poëy) Nature, **2**: 382.
— Night in. Dem. R. **33**: 144.
— Nomenclature of. Lond. M. **4**: 334.
— Pictures in. Chamb. J. **45**: 820.
Clouds and Sunshine. (C. Reade) Bentley, **35**: 604. **36**: 69, 123, 228.
Cloudburst on the Desert. (A. S. Evans) Overland, **3**: 138.
Cloudbursts, Theory of. (J. Chamberlain) Overland, **14**: 464.
Cloud Confines; a Poem. (D. G. Rossetti) Fortn. **17**: 14.
Cloud Forms, Outlines of: Electric Cumulus, Anvil Cloud, and Rain-Ball. (S. Barber) Pop. Sci. R. **12**: 359. **17**: 243.
Cloud Formation in rarefied moist Air. J. Frankl. Inst. **101**: 127.
Clouded Intellect, The. (J. Ingelow) Liv. Age, **85**: 406.
Cloudy Hours in Summer Days. Fraser, **28**: 460.
Clough, Arthur Hugh. (W. Allingham) Fraser, **74**: 525. — (G. W. Curtis) Putnam, **11**: 6. — (J. Dowden) Contemp. **12**: 513. Same art. Liv. Age, **105**: 56. — (C. E. Norton) Atlan. **9**: 462. — (C. E. Norton) No. Am. **105**: 434. — (F. T. Palgrave) Fraser, **65**: 527. — (T. S. Perry) Atlan. **36**: 409. — (G. H. Sass) So. M. **9**: 72. — (J. A. Symonds) Fortn. **10**: 589. — Blackw. **92**: 586. — Bost. R. **3**: 132. — Liv. Age, **76**: 391. — Once a Week, **21**: 237. — Ecl. M. **73**: 719. — Ev. Sat. **8**: 507.
— and Matthew Arnold. Liv. Age, **137**: 410.
— and Charles Kingsley, Poetry of. (S. R. T. Mayer) St. James, **40**: 265.
— Bothie of Toper-na-Fuosich. Fraser, **39**: 103. Same art. Liv. Age, **21**: 197.
— Dipsychus and Letters of. Macmil. **15**: 89.
— Life and Poems. Chr. Rem. **45**: 61. — Cornh. **14**: 410. Same art. Ecl. M. **67**: 735. Same art. Liv. Age, **91**: 259. Same art. Ev. Sat. **2**: 515.
— Poems of. Westm. **92**: 363. — (D. Masson) Macmil. **6**: 318. — (S. Waddington) Tinsley, **22**: 57. — Cornh. **6**: 398. — Ecl. R. **115**: 27. — Nat. R. **15**: 310. — No. Brit. **37**: 323.
— Thyrsis; Poem on. (M. Arnold) Macmil. **13**: 449.
Clough, Simon. Select Writings. (S. Barrett) Chr. Exam. **42**: 227.
Clough Fionn. (M. Banim) Dub. Univ. **40**: 148–639.
Clovelly. Lond. Soc. **10**: 302.
Clover, Lewis P., with portrait. Dem. R. **26**: 260.
Clover, Japan. (H. W. Ravenal) Land We Love, **4**: 405.
— White. (Mrs. Lankester) Pop. Sci. R. **1**: 337.
Clown's real Pigling, The. (R. G. White) Galaxy, **9**: 397.
Clowns. (W. J. Thoms) Bentley, **3**: 617.
— first of Merry Andrews. (E. Walford) Once a Week, **16**: 454.
Club, Beefsteak. Lond. Soc. **11**: 282.
Clubs. Fraser, **64**: 552. — Lond. Soc. **9**: 267. **11**: 101-461. **20**: 154.
— and Clubbists. Blackw. **73**: 265. Same art. Liv. Age, **37**: 354.
— and Club Houses. Chamb. J. **28**: 141.
— and Clubmen. (A. Poyntz) Bentley, **14**: 453. — All the Year, **16**: 283.
— and Co-operation. All the Year, **30**: 268.
— Dinners, etc. Quar. **55**: 445.
— Ladies'. Tinsley, **4**: 368.

Clubs, Literary. (A. H. Rhine) Am. Bibliop. **8**: 23.
— Modern French. (G. M. Towle) Galaxy, **5**: 247.
— of London. (C. W. Reade) Galaxy, **3**: 190. — (D. W. Jobson) No. Am. **81**: 1. — (A. C. Sellar) Nation, **20**: 238. — (W. Thornbury) Belgra. **6**: 30–513. **7**: 49. — Blackw. **3**: 552. — Mo. R. **115**: 223. — Nat. Q. **7**: 233. — Nat. R. **4**: 295. — (R. Wynford) Lippinc. **9**: 712. — New Q. **4**: 133. — Mus. **3**: 68. — Tinsley, **8**: 569. — Colburn, **43**: 10. — Once a Week, **2**: 526. — Penny M. **6**: 137. — Temp. Bar, **51**: 189.
— — and their Ends. Temp. Bar, **34**: 469. Same art. Ev. Sat. **12**: 410.
— — Timbs on. Fraser, **73**: 342.
— — West End. Peop. J. **1**: 162.
— of New York. Galaxy, **22**: 227.
— of Paris. (G. Barmby) Howitt, **3**: 300. — Lond. Soc. **16**: 13.
— People's, of New England. O. & N. **5**: 373.
— Philosophy of. (S. Dell) So. M. **13**: 583.
— Unfashionable. Chamb. J. **17**: 369.
— Working-Men's. Temp. Bar, **8**: 583.
See Burlesque Societies.
Club Books. Chamb. J. **52**: 286.
— Leaves from. Blackw. **91**: 309.
Club Chambers for the Married. (A. Wynter) Peop. J. **3**: 49.
Club Hotels. Victoria, **19**: 555.
Club House, Economy of. Chamb. J. **4**: 265, 276.
Club Houses. Lond. M. **19**: 289.
Club-House Sobriety. Cornh. **9**: 480.
Club Land. (W. B. Ranken) Belgra. **21**: 459.
Club Life. (C. A. Bristed) Nation, **1**: 12. — Chamb. J. **4**: 241. **53**: 305.
— a Poem. (Earl of Dufferin) Canad. Mo. **9**: 360.
— and Society in London. Brit. Q. **43**: 414. Same art. Ecl. M. **67**: 44.
— Family, in England. Temp. Bar, **12**: 396. **13**: 78.
Club-Root. (E. P. Wright) Nature, **18**: 279.
Club Servants. (T. H. S. Escott) Belgra. **25**: 201.
Cluny, France, Congregation of. (A. F. Hewitt) Cath. World, **25**: 691.
Clunys, Corbeship of. Dub. Univ. **89**: 605.
Cluricaun, The; a Poem. Dub. Univ. **63**: 625.
Cluster of Lilies. Tinsley, **19**: 5, 84.
Clutterbuck, Dr. Henry, with portrait. Peop. J. **10**: 245.
Clyde, Lord. *See* Campbell, Sir Colin.
Clyde, River, Adventure on. Chamb. J. **53**: 298, 314.
— Deas's. Nature, **15**: 99.
— Falls of. Penny M. **1**: 253.
— Frith of. Liv. Age, **58**: 705.
— Shipbuilding Trade of. Pract. M. **3**: 2.
— Steamboat Works on, Day at. Penny M. **12**: 377.
Clyffards of Clyff; a Novel. (J. Payn) Chamb. J. **42**: 401–745.
Clymer, George. (W. Dickenson) M. Am. Hist. **5**: 196.
Clytie; a Novel. (J. Hatton) Gent. M. n. s. **10**: 237–613. **11**: 1–707. **12**: 100–607.
Clytie, The; a Tale. Chamb. J. **52**: 825.
Coaches, Four-in-Hand. (J. J. Young) Lippinc. **21**: 683.
— History of. All the Year, **38**: 521.
— Modern. Godey, **61**: 13, 109, 205.
— Notice of. Penny M. **3**: 321.
Coach-Factory, Day at a. Penny M. **10**: 501.
Coaching. All the Year, **13**: 134.
— and Coaches. (W. P. Lennox) Once a Week, **17**: 66.
See Stage-Coaching.
Coachmaker, Who was the first? Fraser, **25**: 584.
Coachmen, Latter-Day. Chamb. J. **30**: 97.
Coal. (W. C. Williamson) Nature, **19**: 238. — House. Words, **1**: 246. — Lond. Q. **42**: 121.
— Acid Products of Combustion of. (M. Vincotte) J. Frankl. Inst. **109**: 180.
Coal, Albert, of New Brunswick. (C. H. Hitchcock) Am. J. Sci. **89**: 267.
— Analysis of some Varieties of. (F. Vaux) J. Frankl. Inst. **47**: 197.
— — Improved, 1854. (J. H. Alexander and C. Morfit) J. Frankl. Inst. **57**: 102, 173.
— and Coal Mines. Dub. Univ. **45**: 515.
— and Coal-Mining. (H. D. Rogers) Harper, **29**: 163. — (D. K. Clark) Pract. M. **1**: 196.
— and Coal Plants. (W. C. Williamson) Macmil. **29**: 404. Same art. Ecl. M. **82**: 592. — Nature, **8**: 446.
— and Colliery Explosions. (C. De Rance) Pop. Sci. R. **17**: 355.
— and Coniferous Wood under Microscope. (J. R. Leifchild) Recr. Sci. **1**: 343.
— and Iron. (J. S. Newberry) Ecl. Engin. **4**: 611. — (J Western) Lakeside, **3**: 197.
— and Iron Ore in Guerero, Mexico. (N. S. Manross) Am. J. Sci. **89**: 309.
— and Iron Trade of Ohio Valley. (C. Whittlesey) Hunt, **16**: 450.
— and Petroleum. (H. D. Rogers) Good Words, **4**: 374.
— and Smoke. Quar. **119**: 435. Same art. Liv. Age, **89**: 515.
— Anthracite, as a Fuel. (P. W. Sheafer) J. Frankl. Inst. **83**: 314.
— — for generating Steam, Power of. J. Frankl. Inst. **32**: 92.
— — in Locomotives. J. Frankl. Inst. **44**: 110. — (G. W. Whistler) J. Frankl. Inst. **48**: 6, 78, 176.
— — in Smelting-Furnaces. (M. Robin) J. Frankl. Inst. **19**: 264, 341.
— — of Pennsylvania. (C. Cushing) No. Am. **42**: 241.
— — Trade in. (J. E. Bloomfield) Hunt, **11**: 541.
— — Use of. (D. Olmsted) Am. Alma. **1837**: 61.
— — When first used. M. Am. Hist. **5**: 452.
— as a Reservoir of Power. (R. Hunt) Pop. Sci. R. **10**: 155. Same art. Pop. Sci. Mo. **1**: 738.
— Assaying by Blowpipe. (E. J. Chapman) Canad. J. n. s. **3**: 208.
— Bituminous, Analysis of. (T. O'C. Sloane) Am. J. Sci. **114**: 286.
— — Chemical Examination of. (B. Silliman) Am. J. Sci. **42**: 369.
— — Origin of. (C. Whittlesey) Hesp. **1**: 111. — (J. W. Foster) Hesp. **2**: 204. **3**: 199.
— — — Varieties, and special Uses of. (E. B. Andrews) J. Frankl. Inst. **95**: 58, 133.
— Bradford's Report on. Am. J. Sci. **39**: 137.
— Cannel, Formation of. (J. S. Newberry) Am. J. Sci. **73**: 212.
— Compressed Slack. (W.W. Smyth) Ecl. Engin. **1**: 157.
— Cost and Consumption of. Ed. R. **137**: 456. — All the Year, **6**: 492.
— Cutting, by Machinery. (J. S. Jeans) Pract. M. **3**: 272. — Pract. M. **6**: 286. — Ecl. Engin. **5**: 527.
— Distribution of. Liv. Age, **44**: 115.
— Duhamel's Communication on. Ed. R. **9**: 67.
— Early Discovery of. (W. J. Buck) Potter Am. Mo. **4**: 180.
— Early Use of, in Penn. J. Frankl. Inst. **109**: 411.
— Few Words about. Cornh. **26**: 460.
— for Illumination, Comparative Value of. (A. Fyfe) Am. J. Sci. **57**: 77, 157.
— Formation of. (T. H. Huxley) Contemp. **15**: 618. Same art. So. M. **8**: 174. — (W. Nicol) Ed. New Philos. J. **46**: 174. — J. Frankl. Inst. **108**: 338.
— — Ancient Forests and modern Fuel. Temp. Bar, **4**: 277. Same art. Ecl. M. **55**: 367.
— — Ancient Vegetation. Lond. Q. **17**: 414.
— — Geological. Temp. Bar, **4**: 277.
— — Theories of. (L. Horner) Ed. New Philos. J. **41**: 97.

Coal, Future. (D. Ker) Geog. M. **3**: 60.
— Geology of. (S. J. Mackie) Recr. Sci. **1**: 233. — Temp. Bar, **4**: 277.
— German. Pract. M. **7**: 337.
— History and Destiny of. (G. W. Anderson) Chr. R. **21**: 267.
— — of Fossil Fuel. Mo. R. **138**: 430.
— in China. (D. J. Macgowan) Am. J. Sci. **61**: 235.
— in Europe, Production of, 1846. J. Frankl. Inst. **42**: 284.
— in the Fire. (C. Kingsley) Ev. Sat. **12**: 492.
— in Great Britain. (P. Bevan) Gent. M. n. s. **9**: 268. — (H. B. Spencer) St. James, **19**: 103. — Ev. Sat. **11**: 267.
— — Britain's Coal Cellars. St. Paul's, **9**: 182.
— — British Diamonds. (R. Hunt) St. James, **1**: 223.
— — Commissioners' Report, 1872. Ecl. Engin. **6**: 417. — Brit. Q. **56**: 66.
— — Exhaustion of. (H. D. Rogers) Good Words, **5**: 334. — (L. Lemoran) Pop. Sci. R. **5**: 290. Same art. Ecl. M. **67**: 341. — Ecl. Engin. **8**: 445. — All the Year, **2**: 488. — (A. S. Harvey) Macmil. **26**: 375. — (L. Levi) Pract. M. **1**: 67.
— in Nebraska. (F. V. Hayden) Am. J. Sci. **95**: 326.
— in New York. (A. Eaton) Am. J. Sci. **19**: 21.
— in Rhode Island. Am. J. Sci. **11**: 78.
— in the United States. (E. Crapsey) Scrib. **1**: 647.
— — Product of. De Bow, **19**: 123.
— — Report on. (W. R. Johnson) Am. J. Sci. **49**: 310. *See* Coal Fields.
— in Ships, Spontaneous Combustion of. Pract. M. **6**: 280.
— Life of a Block of. (G. P. Bevan) Once a Week, **12**: 285–467.
— Mineral, Chemical Composition of. (P. E. Chase) J. Frankl. Inst. **108**: 95.
— Mauch Chunk. (B. Silliman) Am. J. Sci. **19**: 12.
— Natural Hist. of. (S. Calvin) Pop. Sci. Mo. **18**: 610.
— Origin of. (A. Jaquith) Overland, **13**: 503.
— — and Uses of. Pract. M. **7**: 147.
— — Distribution, and mechanical Efficiency of. (H. D. Rogers) Good Words, **4**: 247.
— Phosphorus in. (A. S. McCreath) J. Frankl. Inst. **107**: 389. — (C. H. Roney) J. Frankl. Inst. **108**: 56.
— Products from. Chamb. J. **55**: 121. — West. J. **13**: 186. — (F. C. Calvert) J. Frankl. Inst. **59**: 277, 332.
— Resinous Nature of. (J. E. Teschmacher) Am. J. Sci. **64**: 70.
— Statistics of. (J. MacFarlane) J. Frankl. Inst. **96**: 255. — Ed. R. **90**: 525. — Pract. M. **2**: 406.
— Substitutes for. Penny M. **12**: 278.
— Supply of. (E. B. Andrews) Internat. R. **1**: 458. — (J. Scoffern) St. James, **8**: 301. — (Sir W. Armstrong) Nature, **7**: 270, 291.
— — and Iron Industry. (I. L. Bell) Ecl. Engin. **10**: 401.
— — and reproductive Power of. (Dr. Wilkinson) J. Frankl. Inst. **31**: 279.
— — and Waste of. (D. T. Ansted) Intel. Obs. **4**: 317.
— Testing for Water in. (J. B. Britton) Pract. M. **6**: 301.
— Washing of. (A. Beckwith) Ecl. Engin. **2**: 337.
— What is? Once a Week, **5**: 23.
— Why so dear? Ecl. R. **101**: 21.
Coal-Basin on Lake of the Woods. (H. R. Schoolcraft) Am. J. Sci. **69**: 232.
Coal Companies, and their Growth. Bank. M. (N. Y.) **31**: 925.
Coal Deposit in Brandon, Vt. (E. Hitchcock) Am. J. Sci. **65**: 95.
Coal Dust a dangerous Element in Mining. (H. C. Hovey) Am. J. Sci. **122**: 18.
— Burning. Ecl. Engin. **1**: 750.
Coal Dust, Compressed, as Fuel. Pract. M. **6**: 166.
— Utilization of. (E. F. Loiseau) Ecl. Engin. **6**: 261. *See also* Coal Waste.
Coal Fever. (C. B. Conant) Hunt, **52**: 349.
Coal Field, Alleghany, Ohio and West Virginia Sides of. (E. B. Andrews) Am. J. Sci. **110**: 283.
— of Bristol County, and of Rhode Island. (E. Hitchcock) Am. J. Sci. **66**: 327.
Coal Fields, American. (H. D. Rogers) J. Frankl. Inst. **63**: 363.
— and Mines. Hunt, **31**: 765.
— — Life and Labor in. Cornh. **5**: 343, 426.
— in China, Anthracite and bituminous. (R. C. Taylor) J. Frankl. Inst. **40**: 51.
— Lesley's Manual of. J. Frankl. Inst. **63**: 70.
— of East Indian Archipelago. Am. J. Sci. **73**: 157.
— of Great Britain. Belgra. **5**: 555. — Ed. R. **117**: 406. — Chamb. J. **35**: 164. Same art. Ecl. M. **53**: 176. — Nature, **6**: 283. — Pract. M. **1**: 417. *See above*, Coal in Great Britain.
— of North America and Great Britain. Ed. R. **111**: 68.
— of the North Pacific. Ecl. Engin. **2**: 478.
— of Ohio Valley. (S. P. Hildreth) Am. J. Sci. **29**: 1.
— of Pennsylvania. (H. M. Alden) Harper, **27**: 455. — (E. Bowen) Harper, **15**: 451. — (B. Silliman) Am. J. Sci. **10**: 331. — (M. C. Lea) Hunt, **13**: 67. — (J. Peirce) Am. J. Sci. **12**: 54.
— — Bear Valley. (W. R. Johnson) J. Frankl. Inst. **32**: 318. — Hunt, **14**: 141.
— — Cumberland. Bank. M. (N. Y.) **4**: 394.
— — First. (M. C. Lea) Hunt, **13**: 426.
— — Lackawanna and Wyoming. (J. H. Lanman) Hunt, **19**: 290. — (B. Silliman) Am. J. Sci. **42**: 369. — J. Frankl. Inst. **46**: 280.
— — — Visit to. Knick. **15**: 102.
— — Produce of, 1820–72. Bank. M. (N. Y.) **27**: 721.
— — Region of Schuylkill and Wyoming Valley. Hunt, **14**: 539.
— of Russia. Lippinc. **21**: 361.
— of South Staffordshire. (F. Burr) J. Frankl. Inst. **26**: 375. — Once a Week, **6**: 148.
— of the United States. Penny M. **7**: 227.
— of World, Dimensions of. J. Frankl. Inst. **75**: 421.
— of Wyoming Ter. (E. D. Cope) Am. Natural. **6**: 669.
— of Yorkshire. Chamb. J. **46**: 531.
Coal Fire, True Story of. House. Words, **1**: 26–90.
Coal Formation of China, Age of. (J. S. Newberry) Am. J. Sci. **92**: 151.
Coal Formations of North America. (L. Lesquereux) Am. J. Sci. **78**: 21. **80**: 63, 367. **82**: 15, 193. **83**: 206. **85**: 375.
— of Nova Scotia. (A. Gesner) J. Frankl. Inst. **37**: 399.
— Rocky Mountain, Age of. (L. Lesquereux) Am. J. Sci. **116**: 441.
— United States. U. S. Lit. Gaz. **1**: 307.
Coal Measures. Chamb. J. **28**: 245.
— Exogenous Structures amongst. (W. C. Williamson) Nature, **4**: 408, 490
— in the Southeast of England. (J. Prestwick) Pop. Sci. R. **11**: 225.
— of Cape Breton. (J. P. Lesley) Am. J. Sci. **86**: 179.
— of Indiana. (E. T. Cox) Am. Natural. **5**: 547.
— of Iowa. (C. A. White) Am. J. Sci. **95**: 331.
— of Ohio and Illinois. (R. P. Stevens) Am. J. Sci. **76**: 72.
— Origin of Vegetation of. (J. T. B. Beaumont) J. Frankl. Inst. **29**: 205.
— Plant Remains in. (L. Lesquereux) Am. Natural. **5** 340.
— Tree Ferns of. (W. Carruthers) Nature, **6**: 486.
Coal Mine, Descent into a. Chamb. J. **28**: 110.
— Fire in. All the Year, **5**: 107. — Liv. Age, **30**: 32.
— Hartley, Catastrophe at. Chamb. J. **37**: 215.

Coal Mine, Hour in. Chamb. J. **32**: 343.
Coal Mines. Mo. R. **84**: 311. — Penny M. **4**: 120, 161.
— Accidents in. (J. R. Leifchild) Good Words, **3**: 137. — Brit. Q. **25**: 86. — Ecl. R. **100**: 192. — Ed. R. **125**: 549.
— and Colliers. (Lord Ashley) Quar. **70**: 158. Same art. Am. Ecl. **4**: 316. — Appleton, **1**: supp. — Ev. Sat. **10**: 172–240.
— Fire-Damp in. Cornh. **5**: 426.
— — Explosions of. Chamb. J. **19**: 232. **39**: 72. Same art. Liv. Age, **37**: 758. — Nature, **10**: 224. — J. Frankl. Inst. **43**: 347, 427.
— — — and their Cure. (S. Plimsoll) 19th Cent. **8**: 895. — (J. H. Merivale and Col. Shakespear) 19th Cent. **9**: 237.
— — — and the Weather, Connection between. Nature, **5**: 504. — Pract. M. **5**: 188.
— — — Are they preventible? (F. R. Conder) Fraser, **99**: 557.
— — — Causes and Prevention of. (A. H. Green) Pop. Sci. R. **12**: 14. — Nature, **24**: 512.
— — — Plimsoll's Cure for. (W. Galloway) Nature, **23**: 171.
— — — Prevention of. (J. Harrison) Ecl. Engin. **10**: 272. — (F. R. Conder) Fraser, **99**: 557. Same art. Pop. Sci. Mo. **15**: 200.
— — — Report on Causes of. J. Frankl. Inst. **54**: 323. *See also* Fire-Damp.
— Fires in, Extinction of. Chamb. J. **15**: 399. — J. Frankl. Inst. **48**: 152.
— Gases in. (J. J. Atkinson) Ecl. Engin. **12**: 17.
— Life in. (T. H. Walton) Lippinc. **3**: 517. — Quar. **110**: 329. — Chamb. J. **58**: 577.
— — and Death in. Lond. Q. **5**: 30.
— near Richmond, Va. (A. S. Woolridge) Am. J. Sci. **43**: 1.
— New System of sinking. Ecl. Engin. **16**: 293.
— Northumberland and Durham, 1840. Mo. R. **154**: 136.
— of Alabama. De Bow, **10**: 73.
— of Belgium. (R. C. Taylor) Hunt, **16**: 235, 327.
— of France. Ed. Philos. J. **14**: 252.
— of Sweden. Ecl. Engin. **7**: 240
— of the U. S. (F. M. Lubbren) Intel. Obs. **11**: 34.
— Shafts of. (Sheafer Bros.) J. Frankl. Inst. **84**: 393.
— Temperature of. Ecl. Engin. **2**: 614.
— Ventilation of. (G. G. Andre) Ecl. Engin. **19**: 369. — J. Frankl. Inst. **39**: 366.
— Working and Ventilation of. Ecl. Engin. **2**: 255.
Coal-Miner's Evidence. House. Words, **2**: 245.
Coal-Miners at Home and at Work. (J. R. Leifchild) Good Words, **3**: 213.
— History of Pit Geordie. Once a Week, **17**: 710, 736.
— How to teach and preach to. Liv. Age, **33**: 261.
— in England. Ecl. R. **76**: 201.
— in the North of England. Temp. Bar, **4**: 454.
— — Manners of. Penny M. **5**: 242.
— of Carrick. (A. Geikie) Good Words, **14**: 306.
— of South Wales. All the Year, **34**: 52.
— Plea for. All the Year, **3**: 102.
Coal-Mining. Ecl. Engin. **1**: 23.
— Improvements in. Ecl. Engin. **1**: 501.
— in deep Workings. Ecl. Engin. **3**: 270.
— Perils in. All the Year, **5**: 61. — (P. Bevan) Fortn. **3**: 617. — Ev. Sat. **1**: 212. — Temp. Bar. **1**: 258.
— The Possible in. Ecl. Engin. **11**: 26.
— Relative Safety of Modes of. Ecl. Engin. **3**: 263.
— Sinking the Shaft. Temp. Bar, **5**: 102.
Coal-Mining Districts, In. Temp. Bar, **3**: 132. **4**: 454.
— Life in. Ecl. R. **116**: 80.
Coal-Pit, Adventure in. Chamb. J. **52**: 213.
— and the People in it. Ecl. M. **24**: 249.
— Visit to. All the Year, **19**: 112, 327.
Coal-Pit Accidents. All the Year, **19**: 568.
Coal-Pit Cabin, In the. Chamb. J. **35**: 154.
Coal-Pit Catastrophes and Rescues. Chamb. J. **46**: 298.
Coal Plants, New and interesting. (E. B. Andrews) Am. J. Sci. **110**: 462.
Coal Policy of Pennsylvania. Hunt, **13**: 242.
Coal Question, American View of. Pract. M. **2**: 219.
Coal Seam. (E. B. Andrews) Am. J. Sci. **88**: 194.
Coal Seams, Parallelism of. (J. S. Newberry) Am. J. Sci. **107**: 367. — (E. B. Andrews) Am. J. Sci. **108**: 56.
Coal Strike, 1871. (J. B. Hodgkin) Nation, **12**: 254. — (E. L. Godkin) Nation, **12**: 352.
Coal-Tar and its Products. (E. J. Mills) Stud. & Intel. Obs. **5**: 69, 198.
— Coloring Matters from. (M. E. Kopp) J. Frankl. Inst. **72**: 181–409. — Once a Week, **25**: 194.
Coal Trade of England. Westm. **40**: 392. — Ed. R. **51**: 176. — Mo. R. **123**: 443.
— — Statistics of, 1846. J. Frankl. Inst. **42**: 266.
— of London. Bank. M. (N. Y.) **4**: 898.
— of Pennsylvania. Hunt, **4**: 375. — (F. Hunt) Hunt, **8**: 544. — (C. G. Childs) Hunt, **16**: 202, 327. — (C. Cushing) No. Am. **42**: 241. — Bank. M. (N. Y.) **3**: 146.
— — Statistics of, 1846. J. Frankl. Inst. **42**: 124.
— of Schuylkill, Penn. Hunt, **25**: 644.
— of United States. (J. E. Bloomfield) Hunt, **11**: 541. — (J. Blunt) Hunt, **4**: 62. — (F. Hunt) Hunt, **21**: 266. — Bank. M. (N. Y.) **9**: 467.
Coal Waste, Utilization of. (W. H. Wahl) J. Frankl. Inst. **94**: 419. — J. Frankl. Inst. **96**: 266, 356. — Pract. M. **2**: 409.
Coal-Whipping. Chamb. J. **19**: 170.
Coals, Comparative Value of. (C. B. Stuart) J. Frankl. Inst. **54**: 217.
— Experiments on various, 1871. (B. F. Isherwood) J. Frankl. Inst. **93**: 392. **94**: 31, 115, 178.
— for the Steam Navy. J. Frankl. Inst. **49**: 52.
— Free and cheap. Ecl. R. **99**: 668.
— in the Pool. All the Year, **35**: 129.
— Japanese, Evaporative Efficiency of. J. Frankl. Inst. **70**: 185.
— Russian. (B. F. Isherwood) J. Frankl. Inst. **97**: 404.
— Skore-Cases in. (J. W. Dawson) Am. J. Sci. **101**: 256.
Coalbrookdale. (G. Hill) Sharpe, **38**: 17.
Coalition Ministry proposed, Eng., 1840. Ecl. R **72**: 589.
Coast Defense; Iron-plated Forts, etc. Cornh. **17**: 189. **18**: 181.
Coast Defenses and Rifle Corps. No. Brit. **32**: 26.
— Military Discussion on. Blackw. **63**: 362.
— and F. Thurot (J. K. Laughton) Fraser, **97**: 71. Same art. Liv. Age, **137**: 613.
Coast-Guard, Tales of. Chamb. J. **15**: 369. **16**: 19, 66, 225.
Coast Survey of United States (M. J. Lamb) Harper, **58**: 506. — (C. H. Davis) Am. Alma. **1848**: 65. — (Mr. Ferguson) No. Am. **42**: 75. — (C. H. Davis) No. Am. **54**: 446. — (J. D. Whitney) No. Am. **121**: 37. — (B. Silliman) Am. J. Sci. **49**: 229. — Am J. Sci. **55**: 307. **62**: 158. — (J. Henry) Princ. **17**: 321. — Hunt, **21**: 266. — Am. J. Educ. **1**: 103.
— — and Telegraphic Operations. (S. C. Walker) Am. J. Sci. **59**: 151.
— — Costs, Abuses, and Power of, 1858. J. Frankl. Inst. **67**: 63.
— — Measurement of Base Lines in Florida. (F. Rogers) J. Frankl. Inst. **60**: 361.
— — Operations and Results of. Am. J. Sci. **75**: 75, 249.
— — Report on, 1839. (F. R. Hassler) J. Frankl. Inst. **29**: 91.
— — — 1847. J. Frankl. Inst. **45**: 213, 229.
— — — 1848–50. J. Frankl. Inst. **47**: 141, 209. **51**: 359.

Coast Survey of United States, Report on, 1849. (A. D. Bache) J. Frankl. Inst. **50**: 83, 145, 217.
— — — 1861 and 1862. Am. J. Sci. **87**: 95.
Coasting Trade and Internal Commerce. Niles's Reg. **41**: supp. 54.
Coastwise. (E. Downey) Tinsley, **26**: 440.
Coati, The. Penny M. **6**: 6.
— and its Cousins. (S. Lockwood) Pop. Sci. Mo. **2**: 136.
Cob. Chamb. J. **28**: 14.
Cobb, David, with portrait. (F. Baylies) N. E. Reg. **18**: 5.
Cobb, Howell, with portrait. Dem. R. **25**: 266. **41**: 131.
Cobb, Joseph B., with portrait. Am. Whig R. **13**: 113.
Cobb, T. R. R. (R. K. Porter) Land We Love, **3**: 183.
Cobbe, Frances P. (J. W. Chadwick) Chr. Exam. **83**: 265.
— Broken Lights. (S. Winkworth) Victoria, **3**: 193. — Mo. Rel. M. **32**: 283.
Cobbett, William. Blackw. **14**: 312. — (H. C. Lodge) Internat. R. **8**: 67. — Westm. **23**: 450. — with portrait, Fraser, **12**: 207, 430. — Mus. **4**: 23. — Niles's Reg. **14**: 170. — Cornh. **39**: 427. Same art. Liv. Age, **141**: 323. — Liv. Age, **40**: 121. — Ecl. M. **33**: 412. — Month, **36**: 296. — Ed. R. **149**: 458. Same art. Liv. Age, **141**: 457. — Liv. Age, **41**: 61. — Fraser, **76**: 474. Same art. Liv. Age, **95**: 387. — Mo. R. **138**: 221.
— Comedies of. (G. A. Sala) Belgra. **25**: 465.
— Letter on Tariff. Niles's Reg. **35**: 105.
— Life and Writings of. Tait, n. s. **2**: 491, 583.
— on Corn. Westm. **11**: 54.
— on Cottage Economy. (F. Jeffrey) Ed. R. **38**: 105.
— Political Register. (F. Jeffrey) Ed. R. **10**: 386.
— Political Writings. Ecl. M. **67**: 410.
— A rural Ride. (G. S. Venables and H. Lushington) Macmil. **1**: 40.
Cobbler Keezar's Vision. (J. G. Whittier) Atlan. **7**: 165.
Cobbler of Dort. Bentley, **1**: 403.
Cobbs, Bishop Nicholas H. Am. Church R. **20**: 543.
Cobden, Richard. (A. V. Dicey) Nation, **26**: 13. — (A. L. Chapin) Dial (Ch.), **2**: 206. — (T. C. B. Fraser) New Dom. **19**: 509. — with portrait, Peop. J. **2**: 43. — (Goldwin Smith) Macmil. **12**: 90. — Brit. Q. **43**: 1. Same art. Ecl. M. **66**: 393. Same art. Liv. Age, **88**: 612. — with portrait, Ecl. M. **61**: 395. — St. Paul's, **6**: 262. Same art. Ecl. M. **75**: 129.
— and the Land Question. (R. A. Arnold) Fraser, **76**: 79.
— and Peace and War Agitators. Blackw. **66**: 581.
— and the Peace Congress. Ecl. R. **97**: 589.
— First Pamphlets of. Fortn. **35**: 634.
— Grave of. All the Year, **13**: 342.
— Mission of. (J. P. Edwards) Howitt, **3**: 200 — Lord Hobart) Macmil. **15**: 177. Same art. Liv. Age, **92**: 323.
— Morley's Life of. Blackw. **130**: 793.
— Political Writings of. No. Brit. **46**: 77. Same art. Ecl. M. **68**: 649.
— To, and other public Men in Search of Work. (T. Hughes) Macmil. **4**: 329.
Cobham, Sir John Oldcastle, Lord, Life and Times of. Ecl. R. **80**: 249.
Cobham Hall, Kent. Penny M. **5**: 260.
— Summer Day at. (E. L. Blanchard) Peop. J. **6**: 90.
Coblow Cataract. So. Lit. Mess. **16**: 439.
Cobra de Capello. Bentley, **33**: 155.
— Cure for Bite of. Ev. Sat. **9**: 242.
— of India. Chamb. J. **53**: 822.
Coccium, Situation of. (J. Watson) Arch. **1**: 65.
Cochin China. (J. C. Gray) No. Am. **18**: 140.
— and Cambodia. Quar. **116**: 283.
— Barrow's Voyage to. (F. Jeffrey) Ed. R. **9**: 1.
— French. Temp. Bar, **14**: 38. Same art. Cath. World, **1**: 369. Same art. Ecl. M. **64**: 726.
— French in. (H. A. Browne) Fraser, **94**: 181.
Cochin China, French in, in 1859. Colburn, **116**: 1.
— Language of. (J. Pickering) No. Am. **52**: 404.
— Subjugation of. Colburn, **131**: 127.
— White's Voyage to. Ed. R. **41**: 123. — Mo. R. **106**: 337.
Cochineal, Cultivation of. Hogg, **3**: 132.
Cochineal Insect, and its Produce. Penny M. **10**: 455.
Cochran, Jane, Lady Kilsyth. Once a Week, **17**: 402.
Cochran, Dr. John, with portrait. (W. L. C. Biddle) Pennsyl. M. **3**: 241.
Cochrane, Alex. Baillie. Young Italy. Bentley, **28**: 298. — Quar. **87**: 533.
Cochrane, Grisell. Chamb. J. **51**: 577.
Cochrane, J. D. Pedestrian Journey to Russia. Quar. **31**: 215.
Cochrane, T., Lord. *See* Dundonald, Earl.
Cock, Chapter on the. Knick. **58**: 217.
Cock and Anchor, The. Dub. Univ. **26**: 607.
Cocks and Hens. Chamb. J. **36**: 382.
Cock-Fight, The. (W. L. Tidball) Putnam, **4**: 310.
— in Havana. Knick. **45**: 40.
Cock-Fighting, Memoir on. (S. Pegge) Arch. **3**: 132
— Modest Commendation of. Blackw. **22**: 587.
— Royal Cockpit. (E. Herbert) Lond. M. **6**: 389.
Cockaigne, State Council of. Blackw. **13**: 34.
Cockatoo Islands. Chamb. J. **41**: 830.
Cockburn, Sir Alexander. Lond. Soc. **11**: 86. Same art. Ecl. M. **68**: 280. — (A. V. Dicey) Internat. R. **10**: 397.
— and C. Cushing. (S. T. Wallis) So. M. **12**: 635.
Cockburn, Henry, Lord, Journal of. Quar. **148**: 255. (J. Moncrieff) Ed. R. **140**: 259.
— Memorials of his Times. (T. Durfee) Chr. R. **22**: 60. — Bentley, **40**: 45. Same art. Ecl. M. **39**: 52. — Brit. Q. **24**: 343. — Chamb. J. **25**: 394. — Dub. R. **41**: 279. — Fraser, **54**: 79. — Liv. Age, **50**: 260. — New Q. **5**: 337. — No. Brit. **26**: 228.
Cocked-Hat Gentry. (J. E. Cooke) Putnam, **3**: 261.
Cocker, Edward. "According to Cocker." All the Year, **23**: 590.
— and his Arithmetic. Once a Week, **17**: 324.
Cockney, Archæology of the Word. Chamb. J. **3**: 225.
— Etymology of the Word. Dub. Univ. **74**: 308.
— Meaning of. Sharpe, **5**: 102, 126.
— What is a? (C. Waddy) St. James, **33**: 124.
Cockney Writers. Lond. M. **3**: 69.
Cockney's Rural Sports. Lond. M. **6**: 498.
Cockroach, The, on Shipboard. Chamb. J. **10**: 14.
— Only a. (J. G. Wood) Good Words, **20**: 628.
Cockroaches. (S. H. Scudder) Am. Natural. **10**: 521.
Coca Leaf, The, as a Stimulant. Cornh. **6**: 713.
Cocoa. (J. R. Jackson) Nature, **2**: 497. — Penny M. **2**: 119. — Blackw. **75**: 86.
— Wanklyn's Treatise on. Pract. M. **4**: 234.
Cocoanut and its Uses. (J. R. Jackson) Once a Week, **12**: 485.
— Carving a. Cornh. **36**: 461.
Cocoanut Day. (Mrs. Postans) Sharpe, **7**: 32.
Cocoanut Fiber. Art J. **21**: 74.
Cocoanut Palm and its Uses. (C. R. Low) Pop. Sci. Mo. **2**: 214.
Cocoa Plantation in the West Indies. (M. R. S. Ross) Belgra. **26**: 230.
Cocoa-Tree, and its Products. Penny M. **3**: 116.
— of Solomon. Chamb. J. **17**: 405.
Cocquerel, A. *See* Coquerel.
Cod, Cape, Formation of. (W. Upham) Am. Natural. **13**: 489, 552.
— Ship Channel across. (J. P. Frizell) J. Frankl. Inst. **91**: 386. **92**: 41.
Cod Fishery. (A. H. Baldwin) Once a Week, **7**: 596. — All the Year, **13**: 508.
— in Iceland. Chamb. J. **54**: 662.
— in Labrador. Penny M. **4**: 67.

Cod Fishery on the Banks. (W.V.Wells) Harper, **22**: 456.
— on the Coast of Norway. Penny M. **8**: 310, 326.
— Pacific Coast. (C. M. Scammon) Overland, **4**: 436.
Coddington, William, Governor of Rhode Island, 1640. Am Q. Reg. **15**: 25. — N. E. Reg. **28**: 13.
Code Napoleon. Walsh Am. R. **2**: 359. — (E. Everett) No. Am. **20**: 393. — U. S. Lit. Gaz. **5**: 125. — Niles's Reg. **28**: 303.
Codes, and Arrangement of Law. Am. Law R. **5**: 1.
— Ancient Ideas in Arrangement of. (Sir H. S. Maine) Fortn. **31**: 761.
Codex Sinaiticus, etc. *See* Bible, New Testament, Greek.
Codification. For. Q. **6**: 322. — (T. Walker) West. Law J. **1**: 433. — (W. Van Hamm) West. Law J. **1**: 529. — (H. Brougham) West. Law J. **2**: 32.
— Bentham on. Westm. **12**: 430. — (H. S. Legaré) So. R. **7**: 391. — (Sir S. Romilly) Ed. R. **29**: 217.
— in India and England. (J. F. Stephen) Fortn. **18**: 644.
— of the Law. Lond. Q. **24**: 432.
Codlingbury Races. Chamb. J. **43**: 497.
Codman, John. (L. Capen) Chr. Exam. **59**: 203. — (J. H. Means) Cong. Q. **2**: 1.
— Sermon of. Lit. & Theo. R. **4**: 33.
— Visit to England. Chr. R. **1**: 286. — (J. Walker) Chr. Exam. **20**: 265. — Cong. M. **19**: 612, 685.
Codrington, Admiral Henry John. (J. L. Laughton) Fraser, **103**: 73.
Coeducation of the Sexes. (J. H. Fairchild) Am. J. Educ. **17**: 385. — (W. F. Allen) Nation, **10**: 134. — (E. L. Godkin) Nation, **16**: 349.
— — at Antioch College. Nation, **11**: 24.
— — at Michigan Univ. (M. C. Tyler) Nation, **11**: 383.
— — in College. (A. C. Brackett) Educ. **1**: 156.
See Women, Education of.
Cœlebs in Search of a Bed. Dub. Univ. **27**: 624.
Cœlebs in Search of a Mulready Envelope. Lond. Soc. **7**: 29.
Cœur, Jaques. Penny M. **11**: 75.
Coercion, Policy of. (W. T. Stead) Fortn. **34**: 245.
Coeymans, N. Y., Reminiscences of. (J. Munsell) Am. Bibliop. **7**: 202.
Coffee. (J. R. Jackson) Nature, **2**: 126. — Blackw. **75**: 86. — House. Words, **5**: 562. — Penny M. **1**: 49. — (J. von Liebig) Pop. Sci. R. **5**: 12.
— and Coffee Trade. Hunt, **27**: 39. — (J. Gardner) Hunt, **41**: 165.
— and Crumpets; a Poem. Fraser, **15**: 316.
— and its Adulteration in New York. (J. C. Draper) Galaxy, **7**: 198.
— and Milk as Diet. (D. A. Caron) J. Frankl. Inst. **64**: 349.
— as a Beverage. (A. T. Dalson and C. M. Wetherill) J. Frankl. Inst. **60**: 60, 111.
— Culture of. (J. J. Peatfield) Overland, **13**: 323.
— — in Brazil. (H. H. Smith) Scrib. **19**: 225. — Penny M. **9**: 484.
— — in Ceylon. House. Words, **3**: 109. — (R. Abbay) Nature, **14**: 375.
— — in South Travancore. Fraser, **90**: 64.
— Culture and Use of. (M. S. de Vere) Harper, **44**: 237.
— Cup of. All the Year, **20**: 476.
— — Chemistry of. (J. von Liebig) Ev. Sat. **1**: 135.
— History of. (J. Crawford) J. Statis. Soc. **15**: 50. — (M. Heilprin) Nation, **6**: 275.
— — and Cultivation of. Godey, **54**: 51.
— How to make a Cup of. Godey, **63**: 107. — Sharpe, **44**: 259.
— in its Home. (J. D. Beugless) Overland, **2**: 319.
— Preparation of, for Use. Penny M. **3**: 228.
— Price, Import, and Consumption of. De Bow, **20**: 253.
— Production and Consumption of. (J. Gardner) Hunt, **29**: 194.
— Properties of. (D. W. Cheever) Atlan. **3**: 35.
Coffee, Reduction of Duties on. Ed. R. **41**: 488.
— Wanklyn's Treatise on. Pract. M. **4**: 234.
See Chicory.
Coffee Diseases, Two. (M. C. Cooke) Pop. Sci. R. **15**: 161.
Coffee Grounds of Cuba. All the Year, **24**: 61.
Coffee-House Movement. Chamb. J. **56**: 143.
Coffee-House News. Lond. M. **20**: 563.
Coffee-Houses. (J. Humphreys) St. James, **43**: 598.
— and their Clubs in 18th Century. (A. Andrews) Colburn, **106**: 107.
— of the Restoration. Tait, n. s. **22**: 104. Same art. Ecl. M. **34**: 500.
Coffee-Leaf Disease of Ceylon. (D. Morris) Nature, **20**: 557.
Coffee-Leaf Miner. (B. P. Mann) Am. Natural. **6**: 332, 596.
Coffee Palaces. (H. A. Page) Good Words, **18**: 678.
— English. (W. Sikes) Lippinc. **24**: 728.
Coffee Planter in Southern India, Experiences of. Fraser, **99**: 703.
Coffee Rooms for the People. (Lady Hope) Good Words, **21**: 749, 844.
Coffee Trade. (J. Gardner) West. J. **7**: 301. — Hunt, **13**: 273. — (J. Gardner) Hunt, **25**: 690. Same art. Liv. Age, **27**: 254. — (J. S. Duke) De Bow, **2**: 303.
— in 1850. Hunt, **23**: 59, 172, 451.
Coffer-Dam at Turner's Falls. (J. B. Francis) J. Frankl. Inst. **83**: 317.
— Description of a. Penny M. **5**: 273.
— — of portable, 1860. (E. B. Hunt) J. Frankl. Inst. **70**: 375. **73**: 145. — (T. Stevenson) J. Frankl. Inst. **46**: 217.
Coffer-Dams in Connecticut River. (W. H. Burrall) Ecl. Engin. **14**: 366.
— Relative Economy of. Ecl. Engin. **4**: 166.
— Structures in the Sea without. (D. Miller) J. Frankl Inst. **75**: 371.
— used on the Thames Embankment. Ecl. Engin. **4**: 307.
Coffeyville, Kansas. Chamb. J. **55**: 93.
Coffin, James Henry. Pop. Sci. Mo. **3**: 503.
Coffin, Levi. Chamb. J. **55**: 321. — Internat. R. **9**: 143.
Coffin Family. Am. Hist. Rec. **1**: 8. **2**: 14, 64, 175.
— Name and Armorial Bearings of. (J. C. J. Brown) N. E. Reg. **35**: 376.
— Pedigree of. Hist. M. **14**: 132.
— Records of. Canad. Mo. **8**: 215.
Coffin Genealogy. (N. W. Coffin) N. E. Reg. **2**: 336. — N. E. Reg. **24**: 149, 305.
Coffins, Material for. (W. Chambers) Chamb. J. **52**: 465.
— of Oak found in Northumberland. (T. W. Snagge) Arch. **44**: 8.
Coffin Flowers; a Poem. (A. Young) Cath. World, **21**: 589.
Coffin-Maker, The. Colburn, **34**: 257.
Cog-Wheels, Teeth of. (E. W. Blake) Am. J. Sci. **7**: 86.
Cogers, or Thoughtful Men. All the Year, **19**: 231.
Cogitation, Theory of. (E. Zeller) J. Spec. Philos. **9**: 33.
Cogitations of Mrs. Clarinda Singleheart. Sharpe, **20**: 129–342.
Cogito, ergo sum. (W. G. Davies) Mind, **2**: 412. — (S. H. Hodgson and A. Main) Mind, **2**: 126.
— Matthew Arnold on. (S. H. Hodgson) Mind, **1**: 568
— Meaning of Existence. (A. Bain) Mind, **2**: 259.
Cognition, Psychology of, Jardine on. (D. A. Spalding) Nature, **11**: 422.
Cogswell, Joseph G. (J. G. Wilson) Appleton, **7**: 19.
Cohasset, Mass., Flint's History of the Church of. Chr. Disc. **4**: 121.
— Ministers of. Am. Q. Reg. **8**: 48.
Cohesion and Crushing. Ecl. Engin. **14**: 558.
— Gravitation. (M. Faraday) J. Frankl. Inst. **70**: 103, 169.
Cohesive Attraction. (J. D. Dana) Am. J. Sci. **55**: 100.

Coif, Order of the. Ed. R. **146**: 435.
Coiffeur, The first, of his Age. Chamb. J. **46**: 193.
Coiffeur of Sevres; a Revolutionary Sketch. Dub. Univ. **24**: 412.
Coignard, Pierre. Liv. Age, **42**: 598.
Coignet-Béton. (C. K. Graham) Ecl. Engin. **13**: 203.
Coil-Machine, Ruhmkorff's. (R. Bithell) Recr. Sci. **3**: 202.
Coilin, Duc de. Fraser, **32**: 330.
Coin of Basilis, a City in Arcadia. (T. Combe) Arch. **18**: 344.
— of Nerva, Dissertation on a. (G. Ashby) Arch. **3**: 165.
— of Prince Edmund. (S. Pegge) Arch. **4**: 190.
— of Robert, Earl of Gloucester. (J. Colebrooke) Arch. **4**: 132.
Coin-Current. All the Year, **37**: 294.
Coins, American. (W. C. Prime) Harper, **20**: 468.
— — First. Hist. M. **3**: 197.
— — previous to 1792. Hist. M. **1**: 297.
— — Washington Cents. Hist. M. **1**: 302.
— Ancient and modern, Catalogue of. (H. Scadding) Canad. J. n. s. **9**: 105, 226.
— and Coinage. (W. C. Prime) Harper, **20**: 326.
— — of the United States. Bank. M. (N. Y.) **10**: 614.
— and Medals. Nat. M. **4**: 18, 1826.
— — Ancient, Walsh on. Mo. R. **114**: 457. — Ecl. R. **47**: 37.
— and Tradesmen's Tokens. Antiquary, **4**: 165, 191.
— Anglo-Saxon, discovered at Hexham. (J. Adamson) Arch: **25**: 279. **26**: 346.
— — minted at Derby. (J. S. Doxey) Reliquary, **15**: 129.
— British, found at High Wycombe. (J. Norris) Arch. **22**: 297.
— — Places where they have been found. (J. Y. Akerman) Arch. **33**: 177.
— Cardwell and Akerman on. Quar. **72**: 356. Same art. Ecl. M. **3**: 397.
— Castorland Half-Dollar. (F. B. Hough) Hist. M. **4**: 33.
— Coinage, and Bullion. Bank. M. (N. Y.) **28**: 873.
— Copper, of Vermont. (P. H. White) Hist. M. **13**: 32.
— Cufic, Origin and Use of. (S. Weston) Arch. **18**: 309.
— Curious. Arch. **16**: 272–278.
— discovered in the River Dove near Tutbury. (E. Hawkins) Arch. **24**: 148.
— Eckfeldt and Du Bois on. (C. F. Adams) No. Am. **56**: 208.
Episcopal and monastic. (B. Bartlet) Arch. **5**: 335.
— Foreign Report on. Niles's Reg. **23**: 379.
— found near the Church of S. Mary Hill, London. (G. Griffith) Arch. **4**: 356.
— found in Southern India. (Sir A. Carlisle) Arch. **21**: 1.
— found at Fenwick Castle (O. S. Brereton) Arch. **5**: 160.
— French. Hunt, **5**: 379.
— Gold, of Charles I. (M. Noble) Arch. **13**: 23.
— Greek. (H. V. Tebbs) Portfo. **6**: 26, 35. — (S. Weston and S. B. Howes) Arch. **16**: 9, 14. — Blackw. **79**: 193. — Ed. R. **104**: 161. — Ev. Sat. **15**: 440.
— Jewish. (H. N. Humphreys) Intel. Obs. **4**: 328, 442.
— — and Hebrew Palæography. Theo. R. **5**: 244.
— Manual of Gold and Silver. Hunt, **7**: 267.
— Massachusetts Shilling. (W. Kelby) Hist. M. **15**: 115.
— Mickley Collection. Hist. M. **12**: 113.
— Noted, Origin of. Bank. M. (N. Y.) **26**: 283.
— of Cymbeline and other British Princes. (H. N. Humphreys) Recr. Sci. **3**: 151, 263.
— of Edward I. and II., found at Wyke, Yorkshire. (F. Sharpe and D. H. Haigh) Arch. **28**: 47.
— of Edward III. (S. Pegge) Arch. **3**: 316.
— of England. Penny M. **5**: 275–324.
— — Old. Bank. M. (N. Y.) **28**: 617.
— of Great Britain, Lord Liverpool on. (H. Brougham) Ed. R. **7**: 265. — Ecl. R. **7**: 214, 312.
Coins of Seleucidæ, Kings of Syria. (H. N. Humphreys) Recr. Sci. **1**: 204.
— of William the Conqueror found at Beaworth. (E. Hawkins) Arch. **26**: 1.
— of the World and their Value. Potter Am. Mo. **9**: 145.
— Rare, and their Prices. Cornh. **16**: 576.
— Roman "Consecratio." (H. N. Humphreys) Recr. Sci. **1**: 45, 100.
— Roman Family. (F. P. Brewer) University Q. **2**: 218.
— Saxon Pennies found at Sevington, Wilts. (E. Hawkins) Arch. **27**: 301.
— Seyss Automatic Weighing and Sorting Machine for. (S. James) J. Frankl. Inst. **105**: 97.
— Silver, found at Tutbury, Staffordshire, 1831. Penny M. **3**: 430.
— — of Syracuse. (R. P. Knight) Arch. **19**: 369.
— Small Change. Chamb. J. **30**: 253.
— Tables of. Hunt, **1**: 79, 179, 282.
— Tokens and Abbey Pieces. Antiquary, **4**: 309.
— Weights and Measures. (J. D. Browne) Hunt, **4**: 434. — (J. B. D. De Bow) De Bow, **2**: 281.
Coin Adjusters, Mint. (A. B. Neal) Godey, **45**: 125.
Coin Collecting. (R. S. Poole) Once a Week, **5**: 576. **6**: 326.
Coin Dies, Manufacture of. (J. Newton) Recr. Sci. **2**: 200.
Coin Moulds, Roman. Penny M. **9**: 15.
Coinage. Am. Alma. **1840**: 157.
— British, Condemned. Chamb. J. **34**: 228.
— — Earliest. (H. N. Humphreys) Recr. Sci. **2**: 23, 160.
— Chancellor of Exchequer on. (B. Price) Contemp. **12**: 370.
— Coins and Bullion. Bank. M. (N.Y.) **8**: 736, 784, 887. **9**: 220–927. **16**: 840.
— Debasement of. (E. R. Leland) Pop. Sci. Mo. **12**: 580.
— Decimal. *See* Decimal Coinage.
— Defective State of English Silver. Colburn, **1**: 237.
— English and Foreign. Bank. M. (N. Y.) **27**: 972.
— Frauds in. Chamb. J. **53**: 30.
— Free, and a self-adjusting Ratio. (T. Balch) Penn Mo. **8**: 189.
— French System of. Bank. M. (N. Y.) **8**: 806.
— German. (G. Bradford) Nation, **22**: 294.
— Gold, Process of. (J. Newton) Recr. Sci. **3**: 234.
— History of. (R. Musket) Bank. M (N. Y.) **26**: 1.
— in Tower of London, 1469. (T. Combe) Arch. **15**: 164.
— International. (C. Meredith) Lippinc. **5**: 85. — (E. Seyd) J. Statis. Soc. **33**: 42. — (J. H. Gibbon) De Bow, **17**: 1. — (R. N. Toppan) Am. J. Soc. Sci. **11**: 82. — Bank. M. (N. Y.) **21**: 661. — (D. P. Bailey) Bank. M. (N. Y.) **35**: 339. — Ed. R. **124**: 383. Same art. Liv. Age, **91**: 591. — Hunt, **58**: 63, 139. — Nature, **8**: 229. — St. Paul's, **4**: 306.
— — and British Metallic Currency. (W. S. Jevons) J. Statis. Soc. **31**: 426.
— — Canadian Mint Bill, 1855. J. Frankl. Inst. **60**: 358.
— Loss on, from Abrasion. Bank. M. (L.) **12**: 167. — Chamb. J. **35**: 180. — Penny M. **11**: 335.
— New, of the World. Bank. M. (N. Y.) **28**: 553.
— New Bronze and old Copper. (J. Newton) Recr. Sci. **2**: 41.
— of America, Early Spanish and Portuguese. (J. C. Brevoort) M. Am. Hist. **2**: 334.
— — First. Hist. M. **1**: 225.
— — History of. (J. H. Hickcox) Bank. M. (N. Y.) **16**: 241, 321.
— of England. (S. Pegge) Arch. **5**: 390. — Chamb. J. **47**: 641.
— — and Monetary Conventions. (H. Goodwin) Liv. Age, **95**: 805.
— — History of. (A. De Morgan) Bank. M. (N. Y.) **10**: 936.
— of Great Britain. Bank. M. (N. Y.) **11**: 453.

Coinage of precious Metals. (J. V. C. Smith) Hunt, 5: 321.
— of United States. (R. Hare) Hunt, 27: 64. — Hunt, 10: 240.
— — 1792–1863. Bank. M. (N. Y.) 18: 554.
— — 1792–1870. Bank. M. (N. Y.) 25: 556.
— — Law of. Bank. M. (N. Y.) 32: 791, 873, 942.
— — — Act of 1873. (H. White) Nation, 25: 343. — Bank. M. (N. Y.) 27: 921.
— — Seigniorage on. (W. L. Hodge) West. J. 8: 331.
— — Silver. (F. A. Sawyer) Hunt, 42: 177.
— of United States Mint. Hunt, 37: 52.
— of the World. Hunt, 38: 302.
— Process of. (D. L. Riddell) Hunt, 14: 66.
— — and Statistics of. (D. L. Riddell) De Bow, 3: 528.
— Pyx-Trial of. Chamb. J. 44: 105.
— Regulation of, Lownde's Report. Niles's Reg. 16: 265.
— Report on. Bank. M. (N. Y.) 12: 711.
— Silver. (R. P. Bland and H. V. Poor) No. Am. 127: 117. — (J. S. Moore) No. Am. 124: 289.
— Statistics of. Hunt, 3: 85. 4: 382. 8: 90. 15: 202.
— Theory of. (J. B. Hodgskin) No. Am. 111: 78.
— Unification of. (C. F. McCoy) Bank. M. (N. Y.) 33: 176. — Hunt, 60: 248.
— Uniform. (J. H. Gibbon) Hunt, 31: 63. — (J. A. Tefft) Hunt, 41: 297.
Coincidence, A remarkable. (G. M. Beard) Pop. Sci. Mo. 15: 628.
Coincidences. Chamb. J. 47: 840.
— and Speculations. Cornh. 26: 679.
— Strange. Bentley, 14: 493.
— a Tale of Facts. Fraser, 36: 655. Same art. Liv. Age, 16: 149.
Coipus, The. Penny M. 5: 20.
Coit's Ridge. (A. B. Street) Ecl. M. 20: 255.
Coke, Sir Edward. (C. Cushing) No. Am. 13: 255. — Retros. 8: 105. — Brit. & For. R. 6: 564. — Mus. 5: 496.
— Johnson's Life of. Ecl. 67: 485. — Mo. R. 144: 392.
— Life of. Ed. R. 67: 461.
Coke, Thomas. (C. K. True) No. Am. 90: 181.
— Death of. Am. Meth. M. 1: 36.
— Etheridge's Life of. Lond. Q. 15: 227.
— Journal of Sixth Tour. Meth. M. 21: 313.
— Wesley's Ordination of. (A. Brunson) Meth. Q. 35: 579.
Coke, Anthracite Metallurgical. J. Frankl. Inst. 101: 274.
— Manufacture of. Ecl. Engin. 2: 516.
Cokesbury College, Some Account of. (W. Hamilton) Meth. Q. 19: 173.
Col du Géant, Passage of, from Chamounix, in 1862. Colburn, 127: 436.
Colbert, Jean Baptiste. St. Paul's, 3: 342. — Temp. Bar, 59: 89.
— and Richelieu, France under. Fraser, 75: 537. Same art. Ecl. M. 69: 78.
Colburn, Dana Pond. Am. J. Educ. 11: 289.
Colburn, Warren. (T. Edson) Am. J. Educ. 2: 294.
— Arithmetic. (G. B. Emerson) No. Am. 14: 381.
Colburn, Zerah. New Eng. 5: 342. — Anal. M. 1: 124. — Am. Alma. 1840: 307.
Colburn, Zerah, jr., Obituary of. (A. L. Holley) Ecl. Engin. 2: 654.
Colby University Library. (E W. Hall) Lib. J. 2: 68.
Colchester. (L. S. Costello) Bentley, 18: 62.
— Romans at. Quar. 97: 71.
Colchester, Lord, Diary of. Ed. R. 113: 360.
Colchis, and the German Colonies beyond the Caucasus. Westm. 54: 497.
Cold, Artificial Production of. (R. Walker) J. Frankl. Inst. 8: 396. — (H. Meidinger) J. Frankl. Inst. 101: 266, 347, 413. 102: 49, 135. — Liv. Age, 15: 55. — (A. Kirk) Ecl. Engin. 10: 447.
Cold, Curiosities of. Chamb. J. 35: 81. Same art. Ecl. M. 53: 121.
— Effects of, upon the Human Body. Penny M. 12: 238. — (J. C. Draper) Am. J. Sci. 104: 445.
— Nature and Phenomena of. (F. Winslow) Am. Ecl. 2: 113.
— What is a? Chamb. J. 58: 57. Same art. Ecl. M. 96: 833. — Potter Am. Mo. 17: 37. — Pop. Sci. Mo. 18: 801.
Colds and Cold Water. Tait, n. s. 17: 705. Same art. Liv. Age, 28: 353. — Godey, 50: 503.
— Waves of Heat and Waves of Death. (B. W. Richardson) Pop. Sci. R. 4: 180.
Cold Hands. (C. F. Guernsey) Lippinc. 8: 544.
Cold Harbor, Name of. (W. H. Smyth) Arch. 33: 125.
Cold Harbor, Va., Battle of, Gen. Smith's Report. Hist. M. 15: 240.
Cold Snap; a Tale. (E. Bellamy) Scrib. 10: 619.
Cold-Water Cure; a Story. Ev. Sat. 10: 119.
Colden, Cadwallader, with portrait. Hist. M. 9: 1.
— Letter to Governor of New York. Hist. M. 12: 226.
— Memoir of. Anal. M. 4: 307.
Coldengame, Curse of. Lond. M. 8: 621.
Coldstream Guards. All the Year, 30: 181.
— MacKinnon on. Colburn, 38: 337.
Cole, Sir Henry, with portrait. Pract. M. 7: 321.
— and the Schools of Design. Art J. 4: 103.
— Testimonial to. Nature, 8: 357.
Cole, Jonathan. (J. H. Morison) Unita. R. 9: 93.
Cole, Thomas. Nat. M. 4: 312. — (G. W. Greene) No. Am. 77: 302.
— Paintings of. Dem. R. 12: 598. — So. Lit. Mess. 15: 351.
Cole, Vicat. Art J. 22: 177.
Colebrooke, Henry Thomas. (F. Hall) Nation, 19: 125. — Ed. R. 136: 461.
Coleman Genealogy. (W. C. Folger) N. E. Reg. 12: 129.
Colenso, J. W. (O. S. Stearns) Chr. R. 28: 464. — Cong. 4: 118. — Theo. R. 4: 34.
— and Church of England. (F. P. Cobbe) Chr. Exam. 83: 1.
— and Gibbon. (W. Adams) Am. Presb. R. 14: 77.
— and Spinoza: the Bishop and the Philosopher. (M. Arnold) Macmil. 7: 241.
— Ciphering of, reciphered. Bost. R. 3: 578.
— Controversy on. (E. E. Hale) Chr. Exam. 75: 97.
— Convocation and. Macmil. 8: 249.
— Judgment in Case of. Lond. Q. 24: 492.
— upon Moses and Joshua. Bost. R. 3: 190.
— *vs.* Historical Christianity. (T. Richey) Am. Church R. 15: 90.
— Vindication of. (H. Rogers) Good Words, 4: 85, 205. *See* Bible, Pentateuch.
Coleridge, Hartley. (G. S. Hillard) Liv. Age, 21: 161. — Liv. Age, 29: 235, 555, 605. 30: 337. — Ed. R. 94: 64. Same art. Ecl. M. 24: 289. Same art. Liv. Age, 31: 1. — Ecl. M. 23: 44. — Nat. M. 1: 191. — Bentley, 45: 581. — Tait, n. s. 18: 267. Chamb. J. 16: 327.
— and his Genius. Internat. M. 3: 249.
— and Wordsworth. (J. Dawson, jr.) Macmil. 13: 232.
— as Man, Poet, and Essayist. Fraser, 43: 603. Same art. Ecl. M. 23: 357. Same art. Liv. Age, 30: 145.
— Life and Works of. Ecl. R. 93: 645.
— Lives of Northern Worthies. Prosp. R. 8: 514.
— Memoir of. Colburn, 92: 276.
— — and Poems. Chr. Rem. 22: 102. — Chr. Obs. 51: 529.
— Poems of. Am. Q. 20: 478. — Brit. Q. 15: 293.
— Reminiscences of. Macmil. 13: 31. Same art. Ecl. M. 66: 109. Same art. Liv. Age, 87: 433.
Coleridge, Herbert. (J. D. Coleridge) Macmil. 5: 56.
Coleridge, Sir John, and Mr. Buckle. (J. D. Coleridge) Fraser, 59: 635.

Coleridge, Samuel Taylor. (D. Curry) Meth. Q. **14**: 34. —(T. De Quincey) Tait, n. s. **1**: 509, 588, 685. **2**: 3. — (S. C. Hall) Art J. **17**: 49. Same art. Ecl. M. **64**: 657. — (J. S. Mill) Westm. **33**: 257. — (M. Valentine) Evang. R. **7**: 85. — (G. B. Cheever) No. Am. **40**: 299. — (H. T. Tuckerman) So. Lit. Mess. **7**: 177. — Dub. Univ. **6**: 1, 250. — (L. Withington) Chr. Q. Spec. **6**: 617. — (J. D. Whelpley) Am. Whig R. **10**: 532. — (L. H. Atwater) Princ. **20**: 143. — Brit. & For. R. **8**: 414. — with portrait, Fraser, **8**: 64. — Am. Q. **19**: 1. — with portrait, Hogg, **9**: 129, 158. — Bentley, **40**: 208. Same art. Ecl. M. **39**: 394. — Blackw. **110**: 552. Same art. Ecl. M. **78**: 138. Same art. Liv. Age, **111**: 643. — Canad. Mo. **13**: 362. — Nat. M. **1**: 289. — Colburn, **42**: 55. — No. Brit. **43**: 251. Same art. Liv. Age, **88**: 81, 161.

— Aids to Reflection. New York R. **6**: 477. Blackw. **44**: 135.

— Ancient Mariner. (G. Garrigues) J. Spec. Philos. **14**: 327.

— and American Disciples. (N. Porter) Bib. Sac. **4**: 117.

— and his Followers. (W. M. Hetherington) Ex. H. Lec. **8**: 407.

— and Opium Eating. (T. De Quincey) Blackw. **57**: 117.

— and present Theology. (J. Martineau) Nat. R. **3**: 449.

— and Robert Southey. Ed R. **87**: 368. Same art. Ecl. M. **14**: 195. Same art. Liv. Age, **17**: 310. — Chr. R. **15**: 321.

— as a Poet. Am. Presb. R. **4**: 80. — Quar. **125**: 78. Same art. Liv. Age, **98**: 515.

— as Poet and Man. (G. P. Lathrop) Atlan. **45**: 483.

— as a Thinker. (R. Turnbull) Chr. R. **19**: 321.

— Biographia Literaria. (W. Hazlitt) Ed. R. **28**: 488. — Mo. R. **88**: 124. — Blackw. **2**: 1, 285. **3**: 653.

— Christabel. Ed. R. **27**: 58. — Mo. R. **82**: 22.

— Coleridgeiana. Fraser, **11**: 50. — Mus. **26**: 359.

— Confessions of an Inquiring Spirit. Chr. Obs. **50**: 234.

— Cottle's Recollections of. Cong. M. **20**: 520. — Chr. Obs. **37**: 594, 632. **59**: 374. — (J. Foster) Ecl. R. **66**: 137. — Tait, n. s. **4**: 341.

— Country of. (M. Collins) Belgra. **12**: 197.

— Early Recollections of. Ecl. R. **66**: 137.

— Ethical Works of. New York R. **2**: 96. — Am. Q. **19**: 1. — (J. S. Mill) Westm. **33**: 257.

— The Friend. (J. Foster) Ecl. R. **14**: 912.

— Lamb's Last Words on. Colburn, **43**: 198.

— Lay Sermon. Ed. R. **27**: 444.

— Letters from. Blackw. **10**: 243.

— Letters of. West. Lit. J. **1**: 198.

— — Recollections, and Conversations of. Tait, n. s. **3**: 113. — Mo. R. **139**: 87.

— — to Matilda Betham. Fraser, **98**: 73.

— — to William Godwin. Macmil. **9**: 524. Same art. Liv. Age, **81**: 275.

— Life of. (J. Gilman) Chr. Obs. **59**: 304, 308. — Fraser, **12**: 493.

— Literary Character of. (F. H. Hedge) Chr. Exam. **14**: 109.

— Literary Life of. (W. Hazlitt) Ed. R. **28**: 488.

— Literary Remains of. (J. G. Lockhart) Quar. **59**: 1. — New York R. **2**: 96. **7**: 403. — Dub. Univ. **10**: 257.

— Personal Memories of. (S. C. and A. F. Hall) Atlan. **15**: 213.

— Philosophy of. Fraser, **5**: 585.

— — and Theology of. Ecl. R. **93**: 1.

— — of Christianity. (D. N. Lord) Theo. & Lit. J. **1**: 631.

— Plagiarisms of. Blackw. **47**: 287.

— a Poetical Sphinx. Victoria, **13**: 26.

— Poetical Works of. Blackw. **6**: 1. **36**: 542. — Westm. **12**: 1. — Mus. **25**: 560. — Quar. **11**: 177. — (R. C. Waterston) No. Am. **39**: 437. — (J. G. Lockhart) Quar. **52**: 1, 156.

Coleridge, Samuel Taylor, Recollections of. So. Lit. Mess. **2**: 451. — (C. E. Norton) No. Am. **65**: 401.

— Reminiscences of. Fraser, **10**: 379. — Chr. Obs. **45**: 257.

— Remorse. Chr. Obs. **12**: 228.

— Science and Logic. Fraser, **12**: 619.

— Sibylline Leaves. Mo. R. **88**: 24.

— Sketch of. (T. De Quincey) Tait, n. s. **6**: 515.

— Table Talk. (J. G. Lockhart) Quar. **53**: 79. — Ed. R. **61**: 129. — (G. Putnam) Chr. Exam. **19**: 204. — (T. P. Thompson) Westm. **22**: 531. — Mus. **26**: 443. — Dub. Univ. **6**: 1. — Am. Mo. M. **5**: 454. — Mo. R. **137**: 250.

— Theology of. Chr. Obs. **59**: 634.

— Unpublished Letters of. (G. M. Towle) Lippinc. **13**: 697. — Chr. Obs. **45**: 81–585. — Westm. **93**: 341. **94**: 1.

— with Socinians and Atheists. Cong. M. **18**: 486.

— Works of. (A. N. Littlejohn) Am. Church R. **6**: 489. — Westm. **85**: 106.

See Lake Poets.

Coleridge, Sara. (S. S. Conant) Harper, **47**: 893. — (P. Q. Keegan) Victoria, **36**: 493. — (C. E. Norton) Nation, **17**: 425. — (H. Reed) Penn Mo. **4**: 828.

— Letters of. (J. M. Hoppin) New Eng. **34**: 201.

— Memoir and Letters of. Ed. R. **139**: 44. Same art. Liv. Age, **120**: 515.

Coles, Edward, Washburne's Sketch of. (I. N. Arnold) Dial (Ch.), **2**: 139. — (O. Johnson) Nation, **33**: 495.

Colet, John, Dean of St. Paul's. Am. Church R. **21**: 193. — Antiquary, **4**: 214. — (W. R. W. Stephens) Good Words, **19**: 403. — Chr. Obs. **73**: 589.

— and St. Paul's School, London. Am. J. Educ. **16**: 657. **28**: 729.

Colfax, Schuyler. (V. B. Denslow) Putnam, **11**: 763. — with portrait, Lakeside, **2**: 133.

Colic from Lead. (Dr. Christison) J. Frankl. Inst. **11**: 279.

Coligni, G. de, Admiral. (E. S. Creasy) Bentley, **31**: 107. Same art. Ecl. M. **25**: 493. — Brit. Q. **61**: 297. Same art. Ecl. M. **85**: 257. Same art. Liv. Age, **125**: 707.

Colima, Evening and Morning in. (A. S. Evans) Overland, **5**: 26.

— Rambles in. (F. L. Oswald) Lippinc. **24**: 153.

Colin Clink. Bentley, **5**: 427, 537, 648. **6**: 96–623. **7**: 50, 289, 404. **8**: 277–588. **9**: 65.

Colin Clout; a Story. Argosy, **32**: 371.

Coliseum at Rome. Ecl. Engin. **11**: 522. — Penny M. **1**: 145.

— and Associations. (J. S. Howson) Hours at Home, **4**: 8.

— A Night in. Ev. Sat. **1**: 37.

Coliseum in Regent's Park, London. Penny M. **2**: 121. — Peop. J. **2**: 333.

— Visit to. Lond. M. **23**: 104.

Collamer, Jacob, with portrait. Am. Whig R. **9**: 202.

Collar of Bronze found in Lochar Moss. (A. Way) Arch. **34**: 83.

Collard, Royer, Philosopher and Politician. No. Brit. **39**: 1. — Lond. M. **20**: 38.

Collateral Securities, Law of. (L. A. Jones) Am. Law R. **14**: 465, 689.

Collé, Charles, Journal of. (C. Hervey) Belgra. **37**: 80.

Collects, Liturgies, etc., Comparison of. Chr. Rem. **36**: 18.

Collected by a Valetudinarian. (Mrs. R. H. Stoddard) Harper, **42**: 96.

Collecting Banks, Liability of. Bank. M. (N. Y.) **31**: 140.

Collecting Manias. (J A. Noble) Victoria, **9**: 481.

Collection Paper, Law of. Bank. M. (N. Y.) **21**: 745. **26**: 577, 610.

Collections, Odd. Chamb. J. **48**: 612.

Collective Lessons, Specimen Notes of. Am. J. Educ. **10**: 575.

Collector of Cawnpore; a Tale. Colburn, **17**: 240, 342.

Collector's Mania. All the Year, **5**: 572.

Collectors and Collections. (T. F. Dwight) Overland, **5**: 139.
Colleen Dhyas. (A. M. Williams) Cath. World, **33**: 464.
Colleen Rue; a Tale. (N. Robinson) Appleton, **20**: 73.
College, The. (C. S. Albert) Luth. Q. **10**: 376.
— a Sketch in Verse. Blackw. **65**: 601.
— and the Church. (I. N. Tarbox) New Eng. **11**: 595.
— and New Country. (J. F. Tuttle) Am. Presb. R. **14**: 460.
— and School. Blackw. **128**: 62.
— and University; Pres. Carter's Inaugural. (E. B. Coe) New Eng. **40**: 635.
— Entering. (A. B. Muzzey) Mo. Rel. M. **46**: 156.
— Errors of pious Students in. (J. W. Alexander) Princ. **4**: 230.
— of France, the Sorbonne of 19th Cent. Hogg, **14**: 253.
— of the Holy Cross, Worcester, Mass. Brownson, **6**: 372. — (G. E. Ellis) Chr. Exam. **47**: 51.
— Preparatory Studies for. U. S. Lit. Gaz. **1**: 123.
Colleges. (E. L. Godkin) Nation, **13**: 5.
— American. (C. K. Adams) No. Am. **121**: 365. — (T. G. Apple) Mercersb. **24**: 614. — (B. Bellows) Am. Bib. Repos. **6**: 224. — (D. C. Gilman) No. Am. **122**: 191. — (A. Suydam) University Q. **4**: 196. — O. & N. **3**: 226.
— — and the American Public. (N. Porter) New Eng. **28**: 69-748.
— — — Porter on. (C. Carroll) Nation, **11**: 282. — (M. Valentine) Luth. Q. **1**: 140. — J. Frankl. Inst. **90**: 213, 286.
— — and Christianity. (Dr. Harrington) Meth. Q. **39**: 626.
— — and Churchmen. Nat. Q. **13**: 316.
— — and German Universities. (R. T. Ely) Harper, **61**: 253.
— — and Legislators. (C. C. Nott) Nation, **17**: 141.
— — and Seminaries. (E. I. Sears) Nat. Q. **17**: 294.
— — Annual View of, 1829. Am. Q. Reg. **1**: 224.
— — — 1830. Am. Q. Reg. **2**: 238.
— — — 1831. Am. Q. Reg. **3**: 294.
— — Characteristics of. (C. C. Felton) Am. J. Educ. **9**: 112.
— — Consolidation of. (A. Potter) Am. J. Educ. **1**: 471.
— — Directory of, 1874. O. & N. **10**: 771.
— — Discipline in. (J. McCosh) No. Am. **126**: 428.
— — Early History of. (G. F. Magoun) New Eng. **36**: 445.
— — Improvement of, 1871. (F. A. P. Barnard) Am. J. Educ. **22**: 435.
— — Improvements practicable in, 1855. (F. A. P. Barnard) Am. J. Educ. **1**: 174, 269.
— — in American Revolution. (J. T. Headley) Knick. **57**: 353.
— — Instruction in. (J. G Clark) University Q. **2**: 136.
— — List of Graduates of New York and New Jersey. (J. Farmer) Am. Q. Reg. **11**: 290, 415.
— — List of Graduates of New England, New York, and New Jersey Colleges from 1834; and all other Colleges from their foundation to 1841. (M. Chamberlain) Am. Q. Reg. **15**: 137, 276, 446. *See also* Colleges, New England.
— — on the Defensive. (L. H. Steiner) Mercersb. **18**: 182.
— — Poverty of. Nation, **8**: 207.
— — Reform in. (W. F. Allen) Chr. Exam. **83**: 47.
— — Relation to Christianity. (J. B. Angell) Luth. Q. **8**: 65.
— — Reminiscences of. (C. Benson) Macmil. **2**: 218. **3**: 264.
— — Student in. (J. Cooper) New Eng. **37**: 610.
— — *vs.* American Science. (F. W. Clarke) Pop. Sci. Mo. **9**: 467.
— Ancient Athenian. (W. W. Capes) Am. J. Educ. **27**: 759.
Colleges and the Business Life. (E. Atkinson) Nation, **29**: 57.
— and Classics. (B. L. Gildersleeve) Princ. n. s. **2**: 67.
— and Legislation. (E. L. Godkin) Nation, **28**: 279.
— and the Ministry. Ecl. R. **75**: 1. — (A. B. Chapin) Am. Church R. **4**: 242.
— and Public Schools. (J. R. Dimm) Luth. Q. **9**: 41.
— and State Universities. (J. M. Sturtevant) New Eng. **32**: 453.
— and Universities. Am. J. Educ. **24**: 401.
— — History and Organization of. So. Lit. Mess. **20**: 449, 577, 605.
— — Pencil Sketches of. (E. I. Sears) Nat. Q. **30**: 92.
— as Landlords. Fraser, **103**: 590.
— Atheism in. (J. Bascom) No. Am. **132**: 32.
— Athletics in. (G. W. Green) New Eng. **35**: 548.
— — Intercollegiate Regattas, Hurdle-Races, etc. (B. W. Dwight) New Eng. **35**: 251.
— Beecher's Plea for. Lit. & Theo. R. **3**: 219.
— Catholic. Brownson, **15**: 209.
— Christian, and Home Missions, Mutual Relations of. (J. E. Roy) Cong. Q. **19**: 29.
— — Instruction and Government of. (W. L. Breckenridge) Danv. Q. **4**: 473.
— Commercial. *See* Commercial Colleges.
— Compulsory Attendance in. (F. A. P. Barnard) Pop. Sci. Mo. **3**: 235.
— Congregationalists specially interested in. (C. Cushing) Cong. Q. **11**: 416.
— Conservatism of. (W. M. Nevin) Mercersb. **10**: 45.
— Courses of Study at. (E. E. Hale) O. & N. **8**: 1. — (L. P. Hickok) Bib. Sac. **10**: 151. — So. Lit. Mess. **17**: 155.
— Denominational. (J. M. Sturtevant) New Eng. **18**: 68.
— Endowment of. (C. F. Thwing) Internat. R. **11**: 258.
— English, Incorporation and Endowment of. Chr. Rem. **8**: 72.
— — Congregational. (G. F. Magoun) Cong. R. **7**: 372.
— — Theological. Ecl. R. **109**: 99.
— — Dissenting Theological, 1839. Ecl. R. **71**: 1.
— — — Defects of. Ecl. R. **72**: 547.
— for the People. (N. S. Richardson) Am. Church R. **6**: 349.
— Hedge on Reforms in. (T. D. Woolsey) New Eng. **25**: 695.
— Improvements in. So. Lit. Mess. **23**: 358.
— in 1836. West. M. **5**: 220.
— in Virginia. So. Lit. Mess. **13**: 507.
— Intercollegiate Contests. (J. Smith) New Eng. **34**: 518.
— Method of Culture in. (J. L. Diman) New Eng. **28**: 724.
— New England, 1837. Am. Q. Reg. **9**: 328.
— — 1839. Am. Q. Reg. **12**: 70.
— — and the Public. Chr. R. **10**: 54.
— — Biography of Graduates. N. E. Reg. **1**: 77, 182, 278.
— — List of Graduates of. (J. Farmer) Am. Q. Reg. **7**: 93, 181.
— — Students in, where from, 1855. (I. N. Tarbox) Am. J. Educ. **1**: 405.
— of Christian Brothers. (Brother Noah) Nat. Q. **26**: 331.
— Pastoral Labor in. (J. Edwards) Am. Q. Reg. **3**: 16.
— People's. Howitt, **1**: 85.
— Popular. Westm. **48**: 426.
— Queen's College, London. Quar. **86**: 364.
— Reform in. (I. Butt) Dub. Univ. **2**: 214. — (W. G. Sumner) Nation, **11**: 152.
— — Can they reform themselves? Macmil. **25**: 461.
— — Wayland on. Am. Whig R. **13**: 141.
— Religion in. (L. H. Atwater) Princ. **31**: 29.
— — Public Prayers in. (F. D. Huntington) Am. J. Educ. **4**: 23.
— Religion in relation to. (J. H. Hopkins, Jr.) Am. Church R. **7**: 259.

Colleges, Religious Biblical Instruction and Pastoral Supervision in. (C. E. Stowe) Bib. Sac. **8**: 304.
— Religious Influence of. (J. Crowell) Am. Presb. R. **13**: 611.
— Religious Instruction in. (M. L. Stoever) Evang. R. **11**: 523. — Chr. Mo. Spec. **10**: 23, 75.
— — Method of. (J. McCosh) Princ. **41**: 72.
— Remarks on. (S. F. Smith) Chr. R. **13**: 108.
— Sanctified Literature with. (C. Colton) Am. Q. Reg. **2**: 212.
— Scholarships in, Intercollegiate. (T. W. Higginson) Scrib. **5**: 366. **6**: 115.
— — Open, in American. (T. W. Higginson) Nation, **28**: 148, 181. — (C. W. Eliot) Nation, **28**: 163, 181, 265.
— Scientific Teaching in. Pop. Sci. Mo. **16**: 556.
— Study of Didactics in. (T. Hill) Am. J. Educ. **15**: 177.
— Suggestion on the Management of. Bib. R. **2**: 311.
— Talk about. Cong. R. **11**: 483.
— Value of. (F. W. Conrad) Evang. R. **9**: 220.
— Western, Relative Claims of. (G. F. Magoun) Cong. Q. **15**: 49.
— Who are the best Scholars? (I. N. Tarbox) Cong. Q. **3**: 158.
See Universities.
College Alumni and Ministers. (C. Cushing) Cong. Q. **12**: 567.
College Boat-Clubs. (E. F. Blake) University Q. **2**: 99.
College Breakfast-Party. (George Eliot) Macmil. **38**: 161.
College-bred Men, Obligations of the Country to. (H. W. Bellows) Unita. R. **2**: 477.
College Buildings, with plate of Yale College Library. Am. Lit. M. **1**: 269.
College Celibacy. Liv. Age, **11**: 397.
College Changes. Dub. Univ. **5**: 407.
College Characters and Characteristics. (L. M. Jones) University Q. **1**: 144.
College Code of Honor. (H. Mann) Am. J. Educ. **3**: 65.
College Commencements. (E. I. Sears) Nat. Q. **7**: 369. **9**: 347. **11**: 366. — (D. Y. Heisler) Mercersb. **26**: 537.
— Admonitions for. (E. L. Godkin) Nation, **25**: 5.
College Conference Papers. Cong. M. **28**: 401–881.
College Education. Am. J. Sci. **15**: 297. — (A. S. Packard) No. Am. **28**: 294. — (C. C. Felton) No. Am. **44**: 178. — (W. A. Larned) New Eng. **5**: 201. — (F. Bowen) No. Am. **55**: 302. — Dem. R. **20**: 129. — (W. G. T. Shedd) Bib. Sac. **7**: 132. — (G. H. Calvert) Lippinc. **3**: 377. — (J. B. Helwig) Luth. Q. **5**: 569. — (P. A. Chadbourne) Putnam, **14**: 335. — (F. S. Chatrard) Cath. World, **25**: 814. — (M. L. Stoever) Evang. R. **4**: 443. — So. Q. **24**: 53.
— Æsthetics in. (G. F. Comfort) Meth. Q. **27**: 572.
— and Education of Circumstances. (E. L. Godkin) Nation, **29**: 20.
— and Self-Education. (D. Masson) Am. J. Educ. **4**: 262.
— Coercion in. (J. P. Quincy) O. & N. **8**: 44.
— for the People. Chr. Q. **4**: 527.
— in Northwest. (J. M. Sturtevant) New Eng. **30**: 129.
— in United States, Wayland on. (J. C. Gray) No. Am. **72**: 60. — Chr. R. **15**: 442.
— Plan for. Am. J. Educ. **16**: 539.
— Plan of University of Rochester. (H. P. Tappan) Chr. R. **16**: 126.
— Reforms in. New Eng. **9**: 100.
— Tendency of. (D. Wilson) Canad. J. n. s. **1**: 168.
— Vital Principle of. (E. V. Gerhart) Mercersb. **7**: 72.
— What is the Use of? (E. L. Godkin) Nation, **4**: 275.
College Ethics. University Q. **2**: 61.
College Examinations. (P. G. Tait) Macmil. **25**: 416.
— Audi aliam Partem. (I. Todhunter) Macmil. **26**: 60.
College Expenses. (C. F. Thwing) Scrib. **13**: 83. — Chamb. J. **16**: 355.
College Expenses, Growing Chr. Obs. **13**: 224–707. **14**: 21, 165.
College Fallacies. (J. M. Morris) University Q. **1**: 331.
College Fellowships. (C. F. Thwing) Scrib. **16**: 660.
College Friends, My. Blackw. **56**: 569, 763. **58**: 197. **59**: 73. **60**: 145, 309.
College Government. (E. V. Gerhart) Mercersb. **7**: 349.
— by the Students, Experiment in, at Illinois University. (J. N. Gregory) Internat. R. **10**: 510.
College Honors. New Eng. M. **2**: 107.
College Influence in the West. (C. White) Am. Bib. Repos. 3d s. **4**: 383.
College Instruction. (C. F. Thwing) Scrib. **14**: 706.
— and Discipline. Am. Q. **9**: 283.
— What is successful? (J. Cooper) New Eng. **36**: 725.
College Journalism. (C. F. Thwing) Scrib. **16**: 808.
College Library and the Classes. (J. Winsor) Lib. J. **3**: 5.
College Life a hundred Years ago. Putnam, **9**: 631.
— at Cambridge, England. Westm. **35**: 456.
— at Glasgow. Fraser, **53**: 505.
— of Maître Nablot. (MM. Erckmann-Chatrian) Ev. Sat. **16**: 212–316.
— Qualities needed in. (G. M. Steele) O. & N. **1**: 304.
— Reminiscences of. Knick. **35**: 248.
College Literary Societies, Value of. (D. H. Chamberlain) University Q. **3**: 348.
College Oratory. (E. L. Godkin) Nation, **26**: 38.
College Rank of distinguished Men. (C. F. Thwing) Scrib. **15**: 467.
College Recollections. (D. L. Ogden) New Eng. **5**: 572. — Month, **108**: 200.
College Reminiscences. Overland, **6**: 229. — (F. Buckland) Temp. Bar. **37**: 175.
College Romances. (I. Butt) Dub. Univ. **4**: 486. **5**: 332. **6**: 31, 361. **8**: 264, 435. **10**: 157, 499.
College Scouts. Belgra. **20**: 64.
College Secret Societies. (W. W. Lathrop) University Q. **3**: 273.
College Songs. Hours at Home, **8**: 141.
College Student. (J. M. Hart) Lippinc. **17**: 428.
College Studies and Government. (L. H. Atwater) Princ. **39**: 31.
College Theatricals. (J. K. Hosmer) Nation, **10**: 6. — Blackw. **54**: 737. Same art. Ecl. M. **1**: 253. — Liv. Age, **59**: 278.
— He playing She. Scrib. **17**: 189.
College Youths, Ancient. All the Year, **21**: 303.
Collegian's Guide. Ecl. R. **81**: 651.
Collegians, The. Lond. M. **15**: 60.
Collegiate and Professional Schools, Utility of. (E. A. Park) Bib. Sac. **7**: 626.
Collegiate and Scholastic Quackery. (E. I. Sears) Nat. Q. **23**: 337.
Collegiate System of United States. Chr. R. **7**: 466. — So. Lit. Mess. **11**: 112.
Collembola and Thysanura, Lubbock on. Nature, **8**: 482.
Colles, Abraham, with portrait. Dub. Univ. **23**: 688.
Colles, Christopher. (J. A. Stevens) M. Am. Hist. **2**: 340.
Collet, Anthelme. Sharpe, **37**: 238.
Collier, Arthur, Idealism of. No. Brit. **53**: 368.
Collier, Jeremy, and Opponents of the Drama. Blackw. **7**: 387.
Collier, J. P., the Old Corrector. Fraser, **61**: 176, 722.
— Shaksperian Discovery. Fraser, **61**: 53.
See Shakspere.
Collier-Vessels in England. Cornh. **11**: 461.
Colliers. *See* Coal-Miners.
Collieries. *See* Coal-Mines.
Colling, Mary, Poetry of. (R. Southey) Quar. **47**: 80. — Mo. R. **126**: 552.

Collingwood, Cuthbert, Lord. (F. Jeffrey) Ed. R. **47**: 385. — Quar. **37**: 364. — Mo. R. **115**: 285. — Sharpe, **1**: 321. — Lond. M. **21**: 137.
— Memoir of. Ecl. R. **49**: 547.
Collins, Anthony. (J. Hunt) Contemp. **9**: 357.
Collins, Jemima J., afterwards Mrs. Harvey. *See* Old Loves and old Letters.
Collins, John. (M. Collins) Belgra. **16**: 443.
Collins, John, Gov. of R. I., 1786. Am. Q. Reg. **15**: 162.
Collins, Rev. John, Life of. Meth. Q. **10**: 324.
Collins, Mortimer, Life and Writings of. Dub. Univ. **90**: 340, 474, 561.
— Who s the Heir? Dub. Univ. **66**: 450.
Collins, Wilkie, with portrait. Appleton, **4**: 278.
— Antonina. Dub. Univ. **35**: 661. — So. Lit. Mess. **17**: 104.
— as a Novelist. (J. L. Stewart) Canad. Mo. **14**: 586.
— Basil. Dub. Univ. **41**: 77. — New Q. **2**: 94.
— New Magdalen. Canad. Mo. **4**: 357.
— — dramatized. Dub. Univ. **82**: 371.
— Woman in White. Dub. Univ. **57**: 200.
Collins, William. (T. S. Perry) Atlan. **46**: 810. — Penny M. **8**: 205.
— Gray's Opinion of. Lond. M. **4**: 13.
— Memoir of. Ecl. R. **89**: 709. — Blackw. **67**: 192. — Colburn, **85**: 53.
— Poetical Works of. Liv. Age, **57**: 72.
— Two Poems of. (E. S Nadal) Scrib. **12**: 219.
Collinson, Peter, and J. Bartram. Am. J. Educ. **28**: 872.
Collision, The. Dub. Univ. **8**: 133.
— at Sea. (N. S. Dodge) Galaxy, **6**: 399.
— of Ships, and Rules of the Sea. Westm. **42**: 117. — (A. Nash) Hunt, **9**: 543. *See also* Mercantile Law Cases and Ships.
Collyer, Robert. (M. D. Conway) Harper, **48**: 819. — (J. C. Ambrose) Potter Am. Mo. **17**: 115. — Ev. Sat. **10**: 43.
— and Astrology. (J.W. Thompson) Mo. Rel. M. **43**: 481.
— Sermons on Nature and Life. (B. W. Dwight) New Eng. **27**: 258.
— The Story of a Yorkshire Blacksmith. (M. D. Conway) Fraser, **89**: 574. Same art. Ecl. M. **83**: 92.
Colman, Benjamin, with portrait. (W. T. Harris) N. E. Reg. **3**: 105, 220. — with portrait, (J. Tracy) Am. Q. Reg. **15**: 345.
Colman, George. (T. Hook) Bentley, **1**: 7. — Colburn, **49**: 58.
— Letter to. Colburn, **11**: 554.
— Poetical Vagaries. Quar. **8**: 144. **9**: 346.
— Random Records. Blackw. **28**: 362. — Mo. R. **121**: 347.
Colman, George, the Younger. (T. Woodfall) Bentley, **20**: 126.
— and George Colman, the Elder. Temp. Bar, **46**: 461.
— Ode to. Lond. M. **11**: 104.
— Recollections of. Colburn, **51**: 491.
Colman, Henry. European Life and Manners. (A. M. Wells) Am. Whig R. **10**: 159. — Liv. Age, **29**: 568. — Fraser, **40**: 259.
— Memorial of. (J. W. Thompson) Mo. Rel. M. **6**: 481.
— on Agriculture. Chr. Exam. **30**: 128. **31**: 277. **34**: 117.
— Sermons of. Chr. Disc. **2**: 382. — (A. Walker) Chr. Exam. **15**: 330.
Colman Family. Ed. R. **78**: 389.
— Peake's Memoirs of. Mus. **43**: 49. — Mo. R. **154**: 543.
Colney Hatch Asylum. Westm. **48**: 119.
Cologne. Penny M. **4**: 281. — (M. P. Thompson) Cath. World, **16**: 615.
— Archbishop of, Papal Conspiracy of. Quar. **63**: 88.
— Architecture of. Am. Arch. **6**: 158.
— Carnival at, Feb 3, 1845. Colburn, **74**: 254.
Cologne, Cathedral of. Ecl. Engin. **5**: 486. — Quar. **78**: 425. Same art. Liv. Age, **11**: 568. — Godey, **37**: 292. — Liv. Age, **143**: 118. — Chamb. J. **58**: 111. — Penny M. **11**: 444, 460. — Potter Am. Mo. **13**: 387. — Quar. **78**: 425.
— — Historical Procession on Completion of. Art J. **33**: 270.
— — Mediæval Legend of. Ecl. M. **28**: 556.
— Churches of, and their Legends. Chr. Obs. **66**: 777.
— Day in. All the Year, **46**: 61.
— Hermesian Question at. Dub. R. **8**: 117.
— Legend of. (Bret Harte) Belgra. **38**: 44.
— Reformation under Archbishop Herman. Chr. Obs. **68**: 8–371.
— The Thurnmarket. (G. A. Sala) Temp. Bar, **13**: 34.
— Zoölogical Gardens at. (E. Legge) Belgra. **23**: 353.
Cologne Water, Invention of. Nat. M. **10**: 334.
Colomba; a Tale of Corsican Life. (P. Mérimée) Victoria, **16**: 289–404. **17**: 63–359.
Colombia. Mo. R. **103**: 242. **104**: 1. **113**: 443. — U. S. Lit. Gaz. **1**: 369.
— 1822–23. U. S. Lit. Gaz. **5**: 418.
— 1825. Ann. Reg. **1**: 179. — Niles's Reg. **28**: 46, 221. **29**: 124. **30**: 271.
— 1826. Niles's Reg. **34**: 403. — Ann. Reg. **2**: [181.
— 1827. Ann. Reg. **2**: 183. — Mo. R. **112**: 174.
— 1829. Ann. Reg. **3**: 493. — (C. Cushing) Ann. Reg. **5**: 222.
— 1830. (C. Cushing) Ann. Reg. **6**: 122.
— and Hayti. Niles's Reg. **28**: 158.
— and Mexican Treaty. Niles's Reg. **28**: 222.
— Constitution of. Niles's Reg. **22**: 230, 247. — (R. C. Anderson) No. Am. **23**: 314.
— Convention with, 1825. Niles's Reg. **28**: 61.
— Description of. Meth. M. **48**: 18.
— Journey into. Dub. Univ. **3**: 524.
— President's Message, 1823. Niles's Reg. **24**: 269.
— Republic of. West. Mo. R. **2**: 537.
— — and external Policy of England. Am. Whig R **14**: 258.
— Travels in. (J. Sparks) No. Am. **20**: 441. **21**: 153. — Ecl. R. **42**: 27.
Colonel, The; a Story. (H.W. Lucy) Belgra. **43**: supp. 55.
Colonel and Mrs. Chutney; a Tale. All the Year, **14**: 186, 210.
Colonel Benyon's Entanglement. (M. E. Braddon) Belgra. **18**: 69, 213.
Colonel Campion's Confession. Colburn, **161**: 55.
Colonel Clive's Wife. Tinsley, **9**: 433–541. Same art. Ev. Sat. **12**: 40.
Colonel Eph's Shoe-Buckles. (H. B. Stowe) Atlan. **26**: 424.
Colonel Rannoch. Victoria, **7**: 12–526. **8**: 22–413.
Colonel Van Halen and the Widow. St. James, **12**: 476.
Colonel's Love-Chance. Lond. Soc. **6**: 48.
Colonel's Sentence; an Algerian Story. (D. Ker) Lippinc. **22**: 771.
Colonel's Valentine, and its Fate. Lond. Soc. **7**: 139.
Colonel's Venture. (R. H. Davis) Lippinc. **23**: 186.
Colonel's Ward. Sharpe, **46**: 33–188.
Colonia Camulodunum. (E. A. Freeman) Macmil. **36**: 119.
Colonial Failure, Confessions of a. Tinsley, **12**: 261.
Colonial Policy of the Ancients. Westm. **23**: 387. — Am. Ecl. **1**: 468.
— of European Powers, Brougham on. Chr. Obs. **2**: 618, 688.
— of Great Britain. Quar. **26**: 522. — Ed. R. **54**: 330. — Anal. M. **7**: 508.
Colonial Story; Finding of my Mother. Temp. Bar, **57**: 503.
Colonies, American. *See* American Colonies.
— and Colonization, Merivale on. Blackw. **52**: 206. — Mo. R. **155**: 417.

Colonies, British. *See* Great Britain, Colonies.
Colonization. Ed. R. **91**: 1. — St. James, **46**: 483. — (J. L. Laughlin) Internat. R. **11**: 88.
— African. (J. Sparks) No. Am. **18**: 40. — (B. B. Thatcher) No. Am. **35**: 118. **41**: 265. — (O. W. B. Peabody) No. Am. **63**: 269. — (L. Bacon) Chr. Q. Spec. **2**: 459. **4**: 311. **5**: 145. **6**: 445. — (A. Twining) Chr. Q. Spec. **7**: 503, 521. — (T. Frelinghuysen) Lit. & Theo. R. **1**: 62. — (A. Proudfit) Lit. & Theo. R. **2**: 429. — (B. B. Edwards) Chr. Mo. Spec. **10**: 358. — Am. Q. **4**: 395. **12**: 213. **18**: 245. — So. R. **1**: 219. — (E. Hopkins) Princ. **5**: 257, 281. **13**: 266. — Spirit Pilg. **6**: 322, 396, 569. — Chr. Mo. Spec. **5**: 485, 540. **10**: 493. — (B. B. Thatcher) Chr. Exam. **13**: 96, 200, 287. — Am. Mo. R. **2**: 151. **4**: 282. — Niles's Reg. **13**: 164. **15**: supp. 42. **16**: 165, 233. **17**: 201. **23**: 39, 138. **24**: 333. **25**: 175, 381. **26**: 270, 282, 373. **27**: 29. **29**: 329. **47**: 203. — New Eng. M. **2**: 13, 273. — Meth. Q. **12**: 361. — New Eng. **9**: 70. — (A. Alexander) Princ. **16**: 57. — (D. Curry) Meth. Q. **12**: 361. — Am. Meth. M. **22**: 387. — Brownson, **19**: 220. — (S. J. Baird) Princ. **34**: 686. — West. R. **1**: 142.
— — Colonists *vs.* the Antislavery Society. Fraser, **2**: 334. **3**: 114.
— — Gurley's Mission. (A. Alexander) Princ. **14**: 266.
— and Allotment System. No. Brit. **3**: 406.
— and Christianity, Howitt on. Tait, n. s. **5**: 527. — Mo. R. **146**: 490.
— and Colonial Reform. Ecl. R. **89**: 755.
— and Emigration. Dub. R. **26**: 316.
— British. Dub. Univ. **53**: 498.
— — Romance of. (M. I. Griffin) St. James, **31**: 464.
— Close of the Era of. Bank. M. (N. Y.) **35**: 359.
— Effect on the Parent State. Ox. Prize Ess. **3**: 119.
— European; its Crimes and Improvements. Ecl. R. **68**: 646.
— Freehold Assurance and. Westm. **51**: 408.
— from Great Britain. Blackw. **64**: 66. — Ed. R. **91**: 1. — Brit. & For. R. **6**: 472.
— from Ireland. No. Brit. **8**: 421.
— Grey's Plan of. Fraser, **35**: 736.
— in Algeria. (M. B. Edwards) Fraser, **86**: 422.
— New Theory of. Ed. R. **71**: 517.
— of ancient and modern Nations. Am. Ecl. **1**: 468.
— of New Zealand, Ritter on. Mo. R. **158**: 264.
— only Cure for national Distress. Fraser, **27**: 735.
— Principles of. Dub. R. **4**: 67.
— Wakefield's Theory of. Blackw. **65**: 509. — Fraser, **39**: 245.
See also Emigration; Africa; Liberia; Sierra Leone.
Colonization Society. Cong. M. **22**: 789.
— of America. Chr. Obs. **47**: 275, 349. — Am. Meth. M. **15**: 344.
Colonna, Angelo Michele, the Painter. Blackw. **26**: 351. — Mus. **16**: 55.
Colonna, Vittoria. (E. D. Cheney) Chr. Exam. **84**: 22. — (J. M. Olin) Meth. Q. **20**: 606. — (A. C. Ritchie) Galaxy, **3**: 863. — (R. Seton) Cath. World, **23**: 680. — Argosy, **5**: 346. — Colburn, **116**: 37. — Dub. Univ. **51**: 232. Same art. Ecl. M. **43**: 556.
— Homes and Haunts of. (F. E. Trollope) Belgra. **34**: 450.
— Roscoe's Life and Poems of. Victoria, **11**: 273.
Colonna Infame, La; Milan, 1630. Cornh. **16**: 230.
Color. Hogg, **2**: 320.
— and Form, Hay on. (Sir D. Brewster) Ed. R. **78**: 300.
— — Sir G. Wilkinson on. No. Brit. **32**: 126.
— and Music, Analogy between. Contin. Mo. **2**: 535. — (W. F. Barrett) Nature, **1**: 286.
— Constants of. (O. N. Rood) Pop. Sci. Mo. **9**: 641.
— Distinctions of. (H. Bushnell) Hours at Home, **7**: 81.
Color, Experiments on. (J. W. Strutt) Nature, **3**: 234.
— Geographical Distinctions of. Knick. **10**: 449.
— in Animals. Ev. Sat. **17**: 9. — Chamb. J. **51**: 340. Same art. Pop. Sci. Mo. **5**: 470.
— in Birds and Insects. (Lady Verney) Good Words, **18**: 835.
— in Nature. (A. R. Wallace) Nature, **19**: 501.
— — and in Art. Blackw. **76**: 539.
— in Painting. Cornh. **38**: 476. Same art. Liv. Age, **139**: 287. Same art. Sup. Pop. Sci. Mo. **4**: 14.
— Influence of, on Radiation. (A. D. Bache) J. Frankl. Inst. **20**: 289.
— — upon Reduction of Light. (M. C. Lea) Am J. Sci. **107**: 200. **109**: 355.
— Laws of. J. Frankl. Inst. **64**: 276.
— Mauve and Magenta. (R. Hunt) St. James, **1**: 43.
— of Air and deep Waters. Am. J. Sci. **26**: 65.
— of the Organic World, Action of Light upon. Sup. Pop. Sci. Mo. **2**: 367.
— Organic, Origin and Distribution of. (W. S. Kent) Nature, **18**: 523.
— Perception of, G. S. Hall on. (G. Allen) Mind, **4**: 267.
— Philosophy of. Ed. R. **150**: 368. — Liv. Age, **143**: 643. — Knick. **3**: 218. **13**: 199.
— Science and Æsthetics of. Fraser, **52**: 503.
— Studies of. (G. Turner) Recr. Sci. **1**: 238.
— Uses of. (J. J. Croly) Victoria, **25**: 819.
Color-Blindness. (J. Hogg) Pop. Sci. R. **2**: 497. Same art. Ecl. M. **60**: 95. — (J. G. McKendrick) Mind, **1**: 409. — (W. Pole) Nature, **18**: 676, 700. — (W. Pole) Contemp. **37**: 821. Same art. Ecl. M. **95**: 100. — Chamb. J. **54**: 152. — Cornh. **1**: 403. — (S. R. Koehler) Pop. Sci. Mo. **19**: 91. — Ecl. R. **109**: 261. Same art. Ecl. M. **48**: 513. — House. Words, **8**: 255. **12**: 521. — Ev. Sat. **10**: 539. — Liv. Age, **39**: 797. — (J. Henry) Princ. **17**: 483.
— and Color Vision. (J. C. Maxwell) Nature, **4**: 13. — (J. D. Everett) Nature, **21**: 62.
— in Railway Employés. Ecl. Engin. **23**: 17.
— Jeffries on. (W. Pole) Nature, **20**: 477. — (T. M. Coan) Nation, **29**: 62.
— Researches on. (G. Wilson) Canad. J. n. s. **1**: 146.
— Wilson on. (Sir D. Brewster) No. Brit. **24**: 325.
Color Correction of Achromatic Object-Glasses. (C. A. Young) Am. J. Sci. **119**: 454.
Color-Printing, Novelty in. Chamb. J. **51**: 781.
Color-Sense. (W. E. Gladstone) 19th Cent. **2**: 366. Same art. Liv. Age, **135**: 323. — (C. S. Peirce) Am. J. Sci. **113**: 247.
— Development of. (H. T. Finck) Macmil. **41**: 125. Same art. Liv. Age, **144**: 19.
— in Homeric Poems, Gladstone controverted. (G. Allen) Mind, **3**: 129.
— in Man and Animals, Allen on. (H. T. Finck) Nation, **28**: 373. — (J. Sully) Mind, **4**: 415.
Color Studies with the Microscope. (H. S. Slack) Pop. Sci. R. **14**: 126.
Color Theory, Vogel's. (M. C. Lea) Am. J. Sci. **112**: 48.
Colors. Chamb. J. **46**: 6.
— and Devices, National. Ecl. M. **64**: 293.
— Meaning of. (M. E. G. Gage) Contin. Mo. **6**: 199.
— Artists'. Art J. **32**: 263.
— — Improvements in. Art J. **32**: 37.
— Contrast of. (O. N. Rood) Pop. Sci. Mo. **14**: 1.
— employed in the Arts, Chemistry of. Art J. **1**: 71–369.
— Enamel, for Porcelain, Glass, etc. J. Frankl. Inst. **5**: 80, 168, 221.
— — Manufacture of. J. Frankl. Inst. **10**: 257, 338.
— for Photographic Painting. Art J. **11**: 242.
— Goethe on. (T. Young) Quar. **10**: 427. — Ed. R. **72**: 99. — (J. Tyndall) Fortn. **33**: 471. Same art. Pop. Sci. Mo. **17**: 215, 312.

Colors, Harmony of. (Mrs. Merrifield) Art J. 4: 13, 58, 90. — Art J. 4: 117. — (J. Sully) Mind, 4: 172.
— — and Contrast of. Art J. 6: 285.
— — — Chevreul on. Liv. Age, 43: 141.
— in Art. Nature, 22: 357.
— in Dress, Abuse of. (Mrs. Merrifield) St. James, 1: 289.
— in old Pictures. (S. Laurence) Cornh. 15: 222.
— Loves of; a Poem. (J. H. Clinch) Am. Mo. M. 10: 115.
— Music of. (C. E. S. Smith) J. Spec. Philos. 8: 216. — Once a Week, 21: 578.
— obtained from the Animal Kingdom. Art J. 10: 45.
— of Animals and Plants. (A. Murray) Ed. New Philos. J. 68: 66. — (A. R. Wallace) Macmil. 36: 384, 464. Same art. Liv. Age, 135: 67, 352. Same art. Sup. Pop. Sci. Mo. 1: 522. 2: 43. Same art. Am. Natural. 11: 641, 713.
— of Fibers. (D. Brewster) J. Frankl. Inst. 16: 138.
— of the Sea, Causes of. (J. Tyndall) Nature, 4: 203.
— of Spring Flowers. (A. W. Bennett) Pop. Sci. R. 20: 309.
— of thin Blowpipe Deposits. (C. H. Koyl) Am. J. Sci. 120: 187.
— of Vegetation. (D. S. Jordan) Am. Natural. 7: 65. — Recr. Sci. 2: 222.
— Perception of, in Pictures. Art J. 8: 66.
— Permanent, Bancroft on. (T. Young) Quar. 11: 203.
— Vegetable, used in the Arts. Art J. 10: 70.
— Young's Theory of. (A. M. Mayer) Am. J. Sci. 109: 251.
Colorado. (J. A. Church) Galaxy, 1: 292. — (J. W. Barclay) Fortn. 33: 119. — (Earl Dunraven) 19th Cent. 8: 445. Same art. Liv. Age, 147: 40. Same art. Appleton, 24: 437. — (H. H. Jackson) Scrib. 16: 55. — (A. S. Southworth) Geog. M. 2: 139.
— Adventure of a Digger in. Chamb. J. 51: 365.
— Age of Rocky Mountains in. (J. J. Stevenson) Am. J. Sci. 113: 172, 297.
— Alpine Flora. (E. L. Greene) Am. Natural. 6: 734.
— Ancient Pottery. (E. A. Barber) Am. Natural. 10: 449.
— Animals in. (W. H. Brewer) Am. Natural. 5: 220.
— April Days in. (I. D. Hardy) Belgra. 44: 200.
— as a Field for Geological Study. (G. K. Gilbert) Am. J. Sci. 112: 16, 85.
— Camping in. Lakeside, 8: 376.
— Cattle Ranches. Harper, 59: 277. — Chamb. J. 57: 55.
— Dark Side of Life in. Fraser, 99: 660. Same art. Liv. Age, 141: 820.
— Explorations in. Am. Natural. 11: 73. — (W. H. Rideing) Lippinc. 26: 393.
— — Hayden's. (A. S. Packard, jr.) Am. Natural. 10: 161.
— Flowers of. (H. H. Jackson) Atlan. 40: 401.
— Fox Hills Group of. (J. J. Stevenson) Am. J. Sci. 117: 369.
— Glimpse at. (C. E. Aiken) Am. Natural. 7: 13.
— Glimpses of. (L. I. Dupré) Appleton, 9: 368, 399.
— Grub-Stakes and Millions in. (A. A. Hayes, jr.) Harper, 60: 380.
— Home of the Farmer. Fraser, 98: 622.
— Laramie Group of Southern. (J. J. Stevenson) Am. J. Sci. 118: 129.
— Mountains of. (J. W. Foster) Am. Natural. 6: 64.
— New, and Santa Fé Trail, Hayes's. (C. S. Holt) Dial (Ch.), 1: 128.
— Over the Plains to. (A. W. Hoyt) Harper, 35: 1.
— Parks of. Am. J. Sci. 94: 351.
— Pioneers of the Sierra Madre. (A. A. Hayes, jr.) Internat. R. 10: 518.
— Plants of. (I. C. Martindale) Am. Natural. 13: 675.
— Prehistoric Ruins in Southern. (H. Gannett) Pop. Sci. R. 16: 666.
— Road in. (H. H. Jackson) Atlan. 38: 677.
Colorado, Round up in. (A. T. Bacon) Lippinc. 28: 618.
— Ruins in. (W. H. Jackson) Am. Natural. 10: 31.
— San Luis Park. Hunt, 58: 211.
— Saurians of the Dakota Beds of. (E. D. Cope) Am. Natural. 12: 71.
— Shepherds of. (A. A. Hayes, jr.) Harper, 60: 193.
— South Park. (S. C. Clarke) Lippinc. 12: 332.
— Stage Ride to. (T. R. Davis) Harper, 35: 137.
— Statistics of, 1869. Am. J. Educ. 18: 486.
— Symphony in Yellow and Red. (H. H. Jackson) Atlan. 36: 666.
— Tellurium Ores of. (B. Silliman) Am. J. Sci. 108: 25.
— Tertiary Epoch in. (S. Lockwood) Pop. Sci. Mo. 4: 470.
— To Pike's Peak and Denver. (T. W. Knox) Knick. 58: 115.
— Twin Lakes and Teocalli Mountain. (F. V. Hayden) Am. Natural. 14: 858.
— Vacation Aspects of. (A. A. Hayes, jr.) Harper, 60: 542.
— Veta Pass and Garland City. (H. H. Jackson) Scrib. 15: 386.
— Wheeler Expedition. (W. H. Rideing) Harper, 52: 793.
— Winter Journey in. (N. S. Shaler) Atlan. 47: 46.
See Leadville.
Colorado Beetle. *See* Potato Beetle.
Colorado Desert, Botanizing on. (E. L. Greene) Am. Natural. 14: 787. 15: 24.
— Fossil Shells from. (R. E. C. Stearns) Am. Natural. 13: 141.
— Physical History of. (J. P. Widney) Overland, 10: 44.
Colorado River of the West. (J. C. Ives) Am. J. Sci. 83: 387. — De Bow, 26: 282.
— Cañons of. (E. O. Beaman) Appleton, 11: 481–686. — (J. Clerke) Lippinc. 2: 588. — (J. W. Powell) Scrib. 9: 293–523. 10: 659. — (G. E. Roberts) Intel. Obs. 4: 309. — Once a Week, 23: 184.
— Chasms of. (A. Hyatt) Am. Natural. 2: 359.
— Geological History of. (C. E. Dutton) Nature, 19: 247, 272.
— Scenes along. (L. White) Overland, 9: 360.
— Upper. (A. Geikie) Nature, 15: 337.
Colorado Valley, Great Plateau Region. (H. Gannett) Penn Mo. 7: 852.
— Physical Features of. (J. W. Powell) Pop. Sci. Mo. 7: 385–670.
— Ruins of. (A. T. Bacon) Lippinc. 26: 521.
Colored Citizens, Free. (L. Bacon) Chr. Q. Spec. 4: 311.
— Right to vote. (E. R. Tyler) New Eng. 5: 522.
Colored Member, The. (J. W. De Forest) Galaxy, 13: 293.
Colored Race. (T. P. Thompson) Westm. 20: 168. — (J. Leavitt) Chr. Mo. Spec. 7: 130, 239. — (E. H. Sears) Chr. Exam. 41: 33.
— Prejudice against, in America. (W. Chambers) Chamb. J. 23: 185, 267.
Colored Races, Colonial Policy in the Government of. No. Brit. 44: 388.
— Prejudices against. Mo. R. 165: 227.
See Negroes.
Colored Rain and Snow. Ev. Sat. 3: 180.
Coloring Matters for Calico Printing, Preparation of. (W. H. De Kurrer) J. Frankl. Inst. 50: 327.
— from Coal Tar. (F. C. Calvert) J. Frankl. Inst. 65: 347. — (M. E. Kopp) J. Frankl. Inst. 72: 181–409.
— History of Alizarin and allied. (W. H. Perkin) J. Frankl. Inst. 108: 88.
— Qualitative Analysis of vegetable and animal. (H. C. Sorby) J. Frankl. Inst. 84: 335, 413. 85: 54, 201, 272.
Colossus of Rhodes. St. James, 14: 310. Same art. Cath. World, 2: 544.
Colosseum. *See* Coliseum.
Colporteurs of Bonn. (J. Mulroy) Cath. World, 22: 90.
Colporteur System. (J. M. Sturtevant) Am. Bib. Repos. 2d s. 12: 214.

Colquhoun, Patrick. Lond. Soc. **8**: 461. — with portrait, Colburn, **166**: 142.
— on the State of Ireland. Dub. Univ. **7**: 119.
Colt, John C., Case of. Dem. R. **11**: 651.
Colt, Samuel, with portrait. Dem. R. **38**: 1.
Colter's Escape from Blackfeet Indians. Blackw. **3**: 45.
Coltness Collections. Quar. **70**: 356.
Colton, Caleb C. Lacon. Land We Love, **5**: 309. Same art. N. Ecl. **3**: 129.
Colton, Calvin. Internat. M. **4**: 1.
— Four Years in Great Britain. Ecl. R. **65**: 53. — Lit. & Theo. R. **2**: 614.
— Public Economy. Am. Whig R. **8**: 142. — (F. Bowen) No. Am. **73**: 90.
Colton, Geo. H., Life of. (I. N. Tarbox) New Eng. **7**: 229.
— Poems. Am. Whig R. **1**: 82, 112, 243. **4**: 338, 446. **5**: 157, 405. **7**: 47. — Dem. R. **11**: 496.
— Tecumseh. (I. N. Tarbox) New Eng. **1**: 53. — Dem. R. **11**: 630.
Colton, Walter. Visit to Constantinople. Am. Q. **20**: 351.
Columb, St., and N. W. Coast of Cornwall. (G. F. Jackson) Once a Week, **7**: 527.
Columba, St. Dub. Univ. **50**: 255. — Good Words, **1**: 385, 401.
Columbia, British. *See* British Columbia.
Columbia, District of. *See* District of Columbia.
Columbia, Conn., Early History of. Hist. M. **18**: 297.
Columbia, S. C., Burning of. (E. Dill) Land We Love, **4**: 361. — (G. W. Nichols) Harper, **33**: 363. — (J. McCarter) Harper, **33**: 642. — So. Hist. Pap. **7**: 156, 185, 249. — (J. P. Carroll) So. Hist. Pap. **8**: 202.
Columbia College. (E. I. Sears) Nat. Q. **18**: 303. — Appleton, **5**: 583.
— Dropsy at. (E. I. Sears) Nat. Q. **33**: 286.
— First Century of. Knick. **61**: 170.
— Geological Museum of. (I. C. Russell) Am. Natural. **13**: 502.
— History of. Am. Q. Reg. **7**: 344. — Chr. R. **2**: 115.
— Library of. (B. N. Betts) Lib. J. **2**: 70. — (W. A. Jones) University Q. **3**: 41.
Columbia County, N. Y., Lutheran Church in. (W. Hull) Luth. Q. **10**: 33.
Columbia River. Blackw. **87**: 215. — Mo. R. **126**: 496.
— Adventures on. Am. Meth. M. **14**: 274.
— and Puget Sound. (C. Nordhoff) Harper, **48**: 338.
— Cox's Adventures on. Westm. **16**: 130.
— First Settlement of. Hunt, **14**: 202.
— Missions on. (P. J. De Smet) U. S. Cath. M. **2**: 502–739.
— Mouth of. (F. F. Victor) Overland, **8**: 71.
— Up. (F. F. Victor) Overland, **8**: 146, 229.
See also Astoria; Shoshone.
Columbian Orator. New Eng. M. **7**: 309.
Columbine on Camelback. All the Year, **37**: 470.
Columbkill, St., Life of. Cath. World, **5**: 664.
Columbus, Christopher. (C. Cushing) No. Am. **21**: 398. — Ed. R. **27**: 492. — (T. P. Johnston) Blackw. **81**: 626. — (A. G. Knight) Month, **28**: 168, 257, 389. **29**: 29, 137. — with portrait, Ecl. M. **59**: 359. — Chamb. J. **31**: 44. — Nat. Q. **31**: 91. — (J. S. C. Abbott) Harper, **38**: 721.
— a Dramatic Fragment. St. Paul's, **2**: 179.
— a Poem. Cath. World, **5**: 525.
— Adventures of; a Poem. Dem. R. **22**: 120, 340, 420. **23**: 341.
— and Beatrice Enriquez. Hist. M. **5**: 225.
— and Captain Cook. Am. Ecl. **2**: 536.
— and Discovery of America. (R. H. Major) Am. Bibliop. **2**: 329. **3**: 9.
— and his Discoveries. (L. Hooker) Canad. Mo. **9**: 1.
— at Salamanca. Cath. World, **9**: 433.
— Bibliographical Account of Voyages of. Hist. M. **5**: 33.
Columbus, Christopher, Examination of Claims of. (M Maury) Harper, **42**: 425, 527.
— Genoa, Home of. (O. M. Spencer) Harper, **54**: 1.
— Landing of. (G. Gibbs) Hist. M. **2**: 161.
— Legend of; a Poem. Portfo.(Den.) **25**: 471.
— Letter of. Hist. M. **9**: 114.
— — 1493. Hist. M. **8**: 289.
— Letters of. Liv. Age, **17**: 356.
— Life of. (J. B. Duffey) Godey, **49**: 37–528.
— — and its Lessons. Chr. Obs. **61**: 430. Same art. Liv. Age, **72**: 359.
— — in Giustiniani Psalter, Turin, 1516. Hist. M. **6**: 370.
— — Irving's. (F. Jeffrey) Ed. R. **48**: 1. — (A. H. Everett) No. Am. **28**: 103. — Am. Q. **3**: 173. **9**: 163. — So. R. **2**: 1. **7**: 214. — Mus. **13**: 23. — So. Lit. Mess. **6**: 569. — Mo. R. **115**: 419. **124**: 244. — Colburn, **22**: 288. — Ecl. R. **47**: 224. — Lond. M. **21**: 281.
— Life and Voyages of. (A. C. Ramsey) Nation, **7**: 417.
— Memorials of. (J. Sparks) No. Am. **18**: 415. — Mo. R. **105**: 72.
— New Documents on. (C. Cushing) No. Am. **24**: 265.
— Note on. (J. R. Bartlett) Hist. M. **13**: 100.
— Own Account of his first Voyage. Anal. M. **9**: 513.
— Sketch of. Once a Week, **10**: 699.
— Where are the Remains of? (J. C. Brevoort) M. Am. Hist. **2**: 157.
Columbus, Fernando, Career of. (W. M. Wood) Once a Week, **12**: 165.
Columella auris in the Amphibia. (T. H. Huxley) Nature, **11**: 68.
Columns, Strength of. (E. Hatzel) Ecl. Engin. **17**: 237. — Am. Arch. **6**: 187.
— Wrought-Iron, Strength of. (G. Bouscaren) Am. Arch. **9**: 114.
Colville, Corporal. Lond. M. **7**: 132.
Colvine, M., Cumberland Mariner, Legend of. Lond. M. **4**: 594.
Comans, or Kipchaks. (H. W. Howorth) Geog. M. **4**: 19.
Combs. Chamb. J. **51**: 445.
— Manufacture of, at Aberdeen. Chamb. J. **16**: 70.
Combat, Judicial. (H. C. Lea) No. Am. **88**: 1.
— of the Thirty. (W. H. Ainsworth) Bentley, **45**: 5, 445.
Combe, Andrew, Life and Correspondence of. Liv. Age, **25**: 458.
Combe, George. (B. G. Wilder) Nation, **27**: 304.
— and Andrew. (H. Martineau) Once a Week, **4**: 575. Same art. Liv. Age, **70**: 22.
— Autobiography. (E. A. Youmans) Pop. Sci. Mo. **15**: 109.
— Constitution of Man. Brit. & For. R. **12**: 142. — Westm. **53**: 366. — Am. Mo. R. **3**: 417.
— Moral Philosophy. New York R. **1**: 218.
— Phrenology. Fraser, **22**: 509. — (F. Jeffrey) Ed. R. **44**: 253.
Combe, John, Poems of. Tait, n. s. **23**: 419.
Combe, William, Life and Writings. Dub. Univ. **75**: 316. Same art. Ecl. M. **74**: 611.
Combe, Colonel. Blackw. **77**: 536.
Comber, W. T., on National Subsistence. Ed. R. **13**: 205.
Combermere, S. S. C., Field-Marshal. Chamb. J. **43**: 462. — Fraser, **74**: 564. — Lond. Q. **27**: 177.
Combermere Abbey. (E. Walford) Once a Week, **15**: 514.
Combination and cheap Living. Cornh. **1**: 745. **7**: 189, 252. — Temp. Bar, **9**: 293. **12**: 396.
Combination Laws, Repeal of. Blackw. **18**: 20, 463.
Combinations. Blackw. **35**: 836. — Mo. R. **109**: 1.
Combustion (S. Morey) Am. J. Sci. **25**: 146.
— as applied to Steam Boilers. (W. M. Henderson) J. Frankl. Inst. **87**: 244.
— Chemical Process of. Blackw. **1**: 138. — (W. M. Henderson) J. Frankl. Inst. **87**: 166.
— in compressed Air. (F. Collingwood) J. Frankl. Inst. **95**: 345.

Combustion in rarefied Air. (E. Frankland) Canad. J. n. s. **6**: 380. — (E. Frankland) J. Frankl. Inst. **72**: 159.
— Influence of Pressure on. (L. Cailletet) J. Frankl. Inst. **104**: 127.
— Influence of Solar Light on. (J. L. LeConte) Am. J. Sci. **74**: 317.
— Spontaneous. Blackw. **89**: 385. Same art. Liv. Age, **69**: 728. — (W. Sargent) No. Am. **77**: 409. — Stud. & Intel. Obs. **2**: 128.
— Temperature of. (M. Berthollet) J. Frankl. Inst. **104**: 35.
Come to Grief in the Shires; a Tale. (C. Clarke) Temp. Bar, **18**: 549.
Come-outerism. Brownson, **1**: 367.
Comedians, American. (L. C. Davis) Atlan. **19**: 750.
Comedy, Athenian. Westm. **65**: 188.
— English. Broadw. **2**: 380.
— — in 1873. Dub. Univ. **82**: 747.
— — New School of. (W. Mackay) Colburn, **147**: 222.
— Fitzgerald's Principles of. Colburn, **148**: 49.
— French. (J. Pollock) Contemp. **18**: 43. — (F. Sarcey) 19th Cent. **6**: 182. — Cornh. **40**: 56. — Ev. Sat. **11**: 37. Same art. Appleton, **22**: 146. — Once a Week, **24**: 516. — Quar. **29**: 414.
— — D'Heylli on. (J. B. Matthews) Nation, **29**: 211.
— — Vaudeville. Tait, n. s. **4**: 621.
— Greek. Westm. **64**: 302.
— History of. (J. Mähly) Temp. Bar, **7**: 120.
— in a Courtyard. Chamb. J. **7**: 306. Same art. Liv. Age, **14**: 228.
— Italian. For. R. **3**: 190. **4**: 408.
— — Modern. (W. D. Howells) No. Am. **99**: 364.
— — Old. Dub. Univ. **63**: 67.
— Modern. Fraser, **89**: 235.
— New and old. (P. Fitzgerald) Belgra. **18**: 199.
— of Convocation. (J. R. G. Hassard) Cath. World, **6**: 554. Same art. N. Ecl. **1**: 208.
— of an Umbrella. (E. Dale) Canad. Mo. **11**: 519.
— of Creation; an Indian Poem. Dub. Univ. **91**: 313.
— of Terrors. (J. De Mille) Atlan. **29**: 36–716. **30**: 62–663.
— Principles of. Tinsley, **6**: 86. *See* Drama.
Comedy Writers of the Restoration. Temp. Bar, **57**: 539. Same art. Appleton, **23**: 109.
Comenius, John Amos. (K. von Raumer) Am. J. Educ. **5**: 257. — Chamb. J. **11**: 249.
Comet, Biela's. Intel. Obs. **11**: 208. — (R. A. Proctor) St. Paul's, **11**: 681.
— Brorsen's. (R. A. Proctor) Fraser, **79**: 158. Same art. Ecl. M. **72**: 421.
— — Spectrum of. (C. A. Young) Am. J. Sci. **117**: 373.
— Coggia's. (J. Birmingham) Dub. Univ. **84**: 524. — (W. A. Norton) Am. J. Sci. **115**: 161.
— Donati's, 1858. (G. P. Bond) Math. Mo. **1**: 61, 88. — (J. Williamson) Canad. J. n. s. **3**: 486. — Chamb. J. **31**: 57. — Ecl. M. **45**: 423. **46**: 121. — Ed. New Philos. J. **67**: 60. — (G. P. Bond) Am. Alma. **1860**: 42.
— — Dimensions of. (W. A. Norton) Am. J. Sci. **79**: 79, 383. **82**: 54.
— Encke's. (N. Bowditch) No. Am. **14**: 26. — (L. F. Wartmann) Am. Meth. M. **21**: 113.
— — Observations on. (C. A. Young) Am. J. Sci. **103**: 81.
— Halley's. (E. Loomis) Am. J. Sci. **30**: 209. **55**: 370. — For. Q. **15**: 477. — Ed. R. **61**: 82. — Penny M. **4**: 360. — Quar. **55**: 195.
— In the Trail of a. (J. Carpenter) Once a Week, **17**: 577.
— Journey on a. (W. Leitch) Good Words, **2**: 516.
— Lost, and its Meteor-Train. (R. A. Proctor) Pop. Sci. R. **12**: 139.
— of 1106. Nature, **17**: 189.
Comet of 1744, Multiple Tail of. (J. R. Hind) Stud. & Intel. Obs. **5**: 58.
— of 1812 and of 1846, Origin of. (D. Kirkwood) Am. J. Sci. **98**: 255.
— of 1825, Elements of. (W. Colburn) U. S. Lit. Gaz. **3**: 317.
— of 1832. (F. Arago) J. Frankl. Inst. **14**: 315.
— of 1843. (B. Peirce) Am. Alma. **1844**: 94. — Am. J. Sci. **44**: 412. — (E. O. Kendall) Am. J. Sci. **45**: 188.
— of 1847. (W. Mitchell) Am. J. Sci. **55**: 83.
— of 1858. (J. P. Cherriman) Canad. J. n. s. **8**: 57.
— of 1860, Expected great. (G. W. F. Chambers) Recr. Sci. **1**: 139.
— of 1861. Am. J. Sci. **82**: 252. — Once a Week, **5**: 138. — (J. Breen) Pop. Sci. R. **1**: 111. — Recr. Sci. **3**: 141.
— — Physical Aspects of. (J. M. Gilliss) Am. J. Sci. **82**: 305.
— of 1862. Cornh. **6**: 550.
— of 1862, Sec nd. Intel. Obs. **2**: 198.
— of 1880, Great Southern. (A. M. Clerke) Fraser, **104**: 224. Same art. Liv. Age, **150**: 760. — (B. A. Gould) Am. J. Sci. **119**: 396.
— of *b*, 1881. (L. Boss) Am. J. Sci. **122**: 140, 303. — (H. Draper) Am. J. Sci. **122**: 134. — (C. A. Young) Am. J. Sci. **122**: 135. — (W. Harkness) Am. J. Sci. **122**: 137. — (A. W. Wright) Am. J. Sci. **122**: 142, 372. — (E. S. Holden) Am. J. Sci. **122**: 260.
— Winnecke's. (R. A. Proctor) Fraser, **79**: 739. Same art. Ecl. M. **73**: 413.
Comet of a Season; a Novel. (J. McCarthy) Gent. M. n. s. **26**: 1–641. **27**: 1–641.
Comets. (S r D. Brewster) No. Brit. **35**: 495. — (Sir J. F. W. Herschel) Good Words, **4**: 476, 549. — (J. N. Lockyer) Nature, **10**: 149, 179, 226. — (J. Lovering) Am. Alma. **1853**: 69. — (A. N. Skinner) Pop. Sci. Mo. **19**: 790. — Appleton, **12**: 105. — House. Words, **15**: 481. — Ecl. R. **109**: 30. Same art. Ecl. M. **46**: 407. — Chamb. J. **18**: 102. **20**: 30. **28**: 6. **46**: 361. **58**: 549. — Ecl. M. **31**: 563. — Hogg, **12**: 459. Same art. Ecl. M. **34**: 368. — Fraser, **65**: 95. — Liv. Age, **71**: 139, 207. — Nat. M. **6**: 355, 449. — No. Brit. **35**: 495. — Penny M. **1**: 283, 291. — Quar. **55**: 105. — Am. Alma. **1830**: 88.
— and Meteors. Appleton, **2**: 434, 524. — Ed. R. **140**: 393. — Ev. Sat. **4**: 780.
— — Connection between. Nature, **7**: 468.
— and temporary Stars. (T. W. Tobin) J. Frankl. Inst. **109**: 272.
— and their Orbits. (D. Trowbridge) Nat. Q. **17**: 339.
— and their Phenomena. Ecl. M. **55**: 329.
— Arago on. (J. Farrer) No. Am. **42**: 196. — Am. Mo. R. **2**: 250, 335.
— as Portents. (R. A. Proctor) Belgra. **32**: 195.
— Astronomy of. Fraser, **50**: 47.
— Catalogue of. Am. Alma. **1847**: 82.
— — with Orbits. (G. W. F. Chambers) Recr. Sci. **1**: 195–321.
— Chemistry of. (E. Divers) Pop. Sci. R. **8**: 400.
— Classification of. (R. A. Proctor) Pop. Sci. R. **13**: 350. Same art. Ecl. M. **84**: 87. Same art. Liv. Age, **124**: 54.
— Collision of two. (J. J. Littrow) Am. J. Sci. **24**: 346.
— Dangers from. (R. A. Proctor) Cornh. **44**: 698. — Liv. Age, **114**: 170.
— Disintegration of. (D. Kirkwood) Nature, **6**: 148.
— Distinguishing Features of. (R. V. Marsh) Am. J. Sci. **83**: 89.
— Dynamical Condition of Head of. (W. A. Norton) Am. J. Sci. **77**: 86.
— Essay on. (D. Milne) Ed. New Philos. J. **5**: 343.
— Five. House. Words, **18**: 409.

Comets, Forms of. (H. A. E. Faye) Nature, **10**: 227–287.
— Guillemin's World of. (J. R. Hind) Nature, **16**: 5.
— Lectures on. Gen. Repos. **1**: 160.
— List of. (G. Chambers) Intel. Obs. **2**: 383. **3**: 97, 252. **4**: 218, 381. **5**: 218, 373. **6**: 131, 298, 373. **8**: 125–379. **9**: 64.
— Milne on. Ecl. R. **50**: 286.
— Nature of. Knick. **9**: 34.
— New Theory of. New Eng. M. **7**: 276.
— News about. (R. A. Proctor) Temp. Bar, **21**: 203. Same art. Ecl. M. **69**: 618.
— of 1860. (G. F. Chambers) Recr. Sci. **2**: 99, 212, 283.
— of 1868. (R. A. Proctor) Fraser, **79**: 158, 739. Same art. Ecl. M. **72**: 421. **73**: 413.
— of 1881. Nature, **24**: 197–612.
— of short Period. Chamb. J. **45**: 471. Same art. Ecl. M. **72**: 108.
— Orbits of, Elements of. (C. Abbe) Am. J. Sci. **88**: 79. — (J. C. Watson) Am. J. Sci. **85**: 218.
— Origin of. (H. A. Newton) Am. J. Sci. **116**: 165.
— Periodical. All the Year, **27**: 388.
— Spectra of. (H. Vogel) Nature, **9**: 193.
— Structure and Movements of. (G. F. Chambers) Recr. Sci. **2**: 77–197.
— Tails of. (H. M. Parkhurst) Am. J. Sci. **109**: 37. — (W. Mitchell) Am. J. Sci. **38**: 35. **40**: 59. — (W. A. Norton) Am. J. Sci. **46**: 104. — (R. A. Proctor) St. Paul's, **8**: 547. Same art. Ecl. M. **78**: 55. Same art. Liv. Age, **111**: 44. — Cornh. **30**: 309. Same art. Ecl. M. **83**: 745. Same art. Liv. Age, **123**: 247.
— — and Comas. (W. H. C. Bartlett) Am. J. Sci. **79**: 62.
— — Formation of. (M. Faye) Pop. Sci. R. **20**: 327.
— — Halley on. (B. F. Joslin) Am. J. Sci. **31**: 142, 324.
— Tyndall's Theory of. (R. A. Proctor) Fraser, **80**: 504. Same art. Ecl. M. **74**: 83.
— What are they? Ecl. R. **109**: 30. Same art. Ecl. M. **46**: 407.
Cometary Astronomy. Danv. Q. **1**: 614.
Cometary Universe. So. R. n. s. **8**: 386.
Cometh up as a Flower. (R. Broughton) Dub. Univ. **68**: 24–618. **69**: 38.
Comfort in its Relations to Physical Culture. (S. B. Hunt) Hours at Home, **10**: 123.
Comic, The. Dial, **4**: 247.
Comic Alpenstock. Dub. Univ. **30**: 371, 560, 710.
Comic and Satirical Literature of Middle Ages. For. Q. **37**: 75.
Comic Annuals, 1840. Mo. R. **151**: 109.
— 1842, Hood's. Mo. R. **156**: 600.
Comic Artist. (T. Westwood) Fraser, **52**: 587.
Comic Blackstone. Ecl. M. **1**: 207.
Comic Drama, Modern. Blackw. **19**: 46.
Comic Dramatists of the Restoration. (T. B. Macaulay) Ed. R. **72**: 490. — (J. Pyne) Nat. Q. **34**: 306.
Comic History of England. Ecl. R. **88**: 533.
Comic Literature in England. Temp. Bar, **9**: 590.
Comic Papers. Sharpe, **40**: 260. — (E. L. Godkin) Nation, **11**: 434.
— of Germany. (E. Wilberforce) Once a Week, **14**: 402.
Comic Periodicals in U. S. Am. Bibliop. **7**: 199, 262.
Comic Writers of England. (C. C. Clarke) Gent. M. n. s. **6**: 503, 631. **7**: 27–823. **8**: 38–659.
See Burlesque Writers; Humor.
Comines, Philip de, Memoirs of. (Mrs. B. Hofland) Retros. **7**: 14.
Coming Crisis. Dub. Univ. **2**: 1.
Coming into a Fortune. All the Year, **8**: 354. Same art. Liv. Age, **76**: 168.
Coming Man. Chamb. J. **15**: 216.
Coming Marriage. (A. Rhodes) Galaxy, **16**: 293.
Coming of the Spring; a Poem. (D. M. Craik) Good Words, **2**: 224.
Coming One; a Meditation. (W. R. C. Rogers) Kitto, **38**: 350.
Coming together. Tinsley, **4**: 182.
Commandments of God. (B. F. Bowles) Univ. Q. **36**: 480.
— Ten. *See* Decalogue.
Commencement a Century ago. Penn Mo. **2**: 315.
Commencements of Colleges, Seminaries, etc. (E. I. Sears) Nat. Q. **9**: 347. **11**: 366. *See* College Commencements.
Commentaries. *See* Bible, Commentaries.
Commentator, Old. Chamb. J. **28**: 209.
Commeragh Mountains, Lakes and Legends of. Dub. Univ. **34**: 420, 533.
Commerce. (H. M. Dennison) De Bow, **26**: 149. — (G. M. Weston) Hunt, **36**: 19. — Ox. Prize Ess. **2**: 29. — Westm. **7**: 126. — So. Lit. Mess. **9**: 185.
— Advantages of. (F. Hunt) Hunt, **1**: 200.
— Agriculture and Manufactures, Progress of. (T. P. Kettell) De Bow, **4**: 85.
— American. (F. Gilbert) Lakeside, **5**: 125.
— — Annals of. Hunt, **11**: 65–545. **12**: 365, 459.
— — Domestic. (S. Shellabarger) Internat. R. **1**: 819.
— — Foreign. Hunt, **17**: 153. — Niles's Reg. **31**: 355.
— — New Fields for. (J. D. B. De Bow) De Bow, **4**: 475.
— — Openings for. Hunt, **15**: 137.
— — Progress of. (J. D. B. De Bow) De Bow, **2**: 368. — (J. H. Lanman) Hunt, **5**: 37.
— Ancient, Lindsay's. Ed. R. **143**: 420.
— — and modern. Dub. Univ. **28**: 391.
— and Agriculture, Subjects of University Instruction. (J. D. B. De Bow) De Bow, **3**: 502.
— and Christianity. (R. Bickersteth) Ex. H. Lec. **4**: 79.
— — Chalmers on. Meth. M. **44**: 452.
— and Commercial Biography. (W. Arthur) Hunt, **27**: 570.
— and Commercial Character. (P. Hone) Hunt, **4**: 129. **10**: 65.
— and Finances. De Bow, **15**: 196.
— and the Fine Arts. (G. Cook) De Bow, **1**: 269.
— and great Cities. Hunt, **13**: 245.
— and Manufactures. No. Am. **17**: 186. — Westm. **2**: 280.
— and Missionary Enterprise. Hunt, **16**: 65.
— and Navigation, Academy of, at Trieste. Hunt, **16**: 60.
— — Schools of, Belgium. Am. J. Educ. **21**: 623.
— — of the United States, 1831. Niles's Reg. **43**: 155.
— — — 1833. Niles's Reg. **44**: 241.
— — — 1845. Hunt, **14**: 465.
— and the Navy. (C. A. Washburn) Penn Mo. **8**: 808.
— and Protection. (H. Greeley) Hunt, **1**: 53, 413. — Dem. R. **6**: 249.
— and the Sea, Moral Uses of. (H. Bushnell) Hunt, **14**: 60.
— and War. Nation, **11**: 185.
— Art and Science applied to. Hunt, **11**: 73, 163.
— as a liberal Pursuit. (C. King) Hunt, **2**: 1.
— as connected with Civilization. (D. D. Barnard) Hunt, **1**: 3.
— as connected with Learning. (A. Bradford) Hunt, **3**: 394.
— Bearing of Circumstances on. Westm. **10**: 96.
— before the Christian Era. Hunt, **13**: 307.
— Benefits and Evils of. Hunt, **24**: 147.
— Christianized. (R. T. Jeffrey) Ex. H. Lec. **16**: 287.
— Conquests of. (B. G. Smith) Hunt, **32**: 706.
— Dignity and Importance of. (J. Hall) De Bow, **4**: 1.
— Divine Uses of. (E. L. Magoon) Hunt, **27**: 33.
— Dutch. (M. B. Lecompte) Hunt, **5**: 437.
— Eastern, Old-Time. (W. L. Fawcette) Atlan. **36**: 468.
— Effect of, in abolishing Restrictions on Transfers of Property. (B. F. Porter) Hunt, **22**: 385.
— English, Early. Lond. Soc. **5**: 129. Same art. Ecl. M **63**: 57.
— — in Middle Ages. Ecl. R. **116**: 426.

Commerce, Equitable: Cost the scientific Limit of Price. (S. P. Andrews) Hunt, **24**: 332.
— Evils of. Hunt, **3**: 76.
— Foreign and domestic Industry. (E. Everett) No. Am. **10**: 316.
— Freedom of. Quar. **24**: 281.
— — of belligerent. (J. N. Pomeroy) Nation, **11**: 116.
— Geography of. (J. B. Auld) De Bow, **15**: 385.
— History of. Westm. **60**: 609.
— — Ancient. (J. W. Gilbart) Hunt, **19**: 131–467.
— — McPherson's. (G. Ellis) Ed. R. **8**: 237.
— in Art, Present State of. Art J. **6**: 312.
— in 12th Century. (W. H. Browne) So. M. **9**: 174.
— Influence of. (G. R. Russell) Hunt, **24**: 531, 681. **25**: 39.
— — on Education. (L. Woodbury) Hunt, **10**: 456.
— — on Language. (A. R. Ryder) Hunt, **24**: 174.
— — on Law. Hunt, **27**: 147.
— — on the World. (R. C. Winthrop) Hunt, **14**: 122.
— Inter-State, Congress and. (J. D. Potts) Nation, **28**: 79.
— — Taxation of. (B. Adams) Internat. R. **10**: 428.
— Is it inimical to Art? Art J. **3**: 192.
— McCulloch's Dictionary of. Mo. R. **128**: 389. — Ecl. R. **56**: 209.
— Moral Influence of. (G. Fisk) Ex. H. Lec. **3**: 287.
— Moral Limits of beneficial. (F. W. Newman) Contemp. **36**: 232.
— of Ancient Egypt. (J. W. Gilbart) Hunt, **19**: 131, 243.
— of Ancient Rome. (J. W. Gilbart) Hunt, **19**: 467.
— of Asia and Oceanica. (A. B. Stout) Overland, **8**: 171.
— of Boston. (J. H. Lanman) Hunt, **10**: 421.
— of Canada. Hunt, **6**: 538.
— of Ceylon. Hunt, **16**: 339.
— of Cuba. Hunt, **7**: 319. **9**: 337.
— of Europe. (E. W. Stoughton) Hunt, **1**: 465.
— — Oddy on. (M. Napier) Ed. R. **8**: 128. — Ecl. R. **3**: 38, 134.
— of France. Hunt, **8**: 438. **18**: 497.
— — England and United States, 1827–36. (M. D. L. Rodet) Hunt, **7**: 13.
— — in 1849. Hunt, **24**: 284.
— of Great Britain. (G. M. Weston) Bank. M. (N. Y.) **32**: 266. — Hunt, **8**: 131. — (A. J. Wilson) Fraser, **94**: 269–736. **95**: 82–701. **96**: 204, 382.
— — Reinhard on State of, 1804. Ecl. R. **1**: 291.
— of Italy in the Middle Ages. (R. Seton) Cath. World, **23**: 79.
— of Philadelphia. Hunt, **14**: 423.
— of Rio de Janeiro, 1836–47. Hunt, **16**: 371.
— of St. Louis. Hunt, **15**: 162.
— of Straits of Malacca. (J. Balestier) Hunt, **16**: 351.
— of Syria. (J. W. Jenks) Hunt, **6**: 489.
— of the East. (H. F. Harrington) Hunt, **1**: 202.
— of the Lakes. Hunt, **6**: 439. **18**: 488.
— of the Mississippi. (J. H. Lanman) Hunt, **9**: 154.
— of the Prairies. Hunt, **11**: 501.
— of Tyre and Carthage. (J. W. Gilbart) Hunt, **19**: 355.
— of United States. (J. Quincy) No. Am. **3**: 345. — (J. D. B. De Bow) De Bow, **9**: 365. — (M. Nourse) Bank. M. (N. Y.) **11**: 625, 673, 785. — (L. Sabine) No. Am. **57**: 293.
— — 1790–1847. J. Frankl. Inst. **45**: 350.
— — 1821. Niles's Reg. **22**: 51, 74.
— — 1822. Niles's Reg. **24**: 60.
— — 1823. Niles's Reg. **27**: 124, 142.
— — 1824. Niles's Reg. **28**: 282.
— — 1841. Hunt, **7**: 481, 558.
— — 1847. Hunt, **19**: 87.
— — and the Currency. No. Am. **90**: 39. — Bank. M. (N. Y.) **14**: 689.
— — and Great Britain. Bank. M. (N.Y.) **11**: 1. — Fraser, **94**: 572.
Commerce of United States and Great Britain, Improvement of. (J. Leavitt) Liv. Age, **102**: 195.
— — and West Indies. Quar. **39**: 215.
— — Foreign. Bank. M. (N. Y.) **32**: 200.
— — from 1842 to 1847. Hunt, **18**: 533.
— — Inter-State. *See* Commerce, Inter-State.
— — Pitkin on. Anal. M. **8**: 281, 456. — Mo. R. **139**: 171.
— — with China. Hunt, **11**: 54.
— — with the World. Hunt, **14**: 365.
— of West Indies. (J. R. Williams) Hunt, **19**: 19.
— of Western Asia, Ancient. (A. Barnes) Am. Bib. Repos. **5**: 48. 2d s. **3**: 300.
— of Western Lakes. Hunt, **15**: 348.
— Origin, Progress, and Influences of. (J. D. B. De Bow) De Bow, **1**: 98.
— Physical Conditions and. (R. Edwards) Hunt, **28**: 548.
— Power and Influence of. (S. Beaman) Hunt, **23**: 632.
— Prejudice against. (B. F. Porter) Hunt, **10**: 392.
— Principles of. (G. R. Porter) Bank. M. (L.) **11**: 461.
— — and Tendencies of modern. (G. P. Marsh) Hunt, **33**: 147.
— Professorship of. (J. D. B. De Bow) De Bow, **6**: 110.
— Progress of. (A. H. Ryder) Hunt, **33**: 659.
— Protection to. Niles's Reg. **23**: 305.
— — 1787. Carey's Mus. **2**: 263.
— — 1820. Niles's Reg. **19**: 153.
— Restrictions on foreign. Ed. R. **33**: 331.
— Rise and Progress of. (F. Hunt) Hunt, **1**: 193.
— Romance of. (A. J. Lawson) Lakeside, **9**: 351.
— Scheme for rebuilding Southern. So. Lit. Mess. **5**: 2.
— Sermon on. (J. T. Hendrick) Hunt, **28**: 672.
— Special Schools of, in England. Am. J. Educ. **22**: 177.
— — in France. Am. J. Educ. **21**: 533.
— Speculations on. (W. W. Wheildon) Hunt, **3**: 237.
— Tribunals of. Dub. Univ. **85**: 257.
— with Africa. Fraser, **43**: 30.
— with Eastern Coast of Africa. Hunt, **16**: 29.
— with Japan. (J. Aldrich) Hunt, **1**: 208.
See Trade.
Commercial Activity revived. Bank. M. (N. Y.) **31**: 843.
Commercial Age. (J. D. B. De Bow) De Bow, **7**: 225.
Commercial and Financial Policy. (T. P. Thompson) Westm. **18**: 168, 421.
Commercial and Manufacturing Prosperity. Blackw. **69**: 700.
Commercial Associations of France and England. Hunt, **12**: 409, 500.
Commercial Banking. (W. M. Gouge) Hunt, **8**: 313.
Commercial Change Hours. Hunt, **8**: 389.
Commercial Code of Spain. (A. Nash) Hunt, **15**: 267, 556. **16**: 378. **18**: 614. **19**: 59, 178, 619. **20**: 628. **21**: 528. **22**: 73, 526. **23**: 199, 312.
Commercial Colleges. Hunt, **39**: 410.
Commercial Copartnerships. Hunt, **12**: 361.
Commercial Crisis. *See* Panics.
Commercial Decline in Spain. (F. Wharton) Hunt, **7**: 493.
Commercial Delusions. (J. C. Cotton) Am. Whig R. **2**: 341.
Commercial Distress. Ed. R. **27**: 373. — Quar. **43**: 278.
Commercial Docks. (D. J. Brown) Hunt, **5**: 239.
Commercial Embarrassments, 1819. Ed. R. **32**: 48.
Commercial Events, Sketch of. Bank. M. (N.Y.) **12**: 903.
Commercial Facilities of the American Continent. (A. Whitman) Hunt, **19**: 625.
Commercial Failures in Europe and America. De Bow, **24**: 183.
— of 1847. Ecl. R. **88**: 750.
See Failures.
Commercial Fields, New. (F. Hunt) Hunt, **1**: 142.
Commercial Grief. Once a Week, **2**: 216.
Commercial Growth of the West. (J. Hall) Hunt, **17**: 495.
Commercial Histories. For. Q. **6**: 49.

Commercial History of France. (F. Wharton) Hunt, **5**: 105. **7**: 301.
Commercial Intercourse. Niles's Reg. **14**: 111.
— between Atlantic and Pacific. Blackw. **54**: 658.
— impeding Revolution. (F. Wharton) Hunt, **9**: 321.
— with British Colonies. Hunt, **12**: 262.
Commercial Jurisprudence. (G. Eustis) De Bow, **3**: 56, 160.
Commercial Law. (J. K. Angell) Hunt, **15**: 131.
— Green on. Mo. R. **104**: 23.
Commercial Laws of the State. Bank M. (N. Y.) **25**: 17-911. **26**: 261.
Commercial Lawyers. Hunt, **14**: 63.
Commercial League of Hanse Towns. (E. W. Stoughton) Hunt, **2**: 273.
Commercial Legislation. (G. S. Boutwell) Hunt, **7**: 427.
— American Seamen in foreign Ports. Hunt, **11**: 344.
— English. (G. S. Boutwell) Hunt, **11**: 121. **17**: 241.
— New York. (J. B. Varnum) Hunt, **21**: 25.
— Sketches of. (F. Wharton) Hunt, **9**: 30, 495. **10**: 399, 522.
Commercial Literature. Hunt, **19**: 670.
Commercial Marine of Britain and America. (N. W. Beckwith) Canad. Mo. **5**: 461.
Commercial Morals. (T. Walker) West. J. **1**: 293.—(Dr. Dennison) De Bow, **27**: 444.
— in America and England. (E. L. Godkin) Nation, **6**: 24.
— R. Heber Newton on. (J. Dyer) Penn Mo. **8**: 145.
Commercial Paper, Law of. Bank. M. (N. Y.) **21**: 1-610.
Commercial Papers, British, 1820. Niles's Reg. **18**: 345.
Commercial Philanthropy. No. Brit. **41**: 254.
Commercial Policy, British. (T. P. Kettell) Hunt, **12**: 538. — (J. R. McCulloch) Ed. R. **55**: 421. — Dem. R. **17**: 137. — Westm. **18**: 168.
— — on the Continent. Fraser, **34**: 499.
— European, 1843. Blackw. **54**: 243, 406, 637.
— of ancient and modern Nations. (J. D. B. De Bow) De Bow, **1**: 142.
— of England and Germany. Westm. **43**: 77.
— Russian. Blackw. **53**: 807.
— Spanish, 1843. Blackw. **53**: 673.
Commercial Power of Great Britain. Quar. **30**: 368. — Westm. **4**: 337.
Commercial Practices, Theory and Law in. Dub. Univ. **95**: 53.
Commercial Progress of four Centuries. Hunt, **46**: 17.
Commercial Reciprocity. (C. C. Haven) Hunt, **10**: 354. — Dem. R. **14**: 447.
Commercial Reform. Brit. Q. **1**: 514. — Dem. R. **18**: 214.
Commercial Regulations with China. Hunt, **11**: 365.
— with Mexico, 1847. Hunt, **16**: 455.
— — during the War. (F. O. Dorr) Hunt, **15**: 250.
Commercial Relations of France and England. (T. P. Thompson) Westm. **21**: 257.
— of England and Poland. Brit. & For. R. **6**: 505.
of Great Britain. Westm. **35**: 391.
— of Indian Archipelago. Fraser, **34**: 379.
— of United States. (J. H. Lanman) Hunt, **5**: 507.
Commercial Revulsions. Ed. R. **44**: 70. — Mus. **9**: 412.
Commercial Sermons, Chalmers's. Blackw. **8**: 178.—Chr. Mo Spec. **4**: 19, 82.
Commercial Spirit of the Age. (Dr. Scott) De Bow, **18**: 647.
— — Moral Influence of. (W. A. Scott) Pioneer, **3**: 150.
— of the South. (J. Gadsden) De Bow, **2**: 119.
Commercial Statistics and a Commercial Code. (L. Levi) J. Statis. Soc. **15**: 108.
— Foreign. Bank. M. (N. Y.) **11**: 795, 863, 944. **12**: 17.
— Macgregor's. Ed. R. **82**: 204.—Westm. **42**: 437. Same art. Ecl. M. **5**: 341.
Commercial Supremacy. (G. R. Gibson) Bank. M. (N. Y.) **32**: 113.
— Evils of. (D. R. Hundley) Hunt, **36**: 316.
Commercial Suretyship. (N. Merrill) Hunt, **12**: 330.
Commercial System of East India Co. Mo. R. **134**: 353.
— of France. Ed. R. **50**: 48.
— of United States. (J. H. Lanman) Hunt, **11**: 47.
Commercial Tariffs; German Zollverein. Ed. R. **79**: 105.
Commercial Terms, Dictionary of. Bank. M. (N. Y.) **15**: 545.
Commercial Traveler. Chamb. J. **53**: 813.
Commercial Travelers. (A. L. Stimson) Hunt, **1**: 29. — Chamb. J. **43**: 319.
Commercial Treaty of England with France, 1880. (J. Slagg) Fortn. **27**: 377. — (E. R. Duval) 19th Cent. **8**: 99.
— of United States with France, Proposed, 1880. (G. Schwab) Nation, **30**: 109.
— — with Spain. Brit. & For. R. **5**: 616.
— — with Austria. Brit. & For. R. **8**: 95.
Commercial Treaties. Hunt, **9**: 540. — Dem. R. **20**: 486. — (T. P. Kettell) Hunt, **17**: 339.
— between England and France, 1877 and 1777. Bank M. (L.) **37**: 153.
— between European States, Results of. (L. Levi) J. Statis. Soc. **40**: 1.
— of Reciprocity. (J. L. Tellkampf) Hunt, **14**: 51. — De Bow, **14**: 525.
— Policy of. (J. Morley) Fortn. **35**: 794.
— a Surrender of Principle. (J. Bird) Fortn. **36**: 260.
Commercial Tribunals and Court of Commerce for New York. Hunt, **25**: 174.
Commercial Union from a Canadian Point of View. (Sir F. Hincks) Fortn. **35**: 618.
Commercial Voyages and Discoveries. (W. S. Mayo) Hunt, **6**: 393, 531. **7**: 57, 174.
Commines, P. de. *See* Comines.
Commission Rates adopted by the New York Chamber of Commerce. Hunt, **9**: 280.
Commissions. (A. G. Sedgwick) Nation, **10**: 203.
— Illicit. Westm. **108**: 31.
— Patronage of. Westm. **46**: 222.
— Purchase of. Quar. **124**: 525.
Commissionaires, Corps of. All the Year, **12**: 62.—Chamb. J. **55**: 600.
— Our. Chamb. J. **38**: 28.
Commissioner, or De Lunatico Inquirendo. Dub. Univ. **22**: 340.
Commodus, Bust of. (C. Grindriez) Portfo. **7**: 148.
Commons and open Spaces, Our. Fraser, **73**: 652.
— Enclosure of. (H. Fawcett) Fraser, **81**: 185. — Penny M. **14**: 347, 355.
— Our common Land. (O. Hill) Macmil. **33**: 536.
— Preservation of. Fraser, **84**: 293.
Common Law. *See* Law, Common.
Common Prayer, Book of. Brit. Q. **47**: 70. — (J. Conington) Contemp. **7**: 401. — Blackw. **18**: 573.
— Adaptedness of. (W. Payne) Am. Church R. **8**: 67. — Quar. **149**: 405.
— American. (J. Dowden) Contemp. **21**: 119. — Liv. Age, **116**: 84.
— — Revision of. (W. R. Huntington) Am. Church R. **34**: 11. — (J. Emott) Am. Church R. **35**: 37. — (A. C. A. Hall) Am. Church R. **36**: 113.
— and 39 Articles. (J. M. Capes) Contemp. **17**: 218.
— Blakeney on. Chr. Obs. **65**: 814. **66**: 838.
— Dogmatic Teaching of. Month, **8**: 314.
— History and Merits of. Ecl. R. **72**: 489.
— Principles and Influences of. Chr. Obs. **77**: 93.
— Revision of. Ed. R. **140**: 427. — Blackw. **89**: 20. — Chr. Rem. **30**: 68. **39**: 208. **46**: 58. **50**: 200.
— — and the Act of Uniformity. (F. D. Maurice) Macmil. **1**: 447.
— — in 1661-62. (C. A. Swainson) Chr. Obs. **77**: 545. 595.
— — in Church of Ireland. Chr. Obs. **77**: 681.

Common Prayer, Book of, Revision of, Literary Aspects of. (J. Dowden) Contemp. **18**: 267.
Common Schools. (G. B. Emerson) Chr. Exam. **36**: 411. — (O. Dewey) No. Am. **24**: 156. — (J. Maclean) Princ. **5**: 217. — New Eng. M. **3**: 194. — Chr. Mo. Spec. **9**: 85, 125. — (J. S. Hart) Princ. **38**: 25. — Brownson, **15**: 70.
— and higher Seminaries. (C. Hammond) New Eng. **6**: 313.
— and public Instruction, 1800–70. Am. J. Educ. **24**: 225.
— Duties of Female Teachers. (D. Kimball) Am. Inst. of Instruc. **1836**: 103.
— Female Teachers for. Chr. Exam. **34**: 371.
— Importance of. (S. J. May) Am. Inst. of Instruc. **1843**: 225.
— Improvement of. (S. Farley) Am. Inst. of. Instruc. **1834**: 67. — (W. D. Swan) Am. Inst. of Instruc. **1848**: 125.
— in South Carolina. De Bow, **18**: 119.
— in United States. Am. J. Educ. **2**: 257, 465. — (B. Peters) Univ. Q. **23**: 224. — St. Paul's, **6**: 344.
— Influence of Academies and High Schools on. (W. C. Fowler) Am. Inst. of Instruc. **1831**: 183.
— Management of. (T. Dwight, jr.) Am. Inst. of Instruc. **1835**: 203.
— Means of cultivating a Classic Taste in. (L. B. Lincoln) Am. Inst. of Instruc. **1839**: 75.
— Obligations of Towns to elevate. (L. B. Lincoln) Am. Inst. of Instruc. **1846**: 109.
— Obstacles to. (C. Northend) Am. Inst. of Instruc. **1844**: 64.
— of Connecticut. New York R. **10**: 331. — (J. A. Root) New Eng. **4**: 522.
— of Massachusetts. Ed. R. **73**: 260. — (J. G. Palfrey) No. Am. **44**: 503. — (R. Rantoul, jr.) No. Am. **47**: 274. — (G. B. Emerson) No. Am. **52**: 148. — (E. B. Hall) Chr. Exam. **33**: 97. **34**: 366. — (E. Wigglesworth) Chr. Exam. **38**: 229.
— of New England. (G. Ticknor) No. Am. **19**: 448.
— of Rhode Island. (N. Porter, jr.) No. Am. **67**: 240.
— opposed. (H. Harbaugh) Mercersb. **5**: 32.
— Religious Instruction in. (F. A. Packard) Princ **13**: 315.
— Romanism and. (A. Stevens) Meth. Q. **30**: 204.
— Speech on, at Westminster. (M. Arnold) Macmil. **29**: 361.
— System of. (S. Eliot) No. Am. **106**: 128. — De Bow, **20**: 239.
Common-School Education. (R. Rantoul. jr.) No. Am. **47**: 273. — (G. S. Hillard and J. G. Palfrey) No. Am. **54**: 458. — (J. E. Cabot) No. Am. **103**: 291. — (H. A. Miles) Chr. Exam. **45**: 217. — (O. Dewey) No. Am. **9**: 167. — (T. Dwight) Lit. & Theo. R. **2**: 326. — (G. F. Walker) Radical, **6**: 462.
— Essentials of, and their Attainment. (R. Putnam) Am. Inst. of Instruc. **1846**: 55.
See Education; Schools.
Common-School Journal, Mann's. Chr. Exam. **27**: 320.
Common-School Library of Massachusetts. Chr. Exam. **30**: 263. — (A. P. Peabody) No. Am. **50**: 505.
Common Sense. Unita. R. **12**: 315. — (E. O. Simpson) University Q. **3**: 85. — Ox. Prize Ess. **2**: 85. — Ed. Mo. R. **2**: 670.
— and moral Sense. (T. Harper) Month, **13**: 466.
— Importance of. Am. Meth. M. **10**: 168.
— in Men and Poets. U. S. Lit. Gaz. **2**: 182.
— Philosophy of. Blackw. **62**: 239. — So. Lit. Mess. **5**: 536.
— What is? (B. W. Carpenter) Contemp. **19**: 401.
— Wilson's Prize Essay on. Chr. Obs. **19**: 235, 307.
Commoner's Daughter; a Tale. Sharpe, **43**: 1–281.
Commonplace; a Tale. (I. G. Meredith) O. & N. **2**: 16.
Commonplace, The. Irish Mo. **2**: 589.
Commonplace Book, Plan for a. (W. A. Guy) J. Statis. Soc. **3**: 353.
Commonplace People. Dub. Univ. **77**: 231.
Commons and Charles I., 1642. All the Year, **3**: 150.
— Battle of. (H. King) Once a Week, **15**: 24.
See House of Commons.
Commonwealths, Growth of. (E. A. Freeman) Fortn. **20**: 434. Same art. Liv. Age, **119**: 451.
— Ideal. (S. W. Lewis) Nat. Q. **38**: 1.
— Imaginary. (J. S. Cox) Dem. R. **19**: 175.
— Refinement of Ages before and after. Lond. M. **1**: 263.
Communal Fête. Chamb. J. **23**: 236.
Commune, The, and the Internationale. Quar. **131**: 549.
— and the Nation. (T. Gray) J. Spec. Philos. **12**: 44.
— and English Working Classes. (T. Wright) Fraser, **84**: 62.
— Birth of, 1831–39. (J. H. D. Debar) Internat. R. **6**: 141.
— in Paris, 1871. (J. Andrieu) Fortn. **16**: 571. — (Gen. Cluseret) Fraser, **86**: 782. **87**: 360. — (E. L. Godkin) Nation, **12**: 193, 253. — (F. Harrison) Fortn. **15**: 556. — (A. S. Hill) No. Am. **116**: 90. — Macmil. **24**: 384, 487. — (W. J. Linton) Radical, **9**: 81. — (J. Mazzini) Contemp. **17**: 307. Same art. Liv. Age, **110**: 112. — (G. Ramsay) Month, **16**: 60. — Ed. R. **134**: 250, 511. — Fraser, **83**: 798. **84**: 230. — (Count Orsi) Fraser, **100**: 784. — Liv. Age, **143**: 811. — Blackw. **110**: 118. Same art. Ecl. M. **77**: 274.
— — and the Assembly. (E. L. Godkin) Nation, **12**: 377.
— — and Labor Question. (E. L. Godkin) Nation, **12**: 333.
— — and Martyrs of Arcueil. (J. R. G. Hassard) Cath. World, **14**: 613.
— — Beginning and End of. Cath. World, **14**: 127–347.
— — Celebrities of, with portraits. Ev. Sat. **10**: 573. **11**: 6, 12.
— — Consule Julio, Episode of. Cornh. **24**: 175.
— — Days before. (A. G. Knight) Month, **36**: 502.
— — defended. (H. Sandwith) Fortn. **16**: 35.
— — Distinguished Incendiaries of. (A. G. Knight) Month, **37**: 228.
— — Du Camp's. (A. Laugel) Nation, **26**: 210.
— — Fall of. (F. Harrison) Fortn. **16**: 129.
— — Hostages to. Month, **15**: 286.
— — Interview at Aubervilliers. (Gen. Cluseret) Fraser, **85**: 422.
— — Jesuit Martyrs of. Cath. World, **19**: 505.
— — Last Days of. (J. B. Marsh) Gent. M. n. s. **7**: 234.
— — Military Side of. (Gen. Cluseret) Fortn. **20**: 1, 213, 351.
— — Ministry of War under. (L. Seguin) Fortn. **18**: 136.
— — Paris after. All the Year, **26**: 150, 390.
— — Prisons of. Month, **37**: 22.
— — Story of the Hostages. Liv. Age, **112**: 174.
— — Suum cuique. (W. R. Greg) Fraser, **84**: 115.
— — Vandalism of. Ev. Sat. **10**: 578.
Communicant, Why are you a? Chr. Disc. **2**: 164.
Communication, Cheap and rapid. Penny M. **14**: 394.
Communicative Persons. (T. H. S. Escott) Belgra. **4**: 410. Same art. Ecl. M. **70**: 430.
Communion, Close. (S. L. Harkey) Evang. R. **21**: 111.
— — Baptist. (D. L. Ogden) New Eng. **13**: 562.
— — opposed. (M. Valentine) Luth. Q. **3**: 214.
— Evening. Chr. Obs. **77**: 215.
— — Patristic Writers on. Chr. Rem. **40**: 191.
— Free. Cong. M. **1**: 267, 324.
— in one Kind. Month, **41**: 73.
— — Leicester Conference. (C. Beard) Theo. R. **15**: 366.
— Mason Hall, etc., on. Chr. Mo. Spec. **4**: 476.
— of Churches. Cong. M. **2**: 532.
— of Saints. (T. Apple) Mercersb. **4**: 590. **5**: 326. — (C. A. Hay) Luth. Q. **2**: 377. — (N. Macleod) Good Words, **16**: 162.

Communion of the Soul with God. (F. T. Washburn) Mo. Rel. M. **48**: 97.
— of the unworthy. (C. P. Krauth) Mercersb. **17**: 219.
— Open, controverted. (G. D. B. Pepper) Bapt. Q. **1**: 216.
— Pope's Posture in. (A. P. Stanley) Macmil. **20**: 273.
— Preparatory Service. (H. Wissler) Mercersb. **18**: 563.
— Qualification for. (C. A. Stork) Luth. Q. **7**: 225.
— Sacramental. (N. Porter) Am. Bib. Repos. 2d s. **2**: 1.
— Strict and mixed. Spirit Pilg. **6**: 103.
— Terms of. Ecl. R. **41**: 431, 544. — So. R. n. s. **21**: 170, 453. — (L. W. Bacon) New Eng. **31**: 346.
— — Hall on. Ecl. R. **22**: 338. — Chr. Obs. **14**: 664.
— Uses of. (O. Dewey) Chr. Exam. **31**: 194.
— Weekly. (J. P. Tustin) Chr. R. **18**: 271.
Communion Question. (J. P. Tustin) Chr. R. **16**: 210.
— Dissent on. (H. A. Hart) Bapt. Q. **2**: 228.
Communion Sermon. Chr. Mo. Spec. **8**: 614.
Communion Table, North Side of. Chr. Obs. **74**: 513, 576.
See Lord's Supper.
Communism. Prosp. R. **4**: 351. — (T. B. Browning) Canad. Mo. **13**: 478, 577. — (W. W. Crane, jr.) Overland, **14**: 232.
— and Commune. (J. A. de Cespedes) Galaxy, **18**: 522.
— and Socialism. (J. T. Hecker) Cath. World, **28**: 808.
— Christian. Cong. **2**: 278.
— Duties of the Rich in reference to. (A. F. Hewit) Cath. World, **14**: 578.
— How to deal with. (J. B. Clark) New Eng. **37**: 533.
— in Russia. (R. E. Thompson) Penn Mo. **5**: 791.
— in United States. (A. Bierbrower) Lippinc. **20**: 501. — (J. Crawford) Ref. Q. **26**: 307. — (E. L. Godkin) Nation, **26**: 302.
— Lecture on. (J. L. Davies) Good Words, **13**: 84.
— Political. (D. H. Wheeler) Lakeside, **6**: 26.
— Primitive. (A. G. Sedgwick) Atlan. **42**: 337.
— Sources of. (E. L. Godkin) Nation, **26**: 318.
Communisms of the Old World. (R. E. Thompson) Penn Mo. **5**: 12–557.
Communist and the Railway. (W. M. Grosvenor) Internat. R. **4**: 585.
— An English. (J. H. Friswell) Dark Blue, **2**: 185.
Communist Convicts in New Caledonia. Month, **27**: 312.
Communist's Baby. (J. P. Widney) Overland, **12**: 138.
Communists and Capitalists; a Tale. (O. Thanet) Lippinc. **22**: 485.
— Sentence of. (A. Laugel) Nation, **13**: 415.
See Internationals.
Communistic Morality. (E. L. Godkin) Nation, **12**: 413.
Communistic Societies, Nordhoff on. (H. James, jr.) Nation, **20**: 26.
Community, Ebenezer, in New York. (P. Godwin) Peop. J. **4**: 218.
Community of Property, Apostolic. Theo. & Lit. J. **11**: 675.
Communities, Equitable Villages in America. (W. Pare) J. Statis. Soc. **19**: 127.
— Recent American. (G. Barmby) Peop. J. **3**: 196.
— Religious. (S. B. Smith) Am. Cath. Q. **3**: 235.
— Village. (E. Nasse) Contemp. **19**: 739.
See Brook Farm; Fourierism; Oneida; Shakers; Socialisms.
Comnena, Anna, Grecian Authoress, b. 1083, Sketch of. Colburn, **144**: 667.
Como and Il Medeghino. Cornh. **38**: 342.
— Day at. (H. Brooke) Macmil. **25**: 128.
— Week at. (B. Murphy) Cath. World, **18**: 137.
Compagnoni's America. (C. Cushing) No. Am. **27**: 30.
Companies, Great, and Trading-Houses. Colburn, **169**: 69–494.
— How they are floated. All the Year, **14**: 58–393.
— London Livery. Brit. Q. **70**: 130.
— Public. Bank. M. (L.) **24**: 104, 240, 349.
Companions; a Poem. (R. H. Stoddard) Atlan. **39**: 717.
— of Death; a Tale. Bentley, **64**: 95.
— of my Solitude. Ecl. R. **94**: 284. Same art. Liv. Age, **31**: 174.
— on the Road. (W. W. Story) Blackw. **123**: 755.
Companionship. (H. Pearce) Dub. Univ. **78**: 544.
Comparative Anatomy and Physiology. *See* Anatomy; Physiology.
Comparison. (L. G. Janes) Radical, **10**: 124.
Compass, Mariner's. (W. Thomson) Good Words, **15**: 69. — (B. T. Green) Ecl. Engin. **14**: 298, 401. — Chamb. J. **23**: 132. Same art. Liv. Age, **45**: 202. — Quar. **118**: 339.
— and Terrestrial Magnetism. (W. Thomson) Good Words, **20**: 383, 445.
— Deviation of. (W. Scoresby) J. Frankl. Inst. **16**: 40, 121.
— Effects of Iron Masts on. (E. W. Creak) Ecl. Engin. **15**: 426.
— Errors in. (J. H. Upton) Hunt, **54**: 184.
— How to box. (E. H. Swann) Recr. Sci. **2**: 165.
— in Iron Ships. Hunt, **48**: 53.
— — Adjustment of. (W. Thomson) Nature, **17**: 331, 352, 387. — Ecl. Engin. **6**: 371. **10**: 425, 524.
— — Correction of. (G. B. Airy, etc.) J. Frankl. Inst. **60**: 53–317.
— in Mining Surveys. (W. Linton) Ecl. Engin. **19**: 259.
— Invention of. J. Frankl. Inst. **22**: 68. — Am. J. Sci. **40**: 242.
— Peaucellier's Compound. (W. D. Marks) J. Frankl. Inst. **107**: 361.
— Report on. J. Frankl. Inst. **65**: 404.
Compass Observatory, Charlton. House. Words, **1**: 414.
Compass Plant, Polarity of. Am. Natural. **5**: 1.
Compensation, Theory of. Fraser, **74**: 794.
Compensation Office. (F. B. Perkins) Putnam, **5**: 459. Same art. Broadw. **8**: 227.
Compensations, Comfortable Doctrine of. Fraser, **42**: 473.
Competition. All the Year. **29**: 270.
— and Co-operation. Chamb. J. **15**: 122.
— By. Chamb. J. **39**: 261.
— Endowed, at the Universities, and its Results. (S. Taylor) Macmil. **29**: 378.
— in Trade and Social Economy. (E. Chadwick) J. Statis. Soc. **22**: 381.
— Modern. Fraser, **62**: 767.
— Principle of. Art J. **3**: 105.
Competition-Wallah Extraordinary; Chinese Legend. St. James, **26**: 343.
Competitive Examination. (J. D. Cox) No. Am. **112**: 81. — Quar. **108**: 568.
— and the Civil Service. Quar. **133**: 241.
— and Selection thereby. (A. K. H. Boyd) Fraser, **86**: 67.
Competitive Examinations. Cornh. **4**: 692. — Dub. Univ. **51**: 584. — Nature, **10**: 416.
— Apology for. Fraser, **95**: 470.
— for Military and Naval Schools. (W. E. Crosby) Nation, **1**: 231. *See* West Point.
— for the Public Service. (E. Chadwick) J. Statis. Soc. **21**: 18. **22**: 44. **26**: 72.
— in China. (W. A. P. Martin) No. Am. **111**: 62. — — Macmil. **23**: 216.
— in English Schools. Ed. R. **139**: 330.
— Mental Overwork and. Pop. Sci. Mo. **11**: 105.
See Examinations.
Compiègne. (H. King) St. James, **12**: 51.
— How they kept House in. Galaxy, **8**: 249.
— Retrospect of. (K. O'Meara) Cath. World, **16**: 395, 516.
Complaining Bore, The. Contin. Mo. **3**: 496.
Complaint of Katharina Maria Poppelle; a Poem. (R. T. Cooke) Harper, **18**: 721.

Complaint of Monna Lisa; a Poem. (A. C. Swinburne) Fortn. **13**: 176.
Complaisance. Ev. Sat. **11**: 246.
Complexion and Climate. (J. M. Buchan) Pop. Sci. Mo. **17**: 1.
— Causes of Variety in. Walsh's R. **2**: 128.—(S. S. Smith) Carey's Mus. **6**: 30, 181, 273. **7**: 195, 247
— Touchstone of. Retros. **12**: 336.
— Variety of human. Portfo.(Den) **12**: 8–447.
Compliment, Decay of. Once a Week, **28**: 387.
Compliments, Academy of. Chamb. J. **36**: 362.
Composers, Some Traits of great. (J. Marshall) Macmil. **33**: 340. Same art. Liv. Age, **128**: 810.
Composition, Original. Ox. Prize Ess. **1**: 109.
— Pleasures of. Ecl. R. **18**: 270, 350.
— Teaching of, in Schools. (R. G. Parker) Am. Inst. of Instruc. **1837**: 181.
Compostella, St. James of, Church of. (R. Barker) Cath. World, **26**: 163.
Compound-Interest Curve. (F. D. Y. Carpenter) Ecl. Engin. **25**: 385.
Compounds, Atomic Volumes of solid. (F. W. Clarke) Am. J. Sci. **100**: 174.
Compressed Air. *See* Air.
Compression of Water, Rule for. (D. MacKain) J. Frankl. Inst. **39**: 340.
Compromise. (J. Morley) Fortn. **21**: 425, 720. **22**: 226. —(J. P. Quincy) Unita. R. **10**: 134.
— Curiosities of. (G. J. W. Melville) Fraser, **61**: 593. Same art. Ecl. M. **51**: 28.
Compromises. Dem. R. **34**: 1.
Compromise Measures. New Eng. **8**: 292, 378.—Am. Whig R. **12**: 114, 555.
Compton, Samuel, Life of. Chr. Obs. **60**: 345.
Compton Friars. (A. Manning) Hours at Home, **9**: 253–499. **10**: 42–336.
Compulsory Education. (C. E. Norton) Nation, **5**: 191.
— in Brooklyn. (F. E. Fryatt) Harper, **60**: 218.
Compulsory Hygiene. (E. L. Godkin) Nation, **5**: 376.
Compulsory Military Service. (Maj. Knollys) Dark Blue, **2**: 672.
Compurgation, Canonical. (H. C. Lea) No. Am. **88**: 1.
Comrades, The. (S. W. Kellogg) Lippinc. **16**: 314–692.
Comrie and Environs. (G. Gilfillan) Hogg, **4**: 1, 40, 78, 92.
Comstock Lode. (H. Degroot) Overland, **10**: 488.
— New Feature in. (G. P. Becker) Am. J. Sci. **110**: 459.
— Underground Temperatures on. (J. A. Church) Am. J. Sci. **117**: 289.
Comte, Auguste. (E. Gryzanowski) No. Am. **120**: 237. —(G. H. Lewes) Fortn. **3**: 385.—Blackw. **53**: 397.
— and his Philosophy. (E. A. Lawrence) Hours at Home, **11**: 78.—(J. Rickaby) Month, **12**: 290, 385.
— and Political Economy. (J. E. Cairnes) Fortn. **13**: 579.
— and Positivism. (S. Adams) New Eng. **32**: 56, 323. —(W. Whewell) Macmil. **13**: 353. Same art. Ecl. M. **66**: 603.—No. Brit. **21**: 247.
— Anthropology of. (J. Kaines) Anthrop. J. **1**: 349.
— Definition of Life. (J H. Bridges) Fortn. **35**: 675.
— Disciples and Critics. Brit. Q. **44**: 59.
— Huxley on. (R. Congreve) Fortn. **11**: 407.
— Later Speculations of. (J. S. Mill) Westm. **84**: 1.
— Life and Philosophy of. (J. Martineau) Nat. R. **7**: 184.—Liv. Age, **58**: 883.
— Mill on. (G. H. Lewes) Fortn. **6**: 385.—(C. Wright) Nation, **2**: 20.
— Morning with. (Sir E. Perry) 19th Cent. **2**: 621.
— on Christianity. (B. F. Westcott) Contemp. **6**: 399. **8**: 371.—Theo. Ecl. **7**: 110.
— on International Polity. (W. H. Fremantle) Contemp. **3**: 477.
— Pantheism of. (J. W. Jackson) Kitto, **39**: 174.
Comte, Auguste, Philosophy of. Chr. Obs. **54**: 740, 811. **55**: 83.—(W. S. Jevons) Nature, **12**: 491.—(E. Saisset) New Eng. **27**: 423, 680.—(F. Bowen) No. Am. **79**: 200.—(J. Fiske) No. Am. **102**: 275.—(P. Godwin) Putnam, **3**: 621.—(J. S. Mill) Westm. **83**: 339.—Dub. Univ. **25**: 452.—Meth. Q. **12**: 9, 169, 329.—Ed. R. **67**: 271.—Am. Presb. R. **6**: 311.—Ed. R. **127**: 303.—(L. H. Atwater) Princ. **28**: 59. —Westm. **62**: 173.
See Positivism; Cosmic Philosophy.
— Recollections of. Chamb. J. **29**: 398.
— Religion of. Mo. Rel. M. **36**: 137.
— — and Philosophy of. Brit. Q. **19**: 297.
— Social Philosophy and Religion of. (E. Caird) Contemp. **35**: 193, 520, 648. **36**: 66.
Comtism and George Eliot. Lond. Q. **47**: 446.
Comunidades, Wars of the. Fraser, **40**: 395.
Conan, Michael Edward, Obituary of. Art J. **32**: 107.
Conant, Roger. (J. B. Felt) N. E. Reg. **2**: 233, 329.
Concarneau, At. (J. G. Bertram) Once a Week, **16**: 586.
Conceit. Dub. Univ. **89**: 343.—Liv. Age, **137**: 636.
Concepcion de Arguello; a Poem. (Bret Harte) Atlan. **29**: 603.
Concerning a certain Prodigal. (H. King) Scrib. **15**: 636.
Concerning Charlotte; a Tale. Putnam, **15**: 38–407.
Concert, A. Cornh. **5**: 744.
— for Lancashire; a Tale. Sharpe, **38**: 205.
Concerts in Munich. Temp. Bar, **6**: 184.
— London, and the Songs sung there. Broadw. **1**: 424.
Conchologist at Guernsey and Herne. (J. R. Leifchild) Recr. Sci. **2**: 213.
Conchology. Ecl. R. **72**: 694.
— British. Fraser, **73**: 402.
— Ethnographic Phases of. (D. Wilson) Canad. J. n. s. **3**: 377.
— in the United States, History of. Am. J. Sci. **83**: 161. *See also* Shells.
Concision as distinct from Circumcision. (J. R. Arnold) New Eng. **4**: 333.
Concord, Mass, Annals of. U. S. Lit. Gaz. **1**: 53.
— Books and Authors at. (H. R. Hudson) Harper, **51**: 18.
— Churches and Ministers of. Am Q. Reg. **11**: 182.
— Days and Nights in. (H. D. Thoreau) Scrib. **16**: 721.
— Fight at, April 19, 1775. (F. Hudson) Harper, **50**: 777.—(G. Reynolds) Unita. R. **3**: 383.
— — Centennial of. (S. M. Brady) Appleton, **13**: 523. —N. E. Reg. **29**: 380.
— — — Ode at. (J. R. Lowell) Atlan. **35**: 730.
— History of. (B. B. Thatcher) No. Am. **42**: 448.
— School of Philosophy at. (G. P. Lathrop) Atlan. **46**: 652.—(J. H. Ward) Internat. R. **9**: 459.—(X. Clark) Nation, **31**: 74, 164.—J. Spec. Philos. **14**: 135, 251.
— Transcendentalists of. Fraser, **70**: 245. Same art. Ecl. M. **63**: 231. Same art. Liv. Age, **83**: 99, 178.
Concord, N. H., Reminiscences of. (S. L. Bailey) Lakeside, **8**: 354.
Concordance, Englishman's Greek. Chr. Obs. **39**: 490.
Concordances of Scriptures. Meth. Q. **7**: 451.—(M. W Jacobus) Princ. **17**: 471.
Concordat of 1801. Month, **1**: 245.
Concrete and the Abstract. J. Spec. Philos. **5**: 1.
Concrete. Ecl. Engin. **5**: 275.
— as a Building Material. Am. Arch. **2**: 266.
— Fire-Proof. Ecl. Engin. **16**: 237.
— in Works of Engineering. J. Frankl. Inst. **65**: 86.
Concretes. (C. H. Haswell) J. Frankl. Inst. **79**: 361. **80**: 171. **82**: 295.
— Notes on. Ecl. Engin. **14**: 465.
— Observations on. J. Frankl. Inst. **25**: 145, 234 **26**: 17.
— used in Extension of London Docks. (G. Robertson) J. Frankl. Inst. **73**: 155.

Concrete Building. (A. W. Bromfield) Ecl. Engin. **6:** 281. — (W. C. Homersham) Ecl. Engin. **11:** 437. — (J. H. Owen) Ecl. Engin. **8:** 113.
— in Australia. Am. Arch. **3:** 14.
— Failure of. Am. Arch. **4:** 174.
Concrete Slab Cottages. Pract. M. **5:** 276.
Concrete Towers. (I. Bell) Am. Arch. **8:** 126.
Concussion of metallic Balls. Pract. M. **1:** 198.
Condé, Prince of. (W. B. O. Peabody) No. Am. **63:** 118.
— Mahon's Life of. (J. W. Croker) Quar. **71:** 106.
— Wife of. Chamb. J. **20:** 276. Same art. Ecl. M. **30:** 552.
Condé, Louis de, Duc d'Enghien. *See* Enghien, Duc d'.
Condé, Louise de, a Royal Nun. (A. Young) Cath. World, **6:** 106.
Condé, Princess of, and Henri IV. Cornh. **20:** 292. Same art. Liv. Age, **103:** 33.
— Flight of, from Chantilly to Montrond. Temp. Bar, **50:** 332. Same art. Liv. Age, **134:** 425.
Condé, House of. Fraser, **81:** 806. — Quar. **127:** 176.
— Duc d'Aumale's Lives of the Princes of. Ed. R. **130:** 355. Same art. Ecl. M. **74:** 257.—Liv. Age, **103:** 707.
— Last of. (W. A. Buller) Dem. R. **23:** 13. — Once a Week, **5:** 485. — Chamb. J. **37:** 56. Same art. Ecl. M. **55:** 418.
Condé's Daughter; a Tale. Blackw. **60:** 496.
Condemned Cells. Fraser, **22:** 288. **23:** 21, 224, 339. **24:** 32, 663.
Condemned of Lucerne. (H. F. Harrington) Godey, **21:** 169.
Condemned Soldier; a Tale. Dub. Univ. **2:** 398.
Condemned to Death. House. Words, **14:** 75–205.
Condensed Novel; Lothaw. (B. Harte) Ev. Sat. **10:** 412.
Conder, Josiah. Ecl. R. **106:** 244.
Condillac, and the Principle of Identity. (L. Adams) New Eng. **35:** 440.
Condiments. (J. Scoffern) Belgra. **13:** 313.
— Physiological Influence of. (Prof. Voit) Pop. Sci. Mo. **1:** 701.
Conditioned, Hamilton's Law of the. (F. E. Abbot) No. Am. **99:** 402.
Condor, The. Penny M. **2:** 183.
— Haunts of, in Peru. (W. Bollaert) Intel. Obs. **1:** 278.
Condorcet, Jean de. (J. Morley) Fortn. **13:** 16, 129.
— Arago's Life of. Quar. **87:** 1. Same art. Ecl. M. **21:** 1. Same art. Liv. Age, **26:** 441.
Condottieri, Modern. Fraser, **37:** 16.
Conduct, the Aim of the Bible and Business of the Church. (G. L. Chaney) Unita. R. **14:** 316.
— Instructions for. (W. Raleigh) Am. J. Educ. **27:** 729.
— Probability as the Guide of. (W. E. Gladstone) 19th Cent. **5:** 908. Same art. Liv. Age, **141:** 579.
Conducting Power of solid and liquid Bodies. (M. E. Becquard) Am. J. Sci. **58:** 333.
Cone, Spencer H. (J. Belcher) Chr. R. **21:** 44.
Cones, Phyllotaxis of. (W. J. Beal) Am. Natural. **7:** 449.
Conecte, Father Thomas. Penny M. **14:** 429.
Conewago, Pa , Old Catholic Church at. Hist. M. **21:** 283.
Coney Island. Scrib. **20:** 353. — Chamb. J. **56:** 14.
Confederacy, The. Am. Whig R. **10:** 296.
Confederacies, State, European and American. (N. W. Senior) Ed. R. **83:** 150.
Confederate Bonds. (J. N. Pomeroy) Nation, **13:** 253.
Confederate Boy, Diary of. All the Year, **7:** 224.
Confederate States and their Constitution. (J. L. M. Curry) Galaxy, **17:** 399.
— Army of, Hood's Tennessee Campaign. (W. O. Dodd) So. Hist. Pap. **9:** 518.
— — Longstreet's Division. (E. P. Alexander) So. Hist. Pap. **9:** 512.
— — of Northern Virginia. (J. W. Jones) So. Hist. Pap. **9:** 90–557.
Confederate States, Army of, Northern Virginia, Artillery of. (W. N. Pendleton) So. Hist. Pap. **9:** 418.
— — — Infantry of. (C. S. Stringfellow) So. Hist. Pap. **9:** 500.
— Battle Flag of. (G. T. Beauregard) So. M. **10:** 506.
— — Origin of. (C. McCarthy) So. Hist. Pap. **8:** 497.
— Congress of. (E. A. Pollard) Galaxy, **6:** 749.
— Fallen Heroes of. (A. M. Kelley) So. Hist. Pap. **7:** 373.
— Financial Position of, 1864. Bank. M. (L.) **24:** 934, 1089.
— Flag of. So. Hist. Pap. **8:** 155.
— Foreign Recognition of. (J. Lyons) So. Hist. Pap. **7:** 353.
— Government of. Am. Hist. Rec. **2:** 56.
— Great Seal of. (T. J. Pickett) Am. Hist. Rec. **3:** 360.
— in 1862–63. Dub. Univ. **63:** 214.
— Instructions to James M. Mason, 1861. So. Hist. Pap. **7:** 231.
— State Correspondence. So. Hist. Pap. **7:** 99–333.
— Treasury of, Last Days of. (M. H. Clark) So. Hist. Pap. **9:** 542.
— under Defeat. Dub. Univ. **68:** 635.
— War Poetry of. Dub. Univ. **70:** 424.
Confederation, Imperial. (R. Fisher) Canad. Mo. **8:** 335.
Conference System of New England, Origin of. (A. Cole) Cong. Q. **6:** 187.
Conferences, Religious, in Europe, 1869. (S. Osgood) Mo. Rel. M. **44:** 411.
Confessio Amati; a Poem. St. James, **30:** 683.
Confession. (E. J. O'Reilly) Irish Mo. **2:** 603. — Chr. Obs. **53:** 809. — Chr. Rem. **17:** 430.
— and Absolution. (W. Harrison) Chr. Obs. **75:** 161. — (A. C. Coxe) Am. Church R. **2:** 573. — Dub. Univ. **76:** 331. — Lond. Q. **41:** 370.
— — and the Real Presence, Boyd on. Chr. Obs. **67:** 688.
— Auricular. For. Q. **35:** 188. — Ecl. M. **5:** 413. — Brownson, **3:** 327. — Ecl. R. **71:** 668. — Chr. Rem. **37:** 212. — Kitto, **10:** 407. — Quar. **144:** 539. — Tait, n. s. **25:** 427.
— — in the Church of England. Chr. Obs. **69:** 241. — (O. Shipley) Contemp. **22:** 846. — (F. P. Cobbe) Theo. R. **9:** 17. — Month, **30:** 479.— Quar. **124:** 83.
— — Lasteyrie on. Ecl. R. **87:** 690.
— — Michelet on. For. Q. **35:** 188.
— — Protestant Bishop on. (A. F. Hewit) Cath. World, **23:** 831.
— — Ridsdale Judgment. Quar. **144:** 241.
— — Scientific and medical Aspects of. (G. Cowell) Contemp. **34:** 717.
— Denison's Sermon on. Chr. Obs. **73:** 739.
— Private. Chr. Obs. **73:** 519, 565. — (L. A. Fox) Luth. Q. **11:** 397. — Am. Cath. Q. **5:** 666.
— — and indicative Absolution. Chr. Obs. **74:** 469.
— — Case of Mr. Poole. Chr. Obs. **59:** 251.
— Romish, Protestant, and Scriptural. (F. Springer) Luth. Q. **7:** 81.
— Sacramental. U. S. Cath. M. **7:** 169.
— Value of, as Evidence. Cornh. **11:** 664. — (J. Gallison) No. Am. **10:** 418.
See Absolution; Confessional.
Confession of Faith of Northampton Church. Cong. Q. **3:** 168.
— Philosophical. (S. Alexander) Princ. **39:** 416.
See Creeds.
Confessions and the Confessional Principle. (H. E. Jacobs) Luth. Q. **11:** 14.
— and Opinions of Ralph Restless. (F. Marryat) Colburn, **50:** 322–473. **51:** 20–168.
— of a Candidate. (D. H. Strother) Harper, **52:** 329.
— of a Clarionet-Player. (MM. Erckmann-Chatrian) Eng. Dom. M. **11:** 265–328. **12:** 17–137.
— of a Debutant. (C. W. Stoddard) Overland, **1:** 356.

Confessions of an elderly Gentleman. Bentley, **2**: 445.
— of an English Opium-Eater. (T. De Quincey) Lond. M. **4**: 293, 352. — Tait, n. s. **1**: 18–797. **2**: 3–769. **3**: 350. **4**: 65, 169. **5**: 152–559. **6**: 1–804. **7**: 32–765. **8**: 97.
— of Faith. *See* Creeds.
— of a Green-Tea Drinker. Mo. Rel. M. **25**: 317.
— of a Keyhole. (L. Blanchard) Colburn, **69**: 326. **70**: 447.
— of Literature. (J. Gostick) Peop. J. **3**: 291.
— of a Medium. (B. Taylor) Atlan. **6**: 699.
— of a Patent-Medicine Man. (R. Keeler) Atlan. **26**: 641.
— of Paul Gosslett. St. Paul's, **1**: 582.
— of a Phœnix. (T. Hood) Colburn, **67**: 427.
— of St. Valentine; a Poem. (M. E. Rogers) Once a Week, **4**: 207.
— of a young Artist. Putnam, **3**: 39.
— of Zephyras; a Poem. (M. Junkin) So. Lit. Mess. **16**: 709.
Confessional, The. Dub. R. **45**: 203.—U. S. Cath. M. **5**: 1.
— and Extra-Confessional. (E. J. Koons) Evang. R. **19**: 232.
— Episcopalian. (T. F. Preston) Cath. World, **7**: 372.
— Hopkins's History of. (N. S. Richardson) Am. Church R. **3**: 389.
— New. Fraser, **75**: 501.
— Protestant Ideas of. Dub. R. **31**: 122.
Confidence. (E. E. Hale) O. & N. **6**: 669.
— and Caution. (L. Withington) Bib. Sac. **21**: 180.
Confidence; a Novel. (H. James, jr.) Scrib. **18**: 507–849. **19**: 65–393.
Confidence Games. Cornh. **8**: 250.
Confident Prediction. House. Words, **2**: 465.
Confidential; a Tale. Lippinc. **11**: 214.
Confidential Agent. (J. Payn) Belgra. **40**: 257, 385. **41**: 1–385. **42**: 1–386. **43**: 1, 129.
Confirmation. Cong. **1**: 733. — Chr. Obs. **29**: 71, 142. — Cong. M. **6**: 16.
— and Baptism. (H. Martenson) Mercersb. **5**: 303.
— as a Sacrament. (W. J. Barbee) Chr. Q. **2**: 433.
— Before and after. (G. U. Wenner) Luth. Q. **6**: 436.
— Formula for Mercersb. **6**: 554.
— how soon to be administered. (H. Harbaugh) Evang. R. **17**: 402.
— in the Reformed Church. (J. H. Dubbs) Mercersb. **24**: 387.
— of Bishops Elect, Archiepiscopal. Chr. Obs. **70**: 50.
— of Converts from Papacy. Am. Church R. **5**: 53.
— Smyth against. (W. Johnson) Am. Church R. **2**: 325.
Confirmed Bachelor; a Tale. Chamb. J. **49**: 701–756.
Confiscated Weeds. (J. Payn) Belgra. **31**: 519.
Confiscation, Policy of. (W. C. Church) Galaxy, **3**: 28.
Conflict of Ages. (T. S. King) Univ. Q. **11**: 33.
— Beecher's. Chr. R. **19**: 98.
— — and Concord of Ages. Chr. R. **25**: 244.
— of modern Thought. Brit. Q. **27**: 36. Same art. Ecl. M. **44**: 89.
Conformity, from Nonconformist Point of View. (C. Beard) Theo. R. **5**: 292.
— Obligations of, in Church of England. Theo. R. **5**: 401.
— Some new Attempts at. (J. H. Allen) Chr. Exam. **75**: 387.
Confucianism. (J. K. Wight) Princ. **30**: 226.
— and Taonism, Douglas on. (S. W. Williams) Nation, **29**: 407.
— practical Agnosticism. (C. A. Stork) Luth. Q. **9**: 377.
Confucius. (Sir J. Bowring) Fortn. **9**: 537. — Putnam, **4**: 146. — (M. Dods) Good Words, **22**: 274, 315. — (C. H. Dall) Chr. Exam. **84**: 175. — (J. Pyne) Am. Church R. **29**: 236. — Ed. R. **129**: 303. Same art. Liv. Age, **101**: 771. Same art. Ev. Sat. **7**: 628.
— and Chinese. (J. F. Clarke) Atlan. **24**: 336.
— and his Influence. (J. Pyne) Nat. Q. **30**: 333.
Confucius, Life and Doctrines of. (I. Tracy) Bib. Sac. **3**: 284. — (E. G. Holland) Chr. Exam. **45**: 317. — Anal. M. **1**: 303, 383. — Ecl. Mus. **2**: 507. — (R. H. Graves) Bapt. Q. **6**: 425.
— Morality of. (J. W. Wiley) Nat. M. **8**: 413.
— Philosophy of. Hogg, **2**: 382.
— Works of. Quar. **11**: 332.
Congal; a Historical Poem. Dub. Univ. **80**: 385.
Congo, Kingdom of, and Roman Catholic Missionaries. (J. L. Wilson) Bib. Sac. **9**: 110.
— and Loango, Observations on, in 1790. (G. Maxwell) Ed. Philos. J. **4**: 327. **5**: 45, 268. **6**: 62, 213.
— Burton's Congo-Land. Appleton, **15**: 353.
— Livingstone Expedition to. Geog. M. **2**: 26.
Congo or Zaire River. (S. Agha) Geog. M. **2**: 203. — (W. Brown) Ed. Philos. J. **3**: 102, 205.
— Discovery of Course of. (C. R. Markham) Geog. M. **2**: 225.
— Expedition to, 1816. (H. Salt) Quar. **18**: 335. — (J. Foster) Ecl. R. **28**: 445. — Ecl. R. **28**: 518.
— Stanley's Voyage down. Geog. M. **4**: 318.
Congregational Catechism. (J. Murdock) New Eng. **2**: 180.
Congregational Chapel Extension. Ecl. R. **114**: 71.
Congregational Church, Conference System of. (M. M. G. Dana) New Eng. **27**: 78.
— Constitution of. Chr. Disc. **2**: 257.
— Creed of, Revision of. (E. L. Godkin) Nation, **30**: 413.
— Polity and Theology of. (J. P. Thompson) New Eng. **18**: 627.
— Relation of, to other Churches. (I. Tracy) Cong. R. **9**: 138.
Congregational Churches, American, in Census of 1870. Cong. Q. **16**: 49.
— — Reed and Mattheson's Visit to. Cong. M. **19**: 31, 41, 113.
— — Statistics of, 1858. (A. H. Quint) Cong. Q. **1**: 77.
— — — 1859. (A. H. Quint) Cong. Q. **2**: 97.
— — — 1860. (A. H. Quint) Cong. Q. **3**: 73.
— — — 1861. (I. P. Langworthy) Cong. Q. **4**: 73.
— — — 1862. (I. P. Langworthy) Cong. Q. **5**: 57.
— — — 1863. (I. P. Langworthy) Cong. Q. **6**: 61.
— — — 1864. (A. H. Quint) Cong. Q. **7**: 61.
— — — 1865. (A. H. Quint) Cong. Q. **8**: 57.
— — — 1866. (A. H. Quint) Cong. Q. **9**: 57.
— — — 1867. Cong. Q. **10**: 54.
— — — 1868. Cong. Q. **11**: 81.
— — — 1869. Cong. Q. **12**: 84.
— — — 1870. Cong. Q. **13**: 105.
— — — 1871. Cong. Q. **14**: 113.
— — — 1872. Cong. Q. **15**: 101.
— — — 1873. Cong. Q. **16**: 97.
— — — 1874. Cong. Q. **17**: 97.
— — — 1875. Cong. Q. **18**: 97.
— — — 1876. Cong. Q. **19**: 97.
— — — 1877. Cong. Q. **20**: 81.
— Decaying. Cong. M. **23**: 609–738.
— English, Statistics of. Cong. M. **9**: 697. **10**: 681. **12**: 695. **13**: 685. **24**: 917, 926. — (H. M. Dexter) Cong. Q. **5**: 130.
— — Work and Wants of, 1864. Ecl. R. **119**: 105.
— Fellowship in. (G. N. Boardman) Bib. Sac. **33**: 62.
— of Massachusetts, Rights of. (E. Pond) Cong. Q. **5**: 328. — Spirit Pilg. **1**: 57, 113. **2**: 128, 370. **3**: 539.
— of Portage and Summit Co., O. (J. C. Hart) Cong. Q. **2**: 269, 386. **3**: 149, 285, 329. **4**: 36–332.
— Scottish, Jubilee Memorial of, 1849. Brit. Q. **10**: 267.
— Statistics of foreign, 1859. Cong. Q. **2**: 302.
— — of all Nations. (H. A. Hazen) Cong. Q. **19**: 62.
— Superiority of. (A. H. Ross) Cong. Q. **12**: 557.
— Welsh, in United States. Cong. Q. **2**: 401.

Congregational Conference, Ministerial Membership in. (A. H. Ross) Cong. Q. **14**: 304.
— National. (A. H. Ross) Cong. R. **10**: 425. — (R. B. Thurston) Cong. Q. **12**: 392.
Congregational Convention, General, 1852. (H. D. Kitchel) New Eng. **11**: 72.
— Massachusetts, 1823. Chr. Disc. **5**: 236.
Congregational Council, Ecumenical. (A. H. Ross) Cong. Q. **16**: 291.
— National. (S. W. S. Dutton and W. T. Eustis) New Eng. **24**: 531, 546. — (A. H. Quint) Cong. Q. **14**: 61. — (W. T. Savage) Bost. R. **5**: 285. — Cong. Q. **13**: 234. — (L. H. Atwater) Princ. **37**: 599. — (G. M. Boynton) New Eng. **39**: 215.
— — Doctrinal Basis of. (S. B. Goodenow) New Eng. **31**: 726. — (L. Bacon) New Eng. **31**: 745. — (W. W. Patton) New Eng. **31**: 318.
— — in 1865. Cong. Q. **7**: 47.
— — — Action of. Cong. Q. **8**: 12.
— — — Official Record. Cong. Q. **7**: 238.
— — in 1872 at Oberlin. (S. B. Goodenow) New Eng. **31**: 726.
Congregational Councils. (H. M. Dexter) New Eng. **26**: 235. — (I. Mather) Cong. Q. **12**: 25, 246, 363.
— and Associations. (L. H. Atwater) New Eng. **3**: 161. Same art. Cong. M. **28**: 476.
— and Congregationalism. (E. Beecher) Bib. Sac. **22**: 284.
— Authority of. Cong. Q **2**: 53.
— Composition of. (J. Guernsey) Cong. Q. **11**: 249.
— Judicial Power of. (E. Washburn) Cong. Q. **11**: 491.
— of Advice. Cong. **2**: 624.
Congregational County-Union Administration. Cong. **5**: 499, 513.
Congregational Dissenters. Westm. **28**: 217.
Congregational Deputation to America. (J. Blackburn) Cong. M. **18**: 604.
Congregational House. Cong. Q. **15**: 77.
Congregational Independency. Brit. Q. **7**: 311.
Congregational Institutions, English. Cong. Q. **3**: 240.
Congregational Library Association. (J. S. Clark) Cong. Q. **1**: 70, 327.
— 10th Annual Report. Cong. Q. **5**: 279.
Congregational Literature. (S. D. Clark) Cong. R. **7**: 161.
Congregational May Meetings of 1873. Cong. **2**: 364.
Congregational Ministers, Connecticut, from 1639 to 1832. Am. Q. Reg. **4**: 307.
— Usurpation of Judicial Functions by. (H. P. Arms) Cong. Q. **8**: 35.
— who died in 1875. Cong. Q. **18**: 418.
— — 1876. Cong. Q. **19**: 407.
— — 1877. (H. A. Hazen) Cong. Q. **20**: 438.
Congregational Ministry and its Education. Brit. Q. **52**: 78.
— Andrews's Sermon on leaving. Theo. & Lit. J. **4**: 338.
— of the Future. (R. Palmer) New Eng. **15**: 366.
— vindicated. Cong. M. **25**: 1.
Congregational Nonconformity. Cong. M. **15**: 595.
Congregational Ordination. Chr. Exam. **17**: 177.
Congregational Polity. (A. B. Ely) Cong. Q. **13**: 279. — (M. Hopkins) Cong. Q. **13**: 20.
— Divine Origin and Importance of. Ecl. R. **87**: 649.
— a Polity of the Spirit. (L. Swain) Cong. Q. **6**: 51.
— Relation of, to Church of Future. (T. M. Post) Cong. Q. **15**: 16.
— Rise and Progress of. (H. D. Kitchel) Cong. Q. **14**: 373.
— Usages and Law. (W. Davis) Bost. R. **5**: 321.
Congregational Principles. Ecl. R. **111**: 416.
Congregational Reform. Cong. M. **19**: 781.
Congregational Singing. (F. A. Adams) New Eng. **7**: 55. — (R. T. Robinson) Cong. R. **8**: 260. — Chr. Exam. **65**: 230. — Cornh. **37**: 90.
— How to destroy. (T. DeW. Talmadge) Cong. **2**: 37.
Congregational Theological Seminaries, 1868–69. (A. H. Quint) Cong. Q. **11**: 279.
— 1870–71. Cong. Q. **13**: 307.
— 1875–76. Cong. Q. **18**: 315.
— 1876–77. Cong. Q. **19**: 300.
Congregational Topic in England, 1864. Ecl. R. **119**: 219, 357, 465. **120**: 91–667. **121**: 104.
Congregational Union of England and Wales. Bib. R. **1**: 333. — Cong. M. **14**: 94, 373.
— Address of, 1834. Cong. M. **17**: 394.
— — 1837. Cong. M. **20**: 541.
— — 1838. Cong. M. **21**: 393.
— American Address to. Cong. Q. **4**: 369.
— American Reports on, 1835. Cong. M. **19**: 461.
— and Baptist Union in England, 1836. Ecl. R. **65**: 166.
— Correspondence of. Cong. M. **20**: 827.
— Meeting at Ipswich in 1873. Cong. **2**: 693.
— — in 1876, Finance Debate in. Cong. **5**: 664.
— — in 1877. Cong. **6**: 686.
— — in 1878. Cong. **7**: 326.
— Publications of. (J. S. Clark) Cong. Q. **1**: 178.
Congregationalism. (J. P. Dabney) Chr. Exam. **67**: 215. — (H. M. Dexter) Cong. Q. **1**: 17. — (R. W. Dale) Brit. Q. **73**: 1, 265. — (E. Johnson) Cong. Q. **9**: 25. — (A. P. Marvin) Cong. Q. **2**: 390. — (A. P. Marvin) New Eng. **13**: 530. — (E. R. Tyler) New Eng. **4**: 173. — Cong. **1**: 1. — (L. H. Atwater) Princ. **27**: 239.
— Absorption of. (T. Baldwin) Cong. Q. **12**: 19.
— adapted to Foreign Missions. (A. L. Thompson) Cong. Q. **2**: 28.
— adapted to Home Missions. (I. E. Dwinell) Cong. Q. **1**: 341.
— and Christian Union. (W. W. Patton) Cong. Q. **4**: 335.
— and Church of Eng. (J. L. Davies) Contemp. **17**: 15.
— and Councils. (E. Beecher) Bib. Sac. **22**: 284.
— and Education. (G. F. Magoun) New Eng. **38**: 412.
— and Presbyterianism. (E. R. Tyler) New Eng. **3**: 438. — Cong. M. **28**: 697.
— — Doctrinal Tendencies of. Danv. Q. **1**: 1.
— and religious Communion. Brit. Q. **68**: 192.
— and Revivals. (H. M. Dexter) Cong. Q. **3**: 52.
— and Symbolism. (W. G. T. Shedd) Bib. Sac. **15**: 661.
— Century of, 1876. (W. W. Patton) New Eng. **35**: 634.
— Character and Position of. (S. K. Lothrop) Chr. Exam. **41**: 427.
— Dangerous Principles in. (A. H. Ross) New Eng. **37**: 514.
— defined. Cong. M. **21**: 166.
— Dexter's. (W. L. Ropes) No. Am. **101**: 573. — (W. F. Poole) Dial (Ch.), **1**: 69. — Presb. R. **1**: 762.
— Duty of, to Itself. (E. P. Marvin) Bost. R. **5**: 521.
— Earliest Development of. (L. W. Bacon) Cong. Q. **6**: 276.
— English, Germs of. (A. B. Ely) Cong. R. **11**: 440.
— English and American. Brit. Q. **44**: 91.
— for America. (E. F. Howe) Cong. Q. **9**: 254.
— Forces and Fruits of. Bost. R. **4**: 449.
— History of, Hanbury's, to 1660. Ecl. R. **70**: 335.
— — Waddington's. (H. M. Dexter) Cong. Q. **16**: 420.
— Improvements in. (H. M. Dexter) Cong. Q. **7**: 197.
— in America. (W. W. Patton) Cong. **7**: 449, 513.
— in Apostolic Churches. Cong. Q. **9**: 148. — (D. P. Noyes) New Eng. **38**: 509.
— in E. New York. (J. P. Thompson) Cong. Q. **2**: 33.
— in England. (S. F. Williams) Unita. R. **11**: 295. — Chr. Rem. **40**: 82.
— in 1863–64. Ecl. R. **118**: 316. **119**: 723.
— in four Epochs. Ecl. R. **117**: 263.
— in History and Literature. (J. F. Hurst) Meth. Q. **41**: 286.
— in Kansas. (R. Cordley) Cong. Q. **18**: 367.
— in Massachusetts, 1843. Cong. M. **26**: 157.

Congregationalism in Michigan. (J. D. Pierce) Cong. Q. 2: 190.
— in Minnesota. (D. Burt) Cong. Q. 2: 67.
— in New England. (N. Porter) New Eng. 1: 568. Same art. Cong. M. 27: 171. — Am. Q. Reg. 1: 159. 2: 153. — (L. Hart) Chr. Q. Spec. 2: 321.
— in New Jersey, Early History of. (W. B. Brown) Cong. Q. 19: 531.
— in Norfolk 200 Years ago. Cong. M. 27: 801, 899.
— in Ohio. (H. Cowles) Cong. Q. 5: 132. — (J. C. Hart) Cong. Q. 5: 248. — (J. C. Hart) New Eng. 13: 607.
— in the West. (H. A. Stimson) New Eng. 39: 124.
— in Western New York. (J. H. Dill) Cong. Q. 1: 151.
— New-fangled. New Eng. 37: 1.
— of Dr. Watts. (J. O. Means) Cong. Q. 6: 10.
— Office of. (H. M. Storrs) Cong. Q. 7: 170.
— Organic Development of. Cong. 2: 325.
— Past and Future of. (N. Porter) New Eng. 39: 96.
— Platforms of. (A. H. Ross) New Eng. 39: 368.
— Position of. (J. Williams) Am. Church R. 2: 559.
— Principles of. (O. Dewey) Chr. Exam. 8: 85. — (S. K. Lothrop) Chr. Exam. 41: 230. — Chr. R. 6: 246. — (J. P. Thompson) New Eng. 7: 109. — Cong. M. 13: 516, 586, 631.
— Question in. (L. W. Bacon) New Eng. 31: 346.
— Radical Fallacy of. (L. W. Bacon) Cong. Q. 5: 310.
— Reform in. Cong. Q. 15: 536.
— Savoy Assembly, 1658. Cong. M. 9: 449.
— — Declaration of. Cong. M. 9: 681.
— Situation and Needs of. (T. M. Post) Cong. R. 10: 363.
— Spiritual State of. Brit. Q. 12: 237.
— Spread of. (W. Barrows) Cong. R. 10: 441.
— Vaughan on. Cong. M. 25: 169. — Mo. R. 157: 253. — Ecl. R. 76: 60.
— What it has done. (C. Cushing) Cong. Q. 18: 537.
Congregationalists, Adherence to evangelical Truth. Cong. M. 26: 857.
— and Presbyterians. (B. J. Wallace) Am. Presb. R. 1: 630. — Cong. Q. 4: 38.
— — in the West. (H. D. Kitchel) Cong. Q. 3: 341.
— Denominational Duties of. (S. Pearson) Cong. 7: 615.
— English. (M. P. Lowe) Unita. R. 8: 217, 693. — Cong. M. 25: 34.
— — Condition of, in 1833. Cong. M. 16: 797.
— — Theological Thought among. (S. F. Williams) Unita. R. 11: 295. — (R. W. Dale) Cong. 6: 1.
— Hanbury's Memorials of. Ecl. R. 75: 288.
— in Maryland 200 Years ago. (E. Johnson) Cong. Q. 10: 201.
— Undenominational. (I. P. Langworthy) Cong. Q. 9: 349.
Congress, The, and the Agapedome; a Tale. (W. E. Aytoun) Blackw. 70: 359.
Congress, Continental. *See* Continental Congress.
Congress of Nations. (O. Dewey) Am. Whig R. 5: 341. — No. Brit. 16: 1. — (W. Allen) Am. Q. Obs. 2: 50. — (A. P. Peabody) Chr. Exam. 29: 83. — Meth. Q. 2: 220.
Congress of Peace and Liberty at Lausanne, 1869. (C. E. Norton) Nation, 9: 313, 336.
Congress of Verona, Chateaubriand on. Ed. R. 67: 535. — Mo. R. 146: 579.
Congress of Vienna. *See* Vienna, Congress of.
Congress, United States, Caricature of an early Fracas in. Hist. M. 8: 1.
— A Century of. (J. A. Garfield) Atlan. 40: 49.
— Conduct of Business in. (G. F. Hoar) No. Am. 128: 113.
— Excess of Debate in. (W. Tudor) No. Am. 26: 158.
— Glances at. Dem. R. 1: 68.
— Library of. *See* Congressional Library.
— Lobby of, Cause and Cure of. (A. G. Sedgwick) Atlan. 41: 512.
Congress, United States, Lobby of, "Strikers" of. (J. Parton) Atlan. 24: 216.
— Lobbying in. (J. Parton) Atlan. 24: 361.
— Memoirs of, from 1774 to 1833. Am. Alma. 1834: 98.
— — from 1789 to 1843. Am. Alma. 1844: 149.
— Parliamentary Reforms in. Republic, 1: 129.
— Pressure upon. (J. Parton) Atlan. 25: 145.
— Secret Journals of the Old. Am. Q. 1: 129.
— Small Sins of. (J. Parton) Atlan. 24: 517.
— Speech-Making in. (A. Rhodes) Scrib. 7: 294.
— *vs.* Constitution. (A. T. Bledsoe) So. R. n. s. 4: 67.
— 18th. Dem. R. 42: 191.
— 25th. Dem. R. 5: 347.
— — Extra Session of, 1837. Dem. R. 1: app.
— 28th. (H. Greeley) Am. Whig R. 1: 221.
— 29th. December, 1846. (J. P. Kennedy) Am. Whig R. 4: 543.
— — May, 1846. (C. King) Am Whig R. 5: 433.
— 31st. Dem. R. 28: 289.
— 35th. Dem. R. 42: 365.
— 37th. (J. H. Allen) Chr. Exam. 74: 430.
— 40th. Am. J. Educ. 18: 70.
— — 1st Session, Proceedings. Am. J. Educ. 18: 225.
— — 3d Session. (H. B. Adams) No. Am. 108: 610.
— 43d, Corruption of. (S. Newcomb) No. Am. 117: 182.
— 46th, Some noteworthy Facts about, 1879. (E. L. Godkin) Nation, 28: 160.
See United States.
Congresses and Conferences. All the Year, 37: 342, 364.
— of 1864. Lond. Q. 23: 269.
— of Europe, Great. (F. Martin) Once a Week, 2: 379, 409.
Congressional Burying-Ground. (E. Brooks) So. Lit. Mess. 8: 81. — (G. Waterston) So. Lit. Mess. 9: 652.
Congressional Debates, Benton's. Dem. R. 40: 435.
Congressional Eloquence. (J. G. Palfrey) No. Am. 52: 109.
Congressional Library. (B. P. Poore) Harper, 46: 41. — Republic, 3: 1.
— Building for. Am. Arch. 5: 57, 121. — (J. L. Smithmeyer) Lib. J. 6: 77.
Congressional Oratory. Am. Whig R. 8: 361.
Congressional Reports, Appleton's. Dem. R. 43: 297.
Congressional Rhetoric, Flowers of. Dem. R. 5: 94.
Congreve, Richard, Essays of. Blackw. 116: 166. Same art. Liv. Age, 122: 696.
Congreve, William. (C. C. Clarke) Gent. M. n. s. 7: 823.
— Works of. (T. B. Macaulay) Mus. 42: 40.
Congreve Rocket, What is a? Chamb. J. 21: 264. Same art. Liv. Age, 41: 556.
Conic Sections, Geometrical. Nature, 6: 391.
Conic Section Compasses. (J. P. Frizell) Math. Mo. 1: 262.
Conies; a Sermon out of Church. (D. M. Craik) Good Words, 22: 122.
Conington, Prof. John. (T. H. Ward) Macmil. 21: 146.
Coniferæ, Chapter in History of. (J. S. Gardner) Nature, 22: 199. 23: 412.
Coniferous Forests of the Sierra Nevada. (J. Muir) Scrib. 22: 710, 921.
Conjurer at Home. (D. Ryan) Belgra. 6: 576.
Conjurer's Call; a Poem. Temp. Bar, 23: 539.
Conjurers and Clairvoyants. Tait, n. s. 27: 229.
— and Spiritualists. Chamb. J. 53: 657, 686.
Conjuring, Secrets of. (H. Hatton) Scrib. 21: 65, 304.
Conkling, Roscoe. (F. W. Whitridge) Internat. R. 11: 375.
— and the New York Senatorship, 1878. (E. L. Godkin) Nation, 28: 63.
Connaught, Otway's Tour in. Dub. Univ. 14: 123.
— Province of, 1612, Lansdowne MSS. Arch. 27: 124.
Connaught Circuit, History of. (O. J. Burke) Dub. Univ. 84: 470, 592, 727. 85: 90–690. 86: 87, 182, 437.
Connaught Rangers, Adventures of. (Lt. Col. Steevers) Blackw. 61: 457.

Connaught Rangers, Reminiscences of. Dub. Univ. **15**: 75.
Connecticut. (J. G. E. Learned) New Eng. **10**: 161.
— Aboriginal Inhabitants of. (L. Ray) New Eng. **1**: 312.
— Academy of Arts and Sciences. (E. C. Herrick) Am. Q. Reg. **13**: 23.
— Archives of. (W. S. Porter) N. E. Reg. **3**: 167.
— Atlantic Monthly *versus*. (I. N. Tarbox) New Eng. **24**: 319.
— Blue Laws of. *See* Blue Laws.
— Civil Liberty in. (E. H. Gillett) Hist. M. **14**: 1.
— Colonial Records of, Trumbull's. (L. Ray) New Eng. **10**: 198. — (F. Bowen) No. Am. **71**: 34.
— — 1735–43. No. Am. **119**: 205.
— Colony Rights and State Rights in. Knick. **63**: 265.
— Common Schools of. (J. A. Root) New Eng. **4**: 522. — New York R. **10**: 331. — (H. Barnard) Am. J. Educ. **4**: 657. **5**: 114. — Am. J. Educ. **13**: 725. **14**: 244. **15**: 276.
— Constitution of, 1818. Niles's Reg. **15**: 30, 65.
— Doctrinal and Ecclesiastical Conflicts in. (L. H. Atwater) Princ. **25**: 598.
— Documents relating to. N. E. Reg. **23**: 21, 169, 455. **24**: 124, 324. **25**: 72.
— Early Clergy of. Am. Church R. **2**: 309.
— Early History of. (J. L. Kingsley) New Eng. **1**: 224.
— Education in. Am. Q. Reg. **5**: 297.
— Educational Institutions of. Am. J. Educ. **11**: 305.
— Episcopal Church in Colony of. (C. J. Hoadly) Am. Church R. **10**: 106.
— Founders of, and the Blue Laws. (W. L. Kingsley) New Eng. **30**: 248.
— General Association of. (C. Chapin) Am. Q. Reg. **12**: 20.
— Geol. Survey of. (B. Silliman) Am. J. Sci. **33**: 151.
— Governor's Message, 1818. Niles's Reg. **14**: 250.
— — 1819. Niles's Reg. **16**: 196.
— — 1820. Niles's Reg. **18**: 293.
— — 1821. Niles's Reg. **20**: 212.
— — 1822. Niles's Reg. **22**: 313.
— — 1823. Niles's Reg. **24**: 173.
— — 1829. Niles's Reg. **36**: 189.
— History of, Fenwick's. Anal. M. **4**: 49.
— — Hollister's. (T. C. Pitkin) Am. Church R. **8**: 337.
— — Peters's. New Eng. M. **6**: 121.
— — Trumbull's. Chr. Mo. Spec. **1**: 244, 301. — Anal. M. **13**: 17. — (N. Hale) No. Am. **8**: 72.
— Local Law of. (W. C. Fowler) N. E. Reg. **24**: 33, 137.
— Matters in, in 1644. N. E. Reg. **29**: 237.
— Newgate Prison of. (C. B. Todd) Lippinc. **27**: 290.
— Peep into. Am. Mo. M. **9**: 165.
— Picturesque Views in. (C. U. C. Burton) Nat. M. **12**: 400.
— Pleiades of. (F. Sheldon) Atlan. **15**: 187.
— Poets of. (Mrs. L. Phelps) Am. Church R. **17**: 98.
— Productive Industry of. (J. H. Lanman) Hunt, **15**: 565.
— School Fund of. (J. L. Kingsley and E. Everett) No. Am. **16**: 379. — Am. J. Educ. **6**: 367.
— School Question in, 1867. (D. C. Gilman) New Eng. **26**: 671.
— School System of. (D. Olmsted) Am. Inst. of Instruc. **1838**: 95.
— Statistics of, 1869. Am. J. Educ. **18**: 294.
— Teachers' Association of. Am. J. Educ. **15**: 593.
— Valley of the Naugatuck. (C. U. C. Burton) Nat. M. **11**: 193–491. **12**: 11.
Connecticut Ballad of 1769. Hist. M. **2**: 4.
Connecticut Bar, Statistics of. Am. Q. Reg. **14**: 386.
Connecticut Georgics. (F. B. Perkins) Putnam, **3**: 356.
Connecticut Historical Society. (H. Barnard) Am. Q. Reg. **13**: 284.
Connecticut Medical Society. (T. Miner) Am. Q. Reg. **11**: 279.
Connecticut River, Formation of Bars in. (T. G. Ellis) Ecl. Engin. **11**: 313.
— Fur Trade on, in 17th Century. (S. Judd) N. E. Reg. **11**: 217.
— Valley of. (T. A. Richards) Harper, **13**: 289. — (A. Smith) Am. J. Sci. **22**: 205.
— — Glacier of. (J. D. Dana) Am. J. Sci. **102**: 233.
— — in the Champlain and Terrace Periods. (W. Upham) Am. J. Sci. **114**: 459.
— — Trap Rocks of. (G. W. Hawes) Am. J. Sci. **109**: 185.
Connecting-Rods, Taper of. (W. D. Marks) J. Frankl. Inst. **107**: 31.
Connemara, Adventures in. Once a Week, **10**: 614. **11**: 51, 93.
— Hints for Vagabonds. Fraser, **59**: 452.
— Incursion into. (W. H. Maxwell) Bentley, **25**: 359.
— Naturalist's Notes in. (G. S. Brady) Intel. Obs. **9**: 334.
— A Scare in. Chamb. J. **55**: 361, 377.
Connemara Converts. (H. Billingham) Month, **39**: 446.
Connemara Hills. (J. L. Cloud) Harper, **59**: 664.
Conner, Henry W., with portrait. De Bow, **10**: 578.
Conner, Sheriff, and his Friend Tweed. (E. I. Sears) Nat. Q. **32**: 336.
Connoisseur, Speculation of a. Lond. M. **16**: 243.
Connolly, John, Imprisonment of, 1776. Olden Time, **2**: 105.
Connolly, Richard B., with portrait. Ev. Sat. **11**: 405.
Connor McGloghlin; a Tale. Blackw. **23**: 324. Same art. Liv. Age, **1**: 628.
Conolly, Arthur. (J. W. Kaye) Good Words, **6**: 398.
Conolly, T. L., Archbishop of Halifax. Canad. Mo. **10**: 254. — Cath. World, **24**: 136.
Conquered Prejudice, A. Victoria, **24**: 526.
Conquest, Dr. Edition of the Bible. Cong. M. **24**: 576.
Conquest and Usurpation. Anal. M. **7**: 166.
Conquests. Liv. Age, **13**: 109.
Conrad and Walsburga. (W. Seton) Cath. World, **27**: 163–487.
Conradin, last of the Hohenstaufens; a Poem. Am. Mo. M. **1**: 81.
Consalvi, Cardinal. Month, **1**: 535. **2**: 126.
— Controversy about. Month, **11**: 607.
— Memoirs of. Dub. R. **56**: 396. Same art. Cath. World, **1**: 377.
Consanguinity and primitive Marriage, Systems of. (J. N. Pomeroy) Nation, **17**: 209, 226. *See* Marriage.
Conscience, Hendrik. Chamb. J. **27**: 214. Same art. Liv. Age, **54**: 219.
— Tales. Dub. R. **21**: 163.
Conscience. (A. I. Hobbs) Chr. Q. **4**: 1. — Lond. Q. **44**: 91.
— an Infidel Shield. (D. Gans) Mercersb. **16**: 448.
— Analysis of. (J. Day) New Eng. **14**: 243.
— and the Bible. (R. S. Candlish) Ex. H. Lec. **11**: 461.
— and Evolution. (T. S. Lathrop) Univ. Q. **36**: 303.
— and its proper Function. Chr. Obs. **68**: 830.
— and Revealed Law. (A. Saxe) Univ. Q. **23**: 320.
— and Revelation. Bib. R. **6**: 453.
— — Supremacy of. (L. H. Atwater) Princ. n. s. **3**: 671.
— as a Witness for Christ. (W. D. Killen) Princ. n.s. **3**: 1.
— Christian. (H. Alford) Good Words, **9**: 25. Same art. Theo. Ecl. **5**: 468.
— contrasted with discursive Reason. (L. M. Dorman) New Eng. **21**: 206.
— Development and Growth of. (J. McCosh) Princ. n. s. **6**: 138.
— Edson's Letters on. Chr. Q. Spec. **7**: 629.
— Education of. Chr. R. **12**: 369.
— in Animals. (G. J. Romanes) Pop. Sci. Mo. **9**: 80
— Is it infallible? (M. Valentine) Luth. Q. **10**: 23.
— Is it primitive? (W. Wilkinson) Pop. Sci. Mo. **14**: 647
— Liberty of. Irish Mo. **4**: 163.

Conscience, Liberty of, Plea for. (A. F. Hewit) Cath. World, 7: 433.
— Maurice on. (J. C. Morison) Fortn. 10: 461.
— Moral Faculty and. (J. Haven) Bib. Sac. 13: 229.— (D. J. Noyes) Bib. Sac. 24: 401.
— Natural and spiritual. Chr. Obs. 42: 389.
— Nature and Sphere of. Ecl. M. 43: 186.
— Place of, in Evolution. (T.W. Fowle) 19th Cent. 4: 1. Same art. Pop. Sci. Mo. 13: 513.
— Preaching should appeal to. Bost. R. 1: 421.
— Relations and Office of. (J. Bascom) Bib. Sac. 24: 150.
— Rights of. Chr. Exam. 13: 69.—(D. Peck) Meth. Q. 3: 5.
— — Mivart on. Dub. R. 79: 1.
— — under the Laws of our Republic. (A. F. Hewit) Cath. World, 16: 721.
— seared. (H. Ballou, 2d) Univ. Q. 2: 90. — (T. B. Thayer) Univ. Q. 6: 168.
— Supremacy of. (J. W. Yeomans) Princ. 12: 299.
— under Revelation and Grace. (M. Valentine) Luth. Q. 7: 257.
— What is? Chr. Mo. Spec. 2: 337, 393.
Conscience Clause, The. (G. S. Lefevre) Fortn. 3: 165. — (E. H. Plumptre) Contemp. 1: 577.
Consciousness. (J. Bascom) Bib. Sac. 32: 676.
— and Personality. (A. P. Peabody) Princ. n. s. 8: 273.
— and Unconsciousness. (G. H. Lewes) Mind, 2: 156.
— Authority and Sphere of. (G. H. Emerson) Univ. Q. 13: 277.
— Autobiography of; a Sketch. Fraser, 80: 119.
— Central Innervation and. (W. Wundt) Mind, 1: 161.
— Christian, and the Written Word. (O. Stearns) Chr. Exam. 61: 157.
— Definition of. (W. L. Davidson) Mind, 6: 406.
— Dual. (J. Elliotson) Zoist. 4: 157. — Cornh. 35: 86.
— Facts of. (J. G. Fichte) J. Spec. Philos. 5: 53, 130, 338. 6: 42, 120, 332. 7: 36.
— in Psychology and Morals, Bouillier's. (A. Main) Mind, 3: 258.
— Inquiry concerning. (I. D. Williamson) Univ. Q. 13: 365.
— Interior. (I. E. Crosby) Radical, 4: 98.
— Modern Theories of. (T. M. Stewart) Bapt. Q. 7: 354.
— Murphy on Science of. Mo. R. 147: 407.
— Phenomena of divided. Chr. Rem. 3: 55.
— Philosophy of. Blackw. 43: 187, 437, 784. 44: 234, 539. 45: 201, 419.
— Self. *See* Self-Consciousness.
— Source of the Preacher's Power. (E. E. Bliss) Am. Q. Reg. 15: 317.
— under Chloroform. (H. Spencer) Pop. Sci. Mo. 13: 694.
— Validity of. (Sir W. Hamilton) Canad. J. n. s. 1: 379.
— Veracity of. (W. G. Davies) Mind, 2: 64.
— What is? (J. Bascom) Am. Presb. R. 18: 478.
Conscription in France. Good Words, 4: 733.
Consecration, Christian. Chr. Obs. 75: 429. — So. R. n. s. 21: 363.
Consecration of a Church, Form for. Mercersb. 8: 152.
Conservatism. Am. Whig R. 6: 122, 242. — Brownson, 5: 453.
— American, English View of. (A. V. Dicey) Nation, 30: 228, 282.
— and Radicalism. (O. Dewey) Chr. Exam. 79: 211.
— and Reform in Religion. Bost. Q. 5: 60.
— Genius of. (Sir E. Bulwer-Lytton) Lippinc. 14: 557.
— in England. Dub. Univ. 59: 755.
— or Revolution. Dub. Univ. 5: 114.
— Philosophy of. (W. H. Mallock) 19th Cent. 8: 724.
— Progressive. (I. E. Graeff) Mercersb. 17: 88.
— Some Aspects of. Tinsley, 15: 538.
— True. (E. Dowden) Contemp. 12: 267.
Conservative Associations. Blackw. 38: 1. 64: 632.
Conservative Government, Chief Obstacle to. Fraser, 26: 112.
Conservative Men, and the Union Meetings of the North. De Bow, 28: 514.
Conservative Party in England. Fraser, 39: 224.
— Past and Future of. Quar. 152: 369.
— Reorganization of, 1880. Blackw. 127: 804.
— Weakness and Strength of. Fraser, 15: 515, 646.
Conservative Policy in Parliament. Dub. Univ. 1: 378.
Conservative Prospects, 1835. Dub. Univ. 5: 629.
Conservative Registration Committee, Report of. Dub. Univ. 13: 739.
Conservative Union. Blackw. 64: 632.
Conservatives and Liberals, English. Month, 20: 451.
— and Radicals. (A. Abbott) Univ. Q. 14: 150.
— in Parliament, Word to. Dub. Univ. 10: 520.
— in Power. Fraser, 25: 363.
— Who are the true? Chr. Q. Spec. 10: 601.
Conservatory Building, Plan of. Pract. M. 6: 312.
Conservatories and Greenhouses. (M. B. Adams) Am. Arch. 7: 71.
— at Kew, Wanderings through. Fraser, 40: 127.
— Domestic, for Plants. Penny M. 11: 259.
— Loddiges's, Visit to. Chamb. J. 6: 281.
Consistency. (R. Whately) Good Words, 2: 629. — Colburn, 73: 104.
Consolation. (S. E. Henshaw) Overland, 15: 486.
— Christian. (A. St. John Chambre) Univ. Q. 22: 181.
— Peabody on. (C. Palfrey) Chr. Exam. 42: 240.
Consolations from Nature. Fraser, 103: 771. Same art. Liv. Age, 150: 248.
Consols, English, Price of. Bank. M. (N. Y.) 13: 913.
Conspirator in spite of Myself. Chamb. J. 57: 361-408.
Constable, Archibald. (A. G. Constable) Harper, 48: 501. — (W. Chambers) Chamb. J. 51: 193. — Liv. Age, 121: 242.
— and his Friends. No. Am. 119: 423.
— Memoirs of. Ed. R. 141: 149.
Constable, Henry. Poems. Irish Q. 9: 953.
Constable, John. (P. G. Hamerton) Portfo. 4: 93, 108, 117.
— and Gainsborough. Art J. 33: 150.
— Life of, Leslie's. Ed. R. 87: 472.
— — and English Landscape. Blackw. 58: 257.
Constable de Bourbon. (W. H. Ainsworth) Bentley, 58: 441, 551. 59: 1-551. 60: 91, 203.
— and Sacking of Rome. Fraser, 18: 424.
Constable of the Tower. (W. H. Ainsworth) Bentley, 49: 1-567. 50: 1-314. Same art. Ecl. M. 52: 365, 515. 53: 98-484. 54: 43-484.
Constabulary, Royal Irish. Tinsley, 4: 525.
Constabulary Officer, Leaves from Notebook of a. Dub. Univ. 88: 439. 89: 621, 718.
Constance, Council of. Irish Mo. 4: 228.
— Treaty of, 1183. (E. Creasy) Dub. Univ. 49: 387.
Constance; a Poem. St. James, 26: 646.
Constance Sherwood; a Tale. (G. Fullerton) Month, 1: 16-463. 2: 1-489. 3: 1-251. Same art. Cath. World, 1: 78-748. 2: 37-759.
Constance Woodburn. (C. M. S. Barnes) So. Lit. Mess. 4: 169.
Constancia de Gonsalvo. Liv. Age, 39: 259.
Constant, Benjamin. (J. H. Browne) Lippinc. 14: 501. — Prosp. R. 1: 356.
— and Mad. Recamier. (A. Laugel) Nation, 33: 391.
— on Religion. (O. A. Brownson) Chr. Exam. 17: 63. — Lond. M. 10: 483.
Constant Couple; a Tale. All the Year, 26: 513.
Constantine the Great. (P. Schaff) Bib. Sac. 20: 778. — (P. Schaff) Mercersb. 12: 173. — (P. Schaff) Contin. Mo. 6: 161.
— Church Policy of. No. Brit. 52: 1.
— Life of. Chr. R. 4: 201. — Lit. & Theo. R. 6: 541.

Constantine the Great, Reign of. Dub. R. **42**: 490.
Constantine, Grand Duke of Russia. Colburn, **16**: 194.— Temp. Bar, **8**: 590.
Constantine's Cell. *See* Wetheral Safeguard.
Constantine's Legacy. Chamb. J. **35**: 234, 253.
Constantinople. (A. Archer) Canad. Mo. **11**: 38.—(J. Bryce) Macmil. **37**: 337. Same art. Ecl. M. **90**: 481. Same art. Liv. Age, **136**: 619.—(F. W. Holland) Lippinc. **9**: 631.—(J. O. Noyes) Knick. **48**: 162.—(W. S. Tyler) Hours at Home, **6**: 437.—Brit. Q. **67**: 414. Same art. Liv. Age, **137**: 579.—Colburn, **10**: 137, 275—Fraser, **21**: 90.—Penny M. **1**: 193, 201. **13**: 448.—Sharpe, **48**: 198, 251, 314.
— Account of Walls of. (J. Dallaway) Arch. **14**: 231.
— Adventures of a Queen's Messenger in. St. James, **10**: 492. **11**: 58, 205.
— An American in. (W. C. Prime) Harper, **16**: 289.
— and the Bosphorus. Hogg, **11**: 176.
— and the Danube. (N. Macleod) Good Words, **7**: 267.
— and Decline of the Ottoman Empire. Blackw. **61**: 685.
— and the Eastern Question. Chr. R. **20**: 240.
— and Environs. Am. Q. **18**: 62.
— and Greek Christianity. (R. Burgess) Ex. H. Lec. **10**: 239.
— Architecture of. Am. Arch. **5**: 180.
— At-Meidan and its Pillars. Penny M. **9**: 1.
— — Huldjo's Visit to, 1833. Mo. R. **137**: 378.
— Bazaars of. All the Year, **2**: 457.
— Can it be defended? All the Year, **37**: 462.
— City of the Sultan. Nat. M. **6**: 193, 361, 457.
— Colton's Visit to. Am. Q **20**: 351.
— Council of. Ed. R. **126**: 95.
— Day in. Sharpe, **10**: 340.
— Defenses of. Appleton, **17**: 263.
— Dogs of. Chamb. J. **25**: 267. Same art. Liv. Age, **49**: 664.—All the Year, **2**: 256.
— during Conference of 1877. Macmil. **35**: 397.
— during Crimean War. Sharpe, **51**: 69, 124.
— during the Plague. (H. R. Addison) Peop. J. **5**: 331.
— Fall of. St. James, **20**: 19.
— Fête Champêtre in. (Mrs. P. Sinnet) Bentley, **23**: 121.
— Fire at Pera, 1831. Colburn, **32**: 313.
— A Forenoon at. Tait, n. s. **25**: 149.
— Fortifications of. Brit. & For. R. **5**: 600.
— From Pesth to, by the Danube and Black Sea. Colburn, **110**: 379.
— Glance at. Lond. Soc. **39**: 332.
— Glimpses of. (S. Hale) Lippinc. **17**: 539, 668.
— Grand Mosque of. Penny M. **4**: 419.
— Greece, and Russia. St. James, **44**: 24.
— Guardsman in. Bentley, **44**: 145, 269.
— Historians of the Fall of. (A. Laugel) Nation, **31**: 76.
— in Byzantine Times. Chamb. J. **50**: 734
— in 1851. (F. W. Holland) Am. Whig R. **14**: 429.
— in 4th Century. Quar. **78**: 346. Same art. Ecl. M. **10**: 1. Same art. Liv. Age, **11**: 428.
— in Ramazan, 1852. (J. P. Brown) Knick. **40**: 420.
— Law and Justice in. Chamb. J. **15**: 323.
— Letters from, 1880. Temp. Bar, **58**: 456. **60**: 99. Same art. Ecl. M. **94**: 756. **95**: 617.
— Lunacy in. All the Year, **2**: 329, 339.
— Madhouses of. (W. Goodell) Atlan. **28**: 527.
— Memorial Church at. Dub. Univ. **52**: 709.
— Old Accounts of. All the Year, **33**: 174, 204, 510.
— Miss Pardoe's. Brit. & For. R. **7**: 86.—Mo. R. **143**: 357.
— Patriarchate of. (A. Hewit) Cath. World, **3**: 1.
— Remembrances of. Argosy, **22**: 213.
— St. Sophia, Church and Mosque of. Ed. R. **121**: 456. Same art. Ecl. M. **65**: 385. Same art. abridged, Cath. World, **1**: 641.—(H. Craig) Lippinc. **20**: 629.
— Saunterings about. (C. D. Warner) Scrib. **13**: 238.
Constantinople, Scenes in. (S. C. Massett) Pioneer, **2**: 120, 140, 207.—Knick. **25**: 305.
— Site of. (G. F. Herrick) Galaxy, **22**: 770.
— Sketches from. (J. P. Brown) Knick. **26**: 133, 307, 419. **28**: 26. **32**: 291.
— Slave-Market of. Chamb. J. **4**: 385. Same art. Liv. Age, **8**: 328.
— Smith's Month at. Blackw. **67**: 679. Same art. Liv. Age, **26**: 161.
— Stamboul and Suburbs. (W. Knight) Bentley, **53**: 410.
— State Ball in. (E. Fagnani) Scrib. **14**: 148.
— Story of the Plague at. Colburn, **32**: 166.
— Streets of. Penny M. **7**: 401.
— Street Sights in. All the Year, **2**: 279.
— Suburb of Pera. Temp. Bar, **50**: 211.
— Three Weeks at. Chamb. J. **8**: 104, 123.
— Three Years in. Dub. Univ. **25**: 331.
— Trip to. Gent. M. n. s. **8**: 529.
— Valley of the Sweet Waters. All the Year, **2**: 490.—(E. De Leon) Lippinc. **11**: 454.
— Visit to, 1840. (Marchioness of Londonderry) Colburn, **70**: 25–539.
— Visits to. Chamb. J. **51**: 231.
— Von Hammer's. (E. Everett) No. Am. **16**: 203.
— Walsh's Residence in. Ed. R. **64**: 125.—Mo. R. **140**: 506.—Ecl. R. **64**: 346, 385.—So. R. **3**: 225.—Mus. **31**: 74.
— Water-Supply of. (H. A. Homes) Ecl. Engin. **9**: 407.
— Week in. Bentley, **39**: 304.
— White's Three Years in. Blackw. **58**: 688.—Dub. Univ. **25**: 331.
See Pera.
Constantyne, George. Memorial to Thomas, Lord Cromwell. Arch. **23**: 50.
Constanza, Valley of. (Sir R. H. Schomburgk) Liv. Age, **34**: 518.
Constellation Figures, Origin of. (R. A. Proctor) Belgra. **33**: 416. Same art. Sup. Pop. Sci. Mo. **2**: 49.
Constipation, Epps on. Ecl R. **102**: 736.
Constitution, Frigate. (J. F. Cooper) Putnam, **1**: 473, 593.—Niles's Reg. **44**: 431.—So. Lit. Mess. **4**: 357.
Constitution Makers, Hints for. (C. C. Nott) Nation, **5**: 132–211.
Constitution-Making. (L. Bacon) New Eng. **33**: 16.
— American and English. Liv. Age, **28**: 190.
Constitutions. (W. Tudor) No. Am. **12**: 290.
— English and United States. (G. Bradford) No. Am. **118**: 1.—West. M. **2**: 11.
— State, Reform of. (H. Reed) No. Am. **121**: 1.
— Written. (W. A. Benton) Am. Church R. **19**: 593.
See names of countries, as United States; Great Britain.
Constitutional Association. Ed. R. **37**: 110.
Constitutional Compromises. Dem. R. **28**: 385.
Constitutional Convention of 1776. (W. H. Egle) Pennsyl. M. **3**: 96–438. **4**: 89, 225, 361.
Constitutional Conventions. (C. C. Beaman, Jr.) No. Am. **104**: 646.
— Jameson on. (T. G. Shearman) Nation, **4**: 5.
— Powers of. Penn Mo. **5**: 813.
— Work of. (A S. Biddle) Penn Mo. **4**: 283.
Constitutional Fallacies and unreformed Abuses. Ecl. R. **89**: 730.
Constitutional Government. Portfo.(Den.) **14**: 450, 556.
Constitutional Governments. Bost. Q. **5**: 27.—Dem. R. **20**: 195.
Constitutional History. (E. Brooks) No. Am. **29**: 265.
Constitutional Law. (W. Dutton) No. Am. **10**: 83.
— a Study in Common Schools. (E. A. Lawrence) Am Inst. of Instruc. **1841**: 180.
— Peters's. (C. S. Davis) No. Am. **46**: 126.
— Pomeroy's. (J. C. Hurd) Nation, **7**: 53.

Constitutional Law, Story's. (E. Everett) No. Am. **38**: 63. — Dem. R. **23**: 444. — Niles's Reg. **29**: 165. **38**: 297.
Constitutional Progress, Burrow's Lectures on. Chr. Obs. **69**: 511.
Constitutional Reform. Dem. R. **29**: 1.
— in New York. Dem. R. **13**: 563.
— in Pennsylvania. Am. Q. **19**: 223.
— in United States. Dem. R. **18**; 243, 403.
— Limits of. (A. G. Sedgwick) Nation, **21**: 128.
Construction, Æsthetics of. (G. F. Deacon) Ecl. Engin. **1**: 641.
— Materials for. Ecl. Engin. **7**: 609.
— — Mechanical Properties of. (R. H. Thurston) Ecl. Engin. **11**: 97.
— Papers on. (C. E. Dutton) Ecl. Engin. **1**: 305–674.
Consular Establishments. Westm. **54**: 66.
Consular Service of Great Britain. Cornh. **22**: 546.
Consular Story. (W. J. Stillman) Nation, **8**: 129, 493.
Consular System. (J. D. B. De Bow) De Bow, **1**: 56. — (J. G. Moore) De Bow, **16**: 12.
— of United States. (W. S. Mayo) Hunt, **6**: 297. **13**: 551. — (C. E. Lester) Hunt, **10**: 447. **12**: 211. **17**: 43. **18**: 60.
Consule Julio; an Episode of the Commune. Cornh. **24**: 175. Same art. Liv. Age, **110**: 718.
Consuls. (W. J. Stillman) Nation, **2**: 104.
— in China and elsewhere, Our. (W. D. Howells) Nation, **1**: 551.
— Miltitz on the Duties of. For. Q. **19**: 106.
Consumption. (A. Brigham) Knick. **8**: 1. — Mo. R. **82**: 271. — Chamb. J. **24**: 68.
— and its newest Cure. Month, **38**: 295.
— Andral on. For. Q. **7**: 52.
— Cure of. Mo. R. **123**: 54.
— Hospital at Brompton. Peop. J. **3**: 341.
— — for. Chamb. J. **7**: 246.
— Hygienic Change of Air. Chamb. J. **18**: 6. Same art. Liv. Age, **34**: 372.
— in the Guards. (W. H. Guy) Fraser, **58**: 80.
— Influence of Climate on. Nature, **16**: 59.
— investigated by Auscultation. Quar. **57**: 199.
— Nature, Causes, and Prevention of. (A. S. Thomson) Colburn, **59**: 108–506.
— Oil-Anointing for. Chamb. J. **19**: 164. Same art. Liv. Age, **37**: 401.
— Pulmonary, in America. (H. I. Bowditch) Atlan. **23**: 51, 177, 315.
— — Robertson on. Mo. R. **145**: 244.
— — Southey on. Ecl. R. **21**: 181.
— Relations of Climate to. (W. J. Burnett) Liv. Age, **35**: 314.
— Successful Treatment of. Chamb. J. **58**: 489.
— Sweetser on. No. Am. **43**: 516.
— Victims of. Knick. **8**: 338.
Contact Resistance, Experiments on. (W. A. Norton) Am. J. Sci. **111**: 442.
Contagion. (E. Hale) No. Am. **12**: 174.
— and Fever, 1819. (E. Hale) No. Am. **10**: 386.
— and Quarantine. (Dr. Gooch) Quar. **27**: 524.
— and Sanitary Laws. (S. Smith) Westm. **3**: 134.
— Prevention of. Ed. R. **1**: 237.
Contagious Diseases, Glandular Origin of. (B. W. Richardson) Nature, **16**: 480.
Contagious Diseases Act. Lond. Q. **35**: 128.
— Englishwomen and. (R. D. Webb) Nation, **11**: 40, 136.
— Operation of. (J. Stansfeld) J. Statis. Soc. **39**: 540.
— Results of. (B. Hill) J. Statis. Soc. **33**: 463.
Contagious Fever. Ed. R. **31**: 414.
Contemplative Sentiment, as opposed to Sensation. Blackw. **9**: 393.
Contemporary Criticism; a Poem. (W. W. Story) Fortn. **3**: 330.
Content; new Readings from old Texts. Colburn, **67**: 454.
Content, or not Content. (L. Blanchard) Colburn, **64**: 285.
Continent, European, Bradshaw's Guide in 1852. Chamb. J. **18**: 133.
— British Connections with. For. Q. **19**: 135.
— Englishman on. (G. M. Towle) Lippinc. **3**: 597.
— Gossip about, 1847. (C. Lever) Dub. Univ. **29**: 541.
— Homes of. Eng. Dom. M. **16**: 16–288. **17**: 16–292.
— in 1854. No. Brit. **22**: 289.
— Jottings on. Hogg, **11**: 380, 470. **12**: 106.
— Journal of a Traveler on. Lond. M. **15**: 33–433.
— Letters from. (J. Galt) Blackw. **16**: 555. **17**: 329.
— Life on, Tales of. Lond. M. **18**: 187.
— Prospects on, 1850. Westm. **54**: 415.
— Revolutions on. Bentley, **50**: 49. Same art. Ecl. M. **54**: 540.
— Seven Years on. Temp. Bar, **21**: 38, 245, 404.
— Tour on. Fraser, **28**: 681. **29**: 449.
— — and its Results. Blackw. **46**: 56.
— Travels on. Lond. M. **18**: 201.
— What it costs to see. Chamb. J. **41**: 252.
See Europe.
Continental Army, Plan for Reorganization of. (M. Gist) Hist. M. **13**: 270.
Continental Bills of Credit, Devices of. M. Am. Hist. **1**: 751.
Continental Congress at Philadelphia, Centennial of. N. E. Reg. **29**: 426.
— before Independence. (J. Ward) M. Am. Hist. **2**: 193.
— Members of First. Am. Alma. **1834**: 97. — Bost. Mo. **1**: 603.
— of 1774. New York R. **4**: 324. — Niles's Reg. **18**: 225.
— Protest against. Hist. M. **10**: 144.
Continental Money. Hist. M. **3**: 71.
— First Issue of. (A. S. Bolles) Bank. M. (N. Y.) **33**: 784.
Continental Treasury Board. (A. S. Bolles) Bank. M. (N. Y.) **33**: 860, 955. **34**: 117, 273.
Continents, Growth of. (L. Agassiz) Atlan. **12**: 72.
— Old Age of. (A. Winchell) Lakeside, **1**: 210.
— Origin of. (A. C. Ramsay) Pop. Sci. Mo. **3**: 573. Same art. Liv. Age, **118**: 372.
— Permanence of. (J. S. Gardiner) Pop. Sci. R. **20**: 117. Same art. Ecl. M. **97**: 58.
Continuity, Grove on. Month, **5**: 635.
— in History, Morals, and Religion. (P. W. Clayden) Theo. R. **4**: 572.
— Law of. (G. Iles) Pop. Sci. Mo. **12**: 29.
Contraband of War. Am. Law R. **5**: 247.
Contrabandista. (T. Medwin) Bentley, **8**: 17.
Contrabbandieri, Last of. (L. Mariotti) Colburn, **72**: 150.
Contract, Freedom of. (F. H. Farrer) Fortn. **35**: 44.
Contracts, Doctrine of. Am. Q. **1**: 106. — U. S. Lit. Gaz. **3**: 441.
— Government, of England. Westm. **73**: 1.
— — Faith in. (F. O. G. Smith) Hunt, **13**: 19.
— Law of. (A. S. Stearns) No. Am. **17**: 375.
— Moral Law of. (J. Aldrich) Hunt, **1**: 303.
— Obligation of. (J. M. Krum) West. J. **1**: 68, 199. — Niles's Reg. **16**: 269. **21**: 146. — West. Law J. **4**: 254.
— Verplanck's Essay on. (H. Wheaton) No. Am. **22**: 253.
Contract System in Public Works. (C. C. Nott) Nation, **20**: 324.
Contraction Hypothesis. (C. E. Dutton) Am. J. Sci. **108**: 113.
Contrast, The. (C. Wolfe) Dub. Univ. **2**: 178.
Contrast, The; a Poem. So. Lit. Mess. **16**: 599.
Contrasted Scenes. Lond. M. **10**: 308.

Contrecœur, M. Summons to Ensign Ward, 1754. Olden Time, 1: 83.
Contreras, Battle of. So. Q. 21: 373.
Contributions of the Ungodly for religious Objects. Cong. M. 18: 658.
Controjanni, Greek Robbers, Execution of, 1836. Colburn, 64: 146.
Controversy, Ethics of. Brownson, 10: 262.
— Plague of. Dub. R. 36: 351.
— Religious, Morality of. Kitto, 26: 40.
— Thoughts on. Chr. Disc. 5: 261.
Controversies, Minor, among Christians. (L. Beecher) Cong. M. 15: 585.
Conundrums. (G. Wakeman) Galaxy, 3: 416.
Convalescence. Liv. Age, 135: 446.
Convalescent, The. (C. Lamb) Lond. M. 12: 376.
Convalescent Homes. All the Year, 23: 204.
Convent of the Inquisition. Peop. J. 5: 137.
— of Iona. (E. Pond) Am. Q. Reg. 12: 153.
— of St. Margaret and St. Agnes. Month, 1: 438.
— of San Lazzaro, at Venice. Dub. R. 12: 362.
— Miss Reed's Six Months in a. Chr. Obs. 35: 681, 700. 36: 49. — Dub. R. 1: 313.
— Wilson's Escape from a Portuguese. Chr. Obs. 36: 49, 94.
See also Nunnery.
Convents. Dub. R. 33: 467.
— English, and Conventualities. Colburn, 92: 51.
— — on the Continent. (Abbé Mann) Arch. 13: 251.
— in the U. S. (J. G. McGee) Cath. World, 19: 362.
— of Great Britain. Dub. Univ. 82: 87. 88: 126. — Fraser, 89: 14.
— — Parliamentary Committee on, 1870. Dub. R. 67: 271.
— Romish, and Protestant Sisterhoods. Chr. Obs. 69: 454.
Convent Belles, Those. All the Year, 21: 445.
Convent Boarding-Schools for young Ladies. Fraser, 89: 778.
— Word for. Fraser, 90: 473.
Convent Education. Month, 21: 352.
Convent Life. (C. E. Robins) Putnam, 12: 575. — Blackw. 105: 607.
— and Work. (B. Murphy) Lippinc. 17: 322.
— Behind the Convent Grille. (J. G. Austin) Atlan. 33: 530.
— in England. Dub. R. 73: 115.
— in Ireland. Fraser, 80: 431. 81: 381.
— Sister X's. All the Year, 23: 43, 68.
Convent Question, Two Views of. Macmil. 19: 534.
Convention of 1787, North and South in. (A. T. Bledsoe) So. R. n. s. 2: 359.
Conventions and Conferences. (S. Osgood) Chr. Exam. 38: 145.
— Danger of. (S. W. Cone) Dem. R. 36: 453.
— Nominating. (E. L. Godkin) Nation, 8: 429. 22: 240.
— Politico-Commercial. Dem. R. 40: 299.
See Constitutional Conventions.
Conventionality. Dub. Univ. 88: 764.
Conventionalities of Life. Lond. Soc. 7: 147.
Conversation. New Eng. M. 3: 491. — (T. De Quincey) Ecl. M. 18: 446. — So. Lit. Mess. 1: 547. — (A. Helps) Ev. Sat. 9: 115–325. — (T. De Quincey) Hogg, 4: 65. — (T. De Quincey) Tait, n. s. 14: 678. — (L. Fountain) Putnam, 14: 243. — All the Year, 13: 284. — (E. Hosken) Colburn, 160: 553. — Irish Mo. 2: 633. — Blackw. 102: 555. — Chamb. J. 56: 188. — Ev. Sat. 1: 119. — Liv. Age, 66: 486. 72: 214.
— and Authors. St. James, 49: 258.
— Art of. (L. Withington) Bib. Sac. 24: 74. — Cornh. 16: 719. 17: 90, 168, 370. — Fraser, 26: 224. — So. R. n. s. 9: 812. — Temp. Bar, 27: 487.
— by Friends in Council. (A. Helps) Ecl. M. 78: 492.
Conversation, Decay of. Chamb. J. 40: 177. — Ecl. M. 60: 438.
— Elements of. Colburn, 46: 17. 47: 418.
— Exaggeration in. Blackw. 100: 672. Same art. Liv. Age, 92: 3.
— Gift of the Gab. (W. Maclerie) Tinsley, 18: 271.
— Maxims in. (J. Payn) Chamb. J. 45: 49.
— of Authors. Lond. M. 2: 250.
— Possible Revival of. Belgra. 36: 99.
— Professional. Cornh. 11: 489.
— Professional Religious. (J.C. Learned) Radical, 1: 475.
— Reverence for good Words in. Fraser, 97: 596. Same art. Liv. Age, 137: 563.
— Rhetoric of. Ecl. M. 51: 364.
— Rules for. So. Lit. Mess. 4: 137.
— Simplicity in. (R. A. Stiles) University Q. 2: 117.
— Talk about Talking. Colburn, 60: 55.
— Truth of Intercourse. Cornh. 39: 585. Same art. Liv. Age, 141: 762.
— What it should be. Temp. Bar, 34: 179.
Conversations at Casa Tonti. (E. Howland) Lippinc. 10: 100, 470.
— of our Club. Brownson, 15: 1–425.
Conversational Observances. Lond. Soc. 14: 51. Same art. Ecl. M. 71: 1233.
Conversazione: Science and Art. Cornh. 6: 269.
Conversion. (A. I. Hobbs) Chr. Q. 4: 481. — (H. E. Jacobs) Evang. R. 18: 536. — (T. G. Apple) Mercersb. 24: 452. — (S. E. Shepard) Chr. Q. 6: 87, 189. — Mo. Rel. M. 33: 347.
— and Baptism. (H. S. Lobingier) Chr. Q. 8: 263.
— and Regeneration. Cong. 4: 653.
— and religious Experience. (C. S. Gerhard) Mercersb. 21: 444.
— and Repentance. Chr. Disc. 1: 354.
— Bible Records of. Good Words, 1: 65–587.
— Catholic View of. (L. Bacon) New Eng. 26: 114.
— Human Responsibility in. (A. Phelps) Bib. Sac. 23: 645.
— in primitive and modern Times. (J. Caird) Good Words, 4: 75.
— Nature of. (A. Phelps) Bib. Sac. 23: 48.
— of the Northern Nations, Merivale on. Chr. Obs. 66: 785, 818.
— of the Thief on the Cross. Chr. Mo. Spec. 6: 187.
— of the World. Ecl. R. 112: 573. — (J. A. Brown) Luth. Q. 3: 161.
— — and Church History. (W. De L. Love) New Eng. 40: 86.
— — Christian Obligation for. Princ. 4: 309.
— — Harris's Theory of. Theo. & Lit. J. 12: 1.
— Philosophy of. Cath. World, 4: 459.
— Sudden, Scriptural Argument for. (G. A. Nixdorff) Evang. R. 19: 561.
— Theory of. (H. C. Lay) Am. Church R. 7: 220.
— Tracts on, 1815. Ecl. R. 23: 538.
— Zaccheus, an Example of true. Chr. Disc. 5: 332.
See Regeneration.
Conversion of Property by Purchase. (N. Newmark) Am. Law R. 15: 363.
Conveyancer's Romance. Am Law R. 10: 60.
Conveyancing, English. Ed. R. 35: 190.
— in England, Ancient. (H. Ellis) Arch. 17: 311.
— The Horn as a Charter of. (S. Pegge) Arch. 3: 1.
Conveying and Stealing. (F. Jacox) Temp Bar, 23: 354.
Convict in Australia. Cornh. 4: 229. 10: 722. 13: 489.
Convict's Return; a Poem. Temp. Bar, 55: 118
Convict's Tale. (E. A. Dupuy) Knick. 37: 219.
Convict's Tale. Peop. J. 11: 222.
Convict's Views of penal Discipline. Cornh. 10: 722.
Convicts and Quakers. (J. Service) Good Words, 19: 197, 378, 541.

Convicts, Mary Carpenter on Treatment and Reformation of. (C. F. Barnard) Chr. Exam. **78**: 250. — Month, **3**: 646. — (W. Hincks) Canad. J. n. s. **10**: 412.
— Dialogue concerning. All the Year, **5**: 155.
— Discharged. (W. Gilbert) Good Words, **8**: 622.
— English. (C. Winkworth) Good Words, **6**: 446. — Victoria, **5**: 1.
— — What should be done with them? Westm. **79**: 1.
— Fat. All the Year, **13**: 204.
— Female. (O. H. Dutton) Harper, **28**: 193.
— — on board Ships. Eng. Dom. M. **1**: 311.
— for their Faith. All the Year, **17**: 66.
— in Australia, Escape of. Temp. Bar, **14**: 50.
— on Norfolk Island, 1843. (Capt. Maconochie) J. Statis. Soc. **8**: 1.
— Punishment and Reform of. Cornh. **7**: 189. **10**: 722.
— Rights of. (F. B. Perkins) O. & N. **9**: 495.
— Sketches of. House. Words, **19**: 489-596.
Convict Biography. Dub. Univ. **63**: 440.
Convict Capitalists. All the Year, **3**: 201.
Convict Establishment in Spain. Temp. Bar, **47**: 400.
— in Western Australia. Chamb. J. **18**: 106.
Convict Life. Chamb. J. **57**: 177.
— at Dartmoor. Temp. Bar, **40**: 348.
Convict Literature. Chamb. J. **21**: 388.
Convict Lunatic Asylum. Cornh. **10**: 448.
Convict Management. Brit. Q. **37**: 314.
Convict Prison. Chamb. J. **58**: 497.
Convict Prisons. Month, **5**: 379.
Convict Settlement in India. Good Words, **7**: 305.
Convict System, English. Chamb. J. **51**: 556. — Lond. Q. **53**: 421. — Cornh. **3**: 708. **7**: 189. **10**: 722. **14**: 489. — Temp. Bar, **12**: 225. — Westm. **109**: 407.
— — and Irish. Cornh. **3**: 409, 708. **4**: 229. **10**: 722. — Dub. Univ. **62**: 112. — Ed. R. **117**: 241. — Temp. Bar, **3**: 181.
— — Flaw in. (A. G. Knight) Month, **39**: 548.
— — in the Colonies. Bentley, **51**: 513.
See Ticket of Leave; Transportation.
Convicted by a Dream. (J. J. Beardsley) Lakeside, **6**: 10.
Conviction, Emotion of. (W. Bagehot) Contemp. **17**: 32.
Convictions, Ethical Value of. (J. E. Wells) Canad. Mo. **13**: 503.
Conviviality. Blackw. **127**: 340.
Convivium Templare. Blackw. **115**: 568.
Convocation. *See* Church of England, Convocation.
Convulsionists of St. Médard. (R. D. Owen) Atlan. **13**: 209, 339. — Sharpe, **44**: 240. **45**: 234. — (T. A. Trollope) Temp. Bar, **28**: 183.
Conway, Anne, Viscountess. (T. Cooper) Once a Week, **12**: 218.
— and Valentine Greatrakes. (C. J. Langston) Argosy, **30**: 378.
Conway, H. S. Letters to H. Walpole. Fraser, **41**: 272, 423, 631. **42**: 337.
Conway, M. D. Sacred Anthology. (J. E. Carpenter) Theo. R. **11**: 191. — (S. Longfellow) O. & N. **10**: 747.
Conway, William A., and Mrs. Piozzi. (D. Cook) Gent. M. n. s. **27**: 538.
Conway Castle, Account of. Penny M. **13**: 157.
Cony, Thomas, Household Book of. (E. Turnor) Arch. **11**: 22.
Conybeare, William Daniel, Biographical Notice of. (J. E. Portlock) Am. J. Sci. **77**: 63.
Conybeare, W. J. Perversion; the Hard Church Novel. Nat. R. **3**: 127.
Coo-ee! House. Words, **17**: 232.
Cook, Eliza. Poems. Ecl. M. **17**: 24. — So. Lit. Mess. **10**: 107, 217. — Colburn, **70**: 196. **71**: 298. **72**: 448.
Cook, Captain James. Nature, **19**: 334.
— a Hawaiian Divinity. (J. T. Meagher) Lakeside, **8**: 197.
Cook, Captain James, Scene of Death of. (C. W. Stoddard) Overland, **1**: 436.
— Statue to. Nature, **20**: 7.
Cook, Joseph, with portrait. Ecl. M. **90**: 120.
— Monday Lectures. (H. H. Barber) Unita. R. **7**: 546. — Unita. R. **8**: 202. — (D. A. Wasson) Unita. R. **9**: 11. — (G. S. Hall) Nation, **30**: 364.
— on Biology. New Eng. **37**: 100.
— — and Transcendentalism. Bib. Sac. **35**: 381.
— on Transcendentalism. (M. S. Phelps) New Eng. **37**: 236.
— Spread-Eagle Philosophy. Sup. Pop. Sci. Mo. **3**: 128.
— Theolog. Charlatanism. (J. Fiske) No. Am. **132**: 287.
Cook, Lemuel, Last Pensioner of the Revolution. Am. Hist. Rec. **2**: 357.
Cook, A French. (A. Poyntz) Bentley, **11**: 606. — Lond. M. **11**: 65.
— of Confederate Army. (A. C. Redwood) Scrib. **18**: 560.
Cooks. Chamb. J. **45**: 385. — Cornh. **4**: 601. — Ev. Sat. **6**: 19.
— and Cookery. Dub. Univ. **57**: 696.
— Eccentricities of. All the Year, **20**: 534. Same art. Ev. Sat. **6**: 714.
Cook County, Ill., Land Titles in. (J. B. Adams) Lakeside, **7**: 161.
Cook's Inlet, Alaska. (W. T. Wythe) Overland, **8**: 64.
Cooke, Edward William. Art J. **21**: 253.
Cooke, George F., the Tragedian. (W. Dunlap) Anal. M. **1**: 404, 466. — Mus. **43**: 508. — Portfo. (Den.) **9**: 532. — Temp. Bar, **50**: 189. Same art. Ecl. M. **89**: 197.
— in New York. (J. E. Cooke) Galaxy, **7**: 755.
Cooke, Henry, with portrait. Hogg, **2**: 296.
— Life and Times of. Chr. Obs. **72**: 17.
Cooke, Rev. John, Redford's Memoir of. Ecl. R. **48**: 552 — Cong. M. **10**: 1, 57.
Cooke, John Esten. (J. Craik) Am. Church R. **9**: 226. — So. Lit. Mess. **24**: 286.
Cooke, Nicholas, Gov. of R. I., 1775. Am. Q. Reg. **15**: 162.
Cooke, Parsons. (J. A. Vinton) Cong. Q. **14**: 219.
— Letter to. (I. Parker) Chr. Exam. **5**: 277.
Cooke, Philip P. Internat. M. **4**: 300. — Knick. **64**: 424.
— Florence Vane. (J. Hunt, jr.) So. Lit. Mess. **16**: 369.
— Poetry of. So. Lit. Mess. **13**: 437.
— Recollections of. So. Lit. Mess. **26**: 419.
— Sketch of. So. Lit. Mess. **17**: 669.
Cookery. (L. Fountain) Putnam, **14**: 374. — (A. Hayward) Quar. **52**: 406. — Irish Q. **8**: 461, 1103. — Chamb. J. **39**: 233. — Quar. **52**: 216. — Ed. R. **35**: 43.
— American. (P. Blot) Galaxy, **4**: 748.
— Ancient and modern. (P. Blot) Galaxy, **2**: 215. **4**: 863.
— Ancient Roman. Portfo. (Den.) **12**: 539.
— and Civilization. Blackw. **60**: 238.
— and Confectionery. Mo. R. **96**: 389.
— and Cooks. Chamb. J. **29**: 361.
— and Culinary Literature. For. Q. **33**: 98. — Blackw. **2**: 300. **19**: 651.
— Art of. (A. J. H. Crespe) Victoria, **25**: 719.
— at So. Kensington. (E. R. Lankester) Nature, **8**: 178.
— Chemistry of the Kitchen. Dub. Univ. **77**: 461. — Hogg, **6**: 151-350.
— Conservative. So. Lit. Mess. **16**: 210.
— Cook in History. (A. Fabie) Lippinc. **1**: 91.
— Cook's Oracle. Lond. M. **4**: 432. — Appleton, **24**: 168.
— Cuisine Bourgeoise of Ancient Rome. (H. C. Coote) Arch. **41**: 283.
— Culinary Affairs. Once a Week, **24**: 395.
— Curiosities of. Bentley, **33**: 209. — Chamb. J. **22**: 260.
— Dutch Dishes. Ev. Sat. **11**: 607.
— English and French. Mo. R. **113**: 34.

Cookery, French. Bentley, 11: 97. — Colburn, 65: 6. — Liv. Age, 1: 49. — Lond. M. 10: 178. — Lond. Soc. 4: 555. 16: 170-552.
— — as a Fine Art. Ev. Sat. 12: 262.
— — Rise and Progress of. All the Year, 20: 225.
— French Cottage. Chamb. J. 15: 364.
— French Kitchens. (F. Marshall) Bentley, 54: 43.
— Good old English. All the Year, 30: 65.
— How we should dine. (G. A. Sala) Belgra. 6: 448.
— International School for. Chamb. J. 50: 388.
— The Kitchen. (S. E. Henshaw) Lippinc. 2: 312.
— — and Cellar. Quar. 143: 379. Same art. Liv. Age. 133: 752.
— Learning. All the Year, 33: 366. 41: 40. 43: 156. 44: 89. 45: 14, 79.
— Lessons in. (E. L. Youmans) Nation, 27: 338. — All the Year, 32: 488-611. 35: 420, 471.
— Man who cooks. (P. Mulford) Lippinc. 8: 522.
— Manual of, for Days of Fasting. All the Year, 21: 353.
— Modern. So. R. 3: 416.
— — in all its Branches. Fraser, 31: 465.
— New Practice of. (Sir W. Scott) Ed. R. 6: 350.
— Obsolete. House. Words, 11: 21.
— of our Forefathers. (C. Russell) Sharpe, 32: 123.
— Old Chapter in. (E. R. Seymour) Once a Week, 10: 709.
— Philosophy of. Chamb. J. 28: 280.
— Real School of. (G. A. Sala) Belgra. 25: 192.
— School of. Chamb. J. 44: 817. — Once a Week, 9: 596.
— — German, One Year in. Cornh. 43: 610. Same art. Ecl. M. 97: 124. Same art. Appleton, 26: 67.
— Science of good Cheer. St. James, 8: 488.
— Soyer in Crimea. (W. G. Sewall) Harper, 16: 325.
— with the Poor. All the Year, 37: 275-466.
See Pastry; Kitchen.
Cookery Book, Cromwell's. All the Year, 36: 125.
— Sanscrit. Ev. Sat. 16: 690.
— Soyer's Modern Housewife. Fraser, 44: 199.
Cooking Vessels, Improved. Pract. M. 3: 192.
Cookman, G. G. (A. Stevens) Nat. M. 7: 97.
Cooley, Timothy Mather. (D. B. Coe) Cong. Q. 2: 272.
Coolie, The. (W. P. Garrison) Nation, 13: 131. — (E. Jenkins) Good Words, 12: 45-465.
Coolies, Chinese, Trade in. Tait, n. s. 24: 321.
— Cuba and Emancipation. (T. S. Clingman) De Bow, 22: 414.
— Labor of, and Immigration. Cornh. 16: 74.
— — at the South. (R. A. Johnson) Nation, 1: 264.
— — Eastern. (W. L. Distant) Anthrop. J. 3: 139.
— Traffic in. (D. R. Hundley) Hunt, 36: 570. — (R. Pumpelly) Nation, 8: 449. — (W. W. Wright) De Bow, 27: 296.
— — Chapter on. (E. Holden) Harper, 29: 1.
— — in China. Westm. 100: 75.
Cooling. Am. Arch. 8: 201.
Cooling Earth, Our. (W. Downes) Ecl. M. 97: 275.
Coomans, Joseph. Art J. 18: 302.
Coombs, Leslie, Portrait of. Am. Whig R. 14: 359.
Cooper, Abraham. Art J. 15: 89.
Cooper, Adeline, Sketch of. Good Words, 7: 705.
Cooper, Sir Astley. Blackw. 65: 491. Same art. Ecl. M. 17: 246. — Ecl. Mus. 2: 167. — Dem. R. 12: 368. — Dub. Univ. 21: 411. — Quar. 71: 529. — Mo. R. 160: 254.
— and Dr. Abernethy. Lond. Q. 4: 44. Same art. Ecl. M. 35: 178.
Cooper, A. A., 3d Earl of Shaftesbury. *See* Shaftesbury.
Cooper, Charles H. (L. Jewitt) Reliquary, 7: 34.
Cooper, Sir Daniel, with portrait. Colburn, 166: 146.
Cooper, Edward. Letters to an Inquirer after Divine Truth. Chr. Obs. 16: 714.
Cooper, Edward, Sermons of. Chr. Obs. 3: 287, 353. 5: 497. 8: 177. 10: 372. 14: 317.
Cooper, James Fenimore. (L. G. Clark) Lippinc. 8: 625. — (W. R. Griswold) Bentley, 21: 533. — (G. S. Hillard) Atlan. 9: 52. — (K. Cook) Belgra. 18: 379. — with portrait, Appleton, 7: 549. — with portrait, Colburn, 31: 356. — with portrait, Ecl. M. 37: 313. — with portrait, Internat. M. 3: 1. — Chamb. J. 17: 3.
— American Sailor Authors. Liv. Age, 48: 560.
— and the Quarterly. Knick. 11: 184.
— and Novels. (G. W. Greene) Am. Church R. 14: 243.
— as a Novelist. (H. T. Tuckerman) No. Am. 89: 289.
— Biographical Sketch of. So. Lit. Mess. 4: 373.
— Bravo. So. R. 8: 382. — Westm. 16: 180. — Am. Mo. R. 1: 147.
— Crater; or Vulcan's Peak. Dem. R. 21: 438.
— Death of. Liv. Age, 31: 87.
— Deerslayer. Bentley, 10: 275.
— England. Fraser, 16: 233. — Quar. 59: 85. — Knick. 11: 184.
— Excursions in Switzerland. Mo. R. 26: 155. — Am. Q. 20: 228.
— Fragments from Diary of. Putnam, 11: 167, 730.
— The Headsman. Am. Mo. M. 2: 194.
— Hiedenmauer. Am. Mo. R. 2: 411. — Tait, 1: 660.
— Home as found. So. Lit. Mess. 5: 169.
— Home of, at Cooperstown, N. Y. (C. Fenimore) Harper, 44: 20.
— Homeward-Bound, and Sequel. Dub. R. 6: 490. — So. Lit. Mess. 4: 724. — (F. Bowen) No. Am. 47: 448. — New York R. 4: 209. — Mo. R. 146: 417.
— Indian and Ingin. (C. A. Bristed) Am. Whig R. 4: 276.
— Indians of. (J. E. Cooke) Appleton, 12: 264.
— Last of the Mohicans. Lond. M. 15: 27. — U. S. Lit. Gaz. 4: 87. — Mo. R. 110: 122. — (W. H. Gardiner) No. Am. 23: 155.
— Lionel Lincoln. U. S. Lit. Gaz. 1: 337.
— Memoir of. (W. R. Griswold) Ecl. M. 11: 430.
— Naval History. Dem. R. 10: 409, 513. — (A. S. Mackenzie) No. Am. 49: 432. — Mus. 37: 449.
— Ned Myers. Mo. R. 162: 550.
— Novels of. (F. Bowen) No. Am 46: 5. — (W. H. Gardiner) No. Am. 23: 150. — So. R. 5: 207. — (O. Dewey) Chr. Exam. 12: 78. — Dem. R. 25: 51. — New York R. 4: 209. — Mus. 9: 57. 18: 561.
— on Secession and State Rights. (C. K. Tuckerman) Contin. Mo. 6: 79.
— Pathfinder. So. Lit. Mess. 6: 229.
— Pilot. U. S. Lit. Gaz. 1: 6. — (W. Phillips) No. Am. 18: 314. — Portfo.(Den.) 31: 132.
— Pioneers. (W. H. Gardiner) No. Am. 23: 193. — Portfo (Den.) 29: 230.
— Portrait of. Dem. R. 15: 1.
— Prairie. U. S. Lit. Gaz. 6: 306.
— Public Honors to Memory of. Internat. M. 4: 456.
— Red Rover. (G. Mellen) No. Am. 27: 139. — Colburn, 22: 69. — Lond. M. 21: 101. — West. Mo. R. 1: 603.
— Reminiscences of. (J. W. Francis) Internat. M. 4: 453.
— Residence in France, etc. Quar. 58: 497.
— Sea Stories of. Dub. Univ. 47: 47.
— The Spy. (W. H. Gardiner) No. Am. 15: 250. — Portfo.(Den.) 27: 90.
— Verses to. (T. C Latto) Harper, 41: 293.
— *versus* Sir Walter Scott. Fraser, 19: 371.
— Water Witch. (O. W. B. Peabody) No. Am. 32: 508.
— Ways of the Hour. (F. Bowen) No. Am. 71: 121. — West. Law J. 8: 1.
— Works of. Ecl. R. 95: 410. Same art. Ecl. M. 26: 207. — Am. Q. 17: 407. — (F. Parkman) No. Am. 74: 147. — (E. I. Sears) Nat. Q. 1: 279.

Cooper, James Fenimore. Wyandotte. Mo. R. **162**: 224.
Cooper, Mrs. Mary, Memoirs of. Chr. Disc. **1**: 294. — Chr. Mo. Spec. **2**: 469.
Cooper, Myles, Life of. Anal. M. **14**: 73.
Cooper, Peter, with portrait. Ecl. M. **83**: 373. — with portrait, Ev. Sat. **10**: 385, 402. — with portrait, Dem. R. **42**: 1.
Cooper, Samuel. Art J. **2**: 293.
— Testimonial to, 1871. Ev. Sat. **11**: 396.
Cooper, Samuel. (F. Lee) So. Hist. Pap. **3**: 269.
Cooper, Thomas. Chamb. J. **49**: 373. — Ecl. M. **62**: 214. — Lond. Q. **38**: 445. — Howitt, **3**: 226, 242.
Cooper, Thomas Sidney, Memoir of. Art J. **1**: 336.
Cooper of Thorsund and his Family. Blackw. **22**: 692.
Co-operation. (A. H. Clough) No. Am. **77**: 106. — (R. J. Hinton) O. & N. **11**: 69. — (Marquis of Ripon) Month, **36**: 369. — Chamb. J. **31**: 190. — Hunt, **58**: 249. — Victoria, **11**: 50, 147. — Contemp. **28**: 44.
— and Competition. Victoria, **8**: 215.
— Experiments in. (C. Barnard) Scrib. **12**: 99, 242.
— in England. (G. Iles) Pop. Sci. Mo. **17**: 742. — (J. Samuelson) Am. J. Soc. Sci. **11**: 113.
— in the Slate Quarries of North Wales. (J. E. Cairnes) Macmil. **11**: 181.
— Industrial. Chr. Rem. **27**: 457. — Ev. Sat. **11**: 578. — Penny M. **1**: 327. — Am. Arch. **8**: 54. — St. James, **22**: 719. — (F. Harrison) Fortn. **3**: 477. — (G. J. Holyoake) 19th Cent. **4**: 494. Same art. Sup. Pop. Sci. Mo. **3**: 521.
— — Forms of. (J. M. Ludlow) Good Words, **8**: 240.
— — Leclaire's System of. (S. Taylor) 19th Cent. **8**: 370. **9**: 802.
— — its Rise and Progress in England, 1864. Westm. **81**: 357.
— Plate Locks and Paisley Shawls. (C. Barnard) Scrib. **14**: 370.
— Position and Prospects of. (H. Fawcett) Fortn. **21**: 190.
— Progress of. Chamb. J. **29**: 70. — Good Words, **5**: 660.
— Scottish Loaf Factory. (C. Barnard) Scrib. **13**: 60.
— Toad Lane, Rochdale, England. (C. Barnard) Scrib. **13**: 203.
— Village Improvement Associations. (G. E. Waring, jr.) Scrib. **14**: 97.
— Wages against. (E. L. Godkin) Nation, **5**: 111.
See Labor; Workingmen.
Co-operative Agricultural Societies. Chamb. J. **46**: 97.
Co-operative Agriculture. (A. Church) Contemp. **16**: 71.
— Three Experiments in. Fraser, **91**: 529.
— at Ralahine. (W. P. Garrison) Nation, **12**: 341.
— Lawson's. (G. E. Waring, jr.) Nation, **20**: 245.
Co-operative Apartment Houses. Am. Arch. **9**: 88.
Co-operative Associations. (W. Howitt) Peop. J. **1**: 311.
Co-operative Band; a Story. Howitt, **1**: 144, 156.
Co-operative Building. O. & N. **5**: 505.
Co-operative Feature of Building Associations. (E. Wrigley) Penn Mo. **7**: 497.
Co-operative Community. Chamb. J. **53**: 600.
Co-operative Credit Unions, German. (R. T. Ely) Atlan. **47**: 207.
Co-operative Distribution. (W. A. Hovey) Am. J. Soc. Sci. **11**: 105.
Co-operative Flour-Mill at Leeds. Chamb. J. **22**: 401.
Co-operative Housekeeping. Chamb. J. **46**: 177.
— Practical Side of. (R. Fisher) 19th Cent. **2**: 283. Same art. Sup. Pop. Sci. Mo. **1**: 517.
Co-operative Land Movement. (E. W. Brabrook) J. Statis. Soc. **37**: 327.
Co-operative Life in America. (H. Greeley) Peop. J. **4**: 167.
Co-operative Production. (T. Brassey) Contemp. **24**: 212. — Republic, **4**: 289.
Co-operative Societies. (H. Fawcett) Macmil. **2**: 434. — (W. P. Garrison) Nation, **2**: 360. — (E. W. Brabrook) J. Statis. Soc. **38**: 185. — (M. Howland) Galaxy, **3**: 197. — O. & N. **1**: 701. — Quar. **114**: 418.
— German. (B. S. Blyth) Once a Week, **10**: 457.
— in 1864. Ed. R. **120**: 407.
— in England. (J. Plummer) Once a Week, **7**: 554.
— in Russia. (E. Schuyler) Nation, **7**: 287.
— Notes on. Bank. M. (N. Y.) **24**: 689.
— Trading and Burial, and Post-Office Insurance. (A. J. Wilson) Fraser, **90**: 541.
— Visit to. Chamb. J. **32**: 305.
See Friendly Societies; Building Societies; Rochdale.
Co-operative Stores. (E. L. Godkin) No. Am. **106**: 150. — Chamb. J. **14**: 346. **51**: 7. — Cornh. **28**: 335.
— Common-Sense and. (W. L. Blackley) Contemp. **34**: 553
— Reply to the Shopkeepers. (J. H. Lawson) 19th Cent. **5**: 362.
— Shopkeeper's Rejoinder. (T. Lord) 19th Cent. **5**: 733.
Co-operative Trading. Chamb. J. **19**: 343.
Co-operative Trouble, Beginning of. (G. J. Holyoake) Contemp. **26**: 269.
Coorg, A Day at. Chamb. J. **20**: 94.
Copal, Sources of. (J. R. Jackson) Stud. & Intel. Obs. **3**: 356.
— Trade in. Geog. M. **1**: 181.
Copartnerships. (D. Lord, jr.) Hunt, **1**: 67, 147. — Hunt, **12**: 361.
Co-Pastorates, Plea for. Cong. **5**: 302.
Coke, Charles West. Art J. **21**: 177.
Cope, E. D., with portrait. Pop. Sci. Mo. **19**: 10.
Copenhagen. (R. Romayne) Knick. **57**: 503. — Chamb. J. **13**: 169, 177. — Once a Week, **7**: 52. **10**: 164. — Liv. Age, **14**: 130.
— Antiquarian Society of. Am. Q. Reg. **12**: 63.
— Expedition against. Selec. Ed. R. **4**: 168.
— Insured at. Chamb. J. **40**: 214.
— Morning in. Argosy, **1**: 524.
— Museum at. Chamb. J. **7**: 75.
— One Day in. (G. A. Sala) Temp. Bar, **8**: 111, 372.
— Peep at. Lond. Soc. **36**: 283.
— Traveler's Hand-Book to. Liv. Age, **39**: 625.
— University of. Am. Q. Reg. **12**: 160.
— Visit to. (R. Chambers) Chamb. J. **13**: 169, 177.
— Voyage to. (R. Chambers) Chamb. J. **12**: 273, 294, 306.
Copepod Crustacean, Variations in. (C. F. Gissler) Am. Natural. **15**: 689.
Copernicanism and Pope Paul V. Dub. R. **68**: 351.
Copernicus, Nicolaus. (J. G. Meline) Cath. World, **11**: 806. — (E. I. Sears) Nat. Q. **17**: 201. — Cath. World, **12**: 373. — Lond. Q. **5**: 99.
— and Astronomy. Chamb. J. **7**: 274.
— in Italy. (A. Clerke) Ed. R. **146**: 103. Same art. Sup. Pop. Sci. Mo. **1**: 398.
— Last Days of. Chamb. J. **13**: 332. — Nat. M. **1**: 464.
Copestake, Hughes, Crampton, & Co. Lond. Soc. **35**: 225.
Copleston, Edward, Memoir of. No. Brit. **16**: 492. — Fraser, **44**: 320. — New Q. **1**: 29.
— Remains of. Chr. Obs. **54**: 703.
Copley, John Singleton. Liv. Age, **63**: 119.
— Portraits by. O. & N. **4**: 735.
Copley, John Singleton, Lord Lyndhurst. *See* Lyndhurst.
Coppée, François. Poems. Appleton, **23**: 231.
Copper and Copper Mines in the U. S. So. Q. **28**: 201.
— Bessemer Process in Making of. Ecl. Engin. **1**: 514.
— Chemistry of. (T. S. Hunt) Am. J. Sci. **99**: 153.
— Coating Iron and Steel with. Pract. M. **5**: 230.
— Diffusion of, in the Animal Kingdom. (T. H. Norton) Nature, **21**: 305.

Copper, Effect of Metals on Conducting Power of. J. Frankl. Inst. 73: 337.
— Notes on. Ecl. Engin. 10: 329.
— Paragenesis and Derivation of. (R. Pumpelly) Am. J. Sci. 102: 188, 243, 347.
— Uses of, by the Indians. (E. G. Squier) Am. J. Sci. 59: 314.
Copper-bearing Rocks of Lake Superior. (T. B. Brooks and R. Pumpelly) Am. J. Sci. 103: 428. — (Sir W. E. Logan) Am. J. Sci. 83: 320. — (R. Irving) Am. J. Sci. 108: 46.
Copper District of Lake Superior. (W. Pettit) J. Frankl. Inst. 43: 338.
Copper Factory, Day at a. Penny M. 11: 249.
Copper Implements found at Brockville. (H. Croft) Canad. J. n. s. 1: 334.
Copper Mine at Bristol, Conn. (B. Silliman, jr., and J. D. Whitney) Am. J. Sci. 70: 361.
Copper Mines, Ancient, of Isle Royale. (N. H. Winchell) Pop. Sci. Mo. 19: 601.
— at Duck Town, Tenn. (M. Twomey) Am. J. Sci. 69: 181.
— of Cornwall, Statistics of. (C. Lemon) J. Statis. Soc. 1: 65.
— of Cuba. Hunt, 11: 143.
— of Lake Superior. Hunt, 15: 105. — (D. Ruggles) Am. J. Sci. 49: 64. — (C. T. Jackson) Am. J. Sci. 49: 81. — (J. H. Lanman) Hunt, 14: 439. — (H. Greeley) Hunt, 19: 559. — (H. R. Schoolcraft) Am. J. Sci. 3: 201. 7: 43. — Niles's Reg. 36: 203.
— — Ancient. (A. D. Hager) Atlan. 15: 308. — (D. Wilson) Canad. J. n. s. 1: 225.
Copper Mining in Cornwall, 1844. J. Frankl. Inst. 38: 223.
Copper Ore, Statistics of. Hunt, 18: 111.
— Continental Method of assaying. (S. E. Thomas) J. Frankl. Inst. 32: 105.
— Reduction of gray. (J. L. Kleinschmidt) J. Frankl. Inst. 82: 124, 164, 249.
— Working of. (G. W. Hughes) J. Frankl. Inst. 38: 31–261.
Copper Plates, Engraved, Process of hardening. Art J. 10: 356.
Copper Pyrites, Extraction of Gold and Silver from. (M. F. Claudet) Pract. M. 1: 47.
Copper Range of Lake Superior. (C. P. Williams and J. F. Blandy) Am. J. Sci. 84: 112.
Copper Region of United States. (R. E. Clarke) Harper, 6: 433, 577.
Copper Smelting in U. S. Hunt, 11: 290. — (G. Ditson) Hunt, 12: 551. 13: 256. — Am. J. Sci. 58: 336.
Coppersmith, Ancient Work of. Ecl. Engin. 11: 532.
Copper-Tin-Zinc Alloys. (R. H. Thurston) Ecl. Engin. 25: 374, 479.
Copper Tokens, Old. Chamb. J. 51: 363.
Copper-Works, Swansea. Tait, n. s. 22: 149.
— Visit to. Chamb. J. 18: 234.
Copperas Mine of Vermont. Penny M. 7: 397.
Coppet, Château of. Blackw. 4: 198, 277.
Coppin, Captain William. (W. Chambers) Chamb. J. 55: 241.
Coppinger, S. Irish Q. 8: 626.
Copp's Hill Burial Ground, Boston, Inscriptions in. N. E. Reg. 2: 391.
Coprolite Works at Abington, Visit to. (G. Sandys) Once a Week, 12: 328.
Coptic Church. Dub. R. 28: 314.
Coptic Language. Princ. 27: 388.
Coptic Papyri and other MSS. brought from the East. (C. W. Goodwin) Arch. 39: 447.
Copying, Devices for. All the Year, 45: 160.
Copying Process, New. (R. H. Ridout) Nature, 21: 155.
Copyright. (W. D. Howells) Nation, 1: 774. — (E. L. Godkin) Nation, 4: 520. 6: 147. — (E. A. Walker) Nation, 6: 265. — (W. Collins) Internat. R. 8: 609. — (M. Arnold) Fortn. 33: 319. Same art. Ecl. M. 94: 513. — Westm. 116: 392. — St. James, 47: 71. — (E. Roscoe) Victoria, 19: 340. — (R. Southey) Quar. 21: 196. — Quar. 69: 186. — Pamph. 2: 169, 343. 18: 523. — (A. Alison) Blackw. 51: 634. Same art. Am. Ecl. 3: 376. — So. Lit. Mess. 10: 181. — Am. Mo. M. 9: 153, 283. — Blackw. 51: 634.
— American. Blackw. 62: 534.
— and Land-Owning. (G. Allen) Fraser, 102: 343.
— and Morality. Pop. Sci. Mo. 14: 530.
— Drone on. (A. G. Sedgwick) Nation, 28: 303. — Internat. R. 6: 699.
— Ethics of. (Grant Allen) Macmil. 43: 153.
— for Artists. (W. H. Hunt) 19th Cent. 5: 418. — (F. Leighton and H. T. Wells) 19th Cent. 6: 968. — (A. G. Sedgwick) Nation, 27: 190. — Art J. 6: 25. 10: 53–369. — Westm. 113: 355.
— Foreign. Art J. 2: 94.
— — in Great Britain. Liv. Age, 30: 36, 263.
— in Engravings. Art J. 8: 92.
— in Incidents. Am. Law R. 3: 453.
— in Italy. For. Q. 26: 160. Same art. Am. Ecl. 1: 370.
— in relation to Libraries and Literature. (A. R. Spofford) Lib. J. 1: 84.
— International. (W. Phillips) No. Am. 48: 257. — (G. M. Wharton) No. Am. 52: 385. — (J. G. Palfrey) No. Am. 55: 245. — (C. C. Felton) No. Am. 67: 161. — (W. G. Simms) So. Lit. Mess. 10: 7, 137. — (C. F. Briggs) Putnam, 3: 96. — (C. A. Bristed) Galaxy, 10: 811. — (E. S. Drone) Scrib. 11: 90. — (A. H. Dymond) Canad. Mo. 1: 289. — (E. L. Godkin) Nation, 13: 301. — (J. Parton) Atlan. 20: 430. Ed. R. 95: 145. — Blackw. 51: 107. 62: 534. — Westm. 24: 187. — Brit. & For. R. 8: 333. — Am. Q. 21: 214. — Knick. 6: 285. 22: 360. — Dem. R. 2: 289. 12: 115, 209, 609. — So. Lit. Mess. 3: 37. 5: 663. 6: 69. — Am. Alma. 1836: 97. — So. Q. 4: 1. — (W. F. Rae) 19th Cent. 10: 723. — Am. Law R. 9: 1. — (W. T. Howe) West. Law J. 2: 347. — West. Law J. 10: 515. — (W. F. Allen) Lippinc. 25: 102. — O. & N. 7: 732. — Penn Mo. 1: 118. — Am. Bibliop. 3: 495. — Art J. 3: 240. Same art. Internat. M. 4: 386. — Appleton, 7: 441. — Chamb. J. 47: 107. — Dem. R. 33: 97. 42: 454. — Ev. Sat. 7: 742. — Harper, 46: 906. — Internat. M. 4: 303. — Macmil. 40: 151, 161. — Putnam, 9: 85. — Tinsley, 9: 528.
— — American Efforts for. (C. E. Appleton) Fortn. 27: 237.
— — and Congress. (E. L. Didier) Scrib. 20: 132.
— — and Publishers. (A. G. Sedgwick) Nation, 29: 340.
— — and Tariff on Books. Westm. 57: 525.
— — between Gt. Britain and America. Macmil. 20: 89.
— — by Judicial Decision. (A. G. Sedgwick) Atlan. 43: 217.
— — Carey's Letters on. Liv. Age, 40: 112.
— — English Report on. Pop. Sci. Mo. 13: 618.
— — Publisher's View. (C. J. Longman) Fraser, 103: 372.
— Is it perpetual? Am. Law R. 10: 16.
— Justice to Authors. St. James, 36: 64.
— Law of. (D. Wilson) Canad. J. n. s. 12: 415. — Am. Mo. M. 11: 105. — Lond. M. 22: 645. — Am. Alma. 1833: 98. — Niles's Reg. 40: 188, 391. — So. Lit. J. 4: 109, 179, 281.
— — Case of Reade *vs.* Outram. (W. Chambers) Chamb. J. 53: 545.
— — English, 1837. Ecl. R. 67: 693. — Mo. R. 145: 52.
— — — 1839. Ecl. R. 69: 434.
— — — 1842. Mo. R. 158: 66.

Copyright, Law of, English, Talfourd's Bill. Tait, n. s. **5**: 332.
— — — under Queen Anne. Pamph. **10**: 493.
— Literary and Musical. (R. Blaine) Fraser, **81**: 278.
— of Designs. Art J. **8**: 14–283. **12**: 14, 63, 283.
— Political Economy of. (W. B. Adams) Fortn. **2**: 227.
— Principle of. (T. H. Farrer) Fortn. **30**: 836. — (E. Laflear) Canad. Mo. **18**: 373.
— Produce of, in England. Am. Alma. **1840**: 100.
— Question of. (G. M. Adam) Canad. Mo. **14**: 369. — (E. Dicey) Fortn. **25**: 126. — (E. L. Godkin) Nation, **14**: 101. — Quar. **69**: 186.
— Reply to Mr. Simms. So. Lit. Mess. **10**: 193.
— Report of Royal Commission on. Ed. R. **148**: 295.
— Right of. (S. I. Prime) Putnam, **11**: 635.
— Unreciprocated. Colburn, **93**: 122.
— with respect to Abridgments. West. Law J. **5**: 97.
Copyrights and Patents. (L. Levi) Princ. n. s. **2**: 743.
— Art. Art J. **13**: 88, 189.
See Literary Property; Authors, Rights of.
Copyright Commission, Huxley before. Pop. Sci. Mo. **14**: 166.
— H. Spencer and. Pop. Sci. Mo. **14**: 296, 440.
— Tyndall before. Pop. Sci. Mo. **14**: 39.
Coquerel, Athanase Laurent Charles. (A. R. Abbott) Univ. Q. **25**: 225. — (E. E. Hale) Unita. R. **4**: 283, 320, 511. — (A. Reville) Theo. R. **12**: 500. — Blackw. **43**: 636. — Ev. Sat. **11**: 306.
— and Art-Protestantism. (R. St. J. Tyrwhitt) Dark Blue, **1**: 755.
— Experimental Christianity. (R. Wheaton) Chr. Exam. **44**: 1.
— Life and Work of. (S. W. Bush) Unita. R. **5**: 109.
— Sermons of. (E. E. Hale) Chr. Exam. **40**: 321.
Coquetry, Female. West. M. **5**: 226, 457.
Coquette's Campaign; a Tale. (L. de la Ramé) Broadw. **5**: 97, 289. Same art. Bentley, **48**: 407.
Cora; a Poem. (B. D. Hill) Cath. World, **19**: 418.
Coral. Art J. **12**: 55. — (S. S. Farmer) Nat. M. **9**: 32. — Argosy, **10**: 491.
— and the Coral Fishery. Penny M. **9**: 79.
— Red, Recent Investigations into the Natural History of. (H. Lawson) Pop. Sci. R. **4**: 67.
Corals. (M. Schele de Vere) Putnam, **11**: 25. — Chamb. J. **47**: 325.
— and Coral Architecture. (E. Lewis, jr.) Pop. Sci. Mo. **1**: 257.
— and Coral Fishing. Broadw. **5**: 214.
— and Coral Islands. (Mrs. S. B. Herrick) So. R. n. s. **13**: 387. — (T. H. Huxley) Good Words, **12**: 104. — St. James, **12**: 33. **34**: 228. — Nat. Q. **28**: 207.
— — Blackwood on. Quar. **81**: 468. Same art. Liv. Age, **15**: 577. Same art. Ecl. M. **10**: 151.
— — Brazilian. (R. Rathbun) Am. Natural. **13**: 539.
— — Dana's. (F. W. Putnam) Am. Natural. **6**: 674. — J. Frankl. Inst. **100**: 208. — (P. M. Duncan) Nature, **7**: 119.
— and Coral Makers. Hogg, **14**: 446. Same art. Ecl. M. **37**: 371.
— and their Polypes. (P. M. Duncan) Stud. & Intel. Obs. **3**: 81, 241. **4**: 95, 445.
— at the Galapagos Islands. (L. F. Pourtalés) Am. J. Sci. **110**: 282.
— Devonian. (E. Billings) Canad. J. n. s. **4**: 97.
— dredged in Expedition of the Porcupine. (P. M. Duncan) Nature, **1**: 612.
— from the Gulf of California. (A. E. Verrill) Am. J. Sci. **99**: 93.
— Living. (W. E. Damon) Pop. Sci. Mo. **12**: 737.
— Microscopical. (S. B. Herrick) Scrib. **14**: 689.
— New. (A. E. Verrill) Am. J. Sci. **99**: 370.
— New Genus of. (F. B. Meek) Am. J. Sci. **95**: 62.
Corals, Paleozoic Tabulate, Affinities with existing Species. (A. E. Verrill) Am. J. Sci. **103**: 187.
— Rate of Growth of. (J. L. LeConte) Am. J. Sci. **110**: 34.
— Source of Lime in Growth of. (E. N. Horsford) Am. J. Sci. **64**: 251.
Coral Animals, Structure of. Hogg, **7**: 80.
Coral Fishery. Hunt, **16**: 62.
— at Naples. Pract. M. **3**: 138.
— in the Mediterranean. House. Words, **2**: 379.
Coral Formations, Consolidation of. (J. D. Dana) Am. J. Sci. **66**: 357.
Coral Islands. Chamb. J. **41**: 585. — Mus. **2**: 394.
— and Islanders, Some. (J. D. Hague) Atlan. **22**: 36.
— Formation of. (C. Maclaren) Ed. New Philos. J. **34**: 33. — Cornh. **7**: 415.
— Subsidence of. (J. D. Dana) Am. J. Sci. **104**: 31.
Coral Reefs. Godey, **56**: 239. — (J. D. Dana) Am. J Sci. **59**: 357. **62**: 25, 165, 329.
— and Islands. (J. D. Dana) Am. J. Sci. **63**: 34, 185, 338. **64**: 76.
— Darwin's. Nature, **10**: 353. — (J. D. Dana) Nature, **10**: 408.
— in the Pacific. (Sir H. Holland) Quar. **81**: 468. Same art. Liv. Age, **15**: 577. Same art. Ecl. M. **10**: 151. — Ed. R. **53**: 216.
Coral Rings. Blackw. **74**: 360.
Coralie. House. Words, **12**: 60.
Coram, Captain Thomas. Penny M. **6**: 479.
— and his Hospital. (Mrs. C. A. White) Sharpe, **44**: 11.
Coray, Dr., and the Greek Church. (G. A. Perdicario) Am. Q. Obs. **2**: 199.
Corbet, Bishop Richard. Once a Week, **27**: 122. — Temp. Bar, **2**: 178.
— Poems of. Retros. **12**: 299. — Blackw. **10**: 80.
Corbould, Edward H., with portrait. Colburn, **166**: 653.
Corbridge Altars. (T. Morell) Arch. **5**: 182.
Corcoran, Peter, Poetical Remains of. Lond. M. **2**: 71.
Corcoran, W. W. Appleton, **11**: 9. — So. R. n. s. **11**: 157.
Corcumroe Abbey. (R. H. Horne) Howitt, **1**: 80.
Corda Concordia; a Poem. (E. C. Stedman) Atlan. **48**: 179.
Cordage, Agave-Fiber. Pract. M. **5**: 183.
— Manufacture of. Chamb. J. **24**: 391.
— Materials and Manufacture of. Penny M. **8**: 494.
— Vegetable Materials for. (J. Mease) Am. J. Sci. **21**: 27.
Corday, Charlotte. (M. Forman) Sharpe, **44**: 205. — Peop. J. **9**: 229. — (A. de Lamartine) Bentley, **21**: 570. — (J. Michelet) Knick. **61**: 503. — Fraser, **75**: 735. — Eng. Dom. M. **2**: 8. — Chamb. J. **1**: 125, 238. Same art. Liv. Age, **1**: 560. — So. Lit. Mess. **14**: 142. — Knick. **32**: 304. — with portrait, Ecl. M. **17**: 275.
— Execution of. Quar. **73**: 236.
Cordelia, Shakspere's. (W. R. Casteli) Ecl. M. **14**: 517.
Cordelier of Sisteron. (D. Costello) Ecl. M. **19**: 259.
Corder, William, the Murderer. All the Year, **18**: 397.
Cordière, La belle, Louise Labé. House. Words, **7**: 214.
Cordilleras and the Andes. (G. P. Disosway) Nat. M. **12**: 198, 385. **13**: 114.
— Brand's Passage of. Mus. **15**: 276.
— Heights of. Ed. New Philos. J. **8**: 350.
Cordova. (A. Griffiths) Art J. **33**: 145. — (S. P. Scott) Lippinc. **28**: 334.
— Mosque at. Penny M. **9**: 401.
Cordova Colonist, Adventures of. (T. J. Russell) So. M. **11**: 90, 155.
Corea. Ed. R. **136**: 299. — Geog. M. **4**: 148.
— and Loo-Choo, Hall's Voyage to. Ecl. R. **27**: 513.
— Glimpse of. (C. A. Bridge) Fortn. **25**: 96. Same art. Liv. Age, **129**: 168.
— Mission of. (A. Kim-Hai-Kim) U. S. Cath. M. **7**: 421, 462.

Corea, Oppert's Voyages to. (W. E. Griffis) Nation, **30:** 271. — (S. W. Williams) New Eng. **39:** 509.
— Visit to. Chamb. J. **57:** 598.
What shall we do with? (W. Speer) Galaxy, **13:** 303.
Corean Church, Early Days of. (F. Goldie) Month, **24:** 205, 231.
— Modern History of. (F. Goldie) Month, **25:** 281.
Corfe Castle, Dorsetshire. Penny M. **5:** 476.
— Story of. Fraser, **48:** 551.
Corfu, Island of. Bentley, **46:** 493. — (C. K. Tuckerman) Scrib. **4:** 445. — Blackw. **95:** 583. — Penny M. **3:** 394. — Hogg, **12:** 328.
— Jervis's History of. Ed. R. **97:** 41.
— Life and Customs in. Westm. **67:** 216.
— Sketches of. Ecl. R. **61:** 113.
— to Trieste. Sharpe, **50:** 17, 74.
— University of, Lord Guilford and. Colburn, **20:** 17.
Coriat, Tom, jr. [S. Paterson], Travels of. Retros. **12:** 287. *See* Coryat, Tom.
Corinth, Greece, Isthmus of. Ecl. Engin. **2:** 376.
— — Canal across. Am. Arch. **10:** 196.
Corinth, Miss., Battle of. (F. L. Hubbell) Land We Love, **6:** 97.
Coriolanus, C. M., and Charles, Duke of Bourbon. (J. W. Calcraft) Dub. Univ. **41:** 418. Same art. Ecl. M. **29:** 180.
— Character of. So. Lit. Mess. **2:** 737.
Cork, Richard Boyle, Earl of. Dub. Univ. **54:** 318.
Cork, Countess of. Bentley, **19:** 293.
Cork, and its Citizens. Dub. Univ. **40:** 119.
— Council and Corporation of. Dub. Univ. **6:** 587.
— Etchings from. (Mrs. Hoare) Peop. J. **5:** 163.
— Exhibition at, 1862. Irish Q. **2:** 626.
— Female Industrial Schools in. Sharpe, **16:** 119.
Cork, and the Cork Tree. Penny M. **8:** 210.
Cork-Cutting. Chamb. J. **21:** 29.
Corkran, Alice, Bessie Lang. Dub. Univ. **88:** 791.
Corkran, J. F. An Hour ago; or Time in Dreamland. Dub. Univ. **53:** 300. Same art. Ecl. M. **47:** 388.
Corliss, Geo. H., Presentation of the Rumford Medal to. Ecl. Engin. **2:** 266.
Cormac, The Fortunes of King. Dub. Univ. **69:** 588.
Cormorants. (W. J. Broderip) Fraser, **58:** 292.
Cormorant-Fishing. Chamb. J. **41:** 773.
— Chinese Mode of. Penny M. **4:** 76.
Corn. (J. Buckman) Pop. Sci. R. **1:** 9.
— and Bullion. Brit. Q. **3:** 221.
— and Currency. Pamph. **14:** 285. — Westm. **41:** 319.
— and Money. Ed. R. **26:** 135.
— Sir J. Banks on Blight in. Ed. R. **7:** 148.
— Cause of Disease in. Pamph. **6:** 401.
— Cobbett's. Westm. **11:** 54.
— Disease in, Banks on. Ecl. R. **2:** 538.
— Exported, Bounty on. (F. Horner) Ed. R. **5:** 190.
— History of a Sack of. All the Year, **18:** 516, 535, 565.
— Importation, H. Davis on. Fraser, **3:** 727.
— Indian. *See* Indian Corn.
— Price of foreign. Ed. R. **41:** 55.
— Production of. Pract. M. **2:** 394.
— Threshing in the East. Penny M. **10:** 220.
— Use of, in England. Penny M. **2:** 370.
Corns, Pet. St. James, **34:** 274.
Corn-Fields, Gleanings from. Dub. Univ. **44:** 383.
Corn-Husking in America. Penny M. **5:** 376.
Corn Law and a fixed Duty. Blackw. **29:** 645.
— Project of, 1827. Lond. M. **17:** 525.
Corn Laws. (H. Edwards) Quar. **51:** 228. — (E. Elliott) Tait, **3:** 531. n. s. **1:** 228. Blackw. **21:** 169, 274. **22:** 240. **29:** 645. **35:** 792. **44:** 650. **45:** 170. **51:** 537. **52:** 271. **54:** 538. — Brit. & For. R. **2:** 270. **9:** 507. **12:** 462. **16:** 30. — Westm. **3:** 394. **6:** 373. **7:** 169. **9:** 313.
Corn Laws. (T. P. Thompson) Westm. **11:** 1. **17:** 510. **18:** 108. **20:** 265, 514. — (W. R. Greg) Westm. **37:** 348. **38:** 494. **41:** 319. **46:** 119. — Pamph. **4:** 131, 177, 489. **8:** 127. **10:** 249. — Ed. R. **24:** 491. **26:** 135. **33:** 155. **41:** 55. — **44:** 319. — Quar. **35:** 269. **37:** 426. **51:** 228. **68:** 131. — Ecl. R. **69:** 79. **74:** 344, 489. **75:** 339. — Mo. R. **95:** 198. **111:** 202. — (T. Lyman) No. Am. **1:** 214. — Niles's Reg. **28:** 251. **33:** 10. — (J. M. Whiton) Hunt, **5:** 519. — Selec. Ed. R. **6:** 211. — Dub. Univ. **13:** 334. **19:** 159. — Colburn, **17:** 349. **92:** 62. — Tait, **3:** 41. — Ecl. R. **69:** 79.
— Action of. Tait, n. s. **8:** 626.
— Advocates and Opposers of. Tait, n. s. **6:** 117, 201, 217.
— Agricultural Petition on. Pamph. **14:** 1.
— and the Bread-Taxry. (E. Elliott) Tait, **4:** 260, 446.
— and Catechism. Colburn, **26:** 330–420.
— and Taxation. Ed. R. **33:** 155.
— Combinations and. (E. Elliott) Tait, n. s. **5:** 253.
— and Free Trade. (T. C. B. Fraser) New Dom. **19:** 509.
— — Chalmers on. Chr. Obs. **41:** 459.
— Changes required in. Ed. R. **58:** 271.
— Commerce *versus*. Tait, n. s. **6:** 117.
— Debate on, 1842. Westm. **38:** 494.
— Dilemmas on. Blackw. **45:** 170.
— Distress of the Landed Interest. (T. P. Thompson) Westm. **18:** 108.
— Effect of. Tait, **4:** 344.
— — on Banking. Bank. M. (L.) **1:** 130.
— Historical Examination of. Tait, n. s. **8:** 610.
— History of. Ecl. R. **74:** 489.
— in 1814. Ecl. R. **20:** 1.
— in 1842. Ecl. R. **75:** 339.
— in Parliament, 1838. Tait, n. s. **5:** 201–541.
— Lord Milton on. Ecl. R. **56:** 436. — (T. P. Thompson) Westm. **17:** 510.
— Monopoly of Food. Westm. **20:** 378.
— of Athens and Rome. Ed. R. **83:** 351.
— Peel on. Dub. Univ. **19:** 405.
— Platt's History of. Mo. R. **156:** 101.
— Railway Glance at. Fraser, **19:** 254.
— Repeal of the British. Dem. R. **29:** 385.
— Prospect of, 1846. (W. R. Greg) Westm. **46:** 119.
— Salomans on, 1839. Mo. R. **151:** 54.
— Tariff, and Income Tax, 1842. Ecl. R. **75:** 573.
Corn-Law Agitation. (J. W. Croker) Quar. **71:** 244. — Dub. Univ. **13:** 334. — Tait, n. s. **1:** 72, 140, 281. **7:** 135–273. **8:** 67–746.
Corn-Law Conference, Anti-, Manchester, 1841. Ecl. R. **74:** 344.
Corn-Law Deputation to Sir R. Peel. Blackw. **52:** 271.
Corn-Law Hymn. (E. Elliott) Tait, **4:** 110.
Corn-Law League, Anti-. Fraser, **27:** 503. **29:** 364. — Ecl. R. **77:** 461. **81:** 100.
— History and Prospects of, 1844. Ecl. R. **79:** 194.
— Revenge of. Blackw. **52:** 542.
Corn-Law Orators, pro and con. Fraser, **34:** 91.
Corn-Law Policy of Sir R. Peel. Quar. **70:** 265. **81:** 147. — Blackw. **51:** 537.
Corn-Law Question. Blackw. **35:** 792. — Pamph. **17:** 417.
Corn-Law Rhymes. (T. Carlyle) Ed. R. **55:** 338. — (E. Elliott) Tait, **2:** 83, 765. *See* Elliott, Ebenezer.
Corn-Law Riots. Blackw. **52:** 410.
Corn Trade. Mo. R. **111:** 1. — Penny M. **14:** 452.
— of Great Britain and the U. S. De Bow, **16:** 411.
— of Northern Europe. Penny M. **8:** 221, 242.
— Tracts on. (T. Chalmers) No. Brit. **1:** 67. — Blackw **20:** 359.
— of United States. (C. Hudson) Hunt, **12:** 421. — (R. Fisher) Am. Whig R. **6:** 430.
— with Hungary. Brit. & For. R. **9:** 126.
See Food; Grain; Wheat.

Cornage, Tenure or Service of. (F. M. Nichols) Arch. **39**: 349.
Cornaro, Catherine. *See* Catharine Cornaro.
Cornbury, Lord. (J. R. Brodhead) Hist. M. **13**: 71.
— impeached as a Forger. Hist. M. **7**: 329.
Corneille, Pierre. (F. W. Palfrey) No. Am. **78**: 214.— with portrait, Ecl. M. **75**: 757.—Penny M. **10**: 369.
— and Dryden. Principles of the Drama. Fraser, **66**: 383.
— and French Tragic Drama. Nat. Q. **23**: 256.
— and his Contemporaries. Dub. Univ. **71**: 158.
— and his Times. Bentley, **32**: 89. Same art. Ecl. M. **27**: 66.—Hogg, **9**: 355.—Liv. Age, **34**: 193.
— and the literary Society of his Age. Temp. Bar, **45**: 516. Same art. Liv. Age, **128**: 281.
— and Shakspere, Guizot's. Dub. Univ. **40**: 187.—Blackw. **72**: 396. Same art. Ecl. M. **27**: 535.—No. Brit. **18**: 106.
— Life of. So. Lit. Mess. **8**: 647.
Cornelian, An ancient. (J. Hodgson) Arch. **2**: 42.
Cornelius the Centurion. Kitto, **33**: 46.
Cornelius, Elias, Life of. Am. Q. Reg. **4**: 249. **5**: 1.—(E. G. Smith) Chr. Q. Spec. **6**: 308.
Cornelius, Peter von, German Painter. Art J. **17**: 1.—Cath. World, **6**: 391.—Hours at Home, **1**: 18.
Cornelius, W., Sonnets by. Lond. M. **1**: 423, 531.
Cornelius's Memorial. (W. M. Reily) Mercersb. **14**: 457.
Cornelius O'Dowd upon Men and Women, etc. (C. J. Lever) Blackw. **95**: 172–748. **96**: 1–755. **97**: 57–556. **98**: 24–755. **99**: 67–489. **100**: 109–713. **101**: 54–576. **102**: 99–725. **103**: 180–748. **104**: 97–745. **105**: 174–759. **106**: 125–720. **107**: 237–591. **108**: 351–508. **109**: 230, 580. **110**: 169–728. **111**: 364.
Cornell, Ezra, with portrait. Potter Am. Mo. **4**: 79, 119.
— and Cornell University. Am. J. Educ. **24**: 447.
Cornell University. (D. C. Gilman) Nation, **1**: 44.—(J. M. Hart) Scrib. **6**: 199.—(R. P. Stebbins) Unita. R. **1**: 325.—(T. Hughes) Macmil. **22**: 161.
— Co-education at. (A. C. Brackett) Victoria, **31**: 218.
— History of. (G. Smith) Canad. Mo. **4**: 125.
— Library of. (W. Fiske) Lib. J. **2**: 71.
— Recollections of. (T. Hughes and W. D. Rawlins) Ev. Sat. **10**: 370, 466.
Corners, Commercial. (W. B. Halhed) 19th Cent. **10**: 532.
— Remedies for. (H. White) Nation, **33**: 210.
Corner-Stone, A. (C. Cook) Galaxy, **5**: 144.
Corney, Bolton, and Isaac Disraeli. Cornh. **40**: 687.
Corney Noonan's Courtship. (M. A. Browne) Godey, **21**: 180.
Cornish Customs in May. Chamb. J. **56**: 260.
Cornish Engine. All the Year, **3**: 393.
Cornish Hug. House. Words, **18**: 296.
Cornish Language, Expiration of. (D. Barrington) Arch. **3**: 278.
— Observations on. (D. Barrington) Arch. **5**: 81.
— Vestiges of. (C. M. Ingleby) Once a Week, **14**: 193.
Cornish May Song. (E. Boger) Once a Week, **12**: 559.
Cornish Miners in America. (Sir F. B. Head) Quar. **36**: 81.
Cornish Vicar, Remembrances of. All the Year, **13**: 153.
Cornplanter, Chief of the Seneca Indians. (W. Hall) Potter Am. Mo. **12**: 31.—Olden Time, **1**: 92.
Cornstalk, the Shawanee Chief. (W. H. Foote) So. Lit. Mess. **16**: 533.—(M. M. Jones) Potter Am. Mo. **5**. 583.
Cornu Tribes, Vocabulary of. (W. A. Pechey) Anthrop. J. **1**: 143.
Cornwall, Barry. *See* Procter, B. W.
Cornwall. Quar. **102**: 289.
— Antiquities of. Quar. **123**: 35.
— and the Cornish People. Lond. Q. **19**: 1.
— and Derbyshire, Mining Laws of. Penny M. **12**: 487.
— and Devon. Ed. R. **93**: 71.
Cornwall and Devon, Coast of. (C. W. Wood) Argosy, **27**: 124, 206.—Once a Week, **10**: 645, 673.
— Are there Jews in? (M. Müller) Ecl. M. **69**: 47.
— Budehaven in. Chamb. J. **54**: 449.
— Carnival in. All the Year, **27**: 417.
— Church of England in. Chr. Rem. **47**: 142.
— Coast of, in 1800. (I. Taylor) Good Words **5**: 8. Same art. Liv. Age, **80**: 371.
— Corners in. Lond. Soc. **12**: 502.
— Customs and Traditions of. Brit. Q. **52**: 281.
— Daniel Gumb's Rock. All the Year, **15**: 206.
— Ethnology and Literature of. Lond. Q. **13**: 322.
— Fair Maids of. Chamb. J. **26**: 249.
— Fisherfolk of. Lond. Soc. **40**: 394.
— Folk-Lore of. Ecl. R. **122**: 179.
— in its religious Aspect. Chr. Obs. **75**: 195.
— Laboring Classes of. Penny M. **5**: 196.
— Legend of. (T. A. Harcourt) Overland, **14**: 88.
— Legends of. Chamb. J. **43**: 103.—Dub. Univ. **77**: 481.
— Life in, Week's Study of. (D. M. Craik) Good Words, **8**: 61.
— Mines of, Contracts in. Penny M. **3**: 50.
— — and Miners of. Chamb. J. **2**: 245.—Lond. Q. **6**: 436.
— Mining in, and its Traditions. Good Words, **8**: 126.
— More of. (H. Alford) Good Words, **9**: 673.
— Naturalist's Rambles in. Intel. Obs. **9**: 111.
— North Coast of. (H. Alford) Good Words, **9**: 222, 286.
— Old Haunts and Remains of a Cornish Genius, W. Borlase. Lond. Q. **17**: 385.
— Pilchard Fishery in. Hunt, **49**: 302.
— Rambles in. Fraser, **96**: 575.
— Remarkable Rocks in. Penny M. **5**: 28.
— St. Columb and N. W. Coast of. (G. F. Jackson) Once a Week, **7**: 527.
— Saunter in. (D. C. Macdonald) Appleton, **22**: 112.
— Seas of, Rambles by. (R. Noel) Macmil. **34**: 334.
— Sepulchral Monuments of. Nature, **7**: 337, 378.
— Sketches from. (W. H. Rideing) Harper, **63**: 801.
— a Tale of the West. Colburn, **16**: 393.
— Through. Belgra. **1**: 217.
— Tin Mines of. Dub. Univ. **58**: 32.
— Who owns? Chamb. J. **34**: 183.
Cornwall, N. Y., Circulating Library. Lib. J. **3**: 67.
Cornwallis, Caroline Frances. No. Brit. **42**: 341. Same art. Liv. Age, **85**: 598. Same art. Ecl. M. **65**: 270.
Cornwallis, Charles, Lord. (C. C. Smith) No. Am. **89**: 114.—(J. W. Kaye) Good Words, **6**: 543.—Quar. **105**: 1. Same art. Liv. Age, **61**: 392.
— Administration of, in India. Westm. **89**: 149.
— Biography of. Westm. **72**: 290.
— Correspondence of. Bent. Q. **1**: 375.—Ed. R. **109**: 387.—Dub. R. **46**: 110.—Brit. Q. **30**: 1.
— in America. (E. E. Hale) Chr. Exam. **67**: 31.
— Surrender of. (H. P. Johnston) Harper, **63**: 323. *See* Yorktown, Va.
Cornwallis House, S. C. (M. P. Thatcher) Scrib. **9**: 618
Coronado, Carolina. Life and Poems. Chr. Exam. **77**: 160.
Coronado, Francis Vasquez de. Expedition to Cibola. (L. H. Morgan) No. Am. **108**: 457.
Coronation. Blackw. **9**: 337.
— of George IV. Portfo. (Den.) **26**: 340.—Niles's Reg. **21**: 54.
Coronations. Lond. M. **2**: 56.
— Ceremonies connected with. Lond. M. **2**: 81.
— English. Penny M. **7**: 249.
— of the Queens of England, Planche on. Mo. R. **146**: 109.
Coronation Coronal: Imitations of various Poets. Fraser, **4**: 375.
Coronation Medals, English, from Edward VI., Till on. Mo. R. **155**: 559.
Coronation Oath. Blackw. **24**: 1.—Fraser, **8**: 100.—Mo. R. **113**: 387.

Coroner's Clerk. Bentley, 25: 1-614. 26: 1-617. 27: 49.
Coroner's Inquest; a Tale. Bentley, 41: 282. Same art. Ecl. M. 41: 88.
Coroners. (J. R. Phillips) Fraser, 97: 346.
— Duties of. Irish Q. 9: 268.
— Notes on. (T. H. Tyndale) Am. Law R. 11: 480.
Corot, Jean Baptiste Camille. (A. H. Bicknell) O. & N. 10: 637. — (R. Ménard) Portfo. 6: 146. — Portfo. 1: 60.
— and Millet. (J. C. Carr) Contemp. 26: 157.
— Life of. (J. P. Moore) Overland, 15: 468.
Corporal's Story; a Tale. (M. B.) Temp. Bar, 3: 273.
Corporal Punishment. So. Lit. Mess. 7: 575.
— as a moral Discipline. (J. C. Kimball) Mo. Rel. M. 37: 199.
— Commission on. Fraser, 13: 645.
— in Schools. (B. Kurtz) Evang. R. 1: 131. — West. Mo. R. 1: 377.
— and Penal Reformation. Fraser, 71: 154.
Corporations. Ed. R. 58: 469. — Dem. R. 9: 107.
— Advantages and Disadvantages of. (A. B. Johnson) Hunt, 23: 626.
— and Monopolies. (E. L. Godkin) Nation, 18: 359.
— Borrowing Power of. (J. B. Hodgskin) Nation, 12: 398.
— Decisions relating to. Bank. M. (N. Y.) 27: 21, 97, 172.
— for industrial Purposes. (M. Tarver) West. J. 1: 521.
— History of. Fraser, 11: 309.
— Law of. Bank. M. (N. Y.) 14: 800.
— Legislative Control over. (C. J. Ingersoll) Dem. R. 5: 99.
— Legislative Policy of Maine. (F. O. J. Smith) Hunt, 16: 256.
— Municipal, of Scotland. Westm. 24: 156.
— — Origin and Progress of. Westm. 22: 408.
— of New York, Law of. Hunt, 18: 438.
— — Legislative History of. (A. B. Johnson) Hunt, 23: 610.
— Reform of. Bank M. (N. Y.) 32: 184. — Brit. & For. R. 1: 60, 512. 4: 460. — Westm. 29: 48. — Fraser, 11: 428. — Dub. Univ. 6: 119.
— Unreformed. Cornh. 42: 77.
— Valuation of Property of. (W. Farr) J. Statis. Soc. 39: 464.
See Joint-Stock Corporations.
Corporation and Test Acts. Cong. 7: 367. — Westm. 9: 1, 373.
Corporation Bill. Fraser, 12: 114.
Corporation Plate and Insignia of Office. (L. Jewitt) Art J. 32: 9-361. 33: 105-365.
Corpulency. (W. J. Youmans) Pop. Sci. Mo. 1: 445. — Cornh. 7: 457. — Westm. 10: 169. — Anal. M. 5: 280.
— Art of unfattening. Liv. Age, 54: 69.
— Banting on. Blackw. 96: 607. — Chamb. J. 41: 268.
— — and Harvey on. Colburn, 131: 116.
— Chambers on. Liv. Age, 27: 301.
— Corsets and. Lond. Soc. 16: 312.
— Ward on. Blackw. 17: 69.
Corpus Christi, Festival of. (J. Cordner) Unita. R. 6: 195.
Corpus MSS. Bentley, 8: 153.
Corpus Missal, and its probable Date. (S. Malone) Dub. R. 88: 333.
Corral, The. Gent. M. n. s. 9: 149.
C'rrect Card; a Racing Lyric. Temp. Bar, 38: 366.
Correggio, Antonio da. Ecce Homo. Penny M. 7: 177.
— and Leonardo da Vinci. Blackw. 28: 270.
— Magdalen of. Ev. Sat. 9: 375.
Correlation of Physical Forces. (M. Faraday) J. Frankl. Inst. 70: 399. — (W. R. Grove) Cornh. 6: 707. — Brit. Q. 14: 155.
— Does it presuppose conscious Beings? (W. T. Harris) J. Spec. Philos. 11: 433.
— in its Bearing on Mind. (A. Bain) Macmil. 16: 372.
Correlationists. Do they believe in Self-Movement? (W. T. Harris) J. Spec. Philos. 6: 289.
Correspondant, Le. Brownson, 13: 121.
Correspondents, Distant. (C. Lamb) Lond. M. 5: 282.
— To. Cornh. 7: 801.
See War Correspondents.
Corrie, Daniel, Memoir of. Chr. Obs. 48: 19.
Corrigan, Sir Dominic. (E. D. Mapother) Irish Mo. 8: 160.
Corrosion of Metals. (R. Adie) J. Frankl. Inst. 43: 274.
— of Plate-Iron. (I. Sherwood) J. Frankl. Inst. 108: 80.
Corrupt Practices Bill, 1881. (S. C. Buxton) Contemp. 39: 758.
Corsair's Bride. (W. H. G. Kingston) Bentley, 56: 161, 294.
Corselet, Account of a British Gold. (J. Gage) Arch. 26: 422.
Corsets. Godey, 68: 527.
— and Corpulence. Lond. Soc. 16: 312.
— Use of. Chamb. J. 6: 102. *See* Stays.
Corsica. (R. Nowell) Fraser, 99: 115.
— and Sardinia, Forester's Rambles in. Liv. Age, 58: 778.
— Description and History of. Cornh. 18:
— Fortnight in. Belgra. 4: 87.
— Gregorovius's. Quar. 96: 260.
— in 1867. Eng. Dom. M. 14: 17, 70, 121.
— Traits of Corsican Character. (G. Burdett) Colbur 73: 81-223.
— Vocératrices of. Once a Week 17: 437.
Corsican Highlands, In. (R. Noel) Fraser, 100: 386.
Corso in Carnival Time; a Tale. Knick. 60: 33.
Corson, J. W. Loiterings in Europe. Meth. Q. 8: 613.
Corson, James, Struggles of. Chamb. J. 4: 31.
Cort, Henry. Liv. Age, 52: 667.
Cortez, Fernando, and his Wife. Liv. Age, 71: 51.
— Dispatches of. (W. B. Lawrence) No. Am. 57: 459. — Liv. Age, 4: 236. — Mo. R. 162: 210.
— Letter from. Portfo. (Den.) 18: 127, 190, 280. 19: 18, 108.
— Life and Adventures of. (J. B. Duffey) Godey, 50: 51-534.
— Prescott's Life of. Mo. R. 162: 415.
— Tomb of. (B. Murphy) Cath. World 33: 24.
Cortino, P. de. Sharpe, 37: 153.
Corundum. Pop. Sci. Mo. 4: 452.
— of North Carolina, Georgia, and Montana. (J. L. Smith) Am. J. Sci. 106: 180. — (C. U. Shepard) Am. J. Sci. 104: 109, 175.
Corunna, Battle of. Penny M. 2: 15.
— Retreat to. (H. Curling) Bentley, 18: 74. 19: 52.
Corvées. (G. A. Rogers) Belgra. 41: 322.
Corvinus, Matthias. (J. O. Noyes) Nat. M. 13: 207.
Corwin, Thomas, with portrait. Am. Whig R. 6: 310. — (W. F. G. Shanks) Harper, 35: 80.
Corwine, A. H., Sketch of. West. M. 3: 294.
Coryat, Tom. Penny M. 14: 5, 14, 22.
— Crudities. (T. Roscoe) Retros. 6: 206.
— Travels of. (H. T. Wood) Gent. M. n. s. 11: 183. — Retros. 12: 287.
Cosmetor, Peter. (G. Masson) Kitto, 36: 81.
Cosmetics. (J. Scoffern) Belgra. 4: 208. Same art. Ecl. M. 71: 1132. — Chamb. J. 42: 449. — Hunt, 46: 139.
— Face-Enameling. Chamb. J. 45: 641.
— for the Hair. (J. Scoffern) Belgra. 5: 383.
— Hair-Dyes, etc. Cornh. 7: 391, 738.
— Manufacture of. Penny M. 7: 467, 477.
— Painting the Lily. Chamb. J. 37: 124.
Cosmic and Organic Evolution. (L. T. Ward) Pop. Sci. Mo. 11: 672.
Cosmic Emotion. (W. K. Clifford) 19th Cent. 2: 411. Same art. Sup. Pop. Sci. Mo. 2: 74.

Cosmic Forces. Dub. Univ. **75**: 205.
Cosmic Philosophy. (J. Bascom) Bib. Sac. **33**: 618. — (C. C. Everett) Unita. R. **5**: 482. — (B. P. Browne) Meth. Q. **36**: 655.
— Fiske's. (M. S. Phelps) New Eng. **34**: 530. — (F. Pollock) Fortn. **23**: 725. — (D. A. Spalding) Nature, **12**: 267. — (J. E. Cabot) No. Am. **120**: 200.
Cosmo III. Travels through England in 1669. Lond. M. **4**: 156.
Cosmogony. (T. Appel) Mercersb. **24**: 130. — Brownson, **20**: 29, 204. — Mo. Rel. M. **26**: 69-359. — Lond. Q. **32**: 358.
— according to the Bible and Science. Brownson, **20**: 204.
— Davis's Divine Revelations. Dem. R. **21**: 207.
— Mosaic. (J. D. Dana) New Eng. **16**: 74. — (S. Hopkins) New Eng. **36**: 58.
— — C. W. Goodwin on. (H. A. DuBois) Am. Church R. **14**: 306. — New Eng. **19**: 541.
— — Relation of, to Science. (C. B. Warring) Penn Mo. **9**: 430.
See Bible; Genesis; Creation.
Cosmography, Age of Sun and Earth. Liv. Age, **138**: 796.
Cosmology, Biblical. (W. F. Warren) Bib. Sac. **20**: 752.
— Hickok's Rational. (O. W. Wight) New Eng. **16**: 817. — (W. D. Wilson) Am. Church R. **12**: 239. — Princ. **31**: 305. — Theo. & Lit. J. **11**: 353.
Cosmoramas, Dioramas, and Panoramas. Penny M. **11**: 363.
Cosmos, Humboldt's. (Sir J. W. F. Herschel) Ed. R. **87**: 170. — (A. W. Ely) Quar. **77**: 154. Same art. Ecl. M. **7**: 353. — Ecl. R. **95**: 720. Same art. Ecl. M. **46**: 332. — Am. Whig R. **3**: 598. — (C. G. Forshey) De Bow, **9**: 150, 271. **12**: 370. — Liv. Age, **12**: 327. — Brit. Q. **3**: 320. — (Sir D. Brewster) No. Brit. **4**: 202. *See* Humboldt, A. von.
— Symbolism of. (Brother Azarias) Am. Cath. Q. **2**: 84.
— Tyndall on Origin of. (M. Hopkins) Princ. n. s. **4**: 471.
— Views of. So. R. n. s. **9**: 561.
Cossack Epic of Demetrius Rigmarolovicz. Fraser, **20**: 715.
Cossacks. (C. A. G. Bridge) Geog. M. **5**: 113. Same art. Sup. Pop. Sci. Mo. **3**: 241. — (E. F. Hall) Putnam, **5**: 236. — (Dr. Michelsen) Bentley, **55**: 211. — (J. Pyne) Nat. Q. **30**: 233. — Blackw. **46**: 345.
— Captured by. Lippinc. **20**: 684.
— History and Literature of. For. Q. **26**: 266. Same art. Am. Ecl. **1**: 332.
— of the Don. (D. Ker) Galaxy, **23**: 406.
— — Amongst. Temp. Bar, **50**: 244. Same art. Ecl. M. **89**: 237.
— of the Ukraine, Krasinski's. Brit. Q. **10**: 264. — Tait, n. s. **16**: 468.
— Ride with, at Kertch. Cornh. **7**: 401.
— Songs, History, and Destiny of. (Prince Howra) Sharpe, **18**: 220. — Nat. M. **4**: 35.
See Ukraine.
Cost. Counting the. Dub. Univ. **77**: 171.
— of Living, 1650-51. N. E. Reg. **7**: 189.
Costa Rica and its Railroad. (J. T. Meagher) Overland, **10**: 160.
— Geology of. (W. M. Gabb) Am. J. Sci **109**: 198.
— Holidays in. (T. F. Meagher) Harper, **20**: 18, 145, 304.
— Mission to. (R. M. Walsh) Lippinc. **10**: 511.
— Sketch of Life in. Temp. Bar, **21**: 331.
— Visit to. (W. G. Waller) So. M. **15**: 262, 374.
— Wagner's, 1853-54. Colburn, **108**: 253. — Liv. Age, **51**: 769.
Coste, Pascal, Obituary of. Am. Arch. **8**: 185.
Costebelle, P. de, Expedition against Newfoundland, 1705. M. Am. Hist. **1**: 107.
Costello, Dudley. Bentley, **58**: 543.
— Valley of the Meuse. Dub. Univ. **26**: 298.
Costello, Edward, Life of. Mus. **37**: 248.
Costello, Louisa Stuart. Gabrielle. Mo. R. **161**: 445.
— Redwald; a Tale of Mona. Lond. M. **2**: 631.
— Summer among Bocages and Vines. Mo. R. **153**: 75.
Coster, Anna V. *See* Vallayer Coster.
Costers and their Donkeys. Chamb. J. **54**: 753.
Costermongers' Club. (A. Forbes) Belgra. **10**: 355.
Costume. (H. T. Tuckerman) Godey, **30**: 139.
— and Character. Cornh. **12**: 568.
— Art of. Quar. **79**: 372.
— British. Mo. R. **135**: 10.
— — Mediæval and modern. Lond. Q. **4**: 122.
— Character of. Chamb. J. **9**: 313. Same art. Liv. Age, **18**: 399.
— Curiosities of. (H. Curling) Bentley, **19**: 68.
— Development in. (G. H. Darwin) Pop. Sci. Mo. **2**: 40.
— Eccentricities of. All the Year, **9**: 280.
— in all Ages. Godey, **61**: 59.
— in 18th Century. (A. Andrews) Colburn, **102**: 186.
— in Sculpture. (F. G. Stephens) Fraser, **75**: 382.
— Male, of the Period. Ev. Sat. **10**: 498.
— Modern; Welsh Sketch. (A. Beale) Temp. Bar, **33**: 96.
— National, Brewster's. Am. Mo. M. **11**: 503.
— of all Nations. Godey, **40**: 67-395. **41**: 44-200. **42**: 34-353. **43**: 155-360. **44**: 45-469. **45**: 15-518.
— of Englishwomen. (W. Thornbury) Art J. **28**: 17-237.
— of the Future. Internat. M. **3**: 103.
— of Roman Ladies. Portfo.(Den.) **29**: 21.
— of various Epochs. (Prof. Heideloff) Art J. **4**: 20, 108, 212.
— Old English. Antiquary, **2**: 197.
— Songs and Poems on. Chamb. J. **11**: 349.
— Togas and Toggery. (C. Cook) Scrib. **14**: 783
— Wigs and Ringlets. Tinsley, **9**: 201.
See Dress; Fashions.
Costumes. Antiquary, **3**: 219, 243, 303. **4**: 51.
— Correct. All the Year, **32**: 163.
— Grecian and Albanian. Penny M. **5**: 179, 187, 220.
— of various Epochs. Art J. **3**: 18, 92, 281.
— Stage, History of. Penny M. **6**: 187.
Côte d'Or, Autumn in. (M. B. Edwards) Fraser, **102**: 357. Same art. Liv. Age, **147**: 114.
— Traditions of. St. James, **3**: 105.
— Vineyards of. House. Words, **11**: 28.
Cothren, William. History of Woodbury, Conn., with portrait. (S. G. Drake) N. E. Reg. **8**: 193.
Cotopaxi, Eruptions of. (A. Flores) Nation, **25**: 149.
— First Ascent of. (J. Orton) Nature, **7**: 449.
Cotswold Games. Cornh. **37**: 710.
Cotta, Bernhard von. (R. R. Noel) Nature, **20**: 505.
Cottage and Castle; a Sketch. Dub. Univ. **64**: 566.
Cottage by the River. (T. Wyatt) Blackw. **124**: 735. Same art. Liv. Age, **139**: 803.
Cottage in a Glen; a Tale. So. Lit. Mess. **1**: 78.
Cottages. (J. Wilson) Blackw. **19**: 241. — Chamb. J. **46**: 615.
— Cost of. (H. Martineau) Once a Week, **2**: 61, 169.
— Model. Godey, **33**: 133, 181, 229. **34**: 44-307. **35**: 95-325.
Cottage Allotments, Pauperism and. Chr. Obs. **32**: 574, 842. **33**: 91, 222.
Cottage Building in Norway. Ecl. Engin. **6**: 591.
Cottage Life in England. Temp. Bar, **7**: 55.
— in Scotland; a Tale. Sharpe, **47**: 196. **48**: 134.
Cottage Property in London. (O. Hill) Fortn. **6**: 681.
Cottager's Wife. Chr. Obs. **12**: 129, 201, 273.
Cottagers and Cottages. Cornh. **41**: 683.
Cotter's Birthday. Dub. Univ. **26**: 368.
Cotterill, Thomas, Memoir of. Chr. Obs. **24**: 529, 597.
Cotteswold Hills. Lond. Soc. **24**: 236.
Cottin, Mad. Sophie. (Alice King) Argosy, **18**: 103.
— Amelie Mansfield. Quar. **1**: 304

Cottin, Mad. Sophie. Elizabeth. Ed. R. 11: 448.
Cottle, Joseph. Fall of Cambria; a Poem. Ecl. R. 12: 1073.
Cotton, Agnes, her House for Waifs. Good Words, 14: 65.
Cotton, W. J. Richard, with portrait. Colburn, 166: 518.
Cotton, George Edward L., Bishop of Calcutta. Macmil. 15: 102. — Brit. Q. 45: 214. — Chr. Obs. 71: 241.
Cotton, John. (J. S. Clark) Cong. Q. 3: 133.
— and Boston, England, in 1621. N. E. Reg. 28: 125.
— God's Promise to his Plantation. (C. Deane) N. E. Reg. 2: 151, 318.
— in Church and State. (G. E. Ellis) Internat. R. 9: 370.
— Memoirs of. (F. Parkman) No. Am. 38: 486. — Am. Q. Reg. 10: 245. — (L. Bacon) New Eng. 8: 388.
Cotton Genealogy. (J. W. Thornton) N. E. Reg. 1: 164.
Cotton. (C. P. William) Once a Week, 2: 160. — Chamb. J. 39: 136. — Liv. Age, 68: 546. — Lond. Q. 15: 495. — Niles's Reg. 34: 417. — (S. T. Coit) Hunt, 10: 48.
— Age of. Am. Mo. M. 11: 1.
— American. All the Year, 5: 234.
— — and Indian. Hunt, 17: 325.
— and Civilization of Africa. (J. P. Thompson) New Eng. 19: 829.
— and Cotton Manufactures. (A. W. Ely) De Bow, 12: 337. — (J. G. Dudley) De Bow, 15: 352.
— — Chronology of. (S. Batchelder) J. Frankl. Inst. 95: 355.
— and Cotton Planters. (R. Abbey) De Bow, 3: 1.
— and Cotton Supply. Once a Week, 5: 212, 238.
— and Cotton Trade. (C. F. McCay) Hunt, 19: 594.
— and Currency. Dem. R. 1: 383.
— and Industry, Plea for. (T. Bazley) J. Frankl. Inst. 75: 385.
— and its Culture. (J. E. Bloomfield) Hunt, 45: 561.
— and its Prospects. De Bow, 11: 307.
— and Negroes. (W. W. Wright) De Bow, 29: 136.
— and Protection. Dem. R. 2: 32, 225.
— and Slavery. Hogg, 12: 209.
— and the South. (H. W. Grady) Harper, 63: 719.
— and Specie Payments. (J. B. Hodgskin) Nation, 12: 173.
— and Sugar Cultivation in East Indies. De Bow, 4: 511.
— Annual Reports on, for 1870–72. Bank. M. (N. Y.) 27: 289.
— Atkinson's Report on. Liv. Age, 77: 464.
— Bleaching of. Chamb. J. 11: 66.
— British Competition in Production of. De Bow, 8: 20.
— Brokers in. Hunt, 8: 556.
— Chronology of. Am. Q. Reg. 10: 277.
— Consumption of, in Europe. (J. Claiborne) De Bow, 25: 65.
— Crop of United States. Bank. M. (N. Y.) 10: 378. 23: 619. — De Bow, 17: 538.
— — in 1840. Hunt, 3: 555.
— — in 1857–60. Bank. M. (N. Y.) 15: 571.
— — in 1867–69. Bank. M. (N. Y.) 24: 291.
— — in 1868–70. Bank. M. (N. Y.) 25: 372.
— Cultivation of. (T. B. Thorpe) Harper, 8: 447. — Niles's Reg. 23: 216. — (R. Abbey) De Bow, 2: 133.
— — and Manufacture of. (C. T. James) Hunt, 22: 195, 290.
— — and Supply of. Ho. & For. R. 2: 1.
— — Free or Slave Labor better? (E. Atkinson) Contin. Mo. 1: 247.
— — in America and India. Brit. Q. 9: 354.
— — in Asia. (J. Capper) Bank. M. (N. Y.) 10: 386.
— — Labor in. (J. L. Strong) Overland, 13: 18.
— — Mallet and Gibbs on. Colburn, 126: 1.
— — Origin and Progress of, in America. (J. Rawle) De Bow, 17: 426.
— — Picking, and Cotton Planter's Calendar. Pract. M. 2: 339.
Cotton, Cultivation of, Trade and Manufacture. De Bow, 4: 250.
— Foreign Demand for. Bank. M. (N. Y.) 4: 455.
— from 1825 to 1850. (C. F. McCay) De Bow, 10: 206. — (C. F. McCay) Hunt, 23: 595.
— Growing of. Nat. Q. 29: 107.
— Growth and Consumption of. (J. M. Cardoza) De Bow, 21: 153.
— — and Manufacture of. De Bow, 8: 99. — (C. T. James) Hunt, 21: 492. — Temp. Bar, 3: 431.
— — — Profits compared. (C. Colton) Hunt, 15: 276.
— — and Power of. (R. D. Owen) O. & N. 3: 273.
— — Future. (B. F. Nourse) Hunt, 61: 85.
— — Trade, and Manufacture of. De Bow, 15: 217, 470. — (J. G. Dudley) De Bow, 16: 1.
— History of. Chamb. J. 39: 136. Same art. Ecl. M. 59: 59.
— in Australia; Visit to Queensland Plantation. (C. D Pringle) Once a Week, 14: 501.
— in Brazil. (A. Andrews) Colburn, 132: 175.
— in California. (J. L. Strong) Overland, 6: 326.
— in Egypt. (A. Andrews) Colburn, 132: 70–449.
— — Gliddon on. Mo. R. 156: 46.
— in India. All the Year, 5: 375. — Ecl. R. 96: 391. — Liv. Age, 52: 244. — Cornh. 6: 654.
— — Culture of. De Bow, 9: 314. — Dub. Univ. 49: 678. — Ed. R. 115: 478.
— — — and Irrigation. Ecl. R. 106: 104.
— — — and Commerce of. (J. F. Royle) Hunt, 25: 307, 423, 582. — (J. F. Royle) West. J. 12: 420. — De Bow, 17: 309.
— — in 1852. Ecl. R. 95: 391. 96: 129.
— — Nature and present Condition of. (J. Rawle) De Bow, 17: 466.
— in Peru. (S. F. Glenn) De Bow, 2: 439. — (A. Andrews) Colburn, 132: 75.
— is King. (M. Butler) West. J. 14: 169, 250, 323. — De Bow, 22: 540. — Liv. Age, 75: 3.
— — Is it? Nat. R. 13: 451.
— — King Cotton and his Gin. Atlan. 40: 188.
— Old and new Times. Chamb. J. 15: 89.
— Price of, Advancing and controlling. (H. Smith) De Bow, 7: 48.
— — How to maintain. (M. H. McGehee) De Bow, 7: 73.
— — Influence of, on Consumption of, 1860–70. (W. B. Forwood) J. Statis. Soc. 33: 366.
— — — on Production of. (W. B. Forwood) J. Statis. Soc. 34: 366.
— Speculations in. Chr. Exam. 31: 32.
— Statistics of. Hunt, 6: 179. 17: 417. — Am. Alma. 1837: 92. — Bank. M. (N. Y.) 9: 577. 11: 90.
— Steam and Machinery. (H. Wilson) So. Lit. Mess. 27: 161.
— Supply of. All the Year, 6: 256.
— — and Consumption. (J. N. Cardoza) De Bow, 24: 396. — De Bow, 22: 337.
— — Competition of Algeria. (D. D. Deming) De Bow, 24: 193.
— — Old and new Fields. All the Year, 6: 125.
— — Possibilities of. (A. Andrews) Colburn, 133: 230–443. 134: 105.
— — Present and future. De Bow, 22: 197.
— — Problem of. (E. Spencer) So. M. 13: 680.
— — Question of, 1862. Bank. M. (L.) 22: 690.
— — — 1864. (E. Atkinson) No. Am. 98: 477.
— State and Prospects of. All the Year, 8: 322.
— Varieties of. De Bow, 18: 177.
Cotton Country, Chronicle of a. Cornh. 27: 467.
— Scene in. All the Year, 4: 398.
Cotton Countries. Chamb. J. 35: 172.
Cotton Factory, Day at a. Penny M. 12: 241.
Cotton Famine, 1857. Brit. Q. 26: 416.

Cotton Famine, 1862–64. (J. Holingshead) Good Words, **3**: 593. — (C. Redding) Colburn, **125**: 216. — Lond. Q. **23**: 313. — No. Brit. **39**: 235. — Temp. Bar, **9**: 380. — Westm. **80**: 191. — Bank. M. (L.) **22**: 340. — Liv. Age, **70**: 438. — Brit. Q. **41**: 358.
Cotton Fiber, Action of Silicate and Carbonate of Soda in. (F. C. Calvert) J. Frankl. Inst. **80**: 406.
— Structure of. De Bow, **18**: 40.
Cotton Fibers and Fabrics. (Dr. Sacc) Pop. Sci. Mo. **2**: 161.
Cotton Gin. Niles's Reg. **32**: 332. — (J. Blunt) Hunt, **21**: 633. — (D. Pratt) De Bow, **2**: 153.
— Effect of the Invention of. (D. F. Bacon) Hunt, **16**: 44.
Cotton Goods, Cost of manufacturing. Hunt, **25**: 249, 370.
— Domestics. Hunt, **9**: 191.
— Sail-Duck. Niles's Reg. **37**: 24.
— Thomson's Sizing of. Nature, **17**: 4.
Cotton Gown, History of a. Penny M. **9**: 4, 20, 45.
Cotton Industry, Revolution in. De Bow, **22**: 387.
Cotton Interest. So. R. n. s. **7**: 159.
Cotton Manufacture. Niles's Reg. **35**: 139. — (H. A. Miles) No. Am. **52**: 31. — Brit. & For. R. **2**: 89. — Blackw. **39**: 407. **40**: 100. — Mus. **11**: 340. — Chamb. J. **10**: 372. **11**: 66, 162.
— and the Ring Frame. (F. H. Silsbee) J. Frankl. Inst. **101**: 89, 169.
— British. Ed. R. **46**: 1. Hunt, **17**: 297.
— by its Producers. (S. R. Cockerell) De Bow, **7**: 484.
— History of. Mo. R. **105**: 394.
— — and Condition of, 1861. Westm. **75**: 419.
— — Baines's. Tait, n. s. **2**: 235.
— in France. Hunt, **38**: 761.
— in Germany. Hunt, **38**: 758.
— in Great Britain, 1850. (G. R. Porter) J. Frankl. Inst. **51**: 29.
— in Switzerland. Hunt, **15**: 265.
— in United States. De Bow, **8**: 272.
— Letter on. (H. Lee) Hunt, **9**: 253, 351.
— Life of S. Compton. Chr. Obs. **60**: 345.
— of Dacca. Chamb. J. **18**: 393.
— Progress of. Bank. M. (N. Y.) **7**: 311.
— Prospects of. (A. A. Lawrence) Hunt, **21**: 628.
— Report on, 1832. Niles's Reg. **42**: 4.
— Statistics of, 1861. J. Frankl. Inst. **72**: 119.
Cotton Manufactures. De Bow, **19**: 693.
— and Free Trade. Blackw. **68**: 123.
— at the South. (C. T. James) De Bow, **8**: 307, 462, 556.
— Condition of American. (A. A. Lawrence) Hunt, **22**: 26.
— in United States. De Bow, **7**: 348.
Cotton Plant. (W. Elliott) De Bow, **20**: 571. — (J. D. B. De Bow) De Bow, **1**: 289. — De Bow, **15**: 84. — Penny M. **1**: 156.
— Accidents and Disease of. (T. Glover) De Bow, **21**: 635.
— Diseases of, and the Remedies. (M. H. McGehee) De Bow, **11**: 7.
— Insects belonging to. (C. Taylor) Harper, **21**: 37.
— Natural History of. (E. Lankester) Pop. Sci. R. **1**: 170.
Cotton Planters, Duty of. (M. W. Phillips) De Bow, **7**: 410.
— Embarrassments of. De Bow, **1**: 434.
Cotton-Planters' Convention. De Bow, **11**: 497.
— at Macon. De Bow, **12**: 121.
— at Montgomery. (J. G. Gamble) De Bow, **12**: 275.
Cotton Planting at Port Hudson. (J. O. Noyes) Putnam, **12**: 46.
Cotton Seed. Pract. M. **3**: 267.
— Product of the South. (C. Cist) De Bow, **29**: 510.
Cotton Spinning. (E. L. Plimpton) Potter Am. Mo. **8**: 270, 351.
— Machines and their Inventors. Quar. **107**: 45. Same art. Liv. Age, **65**: 3.
— Science of modern. Pract. M. **3**: 32.
Cotton Trade. (E. H. Derby) No. Am. **92**: 1. — (C. F. McCay) Hunt, **9**: 516. **11**: 517. **13**: 507. **15**: 531. **17**: 559. **21**: 595. **23**: 595. **25**: 659. **28**: 40. **31**: 707. — (C. F. McCay) West. J. **5**: 233. **7**: 234. **9**: 249. **11**: 315. — (J. B. Gribble) Hunt, **35**: 549. **37**: 554. — (J. H. Lanman) Hunt, **4**: 201. — (J. B. Gribble) De Bow, **6**: 126. — De Bow, **12**: 185. — Anal. M. **2**: 298. — Niles's Reg. **17**: 9. — Ecl. M. **42**: 76.
— and Manufacture, and the U. S. Civil War. (L. Levi) J. Statis. Soc. **26**: 26.
— British. Hunt, **8**: 382. **19**: 167, 275. — (R. Burn) Hunt, **18**: 152, 610.
— Difficulties of. (T. Bazley) Liv. Age, **77**: 207.
— in 1857–58. Bank. M. (N. Y.) **13**: 394.
— in 1859. Bank. M. (N. Y.) **15**: 177.
— of the Southwest. De Bow, **21**: 393.
— of the World, 1853. (C. F. McCay) De Bow, **16**: 337. **21**: 292.
Cotton Trees and Vultures of Jamaica. (W. E. Barrett) Recr. Sci. **3**: 193.
Cotton Weaving, and Lancashire Looms. Macmil. **6**: 445.
Cotton Wool, British Trade in. Hunt, **16**: 111.
Cotton Worm. (L. A. Dodge) Am. Natural. **7**: 213. — (D. B. Gorham) De Bow, **3**: 535. — (A. R. Grote) Am. Natural. **8**: 722. — De Bow, **2**: 277. — (J. H. Zimmerman) De Bow, **17**: 451.
Cotton Yarn, Exportation of. Blackw. **1**: 472.
Cougar, The. Chamb. J. **20**: 354.
Cougar Hunting. (J. J. Audubon) Ed. New Philos. J. **11**: 103.
Coulisses in Paris. Liv. Age, **54**: 632.
Coulon, Eugene. Liv. Age, **65**: 382.
Coulter, John, Cruise of. Blackw. **62**: 323.
Council of Church of England and Rome. Ecl. R. **29**: 301, 440, 581.
Councils, Acts of recent Eastern. (J. McSwiney) Month, **28**: 336.
— and Synods. Ecl. R. **104**: 357.
— Early Christian. Chr. Rem. **34**: 457.
— Ecumenical. (B. A. Hinsdale) Chr. Q. **1**: 491. — (P. Schaff) New Eng. **22**: 654. — Brit. Q. **51**: 167.
— — First, A. D. 325. St. James, **26**: 48.
— New Field for. (T. T. Munger) Cong. Q. **13**: 379.
— of Constance and of the Vatican. (G. P. Fisher) New Eng. **29**: 191.
— Some recent. Month, **37**: 584. **38**: 130.
See Congregational Councils; *also* Nice, Trent, etc.
Counsel for Prisoners. (Syd. Smith) Ed. R. **45**: 74.
— License of. Westm. **35**: 1.
Counsel Mal-à-Propos; a Tale. Fraser, **33**: 288.
Counselor, The. (J. Wilmer) Tait, n. s. **15**: 503–793.
Count Burkhardt; a Poem. Once a Week, **7**: 376.
Count Cagliostro. Fraser, **8**: 19, 132.
Count Eberstein; a Poem. (J. L. Uhland) St. James, **33**: 91.
Count Horace's Sporting Exploits. Bentley, **43**: 176.
Count Monte-Leone; a Tale. (H. De St. Georges) Internat. M. **1**: 494. **2**: 45–495. **3**: 58–489. **4**: 42–500
Count of Arco, Story of. Dub. Univ. **17**: 711.
Count Pott's Strategy. (N. P. Willis) Hogg, **1**: 250.
Count Pulaski's strange Power. (H. F. French) Atlan. **41**: 729.
Count Wala, first Prisoner of Chillon. Bentley, **54**: 249.
Count Waldemar. Cornh. **37**: 584. Same art. Liv. Age, **137**: 595.
Count's Daughters. Liv. Age, **124**: 294, 342.
Count's Little Daughter; a Poem. (Mrs. R. S. Greenough) Scrib. **3**: 129.
Count the Cost. Chr. Obs. **34**: 645, 709.
Counterfeit Coin; a Tale. Putnam, **7**: 576.

Counterfeit Coin, Forged Notes and Magsmen. Once a Week, **9**: 383.
Counterfeit Presentment; a Comedy. (W. D. Howells) Atlan. **40**: 148, 296, 448.
Counterfeit Presentments. (Mrs. Gore) Bentley, **4**: 496.
Counterfeits. (C. H. Spurgeon) Ex. H. Lec. **17**: 337.
Counterfeiters, Hunting. (E. Spencer) So. M. **12**: 569.
Counterfeiting and Handwriting. Bank. M. (N. Y.) **34**: 22.
— as a Profession. Bank. M. (N. Y.) **34**: 378.
— in America. Bank. M. (L.) **22**: 621, 659.
— of Names and Marks. (C. Edwards) Hunt, **14**: 330.
— of Trade Marks. West. Law J. **66**: 337.
— Prevention of. Bank. M. (L) **22**: 675. — Bank. M. (N. Y.) **8**: 893. **9**: 705. **10**: 798, 921. **11**: 129. **13**: 131, 693. **14**: 702. — Hunt, **29**: 72. **35**: 731.
— — Seropyan's Plan for. Bank. M. (N. Y.) **10**: 921. **11**: 129–587.
Counter-Syndicate. Chamb. J. **58**: 788–836.
Countess. (M. Browne) Ev. Sat. **11**: 559.
— Three Scenes in the Life of a. So. Lit. Mess. **13**: 37.
Countess Adelcrantz; a Tale. Cornh. **41**: 51.
Countess Felicita's Discovery. (J. Hawthorne) Belgra. **44**: 424. **45**: 64.
Countess Laura; a Poem. (G. H. Boker) Atlan. **16**: 143.
Countess Mélusine; a Tale. Temp. Bar, **1**: 331.
Countess Ruby; a Tale. Cornh. **40**: 171.
Countess's Lover. All the Year, **15**: 379.
Countess's Wedding-Day. Fraser, **49**: 387.
Counting by Aid of the Fingers. (J. Trowbridge) Pop. Sci. Mo. **12**: 430.
Counting-House Romance. Chamb. J. **49**: 129–204.
Counting-House Scene. Dem. R. **28**: 223.
Country, Beauties of, Miller's. Mo. R. **142**: 259.
— Living in; Sparrowgrass Papers. (F. S. Cozzens) Putnam, **4**: 619. **5**: 119, 321, 426. **6**: 166–629. **7**: 166, 295.
— Love of. Ox. Prize Ess. **2**: 229. *See* Patriotism.
— Our, right or wrong? Brownson, **3**: 493. — Am. Whig R. **3**: 284.
— Ramble in. Temp. Bar, **6**: 173.
— Summer Night in. Temp. Bar, **12**: 237.
See titles under Rural *and* Rustic.
Country Annals. (Mrs. M. G. Milward) So. Lit. Mess. **7**: 37, 119.
Country Ball in New England. All the Year, **23**: 108.
Country Board. (E. L. Godkin) Nation, **10**: 381.
Country Cousin. All the Year, **32**: 115, 139. Same art. Liv. Age, **122**: 269.
Country Cousins. Lond. Soc. **4**: 112. — St. James, **25**: 592.
Country Critic, Thoughts of. Cornh. **30**: 717.
Country Curate. Blackw. **18**: 529. **19**: 4, 137, 529.
Country Delights. (G. J. A. Coulson) N. Ecl. **7**: 1.
— Decay of, in England. Temp. Bar. **39**: 474.
Country Doctor. Knick. **41**: 108–536.
— a Welsh Sketch. (A. Beale) Temp. Bar. **33**: 385.
Country Fair. Tinsley, **27**: 497.
Country Gentlemen, Hints to. Blackw. **12**: 482, 624.
— in England. Cornh. **9**: 618.
Country House, In a. (E. Courtenay) Belgra. **18**: 495. **19**: 39, 517. **20**: 454.
— Life in. Cornh. **8**: 710.
— on the Rhine. (B. Auerbach) Liv. Age, **99**: 490–785. **100**: 38–790. **101**: 22–787. **102**: 18–267.
— Something like a. Blackw. **63**: 28.
Country Houses and Country Life. (A. K. H. Boyd) Fraser, **57**: 295.
Country-House Life. Belgra. **7**: 445. — St. James, **25**: 488.
Country Lanes in England. Temp. Bar, **14**: 484.
Country Life. (I. Taylor) Good Words, **5**: 580, 625. — Blackw. **120**: 483.
Country Life, Economics of. Cornh. **11**: 548.
— for Ladies. Chamb. J. **3**: 327.
— incompatible with Literary Labor. So. Lit. J. **4**: 297.
— Jesse's Scenes and Tales of. Mo. R. **164**: 88.
— Modern, in England. Cornh. **16**: 704.
Country Manor-House; a Ghost Story. (Mrs. Harley) Belgra. **28**: 368.
Country Minister; a Story. (Mrs. L. J. Hall) Mo. Rel. M. **38**: 101, 329, 414.
Country Neighbors, My. Blackw. **54**: 431.
Country Overseer. Fraser, **10**: 629.
Country Parson. *See* Boyd, A. K. H.
Country Parsons. Cornh. **42**: 415. Same art. Liv. Age, **147**: 429.
Country Pastor, Characteristics of. (S. G. Bulfinch) Chr. Exam. **53**: 269.
Country Post-Office; a Tale. (Mrs. Abely) Sharpe, **32**: 58.
Country Quarters. Fraser, **11**: 137.
Country Rambles. Chamb. J. **53**: 369. — (C. Raymond) Potter Am. Mo. **15**: 193.
Country Seat; a Poem. Blackw. **34**: 820.
Country Sermon; a Poem. (J. Truman) Liv. Age, **94**: 2.
Country Sights and Sounds. (M. H. Hinckley) O. & N. **7**: 415. **8**: 191, 431, 711. **9**: 444, 671.
Country Tavern in Winter. (M. Dean) Lippinc. **27**: 159.
Country Towns, Old. (A. Rimmer) Belgra. **40**: 333, 434. **41**: 76, 216, 303. **42**: 36–427. **43**: 44, 156.
County Ball, A. Cornh. **4**: 218.
County Boards, English. (C. T. D. Acland) Fortn. **35**: 93.
County-Court Extension. Westm. **54**: 104.
County-Court Practice. Chamb. J. **49**: 497.
County Family; a Tale. Chamb. J. **46**: 273–601. Same art. Liv. Age, **102**: 229–782. **103**: 13–230.
County Franchise and Mr. Lowe. (W. E. Gladstone) 19th Cent. **2**: 537.
County Legends. (R. H. Barham) Bentley, **8**: 171. **9**: 81, 521, 574. **10**: 75.
County Palatine. (J. E. Taylor) Belgra. **12**: 307.
Counties, The; a Poem. Fraser, **16**: 589.
— Contesting. (W. Minto) Fraser, **101**: 504.
— Lord Lieutenants of, Early History of. (Sir H. Ellis) Arch. **35**: 350.
Coup de Jarnac. Chamb. J. **23**: 289, 317.
Coupon Bonds. (J. T. Trowbridge) Atlan. **16**: 257, 399.
Courage. Chr. Exam. **33**: 204.
— Anatomy of. (Prince Pückler Muskau) Bentley, **1**: 398.
— and Cowardice. Dub. Univ. **67**: 586. **68**: 207. Same art. Cath. World, **4**: 160.
— and Death. (L. Tollemache) Fortn. **25**: 103.
— Physical. (T. W. Higginson) Atlan. **2**: 728.
Courbet, Gustave, and his Works. Temp. Bar, **42**: 535.
— A Memory of. (C. Adams) Lippinc. **21**: 631.
Courcelles, E. de. (A. Polenburg) Meth. Q. **23**: 92, 311.
Coureur des Bois. (A. T. Howells) Scrib. **12**: 108.
Courier, Paul Louis, Life and Writings of. (H. D. Traill) Fortn. **27**: 188. — Mo. R. **150**: 185. — Colburn, **37**: 285. — Westm. **85**: 451. — Ed. R. **49**: 34. — Westm. **11**: 9.
Courier's Tale. Chamb. J. **36**: 358.
Course of Love; or, The Quarrel and the Reconciliation. Godey, **22**: 128.
Coursing. Belgra. **18**: 502. **43**: 76.
— Waterloo Cup. St. James, **27**: 750.
Court, Antoine. Ed. R. **138**: 203. — Chr. Obs. **73**: 892.
Court of England, Secret History of. Quar. **61**: 425.
Courts and Court Journals. (Lady S. O. Morgan) Colburn, **64**: 544.
— Ceremony of. Chamb. J. **31**: 318.
— of British Queens. (E. B. Lytton) Westm. **29**: 281 Same art. Mus. **33**: 302.
— of England, Jesse's Memoirs of. Ed. R. **77**: 412.

Courts of Europe, Swinburne on. Ed. R. **73**: 461. — Mo. R. **154**: 494. — Ecl. R. **73**: 563. — (J. W. Croker) Quar. **68**: 145.
Court Festivities, English. Lippinc. **12**: 294.
Court, Central Criminal. Westm. **22**: 195.
— of Chancery *See* Chancery.
— of Justice, English. Cornh. **4**: 195.
— — High. (J. F. Stephen) 19th Cent. **9**: 62.
— of Session, Reform of. (H. Murray) Ed. R. **9**: 462.
Courts, Brown's Northern. Quar. **19**: 379.
— County, their Jurisdiction and Benefits. Ecl. R. **89**: 336.
— — New. (J. B. Kington) Peop. J. **4**: 171, 194.
— Criminal, of London. (J. Fletcher) J. Statis. Soc. **9**: 289.
— Ecclesiastical, 1844. Mo. R. **164**: 230.
— Local. Westm. **36**: 58.
— — and Independence of the Bar. Fraser, **23**: 359.
— of ancient English Common Law. (Sir F. Palgrave) Ed. R. **36**: 287.
— of Conciliation. (J. C. Gray, jr.) No. Am. **102**: 135.
— of Common Law. Chamb. J. **42**: 717.
— of Local Jurisdiction. Mo. R. **124**: 167.
— Proposed Removal of. Fraser, **64**: 635.
— Removal of Suits from State to Federal. (A. B. Magruder) Am. Law R. **13**: 434.
Court Letter-Writer, Complete. Chamb. J. **31**: 281.
Court Martial. All the Year, **10**: 421, 541.
— Late Case of. Blackw. **67**: 269.
— Capt. Evans's Case. Niles's Reg. **24**: 360.
— Capt. Heath's Case. Niles's Reg. **13**: 415. **14**: 29.
— Col. Dawkins's Case. Temp. Bar. **14**: 525.
— Com. Porter's Case. Niles's Reg. **28**: 370, 390, 402. **29**: 90.
— Com. Stewart's Case. Niles's Reg. **28**: 409.
— The; a Tale. Dub. Univ. **2**: 33.
Courts-Martial. Cornh. **5**: 682.
— and Cat-o'-nine-Tails. Fraser, **13**: 539.
— Farce of. Temp. Bar. **5**: 280.
— in the British Army. Temp. Bar, **10**: 412.
— Military. Ho. & For. R. **4**: 19.
Court Netherleigh; a Story. (Mrs. H. Wood) Argosy, **31**: 1–401. **32**: 1–401.
Court Rolls. (J. Amphlett) Gent. M. n. s. **25**: 488.
Court Scandal. Belgra. **13**: 231.
Court of Darkness; a Poem. Blackw. **24**: 481.
Court of Miracles. Dub. Univ. **12**: 361.
Courts of Love. (T. Roscoe) Retros. **5**: 70. — St. James, **13**: 437.
Courtenay, Marie. House. Words, **16**: 523.
Courtenay, Sir William, Knight of Malta. Ev. Sat. **3**: 658.
Courtesy as a Christian Virtue. Cong. **1**: 29. — (W. C. Richards) Chr. R. **19**: 498.
— in School Instruction. (G. F. Thayer) Am. Inst. of Instruc. **1840**: 83.
Courthope, W. J. Ludibria Lunæ. Once a Week, **21**: 62.
Courtier of Misfortune; a Bonapartist Story. Cornh. **29**: 308. Same art. Liv. Age, **121**: 150, 227.
Courtney, Archbishop, Burial-Place of. (S. Denne) Arch. **10**: 261.
Courtship. (S. H. Blanchard) Belgra. **23**: 511. — (T. H. Shreve) West. Lit. J. **1**: 34. — Knick. **9**: 377.
— and Love-Making. Fraser, **25**: 144. — Mus. **45**: 645.
— and Marriage. Lond. M. **14**: 37.
— — among the Portuguese. Tait, **4**: 424.
— — in France. Westm. **107**: 337.
— Curiosities of. Chamb. J. **56**: 158.
— History of. Once a Week, **20**: 558.
— in France. (Lady Pollock) Temp. Bar, **46**: 183.
— in the Time of James I. Blackw. **68**: 141. Same art. Ecl. M. **21**: 186. Same art. Liv. Age, **26**: 558
— of Susan Bell. (A. Trollope) Harper, **21**: 366.
— Old-Time. (F. M. Colby) Potter Am. Mo. **10**: 409.
Courtship under Difficulties. (F. Stolle) Blackw. **78**: 718. *See* Marriage; Wooing.
Courtyard of the Ours d'Or; a Story. (Mrs. A. I. Ritchie) Cornh. **19**: 726. Same art. Ev. Sat. **7**: 801. Same art. Liv. Age, **102**: 49.
Cousin, Germaine, Holy Shepherdess of Pibrach. Cath. World, **7**: 753.
Cousin, Jehan. (E. F. S. Pattison) Portfo. **2**: 7, 76.
Cousin, Victor. Ed. R. **93**: 429. — No. Brit. **46**: 162. — Ecl. M. **31**: 527. — Ev. Sat. **3**: 209.
— and Eclecticism in France. Month, **6**: 346, 439.
— Church Review's Defense of. (O. A. Brownson) Cath. World, **7**: 95.
— Philosophy of. (Mrs. W. Minot) No. Am. **85**: 19. — (F. Bowen) No. Am. **53**: 1. — (O. A. Brownson) Chr. Exam. **21**: 33. — (Sir W. Hamilton) Ed. R. **50**: 194. — (F. Beasley) Meth. Q. **2**: 637. — (C. C. S. Farrar) De Bow, **5**: 58–346. — Brit. Q. **5**: 289. — (A. N. Littlejohn) Am. Church R. **5**: 169. — Am. Q. **10**: 291. — Selec. Ed. R. **3**: 310. — For. Q. **1**: 358. — Chr. R. **3**: 590. **4**: 21. — Mo. R. **119**: 37. — (O. A. Brownson) Cath. World, **5**: 333. — Am. Church R. **20**: 374. — (C. Hodge) Princ. **28**: 331.
— — Brownson on. (F. A. Henry) Am. Church R. **19**: 532.
— Psychology of. (J. Day) Chr. Q. Spec. **7**: 89. — Meth. Q. **1**: 336. — (W. D. Wilson) Am. Church R. **9**: 38, 358.
— Ste. Beuve's Sketch of. Ev. Sat. **3**: 609.
— Works of. Ed. R. **93**: 219. Same art. Ecl. M. **23**: 187. — Dub. Univ. **49**: 428. — No. Brit. **25**: 349.
Cousin Amy. (R. Hannay) St. James, **20**: 384.
Cousin Carl. (C. Bernhard) Colburn, **106**: 368–473. **107**: 75–192.
Cousin Fanny; a Tale. (C. Clarke) Temp. Bar, **23**: 249.
Cousin Felix; a Story. (B. M. Butt) Temp. Bar, **62**: 337.
Cousin Geoffrey. (A. La Forge) Overland, **10**: 403.
Cousin Harry. (M. Norris) Sharpe, **28**: 195.
Cousin Helen; a Tale. So. Lit. Mess. **5**: 606.
Cousin in Need. House. Words, **12**: 381.
Cousin Jean. (E. B. Horsbrugh) Colburn, **160**: 413.
Cousin John's Property. Blackw. **84**: 709. Same art. Liv. Age, **60**: 195.
Cousin Julian; a Story. St. James, **2**: 331.
Cousin Kate. (S. Beauchamp) Tinsley, **24**: 1.
Cousin Phillis; a Story. (E. C. Gaskell) Cornh. **8**: 619, 688. **9**: 51, 187. Same art. Liv. Age, **80**: 3–494.
Cousin Tom. Liv. Age, **20**: 265.
Cousin Tom and the New Curate; a Sketch. (C. Clarke) Temp. Bar, **18**: 113.
Cousins. Liv. Age, **75**: 167. — Dub. Univ. **8**: 27.
— Marriage of. (G. H. Darwin) J. Statis. Soc. **38**: 153, 344.
Coussins, Jonathan. (R. Waddy) Meth. M. **29**: 289.
Coulton, D. T. Fortune. New Q. **1**: 274.
Coutts, Lady Burdett. *See* Burdett-Coutts.
Coutts, Thomas. Bank. M. (N. Y.) **2**: 525.
Coutts & Co.'s Banking House. (W. Chambers) Chamb. J. **51**: 705.
Coutts Family of Edinburgh and Lond. Lond. Soc. **8**: 358
Couture, Thomas, the Painter. Appleton, **18**: 349.
— Letters on. Art J. **31**: 253.
— on Art. Cath. World, **6**: 653.
Covenant, English Church, 1654. Cong. Q. **4**: 21.
— of Church at Taunton, Eng., 1654. Cong. M. **22**: 441.
— — at Windsor, Conn., 1647. Cong. Q. **4**: 168.
— of Greece, Colquhoun on. Cong. M. **1**: 694.
— of Salt. Evang. R. **18**: 532.
— of Works. Cong. M. **5**: 349, 406.
— Old, History of. Ecl. M. **48**: 353.
— or Testament, Is the English Bible a? Lond. Q. **8**: 453.
— Second Set of Tables of. Dub. Univ. **8**: 211.

Covenants, The. (R. B. C. Howell) Chr. R. 19: 590. — Danv. Q. 2: 35.
— Kelly on. Ecl. R. 114: 65.
Covenanter, Perils and Escapes of a. Tait, n. s. 6: 433.
Covenanters, Scottish. (P. Bayne) Contemp. 25: 683. — (E. Lawrence) Harper, 46: 103.
— and the Deeds of Montrose. Tait, n. s. 5: 198, 434.
— and Montrose, Napier on. Ecl. R. 70: 1. — Mo. R. 146: 205.
— and the Cameronians. Blackw. 6: 169.
— Charles II. and Argyll. Contemp. 25: 683. Same art. Liv. Age, 125: 643. — (W. S. Drysdale) Am. Presb. R. 14: 109.
— Fifty Years' Struggle of. Liv. Age, 67: 108.
— Martyrs, Heroes, and Bards of. Ecl. R. 97: 335.
— Mark Macrabin. Blackw. 6: 513, 663. 7: 48, 297, 374.
— of North of Scotland. Brit. Q. 4: 325.
— Simpson on Traditions of. Mo. R. 163: 121.
Covenanters' Night Hymn. (D. M. Moir) Blackw. 65: 244.
Covent Garden, London. All the Year, 28: 461. 29: 54.
— Flower Market of. Once a Week, 28: 566.
— Lease of a Pasture in. Arch. 30: 494.
— Market of. Cornh. 5: 319.
Covent-Garden Theater and the Royal Italian Opera. Macmil. 39: 255.
Coventry, Sophia. Lond. Soc. 5: 353.
— Ancient. Penny M. 13: 129.
— and Wales, Princes of. Antiquary, 2: 89.
— Day at. Tinsley, 3: 376.
— Tapestry in St. Mary's Hall. (G. Scharf) Arch. 36: 438.
Coventry Mysteries. Mo. R. 110: 1. — Penny M. 11: 365.
Coverdale, Miles. Cong. M. 8: 337, 393, 449. 23: 677.
— Life of. (S. F. Smith) Chr. R. 7: 535. — Chr. Obs. 40: 658, 742, 785.
Coverley, Sir Roger de. Quar. 90: 285. Same art. Ecl. M. 26: 76. Same art. Liv. Age, 33: 385. — Penny M. 12: 1-489.
Covetousness. (C. C. Shackford) Mo. Rel. M. 50: 51. — Ecl. R. 64: 189, 248.
— Dick on. (W. Hosmer) Am. Meth. M. 22: 202.
— Harris on. Chr. R. 1: 612.
— Illustrations of. Cong. M. 22: 16, 231, 779.
— in the Christian Church. Cong. M. 19: 633.
Covin's Revenge. Cornh. 38: 445.
Cow, our rural Divinity. (J. Burroughs) Galaxy, 23: 43.
— with the Iron Tail. House. Words, 2: 145.
Cows, Alderney. (H. D. Inglis) Tait, n. s. 1: 351.
— Jersey. Galaxy, 8: 312.
Cow-Chace; a Poem. (J. Andre) Am. Bibliop. 2: 8, 54.
Cow Hunt; an Irish Tale. Dub. Univ. 42: 695.
Cow-Tree of America. Penny M. 5: 166.
Coward by Profession. Dub. Univ. 1: 123.
Coward College, London. Cong. M. 17: 1, 129.
Cowardice and Courage. Dub. Univ. 67: 586. 68: 207.
Cowed People, Thoughts on. (A. K. H. Boyd) Fraser, 65: 35. Same art. Ecl. M. 55: 313.
Cowes and the Amateur Fleet. Belgra. 15: 74.
Cowles, George, Memoirs of. Am. Q. Reg. 10: 278.
Cowles, Samuel H., Memoirs of. (J. Richards) Chr. Mo. Spec. 10: 1.
Cowley, Abraham. (Mrs. S. C. Hall) Nat. M. 2: 201. — Cornh. 34: 718. Same art. Liv. Age, 132: 50. — No. Brit. 6: 365. — (J. H. Bassett) Am. Whig R. 6: 29.
— Familiar Letters of. Fraser, 13: 395. 14: 234.
— a Metaphysical Poet. St. James, 23: 209.
— Poems. (W. C. Bryant) No. Am. 124: 368. — Chr. Rem. 38: 457. — Retros. 15: 351.
Cowley-Wellesley Family. Dub. Univ. 56: 655.
Cowling Castle, Kent. Penny M. 9: 297.
Cowpens, Battle of. Hist. M. 12: 356.
— — a Poem. (T. D. English) Harper, 22: 163.
Cowper, Mary, Lady, Diary of. Fraser, 69: 566. — Tait, n. s. 14: 34.
Cowper, Spencer, Trial of. Blackw. 90: 19. — House. Words, 14: 385.
Cowper, William. (W. H. Barnes) Meth. Q. 28: 580. — (M. M. G. Dana) Hours at Home, 3: 365. — (A. H. Clough) Good Words, 7: 209. — (G. Smith) Canad. Mo. 4: 213. — (G. W. Forrest) Temp. Bar, 59: 212. — Blackw. 109: 763. Same art. Liv Age, 110: 67. — (D. H. Hill) Land We Love, 2: 123, 206. — Ecl. M. 76: 365. — Appleton, 24: 175. — Ecl. R. 113: 335. — Ev. Sat. 1: 106. — Knick. 44: 174. — Nat. M. 6: 537. — Nat. R. 1: 31. — No. Brit. 22: 225. Same art. Ecl. M. 34: 108. — Liv. Age, 43: 483. — Penny M. 10: 149. — Portfo.(Den.) 16: 392.
— and Lady Austen. Chamb. J. 15: 145.
— and Burns, Lecture on. (E. Elliott) Tait, n. s. 9: 357.
— and his Writings. Nat. Q. 7: 246.
— and Pope. Macmil. 24: 217. Same art. Liv. Age, 110: 376.
— and Rousseau. Cornh. 32: 439. Same art. Ecl. M. 85: 660. Same art. Liv. Age, 127: 323.
— and Shelley. Hogg, 4: 257.
— as a Satirist. Temp. Bar, 36: 457. Same art. Ecl. M. 80: 64.
— Bruce's Edition of Works of. Liv. Age, 86: 563. — Ecl. M. 66: 338.
— Cowperiana. Chr. Obs. 17: 585, 790. 18: 226, 363.
— Defense of, against Monthly Review. Colburn, 3: 11.
— Hayley's Life of. (F. Jeffrey) Ed. R. 4: 273. — Chr. Obs. 2: 357, 417. 4: 38, 101, 165. 5: 84.
— Insanity of. Liv. Age, 57: 5.
— Letters of, Quar. Review on. Chr. Obs. 24: 508. 25: 23.
— Life and Works of. (W. B. O. Peabody) No. Am. 38: 1. — (E. T. Channing) No. Am. 44: 29. — (F. Jeffrey) Ed. R. 2: 64. — (W. P. Lunt) Chr. Exam. 27: 333. — (W. Phillips) No. Am. 2: 233. — (M. P. Braman) Chr. Mo. Spec. 7: 452. — (R. Robbins) Chr. Q. Spec. 5: 568. — (H. T. Tuckerman) So. Lit. Mess. 6: 838. — Quar. 16: 117. — Selec. Ed. R. 2: 118. — Mus. 23: 481. 29: 7. — Portfo.(Den.) 22: 95. — Quar. 107: 168. Same art. Ecl. M. 50: 1. Same art. Liv. Age, 64: 579.
— Memoir of early Life. (E. T. Channing) No. Am. 5: 48.
— Memoirs of. Ecl. R. 24: 313. 63: 265.
— Poems. Fraser, 64: 700. Same art. Liv. Age, 72: 259. — St. James, 24: 373.
— — New Aldine Edition. (J. Dennis) Fortn. 3: 337.
— Poetry and Letters of. Am. Bib. Repos. 2d s. 2: 449.
— Private Correspondence of. (H. Ware) No. Am. 19: 435. — Chr. Exam. 1: 454. — Quar. 30: 185. — Westm. 2: 48. — Mus. 4: 121. — Chr. Mo. Spec. 2: 407, 465. 6: 638. — Mo. R. 105: 172. — (R. Heber) Quar. 30: 185. — Colburn, 10: 90. — Ecl. R. 39: 193.
— Recent Lives of. (T. Arnold) Ed. R. 63: 337.
— Southey's Life of. Fraser, 14: 69. — Mo. R. 139: 565.
— The Task, Essays on. Chr. Obs. 17: 300, 374. 18: 21, 87, 162.
— Taylor's Life of. Ecl. R. 58: 89. — Fraser, 7: 482. — Meth. M. 56: 342. — Chr. Obs. 33: 225, 286, 662.
— Visit to the Home of. Ecl. M. 15: 423.
Cowper, William, Bishop, Account of. Chr. Obs. 8: 133.
Cowslip-Gathering. Chamb. J. 23: 258.
Cox, David. (J. T. Bunce) Cong. 6: 665, 736. — (B. Champneys) Portfo. 4: 89. — (F. Wedmore) Gent. M. n. s. 20: 330. — Art J. 9: 123.
— Loan Collection, Liverpool. (J. B. Atkinson) Portfo. 7: 9.
— Paintings of. Dub. Univ. 53: 747.
Cox, Francis A. Address at Newton, Mass., Aug. 19, 1835. Chr. R. 1: 15.
— and Hoby's Travels. Chr. R. 1: 455.

Cox, Melville B. (N. Bangs) Am. Meth. M. **16**: 1.
Cox, Ross. Adventures to Columbia River. Am. Mo. R. **2**: 1.
Cox and Five. Lond. Soc. **7**: 304.
Coxe, Arthur C. Apollos; or the Way of God. (J. W. Nevin) Mercersb. **21**: 5.
— Essay on the Prot. Episcopal Church. O. & N **7**: 311.
Coxe, William, Archdeacon, Life and Works of. Quar. **50**: 88. — Select J. **3**: 185. — Mus. **24**: 168.
Coxsackie, N.Y., Subsidence of Land at. (W. B. Dwight) Am. J. Sci. **91**: 12.
Coyote. (Bret Harte) Overland, **3**: 93.
Coyotes, Adventures with, in Central America. Temp. Bar, **23**: 66.
Coyote Cañon. (L. Kipe) Overland, **9**: 27.
Coyote Hill, Literary Society of. (E. W. Drummond) Lakeside, **5**: 453.
Cozy Nook. (Mrs. S. C. Hall) St. James, **1**: 121.
Crab, Embryology of Limulus. (A. S. Packard, jr.) Am. Natural. **7**: 675.
— Fiddler, Early Larval Stages of. (A. S. Packard, jr.) Am. Natural. **15**: 784.
— Green. (J. G. Wood) Once a Week, **7**: 181.
— Horsefoot. (S. Lockwood) Am. Natural. **4**: 257.
— Spider. (E. Jesse) Once a Week, **1**: 29.
— Why does it go sideways? (R. B. Roosevelt) Appleton, **25**: 325.
Crabs. Sharpe, **40**: 65. — House. Words, **10**: 176. — (S. Lockwood) Pop. Sci. Mo. **5**: 191. — (A. C. Wheeley) Once a Week, **17**: 667. — (A. Wilson) Colburn, **157**: 194.
— and Prawns. Chamb. J. **44**: 504. Same art. Ev. Sat. **4**: 257.
— Gossip about. Chamb. J. **58**: 501.
— Hermit, Instinct in. (A. Agassiz) Am. J. Sci. **110**: 290.
— Something about. (S. Lockwood) Am. Natural. **3**: 261.
— Tree-Climbing. Nat. M. **11**: 443.
Crab Fishing. Penny M. **6**: 324.
Crab Story. Lond. Soc. **40**: 41.
Crabbe, Geo. (G. Gilfillan) Tait, n. s. **14**: 140. Same art. Ecl. M. **11**: 1. — (S. C. Hall) Art J. **17**: 373. Same art. Ecl. M. **66**: 216. Same art. Ev. Sat. **1**: 48. — (G. E. Woodberry) Atlan. **45**: 624. — Peop. J. **11**: 1. — (F. Laurence) Sharpe, **12**: 21. Same art. Ecl. M. **21**: 64. — (L. Stephen) Ev. Sat. **17**: 478. — Ecl. M. **65**: 343.
— The Borough. (W. Gifford) Quar. **4**: 281. — Chr. Obs. **10**: 502. — Ecl. R. **11**: 546. — Portfo.(Den.) **4**: 451.
— Campbell and Southey. Tait, n. s. **1**: 161, 393, 668.
— Life of. (J. G. Lockhart) Quar. **50**: 468. — New Eng. M. **8**: 215.
— Life and Poems. Westm. **30**: 316. — Nat. R. **8**: 1. Same art. Liv. Age, **60**: 529. — Mo. R. **135**: 101. — (O. W. B. Peabody) No. Am. **39**: 135. — New York R. **1**: 96. — Ecl. M. **22**: 424. — Select J. **4**: 1. — Westm. **30**: 316. — Meth. Q. **1**: 460, 514. — Ed. R. **60**: 255. — Ecl. R. **59**: 253.
— Poems. (F. Jeffrey) Ed. R. **12**: 131. **16**: 30. — Mus. **13**: 625. **22**: 626. **23**: 132. **24**: 477. **25**: 579. — (F. Sheldon) No. Am. **115**: 48. — (L. Stephen) Cornh. **30**: 454. Same art. Liv. Age, **123**: 403. — Ecl. R. **9**: 40. — St. James, **23**: 677. — Tait, n. s. **1**: 161. — Lond. M. **3**: 484.
— Posthumous Tales. (J. G. Lockhart) Quar. **52**: 184.
— Subjects of his Poetry. (F. Jeffrey) Selec. Ed. R. **1**: 271.
— Tales of the Hall. Ecl. R. **16**: 1240. **31**: 114. — (F. Jeffrey) Ed. R. **20**: 277. **32**: 118. — Blackw. **5**: 469. — Mo. R. **90**: 225. — Chr. Obs. **18**: 650. — Ecl. M. **63**: 416.
— Works of. Ecl. R. **60**: 305.
Crabbed Age and Youth; an Essay. Cornh. **37**: 351.
Crabbed Age and Youth; a Poem. (E. C. Stedman) Putnam, **16**: 255.
Crack Shot; from the Russian of Pushkin. (J. A. O'Shea) Tinsley, **27**: 314.
Cracked Tumbler; a Tale. Temp. Bar, **54**: 62.
Cracow. (J. Mazzini) Ecl. M. **10**: 424. — Brit. & For. R. **1**: 411. — (J. Mazzini) Peop. J. **3**: 13.
— Fate of. Brit. & For. R. **4**: 498.
— in 1845–46. Ed. R. **85**: 261.
— Occupation of, by Austria. For. Q. **18**: 418. — Brit. & For. R. **2**: 653.
— Recent Occurrences in. Brit. & For. R. **10**: 575.
— Scenes and Customs in. Dub. Univ. **58**: 145.
Cradle and Cross. (E. Cook) Cath. World, **28**: 418.
— Carved, of the Queen. (W. G. Rogers) Art J. **2**: 241.
Cradle Songs, German. (A. Schwartz) Macmil. **35**: 153.
Cradock Family. Hist. M. **1**: 41.
— Notes on. (W. H. Whitmore) N. E. Reg. **10**: 231.
Cradock Genealogy. (F. Brinley) N. E. Reg. **8**: 25. — (W. H. Whitmore) N. E. Reg. **9**: 123.
Cradock Nowell. (R. D. Blackmore) Macmil. **12**: 32–473. **13**: 36–504. **14**: 105–280.
Craft, William and Ellen. Chamb. J. **15**: 174.
Crafts, William, Eulogy on. (J. Sparks) No. Am. **24**: 473.
— Fugitive Writings. So. R. **1**: 503.
Crafts and Craftsmen, Mediæval and modern. Ecl. Engin. **15**: 410.
Craftsmen's Associations in France. (W. H. Browne) So. R. n. s. **1**: 95.
Crag-Fast. Chamb. J. **29**: 280.
Craig, Isabel, Poems of. Dub. Univ. **53**: 403.
Craig, Sir Thomas. Westm. **1**: 274. — Blackw. **2**: 383.
Craigallan Castle. Tait, n. s. **17**: 599, 659. **18**: 11–525.
Craigie, Lawrence. Hogg, **10**: 487.
Craik, Dinah Muloch. (A. B. Harrison) Overland, **11**: 537. — Brit. Q. **44**: 32. Same art. Ecl. M. **67**: 513. — Victoria, **28**: 479. Same art. Liv. Age, **133**: 371. — Colburn, **95**: 399.
— Head of the Family. Agatha's Husband. Ed. R. **97**: 380.
— Life for a Life. Chr. Rem. **38**: 305.
— Novels. No. Brit. **29**: 466.
— Olive; a Novel. Chamb. J. **15**: 4.
— Riverston. New Q. **7**: 62.
Cram. Nature, **9**: 501. — (W. S. Jevons) Mind, **2**: 193. Same art. Sup. Pop. Sci. Mo. **1**: 18.
Crammer, Life with a. Chamb. J. **56**: 139.
Cramming. Colburn, **169**: 267.
Crampton, Sir Philip, with portrait. Dub. Univ. **15**: 613.
Crampton's Clinical Lecture. Dub. Univ. **7**: 163.
Cranach, Lucas. (F. Schaller) So. M. **12**: 78.
Cranberry and its Allies. Once a Week, **9**: 232.
— Culture of. Land We Love, **4**: 156.
Cranborne Chase, Story of. All the Year, **34**: 302. — Lond. M. **17**: 309.
Crane, George, Obituary of. (S. W. Roberts) J. Frankl. Inst. **41**: 214.
Crane Family. N. E. Reg. **27**: 76.
Crane, as a Dish in England. (S. Pegge) Arch. **2**: 171.
— in Britain. Chamb. J. **33**: 355.
— Trumpet of. (F. Buckland) Pop. Sci. Mo. **9**: 137.
Cranes of Ibycus; Poem from Schiller. Blackw. **18**: 302.
— Sandhill and Whooping, Convolution of the Trachea in. (T. S. Roberts) Am. Natural. **14**: 108.
Cranfield, Edward. Am. Q. Reg. **15**: 163.
Cranford. (E. C. Gaskell) House. Words, **4**: 265–588. **5**: 55. **6**: 390, 413. **7**: 108, 277.
— Cage at. (E. C. Gaskell) All the Year, **10**: 332. Same art. Liv. Age, **80**: 17.
Crania, American, Morton's. (J. Wyman) No. Am. **51**: 173. — Am. J. Sci. **38**: 314.
— Ancient Egyptian. (S. G. Morton) Am. J. Sci. **48**: 268.

Crania, Britannica. Anthrop. R. **6**: 52.
— Distortions of. (D. Wilson) Canad. J. n. s. **7**: 399.
— Measurement of. (J. Wyman) Anthrop. R. **6**: 345.
Cranial Forms, Ethnic Significance of. (D. Wilson) Canad. J. n. s. **6**: 414.
Cranial Measurements. (L. Tait) Nature, **5**: 463.
Craniological Controversy. Blackw. **1**: 35, 365. **10**: 73.
Craniologist, A. (J. E. Cooke) Harper, **54**: 227.
Craniologist's Review; Napoleon's Head. Blackw. **3**: 146, 298.
— Greek Heads. Blackw. **3**: 298.
Craniology. U. S. Lit. Gaz. **6**: 124. — Blackw. **10**: 73.
— Results of Rage for. Chr. Obs. **14**: 726. **15**: 22.
See Phrenology.
Cranioscopy. Anthrop. R. **6**: 386. — Portfo.(Den.) **27**: 353.
Cranium, Human, Deformations of. (R. Knox) Anthrop. R. **1**: 271.
Crank, Properties of the. J. Frankl. Inst. **35**: 334.
Crank Pins and Journals. (W. D. Marks) J. Frankl. Inst. **105**: 233.
Cranmer, Thomas, Archbishop. (J. J. Blunt) Quar. **47**: 366. — Penny M. **2**: 103. — Am. Meth. M. **6**: 14.
— and Anglican Church. (O. W. Wight) Univ. Q. **9**: 144.
— and the English Reformation. Lond. Q. **41**: 1.
— Character of. (F. W. Holland) Chr. Exam. **55**: 63. — (T. B. Macaulay) Ed. R. **48**: 106. — (A. P. Peabody) Chr. Exam. **7**: 21.
— Family History of. (J. G. MacLeod) Month, **32**: 46.
— La Bos's Life of. Am. Meth. M. **18**: 1.
— Latimer, and Ridley, with portraits. Ecl. M. **51**: 131.
— Letter relating to Catherine of Arragon and Anne Boleyn. Arch. **18**: 77.
— Life of. Quar. **47**: 366. — Ed. R. **54**: 312. — Chr. Exam. **30**: 115. — Mo. R. **126**: 223. — Liv. Age, **2**: 116.
— Macaulay on. (W. Peet) Am. Church R. **6**: 262.
— Theology of. (J. Hunt) Contemp. **12**: 199.
Crannoge found in Drumkeery Lough, Ireland. (R. Harkness) Arch. **39**: 483.
Cranston, John and Thomas. Am. Q. Reg. **15**: 165.
Cranworth, Lord. Am. Law R. **3**: 178.
Crapelet, G. A. Le Combat de trente Bretons. Retros. **16**: 353.
Crapoune, Adam de. Chamb. J. **32**: 43. — St. James, **47**: 205.
Craque-o'-Doom. (M. H. Catherwood) Lippinc. **27**: 350, 443, 564. **28**: 31, 135.
Crashaw, Richard, Poetry of. (H. Southern) Retros. **1**: 225. — Chr. Disc. **5**: 81. — (M. F. Egan) Cath. World, **32**: 138. — (J. A. Nolan) Am. Cath. Q. **6**: 445.
Crater, Large, in Japan. (J. Milne) Pop. Sci. R. **19**: 336.
— of Asosan, Japan. (J. Milne) Ecl. M. **95**: 746.
Craters, Formation of. (G. P. Scrope) Am. J. Sci. **73**: 346. **74**: 217.
Cravat, Art of tying. Chamb. J. **43**: 43.
Cravats, Concerning. All the Year, **2**: 368.
Craven, Mrs. Augustus. Fleurange, Comparison with Middlemarch. Cath. World, **17**: 775.
— A Sister's Story. (M. C. Bishop) 19th Cent. **5**: 849. Same art. Liv. Age, **141**: 739. — (W. L. Kingsley) New Eng. **31**: 111. — Cath. World, **7**: 707. — Dub. R. **63**: 39. — Blackw. **104**: 165. Same art. Liv. Age, **98**: 579.
— Veil withdrawn. (J. McCarthy) Cath. World, **23**: 158.
Craven, Countess of. (Mrs. Mathews) Bentley, **18**: 249.
Craven, W. Discourses. Ed. R. **2**: 437.
Craven, Legend of. Blackw. **25**: 1.
Cravens of Cravenscroft. St. James, **29**: 1–521. **30**: 1–629. **31**: 1–517. **32**: 1–241.
Craven Co., S. C., History of. So. Q. **25**: 377.
Crawford, Alexander, Lord. Argo. Dub. Univ. **87**: 756
Crawford, George W., Portrait of. Am. Whig R. **10**: 1.
Crawford, John; a Poem. (J. Hogg) Fraser, **4**: 422.
Crawford, Thomas. (S. Eliot) Am. Church R. **11**: 32. — (G. S. Hillard) Atlan. **2**: 64. **24**: 40. — Liv. Age, **56**: 274.
— and his last Works. Art J. **7**: 41.
— Orpheus. (C. Sumner) with plate, Dem. R. **12**: 451.
Crawford, William H., Character and Life of. So. Lit. Mess. **3**: 262, 273. **5**: 361.
— Exposition of, 1831. Niles's Reg. **41**: 41, 65.
— Life and Times of. (J. B. Cobb) Am. Whig R. **13**: 193, 475.
Crawford's Consistency. (H. James, jr.) Scrib. **12**: 569.
Crawley, Lt.-Col., Court-Martial Trial of, 1864. Brit. Q. **39**: 389.
Crawshaw Sisterhood. (G. Percival) St. James, **37**: 551.
Crawshay, Robert, Portrait of. Pract. M. **2**: 81.
Crayfish. (E. R. Lankester) Nature, **21**: 353. Same art. Pop. Sci. Mo. **16**: 789.
— Philosophy of. 19th Cent. **8**: 622.
Crayons, Preparation of. J. Frankl. Inst. **9**: 94.
— Red, How to make. (A. F. Lomet) J. Frankl. Inst. **5**: 157.
Crayon Papers. (W. Irving) Bentley, **6**: 24, 159.
Cream from Milk, Obtaining. (G. Carter) J. Frankl. Inst. **16**: 125.
Creation. (W. K. Clifford) Fortn. **23**: 465. Same art. Pop. Sci. Mo. **7**: 268. — (R. Martineau) Theo. R. **5**: 1, 224, 334. — (E. P. Peabody) Ch. Exam. **16**: 174. — Bib. R. **1**: 89.
— a Series of Supernatural Growths. (T. Lewis) Meth. Q. **25**: 207.
— Agassiz on, and Unity of the Race. Princ. **41**: 5.
— and Cosmogony. (T. G. Apple) Mercersb. **24**: 123.
— and the Fall of Man. Chr. Disc. **1**: 102, 169.
— and the Flood, Colenso's Views on. Theo. R. **1**: 161.
— and modern Science. (C. B. Waring) Scrib. **15**: 817.
— and Universe, Theories of. (G. Tayler) De Bow, **4**: 177.
— Argument from Design. Dub. Univ. **50**: 209. Same art. Ecl. M. **42**: 250.
— Bible Account of. (W. W. Kinsley) University Q. **3**: 240.
— Chaldean Account of. (P. N. Lynch) Cath. World, **24**: 490.
— Cuvier and Blainville on. Brit. Q. **24**: 365.
— Days of, What are they? (W. D. Strappini) Month, **41**: 22.
— de Nihilo. (R. O. Williams) Univ. Q. **34**: 401.
— Divine Plan in. Bib. R. **1**: 5.
— Epoch of. Lit. & Theo. R. **4**: 526.
— — Lord's. New Eng. **9**: 510. — Theo. & Lit. J. **4**: 346.
— Evolution in. (E. S. Wilson) Am. Church R. **27**: 182.
— Faith in. (S. N. Callender) Mercersb. **17**: 593.
— Genealogy of. Ecl. M. **55**: 21.
— Hequembourg's Plan of. Theo. & Lit. J. **12**: 477.
— History of, Haeckel's. Internat. R. **3**: 537. — Nature, **3**: 102.
— in Theology, Philology, and Geology. Kitto, **16**: 66.
— Henry James on. (J. F. Clarke) Chr. Exam. **75**: 212.
— Laws of — Ultimate Science. (T. Gray) J. Spec. Philos. **14**: 219.
— Tayler Lewis on. (J. D. Dana) Bib. Sac. **13**: 80, 631. **14**: 388, 461. — (D. N. Lord) Theo. & Lit. J. **8**: 271, 445, 529.
— Man's Place in. (C. A. Bartol) Radical, **2**: 663.
— Meditations on. (H. Alford) Good Words, **4**: 355.
— Miracle of. (J. H. McIlvaine) Princ n. s. **1**: 830.
— Mosaic Account of. (E. P. Barrows) Bib. Sac. **13**: 743. **14**: 61. — (J. D. Dana) New Eng. **16**: 74. — (J. C. Fisher) Ed. New Philos. J. **67**: 214. — (T Hill) Bib. Sac. **32**: 303.

Creation, Mosaic Account of. (E. A. Lawrence) Bib. Sac. 27: 454. — Kitto, 5: 186. — (S. H. Thompson) Meth. Q. 12: 497. — Chr. Obs. 26: 198. 31: 76. 42: 525. — Meth. M. 36: 425.
— and Geology. (O. Föckler) Meth. Q. 26: 187. — (E. Hitchcock) Cong. M. 19: 82. — (D. C. McLaren) Theo. & Lit. J. 4: 346. 12: 133. — (D. N. Lord) Theo. & Lit. J. 4: 529. 7: 119. 9: 251. — (J. O. Means) Bib. Sac. 12: 83, 323. — New Eng. 9: 510. — Theo. & Lit. J. 7: 119. 10: 97. — Ecl. M. 77: 542. — Westm. 68: 176. 69: 260.
— — and Heathen Accounts of. (J. S. Blackie) Good Words, 2: 553. Same art. Theo. Ecl. 1: 77.
— — and Hugh Miller. (J. Clark) Mercersb. 9: 620.
— — Scientific. Am. Presb. R. 7: 129.
— Natural History of. (E. Lankester) Ex. H. Lec. 3: 1. — U. S. Cath. M. 6: 229.
— — Vestiges of. (F. Bowen) No. Am. 60: 426. — (A. Gray) No. Am. 62: 465. — (J. H. Allen) Chr. Exam. 40: 333. — (Sir D. Brewster) No. Brit. 3: 470. 4: 487. Same art. Liv. Age, 6: 564. — Brit. Q. 1: 490. 3: 178. — (A. Sedgwick) Ed. R. 82: 1. Same art. Ecl. M. 6: 43. — Blackw. 57: 448. — Westm. 44: 152. 48: 130. — (A. B. Dod) Princ. 17: 505. — Ecl. R. 82: 59. — Fraser, 42: 355. — Am. Whig R. 1: 525. — Liv. Age, 4: 60. — (W. H. Allen) Meth. Q. 6: 292. — Chr. Obs. 51: 599. — Prosp. R. 1: 49. 2: 33.
— — — and its Reviewers. New Eng. 4: 113.
— — — Author of. Am. Whig R. 3: 168, 383.
— — — A Precursor of. (G. H. Lewes) Fraser, 56: 526.
— — — Sequel to. Am. J. Sci. 51: 250. — Liv. Age, 8: 442. — (J. H. Allen) Chr. Exam. 40: 333.
— Natural Theory of. (A. Agassiz) Nation, 8: 193.
— Noyes's Lectures on. (T. D. Howard) Unita. R. 13: 481.
— or Creature in Romans viii. 19–23. (A. N. Arnold) Bapt. Q. 1: 143.
— or Evolution, which? (T. Clarke) Lakeside, 1: 91.
— or Foundation. (S. R. Calthrop) Unita. R. 16: 1, 230.
— Powell's Essay on. Theo. & Lit. J. 8: 609.
— Record of. (C. Gooch) Kitto, 29: 339.
— Records of, Sumner's. Mo. R. 82: 276.
— Scientific Theories of. Ev. Sat. 11: 282.
— Scriptural Evidences of. Bib. R. 3: 81.
— Scripture Doctrine of. (M. Sanford) Univ. Q. 4: 392.
— Six Days of. (T. Hill) Chr. Exam. 59: 379. — (W. McCrombie) Kitto, 3: 159. — Am. Ch. Mo. 2: 204. — Brownson, 20: 204. — Good Words, 1: 636. — Meth. Q. 31: 581.
— — T. Lewis's View of. Am. Presb. R. 4: 469.
— Sixth Day of. Bost. R. 3: 68.
— Seventh Day of. (J. W. Colenso and R. Martineau) Theo. R. 10: 175, 599.
— Swedenborg's Theory of. (H. James) No. Am. 105: 89.
— Theory of. (F. Bowen) No. Am. 60: 264.
— Typical Forms in. (J. McCosh) Canad. J. n. s. 1: 528.
— — and Special Ends in, McCosh's. New Q. 5: 262. — Ecl. R. 103: 563. — Theo. & Lit. J. 9: 270. — Dub. Univ. 50: 209. Same art. Ecl. M. 42: 250.
— Week of. (W. Clifford) Dub. R. 88: 311. 89: 498.
— Wonders of. (E. Jesse) Once a Week, 17: 533.
Creations, Natural and spiritual. Theo. Repos. 2: 85.
Creative Forces. (W. W. Kinsley) Penn Mo. 7: 352.
Creator and Creature. (J. Rickaby) Month, 40: 386, 484. 41: 182, 536. 42: 346.
— Indications of, Whewell's. (Sir D. Brewster) No. Brit. 4: 364.
— Wisdom of, in Nature and Revelation. Mo. R. 131: 187.
Creature Worship. Month, 40: 219, 528.
Crebillon, the French Æschylus. Fraser, 44: 267. Same art. Ecl. M. 24: 223. Same art. Liv. Age, 31: 167. Same art. Internat. M. 4: 520.
Credit. (J. S. Crawley) No. Am. 90: 322. — Chamb. J. 40: 280.
— and Cash. Tait, n. s. 26: 17.
— and Crises. (B. Price) Fraser, 80: 207.
— as Substitute for Money. (L. H. Atwater) Princ. 34: 310.
— Currency, and Banking. Brit. Q. 27: 361.
— — and precious Metals. Bank. M. (N. Y.) 14: 417.
— Recent History of. (W. Newmarch) J. Statis. Soc. 21: 444.
— System of. Bank. M. (N. Y.) 11: 5.
— Nature and Power of. Bank. M. (L.) 22: 121.
— or ready Money? Chamb. J. 48: 9.
— Principles of. (C. F. Adams) Hunt, 2: 185.
— Public. (E. L. Godkin) Nation, 10: 52, 137. — (G. M. Weston) Bank. M. (N. Y.) 33: 769.
— — and private. Bank. M. (N. Y.) 24: 241.
Credit Banks, Organization of. (W. T. Thornton) Bank. M. (N. Y.) 30: 210.
Credit Foncier of France. Bank. M. (N. Y.) 29: 191, 666. 30: 5. 31: 7, 930.
Credit Institutions of Italy. (D. P. Bailey) Bank. M. (N. Y.) 35: 775.
Credit Mobilier. Republic, 1: 3, 49. — Mo. Rel. M. 49: 276.
— in Discredit. All the Year, 20: 57.
— in France. Bank. M. (L.) 16: 421, 481, 548. 17: 465. — Bank. M. (N. Y.) 10: 1, 446. 13: 43. 18: 137. — Nat. R. 4: 152.
— of America. (A. G. Sedgwick) Nation, 16: 53. — (S. Newcomb) No. Am. 117: 182. — (E. L. Godkin) Nation, 16: 68, 128, 160. — Scrib 7: 546.
Credit System. (S. Colwell) Bank. M. (N. Y.) 14: 753. — Dem. R. 2: 167. 3: 195. 5: 147. — Hunt, 42: 684.
— and the Currency. Penn Mo. 4: 822.
Creditors, Preferred. (C. A. Stackpole) Hunt, 7: 273, 527.
Credulity and Crime, Modern Instances of. Dub. Univ. Ecl. M. 34: 267.
— and Scepticism in History. (E. D. Sanborn) Am. Bib. Repos. 2d s. 12: 131.
— and Versatility. So. Lit. Mess. 4: 287.
— Modern Absurdities of. Chamb. J. 53: 470.
Credulous People. New Eng. M. 8: 285.
Creed and Doctrine. (T. G. Apple) Mercersb. 24: 99.
— and dogmatic Theology. (E. V. Gerhart) Mercersb. 18: 207.
— and Puritanism. (J. W. Nevin) Mercersb. 1: 585.
— Change of. (S. L. Bailey) Lakeside, 7: 244.
— Church's or Crown's, Foulkes on. Dub. R. 64: 269.
— Congregational, General Association, 1827. New Eng. 4: 153.
— Construction of. (J. W. Nevin) Mercersb. 15: 584.
— Foundations of, G. H. Lewes on. (I. M. Atwood) Univ. Q. 35: 177.
— Hopkins's Primitive. (A. Lamson) Chr. Exam. 20: 342.
— Inconsistency in. (W. R. French) Univ. Q. 20: 202.
— Necessity of. (N. S. Richardson) Am. Church R. 7: 337.
— New and old. (F. P. Cobbe) Theo. R. 4: 1, 241. 5: 26.
— of Christendom. (J. Martineau) Westm. 55: 429.
— — Greg on. Prosp. R. 7: 192.
— of the Early Christians. (A. P. Stanley) 19th Cent. 8: 207.
— of the Future; a Poem. Fraser, 91: 788.
— of a Layman. (F. Harrison) 19th Cent. 9: 455.
— Safest. (J. G. Adams) Univ. Q. 32: 22.
— to Faith, Change From. (G. E. Ellis) Mo. Rel. M. 39: 1.
Creeds. (F. W. Conrad) Evang. R. 18: 351. — (E. W. Gilman) Cong. Q. 4: 179. — (W. T. Moore) Chr. Q. 2: 1. — (B. U. Watkins) Chr. Q. 2: 461. — Bost. R. 1: 489.
— Ancient, and Family Covenants. (E. W. Gilman) Cong. Q. 11: 516.
— and the Church. (J. Martineau) Theo. R. 3: 296.

Creeds and Church Membership. (C. Cushing) Cong. Q. 19: 261.
— and Confessions. (A. M. Machar) Canad. Mo. 9: 134.
— — Use and Abuse of. Cong. M. 20: 382.
— and Creed-Subscription. Fraser, 102: 696.
— and Morality. (W. Kirkus) Theo. R. 4: 534.
— Antagonisms of. (P. Schaff) Contemp. 28: 836.
— as Tests of Church Membership. (K. Twining) New Eng. 32: 670.
— — of Fellowship among Christians. (S. Hayward) Cong. Q. 8: 382.
— Catholic, and Authority and Reason. (W. Adams) Am. Church R. 18: 206.
— Christian, and their Defenders. Westm. 76: 207.
— — Paraphrase of. Theo. Repos. 1: 136.
— Church. (J. F. Kendall) Am. Presb. R. 16: 605. — (J. Orton) Cong. Q. 5: 206. — (E. Pond) Bib. Sac. 29: 538. — (W. W. Woodworth) Cong. Q. 19: 249. — No. Brit. 48: 397.
— Duncan and Miller on. (C. Robinson) Chr. Exam. 2: 364.
— Essential Difference of. (M. G. Darling) Radical, 6: 363.
— Formation of. (J. P. Thompson) New Eng. 4: 265.
— Importance of. Bost. R. 3: 541.
— in Church and Chapel. (G. V. Smith) Contemp. 21: 283, 372.
— in Worship. Theo. R. 8: 237.
— Makers of. (O. A. Burgess) Chr. Q. 6: 62.
— of Christendom, Schaff's. (J. A. Brown) Luth. Q. 7: 618. — Mercersb. 24: 470. — So. R. n. s. 23: 448.
— — Second Advent and. (J.A.Brown) Bib. Sac. 24: 629.
— Old, and new Beliefs. Nat. R. 12: 151.
— Old and new. (W. P. Roberts) Good Words, 22: 522. — (F. Harrison) 19th Cent. 8: 526, 787.
— Origin and Use of. (S. Fuller) Am. Church R. 1: 352.
— Orthodox, Varieties of. Bost. R. 1: 517.
— Panic of. Ecl. R. 113: 480.
— Popular. Chr. Exam. 80: 1.
— Proper Limits of, Blaikie's. (J. A. Brown) Luth. Q. 3: 397.
— Relation of, to Christian Life. (J. M. Whiton) Cong. Q. 11: 28.
— Revision of. (E. L. Godkin) Nation, 30: 413.
— Subscription to, Ethics of. (W. Knight) Contemp. 20: 327. *See* Subscription.
— Swainson on the Nicene and Apostles'. Brit. Q. 28: 74. — Chr. Obs. 75: 728, 808.
— Use of. (J. G. Hall) Am. Bib. Repos. 3d s. 1: 577.
See Apostles'; Athanasian; Nicene; etc.
Creedmore, Story of. (F. Whittaker) Galaxy, 22: 258.
Creek Indians, Controversy with. Ann. Reg. 1: 42. 2: 85. 5: [123. — Niles's Reg. 16: supp. 101. 27: 222. 28: 14-412. 32: 89, 108. 36: 231, 257.
— Intruders on. Niles's Reg. 45: 138, 155, 189.
— Mission among. Am. Meth. M. 5: 232.
— Treaty with. Ann. Reg. 7: [94. — Niles's Reg. 28: 63. 14: 26. 30: 175, 254. 42: 116.
Cregan Curse. (W. H. Burdett) Lakeside, 7: 379.
Creichton, Capt. John. (H. Baldwin) Retros. 5: 238.
Crema and the Crucifix. Cornh. 35: 685. Same art. Liv. Age, 134: 182.
Cremation. (J. P. Pennefather) Dub. Univ. 83: 592. — (H. Thompson) Contemp. 23: 319, 553. — All the Year, 43: 127. — Appleton, 11: 619. — Dub. R. 79: 37. — Ecl. M. 42: 536. — Pract. M. 5: 64. — (W. Cochran) Victoria, 24: 226.
— and its Alternatives. (G. Bayles) Pop. Sci. Mo. 5: 225.
— and Burial of the Dead. (W. M. Wylie) Arch. 37: 455.
— — in the East. (F. R. Feudge) Lippinc. 13: 593.
— and contracted Burials. (R. Pennington) Anthrop. J. 4: 265.
— Chemistry of. Nature, 11: 33.
Cremation, Ethics of. (R. F. Clarke) Month, 24: 25.
— Fire-Burial among our Germanic Forefathers. (K. Blind) Fraser, 91: 730.
— in China. Cornh. 39: 335. Same art. Liv. Age, 141: 309.
— Merits of. (P. Fraser, jr.) Penn Mo. 5: 414.
— or Burial. (P. H. Holland) Contemp. 23: 477.
See Urn Burial.
Crémieux, Isaac Adolphe, with portrait. Ev. Sat. 9: 771.
Cremorne to Westminster, From. (P. Fitzgerald) Gent. M. n. s. 25: 203.
Creole, Case of the. So. Lit. Mess. 9: 11.
Creole, The; a Tale. So. Lit. Mess. 6: 434.
Creole Fancies. (W. C. Bates) O. & N. 7: 304.
Créqui, Marquise de, Souvenirs de. (J. W. Croker) Quar. 51: 391. — Select J. 4: 215.
Cresap, M., and Logan. (J. E. Cooke) N. Ecl. 6: 169.
Crescembeni, Giovanni Mario. Colburn, 11: 490.
Crescent and Cross, Conflict between. (J. I. Swander) Mercersb. 20: 28.
Cressey Family. (G. B. Blodgette) N. E. Reg. 31: 197.
Cressida. (B. Thomas) Lond. Soc. 33: 1-481.
Cresson, Elliott, and Pro-Slavery Colonization. Chr. Obs. 47: 275.
Cressy, Battle of. Penny M. 2: 326.
— and Agincourt, Visit to Fields of. (H. L. Long) Colburn, 83: 334-478. 84: 97-466. Same art. Ecl. M. 15: 362, 478. 16: 189.
— Narratives of. (G. F. Beltz) Arch. 28: 171.
— Poem on. (L. Moseley) Once a Week, 22: 337.
Cretaceous Rocks of England. (P. B. Brodie) Recr. Sci. 2: 297.
Cretans, St. Paul's Character of. Lond. M. 7: 637.
Crete. (E. H. Bunbury) Contemp. 1: 551. — All the Year, 12: 462. — Blackw. 121: 428.
— and the Cretans. (H. J. Warner) Chr. Exam. 82: 224.
— Daughter of. Chamb. J. 9: 181.
— Days in. (W. J. Stillman) Atlan. 20: 533. 21: 326. 22: 221.
— Heart of. Cornh. 22: 49. Same art. Ecl. M. 75: 280.
— Insurrection in, 1867. (W. J. Stillman) Nation, 3: 275. 4: 54, 76, 318. 5: 337. 7: 10. 8: 48. — (H. J. Warner) Nation, 4: 70. — Ev. Sat. 3: 233. — Fraser, 79: 291. — Hours at Home, 4: 554. — Macmil. 15: 257. — Mo. Rel. M. 39: 379.
— Labyrinth of. Penny M. 5: 278.
— Pashley's Travels in, 1834. Mo. R. 143: 45.
— Travels in. Brit. & For. R. 6: 540.
Crêtinism and Goître. Ecl. R. 104: 278.
Cretins and their Benefactor. Bentley, 31: 405. Same art. Ecl. M. 26: 201.
— Hospital for infant. Chamb. J. 9: 296.
— What has been done for. (L. P. Brockit) Atlan. 1: 410.
Cretineau-Joly, Jacques. (J. McSwiney) Month, 25: 205.
Creusot, Le, in France. Chamb. J. 45: 70.
Creuznach and its saline Cure. Lond. Soc. 16: 433.
Crewe, Day at. Chamb. J. 13: 391.
Crewe Hall. Antiquary, 3: 145.
Crichton, James, The Admirable. Bentley, 1: 416. — Colburn, 115: 414. — (J. D. Forbes) Good Words, 5: 67.
Cricket. Lond. Soc. 2: 114-441. 3: 82-530. 18: 422. 21: 319. — St. Paul's, 2: 549.
— as it was and is. Once a Week, 8: 718.
— at Lord's. Belgra. 15: 213.
— Early Forms of. (R. R. Macgregor) Belgra. 39: 450.
— Eton and Harrow at Lord's. (R. Russell) Belgra. 24: 128.
— Fashionable. All the Year, 38: 508.
— History of. Bentley, 36: 171. — Temp. Bar, 6: 273.
— in America. (A. H. Outerbridge) Lippinc. 11: 593.
— in Canada. Canad. Mo. 14: 608.

Cricket in 1839 and 1867. (F. Gale) Once a Week, **17**: 226.
— in England. (H. Silver) Once a Week, **5**. 179.
— Morale of. Chamb. J. **54**: 298.
— on the Goodwins. Chamb. J. **36**: 212. Same art. Liv. Age, **71**: 421.
— Pursuit of, under Difficulties. All the Year, **6**: 33.
— Rural. Chamb. J. **57**: 401.
— Yorkshire Stories of. Lond. Soc. **31**: 411.
Cricket Legislation. Lond. Soc. **6**: 72, 136.
Cricketana. (R. Macgregor) Belgra. **42**: 84.
Cricketer, Fifty Years a. Lond. Soc. **30**: 193-417.
— Reminiscences of a. Lond. Soc. **8**: 248.
Cricketers, English, in Canada. Canad. Mo. **4**: 38.
Crime, Aids of Science in detecting. Chamb. J. **53**: 101.
— and Civilization. (S. Amos) Fortn. **2**: 319.
— and Consequence; a Tale. So. Lit. Mess. **2**: 749.
— and Credulity on the Continent. Dub. Univ. **45**: 27.
— and Creed, Statistics of. Cong. M. **26**: 995.
— and Criminal Law in France. Lond. Q. **8**: 92.
— and Criminals. (J. H. Fyfe) Good Words, **4**: 97. — (A. Shuman) Lakeside, **6**: 316.
— and English Law. Victoria, **32**: 68-240.
— and its Consequences. Dub. Univ. **34**: 383.
— and its Prevention. Lond. M. **23**: 246. — (J. Plummer) Victoria, **3**: 432.
— and its Punishment. (W. C. Taylor) Bentley, **6**: 476. **7**: 131. — Fraser, **20**: 689.
— — Beccaria on. O. & N. **10**: 245.
— — in the East. Hours at Home, **10**: 23.
— — in France in good old Times. St. James, **32**: 681.
— and Remedies. Chamb. J. **19**: 177. — Peop. J. **8**: 106.
— and its Repression. Penny M. **8**: 174.
— and its Treatment. Canad. Mo. **11**: 166.
— and Pauperism. (R. Everest) De Bow, **19**: 268.
— and Poverty in Cities. (J. W. Alexander) Princ. **17**: 606.
— and remarkable Trials in Scotland. Blackw. **63**: 293, 607.
— and Science. All the Year, **44**: 347, 372.
— as affected by good or bad Times. (J. Clay) J. Statis. Soc. **20**: 378.
— Automatism and. (O. W. Holmes) Atlan. **35**: 466.
— Capital, and Poverty. (E. Roscoe) Victoria, **21**: 561.
— Cause and Cure of. (E. C. Wines) Princ. n. s. **1**: 784.
— Causes of. (H. Seymour) Pop. Sci. Mo. **2**: 589.
— — and Prevention of. Ed. R. **48**: 411.
— — of its Increase. Blackw. **3**: 176. **55**: 583. **56**: 1. — Pamph. **15**: 27. **29**: 307.
— Characteristics of. Ecl. R. **85**: 232.
— Criminals, Punishment. (Lord De Mauley) Macmil. **29**: 145.
— Dangerous Classes in large Towns, Frégier on. Mo. R. **155**: 486.
— Dear Food and. Ecl. R. **90**: 393.
— Detection of. Cornh. **2**: 697. — Dub. R. **50**: 150.
— Education and. (J. B. Bittinger) Luth. Q. **5**: 481. — (J. Fletcher) J. Statis. Soc. **10**: 193. **11**: 344. **12**: 151, 189. — (G. R. Porter) J. Statis. Soc. **10**: 316. — (H. Rogers) Ed. R. **86**: 512. — (E. C. Tainsh) Am. J. Educ. **11**: 77. — Tait, n. s. **25**: 29. — Penny M. **4**: 206, 222. — (M. Tarver) West. J. **8**: 297. — De Bow, **18**: 409.
— — at North and South. De Bow, **16**: 578.
— — Church-Going, Intemperance and. (J. Clay) J. Statis. Soc. **20**: 22.
— English State Trials. Cornh. **6**: 351.
— Extenuation of. Cornh. **9**: 210.
— First and last. Blackw. **25**: 303.
— French Police. Colburn, **131**: 372.
— Hints on Increase of. Blackw. **3**: 176.
— How to be treated. (Lord Nugent) Peop. J. **3**: 233, 302, 362. **4**: 62-308. **5**: 107.
Crime in the Army. (P. Beaton) Good Words, **11**: 595.
— in 18th Century. (A. Andrews) Colburn, **105**: 78-175.
— in England, and its Treatment. Nat. R. **3**: 289.
— — in 1857-76. (L. Levi) J. Statis. Soc. **43**: 423.
— — Pike's History of. (H. C. Lea) Nation, **19**: 60.
— — Progress and Character of. Ecl. R. **88**: 645.
— — Statistics of. Penny M. **5**: 359.
— in England, Wales, and Ireland. Dub. R. **41**: 142. — Cong. **3**: 156, 233, 309.
— — Government Returns of. Dub. R. **28**: 330.
— — Judicial Statistics of. (J. T. Hammick) J. Statis. Soc. **30**: 375.
— — Statistics of, 1839-43. (W. Russell) J. Statis. Soc. **10**: 38.
— — — 1842-44. (F. G. P. Neison) J. Statis. Soc. **9**: 223.
— — — 1854-59. (T. B. L. Baker) J. Statis. Soc. **23**: 427.
— in France. Westm. **18**: 353. — Am. Alma. **1836**: 72. — Mo. R. **132**: 23.
— in Great Britain. Am. Alma. **1837**: 69.
— — Progress of. (J. Fletcher) J. Statis. Soc. **6**: 218.
— in large Towns. Tait, n. s. **20**: 165.
— in London, Causes of. Tait, n. s. **17**: 329.
— — Punishment of. Mo. R. **125**: 538.
— in Russia, Statistics of. (T. Michell) J. Statis. Soc. **27**: 369.
— in Scotland, how investigated. (W. Chambers) Fortn. **2**: 79.
— in the United States, Increase of; its Cause and Cure. (E. W. Hutter) Evang. R. **11**: 61.
— Increase and Causes of. Ecl. R. **55**: 313.
— — of Material Prosperity and. (J. H. Elliott) Hunt, **61**: 239.
— Insanity and. *See* Insanity and Crime.
— Machinery of, in England. Colburn, **40**: 487. **41**: 77. — Mus. **25**: 88.
— Material Prosperity, Moral Agents, and. (J. H. Elliott) J. Statis. Soc. **31**: 299.
— Medical Evidence of. Cornh. **7**: 338.
— Modern Philanthropy and. Westm. **91**: 437.
— Origin of. Ed. R. **35**: 342.
— — and Cure of. (J. G. McGee) Cath. World, **18**: 55.
— — in Society. (R. L. Dugdale) Atlan. **48**: 452, 735.
— Pecuniary, Cruelty of. Liv. Age, **136**: 508.
— Philosophy of. (F. G. Fairfield) Appleton, **15**: 15.
— — with Illustrations from History. Fraser, **33**: 7, 235
— Police Force, Consolidated, and Prevention of. (E. Chadwick) Fraser, **77**: 1.
— Prevention of. (E. Hill) J. Statis. Soc. **25**: 497. — No. Am. **9**: 288. — (H. Rogers) Ed. R. **86**: 512. — (W. C. Woodbridge) Chr. Mo. Spec. **8**: 192.
— — by the State. (W. Crofton) Good Words, **16**: 204.
— Progress of. Ecl. M. **10**: 249.
— — and Characteristics of. Ecl. R. **85**: 95, 232.
— Punishment and Prevention of. Cornh. **7**: 189.
— Rationale of. Dem. R. **20**: 49.
— Relation of Ignorance to. (R. Rantoul, jr.) No. Am. **47**: 311.
— Relations of Women to. (E. Van de Warker) Pop. Sci. Mo. **8**: 1, 334, 727.
— Repression of. Irish Q. **7**: 529.
— Responsibility of Society for Causes of. (J. B. Bittinger) Princ. **43**: 18.
— Suggestions for Repression of. Brit. Q. **52**: 57.
— Sources of. (E. C. Wines) Am. Presb. R. **12**: 558. — Irish Q. **3**: 299.
— Spontaneous and imitative. (E. V. Blake) Pop. Sci. Mo. **15**: 656.
— Statistics of. Penny M. **6**: 351. — Quar. **137**: 526.
— Suppression of. (Syd. Smith) Ed. R. **13**: 333.
— Thieves and Thieving. Cornh. **2**: 326. **6**: 640.
See Detection; Detectives; Convicts; Criminals; Juvenile Delinquency.

Crimes against Life, Increase of. (H. Dutton) New Eng. **2**: 346.
— and Trials, Remarkable, in Germany. (N. W. Senior) Ed. R. **82**: 318.
— Celebrated. Chr. Rem. **18**: 288.
— — Dumas's. For. Q. **30**: 36.
— State, Penalty of. (J. H. Allen) Chr. Exam. **79**: 282.
Crime of Abigail Tempest. (S. A. Weiss) Harper, **52**: 490.
Crime-Land Excursion. (A. O. Hall) Galaxy, **7**: 91.
Crimea, The, and its Inhabitants. Colburn, **105**: 127.
— Baktchi-Sarai and the Tartars of. Bentley, **37**: 279.
— Day's Sport in. Temp. Bar, **63**: 177–528.
— Five Days on Horseback in. Bentley, **40**: 64.
— Garrisons of. Fraser, **50**: 356. Same art. Ecl. M. **33** 327.
— History of, Romance of. Putnam, **7**: 144.
— Journal of a Tour in, 1856. Fraser, **54**: 407, 524.
— Letters on. (A. K. H. Boyd) Good Words, **4**: 557.
— A Month in. Bentley, **40**: 221.
— Mud Volcanoes and Salt Lakes in. (D. T. Ansted) Intel. Obs. **8**: 409.
— Notes from. Blackw. **118**: 720. Same art. Ecl. M. **86**: 218.
— Odessa and. Ed. R. **102**: 88.
— Religious Societies in. Chr. Obs. **56**: 412.
— Ten Days in, 1862. Macmil. **5**: 301.
— Tour in. Blackw. **80**: 430.
— Town Life in. Temp. Bar, **63**: 477.
— Travels in. Colburn, **103**: 253.
— Trip to. Bentley, **41**: 67, 190.
Crimean War. (A. W. Kinglake) Cornh. **7**: 268. — (J. H. Perry) Meth. Q. **16**: 51. — Bentley, **36**: 1, 107, 212. **37**: 331. — Blackw. **74**: 633, 769. **75**: 381. **76**: 599, 618. **77**: 112–740. **78**: 91–617. **79**: 232–486. **85**: 291, 449. **93**: 355. **104**: 699. **105**: 71. **117**: 451. — Brownson, **11**: 376. — Colburn, **99**: 379. **100**: 253–487. **102**: 253. — Dem. R. **34**: 373. **35**: 237, 331. — Dub. Univ. **43**: 379. **44**: 1, 509, 635. **45**: 103, 623, 742. **46**: 741. — Ed. R. **100**: 264. **101**: 261. **141**: 522. — Irish Q. **5**: 912. **6**: 140. — Liv. Age, **48**: 440. — Lond. Q. **4**: 203. **5**: 499. — New Q. **4**: 34, 295. **6**: 17. — No. Brit. **20**: 523. — Pioneer, **3**: 291. — Theo. & Lit. J. **7**: 500, 680. **8**: 342. **9**: 163.
— and its Opponents. Fraser, **52**: 479.
— and what is to come of it, 1854. Brit. Q. **20**: 248.
— and the Anglican Clergy. (P. Berry) Am. Church R. **8**: 379.
— Battle of the Alma. (Gen. F. E. Todleben) Cornh. **10**: 282. — Colburn, **127**: 468.
— — of Balaklava. Liv. Age, **49**: 607.
— — — Episode of. Ev. Sat. **5**: 626.
— — of Inkerman. (J. C. Paget) St. James, **36**: 14. — Bentley, **38**: 141.
— Bazancourt's History of. Colburn, **107**: 302. — Dub. Univ. **47**: 626. — Fraser, **54**: 97. — New Q. **5**: 330.
— Campaign in. Bentley, **36**: 431.
— — of 1854. Tait, n. s. **21**: 432–751. — Quar. **96**: 200.
— — — Life at Balaklava in. Liv. Age, **44**: 39.
— — — Soldier's View of. Fraser, **51**: 32.
— — of 1855. Brit. Q. **22**: 347. — Tait, n. s. **22**: 45–690.
— — — Results of. Ed. R. **102**: 584.
— — on the Danube. Bentley, **34**: 555, 575. **35**: 160.
— — with the Russian Army. Fraser, **52**: 549.
— Cause and Objects of. (F. W. Newman) Fraser, **94**: 522.
— Causes of. (F. W. Newman) Fraser, **83**: 1.
— — and Consequences of. (R. Baird) Putnam, **4**: 422, 537.
— Chapter on. Colburn, **103**: 317.
— Character of Russia. Colburn, **101**: 472.
— Comparative Power of Russia and Allies. Westm. **65**: 91. Same art. Liv. Age, **48**: 485.
Crimean War, Conduct of. Bentley, **37**: 318. — Quar. **96**: 277.
— Constantinople in, Supply and Defense of. Bentley, **35**: 301.
— Czar Nicholas on. (J. A. O'Shea) St. James, **40**: 24.
— Diplomacy of. (W. O. Johnson) No. Am. **81**: 477.
— Duberly's Journal kept during. New Q. **5**: 146. — Liv. Age, **48**: 385.
— Effect of, on Russian Produce. (R. Valpy) J. Statis. Soc. **18**: 301.
— Engagement with Cossacks. Cornh. **7**: 401.
— England's Part in. Temp. Bar, **52**: 396.
— Ensign Pepper's Letters from, 1855. Colburn, **104**: 141. **105**: 34.
— Ethics and Object of, 1856. Brit. Q. **23**: 219.
— Heroic Incidents of. Colburn, **102**: 94.
— History of. (E. E. Hale) No. Am. **81**: 458. — Ecl. M. **33**: 509.
— — A Scrap of. (D. C. Murray) Gent. M. n. s. **14**: 171.
— How shall we deal with, 1855. Dub. Univ. **45**: 103. Same art. Liv. Age, **44**: 694.
— Influence of, on Money Market. Bank. M. (L.) **15**: 368.
— Kinglake's History of. (C. C. Hazewell) No. Am. **109**: 612. — (E. H. Lacombe) No. Am. **121**: 408. — Bentley, **53**: 477, 633. **54**: 68, 142. — Blackw. **128**: 689. — Brit. Q. **61**: 421. — Canad. Mo. **7**: 458. — Chr. Rem. **46**: 447. — Colburn, **127**: 364. — Dub. Univ. **61**: 259. — Ecl. R. **117**: 277. — Ed. R. **117**: 307. **128**: 379. Same art. Liv. Age, **77**: 26. — Ed. R. **153**: 241. — Fraser, **78**: 119. — Lond. Q. **20**: 159. Same art. Ecl. M. **59**: 135, 333. — Ho. & For. R. **2**: 398. — No. Brit. **38**: 325. — (R. D. Osborn) Nation, **31**: 379. — Nat. R. **16**: 298. — Penn Mo. **6**: 299. — Quar. **113**: 514. — Westm. **79**: 601.
— — and his Critics. Chr. Exam. **75**: 81.
— Gen. Klapka on. Tait, n. s. **23**: 54.
— Management of. Dub. Univ. **46**: 116.
— Military History of. No. Brit. **25**: 493.
— Month in Camp before Sebastopol. New Q. **4**: 190.
— Mortality of British Officers in. (R. T. Jopling) J. Statis. Soc. **20**: 54.
— Napier's Baltic Campaign. New Q. **6**: 168.
— Object and Occasion of. Tait, n. s. **26**: 248.
— Objects of. Quar. **97**: 245.
— Oliphant's Trans-Caucasian Campaign. Bentley, **39**: 507.
— Origin of. Brit. Q. **21**: 540. **22**: 201.
— The Peace and its Adversaries, 1856. Colburn, **107**: 1.
— Peard's Campaign in the Crimea. New Q. **4**: 303.
— Plan of. Dub. Univ. **46**: 383.
— Policy of. Bentley, **35**: 319.
— Realities of. Dub. Univ **49**: 229.
— Results of. (F. W. Holland) Chr. Exam. **62**: 73. — Quar. **98**: 249.
— Retrospect of, 1854. Fraser, **50**: 711.
— Russian Defeats and their Effects on Europe. Fraser, **50**: 594.
— Sanitary View of. (M. L. Baudens) Colburn, **113**: 415.
— Sebastopol Committee and Vienna Conferences. Ed. R. **102**: 274.
— Significance of. No. Brit. **24**: 268.
— Staff Officer on. Fraser, **55**: 103.
— Story of. Chamb. J. **23**: 353–410.
— Lord Stratford and. Temp. Bar, **62**: 170, 460. **63**: 167–528. Same art. Liv. Age, **150**: 170. **151**: 348.
— Todleben's History of. No. Brit. **41**: 545. Same art. Ecl. M. **64**: 1.
— Turkey and. Fraser, **76**: 503.
— Turkish Poems on. House. Words, **12**: 155.
— Unexpected Results of. (G. Hooper) Fortn. **2**: 310.

Crimean War, Winter in the Crimea. Bentley, **37**: 49.
— Zouaves in. Liv. Age, **45**: 739.
See Sebastopol; Treaty of Paris.
Criminals and the Law. (E. L. Godkin) Nation, **8**: 106.
— and their Treatment. (C. M. O'Leary) Cath. World, **26**: 56.
— at large. Once a Week, **7**: 569.
— Boys as, Plea for. (W. Gilbert) Good Words, **7**: 279.
See Juvenile Delinquency.
— Casual. (E. Crapsey) Galaxy, **11**: 827.
— Dealing with. (W. Chambers) Chamb. J. **56**: 273. — Hogg, **11**: 441. — Temp. Bar, **27**: 390.
— Education and. (R. W. Rawson) J. Statis. Soc. **3**: 331.
— Employment of. (G. Odger) Contemp. **15**: 463.
— Felon Literature. Mus. **44**: 539.
— Female. Cornh. **14**: 152.
— — and their Children's Fate. Good Words, **14**: 170.
— French Treatment of. No. Brit. **27**: 45.
— Habitual, Supervision of. (W. Crofton) Good Words, **16**: 433.
— — Treatment of. (A. G. Sedgwick) Nation, **25**: 23.
— Home for discharged young. Ecl. R. **77**: 523.
— Homes, not Prisons, for young. Ecl. R. **85**: 560.
— Imperfect. (F. Jacox) Bentley, **54**: 486. Same art. Liv. Age, **80**: 23.
— Imprisonment and Transportation. Blackw. **55**: 533.
— Juvenile. No. Brit. **10**: 1. *See* Juvenile Delinquency.
— Legal Responsibilities of. Canad. Mo. **18**: 541.
— Our. Belgra. **27**: 482.
— — and our Judiciary. (E. I. Sears) Nat. Q. **20**: 374.
— Professional, What shall be done with? All the Year, **21**: 414.
— Recruits for the Ranks of Crime. (R. Quiddam) St. James, **37**: 580.
— Reformation of. (B. K. Pierce) Meth. Q. **28**: 387. — Cornh. **3**: 409, 708. **4**: 229. **10**: 722.
— Remarkable, in France. Cornh. **12**: 606.
— Transportation of. *See* Transportation.
— Treatment of. (W. G. Eliot) Am. Soc. Sci. J. **8**: 79.
— What is to be done with our? (H. Rogers) Ed. R. **86**: 214.
See Penal Servitude; Convicts; Transportation.
Criminal Case in Russia. Chamb. J. **24**: 116. — (E. Crapsey) Galaxy, **8**: 345.
Criminal Classes. Chamb. J. **31**: 84.
— and the Government. Temp. Bar, **7**: 505.
— Disposal and Control of. St. Paul's, **3**: 599.
— Excursion with. Cornh. **9**: 627.
— Life in. Ed. R. **122**: 337.
— Management of. Ed. R. **100**: 563.
Criminal Court, Central. Westm. **22**: 195.
Criminal Courts of London. (J. Fletcher) J. Statis. Soc. **9**: 289.
Criminal Jurisprudence. New Eng. M. **7**: 126. — Pamph. **18**: 67.
— a hundred Years ago. Am. Mo. M. **5**: 249.
— of Ohio. Am. Q. **10**: 29.
— Sampson on. Mo. R. **155**: 517.
— Scottish. (J. Cockburn) Ed. R. **83**: 196.
Criminal Justice, Administration of. (G. C. Barrett) Am. Soc. Sci. J. **2**: 167.
— in England. Westm. **1**: 146.
Criminal Law. Quar. **24**: 195. **47**: 170. — Mo. R. **131**: 302. — Chr. Exam. **8**: 338. — Quar. **22**: 247. **37**: 147. — Ed. R. **54**: 183. — Westm. **7**: 91. — (Judge Porter) So. Q. **3**: 389.
— and Detection of Crime. Cornh. **2**: 697.
— and Executions in old Days. Cornh. **17**: 559.
— and Prison Discipline. Westm. **61**: 409.
— in America and Europe. (F. Wharton) Atlan. **26**: 69.
— in 1819. Ecl. R. **30**: 108.
Criminal Law in England. Quar. **7**: 159. — (F. Parkman) Chr. Exam. **12**: 1. — Mo. R. **96**: 510. **104**: 449. — Ed. R. **19**: 389. **150**: 524. — (J. F. Stephen) 19th Cent. **7**: 136. — Zoist, **1**: 101. — Pamph. **16**: 1.
— — Code of, Needed. Am. Law R. **7**: 264.
— — — Proposed. (J. B. Perkins) Am. Law R. **13**: 244.
— — Habitual Criminals Bill. (H. Taylor) Fraser, **79**: 661.
— — in 1836. Mo. R. **142**: 299.
— — Miller on, 1822. Ecl. R. **39**: 481.
— — Romilly on. (J. Davison) Quar. **7**: 159.
— — Severity of. Tait, **3**: 269.
— — Stephens's View of. St. James, **11**: 500.
— — temp. Edw. I. (F. M. Nichols) Arch. **40**: 39.
— in Scotland. (J. Craufurd) No. Brit. **4**: 313. — Ed. R. **41**: 450. — Westm. **22**: 92. — Am. Law R. **6**: 427.
— Influence of Christianity on. So. Lit. Mess. **6**: 129.
— of France. Dub. Univ. **79**: 651.
— — and England, 1824. Ecl. R. **39**: 385.
— of the Jews. Liv. Age, **143**: 498–756.
— Origin of. (W. W. Billson) Pop. Sci. Mo. **16**: 433.
— Reform in. Ed. R. **121**: 109. — Westm. **21**: 353. — Ecl. R. **69**: 350. **89**: 720. — (Sir J. F. Stephen) 19th Cent. **2**: 737.
— Some Topics in. (H. W. Torrey) Am. Soc. Sci. J. **1**: 120.
— J. F. Stephen on. Fraser, **69**: 37.
— Wharton's. Internat. R. **1**: 556.
— Mrs. Winsor's Views on. All the Year, **16**: 540.
Criminal Lunatics. Temp. Bar, **1**: 135.
Criminal Procedure. Ed. R. **101**: 532.
— Amer. and English. (J. N. Pomeroy) No. Am. **92**: 297.
— and License of Counsel. Westm. **35**: 1.
— French System of. Ed. R. **17**: 88.
— German and French. (J. N. Pomeroy) No. Am. **94**: 75.
— in England in Murder Cases. Westm. **91**: 76.
— in Scotland and England. (W. Forsyth) Ed. R. **108**: 443.
— Publicity in. Ed. R. **40**: 169.
Criminal Prosecutors, Public and private. Fortn. **1**: 675.
Criminal Returns, Report on. (W. M. Tartt) J. Statis. Soc. **20**: 365.
Criminal Statistics of England and Wales. (R. W. Rawson) J. Statis. Soc. **2**: 316.
— of Preston, England, 1838. J. Statis. Soc. **2**: 84.
Criminal Trials. Penny M. **1**: 85.
— American. (C. W. Upham) No. Am. **54**: 199.
— Celebrated. Mo. R. **117**: 325, 437.
— French. For. Q. **4**: 139. — Mus. **15**: 211.
— German. For. Q. **8**: 265.
— Modern French. Ed. R. **95**: 281. Same art. Ecl. M. **26**: 247.
— Remarkable. Fraser, **53**: 612. Same art. Ecl. M. **38**: 347.
— Scotch. (Sir W. Scott) Quar. **43**: 438. — Westm. **19**: 332. — Blackw. **63**: 293, 607.
— — Ancient. (Sir W. Scott) Quar. **44**: 438.
— — Burton's. Hogg, **9**: 398.
— — Pitcairn's. Tait, **3**: 511.
Crimson, Blue, Gold. (G. W. Bungay) Putnam, **14**: 711.
Crinoid, New. (G. B. Grinnell) Am. J. Sci. **112**: 81.
Crinoids. (E. Billings) Am. J. Sci. **98**: 69. **99**: 51. **100**: 225.
— Genus Belemnocrinus. (C. Wachsmuth and F. Springer) Am. J. Sci. **113**: 253.
— Palæozoic. (W. Thomson) Nature, **4**: 496. — (F. B. Meek and A. H. Worthen) Am. J. Sci. **98**: 23.
— — Structure of. (C. Wachsmuth) Am. J. Sci. **114**: 115, 181.
Crinoline and Whales. Dub. Univ. **52**: 537. Same art. Ecl. M. **46**: 220.
— Who killed? Once a Week, **20**: 369.

Crinoline Manufactory. Once a Week, **10**: 124.
Cripplegate Morning Exercises. Cong. M. **28**: 889.
Cripples, Munich Asylum for. Dub. Univ. **80**: 322.
Cririe, James. Scottish Scenery; a Poem. (F. Jeffrey) Ed. R. **3**: 328.
Crisis, The, 1835. Dub. Univ. **5**: 459.
— 1841. Dub. Univ. **17**: 777. **18**: 119.
— 1846. Dub. Univ. **27**: 246.
Crisp, Samuel; a condemned Dramatist. All the Year, **31**: 103.
Crispin, St.; a Poem. (F. Parke) Dub. Univ. **87**: 722.
Crispus; a poetic Romance. Gent. M. n. s. **10**: 429, 540, 670.
Criterion in Piccadilly. Pract. M. **3**: 63.
Critic, Qualifications of the. (S. M. Worcester) Am. Q. Obs. **1**: 287.
Critic on the Hearth. (J. Payn) 19th Cent. **5**: 1003. Same art. Liv. Age, **142**: 151.
Critics. Bentley, **3**: 396.
— and Books. (M. Pattison) Ecl. M. **90**: 93.—Liv. Age, **135**: 771.
— and Criticism. (C. A. Bristed) Nation, **1**: 10.—Blackw. **8**: 138.
— — of the 19th Century. Dem. R. **15**: 153.
— and their Prey. Belgra. **20**: 495.
— and Writers. Am. Mo. M. **2**: 1.
— British. (A. H. Everett) No. Am. **31**: 26.—(E. P. Whipple) No. Am. **61**: 468.
— Canons for. Sharpe, **46**: 9.
— English, and Scottish Lawyers. Ed. R. **105**: 219.
— Essay on. Dial, **1**: 5.
— Fallibility of. Ev. Sat. **4**: 596.
— Small, and amateur Authors. Dem. R. **17**: 62.
— *versus* Puffers. (E. I. Sears) Nat. Q. **33**: 62.
— Word with some. (J. Morley) Fortn. **32**: 577.
Critical Blunders. Chamb. J. **43**: 476.
Critical Curiosities. Chamb. J. **48**: 289. Same art. Ecl. M. **77**: 224.
Critical Errors. Chamb. J. **42**: 164.
Critical Method. (A. Kuenen) Mod. R. **1**: 461, 685.
Critical Review, Review of. Chr. Obs. **1**: 250. **2**: 41.
Critical Theology, Decline of. (G. R. Noyes) Chr. Exam. **43**: 325.
Criticism. (W. D. LeSueur) Canad. Mo. **16**: 323.—Blackw. **13**: 686. **101**: 149.—Knick. **14**: 175.—Retros. **1**: 313.
— American. (E. S. Gould) Lit. & Theo. R. **3**: 33.—(W. A. Jones) Dem. R. **15**: 241.
— and Cliques. Temp. Bar, **20**: 321.
— and Creation. (J. C. Shairp) Macmil. **38**: 246. Same art. Liv. Age, **138**: 246.
— and Critics. Am. Mo. M. **3**: 313.—Temp. Bar, **42**: 100.
— Arnold's Essays in. (H. James, jr.) No. Am. **101**: 206.—(W. D. Adams) Gent. M. n. s. **14**: 467. Same art. Ecl. M. **65**: 67. *See* Arnold, Matthew.
— Art and. (T. M. Coan) Lippinc. **13**: 355.—(S. Colvin) Appleton, **22**: 320.
— as one of the Fine Arts. (W. Hutcheson) St. Paul's, **10**: 386.
— Cant of. Fraser, **19**: 95.
— — of modern. (G. A. Sala) Belgra. **4**: 45.
— Christmas Carol of. No. Brit. **8**: 378.
— Coleridge and. Am. Whig R. **3**: **581**.
— Curiosities of. Fraser, **87**: 43. Same art. Liv. Age, **116**: 355.—Gent. M. n. s. **24**: 740.—Ecl. M. **97**: 420.
— Dallas on the Gay Science. (J. Skelton) Fraser, **74**: 771. Same art. Ecl. M. **68**: 230.—St. Paul's, **4**: 739.—Lond. Q. **28**: 140.—Bentley, **61**: 187.
— Dutch School of, and Dr. Badnam. Quar. **120**: 324.
— English, Errors and Abuses of. (G. H. Lewes) Westm. **38**: 466. Same art. Ecl. Mus. **1**: 327.
Criticism, English, German Views of. (T. A. Tellkampf) Am. Whig R. **6**: 497.
— Essay on. West. M. **5**: 10.
— Ethics of. (H. P. Cutting) Mo. Rel. M. **49**: 228.
— False, by true Poets. Chamb. J. **3**: 349.
— First Edinburgh Reviewers. (L. Stephen) Cornh. **38**: 218. Same art. Liv. Age, **138**: 643.
— French. (H. James, jr.) Nation, **1**: 468.
— General and theatrical. (J. W. Calcraft) Dub. Univ. **37**: 727.
— in a Carriage. Sharpe, **38**. 225, 287.
— in Religion, Abuse of. Kitto, **38**: 48.
— Liberty of, and the Law of Libel. Fraser, **68**: 35.
— Literary. (J. R. Dennett) Nation, **7**: 88.—(S. Dyer) Bapt. Q. **1**: 310.—(E. Yates) Temp. Bar, **17**: 528.
— — Aims and Methods of. Westm. **80**: 468.
— — R. H. Hutton on. Penn Mo. **7**: 972.
— — in England. Fraser, **21**: 190.
— — in France. Brit. & For. R. **16**: 327. Same art. Ecl. M. **1**: 515.
— Modern. (E. I. Sears) Nat. Q. **2**: 262.—Am. Whig R. **1**: 617.—Broadw. **4**: 243.—Chamb. J. **42**: 433.
— Mutual. (J. H. Noyes) Cong. Q. **17**: 272
— Need of Caution in. (W. R. C. Rogers) Kitto, **37**: 193.
— New. (N. Porter) New Eng. **29**: 295.
— of Classes. Temp. Bar, **8**: 236.
— on Women. Westm. **32**: 454.
— Past and present. (Lady Pollock) Temp. Bar, **57**: 367. Same art. Liv. Age, **143**: 820.
— Periodical. Anal. M. **5**: 409.—(C. A. Goodrich) Chr. Mo. Spec. **7**: 71.—Ed. R. **38**: 349.
— — Ethics of. Brit. Q. **37**: 277. Same art. Ecl. M. **60**: 441.
— Popular. Lond. Q. **4**: 179.
— Science of. Bentley, **61**: 187.
— Some Hints on. Hogg, **13**: 85.
— Spirit of. Hogg, **3**: 273.
— Strange. All the Year, **33**: 558.
— Textual, Principles of. (F. Gardiner) Bib. Sac. **32**: 209. *See* Bible.
— Thorough. (E. R. Russell) Belgra. **7**: 39.
— Thoughts on, by a Critic. Cornh. **34**: 556. Same art. Liv. Age, **131**: 743.
— True Art of. (Lady Pollock) Temp. Bar, **45**: 391.
— Two Kinds of. Ev. Sat. **9**: 706.
— Verbal. Am. Meth. M. **19**: 29.
— What is? Chamb. J. **11**: 353.
Crittenden, John J. (E. Quincy) Nation, **15**: 320.
Croakers. Fraser, **68**: 730. Same art. Ecl. M. **61**: 192.
Croat and Servian Literature. Westm. **109**: 303.
Croatia and Hungary. (E. Fitzmaurice) Macmil. **36**: 34.
— and Italy, Letters from. For. Q. **7**: 423.
— From Agram to Zara. (A. J. Patterson) Fortn. **17**: 359, 509.
See Jellachlich.
Croats, Bird's-Eye View of. (A. M. Birkbeck) Sharpe, **20**: 133. Same art. Ecl. M. **33**: 346.
Crochet. (A. H. Forrester) Bentley, **24**: 444.
Crockett, Col. David. Fraser, **16**: 610.
— Exploits in Texas. Mo. R. **143**: 215.
— Reminiscences of. Mo. R. **134**: 254.
— Sketches of. Ev. Sat. **11**: 515.
Crockford's Club House. Fraser, **17**: 538.
— and Crockford. Bentley, **17**: 142, 251.
— or Life in the West. Lond. M. **21**: 260.
Crocodile and Gavial. Chamb. J. **54**: 653.
— in Florida. (W. T. Hornaday) Am. Natural. **9**: 498.—(J. Wyman) Am. J. Sci. **99**: 105.
— Is it the Leviathan of Scripture? Penny M. **7**: 209.
— Mode of catching. (Dr. Rüppell) Penny M. **1**: 89.
Crocodiles. Bentley, **31**: 123. Same art. Liv. Age, **33**: 305.—Ev. Sat. **9**: 187.

Crocodiles, Nests of. Once a Week, **22**: 275.
Crocodile Battery. House. Words, **7**: 540.
Crocodile Pets of Maäbdeh, Egypt. St. James, **24**: 324.
Crœsus and Adrastus; a Poem. All the Year, **15**: 61.
Croft, Sir James, Memoirs of. Retros. **15**: 469.
Croga, Fairy Miller of. Lond. M. **7**: 678.
Croghan, Col. George. Portfo.(Den.) **13**: 212.
— Journal from Fort Pitt to Vincennes, 1765. Olden Time, **1**: 403.
Croker, John Wilson, with portrait. Dub. Univ. **19**: 796. — with portrait, Ecl. M. **33**: 242. — with portrait, Fraser, **4**: 240. — Liv. Age, **55**: 182, 317.
— and Montalembert. Fraser, **53**: 563.
— as a Quarterly Reviewer. Bentley, **40**: 327. Same art. Liv. Age, **51**: 240.
— Public Career of. Quar. **142**: 83. Same art. Liv. Age, **132**: 195.
Croker, T. Crofton, with portrait. Fraser, **3**: 67. — Dub. Univ. **34**: 202.
— Fairy Legends. Blackw. **18**: 55.
Croly, George. (G. Gilfillan) Hogg, **1**: 161. Same art. Ecl. M. **14**: 459.
— Angel of the World. Blackw. **8**: 20. — Ed. Mo. R. **4**: 445. — Lond. M. **2**: 542.
— Catiline; a Tragedy. Colburn, **4**: 470. — Blackw. **11**: 698. — Mo. R. **100**: 383.
— Gems from the Antique. Blackw. **12**: 478.
— Letters. Dem. R. **40**: 62–546. **41**: 165, 392, 469.
— Marston, or the Soldier and Statesman. Ecl. R. **85**: 21.
— Paris. Lond. M. **3**: 430, 540.
— Poems. Ecl. R. **51**: 525.
— Pride shall have a Fall. Blackw. **15**: 343.
— Salathiel. Ecl. R. **48**: 27. — Lond. M. **20**: 209.
— Writings of. Colburn, **101**: 284. Same art. Ecl. M. **32**: 556. Same art. Liv. Age, **42**: 318.
Cro-Magnon Cave. Once a Week, **25**: 326.
Cromartie, Earls of. Ed. R. **147**: 1.
— Traditional History of, Miller's. Mo. R. **137**: 127.
Crombie, Alexander, a Universalist. Univ. Q. **34**: 158.
Crome, John. (M. M. Heaton) Portfo. **10**. 33, 48.
Cromlech at Drewsteignton. Antiquary, **1**: 147.
— in the County of Kilkenny. (J. T. Finnegan) Arch. **16**: 264.
Cromot du Bourg, Baron, Diary in America, 1781. M. Am. Hist. **4**: 205–441.
Cromwell, Henry and Elizabeth, Petition to Charles II. (Mrs. E. Green) Arch. **38**: 322.
Cromwell, Oliver. (P. Bayne) Contemp. **21**: 408. — Ecl. M. **80**: 447. Same art. Liv. Age, **116**: 771. — (T. B. Macaulay) Ed. R. **48**: 142. — (W. T. Dwight) Chr. Q. Spec. **1**: 385. — (C. F. Adams) No. Am. **37**: 179. — (J. T. Headley) Am. Whig R. **3**: 396. — (W. P. Lunt) Chr. Exam. **40**: 440. — (S. F. Smith) Chr. R. **12**: 1. — (D. Curry) Meth. Q. **5**: 325. — (S. G. Arnold) Meth. Q. **8**: 51. — (J. W. Brown) Am. Church R. **1**: 413. — Ed. Mo. R. **4**: 627. — Westm. **8**: 328. **33**: 181. — Dem. R. **18**: 336. **21**: 33, 141. — Mo. R. **95**: 1, 126. **117**: 474. — (R. Southey) Quar. **25**: 279. — Ecl. R. **68**: 622. **72**: 604. — Bib. R. **1**: 38, 139. — Dial, **3**: 258, 281. — Penny M. **8**: 340.
— and Cæsar. (F. M. Holland) University Q. **1**: 295.
— and Charles I. Godey, **44**: 141.
— and the Civil Wars. (J. Forster) Ed. R. **103**: 1. Same art. Ecl. M. **37**: 513. — Liv. Age, **51**: 193.
— and his Contemporaries. Liv. Age, **29**: 241.
— and his Correspondents. Bentley, **41**: 371.
— and his Sons, Memoirs of. Ecl. R. **33**: 297.
— and the Jews. Ecl. M. **73**: 80.
— and Napoleon. Selec. Ed. R. **2**: 376.
— and Nonconformist Heroes, Lays and Legends of. Ecl. R. **114**: 84.
Cromwell, Oliver, and the Protectorate in Scotland. Hogg, **3**: 405.
— and the Revolution. (S. G. Arnold) Meth. Q. **30**: 51.
— Carlyle's Letters and Speeches of. Dub. R. **21**: 65. — Westm. **46**: 432. — (R. Vaughan) Brit. Q. **3**: 50. — Liv. Age, **8**: 459. — Blackw. **61**: 393. Same art. Liv. Age, **13**: 385. — Ecl. M. **7**: 452. — Dub. Univ. **27**: 228. — (M. Richardson) New Eng. **4**: 211. — (C. C. Felton) No. Am. **62**: 380. — Chamb. J. **5**: 3, 23, 130. — Chr. Rem. **11**: 243. — (J. Moncrieff) No. Brit. **4**: 505. — Tait, n. s. **13**: 38.
— — and Guizot's Life of. Liv. Age, **44**: 429.
— Character and Government of. Nat. Q. **14**: 244.
— Cornish's Life of. (A. V. Dicey) Nation, **33**: 474.
— Cromwell's Memoirs of. Chr. Obs. **19**: 811.
— Desecration of his Remains. Chamb. J. **25**: 113.
— Diplomacy of. Dub. Univ. **46**: 321.
— Embarkation for New England. N. E. Reg. **20**: 113.
— Forster's Life of. Ecl. R. **72**: 605.
— Funeral and Grave of. Antiquary, **4**: 32–302.
— Granddaughter of. Sharpe, **38**: 229.
— Guizot's Hist. of. Dub. R. **36**: 494. — Ecl. R. **99**: 693.
— Head of. Chamb. J. **52**: 139.
— Headley's Life of. Dem. R. **23**: 333.
— Historical Romance on. Ecl. R. **73**: 315.
— Histories and Historians of. Dem. R. **26**: 17.
— in Ireland. Dub. R. **71**: 49. — Irish Mo. **3**: 158–446.
— Lays and Legends of. Ecl. M. **54**: 62.
— Letters of. (T. Wright) Arch. **32**: 25. All the Year, **35**: 414.
— — and Speeches of. (T. E. Bond, jr.) Meth. Q. **6**: 573. — (J. Moncrieff) No. Brit. **4**: 505. — Ecl. R. **83**: 469. — Prosp. R. **2**: 119.
— — to his Family. Ecl. Mus. **2**: 553.
— Life of. Mus. **41**: 329. — Mo. R. **147**: 549. — Portfo. (Den.) **28**: 99, 193.
— — Merle d'Aubigné's. Am. Lit. M. **1**: 172. — Ecl. R. **88**: 318. — Liv. Age, **14**: 305. — Chamb. J. **8**: 97. — Chr. Obs. **49**: 265. — Tait, n. s. **14**: 459.
— on the Christian Ministry. Cong. M. **25**: 301.
— refusing the Crown. Ecl. M. **64**: 129.
— Theory of Life of. Ecl. R. **116**: 224. Same art. Ecl. M. **57**: 465.
— Unpublished Letters of. (T. Carlyle) Fraser, **36**: 631. Same art. Liv. Age, **16**: 214, 499.
— Vaughan's Protectorate of. Ecl. R. **68**: 622.
— What became of? Gent. M. n. s. **26**: 553.
Cromwell, Richard. Colburn, **127**: 418.
— and his Wife. Penny M. **8**: 461–490.
— Guizot's History of. Dub. R. **41**: 86. — Fraser, **54**: 433. Same art. Ecl. M. **39**: 448.
— Protectorate of. Dub. Univ. **47**: 714.
Cromwell; a Drama. (E. L. Bulwer) So. Lit. Mess. **2**: 605.
Cromwell Doolan; or Life in the Army. Dub. Univ. **34**: 26.
Cromwellian Christianity. (T.G. Apple) Mercersb. **1**: 372.
Cromwellian Settlement of Ireland, Prendergast's. Fraser, **75**: 33. *See* Ireland.
Cronstadt and the Russian Fleet. Fraser, **49**: 493.
— Visit to. Once a Week, **16**: 109.
Crook, Japhet, Case of. Once a Week, **27**: 169.
Crook, John. (J. McDonald) Meth. M. **31**: 3.
Crooked Life. (T. A. Harcourt) Overland, **13**: 478.
Crooked Usage. (D. Costello) Bentley, **49**: 221–660. **50**: 64–641. **51**: 115–550.
Crooked Ways; a Story. (C. Dunning) Lippinc. **28**: 606.
Crooker Genealogy. (M. A. Thomas) N. E. Reg. **12**: 68.
Crookes, William, with portrait. Colburn, **168**: 68.
Crookit Meg; a Story of the Year One. Fraser, **101**: 272–721. Same art. Liv. Age, **145**: 38–545. **146**: 13, 67.
Croon by Coul Goppagh. Dub. Univ. **12**: 472.
Crops, Chemical Principles of Rotation of. (D. P. Gardner) J. Frankl. Inst. 43: 106.

Crops, Effects of good. (J. B. Hodgskin) Nation, **7**: 226, 265, 305.
— of Europe. Dem. R. **20**: 217.
Croppy's Fingers. Dub. Univ. **31**: 228.
Croquet. (L. C. Davis) Galaxy, **4**: 413.—(H. Jones) Gent. M. n. s. **1**: 81.—Chamb. J. **47**: 573.—Godey, **74**: 141, 235, 326.—Lond. Soc. **9**: 507.—Tinsley, **5**: 170. **7**: 188.
— American. (A. Erwine) Nation, **3**: 113.
— and its Laws, 1866. Ev. Sat. **2**: 226.
— History of. Lond. Soc. **8**: 58. Same art. Ecl. M. **65**: 338.
— past, present, and to come. Tinsley, **5**: 681.
— Science of. (H. Jones) Gent. M. n. s. **1**: 225, 389, 497.
Croquet Alphabet. Lond. Soc. **6**: 384.
Crosby, Frederick. (G. Stewart, jr.) Potter Am. Mo. **13**: 210.
Crosby, Howard, with portrait. Ecl. M. **82**: 757.
Crosby Hall, London. Penny M. **1**: 385.
— Nonconformist Recollections of. Cong. M. **16**: 451.
Crosby Place. Ev. Sat. **13**: 438.
Crosland, C. Lydia; a Woman's Book. New Q. **1**: 288.
Cross, The. Cath. World, **7**: 21.
— a Poem. Cath. World, **13**: 14.
— ancient Amer. Symbol. (T. Ewbank) Hist. M. **12**: 159.
— and Crescent. (F. Harrison) Fortn. **26**: 709.
— Attractions of. (J. W. Alexander) Princ. **18**: 158.—(H. Bacon) Univ. Q. **3**: 255.—(S. F. Smith) Chr. R. **11**: 500.
— Christ's, or Criss-Cross. (F. C. Lukis) Reliquary, **11**: 67.
— Fylfot, or Thor's Hammer. (L. Jewitt) Art J. **27**: 369.
— Imperial Byzantine. Antiquary, **1**: 177.
— in the Desert; a Tale. (W. Seton) Cath. World, **21**: 813.
— in Legend, Poetry, and Art. (M. A. Lloyd) Lippinc. **5**: 518. Same art. Broadw. **6**: 559.
— in Nature and in Art. (L. Jewitt) Art J. **26**: 23–365.
— Moral Influence of. (M. Tucker) Princ. **7**: 367.
— of Danzig. Fraser, **32**: 20.
— of St. Anthony. (L. Jewitt) Reliquary, **15**: 65.
— on the Snow Mountains. Dub. Univ. **33**: 169. Same art. Liv. Age, **21**: 1.
— Pre-Christian. Ed. R. **131**: 222.
— — Symbolism of. (J. T. Short) Meth. Q. **36**: 612.
— Punishment of. Am. Q. Obs. **1**: 206.
— Reason of. Chr. Obs. **69**: 178–539.
— Sign of, in early Church. Dub. R. **30**: 113.
— Superscription on. (W. N. Irish) Am. Church R. **28**: 193.
— Symbol of. Hist. M. **11**: 288.
— Tau, as an Emblem and in Art. (L. Jewitt) Art J. **27**: 305.
— through Love. Cath. World, **16**: 412, 523.
— Traditions of. (A. Rhodes) Appleton, **6**: 741.—All the Year, **45**: 114.
— Triumph of. Ecl. R. **124**: 211.
— True. Brownson, **17**: 96.
— — Malan on. Chr. Obs. **33**: 733, 765.
— True Doctrine of. Mo. Rel. M. **14**: 61.
— Various Senses explained. (E. W. Hutter) Evang. R. **16**: 508.
Crosses of England, Ancient Stone. (A. Rimmer) Art J. **27**: 41, 109.
Crosses of Honor, Two. Chamb. J. **56**: 433.
Cross Currents; a Sketch. Dub. Univ. **90**: 599.
Cross Purposes; a Story. (M. Vandergrift) Lippinc. **18**: 227.
Cross Purposes; a Story. Chamb. J. **54**: 441, 457.
Cross Purposes. Lond. Soc. **16**: 150.
Cross Purposes. Lond. Soc. **36**: 425.
Cross-Sectioning, Angular. (F. Z. Schellenberg) Ecl. Engin. **15**: 44.—(R. Bell) Ecl. Engin. **14**: 393.
Crossbill, Change of Plumage in. Intel. Obs. **8**: 188.
Crosse, Andrew, Electrician and Poet. Brit. Q. **26**: 333. Same art. Ecl. M. **43**: 20. Same art. Liv. Age, **56**: 129.—Chamb. J. **28**: 11. Same art. Liv. Age, **55**. 220.—Liv. Age, **54**: 346.
Crosse, Andrew, Memorials of. Lond. Q. **9**: 365.
Crossed in Love. Lond. Soc. **20**: 430, 492.
Crossing the Border. (S. S. Cox) Knick. **38**: 504.
Crossing-Sweepers of London. Chamb. J. **17**: 305.
Crosskey Boys. (M. T. Mott) Overland, **14**: 514. **15**: 23.
Crossness, Well-Boring at. Nature, **1**: 333.
Croswell, Rev. William. (G. W. Doane) Am. Church R. **4**: 591.—(A. C. Coxe) Am. Church R. **7**: 98.—(R. H. Dana, jr.) No. Am. **78**: 424.
Crotchets. Fraser, **56**: 350.
— and Crotchetiness in the Church. Dub. R. **44**: 200.
Crotchety Curate, Diary of. Peop. J. **8**: 55–113.
Crotchety Men and their Counterfeits. Mus. **44**: 320.
Croton Aqueduct, New York. (W. B. Lawrence) Hunt, **10**: 434.—Am. Alma. **1850**: 187.—Chamb. J. **1**: 19.
— Condition and Finances of. Hunt, **25**: 704.
Croton Bug as a Library Pest. (W. Flint) Lib. J. **4**: 376.
Croton Water. (W. H. Rideing) Scrib. **14**: 161.
Crouch, Isaac, Obituary of. Chr. Obs. **37**: 410.
Crow, The. Chamb. J. **46**: 505.
— in Mythology. (W. H. Gardner) Pop. Sci. Mo. **18**: 43.
— of Ceylon. (E. Jesse) Once a Week, **1**: 180.
— of India. Chamb. J. **53**: 477.
Crows and Choughs. (W. J. Broderip) Fraser, **55**: 507.
Crow-Boy's Mind. All the Year, **26**: 61.
Crow Castle, Bird's-Eye View from. Fraser, **83**: 343.
Crow Indians and Neighbors. (P. Koch) Nation, **28**: 116.
Crowds, On. Temp. Bar, **7**: 185.
— Life in. Dub. Univ. **87**: 747.
Crowder's Cove. (C. F. Woolson) Appleton, **15**: 357.
Crowe, Mrs. Catherine. Colburn, **96**: 439. Same art. Liv. Age, **36**: 97.
— Light and Darkness. Tait, n. s. **17**: 695.
— Night Side of Nature. Blackw. **68**: 265.—Liv. Age, **17**: 37.—Chamb. J. **9**: 104, 123. Same art. Liv. Age, **17**: 289.—So. Lit. Mess. **17**: 1.
— Novels of. (P. Q. Keegan) Victoria, **33**: 35.
Crowe, Eyre. Art J. **16**: 205.
Crown, William and John. N. E. Reg. **6**: 46.
Crown, Influence of, Rose on. Ed. R. **16**: 187.
— Prerogative of, in the Colonies. (T. Hodgins) Canad. Mo. **18**: 385.
Crown and Dagger; a Tale. Dub. Univ. **42**: 216.
Crown of Life; James i. 12. (E. Zeller) Am. Presb. R. **12**: 414.
Crowns, About. Chamb. J. **52**: 421.
— and Crowned. Potter Am. Mo. **9**: 381.
Crown Federalism; The late American Colonies. Dub. Univ. **22**: 528.
Crown Jewels. Chamb. J. **44**: 353. Same art. Ecl. M. **69**: 340.—Ecl. M. **74**: 231.
— in 3 Edward III. (C. Ord) Arch. **10**: 241.
— Strange Dealings with. All the Year, **43**: 182. Same art. Liv. Age, **143**: 374.
Crown Lands. Belgra. **12**: 172.
Crown Point, Campaigns against, in 1755-56. (T. Williams) Hist. M. **17**: 209.
— Expedition against, 1755; Chandler's Diary. N. E. Reg. **17**: 346.
Crowned Women of Lormandie. Hogg, **6**: 376, 395, 402.
Crowther, James, the Naturalist. Chamb. J. **7**: 215. Same art. Liv. Age, **13**: 511.
Crowther, Samuel, the Negro Bishop. Chr. Obs. **69**: 641.
Croyland Abbey, Boundary Stones of. (T. Pownall) Arch. **3**: 96. **6**: 395.—(S. Pegge) Arch. **5**: 101.
Crozet Islands. (L. Brine) Geog M. **4**: 266.
Crucifix of Baden; a Legend. Cath. World, **5**: 480, 672.
Cruden, Alexander. Chamb. J. **37**: 47.—Liv. Age, **65**: 640.—Penny M. **10**: 31.
Cruel Barbara Allen. (D. C. Murray) Belgra. **43**: 195.
Cruel Lord; a Poem. (E. Renaud) Scrib. **5**: 734.
Cruelty, On. (F. W. Newman) Fraser, **93**: 523.

Cruelty, Cost of. (H. Bergh) No. Am. **133**: 75.
— on the High Seas. Liv. Age, **56**: 291.
— Scientific. (E. C. Gray) Good Words, **17**: 241.
— to Animals. (A. H. Japp) Good Words, **15**: 531. — (W. S. Jevons) Fortn. **25**: 671. — (J. Hutchinson) Fortn. **26**: 307. — Cornh. **29**: 213. — (A. Chalmers) Am. Meth. M. **9**: 259. — (R. F. Clarke) Month, **25**: 393. — All the Year, **15**: 238. **36**: 326. — Blackw. **107**: 531. — Meth. M. **30**: 547. — Sharpe, **13**: 188. — Lond. M. **6**: 530.
— — Bergh and his Work. (C. C. Buel) Scrib. **17**: 872.
— — Bill to prevent. Nature. **14**: 87, 172.
— — caused by Ignorance. Stud. & Intel. Obs. **4**: 195.
— — Erskine's Speech on. (J. Foster) Ecl. R. **10**: 1150.
— — in Italy. (W. Chambers) Chamb. J. **51**: 62.
— — Prevention of. Penn Mo. **12**: 53.
— — — Society for. Mo. R. **150**: 77.
— — Richmond's Sermon on. Chr. Obs. **1**: 449, 502.
— — Sportsmen's. Temp. Bar, **28**: 359.
— — Windham on. (J. Foster) Ecl. R. **12**: 975.
See Vivisection.
Cruger, Henry, Diary of. M. Am. Hist. **7**: 358.
Cruger, John, with portrait. (J. A. Dix) M. Am. Hist. **1**: 172.
Cruikshank, George. (L. Jewitt) Reliquary, **18**: 231. — (F. G. Stephens) Portfo. **3**: 77. — (R. Sturgis) Scrib. **16**: 161.— (F. Wedmore) Temp. Bar, **52**: 499. Same art. Ecl. M. **90**: 677. — with portrait, Appleton, **8**: 235. — Blackw. **14**: 18. — Mus. **5**: 563. — with portrait, Fraser, **8**: 190. — with plates, Westm. **34**: 1. — Art J. **15**: 25. — Blackw. **94**: 217. — Chamb. J. **55**: 161. Same art. Liv. Age, **137**: 178.
— and English Caricaturists. (W. Thornbury) Art J. **12**: 229.
— Illustrations of Time. Blackw. **21**: 777.
— in Melodrama. St. James, **28**: 645.
— Life in Paris. (G. A. Sala) Atlan. **15**: 54.
— A Life Memory. (G. A. Sala) Gent. M. n. s. **20**: 544.
— Life and Works of. Lond. Q. **40**: 285. Same art. Liv. Age, **119**: 3.
— My Sketch Book. Tait, **4**: 126.
— Worship of Bacchus. Chamb. J. **38**: 298.
Cruise in the Flying Dutchman. (G. W. Curtis) Putnam, **5**: 516.
— of the Anti-Torpedo. Chamb. J. **48**: 561, 578, 596.
— of the Aphrodite. Lond. Soc. **10**: 179.
— of the Balboa. (N. Brooks) Scrib. **3**: 526. Same art. Broadw. **8**: 554.
— of the Coya. Blackw. **129**: 768.
— of the Enterprise. Dem. R. **6**: 33.
— of the Frolic. (W. H. G. Kingston) Colburn, **88**: 293.
— of the Heron. (J. T. McKay) Lippinc. **19**: 231.
— of the Midge. (M. Scott) Blackw. **35**: 311–899. **36**: 29–642. **37**: 319–893.
— of the Tomtit. House. Words, **12**: 491.
— of the Two Deacons. (F. H. Ludlow) Harper, **21**: 194, 334, 480.
— of the Wasp. Chamb. J. **57**: 626–691.
— of the Willing Lass. Bentley, **30**: 603.
— on a Slaver. (J. C. Cremony) Overland, **1**: 398.
Crusade of the Children. Blackw. **62**: 285. — Colburn, **26**: 456. — Once a Week, **22**: 39.
Crusades. (A. St. J. Chambre) Univ. Q. **24**: 411. **25**: 84, 283. **26**: 65. — (G. A. Lintner) Evang. R. **14**: 116. — (C. Mackay) Nat. M. **5**: 75, 266, 358. — (C. C. Read) Land We Love, **3**: 18. — (C. C. Smith) Chr. Exam. **55**: 97. — Nat. M. **4**: 113-533.
— Antioch during. (F. Damiani) Arch. **15**: 234.
— described by Crusaders. Brit. Q. **18**: 63. Same art. Liv. Age, **40**: 251.
Crusades, History of. Ed. Mo. R. **4**: 509. — Blackw. **4**: 303. **59**: 475. — No. Brit. **1**: 114. — For. Q. **5**: 623. **28**: 12. — Ecl. M. **4**: 471. — Anal. M. **3**: 441. — Mo. R. **87**: 519. **97**: 389. **99**: 533. **121**: 65.
— — and Effects of. (D. Moore) Ex. H. Lec. **2**: 237.
— — Michaud's. Chr. R. **19**: 290. — Dub. Univ. **90**: 507. — (Prof. Hamilton) No. Brit. **1**: 114.
— — Mills's. Ecl. R. **31**: 497.
— — Sybel's. For. Q. **28**: 22. Same art. Am. Ecl. **3**: 340. — Liv. Age, **71**: 567.
— Influence of. Hogg, **5**: 251, 280, 360.
— — on Art and Literature. Ox. Prize Ess. **4**: 155.
— — on European Literature. (Mrs. E. F. Ford) New Eng. **35**: 601.
— Last great Dream of. (J. B. Brown) 19th Cent. **10**: 701. Same art. Liv. Age, **151**: 643.
— Philosophy of. (J. A. Mets) Bapt. Q. **8**: 80.
— Sketches of. Am. Mo. M. **1**: 105, 251.
Crusader of Bigorre; a Tale. Dub. Univ. **40**: 108.
Crusaders, The. All the Year, **32**: 445, 508, 588.
— In the Footsteps of. Ecl. R. **120**: 597.
— Joinville's Memoir of St. Louis. (C. E. Norton) No. Am. **98**: 419.
— Last of. (S. C. Read) Land We Love, **2**: 196–403.
Crusading Days; a Poem. Dub. Univ. **62**: 282.
Crusenstolpe, Magnus. Dem. R. **9**: 438.
Crusoes, Genuine. Chamb. J. **45**: 773.
— Two German. Chamb. J. **51**: 573.
Crusoe-Life. (J. R. Browne) Harper, **6**: 300, 470, 588.
Crusoeing. All the Year, **46**: 7.
Crustacea, The. Chamb. J. **25**: 189.
— American Phyllopod. (A. E. Verrill) Am. J. Sci. **98**: 244.
— Choristopoda, Classification of. (J. D. Dana) Am. J. Sci. **64**: 297.
— Classification of. (J. D. Dana) Am. J. Sci. **72**: 14.
— collected by C. F. Hartt, on the Coast of Brazil, 1867. (S. I. Smith) Am. J. Sci. **98**: 388.
— Freshwater, of Norway, Sars's. Nature, **1**: 455.
— Geographical Distribution of. (J. D. Dana) Am. J. Sci. **68**: 314. **69**: 6. **70**: 168, 349.
— Habits of. (A. E. Verrill) Am. Natural. **3**: 239.
— in Custody. Once a Week, **27**: 186.
— Life-Histories of. (A. S. Packard, jr.) Am. Natural. **9**: 583.
— of English Lakes. (G. S. Brady) Intel. Obs. **12**: 416.
— Stridulating. Nature, **18**: 53.
Crutchley Prior. (T. Speight) Once a Week, **6**: 266.
Cruthers and Johnson, or the Outskirts of Life. Fraser, **2**: 191.
Cry of the Children. (E. B. Barrett) Blackw. **53**: 260.
Crying. Mo. Rel. M. **21**: 59.
Cryptogams. (W. R. McNab) Nature, **4**: 427. — Chamb. J. **24**: 134. — Chamb. J. **25**: 175. Same art. Ecl. M. **36**: 1072.
— Evolution of. (J. S. Gardner) Nature, **24**: 73–606.
Cryptography. Appleton, **7**: 627.
— Art of. Pract. M. **1**: 314.
— in Politics. (J. R. G. Hassard) No. Am. **128**: 315.
Crystal Magic. House. Words, **2**: 284.
Crystal, Rock. *See* Rock Crystal.
Crystals from a Cavern. (J. Sterling) Blackw. **42**: 39. **43**: 354.
— in circularly polarized Light. (W. Spottiswoode) Nature, **6**: 91.
— Lettering Figures of. (J. D. Dana) Am. J. Sci. **63**: 399.
— Measurement of Angles of. (A. R. Leeds) J. Frankl. Inst. **92**: 203.
— Morphology of, Maskelyne's. Nature, **11**: 187.
— Stelliform (E. J. Chapman) Canad. J. n. s. **6**: 1.
Crystal Cup. (A. Stoker) Lond. Soc. **22**: 228.

Crystal Palace at Sydenham. (J. Eagles) Blackw. **76**: 317. — Liv. Age, **29**: 110. — Peop. J. **11**: 264. — Quar. **96**: 305. — Fraser, **48**: 607. Same art. Ecl. M. **31**: 161. — Chamb. J. **15**: 129.
— and its Schools. Pract. M. **5**: 193.
— Geology at. Hogg, **11**: 279.
— Opening of. Liv. Age, **29**: 523.
— Private Hist. of. (W. H. Wills) House. Words, **2**: 385.
— Voltaire in. Blackw. **70**: 142.
— What it is, and what it might be. Westm. **62**: 534.
See also London, Exhibition of 1851; Sydenham.
Crystal Palace, New York. (P. Godwin) Putnam, **2**: 121.
— Fire in, 1867. Ev. Sat. **3**: 369.
Crystal Palace of Wieliczka. Chamb. J. **22**: 381.
Crystallization. (J. R. Coxe) Portfo.(Den.) **12**: 485.
— of Silver, Gold, and other Metals. (J. H. Gladstone) Nature, **6**: 66.
— of Metals. (T. J. Gregan) Pop. Sci. Mo. **14**: 434.
Crystallography, Groth's. Nature, **15**: 372.
— Milne's. Nature, **20**: 73.
— Notes on. (W. H. Wahl) J. Frankl. Inst. **90**: 44, 263. **91**: 406.
Csardas; National Dance of Hungary. (F. Foster) Appleton, **20**: 373.
Ctesias. Tinsley, **8**: 412.
Ctesiphon, Arch of. Colburn, **165**: 1074.
Cuba. (R. B. Kimball) Putnam, **1**: 3. — (H. J. Warner) Nation, **3**: 85. — Am. Q. **7**: 475. — Blackw. **40**: 322. — So. R. **4**: 285. — Appleton, **1**: 616. **2**: 1. — Danv. Q. **1**: 260. — De Bow, **18**: 163. — Lippinc. **1**: 423. **11**: 326. — Once a Week, **29**: 394.
— Abbot's Letters on. (W. Phillips) Chr. Exam. **6**: 259. — (W. Phillips) No. Am. **29**: 199. — So. R. **4**: 123.
— Adventures in. (L. Schlesinger) Dem. R. **31**: 209, 352, 553.
— and the Cubans. (H. F. Bond) No. Am. **79**: 109. — Dub. Univ. **37**: 763 — Liv. Age, **25**: 374.
— and the Floridas, 1819. Niles's Reg. **17**: 305.
— and Political Economy. (G. L. Ditson) Hunt, **17**: 265.
— and the Slave States. Colburn, **93**: 218.
— and the South. (S. R. Walker) De Bow, **17**: 519.
— and Spain. Putnam, **15**: 9.
— and the Tripartite Treaty, 1853. So. Q. **25**: 1.
— and the United States. (W. J. Sykes) De Bow, **14**: 63. — (J. S. Thrasher) De Bow, **17**: 43. — Dub. Univ. **37**: 763. — (C. C. Andrews) Atlan. **44**: 81. — Dem. R. **31**: 326, 433. **32**: 36.
— — Annexation of. (A. H. Everett) Scrib. **11**: 876. — (F. O. J. Smyth) Hunt, **40**: 403. — De Bow, **18**: 305. — Dem. R. **43**: 1. — (M. Tarver) West. J. **9**: 295. — Westm. **64**: 180.
— Antiquities of; Caneys of the Dead. (E. W. Balch) M. Am. Hist. **1**: 720.
— Frederika Bremer in. (P. F. André) Victoria, **7**: 1, 97.
— Chinese in. (H. B. Auchincloss) Hunt, **52**: 186.
— Coffee Grounds of. All the Year, **24**: 61.
— Commerce of. Hunt, **7**: 319. **9**: 337. **21**: 34 — Republic, **1**: 325.
— Conquest of (C. C. Hazewell) Atlan. **12**: 462.
— Countess Merlin's Letters from the Havana. (J. F. Otis) Godey, **30**: 211.
— Country Life in. All the Year, **28**: 414.
— Currency of. Hunt, **2**: 523.
— — and Commerce of. Bank. M. (N. Y.) **35**: 697.
— Glances at. (G. A. F. Van Rhyn) Appleton, **13**: 321, 353, 385.
— History of. Am. Q. **10**: 230.
— Humboldt's. For. Q. **3**: 400. — Mus. **14**: 444. — Ecl. R. **52**: 22.
— Impressions of. (W. H. Bishop) Nation, **32**: 312.
— — in 1870. Mo. Rel. M. **43**: 66–562.
— in 1844. Dem. R. **15**: 475.
Cuba in 1849. Dem. R. **25**: 193.
— in 1854. (Dr. Ely) De Bow, **17**: 219.
— in 1855. Liv. Age, **47**: 811.
— in 1872. Dub. Univ. **82**: 635.
— Independence of. (W. J. Sykes) De Bow, **14**: 417.
— Insurrection in 1868–69. (W. J. Starks) Scrib. **6**: 10. — Nation, **8**: 288. — Ed. R. **138**: 395.
— — Our supposed Sympathy with. (A. G. Sedgwick) Nation, **9**: 24.
— — Tale of. (Capt. Bacon) Belgra. **14**: 82.
— — The Virginius. (J. N. Pomeroy and E. L. Godkin) Nation, **17**: 332.
— — What are the Cubans fighting for? (J. M. Macias) St. James, **35**: 191.
— Invasion of. So. Q. **21**: 1.
— Key to Mexican Gulf. (C. Montgomery) Hunt, **21**: 519.
— Letters from. Knick. **24**: 449, 545. **25**: 1. **26**: 36, 449, 545. — Liv. Age, **22**: 11.
— Letters on. Bost. Mo. **1**: 561, 641.
— Life in. (H. S. Conant) Harper, **43**: 350.
— Literature of. Chamb. J. **32**: 290. — Liv. Age, **64**: 37.
— Lopez's Expedition. Fraser, **12**: 107. Same art. Liv. Age, **26**: 347. — (J. D. B. De Bow) De Bow, **9**: 164. — Dem. R. **26**: 97. **29**: 291. — Liv. Age, **26**: 141. **31**: 190, 228, 283.
— Manners and Customs in. West. M. **1**: 330, 412, 501.
— Masquerading in. All the Year, **23**: 461.
— past and present. (A. W. Ely) De Bow, **14**: 93.
— Position, Dimensions, and Population of. (J. C. Reynolds) De Bow, **8**: 313.
— Prison Life in. All the Year, **25**: 222.
— Question of. Dem. R. **35**: 448. — Ev. Sat. **11**: 2. — (W. H. Trescott) So. Q. **25**: 429. — Belgra. **22**: 311. — (E. L. Godkin) Nation, **9**: 264. — (A. G. Sedgwick) Nation, **21**: 335.
— Recollections of, 1850. (W. E. Surtees) Colburn, **94**: 208.
— Reminiscences of. So. Lit. Mess. **21**: 567–745.
— Resources and Destiny of. Nat. Q. **14**: 34.
— — and Prospects of. Hogg, **4**: 285.
— — Progress, and Prospects of. Dub. R. **27**: 123.
— Revolution in. (W. W. Nevin) Lippinc. **3**: 339.
— Sketches in. Blackw. **40**: 322.
— Slavery in. (F. W. P. Greenwood) Chr. Exam. **23**: 82.
— Spanish Bank of. Bank. M. (N. Y.) **36**: 17.
— State and Prospects of, 1856. Lond Q. **7**: 98. Same art. Ecl. M. **39**: 466.
— State of, 1876. (R. B. Minturn) Nation, **22**: 110.
— State of Siege in. All the Year, **25**: 610.
— State Trials in. Dem. R. **30**: 307.
— Sugar-Making in. (H. B. Auchincloss) Harper, **30**: 440.
— Thirty Days in Savannahs of. Hogg, **1**: 104, 115, 131.
— Three Weeks in. Harper, **6**: 161.
— To, and back, Dana's. Liv. Age, **63**: 315.
— Trade and Commerce of. Hunt, **3**: 351. **6**: 81.
— Trip to. (J. W. Howe) Atlan. **3**: 601, 686. **4**: 184–602.
— Truth about St. James, **35**: 414.
— Turnbull's Travels in, 1837–39. Mo. R. **151**: 449.
— The Volante. All the Year, **15**: 566.
Cuban Ball, and how it ended. Chamb. J. **58**: 445.
Cuban Beggars. All the Year, **27**: 346.
Cuban Convent. All the Year, **27**: 33.
Cuban Pirates. All the Year, **23**: 172.
Cuban Theatricals. All the Year, **24**: 413.
Cuban Wedding All the Year, **27**: 198.
Cube, Anatomy of (W. B. Tegetmeier) Recr. Sci. **1**: 271.
— Forms contained in. (W. B. Tegetmeier) Recr. Sci. **3**: 264.
Cubi's Traductor Español. (J. Sparks) No. Am. **22**: 451.
Cubic Equations, Solution of, by the common Logarithmic Tables. Math. Mo. **2**: 85.

Cuckoo, The. (E. Jesse) Once a Week, 6: 516. — Colburn, 62: 475. — Penny M. 8: 124. — St. James, 13: 337.
Cuckoo; a Poem. (C. S. Calverley) Scrib. 5: 365.
Cuckoo and the Nightingale. Cath. World, 3: 543. Chamb. J. 42: 429.
Cuckoo-Bees. (H. N. Humphreys) Intel. Obs. 1: 165.
Cuckoos' Eggs. (A. Newton) Nature, 1: 74, 265.
— Coloring of. (C. Smith) Nature, 1: 242.
Cudworth, James, and New England Toleration. (J. Chaplin) Bapt. Q. 10: 312.
— Letter of, 1634. N. E. Reg. 14: 101.
Cudworth, Ralph. Intellectual System. (T. Parker) Chr. Exam. 27: 289. — (W. P. Seargill) Retros. 6: 49. — (Sir J. Mackintosh) Ed. R. 27: 191.
Cufic Coins, Origin, Antiquity, and Use of. (S. Weston) Arch. 18: 309.
Cui Bono? New Eng. M. 4: 31.
Cui Bono? a Tale. (J. Graham) Belgra. 34: supp. 45.
Cuisine Maigre. (T. Medwin) Bentley, 3: 367.
Culdee Monasteries. (W. M. Blackburn) Princ. 39: 1.
Culdees, The. (E. Pond) Meth. Q. 21: 628. — Dub. Univ. 76: 706.
— of Iona, Jamieson's Account of. Ecl. R. 15: 443.
Culinary Art, Origin of. (F. Schultze) Sup. Pop. Sci. Mo. 4: 24.
Culinary Philosophy. So. Lit. J. 1: 209.
Culinary Poisons. Quar. 24: 341. — Ed. Mo. R. 3: 276. *See* Cookery.
Cullen, Dr. Wm., Life and Writings of. (Sir W. Hamilton) Ed. R. 55: 461. — Mo. R. 130: 444.
Cullet. (J. G. Austin) Atlan. 14: 305.
Culloden; a Poem. (G.W. Thornbury) Dub. Univ. 49: 198.
— Battle of. All the Year, 18: 271. — Ev. Sat. 4: 436.
Culloden Papers. (Sir W. Scott) Quar. 14: 283. — Ed. R. 26: 107.
Culprits, Queer. (S. B. Gould) Once a Week, 5: 91.
Cultivation of Present. (P. Mulford) Overland, 7: 381.
Culture. (R. W. Emerson) Atlan. 6: 343. — (J. P. Wickersham) Lippinc. 1: 276. — Irish Mo. 3: 631.
— Æsthetical. Victoria, 13: 97.
— Alcott on. Bost. Q. 1: 417.
— American. (H. Hartshorne) Lippinc. 1: 645.
— and Action. N. Ecl. 1: 15.
— and Anarchy, Arnold on. (T. M. Coan) Galaxy, 24: 5. — Lond. Q. 33: 209. — No. Brit. 50: 190. — Liv. Age, 102: 67.
— and Art. (R. St. J. Tyrwhitt) Contemp. 13: 362.
— and Christianity. Theo. Ecl. 6: 585.
— and Discipline. (S. H. Emery, jr.) Western, 3: 319.
— — *vs.* Information and Dexterity. (W. T. Harris) Western, 2: 25.
— and Facts. (L. F. Soldan) Western, 2: 623.
— and its Enemies. (M. Arnold) Cornh. 16: 36. Same art. Ecl. M. 69: 232. Same art. Ev. Sat. 4: 97.
— and modern Poetry. Cornh. 34: 664. Same art. Ecl. M. 88: 361.
— and practical Life. (C. D. Warner) Scrib. 4: 470.
— and Religion. (W. M. Bryant) Western, 1: 409. — (J. L. Spalding) Am. Cath. Q. 4: 389.
— — Shairp on. (J. M. Sturtevant) New Eng. 31: 201. — (E. L. Godkin) Nation, 12: 360.
— and Science. (T. H. Huxley) Nature, 22: 545.
— as a Substitute for Christianity. (W. W. Patton) New Eng. 40: 773.
— Basis of true. (G. R. W. Scott) Cong. Q. 17: 50.
— Dialogue on. (F. Harrison) Fortn. 8: 603.
— Early. (R. W. Bailey) So. Lit. Mess. 20: 14.
— a Failure without Christianity. (J. S. Vandersloot) Ref. Q. 28: 220.
— Force of. (J. S. Hittell) Overland, 12: 230.
— in early Ages. (M. P. Case) Bib. Sac. 9: 686.
Culture, Intellectual and moral, in Public Schools. Bost. R. 1: 371.
— Limits of. (B. L. Gildersleeve) So. R. n. s. 2: 421.
— Loose Thoughts on. (J. Burroughs) Sharpe, 41: 96. Same art. Knick. 63: 1.
— Models of. (A. B. Muzzey) Mo. Rel. M. 47: 533.
— Modern. Quar. 137: 389. Same art. Liv. Age, 123: 579. — So. R. n. s. 13: 111.
— — and Christianity. Canad. Mo. 8: 523.
— — Youmans on. (J. Fiske) Nation, 5: 45. — (F. Tiffany) Chr. Exam. 83: 286.
— Modern Doctrine of. Cornh. 13: 434.
— Organization of. (E. L. Godkin) Nation, 6: 486.
— Physical and mental, in Common Schools. (G. F. Walker) Radical, 6: 462.
— Physiological Basis of. (N. Allen) Pop. Sci. Mo. 6: 183.
— Plea for. (E. L. Godkin) Nation, 4: 151. — (T. W. Higginson) Atlan. 19: 29.
— Popular. (J. Morley) Fortn. 26: 632. Same art. Ecl. M. 88: 129.
— Primitive, Tylor's. Nature, 4: 117, 138. — (J. S. Sewall) New Eng. 33: 213.
— School of. Dub. Univ. 93: 740.
— Scientific. (J. P. Cooke, jr.) Pop. Sci. Mo. 7: 513.
— Speculative. (G. Howison) Radical, 1: 459.
— Sweetness and Light. (E. L. Godkin) Nation, 5: 212.
— Tendency of. No. Brit. 50: 190. Same art. Liv. Age, 102: 67.
Culture-Ghost; or Winthrop's Adventure. (V. Lee) Fraser, 103: 1. Same art. Appleton, 25: 330.
Cultus, Christian. (H. Harbaugh) Mercersb. 6: 573. 7: 116.
Cultus Ventris. (W. C. Conant) New Eng. 30: 616.
Cumæ, City of, and Excavations there. (A. Ashpitel) Arch. 37: 316.
Cumberland, Richard. Colburn, 79: 303–515. 80: 38. — Dem. R. 37: 389. — Temp. Bar, 14: 580. 56: 171.
— Life and Writings of. Anal. M. 4: 368. — (F. Jeffrey) Ed. R. 8: 107. — Mus. 7: 273. — Quar. 1: 295.
— Memoir of. Ecl. R. 3: 414.
— Mudford's Life of. (J. Foster) Ecl. R. 16: 840.
Cumberland, William, Duke of. Colburn, 146: 55.
Cumberland County, Me., Association of, History of. (J. Weston) Cong. Q. 9: 334.
— Members of the Bar from 1700 to 1838. (J. D. Hopkins) Am. Q. Reg. 12: 274.
Cumberland and Westmoreland. (J. Dennis) Fortn. 6: 445. — Blackw. 83: 344.
— Dalesfolk of. Fraser, 92: 25.
— Border of, Divine Worship on. (J. H. Hollowell) Cong. 7: 539.
— Manners and Customs in. Penny M. 8: 227.
— Photographs; Character Sketches. St. Paul's, 1: 348.
Cumberland, The; a Poem. (H. W. Longfellow) Atlan. 10: 669.
Cumberland Gap, Mountain Axes near. (N. S. Shaler) Am. Natural. 11: 385.
Cumberland Mare's Nest; a Poem. Cornh. 4: 102.
Cumberland Road. Niles's Reg. 30: 160. 48: 191.
— Mr. Clay's Speech on. Niles's Reg. 27: 357.
— Mr. Munroe's Veto on. Niles's Reg. 22: 171.
Cumberland Univ., Lebanon, Tenn. Am. J. Educ. 4: 765.
Cumming, John. Liv. Age, 47: 397.
— Ecclesiastical Portrait of. St. James, 25: 709.
— Memoir and Confession of Faith. Cong. M. 19: 533.
— Theological Teachings of. Westm. 64: 436.
— Voices of the Night. Kitto, 6: 378.
Cumming, R. G. Hunter's Life in South Africa. Quar. 88: 1. — Ecl R. 92: 476. Same art. Ecl. M. 22: 25. — (F. Bowen) No. Am. 71: 359. — De Bow, 9: 504. — Blackw. 68: 231. — Colburn, 89: 504. — Internat. M. 1: 218. — Chamb. J. 14: 72. *See* Africa, South.

Cumming, W. F. Notes of a Wanderer. Mo. R. **149**: 1.
Cummins, G. D. Movement in the Episcopal Church. So. R. n. s. **14**: 443.
Cumnor, Day at. Once a Week, **13**: 321.
Cumnor Hall. Lond. Soc. **10**: 348.
Cunard Steamship Company. Lond. Soc. **38**: 33.
Cuneator, On the Office of. (R. Ruding) Arch. **17**: 207.
Cuneiform Evidences of Religion. Lond. Q. **16**: 1.
Cuneiform Inscriptions. (G. A. Schmidt) O. & N. **8**: 314.
— and Biblical History. (J. Kenrick) Theo. R. **8**: 495. — Theo. R. **5**: 158.
— at Behistun. (H. Rawlinson) Arch. **34**: 73.
— Decipherment of. Kitto, **33**: 114. **34**: 91. — (O. T. Mason) Bapt. Q. **8**: 191. — Month, **3**: 94, 203.
— — Gobineau *vs.* Rawlinson on. Fraser, **72**: 589.
— described and tested. Kitto, **33**: 114. **34**: 91.
— Interpretation of. Quar. **147**: 430.
Cunliffe-Owen, Sir Philip, with portrait. Colburn, **165**: 1263.
Cunningham, Allan. (S. C. Hall) Art J. **18**: 369. Same art. Ecl. M. **68**: 197. — Brit. Q. **5**: 348. Same art. Ecl. M. **11**: 380. — Ecl. Mus. **1**: 176. —with portrait, Fraser, **6**: 249. — Bentley, **17**: 557. Same art. Liv. Age, **6**: 68.
— and Sir F. Chantrey. Fraser, **27**: 664. Same art. Ecl. Mus. **2**: 481.
— Letters to Croker. Sharpe, **37**: 93.
— Literature of fifty Years. Fraser, **9**: 224.
— Maid of Elvar. Blackw. **31**: 981. — Fraser, **5**: 659. — Tait, **1**: 445.
— Paul Jones. West. Mo. R. **1**: 119. — U. S. Lit. Gaz. **6**: 66.
— Poems and Songs of Scotland. Ed. R. **47**: 184. — Ecl. R. **36**: 259. — Liv. Age, **13**: 467.
— Sir Marmaduke Maxwell. Lond. M. **6**: 460.
— Sir Michael Scott. Lond. M. **21**: 99.
— Works of. Portfo.(Den.) **28**: 503.
Cunningham, J.W. Sancho. (F. Dexter) No. Am. **5**: 239.
— Sermons. Chr. Obs. **22**: 777. **25**: 47.—Ecl. R. **36**: 225.
— Velvet Cushion. Quar. **12**: 433.
Cunningham, William. Am. Hist. Rec. **2**: 441.
— Life of. Lond. Q. **37**: 400.
Cunningham Lecture. (R. S. Candlish) Lond. Q. **25**: 336.
Cunninghame, William. Fraser, **23**: 513.
Cup, The; a Fairy Tale. (A. L. A. D. Dudevant) Ecl. M. **66**: 305, 481.
Cupid; an Episode in the Career of Prof. MacPelvis. (G. A. Sala) Gent. M. n. s. **21**: 257, 385.
— and Death. Lond. M. **16**: 70.
— and Mars; a Tale of the Siege of Boston. (H. E. Scudder) Scrib. **11**: 322.
— at Sea; a Story. (E. Cuthbert) Tinsley, **22**: 95.
— in the Cabinet; a Poem. Blackw. **71**: 231.
— Judgment of; a Song. Dub. Univ. **16**: 119.
Cupid's Conflict; a Poem. (H. More) Dial, **2**: 137.
Cupid's Sport; a Tale. So. Lit. Mess. **1**: 102, 741.
Cupid's Sports. So. Lit. Mess. **18**: 20.
Cupboard Papers. All the Year, **28**: 539–582. **29**: 11–160.
Curacy, Harry Bolton's. Blackw. **69**: 180.
Curare, The Poison. Chamb. J. **42**: 6. — (M. Girard) Pop. Sci. Mo. **14**: 369.
Curate in Charge. (M. Oliphant) Macmil. **32**: 289, 397, 490. **33**: 10, 120, 248. Same art. Liv. Age, **127**: 425–783. **128**: 103–501.
— of Edenholm. Fraser, **56**: 473.
— of St. Matthews. Liv. Age, **144**: 89.
— of Suverdsio. (D. M. Moir) Good Words, **4**: 325.
— Our new. Fraser, **40**: 136.
Curate's Autobiography, A Country. Mo. R. **141**: 547.
Curate's good Match. Colburn, **161**: 689.
Curate's Holiday; a Tale. Chamb. J. **54**: 11–58.
Curate's last Half-Crown. Lond. Soc. **38**: 241.
Curate's Salary Bill. (Syd. Smith) Ed. R. **13**: 25.
Curate's Story. Sharpe, **45**: 128.
Curate's Volume of Poems; a Story. Fraser, **31**: 82–422. **32**: 77–416.
Curate's Wedding Feast. Chamb. J. **25**: 54.
Curates. (M. Davies) Belgra. **29**: 110.
— British. St. James, **23**: 731. — Chamb. J. **28**: 231.
— Case of. All the Year, **42**: 28.
— of the Church of England. Temp. Bar, **33**: 535.
— of Tittlebatington. House. Words, **3**: 381.
Curatives, Curious. Chamb. J. **49**: 456.
Curci, Father Carlo M. Lond. Q. **57**: 281.
— and the Curia. (K. Hillebrand) Nation, **25**: 329.
— and the Roman Question. Dub. R. **82**: 1.
— Case of. (H. J. Coleridge) Month, **33**: 1, 377.
Cure by ye Touch. St. James, **9**: 322.
Cure for Ennui; a Tale. (A. W. Cole) Sharpe, **19**: 279.
Cures, Odd. Chamb. J. **52**: 14.
— Some popular. All the Year, **42**: 250.
Curé of Ars. *See* Ars, Curé of.
Curiosity. (J. Dean) Portfo.(Den.) **6**: 431. — Chamb. J. **7**: 33.
Curiosities of great Men. Ecl. M. **26**: 500.
— of History. Bank. M. (N. Y.) **11**: 268, 340.
— of our Parish. Chamb. J. **19**: 403.
Curious, if true; a Story. (E. C. Gaskell) Cornh. **1**: 208.
Curious Adventures of a Field Cricket. (E. Candèze) Lond. Soc. **33**: 48–533.
Curious Couples. (W. M. Baker) Lippinc. **19**: 750.
Curious History of some misdirected Letters. Lond. Soc. **36**: 529.
Curious Page of Family History. House. Words, **4**: 246.
Curious Reflections. (F. Jacox) Belgra. **10**: 69.
Curl; a Poem. (W. Buchanan) Temp. Bar, **4**: 492.
Curliana. Blackw. **15**: 172.
Curling, Game of. Chamb. J. **3**: 120. **55**: 3. — Liv. Age, **148**: 639. — Penny M. **7**: 478. — St. Paul's, **4**: 185.
— and Curlers. Dub. Univ. **87**: 206.
— A Day's. Fraser, **49**: 269.
— Gossip about. Belgra. **34**: 99.
Curragh Camp. All the Year, **17**: 520.
Curragh Comforts. All the Year, **19**: 58.
Curran, John P. (F. Lawrence) Sharpe, **13**: 202. — (E. Townbridge) Sharpe, **47**: 318. — Chamb. J. **20**: 153. — Dub. Univ. **11**: 404.
— and his Contemporaries. Blackw. **69**: 222. Same art. Ecl. M. **22**: 415. — Irish Q. **1**: 45. — Lond. Q. **8**: 473. Same art. Ecl. M. **42**: 40.
— and Irish Eloquence. (G. Croly) Ex. H. Lec. **8**: 187.
— Eloquence at the Bar. West. Law J. **3**: 245.
— Letters to Weston. Blackw. **5**: 192.
— Life of. (F. Jeffrey) Ed. R. **33**: 259. — West. R. **4**: 1.
— Oratory of. (W. J. Spooner) No. Am. **10**: 62.
— Recollections of. Internat. M. **2**: 519.
— Speeches of. Quar. **1**: 83. — (F. Jeffrey) Ed. R. **13**: 136. — Mo. R. **82**: 391. **87**: 74. — Dub. R. **20**: 273. — (J. Foster) Ecl. R. **23**: 162.
Currency. (W. Phillips) No. Am. **2**: 362. — (G. Wood) Hunt, **4**: 317. — (J. L. Tellkampf) Hunt, **6**: 65, 164. — (G. Tucker) Hunt, **6**: 433. — (J. J. Crocheron) Hunt, **10**: 50. — Brit. Q. **7**: 168. — Quar. **39**: 415. — Westm. **35**: 45. **48**: 448. — Niles's Reg. **36**: 209. — Mo. R. **109**: 315. — Lond. M. **23**: 197. — Penn Mo. **4**: 822.
— and Banking. (R. Sulley) Hunt, **31**: 188. — (E. E. Hale) O. & N. **8**: 513. — Bank. M. (N. Y.) **22**: 737. — Blackw. **49**: 550. — Penn Mo. **5**: 408. — Westm. **35**: 89. — Fraser, **36**: 728. — (T. P. Kettell) De Bow, **9**: 413.
— — American. For. Q. **10**: 214.
— — English and American. Bank. M. (N. Y.) **24**: 321.
— — in New England, History of. Hunt, **34**: 288.

Currency and Banking, B. Price on. (S. Newcomb) Nation, **21**: 420. — Nation, **22**: 79.
— — Systems of. So. R. n. s. **7**: 355.
— and Banks. Republic, **6**: 316.
— and Capital. No. Brit. **28**: 191.
— and Commerce, Relations of. Bank. M. (N.Y.) **14**: 249.
— — Wheatley on. Ed. R. **3**: 231.
— and the Commercial Crisis of 1857. Bent. Q. **1**: 106.
— — of 1874. (W. P. Rosland) Bank. M. (N. Y.) **29**: 572.
— and Credit. (G. A. Butler) Bank. M. (N. Y.) **29**: 307, 375. — Liv. Age, **15**: 427.
— and Finance. (H. Greeley) Am. J. Educ. **18**: 632.
— and Government. (H. Middleton) Hunt, **13**: 211, 311, 412. — So. Q. **18**: 123.
— and History. Brit. Q. **2**: 1.
— and Money. (J. Miller) Nat. Q. **36**: 353. — (R. Sulley) Hunt, **59**: 374.
— and Repeal of Bank Restriction. Ed. Mo. R. **2**: 92.
— and Resumption. (K. Cornwallis) So. M. **14**: 128.
— and Specie. (S. Hooper) Bank. M. (N. Y.) **14**: 715. — (J. A. Lowell) Bank. M. (N. Y.) **14**: 953.
— and the State, 1867. (R. H. Patterson) Fortn. **8**: 77.
— and Tariff. (C. H. Carroll) Hunt, **33**: 191.
— and Trade. (A. Walker) Lippinc. **1**: 87.
— — of the United States. Dem. R. **40**: 385.
— Anomalies of. Bank. M. (N. Y.) **8**: 747.
— as related to Prices. (B. F. Nourse) Bank. M. (N.Y.) **31**: 546. — (G. Walker) Bank. M. (N. Y.) **21**: 761.
— Bailey on. Westm. **5**: 157. — Walsh's Am. R. **2**: 243.
— Banking, and Credit. (J. S. Ropes) New Eng. **16**: 312. Same art. Bank. M. (N. Y.) **14**: 161, 272.
— Cash Payments, etc. Mo. R. **88**: 392.
— Causes of Unsteadiness in. (H. C. Carey) Hunt, **2**: 372. **3**: 47–482.
— Cheap. (C. H. Carroll) Hunt, **38**: 35.
— Chinese. (W. G. Sumner) Nation, **26**: 45.
— — Notes on. Bank. M. (N. Y.) **28**: 713.
— Chronological History of. Westm. **48**: 483.
— — to 1847. De Bow, **5**: 497.
— Conflict on. (J. A. Garfield) Atlan. **37**: 219.
— Contraction of. (E. Atkinson) Nation, **5**: 151.
— — Does it destroy Capital? Bank. M. (N. Y.) **30**: 850.
— Corn, Cotton, and. (A. Walker) Lippinc. **8**: 492.
— depreciated, Evils of. Tait, **2**: 461.
— Depreciation of, at a Discount. Tait, **3**: 479.
— Difficulties in. Brit. Q. **5**: 148.
— Economical and secure. Ed. R. **31**: 53. — Selec. Ed. R. **6**: 41.
— Effect of Variations in. Blackw. **27**: 59.
— Effects of War and Speculation on. (J. B. Lloyd) Nat. Q. **5**: 270.
— Elastic. (A. Walker) Lippinc. **1**: 317.
— Essay on. (J. N. Cardozo) Bank. M. (N. Y.) **23**: 673. — Pamph. **17**: 501.
— Experience of California in. (H. D. Barrows) Nation, **26**: 59.
— Extension Act of Nature, in the recent Gold Discoveries. Blackw. **69**: 1.
— Free Paper. Lond. M. **5**: 185.
— French and American. (A. Walker) Scrib. **11**: 227.
— Gold and Silver. Hunt, **26**: 326.
— — D. Wilder, of Boston, on. (B. Price) Fraser, **84**: 653.
— — Great City Apostasy on. (B. Price) Macmil. **8**: 124.
— Harrowby's Speech on. Quar. **10**: 41.
— History of Opinions on. Bank. M. (L.) **10**: 17–707.
— Huskisson on Depreciation of. Quar. **4**: 414.
— in South Carolina. Bank. M. (N. Y.) **10**: 399.
— inconvertible, Advantages of. Bank. M. (L.) **4**: 13.
— Inflated. Hunt, **58**: 338.
— Inflation of. (E. L. Godkin) Nation, **17**: 350.
— — and Resumption. (J. A. Garfield) Bank. M. (N.Y.) **30**: 698.
Currency, Inflation of, and the West, 1868. (J. B. Hodgskin) Nation, **6**: 187.
— — Congressional Debate on, 1873–74. (C. F. Adams, jr.) No. Am. **119**: 111.
— — The Debtor Class. (E. L. Godkin) Nation, **18**: 262.
— — Democratic Inflationists. (E. L. Godkin) Nation, **21**: 66.
— — in relation to the Money Market. (J. B. Hodgskin) Nation, **6**: 124.
— — means what? 1867. (E. L. Godkin) Nation, **5**: 480.
— — National Schooling in, 1874. (C. C. Nott) Nation, **19**: 84.
— — the Prosperity of Austria. (E. L. Godkin) Nation, **18**: 54.
— — Remedy against. (C. C. Nott) Nation, **19**: 100, 394.
— — Scheme for, 1873. (E. L. Godkin) Nation, **17**: 316.
— — Shame of. (E. L. Godkin) Nation, **17**: 400.
— — Veto of, 1874. (E. L. Godkin) Nation, **18**: 278.
— — Vote on, 1874. (E. L. Godkin) Nation, **18**: 214.
— Influence of convertible Paper. Bank. M. (L.) **9**: 193.
— Instrument of Exchange. Westm. **1**: 174.
— Interest and Production. (J. S. Ropes) Hunt, **22**: 404, 516. **23**: 519. **24**: 181, 707.
— Laws of, in Scotland. (J. W. Gilbart) J. Statis. Soc. **19**: 144.
— Legislation on. Bank. M. (N. Y.) **19**: 593.
— National. Niles's Reg. **14**: 409. — Bank. M. (N. Y.) **23**: 593.
— — Real Estate its Basis. Hunt, **25**: 445.
— New Views on. (C. H. Carroll) Bank. M. (N. Y.) **13**: 673, 833. — (J. A. Dix) Bank. M. (N. Y.) **13**: 513. — (G. D. Lyman) Bank. M. (N. Y.) **13**: 593. — (G. Opdyke) Bank. M. (N. Y.) **13**: 417. — Bank. M. (N. Y.) **17**: 409, 481. **20**: 673.
— of American Colonies. (S. E. Dawson) Bank. M. (N. Y.) **28**: 633. — (A. H. Ward) N. E. Reg. **14**: 261.
— — in Maryland and Va. (S. F. Streeter) Hist. M. **2**: 42.
— — prior to 1739. (L. Neeley) Hunt, **16**: 344. — (S. E. Dawson) Canad. Mo. **1**: 326.
— of Great Britain. Anal. M. **13**: 54, 432.
— — and American. (J. Abbott) Hunt, **26**: 681.
— — Bill on. Bank. M. (L.) **11**: 301. **12**: 71.
— — and its Reform. (R. H. Patterson) Fortn. **6**: 837.
— — Laws of. (J. W. Gilbart) J. Statis. Soc. **17**: 289.
— — Metallic, and International Coinage. (W. S. Jevons) J. Statis. Soc. **31**: 426.
— — Parliamentary Proceedings relating to. Lond. M. **14**: 413.
— — Periodical Fluctuations in. Bank. M. (L.) **9**: 473.
— — State of, 1822. (E. Copleston) Quar. **27**: 239.
— of Japan. (J. Newton) Intel. Obs. **12**: 13.
— of New England, and Suffolk Bank System. (F. O. J. Smith) Hunt, **24**: 316, 439.
— of New York, Report on. Niles's Reg. **14**: 39.
— of United States. (C. H. Carroll) Hunt, **43**: 574. — (S. D. Ingham) West. J. **7**: 91. — (A Oaksmith) So. M. **13**: 733. — (G. A. Potter) Galaxy, **2**: 708. — Bank. M. (N. Y.) **23**: 698. — Bost. Q. **2**: 298. **3**: 80
— — and Congress. Bank. M. (N.Y.) **22**: 505. **28**: 889.
— — and the Constitution. Dem. R. **41**: 1.
— — and National Debt. (S. M. Stillwell) Bank. M. (N. Y.) **22**: 777.
— — and the National Finances, 1863. (L. S. Homans) Contin. Mo. **4**: 419. — Bost. Q. **4**: 371.
— — and Europe. (G. Walker) Bank. M. (N.Y.) **23**: 714.
— — and the Supreme Court. (B. Adams) Internat. R. **6**: 635.
— — and the two Parties. Dem. R. **8**: 157.
— — Bankruptcy in. (C. H. Carroll) Hunt, **40**: 673.
— — Bill on, 1870. (J. B. Hodgskin) Nation, **11**: 37.
— — — and three per cent Certificates. (J. B. Hodgskin) Nation, **10**: 86.

Currency of United States, Bill of 1874, does it contract or inflate? (C. E. Bockus) Nation, **19**: 68.
— — Cause of its Depreciation, 1864. Nat. Q. **10**: 109.
— — Expansion in, and Congress. Bank. M. (N. Y.) **29**: 409.
— — in 1859. (P. Cooper) Bank. M. (N. Y.) **14**: 87.
— — Ingham on. Hunt, **25**: 287.
— — Metallic. (G. Tucker) Hunt, **27**: 174.
— — National. (S. G. Fisher) No. Am. **99**: 204. — (J. S. Ropes) Bank. M. (N. Y.) **23**: 1. — (A. Walker) Internat. R. **1**: 213. — Bank. M. (N. Y.) **19**: 725. — Hunt, **34**: 19. **46**: 113, 119.
— — — Amendment to Law of. Hunt, **52**: 389.
— — — Plan for. (L. Bonnefoux) Bank. M. (N. Y.) **16**: 589.
— — — Uniform. (J. J. Knox) Hunt, **48**: 28.
— — — Withdrawal of. (A. Walker) Bank. M. (N. Y.) **22**: 161.
— — National Bank. (J. B. Hodgskin) Nation, **5**: 394. — (G. Walker) Internat. R. **6**: 248. — Hunt, **58**: 256.
— — Needed Modifications of. (L. H. Atwater) Scrib. **5**: 737.
— — New. (A. Walker) Bank. M. (N. Y.) **17**: 831.
— — New Measures with. Bank. M. (N. Y.) **24**: 409.
— — New York Chamber of Commerce on. Bank. M. (N. Y.) **29**: 970.
— — Reform in. (J. S. Ropes) Bank. M. (N. Y.) **28**: 521.
— — Reforms in. Bank. M. (N. Y.) **28**: 649.
— — Report on. Niles's Reg. **38**: 126. **41**: supp. 41. — Bank. M. (N. Y.) **13**: 482, 977.
— — Southern. Hunt, **6**: 191.
— — State of, 1823. Quar. **27**: 239.
— — — 1839. (C. F. Adams) Hunt, **1**: 44, 505.
— — Sumner's History of. (C. F. Dunbar) No. Am. **119**: 408. — (W. H. Browne) So. M. **14**: 660. — (E. L. Godkin) Nation, **18**: 267. — Canad. Mo. **6**: 572. — O. & N. **10**: 242.
— Overstone on. (A. Walker) Hunt, **40**: 147. — Ed. R. **107**: 248.
— Paper. (J. B. Hodgskin) No. Am. **111**: 78. — Niles's Reg. **14**: 141, 153.
— — Origin of. Hunt, **7**: 354.
— — Theory of State. (R. H. I. Palgrave) Bank. M. (L.) **35**: 381.
— — Unlimited, Effect of. (I. Butts) No. Am. **116**: 56.
See also Paper Money.
— Plan for a domestic convertible. Bank. M. (L.) **8**: 225.
— Principles of. (B. Price) Fraser, **67**: 581. — Fraser, **80**: 40. — (B. Price) Fraser, **80**: 477.
— Progressive Expansion of. (E. Dwight) Hunt, **25**: 147.
— Reform in. Dem. R. **7**: 167, 195. — Bank. M. (N. Y.) **12**: 769.
— Reforms in, Report of New York Chamber of Commerce. Bank. M. (N. Y.) **28**: 541.
— Regulation of. Bank. M. (N. Y.) **19**: 886.
— Remarks on. (J. Gallatin) Bank. M. (N. Y.) **16**: 625.
— Restoration and Reform of. (J. S. Ropes) Am. Soc. Sci. J. **5**: 46.
— Review of Pamphlets on. Bank. M. (N. Y.) **18**: 687.
— Ricardo and Bollman on. Portfo. (Den.) **22**: 135.
— Silver, Restoration of. (W. E. Dubois) Bank. M. (N. Y.) **24**: 166. — (E. L. Godkin) Nation, **22**: 303.
See Bimetallism; Money.
— Sound Views of. (R. B. Minturn) Bank. M. (N. Y.) **28**: 896.
— Speeches on. (Sir R. Peel) Bank. M. (L.) **1**: 177.
— Theories of. (E. Lord) Am. Presb. R. **13**: 452.
— — of the Day on. Bank. M. (N. Y.) **25**: 817.
— Tooke's Theory of. Bank. M. (L.) **6**: 81, 197.
— Trade and Tariff. Blackw. **62**: 744.
— Uniform. (C. F. McCay) Hunt, **35**: 697.
Currency, Value and Regulation of. (A. J. Warner) Nat. Q. **41**: 60.
— Volume of. Galaxy, **17**: 830.
— What is? Bank. M. (N. Y.) **10**: 34-353.
— Who shall issue? Bank. M. (N. Y.) **33**: 528.
— Working of. Blackw. **25**: 135.
See Money; Specie Payment; Gold; Silver.
Currency Juggle. (J. S. Mill) Tait, **2**: 461.
Currency Monopoly, 1848. Prosp. R. **4**: 297.
Currency Question. (A. S. Bolles) Bank. M. (N. Y.) **29**: 33. — (E. L. Godkin) Nation, **16**: 144. **17**: 220. **21**: 112, 208. — Westm. **41**: 579. **48**: 448. — Blackw. **27**: 591, 792. — Fraser, **4**: 686. — (P. B. Marcon) Western, **7**: 160.
— Elements of. Bank. M. (L.) **4**: 189, 321. **5**: 6, 78, 337.
— in Austria. (M. Wirth) Internat. R. **3**: 335.
— in England. Bank. M. (N. Y.) **13**: 295.
— in relation to Debt. Bank. M. (N. Y.) **32**: 779.
— Present Phases of, 1877. (H. White) Internat. R. **4**: 730.
Current Coins somewhat defaced. Belgra. **29**: 544.
Currents at Sea. Blackw. **3**: 579.
— Laws of, Colding's. Nature, **5**: 71, 90, 112.
— Observations on. (G. H. Mann) Ecl. Engin. **6**: 532.
— of Atlantic Coast. (J. E. Hilgard) Am. J. Sci. **110**: 117.
— of the Oceans. (J. D. Dana) Am. J. Sci. **76**: 231.
— — Dynamics of. (E. B. Hunt) Am. J. Sci. **77**: 169.
— on Earth's Surface. (B. Silliman) Am. J. Sci. **11**: 100.
Currey, Frederick, Obituary of. Nature, **24**: 485.
Currie, James, Life and Writings of. Ed. R. **55**: 108. — Mo. R. **124**: 416.
Curse, The; a Tale. So. Lit. Mess. **3**: 371.
— Divine, upon the World. Mercersb. **20**: 295.
— of Kishoge; a Poem. Dub. Univ. **19**: 18.
— of Tyrrell. Tinsley, **10**: 415.
— of Wulfheimberg. (Mrs. Bushby) Colburn, **121**: 52, 207.
Cursitor Baron of the Exchequer, Office and Title of. (E. Foss) Arch. **36**: 23.
Curtis, Benj. R. (J. T. Morse, jr.) Atlan. **45**: 265.
— Memoir of. (A. G. Sedgwick) Nation, **29**: 405. — Internat. R. **7**: 701.
Curtis, George W. (E. Benson) Galaxy, **7**: 327. — with portrait, Appleton, **10**: 321. — with portrait, Ecl. M. **79**: 246. — Colburn, **98**: 476. Same art. Ecl. M. **30**: 344. Same art. Liv. Age, **38**: 801. — Putnam, **9**: 384.
— Writings of. (W. D. Howells) No. Am. **107**: 104. — Dem. R. **33**: 80.
Curtis, Joseph. Knick. **48**: 94.
Curtis, Nathaniel, with portrait. N. E. Reg. **22**: 1.
Curtis House, Jamaica Plain. (B. J. Lossing) Potter Am. Mo. **6**: 162.
Curtius, Ernst, Müller, and Mommsen. (R. P. Keep) Internat. R. **2**: 745.
Curve, Involute. (T. Bakewell) J. Frankl. Inst. **11**: 99.
Curves, Expansion, Method of drawing. (C. S. Wilcox) Ecl. Engin. **21**: 72.
— Experiment of M. Lissajous. (E. C. Pickering) J. Frankl. Inst. **87**: 55.
— for Railroads, Principles of laying out. (J. C. Trautwine) J. Frankl. Inst. **51**: 361.
— — Setting out. (W. Airy) Ecl. Engin. **1**: 143.
— — Vignoles on. J. Frankl. Inst. **35**: 371. **36**: 20.
Curwen, Samuel. House. Words, **7**: 1, 157.
— Journal and Letters of. Chr. Exam. **33**: 259. — So. Lit. Mess. **13**: 48, 422. — Mo. R. **160**: 322.
— Ward's Memoir of. (C. F. Adams) No. Am. **56**: 89.
Curwin Genealogy. (G. R. Curwin) N. E. Reg. **10**: 305.
Curzola. (E. A. Freeman) Macmil. **44**: 372. Same art. Liv. Age, **151**: 59.

Cushing, Caleb and Alexander Cockburn. (S. T. Wallis) So. M. **12**: 635.
— Portrait of. Am. Whig R. **10**: 403.
— Reminiscences of Spain. (A. H. Everett) No. Am. **37**: 84.
Cushing, Jonathan. (G. W. Dana) Am. Q. Reg. **11**: 113.
Cushing, Thomas. (J. S. Loring) Hist. M. **6**: 212.
Cushing, Wm. B., U. S. N., Exploits of. (H. P. Spofford) Harper, **49**: 256.
Cushing Genealogy. (W. H. Whitmore) N. E. Reg. **19**: 39.
Cushman, Charlotte, with portrait. (G. T. Ferris) Appleton, **11**: 353. — (J. D. Stockton) Scrib. **12**: 262. — (R. G. White) Nation, **19**: 314. — (M. Howitt) Peop. J. **2**: 30, 47. — All the Year, **41**: 102. — Victoria, **32**: 468.
— and Rachel. (Mme. de Marguerittes) Sharpe, **15**: 13.
— and Macbeth. (G. T. Ferris) Lakeside, **7**: 407.
— Reminiscences of. (C. Bede) Belgra. **29**: 333.
Cushman, Henry Wyles, with portrait. (G. T. Davis) N. E. Reg. **18**: 321.
Custer, Gen. George A. (F. Whittaker) Galaxy, **22**: 362.
— Defeat of. (J. Gibbon) Am. Cath. Q. **2**: 271, 665. — (E. Jacker) Am. Cath. Q. **1**: 712.
— Last Battle of. (J. J. Talbot) Penn Mo. **8**: 679.
— My Life on the Plains. Galaxy, **13**: 39–748. **14**: 25–751. **15**: 164–780. **16**: 42, 174, 747.
— Whittaker's Life of. (F. W. Palfrey) Nation, **24**: 179.
Custody of Infants. Fraser, **19**: 205. — Brit. & For. R. **7**: 269.
Custom and Sex. (H. Lawrenny) Fortn. **17**: 310.
Customs, Ancient, Blunt on. Ecl. R. **38**: 505.
— Curious old. (A. H. Baldwin) Belgra. **17**: 50.
— Odd, in old Families. (W. Dowe) Nat. Q. **35**: 366.
— past and gone. Temp. Bar, **11**: 387.
— Some quaint. Lond. Soc. **37**: 316.
— Some undesirable old. All the Year, **32**: 580.
— Tenacity of. (A. Fonblanque) Temp. Bar, **52**: 387.
Custom-House, New York, Who is responsible for? (E. L. Godkin) Nation, **28**: 96.
— Passing the. (H. D. Jenkins) Lakeside, **4**: 108.
— Two Hours at. Chamb. J. **30**: 333.
Custom-Houses, Colonial. (E. Langton) Fraser, **98**: 482.
— Colonial and Indian, and Manchester. (A. Michie) Fraser, **97**: 632.
Custom-House Bonds. Niles's Reg. **41**: 119.
Custom-House Laws. (H. D. Hyde) Am. Soc. Sci. J. **9**: 132.
Custom-House Rules at Havana. Hunt, **11**: 87.
Custom-House Sale, A. Chamb. J. **34**: 371.
Customs Laws and their Administration, 1877. (H. D. Hyde) Am. Soc. Sci. J. **9**: 132.
Customs Revenue System. Am. Law R. **2**: 653.
Cut down like Grass. St. James, **23**: 215–769.
Cut up; First Attempt at writing a Book. St. James, **18**: 347.
Cutcherry Intrigue, A. Fraser, **88**: 757.
Cuthbert, St. Fraser, **77**: 233.
— History of. Dub. R. **27**: 512.
— Life and Legend of. Chr. Rem. **44**: 158.
Cutler, Sir John. House. Words, **12**: 427.
Cutler, Manasseh, and the Ordinance of 1787. (W. F. Poole) No. Am. **122**: 229. — (W. F. Poole) N. E. Reg. **27**: 161.
— Journal in New York, 1787. Hist. M. **22**: 25, 82, 142. — Hours at Home, **7**: 455.
Cutler, Samuel, with portrait. (J. M. Gray) N. E. Reg. **35**: 213.
Cutlery Works, Sheffield, Day at. Penny M. **13**: 161.
Cutt, John. Am. Q. Reg. **15**: 165.
Cutting and Boring Machine, Elterich's. Pract. M. **5**: 360.
Cutting Wise Teeth. Temp. Bar, **56**: 333.
Cuttings, Deep, Construction of. (Prof. Hosking) J. Frankl. Inst. **41**: 73.
Cuttle-Fish. (L. L. Hartt) Am. Natural. **3**: 257. — (St. G. Mivart) Pop. Sci. R. **8**: 111. — (A. Wilson) Good Words, **14**: 677. — Chamb. J. **53**: 645. — Penny M. **3**: 324.
— and Nautilus. (H. Woodward) Stud. & Intel. Obs. **4**: 1, 241.
— Giant. (W. S. Kent) Pop. Sci. R. **13**: 113. — (A. S. Packard, jr.) Am. Natural. **7**: 87. — (A. E. Verrill) Am. Natural. **8**: 167. **9**: 21, 78.
Cutts Genealogy. (J. W. Thornton) N. E. Reg. **2**: 276.
Cuvier, G. (A. De Candolle) Am. J. Sci. **23**: 303. — (C. U. Shephard) Chr. Q. Spec. **6**: 291, 456. — For. Q. **14**: 311. **22**: 45. — For. R. **5**: 342. — Ed. R. **62**: 143. — Knick. **3**: 17. — Select J. **1**: [88. **3**: [54. — (Sir D. Brewster) No. Brit. **1**: 1. — Lond. M. **20**: 221. — Mus. **26**: 209. **28**: 477. — Mo. R. **132**: 159.
— and Blainville. Brit. Q. **24**: 365. Same art. Liv. Age, **51**: 417.
— as a Naturalist. (C. L. Laurillard) Ed. New Philos. J. **16**: 340.
— Eulogy on. (Baron Pasquier) Ed. New Philos. J. **14**: 339. **15**: 164.
— Lee's Memoir of. Ecl. R. **58**: 228.
— Life and Works of. Ed. R. **62**: 265.
— Obituary Note on. (A. de Candolle) Ed. New Philos. J. **14**: 209.
— on the Animal Kingdom. Mo. R. **88**: 449.
— Scientific Labors of. Mo. R. **141**: 352.
— Theory of the Earth. Ed. R. **22**: 454. — So. R. **8**: 69. — Anal. M. **4**: 206.
Cuvillier-Fleury, Notes on. Colburn, **105**: 310.
Cuyamaca Mountains, Animals of. (J. G. Cooper) Am. Natural. **8**: 14.
— Botany of. (J. G. Cooper) Am. Natural. **8**: 90.
Cuzco, the City of the Incas. Ecl. M. **38**: 451.
Cuyp, A., and his Paintings. (E. Mason) Harper, **61**: 61.
— Markham's Journey to. Chamb. J. **25**: 261. — Colburn, **106**: 441.
Cyanotype Printing. (J. M. Eder) J. Frankl. Inst. **111**: 469.
Cycads. (J. R. Jackson) Intel. Obs. **5**: 246.
Cycles of the Worlds. (R. H. Patterson) Belgra. **8**: 415.
Cycloid, Note on the. (L. R. Gibbes) Math. Mo. **1**: 297.
Cyclometers and other Paradoxers. Nature, **12**: 558. **13**: 28.
Cyclone at Calcutta, 1864. (L. J. Jennings) Fortn. **2**: 424. — Liv. Age, **84**: 44.
— Bengal, of 1876. (C. Dambeck) Pop. Sci. Mo. **12**: 192. — Geog. M. **4**: 198.
— Contribution to History of. Geog. M. **1**: 238.
— Escape from a Fijian. Macmil. **42**: 27. Same art. Liv. Age, **145**: 627.
— in the Universe. (J. Mackintosh) Pop. Sci. Mo. **7**: 209.
— in the West Indies. (G. W. Westerby) Nature, **5**: 507.
— Signs of a. All the Year, **34**: 247, 449.
— What a Cyclone did. All the Year, **13**: 106.
Cyclones. (A. S. Herschel) Intel. Obs. **8**: 329.
— Avoidance of. (J. Rodgers and A. Schoenborn) Am. J. Sci. **73**: 205.
— in the Indian Ocean. (C. Meldrum) Nature, **6**: 28.
— of the Northern Pacific Ocean. (W. C. Redfield) Am. J. Sci. **74**: 21.
— Phenomena of. Ev. Sat. **11**: 38.
— Storm Waves of. Nature, **15**: 311.
— Tornadoes, and Waterspouts. (W. Ferrell) Am. J. Sci. **122**: 33.
See Hurricanes; Tornadoes; Whirlwinds.
Cyclopædia, English, and Universal Information. (D. Masson) Macmil. **5**: 357.
— New American. (G. B. Taylor) Chr. R. **23**: 596.

Cyclopædias. (G. A. Hudson) Galaxy, **22**: 67. — (A. Hunter) St. Paul's, **12**: 464.
— History of. Quar. **113**: 354.
Cyclopean-Walled Towns. (L. G. Olmstead) Appleton, **5**: 161.
Cylinders and Spheres, Resistance of. (V. D. Dery) Ecl. Engin. **14**: 152.
— Lamé's Formula for Strength of thick hollow. (G. Lanza) J. Frankl. Inst. **102**: 329.
Cylindrical Fitting, Standard Sizes in. (G. Richards) J. Frankl. Inst. **109**: 17.
Cylindrical Surfaces for Calendar or other Rolls. J. Frankl. Inst. **100**: 377.
Cymbaleer's Bride. Dub. Univ. **20**: 400.
Cymbeline in a Hindu Play-House. (H. Littledale) Ecl. M. **95**: 96.
Cymric Literature in Middle Ages. Dub. Univ. **63**: 303.
Cymric Studies in Relation to English History. Dub. Univ. **62**: 243.
Cymry, Habits and Legends of. Dub. Univ. **64**: 464.
— past and present. Victoria, **5**: 497.
Cynic, Memoirs of a. St. Paul's, **13**: 67–639.
— Modern. Once a Week, **22**: 142.
Cynic's Apology. Cornh. **19**: 574.
Cynics and Hero-Worshipers. (G. S. Godkin) Argosy, **32**: 144.
Cynical Spectators; Gulliver, Candide, Teufelsdröckh. Dub. Univ. **67**: 64, 184.
Cynicasterism. (R. G. White) Galaxy, **20**: 837.
Cynicism. Temp. Bar, **14**: 297. — St. Paul's, **6**: 596.
— Modern. Blackw. **102**: 62.
— past and present. Ev. Sat. **17**: 489.
Cynrowski, Count, Reminiscence of. Ev. Sat. **10**: 174.
Cyples, W. Process of Human Experience. (P. Bayne) Contemp. **39**: 548.
Cypress in Poetry. St. James, **17**: 205.
Cypress Crown; a Tale. Blackw. **7**: 156.
Cypress Timber. (M. W. Dickson and A. Brown) Am. J. Sci. **55**: 15.
Cyprian, St. (W. A. Benton) Am. Church R. **19**: 615.
— and early Christianity. (J. W. Nevin) Merscersb. **4**: 259–513.
— and his Times. (J. H. Merle d'Aubigné) New Eng. **31**: 643.
— Life and Times of. Kitto, **17**: 279.
— Nevin on. (A. Varien) Mercersb. **5**: 555.
— Shepherd on. Chr. Obs. **54**: 308.
— Study of his Life. (J. C. Long) Bapt. Q. **11**: 385.
— Tizzani on. Dub. R. **62**: 165.
Cyprus, Island of. (L. Cass) So. Lit. Mess. **7**: 81. — (J. A. Johnson) Scrib. **3**: 177. — (R. H. Lang) Macmil. **38**: 325, 337. Same art. Liv. Age, **138**: 627. **139**: 3. — Blackw. **126**: 150. — Geog. M. **5**: 201. — Lond. Q. **51**: 372.
Cyprus, Island of, Adventure in. (D. Ker) Lippinc. **22**: 504.
— Ancient. Quar. **146**: 414.
— and its Inhabitants. Dub. Univ. **48**: 175–523.
— and Mycenæ. (A. S. Murray) 19th Cent. **5**: 112.
— Discoveries at. (R. S. Poole) Contemp. **31**: 344.
— — Cesnola's. (H. M. Baird) Meth. Q. **39**: 476. — (R. Sturgis) Nation, **26**: 186. — (H. Hitchcock) Harper, **45**: 188. — So. R. n. s. **24**: 442.
— — — Trials in. (G. W. Sheldon) Appleton, **18**: 150.
— — Pottery found in ancient Tombs in. (T. B. Sandwith) Arch. **45**: 126.
— — Unknown Graves in. (R. H. Horne) Macmil. **38**: 403.
— English Occupation of. Liv. Age, **138**: 574.
— Extract from a Letter of Sir Garnet Wolsey's. Macmil. **39**: 96.
— Fiasco of. (A. Forbes) 19th Cent. **4**: 609.
— Folk Lore of. (W. Axon) Dub. Univ. **80**: 25.
— Fortnight in. Temp. Bar, **54**: 48.
— Inscriptions from. (I. H. Hall) Scrib. **20**: 205.
— Is it worth keeping? (R. H. Lang) Macmil. **40**: 441.
— Pilgrimage to, in 1395–96. (J. T. Bent) Fraser, **103**: 818. Same art. Liv. Age, **150**: 126.
— Present and Future of, 1878. (R. S. Poole) Contemp. **33**: 137.
— Recent Researches in Cilicia, 1878. Colburn, **163**: 313.
— Trip to. (W. F. Butler) Good Words, **21**: 518, 807.
Cyprus Wine. (P. J. de Beranger) Bentley, **5**: 426.
Cyrenaica, Hamilton's North Africa. Colburn, **107**: 432.
— Modern. Ed. R. **48**: 220.
Cyrenian Marbles. Art J. **14**: 20.
Cyrenius, Latin Equivalent of. (T. D. Woolsey) Bib. Sac. **35**: 499.
Cyril, St., of Alexandria. Dub. R. **60**: 349.
Cyril, Patriarch of Constantinople. (J. A. Alexander) Princ. **5**: 212. — (A. G. Paspati) Bib. Sac. **23**: 452.
Cyril, St., of Jerusalem, Milman on. (M. Mahan) Am. Church R. **14**: 575.
— Works of. Dub. R. **7**: 1.
Cyril Thornton, Yankee Criticism on. Tait, **4**: 97.
Cyrus, Identity of. Kitto, **13**: 435. **14**: 364. **15**: 157.
— Inscriptions of. (G. Rawlinson) Contemp. **37**: 86. Same art. Liv. Age, **144**: 368.
Czar, and the Sceptic; a Sketch. Dub. Univ. **55**: 66.
Czar Alexander and Czar Mob; a Poem. Fraser, **52**: 717.
Czar's Clemency; a Polish Priest's Story. Cornh. **36**: 561. Same art. Liv. Age, **135**: 812.
Czars, Palace and Tombs of. (N. S. Dodge) Overland, **8**: 125.
Czartoryski, Prince Adam, and Alexander I. of Russia. (M. Heilprin) Nation, **1**: 150.
Czermak, Johann Nepomuk. (M. Foster) Nature, **9**: 63.
Czerny, George. Cornh. **32**: 213. — Penny M. **8**: 179.
Czerski, John, in England. Ecl. R. **84**: 492.

D

Da Capo; a Tale. (A. I. Thackeray) Cornh. **36**: 641. **37**: 1. Same art. Harper, **56**: 119, 289. Same art. Liv. Age, **135**: 422–736.
Dace, The. (A. H. Baldwin) Once a Week, **11**: 153.
— and the Roach. Penny M. **11**: 436.
Da Costa, Isaac. (M. G. Hansen) Ref. Q. **28**: 27.
Dacotah. *See* Dakota.
Dacre, Lady; Tales of the Peerage. Dub. Univ. **7**: 205.
Daddy Dodd; a Tale. All the Year, **14**: 566.
Daddy Will. (C. D. Deshler) Harper, **57**: 238.
Dafforne, James, Obituary of. Art J. **32**: 248.
Daft Days, Tales of. Blackw. **12**: 600, 761. **13**: 324.
Daggett, David. (S. W. S. Dutton) New Eng. **9**: 296.
Daguerre, L. J. M., with portrait. Internat. M. **4**: 283. — Tait, n. s. **17**: 625.

Daguerreotype. Am. J. Sci. 37: 69. — (W. H. Goode) Am. J. Sci. 40: 137. — No. Brit. 7: 248. — For. Q. 23: 213. — Dem. R. 6: 444. — (A. Wynter) Peop. J. 2: 288.
— and Electrotype. Westm. 34: 434.
— Discovery of. Dem. R. 5: 517.
— Experiments with Galvanic Light. (B. Silliman, jr.) Am. J. Sci. 43: 185.
— History of. Mo. R. 150: 321.
— Practical Description of, 1839. (M. Daguerre) J. Frankl. Inst. 28: 303.
Daguerreotypes. Godey, 63: 110, 200, 290.
Daguerreotype Art, Progress and State of, 1844. (M. Claudet) J. Frankl. Inst. 40: 45, 113.
Daguerreotype Pictures for the Stereoscope. (F. A. P. Barnard) Am. J. Sci. 66: 348.
Daguerreotyping. (J. H. Fitzgibbon) West. J. 6: 200, 380.
— Natural. Ecl. Mus. 1: 419.
Dahabiah in Egypt. Fraser, 58: 266.
Dahcotah. *See* Dakota.
Dahome and Abeokuta. (R. F. Burton) Lond. Q. 23: 452.
Dahomey and the Dahomans. Chamb. J. 15: 213. — Tait, n. s. 18: 300. — Ecl. R. 93: 459.
— — Forbes's. Liv. Age, 29: 257. — Fraser, 44: 233.
— Burton's Mission to. (W. W. Reade) Anthrop. R. 2: 335.
— Customs of. All the Year, 12: 414.
— Journal of a Visit to, 1847. (A. R. Ridgway) Colburn, 81: 187–406.
— King of, at Home. Liv. Age, 79: 63.
— Mission to. Ecl. M. 64: 19. — Ecl. R. 120: 506.
— Trip to. (J. W. Watson) Lippinc. 7: 37, 165. — Broadw. 10: 147.
— Wilmot's Visit to King of. Liv. Age, 78: 147.
Dahra, Caves of. (E. Clive) Bentley, 20: 209.
Daille, Pierre. (C. W. Baird) M. Am. Hist. 1: 91.
Daily Flambeau, Rise and Fall of. Chamb. J. 37: 353.
Daily Service. (C. W. Homer) Am. Church R. 16: 106.
Dairy, London, Day at. Penny M. 10: 297.
Dairies, American. (S. Buckland) Fraser, 75: 512. — Penny M. 9: 26.
Dairy-Farming; Butter and Cheese. (E. J. Wickson) Harper, 51: 813.
Dairyman's Daughter. Blackw. 12: 748.
Daisy, The. (Mrs. Lankester) Pop. Sci. R. 1: 17.
— Dissecting a. (G. Allen) Sup. Pop. Sci. Mo. 2: 329.
— in India. (J. Montgomery) Lond. M. 7: 675.
— Pedigree of. Cornh. 44: 168.
Daisy's Choice. Chamb. J. 46: 33, 60, 75.
Daisy's Sergeant. (F. W. Loring) O. & N. 6: 391.
Daisy's Trials. All the Year, 24: 497–614. Same art. Appleton, 5: 2–185.
Daisy Hope. House. Words, 12: 461. Same art. Ecl. M. 37: 352.
Daisy Miller; a Study. (H. James, jr.) Cornh. 37: 678. 38: 44. Same art. Liv. Age, 138: 27–226.
Dakota Indians, Calendar of, Mallery on. (A. L. Riggs) Nation, 25: 124.
— Religion of. Am. Presb. R. 9: 353.
— Who is to blame? (E. Jacker) Am. Cath. Q. 1: 712.
Dakota Territory; Bad Lands. (J. A. Allen) Am. Natural. 10: 207.
— Geology of Northeastern. (F. V. Hayden) Am. J. Sci. 93: 15.
— a Diocese? (J. H. Hopkins) Am. Church R. 34: 135.
— Statistics of, 1869. Am. J. Educ. 18: 489.
— Wheat Fields of. (C. C. Coffin) Harper, 60: 529.
Dal Pozzo's Happiness of Italy. Westm. 21: 118.
Dalby; a Tale. Chamb. J. 33: 241.
Dale, David. Lond. Soc. 8: 461.
Dale, Com. Richard, with portrait. Portfo.(Den.) 11: 499.
Dale, Thos. Blackw. 8: 185. 12: 61. — Mo. R. 99: 241.
Dale Abbey, Derbyshire. (S. Fox) Reliquary, 8: 193.
Dalecarlia, Rambles in. (C. U. C. Burton) Nat. M. 9: 361, 401.
Dalertes, Sect of. Cong. M. 2: 483.
Dalesfolk, The. Chamb. J. 55: 157.
Dalgarno, George, Works of. (Sir W. Hamilton) Ed. R. 61: 407.
Dalhousie, Lord. Fraser, 52: 123.
Dallas, Alexander James. (E. Quincy) Nation, 13: 179.
— Life of. Portfo.(Den.) 17: 181.
Dallas, Alexander R. C., Life of. Chr. Obs. 72: 98.
Dallas, George M., with portrait. Dem. R. 10: 158.
— Letter, July 25, 1851. Am. Whig R. 14: 451.
— Speech on Nullification. Niles's Reg. 43: supp. 124.
Dallas Galbraith. (R. H. Davis) Lippinc. 1: 9–568. 2: 9, 121, 233.
Dalmatia. Brit. Q. 29: 57.
— and Montenegro, Wilkinson's. (F. Bowen) No. Am. 70: 369. — Blackw. 65: 202.
— Day in. Fraser, 36: 127.
— — with the Voivoda. (E. King) Lippinc. 18: 477.
Dalmeny, Lady. Spanish Lady's Love. Ed. R. 83: 339. — Quar. 78: 323.
Dalou, Jules. Portfo. 8: 78.
Dalrymple, Sir James and Sir John. (H. H. Lancaster) Ed. R. 143: 1. Same art. Liv. Age, 128: 579.
Dalrymples, Story of. (W. Chambers) Chamb. J. 52: 705.
Dalstone, Sir George, Character of. (J. Taylor) Chr. Obs. 3: 453.
Dalton, John, with portrait. Pract. M. 6: 257. — Chamb. J. 3: 211.
— and Atomic Chemistry. Quar. 96: 43. Same art. Liv. Age, 44: 707.
— Life and Discoveries of. Brit. Q. 1: 157. Same art. Liv. Age, 5: 115. — Westm. 45: 88. Same art. Ecl. M. 8: 56. — Fraser, 50: 554. — (Sir H. Holland) Ed. R. 96: 43. — (Sir D. Brewster) No. Brit. 27: 465. — Liv. Age, 42: 520. — Westm. 67: 270.
Dalton and Batcheller, Pedigree of. (W. H. Whitmore) N. E. Reg. 27: 364.
Daltonism, or Color-Blindness. (W. Pole) Macmil. 37: 821. Same art. Ecl. M. 95: 100 *See* Color-Blindness.
Daly, Bishop Robert, Memoir of. Chr. Obs. 75: 171.
Dalzell, Downfall of. Lond. M. 6: 27.
Damara, South Africa, Story of Annexation of. (F. R. Statham) Fortn. 34: 617.
Dams, Construction of. (D. S. Howard) J. Frankl. Inst. 88: 233.
— for Reservoirs. (W. J. McAlpine) Ecl. Engin. 16: 54.
— High Masonry, Profiles of. (J. B. McMaster) Ecl. Engin. 14: 259, 289, 385.
Damascus. (C. H. Brigham) Mo. Rel. M. 13: 145. — (C. H. Brigham) No. Am. 83: 30. — (W. S. Tyler) Hours at Home, 4: 314. — Bentley, 39: 48. — Blackw. 126: 387. — Broadw. 7: 226. — Penny M. 9: 353.
— Adventure at. (W. H. Bartlett) Sharpe, 7: 174.
— and Ba'albek, Excursion to. (A. L. Koepper) Am. Whig R. 8: 157, 235.
— and Cairo. (F. W. Holland) Lippinc. 7: 197.
— and Mount Lebanon. (A. L. Koeppen) Mercersb. 7: 513. — Month, 4: 481.
— By Diligence to. (J. H. Johnson) Scrib. 14: 137.
— Castlereagh's Travels to. Dub. Univ. 31: 331.
— Excursions to Environs of. (J. L. Porter) Bib. Sac. 11: 329, 433, 649.
— Hadji Caravan from. (E. T. Rogers) Good Words, 7: 345.
— Massacre of July, 1860, at. (H. J. Warner) Chr. Exam. 70: 325.
— Memoir of. (J. Abbott) Harper, 7: 577.

Damascus, Porter's Five Years in. (J. Forsyth, jr.) Theo. & Lit. J. 10: 146.
— Rambles in. Chamb. J. 20: 105.
— Rivers of. Kitto, 11: 245. 12: 45.
— Round about. Liv. Age, 143: 425.
— Sword-Blades and Gun-Barrels from. J. Frankl. Inst. 2: 1. — Penny M. 8: 138.
Dame Camberback; a Tale. All the Year, 29: 252.
Dame de Margon. Tinsley, 17: 571.
Dame Martha's Well; a Poem. (R. Buchanan) Good Words, 11: 679.
Dame Pugeley's Well. (J. A. St. John) Sharpe, 20: 101.
Dames' Schools. *See* Schools, Dames'.
Damon and Pythias; a Story. (C. Bernhard) Colburn, 127: 55.
Damon, David, Sermon of. Chr. Disc. 5: 241.
Damp, Cause and Cure of. Ecl. Engin. 25: 476. — Am. Arch. 10: 137.
Dampier, William. All the Year, 35: 327.
— Adventures of. Penny M. 2: 414, 429, 434.
— Voyages of. Retros. 9: 73.
Dan Farthing's only Son. All the Year, 44: 396, 419.
Dana, Daniel. Letter on the Atonement. Chr. Mo. Spec. 6: 659.
Dana, Francis. (R. H. Dana, jr.) Pennsyl. M. 1: 86.
Dana, James D. Pop. Sci. Mo. 1: 362.
Dana, Mary S. B., Letters of. (S. Gilman) Chr. Exam. 39: 389.
Dana, Richard Henry. (H. H. Barber) Unita. R. 11: 546. — (R. H. Stoddard) Harper, 58: 769. — (J. H. Ward) Atlan. 43: 518. — (J. G. Wilson) Scrib. 18: 105. — Colburn, 98: 77. Same art. Ecl. M. 29: 397. Same art. Liv. Age, 37: 762.
— Literary Character of. (W. A. Jones) Am. Whig R. 5: 269.
— Poems and Prose Writings of. (E. P. Whipple) Chr. Exam. 48: 247. — (S. G. Brown) No. Am. 72: 115. — (N. Adams) Lit. & Theo. R. 1: 214.
— Poetry of. (W. C. Bryant) No. Am. 26: 239. — (E. C. Tracy) Am. Q. Obs. 2: 149. — Am. Q. 3: 115. — New Eng. M. 5: 327. — Blackw. 37: 416. — Mus. 26: 463.
— Thoughts on the Soul. (F. W. P. Greenwood) No. Am. 30: 274.
— Writings of. (C. C. Felton) Chr. Exam. 15: 392. — Am. Mo. R. 4: 468. — New Eng. 9: 28. — Knick. 38: 542.
Dana, Richard H., jr. Two Years before the Mast. Chr. Exam. 29: 268. — (E. T. Channing) No. Am. 52: 56. — Dem. R. 8: 318. — New York R. 7: 535. — Dub. Univ. 47: 50. Same art. Liv. Age, 48: 560. — Tait, n. s. 8: 430.
Danby, Thomas Osborne, Earl of, Life of. Ecl. R. 79: 373.
Dance, History of the. Liv. Age, 73: 55.
— National, of Hungary. (F. Foster) Appleton, 20: 373.
— of Death. Blackw. 31: 328. — (M. P. Thompson) Cath. World, 33: 55.
— — as a Mystery. Temp. Bar, 12: 292.
— — History of. St. James, 14: 436.
— — in Italian Art. Cornh. 40: 346.
— — Juan de Pedraza's. (D. F. McCarthy) Irish Mo. 4: 326.
— of modern Society. (W. C. Wilkinson) Bapt. Q. 1: 465.
— Physiology of. (Tom Hood) Lond. Soc. 14: 48–367.
Dance-Music. Broadw. 8: 382.
Dances, Characteristic, of the World. (A. E. Barr) Lippinc. 27: 330.
— French scandalous. Internat. M. 2: 333.
— Old English. Temp. Bar, 14: 145.
Dancers, The. (M. Doyle) Penny M. 12: 310.
Dancing. Once a Week, 20: 449. — Penny M. 5: 1. — Sharpe, 44: 178. — Chr. Mo. Spec. 1: 185.
Dancing, Art of. Mo. R. 118: 23.
— as a Fine Art. (W. Bellars) Tinsley, 17: 70.
— at the Opera. Colburn, 47: 299.
— Ball at the Tuileries. Colburn, 61: 222.
— Description of a good Dancer. Tait, n. s. 6: 129.
— in all Ages. St. James, 4: 68.
— in the East. Penny M. 9: 113.
— Polkaphobia; illustr. by Leech. Bentley, 17: 35.
— Lessons in. Once a Week, 20: 257.
— the Poetry of Motion. Colburn, 47: 21.
— Profanity of. Blackw. 6: 43.
— the Schottische. Godey, 65: 74.
— under three Denominations. Victoria, 23: 392.
— Waltzing, etc. So. Lit. Mess. 1: 512.
See Minuet; Polka; Waltz.
Dancing-Girl of India. Chamb. J. 8: 98.
Dancing-Girls of the East. Anal. M. 1: 49.
Dancing Mania. Penny M. 8: 439, 454.
— of the French Revolution. (A. Sadler) Once a Week, 16: 137.
Dancing-Master, Our old. St. James, 14: 508.
Dancing Procession of Echternach. Month, 28: 90.
D'Ancre, Marshal. Liv. Age, 19: 553.
Dandolo, Arigo, Life of. Am. Mo. M. 4: 101.
Dandy, Ancient; a Tale. Blackw. 52: 590.
— of the present Day. Bentley, 8: 40.
Dandies, The. Chamb. J. 36: 205.
— and the Fashionables. (C. J. Langston) Temp. Bar, 63: 471.
— Notes on. (D. Cook) Once a Week, 10: 240, 288.
Dandyism and Beau Brummell. Bentley, 17: 514.
Dane, John, Autobiography of. N. E. Reg. 8: 147.
Dane Genealogy. (J. W. Dean) N. E. Reg. 8: 148.
Danes and Germans, War between. (A. L. Koeppen) Am. Whig R. 8: 453.
— and Norwegians in Great Britain. Dub. R. 32: 184.
— and the Swedes. (Col. Szabo) Colburn, 106: 286. Same art. Ecl. M. 38: 22.
— at Home. All the Year, 13: 115.
— in Ireland. Irish Q. 2: 817.
See Denmark.
Danforth, Samuel, Biography of. Am. Q. Reg. 13: 78.
— Records of. N. E. Reg. 34: 84–359.
Danforth Genealogy. (W. T. Harris) N. E. Reg. 7: 315.
Dangeau, Marquis, Journal of. Ed. R. 119: 61.
— Memoirs of the Court of France. Colburn, 13: 506.
Danger in the Desert. Liv. Age, 109: 415.
— On the Perception of. Colburn, 65: 331.
Danger-Signal, New. Pract. M. 4: 75.
Dangers of the Country. Blackw. 69: 196, 257. — (F. Jeffrey) Ed. R. 10: 1.
Dangerous Classes. (W. Chambers) Chamb. J. 52: 113.
— and Treatment of. (J. F. Richmond) Meth. Q. 33: 455.
— Increase of, in U. S. (J. G. Shea) Am. Cath. Q. 4: 240.
— of London. Brit. Q. 35: 352.
— of New York. (C. L. Brace) Appleton, 3: 211–631. 4: 45–667. 5: 18.
— out West. Chamb. J. 51: 244.
See Criminals.
Dangeville, Mlle., French Actress. All the Year, 41: 185.
D'Angoulême. *See* Angoulême.
Daniel the Prophet. Lond. Q. 43: 292
— Model for young Men. (W. Brock) Ex. H. Lec. 6: 341.
— *versus* Zoroaster. (C. H. Hall) Am. Church R. 16: 355.
Daniel, John M., with portrait. Dem. R. 30: 385.
Daniel, Junius. Land We Love, 5: 97.
Daniel, Luke, and Polperro. (W. Rendle) Temp. Bar, 60: 536.
Daniel, Robert Mackenzie. Tait, n. s. 14: 468.
Daniel, Samuel, Poems of. Retros. 8: 227.
Daniel O'Rourke; an Epic Poem. Blackw. 7: 476. 8: 40, 157. 9: 77, 373. 10: 429.

Daniel Deronda. (George Eliot) Harper, 52: 425–899. 53: 109–745.
Daniel Leary; an Irish Tale. (Mrs. Hoare) Peop. J. 4: 53.
Daniell Family. (M. G. Daniell) N. E. Reg. 28: 185.
Danielo, Prince of Montenegro, Visit to. (A. Baschet) Sharpe, 30: 185.
Danish and Norwegian Literature. For. Q. 6: 48.
Danish and Swedish Poetry. (E. Perhault) Nat. Q. 3: 133.
Danish Ballads. Fraser, 45: 649. 51: 86.
— Old. (R. Buchanan) Fortn. 1: 685.
Danish Camp, In the. All the Year, 11: 269, 484.
Danish Claims. Westm. 22: 439. — Brit. & For. R. 5: 581. — Westm. 31: 462.
Danish Drama. For. Q. 8: 1.
Danish Dressmaker. Chamb. J. 40: 21.
Danish Exploring Expedition. Hunt, 23: 406.
Danish Islands, Treaty of U. S. for. Nation, 8: 248.
Danish Literature. Ecl. R. 122: 545. — (R. Baird) Am. Q. Reg. 14: 59. — For. Q. 21: 132. — Liv. Age, 4: 323. — No. Brit. 38: 133.
— Survey of. (Mrs. Bushby) Colburn, 94: 452. 95: 40–253.
Danish Poetry; Ingemann. For. R. 2: 67. — For. Q. 21: 132.
Danish Popular Tales. (A. Hamilton) Macmil. 8: 43.
Danish Question, 1850. Am. Whig R. 12: 324.
Danish Romances. (N. Neville) St. James, 14: 449.
Danish Sound and Belt-Tolls. (J. F. W. Schlegel) Hunt, 10: 218, 303. — (C. F. Dunbar) No. Am. 84: 48. — Dem. R. 36: 426.
Danish Visit to England 100 Years ago. Once a Week, 8: 497.
Danks, Hart P. (G. Birdseye) Potter Am. Mo. 12: 333.
Danluce Castle. Sharpe, 11: 361.
Dannecker, Recollections of. Art J. 8: 34.
Dante Alighieri. (R. Atkinson) Contemp. 24: 420. — (M. Creighton) Macmil. 29: 554. 30: 56. Same art. Ecl. M. 82: 704. 83: 74. Same art. Liv. Age, 121: 771. — (J. M. Finotti) Cath. World, 8: 213. — (W. W. Fyfe) Sharpe, 19: 111. — (Alice King) Argosy, 9: 350. — (L. F. Soldan) Western, 1: 160, 243. — (F. R. Marvin) Western, 2: 65. — (E. I. Sears) Nat. Q. 1: 1. — (J. C. Gray) No. Am. 8: 322. — (F. Inglis) No. Am. 37: 506. — (S. G. Brown) No. Am. 62: 323. — (R. Wheaton) No. Am. 64: 97. — (Ugo Foscolo) Ed. R. 29: 453. — Ed. R. 30: 317. Same art. Selec. Ed. R. 1: 64. — For. Q. 33: 1. — Knick. 18: 275. — (A. B. Hyde) Meth. Q. 12: 49. — Westm. 7: 153. — Mus. 11: 43. — Mo. R. 113: 109. — Cornh. 12: 243. Same art. Ecl. M. 65: 480. — Ecl. R. 108: 481. 118: 461. — Am. Cath. Q. 5: 715. — Fraser, 57: 426. — Quar. 126: 413.
— a Poem. Cornh. 1: 483.
— and Beatrice. (M. Arnold) Fraser, 67: 665. — Brit. Q. 19: 205. Same art. Ecl. M. 31: 380. — (C. T. Turner) Internat. R. 3: 94. — Tait, n. s. 12: 14.
— and Bunyan. (J. Ferguson) Am. Church R. 16: 337.
— and his Age. (E. M. Clerke) Dub. R. 85: 279. — (P. Dillon) Irish Mo. 9: 307.
— and his Circle. Lond. Q. 42: 299.
— and his Commentators. Ho. & For. R. 3: 574.
— and his Translators. Dub. Univ. 43: 543. — Westm. 75: 202.
— and his latest Translators, 1858. (G. H. Calvert) Putnam, 11: 155. Same art. Broadw. 7: 232.
— and his Times. Blackw. 13: 141.
— and Italian Literature. Meth. Q. 16: 381.
— and Milton. (T. B. Macaulay) Ed. R. 42: 316. — St. James, 15: 243.
— — and Æschylus. Tait, n. s. 20: 513, 577, 641.
— and St. Paul. Univ. Q. 15: 400.
— Beatrice. Ecl. M. 11: 231.
Dante Alighieri. Beatrice, and Lady of the Vita Nuova. (J. R. Lowell) No. Am. 115: 139.
— — as a Type of Womanhood. (E. V. Scherb) Chr. Exam. 64: 39.
— Character of. (W. R. Alger) Chr. Exam. 81: 37.
— Commemoration of, in 1865. (H. T. Tuckerman) Nation, 1: 440. — Lond. Q. 25: 1. Same art. Ecl. M. 66: 1.
— Divine Comedy. (J. A. Smith) Bapt. Q 9: 322. — Cath. World, 1: 268. — Chr. Rem. 19: 187. — Lond. M. 7: 317, 396. — Nat. M. 7: 28. — No. Brit. 21: 451. — St. James, 17: 45. — Sharpe, 23: 332. — Same art. Ecl. M. 38: 567.
— — and New Life. Cornh. 5: 283.
— — Boyd's. Ed. R. 1: 307.
— — Carey's Translation of. Ecl. R. 29: 556.
— — Contemporary Commentary on. Mo. R. 148: 170.
— — in English, French, and German. Chr. Rem. 33: 414.
— — in English Terza Rima. Blackw. 101: 736.
— — Longfellow's Translation of. (G. W. Greene) Atlan. 20: 188. — (C. E. Norton) Nation, 4: 369. 5: 226. — (W. D. Howells) Nation, 4: 492. — (C. E. Norton) No. Am. 105: 124. — (E. I. Sears) Nat. Q. 15: 286.
— — Perez's and Longfellow's. Dub. R. 64: 398.
— — Mrs. Ramsay's Translation of. Chr. Obs. 63: 214.
— — Sources of. (R. Wheaton) No. Am. 64: 97.
— — Translations of. (C. E. Norton) No. Am. 102: 509.
— — Inferno. (F. M. McAllister) Am. Church R. 29: 113.
— — — Dayman's Translation. Mo. R. 163: 43.
— — — Disputed Translations of. Lond. M. 10: 529.
— — — Canto I. (Sir J. F. W. Herschel) Cornh. 18: 38.
— — — Parsons's Translation. (C. E. Norton) Nation, 5: 269. — Dial, 4: 285.
— — — Lord Vernon's. Fraser, 79: 651.
— — — Wright's Translation. Ed. R. 57: 412. — Mo. R. 130: 428.
— — Purgatorio. (L. F. Soldan) Western, 2: 701. 3: 21.
— — — Butler's Trans. (C. E. Norton) Nation, 31: 397.
— — — translated. (T. W. Parsons) Cath. World, 12: 145. 14: 503. 15: 730. 16: 319, 581. 17: 24, 158, 304. 18: 166, 299, 587. 19: 450. 27: 272, 498. 29: 289. 30: 350. 31: 17, 450.
— — Paradiso. St. Paul's, 8: 63.
— — — Wright's. Dub. Univ. 16: 590.
— Early Life of. Dub. Univ. 29: 412. Same art. Ecl. M. 11: 231. — Cornh. 32: 471.
— from the modern Point of View. (S. Osgood) Knick. 58: 340, 505.
— Home and Haunts of. (T. A. Trollope) Belgra. 32: 69.
— in Exile. Cornh. 32: 670.
— Lamennais on. Westm. 86: 371.
— Life of, Balbo's. New Q. 1: 164.
— — and Genius of. (P. Schaff) Am. Whig R. 8: 125.
— Macaulay's Estimate of. Gent. M. n. s. 11: 255.
— Notes on. Dub. Univ. 63: 504.
— Rediscovery of his Remains. Cornh. 13: 665.
— Rossetti's. For. Q. 5: 419. — For. R. 2: 175.
— Miss Rossetti's Shadow of. (J. R. Dennett) Nation, 15: 28.
— Skull of. (H. Welcker) Anthrop. R. 5: 56.
— Spirit of. (A. Gallenga) Colburn, 80: 1.
— Taaffe's Commentary on. Mo. R. 102: 225.
— Translations from. New Eng. M. 5: 474.
— Two Studies in. (E. H. Plumptre) Contemp. 40: 843.
— Vita Nuova. (C. E. Norton) Atlan. 3: 62, 202, 330. — Dub. Univ. 29: 412. Same art. Ecl. M. 11: 231. — (L. G. Ware) Chr. Exam. 73: 363. — Fraser, 65: 580.
— Works and Wanderings of. Fraser, 63: 299.
Danton, Jacques Georges. Temp. Bar, 32: 475. — Dem. R. 24: 401, 523.

Danton, Jacques Georges, and Robespierre. (G. Gilfillan) Hogg, **6**: 65.
— — and Marat. Dem. R. **14**: 223.
Dantzic, Dom of. Internat. M. **1**: 43.
Danube, The River. (J. Bowring) Howitt, **1**: 324. — C. F. F. Clinton) Bentley, **16**: 191, 246, 337. — Fraser, **22**: 560, 684. — Sharpe, **29**: 9.
— Along. (E. King) Lippinc. **22**: 137.
— and the Black Sea. Dub. R. **3**: 198.
— and the Crimea. Fraser, **50**: 296.
— and the Euxine; a Poem. Blackw. **64**: 608
— and the Mountains. Chamb. J. **38**: 65.
— Cruise on, Mansfield's. Fraser, **47**: 190.
— Day on. (P. Godwin) Putnam, **4**: 397.
— Delta of. (Sir C. A. Hartley) Ecl. Engin. **11**: 257. — (C. A. Hartley) J. Frankl. Inst. **74**: 161.
— Down. (J. H. Browne) Harper, **45**: 652, 817. — (J. Hay) Putnam, **15**: 625.
— Engineering on. Ecl. Engin. **13**: 276.
— Fishermen of. Chamb. J. **8**: 195.
— Foreign Influence on the Banks of. Colburn, **90**: 253.
— from Vienna to Constantinople. Fraser, **49**: 571.
— in Hungary. Temp. Bar, **6**: 61, 244, 348.
— Lower. (E. Hull) Dub. Univ. **83**: 257.
— Letters from. Fraser, **37**: 403.
— More Light on. Tait, n. s. **8**: 425.
— Quin's Steam Voyage down. Ed. R. **52**: 109. — (R. Southey) Quar. **54**: 469. — Westm. **23**: 471. — Brit. & For. R. **1**: 427. — Mo. R. **138**: 165.
— Races of. (J. Fiske) Atlan. **39**: 401.
— Reopening of. Dub. Univ. **44**: 625.
— Russia and. Colburn, **91**: 362.
— Scene on. (H. C. Andersen) Howitt, **1**: 209.
— Scenery on. Penny M. **10**: 333, 349, 365.
Danubian Days. (E. King) Lippinc. **22**: 649.
Danubian Principalities. (C. H. Brigham) No. Am. **84**: 70. — (A. Gielgud) Fortn. **6**: 87. — (J. O. Noyes) Nat. M. **8**: 232. — (G. M. Towle) Harper, **52**: 473. — Colburn, **101**: 127. — Dub. Univ. **49**: 1. — Brit. Q. **25**: 391. — Ecl. R. **105**: 563. — Lond. Q. **10**: 213. — Colburn, **109**: 294.
Danvers, Mass., Burial Inscriptions at. N. E. Reg. **8**: 73.
— Centennial Celebration at, 1852. Liv. Age, **34**: 85.
— Church Records. N. E. Reg. **11**: 131, 316. **12**: 245. **13**: 55.
— Peabody Institute. Am. J. Educ. **1**: 237.
Danville, Ky., Men of. Danv. Q. **4**: 151, 274.
Danville Quarterly Review, Origin of. (R. J. Breckinridge) Danv. Q. **2**: 140.
Daponte, Lorenzo. (H. T. Tuckerman) Putnam, **12**: 527. — Same art. Dub. Univ. **80**: 215.
Dapples; a Poem. (P. H. Hayne) So. R. n. s. **7**: 213. Same art. N. Ecl. **6**: 257.
D'Arblay. *See* Arblay, Madame d'.
Darboy, Archb. of Paris, with portrait. Ev. Sat. **11**: 55.
Darby the Swift. (J. A. Wade) Bentley, **1**: 541. **2**: 68, 464.
Darby Sykes. Dub. Univ. **11**: 164.
Dardanelles and Bosphorus, Undercurrent in. (W. B. Carpenter) Nature, **6**: 521.
— and the Suez Canal, Legal Position of. (J. Macdonell) Fraser, **97**: 654.
Dardenne, Antoine, the Hermit. West. Mo. R. **1**: 569.
Dardistan. Geog. M. **2**: 232.
Dargan, Edward S., with portrait. Dem. R. **29**: 67.
Darien, Isthmus of. Dub. Univ. **35**: 221. **41**: 718.
— Map of, 1870. (J. C. Trautwine) J. Frankl. Inst. **91**: 43.
— Routes across. Lippinc. **25**: 358.
— Scottish Colony of, 1698–1700. Retros. **17**: 173.
— Strain's Expedition to. (J. T. Headley) Harper, **10**: 433, 600, 745.
— Survey of. (E. Cullen) Hunt, **46**: 14.
Darien, Isthmus of, Trip across. Liv. Age, **14**: 217.
— Warburton's History of. New Q. **1**: 171.
Darien Expedition. Hogg, **4**: 350.
Darien Language. Am. Hist. Rec. **3**: 54.
Darien Ship Canal. (J. C. Bayles) Hunt, **60**: 168. — (W. H. Bryan) Overland, **2**: 116. — (C. C. Buel) Scrib. **18**: 268. — Blackw. **54**: 658. — Dem. R. **6**: 287, 413. **32**: 458. — Ecl. M. **1**: 88. **4**: 351. — For. Q. **34**: 389. — Liv. Age, **27**: 193. — Niles's Reg. **28**: 152. **31**: 72. — Am. Whig R. **12**: 441. — (L. Dow) Hours at Home, **10**: 349. — (T. W. Osborn) Internat. R. **7**: 481. — Bentley, **34**: 654. — Ecl. Engin. **1**: 553. — Geog. M. **5**: 312. — Lond. Q. **2**: 172. — Mo. R. **107**: 193. — Tait, n. s. **20**: 683.
— Congress at Paris, 1879. (A. G. Menocal) No. Am. **129**: 288.
— Plan for, 1856. Ecl. R. **105**: 443.
— Route of. Putnam, **13**: 329. — Chamb. J. **19**: 183.
Daring Game. (H. Deas) Overland, **12**: 68.
Darius the Mede. Kitto, **21**: 449.
— Inscriptions concerning. Dub. Univ. **29**: 14.
— Who was? Bib. R. **1**: 25. — (I. W. Bosanquet) Kitto, **16**: 393.
Dariuses, The two. Kitto, **40**: 192.
Darjeeling, India, Sanitarium of. Colburn, **129**: 347.
Dark Ages, The. (C. E. Appleton) Contemp. **8**: 208.
— Character of. Blackw. **47**: 65, 273. Same art. Mus. **3**: 393.
— Europe during. Bost. Mo. **1**: 465.
— Maitland's History of. Dub. R. **17**: 159.
Dark Chamber; a Tale. Chamb. J. **11**: 305.
Dark Church in Vienna; a Story. Cornh. **7**: 326.
Dark Days of 1780. N. E. Mag. **4**: 379.
— in United States, Nov. 1819. Ed. Philos. J. **6**: 266.
— in Canada, 1785 and 1814. (H. D. Sewell) Ed. New Philos. J. **14**: 221.
Dark Dennis and his Grandson. (R. Rowe) Liv. Age, **133**: 437.
Dark House on the Moor. Dub. Univ. **90**: 107.
Dark Lady. (F. C. Fisher) Lippinc. **10**: 194.
Dark Lady. (Mrs. S. C. Hall) Liv. Age, **19**: 557.
Dark Night's Work. (E. C. Gaskell) All the Year, **8**: 457–553. **9**: 1–73.
Dark Pond of Châteaulandrin. (C. M. Caddell) Irish Mo. **4**: 303.
Dark Story. Ecl. M. **58**: 351.
Dark Suspicion. House. Words, **2**: 532.
Dark Wagon; a Poem. (D. M. Moir) Blackw. **67**: 71.
Dark Ways. (H. P. Spofford) Atlan. **11**: 545.
Dark Ways; a Story of 1863. Sharpe, **44**: 181.
Dark Wood; a Poem. (W. Norris) Fortn. **15**: 219.
Darkness, Star of; a Song. Dub. Univ. **2**: 41.
Darley, Felix O. C. (R. H. Stoddard) Nat. M. **9**: 193.
Darley, G. Errors of Ecstasie. Lond. M. **10**: 571.
Darling Dorel. *See* Brieg, Dorothea Sybilla, Duchess of.
Darlington, William, Memorial of. Hist. M. **7**: 233.
Darliston; a Tale. Sharpe, **47**: 113–281. **48**: 1–281. **49**: 1–281. **50**: 1–113.
Darmstadt, Alice Ladies' Society of. Contemp. **21**: 138.
— Ducal. Blackw. **94**: 576.
— Polytechnic School of. Nature, **5**: 368.
Darnley, Contemporary Ballad on Murder of. Fraser, **70**: 221.
Darragh, The; a Tale. Dub. Univ. **47**: 566, 682. **48**: 15–424.
D'Artagnan, Capt., Memoirs of. Temp. Bar, **56**: 42.
Darters, Fish. (D. S. Jordan) Am. Natural. **10**: 335.
— Food of. (S. A. Forbes) Am. Natural. **14**: 697.
Dartington, William. (C. Lanman) Hist. M. **21**: 32.
Dartmoor. All the Year, **21**: 283. — Lond. Q. **24**: 341 Quar. **135**: 138.
— Adventure at. Chamb. J. **26**: 358.

Dartmoor and the Dart. (P. H. Gosse) Intel. Obs. 3: 318.
— Convict Life at. Temp. Bar, 40: 348.
— Experiences on. Lond. Soc. 11: 516.
— Forest of. (R. J. King) Fortn. 6: 300.
— Military Maneuvers and Convicts at. Temp. Bar, 40: 346.
— Straight across. (H. Waddington) Temp. Bar, 19: 272.
— Tramp through. (M. G. Watkins) Belgra. 21: 269.
— Winter Day on. St. James, 23: 791.
Dartmoor Prison. (N. Hawthorne) Dem. R. 18: 31–457. 19: 141, 209. — Sharpe, 31: 134.
— as it was and as it is. Fraser, 48: 577. Same art. Ecl. M. 31: 123. — Liv. Age, 39: 671.
— Reminiscences of Prisoner at. Knick. 23: 146, 356, 517. 24: 457, 519.
Dartmouth, Mass., Records of. N. E. Reg. 20: 336. 21: 265. 22: 66. 30: 56. 34: 198, 406. 35: 32.
Dartmouth College. (D. Henshaw) Hist. M. 4: 299. — Am. J. Educ. 27: 277. — Chr. Obs. 13: 17. — (A. D. Smith) O. & N. 4: 381.
— Alumni of. Am. Q. 4: 45, 112, 327.
— and John Thornton. Cong. Q. 3: 371.
— Biographical Sketch of Graduates. (J. Farmer) Am. Q. Reg. 12: 379.
— Law Case. (W. Dutton) No. Am. 10: 83. — Am. Law R. 8: 189. *See* Webster's Speeches; Marshall's Decisions.
— Library of. (C. W. Scott) Lib. J. 2: 68.
— Revivals of Religion in. (H. Wood) Am. Q. Reg. 9: 177.
Darwen, Congregational Church at. Cong. M. 14: 133.
Darwin, Charles Robert. (A. Gray) Nature, 10: 79. Same art. Pop. Sci. Mo. 5: 475. — (A. Gray) Am. Natural. 8: 473. — with portrait, Appleton, 3: 439. — with portrait, Dub. Univ. 92: 154. — with portrait, Ev. Sat. 10: 347. — with portrait, Ecl. M. 76: 757. — with portrait, Once a Week, 26: 520. — Penn Mo. 2: 469. — Pop. Sci. Mo. 2: 497.
— and F. Galiani. (E. Du Bois-Reymond) Pop. Sci. Mo. 14: 409.
— and Haeckel. (T. H. Huxley) Pop. Sci. Mo. 6: 592.
— Animals and Plants under Domestication. (C. R. Bliss) Cong. R. 9: 453.
— answered. Penn Mo. 6: 368.
— before the French Academy. Nature, 2: 298, 309.
— Critics on. (T. H. Huxley) Contemp. 18: 443.
— Descent of Man. *See* Man.
— Expression of Emotion in Man and Animals. (H. Holbeach) St. Paul's, 12: 190. — Ed. R. 137: 492. Same art. Liv. Age, 118: 3.
— Facts and Fancies of. (D. Brewster) Good Words, 3: 3.
— Hypotheses of. (G. H. Lewes) Fortn. 9: 353, 611. 10: 61, 492.
— on his Travels. (R. E. Thompson) Penn Mo. 2: 562.
— Origin of Species. *See* Species.
— Philosophy of Language. (M. Müller) Fraser, 87: 525, 659. 88: 1. Same art. Ecl. M. 81: 75, 148, 257.
— Testimonial to, in the Netherlands. Am. Natural, 11: 295.
— Theories of Variation. Westm. 91: 207.
Darwin, Erasmus. (T. Hill) Bib. Sac. 35: 461. — Temp. Bar, 60: 309. Same art. Ecl. M. 96: 189. Same art. Liv. Age, 147: 720.
— Botanic Garden. Blackw. 5: 153.
— Krause's Life of. (A. G. Sedgwick) Nation, 30: 253. — Nature, 21: 245.
— Life and Writings of. Lond. M. 6: 520. — Portfo. (Den.) 29: 441.
— Memoir of. (T. Thomson) Ed. R. 4: 230.
— Poems of. Ed. R. 2: 491.
— Remarks on Opinions of. Meth. M. 27: 210.
Darwinian Eden. (M. G. Upton) Overland, 7: 159.
Darwinian Idea. Ev. Sat. 10: 414.
Darwinism. (S. Adams) Cong. R. 11: 233, 338. — (L. T. Adams) New Eng. 33: 741. — (G. Axford) O. & N. 6: 655. — (J. Bayma) Cath. World, 26: 496. — (J. B. Drury) Scrib. 10: 348. — (W. H. Furness) Unita. R. 5: 291. — (F. Gardiner) Bib. Sac. 29: 240. — (L. J. Livermore) Unita. R. 3: 237. — (W. H. Penning) Tinsley, 19: 515. — (J. A. Lowell) Chr. Exam. 68: 449. — (W. N. Rice) New Eng. 26: 603. — (F. Smith) Cath. World, 17: 641. — (G. F. Wright) Bib. Sac. 33: 656. — Am. Church R. 21: 525. — Dub. R. 48: 50. — Ecl. R. 117: 337. — So. R. n. s. 12: 406. — Stud. & Intel. Obs. 1: 179. — (C. J. Sprague) Atlan. 18: 415. — (G. M. Kellogg) O. & N. 8: 283.
— Agassiz and. (J. Fiske) Pop. Sci. Mo. 3: 692.
— Analogies with Calvinism. (G. F. Wright) Bib. Sac. 37: 48.
— and Christianity. (E. O. Haven) Lakeside, 7: 302.
— — Man in. Am. Church R. 24: 288.
— and Design, St. Clair on. Dub. R. 75: 232.
— and Divinity. Fraser, 85: 409. Same art. Pop. Sci. Mo. 1: 188.
— and Language. (W. D. Whitney) No. Am. 119: 61.
— — Schleicher on. (F. M. Müller) Nature, 1: 256.
— and Morality. (J. Watson) Canad. Mo. 10: 319.
— and National Life. Nature, 1: 183.
— and Religion. Macmil. 24: 45. Same art. Ecl. M. 77: 25. Same art. Liv. Age, 109: 621.
— Application of. (E. Muller) Am. Natural. 5: 271.
— Attitude of working Naturalists towards. (A. Gray) Nation, 17: 258.
— Bateman on. Dub. R. 83: 139. — (J. Fiske) Nation, 27: 367.
— Dangers of. Pop. Sci. Mo. 15: 68.
— Deduction from. (W. S. Jevons) Nature, 1: 231.
— Ethical Aspect of. (J. Watson) Canad. Mo. 11: 638.
— Fiske's. Nature, 20: 575.
— Frolic in Space. (J. M. Binckley) Lakeside, 8: 446.
— Gray's Darwiniana. (H. W. Holland) Nation, 23: 358. — Sup. Pop. Sci. Mo. 1: 190.
— Great Difficulty of. (L. S. Beale) Nature, 5: 63.
— Haeckel's Reply to Virchow. (H. T. Finck) Nation, 28: 320.
— Historic Development of. (G. W. Samson) Bapt. Q. 11: 29.
— in Germany. (C. L. Brace) No. Am. 110: 284. — (C. Wright) Nation, 21: 168. — Anthrop. R. 6: 21.
— — New York Nation. Pop. Sci. Mo. 8: 235.
— in Morals. (J. A. Allen) Canad. Mo. 11: 490. — (F. P. Cobbe) Theo. R. 8: 167.
— Infallibility in. Dub. Univ. 95: 641.
— Last Attack on. (A. R. Wallace) Nature, 6: 237.
— Last Development of. Lond. Q. 57: 371.
— Missing Links in. (A. Wilson) Gent. M. n. s. 23: 298.
— Mivart on. Dub. R. 68: 482.
— My Cousin the Gorilla. Tinsley, 8: 395. 9: 135.
— Objections to. (E. Nisbet) Bapt. Q. 7: 69, 204.
— or Evolution. (R. P. Stebbins) Mo. Rel. M. 50: 496.
— Ridiculous. (W. Streissguth) Luth. Q. 5: 404.
— Science against. (J. Moore) Univ. Q. 35: 186.
— Strictures on. (H. H. Howorth) Anthrop. J. 2: 21. 3: 208. 4: 101.
— Studies in. (J. F. Garrison) Am. Church R. 27: 197.
— Theological Import of. Chr. Obs. 73: 623.
— Triumph of. (J. Fiske) No. Am. 124: 90.
— True and False in. (E. von Hartmann) J. Spec. Philos. 11: 244, 392. 12: 138. 13: 139.
— *versus* Philosophy. So. R. n. s. 13: 253.
— What is? (A. Gray) Nation, 18: 348.
See Evolution; Development.

Daschkaw, Catherine Woroutzow, Princess. (W. Robinson) Once a Week, **14**: 510. — Tinsley, **14**: 624. Same art. Ev. Sat. **1**: 617. — Mo. R. **152**: 14.
Dasent, G. W. Annals of an eventful Life. Quar. **128**: 546.
— Tales from the Norse. Blackw. **85**: 366.
Dash, Countess. (K. Cook) Lond. Soc. **26**: 386.
Dashmarton's Legacy. Chamb. J. **53**: 425–523.
Dashwood's Drag. (L. de la Ramé) Bentley, **45**: 335, 487.
Date-Palm, The. Chamb. J. **28**: 108. **39**: 113. — Penny M. **4**: 473.
Dates and Dates; a Poem. (R. E. B. Lytton) Blackw. **115**: 625.
— Coincidences in. Chamb. J. **53**: 761.
— Inaccuracies of Historians as regards. (T. Astle) Arch. **14**: 162.
— of Buildings, How to ascertain. (J. A. Repton) Arch. **33**: 136.
Datura, or Thorn-Apple. Chamb. J. **11**: 335.
Datura Fastuosa; a Botanical Tale. (E. T. W. Hoffmann) Dub. Univ. **13**: 707.
Daubeny, Charles. Discourses on various Subjects. Chr. Obs. **5**: 26, 94.
D'Aubigné, J. Agrippa. Colburn, **126**: 294.
— and Madame Maintenon. Blackw. **67**: 174. Same art. Ecl. M. **20**: 44. Same art. Liv. Age, **25**: 49.
D'Aubigné, J. H. Merle. *See* Merle d'Aubigné, J. H.
Daubin's Double; a Story. (F. E. Loop) Galaxy, **17**: 245.
Daud Pasha, Governor of Lebanon, with portrait. Ecl. M. **68**: 513.
Daudet, Alphonse, the French Dickens. (J. L. Heclis) Colburn, **161**: 133, 307.
— Kings in Exile. (A. Laugel) Nation, **29**: 419.
— Le Nabob. (A. Laugel) Nation, **26**: 6.
— — translated by Lucy H. Hooper. Penn Mo. **9**: 557.
— Numa Roumestan. (A. G. Sedgwick) Nation, **33**: 379.
Daughter of Bohemia; a Tale. (F. C. Fisher) Appleton, **10**: 513–801. **11**: 14–452.
— of the Dark. (R. Dowling) Belgra. **38**: 85.
— of Henry Sage Rittenhouse. Scrib. **22**: 498, 770.
— of the Puritans, A. (M. E. Emery) Cath. World, **23**: 92.
— of Stanislaus. Chamb. J. **7**: 101.
— of the Sun. (F. Caballero) Colburn, **146**: 287.
Daughters of the Cross. Am. J. Educ. **26**: 721.
— of Eve; Lives of noted Women. Temp. Bar, **1**: 483. **2**: 241. **3**: 200. **4**: 85. **5**: 414. **8**: 415.
— of the Legend of Honor. (M. E. Blair) Lippinc. **23**: 247.
— of Time; an Eclogue. Dub. Univ. **8**: 298.
Dauntless; a Novel. (S. de Kerkadec) St. James, **46**: 85–437.
Dauphin, Son of Louis XVI. (N. B. Ely) Dem. R. **25**: 11. — Fraser, **19**: 192.
Dauphin Importers, Three. Ecl. M. **26**: 551.
Dauphine, Heroine of. Once a Week, **16**: 685.
Dauphiny. Ed. R. **154**: 397.
Davenant, John, Life and Writings of. Ecl. R. **57**: 124.
— Memoir of. Chr. Obs. **33**: 124.
Davenant, Sir Wm. G. (G. Robinson) Retros. **2**: 304.
— Works of. Retros. **18**: 1.
Davenport, E. L., Recollections of. (H. P. Goddard) Lippinc. **21**: 463.
Davenport, John, Letter of, 1639. N. E. Reg. **9**: 149.
Davenport, Robert. King John and Matilda. (H. Southern) Retros. **4**: 87.
Davenport Brothers. (E. Dicey) Macmil. **11**: 35.
— Cabinet-Trick of. Once a Week, **11**: 689.
Davenport Family. (B. F. Davenport) N. E. Reg. **33**: 25.
Davenport Genealogy. (J. W. Dean) N. E. Reg. **9**: 146. — (H. Davenport) N. E. Reg. **4**: 111, 351.
Davenport Gravel Drift. (S. Fleming) Canad. J. n. s. **6**: 247.
Davezac, Maj. Auguste, with portrait. Dem. R. **16**: 109.
David, King of Israel. Dem. R. **34**: 313. (A. H. Guernsey) Galaxy, **10**: 839. **11**: 29. — (W. R. Smith) Sup. Pop. Sci. Mo. **2**: 13.
— and Goliath. (E. C. Benedict) Hist. M. **15**: 289.
— Character of. (E. E. Hale) Mo. Rel. M. **12**: 94, 121.
— Early Career of. Kitto, **15**: 33. — (D. Macleod) Good Words, **15**: 207.
— Fall of. (D. Macleod) Good Words, **15**: 377
— Imprecations of. Chr. Mo. Spec. **8**: 620.
— Krummacher on. Chr. Obs. **68**: 59, 187.
— Lament for Jonathan. Cong. M. **18**: 209.
— Literary Character of. (G. M. Bell) Kitto, **4**: 335.
— Reign of. Chr. Mo. Spec. **5**: 528, 579, 637. **6**: 23.
— Relation of his Family to the Messiah. (E. P. Barrows, jr.) Bib. Sac. **11**: 306.
— Typical Character of. Kitto, **33**: 14.
— Youth of. (J. Kitto) Kitto, **2**: 59.
David, Jacques-Louis, French Painter. Liv. Age, **49**: 520. **55**: 708. — New Q. **4**: 490. — Westm. **64**: 308. — Bentley, **59**: 321. Same art. Liv. Age, **90**: 728.
David, Pierre-Jean, Sculptor. (T. Karcher) Bentley, **58**: 281. Same art. Ecl. M. **65**: 704. Same art. Liv. Age, **89**: 795. — Fraser, **27**: 151. — Art. J. **32**: 281. — Tait, n. s. **1**: 168.
— Story of a Statue. Am. Arch. **8**: 282.
David, St.; a Poem. (F. Parke) Dub. Univ. **88**: 466.
David Chantrey; a Novel. (W. G. Wills) Temp. Bar, **13**: 5–507. **14**: 119–552. **15**: 116–557. **16**: 117.
David Garth's Night Watch. Liv. Age, **104**: 809.
David Gaunt; a Story. (R. H. Davis) Atlan. **10**: 257, 403. Same art. Sharpe, **36**: 286. **37**: 26.
David the Harper; a Tale of Wales. (J. Downes) Blackw. **58**: 96.
Davidson, Lucretia M. So. Lit. Mess. **1**: 51. **9**: 94, 399. — Mo. R. **160**: 492.
— Life of. (C. M. Sedgwick) Sparks's Am. Biog. **7**: 209.
— Remains of. (R. Southey) Quar. **41**: 289. Same art. Mus. **16**: 108.
Davidson, Lucretia and Margaret. Ecl. M. **34**: 261. — Liv. Age, **45**: 363.
Davidson, Margaret M. (R. Southey) Quar. **69**: 91. — Mo. R. **159**: 378. — Ecl. R. **78**: 64.
— Poems of. Mus. **44**: 324. — Chr. Exam. **31**: 269.
Davidson, Thomas, a Scottish Elia. (J. Service) Macmil. **36**: 307. Same art. Liv. Age, **134**: 561. — Blackw. **123**: 178. Same art. Liv. Age, **136**: 682. — Cong. M. **11**: 449.
Davie, Wm. Richardson, Life of. (F. M. Hubbard) Sparks's Am. Biog. **25**: 3. — So. Lit. Mess. **14**: 510.
Davies, Rev. C. N., Memoir of. Cong. M. **25**: 357.
Davies, John, the Epigrammatist. Retros. **18**: 229.
Davies, Sir John, Poems of. Retros. **5**: 44.
Davies, J. Llewelyn, with portrait. Dub. Univ. **93**: 583.
Davies, Mary, with portrait. Victoria, **35**: 506.
Davies, Maurice. Shakspere's Heroines; Poems. Colburn, **154**: 716. **155**: 8–633.
Davies, Pres. Samuel, Memoir of. Am. Q. Reg. **9**: 305.
— Sermons of. Meth. Q. **6**: 138.
— Theological Opinions of. (C. Hodge) Princ. **14**: 142.
Daviess, Joseph Hamilton. (R. T. Coleman) Harper, **21**: 341. — (M. T. Daviess) Land We Love, **6**: 293.
Davis, Andrew Jackson, the Poughkeepsie Seer. (J. Weiss) Chr. Exam. **43**: 452. — Dem. R. **21**: 207. — (P. Godwin) Peop. J. **4**: 121.
— and his Revelations. Fraser, **37**: 127.
Davis, Mrs. Eleanor, with portrait. Bost. Mo. **1**: 617.
Davis, Francis, Poetry of. (M. Russell) Irish Mo. **5**: 569.
Davis, Gustavus F., Memoir of. Chr. R. **2**: 384.
Davis, H. W. B. (P. G. Hamerton) Portfo. **6**: 159. **7**: 117.
Davis, Jefferson. (T. Jordan) Harper, **31**: 610. — Blackw. **92**: 343. — Land We Love, **6**: 179.

Davis, Jefferson, Address of, July 10, 1878. So. Hist. Pap. **6**: 162.
— Affair of Honor with Col. W. H. Bissell. (H. King) Lakeside, **6**: 43.
— and the Confederacy. (A. H. Guernsey) Appleton, **26**: 172.
— and R. E. Lee. (A. T. Bledsoe) So. R. n. s. **2**: 231.
— and Lincoln. Land We Love, **4**: 391.
— and Repudiation. (R. J. Walker) Contin. Mo. **4**: 207, 352, 390. **5**: 478.
— Capture of. (G. W. Lawton) Atlan. **16**: 342. — (J. H. Parker) So. Hist. Pap. **4**: 91. — (W. T. Walthall) So. Hist. Pap. **5**: 97.
— History of the Confederacy. (J. D. Cox) Nation, **33**: 10, 35. — (W. H. Smith) Dial (Ch.) **2**: 55. — Atlan. **48**: 405. — (J. M. Farrar) Contemp. **40**: 229.
— Jordan on. (C. C. Hazewell) Nation, **1**: 422.
— Prison Life of. Land We Love, **1**: 277. — (M. B. Clarke) Land We Love, **1**: 406. — (S. T. Wallis) So. R. n. s. **1**: 233.
— Release of. (E. I. Sears) Nat. Q. **15**: 106.
— Sincerity of. (E. L. Godkin) Nation, **2**: 776.
Davis, John, Navigator. (B. F. De Costa) Nation, **30**: 459.
Davis, Joseph Barnard, Obituary of. Nature, **24**: 82.
Davis, Matthew L. Liv. Age, **26**: 217.
Davis, Samuel, Reminiscences of. Hesp. **2**: 22.
Davis, Thomas, with portrait. Dub. Univ. **29**: 190.
— Poems. Irish Q. **5**: 697.
Davis Genealogy. (E. W. Peirce) N. E. Reg. **20**: 212, 299. **21**: 65.
Davis's Strait, O'Reilly's Voyage to. Quar. **19**: 208.
Davos-Platz, in Switzerland. (W. Chambers) Chamb. J. **56**: 769.
— in Winter. (J. A. Symonds) Fortn. **30**: 74. Same art. Liv. Age, **138**: 426. — (J. A. Symonds) Cornh. **43**: 446. Same art. Liv. Age, **149**: 432.
Davy, Sir Humphry. (S. Brown) No. Brit. **2**: 53. Same art. Liv. Age, **4**: 3. — Temp. Bar, **58**: 95. Same art. Liv. Age, **144**: 483. — (J. Ferguson) Good Words, **20**: 102, 185, 304. — (T. De Quincey) Tait, n. s. **4**: 169. — Hogg, **2**: 49. — Pop. Sci. Mo. **14**: 813. — Am. J. Sci. **17**: 217. — Ed. R. **63**: 53. — Am. Q. **13**: 403. — Meth. Q. **1**: 551. — Ecl. M. **4**: 56. — Mo. R. **124**: 364. — Mus. **16**: 303. **29**: 413. — Ann. Reg. **4**: 204. — Dub. Univ. **7**: 611.
— Agricultural Chemistry. Quar. **11**: 318. — Ed. R. **22**: 251.
— Bakerian Lecture. Ed. R. **9**: 390. **12**: 394. **14**: 483.
— Chemical Philosophy. Quar. **8**: 65.
— Consolations in Travel. Mo. R. **121**: 391.
— Discoveries of. Mo. R. **113**: 315.
— Elements of Chemistry. Anal. M. **1**: 423.
— Life and Writings of. Dub. R. **2**: 437.
— Memoir of. (G. Cuvier) Ed. New Philos. J. **15**: 1. — Ed. R. **63**: 101. — Tait, n. s. **3**: 246.
— on Oxymuriatic Acid. Ed. R. **17**: 402.
— on Oxymuriatic Gas. Ed. R. **18**: 470.
— on the Earths. Ed. R. **13**: 462.
— on Fire Damp. Ed. R. **26**: 233.
— Paris's Life of. Colburn, **31**: 260. — Ecl. R. **53**: 213.
— Remains of. Liv. Age, **59**: 842.
— Salmonia. (D. Olmsted) Chr. Q. Spec. **2**: 133. — (Sir W. Scott) Quar. **38**: 503. — Blackw. **24**: 248. — Am. Mo. R. **2**: 14. — Mo. R. **116**: 537.
Davy, Wm., Memoir of. Chr. Obs. **27**: 65.
Davy Jones, jr. (D. Cook) Once a Week, **17**: 105, 136.
Davy's Locker; a Tale. All the Year, **35**: supp.
Davyum. (S. Kern) Nature, **17**: 245.
Daw's Reminiscences. Lond. M. **17**: 494.
Dawison, Bogumil. Bentley, **43**: 524.
Dawk Bungalow. (G. O. Trevelyan) Fraser, **73**: 215, 382.
Dawkins, Colonel, Military Trial of. Temp Bar, **14**: 525.
Dawn to Sunset; a Tale. Chamb. J. **54**: 548–708.
Dawson, George. (R. W. Dale) 19th Cent. **2**: 44. — Brit. Q. **11**: 125. — (G. Gilfillan) Tait, n. s. **15**: 279. Same art. Ecl. M. **14**: 356. — (G. Barmby) Ecl. M. **17**: 382. — (G. Barmby) Peop. J. **7**: 85.
Dawson, Lieut. George F., Trial of. Ecl. R. **42**: 1.
Dawson, Henry B., with portrait. (J. W. Dean) Hist. M. **14**: 257.
Dawson, Henry R., Tribute to. Dub. Univ. **16**: 663.
Dawson, John Wm., with portrait. New Dom. **7**: 319. — Pop. Sci. Mo. **8**: 231.
Dax; a Watering-Place. (R. H. Story) Fraser, **102**: 541.
Day, George Edward. Nature, **5**: 383.
Day, Jeremiah, Discourse on. (T. D. Woolsey) New Eng. **26**: 692. — with portrait, Ecl. M. **51**: 426.
— on the Will. *See* Will.
Day, Thomas, Loves of. Once a Week, **9**: 23.
Day & Martin's Blacking, Origin of. Hunt, **19**: 662.
— Factory of. Penny M. **11**: 509.
Day after my Death. (H.D.Traill) Dark Blue, **3**: 206–679.
— and Night. (M. Oliphant) Blackw. **97**: 89.
— — a Poem. (B. Taylor) Galaxy, **1**: 360.
— — among the Mountains. Fraser, **25**: 216.
— at Cherry Patch. (J. A. Harris) Lippinc. **2**: 555.
— by the Sea; a Poem. (T. Hood) St. James, **4**: 65.
— Commencement of, by Saxons and Britons. (S. Pegg) Arch. **6**: 150.
— in June; a Poem. (J. Pennant) St. James, **48**: 419.
— in a Railroad Car. (C. M. Sedgwick) Godey, **25**: 51.
— in Kent. Fraser, **3**: 17.
— Longest. (A. K. H. Boyd) Fraser, **96**: 267. Same art. Liv. Age, **134**: 684.
— of Days; a Tale. (H. James, jr.) Galaxy, **1**: 298.
— of Memories; a Poem. (C. P. Cranch) Galaxy, **15**: 758.
— of my Death. (E. S. Phelps) Harper, **37**: 621.
— of Reckoning. House. Words, **14**: 366, 402. Same art. Ecl. M. **40**: 169. Same art. Liv. Age, **51**: 742.
— of Surprises; a Tale. (V. Vaughan) Putnam, **12**: 607, 652.
— on the Moors. Fraser, **36**: 356.
— too late. Tinsley, **9**: 290.
— with the Babies; a Tale. (L.D.Nichols) Putnam, **12**: 586.
Day's Journey. (L. Claxton) O. & N. **6**: 699.
Day's Pleasure. (W. D. Howells) Atlan. **26**: 107, 223, 341.
Day's Ride; a Life Romance. (C. Lever) All the Year, **3**: 441–601.
Days from a Diary. (A. B. Alcott) Dial, **2**: 409.
— of Derry. Fraser, **72**: 726.
— of Genesis. *See* Creation.
— of the Week. (H. Bradley) Belgra. **41**: 423. Same art. Ecl. M. **95**: 236. — Tait, **1**: 625.
— with the Knapsacks. (J. F. Fitts) Galaxy, **2**: 405.
Daybreak; a Tale. (M.A.Tincker) Cath.World, **9**: 37–721.
Day-Dreaming. (F. Tiffany) O. & N. **4**: 645.
Day-Dreams. (J. Wilson) Blackw. **22**: 724.
— a Poem. (H R. Hudson) Scrib. **13**: 289.
— of a Dawdler. Tinsley, **13**: 43–281. **14**: 51. **15**: 466.
Daylesford; a Story of Oxford Days. Argosy, **29**: 219.
Daylight, Physics of. (R. H. Patterson) Belgra. **6**: 253.
Dayton, William L., with portrait. Am. Whig R. **9**: 68.
D'Azeglio, Massimo. *See* Azeglio.
Dazzled, not blinded; a Tale. Eng. Dom. M. **2**: 257, 360.
D. D., Conferring and receiving Title of. Chr. M. Spec. **2**: 297.
— in Germany, Getting a. Nation, **20**: 343.
De Mortuis. Blackw. **114**: 618.
De Mortuis Omnia. (E. L. Linton) Cornh. **30**: 96.
De Profundis. Month, **4**: 291, 403. **5**: 144.
— a Poem. (A. Tennyson) 19th Cent. **7**: 737. Same art. Ecl. M. **95**: 46.
Deacon's Holocaust. (J. P. Quincy) Atlan. **12**: 420.
Deacons and Diaconate. (J. C. Wightman) Bapt. Q. **3**: 40.
— Appointment of, by early Church. Theo.& Lit. J. **12**: 120.

Deacons, Duties of. (T. W. Aveling) Cong. **6**: 226, 271. — Cong. M. **24**: 525.
— Local. Am. Church R. **25**: 53.
— Office of. (G. Anderson) Bib. Sac. **30**: 29. — (S. L. Blake) Bib. Sac. **27**: 759. — Am. Presb. R. **6**: 409. Cong. M. **12**: 81. — (H. M. Dexter) Cong. Q. **1**: 66.
— — and Duties of. (J. Leavitt) Chr. Mo. Spec. **9**: 281.
— — and Qualifications of. Cong. M. **22**: 172, 434, 499.
— — Extension of. Chr. Obs. **74**: 610.
— — in Congregational Churches. (T. S. Potwin) Cong. Q. **8**: 345.
— Ordination of. (W. W. Patton) Cong. Q. **7**: 185.
— Restoration of primitive Diaconate. (J.H.Hopkins, jr.) Am. Church R. **10**: 88.
— Scriptural. (G. B. Safford) Cong. Q. **11**: 206.
— Term of Office of. Cong. Q. **9**: 241.
— Watts on. (Mrs. S. A. Dwight) Chr. Mo. Spec. **9**: 482.
Deaconesses. (F. Wharton) Bib. Sac. **28**: 1. — Quar. **108**: 342. — Am. Church R. **24**: 47. — Sharpe, **44**: 145. — Cong. **6**: 482. — (A. T. McGill) Presb. R. **1**: 268.
— Anglican. (E. M. Sewell) Macmil. **28**: 463.
— of early Church. (J. M. Ludlow) Good Words, **4**: 133. — Chr. Obs. **62**: 194.
— Office of. (H. Harbaugh) Mercersb. **14**: 193.
— — in Congregational Churches. (J. Anderson) Cong. Q. **16**: 10.
— or Sisters. (L. Coleman) Am. Church R. **14**: 617. — Ed. R. **87**: 430.
— Pastor Fliedner and the Order of. (D. S. Schaff) Mercersb. **22**: 193.
— Protestant. (E. M. Sewell) Macmil. **21**: 229.
Deaconess Institution of Kaiserwerth. (W. F. Stevenson) Good Words, **2**: 121, 143.
Deaconess Life in Germany. Once a Week, **8**: 272.
Dead, The, as described by Homer. Liv. Age, **37**: 666.
— Burial of. (J. Brazer) Chr. Exam. **31**: 137, 281.
— Condition of. (J. Porter) Meth. Q. **10**: 112.
— Defamation of. (H. St. John) St. James, **36**: 498.
— Dialogues of. Fraser, **6**: 728.
— Disposal of. Cornh. **31**: 329. Same art. Ecl. M. **84**: 522. — O. & N. **4**: 752. *See* Burial; Cremation.
— Everything concerning. (E. L. Linton) Cornh. **30**: 96.
— forever alive to God. (J. H. Heywood) Unita. R. **13**: 449.
— Honors to. So. Lit. Mess. **7**: 205.
— Intercourse with. Cong. M. **20**: 549.
— Intermediate State of. *See* Intermediate State.
— Letters from. Blackw. **11**: 207.
— Message to. Blackw. **24**: 353.
— No Preaching to. (N. West) Princ. n. s. **1**: 451.
— Prayers for, and the Liturgy. Am. Church R. **20**: 207.
— Praying to or for. Chr. Obs. **39**: 12.
— Raising, and Materialism. (L. S. Beale) Princ. n. s. **2**: 96.
— restored; a Poem. (E. Phelps) Lakeside, **8**: 48.
— Use of, to the Living. (S. Smith) Westm. **2**: 59.
— *versus* the Living. Westm. **37**: 201.
Dead alive, The. Fraser, **9**: 411.
Dead alive, The. (W. Collins) Canad Mo. **5**: 16, 128.
Dead alive; an Inn Story. Fraser, **26**: 85.
Dead Baby; a Poem. (W. Buchanan) Temp. Bar, **2**: 372.
Dead Boxer; a Legend. Dub. Univ. **2**: 617.
Dead Bride; a Poem. (W. Thornbury) Once a Week, **6**: 461.
Dead Clearing. (W. C. Hoffman) Bentley, **4**: 129.
Dead-Head. (E. F. Dawson) Overland, **14**: 428.
Dead Heart. (C. Chesebrough) Knick. **36**: 268.
Dead in the Sierras. (C. H. Miller) Overland, **8**: 91.
Dead-Letter Office, Washington. (L. Bagger) Appleton, **10**: 593. — (J. Clifford) Overland, **3**: 517.
— Day in. (F. Copcutt) Knick. **55**: 179.
Dead Letters. All the Year, **33**: 246.—New Eng. M. **2**: 55.
Dead Love; a Poem. (A. C. Swinburne) Once a Week, **7**: 432.
Dead Man and still; a Drama. (H. C. Merivale) Dub. Univ. **93**: 346.
Dead Man of St Anne's Chapel. (O. Ludwig) Blackw. **47**: 575.
Dead Man's Bell; a Tale. Eng. Dom. M. **8**: 19.
Dead Man's Hand. (J. Y. Akerman) Bentley, **13**: 234.
Dead Man's Isle; a Poem. Temp. Bar, **3**: 340.
Dead Man's Message; a Poem. (E. Arnold) Once a Week, **15**: 210.
Dead Man's Race; a Poem. (W. G. Blackwood) West. J. **11**: 147.
Dead Man's Revenge. Chamb. J. **30**: 355, 374. Same art. Liv. Age, **60**: 277.
Dead or alive. House. Words, **6**: 37.
Dead Pope; a Poem. All the Year, **7**: 34.
Dead Sea. (B. B. Edwards) No. Am. **53**: 203. — Am. Bib. Repos. **6**: 112. — Am. Presb. R. **20**: 113. — Nat. M. **6**: 495. **7**: 20.
— and Bible Lands. Bentley, **34**: 273.
— — De Saulcy's. Dub. R. **35**: 139.
— and Cities of the Plain. (G. S. Faber) Dub. Univ. **42**: 491.
— and the Desert. (A. L. Koeppen) Mercersb. **5**: 521.
— and Jebel Usdum. All the Year, **11**: 467.
— and Jordan. (C. Ritter) Kitto, **7**: 334. — (J. P. Durbin) Meth. Q. **9**: 633. — No. Brit. **11**: 494.
— and Valley of the Jordan. (E. Robinson) Bib. Sac. **5**: 397. — (J. D. Sherwood) Am. J. Sci. **48**: 1.
— Asphalt of. (L. Lartet) Intel. Obs. **10**: 62.
— Characteristics of its Waters. (T. J. and W. Herapath) Ed. New Philos. J. **48**: 313.
— Day at. (F. P. Cobbe) Fraser, **67**: 226. Same art. Liv. Age, **76**: 483. Same art. Ecl. M. **58**: 489.
— Jordan, and Jericho. All the Year, **25**: 180.
— Journey to. Bentley, **59**: 511.
— Lynch's Expedition to. Am. J. Sci. **58**: 317. — Liv. Age, **22**: 157. — Bib. Sac. **7**: 393. — No. Brit. **11**: 494. Same art. Liv. Age, **23**: 1. — (E. Robinson) Bib. Sac. **5**: 764. — (M. F. Maury) So. Lit. Mess. **14**: 547. — (W. A. Larned) New Eng. **7**: 443. — Meth. Q. **9**: 633. — Theo. & Lit. J. **2**: 288. — Chamb. J. **12**: 103. — Hogg, **3**: 387, 402. — Sharpe, **10**: 65.
— Monastery of. (L. P. Hale) O. & N. **6**: 680.
— Recent Explorations of, 1855. (J. P. Thompson) Bib. Sac. **12**: 528.
— Route to, Allen's. Fraser, **53**: 311.—Liv. Age, **46**: 736.
— Water of. Liv. Age, **31**: 307.
Dead Sea Fruit; a Novel. (M. E. Braddon) Belgra. **3**: 131, 257, 383. **4**: 5–383. **5**: 5–447. **6**: 99–378.
Dead Secret. House. Words, **8**: 27. Same art. Liv. Age, **39**: 276.
Dead Secret. (W. Collins) House. Words, **15**: 12–565. Same art. Liv. Age, **52**: 555, 607, 751. **53**: 46–808. **54**: 94, 184.
Dead Sorrow's Kin; a Tale. (Mrs. C. Reade) Belgra. **22**: 485. **23**: 69–451.
Dead Stranger; from the German of Zschokke. Gent. M. n. s. **10**: 265–554.
Dead Vashti; a Story. (L. Stockton) Galaxy, **23**: 528.
Dead-Watch. Chamb. J. **58**: 733.
Deadly Creek. Chamb. J. **51**: 516.
Deadly Feud. (R. Lindau) Blackw. **126**: 408. Same art. Appleton, **25**: 162. Same art. Liv. Age, **144**: 45.
Deadly Sins, Old Poets on. Cornh. **13**: 624.
Deæ Matres. (R. Gough) Arch. **3**: 105.
Deaf, but not dumb. (B. St. J. Ackers) Sup. Pop. Sci. Mo. **1**: 182.
Deaf, The, Education of. Liv. Age, **140**: 125.
— Horace Mann School for. (M. G. Morrison) Pop. Sci. Mo. **19**: 84.

Deaf, The, Letter to. (H. Martineau) Tait, n. s. **1**: 174. Same art. Mus. **25**: 215.
— Utility of Speech to. Chr. Obs. **27**: 82.
Deaf and Dumb. (E. M. Gallaudet) Internat. R. **2**: 471. —(L. P. Brockett) Nat. M. **11**: 27.—Irish Q. **8**: 1286. —Knick. **30**: 34.
— and L'Abbé de l'Epée. Penny M. **6**: 286.
— and visible Speech. (S. F. A. Caulfield) Victoria, **21**: 193.
— at Lessons. All the Year, **42**: 371.
— College for, at Washington. O. & N. **6**: 492.—(A. G. Draper) Scrib. **3**: 727.—(E. M. Gallaudet) Am. Soc. Sci. J. **6**: 160.
— Education of. (F. B. Sanborn) No. Am. **104**: 512.—(F. A. P. Barnard) No. Am. **38**: 307.—(H. P. Peet) No. Am. **59**: 329.—(F. A. P. Barnard) Lit. & Theo. R. **2**: 365.—(F. A. P. Barnard) Chr. Q. Spec. **9**: 521.—(J. R. Burnet) Am. Bib. Repos. 2d s. **8**: 269. —(S. E. Hull) Education, **1**: 286.—(J. E. Gallagher) Western, **7**: 273.—(E. M. Gallaudet) Internat. R. **11**: 503.—Am. Whig R. **3**: 497.—Quar. **26**: 391. **102**: 116.—Mo. R. **95**: 32. **134**: 378.—Anal. M. **15**: 419.
— — Dalgarno on. (Sir W. Hamilton) Ed. R. **61**: 407.
— — in Europe and America. (A. W. Ely) De Bow, **17**: 435.
— International Convention of Instructors of, at Milan, 1880. (E. M. Gallaudet) Education, **1**: 279.
— Gov. Tazewell's Report on. So. Lit. Mess. **1**: 134, 201.
— Hartford Institute. (J. M. Wainwright) No. Am. **7**: 127.
— in France, Efforts for. (G. E. Day) Am. J. Sci. **30**: 301.
— in Great Britain, Census of, 1851. (D. Buxton) J. Statis. Soc. **18**: 174.
— in Ireland. Dub. R. **20**: 291.
— — Statistics of. (W. R. Wilde) J. Statis. Soc. **16**: 69.
— Institutions for. (L. P. Brockett) Nat. M. **9**: 385, 487.
— Instruction of. (H. L. Peet) Hours at Home, **6**: 237. —(J. E. Zimmerman) Lippinc. **17**: 504.—(S. W. S. Dutton) New Eng. **10**: 415.—Chr. Obs. **26**: 588, 749. **27**: 82.—No. Brit. **6**: 331.—Penny M. **1**: 27.
— — American and European Systems of. (E. M. Gallaudet) New Eng. **27**: 1.
— — at Exeter Institution. Penny M. **4**: 21.
— — Gallaudet on. (O. Tiffany) No. Am. **87**: 517.
— — New York Institution for. Am. J. Educ. **3**: 347.
— Religious Ideas of. (H. P. Peet) Bib. Sac. **12**: 559.
— Schools for. (F. B. Sanborn) Nation, **4**: 249.—Nation, **4**: 339.
— Signs in Education of. (J. R. Keep) New Eng. **26**: 506.
— teaching, Methods of (H. F. Jenks) Mo. Rel. M. **50**: 125.
— Teaching Articulation to. (J. Lesperance) Canad. Mo. **2**: 506.—Cornh. **16**: 693. **17**: 573.—Chamb. J. **51**: 595.—Chr. Obs. **17**: 514, 787. **18**: 29–846. **24**: 226, 487.
— — Belgian Experiment. Ev. Sat. **5**: 48.
— Ten Days with. (M. Barrett) Harper, **47**: 496.
— Training of. (B. K. Pierce) Meth. Q. **30**: 416.
See Sign-Language.
Deaf and Dumb; a Tale. (T. J. Beach) Godey, **22**: 59.
Deaf and Dumb Asylum, Visit to. (W. Gilbert) Good Words, **14**: 252.
Deaf and Dumb Debate. All the Year, **44**: 20.
Deaf, Dumb, and Blind. Liv. Age, **1**: 759.—Chr. Obs. **44**: 409.
Deaf-Mute, Blind, History of. Cath. World, **1**: 326.
Deaf Playmate's Story. (C. Dickens) House. Words, **6**: 598.
Deaf Traveler. Penny M. **2**: 309–406.
Deafness. Penny M. **14**: 151, 155.
— and Blindness. (B. B. Bowen) Univ. Q. **15**: 412.
Deafness and Blindness, Kitto on. No. Brit. **6**: 175. Same art. Liv. Age, **13**: 49.—Liv. Age, **8**: 57.—Westm. **45**: 343.
— Artificial Membrane for. Chamb. J. **23**: 4.
— Notes. (G. Allen) Mind, **3**: 156.—(E. Simcox) Mind, **3**: 401.
— Thirty-five Years off Soundings. Lippinc. **21**: 236.
Deak, Francis. (J. W. Tipping) Dark Blue, **4**: 184.
— Life and Labors of. (K. Blind) Fraser, **93**: 374. Same art. Ecl. M. **86**: 623. Same art. Liv. Age, **129**: 173. —Once a Week, **15**: 57.
Deal-Town, Day at. Once a Week, **14**: 623.
Dealer in Wisdom. House. Words, **3**: 507.
Dean, Amos. Philosophy of human Life. Chr. Exam. **28**: 263.
Dean, F. M. Miscellaneous Poems. Dub. Univ. **88**: 117.
Dean, John Ward. (W. H. Whitmore) Hist. M. **12**: 229.
Dean of Denham. Bentley, **46**: 368.
Dean's Meditation; a Story. Lond. Soc. **39**: supp. 33.
Dean's Watch; a Tale. (MM. Erckmann-Chatrian) Temp. Bar, **43**: 512. Same art. Ecl. M. **84**: 571.
Deans and Chapters, English. Ecl. R. **95**: 731.
— Rural. Chr. M. **9**: 1.
Dean, Forest of. Chamb. J. **41**: 556.—Penny M. **6**: 215, 218.
— Free Miners of. Penny M. **12**: 318.
Deane, Silas. (C. J. Hoadly) Pennsyl. M. **1**: 96.—Liv. Age, **49**: 105.
— and Arthur Lee, Beaumarchais on. M. Am. Hist. **3**: 631.
— Letter to Patrick Henry. Hist. M. **17**: 22.
Deane, Thomas. Letter to Joseph Dudley, 1684. N. E. Reg. **13**: 237.
Deane Family Records. (J. W. Dean) N. E. Reg. **25**: 358.
Deane Genealogy. (J. W. Dean) N. E. Reg. **9**: 93.—(W. R. Deane and J. W. Dean) N. E. Reg. **3**: 375.
Dear Annette. Tinsley, **4**: 44.
Dear Davie. All the Year, **25**: 379.
Dear Food, and Crime. Ecl. R. **90**: 395.
Dear Girl; a Tale. (P. H. Fitzgerald) All the Year, **18**: 385–553. **19**: 1–210.
Dear Lady Disdain. (J. McCarthy) Gent. M. n. s. **14**: 1–649. **15**: 88–735.—Galaxy, **19**: 147–725. **20**: 5–769. **21**: 5.
Dearborn, Fort, Chicago, Sketch of. Hist. M. **6**: 108.
Dearborn, Henry A. S. Hunt, **28**: 60.
Dearborn Genealogy. (E. B. Dearborn) N. E. Reg. **2**: 81, 297
Dearly bought Pleasure. Lond. Soc. **26**: 31.
Dearths and Insects in France. Ecl. R. **100**: 154.
Deas, Charles. Godey, **33**: 250.
Death. (A. D. Vandam) Tinsley, **19**: 377.
— Æs triplex. Cornh. **37**: 432. Same art. Liv. Age, **137**: 307.
— and Burial (J. L. Davies) Good Words, **17**: 205.
— and Children. Lond. M. **3**: 250.
— and the Doctor. Ecl. M. **36**: 1101.
— and Dying in France, Lauvergne on. For. Q. **32**: 76.
— and Glory. (I. C. Knowlton) Univ. Q. **24**: 30.
— and its Agencies. (H. Bacon) Univ. Q. **3**: 395.
— and its Superstitions. Ecl. M. **96**: 396.
— and Immortality; a Poem. Dub. Univ. **89**: 645.
— and Life, Christian Doctrine of. (W. R. Alger) Chr. Exam. **30**: 429.
— and Madness. Mus. **23**: 59.
— — Sir H. Halford on. (W. Ferguson) Quar. **49**: 175.
— and Resurrection, Analogies of. Univ. Q. **20**: 67.
— and Sisyphus. (Sir E. B. Lytton) Harper, **32**: 641.
— Apparent. All the Year, **22**: 109.
— — and Real. Hogg, **3**: 307. Same art. Ev. Sat. **8**: 104.
— — — Distinction of. (W. Fraser) Pop. Sci. Mo. **18**: 401.

Death as connected with the Fall. (J. P. Smith) Kitto, **1**: 167.
— at the Altar. St. James, **4**: 335.
— by Lightning. Cath. World, **1**: 833.
— disarmed. (J. H. Browne) Galaxy, **14**: 686.
— Doubts and Immortality. So. Lit. Mess. **7**: 379.
— Erroneous Views of. Chr. Exam. **2**: 178. — (O. Dewey) Chr. Exam. **9**: 161.
— Fear of. Cornh. **38**: 592. Same art. Sup. Pop. Sci. Mo. **4**: 152. Same art. Liv. Age, **139**: 619, 623.
— Forecast Shadow of. (A. Foxcar) Belgra. **22**: 30.
— Forms of, in ancient Art. Sharpe, **52**: 232.
— Greek Mind in the Presence of. (P. Gardner) Contemp. **31**: 144. Same art. Sup. Pop. Sci. Mo. **2**: 265. Same art. Liv. Age, **136**: 280.
— Imitation of, by Eastern Fakirs. (F. G. Fairfield) Scrib. **21**: 249.
— In Articulo Mortis. (B. W. Richardson) Pop. Sci. R. **8**: 275.
— Is it painful? (E. P. Buffet) Putnam, **15**: 311. — Broadw. **7**: 424.
— Lightning before. (J. C. Browne) Gent. M. n. s. **8**: 150.
— Myths of Sea and River of. (C. F. Keary) Contemp. **36**: 243.
— of Children under five Years of Age. Am. Q. Reg. **10**: 63.
— of Columba; a Poem. (J. S. Blackie) Good Words, **13**: 563.
— of Dominie Quitman. (M. L. Thompson) Atlan. **32**: 720.
— of the Duke de M——; a Sketch. (A. Daudet) Temp. Bar, **53**: 113. Same art. Liv. Age, **137**: 653.
— of the Flowers; a Poem. (W. C. Bryant) Hogg, **9**: 344.
— of a Goblin. House. Words, **2**: 335.
— of Œnone; a Poem. Once a Week, **4**: 14.
— of the old Squire; a Poem. All the Year, **22**: 370. Same art. Liv. Age, **103**: 349.
— of Paris; a Poem. (W. Morris) Ev. Sat. **8**: 625.
— of Slavery; a Poem. (W. C. Bryant) Atlan. **18**: 120.
— of Walter Butler; a Poem. (T. D. English) Harper, **19**: 204.
— Pain and. (Grant Allen) Mind, **5**: 201.
— Phenomena of. (B. W. Richardson) Ecl. M. **73**: 580.
— Philosophy of. Nat. Q. **13**: 236.
— Physical Phenomena of. Quar. **85**: 346. Same art Ecl. M. **19**: 23. Same art. Liv. Age, **23**: 481. Same art. Internat. M. **2**: 425. — (T. D. Spencer) Pop. Sci. Mo. **19**: 394.
— Physiology of. (F. Papillon) Pop. Sci. Mo. **3**: 270.
— Poetical and artistic Conceptions of. Art J. **8**: 365.
— Poetry of. Tait, n. s. **22**: 157.
— Preparation for. (C. K. Whipple) Radical, **1**: 330.
— preventible. (K. Thaler) Tait, n. s. **19**: 129. Same art. Liv. Age, **33**: 209.
— Punishment of. *See* Capital Punishment.
— Reid on Philosophy of. Mo. R. **155**: 229.
— Relations to Life, in Nature. (J. D. Dana) Am. J. Sci. **84**: 316.
— Repose in, True and false. Chr. Obs. **27**: 581, 649.
— Resignation to, False. Chr. Mo. Spec. **2**: 454.
— Riddle of. (F. P. Cobbe) Liv. Age, **134**: 374.
— Sermon on. (E. Finley) Radical, **7**: 114.
— Signs of, Fontenelle on. Quar. **85**: 346.
— Singular Recovery from. Blackw. **10**: 582.
— Sleep and. (S. B. Hunt) Hours at Home, **5**: 448.
— Sudden, Blessedness of. (J. H. Browne) Galaxy, **13**: 251.
— The terrible. Once a Week, **30**: 292.
— The To-morrow of. (A. C. Barry) Univ. Q **35**: 300.
— Verses. Am. Whig R. **13**: 534.
— What is? (C. J. Ellicott) Contemp. **18**: 56. — Ref. Q. **28**: 606. — Westm. **56**: 168.
Death's Choice; a Poem. (G. Halse) Belgra. **16**: 52.
Deaths, Anecdotes of curious. Temp. Bar, **54**: 199.
— Singular. Ecl. M. **31**: 427.
— from Accident, Violence, etc., Statistics of. (C. Walford) J. Statis. Soc. **44**: 444.
Death-Beds, Holy. Cath. World, **10**: 206.
Death-Bed Promise. Chamb. J. **37**: 323.
Death-Bed Scenes, Warton's. Meth. M. **55**: 729.
Death-Bed Secrets; a Poem. (E. Wilberforce) Temp. Bar, **1**: 544.
Death Bell; a Tale. (A. Ford) Putnam, **15**: 216.
Death Blow; a Tale. Dub. Univ. **19**: 245.
Death-Bringer, The. Chamb. J. **31**: 355.
Death Cave. (R. M. Bird) Godey, **27**: 149.
Death Chant of King Regner Lodbrok. Dub. Univ. **30**: 214.
Death Laments of Savages. (Sir G. Grey) Fortn. **13**: 82.
Death Rate. Chamb. J. **31**: 261.
— as a Test of Sanitary Condition. (N. A. Humphreys) J. Statis. Soc. **37**: 437.
— as affected by Migrations. (T. A. Welton) J. Statis. Soc. **38**: 324.
— of St. Louis. (C. A. Todd) Western, **5**: 383.
— Rationale of. (B. F. Underwood) Nat. Q. **36**: 135.
Death Scene; a Poem. (D. M. Moir) Blackw. **21**: 259.
Death Walk; a Poem. (W. Duthrie) Belgra. **1**: 197.
Death Watch worth Reading. (H. Martineau) Once a Week, **2**: 18.
Death Wish; a Tale. Temp. Bar, **3**: 58.
Debating, a Means of educational Discipline. (J. N. McElligott) Am. J. Educ. **1**: 495.
Debating Society, Our. All the Year, **43**: 85.
— Village. Knick. **45**: 156.
Debating Societies. Chamb. J. **9**: 107.
— Dangers of. Bentley, **19**: 615.
Debby's Début. (L. M. Alcott) Atlan. **12**: 160.
Debentures and Deposits, Report on. Niles's Reg. **30**: 5.
Debit and Credit. (J. Harwood) Belgra. **20**: 503.
De Bode, Baron C. A., Travels of, in Luristan and Arabistan. Ecl. R. **82**: 538. — Dub. Univ. **25**: 265.
Deborah, Song of. Chr. Exam. **55**: 390. — Chr. Mo. Spec. **2**: 307. — (R. Robbins) Chr. Mo. Spec. **8**: 70.
— Story of. (J. T. Headley) Hours at Home, **11**: 236.
Deborah's Diary. (A. Manning) Sharpe, **11**: 129. **12**: 207.
De Bow's Southern Review. (C. G. Leland) Contin. Mo. **2**: 466.
Debt. (E. B. Willson) Mo. Rel. M. **50**: 97. — Temp. Bar, **19**: 487.
— and Credit. Chamb. J. **21**: 385.
— and Currency. Bank. M. (N. Y.) **13**: 137.
— and Money, Relations of. (E. Wright) No. Am. **124**: 417.
— Arrest for. Brit. & For. R. **5**: 64.
— — and Bankruptcy. Bank. M. (N. Y.) **3**: 88.
— Being in. All the Year, **11**: 463.
— Imprisonment for. Tait, n. s. **23**: 243. — Hunt, **4**: 72. — (C. F. Daniels) Hunt, **4**: 538. — (A. H. Everett) No. Am. **32**: 490. — Am. Alma. **1848**: 181. — Westm. **9**: 41. **19**: 198. **20**: 354. **44**: 231. — Niles's Reg. **20**: 58. **21**: 123. **23**: 251, 321. **26**: 153. — Broadw. **2**: 227, 309. — Lond. M. **23**: 109. — (J. N. Pomeroy) Nation, **13**: 317. — Bank. M. (L.) **4**: 6. — Bank. M. (N. Y.) **1**: 713. — Fraser, **9**: 645. **17**: 171.
— — Have we abolished? (R. Lowe) Fortn. **27**: 307.
— — in England. Temp. Bar, **12**: 249, 341.
— Payment of. (C. Carroll) Scrib. **6**: 665.
Debts and Constitutional Restrictions. Bank. M. (N. Y.) **30**: 946.
— and Stocks of the several States. (A. C. Flagg) Am. Alma. **1840**: 103.
— Local, and Government Loans. Ed. R. **153**: 548.

Debts, Municipal. (C. Hale) Atlan. 38: 661.
— — and other, Blaine on. Bank. M. (N. Y.) 29: 356. 32: 359.
— National. *See* National Debts.
— Public, in United States. (G. M. Weston) Bank. M. (N. Y.) 32: 806. — (R. P. Porter) Princ. n. s. 8: 205.
— — injure productive Interests. Bank. M. (N. Y.) 31: 958.
— — Modern. (H. C. Adams) Internat. R. 10: 210.
— — Payment of. (H. C. Adams) Internat. R. 11: 246.
— Small, Act on. Quar. 77: 215.
Debtor and Creditor. Colburn, 62: 17. — Fraser, 17: 545.
— Law of. Westm. 19: 198. — Brit. & For. R. 16: 119, 658. — (F. Brinley) Hunt, 2: 321.
Debtors, Laws concerning. Temp. Bar, 12: 249, 341. Same art. Ecl. M. 64: 69.
— — in Alabama. (J. Bond) Hunt, 6: 155. — (B. F. Porter) Hunt, 15: 580. 16: 57.
— — in Connecticut. (J. H. Lanman) Hunt, 3: 132.
— — in England. Hunt, 6: 49.
— — in Illinois. (C. Gilman) Hunt, 6: 446.
— — in Iowa. (E. B. Washburn) Hunt, 7: 443.
— — in Louisiana. (F. H. Upton) Hunt, 15: 70, 471. — (W. S. Upton) Hunt, 16: 53, 165, 281. — (L. Eyma) De Bow, 4: 106.
— — in Maine. (F. Brinley) Hunt, 2: 321.
— — in Massachusetts. (B. F. Porter) Hunt, 16: 379. — (A. C. Spooner) Hunt, 4: 549.
— — in Michigan. (C. Townsend) Hunt, 17: 274.
— — in Mississippi. (B. F. Porter) Hunt, 16: 379. 17: 179.
— — in Missouri. (J. C. Blunt) Hunt, 2: 412. — (C. D. Drake) Hunt, 5: 252. — (C. C. Whittlesey) Hunt, 21: 61.
— — in New Hampshire. (J. C. Moore) Hunt, 3: 63.
— — in N. Jersey. (J. Chetwood) Hunt, 2: 481. 4: 253.
— — in New York. (J. H. Lanman) Hunt, 4: 74.
— — in Ohio. (C. Bryan) Hunt, 16: 469.
— — in Pennsylvania. (P. P. Morris) Hunt, 4: 448.
— — in Tenn. (H. G. Smith) Hunt, 17: 377. 19: 386.
— — in United States. (D. Webster) No. Am. 11: 197.
— — in Vermont. (F. Hunt) Hunt, 3: 333.
— — in Wisconsin. (E. B. Washburn) Hunt, 6: 256.
Debtor's Experience. Colburn, 40: 322–478.
Decalogue. (F. D. Maurice) Victoria, 8: 277. — (A. P. Stanley) Good Words, 21: 351.
— Division of. (C. F. Schaeffer) Evang. R. 7: 102.
— Permanent Obligation of. Cong. M. 26: 793, 893.
Decamps, Alexander G. F. Arts Q. 5: 299.
De Candolle. *See* Candolle.
Decatur, Commodore Stephen. Duel with Commodore Barron. Niles's Reg. 18: 98.
— Life of. (F. Bowen) No. Am. 64: 217. — (A. S. Mackenzie) Sparks's Am. Biog. 21: 3. — Anal. M. 1: 456.
— Operations against Algiers. Anal. M. 7: 113.
Deccan, The. (Sir D. Wedderburn) Fortn. 34: 210. Same art. Liv. Age, 146: 771.
— Hill Forts of. (F. Gell) Good Words, 19: 24, 95.
Deceased Wife's Sister; a Sketch. Dub. Univ. 83: 226.
— — — a Tale. (S. Mostyn) Temp. Bar, 34: 116–546. 35: 130–363.
— — Bill on Marriage of, Poem on. (Col. Colomb) St. James, 34: 50.
See Marriage.
Deceits, Necessary, and agreeable Surprises. (Mrs. V. E. Howard) Godey, 23: 146.
December. (W. Howitt) Howitt, 2: 361. — (I. D. Coolbrith) Overland, 1: 552.
Deception, Science of. Fraser, 44: 332.
Deceptions, Heartless. (J. Crosswaithe) Good Words 4: 518.
Dechamp, Nicholas. Chamb. J. 10: 370.
Dechamps, Cardinal, Writings of. (A. F. Hewit) Cath. World, 32: 394.
Decimals, Circulating. (J. W. L. Glaisher) Nature, 19: 208.
Decimal Coinage. Bank. M. (L.) 13: 81, 864. — Bank. M. (N. Y.) 9: 189. — Chamb. J. 17: 167. Same art. Liv. Age, 33: 270. — Liv. Age, 63: 230. — (J. Bowring) Peop. J. 4: 45. — (J. Bowring) Howitt, 2: 42, 223, 255. — Lond. Q. 8: 373. — Nat. R. 1: 285. — No. Brit. 29: 428.
— and International Coinage. Ed. R. 124: 383.
— Division of. Penny M. 11: 370.
— for Great Britain. (F. J. Minasi) J. Statis. Soc. 17: 243.
— Report on, 1860. J. Frankl. Inst. 69: 279.
— vouched by Scripture. Bank. M. (L.) 22: 197.
— Weights and Measures. Chamb. J. 17: 316. — Hogg, 10: 375.
Decimal Currency. Bank. M. (L.) 15: 138, 200, 430.
— Suggestions for. (H. Taylor) Bank. M. (L.) 4: 328.
Decimal Gauge. (R. Briggs) J. Frankl. Inst. 109: 382.
Decimal Measure, Inch and Meter as Unit of. (J. Fernie) J. Frankl. Inst. 79: 176.
Decimal System for England, Simple. (Royston-Pigott) Pop. Sci. R. 9: 257.
— in bowing and turning Wheels and Axles. (J. Fernie) J. Frankl. Inst. 72: 105.
— of Weights, Measures, and Coins. (L. Levi) Victoria, 2: 349. — Bank. M. (N. Y.) 11: 606. 15: 133. — Chamb. J. 17: 316. — De Bow, 16: 445. — Dub. R. 12: 466.
See Metric System; Weights and Measures.
Decision and Charity. (O. Dewey) Chr. Exam. 14: 200.
Declaration of Independence. (B. J. Lossing) Harper, 3: 145. — (J. Gregg) Am. Q. Obs. 2: 48. — Niles's Reg. 30: 393. 37: 41. — (G. E. Ellis) Unita. R. 6: 1.
— Committee on. Potter Am. Mo. 7: 17.
— in Verse. (W. Young) Dem. R. 15: 191.
— Mahon on. (P. Force) Liv. Age, 44: 387.
— Signers of. (B. J. Lossing) Harper, 7: 153. 47: 258, 424. — (J. Everett) No. Am. 16: 184. — West. Mo. R. 1: 531. — Portfo.(Den.) 32: 293, 441. 33: 71.
— Signing of. Potter Am. Mo. 5: 658. — (B. J. Lossing) Potter Am. Mo. 5: 754. — (T. W. Higginson) Scrib. 12: 289.
— Where it was written. Potter Am. Mo. 6: 341.
— with Letters by Signers. Hist. M. 14: 209.
Decomposing Power of Water at high Temperature. (R. A. Tilghman) J. Frankl. Inst. 45: 142.
Decomposition of Salts by hot Steam. (E. Solly) J. Frankl. Inst. 45: 426.
Decoration as applied to Architecture. (R. Corbett) Am. Arch. 10: 99.
— of Home Cottages. (H. Cox) Potter Am. Mo. 17: 257.
— of Trinity Church. Boston. (H. Van Brunt) Am. Arch. 5: 164.
— — and Capitol at Albany. (H. Van Brunt) Atlan. 43: 633.
See Interiors; Ornament.
Decorations. Blackw. 115: 486. Same art. Liv. Age, 121: 340.
Decoration Day. (S. E. Henshaw) Overland, 14: 478.
Decorative Art. Art J. 5: 37. — (M. M. Mason) Dial (Ch.), 2: 34. — (A. F. Oakey) Am. Arch. 8: 173. — (E. Randolph, jr.) Month, 43: 401.
— Ancient Egyptian Art. Art J. 16: 303.
— and Architecture in England. (M. D. Conway) Harper, 49: 617, 777. 50: 35.
— for Ladies. All the Year, 45: 59.
— Home Decoration. Eng. Dom. M. 26: 50.
— How to adorn Houses externally. Eng. Dom. M. 25: 31, 75.

Decorative Art, Illustrated. (G. B. Griffith) Potter Am. Mo. 13: 295.
— in England. (M. D. Conway) Harper, 49: 617, 777. 50: 35.
— Marine Forms in. (J. C. Beard) Scrib. 21: 809.
— Painted Ceilings. Art J. 4: 79.
— Position and Aims of. (W. Crane) Art J. 33: 227.
— Practical Laws of. (F. T. Palgrave) Fortn. 13: 443.
Decorative Art Society, English. Art J. 30: 51.
— in New York. (W. C. Brownell) Scrib. 22: 697.
Decorative Arts in Germany, France, and Great Britain, 1843. (C. H. Wilson) Ed. New Philos. J. 35: 259.
Decorative Decorations. Cornh. 42: 590. Same art. Appleton, 25: 169. Same art. Ecl. M. 96: 62. — Am. Arch. 8: 284, 296.
Decorative Designing. Art J. 29: 209.
Decorative Painting for our Dwellings. Fraser, 31: 97.
Decorative Stuffs, Ancient. (H. M. Benson) Lippinc. 23: 468.
Decorator, My Work as. (E. Meteyard) Sharpe, 20: 304, 328.
De Courcy's Ride. (W. H. Babcock) Harper, 61: 109.
Decoys. All the Year, 45: 487.
— and Decoying. Blackw. 130: 745.
Decrees, History of Doctrine of Divine. (E. Pond) Am. Bib. Repos. 2d s. 9: 285.
De Cresci; a Poem. Blackw. 51: 242.
Decretals, False. (R. F. Clarke) Month, 41: 354.
Dedham, Mass., Fairbanks House. (B. J. Lossing) Potter Am. Mo. 7: 241.
— Ministers of. Am. Q. Reg. 8: 49.
Dedication of the Temple; a Poem. Dub. Univ. 44: 346.
Dedications. Chamb. J. 47: 211.
— and Prefaces. Liv. Age, 61: 25.
Deduction and Induction in Natural Science. (J. v. Liebig) Cornh. 12: 296.
Dee, Dr. John. Blackw. 51: 626. — Nat. M. 2: 118. — Sharpe, 37: 66, 126.
— and Edward Kelly. (G. F. Holmes) So. M. 16: 373. — Colburn, 164: 467.
See Bit of Alchemy.
Dee, Across the. (G. Hill) Sharpe, 27: 292. 28: 43. — (J. S. Howson) Art J. 24: 1–353.
Deeds of the Time of Henry VI. with Seals appended. (W. S. Walford) Arch. 37: 335.
Deepdale Mystery (M. Sullivan) Colburn, 139: 149–399. 140: 21–396. 141: 22–388. 142: 18–524.
Deephaven Cronies. (S. O. Jewett) Atlan. 36: 316.
Deephaven Excursions. (S. O. Jewett) Atlan. 38: 277.
Deep-Laid Plot. (I. R. Vernon) Tinsley, 18: 471.
Deep Sea and its Contents. (W. B. Carpenter) 19th Cent. 7: 593. Same art. Ecl. M. 94: 641.
Deep-Sea Climates. (W. Thomson) Nature, 2: 257.
Deep-Sea Dredging and Life in the Deep Sea. (H. N. Moseley) Nature, 21: 542–591.
— and Sounding. Pop. Sci. Mo. 3: 257.
— Cruise of the Knight Errant. (C. W. Thomson) Nature, 22: 405.
Deep-Sea Explorations. (W. P. Trowbridge) Am. J. Sci. 76: 386. — (J. G. Jeffreys) Nature, 23: 300. — (A. Wilson) Gent. M. n. s. 18: 109. — Chamb. J. 52: 281–328. — Ecl. Engin. 4: 201.
— in the Bay of Biscay. (J. G. Jeffreys) Nature, 22: 468.
Deep-Sea Investigation and Apparatus. (J. Y. Buchanan) Ecl. Engin. 24: 401.
Deep-Sea Mud, Dr. Gümbel on. Nature, 3: 16.
Deep-Sea Soundings. (W. P. Trowbridge) Am. J. Sci. 76: 157. — Chamb. J. 45: 25. Same art. Ecl. M. 70: 573. — Cornh. 3: 625. 6: 852.
— American. Nature, 5: 324.
— by Wire. Ecl. Engin. 11: 6.
Deep-Sea Soundings for a Cable across the Atlantic. (W. P. Trowbridge) Am. J. Sci. 78: 51.
— Use of the Piezometer in. (J. Y. Buchanan) Ecl. Engin. 18: 61.
See Dredging: Sea.
Deer. (W. J. Broderip) Fraser, 55: 701. 56: 72, 204.
— American, Habits and Associations of. (T. B. Thorpe) Harper, 17: 606.
— and Deer-Hunting. (C. Wright) Am. Natural. 2: 466.
— and Deer Parks. Quar. 125: 366.
— Antlers of. (J. D. Caton) Am. Natural. 8: 348.
— Californian. (J. D. Caton) Am. Natural. 10: 464.
— Domestication of. (A. E. Brown and J. D. Caton) Am. Natural. 14: 393.
— Extinct Species of, Remains of an. (J. A. Allen) Am. J. Sci. 111: 47.
— Fallow, Existence of, in England during Pleistocene Times. (V. Brooke) Nature, 11: 210.
— — Geographical Distribution of. (L. H. Jeitteles) Nature, 11: 71. — Nature, 3: 94.
— — Northern Range of, in Europe. (W. B. Dawkins) Nature, 11: 112.
— Highland. All the Year, 13: 233.
— Horns of extinct. (Dr. Percy) Arch. 7: 158.
— The Mule. (W. J. Hays) Am. Natural. 3: 180.
— of the British Islands. Penny M. 10: 103, 133.
— Red, of Devon. Once a Week, 13: 292.
— Roe, former Existence in England. (J. E. Harting) Pop. Sci. R. 20: 136.
— Senses of. (J. D. Caton) Am. Natural. 3: 28.
— Wild, in Devon. Chamb. J. 37: 348.
Deer Forest. (E. Jesse) Once a Week, 12: 155.
— In the; a Day bewitched. Blackw. 128: 221.
Deer Forests and culpable Luxury. (A. H. Beesly) Fortn. 19: 732.
— Scottish. Blackw. 64: 92.
Deerhounds, Scotch. (G. Cupples) Macmil. 12: 343.
Deer-Hunt in a Dug-Out. Chamb. J. 20: 294.
— on the Bouquet. (P. Martindale) Knick. 45: 577.
Deer-Hunting. (R. St. J. Tyrwhitt) Lond. Soc. 8: 242.
— in America. (J. J. Audubon) Ed. New Philos. J. 11: 103.
— in the Au Sable. (W. M. Laffan) Scrib. 15: 753.
— in the Black Forest. Cornh. 17: 317.
— in the Highlands. Penny M. 9: 449.
— in Louisiana. (H. J. Peck) De Bow, 5: 220.
— in North America. Penny M. 7: 407.
Deer-Park, English. Chamb. J. 44: 520.
Deer-Stalking, Extraordinary. Once a Week, 1: 313.
— in the Highlands. Penny M. 8: 106, 119.
— Scrope on. Quar. 63: 73. — Ed. R. 71: 98. — Mo. R. 148: 259. — Mus. 39: 78.
— with Margraf of Baden. Dub. Univ. 27: 706.
Deerfield, Mass., Ministers of. Am. Q. 10: 268.
— Old Indian House in. N. E. Reg. 2: 110.
Defalcations. Dem. R. 5: 468.
— American Railway, 1854. Bank. M. (L.) 14: 494, 601, 729.
Defamation, Law of. Cornh. 14: 174. 15: 36.
Defaulter, The. (T. Hood) Colburn, 67: 117.
Defaulters. (H. S. Brown) Ex. H. Lec. 18: 115.
— of Controversy. Month, 24: 160.
Defender of the Faith, Signification and Origin of. Cath. World, 6: 257. — (A. Luders) Arch. 19: 1.
Defenders, The. Dub. Univ. 25: 242.
Defense, Carnot's Principles of. Mo. R. 91: 89.
— Harbor. (J. G. Barnard) So. Lit. Mess. 11: 25.
— Insular. Quar. 4: 313.
— Lake, and Western Interests. (M. F. Maury) So. Lit. Mess. 11: 83.
— of fortified Places. Ed. R. 38: 467.

Defenses, National. (Maj. Chase) De Bow, **14**: 54. — (H. L. Scott) Putnam, **5**: 122.
— of Britain. Blackw. **68**: 736.
Defenseless State of Great Britain. Quar. **88**: 269.
Defensible State of the Country. Fraser, **32**: 599.
Defensive Armament of Great Britain. (G. R. Gleig) Ed. R. **96**: 194.
Defensive Force. (T. P. Thompson) Westm. **14**: 1.
Deffand, Madame du, Letters of. (F. Jeffrey) Ed. R. **15**: 458. **17**: 290. — (A. Davezac) Dem. R. **9**: 277. — Quar. **146**: 141. Same art. Liv. Age, **138**: 579. — (K. O'Meara) Cath. World, **19**: 693.—(J. W. Croker) Quar. **5**: 498. — Liv. Age, **33**: 447. —Ed. R. **110**: 495.
Definition in Science and Philosophy. (A. Sidgwick) Mind, **4**: 230.
Definitions. (D. Wilkie) Am. J. Sci. **30**: 28, 266. **31**: 88, 236. — (E. C. Benecke) Mind, **6**: 530.
Deflection of Solids, Formulæ for. (J. B. Francis) J. Frankl. Inst. **73**: 85.
De Foe, Daniel. (J. Forster) Ed. R. **82**: 480. Same art. Ecl. M. **6**: 465. — Blackw. **106**: 457. — Brit. Q. **27**: 85. — Chr. Exam. **71**: 340. — Lond. Q. **57**: 345. — Cong. M. **13**: 1, 57. — Ev. Sat. **10**: 335. — Cornh. **23**: 310. Same art. Liv. Age, **109**: 56. Same art. Ecl. M. **76**: 580. — Tait, n. s. **26**: 389. — All the Year, **22**: 132, 156.
— as a Novelist. Nat. R. **3**: 380.
— Captain Singleton; or Through the Dark Continent in 1720. Macmil. **38**: 459.
— Chadwick's Life of. Colburn, **117**: 115.
— Educational Projects. Am. J. Educ. **26**: 417.
— Lee's Life of, and recently discovered Writings. Brit. Q. **50**: 483.
— Life of. Penny M. **2**: 151.
— — and Times of. Ecl. R. **94**: 27.
— — and Writings of. (W. Hazlitt) Ed. R. **50**: 397. (C. Barker) Retros. **3** : 354. — (H. Southern) Retros. **6**: 1. — Ecl. R. **94**: 27. Same art. Ecl. M. **25**: 365. — So. R. **7**: 68. — Liv. Age, **29**: 49. — Westm. **13**: 69. — Mus. **16**: 113.
— Novels and Style of. Cornh. **17**: 293. Same art. Liv. Age, **97**: 195. — Dub. Univ. **48**: 57. Same art. Ecl. M. **39**: 18. Same art. Liv. Age, **50**: 513. — Ev. Sat. **5**: 453.
— Robinson Crusoe. (H. T. Tuckerman) No. Am. **78**: 265. — Broadw. **4**: 447. **7**: 158. — Liv. Age, **63**: 610.
— — Authorship of. Lond. Soc. **17**: 67. Same art. Ecl. M. **74**: 366.
— in America. (M. E. Ireland) Scrib. **12**: 61.
De Forest, J. B. History of Art. (M. G. Van Rensselaer) Am. Arch. **10**: 181.
De Forest. J. W. The Bloody Chasm. (A. G. Sedgwick) Nation, **33**: 376.
— Novels. (C. Gordon) Atlan. **32**: 611.
Deformed, The, and their mental Characteristics. Liv. Age, **72**: 393.
— and the Stricken. (M. Browne) Good Words, **7**: 737. Same art. Ev. Sat. **2**: 655.
Deformity, Fashion in. (W. H. Flower) Pop. Sci. Mo. **17**: 721.
Degeneration. Chamb. J. **58**: 321. — Lond. Q. **56**: 353. — Ecl. R. **110**: 82. — (A. Wilson) Gent. M. n. s. **26**: 470. — (A. Wilson) Pop. Sci. Mo. **19**: 218, 382.
De Geraude, J. M. (E. P. Peabody) No. Am. **92**: 391.
Degrees, Honorary, conferred by Colleges. (D. C. Gilman) Nation, **5**: 93.
De Grey and Ripon, Geo. F. S. R., Earl of, with portrait. Ev. Sat. **10**: 463.
De Grey; a Tale. Eng. Dom. M. **13**: 137, 193, 252.
De Grey; a Romance. (H. James, jr.) Atlan. **22**: 57.
Dehon, Bp. Theodore, Memoir of. Chr. Obs. **22**: 673, 737.
— Sermons of. Chr. Obs. **22**: 353.
Deinhardstein's Picture of Danaë; poetical translation. Blackw. **50**: 308.
Deism. Meth. M. **30**: 393.
— Horne on. Ed. Mo. R. **2**: 661. — Meth. M. **42**: 902.
— Modern. Dub. R. **35**: 336.
— — Positive Side of. Ecl. R. **107**: 253.
Deists, Duties of Christians towards. Ecl. R. **31**: 1.
— French. Prosp. R. **2**: 48.
— Modern. Lond. Q. **3**: 1.
Deity, Existence of. (A. Arrington) Dem. R. **21**: 102, 253.
— Our Knowledge of. (G. F. Seiler) Evang. R. **1**: 348. *See* God.
Déjazet, Mademoiselle. (E. H. House) Galaxy, **4**: 179. — Temp. Bar, **59**: 108. — Eng. Dom. M. **9**: 350.
De Kalb, Baron. So. Q. **22**: 141. *See* Kalb, Gen. John de.
De Kay, James E., Address at New York, 1826. (G. Bradford) No. Am. **23**: 204.
De La Beche, Sir Henry, Obituary of. Art J. **7**: 156.
— Review of his Life. Fraser, **51**: 694. Same art. Ecl. M. **35**: 505.
Delabussière, Charles; a Hero of the French Revolution. Temp. Bar, **4**: 355.
Delacroix, Eugène. F. Arts Q. **3**: 80, 265.
— Letters of. (H. James, jr.) Internat. R. **8**: 357. — (W J. Stillman) Nation, **30**: 388.
— Talk with. Peop. J. **5**: 26.
Delagoa Bay Arbitration. Colburn, **152**: 254. **154**: 197.
De Lalain, Jacques. (J. Hatton) Tinsley, **22**: 585.
Delamater Genealogy. (R. H. Walworth) N. E. Reg. **14**: 41.
Delane, John Thadeus. Macmil. **41**: 267.
Delano, Capt. Amasa, Voyages and Travels of. (W. P. Mason) No. Am. **5**: 244.
Delany, Mary Granville, Autobiography and Correspondence of. Blackw. **91**: 401. — Bentley, **49**: 436. — (S. D. Clark) Unita. R. **14**: 129. — Liv. Age, **69**: 29, 323. — Sharpe, **39**: 129, 188. — Dub. Univ. **58**: 84. — Chr. Rem. **41**: 325. — Fraser, **65**: 448. — Westm. **77**: 374. — Ed. Mo. R. **4**: 379.
Delany, Patrick. Dub. Univ. **52**: 578. Same art. Liv. Age, **60**: 178.
Delaplaine's Repository. Anal. M. **8**: 193, 380. **10**: 483. **13**: 89.
De la Pole Family. Antiquary, **1**: 139.
— of Hull. Lond. Soc. **5**: 256.
De la Rive, Auguste. Nature, **9**: 143.
Delaroche, Paul. (P. G. Hamerton) Portfo. **6**: 62. — F. Arts Q. **2**: 273. — Knick. **62**: 433. — Sharpe, **42**: 161. — Ecl. M. **40**: 283.
Delarue's Manufactory of fancy Stationery. Chamb. J. **6**: 33, 57.
Delaunay's Deliverance. Tinsley, **8**: 682.
Delavigne, Casimir. Colburn, **10**: 105. — Lond. M. **20**: 224.
— Comedies of. Blackw. **15**: 263. — So. R. **8**: 88.
— Vêpres Siciliennes. Colburn, **5**: 385-497.
Delaware, Historical Discourse on. (J. R. Snowden) Hist. M. **8**: 385.
— Statistics of, 1869. Am. J. Educ. **18**: 303.
Delaware Indians. Olden Time, **1**: 311.
Delaware River. Godey, **33**: 97.
— Down the. (A. Plumasier) Potter Am. Mo. **14**: 81.
— Robert Evelyn, early Explorer of. (E. D. Neill) Hist. M. **14**: 75.
— Swedish Settlements on. Pennsyl. M. **1**: 149.
Delaware Water Gap (J. Bonsall) Potter Am. Mo. **11**: 370.
Delaware, U. S. Ship, in 1833. Nav. M. **2**: 169.
Delesse, Achille, Obituary of. Nature, **23**: 535.
Delhi, Akbar II. and. Blackw. **4**: 121.

Delhi and its Edifices. Potter Am. Mo. **5**: 699.
— and the Mohammedan Rebellion in India. Colburn, **111**: 127. Same art. Ecl. M. **42**: 487.
— as it is. Fraser, **58**: 59.
— Grand Mosque and Imperial Palace of. Bentley, **42**: 546.
— Historical Sketch of. Dub. Univ. **50**: 352. Same art. Ecl. M. **42**: 393.
— How we escaped from. (C. T. Le Bas) Fraser, **57**: 184. Same art. Ecl. M. **43**: 528.
— Imperial, and the English Raj. (W. Simpson) Fraser, **95**: 285.
— Monarchs of. Ecl. M. **44**: 33.
— Observatory at. Penny M. **9**: 217.
— Sack of. Cornh. **6**: 528.
— — First. House. Words, **16**: 276.
— Siege of. House. Words, **18**: 56. — Liv. Age, **55**: 314. — (R. D. Osborn) No. Am. **107**: 594.
— to Cabul, Barr's March from, 1839. Mo. R. **164**: 383.
— to Cawnpore. Ecl. M. **44**: 505.
— Traveling to, by a Dawk. Liv. Age, **40**: 226.
Deliberative Bodies, Procedure of. (A. Bain) Contemp. **38**: 773. Same art. Liv. Age, **147**: 741.
Delicate Health; a Tale. Putnam, **9**: 360, 494.
Delicate Intricacies. Lond. M. **6**: 72.
Delights of a dirty Man. Dub. Univ. **4**: 442.
De Lille, Abbé, Poetry of. (F. Jeffrey) Ed. R. **3**: 26. **7**: 134. **15**: 351. — Mo. R. **94**: 471.
Deliverer, The; a Poem. (J. Thomson) Fortn. **36**: 617.
Deloraine's Holiday. (M. Collins) Belgra. **3**: 460.
Delphi. (A. W. Ward) Cornh. **36**: 36.
Delsarte, François. (F. A. Durivage) Atlan. **27**: 613.
Delsthorpe Sands. (G. M. Fenn) Once a Week, **11**: 582.
Delta, *pseud.* *See* Moir, D. M.
Deluge, The. (J. W. De Forest) O. & N. **6**: 437. — Am. Meth. M. **18**: 231. — (J. Prusoe) Colburn, **167**: 203–462.
— Before the. All the Year, **15**: 7.
— Cause of geological Change. (D. C. McLaren) Theo. & Lit. J. **12**: 263.
— Chaldean Account of. (A. H. Sayce) Theo. R. **10**: 364. — Ecl. M. **80**: 201.
— Colenso's Views on. Theo. R. **1**: 161.
— Extent and Character of. Chr. R. **20**: 108.
— — and its Memorials. Nat. M. **7**: 538. **8**: 28.
— Fairholme on. Mo. R. **143**: 489.
— Historical and Geological, compared. (E. Hitchcock) Am. Bib. Repos. **9**: 78. **10**: 328. **11**: 1.
— Legends of. (T. Hodgins) Canad. Mo. **8**: 132.
— Maori Traditions of. (H. Eley) Recr. Sci. **2**: 195.
— a Miraculous Interposition. Liv. Age, **11**: 109.
— Mosaic History of. Cong. M. **15**: 18, 77.
— of Noah and Deucalion. (Dr. von Schubert) Ed. New Philos. J. **19**: 34.
— Religious Lessons of. (C. W. Shields) Theo. & Lit. J. **11**: 440.
— Traditions of, in ancient Nations. (F. Lenormant) Contemp. **36**: 465.
Deluge at Blissford. House. Words, **7**: 80.
Deluges. All the Year, **3**: 49.
Delusion, Philosophy of. Bentley, **16**: 305.
Delusions, Ancient and modern. Temp. Bar, **13**: 231.
— Epidemic. (W. B. Carpenter) Pop. Sci. Mo. **2**: 15.
— Extraordinary popular. Hogg, **9**: 281.
— Horrible. (S. Bywater) Bentley, **24**: 29.
— Popular. Ed. R. **80**: 203. — Tait, n. s. **25**: 599.
— — Mackay on. Mo. R. **156**: 493.
— Predominant. (W. Chambers) Chamb. J. **54**: 481. — Same art. Sup. Pop. Sci. Mo. **1**: 475.
Delville. All the Year, **34**: 445, 467.
Demagogueism. Brownson, **1**: 84.
Demagogues, Modern. Am. Presb. R. **1**: 406.
Demagogy, Sincere. Atlan. **44**: 488.
Demaillet. (C. Read) Fortn. **20**: 54.
De Maistre, J., Works of. (C. C. Shackford) No. Am **79**: 371.
Demand Notes, Objections to. Bank. M. (N. Y.) **16**: 353.
Demerara. (F. M. Endlich) Am. Natural. **15**: 937.
— Insurrection at. Ed. R. **40**: 226.
— Overseeing at. Chamb. J. **56**: 325, 508.
— Revolt in. Cong. M. **7**: 217, 271, 315.
Demeter and Persephone, Myth of. (W. H. Pater) Fortn. **25**: 82, 260. Same art. Liv. Age, **128**: 480. **129**: 152.
Demetrius, Eustaphieve's. (S. Gilman) No. Am. **7**: 258.
Demetrius, the Cadi's Pipe-Bearer. Sharpe, **24**: 377.
Demetrius, the Diver. House. Words, **10**: 165.
Demetrius, the Impostor. St. Paul's, **10**: 258. — Liv. Age, **37**: 174.
— Merimée's History of. Dub. R. **35**: 492.
Demetrius Galamus. (T. L. Peacock) Fraser, **58**: 596.
Demidoffs and Mining Industry of Ural. Pract. M. **1**: 406.
Democracy. Blackw. **41**: 71. — Dem. R. **7**: 215. **35**: 140. — (H. C. Adams) New Eng. **40**: 752. — Bost. Q. **1**: 33. — Galaxy, **4**: 90. — Prosp. R. **1**: 208. — Quar. **85**: 260.
— American. (J. Leavitt) New Eng. **14**: 52, 385.
— — and French Republicanism. Dem. R. **34**: 272.
— and Foreign Policy. (H. D. Traill) 19th Cent. **4**: 910.
— and Liberty. (O. A. Brownson) Dem. R. **12**: 374.
— and Monarchy. Quar. **149**: 230.
— and Money-Power. Bost. Q. **4**: 41.
— and Reform. Bost. Q. **2**: 478.
— and Republicanism. Dem. R. **42**: 112.
— as a Form of Government. Westm. **88**: 479.
— Athenian. (W. A. Larned) New Eng. **18**: 651.
— Camp's. Dem. R. **10**: 122.
— Christian. (E. S. Porter) Hours at Home, **2**: 177.
— Dangers of. Westm. **89**: 1. Same art. N. Ecl. **2**: 133, 256.
— Defects of. Brownson, **22**: 235.
— De Tocqueville's Theory of. (A. T. Bledsoe) So. R. n. s. **1**: 302.
— Experience of. Blackw. **39**: 655. **40**: 293.
— Grote's Theory of. (F. A. Walker) Bib. Sac. **25**: 687.
— The Historic. (A. R. McDonough) Nation, **15**: 36.
— in America, De Tocqueville's. Dem. R. **2**: 337. — (E. Everett) No. Am. **43**: 178. — (T. M. Post) Am. Bib. Repos. 2d s. **10**: 247 — Chr. Exam. **29**: 105. — (J. S. Mill) Ed. R. **72**: 1. — Quar. **57**: 132. — Am. Q. **19**: 124. — Brit. & For. R. **2**: 304. **10**: 541. — New York R. **7**: 233. — Blackw. **37**: 758. — Dem. R. **1**: 91. — Knick. **12**: 256. — Dub. Univ. **16**: 544. — (J. S. Mill) Westm. **31**: 85. — Mus. **28**: 535. — Blackw. **48**: 463. — Am. Mo. M. **12**: 377. — Mo. R. **138**: 394. **152**: 283. — Ecl. R. **72**: 1. — Tait, n. s. **7**: 506.
— — Poussin's. (F. Bowen) No. Am. **52**: 529.
— in 1838. Dem. R. **3**: 276.
— in England. (S. Amos) Fortn. **1**: 228. — (L. J. Hinton) O. & N. **1**: 551.
— — in 1880. (A. V. Dicey) Nation, **30**: 413.
— in Europe. Westm. **109**: 1. — (J. Mazzini) Peop. J. **2**: 115–361. **3**: 79, 219.
— — History of. Ed. R. **147**: 301.
— — — May's. Fraser, **97**: 200. — Quar. **145**: 112. — Month, **34**: 101.
— — Prince Napoleon and. (K. Blind) Fraser, **100**: 504.
— in France, Guizot on. Chr. Obs. **49**: 475.
— in United States. (E. Everett) No. Am. **23**: 304. — (E. L. Godkin) No. Am. **101**: 103. — Bost. Q. **4**: 512
— Natural. (S. Johnson) Radical, **3**: 593.
— of Christianity. Bost. Q. **1**: 444.
— on its Trial. (H. W. Richardson) Chr. R. **27**: 94.
— Partridge on. (C. E. Norton) No. Am. **104**: 247.

Democracy, Pending Ordeals of. (G. H. Julian) Internat. R. 5: 734.
— Political Economy as a Safeguard of. Westm. 106: 390.
— Progress of. (E. C. Marshall) Dem. R. 30: 289.
— Retrospective and prospective. Dem. R. 36: 437.
— tending to Romanism. (T. Post) Cong. M. 26: 969.
— Travail of. (D. A. Gorton) Nat. Q. 35: 159.
— *versus* Slavery and Nobility. (L. Sherwood) Contin. Mo. 2: 89.
— What is it? Dem. R. 33: 1.
See People.
Democrat and Federalist, The Terms. Niles's Reg. 43: 97.
— American. Bost. Q. 1: 360.
Democrats, Southern, a Word to. Am. Whig R. 10: 190.
Democratic Candidates for President, 1856. Dem. R. 38: 521.
Democratic Deities. (E. Benson) Galaxy, 6: 661.
Democratic Nationality. (J. P. Thompson) Nation, 1: 38.
Democratic Opinion in America. (C. E. Norton) No. Am. 101: 550.
Democratic Party. Dem. R. 36: 179. 38: 87. 42: 257. — Gent. M. n. s. 14: 429.
— and the Constitution. Dem. R. 41: 426.
— and the Press. (E. L. Godkin) Nation, 29: 398.
— and National Office-Holders. Lippinc. 26: 690.
— and Whig Party. Bost. Q. 3: 238.
— Claims of. Dem. R. 38: 244.
— Duty of. Dem. R. 6: 437.
— Five Campaigns of. Dem. R. 7: 475.
— Future Policy of. Bost. Q. 4: 68.
— Home Policy of. Dem. R. 40: 289.
— judged by its History. (E. A. Storrs) No. Am. 131: 285.
— National Conventions of, History of. Knick. 64: 353.
— Platform of, 1868. Am. J. Ed. 18: 265.
— Policy of. Dem. R. 40: 481. 42: 358.
— Prospects of. Bost. Q. 2: 123.
— Rank and File of. Dem. R. 3: 385.
— Rule of. (A. Cameron) No. Am. 126: 485.
— Southern and Northern, 1878. (E. L. Godkin) Nation, 27: 360.
— Southern Demand upon, 1871. Ev. Sat. 10: 458.
— Spirit of. (W. M. Wood) So. Lit. Mess. 9: 671.
— Union of. Dem. R. 33: 84.
Democratic Principle, Progress of. Chr. R. 4: 284. — Dem. R. 1: 1. — Hesp. 3: 213.
— Ultra-, Progress of. Am. Mo. M. 12: 105, 317.
Democritus and Heraclitus. (G. S. Hall) Unita. R. 10: 611.
Demoiselle Anglaise, La; a Story. (C. N. Marston) Dub. Univ. 94: 78.
Demon of the Steppes. Bentley, 24: 338.
— of the Study; a Poem. (J. G. Whittier) New Eng. M. 8: 118.
Demon's Game of Chess; a Tale. So. Lit. Mess. 10: 481.
Demons, Existence and Agency of. Chr. Rem. 44: 22.
— of Derrygonelly. (W. F. Barrett) Dub. Univ. 90: 692.
Demon Chain; a Legend of the Swedish Counts of Piper. Fraser, 48: 170.
Demon Ferry-Boat; a Story of the Thames. Chamb. J. 41: 593.
Demon Ride; a Poem. (J. T. Anthony) Pioneer, 4: 350.
Demon Tower. Colburn, 166: 474.
Demon Wife. Colburn, 135: 244-425. 136: 84.
Demon Worship, Paganism a. Am. Presb. R. 9: 353.
Demon Yager; a Poem. Dub. Univ. 6: 22.
Demonax the Cynic. Ecl. R. 111: 479.
Demoniac, The; a Poem. (T. Aird) Blackw. 28: 812.
Demoniac Ideals in Poetry. Dub. Univ. 63: 29.
Demoniacal Possession. Theo. Repos. 4: 128.
— among the Hindus. Dub. Univ. 31: 315. 37: 52. — (W. Knighton) 19th Cent. 8: 646. Same art. Ecl. M. 95: 701.
Demoniacal Possession in Judea and India. Dub. Univ. 32: 262.
— in Morzine. Cornh. 11: 468.
— Dr. Kerner's Narrative. Temp. Bar, 4: 216.
— of the New Testament. (Z. S. Barstow) Bost. R. 6: 426. — (S. Comfort) Meth. Q. 10: 213. — (J. H. A. Ebrard) Meth. Q. 17: 405. — (S. Hopkins) Am. Presb. R. 14: 495. — (J. J. Owen) Bib. Sac. 16: 119. — Kitto, 7: 394.
— — Christ and. (W. Everett) Unita. R. 10: 53.
— — Scriptural Doctrine of. (W. E. Taylor) Kitto, 4: 1.
Demonism and Convulsionism. (H. White) Stud. & Intel. Obs. 5: 251. — (C. Richet) Pop. Sci. Mo. 17: 86, 376.
Demonolatry, Devil-Dancing, and Demoniacal Possession. (R. C. Caldwell) Contemp. 27: 369. Same art. Ecl. M. 86: 454.
Demonology. (M. D. Conway) Scrib. 5: 63, 233. — Blackw. 99: 502. — Fraser, 86: 596, 697.
— and Angelology. (Mrs. A. B. Garrett) Nat. Q. 5: 25.
— and Devil Lore, Conway's. (S. J. Barrows) Unita. R. 12: 221. — Nature, 21: 28. — (T. W. Higginson) Nation, 28: 203. — Nature, 21: 29.
— and Dreams. Ecl. R. 52: 501.
— and Witchcraft. Mo. R. 123: 286. — For. Q. 6: 1. — Fraser, 2: 507.
— A Hunt after Devils. (M. D. Conway) Harper, 38: 540.
— Mediæval. Colburn, 118: 100.
— Modern. Blackw. 97: 192.
— of Hindus, Buddhists, and Chaldeans. (T. B. Thayer) Univ. Q. 23: 308.
— of Ireland. Dub. Univ. 64: 203, 243.
See Devil; Magic; Satan; Witchcraft.
Demonopathy, Conventual. Fraser, 57: 376.
Demonstrativeness. (F. Parke) Dub. Univ. 82: 68.
De Morgan, Augustus. (W. Mountford) Mo. Rel. M. 49: 263.
De Mortier, a Tale of the French Revolution. So. Lit. Mess. 10: 52
Demosthenes. (E. S. Creasy) Bentley, 30: 426. — Blackw. 122: 570. — Ed. R. 33: 226. 36: 483. — Selec. Ed. R. 2: 328. — Westm. 33: 324. — (J. C. Gray) No. Am. 22: 34. — (H. S. Legaré) New York R. 9: 1. — (E. S. Creasy) Ecl. M. 24: 413. — Hesp. 2: 471. — Nat. R. 12: 99. — Penny M. 7: 445, 453.
— and Cicero. Mo. R. 152: 89.
— and Æschines. Ed. R. 12: 486.
— Archons of. *See* Chronology.
— Brougham's. Fraser, 21: 620. — Ecl. R. 71: 524.
— Eloquence of. Evang. R. 9: 586.
— Kennedy's Translation of. Ecl. R. 75: 182.
— a Model for the Preacher. (D. Steele) Meth. Q. 22: 5.
— Oration on the Crown. Chr. R. 9: 114. — Mo. R. 92: 157.
— Philippics of, Smead's. Chr. R. 17: 346.
— Rhetorical Principles of. (G. Shepard) Bib. Sac. 27: 491.
Dempster, John. (H. Bannister) Meth. Q. 24: 357.
Dene Hollow. (Mrs. H. Wood) Argosy, 11: 1-401. — 12: 1-401.
D'Enghien, Duke. *See* Enghien, D'.
Denis; a Story. Blackwood, 130: 491.
Denis and Mountjoy; God and my Right. Fraser, 45: 261.
Denis Duval; a Novel. (W. M. Thackeray) Cornh. 9: 257-641. Same art. Harper, 28: 675, 815. 29: 213, 358.
Denise Blake: a serial Story. Eng. Dom. M. 3: 1-508.
Denison, Maj.-Gen. D. (D. D. Slade) N. E. Reg. 23: 312.
— Abstract of Will of, 1673. N. E. Reg. 8: 23.
Denison, Edward. (B. Orme) Good Words, 13: 133.
— In Memoriam. (J. R. Green) Macmil. 24: 376.
— Letters of. Blackw. 111: 478. Same art. Liv. Age, 113: 442.

Denison, Edward, Writings of. No. Am. **114**: 426.
Denison, George, Will of, 1693. N. E. Reg. **13**: 73.
Denison, George A., Archdeacon of Taunton. Cong. **4**: 437.
— Ecclesiastical Portrait of. St. James, **26**: 315.
Denison Case. (F. D. Maurice) Fraser, **54**: 732.
Denman, Thomas, Lord. (A. V. Dicey) Nation, **19**: 27. — Ecl. M. **34**: 42.
— Arnould's Memoir of. Chr. Obs. **74**: 177.
— Inaugural Discourse of. Ed. R. **47**: 481.
Denmark. All the Year, **11**: 85. — (D. Wedderburn) Fortn. **36**: 76. Same art. Liv. Age, **150**: 323.
— Ancient Food and Physic in. Once a Week, **9**: 91.
— Ancient History and Constitution of. For. Q. **11**: 128.
— Ancient Horn from, in York Cathedral. (S. Gale) Arch. **1**: 168.
— and the Danes. Broadw. **3**: 117. — Dub. Univ. **61**: 499.
— and Duchies of Holstein and Schleswig. Fraser, **38**: 49. Same art. Ecl. M. **15**: 52. — Westm. **50**: 75. Same art. Ecl. M. **15**: 526. — Bentley, **55**: 245. — Sharpe, **12**: 193.
— — in 1864. (C. Redding) Colburn, **131**: 209. — Dub. Univ. **63**: 344. — Quar. **115**: 236. Same art. Ecl. M. **62**: 79, 164. — Colburn, **130**: 493. — Ecl. M. **63**: 105.
— — — Gallenga on. Dub. Univ. **64**: 341.
— — — Siege of Fredericia. Victoria, **3**: 78.
— and Jutland. Bentley, **51**: 199.
— and Sweden in 1862. (Mrs. Bushby) Bentley, **53**: 589. **54**: 57.
— — Travels in. Anal. M. **2**: 96.
— Antiquities of, Madsen's. (J. Lubbock) Nature, **1**: 15.
— in the early Iron Age. (J. Lubbock) Fortn. **5**: 763.
— Boisgelin's Travels in. Anal. M. **2**: 89.
— Caroline Matilda, Queen of. Blackw. **9**: 142.
— Catteau's. (Syd. Smith) Ed. R. **2**: 287.
— Church of. Colburn, **86**: 232.
— Claims of United States on. Bost. Mo. **1**: 393.
— Commercial Regulations of. Hunt, **8**: 469.
— Domestic Life in. Temp. Bar, **30**: 87.
— Drama of. *See* Danish Drama.
— Feldburg's. Blackw. **10**: 172.
— Fisheries of. Geog. M. **3**: 251.
— History and Literature of. Sharpe, **45**: 290. — Knick. **64**: 48.
— — Leaf of. Hogg, **3**: 395.
— — Legendary. Dub. Univ. **76**: 361.
— — Revolution under Struensee. (Sir J. Macintosh) Ed. R. **44**: 360. Same art. Selec. Ed. R. **4**: 96.
— Home Life in. Nat. R. **16**: 140.
— in 1851, Laing's History of. Ecl. R. **96**: 37.
— Intercourse with Ireland, Ancient. Dub. Univ. **70**: 3.
— King of, in England, 1768. Temp. Bar, **7**: 427.
— Kohl's Travels in. Westm. **48**: 195. — Blackw. **60**: 647.
— Laing's Travels in. Dub. R. **14**: 277.
— Life in. Ecl. R. **92**: 46.
— Literary Education in. (J. C. Brown) Am. Q. **12**: 160.
— Literature of. *See* Danish Literature.
— National Character of the Danes. Temp. Bar, **28**: 436. Same art. Liv. Age, **105**: 259.
— National Theater of. Cornh. **30**: 297.
— Peasants of. (C. Petersen) Putnam, **16**: 318.
— People of, and their Faith. Colburn, **86**: 76. Same art. Ecl. M. **17**: 407.
— Poetry of. *See* Danish Poetry.
— Public Law of. (H. Wheaton) No. Am. **27**: 285.
— Religion in. Theo. R. **2**: 322.
— Russia, Finland, Norway, and the Baltic. Fraser, **49**: 214.
Denmark, Schlegel on State of. Mo. R. **146**: 184.
— Sketches of Life in. (Mrs. P. Sinnett) Peop. J. **4**: 80–274.
— Social and Political State of, 1851. Chr. Obs. **52**: 628.
— Society in, Revival of. (C. Petersen) Atlan. **31**: 679.
— Sweden and Norway. Am. Q. **14**: 308.
— Treaty with. Ann. Reg. **7**: [214. — Niles's Reg. **31**: 119, 220. **38**: 307.
— Winter Pictures of. Ecl. M. **19**: 526.
See also Scandinavia.
Dennelle, Dominique Alexandre, Obituary of. Am. Arch. **7**: 14.
Dennett, John Richard. (E. L. Godkin) Nation, **19**: 362.
Dennie, Joseph, with portrait. Portfo. (Den.) **15**: 361. — Penn Mo. **11**: 722. — Liv. Age, **27**: 168.
Dennis, J., Works of. (T. N. Talfourd) Retros. **1**: 305.
Dennistoun, James, Sketch of. Fraser, **51**: 643.
Denny's Intentions; a Tale. Chamb. J. **51**: 273–333.
Denominations, Ecclesiastical, American. (A. H. Quint) Cong. Q. **1**: 385.
— in New England now and 100 Years ago. (J. S. Clark) Cong. Q **2**: 173.
— of the 19th Century. Ecl. R. **64**: 225.
Denominational Christianity. (G. H. Johnston) Ref. Q. **27**: 139.
Denominational Schools in England, State Support of. (R. W. Dale) Internat. R. **9**: 605. **10**: 1.
Denominational Statistics, American. (A. H. Quint) Cong. Q. **2**: 409.
Denominationalism, Use and Abuse of. (J. A. Brown) Luth. Q. **8**: 101.
Denslow Palace. (J. D. Whelpley) Atlan. **2**: 208.
Dentistry, Materials used in. O. & N. **10**: 35.
Denton, Bailey, with portrait. Colburn, **166**: 270.
Denudation, Modern Views of. (E. Hull) Pop. Sci. R. **5**: 453.
Denver, James W., with portrait. Dem. R. **43**: 93.
Denver, Colorado. (E. Ingersoll) Scrib. **20**: 453.
— Sketch of. Potter Am. Mo. **12**: 81.
— Ute Day at. (J. B. McConnell) Lakeside, **5**: 421.
Denys, St , of France; a Poem. (F. Parke) Dub. Univ. **88**: 216.
Deodand. (W. H. Bishop) Atlan. **46**: 476.
Deodorization. Chamb. J. **28**: 190.
— Dry-Earth System of. Ecl. Engin. **11**: 218.
D'Eon, Chevalier, True History of. (L. Wraxall) Once a Week, **5**: 585.
Departed, The; a Poem. Dub. Univ. **10**: 557.
D'Epinay, Madame. *See* Epinay, Madame d'.
Deposits, Bank, Decisions on. Bank. M. (N. Y.) **28**: 131, 209.
— Interest on. Bank. M. (N. Y.) **12**: 822. **24**: 665. **31**: 108.
— Special, Law of. Bank. M. (N. Y.) **21**: 257.
— — Liability of Banks for. Bank. M. (N. Y.) **22**: 453. **24**: 849. **30**: 53, 85.
— Tax on, Repeal of. Bank. M. (N. Y.) **31**: 670.
Deposit Banking, Development of. Bank. M. (N. Y.) **32**: 100.
Depravity, Human. (O. B. Frothingham and T. W. Chambers) No. Am. **126**: 466. — (S. S. Schmucker) Evang. R. **17**: 100.
— Doctrine of. Chr. Obs. **6**: 715.
— Pauline Use of the Word σαρξ. (F. G. Hibbard) Meth. Q. **21**: 240.
— Sewall on. Chr. Exam. **2**: 285.
— Total and native. (A. W. McClure) Lit. & Theo. R. **4**: 3. — (J. F. Clarke) Chr. Exam. **53**: 402.
— Woods on. (A. Alexander) Princ. **7**: 546.
Depreciation and Dislike. (A. K. H. Boyd) Fraser, **79**. 475.
Depression, Religious. Chr. Obs. **20**: 333, 401, 469.

De Quincey, Thomas. (H. M. Alden) Atlan. **12**: 345. — Ev. Sat. **9**: 82. — (S. A. Allibone) U. S. Serv. M. **1**: 374. — (G. B. Cheever) Chr. Exam. **74**: 77. — (B. P. Drury) Western, **4**: 743. — (H. Giles) Chr. R. **19**: 72, 208. — (J. H. Ingram) Internat. R. **4**: 647. — (D. Masson) Macmil. **12**: 74. — (G. S. Phillips) No. Am. **88**: 113. — (L. Stephen) Fortn. **15**: 310. Same art. Liv. Age, **109**: 278. — (R. H. Stoddard) Appleton, **18**: 166. — Bentley, **37**: 251. — Blackw. **122**: 717. — Brit. Q. **66**: 415. — Canad. Mo. **13**: 359. — Ecl. M. **27**: 565. **71**: 1192. — Liv. Age, **60**: 387. — Lond. Q. **8**: 198. **49**: 35. — No. Brit. **39**: 62. — Peop. J. **8**: 217. Same art. Ecl. M. **60**: 409. — Quar. **110**: 1. Same art. Liv. Age, **70**: 579. — Sharpe, **38**: 63, 119. **49**: 300.
— and his Writings. (L. W. Spring) Contin. Mo. **5**: 650. — Brit. Q. **38**: 1. — Hogg, **12**: 1. — Nat. Q. **22**: 71.
— and Literary Society of Liverpool in 1801. Tait, n. s. **4**: 337.
— and Prose-Writing. Brit. Q. **20**: 163.
— Autobiographic Sketches. Chr. Rem. **29**: 155. — Colburn, **98**: 142. — Liv. Age, **57**: 918.
— Childhood of. Hogg, **6**: 145, 232. **8**: 1-337. — Harper, **2**: 156, 302. — Tait, n. s. **1**: 18. **5**: 153.
— Confessions of an Opium-Eater. Tait, n. s. **1**: 18-797. **2**: 3-769. **3**: 350. **4**: 65, 169. **5**: 152-559. **6**: 1-804. **7**: 32-765. **8**: 97. — (Willard Phillips) No. Am. **18**: 90. — U. S. Lit. Gaz. **1**: 38. — Mo. R. **100**: 288. — Mus. **2**: 269. — (R. Dowling) Tinsley, **27**: 129. — Dub. Univ. **43**: 409. — Hogg, **9**: 57.
— Humor of. Colburn, **96**: 142. Same art. Liv. Age, **36**: 64.
— Life and Writings of. Ecl. R. **91**: 397. Same art. Ecl. M. **20**: 412. Same art. Harper, **1**: 145. — Fraser, **62**: 781. Same art. Liv. Age, **68**: 323, 451. — Penn Mo. **9**: 67.
— Miscellanies. Colburn, **101**: 338. **105**: 87.
— Pathos of. Colburn, **98**: 389.
— Some Aspects of. (G. P. Lathrop) Atlan. **40**: 569.
— Writings of. (S. G. Brown) No. Am. **74**: 425. — (D. Masson) Brit. Q. **20**: 163. — (H. T. Tuckerman) Chr. Exam. **54**: 428. — Dub. Univ. **44**: 331. — Ecl. R. **100**: 385. — Liv. Age, **35**: 442. **66**: 151. — Westm. **61**: 519. Same art. Ecl. M. **32**: 289. Same art. Liv. Age, **41**: 445.
Derby, E. G. S. Stanley, 14th Earl of. Ev. Sat. **8**: 683. — with portrait, Ev. Sat. **9**: 33, 35. — St. James, **25**: 376.
— Administration of. Fraser, **46**: 112.
— Career of. St. James, **25**: 145.
— Derbyism. Fraser, **49**: 118.
— Ministry of, and Protection. Ed. R. **95**: 295.
— Political Portrait of. St. James, **25**: 170.
— Second Ministry of. Ed. R. **107**: 540.
— Three Months of Power of. Fraser, **57**: 764.
Derby, E. H. S. Stanley, 15th Earl of, with portrait. Ecl. M. **87**: 633.
— and the Liberal Party. Nation, **29**: 306.
— at the Foreign Office, 1876-78. (T. W. Reid) Macmil. **40**: 180.
See also Stanley, E. H. S., Lord (his previous title).
Derby, Countess of. (Mrs. Mathews) Bentley, **18**: 54.
Derby, Elias Hasket. Hunt, **36**: 147.
Derby, England. (L. S. Costello) Bentley, **18**: 341. — Penny M. **4**: 476.
— Foot-Ball Play at. Penny M. **8**: 131.
— Porcelain Works of, Hist. of. (L. Jewitt) Art J. **14**: 1.
— St. Alkmund's Church and its oldest Register. (W. Beresford) Reliquary, **10**: 193. **11**: 109, 135. **12**: 9.
Derby Races. (A. Smith) Bentley, **12**: 54. — Lond. Soc. **2**: 79. — All the Year, **13**: 490. — Broadw. **2**: 270. — Ev. Sat. **9**: 401, 418, 424. — Once a Week, **2**: 498. — Chamb. J. **35**: 406. **44**: 321.
Derby Races, Betting on. Temp. Bar, **21**: 187.
— The Dirty. All the Year, **9**: 369.
— An expensive Derby. Belgra. **43**: 61.
— of 1865. (C. Clarke) Fortn. **1**: 277.
— Scenes at. All the Year, **36**: 275.
— Visit to. (S. Hale) O. & N. **8**: 451.
— Week of. Lond. Soc. **19**: 482.
Derbyshire, England, Agriculture and Minerals of, Farey on, 1811. Ecl. R. **16**: 826.
— Antiquities discovered in. (H. Rooke) Arch. **12**: 327.
— — Bateman's. Tait, n. s. **15**: 202.
— Barrows in. (S. Pegge) Arch. **7**: 131.
— — Pennington on. Nature, **16**: 416.
— Dialect of, Glossary of. (J. Sleigh) Reliquary, **5**: 156. **6**: 92, 157.
— Four Days in. (J. Fowler) Howitt, **2**: 3.
— Peak of. Lond. Soc. **34**: 413.
— Peaks and Dales in. Bentley, **55**: 319, 430.
— Rambles in. Dub. Univ. **44**: 73.
— Rhodes's Peak Scenery. (J. Foster) Ecl. R. **29**: 530.
— Songs and Ballads of, Jewitt's. St. James, **21**: 101.
— Traditions of. All the Year, **32**: 134.
Derceto, the Goddess of Ascalon. Kitto, **35**: 1.
Derevaragh; a Legend of the great Lake Serpent. Lond. Soc. **24**: 250.
Derfflinger, George. Tinsley, **23**: 291.
Dermody, Thomas, Raymond's Life of. Ecl. R. **4**: 701
Derrick Van Dam. (J. T. Irving) Knick. **57**: 363.
Dervishes, Eastern. (J. P. Brown) Knick. **48**: 380. — (J. R. Dennett) Nation, **6**: 172. — Ev. Sat. **5**: 214.
— and Hadjis. (A. Vámbéry) Intel. Obs. **7**: 243.
— Dancing and howling. Colburn, **22**: 152.
— Howling. Liv. Age, **49**: 661.
— — Monastery of. Colburn, **22**: 451.
— in Syria. (E. T. Rogers) Good Words, **7**: 843.
Dervish Life, My. (A. Vámbéry) Good Words, **7**: 17.
Dervish Poetry. Brit. Q. **63**: 42.
Derwent River, Valley of. (G. Hill) Sharpe, **36**: 262. **37**: 141.
Derwentwater, James, Earl of. (M. E. Herbert) Temp. Bar, **23**: 18. — Sharpe, **12**: 101.
Desart, Earl of, with portrait. Colburn, **165**: 1388.
Desatir, The; an ancient Religious Book. (E. H. Palmer) Stud. & Intel. Obs. **1**: 406.
Desauges, Louis William. Art J. **16**: 41.
Désaugiers, Marc Antoine, the Predecessor of Béranger. (W. Besant) Temp. Bar, **45**: 465.
Des Autels, Guillaume, early French Poet. Lond. M. **6**: 416.
Descartes, René. (F. Bowen) No. Am. **56**: 81.
— Discourse on Method. (T. H. Huxley) Macmil. **22**: 69. Same art. Ecl. M. **75**: 30. — Dub. R. **38**: 169.
— Genius and Writings of. (H. Rogers) Ed. R. **95**: 1.
— Historical Position and Philosophical Claims of. Ecl. R. **94**: 1. Same art. Ecl. M. **26**: 39.
— Influence of, on English Speculation. Dub. Univ. **88**: 491.
— Meditations. J. Spec. Philos. **4**: 16-304. **5**: 97.
— Philosophy of. Brownson, **23**: 338. — (W. L. Davidson) Mind, **5**: 428.
— System of. Penn Mo. **3**: 10, 147, 334.
Descents, Law of. Lond. M. **20**: 469.
Desclée, Mlle. (C. Barrère) Gent. M. n. s. **14**: 223.
Desdemona, Character of. Blackw. **129**: 325. Same art. Liv. Age, **149**: 206.
Deseret and Nauvoo. Nat. M. **4**: 481. **5**: 343.
Desert, The, and its Adventures. Chamb. J. **12**: 17.
— Caravan in. (A. Vámbéry) Argosy, **1**: 362.
— Chat about. Ev. Sat. **6**: 431.
— Crossing. Blackw. **62**: 21.
— Day in. Once a Week, **9**: 690.

Desert, The, Forty Days in, Bartlett's. Ecl. R. **89**: 313. — Liv. Age, **20**: 244.
— In Danger in. All the Year, **25**: 450.
— Life in an Oasis. (R. A. Arnold) Belgra. **3**: 218.
— Morning in. Ev. Sat. **9**: 587.
— of Exodus, Wanderings in. (E. H. Palmer) Good Words, **11**: 484-698.
— of Sahara. (J. J. Lalor) Lakeside, **10**: 393.
— — Richardson's Travels in. Ecl. R. **87**: 274.
— Scenes in. Fraser, **21**: 346, 473. **22**: 521, 736.
Deserts, Great, of North America. Liv. Age, **66**: 726.
Desert-Storm Adventure. Chamb. J. **43**: 142.
Deserted; a Tale. (E. Bellamy) Lippinc. **22**: 612.
Deserted House. Lond. M. **20**: 386. — Chamb. J. **15**: 290. Same art. Ecl. M. **23**: 469.
Deserted House. Harper, **3**: 241.
Deserted Mansion. Fraser, **44**: 411. Same art. Internat. M. **4**: 227.
Deserted Plantation at Hilton Head. (E. B. Seabrook) Galaxy, **5**: 308.
Deserted Village. (O. Goldsmith) Harper, **2**: 1.
Deserter, The; a Tale. Sharpe, **48**: 48.
Deserter, The; a Tale. So. Lit. Mess. **3**: 549, 609. **4**: 106.
Deserters from Army and Navy. Chamb. J. **31**: 321.
Desfontaines, René L., Life and Writings of. (A. P. Candolle) Am. J. Sci. **27**: 201.
Desgenettes, Abbé Dufriche-, his Life and Works. Chr. Rem. **42**: 113.
Deshoulières, Mme., and Daughter. Portfo.(Den.) **4**: 416.
Design in Nature. (P. A. Chadbourne) Princ. n. s. **1**: 272. — (A. Wilson) Good Words, **19**: 166. Same art. Ecl. M. **90**: 660. — (G. F. Wright) Bib. Sac. **34**: 355.
— — Argument from. (J. T. Bixby) Unita. R. **8**: 1. — (T. Madge) Theo. R. **6**: 581. — (H. Lawrenny) Fortn. **18**: 692. — Dub. Univ. **50**: 209. — Quar. **127**: 134. Same art. Liv. Age, **103**: 323.
— — Evidences of. Westm. **104**: 182.
— — Evolution and the Doctrine of. (W. S. Jevons) Pop. Sci. Mo. **5**: 98.
— Law, Force, and. (N. Porter) Princ. n. s. **3**: 463.
Design as applied to Ladies' Work. (Mrs. Merrifield) Art J. **7**: 37, 73, 133.
— Schools of. *See* Schools of Design.
Designs for Art Manufacture. Art J. **32**: 5-369.
— Original. Art J. **10**: 90.
— — as Suggestions to Manufacturers. Art J. **10**: 22-328.
Designers, Hints to. (F. Furness) Lippinc. **21**: 612.
Designers' Ateliers in Paris. Chamb. J. **27**: 305. Same art. Liv. Age, **55**: 358.
Designing, Art Studies from Nature applied to. Pract. M. **1**: 149.
Designing of Machinery, Practical Papers on. Pract. M. **4**: 138-414. **5**: 92, 241.
Desirable Villa to let; a Tale. Eng. Dom. M. **26**: 298.
Desire and Volition, G. L. Turner on. (T. W. Levin) Mind, **6**: 424.
Desired Boon, denied Bane. (F. Jacox) Bentley, **60**: 57.
Desmids. Recr. Sci. **2**: 205.
— Are they simple Cells? (G. C. Wallich) Pop. Sci. R. **16**: 130.
— External Characteristics of. (E. T. Dixon) Recr. Sci. **2**: 277.
— What are? (A. M. Edwards) Am. Natural. **3**: 313.
Des Moines Valley. (S. R. Curtis) West. J. **10**: 187.
Desmond, Old Countess of. Dub. R. **51**: 51. — Quar. **92**: 329.
Desmond, or the charmed Life. (F. Macarty) Dem. R. **14**: 276.
Desmond Plantation. (D. Murphy) Am. Cath. Q. **3**: 482.
Desmoulins, Camille. (A. Laugel) Nation, **21**: 132. — Temp. Bar, **32**: 486. — Chamb. J. **20**: 214. Same art. Ecl. M. **30**: 562.
Desmoulins, G., and the Bible Historiale. (G. Masson) Kitto, **36**: 81.
Desolata. (A. H. Baldwin) Fraser, **66**: 345.
Desolate; a Sonnet. (P. B. Marston) Cornh. **20**: 214.
Desolation of Jerusalem. (W. W. Story) Blackw. **111**: 83.
Désormais; a Story of Skipton Castle. Bentley, **47**: 405.
De Soto, Hernando, Charter of Charles V. to. Hist. M. **5**: 42.
— Letter of. Hist. M. **2**: 193.
— Will of. Hist. M. **5**: 134.
Despair; a Dramatic Monologue. (A. Tennyson) 19th Cent. **10**: 629. Same art. Liv. Age, **151**: 510.
Despard, Col. Edward, Execution of. Dub. Univ. **65**: 95.
— Plot of. All the Year, **18**: 179.
Desperate Doves; a Story. Tinsley, **27**: 292.
Despine, P. Psychologie Naturelle. (O. W. Holmes) Atlan. **35**: 466.
Despondency and Aspiration. (F. Hemans) Blackw. **37**: 793.
— a Poem. (M. J. Serrano) Scrib. **4**: 424.
— The gray Luik o' Life. (J. Dyer) Penn Mo. **2**: 151.
Desportes, Alexander Francis. Art J. **6**: 242, 264.
Desportes, Philippe, early French Poet. Lond. M. **6**: 204.
Despotism in Europe, Rise of. So. Lit. Mess. **22**: 83.
— Panegyric on. Ed. R. **17**: 409.
Desprez, Philip C. S., a liberal Country Parson. (J. Owen) Mod. R. **1**: 166.
Dessau. *See* Anhalt-Dessau.
Dessert. All the Year, **20**: 321.
Desserts, Summer. Sharpe, **44**: 24.
De Staël. *See* Staël.
D'Esterre, Duel with O'Connell. Bentley, **33**: 538.
Destiny. (T. G. Carey) Hunt, **18**: 391.
— a Poem. Dem. R. **35**: 366.
— Human. (M. Ballou) Univ. Q. **22**: 196. — (A. Traver) Ref. Q. **28**: 615.
— of Léon Grenier; a Tale. Temp. Bar, **20**: 327. Same art. Ecl. M. **69**: 159.
— of the Creature. (E. Fisher) Univ. Q. **30**: 389.
Destroyer and the Deliverer; a Tale. Dub. Univ. **9**: 414.
Destruction, New Aids to. Chamb. J. **23**: 339.
— New Instruments of. Liv. Age, **2**: 664.
— of the World by Fire. (N. L. Frothingham) Chr. Exam. **34**: 75.
Detection of Crime, Scientific. (A. McL. Hamilton) Appleton, **15**: 825.
Detective; a Tale of the old Walton House. (H. Macaulay) Harper, **41**: 696.
— in America. Chamb. J. **36**: 195.
Detective Police. Dub. R. **50**: 150. — (B. S. Brooks) Pioneer, **2**: 321.
Detectives as they are. Chamb. J. **47**: 445.
— English. Quar. **99**: 160.
— Experiences with. (M. L. Meason) Belgra. **19**: 490.
— Private. (E. Crapsey) Galaxy, **11**: 188.
Detective's Story. Chamb. J. **56**: 45, 692.
Detective's Story. Contin. Mo. **4**: 474.
Determinants, Treatise on. Math. Mo. **3**: 86.
Determinism and Duty. (L. S. Bevington) Mind, **5**: 30.
De Ternay, the Chevalier, Memoir of. (S. Everett) N. E. Reg. **27**: 404.
Detmold. (W. H. Bishop) Atlan. **40**: 732. **41**: 76-697.
Detonating Agents. (Prof. Abel) Nature, **20**: 19, 42, 67.
Detonation, Rapidity of. Nature, **8**: 534.
Detroit, Early History of. (C. L. Walker) Hist. M. **15**: 132.
— House of Correction at. (C. H. Brigham) Unita. R. **5**: 315.
— illustrated. Appleton, **8**: 85.
— Schools of, Visit to. (J. M. Buchan) Canad. Mo. **8**: 483.
— Siege of, 1762. (J. T. Headley) Harper, **22**: 437.
— Tunnel at. (E. S. Chesebrough) Ecl. Engin. **7**: 362.

De Trop. Dub. Univ. 11: 689.
Deus, Use of the Word in Plautus and Terence. (E. Abbot) Chr. Exam. 45: 389.
Deutsch, Emanuel. (H. R. Haweis) Contemp. 23: 779. Same art. Liv. Age, 121: 800.
— and Edinburgh Review. (G. Grove) Macmil. 28: 382.
— Literary Remains of. O. & N. 10: 630. — Internat. R. 2: 419.
— Memoir and Writings of. Chr. Obs. 74: 289.
Deutz, Murders at. Fraser, 58: 411.
Devastation, War-Ship. Ecl. Engin. 8: 488.
— On Board of. Chamb. J. 51: 409.
— Ventilation of. (M. Blank) Ecl. Engin. 11: 220.
Development. Chamb. J. 48: 756. 49: 627. — (G. I. Cowan) Peop. J. 5: 255.
— and Causation. (J. McCosh) Princ. n. s. 7: 369.
— and Evolution. (S. Harris) New Eng. 17: 880.
— and Food. (O. Ule) Pop. Sci. Mo. 5: 591.
— Byways of. (A. Wilson) Gent. M. n. s. 27: 429, 584.
— Palæontological and embryological. (A. Agassiz) Nature, 22: 425.
— Theory of. (J. W. Jackson) Anthrop. R. 5: 257.
— — and the Bible. (J. Lillie) Chr. Q. 7: 202. Temp. Bar, 5: 214.
— — Haeckel's. (S. J. Barrows) Unita. R. 6: 281.
— — Modern Physicists on. (G. D. Wolff) Am. Cath. Q. 1: 126.
— — of Life. (F. E. Abbot) No. Am. 107: 377.
See Darwinism; Evolution.
De Vere, Sir Aubrey. (M. Russell) Irish Mo. 5: 645.
— and Swinburne. (J. McCarthy) Cath. World, 20: 346.
— Alexander the Great. Dub. R. 75: 412. — Month, 21: 454.
— Greece and Turkey. Internat. M. 1: 255.
— Inisfail; a Poem. Dub. R. 50: 457.
— Irish Odes. Dub. R. 66: 79.
— Julian; a Poem. Ecl. R. 36: 408.
— Legends of Saxon Saints. Month, 37: 219.
— Letter to Sara Coleridge. Cath. World, 20: 577.
— Mary Tudor. (B. D. Hill) Cath. World, 24: 777. — (J. McCarthy) Cath. World, 25: 261.
— May Carols. Month, 13: 649.
— Poems. Dub. R. 38: 300. — Ecl. R. 39: 163. — Dub. Univ. 36: 209. — (M. F. Sullivan) Am. Cath. Q. 5: 509. — (H. Taylor) Quar. 72: 142. — Temp. Bar, 27: 182.
— St. Thomas of Canterbury, a Poem. Month, 28: 227.
— Song of Faith. Chr. Rem. 5: 92.
— The Waldenses. Chr. Rem. 5: 92.
De Vere, Aubrey T. Infant Bridal, and other Poems. Dub. Univ. 87: 124. — Fraser, 69: 601.
— Poems. Dub. Univ. 21: 199.
— Search after Proserpine, etc. Chr. Rem. 7: 373.
Devereux Hall; a Tale. Blackw. 32: 486.
De Verney's Eton Days. Lond. Soc. 15: 513.
Device, The, in Heraldry. Chamb. J 18: 9.
Devil, The. (F. P. Cobbe) Fortn. 16: 180. — Am. Mo. M. 7: 184.
— and all his Works. (J. B. Matthews) Galaxy, 18: 112.
— and Dr. Faustus. Cornh. 14: 687.
— and his Angels. (W. Harlin) Chr. R. 23: 38.
— and Johnny Dixon. (W. H. Maxwell) Bentley, 1: 251.
— Buddhistic. Univ. Q. 31: 476.
— Did Jesus sanction Jewish Belief in? (T. B. Thayer) Univ. Q. 17: 291.
— Histories of. (P. H. Wicksteed) Theo. R. 16: 398.
— History of. Univ. Q. 28: 335.
— — Roskoff's. (P. H. Wicksteed) Theo. R. 8: 30.
— — and Doctrine of. (E.V. Scherb) Chr. Exam. 66: 351.
— in Leipzig. (M. D. Conway) Fraser, 79: 360.
— in Manuscript. (A. A. Royce) New Eng. M. 9: 340.
— Modern. (T. Parker) Radical, 2: 525.
Devil, Personal, does he exist? (G. Hill) Univ. Q. 36: 286. — (W. T. Moore) Chr. Q. 8: 78.
— — historically considered. Univ. Q. 17: 401.
— — Scott on. Victoria, 23: 562.
— — Theory of (W. R. Alger) Chr. Exam. 71: 157.
— Recent Confession of. Dub. Univ. 2: 470.
— Selling the Soul to. (R. H. Horne) Contemp. 33: 310. Same art. Liv. Age. 139: 104.
— Serpent and Eve. Cong. M. 23: 92, 213. — (L. J. Dudley) Unita. R. 10: 24.
See Demonology; Diabolism; Satan.
Devil-Fish, The. Chamb. J. 44: 781. Same art. Ecl. M. 70: 336. — Ev. Sat. 9: 414.
— and his Relatives. (W. E. Damon) Pop. Sci. Mo. 14: 345.
— of Jamaica. (R. Hill) Intel. Obs. 2: 167.
See Octopus.
Devil Byron; a Ballad. (E. Elliott) Peop. J. 3: 45.
Devil-Puzzlers. (F. B. Perkins) O. & N. 4: 178.
Devil-Worship in India. (M. J. Walhouse) Anthrop. J. 5: 408. — (C. H. Brigham) Unita. R. 5: 543.
Devil-Worshipers. Nat. M. 1: 51.
— of Armenia, Visit to. Fraser, 51: 587. Same art. Ecl. M. 35: 356. Same art. Liv. Age, 46: 240. Same art. Nat. M. 7: 253.
Devil's Arrows, Yorkshire. (A. L. Lewis) Anthrop. J. 8: 180.
Devil's Boots. (W. Gilbert) Good Words, 12: 213.
Devil's Bridge, South Wales. Penny M. 4: 313.
Devil's Diadem; a Tale. Putnam, 10: 390.
Devil's Diary, or Temptations. Fraser, 19: 653. 20: 284.
Devil's Christmas Gift; a Tale. Cath. World, 24: 322.
Devil's Confession; from Cæsarius Heisterbachensis. Fraser, 76: 320.
Devil's Fiddle. Pioneer, 4: 175.
Devil's Frills; a Dutch Water-Cure. Blackw. 54: 225.
Devil's Kitchen. Chamb. J. 42: 689.
Devil's Ladder. Dub. Univ. 25: 658.
Devil's Mark. House. Words, 17: 535.
Devil's Own; a Poem. (W. Jones) Bentley, 63: 82.
Devil's Punch Bowl, Ride to. (C. Mackay) Peop. J. 8: 287.
Devil's Rafter; a Poem. Once a Week, 21: 165.
Devils, Doctrine of. (H. L. Dix) Luth. Q. 8: 550.
— Luther's, Milton's, and Goethe's. (D. Masson) Fraser, 30: 648.
— — Masson on. (H. James, jr.) Nation, 20: 114.
— Scripture Doctrine of. (E. White) Cong. 1: 585, 661.
Deville, Charles Sainte-Claire. Nature, 14: 575. 24: 219.
Devonian System, American. (J. W. Dawson) Am. J. Sci. 85: 309.
— Bearing of, on the Origin of Species. (J. W. Dawson) Am. J. Sci. 102: 410.
Devonshire, Duchess of, Queen of the Whigs. (S. R. T. Mayer) Temp. Bar, 56: 513. Same art. Liv. Age, 142: 732. — Eng. Dom. M. 21: 10.
Devonshire. (J. Dennis) Fortn. 5: 587. — Cornh. 9: 743 — Quar. 105: 422.
— and Cornwall. Ed. R. 93: 71. 94: 37.
— — Fortnight on the Coasts of. St. James, 20: 236.
— — illustrated. Blackw. 33: 689.
— — North Coast of. Once a Week, 10: 645, 673.
— — to Scilly Islands. Bentley, 61: 316.
— and Somerset, Walk through. Temp. Bar, 7: 277.
— Mrs. Bray's Letters on. (R. Southey) Quar. 59: 275. — Mo. R. 139: 417.
— Cavern Exploration in. (W. Pengelly) Am. J. Sci. 114: 299, 387.
— Coast of. (C. W. Wood) Argosy, 27: 124, 206.
— Day's Walk in. Victoria, 5: 421.
— Down into. (J. R. Thompson) Land We Love, 3: 9, 118.
— Festivities and Superstitions of. (Mrs. J. Whittle) Bentley, 21: 301.

Devonshire, Folk-Lore of. (R. J. King) Fraser, **88**: 773.
— Four Southern Headlands of. Cornh. **40**: 697.
— Lanes of, and their Associations. Cornh. **9**: 743.
— North. (C. Kingsley) Fraser, **40**: 1, 652. **41**: 167.
— Rambles in. Fraser, **81**: 59, 197. **96**: 575.
— Savages of. Lond. Soc. **33**: 511.
— South, Week's Angling in. (E. Lethbridge) Once a Week, **10**: 473.
— Summer in. Once a Week, **7**: 121.
— Worthies of. Fraser, **52**: 534. Same art. Ecl. M. **37**: 156.
Devonshire Combe. Argosy, **31**: 381.
Devoted Lives. (W. F. Stevenson) Good Words, **11**: 73–769.
Devotion at Church. (O. Dewey) Chr. Exam. **4**: 281.
— Books of. Chr. Disc. **1**: 449. — Mo. Rel. M. **24**: 1.
— Influence of, on the Intellect. Chr. R. **6**: 477.
— Rules for habitual. Chr. Disc. **3**: 271.
— True Spirit of. (S. R. Andrews) Chr. Q. Spec. **5**: 41.
Devrient, Louis. (Mrs. E. F. Ellet) Dem. R. **16**: 164.
Devrient, Madame. (Mrs. E. F. Ellet) Dem. R. **16**: 262.
Dew, Thomas, Address of. So. Lit. Mess. **2**: 721, 760. **3**: 130, 268, 401.
Dew. Chamb. J. **45**: 659.
— Does it fall? Hogg, **10**: 60.
— Influence of Color on. (J. Brocklesby) Am. J. Sci. **56**: 178.
— Theory of. (M. Melloni) J. Frankl. Inst. **45**: 52.
— Wells on. (T. Young) Quar. **12**: 90.
Dew Point, Influence upon Health of. (J. P. Espy) J. Frankl. Inst. **12**: 389. **13**: 76.
Dew-Point and Wet-Bulb Hygrometers. (J. P. Espy) J. Frankl. Inst. **17**: 81.
De Walstein, the Enthusiast. Blackw. **48**: 338.
Dewangiri, How we retook. Fraser, **73**: 120.
De Wette, Wm. M. L. Canonical Scriptures. No. Brit. **7**: 355.
— Life and Character of. (B. B. Edwards) Bib. Sac. **7**: 772.
— on Old Testament. (S. Osgood) Chr. Exam. **35**: 303.
— Practical Ethics. Chr. Exam. **33**: 252.
— Religion and Theology. (S. Osgood) Chr. Exam. **24**: 137. **25**: 1. — Chr. R. **6**: 537.
— Schleiermacher and Harms. (K. R. Hagenbach) Meth. Q. **21**: 403.
Dewey, C. A. Am. Law R. **1**: 79, 213.
Dewey, George W., Poems by. Internat. M. **3**: 287.
Dewey, Orville, Controversial Writings of. (J. W. Alexander) Princ. **19**: 1. — (B. N. Martin) New Eng. **6**: 67.
— Discourses of. (J. G. Palfrey) No. Am. **47**: 469. — (C. C. Felton) Chr. Exam. **9**: 218. — (F. W. P. Greenwood) Chr. Exam. **18**: 389. — (A. P. Peabody) Chr. Exam. **31**: 382. **41**: 452. — (A. Lamson) Chr. Exam. **42**: 292. — New York R. **3**: 443.
— Sermons of. (J. H. Morison) Unita. R. **7**: 53.
— Travels in Europe. Chr. R. **2**: 64. — Mo. R. **141**: 277.
De Wint House at Tappan, N. Y. (J. A. Stevens) M. Am. Hist. **5**: 105.
De Witt, John. De Bow, **20**: 256.
— Geddes's History of. (M. Heilprin) Nation, **33**: 37.
Dexter, Samuel, Diary of, 1720. (W. B. Trask) N. E. Reg. **13**: 305. **14**: 35, 167, 202.
— Life of. Portfo. (Den.) **16**: 72.
Dexterous Wedding: a Chinese Comedy. Once a Week, **18**: 232, 254. Same art. N. Ecl. **2**: 153.
Dezzenzano. (H. D. Jenkins) Lakeside, **2**: 321.
Dhuleep-Singh, Maharajah. (P. Robinson) Scrib. **10**: 326.
Diabolism and Witchcraft, Literature of. Westm. **95**: 1. *See* Demonology; Devil.
Diacaustics, Notes on. (T. Hill) Math. Mo. **2**: 416.
Dial of Ahaz. Kitto, **15**: 407. **16**: 163.
Dial of Life, or the Bioscope. (J. Foster) Ecl. R. **20**: 373.
— Pocket, made in 1593. (J. Bruce) Arch. **40**: 343.
Dial, The, Emerson's. (N. C. Perkins) Dial (Ch.), **1**: 9.
Dials, Self-Luminous Clock. (H. Morton) J. Frankl. Inst. **107**: 51.
Dialect. Broadw. 6: 424.
Dialects, American. (N. C. Burt) Appleton, **20**: 411.
— Development of. (W. D. Whitney) No. Am. **104**: 30.
Dialectic and the Principle of Contradiction. (C. L. Michelet) J. Spec. Philos. **5**: 319.
— of the Pulpit. (H. W. Wynn) Evang. R. **18**: 380.
— Two Kinds of. (L. P. Hickok) J. Spec. Philos. **10**: 158.
Dialing, Mathematical Principles of. (G. Eastwood) Math. Mo. **1**: 171.
Dialogue on Human Happiness. (W. H. Mallock) 19th Cent. **6**: 425.
Dialogues of the Dead. Colburn, **5**: 140.
Dialogues of the Dead; a Poem. Once a Week, **19**: 271–509. Same art. N. Ecl. **3**: 468.
Dialogues of the Living. Colburn, **41**: 63.
Dialogues of Lydney. Month, **11**: 474–588. **12**: 1–457.
Dialysis, Researches in. (W. Odling) J. Frankl. Inst. **74**: 181, 253.
Diamagnetic Force. (J. Tyndall) Am. J. Sci. **69**: 24.
Diamond, and its Uses. (C. T. Hinckley) Godey, **49**: 297.
— Commercial Value of. Penny M. **13**: 214.
— History and Properties of. (Sir D. Brewster) No. Brit. **18**: 186. Same art. Ecl. M. **28**: 1.
— Notes on. (T. A. Blyth) Recr. Sci. **2**: 351.
— of History and Romance. (G. D. Cowan) Tinsley, **20**: 251.
— Origin of. Sharpe, **7**: 149.
— Pindar's History of. For. R. **5**: 52. — Mo. R. **147**: 400.
Diamonds. (F. M. Endlich) Am. Natural. **12**: 419. — (W. Pole) Macmil. **3**: 179. — Chamb. J. **45**: 360. — Ecl. M. **89**: 466. — No. Brit. **18**: 187.
— and Gems. (J. Bonner) Harper, **32**: 343.
— and Gold; a Tale of the Far West. (E. C. Fellows) Belgra. **37**: 456.
— and Pearls. (J. T. Fields) Atlan. **7**: 361.
— and Precious Stones. Temp. Bar, **3**: 377. Same art. Ecl. M. **55**: 37. — Ecl. M. **49**: 163. **70**: 500. — Ed. R. **124**: 228. — So. R. n. s. **12**: 445.
— Artificial Production of. J. Frankl. Inst. **108**: 212. — (N. S. Maskelyne) Nature, **21**: 203. — (W. Crookes) Nature, **21**: 260. — Nature, **21**: 404. — (J. B. Hannay) Nature, **21**: 421. **22**: 255. — (J. B. Hannay) J. Frankl. Inst. **110**: 123. — (E. J. Houston) J. Frankl. Inst. **110**: 170. — (F. W. Rudler) Pop. Sci. R. **19**: 136. Same art. Liv. Age, **145**: 362. — Belgra. **41**: 186. Same art. Ecl. M. **94**: 699. — Liv. Age, **146**: 438.
— Black. (M. F. Maury) Pop. Sci. Mo. **14**: 337. — Once a Week, **28**: 325.
— Chapter on. Bank. M. (N. Y.) **5**: 270, 369.
— Chapter on. Colburn, **89**: 427.
— Four famous. Appleton, **9**: 339.
— Historical. (G. N. Richards) Overland, **3**: 221.
— in the Exhibition of 1862. Once a Week, **7**: 218.
— in Virginia, Discovery of. Bank. M. (N. Y.) **9**: 44.
— The Koh-i-noor. (L. Ritchie) Chamb. J. **12**: 49. — Liv. Age, **26**: 345.
— Natural and artificial. (A. M. Clerke) Fraser, **101**: 817. Same art. Liv. Age, **146**: 148.
— Our great. Galaxy, **6**: 32.
— Something about. (J. W. Watson) Harper, **19**: 466. — Ev. Sat. **9**: 46, 61.
— South African. (T. R. Jones) Pop. Sci. R. **10**: 169. — Art J. **23**: 117.
— Trade in. Chamb. J. **32**: 424. Same art. Ecl. M. **49**: 419.
— Uses of, in the Arts. Penny M. **13**: 246.

Diamond Bracelets; a Story. (C. Colville) Peop. J. 7: 81.
Diamond Bullet. (W. Sawyer) Belgra. 10: 320.
Diamond Carriers. Penny M. 11: 100.
Diamond Company. (R. Johns) Bentley, 4: 174.
Diamond Cutting. (A. C. Hamlin) Pop. Sci. Mo. 8: 206. — Chamb. J. 18: 199. 44: 689.
— in Amsterdam. Pract. M. 2: 145.
— in New York. Pract. M. 3: 138.
Diamond Digging at Pniel. Chamb. J. 50: 468.
Diamond District of Brazil. Westm. 21: 297. — Mus. 26: 6. — Mo. R. 82: 419.
Diamond Drill, The. Ev. Sat. 11: 119.
Diamond Fields, South African. (A. E. Coleman) Harper, 46: 321. — (R. W. Miller) Scrib. 5: 529. — (W. J. Morton) Scrib. 16: 551, 662. — Argosy, 11: 269. — Chamb. J. 48: 117. 57: 551. — Cornh. 23: 457. — Temp. Bar, 41: 388. — (H. Hall) Ecl. Engin. 4: 59. — (G. F. Harris) Belgra. 13: 224. — Ev. Sat. 10: 251. — All the Year, 25: 617. — (E. B. Biggar) Lippinc. 27: 217. — Cornh. 23: 457. Same art. Liv. Age, 109: 490. — Ed. R. 134: 410. — New Dom. 10: 268, 321. 11: 86-341. 12: 25.
— — Dry Diggins in. Once a Week, 29: 430.
— — End of. Once a Week, 27: 172.
— — Geology of. Nature, 3: 2.
— — Lady's Visit to. Dark Blue, 4: 308.
— Life at. (A. B. Ellis) Good Words, 14: 174.
Diamond Island, N. Y., Fight at, 1777. (B. F. DeCosta) N. E. Reg. 26: 147.
Diamond Lens. (F. J. O'Brien) Atlan. 1: 354.
Diamond Maker of Sacramento. (N. Brooks) Overland, 1: 46. Same art. N. Ecl. 3: 385.
Diamond Maker of Sacramento; a Tale. Broadw. 7: 70.
Diamond Mines, Ancient, in India. (V. Ball) Nature, 23: 491.
— of Sincura. Hunt, 15: 600.
Diamond Necklace. (T. Carlyle) Fraser, 15: 1, 172.
— Case of. (J. B. Perkins) Am. Law R. 13: 463. — Chamb. J. 52: 669.
— Romance of. All the Year, 17: 159.
Diamond Ring; a Story. (E. M. Alford) Tinsley, 28: 327.
Diamond Ring; a Tale. Bentley, 64: 124.
Diamond Ring, Mrs. Fitzpatrick's. Chamb. J. 57: 525.
Diamond Robberies in the Diggings. Chamb. J. 58: 680.
Diamond Washing and Cutting. Chamb. J. 26: 219. Same art. Ecl. M. 40: 137.
Diamond Works of Sumbhulpore. Penny M. 7: 447. — (P. Breton) J. Frankl. Inst. 6: 46.
Diana. Argosy, 1: 340, 442.
— and the Poets. St. James, 15: 390.
— Hymns to. Lond. M. 11: 365.
— Statue of. Penny M. 4: 4.
— Temple of, at Ephesus. (T. Falconer) Arch. 11: 1. — Penny M. 11: 167.
— — Passage in Pliny on. (J. Windham) Arch. 6: 67.
Diana Gay; a Novel. (P. H. Fitzgerald) Belgra. 3: 475. 4: 106-485. 5: 109-514. 6: 51-544.
Diana of Poitiers. Bentley, 48: 604.
Diana Smith. (J. M. Fothergill) Good Words, 21: 485, 533.
Diana Temple. Tinsley, 11: 345-394.
Diarrhœa, Ice Treatment of. Westm. 84: 541. 87: 229.
Diary of Anne Rodway. House. Words, 14: 1, 30. Same art. Liv. Age, 50: 736.
— of a Colonial Parson. Victoria, 14: 52-442.
— of a Dining-Out Man. Bentley, 9: 280.
— of the Dreamer of Gloucester. Colburn, 115: 107-344. 116: 106, 437. 119: 235-435.
— of a dutiful Son. Quar. 86: 449. Same art. Liv. Age, 26: 112.
— of an Invalid. So. Lit. Mess. 2: 428, 489. 4: 114.
Diary of a late Physician. (S. Warren) Blackw. 28: 322, 474, 608. 29: 105, 802. 30: 60, 566. 32: 279, 878. 35: 81. 40: 1, 181. 42: 248.
— of a Lover of Literature. Quar. 4: 153.
— of a Man of Fifty. (H. James, jr.) Harper, 59: 282. — Macmil. 40: 205.
— of Minerva Tattle. (G. W. Curtis) Putnam, 2: 330.
— of an Oxford Man. Sharpe, 5: 19, 264. 6: 24. 7: 49, 107.
— of Sophia Adelan. Tait, n. s. 11: 141.
Diatoms. Chamb. J. 22: 72.
— Are they simple Cells? (G. C. Wallich) Pop. Sci. R. 16: 130.
— Desmids and. (L.W. Bailey) Am. Natural. 1: 505, 587.
— How to examine and prepare. (T. West) Recr. Sci. 1: 7, 69.
— Hunting for. Intel. Obs. 1: 190.
— What are? (T. West) Recr. Sci. 1: 85.
Diatomaceæ, British, Donkin's. Nature, 3: 210.
— Fossil, New Localities of. (J. W. Bailey) Am. J. Sci. 67: 179.
— Movements of. (P. Freeland) Canad. J. n. s. 6: 324. — (E. R. Lankester) Pop. Sci. R. 5: 395.
Diaz, Bernal, Memoir of. Liv. Age, 2: 232.
Diaz, Porfirio, Ruler of Mexico. (F. S. Oswald) Internat. R. 6: 568.
Diaz de Bivar. *See* Cid.
Dibdin, Charles, the Ocean Minstrel. (W. E. Tompkins) St. James, 13: 480. — (J. A. Wade) Bentley, 4: 626.
— and his Songs. Cornh. 17: 578. Same art. Liv. Age, 97: 682. — Temp. Bar, 39: 240.
— Sea Songs. Blackw. 26: 570. — Tait, n. s. 9: 551. — Tinsley, 13: 538. — Penny M. 10: 372.
Dibdin, Thomas, Autobiography of. Lond. M. 18: 221. — Mus. 11: 236.
— Library Companion. (I. Disraeli) Quar. 32: 152. — Westm. 3: 88.
— Reminiscences. Mo. R. 113: 348. 139: 505.
— Tour in France and Germany. Blackw. 27: 306.
Dice, The; from the German. Lond. M. 8: 117.
— Playing Cards and. (C. Nordhoff) Harper, 26: 163.
Dick, Robert, the Thurso Baker-Naturalist. (A. Geikie) Nature, 19: 189. — (W. Chambers) Chamb. J. 56: 2. Same art. Liv. Age, 140: 630. — Argosy, 27: 288. — (A. M. Symington) Good Words, 20: 239. — All the Year, 46: 127.
Dick, Thomas, with portrait. Hogg, 5: 145. — Liv. Age, 61: 131.
— Christian Philosopher. Meth. M. 47: 33. — (D. Olmsted) Chr. Mo. Spec. 9: 149.
Dick Bequest for Scottish Schools. Chamb. J. 22: 148.
Dick. (W. H. Smith) Scrib. 18: 923.
Dick Dafter. (J. Y. Akerman) Bentley, 11: 86.
Dick Dallington. House. Words, 14: 245.
Dick Libby. (G. Jones) Lippinc. 4: 432.
Dick Lyle's Fee. (L. C. Davis) Lippinc. 3: 526.
Dick Mitchel. Liv. Age, 105: 433.
Dick Netherby; a Story. (L. B. Walford) Good Words, 22: 328-767.
Dick Pastel's Story. (C. D. Warner) Putnam, 3: 632.
Dick Sparrow's Evening Out. (C. Whitehead) Bentley, 18: 498.
Dickens, Charles. (E. P. Whipple) No. Am. 69: 383. — No. Brit. 4: 165. Same art. Liv. Age, 5: 601. — (A. P. Peabody) Chr. Exam. 32: 15. — Knick. 34: 443. — Ed. R. 68: 75. — No. Brit. 7: 61. — (J. R. Dennett) Nation, 10: 380. — (P. Godwin) Putnam, 16: 231. — (B. Hill) Lippinc. 6: 288. — (B. Jerrold) N. Ecl. 7: 332. — (D. G. Mitchell) Hours at Home, 11: 363. — (G. B. Smith) Gent. M. n. s. 12: 301. — (G. Stott) Contemp. 10: 203. Same art. Liv. Age, 100: 707.

Dickens, Charles. (A. Trollope) St. Paul's, **6**: 370. Same art. Ecl. M. **75**: 297. — Blackw. **77**: 451. Same art. Ecl. M. **35**: 200. — Blackw. **109**: 673. Same art. Ecl. M. **77**: 257. Same art. Liv. Age, **110**: 29. — Ev. Sat. **1**: 79. — Fraser, **82**: 130. — Liv. Age, **58**: 263. — Lond. Q. **35**: 265. Same art. Liv. Age, **95**: 681. — Nat. R. **7**: 458. Same art. Liv. Age, **59**: 643. — (E. Roscoe) Victoria, **15**: 357. — with portrait, Peop. J. **1**: 8. — with portrait, Ev. Sat. **9**: 225.
— About England with. Scrib. **20**: 494.
— Amateur Theatricals of. Macmil. **23**: 206. Same art. Ecl. M. **76**: 322. Same art. Ev. Sat. **10**: 70.
— American Notes. (C. C. Felton) No. Am. **56**: 212.— (J. P. Thompson) New Eng. **1**: 64. — Quar. **71**: 502. — Ed. R. **76**: 497.— Blackw. **52**: 783.— Westm. **39**: 146. — So. Lit. Mess. **9**: 58. — Fraser, **26**: 617. — Ecl. Mus. **1**: 230. — (T. Hood) Colburn, **66**: 396. — (G. W. Putnam) Atlan. **26**: 476, 591. — (R. Tomes) Putnam, **11**: 112. — (E. P. Whipple) Atlan. **39**: 462. — Mo. R. **159**: 392. **161**: 483.
— — Change for. Quar. **73**: 131. — (C. C. Felton) No. Am. **58**: 211.
— and Bulwer; a Contrast. Temp. Bar, **43**: 168.
— and Criticism. (G. H. Lewes) Fortn. **17**: 141. Same art. Ecl. M. **78**: 445. Same art. Ev. Sat **12**: 246.
— and Disraeli, Styles of. (R. G. White) Galaxy, **10**: 253.
— and his Debt of Honor. Land We Love, **5**: 414.
— and his Works. Fraser, **21**: 381.
— and Thackeray. Dub. R. **68**: 315. — Ecl. M. **16**: 370. — No. Brit. **15**: 57. Same art. Liv. Age, **30**: 97.— Liv. Age, **21**: 224.
— Another Gossip about. Eng. Dom. M. **12**: 78.
— as Capt. Bobadill, with portrait. Ev. Sat. **11**: 295.
— as Dramatist and Poet. (P. Fitzgerald) Gent. M. n. s. **20**: 61.
— as a Humanizer. (A. Quamoclit) St. James, **45**: 281.
— as a Literary Exemplar. (F. A. Walker) University Q. **1**: 91.
— as a moral Teacher. (J. H. Morison) Mo. Rel. M. **44**: 129.
— as a Moralist. O. & N. **3**: 480.
— as a Novelist. Westm. **82**: 414. Same art. Ecl. M. **64**: 42.
— at Home. Ev. Sat. **2**: 396. — Gent. M. n. s. **27**: 562.
— at Idleburg. Knick. **20**: 146.
— Ball given to, in New York. Hist. M. **12**: 291.
— Barnaby Rudge, Grip the Raven in. Ev. Sat. **9**: 542, 742, 749.
— Battle of Life. Tait, n. s. **14**: 55.
— on Bells. (G. D. Cowan) Belgra. **28**: 380.
— a Benefactor of Mankind. (C. E. Norton) No. Am. **106**: 671.
— Bleak House. Ecl. R. **98**: 665. — (C. F. Riggs) Putnam, **2**: 558. — Dem. R. **33**: 276.
— Chimes. Ed. R. **81**: 181. — Dub. R. **17**: 560. — Ecl. M. **5**: 33. — Ecl. R. **81**: 70. — Mo. Rel. M. **3**: 320.
— Christmas Carol. (L. G. Clark) Knick. **23**: 276. — Dub. R. **15**: 510.
— David Copperfield. Fraser, **42**. 698. Same art. Ecl. M. **22**: 247. — Prosp. R. **7**: 157.
— — and Arthur Pendennis. So. Lit. Mess. **17**: 499.
— Death of. Ecl. M. **75**: 217. — Ev. Sat. **9**: 450.
— — English Magazines on, 1870. Ev. Sat. **9**: 482.
— Dictionary of, Pierce & Wheeler's. Ev. Sat. **11**: 258.
— Dogs. Lond. Soc. **4**: 48.
— Dombey and Son. (E. P. Whipple) No. Am. **69**: 383.
— Early Life of. Fraser, **85**: 105. Same art. Ecl. M. **78**: 277. — Chamb. J. **49**: 17, 40. — Ev. Sat. **12**: 60.
— Farewell Banquet to, 1867. Ev. Sat. **4**: 705.
— Farewell Reading in London. Ev. Sat. **9**: 242, 260.
— Faults as a Novelist. (W. Sargent) No. Am. **77**: 409.
— Footprints of. (M. D. Conway) Harper, **41**: 610.
Dickens, Charles, Forster's Life of. (J R. Dennett) Nation, **14**: 42. **16**: 28. **18**: 175. — (G. B. Merrill) Overland, **8**: 443. — (J. H. Stack) Fortn. **17**: 117. — Am. Bibliop. **4**: 125. — Canad. Mo. **1**: 179. **3**: 171. **5**: 364. — Ecl. M. **78**: 237. — Ev. Sat. **14**: 608. — Internat. R. **1**: 417. — Lakeside, **7**: 336. — (F. Sheldon) No. Am. **114**: 413. — Quar. **132**: 125. — Temp. Bar, **38**: 169.
— French Criticism of. Peop. J. **5**: 228. — Ev. Sat. **9**: 478.
— Genius of. (E. P. Whipple) Atlan. **19**: 546. — (F. W. Shelton) Knick. **39**: 421. — (G. F. Talbot) Putnam, **5**: 263. — N. Ecl. **7**: 257. — (A. Austin) Temp. Bar, **29**: 554.
— Good Genie of Fiction. St. Paul's, **10**: 130.
— Great Expectations. (E. P. Whipple) Atlan. **40**: 327. Dub. Univ. **58**: 685. — Ecl. R. **114**: 458.
— Hard Times. (E. P. Whipple) Atlan. **39**: 353.—Westm. **62**: 604.
— Home of. (J. D. Sherwood) Hours at Home, **5**: 239. Ev. Sat. **9**: 228.
— in the Editor's Chair. Gent. M. n. s. **26**: 725.
— in France. (W. M. Thackeray) Ev. Sat. **3**: 737. — Fraser, **25**: 342.
— in London with. (B. E. Martin) Scrib. **21**: 649. **22**: 32.
— In Memoriam. Cornh. **9**: 129. — Macmil. **22**: 236. — (B. Jerrold) Gent. M. n. s. **5**: 228.
— in New York. (J. R. Dennett) Nation, **5**: 482.
— Least known Writings of. Ev. Sat. **9**: 471.
— Letters of. (W. C. Brownell) Nation, **29**: 388. — Appleton, **23**: 72. — Westm. **113**: 423. Same art. Liv. Age, **145**: 707. — (W. Minto) Fortn. **32**: 845. Same art. Ecl. M. **94**: 165. Same art. Liv. Age, **144**: 3. — (J. G. Macleod) Month, **39**: 81. — (M. Browne) Contemp. **37**: 77. Same art. Liv. Age, **144**: 420. — (J. T. Morse, jr.) Internat. R. **8**: 271. — Dub. R. **86**: 409.
— — from Italy. Ecl. M. **7**: 540. **8**: 45-519. **9**: 109, 190.
— Life of. Chamb. J. **51**: 177.
— — and Letters of. (J. R. G. Hassard) Cath. World, **30**: 692.
— Manuscripts of. Chamb. J. **54**: 710. Same art. Liv. Age, **136**: 252. — Potter Am. Mo. **10**: 156.
— Martin Chuzzlewit. Mo. R. **165**: 137. — Nat. R. **13**: 134. — Knick. **24**: 374.
— Master Humphrey's Clock. Mo. R. **152**: 35.
— Memories of. (J. T. Fields) Atlan. **26**: 235.
— Middle Life of. Chamb. J. **50**: 74.
— Moral Service of, to Literature. Ecl. M. **73**: 103.
— Mystery of Edwin Drood. (T. Foster) Belgra. **35**: 453. — (G. B. Woods) O. & N. **2**: 530. — Ev. Sat. **9**: 291, 594. — (W. H. Browne) So. M. **14**: 219.
— Nomenclature of. (W. F. Peacock) Belgra. **20**: 267, 393.
— Notes and Correspondence. Eng. Dom. M. **11**: 91.
— Old Curiosity Shop, Barnaby Rudge. Chr. Rem. **4**: 581.
— Oliver Twist. (E. P. Whipple) Atlan. **38**: 474.—Quar. **64**: 83. — So. Lit. Mess. **3**: 323. **5**: 704. — (J. S. Dwight) Chr. Exam. **27**: 161.— Dub. Univ. **12**: 699. — Mo. R. **148**: 29.
— Our Mutual Friend. Ecl. R. **122**: 455. — Westm. **85**: 582. — (H. James, jr.) Nation, **1**: 786.
— — MS. Notes for. (K. Field) Scrib. **8**: 472.
— Pickwick Papers. (J. W. Croker) Quar. **59**: 484. — (W. Sawyer) Belgra. **12**: 33. — Westm. **27**: 194. — So. Lit. Mess. **2**: 787. **3**: 525. — Mus. **32**: 195. — Mo. R. **142**: 153. — Ecl. R. **65**: 339.
— — and Nicholas Nickleby, Topography of. Scrib. **20**: 641.
— — German Translation of. Dub. R. **8**: 160.
— — Portrait of Mr. Pickwick. (G. A. Sala) Belgra. **12**: 165.

Dickens, Charles. Pictures from Italy. Dub. R. **21**: 184. — Tait, n. s. **13**: 461.
— Place of, in Literature. St. James, **26**: 696.
— Poetic Element in Style of. Ev. Sat. **9**: 811.
— Readings by. (T. C. De Leon) Land We Love, **4**: 421.
— — Kate Field's Pen Photographs of. (E. Rawlinson) Dark Blue, **2**: 516. — Ev. Sat. **11**: 631.
— — New. (E. Yates) Tinsley, **4**: 60.
— Reminiscences of. Eng. Dom. M. **10**: 336.
— Remonstrance with. Blackw. **81**: 490. Same art. Liv. Age, **53**: 480.
— Sale of the Effects of. Chamb. J. **47**: 502. — Ev. Sat. **9**: 557.
— Satire on. (S. Warren) Blackw. **60**: 590. Same art. Ecl. M. **10**: 65.
— Seasonable Words about. (N. S. Dodge) Overland, **6**: 77.
— Sketches. Mus. **31**: 185. — So. Lit. Mess. **2**: 457. — Mo. R. **139**: 350.
— Tale of two Cities. Liv. Age, **64**: 366.
— Tales. Ed. R. **68**: 75.
— Use of the Bible. Temp. Bar, **27**: 225. Same art. Appleton, **2**: 265, 294. Same art. Ev. Sat. **8**: 411.
— Verse of. Liv. Age, **136**: 237.
— Visit to. (H. C. Andersen) Temp. Bar, **31**: 27. Same art. Ecl. M. **76**: 183. Same art. Ev. Sat. **9**: 874.
— — Andersen's. Bentley, **48**: 181. Same art. Ecl. M. **62**: 110. Same art. Liv. Age, **66**: 692.
— Voice of Christmas Past. (Mrs. Z. B. Buddington) Harper, **42**: 187.
— with the News-Venders. Ev. Sat. **9**: 318.
— Works of. (H. Dennison) Nat. Q. **1**: 91. — Brit. Q. **35**: 135. — (J. Cleghorn) No. Brit. **3**: 65.
Dickinson, Anna. (I. B. Hooker) Nation, **7**: 391.
— and the Critics. (E. L. Godkin) Nation, **24**: 232.
— as Writer and Orator. (J. R. Dennett and E. L. Godkin) Nation, **7**: 346, 388.
Dickinson, Austin, and Amherst College. (O. Eastman) Cong. Q. **14**: 282.
Dickinson, Daniel S., Portrait of. Dem. R. **19**: 83. — with portrait, Dem. R. **40**: 1.
— Speech of. Dem. R. **27**: 104.
Dickinson, John, in 1774. Hist. M. **10**: 288.
Dickinson, Jonathan, and Dickinson Hall. (J. O. Murray) Princ. **43**: 93.
Dickinson, Philemon. (W. Dickinson) M. Am. Hist. **7**: 420.
Dickinson College. (Prof. Caldwell) Am. Q. Reg. **9**: 17.
Dicksee, Thomas F. Art J. **24**: 5.
Dicotyledons, Natural Succession of. (L. F. Ward) Am. Natural. **12**: 724.
Dictionary, First Specimen of a new. Fraser, **33**: 127.
Dictionary Definitions, Logic of. (W. L. Davidson) Mind, **6**: 212.
Dictionary Dreams. All the Year, **5**: 549.
Dictionaries, Among. Ecl. M. **97**: 236. Same art. Liv. Age, **150**: 239.
— Form and Arrangement of. (G. P. Marsh) Nation, **3**: 515. **4**: 7. — Liv. Age, **61**: 489.
— Use of. (D. G. Haskins) O. & N. **1**: 755. — (A. Dean) Hours at Home, **5**: 493.
See names of languages; also Arts and Sciences, etc.
Did he dream it? (J. Clifford) Lakeside, **4**: 251.
Did he take the Prince to ride? (E. E. Hale) Atlan. **21**: 603.
Did she love him? (J. Grant) Tinsley, **18**: 89–681. **19**: 41–677.
Didactic Irish Novelists. Dub. Univ. **26**: 737.
Didactics in University of Iowa. (S. N. Fellows) Education, **1**: 393.
— Walsh's. (J. G. Palfrey) No. Am. **43**: 257.
Didcot Junction, Half an Hour at. (J. A. Wilson) Belgra. **38**: 287.
Diderot, Denis. (J. Morley) Fortn. **23**: 151, 485, 680. **24**: 353, 664. — Knick. **56**: 27. — (G. Garrigues) Western, **5**: 542.
— and the Encyclopædists, Morley's. Quar. **150**: 406.
— and Materialism. (C. W. Parkin) Canad. Mo. **20**: 640.
— as an Art Critic. (G. A. Simcox) Portfo **3**: 140.
— at St. Petersburg. Fortn. **29**: 752. Same art. Liv. Age, **137**: 732.
— Life of. (T. Carlyle) For. Q. **11**: 261. — Quar. **47**: 301. — Select J. **1**: 192. — (A. Middleton) Dem. R. **20**: 227, 329.
— Le Neveu de Rameau. Tinsley, **2**: 319.
— Philosophie de. (P. Janet) 19th Cent. **9**: 695.
Dido, Planet, Elements of. (C. H. F. Peters) Am. J. Sci. **119**: 130.
Didot, Firmin, Sale of Library of. (A. Laugel) Nation, **28**: 416.
Didsbury Sermons, by J. D. Geden. Lond. Q. **50**: 174.
Didymus of Alexandria. Ecl. M. **54**: 14.
Die, black Fellow! Rise, white Fellow! a Tale. Eng. Dom. M. **9**: 89.
Dies for Coins and Medals. Penny M. **11**: 231.
Diego the Heretic; a Tale of the Carlist Rising. Cornh. **25**: 48.
Dieppe, France. Argosy, **5**: 64. — Penny M. **4**: 236. — Liv. Age, **143**: 195.
— Excursions in Environs of. Colburn, **54**: 465.
Dies Boreales. (J. Wilson) Blackw. **72**: 133, 373.
Dies Iræ. (P. S. Worsley) Blackw. **87**: 369. — Am. Church R. **25**: 203. — Cath. World, **33**: 15. — So. Lit. Mess. **14**: 106. — (D. Y. Heisler) Ref. Q. **27**: 442.
— translated. (J. A. Dix) Scrib. **11**: 797. — Irish Mo. **2**: 136. — (C. Kent) Month, **22**: 273. — (P. Schaff) Hours at Home, **7**: 39, 261. — (A. P. Stanley) Macmil. **19**: 167. — (C. A. Walworth) Cath. World, **17**: 221.
— On the Sequence. (A. Schwartz) Macmil. **30**: 455, 568.
— with translation. Cong. M. **24**: 167.
Dies Iræ; a Tale. (L. Nelson) Galaxy, **2**: 433.
Dies natalis Christi; a Poem. (R. H. Stoddard) Harper, **48**: 178.
Diet. (C. A. Bristed) Galaxy, **16**: 324. — (F. L. Oswald) Pop. Sci. Mo. **18**: 303, 456. — Chamb. J. **36**: 286. **53**: 216. — Penny M. **6**: 135–159.
— and Dress. No. Brit. **22**: 505. Same art. Ecl. M. **35**: 75.
— and Dyspepsia. Quar. **65**: 315. — Mus. **39**: 305.
— and Regimen, Robertson on. Mo. R. **138**: 271.
— Chambers's Manual of. Nature, **12**: 64.
— Cook or the Doctor. (H. Martineau) Once a Week, **1**: 331.
— Curiosities of. (N. S. Dodge) Appleton, **9**: 12.
— en Masse. (S. B. Hunt) Hours at Home, **11**: 34.
— French and English. Lond. M. **23**: 347, 433.
— Notes on. Hogg, **1**: 7.
— of Charles I. when Duke of York. (E. Turner) Arch. **15**: 1.
— Old English. Appleton, **9**: 747.
— Old Notions on. Retros. **17**: 402.
— Paris's Treatise on. Lond. M. **15**: 481.
— Poetry of. Chamb. J. **9**: 25.
— What shall we drink? (J. Bell) Lippinc. **7**: 428.
Dietaries of Prisoners and others. (W. A. Guy) J. Statis. Soc. **26**: 239.
Dietetics. Dem. R. **24**: 337. — Am. Mo. R. **1**: 193. — Ed. R. **47**: 37.
— of old. Chamb. J. **37**: 373.
See Food.
Dietetic Charlatanry. New York R. **1**: 336.
Diez, Juan Martin, the Empecinado. Blackw. **51**: 521, 756. **52**: 75. **53**: 343.

Diez del Castillo, Bernal. Am. Hist. Rec. 1: 536.
Difficult Circumstances of Captain Mannering. Lond. Soc. 14: 358–542.
Difficult Question. Chamb. J. 54: 808, 819.
Difficulty, Pleasures of. (L. O. Pike) Fraser, 69: 618. Same art. Ecl. M. 62: 294.
Difficulties, In. All the Year, 18: 92, 105, 136.
— in Parishes. Chr. Exam. 9: 1.
Diffraction, Phenomena of. (O. N. Rood) Am. J. Sci. 65: 327.
— produced by Edges of Moon. (E. C. Pickering) J. Frankl. Inst. 89: 264.
Diffraction Experiments. Intel. Obs. 7: 122.
Diffraction Gratings. (J. M. Blake) Am. J. Sci. 108: 33.
Diffraction Spectrum and Wave Lengths. (J. Stuart) Nature, 1: 506.
Diffusion, Loschmidt's Experiments on. (J. C. Maxwell) Nature, 8: 298.
Digamma, Homeric. Dub. Univ. 16: 469.
Digby, Sir Everard, and James I. (S. R. Gardiner) Fraser, 83: 571.
Digby, Sir Kenelm. Compitum. Dub. R. 25: 463.
— Memoirs. (H. T. Tuckerman) So. Lit. Mess. 19: 696.
Digby, Kenelm H. Evenings on the Thames. Dub. R. 48: 526.
Digby Grand, Autobiography of. (G. J. W. Melville) Fraser, 44: 473, 635. 45: 60–673. 46: 68–660.
Digestion, Chemistry of. (Dr. Marcet) J. Frankl. Inst. 74: 404.
— Food and. (A. L. Carroll) Harper, 39: 892.
— of Foods. (Prof. Voit) Pop. Sci. Mo. 1: 308.
— Physiology of. (H. Power) Nature, 2: 238. — (H. L. Fairchild) Pop. Sci. Mo. 17: 600. — Cornh. 4: 75. 7: 141, 542. 8: 35. 9: 219. — Mo. R. 140: 348.
- Sweetser on. No. Am. 46: 538.
— Talk about. (W. J. Conklin) Lakeside, 1: 107.
Digger's Diary. House. Words, 6: 457, 545. 7: 125. 8: 6.
Dighton-Rock Inscription. (C. Rau) M. Am. Hist. 2: 82. 3: 236.
Digital Reduction, Laws of. (J. A. Ryder) Am. Natural. 11: 603.
Dignity. Cornh. 3: 584.
Dijon. Liv. Age, 145: 185. — So. Lit. Mess. 18: 353.
Dikes and Levees of Holland and Louisiana. (A. B. Roman) De Bow, 7: 322.
Dilemma, The. Blackw. 117: 541, 688. 118: 1–629. 119: 1–397. Same art. Liv. Age, 126: 102–665. 127: 17-749. 128: 80–805. 129: 78–333.
Dilemma, A; a Tale. Chamb. J. 53: 394, 411.
Dilemma, A; a Sketch. Dub. Univ. 81: 312.
Dilettanti, Society of. Chamb. J. 33: 179. — Ed. R. 105: 493.
Diligence, The. Blackw. 55: 692.
Dilke, Sir Charles, and English Republicans. (J. McCarthy) Galaxy, 13: 725.
— at Home. (M. E. Beedy) Lakeside, 7: 386.
— Greater Britain. (J. D. Butler) Lakeside, 7: 248. — Once a Week, 21: 128.
Dillard, Mrs. (Mrs. E. F. Ellet) Godey, 36: 323.
Dillingham, Edward, Will of, 1666. N. E. Reg. 7: 225.
Dillon, Henry A., Viscount, Poems of. Mo. R. 116: 359.
Dillon's Sermon on Bartholomew's Fair. Fraser, 2: 342.
Dilly, James, and his Table Talk. Once a Week, 26: 286, 331, 396.
Dilston Hall, and the Radcliffes of Derwentwater. St. James, 23: 428.
Diluvian Period. (F. J. Pictet) Am. J. Sci. 81: 345.
Dime Books. (W. Everett) No. Am. 99: 303.
Dimitri Roudine. (I. Tourgénieff) Ev. Sat. 14: 85, 113, 141.
Dimmick, K. H., with portrait. Am. Whig R. 13: 274.
Dimmick, Luther F. (L. Withington) Cong. Q. 2: 370.
Dinah Blake's Revenge; a Tale. (J. V. Noel) Canad. Mo. 1: 201–497. 2: 10.
Dinan. Once a Week, 16: 735.
Dinant and Liege; Fate of two Cities. (J. W. Sheahan) Lakeside, 9: 35.
Dinely, Sir John. Penny M. 10: 356.
Diner-Out of the Old School. Tait, n. s. 19: 234.
Dingelstedt, Franz. Die Amazone. No. Brit. 49: 427.
— Poems. Tait, n. s. 13: 759.
Dingle, Protestant Colony in. Chr. Obs. 47: 235.
Dingley, Thomas, Gent. St. James, 27: 15.
Dining. (H. Schütz-Wilson) Dark Blue, 4: 114. — Chamb. J. 23: 392. — Knick. 56: 485. — All the Year, 4: 465.
— alone. (F. Jacox) Belgra. 14: 378.
— Art of. (P. Blot) Galaxy, 1: 116–741.
— down the River. Cornh. 5: 105.
— out. (G. W. Curtis) Putnam, 2: 25.—Fraser, 33: 445.
— out and at Home. Belgra. 21: 304.
— with an ancient Roman. All the Year, 20: 104, 127.
— with a Mandarin. (C. F. F. Woods) Belgra. 16: 80.
Dining-Rooms. (E. R. Church) Art J. 31: 285.
Dinner. (P. Blot) Galaxy, 5: 173.—Once a Week, 5: 413.
— At. (J. Harwood) Belgra. 17: 440.
— by Mistake; a Tale. Cath. World, 1: 535.
— First and last. Blackw. 25: 223.
— in London. Temp. Bar, 6: 165.
— Public. Dub. Univ. 94: 91.
— Real and reputed. Blackw. 46: 815.
— Souvenir of a. Chamb. J. 30: 305.
— Time of. Chamb. J. 48: 577.
— Why we eat our. (G. Allen) Pop. Sci. Mo 14: 799.
— with the jolly old Boy. (T. H. S. Escott) Belgra. 13: 337.
Dinners. Once a Week, 6: 541.
— and Diners. (F. A. Dixon) Canad. Mo. 15: 645.
— Clubs, etc. (A. Hayward) Quar. 55: 445.
— French. Ev. Sat. 9: 23.
— Home. All the Year, 11: 63.
— in Literature. Cornh. 40: 590. Same art. Appleton, 23: 31.
— in many Places. Lond. Soc. 39: 510.
— Lectures on. Blackw. 19: 195.
— London. (T. Hankey) Macmil. 25: 370. — Ev. Sat. 12: 355.
— Modern and mediæval. (P. Blot) Galaxy, 3: 717.
— Musical. (G. A. Sala) Belgra. 24: 38.
— Our. St. Paul's, 10: 408. Same art. Ecl. M. 78: 704. Same art. Ev. Sat. 5: 338.
— à la Russe. (E. Schuyler) Nation, 8: 7. — All the Year, 38: 103. — Fraser, 59: 462.
— Science of. (M. Collins) Belgra. 15: 242.
— sent out. (G. A. Sala) Belgra. 23: 54.
— Thoughts upon. Blackw. 71: 734.
— Uncommon. Chamb. J. 40: 367.
Dinner Commissariat. Chamb. J. 29: 55.
Dinner-Givers, Directions to. Dub. Univ. 31: 377.
Dinner-Giving, Art of. Cornh 19: 555. Same art. Ev. Sat. 7: 763.
Dinner Party, A. (J. Eddy) Atlan. 30: 527.
Dinner Table. Chamb. J. 52: 120.
Dinner Tables and Talkers. Ecl. R. 15: 213.
Dinner Time. Ev. Sat. 11: 407. — Ecl. M. 56: 191.
Dinoceras Mirabile, Restoration of. (O. C. Marsh) Am. J. Sci. 122: 31.
Dinornis, The. Chamb. J. 9: 247.
Dinosauria. (H. G. Seeley) Pop. Sci. R. 19: 44.
— American Jurassic. (O. C. Marsh) Am. J. Sci. 119 253, 395.
Dinotherium, The. Penny M. 6: 195.
Dinter, G. F. Am. J. Educ. 7: 153.

Dinton Church, Saxon Arch and Inscription. (J. Claxton) Arch. 10: 167.
Dioceses, Size of primitive. (W. W. Olssen) Am. Church R. 14: 587.
Diocletian, Abdication of. Dub. Univ. 72: 207. Same art. Ecl. M. 71: 1332.
Diodate, William, and his Italian Ancestry. (E. E. Salisbury) N. E. Reg. 35: 167.
Diogenes the Cynic. (E. I. Sears) Nat. Q. 18: 209.
Diogenes in America; a Poem. Scrib. 8: 253.
Diognetus, Epistle to. (B. H. Cowper) Kitto, 9: 175.— Chr. R. 9: 280.—Princ. 25: 44
Dion. Colburn, 117: 292.
— and the Sibyls; a Classic Christian Novel. (M. G. Keon) Cath. World, 11: 15-733. 12: 31-799. 13: 56.
Dionysius the Areopagite. (B. F. Westcott) Contemp. 5: 1.—(W. H. Anderdon) Irish Mo. 8: 427.
Dionysius the Elder. Colburn, 128: 37.
Dionysius the Younger. Colburn, 145: 664.
Dionysius O'Dogherty, Esq. (W. H. Maxwell) Bentley, 26: 227.
Dionysus, Study of. (W. H. Pater) Fortn. 26: 752.
Diophantine Analysis. (A. D. Wheeler) Math. Mo. 3: 325.
Dioramas, Cosmoramas, and Panoramas. Penny M. 11: 363.
— Moving. All the Year, 17: 304.
Dips, Spurs, and Angles. (E. W. Carpenter) Overland, 10: 105.
Dipleidoscope, On the. J. Frankl. Inst. 38: 341.
Diplomacy. (C. Redding) Colburn, 109: 120.
— Adventures of a roving Diplomatist. (H. Wikof) Colburn, 110: 293.
— American. (H. T. Tuckerman) Atlan. 22: 348.
— — Sketch of. (R. H. Dana) Scrib. 20: 616.
— and Cannon-Balls. (E. Tompkins) Putnam, 5: 113.
— and Diplomatic History, Notes on. (H. Ottley) Fraser, 70: 135-781.
— and Diplomatists of England. Fraser, 41: 605. Same art. Liv. Age, 26: 193, 315. Same art. Ecl. M. 20: 425.
— Ceremony and Forms in. Blackw. 114: 667. 115: 55. Same art. Liv. Age, 120: 101, 387.
— eighty Years ago; a Tale. Am. Mo. M. 6: 302, 343, 438.
— Embassies and Foreign Courts. Liv. Age, 47: 434.
— English. Blackw. 122: 66.
— French and English. (D. H. Wheeler) Lakeside, 8: 154.
— Immorality in. Westm. 64: 37.
— Mock. Once a Week, 9: 133.
— Modern. (J. H. Fyfe) Macmil. 36: 238. Same art. Ecl. M. 89: 342.—For. Q. 13: 1.—Mus. 24: 628.
— of the last Century. Fraser, 39: 701.
— of the Sword. Dem. R. 43: 360.
— of the U. S. (J. MacCarthy) Cath. World, 32: 57.
— — from 1783 to 1789. (E. Everett) No. Am. 39: 302.
— — from 1778 to 1814. (C. Cushing) U. S. Lit. Gaz. 5: 1.—(T. Pitkin) No. Am. 24: 92.
— Reform in. Brit. Q. 5: 1.
— Rise and Progress of. Westm. 62: 506.
— — of American. Bost. R. 4: 462.
— Secret. Westm. 21: 484.
Diplomatic and Consular Service Bill, 1868. (G. H. Yeaman) Nation, 7: 498.
Diplomatic Doings. Colburn, 73: 153.
Diplomatic History of the United States. So. Q. 25: 432.
Diplomatic Privileges. Blackw. 116: 346.
Diplomatic Reform. Westm. 55: 173.
Diplomatic Service. (W. D. Howells) Nation, 1: 551.—(W. J. Stillman) Nation, 2: 104.—Nat. R. 12: 300.
— American. (E. L. Godkin) Nation, 4: 132. 6: 165.—Nation, 7: 187.
Diplomatic Service, Dress Question of. (E. L. Godkin) Nation, 6: 267.—Liv. Age, 40: 521.
— English. Chamb. J. 47: 705.
— Sectarian. (P. Girard) Cath. World, 27: 223.
Diplomatist, Diaries of, Sir G. Jackson. Quar. 132: 494.
— Extracts from the Diary and Letters of a. Colburn, 78: 227-455.
Diplomatist's Story. Chamb. J. 42: 761. Same art. Ecl. M. 66: 366.
Diplomatists, American. (E. L. Godkin) Nation, 26: 209.
— Natural. (A. Mitchell) Putnam, 4: 104.
— Talk about. Once a Week, 18: 296.
— Trained and improvised. Dem. R. 43: 185.
Dipplebury Scandal. St. James, 10: 411. 11: 44, 177.
Dipsomania. (T. Carlisle) St. James, 38: 36.—(A. Wynter) Once a Week, 10: 209.—Chamb. J. 29: 201.
Diptych. Fraser, 104: 42.
Directors, Powers and Responsibilities of. Hunt, 58: 432.
Directories, Hints for Improvement of. Ecl. M. 20: 318.—Dub. Univ. 35: 494.
Dirge of Alaric; a Poem. Colburn, 7: 64.
Dirges, Folk. Cornh. 36: 196.
Dirt, Sanctity of. (T. E. Bridgett) Contemp. 25: 417.
Dirt-Eaters. So. Lit. J. 4: 9.
Disadvantages of living in a small Community. (A. K. H. Boyd) Fraser, 86: 770. Same art. Ecl. M. 80: 271.
Disaffection, Rise and Progress of. (R. Southey) Quar. 16: 511.
Disagreeable People. (A. K. H. Boyd) Fraser, 66: 173. Same art. Ecl. M. 57: 208.—(W. Sawyer) Belgra. 5: 315.
Disagreeable Things, Bearing. Temp. Bar, 54: 338.
Disagreeing, Art of. Ev. Sat. 10: 402.
Disappearance of John Ackland; a Tale. All the Year, 22: 380-475.
— of Robert Fairway. (J. Armstrong, jr.) Overland, 7: 121.
Disappearances. Chamb. J. 45: 257. Same art. Ecl. M. 71: 1142.—Ev. Sat. 5: 585.—House. Words, 3: 246. 9: 227.
— Mysterious. Atlan. 44: 622.—Chamb. J. 53: 75.
Disappointment and Success, Concerning. (A. K. H. Boyd) Fraser, 61: 1. Same art. Liv. Age, 64: 451.
Disasters of Jan Nadeltreiber. (W. Howitt) Fraser, 2: 215.
— of three Days. Fraser, 7: 292.
— of a Wedding Day. Temp. Bar, 19: 543.
Discharge of Gas and Steam from Orifices. (G. Zeuner) Ecl. Engin. 7: 10, 200.
Disciples, Church of, not Evangelical. (J. N. Carmon) Bapt. Q. 9: 188.
— and Baptists, Union of. (W. T. Moore) Chr. Q. 3: 335.
Discipleship; a Poem. (G. MacDonald) Good Words, 9: 112.
Discipline. Chamb. J. 58: 305.
— Aphorisms on. Am. J. Educ. 10: 187.
— Book of, Revised Presb. (C. Hodge) Princ. 30: 692.
— Church. (A. W. Lilly) Luth. Q. 8: 229.
— in Literary Institutions. West. M. 2: 540.
— Mental. (P. G. Hamerton) O. & N. 7: 83.
— Moral and mental. (Z. Richards) Am. J. Educ. 1: 107.
— of Life. (A. Traver) Ref. Q. 28: 597.
— of Valerie Gore. Dub. Univ. 66: 580, 651.
— Scholastic. (C. Hoole) Am. J. Educ. 17: 293.
— School. *See* School Discipline.
Disco Bay. (R. Brown) Geog. M. 2: 33.
Discontent. Chr. Disc. 3: 407.
Discontents and Remedies. (E. Hosken) Dub. Univ. 86: 590.
Discontented Journey; a Tale. (Mrs. Montgomery) Cath. World, 29: 592.
Discord in Sound and Color. (E. Gurney) Mind, 4: 22.
Discount, Illustrations of. Fraser, 27: 398.

Discount, Rate of. Blackw. **114**: 92.
— — Fluctuations in. Bank. M. (N. Y.) **15**: 764.
Discounts, Trade. Bank. M. (L.) **9**: 702.
Discount Deposit. (C. H. Carroll) Bank. M. (N. Y.) **31**: 961.
Discoverer, The. (E. C. Stedman) Radical R. **1**: 74.
Discoverers, Fate of. Dub. Univ. **83**: 82.
— How the World treats. Blackw. **90**: 545.
Discovery, Unexplored Fields of. Dub. Univ. **43**: 426.
Discoveries, New and old. Brit. Q. **34**: 382. Same art. Ecl. M. **55**: 381. **56**: 50. Same art. Liv. Age, **72**: 691.
— Singular. Chamb. J. **56**: 745.
Discrowned Jingo. Gent. M. n. s. **26**: 46.
Discussion an Aid to Faith. (A. B. Muzzey) Mo. Rel. M. **39**: 465.
Disease, Alternation in Intensity of. (A. De Candolle) Pop. Sci. Mo. **4**: 569.
— and Health, Geograph. Distribution of. Hogg, **9**: 415.
— and Human Body. (L. H. Steiner) Mercersb. **11**: 63.
— Camp Cure for. (S. W. Mitchell) Lippinc. **14**: 192.
— Conservative Design of organic. (A. F. A. King) Pop. Sci. Mo. **7**: 160.
— Duncan's God in. Hogg, **8**: 219.
— Dust and. (J. Tyndall) Fraser, **81**: 302. Same art. Ecl. M. **74**: 556.
— Germ Theory in. (H. C. Bastian) Sup. Pop. Sci. Mo. **2**: 310.
— Influence of, on Mind and Body. (W. Hooker) New Eng. **3**: 493.
— — of Passions on. (B. W. Richardson) Pop. Sci. Mo. **8**: 60.
— Mental Aspects of. (J. M. Fothergill) Pop. Sci. Mo. **6**: 562.
— Natural Treatment of. Chamb. J. **28**: 135.
— Nature and Art in Cure of. Ecl. R. **106**: 305.
— — in Cure of. (D. W. Cheever) No. Am. **89**: 165.
— of the Body as a mental Stimulant. Cornh. **39**: 412. Same art. Pop. Sci. Mo. **15**: 71.
— Propagation of, by Shipping. Hunt, **50**: 435.
— Reflex Action. (T. L. Brunton) Pop. Sci. Mo. **14**: 639.
— Relation of Fermentation to. (J. Tyndall) Fortn. **26**: 547. Same art. Liv. Age, **131**: 643.
— Removal of inherited Tendencies to. (J. R. Black) Pop. Sci. Mo. **15**: 433.
— Researches on Life and. Ed. R. **136**: 216. Same art. Liv. Age, **114**: 771.
— Spread of, Tyndall on. Nature, **16**: 9.
— Strange mental Faculties in. (H. Butterworth) Pop. Sci. Mo. **8**: 177.
Diseases, Duration of. Penny M. **6**: 15.
— Causes and Effects of, Barlow on. Mo. R. **146**: 78.
— Endemic and Epidemic. Penny M. **10**: 291-346.
— Epidemic, Adams on. Ecl. R. **24**: 456.
— — Prevention of. Pamph. **10**: 443.
— Feigned. Penny M. **9**: 367, 370.
— — and factitious, Gavin on. Mo. R. **162**: 157. **163**: 525.
— from the Air. (M. Wilson) Carey's Mus. **4**: 417.
— Infectious, Compulsory Registration of. (A. Scott) Good Words, **18**: 410.
— Instincts of Nature in. Colburn, **6**: 153.
— Nomenclature of. Nature, **10**: 436.
— of Children, Clark on. Mo. R. **84**: 34.
— of modern Life, Richardson on. Nature, **13**: 508.
— prevalent at Edinburgh, 1817. Blackw. **1**: 394.
— Remittent and intermittent. (J. McCulloch) Am J. Sci. **18**: 338.
— Tyndall on Theories of. Nature, **4**: 164.
Disease Germs. (W. B. Carpenter) 19th Cent. **10**: 538. Same art. Liv. Age, **151**: 323.
Disestablishment. *See* Church of England.
Disfranchisement of the Boroughs. Blackw. **70**: 296.
Disguised Knight, Legend of. (W. E. A. Axon) Reliquary, **10**: 38.
Dish of Lapwings à la Tantale. Lond. Soc. **27**: 298.
Dishonored. House. Words, **19**: 293.
Disinfectants. (C. W. Eliot) Nation, **2**: 698, 713. — Ecl. Engin. **5**: 510. — Tinsley, **9**: 349.
Disinfection. No. Brit. **44**: 458.
— and Disinfectants. (W. Eassie) Pop. Sci. Mo. **1**: 55.
— Purifying infected Air. Ed. R. **1**: 237.
Disinherited; a Mexican Story. St. James, **4**: 257-508. **5**: 105-516. **6**: 100-516.
Disintegration of Empires. No. Brit. **38**: 257. Same art. Ecl. M. **59**: 267, 483.
Disinterment of Human Bodies, Unlawful. Quar. **42**: 1.
— of several Kings. (J. Bigelow) No. Am. **38**: 455.
Dismal Dobbs; a Theatrical Reminiscence. Dub. Univ. **57**: 483.
Dismal Swamp, Virginia. (H. D. Strother) Harper, **13**: 441. — (N. B. Webster) Am. Natural. **9**: 260. — (A. Hunter) Potter Am. Mo. **17**: 1.
— Flora of. (J. W. Chickering, jr.) Am. Natural. **7**: 521.
Disney, David T., with portrait. Dem. R. **26**: 266.
Disorder in Dreamland. Blackw. **115**: 204, 417. Same art. Liv. Age, **120**: 801. **121**: 46-495.
Dispensary, Country, Recollections of. (M. J. Malone) Irish Mo. **6**: 72.
Dispensaries, First London. Fraser, **91**: 598.
— Self-Supporting. Penny M. **3**: 238.
Dispensation, New. Theo. & Lit. J. **9**: 129.
Dispensations, Patriarchal, Lentical, and Christian. Chr. Obs. **24**: 33, 242, 302.
Disputed Identity. House. Words, **12**: 481. Same art. Ecl. M. **37**: 328.
Disputed Wedding-Ring. (N. P. Willis) Godey, **24**: 72.
Disraeli, Benjamin. (H. Holbeach) St. Paul's, **10**: 30. — (L. J. Jennings) Atlan. **32**: 641. — (N. Sheppard) Lakeside, **1**: 338. — with portrait, Appleton, **3**: 604. — with portraits, Appleton, **5**: 703. — with portrait, Colburn, **49**: 532. — with portrait, Fraser, **7**: 602. — Liv. Age, **3**: 188. — Fraser, **31**: 727. **35**: 79. Same art. Ecl. M. **10**: 230, 410. — Liv. Age, **25**: 123. — Blackw. **75**: 255. — Brit. Q. **10**: 118. Same art. Ecl. M. **18**: 170. — Dub. Univ. **80**: 511. — Lond. Soc. **13**: 385. — N. Ecl. **2**: 47. — with portrait, Once a Week, **26**: 322. — (E. S. Nadal) Scrib. **14**: 190. — Colburn, **159**: 387-511.
— and Carlyle. Colburn, **147**: 118.
— and Dickens, Styles of. (R. G. White) Galaxy, **10**: 253.
— and the Dukes. St. Paul's, **6**: 447. Same art. Ecl. M. **75**: 493.
— as a Leader and Legislator, 1852. Fraser, **45**: 127. — Same art. Ecl. M. **25**: 476.
— as a Novelist. (B. Cracroft) Fortn. **10**: 146. Same art. N. Ecl. **3**: 187.
— as Statesman and Novelist. (J. M. Bundy) Putnam, **16**: 87.
— Character and Career of. Ed. R. **97**: 420. Same art. with portrait, Ecl. M. **29**: 285. Same art. Liv. Age, **37**: 579.
— Coningsby. (J. Moncrieff) No. Brit. **1**: 545. — Westm. **42**: 80. — Fraser, **30**: 71. **31**: 211. — Chr. Rem. **7**: 667. — Colburn, **71**: 203. Same art. Ecl. M. **3**: 45. — Ecl. R. **80**: 50. — Tait, n. s. **11**: 447.
— Conservative Premier. St. Paul's, **3**: 14, 185.
— General Preface. (W. Mackay) Colburn, **147**: 720.
— Glasgow Speeches. Ed. R. **139**: 271.
— He grows old. (J. McCarthy) Galaxy, **21**: 325.
— Henrietta Temple. Colburn, **49**: 136.
— in House of Commons. (J. L. Motley) Colburn, **162**: 419.
— The Jew and his Writings. So. R. n. s. **24**: 373.

Disraeli, Benjamin. Letters of Runnymede. Fraser, **90**: 254.
— Literary and Political Biography of. Ecl. R. **99**: 257.
— Literary Character and Works of. Brit. Q. **52**: 121.
— Lothair. (A. F. Hewit) Cath. World, **11**: 537. — (E. Quincy) Nation, **10**: 372. — (J. Skelton) Fraser, **81**: 790. — Blackw. **107**: 773. **108**: 129. — Liv. Age, **106**: 3, 101. — Chr. Obs. **70**: 420. — Dub. R. **67**: 156. — Ed. R. **132**: 275. — Lond. Q. **35**: 162. — Macmil. **22**: 142. — No. Brit. **52**: 453. — O. & N. **2**: 216. — Quar. **129**: 63. — Month, **12**: 727. — Tinsley, **6**: 565.
— — and the Critics. Gent. M. n. s. **5**: 291.
— — and its Author. (H. T. Tuckerman) Hours at Home, **11**: 256.
— New Curiosities of Literature. Fraser, **46**: 637.
— Novels of. (L. Stephen) Fortn. **22**: 430. Same art. Ecl. M. **83**: 675. — Ed. R. **66**: 59.
— Political Career of, 1853. Hogg, **10**: 185. Same art. Ecl. M. **34**: 231.
— Political Novels of. (T. E. Kebbel) 19th Cent. **6**: 504.
— Political Portrait of. St. James, **24**: 385.
— Political Study. (J. B. Hopkins) Gent. M. n. s. **8**: 695.
— Prime Minister of England. (G. M. Towle) Hours at Home, **7**: 309. — St. James, **22**: 119.
— Religious Creed and Opinions of. Fraser, **78**: 363.
— Revolutionary Epic. Am. Mo. M. **3**: 267. — Mo. R. **134**: 54.
— Schoolboy Days of. Canad. Mo. **12**: 154.
— Sybil. (W. R. Greg) Westm. **44**: 141. — Brit. Q. **2**: 159. Same art. Ecl. M. **6**: 120.
— Tancred. (J. R. Lowell) No. Am. **65**: 201. — Ed. R. **86**: 138. — Bentley, **21**: 385. — Chr. Rem. **13**: 514. — Colburn, **79**: 523. — Dub. Univ. **30**: 253.
— Triumph as an Orator, 1855. Tait, n. s. **22**: 370.
— Vivian Grey. Lond. M. **15**: 207. **17**: 472. — (H. W. Lucy) Gent. M. n. s. **17**: 689.
— Vindication of the English Constitution. Westm. **31**: 533.
— Wondrous Tale of Alroy. Am. Mo. R. **4**: 279.
— Young Duke. Westm. **15**: 399.
— Young England. So. Lit. Mess. **10**: 758.
See also Beaconsfield, B., Earl of.
D'Israeli, Isaac. (C. C. Smith) No. Am. **90**: 526. — (W. I. Taylor) Bentley, **23**: 219. — with portrait, Fraser, **5**: 321.
— Amenities of Literature. Am. Ecl. **3**: 127. — Tait, n. s. **8**: 638. — Ecl. R. **74**: 431.
— and Bolton Corney. Cornh. **40**: 687.
— Calamities of Authors. (R. Southey) Quar. **8**: 93. — (J. Foster) Ecl. R. **17**: 496.
— Charles I. Westm. **14**: 486.
— Commentaries. Mo. R. **123**: 193. — Westm. **30**: 533.
— Curiosities of Literature. Blackw. **13**: 162. — Mo. R. **89**: 77. **101**: 254. — Ecl. R. **28**: 587. **61**: 202.
See also Literature.
Dissecting-Room, Night in a. Belgra. **37**: supp. 122.
Dissent. Cong. M. **4**: 147.
— and Church of England. Cong. M. **16**: 167, 287.
— — Curteis on. Chr. Obs. **74**: 362. — Cong. **1**: 502, 553, 618. — (C. Beard) Theo. R. **9**: 487.
— and Manufactures, Worsley on. Ecl. R. **25**: 189.
— Characteristics of. (R. Vaughan) Brit. Q. **6**: 115.
— Consistent, and Rev. J. Dodson. Ecl. R. **90**: 1.
— Dogmatism of. (J. Tulloch) Contemp. **33**: 570.
— — Reply to Tulloch. (F. Harrison) Contemp. **33**: 825.
— English. (W. H. Herford) Theo. R. **5**: 127.
— Evils of, 1827. Ecl. R. **47**: 110.
— in 1830. Ecl. R. **53**: 415, 464.
— in 1835. Ecl. R. **63**: 97, 333.
— in Lancashire in the 18th Century. Cong. **4**: 353.
— Letters on. Cong. M. **2**: 93-609. **3**: 78-535.
Dissent, Oliver's Secret History of. Mo. R. **154**: 67.
— Principles of. Fraser, **3**: 478.
— Progress of. (R. Southey) Quar. **31**: 229.
— Reasons for. Cong. **1**: 307.
— Recollections of the old. (R. Halley) Cong. **3**: 223, 257, 391. **4**: 9-423.
— Scottish, Real and apparent. Ecl. R. **89**: 151.
Dissent. *See* Nonconformity.
Dissenters, Acts of Parliament on. Cong. M. **23**: 909.
— Admission to Universities. Blackw. **35**: 716. — Ecl. R. **61**: 241. — Quar. **52**: 466.
— Alleged Illiteracy of, 1848. Ecl. R. **87**: 257.
— and Matthew Arnold. Cong. **2**: 427.
— and the Bishop of London, 1842. Ecl. R. **76**: 293.
— and the Coalition Government. Ecl. R. **99**: 611.
— and Church of England. (J. B. Brown) Contemp. **16**: 298. — Blackw. **16**: 395. — Ecl. R. **78**: 567. — Tait, n. s. **1**: 44-368. — Ecl. R. **55**: 97.
— and Popery. Ecl. R. **74**: 609.
— and the Papacy. Ecl. R. **92**: 739.
— and Lord John Russell. Ecl. R. **71**: 345.
— and the Universities. Fraser, **12**: 174.
— Assurance Company of. Ecl. R. **69**: 520.
— Batch of voluntary. Fraser, **16**: 308.
— Bennett's History of. Ecl. R. **69**: 438. — Meth. M. **57**: 200.
— Biographies of, List of. Cong. M. **13**: 22.
— Bogue and Bennett's History of, from 1688 to 1808. Chr. Obs. **10**: 92. **12**: 583. — Meth. M. **35**: 256.
— Claims of, on Government. Cong. M. **19**: 239.
— — Thomson on. Mo. R. **139**: 513.
— — and Opinions of. Ecl. R. **59**: 43.
— Conduct and Duty of, 1845. Ecl. R. **81**: 732. **82**: 599.
— Congregational. Westm. **28**: 217.
— De Foe on, with extracts. Cong. M. **24**: 153.
— Duty of, 1837. Ecl. R. **66**: 204.
— Electoral Policy of, Results of, 1847. Ecl. R. **86**: 354.
— English. Bost. R. **4**: 90, 181. — Tait, **2**: 269, 385. — (E. Calamy) Cong. M. **15**: 265.
— Grievances of. Cong. M. **19**: 284.
— — and Policy of, 1849. Ecl. R. **89**: 637.
— History of. (R. Southey) Quar. **10**: 90. — Ecl. R. **19**: 381. **69**: 438.
— in Switzerland, Wyss on. Ecl. R. **50**: 298.
— Marriage Act for. Ecl. R. **77**: 389.
— Marriages of. Ed. R. **35**: 62. — Westm. **23**: 196. — Cong. M. **15**: 487.
— Objections to Ordination among. Theo. Repos. **6**: 322.
— of London, Address of, Dec. 11, 1827. Cong. M. **11**: 6.
— — Recollections of. (R. Halley) Cong. **4**: 9-423.
— Old London. Brit. Q. **48**: 59.
— Palmer's Vindication of. Cong. M. **5**: 208.
— Parsonolatry of. Tait, n. s. **19**: 305, 342.
— Political. Cong. **5**: 439.
— Position of, 1838. Ecl. R. **69**: 1.
— Protestant. Ed. R. **19**: 149. — Mo. R. **113**: 473.
— Toulmin's History of. Ecl. R. **24**: 127.
— Views of. Cong. M. **18**: 53.
Dissenters' Chapels. Cong. M. **16**: 65, 257.
— Registration Act for. Ecl. R. **97**: 453.
Dissenting Academies in England, Statistics of. Cong. M **14**: 799.
Dissenting Agitation, 1847. Ecl R. **86**: 488.
Dissenting Churches, History of. Ecl. R. **76**: 434.
— Wilson's History of. Ecl. R. **23**: 401, 585.
Dissenting Colleges, Defects of. Ecl. R. **72**: 547.
Dissenting Collegiate Institutions. Ecl. R. **81**: 88.
Dissenting Convention at Manchester. Fraser, **24**: 361.
Dissenting Controversy. Cong. M. **22**: 107.
Dissenting Endowments. Westm. **24**: 92.
Dissenting Meeting-Houses in England and Wales, 1836. Ecl. R. **65**: 1.

Dissenting Ministers, Regium Donum to. Ecl. R. **79**: 101.
Dissenting Registers. Cong. M. **24**: 922.
Dissenting Student, Letters to. Cong. M. **15**: 406–752.
Dissenting Theological Colleges. Ecl. R. **71**: 1.
Dissevered. (W. A. Kendall) Overland, **9**: 175.
Distaff, The; a Tale. Cath. World, **16**: 133.
— and Spindle as Insignia of the Female Sex. (J. Y. Akerman) Arch. **37**: 83.
Distance, Can we see? (T. C. Simon) Macmil. **13**: 429.
— Measures of, for Military Use. (P. Henrard) Pract. M. **4**: 56.
Distillery, Day at a. Penny M. **11**: 297.
Distilling, English Patents for, 1827. J. Frankl. Inst. **4**: 324. **5**: 1.
Distilling Apparatus. Pract. M. **3**: 306.
Distracted young Preacher. (T. Hardy) Liv. Age, **141**: 501–595.
Distress, National, England, 1842. Ecl. R. **76**: 214.
— of the Country, Prize Essay on. (S. Laing) Chamb. J. **1**: 233, 254, 260.
See England.
Distressed Gentlewoman. Dub. Univ. **92**: 679.
Distressed Needlewomen and cheap Prison Labor. Westm. **50**: 371.
District of Columbia, Government of. (C. C. Nott) Nation, **15**: 328. **18**: 375. **20**: 5. — (S. Newcomb) Nation, **18**: 407.
— Statistics of, 1869. Am. J. Educ. **18**: 510.
District School; a Poem. (B. F. Taylor) Scrib. **8**: 1.
Ditmarsh, Land of. (B. Williams) Arch. **37**: 371.
Divan, The. Bentley, **15**: 105–527.
Di Vasari; a Tale of Florence. (C. Edwards) Blackw. **20**: 793.
Diversions of the Echo Club. (B. Taylor) Atlan. **29**: 76–710. **30**: 76.
Divided; a Story. (L. E. Ward) Belgra. **42**: 108.
Divination among the Natives of Natal. (H. Callaway) Anthrop. J. **1**: 163.
— by the Rod and by the Arrow. (A. W. Buckland) Anthrop. J. **5**: 436.
— for the Drawing-Room. Eng. Dom. M. **3**: 141–550.
— Witchcraft, and Mesmerism. Dub. Univ. **38**: 687. Same art. Ecl. M. **25**: 199. Same art. Internat. M. **5**: 198.
See Chiromancy; Geomancy.
Divine and human Agency. (H. Ballou, jr.) Univ. Q. **3**: 31. — (D. A. Gorton) Nat. Q. **36**: 310. — (W. Haslam, J. V. O'Conor, D. A. Gorton Nat. Q. **37**: 379.
Divine Authority. (C. P. Cranch) Unita. R. **12**: 465.
Divine Expediency. Good Words, **4**: 737.
Divine Government. *See* God, Government of.
Divine Influence. Ecl. R. **47**: 481.
— Davies, Biddulph, and Mortimer on. Chr. Obs. **24**: 754.
— Doctrine of. (J. Brazer) Chr. Exam. **17**: 311.
— not supernaturally imparted. (J. Brazer) Chr. Exam. **18**: 50, 230.
Divine Life, Way of. (W. R. Alger) Chr. Exam. **80**: 34.
Divine Myths in India, Origin of. (A. C. Lyall) Fortn. **24**: 306.
Divine Passion. (T. M. Griffith) Meth. Q. **26**: 64.
Divine Rule of the Church's Legislation. Am. Church R. **4**: 399.
Divine Teaching. Chr. Mo. Spec. **4**: 400.
Divine Things, Knowledge of. (C. H. Brigham) Unita. R. **2**: 169.
Diving. Chamb. J. **57**: 119. — Liv. Age, **35**: 463.
— Fleuss's New Process of. (B. W. Richardson) Nature, **21**: 62. **22**: 32.
— Submarine. (W. W. Harney) Lippinc. **11**: 200. — Cornh. **17**: 664. Same art. Ecl M. **71**: 1007.
Diving Apparatus. Chamb. J. **46**: 56. — (W. H. James) J. Frankl. Inst. **5**: 306.
Diving Bell. (T. Alden) Am. J. Sci. **22**: 325. — Blackw **17**: 336. — Mus. **6**: 515.
— Down in a. Ecl. R. **111**: 602.
— Experiments with. J. Frankl. Inst. **14**: 54.
Divining Cup. (P. J. Bailey) Lond. Soc. **2**: 561.
Divining Rod. (H. Mayo) Blackw. **61**: 368. — (L. H. Steiner) Mercersb. **13**: 374. — (H. White) Stud. & Intel. Obs. **5**: 20. — (J. T. Crane) Meth. Q. **8**: 202. — Dem. R. **26**: 218, 317. — Am. J. Sci. **3**: 102. **11**: 201. — Worc. M. **1**: 27. — Liv. Age, **13**: 105. — All the Year, **17**: 391. — Chamb. J. **20**: 298. Same art. Ev. Sat. **3**: 581.
Divinity, American New School. Cong. M. **22**: 236.
— Law, and Physic. Am. Mo. M. **1**: 217.
— of Jesus Christ. *See* Jesus Christ.
— revealed and unrevealed. (W. B. Hayden) Mo. Rel. M. **22**: 234.
— Study of, Herder's Letters on. Chr. Disc. **2**: 233, 417. **3**: 1, 81, 171.
Divinity Schools, Danger of. (J. F. Clarke) Nation, **29**: 77.
Division of Labor in civil Life. Westm. **12**: 125.
Divisibility of Matter. (A. McWhorter) Am. J. Sci. **56**: 329.
Divorce. (N. H. Davis) Internat. R. **1**: 794. — (H. D. Evans) Am. Ch. Mo. **1**: 320. — (S. Lee) Chr. R. **3**: 235. — (T. Munnell) Chr. R. **2**: 312. — (W. S. Upton) De Bow, **2**: 155. — Putnam, **8**: 630. — Ed. R. **105**: 181.
— a Vinculo. Once a Week, **2**: 184–317.
— and Divorce Laws. (C. M. O'Leary) Cath. World, **25**: 340. — Brownson, **16**: 473.
— and Marriage. (M. F. Taylor) So. M. **11**: 447. — So. Q. **26**: 332. — So. R. n. s. **9**: 124.
— and some of its Results. (T. A. Becker) Cath. World, **31**: 550.
— and voluntary Separation. Brit. & For. R. **7**: 269.
— Bible Doctrine of. (J. Tracy) Bib. Sac. **23**: 384.
— Döllinger on. (J. Conington) Contemp. **11**: 1.
— Ethics of. (D. A. Gorton) Nat. Q. **37**: 27.
— Free, and Free-Love. Ev. Sat. **11**: 75.
— History and Doctrine of. (T. D. Woolsey) New Eng. **26**: 88, 212, 482. **27**: 12, 517, 764.
— in Italy, Introduction of. (C. F. Gabba) Am. Church R. **33**: 111.
— Indissolubility of Christian Marriage. (A. F. Hewit) Cath. World, **5**: 567, 684.
— Law of. Blackw. **26**: 756. — Fraser, **1**: 427. — Am. Church R. **25**: 323, 465.
— — Decisions in. Quar. **25**: 229.
— — English, 1856. Westm. **65**: 338. — No. Brit. **27**: 162. — Fraser, **52**: 149. — Westm. **82**: 442. — Chamb. J. **28**: 302.
— — in California. (C. T. Hopkins) Pioneer, **1**: 213.
— — Scottish. Blackw. **2**: 176.
— Legislation on, in Connecticut. (A. F. Hewit) Cath. World, **4**: 101. — (H. Loomis) New Eng. **25**: 436.
— Milton's Doctrine of. Mo. R. **93**: 144. — Cong. M. **4**: 544.
— Madame Necker on. (F. Jeffrey) Ed. R. **1**: 456.
— Question of. (W. H. Phillips) Internat. R. **11**: 139.
Divorce Courts, English. No. Brit. **35**: 187.
Divorcée Dévote, The. Colburn, **39**: 25.
Divorces. U. S. Cath. M. **17**: 204.
— in New England. (N. Allen) No. Am. **130**: 547.
— — Frequency of. Am. Church R. **20**: 214.
— in Pennsylvania, 1813. Portfo. (Den.) **10**: 483.
Dix, Dorothea L. (L. J. Bigelow) Galaxy, **3**: 668.
Dix, John A., with portrait. Dem. R. **17**: 321.
Dix Island, Me., Visit to. (E. R. Church) So. M. **16**: 615.
Dix Minutes d'Arrêt. (R. B. Kimball) Galaxy, **17**: 807.
Dixie, In, 1864. Bentley, **63**: 638. **64**: 80.

Dixie, Seeking. (J. Ransome) So. M. **11**: 687.
Dixon, James, Memoir of, with portrait. (R. A. West) Meth. Q. **9**: 9. — Lond. Q. **42**: 368.
Dixon, John, on America. Meth. Q. **9**: 653.
Dixon, William H., with portrait. Once a Week, **26**: 542.
— Spiritual Wives. Fraser, **77**: 655. — St. Paul's, **2**: 66.
— White Conquest. Westm. **105**: 42.
Dixon, William Jerrold. (J. Hawthorne) Belgra. **40**: 193.
Doane, Bishop Geo. W. (E. A. Hoffmann) Am. Church R. **12**: 434. — (S. Eliot) Am. Church R. **14**: 126.
Dobbs his Ferry. A Legend in Verse. (W. A. Butler) Putnam, **11**: 20.
Dobell, Sydney. (R. Buchanan) Temp. Bar, **56**: 80. — (D. M. Craik) Internat. R. **6**: 484. — (Alex. Smith) Argosy, **2**: 313.
— and his Works. Good Words, **20**: 314.
— Balder. Fraser, **50**: 59. — Hogg, **11**: 89.
— in Memoriam. Good Words, **15**: 718.
— Life and Letters of. (M. P. Lowe) Unita. R. **11**: 557. — (G. E. Woodberry) Nation, **28**: 289.
— Poems on the Crimean War. New Q. **5**: 421. — Westm. **66**: 566. — Nat. R. **3**: 442.
Dobschau, Ice Cavern of. (W. B. Lowe) Nature, **20**: 151.
Dobson, Austin. Poems. (F. F. Browne) Dial (Ch.), **1**: 6.
— Vignettes in Rhyme. (W. C. Brownell) Nation, **30**: 330.
Dobson, W. C. T., Technical Notes on. (P. G. Hamerton) Portfo. **7**: 116.
Doche, Madame, Actress. Colburn, **86**: 420.
Dock, Floating, at Nicolaieff. Pract. M. **7**: 202.
— Marine Railway. (J. L. Sullivan) J. Frankl. Inst. **3**: 73.
Docks, Dry, Plans for. J. Frankl. Inst. **3**: 3.
— Floating. Pract. M. **7**: 233.
— — Stability of. (G. B. Rennie) Ecl. Engin. **1**: 635.
— Flotation of Vessels by buoyant. (J. E. Gowen) Ecl. Engin. **4**: 229.
— Tubular Floating. Ecl. Engin. **12**: 28.
Dock Expansion, West England. Pract. M. **4**: 136, 268.
Dock Warrants. (D. Costello) Bentley, **39**: 31, 139, 236.
Docking Vessels, New Mode of. Pract. M. **6**: 169.
Dockyards, Eng., Mismanagement of. Temp. Bar, **14**: 231.
Dockyard Ghost. (R. Johns) Bentley, **3**: 285.
Docteur Lavardin. (M. Cross) Liv. Age, **136**: 525.
Doctor Abroad. Blackw. **113**: 525, 657.
— in Love; a Poem. (A. McFarland) Lakeside, **9**: 426.
— The marvellous. (J. Hogg) Blackw. **22**: 349.
— of Philosophy. Dub. Univ. **48**: 722. **49**: 35, 200.
— Paying the. All the Year, **2**: 566.
Dr. Aar; a Tale. (K. P. Kereven) Lippinc. **2**: 502.
Doctor Barbe-Bleue. Liv. Age, **106**: 268.
Dr. Barberon; a French Trial for Murder. Belgra. **39**: 420.
Dr. Bartholomew; a Story. St. James, **46**: 139.
Doctor Bonomi. Fraser, **76**: 601.
Doctor Book's Chronicle; a Tale. Temp. Bar, **49**: 362.
Dr. Breen's Practice. (W. D. Howells) Atlan. **48**: 145–721.
Doctor Campany's Courtship. (M. B. Edwards) Once a Week, **12**: 351–443.
Dr. Chillingworth's Prescription. House. Words, **6**: 292.
Doctor Dolbie's Experiment. (A. Shackleford) Lakeside, **7**: 290.
Dr. Dollopson's Patient. Eng. Dom. M. **9**: 335.
Doctor Dubois. House. Words, **11**: 429.
Doctor Eisenbart; a Poem. Dub. Univ. **17**: 627.
Dr. Figaro's Establishment. (G. A. Sala) Belgra. **26**: 200.
Dr. Fox's Prescription. Contin. Mo. **5**: 717.
Dr. Garrick. (M. E. Braddon) All the Year, **40**: supp. 1.
Doctor Garrick. House. Words, **16**: 142.
Dr. Gates and the Señoritas; a Tale of Nicaragua. (F. Boyle) Belgra. **42**: 48.
Doctor Hawley. (J. W. De Forest) Harper, **26**: 312, 468.
Doctor Johns. (D. G. Mitchell) Atlan. **15**: 141–681. **16**: 66–713. **17**: 69–707.
Dr. Lorriner. Tinsley, **5**: 395.
Doctor Marigold's Prescriptions. (C. Dickens) All the Year, **14**: supp. 1.
Doctor Middleton's Daughter. Once a Week, **28**: 411–551. **29**: 13–478.
Dr. Molke. (I. I. Hayes) Atlan. **20**: 43. **21**: 36, 198, 485.
Dr. Oliver's Maid. (E. Meteyard) Sharpe, **22**: 148–321.
Doctor Pablo. House. Words, **9**: 280.
Dr. Reinhard; a Tale. Canad. Mo. **2**: 134.
Dr. Steele's Daughters; a Tale. Sharpe, **38**: 11–244.
Doctor Winter's Notions. (Mrs. S. J. Hale) Godey, **21**: 220, 373.
Dr. Wortle's School; a Novel. (A. Trollope) Blackw. **127**: 545–681. **128**: 1–710.
Dr. Wrightson's Enemy. (E. Eden) Liv. Age, **95**: 741.
Doctor's Assistant; a Tale. Putnam, **11**: 569.
Doctor's Book, An old; Læce Boc. Once a Week, **13**: 34.
Doctor's Degree, My. Ecl. M. **6**: 330.
Doctor's Dream; a Story. (F. E. Faithful) St. James, **46**: 245.
Doctor's Fortune. Lond. Soc. **4**: 77.
Doctor's Mixture. All the Year, **24**: 1–601. **25**: 1–211.
Doctor's Story. (E. Phelps) Knick. **61**: 205.
Doctor's Story. Chamb. J. **58**: 824.
Doctor's two Christmases. (G. M. Bussey) Peop. J. **7**: 29, 46.
Doctor's Wife; a Novel. (M. E. Braddon) Temp. Bar, **10**: 155–455. **11**: 5–455. **12**: 5–455. **13**: 117.
Doctor's Wife. Liv. Age, **63**: 422.
Doctors. (H. T. Tuckerman) Putnam, **2**: 66.
— Ancient. All the Year, **30**: 293, 523.
— and Patients, Timbs on. Chamb. J. **50**: 180.
— Anecdotes of. Chamb. J. **51**: 693. **56**: 521. Same art. Ecl. M. **84**: 239.
— Concerning. Chamb. J. **35**: 78. Same art. Ecl. M. **53**: 256.
— Confessions of. Lond. Soc. **25**: 49. Same art. Ecl. M. **82**: 360.
— Liability of. (O. E. Lyman) Pop. Sci. Mo. **18**: 760.
— of Molière's Time. Liv. Age, **78**: 448.
— Our, in the Rebellion. (F. B. Perkins) Galaxy, **4**: 822.
— Quack, and how they thrive. (E. I. Sears) Nat. Q. **24**: 72.
Doctoring under Difficulties. (M. J. Malone) Irish Mo. **7**: 383.
Doctrinal Basis, Union. Cong. Q. **5**: 254.
Doctrinal Discourses. Chr. Exam. **35**: 385.
Doctrinal Divisions in the Church. Am. Presb. R. **7**: 638.
Doctrinal Preaching. (S. L. Blake) Cong. R. **11**: 452. — Bost. R. **1**: 209. — (E. B. Hall) Chr. Exam. **37**: 80 — (E. Peabody) Chr. Exam. **38**: 107. — (O. A. Skinner) Univ. Q. **1**: 37. — (T. J. Sawyer) Univ. Q. **6**: 221.
Doctrinal Subscription. *See* Subscription.
Doctrine and Creed. (T. G. Apple) Mercersb. **24**: 99.
— and Dogma. (G. F. Magoun) Cong. R. **11**: 562. — Lond. Q. **40**: 399.
— and Duty. (E. B. Hall) Chr. Exam. **35**: 209.
— and Life. Chr. R. **24**: 161.
— and Worship, Progressive. (D. Y. Heisler) Mercersb. **21**: 212.
— Christian, Development of. Dub. R. **22**: 325. **23**: 373. **64**: 28.
— — — in Bible. (J. Milliken) Am. Presb. R. **19**: 133.
— — — in N. Testament. (W. Scribner) Princ. **40**: 519.
— — — Theory of. Bib. R. **1**: 182.
— in Sunday School. (J. F. W. Ware) Mo. Rel. M. **7**: 481.
— Standard of. Chr. Obs. **68**: 529.
— Syllabus of. (W. Adams) Am. Church R. **16**: 298. *See* Theology, Doctrinal.
Documents of the Case. (J. B. Matthews and H. C. Bunner) Scrib. **18**: 755.

Docwra, Sir Thomas, Grand Prior of St. John's. (F. Duncan) Gent. M. n. s. **26**: 102.
Dodd, James William. Sir Benjamin Backbite. (D. Cook) Gent. M. n. s. **21**: 204.
Dodd, Thomas, Print Collector and Connoisseur. Temp. Bar, **47**: 315. Same art. Liv. Age, **130**: 361.
Dodd, William, Life of. (P. Fitzgerald) Dub. Univ. **63**: 257, 385. — Liv. Age, **50**: 552. — (A. Marks) Once a Week, **12**: 263.
Doddridge, Philip. (J. Hamilton) No. Brit. **14**: 350. Same art. Liv. Age, **28**: 461. Same art. Ecl. M. **22**: 433. Same art. Internat. M. **3**: 77. — Hogg, **9**: 309.
— as a Hymn Writer. (T. H. Gill) Cong. **5**: 586.
— at Kibworth. Cong. M. **27**: 397.
— Correspondence and Diary of. Mo. R. **121**: 73. **122**: 203. — Chr. Exam. **8**: 66. — Cong. M. **13**: 89–361.
— Five Hymns. Cong. Q. **4**: 23.
— Writings of. (J. W. Alexander) Princ. **29**: 234.
Doddridge's Seminary, History and Character of. Chr. Disc. **1**: 249.
Dodds, Joseph, with portrait. Colburn, **167**: 630.
Dodge Club. (J. de Mille) Harper, **34**: 409, 545, 699. **35**: 22–550.
Dodger Family. Chamb. J. **42**: 353.
Dodington, G. Bubb, Lord Melcombe. Colburn, **121**: 38.
Dodo, The. Penny M. **2**: 209. — (A. Wilson) Good Words, **17**: 427.
— and its Kindred. Westm. **51**: 128. — Blackw. **65**: 81. — (H. E. Strickland and A. G. Melville) Am. J. Sci. **57**: 52. — Liv. Age, **20**: 316.
— Memorials of. Chamb. J. **17**: 360.
Dodos; an Ornithological Sketch. Tait, n. s. **1**: 79.
Dodsley, Robert. House. Words, **11**: 308.
Dodson, I., and Consistent Dissent. Ecl. R. **90**: 1.
Doellinger, John Joseph Ignatius. (J. E. Johnson) O. & N. **4**: 201. — with portrait, Ev. Sat. **11**: 52. — (G. Prentice) Meth. Q. **39**: 605. — with portrait, Ecl. M. **79**: 374. — Cath. World, **14**: 248. — St. James, **28**: 258.
— and Catholicism in Bavaria. Contemp. **17**: 261.
— and Munich Congress. Dub. R. **55**: 200, 483. **56**: 214.
— and the Old Catholic Movement in Germany. Scrib. **22**: 365.
— and the Roman Catholic Church. (F. T. Washburn) O. & N. **4**: 264. — Brownson, **22**: 34.
— Apostasy of. (A. F. Hewit) Cath. World, **13**: 415.
— Gratry and Hyacinthe. O. & N. **5**: 377.
— on the Popes. Dub. R. **70**: 363.
Dog, A, and his Doings. (W. F. Butler) Good Words, **18**: 39. Same art. Ecl. M. **88**: 334.
— and his Shadow. (R. E. Francillon) Gent. M. n. s. **15**: 1–513. **16**: 92–734.
— Anecdotes of. Penny M. **5**: 354.
— Life of. Putnam, **2**: 542.
Dog, The, and its Folk-Lore. (T. F. T. Dyer) Gent. M. n. s. **24**: 489. Same art. Liv. Age, **145**: 504.
— a Russian Tale. (I. Tourgénieff) Temp. Bar, **28**: 474.
— Blaze's History of. (W. J. Broderip) Quar. **72**: 488. Same art. Ecl. Mus. **3**: 145. — Ecl. M. **9**: 476.
— History of. Ecl. R. **84**: 168.
— of Alcibiades. Blackw. **62**: 102. Same art. Liv. Age, **14**: 327.
— of Flanders. (J. de la Ramé) Lippinc. **9**: 79.
— without a Tail. (R. E. Francillon) Blackw. **117**: 321.
Dog's Universe. (G. Allen) Gent. M. n. s. **25**: 287. Same art. Appleton, **24**: 545.
Dogs. (G. L. Henry) N. Ecl. **7**: 291. — Argosy, **19**: 281. — (D. Piatt) Lippinc. **6**: 265. — Chamb. J. **30**: 11. **44**: 81. **50**: 385. — Colburn, **56**: 60. — Ecl. R. **124**: 416. — Ev. Sat. **15**: 62. — Liv. Age, **24**: 539. — Putnam, **9**: 288.
Dogs, Advantages of. West. R. **4**: 367.
— American Sporting. (W. M. Tileston) Scrib. **13**: 768.
— and their Days. All the Year, **35**: 374.
— and their Diet. Once a Week, **25**: 304.
— Anecdotes of. Blackw. **2**: 417, 621. **15**: 177. — Liv. Age, **10**: 197. — Ecl. M. **8**: 495. — Blackw. **45**: 475. — Mus. **4**: 429. — Chamb. J. **56**: 183. — Dub. Univ. **58**: 219. — Sharpe, **45**: 103.
— — Brown's. Ecl. R. **50**: 259.
— as Companions. Broadw. **7**: 65.
— Canine Guests. (P. G. Hamerton) Portfo. **4**: 27.
— Caninology. Bentley, **16**: 431.
— Celebrated. Lond. Soc. **12**: 297. **13**: 172. Same art. Ev. Sat. **4**: 481. **5**: 247.
— Chapter on. Dub. Univ. **58**: 219. Same art. Ecl. M. **54**: 254. — Portfo.(Den.) **25**: 1. — Knick. **59**: 126.
— Consciousness of. Quar. **133**: 419. Same art. Liv. Age, **115**: 579.
— described and illustrated. (T. B. Thorpe) Harper, **10**: 615.
— Eastern. Chamb. J. **48**: 441.
— English. Once a Week, **4**: 381.
— Esquimaux. (H. M. Bannister) Am. Natural. **3**: 522.
— Human. Colburn, **50**: 483.
— Humanity to. Good Words, **2**: 486.
— Homes for houseless. Once a Week, **13**: 543.
— how they retrace a Journey. (F. L. Oswald) Pop. Sci. Mo. **17**: 359.
— Intelligence of. Westm. **86**: 413.
— — Do they understand human Speech? (M. Westcott) Recr. Sci. **1**: 121.
— Japanese Lap. Once a Week, **25**: 434.
— Mad. (W. Chambers) Chamb. J. **51**: 403. — All the Year, **28**: 300. — Blackw. **90**: 222.
— Migratory. Chamb. J. **50**: 791.
— My. Chamb. J. **36**: 106. — (W. T. Greene) Colburn, **161**: 541.
— Natural History and Origin of. No. Brit. **7**: 29. Same art. Liv. Age, **14**: 17.
— New York. (C. D. Shanly) Atlan. **29**: 550.
— of Constantinople. Chamb. J. **25**: 267. Same art. Liv. Age, **49**: 664. Same art. Ecl. M. **38**: 427.
— of History and Romance. Quar. **109**: 177. Same art. Liv. Age, **68**: 780.
— of Literature. Temp. Bar, **61**: 476. Same art. Ecl. M. **97**: 174.
— of St. Bernard. Once a Week, **7**: 363.
— of several of my Acquaintances. Fraser, **24**: 578, 702. **25**: 304, 390.
— Our Charlie. (W. Chambers) Chamb. J. **53**: 817.
— Our Dog Di. Macmil. **35**: 318. Same art. Liv. Age, **132**: 677.
— Our Pets and Protectors. (W. M. Tileston) Scrib. **16**: 95.
— Peninsular. Blackw. **80**: 326.
— Pointer; why do they point? All the Year, **22**: 390.
— Portraiture of. Once a Week, **17**: 170.
— Reasoning in. Penny M. **6**: 486.
— Retrievers. Chamb. J. **51**: 76.
— Sagacity of. Chamb. J. **53**: 126.
— Shaksperian. Once a Week, **27**: 161.
— socially considered. (A. Halbert) Putnam, **16**: 495. Same art. Ev. Sat. **11**: 166.
— Stories about. Chamb. J. **58**: 358.
— Story of Rolf. Chamb. J. **58**: 269.
— Traits of; Dog-Talk. (C. D. Shanly) Atlan. **4**: 590.
— we have had. All the Year, **20**: 208.
— whom I have met. Cornh. **26**: 662. Same art. Liv. Age, **116**: 109.
— Wild, in Van Diemen's Land. Penny M. **3**: 197.
— — and domestic. Penny M. **10**: 7, 56, 77.
— — of the Western Ghauts of India. Penny M. **3**: 205

Dog-Breaking. (Sir F. B. Head) Quar. **84**: 344. Same art. Ecl. M. **17**: 482. Same art. Liv. Age, **22**: 19.
Dog Hospital of Paris. Bentley, **6**: 141.
Dog Show, At a. Chamb. J. **38**: 81.
Dog Shows. All the Year, **7**: 493.
— and Dog Trials. Lond. Soc. **24**: 365.
Dog Sledge, Lake Travel by. (H. M. Robinson) Appleton, **17**: 31.
Dog Star, The. Once a Week, **20**: 277.
Dog-Stealers, London. Chamb. J. **56**: 463.
Dog-Stealing. Fraser, **30**: 322.
Dog-Worshiper, Story of. Fraser **82**: 73.
Dogberry and Verges. Irish Mo. **5**: 687, 747.
Doge and his Consort; a Tale of Venice. (E. T. A. Hoffman) Colburn, **163**: 669.
Dogged by Sin. Knick. **44**: 276.
Dogged in the Streets. Chamb. J. **39**: 202.
Dogget, Thomas, the Actor. Dub. Univ. **63**: 513.
Dogherty's Courtship. Once a Week, **28**: 485–560.
Dogma and Doctrine. (G. F. Magoun) Cong. R. **11**: 562.
— and dogmatic Theology. (J. Tulloch) Contemp. **23**: 919.
— and Liberalism. (M. K. Cross) Cong. Q. **17**: 515.
— and Literature, M. Arnold on. Dub. R. **72**: 357. *See* Arnold, Matthew.
— Reason, and Morality. (W. H. Mallock) 19th Cent. **4**: 1013. Same art. Liv. Age, **140**: 100.
Dogmatic Decay. (E. M. Geldart) Theo. R. **11**: 469.
Dogmatic Extremes. (J. Tulloch) Contemp. **23**: 182.
Dogmatic History, Elements of. (J. Walker) Chr. Exam. **9**: 182.
— Utility of. (J. Murdock) Chr. Mo. Spec. **9**: 27, 249.
Dogmatic Principle, The. Dub. R. **53**: 458.
Dogmatic Standards. (D. R. Goodwin) Am. Church R. **30**: 548. *See* Creeds.
Dogmatics, Christian, Revival of. (J. J. Van Oosterzee) Am. Presb. R. **20**: 401.
Dogmatism. (T. M. Coan) Scrib. **4**: 682. — (W. K. Pendleton) Chr. Q. **5**: 496.
— Vanity of. Retros. **17**: 105.
Dog-Violet and Mignonette. (I. R. Vernon) Tinsley, **18**: 45.
Dogwood Bitters. (J. Woodville) Lippinc. **25**: 612.
Doherty, John, with portrait. Dub. Univ. **29**: 740.
Doherty, M. Legends and Poems. Dub. Univ. **89**: 671.
Doings, and Misdoings of Milston. (Florence Marryat) Victoria, **31**: 16–481.
— at Stamford Hill. (W. L. Gane) Bentley, **21**: 465.
Doineau, Captain. House. Words, **16**: 423.
Dolcino, Fra, and his Times. New Q. **2**: 229.
— — Mariotti on. Prosp. R. **9**: 203.
Dole of Jarl Thorkell. (J. G. Whittier) Atlan. **22**: 10.
Dolet, Etienne. (M. Pattison) Fortn. **35**: 35. — (G. Saintsbury) Macmil. **43**: 273.
Dolgelley and its Attractions. Lond. Soc. **16**: 56.
Doll Land; a Christmas Story. Sharpe, **38**: 326.
Doll Philosophy. Chamb. J. **58**: 721.
Dollar, Origin of the $ Mark. (W. T. R. Saffell) Am. Hist. Rec. **3**: 271, 407, 500.
— Pursuit of the. (A. Rhodes) Galaxy, **21**: 652.
Dollie and the two Smiths. Blackw. **108**: 105.
Döllinger. *See* Doellinger.
Dolly. (R. H. Davis) Scrib. **9**: 89.
Dolly. (N. Perry) Harper, **40**: 37.
Dolly; a Pastoral Tale. (M. R. Godfrey) Temp. Bar, **53**: 377.
Dolly; a Story of the London Sans-Souci. (H. L. Williams) Belgra. **24**: 337.
Dolly Duster, Diary of. Fraser, **18**: 471, 597.
Dolmen Mounds. (S. P. Oliver) Nature, **8**: 344.
— in Japan. (E. S. Morse) Pop. Sci. Mo. **16**: 593.
Dolomite Mountains, The. Brit. Q. **40**: 333.
— Lady's Visit to. All the Year, **24**: 352.
Dolomite Mountains, Sketches among. Good Words, **12**: 782.
— Ten Days among. Argosy, **12**: 227
— Visit to. (W. D. Reed) Canad. Mo. **14**: 257. Same art. Lippinc. **14**: 271, 411.
Dolons, The two. Dial, **3**: 112.
Dolores; a Poem. (A. C. Ketchum) Harper, **43**: 641.
Dom Gueranger and Solesmes. (M. Raymond) Cath. World, **21**: 279.
Dome in Pointed Architecture. Ecl. Engin. **5**: 522.
— of St. Peters. Am. Arch. **2**: 303, 310.
Domes of Stone and Brick. Ecl. Engin. **10**: 527.
— Structure of. (R. Briggs) J. Frankl. Inst. **85**: 305.
Domenech, Abbé, Missionary Adventures in Texas and Mexico. Ecl. R. **108**: 164.
Domenichino. Chamb. J. **16**: 237. — Penny M. **3**: 356.
Domesday Book. Cornh. **8**: 600. — Ecl. M. **68**: 244.
— Ecclesia and Presbyter in. (S. Denne) Arch. **8**: 218.
— New. (E. L. Stanley) Fortn. **25**: 791.
— of Hampshire. Fraser, **73**: 368.
Domestic Accomplishments. Chamb. J. **9**: 241.
Domestic Affairs, Our. (G. Wurts) Contin. Mo. **6**: 241.
Domestic and Social Economies. (S. P. Day) Victoria, **35**: 91–488. **36**: 144.
Domestic and social Life in Mediæval England. Brit. Q. **35**: 428.
Domestic Art. (E. Balfour) Good Words, **20**: 658. *See* Household Art.
Domestic Arts, Ancient. Knick. **52**: 60.
Domestic Constitution. (N. Porter) Chr. Q. Spec. **7**: 185.
Domestic Economy. (Mrs. S. J. Hale) Godey, **20**: 42, 86, 154. — (E. M. King) Victoria, **17**: 251. — Penny M. **11**: 34. — Victoria, **17**: 345.
— for Farmers. De Bow, **18**: 731.
— House and Home Papers. (H. B. Stowe) Atlan. **13**: 40–754. **14**: 93–689.
— Letter to a young Housekeeper. (C. P. Hawes) Atlan. **16**: 535.
— Parlor and Kitchen. Lippinc. **4**: 207.
— The Persecuted Woman. (E. Elcourt) Lippinc. **5**: 27.
— Science of. (E. M. King) Victoria, **24**: 131.
See Housekeeping; Cookery.
Domestic Education. (Z. Crocker) Chr. Q. Spec. **8**: 43.
Domestic Experiences. Victoria, **17**: 502.
Domestic Grievance. St. James, **2**: 229.
Domestic Handicrafts, Interference with. (F. Seebohm) 19th Cent. **3**: 370.
Domestic Harmony. Chamb. J. **57**: 93.
Domestic Hygiene. (D. A. Gorton) Nat. Q. **29**: 316.
Domestic Improvidence. Penny M. **2**: 271.
Domestic Industry. (J. H. Lanman) Hunt, **2**: 353.
Domestic Life. Ecl. M. **13**: 126.
— Past and present. Temp. Bar, **4**: 402.
Domestic Management. Godey, **62**: 313.
— a neglected Art. Macmil. **12**: 494.
Domestic Politics. Eng. Dem. M. **25**: 243, 302.
Domestic Portraiture. (E. G. Smith) Chr. Q. Spec. **5**: 363.
Domestic Romance. Putnam, **15**: 675.
Domestic Scenes in Russia, Venables on. Mo. R. **148**: 403.
Domestic Servants. (R. R. Bowker) O. & N. **4**: 491. — (L. P. Smith) Putnam, **15**: 114. — Fraser, **74**: 129.
— Chinese as. (M. Hosmer) Lippinc. **6**: 355.
— Doings and Goings on of hired Girls. (M. Dean) Lippinc. **20**: 589.
— English, and their Ways. (O. Logan) Lippinc. **20**: 758.
— in Hamburgh. (G. A. Jackson) Once a Week, **1**: 159.
Domestic Service. (F. P. Cobbe) Fraser, **77**: 121. Same art. N. Ecl. **1**: 257. — (H. Martineau) Westm. **29**: 405. — Macmil. **34**: 182. Same art. Ecl. M. **87**: 244. — O. & N. **6**: 361. — Tinsley, **10**: 700.
— Difficulties of. Victoria, **2**: 241.
— for Ladies. (M. P. Lowe) Unita. R. **4**: 90.

Domestic Service in the United States. (F. A. Walker) Scrib. **11**: 273.
— Mistress and Maid, Relations of. (H. Elrington) Eng. Dom. M. **23**: 95, 123.
— Modern. Ed. R. **115**: 409.
— Nelly Armstrong; a Story. No. Brit. **20**: 179.
— Side of the Maids. (E. L. Linton) Cornh. **29**: 298.
— Side of the Mistresses. Cornh. **29**: 459.
— Question of. Once a Week, **5**: 430.
Domestic Servitude. Knick. **19**: 521.
Domestic Taste, Principles of. (E. E. Salisbury) New Eng. **36**: 310.
Domestic Worship, Furness on. (C. Stetson) Chr. Exam. **28**: 199.
Domesticated Animals, History of. No. Brit. **5**: 1.
Domestication, Darwin's Variation of Animals and Plants under. (A. Gray) Nation, **6**: 234.
— of Animals in the Middle Ages. (T. Wright) Intel. Obs. **6**: 318.
Domina Fluvia and the Lion. (G.A.Sala) Belgra. **15**: 220.
Dominic, St., and the Dominicans. (S. L. Caldwell) Bapt. Q. **11**: 247. — Am J. Educ. **24**: 375.
— and his Age. (J. Tulloch) Good Words, **18**: 161.
— and the Inquisition. (E. Lawrence) Harper, **42**: 730.
Dominic Pim's Woodcock. N. Ecl. **4**: 514.
Dominica Island. (F. M. Endlick) Am. Natural. **14**: 761.
— Volcanic Eruption in. Nature, **21**: 372.
Dominican, The; a Story of the Plague of Naples. Colburn, **20**: 37.
Dominican Artist-Monks. Dub. R. **25**: 386.
Dominican Republic of St. Domingo. (S. A. Kendall) Am. Whig R. **9**: 235, 368.
Dominican Schools in ancient Ireland. Dub. R. **19**: 145.
Dominie's Legacy. Fraser, **1**: 318.
Dominie's Sons. Fraser, **82**: 332. Same art. Liv. Age, **107**: 159. Same art. Ev. Sat. **9**: 646, 666, 682.
Dominion and Subordination in Society. (A. Harris) Mercersb. **24**: 520.
Dominique; a Sketch from Life. Blackw. **66**: 77.
Dominis, Antonio de. Retros. **16**: 436.
— Newland's Life of. Dub. R. **47**: 97.
Domitian and the Turbot. Blackw. **87**: 731.
Don, George, the Forfar Botanist. Hogg, **8**: 279.
Don Carlos. *See* Carlos, Don.
Don Esteban. Quar. **33**: 205.
Don Esteban; or Memoirs of a Spaniard. Colburn, **13**: 513.
Don Giovanni. Lond. Soc. **27**: 255. — Dem. R. **20**: 36.
— Mozart's. Colburn, **59**: 533.
Don Gomez and the Cid; a Song. Dub. Univ. **2**: 143.
Don John of Austria. Blackw. **63**: 70. Same art. Liv. Age, **16**: 337.
Don John. (J. Ingelow) Liv. Age, **148**: 491, 525, 595. **149**: 87, 154.
Don Quixote. (W.H. Prescott) No.Am. **45**: 1.— Blackw. **11**: 657. —(R. J. De Cordova) Knick. **38**: 189.
— and Gil Blas. (C. H. Drew) Penn Mo. **3**: 555.
— Extracts from. Ev. Sat. **11**: 215.
— Ramble in the Footsteps of. Dub. Univ. **11**: 574. *See* Cervantes.
Don Quixote's Library. Fraser, **7**: 324, 565. **8**: 445.
Don Ricardo; a Spanish Sketch. Cornh. **17**: 476.
Don Roderick, Ballad of. (S. W. Cone) Dem. R. **16**: 13. **36**: 485.
Don Sebastian: a Romance. Tait, n. s. **23**: 473, 518.
Dona Dalrae. Broadway, **10**: 264.
Doña Paula: a Tale of Peru. Am. Whig R. **13**: 419, 509.
Dona Ramona; a Tale. Cath. World, **16**: 122.
Donaldson, John W. New Cratylus. So. Q. **20**: 390.
Donati, Giovanni Battista. Nature, **8**: 556.
— Comet of. *See* Comet.
Donatist Controversy. (P. Schaff) Princ. **36**: 385.
Doncaster, Miller's History and Antiq. of. Ecl. R. **1**: 175.
Doncaster, Sports and Saturnalia of. Bentley, **20**: 288-622.
— Town and Moor. (J. Wilkins) Once a Week, **15**: 258.
Doncaster Race-Course. All the Year, **37**: 14.
Doncaster Races. Bentley, **31**: 116.
Doncaster St. Leger; a Poem. (F. H. Doyle) Canad. Mo. **4**: 19.
Donegal, Ireland, Among the Wilds of. (P. Q. Keegan) Colburn, **158**: 531.
— Down in. (G. P. Bevan) Once a Week, **6**: 625.
— Folk Lore of. Cornh. **35**: 172.
— Life in. (F. P. Cobbe) Once a Week, **15**: 436.
— Rambles in. Dub. Univ. **52**. 415.
— State of. Dub. Univ. **51**: 731.
Donegal Bay and Irish Chronicles. Fraser, **76**: 741.
Donegal Highlands. Dub. Univ. **41**: 528, 701.
Dongan, Thos., Governor of New York Colony. (R. H. Clarke) Cath. World, **9**: 767.
Donham, Leonard, Character and Death of. (F. D. Huntington) Mo. Rel. M. **17**: 272.
Doniert's Stone. Antiquary, **2**: 13.
Donizetti, Gaëtano. Bentley, **23**: 537. — Ecl. M. **14**: 279, 563. — Sharpe, **51**: 196.
— and Italian Music since Rossini. (P. Scudo) Knick. **57**: 136.
Donkey, Sorrows of the. Lond. M. **13**: 95.
— Story of a. Chamb. J. **50**: 705.
Donkeys. Chamb. J. **42**: 540.
— Exhibition of. All the Year, **12**: 101.
Donkey Power. Ev. Sat. **4**: 52.
Donna è Mobile; a Story. (L. Bigg) Victoria, **36**: 373.
Donna Quixote; a Story. (J. McCarthy) Belgra. **37**: 257, 478. **38**: 1, 225, 478. **39**: 1, 226, 479. **40**: 1, 129.
Donne, John. (W. Minto) 19th Cent. **7**: 845. — Argosy **32**: 299.
— first of English Satirists. Temp. Bar, **47**: 337.
— the Metaphysician. Temp. Bar, **3**: 78.
— Polydoron. Retros. **18**: 270.
Donner Emigrant Party. (H. Degroot) Overland, **5**: 38.
Donnersmarck, Count Henckel von. Fraser, **36**: 677.
Donnington Castle, Berks. (H. Godwin) Arch. **44**: 459.
Donnybrook, Lament for; a Poem. Dub. Univ. **61**: 331.
Donnybrook Fair. Bentley, **10**: 357. — Dub. Univ. **79**: 361.
— Historical Sketch of. Dub. Univ. **58**: 492.
Donovan the Intoxicator. Fraser, **1**: 209.
Doolittle Genealogy. (S. G. Drake) N. E. Reg. **6**: 293.
Doom of the Bell; a Tale. (B. Murphy) Cath. World, **25**: 324.
Doom of the Children; a Poem. (W. O. Bourne) So. Lit. Mess. **10**: 201.
Doom of the Griffiths. (E. C. Gaskell) Harper, **16**: 220.
Doomed Man, The. Lond. M. **8**: 306.
Doomed Ship; a Tale. Chamb. J. **51**: 49.
Doomed Skater. Chamb. J. **32**: 308.
Doom's Day Camp. All the Year, **29**: supp.
Doon, Day on the Banks of. Chamb. J. **2**: 129.
Doorstep, The; a Poem. (E. C. Stedman) Atlan. **23**: 147.
Doorsteps. Chamb. J. **35**: 241.
Dora; or Spirit of Lake George. (W. D. Potter) So. Lit. Mess. **11**: 13.
Dora, Sister; a Biography. Lond. Q. **57**: 49.
Dora d'Istria, *pseud.* *See* Koltzoff-Massalsky, H. G.
Dora's Trial; a Love Story. (W. Thompson) Lippinc **28**: 405.
Doran, Dr. John. (L. Jewitt) Reliquary, **18**: 227.
— Habits and Men. Tait, n. s. **22**: 649.
— Life and Writings of. Temp. Bar **52**: 460.
— New Pictures and old Panels. Brit. Q. **30**: 46.
Dorcas Lindsay; or Bachelor's Writing-Desk. So. Lit. Mess. **5**: 48.

Dorchester, England, Church of. Penny M. **14**: 372.
— Roman Amphitheater at. Penny M. **8**: 397.
Dorchester, Mass., Early Settlers of. (S. G. Drake) N. E. Reg. **5**: 389, 465.
— Inscriptions in Burial-Ground. N. E. Reg. **2**: 312, 381. **4**: 165, 275. **5**: 89, 255. **6**: 179, 236.
— Ministers of. Am. Q. Reg. **8**: 50.
— Records at. N. E. Reg. **16**: 77, 152. **21**: 163, 269, 329. **22**: 48.
Dorchester, S. C., Old Congregational Church at. Am. Q. Reg. **14**: 68.
Doré, P. Gustave. (P. G. Hamerton) F. Arts Q. **3**: 1, 300. — No. Brit. **47**: 127. — (J. McCarthy) Galaxy, **17**: 344. — (R. Sturgis) Nation, **3**: 388. — (J. R. Ware) Sharpe, **36**: 296. — with portrait, Ecl. M. **67**: 631. — with portrait, Once a Week, **26**: 454. — Art J. **19**: 51-166. — Belgra. **2**: 75. — (G. C. Swayne) Once a Week, **11**: 83. — Ev. Sat. **1**: 60. — Galaxy, **1**: 324. — N. Ecl. **5**: 478.
— and Millais. (R. St. J. Tyrwhitt) Contemp. **2**: 482.
— and his latest Works. (L. H. Hooper) Art J. **31**: 185. Same art. Appleton, **12**: 80.
— and Works. St. James, **29**: 353. — Temp. Bar, **16**: 347.
— at Home. (B. Jerrold) Gent. M. n. s. **3**: 439. Same art. Ev. Sat. **8**: 462.
— at Work. (B. Jerrold) Gent. M. n. s. **10**: 299. Same art. Am. Bibliop. **5**: 105.
— Bible illustrated. (P. G. Hamerton) Fortn. **4**: 669.
— Visit to Studio of. Ev. Sat. **4**: 641.
— Wandering Jew. Dub. R. **41**: 183.
— Works of. Brit. Q. **49**: 62. Same art. Liv. Age, **101**: 259.
Doré, Mont, Mineral Springs of. Chamb. J. **56**: 150.
Dorians, Müller's History of. (A. L. Koeppen) Mercersb. **8**: 362. — Ed. R. **53**: 121. — For. R. **4**: 322. — Mo. R. **125**: 159. — Am. Mo. M. **1**: 55.
Doris. Lond. Soc. **33**: 522.
Doris Barugh. (K. S. Macquoid) Good Words, **18**: 1-793. Same art. Liv. Age, **135**: 87-783. **136**: 34-241.
Doris Holt's Valentine. All the Year, **44**: 274, 299.
Dorking, Battle of. *See* Battle of Dorking.
Dornadilla, Dune of. (A. Pope) Arch. **5**: 216.
Dorney and Burnham, Summer Day at. (E. Walford) Once a Week, **12**: 696.
Dorothea, St., Virgin and Martyr. (W. H. Anderdon) Irish Mo. **8**: 81.
Dorothy Fox. (L. Parr) Good Words, **11**: 27-844. Same art. Liv. Age, **104**: 533. **105**: 12, 737. **106**: 218-725. **107**: 145-794.
Dorothy Q.; a Poem. (O. W. Holmes) Atlan. **27**: 120.
Dorothy in the Garret; a Poem. (J. T. Trowbridge) Atlan. **26**: 188.
Dorpat Review. (W. M. Reynolds) Evang. R. **11**: 594.
Dorr, Thomas W., with portrait. Dem. R. **11**: 201.
D'Orsay, Count, with portrait. Fraser, **10**: 645.
Dorsay, John S., with portrait. Anal. M. **13**: 265.
Dorset. Quar. **111**: 281.
Dorsetshire Dialect, Barnes's Poems in. No. Brit. **31**: 339.
— Queen's English in. Once a Week, **30**: 760.
Dort, Synod of. (E. Pond) Theo. & Lit. J. **7**: 33. — (E H. Sears) Chr. Exam. **62**: 1. — Am. Meth. M. **10**: 436.
— — Articles of. (A. Alexander) Princ. **4**: 239.
— — Opening of. (S. M. Hopkins) Princ. n. s. **1**: 322.
Dory; a Story. (C. Gibbon) Good Words, **22**: 56.
Dos Reales. (G. T. Shipley) Overland, **1**: 81. Same art. Broadw. **6**: 433.
Dosia; a Story. (H. Gréville) Temp. Bar, **58**: 477.
Dost, Mohammed, Ameer of Cabul. Mus. **45**: 666. — Temp. Bar, **9**: 338.
— Life and Character of. Fraser, **44**: 539.
Doten, Lizzie, Spiritual Poems of. Temp. Bar, **27**: 464.
Dotterel's Nest, How I found the. (D. Bruce) Macmil. **44**: 347.
Douay and the Fête of Gayaut. Once a Week, **15**: 7.
Douay Diaries. Month, **32**: 451.
Douay Missionaries. Dub. R. **82**: 427.
Double-Bedded Room. Bentley, **4**: 575.
Double Cure. (L. Schücking) N. Ecl. **6**: 315.
Double House. (D. M. Craik) Fraser, **54**: 170.
Double Life of Martin Staples. (C. A. Washburn) Lippinc. **24**: 468.
Double Love; a Tale. (W. Buxton) Sharpe, **50**: 218.
Double Marriage. (C. M. Brame) Cath. World, **6**: 776.
Double People. All the Year, **26**: 103.
Double Stars. Nature, **21**: 53.
Double Veil. (F. B. Perkins) Putnam, **5**: 405.
Double Widowhood. Chamb. J. **30**: 316, 329. Same art. Liv. Age, **60**: 433.
Doubles and Quits. Blackw. **104**: 511, 645. **105**: 50-379
Doubles in Plays. All the Year, **29**: 372.
Doubleday, T. Bubbington; a Tragedy. Blackw. **18**: 119.
Doubleday's Children. (Dr. Cook) All the Year, **37**: 265-553. **38**: 1-544. **39**: 20-227.
Doubt and Unbelief, Modern. (W. S. Balch) Univ. Q. **33**: 338.
— Deliverance from. Univ. Q. **14**: 122.
— Discipline of, in Religion. (J. F. Spalding) Bost. R. **6**: 120.
— Intellectual. (D. A. Wasson) Radical, **3**: 293.
— Modern. (I. Bayne) N. Ecl. **4**: 580.
— — and Christian Belief, Christlieb on. Canad. Mo. **6**: 89. — Chr. Obs. **74**: 537.
Doubt, Philosophic. (L. Stephen) Mind, **5**: 157.
— — Balfour's Defense of. (F. W. Maitland) Mind, **4**: 576.
— Victims of. Month, **5**: 441. Same art. Cath. World, **4**: 550.
Doubts respecting the Battle of Bunker Hill. (C. Hudson) Chr. Exam. **40**: 247.
— respecting Napoleon, Whately's. Anal. M. **14**: 270. — Ed. Mo. R. **1**: 523.
— respecting Archbishop Whately. Dub. Univ. **5**: 528.
Doubting Heart, A. (A. Keary) Macmil. **38**: 82-475. **39**: 32-546. **40**: 68-507. Same art. Liv. Age, **137**: 804. **138**: 10-653. **139**: 343-497. **140**: 208-663. **141**: 20-730. **142**: 156-686. **143**: 93-539.
Doudan, Ximenes. Fraser, **97**: 569. — (A. Laugel) Nation, **23**: 7. — (T. S. Perry) Atlan. **41**: 681. — No. Am. **124**: 126.
— Letters of. Ed. R. **148**: 182. — (H. James, jr.) Nation, **26**: 64.
Douglas, David. (T. Somerville) Overland, **7**: 105.
Douglas, Earl of Philadelphia. Lippinc. **3**: 546.
Douglas, Gawain. (A. Wall) Western, **3**: 724.
Douglas, Sir Howard. Blackw. **93**: 561.
Douglas, Lady Jane. (W. Chambers) Chamb. J. **51**: 385.
Douglas, Stephen A., Political Career of. (G. W. Curtis) No. Am. **103**: 509.
— Reminiscences of. (J. Howard, jr.) Atlan. **8**: 205
— Southerner's Estimate of. Nat. Q. **40**: 173.
Douglas, Sutherland. (A. C. Twining) Chr. Q. Spec. **4**: 567.
Douglas, William. Art J. **21**: 137.
Douglas Family. N. E. Reg. **28**: 69.
Douglass, David Bates, with portrait. (C. B. Stuart) Ecl. Engin. **6**: 1.
Douglass, Frederick. (M. Howitt) Peop. J. **2**: 302.
— Narrative of. Chamb. J. **5**: 56.
Douhault, Marquis de, Strange Story of. Cornh. **7**: 629. — (E. H. Lacombe) So. M. **15**: 386.
Doune, Castle of. Sharpe, **7**: 193.
D'Outre-Mort; a Tale. (H. E. Prescott) Galaxy, **2**: 516.

Dove, Heinrich Wilhelm. Nature, 19: 529. — (F. Hoffman) Pop. Sci. Mo. 16: 261.
Dove, The; paraphrase of Poe's Raven. St. James, 1: 235.
Dove in the Eagle's Nest. (C. M. Yonge) Macmil. 12: 1-510. 13: 13, 81.
Dove Dale. Lond. Soc. 16: 38. — Penny M. 3: 108.
Dove's Nest. (J. Hatton) Lond. Soc. 24: 332, 426.
Dover, Capt. Robert. Cotswold Games. Cornh. 37: 710.
Dover, England. (H. Curling) Bentley, 20: 580.
— Day at. All the Year, 43: 369.
— Shakspere's Cliff. Penny M. 11: 290.
— Snargate Street. (G. A. Sala) Temp. Bar, 10: 479.
— to Calais. Chamb. J. 50: 232. — Dub. Univ. 80: 623.
Dover and Calais Railway. Chamb. J. 43: 566.
Dover Castle. Penny M. 2: 57.
— Roman Antiquities in. Penny M. 8: 472.
Dover Channel, Tides in, B. C. 55. Arch. 39: 277.
Dover Cliff, Explosion of, 1843. J. Frankl. Inst. 35: 270, 325. — (C. W. Pasley) J. Frankl. Inst. 36: 28.
Dover Haven, Account of. (J. Thorpe) Arch. 11: 212.
Dover, Straits of. *See* English Channel.
Dover, N. H., Combination of 1640. (A. H. Quint) N. E. Reg. 33: 91.
— Puritanical Land-Grabbers. Hist. M. 18: 84.
— Records. N. E. Reg. 4: 30, 246. 25: 56. 28: 155. 29: 261. 30: 455. 31: 313.
Dovetailing Machine. Pract. M. 5: 109.
Dow, Gerhard. Art J. 33: 102.
Dow, Rich. W., Biog. of. (F. W. Holland) Hunt, 2: 507.
Dow's Flat. (Bret Harte) Overland, 4: 569.
Dowager, The. Tinsley, 13: 56.
Dowager Countess. Liv. Age, 107: 429, 478.
Dowden, Edward, Poems of. Irish Mo. 9: 419.
Down among the dead Men. House. Words, 8: 418.
Down at Dippington. All the Year, 1: 414.
Down at Red Grange. House. Words, 14: 223.
Down East and Out West. (C. Gardner) Lakeside, 2: 339.
Down in a Chine; a Tale. (M. L. Pool) Galaxy, 2: 261.
Down in Tennessee. (J. R. Gilmore) Contin. Mo. 3: 469.
Down the River. (H. P. Spofford) Atlan. 16: 468.
Downes, John, Life of. Am. Mo. M. 8: 71.
Downes, Joseph. Mountain Decameron. Quar. 57: 162.
Downing, Ellen M. (M. Russell) Irish Mo. 6: 459-661.
Downing, Mrs. Harriet. Satan in Love. Mo. R. 154: 122.
Downing, Helena P. Victoria, 35: 72.
Downs, Solomon U., with portrait. Dem. R. 24: 547.
Downs, The. Once a Week, 10: 640.
Downs Harbor. Westm. 18: 406.
Downshire; a Poem. Dub. Univ. 16: 205.
Downton Castle and the Knights. (T. Wright) Once a Week, 16: 283.
Dowse, Thomas. Am. J. Educ. 3: 284. 9: 355.
— Library of. Hist. M. 1: 7.
Dowton, William. (T. P. Grinsted) Bentley, 41: 318.
Doyle, Sir Francis H., Poems of. (F. Bowen) No. Am. 55: 237. — Mo. R. 153: 69. — Dark Blue, 3: 294. — Ecl. M. 68: 551.
Doyle, James, Bishop of Kildare. Dub. Univ. 58: 237. — (H. Giles) Chr. Exam. 74: 157. — (J. N. Nylan) Cath. World, 7: 44. — Month, 40: 145.
Doyle, John, Memorials of. Month, 8: 392.
Doyle, Martin, with portrait. Dub. Univ. 15: 374.
D'Oyly, G. Letters to Sir W. Drummond. Quar. 9: 329.
Dracontia, Observations on. (J. B. Deane) Arch. 25: 188.
Dracut, Mass., Ministers of. Am. Q. Reg. 11: 276.
Draft in Marine Boilers burning Anthracite Coal. (J. V. Merrick) J. Frankl. Inst. 58: 390.
Draft on the Bank of Spain. Lippinc. 9: 668.
Dragon, Fight with; a Poem. (F. Schiller) Cath. World, 32: 666.
— Natural History of. Chamb. J. 9: 262.
— of Wantley Legend. (L. Jewitt) Reliquary, 18: 193.
Dragon Rouge, Le. Dub. Univ. 2: 386.
Dragon Flies. (A. S. Packard, jr.) Am. Natural. 1: 304.
Dragon Myth, The. Colburn, 154: 541, 673.
Dragon Tree of Teneriffe. (J. R. Jackson) Stud. & Intel. Obs. 1: 150.
Dragon's Head, The. Fraser, 88: 447.
Dragons. Colburn, 68: 449.
— and Dragon-Slayers. Good Words, 11: 274, 348.
— Griffins, and Salamanders. House. Words, 15: 427.
— Sea. Colburn, 69: 38-501.
Dragoons, English, and their Horses. Temp. Bar, 13: 391. Same art. Ecl. M. 64: 563.
Drainage. J. Frankl. Inst. 75: 297, 301. — Westm. 39: 231. — De Bow, 3: 66, 259.
— and Water Supply. (W. A. Corfield) Ecl. Engin. 13: 147-401. — (R. Rawlinson) J. Frankl. Inst. 80: 312.
— — of suburban Houses. (R. Vawser) Ecl. Engin. 22: 366.
— Denton on. Mo. R. 158: 104.
— House. (F. C. Cotton) Ecl. Engin. 16: 113. — (T. M. Reade) Ecl. Engin. 16: 232. — (E S. Philbrick) Am. Arch. 7: 271-283.
— — and Sewage. (G. E. Waring, jr.) Penn Mo. 9: 215.
— — Apparatus for. (E. S. Philbrick) Am. Arch. 8: 4.
— — Disposal of. (E. S. Philbrick) Am. Arch. 10: 167.
— — Double-Check System. (H. Masters) Ecl. Engin. 21: 471.
— Land. Ecl. Engin. 14: 182. — Quar. 86: 79.
— of the Everglades of Florida. Hunt, 19: 401.
— of the Fens of England. Chamb. J. 23: 278. — Brit. Q. 18: 381. — Penny M. 11: 198.
— of London. Ecl. R. 108: 193. — Fraser, 41: 190.
— — Main Drainage Works. (S. J. Mackie) Pop. Sci. R. 3: 56. — Nature, 1: 558.
— of small Towns. Ecl. Engin. 10: 104.
— of Towns. (E. S. Philbrick) Am. Arch. 7: 224, 236.
— of a Village. (G. E. Waring, jr.) Harper, 59: 132.
— Philadelphia System. (R. Herring) Ecl. Engin. 18: 429.
— Pneumatic. (D. Esdaile) Good Words, 15: 404. 17: 773.
— — Liernur's System of. Ecl. Engin. 13: 426.
— Sanitary. (G. S. Morison) Nation, 23: 13.
— — of Houses and Town. (G. E. Waring, jr.) Atlan. 36: 339, 427, 535.
— — Recent Modifications in. (G. E. Waring, jr.) Atlan. 44: 56. — Am. Arch. 6: 27, 36.
Draining. Quar. 86: 43.
— and improving Desert Land. (G. Wilson) Ecl. Engin. 20: 502.
— of Lungern Lake in Unterwalden. Tait, n. s. 4: 289.
— of the Zuiderzee. All the Year, 37: 234.
Drains, Absorption, *versus* Cesspools. (G. E. Waring, jr.) Am. Arch. 5: 103.
— and Typhoid Fever. Am. Arch. 4: 43.
— Clean, and improved Mortars. (H. Y. D. Scott) Ecl. Engin. 7: 246.
— Rivers, and Water Supply. Westm. 54: 368.
— Ventilation and Trapping of. (J. Lovegrove) Ecl. Engin. 1: 731.
Drake, Albert. (E. K. Alden) Cong. Q. 7: 227.
Drake, Sir Francis, Life and Voyages of. Ed. R. 80: 376. Same art. Liv. Age, 3: 289. — Dub. Univ. 23: 551. — (O. W. B. Peabody) No. Am. 59: 70. — (J. B. Brown) Ecl. R. 110: 360.
— and his Familiars: a Poem. (W. Jones) Bentley, 62: 587.
Drake, Joseph Rodman. (J. G Wilson) Harper, 49: 65.
— Grave of. (H. B. Dawson) Hist. M. 21: 705.
— Poems of. Am. Mo. M. 6: 65. — So. Lit. Mess. 2: 326. — Dem. R. 14: 202.

Drake, Nathan, Poems of. Mo. R. **93**: 352. **99**: 302. **116**: 14. — (J. Foster) Ecl. R. **16**: 1141.
Drake, Samuel G., with portrait. (J. H. Sheppard) N. E. Reg. **17**: 197. — with portrait, (W. B. Trask) Potter Am. Mo. **5**: 729.
— Address to New England Historic Genealogical Society, 1858. N. E. Reg. **12**: 97.
Drake Pedigree, of Ashe, Devon. (W. H. H. Rogers) Antiquary, **2**: 237, 282.
Drama, The. (W. H. Pollock) Contemp. **28**: 54. — (Sir C. L. Young) Once a Week, **26**: 318, 348. — Dem. R. **42**: 16. — So. Lit. J. **4**: 289. — Ed. R. **49**: 317. — So. Lit. Mess. **6**: 846. **7**: 181. — Blackw. **11**: 440. **18**: 240. — Brit. & For. R. **2**: 568. — Fraser, **29**: 181.
— About Plays and Players. Appleton, **17**: 174.
— and its Literature. Mo. R. **129**: 461.
— and its Prospects. Fraser, **41**: 69.
— Ancient, and the modern Novel. (K. Cook) Dark Blue, **3**: 709.
— and Music. Blackw. **6**: 430. — Irish Q. **9**: 104.
— and Music Halls. Cornh. **15**: 119.
— Anglo-French. Ed. R. **51**: 225.
— Authors and Managers. (G. H. Lewes) Westm. **37**: 71.
— Bearing on Morals and Religion. Victoria, **25**: 739.
— Behind the Scenes. Tinsley, **10**: 285.
— British. Blackw. **89**: 218. — Mo. R. **150**: 457. **151**: 291. **152**: 347. — Dub. Univ. **28**: 525, 668.
— — Causes of the Decline of. Blackw. **23**: 33. — Mus. **12**: 661.
— — Modern. No. Brit. **29**: 124. Same art. Ecl. M. **46**: 29.
— British Playgoer. Tinsley, **3**: 634.
— Bygone Celebrities. (R. H. Horne) Gent. M. n. s. **6**: 247, 660. **7**: 88, 468.
— Causeries on. (C. Hervey) Colburn, **92**: 484.
— Character and Tendency of. Ecl. R. **90**: 129.
— Church and the Stage. Victoria, **28**: 389.
— Comic, of the Restoration. (J. Pyne) Nat. Q. **34**: 306.
— Conventionalities of. (F. Parke) Dub. Univ. **85**: 503.
— Decadence of. Tait, **2**: 380.
— Decline of. (D. Boucicault) No. Am. **125**: 235. — (J. B. Matthews) Galaxy, **19**: 225. — Chamb. J. **38**: 392. — Tait, n. s. **18**: 600. — Tinsley, **5**: 293.
— Drunken. (O. Logan) Galaxy, **4**: 934.
— Early English. Retros. **16**: 1.
— — and German. (W. J. Thoms) Colburn, **61**: 19.
— English Stage and the Comédie Française. Dub. Univ. **94**: 340.
— First Nights at the Play. Dub. Univ. **90**: 226.
— Footlights of other Days. Tinsley, **10**: 465.
— For and against. (J. Pollock) 19th Cent. **1**: 611.
— French Opinion of. (C. Bonjour) Colburn, **52**: 363.
— German and French. (J. Pollock) Contemp. **21**: 335.
— Girardin on. For. Q. **33**: 33. Same art. Ecl. M. **3**: 33.
— Gods and Galleries. Tinsley, **10**: 592.
— Greek, Ancient. (J. Proudfit) Am. Bib. Repos. 2d s. **1**: 449.
— — and Romantic. Blackw. **59**: 54.
— — Beauties of. So. Lit. Mess. **24**: 58.
— — *versus* French. (L. Tennyson) 19th Cent. **7**: 58.
— Habitué's Note-Book. (C. Hervey) Colburn, **84**: 122-535. **85**: 125-502. **86**: 113-383. **87**: 373-490. **88**: 123-550. **89**: 129-381. **90**: 116-244.
— Hazlitt's Lectures on. (T. N. Talfourd) Ed. R. **34**: 438.
— Hindu. Ed. R. **108**: 253.
— Historical, Revival of. Once a Week, **28**: 170.
— — History and Character of. Westm. **67**: 364.
— History of. Selec. Ed. R. **1**: 139.
— in America. (A. E. Lancaster) Potter Am. Mo. **8**: 23-346. — (E. A. Poe) Am. Whig R. **2**: 117. — Am. Q. **1**: 331. — Dem. R. **40**: 554. — Dub. Univ. **74**: 319. Same art. N. Ecl. **5**: 555. — Lond. M. **16**: 466.
Drama, The, in Colleges. (J. K. Hosmer) Atlan. **30**: 19. — (J. K. Hosmer) Nation, **10**: 6. *See also* College Theatricals.
— in connection with the Fine Arts. Dub. Univ. **28**: 97.
— in England. Quar. **132**: 1. — Sharpe, **39**: 6-231. **40**: 187, 230, 287. **41**: 18.
— — and France. Macmil. **20**: 70. Same art. Ecl. M. **73**: 87.
— — Dawn of. Nat. Q. **28**: 97.
— — Decline of. Cornh. **8**: 172.
— — — and Fall of. Colburn, **153**: 304.
— — in Times of Elizabeth and James. Cornh. **11**: 604, 706. **12**: 86.
— — in 1853. Quar. **95**: 71.
— — in 1873. Dub. Univ. **82**: 240, 492.
— — Modern. Blackw. **79**: 209. — Dub. R. **2**: 367.
— — Notes on. So. Lit. J. **4**: 533.
— — Old. Retros. **2**: 70. **3**: 97, 142. **11**: 123. — Mo. R. **111**: 365. **109**: 388.
— — State of. Victoria, **28**: 520.
— in France. (Vicomte de Calonne) Macmil. **34**: 176. — Lond. M. 2d s. **5**: 44. — For. R. **4**: 309. — Quar. **51**: 177. — (G. H. Lewes) Westm. **34**: 287. — For. Q. **9**: 78. **31**: 140. — Dem. R. **21**: 333.
— — and England. (G. H. Lewes) Cornh. **11**: 33. — New Q. **10**: 127.
— — Classic and romantic. Putnam, **6**: 401.
— — in the 16th Century. Retros. **18**: 396.
— — Modern. (E. I. Sears) Nat. Q. **1**: 64.
— — Morals of. Pamph. **12**: 49.
— — New Classic. For. Q. **36**: 32.
— — Specimens of. Fraser, **18**: 649.
— — under Louis XIV. (H. M. Trollope) Macmil. **31**: 522.
— in Italy. For. Q. **27**: 1. — (F. Inglis) No. Am. **39**: 329. — Blackw. **18**: 545. **19**: 176. **20**: 164. **21**: 727. **22**: 571. — No. Am. **5**: 182. — (R. Davey) Lippinc. **15**: 90. — (C. M. Phillimore) Macmil. **34**: 319, 324, 535. **36**: 218, 376. **39**: 198.
— in London. Fraser, **71**: 124.
— — Acted. Blackw. **2**: 426, 567, 664. **3**: 77, 207, 329. **4**: 443, 708. **5**: 71, 317. **6**: 51-624. **7**: 182, 307. — Fraser, **38**: 41.
— — French. (M. Arnold) 19th Cent. **6**: 228. Same art. Appleton, **22**: 311. — (F. and W. H. Pollock) Dark Blue, **2**: 102.
— — in 1875. Dub. Univ. **85**: 204, 379, 743.
— — in 1876. Dub. Univ. **87**: 108.
— — Recollections of Her Majesty's Theater. (N. D'Arcy) Belgra. **4**: 416.
— in the Middle Ages. (T. Wright) Bentley, **38**: 298. — Nat. M. **2**: 221, 367.
— in Paris. Dub. Univ. **64**: 591. — Fraser, **70**: 678. — Westm. **71**: 416.
— — before Molière. Cornh. **26**: 90.
— — Censorship of. Dub. Univ. **68**: 525. **69**: 243.
— in Russia. So. Lit. Mess. **24**: 250.
— in Scotland, Historical Sketch of. Hogg, **8**: 392, 412.
— in Spain. Quar. **25**: 1.
— — Calderon and de Vega. For. Q. **31**: 502.
— — Early. Am. Q. **4**: 308. — Blackw. **17**: 641. **18**: 680.
— — Interludes of the early. Colburn, **5**: 549.
— — Modern. Colburn, **11**: 87-186.
— Inexplicable Dumb-Shows. (D. Cook) Belgra. **39**: 190.
— Influence of. Ox. Prize Ess. **3**: 245. — Blackw. **7**: 387. — Knick. **7**: 7.
— Leg Business. (O. Logan) Galaxy, **4**: 440.
— Legitimate. Victoria, **17**: 461.
— Lyric. For. Q. **12**: 197.
— — past, present, and future. (C. L. Gruneisen) St. James, **36**: 363.
— Manager's Note-Book. Colburn, **51**: 320-485. **52**: 63-323. **53**: 101-530. **54**: 87-457.

Drama, The, Means of regenerating. Colburn, 1: 5.
— Mediæval Theatricals. Knick. 63: 237.
— Meiningen Realism. (W. Archer) St. James, 49: 71.
— Modern. Dial, 4: 307.
— — and Dramatists. Tinsley, 6: 421.
— — Decline of. New Eng. M. 8: 105.
— — Origin and Development of. Nat. Q. 21: 68.
— — Rise and Progress of. (J. W. Wall) Knick. 44: 59.
— Musical, Hogarth on. Mo. R. 146: 533.
— Mysteries and Moralities. (Lady F. P. Verney) Contemp. 25: 595.
— National, Absence of, in 19th Century. (H. P. Hayman) St. James, 46: 315.
— A National Theater. Victoria, 24: 329.
— Neo-Classical, 1858-67. Chr. Rem. 55: 39.
— New Lights from old Plays. (P. Q. Keegan) Colburn, 167: 337.
— of the Day, 1859. Bent. Q. 1: 550.
— of the Period. (R. G. White) Galaxy, 8: 678.
— Old Dublin Stage. (R. B. Baker) Belgra. 39: 304.
— Past and present. Broadw. 2: 119.
— Players of our Day. Gent. M. n. s. 7: 591, 683, 846. 8: 73-712.
— Principles of; Corneille and Dryden. Fraser, 66: 383.
— Puritans' Opposition to. No. Brit. 25: 1.
— Realism in Plays. (G. S. Bower) Colburn, 169: 10.
— Recent Tragedies. (G. H. Lewes) Westm. 37: 321.
— Recollections of John O'Keefe. Colburn, 16: 345. 17: 17-564. 47: 232.
— Records of a Stage Veteran. Colburn, 41: 454.
— Regeneration of. Westm. 37: 71.
— Religious. (W. Binns) Mod. R. 1: 792.
— — of the Middle Ages. (W. H. Withrow) New Dom. 12: 129, 202.
— Review of, 1800-20. Lond. M. 1: 65.
— Revolution in. Cornh. 39: 442.
— Rise and Fall of European. For. Q. 35: 290.
— Romantic. Blackw. 60: 161.
— Schlegel on. (W. Hazlitt) Ed. R. 26: 67. — Quar. 12: 112. — Am. Mo. R. 4: 1. — Am. Mo. M. 2: 12, 115.
— Stage Exaggerations. Victoria, 24: 457.
— State and Prospects of. Ed. R. 57: 281. — Westm. 20: 151. — Blackw. 17: 727. — Mus. 6: 355.
— Thespian Cartes. Tinsley, 18: 71-587.
— under Canvas. Chamb. J. 42: 321.
— under Difficulties. All the Year, 36: 102. — Chamb. J. 26: 289.
— will it revive? St. James, 48: 174.
— without Footlights; a Tale. Temp. Bar, 32: 180.
— Women in. Victoria, 25: 1126.
— Sir C. Young on. Victoria, 18: 552.
See Actors; Burlesque; Comedy; Tragedy; Theater; Stage; Plays.
Dramas, Modern British. Blackw. 14: 421, 723. 18: 119.
— New. Ecl. R. 71: 163.
Dramatic Adaptation. (A. D. Vandam) Tinsley, 19: 499.
Dramatic and Theatrical, Difference of. (F. A. Kemble) Cornh. 8: 733.
Dramatic Art. (J. Pollock) Contemp. 23: 363.
— Fechter's Realism in. (R. G. White) Nation, 10: 364.
— Influence of the Theater on. Lond. M. 1: 146.
— Meiningen Theater. (C. H. Hawkins) Macmil. 35: 482.
— Past and present. Dub. Univ. 73: 511.
— Schlegel's Lectures on. Portfo. (Den.) 17: 477.
Dramatic Art Representation. (W. B. Donne) Dark Blue, 1: 70.
Dramatic Author, Miseries of a. Cornh. 8: 498.
Dramatic Authors, Actors, and Amateurs. Dub. Univ. 38: 407.
— Rights of; the suppressed Comedy. Colburn, 70: 533.
Dramatic Biography, Jones's. Quar. 7: 282.
Dramatic Canons. (F. Whittaker) Galaxy, 23: 396, 508.
Dramatic Censorship. Chamb. J. 26: 313. Same art. Liv. Age, 52: 26. — Chamb. J. 39: 158. 50: 263.
Dramatic Composition. (D. Boucicault) No. Am. 126: 40. — Ox. Prize Ess. 1: 167.
Dramatic Critics as Actors. (H. Louther) Tinsley, 28: 60.
Dramatic Criticism, Cant in. Blackw. 19: 197.
— Tieck's. Mo. R. 110: 470. 111: 457. — Mus. 10: 289.
Dramatic Doctors. All the Year, 39: 373.
Dramatic Doings. Dub. Univ. 16: 641. 17: 328, 599. 18: 180. 19: 64.
Dramatic Emancipation. Pamph. 2: 369.
Dramatic Failures. Chamb. J. 41: 263.
Dramatic Fictions. Knick. 9: 587.
Dramatic Illusion, Imperfect. (C. Lamb) Lond. M. 12: 599.
Dramatic Literature. Am. Q. 8: 134. — Westm. 18: 31. — So. Q. 16: 377. — Lond. M. 22: 298.
— English, Ward on. (W. B. Donne) Macmil. 33: 314.
— Geoffrey on. (A. H. Everett) No. Am. 10: 291.
— in 1869. Colburn, 146: 92.
— Past and present. (Lady Pollock) Temp. Bar, 44: 331.
— Select Committee on, 1832. Westm. 18: 31.
Dramatic Poetry. Dub. Univ. 23: 19.
— English, History of. Quar. 46: 477. — Mo. R. 125: 377. — Westm. 31: 51.
— of Age of Elizabeth. Brit. Q. 14: 39.
Dramatic Reform. (T. J. Serle) Colburn, 166: 8. — Victoria, 31: 1.
— Classifying Theaters. (G. H. Lewes) Ed. R. 78: 382.
Dramatic Representations, Music at. All the Year, 26: 369.
Dramatic Sensation, A. (W. P. Wood) Lakeside, 9: 9.
Dramatic Situation and Character. Cornh. 26: 155. Same art. Ev. Sat. 13: 229.
Dramatic Treasure-Trove. Fraser, 59: 65.
Dramatic Writers of Age of Elizabeth: Ben Jonson. Brit. Q. 25: 285.
— of Ireland. (J. W. Calcraft) Dub. Univ. 45: 39-527. 46: 38-548. 47: 15, 359.
Dramatic Writings, Decline of. Blackw. 9: 279.
Dramatists, Beauties of living. Lond. M. 5: 27.
— Comic, of the Restoration. (T. B. Macaulay) Ed. R. 72: 490.
— Early English. Am. Whig R. 14: 285.
— French. (J. T. Lomax) So. Lit. Mess. 8: 763. 9: 76.
— Greek. So. Lit. Mess. 8: 606, 793.
— Lady. Eng. Dom. M. 11: 27.
— Minor Elizabethan. (E. P. Whipple) Atlan. 20: 692.
— Modern English. Blackw. 14: 421, 723. 18: 119.
— Old English. (E. P. Whipple) No. Am. 63: 29. — Selec. Ed. R. 2: 14. — So. Lit. Mess. 15: 656. — Westm. 1: 560. — Blackw. 2: 21, 260, 656. 3: 556. 4: 66. 6: 409.
— Songs from, Bell's. Fraser, 50: 583. — Liv. Age, 42: 579. — Chamb. J. 22: 203. Same art. Liv. Age, 43: 255.
— Tales from. (A. H. Bromilow) Colburn, 163: 43-536. 164: 19-414.
Dramatization. Ev. Sat. 9: 835.
— of Novels. (J. N. Porter) Macmil. 40: 244.
Draper, John Wm. Pop. Sci. Mo. 4: 361. — (W. H. Bidwell) Ecl. M. 85: 759.
— Buckle and a Science of History. (E. B. Freeland) Contin. Mo. 4: 529, 610. 5: 161.
— Lecture of. So. Lit. Mess. 3: 693.
— Scientific Memoirs. Nature, 19: 26.
— Writings of. (O. A. Brownson) Cath. World, 7: 155.
Draper, Lyman C., Sketch of. Am. Bibliop. 7: 249.
Draper's Daughter; a Tale. Dem. R. 15: 163, 285.
Draper's Shops, Late Hours in. Penny M. 13: 102.
Drapery in Memorial Sculpture. Art J. 5: 279.
Draperies, Curtains, and Blinds. Godey, 60: 185, 282, 506.

Draught, Power of. J. Frankl. Inst. **13**: 199.
Draughting, Mechanical, for Apprentices, Hints on. (J. Richards) J. Frankl. Inst. **94**: 166, 244.
Dravidian Folk-Songs. Cornh. **24**: 570.
Drawback on Imports; Treasury Circular. Hunt, **15**: 398.
Drawbridge, Applied Forces in a. (H. T. Eddy) Ecl. Engin. **10**: 551.
Drawing. (E. Hentschel) Am. J. Educ. **21**: 227.
— among the Hindus. (A. Hunter) Art J. **12**: 205.
— Graphic Science in Education. (S. E. Warren) Education, **1**: 439.
— Industrial. (C. O. Thompson) Am. Soc. Sci. J. **4**: 105.
— — Free-Hand. Pract. M. **6**: 278.
— Instruction in. (R. Burchett) Am. J. Educ. **22**: 57. — (M. A. Dwight) Am. J. Educ. **4**: 229. — (F. Ravaisson) Am. J. Educ. **2**: 419.
— — Elementary. Art J. **8**: 273.
— — in Belgium. Am. J. Educ. **21**: 658.
— — in France. Am. J. Educ. **21**: 497.
— — in Public Schools. (W. T. Brigham) O. & N. **4**: 103. — (E. Hentschel) Am. J. Educ. **10**: 59. — Am. J. Educ. **22**: 251. — O. & N. **2**: 631.
— — in Wurtemberg. Am. J. Educ. **21**: 347.
— — Rep. of French Commission. Am. J. Educ. **21**: 513.
— Lessons in. Godey, **49**: 27-502. **50**: 45-515. **51**: 25, 218, 417. **52**: 119, 318, 507. **53**: 117, 322, 506. **54**: 130, 315, 503. **55**: 129, 320.
— Linear. (W. R. Johnson) Am. Inst. Instruc. **1830**: 257.
— Pleasures of. Colburn, **6**: 385.
— Ruskin's Elements of. Blackw. **87**: 32.
— Study of. Am. Arch. **8**: 173. — (W. M. R. French) Dial (Ch.), **1**: 154.
— — Methods of. (E. J. Poynter) Am. Arch. **7**: 11.
Drawings by the Old Masters. (F. T. Palgrave) Portfo. **1**: 127.
— Mechanical and Architectural, Art of coloring. Pract. M. **4**: 384. **5**: 27.
— Modern. (J. L. Roget) Art J. **33**: 13.
Drawing-Crayons, Composition of. Penny M. **13**: 264.
Drawing-Instruments, Mathematical. Nature, **19**: 128.
Drawing-Rooms, Philosophy of. Cornh. **41**: 312. Same art. Appleton, **23**: 432.
— Thoughts on. Chamb. J. **44**: 107.
Drawing-Room Performance. (B. Francis) Belgra. **28**: 425.
Drawn at a Venture; a Tale. Temp. Bar, **41**: 222, 361, 497.
Drawn Bet; a Poem. Temp. Bar, **58**: 359.
Draxy Miller's Dowry. (Saxe Holm) Scrib. **4**: 86-290. Same art. Eng. Dom. M. **17**: 237, 296. **18**: 20, 66.
Drayton, Michael. Gen. Repos. **4**: 74. — (A. M. F. Robinson) Dub. Univ. **94**: 56.
— Polyolbion. Retros. **18**: 105.
Dread Reckoning. (E. Jerrold) St. James, **36**: 205-635.
Dreadful Case; a Story. (W. Jameson) Belgra. **43**: 346.
Dreadful Discovery. Lond. Soc. **3**: 504. **4**: 193-421.
Dreadful Ghost, A. (D. M. Craik) Once a Week, **6**: 211. Same art. Ecl. M. **55**: 553.
Dream, A. (W. D. Howells) Knick. **58**: 146. — Dub. Univ. **1**: 145. — Mus. **5**: 163.
— Curious. Dub. Univ. **81**: 130.
— False. Chamb. J. **30**: 73.
— from Heaven. Liv. Age, **53**: 469.
— of the Cavaliers. (J. E. Cooke) Harper, **22**: 252.
— of the Dead. Blackw. **86**: 358.
— of Egypt; a Poem. (J. Goddard) Once a Week, **16**: 238.
— of Faiths; a Poem. St. James, **48**: 344.
— of Gerontius; a Dramatic Poem. (J. H. Newman) Cath. World, **1**: 517, 630.
— of Life. (W. R. Alger) Putnam, **13**: 577. Same art. Broadw. **6**: 252. — Dub. Univ. **80**: 110.
— of Love; a Poem. (S. W. Cone) Dem. R. **36**: 421.
Dream of my Life; a Tale. (W. W. Fenn) Broadw. **2**: 541.
— of Pilate's Wife. (C. P. Cranch) Putnam, **14**: 409.
— of Ravan; a Hindu Episode. Dub. Univ. **42**: 475, 578, 673. **43**: 456.
— of Sappho; a Poem. (M. Mackay) Gent. M. n. s. **19**: 108.
— Remarkable. Blackw. **19**: 736.
— which is not all a Dream. Knick. **61**: 491. **62**: 10.
Dreams. (E. Fitzgerald) Canad. Mo. **13**: 467. — (C. B. Lewis) Galaxy, **24**: 95. — Argosy, **25**: 190. — Temp. Bar, **58**: 503. Same art. Appleton, **23**: 549. — Cornh. **29**: 720. Same art. Ecl. M. **83**: 181. — Dub. Univ. **79**: 392. **84**: 58. — Ecl. R. **122**: 516. — Ev. Sat. **16**: 691. **17**: 438. — Irish Q. **9**: 1148. Liv. Age, **140**: 314. — Lippinc. **5**: 296. — Lond. M. **10**: 125. — Once a Week, **7**: 543. **22**: 544. — Tinsley, **2**: 268. — Westm. **30**: 424.
— and Apparitions. (J. Hogg) Blackw. **21**: 549, 664. **22**: 173. *See also* Apparitions.
— and Demonology. Ecl. R. **52**: 501.
— and Dreaming. (C. Redding) Colburn, **147**: 58. — (Alex. Smith) Argosy, **1**: 390.
— and the Making of Dreams. (J. M. Granville) Gent. M. n. s. **27**: 730.
— and Omens. (R. W. Emerson) No. Am. **124**: 179. — Blackw. **48**: 194. **58**: 735. — Dub. Univ. **67**: 506.
— and Realities. (L. Stephen) Fortn. **30**: 334. Same art. Sup. Pop. Sci. Mo. **3**: 532.
— and Sleep. (N. S. Shaler) Internat. R. **6**: 234. — (J. Cunningham) Macmil. **9**: 473.
— — Maury on. (Sir H. Holland) Ed. R. **137**: 330. Same art. Liv. Age, **117**: 579.
— and their Causes. Once a Week, **23**: 96.
— and their Interpretation. Good Words, **11**: 353.
— and Visions. (J. Cunningham) Macmil. **5**: 506.
— as Illustrations of unconscious Cerebration. (F. P. Cobbe) Macmil. **23**: 512. Same art. Ecl. M. **76**: 726. Same art. Liv. Age, **109**: 363.
— Crimes in. Ev. Sat. **11**: 47.
— Divination by. Eng. Dom. M. **3**: 141, 327.
— Extraordinary. Once a Week, **9**: 623.
— in the Invalides; a Poem. Blackw. **103**: 756. Same art. Liv. Age, **98**: 84.
— in Sleep. Temp. Bar, **7**: 500.
— Land of; a Poem. Dub. Univ. **1**: 201.
— Laws of. Cornh. **34**: 536. Same art. Ecl. M. **88**: 32.
— Literature of. Bentley, **59**: 267. Same art. Ecl. M. **66**: 701.
— Nature and Uses of. (A. S. Patton) Chr. R. **22**: 621.
— Notable. (J. Hatton) Argosy, **5**: 462. Same art. Ev. Sat. **5**: 689.
— Phenomena of. Mo. R. **127**: 287.
— Psychology of. (J. H. Gulliver) J. Spec. Philos. **14**: 204.
— Remarkable; Warnings, etc., in. Howitt. **3**: 136-203.
— Scientific Study of. (J. C. Murray) New Dom. **20**: 481.
— Seafield on. Temp. Bar, **15**: 405.
— Speculation about. (C. B. Radcliffe) Contemp. **40**: 105.
— strangely fulfilled. (R. A. Proctor) Belgra. **43**: 26. Same art. Ecl. M. **96**: 27.
— Stuff they are made of. Atlan. **46**: 402.
— Theory of. Hesp. **3**: 229.
— Visions, and Ecstasies. St. Paul's, **14**: 69. Same art. Ecl. M. **82**: 279.
— Warning. Chr. Obs. **41**: 405, 480.
Dream Children; a Reverie. (C. Lamb) Lond. M. **5**: 21.
Dream Fancy, Laws of. Cornh. **34**: 536. Same art. Liv. Age, **131**: 627. Same art. Ecl. M. **88**: 32.
Dream-Haunted. Chamb. J. **43**: 328.
Dream Interpretation, Art of. Dub. Univ. **76**: 427.
Dreamland. (E. Arnold) Fraser, **52**: 202.
— and Somnambulism. Chamb. J. **58**: 484.

Dreamland of Love. Lond. Soc. **31**: 50–507.
Dream Life, Thoughts touching. (A. K. H. Boyd) Fraser, **68**: 403. Same art. Ecl. M. **61**: 95.
Dream Lore. Lond. Soc. **30**: 343.
Dream Madonna. Irish Mo. **7**: 150.
Dream Music. (F. Boyle) Belgra. **36**: supp. 99.
Dream Painter, The. (J. E. Carpenter) Colburn, **147**: 92–655. **148**: 58–632.
Dream Revelations. Chamb. J. **3**: 314.
Dream Story; a Tale. (K. S. Macquoid) Temp. Bar, **42**: 177. Same art. Scrib. **7**: 612. Same art. Liv. Age, **123**: 173.
Dream Woman; a Mystery. (W. Collins) Temp. Bar, **42**: 547. **43**: 125.
Dreamer, Confessions of a. All the Year, **24**: 569.
Dreamer's Note-Book. Dub. Univ. **19**: 612, 763. **23**: 488. **24**: 40.
Dreamers and Workers. Month, **1**: 551.
Dreaming. Chamb. J. **2**: 113. — Westm. **2**: 123. — (F. W. Holland) Putnam, **15**: 238.
— and Sleep. (Sir W. Molesworth) Westm. **30**: 424. — (E. M. Smalley) Lakeside, **4**: 388.
— and Sleep-Walking. Chamb. J. **53**: 56. — Cath. World, **3**: 418.
— and Waking; a Story. (Mrs. C. A. Mason) Mo. Rel. M. **37**: 349, 433.
— Curiosities of. Sharpe, **32**: 267. Same art. Ecl. M. **52**: 123.
— in Italy; a Poem. Cornh. **6**: 513.
— Mysteries of. (A. B. Garrett) Hours at Home, **10**: 439.
— Notes on. Chamb. J. **56**: 682.
— Philosophy of. Westm. **30**: 424.
— Radestock on. (J. Sully) Mind, **4**: 588.
Dreary Court Sky; a Poem. (E. Cave) Cornh. **10**: 111.
Dred Scott Case. (N. Hale) Chr. Exam. **63**: 65. — (T. Farrar) No. Am. **85**: 392. — (T. D. Woolsey) New Eng. **15**: 345.
Dredging, A Day's. Once a Week, **6**: 466.
— Deep-Sea. (L. Agassiz) Am. Natural. **6**: 1. — (C. W. Thompson) Am. Natural. **7**: 406.
— — Apparatus employed on H. M. S. Porcupine, 1869. (W. L. Carpenter) Pop. Sci. R. **9**: 281.
— — by the Porcupine. (J. G. Jeffreys) Nature, **1**: 135, 166.
— — in the Gulf of St. Lawrence. (J. F. Whiteaves) Nature, **5**: 8.
— in the Gulf of Maine. (A. S. Packard, jr.) Am. Natural. **8**: 145.
— in Salcombe Bay. Chamb. J. **15**: 218. **16**: 74.
— Notes from the Challenger. (G. J. Allman) Nature, **12**: 555.
— on Ocean Bars. (Q. A. Gillmore) Ecl. Engin. **7**: 311.
— Results with Towing-Net, South Coast of Ireland. (Prof. Allman) Nature, **9**: 73.
— Shell. (E. S. Morse) Am. Natural. **3**: 269.
Dredging Expeditions. Nature, **5**: 343.
— off Spain and Portugal. (W. S. Kent) Nature, **4**: 456.
— on the Coast of New England. (A. E. Verrill) Am. J. Sci. **105**: 1, 98. **106**: 435. **107**: 38–498. **109**: 411. **110**: 36, 196.
Dredging-Ground, A. (E. Lawless) 19th Cent. **10**: 131.
Dredging-Machine. (D. S. Howard) J. Frankl. Inst. **87**: 239.
— Howard's, 1855. (J. W. Nystrom) J. Frankl. Inst. **60**: 1.
Dredging Operations in the Gulf of St. Lawrence. (J. F. Whiteaves) Am. J. Sci. **107**: 210.
See Deep-Sea Explorations; Soundings.
Dreepdaily Burghs, How I stood for. Blackw. **62**: 259.
Drei Eichen, Pilgrimage to Shrine at. (A. Seymour) Cath. World, **33**: 706.
Dresden and Saxony, Letters from, 1837. Tait, n. s. **4**: 389, 442.
— Reminiscence of. Temp. Bar, **53**: 545.
— Visit to. (H. Bedford) Month, **38**: 506.
Dresden China. (S Powers) Nation, **2**: 715.
— and its Manufactory at Meissen. Blackw. **122**: 62. Same art. Ecl. M. **89**: 370.
Dress. (L. Fountain) Putnam, **14**: 620. — Blackw. **3**: 301. **97**: 425. — Chamb. J. **37**: 395. — Godey, **20**: 187. — Lond. Soc. **2**: 37, 173. — (J. B. Atkinson) Good Words, **21**: 777. Same art. Appleton, **25**: 37.
— according to Statute. (F. W. Rowsell) Intel. Obs. **12**: 167.
— Æsthetics of. (R. G. White) Harper, **25**: 162. — (Mrs. Haweis) Art J. **32**: 97–205.
— — Bonnets. Blackw. **57**: 242.
— — Cut of a Coat. Blackw. **57**: 608.
— — Hats. Blackw. **57**: 51.
— — Military Costume. Blackw. **59**: 114.
— — Minor Matters. Blackw. **57**: 731. Same art. Liv. Age, **6**: 139.
— American. (M. Schele de Vere) Putnam, **15**: 385.
— and Address. Fraser, **20**: 189.
— and the Age. Once a Week, **9**: 427, 637.
— and Diet. No. Brit. **22**: 505.
— and Food 500 Years ago. All the Year, **4**: 185.
— and its Critics. (C. A. Bristed) Nation, **2**: 10.
— and its Eccentricities. Lond. Soc. **12**: 283. Same art. Ev. Sat. **4**: 369.
— and its Victims. (H. Martineau) Once a Week, **1**: 387.
— and Nature. (J. C. Draper) Galaxy, **9**: 626.
— and Women. (E. Benson) N. Ecl. **4**: 601.
— Art of. (P. Fitzgerald) Art J. **29**: 316, 345. **30**: 23, 58. — Quar. **79**: 372. Same art. Liv. Age, **13**: 337. — Ecl. M. **11**: 145. — Blackw. **27**: 185. — Godey, **54**: 538. **57**: 324. **60**: 230–515.
— as a Fine Art. (Mrs. Merrifield) Art J. **5**: 1–211.
— Bondage of. (L. E. Furniss) Appleton, **9**: 75.
— Clothes Mania. (J. Parton) Atlan. **23**: 531. — Victoria, **25**: 876.
— Common Sense in. Lond. Soc. **21**: 465.
— Curiosities of Fashion. Lond. Soc. **4**: 232.
— Daily Beauty. (R. G. White) Atlan. **4**: 397.
— Dandies, Fashion, etc. Fraser, **15**: 232.
— Development in. (G. H. Darwin) Macmil. **26**: 410. Same art. Liv. Age, **114**: 802. — Ecl. M. **79**: 610. Same art. Ev. Sat. **13**: 348.
— Etymology of Names of Fabrics. All the Year, **30**: 202.
— Exercise, and Sleep, Philosophy of. Lond. M. **23**: 561.
— External Appearance. Colburn, **6**: 381.
— Fashions of. (H. R. Cleveland) No. Am. **47**: 148. — Mo. R. **148**: 380.
— — How made. Ev. Sat. **5**: 175.
— Female. (J. Wilcox) Galaxy, **2**: 570. Same art. Ecl. M. **58**: 370. Same art. Liv. Age, **75**: 42, 71.
— — in 1450–1650. Lond. Soc. **22**: 405.
— — in 1857. Westm. **68**: 315.
— — Ornaments of. (F. Douce) Arch. **12**: 215.
— — Thoughtfulness in. Cornh. **18**: 281.
— Fig Leaves and French Dresses. (L. H. Hooper) Galaxy, **18**: 504.
— French. Canad. Mo. **4**: 438. — Ev. Sat. **13**: 242.
— Greek, for Women. Art J. **26**: 9.
— Hints to Ladies. (M. E. Haweis) St. Paul's, **12**: 42.
— How to dress for £15 a Year. All the Year, **30**: 199.
— in Paris. All the Year, **9**: 7.
— in relation to Health. (B. W. Richardson) Gent. M. n. s. **24**: 469. Same art. Pop. Sci. Mo. **17**: 182.
— Individuality in. Broadw. **6**: 286.
— Men and Coats. Fraser, **24**: 268.
— Modern. (C. R. Corson) Canad. Mo. **1**: 127. — Chamb. J. **58**: 117.

Dress, Natural History of. Cornh. **42**: 560. Same art. Ecl. M. **96**: 123.
— of Elizabethan Age. Blackw. **3**: 534.
— of Gentlemen. (C. Clarke) Temp. Bar, **22**: 63.
— of our Ancestors. Hogg, **8**: 173.
— of our Grandmothers. (F. M. Colby) Potter Am. Mo. **15**: 113.
— Peacockism in. (J. Hollingshead) Good Words, **2**: 198.
— Philosophy of. (W. N. Pendleton) So. Lit. Mess. **22**: 199. — Blackw. **53**: 230.
— Ruff and its Successors. Ev. Sat. **15**: 548.
— Science of. Godey, **56**: 22, 114, 235.
— Sensation in. (H. R. St. John) Victoria, **20**: 239.
— Sense and Fashion in. Bentley, **63**: 292.
— Talk on. (M. R. Oakey) Harper, **62**: 589.
— Taste of the Day. Fraser, **56**: 604.
— True Principles of. Godey, **54**: 325.
— Well-dressed. All the Year, **1**: 490.
— Worship of. N. Ecl. **4**: 190.
See Bloomerism; Clothing; Costume; Fashions.
Dresses, Dangerous. Once a Week, **11**: 719.
Dressed Grave; a Poem. Dub. Univ. **12**: 519.
Dresser's Process of Nature-Printing. Art J. **13**: 213.
Dresser, On the. Chamb. J. **47**: 359.
Dressmaker at Green Harbor. (S. H. Smith) Lippinc. **28**: 289.
Dressmakers. Good Words, **12**: 62, 143. Same art. Liv. Age, **108**: 485, 558.
— and Milliners. All the Year, **10**: 36.
Dressmaking, Lessons in. Eng. Dom. M. **25**: 142–245. **26**: 72.
Drew, Samuel. Hogg, **3**: 8. — Meth. M. **57**: 602. — Nat. M. **1**: 144.
Drift and Alluvium of Ohio and the West. (C. Whittlesey) Am. J. Sci. **55**: 205.
— Geology of. Lond. Q. **13**: 375.
— of the Western and Southern States. (E. W. Hilgard) Am. J. Sci. **92**: 343.
— Phenomena of. (E. Hitchcock) Am. J. Sci. **49**: 258.
Drift Deposits in the Northwest, U. S. (N. H. Winchell) Pop. Sci. Mo. **3**: 202–286.
Drift Ice and Currents of North Atlantic. (W. C. Redfield) Am. J. Sci. **48**: 373.
Drift Log on the Mississippi. Colburn, **87**: 254–485. **88**: 33–452.
Drift Phenomena of Labrador. (A. S. Packard, jr.) Am. J. Sci. **91**: 30.
— of Southwest Iowa. (C. A. White) Am. J. Sci. **93**: 301.
Drifting away; a Tale. All the Year, **32**: 220.
Driftings and Dreamings. Dub. Univ. **18**: 257.
Driftwood. Galaxy, **5**: 645, 782. **6**: 129–747. **7**: 130–904. **8**: 135–851. **9**: 129–845. **10**: 121–862. **11**: 133–877. **12**: 112–855. **13**: 122–837. **14**: 122–852. **15**: 125–483. **16**: 127–843. **17**: 122–840. **18**: 121–839. **19**: 122–843. **20**: 118–846. **21**: 126–843. **22**: 123–843. **23**: 125–842. **24**: 123–839.
Driftwood; a Poem. (G. P. Meade) Dub. Univ. **86**: 737.
Drill under Difficulties. Chamb. J. **37**: 375.
Drill, Diamond. (C. E. Ronaldson) J. Frankl. Inst. **98**: 352. — (Maj. Beaumont) Ecl. Engin. **12**: 44.
— Percussion Rock-. (R. Grimshaw) J. Frankl. Inst. **112**: 50.
Drilling-Machine, Portable Radial. Pract. M. **3**: 143.
— Universal. Pract. M. **1**: 167.
Drink. Bentley, **14**: 129.
— Our national. (B. H. Paul) Nature, **1**: 576.
— What we. All the Year, **35**: 77.
Drinks and Drinkers, French. Ev. Sat. **11**: 511.
— Artificial Cooling of. Penny M. **10**: 319.
— Strange. Chamb. J. **47**: 392.
Drink Difficulty. (Sir W. Lawson) 19th Cent. **5**: 405.
Drinking, In Vino Veritas. St. James, **22**: 551.
— Parton's Smoking and. N. Ecl. **4**: 365. — Ev. Sat. **7**: 669.
— Philosophy of. (A. H. Forrester) Bentley, **11**: 148.
— The Vice and the Disease. Quar. **139**: 396.
Drinking Customs in England. All the Year, **11**: 437.
Drinking Experiences. Fraser, **13**: 727. **14**: 273. — Internat. M. **4**: 621.
Drinking Fountains, Public. Art J. **12**: 113.
— — Iron. Art J. **13**: 25.
Drinking-Habit. (J. W. Palmer) Atlan. **25**: 159.
See Intemperance; Drunkenness; Alcoholism; etc.
Drinking Usages in America. (W. Chambers) Chamb. J. **23**: 42.
— of Great Britain and Ireland. Chr. Obs. **39**: 677.
Drinking Vessels, Ancient. Antiquary, **4**: 258, 284.
Drinkwater House. (Mrs. C. V. Hamilton) Harper, **57**: 49.
Driven overboard: a Tale. Chamb. J. **44**: 715.
Driven to and fro; a Story. (Mrs. L. J. Hall) Mo. Rel. M. **8**: 193–375.
Driven to Despair; a Story. (P. Pastnor) Western, **7**: 395.
Driver, Wanted a. Chamb. J. **43**: 529.
Driver Mike. All the Year, **1**: 374.
Driving-Bands, Experiments on Tension of. Pract. M. **1**: 106.
Droll Acquaintance; a Story. (C. D. Brewer) Galaxy, **16**: 835.
Drôme, Peasant Proprietors of the. Fraser, **70**: 529.
Drommel's Inconsistencies. (V. Cherbuliez) Appleton, **23**: 497. **24**: 1.
Drops. (A. M. Worthington) Nature, **16**: 165.
— and Bubbles. Chamb. J. **42**: 387.
— Liquid, Forms of. (A. M. Worthington) Pop. Sci. Mo. **11**: 544.
Drop-Hammer. Pract. M. **6**: 52.
Dropped in Haste; a Sketch. Dub. Univ. **87**: 675.
Dropping an Acquaintance. Chamb. J. **29**: 305.
Dropsies, Blackall on. (T. Young) Quar. **9**: 466.
Drought, and its Lessons. Chamb. J. **32**: 104.
— at Gaza. Fraser, **54**: 244.
— Great, 1844. Blackw. **56**: 433.
— Proposed Remedy for. Ev. Sat. **9**: 470.
Drouyn de Lhuys, Edouard. Ev. Sat. **2**: 189.
Drover's Carpet-Bag. (C. Dartmoor) Am. Whig R. **10**: 125.
Drovers, Sketches of. Penny M. **12**: 356.
Drowne, Solomon, Biography of. Am. Q. Reg. **11**: 357.
— Fourth of July Oration, 1800. Hist. M. **17**: 228.
Drowned at Sea. Cornh. **3**: 341.
Drowned Persons, How to recover. Chamb. J. **7**: 383.
— Treatment of. Mo. Rel. M. **36**: 269.
Drowning, How to prevent. (H. MacCormac) Nature, **24**: 62. Same art. Pop. Sci. Mo. **19**: 369.
— Instructions in Case of. Chamb. J. **41**: 495.
— Question of Pain in. (R. S. Tracy) Pop. Sci. Mo. **13**: 93.
Drowning the Miller; an Ulster Tale. Lond. M. **21**: 161.
Drugs, Adulteration of. Westm. **91**: 185.
— and Medicines, Importation of. Hunt, **19**: 326.
— as an Indulgence. (J. T. Crane) Meth. Q. **18**: 551. **19**: 188.
— History of. (H. Yule) Geog. M. **2**: 81.
Druids, The. Ed. R. **4**: 391. — (S. L. Knapp) Knick. **2**: 90. — Meth. M. **36**: 304.
— and Druidical Remains. Hogg, **3**: 366.
— and their Religion. Dub. Univ. **76**: 38.
— Bardism of. (A. Vardd) Internat. R. **3**: 161.
— Bards and. Ed. R. **118**: 40.
— Celtic. (E. I. Sears) Nat. Q. **11**: 1.—So. R. **3**: 207. **4**: 1.
— in Wales. Cong. M. **28**: 165, 558, 712.
— Religion of. (E. Ledwich) Arch. **7**: 303.
Druid Stones near Shap. Penny M. **9**: 91.
Druidical Remains. Penny M. **9**: 301–324.

Druidical Remains at Halifax. (J. Watson) Arch. 2: 353.
— at Stanton Drew. Penny M. 5: 115.
— in Cumberland. (H. Rooke) Arch. 10: 105.
— in Derbyshire. (H. Rooke) Arch. 6: 110. 7: 175. 12: 41. — (S. Pegge) Arch 7: 19.
— in Guernsey. (J. Gosselin) Arch. 17: 254.
— on Harborough Rocks. (H. Rooke) Arch. 9: 206.
— on Stanton Moor. (S. Pegge) Arch. 8: 58.
See Stone Monuments.
Druidical Temple discovered in Jersey. (W. Molesworth and H. S. Conway) Arch. 8: 384, 386.
Druidism. (A. Clive) Dub. Univ. 86: 513. — (E. D. Morris) Bib. Sac. 11: 456. — (G. Smith) Ex. H. Lec. 2: 53. — (M. F. Tupper) Sharpe, 9: 156. Same art. Ecl. M. 17: 320. — (J. J. Jarves) Galaxy, 10: 777.
Drum Weirs on the Marne River. (W. Watson) Ecl. Engin. 17: 253.
Drumkelin Bog, Ireland, House dug out of. (W. Mudge) Arch. 26: 361.
Drummer Ghost. (J. W. De Forest) Atlan. 24: 1.
Drummers and Fifers. Chamb. J. 53: 628.
Drummond, D. T. K., Withdrawal from the Episcopal Church. Chr. Rem. 5: 295. 6: 94.
Drummond, Henry. Lond. Q. 15: 255.
Drummond, Thomas, Memoirs of. Ed. R. 126: 524.
— Irish Domiciliary Circular. Dub. Univ. 10: 459.
Drummond, Sir William. Academical Questions. (F. Jeffrey) Ed. R. 7: 163.
Drummond, Sir William, of Hawthornden. Ecl. M. 25: 511. — (E. Bowles) Month, 21: 184. — Penny M. 10: 169. — Liv. Age, 122: 259.
— Odin; a Poem. Ecl. R. 26: 77.
— Poetry of. Lond. M. 22: 476. — Retros. 9: 351. — Mo. R. 88: 33.
Drunk in the Streets. (A. Clerc) Liv. Age, 146: 143.
Drunkard, Confessions of a. (C. Lamb) Lond. M. 6: 117. Same art. Mus. 1: 134.
Drunkard's Bible; a Tale. (Mrs. S. C. Hall) Chamb. J. 21: 369. Same art. Ecl. M. 32 523.
Drunkard's Dream. Dub. Univ. 12: 151.
Drunkard's Wife. (E. Burritt) So. Lit. Mess. 7: 577.
Drunkards, Control and Cure of. (G. R. Wynne) Chr. Obs. 77: 621.
— Rational Treatment of. Macmil. 22: 309.
Drunkenness. (W. Chambers) Chamb. J. 51: 465. — (J. T. Watkins) Overland, 1: 146.
— Anatomy of. So. R. 5: 226. — Blackw. 23: 481. — Mus. 13: 97.
— and Legislation. (C. Beard) Theo. R. 9: 273.
— Can an Inebriate conquer himself? (F. H. Norton) Putnam, 16: 163.
— How to stop. No. Brit. 22: 455.
— in England, and its Remedies. Brit. Q. 64: 98.
— in Scotland. Tait, n. s. 17: 547.
— not curable by Legislation. Westm. 64: 463.
— Philosophy of. (G. Raymond) Bentley, 14: 34.
— Tree of Knowledge. (C. Kingsley) Good Words, 15: 90.
See Alcohol; Intemperance.
Drury, Henry. Arundines Cami. Chr. Rem. 6: 308.
Drury Lane, In and about. Temp. Bar, 16: 540.
Drury Lane Theater: Baddeley's Annual Feast. Temp. Bar, 13: 443.
Drury's Bluff, Battle of. (G. T. Beauregard) Land We Love, 3: 1. — So. M. 10: 288.
Druse Religion, Churchill's Account of. Ecl. R. 98: 444.
Druses. (E. Napier) Sharpe, 17: 141, 201. — (J. A. Alexander) Princ. 1: 210. — Penny M. 9: 97, 106.
— Among. Blackw. 126: 257. Same art. Liv. Age, 143: 288.
— and Assassins. (A. G. Laurie) Univ. Q. 30: 350, 410.
Druses and the Maronites. (W. H. Thomson) New Eng. 19: 32. — Cornh. 2: 370. — Dub. R. 18: 43.
— and their Religion. (C. H. Brigham) No. Am. 81: 69. — Dub. R. 38: 120.
— Creed of, and its Sources. For. Q. 29: 92, 168.
— of Mount Lebanon. (C. H. Brigham) Chr. Exam. 58: 362. — (M. L. Meason) Once a Week, 3: 119. (E. Robinson) Bib. Sac. 1843: 205. — Fraser, 64: 366. — Temp. Bar, 11: 580.
— Story of Caliph Hakem. Ecl. R. 112: 419.
— Visit to. Putnam, 6: 613.
Dry-Earth System of Deodorization. Ecl. Engin. 11: 218.
Dry Rot. (Sir J. Barrow) Quar. 30: 216.
— in Ships, Causes of. (J. Barron) J. Frankl. Inst. 5: 407.
— in Timber. (G. Gibbs) Am. J. Sci. 2: 114. — (P. Rainey) Am. J. Sci. 34: 169. — Westm. 10: 414. — Pamph. 16: 355. — Quar. 12: 227. 30: 216. — Mo. R. 86: 361. 95: 387.
— Kyan's Patent. (Sir J. Barrow) Quar. 49: 125.
— McWilliam on. Ecl. R. 28: 71.
— Nature and Cure of. Chr. Obs. 1: 165. — J. Frankl. Inst. 8: 376. 16: 346. 17: 422. 20: 208.
Dry Sticks. All the Year, 18: 496.
Dry Tortugas. (J. B. Holden) Harper, 37: 260.
— Thirty Months in. Galaxy, 7: 282.
Dry Well; a Tale. Chamb. J. 41: 561, 578.
Dryden, John. (J. A. Heraud) Temp. Bar, 7: 77. — (T. B. Macaulay) Ed. R. 47: 1. — (J. Wilson) Blackw. 57: 133, 503. — Victoria, 26: 313-393.
— and Corneille. Fraser, 66: 383.
— and Purcell, Dialogue between. Fraser, 45: 196.
— and his Times, 1630-1700. Westm. 63: 336. Same art. Liv. Age, 45: 432.
— and Literature of the Restoration. (D. Masson) Brit. Q. 20: 1. Same art. Ecl. M. 32: 537.
— and Pope. (J. Wilson) Blackw. 57: 369. — Blackw. 2: 679.
— and the Restoration. Once a Week, 21: 347-409.
— as a Dramatist. Temp. Bar, 59: 163.
— Bell's Edition of. Colburn, 100: 244.
— Character and Writings of. Ecl. R. 101: 71.
— Dramatic Works of. Dub. Univ. 89: 658. — (H. Southern) Retros. 1: 112.
— Genius of. (J. R. Lowell) No. Am. 107: 186. — Ed. R. 102: 1.
— Life and Times of. Ecl. R. 75: 47.
— — and Works of. Fraser, 50: 157. — Quar. 146: 289. — Liv. Age, 139: 579.
— on Chaucer. (J. Wilson) Blackw. 57: 617, 771.
— Poetical Works. Mus. 13: 162.
— Prose Works. (C. Barker) Retros. 4: 55.
— Relic of. (A. C. Swinburne) Gent. M. n. s. 25: 416.
— Saintsbury on. (W. C. Brownell) Nation, 32: 337.
— Scott's Edition. (H. Hallam) Ed. R. 13: 116. — Anal. M. 2: 148.
— a Vindication. (J. Skelton) Fraser, 72: 160.
Drying of Earth. (J. D. Whitney) Am. Natural. 10: 513.
Drying Process. Chamb. J. 15: 332.
Dualism and Optimism. (F. H. Hedge) Unita. R. 6: 581.
— in Moral Theology, Plea for. (E. Myers) Theo. R. 11: 179.
— Materialism, or Idealism? (F. Bowen) Princ. n. s. 1: 423.
Duane Papers. Hist. M. 14: 60.
Du Bartas, G. de Salluste, Sylvester's. Fraser, 58: 480.
Dublin. (R. Wynford) Lippinc. 11: 54. — Lond. Soc. 26: 521.
— a Poem. Dub. Univ. 34: 102.
— All Hallow's Priory. (O. J. Burke) Dub. Univ. 81: 547, 661.
— and its Corporation. Ecl. R. 86: 328.
— Art in. Irish Q. 3: 791.

Dublin at Bar of House of Lords. Dub. Univ. 16: 108.
— Book Auctions in. Dub. Univ. 71: 280.
— Castle of. All the Year, 15: 462, 495. 49: 259, 515. 50: 105–610. 51: 248.
— City Constituency of. Dub. Univ. 8: 471.
— City Election. Fraser, 4: 241.
— — 1835. Dub. Univ. 5: 237.
— College Life in. Tait, n. s. 11: 20.
— D'Alton on County and Archbishops of. Mo. R. 147: 17.
— Exhibition of 1853. Irish Q. 3: 785. — Dub. Univ. 41: 655. — Chamb. J. 19: 369, 409.
— — of 1861. Dub. Univ. 58: 1.
— — of 1865. (F. P. Cobbe) Fraser, 72: 403.
— — — Fine Arts in. (J. H. Pollen) Month, 3: 186.
— — — Sculpture in. Temp. Bar, 15: 51.
— German in. Bentley, 54: 95.
— History of, Gilbert's. Colburn, 120: 75. — Dub. R. 47: 1. — Dub. Univ. 47: 320. 54: 370.
— Hospital Reports of. Mo. R. 97: 287.
— Hospitals of. Irish Q. 4: 635, 1161.
— in the 18th Century. Dub. Univ. 85: 447, 703.
— in 1822. Colburn, 4: 503.
— Independence of. Dub. Univ. 7: 712.
— Kevin Street College. Dub. Univ. 3: 695.
— Life and Manners in. (T. De Quincey) Tait, n. s. 1: 196.
— — in, in the last Century. All the Year, 30: 155.
— Lounge in. All the Year, 14: 516.
— Mayor's Nest. Fraser, 24: 735.
— Newspapers of, in 18th Century. (P. Kennedy) Dub. Univ. 80: 121, 241.
— ninety Years ago. Irish Mo. 7: 474.
— Old, Lady Morgan's. Colburn, 14: 57.
— Penny Journal. Dub. Univ. 15: 112.
— Political Satire and Satirists of, forty Years ago. Gent. M. n. s. 13: 685. 14: 202.
— Royal Society of, Account of. Dub. R. 2: 226.
— Sackville Street. (G. A. Sala) Belgra. 1: 435.
— St. Martha's Home for Girls. (Mrs. C. Martin) Irish Mo. 9: 57.
— St. Patrick's Cathedral. Penny M. 3: 129.
— Season of 1876. (N. Robinson) Belgra. 29: 182.
— Society of. Dub. Univ. 63: 3.
— — in 1850. (C. P. Mulvany) Canad. Mo. 17: 376.
— Stage in, The old. (R. B. Baker) Belgra. 39: 304.
— — Theater Royal, 1830–51. (J. W. Calcraft) Dub. Univ. 73: 93–428.
— State of Parties in, 1823. Colburn, 6: 553.
— Stock Exchange of. Bank. M. (L.) 10: 37.
— Streets of. Irish Q. 2: 1–701. 3: 17–937.
— Trinity College. (M. Cullinan) Fortn. 14: 429. — (J. P. Mahaffy) Fortn. 14: 703. — (J. P Mahaffy) Macmil. 20: 463. — Dub. R. 4: 281. — Dub. Univ. 51: 623, 752. 52: 106, 228.
— — Celibacy Statute. Dub. Univ. 15: 355.
— — Experimental and Nat. Sciences in. Nature, 3: 361.
— University of. (J. H. MacMahon) Dub. Univ. 87: 444. — Blackw. 26: 153. — Dub. Univ. 7: 342.
— — and Queen Elizabeth. Dub. Univ. 3: 1.
— — and Trinity College. Am. J. Educ. 26: 738.
— — Calendar of. Dub. Univ. 1: 105.
— — Choral Society of. Dub. Univ. 86: 257.
— — Commission of, 1851–53. Dub. Univ. 42: 115.
— — History of, from 1591. (O. J. Burke) Dub. Univ. 82: 51–698.
— — Law School in. Dub. Univ. 1: 93.
— — Reform in. Dub. Univ. 3: 81, 600. — Dub. R. 23: 228.
— What is doing for the People in. (J. Haughton) Peop. J. 2: 232.
Dublin May Morning. All the Year, 13: 421. Same art. Cath. World, 1: 825.
Dublin Review and Dr. Murray. Dub. Univ. 8: 495.
Dublin University Magazine, Past and Future of. Dub. Univ. 41: 1.
Dubois, Edward, Gossip about. Colburn, 81: 83.
Dubois, John. (J. McCaffrey) U. S. Cath. M. 2: 278, 357.
Dubois-Reymond, E., Sketch of. Pop. Sci. Mo. 13: 360.
Du Bosc, P., Memoir of. Cong. M. 6: 617, 673.
Duc, Joseph Louis. Am. Arch. 5: 49.
Duc de l'Omelette. Bentley, 8: 352.
Ducas, T., Travels of. Quar. 28: 365.
Ducatel, Julius T., Obituary of. Am. J. Sci. 58: 146.
Du Chaillu, Paul, and his Detractors. Liv. Age, 70: 473.
— Facts about. (W. W. Reade) Galaxy, 3: 853.
— Travels in Africa. *See* Africa.
Duché, Jacob. (E. D. Neill) Pennsyl. M. 2: 58. — Am. Hist. Rec. 3: 97.
Duchesne, Mme., Réligieuse. (B. Murphy) Cath. World. 28: 685.
Duchesne Estate. (J. W. De Forest) Galaxy, 7: 823.
Duchesnois, Catherine Josephine. (C. Hervey) Temp. Bar, 62: 253.
Duchess of Rosemary Lane. (B. L. Farjeon) Tinsley, 18: 1–633. 19: 1–679.
Duchess Pepitu; a Miniature Drama. (R. Mulholland) Irish Mo. 9: 1, 62.
Duchess's Pocket-Handkerchief. (C. A. Bristed) Knick. 45: 1.
Ducie of the Dale; a Poem. (A. J. Munley) Once a Week, 8: 475.
Ducks and Geese. Once a Week, 20: 404.
— — My. Chamb. J. 49: 747.
— Canvas-Back. Penny M. 8: 403.
— Eider. All the Year, 20: 162.
— Wild. Penny M. 4: 49, 60. — Chamb. J. 26: 337. Same art. Liv. Age, 52: 150.
Duck-Hunting. (W. G. Beers) Canad. Mo. 5: 34.
Duck-Shooting. (W. M. Laffan) Scrib. 15: 1.
— on the Chesapeake. Chamb. J. 20: 138.
Ducking-Stools. (L. Jewitt) Reliquary, 1: 145. — Am. Hist. Rec. 1: 204.
Duckweeds, Winter State of. (T. D. Biscoe) Am. Natural. 7: 257.
Ducornet, L. C. J. Nat. M. 11: 307.
Ducrow, Andrew. All the Year, 27: 223.
Duddon River, Scenery of. Penny M. 12: 236, 268, 316.
Dudevant, Mad. A. L. A. D. (M. Arnold) Fortn. 27: 767. Same art. Ecl. M. 89: 225. Same art. Liv. Age, 134: 195. — Quar. 143: 423. — (K. Hillard) Lippinc. 9: 451. — (R. Davey) Lippinc. 18: 244, 372. — (J. W. Howe) Atlan. 8: 513. — (L. Katscher) Internat. R. 7: 39, 125. — (J. McCarthy) Galaxy, 9: 661. — (H. James, jr.) Galaxy, 24: 45. — (M. F. Miller) Nat. Q. 37: 254. — (F. W. H. Myers) 19th Cent. 1: 221. — (T. S. Perry) Atlan. 38: 444. — Belgra. 5: 156. — Internat. M. 1: 65. — Lond. Soc. 21: 147. Same art. Ecl. M. 78: 465. — Irish Q. 8: 54, 389. — Nat. R. 6: 37. Same art. Liv. Age, 56: 513. — Liv. Age, 77: 131. — Nat. M. 2: 217. — Blackw. 121: 70. — Bent. Q. 2: 369. — Sharpe, 52: 15. — with portrait, Howitt, 1: 128. — with portrait, Peop. J. 3: 131.
— Ancestors of. Westm. 63: 598.
— and the Empress Eugénie. Ev. Sat. 9: 257.
— and George Eliot. Ecl. M. 88: 111.
— and her Works. (E. Benson) Galaxy, 3: 240, 618.
— at Home. Appleton, 16: 543.
— Césarine Dietrich. Dub. Univ. 79: 550.
— Characteristics of. Dub. Univ. 88: 368.
— Consuelo. Blackw. 116: 72.
— — and Virginia. Tait, n. s. 23: 216.
— Elle et lui. Dub. Univ. 53: 664.
— Genius of. Bentley, 27: 506.
— Gabriel. Mo. R. 152: 190.

Dudevant, Mad. A. L. A. D. Histoire de ma Vie. Dub. Univ. 63: 495.—Liv. Age, 47: 382.—(A. de Valvèdre) St. James, 38: 465, 587.
— La Daniella. Liv. Age, 55: 574.
— Life of. Dub. Univ. 61: 217.
— Malgrétout. Broadw. 6: 479.
— Memoirs of. (G. Ripley) Putnam, 9: 175, 598.—Victoria, 27: 343.
— Monograph of. (J. F. Molloy) Tinsley, 29: 530.
— My private Grief against. (C. A. Bristed) Galaxy, 17: 467.
— Novels of. (F. Bowen) No. Am. 37: 156.—(F. D. Hedge) Chr. Exam. 42: 201.—Fraser, 37: 156.—For. Q. 14: 271. 30: 414. 37: 21.—Westm. 38: 487.—Blackw. 64: 580.—Select J. 3: [72.—For. Q. 14: 271. 30: 414. 37: 21.
— on Prince Talleyrand. Dub. Univ. 52: 625. Same art. Liv. Age, 60: 38.
— Spiridion. Mo. R. 159: 351.
Dudley, John. Metamorphosis of Sona; a Poem. (J. Foster) Ecl. R. 13: 432.
Dudley, John W. W. Letters to Bishop of Llandaff. (J. W. Croker) Quar. 67: 79.—Mus. 41: 512.—Mo. R. 151: 486.
Dudley, Joseph. Am. Q. Reg. 15: 302.
Dudley, Paul, Diary of. N. E. Reg. 35: 28.
Dudley, Robert, Earl of. Select J. 2: [274.
— Amy Robsart and Queen Elizabeth. Fraser, 63: 659. Same art. Liv. Age, 70: 50, 659.
Dudley, Thomas. Am. Q. Reg. 15: 298.
— Catalogue of his Library, 1653. N. E. Reg. 12: 355.
Dudley Genealogy. (W. Cogswell) N. E. Reg. 1: 71.—(D. Dudley) N. E. Reg. 10: 130, 337.
Dudley, Mass., Ministers of. Am. Q. 10: 55.
Dudley Castle, Caverns, and Nailers of. Penny M. 12: 83.
Dudley Gallery, London. Victoria, 11: 70.
Dudley Observatory, Albany, N. Y. Am. J. Educ. 2: 593.
— Meridian Instruments of. (B. A. Gould) Am. J. Sci. 73: 404.
Duel, The: a Tale. So. Lit. Mess. 1: 641.
— Comedy of. Appleton, 25: 521.
— How to avoid a. Blackw. 43: 371.
— in the Dark. Chamb. J. 44: 807.
— in Herne Wood. (W. Collins) Belgra. 34: 304.
— My first. Belgra. 17: 481.
— of D'Esterre and O'Connell. Bentley, 33: 538. Same art. Ecl. M. 29: 392.
— on Boston Common. (A. Young) Overland, 13: 330.
— Remarkable, in 1664. Penny M. 5: 31.
Duels. Chamb. J. 45: 630.
— French. All the Year, 9: 189.—Scrib. 11: 546.
— German University. (J. Hawthorne) Galaxy, 16: 405.
— Instances of. (J. Gordon) Overland, 9: 251.
— Judicial, in Germany. (R. L. Pearsall) Arch. 29: 348.
— Two. Chamb. J. 11: 185.
Dueling. (T. De Quincey) Tait, n. s. 8: 97.—(Capt. Medwin) Bentley, 2: 76.—(J. J. Reed) Lippinc. 4: 540.—(T. B. Thorpe) Harper, 37: 401.—(P. H. Cruse) No. Am. 26: 498.—Fraser, 21: 594.—Dem. R. 11: 311, 413. 29: 547.—Chr. Q. Spec. 10: 353.—(W. S. Plumer) Princ. 20: 542.—Knick. 37: 402.—Ed. R. 75: 422.—Mus. 35: 18.—Pamph. 12: 79.—Am. Q. 22: 1.—All the Year, 7: 212. 20: 469, 500.—Am. Mo. M. 11: 331.—Am. Presb. R. 5: 407.—Cong. M. 5: 460.—Dem. R. 36: 116.——Ecl. R. 36: 170.—Ev. Sat. 6: 618, 661. 9: 235.—Liv. Age, 37: 39.—Portfo.(Den.) 28: 60.—West. Mo. R. 1: 453.
— Anecdotes of. Bentley, 30: 137, 255, 353.—Ecl. M. 24: 53, 233, 407.—Knick. 62: 525.
— Beauvoir on. Bentley, 57: 183.
Dueling, British Code of. Lond. M. 11: 198.—Portfo. (Den.) 33: 239, 431.—Westm. 4: 20.—Mus. 7: 317.—Chamb. J. 44: 305.
— Code of Honor. (H. Alger) Harper, 15: 516.
— Common Law on. West. Law J. 4: 433.
— Droll Side of. Chamb. J. 56: 763.
— Dunlop's Anti-Duel. Chr. Obs. 43: 564.—Mo. R. 161: 169.
— French, Curiosities of. Chamb. J. 44: 529. Same art. Ev. Sat. 4: 336.
— — Extraordinary. House. Words, 18: 97.
— German. (T. C. Grattan) Colburn, 40: 470.
— in America. Liv. Age, 15: 467.
— in the 18th Century. (A. Andrews) Colburn, 103: 465.
— in England. Liv. Age, 28: 545.—House. Words, 15: 596, 614.
— in France and the United States. Tait, n. s. 18: 151.
— in Ireland, Reminiscences of. Ev. Sat. 16: 288.
— in olden Times. Colburn, 122: 476.
— in modern Times. Colburn, 123: 116. Same art. Ecl. M. 54: 376.
— in the West Indies. (J. C. Cremony) Overland, 1: 496.
— Laws of. Ev. Sat. 17: 383.—Fraser, 71: 316. Same art. Liv. Age, 85: 17.
— Millingen on. Ed. R. 76: 422.—Mo. R. 155: 72.
— Philosophy of the Pistol. Putnam, 10: 254.
— Reminiscences of, in Ireland. (M. Corr) Macmil. 29: 304.
— Trial by Battle. Cornh. 22: 715. Same art. Ecl. M. 76: 168.
— two hundred and fifty Years ago. (T. Carlyle) Internat. M. 3: 108.
Dueling Ground at Bladensburg, Md. (F. A. Foster) Harper, 16: 471.
Duelist, The. Tait, 3: 355.—Mus. 14: 59.
Duelist's Vow; a Tale. Liv. Age, 4: 178.
Duelists, The. Blackw. 24: 541.
Duer, Col. William. Knick. 40: 95.
Duerer, Albrecht. (S. Colvin) Portfo. 8: 2-182.—(A. H. Guernsey) Harper, 40: 812.—(M. J. Preston) N. Ecl. 7: 427.—Art J. 3: 141, 193.—Blackw. 107: 628.—For. Q. 11: 73.—Select J. 2: [37.—Lond. Q. 34: 328. Same art. Liv. Age, 107: 259.—(J. G. MacLeod) Month, 35: 209.—Nat. M. 3: 385.—Penny M. 2: 118.—Portfo. 1: 111.—Quar. 148: 376.—So. R. n. s. 19: 101.
— and the "Fairford Windows." (T. Taylor) Gent. M. n. s. 1: 593.
— at his Easel. (C. Pebody) Gent. M. n. s. 21: 171.
— and early Engraving. Colburn, 128: 217.
— Drawings by, in the British Museum. (J. W. C. Carr) Portfo. 6: 92.—(C. M. Hewins) O. & N. 10: 639.
— English Lives of. (R. Sturgis) Nation, 10: 92.
— Letters and Journal of. Victoria, 14: 385.
— Life and Works of. Mo. Rel. M. 19: 297.
— Literary Remains of. (C. Dempster) Ed. R. 114: 39.
— Manuscripts of. (W. Bell) Art J. 13: 106.
— Married Life of. Howitt, 3: 378.
— — Schefer's. Prosp. R. 5: 280.
— Notes on. (S. Colvin) Fortn. 13: 333.
— Private Life of. (J. G. MacLeod) Month, 34: 433.
— Sketch of. Hogg, 9: 401.
— Works of. (F. W. Fairholt) Art J. 7: 1-122.
Duerrnberg, Salt Mountain of. Liv. Age, 37: 188.
Duesseldorf, Academy of. Hours at Home, 1: 300.—Art J. 7: 13. 32: 65, 304.
Dufame, J. A. S. Ev. Sat. 13: 626.
Duff, Alexander, with portrait. Hogg, 8: 369.—Lond. Q. 54: 93.
— Educational Work of, in Southern India. (G. Smith) Good Words, 19: 307.

Duff, M. E. Grant, with portrait. Colburn, **165**: 1205, 1258.
Duffers. All the Year, **13**: 538.
Dufferin, Fred. Temple Blackwood, Lord, with portrait. Ecl. M. **83**: 244. — with portrait, Dub. Univ. **86**: 142.
— on Ireland. Dub. Univ. **68**: 116.
— Yacht Voyage of, to Arctic Seas. Dub. Univ. **50**: 723. — Lond. Q. **9**: 174. Same art. Ecl. M. **43**: 33.
Duffy, James, Life of. Am. Bibliop. **3**: 437.
Dugong, The, Notes on. Gent. M. n. s. **27**: 738.
Duitsch, S., Conversion of. Meth. M. **27**: 385.
Du Jardin, Karel. (R. N. Wornum) Portfo. **8**: 133. — Art J. **4**: 209, 241.
Duke of Kent's Lodge. (T. C. Haliburton) Bentley, **8**: 386.
Duke and the Duchess; a Story. (D. Cook) Belgra. **45**: supp. 38.
Duke's Agent. House. Words, **4**: 498.
Duke's Answer. (E. D. Hervey) Lond. Soc. **11**: 173.
Duke's Children; a Tale. (A. Trollope) All the Year, **43**: 361-529. **44**: 1-553. **45**: 1-241.
Duke's Dilemma; a Chronicle of Niesenstein. Blackw. **74**: 325. Same art. Ecl. M. **30**: 397.
Duke's House; a Sketch. (M. Deane) Dub. Univ. **82**: 641.
Duke's Piper; a Tale. Chamb. J. **54**: 376, 392, 410. Same art. Liv. Age, **134**: 411.
Duke's Stratagem; a Poem. (J. G. Saxe) Scrib. **7**: 331.
Dukes, Ignoble. All the Year, **5**: 211.
Dukeries, Among the. All the Year, **41**: 84.
Duke's County, Mass., Court Papers. N. E. Reg. **11**: 242.
— Ministers of. (A. Gannett) Am. Q. Reg. **15**: 492.
Dukesborough Tales, by Philemon Perch. (R. M. Johnson) N. Ecl. **5**: 560, 652. **6**: 12-689. **7**: 39, 415. — So. M. **8**: 565, 701. **9**: 32. **10**: 183-664. **11**: 1, 129.
Dukrah the Dwarf. (W. Hauff) Lakeside, **7**: 233.
Dulany, Daniel. (J. H. B. Latrobe) Pennsyl. M. **3**: 1.
Dulce Domum. (M. E. C. Walcott) Once a Week, **7**: 105.
Dulcie's Delusions. Chamb. J. **48**: 545-622.
Dulcimer; a Story. Colburn, **153**: 515, 639.
Dulcissima! Dilectissima. (R. Ferguson) Liv. Age, **136**: 445.
Dull Boys, Plea for. Fraser, **103**: 123.
Dull People. Am. Mo. M. **12**: 333.
Dullness, Dignity of. (A. K. H. Boyd) Fraser, **61**: 648. Same art. Liv. Age, **66**: 335.
Dulwich College. Colburn, **6**: 67. — Fraser, **87**: 109. — St. James, **27**: 797.
— Proposed Changes in Constitution. Chr. Rem. **31**: 84.
— Story of a Foundation. (J. Goodall) Macmil. **17**: 61. **18**: 130.
Dulwich Picture Gallery. Bentley, **30**: 344. — Chamb. J. **5**: 413. — Penny M. **10**: 137-289.
Duluth, Minn., Week at. (J. T. Trowbridge) Atlan. **25**: 605.
Dum spiro, spero; a Poem. Cath. World, **2**: 159.
Dumaresq, James. (J. H. Sheppard) N. E. Reg. **17**: 320.
Dumaresq Genealogy. (A. T. Perkins) N. E. Reg. **17**: 317.
Dumas, Alexandre. (J.E. Cooke) Appleton, **6**: 577. — (W. H. Pollock) 19th Cent. **8**: 653. Same art. Appleton, **24**: 514. — (A. Hayward) Quar. **131**: 189. — (F. R. Marvin) Western, **2**: 409. — Ev. Sat. **9**: 781. — with portrait, Ev. Sat. **10**: 73, 83. — (G. Saintsbury) Fortn. **30**: 527. — (A. P. Southwick) Galaxy, **10**: 691. — with portrait, Ecl. M. **32**: 417. — Argosy, **27**: 445. — Blackw. **114**: 111. Same art. Ecl. M. **81**: 407. — Chamb. J. **25**: 321 Same art. Ecl. M. **38**: 491. Same art. Liv. Age, **50**: 87. — Chamb. J **27**: 298. Same art. Liv. Age, **55**: 374. — Chamb. J. **50**: 133. — Ev. Sat. **15**: 157. — Galaxy, **20**: 29. — Lond. Soc. **20**: 453. Same art. Ecl. M. **78**: 97. — Tait, n. s. **23**: 99, 152. Same art. Ecl. M. **37**: 537. **38**: 60.
Dumas, Alexandre, and Goethe. (H. James, jr.) Nation, **17**: 292.
— and his Mousquetaire Paper. Hogg, **13**: 35. Same art. Ecl. M. **34**: 349.
— and his Pets. Colburn, **114**: 337.
— and his Scotch Pointer. Bentley, **63**: 273.
— and Auguste Maquet. Ev. Sat. **10**: 214.
— Anecdotes of. Dub. Univ. **72**: 603. Same art. Ecl. M. **72**: 284.
— as a Hero. (H. Ayrault) Potter Am. Mo. **17**: 309.
— Autobiography of. Bentley, **32**: 471. Same art. Ecl. M. **28**: 99. Same art. Liv. Age, **35**: 587. — Colburn, **95**: 66. — Select J. **4**: 58.
— Breakfast with. (J. Bigelow) Scrib. **1**: 597.
— Cookery of. All the Year, **29**: 488.
— Count of Monte Cristo. Irish Q. **5**: 301. — Ecl. M. **39**: 33.
— Crimes Célèbres. For. Q. **30**: 36.
— Dashing Exploit of, 1830. All the Year, **28**: 544.
— Death of. Ev. Sat. **10**: 18.
— Dramas of. (J. B. Matthews) Atlan. **48**: 383.
— Dramatic Genius of. Knick. **3**: 199.
— Entr'Actes. (A. Laugel) Nation, **27**: 237, 282.
— Histoire de mes Bêtes. Dub. Univ. **71**: 205. Same art. Ecl. M. **70**: 412.
— in his Curricle. Blackw. **55**: 347.
— in Italy. Blackw. **53**: 551.
— in St. Petersburg. Bentley, **45**: 317.
— Memoirs of. Irish Q. **3**: 193, 833.
— Le Meneur de Loups. Bentley, **41**: 483, 604.
— Modern Republican Tragedy. Fraser, **39**: 188.
— Les Morts vont vite. Bentley, **51**: 283.
— Novel-Factory of. Appleton, **15**: 813.
— on the Rhine. For. Q. **30**: 105. — Ecl. M. **1**: 90.
— Paris to Cadiz. Westm. **48**: 210.
— Plagiarisms of. (W. Sargent) No. Am. **78**: 305. Irish Q. **8**: 54. — Ev. Sat. **11**: 294.
— Reminiscence of. (B. Phillips) Galaxy, **12**: 503.
— A Supper with. Bentley, **52**: 523.
— Theatrical Experiences of. Dub. Univ. **77**: 241.
— Three Guardsmen. Blackw. **57**: 59.
— Thrush Hunting. Blackw. **55**: 150.
— Traveling Impressions. For. Q. **14**: 119.
— Un Père prodigue. Bentley, **47**: 29.
— Way of Working of. (J. E. Cooke) Appleton, **11**: 554. — So. Lit. Mess. **27**: 303.
— Writings of. (F. Bowen) No. Am. **56**: 109. — Brit. Q. **7**: 181.
Dumas, Alexandre, the Younger. (L. H. Hooper) Lippinc. **21**: 501. — (J. B. Matthews) Internat. R. **10**: 530. — (E. Jerrold) Temp. Bar, **51**: 392. — Bentley, **41**: 347. — Lond. Soc. **25**: 208. Same art. Ecl. M. **82**: 613.
— Diane de Lys, at the Princess's Theater (M. Browne) St. Paul's. **13**: 211.
— Princess of Bagdad. (A. Laugel) Nation, **32**: 127.
Dumas, Prof. J. B. A., with portrait. (A. W. Hoffman) Pop. Sci. Mo. **18**: 257.
Dumas, Count Mathieu, Campaigns of, 1799. For. Q. **1**: 99.
Dumb Men's Speech; Belgian Experiment. Cornh. **16**: 693.
— London Experiment. Cornh. **17**: 573.
Dumb Mouths. (J. Clyne) Once a Week, **1**: 136.
Dumb Oracle, The. Dub. Univ. **91**: 665.
Dumbartonshire, Scotland, Irving's History of. (J. Skeltie) Macmil. **42**: 33.
Dumberdene, The. (L. K. Knatchbull-Hugessen) Belgra. **20**: 513.
Dumesnil, Mlle., French Actress. All the Year, **41**: 400.
Dummer, Jeremy. Letter, May 13, 1720, to Samuel Sewall. N. E. Reg. **2**: 146.

Dummer, Shubael, Memoir of. Am. Q. Reg. **10**: 241.
Dummer, William. Am. Q. Reg. **15**: 306.
Dummer Family. (J. L. Chester) N. E. Reg. **35**: 254, 321.
Dummer, Fort, Papers relating to. Hist. M. **10**: 109, 141, 178.
Dummer School and S. Moody. Am. J. Educ. **28**: 785.
Dumont, M., Notice of. For. Q. **5**: 317.
Dunasker, Orphans of. Dub. Univ. **10**: 636. **11**: 54–736.
Dunbar, William, Memoir of. Liv. Age, **1**: 382.
— Poetry of. Blackw. **37**: 287.
— Thistle and the Rose. (J. G. R. McElroy) Penn Mo. **12**: 533.
Dunbarton Castle. Penny M. **10**: 36.
Dunblane, Legend of. All the Year, **22**: 593, 616.
Dunblane Cathedral; a Poem. (W. C. Smith) Good Words, **16**: 23, 91, 750.
Duncan, Adam, Admiral, and his Victory. Colburn, **47**: 466.
Duncan, F. J. My intimate Friend. Canad. Mo. **13**: 442.
Duncan, James, with portrait. Dem. R. **30**: 193.
Duncan, John, the Alford Weaver and Botanist. (W. Jolly) Good Words, **19**: 261, 353, 385. — (W. Jolly) Nature, **23**: 269. — Nature, **24**: 6.
Duncan, Wm., Shipwreck of. Antiquary, **3**: 14.
Duncan Rea. (F. Davis) Once a Week, **12**: 210.
Dunces in Schools who became Prizemen in Life. (F. Jacox) Bentley, **63**: 70.
Dunciad, Need of a new. (J. V. O'Conor) Cath. World, **30**: 99.
Dunck, Mary, 1670. (C. J. Hoadly) N. E. Reg. **11**: 150.
Duncombe, Thomas S., Challenge to Mr. Fraser. Fraser, **10**: 494.
— Oratory of. Fraser, **34**: 349.
Dundee, John Grahame of Claverhouse, Viscount. Blackw. **88**: 155. Same art. Liv. Age, **66**: 656. — Temp. Bar, **54**: 28. — Ed. R. **118**: 1.
— Last Days of. Dub. Univ. **19**: 479.
Dundee, Anthropol. Conference at. Anthrop. R. **6**: 71.
— Bank Robbery in 1788. (J. Myles) Hogg, **6**: 373.
— Extracts from Lockit Buik. Antiquary, **3**: 15–88.
— Jute and Whale-Oil Trade of. Pract. M. **3**: 168.
— Two Days in. Chamb. J. **7**: 161.
Dundonald, Thomas Cochrane, Earl of. Blackw. **87**: 176. — (W. C. Taylor) Bentley, **22**: 1. — Bent. Q. **2**: 575. Same art. Liv. Age, **64**: 478. — Dub. Univ. **54**: 121. Same art. Ecl. M. **48**: 110. — No. Brit. **34**: 84. — Quar. **109**: 383.
— Case of. (A Arnold) Gent. M. n. s. **19**: 606. Same art. Liv. Age, **135**: 746.
— Chapter in modern Knight-Errantry. (P. Greg) Macmil. **1**: 374.
— Elopement to Gretna. St. Paul's, **10**: 402.
— in South American Waters. Liv. Age, **60**: 619.
Dundreary, Lord. Lond. Soc. **2**: 213–473. **3**: 371.
Dundrearys, Historical. Temp. Bar, **31**: 215.
Dunes and Moving Sands. Nature, **23**: 569.
Dunedin, Glance at. Chamb. J. **41**: 344.
Dunkerque. House. Words, **7**: 357.
Dunlop, William, with portrait. Fraser, **7**: 436.
Dunluce Castle. Penny M. **5**: 105.
Dunmore Lake, Naming of. N. E. Reg. **7**: 253.
Dunmow, England. Dunmow Flitch, 1877. (M. D. Conway) Harper, **56**: 373.
Dunning, Chapter on. Am. Mo. M. **4**: 378.
Dunning, Scotland, Steeple of. Colburn, **127**: 350.
Dunns, Albert Robert. (P. Beaton) Good Words. **10**: 470.
Dunoyer, Madame. Bentley, **32**: 273.
Duns Scotus as a Theologian and Philosopher. (J. E. Erdmann) Am. Presb. R. **14**: 289.
Dunstable Priory, Bedford, Annals of. Chr. Rem. **54**: 382.
— in the 13th Century. Cornh. **6**: 830.
Dunstable, Mass., Fox's History of. (S. Osgood) Chr. Exam. **41**: 18.
— Ministers of. Am. Q. Reg. **11**: 395.
Dunstan, St., and his Contemporaries. Chr. Rem. **4**: 345.
— Ballad from English History. (J. Payn) Colburn, **106**: 485.
— Memorials of. (M. Allies) Cath. World, **29**: 797.
Dunster, Henry. (E. Quincy) Nation, **14**: 375.
Dunster Family. N. E. Reg. **27**: 307.
Dunton, John. House. Words, **9**: 338. — Irish Q. **9**: 905.
— Life of. Blackw. **6**: 24.
Duntroon, Two Pipers of. Good Words, **22**: 201.
Dunwich, a drowned City. (H. King) Once a Week, **12**: 621.
— Romance of the East Coast. (E. L. Cornish) Fraser, **97**: 523. Same art. Liv. Age, **137**: 380.
Dupanloup, Felix, Bishop of Orleans. (K. O'Meara) Cath. World, **28**: 538. — (C. de Warmont) 19th Cent. **5**: 219. Same art. Liv. Age, **140**: 707. — Month, **35**: 436. — Temp. Bar, **55**: 391.
— Speech at Malines. Cath. World, **6**: 587.
Dupin, André M. J. J. Memoirs. Fraser, **51**: 676. — Meth. Q. **16**: 33.
Dupleix, Joseph François. Nat. R. **15**: 203.
Du Plessis-Mornay. *See* Mornay.
Duplicity of Men. Colburn, **71**: 62.
Du Ponceau, Peter S. Address. U. S. Lit. Gaz. **1**: 133.
— — at Philadelphia. (J. C. Gray) No. Am. **14**: 384.
— on Chinese Writing. New York R. **3**: 457. — (J. Pickering) No. Am. **48**: 271. — For. Q. **21**: 316.
— on English Phonology. Anal. M. **14**: 16.
Dupont, Pierre, Poetry of. All the Year, **4**: 31. — Chamb. J. **21**: 280.
Dupré, the young Sculptor, Story of. Ev. Sat. **9**: 135.
Dupuytren, Death of. Sharpe, **27**: 209.
Du Quesne, A., and French Navy of the 17th Century. (J. K. Laughton) Fraser, **90**: 638.
Duquesne, Fort. (Prof. Frost) Godey, **29**: 189.
— Capture of. Olden Time, **1**: 177, 281.
— Description of. (J. McKenney) Olden Time, **1**: 39. *See* Braddock's Defeat.
"Duquesne," Expedition of the. (W. de Fonvielle) Nature, **3**: 370.
Durand, Asher Brown. Godey, **33**: 115.
Durand, Sir Henry. (G. Smith) Good Words, **14**: 575, 706.
Duration. (F. Bayma) Cath. World, **22**: 111, 244.
Durbin, John P. (A. Stevens) Nat. M. **6**: 137.
— Observations in the East. Meth. Q. **4**: 460. **6**: 114. — (J. P. Thompson) New Eng. **2**: 446. — (S. F. Smith) Chr. R. **11**: 88.
Dürer, A. *See* Duerer.
Durfee, Job. (J. M. Mackie) Am. Whig R. **7**: 471.
— Phi Beta Kappa Oration. Chr. Exam. **35**: 377.
— Roger Williams in Banishment; a Poem. (J. Foster) Ecl. R. **68**: 22.
D'Urfey, Thomas. Belgra. **18**: 427. — Bentley, **45**: 95. — House Words, **11**: 186.
Durham, John George, Lord. Fraser, **18**: 361. — Tait, **4**: 88.
— and the Edinburgh Review. Tait, n. s. **1**: 647.
Durham, Cathedral of. All the Year, **33**: 60. — Appleton, **10**: 527. — Penny M. **2**: 196. **4**: 276, 305. — Sharpe, **46**: 232.
— Deeds of. All the Year, **20**: 215.
— Ecclesiastical Controversy in. Cong. M. **13**: 650.
— — Clerical Abuses. Ed. R. **37**: 350.
— Richardson's History of. Mo. R. **157**: 364. **162**: 199. **163**: 582.
— Ritual of. Chr. Rem. **44**: 158.
— Surtees's History of. (R. Southey) Quar. **39**: 360.
— University of. Am. J. Educ. **28**: 545.
Durham, N. H., Documentary Hist. of. Hist. M. **18**: 292.
— Records. N. E. Reg. **30**: 59. **32**: 133. **33**: 80, 345.

Durolevum, Site of. (C. R. Smith) Arch. **29**: 217.
Dury, John, and Pacification of Church. Chr. Rem. **29**: 1.
Duryee, Chauncy, with portrait. Hunt, **25**: 365.
Düsseldorf. *See* Duesseldorf.
Dusselthal Abbey, Count Von der Recke's Institution of. Chr. Obs. **36**: 246, 304.
Dust. (H. P. Malet) Geog. M. **1**: 324, 371.
— and Disease. (J. Tyndall) Fraser, **81**: 302. Same art. Ecl. M. **74**: 556.— Nature, **1**: 327.— Ev. Sat. **9**: 147.
— and Smoke. (J. Tyndall) Nature, **4**: 124. — Once a Week, **27**: 276.
— as an Explosive. Chamb. J. **56**: 95.
— at Sea. Chamb. J. **41**: 369.
— Atmospheric. (G. Tissandier) Pop. Sci. Mo. **17**: 344.
— Cosmical. J. Frankl. Inst. **104**: 278.
— Fogs and Clouds. (J. Aitken) Nature, **23**: 195. —(J. Aitken) Ecl. Engin. **24**: 308.
— in a Sunbeam. Once a Week, **2**: 50.
— Living. St. James, **26**: 113.
— Zoölogical Aspects of. (A. Wilson) Good Words, **15**: 300.
Dustmen of London. (J. Greenwood) Lond. Soc. **19**: 204. Same art. Ecl. M. **76**: 599.
Dust-Showers and Red Rain. Chamb. J. **17**: 230. — Nat. M. **1**: 72.
Dust-Yards in London. (C. Camden) Good Words, **20**: 738.
Dutch, The, History of. (J. C. Moffat) Princ. **33**: 463. *See* Holland.
Dutch and Flemish Masters. (P. G. Hamerton) Internat. R. **4**: 474.
Dutch and German Schools. Westm. **34**: 61.
Dutch Anna. Chamb. J. **4**: 310.
Dutch Colonies and Colonial Policy. Brit. & For. R. **12**: 396.
Dutch Commerce. (M. B. Lecompte) Hunt, **5**: 437.
Dutch Dikes and Polders. Chamb. J. **44**: 793.
Dutch Flag in the Northern Seas. (A. H. Markham) Good Words, **20**: 90, 172, 244.
Dutch Fork, Reminiscences of. (Mrs. E. F. Ellet) Godey, **58**: 220.
Dutch-Gap Canal. (J. W. Ames) Overland, **4**: 30.
Dutch Holidays. All the Year, **16**: 128.
Dutch Houses, Old. Knick. **18**: 150.
Dutch Language, Penn. (P. E. Gibbons) Atlan. **24**: 473.
Dutch Literary Jest, An old. Cornh. **28**: 568.
Dutch Literature. For. Q. **21**: 397. — Ecl. R. **105**: 355.
— Researches in. Fraser, **49**: 185, 349, 578. **50**: 95, 663. Same art. Ecl. M. **32**: 134, 498. **33**: 27.
Dutch Painters, Old. (E. Mason) Harper, **58**: 530.
Dutch Picture. (H. W. Longfellow) Atlan. **39**: 176.
Dutch Poetry. Lond. M. **9**: 300.
Dutch Political Novel, A. (M. Havelaar) No. Brit. **46**: 319. Same art. Ecl. M. **69**: 348.
Dutch Popular Songs. For. Q. **14**: 163.
Dutch Reformed Synod, Albany. Cong. M. **21**: 621.
Dutch Republic. *See* Netherlands.
Dutch Society of Sciences. Nature, **7**: 464.
Dutch War, The. (T. P. Thompson) Westm. **18**: 249.
Dutchess Co., New York, Lutheran Church in. (W. Hull) Luth. Q. **11**: 381.
Dutchman, My Friend the; a Tale. Blackw. **62**: 494.
Duties, British Import. (J. Bowring) Hunt, **5**: 145, 422. — Hunt, **6**: 320.
— Countervailing. (C. Raguet) Hunt, **6**: 9. — (C. C. Whittlesey) Hunt, **9**: 448.
— on Exports. (S. G. Fisher) No. Am. **101**: 147.
— on Imports. (G. W. Tucker) Hunt, **4**: 506.
— on foreign Books. (C. C. Jewett) Hunt, **14**: 456.
— on Railroad Iron. (M. Tarver) West. J. **12**: 77.
— Productiveness of low. Tait, n. s. **6**: 134.
Dutton, Samuel W. S. (I. N. Tarbox) Cong. Q. **8**: 129
— Discourse on. New Eng. **26**: 345.
Duty. Chr. Obs. **35**: 393, 585.
Duty; a Tale. Godey, **24**: 266.
— and Beauty. (H. Holbeach) St. Paul's, **12**: 73.
— and Determinism. (L. S. Bevington) Mind, **5**: 30.
— involving Destiny. (A. A. Miner) Univ. Q. **7**: 31.
— Reality of; illustrated by Mill's Autobiography. Contemp. **28**: 508. Same art. Liv. Age, **131**: 131.
Duties of Ignorance. Cornh. **39**: 455.
— of Man, Pellico on. Mo. R. **134**: 174.
— to Society. Cornh. **28**: 216.
Duxbury, Mass., Ministers of. Am. Q. Reg. **8**: 151.
Duyckinck, E. A., Memoir of, with portrait. (S. Osgood) N. E. Reg. **33**: 133.
Dwarf and the Oak-Tree; a Poem. Blackw. **67**: 411.
Dwarfs. All the Year, **14**: 376. — Colburn, **4**: 49. — Nat. M. **9**: 438.
— and Giants. (W. A. Seaver) Harper, **39**: 202. — Fraser, **54**: 140, 286.
— St. Hilaire on. Ed. New Philos. J. **15**: 142.
— Women in Miniature. (F. G. Baylis) Victoria, **10**: 289.
Dwelling-Houses. (J. Stevenson) Good Words, **14**: 673.
— American. (C. E. Beecher) Harper, **32**: 762.
— Apartment Houses. (P. B. Wight) Putnam, **16**: 306.
— Artisans'. Brit. Q. **51**: 343.
— Choice of. Penny M. **1**: 15.
— City-Leased. Brit. Q. **69**: 301.
— Country, for Town Laborers. (J. T. Danson) J. Statis. Soc. **22**: 362.
— Effect on Health and Morals of. (C. Gatliff) J. Statis. Soc. **38**: 33.
— English. Westm. **103**: 173.
— for Artisans at Mulhouse. St. James, **22**: 109.
— Improvement Question. Good Words, **15**: 515.
— Modern. (H. H. Holly) Harper, **52**: 855. **53**: 49, 217, 354.
— of London Poor. (W. Gilbert) Good Words, **13**: 458.
— of the Poor. Chamb. J. **43**: 252.
— — and Sanitary Legislation. (G. W. Child) Contemp. **32**: 297.
— Overcrowded, Prevention Act, 1857. Tait, n. s. **24**: 559.
— Sanitary Construction of. (W. H. Corfield) Ecl. Engin. **22**: 177, 281.
— Sanitary and constructive Supervision of. (L. Angell) Ecl. Engin. **25**: 388.
— Workingmen's. O. & N. **4**: 749.
See Houses.
Dwight, Edmund. (F. Bowen) Am. J. Educ. **4**: 1.
Dwight, Francis. Am. J. Educ. **5**: 803.
Dwight, John Breed. (S. W. S. Dutton) New Eng. **4**: 127.
Dwight, John S. German Translations. (G. S. Hillard) No. Am. **48**: 505. — (G. Bancroft) Chr. Exam. **26**: 360.
Dwight, Sereno S., Sermon of. Chr. Mo. Spec. **8**: 358.
— Hebrew Wife. (W. Marshall) Lit. & Theo. R. **4**: 182.
— on the Death of Christ. (M. Stuart) Chr. Mo. Spec. **9**: 268, 308.
Dwight, Timothy, with portrait. Am. Lit. M. **2**: 269. — with portrait, (J. L. Kingsley) Anal. M. **9**: 265. — (S. Willard) No. Am. **7**: 347. — (W. B. Sprague) Sparks's Am. Biog. **14**: 225.
— as a Teacher. (D. Olmsted) Am. J. Educ. **5**: 567.
— Interview with. (E. Everett) O. & N. **7**: 48.
— Life of. (Portfo. (Den.) **18**: 355.
— Memoir of. Cong. M. **3**: 289.
— Sermons of. Chr. Obs. **29**: 365.
— Theology. (W. B. Sprague) Meth. Q. **7**: 325. — Spirit Pilg. **2**: 248, 308. — Cong. M. **3**: 30, 98.
— Travels. (R. Southey) Quar. **30**: 1. — Chr. Mo. Spec. **4**: 145, 423.
Dwight, Wilder. Liv. Age, **75**: 142.
Dwight, William T. (E. C. Smyth) Cong. Q. **11**. 181.
Dwight Genealogy. (I. N. Tarbox) New Eng. **35**: 280.
Dwinford, Richard, Bishop of Chichester. Cong. **4**: 23.

Dyaks, The. Chamb. J. **28**: 201. Same art. Nat. M. **11**: 511.
— Encounter with. Temp. Bar, **23**: 499.
Dyce, Alexander. (J. Forster) Fortn. **24**: 731.
Dyeing. (C. T. Hinckley) Godey, **46**: 293.
— and Calico Printing. (R. Meldola) Nature, **13**: 283.
— in permanent Colors. (B. Abbott) Recr. Sci. **3**: 313.
— Mordants used in. J. Frankl. Inst. **7**: 375. **8**: 1.
— Plants used in. Penny M. **12**: 71.
— Recent scientific Applications to. Art J. **10**: 153.
— Red, Blue, and Yellow, Plants used in. Penny M. **11**: 438, 451, 477.
Dye-Works, Glasgow, Day at. Penny M. **13**: 289.
— of Boutarel & Co., Clichy-La-Grenne. Pract. M. **1**: 363, 410.
Dyer, Eliphalet. (J. H. Trumbull) Pennsyl. M. **3**: 174.
Dyer, George. Poetics and Poetry. (J. Foster) Ecl. R. **19**: 366.
Dyes, Ancient. (J. Keen) Potter Am. Mo. **9**: 356.
Dying by Poison. (G. M. Fenn) Belgra. **13**: 342.
— Game. Lond. M. **15**: 385.
— in a Ditch, Advantages of. (B. M. Ranking) Dark Blue, **1**: 685.
Dying Confessions. Chr. Mo. Spec. **1**: 128.
Dying Doytschin; a Poem from the Servian. Dub. Univ. **43**: 588.
Dying Gladiator, Statue of. (T. Lyman) O. & N. **2**: 718. — Penny M. **2**: 10.
Dying Men, Living Words of. (A. S. Miller) Lakeside, **9**: 224.
Dykes, Thomas, Obituary of. Chr. Obs. **48**: 211, 346.
Dykwynkyn at Work. Belgra. **1**: 359.
Dymoke, Sir Henry, Her Majesty's Champion. Once a Week, **12**: 593.
Dymond, Jonathan. Essays on Morality. (R. Southey) Quar. **43**: 83. — (S. J. May) Chr. Exam. **18**: 101. — Am. Mo. M. **3**: 97.
Dynamics, Clifford's. (P. G. Tait) Nature, **18**: 89.
— Speculative. (C. Wright) Nation, **20**: 379.
— Vital. (J. B. Russell) Recr. Sci. **3**: 339.
— Whewell's Treatise on. Westm. **2**: 311.
Dynamical Terms, Use and Abuse of. Ecl. Engin. **8**: 438.
Dynamite. Chamb. J. **47**: 649. Same art. Ecl. M. **76**: 108. — Ev. Sat. **9**: 763.
— and its Manufacture. Ecl. Engin. **6**: 386.
— Experiments with. Ecl. Engin. **1**: 611. **7**: 505, 511, 585. **9**: 179.
— Frozen. (P. Hess) Ecl. Engin. **17**: 417.
— Trauzl on. Nature, **14**: 367.
Dynamo-Electric Current, New Applications of. J. Frankl. Inst. **110**: 112.
Dynamo-Electric Machines. (E. J. Houston and E. Thomson) J. Frankl. Inst. **105**: 289, 361. **107**: 106. *See* Electrical Machine.
Dynamometer at Royal Technological Institute, Stockholm. (J. W. Nystrom) J. Frankl. Inst. **79**: 392.
— for measuring Steam or Water Power. J. Frankl. Inst. **36**: 275.
— The Francis. (S. Webber) J. Frankl. Inst. **95**: 106.
— Froude's. Nature, **16**: 272.
— Improved. (W. P. Tatham) J. Frankl. Inst. **112**: 321.
— New. (T. W. Webb) Nature, **4**: 427.
— Prony's Friction. (E. Morris) J. Frankl. Inst. **35**: 225.
Dyspepsia. Am. Q. **9**: 233. — Quar. **65**: 315. — So. R. **4**: 208. — Spirit Pilg. **2**: 248, 308. — Chr. Exam. **9**: 236.
— Advantages of Traveling for. Colburn, **58**: 260.
— Causes of. (A. Leared) Pop. Sci. Mo. **1**: 75.
— Meditations on. Blackw. **90**: 302, 406.
Dyspeptic Man, The. So. Lit. Mess. **1**: 71.
Dyspeptic Saints. St. James, **23**: 24.
Dyspeptics, Hints to. Ecl. M. **97**: 762.

E

Eachard, John. Contempt of the Clergy. Mus. **14**: 305.
Eadie, John. Dub. Univ. **88**: 276. — Lond. Q. **53**: 87.
— Characteristics of. (A. M. Symington) Good Words, **19**: 470.
Eagle, The. Penny M. **4**: 153, 278.
— Harpy. Penny M. **8**: 441.
— — Home of. (F. L. Oswald) Am. Natural. **12**: 146.
— of the German Empire. Cornh. **15**: 612.
— Washington. (J. A. Allen) Am. Natural. **4**: 524.
— White-headed. Penny M. **1**: 245.
Eagle Rock; a Poem. Mo. Rel. M. **20**: 202.
Eagle's Nest; a Tale. Dub. Univ. **12**: 346.
Eagles. Bentley, **30**: 115. Same art. Liv. Age, **31**: 158.
— and Swans. Once a Week, **22**: 165.
— Destruction of. Once a Week, **20**: 368.
Eagles, John. Bentley, **46**: 594.
Eagleswood Military Academy, Perth Amboy, N. J. Am. J. Educ. **13**: 471.
Ear, Anatomy and Function of. (C. A. Todd) Western, **1**: 359. — (J. D. Macdonald) Nature, **18**: 285.
— and Eye, Human. (D. McAllum) Meth. M. **49**: 675.
— and its Mechanism. (J. McKendrick) Good Words, **21**: 55, 140.
— Cyon's Researches on. (A. C. Brown) Nature, **18**: 633, 657.
— Hygiene of. (J. Hinton) Pop. Sci. Mo. **3**: 139.
Ear, Membrana Tympani, Action of. (J. G. McKendrick) Nature, **14**: 253.
— My Notion about. (G. W. Bagby) Putnam, **15**: 231.
Ears. Eng. Dom. M. **2**: 145.
— Chapter on. (C. Lamb) Lond. M. **3**: 263.
Earlobe, Artificial Enlargement of. (J. P. Harrison) Anthrop. J. **2**: 190.
Ear-Trumpets and Voice-Conductors. Penny M. **11**: 11.
Earl Eirek's Voyage; a Poem. (W. A. Smith) Once a Week, **11**: 545.
Earldoms of Strathern, Monteith, and Airth, Nicolas on. Mo. R. **158**: 31.
Earle, Gilbert. Westm. **2**: 556.
Earle, John. Microcosmography. House. Words, **17**: 469.
Earl's Daughter. Lond. Soc. **8**: 349.
Earl's Dene (R. D. Francillon) Blackw. **106**: 515, 746. **107**: 1-667. **108**: 20-719. Same art. Liv. Age, **103**: 742. **104**: 108-667. **105**: 81-625. **106**: 19-588. **107**: 77-664. **108**: 167, 235.
Earlscourt. (Mrs. F. Grahame) Dub. Univ. **77**: 503, 641. **78**: 21-374.
Early Ages, Non-Historic Times. Quar. **128**: 432.
Early English Text Society's Publications. (P. Kennedy) Dub. Univ. **81**: 481.
Early Friendship. Bentley, **7**: 513.

Early History of William and Louis; a Sketch. Dub. Univ. **77**: 334.
Early Piety, Sermon on. (J. Abbott) Cong. M. **16**: 518.729
Early Rising. Cath. World, **5**: 754.—Liv. Age, **134**: 574.
— English *versus* American Habits. Ev. Sat. **11**: 575.
— Poetry of. Colburn, **50**: 366–490.
— A Word about. Ev. Sat. **10**: 547.
Early Workers. All the Year, **36**: 591. **37**: 539. **38**: 106–462.
Earnest Man, Character of. (E. V. Gerhart) Mercersb. **8**: 606.
Earning a Living; a Comedy. Dem.R. **25**: 161–553. **26**: 50.
Earth, The. All the Year, **12**: 469, 486.
— a Magnet. Ecl. M. **71**: 1100.
— Age of. (W. Chambers) Chamb. J. **53**: 529.—(H. P. Malet) Am. Natural. **11**: 286.—(H. P. Malet) Geog. M. **4**: 38 —(D. Trowbridge) Nat. Q. **23**: 130. —Cornh. **38**: 321.—Dub. Univ. **47**: 580.—Liv. Age, **14**: 516. —Tait, **4**: 165.
— — Geological Evidences of. (D. N. Lord) Theo & Lit. J. **4**: 529. **5**: 1.—Theo. & Lit. J. **5**: 292.
— — Modern Philosophers on. Quar. **142**: 202. Same art. Pop. Sci. Mo. **9**: 649. Same art. Liv. Age, **130**: 771.
— — Old. (J. G. Hargreaves) Ecl. R. **111**: 72. Same art. Ecl. M. **49**: 370.
— and the Heavens, Harmony of. (J. Prusol) Colburn, **167**: 642.
— and Inhabitants. (S. Haughton) Dub. Univ. **58**: 105.
— and Man. (J. Lovering) Chr. Exam. **47**: 96.—(J. D. B. De Bow) De Bow, **10**: 282.—Am. Whig R. **14**: 195.—New Eng. **8**: 365.—Chr. R. **14**: 471.—(E. O'Meara) Canad. Mo. **9**: 254.—Westm. **64**: 151.—(G. Bischof) Ed. New Philos. J. **37**: 44.
— — Story of, Dawson's. Canad. Mo. **3**: 454.—Internat. R. **1**: 413.
— — Unwritten History of. Ecl. M. **58**: 169.
— Arago's Theory of. Mo. R. **134**: 1.
— as a Habitation of Man. (W. Arnot) Ex. H. Lec. **15**: 193.
— as modified by Human Action, Marsh's. Internat. R. **2**: 120.
— as occupied and improved by Man. (W. Arnot) Ex. H. Lec. **18**: 219.
— before Life. (C. H. Hitchcock) Pop. Sci. Mo. **4**: 513.
— Burnet's Theory of. (H. Southern) Retros. **6**: 133.
— Causes of Difference in Temperature. (A. Humboldt) Ed. New Philos. J. **4**: 329.
— Changes in Position of Axis of. (J. Evans) Am. J. Sci. **93**: 230.
— Climate of, in Palæozoic Times. (T. S. Hunt) Am. J. Sci. **86**: 396.
— Conductibility of. (C. Matteucci) J. Frankl. Inst. **50**: 389.
— Conformation of. (G. W. Hill) Math. Mo. **3**: 166.
— considered as a Spheroid of Revolution: Geodetic Formulas. (R. C. Matthewson) Math. Mo. **3**: 71.
— Contraction of. (B. Peirce) Ecl. Engin. **4**: 625.—(B. Peirce) Nature, **3**: 315.
— — Results of. (J. D. Dana) Am. J. Sci. **105**: 423. **106**: 6, 104, 161.
— Creation and Destiny of. (W. K. Clifford) Pop. Sci. Mo. **7**: 268.
— Crust of, Thickness of. (J. H. Pratt) Nature, **4**: 28.
— Cuvier's Theory of. So. R. **8**: 69.—Ed. R. **22**: 454. —Anal. M. **4**: 206.—Chr. Obs. **15**: 105.
— Day-Dream of. All the Year, **26**: 84.
— Density of. Dub. R. **18**: 75.—(G. B. Airy) Am. J. Sci. **71**: 359.
— Division of, into Zoölogical Regions. (E. Blyth) Nature, **3**: 427.
— Does the Earth grow sick? Liv. Age, **103**: 798.
Earth, The, Figure of. (J. Herschel) Nature, **20**: 33.—(H. Y. Hind) Nature, **10**: 165.—(J. Renwick) J. Frankl. Inst. **1**: 164, 203.—Cornh. **6**: 550.
— — Action of Winds in determining. (F. Czerny) Nature, **15**: 239.
— — and Size of. (K. M. Friederici) Nature, **18**: 557, 602.
— — Biot on. Blackw. **3**: 463.—Anal. M. **13**: 26.
— — Employment of the Pendulum for determining. (J. Herschel) Nature, **21**: 599.
— — Sabine on. Mo. R. **108**: 270.
— — True. (J. H. Maedler) Am. J. Sci. **80**: 46.
— Formation of. (D. Deshler) West. J. **4**: 25.
— — Ancient Views of. (C. Flammarion) Pop. Sci. Mo. **10**: 542.
— — Origin of grand Outline Features. (J. D. Dana) Am. J. Sci. **53**: 381. **92**: 205, 252.
— — of Crust of. (D. N. Lord) Theo. & Lit. J. **13**: 400.
— Gruithuisen's Theory of the Beginning of. (H. P. Malet) Geog. M. **5**: 65, 97.
— Higgins on. Mo. R. **138**: 523.
— History of. (S. Haughton) Ecl. M. **54**: 129.—Chr. Obs. **61**: 49.
— — Critical Periods in. (J. L. LeConte) Am. Natural. **11**: 540.—(J. L. LeConte) Am. J. Sci. **114**: 99.
— Huttonian Theory of. Ed. R. **69**: 441.
— — Playfair on. (H. Brougham) Ed. R. **1**: 201.—(F. Jeffrey) Ed. R. **2**: 337.
— Igneous Action in. Sharpe, **49**: 207. **50**: 39.
— Internal and external Fire of. (D. Trowbridge) Nat. Q. **26**: 353.
— Internal Fluidity of. (W. Thomson) Nature, **5**: 257.
— Internal Heat of. Nature, **12**: 545.—Ecl. Engin. **5**: 627.
— — Evidences of. (S. Hibbard) Recr. Sci. **1**: 253, 325.
— — New Theory of. Liv. Age, **29**: 261.
— Interior of. (G. B. Airy) Nature, **18**: 41.—(R. Radau) Pop. Sci. Mo. **17**: 289, 453.—(H. Hennessy) Am. J. Sci. **116**: 461.
— — Nature of. (D. Forbes) Nature, **3**: 296.—(D. Forbes) Pop. Sci. R. **8**: 121. Same art. Ecl. M. **73**: 23.—(D. Forbes) Ecl. Engin. **4**: 538.
— — Temperature of. For. Q. **8**: 303.—Am. J. Sci. **15**: 109.—(E. Hitchcock) No. Am. **28**: 265.—(L. Cordier) Ed. New Philos. J. **4**: 273. **5**: 277. **6**: 32.
— Knight's Theory of. Ed. Mo. R. **1**: 340.
— Land and Water Surface of. Penny M. **10**: 107.
— Life of. Belgra. **21**: 438.
— Man and his Dwelling-Place. (A. K. H. Boyd) Fraser, **59**: 645. Same art. Liv. Age, **66**: 536.
— Man on. Liv. Age, **2**: 186.
— Mother Earth's Biography. Nature, **8**: 259.
— Movements of. (A. Wilson) St. James, **34**: 524.
— New. (L. Bacon) New Eng. **7**: 1.
— Nicholson's Life-History of. Nature, **16**: 39.
— Orbit of, Curve of Eccentricity of. (R. W. McFarland) Am. J. Sci. **111**: 456.
— — Secular Variations. (J. L. Stockwell) Am. J. Sci. **96**: 87.
— Our cooling. (W. Downes) Belgra. **44**: 413. Same art. Ecl. M. **97**: 275.
— past and present. Ecl. M. **49**: 309.
— Past and Future of. (R. A. Proctor) Contemp. **25**: 74. Same art. Canad. Mo. **7**: 82. Same art. Ecl. M. **84**: 182.
— Physical Condition of. (Sir W. Thomson) Am. J Sci. **112**: 339.
— Physical Evolution of. Penn Mo. **7**: 364, 417.
— Physical Geography of, when the Sea was young. Cornh. **34**: 151, 427. Same art. Ecl. M. **87**: 528.
— Physical Theory of. Brit. Q. **9**: 473.
— Place in Nature. (J. N. Lockyer) Good Words, **19**: 129–842. Same art. Ecl. M. **90**: 537.

Earth, Pre-Adamite, Harris's. (A. P. Peabody) No. Am. **70**: 391. — Brit. Q. **5**: 387. — (D. W. Phillips) Chr. R. **14**: 402.
— Reclus on. Nature, **7**: 421.
— Relations with the Sun. (B. Stewart) Nature, **16**: 9, 26, 45.
— Rigidity of. (H. Hennessy) Nature, **5**: 288.
— Rotation of, Effects of. Cornh. **7**: 140.
— — Foucault's Experiment. Chamb. J. **16**: 101.
— — Influence of Geological Changes on Axis of. (G. H. Darwin) Am. J. Sci. **113**: 444.
— — New Proof of. Internat. M. **3**: 296.
— — Variability of. (S. Newcomb) Am. J. Sci. **108**: 161.
— — Period of, losing Time. Chamb. J. **44**: 641. Same art. Ecl. M. **70**: 245.
— — Physical Demonstration of. (C. J. Allen) J. Frankl. Inst. **52**: 38–419. — (M. L. Foucault) J. Frankl. Inst. **51**: 350.
— Rotundity of. Nature, **1**: 581. **2**: 214.
— Shape and Size of. (M. Merriman) Ecl. Engin. **22**: 53, 115, 233.
— Sources of the Materials of the Strata of. (D. N. Lord) Theo. & Lit. J. **5**: 177.
— Structure of. (D. Trowbridge) Nat. Q. **22**: 86.
— Surface of, Formation of. (J. L. LeConte) Am. J. Sci, **104**: 345, 460. **105**: 448.
— — Motions of Fluids and Solids relative to. Math. Mo. **1**: 140–397. **2**: 89, 339, 374.
— Superficial Temperature of, Changes in. (W. Hopkins) Am. J. Sci. **65**: 72, 248, 334.
— Symmes's Theory of. (P. Clark) Atlan. **31**: 471.
— Theories of. (J. Sparks) No. Am. **18**: 266. — Mo. R. **126**: 371.
— Viscosity of Mass of. Nature, **19**: 292.
— Weighing the. Chamb. J. **23**: 219.
See World.
Earth, Edible. J. Frankl. Inst. **90**: 155.
— Infusorial, and its Uses. (W. H. Wahl) J. Frankl. Inst. **102**: 407.
Earth Currents. (W. H. Preece) Nature, **3**: 15.
— and the Aurora. (W. H. Preece) Nature, **5**: 368.
Earth Waves, Transmission of. (H. L. Abbot) Am. J. Sci. **115**: 178.
Earth's worst Tragedy; a Story. Howitt, **1**: 260.
Earthbound; a Story. (M. Oliphant) Fraser, **101**: 118.
Earthen Pitchers. (R. H. Davis) Scrib. **7**: 73–714.
Earthenware and Porcelain. J. Frankl. Inst. **4**: 73–374. *See* Pottery; Porcelain; Ceramic Art.
Earthly Ties, and the Social Economy of another Life. Am. Church R. **4**: 49.
Earthquake, The; a Tale. Lond. M. **3**: 91.
— at Aleppo. Am. Meth. M. **6**: 185.
— at Bogota. (S. A. Hurlbut) Am. J. Sci. **100**: 408.
— at Calabria and Sicily, 1783. Blackw. **26**: 879. — Mus. **16**: 97.
— at Caraccas, 1812. Anal. M. **2**: 163. — Mus. **18**: 121. — Ill. M. **2**: 85.
— at Chiana, Architectural Aspects of. (J. T. Clarke) Am. Arch. **10**: 47.
— at Lisbon, 1755. Blackw. **88**: 195. — N. E. Reg. **8**: 289.
— at Mitylene, 1867. Ecl. M. **70**: 767.
— at Philippine Islands, 1880. Am. J. Sci. **121**: 52.
— at Rhodes. Ecl. M. **60**: 65.
— at St. Thomas, Oct. 1867. Month, **8**: 379.
— in Algeria. Chamb. J. **44**: 200.
— in Chili. Colburn, **34**: 469. — Mus. **21**: 163.
— — April 2, 1851. (J. M. Gilliss) Am. J. Sci. **71**: 388.
— in China. Nature, **4**: 145.
— in Connecticut, Aug. 9, 1840. Am. J. Sci. **39**: 335.
— in England, Nov. 9, 1852. Colburn, **96**: 446.
Earthquake, The, in Honduras, Aug. 1856. (J. V. S. Anthony) Harper, **14**: 164.
— in Ischia. (H. J. J. Lavis) Nature, **23**: 497.
— in Owen's Valley, 1872. (J. D. Whitney) Overland, **9**: 130, 266.
— in Palestine, Jan. 1, 1837. Cong. M. **20**: 405.
— in Venezuela. Anal. M. **4** : 301.
— — in 1878. (I. Anderson) Lippinc. **22**: 774.
— Lands of. (E. Lawrence) Harper, **38**: 466.
— Night of Horror. Chamb. J. **38**: 241.
— of 1727. (W. B. Trask) N. E. Reg. **14**: 205.
— of 1861, at Mendoza. All the Year, **6**: 444. Same art. Liv. Age, **72**: 667. — Intel. Obs. **5**: 85.
— of Oct. 1863, in England. Intel. Obs. **4**: 294.
— of Aug. 13, 1868, Great Sea Wave of. (R. A. Proctor) Fraser, **82**: 93. Same art. Ecl. M. **75**: 301. Same art. Liv. Age, **106**: 310.
— of Oct. 20, 1870, in Northeastern America. (A. C. Twining) Am. J. Sci. **101**: 47. — (E. Colbert) Lakeside, **4**: 372.
— of March 6, 1872, in Germany. (B. K. Emerson) Am. J. Sci. **108**: 405.
— of Dec. 1874. (D. S. Martin) Am. J. Sci. **110**: 191.
— on Coast of Peru, May 9, 1877. Geog. M. **4**: 206.
Earthquakes. (W. T. Brigham) Am. Natural. **2**: 539. — (J. Lea) Am. J. Sci. **9**: 209. — Niles's Reg. **24**: 171. — (J. Scoffern) St. James, **8**: 426. — (N. S. Shaler) Atlan. **23**: 676. — (W. S. Symonds) Pop. Sci. R. **3**: 204. — (J. D. B. Stillman) Overland, **1**: 474. — (C. R. Weld) Fraser, **60**: 708. Same art. Liv. Age, **64**: 289. — (J. D. Whitney) No. Am. **108**: 578. — All the Year, **3**: 197. — Chamb. J. **41**: 11. — All the Year, **18**: 545. — Brit. Q. **13**: 384. — Cornh. **18**: 43. — Dub. Univ. **55**: 493. — Liv. Age, **79**: 341. — Portfo.(Den.) **7**: 421. **12**: 299. — Quar. **126**: 80. Same art. Ecl. M. **73**: 169. — St. Paul's, **3**: 467.
— Advent of a Period of. Am. Arch. **10**: 20.
— and Buildings. Ecl. Engin. **19**: 248, 271.
— and the Earth. (E. B. Smith) So. R n. s. **3**: 387.
— and Results. (W. B. Adams) Once a Week, **9**: 499.
— and Volcanoes. (Sir J. F. W. Herschel) Good Words, **4**: 53, 141. Same art. Ecl. M. **58**: 429. Same art. Liv. Age, **77**: 457. — (M. Schele de Vere) Putnam, **14**: 343. — Blackw. **106**: 74. — Brit. Q. **13**: 358. — (C. R. Weld) Fraser, **77**: 488. Same art. Ecl. M. **70**: 662. — Liv. Age, **30**: 13. — Nat. M. **9**: 169. — So. R. n. s. **9**: 381.
— — Electric Theory of. Liv. Age, **102**: 387.
— — in the Bible. Kitto, **40**: 46.
— — Natural History of. (G. Bischof) Ed. New Philos. J. **26**: 25, 347.
— Anecdotes of. Colburn, **101**: 453. Same art. Ecl. M. **33**: 209. Same art. Liv. Age, **43**: 134.
— at Agram in 1880–81. (Prof. Szabo) Nature, **23**: 530.
— at Fiume during 1870. Nature, **3**: 269.
— Causes of. (J. J. Lake) Pop. Sci. Mo. **7**: 732. — Quar. **152**: 79. — (A. le Plongeon) Ecl. Engin. **6**: 537, 577.
— — and Consequences of. Hogg, **3**: 188. — Nat. Q. **7**: 84.
— Comrie. (G. Gilfillan) Hogg, **4**: 200.
— during 1878. Nature, **20**: 378.
— Experiences in. (L. Van Housel) Scrib. **15**: 662. — Liv. Age, **58**: 42.
— Great, of Old World. (N. S. Shaler) Atlan. **24**: 140.
— in California. (N. S. Shaler) Atlan. **25**: 351.
— — in 1856. (J. B. Trask) Am. J. Sci. **73**: 341.
— in England. Once a Week, **21**: 336. — Ecl. M. **59**: 283.
— in Great Britain, 1608–1839. (D. Milne) Ed. New Philos. J. **31**: 92, 259. **32**: 106, 362. **33**: 372. **34**: 85. **35**: 137. **36**: 72, 362. — Nature, **23**: 117
— in London. Chamb. J. **58**: 229.

Earthquakes in Manila, 1879. (W. B. Pauli) Month, **42**: 22.
— in New England. (W. T. Brigham) O. & N. **1**: 27. — (Prof. Williams) Carey's Mus. **3**: 291, 567.
— in New Zealand. Westm. **51**: 390.
— in Philippine Islands. (A. B. Meyer) Nature, **11**: 194.
— in Sandwich Islands, 1868. Ecl. M. **71**: 968.
— in South America, 1868. (E. G. Squier) Harper, **38**: 603. — Hunt, **59**: 262.
— in Southern Italy. (J. P. Lacaita) Am. J. Sci. **78**: 210.
— in W. New York. (C. E. West) Am. J. Sci. **76**: 177.
— in Western United States. (N. S. Shaler) Atlan. **24**: 549. — (A. R. Barraud) Lakeside, **6**: 144.
— Land of. All the Year, **20**: 510.
— Mental Effect of. Pop. Sci. Mo. **19**: 257.
— My Experiences of. Dub. Univ. **55**: 493. Same art. Ecl. M. **50**: 212.
— Natural History of. (G. Bischof) Am. J. Sci. **37**: 41.
— Notes on. (W. S. Symonds) Pop. Sci. R. **3**: 204. Same art. Ecl. M. **61**: 340.
— Notices of. Am. J. Sci. **90**: 362.
— of American Continents. (N. S. Shaler) Atlan. **24**: 461.
— on the West Coast of South America, 1831–35. (M. Hamilton) Ed. New Philos. J. **30**: 153.
— Phenomena of. (A. von Humboldt) Ecl. M. **71**: 1509. Same art. Lakeside, **1**: 44. — (E. Lewis) Pop. Sci. Mo. **2**: 513. — Ecl. M. **44**: 420. **49**: 239. **58**: 89. — (C. F. Winslow) Am. J. Sci. **92**: 45.
— Philosophy of. Intel. Obs. **4**: 358.
— Recent. (C. G. Rockwood, jr.) Am. J. Sci. **104**: 1. **105**: 260. **106**: 40. **107**: 384. **109**: 331.
— — American. (C. G. Rockwood, jr.) Am. J. Sci. **112**: 25. **115**: 21. **117**: 158. **119**: 295. **121**: 198.
— Something about. Bentley, **30**: 107.
— Study of, in Switzerland. Nature, **21**: 351.
— Theory of. (A. Perrey) Am. J. Sci. **87**: 1. — Colburn, **129**: 354.
— Theories of. (M. G. Upton) Overland, **1**: 516.
— Usefulness of. (R. A. Proctor) Ecl. Engin. **5**: 121. — Chamb. J. **45**: 707. — Ev. Sat. **6**: 676.
Earthquake-Waves in the Pacific. (R. A. Proctor) Nature, **1**: 54.
— Experiments on, at Holyhead. (R. Mallet) J. Frankl. Inst. **75**: 45.
— Measurement of. (G. Forbes) Pop. Sci. Mo. **1**: 586.
— on the Western Coast of the United States, Dec. 23, 25, 1854. (A. D. Bache) Am. J. Sci. **71**: 37.
Earthwork, Calculation of. (N. B. Putnam) Ecl. Engin. **16**: 161. — Ecl. Engin. **15**: 358.
— Center of Gravity of. (J. W. Davis) Ecl. Engin. **17**: 83.
— Computation of. (E. W. Hyde) Ecl. Engin. **15**: 225.
— Formulæ for. (J. Warner) J. Frankl. Inst. **91**: 396. **92**: 188.
— Lateral Pressure of. (B. Baker) Ecl. Engin. **25**: 333, 353, 492.
— Measuring Cross-Section of. (M. H. Willotte) Ecl. Engin. **24**: 153.
— Mechanical Calculation of. (C. Herschell) J. Frankl. Inst. **97**: 262.
— Vignoles's Lectures on. J. Frankl. Inst. **34**: 157.
Earthworm, The. Nature, **17**: 18.
Earthworms. Chamb. J. **58**: 769.
Earwigs, Plague of. Chamb. J. **45**: 281.
Easby Abbey, Yorkshire. Penny M. **5**: 313.
East, The. (H. P. Haynes) Godey, **47**: 30. — (Countess de Gasparin) Good Words, **3**: 399. — (N. Macleod) Good Words, **6**: 33–914. **7**: 134, 172, 267. — Mus. **44**: 490.
— Aiton's Travels in. Blackw. **72**: 745.
— and the West. (G. N. Smith) Lakeside, **1**: 159. — Dem. R. **22**: 401.
— Artisans of. Ecl. Engin. **11**: 136.
East, The, Books on, 1840. Mo. R. **152**: 360.
— Cairo to Athens. (M. B. Edwards) Ecl. M. **79**: 349.
— Carlisle's Diary in. (C. C. Felton) No. Am. **81**: 91.
— Castlereagh's Travels in. Colburn, **80**: 363.
— Christians in. (W. G. Palgrave) Quar. **127**: 1. Same art. Liv. Age, **102**: 515. — (T. J. Lamy) Dub. R. **84**: 397.
— Cities of Cairo and Damascus. Broadw. **7**: 226.
— Clarke's Travels in. Portfo.(Den.) **17**: 59.
— Commerce of, Struggles for. De Bow, **22**: 604.
— Communications with the far. Fraser, **54**: 574. Same art. Liv. Age, **52**: 156.
— Discovery in, Progress and Results of. Lond. Q. **1**: 297.
— Early Travelers in. All the Year, **32**: 445, 508, 588. **33**: 30–508. **34**: 103, 173. — Brit. Q. **17**: 128.
— Forbes's Oriental Memoirs. (R. Southey) Quar. **12**: 180. — Ecl. R. **20**: 405, 440, 631. — Anal. M. **6**: 1.
— From Calcutta to Alexandria. (N. Macleod) Good Words, **11**: 626.
— Funeral Ceremony in. Chr. Rem. **19**: 407.
— Glimpse of. St. James, **19**: 42.
— Greek Civilization in. Quar. **149**: 125. Same art. Liv. Age, **144**: 515.
— Lady Herbert's Cradle Lands. (H. M. Alden) Harper, **36**: 701.
— History of, Early. (G. Rawlinson) Contemp. **14**: 80.
— — Rawlinson's Five Great Monarchies. Brit. Q. **49**: 349. Same art. Ecl. M. **73**: 1, 182. — Ed. R. **125**: 108. — No. Brit. **44**: 331. Same art. Ecl. M. **67**: 385, 548. *See* Rawlinson.
— Home Life in. (L. Abbott) Harper, **53**: 695.
— How I entered and how I left it. Lippinc. **4**: 630.
— Hutton's Five Years in. Ecl. R. **87**: 83.
— Kinglake's Eöthen; or Travels in. Quar. **75**: 54. Same art. Ecl. M. **5**: 321. Same art. Liv. Age, **4**: 467. — Liv. Age, **3**: 726.—Dem. R. **16**: 367.—So. Q. **9**: 285.
— Languages and Literature of. (C. Wells) Gent. M. n. s. **2**: 161.
— Life in. So. Lit. Mess. **26**: 294.
— — Cases illustrative of. Liv. Age, **38**: 611.
— — Miss Martineau's. Prosp. R. **4**: 524. — Tait, n. s. **15**: 604. — Colburn, **83**: 194. — Chr. Obs. **48**: 818.
— — Reminiscences of. Sharpe, **17**: 193, 273. **18**: 81.
— Low Life in. Sharpe, **46**: 294.
— Missions in. (G. B. Cheever) Am. Bib. Repos. 2d s. **3**: 54.
— Moral and Religious State of. Portfo.(Den.) **28**: 329.
— Mummies and Moslems, Warner's. Canad. Mo. **10**: 270.
— New Lines of Communication in. Colburn, **106**: 379.
— Oriental Acquaintance. Putnam. **7**: 415.
— Overland Journey to. So. Lit. Mess. **20**: 33–217.
— Passages of Travel in. (W. C. Prime) Harper, **12**: 224, 371, 482. **13**: 191–772. **14**: 32.
— Peeps at. (N. Macleod) Good Words, **10**: 22–855.
— Petty Warfare in. (W. F. Ainsworth) Colburn, **82**: 281.
— Picture of. Knick. **59**: 567.
— Poetry of. (W. D. Whitney) Nation, **1**: 535.
— R. K. Porter's Travels in. Portfo.(Den.) **28**: 457.
— Prime's Travels in. Liv. Age, **49**: 243.
— Rambles in. Dub. Univ. **33**: 561, 739. **35**: 169, 309, 615.
— Ramblings in. (H. T. Cook) Lakeside, **1**: 362.
— Recollections of. (J. Bowring) Once a Week, **3**: 16.
— Religious Imagination in. (F. R. Conder) Dub. Univ. **91**: 345, 468.
— Religious Life in. Bentley, **36**: 195.
— Routes to. Brit. Q. **27**: 133.
— Gen. Sherman in. (J. C. Audenried) Harper, **47**: 225, 481, 652.
— Sketches of. Knick. **35**: 130. — (J. P. Brown) Contin. Mo. **2**: 179.
— Spencer's Travels in. Am. Church R. **15**: 368.

East, The, Stray Letters from. Colburn, **101**: 344. **102**: 41–454.
— Tischendorf's Travels in. (W. H. Green) Princ. **29**: 34.
— Trade with, and the precious Metals. (R. H. Patterson) Contemp. **35**: 131.
— Traveler in. (A. L. Koeppen) Mercersb. **6**: 258, 435, 531. **7**: 1–513. **8**: 40, 350. **9**: 108, 402. **11**: 149. **12**: 1.
— Travelers in. (F. Walpole) Bentley, **30**: 547. — (A. Barnes) Chr. Q. Spec. **9**: 212.
— Traveling in. Month, **3**: 240.
— Travels in. (F. R. Feudge) Lippinc. **12**: 263, 513, 643. — (M. Stuart) No. Am. **26**: 539. — Blackw. **5**: 527. — (J. S. Buckingham) Dem. R. **1**: 413. **2**: 53, 247. — (A. P. Peabody) No. Am. **81**: 194. — (H. Southgate) Tait, n. s. **7**: 569, 637. — Chr. Rem. **6**: 143. **10**: 498. — Dub. Univ. **41**: 218. — Ecl. R. **86**: 553. — Hogg, **11**: 177–416. **12**: 30–489. — Colburn, **93**: 88. — Once a Week, **11**: 331.
— — Episodes of. Dub. Univ. **22**: 421. **23**: 5, 239.
— — of an Ultramontane in. Colburn, **149**: 148.
— — Southgate's. Mus. **40**: 265, 399.
— under the Caliphs. (W. Spitta) Western, **5**: 291.
— Urquhart's Spirit of. Mo. R. **147**: 81.
East Basham Hall, Norfolk. Penny M. **14**: 245.
East Boston. *See* Boston, East.
East Coast, Romance of. (E. L. Cornish) Fraser, **97**: 523.
East-End Entertainment. (F. W. Robinson) Belgra. **9**: 518.
East Granby, Conn., Old Prison at. (C. B. Todd) Lippinc. **27**: 290.
East India College. Ed. R. **27**: 511. — Quar. **17**: 107. — Pamph. **9**: 469.
East India Company. Brit. & For. R. **8**: 154. — Am. Ecl. **2**: 505. — Quar. **8**: 126. — (F. Brinley) Hunt, **4**: 297. — Pamph. **1**: 185. — Fraser, **1**: 260, 457, 655. **2**: 222. — (N. Allen) No. Am. **82**: 404. — Bentley, **42**: 415. — Penny M. **3**: 84.
— and Juggernaut. Mo. R. **123**: 529.
— Anglo-Indian Lament for. Fraser, **57**: 635.
— Bruce's Annals of. Ecl. R. **13**: 1.
— Charter of. Quar. **8**: 239. — Pamph. **2**: 143. — Tait, **3**: 253, 650. — Colburn, **28**: 276.
— Chinese Question in. Ed. R. **52**: 282. — Selec. Ed. R. **6**: 263.
— Commercial System of. Mo. R. **134**: 353.
— Death of. Knick. **52**: 615.
— Dissolution of. Bank. M. (N. Y.) **13**: 431. — (C. Redding) Colburn, **112**: 243. — Tait, n. s. **25**: 502.
— Ensign of. Hist. M. **11**: 235.
— Government of. No. Brit. **18**: 526.
— Grant's History of. Ecl. R. **18**: 383.
— Hall on Renewal of Charter, 1813. (J. Foster) Ed. R. **17**: 385.
— House and Servants of. Cornh. **2**: 113.
— Kaye's Administration of. Bentley, **34**: 157.
— Museum of. Penny M. **10**: 207.
— — History of. Pract. M. **5**: 68.
— Palmerston's India Bill. Colburn, **112**: 369.
— Postans's Hints to Cadets of. Mo. R. **159**: 299.
— Report on. Pamph. **2**: 93.
East India Gazetteer, Hamilton's. Ed. R. **25**: 220.
East India Monopoly. Ed. R. **19**: 229. **20**: 471.
East India Question. Blackw. **33**: 776.
East India Trade. (T. P. Thompson) Westm. **14**: 93.
— and Opium Trade. (F. Wharton) Hunt, **4**: 9.
East Indies, History of. (J. W. Mann) Mercersb. **2**: **13**.
— Islands of. (A. W. Ely) De Bow, **15**: 14, 243.
— Languages of. (R. Cust) Geog. M. **5**: 1, 25.
— Life in. (H. Copinger) Colburn, **158**: 122. **159**: 36. — New Dom. **14**: 340.
— Life in Cantonment. Liv. Age, **44**: 489.
— Native States of. Mus. **41**: 271.
East Indies. Our manifest Destiny in the East. De Bow, **15**: 541.
— Sketches in. (G. J. Oliver) Harper, **11**: 324.
See Dutch East Indies; India.
East Lynne. (Mrs. H. Wood) Colburn, **118**: 28–428. **119**: 89–405. **120**: 15–393. **121**: 68–401. **122**: 31–393. **123**: 24.
East-River Bridge. *See* Bridge, East-River.
East-Winds, May. Fraser, **63**: 586.
— Threnode to. Fraser, **57**: 517.
Eastburn, Bishop Manton, Criticism of. (J. Wayland) Am. Church R. **12**: 387.
Eastburn, J. W. Yamoyden. Portfo. (Den.) **24**: 456.
Easter. (A. Lamson) Chr. Exam. **38**: 41. — Galaxy, **9**: 700.
— Calculation of. Penny M. **14**: 3.
— Controversies of 2d Century on. (W. Milligan) Contemp. **6**: 101.
— Ecclesiastical Computation of. Quar. **18**: 496. — House. Words, **19**: 325.
— Origin and Celebration of. Colburn, **4**: 270.
— Poem on. (A. D. T. Whitney) Scrib. **3**: 707.
— Three Lifts and other Customs of. St. James, **24**: 130.
Easter Card; a Story. (V. W. Johnson) Harper, **60**: 755.
Easter Day. (J. F. Waller) Dub. Univ. **37**: 624.
— Customs of, Origin of. (G. B. Griffith) Potter Am. Mo. **10**: 306.
— De Morgan on. Chr. Obs. **45**: 41.
— in Russia. Broadw. **10**: 243. — (E. Schuyler) Scrib. **3**: 681.
— Observance and Custom of. (F. R. Diffenderfer) Mercersb. **21**: 259.
Easter Eggs. Ev. Sat. **3**: 615. — (M. A. Hoare) Once a Week, **16**: 450.
Easter Eve; a Tale. (B. Murphy) Cath. World, **15**: 42.
Easter Feasts in Poland. Colburn, **70**: 592.
Easter Flowers. (S. Osgood) Harper, **27**: 189.
Easter Holiday. (J. Payn) Belgra. **36**: supp. 40.
Easter Hymns from old Cloisters. (F. Foxcroft) Atlan. **43**: 417.
Easter Trip of two Ochlophobists. Blackw. **102**: 42, 188.
Easter Island. (J. A. Palmer, jr.) Overland, **2**: 551. — Ev. Sat. **9**: 250. — Macmil. **21**: 449.
— a doomed People. Chamb. J. **46**: 633.
— Hieroglyphics of. (J. P. Harrison) Anthrop. J. **3**: 370.
Eastern Archipelago. *See* Indian Archipelago.
Eastern Christianity. (J. Pyne) Nat. Q. **35**: 313.
Eastern Church. (E. A. Freeman) Ed. R. **107**: 322. — (W. A. McVickar) Am. Church R. **7**: 515. **8**: 78. — Dub. R. **23**: 406.
— Account of. (E. M. Bliss) New Eng. **36**: 568.
— and Anglican, Intercommunion of. (H. Southgate) Am. Church R. **15**: 517. **16**: 1. — Am. Church R. **21**: 236.
— — Obstacles to Union of. Chr. Rem. **47**: 455.
— and Archbishop Lycurgus. Chr. Obs. **70**: 294.
— and Council of Nice. (A. St. J. Chambre) Univ. Q. **21**: 25.
— and divergent Branches. Chr. Rem. **42**: 234.
— Divergence from Rome. Chr. Rem. **26**: 64.
— History of. Chr. Obs. **54**: 40. — Ed. R. **107**: 322. — So. R. n. s. **23**: 176. **24**: 124.
— — Neale's. Dub. R. **24**: 487.
— — Stanley's. Chr. Obs. **61**: 607. — Ecl. R. **113**: 613. — Dub. R. **50**: 92. — No. Brit. **35**: 82. — (H. Southgate) Am. Church R. **15**: 1, 169, 337.
— — in 1856. Chr. Rem. **33**: 200.
— in Russia, State of, 1814. Ecl. R. **20**: 429.
— Missions to. (N. S. Richardson) Am. Church R. **6**: 527.
— Past and Future of. Nat. R. **13**: 27.
— Patterson on. Dub. R. **32**: 407.
— School of Alexandria, etc. Chr. Rem. **17**: 76.

Eastern Church, Translations of Liturgies. Chr. Rem. **50**: 420.
— Union with. Chr. Obs. **76**: 248.
Eastern Churches. (J. C. Moffat) Princ. **39**: 89. — U. S. Cath. M. **5**: 389.
— and the A. B. C. F. M. (N. S. Richardson) Am. Church R. **14**: 417.
Eastern Colonies, Australia, etc. Dub. Univ. **13**: 88.
Eastern Excavations. Nature, **17**: 397.
Eastern Policy, Our. Fraser, **27**: 108.
Eastern Problem. (D. S. Gregory) Princ. n. s. **1**: 49. — Lond. Q. **14**: 85.
Eastern Prodigies. All the Year, **22**: 125.
Eastern Question. (J. S. C. Abbott) Putnam, **13**: 456. (K. Blind) Macmil. **20**: 36. Same art. Ecl. M. **73**: 48. — (M. E. G. Duff) Contemp. **28**: 694. — (E. L. Godkin) No. Am. **124**: 106. — (A. H. Guernsey) Galaxy, **23**: 359. — (G. P. Marsh) Chr. Exam. **64**: 393. — (J. Robertson) Good Words, **18**: 57. — (R. B. Smith) Contemp. **29**: 147. — All the Year, **40**: 9. — Brit. Q. **11**: 230. — Colburn, **98**: 415. — Dem. R. **33**: 353. — Dub. R. **2**: 509. — Dub. Univ. **87**: 634. — Fraser, **83**: 174. — Lond. Q. **29**: 399. Same art. Ecl. M. **70**: 269, 451, 694. — Mus. **40**: 410. — Tait, n. s. **20**: 421.
— and Eastern Christians. Macmil. **35**: 84, 158.
— and Election of 1880. (E. A. Freeman) Contemp. **37**: 956.
— and the English. (E. A. Freeman) Contemp. **29**: 489.
— and European Alliances. Liv. Age, **38**: 304.
— and Future of Russia. Westm. **110**: 469.
— and Prophecy. (G. F. Herrick) Bib. Sac. **27**: 360.
— and Workingmen. (G. Potter and G. Howell) Contemp. **28**: 851.
— as respects Syria. No. Brit. **37**: 422.
— Austria, and Germany. Fraser, **96**: 407. — (E. L. Godkin) Nation, **32**: 453.
— Best Books on. (E. Schuyler) Nation, **25**: 284.
— Bjornstjerna on. Mo. R. **153**: 324.
— British Interests in the East. (M. E. G. Duff) 19th Cent. **7**: 658.
— Charter of our Policy. (M. Maccoll) Gent. M. n. s. **20**: 414.
— Commercial View of, 1854. Brit. Q. **20**: 509.
— Constantinople and our Road to India. (H. M. Havelock) Fortn. **27**: 119.
— Diplomatic History of. Ed. R. **100**: 1.
— England in. (G. Rawlinson) Princ. n. s. **6**: 1. — Colburn, **143**: 347.
— England and Russia in the East. Ed. R. **142**: 264. — (A. Vámbéry) 19th Cent. **7**: 917.
— English Foreign Policy and. Fraser, **93**: 537.
— European Rule in the East. (I. E. Graeff) Mercersb. **25**: 130.
— Four Empires. Westm. **68**: 415. Same art. Liv. Age, **55**: 641.
— Fulfilment of the Berlin Treaty. (E. A. Freeman) Princ. n. s. **5**: 57.
— Geographical Aspect of. (E. A. Freeman) Fortn. **27**: 73. Same art. Liv. Age, **132**: 369.
— German's View of. Colburn, **101**: 291.
— Hellenic Factor in. (W. E. Gladstone) Contemp. **29**: 1. Same art. Liv. Age, **132**: 131.
— Historical Sketch of. West. J. **14**: 24, 92.
— Historical Studies of. Tait, n. s. **22**: 111.
— History of, Argyll's. (M. Maccoll) Contemp. **34**: 763.
— how to settle it. St. Paul's, **2**: 403.
— in 1834. Mo. R. **136**: 50.
— in 1835. Mo. R. **137**: 84. **138**: 50.
— in 1836. Mo. R. **140**: 474.
— — and Non-Intervention. Tait, n. s. **3**: 240, 535.
Eastern Question in 1853. Liv. Age, **39**: 504. — Dub. R. **35**: 69. — Ecl. R. **98**: 225. — New Q. **2**: 458.
— in 1854. (G. H. Emerson) Univ. Q. **11**: 221. — Liv. Age, **39**: 237. — Dub. Univ. **43**: 253, 624. Same art. Liv. Age, **41**: 543. — Fraser, **48**: 711. Same art. Liv. Age, **40**: 99. — New Q. **3**: 21, 135. — Tait, n. s. **21**: 234–565.
— — Austria and the Allied Armies. Liv. Age, **42**: 324.
— — England's Share in the Calamities of War. Liv. Age, **41**: 526.
— — Germany and the War. Liv. Age, **43**: 571.
— — Southern Seat of War. Ecl. R. **100**: 271.
— — Turks in Asia. Ecl. R. **12**: 323.
See Crimean War.
— in 1855, Condition of Hungary. Ecl. R. **102**: 479.
— — New Congress of Vienna. Liv. Age, **45**: 45.
— — Religious Aspects of. Univ. Q. **12**: 25.
— — Reconstruction of Poland. Ecl. R. **101**: 220.
— — Significance of the Struggle. No. Brit. **24**: 268. Same art. Liv. Age, **47**: 785.
— in 1856, Danubian Principalities. Ecl. R. **105**: 563.
— in 1857. Dub. Univ. **49**: 1.
— in 1858. New Q. **7**: 269.
— in 1859. New Q. **8**: 106, 221. — Tait, n. s. **26**: 559.
— in 1861. New Q. **10**: 109.
— in 1870, Anglo-Russian Difficulty. (L. Stephen) Nation, **11**: 399.
— — and Prussia. (F. Kapp) Nation, **11**: 400.
— — Spectacular Theory of War. (E. L. Godkin) Nation, **11**: 416.
— — Turco-Russian Trouble. (E. L. Godkin) Nation, **11**: 345.
— in 1871. (E. L. Godkin) Nation, **12**: 5. — (M. Heilprin) Nation, **12**: 38.
— — and France. (E. L. Godkin) Nation, **13**: 173.
— in 1872. (E. L. Godkin) Nation, **14**: 285.
— — Pan-Hellenic Dream. (S. Powers) Lippinc. **7**: 28.
— in 1875. (E. L. Godkin) Nation, **21**: 128. — (A. Laugel) Nation, **21**: 337. — Nation, **21**: 397.
— — England in Egypt. (E. L. Godkin) Nation, **21**: 352.
— — Is Anglo-Russian Alliance possible? (J. C. Paget) St. James, **36**: 462.
— — Khiva and. (J. C. Paget) St. James, **35**: 527, 590.
— — Mussulman Progress and British Policy. (E. Bell) St. James, **35**: 104.
— in 1876. (E. L. Godkin) Nation, **22**: 361. **23**: 251. — (A. Laugel) Nation, **23**: 88–324. **24**: 219.
— — and the Berlin Conference. Quar. **143**: 276.
— — and the Government. Quar. **142**: 544.
— — Aspect of. Liv. Age, **131**: 414.
— — English Feeling on. (E. L. Godkin) Nation, **23**: 223.
— — Estimate of Russian Power. (E. L. Godkin) Nation, **24**: 36.
— — Germany and Russia in. (H. von Holst) Nation, **23**: 226.
— — Montenegro's Importance. (W. J. Stillman) Nation, **22**: 380.
— — Prospect of general War in Europe. (E. L. Godkin) Nation, **22**: 288.
— — Religion in. (E. L. Godkin) Nation, **23**: 176.
— — Russian Finances. (E. L. Godkin) Nation, **24**: 83.
— — Three Emperors' Policy. (W. H. Dixon) Gent. M. n. s. **17**: 51.
— in 1877. (E. L. Godkin) Nation, **24**: 5. — Westm. **108**: 200.
— — American Opinion on. (E. L. Godkin) Nation, **24**: 260.
— — Balance of Power. Quar. **143**: 526.
— — France and. (A. Laugel) Nation, **24**: 277.
— — Neutrality, — real or pretended? (E. A. Freeman) Contemp. **30**: 877.
— — Part of England in. (A. Laugel) Nation, **24**: 289.

Eastern Question in 1877, Plevna Defeat. (E. L. Godkin) Nation, **25**: 115, 361.
— — Prospect in Turkey. (E. L. Godkin) Nation, **24**: 275.
— — Relation of England to the War. (E. A. Freeman) Contemp. **30**: 481.
— — Terms of Peace. (E. L. Godkin) Nation, **25**: 361.
— — Turco-Russian Complication. (E. L. Godkin) Nation, **24**: 231.
— — Turkish Navy. (H. H. Gorringe) Nation, **24**: 307. *See* Turco-Russian War.
— in 1878. (E. L. Godkin) Nation, **27**: 234. — Ed. R. **147**: 559. — Brit. Q. **67**: 506.
— — Austria in. (E. L. Godkin) Nation, **26**: 194.
— — Agreement of England and Russia. (E. L. Godkin) Nation, **26**: 398.
— — Anglo-Russian Agreement. (A. C. Sellar) Nation, **27**: 6.
— — England and Russia. (E. L. Godkin) Nation, **27**: 65.
— — European Congress. (E. L. Godkin) Nation, **26**: 237.
— — What is in Store. (L. Kossuth) Contemp. **31**: 555.
— in 1879, Newest Phases of. (A. Laugel) Nation, **28**: 348.
— in 1880. (A. Laugel) Nation, **31**: 43. — Nat. Q. **40**: 140. — Month, **39**: 126.
— in 1881, English and French Relations to. (J. R. Holland, A. Laugel, and S. Amos) Nation, **33**: 311, 490.
— Irrepressible Conflict in. (T. M. Anderson) Galaxy, **24**: 689.
— Kings of the East in Rev. xvi. 12. Liv. Age, **48**: 65.
— long ago. (S. Robjohns) St. James, **37**: 640.
— Peace of the Dardanelles. Ecl. R. **82**: 324.
— Relations to Europe. Knick. **41**: 479.
— Russian Campaigns of 1853–54 and 1877. (E. L. Godkin) Nation, **24**: 347.
— Treaties of 1856 and 1867. Ed. R. **133**: 267.
— — and of 1878. Brit. Q. **68**: 465.
— The True. (E. A. Freeman) Fortn. **24**: 747. Same art. Ecl. M. **86**: 159. Same art. Liv. Age, **128**: 67.
— Turkey, Egypt, and. Fraser, **93**: 1.
— What has the United States to do with? (P. Godwin) Putnam, **3**: 514.
— Position of the United States in Case of War, 1878. (A. G. Sedgwick) Nation, **26**: 270.
— What is it? St. Paul's, **2**: 274.
See Asia, Central; Egypt; Russia; Turkey; Greece; Crimean War.
Eastern Sketches. *See* Oriental Sketches.
Eastern States, Effect of Western Competition on. (L. Playfair) Fraser, **101**: 747.
— First Impressions of. (J. T. Watkins) Overland, **5**: 352.
— Letters on. (E. and J. Everett) No. Am. **11**: 68.
Eastern Stories. Blackw. **18**: 61.
Eastern Story-Tellers. Lond. M. **20**: 183.
Eastern Stratagem. (N. S. Dodge) Lippinc. **10**: 231.
East Haddam, Land Records. N. E. Reg. **11**: 273, 311. **12**: 42. **13**: 125.
Eastham, Mass., Records of. N. E. Reg. **6**: 41, 167, 234. **7**: 279, 347.
East Hampton, Long Island. Dem. R. **1**: 297.
— Romance of. (A. A. Hayes, jr.) Harper, **59**: 219.
Eastlake, Sir C. L. Ed. R. **131**: 392. — F. Arts Q. **4**: 52.
— Literature of the Fine Arts. Blackw. **64**: 753.
Eastman, Mary. Dahcota. Peop. J. **7**: 340.
Eastman Genealogy. (L. R. Eastman) N. E. Reg. **21**: 229.
Easton, Mass., Ministers of. Am. Q. Reg. **12**: 141.
Eastward; a Poem. Broadw. **7**: 463.
Eastward Ho! Lond. Soc. **7**: 370.
Easy-Chairs, Science of. Nature, **18**: 637. Same art. Pop. Sci. Mo. **14**: 186.
Easy Methods. (T. E. C. Leslie) Fraser, **102**: 425.
Eaters, Great. All the Year, **23**: 343. Same art. Ev. Sat. **9**: 215.
Eating. (C. W. Dulles) Lippinc. **25**: 502.
Eating among the Greeks and Romans. So. Lit. Mess. **21**: 713.
— Ancient. Penny M. **4**: 324.
— and Drinking. (A. Flint, jr.) Nation, **3**: 354. — Mus. **7**: 89.
— — Rules for. Lond. M. **12**: 225.
— Art of. (T. W. Storrow) Putnam, **4**: 581. Same art. Broadw. **9**: 518.
— — Chapter on. Fraser, **36**: 610.
— — from the earliest Ages, etc. Broadw. **8**: 519.
— Enjoyment of. Cornh. **8**: 613.
— Gastronomy in all Ages. Colburn, **130**: 451.
— Gossip about. Dub. Univ. **58**: 448.
— How Animals eat. (H. L. Fairchild) Pop. Sci. Mo. **17**: 224.
— in England. Lond. M. **4**: 246.
— Over- and under-Eating. Cornh. **8**: 35.
— Question of. (W. Browning) Pop. Sci. Mo. **15**: 345.
— Society for the Suppression of. New Eng. M. **2**: 313.
— Why do we eat our Dinner? (G. Allen) Pop. Sci. Mo. **14**: 799.
Eaton, Cyrus, Account of. (J. L. Sibley) Unita. R. **3**: 373.
Eaton, Mrs. M. O'Neill. (S. Hutchins) Internat. R. **8**: 126.
Eaton, Peter, Life of. Chr. Exam. **45**: 314.
Eaton, Gen. William, Life of. (C. C. Felton) Sparks's Am. Biog. **9**: 165. — Anal. M. **5**: 299, 398. — Gen. Repos. **4**: 174.
Eaux Bonnes, Les. Chamb. J. **43**: 779.
Ebba; or the Emigrants in Sweden; a Tale. (E. Marmier) Internat. M. **1**: 345.
Ebel, Johann Wm. (E. C. Towne) Chr. Exam. **84**: 287.
Eben; a true Story. (M. Oliphant) Liv. Age, **55**: 790.
Eben Jackson; a Story. (R. T. Cooke) Atlan. **1**: 524.
Ebenezer; a Tale. (C. G. Leland) Temp. Bar, **55**: 204, 354, 543.
Eber, J. Seven Years in King's Theater. Mo. R. **117**: 53.
Ebers, Georg. Homo Sum. (F. Carter) New Eng. **38**: 75. — (E. F. Williams) Dial (Ch.), **1**: 28.
Ebert, F. A. Bibliographisches Lexikon. Lond. M. **2**: 41.
Ebionitism and Christianity of Sub-Apostolic Age. (G. P. Fisher) Am. Presb. R. **13**: 529.
Ebon, Atoll of, in Micronesia. (E. T. Doane) Am. J. Sci. **81**: 318.
Ebony and its Varieties. (P. L. Simmonds) Art J. **24**: 66.
Ebrard, J. H. A., and the Church Question. (W. M. Reily) Mercersb. **17**: 5.
Ecce Deus. Chr. Obs. **67**: 585. — Dub. Univ. **70**: 72.
Ecce Homo; a Sketch. Chr. Obs. **67**: 1.
See Jesus Christ.
Eccentrics and Eccentricities. Potter Am. Mo. **12**: 114.
— Modern. Temp. Bar, **16**: 558. **17**: 270–562. **18**: 132. Same art. Ecl. M. **67**: 105. Same art. Ev. Sat. **1**: 331.
— of the 16th Century. Dub. Univ. **69**: 297.
Eccentric Biography, Curiosities of. (F. W. Fairholt) Bentley, **29**: 15, 180. Same art. Ecl. M. **22**: 278, 401.
Eccentric People. Chamb. J. **54**: 535. Same art. Ev. Sat. **1**: 613.
Eccentric Village; a Story. Peop. J. **8**: 193.
Eccentricity. (I. F. Mayo) Good Words, **17**: 525. Same art. Liv. Age, **70**: 216.
— as a Pursuit. (W. E. McCann) Lippinc. **5**: 524.
Eccentricities in a Basket. Cornh. **13**: 345.
Ecclesiastical and Denominational Organization. (O. A. Skinner) Univ. Q. **7**: 43.
Ecclesiastical Antiquities. Dub. Univ. **31**: 207.
Ecclesiastical Authority *versus* Protestantism. (G. E. Ellis) Chr. Exam. **35**: 273.
Ecclesiastical Biography, Dr. Wordsworth's Quar. **4**: 93. — (J. Foster) Ecl. R. **11**: 428.
Ecclesiastical Christendom. (F. H. Hedge) Chr. Exam. **51**: 112.

Ecclesiastical Commission and Church Rates. Fraser, **11**: 457.
Ecclesiastical Continuity. (C. D. B. Mills) Radical, **2**: 481.
Ecclesiastical Councils of early Ages. Chr. Mo. Spec. **6**: 520. *See* Councils.
Ecclesiastical Courts. Westm. **14**: 316. — Ecl. R. **71**: 197. — (F. W. Rowsell) Macmil. **21**: 73. — Tait, n. s. **6**: 781.
— Bill on, 1844. Mo. R. **164**: 230.
— Seals of; Edw. I. (Sir W. Blackstone) Arch **3**: 414.
Ecclesiastical Denominations, American. (A. H. Quint) Cong. Q. **1**: 124, 296.
Ecclesiastical Discipline. Chr. Mo. Spec. **2**: 288, 567. **3**: 281.
Ecclesiastical Discoveries of the Puritans. (G. B. Cheever) Am. Bib. Repos. 3d s. **4**: 1.
Ecclesiastical Economy. Ed. R. **99**: 94. — (J. W. Alexander) Princ. **14**: 562.
Ecclesiastical Endowments; Tithe Laws. (R. Southey) Quar. **42**: 105.
Ecclesiastical Establishments. Westm. **5**: 404. — (E. Everett) No. Am. **15**: 431. — Ecl. R. **80**: 149.
Ecclesiastical Functions, Nature of. (I. E. Graeff) Mercersb. **7**: 290.
Ecclesiastical History. *See* Church.
Ecclesiastical Infallibility. (M. Gavin) Month, **43**: 109.
Ecclesiastical Jurisprudence and American Civil Law. (H. D. Jenkins) Presb. R. **1**: 549.
Ecclesiastical Law. (S. Miller) Princ. **7**: 89, 186. — Brit. & For. R. **8**: 1.
— Curates and Curacies. Chr. Rem. **4**: 293.
— Dilapidations. Chr. Rem. **2**: 184.
— Historical Sketch of. Chr. Obs. **63**: 854.
— in the United States. Brit. Q. **64**: 414.
— Residence of the Clergy. Chr. Rem. **3**: 200.
Ecclesiastical Lectures, Hillyard's. Ecl. R. **80**: 574.
Ecclesiastical Legislation in New England. (L. E. Smith) Bapt. Q. **1**: 81.
Ecclesiastical Legislature. Dub. Univ. **22**: 720. **23**: 183.
Ecclesiastical Miracles, Newman on. No. Brit. **4**: 451.
Ecclesiastical Opinions, Gladstone on. Lond. Q. **43**: 382.
Ecclesiastical Organizations and Foreign Missions. (J. Van Vechten) Am. Presb. R. **13**: 626.
— of English Dissent. (P. W. Clayden) Fortn. **9**: 497.
Ecclesiastical Polity, Davidson's. (G. E. Day) Bib. Sac. **5**: 513.
Ecclesiastical Power. (H. Giles) Chr. Exam. **31**: 203.
Ecclesiastical Prime Ministers. Dem. R. **43**: 49.
Ecclesiastical Prudence, Newman on. Dub. R. **77**: 273, 500.
Ecclesiastical Question, Facts and Phantasms on the. Fraser, **78**: 567.
Ecclesiastical Reform in England. Brit. & For. R. **1**: 172. **2**: 201. **3**: 201.
Ecclesiastical Revenues. (R. Southey) Quar. **29**: 524.
Ecclesiastical Standards. (H. Giles) Chr. Exam. **31**: 209.
Ecclesiastical State of the Colonies. Quar. **75**: 201.
Ecclesiastical Statistics, 1859. (A. H. Quint) Cong. Q. **2**: 220.
— American. (A. H. Quint) Cong. Q. **8**: 199. — Cong. Q. **9**: 195, 291.
— Hints on. Cong. Q. **9**: 174.
— Lessons from. (I. P. Langworthy) Cong. Q. **4**: 293.
Ecclesiastical Symbolism. Temp. Bar, **19**: 260.
Ecclesiastical Theses. (L. Bacon) Cong. Q. **5**: 211.
Ecclesiastical Tribunals. Gen. Repos. **2**: 288.
Ecclesiastical Unity, Principle of. (I. E. Graeff) Mercersb. **10**: 265.
Ecclesiasticism, or false Authority. (J. W. Nevin) Mercersb. **19**: 364.
Echinoderms and Corals from the Gulf of California. (A. E. Verrill) Am. J. Sci. **99**: 93.
— Morphology of. Nature, **19**: 406.
— Nursing. Pop. Sci. R. **16**: 51.
— Recent Works on. (E. P. Wright) Nature, **8**: 103.
Echinoid Fauna of Brazil. (R. Rathbun) Am. J. Sci. **115**: 82.
Echinoids. *See* Hedgehogs.
Echo. So. Lit. Mess. **13**: 215.
— in two Political Dialogues. Blackw. **3**: 55.
Echo Farm, Litchfield, Conn. (W. H. Rideing) Harper, **57**: 641.
Echo Verses. All the Year, **27**: 247.
Echoes, Aerial. (J. Henry) J. Frankl. Inst. **105**: 189.
— Harmonic. (Lord Rayleigh) Nature, **8**: 319.
— Mountain. Penny M. **14**: 55.
Echternach, Dancing Procession of. (Miss Curry) Cath. World, **25**: 626.
Eckel, Mrs. L. St. J., Autobiography of. Brownson, **24**: 43.
Eckermann and Goethe. (A. M. Machar) Canad. Mo. **16**: 230, 386. — Dub. Univ. **37**: 732. Same art. Ecl. M. **23**: 454.
Eckley, Sophia May. Minor Chords, and other Poems. Victoria, **12**: 276.
Eclectic, The. Knick. **8**: 168, 397.
Eclectic Philosophy. Bost. Q. **2**: 27.
Eclecticism. (W. Knight) Theo. R. **16**: 74.
— and Brahmoism. (R. Milman) Good Words, **11**: 792.
— Fragments Philosophiques. Bost. Q. **2**: 435.
— Ontology. Bost. Q. **2**: 169.
— or the Philosophy of Cousin. Chr. R. **3**: 590. **4**: 21.
Eclipse of the Moon, February, 1860. (Mrs. Ward) Recr. Sci. **1**: 279.
— of the Sun. (J. N. Lockyer) Nature, **17**: 481, 501. — Nature, **18**: 353.
— — of Agathocles. (S. Haughton) Nature, **16**: 563.
— — of 1806. (J. F. Cooper) Putnam, **14**: 352.
— — of May, 1836, Note on. (S. C. Walker) J. Frankl. Inst. **26**: 148.
— — of July 8, 1842. Am. J. Sci. **42**: 175. — J. Frankl. Inst. **35**: 248.
— — of July 18, 1860. (E. J. Lowe) Recr. Sci. **2**: 16. — Chamb. J. **34**: 133, 248, 265. Same art. Liv. Age, **67**: 224.
— — — Expedition to Spain. (Prof. Pole) Macmil. **2**: 406. — (C. Pritchard) Good Words, **8**: 609, 694.
— — of Aug. 17, 1868. Once a Week, **19**: 37. — (M. Janssen) Cath. World, **8**: 697. — (R. A. Proctor) Pop. Sci. R. **7**: 263. Same art. Ecl. M. **71**: 1152. — (A. Secchi) Month, **10**: 266. — Nature, **1**: 536. — Cornh. **23**: 158. Same art. Ecl. M. **76**: 412. — J. Frankl. Inst. **87**: 268.
— — — Hindu View of. Chamb. J. **45**: 676. Same art. Ecl. M. **72**: 22.
— — — Our Efforts in. (J. Carpenter) Belgra. **14**: 297.
— — — seen in India. All the Year, **21**: 250.
— — of 1869. (C. Abbe) Am. J. Sci. **103**: 264. — (R. S. Franklin) Overland, **6**: 519. — (M. Mitchell) Hours at Home, **9**: 555. — (Morton, Mayer, Himes, etc.) J. Frankl. Inst. **88**: 200, 249, 354. **89**: 58. — (G. Searle) Cath. World, **10**: 106.
— — — Anvil Protuberance of. (W. S. Gilman) J. Frankl. Inst. **89**: 417.
— — — as seen from Villasmunda. (H. Samuelson) Nature, **3**: 310.
— — — at the Mediterranean. Galaxy, **12**: 179.
— — — Augusta Expedition. (W. G. Adams) Nature, **3**: 249.
— — — Stellar Objects seen during. (J. R. Hind) Nature, **18**: 663.

Eclipse of the Sun of Dec. 22, 1870. Cornh. **23**: 158. — (E. Colbert) Lakeside, **5**: 226. — (J. N. Lockyer) Nature, **3**: 221, 321. **4**: 230, 248. — (S. Perry) Month, **14**: 272. — Ev. Sat. **10**: 108, 150. — (E. C. Pickering) O. & N. **3**: 634. — (R. A. Proctor) Fraser, **82**: 724.

— — — as observed at Jerez. (C. A. Young) J. Frankl. Inst. **91**: 82.

— — — Expedition to observe. (A. Weld) Month, **14**: 109. — (R. A. Proctor) Pop. Sci. R. **10**: 37.

— — — — Government and. Nature, **2**: 409.

— — — — Spain and. (A. Aguilar) Nature, **3**: 69.

— — — Issues of. (J. Carpenter) Pop. Sci. R. **10**: 130.

— — — Italian Report on. (J. Brett) Nature, **7**: 308.

— — — Lessons of. So. M. **8**: 496.

— — — Reports from United States Parties. J. Frankl. Inst. **91**: 137.

— — — To Oran to see. (J. Tyndall) Fortn. **15**: 330.

— — — What we may learn by. St. Paul's, **6**: 551. Same art. Ecl. M. **75**: 551.

— — of December, 1871. (J. N. Lockyer) Nature, **5**: 217, 259. Same art. Liv. Age, **112**: 483. — (R. A. Proctor) Good Words, **13**: 416. Same art. Ecl. M. **79**: 227. — (R. A. Proctor) Pop. Sci. R. **11**: 136. — (L. Respighi) Nature, **5**: 237. — Nature, **4**: 197. — (R. A. Proctor) Cornh. **23**: 158. Same art. Liv. Age, **112**: 88. — St. Paul's, **9**: 280.

— — — Australian Preparations for. (R. L. J. Ellery) Nature, **5**: 205, 351.

— — — English Government Expedition. Nature, **5**: 163. — (J. N. Lockyer) Nature, **7**: 57, 92. — Nature **4**: 516. **5**: 18.

— — — Observations of. (J. P. Maclear) Nature, **5**: 219.

— — of 1872. Pop. Sci. Mo. **1**: 17.

— — of 1874, African. Nature, **10**: 59.

— — of 1875. Nature, **11**: 201, 452, 490.

— — — Expedition to Siam. (F. E. Lott) Nature, **12**: 172.

— — — — Instructions to Observers. Nature, **11**: 351.

— — of 1878. (H. Draper) J. Frankl. Inst. **106**: 217. — (J. Degni) Am. Cath. Q. **3**: 635. — (R. A. Proctor) Gent. M. n. s. **21**: 50. — (C. A. Young) Princ. n. s. **2**: 865. — (J. N. Lockyer) Nature, **18**: 457. Same art. Liv. Age, **137**: 557. — (H. Draper) Am. J. Sci. **116**: 227. — (C. A. Young) Am. J. Sci. **116**: 279. — (G. F. Barker) Am. J. Sci. **117**: 121.

— — — First Fruits of Observations of. (R. A. Proctor) Gent. M. n. s. **21**: 288. Same art. Sup. Pop. Sci. Mo. **3**: 289.

— — of 1880. (D. P. Todd) Nation, **32**: 171.

— Prediction of the first. (O. Mitchell) Hogg, **8**: 200.

Eclipses. (T. H. Safford) Lakeside Mo. **2**: 119.

— and Phenomena. (D. Trowbridge) Nat. Q. **20**: 151.

— Arrangement for observing the Corona. (S. Newcomb) Am. J. Sci. **97**: 413.

— Celestial and terrestrial. Bentley, **58**: 364.

— in China. All the Year, **33**: 426.

— Great Solar. (C. F. Himes) Evang. R. **21**: 134. — (S. Newcomb) Princ. n. s. **2**: 848. — Cornh. **18**: 155. Same art. Liv. Age, **98**: 745. Same art. Ecl. M. **71**: 1181.

— Historical. (J. R. Hind) Nature, **6**: 251.

— Historical Notes on. Dub. Univ. **52**: 568.

— Hist. Sketch of. (C. Pritchard) Good Words, **12**: 628.

— Phenomenon in. (F. Bailey) J. Frankl. Inst. **26**: 154.

— Polarization of the Corona. (E. C. Pickering) J. Frankl. Inst. **91**: 58.

Eclipse Camera, Improved. Nature, **1**: 313.

Eclipse Photographs. (A. Brothers) Nature, **3**: 327, 369.

Eclipse Photography. (A. Brothers) Nature, **4**: 327.

Eclipse, the Racer. All the Year, **19**: 223. — Ev. Sat. **5**: 327.

Eclipse of Faith. Quar. **95**: 448. — (N. Porter) New Eng. **11**: 277.

Economic Address. (J. Morley) Fortn. **30**: 547.

Economic Contradictions, System of. (P. J. Proudhon) Radical R. **1**: 76–721.

Economic Education, Progress in. Am. Soc. Sci. J. **1**: 137.

Economic Law and Land Ownership, Froude on. (G. S. Lefevre) Fortn. **27**: 32.

Economic Legislation, Inefficiency of. (E. Atkinson) Am. Soc. Sci. J. **4**: 123.

Economic Method. (H. Sidgwick) Fortn. **31**: 301.

Economic Science, Elementary Instruction in. Am. J. Educ. **10**: 105.

— Notes on. (W. Hincks) Canad. J. n. s. **11**: 96.

Economic Sketches. Bank. M. (N. Y.) **30**: 257.

Economy and Trade. (J. Bowring) Bank. M. (N. Y.) **28**: 28.

— Bentham's Defense of. Pamph. **9**: 1. **10**: 281.

— Christian and Civic, Chalmers on. Chr. Obs. **20**: 490–707. **22**: 39, 105. **23**: 627.

— Cobbett's Cottage. Ed. R. **38**: 105.

— Compulsory, to cure Pauperism. (W. L. Blackley) Contemp. **35**: 608.

— How to live on a reduced Income. Good Words, **19**: 339. Same art. Liv. Age, **137**: 699.

— in Machine Shops. Pract. M. **6**: 74.

— Living in Perspective. (D. M. Craik) Fraser, **74**: 501. Same art. Liv. Age, **91**: 329.

— of the Earth. Dub. R. **1**: 1.

— of Life. So. Lit. Mess. **10**: 648, 714.

— of Paying twice. (T. P. Thompson) Westm. **20**: 238.

— Political. *See* Political Economy.

— Popular, Symons on. Mo. R. **153**: 405.

— Possibilities of. Galaxy, **1**: 719.

— Private. Once a Week, **8**: 79.

— Profitable and unprofitable. (E. L. Godkin) Nation, **21**: 97.

— Public and private. Niles's Reg. **19**: 37.

— Secret of. St. James, **22**: 537.

— Sermon on. (C. J. Vaughan) Good Words, **12**: 778.

— True and false. (C. Walbey) Peop. J. **10**: 205.

Economies. (H. Giles) Chr. Exam. **46**: 236.

Ecrivain Public; Sketch of Parisian Life. Fraser, **34**: 301. Same art. Ecl. M. **9**: 262. Same art. Liv. Age, **11**: 41.

Ecstatics of Genius. (J. W. Jackson) Zoist, **13**: 149–351.

Ecuador, Barometrical Measurements in. (W. Reiss and A. Stuebel) Am. J. Sci **102**: 267.

Ecumenical Councils. *See* Councils; *also, names of places where held, as* Nice, Trieste, Vatican.

Edda, The. (C. Lottner) Fraser, **64**: 190.

— Ethical Ideas of. (K. Blind) Dub. Univ. **91**: 392, 520.

— Free Translation from the Icelandic of. (E. Head) Fraser, **72**: 370.

— Rhymes from. Dub. Univ. **41**: 578.

Eddas, The. Prosp. R. **8**: 456. **9**: 488.

— Symbolism of. Nat. Q. **12**: 67.

See Scandinavian Poetry.

Edda Doctrine, and its Origin. For. Q. **2**: 210.

Eddies round the Rectory. (O. Varra) Liv. Age, **57**: 37–751. **58**: 49, 413.

Eddy, Joshua, with portrait. (Z. Eddy) N. E. Reg. **8**: 201.

Eddy, S. Reasons for becoming a Unitarian. (J. G. Palfrey) Chr. Disc. **1**: 62.

Eddy, Zechariah. (H. M. Dexter) Cong. Q. **4**: 223.

Eddystone Lighthouse. Fraser, **39**: 432. Same art. Ecl. M. **17**: 212. Same art. Liv. Age, **21**: 460. — Am. Arch. **5**: 103, 207. — Chamb. J. **37**: 91. — Penny M. **1**: 163. — Sharpe, **10**: 321.

— Last Days of. All the Year, **43**: 82.

— New. Ecl. Engin. **19**: 379.

Eden, Wm., Lord Auckland. *See* **Auckland.**

Eden, Garden of. Bentley, **64**: 230. — Sharpe, **17**: 11. Same art. Liv Age, **37**: 61.
— Expulsion from. Kitto, **39**: 331.
— Literality of. (L. Lee) Meth. Q. **29**: 338.
— Serpent of. (J. Duns) Bib. Sac. **21**: 163.
— Site and Rivers of. Kitto, **39**: 363. — Ev. Sat. **9**: 763. *See* Ararat and Eden.
Edenic Period of Man. (A. McWhorter) Princ. n. s. **6**: 62.
Edes, Edward H. Sermons. Chr. Exam. **41**: 297.
Edfou, and its Neighborhood. Chamb. J. **17**: 170. Same art. Liv. Age, **33**: 238.
Edgar, Charter of. (T. Astle) Arch. **10**: 232.
Edgar Wayne's Escape. (M. Oliphant) Blackw. **114**: 459. Same art. Liv. Age, **119**: 465.
Edge-Tools, Manufacture of. (S. Parkes) J. Frankl. Inst. **5**: 198, 226.
Edge-Tools; a Story. Appleton, **24**: 97, 193.
Edgerly Genealogy. (N. F. Edgerly) N. E. Reg. **15**: 337. — (J. A. Edgerly) N. E. Reg. **34**: 282.
Edgcumbes of Edgcumbe and Cothele. (E. Walford) Gent. M. n. s. **18**: 500.
Edgeworth, H. E. E., Abbé. *See* Firmont, H. E. E. de.
Edgeworth, Maria. So. Lit. Mess. **15**: 578. — Selec. Ed. R. **2**: 464, and app. — Dub. Univ. **33**: 795. — Blackw. **1**: 519. — (S. C. Hall and Mrs. S. C. Hall) Art J. **18**: 345. Same art. Ecl. M. **68**: 120. — Bentley, **24**: 477. Same art. Ecl. M. **16**: 88. Same art. Liv. Age, **19**: 488. — Eng. Dom. M. **13**: 28. **25**: 43. — Irish Q. **1**: 548. — Liv. Age, **59**: 290. — Sharpe, **50**: 326.
— at Edgeworthstown. Ecl. Mus. **1**: 162.
— Comic Dramas. Quar. **17**: 96. — Mo. R. **83**: 315.
— Harrington and Ormond. (W. Phillips) No. Am. **6**: 153. — Blackw. **1**: 519, 631.
— Harry and Lucy. Lond. M. **14**: 49. — Mo. R. **109**: 225.
— Helen. (W. B. O. Peabody) No. Am. **39**: 167. — Quar. **51**: 481. — So. Lit. Mess. **3**: 465, 532. — Am. Mo. M. **3**: 193.
— Kennedy. Chr. Rem. **3**: 74.
— Leonora. (F. Jeffrey) Ed. R. **8**: 206.
— Letters to Croker. Sharpe, **36**: 306.
— Life and Letters. Godey, **76**: 161.
— — and Writings. (A. Hayward) Ed. R. **126**: 458. Same art. Liv. Age, **95**: 451.
— Memoirs of. Lond. M. **1**: 555. — with portrait, Bost. Mo. **1**: 539.
— Memories of. (Mrs. S. C. Hall) Art J. **1**: 225.
— Patronage. (Sir W. Scott) Ed. R. **22**: 416. — (Earl of Dudley) Quar. **10**: 301.
— Tales of Fashionable Life. (W. Gifford) Quar. **2**: 135. **7**: 329. **10**: 301. — (F. Jeffrey) Ed. R. **14**: 375. **20**: 100. **28**: 390. — Fraser, **6**: 541. — Anal. M. **1**: 22. **4**: 1. — Chr. Obs. **8**: 781. **11**: 781. — (J. Foster) Ecl. R. **12**: 879. — Ecl. R. **16**: 979.
— Works of. (E. Everett) No. Am. **17**: 383. — U. S. Lit. Gaz. **1**: 281.
Edgeworth, Richard L. (T. Parsons) No. Am. **11**: 340. — (W. B. O. Peabody) No. Am. **42**: 148. — Quar. **23**: 510. — (F. Jeffrey) Ed. R. **34**: 121. — Mo. R. **92**: 387.
— Essays on Professional Education. (J. Davison) Quar. **6**: 166.
— Memoir of. Ecl. R. **32**: 359.
Edgeworth, Roger. Dub. R. **84**: 73.
Edgeworthstown, Visit to. (W. Howitt) Howitt, **3**: 89. Same art. Ecl. M. **14**: 57.
— To, and back. Ecl. R. **111**: 380.
— with Memoirs of Maria Edgeworth. (Mrs. S. C. Hall) Art. J. **1**: 224. Same art. Liv. Age, **22**: 320.
Edict of Nantes, Revocation of. Fraser, **22**: 307.
— — Suffering caused by. Meth. M. **35**: 60.
Edina. (Mrs. H. Wood) Argosy, 21: 1-401. 22: 1-401.
Edinburgh, Duke of. *See* Alfred Ernest Albert, Prince.
Edinburgh. Mo. R. **108**: 125. — All the Year, **24**: 560. — Fraser, **56**: 505.
— after Flodden. (W. E. Aytoun) Blackw. **63**: 165.
— and its Associations. (D. S. Stephens) Lakeside, **9**: 319.
— and its Surroundings. Galaxy, **12**: 91.
— and Glasgow. (W. Chambers) Chamb. J. **9**: 145.
— Art and Landscape in. (F. Wedmore) Temp. Bar, **63**: 502.
— as a Place of Education. Tait, n. s. **8**: 736.
— Cockburn on the best Ways of spoiling the Beauty of. No. Brit. **12**: 283. Same art. Ecl. M. **20**: 25.
— Convivialia in past Times. Chamb. J. **8**: 200.
— Decorations of. Blackw. **6**: 76.
— Description of. Colburn, **1**: 16–137.
— Donaldson's Hospital. Hogg, **5**: 103.
— during the General Assembly. Fraser, **54**: 1. Same art. Ecl. M. **39**: 86.
— Election of 1831. Blackw. **29**: 867.
— Fine Arts in. No. Brit. **16**: 89.
— First Glance at. Penny M. **12**: 417.
— Gossip about. Ecl. R. **110**: 56.
— Grant's Memorials of. Hogg, **6**: 34.
— Great Fire of 1824. Blackw. **16**: 698.
— Hogmanay and New Year's in. Dub. Univ. **77**: 1.
— in 1800. Westm. **66**: 407. Same art. Ecl. M. **39**: 516.
— King's Visit to. Blackw. **12**: 253, 306.
— Letters from. (T. Lyman) No. Am. **1**: 182, 338.
— Literary and Philosophical Societies of, in 18th Century. Hogg, **8**: 43. Same art. Ecl. M. **24**: 565.
— — 1849. Tait, n. s. **16**: 47. Same art. Ecl. M. **16**: 554.
— Medical Report of. Blackw. **1**: 266. **2**: 48, 550.
— the modern Athens. Lond. M. **12**: 488.
— Monument to Lord Melville. Blackw. **6**: 562, 690.
— National Monument of. (A. Alison) Blackw. **5**: 377.
— New College. Cunningham Lecture. Lond. Q. **25**: 336.
— Notes on. (R. L. Stevenson) Portfo. **9**: 80–189.
— Old Stage of. (E. B. Baker) Belgra. **41**: 167.
— Picturesque. (H. S. Conant) Harper, **58**: 673.
— Public Buildings of. Blackw. **6**: 370.
— Ragged School. (T. Guthrie) Good Words, **2**: 3.
— Rambles in. Fraser, **84**: 458.
— Restoration of Parthenon. Blackw. **5**: 509. **6**: 137.
— Sketches in. (A. S. Gibbs) Canad. Mo. **14**: 129.
— Society in, 1848. (G. A. Rogers) Belgra. **37**: 423.
— —.one hundred and fifty Years ago Sharpe, **25**: 124.
— Student Life in. Tait, n. s. **21**: 29. — Temp Bar, **3**: 513.
— Trinity College Church. Fraser, **56**: 650.
— Truman's Visit to, in 1840. Tait, n. s. **8**: 393.
— Views of. Fraser, **38**: 481. Same art. Ecl. M. **16**: 114.
Edinburgh Academy. O. & N. **4**: 629.
Edinburgh Annuity Tax. Ecl. R. **68**: 160.
Edinburgh Castle. Penny M. **2**: 145.
— Crown and Scepter in. (R. Kempt) Belgra. **29**: 142.
Edinburgh Courant, Feb. 14–19, 1705, reprinted. Antiquary, **2**: 296.
Edinburgh Doctors, Old. All the Year, **29**: 389.
Edinburgh High School. Penny M. **8**: 361.
— History of. Chamb. J. **11**: 151.
Edinburgh Jottings. (A. S. Gibbs) Lippinc. **20**: 28.
Edinburgh Literati, Sketches of. (W. Frothingham) Contin. Mo. **1**: 453.
Edinburgh Portraits, Kay's. Mo. R. **144**: 363.
Edinburgh Review. (I. T. Brooks) University Q. **4**: 9. — Westm. **1**: 206, 505. — Anal. M. **14**: 40. — Dem. R. **27**: 320. — Chr. Obs. **1**: 250. **2**: 41. — Portfo. (Den.) **7**: 323.
— and its Contributors. Ecl. M. **24**: 141. — (C. Pebody) Gent. M. n. s. **24**: 355.
— and the Irish Government. Dub. Univ. **11**: 358.
— and the Quarterly Review. Anal. M. **13**: 116. — Portfo.(Den.) **13**: 59, 263.

Edinburgh Review, Character and Influence of. Westm. **58**: 105.
— How it was started. Ev. Sat. **10**: 322.
— Jeffrey's Contributions to. (J. Moncrieff) No. Brit. **1**: 252. Same art. Ecl. M. **3**: 542. Same art. Liv. Age, **3**: 529. — Mo. R. **163**: 1
— Politics of. Westm. **1**: 505. — Blackw. **14**: 212. **22**: 403.
— Projection of. (J. Clark) Mercersb. **5**: 221.
— Religion and Patriotism of. Ed. R. **4**: 228.
— Review of. Chr. Obs. **4**: 758.
— — 1806, 1808. Chr. Obs. **5**: 572, 635. **8**: 598.
— Rise and Fall of. Blackw. **10**: 668.
Edinburgh Reviewers. (T. L. Cuyler) New Eng. **2**: 56. — N. Ecl. **7**: 156.
— First. (L. Stephen) Cornh. **38**: 218. Same art. Liv. Age, **138**: 643. — Nat. R. **1**: 253. Same art. Liv. Age, **47**: 449.
Edinburgh Sessional School. Blackw. **25**: 106.
Edinburgh University. Am. Q. Reg. **13**: 328.
— Chair vacant in. Fraser, **45**: 624. Same art. Ecl. M. **26**: 388.
— Reminiscences of. (D. Masson) Macmil. **11**: 123. Same art. Liv. Age, **84**: 99. Same art. Ecl. M. **64**: 572.
— Statement of Facts. (F. Horner) Ed. R. **7**: 113.
Edison, Thomas A., with portrait. Dub. Univ. **94**: 585.
— and his Inventions. (E. M. Fox) Scrib. **18**: 297–840. — Nature, **18**: 674.
— and the Electric Light. (F. R. Upton) Scrib. **19**: 531. — Nature, **21**: 341.
— Dynamometer. (C. F. Brackett and C. A. Young) Am. J. Sci. **119**: 475.
— his System of fast Telegraphy. (E. M. Fox) Scrib. **18**: 840.
— A Night with. (W. H. Bishop) Scrib. **17**: 88.
— Paper Carbon Horse-Shoe Lamp. Ecl. Engin. **23**: 1.
— Sketch of. (G. M. Shaw) Pop. Sci. Mo. **13**: 487.
— Telephonic and Acoustic Inventions of. (G. B. Prescott) Pop. Sci. Mo. **14**: 129.
Edith. (F. Copcutt) Knick. **39**: 246.
Edith; a Poem. (T. Ashe) Once a Week, **23**: 163–470. **24**: 34–231.
Edith Dewar. (C. R. Brown) St. James, **33**: 384, 463, 590. **34**: 33–505. **35**: 1–353.
Edith Falconer. (J. M. Wharton) Argosy, **32**: 148.
Edith Ludlow. Fraser, **22**: 455.
Editor, The. (F. Gilbert) Lakeside, **8**: 113. — St. James, **49**: 253.
— at large. (F. J. O'Brien) Putnam, **4**: 331, 434.
— Experience of an. Once a Week, **27**: 477, 523.
— The First. (A. Gilman) Putnam, **13**: 273.
— Recollections of a provincial. (J. Hannay) Temp. Bar, **23**: 175.
— Specimen Leaders of a would-be. Fraser, **23**: 433.
Editor's Tales. (A. Trollope) Galaxy, **8**: 689, 825. **9**: 252–611.
Editors and Newspaper Writers of the last Generation. (A. V. Kirwan) Fraser, **65**: 169, 595. **66**: 32.
— Fallacies about. Knick. **45**: 243.
— London. Lond. Soc. **3**: 518.
Editorial Profession. (D. C. Gilman) New Eng. **11**: 210.
Editorial Visit; a Tale. (T. S. Fay) Internat. M. **2**: 421.
Edmund, St., of Canterbury, Martyrdom of; a Poem. (F. Parke) Dub. Univ. **87**: 605. *See* Rich, E.
Edmund, Prince, Coin of. (S. Pegge) Arch. **4**: 190.
— Grant of Sicily to. (T. Astle) Arch. **4**: 195.
— Seal of. (T. Astle) Arch. **4**: 195.
Edmund Ironside and Canute, Battles between. (B. Willis) Arch. **8**: 106.
Edmund; a Drama. (G. Smith) Colburn, **140**: 230.
Edmund Brook. (E. P. Campbell) Atlan. **22**: 450.
Edmundsbury Abbey, Great Bell Tower of. (J. Gage) Arch. **23**: 327.
Edom, Desolation of. Theo. & Lit. J. **12**: 685.
Edrehi, Moses. River Sambatyon. Fraser, **15**: 477.
Edson's Mother. (S. C. Woolsey) Scrib. **2**: 296.
Educated Classes, in which Party? Fraser, **16**: 513.
Educated Men, Character in. Chr. R. **8**: 283.
— in Politics. (E. L. Godkin) Nation, **23**: 5.
— Mistakes of. (S. A. Allibone) Evang. R. **15**: 375.
Education. (T. Dwight) Chr. Mo. Spec. **2**: 349. — (L. Minor) So. Lit. Mess. **2**: 17. — (G. H. Bode) No. Am. **27**: 67. — (S. E. Sewall) No. Am. **30**: 323. — (H. N. Hudson) Dem. R. **16**: 468. **17**: 40. — (Z. Crocker) Chr. Q. Spec. **8**: 43, 394. — (T. Dwight) Lit. & Theo. R. **2**: 326. — (G. Tucker) Hunt, **9**: 53. — U. S. Lit. Gaz. **3**: 171, 218. — Dem. R. **25**: 149. — Fraser, **75**: 691. — So. Lit. Mess. **5**: 441. — Carey's Mus. **4**: 25–310. — Anf. Q. **6**: 145. — Westm. **1**: 43. — So. Lit. J. **1**: 50. — Am. Whig R. **12**: 87. — (F. Wayland) Am. Inst. of Instruc. **1830**: 1. — (J. Walker) Am. Inst. of Instruc. **1831**: 1. — (W. Sullivan) Am. Inst. of Instruc. **1833**: 1. — (C. Cushing) Am. Inst. of Instruc. **1834**: 1. — (W. H. Furness) Am. Inst. of Instruc. **1835**: 1. — (E. White) Am. Inst. of Instruc. **1837**: 1. — (R. Rantoul, jr.) Am. Inst. of Instruc. **1839**: 1. — (E. L. Godkin) Nation, **17**: 4. — (W. B. Hodgson) Am. J. Educ. **26**: 473. — (E. S. Janes) Am. Meth. M. **22**: 401. — (W. Johnson) Hesp. **2**: 337. — (A. B. Koplin) Ref. Q. **26**: 126. — (H. Moore) West. M. **5**: 414. — (F. A. Rauch) Mercersb. **10**: 443. — (L. Reuben) Contin. Mo. **1**: 592, 662. — (A. Schopenhauer) Education, **1**: 138. — (M. Tarver) West. J. **1**: 405, 463. — (J. H. Tice) West. J. **1**: 540, 614. — Am. Meth. M. **13**: 160. — Bost. Q. **3**: 137. — Chr. Rem. **4**: 490. — Nature, **20**: 549. — New Q. **3**: 285. — So. Lit. Mess. **28**: 307. — West. M. **1**: 10. **2**: 30. **3**: 259.
— Address on. (T. Binney) Cong. M. **25**: 505. — (R. W. Hamilton) Cong. M. **27**: 565.
— Adult. Chamb. J. **44**: 120. — Irish Q. **5**: 1.
— Aims and Results of. (W. M. Baum) Luth. Q. **1**: 384.
— American Side of the Question. (J. Nevins) Cath. World, **30**: 515.
— among different European Nations. Ev. Sat. **11**: 587.
— among the Jews. (M. J. Raphall) Am. J. Educ. **1**: 243. — Bib. R. **5**: 70. — St. James, **26**: 683.
— Ancient and modern. Temp. Bar, **7**: 295.
— and Advancement in Life. (E. Strachey) Good Words, **13**: 606.
— and Agriculture. Dem. R. **37**: 411, 448.
— and Athletics. (H. H. Almond) Ecl. M. **96**: 554.
— and Crime. *See* Crime.
— and Culture of Youth. Lond. Q. **7**: 519.
— and Liberal Christianity. (C. H. Brigham) Chr. Exam. **84**: 1.
— and Life. (W. G. Todd) Unita. R. **4**: 286.
— — Theories of. (J. L. Spalding) Am. Cath. Q. **4**: 1.
— and Literary Institutions, 1832. Am. J. Educ. **27**: 289.
— and Morals in England. (J. Fletcher) J. Statis. Soc. **10**: 193. **11**: 344. **12**: 151, 189.
— and Religion in America, Lang on, 1840. Mo. R. **153**: 307.
— and religious Sentiment. (C. H. Super) Nat. Q. **37**: 289.
— and School. Contemp. **1**: 80.
— and Schoolrooms. Mo. R. **163**: 570.
— and Science, Liberty of. Pop. Sci. Mo. **13**: 107.
— and the State. (G. W. Doane) Am. J. Educ. **15**: 5. — (D. C. Gilman) New Eng. **27**: 99. — Am. J. Educ. **11**: 323. **13**: 717. **14**: 403. — West. J. **6**: 309, 356.
— — in England and Ireland. Dub. R. **52**: 106.

Education and the State. Relation of the free State to Education. (H. M. King) Bapt. Q. **11**: 337.
— and Teachers. (W. E. Channing) Am. J. Educ. **12**: 453.
— Aphorisms on. Am. J. Educ. **10**: 116. **13**: 7.
— — and Suggestions on. Am. J. Educ. **8**: 7.
— applicable to emotive Nature. (C. Long) Q. Obs. **3**: 248.
— Art. *See* Art Education.
— Art of. (H. Spencer) No. Brit. **21**: 137.
— as an Adjustment. (J. M. Long) Western, **4**: 765.
— as a Science. (A. Bain) Mind, **2**: 1, 294. **3**: 304, 451. Same art. Pop. Sci. Mo. **10**: 418, 513. **11**: 391. **14**: 55, 152. — (W. T. Harris) Western, **3**: 272.
— as it is. Zoist, **1**: 351.
— — and ought to be. Zoist, **2**: 1.
— at Home and abroad. (S. H. McCollester) Univ. Q. **28**: 469.
— at Oxford and Cambridge. (B. B. Edwards) Bib. Sac. **7**: 586. — (R. Lowe) Liv. Age, **96**: 131.
— at the Vienna Exhibition. Penn Mo. **7**: 814.
— Babbington on. Chr. Mo. Spec. **1**: 355.
— Bache's Report on. (W. B. Reed) No. Am. **51**: 23.
— Basis of. (T. R. Price) N. Ecl. **7**: 385.
— Bell and Lancaster's System. (R. Southey) Quar. **6**: 264. — Ecl. R. **81**: 249.
— Benefactors of. (H. Barnard) Am. J. Educ. **1**: 202.
— Beneficiary. (H. L. Baugher) Evang. R. **4**: 151. — (M. L. Stoever) Evang. R. **13**: 111.
— Berkeley's Scheme of. (H. T. Tuckerman) No. Am. **80**: 171.
— Best Mode of fixing the Attention of the Young. (W. Burton) Am. Inst. of Instruc. **1834**: 41.
— Bigelow on. (J. E. Cabot) No. Am. **102**: 592.
— Bombastic Element in. (E. I. Sears) Nat. Q. **34**: 162.
— Lord Brougham on. Penny M. **6**: 315.
— by Post. (T. M. Lindsay) Good Words, **20**: 805. — Temp. Bar, **36**: 518.
— Carpenter's Principles of. Mo. R. **95**: 249.
— Carter's Letters on. U. S. Lit. Gaz. **1**: 185.
— Catholic, Intermediate. Dub. R. **78**: 322.
— — Prospects of. Month, **11**: 1.
— — Rights of the Church over. Cath. World, **21**: 721.
— — Teaching Orders in. Am. J. Educ. **24**: 742.
— Catholic College in England. Dub. R. **82**: 327.
— Cheap and social. Tait, n. s. **4**: 801.
— Church and. (G. D. B. Pepper) Bapt. Q. **10**: 19.
— — Relation of. So. R. n. s. **15**: 37.
— — and State in. (E. H. Plumptre) Contemp. **9**: 381. — Ed. R. **92**: 94. — (O. A. Brownson) Cath. World, **14**: 433.
— — State, and School in. (W. T. Harris) No. Am. **133**: 215.
— Classical. *See* Classical Education.
— Clerical. *See* Ministry, Education for.
— Co-. *See* Co-Education of the Sexes.
— Collegiate. *See* College Education.
— Committee, and Abuse of Charities. Ed. R. **31**: 497.
— Common School. *See* Common School.
— Comparative Results of. (T. P. Rodman) Am. Inst. of Instruc. **1839**: 181.
— Compulsory. (D. A. Hawkins) O. & N. **9**: 272. — (W. Jack) Macmil. **35**: 73. — (C. E. Norton) Nation, **5**: 191. — (F. Seebohm) Fortn. **14**: 103. — (J. Simpson) Peop. J. **5**: 17. — Canad. Mo. **20**: 174. — Chamb. J. **30**: 45. **45**: 171. — Chr. Obs. **69**: 568. — Penn Mo. **2**: 53. — (J. C. Ayrton) Victoria, **16**: 271.
— — defended. (D. Campbell) Westm. **92** : 550.
— — Laws on. (J. White) Fortn. **25**: 897.
— — Primary. (D. Campbell) Fortn. **9**: 570. — Westm. **91**: 458.
— Congregationalism and. (G. F. Magoun) New Eng. **38**: 412.
Education, Covenant. (J. H. McIlvaine) Princ. **33**: 238.
— Crime, and Insanity. Mo. R. **134**: 295. *See* Crime.
— Crosby Hall Lectures on, 1848. Ecl. R. **88**: 596.
— Cultivation of expressive Faculties. (W. Russell) Am. J. Educ. **3**: 47, 321.
— Dangers in. Month, **6**: 385.
— Dangerous Tendency of Innovations and Extremes in. (H. Winslow) Am. Inst. of Instruc. **1834**: 167.
— Day-School, Advantages and Disadvantages of. (A. Church) Contemp. **15**: 225.
— Defects in, Quain on. Nature, **3**: 103.
— — in our System of. (R. B. Hubbard) Am. Inst. of Instruc. **1843**: 203.
— Deficiencies in modern Systems of. (J. Frankel) Penn Mo. **5**: 672.
— Deflective. Fraser, **83**: 718.
— Demands of the Age in. (Z. G. Wilson) Western, **1**: 626, 688.
— Denominational. Dub. R. **66**: 1.
— — and national. Lond. Q. **33**: 265.
— Detached Notes on. Tinsley, **21**: 190.
— Didactical, in University of Iowa. (S. N. Fellows) Education, **1**: 393.
— Discipline in, Aphorisms on. Am. J. Educ. **10**: 187.
— Duties and Rights of Society as to. (W. J. Fox) Howitt, **1**: 241.
— — of an Educator. Mo. R. **151**: 566.
— — of the Hour. (S. S. Greene) Am. J. Educ. **16**: 229.
— Early, Aphorisms on. Am. J. Educ. **13**: 79.
— — Hints for Improvement of. Chr. Obs. **18**: 518.
— — Methods of. (J. Currie) Am. J. Educ. **9**: 229. — (T. U. Young) Am. J. Educ. **13**: 155.
— — Moral. Ed. R. **38**: 437.
— Elementary. (W. T. Harris) J. Spec. Philos. **3**: 181. — (Sir J. Lubbock) Contemp. **28**: 78. — (J. Pickering) No. Am. **28**: 489. — For. Q. **20**: 254. — Lond. M. **22**: 303, 504.
— — and Catholic Poor Schools. (J. B. Rowe) Month, **28**: 1, 225.
— — — in England. (F. Curran) Cath. World, **31**: 603.
— — in new Colleges of London. (R. Southey) Quar. **39**: 100.
— — Progress of (W. L. Sargent) J. Statis Soc. **30**: 80.
— — Public, in England. (J. A. Picton) Theo. R. **10**: 475.
— — Secularism in. Dub. R. **77**: 63.
— Endowed Schools. (D. R. Fearon) Contemp. **12**: 559.
— Endowment of. (C. E. Appleton) Theo. R. **12**: 36.
— Essay on. (Mrs. Day) Good Words, **19**: 69. — (O. Goldsmith) Am. J. Educ. **13**: 347.
— Essays on, Thomson's. Ecl. M. **41**: 49.
— Essential Phases of. (W. M. Bryant) Western, **5**: 353.
— Expensiveness of. Pop. Sci. Mo. **7**: 746.
— Explanations on. Westm. **55**: 454.
— Fallacies in. Ecl. R. **71**: 241.
— False Schooling. Tinsley, **11**: 237.
— Female. *See* Women, Education of.
— Fénelon's Views on. Am. J. Educ. **13**: 477.
— Flight on. (Mrs. White) Colburn, **78**: 438.
— for Journalists. (E. L. Godkin) Nation, **9**: 311.
— for Manufacturing Towns. No. Brit. **24**: 1.
— for the Masses. (W. H. Dixon) Peop. J. **3**: 275.
— for practical Life. (F. W. Capers) De Bow, **7**: 317.
— for the Times. (T. M. Clark) Am. J. Educ. **2**: 375.
— for unlearned Professions. (E. Atkinson) Atlan. **45**: 742.
— for the upper Classes. Colburn, **52**: 109.
— Foreign, Facts as to. Month, **11**: 425.
— — for young Republicans. Lippinc. **24**: 739.
— Fourfold Culture of Man. (C. Z. Weiser) Mercersb. **18**: 343.
— Free Schools. (J. Chamberlain) Fortn. **27**: 54. — (Sir C. W. Dilke) Fortn. **20**: 789.
— — Success of. (J. D. Philbrick) No. Am. **132**: 249.

Education, Friends of. (L. Rosecrans) Cath. World, **22**: 758.
— from without and from within. (J. W. Nevin) Mercersb. **18**: 5.
— Function of the Thinker in. (H. H. Morgan) Education, **1**: 229.
— Gall's Lesson System. (H. A. Boardman) Princ. **5**: 113.
— General Means of. (H. Kruesi) Am. J. Educ. **5**: 187.
— German Writers on. (G. Baur) Bib. Sac. **12**: 1.
— Greek Views of. (Plutarch) Am. J. Educ. **11**: 99.
— Pres. Hayes on. (A. D. Mayo) Education, **1**: 84.
— Herbart on. (K. Schimdt) J. Spec. Philos. **10**: 166.
— Higher. (O. A. Brownson) Cath. World, **13**: 115. — (F. W. Clarke) Pop. Sci. Mo. **7**: 402. — (B. W. Dwight) New Eng. **17**: 1. — (J. M. Hart) Lippinc. **18**: 573. — (A. F. Hewit) Cath. World, **12**: 720. — (A. B. Muzzey) Mo. Rel. M. **46**: 440. — Cath. World, **13**: 281.
— — and Methodism. Lond. Q. **40**: 369.
— — and Parliament. (J. E. T. Rogers) Fraser, **104**: 68.
— — and the State. (C. K. Adams) New Eng. **37**: 362. — (N. S. Burton) Bapt. Q. **8**: 481. — (H. G. Robinson) Macmil. **4**: 1. — (A. D. White) Am. Soc. Sci. J. **7**: 299. — (A. D. White) O. & N. **10**: 475. —(E. V. Gerhart) Mercersb. **6**: 275.
— — Catholic. Dub. R. **64**: 86. **65**: 88, 515.
— — Historical Development of. (E. Kirkpatrick) Am. J. Educ. **24**: 453.
— — in United States. (E. E. Hale) O. & N. **10**: 649. — Galaxy, **11**: 369. — Brit. Q. **52**: 420.
— — on the Continent. Month, **8**: 425.
— — Philosophy the Basis of. (G. Ramieu) Cath. World, **15**: 632, 815.
— — Puffing Element in. (E. I. Sears) Nat. Q. **31**: 281.
— — Reform in. Internat. R. **3**: 289.
— — without God. (C. A. Stork) Luth. Q. **8**: 278.
— History of, Movements in, A. D. 174 to 1785. Am. J. Educ. **27**: 459.
— — Sketches of. Chamb. J. **8**: 372. **11**: 22, 249.
— — Thoughts on. (W. T. Harris) Western, **3**: 332.
— Home. (B. Murphy) Cath. World, **17**: 91. — (Z. Crocker) Chr. Q. Spec. **8**: 43. — (F. A. Farley) Chr. Exam. **46**: 443. — No. Am. **48**: 380. — Brownson, **15**: 523.
— — and School. De Bow, **29**: 716. — (W. E. Jeff) Contemp. **3**: 220.
— — or Kindergartens. (K.G.Wells) Mo. Rel. M. **50**: 334.
— Hook on, 1846. Chr. Obs. **46**: 545, 611.
— Household. (H. Martineau) Peop. J. **2**: 36–345. **3**: 23, 90. **4**: 36–337. **5**: 3, 122, 145.
— Human Nature Basis of. (W. J. Fox) Peop. J. **1**: 60.
— impeded by our Legislators. Nat. Q. **14**: 134.
— Importance of. (W. G. Bates) Am. J. Educ. **16**: 453.
— in Australia. (J. Allen) Dub. Univ. **82**: 572.
— in Austria. Am. J. Educ. **9**: 589. **16**: 5, 337, 609. **17**: 129. — U. S. Cath. M. **4**: 318, 364.
— — Legislation for. Am. J. Educ. **22**: 879.
— — Special. Am. J. Educ. **21**: 33.
— in Baden. Am. J. Educ. **10**: 201. **11**: 232.
— — Special. Am. J. Educ. **21**: 81.
— in Basle. Am. J. Educ. **20**: 41.
— in Bavaria. Am. J. Educ. **6**: 273, 572. **8**: 491, 581.
— — Special. Am. J. Educ. **21**: 97.
— in Belgium. Am. J. Educ. **20**: 445. **22**: 387.
— — Civil and religious. Dub. R. **8**: 373.
— — Decline of popular. (R. W. Rawson) J. Statis. Soc. **2**: 385.
— — New Law on. (Mrs. R. Barker) Cath. World, **30**: 481.
— — Question of, 1879. Dub. R. **85**: 154. — (I. T. Hecker) Cath. World, **33**: 119.
— — Special. Am. J. Educ. **21**: 607.
Education in Berne. Am. J. Educ. **20**: 51.
— in Birmingham, Report on, 1840. J. Statis. Soc. **3**: 25.
— in Bristol, England. J. Statis. Soc. **4**: 250.
— in Brunswick, Ger., Special. Am. J. Educ. **21**: 137.
— in California. Am. J. Educ. **16**: 625.
— in Canada. Canad. Mo. **11**: 339.
— — Popular, in Upper. (J. G. Hodgins) Am. J. Educ. **1**: 186.
— in Connecticut, Common School. Am. J. Educ. **28**: 163.
— in Denmark. Am. J. Educ. **20**: 455. **21**: 698.
— in Egypt. (J. C. McCoom) Fraser, **95**: 187.
— in England. (J. H. Morison) Unita. R. **5**: 73. — Am. J. Educ. **28**: 726. — Broadw. **3**: 395.
— — Act of 1870, Results of. Ed. R. **139**: 213. — Lond. Q. **35**: 452. **39**: 429.
— — and in America. Blackw. **103**: 111.
— — and Nonconformity, Conder on. Cong. **1**: 441.
— — and the State. Chr. Rem. **20**: 84.
— — Aristocratic. Westm. **23**: 303.
— — at the great Public Schools. (C. E. Norton) Nation, **1**: 149.
— — Barbarism in English Schools. (E. E. White) Pop. Sci. Mo. **2**: 671.
— — Bill for Factory Children, 1843. Ecl. R. **77**: 573, 697.
— — Binney on Question of. Cong. **1**: 562.
— — Colleges and Schools in. (S. R. Calthrop) Chr. Exam. **79**: 373.
— — Defects of Public. Cornh. **2**: 641. **10**: 113.
— — Denominational. (J. A. Picton) Macmil. **29**: 542.
— — — and Board Schools. Cong. **6**: 305.
— — Dissenters' Institutions for. (J. Blackburn) Cong. M. **26**: 545.
— — Elementary. (H. G. Taylor) Scrib. **11**: 397. — Am. J. Educ. **10**: 323. **26**: 577.
— — — Act of 1874. (J. A. Picton) Theo. R. **14**: 49.
— — Elementary Schools. Am. J. Educ. **24**: 659.
— — — in 1875. Am. J. Educ. **26**: 625.
— — — in 1879. Dub. R. **85**: 417.
— — English Schools and Schoolmasters. Quar. **147**: 155.
— — Eton School. Quar. **52**: 128. — Westm. **23**: 303. — Ed. R. **53**: 64. *See* Eton.
— — free from State Control, 1847. Ecl. R. **86**: 589.
— — Froude's Attack on. (J. R. Price) So. M. **9**: 452.
— — Funds available for. J. Statis. Soc. **30**: 557.
— — Government. (J. H. Rigg) Contemp. **31**: 322.
— — Home Life and. Am. J. Educ. **26**: 369.
— — in 1815, Committee on. (J. H. Monk) Quar. **19**: 492.
— — in 1822, Bill for. Ed. R. **35**: 214.
— — in 1825, System of. Westm. **4**: 147.
— — in 1836. Dub. R. **2**: 1.
— — in 1837, Village Schools, Brougham's Bill. (J. J. Blunt) Quar. **61**: 451.
— — in 1839, Ministerial Plan of. (Lord Monteagle) Ed. R. **70**: 149, 281.
— — in 1842, Committee of Council on. Ed. R. **75**: 105.
— — in 1843, Bill for, Conduct of Dissenters on. Ecl. R. **77**: 697.
— — — Government Plan of. Fraser, **27**: 620.
— — in 1846, Secular and religious. Prosp. R. **3**: 238.
— — in 1851, Rival Projects. Ecl. R. **93**: 471.
— — in 1852. Chr. Obs. **52**: 398.
— — — German Letters on, Wiese's. Prosp. R. **8**: 186.
— — in 1855, Lord John Russell's Bill to promote. Dub. R. **38**: 212.
— — in 1858, Commission on. Chr. Rem. **43**: 90.
— — in 1861. Ecl. R. **114**: 478.
— — — Report of Commissioners. St. James, **2**: 459.
— — in 1862, Re-revised Code. Fraser, **65**: 347. — Lond. Q. **17**: 583. **18**: 234. — Quar. **111**: 72. — Temp Bar, **4**: 75.
— — — — in Practice. (J. Wisker) Fortn. **5**: 63.

Education in England in 1870, Ministerial Bill for. Chr. Obs. **70**: 619. — Dub. R. **66**: 430. **67**: 122.
— — — — and the Catholics. (T. W. Allies) Month, **13**: 609. — Month, **13**: 374.
— — — — Mr. Forster's proposed Amendments. Cong. **2**: 385. — Lond. Q. **34**: 1.
— — — — Results of. (G. Porter) Month, **16**: 121, 322. — (Sir J. K. Shuttleworth) Fortn. **25**: 685.
— — in 1872, Controversy on. Cong. **2**: 312.
— — — Difficulty about. (F. Seebohm) Contemp. **19**: 281.
— — — Working of the Act. Brit. Q. **55**: 166.
— — in 1872–73, Report of Committee of Council. (S. A. Steinthal) Theo. R. **11**: 206.
— — in 1875, Controversy on. Am. J. Educ. **26**: 599. — Westm. R. **104**: 105.
— — — Public Schools' Commission. Chamb. J. **41**: 659.
— — in 1876, New Bill for. (A. H. A. Hamilton) Fraser, **94**: 39. — Am. J. Educ. **28**: 901. — Dub. R. **81**: 147.
— — Liberal. Ed. R. **127**: 131.
— — Middle-Class. (M. Arnold) Fortn. **30**: 589. — Cong. **2**: 155, 221. — Cornh. **10**: 409, 549.
— — — and Higher Class. Chr. Obs. **73**: 758. — Lond. Q. **31**: 1.
— — — and Primary. Cornh. **4**: 50.
— — — Experiment in. (M. A. Sewell) Macmil. **25**: 243.
— — — in 1857. Chr. Rem. **35**: 259.
— — — University of London and. Nat. R. **5**: 222.
— — National. (H. Brougham) Ed. R. **66**: 439, 523. — (G. Canning) Quar. **8**: 1. — (T. Hughes) Macmil. **35**: 30. — (Mrs. S. Parkman) Am. Soc. Sci. J. **4**: 150. — Dub. Univ. **9**: 196. **19**: 286, 414. — Ecl. R. **97**: 129. — Meth. M. **54**: 472.
— — — and Established Church. Dub. Univ. **24**: 615.
— — — and Government. (W. Howitt) Howitt, **1**: 201.
— — — and Government Bill of 1876. Chr. Obs. **76**: 520.
— — — and London School Board, 1879. (E. L. Stanley) Fortn. **32**: 530.
— — — Brougham on. Dub. Univ. **14**: 619.
— — — from a Denominationalist's Point of View. Macmil. **29**: 270.
— — — High Church. Ed. R. **35**: 509.
— — — in 1812. Ecl. R. **16**: 783.
— — — in 1824. Ecl. R. **41**: 97.
— — — in 1833. Ecl. R. **59**: 1.
— — — in 1846. Ecl. R. **85**: 102–635.
— — — in 1847, Government Plan. Ecl. R. **85**: 355.
— — — in 1854. Chr. Obs. **54**: 15, 163. — Ecl. R. **100**: 482.
— — — in 1856. Chr. Rem. **33**: 187.
— — — in 1859. Chr. Obs. **59**: 21, 744, 807. **60**: 708.
— — — New Plan of. Ed. R. **34**: 214.
— — — New Problem in. Macmil. **35**: 467.
— — — School Method of. Am. J. Educ. **10**: 501.
— — of the Infant Poor. Temp. Bar, **3**: 329. — (E. C. Tufnell) Macmil. **32**: 350. — Month, **11**: 217. — Chr. Rem. **55**: 161.
— — — Facts and Fallacies of. (W. R. Browne) Fraser, **98**: 197.
— — of the Poor. (Lord Brougham) Pamph. **16**: 173, 200. — Ed. R. **9**: 61. **17**: 58. **19**: 1. **21**: 207. **30**: 486. **32**: 89. — Blackw. **7**: 419.
— — — in 1812. Ecl. R. **16**: 651.
— — of the Working-Classes. Cornh. **14**: 283. — Dub. R. **14**: 141.
— — Policy of English Government. (R. W. Dale) Contemp. **22**: 643.
— — Popular. (J. H. Rigg) Am. J. Educ. **26**: 561. — Ed. R. **114**: 1. — Blackw. **91**: 77. — (J. H. Morison) Unita. R. **5**: 73. — Dub. R. **50**: 60. **62**: 131.
— — — and Pauper. Chr. Obs. **61**: 374.
— — — Crisis of, 1848. Ecl. R **87**: 94.
— — — Resources of. (H. Mann) J. Statis. Soc. **25**: 50.
Education in England, Progress of. (F. Peek) Contemp. **35**: 862. — Cornh. **1**: 608.
— — Public, Expense of. Ed. R. **111**: 348. Same art. Ecl. M. **50**: 481.
— — Public Schools of England. (Syd. Smith) Ed. R. **16**: 326. — Ed. R. **51**: 65.
— — Public School Types. Lond. Soc. **16**: 33.
— in Europe. (S. W. McDaniel) O. & N. **3**: 112. — (J. Hall) Princ. **12**: 244. — Am. J. Educ. **20**: 1.
— — Academic Teaching. (J. McCosh) Liv. Age, **100**: 323.
— — in 1840, Report on. (A. D. Bache) J. Frankl. Inst. **29**: 37.
— — in 1850. Brit. Q. **13**: 408.
— — — Popular. Chr. Obs. **54**: 252.
— — Mann on. So. Q. **7**: 1.
— — Progress of Development in. (H. P. Tappan) Am. J. Educ. **1**: 247.
— in Finland. Am. J. Educ. **24**: 209.
— in France. (H. L. Jones) J. Statis. Soc. **5**: 1. — Quar. **117**: 396. — Blackw. **38**: 16. **40**: 579. — (C. Montalembert) U. S. Cath. M. **7**: 592, 693. — U. S. Lit. Gaz. **3**: 281.
— — and the Church. Chr. Rem. **18**: 151.
— — and French Press. Anal. M. **10**: 25.
— — Arnold's Report on. Quar. **125**: 473.
— — Crisis in, 1879. (E. L. Godkin) Nation, **28**: 313. — (T. A. Finlay) Month, **36**: 100.
— — Early Christian. Am. J. Educ. **24**: 737.
— — Expenditures for, compared with Germany. (E. Rendu) Am. J. Educ. **2**: 337.
— — Ferry Bill, 1880. (A. J. Thebaud) Am. Cath. Q. **5**: 193.
— — Freedom of, under Louis Philippe. (A. C. Knight) Month, **38**: 219.
— — German Views of. (E. Renan) Am. J. Educ. **22**: 577.
— — German and American. Chr. Rem. **55**: 90.
— — Guizot's Ministry of. Am. J. Educ. **20**: 253. — Quar. **84**: 238.
— — Infant Schools and Asylums. Am. J. Educ. **26**: 649.
— — Law of 1849. (A. Laugel) Nation, **28**: 383.
— — — of M. de Falloux. Month, **38**: 567.
— — Normal Schools in. Am. J. Educ. **13**: 281. **20**: 323.
— — of Boys. Chr. Obs. **74**: 753.
— — of the Poor. Ed. R. **33**: 494.
— — Old and new Pedagogy in. Am. J. Educ. **30**: 449.
— — Peep at French Schools. (J. Bonar) Macmil. **44**: 199. Same art. Appleton, **26**: 208. Same art. Ecl. M. **97**: 413.
— — Primary and secondary. (C. H. Harding) Lippinc. **20**: 69.
— — Public. Am. J. Educ. **6**: 293. **9**: 381. — (F. Guizot) Am. J. Educ. **11**: 254, 357. — Am. J. Educ. **20**: 209. **21**: 401. **22**: 331, 651. — Blackw. **38**: 16. — Chamb. J. **50**: 664. — Penn Mo. **4**: 164.
— — — Secondary. (M. Arnold) Liv. Age, **79**: 83.
— — — under Guizot. Quar. **84**: 238.
— — — under the new Law, 1851. Dub. R. **31**: 89.
— — Reform in, 1880. Penn Mo. **11**: 572.
— — Special. Am. J. Educ. **9**: 405.
— — — Secondary Schools for. Am. J. Educ. **24**: 64.
— — State. Blackw. **40**: 579. — Mus. **31**: 26.
— — System of universal. Fraser, **11**: 680.
— — University and the Church in. (H. Merivale) Ed. R. **81**: 399.
— in Fribourg. Am. J. Educ. **20**: 69.
— in Germany. (A. Lamb, jr.) Bib. Sac. **12**: 312. — So. R. **4**: 86.
— — Cousin on. (Sir W. Hamilton) Ed. R. **57**: 505.
— — Early School Codes of. (K. von Raumer) Am. J. Educ. **6**: 426.
— — English Views of. Am. J. Educ. **27**: 249.

Education in Germany, French View of. (G. Pouchet) Am. J. Educ. **27**: 241.
— — German Schools. (W. C. Perry) Macmil. **36**: 155. Same art. Ecl. M. **89**: 279.
— — — and Universities. (Prof. Zander) Dub. Univ. **67**: 451.
— — in free Cities. Am. J. Educ. **15**: 333. **20**: 731.
— — — Special. Am. J. Educ. **21**: 149.
— — in Gymnasia. (R. P. Keep) New Eng. **35**: 145.— Princ. **25**: 564.
— — James on, 1835. Mo. R. **138**: 569.
— — Primary. Am. J. Educ. **8**: 371. **22**: 767.
— — — History of. Am. J. Educ. **8**: 348.
— — Public. Am. J. Educ. **22**: 743.
— — Real Schools. (K. von Raumer) Am. J. Educ. **5**: 689.
— — Reform in. Tait, n. s. **20**: 220.
— — Two German Schools. Fraser, **84**: 446.
— — Village School in. (C. M. Martin) Lippinc. **1**: 494.
— in Great Britain and Ireland. No. Brit. **29**: 482.
— — Elementary. (H. G. Taylor) Scrib. **11**: 397.
— — Popular. No. Brit. **16**: 285.
— — Special. Am. J. Educ. **22**: 21.
— in Greece, Ancient. Am. J. Educ. **27**: 737.
— — Modern. (H. P. Peabody) No. Am **93**: 277.—(P. Johannis) Am. J. Educ. **12**: 571.
— — — and University of Otho. (H. M. Baird) Meth. Q. **22**: 377.
— in Hamburg, Special. Am. J. Educ. **21**: 149.
— in Hanover, Special. Am. J. Educ. **21**: 163.
— in Holland. (C. K. Altmann) Fortn. **12**: 338.—Am. J. Educ. **8**: 595. **14**: 495.—(A. Leroy) Am. J. Educ. **14**: 64.
— — Middle-Class. Nature, **13**: 528.
— — Public Schools and Van der Palm. (N. Bests) Am. J. Educ. **27**: 691.
— — Question of. Contemp. **7**: 386. **8**: 98.
— — Schoolmaster abroad. (M. P. Lindo) Fraser, **83**: 55.
— — Special. Am. J. Educ. **21**: 691.
— — in Hull, England. J. Statis. Soc. **4**: 156.
— in India, British. Ecl. R. **117**: 535.
— — Government. Chr. Obs. **69**: 337, 501.—Ecl. R. **102**: 227.
— — Missions for. (P. Hordern) Fraser, **97**: 207.
— — National. (W. T. Thornton) Cornh. **23**: 282.
— — Trevelyan on, 1838. Ecl. R. **70**: 393.
— in Ireland. Month, **11**: 321.—Brit. Q. **4**: 509.—Blackw. **7**: 534. **23**: 351. **31**: 289.—Dub. R. **6**: 74. **70**: 409.—Irish Q. **8**: 300.—Tait, **1**: 321.—Dub. Univ. **39**: 707.—(E. J. O'Reilly) Month, **16**: 169.—Month, **18**: 411.
— — Ancient Schools. (B. Hauréan) Am. Presb. R. **13**: 652.
— — and the State. Dub. R. **52**: 106.
— — Compulsory, Feasibility of. (W. N. Hancock) J. Statis. Soc. **42**: 456.
— — Elementary. Am. J. Educ. **11**: 133.
— — Experiments in. Dub. Univ. **45**: 70.
— — Fall and Rise of. (T. Quigley) Am. Cath. Q. **4**: 288.
— — History of. No. Brit. **53**: 479.
— — in 1818. Chr. Obs. **16**: 701. **17**: 26, 165, 589.—Ecl. R. **27**: 119.
— — in 1860. Westm. **74**: 94.
— — in 1864. Dub. Univ. **63**: 603.
— — Intermediate. (W. G. Huband) Fraser, **97**: 374.
— — Middle-Class. Month, **9**: 105.
— — National. Dub. Univ. **33**: 366. **42**: 245.—Am. J. Educ. **4**: 363. **13**: 145.—Brit. Q. **50**: 305.—Dub. R. **47**: 345.—Brit. & For. R. **5**: 210.—Irish Q. **4**: 1042.
— — of Gentlemen. (J. M. Capes) Contemp. **20**: 516.
— — Popular, English Policy for. (J. N. Murray) Am. J. Educ. **24**: 673.
Education in Ireland, Primary. Quar. **132**: 228.—Fraser, **90**: 728. **91**: 686.—Lond. Q. **38**: 150.
— — Project for. Dub. Univ. **13**: 115.
— — Question of. Dub. Univ. **1**: 595. **63**: 603. **82**: 1.
— — School System of. (F. A. Packard) Princ. **14**: 88.
— — Special. Am. J. Educ. **27**: 769.
— — State of, 1860. Westm. **74**: 94.
— — Statistics of. Dub. Univ. **62**: 596.
— — Superior. Am. J. Educ. **24**: 825. **26**: 737.
— — Whately and. Dub. R. **35**: 229.
— in Italy. (J. W. Mario) Nation, **6**: 167.—For. Q. **27**: 297.—(M. E. Chambers) Victoria, **13**: 347–543.—(C. Tommasi-Crudeli) Contemp. **11**: 375.—Am. J. Educ. **16**: 689.—Mus. **43**: 360.—O. & N. **1**: 136.
— — Elementary. Macmil. **32**: 151. Same art. Liv. Age, **126**: 223.
— — Female. (G. P. Marsh) Nation, **3**: 5.
— — History of. (K. von Raumer) Am. J. Educ. **7**: 413.
— — in 1863–64. Brit. Q. **39**: 145.
— — Progress of. Lond. Q. **26**: 367.
— — Public. Am. J. Educ. **20**: 145.—(J. W. Mario) Nation, **6**: 167.
— — — Special Instruction in. Am. J. Educ. **21**: 777.
— — — Superior. Am. J. Educ. **20**: 181.
— in London, 1875. (C. Reed) Am. J. Educ. **26**: 609.
— — in Westminster, 1838. J. Statis. Soc. **1**: 193, 298, 449.
— in Louisiana. De Bow, **18**: 421.
— in Maryland. (J. Sparks) No. Am. **13**: 338.
— in Massachusetts. Chr. R. **5**: 396.—Ed. R. **73**: 486.
— — Board of. (E. Wigglesworth) Chr. Exam. **38**: 229.
— — School Legislation on. Am. J. Educ. **24**: 697.
— — — Early. Am. J. Educ. **27**: 59.
— — Schools in Roxbury and Charlestown, Early. Am. J. Educ. **28**: 127.
— — — Ipswich Grammar. (A. Hammatt) Am. J. Educ. **28**: 135.
— — System of. Ed. R. **73**: 260.
— in Mecklenburg. Am. J. Educ. **15**: 459.
— in the Middle Ages. (E. Lawrence) Harper, **43**: 559.
— in Nassau, Special Instruction in. Am. J. Educ. **2**: 444. **21**: 172.
— in New England. (R. Rantoul) No. Am. **47**: 297.
— — Early Schools. Am. J. Educ. **27**: 105.
— — Genesis of. (H. Barnard) Am. J. Educ. **30**: 737.
— in New Hampshire. (J. W. Simonds) Am. J. Educ. **28**: 353.
— in New York. Anal. M. **13**: 452.—Am. Q. Reg. **5**: 303.
— in New York City, 1867. Nation, **4**: 192, 279.
— in North Carolina, Report on. Niles's Reg. **15**: supp. 47.
— in Norway. (H. Nissen) Am. J. Educ. **8**: 295.
— — Special. Am. J. Educ. **21**: 705.
— in the Papal States, 1827. Colburn, **19**: 313–433.
— in Paris, Report on superior. J. Statis. Soc. **4**: 50.
— in Pendleton, England, 1838. J. Statis. Soc. **2**: 65.
— in Pennsylvania, among the Germans. (J. W. Nevin) Mercersb. **5**: 395.
— in Periods of War and Peace. (K. von Raumer) Am. J. Educ. **7**: 367.
— in Philadelphia Public Schools. So. Q. **20**: 480.
— in Poland. Brit. & For. R. **4**: 256.
— in Portugal. Am. J. Educ. **20**: 513.
— — Special. Am. J. Educ. **21**: 797.
— in Presbyterian Church. (S. W. Fisher) Am. Presb. R. **13**: 63.
— in Prussia. Am. Mo. M. **5**: 111.—Colburn, **53**: 205.—Am. J. Educ. **17**: 435. **20**: 333.—Westm. **104**: 105.—So. Lit. Mess. **25**: 241.
— — and in England, 1875. Westm. **104**: 105.
— — and Religion, 1842. Chr. Rem. **3**: 385.
— — Cousin on. Mo. R. **134**: 60.
— — Expenditure for, compared with France. (E. Rendu) Am. J. Educ. **2**: 337.

Education in Prussia, Normal School. Am. J. Educ. **20**: 435.
— — Popular, 1862. Westm. **77**: 169.
— — Primary. Am. J. Educ. **22**: 745.
— — Reforms of Frederick II. Am. J. Educ. **26**: 305.
— — Special. Am. J. Educ. **21**: 177.
— — System of. For. Q. **11**: 273. — Mus. **24**: 261. — (T. Dwight) Lit. & Theo. R. **2**. 326.
— in Rhode Island prior to 1800. Am. J. Educ. **27**: 705.
— in Roman Catholic Church, Question of. (E. J. O'Reilly) Irish Mo. **3**: 108, 228.
— — Teaching Orders. Am. J. Educ. **30**: 705.
— in Russia. Am. J. Educ. **12**: 725. **20**: 461. — Brit. & For. R. **4**: 254. — Am. Q. Reg. **5**: 59.
— — Special. Am. J. Educ. **21**: 717.
— — System of. Brit. & For. R. **4**: 254.
— — University. Am. J. Educ. **20**: 499.
— in St. Gall. Am. J. Educ. **20**: 105.
— in St. Louis. Am. J. Educ. **1**: 348. **30**: 621. — (H. Barnard) Am. J. Educ. **30**: 625.
— in Salem, Mass. Am. J. Educ. **27**: 97.
— in Sardinia. (V. Botta) Am. J. Educ. **3**: 512. **4**: 37, 479.
— in Saxe-Altenburg. Am. J. Educ. **20**: 567.
— in Saxe-Coburg-Gotha. Am. J. Educ. **20**: 573.
— in Saxe-Gotha, Common-School Law. Am. J. Educ. **22**: 894.
— in Saxe-Meiningen. Am. J. Educ. **20**: 605.
— in Saxony. (H. Wimmer) Am. J. Educ. **5**: 350. **20**: 529.
— — Secondary. Am. J. Educ. **9**: 201.
— — Special. Am. J. Educ. **21**: 287.
— — Training of Teachers. Am. J. Educ. **13**: 523.
— in Schleswig-Holstein. Am. J. Educ. **20**: 635.
— in Schwarzburg. Am. J. Educ. **20**: 649.
— in Scotland. Cornh. **4**: 220. — Am. J. Educ. **22**: 267. **36**: 641. — All the Year, **14**: 349.
— — before the Reformation. Hogg, **4**: 124.
— — Bill for. Cong. **1**: 193.
— — Elementary. Am. J. Educ. **9**: 215.
— — Four Centuries of. (J. Russell) Education, **1**: 205.
— — Higher. (A. C. Sellar) Nation, **21**: 258.
— — National. Blackw. **65**: 567. — No. Brit. **12**: 482.
— — Parish Schools. Dub. Univ. **69**: 553. — Ed. R. **46**: 107. — Chamb. J. **8**: 136.
— — Popular. No. Brit. **22**: 57.
— — Question of. No. Brit. **34**: 495.
— — School and University System. Fraser, **78**: 333.
— — Schools for Middle Classes. No. Brit. **24**: 359.
— — Secondary. (G. G. Ramsay) Fraser, **93**: 403, 588. — Blackw. **119**: 284. — Ed. R. **143**: 511. — Am. J. Educ. **22**: 453, 677.
— — Superior. Am. J. Educ. **24**: 801. **27**: 673.
— in the South. (C. Lowe) O. & N. **1**: 775. — (C. G. Fairchild) O. & N. **9**: 223. — (J. H. Morison) Unita. R. **7**: 424. — (T. M. Logan) Am. Soc. Sci. J. **9**: 92. — (D. H. Hill) Land We Love, **1**: 1, 83, 235. — N. Ecl. **6**: 38.
— in South Carolina. (J. Cooper) No. Am. **14**: 310.
— — Common School. So. Q. **25**: 470.
— in Spain, and Alfonso X. Am. J. Educ. **27**: 157.
— — Special. Am. J. Educ. **21**: 799.
— — Superior. Am. J. Educ. **24**: 777.
— in Sweden. Am. J. Educ. **22**: 697.
— — Special. Am. J. Educ. **21**: 711.
— in Switzerland. Am. J. Educ. **20**: 32.
— — Federal Polytechicum at Zurich. Am. J. Educ. **21**: 743.
— — in Lucerne. Am. J. Educ. **20**: 85.
— — Special. Am. J. Educ. **21**: 735.
— in Turkey. Am. J. Educ. **20**: 1. — Fraser, **99**: 63. — Chr. R. **18**: 342. — (H. Clarke) J. Statis. Soc. **30**: 502.
Education in United States. (J. P. Bodfish) Cath. World, **9**: 121. — (E. O. Haven) Lakeside, **1**: 261. — (N. Webster) Carey's Mus. **12**: 41-237. — (S. Willard) No. Am. **9**: 240. — Blackw. **4**: 546. — Anal. M. **2**: 303. **9**: 285. — (D. C. Gilman) Am. J. Soc. Sci. **10**: 1. — Blackw. **4**: 546, 641. — Month. **8**: 261. — So. R. n. s. **9**: 140.
— — and the Republic. Brownson, **23**: 37.
— — Bill in Congress, 1872. (G. F. Hoar) O. & N. **5**: 599.
— — Catholic View of. (A. Young) Cath. World, **8**: 686.
— — Constitutional Provision for. Am. J. Educ. **17**: 81. **24**: 713.
— — Department of, 1869. Am. J. Educ. **18**: 190.
— — Faults in. (T. H. Rearden) Overland, **1**: 311.
— — Ideal. (W. T. Harris) Western, **2**: 193.
— — in Congress. Nat. Q. **14**: 159.
— — in its Relations to the Republic. (J. W. Patterson) Cong. R. **10**: 511.
— — in 1776–1876. (D. C. Gilman) No. Am. **122**: 191.
— — in 1796. (W. Winterbotham) Am. J. Educ. **24**: 137.
— — in 1800–70. Am. J. Educ. **24**: 225.
— — in 1806. (N. Webster) Am. J. Educ. **24**: 159.
— — in 1857. Chr. Obs. **57**: 222.
— — in 1868. Brit. Q. **48**: 429.
— — Mansfield on. So. Q. **27**: 451.
— — National. (H. Barnard) Am. J. Educ. **30**: 193. — Quar. **138**: 420.
— — — H Wilson's Scheme of. Cath. World, **13**: 1.
— — Outlook of. (P. R. Burchard) Scrib. **4**: 97.
— — Popular. Ed. R. **98**: 170. Same art. Ecl. M. **30**: 109. — Chr. Obs. **53**: 819. — (R. W. Dale) Sup. Pop. Sci. Mo. **3**: 206, 339.
— — — the Genius of American Institutions. (B. Hawley) Meth. Q. **41**: 635.
— — Problem of, 1868. (J. R. Boise) Bapt. Q. **2**: 8.
— — Progress of. Harper, **51**: 845.
— — — 1830–80. (B. Sears) Education, **1**: 21.
— — School Life in 1760. Am. J. Educ. **28**: 157.
— — Schools and Universities, North and South. De Bow, **18**: 545.
— — Source of. (G. F. Magoun) New Eng. **36**: 445.
— — Southern View of. (E. S. Joynes) Education, **1**: 70.
— — Statistics of, 1840. (G. Tucker) Am. J. Educ. **24**: 171.
— — — 1855. (H. Barnard) Am. J. Educ. **1**: 364, 445.
— — System of. (G. W. Williard) Mercersb. **25**: 508.
— — — Ought it to be sustained? (D. R. Cady) Cong. Q. **12**: 524.
— in Vaud. Am. J. Educ. **20**: 129.
— in Virginia. (G. E. Dabney) So. Lit. Mess. **7**: 631. **13**: 685. — (J. W. Johnston) Nation, **24**: 233.
— — Colonial Period. Am. J. Educ. **27**: 33.
— in Waldeck. Am. J. Educ. **20**: 651.
— in Wales. Westm. **49**: 36. — Blackw. **63**: 540.
— in the West. (S. Osgood) Chr. Exam. **23**: 194. — West. R. **1**: 53.
— — Female Teachers. (S. W. S. Dutton) New Eng. **7**: 593.
— in Wurtemberg. Am. J. Educ. **20**: 653. **22**: 709.
— — Special. Am. J. Educ. **21**: 337.
— Industrial. *See* Industrial Education.
— Infant, Wilderspin on. Chr. Obs. **23**: 304. **25**: 684.
— Infant School System. (W. Russell) Am. Inst. of Instruc. **1830**: 97.
— Infant Schools, Management of. (M. M. Carll) Am. Inst. of Instruc. **1834**: 99.
— Influence of. (E. Casselberry) West. J. **1**: 253.
— — on Character. (T. Flint) Knick. **2**: 401.
— Influence of moral. (R. Rantoul) No. Am. **47**: 297.
— International Congress on, Belgium, 1880. (W. T. Harris) Education, **1**: 623.
— Italian View of. Lond. M. **4**: 180.

Education, Jacotot's Method of. (G. W. Greene) Am. Inst. of Instruc. **1833**: 175. — For. Q. **5**: 655. — Westm. **17**: 62.
— Lancaster's Plan of. (Syd. Smith) Ed. R. **9**: 177. — (J. Griscom) No. Am. **18**: 184. — (R. Southey) Quar. **6**: 264.
— Landmarks in. (L. F. Soldan) Western, **2**: 1.
— Language in. (W. D. Whitney) No. Am. **113**: 343.
— Laws of. (C. de Montesquieu) Am. J. Educ. **24**: 59.
— Learning or Training? (A. P. Marble) Education, **1**: 173.
— Legal. *See* Legal Education.
— Leyendecker on. Select J. **3**: 189.
— Liberal. (E. P. Evans) No. Am. **105**: 291. — (T. Lewis) Mercersb. **16**: 497. — (F. Oakeley) Dub. R. **65**: 246. — Dem. R. **35**: 250. — Macmil. **15**. 464. — No. Brit. **48**: 291.
— — Dispute about. (C A. Bristed) Lippinc. **2**: 295, 389.
— — Essays on. (J. Conington) Contemp. **7**: 1.
— — in the 19th Century. (W. P. Atkinson) Pop. Sci. Mo. **4**: 1.
— — Methods of. Princ. **42**: 622.
— — Necessity of. Brownson, **1**: 194.
— — Objects and Claims of. (B. F. Tweed) Univ. Q. **23**: 393.
— — Recent Discussions on. (L. H. Atwater) Princ. **39**: 585.
— — Where to find it. (T. H. Huxley) Macmil. **17**: 367. Same art. Ev. Sat. **5**: 466.
— Limits of. (J. Bigelow) Liv. Age, **88**: 1.
— Literature of. (F. W. Clarke) Pop. Sci. Mo. **11**: 713.
— Love of Excellence an Aim in. (E. Q. Sewall) Chr. Exam. **23**: 215.
— Luther on. (K. von Raumer) Am. J. Educ. **4**: 421.
— Man the Subject of. (S. G. Goodrich) Am. Inst. of Instruc. **1838**: 163. — Am. J. Educ. **22**: 559.
— Manchester Scheme of. Tait, n. s. **19**: 65.
— Mann's Report on. Liv. Age, **1**: 425.
— Martineau on. Am. Whig R. **9**: 604.
— Maurice's Lectures on. New Q. **4**: 353. — Mo. R. **150**: 563.
— Mayhew on. Mo. R. **157**: 502.
— Meaning and Objects of. (T. B. Fox) Am. Inst. of Instruc. **1835**: 181.
— Meditation on. (J. H. Pestalozzi) Am. J. Educ. **6**: 169.
— Mental Discipline in. (J. E. Cabot) No. Am. **105**: 629. — (A. G. Merwin) Pop. Sci. Mo. **7**: 699.
— Method of. (K. von Raumer) Am. J. Educ. **7**: 381.
— Method of Academic Culture. (J. L. Diman) New Eng. **28**: 724.
— Methods in. (J. Fiske) No. Am. **107**: 117.
— Military. *See* Military Education.
— Milton on. Am. J. Educ. **2**: 61. — Pamph. **17**: 121.
— Mis-Education. (T. Wright) Fraser, **86**: 641.
— Modern. (A. P. Boller) Ecl. Engin. **17**: 247. — (L. P. Hale) O. & N. **7**: 628. — Lond. M. **23**: 367.
— — Opportunities and Perils of. (N. Porter) New Eng. **38**: 766.
— Modern Ideas of. So. Lit. Mess. **8**: 625.
— Montaigne on. (K. von Raumer) Am. J. Educ. **4**: 461.
— Moral. (J. Dymond) Am. Meth. M. **18**: 219. — (J. Abbott) Am. Inst. of Instruc. **1831**: 43. — (F. W. P. Greenwood) Chr. Exam. **10**: 1.
— — and religious. (S. Osgood) Chr. Exam. **26**: 163.
— — — with the intellectual. (J. W. Richard) Luth. Q. **11**: 209.
— — and spiritual. (E. H. Clarke) Mo. Rel. M. **11**: 314.
— — — Early. (R. C. Waterston) Am. Inst. of Instruc. **1835**: 233.
— — in Public Schools. (G. Howland) Education, **1**: 144.
— Moral Problem of. (J. H. Allen) Chr. Exam. **76**: 205.
— Morality and. (A. E. Kroeger) So. M. **10**: 202.
Education, Mother Tongue in. (T. R. Price) So. M. **15**: 346, 472.
— Museums as Instruments of. (H. Scadding) Canad. J. n. s. **13**: 1.
— Mutual Duties of Parents and Teachers. (D. P. Page) Am. Inst. of Instruc. **1838**: 141.
— National. (G. Canning) Quar. **6**: 419. — (H. Crosskey) Macmil. **35**: 139. — (J. Simpson) Peop. J. **5**: 17, 87, 129. — (T. L. Spalding) Cath. World, **31**: 398. — Ev. Sat. **9**: 858. — New York R. **3**: 149. — Dub. Univ. **10**: 1. **11**: 195. — Brit. & For. R. **3**: 564. **10**: 50. — Ecl. R. **84**: 280. **85**: 102, 355, 507. — Quar. **6**: 419. **8**: 1. — Niles's Reg. **13**: 145. **17**: 322. — Ed. R. **58**: 1. **65**: 129. **95**: 321. — Westm. **20**: 296. — Fraser, **34**: 370. — Brit. Q. **34**: 218. **48**: 431. **49**: 207. — Irish Q. **7**: passim. — Nat. R. **12**: 311. — Penn Mo. **6**: 95-327. — Prosp. R. **3**: 115. — Republic, **1**: 34. — St. James, **5**: 90. — Tait, **2**: 755.
— — as a National Duty. (M. Müller) Contemp. **27**: 70. Same art. Liv. Age, **128**: 676.
— — Brougham on. Quar. **19**: 493. **61**: 451. — Blackw. **17**: 534.
— — English and Continental. Lond. Q. **55**: 314.
— — Hook on. Ecl. R. **84**: 280.
— — in England and Ireland. (H. Brougham) Ed. R. **65**: 245.
— — Struggle for. (J. Morley) Fortn. **20**: 143, 303, 411.
— — Unsolved Problems in. (J. G. Fitch) Fortn. **22**: 754.
— — *versus* State. Tait, n. s. **4**: 714.
— — Works on. Chr. Obs. **38**: 266, 378.
— National Aid to. (J. W. Patterson) Education, **1**: 413.
— a National Interest. Am. J. Educ. **17**: 41. **28**: 305.
— National University. (C. W. Eliot) Pop. Sci. Mo. **3**: 689.
— Natural Sciences in popular. (A. Gray) Am. Inst. of Instruc. **1841**: 91.
— Nature and Value of. (J. Lalor) Am. J. Educ. **16**: 33.
— Necessity of, in a Republic. (J. P. Wickersham) Lippinc. **1**: 57. — (H. Mann) Am. Inst. of Instruc. **1844**: 261.
— Neighborhood as a Starting-Point in. (R. E. Thompson) Penn Mo. **10**: 664.
— New. (C. E. Eliot) Atlan. **23**: 203, 358. — (H. Bushnell) Hours at Home, **11**: 421.
— New Schoolmaster abroad. (B. Jerrold) Gent. M. n. s. **5**: 722.
— New System of. Dub. Univ. **1**: 156.
— Newnham on. Chr. Obs. **28**: 515, 571.
— Notes on. (E. I. Sears) Nat. Q. **30**: 351.
— Objects of. Ev. Sat. **4**: 789. — Penny M. **2**: 174. — N. Ecl. **1**: 74.
— — and Means of. (C. Wright) No. Am. **121**: 86. — (F. Wayland) Am. J. Educ. **13**: 801.
— Observations on. U. S. Cath. M. **7**: 449.
— Obstacles to. (J. M. Garnett) So. Lit. Mess. **1**: 725.
— — Faults of Parents. So. Lit. Mess. **2**: 436.
— — — of Teachers. So. Lit. Mess. **2**: 477.
— — — of Scholars. So. Lit. Mess. **2**: 561.
— — — of the Public. So. Lit. Mess. **2**: 613.
— of after Life. (A. P. Stanley) Macmil. **37**: 97. Same art. Sup. Pop. Sci. Mo. **2**: 257.
— of an agricultural People. (S. Nott, jr.) Am. Inst. of Instruc. **1835**: 34.
— of the Blood. Am. Mo. M. **9**: 1.
— of Boys. Lond. M. **9**: 410, 503.
— of the English Aristocracy. Brit. & For. R. **1**: 298. Westm. **23**: 303.
— of Example, Aphorisms on. Am. J. Educ. **10**: 194.
— of the Faculties. (S. J. May) Am. Inst. of Instruc. **1846**: 87.
— of the Five Senses. (W. H. Brooks) Am. Inst. of Instruc. **1831**: 103.

Education of the Future. Once a Week, **22**: 456.
— of the Heart. (S. Colfax) Lakeside, **1**: 20.
— of the Highways. Chamb. J. **20**: 86.
— of the Intellect in English Schools. Am. Ecl. **1**: 428.
— — Spencer on. (A. T. Bledsoe) So. R. n. s. **2**: 316.
— of a Man of Business. Hunt, **15**: 381.
— of perceptive Faculties. (W. Russell) Am. J. Educ. **2**: 113, 317.
— of pious Youth. Am. Q. Reg. **7**: 371.
— of Scepticus. (H. D. Traill) Dark Blue, **1**: 164.
— of Women. *See* Women, Education of.
— of the World. (A. T. Bledsoe) So. R. n. s. **1**: 1.
— of a young Princess. (W. Drummond) Ed. R. **7**: 91.
— The Old. (R. E. Thompson) Penn Mo. **1**: 52.
— outside the Schoolroom. (R. O'Shaughnessy) Irish Mo. **5**: 381.
— Over-. (E. H. Clarke) Pop. Sci. Mo. **6**: 57.
— Paganism in. (C. Z. Weiser) Mercersb. **24**: 232.
— Philosophical Survey of. (H. Wotton) Am. J. Educ. **15**: 131.
— Philosophy of. (S. S. Laurie) Princ. n. s. **6**: 115. — West. Mo. R. **3**: 393, 449.
— Physical. *See* Physical Education.
— Plea for our dull Boys. Fraser, **103**: 123.
— Political. (J. C. Moffatt) Princ. **31**: 207.
— — Our. (A. White) Nation, **28**: 283, 386.
— Popular. (O. A. Brownson) Cath. World, **7**: 228.—(Sir W. Hamilton) Ed. R. **57**: 505.—(A. Lewis) Dark Blue, **1**: 221. — (H. H. Milman) Quar. **78**: 377. — Quar. **128**: 473. — (M. A. Garvey) Peop. J. **8**: 189. — (T. Walker) No. Am. **29**: 241. — (O. Dewey) No. Am. **23**: 49. **36**: 73. — (A. H. Everett) No. Am. **40**: 511. — Am. Q. **20**: 315. — For. Q. **20**: 147. — Ed. R. **86**: 270. — Mass. Q. **1**: 198. — So. Lit. Mess. **14**: 597. — Chr. R. **5**: 218. — Ecl. R. **87**: 94. — (J. W. Alexander) Princ. **7**: 41. — Brit. Q. **2**: 143. **6**: 257, 528. **7**: 41. — So. Quar. **20**: 480. — So. Lit. J. **1**: 177. — So. Lit. Mess. **2**: 88. **8**: 115. — Brit. & For. R. **10**: 50. — Westm. **7**: 269. **46**: 182. — Blackw. **27**: 1. — Ed. R. **41**: 508. **43**: 242. — Liv. Age, **12**: 153. — Mo. R. **113**: 103. — U. S. Lit. Gaz. **5**: 346. **6**: 264. — (O. A. Brownson) Chr. Exam. **20**: 153. — Fraser, **35**: 253. **36**: 169. — Bost. Q. **2**: 393. — Chamb. J. **8**: 217. — Cong. M. **28**: 128. — Fraser, **70**: 582. — Lond. M. **20**: 1. **23**: 447. — Lond. Q. **12**: 462. **16**: 503. — (J. C. Moffatt) Princ. **29**: 609.
— — and the Clergy. Am. J. Educ. **17**: 211.
— — and Government. (E. C. Wines) Bib. Sac. **8**: 737.
— — and House of Lords. Fraser, **102**: 261.
— — and Liberal. Knick. **9**: 209.
— — and Prevention of Crime. (H. Rogers) Ed. R. **86**: 512.
— — Are the People educated? Chamb. J. **6**: 233.
— — as a Safeguard for popular Suffrage. (R. L. Dabney) Princ. n. s. **6**: 186.
— — Delusions in. (D. McCauley) De Bow, **1**: 528.
— — Development of Character under. Chr. R. **8**: 514.
— — Dry Bones of. (M. E. Christie) Fortn. **36**: 355. — (Reply by T. S. Dalgleish) Fortn. **36**: 513.
— — Hamilton's Essay on. Brit. Q. **2**: 143. Same art. Ecl. M. **6**: 229. — Mus. **7**: 327, 492. — Ecl. R. **82**: 22.
— — High-Church Opinions of. Ed. R. **42**: 206.
— — Hook's Letter on. Prosp. R. **2**: 428.
— — how obtainable. Prosp. R. **8**: 10.
— — in the British Empire. Dub. Univ. **48**: 240.
— — in common Things. Am. J. Educ. **10**: 93.
— — in England. Brit. Q. **4**: 444. — (M. J. Higgins) Ed. R. **114**: 1.
— — — Progress of. No. Brit. **16**: 537.
— — in Germany and England. Penny M. **9**: 417.
— — in Prussia, 1862. Westm. **77**: 169.
Education, Popular, Legislative Provision for. Selec. Ed. R. **3**: 386, 409.
— — Mechanics' Institutions. Ecl. R. **102**: 204.
— — Problem of. (J. H. von Fichte) Am. J. Educ. **28**: 59.
— — Societies in Great Britain for. Westm. **89**: 421.
— — States' Duties in regard to. De Bow, **20**: 143.
— — *versus* Sectarianism. (S. S. Randall) Hours at Home, **11**: 5.
— Popular Fallacies in. Ecl. R. **124**: 23.
— Practical, English Works on. Chr. Rem. **4**: 1.
— — Need and Mode of. Westm. **58**: 1.
— — School, 1842. Chr. Rem. **3**: 317.
— — with a Liberal. (W. R. Johnson) J. Frankl. Inst. **6**: 55–367.
— Premature Use of Books in. So. Lit. Mess. **13**: 315.
— Primary. (G. B. Perry) Am. Inst. of Instruc. **1833**: 95. — (R. Mulcaster) Am. J. Educ. **24**: 179. — Quar. **135**: 374.
— — and the Church. (J. Oakley) Contemp. **14**: 192.
— — and German Method of teaching Reading and Writing. Macmil. **18**: 297.
— — and the Laws of the Universe. St. James, **43**: 858.
— — in Boston. Am. J. Educ. **27**: 93.
— — in Ontario. (J. Potter) Canad. Mo. **1**: 483.
— — National. Chr. Obs. **70**: 167, 286.
— — Problem of. (J. M. Gregory) Am. J. Educ. **14**: 431. — (H. H. Morgan) Western, **2**: 87.
— — to University. (W. T. Harris) Western, **2**: 521.
— Professional. *See* Professional Education.
— Professor and Teacher. (J. M. Hart) Lippinc. **17**: 193.
— Progress in. (T. Walker) Good Words, **21**: 136.
— — of, in the U. S. and Europe. De Bow, **18**: 132.
— Psychology of. (W. T. Harris) J. Spec. Philos. **14**: 225.
— Public. Am. Mo. M. **5**: 111, 329, 409. — Chr. Mo. Spec. **8**: 456. — Ed. R. **97**: 461. — Am. Mo. M. **6**: 1, 295. — (C. Hodge) Princ. **1**: 370. — Lond. Q. **1**: 189. — Brownson, **14**: 375.
— — before the Reformation. (R. Rea) Cath. World. **32**: 262, 354.
— — Government Measures for Rich and Poor. Ed. R. **99**: 158.
— — Hazlewood School. Ed. R. **41**: 315.
— — Lack in System of. (G. H. Emerson) Univ. Q. **20**: 5.
— — Means and Methods of. (D. P. Page) Am. Inst. of Instruc. **1843**: 107.
— — Shall it be exclusively secular? (C. H. Payne) Meth. Q. **40**: 299.
— — Statistical Fallacies. (J. G. Fitch) Fortn. **20**: 614.
— Public School. (F. W. Farrar) Fortn. **9**: 233. — (M. J. Higgins) Ed. R. **120**: 147. — (J. Lubbock) Contemp. **27**: 163. — (Syd. Smith) Ed. R. **16**: 326. — Dub. R. **57**: 1. — Tinsley, **16**: 420. — Quar. **108**: 387.
— — Thoughts of an Outsider. Cornh. **27**: 281. **28**: 605.
— Purposes of Study. (J. G. Fitch) Victoria, **20**: 323.
— Quar. Journal of. (T. P. Thompson) Westm. **15**: 495.
— Question of. (J. Simpson) Peop. J. **4**: 15–324. **5**: 17–129.
— Racing Season. Once a Week, **5**: 607.
— Radical Defect in. (J. R. Herrick) Am. Presb. R. **12**: 587.
— Radical System of. Fraser, **24**: 584.
— Rational, Plea for. (M. E. G. Duff) Fortn. **28**: 170. Same art. Liv. Age, **134**: 745.
— Real. (W. Jolly) Education, **1**: 356, 531.
— Realism and Idealism in. (J M. Long) Western, **6**: 196.
— Reform in. (G. F. Walker) Radical, **7**: 306. **9**: 192. — Dub. Univ. **46**: 499.
— — Wyse on, 1836. Mo. R. **142**: 381.
— Reforms in. (W. T. Harris) Western, **1**: 304. — (L. Soldan) Western, **5**: 274.
— — and Reformers. Penn Mo. **6**: 576–793.

Education, Reforms in, in School and College. (W. P. Atkinson) Nation, 4: 359, 380, 399.
— Relation of, to the Well-Being of States. New Eng. 6: 207, 312.
— Religion, and Morality in the State. (L. H. Atwater) Princ. n. s. 1: 395.
— Religion in. Westm. 99: 111. — Cath. World, 11: 782. — Cong. M. 27: 39.
— — and Public School System. (W. W. Patton) New Eng. 32: 201.
— — and Science. (R. Fisk) Univ. Q. 26: 5.
— — — Harmony of. (S. P. Hill) Chr. R. 11: 57.
— — Philosophy of. Prosp. R. 10: 261.
— Religion in Systems of. Chr. Obs. 11: 424.
— Religious. *See* Religious Education.
— — and moral, Aphorisms on. Am. J. Educ. 10: 166.
— — and secular. (J. Simpson) Peop. J. 4: 157, 227.
— — in Public Schools. (J. Monteith) Cong. 4: 537, 620. — Brit. & For. R. 11: 416. — (J. A. Picton) Fortn. 22: 308.
— — — *vs.* Ethical. (W. Mackintosh) Contemp. 23: 245.
— — or secular? (C. Hodge) Princ. 26: 504.
— — State Aid to. Cong. 1: 65.
— Religious Difficulty in. (J. P. Hopps) Theo. R. 5: 277.
— Religious Element in. (C. E. Stowe) Am. Inst. of Instruc. 1844: 1.
— Renaissance and. (R. H. Quick) Education, 1: 37, 177.
— Restoration of, in 9th Century. Ed. R. 151: 380.
— Richter's Levana. Prosp. R. 5: 317. — Westm. 49: 207.
— Roman Thoughts on. Am. J. Educ. 11: 111.
— Rosenkranz's Pedagogics, Analysis of. (W. T. Harris) J. Spec. Philos. 15: 52.
— Schelling's Idea of. (T. Apple) Mercersb. 15: 290.
— School. (J. Pickering) No. Am. 9: 167.
— — College, and University. (J. L. LeConte) Princ. n. s. 5: 177.
— Schools of the Future. (H. Spencer) Contemp. 17: 443.
— Science in. (B. V. B. Dixon) Western, 7: 420.
— Science of. (J. Donaldson) Am. J. Educ. 26: 481. — (W. Fisk) Am. Meth. M. 13: 419. — (W. T. Harris) J. Spec. Philos. 13: 205. — (R. Rosenkranz) J. Spec. Philos. 12: 67, 297. 14: 191. — (A. C. Brackett) J. Spec. Philos. 15: 35.
— — Is there a? (J. M. Gregory) Education, 1: 384.
— Scientific. *See* Scientific Education.
— Secondary, M. Arnold on. Brit. Q. 69: 120.
— Secular. U. S. Cath. M. 7: 34. — Peop. J. 9: 155. — (A. A. E. Taylor) Luth. Q. 10: 55.
— — and compulsory. (I. Washburn, jr.) Univ. Q. 34: 59.
— — and religious. Blackw. 45: 275.
— — and Sects. Westm. 60: 112.
— — in England and United States. (T. W. M. Marshall) Am. Cath. Q. 1: 278. — Dub. R. 78: 442.
— Secularism in elementary. Dub. R. 77: 63.
— Secularized. (R. L. Dabney) Princ. n. s. 4: 377.
— Sedative Value of. (B. Murphy) Penn Mo. 11: 220.
— Self. (J. T. Brantley) Chr. R. 18: 51. — (G. Ripley) Chr. Exam. 9: 70. — (J. Brazer) 11: 259. — (R. Usher) Sharpe, 25: 32. — Westm. 64: 73.
— of young Men. (C. Kingsley) Ev. Sat. 7: 346.
— Miss Sewell's Principles of. (S. Eliot) Nation, 2: 311.
— Sex in. *See* Co-education; Women, Education of.
— Special. (H. H. Morgan) Western, 1: 199.
— Spencer on. (E. Cary) University Q. 4: 99. — Ecl. R. 114: 155.
— Sphinx Riddles of. (W. T. Harris) Western, 3: 639.
— State. Ed. R. 142: 89. — Chamb. J. 7: 297.
— — a Necessity. (C. S. Bryant) Pop. Sci. Mo. 19: 635.
— — in England, France, Germany. Chr. Rem. 12: 411.
— — Past and Future of. (H. G. Robinson) Macmil. 5: 72.
— State Agency in. Brit. Q. 5: 540.
Education a State Duty. (D. B. Duffield) Am. J. Educ. 3: 81.
— States' Duties in regard to. De Bow, 25: 417.
— Suffrage and. (S. F. McCleary) O. & N. 2: 542.
— Superficial. Am. Church R. 25: 425.
— Supervisors and Assistants in. (W. M. Bryant) Western, 7: 88.
— Systems of, Harmony in. (J. McCosh) Education, 1: 10.
— Tale of ripe Scholar. (F. Parkman) Nation, 9: 558.
— Teaching to read. (J. Spedding) 19th Cent. 1: 637. Same art. Ecl. M. 89: 241.
— Technical. *See* Technical Education.
— that we need. (H. L. Wayland) Bapt. Q. 3: 1. — (W. A. Scott) Pioneer, 4: 359.
— Theological. *See* Theological Education.
— Theory and Practice of. For. Q. 34: 130. Same art. Ecl. M. 3: 532.
— Theories of. (J. A. Alexander) Princ. 5: 165. — (B. R. Hall) Princ. 14: 215.
— Thompson's Day-Dreams of a Schoolmaster. No. Brit. 40: 402.
— Thoughts on. (C. B. Haddock) Bib. Sac. 2: 1. — (J. Henry) Am. J. Educ. 1: 17. — (J. Locke) Am. J. Educ. 11: 461. 13: 548. 14: 305. — (S. Johnson) Am. J. Educ. 13: 359. — (H. Spencer) Am. J. Educ. 11: 485. 13: 372. — Ill. M. 1: 111.
— Tractate on. (J. Milton) Am. J. Educ. 22: 181.
— True. Month, 21: 170.
— Union of manual and mental Labor in. (B. Green) Am. Inst. of Instruc. 1834: 189.
— University. *See* University Education.
— University Chairs of, Edinburgh. (S. S. Laurie) Am. J. Educ. 27: 193, 220.
— Universal. (R. Palmer) Internat. R. 1: 58. — (J. C. Young) West. M. 2: 463.
— Use of modern Literatures in. (J. R. Mozley) Contemp. 17: 559.
— Value and Essence of a good. Am. J. Educ. 8: 38.
— What Knowledge is of most Worth? Westm. 72: 1.
— What is? Am. J. Educ. 11: 11. — Penny M. 1: 109.
— Woodbridge's Annals of. (W. E. Channing) Chr. Exam. 15: 257.
— Word to the Schoolmaster. Colburn, 62: 172.
— Works on, 1879. (T. M. Coan and B. G. Wilder) Nation, 29: 130.
— — American. So. Q. 25: 57.
See Common Schools; Schools; College Education. *See, also, names of educators, as* Pestalozzi; Froebel; etc. *Also, names of specialties, as* Art Education; Industrial Education; Women, Education of; etc.
Educational Associations. Am. J. Educ. 16: 311.
— in Southern States. Am. J. Educ. 16: 353.
— Town, County, and State. Am. J. Educ. 15: 185.
Educational Benefactions in Boston, Mass. Am. J. Educ. 9: 606.
Educational Census of England and Wales, 1851. Chr. Obs. 54: 687.
Educational Charities. Penny M. 6: 420.
Educational Development. (K. von Raumer) Am. J. Educ. 8: 216.
Educational Endowments. (J. G. Fitch) Fraser, 79: 1.
— Worth of. Macmil. 19: 517.
Educational Exhibition at St. Martin's Hall. Chamb. J. 22: 97.
Educational Facilities. Dem. R. 25: 433.
Educational Fallacies. Ecl. R. 71: 241.
Educational Grant, Conscience Clause. (G. S. Lefevre) Fortn. 3: 165.
Educational Humbug. All the Year, 43: 199.
Educational Ideas, Growth of some great. Pract. M. 2: 12.
Educational Institute of Scotland. Chamb. J. 8: 409.

Educational Institutions, Excursion among. (E. I. Sears) Nat. Q. **29**: 120.
— Higher, of New England. (D. Dorchester) Meth. Q. **32**: 181, 399.
— — of United States. (E. I. Sears) Nat. Q. **19**: 348.
— on the Hudson. (E. I. Sears) Nat. Q. **28**: 330.
Educational Land Policy of United States. Am. J. Educ. **17**: 65. **28**: 929.
Educational Movements, 1851. Westm. **54**: 388.
Educational Museum, S. Kensington. Am. J. Educ. **22**: 89.
Educational Notions, Some. (E. C. Dawes) University Q. **4**: 49.
Educational Periodicals, List of. Am. J. Educ. **15**: 383.
Educational Policy of German Reformed Church. (T. G. Apple) Mercersb. **19**: 153.
Educational Society, American. (J. Carnahan) Princ. **1**: 344. — (M. Stuart) Princ. **1**: 560. — (C. Hodge) Princ. **1**: 602.
— — Stuart on. (C. Hodge) Princ. **2**: 122.
Educational Societies. (H. Humphrey) Am. Q. Reg. **2**: 129. — (R. Babcock, jr.) Am. Q. Reg. **2**: 145. — (J. Bates) Am. Q. Reg. **3**: 81. — (J. P. Durbin) Am. Q. Reg. **4**: 10. — (E. Cornelius) Am. Q. Reg. **4**: 153. — (B. B. Edwards) Am. Bib. Repos. 2d s. **8**: 444. — (J. M. Sturtevant) Am. Bib. Repos. 2d s. **10**: 462. — (L. Bacon) Chr. Mo. Spec. **9**: 92. — (J. Emerson) Chr. Mo. Spec. **9**: 241. — (M. Stuart) Am. Q. Reg. **2**: 79, 134. — (Dr. Scudder) Am. Q. Reg. **10**: 81. — Spirit Pilg. **3**: 301. — Chr. R. **3**: 343.
Educational Tests for Voting. (E. L. Godkin) Nation, **3**: 497. **8**: 125.
Educators. Blackw. **98**: 742.
— Dead and living. (E. I. Sears) Nat. Q. **27**: 272.
— a model Head Master. (E. I. Sears) Nat. Q. **29**: 325.
— Some specimen. (P. Girard) Cath. World, **29**: 292.
Edward the Confessor, Monument of, at Westminster Abbey. (G. Vertue) Arch. **1**: 32.
Edward I., with portrait. (N. H. Morris) Potter Am. Mo. **6**: 297.
— Account of opening his Tomb. (J. Ayloffe) Arch. **3**: 376.
— as a military Leader. Cornh. **15**: 281.
— greatest of all the Plantagenets. Chr. Obs. **61**: 302. — Liv. Age, **69**: 171.
— Invasion of Scotland by. (N. H. Nicolas) Arch. **21**: 478.
— Parliament of. Penny M. **3**: 493.
— Portraiture of. Chr. Obs. **59**: 33, 186, 334.
— Roll of Expenses of, at Rhuddlan Castle. (S. Lysons) Arch. **16**: 32.
— Rotulus Familiæ. (J. Brand) Arch. **15**: 350.
— Wardrobe Account of. (J. Topham) Arch. supp. vol.
— Writs inviting to his Daughter's Wedding. (S. Lysons) Arch. **15**: 347.
Edward II., Last Days of Isabella, his Queen. (E. A. Bond) Arch. **35**: 453.
— Murder of. Arch. **27**: 274.
— Wardrobe Accounts of. (T. Stapleton) Arch. **26**: 318.
— Where did he die? (J. T. Bent) Macmil. **41**: 393.
Edward III., Age of. Dub. R. **39**: 328.
— Coins of. (S. Pegge) Arch. **3**: 316.
— Copy of a Harleian MS. on. (T. Amyot) Arch. **22**: 204.
— Elegy on the Death of. Arch. **18**: 21.
— Foreign Wars of. Mo. R. **160**: 213.
— Issue Roll, 1370. Mo. R. **139**: 252.
— Life and Times of. Ed. R. **129**: 534.
— — Longman's. (E. A. Freemain) Fortn. **11**: 586. — Fraser, **79**: 511.
— Subsidy Roll of. (J. Topham) Arch. **7**: 337.
— Wardrobe Accounts of. (Sir N. H. Nicolas) Arch. **31**: 1.
Edward IV., Bruce's History of. Mo. R. **146**: 568.
— Burial of. Arch. **1**: 348.
— Chapel of, on Wakefield Bridge. Penny M. **8**: 496.
Edward IV., History of Part of Reign of. (J. O. Halliwell) Arch. **29**: 127.
— Second Invasion of England. (E. Jerningham) Arch. **21**: 11.
Edward V. Liv. Age, **45**: 208.
Edward VI., Accounts for the Burial of. (C. Ord) Arch. **12**: 334.
— and Elizabeth, Church of England and Romanists under. Chr. Rem. **50**: 51.
— and Mary. Brit. & For. R. **9**: 590.
— — Froude's History of. Dub. R. **49**: 263.
— — Tytler's History of. Ecl. R. **69**: 676. — Ed. R. **70**: 446.
— Picture of his Procession to Westminster. (J. Topham) Arch. **8**: 406.
See England, History of.
Edward the Black Prince, James's Life of. Mo. R. **141**: 85.
Edward, Thomas, the Naturalist. (S. S. Conant) Harper, **54**: 697. — Chamb. J. **30**: 79. **54**: 49. — Ed. R. **146**: 118. — Nature, **15**: 349. — Pop. Sci. Mo. **10**: 594.
— Life of. Blackw. **121**: 175. Same art. Ecl. M. **88**: 698.
— Science under Difficulties. All the Year, **45**: 7.
— Scientific Labors of. Liv. Age, **132**: 311.
Edward, Fort, in 1779–80. Hist. M. **12**: 373.
— Massacre at. (Mrs. E. F. Ellet) Godey, **46**: 435.
Edward Lonsdale. Blackw. **39**: 80.
Edward Saville. (C. Whitehead) Bentley, **1**: 155.
Edward Weston. (Mrs. T. A. Davis) Godey, **21**: 35.
Edwardes, Herbert. (A. H. Forrester) Bentley, **27**: 400.
Edwards, Bela B. (S. G. Brown) No. Am. **77**: 219. — (E. A. Park) Bib. Sac. **9**: 783. — (W. A. Stearns) New Eng. **11**: 411.
— Life and Writings of. (J. N. Putnam) Bib. Sac. **10**: 672.
— Park's Memoir of. (A. Hovey) Chr. R. **19**: 233.
Edwards, Charles, Last Words of. Blackw. **14**: 396.
— Posthumous Letters of. Blackw. **15**: 154. **16**: 45, 658. **19**: 18.
Edwards, John, Poems of. Ecl. R. **37**: 459.
Edwards, Jonathan. (S. Osgood) Chr. Exam. **44**: 367. — (J. P. Thompson) Bib. Sac. **18**: 809. — (O. W. Holmes) Internat. R. **9**: 1. — (I. N. Tarbox) Bib. Sac. **26**: 243. — Am. J. Educ. **27**: 721.
— and the new Divinity. (L. H. Atwater) Princ. **30**: 585.
— and old Clergy. (W. Frothingham) Contin. Mo. **1**: 265.
— and the Revivalists. (W. H. Channing) Chr. Exam. **43**: 374.
— as a Sermonizer. Chr. R. **10**: 32.
— Dismissal from Northampton. (E. H. Gillett) Hist. M. **11**: 333.
— Letters of. Bib. R. **1**: 223.
— Life of. (S. Miller) Sparks's Am. Biog. **8**: 3. — with portrait, Am. Q. Reg. **8**: 287.
— — and Works of. Ecl. R. **60**: 181.
— Manuscripts of. Liv. Age, **36**: 181.
— Narrative of Revival in New England, 1736. (J. Foster) Ecl. R. **7**: 548.
— on original Sin. Chr. Mo. Spec. **6**: 567. **10**: 16.
— on Revivals. (N. Porter) Chr. Mo. Spec. **9**: 295.
— on the Affections. Chr. Disc. **4**: 445.
— on the Trinity. (E. A. Park) Bib. Sac. **38**: 147, 333.
— on the Will, Bledsoe's Examination of. (B. N. Martin) New Eng. **5**: 337. *See also* Will.
— Original Letter of. Bib. Sac. **1**: 579.
— Parish of. (Mrs. M. W. Lawrence) Putnam, **14**: 166.
— Philosophy of. (G. P. Fisher) No. Am. **128**: 284.
— Resolution of. (T. D. Woolsey) Chr. Mo. Spec. **7**: 14.
— Sermons of. Chr. Mo. Spec. **5**: 39.
— N. W. Taylor and Theology of. (N. Porter) New Eng. **18**: 726.
— Unpublished Writings of. (G. F. Magoun) Cong. R. **10**: 19.

Edwards, Jonathan, Works of. Chr. Exam. **32**: 396. — Chr. Mo. Spec. **3**: 298, 357. — (L. H. Atwater) Princ. **15**: 42. — (N. Porter) Chr. Q. Spec. **3**: 337.
Edwards, Jonathan, President. (L. Stephen) Fraser, **88**: 529. Same art. Liv. Age, **120**: 219.
— as a Reformer. (G. F. Magoun) Cong. Q. **11**: 259.
— on Virtue. Bib. Sac. **10**: 705
Edwards, Rev. P., Memoir of. Cong. M. **16**: 705.
Edwards, Sarah Pierpont. *See* Pierpont, Sarah.
Edwards, Timothy, and his Parishioners. (I. N. Tarbox) Cong. Q. **13**: 256.
Edwards, Wm. Personal Adventures. Liv. Age, **58**: 867.
Edwards Family. (W. Frothingham) Contin. Mo. **1**: 11.
Edwin, John, Actor, Recollections of. Colburn, **53**: 400.
Edwin Drood. *See* Mystery of Edwin Drood.
Edwin of Deira; a Poem. (A. Smith) Harper. **23**: 665.
Edwy and Edgar. (B. F. Baer) Potter Am. Mo. **10**: 51.
Eel, The. Penny M. **11**: 37
— Breeding Habits of. (A. S. Packard, jr.) Am. Natural. **13**: 25.
— Skull of, Structure of. (W. K. Parker) Nature, **4**: 146.
Eels. Chamb. J. **28**: 254. **53**: 575. — Quar. **115**: 173.
— Chat about. Good Words, **18**: 479.
— Notes about. (A. H. Baldwin) Once a Week, **8**: 332.
— Vinegar. (J. Hogg) Pop. Sci. R. **2**: 213.
Eel Culture, Curiosities of. Once a Week, **7**: 206.
Effie; a Poem. (T. Irwin) Dub. Univ. **87**: 195.
Effie Gordon. (B. S. Montgomery) Once a Week, **4**: 406.
Effie's Dream; a Poem. (R. C. F. Hannay) Dub. Univ. **78**: 423.
Efficiency as a proximate End in Morals. (J. T. Punnett) Mind, **6**: 350.
Effigies in Brass and Stone. (N. H. Morris) Potter Am. Mo. **8**: 32.
Effigies Poetica. Westm. **2**: 279.
Effigy, Punishment in. Chamb. J. **51**: 126.
Egan, Pierce. Sporting Anecdotes. Lond. M. **2**: 155, 268.
Egbert Stanway; a Tale. Cath. World, **13**: 377.
Egede, Hans, Apostle of Greenland. (W. F. Stevenson) Good Words, **11**: 73. — Cong. M. **4**: 1, 57.
Egerton, Lord Francis, with portrait. Fraser, **12**: 43.
Egerton, Sir Philip de Malpas Grey. Nature, **23**: 579.
Egg, Incubated, Towne on the. Ecl. R. **71**: 203.
— What is an? Stud. & Intel. Obs. **2**: 189.
Eggs. Chamb. J. **36**: 241. Same art. Ev. Sat. **1**: 555.
— and Duckers. Once a Week, **12**: 431.
— and Feathers. Chamb. J. **42**: 638.
— Collections of, Methods of labeling. (W. H. Ballou) Am. Natural. **12**: 306.
— Composition of. (A. Valenciennes and E. Frémy) Am. J. Sci. **69**: 38, 238. **70**: 65.
— Culture of. Chamb. J. **55**: 191.
— Price of, 1314–1850. House. Words, **1**: 159.
— Retention and Coloring. (T. H. Potts) Nature, **6**: 457.
— Trade in. Penny M. **6**: 110.
— — Lucrative. Pract. M. **1**: 318.
Egg Development. Month, **13**: 79.
Eggleston, Edward. (W. Gladden) Scrib. **6**: 561.
— Hoosier Schoolmaster. (J. R. Dennett) Nation, **14**: 44.
Eglinton, Lord. Dub. Univ. **58**: 630.
Eglintoun, Susannah, Countess of. (W. Chambers) Chamb. J. **52**: 145.
Egmont, I. F., Comte de Chasot. *See* Chasot.
Egoism. Blackw. **102**: 342.
— Suppression of. (A. Barratt and H. Sidgwick) Mind, **2**: 167, 411.
Egoity. Radical, **4**: 194.
Egotheism the Atheism of To-Day. Mo. Rel. M. **21**: 165.
Egotism and its Philosophy. Broadw. **5**: 84.
— Literary. Am. Mo. M. **12**: 37.
— or Bosom Serpent. (N. Hawthorne) Dem. R. **12**: 255.
Egotizing. (E. C. Bissell) Overland, **1**: 269.
Egrets, White, at Trenton. (C. C. Abbott) Am. Natural. **10**: 473.
Egypt. (H. W. Bellows) O. & N. **1**: 71. — (Sir G. Campbell) Fortn. **31**: 787. — (G. J. Chester) Fortn. **25**: 580. Same art. Ecl. M. **86**: 684. — (M. E. G. Duff) Contemp. **23**: 407. — Lond. Q. **52**: 286. — Am. J. Sci. **28**: 23. — Kitto, **7**: 257. — Brit. & For. R. **2**: 534. — Westm. **6**: 158. — (T. W. Greenwell) St. James, **46**: 296.
— About's. Dub. Univ. **74**: 192.
— Administrative Machinery of. (F. W. Rowsell) 19th Cent. **10**: 641.
— Adventures in. (F. C. Roka) Penny M. **5**: 438. **6**: 90–222.
— Aggression on. (W. E. Gladstone) 19th Cent. **2**: 149.
— American Influence in. (F. V. Greene) Nation, **32**: 77.
— American Trade to. (E. Weiss) De Bow, **20**: 221.
— Among the Egyptians. Chamb. J. **42**: 635.
— Ancient. (R. S. Poole) Contemp. **34**: 304, 570, 741. **35**: 107, 237. Same art. Liv. Age, **140**: 470. **141**: 237. — (C. W. Chalklen) Westm. **50**: 395. — For. Q. **21**: 92. — Ed. R. **83**: 204. — Ecl. R. **61**: 448.
— — and the Bible. (C. Geikie) Am. Church R. **33**: 1. **36**: 13.
— — and modern. Ed. R. **18**: 435. — (A. B. Chapin) Chr. Q. Spec. **9**: 393.
— — and Pre-Homeric Greeks. (A. Lang) Fraser, **100**: 171.
— — Art of, Oldest. (W. J. Loftie) Macmil. **40**: 354.
— — Art and Literature in, 1320 B. C. (J. E. Carpenter) Unita. R. **4**: 441.
— — Arts of. Penny M. **5**: 237.
— — — and Antiquities of. Ecl. R. **79**: 569.
— — — and Sciences of. (E. I. Sears) Nat. Q. **6**: 1.
— — Burial Customs in. (Col. Streton) Ed. Philos. J. **3**: 345.
— — Civilization of. Cath. World, **13**: 804. **14**: 63.
— — Commerce of. (F. M. Hubbard) Am. Bib. Repos. **10**: 33.
— — Day in the Life of a Dandy of. Colburn, **84**: 1.
— — Dinner in. Fraser, **33**: 229.
— — Gentleman at Home in. Appleton, **5**: 14–166.
— — Glass and Porcelain of. Ed. New Philos. J. **25**: 101.
— — Gliddon's. (A. B. Chapin) Am. Bib. Repos. 2d s. **10**: 134. — Mo. R. **162**: 275.
— — in its comparative Relations. (R. S. Poole) Contemp. **39**: 804. **40**: 45, 282, 361.
— — Kings of. Westm. **14**: 505.
— — Life in, 3000 Years ago. Sharpe, **26**: 8.
— — Literature and People of. (W. M. Reynolds) Evang. R. **4**: 35. — Blackw. **108**: 220, 302. Same art. Ecl. M. **75**: 401, 535. Same art. Liv. Age, **106**: 682. **107**: 97.
— — Manners and Customs of. (R. P. Stebbins) Chr. Exam. **31**: 39. — Quar. **63**: 120. — Ed. R. **68**: 315.
— — — Customs, Trades, Arts, and Manufactures of. Westm. **36**: 1. Same art. Am. Ecl. **2**: 291.
— — Night with King Pharaoh. Belgra. **9**: 196.
— — Nursery Tale of. (J. P. Lesley) Penn Mo. **4**: 19.
— — Rawlinson's. (C. H. Toy) Nation, **33**: 155, 178.
— — Religion of. (K. Cook) Dub. Univ. **90**: 27. — (J. N. Hoare) 19th Cent. **4**: 1105. Same art. Liv. Age, **140**: 33.
— — Romances of. Appleton, **25**: 176.
— — Science of. (G. Cuvier) Ed. New Philos. J. **8**: 334. **13**: 41.
— — — and Art of. (R. S. Poole) Am. Arch. **10**: 169.
— — State Trial in. (J. P. Thompson) Bib. Sac. **26**: 577.
— — under the Pharaohs. (F. H. Underwood) Atlan. **45**: 315.
— — — Kenrick's. Brit. Q. **13**: 92.
— — Wisdom in. (J. Woodward) Arch. **4**: 212.
— — Woman in. Cath. World, **32**: 563.

Egypt and the Bible. (A. Sutherland) Meth. Q. **35**: 221. — Dub. Univ. **32**: 371. — So. R. n. s. **8**: 20. — (W. H. Ryder) Univ. Q. **10**: 329.
— and the Eastern Question. (F. G. Peabody) Unita. R. **12**: 139.
— — and Turkey. Fraser, **93**: 1.
— and Germany. (G. von Bunsen) 19th Cent. **2**: 167.
— and Great Britain. (S. P. Dinsmore) No. Am. **65**: 56.
— — Dealings of. (Sir G. Campbell) Fortn. **25**: 157.
— and the Holy Land, Clarke's Travels in. (R. Southey) Quar. **17**: 160.
— and Italy. (F. Jeffrey) Ed. R. **41**: 42.
— and its Government. Sharpe, **12**: 167. Same art. Liv. Age, **27**: 201. Same art. Internat. M. **1**: 524.
— and a Journey to Palestine. (R. H. Miles) Colburn, **138**: 196–489. **139**: 200, 447. **142**: 188, 346.
— and the Khedive. (E. Dicey) 19th Cent. **2**: 854. — (A. McEwen) 19th Cent. **3**: 423.
— — and our Route to India. Blackw. **122**: 477. Same art. Ecl. M. **89**: 677.
— and Mohammed Ali. Am. Q. **16**: 212. — Dub. R. **19**: 174. — Ed. R. **59**: 404. — Mo. R. **154**: 329.
— and the Nile, Southworth's. Nature, **13**: 43.
— and Nubia, Legh's. Quar. **16**: 1. — Mo. R. **84**: 337.
— — Berber, and Sennaar. (Sir J. Barrow) Quar. **28**: 59. — Quar. **19**: 178.
— and the Suez Canal. Fraser, **61**: 134. — (R. M. Milnes) Colburn, **136**: 114–486. **137**: 114–468.
— and Syria. No. Brit. **29**: 149. — Westm. **95**: 187.
— and Thebes. Quar. **53**: 104.
— Antiquities of. (H. Salt) Quar. **19**: 391. — (H. Wheaton) No. Am. **29**: 361. — For. Q. **4**: 438. **12**: 352. **16**: 303. — Quar. **43**: 112. — Ecl. R. **86**: 416. — (W. E. R. Boughton) Arch. **18**: 59. — Mus. **45**: 668. — (G. W. Samson) Chr. R. **18**: 258.
— — in British Museum. (S. Birch) Arch. **29**: 111. — Month, **3**: 279, 587. **4**: 279, 366, 629. — (R. S. Poole) Temp. Bar, **4**: 227.
— — Museum of, at Leyden. Ed. R. **53**: 370.
— — — at Liverpool. Chamb. J. **18**: 184.
— — New Discovery in, 1881. (C. I. Barnard) Nation, **32**: 313.
— — Osborn on. Ecl. R. **86**: 416.
— — Religious Tract Society's. Chr. Obs. **41**: 355.
— — St. John's Isis. Liv. Age, **35**: 609. — Chamb. J. **18**: 365. Same art. Liv. Age, **36**: 337.
— — Seyffarth on. Evang. R. **8**: 34, 415. **9**: 58.
— — Sharpe's. Liv. Age, **77**: 510.
— — Statue of Memnon at Thebes. Quar. **138**: 529. Same art. Liv. Age, **125**: 475.
— — Wathen on. Ecl. R. **70**: 569.
— Arab Monuments of. (F. Dillon) 19th Cent. **10**: 276.
— At Gates of the East. (C. D. Warner) Atlan. **36**: 523.
— Baldwin's. (F. Jeffrey and H. Brougham) Ed. R. **1**: 59.
— Bartlett's Nile Boat. Tait, n. s. **17**: 60.
— Beaufort's Sepulchers of. Chr. Obs. **61**: 711.
— Belzoni's Operations and Discoveries in. (H. Salt) Quar. **24**: 139. — Ecl. R. **33**: 489. — Lond. M. **3**: 85. — Portfo. (Den.) **29**: 119.
— Book of the Dead. (R. O. Williams) Univ. Q. **33**: 398. — Lond. Q. **43**: 1. Same art. Liv. Age, **123**: 707. — Penny M. **6**: 388.
— bound and unbound, 1881. Ed. R. **153**: 336.
— Bridal Reception in the Harem of the Queen. (E. De Leon) Lippinc. **16**: 379.
— Brides for Sale in. Liv. Age, **46**: 676.
— Bunsen's Place of, in History. Ed. R. **83**: 391. — Quar. **78**: 1. **105**: 382. — Brit. Q. **23**: 333. — (F. G. Peabody) Unita. R. **12**: 581. — (Dr. Hincks) Dub. Univ. **54**: 20. — Dub. Univ. **46**: 273. — (O. T. Dobbin) Hogg, **14**: 177. — Bib. R. **5**: 377.
Egypt, Bunsen's Place of, in History. (Mrs. C. H. Dall) Chr. Exam. **83**: 305. — Ecl. R. **112**: 385. — Lond. Q. **5**: 1. — Kitto, **24**: 53. — Prosp. R. **2**: 1. — Ecl. M. **69**: 564.
— Business in. Chamb. J. **28**: 28.
— Cailliaud's Travels to Meroé. For. Q. **2**: 461.
— Christian Work in. (W. K. Muir) Princ. **40**: 547. **41**: 53, 360, 511.
— Christianity in. (F. G. Peabody) Unita. R. **12**: 233.
— Chronology of. (C. W. Chalklen) Westm. **43**: 104. — (J. Strong) Meth. Q. **38**: 197, 462. — (J. P. Thompson) No. Am. **96**: 111. — Am. Q. **2**: 509. — Kitto, **12**: 109. — Prosp. R. **6**: 193.
— — analyzed, Nolan on. Chr. Obs. **48**: 603.
— — and Sacred Chronology. Lond. Q. **53**: 265.
— — Place of Homer in. (W. E. Gladstone) Contemp. **24**: 1, 175. Same art. Liv. Age, **122**: 361, 742.
— Clark's Illustrations of. Bost. R. **4**: 273.
— Climate, Agriculture, and Commerce of. J. Statis. Soc. **39**: 218.
— Clot-Bey's Observations on. For. Q. **27**: 362.
— Coast of. (H. Mitchell) No. Am. **109**: 476.
— Commerce of. (J. E. Cooley) Hunt, **7**: 416. — (J. W. Jenks) Hunt, **8**: 13.
— Consular Service and Society in. (C. Hale) Atlan. **40**: 280.
— Cotton-Growing in. (A. Andrew) Colburn, **132**: 70.
— Court of the Khedive. (A. Freeland) St. James, **36**: 419.
— Courts in, New. Am. Law R. **10**: 440.
— Crocodile Pits of Maäbdeh. St. James, **24**: 324.
— Denon's Travels in. (F. Jeffrey) Ed. R. **1**: 320. — (J. Foster) Ecl. R. **24**: 562.
— Description of. (J. S. Buckingham) Hesp. **2**: 299.
— Desert of. Chamb. J. **58**: 257.
— Discovery in. Brit. & For. R. **2**: 156.
— Dynasties of. Kitto, **15**: 75. **19**: 305. **20**: 345. — (E. Hincks) Kitto, **30**: 33. **32**: 421. — (J. W. Bosanquet) Kitto, **34**: 191.
— Education in. (E. T. and M. E. Rogers) Art J. **32**: 341.
— Egg-Ovens in. Penny M. **2**: 311. — Tinsley, **6**: 395.
— English Expedition to, 1800. (Syd. Smith) Ed. R. **2**: 53.
— Englishwoman in, Mrs. Poole's. Blackw. **57**: 286. — Penny M. **13**: 300.
— Fellahs of. Ecl. M. **89**: 450.
— Financial Position of. (A. J. Wilson) Fraser, **93**: 786. **99**: 533.
— Finances of, 1879. (C. I. Barnard) Nation, **29**: 291.
— — 1880. (E. Dicey) 19th Cent. **8**: 458.
— France and England in. (A. Laugel) Nation, **29**: 74.
— French in. Colburn, **135**: 1.
— From Cairo to Heliopolis. Nat. M. **9**: 105.
— From Cairo to Pyramids. (J. O. Noyes) Nat. M. **9**: 73.
— From Cairo to Stamboul with Ismail Pasha. St. James, **35**: 506.
— From Thebes to the Pyramids. (W. C. Prime) Harper, **14**: 463.
— Future of. (E. Dicey) 19th Cent. **2**: 3. — Chr. Obs. **65**: 241.
— Gentz's Letters from. Colburn, **98**: 184.
— Lady Gordon's Life in, 1863–65. Ed. R. **122**: 217. Same art. Liv. Age, **86**: 374. Same art. Ecl. M. **65**: 529. — Fraser, **72**: 580. — Mo. Rel. M. **45**: 467.
— Gossip from. Lond. Soc. **14**: 508. Same art. Ecl. M. **72**: 203.
— Henniker's Notes on. Mo. R. **102**: 355. Same art. Portfo. (Den.) **31**: 407.
— High Life in. Temp. Bar, **6**: 404.
— Hints to a Tourist at Grand Cairo. Dub. Univ. **32**: 200.
— History of, and Jewish History. (A. B. Chapin) Chr. Q. Spec. **8**: 337.
— — Brugsch Bey's. (F. G. Peabody) Unita. R. **12**: 581.
— — Herodotus's. Ecl. R. **78**: 430.

Egypt, History of, Monumental. Westm. **63**: 577.
— — Pharaonic Tablets of Memphis. Brit. Q. **41**: 170.
— — Sharpe's. Ed. R. **88**: 32. — Mo. R. **140**: 161. **148**: 112. **162**: 358.
— — Shepherd Kings. (J. Campbell) Canad. J. n. s. **14**: 158, 219. — Antiquary, **4**: 91, 128.
— — since the Christian Era. Chr. Mo. Spec. **5**: 463.
— — Sketch of. Chr. Rem. **19**: 373.
— — Sources of ancient. Dub. R. **47**: 501.
— — Tablets of the Ptolemaic Period. (S. Birch) Arch. **39**: 315.
— — Trojan War and Homer. Blackw. **45**: 366.
— — Two Exodes. Brit. Q. **32**: 440.
— — under Abbas Pasha. (B. St. John) Sharpe, **14**: 71. Same art. Internat. M. **4**: 259. Same art. Ecl. M. **24**: 171.
— — under Mehemet Ali, Leaf of. Fortn. **27**: 875. Same art. Liv. Age, **134**: 174. Same art. Sup. Pop. Sci. **1**: 204.
— — under the Pharaohs, Kenrick's. Brit. Q. **13**: 92. — Ed. R. **150**: 77. — Quar. **147**: 430. — Prosp. R. **7**: 1.
— — — and under the Khedive, Zincke on. Chr. Obs. **72**: 295.
— — under the Romans. Ecl. Mus. **3**: 518.
— — Wilson's. Ecl. R. **3**: 64, 141.
— Hopes and Recollections of; a Poem. Dub. Univ. **5**: 520.
— Houses in. Penny M. **3**: 198.
— How I became an Egyptian. Dub. Univ. **46**: 610. Same art. Liv. Age, **48**: 97.
— illustrated. (E. T. and E. Rogers) Art J. **31**: 37–356. — Art J. **10**: 229.
— in a Caravan in, with Gérome. Lippinc. **13**: 279.
— in the Time of Abraham. (J. C. Moffat) Princ. **29**: 391.
— in 1835. Meth. M. **58**: 833.
— in 1850. Sharpe, **10**: 217.
— in 1852. (F. W. Holland) Chr. Exam. **52**: 51.
— in 1858. Colburn, **114**: 444.
— in 1864. Once a Week, **11**: 179.
— in 1865. Westm. **84**: 482.
— in 1878. (J. C. McCoan) Penn Mo. **9**: 72.
— in 1879. (M. Heilprin) Nation, **26**: 44.
— — Coup d'État in. (C. I. Barnard) Nation, **28**: 384. — (E. De Leon) Internat. R. **7**: 59. — (E. Dicey) 19th Cent. **5**: 670.
— — Emeute in Cairo. (C. I. Barnard) Nation, **28**: 199.
— — Deposition of the Khedive. (C. I. Barnard) Nation, **29**: 73.
— in 1881, Religious Agitation in. (S. Amos and C. I. Barnard) Nation, **33**: 411.
— Inside View of. (Sir G. Campbell) Fortn. **29**: 25.
— International Tribunals of. (P. H. Morgan) Appleton, **24**: 242, 308.
— Israel in. (G. E. Day) New Eng. **16**: 65. — Kitto, **34**: 1.
— — Despoiling of Egyptians by. (G. M. Weston) Bank. M. (N. Y.) **33**: 691.
— — Monumental Testimonies of. (J. Cumming) Ex. H. Lec. **19**: 319.
— Journal in, 1855–56. (N. W. Senior) Victoria, **1**: 60–542. **2**: 74–552. **3**: 69–555.
— Jurisprudence in. (J. Pickering) No. Am. **51**: 308.
— Khedive of, and his Court. (C. Hale) Atlan. **37**: 513.
— the Land of Kemi. Blackw. **129**: 683. **130**: 36–572.
— Language of. (C. Abel) New Eng. **38**: 815.
— — Ancient. (R. D. C. Robbins) Am. Bib. Repos 2d s. **11**: 137.
— — Demotic Grammar. (W. H. Green) Princ. **27**: 649.
— Sir G. de Lanney's Survey of, 1422. (J. Webb) Arch. **21**: 281.
— Legh's Travels in, 1812. (J. Foster) Ecl. R. **25**: 205.
— Lepsius on. Kitto, **13**: 314. — Prosp. R. **9**: 449.
— — and Brugsch on. (W. H. Green) Princ. **27**: 655.
Egypt, Letters from. Knick. **28**: 385, 487. **30**: 50, 316, 500. **31**: 132, 236, 422.
— Life in, past and present. Chr. Rem. **16**: 62.
— Lord Lindsay's Letters on. Tait, n. s. **5**: 655.
— Light's Travels in. (H. Salt) Quar. **19**: 178.
— Mariette's Discoveries in. Ecl. M. **64**: 89.
— Magic in. Dub. Univ. **12**: 568.
— Method of Notation in. Westm. **13**: 227.
— Miot's Expedition to. (R. Southey) Quar. **13**: 1.
— Modern. Westm. **6**: 158. — Quar. **30**: 481. — Am. Q. Reg. **6**: 50. — For. Q. **7**: 307. — Fraser, **21**: 319. — Mus. **10**: 97. **19**: 285. **39**: 44. — Penny M. **5**: 427. — So. R. n. s. **19**: 407.
— — and modern Egyptians. Ed. R. **65**: 146.
— — — Lane's. Dub. R. **4**: 440. — Quar. **59**: 165. — Mus. **31**: 193.
— — Manners and Customs of. Ecl. R. **66**: 345.
— Mohammedan History of. (E. H. Palmer) Stud. & Intel. Obs. **4**: 107–436.
— Monasteries of, MSS. from. Quar. **77**: 39. Same art. Liv. Age, **8**: 393. Same art. Ecl. M. **7**: 289.
— Month in. (W. T. Savage) Cong. R. **8**: 140.
— Monuments of. Ecl. R. **88**: 69. — Meth. Q. **10**: 130. — New Eng. **9**: 1. — For. Q. **17**: 110. *See above*, Egypt, Antiquities of.
— Mummies of. Am. Q. **18**: 170. — Mo. R. **134**: 234.
— My Window in. Chamb. J. **33**: 97.
— Mythology of. Mo. R. **92**: 225. — Fraser, **20**: 1, 200, 326.
— New. (C. H. Woodman) Appleton, **18**: 543.
— New Régime in, 1881. (C. I. Barnard) Nation, **33**: 30.
— Nile as a Sanatorium. (F. W. Fairholt) Intel. Obs. **7**: 4.
— Nile-Boat Recreations. (A. L. Adams) Colburn, **157**: 631. **158**: 29, 199.
— Nile-Notes of a Howadji, Curtis's. Nat. M. **4**: 24. — Tait, n. s. **18**: 470. *See also* Nile.
— Our Protectorate in. (E. Dicey) 19th Cent. **7**: 333.
— Palmer's Chronicles of. Dub. R. **51**: 25. — Ecl. R. **116**: 62.
— Petherick's Travels in. Colburn, **122**: 16.
— Plagues of. Danv. Q. **2**: 640.
— Progress of, 1870. Bank. M. (L.) **30**: 503.
— Pyramids and Temples of. (W. Blackwood) Potter Am. Mo. **8**: 104. *See* Pyramids.
— Public Works in, 1858. Colburn, **113**: 1.
— Races of ancient. (S. G. Morton) Ed. New Philos. J. **37**: 305. — (R. Owen) Anthrop. J. **4**: 223.
— Ramble from Valetta to Alexandria. Dub. Univ. **32**: 68.
— Resources of. Ecl. Engin. **14**: 50.
— Royal Family of. (R. L. N. Michel) Macmil. **39**: 481.
— St. John's Travels in Valley of the Nile. Mo. R. **134**: 197, 279.
— Schlegel's Essay on. For. Q. **22**: 167.
— Sketches of Travel in. (W. Knighton) Dub. Univ. **89**: 507. — (J. De Normandie) Mo. Rel. M. **39**: 453. **40**: 45, 133. — (J. A. St. John) Tait, n. s. **16**: 509–779. **17**: 17–344. — Dub. Univ. **52**: 65–695. — Fraser, **58**: 266.
— — Spencer's. Hogg, **5**: 317.
— Slavery in. (J. C. McCoan) Fraser, **95**: 563. Same art. Ecl. M. **89**: 111.
— Southern Gates of. Chamb. J. **15**: 378.
— Stephens's Travels in. Hesp. **1**: 174.
— Stone Implements in. (Sir J. Lubbock) Anthrop. J. **4**: 215.
— Stones and Bones from. (R. F. Burton) Anthrop. J. **8**: 290.
— Superstition in. Blackw. **37**: 534.
— Syria, and Turkey, Works on. Chr. Obs. **40**: 683, 791.
— Temples and Tombs of. Dub. R. **21**: 401.
— Through, to Bombay. (Miss Roberts) Tait, n. s. **8**: 235.

Egypt, Tombs of, Language of. Chamb. J. **12**: 41. Same art. Liv. Age, **23**: 256.
— Travel in. (R. W. Allen) Am. Meth. M. **22**: 71. — (R. W. Dale) Cong. **3**: 202–743. — (M. E. G. Duff) Contemp. **23**: 407. Same art. Ecl. M. **82**: 417.
— Upper. (M. Heilprin) Nation, **26**: 153.
— — Visit to, in the hot Season. (W. G. Palgrave) Macmil. **15**: 247. Same art. Ecl. M. **68**: 323. Same art. Liv. Age, **92**: 333.
— Village Life in. (F. W. Fairholt) Intel. Obs. **7**: 323.
— — St. John's. New Q. **2**: 64. — Ed. R. **59**: 404. — Colburn, **96**: 367.
— Villagers of. Sharpe, **20**: 120.
— Visit to. Lond. M. **2**: 563.
— — to Convent of Sittna Damiane. (G. Lansing) Harper, **28**: 757.
— Voice from, 1864. (B. W. Saville) Kitto, **35**: 273.
— Way to. (W. H. Dixon) Gent. M. n. s. **16**: 166.
— Western Influence in. No. Brit. **29**: 149. Same art. Ecl. M. **45**: 433.
— Wilson's Travels in. Mo. R. **100**: 240.
— Wintering in. (J. L. Farley) Belgra. **20**: 69.
Egyptian Anaglyphs, Biblical Illustrations from. Westm. **37**: 368.
Egyptian and Assyrian Art. (C. Boutell) Art J. **9**: 244.
Egyptian and Mosaic Records, Harmony of. Lond. Q. **53**: 265. Same art. Meth. Q. **40**: 709.
Egyptian Excavations and Mummies. Nature, **24**: 481.
Egyptian Hieroglyphics. *See* Hieroglyphics.
Egyptian Martyr; a Tale. Temp. Bar, **48**: 258.
Egyptian Story, A remarkable. (J. Hogg) Fraser, **7**: 147.
Egyptians and Turks at Home. (A. Freeland) St. James, **38**: 65.
— at Home. (A. Rhodes) Galaxy, **14**: 149.
— Turks, Spaniards, and. Tinsley, **19**: 141.
Egyptology. (J. P. Thompson) Bib. Sac. **27**: 180. **28**: 397. **29**: 771. **30**: 775. **32**: 185. **34**: 537. — Ecl. R. **105**: 384. — (J. C. Moffat) Princ. **28**: 715.
— Definite Results of. (J. P. Thompson) Nation, **5**: 5.
— Studies in. (F. Gilbert) Dial (Ch.), **1**: 103.
Ehrenberg, Christ. G., Sketch of. (F. Hoffman) Pop. Sci. Mo. **14**: 668.
— Travels in North Africa. For. R. **2**: 465.
Ehrenbreitstein, Castle of. (W. Pickersgill) Colburn, **120**: 444. Same art. Ecl. M. **52**: 258. — Penny M. **2**: 68.
Eider Down. Chamb. J. **36**: 76.
Eifel, The; Hints for Vagabonds. Fraser, **58**: 160.
— Lava Mountains of. Once a Week, **17**: 193, 239.
— Sketcher in. Fraser, **73**: 129.
Eight Castles in Spain. (R. B. Coffin) Harper, **35**: 350.
Eight-Hour Movement. (S. G. Fisher) Nation, **1**: 517. — (E. L. Godkin) Nation, **1**: 615. — (F. J. Kingsbury) Nation, **3**: 412. — (E. L. Godkin) Nation, **7**: 6. **14**: 333. — (J. B. Hodgskin) Nation, **10**: 399.
Eight-Hour Question, Solution of. (F. Lockley) Lakeside, **2**: 149.
Eighteen Christian Centuries, White's. Blackw. **84**: 165. Same art. Ecl. M. **45**: 229.
1801, Remarkable Events in. Chr. Obs. **1**: 64.
1812; a Retrospect. Blackw. **64**: 190.
1820; a Poem. (E. Everett) No. Am. **14**: 360.
1848, the Year of Reaction. Blackw. **67**: 1.
1851. Fraser, **45**: 17.
1852, Events in. Colburn, **96**: 497.
1865, Review of. (E. L. Godkin) Nation, **3**: 518.
1876, Review of. (J. McCarthy) Cath. World, **24**: 562.
1877, Review of. (J. McCarthy) Cath. World, **26**: 560.
1878, Review of. (J. McCarthy) Cath. World, **28**: 563.
1879, Current Events. (J. McCarthy) Cath. World, **29**: 417–849. **30**: 132, 280, 701.
— Review of. (J. McCarthy) Cath. World, **30**: 562.
1895. Blackw. **119**: 453. Same art. Liv. Age, **129**: 398, 472.
Eighteen Years alone. (E. C. Hardacre) Scrib. **20**: 657.
Eighteenth Brumaire. Dub. Univ. **23**: 1.
Eighteenth Century. (W. S. Lilly) Dub. R. **84**: 477. **85**: 330. **86**: 741. **89**: 307. — (T. E. Kebbel) Cornh. **38**: 540. Same art. Liv. Age, **139**: 515. Same art. Appleton, **21**: 19.
— England in. (G. M. Towle) Appleton, **19**: 260. — (K. Hillebrand) Contemp. **37**: 1.
— — Lecky's. Quar. **145**: 498.
— Manners and Customs of. (A. Andrews) Colburn, **102**: 70–465. **103**: 223–465. **104**: 49–485.
— Plea for. (W. Stebbing) 19th Cent. **6**: 1082. Same art. Liv. Age, **144**: 67.
— Review of. Temp. Bar, **45**: 198.
— Schlosser's History of. For. Q. **31**: 24. — Westm. **44**: 79 — Ecl. R. **84**: 64.
Eikon Basilike, Author of. (W. B. Odgers) Mod. R. **1**: 617. *See* Charles I.
Eiley O'Connor. Tinsley, **12**: 221.
Eine junge Amerikanerin. (C. DeKay) Scrib. **16**: 652.
Einsiedeln, a Swiss Sanctuary. Macmil. **26**: 450. Same art. Liv. Age, **115**: 544.
Εἰς, The Preposition. (W. R. C. Rogers) Kitto, **35**: 419.
Eisenberg, Many Tales from. All the Year, **24**: 461.
Eisteddfod. (J. Hullah) Good Words, **9**: 636. — (B. F. Lewis) Nation, **3**: 494.
Ἐκκλησία, Import of the Word. (J. M. C. Breaker) Chr. R. **22**: 593. — (R. Jeffery) Chr. Q. **4**: 343.
El Buscapie. (M. de Cervantes) Bentley, **24**: 199, 295.
El Dorado, Raleigh's original. Chamb. J. **20**: 70. — Sharpe, **26**: 222.
El Empecinado, Passages in the Career of. Blackw. **51**: 521, 756. **52**: 75. **53**: 343.
El Medinah, Burton's Pilgrimage to. Dub. R. **39**: 76.
El Tesoro. (F. F. Victor) Overland, **7**: 560.
El Vaquero. (C. H. Miller) Overland, **10**: 279.
Elachnave, Early Celtic College at. (H. Macmillan) Fraser, **102**: 578.
Elam, Joseph. (W. C. Elam) Penn Mo. **10**: 618.
Eland, The. Chamb. J. **31**: 183.
— Notes on. (H. N. Humphreys) Recr. Sci. **1**: 224.
Eland-Hunting. (M. L. Meason) Broadw. **2**: 138. — Once a Week, **27**: 118.
Elasmobranch Fishes, Balfour on. (E. R. Lankester) Nature, **18**: 113.
Elasmotherium, The. Nature, **18**: 387.
Elastic Tires, Properties of. Ecl. Engin. **4**: 503.
Elasticity of Building Materials. Ecl. Engin. **11**: 421.
— of Solids, Laws of. (W. J. M. Rankine) J. Frankl. Inst. **50**: 348.
Elba, Island of, 1814. Ecl. R. **21**: 301.
— Six Weeks in. Temp. Bar, **42**: 362. Same art. Liv. Age, **123**: 372.
— Visit to. Bentley, **42**: 221.
Elba of the Thames; a Story. (R. Dowling) Belgra. **36**: 83.
Elbe River, Along the. (J. H. Browne) Harper, **46**: 495.
Elberfeld, Germany. (M. Eyre) Victoria, **25**: 614.
— Poor-Law Experiment at. (W. W. Edwards) Contemp. **32**: 675.
Elbert, Gen. Samuel. (W. G. Simms) Hist. M. **13**: 34.
Elbow-Room. All the Year, **31**: 292.
Elden Family in Maryland and Kentucky. (B. J. Webb) Am. Cath. Q. **5**: 653.
Elder in Love. (J. Hogg) Fraser, **5**: 234.
Elder's Death-Bed. (J. Wilson) Blackw. **6**: 682. **7**: 171.
Elder's Wife. (Saxe Holm) Scrib. **5**: 747. **6**: 87.
Elders. (E. Zeller) Evang. R. **16**: 188.
— Plurality of. (T. S. Potwin) Cong. Q. **6**: 38.
— — in primitive Churches. (W. W. Patton) Cong. Q. **5**: *277.

Elders, Presiding, Election of. (J. Cummings) Meth. Q. 31: 685. — (G. Prentice) Meth. Q. 31: 300.
— — Should they be elected? (W. N. McElroy) Meth. Q. 36: 257.
— Rights of. (A. B. Dod) Princ. 15: 313. — (C. Hodge) Princ. 16: 276.
— Ruling. (C. Hodge) Princ. 15: 432.
— — in early New England Churches. (I. N. Tarbox) Cong. Q. 14: 401.
— — Lay. (H. M. Dexter) Cong. Q. 5: 173.
Elder Brother, Inconvenience of an. Lond. M. 23: 224.
Elderly Romance, An. Cornh. 40: 549. Same art. Liv. Age, 143: 675.
Eldership, The. (J. A. Alexander) Princ. 19: 42. — (J. Blanchard) Cong. Q. 5: 306. 6: 9.
— Lay. (R. D. Hitchcock) Am. Presb. R. 17: 253.
— of the New Testament. (J. A. Brown) Luth. Q. 7: 161.
— Presiding. (W. R. Goodwin) Meth. Q. 35: 67.
— Primitive. (E. F. Hatfield) Am. Presb. R. 17: 506.
— Theories of. (T. Smyth) Princ. 32: 185, 449, 702.
Eldon, John Scott, Lord. (A. C. Ewald) Temp. Bar, 49: 58. — Cong. M. 28: 45, 292. — Dub. Univ. 24: 301. — Colburn, 11: 17. 74: 270. — Chamb. J. 2: 88. — Tait, n. s. 13: 674. — Fraser, 30: 211.
— and Chances of the Bar. Ed. R. 81: 131. Same art. Ecl. M. 4: 433.
— and Edinburgh Review. Blackw. 14: 627.
— and Lord Stowell. (T. N. Talfourd) Quar. 75: 32.
— Attacks on. Blackw. 14: 202, 627. 18: 212.
— Character of. Tait, 1: 684.
— Life of. (J. Moncrieff) No. Brit. 2: 212. — (N. W. Senior) Quar. 74: 71. Same art. Liv. Age, 1: 717. — (S. F. Smith) Chr. R. 10: 181. — Brit. Q. 1: 277. — Westm. 42: 456. — Blackw. 56: 245. — Dem. R. 17: 94. — Ecl. R. 80: 718. — Ed. R. 67: 19. — Mo. R. 165: 161. — Tait, n. s. 11: 654. — Lond. M. 18: 477.
— — Public and private. Chr. Rem. 8: 274.
— Phrenological Examination of. (H. G. Atkinson) Zoist. 1: 277.
Eleanor, Queen of Castile, Death of. (J. Hunter) Arch. 29: 167.
Eleanor, Funeral of; a Ballad. Lond. M. 6: 172.
Eleanor Bingley. (C. Whitehead) Bentley, 10: 261.
Eleanor Clare's Journal. House. Words, 16: 197–271.
Eleanor Manton. Knick. 47: 64–586. 48: 14–574. 49: 45–567.
Eleanor Vaughan; or, Twice avenged. Ecl. M. 45: 380. 46: 106.
Eleanor's Career. (I. A. Prokop) Lippinc. 15: 463.
Eleanor's Story. (K. Roche) Irish Mo. 6: 1–212.
Eleänore; a Poem. Dub. Univ. 51: 255.
Eleanour; a Tale of Non-Performers. Blackw. 127: 479. Same art. Liv. Age, 145: 462.
Eleatic Fragments. (J. A. Symonds) Fortn. 24: 228.
Eleatic School. (C. D. B. Mills) Radical, 6: 301, 371.
Election of Representatives, Mode of. (H. R. Droop) J. Statis. Soc. 44: 141.
— The Tattleton. Chamb. J. 18: 150.
Elections, Bribery at English. (Lord Hobart) Macmil. 15: 14. — (H. George) Overland, 7: 497. — Westm. 25: 485. 48: 331. 51: 78. — Dem. R. 13: 227. — Ecl. R. 90: 335.
— Congressional Control of Federal. (E. L. Godkin) Nation, 28: 226.
— Contested, in Great Britain. Dub. R. 7: 36.
— — Law of. Mo. R. 123: 585.
— — Political Dangers from. (S. Newcomb) No. Am. 130: 261.
— — Procedure in. (H. L. Dawes) Am. Soc. Sci. J. 2: 56.
— Corrupt, in England. Temp. Bar, 15: 189.
Elections, Corruption at. (F. D. Maurice) Macmil. 10: 192. — (W. D. Christie) Macmil. 10: 517.
— Cost of, in England. (S. C. Buxton) Fortn. 33: 249. — Chamb. J. 58: 363.
— Critical, in England. Cornh. 18: 601.
— Duty of the Citizen at. Putnam, 8: 533.
— English. Gent. M. n. s. 1: 743.
— — of 1837. Dub. Univ. 10: 243.
— — of 1841. Dub. Univ. 18: 237.
— Frauds in New York. (D. F. Bacon) Am. Whig R. 1: 441, 551.
— Malpractices at (W. M. Torrens) Fraser, 103: 783.
— New York, 1846. Dem. R. 19: 420.
— Old Parliamentary. Chamb. J. 58: 710.
— Statistics of. (A. Frisby) Contemp. 38: 635.
— Supervision of, Democrats and. Nation, 28: 199.
— Theory and Practice of. (W. G. Sumner) Princ. n. s. 5: 262. 6: 24.
— Westminster. House. Words, 14: 361.
— — History of. Temp. Bar, 15: 86.
Election Committees. Quar. 71: 478.
Election Compromises. Westm. 39: 113.
Election Contest in Australia. Cornh. 5: 25.
Election Days, Old, in Ireland. Cornh. 12: 165.
Election Expenses in England. Westm. 78: 62.
Election Laws. (G. W. McCrary) No. Am. 28: 450.
Election Row in New York. (C. A. Bristed) Internat. M. 5: 341.
Election Sermons. (A. Barnes) Chr. Mo. Spec. 10: 418.
Election Story. Chamb. J. 53: 329, 347.
Election Time in America. All the Year, 5: 67.
Election, Doctrine of. (R. Gilbert) Am. Meth. M. 21: 400. — Chr. Mo. Spec. 10: 273. — (N. Bouton) Lit. & Theo. R. 2: 307. 4: 250, 326. — (O. A. Brownson) Brownson, 4: 190, 538.
— Erskine on. Ecl. R. 68: 100.
— Fletcher on. Cong. M. 8: 251, 312.
— Hamilton on. Ecl. R. 41: 169.
— Limited, controverted. (J. W. Nevin) Mercersb. 9: 197.
— Lutheran. (C. F. Schaeffer) Evang. R. 3: 359.
— Perseverance of the Elect. So. R. n. s. 19: 120.
— Preaching. (S. C. Bartlett) Cong. R. 10: 54.
Electioneering. (J. Hannay) Quar. 102: 32. — (J. E. Ritchie) Tinsley, 26: 373. — Lond. M. 15: 362.
Electioneering Experiences. Chamb. J. 42: 657.
Elective Franchise. Dem. R. 22: 97.
Elective Studies in American Colleges. (F. A. P. Barnard) Am. J. Educ. 22: 435.
Electoral Criminalities, England, 1848. Ecl. R. 88: 335.
Electoral Facts. (W. E. Gladstone) 19th Cent. 4: 955.
Electoral Reform. (T. Hare) Fortn. 2: 439. 3: 559. — (J. B. Kinnear) Fortn. 4: 49.
— Bribery and the Ballot. Westm. 115: 443.
Electoral System, French. Tait, n. s. 4: 729.
Electoral Vote. *See* Presidential Election.
Electra. Blackw. 130: 306.
Electric Animals. Ecl. M. 42: 346.
Electric Apparatus, Dynamo-. Ecl. Engin. 18: 355.
Electric Arc. (E. Thomson and E. J. Houston) J. Frankl. Inst. 108: 46.
Electric Conduction. (M. Faraday) Am. J. Sci. 71: 368. — J. Frankl. Inst. 37: 392.
— and the Nature of Matter, Faraday on. (R. Laming) J. Frankl. Inst. 41: 184.
— of Metals. (J. H. Lane) Am. J. Sci. 51: 230.
— on Telegraph Wires. (J. Henry) Am. J. Sci. 53: 25.
— Resistance by Fluids to. (E. N. Horsford) Am. J. Sci. 55: 36.
Electric Conductivities, Method of Measuring. (A. M. Mayer) Am. J. Sci. 100: 307.
Electric Convection, Magnetic Effect of. (H. A. Rowland) Am. J. Sci. 115: 30.

Electric Current, Law of Induction upon itself. (J. H. Lane) Am. J. Sci. 61: 17. — (J. W. Strutt) Nature, 6: 64.
— Velocity of. (E. H. Hall) Am. J. Sci. 120: 52.
Electric Currents circulating near the Earth's Surface. (E. Loomis) Am. J. Sci. 84: 34.
— Molecular Change by passing through Iron Bars. (J. Trowbridge) Am. J. Sci. 108: 18.
— New Action of the Magnet on. (E. H. Hall) Am. J. Sci. 119: 200.
— Terrestrial. (W. Le R. Broun) Am. J. Sci. 115: 385.
Electric Discharge, Form and Function of. (W. Spottiswoode) Nature, 24: 547, 569.
— from circular Disks. (C. J. Bell) Am. J. Sci. 109: 458.
— in Air. (A. W. Wright) Am. J. Sci. 101: 437.
— in Gases. Nature, 18: 525, 547.
— Method of investigating. (A. M. Mayer) Am. J. Sci. 108: 436.
— of a Leyden Jar, Nature of. (O. N. Rood) Am. J. Sci. 98: 153. 102: 160. 104: 249, 371.
— Tubes for silent. Nature, 9: 244.
— with Chloride of Silver Battery. Nature, 20: 174, 199.
Electric Fishes. (F. W. Clarke) Penn Mo. 6: 808.
— Natural History of. (A. Murray) Ed. New Philos. J. 59: 35, 379. 63: 267.
Electric Girl of La Perrière. (R. D. Owen) Atlan. 14: 284. — Sharpe, 51: 14.
Electric Induction. (M. Faraday) Am. J. Sci. 68: 84. — (M. Faraday) J. Frankl. Inst. 25: 418. 26: 389. — (P. Volpicelli) Nature, 13: 437, 475.
— Faraday on. J. Frankl. Inst. 57: 408. 59: 402.
Electric Light. (J. Abbott) Harper, 41: 354. — (R. K. Browne) Galaxy, 3: 365. — (J. Jamin) J. Frankl. Inst. 105: 403. — (F. R. Conder) Dub. Univ. 93: 129. — Dub. Univ. 94: 385. — (J. Munro) Nature, 16: 422. — (A. Niaudet) Pop. Sci. Mo. 11: 429. — (C. W. Siemens) Nature, 18: 650. — (J. T. Sprague) Ecl. Engin. 21: 384. — (W. H. Stone) Pop. Sci. R. 18: 25. — (S. P. Thompson) Nature, 20: 165. — (J. Tyndall) Fortn. 31: 197. — (J. Tyndall) Pop. Sci. Mo. 14: 553. — (H. Wilde) Nature, 19: 78, 152. — (J. Hopkinson) Nature, 22: 42. — Nature, 24: 6–60. — Am. J. Sci. 119: 141. — Chamb. J. 10: 419. 40: 19, 44, 278. — Chamb. J. 54: 667. Same art. Ecl. M. 60: 115. — Cornh. 39: 157, 164. — Ecl. Engin. 17: 15, 277. 18: 146. 20: 70. — Ed. R. 149: 289. — (G. Molloy) Irish Mo. 7: 295. — Liv. Age, 46: 61. — Nature, 19: 230. 20: 39, 85, 190. — (W. Crookes) Pop. Sci. Mo. 3: 584. — Pop. Sci. Mo. 14: 234. — Pract. M. 6: 261, 356. 7: 105.
— Action of, on the iodized Plate. (O. N. Rood) Am. J. Sci. 87: 207.
— Actual Cost of, 1858. (E. Becquerel) J. Frankl. Inst. 66: 204.
— and Gas. (J. T. Sprague) J. Frankl. Inst. 108: 187.
— — in Paris. (W. de Fonvielle) Nature, 21: 282.
— Apparatus for producing. (G. Trouvé) J. Frankl. Inst. 105: 44.
— — Siemens's. Nature, 14: 133.
— as applied to Photo-Micrography. (J. J. Woodward) Am. J. Sci. 99: 294.
— at the Paris Exhibition, 1881. Ecl. Engin. 25: 439.
— Brush System of. (C. F. Brush) Ecl. Engin. 21: 395.
— Candle for. (A. Niaudet) Pop. Sci. Mo. 11: 429.
— Collapse of. (W. H. Stone) Pop. Sci R. 18: 155.
— Dangers incident to. J. Frankl. Inst. 112: 401.
— Development of. Quar. 152: 441.
— Divisibility of. J. Frankl. Inst. 103: 371.
— Division and Regulation of. (W. E. Sawyer) Ecl. Engin. 24: 220.
— Economy of. (R. Briggs) J. Frankl. Inst. 110: 164.
Electric Light, Edison's. (F. R. Upton) Scrib. 19: 531. — (H. A. Rowland and G. F. Barker) Am. J. Sci. 119: 337. — Nature, 21: 261. — J. Frankl. Inst. 109: 145.
— Experiments with. J. Frankl. Inst. 108: 60.
— for Lighthouses. (J. W. McGauley) Intel. Obs. 11: 325. — Nature, 16: 552.
— — and Ships. (E. St. Edme) Ecl. Engin. 1: 119.
— for Ships. Pract. M. 6: 232.
— for Steamships. (J. Trowbridge) Pop. Sci. Mo. 5: 720.
— for Street Lamps. Pract. M. 7: 338, 367.
— History of. (W. M. Williams) Ecl. Engin. 20: 298.
— in the British Museum. (R. Garnett) Lib. J. 4: 444. — J. Frankl. Inst. 109: 59.
— in Collieries. (W. H. Preece) J. Frankl. Inst. 110: 408.
— in 1858. (H. Chapman) J. Frankl. Inst. 66: 119.
— in 1867. (H. Morton) J. Frankl. Inst. 83: 289.
— in 1877. (A. Sartiaux) J. Frankl. Inst. 104: 158.
— in 1878. J. Frankl. Inst. 106: 421.
— in England. Ecl. Engin. 21: 25.
— in London, on the Clock Tower, Westminster. (M. F. O'Reilly) Pop. Sci. R. 12: 265.
— in Medicine. Chamb. J. 58: 314.
— in Paris. All the Year, 41: 495.
— — Cost of. J. Frankl. Inst. 107: 63.
— Incandescent. Nature, 23: 104.
— Influence upon Vegetation. (C. W. Siemens) Nature, 21: 456.
— Invisible Radiation of. (J. Tyndall) J. Frankl. Inst. 79: 390.
— Jablochkoff. J. Frankl. Inst. 104: 142.
— Lamp for, Carbons in. (H. W. Wiley) Am. J. Sci. 118: 55.
— — New. (E. Thomson and E. J. Houston) J. Frankl. Inst. 106: 252.
— — with continuous Circuit. (E. Reynier) J. Frankl. Inst. 106: 275.
— Memoranda on. (J. K. Whilldin) J. Frankl. Inst. 73: 217.
— New Method of. Nature, 8: 372.
— New System of. (E Thomson and E. J. Houston) J. Frankl. Inst 106: 251.
— of the Future. Am. Arch. 4: 164.
— Recent Advances of, 1880. (W. H. Preece) Ecl Engin. 24: 504.
— Regulator for. (M. Serrin) J. Frankl. Inst. 74: 415.
— Sawyer's. J. Frankl. Inst. 110: 395.
— Scientific Principles involved in. (W. G. Adams) Nature, 23: 580–605. — (W. G. Adams) J. Frankl. Inst. 112: 279, 364, 445.
— Siemens's. Nature, 5: 172.
— Staite's. J. Frankl. Inst. 47: 263.
— Success of. (T. A. Edison) No. Am. 131: 295.
— Vegetation under. Nature, 21: 438.
— Werdermann's. Nature, 19: 16, 37.
Electric Motor. (W. W. Griscom) J. Frankl. Inst. 110: 388.
— Griscom's. J. Frankl. Inst. 112: 440.
Electric Power. Ecl. Engin. 25: 371.
Electric Railways. Ecl. Engin. 25: 111. — (A. Siemens) Ecl. Engin. 25: 37.
Electric Signaling on English Railroads. (C. E. Pascoe) Pop. Sci. Mo. 4: 581.
Electric Spark, Method of producing Figures by. (E. W. Blake, jr.) Am. J. Sci. 99: 289.
— Physical Properties of the Light of. (D. Alter) Am. J. Sci. 69: 213.
— Study of. (O. N. Rood) Am. J. Sci. 83: 219. 88: 361.
Electric Time Signals, Alleghany System of. (S. P. Langley) Am. J. Sci. 104: 377.
Electrical Appliances, Future of. (J. Perry) Nature, 24: 19. Same art. Ecl. Engin. 25: 89.
Electrical Battery. (J. F. Dana) Am. J. Sci. 1: 292.

Electrical Batteries. (E. G. Bartholomew) Ecl. Engin. **8**: 58.
Electrical Condition of Gas Flames. (J. Trowbridge) Am. J. Sci. **104**: 4.
Electrical Experiment with an insulated Room. (F. C. Webb) Ecl. Engin. **7**: 583.
Electrical Excitation, New Source of. (Mrs. E. Foote) Am. J. Sci. **74**: 386.
Electrical Fluctuations as a Cause of Disease. Liv. Age, **55**: 65.
Electrical Machine. (Dr. Andrews) Nature, **12**: 90, 130, 170. — (W. H. Walenn) Ecl. Engin. **10**: 442. — (C. G. Page) Am. J. Sci. **34**: 163. — Am. J. Sci. **33**: 213.
— Dr. Robert Hare's. Am. J. Sci. **32**: 272.
— — for continuous Currents, Gramme's. J. Frankl. Inst. **97**: 55.
— — for alternating Currents, Gramme's. J. Frankl. Inst. **106**: 181.
— Holtz's. (J. C. Poggendorff) J. Frankl. Inst. **90**: 58, 117. — (E. Thomson) J. Frankl. Inst. **103**: 207.
— — Modification of. (C. Van Brunt) J. Frankl. Inst. **93**: 347.
— — Theory of. (D. S. Stroumbo) J. Frankl. Inst. **101**: 356.
— Locomotive. Pract. M. **5**: 356.
— Magnetic Currents in. Ecl. Engin. **23**: 31.
— Peculiar Discharge between Poles of. (A.W.Wright) Am. J. Sci. **99**: 381.
— Wilde's. (W. Crookes) J. Frankl. Inst. **82**: 400. — J. Frankl. Inst. **84**: 252.
Electrical Machines. (R. Hare) Am. J. Sci. **24**: 253.
— Report on. J. Frankl. Inst. **105**: 289, 361.
See Electro-Magnetic.
Electrical Measurements. (B. A. Gould) J. Frankl. Inst. **89**: 37, 120, 203.
— Absolute System of. (J. P. Cooke) J. Frankl. Inst. **90**: 138–411.
Electrical Nerves, Social. Nature, **17**: 305, 346.
Electrical Novelties. Ev. Sat. **6**: 328.
Electrical Phenomena. (E. J. Houston and E. Thomson) J. Frankl. Inst. **101**: 270.
— in Rocky Mountains. (F. M. Endlich) Penn Mo. **6**: 403.
— in Houses. (E. Loomis and S. St. John) Am. J. Sci. **76**: 58.
— Theories of. (R. Hare) Am. J. Sci. **55**: 230, 343. **56**: 45.
— Franklin's, Objections to. (R. Hare) J. Frankl. Inst. **45**: 188, 264.
— Tyndall's Lectures on. Nature, **2**: 243.
Electrical Quantities and Resistance. J. Frankl. Inst. **73**: 129.
Electrical Register and Koenig's Tuning Forks. (L. C. Cooley) J. Frankl. Inst. **104**: 199.
Electrical Resistance. (E. L. Nichols) Am. J. Sci. **122**: 363.
— Absolute Unit of. (H. A. Rowland) Am. J. Sci. **115**: 281, 325, 430.
Electrical Science, De la Rive on. Ed. R. **106**: 26. Same art. Ecl. M. **42**: 153.
Electrical Shadows, Holtz's. Nature, **24**: 131.
Electrical Transmission of motive Power. Ecl. Engin. **22**: 196.
Electricity. Chamb. J. **56**: 107. — Liv. Age, **2**: 323.
— Address to the Society of Telegraphic Engineers. (Sir W. Thomson) Nature, **9**: 269.
— Analogies with Phenomena of. Nature, **17**: 226, 385.
— and the Electric Telegraph. Cornh. **2**: 61.
— — Prescott on. Pract. M. **7**: 127.
— and Light, Lectures on. (H. Morton) J. Frankl. Inst. **83**: 48–413. **84**: 52, 209, 281.
— — Relation between. (O. J. Lodge) Nature, **23**: 302.
Electricity and Magnetism. (M. Faraday) J. Frankl. Inst. **70**: 313. — Brit. Q. **18**: 101.
— — Clerk Maxwell's. Nature, **7**: 478.
— — Hydrodynamic Analogies to. (G. Forbes) Nature, **24**: 361.
— and Thunderstorms. (E. Foote) Pop. Sci. Mo. **13**: 689.
— and Water-Drops. (Lord Rayleigh) Nature, **19**: 486.
— Animal. (J. Lovering) Chr. Exam. **55**: 1.
— — Electric Girl of La Perrière. (R. D. Owen) Atlan. **14**: 284. — Sharpe, **51**: 14.
— Applications of, at Paris Exhibition, 1867. Nation, **5**: 521. **6**: 112.
— — to Horticulture. (C. W. Siemens) Nature, **24**: 567.
— applied. Ecl. Engin. **10**: 50.
— — in Peace and War. Quar. **144**: 138. Same art. Ecl. M. **90**: 1. Same art. Liv. Age, **135**: 195.
— — to ascertain Longitude. (A. Jones) Hunt, **17**: 390.
— — to registering Vibrations. J. Frankl. Inst. **87**: 44. **88**: 341.
— as a Factor in Happiness. Appleton, **26**: 467.
— as a motive Power. (W. E. Ayrton) Nature, **20**: 568. — (W. E. Ayrton) Ecl. Engin. **21**: 478. — Ecl. Engin. **1**: 630.
— at Work. (T. L. Phipson) Macmil. **6**: 163. Same art. Ecl. M. **56**: 478.
— Atmospheric. Knick. **4**: 462. — (H. S. Carhart) Pop. Sci. Mo. **18**: 513. — (J. Lovering) Am. Alma. **1854**: 70. **1855**: 65. **1856**: 55.
— — Effect of Temperature upon. (H. Goldmark) Am. J. Sci. **116**: 52.
— — Experiments on. J. Frankl. Inst. **22**: 166.
— Cumming's Theory of. (A. Schuster) Nature, **15**: 526.
— Dissipation of, in Gases. (D. Boboulieff) Am. J. Sci. **107**: 118.
— Dynamic, Faraday on. J. Frankl. Inst. **57**: 276.
— Earth as a Conductor of. (J. Trowbridge) Am. J. Sci. **120**: 138.
— Edison's Results in. (C. Lever) St. James, **45**: 166.
— Elementary Laws of. (W. S. Harris) J. Frankl. Inst. **21**: 68, 143.
— Energy of. Ecl. Engin. **9**: 513.
— Evolution of the Science, 1842. Chr. Rem. **3**: 631.
— Experimental Researches in. (M. Faraday) J. Frankl. Inst. **21**: 282, 362. **22**: 55. — (W. De la Rive and H. W. Müller) Nature, **22**: 149–196.
— Experiments in. (M. Faraday) Am. J. Sci. **59**: 188.
— Faraday's Conception of, Modern Development of. (H. Helmholtz) Pop. Sci. Mo. **19**: 242.
— Faraday's Experiments in. Quar. **79**: 93.
— Faraday's Law of. (H. Helmholtz) J. Frankl. Inst. **111**: 452.
— Force of the Future. (J. A. Bower) Good Words, **22**: 629. Same art. Potter Am. Mo. **17**: 399.
— Franklin's Discoveries in. (W. H. Allen) Meth. Q. **7**: 101.
— Free. (R. Hare) Am. J. Sci. **53**: 334.
— from Steam. J. Frankl. Inst. **31**: 123.
— Generation of Economy in. (S. W. Robinson) Ecl. Engin. **23**: 204.
— Human, Rutter on. Zoist. **12**: 80. *See* Electric Girl.
— in Medicine, Adams on. Canad. Mo. **11**: 674.
— in Plants. (M. Becquerel) Am. J. Sci. **62**: 83. — (E. Smith) J. Frankl. Inst. **89**: 69.
— in Theory and Practice. (Sir D. Brewster) No. Brit. **30**: 160. Same art. Ecl. M. **47**: 39, 200. — Ecl. Engin. **15**: 531.
— International Exhibition at Paris, 1880. Nature, **24**: 39–607.
— Is it Life? (H. Lake) Belgra. **19**: 188. Same art. Pop. Sci. Mo. **2**: 477. — (F. Papillon) Pop. Sci Mo **2**: 526.
— Leithead on. Ecl. R. **69**: 427.

Electricity, Lessons in. (J. Tyndall) Pop. Sci. Mo. **8**: 607. **9**: 30–331.
— Measurement of inductive Resistances. J. Frankl. Inst. **80**: 261.
— Nature of. (W. H. Preece) Nature, **21**: 335. Same art. Ecl. Engin. **22**: 298.
— New and economical Sources of. (A. Moigno) Pract. M. **4**: 239.
— New Kind of electric Repulsion. (A. Schuster) Nature, **22**: 535.
— Noad on. (S. P. Thompson) Nature, **20**: 118. — Mo. R. **164**: 240.
— of Fire in the Earth. (J. R. Loomis) Am. J. Sci. **59**: 1.
— of mineral Veins. (R. Hunt) J. Frankl. Inst. **46**: 129.
— Origin of. Westm. **89**: 130.
— Phenomena of. Ecl. M. **45**: 404.
— Planté's Researches in. (S. P. Thompson) Nature, **21**: 150.
— Practical Uses of. (C. A. Young) Princ. n. s. **7**: 293.
— Production and Transmission of Power by. (G. W. Blodgett) Ecl. Engin. **23**: 24.
— Progress of. (E. Laurence) Harper, **39**: 548.
— Relation of common and Voltaic. (J. J. Waterston) J. Frankl. Inst. **68**: 122.
— — with Light. (O. J. Lodge) Ecl. Engin. **24**: 299.
— the Source of Light, Heat, etc. (C. E. Townsend) Contin. Mo. **6**: 531.
— Sprague's. Nature, **12**: 144.
— Static or Franklinic. (M. Faraday) J. Frankl. Inst. **48**: 319, 387.
— — Generation of. (G. W. Rains) Am. J. Sci. **49**: 93.
— Storage of. Ed. R. **154**: 265. — Nature, **24**: 105. — (W. Thomson) Nature, **24**: 156. — (J. Monro) Pop. Sci. R. **20**: 320. — Pop. Sci. Mo. **19**: 546. — (E. J. Houston and E. Thomson) J. Frankl. Inst. **108**: 388. — J. Frankl. Inst. **112**: 68. — Ecl. Engin. **25**: 219.
— Terrestrial. Ecl. Engin. **10**: 440.
— Thermo-. (P. G. Tait) Nature, **8**: 86, 122.
— Uses of. Chamb. J. **55**: 669.
— — in War. (H. B. Pritchard) Nature, **16**: 281. Same art. Liv. Age, **134**: 700.
— Velocity of, New Method of measuring. (J. Lovering) Am. J. Sci. **111**: 211.
— Voltaic. Chr. Rem. **6**: 58.
— — Conducting Powers of Wires for. (C. L. Dresser) J. Frankl. Inst. **53**: 29.
— What is? Once a Week, **4**: 163. Same art. Ecl. M. **53**: 127. — Ecl. M. **64**: 297.
Electrification of an Island. (F. Jenkin) Nature, **2**: 12.
Electro-Biology. Chamb. J. **18**: 44, 379. — Westm. **55**: 312.
— and Mesmerism. Quar. **93**: 501. Same art. Liv. Age, **39**: 707.
— Experiments in. Chamb. J. **15**: 81.
— Smee on. Chamb. J. **11**: 298.
Electro-Chronograph. (J. Locke) Am. J. Sci. **58**: 231.
Electro-dynamic Induction. (J. Henry) Am. J. Sci. **38**: 209. **41**: 117.
— in Liquids. (M. Faraday) J. Frankl. Inst. **57**: 411.
Electro-Dynamometer for measuring large Currents. (W. N. Hill) Nature, **21**: 327. — (W. N. Hill) Am. J. Sci. **119**: 10.
Electro-Heating. (W. L. Burton) Ecl. Engin. **3**: 289.
Electrolytic Phenomena. (W. G. Levison) Am. J. Sci. **119**: 29.
Electro-Magnets, Armatures for, Thin Iron Plates as. (J. Trowbridge) Am. J. Sci. **11**: 361.
— New Kind of. (J. Nicklès) Am. J. Sci. **65**: 104, 380.
Electro-magnetic Apparatus. (B. F. Joslin) Am. J. Sci. **21**: 86. — (C. G. Page) Am. J. Sci. **35**: 252.
Electro-magnetic Engine. (J. P. Joule) Nature, **3**: 474.
— New. (C. G. Page) Am. J. Sci. **49**: 131.
Electro-magnetic Experiments. (G. Moll) Am. J. Sci. **19**: 329. — (J. H. Abbot) Am. J. Sci. **40**: 104.
Electro-magnetic Induction, Molecular. (D. E. Hughes) Nature, **23**: 519. — Ecl. Engin. **25**: 14.
Electro-magnetic Machine constructed at Cornell Univ. Workshop. (W. A. Anthony) Am. J. Sci. **112**: 251.
— Davenport's. Am. J. Sci. **32**: 217.
Electro-mag. Machines. (J. Locke) Am. J. Sci. **34**: 125.
— Armatures of. (H. Wilde) J. Frankl. Inst. **88**: 121.
— New. (S. J. Mackie) Pop. Sci. R. **6**: 281.
Electro-magnetic Rotations. (G. Gore) Ecl. Engin. **24**: 379.
Electro-Magnetism. (A. M. Mayer) Am. J. Sci. **100**: 195. — (C. G. Page) Am. J. Sci. **36**: 350. — Quar. **35**: 237. — Knick. **9**: 533. — (A. M. Mayer) J. Frankl. Inst. **90**: 403. — Am. Mo. M. **10**: 409.
— and kindred Sciences. Nat. Q. **6**: 284.
— as a moving Power. (R. Hunt) J. Frankl. Inst. **50**: 334. — (C. G. Page) Am. J. Sci. **35**: 106. — (C. G. Page) J. Frankl. Inst. **50**: 267.
Electro-Metallurgy. Art J. **21**: 335. — (A. W. Wright) Am. J. Sci. **114**: 169. — (A. W. Wright) J. Frankl. Inst. **104**: 242. — Chamb. J. **28**: 222. — J. Frankl. Inst. **37**: 402.
— Gore's. Nature, **16**: 263.
— New Process for. Pract. M. **7**: 233.
Electro-motive Force of fluid Batteries. Ecl. Engin. **11**: 358.
Electro-Motors and Electric Light. (H. Morton) Ecl. Engin. **22**: 397, 441.
Electrophysiologica. (C. B. Radcliffe) Nature, **5**: 186, 206, 226.
Electro-Plate Factory, Day at. Penny M. **13**: 417.
Electro-Plating, Application of Science to. (G. Gore) Pop. Sci. R. **1**: 327.
— at Home. Chamb. J. **25**: 28, 364.
— Process of. (G. Gore) Pop. Sci. R. **2**: 37.
Electro-Printing Block Co. Once a Week, **3**: 239.
Electro-Science. Ecl. Engin. **7**: 524.
Electrostatics and Magnetism. Nature, **7**: 218.
Electrotype, The. (R. Bithell) Recr. Sci. **1**: 275. — Liv. Age, **4**: 213.
— and Daguerreotype. Westm. **34**: 434.
— applied to Art-Manufactures. Art J. **2**: 205, 238.
— applied to Printing. (W. Filmer) Overland, **8**: 524.
— Domestic. Chamb. J. **33**: 150.
— in Operations of the United States Coast Survey. (G Mathiot) Am. J. Sci. **65**: 305.
Elegant Tom Dillar. (C. F. Briggs) Putnam, **1**: 525.
Elegy, Greek. (H. N. Coleridge) Quar. **48**: 69.
— in a Country Churchyard. (T. Gray) Harper, **7**: 1.
Elegies. Blackw. **118**: 345. Same art. Liv. Age, **127**: 219.
— Heroic. Dub. Univ. **2**: 202.
Elements, Are they elementary? (F. W. Clarke) Pop. Sci. Mo. **8**: 463. — (M. M. P. Muir) Nature, **18**: 592, 625.
— Atomic Volumes of. (F. W. Clarke) Am. J. Sci. **97**: 308.
— Chemical. (J. N. Lockyer) Pop. Sci. Mo. **14**: 600.
— Compound Nature of. (J. N. Lockyer) Nature, **19**: 157, 197, 225. — (J. N. Lockyer) Am. J. Sci. **117**: 93.
— Evolution of. (M. M. Pattison) Pop. Sci. R. **18**: 125.
Elephant, The. Chamb. J. **44**: 285. — Colburn, **71**: 83–255.
— at Home. All the Year, **2**: 129.
— at Oxford Museum. (H. N. Moseley) Nature, **6**: 183.
— Destruction of an, in Geneva, 1820. Lond. M. **14**: 451.
— in Exeter Exchange. Once a Week, **9**: 586.
— Raffle for an. Chamb. J. **39**: 150.
Elephants. Bentley, **33**: 297. — Colburn, **70**: 515. **71**: 83, 255. — Ev. Sat. **15**: 444. — House. Words, **3**: 229.
— African. Once a Week, **15**: 108.
— Capture of. (C. Nordhoff) Harper, **20**: 455. — Quar. **146**: 361. Same art. Appleton, **21**: 51. — Penny M. **1**: 159, 267. — House. Words, **4**: 305.

Elephants, Chapter on. (J. Bowring) St. James, **28**: 580.
— Military. Chamb. J. **26**: 6.
— Natural History of. Colburn, **74**: 371-631.
— Use of, in War. Dub. Univ. **21**: 117.
— White. All the Year, **8**: 488.
— — Small. Chamb. J. **41**: 545.
Elephant-Back in Burmah. Putnam, **8**: 43.
Elephant-Hunting in Siam. (G. d'Abain) Scrib. **8**: 223.
— in Ceylon. (A. H. Guernsey) Harper, **8**: 758.—Fraser, **33**: 561.
— Modes of. Hogg, **2**: 266.
Elephant Kraal, The. Gent. M. n. s. **9**: 149.—Howitt, **3**: 339.—Macmil. **29**: 466. Same art. Ecl. M. **82**: 574.
Elephant-Shooting. (M. L. Meason) Broadw. **2**: 424.—Ev. Sat. **8**: 198.
Elephant-Stalking in Abyssinia. Ecl. M. **61**: 465.
Elephanta Caves. Penny M. **1**: 121.
Eleusinian Mysteries. (F. Lenormant) Contemp. **37**: 847. **38**: 121, 412.—Blackw. **73**: 185.—(J. Cooper) New Eng. **35**: 467.—(T. De Quincey) Tait, n. s. **14**: 519, 661.
— and Bacchic Mysteries. Pamph. **8**: 33, 455.
Elevated Railway. *See* Railroad, Elevated.
Elevator, Hydraulic, Fall of, at Grand Hotel, Paris, 1878. (W. B. Le Van) J. Frankl. Inst. **105**: 345.
— Improved portable. Pract. M. **5**: 302.
Elevators, Notes on. Am. Arch. **7**: 245. **8**: 3-160.
Elevator Shafts. Am. Arch. **7**: 45-101.
Eleven Hundred Pounds; a Tale. All the Year, **12**: 15.
Eleventh Cot. (A. Webster, jr.) Scrib. **2**: 607.
Eleventh Hour. (E. Lazarus) Scrib. **16**: 242.
Eleventh Hour; a Poem. (C. G. Rossetti) Victoria, **2**: 317.
Elf's Ring. Victoria, **3**: 508. **4**: 26, 129.
Elf King's youngest Daughter. Blackw. **118**: 610.
Elfin Exile. So. Lit. Mess. **11**: 6.
Elgin, James Bruce, 8th Earl of, with portrait. Ecl. M. **50**: 428.—Canad. Mo. **2**: 211.
— and Sir Henry Lawrence. Lond. Q. **39**: 311.
— In Memoriam. No. Brit. **40**: 267.
— Letters and Journals of. Chr. Obs. **73**: 599.—Ed. R. **137**: 38.—Month, **17**: 144.
— Pursuits in Greece. (J. Foster) Ecl. R. **15**: 355.
Elgin, Thomas, 7th Earl of. Quar. **14**: 257.
Elgin Cathedral. Hogg, **7**: 223.—Penny M. **4**: 26.
Elgin Marbles. (J. W. Croker) Quar. **14**: 513.—Lond. M. **5**: 153, 445. **8**: 24.—Pamph. **8**: 431.
Elias, J., Memoir of. Ecl. R. **83**: 316.
Elie de Beaumont, J. B. A. L. L. (A. Geikie) Nature, **11**: 41.
Eliezer the Sage and Eliezer the Simple. Blackw. **32**: 193.
Elijah the Prophet. (J. F. Mackarness) Good Words, **10**: 59.—(W. M. Punshon) Ex. H. Lec. **9**: 229.
— and John the Baptist. Kitto, **9**: 420. **38**: 371.
— at Cherith and Zarephath. Kitto, **26**: 1.
— Character and History of. Chr. Obs. **34**: 348, 406. **37**: 551-754.
— Coming of. (J. Richards) Theo. & Lit. J. **9**: 587.
— Lectures on History of. Chr. Obs. **66**: 330.
— Sacrifice of, Place of. (C. M. Mead) Bib. Sac. **30**: 672.
Elinor Dane. (A. Trafton) Scrib. **6**: 320.
Elinor Travis; a Tale. Blackw. **59**: 718. **60**: 83, 444.
Elinor's Trial. (J. W. Waterbury) Cath. World, **14**: 790.
Eliot, Andrew, Letter of, 1775. N. E. Reg. **8**: 373.
Eliot, Ann, wife of John the Missionary. Knick. **39**: 68.
Eliot, Charles, Obituary of. Gen. Repos. **4**: 357.
Eliot, Charles W., with portrait. Ecl. M. **83**: 759.
Eliot, George. *See* George Eliot.
Eliot, Jacob, Diary of. Hist. M. **15**: 38.
Eliot, Sir John. Ecl. R. **119**: 493.
— Life of. Ecl. R. **70**: 365.
— — Forster's. Chr. Obs. **65**: 212.—Ed. R. **120**: 1.—Quar. **117**: 58. Same art. Liv. Age, **84**: 385.
Eliot, John, Apostle to the Indians. (C. K. Dillaway) Unita. R. **12**: 182.—Am. J. Educ. **28**: 125.
— and the Indians. (M. Moore) Am. Q. Reg. **15**: 319.—Am. J. Educ. **27**: 25.
— Bureau of. (W. H. Sumner) N. E. Reg. **9**: 329.
— Labors among the Indians. Am. Q. Reg. **4**: 198.
— Letter of 1664. N. E. Reg. **9**: 131.
— Life of. (C. Francis) Sparks's Am. Biog. **5**: 1.—(G. Putnam) Chr. Exam. **21**: 119.—Chr. R. **2**: 41.—Am. Q. Reg. **10**: 243.—Mo. R. **164**: 475.
— Memoir of. Cong. M. **7**: 449.
— Petition, 1675, against selling Indians for Slaves. N. E. Reg. **6**: 297.
— Record of Roxbury Church Members. N. E. Reg. **35**: 21, 241.
— Tomb of. (J. W. Thornton) N. E. Reg. **14**: 219.
— Wife of. Knick. **39**: 68.
Eliot, William G. (H. H. Barber) Unita. R. **11**: 544.
Eliot Genealogy. (W. H. Whitmore) N. E. Reg. **10**: 355.
Elis Fröbom. (E. T. A. Hoffmann) Dub. Univ. **88**: 156.
Elisha. (J. F. Mackarness) Good Words, **10**: 122.
Elisabetta's Christmas. (H. P. Spofford) Galaxy, **5**: 60.
Elisabetta Sirani; a Poem. (R. B. Lytton) Cornh. **3**: 500.
Eliza. (H. B. Stowe) Godey, **20**: 24.
Eliza Farnham. (Miss Leslie) Godey, **22**: 217, 245.
Elizabeth, St., of Hungary. (Mrs. H. C. Conant) Hours at Home, **1**: 5, 105.—(J. P. Lacroix) Bib. Sac. **30**: 204.
— Montalembert's Life of. Dub. R. **3**: 384.
Elizabeth, Queen. (H. R. Cleveland) No. Am. **50**: 175.—(H. Stowell) Ex. H. Lec. **15**: 107.—with portrait, Ecl. M. **48**: 289.—Penny M. **8**: 76.
— Age of. Dub. R. **81**: 29.
— — History and Manners of. Retros. **16**: 23.
— — Society in. Brit. Q. **5**: 412. Same art. Ecl. M. **11**: 335.
— Aikin's Court of. Ecl. R. **29**: 105.—Mo. R. **87**: 225.
— Amour with Sir C. Hatton. Ecl. M. **10**: 401.
— and the Continental Protestants. (H. M. Baird) Meth. Q. **28**: 57.
— and the Earl of Essex. Ed. R. **98**: 134. Same art. Ecl. M. **30**: 289.
— — Dr. Abbott on. (J. Spedding) 19th Cent. **7**: 107.
— and her Courtiers. Nat. Q. **9**: 263.
— and her England. (W. Kirkus) Fortn. **6**: 641.
— and her Times. Bentley, **61**: 530, 639.—Mo. R. **145**: 601.
— and the Huguenots. (A. Laugel) Nation, **29**: 110, 140.
— and Leicester. Liv. Age, **81**: 80.
— and Mary Stuart. (J. A. Froude) Temp. Bar, **10**: 199.—Blackw. **101**: 389. Same art. Liv. Age, **93**: 259.
— — Private History of. Tait, n. s. **4**: 118.
— and the Puritans. Liv. Age, **67**: 238.
— and Queen Victoria; a Woman's View. Victoria, **3**: 97.
— and the Reformation. (J. W. Santee) Mercersb. **16**: 368.—Chr. Obs. **64**: 27, 121.
— Archives of Simancas. (J. A. Froude) Fraser, **64**: 135.
— as the Princess Elizabeth. Chr. Rem. **6**: 372.
— Birthplace of. St. James, **11**: 491. Same art. Ecl. M. **64**: 184.
— Character of. (E. Bohan) So. Lit. Mess. **6**: 53.—(J. W. Calcraft) Dub. Univ. **40**: 216.—St. James, **46**: 78.
— Collections on the Times of. Quar. **62**: 452.
— Court of. (Sir E. B. Lytton) Westm. **29**: 281.—Ecl. M. **70**: 133.
— Death of. U. S. Cath. M. **7**: 143.
— Dudley, and Amy Robsart. (J. A. Froude) Fraser, **63**: 659. Same art. Liv. Age, **70**: 50, 659.
— England of. Ed. R. **146**: 199. Same art. Liv. Age, **134**: 579.
— Expeditions of Time of. (A. Woodbury) No. Am. **81**: 289.

Elizabeth, Queen, Favorites of. (E. A. Freeman) Quar. **95**: 207. Same art. Liv. Age, **42**: 435. Same art. Ecl. M. **33**: 145. — (C. B. Gibson) Once a Week, **12**: 510, 543.
— Fragment on Reign of. (H. T. Buckle) Fraser, **75**: 163. **76**: 135, 284.
— Froude on First Years of. Nat. R. **18**: 230.
— Froude's Hist. of. *See* England, Froude's History of.
— Last Parliaments of. Dub. Univ. **75**: 672. — St. James, **16**: 154.
— Letters of. All the Year, **35**: 563.
— — concerning Marriage with the Duc d'Alençon. Arch. **28**: 393.
— Morals of. Fraser, **48**: 371, 489. Same art. Liv. Age, **39**: 387, 643.
— Papers relating to her proposed Marriage. (Sir H. Ellis) Arch. **35**: 202.
— Parpaglia's Mission to. No. Brit. **52**: 366.
— Persecuting Character of. Selec. Ed. R. **4**: 159.
— Progresses of. Penny M. **12**: 12-473.
— Reign of. Chr. Rem. **47**: 383. — Lond. Q. **22**: 158. Same art. Ecl. M. **61**: 405.
— — Philosophy of. Chr. Obs. **35**: 475, 543.
— Visit to Sandwich. (H. Curling) Bentley, **15**: 202-603.
— Wise Policy of. Ed. R. **2**: 482.
— Writings of. Lond. M. **6**: 553.
— Youth of. Temp. Bar, **59**: 451.
Elizabeth, Queen of Henry VII., Directions for receiving her Corpse. Arch. **32**: 126.
Elizabeth, Princess, Marriage of, Expenses of. (W. H. Smyth) Arch. **35**: 1.
— — Wardrobe Account for. (Sir F. Madden) Arch. **26**: 380.
Elizabeth, Empress of Austria, Sketch of. St. James, **7**: 66.
Elizabeth, Queen of Bohemia, 1596-1662. Tait, n. s. **26**: 275. — No. Brit. **31**: 218. Same art. Ecl. M. **48**: 295.
Elizabeth of France. (E. G. Halsey) Potter Am. Mo. **10**: 113.
Elizabeth of Prussia and Victoria of England. Bentley, **62**: 260. Same art. Ecl. M. **69**: 627.
Elizabeth de Valois, Queen of Spain, Freer's. Liv. Age, **53**: 366. **54**: 247.
Elizabeth Charlotte, Duchess of Orleans. Temp. Bar, **59**: 237. Same art. Liv. Age, **146**: 35. — Colburn, **134**: 90.
Elizabeth Petrovna, Empress of Russia. (J. Forfar) Gent. M. n. s. **26**: 598.
— and her Court. Temp. Bar, **53**: 494.
Elizabeth; a Poem. Blackw. **118**: 730.
Elizabeth; a Story. Galaxy, **21**: 176.
Elizabeth Brownrigge; a Tale. Fraser, **6**: 67, 131.
Elizabeth Evanshaw; a Novel. Lond. M. **21**: 84.
Elizabeth Castle, Jersey. Penny M. **5**: 76.
Elizabeth Islands, Visit to. (F. C. Gray) No. Am. **5**: 313.
Elizabethan Days; a Poem. (T. Irwin) Dub. Univ. **49**: 486.
Elk, North American. Penny M. **9**: 239.
Elks. Once a Week, **17**: 216.
Elkanah Brewster's Temptation. (C. Nordhoff) Atlan. **4**: 710.
Elkhorn Campaign, Van Dorn's Report. So. Hist. Pap. **6**: 37.
Elleelah and Kissore. Bentley, **30**: 608.
Ellen Campbell. Godey, **22**: 161.
Ellen Cavanagh. Tinsley, **20**: 81.
Ellen Dean; a Pastoral Story in Verse. St. James, **1**: 427.
Ellen Laning. (Mrs. M. H. Parsons) Godey, **24**: 304.
Ellen Leicester. Bentley, **41**: 626.
Ellen Linn, the Needlewoman. Liv. Age, **27**: 40.
Ellen Tranverse; a Tale. So. Lit. Mess. **5**: 89
Ellenborough, Lord. Mus. **44**: 171. — Anal. M. **13**: 491.
— and Affairs of India. Fraser, **29**: 472.
— and Lord Ashley. Fraser, **29**: 740.
— and the Whigs. Blackw. **53**: 539.
Ellenwood, Henry S. New Eng. M. **4**: 433.
Ellery, William, Life of. (E. T. Channing) Sparks's Am. Biog. **6**: 87. — (T. W. Higginson) Pennsyl. M. **2**: 433.
— Ride to Congress on Horseback, 1777. (T. W. Higginson) Scrib. **19**: 412.
Ellesmere, Earl of. Fraser, **35**: 714.
Ellet, Charles, jr. Liv. Age, **74**: 239.
Ellet, Mrs. E. F. So. Lit. Mess. **2**: 116. — Godey, **34**: 61.
Ellice. (I. Tourgénieff) Dub. Univ. **81**: 679. **82**: 61. Same art. Ev. Sat. **15**: 293.
Ellicott, Charles J., Bishop of Gloucester. Cong. **2**: 752.
Ellinthorpe, England, Dissenting Church at. Cong. M. **14**: 709.
Elliot, Hugh, Memoirs of. No. Brit. **49**: 257. Same art. Ecl. M. **72**: 514. — Quar. **125**: 329. Same art. Liv. Age, **99**: 707.
Elliot, Comm. Jesse D. Portfo. (Den.) **12**: 529.
Elliot, John. Meth. M. **38**: 3. — Am. Meth. M. **1**: 329.
Elliot, Capt. John, Story of. Bost. Mo. **1**: 38, 208, 425.
Elliott, Mrs. Charles. (E. F. Ellet) Godey, **36**: 77.
Elliott, Charles B. Travels in Austria, Russia, and Turkey. Fraser, **18**: 708.
Elliott, Charles L., American Painter. (L. G. Clark) Lippinc. **2**: 652. — (C. E. Lester) Harper, **38**: 42. — with portrait, Ecl. M. **71**: 1409.
Elliott, Charlotte. Chr. Obs. **71**: 941.
— Hymns. Bost. R. **2**: 156.
Elliott, Ebenezer. (S. C. Hall) Art J. **17**: 245. Same art. Ecl. M. **65**: 573. — (J. Watkins) Bentley, **28**: 416. — House. Words, **1**: 310. — Nat. M. **3**: 214. — Hogg, **5**: 23. — Tait, n. s. **17**: 69. — with portrait, Howitt, **1**: 184.
— Corn-Law Rhymes. Tait, **2**: 137.
— Last Days of. (J. Watkins) Peop. J. **10**: 147.
— Obituary of. Westm. **52**: 495.
— Poems of. (T. Carlyle) Ed. R. **55**: 338. **60**: 67. — Ecl. M. **20**: 68. — Blackw. **13**: 321. **35**: 815. — Liv. Age, **26**: 59. — (W. J. Fox) Westm. **30**: 187 — Mus. **25**: 359. — Westm. **53**: 115. Same art. Ecl. M. **20**: 263. — Ecl. R. **37**: 342. — Dub. Univ **89**: 148.
Elliott, Edward, Bishop. Chr. Obs. **75**: 787.
Elliott, Henry V., Bateman's Life of. Chr. Obs. **68**: 800.
— Obituary of. Chr. Obs. **65**: 303.
— Sermons of. Chr. Obs. **66**: 288.
Elliott, Stephen. (J. A. Hamilton) So. Hist. Pap. **9**: 476.
— Address of. Anal. M. **8**: 154. — U. S. Lit. Gaz. **6**: 368.
Elliott, Stephen, Bishop. Am. Church R. **20**: 45.
Elliott, Gen. Stephen. N. Ecl. **6**: 211. — Land We Love, **4**: 453.
Elliott, Wm. Carolina Sports. So. Q. **12**: 67. — (T. G. Cary) No. Am. **63**: 316.
Ellipse and Hyperbola, Properties of Curvature in. (C. Wright) Math. Mo. **2**: 198.
— Rules for Circumference of. (T. W. Bakewell) J. Frankl. Inst. **59**: 369.
Ellipses, Construction of. (J. H. Gill) Ecl. Engin. **13**: 518.
Ellipsoids, Attractions of homogeneous. Ed. R. **17**: 480.
Elliptic Functions. (C. W. Merrifield) Nature, **15**: 252.
Ellis, Alex. John. Sermons. (T. Hill) Unita. R. **6**: 134.
Ellis, Clement. Discourses. Cong. M. **6**: 210.
Ellis, Henry. Historical Letters. Mo. R. **113**: 220. — Ed. R. **41**: 427. **46**: 195.
Ellis, H. W., the Liberian Blacksmith. Liv. Age, **37**: 445.
Ellis, James. (E. Parmer) So. M. **10**: 32.
Ellis, R. L. (G. Grote) Contemp. **20**: 56.
Ellis, Mrs. Sarah. Godey, **45**: 453.
— Sons of the Soil; a Poem. Tait, n. s. **7**: 147.
— Temper and Temperament. Ecl. R. **85**: 625.
— Wives of England. Ecl. R. **77**: 694. — Tait, n. s. **10**: 264.
— Women of England. Dub. Univ. **13**: 419.

Ellis, William, Educationalist, with portrait. (W. Jolly) Good Words, **22**: 543.
Ellis, Sir Wm. C., on Insanity. Dub. Univ. **12**: 459.
Ellis Correspondence. Mo. R. **118**: 354.
Elliston, Robt. Wm., Manager of Drury Lane Theater. Lond. M. **1**: 609. — Temp. Bar, **48**: 315.
— Ellistoniana. (W. T. Moncrieff) Colburn, **67**: 22–532. **68**: 99–529. **69**: 129–557.
Ellora. *See* Elora.
Ellsworth, Col. Ephraim E. (J. Hay) Atlan. **8**: 119.
— and his Zouaves. Chamb. J. **42**: 469.
Ellsworth, Oliver, with portrait. Portfo.(Den.) **34**: 185. — with portrait, Am. Lit. M. **1**: 195.
— Biography of. Anal. M. **3**: 382.
— Speech of, 1788. Carey's Mus. **3**: 334.
Ellwood, Thomas, Life of. Retros. **13**: 109. — Mus. **8**: 309. — (J. G. Whittier) Liv. Age, **15**: 193. — Liv. Age, **126**: 695. — Tait, n. s. **22**: 445.
Elm, Switzerland, Landslip at. (W. Pole) Fortn. **36**: 730. Same art. Am. Arch. **10**: 302.
Elm-Tree. Penny M. **11**: 60.
— a Poem. (J. C. Yule) Canad. Mo. **5**: 400.
— and its Insect Enemies. Intel. Obs. **2**: 191.
— Uses of. Penny M. **13**: 54.
Elms of Old Trinity. (H. T. Tuckerman) Scrib. **2**: 517.
Elmer, Jonathan. (L. Q. C. Elmer) Pennsyl. M. **1**: 443.
Elocution. (Prof. Caldwell) Meth. Q. **4**: 503. — (D. Fosdick, jr.) Am. Inst. of Instruc. **1837**: 109.
— Barber's. Am. Mo. R. **4**: 368.
— Best Method of teaching, in Schools. (T. D. P. Stone) Am. Inst. of Instruc. **1836**: 125.
— Porter's Analysis of. (G. Howe) Chr. Mo. Spec. **9**: 363. — U. S. Lit. Gaz. **6**: 333.
— Principles of. (O. Dewey) No. Am. **29**: 38.
— Pulpit. (A. F. T. Monod) Princ. **15**: 192. — (E. Peabody) Chr. Exam. **41**: 49.
Elohim, Interpretation of the Word. (G. B. Kidd) Kitto, **2**: 332.
— and Jehovah in Genesis. (W. Aikman) Meth. Q. **37**: 610.
Elopement; Wakefield case. Blackw. **21**: 552.
— an Adventure in Old Castile. Blackw. **52**: 312.
Elopement, The; a Tale. So. Lit. Mess. **8**: 716. — U. S. Lit. Gaz. **6**: 209.
Eloquence. (H. L. Baugher) Evang. R. **9**: 586. — (J. Dempster) Am. Meth. M. **18**: 110. — (R. W. Emerson) Atlan. **2**: 385. — (A. M. Judson) So. Lit. Mess. **20**: 535. — (H. Colman) New Eng. M. **2**: 374. — Am. Q. **21**: 287. — Fraser, **21**: 255, 659. — So. Lit. Mess. **1**: 165. — Blackw. **7**: 644.
— American. Dem. R. **34**: 40. — West. R. **2**: 106.
— Ancient. (W. G. Howard) So. Lit. Mess. **6**: 703. **7**: 68. — Mo. R. **149**: 68.
— — and modern. (W. G. Howard) So. Lit. Mess. **8**: 169. — Blackw. **68**: 645. Same art. Ecl. M. **23**: 17. Same art. Liv. Age, **29**: 193.
— and eloquent Men. New Eng. M. **2**: 374.
— and good Sense. (G. F. Simmons) Chr. Exam. **25**: 255.
— and Oratory. Dub. Univ. **62**: 296. Same art. Ecl. M. **60**: 344.
— at the Bar; Grattan and Curran. West. Law J. **3**: 241.
— British. Chr. R. **18**: 481. — (G. Shepard) Bib. Sac. **29**: 22.
— — Parliamentary. Portfo.(Den.) **15**: 375, 492. — Brit. & For. R. **2**: 35.
— Forensic. Knick. **20**: 530.
— Maury on. Am. Meth. M. **15**: 224.
— of the Camp. Dub. Univ. **30**: 646.
— of Debate. New Eng. M. **7**: 105.
— of the French Bar. For. R. **4**: 1.
— of the Romans. (J. L. Kingsley) No. Am. **30**: 259.
— Parliamentary. Westm. **99**: 36.
Eloquence, Popular. So. Lit. Mess. **13**: 735.
— Principles of. Univ. Q. **20**: 26.
— Pulpit. *See* Pulpit.
— Silent. (L. J. B. Case) Univ. Q. **5**: 358.
— Species of. (J. O'Connell) Meth. Q. **8**: 514.
— Study of, in Theological Seminaries. Dub. R. **39**: 433.
Elora, India, Caves of, in 1850. Bentley, **52**: 240.
— Seely's Wonders of. Ecl. R. **43**: 49.
Elphinstone, Mountstuart, In Memoriam. (J. W. Kaye) Once a Week, **1**: 502. — (J. W. Kaye) Good Words, **6**: 165.
Elsie; a Story. (K. M. Grey) Irish Mo. **8**: 405.
Elsie's Child; a Poem. Putnam, **8**: 240.
Elssler, Fanny, and the Tarantula. So. Lit. Mess. **6**: 700.
— in London, Paris, and Havana. Fraser, **28**: 713. **29**: 78, 144, 274.
Elstob, Elizabeth. (Mrs. C. A. White) Sharpe, **50**: 180–304. **51**: 26–251.
Elten, K. van, and his Paintings. Art J. **29**: 340.
Eltham, Churchwardens' Accounts of. (G. R. Corner) Arch. **34**: 51.
— Visit to Old Hall at. Once a Week, **3**: 401. — Penny M. **1**: 263.
Elton, Charles A. Brothers; a Monody. Lond. M. **2**: 310.
— Poems of. Ecl. R. **12**: 1124. — Blackw. **38**: 731. — Mus. **28**: 262.
— Translations of the Classic Poets. Quar. **13**: 151.
— Translation of Hesiod. Blackw. **32**: 165, 505, 807.
Eluen; a Poem. (W. Black) Once a Week, **12**: 704.
Elves, The; a Poem. (R. L. Gerhart) Mercersb. **19**: 278.
Elwes, John, the Miser. Dub. Univ. **73**: 679. — Penny M. **9**: 49, 62, 66.
— Topham's Life of. Retros. **9**: 141.
Elwyn, John, Will of. Am. Law R. **10**: 604.
Ely, Alfred. (C. Hammond) Cong. Q. **9**: 137.
Ely, John, Posthumous Works of. Ecl. R. **87**: 719.
Ely, Smith, jr., with portrait. Dem. R. **43**: 122.
Ely Cathedral. All the Year, **34**: 413. — Penny M. **3**: 245.
— Prior's Chapel at. (W. Wilkins) Arch. **14**: 105.
— — Mosaic in. (R. Gough) Arch. **10**: 151.
— Removal of Remains of Brithnoth. (J. Bentham) Arch. **2**: 364.
Ely, Dean of. *See* Peacock, Geo.
Elyot, Sir Thomas. Am. J. Educ. **16**: 483.
Elysée, Ems, and Claremont. Fraser, **40**: 573.
Emancipation (G. Welles) Galaxy, **14**: 838.
— Channing on, 1841. Mo. R. **154**: 251.
— Effects of, 1823. Chr. Obs. **23**: 684, 760. — Colburn, **26**: 467.
— examined. De Bow, **21**: 265.
— in French Colonies. Westm. **22**: 520.
— in Jamaica. (C. S. Renshaw) New Eng. **6**: 557.
— in Kentucky. (C. Hodge) Princ. **21**: 582.
— in Trinidad, Burnley on, 1842. Mo. R. **157**: 311.
— in West Indies. (R. W. Emerson) Prosp. R. **1**: 159. — (F. W. Newman) Radical, **2**: 193, 507. — (G. W. Perkins) New Eng. **2**: 560. — (W. Ware) Chr. Exam. **33**: 382. — Chr. Q. Spec. **10**: 440. — Ecl. R. **68**: 450, 532. — So. Q. **23**: 422.
— — Results of. (H. Bleby) Meth. Q. **20**: 33, 201. — Ecl. R. **73**: 471. **87**: 197.
— Lincoln's Proclamation of. (A. C. Twining) New Eng. **24**: 178. — (J. C. Welling) No. Am. **130**: 163.
— — Nullity of. (R. H. Dana) No. Am. **131**: 128.
— — Validity of. (A. A. Ferris) No. Am. **131**: 551.
— Practical Effects of. De Bow, **18**: 474, 591.
— Results of. (N. H. Eggleston) New Eng. **21**: 783 (J. R. Sparkman) Land We Love, **4**: 16.
— — in French and English Colonies. (G. H. Emerson) Univ. Q. **20**: 100.
— Root of the Matter. (H. W. Bucher) Liv. Age, **74**: 423.

Emancipation, Who will be harmed by? Univ. Q. **19**: 329.
See Serfs; Slavery.
Emanuel Hospital, London. Antiquary, **4**: 153, 177.
Embalming, Ancient Modes of. Liv. Age, **134**: 447.
— Art of. Hogg, **3**: 142.
— Egyptian Mode of. J. Frankl. Inst. **14**: 20.
— of Jacob, illustrated from Herodotus. Cong. M. **19**: 152.
Embankment across Valley of the Brent. J. Frankl. Inst. **40**: 226.
Embankments and Excavations, Calculating Cubic Contents of. (J. C. Trautwine) J. Frankl. Inst. **52**: 1, 80, 146.
— and Reservoirs. Ecl. Engin. **13**: 491.
— Mensuration and Cost of. (E. Morris) J. Frankl. Inst. **29**: 21, 381. **32**: 164, 236.
— Railroad Cuttings and. (O. Byrne) J. Frankl. Inst. **77**: 145, 229.
Embarking for the Colonies. Fraser, **15**: 339.
Embassies and Foreign Courts. Ecl. R. **102**: 555.
— to Eastern Asia. (J. Brown) No. Am. **47**: 395.
Emblems. Blackw. **115**: 607. Same art. Liv. Age, **121**: 726. — Retros. **9**: 122.
— National. (H. K. W. Wilcox) Harper, **47**: 171.
Embroidered Handkerchief; a Tale. Putnam, **10**: 23.
Embroidery, An old Spanish. (E. Stowe) Art J. **33**: 374.
— Art. (A. F. Oakey) Harper, **62**: 693.
— Art of. Godey, **47**: 67.
— by Machinery. (G. Wallis) J. Frankl. Inst. **68**: 181, 273, 337.
— Ecclesiastical. (E. L. Cutts) Art J. **17**: 357.
— for Home Decoration. (M. Ford) Potter Am. Mo. **16**: 214, 363, 458. **17**: 76–557.
— Swiss. Pract. M. **5**: 281.
Embryology, Comparative, Sketch of. (C. S. Minot) Am. Natural. **14**: 96–871.
— Foster and Balfour's. Nature, **11**: 126.
Embryonic Law in Plants and Animals. Am. Natural. **9**: 257.
Emerald, The. (A. C. Hamlin) Lippinc. **11**: 688.
Emeralds and Beryls. (J. H. Snively) Appleton, **7**: 48.
— Researches on. Nature, **8**: 254.
Emerald Beetles. (T. F. Crane) Galaxy, **1**: 689.
Emerald Mines of Muzo. Ecl. Engin. **6**: 506.
Emerald Studs; a Tale. Blackw. **62**: 214. Same art. Liv. Age, **14**: 561.
Emergencies. Chamb. J. **54**: 703.
Emerson, George B. Am. J. Educ. **5**: 417. — (J. H. Morison) Unita. R. **16**: 59.
— Reminiscences of. Am. J. Educ. **28**: 257.
Emerson, John, Memoir of. Am. Q. Reg. **10**: 244.
Emerson, Luther O. (G. Birdseye) Potter Am. Mo. **13**: 139.
Emerson, Ralph Waldo. (R. Buchanan) Broadw. **2**: 223. — (J. Burroughs) Galaxy, **21**: 254, 543 — (D. M. Colton) Contin. Mo. **1**: 49. — (G. Gilfillan) Tait, n. s. **15**: 17. Same art. Liv. Age, **17**: 97. — (J. O'Connor) Cath. World, **27**: 90. — (G. Prentice) Meth. Q. **34**: 357. — Dub. R. **26**: 152. — No. Brit. **47**: 319. — Westm. **33**: 345. — Blackw. **62**: 643. Same art. Liv. Age, **16**: 97. — (F. H. Underwood) No. Am. **130**: 479. — (B. Herford) Dial (Ch.), **2**: 114. — (E. P. Whipple) Harper, **52**: 417. — (N. P. Willis) Liv. Age, **24**: 457. — (P. Godwin) Peop. J. **4**: 305.
— Address, July, 1838. Bost. Q. **1**: 500.
— — on Forefathers' Day, 1870. (I. N. Tarbox) New Eng. **30**: 175.
— and his Writings. (G. Barmby) Howitt, **2**: 315. — Chr. R. **26**: 640.
— and History. So. Lit. Mess. **18**: 249.
— and Landor. Liv. Age, **52**: 371.
Emerson, Ralph Waldo, and the Pantheists. (H. Heming) New Dom. **8**: 65.
— and Spencer and Martineau. (W. R. Alger) Chr. Exam. **84**: 257.
— and Transcendentalism. Am. Whig R. **1**: 233. *See* Transcendentalism.
— Conduct of Life. (N. Porter) New Eng. **19**: 496. — Ecl. R. **116**: 365. — Liv. Age, **68**: 240. — (F. H. Hedge) Chr. Exam. **70**: 149.
— Culture. Fraser, **78**: 1. Same art. Liv. Age, **98**: 358.
— English Traits. *See* England.
— Essays. Dem. R. **16**: 589. — Ecl. M. **18**: 546. — Liv. Age, **4**: 139. **23**: 344. — (C. C. Felton) Chr. Exam. **30**: 253. — Ecl. R. **76**: 667. — Bost. Q. **4**: 391. — Bib. R. **1**: 148. — Prosp. R. **1**: 232. — Tait, n. s. **8**: 666. — Mo. R. **156**: 274.
— Homes and Haunts of. (F. B. Sanborn) Scrib. **17**: 496.
— Lectures at Manchester. Howitt, **2**: 370.
— — and Writings of. Fraser, **75**: 586. Same art. Liv. Age, **93**: 581. — Ev. Sat. **3**: 680. **4**: 381. — Chr. R. **15**: 249.
— Letters and Social Aims. Internat. R. **3**: 249.
— Philosophy of. (H. W. Holland) Nation, **33**: 396.
— Poems. (C. E. Norton) Nation, **4**: 430. — Am. Whig R. **6**: 197. — (C. A. Bartol) Chr. Exam. **42**: 255. — So. Lit. Mess. **13**: 292. — Brownson, **4**: 262. — Dem. R. **1**: 319. — Chr. Rem. **15**: 300.
— Prose Works. Cath. World, **11**: 202.
— Representative Men. (C. A. Bartol) Chr. Exam. **48**: 314. — Ecl. R. **95**: 568. — Brit. Q. **11**: 281. Same art. Liv. Age, **26**: 1. — (C. E. Norton) No. Am. **70**: 520. — (D. March) New Eng. **8**: 186.
— Residence of. Art J. **32**: 55.
— Society and Solitude. Fraser, **82**: 1. — Liv. Age, **105**: 161.
— Writings. (F. H. Hedge) Chr. Exam. **38**: 87. — (J. W. Alexander) Princ. **13**: 539.
Emerson, William, the Hurworth Mathematician. Sharpe, **36**: 254.
Emery, John, Actor, Recollections of. Colburn, **53**: 530.
Emery. (J. Lawrence Smith) Am. J. Sci. **59**: 53, 354. Same art. Ed. New Philos. J. **50**: 318. — Ecl. Engin. **12**: 472. — Chamb. J. **21**: 382.
— Mine of, Chester, Mass. (C. T. Jackson) Am. J. Sci. **89**: 87. — (J. L. Smith) Am. J. Sci. **92**: 83.
Emery and Corundum Wheels. (A. H. Bateman) Ecl. Engin. **18**: 502.
Emery Grinder, Improved universal. Pract. M. **6**: 175.
Emigrant, The. Cath. World, **11**: 800. — (J. Russell) West. M. **3**: 67.
— Adventures of an. Mo. R. **161**: 402, 549.
— Gentleman-. Chamb. J. **51**: 650. Same art. Canad. Mo. **6**: 515.
Emigrant's Daughter; a Poem. (D. Greenwell) Good Words, **2**: 447.
Emigrant's Guide. Anal. M. **10**: 52.
Emigrant's Story. (J. T. Trowbridge) Harper, **49**: 609.
Emigrant's Tale. Dub. Univ. **8**: 38.
Emigrant's Voyage to Canada. Blackw. **10**: 455.
Emigrants, The. (G. Neiritz) Peop. J. **9**: 82–229.
— a Story of the Backwoods. Chamb. J. **11**: 387.
— Advice to. Penny M. **1**: 158.
— Allegiance of. (J. T. Morse, jr.) No. Am. **106**: 612.
— Church Work among. (J. V. Campbell) Am. Church R. **11**: 233.
— Entrappers. (W. Chambers) Chamb. J. **23**: 141.
— Warning to. Chamb. J. **50**: 644.
Emigrant Family in Australia. Ecl. R. **89**: 699.
Emigrant Lassie; a Poem. (J. S. Blackie) Good Words, **15**: 823.
Emigrant Ship, Aboard an. All the Year, **7**: 111.
— Trip in. Chamb. J. **1**: 228, 262, 302.

Emigrant Ship Washington. Chamb. J. 16: 27.
Emigrant Ships. Irish Q. 4: 430.
— Scenes in. Liv. Age, 26: 492.
Emigrant Train, Day with. (J. Applegate) Overland, 1: 127.
Emigration. (J. D. Cartwright) Sharpe, 38: 37. — (A. Helps) Good Words, 11: 360. — (E. Jenkins) Victoria, 15: 12. — (C. E. Norton) Fortn. 12: 189. — (W. Robinson) Geog. M. 1: 151. — (M. Tarver) West. J. 3: 211. 6: 211. — (G. Tucker) Hunt, 8: 157. — Ed. R. 45: 49. 47: 204. — Brit. & For. R. 10: 493. — Westm. 3: 449. 6: 342. 35: 131. 40: 53. — Blackw. 15: 433. 20: 470. 21: 377. 23: 191, 615. — Dub. Univ. 21: 506. — Knick. 16: 470. — Anal. M. 11: 361. — Mo. R. 112: 113. 129: 478. — Mus. 45: 594. — (T. H. Yeoman) Peop. J. 3: 193. — (J. C. Bryne) Peop. J. 5: 115. 7: 375. — Ill. M. 1: 417. 2: 115. — Lond. M. 18: 263. — Sharpe, 16: 352. — West. M. 5: 743.
— American View of. (A. B. Mason) Fortn. 22: 273.
— and Canadas. Fraser, 16: 683 — Lond. M. 10: 577.
— and Gold. Blackw. 74: 117. — Fraser, 46: 127.
— and Industrial Training. Ed. R. 92: 491.
— and Lutheran Church. (S. Aughey) Luth. Q. 8: 382.
— and Polit. Economy. (T. E. C. Leslie) Fraser, 77: 611.
— and Poor Laws. Lond. M. 20: 227.
— and Public Wealth. Bank. M. (N. Y.) 30: 763.
— and the Sexes. Tait, n. s. 25: 509. 26: 626.
— Causes of. (E. Spiess) Luth. Q. 5: 363.
— Decline of. Bank. M. (N. Y.) 29: 340, 578.
— Distribution and Importance of. Ecl. R. 93: 179.
— Doyle's Hints on. Penny M. 1: 261.
— from England. Victoria, 22: 277.
— from Europe to America. (R. Everest) J. Statis. Soc. 19: 49. — Cath. World, 25: 433.
— from Great Britain. Liv. Age, 31: 284–519.
— — 1838. J. Statis. Soc. 1: 155.
— — to 1843–44. Hunt, 14: 293.
— — to the Colonies. (W. M. Torrens) 19th Cent. 9: 536. — Dub. R. 22: 388. 26: 316.
— — — Bounty System and its Frauds. Fraser, 28: 426.
— German. Liv. Age, 11: 201.
— — to America. (J. D. Angell) No. Am. 82: 248.
— in 1847. (W. Howitt) Howitt, 2: 351.
— in its Effects on the British Islands. No. Brit. 18: 259.
— in the 17th Century. Retros. 17: 44.
— in the 19th Century. Ho. & For. R. 3: 472.
— in the West Indies. Liv. Age, 75: 130.
— Irish. (H. Giles) Chr Exam 52: 361.
— Letters from Canada. Quar. 54: 413.
— Limits of. (F. Wharton) No. Am. 87: 66.
— National. Mus. 44: 449.
— Notes on. (F. Whitehead) St. James, 32: 360.
— of Protestants from Ireland. Dub. Univ. 1: 471.
— or Manufactures. (W. R. Greg) Westm. 40: 101.
— Question of general. Colburn, 83: 523.
— Rationale of. (E. L. Godkin) Nation, 19: 117.
— Report on, 1826. (R. Southey) Quar. 37: 539. — Ecl. R. 46: 229.
— Restraints on. Ed. R. 39: 315.
— Results and future Policy of. (J. E. Mathews) De Bow, 13: 455.
— Lord Selkirk on. (F. Horner) Ed. R. 7: 185.
— Spirit of. So. Lit. Mess. 2: 259.
— to Africa and Hayti. (J. Sparks) No. Am. 20: 191.
— to Canada. Quar. 23: 373. — Dub. Univ. 1: 287.
— to Cape of Good Hope. Blackw. 5: 523. 6: 78.
— to the United States. (J. C. Hutcheson) Belgra. 25: 501. — Fraser, 16: 562. — Ed. R. 100: 236. Same art. Liv. Age, 43: 99.
— — as influenced by the War. Nat. Q. 9: 369.
— — Castle Garden, N. Y. (L. Bagger) Harper, 42: 547.
Emigration to the United States, Utopian. Chamb. J 23: 1.
— — Western. O. & N. 2: 754.
— The Why and How. (J. Saunders) Peop. J. 5: 345. *See* Immigration.
Emilie de Coigny. (R. B. Kimball) Internat. M. 5: 444.
Emillianne, G. d', Life and Works of. Cong. M. 4: 375.
Emily; a Poem. (F. Soule) Pioneer, 2: 158.
Emily Orford. Fraser, 48: 98–659.
Emlyn, Thomas, Character of. Chr. Disc. 1: 26.
Emma; Fragment of a Story. (C. Brontë) Cornh. 1: 487. Same art. Harper, 20: 825.
Emma Mine Co. and R. C. Schenck. (E. L. Godkin) Nation, 22: 5.
— Case of J. W. Park. Nation, 22: 345.
— True History of. Nation, 17: 402.
Emmaus, Journey to. (A. Watson) Good Words, 22: 777.
Emmaus Orphan House, Middletown, Penn. (C. J. Ehrehart) Evang. R. 12: 574.
Emmerich, Anne C., Visions of. Dub. R. 5: 407.
— Youth of. Month, 18: 87.
Emmet, Robert. So. R. n. s. 20: 370. — Liv. Age, 58: 30.
— and Arthur Aylmer. (W. H. Maxwell) Bentley, 23: 470, 551. 24: 15.
— Insurrection of. All the Year, 17: 537. Same art. Ev. Sat. 3: 772.
— — Discovery of. Dub. Univ. 1: 541.
Emmett, Thomas A., Biography of. Ann. Reg. 4: 139.
— Madden's Life of. Dub. Univ. 28: 681.
Emmons, Nathanael. (J. W. Harding) Cong. Q. 3: 225. — with portrait (A. R. Baker) Am. Q. Reg. 15: 113. — (E. T. Fitch) New Eng. 1: 110. — Chr. Exam. 33: 169.
— Park's Life of. Bost. R. 2: 38. — (G. P. Fisher) New Eng. 19: 709.
— Sermon of. (L. Withington) Bib. Sac. 5: 625.
— Theology of. (E. Smalley) Bib. Sac. 7: 254, 479.
— Theory of Divine Agency. (A. Bullard) Am. Bib. Repos. 2d s. 10: 352.
— Works of. Am. Bib. Repos. 2d s. 8: 314. — (A. and J. A. Alexander) Princ. 14: 529. — Chr. R. 7: 520. 8: 7.
Emmons, Richard. The Fredoniad. West. Mo. R. 2: 176.
Emory, John, Memoir of. Meth. Q. 2: 62.
Emotion. (St. G. Mivart) Am. Cath. Q. 3: 301.
— Cosmic. (W. K. Clifford) 19th Cent. 2: 411.
— in primitive Man. (H. Spencer) Pop. Sci. Mo. 6: 331.
— Infectious Expressions of. Once a Week, 28: 407.
— Nature of. (G. F. Blandford) Fortn. 12: 103. Same art. Pop. Sci. Mo. 1: 274.
— Physical Effects of, on the Heart. (H. C. Wood, jr.) Lippinc. 14: 699.
— Voluntary. (P. Spence) Pop. Sci. Mo. 13: 444.
Emotions, Brain-Work and. Pop. Sci. Mo. 2: 420.
— Expression of, Darwin on. Ed. R. 137: 492. — Pop. Sci. Mo. 2: 434. — Canad. Mo. 3: 166. *See* Darwin.
— Language and. (C. Walstein) Pop. Sci. Mo. 14: 190.
— McCosh on. (H. W. Holland) Nation, 30: 196.
— New Theory of. (W. Hincks) Canad. J. n. s. 7: 103.
— Psychology of. Brit. Q. 70: 27.
Emotional Culture. Fraser, 29: 528.
Empedocles. No. Brit. 45: 420.
Emperor and the Pope; a Poem. (E. H. Plumptre) Good Words, 8: 261.
Emperor's Eye; a Tale. (A. Towner) Putnam, 13: 563.
Emperor's Night Adventure. (L. Pardoe) Sharpe, 10: 7. Same art. Ecl. M. 19: 425.
Empire, L', c'est la Paix; Zouave Story. Cornh. 22: 297.
Empires, Disintegration of. No. Brit. 38: 257. Same art. Ecl. M. 59: 267, 483.
— Dissolution of. (W. H. Lowrie) Princ. 32: 236.
Empiric, Two Events in Life of a. Fraser, 31: 482.

Empiricism and Common Logic. (J. Watson) J. Spec. Philos. **10**: 17.
Employers and Employed. (H. Martineau) Westm. **29**: 405. **57**: 61.
— and Working Classes. (R. H. Patterson) Brit. Q. **72**: 1.
Employment Wanted. Belgra. **25**: 81.
Employments and Health. (W. A. Guy) J. Statis. Soc. **6**: 197, 283. **7**: 232.
— Division of. Penny M. **14**: 246.
Empress Giulia's Abdication. Temp. Bar, **4**: 496.
Empress of Spinetta. (P. Heyse) Appleton, **14**: 392.
Em's first and last Lodger. Fraser, **74**: 456.
Empty House. Colburn, **162**: 177.
Ems and its Neighborhood. Bentley, **46**: 249.
— Peep at. (N. Macleod) Good Words, **12**: 649.
— Summer Visitors to. Chamb. J. **56**: 401.
Emulation. Ox. Prize Ess. **5**: 89. — New Eng. M. **2**: 107. — Am. Q. Reg. **5**: 65. — (N. Lord) Am. Bib. Repos. 2d Ser. **5**: 393. — (A. Caswell) No. Am. **43**: 496. — Chr. Obs. **13**: 81–706.
— in Schools. (L. Withington) Am. Inst. of Instruc. **1833**: 131.
— Means of Stimulation without. (J. L. Parkhurst) Am. Inst. of Instruc. **1831**: 131.
Enamel and Enameling. (C. T. Hinckley) Godey, **47**: 489.
— of the Heart. (J. D. Smith) Knick. **30**: 145.
Enamels by Charles Lepec. Pract. M. **1**: 261.
— Celebrated, and their Prices. Cornh. **16**: 688.
Enamel Mosaics, Modern Venetian. Cornh. **19**: 459.
Enameled Cooking Vessels. Pract. M. **6**: 350.
Enameling, Face. Ev. Sat. **6**: 522.
— of Dial-Plates. Penny M. **7**: 434.
— on Metal. Pract. M. **6**: 60.
— on precious Metals in India. (A. Hunter) Art J. **28**: 89.
Enchanted Bridle; a Legendary Ballad. Blackw. **128**: 436.
Enchanted Cave; a Poem. Dub. Univ. **13**: 614.
Enchanted Domain; a Poem. Blackw. **35**: 666.
Enchanted Hare of the Ardennes. Bentley, **41**: 54.
Enchanted Island. (W. Irving) Bentley, **6**: 274. — (G. Roslyn) Colburn, **165**: 920.
Enchanted Isles. (H. Melville) Putnam, **3**: 311, 345, 460.
Enchanted Mule. (R. G. White) Putnam, **2**: 147.
Enchanted Throne. (J. Everett) No. Am. **12**: 365.
Enchantress, The; or Notes from Kit Kelson's Log. Ecl. M. **70**: 712.
Enchantress of Syracuse; a Poem. (T. Sheehan) Temp. Bar, **33**: 312.
Encke, Johann Franz. (W. T. Lynn) Good Words, **8**: 197. — (R. A. Proctor) Nature, **1**: 479. — Am. J. Sci. **93**: 10.
Encumbered Estate. House. Words, **16**: 84.
Encumbered Estates Court. Chamb. J. **30**: 249.
Encyclical of Pius IX., 1865, Text and Commentary. Dub. R. **56**: 441, 560. — (T. Harper) Month, **37**: 356.
Encyclopædia Americana. Am. Mo. R. **2**: 132. **4**: 322. — No. Am. **34**: 262.
— Britannica. Blackw. **1**: 180.
— — 7th Edition. Quar. **70**: 44. Same art. Am. Ecl. **4**: 577.
— — 8th Edition. Westm. **78**: 394.
— — 9th Edition. Nature, **11**: 343. **12**: 308. — (A. H. Garrod) Nature, **13**: 221. **14**: 390.
— Chambers's. Month, **9**: 82.
— Edinburgh. Blackw. **1**: 186.
— London. Mo. R. **112**: 348.
— Metropolitana. Mo. R. **89**: 187.
— New American. Liv. Age, **57**: 551.
Encyclopædias. Am. Q. **6**: 331.
— History of. Quar. **113**: 354. Same art. Liv. Age, **77**: 387.
End of the Banquet. (W. W. Story) Blackw. **112**: 626.
— of Fordyce Brothers. House. Words, **18**: 73.
End of a Month; a Poem. (A. C. Swinburne) Dark Blue, **1**: 217.
— of the World. All the Year, **2**: 270.
Endicott, John, with portrait. (C. M. Endicott). N. E. Reg. **1**: 201.
Endicott Rock. (P. Carrigain) N. E. Reg. **1**: 311.
Endicott Genealogy. (C. M. Endicott) N. E. Reg. **1**: 335.
Endicott Pear-Tree. (C. M. Endicott) N. E. Reg. **2**: 402.
Endless Punishment, Did the Jews believe in? Univ. Q. **35**: 359, 483. *See* Eternal Punishment.
Endor, Apparition at. (L. A. Gotwald) Luth. Q. **8**: 321. — (E. C. Jones) New Eng. **14**: 75.
Endorsement of Notes. Bank. M. (N. Y.) **32**: 475.
— Liability of Endorsers. Bank. M. (N. Y.) **30**: 975.
Endosmosis, Experiments on. (J. W. Draper) J. Frankl. Inst. **21**: 177. **22**: 27.
Endowment of Research. Nature, **8**: 157–377.
— — Essays on. Dub. Univ. **88**: 122.
— — in Birmingham. Nature, **23**: 304.
— — Local. Nature, **21**: 487.
— of Romanism. Brit. Q. **8**: 472.
Endowments. (J. S. Mill) Fortn. **11**: 377. — (C. Neate) Macmil. **22**: 387.
— and the State. Cong. **3**: 107.
— Effect of. Westm. **22**: 119.
— Religious. (F. W. Newman) Theo. R. **12**: 335. — (G. Sharswood) Princ. **25**: 545.
Endurance, Sermon on. (A. Fonblanque) Temp. Bar, **52**: 204.
Energy. (B. Stewart) Nature, **1**: 647. **2**: 78, 183, 270. — (W. Thomson) No. Brit. **40**: 337. — Good Words, **3**: 601.
— and Force. (G. Allen) Canad. Mo. **10**: 20. — (W. K. Clifford) Nature, **22**: 122.
— Availability of. (W. D. Miller) Pop. Sci. Mo. **17**: 244.
— Conservation of, Stewart's. Nature, **9**: 198. *See* Conservation; Forces.
— Dissipation of. (Lord Rayleigh) Nature, **11**: 454. — Pop. Sci. Mo. **12**: 701.
— — Kinetic Theory of. (W. Thomson) Nature, **9**: 441.
— in Life, Importance of. Fraser, **62**: 63. Same art. Ecl. M. **51**: 193.
— in Nature, Sources of. (Sir W. Thomson) J. Frankl. Inst. **112**: 376.
— Theory of. (A. M. Mayer) J. Frankl. Inst. **86**: 109.
— What is? (B. Stewart) Ecl. Engin. **3**: 380.
Energies, Dissipated. Victoria, **16**: 193.
— Specific, Dependence of Quality on. (E. Montgomery) Mind, **5**: 1.
Enfans trouvés, Les. Colburn, **48**: 71.
Enfantin and St.-Simon. (E. S. Howse) Theo. R. **9**: 39.
Engadine Pass. (H. Bedford) Month, **30**: 162. — (G. B. McClellan) Scrib. **16**: 639.
— Overlooking the. Argosy, **16**: 118.
— Romance of. Lond. Soc. **37**: supp. 42.
— Upper. (L. Tollemache) Fortn. **25**: 340.
Engaged. Tinsley, **7**: 303.
Engaged Man; a Tale. Chamb. J. **47**: 497–587. Same art. Ev. Sat. **9**: 554–650.
Engagements. Ev. Sat. **3**: 668.
— Long. Ev. Sat. **9**: 77.
Engedi, Cave of. Chr. Obs. **72**: 280.
Engelbert of Nassau, and his Tomb. Penny M. **6**: 353.
Enghien, Duc d'. Chamb. J. **16**: 276. — Colburn, **1**: 513. — So. Lit. Mess. **3**: 125.
— Murder of. For. R. **5**: 250. — Bentley, **16**: 19. Same art. Liv. Age, **1**: 739.
Engine for producing Motive Power, 1851. (E. Dunn) J. Frankl. Inst. **52**: 228.
Engineer's Adventure. Chamb. J. **41**: 129. Same art. Ecl. M. **61**: 504.

Engineers and Public Health. (W. Donaldson) Ecl. Engin. **19**: 183.
— Early, and James Brindley. Lond. Q. **25**: 58.
— Education of. (R. H. Thurston) J. Frankl. Inst. **94**: 17. — Macmil. **23**: 423.
— in India. Ecl. Engin. **21**: 285.
— Institute of Mechanical, Address, 1856. (J. Whitworth) J. Frankl. Inst. **63**: 257.
— Lives of. Brit. Q. **35**: 263.
— — Smiles's. Lond. Q. **27**: 427. — Ecl. M. **56**: 323, 464. — Fraser, **65**: 519.
— Locomotive, Brotherhood of. (H. Adams) Nation, **24**: 158, 173.
— of Britain. Ed. R. **150**: 437.
— Professional Training of. Ecl. Engin, **9**: 148. — (R. Briggs) J. Frankl. Inst. **102**: 1, 145.
— Royal. No. Brit. **50**: 1.
— Status of. (G. Smith) Ecl. Engin. **18**: 173.
Engineering, Æsthetics of. (R. Gerner) Ecl. Engin. **20**: 472.
— Amateur. Hunt, **53**: 80.
— American; Locomotives. (M. Passavant) J. Frankl. Inst. **49**: 145, 221. **50**: 231, 294.
— among the Alps. Penny M. **13**: 407, 410.
— Ancient, Features of. (G. Burnham) Am. Arch. **6**: 46.
— — and modern. Chamb. J. **26**: 109.
— and Architecture, Studies in. Ecl. Engin. **20**: 85.
— and Art. (C. H. Driver) Ecl. Engin. **20**: 484.
— and Engineers. (Sir D. Brewster) No. Brit. **34**: 142.
— as a Profession. (O. Reynolds) Ecl. Engin. **15**: 555.
— at the Crystal Palace. Pract. M. **1**: 75.
— Civil, Scope, Aim, and Professorship of. (S. E. Warren) J. Frankl. Inst. **85**: 134.
— — Vignoles's Lectures on. J. Frankl. Inst. **34**: 79, 157, 243. **35**: 25–371. **36**: 20–390. **37**: 8.
— Egyptian and modern. Ecl. Engin. **4**: 158.
— French, before the War. Ecl. Engin. **4**: 211.
— Hydraulic. (S. McElroy) J. Frankl. Inst. **73**: 289, 361. **74**: 13–361. **75**: 1, 217, 303. **76**: 217, 289, 361. **77**: 1. **79**: 81–289. **81**: 145.
— in India, Peculiarities of. (J. G. Medley) J. Frankl. Inst. **80**: 375.
— Metallic Constructions. (W. Fairbairn) J. Frankl. Inst. **54**: 1, 73.
— Notes on. (W. Cain) Ecl. Engin. **17**: 452.
— of the Period, 1870. (W. M. Henderson) J. Frankl. Inst. **90**: 382. **91**: 45.
— Origin and Development of. (Sir J. Hawkshaw) Pop. Sci. Mo. **8**: 33.
— Pioneer, Dobson's. Pract. M. **7**: 64.
— Progress in. (G. W. Siemens) Ecl. Engin. **2**: 150. — (T. Wrightson) Ecl. Engin. **12**: 113. — Pract. M. **2**: 464.
— — in last fifty Years. (W. H. Barlow) Ecl. Engin. **22**: 328.
— — in 1880. (L. F. Harcourt) Ecl. Engin **22**: 7.
— Public Works in the United States. (M. Malézieux) Ecl. Engin. **20**: 394.
— Record of, in 1877. Ecl. Engin. **18**: 225.
— Subaqueous. Pract. M. **4**: 272.
— Weisbach's. (P. E. Dove) Nature, **16**: 81.
— Works in. Ecl. Engin. **16**: 177.
Engineering Apprentices, Principles of Shop Manipulation for. (J. Richards) J. Frankl. Inst. **96**: 305, 379. **97**: 31–392. **98**: 25–415. **99**: 59, 132.
Engineering Archæology. J. Frankl. Inst. **79**: 299.
Engineering Geology. (W. H. Penning) Ecl. Engin. **20**: 473. **21**: 40.
Engineering Precedents, Isherwood on. J. Frankl. Inst. **69**: 284.
Engineering Science, History of. (Sir J. Hawkshaw) Ecl. Engin. **13**: 456.
Engineering Science, Progress of. Quar. **114**: 289.
Engineering Structures, Factor of Safety in. (R. H Buel) Ecl. Engin. **11**: 56.
England, John. (W. G. Read) Rel. Cab. **1**: 361
England, Richard. Once a Week, **27**: 7, 39, 53.
England, Abbeys and Castles of. (H. James, jr.) Lippinc. **20**: 434.
— Admirals of. Cornh. **38**: 36.
— Admiralty in, 1870. Ed. R. **133**: 122.
— Æsthetical Condition of. Dub. Univ. **26**: 420.
— Agriculture of. *See* Agriculture.
— America in. (C. Logan) Galaxy, **3**: 105.
— — Slidell's. Am. Mo. M. **7**: 195.
— American View of. (W. H. Pollock) Macmil. **39**: 299.
— American's Impressions of. (H. White) Fortn. **24**: 291. Same art. Ecl. M. **85**: 548.
— Ancient. Chamb. J. **21**: 373.
— Ancient Fortifications in. (J. Watson) Arch. **5**: 87.
— Ancient Streets and Homesteads of. Chamb. J. **54**: 780.
— and America. Ecl. R. **82**: 427. — (E. Everett) No. Am. **13**: 20. — Mo. R. **132**: 574. — Am. Q. **15**: 240. Blackw. **16**: 474. — Mus. **6**: 13. **13**: 738.
— — and France. (W. O. Johnson) No. Am. **77**: 118. — (M. D. Conway) Fortn. **3**: 442. — Liv. Age, **88**: 545.
— — Dispositions of, 1820. (F. Jeffrey) Ed. R. **33**: 395. Same art. Anal. M. **16**: 302, 355.
— — — American Feeling towards England. Blackw. **63**: 780. — (E. Dicey) Fortn. **11**: 704.
— — — English Feeling towards America, 1865. (E. Dicey) Nation, **1**: 336.
— — Future of. (J. Foster) Ecl. R. **5**: 461.
— — in 1855. Liv. Age, **47**: 805.
— — Relation of. (C. Hodge) Princ. **34**: 147.
— — Social Relations of. Quar. **142**: 251. Same art. Liv. Age, **130**: 707.
— and Christendom, Manning on. Ecl. R. **125**: 459.
— and Continent. No. Brit. **21**: 45. Same art. Liv. Age, **42**: 547.
— and the English, American Impressions of. Chr. Rem. **47**: 165.
— — Bulwer's. Am. Mo. M. **2**: 73. — Colburn, **39**: 206.
— — by a Chinaman. Chamb. J. **23**: 153.
— and France. (J. W. Croker) Quar. **25**: 534. — (J. P. Edwards) Peop. J. **6**: 169.
— — Customs and Manners in. Liv. Age, **114**: 579.
— and Greek Question, 1879. (J. Rea) Brit. Q. **70**: 177.
— and Italy, Mme. Craven on. (J. G. Rosengarten) Nation, **29**: 245.
— — and Germany, 1851. Brit. Q. **13**: 190.
— and the Papacy, 1851. Brit. Q. **13**: 234.
— and Russia and Turkey in the Past. (G. L. Gomme) Colburn, **160**: 379, 523.
— and Scotland, Crowns of, Relations of. (E. A. Freeman) Fortn. **7**: 697.
— — Scenes in. (B. Murphy) Cath. World, **20**: 529.
— — Travels in, Blanqui's. Westm. **4**: 32.
— and United States. New York R. **10**: 375. — New Eng. **6**: 281. — Liv. Age, **47**: 570.
— — Address of John to Jonathan, Boston, Oct. 11, 1870. (T. Hughes) Macmil. **23**: 81.
— — Commercial Relations of. (W. C. Miller) Tinsley, **26**: 116.
— — Mutual Interests of. Penny M. **10**: 152.
— — Relationship of. (W. E. Gladstone) No. Am. **127**: 179. *See also* Great Britain.
— and Wales, Kohl's. Liv. Age, **3**: 314.
— — Mackintosh's Scenery of. Nature, **1**: 306.
— — Turner's Illustr. of. (J. Foster) Ecl. R. **67**: 663.
— and Yankee Land. Fraser, **32**: 485. Same art. Ecl M. **6**: 372.
— Antiquarianism in. Ed. R. **86**: 307.

England, Antiquity of Building in. (J. Essex) Arch. 4: 73.
— Antiquities of. (J. H. Norden) Potter Am. Mo. 5: 859, 937. 6: 57, 217.
— — Barrow opened in Yorkshire, 1864. (J. B. Davis) Reliquary, 6: 1, 185.
— — Cemetery at King's Newton. (J. J. Briggs and L. Jewitt) Reliquary, 9: 1, 6.
— — discovered in Cornwall. (P. Rashleigh) Arch. 9: 187.
— — — at Blandford St. Mary, Dorset. (T. Rackett) Arch. 25: 576.
— — — near Chilgrove, Sussex. (L. V. Harcourt) Arch. 31: 312.
— — — at Mentmore, Bucks. (F. Ouvry) Arch. 35: 379.
— — — in Gloucestershire. (T. Mutlow) Arch. 7: 379.
— — — in Lancashire. (W. Hutchinson) Arch. 9: 211.
— — — in Quantock Hills. (C. J. Harford) Arch. 14: 94.
— — — at Sandwich, Kent. (C. R. Smith) Arch. 30: 132.
— — — in Ehenside Tarn, Cumberland. (R. D. Darbishire) Arch. 44: 272.
— — — in Somersetshire. (C. J. Harford) Arch. 14: 90.
— — — in Yorkshire. (J. M. N. Colls) Arch. 31: 299.
— — Eccleston's. Ecl. R. 86: 316.
— — Grave at Grimthorpe, Yorkshire. (J. R. Mortimer) Reliquary, 9: 180.
— — Museum of National. Quar. 37: 485.
— — National. Art J. 6: 121.
— — Prehistoric. Brit. Q. 50: 396. Same art. Ecl. M. 74: 385.
— — Roman, around Faversham, Kent. (G. Bedo) Reliquary, 13: 141.
— — — at Barrow-upon-Soar, Leicestershire. (J. Thompson) Reliquary, 13: 17.
— — Roman City of Uriconium. Once a Week, 2: 39.
— — Roman Monuments. Canad. J. n. s. 14: 543.
— — Roman Station at Wilderspool. (J. Kendrick) Reliquary, 10: 88. 11: 43.
— — Roman Vestiges near Wetton, Staffordshire. Reliquary, 5: 217.
— — Roman Villa at Walesby, Lincolnshire. (W. B. Philpot) Reliquary, 2: 49.
— — Thor's Cave, Derbyshire. (S. Carrington) Reliquary, 6: 201.
— — Traces of Danes and Norwegians in. Chamb. J. 17: 286.
— — Tumulus near Fimber, Yorkshire. (J. R. and B. Mortimer) Reliquary, 9: 65.
— Aristocracy of. (W. E. H. Lecky) No. Am. 126: 62. — Colburn, 41: 1.
— — and Nobility of. Colburn, 128: 183.
— — Illustrious Families, Drummond's. Quar. 72: 165.
— — Nobility and Gentry. (R. G. White) Atlan. 44: 370.
— — Old Nobility. Nat. R. 6: 360.
— — Ruling Class in. (R. S. Mackenzie) Nat. Q. 18: 321.
— Army of. *See* Great Britain, Army.
— Art in. *See* Art in England.
— as it is, 1851. (W. R. Greg) Ed. R. 93: 305. Same art. Ecl. M. 23: 342.
— — Johnston's. Dub. Univ. 37: 351.
— as seen by an Italian. Dub. Univ. 79: 290.
— as seen by Voltaire. (J. Parton) No. Am. 100: 347.
— Australian's Impressions of. Cornh. 13: 110.
— Bar of, and Inns of Court. Blackw. 79: 61. — Quar. 138: 139. Same art. Liv. Age, 124: 707.
— — Kingsdowne's Recollections of. Ed. R. 129: 40.
— — Sketches of. Colburn, 31: 1–426. 32: 129.
— Best's Cosmopolite in. Mo. R. 149: 61.
— Biographical History of, Noble's. Ecl. R. 6: 707.
— Bye-Lanes and Downs of. Bentley, 24: 541. 25: 38–603. 26: 57–572. 27: 73.
England, Campbell's Visit to, 1775. Ed. R. 110: 322. Same art. Liv. Age, 63: 673.
— Canterbury to London. (H. Curling) Bentley, 23: 111, 266.
— Cathedrals of. Quar. 118: 297. Same art. Ecl. M. 66: 222, 326.
— Census. *See* Census; Great Britain, Population.
— Chancellors of. *See* Chancellors.
— Changes in, in half a Century. Am. Church R. 24: 108.
— Chartism in. *See* Chartism.
— Church of. *See* Church of England.
— Churches of. Contemp. 14: 125.
— — and People of England. Brit. Q. 12: 217.
— — Free. Brit. Q. 35: 206.
— Civil Service of. *See* Civil Service; Great Britain.
— Civilization in. De Bow, 27: 403. *See* Civilization.
— Clergy of, and A. Trollope. Contemp. 2: 240.
— Colonies of. *See* Great Britain.
— Commerce of. *See* Great Britain.
— Commonplaces on. Cornh. 8: 83.
— Conflict between Land and Water in. Chamb. J. 22: 182. Same art. Liv. Age, 43: 205.
— J. F. Cooper's. (J. W. Croker) Quar. 59: 327. — Knick. 11: 184.
— Counties of, Formation of. Ho. & For. R. 3: 550. — Chamb. J. 41: 29.
— — Legends and Traditions. All the Year, 31: 445–542.
— — Names of. (H. Bradley) Gent. M. n. s. 26: 712.
— — Richardson's Table-Book on. Mo. R. 157: 364. 162: 199.
— — Traditions of. All the Year, 32: 12–277.
— Country-House Life in. (R. Wynford) Lippinc. 11: 176.
— Country Lanes in. Temp. Bar, 14: 484.
— Country Life in. (A. D. Gridley) New Eng. 25: 1. — (T. L. Cuyler) Godey, 28: 275. — (W. Howitt) Tait, n. s. 2: 526. — (B. Murphy) Cath. World, 17: 319. — (B. Murray) Galaxy, 17: 679. — Colburn, 5: 305–436. — No. Brit. 40: 1.
— — Ancient Country Gentlemen. Fraser, 7: 633.
— — and Country Folk. Bost. R. 2: 284.
— — Modern. Cornh. 16: 704.
— Court Festivities in. Lippinc. 12: 294.
— Coxe's Impressions of. Am. Church R. 10: 392.
— Crime in. *See* Crime.
— Culture in, Ancient. Dub. Univ. 71: 603.
— Customs of, Old. Penny M. 11: 49–305.
— Decline of. (S. J. Bayard) Contin. Mo. 5: 48.
— — Ledru Rollin on. Fraser, 42: 74. — Dem. R. 28: 229. — Dub. R. 29: 271.
— Decline of the National Spirit in. Temp. Bar, 44: 167.
— Deer Parks of. (R. Wynford) Lippinc. 12: 189.
— Defenses of. *See* Great Britain.
— Democracy in. (S. Amos) Fortn. 1: 228. — (L. J. Hinton) O. & N. 1: 551. — Colburn, 41: 409.
— — in 1880. (A. V. Dicey) Nation, 30: 413.
— Dewey's Old World and New. Tait, n. s. 3: 673.
— Dickens's Localities in. Scrib. 20: 494.
— Distress in Manufacturing Districts, in 1862. (J. H. Thom) Mo. Rel. M. 29: 78.
— — National. Ecl. R. 76: 214.
— — Owen's Plan for relieving. Ed. R. 32: 453.
— — Public. Blackw. 19: 429.
— Domestic Life in, Progress of. Peop. J. 7: 146.
— Down the Thames in a Birch-Bark Canoe. (J. S. Whitman) Harper, 62: 211.
— Easter in. (H. James, jr) Lippinc. 20: 50.
— Ecclesiastical Events. (C. Beard) Theo. R. 10: 135–555. 11: 157–436. 12: 146, 436. 13: 119, 302, 566.
— Ecclesiastical History of. So. Q. 12: 170.
— — Ancient Churches of. U. S. Cath. M. 4: 569.
— — Conversion of, to Christianity. Blackw. 102: 702.
— — Cost of Mediæval Church. Fortn. 33: 848.

England, Ecclesiastical History of, Early. Brownson, **18**: 188. — Chr. Rem. **32**: 64. — Dub. R. **18**: 128. — Lond. Q. **53**: 71.
— — — Ancient, British Church discontinuous with the Anglo-Saxon. Chr. Rem. **3**: 47.
— — Sects of the Commonwealth. Brit. Q. **66**: 326.
— — Stoughton's. Brit. Q. **45**: 477. **52**: 304. — Chr. Obs. **70**: 351. **74**: 488. — Ecl. R. **125**: 266.
— — Tractarian, Romish and Rationalizing Developments of last Half-Century. (E. B. Elliott) Chr. Obs. **67**: 316–971. **68**: 376, 945.
— Electoral Statistics of, 1832–58. (W. Newmarch) J. Statis. Soc. **20**: 169–314. **22**: 101, 297.
— Emancipation in. (S. D. Collett) Atlan. **8**: 742.
— Emerson's English Traits. (N. Porter) New Eng. **14**: 573. — Lond. Q. **7**: 381. — New Q. **5**: 449. — Dub. Univ. **48**: 569. — Putnam, **8**: 407. — Westm. **66**: 494. Same art. Ecl. M. **39**: 503.
— English or British? (J. Foster) Gent. M. n. s. **22**: 195.
— Espriella's Letters from. (F. Jeffrey) Ed. R. **11**: 370.
— Esquiros's L'Angleterre. Bentley, **46**: 383.
— Ethnology of. (G. Allen) Fortn. **34**: 472.
— Extracts from Diary of a Diplomatist in. Colburn, **78**: 227–455.
— Feudal Tenures in. (F. Seebohm) Fortn. **13**: 89.
— Field Sports of. Bent. Q. **2**: 267.
— Finances of. *See* Great Britain.
— First Eight Days in. (Judge Carleton) Dem. R. **16**: 175.
— Foreign Relations of. *See* Great Britain.
— Foreigners' Opinion of. (E. Brooks) No. Am. **15**: 51. — Chr. Mo. Spec. **5**: 318.
— Forgotten Worthies of. Westm. **58**: 32. Same art. Ecl. M. **27**: 1. Same art. Liv. Age, **46**: 131.
— French Clergy in. U. S. Cath. M. **5**: 156.
— French Judgments of. Ed. R. **103**: 558.
— Frenchman's Impressions of, a Century ago. (H. Alford) Good Words, **7**: 121.
— Fresh Fields and Pastures new. Liv. Age, **58**: 329.
— Future of. Liv. Age, **134**: 767. — (R. W. Boodle) Canad. Mo. **20**: 442. *See* Great Britain.
— Future Bulwarks of. Cornh. **2**: 493. **5**: 550.
— Game Laws of. Colburn, **42**: 417. *See* Game Laws.
— German's Impressions of. Quar. **46**: 518.
— Governing Families of. Brit. Q. **42**: 98. Same art. Ecl. M. **65**: 641.
— Greatness of. (Goldwin Smith) Contemp. **34**: 1. Same art. Liv. Age, **140**: 131.
— Hawthorne's Our Old Home. Blackw. **94**: 610. — Liv. Age, **79**: 243, 344. **81**: 99. — Lond. Soc. **6**: 405.
— Heart of. (R. G. White) Galaxy, **24**: 115.
— Hereditary Republic of. (Marquis of Blandford) No. Am. **133**: 447.
— History of, *in general*: —
— — Apocryphal. Dub. R. **24**: 143.
— — Bonnechose's. Colburn, **112**: 303.
— — Capgrave's Chronicle of. Dub. Univ. **53**: 551.
— — — Gleanings from. Colburn, **116**: 344.
— — Catholic, McCabe's. Ecl. R. **86**: 200. **90**: 683. — Dub. R. **22**: 92. **27**: 128.
— — Characteristics of. Quar. **123**: 144.
— — Child's. (C. Dickens) House. Words, **2**: 409–524. **3**: 19–616. **4**: 117–570. **5**: 89–613. **6**: 93–524. **7**: 45–597. **8**: 69–360.
— — Civil. Am. Q. Reg. **4**: 22.
— — Comic. Ecl. R. **84**: 533.
— — Ellis's Letters illustrative of. Ed. R. **41**: 427. **46**: 195. — Mo. R. **113**: 220.
— — Falsification of. (T. De Quincey) Lond. M. **10**: 625.
— — for Children, Neale's. Chr. Obs. **51**: 88.
— — Georgiana; or Royal Anecdotes illustrative of. Colburn, **1**: 252–544. **2**: 38–528.
England, History of, *in general*: Government, from Henry the Eighth's Reign to 1865. Ed. R. **122**, 257.
— — Green's. Dub. R. **77**: 308. — (B. Herford) Dial (Ch.), **1**: 105. — (A. V. Dicey) Nation, **31**: 174, 188.
— — Green's Short. (H. Adams) No. Am. **121**: 216. — (A. V. Dicey) Nation, **27**: 227. — (M. P. Lowe) Unita. R. **10**: 452. — (J. Rowley) Fraser, **92**: 395, 710. — Dub. R. **77**: 308. — Quar. **141**: 385.
— — Invasions in. Dub. Univ. **55**: 708.
— — Keightley's. Dub. Univ. **11**: 183.
— — Knight's Pictorial. Ecl. R. **69**: 542. **74**: 53.
— — Lecky's. (F. R. Conder) Dub. Univ. **91**: 513.
— — Letters on. Fraser, **3**: 163.
— — Lingard's. Ed. R. **42**: 1. — (H. Hallam) Ed. R. **53**: 1. — Westm. **7**: 87. — Blackw. **19**: 313. — Mo. R. **89**: 293. **90**: 43. **108**: 1. **112**: 159. **118**: 389. **143**: 290. — Ecl. R. **34**: 1. **45**: 237. — Dub. R. **12**: 295. **41**: 1. — Rel. Cab. **1**: 471, 561.
— — Mackintosh's. (S. A. Eliot) Chr. Exam. **11**: 337. — Mo. R. **122**: 546. **125**: 187. — Westm. **21**: 399. — Ecl. R. **57**: 97.
— — New Sources of. Quar. **130**: 373.
— — New Way of writing. Lond. Q. **50**: 302.
— — Pauli's. Fraser, **54**: 665. — Westm. **61**: 602.
— — Periods of Transition in. Am. Church R. **26**: 172.
— — Pictorial. Ed. R. **74**: 430. — (Dr. McVicker) Meth. Q. **7**: 485. — Ecl. R. **67**: 579. **69**: 542. **74**: 53. **84**: 205.
— — Raumer's Political. Ecl. R. **65**: 151.
— — Records as a Source of. Month, **3**: 173.
— — Revolutions in, Vaughan's. (E. A. Freeman) Ed. R. **112**: 136. — Dub. Univ. **58**: 540. — Fraser, **69**: 199. — Ecl. M. **61**: 469. — Ecl. R. **73**: 249.
— — — Vol. I., Race. Dub. Univ. **54**: 730. — Ecl. M. **50**: 86. — Blackw. **86**: 537. — Fraser, **61**: 485. — Ecl. M. **50**: 214.
— — — Vol. II., Religion. Blackw. **90**: 166. — Brit. Q. **34**: 65. — Ecl. M. **54**: 289. **55**: 98.
— — — Vol. III., Government. Brit. Q. **39**: 160. Same art. Ecl. M. **62**: 144.
— — Scheme for Manual of. Dub. R. **57**: 173.
— — State Papers and Calendars. Chr. Rem. **47**: 72.
— — Storms in. (T. De Quincey) Ecl. M. **39**: 405.
— — Turner's. Ecl. R. **45**: 237.
— — Tytler's. Mus. **38**: 179, 259.
— History of, *Early*: —
— — Dub. Univ. **1**: 663. — No. Brit. **21**: 375. — Quar. **147**: 511.
— — Anglo-Saxon Chronicle. Blackw. **91**: 629.
— — before the Norman Conquest. (W. F. Allen) No. Am. **110**: 349.
— — Chroniclers of. Cornh. **15**: 154. — Chr. Rem. **37**: 1.
— — — English Chronicle. (G. Allen) Gent. M. n. s. **24**: 543.
— — — Froissart's Chronicle. Mo. R. **160**: 1.
— — — Raymond's Metrical History. Mo. R. **158**: 57.
— — Colonization of Northumbria. Ho. & For. R. **4**: 577.
— — Danes and Norwegians in. Dub. R. **32**: 184.
— — Julius Cæsar's Landing-Place in. (Major Rennell) Arch. **21**: 501. *See* Cæsar.
— — History of Kings of East Angles, 792–855. (T. Amyot) Arch. **19**: 302.
— — Monastic Historians of. Dub. R. **37**: 273.
— — Mythical and Romantic Elements in. (E. A. Freeman) Fortn. **4**: 641.
— — Norse Element in. (R. E. Thompson) Penn Mo. **1**: 241.
— — Northmen in Cumberland and Westmoreland, Ferguson's. Colburn, **108**: 165.
— — Norway and, in the 11th Century. (G. N. Dasent) No. Brit. **42**: 357.

England, History of, *Early:* Pearson's Early and Middle Ages. (E. A. Freeman) Fortn. **9**: 397.
— — Pictures of. (J. Ayloffe) Arch. **3**: 239.
— — Races of Men in. (H. Coppée) Evang. R. **13**: 93.
— — Saxons in. Ed. R. **89**: 151. — Lond. Q. **12**: 355.
— — The Shire and the Gá. (E. A. Freeman) Macmil. **41**: 452.
— — Teutonic Tribes in. Ecl. M. **48**: 76, 170.
— — Yeatman's. Dub. Univ. **86**: 753.
— History of, *Norman Conquest:* —
— — (C. C. Hazewell) Atlan. **18**: 461. — Mus. **18**: 290. — Quar. **74**: 281. Same art. Liv. Age, **3**: 131. — For. Q. **6**: 283. — Lond. Q. **48**: 1.
— — and Archæological Research. (G. Rolleston) Nature, **1**: 661.
— — as exhibited in Domesday Book. Cornh. **8**: 600.
— — Freeman's History of. (G. W. Cox) Fortn. **13**: 318. — Brit. Q. **52**: 1. — (W. Hunt) Contemp. **9**: 405. — Chr. Rem. **55**: 296. — (W. F. Allen) Nation, **10**: 45. **14**: 341. **23**: 331. — (C. E. Norton) No. Am. **105**: 640. — Ed. R. **130**: 186. — Lond. Q. **34**: 355. — Quar. **123**: 144. Same art. Liv. Age, **94**: 451. — (H. Coppée) Internat. R. **2**: 433.
— — Maclise's Designs of. Dub. Univ. **53**: 712.
— — Palgrave's History of. Brit. Q. **26**: 1. — Ed. R. **95**: 153. **109**: 486. **121**: 1. — Internat. M. **4**: 169.
— — Thierry's History of. Quar. **74**: 281. — Ecl. R. **44**: 385.
— History of, 11*th to* 15*th Centuries:* —
— — Barons' War, 13th Century, Blaauw on. Mo. R. **163**: 491.
— — Cobbe's Norman Kings of. Victoria, **14**: 184.
— — Foreign Wars in Reign of Edward III. Mo. R. **160**: 213.
— — Invasion of, by Edward IV. (E. Jerningham) Arch. **21**: 11.
— — Middle Ages in. Nat. R. **11**: 348. Same art. Liv. Age, **67**: 400.
— — Pre-Reformation Period. No. Brit. **29**: 48.
— — Troubles of the Lancasterian Kings. (J. S. Stone) Canad. Mo. **20**: 593.
— — under the House of Lancaster, Brougham's. Dub. Univ. **58**: 535.
— — Wars under Edward I. Cornh. **15**: 281.
— History of, 16*th Century:* —
— — Froude's. (E. E. Hale) Chr. Exam. **80**: 90. — (C. C. Hazewell) Nation, **1**: 591. — (C. Kingsley) No. Brit. **26**: 72. — (J. G. Meline) Cath. World, **11**: 289, 577. **12**: 60, 356, 474. — (R. Nugent) Contemp. **4**: 437. — (N. Porter) Hours at Home, **3**: 426. — Dub. R. **44**: 445. **49**: 263. — Dub. Univ. **51**: 669. **57**: 289. — Ecl. M. **54**: 358. — Ed. R. **108**: 206. **119**: 243. — Chr. Obs. **57**: 401. **58**: 631, 723. **60**: 539, 601. **64**: 27, 121. **67**: 201, 277. — New Q. **5**: 312. **7**: 143. **9**: 210. — No. Brit. **26**: 72. — Princ. **41**: 248. — Westm. **66**: 113.
— — — Vols. I., II. Colburn, **107**: 446. Same art. Liv Age, **50**: 769. — Colburn, **110**: 235. Same art. Ecl. M. **42**: 85. — Colburn, **113**: 34. — No. Brit. **26**: 72. — (C. C. Hazewell) Atlan. **10**: 16. — Ecl. M. **54**: 358. — Liv. Age, **59**: 163. — Fraser, **54**: 31. — Sharpe, **40**: 177. — Nat. R. **3**: 107.
— — — Vols. III., IV., Henry VIII. Brit. Q. **28**: 265. Same art. Liv. Age, **60**: 75. — Fraser, **58**: 15. — Lond. Q. **16**: 473.
— — — Vols. V., VI., Edward VI. and Mary. (F. D. Maurice) Macmil. **2**: 276. — Ecl. M. **57**: 50, 200. — Fraser, **62**: 1. — Liv. Age, **67**: 22. — Dub. Univ. **57**: 289. Same art. Liv. Age, **69**: 174. — Lond. Q. **18**: 318. — Nat. R. **11**: 165. Same art. Ecl. M. **51**: 145.
England, History of, 16*th Century:* Froude's, Vols. VII., VIII., Elizabeth. Brit. Q. **45**: 1. — Chr. Obs. **67**: 201, 277. — (N. H. Chamberlain) Am. Church R. **19**: 281. — Am. Church R. **20**: 113. — Ed. R. **124**: 476. Same art. Liv. Age, **91**: 515. — Ed. R. **131**: 1. Same art. Ecl. M. **74**: 515. Same art. Liv. Age, **104**: 451. — Ho. & For. R. **4**: 191. — Liv. Age, **70**: 347. — Quar. **114**: 510. Same art. Liv. Age, **79**: 387. — Quar. **128**: 506. — Victoria, **2**: 174. — Dub. R. **55**: 97. — Ecl. R. **119**: 140. — (Prof. Kingsley) Macmil. **9**: 211. Same art. Liv. Age, **80**: 270. — Victoria, **2**: 174.
— — — Edinburgh Review and. Fraser, **58**: 359.
— — Letters in Reigns of Edward VI. and Mary. Quar. **65**: 52.
— — Rebellion of 1569. Mo. R. **153**: 1.
— — Somerset's Administ., 1547–49. Chr. Rem. **42**: 1.
— — State Papers, 1542–96. Retros. **15**. 204, 419.
— — under Edward VI. and Mary, Tytler on. Mo. R. **149**: 116.
— — under Elizabeth. Ed. R. **146**: 199.
— — under Plantagenets and Tudors (after Froude). Sharpe, **31**: 253.
— — under the Tudors. Nat. Q. **23**: 228.
— — under Henry VII. Ed. R. **117**: 378. — No. Brit. **31**: 287.
— — under Henry VIII. Lond. Q. **2**: 501. — Fraser, **77**: 466.
— — — Social Condition of. Westm. **95**: 92.
— History of, 1600–60: —
— — Bisset's Omitted Chapters of. Chr. Obs. **65**: 502.
— — Civil War, 1640–53. Dem. R. **21**: 33, 141. — (L. Bacon) New Eng. **1**: 250. — (W. Dowe) No. Am. **76**: 334. — (J. Webb) Arch. **37**: 189. — Liv. Age, **59**: 851.
— — — and grand Remonstrance, 1641. Ed. R. **112**: 460.
— — — and Oliver Cromwell. (J. Forster) Ed. R. **103**: 1.
— — — Cary's. Ecl. R. **75**: 167.
— — — Cattermole's History of. Mo. R. **154**: 90.
— — — Causes of, Guizot on. Quar. **99**: 105.
— — — History and Literature of. St. James, **20**: 218, 351, 473.
— — — Illustrations of. Mo. R. **157**: 25.
— — — Memorials of, Bell's Edition. Colburn, **86**: 171.
— — — Outbreak of. Westm. **70**: 519.
— — — Sanford's Studies of. Dub. Univ. **53**: 288.
— — — — and Mr. Forster on. Nat. R. **7**: 382.
— — — State Papers on, 1639–41. Ed. R. **137**: 182.
— — — Studies of. Fraser, **58**: 618.
— — Commonwealth. Ed. R. **55**: 305. — Am. Q. **13**: 485. — Westm. **8**: 328. — Mus. **12**: 55. — Mo. R. **110**: 146. **114**: 287. **117**: 474.
— — — Burton's Diary. Colburn, **23**: 193.
— — — Godwin's Hist. of Commonwealth. Colburn, **10**: 570. **25**: 119. — Ecl. R. **40**: 193. — Lond. M. **10**: 57.
— — — Great Seals in, 1648–60. (W. D. Cooper) Arch **30**: 77.
— — — Green's Hist. of. (A. V. Dicey) Nation, **29**: 210.
— — — Kemble's. Hogg, **3**: 45.
— — — Legislation of. Quar. **145**: 449.
— — — not a Republic. (J. H. Morris) Potter Am. Mo. **7**: 247.
— — — Palgrave's Hist. of. (H. Hallam) Ed. R. **55**: 305.
— — — Republicans of. Westm. **96**: 106. **99**: 146.
— — Gardiner's History of James I. Ed. R. **143**: 101. — Fraser, **69**: 419.
— — Gardiner's History, 1628–37. Ed. R. **148**: 379.
— — Guizot's Revolution of 1640–88. Ecl. R. **91**: 615. — Ed. R. **92**: 220. — Westm. **22**: 488.
— — Ranke's. Dub. R. **75**: 308. **78**: 332. — Brit. Q. **61**: 514. — Ed. R. **144**: 52.
— — under the Stuarts. (A. L. Phelps) Nat. Q. **2**: 64.

England, History of, 1660–1714: —
— — Annalists of the Restoration. Dub. Univ. **35**: 333. Same art. Liv. Age, **23**: 556.
— — Counter Revolution under Charles II. and James II. Ecl. R. **84**: 726.
— — Macaulay's. (A. Alison) Blackw. **65**: 383. Same art. Liv. Age, **21**: 295. — (G. E. Ellis) Chr. Exam. **46**: 253. — (J. Williams) Am. Church R. **2**: 1. — (C. C. Smith) Chr. Exam. **60**: 373. — (L. E. Smith) Chr. R. **21**: 356. — Am. Presb. R. **5**: 48. — Bentley, **39**: 206. — Brit. Q. **9**: 1. — Chamb. J. **10**: 425. **25**: 40. — Chr. Obs. **50**: 50. **56**: 594. **61**: 345. — Chr. Rem. **31**: 377. — Dub. R. **26**: 390. **40**: 156. — Dub. Univ. **47**: 149. — Ecl. M. **53**: 208, 365. — Ecl. R. **89**: 1. **103**: 77, 119. **113**: 365. — (J. Moncrieff) Ed. R. **90**: 131. Same art. Ecl. M. **18**: 116. Same art. Liv. Age, **22**: 441. — Ed. R. **105**: 142. — (Sir J. Moncrieff) Ed. R. **114**: 279. Same art. Ecl. M. **55**: 156. Same art. Liv. Age, **71**: 606. — Fraser, **39**: 1. **53**: 147. — Liv. Age, **48**: 405. **69**: 249, 302. — Lond. Q. **6**: 205. — Nat. R. **2**: 357. **13**: 86. — New Q. **5**: 9. **10**: 177. — No. Am. **68**: 511. — (Sir D. Brewster) No. Brit. **10**: 367. Same art. Ecl. M. **16**: 522. Same art. Liv. Age, **21**: 49. — (J. C. Moffat) Princ. **28**: 286. — Prosp. R. **5**: 133. — Putnam, **7**: 255. — Quar. **84**: 549. Same art. Ecl. M. **17**: 326. Same art. Liv. Age, **21**: 481. — Tait, n. s. **16**: 84. **23**: 45, 70. — So. Q. **15**: 374. — Brownson, **6**: 274. — Princ. **22**: 101. — Ecl. M. **16**: 405, 500. — Dem. R. **24**: 205. — Liv. Age, **20**: 298, 408. — Mass. Q. **2**: 326.
— — — Blemishes in. No. Brit. **25**: 77.
— — Revolution of 1688. (T. B. Macaulay) Ed. R. **67**: 415. — (S. G. Arnold) Meth. Q. **8**: 51. — (C. C. Smith) Chr. Exam. **44**: 205. — Quar. **51**: 493. — For. R. **3**: 489. — Westm. **21**: 399. — Mus. **14**: 280. — Dem. R. **21**: 301. — For. Q. **33**: 321. — Am. Q. **12**: 153. — Mus. **25**: 118. — Ecl. R. **80**: 593. — Ecl. M. **10**: 145.
— — — and the Anti-Catholic Faction. Dub. R. **41**: 383.
— — — and Bishop Burnet. (G. W. Conder) Ex. H. Lec. **18**: 277.
— — — Conspiracy of an Oligarchy. Dub. R. **41**: 26.
— — — French Histories of. For. Q. **3**: 76. — For. R. **3**: 489.
— — — Guizot's History of. Dub. R. **28**: 277. — Westm. **22**: 488. — Ed. R. **92**: 115. — Ecl. R. **91**: 615.
— — — Mackintosh's History of. Dub. R. **53**: 247. — Ed. R. **61**: 265. — (J. W. Croker) Quar. **51**: 493. — Mo. R. **138**: 183.
— — — Sequel of. Dub. R. **43**: 1.
— — — Ward on. (J. Allen) Ed. R. **67**: 415.
— History of, *18th Century*: —
— — Blackw. **57**: 353. — Ed. R. **148**: 81.
— — Adolphus's. Ed. R. **1**: 317.
— — Burnet's, of his Time. (R. Southey) Quar. **29**: 165.
— — Cabinet Changes, 1754–1841. Westm. **37**: 171.
— — Court of, 1688–1760. Ecl. Mus. **1**: 397. **2**: 290.
— — Historical Sketches of the Reign of George II. (M. Oliphant) Blackw. **103**: 195–511 **104**: 1–676. **105**: 1–665. **106**: 140.
— — in 1738. Chr. Obs. **62**: 217.
— — Lecky's. (A. V. Dicey) Nation, **26**: 261, 279. — (J. Dyer) Penn Mo. **9**: 479. — (C. C. Smith) Unita. R. **9**: 643. — Quar. **145**: 498. Same art. Liv. Age, **137**: 451.
— — Mahon's. Quar. **57**: 330. **63**: 151. — Ecl. R. **82**: 551. **95**: 342. **100**: 450. — (J. G. Palfrey) No. Am. **75**: 125. — Ed. R. **64**: 232. — (W. Sargent) No. Am. **80**: 236. — Chr. Obs. **70**: 673. — Fraser, **45**: 494. — Liv. Age, **32**: 246. — Mo. R. **143**: 290. **148**: 136. — New Q. **1**: 17. — No. Brit. **28**: 1.
England, History of, *18th Century*: Memoirs illustrative of. (Sir J. Mackintosh) Ed. R. **25**: 168.
— — Political Parties in, under Queen Anne. (Sir H. Ellis) Arch. **38**: 1.
— — Rebellion of 1715. Mus. **10**: 193.
— — — of 1745. Ed. Mo. R. **5**: 515. — Ecl. M. **8**: 307. — Dem. R. **22**: 433. — Liv. Age, **6**: 11. — Mo. R. **98**: 36. — Retros. **11**: 220. — Ecl. R. **82**: 686. — Portfo. (Den.) **27**: 23.
— — Reign of Queen Anne. Ed. R. **132**: 519.
— — — Burton's. (A. V. Dicey) Nation, **30**: 215, 238. — Fraser, **101**: 337.
— — — Historians of. Blackw. **115**: 301. Same art. Ecl. M. **94**: 385.
— — Reign of George III. Chr. Rem. **47**: 121.
— — — England at his Accession. Lond. Q. **15**: 213. Same art. Ecl. M. **51**: 462.
— — — Massey's. Colburn, **114**: 85. — Dub. Univ. **53**: 192. — Fraser, **51**: 127. — Liv. Age, **59**: 518. **66**: 451. — New Q. **7**: 229.
— — — Phillimore's. Liv. Age, **78**: 157.
— — — Pictorial. Mo. R. **156**: 392.
— — Union of England and Scotland. No. Brit. **21**: 69.
— History of, *19th Century*: —
— — (T. Bacon) New Eng. **25**: 618. — Ed. R. **103**: 305.
— — Administration of, 1783–1830. Chr. Rem. **48**: 128.
— — — 1815–30. Bentley, **31**: 320.
— — Court of, during Regency, 1811–20. Ed. R. **108**: 299.
— — — Buckingham's Memoirs of. New Q. **5**: 325.
— — in 1760–1860. (G. M. Towle) New Eng. **21**: 457.
— — in 1816–46. Quar. **91**: 161.
— — in 1830–41. Am. Ecl. **4**: 124.
— — McCarthy's. (J. V. O'Conor) Cath. World, **29**: 650.
— — Martineau's. (E. E. Hale) Chr. Exam. **81**: 78. — Ecl. R. **21**: 443. — Brit. Q. **11**: 359.
— — Parties in England, 1760–1860. (G. M. Towle) New Eng. **23**: 627.
— — Roebuck on Whig Ministry of 1830. Fraser, **45**: 245.
— — under seven Administrations. (J. S. Mill) Westm. **27**: 60. — So. Q. **8**: 480. — (W. Empson) Ed. R. **65**: 196. — Mo. R. **143**: 127.
— — Walpole's, from 1815. (A. V. Dicey) Nation, **29**: 294. — Ed. R. **149**: 168.
— — Walsh's Contemporary History. Mo. R. **139**: 340.
— Home Life in. (A. Esquiros) Lond. Q. **18**: 461. — (A. Rhodes) Galaxy, **13**: 772. — Ecl. M. **57**: 39, 263. — So. R. n. s. **15**: 68.
— — before the Norman Conquest. (G. Harris) Canad. Mo. **13**: 630.
— — Comforts of. (F. Kottenkamp) Bentley, **3**: 167.
— — described in Danish Literature. Temp. Bar, **26**: 85.
— — Domestic Festivities. (B. Murphy) Cath. World, **17**: 630.
— — French Views of. Once a Week, **25**: 382.
— — in Middle Ages. (T. Wright) Art J. **4**: 92, 247, 310. **5**: 4, 168, 245. **6**: 17–297.
— — in 1645. Chamb. J. **4**: 313.
— — Modern, Malot's. St. James, **5**: 500.
— — Old Houses and Households. Brit. Q. **14**: 369.
— — Phases of old. Dub. Univ. **69**: 681.
— Impressions in. (J. H. Morison) Unita. R. **6**: 525. — (P. Schaff) Mercersb. **9**: 329.
— in Age of Chaucer. Chamb. J. **46**: 282, 294.
— in Age of Spenser. (A. Kerr) Western, **5**: 535.
— in Middle Ages. Nat. R. **11**: 348. Same art. Ecl. M. **52**: 289.
— — Distribution of Wealth in. (J. E. T. Rogers) Macmil. **13**: 249. Same art. Ecl. M. **66**: 555.
— in the Olden Time. (G. Daniel) Bentley, **8**: 441, 545. **9**: 17–593. **10**: 33–589. — All the Year, **2**: 562. — Art J. **11**: 18. — Bentley, **5**: 98. — Chamb. J. **43**: 28. — (J. H. Gurney) Ex. H. Lec. **16**: 135.

England in 14th Century, Religion and Morals in. Chr. Obs. 76: 822.
— in Time of Elizabeth. Ed. R. 146: 199. Same art. Liv. Age, 134: 579.
— — People for whom Shakspere wrote. (C. D. Warner) Atlan. 43: 729. 44: 44.
— — Thornbury's Shakspere's England. Colburn, 107: 323. See Shakspere.
— in 18th Century. Appleton, 19: 260. — (K. Hillebrand) Contemp. 37: 1.
— — Letters and the Public in. (W. H. Browne) Nation, 33: 416.
— — Manners and Customs. (A. Andrews) Colburn, 105: 78–490. 106: 107–321. Same art. Liv. Age, 43: 187. — Temp. Bar, 34: 225.
— in 1745 and 1842. Liv. Age, 5: 70.
— in 1766, State of. Cong. 5: 406.
— in 1776. Liv. Age, 37: 178, 549.
— in 1782. Chamb. J. 50: 521.
— in 19th Century, Walpole on. (G. B. Smith) Fraser, 98: 713.
— — Social and Political Life in 1825. (A. V. Kirwan) Fraser, 62: 113.
— in 1835, Raumer's. Dub. R. 1: 131. — Mo. R. 140: 1.
— in 1840. Mus. 41: 321.
— in 1851. (F. Bremer) Sharpe, 15: 119–351. — Chr. Rem. 20: 400.
— in June. Galaxy, 11: 447.
— Incidents in. (J. P. Anthony) Pioneer, 4: 141–335.
— Income Tax and Tariff of 1842. Dub. Univ. 20: 364.
— Institutions of. Quar. 120: 536.
— Inundation of Land in. (G. P. Bevan) Once a Week, 3: 187.
— Invasion of. Cornh. 25: 21.
— — French Schemes for. Month, 7: 148, 359. — Dub. Univ. 52: 100. — House. Words, 19: 337. — Sharpe, 13: 33.
— — Mr. Jolly Green on. Colburn, 82: 258.
— — Napoleon's Projected, 1803–5. Temp. Bar, 35: 346. — Colburn, 127: 237.
— — Possible, 1859. Quar. 126: 245. Same art. Liv. Age, 62: 515.
— — Precautions against, 1586. (Sir W. Musgrave) Arch. 13: 100.
— Invasion Panic of 1871 and its Lessons. (E. A. Freeman) Macmil. 24: 1.
— Invasion Panics. (C. F. Adams, jr.) No. Am. 113: 473. — Cornh. 1: 135. — Once a Week, 27: 205.
— Islands of. Penny M. 10: 398–420.
— Journey in. (J. Burroughs) Scrib. 8: 560.
— Judges of. Quar. 119: 326. — Brit. Q. 42: 33. — Tait, n. s. 16: 163.
— — Foss's. Tait, n. s. 25: 118.
— Judicial Policy of. (A. V. Dicey) Macmil. 29: 473.
— King of Saxony's Sketches of. Tait, n. s. 13: 301.
— Laboring Class, and Families. Tait, n. s. 25: 72, 166.
— — Condition of. (T. Wright) Fraser, 84: 426. Same art. Ecl. M. 78: 84.
— — — in 1833. Colburn, 38: 46.
— — How do they live? Tait, n. s. 6: 13.
— Lake Country of. (J. R. Thompson) Land We Love, 4: 307. — Art J. 3: 132. — Dub. Univ. 30: 33. — Brit. Q. 41: 476. Same art. Ecl. M. 67: 129. — Tinsley, 1: 178.
— — and Poets. (W. Howitt) Tait, n. s. 6: 365.
— — and their Genii. (M. D. Conway) Harper, 62: 7, 161, 339.
— — and Wordsworth. (T. L. Cuyler) Godey, 28: 30.
— — Descriptive Tours of. Penny M. 6: 241, 289.
— — Notabilities of. (H. Martineau) Harper, 7: 541.
— — Papers on. (L. Cross) Colburn, 163: 172–655.
— — Society of. (T. DeQuincey) Tait, n.s. 7: 34, 346, 525.
England, Land System of. See Land.
— Landed Gentry of. Cornh. 9: 618.
— Land-Owners in. (R. Wynford) Lippinc. 10: 710.
— Landscape in, Constable and. Blackw. 58: 257.
— Larcher's Les Anglais, Londres, etc. Tinsley, 2: 385.
— Law of, and Moral Theology. Dub. R. 35: 172.
— — Criminal. Ed. R. 19: 389. — Selec. Ed. R. 6: 10.
— — Curiosities of English Courts. (G. M. Towle) Appleton, 13: 465-717.
— — Early. Once a Week, 7: 318.
— — Inns of Court and of Chancery. Ed. R. 134: 483.
— — Property and the Poor-Laws. Colburn, 31: 150.
— — Statutes at large. Nat. R. 12: 69.
— — Supreme Court and Law Reform. Am. LawR. 8: 256.
— — System and Administration of. Ed. R. 45: 458.
— Ledru-Rollin on. Brit. Q. 12: 262.
— Lester's Glory and Shame of. Mo. R. 157: 72.
— Letters from. (R. G. White) Atlan. 46: 685.
— — on. (De St. Foix) Colburn, 4: 164–573. 5: 145–552.
— Life in, Habits of. (R. G. White) Atlan. 45: 86.
— Loyalty in, 1876. (J. McCarthy) Galaxy, 21: 83.
— Malo's Panorama. (J.W. Croker) Quar. 18: 223.
— Manners in. (R. G. White) Atlan. 44: 774. — Blackw. 5: 38.
— — and Habits in 16th Century. Hogg, 7: 411.
— — and Customs in 18th Century. (A. Andrews) Colburn, 102: 70–465. 103: 223–465. 104: 49–485.
— — by a Frenchman. Fraser, 1: 479.
— — Illustrations of. Select J. 3: 58.
— — Morals and Poetry of. (C. C. Felton and F. Bowen) No. Am. 59: 1.
— — Progress of. West. J. 3: 107.
— — Some Faults of. Blackw. 5: 38.
— Manufactures of. (J. Hatton) Tinsley, 24: 415. — Bank. M. (N. Y.) 16: 742.
— — American Competition with. (J. Hatton) Tinsley, 24: 381.
— — Districts of, Head's Tour in. Tait, n. s. 3: 401.
— Middle Class in. (M. Arnold) Cornh. 13: 153.
— Mission of. (W. E. Gladstone) 19th Cent. 4: 560.
— Modern, Familiar Letters on. (K. Hillebrand) 19th Cent. 6: 615.
— Montalembert on. Irish Q. 8: 1381. — Brownson, 13: 225.
— Moorland Village in. (Mrs. J. Lillie) Harper, 61: 1.
— Music in. Cornh. 18: 344.
— Name of, Origin of. Fraser, 56: 114.
— — Why called Logris. (E. L. Hervey) Once a Week, 15: 428.
— Names of Places in. Dub. Univ. 75: 377. — Hogg, 1: 383. 2: 46–390. 4: 284, 350, 376. 5: 94–374. 6: 127–327. 7: 15–366.
— — of Rivers in. All the Year, 10: 306.
— Navy of. See Great Britain.
— New-Englanders and the old Home. Quar. 115: 42. Same art. Liv. Age, 80: 339.
— Nicander Nucius in, 1545. Chr. Rem. 3: 522.
— Niemeyer's Travels in. (E. Everett) No. Am. 17: 311.
— Nobility of. See above, England, Aristocracy of.
— Northern, First Week in. (Mrs. E. C. Walton) Harper, 57: 229.
— Notes on the Road in. Am. Whig R. 3: 145.
— Observations in. (A. P. Peabody) No. Am. 83: 503. — Chr. Mo. Spec. 8: 18, 131.
— of To-Day. (H. D. Traill; J. Morley) Fortn. 33: 130.
— Old Boroughs in. Cornh. 18: 299.
— Old Shrines and Pilgrimages in. Cornh. 20: 81.
— Old Streets and Houses. Scrib. 14: 637.
— On Foot from Oxford to London. St. James, 25: 23.
— On the South Coast. (C. W. Wood) Argosy, 31: 278.
— Passavant's Tour in, 1831. Mo. R. 140: 465.
— Parliament of. See Great Britain.

England, Pauperism in. Lond. Q. **37**: 118.
— — Outside Glimpses of English Poverty. (N. Hawthorne) Atlan. **12**: 36.
See Poor-Laws.
— Past and present State of. (R. Southey) Quar. **32**: 160.
— Peasant of. All the Year, **21**: 132.
— Peasantry of. Bost. R. **2**: 406.
— — Condition of. (R. Southey) Quar. **41**: 240.
— — during Middle Ages. (T. Wright) Arch. **30**: 205. — Chamb. J. **3**: 180.
— — of the South of. Fraser, **87**: 542, 679. **88**: 57.
— Pecchio's Observations on. Quar. **48**: 222. — For. Q. **11**: 171. — Colburn, **37**: 13.
— Peerage of. (E. C. G. Murray) Galaxy, **23**: 293.
— — Nicolas on. Quar. **103**: 28. Same art. Liv. Age, **56**: 705.
— Photographs of, by an American. (S. R. Fiske) Harper, **36**: 654. **37**: 111, 253, 415.
— Pictet's Travels in. (F. Jeffrey) Ed. R. **3**: 287.
— Pilgrimages to English Shrines. (Mrs. S. C. Hall) Art J. **1**: 21–120. **2**: 21–349. **3**: 133, 287. **4**: 84–307. — Quar. **133**: 1.
— Political Memoirs, 1795–1840. Dub. Univ. **58**: 672.
— Politics of. *See* Great Britain.
— Popular Progress in. Ed. R. **93**: 157. Same art. Ecl. M. **23**: 342.
— Population of; Census of 1881. Cornh. **43**: 468.
— — Increase of. (R. P. Williams) J. Statis. Soc. **43**: 462. *See* Census; Great Britain.
— Position and Prospects of. *See* Great Britain.
— Post-Office of. *See* Great Britain.
— Princesses of, Mary A. E. Green's. Lond. Q. **5**: 334.
— Prison Discipline in. (F. W. Holland) Chr. Exam. **74**: 232.
— — An English Jail. (K. O'Meara) Cath. World, **18**: 279.
— — Two Hours in Gaol. (J. Greenwood) Lond. Soc. **14**: 178, 246.
— Protection and Free Trade in. (A. J. Wilson) Fraser, **104**: 604. *See* Free Trade.
— Public Monuments of. Brit. & For. R. **8**: 59.
— Queens of, Chapter from Chronicles of. (C. F. Gore) Tait, n. s. **5**: 707.
— — Doran's. New Q. **4**: 454.
— — Historical Memoirs of. Tait, n. s. **5**: 257. **7**: 111.
— — Strickland's. Colburn, **64**: 389.
— Radical Leaders of, Hinton's. Canad. Mo. **9**: 280.
— Reformation in. *See* Reformation in England.
— Religion in. Westm. **61**: 72.
— — Herford's. (D. Swing) Dial (Ch.), **1**: 3.
— Religions in, Census of. (J. G. Hubbard) 19th Cent. **9**: 131.
— Religious and Ecclesiastical Condition of. Am. Bib. Repos. 2d s. **4**: 147. **5**: 126.
— Religious Bodies in, Statistics of. (H. Mann) J. Statis. Soc. **18**: 141.
— Religious Life in. (A. Lamson) Chr. Exam. **40**: 284.
— — Spiritual Destitution of. Westm. **71**: 146.
— — Tayler's Retrospect. (J. H. Thom) Theo. R. **13**: 201.
— Religious Thought in. (J. Tulloch) Contemp. **5**: 190. **6**: 32. — Contemp. **24**: 453.
— Religious Worship in. Ecl. R. **99**: 475.
— Republicanism in. (J. McCarthy) Galaxy, **12**: 30. — Lakeside, **8**: 233.
— Roman Civilization in, Alleged Permanence of. (E. A. Freeman) Macmil. **22**: 211.
— Rubichon's. Quar. **23**: 174.
— Rural. (R. G. White) Atlan. **44**: 241. — Ed. R. **150**: 253.
— — 1500–50. St. Paul's, **5**: 327.
— Rural Life in, Anecdotes of. Appleton, **24**: 473, 570.
— — Howitt's. (C. C. Felton) No. Am. **51**: 457. — New York R. **6**: 170. — Tait, n. s. **15**: 62.
England, Rural Population of, Physique of. (C. Merivale) Contemp. **10**: 255.
— Rural Walk in. (T. E. Kebbel) Fraser, **102**: 686.
— Russian Opinions on. Liv. Age, **55**: 507.
— Scenes in Central. (C. H. Miller) Overland, **6**: 409. **7**: 325.
— Science in, and in France. (M. Chevenix) Ed. R. **34**: 383.
— Seaside Resorts in. (W. H. Rideing) Harper, **63**: 484.
— Shrines of, and their Devotees. Chamb. J. **31**: 61.
— Sketches in. Am. Mo. M. **4**: 225, 299.
— Skies of. (R. G. White) Atlan. **44**: 107.
— Slidell's. Am. Q. **19**: 207.
— Social and Artistic, in Hogarth's Time. (G. A. Sala) Cornh. **1**: 177–716. **2**: 97–438.
— Social and Literary Sketches of, 1783–85. Cornh. **17**: 610.
— Social Condition of. (F. Bowen) No. Am. **65**: 461. — Chamb. J. **14**: 129.
— — under Henry VIII. Westm. **95**: 92. Same art. Liv. Age, **108**: 387.
— Social Dangers of. Westm. **103**: 65.
— Social History of. Colburn, **108**: 473.
— Social Legislation under the Tudors. Lond. Q. **17**: 117.
— Social Life in, Mediæval. Liv. Age, **73**: 403. Same art. Ecl. M. **56**: 289, 513.
— — from 13th to 16th Centuries. Fraser, **56**: 222.
— Social System of. (B. Murphy) So. M. **17**: 665.
— Social Tendencies of, 1852. Westm. **58**: 110.
— Society in. Chr. Exam. **13**: 1. — Nation, **28**: 245. — Tait, **1**: 399.
— — British Cubs. Sharpe, **32**: 293.
— — Fashionable. Am. Q. **1**: 222.
— — — in the Time of Byron. Tinsley, **9**: 298.
— — in France and. So. R. **6**: 379. — Mo. R. **125**: 204. — Westm. **15**: 221.
— — — Miss Berry's. Quar. **75**: 48
— — in 1773. Temp. Bar, **37**: 240.
— — Lester's Glory and Shame of. Dem. R. **12**: 1.
— — near London. (W. Howitt) Tait, n. s. **5**: 756.
— — under Elizabeth. Temp. Bar, **14**: 540.
— — under James I. Brit. Q. **7**: 73. Same art. Ecl. M. **14**: 296. Same art. Liv. Age, **17**: 103.
— — Villari on, 1862. Victoria, **1**: 97.
— — West Country Exclusives. Tait, n. s. **1**: 598. **2**: 335, 390, 602.
— South Coast Saunterings. (M. D. Conway) Harper, **38**: 24, 175, 449. **39**: 330. **40**: 359, 523. **41**: 339, 499. **47**: 843. **48**: 73, 183.
— Squire of Old. Colburn, **41**: 285.
— — Holtzendorff on. (J. Davies) Contemp. **34**: 524.
— State and Scientific Morality. (H. Holbeach) Contemp. **19**: 498, 647.
— Stately Homes of. (S. C. Hall; L. Jewitt) Art J. **29**: 24.
— Statesmen of the 18th Century. Chr. Rem. **37**: 253.
— Statistics of, Moral and Educational. (J. Fletcher) J. Statis. Soc. **10**: 193. **11**: 343. **12**: 151, 189.
— Summer between the four Seas. (S. B. Wister) Lippinc. **10**: 303, 427.
— Sunday in. Lippinc. **24**: 434.
— — and London Churches. (E. S. Nadal) Scrib. **7**: 483.
— Taine's Notes on. (H. James, jr.) Nation, **14**: 58. — Quar. **133**: 199.
— Taurus Centaurus. (R. G. White) Atlan. **46**: 249.
— Three Excursions in. (H. James, jr.) Galaxy, **24**: 346.
— Tour through all. Art J. **13**: 7.
— Towns in, Municipal Institutions of. (J. Fletcher) J. Statis. Soc. **5**: 97.
— Transformations of South Coast. Once a Week, **8**: 221.
— Travels in. (W. Tudor) No. Am. **2**: 242, 346.
— Travelers in, Foreign. (R. Southey) Quar. **15**: 537.
— Traveling in. Quar. **116**: 212.

England, Traveling in, by Railway. Hunt, **49**: 203. — (T. L. Cuyler) Godey, **33**: 7.
— — in olden Times. Temp. Bar, **33**: 320.
— — Modern. Mus. **22**: 534.
— Turtle's Travels in. Dem. R. **36**: 366.
— Louis Viardot in. Colburn, **105**: 185.
— Vignettes in. (H. James, jr.) Lippinc. **23**: 407.
— Village Life in. Bentley, **52**: 593. — No. Brit. **17**: 71.
— Visit to, in 1775. Ed. R. **110**: 322.
— Wages in. (T. Brassey) Internat. R. **3**: 577.
— Walks in. Quar. **152**: 141.
— Wey's. Blackw. **75**: 37.
— What strikes an American in. (Mrs. W. Kirkland) Bentley, **26**: 49.
— Wheaton's Travels in. (S. Gilman) Chr. Exam **9**: 304.
— White's Walk to Land's End. Colburn, **105**: 71.
— Yeomanry of. Colburn, **48**: 425.
— Young, and the political Future. (J. Morley) Fortn. **7**: 491. — Brit. Q. **12**: 169.
— — George Sydney Smythe's Historic Fancies. (C. C. Felton) No. Am. **61**: 231.
Englewood Mystery. Scrib. **10**: 488.
English or British? (T. Foster) Gent. M. n. s. **22**: 195.
English, The, abroad. (E. A. Grattan) No. Am. **56**: 17.
— French Libels on. Colburn, **39**: 401.
— French Opinions and Descriptions of. For. Q. **36**: 474. — Westm. **85**: 390.
— Germans, and French. Brit. Q. **13**: 331.
— in their Continental Homestead. (Bro. Azarias) Am. Cath. Q. **2**: 385.
— My Countrymen. (M. Arnold) Cornh. **13**: 153. Same art. Liv. Age, **88**: 784.
— of the 19th Century. Fraser, **42**: 1.
— on Continent. For. Q. **32**: 90. Same art. Ecl. M. **3**: 447. *See* English People.
English Acquaintance, My. Blackw. **63**: 94.
English Adventure, Records of early. Ed. R. **152**: 379.
English Agriculture. *See* Agriculture of England.
English Ancestors, Our. (T. C. Amory) N. E. Reg. **26**: 405. — (Lady Verney) Good Words, **14**: 127.
English Authors. Mus. **32**: 74.
— in Florence, 1855. Scrib. **4**: 616.
English Ballads, Early. Temp. Bar, **57**: 493. *See* Ballads.
English Ballad-Singers. Colburn, **5**: 212.
English Capital, Employment of. (F. R. Conder) Fraser, **98**: 326.
English Cathedral Establishments. Blackw. **34**: 677. — Quar. **58**: 108.
English Channel, Communication across. Ecl. Engin. **7**: 244.
— Crossing the. Chamb. J. **50**: 232. **47**: 423. — Ecl. Engin. **6**: 510. **8**: 86.
— — Improved Service in. (M. Scott) Ecl. Engin. **5**: 37.
— — Ships for. (A. Strangs) Ecl. Engin. **8**: 417.
— Depth of. Once a Week, **19**: 339.
— Railway across, Projected. Nature, **1**: 160, 303, 631. — Ecl. Engin. **3**: 29. — J. Frankl. Inst. **65**: 295.
— Tunnel under. (W. Topley) Pop. Sci. R. **13**: 394. — (F. C. Danvers) Ecl. Engin. **14**: 216. — Ecl. Engin. **2**: 172. **5**: 574. **11**: 53, 375. **13**: 541. — Ev. Sat. **8**: 208. — Nature, **10**: 181. — All the Year, **22**: 173. — Chamb. J. **53**: 521.
— — and Bridge across. Good Words, **22**: 210.
— — Proposed Floating. J. Frankl. Inst. **65**: 159.
— Winter Gale in. (T. Guthrie) Good Words, **5**: 320.
— Yacht-Cruise in. Temp. Bar, **15**: 444.
English Character. Dem. R. **32**: 236.
— and American compared. Portfo. (Den.) **7**: 337.
— and Scotch and Irish. Blackw. **26**: 818.
— Formation of. (J. Bardsley) Ex. H. Lec. **16**: 349.
— in English Art. Quar. **147**: 81. Same art. Liv. Age, **141**: 3.
English Characteristics. Western, **3**: 84.
— and Scotch. Chr. Rem. **14**: 290.
English Charity. (Sir F. B. Head) Quar. **53**: 473.
English Classics. Nat. Q. **40**: 41.
English Composition. Penn Mo. **7**: 224, 313. — Mo. R. **159**: 115.
English Corporations and Endowments. Ed. R. **58**: 469.
English Crazes, Two. (W. D. Rawlins) Penn Mo. **11**: 117.
English Criticism, Errors and Abuses of. (G. H. Lewes) Westm. **38**: 466. — Ecl. Mus. **1**: 327.
— German Views of. (T. A. Tellkampf) Am. Whig R. **6**: 497.
English Diction. (W. M. Scott) Princ. **22**: 88.
English Dissenting Academies. Am. Q. Reg. **13**: 195.
English Drama, Censorship of. Colburn, **70**: 345.
— Early. Retros. **2**: 70. **3**: 97, 142. **16**: 1.
— — and German. (W. J. Thoms) Colburn, **61**: 19.
English Dramatic Poetry. Quar. **46**: 477.
English Dramatists of the Restoration. (T. B. Macaulay) Mus. **42**: 31.
English Economy. Penny M. **6**: 5.
English Families, Vicissitudes of. Ecl. M. **59**: 85.
English Flower-Garden. Quar. **149**: 331.
English Gentleman's own Profession. All the Year, **19**: 444, 492.
English Gentlewomen of 17th Cent. Dub. Univ. **88**: 71.
English Girls at Home. (I. Reaney) Cong. **7**: 19.
— in Society. (I. Reaney) Cong. **7**: 88.
English Grammar. *See* English Language.
English Historical Society. Brit. & For. R. **7**: 167.
English Home, An old. Lippinc. **26**: 163.
English Humorists, Thackeray's. So. Lit. Mess. **19**: 437. — Liv. Age, **38**: 292.
English Industry, History and Prospects of. (R. Southey) Quar. **34**: 45.
English Intellect in Victoria's Reign. Nat. Q. **23**: 106.
English Interior in the 17th Century. Liv. Age, **113**: 67.
English Kitchen. (J. Sanderson) Godey, **28**: 281.
English Language. (E. Emerson) Mercersb. **12**: 216. — (E. B. Humphreys) Nat. Q. **1**: 401. — (R. G. White) Galaxy, **3**: 62. — (J. W. Lindsay) Meth. Q. **21**: 254. — So. Lit. Mess. **3**: 766. — Meth. Q. **4**: 543. — Knick. **15**: 89, 212. — No. Brit. **13**: 373. Same art. Ecl. M. **21**: 232. — Chr. R. **19**: 529. — Lond. Q. **28**: 269. — Meth. M. **51**: 743. — (J. S. Hart) Princ. **40**: 1.
— against the Classics. Pop. Sci. Mo. **1**: 707.
— and American English. (R. A. Proctor) Gent. M. n. s. **27**: 156. Same art. Appleton, **26**: 315.
— and Literature. Am. J. Educ. **16**: 555.
— — Early. So. Lit. Mess. **13**: 307, 373.
— — Origin and History of. Chr. Rem. **48**: 194.
— — Study of. (W. Calkins) University Q. **1**: 127.
— Anecdotes of. Penny M. **4**: 19.
— as spoken and written. (F. W. Newman) Contemp. **31**: 689. Same art. Liv. Age, **137**: 94.
— as spoken in England. (R. G. White) Atlan. **45**: 374.
— as spoken at Radha Bazar. All the Year, **46**: 343.
— as a universal One. (M. G. Upton) Overland, **11**: 324. — Dem. R. **35**: 306.
— Bad. (H. Estridge) Sharpe, **36**: 207.
— Changes in. Am. Bib. Repos. 3d s. **2**: 160.
— Claims of. So. Lit. Mess. **21**: 145. — Tait, n. s. **22**: 385.
— Composition of. Chamb. J. **24**: 275. *See* English Composition.
— Curiosities of. (G. L. Craik) Dub. Univ. **50**: 114, 437. **51**: 225, 693.
— defiled. (R. G. White) Galaxy, **17**: 175.
— Derivation of. (W. Drake) Arch. **9**: 332.
— — Tooke on. Ecl. R. **3**: 245, 353.
— De Vere's Studies in. (W. D. Whitney) No. Am. **104**: 631.

English Language, Dialects of. Am. Ecl. 3: 566. — Quar. 55: 354. — Good Words, 8: 557. *See* Cheshire; etc.
— Dictionaries of. (T. De Quincey) Lond. M. 8: 493. — Ed. R. 128: 48. — Quar. 135: 445. Same art. Ecl. M. 82: 99. Same art. Liv. Age, 119: 643. — Chr. R. 25: 384. — Lond. Q. 11: 71.
— — and the Language. (A. Roane) So. Lit. Mess. 22: 168.
— — Denunciation of. (R. G. White) Galaxy, 7: 655.
— — Trench on. Ed. R. 109: 365. Same art. Liv. Age, 61: 489.
— Dictionary of, Johnson's, Boucher's Supplement to. Ecl. R. 5: 303. 6: 994.
— — — Latham's Edition. No. Brit. 41: 285.
— — Philological Society's. Dub. Univ. 93: 393.
— — Pytches's. Ecl. R. 9: 81.
— — Richardson's. Mo. R. 146: 514.
— — Walker's. Liv. Age, 58: 16.
— — Webster's. Ecl. R. 5: 82. 7: 469. — Dem. R. 37: 189, 497. 38: 541. *See* Webster, Noah.
— — — Edition of 1859. (P. Schaff) Mercersb. 11: 264.
— — — — of 1864. (J. S. Hart) Princ. 37: 374. — (G. P. Marsh) Nation, 3: 125–268.
— — — — of 1879. (W. Cook) Nation, 29: 99.
— — Worcester's. (C. S. Lyman) New Eng. 18: 412. *See* Worcester, Jos. E.
— — — and Webster's. (A. Roane) De Bow, 28: 566. — So. R. n. s. 6: 34.
— Disguised Verbal Roots in. (J. W. Gibbs) Am. Q. Reg. 15: 173.
— Dutchman's Difficulty with. Good Words, 4: 867. Same art. Liv. Age, 80: 73.
— Early. (J. W. Hales) Macmil. 16: 128.
— Elizabethan Formation of. So. R. n. s. 11: 393.
— Errata. (G. H. Calvert) Lippinc. 6: 527.
— Ethnological Origin of. Westm. 86: 340.
— Etymology of. (H. Coleridge) Macmil. 1: 347.
— — Minute. (W. L. Blackley) Contemp. 5: 284.
— — Talbot's. Quar. 81: 500.
— — Wedgwood's. (W. D. Whitney) No. Am. 115: 423.
— Fine English, Samples of. Cornh. 3: 205.
— Foreigners'. Chamb. J. 54: 561.
— Grammar of. (H. Corson) Canad. Mo. 2: 68. — (S. Hale) Chr. Exam. 52: 335. — (A. Ingraham) University Q. 4: 228. — (J. H. Nutting) No. Am. 89: 245. — (J. Strong) Meth. Q. 14: 368. — (R. G. White) Galaxy, 7: 100. — New Eng. M. 9: 336.
— — and Composition. (J. G. R. McElroy) Penn Mo. 1: 882.
— — Auxiliaries in. Am. Mo. M. 6: 374.
— — Bailey's. So. Lit. Mess. 20: 145.
— — Barrett's. (E. Everett) No. Am. 12: 310.
— — Becker's Philosophical. (N. Porter) Bib. Sac. 12: 661.
— — Booth's. Ecl. R. 66: 393.
— — Brown's. U. S. Lit. Gaz. 1: 100.
— — Common System. U. S. Lit. Gaz. 1: 220, 249, 283.
— — Conjugations in. Am. J. Educ. 3: 101.
— — Elementary. Ecl. R. 73: 693.
— — Fowler's. (D. R. Goodwin) No. Am. 73: 310.
— — Greene's. (E. S. Gallup) No. Am. 107: 337.
— — Mätzner's. (H. Morley) Fortn. 9: 110.
— — Methods of teaching. (W. H. Wells) Am. J. Educ. 15: 145.
— — Murray's. Ecl. R. 2: 673.
— — Points in. Lond. Q. 10: 358.
— — Teaching of. (R. G. Parker) Am. Inst. of Instruc. 1838: 111.
— — Webber's. Am. Mo. R. 4: 271.
— Grammars of. Lond. Q. 42: 147.

English Language. Guesses and Queries. (N. S. Dodge) Lippinc. 5: 545, 627.
— Hall's Modern. (F. A. March) Nation, 18: 158.
— Harrison's History of. (M. B. Hope) Princ. 22: 321. — (D. R. Goodwin) Bib. Sac. 8 715.
— History of. (H. Rogers) Ed. R. 92: 293. Same art. Liv. Age, 28: 285.
— — Early. (E. Moore) No. Am. 65: 31.
— — Periods in, Terminology of. (T. R. Lounsbury) New Eng. 35: 77.
— — Shepherd's. (F. A. March) Nation, 19: 366. — (S. S. Haldeman) So. M. 16: 96.
— How to write. (T. De Quincey) Hogg, 10: 79.
— Icelandic Illustrations of. Quar. 139: 434.
— Idioms and Provincialisms of. Am. Whig R. 9: 251.
— in America. (M. H. Buckham) No. Am. 91: 507. — Chamb. J. 25: 249. 50: 801. 52: 609. — (A. de Fonblanque) Tinsley, 29: 330. — Penny M. 7: 278. — So. Lit. Mess. 2: 110.
— — Pronunciation of. (R. G. White) Galaxy, 21: 521.
— in Canada. (A. C. Geikie) Canad. J. n. s. 2: 344.
— in Paris. (E. G. Buffum) Galaxy, 4: 45.
— in Society and in School. (M. H. Buckham) Am. J. Educ. 14: 343.
— Inroads upon. Blackw. 102: 399. Same art. Liv. Age, 95: 218.
— Japanning the. (C. Kinney) Galaxy, 16: 188.
— Latham on. (D. R. Goodwin) No. Am. 74: 1. — Ecl. R. 75: 519.
— Lewis's Outlines of. (S. Willard) No. Am. 23: 109.
— Lexicography of. (I. Dole) Am. J. Educ. 3: 161. — (N. Porter) Bib. Sac. 20: 78. — (S. Willard) No. Am. 45: 186. — Quar. 54: 295. — Gen. Repos. 4: 150. — Am. Mo. R. 1: 93.
— Lexicon of, Metropolitan. Fraser, 4: 41.
— Literary and vernacular. Lond. Q. 15: 1.
— Lost Beauties of. (R. G. White) Galaxy, 17: 629.
— Lost Preterites. Blackw. 106: 257.
— Marsh's Lectures on. (E. E. Hale) Chr. Exam. 69: 1. — Liv. Age. 65: 776. 71: 560. — Nat. R. 14: 348.
— Modern. Ed. R. 140: 143. — (E. A. Freeman) Bent. Q. 2: 518. Same art. Liv. Age, 64: 389.
— Modern Corruptions of. St. James, 30: 201.
— Nares's Glossary of. Penny M. 4: 191.
— Nature and Destiny of. (B. J. Wallace) Am. Presb. R. 10: 177.
— New Slang in. All the Year, 10: 179.
— Observations on. (J. Bossard) Mercersb. 9: 539. — Am. Meth. M. 16: 381.
— Odell on. Ecl. R. 5: 131.
— Origin of. (G. W. Cox) Fortn. 6: 407. — (W. Drake) Arch. 5: 306, 379.
— — and History of. (G. P. Marsh) Cornh. 7: 138.
— — Weisse on. (F. A. March) Nation, 28: 153. — Internat. R. 6: 334.
— Orthoepy of. Am. Q. 4: 191.
— Orthography of. (F. W. Newman) Fraser, 96: 565. — Am. Q. 22: 172. — So. Lit. Mess. 10: 544.
— Our Mother Tongue. Lond. Q. 22: 429.
— Our spoken. (D. H. Wheeler) Meth. Q. 30: 526.
— past and present, Trench on. Chr. Obs. 55: 664. — Fraser, 52: 340.
— Philology of. (H. N. Day) New Eng. 2: 350.
— — Earle's. (J. Hadley) Nation, 14: 155.
— — Richardson's. Mo. R. 82: 81.
— Phonology of. (H. N. Day) Am. Bib. Repos. 2d s. 10: 432.
— Du Ponceau on. Anal. M. 14: 16.
— Place of, in Education. (J. Crompton) Victoria, 7: 533.
— — in higher Education. (A. B. Stark) Pop. Sci. Mo. 14: 81.
— Plain English. All the Year, 20: 205.

English Language, Portuguese Guide to. All the Year, **23**: 348.
— Present State of. (T. De Quincey) Hogg, **6**: 97.
— Pronunciation of. (F. Hall) Nation, **22**: 94. — (C. S. Peirce) No. Am. **98**: 342. — (R. G. White) Galaxy, **20**: 110, 547.
— — and Spelling of. (W. D. Whitney) New Eng. **19**: 913.
— — Early. (J. Hadley) No. Am. **110**: 420.
— Purity of. (F. Hall) No. Am. **119**: 308.
— Queen's English. Ed. R. **120**: 39. — Ecl. M. **63**: 406. — (H. Alford) Good Words, **4**: 191, 428, 756. **8**: 21. Same art. Liv. Age, **93**: 367.
— — Alford on. (W. D. Whitney) No. Am. **103**: 563. — Chr. Obs. **64**: 613.
— — Plea for. (E. L. Godkin) Nation, **2**: 340.
— — *vs.* Dean's English. (H.C.Cameron) Princ. **39**: 558.
— Rambles over the Realms of Verbs and Substantives. (W. Swinton) Putnam, **4**: 472, 602.
— Rational and irrational. (F. E. Hall) 19th Cent. **8**: 424. Same art. Ecl. M. **95**: 526.
— Remarks on. (W. Blair) Land We Love, **4**: 114.
— Revolutions in. No. Brit. **50**: 65. Same art. Liv. Age, **101**: 515.
— Saxon Element in. House. Words, **18**: 89.
— Spelling of. *See* Spelling.
— Structure of. (H. Rogers) Ed. R. **70**: 221. — Blackw. **45**: 455.
— — Mulligan on. Ecl. R. **99**: 13.
— Study of. (H. N. Day) Am. J. Educ. **16**: 641. — (D. Huntington) Am. Inst. of Instruc. **1846**: 83. — (G. F. Holmes) N. Ecl. **7**: 400. — Liv. Age, **65**: 218. — Macmil. **15**: 520.
— — in Common Schools. (J. W. Gibbs) New Eng. **18**: 429.
— — in Germany. (H. M. Kennedy) Lippinc. **24**: 491.
— — in Schools. (J. R. Seeley) Macmil. **17**: 75.
— — Method of. (E. Ferrier) Luth. Q. **1**: 57.
— Synonyms of. Quar. **35**: 403. — Fraser, **44**: 256. Same art. Liv. Age, **31**: 196. Same art. Ecl. M. **24**: 270.
— Teaching of. (E. A. Abbott) Macmil. **18**: 33. Same art. Ev. Sat. **5**: 655. Same art. Liv. Age, **97**: 596. — (A. Bain) Fortn. **12**: 200. Same art. Appleton, **2**: 49, 85, 115. — (A. B. Stark) Education, **1**: 492. — (F. W. Newman) Fraser, **97**: 18. Same art. Liv. Age, **137**: 115.
— Technical and slang Terms. (G. Wakeman) Putnam, **15**. 294.
— Teutonic, and its Debasers. (H. Thurston) Month, **32**: 358. **33**: 301.
— Trench's Select Glossary of. Liv. Age, **62**: 747.
— True Means of Education. (P. R. Shipman) Pop. Sci. Mo. **17**: 145.
— Two Tongues. (W. Mitchell) Atlan. **6**: 667.
— White's Every-Day. (F. Hall) Nation, **31**: 275.
— Words of. Chamb. J. **44**: 737, 758.
— — Trench's Study of. New Eng. **10**: 438.
— — White on. (C. A. Bristed) No. Am. **112**: 469. — New Eng. **30**: 305. — Atlan. **46**: 427. — O. & N. **3**: 223. *See* Words.
English Law, Story of. Chamb. J. **26**: 18.
English Lecturers in America. (W. C. Brownell) Galaxy, **20**: 62.
English Letters, Four Centuries of. (Sir H. Taylor) 19th Cent. **10**: 405. Same art. Ecl. M. **97**: 721. Same art. Liv. Age, **151**: 131. — (N. C. Perkins) Dial (Ch.), **1**: 129.
English Liberals and Continental. Fraser, **101**: 222.
English Literary Men, Reminiscences of. Dem. R. **14**: 492.
English Literati. So. Lit. Mess. **15**: 744.
English Literature. (W. H. Prescott) No. Am. **49**: 317. — Brit. & For. R. **1**: 190. — For. Q. **15**: 347. **18**: 392. **24**: 174. — Ed. R. **64**: 269. — Westm. **25**: 234. — U. S. Cath. M. **6**: 13. — West. M. **1**: 289.
— and Anglicanism in 1841. Chr. Rem. **1**: 432.
— and French Literature. Ed. R. **35**: 158.
— and Reformation. (E. E. Higbee) Mercersb. **14**: 508.
— Angus's Handbook of. Chr. Obs. **65**: 927. **67**: 952.
— Brief Notes on. (J. G. Cazenove) Am. Church R. **19**: 302.
— Characteristics of. (N. Porter) Am. Bib. Repos. 2d s. **3**: 329.
— Chateaubriand on. (Sir E. B. Lytton) Ed. R. **64**: 506. — Dem. R. **26**: 113.
— Classical. Nat. Q. **40**: 41.
— — Use of. (H. G. Robinson) Macmil. **2**: 425.
— Contemporary, 1851. Westm. **57**: 247, 625.
— Early. (A. Gilman) Atlan. **40**: 430. — New York R. **2**: 431. — Colburn, **35**: 115–243. — Kitto, **40**: 1. — Westm. **96**: 156. Same art. Liv. Age, **111**: 195.
— — and later. (T. Parsons) No. Am. **10**: 19.
— — Anglo-Saxon Bookmen. House. Words, **17**: 498.
— — before Chaucer, Morley's. Brit. Q. **40**: 199. Same art. Ecl. M. **63**: 200.
— — Beowulf. House. Words, **17**: 459.
— — Havelok the Dane. House. Words, **17**: 543.
— — Hippisley on. Mo. R. **144**: 97.
— — Marsh on. (E. Schuyler) New Eng. **22**: 172.
— — Prose Writers. Am. Mo. R. **1**: 24. — (C. Francis) Chr. Exam. **11**: 1.
— — Study of. (J. Alden) Lit. & Theo. R. **4**: 423.
— — Three Interests in. (D. Masson) Contemp. **21**: 199. Same art. Liv. Age, **116**: 323.
— Early English Texts. Ed. R. **125**: 219. Same art. Liv. Age, **92**: 707.
— Early English religious Writings. Chr. Rem. **55**: 113.
— Early English Treatises. Kitto, **40**: 1.
— Early Writers and Speakers. Colburn, **13**: 49.
— Elizabethan. (F. Jeffrey) Ed. R. **18**: 275. — Selec. Ed. R. **1**: 170.
— — Characteristics of. (E. P. Whipple) Atlan. **19**: 144.
— — Pastoral Writers of. Tait, n. s. **22**: 577.
— German Influence in. (T. S. Perry) Atlan. **40**: 129.
— Gothic Renaissance in. No. Brit. **43**: 461. Same art. Liv. Age, **88**: 241.
— Guide to. (M. Arnold) 19th Cent. **2**: 843. Same art. Ecl. M. **90**: 142.
— History of, Craik's. (E. Schuyler) No. Am. **98**: 576.
— — Morley's. Canad. Mo. **4**: 455. — (J. V. O'Conor) Cath. World, **29**: 337.
— — Scoones's Four Centuries of. (W. C. Brownell) Nation, **31**: 241.
— — Taine's. (J. Bascom) Bib. Sac. **30**: 628. — (W. H. Browne) So. M. **10**: 105. — (W. L. Kingsley) New Eng. **31**: 542. — (T. R. Lounsbury) Nation, **14**: 10 — (A. D. Mayo) Mo. Rel. M. **47**: 486. — (J. G. Meline) Cath. World, **15**: 1. — (L. Stephen) Fortn. **20**: 693. Same art. Ev. Sat. **16**: 61. — Dub. R. **74**: 39. — Ed. R. **121**: 252. Same art. Ecl. M. **65**: 44, 146. — Fraser, **85**: 370. — Westm. **81**: 473. **83**: 1.
— — Yonge's. (T. R. Lounsbury) Nation, **14**: 308.
— in 17th and 18th Centuries. Ox. Prize Ess. **3**: 81.
— in 18th Century. (A. Andrews) Colburn, **102**: 70. Temp. Bar, **3**: 402.
— — Twickenham and. Fraser, **61**: 124–834. Same art. Liv. Age, **65**: 283, 330.
— in 19th Century. (W. H. Prescott) No. Am. **35**: 165. — Hogg, **9**: 41. Same art. Ecl. M. **26**: 137.
— — 1815–40. (S. Walpole) Appleton, **21**: 137, 214.
— — under Victoria. (J. McCarthy) Appleton, **21**: 498.
— in Germany. (J. B. Angell) No. Am. **84**: 311.

English Literature, Influence of the Reformation upon. Lond. Q. **4**: 289.
— Italian Influence on. Fraser, **60**: 697. — (J. A. Symonds) Fortn. **23**: 371. Same art. Liv. Age, **125**: 131.
— Modern. Fraser, **60**: 97. Same art. Ecl. M. **48**: 84.
— Modern Prose. (G. Saintsbury) Fortn. **25**: 243. Same art. Ecl. M. **86**: 400. Same art. Liv. Age, **128**: 707.
— Monkish. Lond. Q. **1**: 393.
— Musæ Britannicæ. Ed. R. **123**: 365.
— Notes on. Cornh. **22**: 437, 595, 700.
— of the Restoration. Dryden. Brit. Q. **20**: 1.
— Outlook of. (J. M. Hoppin) Putnam, **15**: 649.
— Personalities of the Augustan Age. Blackw. **10**: 312.
— Recent Works on. (E. Ferrier) Luth. Q. **2**: 435.
— Reed's Lectures on. (C. C. Felton) No. Am. **81**: 252. — Liv. Age, **46**: 559.
— Rise and Progress of. Am. Cath. Q. **4**: 456.
— Sir Walter Scott and the Romantic Reaction. (J. Wedgwood) Contemp. **33**: 514. Same art. Liv. Age, **139**: 298.
— Scottish Influence on. (D. Masson) No. Brit. **17**: 283, Same art. Liv. Age, **35**: 1.
— Study of. (R. P. Dunn) Bib. Sac. **23**: 235. — (T. R. Lounsbury) New Eng. **29**: 572.
See English Poets.
English Loyalty, Liberal's View of. (E. Faithful) O. & N. **7**: 567.
English Lutheran Church in New York City, History of. (G. P. Ockershausen) Luth. Q. **7**: 269.
English Maiden's Love; a Poem. Cath. World, **2**: 27.
English Maiden's Love; a Tale. (G. A. Salter) Cath. World, **18**: 694.
English Mail-Coach; or the Glory of Motion. Blackw. **66**: 485, 741.
English Manners. (A. F. Marshall) Am. Cath. Q. **5**: 105.
English Metrical Romances. (J. W. Hales) Fraser, **92**: 285. — (H. W. Longfellow) No. Am. **37**: 374.
— Ellis's Specimens. (Sir W. Scott) Ed. R. **7**: 387.
English Monasteries, Dissolution of. Ho. & For. R. **4**: 165.
English Moral Songs and Poems, Earlier. Blackw. **44**: 453. **45**: 303.
English National Airs, Chappell's Collection of. Dub. R. **11**: 263.
English Navigators, Early. Westm. **58**: 32.
English Newspapers and Printing of 17th Century. Nat. Q. **16**: 234. *See* Newspapers.
English Opera. Colburn, **45**: 478.
English People, Forefathers of. (T. H. Huxley) Nature, **1**: 514.
— Green's History of. Nature, **11**: 164. *See* England.
— of To-Day. (J. MacCarthy) Cath. World, **32**: 491.
— Origin of. (E. A. Freeman) Macmil. **21**: 415, 509. **22**: 31. Same art. Liv. Age, **105**: 67-771. — Anthrop. R. **7**: 279.
— — Pike on. Anthrop. R. **5**: 49.
— Origin and Political Life of. (M. B. Anderson) Chr. R. **15**: 28.
— Who are they? Fraser, **5**: 98.
English Photographs. Tinsley, **2**: 101-656. **3**: 88-654.
English Physique. (F. N. Broome) Macmil. **22**: 128.
— and American. (G. M. Beard) No. Am. **129**: 588.
English Plagiarism. Chr. Exam. **37**: 423.
English-plated Americans. Ev. Sat. **11**: 43.
English Poetry. Knick. **27**: 1. — So. Lit. Mess. **1**: 397, 557. **2**: 101. — Ed. R. **42**: 47. — Fraser, **7**: 198.
— Ancient. Retros. **17**: 144, 209.
— at the Close of last Century. (O. W. B. Peabody) No. Am. **42**: 52.
— Campbell's Specimens of. Blackw. **4**: 696. **5**: 217. — Mo. R. **90**: 393. — (F. Jeffrey) Ed. R. **26**: 181. — Fraser, **25**: 353. — Anal. M. **14**: 111.
English Poetry, Century of. (A. C. Swinburne) Ecl. M. **95**: 641.
— Chapters on. Tait, n. s. **8**: 303-681.
— Cycle of. Temp. Bar, **38**: 217-451. **39**: 201, 457. **40**: 169, 478.
— Descriptive. Blackw. **45**: 573.
— — from Anne to Victoria. (E. T. Palgrave) Fortn. **5**: 298.
— Early. Brit. Q. **6**: 333. — New York R. **7**: 366. — Ed. Mo. R. **5**: 456. — Retros. **15**: 147. — Dub. Univ. **47**: 611. — No. Brit. **36**: 412.
— Elizabethan. Brit. Q. **42**: 29. Same art. Ecl. M. **65**: 465.
— Ellis's Specimens of. (Sir W. Scott) Ed. R. **42**: 31. — Ed. R. **4**: 151.
— from Dryden to Cowper. Quar. **112**: 146.
— from Queen Anne. (F. Jeffrey) Ed. R. **27**: 1. — Selec. Ed. R. **1**: 180.
— Fugitive Songs and Lyrics. Ed. R. **140**: 355. Same art. Liv. Age, **123**: 515.
— Gems of. Hogg, **4**: 193. **5**: 321.
— Growth of. Quar. **110**: 435.
— Hazlitt's Lectures on. Blackw. **2**: 556, 679. **3**: 71.
— Lanier's Science of. (W. M. Ferriss) Nation, **31**: 310.
— Latest Songs of Chivalry. (H. W. Preston) Atlan. **43**: 12.
— Lyrical. Cornh. **29**: 698. Same art. Liv. Age, **122**: 195.
— Modern. Am. Bib. Repos. 2d s. **1**: 206. — Irish Q. **1**: 351. — Dub. Univ. **64**: 386.
— of the 19th Century. (O. W. B. Peabody) No. Am. **50**: 488. — (G. S. Hillard) No. Am. **55**: 200.
— of 1849-53. (A. H. Clough) No. Am. **77**: 1.
— of 1851. Fraser, **43**: 492.
— of 1853. Dub. Univ. **42**: 253.
— of 1874. Dub. Univ. **84**: 181.
— Old. (J. R. Lowell) No. Am. **110**: 444. — U. S. Lit. Gaz. **1**: 321.
— Pastoral. Knick. **30**: 67.
— Present State of, 1873. St. James, **33**: 261. — Quar. **135**: 1. Same art. Liv. Age, **119**: 131. Same art. Ecl. M. **81**: 385.
— Rural. Cornh. **25**: 164. Same art. Liv. Age, **112**: 756.
— Shelley and Dialect Schools in. (E. Phelps) Lakeside, **8**: 331.
— Southey's Specimens of. Ed. R. **11**: 31.
— Stockdale's Lectures on. Ed. R. **12**: 62.
— Thoughts upon. So. Lit. Mess. **16**: 327, 509.
— under the Stuarts. Chr. Rem. **53**: 328.
— Vers de Société. (C. Dempster) No. Brit. **47**: 47.
— Versification in. Lond. M. **7**: 29-661. **10**: 29. — Mo. R. **114**: 14.
— *vs.* Cardinal Wiseman. (J. H. L. Hunt) Fraser, **60**: 747.
English Poets and Poetry. (E. P. Whipple) Am. Whig R. **2**: 30.
— Bell's Biography of. Fraser, **23**: 402.
— between Milton and Cowper. (E. Elliott) Tait, n. s. **9**: 221.
— Chalmers's. (R. Southey) Quar. **11**: 480. **12**: 60.
— Contemporary. (E. C. Stedman) No. Am. **103**: 221.
— Criticism on. (J. Foster) Ecl. R. **7**: 220.
— Descriptive, of last Century. (E. Maitland) No. Brit. **1**: 397.
— Early, Study of. (W. J. Walter) Godey, **21**: 31.
— Elizabethan, Minor. (E. P. Whipple) Atlan. **22**: 26. — Lond. Q. **19**: 43.
— Evenings with the younger. Dub. Univ. **28**: 383.
— — with the later. Dub. Univ. **29**: 573.
— Gossip with some old. (C. Ollier) Bentley, **1**: 98.
— Hazlitt's Lectures on. Quar. **19**: 424.
— Howitt's Homes and Haunts of. Tait, n. s. **14**: 190.

English Poets, Johnson's Lives of. (D. Dana) Lit. & Theo. R. 5: 72.—Liv. Age, 138: 86.
— Laureate. *See* Poets Laureate.
— Living, 1861. Dub. R. 49: 503.
— Minor. St. James, 24: 839.
— — in 1850. Chr. Rem. 20: 346.
— Modern. Quar. 126: 328. Same art. Liv. Age, 101: 579.
— — Forman's. (Goldwin Smith) Canad. Mo. 1: 278.
— Modern Female. (H. N. Coleridge) Quar. 66: 374.—Mus. 41: 41.
— New. Ed. R. 104: 337.—Putnam, 6: 225.
— Notes on. (A. C. Swinburne) Ecl. M. 96: 156.
— of the Melbourne Ministry. Westm. 29: 193.
— Preachers, and Politicians. Ecl. M. 9: 281.
— Victorian. (E. C. Stedman) Scrib. 5: 357. 6: 49. 7: 101, 463. 8: 100, 160. 9: 167, 426, 585. 10: 609, 679.
— — Stedman's. (W. H. Browne) So. M. 17: 754.—Canad. Mo. 9: 250.
— Ward's. (W. C. Brownell) Nation, 30: 439. 32: 209.—(H. N. Powers) Dial (Ch.), 1: 84, 258.
See British Poets.
English Political Poems, temp. Henry VI. and Edward IV. (Sir F. Madden) Arch. 29: 318.
English Political Satires. (J. Hannay) Quar. 101: 394.
English Political Songs and Satires. Retros. 18: 48.
— — 1199–1327. Mo. R. 151: 322.
English Politico-Commercial Companies. Dem.R. 17: 403.
English Preachers, Amer. Accounts of. Chr. Rem. 14: 178.
English Precursors of Newton. Liv. Age, 147: 131.
English Prefixes derived from the Greek. (J. W. Gibbs) Am. J. Sci. 56: 206.
English Press. (A. Marshall) Cath. World, 29: 544.—(N. Rowe) Contin. Mo. 5: 100, 139, 564. 6: 36, 135.
English Pride. Sharpe, 43: 318.
English Romanist Martyrs, 17th Century. (J. Morris) Month, 12: 478.
English Satire in 19th Cent. (E. Myers) Fraser, 104: 753.
English Scholars of 17th Century. (B. B. Thacher) Am. Bib. Repos. 10: 1.
English Science. Brit. & For. R. 1: 134.
English Society Journals. (A. Marshall) Cath. World, 30: 660.
English Songs. (W. Maginn) Blackw. 17: 480.
— and Ballads, Old. Am. Ecl. 1: 499.
English Sonnets, Treasury of. Ecl. M. 94: 499.
English Stage, Fitzgerald on. (W. H. Browne) So. M. 16: 423.
— Present State of. Temp. Bar, 33: 456.
English Statesmanship, Phases of. Nat. Q. 11: 96.
English Statesmen in Undress. (P. Girard) Cath. World, 27: 549.
English Studies, Influence and Method of. (W. G. T. Shedd) Bib. Sac. 13: 325.
English Thought in 18th Century, Leslie Stephen on. (J. Hunt) Contemp. 29: 410.—(M. Pattison) Fortn. 27: 342.
— in 19th Century. (Prof. Winchester) Meth. Q. 41: 246.
English Trade and foreign Competition. Quar. 152: 271.
English Tragedy. Ed. R. 38: 177.
English Traits. (R. G. White) Galaxy, 23: 520.
— Emerson's. *See* England.
English Travelers. (E. Wigglesworth) Am. Q. Obs. 1: 270.
— in America. Dem. R. 6: 255.
English Views. So. Lit. J. 1: 415.
English Volunteer; a Tale of Carlist War. Peop. J. 4: 276.
English Women. (R. G. White) Galaxy, 23: 675.
— at Home. Bost. R. 2: 525. 3: 25.
English Work and Workers compared with French. (J. M. Ludlow) Good Words, 5: 728, 874.
Englishmen as a natural Curiosity. Lippinc. 2: 441.
Englishmen, Eccentric. (B. Murphy) Lippinc. 10: 155.
— Foreigners' Portraits of. House. Words, 1: 601.
Englishmen, Manners of. (R. G. White) Atlan. 42: 223.
— Old, painted by themselves. Month, 8: 599.
Engraving. (C. T. Hinckley) Sharpe, 30: 296. 31: 18.
— (C. F. Partington) J. Frankl. Inst. 1: 327. 2: 8–336. 3: 15.—No. Brit. 6: 141.—(H. R. Cleveland) No. Am. 49: 118.
— Ancient and modern. For. Q. 26: 312. 27: 40.
— and Burnet's Cartoons. Blackw. 45: 382.
— and multiplying Prints, New Method of. Art J. 16: 26.
— Art of. (C. T. Hinckley) Godey, 59: 109, 205.—(B. J. Lossing) Scrib. 4: 398.—Ecl. M. 53: 260.
— by Light and Electricity. J. Frankl. Inst. 64: 130.
— Dürer and early. Colburn, 128: 217.
— The Engraver. (W. J. Linton) Scrib. 16: 237.
— Golden Age of. (F. Keppel) Harper, 57: 321.
— History of. Cornh. 16: 295.
— Improvements in, 1858. (W. H. F. Talbot) J. Frankl. Inst. 67: 193.
— in Aquatinta. (C. F. Partington) J. Frankl. Inst. 2: 310, 336.
— in Mezzotinto. (C.F. Partington) J. Frankl. Inst. 2: 201.
— Ivory or Dürertype. (H. Dircks) J. Frankl. Inst. 40: 137.
— on Metal. (J. Sartain) J. Frankl. Inst. 109: 245.
— on Steel. All the Year, 16: 372.
— — Improvements in, 1829, Warren on. J. Frankl. Inst. 7: 166.
— on Wood. *See* Wood Engraving.
— Origin and early History of. Ecl. R. 46: 363.
— State of, 1825. Ecl. R. 42: 519.
— Substitutes for. Art J. 18: 87.
Engraving Plates for Typographic Presses, New System of, 1873. (J. L. Ringwalt) J. Frankl. Inst. 97: 39.
Engravings, Ancient Portfolio of. (W. B. Scott) Fraser, 99: 256, 289.
— Collection of. Chr. Rem. 8: 506.
— Thomas Dodd's Collection of. Temp. Bar, 47: 322.
— Old, Cleaning and Restoration of. Art J. 4: 332.
— Rare, and their Prices. Cornh. 16: 295.
Enharmonic of the Ancients. (T. P. Thompson) Westm. 16: 429. 17: 260, 522.
Enharmonic Organ. (T. P. Thompson) Westm. 22: 56.
See also Music, Perfect Intonation in.
Enigma, An. (A. de Fonblanque) Belgra. 45: supp. 103.
Enigma, An. Colburn, 63: 286.
Enigmas. Victoria, 32: 210.—All the Year, 37: 318.
— of Life. *See* Greg, W. R.
Enjoyment, Duty of. Pop. Sci. Mo. 16: 640.
Enlightenment and Religion. (D. van Pelt) Ref. Q. 28: 85.
Ennius, Poems of. Chr. Rem. 38: 489.
Ennui. Colburn, 5: 574.—Am. Q. 9: 33.
— Cure for. So. Lit. Mess. 9: 391.
Enoch, Book of. (M. J. Cramer) Meth. Q. 29: 424.—(A. G. Laurie) Univ. Q. 35: 163.—For. Q. 24: 351.—Fraser, 8: 511.
— and Apocrypha. (A. G. Laurie) Univ. Q. 35: 163, 339.
— Works on. Chr. Obs. 29: 417, 496.
Enoch Reade. (J. D. Cartwright) Sharpe, 35: 257.
Enough at Christmas. (W. B. Jerrold) Belgra. 1: 291.
Ense, Varnhagen von, Autobiog. of. Liv. Age, 14: 413.
— Memoirs of. Westm. 32: 60.—(T. Carlyle) For. Q. 26: 241.
Ensign O'Donoghue's first Love. Fraser, 4: 79.
Ensign Rollynge's Christmas Guard in the Jungle. Lond. Soc. 21: 75.
Ensor, George, Independent Man. (J. Foster) Ecl. R. 5: 289, 380.
Entail and Primogeniture. Dem. R. 25: 17.—(G. Fitzhugh) De Bow, 27: 172.—Mo. R. 163: 535.
— English Law of. Blackw. 64: 1.—All the Year, 44: 539, 558.
— French Law of. Ed. R. 40: 350.

Entail, Scotch Law of. (J. Moncrieff) No. Brit. **7**: 441. — Ed. R. **43**: 442.
Entails of Land. Quar. **83**: 178.
Entertaining, Art of. Eng. Dom. M. **18**: 247–298. **19**: 22–132. **20**: 9.
Entertainment made easy. All the Year, **44**: 130.
Entertainments of the past Winter, 1842. Dial, **3**: 45.
— Out-of-Door. All the Year, **42**: 447, 463.
Enthusiasm. So. Lit. Mess. **27**: 292.
— Influence of, on Happiness. (M. de Staël) West. J. **7**: 138.
— Natural Hist. of. Ecl. R. **49**: 469. — West. M. **2**: 521.
— — Taylor's. (R. Robbins) Chr. Q. Spec. **4**: 418. — Spirit Pilg. **3**: 256, 330. — Mo. R. **119**: 159.
— Nature and Conditions of. (G. H. Emerson) Univ. Q. **16**: 5.
— of Genius. (J. H. Hartzell) Univ. Q. **22**: 93.
— Religious, Nott's Sermons on. Chr. Obs. **4**: 553, 619.
— *versus* Impediment. (H. Lake) Belgra. **17**: 122.
Enthusiasm; or the Young Pastor. (Mrs. J. Thayer) Godey, **23**: 109, 157.
Enthusiast, The; an Autobiography. (J. R. Brown) So. Lit. Mess. **8**: 261.
Enticed; a Poem. (W. C. Wilkinson) Putnam, **14**: 154.
Entomologist in the South. All the Year, **11**: 440.
Entomology. Westm. **50**: 57. Same art. Ecl. M. **15**: 458. Same art. Liv. Age, **20**: 1. — Mo. R. **84**: 268. **109**: 241. — Dub. Univ. **1**: 318. — (W. S. Dallas) Pop. Sci. R. **18**: 147.
— Address before American Association. (J. L. LeConte) Am. Natural. **9**: 481.
— Anniversary Address. (A. R. Wallace) Nature, **3**: 435.
— Australian. Colburn, **162**: 195.
— Economic. (J. L. LeConte) Am. Natural. **7**: 710. — Nature, **6**: 197.
— Every-Day. Chamb. J. **8**: 118, 183, 220.
— in America. Nature, **1**: 379. **17**: 229. **19**: 309.
— Indian, Atkinson's. (R. McLachlan) Nature, **21**: 173.
— Kirby and Spence on. Ecl. R. **23**: 572. **28**: 116. **104**: 382.
— Modern. (S. H. Scudder) Nature, **22**: 550.
— of Massachusetts. (W. B. O. Peabody) No. Am. **54**: 73.
— of United States. (J. G. Morris) Am. J. Sci. **51**: 17.
— Progress and Prospects of. For. Q. **15**: 195.
See also Insects.
Entomostraca, Fresh-Water. (C. L. Herrick) Am. Natural. **13**: 620.
— Method of collecting. (G. S. Brady) Nature, **8**: 68.
Entozoa, Migration of. (A. Pouchet) Canad. J. n. s. **7**: 372.
— Natural History of. Intel. Obs. **6**: 190.
— New Researches in. (T. S. Cobbold) Nature, **6**: 278.
— Vegetables, Fruit, and Water as Sources of Intestinal Worms. (T. S. Cobbold) Pop. Sci. R. **4**: 163.
Entozoon from the Eel. (S. Lockwood) Am. Natural. **6**: 449.
Entr'acte. Lond. Soc. **39**: 248.
Entrapped. (Mrs. A. Fraser) Tinsley, **17**: 531.
Entwisle, Joseph. Meth. Q. **11**: 305.
Envelopes, Commercial. Chamb. J. **32**: 280.
Envy and Scandal. Knick. **33**: 527.
Enyed, Transylvania, Sack of, 1849. Colburn, **92**: 97.
Eocenes of England, how deposited? (J. S. Gardner) Pop. Sci. R. **17**: 282.
Eocene Flora in the Arctic Regions. (J. S. Gardner) Nature, **20**: 10.
— of Bournemouth. (J. S. Gardner) Nature, **21**: 181.
Eon de Beaumont, Chevalier, Ambassador of doubtful Sex. St. James, **30**: 41. — Lond. Soc. **40**: 528.
— and the Will of Peter the Great. (O. C. D. Ross) Gent. M. n. s. **18**: 159.
Eothen. *See* East, The.
Eozöon Canadense. (W. B. Carpenter) Intel. Obs. **7**: 278. — (L. S. Burbank) Am. Natural. **5**: 535. — (W. B. Carpenter and J. W. Dawson) Nature, **20**: 328.
— New Specimens of. (J. W. Dawson) Am. J. Sci. **96**: 245.
Eozöon Question, Möbius on. Nature, **20**: 272, 297. — (J. W. Dawson) Am. J. Sci. **117**: 196.
— Reply to Dawson on. (K. Möbius) Am. J. Sci. **118**: 177.
Epaminondas of Thebes. (J. W. Calcraft) Dub. Univ. **40**: 34.
— and Gustavus Adolphus. Ecl. M. **27**: 106.
Ephesus. Art J. **14**: 172.
— Church at. (J. M. Bellew) Art J. **16**: 10.
— Council of, A. D. 431. (H. A. Miles) Chr. Exam. **54**: 49.
— Cyprus, and Mycenæ, Excavations at. (J. B. Taylor) No. Am. **126**: 111.
— Letter from. Am. Arch. **6**: 118.
— of the Church History. (J. Young) O. & N. **6**: 538. — Broadw. **10**: 547.
— Pagan and Christian. Dub. Univ. **74**: 377.
— Robber Synod of, A. D. 449. Month, **23**: 239.
— Temple of Diana at. Arch. **11**: 1. — Westm. **79**: 310. — Penny M. **11**: 167.
— Topography of. (J. S. Jewell) Meth. Q. **31**: 279.
— Visit to. (J. L. Porter) Good Words, **22**: 781, 822.
— Wood's Discoveries at. (F. A. Paley) Am. Cath. Q. **2**: 460. — Am. Arch. **2**: 26. — Brit. Q. **65**: 366. Same art. Liv. Age, **133**: 387. — Ed. R. **145**: 204. Same art. Liv. Age, **132**: 626. — Pop. Sci. Mo. **7**: 223.
Ephod, Robe of the. (J. A. Seiss) Evang. R. **6**: 114.
Ephphatha; a Poem. (H. E. Warner) Scrib. **10**: 168.
Ephrata, Penn., Brethren of. (M. Schele de Vere) Hours at Home, **4**: 458.
Epic and the Romantic, The. Lond. M. **16**: 309.
— Our earliest. (A. Gilman) Lakeside, **5**: 306.
— of Hades. Dub. Univ. **87**: 627.
— of the Lion. (V. Hugo) Blackw. **123**: 703.
Epics, Recent. Quar. **90**: 333.
Epic Composition, Art of. Blackw. **42**: 737.
Epic Poetry, National. (W. A. Stevens) Bib. Sac. **28**: 613.
— of India. Ho. & For. R. **4**: 512.
— Philosophy of. (D. A. Wasson) No. Am. **107**: 501.
Epicene Gender on the Stage. (F. Parke) Dub. Univ. **85**: 248.
Epicier, The. Westm. **31**: 355.
Epictetus. Colburn, **118**: 296. — (C. P. Hawes) Radical, **2**: 33.
— Higginson's. (H. James, jr.) No. Am. **102**: 599.
— Works of. (O. B. Frothingham) Nation, **1**: 502.
Epicure's Christmas Story. (W. Maynard) Gent. M. n. s. **2**: 227.
Epicurean Philosophy. Am. Q. **1**: 357. — (C. A. Aiken) Princ. **39**: 196.
Epicurean Theory of Life. (W. R. Alger) Mo. Rel. M. **7**: 361.
Epicurean Tour. Belgra. **35**: 154.
Epicureanism, Ancient and modern. (F. W. Newman) Fraser, **84**: 606. Same art. Liv. Age, **111**: 771.
— True. New Eng. M. **3**: 353.
Epicurus. (E. Pond) Chr. R. **17**: 33.
— and Epicureans. (O. B. Frothingham) Chr. Exam. **71**: 1.
— and his Philosophy. (E. I. Sears) Nat. Q. **16**: 209.
— Guyau's Ethical System of. (H. Sidgwick) Mind, **4**: 582.
Epidemics. (D. W. Cheever) No. Am. **91**: 438. — (J. Fayrer) Nature, **21**: 229. — House. Words, **13**: 397. Same art. Liv. Age, **50**: 181. — Westm. **52**: 301. Same art. Ecl. M. **19**: 455.
— affecting Vegetation. No. Brit. **38**: 366.
— Ancient and modern. Nat. Q. **17**: 247.

Epidemics and their Causes; Cholera. Nat. Q. **12**: 105.
— British. Brit. Q. **43**: 29.
— Cause of. Mus. **44**: 373.
— — and Prevention of. (A. N. Bell) Harper, **15**: 194.
— Great. (R. H. Patterson) Belgra. **10**: 35.
— History of. Cornh. **11**: 591.
— in Ireland. Dub. R. **41**: 76.
— Mental. Fraser, **65**: 490.
— of the Middle Ages. Blackw. **75**: 352. Same art. Ecl. M. **32**: 83. — Chamb. J. **12**: 132. **32**: 375. *See* Black Death.
— Origin of, Forster on. Ecl. R. **50**: 132.
— — and Distribution of. Pop. Sci. R. **4**: 593. Same art. Cath. World, **2**: 420. Same art. Ecl. M. **66**: 297.
— Propagation and Prevention of. Month, **11**: 436.
— Sun-Spots and. (E. W. Cushing) Internat. Q. **8**: 417.
Epidemic Monomania. (I. Ray) Chr. Exam. **50**: 457.
Epigram, The. (R. M. Walsh) Lippinc. **6**: 74. — So. Lit. Mess. **14**: 663, 718.
Epigrams. (J. Hannay) Temp. Bar, **21**: 465. — (M. Collins) Belgra. **14**: 498. — (W. Mathews) Lakeside, **3**: 129. — (C. A. Ward) Gent. M. n. s. **20**: 235. — Blackw. **93**: 750. Same art. Liv. Age, **78**: 3. — Chamb. J. **39**: 404. — Colburn, **5**: 35. — Ho. & For. R. **3**: 84. — No. Brit. **42**: 42. — Quar. **117**: 204.
— Ancient and modern. Liv. Age, **76**: 516.
— and Epigrammatists. Ecl. M. **35**: 542.
— Essay on. (M. W. Hazletine) Cath. World, **15**: 467.
— German. Lond. M. **9**: 237, 297, 517.
— Gossip on. Sharpe, **10**: 283.
— Greek, translated. Temp. Bar, **41**: 493.
— a lost literary Art. All the Year, **25**: 34.
— Some modern. Ev. Sat. **11**: 95.
Epigrammatists and Epigrams. (J. Davies) Contemp. **14**: 616.
Epilepsy, Cooke's History of. Mo. R. **103**: 407.
Epileptics, Treatment of, in France. (S. I. Lesley) O. & N. **4**: 502.
Epilogues. All the Year, **32**: 80.
Epimanes. (E. A. Poe) So. Lit. Mess. **2**: 235.
Epinay, Mme. d', Memoirs of. (Syd. Smith) Ed. R. **31**: 44. Same art. Anal. M. **13**: 326. — Mo. R. **88**: 515.
Epiphany. (W. P. Lunt) Mo. Rel. M. **7**: 83. — (J. A. Shea) U. S. Cath. M. **4**: 29. — Cath. World, **12**: 557.
— in Provence. Once a Week, **21**: 512.
— the Supreme. (J. W. Nevin) Mercersb. **25**: 211.
Epirus, Notes of Travel in. (W. V. Chirol) Fortn. **35**: 302.
— South, Among the Albanians of. Blackw. **129**: 304.
Episcopacy. (L. Bacon) New Eng. **1**: 390, 545, 586. — (H. Bushnell) New Eng. **2**: 143. — (L. Bacon) New Eng. **2**: 309, 440. — (A. V. Griswold) Am. Church R. **13**: 69. **23**: 53.
— and the Apostolic Succession. Chr. Rem. **5**: 341. — — Cong. M. **22**: 189.
— and Congregationalism. Cong. M. **21**: 529.
— anti-republican and unevangelical. (A. D. Eddy) Am. Bib. Repos. 3d s. **1**: 315.
— as a Bond of Unity. (J. W. Nevin) Mercersb. **21**: 406.
— Brittan on. (S. Miller) Princ. **5**: 333.
— Claims of, examined. (G. R. Noyes) Chr. Exam. **25**: 190.
— Clementine Comment. Am. Church R. **23**: 53.
— Colton's Reasons for. (L. Bacon) Chr. Q. Spec. **8**: 591. — (J. A. Alexander) Princ. **8**: 390. — Chr. R. **1**: 552. — So. Lit. Mess. **2**: 453.
— from 1829 to 1850. Am. Church R. **4**: 22.
— High Church. (J. A. Alexander) Princ. **14**: 129.
— President Hopkins on. (M. A. Curtis) Am. Church R. **12**: 48, 263.
— in the Apostolic Constitutions. Am. Church R. **24**: 489.
— in 1844. (J. P. Thompson) New Eng. **3**: 140.
— in 1st Cent., Evidence for. Chr. Obs. **2**: 709. **3**: 1, 129.
Episcopacy in Massachusetts. (N. Porter) New Eng. **2**: 619.
— in the Primitive Church. Am. Church R. **29**: 388. — Chr. Q. **4**: 78.
— in the Rough. All the Year, **4**: 470.
— in Scotland. (E. Maitland) No. Brit. **5**: 66.
— its Claim to Divine Right examined. Ecl. R. **82**: 621.
— its Harmony with Cyprian. (A. Varien) Mercersb. **5**: 555.
— New Theory of. (J. A. Alexander) Princ. **7**: 573.
— Origin of. Am. Presb. R. **3**: 28.
— — and Growth of. (R. D. Hitchcock) Am. Presb. R. **16**: 133.
— Primitive and English. Ecl. R. **65**: 305.
— Schisms of. Ecl. R. **114**: 633.
— Scotch, 1866. Chr. Obs. **66**: 946
— Sparks on. Brownson, **1**: 386.
— tested by Scripture. (S. Miller) Princ. **7**: 239. — (A. Barnes) Chr. Q. Spec. **6**: 1.
— Unity in. (A. J. Gordon) Bost. R. **5**: 389.
— with reference to modern Popular Societies. Pamph. **16**: 421.
— Wyatt and Sparks on. Chr. Disc. **2**: 287.
See Bishops.
Episcopal Amenities a Century ago. Once a Week, **22**: 229.
Episcopal Catholicism. (S. W. S. Dutton) New Eng. **5**: 247.
Episcopal Chairs. (C. Clarke) Arch. **11**: 317.
Episcopal Church. (A. Barnes) New Eng. **3**: 333.
— African Mission of. (H. R. Scott) Am. Church R. **30**: 304.
— American, in Continental Europe. Am. Church R. **20**: 96.
— and Church of England. (J. Williams) Am. Church R. **10**: 481. — (A. C. Coxe) Am. Church R. **11**: 624
— and Church of Rome. (H. M. Thompson) Am. Church R. **19**: 63.
— and the Denominations. (H. M. Thompson) Am. Church R. **13**: 220.
— and the Freedmen, 1865. (O. B. Frothingham) Nation, **1**: 742.
— and the Times. (T. M. Clark) Am. Church R. **5**: 75.
— and Unitarianism. (N. H. Chamberlain) Am. Church R. **18**: 566.
— and John Wesley. (A. Stevens) Meth. Q. **22**: 41.
— Chanting in, and its Author. Am. Hist. Rec. **3**: 18.
— Congregationalism in. (J. F. Spalding) Am. Church R. **28**: 261.
— Congress of, 1875. (A. F. Hewit) Cath. World, **22**: 473.
— — 1877. (G. Leeds) Am. Church R. **30**: 284.
— — Utility of. (J. H. Ward) Am. Church R. **27**: 56.
— Constitution and Canons of. Am. Church R. **23**: 15.
— Crisis in, 1871. (W. G. Sumner) Nation, **13**: 222.
— Differences in. (G. W. Burnap) Chr. Exam. **34**: 1.
— Dioceses of, Division of. (H. D. Evans) Am. Ch. Mo. **3**: 368, 414.
— Doctrine of. (G. Burgess) Bib. Sac. **20**: 856.
— Extension of, in the West. (C. B. Stout) Am. Church R. **9**: 98.
— Evangelical Party in. (A. Barnes) New Eng. **2**: 113.
— Hawks's History of. Am. Q. **19**: 254.
— High Church and Arminian Principles. (C. A. Goodrich) Chr. Q. Spec. **2**: 720.
— High Low Church. (J. A. Alexander) Princ. **16**: 517.
— History of. (C. R. Hale) Am. Church R. **28**: 130.
— identified with the Primitive, Wilson on. (I. M. Ely) New Eng. **9**: 564.
— in American Colonies. (J. Williams) Am. Church R. **6**: 591. — (S. M. Hopkins) Am. Presb. R. **9**: 1. — Chr. Rem. **8**: 149. **12**: 184.
— — Clergy of. (E. Allen) Am. Church R. **6**: 591.
— — in 1776. Cong. Q. **2**: 311.
See American Episcopate.

Episcopal Church in Canada. (W. Q. Ketchum) Am. Church R. **28**: 59.
— in Connecticut Colony. (C. J. Hoadly) Am. Church R. **10**: 106.
— in Connecticut, Beardsley's History. (J. Williams) Am. Church R. **18**: 43. — (L. Bacon) New Eng. **25**: 283. — Chr. Obs. **67**: 354.
— in England and America. New York R. **8**: 285.
— in Ireland. Dub. Univ. **1**: 385, 400.
— in Kentucky. (J. A. Merrick) Am. Church R. **10**: 116.
— in Maryland. (E. Allen) Am. Church R. **7**: 302, 595. **8**: 264. — (E. D. Neill) Hist. M. **13**: 82. — Hist. M. **13**: 151.
— in Massachusetts Colony. Am. Church R. **26**: 1.
— in New England. (L. Bacon) New Eng. **25**: 454. — (T. C. Pitkin) Am. Church R. **2**: 405.
— in New Hampshire. Hist. M. **17**: 353.
— — Position and Wants of. (E. B. Boggs) Am. Church R. **16**: 612.
— in N. Y. City, Early Hist. of. Am. Church R. **20**: 507.
— in No. Carolina. (F. L. Hawks) Am. Church R. **3**: 300.
— — Early Hist. of. (J. Buxton) Am. Church R. **28**: 445.
— in Pennsylvania. (F. L. Hawks) Am. Church R. **3**: 276. — (E. Evans) Hist. M. **19**: 380.
— in Scotland, Constitution of. Chr. Obs. **45**: 599.
— — Review of. Chr. Obs. **44**: 224, 469.
— — Works on. Chr. Obs. **46**: 231.
— in the United States, Adaptedness to the People. (A. B. Carter) Am. Church R. **7**: 399. — Chr. Obs. **70**: 343. — O. & N. **10**: 593.
— — and in Canada. Am. Church R. **30**: 106.
— — and Nation. (E. B. Boggs) Am. Church R. **28**: 620.
— — Baptismal Regeneration and Ritualism in. Chr. Obs. **72**: 326.
— — Characteristics of. (G. W. Ridgely) Am. Church R. **31**: 291.
— — Coxe on. O. & N. **7**: 311.
— — General Convention of. (T. S. Preston) Cath. World, **8**: 461. **20**: 465. — Cath. World, **32**: 289.
— — — in 1785. (J. F. Howe) Am. Hist. Rec. **2**: 387.
— — — in 1853. (N. S. Richardson) Am. Church R. **6**: 234. — (J. H. Hobart) Am. Church R. **6**: 567.
— — — in 1856. (A. N. Littlejohn) Am. Church R. **9**: 561.
— — — in 1859. (R. A. Hallam) Am. Church R. **12**: 629.
— — — in 1862. (W. C. Doane) Am. Church R. **15**: 104.
— — — in 1865. (N. S. Richardson) Am. Church R. **17**: 452. — (R. A. Hallam) Am. Church R. **18**: 86.
— — — in 1871. Am. Church R. **23**: 122. — O. & N. **4**: 460. — (T. S. Preston) Cath. World, **14**: 506.
— — — in 1874. (C. W. Andrews) Am. Church R. **27**: 33.
— — — in 1877. (E. B. Boggs) Am. Church R. **29**: 446. — (G. Leeds) Am. Church R. **30**: 284. — (P. Girard) Cath. World, **26**: 395.
— — — in 1880. (J. H. Hopkins) Am. Church R. **33**: 65.
— — — Journals of. Am. Church R. **11**: 642. **12**: 139–648. **13**: 138–659.
— — History of. Chr. Rem. **7**: 317.
— — How governed. (H. Burgwin) Am. Church R. **35**: 111.
— — in 1859–62. Chr. Rem. **45**: 162.
— — Law of, Hoffman's. (J. H. Hopkins) Am. Church R. **3**: 533.
— — Bishop Potter's Pastoral Letter, 1866. New Eng. **25**: 377.
— — Remarks on. (A. C. Coxe) Am. Church R. **24**: 26.
— — Service Book of. Chr. Rem. **45**: 162.
— — Wilberforce on. Chr. Obs. **45**: 418.
— in Virginia. So. Lit. Mess. **2**: 282. — Chr. Obs. **45**: 705, 792. — (J. C. McCabe) Am. Church R. **6**: 119, 272, 436. **7**: 113. **8**: 125, 587. — (B. W. Morris) Am. Church R. **14**: 75, 448. **15**: 210, 585.
Episcopal Church, Increase of Efficiency in. (A. C. Coxe) Am. Church R. **9**: 415.
— Notes of. (G. F. Cushman) Am. Church R. **5**: 253.
— Organization of. Am. Church R. **20**: 257.
— Parties in. (T. M. Clark) Am. Church R. **5**: 219. **9**: 161. — (N. S. Richardson) Am. Church R. **18**: 597.
— Penal Law of. (J. V. Campbell) Am. Church R. **7**: 530.
— A Policy for. (W. Adams) Am. Church R. **29**: 529.
— Position and Duty of. New York R. **1**: 419.
— Question of the Day in, 1855. (P. Berry) Mercersb. **7**: 361.
— Relation to other Churches. (L. W. Bacon) New Eng. **33**: 239. — (A. C. Coxe) New Eng. **33**: 722.
— Religion in. (R. A. Hallam) Am. Church R. **7**: 71.
— Schisms in. Chr. Rem. **7**: 298.
— Status of. Am. Church R. **21**: 117.
— Stranger in. (L. Bacon) New Eng. **7**: 143.
— Toleration in. (E. B. Boggs) Am. Church R. **30**: 450.
Episcopal Churches, Protestant non-established. Chr. Obs. **70**: 343–927.
— Union of. Cath. World, **22**: 502.
Episcopal Clergy. (T. C. Pitkin) Am. Church R. **12**: 126.
Episcopal Controversy, Smyth on. Chr. Exam. **35**: 257.
Episcopal Missions and Bishop Southgate. (N. Porter) New Eng. **3**: 244.
Episcopal Ordination and the English Reformation. (J. H. Drumm) Am. Church R. **26**: 268, 321.
— Need of. (N. S. Richardson) Am. Church R. **17**: 367.
Episcopal Revenues. Ecl. R. **94**: 480.
Episcopal Rings of Investiture. (O. Morgan) Arch. **36**: 392.
Episcopal Visitations. Chr. Rem. **1**: 38, 271. **2**: 18.
— Ancient Mode of proceeding in. Chr. Rem. **3**: 562.
— History of, in England. Chr. Rem. **3**: 112.
Episcopate, The primitive. Ecl. R. **86**: 47.
— Tractarian and Ritualistic View of. Month, **34**: 1, 246.
— viewed as a Center of Unity. (P. Berry) Mercersb. **8**: 297.
— Yale on. (J. Anketell) Am. Church R. **19**: 437.
Episcopius, Simon. (E. de Courcelles) Meth. Q. **23**: 612.
— Calder's Memoirs of. Am. Meth. M. **19**: 75. — Ecl. R. **65**: 549.
Episode in the Life of Charles Mordaunt. (H. Kingsley) Lond. Soc. **21**: 1. Same art. Ev. Sat. **12**: 103.
— in the Life of a Strong-minded Woman. (M. Neil) Lippinc. **12**: 398.
— of Fiddletown. (Bret Harte) Scrib. **6**: 433–696.
— of Fort Desolation. (J. Clifford) Overland, **6**: 207.
— of the little Widow. (M. McConnell) Lakeside, **10**: 116.
— of Reign of Terror. (H. Balzac) Dub. Univ. **85**: 185.
Episodes in the Life of a Musician. (M. Betham-Edwards) Fraser, **87**: 422. Same art. Ecl. M. **80**: 652.
Epistles throughout the Year, McCarthy on. Month, **4**: 196.
Epistolæ obscurorum Virorum. (Sir W. Hamilton) Ed. R. **53**: 180. — Fraser, **59**: 114.
Epistolary Courtesies. All the Year, **30**: 136.
Epitaph, A curious. Temp. Bar, **27**: 234.
— Vicissitudes of an. (S. G. Drake) N. E. Reg. **11**: 67.
Epitaphs. (J. B. Hagany) Nat. M. **7**: 352. — Chamb. J. **46**: 124. — Chr. Obs. **69**: 609. — House. Words, **17**: 372. — Lond. M. **4**: 274.
— Ancient and modern. Chamb. J. **37**: 141.
— and Burial. (D. H. Strother) Harper, **17**: 799.
— and Churchyards. Sharpe, **32**: 156. **33**: 157. **34**: 252.
— and Elegiac Inscriptions. (J. W. Calcraft) Dub. Univ. **40**: 206.
— and Graveyards. (F. Lawrence) Sharpe, **14**: 345. Same art. Ecl. M. **25**: 229. Same art. Internat. M. **5**: 213.
— Christian. (J. McCaul) Canad. J. n. s. **11**: 272, 351. **12**: 1.
— Churchyard Wanderings. Colburn, **5**: 84.

Epitaphs, Curious. Chamb. J. **55**: 570. **57**: 666. — Hist. M. **5**: 372.
— English. Tait, n. s. **26**: 399.
— A few. Mo. Rel. M. **41**: 187.
— French and English. (F. P. Cobbe) Temp. Bar, **22**: 349. Same art. Ev. Sat. **5**: 271.
— Graveyard Literature. (W. N. Granger) Overland, **6**: 134.
— Old. Dub. Univ. **55**: 580.
— Pagan. (S. Northcote) Month, **14**: 185.
— Traders'. Chamb. J. **50**: 377.
— Writing their own. Chamb. J. **49**: 229.
Epizoötic, The American. All the Year, **29**: 105.
Epochs, Three great, 1830, 1840, 1850. Fraser, **22**: 534, 645.
Eppelein von Gailingen. Cornh. **41**: 452.
Epping Forest. (A. R. Wallace) Fortn. **30**: 628 Same art. Liv. Age, **139**: 707.
— History of. Ev. Sat. **11**: 247.
— Ivy Leaves from the Hermitage in. Fraser, **97**: 127-799. **98**: 130-796.
— Rescue of. (G. S. Lefevre) Contemp. **34**: 45.
Epping Hunt, Origin of. Tait, n. s. **17**: 528. Same art. Liv. Age, **27**: 159.
Epsom, At. All the Year, **22**: 273.
Epsom Downs. (A. H. Forrester) Bentley, **12**: 94.
Epsom Races. (H. James, jr.) Galaxy, **24**: 346. — House. Words, **3**: 241.
Epsom Salts. Penny M. **9**: 223.
— and Epsom Sports. (J. Wilkins) Once a Week, **14**: 526.
Epworth Disturbances and the Wesley Family. Chr. Obs. **41**: 482.
Equador, Halinski's Travels in. Bentley, **51**: 371.
Equality. (M. Arnold) Fortn. **29**: 313. Same art. Liv. Age, **137**: 67. — Atlan. **45**: 19.
— and Civilization. (W. H. Mallock) Contemp. **40**: 651.
— at Home. St. Paul's, **1**: 318.
— Human, an Absurdity. (A. Harris) Mercersb. **24**: 526.
Equation of Payments. (C. C. Gordon) Hunt, **6**: 212. — (T. P. Thompson) Westm. **18**: 263.
Equations, Earnshaw's Differential. Nature, **5**: 199.
— Numerical. (A. Vallas) Math. Mo. **3**: 10.
— — of Third Degree. (J. C. Porter) Math. Mo. **3**: 198.
— Reduction of. (J. B. Cherriman) Canad. J. n. s. **1**: 286.
— Solution of. (J. Borden) Math. Mo. **1**: 373.
Equestrians, Lady, Hints to. St. James, **1**: 348.
Equestrian Manager, Recollections of. Chamb. J. **57**: 49-826.
Equigraphic Projections of the Globe. (R. A. Proctor) Intel. Obs. **9**: 429.
Equilibrium, Law of, in the Lever. (T. Strong) Math. Mo. **3**: 283.
Equilibrium and Minimum, Relation between the States of. (J. Patterson) Math. Mo. **1**: 12, 38.
— of pulverulent Bodies. (J. Boussin) Ecl. Engin. **25**: 107.
Equipages of the present Day. Colburn, **61**: 95.
Equitable Adjustment Jurisdiction, Origin of. Quar. **32**: 92.
Equitable Villages in America. (W. Pare) J. Statis. Soc. **19**: 127.
Equity Courts, State of. Quar. **65**: 272.
Equity Jurisdiction. West. Law J. **3**: 49.
Equity Jurisprudence. (P. W. Chandler) West. Law J. **2**: 1.
— Story's. Brit. & For. R. **14**: 154. — Mo. R. **161**: 466.
Equity Reform, Probate Courts. Westm. **53**: 100.
Equivalents, Law of. (E. Payson) Nat. Q. **25**: 29.
Eras, Explanation of certain ancient and modern. Am. Q. Reg. **5**: 194.
Erard, Pierre, Piano-Maker. House. Words, **12**: 238. Same art. Liv. Age, **47**: 523. — Ecl. M. **37**: 125.
Erard, Sebastian and Pierre, Pianos. Colburn, **169**: 273.
Erasmus, Desiderius. (H. H. Milman) Quar. **106**: 1. Same art. Liv. Age, **62**: 643. — (C. T. Brooks) Chr. Exam. **49**: 80. — (J. Hamilton) Ex. H. Lec. **16**: 37. — (J. H. Wynne) Month, **18**: 348. — Cornh. **12**: 116. — Ecl. R. **100**: 341. Same art. Ecl. M. **33**: 310. Same art. Liv. Age, **43**: 28. — Fraser, **93**: 32, 178.
— and Greek Text of the Apocalypse. (Prof. Herzog) Kitto, **29**: 64.
— and his Influence. (E. I. Sears) Nat. Q. **20**: 311.
— and Luther. (B. Sadtler) Luth. Q. **5**: 547.
— and Sir Thomas More. (J. Tulloch) Good Words, **19**: 532, 594. — Sharpe, **14**: 233.
— and the Reformation. (R. B. Drummond) Theo. R. **7**: 331. — (H. Rogers) Good Words, **9**: 162, 227.
— as a Satirist. Cornh. **16**: 610. — No. Brit. **32**: 49. Same art. Ecl. M. **50**: 120. Same art. Liv. Age, **64**: 707.
— Character of. Brit. Q. **61**: 183. Same art. Liv. Age, **124**: 451.
— — and Literary Influence. (W. C. Wilkinson) Chr. R. **23**: 169.
— — and Writings. Temp. Bar, **38**: 23.
— Colloquies of. Chr. Obs. **77**: 373. — Dub. Univ. **89**: 662. — Ecl. R. **116**: 187. — Hogg, **1**: 53.
— — Translations. Dub. Univ. **42**: 545. **43**: 283, 684. **47**: 435.
— Days of. Fraser, **11**: 559.
— Early Years of. (J. Hamilton) Macmil. **11**: 351. Same art. Liv. Age, **85**: 54.
— in England. (R. B. Drummond) Theo. R. **5**: 163. — (J. Hamilton) Macmil. **12**: 397. — Penny M. **7**: 59-119.
— Letters of. (H. Southern) Retros. **5**: 249.
— Life of. So. R. **3**: 77. — Mo. R. **108**: 329. — (E. Pond) Bib. Sac. **19**: 106. — (J. A. Alexander) Princ. **1**: 267. — West. Mo. R. **2**: 550.
— — Butler's. Chr. Obs. **26**: 429.
— — Drummond's. (C. K. Paul) Theo. R. **10**: 405.
— — Passages from. Nat. R. **16**: 326. Same art. Liv. Age, **77**: 531.
— Praise of Folly. (S. Waddington) Tinsley, **20**: 502.
— Story of. (H. Rogers) Good Words, **9**: 122.
— Youth of. (R. B. Drummond) Theo. R. **4**: 331.
Erastianism *versus* Ecclesiasticism. (J. L. Davies) Contemp. **30**: 142.
Erastus and Excommunication. (J. L. Davies) Contemp. **18**: 527.
Erauso, Catalina de, Life of. Mus. **42**: 241.
Erbach, Count E. von, and Luther. Nat. M. **3**: 81.
Erckmann, E., and Chatrian, A. (C. A. Bristed) Lippinc. **1**: 325. — with portraits, Appleton, **4**: 79. — Ev. Sat. **9**: 779. — with portraits, Ev. Sat. **9**: 846. Lond. Soc. **25**: 490. Same art. Ev. Sat. **16**: 716.
— Conscript. Colburn, **135**: 57.
— Double Literary Career. (H. Villard) Hours at Home, **9**: 389.
— Novels of. Dub. R. **68**: 138. — Dub. Univ. **74**: 363. Same art. Ecl. M. **73**: 683. — Ed. R. **123**: 225. — Month, **5**: 196.
Erema; or, My Father's Sin. (R. D. Blackmore) Cornh. **34**: 513, 738. **35**: 1-617. **36**: 101, 257, 495. Same art. Harper, **54**: 49-879. **55**: 51-885.
Ereré, Brazil. (H. H. Smith) Scrib. **18**: 352.
Erfurt and Tilsit. Bentley, **55**: 53.
Ergot. (W. Carruthers) Am. Natural. **9**: 450.
Eric Waldershorn. House. Words, **13**: 590. Same art. Ecl. M. **39**: 302.
Eric's Funeral; a Poem. (M. Sangster) Harper, **51**: 15.
Erica (E. von Ingersleben) Liv. Age, **135**: 495-799. **136**: 14-785. **137**: 35-286.
Ericksons, The; a Tale. Dub. Univ. **51**: 344. Same art. Ecl. M. **44**: 79.

Ericsson, Capt. John. (W. C. Church) Scrib. **17**: 835. — with portrait, Ecl. M. **56**: 566.
— Caloric Ship. (A. Maverick) Putnam, **1**: 102.
— his "Destroyer" and her Gun. (C. Barnard) Scrib. **21**: 689.
— Inventions of. (E. Sargent) Atlan. **10**: 68.
— Propeller of. Nav. M. **2**: 581.
Erie Canal. (J. G. Stevens) Scrib. **15**: 117. — Am. Hist. Rec. **2**: 395. — Penny M. **8**: 262.
— Enlargement of. (J. B. Jervis) Hunt, **12**: 432.
— Future of. (J. B. Jervis) Internat. R. **5**: 379.
— Life on. (W. H. Rideing) Harper, **48**: 1.
— List of Places on. Hunt, **8**: 570.
— Opening of. Niles's Reg. **25**: 103.
— Origin of. (B. H. Wright) Hist. M. **15**: 323.
— — Trade and Tonnage of. (H. S. Dexter) Hunt, **9**: 148.
— Steam on. Hunt, **39**: 531.
Erie, Fort, Assault on, 1814. Mus. **43**: 427.
— Attack on. Portfo.(Den.) **15**: 97.
— Sortie from, 1814. (G. W. Holley) M. Am. Hist. **6**: 401.
Erie, Lake, Battle of. Anal. M. **3**: 252.
— — Sketches of Officers in. (U. Parsons) N. E. Reg. **17**: 17.
— — Speech at Celebration of, 1858. (U. Parsons) N. E. Reg. **13**: 171.
— Commerce of. Am. Whig R. **2**: 189.
— South Shore of. (J. P. Kirtland) Am. J. Sci. **63**: 215.
Erie Railroad. (J. N. Pomeroy) Nation, **13**: 85.
— and English Stock. Am. Law R. **6**: 230.
— Campaigns in 1868, and New York Stock Exchange. Fraser, **79**: 569.
— in 1835. (B. Wright) J. Frankl. Inst. **19**: 358, 423.
— in 1841. J. Frankl. Inst. **31**: 186–380.
— in 1846, Report of Committee on. J. Frankl. Inst. **43**: 217, 289.
— Lawsuit of. (J. S. Black) Galaxy, **13**: 376.
— Raid of. (C. F. Adams, jr.) No. Am. **112**: 241.
— Row of. (C. F. Adams, jr.) Am. Law R. **3**: 41. — No. Am. **108**: 305.
— Swindle of. (J. B. Hodgskin) Nation, **7**: 432.
— War of. (C. F. Adams, jr.) No. Am. **109**: 30.
Erie Tribe of Indians, Destruction of. Olden Time, **1**: 225.
Erigena, John Scotus. (T. Hill) Chr. Exam. **46**: 22.
— and Universalism. (S. S. Hebberd) Univ. Q. **35**: 133.
— Philosophy and Doctrines of. (H. Ballou, 2d) Univ. Q. **7**: 90.
Erin, Transfer of. (T. C. Amory) N. E. Reg. **28**: 163, 291, 423. **29**: 81, 185.
Erinnys. (P. S. Worsley) Blackw. **88**: 122.
Eriphanis; a Poem. Once a Week, **11**: 659.
Erkaempft. (J. Ring) Colburn, **155**: 302.
Ermengarde; a Legend of the Rhine. Tait, n. s. **18**: 339.
Erna; a Story. Argosy, **32**: 289.
Erne, The winding Banks of. Fraser, **78**: 195.
Ernest; or, Political Regeneration. Quar. **65**: 153.
Ernest the Seeker. Dial, **1**: 48, 233.
Ernest Steiner; a Tale of the ideal and real. (J. L. Swift) Dem. R. **13**: 38.
Ernest's Trance; a Poem. (S. Palfrey) Chr. Exam. **59**: 52.
Ernesti, J. Aug. (K. von Raumer) Am. J. Educ. **5**: 750.
Ernestine. (E. Wetherald) Godey, **22**: 34.
Ernst of Edelsheim; a Poem. (J. Hay) Scrib. **4**: 650.
Erôs Athanatos. (R. Buchanan) Gent. M. n. s. **12**: 555.
Erosion. (J. D. Dana) Am. J. Sci. **112**: 192.
Erostratus. So. Lit. Mess. **2**: 467.
Erotion; a Tale of Ancient Greece. Dub. Univ. **30**: 453.
Errand to the Iron Works; from Schiller's Fridolin. Temp. Bar, **53**: 426.
Erris and Tyrawly, Sketches in. Dub. Univ. **18**: 289.
Error, Attractions of. (J. Richardson) Chr. Obs. **75**: 401.
— Conscientious, Moral Quality of. (J. W. Yeomans) Mercersb. **7**: 273.
Error, Constitutional Predisposition to. Cong. M. **24**: 89.
— Genesis of. (T. A. Finlay) Month, **39**: 51. **40**: 93.
— Human Liability to. (G. N. Abbott) Mercersb. **22**: 258.
Errors, Common. (H. Scadding) Canad. J. n. s. **9**: 137, 317. **10**: 31, 223, 386. **11**: 45.
— concerning Animals and Plants. Chamb. J. **54**: 110.
— from false Associations. Penny M. **4**: 371.
— of Speech. All the Year, **32**: 460.
— of the Times, Bishop Brownell's. (H. Bushnell) New Eng. **2**: 143.
— Typographical. (J. J. Belcher) Harper, **32**: 228. — Ev. Sat. **10**: 331.
— Venerable. Chamb. J. **52**: 122.
Erskine, John, of Edinburgh. Cong. M. **1**: 449, 505, 560.
Erskine, Thomas, Lord. Blackw. **2**: 86. — Mus. **4**: 137. — Fraser, **7**: 178. — Pamph. **23**: 413. — Blackw. **122**: 283.
— Armata. Mo. R. **82**: 297. **83**: 359.
— Defender of the Whigs. Pamph. **15**: 287.
— Dinner to. Blackw. **6**: 615.
— Evidences of revealed Religion. Chr. Mo. Spec. **4**: 299.
— Letters of. Ed. R. **147**: 386. — Canad. Mo. **13**: 680.
— Speeches. Ed. R. **16**: 102. **19**: 339. — Lakeside, **5**: 83.
— Story of. (W. Chambers) Chamb. J. **51**: 353.
Erskine, Thomas, of Linlethan. (W. C. Smith) Theo. R. **12**: 353.
— Character of. Contemp. **14**: 260. Same art. Liv. Age, **106**: 174.
— Life and Theology of. (V. Lincoln) Univ. Q. **36**: 149.
Erzeroum. (R. Curzon) Nat. M. **13**: 1.
Escape, The. (L. H. Sigourney) Godey, **20**: 264.
Escapes, Remarkable. (J. R. Thompson) Scrib. **1**: 129.
Escarpacio, St., Bones of. Internat. M. **4**: 483.
Eschatological Studies. (J. A. Reubelt) Bib. Sac. **27**: 647.
Eschatology; Cumming's Great Tribulation. Tait, n. s. **26**: 655.
— A new. Scrib. **8**: 331.
— of O. T. Apocrypha. (E. C. Bissell) Bib. Sac. **36**: 320.
— Olshausen's. Theo. & Lit. J. **11**: 635.
Eschenbach. *See* Wolfram von Eschenbach.
Escobedo, General, Interview with. Galaxy, **4**: 322.
— Murder of. Cornh. **18**: 551. — Harper, **38**: 238.
Escurial, The. Am. Arch. **4**: 64. — Chamb. J. **49**: 755.
— Vicissitudes of. Cornh. **26**: 610. Same art. Ecl. M. **80**: 60. Same art. Ev. Sat. **13**: 641. — Same art. Liv. Age, **115**: 808.
Escutcheons and Shields. (J. A. Repton) Arch. **16**: 194.
Esdraelon, Plain of. (C. H. Brigham) Mo. Rel. M. **14**: 11.
Esdras, First Book of. (E. C. Bissell) Bib. Sac. **34**: 209.
Eskimo. *See* Esquimaux.
Esmé's Visit; a Tale. Bentley, **61**: 503.
Esmée. (Mrs. A. Fraser) Tinsley, **23**: 186–416.
Esmeralda. (F. H. Burnett) Scrib. **14**: 80.
Esnecca, The Word. (J. Topham) Arch. **6**: 116.
España, Count de. Mus. **41**: 211.
Espartero, Baldomero. For. Q. **32**: 247. Same art. with portrait, Ecl. M. **33**: 128. Same art. Ecl. Mus. **3**: 507. — Mus. **41**: 56.
Esperanza; an Incident at Spa. Chamb. J. **50**: 177.
Espinasse, Madame l', Letters of. Anal. M. **5**: 31.
Esprit, Physiology of. (C. Barrère) Gent. M. n. s. **14**: 441.
Esquimaux, The. Cath. World, **1**: 708. — Cornh. **20**: 52. — Anal. M. **14**: 63. — Ev. Sat. **8**: 174. — Quar. **142**: 346. Same art. Ecl. M. **88**: 1. Same art. Liv. Age, **131**: 515.
— and Indians of British America. Month, **4**: 357, 493. Same art. Cath. World, **3**: 557.
— and Loncheux. Hist. M. **8**: 165.
— At Home with. (A. H. Guernsey) Harper, **29**: 432.
— Industrial Arts of. (R. King) Ed. New Philos. J. **42**: 112. Same art. Liv. Age, **13**: 161.

Esquimaux, The, Intellectual Character of. (R. King) Ed. New Philos. J. 38: 306.
— John Sackeouse. Blackw. 4: 656.
— Life with. (W. P. Snow) Harper, 28: 721.
— — Hall's. Dub. Univ. 66: 322. — Month. 4: 357. — Temp. Bar, 16: 144.
— Manners and Customs of. (I. I. Hayes) Hist. M. 1: 5.
— Migrations of. (J. Rae) Anthrop. J. 7: 125.
— Mode of Life of. (A. Woodbury) No. Am. 84: 95.
— of Greenland. (A. Bordier) Nature, 18: 16.
— Physical Character of. (R. King) Ed. New Philos. J. 36: 296.
— Social Life among. (W. H. Dall) Am. Natural. 12: 1. — Chamb. J. 58: 625.
— Tales and Traditions of, Rink's. Nature, 13: 103.
— Traditions of. Chamb. J. 36: 216–365. 53: 134.
— With Schwatka among. (W. H. Gilder) Scrib. 22: 76.
Esquire, Title of. Anal. M. 2: 259.
Essay, An, considered as tentative. Ecl. R. 124: 288.
— without End. Cornh. 1: 248.
Essays and Essay Writing. Galaxy, 1: 677.
— by a Virginian. (E. Everett) No. Am. 16: 45.
— by an Invalid. Dub. Univ. 23: 373.
— Hints for. (A. Helps) Good Words, 13: 11, 141. Same art. Ecl. M. 78: 363.
— on French Themes, 1853. Chr. Rem. 40: 130.
Essays and Reviews. (G. E. Ellis) Chr. Exam. 69: 351. — (S. Wilberforce) Quar. 109: 248. — Liv. Age, 68: 643. — Brit. Q. 33: 1. — Chr. Rem. 40: 327. 41: 439. 44: 68. — Dub. R. 49: 457. — Dub. Univ. 55: 643. 57: 385, 513. — Ed. R. 113: 461. — Fraser, 62: 228. — Kitto, 27: 77. — Lond. Q. 14: 512. — No. Brit. 33: 217. — (H. A. Dubois) Am. Church R. 14: 275.
— in the Church Convocation. Dub. R. 50: 242.
— Judgment of Privy Council on. Quar. 115: 530.
— Letter to the Editor. Macmil. 4: 41.
— Note on. (J. O. Halliwell) St. James, 1: 61.
— Replies to. No. Brit. 36: 273.
Essay Writing. (W. H. Prescott) No. Am. 14: 319. — (T. Dwight) Carey's Mus. 5: 69. — Macmil. 11: 321.
— and Essay Writers in France. New Q. 10: 194.
— and the Press. (J. T. Nesbit) De Bow, 5: 303.
Essayist, Advice to a young. Lond. M. 9: 501.
Essayists. Cornh. 44: 278. Same art. Liv. Age, 151: 67. Same art. Ecl. M. 97: 610. Same art. Appleton, 26: 411.
— British, Literary Reform effected by. (A. P. Peabody) No. Am. 84: 502.
— English. (C. C. Clarke) Ev. Sat. 12: 536.
— Old and new. No. Brit. 37: 132. Same art. Liv. Age, 75: 260.
Essenes. (T. De Quincey) Blackw. 47: 105, 463, 639. — (W. Hall) Am. Bib. Repos. 3d s. 3: 162. — Kitto, 10: 176.
— Traditions of. (K. Cook) Dub. Univ. 96: 146.
Essenism and Christianity. (R. Wahl) Unita. R. 11: 595.
Essex, Robert, 2d Earl of, Defense of Gorges for betraying. (J. Bruce) Arch. 33: 241.
— Rebellion of. (A. C. Ewald) Gent. M. n. s. 27: 43.
Essex, Wm., 3d Earl of, Letters from his Army, 1642. (Sir H. Ellis) Arch. 35: 310.
Essex, Devereux Earls of. Dub. Univ. 41: 583. — Ed. R. 98: 132.
Essex Co., England, revisited. Once a Week, 11: 515.
— Forest of. Cornh. 9: 350.
Essex Co., Mass., Ministers of, to 1834. (J. B. Felt) Am. Q. Reg. 7: 246.
North Association of, History of. (S. J. Spalding) Cong. Q. 6: 161, 245.
Essex Co., Vermont, Ministers of. (J. Glines) Am. Q. Reg. 13: 448.
Essex, U. S. Ship, Cruise of. (R. Tomes) Harper, 19: 289. — (C. E. Lester) Harper, 26: 397.
Essex-Street, Strand. All the Year, 26: 397.
Established Church Society. Dub. Univ. 7: 704.
Established Churches. (H. Giles) Chr. Exam. 31: 209.
Estancia, Life in an. House. Words, 2: 190–233.
Estates of Endowments. (T. Hare) Fortn. 13: 309.
Estates, Proceedings in Rhode Island, in early Times, in settling. (G. A. Brayton) N. E. Reg. 12: 303.
Estatica of Youghal. Chr. Obs. 43: 442, 461.
Estelle. Bentley, 60: 249. Same art. Ecl. M. 67: 589.
Estelle Russell. Macmil. 19: 188–480. 20: 43–537. 21: 51–324.
Estephania de Gautelines; a Tale of the Middle Ages. Lond. M. 4: 379.
Esther Hammond's Wedding-Day. House. Words, 4: 425.
Esther the Jewess; a Tale. So. Lit. Mess. 13: 345, 409.
Esther Lee's Holiday. (G. C. Munro) Peop. J. 8: 7.
Esther Wynn's Love-Letters. (Saxe Holm) Scrib. 3: 164.
Esthonia, History and Condition of. Ecl. R. 75: 272.
Esthonians, Customs among. Penny M. 9: 437.
— Domestic Economy of. Penny M. 10: 403.
Estienne, Henri, and Family, Printers, and Classical Learning in France. Quar. 117: 323.
Estimate of Human Beings. (A. K. H. Boyd) Fraser, 67: 540. Same art. Ecl. M. 59: 209.
Estrées, Gabrielle d'. (C. A. Sainte-Beuve) Bentley, 35: 98. Same art. Ecl. M. 31: 345.
— and Henry IV. Temp. Bar, 48: 461 Same art. Ecl. M. 39: 62.
— Capefigue on. Colburn, 123: 347.
Etching. (G. L. Austin) Galaxy, 18: 639, 768. — (P. G. Hamerton) Art J. 18: 293. — (C. F. Partington) J. Frankl. Inst. 2: 65. — (J. B. Atkinson) Art J. 32: 129–199. — F. Arts Q. 4: 145. — J. Frankl. Inst. 70: 412.
— and Etchers. (W. S. Baker) Penn Mo. 6: 110.
— — P. G. Hamerton's. (R. Sturgis) Nation, 22: 131. — So. R. n. s. 21: 74.
— in France, Modern. (P. G. Hamerton) F. Arts Q. 2: 69.
— Lalanne on. (J. MacAlister) Dial (Ch.), 1: 86.
— Masters of. (F. Wedmore) Macmil. 30: 151. Same art. Ecl. M. 83: 211. Same art. Ev. Sat. 17: 19. 41. Same art. Liv. Age, 122: 215.
— Modern, Examples of. (P. G. Hamerton) Portfo. 3: 1–161. 4: 1–177.
— of Steel Plates. (W. Cooke) J. Frankl. Inst. 3: 250.
— Philosophy of. (P. G. Hamerton) Fortn. 11: 579. Same art. Ev. Sat. 7: 696.
— Recent Improvements in the Process of. (P. G. Hamerton) Portfo. 1: 188.
— Ruskin on. (P. G. Hamerton) Portfo. 5: 25.
Etchings by the great Masters. (P. G. Hamerton) Portfo. 9: 15–188. 10: 87–199.
— from Pictures by contemporary Artists. Portfo. 9: 17–177. 10: 1–193.
— Italian. Dub. Univ. 30: 81.
— Painters'. Portfo. 10: 41–187.
— Seymour Haden's. (F. T. Palgrave) F. Arts Q. 5: 119. — (P. G. Hamerton) Scrib. 20: 586.
— Unger's. (P. G. Hamerton) Internat. R. 3: 37.
— with a Chisel. (H. Greenough) Dem. R. 18: 118.
Etching-Club, Etched Thoughts by. Blackw. 56: 153.
— Illustrated Deserted Village. Blackw. 51: 122.
— Illustrated Thomson's Seasons. Blackw. 52: 674.
Etching-Ground for Engravers. (E. Turrell) J. Frankl. Inst. 2: 83.
Eternal Life and eternal Death. (J. W. Santee) Mercersb. 23: 617.
— in the Gospel of St. John. Lond. Q. 49: 358.

Eternal Punishment. (L. G. M. Miller) Luth. Q. **9**: 1. — (G. Porter) Month, **33**: 358. — (C. H. Robertson) Kitto, **39**: 56. — (T. J. Sawyer) Univ. Q. **25**: 205. **27**: 40. — (A. Wolfe) Kitto, **39**: 299. — Kitto, **40**: 152. — Chr. Obs. **54**: 433. — Nat. R. **16**: 88. — (C. Long) Bib. Sac. **17**: 111. — Meth. M. **25**: 402. — Theo. R. **1**: 559.
— and Evil. Kitto, **40**: 152.
— and Immortality. Kitto, **36**: 433.
— and Universalism. (H. N. Oxenham) Contemp. **27**: 222–724. — Chr. Rem. **45**: 433.
— and the Word *Eternal*. Chr. Rem. **27**: 200. *See* Αἰών.
— Barnes on. Univ. Q. **9**: 377.
— Belief in, essential to Ordination. (D. Merriman) Cong. Q. **15**: 225.
— Christ's Testimony on. (J. Leavitt) Chr. Mo. Spec. **9**: 617.
— Doctrine of. (M. Ballou) Univ. Q. **11**: 72. — (F. H. Hedge) Chr. Exam. **67**: 98.
— Farrar's Eternal Hope. Bib. Sac. **35**: 779. — (C. G. Thompson) St. James, **42**: 514. — (E. V. Gerhart) Mercersb. **25**: 600.
— — Papers on, by seventeen Writers. Contemp. **32**: 153, 338, 545.
— — Reply to Critics. (F. W. Farrar) Contemp. **32**: 569.
— — Sequel to Discussion. (F. Peck) Contemp. **32**: 694.
— Grounds of, considered. (T. J. Sawyer) Univ. Q. **29**: 182. **31**: 306. **32**: 458.
— in Church of England. Contemp. **19**: 573.
— in Old and New Testaments. (W. E. Manley) Univ. Q. **23**: 281.
— Is it endless? (F. H. Foster) Bib. Sac. **35**: 353.
— Matthew xxv. 46. (A. R. Abbott) Univ. Q. **20**: 42.
— Mosheim's Thoughts on. (T. J. Sawyer) Univ. Q. **12**: 69.
— Oxenham on. Canad. Mo. **8**: 548.
— Preaching. Chr. R. **25**: 576.
— a Result of Character. New Eng. **9**: 186.
— Unreasonableness of. (T. C. Druley) Univ. Q. **30**: 215.
— Untrue. (M. Goodrich) Univ. Q. **13**: 329.
See also Future Punishment.
Eternity, Metaphysical Idea of. (C. M. Mead) New Eng. **34**: 222.
— realized. (S. R. Andrew) Chr. Q. Spec. **6**: 73.
Ethel Marchmont. (A. J. Graham) Canad. Mo. **17**: 125.
Etheldreda, St., and the Anglicans. (W. S. L.) Month, **21**: 77.
Ether. (C. Brooke) Nature, **3**: 109.
— and Chloroform. Dub. R. **29**: 226.
— Discovery of. (Sir J. Paget) 19th Cent. **6**: 1119. Same art. Ecl. M. **94**: 219. — Peop. J. **25**: 318.
— Hypothesis relative to luminous. (M. H. Fizeau) J. Frankl. Inst. **52**: 422.
— Physics of. (W. B. Taylor) J. Frankl. Inst. **101**: 405. **102**: 61, 284. — (S. T. Preston) J. Frankl. Inst. **102**: 278.
— Theory of a nervous. (B. W. Richardson) Pop. Sci. R. **10**: 379.
Ether-Drinking and Extra-Alcoholic Intoxication. (B. W. Richardson) Gent. M. n. s. **21**: 440. Same art. Sup. Pop. Sci. Mo. **4**: 31.
Ethereal Cusses. (F. Parke) Dub. Univ. **84**: 665.
Etheridge, Sir George. (E. W. Gosse) Cornh. **43**: 284. Same art. Liv. Age, **149**: 259.
— Comedies of. (R. Bell) Fortn. **3**: 298.
Etheric Force, Identity with induced Electricity. (Houston and Thomson) J. Frankl. Inst. **101**: 270.
Etheridge, John Wesley, Memoir of. Chr. Obs. **71**: 864.
Etherification, Observations on. (T. Graham) J. Frankl. Inst. **54**: 103.
Etherization, Discovery of. (J. H. Abbott) Atlan. **21**: 718. — All the Year, **20**: 298. — Chamb. J. **7**: 140, 398.
Etherization, Discovery of, and Etherton Cottage. (Mrs. S. J. Hale) Godey, **46**: 206.
— — Dr. Jackson's Claims to. (J. L. Lord and H. C. Lord) Liv. Age, **17**: 491. — (J. H. Abbott) Liv. Age, **17**: 565.
— — Dr. Morton's Claims to. (R. H. Dana, jr.) Liv. Age, **16**: 529.
— in Childbirth. (E. Warren) No. Am. **68**: 300.
— Painless Operations in Surgery, by the Use of. No. Brit. **7**: 169. Same art. Ecl. M. **11**: 299. Same art. Liv. Age, **13**: 481.
See Anæsthetics.
Ethical and Social Studies, Cobbe's. Ecl. M. **65**: 323. *See* Cobbe.
Ethical Element in our earlier Literature. (T. W. Hunt) Presb. R. **2**: 530.
Ethical Ideas, Origin of. (G. Batchelor) Unita. R. **8**: 375.
Ethical Law and Social Order. (G. Batchelor) Unita. R. **12**: 624.
Ethical Philosophy. (A. J. Balfour) Mind, **3**: 67. — New Eng. M. **4**: 208, 290. — Princ. **5**: 33. — Am. Q. **12**: 133. — Mo. R. **123**: 213.
— of Plato. Am. Church R. **22**: 175.
Ethical Prolegomena. (S. Talbott) Bapt. Q. **11**: 257.
Ethical Questions, Cogan's. Mo. R. **89**: 130.
Ethical Revival, Necessity of. Cong. **7**: 1. — (H. M. Goodwin) New Eng. **39**: 686.
Ethical Science. Am. Mo. R. **2**: 50.
— Jouffroy's. Brownson, **2**: 53. — (S. Osgood) Chr. Exam. **28**: 137.
— Present Study of. (D. Peabody) Am. Q. Obs. **2**: 247.
Ethical Studies, Bradley on. Dub. Univ. **88**: 239.
Ethical System of the Bible. Theo. & Lit. J. **7**: 666.
Ethics. Danv. Q. **2**: 595.
— Ancient and modern. (Z. G. Wilson) Western, **1**: 109.
— and Christianity. Lond. Q. **11**: 492. Same art. Ecl. M. **46**: 445.
— — British and Continental. No. Brit. **14**: 289.
— and Evolution. (D. M. Hodge) Univ. Q. **36**: 175. — (F. Pollock) Mind, **1**: 334. — (W. Knight) 19th Cent. **4**: 432.
— and Politics. (A. Barrett) Mind, **2**: 453.
— and Psychogony. (A. Barrett) Mind, **3**: 277.
— and Psychology. (F. A. Adams) Am. Presb. R. **18**: 535.
— and Theism. (W. G. Ward) Dub. R. **86**: 101.
— and Unity of Nature. (Duke of Argyll) Contemp. **39**: 186, 333. Same art. Liv. Age, **148**: 579. **149**: 67.
— Aristotle's Nicomachean. (F. Pollock) Mind, **6**: 433.
— as a Science. (N. P. Gilman) Unita. R. **10**: 1.
— Atheistic Methodism. (W. H. Mallock) 19th Cent. **7**: 161.
— Bradley's Ethical Studies. (H. Sidgwick) Mind, **1**: 544.
— Brown's Lectures on. Tait, n. s. **13**: 699.
— Butler's. (W. H. S. Monck) Mind, **3**: 369.
— Chinese. (F. Gilbert) Lakeside, **2**: 191. — (W. A. P. Martin) Princ. **34**: 193.
— Christian. (S. Osgood) Chr. Exam. **29**: 153. **30**: 145. — Brownson, **3**: 137. — (N. Porter) Chr. Q. Spec. **7**: 392. — (L. H. Atwater) Princ. n. s. **7**: 61.
— — and moral Theories. Theo. Ecl. **5**: 401. Same art. Liv. Age, **95**: 67.
— — Culman's Theory. (J. P. Lacroix) Bib. Sac. **30**: 361.
— — Gregory's. So. R. n. s. **21**: 420.
— — Lange on. Bib. Sac. **36**: 373.
— — Wardlaw on. Cong. M. **17**: 285. — Ecl. R. **59**: 21.
— Elements of. Chr. Rem. **10**: 332.
— First Principles in. (H. Sidgwick) Mind, **4**: 106.
— Forcing Truths and Duties into Antagonism. (F. A. Noble) New Eng. **39**: 675.
— Foundation of moral Obligation. (J. H. Jones) New Eng. **24**: 276. — (M. Grosvenor) New Eng. **31**: 469.

Ethics; God and Immortality. (F. W. Newman and M. G. Grey) Theo. R. 16: 1, 208.
— Grecian and Christian. (A. Neander) Bib. Sac. 10: 476, 789.
— — in their Golden Age. (Prof. Wuttke) Meth. Q. 30: 573.
— Grote on moral Ideals. (H. Sidgwick) Mind, 2: 239.
— Hartmann's New System of Pessimistic. (G. S. Hall) Nation, 28: 102.
— Illogical. (H. W. Everest) Chr. Q. 7: 175.
— Jouffroy's; Channing's Translation. Dial, 1: 99.
— Kant's. (J. Edmunds) J. Spec. Philos. 5: 27–289.
— J. S. Mill on. (J. B. Thayer) No. Am. 100: 259.
— Modern. Month, 11: 259.
— A moral Argument. (J. P. Coyle) Princ. n. s. 7: 175.
— Natural. (M. J. Savage) No. Am. 133: 228. — Radical R. 1: 781.
— — Simcox's Essay on. (R. Adamson) Mind, 2: 552.
— The New. (C. C. Everett) Unita. R. 10: 408. — (Prof. Lacroix) Meth. Q. 38: 631.
— of Art. Brit. Q. 10: 441.
— of Christendom. Westm. 57: 182.
— of civil Government. (D. A. Gorton) Nat. Q. 37: 209.
— of Evolution. (B. P. Bowne) Meth. Q. 40: 436.
— of Jesus Christ. (J. L. Stoddard) Radical R. 1: 661.
— of Life. (R. W. Emerson) No. Am. 126: 404.
— of Religion. (W. K. Clifford) Fortn. 28: 35. Same art. Sup. Pop. Sci. Mo. 1: 335.
— of revealed Theology. Brit. Q. 26: 307. Same art. Ecl. M. 43: 1.
— of Sentiment and Science. (O. B. Frothingham) Radical, 7: 186.
— of Sincerity. (J. C. Granberry) Meth. Q. 40: 625.
— of Taste. (J. J. Jarves) Art J. 27: 293.
— of Trade. (D. A. Gorton) Nat. Q. 33: 242.
— of Utilitarianism. (W. Haslam) Nat. Q. 39: 335.
— Political, Lieber's Manual of. Ecl. R. 72: 401.
— Pre-Platonic. (Prof. Wuttke) Meth. Q. 29: 505.
— Professional, and legal Practice. Princ. 43: 286.
— Pure and applied. (T. Hill) Chr. Exam. 52: 188.
— Radical Question of. (A. T. Innes) Contemp. 20: 269. — Liv. Age, 114: 451.
— Recent English Thought on. (G. F. Magoun) J. Spec. Philos. 11: 198.
— Recent Views on. (M. J. Savage) Unita. R. 13: 203.
— Reforms in public. (J. Hayes) Overland, 13: 417.
— Religion, and the Church. Westm. 100: 424.
— R. Rothe's Theologische Ethik. (C. C. Tiffany) Bib. Sac. 17: 241.
— Scientific, Vindication of. (W. D. Le Sueur) Pop. Sci. Mo. 17: 324.
— Sidgwick's Methods of. (A. Bain) Mind, 1: 179. — (J. E. Cabot) No. Am. 122: 446. — (A. V. Dicey) Nation, 22: 162, 180. — (L. Stephen) Fraser, 91: 306.
— Some Views in. (T. F. Brownell) Radical R. 1: 707.
— Spencer's Data of. (A. Bain) Mind, 4: 561. Same art. Pop. Sci. Mo. 16: 210. — (H. Calderwood) Contemp. 37: 64. — (H. Wace) Contemp. 38: 254. — (A. W. Gundry) Canad. Mo. 16: 646. — (C. C. Everett) Unita. R. 13: 43. — (H. Sidgwick) Mind, 5: 216. — (A. W. Benn) Mind, 5: 489. — (H. Spencer) Mind, 6: 82. — (W. James) Nation, 29: 178. — (J. McCosh) Princ. n. s. 4: 607. — (T. G. Apple) Ref. Q. 28: 165.
— Study of. (H. W. Lucas) Month, 34: 236, 346.
— Theoretical. Brit. Q. 6: 407.
— What Morality have we left? No. Am. 132: 497.
See Intuition, Moral; Morals; Utilitarianism.
Ethilwald, Bishop of Dunwich, Seal of. (H. Gurney) Arch. 20: 479.
Ethiopia, Geography of. Ed. R. 41: 181.
— Gold Mines of. (S. Birch) Arch. 34: 357.
Ethiopia, Harris's Highlands of. (A. C. Dick) No. Brit. 1: 41. Same art. Ecl. M. 3: 433. — Ed. R. 80: 43. — Tait, n. s. 11: 182, 232. Same art. Liv. Age, 1: 366. — Westm. 41: 183. — Chr. R. 9: 396. — Ecl. R. 79: 289. — Blackw. 55: 269. — Fraser, 29: 442. — Ecl. M. 2: 183.
— Journey to. Ecl. R. 36: 193.
— Travels in, Hoskins's. Ed. R. 62: 45. — Am. Q. 18: 423.
— Waddington's Visit to. Quar. 27: 215.
Ethiopian Church. (J. A. Reubelt) Mercersb. 11: 590.
Ethiopian Manuscript in Astor Library. (L. Lund) Am. Church R. 36: 189.
Ethiopian Nights' Entertainments. (B. Taylor) Putnam, 4: 205.
Ethiopians, Origin of, and the Apocryphal Books of Isaiah and Enoch. For. Q. 24: 351.
Ethiopic Literature. Dub. R. 51: 133.
Ethiopic Liturgies and Hymns. (J. M. Rodwell) Kitto, 31: 337. 32: 108, 363.
Ethiopic Prayers. (J. M. Rodwell) Kitto, 33: 361. 35: 301. 36: 321.
Ethna's Dowry. Irish Mo. 2: 328, 402.
Ethnical Scriptures. Dial, 4: 59, 205, 402.
Ethnography. *See* Races.
Ethnological Inquiries. (R. Knox) Anthrop. R. 1: 246.
Ethnological Society, Transactions of. Dem. R. 17: 50.
Ethnological Societies of London and Paris. For. Q. 32: 424. Same art. Ecl. M. 1: 419.
Ethnologists, Battle of the. Temp. Bar, 5: 214. Same art. Ecl. M. 56: 331.
Ethnology. Chr. Rem. 7: 15. — New Q. 4: 147.
— American School of. Lond. Q. 3: 68.
— and Anthropology. (J. B. Davis) Anthrop. R. 6: 394.
— and Phrenology an Aid to the Biographer. (J. W. Jackson) Anthrop. R. 2: 126.
— — Jackson's. Anthrop. R. 1: 118.
— and Religion. Dub. Univ. 45: 721.
— and Revelation. Brit. Q. 22: 1.
— and Spiritualism. (E. B. Tylor) Nature, 5: 343.
— English, and English Genius. (W. Larminie) Gent. M. n. s. 26: 233.
— Finnic. (A. H. Keane) Nature, 21: 180.
— Indo-Chinese and Oceanic Races. (A. H. Keane) Nature, 23: 199–271.
— North American. (W. L. Distant) Nature, 21: 247.
— Methods and Results of. (T. H. Huxley) Fortn. 1: 257.
— Progress of. (Dr. Hodgkin) Ed. New Philos. J. 36: 118.
— — Bartlett's. (G. W. Schenk) Mercersb. 1: 127.
— Unity of Mankind. Brit. Q. 10: 408.
— Linguistic Science and. (W. D. Whitney) New Eng. 26: 30.
— Relations to History. (J. C. Prichard) Ed. Philos. J. 43: 307.
See Man; Races.
Ethramonia. (L. S. Dorr) Lippinc. 5: 553.
Etienne. (E. About) So. M. 12: 63–340.
Etienne-du-Mont, St., Parish of, in Paris. Dub. R. 12: 419.
Etiquette. Chamb. J. 39: 211. — Colburn, 54: 21. — Hogg, 2: 161.
— J. Q. Adams's Letter on. Niles's Reg. 21: 327.
— Ancient Guides to. All the Year, 19: 284.
— and Manners, Codes of. Quar. 59: 395.
— and Precedence. Cong. 2: 20, 91.
— Blunders in Behavior corrected. Godey, 60: 30–413.
— Chit-Chat about. (B. Murphy) Galaxy, 16: 533.
— Codes of. Chamb. J. 1: 235.
— Company Manners. Tinsley, 12: 286. — Liv. Age, 42: 126.
— Dinner-Table. Once a Week, 19: 73.
— Drawing-Room Tactics. Lippinc. 10: 464.
— Few Words on. Godey, 33: 87.

Etiquette, French. All the Year, **11**: 616. — Belgra. **5**: 538. Same art. Liv. Age, **98**: 175.
— Gentlewomen's, 1662. House. Words, **12**: 18.
— Hints on. Colburn, **82**: 360. — Mo. R. **139**: 390.
— How to be a Gentleman. Colburn, **11**: 462.
— Legal. Cornh. **8**: 105.
— Medical. Cornh. **8**: 154.
— Moral Influence of. Lond. M. **6**: 456.
— Professional. Cornh. **8**: 101, 154.
— Rules of, in 1679. Retros. **16**: 375.
— Social. All the Year, **46**: 473.
— — of New York. (A. G. Sedgwick) Nation, **28**: 34.
— Unsettled Points of. Lippinc. **11**: 344.
See Manners.
Etna, Mount. (J. H. Hayes) Am. J. Sci. **52**: 157. — Mo. R. **93**: 511. — (R. A. Proctor) Gent. M. n. s. **23**: 73. — Broadw. **4**: 230. — Nature, **20**: 544.
— Ascent of. (S. L. Johnson) Am. J. Sci. **26**: 1. — (W. R. Harris) Colburn, **86**: 341. — Chamb. J. **7**: 188. — Ecl. M. **41**: 133. — Liv. Age, **39**: 632. — Penny M. **2**: 357, 365. — Sharpe, **10**: 177.
— Astronomical Observations on. (S. P. Langley) Am. J. Sci. **120**: 33.
— Eruption of, in 1832. Penny M. **2**: 302. — (S. J. Mackie) Pop. Sci. R. **4**: 447. — Nature, **10**: 522. — (G. F. Rodwell) Nature, **20**: 158, 198.
— Excursion on. (B. Silliman, jr.) Am. J. Sci. **63**: 178.
— How I did not ascend. Sharpe, **40**: 210.
— in Eruption, 1864. Cornh. **12**: 178.
— Observatory on. (G. F. Rodwell) Nature, **19**: 557.
— Rodwell's. Nature, **19**: 480.
— Twenty-four Hours on. Bentley, **47**: 287.
— Visit to. St. James, **17**: 292.
— Winter Visit to. (D. T. Ansted) Intel. Obs. **9**: 125, 268.
— Wintering on. (S. P. Langley) Atlan. **46**: 38.
Eton College. (E. Jesse) Bentley, **7**: 587. — (G. C. Lewis) Ed. R. **51**: 65. — (E. S. Nadal) Harper, **53**: 519. — (C. E. Pascoe) Appleton, **18**: 206. — All the Year, **36**: 229. — Blackw. **95**: 707. — Blackw. **119**: 314. Same art. Liv. Age, **129**: 259. — Brit. Q. **47**: 34. — Ed. R. **113**: 387. **146**: 489. — Macmil. **3**: 292. **15**: 353. — Penny M. **2**: 441. — Prosp. R. **4**: 338.
— and Education in England. Quar. **52**: 128.
— and its Celebrities. (E. R. Creasy) Bentley, **28**: 92.
— and Oxford, Our Sons at. Fraser, **100**: 831.
— and Westminster. (G. C. Lewis) Ed. R. **53**: 64.
— Annals of. Chamb. J. **43**: 348.
— Matthew Arnold and the great Public Schools. (D. Masson) Macmil. **10**: 175.
— as it is. Victoria, **4**: 9, 228.
— Colleges *versus* Oppidans. Cornh. **24**: 688.
— Criticism of. Cornh. **3**: 257. **10**: 113.
— Days at, De Verney's. Lond. Soc. **15**: 513.
— Football at. Lond. Soc. **5**: 216.
— History, Condition, and Influence of. Westm. **75**: 477.
— in 1845. (J. D. Lewis) Macmil. **32**: 42, 273. Same art. Liv. Age, **125**: 666.
— Lyte's History of. (G. Smith) Nation, **22**: 231.
— Parliamentary Report on. Cornh. **10**: 113.
— Rambles about. (A. Rimmer) Belgra. **43**: 325, 423. **44**: 63–446.
— Recent Troubles at, 1876. (R. P. Keep) New Eng. **35**: 314.
— Recollections of. Colburn, **64**: 63. **65**: 79.
— Reform at. (W. E. Jelf) Contemp. **3**: 556. — Nat. R. **18**: 114.
— revisited, August, 1836. Colburn, **48**: 155.
— Scenes and Men at. Bentley, **16**: 36, 181, 434.
— Science at. Nature, **24**: 287.
— sixty Years since. Chamb. J. **43**: 545, 569.
— Something about. Lippinc. **10**: 454.
Eton College, Studies and Management at, 1834. Mo. R. **133**: 212.
— Tutorial System at. (J. Walford) Month, **12**: 443.
— Visit to. Fraser, **56**: 296.
Eton Tradition, The. (T. H. S. Escott) Belgra. **29**: 43.
Etonian, The. Quar. **25**: 95. — Mo. R. **100**: 157.
Etonians, Eminent. Fraser, **42**: 296.
Etoniana, Ancient and modern. Blackw. **97**: 209–471.
Étretat, a French Watering-Place. Temp. Bar, **18**: 457.
— Wintering and Bathing Season at. (J. Banks) Argosy, **1**: 165, 315. **2**: 243.
Etruria, Ancient. Nat. Q. **18**: 144.
— Antiquities of. Lit. & Theo. J. **2**: 133. — Quar. **54**: 429. **76**: 38.
— Architectural Monuments of. Westm. **41**: 145.
— Betham's Celtica. Blackw. **57**: 474. — Dub. R. **15**: 1.
— Dennis's Cities and Cemeteries of. Chr. Obs. **50**: 539. — Ed. R. **90**: 107. — Brit. Q. **9**: 517. Same art. Ecl. M. **17**: 507. — Dub. Univ. **33**: 281. — Lit. & Theo. J. **2**: 133.
— History of, Gray's. Fraser, **34**: 505, 676. — No. Brit. **3**: 454. Same art. Ecl. M. **6**: 196. — Month, **162**: 152. — Dub. Univ. **24**: 527. — So. Q. **7**: 211, 261.
— History and Antiquities of. Ed. R. **50**: 372.
— Literature and Antiquities of, Betham on. Mo. R. **160**: 95.
— Peep at ancient. Fraser, **87**: 500.
— Sepulchers of. Ecl. Mus. **1**: 213. — So. Lit. Mess. **2**: 81. — Ed. R. **73**: 121.
— — Mrs. Gray's. Dub. R. **13**: 485. — Quar. **67**: 375.
— Unburied. (W. R. Alger) Univ. Q. **8**: 113.
Etruscans, Ancient. (J. Tyne) Nat. Q. **32**: 315. — Cornh. **19**: 600.
Etruscan Cities and their Ruins. Ecl. M. **59**: 496.
Etruscan Interpretation. (F. W. Newman) Fraser, **95**: 302, 540. — (I. Taylor) Fraser, **95**: 537.
Etruscan Jewelry. Once a Week, **8**: 218.
Etruscan Researches, Taylor's. Internat. R. **1**: 704.
Etruscan Translations. (F. W. Newman) Fraser, **94**: 104.
Etruscan Vase, The. Recr. Sci. **1**: 129.
Etruscan Vases, Ancient, Composition of. (Prof. Hausmann) Ed. Philos. J. **12**: 360. **13**: 45.
— found at Canino. Arch. **23**: 131.
Ettingshausen, Andreas von. Nature, **18**: 197.
Ettrick Forest. Sharpe, **15**: 165.
Etty, William, Painter. (T. Gautier) Temp. Bar, **6**: 431. — (P. G. Hamerton) Portfo. **6**: 88–180. — (T. W. Newton) Sharpe, **11**: 76. — Temp. Bar, **55**: 233. Same art. Liv. Age, **140**: 757.
— Autobiography of. Art J. **1**: 13, 37, 99.
— Life of. Dub. Univ. **45**: 509. — Ecl. R. **101**: 658. — Westm. **64**: 615.
— — Gilchrist's. Fraser, **52**: 232. — New Q. **4**: 165.
— Sketch of. Hogg, **13**: 261.
— Technical Notes on. (P. G. Hamerton) Portfo. **7**: 105.
— Works of. Art J. **2**: 161. — Ecl. R. **90**: 324.
Etymological Notes. Dub. Univ. **51**: 552.
Etymological Remarks and Derivatives. So. Lit. Mess. **20**: 624.
Etymology. (G. P. Marsh) Nation, **3**: 225–369. — Ox. Prize Ess. **3**: 55. — So. R. **5**: 337. **6**: app.
— and Criticism. (N. Webster) Chr. Q. Spec. **8**: 311.
— English. (B. W. Dwight) Bib. Sac. **19**: 274, 801.
— — Wedgwood on. (E. Schuyler) Bib. Sac. **19**: 726.
— Few curious Derivatives. (H. Coppée) Lippinc. **3**: 521.
— Local. All the Year, **3**: 390.
— Science of. (B. W. Dwight) Bib. Sac. **15**: 401.
— Speculations in. Colburn, **1**: 221–339. **2**: 226–523.
Etymologies, Eccentric. Ecl. M. **65**: 87.
Etzler, J. A. Paradise [to be] Regained. Dem. R. **13**: 451.
'Εν, the Preposition. (W. R. C. Rogers) Kitto, **34**: 183.
Eu, Castle of. (T. F. Wedmore) Once a Week, **15**: 193.

Eucalyptus in the Future. (S. Lockwood) Pop. Sci. Mo. **12**: 662.
— in the Roman Campagna. (H. N. Draper) Chamb. J. **58**: 193. Same art. Liv. Age, **149**: 376.
— Products of Trees of the Genus. (J. R. Jackson) Intel. Obs. **9**: 241.
Eucharist. *See* Lord's Supper.
Euclid and his modern Rivals. Nature, **20**: 240.
— Forty-Seventh Proposition of. (J. M. Richardson) Math. Mo. **2**: 45.
— Horsley's Edition of. (J. Playfair) Ed. R. **4**: 257.
— Peyrard's Edition of. Dub. R. **11**: 330.
— simplified, Morell's. Nature, **13**: 202.
See Geometry.
Eudoxia; a Picture of the 5th Century. Month, 8: 33-606. **9**: 47-543.
Eugene, Prince of Savoy. Ed. R. **116**: 504.—Mus. **42**: 364.
— Marlborough, Frederick, and Napoleon. Blackw. **61**: 34. Same art. Liv. Age, **12**: 489.
— Memoirs of. (J. Mill) Ed. R. **17**: 39. — Fraser, **23**: 187. — Colburn, **114**: 379.
Eugene, François, Life of. (J. G. Wilson) U. S. Serv. M. **5**: 532.
Eugene Aram; a Tragedy. (E. B. Lytton) Colburn, **38**: 401.
Eugene Pickering. (H. James, jr.) Atlan. **34**: 397, 513.
Eugenia, Strange Story of. Chamb. J. **58**: 330, 345.
Eugénie, Empress. (L. H. Hooper) Lippinc. **22**: 247. — (J. McCarthy) Galaxy, **9**: 512. — St. James, **5**: 209. Same art. Ecl. M. **57**: 331. — with portrait, Ecl. M. **46**: 437. — with portrait, Ev. Sat. **9**: 685.
— and the French Artists. Ev. Sat. **9**: 534.
— and George Sand. Ev. Sat. **9**: 257. **11**: 367.
— and Maids of Honor, with engraving. Ecl. M. **49**: 121.
— at Chiselhurst. Ev. Sat. **10**: 415.
— Peep into Boudoir of. Ev. Sat. **9**: 190.
— sketched by Napoleon III. Fraser, **90**: 420.
Euharmonic Organ. (H. W. Poole) Am. J. Sci. **59**: 68, 199. — (E. T. Fitch) New Eng. **8**: 278. — (S. A. Eliot) Liv. Age, **26**: 473.
Eulenstein, Charles, the Jew's-Harp Performer. (T. P. Thompson) Westm. **20**: 74. Same art. Select J. **4**: [17. — Penny M. **7**: 363.
Euler, and his Discoveries. (D. Trowbridge) Nat Q. **15**: 161.
— Letters of. Am. Q. **14**: 255.
Eulœus, or Pasitigris. (W. F. Ainsworth) Colburn, **82**: 165.
Eunice Rookley. (E. Leslie) Godey, **27**: 113-278.
Euphemia; a Story. (A. Levy) Victoria, **36**: 129, 200.
Euphemisms. Liv. Age, **74**: 215. — Chamb. J. **31**: 403.
Euphranor; a Dialogue on Youth. (G. Putnam) Chr. Exam. **51**: 75.
Euphrates, Expedition to the. Colburn, **89**: 122-144. **144**: 347. — Ed. R. **92**: 436. — Dub. Univ. **36**: 379. — Westm. **53**: 332.
— Steam Navigation on. Brit. & For. R. **6**: 235.
Euphrates Valley Railway. (J. C. Paget) St. James, **33**: 406. — Colburn, **149**: 611. **150**: 34, 112. — Dub. Univ. **51**: 239. — Ecl. Engin. **6**: 35. **8**: 494. — Pract. M. **1**: 177.
Euphrates Valley Route. (M. Davies) Colburn, **150**: 381. **151**: 201. — (W. P. Andrew) Ecl. Engin. **22**: 474.
— From India by. (W. B. Keer) Fraser, **90**: 424.
Euphrosyne; a Story. Galaxy, **20**: 800.
Euphrosyne; a Tale of the New World. Chamb. J. **24**: 136, 148.
Euphrosyne and Melidore. (O. Digby) Lond. M. **1**: 501.
Euphuism; Works of John Lilly. Quar. **109**: 350.
Eureka; a Poem. Mo. Rel. M. **36**: 19.
Euripides. So. Lit. Mess. **9**: 96.
— Alcestis. Mo. R. **144**: 416.
— — poetical trans. (M. J. Chapman) Blackw. **44**: 408.
— — Woolsey's. (C. C. Felton) No. Am. **42**: 369.
Euripides and the Greek Drama. (L. S. Blackie) For. Q. **24**: 229. — Chr. Rem. **20**: 1. — Westm. **97**: 1.
— Bacchæ; Tyrrell's Revision. (R. C. Jebb) Dark Blue, **1**: 651.
— Badham's. Quar. **89**: 196.
— Burges's. Quar. **3**: 167.
— Characteristics of. Month, **5**: 385.
— Cyclops of; poetical translation. Blackw. **32**: 652.
— Elmsley's Heraclidæ. Quar. **9**: 348.
— Hecuba. Lond. M. **23**: 469.
— — Porson's. (P. Elmsley) Ed. R. **19**: 64.
— — translated. (A. de Vere) Cath. World, **25**: 353, 550.
— Helena. Blackw. **122**: 420.
— in modern English. (E. J. Hasell) St. Paul's, **12**: 680.
— Iphigenia in Aulis. Blackw. **92**: 94.
— — in Tauris. Blackw. **92**: 462.
— Markland's. (P. Elmsley) Quar. **7**: 441.
— Medea; translated. (A. de Vere) Cath. World, **25**: 638.
— — Translation from. Lond. M. **8**: 611.
— Monk's Hippolytus. Quar. **8**: 215.
— Orestes, Translation of a Scene from. Lond. M. **8**: 503.
— Phaëthon. Fraser, **45**: 448.
— Sea Studies. (J. A. Froude) Fraser, **91**: 541. Same art. Ecl. M. **85**: 24.
— Song from. Fraser, **79**: 79.
— Tragedies and Fragments of. For. R. **5**: 235.
— Troades of. Westm. **13**: 375.
— Vindication of. (E. I. Sears) Nat. Q. **19**: 1.
Euroclydon; a Tale. (F. Copcutt) Putnam, **13**: 683. Same art. Broadw. **6**: 513.
Europe. New Eng. M. **3**: 177. — (F. C. Gray) No. Am. **15**: 177.
— Agriculture in, Colman's. Brownson, **6**: 132.
— American Travelers in. Ecl. M. **31**: 460.
— and America. Am. Q. **9**: 398.
— — Beltrami's. Lond. M. **20**: 157.
— — Chevalier and Cooper on. (J. W. Croker) Quar. **58**: 497.
— — Gurowski's. (J. H. Allen) Chr. Exam. **63**: 231.
— — in 1864. Brit. Q. **39**: 459. Same art. Ecl. M. **62**: 257.
— and Asia, Unexplored Parts of. Nature, **24**: 312.
— and the East, Prime's Travels in. Liv. Age, **49**: 243.
— — Travels in. (A. P. Peabody) No. Am. **81**: 194.
— and France, 1859. Brit. Q. **29**: 215. Same art. Liv. Age, **63**: 515. — Bent. Q. **2**: 1.
— and Peace, 1875. Brit. Q. **61**: 168.
— Armies of, 1856. Putnam, **6**: 196-569.
— Autumn Ramble in. (Lady Verney) Contemp. **38**: 956. Same art. Liv. Age, **148**: 149.
— Autumn Wanderings in. Liv. Age, **149**: 117.
— Balance of Power in. Ed. R. **1**: 345. **9**: 253. — Selec. Ed. R. **5**: 1. — Ev. Sat. **9**: 578.
— — Elements of. Fraser, **73**: 192.
— — in 1853. Bentley, **34**: 208.
— — in 1854. Westm. **61**: 537.
— — in 1878. (T. D. Woolsey) Princ. n. s. **2**: 717.
— Bartol's Pictures of. (F. H. Hedge) Chr. Exam. **59**: 427.
— Baxter's Impressions of. Quar. **86**: 492.
— Boundary Map of. Dub. Univ. **45**: 127. Same art. Liv. Age, **44**: 725.
— British and Continental Characteristics. Liv. Age, **42**: 547.
— By-Ways of. (B. Taylor) Atlan. **20**: 495, 680.
— Central, High and low Life in. (J. O. Noyes) Nat. M. **13**: 7.
— Christian Nations of, Present and Future of. Cath. World, **13**: 452.
— Cities of. Appleton, **11**: 47-720.
— Coblentz *via* Rotterdam. Victoria, **9**: 547.
— Concert of, 1880. Fortn. **34**: 200.

Europe, Cooper's Recollections of. Am. Mo. M. 12: 75. — Mo. R. 142: 321.
— Courts of, Swinburne's. Mus. 42: 160.
— Despotism in, Rise of. So. Lit. Mess. 21: 610.
— Dewey's Old World and New. West. Lit. J. 1: 272.
— Drift of, Christian and social. (J. P. Thompson) Princ. n. s. 1: 733.
— Early Settlement of. (C. W. Hutson) So. M. 13: 183–513.
— East and South of. Blackw. 53: 101. Same art. Ecl. Mus. 1: 267.
— Eastern, and British Policy. Liv. Age, 25: 337.
— — Peoples and Prospects of. Chamb. J. 22: 24, 44.
— — Western Civilization in. Liv. Age, 115: 259. *See* Eastern Question.
— Emigration from, to the U. S. Ed. R. 100: 236.
— Encyclicals of a Traveler. (H. Hunt) Atlan. 27: 758. 28: 215, 340.
— Ethnology of. Blackw. 76: 165.
— — Primeval Inhabitants. St. James, 10: 501.
— Farming and Peasantry on the Continent. Blackw. 107: 23.
— Federative Policy of. Mus. 13: 524.
— Fighting Power of. Temp. Bar, 12: 77. Same art. Ecl. M. 63: 161. — (H. M. Hozier) Gent. M. n. s. 14: 58.
— Fiske's Travels in. Am. Meth. Mo. 20: 449. — Chr. Q. Spec. 10: 468.
— Four Weeks on the Continent. (Duke of Argyll) Contemp. 38: 1. Same art. Liv. Age, 146: 259.
— Fuller's Sparks from a Locomotive. Liv. Age, 63: 508.
— Future of, Political. Brit. Q. 53: 516. Same art. Ecl. M. 76: 641. — Cath. World, 13: 76.
— — foretold in History. (T. E. C. Leslie) Macmil. 2: 329.
— Future Destinies of. Mo. R. 117: 336.
— General View of the States of. West. J. 5: 308.
— Governments of Continental. Tait, n. s. 19: 193–705.
— Great Fairs of. (R. H. Horne) Harper, 46: 376.
— Grain Market of. (R. Fisher) Am. Whig R. 5: 642.
— The grand Tour. Dub. Univ. 62: 311, 645.
— Greeley's Travels in. New Q. 1: 366.
— Historical Geography of. (A. V. Dicey) Nation, 33: 256. — (W. M. Blackburn) Dial (Ch.), 2: 61.
— History of, Alison's, 1789–1815. — (W. R. Greg) Ed. R. 76: 1. — (W. R. Greg) Westm. 41: 388. — Blackw. 48: 64. 50: 419. 52: 419. 79: 404. — Dub. Univ. 36: 631. — (J. Kennard) Chr. Exam. 38: 1. — (J. T. Headley) Am. Whig R. 1: 151. — (A. McVicker) Meth. Q. 3: 350. — So. Q. 5: 259. — (J. Forsyth) Princ. 15: 250. — Chr. R. 8: 77, 249. — So. Lit. Mess. 9: 136, 281. — Chr. Obs. 53: 524. — Mus. 39: 334. 44: 58. — Mo. R. 136: 281. 158: 420. — Ecl. Mus. 1: 1. — Liv. Age, 2: 370. — (P. Godwin) Putnam, 1: 561.
— — — 1815–1852. Ed. R. 97: 269. 111: 119. — Brit. Q. 29: 346. — Fraser, 53: 597. — Dub. Univ. 1: 619. 14: 275. 43: 635. 46: 1. 53: 368. Same art. Ecl. M. 45: 316. — Dub. Univ. 79: 404. — Dub. R. 33: 408. — Bentley, 43: 465. — No. Brit. 27: 277. — Blackw. 87: 441. 100: 475. — (J. K. Kendrick) Chr. R. 22: 110. — Chr. Rem. 27: 174. — Tait, 3: 496. — Ecl. R. 97: 279. 100: 58. — Fraser, 54: 154. 60: 211, 603. 62: 660. — Irish Q. 5: 633. 7: 552. 8: 213. — New Q. 2: 34. 4: 249. 5: 224.
— — Campaign of 1815. Ed. R. 117: 147.
— — Fyfe's Modern. (A. V. Dicey) Nation, 32: 76.
— — in the Dark Ages. Bost. Mo. 1: 465.
— — in the Middle Ages. Fraser, 11: 28.
— — — Hallam's. Ecl. R. 30: 517.
— — Ottoman Rule in. Ecl. M. 74: 409.
Europe, History of, Revolutions in, 1789–1848, Springer's. (E. D. Cheny) Chr. Exam. 83: 157.
— — since the Accession of Louis Philippe. Ecl. M. 7: 323. — For Q. 36: 437. — Liv. Age, 4: 191.
— — since the Peace of Utrecht. Westm. 4: 178.
— — Swedish Invasion of Germany, 1614–30, Negotiations on. (B. Moses) New Eng. 33: 421.
— Humphrey's Travels in. Chr. Q. Spec. 10: 468.
— Intellectual Development of. Westm. 83: 94.
— Internal Improvements in, 1842. (L. Klein) J. Frankl. Inst. 33: 1–217.
— Internal Relations of. (F. W. Newman) Fraser, 82: 443. Same art. Liv. Age, 107: 323.
— Karamsin's Travels. Ed. R. 3: 321.
— Laing's Notes of a Traveler, 1841. Tait, n. s. 9: 169. — Blackw. 68: 671. — (F. Bowen) No. Am. 71: 479.
— Later Stone Age in. (E. Clodd) Mod. R. 1: 489.
— Letters from. So. Lit. Mess. 20: 441–763.
— Liberalism in. New Eng. 8: 329.
— Liberties of the People of. So. Lit. Mess. 8: 613.
— Life in. Hogg, 5: 113–360. 6: 9–317.
— — and Manners in, Colman's. Colburn, 87: 10.
— Literature of South of, Hallam's. Colburn, 49: 436. Same art. Mus. 39: 315.
— long ago. Dem. R. 5: 61.
— Manners and Customs of. So. R. n. s. 20: 116.
— Map of. Once a Week, 28: 533.
— — New, 1860. (E. About) Liv. Age, 65: 724.
— Maritime Powers of. Pract. M. 2: 463.
— Matters and Things in. (G. Peck) Meth. Q. 7: 459, 607. 8: 122.
— Military Topography of. (H. Vethake) U. S. Serv. M. 1: 145, 284.
— Modern. Mo. R. 118: 197.
— Morals of, Lecky's History of. Quar. 128: 49. *See* Morals.
— Museums of. (T. M. Brewer) Pop. Sci. Mo. 11: 472.
— Navies of. Ed. R. 147: 495.
— North of, Barrow's Excursions in. Ed. R. 59: 372.
— — Hurton's Winter Pictures from. Tait, n. s. 17: 37, 88, 154.
— — Notes from. Pract. M. 1: 72–292. 2: 258.
— — Pictures of. De Bow, 26: 286.
— — Tracings in. (R. Chambers) Chamb. J. 12: 273–407. 13: 4–177.
— Notes for Travelers in. (A. Abbott) Harper, 39: 244.
— — of Travel in. (J. R. Thompson) So. Lit. Mess. 21: 303–630. 22: 416.
— Old, Religion and Ethnology of. Brit. Q. 10: 99.
— Pankapog to Pesth. (T. B. Aldrich) Atlan. 39: 19. 41: 596.
— Past and present State of. Walsh's Am. R. 4: 354.
— Political and social Outlook, 1878. Am. Cath. Q. 4: 193.
— Political Changes in, 1847–76. (M. E. G. Duff) Contemp. 27: 694. Same art. Liv. Age, 129: 323.
— Political Management in. (P. Godwin) Putnam, 1: 427.
— Politics of, Forces in. (G. E. Pond) Galaxy, 24: 229.
— — in 1814. (F. Jeffrey) Ed. R. 23: 1.
— — in 1823. (E. Robinson) No. Am. 17: 340.
— — in 1825. (A. H. Everett) No. Am. 21: 141.
— — in 1828. (A. H. Everett) No. Am. 27: 215.
— — in 1830. (A. H. Everett) No. Am. 30: 399.
— — in 1831. (T. P. Thompson) Westm. 14: 245.
— — in 1832. Fraser, 4: 25.
— — in 1834. (H. R. Cleveland) No. Am. 40: 269.
— — in 1844. Mus. 44: 356.
— — in 1847. (J. Mazzini) Peop. J. 3: 17.
— — in 1848. (F. Bowen) No. Am. 70: 473. — Brit. Q. 8: 516. — Ed. R. 88: 514. Same art. Ecl. M. 15: 433. Same art. Liv. Age, 19: 577. — Am. Lit. M. 2: 320. — So. Q. 16: 277. — So. Lit. Mess. 15: 129, 193, 313.

Europe, Politics of, in 1849. Chr. R. **14**: 505.
— — in 1852. Dem. R. **31**: 592. **32**: 481. — Westm. **57**: 442.
— — in 1854. No. Brit. **22**: 289. Same art. Liv. Age, **45**: 131.
— — — and in 1878. Month, **32**: 129.
— — in 1855. Fraser, **52**: 330.
— — in 1856, Kossuth's Speech on. Liv. Age, **44**: 131.
— — — Peace and its political Duties. No. Brit. **25**: 257.
— — in 1857. Dub. Univ. **49**: 246.
— — in 1859. Ecl. R. **110**: 264.
— — in 1860. Brit. Q. **33**: 509. — Dub. Univ. **56**: 123–577. — No. Brit. **32**: 520. Same art. Ecl. M. **50**: 367. — (C. C. Hazewell) Atlan. **7**: 100.
— — — Sicilian Game. No. Brit. **33**: 549.
— — in 1861. Dub. Univ. **57**: 248–750. **58**: 119–753.
— — in 1864. Nat. R. **18**: 293. Same art. Ecl. M. **61**: 366. — No. Brit. **39**: 538.
— — in 1865. Brit. Q. **42**: 385.
— — in 1866. Lond. Q. **27**: 125. — Dub. R. **74**: 267. — Ed. R. **124**: 275.
— — in 1868. (L. Blanc) Lippinc. **1**: 385. — Macmil. **19**: 219. Same art. Ecl. M. **72**: 323.
— — in 1871. Brit. Q. **53**: 516. — Dub. Univ. **77**: 322.
— — in 1873. Brownson, **22**: 111.
— — in 1875. (E. de Laveleye) Fortn. **24**: 1. — Brit. Q. **61**: 168. — Dub. R. **77**: 189.
— — — Armed Peace. Quar. **141**: 81. Same art. Ecl. M. **86**: 513.
— — — Congress of St. Petersburg. (J. N. Pomeroy) Nation, **20**: 21.
— — in 1877, General View of. (A. Laugel) Nation, **25**: 117.
— — in 1878, from a French Standpoint. (E. Pressensé) Internat. R. **5**: 607.
— — in 1880. Blackw. **127**: 518.
— — — Outlook of. Contemp. **37**: 691.
— — Secret of. St. James, **33**: 677.
— — since the Congress of Vienna. Dem. R. **1**: 123.
— Population, Comparative, of States of. (S. Brown) J. Statis. Soc. **31**: 146.
— — of larger Towns of. J. Statis. Soc. **38**: 379.
— Prehistoric. (W. B. Dawkins) Nature, **23**: 309.
— — and Man. Lond. Q. **56**: 408.
— — Fragment of. (A. Geikie) Nature, **22**: 400.
— Progress of, in principal Countries. (F. Martin) J. Statis. Soc. **40**: 593.
— — and Retrogression in. Dub. Univ. **37**: 67.
— — of Opinions in. West. Mo. R. **3**: 266.
— Prospects of. Liv. Age, **29**: 359.
— — of the popular Cause in. Ecl. R. **89**: 375.
— — of Reform in. (E. Everett) No. Am **33**: 154.
— Pulse of, 1816. (M. E. G. Duff) Contemp. **28**: 338.
— Race for Empire in. So. R. n. s. **15**: 1.
— Rationalism in, Lecky's. (J. Fiske) Chr. Exam. **81**: 171. *See* Rationalism.
— Religious Movements in. (A. Ewing) Contemp. **19**: 752.
— Religious Outlook in, 1881. (A. J. Thebaud) Am. Cath. Q. **6**: 132.
— Republican Movement in. (E. Castelar) Fortn. **17**: 668. **18**: 1, 166, 325. — (E. Castelar) Harper, **45**: 47–849. **47**: 282–915. **49**: 716, 814. **50**: 97–867. **51**: 420, 699.
— Republicanism in, Difficulties of. (E. A. Freeman) Internat. R. **2**: 371.
— Revolutions in. Blackw. **71**: 242.
— Royal Families of. Liv. Age, **56**: 769.
— Scots Traveler in, in 1609. Blackw. **124**: 416. Same art. Liv. Age, **139**: 359.
— Miss Sedgwick's Letters from. Tait, n. s. **8**: 590.
Europe, General Sherman in. (J. C. Audenried) Harper, **47**: 225, 481, 652.
— Sight-Seeing in. Am. Mo. M. **4**: 157.
— Silliman's Visit to, 1851. (D. Olmsted) New Eng. **12**: 24.
— Sketches of Travel in. (J. Eldredge) New Eng. **12**: 457.
— Slavonian. Republic, **6**: 27.
— Socialism in. (A. Bierbower) O. & N. **8**: 525.
— Southern, Debts and Tariffs of. (F. Wharton) Hunt, **9**: 207.
— — Spirit of Change in. (J. H. Skene) Colburn, **86**: 288–445. **87**: 34–305. **88**: 468.
— — Symonds's Sketches of. (W. M. Ferriss) Nation, **31**: 189. — (J. MacAlister) Dial (Ch.), **1**: 25.
— Stamboul to Pesth. Bentley, **40**: 331.
— Statesmen of. Colburn, **73**: 1–441.
— Statistics of, 1869. Am. J. Educ. **18**: 538.
— Stowe's Sunny Memories of. (A. P. Peabody) No. Am. **79**: 423. — Liv. Age, **42**: 370, 457. **43**: 40.
— B. Taylor's Travels in. De Bow, **27**: 648.
— Tendencies in. Am. Q. **22**: 257.
— Thrones of, the Farm of the Coburgs. Dem. R. **43**: 217.
— Tour in. (S. J. Lippincott) Bentley, **35**: 198–563. **36**: 33–463.
— Travel in. (F. H. Hedge) Chr. Exam. **53**: 239. — Dub. Univ. **75**: 508.
— — Art of. Nat. R. **17**: 103.
— — Bartol's Essays on. (H. W. Bellows) No. Am. **82**: 33.
— — Expense of. (W. L. Gage) New Eng. **22**: 445. — Contin. Mo. **3**: 730.
— — — Tour of Europe for $181 in Currency. (R. Keeler) Atlan. **26**: 92.
— — in the 18th Century. Dub. Univ. **64**: 91.
— Travels in. (C. C. Shackford) No. Am. **92**: 529.
— Turkish Invasions of, 1670–83. (Lady Verney) Contemp. **29**: 635.
— United States of; a Lecture. (J. R. Seeley) Macmil. **23**: 436. Same art. Ecl. M. **76**: 535.
— — Seeley on. Ev. Sat. **10**: 314. — O. & N. **3**: 260.
— Vale and City. Colburn, **146**: 44–651. **147**: 77–689.
— Visit to; Things generally overlooked. (E. I. Sears) Nat. Q. **21**: 130.
— Wallace's Art, Scenery, and Philosophy in. (H. Binney) Putnam, **6**: 267.
— Western, Celtic Traditions of. Rel. Cab. **1**: 58–241.
Europe's Angels; a Tale. (B. Murphy) Cath. World, **16**: 533.
European Americanized. (O. W. Holmes) Atlan. **35**: 75.
Europeans, Chinese Opinions of. Fraser, **83**: 395. Same art. Ecl. M. **76**: 615.
Europeans, The. (H. James, jr.) Atlan. **42**: 52–404.
European Finance and American Securities, 1869. (J. B. Hodgskin) Nation, **8**: 428.
European Monarchy, Cass on. Dem. R. **30**: 456.
European Nationalities and Races. (K. Blind) Nat. Q. **23**: 1.
European People, Progress and Retrogression of. Dub. Univ. **37**: 67.
Eurydice, H. M. S., Loss of; a Poem. (F. T. Palgrave) Contemp. **32**: 257.
Eusebius Pamphilus. (A. Lamson) Chr. Exam. **18**: 84. — (J. B. Lightfoot) Contemp. **25**: 169.
— Armenian Translation of. Kitto, **11**: 263. **12**: 317.
— as a Historian. (L. Coleman) Bib. Sac. **15**: 79.
— Ecclesiastical History. Ecl. R. **68**: 369.
— Historical Credit of. (A. Lamson) Chr. Exam. **18**: 291.
— Life and Writings of. Chr. Obs. **33**: 523.
— Recovery of a lost Work of. Liv. Age, **71**: 571.
— The Star of Bethlehem. (Syriac text, ed. by W Wright) Kitto, **37**: 117. **38**: 150.
Eustace the Monk. Fraser, **15**: 75.
Eustace the Negro. Chamb. J. **4**: 332.

Eustace de Ribaumont; a Ballad. Lond. M. 6: 325.
Eustace, John C., Vindication of, from Hobhouse's Charges. Lond. M. 1: 532.
Eustace Diamonds. (A. Trollope) Fortn. 16: 1-668. 17: 90-705. 18: 89-723. Same art. Galaxy, 12: 395-804. 13: 61-787. 14: 49-798.
Eustathius as a Reformer. (A. Neander) Kitto, 4: 101.
Eustis, William, Governor, Letter of, 1776, with Notes. N. E. Reg. 23: 205.
Eustis Family. (H. L. Eustis) N. E. Reg. 32: 204.
Euston Square in the Dog-Days. Hogg, 14: 271.
Euthanasia. (J. Scoffern) Belgra. 7: 221. Same art. Canad. Mo. 2: 461. — Pop. Sci. Mo. 3: 90.
— Natural. (B. W. Richardson) Pop. Sci. Mo. 8: 617.
Euthanasia; a Poem. (C. F. Alexander) Dub. Univ. 40: 478.
Euthanasia; a Poem. (A. Austin) Temp. Bar, 3: 472.
Eutrapelia; illustrative of Barrow on Wit. Colburn, 108: 362-460. 109: 176-451. 110: 78-424.
Eutychian Churches. (J. A. Reubelt) Mercersb. 11: 585.
Eutychian Controversy about Heresies. (R. Mochler) Month, 25: 318. 26: 87.
Euxine, Etchings from the. Fraser, 50: 28, 296.
Eva D'Alton's Revenge. (R. W. MacDonnell) Tinsley, 29: 366.
Evading the Law. All the Year, 38: 155.
Evalla. (W. B. Bateman) Colburn, 113: 438. 115: 232, 352. 116: 93-468. 117: 83-474.
Evan Harrington. (G. Meredith) Once a Week, 2: 133-399. 3: 1-421.
Evangelical Alliance. (H. Bushnell) New Eng. 5: 102. — (J. H. Raymond) Chr. R. 12: 155, 477. — (J. Forsythe) Princ. 18: 568. — (G. Peck) Meth. Q. 7: 151. — (L. Bacon) New Eng. 10: 309. — (J. R. G. Hassard) Cath. World, 18: 353. — (J. McCosh) Princ. 42: 455. — Bib. R. 1: 300. — Brownson, 23: 93. — Internat. R. 1: 140, 574. — Lond. Q. 43: 265.
— and the American War, 1863. New Eng. 22: 288.
— and Dr. Whately. Brit. Q. 3: 525.
— in 1845, Proposed. Ecl. R. 83: 487.
— — and Fellowship with Slaveholders. Ecl. R. 84: 747.
— in 1846, Proposed. Chr. Obs. 46: 29, 105, 244.
— — — Whately on. Chr. Obs. 46: 173.
— — Publications on, 1846. Chr. Obs. 46: 439, 494.
— in 1857, at Berlin. (P. Schaff) Mercersb. 9: 318.
— in 1861, at Geneva. Mo. Rel. M. 27: 110, 151.
— in 1867, Report to. (H. B. Smith) Am. Presb. R. 16: 555.
— in 1873, at New York. (P. Schaff) Am. Presb. R. 19: 68. — (J. W. Nevin) Mercersb. 21: 399. — (M. Valentine) Luth. Q. 4: 233. — Canad. Mo. 4: 452, 548. — Mo. Rel. M. 50: 465, 475.
— in 1879, at Basle. Lond. Q. 53: 152. — (J. F. Hurst) Meth. Q. 40: 257.
Evangelical Character. (F. P. Cobbe) Theo. R. 11: 447.
Evangelical Clergy, English. Macmil. 3: 113.
— and Baptismal Regeneration. Ecl. R. 90: 478.
Evangelical Doctrines, Tripartite Nature of Man in relation to. Kitto, 39: 65.
Evangelical Drawing-Rooms. Tinsley, 9: 111.
Evangelical Faith. (E. C. Smyth) Bib. Sac. 17: 494.
Evangelical Homiletics. Meth. Q. 7: 63.
Evangelical Knowledge Society. (N. S. Richardson) Am. Church R. 18: 597.
Evangelical Lutheran Church in United States. (J. A. Brown) Bib. Sac. 25: 435.
Evangelical Movement, History of. (W. E. H. Lecky) 19th Cent. 6: 280. — (W. E. Gladstone) Brit. Q. 70: 1. Same art. Liv. Age, 142: 387.
Evangelical Preachers. (H. J. Coleridge) Month, 24: 265.
Evangelical Preaching. Ed. R. 64: 428.
Evangelical Religious Principles. Chr. Obs. 18: 169.
Evangelical Review. (W. M. Reynolds) Evang. R. 1: 1.
Evangelical Sects. (R. Southey) Quar. 4: 480.
Evangelical Succession. (Sir J. Stephen) Ed. R. 67: 500.
Evangelical Voluntary Church Association. Ecl. R. 71: 365. 74: 1.
Evangelicalism. (J. M. Capes) Contemp. 23: 747.
Evangeline, Story of, in Prose. (M. Walsh) Cath. World, 22: 604.
Evangelism, Modern. (J. A. Singmaster) Luth. Q. 7: 400.
— of the 18th Century. Am. Presb. R. 9: 476.
Evangelist, Work of an. (E. Greenwald) Evang. R. 2: 84.
Evangelists. (E. Pond) New Eng. 2: 297. — (C. Colton) Chr. Mo. Spec. 10: 292, 337.
— in our Churches. (J. M. Chamberlin) Cong. Q. 8: 354. — (M. K. Cross) Cong. R. 10: 566. — (S. D. Cochran) Cong. R. 11: 253.
— — Utility of. (W. Mitchell) Lit. & Theo. R. 2: 494.
— Office and Work of. (S. E. Shepard) Chr. Q. 8: 99.
Evangelists, The, Symbols of, as a Key to the Gospels. Ho. & For. R. 1: 195.
Evangelization, Home. Ecl. R. 112: 413, 514.
— — Methods of. (W. G. Blaikie) Princ. n. s. 2: 169.
— Modes of. (J. K. Wight) Princ. 36: 395.
— Popular. (C. L. Woodworth) Bost. R. 6: 477. — (A. J. Pierson) Presb. R. 1: 446.
— Primitive, and its Lessons. (J. P. Thompson) New Eng. 18: 942.
Evangelizing England, Plans for. Cong. M. 21: 665
Evans, Augusta J. *See* Wilson, Mrs. A. J.
Evans, Rev. B., Memoir of. Cong. M. 6: 169, 225.
Evans, Christmas, of Wales. Ecl. R. 114: 385.
— and Welsh Preaching. Theo. Ecl. 1: 147.
— Memoir of. Ecl. R. 85: 339.
— Sketch of. (A. Mursell) Good Words, 4: 411. Same art. Liv. Age, 78: 114.
Evans, Sir De Lacy. Dem. R. 35: 222. — Ev. Sat. 9: 110.
Evans, Fred., the Shaker Elder. Ev. Sat. 11: 295.
Evans, George, with portrait. Am. Whig R. 6: 19.
Evans, John. (E. D. Neill) N. E. Reg. 26: 421. — (C. T. Jackson) Am. J. Sci. 82: 311.
Evans, Sebastian, Poetry of. St. James, 37: 52.
Evans, R. W., Sermons of. Chr. Obs. 31: 29.
Evaporating Sugar, Kneller's Improvements in. J. Frankl. Inst. 10: 163.
Evaporation and Distillation, Apparatus for. J. Frankl. Inst. 5: 1.
— and Percolation. (C. Greaves) Ecl. Engin. 16: 48.
— on the Tulare Lakes, Cal. (W. P. Blake) Am. J. Sci. 71: 365.
— Rain, etc., Cause of. (G. A. Rowell) J. Frankl. Inst. 44: 340.
— Researches on. (Prof. Marcet) J. Frankl. Inst. 57: 278.
— Where does the Water come from? (G. M. Kellogg) Lakeside, 1: 135.
Evarts, Jeremiah. Am. Q. Reg. 4: 73. — Spirit Pilg. 4: 599. — (S. F. Smith) Chr. R. 11: 20.
Evarts, William M., with portrait. Ecl. M. 86: 248.
Eve, Temptation of. Cong. M. 23: 92, 213.
— Why a Rib? Recr. Sci. 2: 151.
Eve, Sarah, Journal of, 1772-73. Pennsyl. M. 5: 19, 191.
Eve of a Journey. House. Words, 8: 173.
— of the Flood; a Poem. (S. Clarkson) Hogg, 15: 206.
— of St. Andrew. Bentley, 15: 235.
— of St. Bartholomew; a Tale. (H. W. Herbert) Am. Mo. M. 2: 297, 377.
— of St. John: a Masque for Music. (J. F. Waller) Dub. Univ. 57: 446.
— of St. Silvester; a Poem. Dub. Univ. 31: 781.
Eveleen O'Connor; a Story. Cornh. 8: 488.
Eveleigh, John, Sermons of. Quar. 7: 293.
Eveline's Visitant; a Ghost Story. (M. E. Braddon) Belgra. 1: 351.

Evelyn, John. Sharpe, **12**: 351. Same art. Liv. Age, **28**: 222
— and Samuel Pepys. Blackw. **76**: 35. Same art. Ecl. M. **33**: 106. Same art. Liv. Age, **42**: 291.
— Life and Times of. Ecl. R. **110**: 242.
— a Lover of Trees. All the Year. **24**: 294.
— Memoirs of. (R. Southey) Quar. **19**: 1. Same art. Anal. M. **13**: 92. — Mo. R. **91**: 113, 269. — Ecl. R. **32**: 137, 582.
— Miscellaneous Writings. Colburn, **16**: 43-267.
— Original Letter of. Lond. M. **10**: 589.
— Writings of. Mo. R. **108**: 298. — Quar. **9**: 45.
Evelyn, Robert, Explorer of the Delaware. (E. D. Niell) Hist. M. **14**: 75.
Evelyn Family. Am. J. Educ. **26**: 369.
Evelyn Vaughan; a Tale. (A. Clyde) Sharpe, **44**: 304.
Evenheart, Lawrence, Sketch of. So. Lit. Mess. **4**: 590.
Even-Song. (O. W. Holmes) Atlan. **25**: 349.
Evening; an Ode. Blackw. **24**: 37.
— Hymn to. Dub. Univ. **1**: 498.
— in Furness Abbey. (J. Wilson) Blackw. **26**: 540.
— with a Spiritualist. Lippinc. **16**: 557.
— with my Uncle. (J. Greenwood) Lond. Soc. **11**: 139.
Evenings at a Friend's. (S. E. Farley) Godey, **23**: 281.
— at Home. (J. F. W. Ware) Mo. Rel. M. **26**: 151.
— at Sea. Blackw. **62**: 96, 547. **63**: 33.
— in New England. U. S. Lit. Mess. **1**: 275.
Evening Hexameters. (H. Alford) Good Words, **4**: 416.
Evening Shadows; a Poem. Putnam, **14**: 38.
Evening Walk; a Poem. Blackw. **51**: 653.
Evening Walks in the City. (C. Lanman) So. Lit. Mess. **6**: 720.
Events that never happened. Chamb. J. **56**: 91.
Everard, Edward C., Comedian. Blackw. **4**: 51.
Everett, Alexander H. Dem. R. **21**: 395. — with portrait, Dem. R. **10**: 460.
— Essays of. Dem. R. **18**: 126. — So. Q. **10**: 329.
— Obituary of. (E. E. Hale) Chr. Exam. **44**: 155.
Everett, Edward. (E. E. Hale) Atlan. **15**: 342. — (G. W. Searle) Nat. Q. **10**: 293. — with portrait, Ecl. M. **47**: 279. — with portrait, Hist. M. **9**: 73. — Am. J. Educ. **7**: 325. — New Eng. M. **5**: 185.
— Address at Williams College. So. Lit. Mess. **4**: 426.
— — before Mechanics' Association. So. Lit. Mess. **4**: 61.
— — Fourth of July, 1833. New Eng. M. **5**: 143.
— Birthplace of. Appleton, **9**: 719.
— Character of. No. Am. **100**: 560.
— College Life of. (E. Everett) O. & N. **4**: 18, 194.
— Dinner to, at Nashville, 1829. Niles's Reg. **37**: 14.
— Mount Vernon Papers. All the Year, **4**: 138.
— Oration at Charlestown, June 17, 1850. So. Q. **18**: 251.
— Orations and Speeches. So. Lit. Mess. **16**: 659. — (G. S. Hillard) No. Am. **44**: 138. — (L. Withington) Chr. Mo. Spec. **7**: 534. — (J. Sparks) No. Am. **20**: 417. — (C. C. Felton) No. Am. **71**: 445. — U. S. Lit. Gaz. **2**: 293. — New Eng. **9**: 44. — So. Q. **19**: 456.
— Phi Beta Kappa Address. (F. H. Hedge) Chr. Exam. **16**: 1.
— Plymouth Oration. U. S. Lit. Gaz. **1**: 311.
— Public Life of. Am. Whig R. **12**: 484.
Everett, John, Life and Actions of. (H. Southern) Retros. **6**: 237.
Everett, Thomas Chivers, Memoir of. Ecl. R. **72**: 101.
Everett Genealogy. (E. F. Everett) N. E. Reg. **14**: 215.
Evergreen Beauty. (H. S. Hurst) Contin. Mo. **4**: 227.
Eversley, Charles S. L. Mus. **44**: 317.
Everstone. Am. Whig R. **12**: 47, 152.
Every-Day Adventures. (A. Halliday) Lond. Soc. **14**: 97-530.
Everything is good for Something. Chamb. J. **32**: 116.
Evesham, Abbey of. (G. G. Perry) Contemp. **5**: 304. — Penny M. **11**: 404.
Evesham, Chronicle of. Dub. R. **67**: 26.
— Reading-Desk in. (E. Rudge) Arch. **17**: 273.
— Seal of. (W. Hamper) Arch. **19**: 66.
Eviction, An. Chamb. J. **52**: 554.
— and what came of it; a Story. Chamb. J. **57**: 282-345.
— at Ballyhack; a Sketch. Tinsley, **27**: 324.
Evidence. Chamb. J. **36**: 289.
— Bentham's Rationale of Judicial. Westm. **9**: 198. **10**: 367. — Ed. R. **48**: 457. — So. R. **5**: 381.
— Circumstantial. *See* Circumstantial Evidence.
— Confessions in. (J. Gallison) No. Am. **10**: 418.
— Historical, as affected by Time. (A. Barnes) Am. Presb. R. **16**: 189.
— — Religious, and Scientific. Fraser, **84**: 512.
— How to estimate. Cornh. **8**: 438.
— Laws of. (G. S. Hillard) No. Am. **92**: 515. — Mass. Q. **2**: 39.
— — Stephen's Digest of. (F. Pollock) Fortn. **26**: 383.
— of the Senses, Fallacious. Dub. R. **3**: 525.
— of Testimony. (E. Pond) Am. Bib. Repos. 2d s. **2**: 14.
— Rules of, and the New York Bar Association. (E. L. Godkin) Nation, **12**: 256.
— Scottish Law of. Ed. R. **57**: 96.
Evil. (J. De Concilio) Cath. World, **29**: 510. — Chr. Exam. **33**: 197. — (A. P. Peabody) Chr. Exam. **47**: 227.
— and eternal Punishment. Kitto, **40**: 152.
— and God, Young on. Ecl. R. **104**: 177.
— Catholic and Pantheistic View of. (J. De Concilio) Cath. World, **29**: 54.
— Existence of, consistent with God's Goodness. Am. Presb. R. **8**: 192.
— — and moral Utility of. Westm. **83**: 195.
— The greatest. (J. P. Edwards) Peop. J. **6**: 282.
— made subservient to Good. Chr. R. **25**: 433.
— Ministry of. (M. L. Hurlbut) Chr. Exam. **35**: 32.
— Moral. Lond. Q. **52**: 361.
— — Smith and Williams on. Chr. Obs. **5**: 172.
— Nature of, James on. (J. F. Clarke) Chr. Exam. **59**: 116.
— often a Stimulant to Good. (G. H. Emerson) Univ. Q. **19**: 312.
— Origin of. Theo. Repos. **1**: 443.
— — and the Fall. (Dr. Rinck) Meth. Q. **13**: 568.
— Problem of. (E. Naville) Theo. Ecl. **6**: 430. — So. R. n. s. **9**: 745.
— Theories of. Am. Whig R. **14**: 516. — (J. M. Clark) Am. Church R. **32**: 354.
— — of the End of. Lond. Q. **44**: 171.
— Uses of. (T. B. Thayer) Univ. Q. **3**: 167.
— Utilization of. (J. S. Blakie) Good Words, **20**: 770.
"Evil is wrought by want of thought." House. Words, **1**: 580.
Evils, Satan the Source of. (H. L. Dox) Luth. Q. **8**: 566.
Evil Eye. Cornh. **39**: 184. Same art. Appleton, **21**: 247
Evil Eye; a Tale. Temp. Bar, **7**: 560.
Evil May-Day. Fraser, **98**: 381, 537.
Evil Thursday, on Record in Venice. All the Year, **17**: 16. Same art. Ecl. M. **68**: 462.
Evolution. (J. W. Draper) Unita. R. **8**: 536. — (J. Tyndall) Ev. Sat. **17**: 319. — (G. J. Romanes) Nature, **24**: 1.
— a Poem. (H. H. Boyesen) Atlan. **41**: 565.
— American Zoölogists and. (E. S. Morse) Pop. Sci. Mo. **10**: 1, 181.
— and the After-Life. (R. O. Mason) Pop. Sci. Mo. **7**: 46.
— and Apparition of Animal Forms. (J. W. Dawson) Princ. n. s. **1**: 262.
— and Automatism. (C. Elam) Contemp. **28**: 537, 725. **29**: 117. Same art. Ecl. M. **87**: 640. **88**: 166, 342.
— and Christian Doctrine of the Fall. (F. D. Hoskins) Am. Church R. **36**: 25.

Evolution and Conscience. (T. S. Lathrop) Univ. Q. **36**: 303.
— and the Doctrine of Design. (W. S. Jevons) Pop. Sci. Mo. **5**: 98.
— and Ethical Philosophy. (W. Knight) 19th Cent. **4**: 432.
— and Ethics. (H. Calderwood) Contemp. **31**: 123. — (D. M. Hodge) Univ. Q. **36**: 175. — Brit. Q. **68**: 30.
— and Faith. Dub. R. **69**: 1.
— and Female Education. (S.T. Preston) Nature, **22**: 485.
— and Geological Time. (G. Allen) Gent. M. n. s. **25**: 563.
— and Huxley. (A. Winchell) Meth. Q. **37**: 289.
— and Immortality. (S. S. Hebberd) Univ. Q. **34**: 22.
— and Intellect. (St. G. Mivart) Brit. Q. **74**: 298.
— and Involution. (W. H. Butterfield) Western, **5**: 190. — (J. Rickaby) Month, **29**: 269.
— and its Consequences. (E. D. Cope) Penn Mo. **3**: 222-461. — (St. G. Mivart) Contemp. **19**: 168.
— and Materialism. (O. A. Rounds) Univ. Q. **36**: 400. — (J. LeConte) Princ. n. s. **7**: 149.
— and Mind. (C. B. Radcliffe) Pop. Sci. Mo. **3**: 359.
— and Natural Selection. (W. F. Ainsworth) Colburn, **165**: 1246.
— and the Origin of Life. (H. C. Bastian) Pop. Sci. Mo. **4**: 713.
— and Pantheism. (St. J. Tyrwhitt) Contemp. **33**: 81.
— and the physical Forces. (W. F. Ainsworth) Colburn, **166**: 1, 115.
— and Positivism. (J. H. Bridges) Fortn. **27**: 853. **28**: 89. — (M. Pattison) Fortn. **28**: 285.
— and the Problem of Life. (E. Montgomery) Pop. Sci. Mo. **13**: 455-677.
— and Providence. (N. H. Fisher) Mercersb. **24**: 427.
— and Religion. (S. R. Calthrop) Mo. Rel. M. **50**: 193. — (C. B. Upton) Theo. R. **9**: 561.
— — of Future. (A. Swanwick) Contemp. **28**: 110.
— and Species. (J. H. McIlvaine) Presb. R. **1**: 611.
— and Spiritualism. (W. F. Ainsworth) Colburn, **165**: 1081.
— and Theism. (M. J. Savage) Mod. R. **2**: 468.
— and Theology. (A. Gray) Nation, **18**: 44. — (S. Newcomb) No. Am. **128**: 647. — Radical, **9**: 375. — (J. Robinson) Brit. Q. **72**: 78.
— and Thought, Spencer and Lewes on. (T. H. Green) Contemp. **31**: 25.
— and Vegetable Kingdom. (W. Carruthers) Contemp. **29**: 397.
— and Volition. (W. Haslam) Nat. Q. **37**: 127.
— and Zoölogical Formulation. (A. H. Garrod) Nature, **10**: 465.
— as affecting the Earth's Crust. (A. R. Leeds) J. Frankl. Inst. **91**: 129, 202.
— Atheism, and Theology. Lond. Q. **49**: 322.
— Bathybius and the Moners. (E. Haeckel) Pop. Sci. Mo. **11**: 641.
— Bibliography of Theory of. (C. Wright) Nation, **20**: 113.
— Büchner's Force and Matter. (A. Bayma) Cath. World, **19**: 433, 637, 823. **20**: 73, 175, 405.
— by the Spirit. (N. P. Gilman) Unita. R. **10**: 512.
— Catastrophism and. (C. King) Am. Natural. **11**: 449.
— Consciousness in. (E. D. Cope) Penn Mo. **6**: 560.
— Contemporary. (St. G. Mivart) Contemp. **22**: 595. **23**: 345, 599. **24**: 360, 772.
— Controversy of Haeckel and Virchow. (C. Elam) Contemp. **33**: 540.
— controverted. (C. A. Stork) Luth. Q. **3**: 325.
— Cosmic and organic. (L. F. Ward) Pop. Sci. Mo. **11**: 672.
— Critical Periods in the Earth's History and their Relation to. (J. LeConte) Am. Natural. **11**: 540. — (J. LeConte) Am. J. Sci. **114**: 99.
Evolution, Critics of. (J. S. Lippincott) Am. Natural **14**: 319, 398.
— Criticisms corrected. (H. Spencer) Pop. Sci. Mo. **17**: 795. **18**: 101.
— Darwin's Theory of. (F. Bowen) No. Am. **90**: 474. — (A. Weld) Month, **15**: 71. — (R. P. Stebbins) Mo. Rel. M. **50**: 496. *See* Darwinism.
— Development *vs.* Creation. (H. Lincoln) Bapt. Q. **2**: 257.
— Development Hypothesis. (J. McCosh) Pop. Sci. Mo. **10**: 86.
— Doctrine of. (J. Martineau) O. & N. **5**: 545. — Pop. Sci. Mo. **2**: 110.
— Draper on. (J. Bayma) Cath. World, **26**: 774. — Pop. Sci. Mo. **12**: 175.
— Earth's physical. (C. E. Dutton) Penn Mo. **7**: 364, 417.
— Ethical Method of. (D. McG. Means) Mind, **5**: 396.
— Ethics of. (B. P. Bowne) Meth. Q. **40**: 430.
— — Postulates of. (C. A. Stork) Luth. Q. **11**: 42.
— — Savage on. (N. P. Gilman) Unita. R. **15**: 44.
— Evidence of. (T. H. Huxley) Pop. Sci. Mo. **10**: 207, 285.
— Facts and Logic of. (W. D. Wilson) Am. Church R. **31**: 177.
— Fallacies of. (G. J. Romanes) Fortn. **32**: 492. Same art. Pop. Sci. Mo. **16**: 101. — Ed. R. **150**: 219. — Meth. Q. **31**: 753.
— Formula of. (P. G. Tait) Nature, **23**: 80.
— from mechanical Force. (L. P. Hickok) Princ. n. s. **1**: 567.
— Genesis, Geology, and. (G. Henslow) Pop. Sci. Mo. **4**: 324.
— Geographical. (A. Geikie) Pop. Sci. Mo. **15**: 548, 593.
— Geography and. (R. Strachey) Pop. Sci. Mo. **8**: 192.
— Gospel of. (C. Elam) Contemp. **37**: 713. Same art. Ecl. M. **95**: 1.
— Haeckel's Anthropogenie. (R. R. Wright) Canad. J. n. s. **15**: 231.
— Huxley's Lectures on. Nature, **23**: 203, 227. — (J. Bayma) Cath. World, **24**: 616. — (A. M. Kirsch) Am. Cath. Q. **2**: 644.
— Hypothesis of. (H. C. Bastian) Contemp. **23**: 528, 703. — (J. L. Cabell) So. R. n. s. **3**: 408. — (E. D. Cope) Lippinc. **6**: 29, 173, 310. — Nature, **8**: 509.
— in the Netherlands. Am. Natural. **11**: 295.
— in Religion. (A. Reville) Theo. R. **12**: 230.
— Involution before. (M. H. Slosson) Chr. Q. **8**: 331.
— Logic of. (E. F. X. McSweeny) Am. Cath. Q. **4**: 551.
— Martineau on. (H. Spencer) Contemp. **20**: 141.
— Mathematician's View of. (W. H. L. Russell) Macmil. **41**: 55. Same art. Liv. Age, **143**: 567. Same art. Ecl. M. **94**: 115.
— Mathematics in. (G. Iles) Pop. Sci. Mo. **9**: 202.
— Metaphysics of, Spencer on. (L. Adams) New Eng. **34**: 419.
— Missing Links. (H. S. Fagan) St. James, **43**: 764.
— Mivart's Contemporary. (C. W. Ernst) Unita. R. **7**: 15.
— Modern Doctrine of. (E. D. Cope) Am. Natural. **14**: 166, 260.
— Monboddo and Darwin. (A. Weld) Month, **15**: 440.
— New Aspects of. Dub. Univ. **94**: 236.
— of Beauty. (F. T. Mott) Sup. Pop. Sci. Mo. **3**: 361.
— of Ceremonial Government. *See* Ceremonial.
— of Chemical Elements. (L. T. Ward) Pop. Sci. Mo. **18**: 256.
— of Genera and Species. (J. W. Dawson) Canad. Mo **2**: 154.
— of Life, Chapman's. (J. Fiske) Nation, **16**: 168. — (J. J. Lalor) Cath. World, **17**: 145.
— of living Things, Heterogeneous. (H. C. Bastian) Nature, **2**: 170, 193, 219.

Evolution of Man. (H. A. Du Bois) Am. Church R. **17**: 169, 337, 505.
— — and Stone Age. (J. P. Thompson) Bib. Sac. **34**: 70.
— — Haeckel on. (E. Coues) Nation, **29**: 429.
— of Morality. (J. A. Allen) Canad. Mo. **11**: 490.
— of Structure in Seedlings. (J. C. Draper) Am. J. Sci. **104**: 392.
— of Thought, A Law of. (J. LeConte) Princ. n. s. **8**: 373.
— Old and new, Darwin's. (A. R. Wallace) Nature, **20**: 141.
— Opinions of. (W. Hull) Luth. Q. **5**: 91.
— or Creation, which? (T. Clarke) Lakeside, **1**: 91.
— or Teleology, What to believe in Science? (T. R. R. Stebbing) Pop. Sci. R. **13**: 11. Same art. Ecl. M. **82**: 315.
— Organic, Scientific Evidence of. (G. J. Romanes) Fortn. **36**: 739.
— Permanence of Type and. (L. Agassiz) Atlan. **33**: 92.
— Philosophy of. (J. P. Bland) Unita. R. **3**: 576. — (S. H. Carpenter) Bapt. Q. **9**: 149.
— — Spencer's. (E. L. Youmans) No. Am. **129**: 389. — (E. L. Youmans) Pop. Sci. Mo. **6**: 20.
— Physical and Dialectic. (H. Calderwood) Contemp. **40**: 865.
— Place of, in Philosophy. Am. Church R. **25**: 409.
— — of Conscience in. (T. W. Fowle) Pop. Sci. Mo. **13**: 513.
— — of Will in. (T. W. Fowle) 19th Cent. **5**: 385. Same art. Ecl. M. **97**: 577.
— Progress and Poverty. (W. D. Le Sueur) Canad. Mo. **19**: 287.
— — of Discovery of. (A. S. Packard, jr.) Am. Natural. **10**: 218.
— Psychology of. (J. Fiske) No. Am. **117**: 251.
— Reasonableness of. (A. Wilson) Mod. R. **2**: 368.
— Saltatory, Provisional Hypothesis of. (W. H. Dall) Am. Natural. **11**: 35.
— Science and Theology. (W. Binns) Mod. R. **1**: 245.
— Shall it be atheistic? (W. E. Parson) Luth. Q. **9**: 179.
— Speculation on. (A. J. Balfour) Fortn. **28**: 698.
— Spectroscope and. (F.W. Clarke) Pop. Sci. Mo. **2**: 320.
— Spirit of. (J. Watson) Canad. Mo. **16**: 457.
— Theory of. (E. Haeckel) Nature, **16**: 492. Same art. Sup. Pop. Sci. Mo. **2**: 289. — (S. A. Eliot) No. Am. **91**: 528. — (G. Iles) New Dom. **21**: 408. — (A. P. Sprague) Nat. Q. **24**: 256.
— — and the Argument from Design. Cong. **4**: 728.
— — and the Soul. Dub. Univ. **93**: 1.
— — Current. (S. N. Callender) Ref. Q. **28**: 434.
— — Great Men and. (W. James) Atlan. **46**: 441. — (J. Fiske) Atlan. **47**: 75.
— — in Germany. (L. Dumont) Nature, **7**: 352, 433. **8**: 37.
— — in its application to Practice. (H. Sidgwick) Mind, **1**: 52.
— — Modern Philosophy and. (L. Adams) New Eng. **34**: 329.
— — Relation to Christianity and rational Truth. (L. Curtis) New Eng. **39**: 653.
— Theories of, and Theology. (J. S. Stahr) Mercersb. **19**: 439.
— — Modern. (G. W. Samson) Bapt. Q. **10**: 490. **11**: 24, 148.
— Three Hypotheses of History of Nature. (T. H. Huxley) Pop. Sci. Mo. **10**: 43.
— Threshold of. (Maj. Wallich) Pop. Sci. R. **19**: 143.
— Virchow on. (J. Tyndall) 19th Cent. **4**: 809. — (J. Tyndall) Pop. Sci. Mo. **14**: 266.
— Winchell on. (T. Gill) Nation, **19**: 105.
See Apes; Darwinism; Development; Man; Species, Origin of; etc.

Evolutionism and Christianity. (J. B. Tyler) New Eng. **30**: 464.
— and Positivism. Am. Cath. Q. **2**: 598.
— respecting Man, and the Bible. (J. T. Duffield) Princ. n. s. **1**: 150.
— *versus* Theism. (B. A. Smith) New Eng. **33**: 75.
Evolutionists, English. (W. Myall) Internat. R. **11**: 51.
Evora, Portugal, Antiquities at. Penny M. **4**: 217, 233.
Ewald, G. H. Aug. von. (A. Duff) Bib. Sac. **33**: 194. — Brit. Q **57**: 151.
Ewan McGabhar. (J. Hogg) Fraser, **6**: 450.
Ewell, Gen. R. S. Strength of his Division, 1862. (J. A. Early) So. Hist. Pap. **8**: 301.
Ewing, Bp. Alex. Ed. R. **147**: 386. — Liv. Age, **137**: 131.
Ewing, Greville. Ecl. R. **79**: 681. — Cong. M. **26**: 926. — with portrait, Cong. M. **8**: 1.
— Sermon on Death of. Ecl. R. **74**: 623.
Ewing, John. Portfo.(Den.) **9**: 214.
Ewing, Samuel, Life of. Portfo.(Den.) **34**: 443.
Ewing, Thos. New Eng. M. **8**: 382. — Ev. Sat. **11**: 515.
Exaggeration, and Matter-of-Fact People. Lond. M. **7**: 8.
Exaggerations. Chamb. J. **58**: 617.
Exalted Horn, An. (H. Schütz-Wilson) Dark Blue, **1**: 434.
Examinations, Competitive. *See* Competitive.
— Good and Evil of. (A. Barry) 19th Cent. **3**: 647.
— Evils of. (A. R. Grant) 19th Cent. **8**: 715.
— Latham on. (C. P. Mason) Brit. Q. **72**: 362.
— School. (J. Bascom) Western, **6**: 497.
— University. (T. Fowler) Fortn. **25**: 418.
— Use and Abuse of. (R. E. Thompson) Penn Mo. **9**: 379.
Examination Papers in Schools. (M. P. Lowe) Unita. R. **11**: 552.
Examination System. (W. S. Jevons) Mind, **2**: 193. — (W. Brown) Atlan. **45**: 594.
— at Cambridge. Am. J. Educ. **28**: 609.
— at Universities. (A. H. Sayce) Fortn. **23**: 835.
Examiner, The. Ecl. M. **27**: 230.
Example better than Precept. So. Lit. Mess. **1**: 39.
— Power of. (J. B. Gough) Ex. H. Lec. **15**: 431.
Excavations and Embankments, Calculations of. (W. M. Gillespie) J. Frankl. Inst. **64**: 372. — (J. C. Trautwine) J. Frankl. Inst. **52**: 1, 80, 146. — (E. Morris) J. Frankl. Inst. **29**: 21, 381. **32**: 232. — (G. A. Simonson) J. Frankl. Inst. **61**: 1.
— at Cissbury and Highdown. (A. H. L. Fox) Arch. **42**: 53.
— at the Madeleine at Bernay. (Abbé Cochet) Arch. **38**: 66.
— in a Cemetery at Frilford, Berks. (G. Rolleston) Arch. **42**: 417.
— in Quicksand. (W. J. McAlpine) Ecl. Engin. **1**: 8.
Excellence, Love of, in Education. (E. Q. Sewall) Chr. Exam. **23**: 215.
— Price of. So. Lit. Mess. **13**: 631.
Excellency and Accidency. (C. Z. Weiser) Mercersb. **19**: 325.
Excellent Offer. (M. Blake) Bentley, **2**: 340.
Excellent Opportunity; a Tale. House. Words, **1**: 421. Same art. Internat. M. **1**: 249.
Exchange. (J. R. McCulloch) Bank. M. (N. Y.) **4**: 602, 836.
— and Production. (J. B. Howe) Bank. M.(N.Y.) **32**: 609.
— Artificial Agents of. (M. Tarver) West. J. **1**: 289, 347.
— Bills of, Law of. Bank. M. (N. Y.) **8**: 5–281. **10**: 18. **11**: 50–765.
— — — English. (H. Brougham) Bank. M.(N.Y.) **9**: 253.
— Equalization of. Niles's Reg. **15**: 25. **16**: 289.
— Foster on. Ed. R. **9**: 111.
— Instrument of. (T. P. Thompson) Westm. **1**: 171.
— on England, Mystery of. Hunt, **34**: 702.
— Principles of. (J. R. McCulloch) Bank. M. (N. Y.) **1**: 284.

Exchange, Rate of. Niles's Reg. **23**: 293, 356, 374.
Exchange no Robbery. Lond. Soc. **27**: 268.
Exchange of Pulpits. (A. J. Weddell) Evang. R. **21**: 224.
Exchange Alley, Anatomy of. Bank. M. (N. Y.) **5**: 151.
Exchange Tables. Bank. M. (N. Y.) **7**: 360.
Exchanges between England and the Continent. Bank. M. (N. Y.) **1**: 50.
— Foreign. Bank. M. (N. Y.) **30**: 274.
— — Effect of Gold Supplies on. (F. Jourdan) J. Statis. Soc. **24**: 38.
Exchequer Bills and our War Finance. Bank. M (N. Y.) **30**: 123.
Excise, Meaning of. Niles's Reg. **20**: 210.
Excise Laws. (H. Smyth) Macmil. **27**: 61.
Exclusivism in Religion. Am. Presb. R. **5**: 551. **6**: 1.
Excommunication. (I. Errett) Chr. Q. **5**: 1.
— Methodist Theory of. Ecl. R. **97**: 227.
— of Animals and Vermin. (H. White) Stud. & Intel. Obs. **3**: 210.
— of noxious Animals by the Catholic Church. (G. P. Marsh) Nation, **2**: 763.
— Papal; a Dialogue. Macmil. **2**: 68.
— — Bull of Pius IX. (H. C. Lea) Nation, **10**: 71.
Excursion to the Limbos. (M. W. Savage) Dub. Univ. **42**: 570, 666. **43**: 155.
Excursion to Port Arthur. Fraser, **26**: 281.
Excursions for practical People. St. James, **1**: 99.
— of To-Day. (C. C. Hopley) St. James, **32**: 635.
Excursion Train. Cornh. **4**: 727.
Excuses. Chamb. J. **50**: 657.
Execution in Spain. (P. Merimée) New Eng. M. **9**: 410.
Executions in England. Mus. **20**: 567.
— for Murder in England and Wales, 1800-75. (W. A. Guy) J. Statis. Soc. **38**: 463.
— Public. (H. Rogers) Good Words, **6**: 104. — Niles's Reg. **48**: 213.
— — in Manchester. (W. E. A. Axon) Reliquary, **9**: 209.
Executioner, The. Blackw. **31**: 306, 483.
Executioners, Seven Generations of; Sanson Family. Colburn, **127**: 253.
Executor, The. Blackw. **89**: 595. Same art. Liv. Age, **69**: 707.
Executorship, Laws of. Dub. Univ. **11**: 555.
Exegesis of difficult Texts. Kitto, **33**: 65, 275. **34**: 344. **35**: 335. **36**: 107. **37**: 137. **38**: 87. **40**: 349.
— Practical. (A. Neander) Mercersb. **3**: 152.
Exercise. (E. E. Hale) O. & N. **9**: 232.
— and Health. Cornh. **9**: 227.
— Insufficient, by young Women. Penny M. **2**: 77.
— Philosophy of. (R. K. Philp) Peop. J. **5**: 76.
See Gymnastics; Physical Education.
Exeter, England. All the Year, **21**: 257.
— in English History. (E. A. Freeman) Macmil. **28**: 468. Same art. Nature, **8**: 289.
— sixty Years ago. All the Year, **14**: 319.
Exeter Cathedral. Mo. R. **114**: 497. — Penny M. **3**: 157.
— Ancient Constitution of. (J. Jones) Arch. **18**: 385.
— Saxon MS. in. (J. J. Conybeare) Arch. **17**: 180.
Exeter College. Ed. R. **152**: 344.
Exeter, N. H., Burial Inscriptions at. N. E. Reg. **16**: 258.
— Documentary History of. Hist. M. **17**: 367. **18**: 6.
— Early Settlers of. N. E. Reg. **25**: 59.
— Phillips Academy. (H. E. Scudder) Harper, **55**: 562. — (J. G. Hoyt) No. Am. **87**: 119.
— Riot in 1734. Hist. M. **14**: 190.
Exeter Hall, London, Recollections of. Fraser, **19**: 23.
Exhibitions, French Hogg, **6**: 372.
— Industrial, Buildings for. Pract. M. **1**: 157.
— — of the Past. Potter Am. Mo. **6**: 375.
— International. (T. C. Archer) Penn Mo. **7**: 343. — (L. Levi) Ex. H. Lec. **11**: 249.
Exhibitions, International, and technical Instruction. Am. J. Educ. **21**: 29. **22**: 225.
— — Arrangement of great. (J. M. Hart) Nation, **21**: 336.
— — from 1851 to 1874. Pract. M. **4**: 448.
— — Lessons from. (J. S. Russell) Am. J. Educ. **21**: 383.
See London; Paris; Philadelphia; Vienna.
— of Paintings. Blackw. **54**: 188.
Exhibition Season, Memorabilia of. Fraser, **44**: 129.
Ex Humo; a Poem. (B. F. Proctor) Cath. World, **1**: 33.
Exile; a Poem. Broadw. **5**: 222.
Exile, The; a Tale. Am. Mo. M. **1**: 72-379. **2**: 57-409.
Exile of Louisiana. Bentley, **13**: 612.
Exmoor. (Lady Barker) Macmil. **42**: 368. Same art. Liv. Age, **147**: 53. — Lond. Soc. **12**: 144.
— Wanderings on. Fraser, **56**: 489.
— Wild Sport on. Belgra. **21**: 395.
Exmoor Courtship, The. Blackw. **4**: 530.
Exmouth, Lord Admiral. Quar. **55**: 129. — Mus. **28**: 217. — Chamb. J. **4**: 346. Same art. Liv. Age, **8**: 339. — Tait, n. s. **3**: 133. — Mo. R. **138**: 147.
— Life of. Penny M. **2**: 123. Quar. **55**: 129.
Exodus of Israelites. Danv. Q. **3**: 181. — Ecl. R. **121**: 176.
— Brugsch on. (J. P. Thompson) Bib. Sac. **32**: 185.
— on Monuments of Egypt. (W. Osburn) Kitto, **25**: 257.
— Route of. Kitto, **25**: 1.
See Bible; Israel.
Exodus of Negroes from the South to Kansas. (H. King) Scrib. **20**: 211.
Exodi of the Jews and Greeks. Fraser, **14**: 461.
Exogamy and Endogamy. (J. F. McLellan) Fortn. **27**: 884.
Exorcism, Ancient Formula of, translated. (G. Dodds) Reliquary, **10**: 129.
— Specimens of. (A. Wallis) Reliquary, **17**: 141.
Exotic Forage Plants, Spontaneous Growth of, in France. Nature, **6**: 263.
Expansion of isolated Steam, and total Heat of Steam. (C. W. Siemens) J. Frankl. Inst. **54**: 360.
— of solid Bodies by Heat. (H. Kopp) J. Frankl. Inst. **54**: 63.
— of Substances on Solidification. (R. Mallet) Ecl. Engin. **13**: 521.
Expansion Table, Mechanical. (J. H. Warner) J. Frankl. Inst. **68**: 4.
Expatriation. (A. J. H. Crespi) Colburn, **158**: 215.
— Right of. (S. Dutcher) Am. Law R. **11**: 447. — De Bow, **27**: 387.
Expediency, Doctrine of. (F. Wayland) Bib. Sac. **1843**: 301. — (J. Whitman) Chr. Exam. **22**: 13. — (D. Peabody) Chr. Q. Spec. **6**: 410.
Expeditions in War. U. S. Serv. M. **2**: 530.
Expensive Journey. Lond. Soc. **11**: 35.
Experience. Irish Mo. **4**: 595.
— An. All the Year, **22**: 257, 280.
— Human, Four new Philosophical Terms in. (W. Cyples) Mind, **5**: 390.
— Lewes's Account of. (T. H. Green) Contemp. **32**: 751.
— Lewes's Postulates of. (A. Bain) Mind, **1**: 146.
— Postulates of. (R. Noel) Mind, **1**: 427.
— Process of, Cyples on. (J. Sully) Mind, **5**: 273.
Experience of an Heiress. Tinsley, **12**: 169.
Experiences of the A. C. (B. Taylor) Atlan. **9**: 170.
— of Richard Taylor, Esq. Tait, n. s. **1**: 380, 540. **2**: 180, 253, 791.
Experiment in Mesmerism; a Story. Temp. Bar, **60**: 338.
Experiments. (C. A. Hopkinson) Atlan. **26**: 542.
— Trustworthiness of. (G. M. Beard) Pop. Sci. Mo. **14**: 611, 751.
Experts, Testimony of. (E. Washburn) Am. Law R. **1**: 45. — Am. Law R. **5**: 227, 428.
Expiation. Tinsley, **20**: 517.
Expiation; a Tale. Blackw. **28**: 628.
Ex-Pirate. (J. C. Cremony) Overland, **2**: 351.

Explicit and implicit Thought. Dub. R. **65**: 421.
Explorers, Early English. Nat. R. **2**: 297. Same art. Liv. Age, **50**: 65.
— Lost. All the Year, **27**: 342, 376.
Exploring Adventure. House. Words, **1**: 418.
Exploring Expedition, Wilkes's United States. (N. Hale) No. Am. **45**: 369. — (J. R. Poinsett) No. Am. **56**: 257. — (C. H. Davis) No. Am. **61**: 54. — Ed. R. **83**: 431. Same art. Ecl. M. **8**: 352. — So. Q. **8**: 1, 265. — So. Lit. Mess. **2**: 587. **3**: 68, 698. **4**: 566. — — Westm. **44**: 469. — Am. J. Sci. **44**: 393. — Hunt, **12**: 444. — Liv. Age, **4**: 579, 692. **5**: 59. — Brit. Q. **17**: 627. — Nav. M. **2**: 64. — (T. R. Peale) Am. Hist. Rec. **3**: 244, 305.
— Scientific Results of. (A. Gray and C. C. Felton) No. Am. **63**: 211.
Explosion at Erith. (L. Moore) J. Frankl. Inst. **80**: 164.
— of Dover Cliff, 1843. J. Frankl. Inst. **35**: 270, 325. — (C. W. Pasley) J. Frankl. Inst. **36**: 28.
— of Fire Damp. (J. Richardson) J. Frankl. Inst. **48**: 156.
— of Gun on board the Princeton, 1844. (W. Hamilton) J. Frankl. Inst. **38**: 206.
— of Telegraph Steamer, 1843. J. Frankl. Inst. **37**: 133.
— Phenomena of. Ecl. Engin. **25**: 159.
Explosions, Accidental. (F. A. Abel) Nature, **11**: 436, 477, 498.
— and explosive Compounds. Liv. Age, **3**: 43. **5**: 222. — Ecl. Engin. **23**: 92.
— from combustible Dust. (L. W. Peck) Pop. Sci. Mo. **14**: 159.
— in Coal-Mines. *See* Coal-Mines.
— of Niter. (U. A. Boyden) J. Frankl. Inst. **74**: 32.
— of Steam-Boilers. *See* Boilers.
Explosive Agents. (F. A. Abel) Ecl. Engin. **2**: 524.
— applied to industrial Processes. (F. A. Abel) Ecl. Engin. **7**: 124. **9**: 332.
— Development of Force from. Ecl. Engin. **10**: 506.
— History of. (F. A. Abel) Nature, **2**: 326.
— New. Ecl. Engin. **1**: 153. — (F. Papillon) Pract. M. **2**: 296, 327.
— Safety in Manufacture and Storage of. Ecl. Engin. **10**: 369.
Explosive Compounds. Ecl. Engin. **5**: 172.
Explosive Gases, warning Apparatus. Pract. M. **6**: 136.
Explosive Gelatine. Ecl. Engin. **24**: 160.
Explosive Substances, Trade in. Pract. M. **4**: 304.
Explosives applied to warlike Purposes. Nature, **1**: 656. **2**: 49.
— Cotton Powder or Tonite. Ecl. Engin. **19**: 321.
— High, Transportation of. Ecl. Engin. **17**: 300.
— Modern. (C. A. Joy) Nation, **22**: 42.
— Modern blasting. Ecl. Engin. **18**: 561.
— New. Chamb. J. **55**: 247. *See* Dynamite; etc.
Export Trade of U. S. (F. H. Morse) Internat. R. **6**: 39.
Exports of Breadstuffs from United States. (R. H. Edmonds) Internat. R. **11**: 540.
— of United States for fifty-one Years. Hunt, **9**: 85.
— and Imports of United States, 1825, 1830, 1835, 1840. Hunt, **7**: 193.
Express Agent's Story. (W. S. Walker) Lakeside, **5**: 29.
Express Business, History of. (A. S. Stimson) Bank. M. (N. Y.) **12**: 289.
Express Companies; an American Enterprise. (W. H. Rideing) Harper, **51**: 314.
— Liability of. Bank. M. (N. Y.) **15**: 346.
Express System of United States. (C. F. Adams, jr.) No. Am. **110**: 116.
Expression. (R. W. Emerson) Atlan. **6**: 572.
— Anatomists and Artists. (H. Lawreny) St. Paul's, **12**: 222.
— Anatomy and Philosophy of. Chr. Rem. **8**: 130. — Liv. Age, **1**: 289.
Expression, Darwin on. (T. Gill) Nation, **16**: 357. *See* Darwin.
— of Emotions. (H. Calderwood) Internat. R. **6**: 195.
— Unconscious comic. (H. Jennings) Once a Week, **24**: 527.
Expressions. (T. M. Coan) Galaxy, **9**: 171.
Extemporaneous Preaching. Chr. Mo. Spec. **6**: 131. — (T. C. Upham) No. Am. **19**: 297.
Extemporaneous Speaking. (M. Laboulaye) Cong. **2**: 543, 596. — So. Lit. Mess. **1**: 7.
— Reflex Effects of. (D. Macgregor) Mind, **6**: 546.
Extension and Space, Distinction between. (F. E. Abbott) No. Am. **99**: 64.
Extenuating Circumstances. Cornh. **9**: 210.
Extradition. (T. M. Cooley) Internat. R. **3**: 433. — (S. Amos) Am. J. Soc. Sci. **11**: 117. — Westm. **89**: 110.
— between States. (I. T. Hoague) Am. Law R. **13**: 181. — Nat. Q. **40**: 128. — (I. T. Hoague) Nation, **28**: 98.
— Difficulty about, 1876. (A. G. Sedgwick) Nation, **23**: 101.
— Law of. (I. T. Hoague) Nation, **28**: 250.
— of Criminals. (E. S. Roscoe) Fraser, **94**: 163. — (A. G. Sedgwick) Nation, **28**: 25. — (T. D. Woolsey) New Eng. **23**: 133.
Extradition Treaty with England, 1876. (E. L. Godkin). Nation, **22**: 331.
Extraordinary Red Book. (D. Webster) No. Am. **4**: 107.
Extravagance, Microscopic. Liv. Age, **133**: 378.
— Popular. (C. A. Bristed) U. S. Serv. M. **2**: 435.
Extravagant Shepherd; an Anti-Romance. Retros. **7**: 291.
Extreme Unction. Princ. **37**: 188.
Extremes. (J. N. Willan) Belgra. **22**: 298.
— Law of the Mean and of the. (G. W. Hosmer) Unita. R. **3**: 113.
Extremes meet, Philosophy of. Colburn, **87**: 239.
Eye and Ear, Human. (D. McAllum) Meth. M. **49**: 675.
— and Vision. Ev. Sat. **6**: 686.
— Circulation in. (O. N. Rood) Am. J. Sci. **80**: 264, 385.
— Curiosities of Vision. (T. E. Clark) Hours at Home, **10**: 344.
— Education of. (W. C. Woodbridge) Am. Mo. M. **12**: 65, 134.
— Expression of. (C. A. Collins) Macmil. **14**: 357. Same art. Ev. Sat. **2**: 168.
— The Human. (H. C. Rose) Once a Week, **13**: 180. — (D. B. St. J. Roosa) Hours at Home, **8**: 264.
— — and Cysticercus. Sharpe, **11**: 157.
— — Diseases of. Mo. R. **94**: 483.
— — — Adams on. (T. Young) Quar. **11**: 347. — Quar. **18**: 158.
— — — Saunders on, 1811. Ecl. R. **16**: 898.
— Hygiene of. Penn Mo. **6**: 188.
— Illusions of. (Sir D. Brewster) Good Words, **3**: 498. — (Sir D. Brewster) J. Frankl. Inst. **15**: 138, 210.
— Interior of. (J. Burnstein) Pop. Sci. Mo. **9**: 684.
— Minute Nerve of. (Dr. Mann) Ev. Sat. **8**: 339.
— Myope. Bentley, **62**: 592.
— of the Cod-Fish. (T. S. Cobbold) Intel. Obs. **1**: 199.
— of Insects and Crustacea. (H. Fripp) Pop. Sci. R. **8**: 12.
— of the Ox and its Structure. (E. B. Truman) Pop. Sci. R. **2**: 220.
— Optical Defects of. (A. M. Rosebrugh) Canad. J. n. s. **11**: 1.
— Structure and Powers of. (D. Brewster) Good Words, **3**: 170.
— Ware on. Ecl. R. **2**: 755.
See below Eyesight; *also* Sight; Vision.
Eyes and Eye-Glasses. (R. H. Horne) Fraser, **94**: 698. Same art. Ecl. M. **88**: 257.
— and no Eyes. Once a Week, **25**: 485, 511.
— and School-Books. (H. Cohn) Pop. Sci. Mo. **19**: 54.
— Artificial. Once a Week, **20**: 545.

Eyes, Artificial Pupil for. Mo. R. **94**: 423.
— Chapter on. Chamb. J. **30**: 378.
— Color of. St. James, **28**: 59.
— Conservative Use of. (G.A. Bethune) Bib. Sac. **12**: 385.
— Economy of. Portfo.(Den.) **33**: 401.
— Faceted, Mode of Action of. (S. Exner) Pop. Sci. R. **20**: 337.
— Hints on Use of. (S. M. Burnett) Scrib. **14**: 700.
— — to Students on Use of. (E. Reynolds) Am. Bib. Repos. **3**: 518.
— How to care for. (H.W. Williams) Atlan. **27**: 62–636.
— Old, and Spectacles. (S. M. Burnett) Scrib. **13**: 782.
— Plea for. Chamb. J. **29**: 357.
— Reynolds on Use of. Mo. R. **158**: 297.
— Take Care of your. Godey, **50**: 513. **51**: 238.
— Windows of the Soul. (T. Ballantyne) Once a Week, **11**: 344.
Eye and Ear Impressions. (R. St. J. Tyrwhitt) Dark Blue, **1**: 582.
Eye and Ear Infirmary. New Eng. M. **8**: 129.
Eye-Memory. All the Year, **19**: 545. — (C. G. Leland) J. Frankl. Inst. **109**: 327, 391.
Eye-Glasses, Sorrows and Solaces of. (F. B. Crofton) Canad. Mo. **20**: 84.
Eyesight, Economy of. Chamb. J. **31**: 327.
— Effects of Study on. (W. McLean) Pop. Sci. Mo. **12**: 74.
— Helmholtz and Carter on. Ed. R. **154**: 516. Same art. Liv. Age, **151**: 451.
— injured by glaring white Paper and Print. Nation, **29**: 207, 239.
— Use and Abuse of. (S. H. Clark) Meth. Q. **21**: 104.
Eyesores. (W. Chambers) Chamb. J. **57**: 17.
Eylau and Friedland, Campaign of, 1807. Temp. Bar, **40**: 528.
Eyrbyggja Saga, The. Cornh. **41**: 712.
Eyre, E. J., the South Australian Explorer. (H. Kingsley) Macmil. **12**: 501. **13**: 55. Same art. Liv. Age, **87**: 481.
Eyre Hall, Va. (F. Fielding) Land We Love, **3**: 504.
Eytinge, S. Cartoons of most famous Characters of Dickens. Ev. Sat. **9**: 227–865.
Ezekiel, Last Vision of. Chr. Obs. **45**: 721, 783.
— Vision of. (H. A. C. Hävernick) Bib. Sac. **5**: 434, 700. — (M. S. Terry) Meth. Q. **31**: 260.
Ezra the Scribe, his Life and Work. (C. H. Toy) Bapt. Q. **9**: 339.
Ezzelino da Romano, the Cruel. Am. Whig R. **8**: 53.

F

Faber, Cecilia Bohl da. *See* Caballero, F.
Faber, Fred. Wm. Theo. R. **6**: 559. — Blackw. **106**: 693.
— and modern ascetic Divinity. Dub. R. **36**: 194.
— as a Writer. Month, **11**: 154.
— Catholic Hymns. Dub. R. **27**: 163.
— Creator and the Creature. Dub. R. **43**: 235.
— Life and Letters of. (A. F. Hewit) Cath. World, **10**: 145. — (W. Scribner) Princ. **43**: 515. — Dub. R. **65**: 109. — Liv. Age, **104**: 133.
— Poetry of. No. Brit. **1**: 146. — Temp. Bar, **27**: 184.
— Princeton Rev. on. (A. F. Hewit) Cath. World, **14**: 400.
— Sir Lancelot; a Poem. Dub. R. **18**: 320.
— Work of, in the Church. Dub. R. **66**: 95.
Faber, George Stanley. Chr. Rem. **29**: 310.
— Poems of. Ecl. R. **81**: 436.
— Sermons of. Chr. Obs. **16**: 375.
Fable, Origin and History of. Cornh. **2**: 677.
— of the Bees, Mandeville's. (L. Stephen) Fraser, **87**: 713.
Fables. (W. A. Jones) Godey, **44**: 181.
— Æsop illustrated. (J. Hewlett) Colburn, **73**: 13–563. **74**: 70–642. **75**: 68–345.
— and Fabulists. (F. C. Woodworth) Knick. **35**: 421.
— and Facts. (H. B. Spencer) St. James, **20**: 377.
— and their Sequels. (S. L. Clemens) Belgra. **35**: 326.
— for Old and Young. (H. A. Page) Good Words, **14**: 721, 750.
— from Yriarte; translated. Blackw. **46**: 202.
— in different Countries. Penny M. **4**: 286.
— Migration of. (M. Müller) Contemp. **14**: 572.
— Notes on. Penny M. **4**: 262.
— of Bidpai. Dub. Univ. **78**: 601.
— The old. Colburn, **4**: 373.
— Romantic, and popular Superstitions. Fraser, **45**: 215. — Nat. M. **1**: 32.
Fabliaux of France. Dub. Univ. **74**: 637.
Fabrics, Textile, of India. Art J. **19**: 82.
Fabulists; Æsop, Phædrus, and Fontaine. Fraser, **17**: 188, 447.
Fabulous, The, in History. Ecl. M. **46**: 512.
Fabulous Animals. (F. P. Cobbe) Liv. Age, **123**: 354.
Face, Brutish Affinities of the Human. Colburn, **132**: 35.
— Transformation of the British. (G. A. Simcox) Art. J. **26**: 21–345.
— in the Glass. (J. E. Penrhyn) Atlan. **22**: 320–663.
Face to Face with ——. Lond. Soc. **24**: 526.
Faces, A Word about. Ev. Sat. **11**: 186.
— in the Crowd. Temp. Bar, **14**: 530.
Facetiæ. No. Brit. **46**: 381. Same art. Liv. Age, **94**: 100.
— of the War. (J. F. Fitts) Galaxy, **6**: 320.
Facetious, Hints to Authors on the. Blackw. **39**: 166.
Facial Angle. (R. Dexter) Pop. Sci. Mo. **4**: 587.
Facial Anomalies. (K. Müller) Pop. Sci. Mo. **6**: 73.
Facing a Woman. (T. C. Haliburton) Bentley, **8**: 503.
Fact and Fiction. Blackw. **20**: 681. — Mus. **4**: 64.
— What is a? (E. S. Phelps) Atlan. **46**: 676.
Facts in Figures. Quar. **86**: 437.
— not Fiction. (S. A. Downer) Pioneer, **3**: 332.
— Science and. Western, **2**: 235.
Factions. Dem. R. **36**: 70.
Faction Fights in Parliament. Bent. Q. **1**: 343.
Factory Act, The new. (W. C. Taylor) Fraser, **99**: 55.
— and Workshop Act, 1876. Westm. **107**: 36, 462.
Factory Bill, English, 1833. Tait, **3**: 250–672. — Westm. **18**: 380.
— — 1834. Tait, **4**: 114.
— — 1845. Fraser, **29**: 617.
Factory Children, Physical Requirements of. (C. Roberts) J. Statis. Soc. **39**: 681.
Factory Labor, Influence on Health. Mo. R. **132**: 78.
Factory Legislation, English. (J. T. Platt) New Eng. **38**: 224.
Factory Life; Mary Barton. Brit. Q. **9**: 117.
— and Management. (R. Baker) Pract. M. **3**: 340.
— in Lancashire. Chamb. J. **52**: 545.
— in New England. Knick. **30**: 511.
— Influence of, on Health. (A. G. Malcolm) J. Statis. Soc. **19**: 170.
Factory Movement, Hist. of English. Tait, n. s. **24**: 699.

Factory Operatives. (H. A. Miles) No. Am. 52: 31. — Blackw. 33: 419. — Westm. 18: 380.
Factory Populations and Robert Owen. (R. D. Owen) Am. J. Educ. 26: 403.
— Modes of improving. (E. Akroyd) Am. J. Educ. 8: 305.
Factory Schools. Irish Q. 4: 1042. 5: 79.
— at Vauxhall. Quar. 92: 1.
Factory System. (Lord Ashley) Quar. 57: 396. — Fraser, 7: 707. — Westm. 26: 174. 47: 251. — Blackw. 33: 419. 40: 100.
— of England. Dub. Univ. 22: 435. — Tait, n. s. 2: 251.
— and Factory Legislation. Brit. Q. 1: 117.
— Ten Hours' Bill. Fraser, 7: 377.
— Wing on Evils of, 1837. Mo. R. 142: 330.
Factory Town, Study of a New England. Atlan. 43: 689.
Factory Village, New England, People of. Atlan. 46: 460.
Factory Women. (M. L. Gillies) Peop. J. 2: 131. — (S. Smiles) Peop. J. 2: 258. 3: 52, 143.
Factories and Workshops. Pract. M. 7: 178.
— Employment of Children in. Chr. Rem. 5: 675.
— — of Mothers in. (W. C. Taylor) Fortn. 23: 664.
— Order and Cleanliness in. Pract. M. 7: 175.
— Ten-Hour System in. (W. Gray) O. & N. 3: 629.
Factories Education Bill. Ecl. R. 77: 573.
Faculties claimed for Man, Questions concerning. (C. S. Peirce) J. Spec. Philos. 2: 103, 140.
— Play of. (W. F. Ainsworth) Colburn, 167: 262.
Fadlallah. Chamb. J. 16: 114.
Faed, Thomas. Art J. 23: 1, 237.
Fagging in Public Schools. (T. P. Thompson) Westm. 10: 244. — Fraser, 40: 292. — Lond. M. 22: 633. — Tinsley, 9: 410.
Fags and Fagging. Lond. Soc. 4: 350.
Faience, Dutch. (W. Sikes) Harper, 57: 15.
— French. (C. W. Elliott) Art J. 29: 273.
Faience Violin, The. (W. H. Bishop) Atlan. 43: 609.
Failures, Mercantile. (G. Marsland) Bank. M. (N. Y.) 31: 334. — Bank. M. (N. Y.) 29: 429.
— and Improvement in Business. Bank. M. (N. Y.) 32: 365.
— and their Causes. Bank. M. (N. Y.) 31: 591. — Hunt, 15: 260.
— and their Indications. Bank. M. (N. Y.) 30: 847.
— Destruction of Capital by. Bank. M. (N. Y.) 30: 416.
— from 1857 to 1875. Nation, 21: 81.
— in 1847. Ecl. R. 86: 750.
— Increase of. (G. Marsland) Bank. M. (N. Y.) 33: 103.
— Our. Fraser, 58: 505.
— Statistics of, 1876. Bank. M. (N. Y.) 32: 175.
Fain, A. J. F., Baron, Manuscript of, 1814. Colburn, 8: 360.
Faint Heart never won fair Lady. (D. Costello) Bentley, 43: 5-551. 44: 95-637. 45: 64, 189.
Fair, James, the Silver-King. Chamb. J. 55: 205.
Fair at Keady. (A. Smith) Macmil. 2: 179.
Fairs and Markets of Europe, Great. (R. H. Horne) St. Paul's, 12: 169. Same art. Ev. Sat. 14: 268. Same art. Ecl. M. 80: 436.
— and Pilgrimages in India and Russia. (G. Smith) Good Words, 14: 58, 192.
— Great, of Europe. (R. H. Horne) Harper, 46: 376.
— in Russia. Bank. M. (L.) 18: 778, 885.
— Street, of 18th Cent. (A. Andrews) Colburn, 102: 478.
Fair Barbarian. (F. H. Burnett) Scrib. 21: 561, 665, 841.
Fair Compensation. (A. F. Webster) Atlan. 38: 342.
Fair Face; a Tale. (C. Chesebrough) Putnam, 11: 723.
Fair Face in the Yellow Chariot. Lond. Soc. 32: 1.
Fair Gurtha; a Tale. (W. Carleton) Dub. Univ. 47: 414.
Fair Humanities of old Religion. (L. Cross) Colburn, 169: 225.
Fair Inez. (T. Hood) Lond. M. 7: 96.
Fair Man of dark Fortune. All the Year, 6: 153.
Fair Margaret, the Belle of Ashgate. (L. Parr) Lippinc. 9: 379.
Fair May of Mayfair. (W. W. Fenn) Lond. Soc. 35: 385.
Fair One with Velvet Mask. (G. A. Sala) Belgra. 16: 175.
Fair Patriot of the Revolution. (D. Murdoch) Potter Am. Mo. 7: 33-435. 8: 41-441. 9: 41-441.
Fair Rosamond; a Poem. (E. R. B. Lytton) Once a Week, 4: 293.
Fair Stowaway. Chamb. J. 55: 713.
Fair to see. (L. M. W. Lockhart) Blackw. 109: 74-740. 110: 1-531.
Fair Unknown; a Yachting Tale. Bentley, 60: 221.
Fairbairn, Sir Andrew. Lond. Soc. 35: 415. — Colburn, 168: 508.
Fairbairn, Sir Peter. Lond. Soc. 35: 406.
Fairbairn, Sir Thomas. Lond. Soc. 35: 405.
Fairbairn, Sir William, with portrait. Pract. M. 4: 241. — Lond. Soc. 35: 402. — Nature, 15: 370.
Fairbairns, The, Story of. (W. Chambers) Chamb. J. 54: 417.
Fairbanks, Erastus. (C. L. Goodell) Cong. Q. 9: 1.
Fairbanks, George, Will of, 1650. N. E. Reg. 7: 303.
Fairchild, Lucius, with portrait. Lakeside, 1: 65.
Fairer than a Fairy. (J. Grant) Tinsley, 14: 84-601.
Fairfax, Sarah, of Va. (C. C. Harrison) Scrib. 12: 301.
Fairfax, Thomas, Lord. (C. C. Harrison) Scrib. 18: 715. — (F. M. Colby) Potter Am. Mo. 15: 176.
— at Colchester. (C. R. Markham) Fortn. 26: 374.
— Life of. (G. Smith) Nation, 10: 305.
Fairfax Correspondence. Colburn, 84: 336. — Dub. Univ. 33: 63. — Fraser, 38: 573. — Ecl. R. 89: 99.
Fairfax Manuscripts. Bentley, 24: 498.
Fairfield, John, Portrait of. Dem. R. 18: 163.
Fairfield, Sumner L., Poems of. Am. Mo. R. 2: 235. — U. S. Lit. Gaz. 1: 326.
Fairfield County, Ct., Minerals of. (G. J. Brush and E. S. Dana) Am. J. Sci. 116: 33, 114. 117: 359. 118: 45.
Fairhaven, Mass., Ministers of. Am. Q. Reg. 12: 141.
Fairholt, Frederick W. Art J. 18: 179. — (L. Jewitt) Reliquary, 7: 40.
Fairland, Lord, Secret of; a Tale Cornh. 33: 709.
Fairman, James, Works of. Art J. 32: 229.
Fairmount Park. *See* Philadelphia.
Fairy Alice; a Sketch. Dub. Univ. 64: 551.
Fairy and the Ghost. (F. R. Stockton) Lippinc. 5: 33.
Fairy Fenella; a Story. Colburn, 152: 1-313. 153: 107-685. 154: 106-319.
Fairies. (W. Dowe) Sharpe, 17: 329. — Irish Q. 8: 885. — Knick. 36: 430.
— Deils, and Witches. (J. Hogg) Blackw. 23: 509.
— in New England. (J. G. Whittier) Howitt, 3: 278.
— of England. Knick. 40: 484.
— Origin of. (J. Hogg) Blackw. 28: 209.
— Where they hide. (I. D. Fenton) Once a Week, 14: 151.
— Who were they? Cornh. 43: 335.
Fairy Folk, The. Chamb. J. 52: 574.
Fairy Island. (C. F. Woolson) Putnam, 16: 62.
Fairy Ladder; a Poem. Once a Week, 19: 250.
Fairy Land. (J. G. Wood) St. James, 9: 167. — Dub. Univ. 76: 590.
— Great Fair of. Dub. Univ. 47: 740.
— Key to. (J. Dyer) Penn Mo. 1: 61.
— of Science. Cornh. 5: 36.
Fairy Legends, Hindu. Ed. R. 128: 350
Fairy Literature. Hogg, 15: 288.
Fairy Lore in Ireland. Dub. Univ. 59: 239. 63: 640. 64: 203, 243. 90: 70, 193. — Colburn, 122: 329.
— of Savages. (J. A. Farrar) Gent. M. n. s. 21: 673.
Fairy Man and Lady of the Rock. (C. Bede) Belgra. 34: 59.
Fairy Mythology. Am. Mo. M. 9: 478. — Westm. 19: 74. 45: 454.

Fairy Mythology of England. Fraser, **10**: 51. — (W. C. Stafford) Peop. J. **4**: 215.
— of Europe. Ecl. R. **106**: 557.
Fairy Pipes. (L. Jewitt) Reliquary, **3**: 74.
Fairy Plays. (E. Rose) Fraser, **94**: 285.
Fairy Prince, A. Tinsley, **11**: 501.
Fairy Queen. Chamb. J. **15**: 19.
Fairy Reaper. (R. Buchanan) Gent. M. n. s. **14**: 312.
Fairy Serenade. Dub. Univ. **34**: 591.
Fairy Shoe. Dub. Univ. **13**: 38.
Fairy Superstitions in Donegal. Dub. Univ. **94**: 101, 214.
Fairy Tale. So. Lit. Mess. **2**: 77.
— Egyptian, oldest in the World. Macmil. **31**: 39. Same art. Ecl. M. **84**: 101.
Fairy Tales, Diffusion of. (J. Fiske) Atlan. **48**: 310.
— Few Words on. Putnam, **10**: 58.
— in Verse. (A. J. Carden) Colburn, **169**: 282, 370, 535.
— Myths and. St. Paul's, **9**: 143.
— Planché's Translation of Countess d'Aulnoy's. House. Words, **11**: 509.
— Popular Legends and. Nat. R. **5**: 396.
— Sicilian. (W. R. S. Ralston) Fraser, **93**: 423.
— Tartar. (J. P. Lesley) O. & N. **1**: 460.
Faith. (O. A. Burgess) Chr. Q. **8**: 480. — (R. Ellis) Unita. R. **8**: 75. — (M. Hopkins) Princ. n. s. **2**: 511. — (T. Munnell) Chr. Q. **8**: 500. — (S. E. Shepard) Chr. Q. **7**: 246. — Chr. Obs. **12**: 1. — Cong. M. **23**: 11, 97. — Mo. Rel. M. **47**: 580. — Chr. Mo. Spec. **1**: 109. — (C. D. Pigeon) Lit. & Theo. R. **5**: 437.
— a mental Discipline. (H. T. Cheever) Am. Bib. Repos. 3d s. **4**: 315.
— a normal Activity of the Soul. (G. N. Abbott) Mercersb. **19**: 581.
— a Source of Knowledge. (J. M. Macdonald) Princ. **35**: 403.
— Accountability of Men for their. (A. T. Bledsoe) Princ. **18**: 53.
— Aids to. Brit. Q. **35**: 453. — Quar. **112**: 445. Same art. Liv. Age, **75**: 399, 435.
— and Evidences. (J. L. Davies) Good Words, **16**: 812.
— and Feeling. (M. Loy) Luth. Q. **3**: 1.
— and good Works, Beresford's. Chr. Obs. **13**: 645.
— and its Objects. (T. G. Apple) Mercersb. **22**: 618.
— and Knowledge. Broadw. **8**: 149. — (H. Harbaugh) Mercersb. **11**: 556. — (H. Matson) University Q. **2**: 34. — (W. Silsbee) O. & N. **2**: 447
— and Life, Connection of. Chr. Rem. **50**: 437.
— and Politics. Nat. R. **12**: 432.
— and Reason. (F. A. Rauch) Mercersb. **8**: 80 — Am. Church R. **21**: 184. — Danv Q. **2**: 1. — (G. E. Ellis) Chr. Exam. **61**: 412. — (F. H. Hedge) Chr. Exam. **70**: 204. — Princ. **32**: 648.
— — Claims and Conflicts of. (H. Rogers) Ed. R. **90**: 293. Same art. Ecl. M. **19**: 289. — Westm. **56**: 64.
— — Harmony of. Brownson, **18**: 117.
— and right Living. (M. Valentine) Luth. Q. **2**: 585.
— and Salvation. (W. J. Barbee) Chr. Q. **3**: 192.
— and Science. (S. B. Kieffer) Mercersb. **22**: 510. — Liv. Age, **141**: 376. — (C. C. Everett) Chr. Exam. **85**: 61.
— — and Nescience. (J. Martineau) Nat. R. **15**: 394.
— — Comte's Positive Philosophy. Meth. Q. **12**: 9, 169.
— and Skepticism. Westm. **52**: 379.
— — as motive Powers. (J. W. Armstrong) Meth. Q. **34**: 374.
— and Theology. (E. A. Horton) O. & N. **2**: 579.
— and Unbelief, Fields of Conflict. (E. H. Plumptre) Contemp. **40**: 169. Same art. Ecl. M. **97**: 433.
— and Utilitarianism. (H. L. Baugher) Evang. R. **6**: 209.
— and Verification. (W. H. Mallock) 19th Cent. **4**: 673. Same art. Liv. Age, **139**: 410. Same art Sup. Pop Sci. Mo. **4**: 1.
Faith and Virtue. Good Words, **21**: 170.
— and Works. (T. S. Lathrop) Univ. Q. **21**: 322. — Chr. R. **1**: 511. — (J. D. Williamson) Univ. Q. **7**: 322.
— — Importance and Connection of. (E. B. Webb) Evang. R. **21**: 1.
— Appeal of. (J. D. Williamson) Univ. Q. **22**: 169.
— as opposed to Sense. Cong. M. **18**: 335.
— as a Principle of Action. Chr. Disc. **1**: 114.
— Assurance of. (M. Chemnitz) Luth. Q. **1**: 280.
— Authority in Matters of. (O. A. Brownson) Cath. World, **14**: 145.
— Authority of. (G. F. Herrick) Bib. Sac. **26**: 268. — (G. B. Stevens) New Eng. **40**: 432.
— Basis of, Conder on. Cong. **7**: 348.
— the Basis of Science and Religion. (J. M. Sterrett) Bib. Sac. **31**: 74.
— Bases of, Miall's. Prosp. R. **9**: 183.
— Criteria of. Am. Church R. **22**: 417.
— Decay of, Goldwin Smith on. (J. A. Clutz) Luth. Q. **10**: 252.
— Decline of, in Europe, Political Effect of. (J. W. Draper) Princ. n. s. **3**: 78.
— Defense of, Gladstone's. Westm. **99**: 367.
— Doctrines of Paul and James. (A. Neander) Am. Bib. Repos. **3**: 189.
— Dogmatic, Garbett on. Chr. Obs. **68**: 1.
— Doubt, and Reason. (W. B. Clarke) New Eng. **22**: 79.
— Dove's Logic of. Ecl. R. **105**: 68.
— Eclipse of, Rogers's. (J. Floy) Meth. Q. **13**: 169. — Chr. R. **18**: 59. — Liv. Age, **45**: 3. — Prosp. R. **8**: 393. — Theo. & Lit. J. **6**: 279. — Brownson, **10**: 417.
— — and its Author's Defense. Prosp. R. **10**: 195.
— — Rogers's Defense of. Theo. & Lit. J. **7**: 350.
— Erskine and Carlile on. Ecl. R. **37**: 327.
— Erskine's Essay on. Chr. Mo. Spec. **7**: 141, 192. — Chr. Obs. **23**: 502. — Meth. M. **51**: 531.
— the everlasting Bond. (I. Merceir) Meth. Q. **18**: 356.
— exemplified in Life of Moses. Chr. Mo. Spec. **5**: 458.
— False and true Definitions of. (L. W. Bacon) New Eng. **28**: 249.
— Foundation of a living. (J. I. T. Coolidge) Mo. Rel. M. **16**: 289.
— Foundations of. (J. Walker) Chr. Exam. **17**: 1.
— From Doubt to. (R. W. Dale) Ex. H. Lec. **20**: 119.
— Froude's Nemesis of. Tait, n. s. **16**: 376, 421.
— Future of. (W. H. Mallock) Contemp. **31**: 707.
— — Mallock's. (J. McCarthy) Cath. World, **27**: 417.
— Genesis of. (A. F. Hewit) Cath. World, **32**: 433, 577.
— Gladstone on. Am. Church R. **26**: 126.
— Godwin on. Ecl. R. **116**: 208.
— Gospel, Continuity of. Chr. Exam. **80**: 145.
— Guarantees to. (S. A. Repass) Luth. Q. **8**: 218.
— Historical and saving. Chr. Obs. **48**: 1.
— Impossibilities of Unbelief. Am. Cath. Q. **6**: 709.
— in Christ. (J. Priestley) Theo. Repos. **3**: 239.
— — and Faith in Doctrine. (J. McCosh) Mercersb. **19**: 414.
— in Definition and Relations. (G. F. Magoun) Cong. R. **9**: 337.
— in God and his Word. (G. B. Cheever) Am. Bib. Repos. 3d s. **4**: 644.
— — Sermon on. (R. Ellis) Mo. Rel. M. **25**: 93. — (J Weiss) Mo. Rel. M. **4**: 561.
— Influence of, on the Intellect. (C. B. Boynton) Am. Bib. Repos. 3d s. **1**: 391.
— Intrepid. Chr. R. **10**: 591.
— Justification by. (D. Curry) Meth. Q. **4**: 5. **5**: 5. — (O. B. Frothingham) Chr. Exam. **41**: 272. — Meth M. **33**: 11.
— — Whittaker's Sermons on. Chr. Obs. **26**: 152.
— Justifying, Nature and Effects of. Dub. R. **63**: 317.

Faith, Knowledge, and Feeling in their mutual Relations. (L. H. Atwater) Princ. **33**: 421.
— Lay Sermon on. (J. S. Blackie) Good Words, **20**: 178.
— A living. (G. S. Merriam) Canad. Mo. **11**: 222.
— Modern Thought and ancient. (H. W. Bellows) O. & N. **5**: 394.
— Nature of. (J. W. Nevin) Mercersb. **1**: 206.
— — and Effects of, O'Brien on. Chr. Obs. **36**: 285.
— — and Efficacy of. (N. Van Alstine) Evang. R. **20**: 194.
— no Element in Evidences of Christianity. (A. Bierbower) Mo. Rel. M. **49**: 244.
— Normal and abnormal. (C. Z. Weiser) Mercersb. **20**: 346.
— not possible without the Church. Brownson, **3**: 1.
— Object and Confirmation of. (T. G. Apple) Mercersb. **25**: 635.
— of Abraham and of Christians, identical. Chr. Obs. **33**: 262, 339.
— of Christ. (G. B. Russell) Mercersb. **15**: 448.
— of Old Testament Believers. Chr. Obs. **18**: 1–495.
— of Reason. (F. H. Hedge) Unita. R. **13**: 30.
— One, in many Forms; a Poem. (M. A. Jevons) Ecl. M. **97**: 756.
— or Faithfulness? (A. Bierbower) Univ. Q. **37**: 26.
— Order of. (J. Craik) Am. Church R. **15**: 76.
— Orthodox, and modern Error. Bost. R. **1**: 313.
— perfected by Works. (J. E. Rankin) Cong. R. **9**: 449.
— Perversion of. (W. J. Barbee) Chr. Q. **4**: 180.
— Phases and Eclipse of, Newman's. Prosp. R. **6**: 359. **9**: 534. — Brit. Q. **19**: 525.
— Place and Prerogative of. (R. B. Welch) Am. Presb. R. **20**: 509.
— Popular. (C. K. Whipple) Radical, **1**: 381.
— Practical Influence of. Chr. Mo. Spec. **1**: 591.
— Province and Functions of. (W. P. Lunt) Chr. Exam. **59**: 157.
— Radical Religious. (H. James) Radical, **2**: 84.
— Realm of. (G. I. Chace) Bapt. Q. **5**: 42.
— Reasonable. (F. Peek) Contemp. **29**: 660.
— Reasonableness of. (J. C. Shairp) Princ. n. s. **7**: 260.
— Religious, Harmony of the intuitional and logical Elements in. Prosp. R. **7**: 472.
— repenting and Faith resolving. (C. J. Vaughan) Good Words, **7**: 756.
— Repose of. Bost. R. **1**: 273.
— requisite to Christian Fellowship. (H. Ballou, 2d) Univ. Q. **5**: 366.
— Requisitions of. (A. P. Peabody) No. Am. **85**: 237.
— Reverence and Freedom. (J. W. Nevin) Mercersb. **2**: 97.
— Rogers's Reason and. Theo. & Lit. J. **?**: 177.
— Rule of. Meth. Q. **3**: 250.
— — Peck on. (C. Hodge) Princ. **14**: 598. — (S. W. S. Dutton) New Eng. **2**: 304.
— Saving, Chamberlayne on. (D. D. D. Buck) Meth. Q. **33**: 609. — (J. Noon) Meth. Q. **34**: 97.
— Scientific Basis of. (J. J. Murphy) Dub. Univ. **83**: 249.
— Sliding Scale of. (J. Pike) Bost. R. **5**: 213.
— a Source of Knowledge. Bost. R. **4**: 38.
— Thoughts in Aid of. Westm. **74**: 168.
— Translation of. N. Ecl. **6**: 416.
— True Meaning of the Word. (F. Guizot) Kitto, **12**: 430.
— Unity of. (G. T. Flanders) Univ. Q. **24**: 85.
— Use and Abuse of Reason in. Chr. Obs. **26**: 65, 121.
— *versus* Philosophy. (P. Bayne) Theo. Ecl. **2**: 224.
— Victory of. (J. Challen) Chr. Q. **5**: 236.
— Vital. Dub. Univ. **71**: 243.
— What is? Chr. Disc. **1**: 4.
— What it is, and how it comes. (E. G. Evelyn) Good Words, **7**: 194.
See Belief; Certainty.
Faithful and true. Lond. Soc. **8**: 41–254. Same art. Ecl. M. **65**: 607, 678. **66**: 83.
Faithful Fido; a Story. (J. Hutton) Tinsley, **28**: 454.
Faithful Margaret. House. Words, **10**: 12. Same art. Ecl. M. **33**: 272.
Faithful to the last. (W. W. Fenn) Tinsley, **20**: 96.
Faithfull, Emily, with portrait. Dub. Univ. **93**: 173.
Faithless Sally Brown. (T. Hood) Lond. M. **5**: 202.
Falashas, The. (S. Morais) Penn Mo. **11**: 323.
Falco of the Rock, etc. (Mrs. E. F. Ellet) Godey, **21**: 70.
Falcon, The; a Poem. (E. Pollock) Pioneer, **1**: 81.
Falcon Family, The. Dub. Univ. **27**: 58.
Falcons, Game, of New England. (W. Wood) Am. Natural. **5**: 80. **8**: 266. **10**: 132.
Falcon's Flight; a Tale. Eng. Dom. M. **6**: 169–288. **7**. 1–66.
Falconberg. (H. H. Boyesen) Scrib. **16**: 496–824. **17**: 20–816.
Falconer's Bride; a Tale. Dub. Univ. **12**: 523.
Falconry. (W. Wood) Am. Natural. **4**: 74. — Once a Week, **9**: 45. **26**: 130.
— in America. (W. Paton) Overland, **14**: 356.
— in the British Isles. Quar. **139**: 169.
— in the Valley of the Indus. Colburn, **97**: 295. Same art. Liv. Age, **37**: 273.
— Modern. Cornh. **11**: 619. Same art. Cath. World, **1**: 493.
— Revival of. (C. Pebody) Gent. M. n. s. **22**: 179.
Faliero, Marino. (Prof. de Vericour) Dub. Univ. **55**: 461.
Faliscan Inscriptions. (R. Garrucci) Arch. **43**: 43, 259.
Falk, Adalbert, Author of the Falk Laws. (H. Tuttle) Gent. M. n. s. **16**: 56.
Falk, John. (W. F. Stevenson) Good Words, **2**: 560.
Falk Laws. Chr. Q. **7**: 449. — (J. F. Smith) Theo. R. **12**: 552.
— English. (F. W. Roswell) Macmil. **33**: 179.
— Philosophy of. (H. Tuttle) Gent. M. n. s. **15**: 672.
— A Victim of. Lond. Q. **53**: 335.
— What are? (J. B. Paton) Fortn. **21**: 674.
Falkland, Lucius Carey, Viscount. (M. Arnold) 19th Cent. **1**: 141. Same art. Liv. Age, **133**: 34. — (Reply by Goldwin Smith) Contemp. **29**: 925. — Colburn, **125**: 161.
— and his modern Critics. Liv. Age, **135**: 131.
— Chillingworth, and Hales; the earlier Latitudinarians. Nat. R. **17**: 1.
Falkland, Lady. Chr. Rem. **10**: 26. — Meth. M. **35**: 517.
— Journal of. Dub. Univ. **50**: 360.
Falkland Islands. (R. Greenhow) Hunt, **6**: 105. — (Capt. Sullivan) Colburn, **86**: 17. — (C. W. Thomson) Good Words, **18**: 120.
— Mackinnon's Account of, 1838. Mo. R. **152**: 272.
— Picnic at, 1864. (T. Gift) St. James, **34**: 239. **35**: 24.
— Wild Sports of. (Capt. Mackinnon) Colburn, **87**: 139. Same art. Liv. Age, **23**: 337.
Falkland Palace, Fifeshire. Penny M. **12**: 361.
Fall of Adam, and the Penalty of the Law. (S. M. Merrill) Meth. Q **27**: 249.
— and the present Human Mind. Cong. M. **12**: 301.
— Cosmical Effects of. (D. R. Goodwin) Penn Mo. **4**: 171.
— Relation to the Fall of the Race. Princ. **42**: 239.
Fall of the Angels; a Poem. (R. G. Haliburton) St. James, **30**: 206.
Fall of Eve. (M. M. Turner) Lakeside, **9**: 401.
Fall of the House of Usher. (E. A. Poe) Bentley, **8**: 158.
Fall of Katharia; a Tale. Sharpe, **45**: 255.
Fall of Man. (J. De Concilio) Cath. World, **30**: 838. — Chr. Obs. **35**: 65, 137.
— and Evolution. (F. D. Hoskins) Am. Church R. **36**: 25.
— and its Import. (D. F. Bundle) Mercersb. **20**: 376.
— and its Transmission. (J. De Concilio) Cath. World, **30**: 838.
— and Redemption, Arminian View of. (D. D. Whedon) Meth. Q. **21**: 647.

Fall of Man, Effects of, upon the Creation. (B. S. Taylor) Meth. Q. **22**: 289. — (E. V. Gerhart) Mercersb. **12**: 505.
— — Fallen Man in an unfallen World. (E. C. Anderson) Bapt. Q. **2**: 275.
— Psychologico-Moral. (K. H. Sack) Mercersb. **16**: 413.
— Scenes in Eden not a Fall. (V. Lincoln) Univ. Q. **24**: 75.
— Temptation in Eden. Bost. R. **4**: 282.
See Sin, The First.
Fall of Maubila; a Poem. (T. D. English) Harper, **19**: 786.
Fall of Murray; a Tale. (H. W. Herbert) Am. Mo. M. **2**: 157, 225.
Fall of the Yburg. (H. Thompson) Once a Week, **14**: 416.
Fall River, Mass. Hunt, **17**: 303.
— Ministers of. Am. Q. Reg. **12**: 142.
Falls of the Bounding Deer; a Tale. (A. B. Street) Internat. M. **5**: 49.
— of Teycandama; a Poem. (A. Fonblanque) Temp. Bar, **34**: 113.
Fallacies, Antithetic. (F. H. Hill) Fortn. **28**: 395.
— Bentham's Book of. (Syd. Smith) Ed. R. **42**: 367.
— Chapter on. (S. S. Cox) Knick. **30**: 302.
— Fashionable. Dub. Univ. **54**: 117.
— of Faith. All the Year, **3**: 540.
— of the Fallacies. Dub. Univ. **34**: 640.
— of the Learned. All the Year, **45**: 186.
— Old, become new Facts. (H. L. Harrison) Peop. J. **5**: 117, 131.
— Popular. (J. G. Hoyt) No. Am. **96**: 87. — (W. Landels) Ex. H. Lec. **10**: 79.
Fallen among Flunkeys. (G. A. Sala) Belgra. **5**: 505.
Fallen among Thieves; a Story. Galaxy, **23**: 809.
Fallen among Thieves; a Story. House. Words, **13**: 413.
Fallen Fortunes; a Novel. (J. Payn) Chamb. J. **53**: 1–675. Same art. Appleton, **15**: 36–811. **16**: 64–559.
Fallen Leaves. (W. Collins) Canad. Mo. **15**: 130–633. **16**: 63–602. **17**: 47, 150, 253.
Fallen Star. Lond. M. **11**: 22.
Falling Bodies, Force of. (J. W. Nystrom) J. Frankl. Inst. **104**: 130.
— Law of. (T. Sherwin) Math. Mo. **2**: 166.
— Theory of. (T. W. Bakewell) J. Frankl. Inst. **4**: 34.
Falling from Grace. Cong. M. **24**: 315–602.
Falling in Love. Cornh. **3**: 41. **42**: 471.
Falling of a Mill at Oldham, 1844. J. Frankl. Inst. **39**: 289.
Fallmerayer, J. P., Works of. (H. Warner) No. Am. **99**: 281.
Falmouth, Me., Burning of, 1775. (W. Goold) N. E. Reg. **27**: 256. — Am. Mo. M. **11**: 543.
False Colors. (Mrs. P. Cudlip) Broadw. **1**: 46–560. **2**: 9, 528.
False Decretals, The. Month, **7**: 78.
False Distinctions. (T. De Quincey) Lond. M. **9**: 642. — Mus. **5**: 182.
False Friends and true. (T. S. Arthur) Godey, **23**: 207.
False Ground and firm. Fraser, **67**: 797. Same art. Liv. Age, **78**: 28.
False Love. (A. Cambridge) Once a Week, **17**: 475.
False Medium. Blackw. **34**: 440.
False Position, or the Undercurrent. Knick. **37**: 320.
False Pride. (M. W. Hale) Godey, **22**: 7
False Start; a moral Comedy. Blackw. **130**: 331. — Ecl. M. **97**: 698.
False Steps and wrong Roads. Temp. Bar, **6**: 539.
False Telegram, The. Eng. Dom. M. **12**: 147.
Falsehoods, Conventional. (O'D. T. Hill) St. James, **12**: 349.
Falstaff, Sir John, Character of. Fraser, **46**: 403.
Falstaff, Dramatic Character of. Lond. M. **1**: 194. — (J. G. Keily) Overland, **13**: 352.
Falstaff, Dramatic Character of, Historical Element in. (J. Gairdner) Fortn. **19**: 333. *See* Shakspere.
Falstaff's Wake; a Dramatic Scene. (T. Irwin) Dub. Univ. **63**: 222.
Fame and its Accessories. Dem. R. **20**: 431.
— and Monuments. Lond. M. **8**: 37.
— and Popularity. (J. R. Lowell) Ev. Sat. **10**: 166.
— Influence of, on Genius. Blackw. **3**: 701.
— Literary. Brit. Q. **10**: 75.
— Posthumous. Ox. Prize Ess. **2**: 191.
Familiar Epistle from a Parent to a Child. (C. Dickens) Bentley, **5**: 219.
Familiar Sayings. Canad. Mo. **13**: 532.
Familiar Spirit. (M. Hosmer) Overland, **10**: 142.
— Account of a. Anal. M. **4**: 313.
Familiarity, Effects of. Knick. **11**: 305. — (T. H. Shreve) Hesp. **1**: 149.
Familist's Hymn. (J. G. Whittier) Dem. R. **1**: 172.
Family, The. (J. W. Santee) Mercersb. **20**: 401.
— as influenced by Christianity. (P. Schaff) Mercersb. **5**: 473.
— as related to the Church. (M. Valentine) Evang. R. **10**: 360.
— as related to the State. (E. McPherson) Evang. R. **11**: 43.
— at Entenbruch. Radical, **7**: 51, 128.
— at Fenhouse. All the Year, **4**: 260. Same art. Liv. Age, **69**: 784.
— Christian and pagan. Brownson, **24**: 469.
— the domestic Constitution. Chr. R. **24**: 46.
— Evolution of. (H. Spencer) Pop. Sci. Mo. **11**: 129, 257.
— Future of. (E. L. Godkin) Nation, **7**: 453.
— of the cold Feet; an Irish Tale. Tait, **1**: 531.
— of the Rue de Sèvres. (A. A. Harwood) Godey, **24**: 207.
— typical of the State. (J. F. Rowe) Chr. Q. **7**: 507.
Families, Extinction of. (Watson and Galton) Anthrop. J. **4**: 138.
— Luck in. Lond. Soc. **13**: 529. **15**: 23.
— Noble, Vicissitudes of. Quar. **107**: 324.
— Old. (W. Chambers) Chamb. J. **56**: 129.
— Rise of great English, Burke's. Dub. Univ **81**: 457.
— Vicissitudes of, Burke's. Dub. R. **47**: 111.
Family Affections, Decay of. (A. G. Sedgwick) Nation, **8**: 291.
Family Antiquity, The Sentiment of. Blackw. **44**: 403.
Family Associations, United Service. (G. Barmby) Howitt, **1**: 344.
Family Circle, how preserved? Dem. R. **43**: 243.
Family Colors; a Tale. Bentley, **61**: 419.
Family Diamonds; a Story. Chamb. J. **58**: 377, 393, 407.
Family Features, Persistency of. Chamb. J. **4**: 1.
Family Feud; a Tale. (G. Kinkel) Blackw. **68**: 174.
Family Gamp; a Story. (S. Gibney) Tinsley, **28**: 419.
Family Ghost. (F. Talbot) Belgra. **26**: 367.
Family History. Blackw. **80**: 456. Same art. Liv. Age, **51**: 368.
— and Genealogical History. Ed. Mo. R. **4**: 530.
— Ups and Downs of Dub. Univ. **58**: 459.
Family History, A. (H. Martineau) Once a Week, **12**: 531–701. **13**: 1, 29.
Family Histories, British. Dub. Univ. **61**: 324. — Quar. **98**: 289.
See Genealogy.
Family Institutions. Chamb. J. **25**: 145.
Family Paper. (J. R. Dennett) Nation, **5**: 317.
Family Party in the Piazza of St. Peter. (T. A. Trollope) Belgra. **31**: 210, 333, 437.
Family Picture. (A. B. Longstreet) So. M. **8**: 155.
Family Portraits. Lond. M. **20**: 67, 242, 591.
Family Prayers. Chr. Disc. **4**: 1.
— Manuals of. (H. Alford) Contemp. **10**: 196.
— Review of Short Readings for. Chr. Obs. **48**: 189.

Family Register, Form of. N. E. Reg. 1: 67.
Family Religion. Cong. M. 5: 237, 289.
Family Resemblances. Hogg, 7: 65. 10: 90.
Family Scapegrace; a Story. (J. Payn) Chamb. J. 35: 1–262.
Family Worship. (A. B. Muzzey) Chr. Exam. 61: 182.
— (J. W. Yeomans) Princ. 20: 57.
Famine and Pestilence in Egypt, 1200 A. D. Am. Bib. Repos. 2: 657.
— and Poor-Laws. Pamph. 8: 157.
— in Bengal, 1866. No. Brit. 46: 242. Same art. Ecl. M. 68: 746.
— — 1874. Chr. Obs. 75: 667. — (H. Copinger) Colburn, 155: 93.
— in the East. (F. R. Feudge) Lippinc. 13: 249.
— in Ireland, 1847. Dem. R. 20: 424. — (O. C. Gardiner) Am. Whig R. 6: 455, 663.
— — Lessons from. Blackw. 61: 515.
— in Orissa. Fraser, 76: 373.
— in Persia, 1871. Ev. Sat. 11: 563.
— in Samaria; a Poem. Cong. M. 27: 729.
— Political Economy of. No. Brit. 7: 247.
— Sketch of a. (Mrs. Hoare) Howitt, 1: 233.
Famines and Sun-Spots. (R. A. Proctor) Gent. M. n. s. 19: 693. — (J. N. Lockyer and W. W. Hunter) 19th Cent. 2: 583. Same art. Sup. Pop. Sci. Mo. 2: 128.
— in India. (H. P. Malet) Geog. M. 2: 73, 136. — Westm. 109: 139.
— — and Sun-Spots. Geog. M. 4: 311.
— — in 1877. (A. C. Sellar) Nation, 25: 209.
— of the World. (C. Walford) J. Statis. Soc. 41: 433. 42: 79.
— — Walford on. Nation, 28: 15.
Famous Excommunication; a Peruvian Tale. Temp. Bar, 47: 550.
Famous Quire of Earndale; a Sketch. Cornh. 12: 99.
Famous Victory; a Story. (F. Mac Veagh) Dial (Ch.), 1: 33.
Fan, The. (M. Mauris) Scrib. 14: 589. — Chamb. J. 42: 329.
— and Associations. (Mrs. C. A. White) Sharpe, 29: 263.
— Art History of. Penn Mo. 3: 359.
Fans. (Mrs. C. A. White) Godey, 45: 11. 49: 230. — Lond. Soc. 18: 79. — (A. M. Benedict) Potter Am. Mo. 16: 319.
— Amongst the. (R. F. Burton) Anthrop. R. 1: 43.
— Chinese. (H. A. Giles) Fraser, 99: 548. Same art. Appleton, 21: 558. Same art. Liv. Age, 141: 696.
— Exhibition of, at S. Kensington. All the Year, 24: 66.
— Japanese. (N. Brooks) Scrib. 6: 616.
— where they come from. Godey, 58: 205, 301, 401.
Fanariotes of Constantinople. Lond. M. 10: 561.
Fanatical Guides. Am. Q. 8: 227.
Fanaticism. Ed. R. 59: 30. — Mo. R. 133: 73. — Ecl. R. 61: 1. — West. M. 3: 2. 4: 339. — (R. Robbins) Chr. Q. Spec. 6: 118. — (S. Eells) West. Lit. J. 1: 217.
— and Natural Historian of Enthusiasm. Fraser, 9: 159.
— Conspiracy of. Dem. R. 26: 385.
— Modern. Cong. M. 14: 293. — Chr. Obs. 31: 109.
— Page in the History of. Fraser, 37: 312, 441, 549.
— I. Taylor on. Cong. M. 17: 539.
Fanchette, the Goat of Boulainvilliers. Chamb. J. 54: 365. Same art. Liv. Age, 134: 467.
Fancourt, Miss, Extraordinary Cure of. Chr. Obs. 30: 708, 775. 31: 154.
Fancy and the Sense of Beauty. (W. M. Reily) Ref. Q. 28: 417.
— Wit, and Common Sense; a Poem. (F. Rückert) Mercersb. 9: 444.
Fancies of Spray and Petal; a Poem. (E. Fawcett) Atlan. 36: 47.
Fancies on Foot-Paths. (E. L. Blanchard) Peop. J. 5: 272.
Fancy Fair, A. Chamb. J. 34: 116.
— at Mopetown. All the Year, 27: 153.
Fancy Sketch. Contin. Mo. 3: 482.
Fancy-Work, Novelties in. (M. Ford) Potter Am. Mo. 16: 363, 458, 524. 17: 76–557.
Fane, Julian. (G. H. Sass) So. M. 11: 412.
Faneuil, Peter. Am. J. Educ. 9: 603.
— Letter of, 1739. N. E. Reg. 4: 260.
Fanning, Edmund. Voyages round the World, 1792–1832. Mo. R. 134: 137.
Fanning Islands, Natural History of. (T. H. Streets) Am. Natural. 11: 65.
Fanny Bentley; a Tale. Peop. J. 9: 305, 330.
Fanny Fairfield; a Tale. Blackw. 39: 198, 391, 497.
Fanny Fern. *See* Parton, Sarah P. W.
Fanny Forester. *See* Judson, Emily C.
Fanny Graham's Dreams. Fraser, 40: 444, 546, 645.
Fanny Lincoln; or the Village Amanuensis. (T. S. Arthur) Godey, 24: 289.
Fanny Waite; a Story. New Eng. M. 6: 293.
Fanny Winthrop's Treat. (E. A. Walker) Scrib. 4: 24.
Fanö, Island of, in the North Sea. (Mrs. Bushby) Bentley, 48: 588.
Fanshawe, Ann Harrison, Lady. Temp. Bar, 3: 200. — (J. Hutton) Belgra. 35: 204.
— Memoirs of. (F. Jeffrey) Ed. R. 50: 75.
Fantasia Improvisation. Cornh. 27: 447.
Fantasy of Hades; a Poem. (G. Bloede) Western, 5: 367.
Fantasy Piece. (G. W. Peck) Am. Whig R. 8: 179.
Fanti Land. Once a Week, 29: 160–314.
Fantis and Ashantis, Future of. (G. A. Henty) Geog. M. 1: 148.
Far from the madding Crowd; a Tale. (T. Hardy) Cornh. 29: 1–641. 30: 1–617. Same art. Ecl. M. 82: 288–687. 83: 56–715. 84: 72, 200. Same art. Ev. Sat. 16: 113–225. Same art. Liv. Age, 120: 299–597. 121: 19–536. 122: 165–659. 123: 38–790. 124: 49, 99.
Faraday, Michael. (A. de La Rive) Am. J. Sci. 95: 145. — (G. E. Ellis) Mo. Rel. M. 43: 355. — (J. H. Gladstone) Nature, 1: 401. — (J. Lovering) O. & N. 1: 47. — (J. Scoffern) Belgra. 3: 421. Same art. Ecl. M. 70: 61. — (J. Tyndall) Ecl. M. 75: 230, 353. — with portrait, Fraser, 13, 224. — All the Year, 19: 399. — Brit. Q. 47: 434. — Am. Church R. 23: 104. — Ecl. M. 28: 120. — with portrait, Ecl. M. 70: 514. — Ev. Sat. 14: 175. — Fraser, 81: 326. — Lond. Q. 34: 265. — Nature, 8: 397. — (I. Scott) Once a Week, 3: 205. — with portrait, Appleton, 2: 436. — with portrait, Pract. M. 6: 352. — St. James, 20: 501. Same art. N. Ecl. 1: 68. — St. Paul's, 6: 292. — Victoria, 14: 331.
— and his Philosophy. Good Words, 12: 121.
— as a Discoverer. (J. S. Russell) Macmil. 18: 184. Same art. Liv. Age, 98: 67. — (J. Tyndall) Am. J. Sci. 96: 34, 180.
— as a Man. Stud. & Intel. Obs. 4: 436. — Ev. Sat. 9: 92.
— Discoveries in Light and Magnetism. Ecl. M. 11: 353.
— Experiments in Electricity. Quar. 79: 49.
— Helmholtz on. Nature, 3: 51.
— Life of. (W. F. Barrett) Nature, 6: 411. — Ed. R. 132: 176. Same art. Liv. Age, 106: 707. — Westm. 96: 362. Same art. Liv. Age, 112: 278.
— Religious Character of. (G. P. Fisher) New Eng. 32: 311.
— the Scientist and Christian. (P. M. Biklé) Luth. Q. 5: 420.
Faraday Lecture. (H. Helmholtz) Nature, 23: 535.
Farallon Islands, California. (C. Nordhoff) Harper, 48: 617. — (C. M. Scammon) Overland, 15: 54.

Farces, Fashionable. Contemp. 30: 1041.
Farcy, George, Poet and Scientist. (C. E. Meetkerke) Argosy, 30: 266.
Fardorougha, the Miser. (W. Carleton) Dub. Univ. 9: 212–521 10: 671. 11: 95, 250. Same art. Liv. Age, 34: 1–363.
Farewell; a Song. Dub. Univ. 5: 183.
Farewell Valentine. Lond. Soc. 7: 181.
Farina, Jean Maria, and his Eau de Cologne. Chamb. J. 15: 209. Same art. Liv. Age, 29: 465.
Farinelli, the Singer. All the Year, 7: 21.
Farish, Wm., Obituary of. Chr. Obs. 37: 611, 674, 737.
Faristan and Fatima; a Poem. (E. A. Bowring) Once a Week, 3: 377.
Farjeon, B. L., with portrait. Victoria, 32: 81.
— Bread and Cheese and Kisses. Dub. Univ. 80: 694.
— Joshua Marvel. Dub. Univ. 78: 348.
— London's Heart. Victoria, 20: 552.
Farleigh Castle, Legend of; a Poem. Bentley, 63: 619.
Farm and College. All the Year, 20: 414.
— How to treat a. Pract. M. 7: 332.
— of four Acres. Chamb. J. 32: 3.
— of Muiceron; a Tale. (W. M. Storrs) Cath. World, 18: 171–734. — Cath. World, 19: 39, 187, 308.
— of two Acres, Our. (H. Martineau) Once a Week, 1: 37, 44, 96.
— Stephens's Book of. Blackw. 57: 298. 69: 588. — Quar. 84: 389.
— to the Shop. Lippinc. 25: 68.
Farms and Farmers, English. Once a Week, 11: 580. — Cornh. 41: 337.
— Great, of the West. Atlan. 45: 33.
Farm Implements, Mechanical Engineering applied to. (H. Howson) J. Frankl. Inst. 60: 339, 401. 61: 41–401. 62: 45, 197.
Farm Laborer, Life of a. Cornh. 9: 178. 10: 609.
Farm Laborers and Cow Plots. (H. Evershed) Fortn. 20: 79.
Farm Laborers, Strike of. (W. E. Bear) Fortn. 18: 76. *See* Agricultural Laborers,
Farm Life; Boy on a Hill-Farm. (M. Dean) Lippinc. 22: 310.
— Glimpses of New England. (R. E. Robinson) Scrib. 16: 510.
— — of Western. (M. Thompson) Scrib. 16: 676.
— in New York, Picturesque Aspects of. (J. Burroughs) Scrib. 17: 41.
Farm Overseers and their Servants. Blackw. 3: 83.
Farm Produce in America, Depredators on. Penny M. 7: 195.
Farm School at Redhill. Chamb. J. 25: 407.
— of Glasnevin. Chamb. J. 28: 252.
Farm School System of Europe. (J. Fletcher) J. Statis. Soc. 15: 1.
Farm Servants and their Earnings. Chamb. J. 47: 660.
Farm Villages. (G. E. Waring, jr.) Scrib. 13: 756.
Farmer, Hugh, Memoir of. Ecl. R. 1: 139.
Farmer, John, with portrait. (W. Cogswell) N. E. Reg. 1: 9.
— Biography of. (J. B. Moore) Am. Q. Reg. 11: 229. — Am. Alma. 1836: 291.
— Letters of. N. E. Reg. 1: 33.
Farmer Family, Arms of. N. E. Reg. 1: 360.
— Genealogy of. (S. G. Drake) N. E. Reg. 1: 21.
Farmer's Theorem discussed. (F. E. Stimpson) Am. J. Sci. 100: 372.
— Stimpson on. (B. Silliman) Am. J. Sci. 100: 377.
Farmer at Home. (R. Jefferies) Fraser, 90: 135.
Farmer Basset's Romance. (Saxe Holm) Scrib. 13: 484–609.
Farmer Hill's Diary. (A. M. Diaz) Atlan. 18: 397.
Farmer Tubbs's Revenge. All the Year, 46: 349.
Farmer's Encyclopædia. So. Lit. Mess. 9: 356.
Farmer's Guide, Stephen's. New Eng. 9: 553.
Farmer's Wife at St. Fiacre. (K. S. Macquoid) Belgra. 45: supp. 65.
Farmers. Cornh. 8: 164.
— and the Liberal Party. (W. E. Bear) Fortn. 31: 435.
— and Railroads. (E. Stanwood) O. & N. 8: 335.
— English. Land We Love, 1: 100, 209.
— — Great. (C. W. Elliott) Galaxy, 7: 413, 558. 8: 70.
— — Plight of, 1879. (E. L. Godkin) Nation, 28: 212.
— Power of. (R. Jefferies) Fortn. 21: 808.
— Satyrs and sylvan Boys. (M. Dean) Lippinc. 16: 224.
— Tenant, Increasing Difficulties of. (W. E. Bear) Fortn. 18: 309.
Farmers' Movement. *See* Grangers.
Farmhouse Dirge; a Poem. (A. Austin) Contemp. 34: 277. Same art. Liv. Age, 140: 381.
Farming. Dem. R. 29: 217.
— by Steam. All the Year, 1: 66. 11: 67. — Chamb. J. 21: 4.
— Co-operative, Lawson's. (G. E. Waring, jr.) Nation, 20: 245. — (W. H. Roberts) Fortn. 36: 195.
— Fortunatus Agricola. St. James, 49: 173.
— French and English. Dub. Univ. 91: 661.
— Future of. (R. Jefferies) Fraser, 88: 687.
— Greeley's What I know about. (G. E. Waring, jr.) Nation, 13: 108.
— in France. (P. E. Gibbons) Harper, 58: 449.
— in Holland. Pract. M. 4: 260.
— in Kansas, Picturesque Aspects of. (H. King) Scrib. 19: 132.
— in Los Angeles, Skilled. (J. Hayes) Overland, 7: 448.
— in Pajaro Valley. (J. Hayes) Overland, 5: 345.
— Neapolitan Systems of. Brit. & For. R. 9: 507.
— Old Authors on. Sharpe, 38: 30, 91, 262.
— on Thirteen Acres. Cornh. 11: 548.
— past and present. Chamb. J. 4: 19.
— Sanitary. Ecl. R. 99: 310.
— Smith's Productive. Ecl. Mus. 3: 53.
See Agriculture.
Farmington, Conn., Old Meeting-House at. (N. Porter) Mo. Rel. M. 50: 510.
— Records. N. E. Reg. 11: 323. 12: 34, 147, 327. 13: 57.
Farmsley House. (H. Rosevelt) Overland, 5: 68.
Farnam, Henry, and Farnam Hall, Yale College. Am. J. Educ. 28: 895.
Farne Islands. (E. Greatorex) Reliquary, 13: 23. — Penny M. 10: 199.
Farnese, Alexander, Prince of Parma. (W. C. Robinson) Month, 33: 266.
— Sketch of. (J. G. Wilson) U. S. Serv. M. 4: 520.
Farnham Castle. Penny M. 4: 444.
Farnsworth, Seth. (H. Wood) Am. Q. Reg. 12: 131.
Farnum, Alexander, Library of. Am. Bibliop. 7: 92.
Farnum Preparatory School, N. J. Am. J. Educ. 3: 397.
Faro-Gambling. (E. Crapsey) Galaxy, 12: 57.
Faro-Table; transl. from Hoffmann. Dem. R. 16: 555.
Faroe Islands. (R. Southey) Quar. 4: 333. — Penny M. 1: 210. — Ecl. R. 11: 450.
— and Shetland, Fowling in. Chamb. J. 10: 180.
— Fortnight in. No. Brit. 40: 287.
— Holiday in. Once a Week, 30: 454–656.
— Saga of. Blackw. 106: 618, 701.
— Visit to. (R. Chambers) Chamb. J. 24: 129–282.
— Zoölogy of. (R. v. Willemoes-Suhm) Nature, 7: 105.
Farquhar, George. (C. C. Clarke) Gent. M. n. s. 8: 38.
Farr, Jonathan. (A. Hall) Chr. Exam. 39: 379.
— Plain Letters. (F. W. P. Greenwood) Chr. Exam. 12: 32.
Farragut, David G., Admiral, with portrait. (R. B. Irwin) U. S. Serv. M. 3: 5.
— and New Orleans. (G. Welles) Galaxy, 12: 669, 817.

Farragut, David G., Admiral, and D. Porter, and U. S. Navy. (C. C. Chesney) Ed. R. **124**: 185.
— in Mobile Bay. Scrib. **13**: 539.
— — August Morning with. (J. C. Kinney) Scrib. **22**: 199.
— Life of. (J. C. Palfrey) Nation, **30**: 13.
— Monument to, in New York. (R. W. Gilder) Scrib. **22**: 161.—(M. G. v. Rensselaer) Am. Arch. **10**: 119.
Farrar, F. W. Eternal Hope. *See* Eternal Punishment.
— Life of Christ. *See* Jesus Christ.
— St. Paul. *See* Paul.
— Seekers after God. Chr. Obs. **69**: 197.
Farrar, John. (J. G. Palfrey) Chr. Exam. **55**: 121.
Farrar, Joseph. N. E. Reg. **3**: 185, 211.
Farrar, Timo., with portrait. (S. Lee) N. E. Reg. **29**: 225.
Farrar Genealogy. (T. Farrar) N. E. Reg. **6**: 313.
Farren, Elizabeth, the Actress. Dub. Univ. **65**: 68, 202.
Farren, William, an English actor. (D. Cook) Gent. M. n. s. **24**: 213.—(T. P. Grinsted) Bentley, **41**: 80.
Farthings of Queen Anne. Penny M. **9**: 436.
Fascination. All the Year, **30**: 103.
— and the Evil Eye. All the Year, **35**: 41.
— Personal. St. Paul's, **6**: 489.
Fascinum, or Evil Eye, represented on a Bas-Relief. (J. Millingen and S. Weston) Arch. **19**: 70, 99.
Fashion. (G. W. Curtis) Putnam, **1**: 68.—(C. H. Gregory) Am. Lit. M. **1**: 184.—(J. K. Paulding) Dem. R. **2**: 265.—New Eng. M. **4**: 345.—Mus. **2**: 472. **15**: 538.—Sharpe, **38**: 247.
— Amateur of. St. James, **5**: 489.
— and its Follies. Temp. Bar, **43**: 531.
— and Manners. (H. Spencer) Westm. **61**: 357.
— and Popularity. Godey, **54**: 249.
— and Taste. (H. Bushnell) New Eng. **1**: 153.
— Change of. Am. Mo. M. **11**: 503.
— Chatterings on. St. James, **22**: 668.
— Crumpled Rose-Leaves. Chamb. J. **45**: 497.
— Cycles of. Chamb. J. **40**: 187.
— Domain of. (G. Fitzhugh) De Bow, **29**: 695.
— Empire of. Tait, n. s. **1**: 54.
— Examination of young Pretender to. Lond. M. **12**: 46.
— Fancy and. Blackw. **123**: 412.
— Follies of. (C. Nordhoff) Harper, **18**: 310.
— Fools of. All the Year, **38**: 62.
— Freaks of. Dub. Univ. **59**: 633.—Victoria, **11**: 222.
— Frenzies of. (W. Chambers) Chamb. J. **53**: 177.
— Frolics of. Temp. Bar, **35**: 91.
— in Deformity. (W. H. Flower) Pop. Sci. Mo. **17**: 721.
— in Dress. (H. R. Cleveland) No. Am. **47**: 148.—All the Year, **28**: 319.
— — Curiosities in. Lond. Soc. **4**: 232. Same art. Ecl. M. **60**: 357.
— in Religion. (E. Strong) New Eng. **11**: 171.
— in a Village. (H. S. Totten) Godey, **30**: 205.
— Paint, Powder, Patches. Cornh. **7**: 738. Same art. Liv. Age, **78**: 206.
— Philosophy of. Colburn, **7**: 238.—So. Lit. Mess. **23**: 226.
— Poets of. Irish Q. **3**: 626.
— Tyranny of. Cornh. **38**: 83.
— the uglifying Process. Ev. Sat. **9**: 77.
— Votary of. (Mrs. A. J. Hippisley) Peop. J. **5**: 328.
— Word about. Victoria, **14**: 400.
Fashions. All the Year, **4**: 125.—Dem. R. **34**: 210.—Lond. M. **12**: 585. **13**: 88.
— and their Follies. Hogg, **14**: 152.
— Follies in. Chamb. J. **53**: 33.
— Foolish. All the Year, **20**: 65.
— Generations of. (J. J. Jarves) Harper, **9**: 749.
— in Dress. Mo. R. **148**: 380.—So. Lit. J. **4**: 525.
— in Physic. Mus. **8**: 11.
— of the Future. All the Year, **35**: 180.
Fashions, Old. Once a Week, **30**: 735.
— Rationale of. (E. L. Godkin) Nation, **5**: 418.
— Where they come from. Ev. Sat. **9**: 779.
See Dress.
Fashionable and unfashionable New England Wife; a Tale. So. Lit. Mess. **1**: 290.
Fashionable Crazes. Dub. Univ. **94**: 206.
Fashionable Forger. House. Words, **4**: 178.
Fashionable Hospitality. St. James, **16**: 202.
Fashionable Life in England. Am. Q. **1**: 222.—Mus. **22**: 349.
Fashionable Marriage. Argosy, **32**: 55.
Fashionable Monthlies. (D.G. Mitchell) New Eng. **2**: 96.
Fashionable Mother. Knick. **9**: 386.
Fashionable Society in United States. Liv. Age, **31**: 273.
Fashionable Vagaries. (W. Chambers) Chamb. J. **56**: 417.
Fast and firm. Lond. Soc. **8**: 547.
Fast and loose. Lond. Soc. **10**: 459.
Fast-Day at Foxden, (J. P. Quincy) Atlan. **13**: 676.
Fast Friends. (F. W. Currey) Dub. Univ. **88**: 543.
Fast Friends; a Tale. (F. Harrison) St. James, **35**: 640.
Fast Run and a double Kill. Lond. Soc. **7**: 71.
Fasti; Calendars of Church of Christ. Chr. Rem. **40**: 386.
Fasti Hellenici, Clinton's. Westm. **5**: 269.
Fastidious Man, The. So. Lit. Mess. **13**: 147, 230.
Fastidiousness, Miseries of. (T. H. Shreve) Hesp. **3**: 41.
Fasting. Bost. R. **3**: 262.—Cong. M. **2**: 528.—Irish Q. **9**: 1028.
— Cases of long. Ev. Sat. **9**: 13.
— Christian View of. (M. Valentine) Evang. R. **15**: 113.
— Duty of. (T. A. Morris) Meth. Q. **9**: 205.
— Nature, Obligations and Ends of. Chr. Obs. **2**: 74.
— Philosophy of. (B. W. Richardson) Gent. M. n. s. **25**: 348.
Fasting Communion. Chr. Obs. **75**: 410.
Fasting Girls. All the Year, **22**: 442.
Fastolf, Sir J. Sharpe, **1**: 123.
— Appointment as Keeper of the Bastille, 1421. (J. G. Nichols) Arch. **44**: 112.
— Inventory of Effects of. (T. Amyot) Arch. **21**: 232.
Fat People. All the Year, **12**: 352.
Fata Morgana, in the Bay of Reggio. Penny M. **2**: 351.
Fatal Abduction; a Poem. (J. Sheehan) Temp. Bar, **36**: 537.
Fatal Accidents, how preventible. Ed. R. **94**: 98. Same art. Ecl. M. **24**: 1.
Fatal Bride; a Tale. Dub. Univ. **31**: 15.
Fatal Curiosity; a Tale. (J. Payn) Belgra. **34**: supp. 94.
Fatal Fortune; a Tale. (W. Collins) All the Year, **33**: 13, 37.
Fatal Inheritance. (Mrs. S. R. T. Mayer) St. James, **30**: 558, 661. **31**: 69–408.
Fatal Jewels. (A. Fonblanque) Belgra. **9**: 557.
Fatal Letter. (J. Hatton) Lond. Soc. **27**: 521.
Fatal Marriage of Bill the Soundser. (W. L. Tiffany) Contin. Mo. **1**: 395.
Fatal Mark. (H. R. Addison) Bentley, **15**: 501.
Fatal Passion; a Dramatic Sketch. (W. E. Channing) Dial, **4**: 364.
Fatal Picture; a Story. (H.C. Appleby) St. James, **46**: 69.
Fatal Presentiments. Fraser, **3**: 34.—Liv. Age, **24**: 536.
Fatal Unction; a Coronation Tragedy. Blackw. **10**: 53.
Fatal Zero; Diary kept at Homburg. All the Year, **21**: 19–356.
Fatalism and Free Will. (M. A. Castle) Zoist, **13**: 70.
— not Evangelism. Am. Church R. **8**: 207.
— Statistical Variety of. Lond. Q. **12**: 1.
— Servian popular Tale on. House. Words, **11**: 167
Fatalist, The. (I. Tourgénieff) O. & N. **9**: 565.
Fate in the Religion of the Ancients.. Dub. R. **4**: 32.
Fate and a Heart; a Poem. Cornh. **2**: 287.
Fate Ferguston. Galaxy, **3**: 87.

Fate of the Fairleighs; a Tale. Putnam, **8**: 384.
— of Fauriel. (D. Costello) Bentley, **49**: 112.
— of Genius; a Poem. (R. St. Chelt) Hogg, **8**: 316.
— of the Heather Belle. Tinsley, **8**: 401.
— of Hutchinson Wemble. (S. L. Simpson) Overland, **14**: 532.
— of John Wortley. (G. Grant) Tinsley, **18**: 153.
— of Lady Grale. Colburn, **138**: 472.
— of the O'Learys. (Mrs. S. C. Hall) Dub. Univ. **17**: 76.
— of two Cities, Liege and Dinant. (J. W. Sheahan) Lakeside, **9**: 35.
— of a Water Lily; a Poem. Dub. Univ. **82**: 35.
Fate's Choice; a Story. (C. B. Lewis) Galaxy, **21**: 493.
Fates, The. (W. T. Harris) J. Spec. Philos. **11**: 265.
Fates of a Family. (C. H. M. Bridge) Colburn, **168**: 490.
Fated to be free. (J. Ingelow) Good Words, **16**: 33–825. Same art. Liv. Age, **124**: 369, 728. **125**: 160–660. **126**: 165, 744.
Fatello, Sigismund. Blackw. **64**: 714.
Father and Son. House. Words, **1**: 213.
Father Gabriel. House. Words, **2**: 67, 85.
Father Mériel's Bell. (J. K. Hosmer) Atlan. **25**: 179.
Father of the Regiment; a Poem. (W. Thornbury) Once a Week, **5**: 70.
Father Oswald; a Catholic Story. Ed. R. **77**: 482.
Father Prout's Inaugurative Ode. (F. Mahoney) Cornh. **1**: 75.
— Last Book. Dub. Univ. **30**: 442.
Father Stilling's Sunset. (J. H. Jung-Stilling) Colburn, **157**: 594, 793. **158**: 79–319.
Father Tolo's Umbrella; a Story. (L. W. Champney) Galaxy, **22**: 61.
Father Tom and the Pope; or a Night at the Vatican. (J. F. Murray; also attributed to S. Ferguson, and to F. Mahoney) Blackw. **43**: 607.
Father Tudkin's Malediction. Blackw. **51**: 248.
Father's Revenge. (E. A. Dupuy) Godey, **23**: 175.
Father's Story. (M. C. Hay) Belgra. **26**: 497.
Fathers of the Church. Knick. **39**: 205, 493.
— and early Christians. (F. J. Sharr) Ex. H. Lec. **19**: 117.
— Ante-Nicene. Am. Church R. **21**: 228.
— — Boyd's Translation of. (T. Moore) Ed. R. **24**: 58.
— — Difficulties of. Dub. R. **18**: 331.
— of the Desert. Brownson, **10**: 379.
— Value of. (T. W. Coit) Am. Church R. **4**: 497.
Fathers and Sons. (T. E. Hook) Colburn, **58**: 1–441. **59**: 1–289. **60**: 1–425. **61**: 1–417. **62**: 1–429 **63**: 142–417.
Fatherless Daughter; a Tale. So. Lit. Mess. **7**: 452.
Fatma Zaida's Koran. Ev. Sat. **9**: 193.
Faucher Léon. Belgra. **5**: 194.
— Letters and Speeches of. Ed. R. **128**: 191.
— Memoir of. Bank. M. (L.) **15**: 133.
Fauconberg, Lord, Embassy to Italy, 1669. (Sir H. Ellis) Arch. **37**: 158.
Faulder, Richard, Legend of. Lond. M. **3**: 29, 166, 255.
Faulkner, Arthur Brooke, Letters to Lord Brougham. Mo. R. **142**: 514.
Faulkner, Charles J., with portrait. Dem. R. **41**: 207.
Faults on both Sides. (L. Blanchard) Colburn, **71**: 390.
Fault-Finding. Eng. Dom. M. **13**: 76.
Fauna. *See* Animals.
Fauntleroy, Henry, Trial and Execution of. All the Year, **16**: 470.
Fauntleroy Verrian's Fate. (H. E. Prescott) Knick. **57**: 57–465.
Faussett Collection of Antiquities. Chamb. J. **30**: 148, 169. — Art J. **6**: 227.
Faust of Wittenberg and Fust of Mentz. Internat. M. **5**: 172.
Faust; a Story. (I. Tourgénieff) Galaxy, 13: 621, 734.
Faust; Dramatic and Legendary. (J. Oxenford) Belgra. **1**: 88.
— From, to Pickwick. (M. Browne) Contemp. **38**: 162.
— Goethe's and Marlowe's. (C. Grant) Contemp. **40**: 1.
— Legend of. (H. S. Edwards) Macmil. **34**: 268. Same art. Ecl. M. **87**: 351.
— Myth of. (E. G. Holland) Appleton, **14**: 80.
— on the Stage. All the Year, **43**: 39.
— The Supernatural in Art. (V. Lee) Cornh. **42**: 212. *See* Goethe.
Fausts, The two. Dem. R. **13**: 315.
Faustus, Dr. (E. H. Malcolm) Sharpe, **45**: 155.
— and the Devil. Cornh. **14**: 687.
— German popular Legend of. (J. A. L. Robinson) Atlan. **2**: 551.
— how he became a Dancer. (H. S. Edwards) Macmil. **35**: 403.
— Legend of. (R. H. Horne) Contemp. **33**: 310.
Favart, Mons. and Madame. All the Year, **37**: 412.
Favell, S., Memoir of. Cong. M. **13**: 392, 561.
Faversham Church. Antiquary, **3**: 42, 64, 183.
Favette and Thargelie. (L. de la Ramé) Bentley, **51**: 333.
Favorite of the Harem. (Mrs. Leonowens) Atlan. **30**: 335.
Favorites, Royal. St. James, **6**: 330, 485. **7**: 81–476. **8**: 79, 183.
Favorite Haunts and rural Studies. Fraser, **35**: 29.
Favras, Marquis de. Bentley, **30**: 307. Same art. Ecl. M. **24**: 330.
Favre, J., with portrait. Appleton, **2**: 212. — with portrait, Ev. Sat. **9**: 611, 621.
Favre, P., first Disciple of Loyola. (H. J. Coleridge) Month, **20**: 62.
Favre, Pierre Antoine, Obituary of. Nature, **21**: 417.
Fawcett, Edgar. Fantasy and Passion. Canad. Mo. **14**: 760.
Fawcett, Henry. (M. D. Conway) Harper, **50**: 352.
— and Mrs. Henry. (H. Holbeach) St. Paul's, **11**: 74.
Fawcett, John, Life of. (J. Foster) Ecl. R. **28**: 240. — Ecl. R. **30**: 93. — Cong. M. **5**: 1.
— Sermons of. Chr. Obs. **16**: 790.
Fawcett, John, Actor, Recollections of. Colburn, **53**: 101.
Fawkes, Guy. (J. Mew) St. James, **41**: 567.
— Recollections of. (D. Jerrold) Colburn, **51**: 316.
Fawn of Sertorius. Ecl. R. **85**: 155.
Fay, Theodore S. Countess Ida. (C. C. Felton) No. Am. **51**: 434.
— Norman Leslie. So. Lit. Mess. **2**: 54.
Fayal, Portuguese and. (T. W. Higginson) Atlan. **6**: 526.
Fazy, James, and the Politics of Geneva. Cornh. **13**: 409.
Fear and Joy, Scientific Aspects of. (A. Wilson) Colburn, **159**: 67.
— as a Christian Motive. Bost. R. **1**: 165.
Fearful Responsibility; a Story. (W. D. Howells) Scrib. **22**: 276–390. Same art. Canad. Mo. **20**: 59, 134.
Feast and a Battle, Old Story of a. Fraser, **91**: 642.
— of Belshazzar; a Poem. (E. Arnold) Liv. Age, **103**: 93.
— of Fools. (F. Douce) Arch. **15**: 225.
— of Harvest; a Poem. (E. C. Stedman) Atlan. **20**: 616.
— of the Ingathering. Chamb. J. **20**: 324.
— of the Roofs. Liv. Age, **132**: 180.
— of St. Partridge at Park Hall. Belgra. **1**: 103.
— of Tabernacles. Chr. Obs. **63**: 79.
Feasts. Chamb. J. **10**: 361.
— and Festivals. (Mrs. White) Godey, **46**: 430. *See* Festival Days.
Feast-Day Literature in Mexico. Cath. World, **12**: 786.
Feats of Endurance. Chamb. J. **54**: 806.
Feathers. Cornh. **39**: 712.
— and their Uses. Chamb. J. **39**: 127. Same art. Ev. Sat. **14**: 300. Same art. Ecl. M. **59**: 128.
— Nature and Uses of. Penny M. **10**: 357, 363.
— Ostrich. Lond. Soc. **35**: 186.

Feathers; Pleased with a Feather. (G. Allen) Cornh. 39: 712. Same art. Pop. Sci. Mo. 15: 366.
— Symmetry in. (G. A. Lewis) Am. Natural. 5: 675.
Feather-Stars (Comatulæ), Recent and fossil. (P. H. Carpenter) Pop. Sci. R. 19: 193.
Feathered Fossil, A. (H. Woodward) Intel. Obs. 2: 313.
Featherstonhaugh, Charles F., Memoirs and Remains of. Lond. M. 9: 133.
Feathertop; a moralized Legend. (N. Hawthorne) Internat. M. 5: 182, 333.
Febiger, Christian. (H. P. Johnston) M. Am. Hist. 6: 188.
February. (W. Howitt) Howitt, 1: 79.
— Extra Day in. (T. Smith) Good Words, 4: 292.
February Post-Bag; a French Tale. Cornh. 21: 204.
Fechner's Psychophysical Law. (J. Ward) Mind, 1: 452.
Fechter, Charles A. (K. Field) Atlan. 26: 285.—(G. B. Woods) O. & N. 1: 514.—Cornh. 8: 172.—Galaxy, 9: 554.
— as an Actor. Ev. Sat. 10: 138.
— as Hamlet. (K. Field) Atlan. 26: 558.—(R. G. White) Nation, 10: 118.—Ev. Sat. 9: 274, 289.—O. & N. 3: 359.—St. James, 2: 371.
— — and Othello. Blackw. 90: 744.—Fraser, 64: 772.
— Realism in Dramatic Art. (R. G. White) Nation, 10: 364.
Federal and State Decisions, Conflict between. (W. B. Hornblower) Am. Law R. 14: 211.
Federal Constitution. So. R. 2: 432.
Federal Convention of 1787, Anecdotes of. Liv. Age, 25: 557.
Federal Finances. Dem. R. 26: 193.
Federal Government. Portfo. (Den.) 14: 556.
— Defects and Remedy of. Carey's Mus. 1: 269.
— Freeman's History of. Nat. R. 17: 339.
— Gillett's. (J. N. Pomeroy) Nation, 13: 242.
— Letters on. (T. Coxe) Carey's Mus. 2: 300, 387.
— Theory of. (J. G. Palfrey) No. Am. 54: 212.
Federal Procession in Philadelphia, July 4, 1788. Carey's Mus. 4: 57.
Federal Recruit, Adventures of. All the Year, 10: 512.
Federalism and Home Rule. (E. A. Freeman) Fortn. 22: 204.
— in New England, 1800–15. (H. C. Lodge) Nation, 26: 11.
— in Spain. (E. L. Godkin) Nation, 16: 264.
— Present Tasks of, 1864. (J. H. Allen) Chr. Exam. 76: 250.
Federalist, The. Brownson, 21: 385.—Carey's Mus. 2: 441, 523.—Mo. R. 111: 516.
— and the Constitution. (W. A. Cocke) So. M. 8: 77.
— Authorship of disputed Numbers of. Hist. M. 8: 305.
— Dawson's Edition of. (H. W. Torrey) No. Am. 98: 586.
— Life and Character of John Jay. (H. T. Tuckerman) Contin. Mo. 6: 336.
— No. 63, Jay's original Draft. Hist. M. 11: 257.
Federalist Party, Destruction of. (H. C. Lodge) No. Am. 123: 113.
Federalists, Address to. Carey's Mus. 2: 381.
Federative Policy of Europe. Quar. 38: 172.
Federative System of the United States. (B. Tucker) So. Lit. Mess. 4: 761.
Feed my Lambs; a Tale. Contin. Mo. 5: 663.
Feed-Water Heater, Berryman's. Pract. M. 2: 123.
Fees, Gossip about. Chamb. J. 56: 411.
See also Tips; Backsheesh.
Feejee. *See* Fiji.
Feeling and Energy. (W. S. Duncan) Sup. Pop. Sci. Mo. 3: 464.
— and Sentiment. New Eng. M. 2: 24.
— and Thought, Distinctions in. (R. Flint) Mind, 2: 112.
— as related to Faith. (M. Loy) Luth. Q. 3: 1.
— Faith, and Knowledge in their mutual Relations. (L. H. Atwater) Princ. 33: 421.
— of Effort, James on. (W. M. Salter) Unita. R. 16: 544.
Feeling, Religious, Smyth on. (S. Harris) New Eng. 37: 72.
Feelings. Ev. Sat. 4: 60.
— and the Intellect. Brit. Q. 70: 27.
— and the Will. (A. Bain) Fortn. 3: 575.
— Comicalities of. Bentley, 11: 51.
— Psychology of. Brit. Q. 70: 27.
— Survival of. (G. F. Magoun) Luth. Q. 11: 354.
Feet. Eng. Dom. M. 2: 240.
— Distortion of, in China. Chamb. J. 57: 191.
— of Insects. (L. L. Clarke) Intel. Obs. 2: 393. 3: 167, 350.
— of Mammalia, Effect of Impacts and Strains on. (E. D. Cope) Am. Natural. 15: 542.
Feet-Washing. (C. P. Krauth, jr.) Evang. R. 1: 434.
Felbiger, Johann Ignaz von. Am. J. Educ. 9: 600.
Feigning-Face. (M. Collins) Dub. Univ. 93: 279.
Felicia Crompton. All the Year, 8: 425. Same art. Liv. Age, 76: 355.
Félicie Mordaunt's World. (L. P. Hale) O. & N. 1: 439.
Felicita. Blackw. 86: 189, 273. Same art. Liv. Age, 63: 76, 165.
Felipa. (C. F. Woolson) Lippinc. 17: 702.
Felix, Eliza Rachel. *See* Rachel.
Felix, Father, at Notre Dame. (W. C. Wilkinson) Putnam, 15: 177.—Chr. R. 43: 67.
Felix Binocular; a Legal Sketch. Fraser, 3: 472.
Felixston, An August in. (D. C. Badham) Fraser, 51: 259.
Fellenberg, Emanuel, Character and Works of. West. M. 1: 176, 368.
— his Institution at Hofwyl. (W. C. Woodbridge) Chr. Q. Spec. 1: 625. 2: 358.—Ed. R. 31: 150. 32: 488.—Mo. R. 94: 195.—Am. J. Educ. 3: 591.
— Pestalozzi, and Wehrli. (W. de Fellenberg) Am. J. Educ. 10: 81. 21: 765.
— Schools and Plans of. Chr. Obs. 30: 150–481.
Feller, F. X. de. (W. C. Robinson) Month, 39: 574.
Feller, Mme., Sketch of. (Mrs. S. J. Hale) Godey, 21: 134.
Fellowes, Robert, Poems of. Chr. Obs. 5: 755.
Fellowes, W. D. Historical Sketches. Mo. R. 117: 14.
Fellowship, Christian. (G. W. Cox) Theo. R. 13: 499.
— Church. (G. N. Boardman) Bib. Sac. 33: 62.
— denied by Galesburg Declaration. (J. A. Brown) Luth. Q. 7: 595.
Fellowships and national Culture. (S. Colvin) Macmil. 34: 136.
— Idle. (H. Sidgwick) Contemp. 27: 679.
— Oxford; Strike, but hear. Macmil. 25: 300.
Felltham, Owen. Resolves. Retros. 10: 343.—Cong. M. 6: 375.
— Works of. Am. Mo. R. 1: 451.
Fels, Egon. Titania. O. & N. 7: 744.
Felspars and their Derivatives. (T. Smyth) Ecl. Engin. 16: 509.
Felt, Joseph Barlow. (C. W. Upham) Hist. M. 17: 107.
— Memoir of, with portrait. (J. B. F. Osgood) N. E. Reg. 24: 1.
Feltham Reformatory. Chamb. J. 44: 734.
Felting Power, Discovery of Cause of. (P. A. Browne) J. Frankl. Inst. 50: 205.
Felton, Cornelius Conway. Am. J. Educ. 10: 265.
— Agamemnon. *See* Æschylus.
— Greek Reader. New York R. 8: 261.
— Homer. Am. Mo. R. 4: 93.—Am. Q. 14: 143.
Female Artists. Chamb. J. 33: 137.—Nat. Q. 22: 1.
Female Authors. (G. Gilfillan) Tait, n. s. 14: 359, 620, 850.—(A. W. Abbot) No. Am. 72: 151.
Female Beauty, English *vs.* French Ideas of. St. James, 48: 269. *See* Beauty.
Female Character. Knick. 6: 204, 381.—Fraser, 7: 591.
— Formation and Excellence of. (J. Hawes) Am. Inst. of Instruc. 1845: 27.

Female Characters of Goethe and Shakspere. No. Brit. **8**: 265.
— of modern Poetry. Blackw. **37**: 815. **38**: 128.
— of Scripture. (F. Hemans) Blackw. **33**: 593, 804. Same art. Ecl. M. **14**: 1.
— of Shakspere. Blackw. **33**: 124, 391, 539.
Female Convicts, Treatment of. (M. Carpenter) Fraser, **67**: 31.
Female Convict Prisons. Victoria, **31**: 331.
Female Criminals, American. Nat. Q. **11**: 268.
— Remarkable. Dub. Univ. **29**: 51.
Female Deacons. *See* Deaconesses.
Female Education. *See* Women, Education of.
Female Fanaticism in Scotland. Dub. Univ. **30**: 349. Same art. Liv. Age, **15**: 123.
Female Felons. Chamb. J. **38**: 310.
Female Freemasonry. Once a Week, **19**: 105.
Female Friendships. Ecl. M. **42**: 404.
— Skakspere's Delineations of. Penny M. **10**: 109.
Female Funambulist. Sharpe, **37**: 71.
Female Genius, Plea for. Lond. M. **10**: 53, 184.
Female Heroism. Chamb. J. **10**: 108.
Female Immorality, Causes and Remedies of. Ecl. M. **17**: 267. Same art. Liv. Age, **21**: 385. — Westm. **53**: 448, 516.
Female Kinship and maternal Filiation. (E. Reclus) Radical R. **1**: 205.
Female Life in Jail. Chr. Rem. **44**: 365.
Female Literature. (F. W. P. Greenwood) No. Am. **26**: 403. — (M. de Staël) Anal. M. **1**: 313.
Female Nail-Makers at Birmingham. Chamb. J. **52**: 799.
Female Novelists. (W. A. Jones) Dem. R. **14**: 484.
Female Penitentiaries. Quar. **83**: 359. Same art. Liv. Age, **19**: 433.
Female Philanthropists, Group of. Lond. Q. **57**: 49.
Female Poetry. So. Lit. Mess. **7**: 377.
Female Poets, Evenings with some. Am. Whig R. **14**: 217, 418.
— of America. Dem. R. **24**: 232. — (Mrs. E. F. Ellet) No. Am. **68**: 413.
— of England. (C. L. Balfour) Peop. J. **10**: 265.
Female Portraits. Dub. Univ. **13**: 156, 278, 633.
Female Preaching. Chr. Mo. Spec. **4**: 291.
Female Professionals. Chamb. J. **54**: 65.
Female Prose Writers of America. So. Q. **21**: 114. — So. Lit. Mess. **13**: 249, 381.
Female Religious of America. (J. G. McGee) Cath. World, **19**: 362.
Female Revenge; a Tale. So. Lit. Mess. **9**: 171.
Female Rule; or Scenes in New York. Godey, **26**: 184.
Female Sovereigns, Mrs. Jameson's. Am. Mo. R. **4**: 441.
Female Teachers in Common Schools, Duties of. (D. Kimball) Am. Inst. of Instruc. **1836**: 103. – (E. Jarvis) Chr. Exam. **34**: 371.
Female Uhlan, an Episode. (J. A. O'Shea) Tinsley, **27**: 465.
Females, an offensive Word. Ev. Sat. **3**: 61.
Feminine Feud. Colburn, **164**: 574.
Feminine Perfections; or the unreasonable Bachelor. (A. B. Johnson) Knick. **35**: 15.
Feminine Philanthropy. (H. Rosevelt) Overland, **5**: 181.
Fen Country of England. (C. Kingsley) Good Words, **8**: 302. — Chamb. J. **22**: 321.
— Drainage of. Chamb. J. **23**: 278.
— Miller and Skertchly on. Nature, **18**: 514.
— of the Past and of To-Day. Chamb. J. **58**: 145, 279.
Fens and their Fickleness. Once a Week, **6**: 654.
— Origin and Improvement of. Brit. Q. **18**: 381.
Fences, New England. (R. E. Robinson) Scrib. **19**: 502.
Fencing, Parisian. All the Year, **23**: 330. — Ev. Sat. **9**: 199.
Feneberg, John Michael, Memoir of. Chr. Obs. **29**: 445.
Feneberg, John Michael, Sketch of. (W. F. Stevenson) Good Words, **3**: 132.
Fénelon, Bertrand de S. de la Mothe. Diplomatic Correspondence. Ed. R. **69**: 365. — For. Q. **22**: 276.
Fénelon, Archb. François de S. de la Mothe. (J. W. Cummins) Cath. World, **11**: 613. — Chr. Disc. **4**: 421. — (W. E. Channing) Chr. Exam. **6**: 1. — Ecl. M. **75**: 526. — Mo. Rel. M. **28**: 172.
— and Bossuet, Butler's Lives of. Quar. **10**: 409.
— and his Connection with America. (C. D. Bradlee) N. E. Reg. **16**: 344. — (J. G. Shea) N. E. Reg. **17**: 246.
— and his educational Views. Am. J. Educ. **13**: 477.
— and Toleration. (C. L. Loos) Chr. Q. **5**: 365, 513.
— Anecdotes of. (W. J. Walter) U. S. Cath. M. **2**: 65, 141.
— Character and Writings of. (S. K. Kollock) Princ. **25**: 165.
— De Bausset's Life of. Chr. Obs. **9**: 687.
— Letters of. Chr. Obs. **77**: 705.
— Missionary Sermon of. Chr. Obs. **26**: 513, 577.
Fenestration, Scientific. Am. Arch. **9**: 52.
Fenestrelle, Walk up. (H. F. Amedroz) Once a Week, **2**: 48.
Feng-Shui in China. Cornh. **29**: 337.
Fenians, The. All the Year, **14**: 300.
— Ancient. (L. C. Seelye) Scrib. **1**: 517.
— — and Fenian Literature. Cornh. **13**: 121. Same art. Ecl. M. **66**: 361.
— in England, Ireland, and America. Tinsley, **1**: 700.
— in Ireland. All the Year, **17**: 342–520.
— Ireland for the Irish. (An American Fenian) Tinsley, **1**: 607. — (F. P. Cobbe) Tinsley, **2**: 39.
— Irish Conspiracy, 1867. Tinsley, **2**: 143.
— Night with. Chamb. J. **44**: 347.
— of Ballybogmucky. (F. P. Cobbe) Ev. Sat. **1**: 30.
— on Trial. All the Year, **17**: 582.
Fenian Alarm. Blackw. **103**: 308.
Fenian Assassinations. Colburn, **142**: 107.
Fenian Brothers. All the Year, **11**: 391.
Fenian Conspiracies. (C. Redding) Colburn, **142**: 208.
Fenian Convicts. Dub. Univ. **83**: 633.
Fenian Invasion of Canada, 1870. (C. H. Tuttle) O. & N. **2**: 208. — Temp. Bar, **18**: 177.
Fenian Question, 1866. (E. L. Godkin) Nation, **3**: 270.
Fenian Rising in Ireland, 1867. (E. L. Godkin) Nation, **4**: 213.
Fenian Song-Writing. Chamb. J. **50**: 168.
Fenianism. (L. Blanc) Lippinc. **1**: 168. — (C. Redding) Colburn, **137**: 86. — (J. H. Stack) Macmil. **13**: 506. — Blackw. **103**: 222. — Contemp. **19**: 301, 624. — Dub. Univ. **67**: 116, 464.
— An American Opinion of. Dub. Univ. **78**: 492.
— and English Democracy. Quar. **122**: 237.
— and the Irish Church. (J. Godkin) Fortn. **9**: 191.
— as a Swindle. (E. L. Godkin) Nation, **10**: 347.
— British Confederation and. Hunt, **54**: 301.
— in America. Bentley, **63**: 129. — Blackw. **101**: 590. — Dub. Univ. **71**: 115.
— in 1868. (E. L. Godkin) Nation, **6**: 5.
— My Connection with. (G. Cluseret) Fraser, **86**: 31. Same art. Ecl. M. **79**: 271. Same art. Ev. Sat. **13**: 145. Same art. Liv. Age, **114**: 353.
— Why is it? (P. Giraud) Putnam, **11**: 543.
Fenland. *See* Fen Country.
Fenning, Eliza, condemned on Circumstantial Evidence. All the Year, **18**: 66.
— Trial of. Blackw. **89**: 236.
Fenton, Elijah. House. Words, **11**: 43.
Fenton, Lavinia, the Actress. (D. Cook) Once a Week, **8**: 651. — Dub. Univ. **74**: 310.
Fenton Grammar School, Recollections of. Belgra. **23**: 33
— Sketch of. Canad. Mo. **5**: 353, 446.

Fenton's Quest; a Novel. (M. E. Braddon) Belgra. 11: 133–389. 12: 5–389. 13: 68–485. 14: 99–225.
Fenwick, Benedict J., Bishop. Brownson, 3: 518.
Fenwick, Lady A. A., Reinterment of Remains of. Hist. M. 19: 151.
Fenwick, Sir John. (E. B. Seabrook) Galaxy, 3: 256.
Ferdinand II. and the Elector Frederick. Month, 9: 176.
— and Wallenstein. (R. Cardwell) Month, 28: 24, 144.
Ferdinand V. and Isabella, Prescott's. (R. Ford) Quar. 64: 1. — (P. de Gayangos) Ed. R. 68: 376. — (W. H. Gardiner) No. Am. 46: 203. — (F.W. P. Greenwood) Chr. Exam. 24: 99. — (J. Pickering) New York R. 2: 308. — (R. W. Hamilton) Brit. Q. 1: 232. Same art. Ecl. M. 5: 145. — Mus. 36: 451. — Dem. R. 2: 160. — Dub. R. 13: 308. — (P. Fredet) U. S. Cath. M. 2: 449. — Mo. R. 145: 295.
Ferdinand VII. of Spain. Colburn, 39: 324.
— Memoir of. Ecl. R. 39: 355.
Ferdinand, King of Naples. Penny M. 1: 102. — Colburn, 120: 245.
Féreol, Martin. St. Paul's, 4: 452. — Ev. Sat. 8: 137.
Ferghana. (R. Michell) Geog. M. 3: 124, 149.
Ferguson, Sir Adam. Chamb. J. 23: 113. Same art. Liv. Age, 45: 164. Same art. Ecl. M. 34: 554.
— Life and Writings of. Ed. R. 125: 49.
Ferguson, Robert, the Plotter. Blackw. 71: 703. Same art. Ecl. M. 26: 439.
Ferguson, Samuel. Lays of the Western Gael, etc. Dub. R. 56: 302. Same art. Cath. World, 1: 466.
Ferguson, Major William. Am. Hist. Rec. 2: 217.
Fergusson, Robert, Poems of. Dub. Univ. 88: 173.
Ferland, Abbé J. B. A., with portrait. Hist. M. 9: 201.
Fermentation. (C. Graham) Nature, 15: 213, 249.
— and Disease. (J. Tyndall) Pop. Sci. Mo. 10: 129. — (J. Tyndall) Fortn. 26: 547. Same art. Liv. Age, 131: 643.
— and Life. (F. Papillon) Pop. Sci. Mo. 5: 542.
— and Putrefaction. (W. Thomson) Nature, 7: 61, 78.
— Curiosities of. Chamb. J. 50: 711.
— Pasteur on. Pop. Sci. Mo. 7: 709.
— Schützenberger on. Dub. Univ. 88: 124.
Ferments, Means of distinguishing. (C. B. Dudley) J. Frankl. Inst. 101: 129.
Fernando; a Tale. (Lady Herbert) Cath. World, 28: 828.
Fernando Noronha, Penal Settlement of. Scrib. 11: 534.
— Challenger Expedition to. Nature, 9: 388.
Fernando Po and the Slave Trade. Quar. 26: 51.
Ferns. (Mrs. L. A. Millington) O. & N. 8: 694. — (J. L. Russell) Am. Natural. 2: 517. — Chamb. J. 51: 541. — Hogg, 4: 360. — Lond. Q. 19: 91. — Once a Week, 19: 131.
— and Liverworts. (S. B. Herrick) Scrib. 13: 329.
— and their Allies. Colburn, 107: 235.
— and their Portraits. Quar. 101: 57.
— and Wild Oats. (J. Neall) Overland, 8: 238.
— British. Westm. 46: 415. — Peop. J. 6: 260. — Ecl. R. 102: 658.
— Collecting. All the Year, 18: 39.
— Few Pet. Ev. Sat. 14: 683.
— Few Words about. Canad. Mo. 7: 163.
— in their Homes. Dub. Univ. 77: 438.
— Notes on. Chamb. J. 11: 38.
— of Great Britain and Ireland. New Q. 4: 462.
— Pet. All the Year, 30: 90.
— Physiology of. (H. Goode) Reliquary, 1: 34.
— Preservative Power of. Pract. M. 7: 280.
— Recent Studies among. Belgra. 15: 249.
— Smith on. Nature, 14: 286.
— Summer Study of. Good Words, 1: 321–423.
— Superstitions concerning. (L. Jewitt) Reliquary, 1: 39.
Fern Devilry. St. James, 24: 514.
Fern Forests of Carboniferous Period. Sharpe, 43: 190.
Fernery, A Fairy. (B. Medhurst) Victoria, 19: 420.
— How to make a. Once a Week, 6: 240.
Fernley Lecture for 1878. Lond. Q. 51: 265.
Fernyhurst Court. Good Words, 11: 297–801. Same art. Liv. Age, 107: 207–588. 108: 43.
Feroe Islands. *See* Faroe Islands.
Ferrar, Nicholas. (G. A. Ellis) Atlan. 28: 176.
— Life of. Chr. Obs. 16: 481.
Ferrara, Andrea. Cornh. 12: 189.
Ferrara, Vincent. Am. Presb. R. 9: 46.
Ferrara to Genoa, Men and Manners on the Way from. (W. D. Howells) Nation, 2: 205.
Ferrara Marshes reclaimed. Pract. M. 3: 153.
Ferrari, Guadenzio, Painter, Life of. Colburn, 79: 80.
Ferrers, Earl, Execution of, 1760. All the Year, 27: 175. — Temp. Bar, 53: 316.
Ferrets, Human. Ev. Sat. 10: 191.
Ferrier, James Frederick. Blackw. 101: 280.
— Philosophical Life of. (A. C. Fraser) Macmil. 17: 193.
— Philosophical Works. Ed. R. 126: 71.
Ferrier, Susan Edmonstone. Novels. Ed. R. 74: 498. — Temp. Bar, 54: 308. Same art. Liv. Age, 139: 693.
— The Inheritance. Portfo.(Den.) 33: 129.
Ferris, H. W. Poems. Dub. Univ. 89: 542.
Ferro-Manganese. Ecl. Engin. 3: 620.
Ferronays Family. *See* La Ferronays Family.
Ferrucci, Francesco. Colburn, 168: 1.
Ferrucci, Rosa, Letters of. Cath. World, 7: 364, 543.
— Life and Letters of. Dub. R. 53: 111. — Irish Mo. 8: 340.
Ferry, Orris Sanford. (J. A. Hamilton) Cong. Q. 19: 219.
Ferry of Carnoet. (K. S. Macquoid) Liv. Age, 138: 211.
Ferry Laws in France. Month, 36: 417.
Ferries and Bridges. J. Frankl. Inst. 13: 412.
— Steam, for wide Rivers. Pract. M. 6: 110.
Fersen, Jean Axel de. (A. Laugel) Nation, 27: 128, 142.
— and Marie Antoinette. Temp. Bar, 55: 76. Same art. Liv. Age, 140: 367.
Fertility and Sterility. (H. H. Howorth) Anthrop. J. 2: 21.
Fertilization, Darwin on. (W. T. T. Dyer) Nature, 15: 329.
— Darwin on Cross- and Self-. (A. Gray) Am. J. Sci. 113: 125.
— of Calamintha nepeta. (W. Trelease) Am. Natural. 15: 11.
— of certain Labiatæ. (A. W. Bennett) Nature, 10: 92.
— of Clitoria and Centrosema. (W. Trelease) Am. Natural. 13: 688.
— of Flowers by Insects. (A. W. Bennett) Am. Natural. 7: 680. — (A. Wilson) Gent. M. n. s. 27: 696. — (H. Müller) Nature, 8: 187, 205, 433. 9: 44, 164. 10: 129. 11: 32, 110, 169. 12: 50, 190, 444. 13: 210, 289. 14: 173.
— — Darwin on. (T. Meehan) Penn Mo. 8: 463.
— of Land by Warping. Penny M. 13: 221.
— of papilionaceous Flowers. (T. H. Farrer) Nature, 6: 478, 498. 10: 169.
— of Salvia splendens by Birds. (W. Trelease) Am. Natural. 15: 265.
— of wild Pansy. (A. W. Bennett) Nature, 8: 49.
— of winter-flowering Plants. (A. W. Bennett) Nature, 1: 11.
— Self-, of Plants. Nature, 14: 475.
Fertilizers, Morfit on Pure. Nation, 16: 420.
— Phosphatic, Morfit's. Pract. M. 1: 70.
— used by Indians and early Colonists. (G. B. Good) Am. Natural. 14: 473.
Fessen-Penny, The. Once a Week, 22: 392.
Fessenden, Thos. G. (N. Hawthorne) Am. Mo. M. 11: 30.
Fessenden, William Pitt, with portrait. (G. H. Preble) N. E. Reg. 25: 105.
Festa of Madonna della Vita. Once a Week, 16: 434.

Festiniog Railway. (W. H. Bishop) Scrib. 18: 593.—Ecl. Engin. 2: 216, 548.—J. Frankl. Inst. 82: 314, 361. 88: 425.
— as a Type. Ecl. Engin. 8: 305.
Festival upon the Neva; a Tale. Internat. M. 3: 357.
Festival Days of the Church. Mercersb. 10: 251.
Festival Seasons, Prayers for. Mercersb. 8: 415.
Festivals and Holidays. Chamb. J. 11: 220.
— of ancient Christians. (A. Lamson) Chr. Exam. 38: 35.
— of Church of England, Marsden on. Chr. Obs. 48: 107.
— Public Illuminations of the Ancients. Colburn, 2: 325.
Festive Demoralization. (W. Chambers) Chamb. J. 57: 481.
Festivities, Ancient. Fraser, 47: 673.
Fête Dieu. Lond. M. 7: 94.
Fête of the Eagles, Paris, 1852. Colburn, 95: 243.
Fêtes of Italy. Fraser, 20: 348.
Fetish, Tried by. All the Year, 43: 356.
Fetishes. All the Year, 11: 569.
Fetish Worship. (H. Spencer) Pop. Sci. Mo. 8: 158.
Fetishism. (H. H. Barber) Unita. R. 10: 199.
— and Max Müller. (A. Lang) Mind, 4: 453.
— at Home and abroad. (D. Bowen) Radical, 1: 247.
— in Animals. (G. J. Romanes) Nature, 17: 168.
— Is it a primitive Form of Religion? (M. Müller) Macmil. 38: 110, 196.
— Philosophy of. (F. H. Hedge) Unita. R. 15: 193.
Fetishist's Poem to his God. (W. P. Lancaster) Temp. Bar, 29: 347.
Fetters and Lures. (E. Roland) Galaxy, 11: 867.
Feudal Armies of France and England. So. Lit. Mess. 14: 62.
Feudal Epic; La Chanson d'Antioche. (J. G. Sheppard) Fortn. 4: 700.
Feudal Laws, Reform of. (Marquis of Blandford) 19th Cent. 9: 664.
Feudal Property, Decay of, in France and England. (H. S. Maine) Fortn. 27: 460.
Feudal System and the Carlovingian Dynasty. Lond. Q. 25: 32.
— of Middle Ages. Dem. R. 27: 457.
Feudalism and Chivalry. Nat. Q. 7: 265.
— in America. (J. Q. Moore) De Bow, 28: 615.
— of the 19th Century. Blackw. 65: 713.
Feuillancourt, near St. Germain-en-Laye. (A. T. Wilbur) Liv. Age, 39: 496.
Feuillet, Octave. (A. Rhodes) Galaxy, 20: 519.—(G. Saintsbury) Fortn. 30: 102.—Ev. Sat. 16: 710.
— Plays. (J. B. Matthews) Internat. R. 11: 428.
Feuilleton, A. Blackw. 87: 629.
Feuilletonists of France. Dub. Univ. 22: 701.
Feval, Paul, Novels of. Colburn, 109: 170.—Dub. Univ. 63: 226.
Fever. (H. C. Wood, jr.) Lippinc. 15: 197.
— Contagious. Ed. R. 31: 414.—Mo. R. 87: 88. 96: 50.
— Continued. Westm. 12: 195.
— Epidemic. Ecl. R. 41: 254, 537.
— Infectious. Ed. R. 1: 245.
— Intermittent, of New England. (E. Hale) No. Am. 47: 161.
— of 1795. Knick. 13: 52, 135.
— Smith and Stoker on. Westm. 12: 494.
— Typhus. Mo. R. 85: 63.
— — and Typhoid. Dub. Univ. 79: 184.
— Walcheren, Davis on. Ecl. R. 13: 118
— West India. Chamb. J. 55: 716.
— Yellow. Mo. R. 85: 142.
— — at Barcelona. Mo. R. 100: 503.
— — at New York, 1803. Dem. R. 8: 373.
— — in U. S. (A. S. Pigott) Harper, 13: 784. 15: 61.
Fever Factories. (F. L. Oswald) Pop. Sci. Mo. 14: 143.
Fever Hospital. All the Year, 13: 16.
Fever Infection, Curiosities of. (W. Chambers) Chamb. J. 52: 561.
Fever Poisons. Liv. Age, 54: 355.
Fever-Tree. (T. S. Sozinskey) Potter Am. Mo. 13: 452.
Few, William, with portrait. (C. C. Jones, jr.) M. Am. Hist. 7: 340.
Few Letters. (E. C. Hewitt) Lippinc. 20: 111.
Few Spiritual Manifestations revealed to Mr. Jolly Green. Colburn, 98: 127.
Few Tickets from the Matrimonial Lottery. Temp. Bar, 19: 138.
Fezensac, R. E. P. J. de M., Duke of, Military Memoirs of. Colburn, 129: 428.
— Recollections of the Grand Army. (C. C. Chesney) Ed. R. 127: 213.
Ffennell, R. A. B. (H. C. Potter) Am. Church R. 29: 130.
Ffoulkes, T., Answer to. (H. I. D. Ryder) Month, 12: 123.
— Case of. Month, 10: 201. 23: 122.
Fiammetta and Boccaccio. Lond. M. 1: 622.
Fiat Faciendum. (F. B. Perkins) Galaxy, 1: 229.
Fibers of India, Undeveloped. (G. Bidie) Good Words, 4: 656.
Fichte, John Gottlieb. Chamb. J. 3: 361. Same art. Liv. Age, 6: 162.—Liv. Age, 30: 193.—Evang. R. 13: 386.
— Adamson's Study of. (A. Seth) Mind, 6: 586.
— and his Philosophy. (A. E. Kroeger) Nat. Q. 15: 113.
— and Kant, Relations between. (R. C. Ware) J. Spec. Philos. 11: 145.
— Life and Correspondence of. For. Q. 36: 108.—Select J. 2: [244.
— — and Works of. (C. D. B. Mills) Chr. Exam. 81: 16.
— on the Nature of the Scholar. Dub. Univ. 62: 60.
— Science of Knowledge; translated by A. E. Kroeger. J. Spec. Philos. 1: 23, 79, 137. 3: 1–289.
— Sun-clear Statement of the new Philosophy. J. Spec. Philos. 2: 1, 65, 129.
Fiction. (S. E. Pearre) Chr. Q. 3: 110.—Mo. R. 164: 358.—Irish Q. 6: 94.—So. R. n. s. 10: 445.
— American. (J. Pollock) Ev. Sat. 15: 284.—(M. G. Van Rensselaer) Lippinc. 23: 753.—Liv. Age, 2: 643.
— American Heroine in. (A. Macdonell) Macmil. 32: 544. Same art. Liv. Age, 127: 313.
— and Fact. Dub. Univ. 50: 191.
— and History. Once a Week, 18: 106.
— and Reality. Mo. Rel. M. 35: 345.
— and the Stage. (L. Cross) Colburn, 167: 225, 366.
— Art and Religion in Works of. (Mrs. J. L. Jones) Nat. Q. 36: 249. 37: 50.
— as an Art, its History and Progress. Westm. 60: 342. Same art. Liv. Age, 39: 356.
— as an Educator. Blackw. 108: 449. Same art. Ecl. M. 75: 706. Same art. Liv. Age, 107: 307.
— as a Vehicle of Truth. (J. Abbott) Am. Q. Obs. 1: 25.
— Catholic. Dub. R. 83: 439.
— Chinese. Mo. R. 161: 215.
— Church. Ecl. R. 114: 105.
— Didactic, in 1842. Chr. Rem. 3: 74, 145.
— during the Middle Ages. Chr. Rem. 6: 465.
— Ethical and dogmatic. Nat. R. 12: 211.
— Fair and foul. (J. Ruskin) 19th Cent. 7: 941. 8: 195, 394, 748. 10: 516. Same art. Ecl. M. 95: 129, 441, 586. 96: 70. 97: 785.
— for Children. Quar. 122: 55. Same art. Liv. Age, 92: 579.
— Forms of publishing. Tinsley, 10: 411.
— Freedom in the Use of. (M. A. Bean) Lib. J. 4: 341.
— French; the lowest Deep. Nat. R. 11: 400. Same art. Liv. Age, 67: 451. *See* French Novels.
— — German. Brit. & For. R. 5: 442.
— Glut in the Market. (J. R. Dennett) Nation, 3: 453.
— History in. Dub. R. 45: 328.

Fiction, History of, Dunlop's. Quar. 13: 384. — (W. Hazlitt) Ed. R. 24: 38. — Brit. & For. R. 11: 224.
— Imaginative Literature. No. Brit. 33: 165.
— in Public Libraries. (W. F. Poole) Lib. J. 1: 48. — (W. Kite) Lib. J. 1: 277. — (P. Cowell) Lib. J. 2: 152. — (C. F. Adams, jr.) Lib. J. 4: 330. — (S. S. Green) Lib. J. 4: 345. — (J. F. Clarke) Lib. J. 4: 355. — (T. W. Higginson) Lib. J. 4: 357. — (W. P. Atkinson) Lib. J. 4: 359. — (M. Chamberlain) Lib. J. 4: 362. — (J. M. Hubbard) Internat. R. 10: 168.
— — Classification of. (A. P. Massey) Lib. J. 6: 7.
— — Discussion on. Lib. J. 2: 255.
— — — at Manchester. Lib. J. 4: 411.
— — Hubbard on. (C. A. Cutter) Nation, 33: 370.
— — in Boston. (J. M. Hubbard) Lib. J. 6: 11. — Lib. J. 6: 204, 223.
— in two Aspects. Chamb. J. 56: 513.
— Is a rude or refined Age more favorable to the Production of Works of? Ox. Prize Ess. 4: 131.
— Justifiable. (P. Mulford) Overland, 11: 39.
— Literature of. Brit. Q. 2: 527. — (A. Davezac) Dem. R. 16: 268. — (H. T. Tuckerman) Appleton, 6: 319, 455, 511.
— Masson's British. (D. C. Brooks) No. Am. 92: 465.
— Modern. So. Lit. Mess. 8: 342. — So. Q. 15: 41.
— — Ideals in. Putnam, 10: 90.
— — Melancholy Heroines of. Cornh. 11: 630.
— — Philanthropic Aims of. (J. A. Cram) Univ. Q. 2: 70.
— — Seventh Commandment in. (W. L. Alden) Galaxy, 2: 373.
— — Sociological. (J. Pratt) De Bow, 29: 334.
— — Thackeray and. Lond. Q. 22: 375.
— Modern French. (F. Asheton) Lippinc. 13: 237.
— Modern Schools of. Prosp. 10: 460.
— Moral, Advantages of. West. R. 4: 96.
— Morality of. Hesp. 1: 295. — (J. Foster) Ecl. R. 12: 879.
— The new. (H. Holbeach) Contemp. 37: 247. Same art. Liv. Age, 144: 688. Same art. Appleton, 23: 345.
— New School of philosophical. (J. V. O'Conor) Cath. World, 28: 837.
— Noble School of. (H. James, jr.) Nation, 1: 21.
— Penny. (J. Payn) 19th Cent. 9: 145. Same art. Ecl. M. 96: 412.
— Philosophy of. (A. P. Peabody) Chr. Exam. 32: 1. — (F. Burditt) Westm. 29: 73.
— Polar Opposites in. Dub. Univ. 94: 437.
— Polemical. Prosp. R. 7: 404.
— Problem of Suffering in. Once a Week, 23: 52.
— Profligacy in. (A. K. Fiske) No. Am. 131: 79.
— Prose, and its Varieties. Westm. 30: 477.
— Reality of. (T. B. Fox) Chr. Exam. 75: 176.
— Recent English. (W. C. Brownell) Galaxy, 22: 624.
— Recent German, 1858. Westm. 70: 488.
— Religious. Chr. Rem. 33: 124.
— Responsibility of Writers of. (H. S. Burrage) Univ. Q. 1: 109.
— Sectional. (C. H. Jones) Appleton, 24: 563.
— Spirit of. All the Year, 18: 118.
— Stock Incidents in. Once a Week, 5: 182.
— Tendency of Works of. (C. Walby) Peop. J. 7: 199.
— Theory of. Tinsley, 13: 88.
— Uses of. Fraser, 72: 746. Same art. Ecl. M. 66: 192. Same art. Liv. Age, 88: 183. — Ecl. M. 68: 32. — Tinsley, 6: 180.
— — and Abuses of. (J. Ferguson) Am. Church R. 16: 230.
— Value of. (W. Besant) Belgra. 16: 48.
— Welsh. Mo. R. 160: 431. 163: 64.
— Works of. (J. Aldis) Ex. H. Lec. 2: 165.
— World of. Liv. Age, 133: 667.
— Youth as depicted in modern. Liv. Age, 90: 323.
See also Novels.

Fictions, Bohemian. Quar. 103: 328.
— Force of. Fraser, 43: 286.
— Modern. Irish Q. 6: 766.
— of the Future. Dub. R. 70: 76.
Fictitious Letter; a Story. (E. Ingersoll) Potter Am. Mo. 16: 159.
Ficulea, Old. (F. Carton) Once a Week, 4: 26.
Fiddler of Marseilles. Bentley, 12: 262.
— of the Rhine; a Tale. (H. Augu) Bentley, 64: 190.
Fiddlers. All the Year, 40: 32.
Fidelia; a Poem. (B. Taylor) Putnam, 11: 666.
Field, Cyrus W., with portrait Dem. R. 42: 241. — with portrait, Ecl. M. 67: 501.
Field, David Dudley. Hist. M. 11: 351.
Field, Edwin Wilkins. (J. H. Morison) Mo. Rel. M. 48: 50.
Field, Kate, as a Lecturer. (E. L. Godkin) Nation, 8: 371.
Field, Pindar. (G. Hardy) Cong. Q. 18: 493.
Field, Thomas W., Library of. Am. Bibliop. 7: 145.
Field Family of N. Jersey. (O. Field) N. E. Reg. 30: 406.
Field Genealogy. (O. Field) N. E. Reg. 17: 108. — N. E. Reg. 22: 166.
Field of the Cloth of Gold. Hogg, 7: 122.
Field Day. All the Year, 6: 61.
Field-faring Women. (R. Jefferies) Fraser, 92: 382.
Field Flowers; a Poem. (C. Bowles) Blackw. 48: 674.
Field Gardens for Laborers. Chamb. J. 46: 788.
Field Inspector, On Duty with. (C. Dickens) House. Words, 3: 265.
Field Lane, Reminiscence of. Chamb. J. 29: 231.
Field Sports. (D. G. Mitchell) No. Am. 55: 343. — Dub. Univ. 18: 226. — Mo. R. 153: 20.
— and Vivisection. (E. A. Freeman) Fortn. 21: 618. Same art. Canad. Mo. 5: 543.
— British. Sharpe, 23: 368. Same art. Ecl. M. 38: 553. — Ed. R. 74: 68. — Mus. 44: 73. — Bent. Q. 2: 267.
— Controversy on. Fortn. 14: 674.
— in Africa, India, and at Home. Colburn, 112: 343.
— in Madras. Fraser, 95: 43.
— in Minnesota. (C. A. Zimmerman) Scrib. 18: 826.
— in North of Europe, Lloyd's. Blackw. 27: 807. 28: 1.
— Influence of, on Character. Lond. Soc. 22: 126.
— Lawfulness of. Chr. Obs. 4: 284–737.
— Morality of. (E. A. Freeman) Fortn. 12: 353. — (A. Trollope) Fortn. 12: 616. — (H. Taylor) Fortn. 13: 63.
— Poetry of. Chamb. J. 26: 362.
— Season of. Colburn, 42: 417.
Fielding, Henry. Quar. 98: 100. Same art. Liv. Age, 48: 705. — (C. C. Clarke) Gent. M. n. s. 8: 556. — (F. Lawrence) Sharpe, 19: 73–337. — Ev. Sat. 16: 625.
— and Thackeray. No. Brit. 24: 197. Same art. Liv. Age, 47: 769. Same art. Ecl. M. 37: 57.
— Grave of. Once a Week, 10: 559.
— Life and Works of. Bentley, 39: 154. — (E. P. Whipple) No. Am. 68: 41. — Mus. 5: 121. — (F. Keightley) Fraser, 57: 1, 205, 762.
— Newspapers of. Chamb. J. 34: 142.
— Novels of. (L. Stephen) Cornh. 35: 154. Same art. Liv. Age, 133: 3.
— Our first great Novelist. (G. B. Smith) Macmil. 30: 1. Same art. Liv. Age, 121: 643.
— Sterne, and Smollett. Portfo. (Den.) 6: 412.
— Tom Jones. Blackw. 87: 331.
— Works of. Internat. M. 5: 71.
Fielding, Robert, at the Old Bailey. (G. A. Sala) Belgra. 30: 396.
Fields, James T. Nat. M. 7: 462. — (R. Collyer) Dial (Ch.), 2: 203.
— Memoir of. (A. G. Sedgwick) Nation, 33: 514.
— Recollections of. (E. P. Whipple) Atlan. 48: 253.
— Yesterdays with Authors. Chamb. J. 49: 343.

Fiery Colliery of Fiennes. (K. E. Prescott) Harper, 27: 613.
Fiery Furnace, A. (C. Dewees) Lippinc. 18: 426.
Fieschi, G., Conspiracy of. (O. M. Spencer) Harper, 56: 339. — All the Year, 17: 322. Same art. Ev. Sat. 3: 499.
— Morey, and Pepin, Execution of. Bentley, 29: 418.
Fiesole, Fra Angelico da. *See* Angelico, Fra.
Fiesole, Theater Spence at. Temp. Bar, 13: 258.
Fievée, J. Letters on England. (Syd. Smith) Ed. R. 2: 86.
Fife, Kingdom of. (T. Hutchinson) Fraser, 97: 93.
Fife Gypsies, Anecdotes of. Blackw. 2: 282, 523. 3: 14, 393.
Fifæana. Blackw. 10: 60.
Fifine; a Story of Malines. (K. S. Macquoid) Macmil. 22: 119. Same art. Liv. Age, 106: 431, 492.
Fifine and her Ménage. (L. S. Costello) Bentley, 24: 119.
Fifteen Puzzle, The. (R. A. Proctor) Gent. M. n. s. 26: 30.
— Clew to. (G. W. Warren) Nation, 30: 326.
Fifteen Years at the Galleys. Chamb. J. 39: 6. Same art. Liv. Age, 76: 316.
Fifteenth Amendment; Revocation of Ratifications. (G. H. Yeaman) Nation, 10: 84.
Fifth-Monarchy Man, What is a? Ecl. R. 125: 163.
Fifth of November, Celebration of. St. James, 25: 271.
Fifty Brides; a Tale. Cornh. 19: 469.
Fifty-two Wriothesley Place. House. Words, 11: 36.
Fifty Years hence. (G. J. A. Coulson) N. Ecl. 6: 467.
Fig and Fig-Tree. (J. R. Jackson) Intel. Obs. 10: 112.
Fight for the Belt. Blackw. 87: 753.
— for a Locomotive. Lond. Soc. 21: 259.
— of the Falls. (G. T. Curtis) New Eng. M. 9: 181.
— Sea; a Poem. (S. J. Stone) Once a Week, 11: 687.
Fighting, by a Gentleman of the Fancy. Lond. M. 1: 519, 640.
— by Machinery. (T. M. Coan) Galaxy, 22: 675.
— Philosophy of. (A. H. Forrester) Bentley, 12: 544.
Fighting Eighty-eighth Regiment. Blackw. 61: 457.
Fighting Fitzgerald; a Tale. (A. M. Williams) Cath. World, 29: 701.
Figueras, Estanislas. (E. Castelar) Fortn. 17: 303. Same art. Ecl. M. 78: 608.
Figurative Language. Chr. Disc. 5: 178. — (W. P. Lunt) Chr. Exam. 68: 390.
— Ancient. For. Q. 23: 62.
— Laws of. (D. N. Lord) Theo. & Lit. J. 7: 352.
— — Objections to. Theo. & Lit. J. 3: 613.
— of Scripture. (E. Pond) Theo. & Lit. J. 4: 687.
Figure, The, Study of. Art J. 11: 277.
Figure-Casting in Bronze. Penny M. 13: 259.
Figure-Making with Bundles of Wood. Once a Week, 26: 113.
Figures, Facts about. Once a Week, 28: 249.
Figures of Speech. (H. W. Frost) Galaxy, 24: 204.
Fiji Islands. (E. G. Ravenstein) Geog. M. 1: 57. — Ed. R. 136: 429. — Lond. Q. 57: 323. — Fraser, 90: 32. Same art. Ecl. M. 83: 342. — Liv. Age, 121: 510–635.
— and the Fijians. Ecl. R. 108: 520. — Knick. 53: 267. — Lond. Q. 11: 524. — No. Brit. 30: 44. — Liv. Age, 60: 430.
— and the Labor Trade. (Earl of Pembroke) Temp. Bar, 36: 22.
— At Home in. Appleton, 26: 71.
— Cannibalism and Christianity in. (E. House) Meth. Q. 19: 601.
— Cannibals of. (A. H. Guernsey) Harper, 7: 455.
— Colony at. Colburn, 154: 590. 155: 7–265.
— Consulate among. (W. T. Pritchard) Overland, 2: 325.
— Day at Loma Loma. (G. de Robeck) Gent. M. n. s. 23: 363.
Fiji Islands, First Impressions of. (C. F. G. Cumming) Good Words, 22: 600, 669.
— Miss Gordon Cumming on. Nature, 24: 281. — (J. M. Hubbard) Nation, 33: 318.
— in 1868–70. Fraser, 82: 631. Same art. Ecl. M. 76: 82.
— Love in. (T. M. Coan) Putnam, 16: 30, 129, 408.
— Mission to. Theo. & Lit. J. 13: 255.
— Newspaper in. (T. F. O'Donnell) Belgra. 17: 465.
— past and present. (F. W. Chesson) St. James, 35: 552.
— Rejection of, by Great Britain. Lond. Q. 20: 35.
— Seemann's. (A. A. Fraser) Anthrop. R. 1: 355.
— Sketch from. Sharpe, 46: 147.
— Trade in. (E. A. Rockwell) Overland, 2: 240.
— Vacation Tour in. (J. Gorrie) Contemp. 38: 486.
— What has been done on. Good Words, 1: 337–408.
Fijian Cyclone, Escape from. Ecl. M. 95: 51.
Fijian Pottery. (Miss G. Cumming) Art J. 33: 362.
Filaria in a Horse's Eye. (C. A. Gee) Am. J. Sci. 39: 278.
Files and Filing. (J. Rose) Pract. M. 7: 36.
Filey and its Fishermen. (M. E. C. Walcott) Once a Week, 6: 353.
Filey Bay identified as Portus Felix, or Sinus Salutaris. (J. Walker) Arch. 25: 127.
Filial Duty. (W. E. Channing) Am. J. Educ. 28: 820.
Filibusters in Nicaragua. Blackw. 79: 314. Same art. Liv. Age, 49: 129. — Dub. R. 43: 355. — Putnam, 9: 425.
Filibusterism. (Judge Lott) Pioneer, 1: 30.
See Miranda; Nicaragua.
Filicarja, Vincenzo da, Works of. Retros. 10: 314.
Filioque Controversy. Chr. Rem. 48. 468. *See* Holy Ghost.
Fillan, St.; a Poem. (F. Parke) Dub. Univ. 88: 332.
Fillmore, John. (A. Woodward) N. E. Reg. 11: 61.
Fillmore, Millard, with portrait. Am. Whig R. 8: 341.
— Address to Buffalo Hist. Society. Hist. M. 6: 297.
— Life of, with portrait. (G. W. Hosmer) N. E. Reg. 31: 1.
Fillmore Family Genealogy. (A. Woodward) N. E. Reg. 11: 61, 141.
Film of Gossamer; a Story. (E. M. Clerke) Fraser, 104: 235.
Filters, Charcoal. Once a Week, 14: 358.
— — and Water. (A. T. Partington) Pract. M. 5: 28.
Filtering Apparatus, Automatic. (H. W. Wiley) Am. J. Sci. 105: 350.
— Hydrometric, Teller's. Pract. M. 5: 238.
— of H. de Fonvielle. (F. Arago) J. Frankl. Inst. 26: 206. 27: 350.
Filtration, Ancient Methods of. (H. C. Bolton) Pop. Sci. Mo. 16: 495.
— and Media. (J. Dahlke) J. Frankl. Inst. 72: 222.
— by Sand. (W. R. Nichols) J. Frankl. Inst. 112: 436.
— — and Charcoal. (H. M. Witt) J. Frankl. Inst. 62: 257.
— Hot, Apparatus for. (H. C. Bolton) Pract. M. 5: 337.
— Rapid, Apparatus for. (E. W. Morley) Am. J. Sci. 106: 214.
— through spongy Iron. Ecl. Engin. 24: 72.
See Water, Filtration of.
Final Cause. (G. Burke) Overland, 6: 469.
— in Nature. (G. F. Wright) Bib. Sac. 34: 355.
— Porter on. (M. M. Cohn) J. Spec. Philos. 11: 324.
— Taylor's Natural Evidences of. Theo. & Lit. J. 4: 342.
Final Causes. (T. Hill) Mo. Rel. M. 39: 253. — (G. Henslow) Mod. R. 2: 44.
— Doctrine of. No. Brit. 7: 1.
— W. J. Irons on. Fraser, 16: 254.
— Janet on. (J. Sully) Mind, 2: 244.
— Philosophy of. (J. McL. Smith) Nat. Q. 41: 40.
— Problem of. (P. Janet) Sup. Pop. Sci. Mo. 3: 370.
— Theistic Argument from. (M. Valentine) Luth. Q. 1 165.

Finality, Dialogue on. Cornh. **18**: 473. — (G. I. Cowan) Peop. J. **5**: 358.
Finance. Ed. R. **33**: 55. — West. M. **2**: 410.
— American. (S. Bonnefoux) Bank. M. (N. Y.) **19**: 904, 945.
— — and European. Bank. M. (N. Y.) **34**: 760.
— and Banking. (J. E. Williams) O. & N. **8**: 589.
— and Currency. (H. Greeley) Am. J. Educ. **18**: 632.
— and Economy, Wharton School of. (F. Rogers) Penn Mo. **12**: 354.
— Apostolic Principles of. Ecl. R. **112**: 522.
— Black Friday. (W. R. Hooper) Galaxy, **12**: 753.
— Bubbles in. All the Year, **14**: 56–368.
— Changes in Value of Money, 1833. Colburn, **38**: 179.
— Free-Trade. Blackw. **67**: 513.
— German and French, Effects of the War on. (E. L. Godkin) Nation, **23**: 129.
— Gladstone on. (R. Giffen) Fortn. **11**: 101.
— Government Loan on accumulative Bonds. (Sir H. Barron) J. Statis. Soc. **36**: 375.
— President Grant on. Penn Mo. **6**: 63.
— Human Nature in. (E. L. Godkin) Nation, **21**: 272.
— National Appropriations and Misappropriations. (J. A. Garfield) No. Am. **128**: 572.
— Plan of. (A. J. Willard) Am. Whig. R. **9**: 193. — Ed. R. **10**: 72. — Pamph. **1**: 255.
— Patterson's Science of. Bank. M. (N. Y.) **23**: 937.
— Principles of. (S. Colwell) Bank. M. (N. Y.) **13**: 781, 849.
— Public. Bank. M. (N. Y.) **35**: 164.
— — Schemes of. Nation, **21**: 243, 275, 292.
— Substance and Shadow in. (G. S. Boutwell) No. Am. **128**: 74.
Finances, Administration of. (G. Bradford) Am. Soc. Sci. J. **6**: 46.
— Government. Bank. M. (N. Y.) **7**: 169.
— Loans of the Future. (F. N. Newcome) St. James, **39**: 24, 129, 242.
— Morgan's Comparative View of. Ed. R. **4**: 75.
— National. (A. Walker) Hunt, **52**: 22. — Nat. Q. **24**: 110.
— — Elements of. (E. N. Boynton) Nat. Q. **38**: 328.
— — with legal Tender. (C. H. Carroll) Hunt, **52**: 271.
— of Cities. Bank. M. (N. Y.) **8**: 630.
— of Paris, 1879. (A. Laugel) Nation, **28**: 281, 315.
— of States. Bank. M. (N. Y.) **8**: 619, 726, 793. **9**: 754. **10**: 583.
Finance Companies, Fraudulent, in London. Temp. Bar, **17**: 381, 473.
Financial Affairs, 1877. (B. Price) Contemp. **29**: 778.
— of Europe. Bank. M. (N. Y.) **9**: 950.
Financial Basis of Society. (A. P. Sprague) Nat. Q **23**: 88.
Financial Condition of Europe under War. Bank. M. (N. Y.) **8**: 575.
Financial Crisis. *See* Panic.
Financial Difficulty; a Tale. Temp. Bar, **1**: 188.
Financial Education. (E. L. Godkin) Nation, **31**: 249.
Financial Engineering. Bank. M. (N. Y.) **29**: 888. **30**: 189, 353.
Financial Expansions, Theory of. (J. S. Crawley) Bank. M. (N. Y.) **14**: 334.
Financial Heresies. (C. H. Carroll) Hunt, **43**: 317.
Financial History of England. No. Brit. **7**: 337.
— of Europe, 1860–62. Bank. M. (N. Y.) **17**: 630.
— — in 1848. Bank. M. (N. Y.) **3**: 545.
— — in 1853. Bank. M. (N. Y.) **8**: 695, 770.
— — in 1860. Bank. M. (N. Y.) **15**: 673.
— — in 1861. Bank. M. (N. Y.) **16**: 481.
— — in 1875. Bank. M. (Lond.) **36**: 272.
Financial Law, International. Bank. M. (N. Y.) **30**: 448, 632.
— System of. Dem. R. **5**: 324.
Financial Operation, My. Chamb. J. **43**: 385.
Financial Operations, Capefigue's History of. Bentley, **40**: 567. **43**: 246.
— of London. Temp. Bar, **11**: 491.
Financial Policy, Talk about. Penn Mo. **7**: 128.
— of England and United States. (G. Bradford) Am. Soc. Sci. J. **8**: 128.
Financial Pressure in New York. Bank. M. (N.Y.) **8**: 579.
Financial Problems. (C. J. Hutchins) Overland, **14**: 524.
Financial Projects and Calculations. Fraser, **43**: 476.
Financial Propositions, Pebier's. Mo. R. **144**: 402.
Financial Prospects, 1849. Ed. R. **89**: 518.
Financial Reform. No. Brit. **9**: 269. — Blackw. **30**: 457. — Westm. **12**: 394. — Quar. **42**: 505. — Mo. R. **121**: 544. — Ecl. R. **89**: 273.
Financial Troubles, Remedy for. (T. T. Gantt) Western, **4**: 604.
Financier, Memoir of a; G. I. Ouvrard. (J. D. Wallenstein) No. Am. **29**: 1.
Financiers, Ignorance, Usurpations, and Frauds of. (L. Spooner) Radical R. **1**: 141.
— Noted. Ecl. M. **70**: 579.
Finati, Life and Adventures of. Mo. R. **123**: 510.
Findelkind; a Child's Story. (L. de la Ramé) Belgra. **42**: 320. Same art. Lippinc. **26**: 438.
Findern, Derbyshire. (L. Jewitt) Reliquary, **3**: 185.
Finding his Level. (J. Payn) Belgra. **31**: 344.
Finding the Leak. (A. B. Neal) Sharpe, **38**: 72.
Finding one's Occupation gone. (F. Jacox) Bentley, **62**: 378.
Finding out, On. Dub. Univ. **58**: 71.
Fine Art. (T. G. Appleton) O. & N. **7**: 633.
Fine Arts. (W. Channing) No. Am. **3**: 194. — (F. Dexter) No. Am. **26**: 208. — So. R. **4**: 70. **7**: 121. — For. Q. **5**: 256. — Blackw. **6**: 89, 276. **15**: 566. **29**: 214. **30**: 655. **50**: 585. — Colburn, **61**: 273. Am. Mo. M. **4**: 242.
— Administrative Economy of. Ecl. R. **74**: 241.
— among the Anglo-Saxons. Penny M. **13**: 25.
— among the Jews. (J. S. Memes) Kitto, **3**: 50.
— and Death. Sharpe, **47**: 291.
— and Religion and Morals. Dub. Univ. **85**: 385.
— as Educators. Knick. **64**: 102.
— Catholicism and Protestantism in relation to. Ecl. R. **107**: 1.
— Characteristics of artistic Movements. (G. A. Simcox) Portfo. **6**: 103.
— Claims of the Beautiful in. Dem. R. **3**: 253.
— Culture of. (J. R. Fisher) So. Lit. Mess. **6**: 842.
— Eastlake's Literature of. Blackw. **64**: 753.
— Exposition of, in Paris, 1855. Lond. Q. **5**: 230.
— Glance at. (Mrs. A. L. Phelps) Nat. Q. **1**: 146.
— Ignoramus on. (H. Coleridge) Blackw. **29**: 214, 508. **30**: 655.
— Imitation in, De Quincey on. Mo. R. **141**: 563.
— in America. (J. H. Mifflin) Knick. **2**: 30. — (F. R. Hofland) Knick. **14**: 39. — Blackw. **16**: 129. — (D. Clapp) Chr. Exam. **39**: 314. — So. Q. **15**: 333. — Am. Mo. M. **5**: 312, 391.
— in Captivity; French Robberies, in 1789–1813. Macmil. **25**: 137.
— in the Crystal Palace, 1854. Brit. Q. **20**: 301.
— in the Colonies. Ecl. R. **90**: 423.
— in Edinburgh. No. Brit. **16**: 89.
— in Florence. Quar. **66**: 313.
— in France. Ed. Mo. R. **5**: 689.
— — in the 14th Century. Dub. Univ. **74**: 243.
— — in the Middle Ages. For. Q. **22**: 356.
— — in 1855. Ecl. R. **103**: 219.
— in Great Britain, Report of Select Committee on. Blackw. **50**: 585.
— in Italy. Ecl. R. **114**: 410.

Fine Arts in Italy, in the Middle Ages. For. Q. 7: 92.
— — — Restoration of. For. Q. 22: 1.
— in New York. O. & N. 3: 355.
— Influence of. (W. Dunlap) Am. Mo. M. 7: 113.
— — on the moral Sensibilities. (J. N. Danforth) So. Lit. Mess. 10: 109.
— Institution for. (W. Tudor) No. Am. 2: 153.
— Intellectual and moral Relations of. So. Lit. J. 4: 481.
— Landscape Painting among. (P. G. Hamerton) Fortn. 3: 197.
— Lawrence's Address on. U. S. Lit. Gaz. 3: 41, 81.
— Lecture on. (W. M. Thackeray) Fraser, 19: 743.
— Lectures on. Blackw. 14: 18. 15: 219. 54: 691.
— Legends of the Monastic Orders as represented in. Blackw. 69: 305.
— Moral Influence of. (E. Otheman) Am. Meth. M. 17: 318.
— Nature, Necessity, and Offices of. (G. L. Taylor) Meth. Q. 34: 231.
— Origin of. Blackw. 44: 124.
— of Society. (L. Fountain) Putnam, 14: 113–620.
— Over-Production in. (G. A. Simcox) Portfo. 7: 34.
— Patronage of. Tait, 2: 799.
— Philosophy of. (E. P. Evans) No. Am. 103: 346.
— Progress of, in the United States. Harper, 52: 691.
— Proper Sphere and Sources of Excellence of. (G. McClelland) New Eng. 18: 605.
— Rise, Progress, and Influence of. (A. S. Waugh) West. J. 1: 309–672.
— Science of. (F. W. J. Schelling) J. Spec. Philos. 15: 152.
See Arts; Painting; Sculpture; etc.
Fingal's Cave. Penny M. 1: 236.
Finger and Thumb, Human. Belgra. 8: 220.
Finger of Fate, The. (W. S. Gilbert) Ev. Sat. 11: 562.
Fingers and Toes. (B. G. Wilder) Hours at Home, 11: 241–537.
— Index- and Ring-, Relative Lengths of the. (J. C. Galton) Nature, 16: 444.
Finger-Nails. Chamb. J. 41: 148.
Finger-Rings. *See* Rings.
Finishing School; a Poem. Harper, 17: 433.
Finite and the Infinite. (F. A. Henry) J. Spec. Philos. 4: 193, 289. — (N. J. Gates) Pop. Sci. Mo. 13: 73. — (J. Scoffern) St. James, 9: 101.
Finland. (W. Hoffman) Penn Mo. 11: 387.
— and the Finlanders. Colburn, 103: 379.
— and Lapland. Dub. R. 46: 269.
— Day's March through. (D. Ker) Lippinc. 20: 116.
— Epic Poem of. (W. Hoffman) Penn Mo. 11: 677, 778.
— Fortnight in. Colburn, 100: 423.
— Gulf of. Colburn, 101: 112.
— Literature and Language of. Ecl. R. 102: 385. *See* Kalevala.
— Mythology of. Fraser, 55: 523. Same art. Ecl. M. 42: 354. — House. Words, 17: 353.
— North, Western Frontier of, 1855. Fraser, 53: 379.
— Poetry of. House. Words, 9: 583.
— Runes of. Westm. 7: 317.
— Russia, Norway, and the Baltic. Fraser, 49: 214.
— Russian Conquest of, in 1808–9. Liv. Age, 42: 511.
— Summer Tour in. (A. Delmar) Appleton, 10: 653–819. 11: 11–497.
Finlay, John, and his Poetry. Blackw. 2: 186.
Finley, Francis, Death of. Chr. Obs. 2: 125, 190.
Finney, Charles Grandison. (H. Mead) Cong. Q. 19: 1. — Lond. Q. 47: 339.
— Ministerial Test. (C. A. Stork) Luth. Q. 2: 600.
— on Revivals of Religion. Lit. & Theo. R. 2: 667.
— Preaching of. (W. C. Wilkinson) Cong. 4: 725.
— Sermon on a new Heart. Princ. 4: 278.
— Sermons. (A. B. Dod) Princ. 7: 482.
Finney, Charles Grandison, Theology of. (G. Duffield) Am. Bib. Repos. 3d s. 4: 212, 412. — (C. Hodge and M. B. Hope) Princ. 19: 237. — Spirit Pilg. 5: 161. — (J. J. Foot) Lit. & Theo. R. 5: 38. — (G. F. Wright) Bib. Sac. 33: 381. 34: 708.
Finnic Ethnology. (A. H. Keane) Nature, 21: 179.
Finnish Nationality and Literature. Chamb. J. 22: 388.
Fiorella; a Waif. Tinsley, 9: 656. 10: 103–223.
Fioretti di San Francesco d'Assisi. (H. J. Coleridge) Month, 15: 1.
Firdausi, Persian Poet. (E. H. Palmer) Argosy, 4: 62. — Am. Whig R. 9: 54. — Mo. R. 93: 449.
Fire and Frost, Geological Work of. Intel. Obs. 8: 9.
— and its Extinction, Altitude of Buildings in reference to. Pract. M. 4: 134.
— and Snow; a Tale. (W. Thornbury) Belgra. 8: 87.
— and then Rain. All the Year, 26: 539.
— at Grantley Mills. (F. H. Burnett) Scrib. 8: 346.
— at London Bridge, 1861. Once a Week, 5: 40.
— Chemistry of. (L. H. Steiner) Mercersb. 7: 249.
— Deaths by. Once a Week, 5: 63.
— Early History of. (N. Joly) Pop. Sci. Mo. 10: 17.
— from Heaven; a Tale. (E. B. Cobb) Galaxy, 13: 114.
— in the Backwoods. Fraser, 40: 42.
— in Cotton Ships. Bank. M. (N. Y.) 15: 182.
— in Tooley Street, Another. Chamb. J. 43: 58.
— in the Woods. (N. Macleod) Good Words, 2: 512.
— in the Woods; a Tale. (S. F. Cooper) Internat. M. 1: 95.
— Loss of Vessels by. Hogg, 8: 404.
— Means of procuring. Penny M. 3: 284.
— Protection against. Am. J. Sci. 20: 96. 25: 291.
— — Bird's. Nation, 17: 132.
— Weapons for Combat with. (C. W. Wyckoff) Putnam, 15: 226.
Fires and Fire Departments. (J. M. Bugbee) No. Am. 117: 108.
— and Fire Insurance, and Firemen. (A. Wynter) Quar. 96: 1. Same art. Ecl. M. 35: 1.
— and how to deal with them. Temp. Bar, 3: 48.
— and Incendiarism. Lond. M. 12: 545.
— and their Causes. Chamb. J. 54: 772. Same art. Pop. Sci. Mo. 14: 653.
— and Rain-Storms. (J. Trowbridge) Pop. Sci. Mo. 2: 206.
— Chicago and Prairie, Justin McCarthy on. (K. Field) Ev. Sat. 11: 594.
— Extinction of, and Hydrants. (S. McElroy) J. Frankl. Inst. 79: 81–289.
— — by Steam. (A. Moigno) Pract. M. 4: 236.
— Fire Underwriters' Responsibility for. Am. Arch. 10: 41.
— Great. All the Year, 5: 380.
— — Record of. Am. Arch. 6: 151.
— in America. Chamb. J. 55: 166.
— in American Cities. (A. P. Peabody) Internat. R. 1: 17.
— in commercial Cities. (R. Hare) Hunt, 26: 709.
— in Factories. J. Frankl. Inst. 13: 355.
— — at Lowell. (J. B. Francis) J. Frankl. Inst. 79: 268.
— in London. J. Statis. Soc. 1: 283. 7: 255. — Penny M. 7: 387.
— — and Fire Brigades. Temp. Bar, 20: 135.
— — and New York. (D. Hale, jr.) Hunt, 35: 289.
— — in 1832. J. Frankl. Inst. 15: 341.
— — in 1833–65. J. Statis. Soc. 33: 144.
— in Russia. Penny M. 4: 146.
— in Theaters, Provision against. (E. M. Shaw) Pract. M. 2: 84.
— Methods of preventing. (J. W. Boswell) J. Frankl. Inst. 3: 166, 303.
— of 1871 in the Northwest. (I. A. Lapham) J. Frankl. Inst. 93: 413. 94: 46.
— of the Paris Opera House. Pract. M. 3: 8.

Fires on board Steam Vessels. (C. H. Haswell) J. Frankl. Inst. **63**: 289.
— on Shipboard, Extinguishing. Pract. M. **5**: 150.
— Prevention and Extinction of. Penny M. **9**: 269, 277. — (W. H. Wahl) J. Frankl. Inst. **95**: 261.
— Statistics of. Chamb. J. **23**: 73.
Fire-Alarm Telegraph of New York City, 1870. J. Frankl. Inst. **89**: 345, 413.
Fire-Arms; Breech-Loaders and their Inventors. (C. Waddy) Belgra. **17**: 325.
— Cannon, Musket, and Rifle. Quar. **90**: 445.
— Chesney on. Colburn, **94**: 173.
— Gatling System of. Pract. M. **1**: 344.
— History of Hand. (S. R. Meyrick) Arch. **22**: 59.
— — of military. Ecl. Engin. **3**: 639.
— Maynard's. (W. N. Jeffers) J. Frankl. Inst. **54**: 339.
— Modern. Ecl. Engin. **3**: 463, 494.
— of the olden Time. Once a Week, **6**: 558.
— Rifled. Ecl. M. **53**: 556.
— — Elongated Projectiles. J. Frankl. Inst. **72**: 375.
— Small. Dub. Univ. **51**: 506. **53**: 159.
— Visit to Scott's Factory. (C. Waddy) Belgra. **18**: 239.
Firebell, The. Chamb. J. **40**: 311.
Fire-Boat, New Orleans. Pract. M. **6**: 73.
Fire-Bricks. (J. Dunnachie) Ecl. Engin. **16**: 6.
— Dinas's. Pract. M. **4**: 315.
— Notes on. (G. F. Grover) Ecl. Engin. **6**: 6.
Fire Brigade, London. All the Year, **14**: 126. — House. Words, **1**: 145. — Pract. M. **7**: 174.
Fire-Clay and other refractory Materials. (G. J. Snelus) Ecl. Engin. **13**: 497.
Fire-Clay Goods, Manufacture of. Ecl. Engin. **11**: 60.
— — in Scotland. Ecl. Engin. **9**: 353.
Fire-Damp. Chamb. J. **56**: 29.
— and its Victims. Cornh **5**: 426.
— and Safety Lamps. Dub. Univ. **50**: 185, 345. — Liv. Age, **4**: 283.
— Composition of. (T. Graham) J. Frankl. Inst. **41**: 64.
— Explosion of. (J. Richardson) J. Frankl. Inst. **48**: 156.
— of Coal Mines. Ed. R. **26**: 233. — (E. Turner) Am. J. Sci. **37**: 201. *See* Coal Mines.
Fire-Doomed Cities. Ecl. M. **55**: 128.
Fire-Engine, Steam, 1853. J. Frankl. Inst. **56**: 54.
Fire-Engines, Hose, etc., 1827. J. Frankl. Inst. **3**: 281.
Fire-Escape, Buttkereit's. Pract. M. **1**: 205.
Fire-Escapes and Elevators. J. Frankl. Inst. **112**: 408.
— — Franklin Institute on. Am. Arch. **10**: 312.
Fire-Fiend, The. (E. Benson) Galaxy, **8**: 647.
Fireflies and their Phenomena. (Mrs. V. O. King) Am. Natural. **12**: 662.
Fire Island, A Night at. Chamb. J. **45**: 823.
Fire-Kings and Fire-Eaters. Chamb. J. **53**: 732.
Fireman, New York, Life of a. (W. H. Rideing) Harper, **55**: 659.
Firemen, American Volunteer. All the Year, **4**: 537.
Fireman's Defense, Aldini's. J. Frankl. Inst. **16**: 141.
Fireman's Respirator. Pract. M. **5**: 86. — (Capt. Shaw) Ecl. Engin. **12**: 426.
— Experiments with a. (J. Tyndall) Pract. M. **4**: 308.
Fireplace, History of the. Chamb. J. **3**: 274.
— Open. (J. P. Putnam) Am. Arch. **4**: 116–210. — Am. Arch. **5**: 35–187. **6**: 50–183. **7**: 19–257. — Quar. **96**: 145.
Fireplaces, and how to make them good. Pract. M. **7**: 168.
— and the Use of Fuel. Westm. **91**: 399.
— Edwards on. Nature, **1**: 624.
— History of. Niles's Reg. **17**: 207. — Liv. Age, **5**: 545.
Fire-Proof Building in Vienna. (H. A. Hill) Am. Arch. **7**: 57.
— Ventilating. Am. Arch. **7**: 233–282. **8**: 18–238.
Fire-Proof Buildings. (J. S. Baldwin) Nation, **4**: 298. — (E. M. Shaw) Pract. M. **1**: 25. — Ecl. Engin. **17**: 439. — Ev. Sat. **14**: 88.
— Mullet on. Ev. Sat. **11**: 463.
Fire-Proof Construction. (N. H. Hutton) Am. Arch. **1**: 43, 111. — (T. H. Lewis) J. Frankl. Inst. **81**: 295. — (P. B. Wight) Ecl. Engin. **1**: 1017. — Ecl. Engin. **10**: 515, 533. **11**: 74. — J. Frankl. Inst. **41**: 153. — (L. Hornblower) Ecl. Engin. **10**: 33.
Fire-Proof Homes and Forest Economies. Am. Arch. **9**: 149.
Fire-Proof Library, Description of. (J. Travers) J. Frankl. Inst. **42**: 337.
Fire-Proof Materials, Tests of. Am. Arch. **10**: 265.
Fire-Proofing Fabrics and Wood. Pract. M. **6**: 74.
Fireside Chat. (H. M. Rathbone) Peop. J. **11**: 138–258.
Fireside Essay. (C. Lanman) So. Lit. Mess. **7**: 129.
Fireside Fancies. Dub. Univ. **42**: 635.
Fireside Horrors for Christmas. Dub. Univ. **30**: 361. Same art. Liv. Age, **16**: 180.
Fireside Reminiscences. Knick. **36**: 436.
Fireside Story told by a Poker. Belgra. **1**: 83.
Fire-Tank, Self-Acting. Pract. M. **2**: 220.
Fireworks. All the Year, **33**: 84.
— a Story. (A. T. Howells) Galaxy, **14**: 398.
— Art of making, at little Cost. Pract. M. **5**: 95.
— in their chemical and mechanical Relations. Pract. M. **5**: 295.
See Pyrotechnics.
Fire-Worshipers, Persian. Hogg, **7**: 21.
— Temple of, at Baku. Internat. M. **5**: 160.
See Parsees.
Firm of Ah-Why & Co. Chamb. J. **58**: 137.
Firmament, in Gen. i. (C. B. Warring) Bib. Sac. **36**: 459.
Firmilian; a spasmodic Tragedy. (W. E. Aytoun) Colburn, **102**: 140.
Firmin, Giles. (J. W. Dean) N. E. Reg. **20**: 47. **25**: 52.
Firmin, Thomas, Life of. Retros. **12**: 165.
Firmont, A. E. E. de, Abbé Edgeworth, and Louis XVI. St. James, **27**: 65. Same art. Liv. Age, **107**: 547.
— Memoir of. Mo. R. **82**: 135.
Firozpur, Irrigation Works at. (C. R. Markham) Geog. M. **3**: 58.
First of April; a Story. (G. C. Munro) Peop. J. **7**: 173.
First Atlantic Telegraph; a Tale. (E. Spencer) Atlan. **7**: 170.
First Attempt. Lond. Soc. **4**: 205.
First Baby. (Mrs. S. A. Downer) Pioneer, **4**: 326.
First-Born as a Title of Jesus Christ. Kitto, **27**: 17.
First Brick. Knick. **37**: 127.
First Cause, Attributes of. (T. Hill) Bib. Sac. **36**: 3.
First Fan; a Poem. (O. W. Holmes) Atlan. **39**: 659.
First-Fiddles and Top-Sawyers. Temp. Bar, **2**: 404.
First Friendship. Fraser, **66**: 1–679. **67**: 17–290.
First Love; a Tale. Temp. Bar, **29**: 24.
First Meet of the Season. (J. Hewlett) Colburn, **72**: 300–453.
First Morning of 1860; a Poem. Cornh. **1**: 122.
First Mrs. Petersham. (H. P. Spofford) Harper, **59**: 361.
First Picture. Chamb. J. **33**: 371. Same art. Liv. Age. **66**: 223.
First Principles. Dial, **2**: 273.
First Recordership. (J. Payn) Belgra. **36**: 77.
First Ship in the Niger; a Poem. (W. R. Russell) Internat. M. **3**: 128.
First Time I saw her. Lond. Soc. **4**: 1–255.
First Time of Asking. Lond. M. **22**: 231.
First Violin; a Novel. Temp. Bar, **52**: 1–433. **53**: 1–433. **54**: 1–433.
First Vow; a Tale. (W. R. Barker) Cath. World, **28**: 368.
Firth, Mark, with portrait, and Notes on Sheffield. Pract. M. **6**: 289.

Firth, Notes on the. (W. E. Henley) Macmil. **32**: 563.
Fisgrave, Anthony. Midas; on Taste, Genius, Art, etc. (J. Foster) Ecl. R. **8**: 1100.
Fish, Hamilton, with portrait. Ev. Sat. **10**: 266.—with portrait, Ecl. M. **78**: 632.
Fish, Preserved, Biography of. Hunt, **15**: 582.—Bank. M. **1**: 133.
Fish and Oysters. (W. Chambers) Chamb. J. **51**: 43.
— as Food. Chamb. J. **51**: 653.—Liv. Age, **39**: 569.—Penny M. **7**: 175, 183, 191.
— — and Physic. (J. M. Granville) Good Words, **22**: 676.
— Cooking of. All the Year, **20**: 54.—Eng. Dom. M. **15**: 294.
— Fresh. All the Year, **5**: 260.
— — Trade of Boston. Hunt, **11**: 288.
— out of Water. All the Year, **16**: 104.
— used as Food in America. Penny M. **10**: 135.
— Value as Food. All the Year, **35**: 211, 357.
— When in Season, and why. Chamb. J. **15**: 414.
Fishes. Ev. Sat. **13**: 126.—So. Lit. Mess. **14**: 229.
— Air or Swimming Bladder of. (W. Houghton) Pop. Sci. R. **7**: 378.
— Amphibious. (E. Sauvage) Pop. Sci. Mo. **9**: 546.
— and Fishermen. (Dr. A. W. Ely) De Bow, **15**: 143.
— and Fish Ponds. Chamb. J. **40**: 324.—De Bow, **25**: 442.
— and Fisheries of the Pacific Coast. (W. N. Lockington) Am. Natural. **13**: 684.
— Animal Heat of. Nature, **21**: 156.
— Armored. (H. Woodward) Pop. Sci. R. **17**: 1.
— Blind. (F. W. Putnam) Am. Natural. **6**: 6.—Chamb. J. **53**: 326.
— — of the Mammoth Cave. (F. W. Putnam) Nature, **6**: 246, 415.—(J. Wyman) Am. J. Sci. **67**: 258.
— Boccius on Management of Fresh-Water. Mo. R. **156**: 556.
— Character of. Am. Mo. M. **3**: 92.
— Clever. (F. Francis) Fraser, **86**: 11. Same art. Ecl. M. **79**: 312. Same art. Liv. Age, **114**: 309. Same art. Pop. Sci. Mo. **1**: 520.
— — Edible, and otherwise. Galaxy, **17**: 816.
— Death of, in the Bay of Fundy. (A. L. Adams) Am. Natural. **2**: 337.
— distinguished by their Action. (W. S. Kent) Nature, **8**: 263.
— Distribution of Fresh-Water. (D. S. Jordan) Am. Natural. **11**: 607.
— Eel-Pout. (W. Wood) Am. Natural. **3**: 17.
— Electric. (F. W. Clarke) Penn Mo. **6**: 808.—(A. Murray) Ed. New Philos. J. **59**: 35, 379. **63**: 267.
— Electric Organ in. Cornh. **6**: 711.
— Etheostomoids. (F. W. Putnam) Am. Natural. **6**: 109.
— Eye-like Spots in. (H. J. Bell) Pop. Sci. R. **20**: 221.
— Flat. (A. H. Baldwin) Once a Week, **9**: 38.—Chamb. J. **56**: 76.
— Food, Propagation of. Good Words, **21**: 771.
— Food of the Herring and Salmon. Blackw. **44**: 175.
— Fossil. *See* Fossil Fishes.
— from California. (L. Agassiz) Am. J. Sci. **66**: 380.
— from the Tennessee River. (L. Agassiz) Am. J. Sci. **67**: 297, 353.
— Game, of Northern United States. Bost. R. **3**: 389.
— Ganoid, in Queensland. (A. Günther) Nature, **4**: 406, 428.
— Geographical Distribution and Migration of. Hogg, **4**: 347.
— Growth of. Once a Week, **8**: 678.—Penny M. **11**: 55.
— Günther on Study of. (T. Gill) Nation, **33**: 120.
— Habits of. Intel. Obs. **10**: 99.
— Heads of. (E. P. Wright) Nature, **19**: 149.
— Heraldry of, Moule on. Mo. R. **158**: 332.
— How they breathe. (J. C. Galton) Pop. Sci. R. **10**: 341.
Fishes, How they live and grow. Fraser, **68**: 619.
— in the British Museum, Günther's Catalogue of. Nature, **3**: 342.
— in the Tropics, Instincts of. St. James, **3**: 349.
— Irregularities of Structure in. (J. Couch) Stud. & Intel. Obs. **1**: 328.
— Last of the Scombers. (D. C. Badham) Fraser, **47**: 257.
— Limits of the Class. (T. Gill) Am. Natural. **7**: 71.
— Management and History of. Mus. **44**: 266.
— Marine, Food of. (A. E. Verrill) Am. Natural. **5**: 397.
— Migrations of. (F. Heincke) Pop. Sci. Mo. **18**: 212.—Penny M. **1**: 243.—West. Mo. R. **3**: 625.
— — Strange Wanderers. (M. Schele de Vere) Hours at Home, **10**: 533.
— Mud-Loving. (C. C. Abbott) Am. Natural. **4**: 385.
— Musical. All the Year, **48**: 208.
— Natural History of. (D. H. Storer) Am. J. Sci. **36**: 337.—Am. Mo. R. **4**: 133.
— Nest-Building. (C. Strange) Once a Week, **1**: 145.
— Nests of. Chamb. J. **8**: 387.
— New Species of, from the Bermuda Islands. (G. B. Goode) Am. J. Sci. **108**: 123.
— Notes on a few River. (W. C. L. Martin) Recr. Sci. **2**: 8.
— Ocean. (B. G. Wilder) Harper, **40**: 21.
— Odd. All the Year, **2**: 516.—House. Words, **15**: 43.
— — and curious Waters. All the Year, **44**: 494.
— Odd Forms among. (S. Tenney) Pop. Sci. Mo. **11**: 525.
— of America. (C. Lanman) Am. Whig R. **6**: 490, 561.—(C. Lanman) So. Lit. Mess. **14**: 682.
— of Canada. (A. Rimmer) Gent. M. n. s. **24**: 724. **25**: 315.
— of the Coast of California. (W. N. Lockington) Am. Natural. **13**: 299.
— of Connecticut. (J. H. Linsley) Am. J. Sci. **47**: 55.
— of Eastern Seas. All the Year, **14**: 101.
— of Great Britain, Yarrell's History of. Ecl. R. **66**: 598.—Mo. R. **141**: 120.—Quar. **58**: 334.
— of Guiana, Schomburgk's Natural History of. Mo. R. **156**: 433.
— of India and Burmah, Fresh-Water. (A. Günther) Nature, **9**: 159.
— of Massachusetts. (J. H. Blake) Am. Natural. **4**: 513.
— of New Jersey. (C. C. Abbott) Am. Natural. **4**: 717.
— — Fresh-Water. (C. C. Abbott) Am. Natural. **4**: 99. **8**: 326.
— of Ohio River. (C. S. Rafinesque) West. R. **1**: 305, 368. **2**: 49–355. **3**: 165–244.
— of the Pacific, Garrett's. Nature, **9**: 120.
— of Pacific Slope of North America. Am. J. Sci. **69**: 71, 215.
— of Palestine. (A. Günther) Stud. & Intel. Obs. **3**: 409.
— of South Carolina, Holbrook's. (T. Gill) Am. J. Sci. **87**: 89.
— of United States, Notices of 50 Species of East Coast. (G. B. Goode and T. H. Bean) Am. J. Sci. **117**: 39.
— Pelagic. West. M. **5**: 523, 581.
— Pike, Salmon, Silurus, and Herring. (D. C. Badham) Fraser, **48**: 467.
— Poisonous. All the Year, **25**: 366.
— the real Lords of Creation. Colburn, **84**: 330.
— Respiration of. Ed. R. **15**: 374.
— Rumination in. (W. Houghton) Intel. Obs. **11**: 190.
— Scales of. (J. Couch) Intel. Obs. **12**: 246.
— Showers of. Liv. Age, **52**: 186.
— Silk-Producing. Penny M. **9**: 47.
— Some Facts about. (W. S. Dallas) Pop. Sci. R. **20**: 40. Same art. Ecl. M. **96**: 472.
— Some odd. Chamb. J. **54**: 78.
— Something about. (J. V. C. Smith) Harper, **34**: 286.
— Song of. (J. C. Galton) Pop. Sci. R. **13**: 337. Same art. Liv. Age, **123**: 313.
— Sporting. Chamb. J. **13**: 289.

Fishes, Strange. Dub. Univ. 80: 329.
— Systematic Relations of. (E. D. Cope) Am. Natural. 5: 579.
— Tails of. (E. P. Wright) Nature, 17: 286.
— Tame. Recr. Sci. 1: 14.
— Thoughts of. All the Year, 25: 535.
— Traces of a Voice in. (C. C. Abbott) Am. Natural. 11: 147.
— Two new Species. (G. B. Goode and T. H. Bean) Am. J. Sci. 114: 470.
— Viviparous, of the Pacific. (W. Farwell) Pioneer, 1: 45.
— Voracity of. (A. H. Baldwin) Once a Week, 7: 332.
— Walking. All the Year, 24: 32.
Fish Culture. (C. G. Atkins) Am. Natural. 1: 296. — (C. W. Eliot) Nation, 2: 537. — (E. Quincy) Nation, 8: 71. — All the Year, 36: 159. — Chamb. J. 51: 85. — Cornh. 5: 195. — Ecl. M. 40: 211. — Dub. Univ. 40: 619. 62: 354. — Fraser, 72: 105. Liv. Age, 44: 24. — Lond. Q. 20: 454. — Lond. Soc. 2: 123.
— Collecting Salmon Spawn in Maine. Harper, 49: 29.
— in America. (W. F. G. Shanks) Harper, 37: 721.
— in Europe. Intel. Obs. 9: 85, 209.
— in France. (A. Blackwell) Once a Week, 4: 427.
— in Switzerland. Harper, 24: 721.
— in the U. S. Nature, 23: 532. — Pract. M. 1: 236.
— — on McCloud River. (W. M. Turner) Overland, 14: 79.
— — Trout. (A. S. Collins) Am. Natural. 4: 601.
— — Work of U. S. Fish Commission. (W. C. Wyckoff) Harper, 49: 213.—(G. B. Goode) Nature, 22: 597.
— Progress of. Chamb. J. 29: 372.
See Aquarium Car; Trout; Salmon; Herring; etc.
Fish-Dealers, Ancient. (D. C. Badham) Fraser, 47: 548.
Fish Dinners. House. Words, 3: 421.
Fish Eaters. All the Year, 24: 608.
Fish Exhibition in the Zoölogical Gardens. Hogg, 10: 7.
Fish Farm. (E. Dexter) Am. Natural. 3: 202.
Fish Farms of the World. (A. Wynter) Once a Week, 14: 609.
Fish Hawks and Falcons. (H.W. Herbert) Putnam, 2: 35.
— The Osprey. (A. Fowler) Am. Natural. 2: 192.
Fish Hooks. Penny M. 12: 175.
— how made. Ev. Sat. 1: 528.
Fish Manure. Chamb. J. 23: 147.
Fish Markets and Fish Ponds. Quar. 69: 228.
Fish Poisoning in the West Indies. Penny M. 6: 370.
Fish Ponds and Fish Breeding. Once a Week, 9: 654.
— and Fishing-Boats. Blackw. 79: 521. Same art. Liv. Age, 50: 385.
— Domestic. Penny M. 14: 486.
Fish Remains, Beds of, in Western New York. (F. H. Bradley) Am. J. Sci. 92: 70.
Fish Skins, Uses of. Pract. M. 7: 187.
Fish Soup. All the Year, 35: 353.
Fish Stories, Traditional. (W.W. Crane) Lippinc. 3: 407.
Fish Tattle. (D. C. Badham) Fraser, 46: 83.
Fish World at Home. Ecl. M. 57: 387.
Fisher, Alex. M., with portrait. (D. Olmsted) New Eng. 1: 457. — (J. L. Kingsley) Am. J. Sci. 5: 367. — Chr. Mo. Spec. 4: 389, 432.
Fisher, Miss Clara. Mus. 2: 335.
Fisher, Jabez P. (H. Wood) Am. Q. Reg. 12: 127.
Fisher, John, Bishop of Rochester, Death of. (J. Bruce) Arch. 25: 61
Fisher, Jonathan, of Blue Island, Me. (W. R. Deane) Hist. M. 14: 273.
Fisher, The, and Charon; a Poem. Putnam, 8: 493.
Fisher, King. Chamb. J. 41: 101.
Fisher Girl of Newhaven. Sharpe, 19: 240.
Fisher Life, Round of. Good Words, 8: 673.
Fisher's Ghost. House. Words, 7: 6.
Fisher's Hill, Fight at. (J. F. Fitts) Galaxy, 5: 426.
Fishers, The; a Poem. (C. Sangster) Canad. Mo. 8: 222.
Fisher, Fort, Capture of. (H. C. Lockwood) Atlan. 27: 622, 684.
— Ironsides at. Lippinc. 21: 315.
— Naval Battles at, 1864. (K. Kelvin) Hist. M. 22: 368.
— Powder-Boat Explosion at. Galaxy, 9: 77.
— Terry's Expedition against. O. & N. 11: 290.
— Victory at. (J. W. Ames) Overland, 9: 323.
Fisheries. Penny M. 14: 397.
— and Sea Fish. Quar. 122: 310.
— Cod, Herring, Mackerel. (L. Sabine) No. Am. 57: 58.
— Cornish Pilchard. (J. Quick) Fraser, 95: 219.
— Danish. Geog. M. 3: 251.
— Dominion of Seas and. (D. F. Parker) Hunt, 29: 275, 420.
— Dutch. Once a Week, 18: 410, 434.
— Exhibitions of, Recent foreign, and their Lessons. (J. G. Bertram) Macmil. 16: 406.
— — Exposition of Arcachon, 1866. Fraser, 74: 297.
— Facts and Figures about. (J. G. Bertram) Fortn. 4: 745.
— French Claims to, on Coast of Newfoundland. (J. Whitman) Fraser, 93: 22.
— Herring. Chamb. J. 26: 23. *See* Herring.
— International Conference on. All the Year, 16: 493.
— Lloyd's Report on, 1825. Niles's Reg. 29: 377.
— of British America. Chamb. J. 42: 45. — (W. B. Carpenter) Nature, 18: 170, 232.
— of the British Channel. Tait, n. s. 1: 125.
— of California. (C. J. W. Russell) Hunt, 36: 573. 37: 186.
— of Great Britain. (Sir J. Barrow) Quar. 9: 265. — Blackw. 118: 441. — Mo. R. 90: 353. — Penny M. 6: 43-465.
— — Deep-Sea. Fraser, 75: 618. — Once a Week, 8: 442. — Westm. 78: 316.
— — Sea-Fish, Fishermen, and. Fraser, 71: 507.
— of Ireland. Colburn, 106: 37. — Dub. R. 3: 133. Dub. Univ. 31: 771. — Nature, 12: 392. — (Sir J. Barrow) Quar. 72: 473.
— of New England. Nature, 10: 201.
— of North America. Blackw. 123: 287.
— — River. Putnam, 6: 149.
— — Sabine's. Fraser, 48: 587.
— of the Pacific. Chamb. J. 38: 249.
— of Scotland. Blackw. 79: 328. — Hogg, 4: 26. — Quar. 69: 419.
— of Shetland. Blackw. 10: 728.
— of United States. (E. Hale, jr.) Hunt, 26: 19-416. — Hunt, 29: 147. — (L. Sabine) No. Am. 62: 350. — De Bow, 16: 531. — Nature, 19: 429.
— — President Adams on. Niles's Reg. 23: 25.
— — and British American. Tait, n. s. 19: 547. Same art. Liv. Age, 35: 236.
— — — Question of, 1879. (C. Almy, jr.) Nation, 29: 219. — (C. Lindsey) Canad. Mo. 1: 5. — Liv. Age, 35: 42, 90.
— — — American Diplomacy on. Fraser, 48: 587. Same art. Liv. Age, 39: 167.
— — — Anglo-American Association on. (J. N. Pomeroy) Nation, 12: 232.
— — — Award on. (C. Almy, jr., and E. L. Godkin) Nation, 26: 145, 178. — (G. F. Edmunds) No. Am. 128: 1.
— — Internal. O. & N. 3: 750.
— — Northeastern. (J. N. Pomeroy) Nation, 11: 166. — Am. Law R. 5: 389.
— — What of our? (J. G. Scammon) Cath. World, 12: 735.
— Sea. (F. B. Perkins) Galaxy, 1: 430. — Dub. Univ. 38: 509.
— — and Salmon. Chamb. J. 55: 134.

Fisheries, White and Shell. Chamb. J. 26: 44.
See names of kinds of fish, as Cod, Herring, Salmon, etc.
Fisherman, The; a Poem. (J. W. v. Goethe) Dub. Univ. 40: 581.
— of Lake Sunapee. Once a Week, 9: 225. Same art. Liv. Age, 78: 588.
— of St. Auge. St. Paul's, 6: 572, 7: 1, 146. Same art. Ecl. M. 75: 600, 666. 76: 40.
— Scottish. (H. Miller) No. Brit. 1: 326. Same art. Liv. Age, 2: 291. — Blackw. 51: 296. — Quar. 69: 419.
Fisherman's Budget. Blackw. 9: 249, 378.
Fisherman's Daughter; a Tale. (Mrs. A. J. Hippisley) Peop. J. 6: 233, 249.
Fisherman's Daughter. Victoria, 5: 481. 6: 56–299.
Fisherman's Grievances. Chamb. J. 58. 652.
Fisherman's Home, Brighton. Once a Week, 9: 347.
Fishermen. Chamb. J. 7: 53.
— of Boulogne. Once a Week, 19: 14.
Fisher-Wife's Dream; a Poem. (R. Steggall) Colburn, 168: 515.
Fishguard, How the French fared at. Chamb. J. 33: 17.
Fishing. St. Paul's, 2: 330.
— and Fish, Ancient. Fraser, 43: 249.
— and Fishers. (Prof. Leebody) Gent. M. n. s. 9: 45.
— and Fishing Literature. Blackw. 127: 736. Same art. Liv. Age, 146: 226. Same art. Ecl. M. 95: 165.
— at the West. Putnam, 2: 433.
— Chalk-Stream Studies. (C. Kingsley) Fraser, 58: 323.
— Deep-Sea, Holdsworth's. Nature, 11: 421.
— A few Days'. Belgra. 17: 492.
— Flat-Fish Trawling off the Wight. (J. C. Hutcheson) Belgra. 21: 235.
— A French Isaac Walton. Gent. M. n. s. 5: 15.
— Fly-Fisher in Winter Quarters. Cornh. 27: 436.
— Fly-Fishing. Blackw. 5: 123, 281. 7: 137. — Fraser, 42: 136. — Bentley, 13: 257.
— — Dick's. Nature, 8: 220.
— — in Brittany. Colburn, 157: 301.
— — Scenes and Recollections of. Blackw. 35: 775.
— Girl's Attempt at. (J. M. Toes) Canad. Mo. 18: 476.
— in North America. Penny M. 6: 193, 209.
— in Norway. (Sir C. Taylor) Fortn. 2: 443.
— in the Tropics. Chamb. J. 51: 161.
— in Virginia Waters. (J. C. Carpenter) Lippinc. 28: 529.
— in Wales, Trout and Salmon, Hansard on. Mo. R. 135: 467.
— Legislation on. No. Brit. 43: 167.
— Literature of. Ecl. R. 98: 15. 99: 21.
— Piscatory Reflections. Knick. 48: 149.
— Spring-Tide; or the Angler and his Friends. Bentley, 20: 552. 21: 333. 26: 255, 600. 27: 246.
— Trawls and Trawlers. (A. H. Baldwin) Belgra. 18: 97.
See Angling; Trawling; *also names of varieties of fish, as* Salmon, Trout, etc.
Fishing-Banks, New York Harbor, Excursion to. (C. D. Shanly) Atlan. 7: 152.
Fishing-Excursion in County Galway. Fraser, 12: 437.
Fishing-Tour in Scotland. (A. Kinnear) Belgra. 27: 358.
Fishing-Tourist, Hallock's. Canad. Mo. 4: 273.
Fishing-Grounds, Happy. All the Year, 2: 113.
Fishmongers' Company. Penny M. 3: 57.
Fisk, James, jr., Use of. (E. L. Godkin) Nation, 14: 21.
Fisk, Pliny, Bond's Memoir of. Ecl. R. 50: 169.
Fisk, Saml. (B. Hart) New Eng. 25: 75. — Cong. Q. 8: 1.
Fisk, Wilbur. Am. J. Educ. 6: 297.
— Eulogy on. (D. D. Whedon) Am. Meth. M. 21: 384.
— Life of. Meth. Q. 2: 579. — Chr. R. 7: 400.
Fiske, John. Cosmic Philosophy. (J. Bascom) Bib. Sac. 33: 618.
— Myths and Myth-Makers. (J. R. G. Hassard) Cath. World, 17: 209.
Fiske, John. Unseen World. (H. W. Holland) Nation, 23: 214.
Fiske, Nathan W. New Eng. 8: 67.
Fit of Jealousy; a Story. Cornh. 5: 438.
Fitch, Asa. (E. P. Thurston) Pop. Sci. Mo. 16: 116.
Fitch, Ebenezer. (C. Durfee) Am. Q. Reg. 15: 353.
Fitch, Eleazer T., as a Preacher. (J. M. Hoppin) New Eng. 30: 215.
— on the Nature of Sin. (W. E. Channing) Chr. Exam. 4: 77.
— Sermon of. Am. Mo. R. 9: 390.
Fitch, James. (D. M. Leonard) N. E. Reg. 2: 269.
Fitch, James Mason. (C. W. Torrey) Cong. Q. 10: 141.
Fitch, John. (N. Webster) Internat. M. 1: 68.
— Life of. (C. Whittlesey) Sparks's Am. Biog. 16. 83.
Fitchburg, Mass., Ministers of. Am. Q. Reg. 10: 55.
Fitchett, J. King Alfred. (J. T. Gordon) No. Brit. 2: 390.
Fitful Fever in four Stages. (S. J. MacKenna) St. James, 41: 213, 300.
Fitts and Fitz Genealogy. N. E. Reg. 22: 70, 161.
Fitzadam, Ismael. (K. R. Cook) Gent. M. n. s. 4: 400.
Fitz Adam's Story; a Poem. (J. R. Lowell) Atlan. 19: 17.
Fitz-Boodle's Confessions. (W. M. Thackeray) Fraser, 25: 707. 26: 43, 395. 27: 76–465
Fitzgerald, Lord Edward. Temp. Bar, 61: 28. Same art. Liv. Age, 148: 242.
— Moore's Life of. (J. W. Croker) Quar. 46: 213. Same art. Mus. 19: 693. — (R. L. Sheil) Ed. R. 54: 114. — Westm. 16: 110. — Blackw. 30: 631. — Am. Mo. R. 1: 50. — Mo. R. 126: 46.
Fitzgerald, Lady Elizabeth. House. Words, 17: 343.
Fitzgerald, George Robert. Dub. Univ. 16: 1–370. — Cornh. 41: 82. Same art. Liv. Age, 144: 436. Same art. Ecl. M. 94: 326.
Fitzgerald, Hardress, Adventure of. Mus. 40: 104.
Fitzgerald, James, Earl of Desmond, Secret History of. Dub. R. 50: 499. 51: 1.
Fitzgerald, William, Bp. of Cork. Dub. Univ. 49: 416.
Fitzhenry, Mrs. Mary, the Actress. Dub. Univ. 62: 324.
Fitzherbert, Mary. Liv. Age, 49: 275.
— An Evening with. St. James, 5: 285.
— Marriage with the Prince of Wales. Dub. R. 40: 252.
— Memoirs of. Ed. R. 103: 591. — Dub. Univ. 47: 481.
Fitz-James, Bishop, and the Lord Chief Justice, Relationship between. (E. Foss) Arch. 35: 305.
Fitz-James and the Widow; a Story. Galaxy, 24: 640.
Fitz-Osbert, William. Penny M. 14: 365.
Fitzpatrick, James, Fenian. All the Year, 17: 488.
Fitzpatrick, W. J. Life of Bishop Doyle. (J. N. Nylan) Cath. World, 7: 44.
Fitz-Roy, Robert, Sketch of. Good Words, 7: 406.
Fitzroy, Thaddeus T. (N. Macleod) Good Words, 2: 201.
Fitz-Roys in New York. (T. B. Myers) Hist. M. 17: 309.
Fitz-Simeon, Itinerary of, 1322. Retros. 16: 232.
Fitzsimmons, Thomas. (H. Flanders) Pennsyl. M. 2: 306.
Fitzwilliam, Fanny. (T. P. Grinsted) Bentley, 42: 320.
Five Brothers' five Fixes. Chamb. J. 45: 283–339.
Five Cobblers of Brescia. All the Year, 32: 324.
Five Hundred Pounds' Reward. Tinsley, 8: 52.
Five Hundred Years ago. All the Year, 4: 53, 185.
Five Incumbents. (J. Hewlett) Colburn, 65: 498. 66: 95–507.
Five Miles on a Keel. (J. K. Goodrich) Overland, 15: 516.
Five Minutes too late; a Tale. Chamb. J. 15: 107.
Five Months in an ancient Irish City; a Tale. Dub. Univ. 38: 49.
Five Nations, Character of. (F. Post) Olden Time, 1: 134.
— Laws, Customs, etc., of. (C. Colden) Olden Time, 1: 297. *See also* Iroquois.
Five Points, New York. Nat. M. 2: 169, 267, 376.
Five Scenes. (W. S. Landor) Fraser, 43: 59.

Five Sisters Court at Christmas-Tide. (H. E. Scudder) Atlan. **15**: 22.
Fixed Period; a Novel. Blackw. **130**: 413–681.
Flaccus, Poems by. Knick. **15**: 61, 119, 472. **18**: 27, 384. **20**: 42, 117.
Flacius Illyricus and his Times. (C. F. Schaeffer) Evang. R. **14**: 481.
Flag, United States. (C. H. Woodman) Appleton, **15**: 19. — Bost. R. **4**: 581. — Hist. M. **9**: 113.
— — Origin of. (J. C. Conybeare) Potter Am. Mo. **8**: 89.
— — Preble's History of. (J.C. Palfrey) Nation, **31**: 446.
Flags. Good Words, **21**: 194.
— National, of England. (C. Boutell) Art J. **11**: 249–373. **13**: 49.
— Three historic. (G. H. Preble) N. E. Reg. **28**: 17.
Flag of Distress; a Story of the South Sea. (M. Reid) Chamb. J. **52**: 497–818.
Flag Code at Sea. All the Year, **36**: 463.
Flagellants, Pilgrimage of. Blackw. **72**: 596.
Flagellation; Considering one's self horsewhipped. (L. Blanchard) Colburn, **72**: 273.
Flagellum Parliamentarium. Lond. M. **18**: 115.
Flagg, A. C., with portrait. Dem. R. **36**: 91.
Flagg, George W. Godey, **33**: 253.
Flagstaffe, Francis, Passages in Life of. Blackw. **23**: 273.
Flamborough Head. (M. G. Watkins) Once a Week, **14**: 427.
— identified as Ocellum Promontorium. (J. Walker) Arch. **25**: 127.
Flame, Cause of Light of. (W. Stein) Pop. Sci. Mo. **7**: 696. Same art. J. Frankl. Inst. **99**: 296.
— Diathermancy of. (J. Ericsson) Nature, **7**: 149. — (W. M. Williams) Nature, **6**: 506.
— Electrical Properties of. (H. Buff) Am. J. Sci. **64**: 88.
— New sensitive singing. (W. E. Geyer) Am. J. Sci. **103**: 340.
— Sensitive, New Form of. (P. Barry) Nature, **5**: 30.
Flames, Luminous. (E. W. Hilgard) Am. J. Sci. **97**: 218.
— Sounding and sensitive. (A. S. Herschel) Nature, **11**: 6, 45. — (J. Tyndall) J. Frankl. Inst. **83**: 260, 346.
— Temperatures of. (B. Silliman and H. Wurtz) J. Frankl. Inst. **89**: 337.
— Theory of illuminating. (K. Heumann) J. Frankl. Inst. **100**: 419.
Flame Reactions. (Prof. Bunsen) J. Frankl. Inst. **84**: 330. **85**: 49–405.
Flamel, Nicholas, Alchemist. Colburn, **164**: 109.
Flamenca, Story of. (F. Hueffer) Macmil. **36**: 211.
Flamingo, The. Penny M. **3**: 224.
Flaminia. (A. De Bar) Cath. World, **7**: 795. **8**: 76.
Flaminio, Marc Antonio, and the suppressed Reformation in Italy. Chr. Obs. **46**: 532.
Flamsteed, John. (J. M. J. Fletcher) Reliquary, **14**: 149. **15**: 34. — Quar. **55**: 96, 568.
— Biographical Memoir of. (F. Baily) Ed. New Philos. J. **20**: 131.
— Life and Observations of. Ed. R. **62**: 359.
Flanders by the Sea. (J. Hutton) Belgra. **21**: 108.
— Freaks in. All the Year, **19**: 417.
— Free Cities of. (C. Cushing) No. Am. **39**: 112.
— History of the Courts of. For. Q. **35**: 269.
— Journey to, So. Lit. Mess. **3**: 181.
— Tour in. Fraser, **27**: 166.
Flanders Family. N. E. Reg. **27**: 170.
Flandrin, Hippolyte. Month, **2**: 426. — (F. Wedmore) Macmil. **26**: 304. — F. Arts Q. **4**: 115, 284. — (T. F. Wedmore) Contemp. **4**: 488.
Flats. *See* Apartment Houses.
Flats and Sharps. (J. D. Cartwright) Sharpe, **36**: 151.
Flath Innis; a Poem. (G. Moultrie) Once a Week, **16**: 34.
Flattery. (L. Fountain) Putnam, **14**: 113. — Broadw. **6**: 189. — Chr. Obs. **5**: 217, 280.
Flattery, Innocence of. Temp. Bar, **27**: 244.
Flaubert, Gustave. (W. P. Morris) Lippinc. **6**: 439. — (G. Saintsbury) Fortn. **29**: 575.
Flavel, John. Treatise on keeping the Heart. Retros. **7**: 251.
Flavia. (A. L. A. D. Dudevant) Ecl. M. **68**: 101–422.
Flaws in great Characters. Chamb. J. **23**: 286.
Flax. (J. Titus) Hunt, **49**: 102, 179.
— and Flax Cotton. Fraser, **44**: 550.
— and its Machinery. Pract. M. **1**: 249.
— and Linen Trade. Bank. M. (N. Y.) **11**: 438.
— Culture of. (M. Tarver) West. J. **5**: 213. — West. J. **11**: 241.
— Fortunes of. Chamb. J. **38**: 288.
— New Zealand. (J. C. Russell) Am. Natural. **10**: 18. — Ecl. Engin. **6**: 584.
— Preparation of. West. J. **6**: 77.
Flax Cotton. Liv. Age, **27**: 615.
Flax-Mill, Leeds, Day at. Penny M. **12**: 501.
Flax Movement. Ecl. R. **94**: 729.
Flaxman, John. (A. G. Atkinson) Good Words, **22**: 740.
— as a Designer. (G. F. Teniswood) Art J. **24**: 189–278.
— Career of. Liv. Age, **37**: 538, 620.
— Memorials of. (G. F. Teniswood) Art J. **19**: 101–241. **20**: 1–241.
Flea and the Professor. (H. C. Andersen) Scrib. **5**: 759.
Fleas. (M. Schele de Vere) Putnam, **12**: 350. — Broadw. **7**: 332.
— Educated. (W. H. Dall) Am. Natural. **11**: 7.
— Varieties of. (C. Taylor) Harper, **19**: 178.
Flechère, J. W. de la. *See* Fletcher, J. W.
Fléchier, Esprit, Works of. Ecl. R. **98**: 322. Same art. Ecl. M. **30**: 543.
— Chronicles of Clermont Assizes. Blackw. **63**: 47.
Flecknoe's Enigmas. Retros. **5**: 266.
Fleeing from Fate. (Mrs. Parr) Gent. M. n. s. **17**: 727.
Fleet of the Future. (J. Scott Russell) Ecl. Engin. **3**: 147.
Fleets and Navies. Blackw. **85**: 643. **86**: 324, 758. **87**: 226.
— *versus* Forts. Dem. R. **13**: 577.
Fleet Parsons and Marriages. Cornh. **15**: 555.
Fleet-Street. All the Year, **27**: 127.
— Fine Day in. Fraser, **29**: 68.
Fleet-Street Biography. Lond. M. **9**: 417.
Fleet-Street Taverns. All the Year, **26**: 349.
— Dr. Johnson and. (P. Fitzgerald) Gent. M. n. s. **26**: 305.
Fleetwood, Serjeant, Itinerarium ad Windsor. (J. Bruce) Arch. **37**: 350.
Fleetwood, School of Musketry at. Lond. Soc. **5**: 81.
Fleming, John, Works of. Ecl. R. **107**: 118.
Fleming, Marjory; Pet Marjorie. (J. Brown) No. Brit. **39**: 379. Same art. Liv. Age, **79**: 465. — Liv. Age, **80**: 177.
Fleming, Wm., Metaphysical Works of. (A. K. H. Boyd) Fraser, **56**: 657.
Flemings, Defeat of, before Calais in 1436. (B. Williams) Arch. **33**: 129.
Flemings and the Walloons of Belgium. (K. Blind) Fraser, **93**: 69.
Flemish Fair. All the Year, **32**: 468.
Flemish Institutions and Art. (H. Bellingham) Month **30**: 55.
Flemish Interiors. Dub. R. **41**: 230.
Flemish Language. Penny M. **1**: 273, 282.
Flemish Market. All the Year, **28**: 582.
Flemish Painters, Early. Ecl. R. **106**: 393.
— Old. (E. Mason) Harper, **57**: 190, 807. **58**: 401.
Flemish popular Traditions. Ecl. R. **83**: 353.
Flemish Town, Old. (R. Bell) Once a Week, **3**: 463.
Flesh Color. All the Year, **44**: 160. Same art. Appleton, **23**: 268.

Flesh-Worm Disease. Once a Week, **14**: 385.
Fletcher, Andrew. Poetical Works. Retros. **4**: 100.
Fletcher, Calvin, with portrait. (W. B. Trask) N. E. Reg. **23**: 377.
Fletcher, Mrs. Eliza D. Chamb. J. **52**: 443.
Fletcher, Giles. New York R. **2**: 431.
Fletcher, John, and F. Beaumont. Temp. Bar, **42**: 460.
— Life and Works of. Brit. Q. **5**: 50.
Fletcher, John Wm., of Madeley. Mo. Rel. M. **24**: 328.
— Anecdotes of. Meth. M. **48**: 605.
— Benson's Life of. Chr. Obs. **4**: 349. — Ecl. R. **1**: 407.
— Life of. Chr. Obs. **22**: 193. New York R. **1**: 76.
— Works. Am. Meth. M. **15**: 406.
Fletcher, Joseph, Life and Writings of. Bib. R. **2**: 130.
— Memoir of. Cong. M. **26**: 701. — Ecl. R. **84**: 660.
Fletcher, Phineas. Purple Island. Retros. **2**: 341.
Fletcher, Richard. Am. Law R. **4**: 183.
Fletcher, Rev. Richard, Memoir of. Cong. M. **15**: 705.
Fletcher, Samuel, Sketch of. Good Words, **5**: 570.
Fletcher Genealogy. N. E. Reg. **22**: 389.
Fleur-de-Lys. House. Words, **18**: 438.
Fleur-de-Lys; a Tale. (L. de la Ramé) Broadw. **6**: 1.
Fleur-de-Lys; a Story of the Franco-Prussian War. Cornh. **24**: 294. Same art. Liv. Age, **111**: 169. Same art. Ev. Sat. **11**: 310, 334.
Fleur-de-Lys and the two Viscounts. (L. de la Ramé) Bentley, **48**: 227.
Fleur de Sillery. (J. De Legare) Knick. **44**: 390, 494.
Fleurange. (Mrs. R. Craven) Cath. World, **14**: 651, 813. **15**: 60–734. **16**: 18–737.
Fleuriste, La; an o'er-true Tale. Fraser, **32**: 268.
Fleury, André Hercule, Cardinal. Colburn, **128**: 291.
Fleury, A. J. Bénard, and French Stage. Mo. R. **155**: 43.
Flibustier, The; a German Tale. Dub. Univ. **2**: 179.
Fliedner, T., and the Order of Deaconesses. (D. S. Schaff) Mercersb. **22**: 193.
— Institution of, at Kaiserswerth. Am. J. Educ. **3**: 487.
Flies. *See after* Fly.
Flight, Natural and artificial. (J. B. Pettigrew) Fraser, **103**: 227.
— in the Dark; a Tale. Chamb. J. **42**: 273. Same art. Ecl. M. **65**: 227.
— of Diomed. (W. C. Bryant) Galaxy, **7**: 88.
— of Lady-Birds. Dub. Univ. **36**: 77.
Flinder, M. Voyage to Terra Australis. Quar. **12**: 1.
Flint, Austin, jr., Sketch of. Pop. Sci. Mo. **9**: 103.
Flint, Jacob. Historical Discourses. Chr. Disc. **4**: 121.
Flint, James. (J. W. Thompson) Chr. Exam. **58**: 443.
— Character of. (G. W. Briggs) Mo. Rel. M. **13**: 213.
— Lectures to Young. (E. B. Hall) Chr. Exam. **36**: 319.
Flint, Micah P. Poems. U. S. Lit. Gaz. **5**: 245.
Flint, Timothy. Journey from Cincinnati to Boston. Knick. **2**: 242.
— Lectures. Am. Mo. R. **3**: 261.
— Mississippi Valley. So. R. **2**: 192. — Quar. **48**: 201. — Mus. **22**: 218. — U. S. Lit. Gaz. **4**: 133. — Am. Mo. R. **4**: 460. — (J. Flint) No. Am. **23**: 355.
— Shoshonee Valley. West. Mo. R. **2**: 137, 420.
Flint, Ancient Family of. (H. Wright) Once a Week, **14**: 719.
Flint Genealogy. (J. L. Bass) N. E. Reg. **14**: 58.
Flint. (M. Schele de Vere) Putnam, **5**: 490.
— Age of; Chippers of Flint. Cornh. **41**: 189. Same art. Ecl. M. **94**: 599.
— Uses, in the Arts. Art J. **6**: 197.
— What is? Once a Week, **5**: 372.
Flints and their Evidence. Lond. Q. **37**: 150.
— of the upper Chalk. (J. R. Leifchild) Recr. Sci. **1**: 113.
— Worked, of Persigny le Grand. (J. Evans) Arch. **40**: 381.
Flint Chips. (A. Weld) Month, **12**: 736. **13**: 129, 583.
Flint Flakes of Devon and Cornwall, Date of. (S. Bate) Pop. Sci. R. **6**: 169. Same art. Ecl. M. **68**: 759.
Flint Implements. (C. C. King) Pop. Sci. R. **16**: 342.
— Evans on. Lond. Q. **40**: 80.
— from the Drift of Richmond, Va. (C. M. Wallace) Am. J. Sci. **111**: 195.
— from Egypt. (A. J. J. Brown) Anthrop. J. **7**: 396.
— in Beds of Gravel, etc. (J. Evans) Arch. **38**: 280.
— in the Drift. (J. Evans) Arch. **39**: 57.
See Stone Implements.
Flint Implement Station. (C. C. King) Anthrop. J. **2**: 365.
Flint Jack, *alias* Edward Simpson. (L. Jewitt) Reliquary, **8**: 65. — Chamb. J. **16**: 306. Same art. Ecl. M. **25**: 134. — All the Year, **17**: 259. — Internat. M. **5**: 74.
Flint Scalping-Knives in New Jersey. (C. C. Abbott) Nature, **12**: 368. **13**: 270.
Flint Tools of North Devon. Intel. Obs. **8**: 350.
Flint Weapons, True and false. (N. Whitley) Pop. Sci. R. **8**: 30.
Flirt's Failures; a Story. All the Year, **40**: 86.
Flirts and Flirtation. Chamb. J. **56**: 572. — Temp. Bar, **26**: 58.
— and their Ways. (R. E. Dembrey) Lippinc. **13**: 629.
— Didactic. Liv. Age, **140**: 574.
— Male. Tinsley, **1**: 352. — Liv. Age, **74**: 163.
Flirtation. Colburn, **50**: 53.
— and Fox-Chasing. (N. P. Willis) Godey, **25**: 224.
— Philosophy of. Fraser, **23**: 53. Same art. Mus. **42**: 340.
— Theory of. Cornh. **14**: 192. Same art. Ev. Sat. **2**: 210.
Flirtations of Captain Cavendish. Lond. Soc. **8**: 1.
Flirting. (L. M. Anderson) Potter Am. Mo. **13**: 379.
— an even Game. (A. Gould) Lakeside, **9**: 311.
Flitch of Bacon. (W. H. Ainsworth) Colburn, **97**: 3-395. **98**: 1. **100**: 379. **101**: 1.
Flitters, Tatters, and the Counselor. (M. Laffan) Lippinc. **23**: 50.
Flittermouse Well. Chamb. J. **52**: 779, 796.
Floating Beacon. Blackw. **10**: 270.
Floating Bodies, Equilibrium of. Ecl. Engin. **2**: 514.
Floating Islands. Chamb. J. **13**: 237.
— and Gardens. Penny M. **12**: 326.
Floating Martyr; a Poem. Temp. Bar, **9**: 600.
Flockhart, R., the Street Preacher. Tait, n. s. **25**: 470.
Flodden Field. (W. J. Walter) Godey, **20**: 220. — All the Year, **24**: 221.
— Legend of. Fraser, **32**: 469.
Floe; a Poem. (M. Seton) Colburn, **161**: 347.
Flogging, Punishment of. (J. R. Phillips) Gent. M. n. s. **14**: 355.
— and Impressment of Seamen. (T. P. Thompson) Westm. **20**: 489.
— Chapter on. Mus. **25**: 171.
— in the Army. (A. Forbes) 19th Cent. **6**: 604. — (W. Howitt) Peop. J. **2**: 78. — Fraser, **13**: 539, 645.
— — and Navy. Tait, n.s. **1**: 316, 573, 635. **3**: 675. **4**: 385.
— Napier's Experience in. Tait, n. s. **4**: 462.
— Napier on Military Law and. Mo. R. **143**: 380.
Flood, Henry, Letters of. Mo. R. **97**: 187. — Dub. Univ. **7**: 652, 880.
— Life of. Dub. R. **13**: 100.
— Public Career of. (G. L. Phillips) No. Am. **116**: 44.
Flood of 1859 and its Lessons. Chamb. J. **32**: 81.
— of Years; a Poem. (W. C. Bryant) Scrib. **12**: 560.
Floods. Once a Week, **5**: 520.
— of Morayshire, 1829. Westm. **13**: 350.
— Prevention of. Ecl. Engin. **9**: 65. **24**: 131. — (U. A. Forbes) Macmil. **43**: 321.
Floors and Floor Coverings. (R. Sturgis) Nation, **2**: 363.
— Fire-Proof. Ecl. Engin. **6**: 353.
— Lime, Mexican Method of making hard. (T. G. Ellis) Pract. M. **2**: 155. — (T. G. Ellis) J. Frankl. Inst. **95**: 339.

Floors of Paris, Pottery and Iron. (G. R. Burnell) J. Frankl. Inst. **49**: 55.
Floor Cloth, Manufacture of. Chamb. J. **11**: 392.— Penny M. **11**: 337. *See also* Carpets.
Flooring Boards. Am. Arch. **8**: 271.
Flor, Roger de; the Catalan Rover. Cornh. **20**: 452. Same art. Ecl. M. **74**: 17.
Flora. *See* Botany.
Floral Games. Tinsley, **15**: 139.
Floral Gems. (C. Sarbiewski) Temp. Bar, **34**: 346.
Floreal, The; May. Fraser, **45**: 501.
Floreal; a Poem. Dub. Univ. **52**: 153.
Floreen's golden Hair; a Story. (R. Mulholland) Irish Mo. **9**: 180.
Florence, Thomas B , with portrait. Dem. R. **28**: 173.
Florence, William J., with portrait. Colburn, **167**: 297.
Florence. Galaxy, **14**: 529. — (O. M. Spencer) Harper, **54**: 849. — Quar. **152**: 164. Same art. Liv. Age, **150**: 643. — (C. Gearcy) Victoria, **35**: 18–266.— (N. Colgan) Irish Mo. **6**: 325.
— Ancient Portraits in Gallery of. New Eng. M. **9**: 239.
— and the Medici. (J. A. Symonds) Fortn. **28**: 827. **29**: 277. Same art. Liv. Age, **136**: 67. **137**: 3.— Penny M. **13**: 210.
— architecturally and historically. Harper, **8**: 744.
— as it was, and as it is. (J. B. Atkinson) Art J. **27**: 133, 166, 197.
— At. Temp. Bar, **4**: 122.
— Cathedral of. Penny M. **4**: 180.
— Celebrities of, Mrs. Oliphant's. Lond. Q. **48**: 29.
— Christmas Eve at. (C. H. M. Bridge) Colburn, **168**: 229.
— Church of St. Mary of the Flower. (C. E. Norton) Atlan. **42**: 564, 657.
— the City of Lilies. Temp. Bar, **37**: 471.
— Council of. (P. Anderson) Month, **36**: 66. — Dub. R. **58**: 496.
— Description of. So. Lit. Mess. **19**: 229.
— Designs of the old Masters at. (A. C. Swinburne) Fortn. **10**: 16.
— Early Artists of. Art J. **10**: 289, 328.
— English Authors in. (K. Field) Atlan. **14**: 660.
— — in 1855. Scrib. **4**: 616.
— Fine Arts in. Quar. **66**: 313.
— Gallery of the Ponte Vecchio. Broadw. **7**: 19. — O. & N. **2**: 57.
— Gossip from, 1853. Colburn, **99**: 442.
— History of, Capponi's. (T. F. Crane) No. Am. **121**: 450.
— — Napier's. Ed. R. **86**: 465.
— — Trollope's. (O. Browning) Fortn. **4**: 70. — (H. T. Tuckerman) Chr. Exam. **81**: 332. — Victoria, **5**: 268, 324.
— — Villani's. Quar. **9**: 444.
— Horseback Ride from Calais to, 1839. Mo. R. **157**: 456.
— in 1858. Temp. Bar, **21**: 404.
— in Time of Dante. (E. M. Clerke) Dub. R. **85**: 279.
— Journey to. (N. Hawthorne) Ev. Sat. **11**: 438.
— Life in. Scrib. **20**: 283.
— Mosaics of. (F. M. Colby) Potter Am. Mo. **12**: 194. — (J. W. Mario) Nation, **3**: 476. — (J. L. Motley) Atlan. **1**: 12, 129.
— New Capital of Italy. Ecl. M. **65**: 90.
— Notes on. Fraser, **74**: 411. Same art. Ecl. M. **68**: 83.
— Orphanage at. (E. L. Linton) Belgra. **37**: 334.
— Painters of the second Period. Art J. **11**: 33.
— Protestant Cemetery at. (O. M. Spencer) Harper, **47**: 507. — Liv. Age, **147**: 124.
— Reminiscences of. (M. Howland) Lippinc. **11**: 95.
— Republic of. Ed. R. **143**: 474.
— Revolution in. All the Year, **1**: 221.
— Romance of. (T. A. Trollope) Ev. Sat. **8**: 257.
— Romola and. Ev. Sat. **17**: 149.
— St. Pancras in. All the Year, **23**: 368.
Florence, Schools in. (F. H. Muller) Macmil. **44**: 480. Same art. Liv. Age, **151**: 341. Same art. Appleton, **26**: 507.
— Seventeenth-Century Chronicle of. (T. A. Trollope) Temp. Bar, **29**: 97.
— Siege of, 1529–60. Cornh. **31**: 316. Same art. Ecl. M. **84**: 561. Same art. Liv. Age, **125**: 46.
— Studios in. Once a Week, **9**: 721. **10**: 388.
— A Tale of. Dub. Univ. **49**: 689.
— Visit to. (R. W. Dale) Cong. **3**: 75. — (W. Hague) Knick. **20**: 295.
— Walks in. Macmil. **29**: 206. Same art. Ecl. M. **82**: 357.
— Week in. Blackw. **86**: 583.
Florence Athern's Trial; a Tale. (M. Meline) Cath. World, **7**: 213.
Florence O'Brien. Tait, n. s. **3**: 46–361.
Florentine Arithmetician. (R. G. White) Galaxy, **24**: 806.
Florentine Bridal Chamber. (J. Cartwright) Portfo. **9**: 21.
Florentine Experiment. (C. F. Woolson) Atlan. **46**: 502.
Florentine Family of 15th Century. *See* Strozzi.
Flores Poetici. Blackw. **8**: 395.
Florescence, Nature of. (E. Sommel) Pop. Sci Mo. **8**: 471.
Floretta; or the first Love of Henry IV. (H. Zschokke) So. Lit. Mess. **9**: 149.
Florian's William Tell. Quar. **2**: 338.
Floriculture. *See* Flowers; Gardening.
Florida. (E. King) Scrib. **9**: 1. — (N. Hale) No. Am. **13**: 62. — (J. Gadsden) No. Am. **26**: 478. — Am. Q. **2**: 214. — So. R. **6**: 410. — Anal. M. **14**: 203. — De Bow, **4**: 244. — (E. R. Fairbanks) De Bow, **5**: 9. — (J. D. B. De Bow) De Bow, **7**: 297. — De Bow, **10**: 404. — Portfo. (Den.) **25**: 99. — (J. P. Little) Lippinc. **5**: 420. **8**: 487.
— Agency of the Gulf Stream in the Formation of. (J. LeConte) Am. J. Sci. **73**: 46.
— Among the Alligators. (S. C. Clarke) Lippinc. **13**: 220.
— and Carolina, 1688. Hist. M. **3**: 298.
— Bow-Shots on the St. John's. (M. Thompson) Appleton, **15**: 328.
— Canal across. (R. Fairbanks) De Bow, **14**: 123.
— Cession of. Pamph. **15**: 261. — Niles's Reg. **16**: 314.
— Climate, Soil, and Productions of. De Bow, **11**: 409.
— Conquest of, Irving's. Mo. R. **138**: 284. — Am. Mo. M. **5**: 319.
— Day's Sport in East. (S. C. Clarke) Lippinc. **12**: 663.
— Diary of a Campaign in, 1837–38. (E. Backus) Hist. M. **10**: 279.
— Early Settlement of. (J. B. Allston) So. M. **11**: 113.
— East. Niles's Reg. **13**: 189. — (H. Whiting) Am. J. Sci. **35**: 47. — Knick. **23**: 45.
— — Lands of. So. Q. **26**: 304.
— Election Frauds, 1876. (E. L. Godkin) Nation, **26**: 286.
— English Sportsman in. Appleton, **13**: 257, 296, 334.
— Expedition of Narvaez to. Hist. M. **11**: 24. **12**: 109–347.
— Expedition to, 1864. U. S. Serv. M. **2**: 150.
— Fairbanks's History of. (J. F. Meline) Nation, **12**: 438.
— First Colonists of. (J. T. Headley) Harper, **20**: 503.
— Flora of Southern. (F. Brendel) Am. Natural. **8**: 449.
— Geology of. (E. A. Smith) Am. J. Sci. **121**: 292.
— Glance at. (K. N. Doggett) Lakeside, **2**: 223.
— Gulf Stream off, Anomalies in. (E. B. Hunt) Am. J. Sci. **77**: 206.
— How to go to, and where to stay. (J. P. Little) Lippinc. **6**: 605.
— Huguenots in. (F. Parkman) Atlan. **12**: 225, 536.
— in 1821. Niles's Reg. **20**: 353, 404. **21**: 135, 149.
— the Key of the Gulf. De Bow, **21**: 283.
— Lakes of. (L. S. Houghton) Lippinc. **26**: 265.
— Land of Flowers. (A. Plumassier) Potter Am. Mo. **12**: 401.
— Laws of 1821. Niles's Reg. **21**: 89.

Florida, Legislature of, 1822. Niles's Reg. 23: 23.
— Life in. Knick. 8: 150, 276, 552.
— — Phase of. (M. Treat) Lippinc. 25: 460.
— Maroons of. (S. G. Arnold) Meth. Q. 20: 554.
— Medical Topography of. (E. T. Gaillard) De Bow, 19: 255. 20: 315.
— Memorial of Alonzo Vasquez on. Hist. M. 4: 257.
— Military Command in, 1822. Niles's Reg. 22: 121.
— Mission in, Rogel's Acct. of, 1569–70. Hist. M. 5: 327.
— Physical Features of. (W. I. Burnett) Am. J. Sci. 67: 407.
— Plantation in, Our. (H. B. Stowe) Atlan. 43: 641.
— Position, Resources, and Destiny of. De Bow, 14: 312.
— Rambles in. (R. E. C. Stearns) Am. Natural. 3: 281–455.
— Romantic History of. (G. R. Fairbanks) De Bow, 24: 245, 274, 376.
— Shell Mounds of, Wyman on. Nature, 14: 531.
— Seizure of, 1820. Niles's Reg. 18: 46.
— Six Weeks in. (G. W. Nichols) Harper, 41: 655.
— Soil and Products of. West. J. 6: 178.
— Statistics of, 1869. Am. J. Educ. 18: 306.
— Treaty. Niles's Reg. 22: 120.
— Truth about. (L. S. Houghton) Lippinc. 27: 508.
— Vengeance of Gourgues. (F. Parkman) Atlan. 14: 530.
— War in. (H. Whiting) No. Am. 54: 1. — Niles's Reg. 14: 33, 79, 98.
See Ocklawaha.
Florida Keys. Putnam, 8: 561.
— and Southern Coast, Geology of. (M. Tuomey) Am. J. Sci. 61: 390.
— Flora and Fauna of. (L. F. de Pourtalès) Am. Natural. 11: 137.
Florida Pirate. Blackw. 9: 516.
Florida Reef, Along the. (J. B. Holder) Harper, 42: 355–820. 43: 26, 187.
— Origin of. (E. B. Hunt) Am. J. Sci. 85: 197.
— Out on. (J. Wilder) Atlan. 22: 176.
Florida Reefs and Keys. (S. C. Clarke) Lippinc. 13: 484.
— Solidification of the Rocks of. (E. N. Horsford) Am. J. Sci. 64: 245.
— Wrecks on. Hunt, 6: 349.
— — in 1846. Hunt, 19: 427.
— — in 1847. Hunt, 18: 552.
Florio; a little Tragedy. Blackw. 130: 179. Same art. Ecl. M. 97: 486.
Flossy Venner. (A. A. Farmer) Canad. Mo. 8: 413.
Flotow, Friederich von, and Wagner. Ev. Sat. 9: 535.
Flotsam and Jetsam. (H. P. Spofford) Atlan. 21: 7, 186, 313. — Chamb. J. 37: 296.
Flounders, Development of. (A. Agassiz) Am. Natural. 10: 705.
Flour and Wheat, Export of, 1843. Hunt, 9: 91.
— — Prices of, from 1839 to 1846. Hunt, 15: 214.
— Price of, in New York, 1823–45. Hunt, 13: 290.
— Prices of, for the last twenty Years. Hunt, 19: 547.
Flour-Mill, Aubin's. Pract. M. 6: 6.
Flour-Mill Explosions. (S. Macadam) Ecl. Engin. 9: 364. — Pract. M. 1: 464.
Flourishing. (W. Sawyer) Belgra. 6: 117.
Flow of Solids. (H. Tresca) Ecl. Engin. 19: 326. 20: 15. — (H. Tresca) J. Frankl. Inst. 106: 263, 326, 396.
— — through Apertures. J. Frankl. Inst. 81: 271.
Flower, Edward F., with portrait. Victoria, 31: 67.
Flower in a dark Place. (M. B. Williams) Lakeside, 10: 408.
— of Berney; a Tale. (K. S. Macquoid) Temp. Bar, 42: 334.
— of Liberty; a Poem. (O. W. Holmes) Atlan. 8: 550.
— of Love lies bleeding; a Poem. (R. H. Stoddard) Scrib. 7: 545.
— of the Ruins. (F. Caballero) Colburn, 146: 168.
Flower of Souvenance. (W. J. Walter) Godey, 22: 157.
Flowers. (H. T. Tuckerman) Godey, 40: 13. — Cath. World, 13: 305. — Chamb. J. 55: 566. — Once a Week, 18: 141. — West. M. 2: 435.
— and Birds in Poetry. Canad. Mo. 6: 78.
— and Exotics at Sydenham. Chamb. J. 22: 211.
— and foreign Flower-Fashions. Lond. Soc. 7: 489. Same art. Ecl. M. 65: 189.
— and Insects. (G. W. Bennett) Pop. Sci. R. 14: 113.
— — Geological Antiquity of. (J. E. Taylor) Pop. Sci. R. 17: 36.
— — Relation between. (H. Müller) Nature, 15: 178.
— and old Customs. St. James, 25: 533.
— and their unbidden Guests, Kerner's. (A. W. Bennett) Nature, 19: 214. — Chamb. J. 56: 289.
— Arrangement of. Lond. Soc. 1: 11, 251. 2: 30, 314. 3: 62–552. — Contin. Mo. 2: 444.
— Artificial. *See* Artificial Flowers.
— Artificial Fecundation of. (C. G. Page) West. J. 11: 408.
— as religious Emblems. Cath. World, 9: 541.
— Ceremonial Use of. (A. Lambert) 19th Cent. 4: 457. Same art. Liv. Age, 139: 131. — (A. Lambert) 19th Cent. 7: 808.
— Colors of. Chamb. J. 31: 17.
— Cultivation of. (M. Howland) O. & N. 8: 435. — (P. Henderson) Scrib. 22: 219. — All the Year, 28: 112. — Lond. Q. 24: 50.
— Darwin's Different Forms of. Nature, 17: 445.
— Decoration with. Art J. 30: 345.
— Economic Uses of. (P. L. Simonds) Pract. M. 7: 299.
— Facts and Fables about. Chamb. J. 22: 117.
— Feast of. (L. Jewitt) Belgra. 8: 567.
— Fertilization of. (T. C. Gentry) Am. Natural. 9: 263. — (T. Meehan) Penn Mo. 7: 834.
— — by Insects. (E. Muller) Am. Natural. 5: 271. — (H. Müller) Nature, 15: 317, 473. 16: 507. — (W. Ogle) Pop. Sci. R. 9: 160.
— — Contrivances for Cross-Fertilization. (J. E. Todd) Am. Natural. 13: 1.
See Fertilization.
— for a Child's Grave. Irish Mo. 8: 545, 601, 649.
— for the Poor. (I. E. Clarke) Good Words, 2: 551. — (M. Stanley) Macmil. 27: 525.
— Fruits and Trees, Freaks upon. Liv. Age, 20: 178.
— Gossip about. All the Year, 7: 414.
— Home. Chamb. J. 53: 241.
— How to dissect. (M. C. Cooke) Pop. Sci. R. 7: 142.
— in Churches. Chr. Rem. 14: 115.
— in London. (Lady Pollock) Temp. Bar, 56: 188.
— in Paris. Lond. Soc. 18: 129. — Ev. Sat. 9: 551.
— in the Snow; a Story. (C. F. Woolson) Galaxy, 17: 76.
— Language of. So. Lit. Mess, 7: 385.
— Legends of. (S. Wohl) Good Words, 14: 489, 543.
— Life of. Brit. Q. 34: 95.
— May, near London. (C. A. White) St. James, 10: 191.
— Means of Protection in. Nature, 15: 237.
— Microscope among. (S. B. Herrick) Scrib. 13: 530.
— Odors of. (B. Abbott) Recr. Sci. 1: 340. — Contin. Mo. 6: 469.
— of the Affections. Dub. Univ. 42: 276.
— of the Bible. (L. H. Grindon) Dub. Univ. 90: 84.
— of February. Dub. Univ. 41: 184.
— of early Spring. (J. W. Chickering, jr.) Am. Natural. 3: 128.
— of New England. (C. J. Sprague) Putnam, 3: 535.
— of St. Chad; a Tale. Sharpe, 30: 196.
— Origin of. (G. Allen) Cornh. 37: 534. Same art. Sup. Pop. Sci. Mo. 3: 151.
— Peculiarities of. Hogg, 6: 144.
— Poetry of. Colburn, 5: 401.
— Poisonous. House. Words, 14: 234.

Flowers, Preservation of. Penny M. **14**: 262.
— Procession of. (T. W. Higginson) Atlan. **10**: 649.
— Romance of. Hours at Home, **1**: 266.
— Sacred. (M. D. Conway) Harper, **41**: 731, 891. **42**: 87. — Quar. **114**: 210.
— Sea-Side. Cath. World, **4**: 621.
— Spring, of Colorado. (E. L. Greene) Am. Natural. **5**: 65.
— — of New England. (C. J. Sprague) Putnam, **5**: 398.
— Talk about. (M. Morgan) Canad. Mo. **20**: 459.
— Use of. Chamb. J. **58**: 383.
— Utility to, of their Beauty. (E. Fry) Contemp. **36**: 574. Same art. Liv. Age, **144**: 151.
— Wild, Associations of. (H. G. Adams) Hogg, **1**: 278.
— — and Insects. (Sir J. Lubbock) Nature, **10**: 402, 422.
— — Cultivation of. (S. Lockwood) Pop. Sci. Mo. **2**: 356.
— — of January and Feb. (H. G. Adams) Hogg, **2**: 413.
— — of March. Temp. Bar, **28**: 510.
— — of July. (H. G. Adams) Hogg, **1**: 361.
— — of September. (H. G. Adams) Hogg, **2**: 61.
— — of October. (H. G. Adams) Hogg. **2**: 152.
— Worship of. Chamb. J. **8**: 165.
Flower-Bells. House. Words, **8**: 196.
Flower-Farming in South of France. Cornh. **10**: 427.
Flower Garden. (T. James) Quar. **70**: 196. Same art. Liv. Age, **19**: 241.
— English. Quar. **149**: 331. Same art. Liv. Age, **145**: 771.
— near the Alps. St. James, **28**: 584.
Flower Markets of Paris, Three. Fraser, **39**: 259.
Flower Mission. (M. B. Carret) Unita. R. **1**: 456. — Chamb. J. **53**: 678. — (Miss Stanley) Macmil. **29**: 564.
— Boston. (E. Gray) Harper, **48**: 787.
Flower Missions and Missions of Flowers. (A. H. Japp) Good Words, **19**: 646.
Flower-Painter, First; a Legend of Sicyon. Fraser, **33**: 72.
Flower-Show at West End. (R. Rowe) Good Words, **9**: 515.
Flower-Shows, Workingmen's. (C. Barnard) O. & N. **5**: 507.
Flower-Spirit; a Faëry Tale. Lond. M. **8**: 131.
Flower Story. (R. Quiddam) St. James, **40**: 542.
Flowering Sunday. Belgra. **16**: 65.
Floy, James. (D. Curry) Meth. Q. **24**: 111.
Floyd, William. (F. De Peyster) M. Am. Hist. **1**: 429.
Fluctuations of Markets, Rationale of. (G. Walker) Nation, **22**: 398.
Flues, Collapse of. (C. R. Roelker) Ecl. Engin. **24**: 208.
Fluids, Elastic, Expansion of. (E. W. Blake) Am. J. Sci. **59**: 334. — J. Frankl. Inst. **9**: 339.
— — Flow of. (J. E. Hendricks) Am. J. Sci. **65**: 378. — (E. W. Blake) Am. J. Sci. **66**: 80.
— — — through Orifices. (E. W Blake) Am. J. Sci. **55**: 78. **62**: 186.
— Ellipsoid Revolution of. (T. Craig) J. Frankl. Inst. **111**: 500.
— Flow of, through Nozzles. (R. D. Napier) Ecl. Engin. **15**: 240.
— Friction of. (W. Froude) Ecl. Engin. **2**: 480.
— — Resistance of. (G. Rennie) J. Frankl. Inst. **13**: 271.
— in Minerals. Hogg, **2**: 113.
— Motion of. (O. Reynolds) Nature, **21**: 343.
— — Mathematical Theory of. (T. Craig) Ecl. Engin. **20**: 113–506. **21**: 146–486.
— Pressure Regulator for, Casement's. Pract. M. **3**: 459.
— Resistance of. Ecl. Engin. **4**: 431, 546. — (L. R. Gibbes) Am. J. Sci. **27**: 135. — (A. Bourne) Am. J. Sci. **28**: 231. — (E. W. Blake) Am. J. Sci. **29**: 274. **30**: 359. — (G. W. Keely) Am. J. Sci. **30**: 164. — So. R. **8**: 114.
— — to a Ship's Motion. Ecl. Engin. **13**: 438.
— Upward Forces of. (F. Pascalis) Am. J. Sci. **11**: 110. — (E. C. Genet) Am. J. Sci. **12**: 94, 310. — (T. P. Jones) Am. J. Sci. **13**: 79.
Fluids, Upward Forces of, Genet on. J. Frankl. Inst. **2**: 41. **3**: 33. **4**: 104, 170.
— Viscous Motion of. (T. Craig) J. Frankl. Inst. **110**: 217.
Flukes. (T. S. Cobbold) Intel. Obs. **1**: 24.
Flunkey. Chamb. J. **15**: 92.
Flunkeyism, Intellectual. (T. H. S. Escott) Temp. Bar, **17**: 539.
Fluorescence. (H. Morton) J. Frankl. Inst. **92**: 140, 426. — Nature, **18**: 107.
— and Phosphorescence. (M. Faraday) J. Frankl. Inst. **69**: 270.
— — shown by Photography. (M. N. de St. Victor) J. Frankl. Inst. **65**: 50.
Fluorescent Relations of Anthracene and Chrysogen. (H. Morton) J. Frankl. Inst. **94**: 269.
Fluorine. (E. Mylius) J. Frankl. Inst. **103**: 71, 212.
Flush Times in Alabama and Mississippi. (J. G. Baldwin) So. Lit. Mess. **18**: 433, 558, 746. **19**: 10–599.
Flushing, Fast in. Tinsley, **4**: 410.
Flute, The. Penny M. **9**: 170.
Fluxions, Dealtry's. Quar. **5**: 340. — Ed. R. **27**: 87. — Ecl. R. **13**: 390.
— Theory of. (E. Wright) Am. J. Sci. **14**: 330.
Fly, Abyssinian, or Tsaltzala. Colburn, **142**: 444.
— Blow, Structure of. Stud. & Intel. Obs. **5**: 28.
— House. (A. S. Packard, jr.) Am. Natural. **10**: 476. — (C. Taylor) Harper, **18**: 729.
— — Development of. (M. H. Robson) Pop. Sci. Mo. **15**: 618.
— Viviparous. (S. Lockwood) Am. Natural. **7**: 193.
Flies. All the Year, **8**: 6. — Blackw. **24**: 832.
— Antennæ of. (Mrs. L. L. Clarke) Recr. Sci. **2**: 134.
— Chapter on. (A. S. Packard, jr.) Am. Natural. **2**: 586, 638. — (J. P. Anthony) Pioneer, **2**: 348.
— Heads of. (Mrs. L. L. Clarke) Recr. Sci. **2**: 95.
— in Amber. (R. Hunt) Sharpe, **17**: 157, 301. **18**: 65. Same art. Ecl. M. **35**: 140.
— Metamorphosis of. (A. Weissman) Am. Natural. **8**: 603, 661, 713.
— Structure and Habits of. (L. M. Peterselia) Scrib. **1**: 621.
Fly-Bees. (H. N. Humphreys) Intel. Obs. **1**: 165.
Fly-Fishing. *See* Fishing.
Flying. All the Year, **19**: 281, 300.
— and Flying-Machines. Cornh. **24**: 438. Same art Ecl. M. **78**: 11.
— Flight and its Imitation. (F. W. Brearey) Pop. Sci. R **18**: 395.
— Mechanics of. (L. Kargl) Ecl. Engin. **4**: 346, 530.
— Mechanism of Flight. (W. K. Brooks) Pop. Sci. Mo. **4**: 686.
— Modes of. Penny M. **2**: 11.
— Notes on. Temp. Bar, **3**: 564.
— Researches on. (J. Murie) Nature, **4**: 516.
Flying Artist. House. Words, **3**: 557.
Flying Bridge. House. Words, **5**: 466.
Flying Dutchman. Ev. Sat. **11**: 343.
Flying Fish, Movements of. Nature, **18**: 373. — (C. O. Whitman) Am. Natural. **14**: 641.
Flying Island; a Legend of New England. Colburn, **45**: 38.
Flying-Machines. (F. W. Brearey) Pop. Sci. R. **8**: 1. Same art. Ecl. Engin. **1**: 324. — (A. M. Mayer) Pop. Sci. Mo. **8**: 453. — Chamb. J. **9**: 300. **51**: 590.
— and Birds. So. R. n. s. **8**: 78.
— and Penaud's Artificial Bird. (A. M. Mayer) J. Frankl. Inst. **101**: 193.
— First Principles of Aerial Transit. (F. H. Wenham) Pop. Sci. R. **13**: 362. Same art. Ecl. M. **84**: 111.
See also Aerostation; Balloons.
Flying Men, Race of. So. R. n. s. **10**: 272.
Flying Post; a Tale from the Danish. Temp. Bar, **44**: 59.

Fly-Wheels, Deviating Forces of. (A. Briggs) J. Frankl. Inst. **104**: 349.
— Strength of. (O. Kruger) Ecl. Engin. **8**: 171.
Fly-Wheel Bob; a Tale. (W. Seton) Cath. World, **24**: 198.
Foe in the Household. (C. Chesebrough) Atlan. **23**: 323–686. **24**: 26–722.
Foerster, Friedrich. (E. V. Valentine) So. M. **14**: 144.
Foerster, Wm. Philosophical Discourses. (C. W. Ernst) Radical R. **1**: 361.
Fog. (W. H. Stone) Pop. Sci. R. **20**: 27.
— London. (J. V. Blake) Am. Natural. **5**: 76.
— — Observations in. Hogg, **15**: 53.
Fogs. All the Year, **28**: 175. — Nature, **21**: 355. — Colburn, **162**: 55.
— Clouds, and Dust. (J. Aitken) Nature, **23**: 195.
— Dry. Chamb. J. **9**: 307.
Fog-Signals. (J. Tyndall) Nature, **17**: 456. — Chamb. J. **40**: 269.
— American. J. Frankl. Inst. **101**: 37.
— at Sea. Chamb. J. **50**: 453.
— by Land and Sea. Cornh. **21**: 477.
— Investigations on. (W. B. Tayler) No. Am. **122**: 403. — (J. Tyndall) Pop. Sci. Mo. **13**: 275.
Fog-Signaling. (J. Tyndall) Contemp. **24**: 819. **25**: 148. Same art. Pop. Sci. Mo. **6**: 541, 685.
Fogie Club, Prospectus of. Blackw. **59**: 621.
Foley, John Henry. Irish Mo. **9**: 165, 221.
Foley, Richard, Sketch of. Once a Week, **21**: 448.
Folger, Walter. (W. Mitchell) Am. J. Sci. **59**: 313.
Folger Genealogy. (W. C. Folger) N. E. Reg. **16**: 269.
Folger Surname. (G. Woods) N. E. Reg. **9**: 308.
Folia sibyllina. Dub. Univ. **1**: 139, 317.
Foliage, Various Tints of. (H. C. Sorby) Nature, **4**: 341.
Folingsby's Pond. (J. T. Headley) Hours at Home, **9**: 352, 427.
Folios, In Praise of. So. Lit. J. **4**: 59.
Folk Books of France. Dub. Univ. **66**: 516. **67**: 243.
— of Ireland. Dub. Univ. **67**: 532.
Folk Dirges. Cornh. **36**: 196.
Folk Lore. Colburn, **89**: 162. — Ecl. R. **113**: 637. — Month, **8**: 370. — So. R. n. s. **13**: 153.
— Comparative. (J. A. Farrar) Cornh. **33**: 41.
— Contributions to. Ecl. R. **124**: 461.
— Cornish. Ecl. R. **122**: 179.
— in Aubrey's Miscellanies. (T. T. Wilkinson) Reliquary, **10**: 147.
— Lip-Lore of our Forefathers. (S. Wilson) Victoria, **12**: 507.
— of British Plants. (J. Mason) Dub. Univ. **82**: 313–668. **83**: 63, 179.
— of Christianity. (F. R. Conder) Dub. Univ. **90**: 641.
— of a Country Parson. (E. Bradley) Once a Week, **2**: 72.
— of Cyprus. (W. Axon) Dub. Univ. **80**: 25.
— of Devonshire. (R. J. King) Fraser, **88**: 773.
— of Donegal. (L. McClintock) Dub. Univ. **88**: 607. **89**: 241. — Cornh. **35**: 172.
— of Esthonia. Dub. Univ. **70**: 704.
— of Europe. Dub. Univ. **71**: 317.
— of far-off Lands. (H. S. Fagan) Belgra. **22**: 285.
— of Germany. Dub. Univ. **72**: 347.
— of the Hindus. Dub. Univ. **71**: 455.
— of Hungary. Dub. Univ. **70**: 141, 575.
— of Ireland. Dub. Univ. **68**: 699. **69**: 3, 347, 639.
— — Poetic. (W. Barry) St. Paul's, **12**: 449. Same art. Ecl. M. **80**: 707. Same art. Ev. Sat. **14**: 471.
— of Italy. Dub. Univ. **72**: 705. **73**: 184.
— of the Mongols. Dub. Univ. **73**: 591.
— of the North American Indians. Ecl. M. **71**: 1460.
— of the Northern Counties. Bentley, **61**: 169.
— of Norway. (P. Toft) Overland, **9**: 419.
— of Russia. Quar. **136**: 235. — St. James. **30**: 357.
Folk Lore of Scotland. Ecl. R. **113**: 506.
— — of the West Highlands. Dub. Univ. **69**: 182. — Chamb. J. **56**: 501.
— of the Sclavonic Races. Dub. Univ. **70**: 123, 473, 710.
— of Servia. Good Words, **13**: 579–822.
— of Sicily. All the Year, **36**: 582.
— of Southern Negroes. (W. Owens) Lippinc. **20**: 748.
— — Uncle Remus. (T. F. Crane) Pop. Sci. Mo. **18**: 824.
— of Ulster. Dub. Univ. **89**: 747.
— of various Races. Chr. Rem. **54**: 33.—Lond. Q. **31**: 45.
— Oriental. Dub. Univ. **74**: 120.
— Origin and Meaning of. Temp. Bar, **6**: 549. **7**: 438.
— Origins of. (J. Fiske) Atlan. **27**: 145.
— Sicilian. (T. F. Crane) Lippinc. **18**: 433.
— Some Representative. Dub. Univ. **77**: 8.
— Study of. Liv. Age, **94**: 707.
See Water-Tales.
Folk Lullabies. (E. Carrington) Fraser, **103**: 87. Same art. Ecl. M. **96**: 405. Same art. Potter Am. Mo. **16**: 252.
Folk Songs. (J. V. Blake) Putnam, **16**: 441.
— Armenian. Fraser, **93**: 283.
— Dravidian. Cornh. **24**: 570. Same art. Liv. Age, **111**: 672.
— English. (J. V. Blake) Atlan. **31**: 129.
— of Sicily. Cornh. **35**: 443.
— of Southern India. (J. Avery) New Eng. **32**: 507.
Follen, Charles. Inaugural Discourse. (G. Ripley) Chr. Exam. **11**: 373. — Am. Mo. R. **1**: 104.
— Discourse on. (W. E. Channing) Chr. Exam. **28**: 68.
— Life and Character of. Dial, **3**: 343.
— — and Writings of. Dem. R. **7**: 466. — (W. Ware) Chr. Exam. **28**: 87. — (W. H. Channing) Chr. Exam. **33**: 33.
Follen, Mrs. E. L. Gammer Grethel. Chr. Exam. **28**: 267.
Follett, Sir William. (S. Warren) Blackw. **59**: 1. — Fraser, **32**: 165. — Dub. Univ. **20**: 117.
Follette; a Tale. (K. O'Meara) Cath. World, **30**: 201–753. **31**: 65, 172.
Folly, Sketches of. Colburn, **41**: 181.
Follies of the Wise. (W. C. Russell) Temp. Bar, **44**: 85. Same art. Ecl. M. **85**: 186.
Following up the Track; a Tale. Chamb. J. **53**: 569–667.
Folquet de Marseille, Bishop. Colburn, **157**: 357.
Folsom, Nathaniel. (C. H. Bell) Pennsyl. M. **2**: 436.
Folsom Family. (N. S. Folsom) N. E. Reg. **30**: 207.
Fonblanque, Albany, his Place in English Journalism. (T. H. S. Escott) Fraser, **89**: 635.—Ev. Sat. **13**: 550.
Font, Ancient, at Bridekirk. (C. Lyttelton) Arch. **2**: 131. — (H. Howard) Arch. **14**: 113.
— at Burnham Deepdale. (S. Pegge) Arch. **10**: 177.
— in South Kilvington Church. (R. D. Waddilove) Arch. **16**: 341.
— in Thorpe Salvin Church. (R. Holden and F. Douce) Arch. **12**: 207.
Fonts, Ancient, Letters on. (S. Carte) Arch. **10**: 208.
— Observations on. (S. Denne) Arch. **11**: 108. — (R. Gough) Arch. **10**: 183.
— Specimens of, from different Churches. (J. A. Repton) Arch. **16**: 335.
Fontain, James. Story of a French Refugee. (W. Chambers) Chamb. J. **50**: 260.
Fontainebleau. (K. O'Meara) Cath. World, **17**: 241, 382. — (A. L. Bassett) Potter Am. Mo. **16**: 149. — Bentley, **56**: 499. — Lond. Soc. **38**: 224.
— Chateau and Forest of. (A. Ladley) Harper, **44**: 30.
— Forest of. Bentley, **56**: 303. Same art. Ecl. M. **63**: 342. — Westm. **86**: 445.
— From. Belgra. **33**: 92.
— Old; a Poem. St. James, **28**: 658.
— Palace of. Colburn, **105**: 462. Same art. Ecl. M. **37**: 145. — Liv. Age, **21**: 113.

Fontainebleau, Scene at. Chamb. J. **15**: 137.
— under Louis XIII. and Napoleon I. Colburn, **106**: 223. Same art. Ecl. M. **37**: 481.
Fontainebleau; a Poem. (B. R. Parkes) Good Words, **5**: 224.
Fontenaye, Battle of, A. D. 841. (Sir E. Creasy) Temp. Bar, **30**: 109. Same art. Ecl. M. **75**: 458. Same art. Liv. Age, **106**: 643.
Fontenoy, Battle of, Irish Brigade in. Fraser, **86**: 732.
Fonthill Abbey. Dub. Univ. **76**: 196. — Lond. M. **6**: 405.
— Day at. Colburn, **6**: 368–403.
Foochow. Penny M. **12**: 108.
— Street Scene in. All the Year, **47**: 129.
Food. Victoria, **16**: 386. — Chamb. J. **52**: 268. — Irish Q. **8**: 1103. — (T. Robinson) St. James, **49**: 128. — Tait, n. s. **20**: 659.
— Adulterations of. *See* Adulterations.
— and Animal Force. (J. Broughton) Intel. Obs. **9**: 432.
— and Development. (O. Ule) Pop. Sci. Mo. **5**: 591.
— and Dietetics, Pavy's. Nature, **10**: 60.
— and Drink. Blackw. **83**: 325–515. — Liv. Age, **57**: 323, 674, 850.
— — in Shakspere's Time. House. Words, **17**: 304.
— and Fasting. Chamb. J. **57**: 545.
— and Feeding. (Sir H. Thompson) 19th Cent. **5**: 971. **6**: 99. Same art. Pop. Sci. Mo. **15**: 377–620. Same art. Month, **36**: 587. Same art. Liv. Age, **142**: 243, 337.
— and Health. Cornh. **9**: 224.
— and its Effects, Drewry on. Dub. Univ. **88**: 248.
— and its Preparation. Nat. Q. **14**: 84.
— and Medicine, Frauds in. Ecl. M. **42**: 81.
— and Numbers of animated Nature. Blackw. **38**: 109.
— Animal. *See* Animal Food.
— Animals killed or dying of Disease as. Cornh. **7**: 414.
— Articles of. (R. Whately) Good Words, **3**: 30.
— Consumption of, in United Kingdom. Ed. R. **99**: 581.
— Cosmopolite Bill of Fare. (C. Nordhoff) Harper, **18**: 653.
— Curiosities of. (F. L. Oswald) Pop. Sci. Mo. **14**: 721. **15**: 30.
— — of Fashion in. Lond. Soc. **11**: 334. Same art. Ev. Sat. **3**: 472.
— Curious Ways of getting. (H. L. Fairchild) Pop. Sci. Mo. **16**: 770.
— Dependence of Life upon. (W. B. Carpenter) Howitt, **2**: 56, 102, 138.
— Deficiency of, Howard on. Mo. R. **151**: 44.
— Development of human. (W. B. Adams) Once a Week, **8**: 138.
— Dietary Schools. Pop. Sci. Mo. **1**: 590.
— Digestibility of. (C. Voit) Pop. Sci. Mo. **1**: 308.
— Digestion and. (A. L. Carroll) Harper, **39**: 892.
— Dinner Question. Bentley, **45**: 166.
— Economical. (J. M. Fothergill) Good Words, **21**: 18, 123.
— Economizers of. Chamb. J. **48**: 503.
— Excess and Want of. Cornh. **8**: 35.
— Fat and lean. Irish Q. **8**: 865.
— Follies in. (H. Martineau) Once a Week, **1**: 299.
— French. Blackw. **111**: 121. Same art. Liv. Age, **112**: 800.
— Fruits and Vegetables as. (A. J. H. Crespi) Tinsley, **19**: 179.
— Functions of. (G. Allen) Belgra. **38**: 31.
— Future Supply of Great Britain. (R. Wilkes) Canad. Mo. **18**: 113.
— Good. (E. Lankester) Pop. Sci. R. **4**: 14.
— Grisenthwaite on. Mo. R. **147**: 340.
— Hassall on. Nature, **13**: 345.
— History of. (G. B. Griffith) Potter Am. Mo. **10**: 433.
Food; how to eat Bread. (L. S. Bevington) 19th Cent. **10**: 341. Same art. Ecl. M. **97**: 688.
— how to take it. Cornh. **4**: 281.
— in all Ages and Countries. Nat. M. **4**: 147.
— John Bull at Feed. (W. J. Stillman) Atlan. **26**: 748.
— Liebig's Chemistry of. Dub. R. **25**: 179. — Chamb. J. **8**: 293.
— Liebig's Theory of. Cornh. **6**: 547.
— Man and his. (L. Withington) Bib. Sac. **11**: 139.
— Metamorphoses of. All the Year, **5**: 6.
— Modern Bill of Fare. (T. B. Thorpe) Harper, **41**: 606.
— Monopoly of. Westm. **20**: 378.
— Nature and Composition of. (L. Playfair) Good Words, **6**: 24, 156.
— — and Influence of. (E. Smith) Pop. Sci. Mo. **3**: 441.
— Nutritive Salts of. (C. Voit) Pop. Sci. Mo. **1**: 405.
— Nutritive Value of different Sorts of. (J. Liebig) Ev. Sat. **7**: 137–537.
— of the agricultural Laborer. (R. S. Skirving) Good Words, **8**: 387.
— of Australian Aborigines. Bentley, **51**: 544.
— of great Men. (W. G. Murray) Belgra. **26**: 397.
— of the Irish. (W. R. Wilde) Dub. Univ. **43**: 127, 317.
— of London. Chamb. J. **25**: 201. — Ecl. R. **103**: 518.
— of Man, in relation to his muscular Power. No. Brit. **45**: 321.
— of oceanic Animals. (C. C. Wallich) Nature, **1**: 241.
— of the People. (H. Chester) Macmil. **18**: 476. **19**: 13. — (B. Shaw) Contemp. **7**: 174.
— Physiological Influence of Condiments. (Prof. Voit) Pop. Sci. Mo. **1**: 701.
— Pleasures of the Table. Bentley, **45**: 40.
— Preservation of. Westm. **48**: 303. Same art. Liv. Age, **16**: 355. — (J. T. Brondgeest) Westm. **50**: 276.
— Prices of. *See* Prices.
— Queer Dishes. (A. Stradling) Chamb. J. **58**: 731, 748.
— Ramble through the Market. (B. W. Ball) Atlan. **17**: 268.
— Reform in. Chamb. J. **57**: 359.
— Smith on. Nature, **8**: 301.
— Some Talk about. Fraser, **55**: 474. Same art. Ecl. M. **41**: 204.
— Sugar in, Importance of. Cornh. **7**: 141.
— Supply of large Capitals. Penny M. **6**: 1–30.
— Supplies of, American. Chamb. J. **56**: 438.
— — Foreign. (A. J. Wilson) Macmil. **38**: 143.
— Temperance in. (E. Hitchcock) Meth. M. **59**: 660.
— Theory of human. Ecl. R. **99**: 274.
— Theories of. (G. H. Lewes) Blackw. **88**: 676.
— Things we have eaten. (J. F. Hardy) Fraser, **89**: 787. Same art. Ecl. M. **83**: 238.
— Use and Abuse of. (R. A. Proctor) Gent. M. n. s. **19**: 212.
— Vegetable, in the United States. De Bow, **20**: 263.
— — best for Man. (N. Kingsford) Westm. **102**: 500.
— What is? Cornh. **3**: 460.
— What it does. Cornh. **4**: 75.
— What shall we eat? (A. Rhodes) Galaxy, **22**: 665.
— What will our Grandsons eat? All the Year, **8**: 224.
Fool, and his Money. (L. Blanchard) Colburn, **68**: 52.
— of Five Forks. (Bret Harte) Liv. Age, **123**: 416.
— of 19th Cent. (H. Zschokke) Dem. R. **11**: 289, 387.
Fool's Errand. (J. L. Ver Mehr) Overland, **6**: 25.
Fool's Mosaic. (A. D. Vandam) Tinsley, **16**: 269.
Fools. Liv. Age, **65**: 195.
— and Fooling. Chamb. J. **39**: 121.
— Efforts toward a Museum of. Putnam, **9**: 260.
— Feast of. (F. Douce) Arch. **15**: 225.
— of Shakspere. (J. N. Hetherington) Cornh. **40**: 722
— Professional. Liv. Age, **145**: 702.
Foolish Girl; a Story. (N. Perry) Galaxy, **16**: 507.
Foolometers, Construction of. So. Lit. Mess. **22**: 299.
Foot and Leg, The human. Blackw. **5**: 532.

Foot, The, Hints regarding. Chamb. J. **58**: 565.
Foot Coverings. Penny M. **7**: 172, 180, 188.
Foot Structures of the Ungulates, Origin of. (E. D. Cope) Am. Natural. **15**: 269.
Foot's Resolution. Hayne's Speech. Niles's Reg. **37**: 415. **38**: 10.
— Webster's Speech. Niles's Reg. **37**: 435. **38**: 25, supp. — (A. H. Everett) Ann. Reg. **5**: 62. *See also* Webster and Hayne.
Foot, Solomon. (E. H. Gillett) Hours at Home, **3**: 238.
Foote, Andrew Hull, Admiral. (L. W. Bacon) Hours at Home, **1**: 83. — Nation, **19**: 353.
Foote, Sir Edw. James. Vindication of Conduct in 1799. (J. Foster) Ecl. R. **15**: 464.
Foote, Henry S., Portrait of. Dem. R. **29**: 195.
Foote, Maria, Countess of Harrington. Eng. Dom. M. **5**: 70.
Foote, Samuel. (J. Forster) Quar. **95**: 483. Same art. Ecl. M. **34**: 50. Same art. Liv. Age, **43**: 387. — Dub. Univ. **69**: 465. — Temp. Bar, **45**: 448. Same art. Ecl. M. **86**: 207. Same art. Liv. Age, **128**: 303.
— and Farce-Writers. (C. C. Clarke) Gent. M. n. s. **8**: 303.
— as a dramatic Writer. Blackw. **9**: 39.
— Letters of. Lond. M. **3**: 202.
— Memoirs of. Bentley, **1**: 298.
Foote, W. H. Sketches of Virginia. So. Lit. Mess. **17**: 8.
Foote Genealogy. (J. W. Dean) N. E. Reg. **9**: 272.
Football. Chamb. J. **41**: 173. **52**: 734.
— at Eton and Harrow. Lond. Soc. **5**: 246.
— at Rugby. Lond. Soc. **5**: 246. **12**: 565. — Ev. Sat. **9**: 98.
Football Gossip, Old. (R. R. Macgregor) Belgra. **34**: 473.
Football Play, Wirksworth; an old Ballad. (J. S. Doxey) Reliquary, **9**: 93.
Footlights. (D. Cook) Once a Week, **16**: 22. Ev. Sat. **3**: 144.
Footmarks, Fossil. With plates (E. Hitchcock) Am. J. Sci. **47**: 292, 390. **48**: 61. — (J. Deane) Am. J. Sci. **46**: 73. **47**: 381, 399. **48**: 158. **49**: 79. **53**: 74. — (A. T. King) Am. J. Sci. **48**: 343. — (I. C. Russell) Am. Natural. **11**: 406. — Chamb. J. **8**: 329. **31**: 28. — Ed. R. **110**: 109.
— — in New England, Hitchcock on. No. Brit. **32**: 247. Same art. Ecl. M. **50**: 28.
— — — in Connecticut Valley. (E. Hitchcock) Am. J. Sci. **86**: 46.
— — in Pennsylv. (W. D. Moore) Am. J. Sci. **105**: 292.
— — in Kansas. (B. F. Mudge) Am. J. Sci. **91**: 174.
— — in Carboniferous Rocks. (J. W. Dawson) Am. J. Sci. **105**: 16.
— — in Coal Strata. (C. Lyell) Am J. Sci. **52**: 25.
— of Birds. Knick. **7**: 578.
Foot-Notes from Sand. (E. Coues) Am. Natural. **4**: 297.
Footpads. (H. P. Spofford) Atlan. **27**: 401.
Footprints in the Sand; a Poem. (C. Thaxter) Atlan. **29**: 694.
— in the Snow; a New-Year's Story. (C. A. Munger) Knick. **47**: 144.
— of the Creator, Miller's. No. Brit. **12**: 443. Same art. Liv. Age, **25**: 145.
— on the Sea-Shore. (N. Hawthorne) Dem. R. **1**: 190.
For an Album; a Poem. (W. Motherwell) Scrib. **10**: 707.
For and against; a Tale. Contin. Mo. **3**: 334.
For Better, for Worse; a Tale. (C. Chesebrough) Harper, **26**: 501, 647, 747.
For Better, for Worse; a Tale. (S. J. Waterbury) Cath. World, **17**: 257.
For Better, for Worse; a Tale. (L. Wood) Tinsley, **23**: 96.
For Better, for Worse; a Tale. Temp. Bar, **1**: 1–496. **2**: 62–520. **3**: 92, 215.
For Billy's Sake; a Christmas Story. (R. C. Myers) Potter Am. Mo. **16**: 73.
For Cupid dead; a Poem. (L. C. Moulton) Scrib. **9**: 393.
For Father's Sake; a Sketch. Canad. Mo. **20**: 27.
For his Country; a Tale of the U. S. Civil War. Dub. Univ. **82**: 72–703.
For the King; a Poem. (Bret Harte) Atlan. **34**: 15.
For King and Country; a Tale. (A. M. Machar) Canad. Mo. **5**: 102–492.
For Ladies only; a Tale. Temp. Bar, **20**: 542.
For the last Time. (Dudu Fletcher) Atlan. **37**: 521.
For Life. St. James, **27**: 1–707. **28**: 33. 161, 263.
For Life; a Tale. (M. L. Pool) Galaxy, **6**: 329.
For Life or Death; a Tale. All the Year, **12**: 497.
For Life or Death; a Tale. Chamb. J. **52**: 715.
For Pastime. (L. C. Moulton) Scrib. **7**: 34.
For Percival; a Novel. (M. Veley) Cornh. **36**: 359, 615, 740. **37**: 106–738. **38**: 1–733. Same art. Lippinc. **20**: 416, 546, 665. **21**: 26–576. **22**: 57–666.
For Pity's Sake. Liv. Age, **129**: 694–817. **130**: 82.
For Sale, a thoroughbred Nag, unbroken. Lond. Soc. **32**: 66.
For Substance of Doctrine, The Phrase. (N. Worcester) Chr. Exam. **17**: 381.
For the Year. (A. Thomas) Galaxy, **6**: 97.
Foraminifera, Anatomy and Physiology of. (W. C. Williamson) Pop. Sci. R. **4**: 171.
— and Protozoa. Westm. **78**: 171.
— from the St. Lawrence. (G. M. Dawson) Am. J. Sci. **101**: 204.
— Life in the Depths. (A. Wilson) Colburn, **157**: 562.
— Microscopic Geology. (S. J. Mackie) Recr. Sci. **1**: 145.
— Schlicht's. (H. B. Brady) Nature, **1**: 477.
Foray of Con O'Donnell. Dub. Univ. **29**: 488.
Forbes, Archibald. Chamb. J. **50**: 597.—(K. Field) Scrib. **21**: 297. — with portrait, Ecl. M. **95**: 632.
— and his Canadian Experiences. (G. W. Field) Canad. Mo. **17**: 511.
Forbes, David. Nature, **15**: 139.
Forbes, Duncan. No. Brit. **7**: 92. — Ed. R. **26**: 107.
Forbes, Edward, the Naturalist. Bentley, **51**: 323. Same art. Ecl. M. **56**: 166. — Brit. Q. **34**: 293. — Fraser, **51**: 39. — Lond. Q. **17**: 138.— (W. J. Hamilton) Am. J. Sci. **70**: 375. — Ecl. R. **101**: 385. — St. James, **4**: 321. *See* Glaciers.
Forbes, James, Oriental Memoirs. Ecl. R. **20**: 405, 440, 631.
Forbes, James David. (A. Agassiz) Nation, **16**: 369.
— and his Biographers (J. Tyndall) Contemp. **22**: 484.
— and his glacial Explorations. (W. Chambers) Chamb. J. **50**: 811.
— Life and Letters of. Pract. M. **3**: 146.
— Travels through the Alps. No. Brit. **1**: 527. *See* Alps.
Forbes, Gen. John, Death of. Olden Time, **1**: 189.
Forbes, Lady, Story of. Chamb. J. **52**: 785.
Forbidden Fruit; a Novel. Dub. Univ. **78**: 498, 614. **79**: 10–378.
Forbidden Fruit. House. Words, **14**: 436.
Forbin, C. de. Voyage dans le Levant. Quar. **23**: 83.
Force, Peter. Am. Hist. Rec. **3**: 1. — (G. W. Greene) No. Am. **92**: 364. — (G. W. Greene) M. Am. Hist. **2**: 221.
— and his Library. Hist. M. **9**: 335.
— Historical Tracts. (J. G. Palfrey) No. Am. **43**: 274. — (T. W. White) So. Lit. Mess. **6**: 574.
— National Calendar. Am. Mo. R. **2**: 71.
Force. Cornh. **4**: 409. — (W. W. Kinsley) Penn Mo. **7**: 873. — (A. M. Mayer) J. Frankl. Inst. **86**: 45. — (P. G. Tait) Nature, **14**: 459. — (P. G. Tait) Ecl. Engin. **15**: 446. — (J. Tyndall) J. Frankl. Inst. **74**: 266, 331. — (De V. Wood) J. Frankl. Inst. **74**: 351. — (De V. Wood) Ecl. Engin. **16**: 28.
— and Energy. (C. Brooke) Nature, **6**: 122. — (C. Brooke) Ecl. Engin. **7**: 260. — (R. H. Smith) Nature, **19**: 194, 217, 242.

Force and Matter. All the Year, 16: 35. — Ecl. Engin. 10: 393. — Ev. Sat. 2: 157.
— — Büchner on. Anthrop. R. 3: 22.
— — B. Jones on. (D. D. Heath) Contemp. 11: 321.
— and Mind, Bain on. Contemp. 8: 57.
— and Nature, Winslow's. So. R. n. s. 7: 484.
— as a Power in Nature. (W. F. Ainsworth) Colburn, 166: 231.
— behind Nature. (W. B. Carpenter) Mod. R. 1: 34. Same art. Liv. Age, 144: 323. Same art. Pop. Sci. Mo. 16: 614.
— Correlation of, in its Bearing on Mind. (A. Bain) Macmil. 16: 372. Same art. Ecl. M. 69: 571. Same art. Liv. Age, 95: 131.
— Energy, and Will. (St.G. Mivart) 19th Cent. 3: 933.
— Indestructibility of. Macmil. 6: 337.
— Law, and Design. (N. Porter) Princ. n. s. 3: 463.
— Measurement of. (R. Moore) Ecl. Engin. 16: 335.
— Mechanical, Evolution from. (L. P. Hickok) Princ. n. s. 1: 567.
— Momentum and *Vis viva*. (De V. Wood) Ecl. Engin. 18: 33, 241, 467.
— Motion, Inertia, and. (J. C. Trautwine) J. Frankl. Inst. 74: 109, 194.
— Nature of. (E. B. Hunt) Am. J. Sci. 68: 237.
— Newton on. (P. T. Main) Nature, 15: 8.
— not the Equivalent of Personality. (G. E. Watson) Univ. Q. 34: 439.
— Observations on. (J. A. Davies) Recr. Sci. 2: 64.
— or God. (O. Cone) Univ. Q. 36: 424.
— Origin of. (Sir J. W. F. Herschel) Fortn. 1: 435.
— Persistence of. (F. Gardiner) Bib. Sac. 38: 1.
— a Phantom. (A. S. Herschel) Nature, 17: 302, 321, 340.
— Phasis of. Nat. R. 4: 359.
— Psychic, Crooke's Experiments on. (P. H. Vanderweyde) J. Frankl. Inst. 92: 423. — (C. Sellers) J. Frankl. Inst. 92: 211.
— Spatial Quale. (J. E. Cabot) J. Spec. Philos. 13: 199.
— Transformation of. (M. Foster) Nature, 1: 53.
— Transmission by Belts and Pulleys. J. Frankl. Inst. 85: 17.
— Tyndall's Lecture on. (E. W. Blake) J. Frankl. Inst. 75: 87.
— Vital. *See* Vital Force.
See Energy.
Forces. (T. Lyman) Am. J. Sci. 79: 185.
— Composition and Resolution of. (W. R. Johnson) J. Frankl. Inst. 7: 354. — (J. C. Trautwine) J. Frankl. Inst. 87: 121.
— Conservation of. (J. Henry) Am. J. Sci. 80: 32.
— — Correlation, and Origin of. (J. S. Jewell) Meth. Q. 32: 5, 414.
— Correlation of. (S. H. Dickson) Lippinc. 1: 306, 371. — Brit. Q. 14: 155. — Galaxy, 2: 424. — (M. Faraday) J. Frankl. Inst. 70: 399. — (H. C. Sorby) J. Frankl. Inst. 77: 97. — (J. L. LeConte) Am. J. Sci. 78: 305. — (J. L. LeConte) Pop. Sci. Mo. 4: 156.
— — Grove on. (J. C. Clerk-Maxwell) Nature, 10: 302.
— Crystalline and molecular. (J. Tyndall) Pop. Sci. Mo. 6: 257.
— Initiatory. (G. Iles) Pop. Sci. Mo. 11: 156.
— Interaction of natural. (H. L. F. Helmholtz) Am. J. Sci. 74: 189.
— Permanence of material. (C. Mills) No. Am. 129: 604.
— Proof of Parallelogram of. (G. P. Young) Canad. J. n. s. 1: 357.
— Wasted. (W. H. Wahl) Pop. Sci. Mo. 15: 289.
See Physical Forces.
Force Bill, 1871. (E. L. Godkin) Nation, 12: 284. — (J N. Pomeroy) Nation, 12: 286.
Forced Marches. (J. W. DeForest) Galaxy, 5: 708.
Forced Marriage; a Story. Lond. Soc. 40: 251.
Forced Recruit at Solferino; a Poem. (E. B. Browning) Cornh. 2: 419.
Forced Sale. Blackw. 57: 99.
Ford, John. So. Lit. Mess. 15: 656. — Am. Whig R. 14: 285. — (A. C. Swinburne) Fortn. 16: 42.
— Dramatic Works. (W. Gifford) Quar. 6: 462. — (F. Jeffrey) Ed. R. 18: 275. — Mo. R. 113: 497.
— Witch of Edmonton. Blackw. 6: 409.
Ford, Richard, In Memoriam. Fraser, 58: 422.
Forde, Samuel. Dub. Univ. 25: 338.
Fords of Jordan, 1859; a Poem. Cornh. 12: 629.
Foregone Conclusion. (W. D. Howells) Atlan. 34: 1-641.
Foreign Affairs. New Eng. 1: 451.
— British, in 1850. Blackw. 68: 319.
Foreign Competition and British Agriculture. Fraser, 43: 236.
Foreign Debt of U. S. (J. B. Hodgskin) Nation, 7: 520.
Foreign Invaders. All the Year, 25: 133.
Foreign Loans. (E. L. Godkin) Nation, 12: 316.
Foreign Prince, The. Fraser, 42: 400.
Foreign Scenery and Manners. Blackw. 1: 251-582.
Foreign Trade no Cure for hard Times. Atlan. 44: 472.
Foreigner, Intelligent. All the Year, 38: 245.
Foreigners, These. (J. Kirkland) Lakeside, 2: 56, 249.
Foreknowledge, Bromley on. Meth. M. 43: 345.
— and Free Will. So. R. n. s. 15: 91.
— Limitations of. (J. P. Lacroix) Bib. Sac. 32: 137.
Forensic Ethics. (E. L. Godkin) Nation, 12: 56.
Forensic Imputation. Kitto, 40: 160.
Forest, Cuisine in. (H. Vizetelly) Once a Week, 16: 624.
— Law of. (C. S. Maine) Macmil. 38: 58.
— of Arden; a Tale. (H. A. Prokop) Lippinc. 11: 188.
— of the Dartmoors. Fraser, 56: 242.
— of Dean, Rambles in. Once a Week, 1: 167.
Forests. (M. de Vere) Hours at Home, 3: 398.
— American. (I. James) Lippinc. 1: 596.
— — Dangers to. (L. L. Dame) Education, 1: 593.
— — Destruction of. (T. Evans) Overland, 6: 224. — (J. W. Dawson) Ed. New Philos. J. 42: 259.
— — Recreation and Solitude. (W. J. Stillman) Atlan. 40: 10.
— Ancient, and modern Fuel. Ecl. M. 55: 367.
— and Fruit-Culture. (J. S. Patterson) Pop. Sci. Mo. 2: 194.
— Climatic Influence of. (F. L. Oswald) Pop. Sci. Mo. 11: 385.
— Destruction of. Pract. M. 7: 217. — Canad. Mo. 16: 136.
— — Effects of, on Lakes and Streams. Penny M. 11: 502.
— — in Canada. (N. W. Beckwith) Canad. Mo. 1: 527.
— Foes and Friends of. Chamb. J. 51: 8.
— Great, of Antiquity and the present Time. Colburn, 91: 378.
— Influence of, on Climate. Intel. Obs. 7: 448. — (F. Ebener) So. M. 9: 356.
— — on the Rainfall. Chamb. J. 25: 52. — (J. B. Boussingault) Ed. New Philos. J. 24: 85.
— Management of. Ed. R. 142: 359.
— Moisture in. Ecl. Engin. 9: 248.
— Necessity of cultivating. Ed. New Philos. J. 36: 236.
— of Nevada. (C. S. Sargent) Am. J. Sci. 117: 417.
— of North America, Edible Productions of. Penny M. 9: 495.
— Preservation of. (F. L. Oswald) No. Am. 128: 35. — Appleton, 16: 470.
— Tropical. Chamb. J. 48: 206.
— Use of. Chamb. J. 38: 108. Same art. Ecl. M. 59: 502. — Chamb. J. 53: 590. — (N. H. Egleston) Pop. Sci. Mo. 19: 176.
See Timber.
Forest and Game Laws. Westm. 45: 405.
— Martineau's. Ecl. R. 84: 230.
Forest Chase. Belgra. 19: 503.

Forest Clearing by Steam. Pract. M. 4: 315.
Forest Culture, English. Brit. Q. 38: 81.
— in Alpine Ravines. (M. J. Cleve) Pop. Sci. Mo. 19: 830.
— in Germany. Ev. Sat. 3: 589.
Forest Dreams. Dub. Univ. 27: 643.
Forest Economies and Fire-Proof Homes. Am. Arch. 9: 149.
Forest Geography. (A. Gray) Nature, 19: 327.
— and Archæology. (A. Gray) Am. J. Sci. 116: 85, 183.
Forest King; a Christmas Carol. (J. Sheehan) Temp. Bar, 34: 252.
Forest Lands of Maine. (L. Sabine) No. Am. 58: 299.
Forest Laws. Chamb. J. 43: 259.
— Charter of Exemption from. Arch. 15: 209.
Forest Life; a Tale. Fraser, 73: 632.
Forest Life and Forest Trees. Blackw. 70: 669. — De Bow, 12: 296.
— in the West. (C. C. Felton) No. Am. 55: 510.
Forest Music; a Poem. (A. Beaufain) So. Lit. Mess. 22: 211.
Forest Notes in France. Cornh. 33: 545.
Forest Recollections. (C. Lanman) Lippinc. 2: 516.
Forest Scenes in America. Westm. 12: 103.
Forest Trees. Dub. Univ. 46: 236.
— in America. (W. B. O. Peabody) No. Am. 35: 399. — (J. C. Gray) No. Am. 44: 334. — Am. Mo. R. 2: 273.
— Management of. Penny M. 11: 373.
— of Britain. Quar. 96: 431.
Forest Wonders. Sharpe, 41: 8.
Forest World, Subjects of. (G. B. Griffith) Potter Am. Mo. 16: 481.
Forester, Fanny. *See* Judson, Mrs. E. C.
Forester, Frank. *See* Herbert, H. W.
Foresti, E. F. (H. T. Tuckerman) Atlan. 4: 525. — Liv. Age, 59: 366.
Forestry. (H. W. S. Cleveland) Nation, 33: 432. — (T. Meehan) Penn Mo. 8: 141. — Republic, 3: 97.
— European and American. Penn Mo. 7: 431, 527, 727.
— in its economical Bearings. Nature, 7: 118.
— in France. Ecl. Engin. 23: 186.
— in the United States. Am. Arch. 10: 74. — (C. S. Sargent) Nation, 28: 87.
— Schools of. (J. C. Brown) Ecl. Engin. 18: 468. — (C. S. Sargent) Nation, 33: 370.
— — European. (N. H. Egleston) Pop. Sci. Mo. 19: 311.
— Work of 10th Census on. (S. Baxter) Atlan. 48: 682.
Forestalling. Chamb. J. 36: 49.
Forewarning, The; a Tale. Colburn, 31: 529.
Forfarshire, History of. Ed. R. 120: 309.
Forge, The. Atlan. 16: 586, 684.
Forged and altered Paper. Bank. M. (N. Y.) 30: 279.
Forged Bank-Notes. Fraser, 22: 482.
Forged Checks, Recovery on. Bank. M. (N. Y.) 30: 385.
Forger's Bride; a Tale. (R. Terry) Lippinc. 5: 325.
Forgers, Distinguished. (A. Marks) Once a Week, 16: 35.
— History of. Bank. M. (N. Y.) 16: 512.
Forgers, The. Blackw. 9: 572.
Forgers, The; a Dramatic Poem. (J. B. White) So. Lit. J. 4: 118–409.
Forgery. Hunt, 43: 306. — Mus. 36: 108.
— and its Punishment. Fraser, 11: 301.
— Capital Punishment for. Ed. R. 52: 398. — Selec. Ed. R. 6: 293. — Cong. M. 1: 373.
— History and Anecdotes of. Ecl. M. 21: 560.
— Increase of. Ed. R. 31: 203.
— of Bank Notes, Prevention of. Bank. M. (L.) 1: 295.
— of United States Notes. Bank. M. (N. Y.) 18: 207.
— Prevention of. Bank. M. (L.) 20: 355, 412.
— Punishment of. Ed. Mo. R. 1: 260.
— Romance of modern State Trials. Blackw. 69: 461, 605.
Forgeries, Bank-Note. House. Words, 1: 555, 615.
— Ecclesiastical, Shepherd on. Quar. 93: 83.
Forgeries, Great Bank. Bank. M. (L.) 33: 781, 889.
— Literary. Harper, 41: 772, 923.—Portfo.(Den.) 16: 244.
— — Pascal Forgeries in the French Academy. Penn Mo. 1: 151, 191.
— Printed. House Words, 5: 374, 444. Same art. Liv. Age, 34: 477.
— Roman. (J. A. Corcoran) Am. Cath. Q. 2: 532.
Forget-me-not; a Christmas Story. (G. zu Putlitz) Lippinc. 1: 39.
Forget-me-not; a Story. (E. Noble) Colburn, 163: 481.
Forget-me-not; a Tale. Cath. World, 6: 639.
Forget-me-not, The; a Tale. Hogg, 1: 69.
Forget-me-not Flower. Peop. J. 10: 57.
Forgetfulness. (R. Verdon) Mind, 2: 437. — Liv. Age, 136: 62.
Forgiven at last. Temp. Bar, 19: 390.
Forgiveness. (L. R. Page) Univ. Q. 2: 341. — (W. Spaulding) Univ. Q. 23: 330.
— and Law, Bushnell's. (J. A. Brown) Luth. Q. 4: 457. — (D. T. Fiske) Bib. Sac. 32: 179. — (J. B. Thomas) Bapt. Q. 10: 214. — Lond. Q. 43: 411.
— Christian. (A. Dean) Am. Presb. R. 16: 533.
— of Sins. (C. H. Brigham) O. & N. 4: 570.
— — Clarke on. (G. M. Porter) New Eng. 11: 24.
— — Doctrine of. (H. Harbaugh) Mercersb. 15: 22.
— or Justification, Hist. of Doctrine of. Chr. R. 20: 536.
— Salvation, Punishment. (W. H. Ryder) Univ. Q. 36: 387.
Forgotten Crime, A. Argosy, 30: 27. Same art. Liv. Age, 146: 419.
Forgotten Lives; a Tale. (Mrs. Notley) Eng. Dom. M. 16: 1–285. 17: 1–288. 18: 11–294. 19: 15–295.
Forgotten Shrine. (F. M. Ryan) Irish Mo. 7: 369, 437.
Forgotten Sin. (E. E. Hamilton) Colburn, 155: 659. 156: 31.
Forgotten Valentine. Lond. Soc. 11: 120.
Forks, Use of. Penny M. 1: 79, 139.
Form and Color, Wilkinson on. (Sir D. Brewster) No. Brit. 32: 126.
— Coincidence of. Fraser, 39: 660.
— in Nature, as revealing God. (T. Hill) Bib. Sac. 36: 1.
— Matters of. Once a Week, 18: 212.
— Pleasure of visual. (J. Sully) Pop. Sci. Mo. 16: 780.
Forms, Diplomatic. Blackw. 115: 55. Same art. Liv. Age, 120: 387.
— Doctrine of. Mo. Rel. M. 18: 50.
Form-Sickness. All the Year, 15: 41.
Formalism charged against the Catholic Church. Dub. R. 43: 391.
Forman, Samuel S., Autobiography of. Hist. M. 16: 321.
Forman, Capt., Lords Brougham and Russell. Fraser, 6: 680.
Formosa. (E. G. Ravenstein) Geog. M. 1: 292. — (J. Morrison) Geog. M. 4: 260, 293, 319. — St. Paul's, 5: 75. — Cornh. 30: 448. Same art. Ecl. M. 83: 730. — Colburn, 144: 226. — Ev. Sat. 17: 487.
— and the Japanese. All the Year, 33: 463.
— Excursion in. (C. Bridge) Fortn. 26: 214. Same art. Ecl. M. 87: 490. Same art. Liv. Age, 130: 816.
Formosa; a Satire. Temp. Bar, 5: 32.
Formularies, Interpretation of the English. Chr. Obs. 74: 448.
Fornarina, La. (J. I. Mombert) Bib. Sac. 33: 608.
Fornovo, Battle of. Cornh. 37: 290.
Forrest, Edwin. (L. Barrett) Galaxy, 24: 526. — with portrait (A. E. Lancaster) Potter Am. Mo. 8: 161. — Am. Bibliop. 4: 634. — Knick. 11: 85.
— Alger's Life of. (J. B. Matthews) Nation, 25: 124.
— in England. Dem. R. 16: 385. 19: 186.
— Oration of. Dem. R. 3: 51.
— Reminiscences of. Potter Am. Mo. 12: 369.
Forrest, N. B. Land We Love, 1: 268.

Forrest, N. B., and his Campaigns. (J. B. Chalmers) So. Hist. Pap. **7**: 451.
— Operations against W. Sooy Smith, 1864. So. Hist. Pap. **8**: 9.
Forrester, A. H. Bentley, **19**: 99.
Forrester's Lodger. Argosy, **31**: 186.
Forrestt & Son's Boat-Building Yards. Colburn, **169**: 498.
Forsaken: a Sonnet. (P. B. Marston) Cornh. **20**: 355.
Forsaken, The. Fraser, **27**: 571.
Forster, Anthony. Chr. Disc. **3**: 280.
Forster, George, Life and Misfortunes of. Westm. **66**: 360.
Forster, John. (B. Jerrold) Gent. M. n. s. **16**: 313.
— Early Life and Friendships of. (R. H. Horne) Temp. Bar, **46**: 491. Same art. Appleton, **15**: 467, 500.
— Essays. Liv. Age, **58**: 692.
Forster, J. G., Letters of. Mo. R. **120**: 221.
Forster, Maria, Story of. Sharpe, **12**: 327.
Forster, Wm., with portrait. Ev. Sat. **9**: 370.
— Political Portrait of. St. James, **26**: 249.
Förster. *See* Foerster.
Forsthaus in the Solling. Fraser, **25**: 264.
Forsyth, John, with portrait. Dem. R. **2**: 273.
Forsyth, J. H. Memoir and Sermons. Chr. Obs. **49**: 708.
Forsyth, J. S. The Natural and Medical Dieteticon. Lond. M. **12**: 225.
Forsyth, Robert. Autobiography. Tait, n. s. **13**: 359.
Fort Edward, Fort George, etc. *See* Edward, George, etc.
Fort, Oldest, in the United States. O. & N. **2**: 271.
Forts in the U. S. (F. Morton) Once a Week, **4**: 604.
— and Iron Shields. (S. J. Mackie) Pop. Sci. R. **7**: 363.
— Hill, of Sussex, Character and Origin of. (A. H. L. Fox) Arch. **42**: 27.
Fort George Island, Florida. (J. E. Dodge) Scrib. **14**: 652.
Fortescue Family. Ed. R. **145**: 299. Same art. Liv. Age, **133**: 707.
Fortification. Westm. **21**: 480. — Niles's Reg. **20**: 263, 285.
— and Sieges. Am. Q. **13**: 337.
— Bordwine's System of. (T. P. Thompson) Westm. **21**: 480.
— Fergusson on. Dub. Univ. **34**: 243.
— Modern. Ed. R. **102**: 202.
— of the Western Country. (N. Webster) Carey's Mus. **6**: 27, 136. **7**: 323.
— Permanent. Quar. **127**: 212.
— — and Field. Chamb. J. **45**: 492, 500.
— President's Message on, 1822. Niles's Reg. **22**: 87.
— Report on, 1822. Niles's Reg. **22**: 153.
— Systems of. U. S. Serv. M. **5**: 34–328.
— Use of Iron in. (J. G. Barnard) U. S. Serv. M. **1**: 25.
Fortifications, Ancient, in England. (J. Watson) Arch. **5**: 87.
— — of Scotland. (J. Anderson) Arch. **5**: 241. **6**: 87. — (R. Riddell) Arch. **10**: 99.
— in England. St. Paul's, **1**: 438.
— in Hampshire. (F. Grose) Arch. **5**: 237.
— Vitrified, in Galloway. (R. Riddell) Arch. **10**: 147.
Fortified Cities. Nat. Q. **24**: 86.
Fortresses. Blackw. **110**: 584.
— Ancient and modern. Blackw. **75**: 522. Same art. Ecl. M. **34**: 239.
— of ancient Greece. (W. Hamilton) Arch. **15**: 315.
Fortunata's Pocket. (K. P. Osgood) Scrib. **11**: 542.
Fortunate Man. Sharpe, **12**: 141, 203.
Fortunate Shop. Chamb. J. **24**: 209.
Fortune and Misfortune. Dub. Univ. **48**: 234.
— coming Single-Handed. (F. Jacox) Bentley, **62**: 290.
— in a Name; a Tale. Chamb. J. **44**: 533, 547.
— of France; or the Hôtel de Cluny. (D. Costello) Colburn, **74**: 551. **75**: 80.
Fortunes and Misfortunes of Co. C. (A. C. Redwood) Scrib. **17**: 528.
Fortunes, Great. Chamb. J. **50**: 302.
— made in Business. Lond. Soc. **37**: 74–481. **38**: 33, 446. **39**: 39, 171, 569. **40**: 233, 433.
— of Ahmed. (J. W. Morris) Putnam, **16**: 502.
— of Bertram Oakley. (J. B. Harwood) Chamb. J. **58**: 1–830.
— of Glencore. (C. Lever) Dub. Univ. **46**: 164–700. **47**: 141–649. **48**: 98–690. **49**: 55–399. Same art. Liv. Age, **47**: 32. **48**: 80, 687. **49**: 538, 791. **50**: 220. **51**: 349, 784. **52**: 415, 539, 806. **53**: 269, 352.
— of Jessy and Margaret Trevor. (Mrs. Crawford) Sharpe, **39**: 39. **40**: 57.
— of Nara; a Japanese Story. All the Year, **38**: 437.
— of the Reverend Caleb Ellison. House. Words, **3**: 533.
— of the Scattergood Family. (A. Smith) Bentley, **15**: 1–535. **16**: 1–617. **17**: 89, 201.
Fortune-Hunting. (W. H. Whitmore) Galaxy, **4**: 658.
— Extraordinary. Blackw. **71**: 685.
Fortune Seekers and Makers; a Tale. (A. Sargeant) Chamb. J. **9**: 131.
Fortune-Teller. (Mrs. S. J. Hale) Godey, **25**: 61.
— an American Story. (F. E. Wadleigh) Argosy, **31**: 469.
— Parisian. (W. E. McCann) Putnam, **14**: 106.
Fortune-Telling. (J. H. Fyfe) Once a Week, **6**: 375. — Dub. Univ. **11**: 730. — Colburn, **6**: 336. **8**: 337. *See* Palmistry; Chiromancy.
Fortuny, Mariano. (A. Brewster) O. & N. **11**: 357.
Forty Days in the Desert. (W. P. Lunt) Chr. Exam. **46**: 383.
Forty-Seven Rônins; a Japanese Tale. (A. B. Mitford) Fortn. **13**: 668. Same art. Liv. Age, **106**: 349.
Foscolo, Ugo. (H. T. Tuckerman) No. Am. **91**: 213.
— and English Hospitality. Fraser, **31**: 401.
— and his Age. (J. Picciotto) Dub. Univ. **78**: 87.
— and his Times. For. Q. **9**: 312.
— Life and Writings of. Westm. **55**: 237.
— Memoirs of. Lond. M. **19**: 238.
— Pecchio's Life of. Colburn, **34**: 153.
— Ricciarda. (R. P. Gillies) Blackw. **22**: 571.
— Works of. For. R. **2**: 410.
Fossils; Among the stone Lillies. (G. M. Kellogg) Lakeside, **6**: 242.
— and their Teachings. Temp. Bar, **3**: 363.
— British, and what they teach. Ecl. R. **101**: 680.
— Devonian, of N. Y. (C. Barrois) Am. J. Sci. **121**: 44.
— from the Cincinnati Group of Ohio. (F. B. Meek) Am. J. Sci. **103**: 423.
— from Kennedy Channel. (F. B. Meek) Am. J. Sci. **90**: 31.
— from the Laurentian Rocks of Canada. (J. W. Dawson) Am. J. Sci. **94**: 367.
— from Lower Potsdam Rocks at Troy, N. Y. (S. W. Ford) Am. J. Sci. **106**: 134.
— from Potsdam Sandstone of Wisconsin. (A. Winchell) Am. J. Sci. **87**: 226.
— in Illinois Geological Reports. (F. B. Meek) Am. J. Sci. **107**: 189–580.
— Mantell's Petrifactions. (B. Silliman) Am. J. Sci. **63**: 407.
— New Carboniferous. (R. P. Stevens) Am. J. Sci. **75**: 258.
— New Vertebrate. (O. C. Marsh) Am. J. Sci. **114**: 249.
— of New York. (J. Hall) Am. J. Sci. **55**: 243.
— of the Wappinger Valley, N. Y. (W. B. Dwight) Am. J. Sci. **117**: 389.
— Paleozoic, New Species of. (E. Billings) Am. J. Sci. **103**: 352.
— Post-Pliocene, in a Cave. (C. M. Wheatley) Am. J. Sci. **101**: 235.
— — of Sankoty Head. (A. E. Verrill) Am. J. Sci. **110**: 364.

Fossils, Primordial, from Newfoundland. (J. F. Whiteaves) Am. J. Sci. **116**: 224.
— — New Species of. (S. W. Ford) Am. J. Sci. **103**: 419. **115**: 124.
— — of Rensselaer County, N. Y. (S. W. Ford) Am. J. Sci. **105**: 211. **109**: 204.
— — of Troy, N. Y. (S. W. Ford) Am. J. Sci. **111**: 369.
— Silurian, from Ohio. (F. B. Meek) Am. J. Sci. **104**: 274.
— — Lower. (F. Prime, jr.) Am. J. Sci. **115**: 261.
Fossil Birds, Cretaceous and Tertiary. (O. C. Marsh) Am. J. Sci. **99**: 205.
— from New Zealand. (G. A. Mantell) Am. J. Sci. **57**: 28.
— from Solenhofen. (H. Woodward) Intel. Obs. **2**: 313.
— Geologist's Aviary. (A. Wilson) Colburn, **157**: 340.
— Tertiary and Post-Tertiary. (O. C. Marsh) Am. J. Sci. **104**: 256.
Fossil Bones. Ed. R. **6**: 324. — Quar. **27**: 459. — Mus. **1**: 229. — (E. Hitchcock, jr.) No. Am. **97**: 451.
— Cuvier on. Ed. R. **18**: 214.
— found in Vermont. (Z. Thompson) Am. J. Sci. **59**: 256.
— from the Red Sandstone of the Connecticut River Valley. (J. Wyman) Am. J. Sci. **70**: 394.
— from Tennessee. (J. Wyman) Am. J. Sci. **59**: 56.
— — and Texas. (W. Carpenter) Am. J. Sci. **51**: 244.
Fossil Butterflies, Scudder's. Nature, **13**: 222.
Fossil Corals from North Carolina. (E. Emmons) Am. J. Sci. **72**: 389.
Fossil Crustaceans in Upper Devonian Rocks of Ohio. (R. P. Whitfield) Am. J. Sci. **119**: 33.
Fossil Elk of Ireland. Penny M. **4**: 299.
Fossil-Finder of Lyme-Regis. Chamb. J. **28**: 382.
Fossil Fishes. Am. J. Sci. **30**: 33. — Ed. R. **37**: 47.
— Agassiz on. Quar. **55**: 433.
— American. (J. S. Newberry) Am. J. Sci. **84**: 73.
— and fossil Footmarks. (E. Hitchcock) Am. J. Sci. **71**: 96.
— of the Sandstone of Connecticut. (W. C. Redfield) Am. J. Sci. **72**: 357.
— of Scotland. (R. H. Traquair) Nature, **21**: 428.
Fossil Footmarks. *See* Footmarks.
Fossil Forest in the Tertiary of California. (O. C. Marsh) Am. J. Sci. **101**: 266.
Fossil Fruits of Brandon, Vt. (L. Lesquereux) Am. J. Sci. **82**: 355.
Fossil Horses in America. (O. C. Marsh) Am. Natural. **8**: 288.
Fossil Infusoria. (J. W. Bailey) Am. J. Sci. **46**: 137.
— Recent. (J. W. Bailey) Am. J. Sci. **48**: 321.
Fossil Insects from the Carboniferous Formation in Illinois. (J. D. Dana) Am. J. Sci. **87**: 34.
— — — in Indiana. (S. I. Smith) Am. J. Sci. **101**: 44.
— of America. (S. H. Scudder) Am. Natural. **1**: 625.
Fossil Mammals. (O. C. Marsh) Am Natural. **7**: 146. — (F. V. Greene) Am. J. Sci. **66**: 16.
— from the Tertiary Formation. (O. C. Marsh) Am. J. Sci. **102**: 35, 120.
— — New. (O. C. Marsh) Am. J. Sci. **104**: 122, 202. **107**: 531. **109**: 239. **112**: 401.
— — New Equine. (O. C. Marsh) Am. J. Sci. **107**: 247.
— of Australia. Nature, **5**: 503.
— of North America. (J. P. Lesley) O. & N. **1**: 563.
— — Leidy on. (W. B. Dawkins) Nature, **2**: 119, 232.
— of the Genus Coryphodon. (O. C. Marsh) Am. J. Sci. **111**: 425.
— of the Order Brontotherida. (O. G. Marsh) Am. J. Sci. **107**: 81. **111**: 335.
— of the Order Dinocerata. (O. C. Marsh) Am. J. Sci. **105**: 117, 293.
— — Existence or not of Horns in. (R. Owen) Am. J. Sci. **111**: 401.
— — Observations on. (O. C. Marsh) Am. J. Sci. **106**: 300.
Fossil Mammals of the Order Dinocerata, Principal Characters of. (O. C. Marsh) Am. J. Sci. **111**: 163.
— of the Order Tillodontia. (O. C. Marsh) Am. J. Sci. **111**: 249.
Fossil Organic Remains. (J. E. Doornik) Am. J. Sci. **15**: 90.
Fossil Osteography, Zoölogy, and Geology. For. Q. **25**: 318.
Fossil Oysters, Coquand's. (J. W. Flower) Nature, **2**: 22.
Fossil Piano, A. (A. Blackwell) Once a Week, **4**: 451.
Fossil Plant. (E. W. Binney) Nature, **18**: 555.
Fossil Plants. (H. Coultas) Sharpe, **47**: 20. — Am. J. Sci. **31**: 28. — Putnam, **6**: 26.
— and their Lessons. Chamb. J. **38**: 244.
— Arctic. (J. S. Gardner) Nature, **22**: 341.
— Carboniferous, of France. (W. C. Williamson) Nature, **16**: 138.
— Cryptogamous. (W. R. McNab) Nature, **7**: 207.
— and Glacial Periods. (J. W. Dawson) Nature, **16**: 67.
— in the Lower Silurian. (L. Lesquereux) Am. J. Sc. **107**: 31.
— — in Ohio. (J. S. Newberry) Am. J. Sci. **108**: 110.
— of Vancouver Island. (L. Lesquereux) Am. J. Sci. **78**: 85.
— of Great Britain. (W. C. Williamson) Nature, **18**: 35.
— of North America. (L. Lesquereux) Penn Mo. **6**: 591, 642. — Geog. M. **3**: 152.
— of recent Formations. (L. Lesquereux) Am. J. Sci. **77**: 359.
Fossil Reptiles from the Cretaceous Formation. (O. C. Marsh) Am. J. Sci. **101**: 447.
— New Sub-order of Pterosauria. (O. C. Marsh) Am. J. Sci. **111**: 507.
— New Tertiary. (O. C. Marsh) Am. J. Sci. **104**: 298.
— of New Jersey. (E. D. Cope) Am. Natural. **1**: 23. **3**: 84.
— of Nova Scotia. (Sir C. Lyell) Am. J. Sci. **66**: 33.
Fossil Serpents from the Tertiary of Wyoming. (O. C. Marsh) Am. J. Sci. **101**: 322.
Fossil Shell; a Poem. Chr. Obs. **34**: 219.
Fossil Sparrow-like Bird. Nature, **18**: 204.
Fossil Spider from the Coal Measures of Illinois. (O. Harger) Am. J. Sci. **107**: 219.
Fossil Sponges from the Lower Silurian. (O. C. Marsh) Am. J. Sci. **94**: 88.
Fossil Vegetables. Am. J. Sci. **25**: 108. — (J. E. Teschemacher) Am. J. Sci. **53**: 86.
Fossil Woods from British Columbia. (J. W. Dawson) Am. J. Sci. **107**: 47.
Fossiliferous Strata, American. (T. A. Conrad) Am. J. Sci. **97**: 358.
Foster, Balthazar. Colburn, **167**: 638.
Foster, Birket. Art J. **23**: 157.
— and his Works. Art J. **29**: 193.
Foster, Charles. Three Heavenly Witnesses. Chr. Obs. **67**: 941.
Foster, John. (G. B. Cheever) Am. Bib. Repos. 3d s. **3**: 1. — (A. P. Peabody) No. Am. **62**: 141. — (G. Gilfillan) Tait, n. s. **14**: 4. — Ecl. M. **33**: 337. — (G. M. Miller) Nat. M. **10**: 127. — (F. Parkman) Chr. Exam. **42**: 82. — (G. Peck) Meth. Q. **7**: 308. — (H. Bacon) Univ. Q. **4**: 128. — (S. F. Smith) Chr. R. **11**: 437. — (A. McWhorter) New Eng. **5**: 259. — Brit. Q. **4**: 197. Same art. Ecl. M. **9**: 293. Same art. Liv. Age, **14**: 97. — (I. Taylor) No. Brit. **5**: 281. Same art. Liv. Age, **10**: 507. — Tait, n. s. **12**: 727. Same art. Ecl. M. **7**: 225. — Chamb. J. **10**: 249. Same art. Liv. Age, **20**: 21. — Ecl. M. **33**: 246. — Liv. Age, **59**: 45. — Sharpe, **3**: 398, 413.
— and his Reviewers. (D. W. Phillips) Chr. R. **14**: 35, 178.
— and Robert Hall. (R. Vaughan) Brit. Q. **4**: 197.
— as an Essayist. (W. E. Screven) So. Lit. Mess. **18**: 439
— Contributions to Eclectic Review. Ecl. R. **79**: 584.

Foster, John. Essays. Chr. Obs. **5**: 40-186. — Ecl. R. **2**: 801, 930.
— Introduction to Doddridge. (L. Bacon) Chr. Mo. Spec. **10**: 411.
— Lectures. (I. Taylor) No. Brit. **2**: 87. — Ecl. R. **80**: 309.
— Letter on endless Punishment. (H. Ballou, 2d) Univ. Q. **6**: 391.
— Life and Correspondence of. Bib. R. **2**: 268. — Dub. Univ. **28**: 491. — Ecl. R. **84**: 346. — Prosp. R. **2**: 441. — Fraser, **34**: 127, 529. Same art. Ecl. M. **10**: 33. — So. Q. **11**: 321.
— on Missions. (L. Griggs) Chr. Q. Spec. **5**: 400. — Ed. Mo. R. **2**: 345. — Blackw. **5**: 453.
— on Popular Ignorance. Ed. Mo. R. **4**: 353. — Chr. Mo. Spec. **4**: 33.
— Writings of. Fraser, **30**: 684.
— Sermon on Death of. Ecl. R. **79**: 223.
Foster, John and William, of Queensbury. Lond. Soc. **37**: 75.
Foster, Luke, Sermons of. Ecl. R. **75**: 567.
Foster, P. Le Neve. Nature, **19**: 385.
Foster, Stephen C. Liv. Age, **80**: 333.
— and Negro Minstrelsy. (R. P. Nevin) Atlan. **20**: 608.
— Sketch of. (G. Birdseye) Potter Am. Mo. **12**: 28.
Foster, Thomas, Family of. N. E. Reg. **26**: 394.
Foster Family of Charlestown, Mass. N. E. Reg. **25**: 67.
Foster Genealogy. N. E. Reg. **1**: 352. **20**: 227, 308.
— and Forster Geneal. (E. J. Forster) N. E. Reg. **30**: 83.
Foster-Child. Bentley, **2**: 37.
Fothergill, Jessie. Wellfields. (F. F. Browne) Dial (Ch.), **1**: 135.
Fotheringay, England. (J. Jeans) Dark Blue, **3**: 727. — Penny M. **7**: 393.
— Day at. (R. J. King) Fraser, **90**: 284.
Foucault, the Academician. Putnam, **8**: 416.
Fouché, Joseph, Memoirs of. U. S. Lit. Gaz. **3**: 288. — Mo. R. **105**: 500. **106**: 467. — Mus. **7**: 204.
Foudras, T. L. A., Marquis le Chevalier d'Estagnol. New Q. **2**: 417.
Foul Play. (C. Reade; D. Boucicault) Ev. Sat. **5**: 1-129.
Foulke, Samuel. Journal, 1762-64. Pennsyl. M. **5**: 60.
Found and lost. Atlan. **5**: 391.
Found and lost; a Tale. Broadw. **8**: 349.
Found at Sea; a Sketch. Dub. Univ. **56**: 104.
Found by the Fairies; a Nursery Tale from Shakspere. (G. Roslyn) Colburn, **165**: 717.
Found dead; a Tale. (J. Payn) Chamb. J. **45**: 561-804.
Found drowned. (A. T. Freed) Lakeside, **1**: 375.
Found drowned; a Tale. (R. A. Arnold) Once a Week, **13**: 14-98.
Found drowned; a Tale. All the Year, **15**: 321.
Found faithful; a Story. Potter Am. Mo. **14**: 25, 121.
Found in the Snow. (H. Mar) Tinsley, **21**: 430.
Found out; a Tale. Sharpe, **39**: 225.
Found wanting. Knick. **63**: 330, 401, 494. **64**: 68-536.
Foundations. (J. Gaudand) Ecl. Engin. **18**: 68, 113. — Ecl. Engin. **8**: 40.
— in compressible Soils. (F. Baumann) Am. Arch. **7**: 140.
— in Concrete, Brickwork, and Stonework. Ecl. Engin. **8**: 336.
— of Albany Capitol. (W. J. McAlpin) Ecl. Engin. **21**: 388.
— on Sand. J. Frankl. Inst. **37**: 361.
— Pneumatic. (A. Heimercheidt) Ecl. Engin. **22**: 151.
— — Frictional Resistances of. (A. Schmoll) Ecl. Engin. **20**: 119.
— Pressure on. Ecl. Engin. **7**: 58. **18**: 274.
— under Water. (G. Jordan) Ecl. Engin. **10**: 360. — (A. Mitchell) J. Frankl. Inst. **45**: 393.
Founded on Fact. House. Words, **9**: 4.
Founders of Globe City; a Tale. (J. O. Culver) Putnam, **12**: 562, 672.
Founding in Brass, Copper, and Bronze. (E. Tuck) Ecl. Engin. **25**: 304.
Foundling. (Mrs. J. Thayer) Godey, **20**: 202.
Foundlings. Ho. & For. R. **3**: 497.
— and Infanticide. Once a Week, **13**: 332.
— of Paris. (A. Rhodes) Galaxy, **18**: 659.
Foundling Hospital. Chamb. J. **47**: 14.
— at Moscow. Once a Week, **10**: 330.
— in London. (N. E. Dodge) Lippinc. **3**: 293. — (W. H. Wills) House. Words, **7**: 49. Same art. Liv. Age, **37**: 314.
Foundling Hospitals. Ecl. R. **73**: 421. — Am. Church R. **24**: 596. — Penny M. **14**: 345.
— in China. Chamb. J. **26**: 78. Same art. Liv. Age, **51**: 316.
— in Italy. (Lady Amberley) Macmil. **30**: 351. Same art. Ecl. M. **83**: 442.
Fountain of Youth, Search after; Romance of 16th Cent. St. Paul's, **4**: 32, 198, 299.
Fountain of Youth; a Poem. Blackw. **129**: 720.
Fountain Violet; a Story. All the Year, **39**: 84, 106.
Fountains. Penny M. **4**: 246. Pract. M. **7**: 229.
— Drinking. *See* Drinking Fountains.
Fouqué. *See* La Motte Fouqué, F. de.
Fouquet, J., and the Brentano Miniatures. (C. Ruland) F. Arts Q. **4**: 27, 311.
Fouquet, Nicolas, the Magnificent. (F. Sheldon) Atlan. **13**: 467. — Bentley, **53**: 147. — Sharpe, **45**: 179. — Colburn, **125**: 227.
Four Bells of Chartres; a Tale. (F. Wedmore) Temp. Bar, **50**: 48.
Four Days with Sanna. (H. H. Jackson) Atlan. **48**: 39.
"411." (A. La Forge) Overland, **13**: 79.
Four-Leaved Clover. (Saxe Holm) Scrib. **8**: 213, 294.
Four Meetings. (H. James, jr.) Scrib. **15**: 44.
Four Sisters; a Story. Chamb. J. **25**: 358, 374, 391. Same art. Liv. Age, **50**: 347.
Four Suits; a Poem. (A. H. Baldwin) Belgra. **1**: 463.
Four Tombstones. (J. B. Holmes) Lakeside, **5**: 395.
Fourcroy, Anthony Francis. Anal. M. **2**: 328.
Fourfold Alibi; a Story. (W. L. Alden) Galaxy, **15**: 823.
Fourfold Dream. House. Words, **17**: 467.
Fourier, Charles. (A. J. Booth) Fortn. **18**: 530, 673. — Ev. Sat. **13**: 638, 649. **14**: 23, 44. — Tait, n. s. **15**: 700.
— and his Philosophy. (H. Doherty) Peop. J. **3**: 262. — Chr. Rem. **5**: 15.
Fourier, Joseph. (S. Osgood) Chr. Exam. **45**: 204.
— Arago's Eulogy on. No. Brit. **4**: 380.
Fourierism. (J. F. Clarke) Chr. Exam. **37**: 57. — (D. W. Clark) Meth. Q. **5**: 545. — Dial, **4**: 473. — Prosp. R. **4**: 366. — (A. Brisbane) Bost. Q. **4**: 494. **5**: 183
— and the Church. Brownson, **6**: 91.
— and Communism. (J. Mazzini) Peop. J. **3**: 345.
— and similar Schemes. (H. Ballou, 2d) Univ. Q. **2**: 52.
— and the Socialists. Dial, **3**: 86.
— W. H. Channing on. Brownson, **6**: 438.
Fournais, Jacob, the oldest Man. Ev. Sat. **11**: 226.
Fourrière, The. (Mrs. W. P. Byrne) Fraser, **88**: 226.
Fourteen Stars, The. Victoria, **18**: 381.
Fourteenth of the Month; a Memorable Day. Temp. Bar, **16**: 395.
Fourth Commandment. (A. Trollope) Fortn. **3**: 529.
Fourth Dimension, What is? (C. H. Hinton) Dub. Univ. **96**: 15.
Fourth of July. Penn Mo. **6**: 510. — Ev. Sat. **9**: 434, 441.
— Celebration at Dozeyvale. Godey, **57**: 17, 115, 223.
— in America. Cong. M. **22**: 427.
— Thoughts for. (L. R. Hamersly) Godey, **27**: 41.
Fourth Waits. (F. D. Millet) Atlan. **38**: 578.
Fowle, William Bentley. Am. J. Educ. **10**: 597.

Fowle, William Bentley, Memoir of, with portrait. (E. Nason) N. E. Reg. **23**: 109.
Fowler, Absalom, with portrait. De Bow, **11**: 674.
Fowler, Isaac V., Portrait of. Dem. R. **38**: 173.
Fowler, John, and the Steam Plow, with portrait. Pract. M. **5**: 257.
Fowler Genealogy. (H. N. Otis) N. E. Reg. **7**: 131. — (J. Fowler) N. E. Reg. **11**: 247.
Fowling; a Poem. (F. Jeffrey) Ed. R. **13**: 69.
— in Faro and Shetland. Liv. Age, **19**: 580.
Fox, Sir Charles, with portrait. Pract. M. **6**: 129.
Fox, Charles James. Blackw. **116**: 511. — Liv. Age, **2**: 483. **41**: 339. — Month, **6**: 33, 141.
— and George III. Quar. **105**: 463.
— and Pitt. Blackw. **3**: 456. Same art. So. Lit. Mess. **4**: 84. — Quar. **97**: 513. Same art. Liv. Age, **47**: 705. — Ecl. R. **83**: 595.
— as an Orator. (G. Shepard) Bib. Sac. **34**: 447.
— at St. Anne's Hill. Liv. Age, **56**: 619.
— Character of. (Syd. Smith) Ed. R. **14**: 353. — (J. H. Frere) Quar. **2**: 375. — Ecl. R. **8**: 800. — (J. Foster) Ecl. R. **10**: 1113.
— Correspondence with Wakefield. Quar. **9**: 313. — Anal. M. **4**: 89.
— Day with. Liv. Age, **38**: 250.
— Early History of. (J. Bigelow) Harper, **62**: 419. — Appleton, **25**: 17.
— Episode of. All the Year, **18**: 173.
— History of James II. (J. Foster) Ecl. R. **8**: 900. **10**: 638.
— — French translation of. Ed. R. **15**: 190.
— — Heywood's Vindication of. (Syd. Smith) Ed. R. **18**: 325. — Ecl. R. **14**: 1041.
— — Rose's Observations on. Quar. **2**: 243. — Ecl. R. **10**: 638.
— Obituary of. Chr. Obs. **5**: 721, 787. **6**: 60–826.
— Political Career of. (W. O. Johnson) No. Am. **77**: 373.
— Russell's Memorials of. Ed. R. **99**: 1. Same art. Ecl. M. **31**: 289. — Ed. R. **107**: 134. — Chr. Obs. **59**: 685. — Fraser, **47**: 714. **56**: 698. **75**: 395. — Liv. Age, **44**: 286. **61**: 318. — Colburn, **103**: 291. **111**: 157. — Bentley, **46**: 285. — Ecl. R. **98**: 563.
— Trevelyan's Life of. Ed. R. **152**: 540. — Westm. **115**: 71. — Blackw. **129**: 151. — (A. V. Dicey) Nation, **31**: 412, 428. — (H. C. Lodge) Internat. R. **10**: 274. — Ecl. M. **96**: 78.
— Trotter's Memoirs of. (J. H. Frere) Quar. **6**: 518.
Fox, George. Ecl. R. **113**: 225.
— an Ecstatic. (J. W. Jackson) Zoist, **13**: 361.
— and the early Quakers. (J. R. Anderson) Nat M. **5**: 322. — (N. Fox) Bapt. Q. **11**: 433. — (W. R. G. Mellen) Canad. Mo. **19**: 400. — (W. Howitt) Tait, n. s. **1**: 577.
— Character and Experiences of. Westm. **57**: 599.
— Life of. Westm. **47**: 371. Same art. Liv. Age, **15**: 1. Same art. Ecl. M. **12**: 1. — Retros. **11**: 1. — Ecl. R. **86**: 649. — Chr. Obs. **52**: 454, 522.
— Principles and Influence of. (J. Lord) Bost. R. **6**: 19.
Fox, George Croker. Poems. Dub. R. **7**: 484.
Fox, George Townshend. Sermons. Chr. Obs. **67**: 676.
Fox, Henry Watson, Memoir of. Chr. Obs. **50**: 779.
— Posthumous Fragment by. Chr. Obs. **52**: 297.
Fox, Thomas B., Obituary Notice of. (A. P. Peabody) Unita. R. **6**: 325.
Fox, William J. (M. D. Conway) Radical, **5**: 22. — (J. Bowring) Theo. R. **3**: 413. — with portrait (J. Saunders) Peop. J. **3**: 69.
— Reminiscences of. (J. H. Osborne) Univ. Q. **29**: 293.
— Writings of. Ecl. R. **92**: 158.
— Sermons. (H. Ware, jr.) Chr. Exam. **11**: 168. — (O. A. Brownson) Chr. Exam. **17**: 15, 283.
Fox, The. (J. Burroughs) Putnam, **16**: 371. — Sharpe, **51**: 47.
— Chapter on. Knick. **64**: 515.
— Flying, City of. Once a Week, **5**: 639.
— and Fox-Hunters. (T. B. Thorpe) Harper, **23**: 749.
Foxes and Fox-Hunting. (M. Schele de Vere) Hours at Home, **8**: 423.
— Fur-Bearing. (J. K. Lord) Intel. Obs. **12**: 354.
— North American. So. Q. **13**: 403.
Fox Chase in Old England. Knick. **12**: 133.
Fox-Hunter, Recollections of a. Belgra. **16**: 55, 472.
Fox-Hunters; a Poem. (G. H. Barnes) Scrib. **3**: 385.
Fox-Hunting. Quar. **107**: 422. — Once a Week, **17**: 551.
— at Home. (F. A. Eaton) Macmil. **19**: 115.
— at Pytchley. (J. Plummer) Once a Week, **11**: 291.
— in England. (C. J. Apperley) Quar. **47**: 216. — (G. E. Waring) Atlan. **33**: 15. — Broadw. **1**: 234.
— in France. Tait, n. s. **2**: 680.
— in Ireland. Temp. Bar, **16**: 97.
— in New England. (R. E. Robinson) Scrib. **15**: 293.
— on the Mountains of Scotland. Chamb. J. **54**: 473.
— Trollope's Defense of. (H. Taylor) Fortn. **13**: 63.
— White Day and a red Fox. (J. Burroughs) Scrib. **16**: 188.
Foxe, John, his Book of Martyrs. Lond. Q. **50**: 409.
Foxton, F. J., Froude, and Newman. Ecl. R. **92**: 257.
Foxvilles of Foxville; a Tale. (J. Milner) Cath. World, **14**: 604.
Foy Family. Tinsley, **14**: 507.
Fra Aloysius. (E. Lazarus) Lippinc. **17**: 183.
Fra Angelico. *See* Angelico.
Fra Angelico; a Tale. (E. Polko) Argosy, **16**: 462.
Fra Giacomo; a Poem. (R. Buchanan) Temp. Bar, **16**: 391.
Fractions, Nature and Use of. Penny M. **1**: 285.
Fragments from a young Wife's Diary. Liv. Age, **34**: 610.
— of a broken Life. Tinsley, **6**: 470.
— of a Continental Tour. Dub. Univ. **2**: 289, 548.
— of an old Romanza. Dub. Univ. **64**: 47.
Fragonard, Jean-Honoré. (S. Colvin) Portfo. **4**: 2. — Art J. **5**: 189.
Framingham, Mass., Ministers of. Am. Q. Reg. **11**: 270.
Framley Parsonage; a Novel. (A. Trollope) Cornh. **1**: 1–691. **2**: 34–650. **3**: 48–473.
France. (F. Harrison) Fortn. **21**: 841. — Bentley, **1**: 508. — Brit. & For. R. **1**: 17, 492. — New Eng. M. **3**: 316. — Hogg, **7**: 273. — Liv. Age, **32**: 612. — Mus. **41**: 533.
— Administration of the Seine, 1789–1815. Chr. Rem. **56**: 96.
— Africa in; or the Beard and Pipe. Colburn, **72**: 142.
— Aggressions against Spain. Selec. Ed. R. **4**: 325. — Pamph. **22**: 521.
— Agricultural Population of, 1852. Westm. **57**: 230.
— American Colony in. (G. A. Townsend) Galaxy, **1**: 387.
— American Life in. (M. L. Putnam) Atlan. **27**: 92–715. **28**: 276.
— Ancient, Coulange's Political Institutions of. (M. Thevenin) No. Am. **120**: 455.
— and Argentine and Oriental Republics. New York R. **6**: 74.
— and Austria, 1859. Colburn, **115**: 366.
— — and Italy, 1859. Ed. R. **109**: 558. — Ecl. R. **109**: 205. Same art. Ecl. M. **46**: 547.
— and the East, 1841. Ed. R. **72**: 529.
— and England. For. Q. **26**: 234. — Fraser, **2**: 469.
— — Alliances of. Westm. **63**: 1.
— — Characteristics of. No. Brit. **21**: 45.
— — Comparative Sketches of. Ecl. R. **88**: 323.

France and England, Comparative Skill and Industry of. (M. Chevenix) Ed. R. **32**: 340.
— — Customs and Manners in. Quar. **133**: 199. Same art. Liv. Age, **114**: 579.
— — Earl of Portland's Mission, 1698. Blackw. **80**: 104.
— — Germany, and Russia. Liv. Age, **42**: 376.
— — in the 17th Century. Blackw. **48**: 259.
— — in 1781. (I. Taylor) Ex. H. Lec. **17**: 1.
— — in 19th Century. (W. O. Johnson) No. Am. **77**: 118.
— — in 1811. Walsh's R. **1**: 101, 297.
— — in 1812. Walsh's R. **3**: 161.
— — in 1830. Blackw. **28**: 699.
— — in 1840. Blackw. **49**: 457. — Mo. R. **154**: 173.
— — in 1848. Quar. **83**: 135.
— — in 1852. No. Brit. **18**: 302.
— — in 1870. (C. C. Chesney) Fortn. **14**: 581.
— — Political Prospects, 1848. Quar. **83**: 250.
— — Relations of. Nat. R. **7**: 280.
— — Russia, and Turkey, 1857. Westm. **68**: 415.
— — Social and historical, 1858. Brit. Q. **29**: 215.
— — Social Character of. Mo. R. **117**: 24.
— — State of Science in. (M. Chevenix) Ed. R. **34**: 383.
— and Europe. For. Q. **27**: 419.
— — in 1859. Bent. Q. **2**: 1. Same art. Liv. Age, **63**: 515.
— and Free Trade. All the Year, **2**: 466.
— and Germany. Blackw. **117**: 765. Same art. Ecl. M. **85**: 196.
— — and England, 1870. Ed. R. **132**: 554. Same art. Liv. Age, **107**: 515.
— — Strength of, compared (A. V. Fircks) J. Statis. Soc. **38**: 112.
— and her Organization. Mo. R. **163**: 226.
— and Ireland, Sympathy of. Tinsley, **7**: 266.
— — Trade between. Dub. Univ. **57**: 208.
— and Italy, 1862. Brit. Q. **36**: 103. Same art. Ecl. M. **57**: 145.
— — Condition of, 1863. Ecl. M. **60**: 125.
— — First Impressions of. (N. Hawthorne) Good Words, **12**: 25–830.
— — Pedestrian Tour through. Mo. R. **133**: 115.
— — Wilson's Records of a Route through. Mo. R. **137**: 518.
— and Mexico, 1867. (C. S. F. Weld) Radical, **3**: 193.
— and Morocco. Liv. Age, **2**: 277.
— and Napoleon III. Westm. **78**: 433. Same art. Ecl. M. **57**: 20.
— and the Œcumenical Council of 1869. Brit. Q. **49**: 391. Same art. Ecl. M. **73**: 641.
— and Paris, in 1820, 1830, and 1840. (A. V. Kirwan) Fraser, **62**: 389, 569. **63**: 184.
— and Prussia, 1867. Colburn, **141**: 1.
— — and Germany, 1869. St. Paul's, **3**: 147.
— — in 1874. (E. Dowden) Contemp. **16**: 618.
— — Old Scores. All the Year, **24**: 251.
— and Russia, 1804. (H. Brougham) Ed. R. **4**: 43.
— and Savoy and Switzerland. Ed. R. **111**: 533.
— and Scotland. No. Brit. **24**: 289.
— — Michel on. No. Brit. **37**: 369.
— and Spain, Proscribed Races of. Ed. R. **87**: 491.
— and Syria. Mus. **40**: 185.
— and the United States. (G. M. Towle) Hours at Home, **2**: 101.
— — in 1811. Walsh's Am. R. **1**: 1. **2**: 189.
— — in 1835. Niles's Reg. **47**: 334. **48**: 13, 22.
— — in 1836. Niles's Reg. **49**: 346.
— — in 1842. Ed. R. **75**: 1.
— — in 1866. (M. D. Conway) Fortn. **3**: 442. Same art. Liv. Age. **88**: 545.
— — Proposed Treaty between, 1879. (R. E. Thompson) Penn Mo. **10**: 772.
France, Antiquities of. Penny M. **9**: 204.
— Armament of, compared with England. Dub. Univ. **56**: 387.
— Army of. (E. Laboulaye) O. & N. **2**: 516.
— — British Troops in. Colburn, **103**: 370.
— — Conscription for. (G. Balfour) J. Statis. Soc. **30**: 216.
— — Cost of. (W. H. Sykes) J. Statis. Soc. **27**: 1. — Cornh. **7**: 310.
— — The French Soldier, 1861. Colburn, **122**: 239.
— — History of. Colburn, **123**: 367, 487. **124**: 112, 240.
— — in 1734. Fraser, **78**: 249.
— — in 1852. Tait, n. s. **19**: 157.
— — in 1860. Colburn, **118**: 379.
— — in 1867. Month, **7**: 253.
— — in 1875. (C. I. Barnard) Nation, **21**: 167. — Fraser, **91**: 581. Same art. Ecl. M. **85**: 39.
— — in 1877. Blackw. **121**: 391. Same art. Ecl. M. **88**: 665. Same art. Liv. Age, **133**: 291.
— — Organization of. (J. Picciotto) Dub. Univ. **77**: 66.
— — Promotion and Discipline in. Month, **6**: 493. **7**: 12.
— — Subsistence of. (B. E. Martin) U. S. Serv. M. **5**: 143.
— — Trochu on. (M. Heilprin) Nation, **11**: 263.
— Arts and Manufactures in. For. Q. **3**: 359.
— At the Land's End of. Cornh. **32**: 540.
— Autumn in Western. (M. B. Edwards) Fraser, **92**: 652. **93**: 51–514.
— Bank of. *See* Bank of France.
— Bains-de-Mer. Tinsley, **1**: 221.
— Bayonne to Fuenterrabia. (L. G. F. March) Bentley, **28**: 640. **29**: 88, 213.
— Bench and Bar in. (G. Merrill) Am. Law R. **11**: 672.
— Best's Four Years in. Lond. M. **16**: 91.
— Lady Blessington's Idler in. Mo. R. **155**: 407.
— Bulwer's France and the French. Colburn, **46**: 213. — Tait, n. s. **3**: 208.
— By Rail through. (S. L. Clemens) Overland, **1**: 18.
— Castles of. Once a Week, **8**: 557, 585.
— Celebrities of. (J. H. Browne) Harper, **47**: 833. — Brit. Q. **20**: 220. — Westm. **77**: 461.
— Champagne Districts of. Penny M. **13**: 399.
— Château of, and its Dependencies. (Mrs. C. Cook) Putnam, **15**: 606.
— Châteaux of, Old. Colburn, **112**. 291.
— Children in. Liv. Age, **112**: 259.
— Church of. (E. Laboulaye) Am. Presb. R. **9**: 259. — (Mme. Blaze de Bury) Nation, **9**: 288. — (S. Wilberforce) Quar. **118**: 498. Same art. Ecl. M. **66**: 265. — Westm. **7**: 67.
— — and Education. Chr. Rem. **10**: 356.
— — and the Revolution, Pressense on. Chr. Obs. **69**: 857, 897.
— — and the Papacy in 1682. Dub. R. **65**: 328.
— — during the Revolution. Chr. Obs. **76**: 97, 205.
— — Jervis's History of. Chr. Obs. **73**: 9. — Dub. R. **72**: 259. **74**: 100, 362. — Quar. **135**: 40.
— — Liberties of. (Dr. Cunningham) No. Brit. **13**: 447. — Westm. **12**: 213. — Princ. **35**: 21.
— — Present State of, 1856. Chr. Rem. **32**: 423.
— — — 1879. (Abbé Martin) 19th Cent. **6**: 1093.
— — Reform in. Am. Church R. **32**: 161.
— — Reformed. *See below*, France, Reformed Church of.
— Church and School in, 1879. Dub. R. **84**: 493.
— Church and State in. (D. Charraud) Unita. R. **9**: 214.
— — since 1798. Brit. Q. **42**: 178.
— — Perrens on. Chr. Obs. **74**: 570.
— Churches of, Lutheran, Methodist, and Free. Cong. **5**: 103.
— — Three Weeks among. (H. Alford) Good Words, **6**: 688.
— — Vandalism and Restoration. Chr. Rem. **3**: 188.

France, Claim against, for Spoliations. (E. Everett) No. Am. 22: 136. — Hunt, 12: 115. — Am. Q. 10: 156. 17: 431. — Dem. R. 14: 133. — Niles's Reg. 32: 45. 34: 371. — (F. B. Perkins) O. & N. 7: 205. — (C. M. Gibbins) Galaxy, 17: 620. — Am. Q. 17: 431. — (J. Q. Adams) Ann. Reg. 6: 39. — (E. Everett) Ann. Reg. 5: 26. — (W. C. Rives) Ann. Reg. 8: 22. — (H. G. Rice) Hunt, 15: 366. — Niles's Reg. 26: 203.
— Claret and Burgundy Districts of. Penny M. 13: 450.
— Clergy of. No. Brit. 36: 433.
— — Manners and Miseries of. Fraser, 47: 590. Same art. Liv. Age, 38: 67.
— Clerical Question in. Nat. Q. 40: 253.
— Colonial Duties and German League. For. Q. 22: 299.
— Colonial Enterprise of. Pract. M. 5: 220.
— Colonies of, in Africa. No. Brit. 49: 125.
— — Cost of maintaining. Tait, n. s. 1: 287.
— — French Schemes of, 1838. Tait, n. s. 4: 233.
— Commercial and Industrial Reform in, 1860. Colburn, 118: 253.
— Commercial Capabilities of. Penny M. 8: 60.
— Commercial History of. (F. Wharton) Hunt, 5: 105. 7: 301.
— Commercial Policy of. (T. L. Dunvell) Hunt, 17: 19. — For. Q. 14: 172. — Ed. R. 50: 48.
— Commercial Relations of, with England. Ed. R. 111: 277. — Tait, n. s. 21: 1.
— Commercial System of. (J. R. McCulloch) Ed. R. 50: 48. — Bank. M. (N. Y.) 16: 124.
— Commercial Treaty with, 1860. Dub. Univ. 56: 3.
— Commerce of. (T. P. Thompson) Westm. 16: 534. — — Putnam, 11: 746. — De Bow, 18: 366. — Hunt, 7: 229. 8: 131, 438. 13: 26.
— — 1830–48. (J. T. Danson) J. Statis. Soc. 13: 289.
— — 1844. Hunt, 16: 476, 547.
— — 1846. Hunt, 18: 497.
— — 1848. (F. Hunt) Hunt, 22: 259.
— — 1849. Hunt, 24: 284.
— — with Great Britain. Dub. R. 6: 357.
— — with the U. S. (J. S. Moore) No. Am. 126: 421.
— Communism in, 1877. No. Am. 125: 529. *See* Commune in Paris.
— Constituent Assembly of. Quar. 28: 271.
— Constitution of. Mo. R. 109: 512.
— — 1848. Westm. 50: 282.
— Constitutions of. Mo. R. 90: 449. — So. Q. 16: 502.
— — Modern. (E. C. G. Murray) Lippinc. 16: 179.
— Constit. Government in. (C. J. Wallis) Macmil. 27: 212.
— Constitutionalists in. Quar. 102: 1.
— Corps Legislatif of. Once a Week, 20: 211.
— Country Towns and Inns of. (J. Marvel) Bentley, 23: 11, 143.
— Court of. Ed. R. 44: 413.
— — Extravagance of. Galaxy, 2: 257.
— — in 1830. Cath. World, 18: 403.
— — Manners and Morals of. Brit. & For. R. 2: 397.
— Court Life in Old. (Mrs. Elliot) Canad. Mo. 4: 75. — All the Year, 30: 343.
— Court of the Tuileries. N. Ecl. 2: 196.
— Courts of Justice in. All the Year, 21: 604.
— Craftsmen's Associations in. (W. H. Browne) So. R. n. s. 1: 95.
— Crime and Criminal Law in. Lond. Q. 8: 92. — Cornh. 12: 604. — Westm. 18: 353.
— Criminal Court in, Day in. (J. Pardoe) Sharpe, 16: 147. Same art. Ecl. M. 27: 264. Same art. Liv. Age, 35: 298.
— Criminal Jurisprudence in. Ed. R. 75: 359.
— Criminal Justice in. Dub. Univ. 79: 651.
— Criminal Trials in. For. Q. 4: 139. — Mus. 15: 211.
— — Modern. Ecl. M. 26: 247.
France, Crown Matrimonial of. Dub. Univ. 41: 269. Same art. Ecl. M. 29: 56. Same art. Liv. Age, 37: 283.
— Death and Dying in. For. Q. 32: 42.
— Decline of. Colburn, 89: 452.
— Democracy in, Guizot's. Ed. R. 89: 554. — Tait, n. s. 16: 73. — So. Q. 15: 14.
— — Adams on. (W. H. Browne) So. M. 16: 314.
— — during the Middle Ages. No. Am. 119: 185.
— Democratic Movement in, 1869. (K. Blind) Lippinc. 4: 449.
— — American Influence on. (J. McCarthy) Am. Cath. Q. 5: 636.
— Dick Moon in, Wey's. St. James, 4: 326.
— Dress in. Blackw. 112: 154. Same art. Liv. Age, 114: 549.
— Drives from a French Farm. (P. G. Hamerton) Atlan. 25: 656. 26: 23.
— Dynastic Fusion in. (M. Heilprin) Nation, 12: 430.
— Ecclesiastical Power in. For. R. 5: 461.
— Education in. *See* Education.
— Elective System in. Brit. & For. R. 2: 496.
— — in 1837. Tait, n. s. 4: 729.
— Encouragement of Art in. Niles's Reg. 20: 399.
— English in. (J. P. Edwards) Peop. J. 7: 250.
— English Journalism in. St. James, 7: 230.
— Etiquette in. Belgra. 5: 538.
— Experience in. Lond. Soc. 36: 61.
— Family Life and Manners in. (K. Hillebrand) Appleton, 82: 120.
— Fashionable Life in. Bentley, 42: 466.
— — two hundred Years ago. Fraser, 30: 294.
— Financial Example of. Bank. M. (N. Y.) 33: 365.
— Financial History of Reign of Louis Philippe. (M. S. Dumon) Hunt, 28: 659. 29: 19.
— Finance in. For. Q. 7: 388. — Mo. R. 89: 449. — Ecl. M. 77: 746. — Bank. M. (N. Y.) 34: 679. — (Lord Hobart) Macmil. 11: 253. — Ho. & For. R. 2: 374.
— — History of the French Assignats. Chamb. J. 41: 817. Same art. Ecl. M. 64: 441.
— — in 1853. Bank. M. (L.) 13: 196.
— — in 1854. (L. Faucher) Bank. M. (L.) 15: 82.
— — in 1863. Ho. & For. R. 2: 374.
— — in 1866, compared with England. (G. Balfour) J. Statis. Soc. 29: 323.
— — in 1871. Bank. M. (L.) 31: 1049. — Blackw. 110: 215. Same art. Bank. M. (N. Y.) 26: 337. Same art. Liv. Age, 110: 707. — Ev. Sat. 11: 74.
— — — German War Indemnity. (G. Marsland) Bank. M. (N. Y.) 29: 14. — Bank. M. (L.) 31: 975. 34: 888.
— — — — How paid. (L. Wolowski) Bank. M. (N. Y.) 29: 769, 857. — Bank. M. (N. Y.) 29: 510.
— — — — Results of. Bank. M. (N. Y.) 29: 93.
— — in 1875. Bank. M. (N. Y.) 29: 945.
— — Problems in. Bank. M. (N. Y.) 30: 361.
— Five Months in a Pine Forest in. Bentley, 51: 78.
— Flower-Farms in Southern. Cornh. 10: 427.
— Food in. Blackw. 111: 120. Same art. Liv. Age, 112: 800. — Liv. Age, 54: 34.
— Four Years in. Colburn, 17: 268. — Lond. M. 16: 91.
— From London Bridge to Cabourg. Fraser, 89: 61.
— From Cabourg to St. Malo. Fraser, 89: 210.
— From Paris to Marley; the new Hyperion. Lippinc. 12: 9–625. 13: 9–649. 14: 9–649.
— Frontiers of. Colburn, 141: 253.
— Future of. (E. de Laveleye) Fortn. 14: 615. Same art. Liv. Age, 108: 131. Same art. Ecl. M. 76: 129.
— — Renan on. (A. Laugel) Nation, 26: 238.
— Glimpse of. (D. M. Craik) Good Words, 8: 591, 681.

France, Government of, Genius and Disposition of. Quar. 3: 320. — Chr. Obs. 9: 570.
— — in 1809, Walsh's Letter on. (F. Jeffrey) Ed. R. 16: 1.
— — in 1824, Stability of. Ed. R. 40: 517.
— — Instability of any possible. Ev. Sat. 11: 122.
— Government and social Organization of. Ecl. R. 79: 249.
— Head's Fagot of French Sticks. Chamb. J. 17: 54.
— Heine's Letters from, 1840–44. (Countess de Bury) No. Am. 83: 287.
— Highlanders of. (H. S. Fagan) Good Words, 8: 97.
— Historians of. Blackw. 30: 230, 731.
— — Modern. Ecl. M. 54: 119.
— Historical Inquiry in. Ed. R. 73: 44.
— Histories of. (H. Harrisse) No. Am. 96: 239.
— — Modern. Ed. R. 79: 1. — Westm. 6: 62. — (G. H. Lewes) Westm. 36: 273. — Blackw. 30: 230.
— — by modern Frenchmen. Brit. Q. 14: 405.
— History of, *General and Early:* —
— — Crowe and Guizot on. Westm. 19: 283.
— — Early. Dub. Univ. 72: 99.
— — Godwin's. Chr. R. 25: 589. — (F. Williams) Meth. Q. 21: 127. — Nat. Q. 1: 30.
— — Great Monarchs of. So. Lit. Mess. 25: 401.
— — Guizot's. (M. Thevenin) No. Am. 123: 145. — Brit. Q. 65: 165. — Ed. R. 140: 201.
— — Kitchin's, to the Year 1453. (A. V. Dicey) Nation, 18: 268. 26: 215. — No. Am. 119: 442.
— — Martin's. Ed. R. 106: 382. Same art. Ecl. M. 43: 172.
— — Michelet's. Bentley, 41: 529. 42: 101. 43: 566. — Brit. & For. R. 13: 415. — Blackw. 49: 141. 52: 386, 530. — For. Q. 25: 420. — (J. S. Mill) Ed. R. 79: 1. — Prosp. R. 1: 228.
— — Monteil's. Mo. R. 158: 516.
— — Philosophy of. Tait, 4: 341.
— — Pictures from. Dub. Univ. 73: 396.
— — Pleasant Passages from. Dub. Univ. 72: 99. Same art. Ecl. M. 71: 1220.
— — Ranken's. (H. Hallam) Ed. R. 6: 209.
— — Restoration and Revolution compared. Fraser, 35: 418.
— — Revolutions of. Westm. 15: 406. — (A. Featherman) De Bow, 29: 673.
— — — Abortiveness of. (J. C. Morison) Fortn. 20: 41.
— — — Republics, National Assemblies, etc. Fraser, 37: 615.
— — Sismondi's. Ed. R. 35: 488.
— — Stephen's Lectures on. (A. N. Littlejohn) Am. Church R. 5: 88. — So. Q. 22: 443. — (F. Bowen) No. Am. 75: 247. — Ecl. R. 95: 301. — Fraser, 45: 170, 261. — Brit. Q. 15: 1. Same art. Ecl. M. 25: 515. — Chr. Obs. 52: 308. 53: 176. — Dub. Univ. 39: 570. — New Q. 1: 14.
— — Struggles of the 16th Century. (K. O'Meara) Cath. World, 30: 145.
— — Thierry's. Ecl. R. 49: 431.
— — under the Merovingians and Carlovingians. Chr. Rem. 9: 66. 32: 1. 33: 380.
— — under the Bourbons. Chr. Rem. 54: 187.
— — under the Roman Emperors. Dub. Univ. 73: 33.
— — Wars in, 1327–77. Mo. R. 160: 213.
— History of, *18th Century:* —
— — The ancient Régime. Westm. 66: 462. Same art. Liv. Age, 52: 129. — (H. Taine) Contemp. 31: 538. Same art. Ecl. M. 90: 450. — Dub. Univ. 48: 442. — Ed. R. 104: 531.
— — — Influence of. Chr. Rem. 48: 255.
— — — Last Days of. Month, 40: 497.
— — — Life under. (H. Taine) Galaxy, 21: 234.
France, History of, *18th Century:* The ancient Régime, Taine on. (M. Allies) Cath. World, 30: 170. — (J. Morley) Fortn. 25: 370. — (J. C. Morrison) Macmil. 33: 470. — Quar. 141: 386.
— — — Tocqueville on. Dub. R. 80: 111. — (J. T. Crane) Meth. Q. 17: 394.
— — Decline of the Monarchy. Westm. 99: 70.
— — Lacretelle's. Quar. 11: 138. 28: 271. — Ecl. R. 22: 101, 240.
— — Paris before the Outbreak. (H. Taine) Contemp. 32: 234.
— — Regency of the Duke of Orleans, 1715. Temp. Bar, 39: 181. Same art. Liv. Age, 119: 233.
— — Reign of Louis XV. Ed. R. 90: 77. — Ecl. M. 74: 225.
— — — Miss Pardoe's. Bib. R. 5: 253.
— — under Richelieu and Colbert, J. H. Bridges's. Fraser, 75: 537. Same art. Ecl. M. 69: 78.
— History of, *Revolution of* 1789: —
— — (J. S. C. Abbott) Harper, 16: 35. — (W. Sargent) No. Am. 78: 105. — (F. Jeffrey) Ed. R. 1: 1. Same art. Selec. Ed. R. 5: 110. — (Syd. Smith) Ed. R. 1: 122. — (F. Jeffrey) Ed. R. 2: 1. — (J. A. Murray) Ed. R. 3: 486. — Ed. R. 4: 99. 5: 421. — (F. Jeffrey) Ed. R. 6: 137. Same art. Selec. Ed. R. 5: 120. — Ed. R. 14: 211. — Mo. R. 107: 445. — So. Lit. Mess. 7: 609. — Quar. 26: 229. — Am. Q. 1: 189. — Irish Q. 9: 1. — (M. Allies) Cath. World, 30: 675. — Chr. Rem. 16: 165.
— — Alison's. (F. Bowen) No. Am. 56: 363. — Blackw. 42: 715. 46: 272. — Mus. 2: 61. 32: 305. 37: 41. — Dub. Univ. 1: 619. 8: 230, 505. 10: 600. 11: 582. 14: 275. 20: 583. — (J. T. Headley) Am. Whig R. 1: 341. — Tait, 3: 496. — Mo. R. 136: 281. 158: 420. *See* Europe, History of, Alison's.
— — and the ancient Régime. (H. von Sybel) Contemp. 36: 432.
— — and Catholic Doctrine. Dub. R. 55: 253. 56: 279.
— — and Catholic Reform. (C. Loyson) Am. Church R. 35: 21.
— — and its Causes, Sybel on. Chr. Obs. 68: 456, 672, 784. 70: 770.
— — and Empire. Dem. R. 20: 407.
— — and Literature. (E. Dowden) Contemp. 30: 120.
— — and Religion. (Mrs. M. R. Butler) Chr. Q. 2: 381.
— — Anecdotes of. Chr. Obs. 8: 701.
— — Babeuf's Conspiracy. (J. W. Croker) Quar. 45: 167.
— — Bailly's Memoirs. (F. Jeffrey) Ed. R. 6: 137.
— — Barante's Histoire de la Convention of 1792. Colburn, 92: 402.
— — Blanc's. Ed. R. 118: 101. — Westm. 80: 147. — Colburn, 111: 369.
— — Bright Tints of. Liv. Age, 39: 687.
— — Carlyle's. (C. A. Bartol) Chr. Exam. 24: 345. — Ed. R. 71: 411. — Fraser, 16: 85. — (J. S. Mill) Westm. 27: 17. — Bost. Q. 1: 407. — Mus. 40: 385. — Dub. R. 5: 349. — Mo. R. 143: 543.
— — Carrichon's Narrative. Blackw. 112: 361.
— — Causes of. (Lord Mahon) Quar. 49: 152. — Ecl. R. 57: 361. — Putnam, 8: 471.
— — Church and, Pressensé on. Chr. Obs. 69: 857, 897.
— — Close of. Irish Q. 9: 1092.
— — Com. of Public Safety. (J. W. Croker) Quar. 67: 431.
— — Condorcet's Memoirs on. Portfo. (Den.) 33: 33.
— — Constituent Assembly of. (J. W. Croker) Quar 28: 271. — Liv. Age, 40: 283.
— — Count Miot de Melito and. Nat. R. 8: 112.
— — Croker's Essays on. New Q. 7: 3.
— — Mrs. Elliott's Narrative of. Chamb. J. 31: 307.
— — Episode of. (H. Schütz-Wilson) Dark Blue, 2: 738.
— — Feast of the Supreme Being, 1794. (A. Adam) Liv. Age, 142: 470.

France, History of, *Revolution of* 1789: France before and since. Fraser, **54**: 363.
— — Goddesses of Reign of Terror. (O. S. Leland) Knick. **56**: 113.
— — Historians of. Brit. Q. **10**: 168.
— — Historical Data of. Westm. **38**: 193.
— — History of. Ed. R. **128**: 289.
— — in a Country Town. (J. R. Green) Contemp. **7**: 416.
— — Incident of. Chamb. J. **52**: 331. — Hogg, **6**: 286.
— — Invasion of France in 1792. Colburn, **134**: 369.
— — Jacobin Club. (G. Bliss, jr.) No. Am. **82**: 128.
— — Jacobin View of. (R. D. Osborn) Nation, **33**: 497.
— — Lamartine's History of Girondists. Ed. R. **87**: 1. Same art. Liv. Age, **16**: 289. — (C. W. Upham) No. Am. **66**: 288. — (K. Armstrong) Am. Whig R. **7**: 358. — Ecl. M. **13**: 219. — Fraser, **36**: 253. — Ecl. R. **87**: 291, 486. — So. Q. **16**: 53. — Liv. Age, **18**: 577. *See* Girondists.
— — Lessons of. Quar. **135**: 265. — (A. V. Dicey) Nation, **17**: 307, 322.
— — Lives of Revolutionists. (R. Southey) Quar. **7**: 412.
— — Mallet du Pan's Memoirs and Correspondence of. Ed. R. **95**: 481.
— — Miguet's History of. Ecl. R. **44**: 231.
— — National Assembly. (J. S. C. Abbott) Harper, **15**: 606.
— — National Convention. For. Q. **13**: 35. Same art. Selec. J. **4**: 36. Same art. Mus. **24**: 644.
— — Parliamentary History of. (T. Carlyle) Westm. **27**: 233.
— — Philosophy of. (P. Janet) Penn Mo. **3**: 171–448.
— — Principles of. (W. S. Lilly) Contemp. **39**: 944.
— — Quinet on. Lond. Q. **28**: 88. — Ecl. M. **69**: 296.
— — Reign of Terror. (Sir E. B. Lytton) For. Q. **29**: 275. Same art. Am. Ecl. **4**: 285. — Fraser, **65**: 733. **66**: 153. Same art. Ecl. M. **56**: 483. **57**: 221. Same art. Liv. Age, **74**: 171, 483. — Colburn, **126**: 379. **131**: 343.
— — — and its secret Police. Quar. **133**: 43.
— — — Imprisonment during. Blackw. **30**: 920.
— — — Incident of. (K. O'Meara) Cath. World, **22**: 260.
— — Religious Origin of. Dub. R. **37**: 98.
— — Saturnalia of a Republic. Colburn, **129**: 253.
— — Saint-Pierre and D'Argenson, Precursors of. Westm. **85**: 39.
— — Scenes and Characters from. (A. de Lamartine) Howitt, **3**: 99–313.
— — Madame de Staël on. (F. Jeffrey) Ed. R. **30**: 275. — (A. Ritchie) No. Am. **8**: 26. — Mo. R. **88**: 1, 138. — Mus. **18**: 37. — Ecl. R. **29**: 201, 316, 488.
— — States General. (J. S. C. Abbott) Harper, **15**: 314.
— — Sybel's History of. St. Paul's, **2**: 202.
— — Taine on. (A. V. Dicey) Nation, **27**: 44. **33**: 198, 218. — (J. Durand) Penn Mo. **12**: 851. — Cath. World, **30**: 675.
— — Thiers's History of. (J. W. Croker) Quar. **76**: 521. — Am. Whig R. **1**: 341. — So. Lit. Mess. **9**: 341. — Mo. R. **116**: 44.
— — Tocqueville on. (J. C. Fernald) No. Am. **93**: 391. — (M. Heilprin) Nation, **1**: 281.
— — 10th of August, 1792. (J. W. Croker) Quar. **55**: 323.
— — Tribunal of, 1789–93. (J. W. Croker) Quar. **73**: 375.
— — Van Laun on. Canad. Mo. **15**: 126.
— History of, *since the Revolution, in general*: —
— — France during the last fifty Years, 1800–50. (A. Wheaton) Chr. R. **17**: 425.
— — Guizot's Memoirs of his own Time. Brit. Q. **28**: 149. *See* Guizot.
— — Last 100 Years of French History. (A. Gallenga) Contemp. **30**: 661.

France, History of, *since the Revolution, in general*: Ninety Years' Agony, 1787–1877. (Goldwin Smith) Contemp. **31**: 103. Same art. Ecl. M. **90**: 162. Same art. Liv. Age, **136**: 131. Same art. Sup. Pop. Sci. Mo. **2**: 193.
— — Ninety Years of Probation. (M. L. A. Dessaulles) Nat. Q. **38**: 295.
— — Progress since the Revolution. Ed. R. **133**: 1.
— — Ups and Downs of Bonapartes and Bourbons. (J. Amory) Atlan. **27**: 287.
— History of, *under Napoleon I.*: —
— — Anal. M. **8**: 69.
— — Consulate and Empire, Thiers's. (R. Wheaton) No. Am. **74**: 280. — Ed. R. **107**: 358. **108**: 32. **112**: 237. **114**: 486. — Westm. **49**: 386. Same art. Liv. Age, **19**: 193. — For. Q. **35**: 109. — (D. Lardner) Am. Whig R. **1**: 300, 455. — Quar. **76**: 521. — Liv. Age, **5**: 257, 614. — Fraser, **31**: 505. — Dub. Univ. **25**: 493. — Chr. Rem. **10**: 105. — Ecl. R. **83**: 1. — No. Brit. **33**: 133. Same art. Ecl. M. **51**: 289, 451. — (A. V. Kirnan) Fraser, **45**: 603. — Liv. Age, **71**: 40. — Tait, n. s. **12**: 310, 566. Same art. Liv. Age, **5**: 614.
— — Secret. (W. H. Browne) So. M. **9**: 275. *See* Napoleon I.
— History of, 1815–29, *the Restoration*: —
— — Fall of the First Empire. Liv. Age, **110**: 800.
— — from 1815 to Restoration of Louis XVIII. (W. Tudor) No. Am. **3**: 106.
— — Hundred Days. (G. B. Russell) Atlan. **1**: 641, 836.
— — — Lamartine on. Quar. **90**: 543.
— — Restoration of Bourbons, Capefigue's. Quar. **73**: 68.
— — — Lamartine's. Fraser, **44**: 355. — Ecl. R. **94**: 385. — Liv. Age, **30**: 567, 600. **35**: 577.
— — — Marcellus's Memoirs of. Ed. R. **97**: 511. Same art. Ecl. M. **29**: 196.
— History of, *Revolution of* 1830: —
— — (J. W. Croker) Quar. **48**: 234. — (H. Brougham) Ed. R. **52**: 1. Same art. Selec. Ed. R. **4**: 374. — Quar. **43**: 215. **45**: 167. **46**: 313. — For. Q. **6**: 473. **10**: 420, 514. **13**: 35. **29**: 275. **36**: 371. — (T. P. Thompson) Westm. **13**: 475. — Westm. **15**: 406. **38**: 193. — Am. Q. **1**: 189. — (A. H. Everett) New Eng. M. **1**: 190. — Fraser, **2**: 233. **25**: 470. **26**: 142. — (J. Q. Adams) Ann. Reg. **5**: 328, 380. — Dem. R. **2**: 323. — Am. Q. Reg. **4**: 54. — So. Q. **5**: 1. — Dub. Univ. **1**: 619. **2**: 65. **20**: 583. — Blackw. **28**: 542. **33**: 889. **36**: 209. **63**: 393. **64**: 595. — Brit. & For. R. **4**: 294. — Colburn, **29**: 284.
— — and Lafayette. (J. W. Croker) Quar. **48**: 523. — Ed. R. **56**: 481.
— — and Parliamentary Reform. (A. Alison) Blackw. **29**: 36–919. **30**: 17–600. **31**: 103. **32**: 931.
— — Louis Blanc's. (H. Smales) Am. Whig R. **8**: 90. — Liv. Age, **17**: 155.
— — Bonnellier's Memorial. (J. W. Croker) Quar. **55**: 416.
— — Mignet's. Westm. **5**: 385.
— — Military Events of. Quar. **44**: 226.
— — Narratives of. Fraser, **2**: 673.
— — Naval War of. Blackw. **64**: 595.
— — Polignac's Three Days. Quar. **48**: 234.
— History of, 1830–48, *Louis Philippe*: —
— — Dem. R. **22**: 545. — Ecl. R. **76**: 335. — Dub. Univ. **50**: 513.
— — Constitutional Charter, Aug. 1830. Ann. Reg. **6**: 169.
— — Constitutional Monarchy of 1830. (Lord R. Lytton) Contemp. **24**: 856. Same art. Canad. Mo. **6**: 531.
— — Convention of July 13, 1841. For. Q. **28**: 206.
— — from 1830–40, Louis Blanc's. For. Q. **32**: 61. — Ecl. Mus. **3**: 522. — (H. Smales) Am. Whig R. **8**: 90. — Ecl. R. **80**: 88.

France, History of, 1830–48, *Louis Philippe*: Hillebrand's. (J. M. Hart) Nation, 26: 101.
— — Last Campaign of Legitimacy, 1834. Tait, 4: 404.
— History of, *Revolution of* 1848: —
— — (F. Bowen) No. Am. 67: 194. — Ed. R. 88: 225. 89: 554. — Quar. 82: 541. 83: 250. — No. Brit. 9: 1. — Westm. 49: 137. Same art. Ecl. M. 14: 109. — Blackw. 63: 395, 638, 767. 64: 31-687. 65: 1–529. 66: 219. — (J. M. Mackie) Am. Whig R. 9: 299, 358. — (S. W. S. Dutton) New Eng. 6: 431. — (W. A. Larned) New Eng. 7: 153. — Brownson, 5: 380. — Dem. R. 22: 289. — Brit. Q. 7: 496. — Liv. Age, 17: 141–463. — (W. Arthur) Ex. H. Lec. 4: 231. — (Countess de Bury) No. Am. 87: 184. — (W. H. Hurlbut) No. Am. 80: 273. — (J. S. Mill) Westm. 51: 1. — (W. Paul) No. Brit. 9: 1. — (Mrs. Romer) Bentley, 23: 325, 422. — Chr. Rem. 16: 202. — Colburn, 92: 316. — Dub. Univ. 31: 523. 51: 50. — Ecl. R. 107: 101. — Fraser, 38: 461. — Lond. Q. 17: 477. 19: 393. — New Q. 6: 339. — Sharpe, 8: 168. — (P. B. St. John) Tait, n. s. 15: 266–523. — Tait, n. s. 15: 686, 730, 840. 17: 299, 414.
— — Louis Blanc's. (M. Heilprin) Nation, 11: 107.
— — — and national Workshops. (C. Barrère) Fraser, 90: 437.
— — Capefigue on. Colburn, 88: 114–229.
— — Cassagnac's Fall of the Monarchy of July. Colburn, 113: 58.
— — Causes and Consequences of. Fraser, 37: 371. — Tait, n. s. 15: 207.
— — Different Views on. Brit. Q. 13: 408.
— — Episodes of. So. Lit. Mess. 29: 297.
— — Fall of the Throne of the Barricades. Blackw. 63: 393. Same art. Liv. Age, 17: 262.
— — Garnier-Pages's. Bentley, 50: 49.
— — Lamartine's. Ed. R. 91: 228. — Colburn, 86: 484. 93: 48.
— — Lord Normanby's Year of Revolution. Colburn, 112: 104. Same art. Ecl. M. 43: 402. — Fraser, 56: 724. — Liv. Age, 56: 204. — New Q. 7: 52.
— — Order restored. Fraser, 40: 605.
— — Paris in. Colburn, 82: 474. 89: 324.
— — Press of. Ecl. R. 89: 451.
— — Provisional Government. Quar. 87: 502. — Colburn, 113: 236.
— — Public Men of. Brit. Q. 7: 123. Same art. Ecl. M. 14: 145.
— — Retrospect of the Year. Dub. Univ. 33: 134.
— — Reybaud's Jérome Paturot. Quar. 83: 516.
— — Three Epochs of. Fraser, 32: 91, 478.
— — Triumph of the Barricades, Results of. Blackw. 36: 209.
— History of, *Republic*, 1848–51: —
— — Westm. 50: 188. Same art. Ecl. M. 15: 483. — Brownson, 8: 363. — Ed. R. 87: 565. 88: 225. — So. Q. 14: 197. — Dem. R. 23: 61. — Dub. R. 27: 91. — (J. Saunders) Peop. J. 5: 143–274.
— — Difficulties of the Republic. Ed. R. 92: 504.
— — in 1848. Blackw. 64: 51.
— — in 1849. Blackw. 65: 275.
— — Inauguration of 1849. Dub. Univ. 33: 265.
— — Model Republic. Colburn, 82: 502.
— — Prospects of the Legitimists. Colburn, 88: 220.
— — Republic in the King's Coaches. Quar. 88: 416. — Liv. Age, 29: 596.
— — Republican First Fruits, 1848. Blackw. 64: 687.
— — Sentiments and Symbols of. Blackw. 63: 767.
— History of, *Coup-d'Etat and Second Empire*, 1851–70:
— — Coup-d'Etat of Dec. 2, 1851. (A. Irwin) No. Am. 110: 377. — Westm. 58: 622. — Ecl. R. 95: 100. — (A. V. Kirwan) Fraser, 45: 110.
— — — Reminiscence of. Cornh. 20: 555.

France, History of, *Coup-d'Etat and Second Empire*, 1851–70: Downfall of the Republic. Colburn, 85: 122.
— — History of Imperialism, 1870. Fraser, 82: 637. Same art. Liv. Age, 108: 223.
— — Idées Napoleoniennes; the Second Empire. Westm. 78: 433. Same art. Ecl. M. 58: 211.
— — Internal Policy of Napoleon III. Westm. 77: 472. 78: 433.
— — Plébiscite, 1870. (E. L. Godkin) Nation, 10: 284.
— — Re-establishment of Napoleon Dynasty. Theo. & Lit. J. 5: 513.
— — Second Empire. (H. W. Hemans) No. Am. 111: 402. — (M. P. Thompson) Cath. World, 17: 606. — (G. M. Towle) Lippinc. 2: 490. — Bentley, 56: 111. Same art. Ecl. M. 62: 420. — Lakeside, 5: 359. — Fraser, 46: 704. — Dub. Univ. 60: 498. — Westm. 70: 301.
— — — Fortunes of. St. Paul's, 5: 158. Same art. Ecl. M. 74: 46.
— — — Recent History of. Temp. Bar, 63: 55.
— — — Secret Papers of, 1850–70. Fraser, 91: 502. Same art. Ecl. M. 84: 724. Same art. Liv. Age, 125: 308.
— — 10 Years of Imperialism, 1851–61. Lond. Q. 19: 426.
— History of, *Franco-Prussian War*: —
— — (R. S. Dewey) Nation, 12: 58. — (E. L. Godkin) Nation, 11: 288. 12: 20. — Quar. 129: 293. — (W. R. Greg) Contemp. 16: 142. — (F. Kapp) Nation, 12: 88. — (J. Mazzini) Contemp. 17: 1. — (W. P. Morras) Lakeside, 7: 442. — (F. Schaller) So. M. 11: 230, 257. — (E. Scherer) Lippinc. 8: 113. — All the Year, 24: 251–582. — Blackw. 108: 362–657. 109: 131–696. 118: 507. — Brit. Q. 52: 480. 53: 190, 458. — Dub. Univ. 76: 646. — Fraser, 82: 385, 519, 653. — Lond. Soc. 18: 321–513. — Macmil. 22: 321. Same art. Ecl. M. 75: 558. Same art. N. Ecl. 7: 538. — Nat. Q. 21: 365. — Hunt, 63: 125. — So. R. n. s. 9: 460. — Ev. Sat. 9: 707.
— — Alsace and Lorraine. (M. Heilprin) Nation, 11: 232. — (J. N. Pomeroy) Nation, 11: 253.
— — American Surgeon in. (R. S. Dewey) Nation, 11: 327.
— — and American Finance. (J. B. Hodgskin) Nation, 11: 84.
— — and Bismarck. (K. Hillebrand) Internat. R. 6: 425.
— — and Europe. (J. M. Ludlow) Contemp. 15: 648. — Ed. R. 132: 555.
— — and general Culture. (A. Helps) Contemp. 15: 440, 588. 16: 44-571.
— — and the U.S. Civil War. (A. Badeau) Fraser, 82: 793.
— — and the Wars of 1859 and 1866. Fraser, 84: 251.
— — Battles of Speichern, Gorze, and Gravelotte. Colburn, 148: 204.
— — Campaign of August, 1870. Ed. R. 132: 480.
— — Campaign on the Loire. Dub. Univ. 81: 631, 689.
— — — Secret History of. Ecl. M. 77: 612.
— — — Souvenirs of. (G. Monod) Macmil. 24: 69, 134.
— — Carlyle on. Ev. Sat. 9: 834.
— — Catastrophe in. (E. L. Godkin) Nation, 11: 148.
— — Cause of, True. (C. A. Eggert) Putnam, 16: 450.
— — Causes of. (C. K. Adams) No. Am. 114: 233. — (H. von Holst) New Eng. 30: 56. — (M. Heilprin) Nation, 11: 68. — (F. Lieber) Nation, 11: 420. — (J. Morley) Fortn. 14: 367. — Dark Blue, 1: 97. — Nat. Q. 22: 118. — Fraser, 82: 266. — Westm. 95: 160.
— — Chronological Table of Events. Ev. Sat. 10: 359.
— — Decoration of the Iron Cross. Ev. Sat. 9: 612.
— — Effects of, on England. Colburn, 147: 483.
— — — on Finance. (E. L. Godkin) Nation, 23: 129.
— — — on France. (A. F. Hewit) Cath. World, 14: 289.
— — — on other Nations. (M. Heilprin) Nation, 11: 217.
— — England and. (J. Morley) Fortn. 14: 479.

France, History of, *Franco-Prussian War:* England's Aid to the Sick and Wounded. Good Words, **12**: 34.
— — English Aspect of. St. Paul's, **6**: 562.
— — English Neutrality in. Nation, **11**: 68.
— — English Sympathy with. (E. L. Godkin) Nation, **11**: 52.
— — Episode of. (F. M. F. Skene) Temp. Bar, **32**: 270.
— — European Suspension of Specie Payments. (J. B. Hodgskin) Nation, **11**: 100.
— — Expenses of. (F. Kapp) Nation, **11**: 293.
— — Feeling in Germany at Close of. (F. Kapp) Nation, **11**: 203.
— — Freedom of belligerent Commerce. (J. N. Pomeroy) Nation, **11**: 116.
— — French Clergy during. Cath. World, **25**: 247.
— — French Notables of. Ecl. M. **76**: 87.
— — French Opposition to. (M. Heilprin) Nation, **11**: 100.
— — Gambetta and. (E. L. Godkin) Nation, **12**: 36.
— — German and French Armies. Quar. **129**: 415.
— — German Peace Festival, in London, 1871. Good Words, **12**: 489.
— — Gravelotte revisited. (M. D. Conway) Fraser, **88**: 418. Same art. Liv. Age, **119**: 620.
— — Hospital Experiences in. Canad. Mo. **3**: 100.
— — Indemnity. *See* France, Finances of.
— — In the Field with the Prussians, 1870. All the Year, **25**: 104, 157, 205.
— — Industrial and financial Effects of. Lippinc. **6**: 663.
— — — Why not more disastrous? Nation, **11**: 185.
— — Invasion of France. Quar. **130**: 122.
— — Lazareth for the Wounded at Metz. (F. Lees) Good Words, **14**: 500.
— — Lessons of. (E. Ferrier) Luth. Q. **2**: 15. — Temp. Bar, **32**: 54.
— — Lights and Shadows of. (W. Wells) Scrib. **2**: 128.
— — Mansion-House Relief Fund in Paris. (G. Moore) Good Words, **12**: 403.
— — Meaning of Prussian Triumph. (F. Harrison) Fortn. **15**: 145. Same art. Ecl. M. **76**: 465.
— — Military Humiliation of France. Ev. Sat. **9**: 754.
— — Military Resources of the Belligerents, Chesney on. (C. I. Barnard) Nation, **11**: 239.
— — Month with the Belligerents. Fraser, **82**: 483.
— — Moral of. (A. Walker) Lippinc. **7**: 321.
— — My Adventures in. Chamb. J. **51**: 641, 668.
— — Neutrals and Contraband. (E. L. Godkin) Nation, **11**: 165.
— — Notes on. (D. H. Mahan) Nation, **11**: 167–256.
— — Paris after. Temp. Bar, **32**: 91.
— — Personal Adventures in. Gent. M. n. s. **18**: 34.
— — Personal Reminiscences of. (Earl of Dunraven) Dark Blue, **2**: 549, 715.
— — Pictures from. Temp. Bar. **30**: 270, 400, 534.
— — Politics of. (R. H. Hutton) Contemp. **15**: 167.
— — Political Lessons of. Quar. **130**: 256. — Liv. Age, **108**: 579.
— — Preparations for, in 1870. Blackw. **118**: 507. Same art. Liv. Age, **128**: 3.
— — Principles and Issues of. (J. M. Ludlow) Contemp. **15**: 348. Same art. N. Ecl. **7**: 702.
— — Prussians at Versailles. (R. W. Curtis) Nation, **11**: 294.
— — Prussian Losses. (F. Kapp) Nation, **11**: 169.
— — Racial Aspects of. (J. W. Jackson) Anthrop. J. **1**: 1, 30.
— — Reminiscences from Versailles. Ev. Sat. **12**: 93.
— — Results of. (E. L. Godkin) Nation, **12**: 137.
— — Retrospect of. Blackw. **109**: 131. Same art. Ecl. M. **76**: 604.
— — Rhine as a Boundary. Colburn, **147**: 611.
— — Scenes in. All the Year, **25**: 104–399.
— — Second Stage of, 1871. Ev. Sat. **10**: 74.
France, History of, *Franco-Prussian War:* Siege of Metz. (J. L. Hance) Nation, **12**: 104, 176.
— — — of Paris. *See* Paris.
— — Sketches of. Ecl. M. **76**: 87. — Lond. Soc. **18**: 321, 450, 513.
— — Soldier's Story of Sedan. Temp. Bar, **33**: 247.
— — Story of. Cornh. **22**: 566.
— — Studies of. Ed. R. **133**: 545.
— — Surrender of Paris. (E. L. Godkin) Nation, **12**: 69.
— — Terms of Peace. (E. L. Godkin) Nation, **11**: 164. — (F. Kapp) Nation, **12**: 141, 215.—Quar. **129**: 540.
— — — compared with 1815. (J. Bigelow) Scrib. **1**: 290.
— — Three Days with Franc-Tireurs. Lond. Soc. **19**: 130. Same art. Ecl. M. **76**: 437.
— — Transfer of Power in Europe. (E. L. Godkin) Nation, **11**: 117.
— — Triumph at Berlin, 1871. Liv. Age, **110**: 747. — Good Words, **12**: 489. Same art. Liv. Age, **110**: 757.
— — Two Days before Paris. (J. de Liefde) Good Words, **12**: 682, 741.
— — Victim of Paris and Versailles. Macmil. **24**: 384, 487. Same art. Liv. Age, **111**: 222, 346.
— — Week in Paris after the Peace. Cornh. **23**: 475. Same art. Ecl. M. **76**: 698.
— — Will 1792 be repeated? (M. Heilprin) Nation, **11**: 184.
— — With the American Ambulance Corps at Paris. (R. Keeler) Lippinc. **12**: 84.
— — Why was Prussia victorious? Blackw. **108**: 657. Same art. Ecl. M. **76**: 211.
— History of, 1870–1881: —
— — Assembly and the Commune. (E. L. Godkin) Nation, **12**: 377.
— — Chances for Third Empire. Once a Week, **28**: 101.
— — Commune. *See* Commune in Paris.
— — Crisis of 1870. (C. G. Greene, jr.) Nat. Q. **20**: 339. — (B. de Bury) Nation, **10**: 37, 55.
— — Du Noyer on a new Restoration. Colburn, **134**: 175.
— — Dissolution of Waddington Ministry, 1880. (E. L. Godkin) Nation, **30**: 59.
— — Fall of the Empire. (E. L. Godkin) Nation, **11**: 149. — Dub. R. **67**: 479. — Lond. Q. **35**: 21.
— — Government of national Defense. Month, **21**: 43. — Fraser, **83**: 529. — (F. Guizot) Macmil. **23**: 177.
— — International Ignorance of France. (E. Gryzanovski) Nation, **11**: 216.
— — Marshalate, May, 1873–Oct. 1877. (E. D. J. Wilson) 19th Cent. **2**: 647. Same art. Liv. Age, **135**: 600. — Dub. R. **73**: 462.
— — New Régime in, 1879. (E. L. Godkin) Nation, **28**: 97.
— — Republic, 1870. (E. L. Godkin) Nation, **11**: 272. — Ev. Sat. **9**: 643.
— — — begun, 1879. (Mrs. G. M. Crawford) Nation, **28**: 134.
— — — proclaimed in Paris. Putnam, **16**: 553.
— — Republican Burden. (E. L. Godkin) Nation, **28**: 43.
— — Republican Rising in Paris, 1871. (E. L. Godkin) Nation, **12**: 193.
— — Revolution of September, 1870. (H. Rochefort) Fortn. **22**: 216.
— — — of the Commune. (F. Harrison) Fortn. **15**: 556. — (E. L. Godkin) Nation, **12**: 397.
— — Six Months of Prefecture under Gambetta. Fraser, **86**: 651.
— — Third French Republic. (E. S. Beesly) Fortn. **22**: 605.
— — — and Second German Empire. Quar. **130**: 351.
— — — how it was made. Month, **20**: 193.
— — — Year One of. (F. M. Whitehurst) Belgra. **13**: 345.
— Holidays in Eastern. (M. B. Edwards) Fraser, **98**: 362–737. Same art. Liv. Age, **139**: 172–666.

France, Home Life in. Blackw. **110**: 622, 739. **111**: 30–519. **112**: 154. **114**: 23. **123**: 53, 328. Same art. Ecl. M. **90**: 298, 558. Same art. Liv. Age, **136**: 559. **137**: 236. **139**: 152. **140**: 46. — (J. Durand) Atlan. **48**: 164. — Chr. Obs. **74**: 332. — Fraser, **86**: 310. Same art. Ecl. M. **79**: 595. Same art. Liv. Age, **115**: 55. — House. Words, **9**: 434. Same art. Liv. Age, **42**: 236. — (B. Murphy) Cath. World, **26**: 759.
— Horses in. (F. Marshall) Bentley, **53**: 646.
— — and Studs in. Bentley, **53**: 85.
— — Sporting in. (C. J. Apperley) Colburn, **58**: 17–503. **59**: 46. **60**: 16–474.
— Ideal and religious. Ecl. R. **117**: 295.
— Imperial. (G. M. Towle) Galaxy, **3**: 180. — Bentley, **57**: 250.
— — Imperial and Republican Diplomacy in, 1866–70. Dub. R. **70**: 103.
— — Imperial Policy of. Colburn, **117**: 244.
— in the Dikes. Temp. Bar, **60**: 507.
— in the 17th Century. (J. Morley) Fortn. **7**: 1. — Brit. & For. R. **13**: 206.
— in 1715, adrift. Belgra. **9**: 321.
— in 1811. Walsh's Am. R. **1**: 259.
— in 1815. (Sir J. Mackintosh) Ed. R. **24**: 505. — Ed. R. **25**: 501.
— in 1815–20, Williams on Events in. Chr. Obs. **19**: 521.
— in 1816, Financial Situation of. Pamph. **7**: 225.
— in 1820. Ed. R. **34**: 1.
— in 1825. Ann. Reg. **1**: 227.
— — Men, Measures, and Manners in. Lond. M. **11**: 157. Same art. Portfo.(Den.) **33**: 363, 441.
— in 1827. Ann. Reg. **2**: 335.
— in 1829. Ann. Reg. **3**: 223, 243. — Ed. R. **49**: 34.
— in 1829–30, Lady Morgan's. Am. Q. **9**: 1. — Fraser, **3**: 73. — Quar. **17**: 260. — Mo. R. **84**: 113, 225. **123**: 159.
— in 1830. (J. Q. Adams) Ann. Reg. **5**: 251, 285, 307. — (W. C. Rives) Ann. Reg. **6**: 293.
— — Political Condition and Prospects of. (B. Hall) Quar. **43**: 215.
— in 1831. (W. C. Rives) Ann. Reg. **7**: 178.
— in 1832. (J. Q. Adams) Ann. Reg. **8**: 210. — Westm. **17**: 211.
— in 1833. Blackw. **34**: 95. — (A. Alison) Blackw. **34**: 641, 902.
— in 1834. (J. W. Croker) Quar. **52**: 262.
— in 1838, Equality and Centralization in. Dub. R. **5**: 310.
— — Political and social Condition of. Westm. **25**: 137.
— in 1840. Blackw. **48**: 522.
— in 1848. Dub. Univ. **33**: 134.
— — Signs of the Times. Fraser, **37**: 457.
— in 1849, Opinion and Parties in. Brit. Q. **9**: 272.
— in January, 1852. (W. R. Greg) No. Brit. **16**: 559.
— in 1852, State and Prospects of. Fraser, **45**: 352.
— in 1853. Dub. Univ. **42**: 429. Same art. Liv. Age, **39**: 545.
— — Larochejaquelein's. Blackw. **74**: 245.
— in 1855. De Bow, **19**: 440. — Fraser, **52**: 594.
— in 1856. Nat. R. **2**: 123.
— in 1858. No. Brit. **29**: 289. — Liv. Age, **58**: 549.
— — Few Words on Affairs of. Fraser, **56**: 157.
— in 1859. Bent. Q. **1**: 508. Same art. Liv. Age, **62**: 473.
— in 1861. Bentley, **28**: 172.
— in 1865. (A. Gurney) Fortn. **1**: 721.
— in 1868. (E. L. Godkin) Nation, **6**: 325.
— in 1870; a Poem. (G. Meredith) Fortn. **15**: 86.
— in 1871, American Relief to. O. & N. **7**: 114.
— — Condition of. (K. Blind) Fortn. **12**: 651.
— — Phase of Affairs in. Ev. Sat. **10**: 386.
— — Provisional Government and the French Nation. Ev. Sat. **10**: 50.
France in 1871, Rejuvenescent. Dark Blue, **1**: 190, 352.
— in 1872. Westm. **98**: 414.
— in 1873. Dub. Univ. **82**: 513.
— in 1879, Politics and Literature in. (E. de Pressensé) Internat. R. **7**: 113.
— — First Impressions of the new Republic. (F. Harrison) Fortn. **31**: 353.
— in 1880. (A. Talandier) Internat. R. **8**: 150. **9**: 438.
— — Clerical Question. (A. Laugel) Nation, **30**: 303. — (Abbé Martin) 19th Cent. **8**: 119.
— — New Persecution in. Month, **39**: 106.
— — Will the Republic last? (J. Lamber) Scrib. **20**: 522. — Am. Cath. Q. **6**: 164.
— in 1881. (H. Bellingham) Month, **43**: 375.
— — Constitutional Tendencies in. (I. N. Ford) Internat. R. **10**: 468.
— — Is the Revolution over ? (A. V. Dicey) Nation, **31**: 149.
— — The Republic. (G. Merrill) Harper, **62**: 573. — (C. J. Wallis) Brit. Q. **74**: 144.
— Industrial Experience since 1827. (E. L. Godkin) Nation, **24**: 216.
— Industry and Commerce in. Dub. Univ. **51**: 360.
— — Brabazon's Report on. Pract. M. **1**: 226, 284.
— Industries and Artisans of. Dub. Univ. **56**: 34–718. **57**: 230–605. **58**: 74, 322.
— Infidelity in, Modern. Liv. Age, **36**: 439.
— Institute of. Quar. **93**: 315.
— Internal State of, Faber's. Quar. **6**: 235.
— Jesuits in. (A. Panizzi) No. Brit. **2**: 589.
— — in 1880. (E. de Pressensé) Internat. R. **9**: 499. — (L. W. E. Rauwenhoff) Mod. R. **1**: 559.
— Jurisprudence of, Ancient, Curiosities of. (J. Pyne) Nat. Q. **34**: 98.
— King, Church, Nobles, and Sinecures in. (H. Taine) Galaxy, **21**: 91.
— La belle France. (D. M. Craik) Harper, **35**: 497, 606.
— La Délivrande. (F. G. Wheatcroft) Contemp. **12**: 525.
— Land in. Quar. **128**: 81.
— — cultivated by Owners. (G. W. Norman) J. Statis. Soc. **36**: 362.
— — Division of, Gimel on. (F. B. Zincke) Fortn. **34**: 8.
— Landes of. Hogg, **6**: 391.
— — Life in. Liv. Age, **94**: 622.
— Law of Succession in. Ed. R. **40**: 350. — (A. Laugel) Nation, **20**: 312.
— Legitimacy in, 1849. Blackw. **65**: 590.
— Letters from. Mus. **41**: 63, 200. — Am. Mo. M. **6**: 105. — (Miss Raymond) Cath. World, **23**: 464–787. **24**: 108–760. **25**: 56–377.
— Life in. Fraser, **69**: 435, 575, 739 — Once a Week, **2**: 92–237.
— — Glimpses of. (J. D. Osborne) Putnam, **5**: 155.
— — Minor Aspects of. Chamb. J. **33**: 273.
— Life and Thought in, 1879. (G. Monod) Contemp. **35**: 923. Same art. Liv. Age, **141**: 683.
— Literary Institutions of. (R. Baird) Am. Q. **9**: 238,
— Literary Ladies of. (G. Hogarth) Bentley, **3**: 17.
— Literary Statistics of. Bentley, **23**: 456.
— Little Tour in. (H. James, jr.) Atlan. **41**: 67.
— Living in. (A. Rhodes) Galaxy, **15**: 351. — Mo. R. **120**: 523.
— Loitering about a Château in. (A. Rhodes) Scrib. **4**: 743.
— Loiterings in, 1844. Chamb. J. **2**: 273–412. **3**: 91, 236
— Love in. Liv. Age, **46**: 175.
— Manners in. Blackw. **111**: 441. Same art. Liv. Age, **113**: 300.
— — and Customs of, Early. For. R. **2**: 127.
— — and Dress in, 1828. West. Mo. R. **3**: 33.
— — and Politics in. New Eng. M. **4**: 276.

France, Manufactures of. (M. D. L. Rodet) Hunt, 12: 19. — For. Q. 27: 162.
— Map of. Penny M. 8: 270.
— Marriage in. Liv. Age, 118: 259. — Lond. Soc. 8: 294.
— — Courtship and. Westm. 107: 337.
— Material Interests in. (J. B. Hodgskin) Nation, 12: 213.
— Military Conscription in. Ed. R. 13: 427.
— Military Institutions of. Ed. R. 126: 269.
— Military Life under the Empire. Mo. R. 151: 399.
— Military Matters in. Dub. Univ. 54: 515.
— Military Power of. (Sir G. Wolseley) 19th Cent. 3: 1. — (F. J. Lippitt) O. & N. 7: 491. Same art. Ecl. M. 90: 257. Same art. Liv. Age, 136: 259.
— Military System of. Walsh's Am. R. 3: 121. — Brit. Q. 21: 467.
— — and Military Schools of. Am. J. Educ. 12: 7.
— — in 1851. Tait, n. s. 18: 1.
— Mining Resources of, 1841–52. (H. R. Lack) J. Statis. Soc. 18: 345.
— — 1844. (G. R. Porter) J. Statis. Soc. 7: 281.
— Modern, Journalism, Literature, and Society in. Brit. Q. 39: 191.
— — Treitschke on. (M. Heilprin) Nation, 12: 402.
— Monetary Results in. (E. L. Godkin) Nation, 25: 313.
— Money Standard in. Bank. M. (L.) 15: 687.
— Montlosier's. Quar. 27: 146.
— Moral Condition of. (E. de Pressensé) Internat. R. 1: 647. — Bentley, 51: 55.
— Moral and religious Condition of. Blackw. 48: 252.
— Morals and Jurisprudence in. Anal. M. 12: 135.
— — and Manners in. Appleton, 1: 114, 245, 277.
— Morality in. (E. de Pressensé) Internat. R. 6: 54.
— Lady Morgan's. (J. W. Croker) Quar. 17: 260. — Portfo.(Den.) 19: 59.
— Morning Call on. (R. C. Bacon) Belgra. 13: 97.
— Municipal Institutions of, Ancient. For. Q. 8: 140.
— Murdoch's Family Tour in. Tait, n. s. 13: 451.
— Music and Manners in, Chorley's. Tait, n. s. 8: 506.
— Mystery of. Chamb. J. 11: 385.
— National Assemblies of. (J. Ward) Bentley, 23: 615. 24: 69.
— National Guard and Lafayette. Temp. Bar, 39: 479. Same art. Liv. Age, 119: 800.
— National Guards of. Brit. & For. R. 2: 299.
— Natural Boundaries of. (M. Heilprin) Nation, 11: 133.
— Navy of. Blackw. 85: 643. 94: 697.—Ed. R. 98: 240.
— — and of England. Ed. R. 118: 166.
— — and Prince de Joinville. For. Q. 33: 271.
— — in 17th Century. (J. K. Laughton) Fraser, 90: 638.
— — in 1853. Fraser, 48: 1, 205.
— — in 1861. Dub. Univ. 57: 490.
— — in 1865. (W. H. Sykes) J. Statis. Soc. 29: 36.
— — Iron-Clad Squadron of. (H. Raymond) Canad J. n. s. 9: 186.
— Newspapers and Newspaper Writers of. Fraser, 33: 674. — Bentley, 40: 457. Same art. Ecl. M. 40: 64.
— Newspaper Press in. Brit. Q. 3: 468. Same art. Ecl. M. 8: 372. — Quar. 65: 422. — Colburn, 130: 244.
— — Political. (C. J. Wallis) Dub. Univ. 89: 289.
— Observations in. All the Year, 30: 4–393.
— Old-Time. (G. M. Towle) Appleton, 16: 347, 405, 492.
— On the Road. All the Year, 45: 152–278. 46: 31–271.
— or Belgium, What could we have done for? Fortn. 23: 763.
— Pagan Element in. (E. Benson) Galaxy, 1: 203.
— Paganism in Paris. (C. Loyson) 19th Cent. 7: 256.
— Palaces of. (J. S. C. Abbott) Harper, 5: 319, 596, 739.
— — Pilgrimages to. Colburn, 106: 337–458. 107: 46–478. 108: 111.
— Pariahs of. Colburn, 82: 355.
— Parliamentary Institutions in. No. Brit. 35: 31.
France, Parliaments of. (J. B. Perkins) Am. Law R. 12: 262.
— Parties in. Brit. & For. R. 3: 167.
— Passports, Gentlemen! Lippinc. 11: 227.
— past and present. (J. W. Calcraft) Dub. Univ. 42: 429.
— Patriotic Songs of. Quar. 130: 204. Same art. Liv. Age, 108: 791.
— Peasant Life in. Westm. 90: 216. 109: 393. — All the Year, 46: 31–271.
— Peasants of, Bonnemère's History of. (W. F. Allen) No. Am. 121: 202.
— Physical-Force Era in. Westm. 36: 151.
— Plumptre's Narrative of Residence in, 1802–5. (J. Foster) Ecl. R. 15: 478.
— Police of. Ev. Sat. 3: 149.
— Police System of. Bentley, 52: 167.
— Political and criminal Trials in. Mo. R 115: 457.
— Political and social, Laugel on. (H. James, jr.) Nation, 25: 244.
— Political Future of. (A. Talandier) Internat. R. 6: 21.
— Political History of, since the Restoration. Quar. 43: 564.
— Political Preachers of, in the 16th Century. For. Q. 37: 321. Same art. Liv. Age, 10: 441.
— Political Press in. Brit. & For. R. 4: 110. — (C. J. Wallis) Dub. Univ. 89: 289.
— Politics of. Dub. Univ. 35: 532. — (E. L. Godkin) Nation, 8: 126.
— — and Philosophy. Dub. Univ. 52: 165.
— — Decentralization in. No. Brit. 51: 415.
— — Duveyrier's Political Views. (J. S. Mill) Ed. R. 83: 453.
— — Factions in, History of. Anal. M. 9: 213.
— — in 1829, Change of the Ministry. Westm. 11: 494.
— — in 1835. (H. Brougham) Ed. R. 61: 216.
— — in 1836, Ministerial Changes. Brit. & For. R. 3: 551.
— — in 1837; Elections. Brit. & For. R. 6: 371, 712.
— — in 1839; Elections. Blackw. 45: 431.
— — — Parties and Prospects. Fraser, 19: 502.
— — in 1840; Cabinet Policy. (M. Guizot) Mus. 41: 265.
— — in 1841; Chamber of Deputies. Colburn, 61: 508.
— — — Hour or two with Berryer. Colburn, 62: 228.
— — in 1851; Ministerial Crisis. Fraser, 44: 572.
— — in 1852, Questions and Parties in. Westm. 57: 227.
— — — Romier's Le Spectre rouge. Colburn, 92: 67.
— — in 1853. Westm. 59: 451.
— — in 1857. New Q. 6: 455. — Westm. 68: 79.
— — in 1860; Election. (W. Forsyth) Blackw. 88: 107.
— — in 1861. Dub. Univ. 57: 721.
— — in 1863; Elections. Dub. R. 53: 191.
— — in 1867; Franco-Prussian Alliance. Colburn, 141: 1243.
— — in 1868; Visit to the Corps Legislatif. (T. Johnson) Harper, 37: 379.
— — — Corps Legislatif and its Leaders. (G. M. Towle) Hours at Home, 6: 9. Same art. Broadw. 1: 72–446.
— — in 1869. (E. L. Godkin) Nation, 8: 126.
— — in 1870. (E. L. Godkin) Nation, 11: 360.
— — — French Leaders. (M. C. Putnam) Scrib. 2: 366.
— — — Will the Miracle of 1792 repeat itself? (M. Heilprin) Nation, 11: 184.
— — in 1871. (L. Veer) Fraser, 84: 525.
— — — Condition of. (W. R. Greg) Fraser, 83: 541.
— — — Crisis in. Fraser, 83: 257.
— — — National Assembly at Versailles. (J. McCarthy) Galaxy, 15: 581.
— — — Peasantry the Voters in. (E. L. Godkin) Nation, 12: 85.
— — — Why so conservative? (E. L. Godkin) Nation, 12: 301.
— — in 1872. (E. L. Godkin) Nation, 15: 401.
— — — Crisis in. (A. Laugel) Nation, 15: 424.

France, Politics of, in 1873. (E. Michaud) Contemp. 22: 957. — Westm. 100: 173.
— — — and Napoleon III. (R. B. Kimball) Galaxy, 15: 481.
— — — The Assembly. (A. Rhodes) Scrib. 6: 717.
— — — Crisis in. (E. L. Godkin) Nation, 16: 364.
— — in 1874. (E. L. Godkin) Nation, 19: 165. — Temp. Bar, 43: 110.
— — — Crisis in. Dub. R. 75: 132.
— — — Republic and the Suffrage. Fortn. 16: 28.
— — in 1876. (E. L. Godkin) Nation, 22: 141.
— — — Republican Victory. Dub. R. 79: 198.
— — in 1877, Assembly and Army. (E. L. Godkin) Nation, 25: 22.
— — — Crisis in. (I. T. Hecker) Cath. World, 25: 577. — Cong. 6: 623.
— — — Electoral Issue in. (A. Laugel and E. L. Godkin) Nation, 25: 38, 281.
— — — Outlook in. (R. L. Stanton) Princ. n. s. 2: 541.
— — — Republic and the Marshal. (F. Harrison) Fortn. 28: 747.
— — — Republican Victory in. Dub. R. 79: 198.
— — in 1878, Senatorial Election. (E. L. Godkin) Nation, 27: 266.
— — in 1879. (A. Talandier) Internat. R. 7: 391.
— — — Clerical Forces in. (Mrs. G. M. Crawford) Nation, 28: 368.
— — — Ferry Persecution. Month, 37: 134.
— — — Some Aspects of the Republic. Blackw. 125: 551. Same art. Appleton, 21: 546.
— — in 1881. (A. V. Dicey) Nation, 33: 251.
— The Poor in. (W. W. Edwards) 19th Cent. 5: 320.
— Population and Trade in. (F. Marshall) Bentley, 49: 393, 503, 605. 50: 40–632. 51: 104.
— — Census of 1856. Ed. R. 105: 305. Same art. Liv. Age, 53: 612.
— — — of 1872. Ed. R. 140: 383.
— — compared with Great Britain. (C. M. Willich) J. Statis. Soc. 21: 297.
— — Dangers and Decay of. J. Statis. Soc. 30: 343.
— — On Statistics of. (T. A. Welton) J. Statis. Soc. 29: 254.
— Postal Service in, Curiosities of. Bentley, 61: 592.
— Present and Future of. (Mme. Dudevant) Dub. Univ. 88: 224.
— Press of. (A. Rhodes) Galaxy, 17: 31. — All the Year, 19: 127. — Brit. Q. 38: 126. — Colburn, 61: 371.
— — to the Death of Mazarin. Cornh. 27: 703. Same art. Liv. Age, 118: 195.
— — Reigns of Louis XIV. and XV. Cornh. 28: 411. Same art. Liv. Age, 119: 387.
— — Reign of Louis XVI. Cornh. 29: 154. Same art. Liv. Age, 120: 662.
— — Newspapers under the Revolution. Cornh. 29: 535. Same art. Liv. Age, 121: 579.
— — History of, 1789–1860. Ecl. R. 112: 624.
— — "Petite." Lond. Soc. 13: 212.
— — State of. Portfo.(Den.) 22: 404.
See France, Newspaper Press.
— Prizes of Virtue in. (J. Kavanagh) Peop. J. 2: 285.
— Productive and commercial Powers of. For. Q. 1: 472.
— Progress of. De Bow, 15: 90.
— — Scientific and geographical. Ecl. M. 55: 223.
— — towards Liberty. Dub. Univ. 55: 131.
— Progress of Historical Inquiry in. (Sir F. Palgrave) Ed. R. 73: 84.
— Progressive Wealth of. Mo. R. 114: 47.
— Protestant Churches in. Cong. 3: 305.
— Protestant Clergy in, Education of. (F. G. Wheatcroft) Contemp. 9: 98.
— Protestant Martyr of. Temp. Bar, 27: 187.
France, Protestant Synod of. Blackw. 113: 35. Same art. Ecl. M. 80: 257.
— Protestantism in. (R. Burgess) Ex. H. Lec. 5: 475. — (J. Hunt) Contemp. 20: 594. — (R. Wheaton) No. Am. 67: 445. — (S. Willard) Chr. Exam. 3: 498. — (G. Ripley) Chr. Exam. 10: 272. — (C. Brooks) Chr. Exam. 37: 289. — Blackw. 39: 113, 462. 47: 763. — Mus. 28: 505. — Fraser, 18: 563. — Am. Meth. M. 18: 185. — Brit. Q. 36: 338. — Cong. 7: 233. — Ecl. R. 113: 416. — Lond. M. 2: 521. — Lond. Q. 4: 448. — (T. B. Thayer) Univ. Q. 5: 165.
— — Battle of Creed and Freedom. Brit. Q. 57: 430.
— — in 1874. (E. Coquerel) Theo. R. 11: 370.
— — Memoirs of. No. Brit. 19: 175.
— — Plea for. (W. Wells) Meth. Q. 39: 501.
— — Puritans of France. Prosp. R. 9: 72.
— — Restoration of. Fraser, 88: 383. Same art. Liv. Age, 119: 195. Same art. Ecl. M. 81: 699.
— — Revival of. Ecl. R. 86: 570.
— Provincial Assemblies of. Nat. R. 18: 381.
— Provincial Ball in. Lond. Soc. 16: 455.
— Provincial Towns of. (A. A. Bartlett) O. & N. 7: 323.
— Provinces of, Tours in. Quar. 65: 76.
— Public Charities in. Westm. 12: 449.
— Public Meetings in. (E. L. Godkin) Nation, 7: 546. — Once a Week, 20: 35.
— Public Works of. Bank. M. (N. Y.) 34: 695. — (G. R. Burnell) J. Frankl. Inst. 78: 1, 73.
— Pulpit of. (A. Schwartz) Contemp. 28: 587. Same art. Liv. Age, 131: 259.
— — Modern. (C. H. Brigham) Chr. Exam. 67: 71, 409.
— Queens of, of Spanish Origin. Colburn, 117: 233.
— Races of. Westm. 97: 434. Same art. Liv. Age, 114: 195.
— Reformed Church of. (E. Coquerel) Theo. R. 9: 536. — (D. Charruaud) Unita. R. 15: 531. 16: 44, 417. — (F. G. Wheatcroft) Contemp. 7: 368. — Am. Presb. R. 15: 424. — Cong. 5: 27. — Lond. Q. 42: 182, 265. — No. Brit. 14: 122.
— — General Synod of. (A. Laugel) Nation, 15: 23, 56.
— — — in 1872. (E. B. Otheman) Meth. Q. 39: 660. 40: 455.
— — — Revival of. Chr. Obs. 72: 728.
— — in 1866. Brit. Q. 43: 479.
— — in 1880. (D. Charruaud) Mod. R. 1: 125.
— Religion in. (G. Ripley) Chr. Exam. 10: 272. — Quar. 83: 199. — Ecl. R. 80: 535. — Cong. M. 23: 851.
— — after War of 1870–71. (A. Reville) Theo. R. 10: 115.
— — and Politics. (J. Milsand) Contemp. 26: 25.
— — Catholicism and Protestantism. (A. Coquerel) Chr. Exam. 45: 363. — Blackw. 44: 524.
— — Christianity in France. (C. Colton) Knick. 7: 358.
— — — Philosophical. Prosp. R. 4: 105.
— — — Present Condition of. (L. Vitet) Cath. World, 6: 275, 360.
— — Gospel in. (B. W. Noel) Ex. H. Lec. 7: 1.
— — Guizot on. (J. P. Lacroix) Meth. Q. 28: 368.
— — in 1802. Meth. M. 26: 66.
— — in 1848. Quar. 83: 199.
— — New Movement in, 1878. (J. E. Butler) Contemp. 34: 781.
— Religious and political Centralization in. Lond. Q. 17: 1. — Ecl. M. 54: 455.
— Religious and social Condition of. Dub. R. 16: 1, 261.
— Religious Ceremonies and Churches in. Chr. Rem. 46: 420.
— Religious Condition of, in 1865. (R. Burgess) Ex. H. Lec. 20: 205.
— — in 1873. (E. Michaud) Contemp. 23: 303.
— — in 1877. (E. de Pressensé) Princ. n. s. 1: 633.
— Religious Controversy in. (H. H. Milman) Quar. 76: 299.

France, Religious Liberty in. Am. Bib. Repos. 2d s. **4**: 429. — Blackw. **40**: 772. — Ed. R. **16**: 413. — Dub. Univ. **12**: 64. — Am. Meth. M. **18**: 464. — Brownson, **14**: 389.
— Religious Parties in. (J. Parkman) Chr. Exam. **47**: 32.
— Religious Policy of Second Empire. Cath. World, **18**: 793.
— Religious Prospects in. Lond. Q. **27**: 261.
— Religious Struggles in 16th Century. (K. O'Meara) Cath. World, **30**: 145.
— Religious Wars of. Blackw. **68**: 456. Same art. Liv. Age, **27**: 529. Same art. Ecl. M. **21**: 458. — Quar. **126**: 499. Same art. Ecl. M. **73**: 129.
— Renaissance in. (W. Lamoroux) Scrib. **11**: 387.
— — Chapter on. (E. F. S. Pattison) Contemp. **30**: 466. Same art. Liv. Age, **134**: 643.
— Republican Life in. Colburn, **89**: 94.
— Republican Movement in. (E. Castelar) Fortn. **18**: 1.
— Republicanism in, History of. (E. S. Beesly) Fortn. **22**: 471.
— — Is a Republic possible in? (J. C. Morison) Fortn. **22**: 1.
— Rivers of. Ecl. Engin. **6**: 98.
— — Three. Chamb. J. **16**: 81.
— Royal Family of, Memoirs of. (J. W. Croker) Quar. **28**: 464.
— Royal Favorites of. (C. Louandre) Ecl. M. **80**: 144.
— Royal Marriage in. Dem. R. **22**: 256.
— Rural Economy of. Ed. R. **103**: 82.
— Rural Life in. Chr. Obs. **76**: 294.
— Salic Law in. Liv. Age, **48**: 23.
— Scenes, Customs, and Characters in. (J. Durand) Galaxy, **14**: 741. **15**: 30.
— Science in. Ed. R. **15**: 1. — Am. Ecl. **1**: 544.
— Scot in. Blackw. **92**: 543.
— Scotch in. Ed. R. **118**: 230.
— Scrope's Geology and Extinct Volcanoes of. Fraser, **58**: 190.
— Sea-Bathing in. (H. Jones) Once a Week, **5**: 546.
— Sketch in, 1865. Month, **2**: 440.
— Social, literary, and political. Fraser, **11**: 59.
— Social and political Life in. (A. Orr) Contemp. **29**: 448.
— Social Life in. Irish Q. **3**: 497. **4**: 72. — Chamb. J. **13**: 273, 305, 394.
— Social Reform in. (M. C. O'C. Morris) Contemp. **22**: 754. — (F. Ramière) Cath. World, **17**: 348.
— Socialism in. (F. Bowen) No. Am. **69**: 277. — No. Brit. **9**: 213. Same art. Ecl. M. **16**: 470. Same art. Liv. Age, **18**: 4. — Colburn, **86**: 171. Same art. Ecl. M. **17**: 545.
— — Chenu's Les Conspirateurs. Colburn, **88**: 539.
— Socialist Party in, 1849. No. Brit. **10**: 261. Same art. Ecl. M. **14**: 333.
— Socialists of. Blackw. **56**: 588.
— — and Red Republicans. Am. Whig R. **10**: 401. *See also* Socialists.
— Society and Education in. Quar. **67**: 394. Same art. Am. Ecl. **1**: 515.
— — and English Society. (H. Brougham) Quar. **75**: 485. Same art. Ecl. M. **5**: 265.
— — and Salons before the Revolution. Blackw. **128**: 498.
— — before 1789, Tocqueville's. New Q. **5**: 369.
— — before 1848. Chr. Rem. **16**: 202.
— — during the Regency. Irish Q. **4**: 328.
— — in the 18th Century Lond. Soc. **22**: 206.
— — La grande Dame de. (Lady A. Cadogan) Macmil. **36**: 494. Same art. Ecl. M. **90**: 54.
— — Mediæval. St. James, **22**: 417.
— — Modern. St. James, **4**: 326.
— — Respectable Poverty in. (Mrs. R. Barker) Cath. World, **27**: 276.
France, Society in, Sketches of. Tinsley, **15**: 228–561.
— — State of. Mus. **42**: 215.
— — under the Directory. Ed. R. **105**: 205.
— Somerville's Letters on. (G. Bancroft) No. Am. **19**: 50.
— South of, Cooke's. Mo. R. **136**: 27.
— — Johnson's Travels in. New Q. **6**: 328.
— — Martin Summer in. (M. D. Conway) Harper, **61**: 383–820.
— — Rambles in. (S. G. W. Benjamin) Harper, **58**: 193, 337.
— — Sketches of Manners in. Lond. M. **17**: 19, 145.
— — in Winter. (W. F. Rae) Macmil. **15**: 44. Same art. Ecl. M. **68**: 159.
— — Town Life in. Fraser, **72**: 644.
— Southwestern, Small Farmers in. (W. Webster) Fortn. **35**: 206.
— State Papers of. (J. P. Byrne) Macmil. **24**: 314. Same art. Ecl. M. **77**: 468.
— Statistics of. Mo. R. **129**: 325.
— — in 1869. Am. J. Educ. **18**: 547.
— — Moral and intellectual. Ed. R. **69**: 49.
— — Report on, 1867. (W. H. Sykes) J. Statis. Soc. **31**: 49.
— Struggle for naval and colonial Power. (G. Reynolds) Atlan. **12**: 626.
— Summer Loiterings in. Chamb. J. **1**: 17–247.
— Summer Pictures in. (H. M. Field) So. Lit. Mess. **29**: 30.
— Superstitions of Western. Blackw. **71**: 55.
— Tariff in, and Duke of Harcourt. (H. Wikoff) Dem. R. **24**: 110.
— — History of. Westm. **62**: 564.
— Taste in. (F. T. Palgrave) Fraser, **55**: 583.
— Taxation in. Ed. R. **131**: 370.
— Travel in. (S. G. Brown) No. Am. **76**: 397. — (J. Hutton) Belgra. **21**: 179. — De Bow, **20**: 375. — Chr. Rem. **10**: 61.
— Travels in, 1814–15. Anal. M. **9**: 467.
— — 1818. Blackw. **4**: 594.
— Trip to, 1853. Hogg, **10**: 256.
— Mme. Tussaud's Reminiscences of. Mo. R. **146**: 244.
— Unity of. (W. Stigand) Contemp. **16**: 321.
— Universal Suffrage in. (J. Reinach) 19th Cent. **10**: 357.
— Vacation Tourist in. Temp. Bar, **20**: 179.
— Village Life in. Chamb. J. **25**: 140, 157. — Once a Week, **8**: 543.
— Visit to, in 1834. (T. G. Appleton) O. & N. **9**: 675.
— Visit to Bluebeard's Castle. Temp. Bar, **9**: 486.
— Watering-Places of. Bentley, **42**: 148.
— Wayside Pictures in. Bentley, **24**: 128–568. **25**: 57–624. **26**: 35–145.
— Woman in, Kavanagh's. Quar. **88**: 352. — So. Q. **20**: 433. *See* Kavanagh, Julia.
— Women of. Colburn, **134**: 54. — So. Lit. Mess. **5**: 297. — Dark Blue, **2**: 213.
— — and Literature. Internat. M. **1**: 193.
— — and the Salons. Colburn, **104**: 88. Same art. Liv. Age, **45**: 694.
— — Condition of. (J. Boucherett) Contemp. **5**: 98.
— — Decadence of. Blackw. **130**: 429 Same art. Liv. Age, **151**: 671. Same art. Ecl. M. **97**: 831. Same art. Appleton, **26**: 514.
— — of the Past. (A. Kinloch) Victoria, **34**: 53.
— — under the Empire. Temp. Bar, **17**: 320. Same art. Ecl. M. **67**: 240.
— Working-Classes of. (J. Kavanagh) Peop. J. **2**: 159.
— — Literature of. (J Kavanagh) Peop. J. **3**: 46.
— Yankee on the Throne of. Lippinc. **6**: 487.
— Young. (H. Frederic) Appleton, **26**: 555.
— — One or two Habits of. Liv. Age, **45**: 658.
— — Thoughts on. Hogg, **5**: 49.
Frances and Fanny; a Tale. So. Lit. Mess. **8**: 704, 748.

Frances Kendrick, Mistress of Calcot House. (K. S. Macquoid) Liv. Age, **141**: 553-669.
Francesca, Lady; a Legend of Sorrento. Fraser, **28**: 362.
Francesca, Pietro della, Italian Painter. Cornh. **31**: 167.
Francesca; a Song. Dub. Univ. **7**: 408.
Francesca Evelyn; a Story. (E. F. Mosby) Western, **6**: 328, 453. **7**: 55, 146, 239.
Francesco da Bologna, Who was? (A. Panizzi) F. Arts Q. **1**: 372. **2**: 181.
Franchise, Elective. Dem. R. **22**: 97.
— in England. (A. Fonblanque, jr.) Once a Week, **2**: 335. — No. Brit. **30**: 228.
— — County. (E. A. Freeman) Contemp. **31**: 365. — (W. E. Gladstone) 19th Cent. **2**: 537. **3**: 196.
— — Extension of. (H. Pric 1ait, n. s. **3**: 668. — (J. Moncrieff) Ed. R. **123**: 203. — Contemp. **3**: 435.
— — The Laborers and the Vote. (J. Arde and G. Potter) 19th Cent. **3**: 48.
— — The new. (R. Ellerton) Fortn. **1**: 602.
Francia, José G. R. de, Dictator of Paraguay. (T. Carlyle) For. Q. **31**: 544. Same art. Ecl. Mus. **3**: 75. — (A. H. Everett) No. Am. **26**: 445. — Mo. R. **113**: 374. — Mus. **20**: 387. **26**: 579. — (Mrs. C. E. Norton) Colburn, **43**: 331. **44**: 189. — Hesp. **3**: 484. — Chamb. J. **8**: 17. — Quar. **63**: 342. — Lond M. **19**: 11.
— Robertson's Reign of Terror of. Mo. R. **148**: 241.
Francis I. and Charles V., Mignet's. Fraser, **74**: 489. Same art. Ecl. M. **68**: 22.
— and the Countess of Chateaubriand. (O. Delepierre) St. James, **15**: 98.
— and his Times. Brit. Q. **11**: 441.
— and Louis XII., Memoirs of. Lond. M. **19**: 151.
— Court and Reign of. Temp. Bar, **48**: 88. Same art. Liv. Age, **131**: 96.
— Interview of, with Henry VIII. (J. Caley) Arch. **21**: 175.
— Life and Times of. Mo. R. **119**: 565. — Liv. Age, **23**: 577. **27**: 49.
Francis II., Frederick William III., and Alexander I., Meeting of. (J. Clifford) Overland, **6**: 446.
Francis Joseph, Emperor of Austria, with portrait. Ecl. M. **57**: 279, 511.
— Coronation of, at Pesth, 1867. Cornh. **16**: 212.
Francis, St., of Assisi. (Sir J. Stephen) Ed. R. **86**: 1. Same art. Ecl. M. **12**: 83. Same art. Liv. Age, **14**: 348. — (S. Farrington) O. & N. **2**: 159. — (M. G. Gage) Chr. Exam. **78**: 47. — (W. Stigand) Belgra. **10**: 75. — Good Words, **18**: 418, 449. — Broadw. **6**: 541. — Dub. Univ. **59**: 434, 562. Same art. Cath. World, **5**: 495.
— and the Ecstatics. Chr. Rem. **3**: 55.
— and the Franciscans. (S. L. Caldwell) Bapt. Q. **11**: 238. — Am. J. Educ. **24**: 393.
— and his Time. (C. K. Adams) New Eng. **29**: 371.
— Pilgrimage to the Sanctuaries of. Belgra. **18**: 206.
— Preaching to the Birds. Ev. Sat. **9**: 364.
— Sketch of. So. R. n. s. **24**: 291.
— Three Canticles of. Month, **31**: 179.
Francis de Sales, St. (L. W. Bacon) Macmil. **38**: 385. — (C. Teebay) Month, **17**: 201.
Francis, Ebenezer. (R. M. Mason) Hunt, **40**: 436.
Francis, John Wakefield. (S. L. Knapp) New Eng. M. **7**: 210. — Liv. Age, **68**: 689.
— Memoir of. Hist. M. **5**: 97.
— Obituary Notice of. Knick. **57**: 430.
— Recollections of. (J. E. Cooke) Hours at Home, **2**: 559.
— Writings of. So. Q. **19**: 226.
Francis, Sir Philip. Blackw. **103**: 150.
— and Pope Ganganelli in 1772. Liv. Age, **56**: 625.
— Memoir of. Ed. R. **127**: 166. — Anal. M. **13**: 493.
— More about Junius. (A. Hayward) Fraser, **76**: 794.
Francisca da Rimini. Dub. Univ. **13**: 78.
Franciscan Friars. Dub. Univ. **69**: 434, 562.
— Convent of. Blackw. **50**: 288.
— Migration from Bruges to Winchester, 1794. Month, **33**: 430.
Franciscan Missions on the Nile. Cath. World, **3**: 768.
Franciscan Monasteries, Meehan's. Dub. Univ. **82**: 249.
Franck, Augustus Hermann. Meth. M. **33**: 350. — (K. von Raumer) Am. J. Educ. **5**: 441.
— Life of. (J. A. Alexander) Princ. **2**: 408. — (M. L. Stoever) Evang. R. **19**: 277. — Am. Meth. M. **11**: 288.
Franck, Richard. Northern Memoirs. Retros. **8**: 170.
Franck, Sebastian. (J. F. Smith) Theo. R. **11**: 163.
Franckenberg, Cardinal de. (W. C. Robinson) Month, **34**: 305.
Franconia, Scene in. Fraser, **40**: 310.
Franconia Case. (D. Foster) Am. Law R. **11**: 625.
Franconian Switzerland. Temp. Bar, **3**: 492.
Frank Fairlegh. (F. E. Smedley) Sharpe, **2**: 3. **6**: 165.
Frank Hamilton; or, Confessions of an only Son. (W. H. Maxwell) Bentley, **25**: 124. Same art. Internat. M. **1**: 145.
Frank Marshall. Blackw. **109**: 145, 315.
Franks and the Gauls. (E. A. Freeman) Nat. R. **11**: 247.
— and their Metropolitan. Kitto, **22**: 241. **23**: 296.
— History of. For. Q. **17**: 139.
Frankenstein, The new. Fraser, **17**: 21.
Frankfort-on-the-Main. (G. A. Sala) Temp. Bar, **12**: 333. — Fraser, **62**: 409. — Penny M. **9**: 225.
— Modern. Fraser, **38**: 334.
— Statistics of. (W. H. Sykes) J. Statis. Soc. **7**: 318.
Frankincense and Coffee Mountains. Chamb. J. **37**: 378. — Same art. Ecl. M. **57**: 12.
— and Myrrh. All the Year, **34**: 541. — Penny M. **13**: 71.
Franking Privilege. Penn Mo. **2**: 266. — St. James, **5**: 43.
Frankland, Sir C. H. (A. Young) Appleton, **10**: 273.
Frankland, Edward, Sketch of. Pop. Sci. Mo. **15**: 838.
Frankland the Barrister; a Tale. Liv. Age, **6**: 27.
Franklin, Benjamin. (J. Abbott) Harper, **4**: 145, 289. — (T. Hughes) Contemp. **35**: 581. Same art. Liv. Age, **142**: 298. — (A. Norton) No. Am. **7**: 289. — So. Lit. Mess. **7**: 593. — Carey's Mus. **8**: 12. — (C. C. Smith) Unita. R. **3**: 41. — with portrait, Ecl. M. **62**: 367. — Lond. Q. **23**: 483. — Argosy, **32**: 123.
— and Madame Helvetius. Howitt, **3**: 322.
— and Science of the 18th Century. (J. W. Draper) Harper, **61**: 265.
— Autobiography of. Sharpe, **13**: 133. — (S. A. Green) Atlan. **27**: 207.
— Bigelow's Life of. Ed. R. **151**: 321. — Internat. R. **2**: 692.
— Character of. (H. T. Tuckerman) No. Am. **83**: 402.
— Charles Thompson and Mrs. Logan. (W. Willis) Hist. M. **14**: 280.
— Correspondence of. (F. Jeffrey) Ed. R. **28**: 275. — Mus. **6**: 359. — Mo. R. **83**: 18, 133. — (J. Foster) Ecl. R. **27**: 433. — Portfo. (Den.) **22**: 313. — Colburn, **38**: 457.
— Death and Funeral of. (W. J. Bruce) Am. Hist. Rec **3**: 13.
— Discoveries in Electricity. (W H. Allen) Meth. Q. **7**: 101.
— Education, and educational Work of. Am. J Educ. **27**: 401. **28**: 809.
— English Views of. (T. Hughes) Lippinc. **24**: 108.
— Familiar Letters. (W. B. O. Peabody) No. Am. **37**: 249. — Mo. R. **132**: 239. — Am. Mo. R. **4**: 124. — Liv. Age, **25**: 79.
— Family and Friends of. Liv. Age, **61**: 110.
— Last Love-Episode of. Once a Week, **14**: 653. Same art. Ev. Sat. **2**: 34.
— Letter of. Hist. M. **2**: 163. — N. E. Reg. **27**: 246.

Franklin, Benjamin, Letters of, Unpublished. Lond. M. **12**: 606.
— Life and Works of. (F. Bowen) No. Am. **59**: 446. — Anal. M. **12**: 462. — with portrait, Anal. M. **11**: 449. — Mo. R. **88**: 409. — with facsimile of handwriting, Anal. M. **9**: 353.
— Manuscripts of. (J. S. Loring) Hist. M. **3**: 9. — So. Lit. Mess. **2**: 293, 349, 411.
— Memoirs of. Portfo. (Den.) **30**: 441.
— Parton's Life of. Lond. Q. **23**: 483. Same art. Liv. Age, **84**: 289.
— Personal Recollections of. (R Carr) Hist. M. **14**: 59.
— Religious Opinions of. So. Lit. Mess. **8**: 700.
— Remarks proposing Prayers in Congress. Niles's Reg. **15**: 108.
— Return from France in 1785. Hist. M. **10**: 213.
— Supposed Author of the "Parable on Persecution." Lit. & Theo. R. **3**: 51.
— What made? (E. E. Hale) Chr. Exam. **66**: 265.
— Works of. (F. Jeffrey) Ed. R. **8**: 327. — Ecl. R. **78**: 19.
Franklin, Lady Eleanor Ann. (H. St. John) Victoria, **25**: 1076.
Franklin, Sir John, with portrait. Hogg, **5**: 289. — with portrait, Ecl. M. **31**: 283. — (W. Dowe) Putnam, **1**: 629. — (Sir J. Richardson) Liv. Age, **53**: 769.
— and Arctic Regions. (M. F. Force) No. Am. **71**: 168. — Ecl. M. **19**: 414. **20**: 60. — Liv. Age, **24**: 275, 279.
— and his Men, Last of. St. James, **47**: 405. — Liv. Age, **43**: 311.
— and the Northwest Passage. Brit. Q. **11**: 102.
— Character of. So. Lit. Mess. **20**: 404.
— End of an Epic. Sharpe, **30**: 242.
— Esquimaux Reports on. Geog. M. **5**: 82.
— Fate of. Bentley, **36**: 580. — Ecl. R. **111**: 113. — Good Words, **1**: 113, 137, 148. — Liv. Age, **43**: 78. **63**: 414.
— — and the Voyage of the Fox. Fraser, **61**: 221.
— Grave of. Internat. M. **5**: 30.
— Last Voyage of. (S. Osborn) Once a Week, **1**: 338, 361. Same art. Liv. Age, **64**: 25.
— Phase of the Mystery of. Once a Week, **2**: 13.
— Rae's Report on. House. Words, **11**: 12. — Liv. Age, **53**: 89.
— Search for. Fraser, **43**: 198. Same art. Ecl. M. **22**: 420. — Fraser, **44**: 502. — Liv. Age, **31**: 291. — (C. F. Dunbar) Chr. Exam. **68**: 430. — (A. Petermann) Liv. Age, **40**: 161. — (S. Osborn) Once a Week, **1**: 383. Same art. Liv. Age, **64**: 114. — (A. Woodbury) No. Am. **80**: 307. — Harper, **2**: 588. — Liv. Age, **37**: 451. **39**: 131. — Quar. **92**: 386. — Cornh. **1**: 96. — Colburn, **90**: 372. **93**: 193–483. **112**: 288 — Ecl. M. **29**: 307. — De Bow, **13**: 1.
— — The final, 1858. Colburn, **112**: 288.
— — McCormick's Expedition. Fraser, **49**: 633.
— — Penny's Voyage. Liv. Age, **35**: 30.
— — Snow's Voyage of the Albert. Colburn, **91**: 234.
— — Thirty Years of. Chamb. J. **58**: 129.
— — Track of. Colburn, **90**: 372. Same art. Ecl. M. **22**: 112.
See Arctic Voyages.
Franklin Genealogy. (W. Bache and J. W. Dean) N. E. Reg. **11**: 17.
Franklin, Mass., Ministers of Am. Q. Reg. **8**: 51.
Franklin, Tenn., Battle of. (H. Judd) Lakeside, **11**: 81.
Franklin County, Me., Juridical Statistics of. (A. Reddington) Am. Q. Reg. **13**: 293.
Franklin County, Vt., Ministers of. (P Kingsley) Am. Q. Reg. **12**: 352.
Franklin and Marshall College. (J. W. Nevin) Mercersb. **5**: 395.
— Dedication of. Mercersb. **8**: 436.
Franklin Bacon's Republic; Diary of an Inventor. Cornh. **27**: 562.
Franklin Institute, Exh. of 1826. J. Frankl. Inst. **1**: 5.
— 10th Exhibition, 1840, Address before. (F. Fraley) J. Frankl. Inst. **30**: 308.
— 12th Exhibition, 1842, Address. (A. D. Bache) J. Frankl. Inst. **34**: 379.
— 13th Exhibition, 1843, Address, Report, etc. J. Frankl. Inst. **36**: 394.
— — Address. (R. M. Patterson) J. Frankl. Inst. **37**: 36.
— 14th Exhibition, 1844, Address. (J. Wiegand) J. Frankl. Inst. **38**: 372.
— — Address. (F. Fraley) J. Frankl. Inst. **39**: 34.
— 15th Exhibition, 1845, Address. (P. Frazer) J. Frankl. Inst. **41**: 15.
— 16th Exh., 1846, Address, etc. J. Frankl. Inst. **42**: 392.
— 17th Exhibition, 1847, Address. (J. R. Chandler) J. Frankl. Inst. **44**: 327.
— 18th Exhibition, 1848, Address. (J. R. Ingersoll) J. Frankl. Inst. **46**: 435.
— 19th Exhibition, 1849, Address. (J. K. Kane) J. Frankl. Inst. **49**: 65.
— 23d Exhibition, 1853, Address. (G. Harding) J. Frankl. Inst. **56**: 417.
— List of Members, 1876. J. Frankl. Inst. **101**: 73.
— — 1877. J. Frankl. Inst. **103**: 73.
— Report, 1826. J. Frankl. Inst. **1**: 3.
— Rise and Progress of. J. Frankl. Inst. **1**: 66, 129.
Franklin Society of Paris. (C. A. Cutter) Lib. J. **1**: 3.
Franklin's Confession. (A. Thomas) Belgra. **10**: 377.
Franklinite. *See* Zinc.
Franz the great Tragedian. Blackw. **64**: 345.
Franz and Victorine. (J. L. Ver Mehr) Overland, **6**: 542.
Fraser, James, Death of. Fraser, **24**: 628.
— *versus* Berkeley, for Assault. Fraser, **15**: 100.
Fraser, James, Bishop of Manchester, with portrait. Dub. Univ. **95**: 452. — Cong. **2**: 435.
Fraser, J. B. Journey in Persia. Dub. Univ. **13**: 26. — Ed. R. **43**: 87. — (T. P. Thompson) Westm. **5**: 202.
Fraser, William, Murder of, Delhi, 1835. Blackw. **123**: 32. Same art. Liv. Age, **136**: 440.
Fraser's Magazine. Ecl. M. **26**: 238.
— fifty Years ago. Fraser, **99**: 790.
— Past and Future of. (J. Tulloch) Fraser, **100**: 1.
Fraternity. (C. E. Maurice) Contemp. **18**: 407.
Fratricide; a Poem. (A. C. Swinburne) Once a Week, **6**: 215.
Fratricide's Death; a Poem. Am. Mo. M. **6**: 389.
Frau Trüdchen's Dream. (J. L. Ver Mehr) Overland, **4**: 43.
Frau Sommer's Pleasure-Trip. (E. E. Evans) Lippinc. **16**: 191.
Fraud in Subscriptions to Stock. (S. D. Thompson) Am. Law R. **14**: 177.
Frauds, Commercial. Irish Q. **9**: 193.
— Legislative Protection against. Chamb. J. **17**: 408.
— Modern. Dub. R. **31**: 589.
— on Bankers. Bank. M. (N. Y.) **9**: 161.
— on national Flags. (F. Jeffrey) Ed. R. **8**: 1.
— on N. Y. & N. H. R. R. Co. Bank. M. (N. Y.) **9**: 385, 414.
— on Railroad Companies. Bank. M. (N. Y.) **9**: 81. **10**: 97.
— on Union Bank, London. Bank. M. (L.) **20**: 283, 396.
— Pious. (C. K. Whipple) Radical, **4**: 285.
— Statute of. (F. Brinley) Hunt, **21**: 502.
See Imposture.
Fraudulent Piety. Temp. Bar, **14**: 194.
Fraudulent Transfers of Stock. Bank. M. (N. Y.) **34**: 448.
Frauenlob. (A. E. Kroeger) So. M. **11**: 328.
Fraülein. (A. Trafton) Scrib. **17**: 885.
Frauenhofer, Joseph von. Pop. Sci. Mo. **6**: 739. — J. Frankl. Inst. **8**: 96.
Frauenhofer's Lines, Discovery of. Ed. Philos. J. **9**: 296. **10**: 26.
— Note on Theoretical Explanation of. (H. Hartshorne) J. Frankl. Inst. **105**: 38.

Fraysinous, Abbé de, Sketch of. Lond. M. **20**: 34.
Frazer, John F. Penn Mo. **3**: 678.
Freak of Fortune; a Story. Argosy, **31**: 313.
— of Nature. Tinsley, **21**: 654.
Freaks upon Flowers, Fruits, and Trees. Chamb. J. **10**: 309.
Fréchette, Louis. (M. F. Egan) Cath. World, **32**: 550.
Fred; a Tale of Japan. Blackw. **124**: 475. Same art. Liv. Age, **139**: 283.
Fred, and Maria, and Me. (E. Prentiss) Hours at Home, **1**: 30, 130.
Fred's Folly. Tinsley, **7**: 514.
Fred Redestone's Escapade; a Tale. Temp. Bar, **34**: 370.
Fred Shirley's May-Day. Sharpe, **11**: 261.
Fred Trover's little Iron-Clads. (J. T. Trowbridge) Scrib. **6**: 479.
Freddy's Aunt. All the Year, **17**: 211.
Frederica Sophia Wilhelmina, Princess of Prussia. (F. Jeffrey) Ed. R. **20**: 255. — Portfo.(Den.) **8**: 233.
Fredericia, Denmark, Siege of, 1864. Victoria, **3**: 78.
Frederick I., Barbarossa. Fraser, **64**: 217. **84**: 334. — (A. E. Kroeger) Western, **4**: 25, 119, 302. — Colburn, **122**: 417.
— Legend of. Cornh. **21**: 424. Same art. Ecl. M. **74**: 656.
Frederick II., Emperor of the Romans. Colburn, **118**: 446. — Nat. R. **16**: 507. Same art. Ecl. M. **59**: 346. — No. Brit. **45**: 370. Same art. Ecl. M. **68**: 521.
Frederick I. of Prussia. For. Q. **16**: 26.
Frederick II. of Prussia. (J. S. C. Abbott) Harper, **40**: 1–864. **41**: 35–869. **42**: 41–874. — (A. Bissett) Bentley, **28**: 636. — (R. Cardwell) Month, **30**: 299. — (T. Carlyle) Cornh. **6**: 107. — (A. E. Kroeger) Western, **6**: 125, 213. — (G. Bancroft) No. Am. **26**: 287. — (W. Darby) Am. Whig R. **2**: 292. — (T. B. Macaulay) Ed. R. **75**: 218. Same art. Liv. Age, **19**: 97. — Am. Q. **11**: 309. — For. Q. **14**: 245. — Westm. **17**: 118. **38**: 58. — Mus. **20**: 402. **28**: 135. **42**: 493. — Ed. R. **7**: 218. — Mo. R. **127**: 122. — Fraser, **23**: 559. — with portrait, Ecl. M. **54**: 421. — Ecl. M. **38**: 187, 543. — Penny M. **8**: 292.
— Advice from the Throne. Mo. R. **101**: 489. **102**: 549.
— and Catherine II. Bentley, **46**: 307.
— and the Emperor Frederick II. Quar. **134**: 56. Same art. Liv. Age, **117**: 160.
— and Fleury. Colburn, **55**: 215.
— and his School Reforms. Am. J. Educ. **26**: 305.
— and his Times. Ecl. R. **75**: 311. **77**: 630.
— and the Miller. Dub. Univ. **75**: 101.
— and Pietro delle Vigne. Colburn, **4**: 455.
— and Voltaire. Colburn, **116**: 475. Same art. Liv. Age, **63**: 259. — Knick. **55**: 522.
— Anecdotes of. Ecl. R. **3**: 121.
— Campbell's History of. Colburn, **63**: 516. — Dub. R. **12**: 493. — Mo. R. **157**: 122. **160**: 390.
— Carlyle's History of. (A. H. Guernsey) Harper, **25**: 523. — (E. E. Hale) Chr. Exam. **66**: 78. — Ed. R. **110**: 376. — Quar. **105**: 275. **118**: 225. — Westm. R. **71**: 174. — No. Brit. **30**: 22. — (H. H Lancaster) No. Brit. **43**: 79. — (G. H. Lewes) Fraser, **58**: 631. — Fraser, **69**: 539. Same art. Ecl. M. **62**: 321. — Fraser, **72**: 778. — (O. Tiffany) No. Am. **88**: 503. — Blackw. **98**: 38. — Brit. Q. **29**: 239. — Chamb. J. **31**: 51, 73. — Colburn, **114**: 253. — Dub. R. **47**: 132. **51**: 404. — Dub. Univ. **53**: 12. **60**: 110. — Ecl. R. **115**: 409, 703. **122**: 299. — Nat. R. **7**: 247. Same art. Ecl. M. **46**: 49. Same art. Liv. Age, **59**: 403. — Tait, n. s. **25**: 743. **26**: 41. — (G. Fitzhugh) De Bow, **29**: 151.
— Character of. Hogg, **15**: 241, 428. Same art. Ecl. M. **26**: 68.
— Confessions of. Ho. & For. R. **2**: 152.
— Court and Times. Ecl. R. **77**: 630.
Frederick II. of Prussia, Kapp's History of. (H. von Holst) Nation, **13**: 106.
— Last Days of. Quar. **82**: 1. Same art. Liv. Age, **16**: 453. Same art. Ecl. M. **13**: 329.
— Life of. New Q. **7**: 298.
— Mornings of. Hogg, **7**: 28–69.
— Mundt's. (J. L. T. Preston) Land We Love, **4**: 8.
— Raumer's History of. Mo. R. **142**: 591.
— Sketch of. Hogg, **8**: 340.
— Thiebault's Memoirs. Colburn, **121**: 364.
— White Lady of Brandenburg. Chamb. J. **21**: 266. Same art. Liv. Age, **42**: 28.
— Youth of. House. Words, **18**: 398.
Frederick William I., of Prussia. Temp. Bar, **7**: 589.
Frederick William III., of Prussia. For. Q. **36**: 354. Same art. Liv. Age, **2**: 625. Same art. Ecl M. **7**: 334. — Ecl. M. **34**: 278.
— Domestic Life of. Chr. Obs. **45**: 542, 615.
— on Education. Chr. Obs. **44**: 336.
— Religious Life of. Chr. Rem. **8**: 113.
— Religious Opinions of. Chr. Obs. **44**: 307.
Frederick William IV., of Prussia. Am. Whig R. **7**: 79. *See also* William I., Emperor of Germany.
Frederick William, Crown Prince of Germany, with portrait. Ev. Sat. **9**: 599.
— Marriage with Princess Royal of England. Ecl. M. **43**: 563.
Frederick I., King of Italy. Nat. R. **12**: 45.
Frederick VII., of Denmark. Liv. Age, **79**: 572.
Frederick, Prince of Wales, Sketch of. Colburn, **127**: 39. — (H. B. Baker) Gent. M. n. s. **18**: 466.
Frederick Augustus, Prince, Loves of. (P. Fitzgerald) Belgra. **13**: 252.
Frederic Hohenstauffen. (A. E. Kroeger) Western, **5**: 413.
Fredericksburg, Va., in the War. (R. R. Howison) So. M. **16**: supp. 9.
— Battle of. (B. G. Humphreys) Land We Love, **3**: 443. — (J. Longstreet) So. M. **14**: supp. 41.
— — Episode of. (J. W. Ames) Overland, **3**: 432.
— — General Humphreys at. Hist. M. **15**: 353.
— — Sixth Army Corps at. (Gen. Sedgwick) Hist. M. **21**: 102.
— — Stonewall Jackson at. (J. A. Early) Hist. M. **18**: 32.
Fredericksburg; a Poem. (D. A. Casserly) Putnam, **11**: 45.
Free Agency. Chr. Exam. **35**: 198. — (L. Hedge) No. Am. **13**: 384. — (C. Hodge) Princ. **29**: 101.
— and human Liberty. (S. Helfenstein, jr.) Mercersb. **2**: 141.
Free Church of Christendom, Cooper on. Ecl. R. **96**: 585.
— and free Government. (E. Washburn) Cong. Q. **2**: 313.
— in the free American State. (J. W. Kramer) Am. Church R. **29**: 258, 321.
Free-Church System. (J. A. Bolles) Am. Church R. **13**: 484.
Free Churches. (R. A. Hallam) Am. Church R. **8**: 520. **9**: 375. — (E. A. Hoffmann) Am. Church R. **8**: 352. — (J. H. Hopkins, jr.) Am. Church R. **9**: 252, 581. **10**: 88. — (J. M. Whiton) Cong. R. **9**: 551. — (H. Southgate) Am. Church R. **13**: 118, 284.
Free Cities of Flanders. (C. Cushing) No. Am. **39**: 112.
— of Germany, Public Instruction in. Am. J. Educ. **22**: 731.
Free Discussion, Right of. Am. Bib. Repos. **9**: 368.
Free Inquiry. (C. Bois) Cong. **2**: 675, 718.
Free Institutions, Grimke on. (J. H. Perkins) No. Am. **69**: 440.
— Permanence of. (C. Dewey) Am. Bib. Repos. **8**: 193.
Free Labor in British West Indies. (C. L. Brace) Atlan. **9**: 273.

Free Labor in Puerto Rico. Westm. 22: 123.
Free Love. Westm. 89: 456. — Liv. Age, 46: 815.
— and free Divorce. Ev. Sat. 11: 75.
Free Negro Population. Anal. M. 13: 276. — Niles's Reg. 24: 31. 31: 343.
Free Religion. (O. A. Brownson) Cath. World, 10: 195. — (J. Weiss) Radical, 8: 441.
— and the Free State. (S. Johnson) Radical, 6: 265.
— in the West. (A. D. Mayo) Univ. Q. 28: 389.
Free Religionists. Cath. World, 26: 145.
Free Schools, Early, in New England. (H. Barnard) Am. J. Educ. 1: 297.
Free Society, Problem of. So. Lit. Mess. 26: 401. 27: 1, 81.
Free Societies, Failure of. So. Lit. Mess. 21: 129.
Free-Soil Movement, 1848–49. Mass. Q. 2: 105.
Free-Soil Party, 1848–49. Am. Whig R. 8: 193.
— Appeal to. Dem. R. 23: 399.
Free Soup, Educational Influences of. (R. Connor) Nation, 22: 155.
Free-Thinker, Death-Bed of a modern. Chr. Obs. 4: 645. 10: 696.
— The; a Tale. Blackw. 55: 593. — Liv. Age, 1: 145.
Free Thinkers and free Schools. (R. Patterson) Cong. R. 10: 105.
— English. Theo. R. 1: 491.
Free Thinking and plain Speaking, Stephen on. (H. W. Holland) Nation, 26: 79.
— History and Tendencies of. Quar. 116: 59.
Free-Thinking Christian's Magazine. (C. K. Whipple) Radical, 6: 476.
Free Thought, Education and. (G. F. Magoun) Scrib. 10: 450
— Farrar on Chr. Obs. 63: 488. — Lond. Q. 21: 127.
— in England. (A. F. Marshall) Am. Cath. Q. 5: 577.
— in Geography. (W. S. Smith) Cong. R. 9: 371.
— in Religion. Temp. Bar, 37: 107–534.
— Practical View of. (G. Hague) Canad. Mo. 10: 37.
Free Trade. (A. Beatty) West. J. 2: 121. — (F. Lieber) De Bow, 15: 53. — (A. H. Everett) No. Am. 40: 122. — (S. G. Arnold) Hunt, 4: 227. — (H. Greeley) Hunt, 4: 425. 5: 166. — (C. C. Haven) Hunt, 6: 220. — (L. Woodbury) Hunt, 8: 407. — (J. B. Fisher) Hunt, 9: 161. — Hunt, 10: 399, 522. 11: 27. — (S. Beman) Hunt, 24: 53. — Am. Q. 10: 444. — Dem. R. 7: 341. 9: 329. 14: 391, 447. 28: 97. — Ed. R. 33: 331. 78: 1. 90: 133. — Am. Whig R. 5: 201. 13: 233, 329, 443. — Niles's Reg. 28: 186. 29: 289. 41: 135, 156. — Fraser, 5: 577. 8: 103, 222, 604. 9: 356. — (J. Galt) Fraser, 6: 593. 7: 106. — Quar. 86: 148. — For. Q. 9: 261. 10: 68. 11: 140. — (T. P. Thompson) Westm. 12: 138. 18: 366. 19: 269. 22: 226. 40: 1. — Blackw. 17: 551. 19: 474. 21: 1. 24: 370. 27: 553. 44: 317. 55: 259, 385. 67: 94, 222, 447. 70: 106, 448, 629. — Pamph. 17: 457. — Mus. 21: 412. — Carey's Mus. 6: 133. — Colburn, 92: 62. — Mo. R. 163: 368. — So. Q. 25: 115.
— and the Census. Blackw. 70: 123.
— and Cotton Manufactures. Blackw. 68: 123.
— and Currency Reform. Dub. Univ. 29: 785.
— and direct Taxes. De Bow, 22: 645.
— and Elections of 1852 in England. Ed. R. 96: 526.
— and Fair Trade. (W. F. Ecroyd and T. P. Whittaker) 19th Cent. 10: 588, 606. — (S. C. Buxton) Contemp. 40: 959.
— and France. All the Year, 2: 466.
— and the Granges. Republic, 1: 513.
— and Industry of the People. Blackw. 68: 106.
— and low Duties. De Bow, 26: 447.
— and the Poor Law incompatible. Dub. Univ. 35: 270.
Free Trade and Protection. (H. Bushnell) Scrib. 2: 266. — Brit. Q. 69: 369. — (G. Bacon) Hunt, 22: 635. — (R. Sulley) Hunt, 22: 406. 23: 79. 24: 569. 25: 322. 40: 529. 41: 228. — (E. P. Smith) Hunt, 26: 31. 27: 51, 178. — (H. C. Baird) Hunt, 41: 63, 697. — West. J. 7: 152. — (J. T. Champlin) Bapt. Q. 7: 407. — (J. Hatton) Tinsley, 24: 526. — (G. Manigault) Canad. Mo. 5: 214.
— — Fawcett on. Brit. Q. 69: 369.
— and Reciprocity. (A. Arnold) Gent. M. n. s. 22: 310. — (R. Lowe) 19th Cent. 5: 992. — (B. Price) Contemp. 13: 321. — (C. H. Thompson) Fraser, 97: 89.
— — and foreign Competition. Westm. 112: 1.
— and Retaliation. (N. W. Senior) Ed. R. 78: 1.
— at its Zenith, 1849. Blackw. 66: 756.
— Atkinson on. (G. Walker) No. Am. 105: 280.
— Attack upon, 1881. (W. Summers) Brit. Q. 74: 417.
— Autumn Politics, 1851. Blackw. 70: 607.
— Bastiat on. Ed. R. 149: 355. *See* Bastiat.
— British and American Reciprocity. (D. R. James) Hunt, 23: 410.
— British Policy. Am. Whig R. 12: 518, 633.
— Byles's Sophisms of. Dub. R. 32: 343.
— Congress on, at Brussels, 1847. Howitt, 2: 239.
— Downward Tendencies under. Blackw. 70: 106.
— Economy of paying twice over. (T. P. Thompson) Westm. 20: 238.
— Economic Fallacies. (Sir A. Musgrave) Contemp. 29: 310.
— Experiences of. Blackw. 69: 748.
— Experiment of. Blackw. 70: 488.
— Farmer's Question as to. Penn Mo. 4: 421.
— from an American Standpoint. (A. J. Leffingwell) Contemp. 38: 55.
— in Banking. Bank. M. (L.) 1: 67.
— in England, 1841. Ecl. R. 74: 95.
— in France, 1846. Ecl. R. 85: 68.
— in Great Britain, History of. (G. Walker) No. Am. 95: 463.
— Is it a Mistake after all? (F. Watt) St. James, 49: 139.
— Isolated. (E. Sullivan and Duke of Manchester) 19th Cent. 10: 161.
— The let-alone Principle. (W. Elder) Penn Mo. 1: 79.
— Onward Tendencies, 1851. Blackw. 69: 564.
— Plea for. (A. Arnold) Princ. n. s. 3: 649.
— Policy of England and its Results. (H. C. Carey) Am. Whig R. 9: 34.
— Railways, and Growth of Commerce. (W. E. Gladstone) 19th Cent. 7: 367.
— Real Obstacles to. (E. L. Godkin) Nation, 29: 338.
— Reciprocity the true. (A. R. Wallace) 19th Cent. 5: 638.
— Recollections of. (J. Bowring) Howitt, 1: 31–324. 2: 123, 362, 376. 3: 55.
— Story of. Fraser, 43: 716.
— To the Shopkeepers of Great Britain. Blackw. 70: 629.
— Trade Rivalry of Nations. Tinsley, 5: 384.
— with France, Prospects of, 1846. Ecl. R. 83: 440.
— What constitutes real. Am. Whig R. 12: 127–353.
— Workman's View of fair Trade. (G. Potter) 19th Cent. 10: 430.
See also Protection; Tariff.
Free-Trade Finance. Blackw. 67: 513.
Free-Trade Ministry, Latter Days of. Blackw. 69: 491.
Free-Trade Principles and Taxation. (F. Romilly) Fraser, 101: 314.
Free-Trader, The penitent; a Poem. Blackw. 67: 585.
Free Will. (J. D. Williamson) Univ. Q. 16: 138.
— and Authority. (S. Johnson) Radical, 2: 116.
— and Christianity. Westm. 105: 424.
— and modern Science. Month, 33: 243.

Free Will and Necessity. (W. M. Fernald) Univ. Q. **19**: 157. — (A. E. Kroeger) Radical, **2**: 22.
— and Responsibility. (R. Noel) Theo. R. **13**: 366.
— Empirical Theory of. (G. A. Simcox) Mind, **4**: 469.
— Genesis of the Doctrine of. Westm. **96**: 68.
— Scientific Aspect of. (A. J. Leffingwell) Pop. Sci. Mo. **16**: 745.
See Will, Freedom of.
Free-Will Baptists and Elder Randall. (P. Richardson) Chr. Rem. **23**: 372.
Freedman's Story. (W. Parker) Atlan. **17**: 152, 276.
Freedmen at the South. (C. Gayarré) No. Am. **125**: 472. — (J. M. Ludlow) Good Words, **5**: 116. — (T. H. Pearne) Meth. Q. **37**: 462. — (F. B. Stanton) Contin. Mo. **2**: 730.
— and free Labor in the South. (W. F. Allen) Chr. Exam. **76**: 344.
— and the new Administration, 1869. (E. L. Godkin) Nation, **8**: 144.
— at Fortress Monroe. (E. L. Pierce) Atlan. **8**: 626.
— at Port Royal. (E. L. Pierce) Atlan. **12**: 291.
— Church and. (W. C. Williams) Am. Church R. **27**: 559.
— Condition of. (N. S. Shaler) No. Am. **116**: 150.
— Education of. (S. G. Arnold) Meth. Q. **38**: 43. — (D. H. Strother) Harper, **49**: 457.
— — and Civilization of. (E. E. Hale) No. Am. **101**: 528.
— Life on the Sea Islands. (C. L. Forten) Atlan. **13**: 587, 666. — (W. C. Gannett) No. Am. **101**: 1.
— Puritanism and. (N. S. Richardson) Am. Church R. **18**: 63.
— Sketches of. (H. G. Spalding) Contin. Mo. **4**: 188.
— Southern Labor Problem. N. Ecl. **3**: 257.
Freedmen's Bureau. (S. Andrews) O. & N. **1**: 200, 373. — Am. J. Educ. **18**: 125.
— O. O. Howard and. (E. Spencer) So. M. **13**: 633.
Freedmen's Savings-Bank. Bank. M. (N. Y.) **29**: 936. **36**: 14. — O. & N **2**: 245.
— Story of. (C. C. Nott) Nation, **20**: 253, 289.
Freedom. (Max Müller) Contemp. **36**: 369. Same art. Ecl. M. **94**: 1.
— and Authority. (M. Kieffer) Mercersb. **17**: 42.
— Christian. (R. Ellis) Unita. R. **3**: 602.
— Civil and religious. Brownson, **21**: 257.
— Crisis of, 1848. (O. Dewey) Chr. Exam. **46**: 1.
— Human. (J. W. Nevin) Am. Whig R. **7**: 406.
— in the Truth. (T. G. Apple) Mercersb. **25**: 560.
— Individual. (J. P. Blanchard) Radical, **4**: 39.
— Intellectual. Zoist, **2**: 431.
— Moral, Determinism and. (P. Janet) Contemp. **32**: 445.
— Moral and political. (H. W. Bellows) Hunt, **2**: 365.
— of Choice. (J. Miley) Meth. Q. **41**: 434.
— of Opinion. Am. Whig R. **9**: 551.
— of the Press. *See* Liberty of the Press.
— Political, Has it receded? Fraser, **60**: 631.
— Religious. *See* Religious Freedom.
— Social Restraints on. (B. Murphy) Cath. World, **18**: 702.
— What is? Tait, n. s. **22**: 15.
Freedom Wheeler's Controversy with Providence. (R. T. Cooke) Atlan. **40**: 65.
Freehold Assurance and Colonization. Westm. **51**: 408.
Freehold Land Movement, 1849. Ecl. R. **91**: 95.
— Rationale of. Ecl. R. **98**: 499.
Freehold Land Societies. Chamb. J. **20**: 377.
Freeman, Constant, Services of. M. Am. Hist. **2**: 349.
Freeman, Edward Augustus, and Froude. (A. V. Dicey) Nation, **13**: 387, 403.
— Few Words to. (J. A. Froude) 19th Cent. **5**: 618. Same art. Liv. Age, **141**: 800.
— Historical Essays. (W. F. Allen) Nation, **30**: 331. — (Goldwin Smith) Canad. Mo. **1**: 176.
Freeman, Edward Augustus, Historical Prejudices of. (H. Adams) No. Am. **118**: 176.
Freeman, James. (F. Parkman) Chr. Exam. **19**: 383.
— and King's Chapel, 1782–87. (H. W. Foote) Mo. Rel. M. **49**: 505.
— Sermons. (F. Parkman) Chr. Exam. **6**: 273.
Freeman, James E. Godey, **33**: 213.
Freeman, John, Family of. (J. Paine) N. E. Reg. **20**: 59, 353.
Freemantle Divorce. Tinsley, **15**: 65.
Freemasonry. (S. B. Harper) Cath. World, **22**: 145. — (A. J. Thebaud) Am. Cath. Q. **6**: 577. — Cath. World, **32**: 610. — (E. F. Willoughby) Macmil. **38**: 125. — Sup. Pop. Sci. Mo. **3**: 255. — Chamb. J. **43**: 581. — Month, **25**: 90. — West. R. **1**: 74. — Mo. R. **149**: 433.
— and the Eleusinian Mysteries. (T. De Quincey) Tait, n. s. **14**: 519, 661. — Am. Q. **12**: 57.
— Anti-. Am. Q. **7**: 162. — Niles's Reg. **41**: 83, 166.
— — Excitement in 1826–28. West. Mo. R. **3**: 169.
— Arcana of. Fraser, **8**: 568.
— Historical Pretensions of. (J. Clark) Mercersb. **8**: 587.
— in England, Halliwell's Early Hist. of. Mo. R. **163**: 437.
— Italian Documents of. (J. A. Campbell) Cath. World, **20**: 721.
— Monomania, and Witchcraft. Ecl. R. **63**: 30.
— Origin of. (T. De Quincey) Lond. M. **9**: 5. — (T. Pownall) Arch. **9**: 110. — (R. E. Thompson) Penn Mo. **2**: 617.
— — and religious Aspect of. Chr. Rem. **14**: 1.
— Papal Allocution on. Dub. R. **58**: 137.
— Recent Italian. Month, **21**: 121.
— Reid on. Mo. R. **135**: 529.
— What is the Good of? All the Year, **16**: 14.
See Knights of Malta.
Freetown, Mass., Burial Inscriptions. N. E. Reg. **8**: 285. **10**: 53.
Freezing of Plants and Animals. (F. Mohr) Pop. Sci. Mo. **3**: 96.
— of Vegetables. (J. L. LeConte) Am. J. Sci. **63**: 84, 195.
Freezing Mixtures. J. Frankl. Inst. **101**: 142.
Freia-Holda, the Teutonic Goddess of Love. Cornh. **25**: 599. Same art. Liv. Age, **113**: 802.
Freiberg, Saxony, Silver Mines of. St. James, **10**: 48.
— School of Mines. Am. J. Educ. **9**: 167.
Freiburg in Breisgau. (G. C. Swayne) Once a Week, **12**: 666. — Penny M. **3**: 177.
Freight Competition of 1876. Ecl. Engin. **16**: 351.
Freight of the Jacobina. Fraser, **49**: 54.
Freiligrath, Ferdinand. (W. Barker) Am. Whig R. **10**: 361. — Prosp. R. **4**: 34.
— and German minor Poets. Nat. Q. **22**: 341.
— in England. (W. Howitt) Liv. Age, **12**: 598. — (W. Howitt) Peop. J. **2**: 330.
— Life and Lays of. (K. Blind) Fraser, **93**: 659.
— Memoir of. (W. Howitt) Howitt, **3**: 336.
— Poems. Dub. Univ. **21**: 29. — For. Q. **34**: 352. Same art. Liv. Age, **4**: 653. — Lond. Q. **12**: 424. Same art. Ecl. M. **48**: 182. — Tait, n. s. **12**: 205.
Fréjus. Am. Arch. **8**: 198.
Frelinghuysen, Theo., with portrait. Am. Whig R. **1**: 99.
— Speech on Nullification. Niles's Reg. **43**: supp. 80.
Fremont, John Charles. Ecl. R. **104**: 486. — Liv. Age, **26**: 207.
— Expeditions of. Dem. R. **17**: 68. — So. Lit. Mess. **15**: 52. — Am. J. Sci. **53**: 192. — Ecl. R. **83**: 739.
— Geography of California. So. Q. **16**: 82.
French, J. S. Elkswatawa. So. Lit. Mess. **2**: 589.
French and Gordon Families. (C. Sotheran) Antiquary, **4**: 129.
French, The, at Home. (A Rhodes) Galaxy, **13**: 447. — Once a Week, **30**: 687.

French, The, described by themselves. For. Q. **25**: 337.
— Germans, and English. Brit. Q. **13**: 331.
— in Algiers. Mus. **24**: 656. — For. Q. **13**: 74. — Blackw. **50**: 183.
— in England. (J. Humphreys) St. James, **48**: 458.
— in Russia, 1812. Quar. **8**: 445. **12**: 466.
— Pictures of. Mo. R. **152**: 292.
French Academy. (A. Rhodes) Galaxy, **17**: 743.
— Prizes of. Nature, **12**: 177. **13**: 195.
French Actors and Actresses. (C. Hervey) Colburn, **83**: 527.
— Old. All the Year, **38**: 173, 413. **39**: 160, 489. **40**: 183, 541.
French Actresses, Line of. Temp. Bar, **39**: 369.
French Æsthetics. (E. Dowden) Contemp. **1**: 279.
French Aggressions in the Pacific. For. Q. **34**: 166. Same art. Ecl. Mus. **2**: 265.
French Almanacs. Colburn, **81**: 456. **90**: 283.
— for 1852. Colburn, **93**: 330.
— for 1853. Colburn, **96**: 323.
— for 1854. Colburn, **99**: 312.
— for 1867. Bentley, **60**: 597.
— for 1868. Bentley, **62**: 598.
French and English Gaiety. Bentley, **4**: 512.
French and English Industry compared. Ed. R. **32**: 340.
French and English Pictures. Cornh. **40**: 92.
French and English Propagandism. So. Lit. Mess. **10**: 577.
French and German Belles-Lettres. Blackw. **37**: 513.
French and German national Characteristics. (C. G. Greene, jr.) Nat. Q. **22**: 270.
French and Indian War, 1758. N. E. Reg. **16**: 217. — New Eng. M. **8**: 170.
French and Italian Nobility. Dub. Univ. **54**: 720.
French Anti-Socialist Publications. Colburn, **86**: 171. Same art. Ecl. M. **17**: 545.
French April Fool Day. Fraser, **25**: 457.
French Arabs. St. James, **27**: 531.
French Aristocracy at Home. Bentley, **60**: 82.
French Arms Investigation. (E. S. Nadal) Nation, **14**: 212.
French Artists of To-Day. (R. Ménard) Portfo. **6**: 2–178.
French Artisan during the Revolution. Blackw. **28**: 951.
French Assize Courts. Chamb. J. **41**: 786.
French Association for Advancement of Science. Nature, **5**: 357. **9**: 497. **12**: 423. **14**: 357, 379.
French Authors and the Academy in 1861. Dub. Univ. **57**: 641.
— of 1847. Fraser, **35**: 545. Same art. Ecl. M. **11**: 363.
French Authoresses of the 17th Century. Bentley, **31**: 565. 705. **32**: 273.
French Bar, Eloquence of. For. R. **5**: 56.
French Barrack-Yard. All the Year, **17**: 367.
French Benedictines. Ed. R. **89**: 1.
French Bibliomania. Am. Bibliop. **7**: 234.
French Bournemouth. Temp. Bar, **57**: 50.
French Brigands; Les Chauffeurs. All the Year, **27**: 253.
French Building Laws. (T. M. Clark) Am. Arch. **9**: 51.
French Carlists and Prince Polignac. (A. Panizzi) No. Brit. **3**: 130. Same art. Ecl. M. **5**: 396.
French Catholic Universities. Dub. R. **78**: 185.
French Celebrities, portraits of. Brit. Q. **20**: 220. Same art. Ecl. M. **33**: 91.
French Charity Schools. Lond. M. **21**: 14.
French Character. (H. T. Tuckerman) Atlan. **5**: 256. — Blackw. **26**: 309.
French Charter, 1830. Niles's Reg. **29**: 112.
French Château and its Dependencies. Broadw. **5**: 184.
— Few Days in. Chamb. J. **3**: 145. Same art. Liv. Age, **5**: 329.
French Children. (M. de Witt) Macmil. **25**: 103, 295.
French Clergy, Movements of, 1862. No. Brit. **36**: 433. Same art. Ecl. M. **56**: 364.
French Comedy. (J. Pollock) Contemp. **18**: 43. — (T. Sarcey) 19th Cent. **6**: 182. — Quar. **29**: 414. — Westm. **31**: 69. — Cornh. **40**: 56.
— after Molière's Day. Dub. Univ. **75**: 123.
— and Comedians in. Bentley, **47**: 368.
French Comic Romances. Westm. **31**: 69.
French Conquerors and Colonists. Blackw. **65**: 20.
French Cooking. *See* Cooking.
French Country-House, Day in. Chamb. J. **24**: 121.
French Critics and Yankee Foibles. Dem. R. **22**: 171.
French Criticism of the English; the Vengeur Affair. Fraser, **21**: 332.
— of English Writers. For. Q. **30**: 1.
French Detective. All the Year, **3**: 331, 355, 521.
— Autobiography of a. Chamb. J. **38**: 284.
French Detective Story. All the Year, **39**: 368.
French Dinners. Liv. Age, **136**: 317.
French Diplomacy. Brit. & For. R. **2**: 232.
French Drama. (J. Pollock) Contemp. **21**: 335. — Lond. M. **5**: 44. — Putnam, **6**: 401.
— in 16th Century. Retros. **18**: 396.
— in 1875. Quar. **139**: 138.
— Modern. (E. I. Sears) Nat. Q. **1**: 64.
— Portraits of French Players. Colburn, **20**: 545. **25**: 327, 415. **28**: 271. **29**: 66.
— Tendencies of. (J. B. Matthews) Lippinc. **27**: 383.
French Dramatists and Actors. (J. W. Calcraft) Dub. Univ. **43**: 594, 652.
French Economists. Westm. **43**: 1.
French Emigrants. Niles's Reg. **14**: 393.
French Epicurism. Mo. R. **116**: 493.
French Female Celebrities. Ecl. M. **29**: 167.
French Fever. (T. C. de Leon) Lippinc. **4**: 384.
French Fisher-Folk. Chamb. J. **54**: 701.
French Flower-Farms. Chamb. J. **34**: 221.
French Flower-Girl. House. Words, **4**: 10.
French Forts, Early, in Mississippi Valley, U. S. Serv. M. **1**: 356.
French Friends, Group of. (C. Beard) Theo. R. **10**: 339. **11**: 70.
French Gaming-Houses. Westm. **11**: 303.
French Governess. Victoria, **28**: 500.
French Hero; a Tale. (L. Wraxall) St. James, **14**: 490.
French Humorists. (W. H. Browne) So. M. **15**: 641.
French Hill, Westchester Co., N. Y. (W. J. Cumming) M. Am. Hist. **5**: 442.
French Ideas of Democracy and Community. (F. Bowen) No. Am. **69**: 277.
French Industries and Artisans. Dub. Univ. **55**: 629.
— Some queer. Chamb. J. **56**: 279.
French Institute, Transactions of, 1813–14. No. Am. **2**: 51.
French Institution for Experimental Sciences. Nature, **7**: 485.
French Intellectual Life. (K. Hillebrand) Appleton, **26**: 326.
French Island, Six Months on. Once a Week, **6**: 697, 718.
French Journals and Journalists. Fraser, **43**: 350. Same art. Ecl. M. **22**: 511.
French Journalist, Biography of a. Internat. M. **3**: 239.
French Judicature, Modern. Dem. R. **11**: 1.
French Ladies, La grande Dame de l'ancien Régime. (A. L. Cadogan) Macmil. **36**: 494.
French Lake, The Mediterranean as a. Quar. **75**: 532. Same art. Ecl. M. **5**: 83. Same art. Liv. Age, **5**: 361.
French Language. (F. Marshall) Bentley, **54**: 168. — Blackw. **111**: 519. Same art. Liv. Age, **113**: 601.
— Ancient Pronunciation of. (J. Bowle) Arch. **6**: 76.
— Grammar of, Brachet's. (E. B. Cox) No. Am. **111**: 230.
— in England. (H. W. Longfellow) No. Am. **51**: 285.
— Littré's Dictionary of. (F. Bôcher) Nation, **21**: 11.
— Origin and Progress of. (H. W. Longfellow) No. Am **32**: 277. — For. Q. **23**: 339.

French Language, Picking up, in France. Temp. Bar, 8: 484.
— Translations into, Specimens of. Chr. Rem. 44: 1.
French Literary Journals. For. Q. 36: 70.
French Literature. (T.W. Storrow) Knick. 26: 1. — Am. Q. 1: 550. — For. Q. 9: 345. 11: 181. — Blackw. 18: 715. 26: 205. — Quar. 8: 287. — Mo. R. 82: 522. — Select J. 2: 1. — Mo. R. 113: 488. — Dem. R. 42: 388. — West. Mo. R. 3: 25. — Irish Q. 3: 193, 833.
— Ancient. Quar. 120: 283.
— and History, Villemain's Recollec. of. Ed. R. 102: 62.
— and Pulpit. (W. H. Hurlbut) Chr. Exam. 45: 413.
— before the Revolution. Bost. R. 2: 240.
— Classics of, Sainte-Beuve on. Ev. Sat. 9: 337.
— Bohemianism in. (E. Caro) Canad. Mo. 1: 72.
— Current, 1880. (E. de Pressensé) Internat. R. 8: 56.
— Demoralizing, Poitou's Work on. Colburn, 111: 289.
— Early. (A. H. Everett) No. Am. 38: 358.
— English Influence on. (J. B. Angell) No. Am. 86: 412.
— Hawker's. Ed. R. 107: 232. Same art. Liv. Age, 56: 610.
— History of, Nisard's. Fraser, 75: 435.
— — Schmidt's. (T. S. Perry) No. Am. 119: 89.
— — Van Laun's. Radical R. 1: 592. — Lond. Q. 49: 375. — Penn Mo. 8: 715.
— in 1871. Lond. Q. 38: 60.
— in 1873. (G. Masson) Ev. Sat. 16: 152.
— Light, 1550–1700. Dub. Univ. 63: 243.
— Mediæval. (T. F. Crane) No. Am. 128: 212.
— Modern. New Eng. 6: 590. — Ecl. R. 72: 534. — Gen. Repos. 3: 89. — Brit. Q. 13: 561. — Ed. R. 101: 92. — Bost. Q. 5: 230.
— — Classics of. (A. Alison) Blackw. 41: 715. 43: 33.
— — Reynolds on. Mo. R. 149: 457.
— of the Reformation. (D. d'Istria) Internat. R. 3: 799.
— of the 16th and 17th Centuries. Westm. 25: 514.
— of the 18th Century. Blackw. 46: 1, 321.
— — Vinet on. Ecl. R. 100: 553.
— Recent. (F. Bôcher) Nat. Q. 3: 88. — Lond. Q. 21: 161.
— Republican. Fraser, 38: 136.
— Retrospect of. Ecl. R. 1: 149, 228, 308. 3: 237, 315. 4: 847.
— Revolutionary. Quar. 89: 491.
— since the Revolution of 1848. Bentley, 24: 11. Same art. Ecl. M. 15: 114.
— Thirty Years of. Lond. Q. 5: 431.
— under First Empire. (D. d'Istria) Internat. R. 2: 513.
— under the Restoration. Brit. Q. 19: 233.
— under the Empire. (Countess de Bury) No. Am. 83: 476.
— Wits of the Revolution. Nat. R. 17: 38.
French Littérateurs, Personal Sketches of. (A. Venner) Lippinc. 22: 335.
French Marriage Code. Temp. Bar, 36: 279.
French Memoirs. (J. H. Browne) Appleton, 20: 362.
— Collections of. Quar. 69: 281.
— from 1700. Brit. Q. 17: 441.
— from 1789. Fraser, 47: 401. 48: 418. Same art. Ecl. M. 29: 360.
— Old. Brit. Q. 16: 102.
— Recent. Fraser, 57: 673.
French Metrical Romances. For. Q. 17: 97.
French Modern Philosophy. Brit. Q. 2: 130. Same art. Ecl. M. 6: 217.
French Moralists. Am. Whig R. 2: 498.
French Morals and French Politics. (E. L. Godkin) Nation, 1: 647.
French Nation, Appeal to. (T. P. Thompson) Westm. 15: 522.
French National Workshops, 1848. No. Brit. 9: 213. 10: 261. — Quar. 87: 118.
French Naval Romances. For. Q. 21: 422.
French Novel, An unpublished. (Mad. d'Arbouville) Blackw. 62: 671. Same art. Liv. Age, 16: 122.
— Passages from an unpublished. Fraser, 34: 664.
French Novels. (J. W. Croker) Quar. 56: 65. — Belgra. 3: 68. — For. Q. 10: 474. — So. R. 7: 319. — Mus. 29: 47. — Westm. 25: 300. — Ed. R. 34: 372. — For. R. 2: 196. — Blackw. 61: 589. 66: 607. — Colburn, 153: 589. — Blackw. 126: 337. Same art. Liv. Age, 142: 67.
— and French Life. (H. de Lagardie) Macmil. 35: 386. Same art. Ecl. M 88: 587.
— and Novelists. Dub. Univ. 36: 349. Same art. Liv. Age, 27: 99. Same art. Ecl. M. 21: 305.
— — Anti-Clerical. Ed. R. 120: 437. Same art. Ecl. M. 64: 236.
— Better Aspects of. Brit. Q. 33: 81.
— Lowest Deep in. Nat. R. 11: 400. Same art. Liv. Age, 67: 451.
— Modern. (F. Asheton) Lippinc. 13: 237.
— Recent, 1878. Colburn, 162: 307.
French Novelists. Am. Whig R. 3: 239. — Am. Q. 20: 395. — Brit. & For. R. 11: 74. — Ed. R. 57: 330. — Select J. 3: 1.
— Minor. (H. James, jr.) Galaxy, 21: 219.
— Modern. (L. H. Hooper) Lippinc. 20: 379.
French Officers who served in the American Revolution. M. Am. Hist. 3: 364.
French Official Life. Ed. R. 44: 156.
French Opera. Am. Q. 11: 30. — Fraser, 5: 731.
French Oratorians; Nicholas Malebranche. (G. Masson) Kitto, 39: 265.
— Richard Simon. (G. Masson) Kitto, 37: 249.
French Orators and Oratory. (A. Hayward) Quar. 64: 411. — Mus. 38: 129.
French Painters, Day with. (A. Rhodes) Galaxy, 16: 5.
— of the 17th Century. (B. Murphy) Penn Mo. 11: 453.
French Parties and English Sympathies. Month, 31: 129.
French Pawnbroking, Curiosities of. Chamb. J. 51: 732.
French Peasant Songs. Cornh. 33: 596.
French Peasantry. Chamb. J. 21: 225.
French Pedlers in Italy. Liv. Age, 24: 257.
French Peerage, Ancient and modern. Fraser, 8: 413.
French People, Character of. Blackw. 26: 309.
— described by themselves. Mo. R. 164: 13.
French Philosophers of 19th Century. For. Q. 3: 185.
French Philosophy, Modern. Brit. & For. R. 2: 130. — Ecl. M. 6: 217.
French Play in London. (M. Arnold) 19th Cent. 6: 228.
French Plays. (A. Rhodes) Galaxy, 20: 372.
French Players and Playhouses. Blackw. 61: 177.
French Poetry. (C. Mackay) Bentley, 3: 251. — (F. Jeffrey) Ed. R. 37: 407.
— and Translation. For. Q. 31: 82.
— Contemporary. (M. B. Edwards) Fraser, 95: 589.
— Early. (Mrs. T. Robinson) Putnam, 2: 361. — (F. W. Palfrey) No. Am. 78: 214.
— — Besant's. (E. B. Cox) No. Am. 108: 663.
— in English. (W. M. Hardinge) 19th Cent. 9: 812.
— Minor. Retros. 8: 257. 10: 198.
— Modern. (Mrs. E. F. Ellet) No. Am. 44: 361.
— — with translations. (T. De Quincey) Lond. M. 8: 577.
French Poets. Colburn, 6: 305–467.
— Early. Lond. M. 1: 241.
— Minor. Tait, n. s. 10: 21.
— Modern. Dub. Univ. 42: 704. Same art. Ecl. M. 31: 205.
— — Minor. Dub. R. 89: 377.
— — Specimens of. Tait, n. s. 10: 131.
— Neglected; Du Bartas. Fraser, 26: 312.
— of 19th Century. Blackw. 13: 517. — Mo. R. 113: 237.
— Recent. (C. Mendès) Gent. M. n. s. 23: 478, 563.

French Poets, Trio of. Once a Week, **15**: 370.
French Police. For. Q. **29**: 59. — Westm. **10**: 507. — Colburn, **131**: 372.
— before 1789. Chamb. J. **13**: 252.
— System of. Bentley, **52**: 167. Same art. Ecl. M. **57**: 248.
French, Popular Chansons of. (J. F. Waller) Dub. Univ. **36**: 294.
French Preachers. (A. Schwartz) Contemp. **28**: 587.
French Preaching. (R. Baird) Am. Bib. Repos. 2d s. **2**: 332.
French Pretensions. Lond. M. **6**: 293.
French Priests and Bishop of Oxford. Chr. Rem. **50**: 149.
French Prohibition System. For. Q. **6**: 393.
French Protestant Academies. Good Words, **9**: 574.
French Public School. Chamb. J. **47**: 672.
French Railway Literature. Hogg, **13**: 437.
French Renaissance, Châteaux of. (E. F. S. Pattison) Contemp. **30**: 579.
French Reporting. Westm. **20**: 371.
French Roadside Tales. Lond. M. **11**: 189.
French Romance. (E. Everett) No. Am. **22**: 136. — (H. G. Rice) Hunt, **15**: 366. — New York R. **4**: 441. — Fraser, **27**: 184. — Mus. **8**: 209. — Ed. R. **40**: 158. Mo. R. **116**: 1. — Select J. **1**: 125.
— Modern. Dub. R. **9**: 353.
French Romancers on England. For. Q. **32**: 226.
French Romances. Fraser, **27**: 184.
— and American Morals. (E. I. Sears) Nat. Q. **2**: 143.
— of the 13th Century. Brit. Q. **26**: 119.
French Romantic Literature, Decline of. Fraser, **53**: 711. Same art. Liv. Age, **50**: 475. Same art. Ecl. M. **38**: 505.
French Saloon; a Tale. Broadw. **5**: 317.
French Sergeant, Adventures of, in the Wars, 1805–23. Lond. M. **15**: 500.
French Soldier at Inkermann; a Tale. (Mrs. T. S. Fay) Putnam, **14**: 201.
French Songs, Popular. Chamb. J. **1**: 38–365.
— Select Committee on. All the Year, **6**: 448, 561.
French Spectacles. All the Year, **41**: 369.
French Stage. Macmil. **21**: 400. — Penny M. **14**: 271–278. — Ev. Sat. **9**: 214.
— Eccentricities of. Temp. Bar, **41**: 263.
— English History and Character of. For. Q. **31**: 140.
— of To-Day. (E. Jerrold) Gent. M. n. s. **12**: 704.
— Old. All the Year, **41**: 185, 400. **42**: 160, 390.
French Theater. (H. James, jr.) Galaxy, **23**: 437. — (A. Rhodes) Galaxy, **19**: 22.
— before Molière. Dub. Univ. **70**: 243.
— Green Room of. Colburn, **4**: 309.
— Minor. For. Q. **9**: 447.
French Theaters. Quar. **17**: 441.
French Theatricals. All the Year, **42**: 570.
— 1850. Dub. Univ. **35**: 769.
French Titles. Chamb. J. **35**: 305.
French Tragedy. (R. G. White) Atlan. **47**: 827. — Quar. **29**: 25.
— before Corneille. (G. Saintsbury) Fraser, **100**: 456.
French Tragic Drama; Corneille. Nat. Q. **23**: 256.
French Travelers in the West, Early. (J. H. Perkins) No. Am. **48**: 63.
French Trial, A. All the Year, **19**: 535.
— A late. Fraser, **33**: 621.
French Tribunals of Commerce. Am. Law R. **10**: 68.
French University Writers. Fraser, **29**: 127.
French Verse-Writers, 1830–77. Cornh. **36**: 278.
French Versions of Chaucer and Gay. Lond. Q. **10**: 110.
French Village, Rustication in a. Chamb. J. **17**: 311. Same art. Liv. Age, **33**: 573.
French War in Spain. Ed. R. **25**: 63.
French War Letters. N. E. Reg. **4**: 27.
French Widow, Autobiog. of a young. Fraser, **38**: 59, 169.
French Wolf, A. All the Year, **7**: 280.
French Woman, A charming. Fraser, **37**: 509. Same art. Ecl. M. **14**: 401.
French Women, Literary. All the Year, **9**: 489.
— under the Second Empire. Temp. Bar, **17**: 320. *See* France, Women in.
French Words and Phrases. (A. Rhodes) Galaxy, **16**: 472.
French Work, English Eyes on. All the Year, **19**: 560.
— and Workers, judged by English Workingmen. (J. M. Ludlow) Good Words, **9**: 467.
French Workmen's Congress. (F. Harrison) Fortn. **29**: 662.
French Yeoman. Chamb. J. **47**: 785.
Frenchmen in London. All the Year, **27**: 270.
— The slaughtered. (P. Asperge) Galaxy, **5**: 472.
Frenchtown, Mich., Massacre at, 1812. (T. P. Dudley) Hist. M. **19**: 28.
Freneau, Philip. (C. C. Smith) No. Am. **93**: 570.
Frère, E., and Sympathetic Art in France. (M. D. Conway) Harper, **43**: 801.
Frere, John Hookham. (J. Davies) Contemp. **19**: 512. — (C. E. Norton) Nation, **19**: 270. — Fraser, **85**: 491.
— and George Canning, Literary Partnership of. Fraser, **90**: 714. Same art. Liv. Age, **124**: 358.
— Month at Seaford in 1825 with. (A. G. Stapleton) Macmil. **26**: 25. Same art. Liv. Age, **113**: 691.
— Life and Writings. Quar. **132**: 26. Same art. Liv. Age, **112**: 515.
— Poems. (C. E. Norton) No. Am. **107**: 136.
— Works of. Ed. R. **135**: 472.
Freres, The; a Novel. (Mrs. Alexander) Temp. Bar, **63**: 115–540. Same art. Liv. Age, **148**: 361–656. **149**: 41–595. **150**: 20–625. **151**: 39–805.
Fresco discovered at Preston, Sussex. (C. Townshend) Arch. **23**: 309.
— Doings in. Fraser, **25**: 669.
Frescos by German Students at Rome. Lond. M. **2**: 149.
— of the new Houses of Parliament. Art J. **2**: 16.
Fresco Painting. Quar. **74**: 447. — Art J. **3**: 108. — (A. Farley) Penn Mo. **12**: 304. — Quar. **104**: 277.
— in modern Times. Ed. R. **123**: 1.
— Modern, Process of. Art J. **32**: 345.
— of Italy. Blackw. **88**: 458.
— on Room Walls. (R. Sturgis) Nation, **2**: 236.
— Practice of. J. Frankl. Inst. **35**: 57, 126, 185.
Fresh-Water Cure; a Tale. (N. W. Racey) Canad. Mo. **16**: 242.
Fresh-Water Sketches. (L. W. Bailey) Am. Natural. **5**: 334.
Freydank's Poems. Brit. & For. R. **3**: 23.
Freytag, Gustav. Eng. Dom. M. **12**: 144, 218.
— Debit and Credit. Brit. Q. **27**: 152. — Blackw. **83**: 57. — Hogg, **15**: 401.
— Ingo and Ingraban. (W. W. Newell) O. & N. **7**: 610.
— Lost Manuscript. No. Brit. **43**: 323.
— Novels. (H. H. Boyesen) No. Am. **119**: 476. **120**: 444.
Freytag, Georg Wm. F. Arabic Lexicon. (H. P. Goodrich) No. Am. **48**: 461.
Friar Gerund, the famous Preacher. Retros. **7**: 239.
Friar Jerome's beautiful Book; a Poem. (T. B. Aldrich) Atlan. **14**: 195.
Friar of St. Albans; a Tale. (J. G. Gervans) Sharpe, **41**: 273.
Friar Pedro's Ride. (Bret Harte) Overland, **2**: 375.
Friars and Scholars in Paris, 1230. (G. L. B. Wildig) Macmil. **30**: 511. Same art. Liv. Age, **123**: 304.
— in England. Chr. Rem. **52**: 324.
— — Black, or Friar-Preachers. (C. F. R. Palmer) Reliquary, **17**: 33, 130. **18**: 17, 71, 161. **19**: 37.
— of Berwick; a Poetical Tale. Dub. Univ. **13**: 369.
Friction. Ecl. Engin. **4**: 179.

Friction, and Bodies in Motion. J. Frankl. Inst. **8**: 138–285.
— and Pressure. (F. J. J. Nicklès) Am. J. Sci. **67**: 252.
— Anti-Friction Composition. Pract. M. **5**: 333.
— at high Velocities. (D. Galton) Nature, **20**: 292, 316. — Ecl. Engin. **23**: 245.
— at low Speeds. Ecl. Engin. **17**: 124.
— between Air and Water. (R. von Lang) Ecl. Engin. **15**: 181.
— between a Cord and Pulley. (I. O. Baker) Ecl. Engin. **19**: 395.
— Experiments on. (E. Morris) J. Frankl. Inst. **66**: 217.
— Free. (C. T. Congdon) Nation, **2**: 138.
— Laws of. (A. S. Kimball) Am. J. Sci. **113**: 353.
— Morin's Experiments on. (J. F. Frazer) J. Frankl. Inst. **35**: 412.
— of Journals at low Speeds. (A. S. Kimball) Am. J. Sci. **115**: 192.
— — Coefficients of. (R. H. Thurston) J. Frankl. Inst. **106**: 289.
— of Screw-Propellers. (J. W. Nystrom) J. Frankl. Inst. **96**: 338.
— of Solids. (G. Rennie) J. Frankl. Inst. **8**: 289, 388. **9**: 1, 73.
— One of the Laws of. (A. S. Kimball) Ecl. Engin. **17**: 86.
— Rolling. (O. Reynolds) Ecl. Engin. **14**: 42.
— — and Dragging. J. Frankl. Inst. **9**: 57.
— Sliding, on an inclined Plane. (A. S. Kimball) Am. J. Sci. **111**: 181. — (A. S. Kimball) Ecl. Engin. **14**: 497.
— upon Railroads. (M. Ward) J. Frankl. Inst. **9**: 46.
Friction Brake as a Dynamometer. Ecl. Engin. **19**: 277.
Friction Clutches for Rolling-Mills. Ecl. Engin. **7**: 508.
Frictional Resistances of pneumatic Foundations. (A. Schmoll) Ecl. Engin. **20**: 119.
Frida and her Poet. (P. H. Hayne) So. M. **12**: 661.
Friedland, Battle of; 1807. Temp. Bar, **40**: 542.
Friend Barton's Concern. (M. H. Foote) Scrib. **18**: 334.
Friend Eli's Daughter. (B. Taylor) Atlan. **10**: 99. Same art. Eng. Dom. M. **21**: 17, 74. Same art. Sharpe, **37**: 244.
Friend Fritz. (MM. Erckmann-Chatrian) Eng. Dom. M. **10**: 8–330. **11**: 11–207.
Friend in Need; an Extravaganza, after Sterne. (T. Hood) Colburn, **61**: 389–520.
Friend in Need is a Friend indeed. (L. E. Landon) Colburn, **47**: 41.
Friend of the Hero. Blackw. **120**: 417. Same art. Liv. Age, **131**: 359.
— of my Youth. (T. B. Aldrich) Atlan. **27**: 169.
Friend's Burial; a Poem. (J. G. Whittier) Atlan. **32**: 64.
Friends, Essay on. Cong. **2**: 735.
— and Friendship. Colburn, **7**: 321.
— Quarrels of. Macmil. **18**: 353.
Friends; a Duet. (E. S. Phelps) Atlan. **47**: 86–836. **48**: 98.
Friends; a Duet in a minor Key. Lond. Soc. **39**: 580.
Friends; a Story. Victoria, **35**: 276.
Friends at Court. Irish Mo. **7**: 561, 651.
Friends in Council, Helps's. Brit. Q. **6**: 134. — Fraser, **40**: 636.
— — abroad. Fraser, **52**: 607. **53**: 1, 127. Same art. Liv. Age, **48**: 129, 232.
— — Concerning. (A. K. H. Boyd) Fraser, **60**: 334.
"Friends of the Foreigner" seventy Years ago. (E. D. J. Wilson) 19th Cent. **4**: 327.
Friends, Society of. *See* Quakers.
Friendly Islands, Affinity of the Language with Hebrew. (G. H. Glass) Arch. **8**: 81.
— Mariner's Account of. Portfo.(Den) **23**: 61.
Friendly Lead, A. All the Year, **2**: 472.
Friendly Societies. (E. W. Brabrook) J. Statis. Soc. **38**: 185. — Ed. R. **138**: 94. — Quar. **138**: 206. — (W. Webster) Good Words, **5**: 258. — (J. Randall) Fortn. **34**: 188. — Chamb. J. **19**: 199. **32**: 355. — Hogg, **15**: 265.
— Antiquity of. Penny M. **11**: 279.
— History, Functions, and Prospects of. (W. W. Edwards) Contemp. **29**: 187.
— Improved. Penny M. **11**: 387.
— Legislation on, Principles of. (A. J. Wilson) Fraser, **90**: 269.
— Statistics of. (F. G. P. Neison) J. Statis. Soc. **40**: 42.
Friendship. (W. R. Alger) No. Am. **83**: 104. — Knick. **61**: 149. — So. Lit. Mess. **2**: 735. — Tinsley, **13**: 454. — Victoria, **17**: 544.
— Æsthetics of. So. R. n. s. **8**: 50.
— Amicitiæ Shaksperianæ. Tait, n. s. **16**: 696, 796.
— an Idyll. St. James, **27**: 473.
— Blossomings from a sheltering Tree. (E. Spencer) Hours at Home, **11**: 403.
— Debate on. Knick. **34**: 27.
— Ethics of. Cornh. **10**: 299.
— Maxims on. (J. Payn) Chamb. J. **44**: 753.
— of Books, Maurice's. (A. V. Dicey) Nation, **18**: 285.
— Our best Friend. Colburn, **63**: 39.
— Some Aspects of. Blackw. **119**: 297. Same art. Liv. Age, **129**: 214.
— Thoughts about. Victoria, **23**: 232, 379.
Friendship's Triumph; a Tale. (W. Reade) Sharpe, **38**: 318.
Friendships of the great Men of Literature. Westm. **78**: 140.
— of Men and Women. (S. B. Cooper) Overland, **14**: 278.
— — Pure. (W. R. Alger) Mo. Rel. M. **38**: 361.
— Women's. Ev. Sat. **1**: 582.
Fries, Elias Magnus. Nature, **17**: 343.
Friesland, Ancient Laws and Constitution of. Ed. R. **32**: 1.
— Language and Literature of. For. Q. **3**: 602. — Westm. **12**: 186.
— — Oera Linda Book. Cornh. **34**: 181.
Friesland Cap, Strange Origin of. (J. de Liefde) Good Words, **2**: 665.
Frietchie, Barbara; Refutation of Whittier's Myth. So. Hist. Pap. **7**: 435.
Frighted with false Fire. (D. C. Murray) Belgra. **33**: 54.
Frightened to Death. (M. Hosmer) Lippinc. **8**: 62.
Frippery; a Tale. Putnam, **9**: 464.
Frisbie, Levi. Inaugural Address. (A. Norton) No. Am. **6**: 224.
— Writings of. Chr. Disc. **5**: 276.
'Frisco. Fraser, **98**: 679.
Friswell, J. Hain, and G. A. Sala. Ev. Sat. **11**: 210, 571.
Frithiof the Bold, Story of; (transl. by W. Morris) Dark Blue, **1**: 42, 176.
Fritz, George. Ecl. Engin. **9**: 445.
Frobisher, Martin, with portrait. (S. G. Drake) N. E. Reg. **3**: 9.
— Instructions to. (H. Ellis) Arch. **18**: 287.
Froebel, Friedrich, with portrait. Am. J. Educ. **30**: 641.
— and the Kindergarten System. Am. J. Educ. **28**: 33. — (B. W. Richardson) Gent. M. n. s. **26**: 157.
— Educational Views of. (B. von Marenholtz-Bülow) Am. J. Educ. **30**: 81, 323, 673.
— Individuality and Personality in his System. (E. P. Peabody) Education, **1**: 616.
Frog and Toad Families. Chamb. J. **13**: 277.
— Common. (St. G. Mivart) Nature, **8**: 470, 510. **9**: 10–406. — Chamb. J. **52**: 106.
— Green Tree. (S. Hibberd) Recr. Sci. **1**: 49.
— Horned. (F. Buckland) Pop. Sci. Mo. **2**: 676.
Frogs. All the Year, **32**: 369. — Ev. Sat. **17**: 238. — House. Words, **14**: 25.

Frogs and their Allies. Sharpe, **27**: 14.
— and Snails. Once a Week, **20**: 185.
— Bull-, of America. Penny M. **5**: 319.
— Chapter on. Knick. **57**: 484.
— Coagulation in Blood of. Nature, **6**: 447.
— Edible. (S. Hibberd) Stud. & Intel. Obs. **5**: 449.
— — of France. Chamb. J. **34**: 71.
— Formation of. (W. M. Carpenter) Am. J. Sci. **44**: 40.
— Pseudis, the paradoxical. (S. W. Garman) Am. Natural. **11**: 587.
Froissart, Jean, and his Chronicles. Hogg, **3**: 414. — Penny M. **11**: 9–493.
— and his Times. Am. Q. **13**: 261.
— Chronicles of. Ecl. R. **70**: 515. — Fraser, **88**: 37. — Mo. R. **160**: 1. — Westm. **4**: 1. — Dem. R. **13**: 499.
— — Johnes's Translation. (Sir W. Scott) Ed. R. **5**: 347. — Ecl. R. **6**: 749, 1003.
— Love Story of. (W. Besant) Temp. Bar, **56**: 194.
Frolic in Space; a Darwinian Forecast. (J. M. Binckley) Lakeside, **8**: 446.
From the Altar to the Bar; a Tale. Dark Blue, **3**: 86–342.
From Belfry to Porch. (L. Kip) Overland, **6**: 399.
From the Chapel Roof; a Tale. (H. W. Lucy) Belgra. **38**: 322.
From Colchis back to Argos. (J. D. B. Stillman) Overland, **12**: 343, 453, 546. **13**: 56, 146.
From a Convent; a Poem. (N. Perry) Galaxy, **20**: 26.
From the Country; Carl Wrensler's Report. Radical, **5**: 321–499. **6**: 57, 211.
From Dreams to Wishing; a Story. (E. L. Linton) Belgra. **30**: 75–450. **31**: 82.
From the Earth to the Moon. (J. Verne) St. James, **32**: 67–663. **33**: 50. **34**: 1.
From Fable to Fact. (C. M. Ingleby) Fortn. **1**: 733.
From First to Last. House. Words, **19**: 457–527. Same art. Liv. Age, **61**: 713.
From Generation to Generation. (C. Chesebrough) Atlan. **27**: 691. **28**: 9.
From Generation to Generation. Temp. Bar, **2**: 101.
From India; a Poem. (M. Oliphant) Blackw. **82**: 505.
From an Island; a Tale. (A. I. Thackeray) Cornh. **18**: 610, 739. **19**: 62. Same art. Liv. Age, **100**: 756, 804. **101**: 44.
From May till November. (M. Durfee) Godey, **64**: 467, 563. **65**: 55–369.
From May to Martinmas. (Mrs. W. H. Palmer) Galaxy, **5**: 455.
From San Francisco to Sonora; a Tale. St. James, **16**: 54, 237, 337.
From Sea to Sea; a Poem. (J. Miller) Scrib. **3**: 95.
From Thistle Patch to Cincinnati. (J. B. L. Soule) Lakeside, **2**: 309.
From the Trent Gallery. (L. Sand) Sharpe, **36**: 13.
From the Wings; a Novel. (B. H. Buxton) Tinsley, **26**: 1–533. **27**: 1–437.
From the Wisp; a Story. Tinsley, **6**: 348.
From Year to Year; a Poem. (I. D. Coolbrith) Overland, **7**: 385.
Fromentin, Eugène. (E. Benson) Galaxy, **2**: 533.
— Gonse's Life of. (W. C. Brownell) Nation, **32**: 462.
— Montefiore's Etchings after. Portfo. **9**: 32.
F'rona; a Tale. Temp. Bar, **44**: 514. Same art. Liv. Age, **126**: 788.
Fronde, The, and Cardinal de Retz. Temp. Bar, **38**: 524.
— Days of. Blackw. **58**: 596.
— History of. Mo. R. **113**: 430.
— — St. Aulaire's. Mo. R. **164**: 273.
— Wars of. Bentley, **21**: 213.
Frontenac, Count, and New France, Parkman's. (W. F. Allen) Nation, **25**: 259. — (M. P. Lowe) Unita. R. **9**: 210. — Canad. Mo. **12**: 541.
Frontiers. Chamb. J. **36**: 385.
Frontier Folk. (G. Booth) Internat. R. **9**: 29.
Frontier Land, Campion's. Chamb. J. **56**: 421.
Frontier Law. Chamb. J. **49**: 305.
Frontier Life, Webber's. Dem. R. **22**: 324.
Frontier Outrages in America. Chamb. J. **50**: 513.
Frontier Warfare, Trait of. West. M. **5**: 139.
Fronto, M. C., the Orator. So. Q. **22**: 365.
Froschammer, Julius, a Forerunner of Old Catholicism. Cong. **5**: 34.
Frost, Charles. (U. Parsons) N. E. Reg. **3**: 249.
Frost, Richard, Memoir of. Cong. M. **8**: 505.
Frost Genealogy. (U. Parsons) N. E. Reg. **5**: 165.
Frost. Ecl. R. **109**: 476.
— Action on earthy Material. (W. C. Kerr) Am. J. Sci. **121**: 345.
— and Fire, Geological Work of. Intel. Obs. **8**: 9.
— Effect on Plants. (J. Lindley) Am. J. Sci. **39**: 18.
— of 1814. All the Year, **17**: 299.
Frosts, Hard. All the Year, **4**: 396.
— on the Thames. (R. Bell) Once a Week, **4**: 180.
Frothingham, Ebenezer. Chr. Mo. Spec. **2**: 449, 505.
Frothingham, Nathaniel L. Sermon on All Saints Day. Chr. Exam. **29**: 385.
— Sermons. (C. Robbins) Chr. Exam. **53**: 258.
Frothingham, Octavius Brooks. (E. C. Stedman) Galaxy, **22**: 478.
— Transcendentalism of. (I. T. Hecker) Cath. World, **23**: 528.
— Visions of Future. (G. Reynolds) Unita. R. **12**: 227.
Froude, James Anthony. (J. McCarthy) Galaxy, **14**: 293. — with portrait, Ecl. M. **79**: 632. — with portrait, Ev. Sat. **11**: 206. — with portrait, Once a Week, **27**: 540. — with portrait, Appleton, **2**: 399.
— and Mr. Amos, on Tudor Legislation. Nat. R. **9**: 423.
— and Calvinism. (J. Young) Contemp. **21**: 431. Same art. Liv. Age, **116**: 746. — (J. G. Meline) Cath. World, **13**: 541.
— and E. A. Freeman. (A. V. Dicey) Nation, **13**: 387, 403. — Month, **36**: 138.
— and Ireland. Brit. Q. **57**: 481.
— and the Saturday Review. Ev. Sat. **9**: 178.
— as a Biographer. (J. Wedgwood) Contemp. **39**: 821. Same art. Ecl. M. **97**: 159.
— Essay on Progress. (C. D. Warner) Scrib. **7**: 351.
— Historical Method of. (J. L. Spalding) No. Am. **130**: 280.
— History of England. *See* England, History.
— Is he a Historian? (J. G. Shea) Am. Cath. Q. **5**: 113.
— Last Words on. (E. A. Freeman) Contemp. **35**: 214.
— Nemesis of Faith. Chr. Obs. **50**: 16. — Fraser, **39**: 545. — (S. Osgood) Chr. Exam. **47**: 93.
— Philosophical Novels of. Prosp. R. **5**: 163.
— Short Studies on great Subjects. (A. V. Dicey) Nation, **25**: 215. — (E. E. Hale) Chr. Exam. **84**: 237.
Froude, Richard H., Remains of. Dub. R. **6**: 416. — U. S. Cath. M. **2**: 1.
Froude, William. Nature, **20**: 148, 169.
Froufrou, Authors of the Play. (J. B. Matthews) Lippinc. **26**: 711.
Frozen and thawed. House. Words, **8**: 533.
Frozen Deep; a Dramatic Story. (W. Collins) Temp. Bar, **42**: 1, 145, 289.
Frozen Harbor. (J. T. Trowbridge) Atlan. **15**: 281.
Frozen Truth. (J. W. Gally) Overland, **15**: 320.
Frozen Well in Brandon, Vt. Cornh. **7**: 279.
Fructidor; a Poem. Dub. Univ. **52**: 412.
Frugal Marriage; a Tale. Temp. Bar, **3**: 140.
Fruit. Chamb. J. **45**: 353. — Ev. Sat. **6**: 493.
— and Fruit-Trees of America. (A. C. Baldwin) New Eng. **4**: 229.
— Dish of, for Dessert. All the Year, **20**: 367.
— from Plates and Dishes; a Story. Howitt, **3**: 20–76.

Fruits and Flowers; a Summer Symposium. (J. F. Waller) Dub. Univ. **38**: 127.
— — of the East. Chamb. J. **36**: 85.
— and Seeds. (Sir J. Lubbock) Fortn. **35**: 426. Same art. Pop. Sci. Mo. **19**: 156, 354. Same art. Ecl. M. **96**: 756.
— Classification of. (W. R. McNab) Nature, **4**: 475.
— — Dickson's. Nature, **4**: 347.
— — Improved. (W. Hincks) Canad. J. n. s. **6**: 495.
— Curious Forms of. (J. R. Jackson) Good Words, **7**: 525.
— Dried, of the Levant. Penny M. **13**: 359.
— — of Malaga. Penny M. **13**: 374.
— Flowers, and Farming, Beecher's. Liv. Age, **63**: 295.
— of England, Wild. Chamb. J. **18**: 203, 298.
— — Garden. Chamb. J. **19**: 312.
— of the United States. (W. Flagg) No. Am. **96**: 407.
— Origin of. (Grant Allen) Cornh. **38**: 174. Same art. Pop. Sci. Mo. **13**: 597.
— Preservation of. Penny M. **8**: 382.
— Success with small. (E. P. Roe) Scrib. **19**: 9–803.
— Tropical. (W. T. Brigham) Am. Natural. **2**: 183, 307, 405. — Chamb. J. **19**: 55.
Fruit Culture. Land We Love, **1**: 299.
— and Forests. (J. S. Patterson) Pop. Sci. Mo. **2**: 194.
— for the South. De Bow, **12**: 535, 664. **18**: 327.
— Use of. Am. Alma. **1830**: 121.
Fruit Drying. (C. Barnard) Scrib. **16**: 206.
Fruit Farming and Fruit Trade. Chamb. J. **56**: 247.
Fruit Ripening, Chemistry of. (A. B. Prescott) Pop. Sci. Mo. **12**: 460.
Fry, Caroline, Literary Remains of. Hogg, **4**: 107.
Fry, Elizabeth. (F. D. Huntington) Hours at Home, **1**: 534. — Chamb. J. **11**: 202. — with portrait, Peop. J. **5**: 260. — Meth. Q. **11**: 226.
— Life of. Liv. Age, **14**: 183, 199.
— — and Labors of. No. Brit. **9**: 252. — Quar. **82**: 109. Same art. Ecl. M. **13**: 399. Same art. Liv. Age, **16**: 492. — (J. Hall) Princ. **20**: 31. — Prosp. R. **4**: 77.
— Memoir of. Chr. Obs. **48**: 262. — Howitt, **3**: 61. — Ed. R. **150**: 41. — Ecl. R. **87**: 521. — Liv. Age, **17**: 21.
— on the State of Ireland. Mo. R. **115**: 22.
— Verses on. Knick. **44**: 570.
Frye Genealogy. (J. W. Dean) N. E. Reg. **8**: 226.
Fualdès, M., Assassination of. (E. H. Lacombe) So. M. **15**: 239. All the Year, **9**: 549.
Fuchs, Johann Nepomuk von, Biography of. (F. von Kobell) Am. J. Sci. **73**: 95, 225.
Fuchsia, Story of the. House. Words, **8**: 196.
Fucino, Lake, Drainage of. Ecl. Engin. **18**: 433. — (T. Bacon) Atlan. **19**: 465. — Liv. Age, **144**: 493.
Fudge Papers. (D. G. Mitchell) Knick. **39**: 48–448. **40**: 56–512. **41**: 1–529. **42**: 274, 567. **43**: 123–452. **44**: 50–460.
Fudges in England. Westm. **24**: 79. — Brit. & For. R. **1**: 443. — Dub. Univ. **6**: 297.
— in Paris. Blackw. **3**: 129.
Fuegians, The. Chamb. J. **4**: 12. — Colburn, **57**: 77.
Fuehrich, Joseph. Art J. **17**: 201.
Fuel. (C. Morris) Lippinc. **4**: 509. — (E. North) Am. J. Sci. **11**: 66. — (C. W. Siemens) Ecl. Engin. **10**: 235. **16**: 438. — (C. W. Siemens) Nature, **8**: 441. — (C. W. Siemens) Pract. M. **2**: 380.
— and its Use. (H. Fritz) J. Frankl. Inst. **102**: 156.
— Artificial. (E. F. Loiseau) J. Frankl. Inst. **97**: 111. — (E. F. Loiseau) Pract. M. **3**: 292. — Ecl. Engin. **9**: 81.
— — Manufacture of. (E. F. Loiseau) Ecl. Engin. **19**: 544. **23**: 41. — Pract. M. **4**: 156.
— — — in Europe. (R. Grimshaw) J. Frankl. Inst. **108**: 145.
— — Value of. (J. Wormald) Ecl. Engin. **10**: 320.
Fuel, Casement's Method of burning. Pract. M. **3**: 338.
— Coal Oil for. Chamb. J. **46**: 441.
— Combustion of, in Boilers. (H. Geary) Ecl. Engin. **18**: 265.
— — of different Kinds of. (I. L. Bell) Nature, **19**: 175.
— Compressed Coal-Dust. Pract. M. **6**: 166.
— Consumption of, in France and England. Penny M. **5**: 462.
— Domestic Economy of. (D. Galton) Pop. Sci. Mo. **3**: 193–297.
— Dust as. Ecl. Engin. **3**: 647.
— Economizer of. Pract. M. **1**: 238.
— Economy of. Ecl. Engin. **10**: 65. — (W. R. Johnson) Am. J. Sci. **23**: 318. — (L. Shoest) Ecl. Engin. **15**: 228, 346. — Pract. M. **5**: 358. **7**: 150. — Westm. **91**: 399.
— — for Steam. (A. Brunel) Canad. J. n. s. **1**: 336.
— Fossil, History of. Mo. R. **138**: 430.
— Heat evolved and lost. (M. Bull) J. Frankl. Inst. **2**: 257, 281, 360. **3**: 47. **5**: 273.
— Lecture on. (C. W. Siemens) Ecl. Engin. **9**: 458.
— Liquid. Ecl. Engin. **1**: 548.
— — or concentrated. (J. H. Selwyn) Ecl. Engin. **3**: 593.
— of the Future. All the Year, **39**: 448.
— Patent. Ecl. Engin. **6**: 160.
— Petroleum as. J. Frankl. Inst. **108**: 210.
— Pulverized. (C. E. Dutton) J. Frankl. Inst. **91**: 377. **92**: 17. **94**: 337.
— Sulphides as. (J. Hollway) J. Frankl. Inst. **108**: 180.
— Use of, in reheating Furnaces. (R. Akerman) Ecl. Engin. **15**: 464.
— Use and Abuse of, in Cooking. Pract M. **6**: 22.
— Value of different Kinds of. Ecl. Engin. **5**: 21.
— Water as. (W. C. Conant) Pop. Sci. Mo. **16**: 653.
— Wet, Combustion of. (B. Silliman, jr.) Am. J. Sci. **80**: 243.
— — Furnaces for burning. (R. H. Thurston) Ecl. Engin. **12**: 81, 123.
— — in Gas Furnaces. (R. Akerman) Ecl. Engin. **14**: 468.
Fuel-Gas and Strong-Water Gas System. (H. Wurtz) Ecl. Engin. **23**: 376.
Fugger Family. Penny M. **3**: 269.
Fugitive Slave Law. (E. G. Brooks) Univ. Q. **8**: 169. — New Eng. **8**: 378, 615. — Brownson, **8**: 383. — Am. Whig R. **13**: 383. — Dem. R. **28**: 352. — Ecl. R. **93**: 661. — West. Law J. **8**: 57. — Prosp. R. **7**: 424.
— Oberlin-Wellington Rescue. New Eng. **17**: 687.
Fugitive Slaves. Dem. R. **27**: 57.
Fugitives from Justice, Surrender of. (T. M. Cooley) Princ. n. s. **3**: 156.
Fugue in Canon Form. (R. G. White) Galaxy, **19**: 111.
Fuji-Yama, Mt. *See* Fusiyama.
Fulda, Monastery of. (A. F. Hewit) Cath. World, **28**: 301.
Fulfilment. (C. R. Moor) Univ. Q. **31**: 152.
— the true Method of Reform in Religion. (F. W. Clayden) Unita. R. **14**: 385.
Fulham Lawn; a Tale. (A. I. Thackeray) Cornh. **22**: 62. Same art. Liv. Age, **106**: 529. Same art. Ev. Sat. **9**: 506, 522, 538.
Full Heart, few Words. (F. Jacox) Bentley, **61**: 602.
Full Measure. (M Young) Tinsley, **16**: 207.
Fuller, Andrew, Character of. (J. D. Knowles) Am. Q. Obs. **2**: 110. — Ecl. M. **41**: 326.
— Life of. (J. Foster) Ecl. R. **27**: 181. — (A. Alexander) Princ. **18**: 547.
— — and Writings of. (E. Pond) Chr. R. **17**: 161.
— Morris's Memoir of. Ecl. R. **23**: 478.
— Works of. Cong. M. **7**: 642. — Ecl. R. **41**: 505.
Fuller, Margaret. *See* Ossoli, Countess.
Fuller, Thomas. (L. Stephen) Cornh. **25**: 28. — Chr. Obs. **4**: 453. — Lond. Q. **52**: 80. — Penny M. **14**: 135–178.

Fuller, Thomas. Andronicus. Retros. **15**: 396.
— Bailey's Life of. Chr. Obs. **75**: 100.
— Good Thoughts. Cong. M. **7**: 434.
— Holy and profane States. Retros. **3**: 50.—Mus. **31**: 328.
— Life and Writings of. (H. Rogers) Ed. R. **74**: 328. Same art. Liv. Age, **55**: 1. Same art. Mus. **45**: 582.
— Prose of. Am. Mo. M. **7**: 373.
— Writings of. (L. Stephen) Cornh. **25**: 28. Same art. Liv. Age, **112**: 323. — Retros. **15**: 396.
Fuller, William, the Plotter. House. Words, **18**: 64.
Fuller Genealogy. (A. B. Fuller) N. E. Reg. **13**: 351.
Fullerton, Georgiana. Ellen Middleton. (J. Moncrieff) No. Brit. **1**: 545. — Ed. R. **80**: 199. — Chr. Rem. **8**: 81.
— Grantley Manor. Brownson, **5**: 482. — Tait, n. s. **14**: 584.
— Lady Bird. Chr. Rem. **25**: 401.
— Novels. (J. McCarthy) Cath. World, **12**: 546. — Dub. R. **23**: 178.
Fullness of Time. (J. B. Brown) Ex. H. Lec. **11**: 27. — (E. E. Hale) Unita. R. **13**: 433.
Fulminating Powders, Experiments on. J. Frankl. Inst. **10**: 130, 201.
Fulton, Robert. (C. D. Drake) Hesp. **2**: 283. — Anal. M. **5**: 394. **10**: 177. — (J. Renwick) Sparks's Am. Biog. **10**: 3. — Quar. **19**: 347. — Mus. **33**: 340. — Niles's Reg. **13**: 51. **33**: 15. — Tait, n. s. **27**: 215.
— and submarine Gunnery. (R. Fulton) Scrib. **22**: 563.
— Anecdote of. (A. Michaux) J. Frankl. Inst. **48**: 37.
— First Voyage of. Hunt, **15**: 468.
Fulwood, Christopher. Reliquary, **1**: 89.
Fun, The Age of. Chamb. J. **7**: 73.
Fundholders, Poor Folks as. Chamb. J. **58**: 49.
Funding the National Debt, 1870. (E. L. Godkin) Nation, **10**: 150.
— Bill for. (J. B. Hodgskin) Nation, **10**: 267.
— — and Rate of Interest. (J. B. Hodgskin) Nation, **11**: 273.
Funding System. (J. R. McCulloch) Ed. R. **39**: 1. **47**: 59. — Quar. **31**: 311. — Carey's Mus. **6**: 93.
Funds, Public, and Stocks. Blackw. **4**: 55, 287.
Fundy, Bay of, Expedition to. (C. P. Mattocks) Univ. Q. **4**: 236.
— Ice Drifts and Tides of. (H. Y. Hind) Canad. Mo. **8**: 189.
Funeral at Sea. Fraser, **40**: 188.
— of Time; a Poem. (H. B. Hirst) So. Lit. Mess. **10**: 525.
— Roman. Macmil. **30**: 429.
Funerals. Blackw. **44**: 469. — Knick. **10**: 229.
— and Funeral Expenses. Quar. **73**: 441.
— — Reform in. Ev. Sat. **10**: 427, 455.
— and Graveyards, Fashion in. So. R. n. s. **22**: 326.
— Expense of. Penny M. **13**: 94.
— Garlands at. Antiquary, **3**: 207. — (L. Jewitt) Reliquary, **1**: 5.
— Viennese. Chamb. J. **32**: 87.
— Village, in Naples. House. Words, **5**: 19.
— Whimsical. Chamb. J. **56**: 363.
Funeral and sepulchral Honors. Ox. Prize Ess. **3**: 1.
Funeral Ceremonies and Usages. Penny M. **13**: 45.
See Burial Rites.
Funeral Charges in England in the 16th Century. N. E. Reg. **11**: 279.
Funeral Customs. Hogg, **1**: 13, 27.
— Aboriginal, in the United States. (E. A. Barber) Am. Natural. **11**: 197.
Funeral Expenses of the Bishop of Winchester, 1618. (E. P. Shirley) Arch. **44**: 393.
Funeral Farces. All the Year, **37**: 105.
Funeral Follies. O. & N. **1**: 474.
Funeral Fashions. (Mrs. C. A. White) Sharpe, **46**. 89.
Funeral Orations. Chr. R. **7**: 124.
Funeral Rites in China. Ev. Sat. **15**: 61.
— in the East. Chr. Rem. **19**: 407. — Meth. M. **55**: 264. — So. Lit. Mess. **28**: 279.
See Burial.
Funeral Sermons, Researches among. N. E. Reg. **7**: 241, 305. **8**: 29, 179, 363. **9**: 69, 173, 355. **10**: 29. **12**: 151. **15**: 288. **18**: 288, 345. **19**: 159, 245. **20**: 315.
Funeral Services, Form of. Mercersb. **7**: 462.
Fungi. (B. Halsted) Scrib. **10**: 710. — (E. C. Wright) Putnam, **14**: 431. — All the Year, **1**: 341, 437. — Chamb. J. **4**: 244. **21**: 347. **52**: 365. — Sharpe, **6**: 185.
— Alternation of Generations in. (M. C. Cooke) Nature, **5**: 108.
— and their Uses. (D. Esdaile) Good Words, **19**: 565.
— Badham and Hussey on. Ecl. R. **92**: 490. Same art. Liv. Age, **28**: 49.
— British. (M. Plues) Pop. Sci. R. **2**: 322.
— — Cooke's. Nature, **4**: 321. **11**: 462.
— Chignon Fungus. (T. Fox) Am. Natural. **1**: 379.
— Collecting and preserving. (F. T. Brocas) Recr. Sci. **1**: 65.
— Coloring-Matters in. (H. C. Sorby) Nature, **5**: 298.
— Common Molds. (B. D. Halstead) Pop. Sci. Mo. **9**: 398.
— Edible. (R. M. Copeland) Atlan. **31**: 223. — Ed. R. **127**: 333. — (C. J. Robinson) Nature, **2**: 518.
— Folk-Lore of. (L. Jewitt) Reliquary, **1**: 112.
— Growth and History of. (R. Denkin) Recr. Sci. **2**: 189.
— Hybernation of. (M. J. Berkeley) Intel. Obs. **1**: 288.
— Hysterium and Allies. (J. S. Billings) Am. Natural. **5**: 626.
— Life of. Sharpe, **28**: 101, 235.
— Microscopic. (M. C. Cooke) Pop. Sci. R. **3**: 20–469. — All the Year, **15**: 318.
— — infesting Cereals. (W. Barbeck) Am. Natural. **13**: 612.
— — Study of. (J. S. Billings) Am. Natural. **5**: 323.
— Notes on. (M. J. Berkeley) Intel. Obs. **7**: 45, 163, 349. **8**: 183, **9**: 93, 401. **10**: 32.
— of North Germany. (M. J. Berkeley) Nature, **9**: 200.
— of Plains of India. (M. J. Berkeley) Intel. Obs. **12**: 18.
— Parasitic. (E. Sidney) West. J. **6**: 218.
— — Structure of. (R. Denkin) Recr. Sci. **2**: 334.
— Polymorphic. (M. C. Cooke) Am. Natural. **5**: 400. — (M. C. Cooke) Pop. Sci. R. **10**: 25.
— Roumeguère's. (M. J. Berkeley) Nature, **2**: 185.
— Smaller. (J. L. Russell) Am. Natural. **2**: 561, 623.
See also Mushrooms.
Fungus Disease of India, Lewis on. (M. J. Berkeley) Nature, **15**: 21. — (M. J. Berkeley) Intel. Obs. **2**: 248.
Fuqueer's Curse. House. Words, **3**: 310.
Fur and Feather Auction Sales. All the Year, **34**: 515.
Furs. (A. Forbes) Belgra. **14**: 60.
— American; how trapped and traded. Ecl. M. **66**: 445.
— and the Fur-Trade. Appleton, **4**: 749.
— and their Wearers. (J. H. Partridge) Pop. Sci. Mo. **4**: 143.
— Dressing of. Penny M. **14**: 390.
— for the Ladies; how obtained. Godey, **50**: 105–489.
— Hudson's Bay Company. No. Brit. **50**: 159.
— Where they come from. Sharpe, **27**: 20.
Fur-Hunters of the Far West. Chamb. J. **25**: 338. — Ecl. R. **102**: 665. Same art. Ecl. M. **37**: 406.
Fur-Trade, American. (J. H. Lanman) Hunt, **3**: 185.
— and Fur-Bearing Animals. Am. J. Sci. **25**: 311.
— Canada. Ed. R. **1**: 142.
— Northwest. (W. Sturgis) Hunt, **14**: 532.
— Russian. Pract. M. **1**: 332.
— Statistics of. (H. Murray) Hunt, **3**: 252.
Fur-Trade Co., American, History of. (J. Loughborough) West. J. **2**: 305, 365. **3**: 29.
Fur-Trader. (J. C. Smalley) Cath. World, **18**: 412, 502.

Fur-Traders and Trappers. Liv. Age, **143**: 764.
Fur-Trading with the Indians. Penny M. **6**: 303.
Füred, Hungary. Temp. Bar, **59**: 385.
Furel, William, Life of. (J.W. Alexander) Princ. **5**: 145.
Furnaces and Furnace Materials. Am. Arch. **7**: 56.
— Blast. (G. Thomson) J. Frankl. Inst. **37**: 118.
— — and Pig Iron, Construction of. (J. G. Beckton) J. Frankl. Inst. **81**: 37.
— — Arrangement of Materials in. (S. H. Blackwell) J. Frankl. Inst. **55**: 188, 243.
— — Caustic Lime in. J. Frankl. Inst. **51**: 255, 327.
— — Theory of. (Bunsen and Playfair) J. Frankl. Inst. **48**: 136.
See Iron.
— Burning Wet Fuel, Efficiency of. (R. H. Thurston) J. Frankl. Inst. **98**: 397. **99**: 49, 120.
— Construction and Management of. (M. C. Fairbairn) Ecl. Engin. **11**: 349.
— Gas. (C. Schinz) J. Frankl. Inst. **61**: 269, 326.
— — Patent Blast, 1860. (J. J. Griffin) J. Frankl. Inst. **70**: 97, 181.
— — Regenerative. (C. W. Siemens) J. Frankl. Inst. **74**: 243.
— Melting. (R. Grimshaw) J. Frankl. Inst. **108**: 48.
— Pernot, Description of. (M. Armengaud) J. Frankl. Inst. **100**: 89, 180.
— Supply of Air to. Ecl. Engin. **16**: 205.
Furnace Bars, Rotary. Pract. M. **5**: 164.
Furness, William H. (J. H. Morison) Unita. R. **3**: 180.
Furnishing, Art of. Cornh. **31**: 535. Same art. Ecl. M. **85**: 48. — Lond. Soc. **7**: 500. — (E. M. Hiestand) Potter Am. Mo. **16**: 525.
— Books on. Fraser, **59**: 95.
— Chapters on a Chair. Tinsley, **7**: 78–222.
— Decoration of, in Renaissance. (H. P. Spofford) Harper, **54**: 633.
— Decorative. Art J. **30**: 12.
— — Exhibition of, at Gore House. Art J. **5**: 237.
— Elizabethan and Later English. (H. P. Spofford) Harper, **56**: 18.
— English. (A. Wynter) Once a Week, **11**: 90.
— Fashion of. Cornh. **9**: 337.
— French. Canad. Mo. **5**: 78.
— Good and bad. All the Year, **28**: 42.
— Gothic. (Prof. Heideloff) Art J. **4**: 49.—Art J. **19**: 25.
— History of. Chamb. J. **12**: 396.
— Household. Once a Week, **29**: 269. — (G. T. Robinson) Art J. **33**: 23–369.
— Household Taste, Eastlake's. (P. W. Clayden) Fortn. **11**: 375.
— How to furnish Houses. Eng. Dom. M. **25**: 120–287. **26**: 8–132.
— in solid Wood, Manufacture of. Pract. M. **2**: 355.
— Mediæval. (P. Spofford) Harper, **53**: 809.
— of our Forefathers. Sharpe, **33**: 85.
— Original Designs for. (C. Heideloff) Art J. **3**: 25.
— Tables and Chairs. Victoria, **27**: 236.
Furniture. (C. Cook) Scrib. **10**: 169. **11**: 342–809. **12**: 168–796. **13**: 86–816. **14**: 1. — (P. G. Hamerton) Macmil. **8**: 138. — All the Year, **35**: 59.
— and Decoration. Pract. M. **7**: 243.
— Art-Fever. Tinsley, **12**: 648.
Fürstenruhe. (J. Wilmer) Tait, n. s. **14**: 748, 821. **15**: 23, 99.
Fuses of Projectiles. Pract. M. **2**: 409.
Fuseli, Henry. (S. Colvin) Portfo. **4**: 50. — Blackw. **23**: 572.
— Knowles's Life of. Colburn, **31**: 432.—Ecl. R. **53**: 396.
— Lectures at Royal Academy. Blackw. **54**: 691.
Fusi-Yama, Mt., Japan. Colburn, **153**: 475.
— Pilgrimage to. (C. F. G. Cumming) Gent. M. n. s. **27**: 481.
Fuss and Feathers. Temp. Bar, **17**: 192.
Fust, Sir H. J., Judgment in Case of Gorham *versus* Bishop of Exeter. Chr. Obs. **49**: 809. **50**: 698.
Fust, John, and the Invention of Printing. Internat. M. **5**: 172.
Future, The. No. Brit. **9**: 472. — So. Lit. Mess. **7**: 160. — Mus. **28**: 364.
— as it was. (E. M. Smalley) Lakeside, **5**: 48.
— Fictions of. Dub. R. **70**: 76.
Future Generations, Claim on the Present. (W. Sullivan) Chr. Exam. **1**: 427.
Future Judgment and Retribution. (G. B. Cheever) Bib. Sac. **8**: 471.
Future Life. (G. Bailey) Univ. Q. **34**: 78. — (A. C. Barry) Univ. Q. **35**: 300.— (J. Bayma) Cath. World, **25**: 494. — (P. Felts) Luth. Q. **6**: 62. — (C. S. Gerhard) Mercersb. **25**: 192. — (J. H. Morison) Unita. R. **3**: 152. — (J. W. Willmarth) Bapt. Q. **4**: 198. — So. R. n. s. **20**: 459.
— Ancient and modern Belief in. (H. Giles) Nat. Q. **8**: 358.
— and future Punishment, H. W. Beecher on. (H. R. Nye) Univ. Q. **35**: 83.
— and the Soul. (F. Harrison) 19th Cent. **1**: 623, 832. Same art. Sup. Pop. Sci. Mo. **1**: 237, 309.
— — Symposium on. 19th Cent. **2**: 329, 497. Same art. Sup. Pop. Sci. Mo. **1**: 499. **2**: 20.
— Apostolic Doctrine of. So. R. n. s. **24**: 404.
— Bakewell on. (E. Peabody) Chr. Exam. **49**: 37.
— The Bible and. (J. Boyden) Univ. Q. **24**: 397.
— Chaldæo-Assyrian Doctrine of. (O. D. Miller) Univ. Q. **36**: 318.
— confirmed by Nature and Science. (G. W. Quimby) Univ. Q. **8**: 381.
— Daniel *versus* Zoroaster. (C. H. Hall) Am. Church R. **16**: 355.
— Degrees of Happiness in. (T. B. Thayer) Univ. Q. **14**: 129.
— Destiny of Man in. (A. F. Hewit) Cath. World, **27**: 145.
— Druidical Doctrine of. (W. R. Alger) Chr. Exam. **62**: 88.
— Egyptian Doctrine of. (W. R. Alger) Univ. Q. **13**: 136.
— Figuier on. O. & N. **6**: 462. — Temp. Bar, **35**: 104.
— Great Future. Hours at Home, **7**: 344.
— Hebrew Doctrine of. (W. R. Alger) Chr. Exam. **60**: 1.
— History of Doctrine of. (W.T. Clarke) Univ. Q. **21**: 72.
— — Alger's. (O. B. Frothingham) Chr. Exam. **70**: 1.
— Hudson on. (J. Strong) Meth. Q. **18**: 404.
— in Brahmanism and Buddhism. (W. R. Alger) No. Am. **86**: 435.
— Inductive Argument for. (T. B. Thayer) Univ. Q. **22**: 36.
— Life after Death. (F. P. Cobbe) Theo. R. **10**: 438.
— Life in Death. (W. Walford) Bib. R. **2**: 19.
— — Natural Evidence for. (W. Walford) Bib. R. **2**: 108.
— of the Good. (A. Norton) Chr. Exam. **1**: 350.
— of Man and Brute. (C. C. Everett) Chr. Exam. **67**: 157.
— Personal Identity in. (G. H. Emerson) Univ. Q. **11**: 407.
— Physical Theory of, Taylor's. (Sir J. Stephen) Ed. R. **71**: 220. Same art. Liv. Age, **87**: 385. — Ecl. R. **64**: 85. — (W. A. Stearns) Am. Bib. Repos. **8**: 494. — Fraser, **14**: 407.
— Positive Creed on. (F. B. Lockwood) Penn Mo. **9**: 177.
— Practical Value of Belief in. (C. H. Brigham) Chr. Exam. **86**: 158.
— Progressive Knowledge of. Mo. Rel. M. **28**: 19.
— Rabbinical Doctrine of. (W. R. Alger) Chr. Exam. **60**: 189.
— Spiritual Theory of. (J. Service) Contemp. **17**: 127.
— **What can we know of?** Canad. Mo. **13**: 626.

Future Life, What shall we be in? (W. R. French) Univ. Q. **17**: 167. **18**: 67.
Future Punishment. (E. T. Fitch) Chr. Q. Spec. **1**: 598. — (M. Stuart) Am. Bib. Repos. 2d s. **3**: 1. — Brit. Q. **7**: 105. — Chr. Exam. **8**: 392. — Am. Church R. **2**: 359. — Chr. Mo. Spec. **3**: 505. — (W. S. Edwards) Meth. Q. **32**: 546. — (G. P. Fisher, J. M. Whiton, and W. S. Tyler) New Eng. **37**: 169, 311. — (T. Meritt) Am. Meth. M. **6**: 201. — (G. S. Mott) Princ. **43**: 532. — (G. Salmon) Contemp. **32**: 182. Same art. Ecl. M. **90**: 689. — (A. Woodbury) Unita. R. **9**: 673. — (S. Whiting) Meth. Q. **19**: 414, 614. — Am. Meth. M. **3**: 112. — Bentley, **18**: 183. — Bost. R. **1**: 113. — Brit. Q. **68**: 107. — Brownson, **19**: 85.
— and future Life, H. W. Beecher on. (H. R. Nye) Univ. Q. **35**: 83.
— and Rationalism. (E. P. Tenney) Cong. R. **8**: 161.
— and Reward, Doctrine of. Ecl. R. **86**: 385.
— Christ on Duration of. (C. Kent) Bib. Sac. **35**: 290.
— Cudworth's MS. on. (C. Kenny) Theo. R. **15**: 267.
— Dobney on. Theo. & Lit. J. **3**: 395. — Ecl. R. **82**: 153.
— Doctrine of. Ecl. R. **85**: 39.
— Duration of. (E. P. Gould) Bib. Sac. **37**: 221.
— Everlasting. Dub. R. **88**: 117.
— — Decline of Faith in. (A. S. Chesebrough) New Eng. **39**: 308*.
— — Pusey on. (J. B. Mayor) Contemp. **38**: 1025.
— Foster on. (R. A. Hallam) Am. Church R. **2**: 359. — (F. Wayland) Am. Presb. R. **14**: 61.
— in the Old Testament. (H. Cowles) Bib. Sac. **35**: 514.
— of Infants, *not* Calvinism. (L. Beecher) Spirit Pilg. **1**: 42, 78, 149
— Probation after Death. (J. T. Tucker) Cong. R. **10**: 330. — (J. E. Roy) New Eng. **29**: 400.
— — and the New Testament. (R. D. C. Robbins) Bib. Sac. **38**: 460.
— Result of Character. (S. Harris) New Eng. **9**: 186.
— Symposium on. Contemp. **32**: 153–182.
— Verdict of Reason on. (S. Cobb) Univ. Q. **23**: 151.
See Annihilation; Eternal Punishment; Retribution; Hell.
Future State. (G. Grote) Contemp. **18**: 133. — (W. H. Browne) So. M. **17**: 250. — (C. Follen) Chr. Exam. **7**: 390. **8**: 115, 265. — (J. M. Hoppin) Bib. Sac. **15**: 381. — (C. G. Lyttleton) Contemp. **21**: 915. — Liv. Age, **110**: 664. — (J. M. C. Breaker) Chr. R. **22**: 1. — Univ. Q. **9**: 160. — (H. Ballou, 2d) Univ. Q. **10**: 29. — (T. S. Lothrop) Univ. Q. **30**: 207.
— Analogy between the Present and. (H. Ballou, 2d) Univ. Q. **4**: 113.
— Analogies of, in Nature. (A. Traver) Evang. R. **18**: 249.
Future State, Ancient Idea of. (A. Yerrington) Hogg, **1**: 171. — Am. Bib. Repos. 3d s. **2**: 686.
— and Science. (B. Stewart) Princ. n. s. **2**: 399. **3**: 537.
— Antepasts of. Chr. Obs. **46**: 513.
— Apocalyptic Doctrine of. (W. R. Alger) Chr. Exam. **57**: 1.
— Buddhistic Idea of. (G. T. Flanders) Univ. Q. **32**: 428.
— Clark and Mattison on. (C. T. Moss) Meth. Q. **27**: 236.
— Doctrine of, in the Epistle to the Hebrews. (W. R. Alger) Chr. Exam. **53**: 157.
— Doctrine of Rewards and Punishments. Bib. R. **5**: 352.
— Effect of present Conduct on. (H. Ballou) Univ. Q. **2**: 39, 251.
— Egyptian Doctrine of. (J. P. Thompson) Bib. Sac. **25**: 69.
— Harpings upon Hades. (C. A. Alexander) Knick. **42**: 465.
— Homeric Ideas of. (J. Proudfit) Bib. Sac. **15**: 753.
— Hudson's Doctrine of. Theo. & Lit. J. **10**: 592.
— Life after Death. (F. P. Cobbe) Theo. R. **9**: 506. **10**: 438.
— Mythology of. Tait, n. s. **21**: 100, 129, 198.
— Opinions of Contemporaries of the Evangelists on. (F. R. Conder) Fraser, **91**: 100.
— Paul's Doctrine of. (W. R. Alger) Chr. Exam. **54**: 202.
— Peter's Doctrine of. (W. R. Alger) Chr. Exam. **55**: 217.
— Philosophy of, Dick's. West. Mo. R. **3**: 596.
— Physical Speculations on. (W. James) Nation, **20**: 366. — Brit. Q. **64**: 35. — Lond. Q. **45**: 49.
— Place of the Departed. (Mrs. H. A. Bingham) Univ. Q. **24**: 477. — (N. H. Griffin) Bib. Sac. **13**: 153.
— Progressive Revelation of. Chr. Obs. **74**: 161.
— proved from Light of Nature. Theo. Repos. **1**: 236. **2**: 22. **3**: 219.
— Purgatory, Heaven, and Hell. (J. M. Capes) Contemp. **22**: 731.
— Scriptural Doctrine of. (E. P. Barrows) Bib. Sac. **15**: 625.
— J. P. Thompson on. (E. C. Towne) Chr. Exam. **70**: 169.
— The unseen Universe. Brit. Q. **64**: 35. Same art. Liv. Age, **131**: 195.
— Vedic Doctrine of. (W. D. Whitney) Bib. Sac. **16**: 404.
— Whately on. Mercersb **8**: 384. — Theo. & Lit. J. **8**: 640. **9**: 1.
See Hades; Immortality; Intermediate State.
Future Years, Concerning. (A. K. H. Boyd) Fraser, **63**: 441. Same art. Ecl. M. **53**: 499. Same art. Liv. Age, **69**: 475.
Futurity, Prying into. Once a Week, **21**: 580.
Fyster, J. S., Sermons of. Chr. Obs. **26**: 415.

G

Gabb, William M. Nature, **18**: 285.
Gaboon, Late Explorations in. (H. von Koppenfels) Am. Natural. **15**: 447.
Gabriel Conroy. (Bret Harte) Scrib. **11**: 16–840. **12**: 29–512.
Gabriel's Appointment. (M. E. Edwards) Argosy, **23**: 1–401. **24**: 1–401.
Gabriel's Marriage. (W. Collins) House. Words, **7**: 149, 181. Same art. Liv. Age, **37**: 557.
Gabrielle. (C. Reybaud) Colburn, **134**: 183–476.
Gabrielle, or the Sisters. Fraser, **43**: 295. Same art. Ecl. M. **23**: 57. Same art. Liv. Age, **29**: 132.
Gabrielle de Belle Isle; a Tale. Blackw. **51**: 609.
Gabrielle de Bergerac. (H. James, jr.) Atlan. **24**: 55, 231, 352.
Gabrielle, La belle, and Henry IV. Temp. Bar, **48**: 461. Same art. Ecl. M. **88**: 221.
Gabrielle of Wurzburg. (Lady Hardy) Tinsley, **6**: 24.
Gabriello and Adriana; a Dramatic Sketch. (B. W. Procter) St. James, **38**: 143.
Gachet, Gassett, Gushee Genealogy. N. E. Reg. **1**: 344
Gadsden, Christopher. (G. S. Hillard) Pennsyl. M **3**: 186.
— Letter of, 1766. Hist. M. **5**: 260.

Gadsden, Christopher E. Discourse on Pinckney. (J. Sparks) No. Am. **22**: 222.
— Life and Character of. (C. Wallace) Am. Church R. **5**: 577.
Gael, Early Vestiges of the. Dub. Univ. **65**: 466.
— and Sassenach. Blackw. **33**: 505, 763.
Gaels, Celts, and Kymri. (J. Pyne) Nat. Q. **33**: 81.
Gaelic and Norse Popular Tales. (D. Masson) Macmil. **3**: 213. Same art. Liv. Age, **68**: 387.
Gaelic Culture, Old. Westm. **108**: 127.
Gaelic Dictionary. Blackw. **1**: 256.
Gaelic Nuisance. (W. Chambers) Chamb. J. **54**: 689. **55**: 129.
Gaelic Revival. (T. F. Galwey) Western, **5**: 45.
Gaelic Stories, Old. Dub. Univ. **64**: 680.
Gaffney, James. Irish Mo. **4**: 172.
Gaillon, Normandy, Reform School at. (R. Hall) Am. J. Educ. **3**: 744.
Gaines, Maj.-Gen. Edmund P., with portrait. Dem. R. **22**: 549.
Gaines, Mrs. M. S., Case of. So. Q. **25**: 273.
— — Romance of. (H. M. Jenkins) Putnam, **12**: 201.
Gains, Institutions of. (E. Everett) No. Am. **12**: 385. *See* Savings-Banks.
Gainsborough, Humphrey. Cong. **7**: 214.
Gainsborough, Thomas. (T. Gautier) Temp. Bar, **5**: 324. **6**: 425. — Dub. Univ. **48**: 607. — (S. Colvin) Portfo. **3**: 169, 178. — Lond. Q. **7**: 141. Same art. Ecl. M. **39**: 539.
— and Constable. Art J. **33**: 150.
— Eccentricities of. (R. H. Hoare) Peop. J. **6**: 106.
— in green Lanes. (G. W. Thornbury) Art J. **11**: 65.
— Fulcher's Life of. Liv. Age, **50**: 754.
— Life of. New Q. **5**: 413.
Gajani, G., and the Roman Republic. (J. P. Thompson) Putnam, **13**: 595.
Gala Days. (M. A. Dodge) Atlan. **11**: 629. **12**: 17.
Galanti Show. Bentley, **13**: 63, 151, 453.
Galapagos Islands. Nature, **6**: 352.
— Cruise through. (E. C. Agassiz) Atlan. **31**: 579.
— Trip to, 1850. (C. T. Hopkins) Pioneer, **1**: 97.
Galatea, Cruise in the, in 1867. Once a Week, **14**: 370. — Dub. Univ. **73**: 72.
Galdos, B. Perez. Doña Perfecta. (D. Hanning) Temp. Bar, **58**: 326.
Gale, James, the blind Inventor. (B. G. Johns) Good Words, **10**: 466.
Gale, William. Art J. **21**: 373.
Gale Genealogy. (G. Gale) N. E. Reg. **18**: 189.
Gale in the Channel. (C. J. Peterson) Hogg, **5**: 333.
— of June, 1841. Blackw. **50**: 72.
— of August. (J. Pettingal) Arch. **2**: 60.
Gales and Hurricanes in Western Atlantic. (W. C. Redfield) Am. J. Sci. **31**: 115.
— in the Atlantic, Maury on. Canad. J. n. s. **2**: 280.
— of November and December, 1865. (A. S. Herschel) Intel. Obs. **9**: 198.
Galena, Ill., Lead-Mining at. Harper, **32**: 681.
Galera. (T. A. Trollope) Lippinc. **14**: 611.
Gales and Seaton, Charge against, 1823. Niles's Reg. **23**: 333, 358.
— Register of Debates. (J. Sparks) No. Am. **22**: 224.
Galesburg Declaration, Theses on, Krauth's. (J. A. Brown) Luth. Q. **7**: 595.
Galesburg, Ill., Lombard University. O. & N. **4**: 271.
Galgano; a Poem. (H. W. Longfellow) Putnam, **1**: 512.
Galiani, Ferdinand. (E. Howland) Atlan. **31**: 299.
— and Darwin. (E. Du Bois-Reymond) Pop. Sci. Mo. **14**: 409.
— Letters. (A. Laugel) Nation, **33**: 230.
Galilee. (C. R. Conder) Good Words, **19**: 635.
— in Time of Christ. (S. Merritt) Bib. Sac. **31**: 29, 235.
Galilee, Sea of. (W. C. Prime) Hours at Home, **1**: 438. — (C. H. Brigham) Mo. Rel. M. **13**: 256.
Galilei, Galileo. (O. Delapurne) St. James, **13**: 64. — (L. Hunt) Lond. M. **3**: 62. — (A. King) Argosy, **11**: 29. — (J. G. Meline) Cath. World, **8**: 321, 433. — with portrait, Ecl. M. **51**: 423. — Colburn, **131**: 50. — Ecl. M. **60**: 463. — Ed. R. **80**: 164. — Mo. Rel. M. **10**: 337. — Penny M. **2**: 63.
— and Application of Mathematics to Physics. (W. Jack) Nature, **21**: 40, 58. Same art. Liv. Age, **143**: 727.
— and G. Bruno. Quar. **145**: 362. Same art. Liv. Age, **138**: 323. Same art. Sup. Pop. Sci. Mo. **3**: 111. — (B. A. Hinsdale) Chr. Q. **1**: 145.
— and his Discoveries. (E. I. Sears) Nat. Q. **12**: 207.
— and the Inquisition, Gebler on. (S. Taylor) Nature, **14**: 226. — (Prof. Reusch) Contemp. **38**: 665. — Dub. R. **5**: 72.
— and Milton. (R. Owen) Fraser, **79**: 678.
— and Papal Infallibility. (E. Lawrence) Harper, **49**: 417. — (S. Taylor) Macmil. **29**: 89. Same art. Ecl. M. **82**: 187.
— and the Pontifical Congregations. Dub. R. **69**: 140.
— Brown's Tragedy of. Tait, n. s. **17**: 106.
— Case of. Dub. R. **57**: 376. **58**: 260.
— Contemporaries and Predecessors of. New York R. **9**: 444.
— Dream of. Godey, **24**: 44.
— History of. Month, **7**: 262, 348. **8**: 247, 359.
— Life of. Am. Mo. R. **3**: 14.
— Martyrdom of. (Sir D. Brewster) No. Brit. **33**: 513. Same art. Ecl. M. **52**: 199, 303.
— Persecution of. Lond. M. **19**: 112.
— Private Life of. (G. F. Rodwell) Nature, **1**: 529. — Lakeside, **5**: 179.
— Trial of. (A. Mézières) Pop. Sci. Mo. **10**: 385.
— Tuscan Memorial to. (G. F. Rodwell) Nature, **8**: 329.
— Was he tortured? (S. Taylor) Nature, **17**: 299.
Galisteo Creek, New Mexico, Geology of. (J. J. Stevenson) Am. J. Sci. **118**: 471.
Galitzin. *See* Gallitzin.
Gall, François J., and G. Spurzheim. (R. Gordon) Ed. R. **25**: 227.
— Some Particulars about. Zoist, **2**: 455.
Gallagher, Wm. D., Poems of. Am. Mo. M. **8**: 89.
— Sketch of. So. Lit. Mess. **4**: 452.
Gallait, Louis. Art J. **18**: 101.
Galland, Pierre V., Life of. Am. Arch. **8**: 233.
Gallantry, Modern. (F. Jacox) Colburn, **134**: 164. — (C. Lamb) Lond. M. **6**: 453.
Gallatin, Albert. (H. C. Lodge) Internat. R. **7**: 250. — (J. T. Morse, jr.) Atlan. **44**: 513. — (C. C. Smith) Unita. R. **12**: 303. — with portrait, Dem. R. **12**: 641. — Bank. M. (N. Y.) **4**: 773. — Liv. Age, **23**: 324.
— Adams's Life of. Nation, **29**: 128, 144.
— Writings of. M. Am. Hist. **3**: 697.
Gallaudet, Thomas H. (H. Barnard) Am. J. Educ. **1**: 417. — (J. Harrington) Chr. Exam. **53**: 105. — (O. Tiffany) No. Am. **87**: 517.
— and Deaf-Mute Instruction. (S. W. S. Dutton) New Eng. **10**: 415.
— Discourses of. Chr. Obs. **17**: 456.
— Sermons. Chr. Mo. Spec. **1**: 27.
Gallery of Apelles. Colburn, **4**: 1. **5**: 111–193.
Gallery Training-Lessons. (D. Stow) Am. J. Educ. **9**: 413.
Galleys, Ancient War. (L. C. Allison) Canad. Mo. **14**: 574.
— Fifteen Years in. Chamb. J. **39**: 6.
— French, in the 17th Century. House. Words, **17**: 562. Same art. Liv. Age, **58**: 216.
— Huguenots at. Quar. **120**: 39.
Galley Life of France. Ecl. M. **23**: 539.
Galley Slave; a Poem. (H. Abbey) Galaxy, **10**: 520.
Galley Slaves. Penny M. **14**: 134.

Gallic Antiquities. Colburn, **54**: 273.
Gallican Church. *See* France, Church of.
Gallicanism and Infallibility. (J. A. Dorner) Contemp. **17**: 591.
— and Ultramontanism. Brownson, **23**: 313.
— True Origin of. (J. A. Keogh) Cath. World, **10**: 527.
Gallinaceana; Peacocks, Guinea Fowls. Fraser, **49**: 101, 275.
Gallison, John, Character of. (W. Phillips) No. Am. **12**: 489.
— Memoir of. Chr. Disc. **3**: 15.
Gallitzin, Princess Amelia. Cath. World, **13**: 367. — Cornh. **24**: 553. Same art. Liv. Age, **111**: 609.
Gallitzin, Demetrius A. (Mrs. I. James) No. Am. **88**: 349.
— and Catholic Settlements in Pennsylvania. Cath. World, **2**: 145. — Cath. World, **1**: 306.
Gallium, a new Metal. (R. Meldola) Nature, **12**: 481. — Pract. M. **7**: 366.
Gallop for Life. House. Words, **3**: 577. Same art. Liv. Age, **31**: 205.
Galloping Dick. All the Year, **29**: 324.
Galloway, Ancient Lordship of. (R. Riddell) Arch. **9**: 49.
— Thrieve Castle. Fraser, **43**: 152.
Gallows Literature. Am. Bibliop. **5**: 91.
Gallus, Caius Cornelius, Paraphrases from. Ev. Sat. **9**: 101.
Gallwey, T. Lays of Killarney Lakes. Dub. Univ. **77**: 599.
Galongoon, Volcano of. Penny M. **6**: 431.
Galt, Sir Alex. T., with portrait. New Dom. **19**: 188.
Galt, John, with portrait. Fraser, **2**: 555. — Bentley, **18**: 285.
— Annals of the Parish. Blackw. **9**: 203. **10**: 665. **11**: 741. — Portfo.(Den.) **27**: 52.
— Autobiography. Ecl. R. **58**: 343. — Mo. R. **132**: 249. — Westm. **16**: 321. **17**: 182.
— Ayrshire Legatees. Blackw. **11**: 742.
— The Earthquake. Blackw. **8**: 450.
— The Entail. Blackw. **13**: 77.
— Lawrie Todd. Fraser, **1**: 236. — (W. Phillips) No. Am. **31**: 380. — Westm. **12**: 405.
— Life in Pennsylvania. Quar. **26**: 364.
— Literary Life of. Mo. R. **135**: 368.
— Novels. Dub. Univ. **89**: 495.
— Southennan. Westm. **13**: 345.
— Tragedies. Quar. **11**: 33.
— Voyages and Travels. Quar. **7**: 297. — Ed. R. **23**: 40.
Galtees, May-Time on. (J. M. Crothe) Cath. World, **33**: 208.
Galvanic Battery. (G. W. Hough) Am. J. Sci. **98**: 182. — (S. P. Sharples) Am. J. Sci. **101**: 247.
— Cheap. Pract. M. **5**: 131.
— Daniell's, Constant Form of. (W. Thomson) Nature, **3**: 350.
— Economical Constant. (C. G. Page) Am. J. Sci. **63**: 257.
— Smee's. (R. Bithell) Recr. Sci. **3**: 346.
— Some Forms of. (S. B. Sharples) Ecl. Engin. **5**: 189.
Galvanic Batteries. (R. Bithell) Recr. Sci. **3**: 20. — (H. Highton) Ecl. Engin. **8**: 215. — (C. G. Page) Am. J. Sci. **36**: 137.
— Jablochkoff's. Pract. M. **7**: 247.
— of four Elements. (J. W. Draper) J. Frankl. Inst. **18**: 289.
— Simplification in. Pract. M. **6**: 255.
Galvanic Circuit, Electro-motive Force and Resistance of. (H. Haug) Am. J. Sci. **92**: 381. **93**: 43.
Galvanic Current, Conduction and Distribution of. (C. G. Page) Am. J. Sci. **61**: 192.
— in Telegraph Wires, Velocity of. (B. A. Gould, jr.) Am. J. Sci. **61**: 67, 153.
— Vibrations of Trevelyan's Bars by. (C. G. Page) Am. J. Sci. **59**: 105.
Galvanic Deflagrator. (R. Hare) Am. J. Sci. **4**: 201. **5**: 94, 357. **7**: 347. **8**: 99.
Galvanic Electricity, Conduction of, through moist Air. (C. G. Page) Am. J. Sci. **52**: 204.
Galvanic Light, Polarization of. (C. G. Page) Am. J. Sci. **57**: 375.
Galvanic Results. (W. Sturgeon) Am. J. Sci. **39**: 28.
Galvanism, Aldini on. Ed. R. **3**: 194.
— New Theory of. (R. Hare) Am. J. Sci. **1**: 413. **3**: 105.
Galvanometer for powerful Currents. (C. F. Brackett) Am. J. Sci. **121**: 395.
— New Form of. (J. Trowbridge) Am. J. Sci. **102**: 118.
— New Form of Lantern. (A. M. Mayer) Am. J. Sci. **103**: 414. — (G. F. Barker) Am. J. Sci. **110**: 207. — (F. E. Nipher) Am. J. Sci. **111**: 111. — (A. M. Mayer) J. Frankl. Inst. **93**: 421. — (G. F. Barker) J. Frankl. Inst. **99**: 431.
— New Absolute. (M. D. C. Hodges) Am. J. Sci. **117**: 475.
Galway. (D'Arcy W. Thompson) Macmil. **12**: 411. — Irish Q. **1**: 268.
— the City of the Tribes. Once a Week, **5**: 389.
— The Claddagh and its People. Temp. Bar, **10**: 266.
Galway Judgment, The. (E. S. Beesly) Fortn. **18**: 39.
Gama, Vasco da. Month, **12**: 176.
Gamahes, or painted Stones. Chamb. J. **42**: 488.
Gambetta, Léon. (J. McCarthy) Galaxy, **15**: 725. — (G. M. Towle) Appleton, **5**: 223. **20**: 523. — Fraser, **104**: 28. — Ecl. M. **97**: 345. — with portrait, Ecl. M. **76**: 502. — Ev. Sat. **13**: 586. — Gent. M. n. s. **14**: 559.
— and the French Elections, 1881. (Y. Guyot) Contemp. **40**: 616.
— and Thiers. (A. Laugel) Nation, **15**: 278.
— Six Months of Prefecture under. Fraser, **86**: 651.
— Von der Goltz on. (H. von Holst) Nation, **25**: 87, 102.
— What he is doing for France. (E. L. Godkin) Nation, **12**: 36.
Gambia, Royalty on the. (H. V. Huntley) Bentley, **25**: 589.
— Up the. Chamb. J. **16**: 273.
Gambier on Moral Evidence. Ed. R. **12**: 202. — (J. Foster) Ecl. R. **5**: 422.
Gamble, Thomas, with portrait. Anal. M. **13**: 413.
Gambler's Life in last Century. All the Year, **18**: 324.
Gambler's Luck; a Tale. Dub. Univ. **7**: 302.
Gamblers. Godey, **20**: 225.
Gambling. (S. Martin) Ex. H. Lec. **12**: 45, 83. — (G. I. Cowan) Peop. J. **6**: 244. — Chamb. J. **28**: 369.
— among the Utah Indians. (E. A. Barber) Am. Natural. **11**: 351.
— Anatomy of. Fraser, **16**: 9, 368, 748. **17**: 269, 538.
— at Homburg. (E. G. Buffum) Galaxy, **3**: 493. — All the Year, **2**: 517. — Broadw. **5**: 54. — Cornh. **12**: 221.
— Betting, Lotteries, etc. Chamb. J. **18**: 353.
— Card-Sharping. (L. Wraxall) Once a Week, **4**: 597.
— Chapter on. Colburn, **94**: 56. Same art. Internat. M. **5**: 337.
— Chinese. Ev. Sat. **13**: 636.
— Faro. (E. Crapsey) Galaxy, **12**: 57.
— Gaming-Table. (W. A. Seaver) Harper, **41**: 130.
— in the 18th Century. (A. Andrews) Colburn, **103**: 361. Same art. Ecl. M. **35**: 13.
— in London. Fraser, **8**: 191.
— Paris Bourse. Colburn, **62**: 105.
— Paris Gambling-Houses. (J. D. Osborne) Putnam, **3**: 303. — Broadw. **9**: 528.
— Roulette, Trente et Quarante, etc. Ev. Sat. **9**: 58.
— Spas of Germany. (J. H. Browne) Harper, **45**: 1.

Gambling, Superstitions of. (R. A. Proctor) Gent. M. n. s. **22**: 219. — Cornh. **25**: 704. Same art. Ecl. M. **79**: 157. Same art. Liv. Age, **114**: 105. Same art. Ev. Sat. **12**: 680.
Gambling-Hell, Chinese. (E. H. Hall) Lippinc. **4**: 59.
Gambling-House, Fashionable. Bentley, **15**: 552.
Gambling-Houses and Gamesters. Bentley, **18**: 333, 489, 593. **19**: 44–397. **20**: 288–622.
— French. Westm. **11**: 303.
— in Germany. Dub. Univ. **77**: 466. — St. James, **4**: 441.
— of New York. St. James, **20**: 252.
Gambling Speculations. Bank. M. (N. Y.) **34**: 19.
Gamboge. Penny M. **9**: 315.
Gambold, John. Meth. M. **37**: 3.
— Works of. (J. Brazer) Chr. Exam. **21**: 137.
Gambrel Roof; a Poem. (L. Larcom) Atlan. **33**: 141.
Game, and Game Laws in England. Ed. R. **134**: 390. — Quar. **122**: 136.
— and its Cooking. All the Year, **20**: 559.
— Autumn, on the Prairies. (J. Cooke) Scrib. **4**: 697.
— Cost of a Battue. All the Year, **3**: 484.
— Gallinaceous Game-Birds. Penny M. **10**: 401, 414.
— in England. Cornh. **42**: 294.
— of North America. (H. W. Herbert) Dem. R. **18**: 17–282. — Am. Whig R. **10**: 461.
— of South Africa, Drummond's. Nature, **12**: 182.
— Proprietor of, Troubles of a. Lond. M. **17**: 152.
— Water-Fowl of the West. (M. A. Howell, jr.) Harper, **49**: 790.
Game of Bowls. (R. R. Macgregor) Belgra. **36**: 352.
— of the Celts. Belgra. **35**: 184.
— of Checkers; a Comedy. Canad. Mo. **2**: 534.
— of Chess; a Tale. So. Lit. Mess. **4**: 233.
— of Ecarté; a Story. All the Year, **17**: 44.
— of Hazard; a Story. (S. Wilson) Belgra. **42**: 97.
— of Knur and Spell. (J. Holland) Reliquary, **6**: 233.
— of Pall Mall. (R. R. Macgregor) Belgra. **36**: 70.
— of Quintain. (R. R. Macgregor) Belgra. **38**: 313.
— of twenty Questions. Liv. Age, **25**: 40.
Games. Chamb. J. **41**: 796.
— and Amusements, Domestic, of the Middle Ages. Art J. **11**: 9, 79.
— and Play in the Classical Period. Cornh. **20**: 285.
— Development of. (A. G. Sedgwick) Nation, **33**: 131.
— Capt. Dover's Cotswold. Cornh. **37**: 710.
— Drawing-Room. Chamb. J. **49**: 241.
— Evolution of. Liv. Age, **141**: 572.
— Garden. Chamb. J. **40**: 251. — House. Words, **7**: 538. — Lond. Soc. **5**: 473.
— History of. (E. B. Tylor) Fortn. **31**: 735. Same art. Pop. Sci. Mo. **15**: 225.
— of the Ancients. (R. F. Clarke) Month, **13**: 197. — Ecl. M. **28**: 40.
— on Horseback. Chamb. J. **53**: 492.
— Shakspere's. Belgra. **22**: 482.
Game Book, Leaves from. (W. H. Maxwell) Dub. Univ. **3**: 563.
Game Food of America. (W. Minot) Internat. R. **9**: 136.
Game Laws. (Syd. Smith) Ed. R. **31**: 295. **39**: 43. **43**: 248. **49**: 55. — (W. Empson) Ed. R. **54**: 277. — Ed. R. **134**: 390. — Quar. **122**: 136. — Selec. Ed. R. **6**: 240. — Blackw. **22**: 643. **60**: 754. — Westm. **5**: 1. **45**: 405. — Mo. R. **85**: 74, 171. — Niles's Reg. **21**: 92. — Pamph. **9**: 171. **10**: 19. **11**: 325. — Ecl. R. **81**: 463. — Tait, **3**: 632.
— and Committee of 1872. (A. H. Beesly) Fortn. **19**: 352.
— and Game Preserving. Westm. **114**: 131.
— and our Food Supply. Fraser, **88**: 135.
— and Poaching in England. Cornh. **16**: 346.
— Evils of. Howitt, **3**: 226.
— History and Effects of. Mo. R. **165**: 284.
— of Scotland. Blackw. **66**: 63.
Game-Law Committee. (A. H. Beesly) Fortn. **21**: 385.
Game-Law Tactics. (W. Howitt) Howitt, **2**: 50–322.
Game-Keeper's Natural History. All the Year, **1**: 473.
Gamester, Confessions of a. Chr. Obs. **27**: 282.
Gamesters and Gaming. Colburn, **10**: 256.
— in Europe. Westm. **80**: 68. Same art. Liv. Age, **78**: 305.
Gamin de Paris. Once a Week, **15**: 660.
— A London. Temp. Bar, **20**: 257.
Gamut in major and minor Modes. J. Frankl. Inst. **73**: 175, 232, 347.
Gandler's Annuity; a Tale. Temp. Bar, **11**: 447.
Ganganelli, Cardinal, and Carlini. Colburn, **28**: 318.
Ganges, Madame de. Sharpe, **38**: 57.
Ganges River. All the Year, **22**: 392.
— Fair on. All the Year, **5**: 523.
— Scenes on. Penny M. **11**: 165.
Ganges Canal. (C. E. Norton) No. Am. **81**: 531.
Gannett, Observations on the. (W. Hincks) Canad. J. n. s. **7**: 329.
Gannett, Deborah. Am. Hist. Rec. **2**: 562. **3**: 79.
Gannett, Ezra S. (E. E. Hale) O. & N. **4**: 385.
— and his Contemporaries. (J. H. Morison) Mo. Rel. M. **46**: 502 552.
— Memoir of. (J. H. Morison) Unita. R. **3**: 488.
Gano, John, Memoirs of. Hist. M. **5**: 330.
Ganoid Fish from Queensland. (A. Günther) Pop. Sci. R. **11**: 257.
Gansvort, Wessel, the Reformer. (M. G. Hanson) Ref. Q. **28**: 246.
Gaol. *See* Jail.
Gaol Chaplain; a Novel. Bentley, **13**: 508, 568. **14**: 94–572. **15**: 39–522. **16**: 173–615. **17**: 45–565. **18**: 95–563. **19**: 58.
Gap of Barnesmore; a Tale. Dub. Univ. **32**: 219.
Garbett, James, Bampton Lectures of. Chr. Obs. **43**: 350.
— Sermons of. Chr. Obs. **48**: 53. — Chr. Rem. **8**: 1.
Garcia, Madame. Bentley, **24**: 35.
Garcin de Tassy, J. H., Life and Works of. (J. v. Döllinger) Contemp. **35**: 385.
Garde, Roger. (C. E. Banks) N. E. Reg. **35**: 343.
Garden. Sir Robert W., with portrait. Colburn, **168**: 412.
Garden, The. New Eng. M. **9**: 81.
— and Neighborhood. (L. Cross) Colburn, **164**: 181, 391.
— and Spring. Colburn, **152**: 139–286.
— Bits of. (Miss Maling) Good Words, **4**: 589.
— Flower. (T. James) Quar. **70**: 196.
— McIntosh's Book of. Blackw. **73**: 129.
— The Manse. Mo. R. **140**: 206.
— My Town-Garden. Chamb. J. **42**: 417.
— of Flowers. Chamb. J. **29**: 402.
— of Nutmeg-Trees. House. Words, **4**: 147.
— of Plants at Paris, History of. Blackw. **13**: 121. **14**: 577. Same art. Portfo. (Den.) **31**: 190, 274, 353.
— on the Hill. (W. C. Bartlett) Overland, **12**: 364.
Gardens. (J. Emmet) Peop. J. **8**: 21. — Chamb. J. **10**: 221.
— Ancient. Appleton, **2**: 384, supp.
— and Gardeners, Tiny. Once a Week, **17**: 38.
— by Gas-Light. All the Year, **24**: 487, 519.
— Fashions in. (E. C. G.) Lippinc. **18**: 257.
— Hints on planning and planting. Lond. Soc. **12**: 324, 530.
— Hornby Mills, Gossip about. (H. Kingsley) Argosy, **1**: 394.
— in March. Lond. Soc. **13**: 236.
— Kew. Quar. **90**: 34. — Fraser, **40**: 127. — (J. Saunders) Peop. J. **6**: 177.
— Market. House. Words, **7**: 409.
— Modern French. Appleton, **3**: 364, supp.
— of ancient America. Appleton, **3**: 504, supp.
— of the Greeks. Chamb J. **41**: 541.
— of North America. All the Year, **41**: 270.

Gardens of Old Rome. Chamb. J. 25: 284.
— of our Forefathers. Sharpe, 36: 238.
— Paris. (R. M. Copeland) Nation, 10: 44.
— Town. Chamb. J. 37: 188.
— Wild. (M. G. Watkins) Belgra. 20: 240.
Garden Favorites. Chamb. J. 3: 162.
Garden Gate; a Poem. (C. Mackay) Internat. M. 1: 29.
Garden Parties. All the Year, 38: 533.
Garden Reverie; a Poem. (P. B. Marston) Cornh. 23: 221.
Garden Whimsies. Chamb. J. 8: 357.
Gardener and the Manor. (H. C. Andersen) Scrib. 4: 457.
Gardeners, Education of. Blackw. 35: 691.
Gardener Bird. Liv. Age, 137: 189.
Gardening. Lond. Soc. 32: 163. — (C. Fraser) De Bow, 25: 56. — Quar. 89: 1. Same art. Ecl. M. 24: 17. Same art. Liv. Age, 115: 303. — Cornh. 26: 424. — Sharpe, 2: 149.
— at Lille. All the Year, 27: 537.
— Chapter on. (A. Davezac) Dem. R. 12: 121
— Color on Lawns. Broadw. 8: 289.
— Elizabethan. Fraser, 70: 179.
— English and French Mode compared. Westm. 86: 445.
— Landscape. *See* Landscape Gardening.
— My Garden. (M. A. Dodge) Atlan. 9: 540.
— — Smee's. Nature, 6: 186.
— Old-Fashioned. (Mrs. Paul) 19th Cent. 7: 128.
— Old Practice of. Retros. 18: 40.
— Ornamental. (W. Ely) Chr. Mo. Spec. 9: 354.
— Pleasures of. Penny M. 6: 326.
— Popular Taste in. (F. D. Huntington) Chr. Exam. 31: 60.
— Progress of. (D. Barrington) Arch. 7: 113.
— Revolution in. Lond. Soc. 20: 46. Same art. Liv. Age, 110: 367.
— Window. All the Year, 36: 545. — Lond. Soc. 31: 377. — (Mrs. J. W. Loudon) Peop. J. 4: 176, 231.
— Winter. Lond. Soc. 34: 370.
Gardiner, Allen F. Journey to the Zulu Country. Fraser, 14: 332.
— Memoir of. Chr. Obs. 57: 517.
Gardiner, H. W. (W. Walford) Cong. M. 24: 225.
Gardiner, Col. James. Penny M. 13: 353.
Gardiner, Margaret. *See* Blessington, Countess.
Gardiner, Sylvester. (E. B. Carpenter) O. & N. 10: 285.
Gardiner, William, the Botanist. Chamb. J. 7: 248.
Gardiner, William. Music of Nature. (J. S. Dwight) Chr. Exam. 25: 23. — (T. P. Thompson) Westm. 17: 345. — (J. W. Alexander) Princ. 10: 346. — New York R. 3: 44. — Mo. R. 128: 495.
Gardiner, Maine, Lyceum of. U. S. Lit. Gaz. 2: 361.
Gardner, Mass., Ministers of. Am. Q. Reg. 10: 56.
Garfield, James Abram. (R. Shindler) 19th Cent. 10: 236. Same art. Ecl. M. 97: 544. — Atlan. 46: 258. — (C. E. Fitch) Internat. R. 9: 447.
— and the Bosses, Feb., 1881. (E. L. Godkin) Nation, 32: 124.
— and Credit Mobilier. (E. L. Godkin) Nation, 30: 467.
— and the De Golyer Contract. Nation, 31: 5.
— Assassination of. Canad. Mo. 20: 538, 554. — (L. H. Atwater) Presb. R. 2: 775. — (E. L. Godkin) Atlan. 48: 395.
— — Lesson of. (J. G. Shea) Am. Cath. Q. 6: 683.
— Biographies of. (W. H. Smith) Dial (Ch.), 1: 81.
— Death of. (N. F. Davin) Canad. Mo. 20: 607. — Nation, 33: 228.
— — in London. (J. Hawthorne) Nation, 33: 289.
— England and America over the Grave of. (P. Bayne) Contemp. 40: 673.
— Surgical Treatment of. (W. A. Hammond, J. Ashhurst, jr., J. M. Sims, and J. T. Hodgen) No. Am. 133: 578.
Garibaldi, Giuseppe. (H. T. Tuckerman) No. Am. 92: 15. — Argosy, 2: 207, 269, 349. — Chamb. J. 26: 215, 233, 246. 32: 243. — (J. B. Torricelli) Chr. Exam. 70: 108. — Cornh. 2: 591. — with portrait, Ev. Sat. 10: 6. — with portrait, Dem. R. 31: 193. — Liv. Age, 63: 223. 67: 48, 126. 68: 55.
— a Poem. (G. Massey) Good Words, 1: 665. 3: 625.
— Adventure in Search of. (J. Harwood) Once a Week, 4: 209.
— and Cavour. Westm. 75: 172.
— and the Italian Crisis, 1859. Ecl. R. 110: 503.
— and the Italian Volunteers. Westm. 72: 478. Same art. Ecl. M. 49: 89.
— and Paëz. Am. Whig R. 13: 173.
— and Sicilian Revolution. (A. Saffi) Macmil. 2: 235.
— at Varegnano. Once a Week, 7: 386.
— Career of. Dub. Univ. 63: 483.
— Clelia. O. & N. 2: 735.
— Conscience-Stricken. (A. Dumas) Ev. Sat. 2: 235.
— Glimpses of. (L. Parks, jr.) Atlan. 7: 465.
— Headquarters of, Week at, 1866. Sharpe, 45: 68.
— Hero of 1860. St. James, 1: 329.
— in Calabria. Cornh. 9: 666.
— in England. Dub. R. 55: 132.
— in France. (J. W. Mario) Fraser, 96: 452, 602, 720. — Month, 16: 261.
— in Naples, 1860. Cornh. 10: 33. 11: 365.
— in Palermo, 1860. Cornh. 9: 537.
— Last Attempt of. All the Year, 8: 211, 235.
— Last Campaign of. Cornh. 17: 111.
— Life and Times of. Colburn, 119: 363. Same art. Ecl. M. 51: 181. — Liv. Age, 62: 763.
— Love-Episode in Life of. Ev. Sat. 3: 172.
— On the Rock with. Chamb. J. 35: 401.
— Position of, in 1867. (J. W. Mario) Nation, 5: 378.
— Resignation of, 1859. Tait, n. s. 26: 743
— Retirement of, 1861. Macmil. 3: 160.
— Retreat from Rome. Good Words, 8: 493, 518.
— Rule of the Monk. Ev. Sat. 9: 222.
— Sketch of. (A. A. Knox) Once a Week, 1: 24.
— To; a Sonnet. (J. S. Blackie) Fraser, 100: 142.
— Visit to. Chamb. J. 52: 264.
— Wife of. (L. Leslie) Lakeside, 3: 460.
Garibaldian Faith; a Poem. (M. Brotherton) Temp. Bar, 12: 352.
Garland, Fort, Colorado. (G. Gwyther) Overland, 5: 520.
Garland City, Colorado. (H. H. Jackson) Scrib. 15: 386.
Garlands and their Uses. (Mrs. White) Sharpe, 11: 137.
Garlandine and the Tutor; a Legend of the Rhine. Dub. Univ. 31: 513.
Garnaut Hall; a Poem. (T. B. Aldrich) Atlan. 15: 182.
Garnet's Straw, The Imposture of. Penny M. 4: 244.
Garnets from the Trap-Rocks of New Haven. (E. S. Dana) Am. J. Sci. 114: 215.
Garnett, Henry, Life and Martyrdom of. Month, 34: 202.
Garnett, Gen. Robert S., Escape of. (C. Whittlesey) O. & N. 8: 302.
Garnier, Anthony. U. S. Cath. M. 4: 396.
Garnier, Robert, early French Poet. Lond. M. 7: 41, 162.
Garnier-Pagès, Louis A., with portrait. Ev. Sat. 9: 683.
Garnkirk and Glasgow Railroad, 1835. (G. Martin) Ed. New Philos. J. 19: 48.
Garo Hill Tribes. (H. H. G. Austen) Anthrop. J. 2: 391.
Garonne River, Engineering Works on. (J. Bennett) J. Frankl. Inst. 72: 23, 73.
Garpike, Development of. (E. P. Wright) Nature, 19: 100.
— Old and young. (B. G. Wilder) Pop. Sci. Mo. 11: 1, 186.
Garraway's. Chamb. J. 43: 629.
Garrets, Essay on. New Eng. M. 4: 399.
Garrettson, F. Am. Meth. M. 11: 93. 12: 341.

Garrick, David. (J. Winsor) Atlan. **22**: 79. — All the Year, **19**: 346. — Belgra. **5**: 99. — Chamb. J. **45**: 294. — Chamb. J. **57**: 364. Same art. Littell, **146**: 63. — (R. B. S. Knowles) Dub. Univ. **95**: 207. — Quar. **125**: 1. Same art. Liv. Age, **98**: 451. — Temp. Bar, **52**: 70. Same art. Ecl. M. **90**: 336. — Dub. Univ. **70**: 339. Same art. Liv. Age, **96**: 219.
— and Acting. Anal. M. **5**: 65.
— and his Contemporaries. Colburn, **32**: 273.
— and Mrs. Siddons, Theatrical Farewells of. Ev. Sat. **4**: 161.
— and the Shakspere Jubilee. (D. Cook) Once a Week, **10**: 104.
— and his Wife. Ecl. M. **45**: 139.
— as Actor and Manager. Temp. Bar, **11**: 336.
— as Hamlet. (Lord R. Lytton) Fortn. **15**: 221. Same art. Liv. Age, **109**: 67, 236.
— Correspondence of. Mo. R. **126**: 167. **127**: 321.
— Delivery of a Passage of Shakspere. Colburn, **4**: 551.
— Farewell to the Stage. All the Year, **18**: 87.
— Letters of. Lond. M. **2**: 647. **3**: 202. — Colburn, **34**: 196.
— Life of. (P. Fitzgerald) Dub. Univ. **65**: 243, 396, 603. **66**: 553. **67**: 85, 274, 384. **68**: 434, 560, 678. **69**: 65, 212, 573. **70**: 84, 213, 339. — So. R. n. s. **7**: 31.
— Mulberry-Tree of. (J. Plummer) Once a Week, **10**: 571.
— New Facts regarding. Colburn, **34**: 568.
— Recollections of. Westm. **17**: 67. — Blackw. **18**: 488. — Mus. **8**: 78.
— Rivals and Associates of. Temp. Bar, **54**: 86.
— Villa of, Hampton Court. Antiquary, **1**: 32.
Garrick for this Night only; a Story. (H. Louther) Tinsley, **27**: 114.
Garrick, Mrs. David. (D. Cook) Once a Week, **10**: 622.
Garrick Club Theatrical Portraits. (J.W. Calcraft) Dub. Univ. **42**: 643. **43**: 223, 393. — (P. Fitzgerald) Gent. M. n. s. **18**: 561.
Garrison, William Lloyd. (H. H. Barber) Unita. R. **12**: 423. — (L. M. Child) Atlan. **44**: 234. — (T. W. Higginson) Internat. R. **9**: 143. — (W. Phillips) No. Am. **129**: 141. — Nation, **28**: 382. — with portrait (M. Howitt) Peop. J. **2**: 141–185. — (W. Dorling) Mod. R. **1**: 355.
— and the Liberator. (F. J. Garrison) Mod. R. **1**: 645.
— Relation to Abolitionism. (D. Dorchester) Meth. Q. **41**: 270, 474.
Garrison Family of Massachusetts. (W. P. Garrison) N. E. Reg. **30**: 418.
Garrod, Alfred Henry. Nature, **20**: 613.
Garroting, Moral Philosophy of. Fraser, **67**: 258.
— Science of. Cornh. **7**: 79.
Garsoppa, Falls of, India. (M. J. Walhouse) Fraser, **97**: 32. Same art. Liv. Age, **136**: 493.
Garter, Order of. (J. Saunders) Peop. J. **7**: 65. — Gent. M. n. s. **9**: 645. — Once a Week, **26**: 523. — Quar. **68**: 413.
— Beltz's Memorials of. Mo. R. **156**: 178.
— Institution of. (Sir N. H. Nicolas) Arch. **31**: 1.
— Stall-Plates of. (T. W. King) Arch. **31**: 164.
Garth. (J. Hawthorne) Harper, **51**: 100–871. **52**: 100–846. **53**: 65–911. **54**: 112–735. **55**: 123.
Gary Magnetic Motor. (E. M. Bacon) Harper, **58**: 601.
Gas and Electricity as heating Agents. (C. W. Siemens) Nature, **23**: 326, 351. Same art. Ecl. Engin. **24**: 477.
— — in Paris. (W. de Fonvielle) Nature, **21**: 282.
— — Light and Energy of. (J. T. Sprague) J. Frankl. Inst. **108**: 187.
— as Fuel. (M. M. P. Muir) Nature, **18**: 34. Same art. Ecl. Engin. **19**: 39. — Ecl. Engin. **25**: 450.
— Carburetted. Once a Week, **5**: 329.
— Carburation of. J. Frankl. Inst. **73**: 193.
Gas, Coal. (S. A. Eliot) No. Am. **92**: 133. — (T. Thomson) J. Frankl. Inst. **39**: 127. — Anal. M. **8**: 90. — Once a Week, **27**: 470.
— — Air in. Ecl. Engin. **2**: 306.
— — Distillation from. Pract. M. **2**: 314.
— — Engineering of. (R. Briggs) J. Frankl. Inst. **105**: 217, 415. **110**: 233.
— — Experiments on Carburation of. J. Frankl. Inst. **80**: 414.
— — Heating Power of. (W. Wallace) J. Frankl. Inst. **109**: 194.
— — Illuminating Power of. (W. E. A. Aikin) Am. J. Sci. **77**: 82. — (T. N. Kirkham) Ecl. Engin. **1**: 652. — (S. Macadam) Pract. M. **2**: 27.
— — Improvement and new Uses of. Nat. Q. **4**: 303.
— — Manufacture of. Ecl. Engin. **1**: 70.
— — Power and Purity of. (A. V. Harcourt) Ecl. Engin. **15**: 361.
— — Sulphurous Impurity in. (A. V. Harcourt) Nature, **6**: 7.
— Effect of mixing Air with. (B. Silliman and H. Wurtz) Am. J. Sci. **98**: 40.
— First Use of, in London. All the Year, **18**: 349. Same art. Ev. Sat. **4**: 532.
— Flow of, through Pipes. J. Frankl. Inst. **59**: 42, 121.
— for economic Purposes, Combustion of. (Dr. Letheby) J. Frankl. Inst. **82**: 205, 242, 331.
— for Light and Heat. (C. W. Siemens) Ecl. Engin. **25**: 321.
— from Boghead Coal. (A. Fyfe) J. Frankl. Inst. **54**: 347, 399.
— History of. Penny M. **3**: 373–492.
— — and Statistics of. Bank. M. (N. Y.) **13**: 54.
— Igniting Point of. (E. Frankland) J. Frankl. Inst. **74**: 90.
— Illuminating, from Cork. Pract. M. **5**: 348.
— — History of. Ecl. Engin. **6**: 398.
— — London's Supply of. Brit. Q. **69**: 1. — (H. Chubb) J. Statis Soc. **39**: 350.
— — Manufacture of. (J. W. Watson) Harper, **26**: 14. — J. Frankl. Inst. **44**: 352.
— — — from Water. J. Frankl. Inst. **43**: 52.
— — Preparation of, 1827. J. Frankl. Inst. **4**: 361. **5**: 13.
— — Reduction of Light due to Carbonic Acid in. (F. E. Stimpson) J. Frankl. Inst. **91**: 54.
— Manufacture of. (W. E. Simmons) Pop. Sci. Mo **10**: 478.
— — in 1854. (T. I. Dimsdale) J. Frankl. Inst. **61**: 25.
— Measurement of, and Meters, National Standards for. (G. Glover) J. Frankl. Inst. **82**: 117, 180, 261.
— New Hydrocarbon. Nature, **7**: 329.
— obtained from Petroleum Naphtha. (H. H. Edgerton) Am. J. Sci. **101**: 408.
— Photometric Power of. (B. Silliman) Am. J. Sci. **100**: 379.
— Resin and Water. (A. Fife) J. Frankl. Inst. **50**: 271–411.
— Substitutes for Coal in. (H. Gore) Ecl. Engin. **9**: 321.
— Supply for heating and illuminating Purposes. (C. W. Siemens) Nature, **24**: 153.
— — from Works without Gasholder. (M. Servier) J. Frankl. Inst. **103**: 188.
— *versus* Electricity. (W. H. Preece) Nature, **19**: 261. Same art. Ecl. Engin. **20**: 310.
— Water, in Narbonne from 1855–65. (A. Oppenheim) J. Frankl. Inst. **101**: 123.
— Wood, Experiments on Value of. J. Frankl. Inst. **64**: 126.
Gas Analysis, New Apparatus for. (C. W. Hinman) Am. J. Sci. **108**: 182.
— — Orsat's. Pract. M. **6**: 232.
— New Processes in proximate. (H. Wurtz) J. Frankl. Inst. **99**: 146, 218, 286.

Gas Blowpipe, Clarke on. Quar. **23**: 466.
Gas Buoys. Am. Arch. **5**: 31.
Gas Burners, Ventilation of. Am. Arch. **7**: 138, 223.
Gas Burning and its Consequences. (G. J. Varney) Lippinc. **26**: 734.
Gas Cooking Apparatus. Pract. M. **4**: 111.
Gas Engine, Otto's. Ecl. Engin. **18**: 66.
Gas Engines. J. Frankl. Inst. **5**: 18. **109**: 340. — (F. J. Bramwell) Am. Arch. **10**: 291.
— at the Paris Exhibition. (M. Armengaud, jr.) Ecl. Engin. **20**: 148.
— Furnace of. Ecl. Engin. **8**: 424.
Gas Flames, Electrical Condition of. (J. Trowbridge) Am. J. Sci. **104**: 4.
Gas Furnace, Heat-Restoring. Ecl. Engin. **5**: 341.
Gas-Heating Furnace. (C. Schintz) Ecl. Engin. **1**: 328.
Gas Holder, New. (W. F. Barrett) Nature, **17**: 253.
— Collapsed, Novel Method of repairing. Pract. M. **6**: 5.
Gas Light, Accum's Treatise on, 1815. Ecl. R. **24**: 61.
— Inventors and Improvers of. Chamb. J. **15**: 171. Same art. Liv. Age, **29**: 351.
— Intensity of, and the Volume consumed. (B. Silliman) Am. J. Sci. **99**: 17.
Gas Lights. Ed. R. **13**: 477. — Am. J. Sci. **3**: 170. — Westm. **11**: 290.
Gas Lighting. (W. Wallace) Ecl. Engin. **20**: 318. — All the Year, **6**: 55.
— Automatic. Pract. M. **7**: 338, 367.
— by Electricity. Nature, **17**: 495.
— Chemistry of. (Dr. Letheby) J. Frankl. Inst. **82**: 37.
— Early History of. Once a Week, **27**: 360.
— History of. Lond. M. **19**: 502.
Gas Meters. Chamb. J. **52**: 543.
— Glycerine in. Pract. M. **1**: 104.
Gas Monopolies. Nat. Q. **10**: 278.
Gas Pipes, Copper for. Pract. M. **3**: 360.
Gas Poisons of our Dwellings. Once a Week, **13**: 433.
Gas Retorts, Charging and discharging. Pract. M. **1**: 213.
Gas Stock. (J. Trowbridge) Internat. R. **6**: 133.
Gas Stove, and Manufacture of Water. (C. P. Smyth) Ecl. Engin. **2**: 351.
Gas Well in New York. (H. Wurtz) Am. J. Sci. **99**: 336.
Gas Works, Day at. Penny M. **11**: 81.
— Engineering of. (R. Briggs) J. Frankl. Inst. **100**: 242, 324. **101**: 113, 297. **102**: 32–335. **105**: 415.
— of Philadelphia. (C. M. Wetherill) J. Frankl. Inst. **58**: 35.
— — Report on, 1841. (J. C. Cresson) J. Frankl. Inst. **31**: 231.
— — — 1850. J. Frankl. Inst. **51**: 289.
— — — 1852. J. Frankl. Inst. **53**: 385. **55**: 207.
— — — 1853. (J. C. Cresson) J. Frankl. Inst. **57**: 235.
— — — 1856. (J. C. Cresson) J. Frankl. Inst. **63**: 309.
— — — 1857. (J. C. Cresson) J. Frankl. Inst. **65**: 228.
— — — 1860. J. Frankl. Inst. **70**: 13.
— Stokers of. All the Year, **17**: 271.
Gases, Absorption of. (S. Wroblewski) Nature. **21**: 192.
— — by Water. (G. W. Baird) J. Frankl. Inst. **93**: 61.
— accompanying Meteorites. (J. W. Mallet) Am. J. Sci. **110**: 206.
— Avogadro's Law of mechanical Theory of. (A. Neumann) J. Frankl. Inst. **89**: 353.
— Chemistry of. (J. Jones) Recr. Sci. **3**: 231.
— Condensation of. (J. Jamin and A. Bertrand) J. Frankl. Inst. **56**: 405.
— Density of. (M. V. Regnault) J. Frankl. Inst. **45**: 356.
— Diffusion of, in relation to social Life. Fraser, **65**: 643. Same art. Ecl. M. **56**: 335.
— — through absorbing Substances. (J. C. Maxwell) Nature, **14**: 24.
evolved from Iron Furnaces. (Bunsen and Playfair) J. Frankl. Inst. **47**: 268, 338, 387. **48**: 24, 136, 218.
Gases, Flow through Tubes. (S. W. Robinson) Ecl. Engin. **24**: 370.
— from Blast Furnaces, Application of Waste. (D. Mushet) J. Frankl. Inst. **51**: 324, 421. **52**: 271. — (H. L. Damrel) J. Frankl. Inst. **50**: 277. — (Bunsen and Playfair) J. Frankl. Inst. **48**: 218. — (P. Budd) J. Frankl. Inst. **50**: 396.
— from meteoric Iron. (A. W. Wright) Am. J. Sci. **109**: 294, 459. **110**: 44. **111**: 253. **112**: 165.
— Heat Conduction in. J. Frankl. Inst. **102**: 302.
— in relation to Health. (S. T. Preston) Nature, **20**: 366.
— Inflammable, Brande on. Ed. R. **34**: 431.
— Kinetic Theory of. (J. C. Maxwell) Nature, **16**: 242.
— Liquefaction of. (G. Tissandier) Pop. Sci. Mo. **12**: 616. **13**: 78. — Nature, **17**: 177, 265. Same art. Liv. Age, **137**: 121. — Sharpe, **7**: 243. — J. Frankl. Inst. **105**: 187.
— Measurement of, in Analysis. (Williamson and Russell) J. Frankl. Inst. **66**: 400.
— Molecular Mobility of. (T. Graham) J. Frankl. Inst. **78**: 191.
— Occlusion of. Intel. Obs. **11**: 452.
— Sounds produced by Combustion of, in Tubes. (J. Tyndall) J. Frankl. Inst. **64**: 404.
— Subjugation of. Ecl. Engin. **18**: 251.
— Ultra-Gaseous State of Matter. Ecl. Engin. **20**: 303.
— Viscosity of, at high Exhaustions. (W. Crookes) Nature, **23**: 421, 443.
Gascon O'Driscol. (T. Ferguson) Blackw. **123**: 545.
Gascon Stories. (J. Durand) Galaxy, **11**: 861. — **15**: 815.
Gaseous and liquid States, Van der Waals on. (J. C. Maxwell) Nature, **10**: 477.
Gaskell, Mrs. E. C. (E. Dicey) Nation, **1**: 716. — Cornh. **13**: 12. — Eng. Dom. M. **2**: 90. — (M. Barton) Ed. R. 89: 402. — Brit. Q. **9**: 117. — (M. Barton) Prosp. R. **5**: 36.
— Novels of. (P. Q. Keegan) Victoria. **33**: 35. — (W. Minto) Fortn. **30**: 353. — Cornh. **29**: 191. Same art. Ecl. M. **82**: 468. Same art. Liv. Age, **120**: 787. Macmil. **13**: 153. Same art. Liv. Age, **88**: 23. — Colburn, **105**: 427. Same art. Ecl. M. **37**: 259. — Ev. Sat. **16**: 233.
— Recantation. Liv. Age, **54**: 721.
— Ruth. (G. W. Curtis) Putnam, **1**: 535. — Liv. Age, **36**: 543. — No. Brit. **19**: 151. — Tait, n. s. **20**: 217. — Westm. **59**: 474.
— Works of. Brit. Q. **45**: 399. Same art. Ecl. M. **69**: 1. Same art. Liv. Age, **93**: 237.
Gaspar the Pirate. Dub. Univ. **18**: 451, 581, 725. **19**: 56–661.
Gaspar Mendez, Story of. (C. Crowe) Internat. M. **5**: 362.
Gaspard de Besse. (L. S. Costello) Bentley, **8**: 181.
Gasparin, Agénor E., Count de. Ev. Sat. **11**: 23.
— Liberal Principles of. (J. P. Thompson) No. Am. **95**: 437.
— Schools of Doubt and of Faith. Chr. Obs. **55**: 173.
Gasparin, Mme. V. B. de. (J. M. Ludlow) Macmil. **2**: 170.
— Near and heavenly Horizons. Lond. Q. **18**: 273. Same art. Ecl. M. **56**: 304.
— Writings of. Dub. Univ. **64**: 337.
Gasparo Bandollo; a Poem. Dub. Univ. **33**: 650.
Gass, Patrick, Voyages and Travels of. Quar. **1**: 293. — (J. Foster) Ecl. R. **9**: 105.
Gassion, Jean de. Fraser, **32**: 141.
Gassiot, J. P. Nature, **16**: 399.
Gastaldi, Bartolomeo. Nature, **19**: 275.
Gastein, Austria, Valley of. (H. Hunt) Atlan. **27**: 27
— as a Watering-Place. Once a Week, **27**: 32.
— Legends of. (J. Oxenford) Colburn, **82**: 316.
Gastein Papers. Argosy, **15**: 51–442.
Gaston, Jane. (Mrs. E. F. Ellet) Godey, **40**: 183.
Gaston, the little Wolf. House. Words, **16**: 28.

Gaston Phœbus; or Forest of Sauve Terre. Peop. J. **7**: 11–62.
Gastronome, Reveries of a. Fraser, **37**: 388.
Gastronomical Dialogue. (J. Popham) Galaxy, **22**: 187.
Gastronomy. St. James, **31**: 570, 731. — Hogg, **2**: 129.— Blackw. **23**: 581. — For. Q. **1**: 171. — So. R. **3**: 416.
— and Civilization. Fraser, **44**: 591.
— and Gastronomers. (A. Hayward) Quar. **54**: 117.
— Chapter on. Colburn, **59**: 196.
— Classics of the Table. Fraser, **29**: 604. **30**: 48, 269, 427. **31**: 223, 355.
— Moorish. (G. D. Cowan) Tinsley, **25**: 224.
— of the Romans. Am. Q. **2**: 422.
— Recollections à la Fourchette. Blackw. **130**: 106.
Gates, Gen. Horatio. (R. H. Stoddard) Nat. M. **13**: 289. —Portfo.(Den.) **2**: 385.
— at Camden, S. C., 1780. (J. A. Stevens) M. Am. Hist. **5**: 241, 425.
— Letter of. Hist. M. **4**: 9.
— Letters, June–August, 1780. M. Am. Hist. **5**: 281.
— Memoir of. (I. T. Greenwood) N. E. Reg. **21**: 252.
— Orders to, 1780. M. Am. Hist. **5**: 310.
— Southern Campaign. (T. Pinckney) Hist. M. **10**: 244.
Gateway of the Oceans. Internat. M. **2**: 124.
Gathering of the West. (J. Galt) Blackw. **12**: 306.
Gatherings from an Artist's Portfolio. (J. E. Freeman) Appleton, **15**: 12–657.
Gatling, Richard J., and Gatling Gun. (C. H. Foster) Potter Am. Mo. **12**: 321.
Gatling Gun. Once a Week, **26**: 28.
Gatling System of Fire-Arms. Pract. M. **1**: 344.
Gaubil, Anthony. Month, **42**: 428.
Gaucho, The. (W. F. Mayer) Atlan. **2**: 178.
Gauchos, The; a Tale of the Pampas. Colburn, **40**: 137.
Gaudentio di Lucca, Memoirs of. Retros. **4**: 316.
Gauges for Wire and Sheet Metals. (C. Holtzapffel) J. Frankl. Inst. **44**: 116, 204. — (R. Briggs) J. Frankl. Inst. **104**: 407.
— Report on Standard Wire. J. Frankl. Inst. **105**: 103.
— Steam and Water Pressure. J. Frankl. Inst. **78**: 289.
Gauge Pipe for measuring a Flow of Water. J. Frankl. Inst. **45**: 402.
Gauging of Water by triangular Notches. (J. Thomson) J. Frankl. Inst. **73**: 91. **75**: 369.
Gauging and measuring Implements. (J. Richards) J. Frankl. Inst. **107**: 172.
Gaul, Christian Inscriptions in. (W. G. Humphry) Contemp. **3**: 410.
— Old, Memorabilia of. Dub. Univ. **73**: 33. Same art. Ecl. M. **72**: 426.
Gauls and the Franks. (E. A. Freeman) Nat. R. **11**: 247.
— and Germans under the Romans. Dub. Univ. **77**: 601.
— Belloquet on the Origin of. Anthrop. R. **7**: 245.
— History of. For. Q. **10**: 138. — Blackw. **56**: 466.
Gaule, John. Distractions, or the Holy Madnesse. (H. Baldwin) Retros. **4**: 223.
Gauntlett, Henry, Sermons and Life of. Chr.Obs. **35**: 180.
Gauntry, Heirs of. Fraser, **42**: 95, 175, 305. Same art. Liv. Age, **26**: 357, 498. **29**: 208.
Gaur, India, Ruins and Inscriptions of. Liv. Age, **140**: 505.
Gaures in Persia. Chr. Obs. **29**: 607, 677, 755.
Gauss, Carl Friedrich. (R. Tucker) Nature, **15**: 533.
Gaussin, Mlle., French Actress. All the Year, **42**: 160.
Gautama. *See* Buddha.
Gautier, Mademoiselle. House. Words, **16**: 55.
— Strange Confessions of. Blackw. **42**: 444.
Gautier, Théophile. (H. James, Jr.) No. Am. **116**: 310.— (E. Jerrold) Dark Blue, **4**: 277.— with portrait, Ev. Sat. **9**: 403, 413. — (A. Lang) Dark Blue, **1**: 26.— Temp. Bar, **58**: 58. Same art. Appleton, **23**: 239.— (G. Saintsbury) Fortn. **29**: 429.
Gautier, Théophile. (G. Saintsbury) Fortn. **32**: 385. Same art. Appleton, **22**: 415. Same art. Liv. Age, **143**: 108. — Cornh. **27**: 151. — Ev. Sat. **14**: 229.— Dub. Univ. **92**: 70.
— Chanson de Roland. (E. B. Cox) No. Am. **118**: 194.
— Character of. (H. James, jr.) No. Am. **119**: 416.
— a literary Artist. (E. Benson) Atlan. **21**: 664.
— Memorial Verses on. (A.C.Swinburne) Ev. Sat.**14**: 55.
— Spirite; a Fantasy. Canad. Mo. **12**: 544.
Gavarni, Paul Chevalier. (A. Rhodes) Scrib. **6**: 2. — (G. A. Simcox) Portfo. **5**: 56. — Belgra. **1**: 416. — Ev. Sat. **14**: 70. **15**: 278.
Gavazzi, A., Father. (J. B. Thompson) Scrib. **21**: 274.
— *vs.* See of St. Peter. (A. J. Faust) Cath.World,**16**: 55.
Gaveston, Piers, Death of. Penny M. **3**: 363.
Gavial, New Species of. (O.C.Marsh) Am. J. Sci. **100**: 97.
Gavotte. Dub. Univ. **94**: 51.
Gay, Delphine. *See* Girardin, D. G.
Gay, John. Beggar's Opera. Eng. Dom. M. **14**: 290.— (J. B. Matthews) Harper, **60**: 501.
Gay Genealogy. (F. L. Gay) N. E. Reg. **33**: 45.
Gayer Family. N. E. Reg. **31**: 297.
Gayferos and Melisendra. Ev. Sat. **5**: 78.
Gaza and Jerusalem. (W. T. Savage) Cong. R. **9**: 164.
— Three Months at. Blackw. **62**: 334.
Gazelle, The Home of. Chamb. J. **38**: 281.
Gazet, Father. Pia Hilaria. Month, **12**: 279.
Gazetteer, Lippincott's. (M. Heilprin) Nation, **30**: 438.
Gazul, Clara, Plays of. Lond. M. **12**: 401.
Gearing, Laying out. (S.W.Robinson) Ecl.Engin. **19**: 312.
Gears, Teeth of internal. (A. K. Mansfield) J. Frankl. Inst. **103**: 17.
Gebri. *See* Gaures.
Geddes, Alexander, Good's Life of. Ed. R. **3**: 374.
Geddington Cross. (J. Plummer) Once a Week, **9**: 152.
Geese. Cornh. **8**: 203.
Geffrard, Fabre, the Haytien President. (J. M. Ludlow) Good Words, **3**: 523.
Gehenna. (A. R. Abbott) Univ. Q. **17**: 56. — (W. E. Manley) Univ. Q. **23**: 424.
Geibel, E. (J. B. Angell) B b. Sac. **12**: 770.
Geissler, Heinrich. Nature, **19**: 372.
Geist's Grave; a Poem. (M. Arnold) Fortn. **35**: 1. Same art. Ecl. M. **96**: 331.
Geistertodenglocke, Die; a Sketch. Dub. Univ. **59**: 473.
Gelatine as a Food-Preserver. (A. H. Church) Nature, **18**: 546.
— Applications to Art. Art J. **23**: 27.
Gelhausen, Legend of. Fraser, **33**: 143.
Gellert, Christian F., Life of. Ecl. R. **2**: 721. — Chr. Obs. **4**: 417, 479.
— Story of a Hymn. Hours at Home. **2**: 88, 159.
— Tales and Fables. Dub. Univ. **13**: 44.
Gellert; a Story. (Mrs. J. Melville) Overland, **6**: 496.
Gellius, Aulus, and his Contemporaries. Cornh. **37**: 316.
Gems, Ancient engraved. (S. F.Corkran) Nat. Q. **25**: 265.
— — and modern. (L. G. Robinson) Art J. **33**: 165.
— and Gem-Digging in Ceylon. Once a Week, **21**: 383, 402.
— and Jewels. Chamb. J. **35**: 94. Same art. Ecl. M. **53**: 63.
— and Pearls. (J. W. Watson) Harper, **21**: 764.
— and Reptiles. (Mrs. Seba Smith) Godey, **22**: 79.
— Antique. (C. D. Badham) Fraser, **54**: 421, 560.—Art J. **13**: 53. — Chamb. J. **35**: 346. Same art. Ecl. M. **53**: 552. — Dub. Univ. **84**: 513. — Ed. R. **124**: 511.
— — Poniatowski's Collection. Brit. & For. R. **13**: 66.
— Artificial, Manufacture of. Penny M. **7**: 450.
— Australian. Pract. M. **5**: 291.
— brought from Babylon by A. Lockett. (J. Landseer) Arch. **18**: 371.
— Chapter on. (W. H. Strobridge) Harper, **42**: 223.

Gems, Commercial Value of. Hunt, 3: 504.
— Curiosities of. Ecl. M. 37: 169.
— Engraved, Rare, and their Prices. Cornh. 17: 572.
— King Collection. Harper, 59: 532.
— Practical Remarks on. (C. A. Lee) Am. J. Sci. 38: 61.
— Secrets of. Chamb. J. 24: 211. Same art. Liv. Age, 47: 593.
— Useful Application of. Penny M. 11: 474.
See Precious Stones.
Gemmation, Phenomena of. (T. H. Huxley) Am. J. Sci. 78: 206.
Gena. (S. Tytler) Ev. Sat. 14: 59.
Genealogical Dictionary, Circular for. (E. Armstrong) N. E. Reg. 4: 76.
Genealogical Investigations, Reasons for. N. E. Reg. 1: 147.
Genealogy. (J. Amphlett) Pop. Sci. Mo. 13: 583. — N. E. Reg. 1: 334. — Retros. 17: 387.
— American. (C. Sotheran) Am. Bibliop. 7: 46.
— Nomenclature for Relationship. (L. Shattuck) N. E. Reg. 1: 355.
— Origin of Families. Colburn, 138: 290.
— Scottish, Works on. Colburn, 155: 195.
See Pedigrees.
Genealogies. (G. E. Ellis) No. Am. 83: 52.
— American. (W. H. Whitmore) No. Am. 82: 469. — (C. H. Hill) No. Am. 97: 36.
— — List of. (W. H. Whitmore) N. E. Reg. 11: 354. 12: 6. 13: 6. 18: 242.
Genera, Origin of, Cope on. Nature, 5: 21.
General and Mrs. Delormo. House. Words, 9: 449.
General Bounce. (G. J. W. Melville) Fraser, 49: 31-657. 50: 31-651.
General Grant, Shipwreck of the. (H. D. Jarvis) Harper, 38: 535.
General Ogle; a Character. (W. Elder) Putnam, 1: 661.
General's Cousin. Tinsley, 13: 93.
General's Nephew. Chamb. J. 29: 321.
Generals, British, of the Peninsular War. Lond. Q. 6: 32.
— Celebrated. Blackw. 61: 34. Same art. Ecl. M. 10: 253.
— Great, Sketches of. (J. G. Wilson) U. S. Serv. M. 4: 520. 5: 114, 333, 532.
General Assembly, At the. Fraser, 94: 53.
General Association of Connecticut, History of. (C. Chapin) Am. Q. Reg. 12: 20.
— of Massachusetts, History of. (T. Snell) Am. Q. Reg. 11: 166.
General Average; a Poem. (W. A. Butler) Harper, 43: 1.
General Harcourt; a Tale. Fraser, 14: 531.
General Trader. Lond. M. 17: 92.
Generation, Spontaneous. *See* Spontaneous.
Generic Images. (F. Galton) 19th Cent. 6: 157. Same art. Pop. Sci. Mo. 15: 532.
Genesee Country, Gen. Sullivan's Expedition to, 1779. Hist. M. 6: 233, 273.
Genesee Falls, Verses on. (H. J. Brent) Knick. 45: 38.
Genesis and Geology. *See* Geology.
— Chaldean Account of. (J. W. Dawson) Internat. R. 3: 392.
— of Earth and Man, Poole on. (B. H. Cowper) Kitto, 26: 123.
— of Things. (A. B. Alcott) J. Spec. Philos. 1: 165.
— Science and Laws of. Temp. Bar, 41: 175.
Genet, Edmond C. Knick. 35: 283. — Am. Hist. Rec. 3: 49. — Liv. Age, 72: 729. — Hist. M. 10: 329.
— Exploits of, in U. S. (J. Parton) Atlan. 31: 385.
— Selections from Papers of. Hist. M. 12: 154.
Genetic Cycle in organic Nature. (W. Hincks) Canad. J. n. s. 7: 515.
Geneva, Switzerland. (R. Keeler) Harper, 45: 867. — New Eng. M. 8: 348. — Chr. Mo. Spec. 4: 112. — (J. G. Palfrey) Chr. Exam. 4: 37.
— a Poem. Blackw. 17: 385.
Geneva and Chillon, Switzerland. (C. H. Miller) Overland, 11: 493.
— and France, Letters from. (E. Everett) No. Am. 11: 19.
— and Mont Blanc. So. Lit. Mess. 25: 309.
— and the Socinians. Cong. M. 8: 195.
— before Calvin. Dub. Univ. 64: 350. Same art. Ecl. M. 63: 326.
— Catholic Church in. Cath. World, 13: 847.
— Catholicism in. Dub. R. 57: 352.
— — restored in. Dub. R. 58: 325.
— Chronicles of. Lond. Q. 9: 190.
— Church of. Chr. Disc. 3: 215.
— Concerning the Use of Fagots at. (L. W. Bacon) Scrib. 16: 116.
— Description of. (W. Walther) Colburn, 3: 224.
— in History. Brit. Q. 42: 48.
— Jubilee at, August, 1835. (H. Ware, jr.) Chr. Exam. 20: 106.
— Memories and Martyrs of. Ecl M. 71: 925.
— Modern History of. Cornh. 13: 409.
— past and present. Chr. Obs. 72: 696.
— Protestantism in. Blackw. 51: 162.
— Recent Events at. (H. Ware) Chr. Exam. 11: 225.
— Recollections of. (J. Kavanagh) Mon h, 1: 25.
— Religious Instruction at. Chr. Exam. 2: 271.
— Republic of, Earlier Heroes of. Dub. Univ. 61: 568. Same art. Ecl. M. 60: 508.
— School of Theology at. Chr. R. 12: 321. — Am. Q. Reg. 9: 273.
— See of St. Francis of Sales. (B. Murphy) Cath. World, 18: 249.
— Thourel's History of. Brit. & For. R. 6: 122.
— Three Months in, 1871-72. Once a Week. 27: 73.
— Unitarian Persecutions at. (M. Bruen) Chr. Mo. Spec. 10: 86.
Geneva Congress of Arbitration. O. & N. 6: 126. — (E. E. Hale) O. & N. 9: 529. — (J. Moncrieff) Ed. R. 137: 264.
— American Case at. Fraser, 85: 381.
— Award of. Quar. 132: 535. — Am. Law R. 7: 193, 348.
— — Balance of. (W. G. Low) Internat. R. 10: 436.
— — Distribution of the Money. (U. H. Crocker) Nation, 17: 271. — Am. Law R. 8: 13.
— — — Bill for, 1876. (A. G. Sedgwick and E. L. Godkin) Nation, 23: 53.
— — Sir Alexander Cockburn's Dissent. (E. L. Godkin) Nation, 15: 245.
— Results of Decision at. (J. N. Pomeroy) Nation, 15: 377.
— South America in. Radical, 3: 558.
— Treaty of Washington. (J. N. Pomeroy) Nation, 12: 332.
— Uses of. (E. L. Godkin) Nation, 15: 133.
— Verdict of. (E. L. Godkin) Nation, 15: 180.
Geneva Controversy, Review of, 1824. Chr. Obs. 26: 693, 756.
Geneva Lake, and its Associations. (Mrs. S. S. Robbins) Hours at Home, 1: 164.
— and Mediterranean Sea, Color of. (J. Tyndall) Nature, 2: 489.
Geneviève, Saint. House. Words, 15: 558.
— a Poem. (F. Parke) Dub. Univ. 88: 102.
Genius. (J. B. Brown) Atlan. 13: 137. — (W. S. Tyler) Bib. Sac. 12: 283. — (E. W. Wiltbank) Godey, 47: 165. — Chamb. J. 52: 17. — So. Lit. Mess. 1: 337. 2: 297.
— and Industry in their Results. (J. C. Hope) De Bow, 29: 269.
— and Labor, Examples of. (J. H. Browne) Appleton, 20: 173.
— and Method. Temp. Bar, 61: 364.
— and the Public. Fraser, 18: 379.

Genius and Vanity. Cornh. 35: 670. Same art. Sup. Pop. Sci. Mo. 1: 213. Same art. Liv. Age, 134: 52.
— at the Hammer. Belgra. 34: 434.
— Barriers against. Mo. R. 131: 569.
— Before. (J. Burroughs) Galaxy, 5: 421.
— Diversity of. Blackw. 6: 674.
— Early Maturity of. (W. A. Jones) Dem. R. 14: 634.
— Encomiums on unsanctified. (R. Robbins) Chr. Mo. Spec. 8: 113.
— English. (W. Larminie) Gent. M. n. s. 26: 233.
— Enthusiasm of. (J. H. Hartzell) Univ. Q. 22: 93.
— exempt from ordinary Laws. (E. Helfenstein) Godey, 28: 98.
— Genesis of. (G. Allen) Atlan. 47: 371.
— Hereditary and scientific. (F. Galton) Fortn. 19: 345. Same art. Pop. Sci. Mo. 3: 65.
— — Galton on. Ed. R. 132: 100. Same art. Liv. Age, 106: 668. — (A. R. Wallace) Nature, 1: 501.
— Individual and national. Blackw. 6: 375.
— Individuality of. Ev. Sat. 10: 66.
— Infirmities of. Am. Q. 15: 214. — Quar. 50: 34. — Mo. R. 131: 347. — West. M. 2: 603.
— — Madden's. Tait, 4: 49.
— Influence of Love and Fame on. Blackw. 3: 701.
— Insanity of. St. James, 23: 378.
— Instinct of. Chamb. J. 7: 360.
— Marks of. All the Year, 6: 281.
— Men of, Characteristics of. Prosp. R. 3: 231.
— — Marriages among. (J. G. Wilson) Hours at Home, 10: 34.
— — wanting Judgment. (Sir E. Brydges) Fraser, 13: 673.
— Obligations of. Chr. Obs. 29: 485, 543.
— of Men and Women. Blackw. 16: 387.
— Original. Blackw. 1: 347.
— Penalty of. (S. A. Wyllie) Argosy, 19: 363.
— Plea for. So. R. n. s. 9: 628.
— Sources of. Ill. M. 2: 300.
— Study of Works of. New York R. 1: 161.
— Tale of a modern. Lond. M. 19: 433.
— Talent, Science, and Learning. Tait, 4: 483.
— — and Tact. (J. T. Powers) Nat. Q. 6: 43.
— Triumphs of. Peop. J. 8: 235.
— What it is. Temp. Bar, 46: 68. Same art. Ecl. M. 72: 671. — Canad. Mo. 18: 637.
Genius in Love, A. Lond. Soc. 15: 333.
Genius of America; a Poem. Putnam, 8: 121.
Genius of the Library. New Eng. M. 7: 193.
General outflanked. (A. Robbins) Overland, 8: 28.
Genlis, Madame de. (J. W. Croker) Quar. 34: 421. — (H. M. Walters) Nat. Q. 33: 273. — (W. B. O. Peabody) No. Am. 32: 196. — (J. T. Lomax) So. Lit. Mess. 8: 591. — Westm. 6: 134. — Blackw. 27: 481. — Mo. R. 105: 475. 107: 487. 109: 256. — Anal. M. 1: 93. 14: 311. — U. S. Lit. Gaz. 2: 307. 3: 251. — Eng. Dom. M. 2: 312, 343, 375. — Portfo. (Den.) 25: 19. — Tinsley, 6: 320. — Temp. Bar, 53: 28.
— and Madame de Staël. Chamb. J. 15: 221. — Internat. M. 3: 392.
— Character of. Lond. M. 22: 76.
— Memoirs of. Colburn, 14: 78. — Fraser, 47: 401. — Portfo. (Den.) 34: 280.
— Zuma. Portfo. (Den.) 25: 215.
Gennesaret; a Poem. Cornh. 14: 747.
Genoa. Godey, 45: 80. — Penny M. 8: 281. — So. Lit. Mess. 3: 571. — (G. F. S. de Casali) Hunt, 19: 375.
— and the Genoese. (W. Colton) Knick. 13: 337, 393.
— Bank of St. George. (O. M. Spencer) Harper, 42: 392.
— Charitable Institutions of. Dub. R. 14: 97.
— Day in. (W. H. Russell) Bentley, 33: 111.
— From Feder's to Le Fontane Amorose. (G. A. Sala) Temp. Bar, 15: 489.
Genoa, Glimpses of. (R. Davey) Lippinc. 14: 301. — (W. D. Howells) Atlan. 19: 359.
— Home of Columbus. (O. M. Spencer) Harper, 54: 1.
— School for young Ladies in. Fraser, 77: 521.
— under two Aspects. Chamb. J. 22: 273.
Genora, or the Grave-Robber; a Poem. Mus. 42: 538.
Genre Painters, Dutch. (F. W. Fairholt) Art J. 8: 209, 245.
Gent, Thomas, of York, Printer. Penny M. 10: 142.
— Poems. Blackw. 8: 448. — Lond. M. 3: 427.
Genteel Establishment. House. Words, 4: 560.
Genteel Pigeons. (D. Jerrold) Colburn, 52: 321.
Gentile, A, Life of. Dub. R. 31: 365.
Gentiles, Admission of, to the Church. (C. W. Schaeffer) Evang. R. 2: 371.
— Calling of. Chr. Obs. 7: 80-769.
Gentility. (T. S. Arthur) Godey, 22: 267.
— and Vulgarity. (J. Poole) Colburn, 70: 130.
Gentle Belle, A. (F. C. Fisher) Godey, 98: 33-523.
Gentle Euphemia. (A. Trollope) Fortn. 4: 692.
Gentle Fire-Eater. (C. Gordon) Atlan. 41: 43.
Gentle Giantess. (C. Lamb) Lond. M. 6: 529.
Gentle Reader. Chamb. J. 29: 401.
Gentleman, The American. Am. Meth. M. 21: 84.
— Character of, Lieber's. So. Q. 23: 53.
— English. Cong. 2: 464.
— from Reno. (N. Brooks) Overland, 1: 379.
— from Siskiyou. (J. Clifford) Lakeside, 9: 463.
— Grand old Name of. (J. R. Vernon) Contemp. 11: 561. — N. Ecl. 5: 403.
— High-Toned Southern. (J. W. De Forest) Nation, 6: 206.
— in a red Coat, Experiences of. (S. L. Blanchard) Belgra. 9: 399.
— Look of a. Lond. M. 3: 39.
— of La Porte; a Story. (Bret Harte) Belgra. 42: 50.
— of an Old School. (J. W. De Forest) Atlan. 21: 546.
— of the Old School. (J. R. Dennett) Nation, 5: 397.
— Shakspere's Delineation of. Temp. Bar, 23: 104.
— True. (T. D. Woolsey) New Eng. 5: 481.
— What is a? Colburn, 56: 449. — Tait, n. s. 11: 417.
— Who is a? (J. D. Champlin) N. E. Reg. 34: 154.
Gentleman's Magazine. Putnam, 10: 355.
Gentleman's Shawl. Putnam, 7: 301.
Gentleman Beggar. House. Words, 1: 510.
Gentleman Dick. (W. M. Laffan) Lippinc. 15: 220.
Gentleman Hanse. (J. Neall) Overland, 11: 149, 242.
Gentlemen, Educated. (W. M. Pomeroy) University Q. 2: 262.
— Gentilhomme and. (G. Colmache) Lippinc. 17: 81.
— in History. Liv. Age, 38: 418.
— past and present. Dub. Univ. 65: 3.
Gentlewoman of the last Century. Chamb. J. 20: 225
Gentlewomen in Difficulties. Good Words, 20: 69.
Gentry and Peerage. Westm. 27: 95*.
Gentz, Friedrich von, Diaries of. (A. Hayward) Ed. R. 117: 42. — Nat. R. 14: 271. Same art. Liv. Age, 74: 3.
Genzano and Frascati. (M. P. Thompson) Cath. World, 13: 737.
— Infiorata of. Argosy, 1: 39.
Geodes of Illinois. (G. H. Perkins) Am. Natural. 5: 698.
Geodesy. Nature, 19: 505. — (J. Herschel) Nature, 21: 604. — All the Year, 36: 136. — (L. B. Francolur) J. Frankl. Inst. 31: 309, 369. 32: 15-289.
Geodetic Operations in Algeria. (M. Cornu) Nature, 7: 450.
Geoffrey Luttrell's Narrative. All the Year, 26: 524-616. 27: 18, 42.
Geoffrey of Monmouth's History of the Britons. (T. Wright) Arch. 32: 335.
Geoffrey the Lollard; a Historical Romance. (F. Eastwood) Hours at Home, 1: 305, 396, 495. 2: 22-304.

Geoffrin, Madame. (A. Laugel) Nation, **22**: 77.
— Correspondence with King of Poland. (H. James, jr.) Galaxy, **21**: 548.
Geographical and Statistical Science. Meth. Q. **13**: 249.
Geographical Congress, International. Nature, **10**: 267.
Geographical Curiosities. Nature, **15**: 233.
Geographical Exhibition, International. Nature, **12**: 257, 278, 293.
— Curiosities of. Gent. M. n. s. **15**: 328.
Geographical Evolution. (A. Geikie) Nature, **19**: 490. — Pop. Sci. Mo. **15**: 548, 593.
Geographical Explorations west of the 100th Meridian. (G. M. Wheeler) Am. J. Sci. **107**: 388.
Geographical Morality. Dem. R. **28**: 413.
Geographical Notices. (D. C. Gilman) Am. J. Sci. **75**: 305. **76**: 86, 219, 370. **77**: 53, 227, 368. **78**: 89, 411. **79**: 82, 221, 400. **80**: 217, 391. **81**: 51. **83**: 259. **84**: 87, 356. **85**: 223. **87**: 75. **94**: 377. **97**: 98, 377.
Geographical Society, Royal. Quar. **46**: 55. — Ed. R. **28**: 174. **29**: 70.
Geographical Society of London, Formation of. Ed. New Philos. J. **9**: 152.
Geography. (K. von Raumer) Am. J. Educ. **8**: 111.
— Ancient, Bunbury's History of. Nature, **22**: 333.
— and Evolution. (R. Strachey) Pop. Sci. Mo. **8**: 192.
— and History, Connection between. (G. S. Hillard) Am. Inst. of Instruc. **1845**: 269.
— and the Universities. (G. Butler) Contemp. **35**: 671.
— Anniversary Address. (Sir R. I. Murchison) Am. J. Sci. **95**: 14.
— Beginnings of Geographical Science. (G. A. Jackson) Pop. Sci. Mo. **16**: 236.
— Bible, Works on. Chr. Obs. **72**: 850.
— Geikie's Physical. Nature, **16**: 158.
— Goodrich's. Am. Q. **12**: 126. — Am. Mo. R. **2**: 349.
— Grecian and Roman. (S. Willard) No. Am. **29**: 479.
— Hale's. (A. H. Everett) No. Am. **31**: 460.
— Historical. (F. de Rougemont) Bib. Sac. **11**: 217.
— — of 17th Century. Month, **29**: 475. **30**: 339. **31**: 152, 306, 457. **32**: 307.
— Humboldt and Ritter on. (D. C. Gilman) New Eng. **18**: 277.
— Malte-Brun's. U. S. Lit. Gaz. **6**: 102.
— Modern. (N. Hale) No. Am. **7**: 39. — Dub. Univ. **1**: 679.
— — Scientific. (H. J. Klein) Pop. Sci. Mo. **9**: 713.
— Morse's. (N. Hale) No. Am. **16**: 176. — Chr. Mo. Spec. **7**: 664.
— Murray's Encyclopædia of. So. Lit. Mess. **9**: 307, 353.
— National and International. Nature, **24**: 577.
— Northern. So. R. n. s. **5**: 229.
— of Ancient Asia. (Sir D. K. Sandford) Ed. R. **53**: 306.
— of the 19th Century. Chamb. J. **28**: 291.
— Old Book of. House. Words, **9**: 75, 228.
— Our Geographical Sponsors. (W. W. Crane) Lippinc. **5**: 212.
— Our Globe in 1868. (M. Schele de Vere) Lippinc. **2**: 157. **3**: 400.
— Physical. *See* Physical Geography.
— Pinkerton's. Ed. R. **3**: 67. **10**: 154.
— Place of, in Physical Science. (R. Strachey) Fortn. **24**: 536. Same art. Ecl. M. **85**: 683. Same art. Liv. Age, **127**: 552.
— Progress of. De Bow, **17**: 569. — Penny M. **6**: 278.
— Recent Researches in, 1860. Ed. R. **112**: 295. Same art. Ecl. M. **52**: 171, 316. Same art. Liv. Age, **67**: 549.
— — in 1864. No. Brit. **39**: 357. — So. R. n. s. **5**: 275.
— — in 1880. (C. P. Daly) Pop. Sci. Mo. **17**: 171.
— — in the U. S. Am. J. Sci. **103**: 321.
— Scientific and Artistic. Brit. Q. **15**: 373.
— Smith's Dictionary of. (G. M. Lane) Bib. Sac. **15**: 202.
Geography, Study of. (G. F. Thayer) Am. J. Educ. **8**: 81.
— Teaching of. (J. G. Carter) Am. Inst. of Instruc. **1830**: 53. — Am. J. Educ. **9**: 623.
— — Best Method of. (W. C. Woodbridge) Am. Inst. of Instruc. **1833**: 209. — (W. B. Fowle) Am. Inst. of Instruc. **1845**: 219.
— Woodbridge's. Chr. Mo. Spec. **6**: 493.
Geological and Mineralogical Papers. Gen. Repos. **2**: 327.
Geological Calculus. (W. B. Dawkins) Nature, **1**: 505.
Geological Changes, Influence of, on the Earth's Axis. (G. H. Darwin) Am. J. Sci. **113**: 444.
— Influence of, on the Earth's Rotation. (Sir W. Thomson) Nature, **9**: 345.
Geological Continuity. (H. A. Nicholson) Canad. J. n. s. **13**: 269.
Geological Evidence of the Deity. (T. Archer) Ex. H. Lec. **3**: 181.
Geological History. (D. Trowbridge) Nat. Q. **29**: 284.
— American. (J. D. Dana) Am. J. Sci. **72**: 305.
— Missing Chapters of. (D. T. Ansted) Intel. Obs. **6**: 12.
— of the Earth. (Prof. Esmark) Ed. New Philos. J. **2**: 107.
Geological Inquiry, Importance of. So. Lit. Mess. **1**: 484.
Geological Inquiries, McClelland's. No. Am. **46**: 533.
Geological Knot, Attempt to untie. Brit. Q. **27**: 557. Same art. Ecl. M. **44**: 187.
Geological Map, How to make a. (H. B. Woodward) Pop. Sci. R. **12**: 26.
— of the World. (J. Marcou) Am. Natural. **7**: 345.
Geological Maps, On coloring. (W. Whewell) Nature, **24**: 14.
Geological Odors. Chamb. J. **31**: 126.
Geological Observation; Survey of Great Britain. Brit. Q. **14**: 455.
Geological Phenomena in the Solar System. (L. Saemann) Am. J. Sci. **83**: 36.
Geological Problems, Solution of. (W. H. Barton) Overland, **12**: 526.
Geological Record. Nature, **13**: 322.
Geological Results of the Earth's Contraction by Cooling. (J. D. Dana) Am. J. Sci. **53**: 176.
Geological Science and deceased Geologists. Lond. Q. **7**: 71.
— Phases of. (J. R. Loomis) Chr. R. **16**: 114.
— Progress of. Ed. R. **52**: 43.
Geological Section, How to make a. (D. T. Ansted) Pop. Sci. R. **7**: 386.
Geological Society, Address of the President. (J. Prestwich) Nature, **5**: 431–490. — (J. Evans) Nature, **13**: 334, 377.
— Transactions of. (J. Playfair) Ed. R. **19**: 207. **28**: 174. **29**: 70. — Quar. **34**: 507. — Mo. R. **84**: 86.
Geological Speculations. Dub. Univ. **29**: 447.
Geological Strata, Occurrence and Age of. Westm. **64**: 565.
Geological Studies. (H. Pearce) Dub. Univ. **84**: 321.
Geological Survey, Story of the. Chamb. J. **36**: 356.
Geological Surveys. (A. Williams, jr.) Overland, **12**: 261. — (F. Alger) Chr. Exam. **24**: 363. — Am. J. Sci. **40**: 126. — Dub. Univ. **46**: 679. — (A. R. Leeds) Pop. Sci. Mo. **3**: 226.
— American. (A. Geikie) Nature, **12**: 265. **13**: 1. — (J. D. Whitney) No. Am. **121**: 270.
— of the Territories, 1872. (F. H. Bradley) Am. J. Sci. **106**: 194.
— Utility of, by Government. (J. P. Lesley) Penn Mo. **5**: 199.
Geological Theory in Great Britain, 1870. Ed. R. **131**: 39. Same art. Ecl. M. **74**: 641. Same art. Liv. Age, **104**: 643.
Geological Theories. Chr. Obs. **56**: 161.
Geological Time. (G. H. Darwin) Nature, **17**: 509. — No. Brit. **50**: 406.
— and Evolution. (G. Allen) Gent. M. n. s. **25**: 563.

Geological Time, Chain of Life in. Ecl. M. 96: 200.
— Grasp of. (A. Winchell) Lakeside, 1: 369.
— Measurement of. (A. R. Wallace) Nature, 1: 399, 452.
Geological Works, French. Nature, 10: 100.
Geologist, Personal Recollections of a. Temp. Bar, 4: 473.
Geologists, American. First Meeting. Am. J. Sci. 39: 189.
— Second Meeting. Am. J. Sci. 41: 158.
— — Prof. Hitchcock's Address. Am. J. Sci. 41: 232. — Westm. 38: 40.
— Third Meeting. Am. J. Sci. 43: 146.
— — Prof. Silliman's Address. Am. J. Sci. 43: 216.
— Fourth Meeting. Am. J. Sci. 45: 135, 310.
— Fifth Meeting. Am. J. Sci. 47: 94.
— — Prof. Rogers's Address. Am. J. Sci. 47: 137.
Geologists, Discoveries of modern. Fraser, 5: 552. 6: 54, 278. 7: 139, 578.
Geology. (L. Lincklaen) Putnam, 5: 449. — (G. W. Featherstonhaugh) No. Am. 32: 471. — So. R. 6: 284. — Am. Q. 6: 73. 7: 361. — Dub. Univ. 45: 679.
— Address at Montreal, 1864. (J. W. Dawson) Am. J. Sci. 88: 231.
— Age of the Laramie Group. (H. M. Bannister) Am. J. Sci. 117: 243.
— and Agriculture. (H. Woodward) Nature, 1: 46. — No. Brit. 16: 390.
— — Burat's. Nature, 10: 458.
— and Anthropology, Ramsay on. Anthrop. R. 1: 484.
— and Astronomy, Testimony of. So. Lit. Mess. 21: 257.
— and the Bible. (J. T. Dutton) Nat. M. 10: 515. — (W. Fishbough) Univ. Q. 2: 349. — (M. Jacobs) Evang. R. 1: 363. — (D. N. Lord) Theo. & Lit. J. 5: 588. — (D. R. Malone) Chr. Q. 8: 13. — (D. Wortman) Am. Presb. R. 14: 613. — Am. Ecl. 2: 87. — (D. W. Clark) Meth. Q. 5: 198. — (M. B. Hope) Princ. 13: 368. — (R. P. Stebbins) Chr. Exam. 29: 335. — Mo. R. 126: 133. — (J. J. Dana) Am. Bib. Repos. 3d s. 2: 296. — Ecl. R. 71: 426. — Am. J. Sci. 25: 26. — Chr. R. 15: 380. — Am. Bib. Repos. 7: 210. — (E. Hitchcock) Am. Bib. Repos. 5: 439. 6: 261. 7: 448. 9: 78. 10: 328. 11: 1. — (M. Stuart) Am. Bib. Repos. 6: 46. — (E. Pond) Am. Bib. Repos. 12: 1. — (J. L. Kingsley) Am. J. Sci. 30: 114. — Lit. & Theo. R. 1: 120. — Knick. 7: 441. — Chr. Obs. 28: 235–750. 29: 91, 160. 34: 369, 479. 37: 308, 446. 70: 502. — Cong. M. 20: 496–706. — Dub. R. 16: 345. Same art. Ecl. M. 3: 185. — Dub. Univ. 75: 477, 550. — Ecl. R. 49: 39. — Hogg, 1: 220. — Theo. & Lit. J. 8: 108. 9: 215. 10: 350, 696. 11: 694. 12: 133. 13: 76. — U. S. Cath. M. 4: 431. 5: 306.
— — Malloy on. Dub. R. 66: 403.
— — H. Miller on. Theo. & Lit. J. 7: 119. 10: 97.
— — J. P. Smith's Lectures on. Cong. M. 23: 292, 299, 613. — (D. N. Lord) Theo. & Lit. J. 5: 588. 6: 1. — Ecl. R. 71: 426.
— — Young on. Cong. M. 22: 121, 243.
— and Chemistry. So. Q. 3: 182.
— and the Development Theory. Dub. Univ. 39: 81.
— and the Fall. (E. Fisher) Univ. Q. 14: 373.
— and Genesis. (S. E. Shepard) Chr. Q. 8: 243. — Blackw. 82: 312. — Am. Church R. 23: 343. — Kitto, 6: 261. — No. Brit. 27: 325. *See* Bible; Genesis; Creation.
— and History. (G. Allen) Fraser, 101: 769. Same art. Ecl. M. 95: 228. Same art. Pop. Sci. Mo. 17: 495.
— and Man. (E. C. Bolles) Univ. Q. 21: 413.
— and Mineralogy. Dub. Univ. 54: 455.
— — Buckland on. Ed. R. 65: 1.
— and Mosaic Records. (S. Comfort) Nat. M. 5: 540. — (O. Föckler) Meth. Q. 26: 187. — (E. Hitchcock) Cong. M. 19: 82. — (H. Miller) Ex. H. Lec. 9: 377. — (L. Sternberg) Evang. R. 19: 138. — Brit. Q. 54: 90. Same art. Ecl. M. 77: 542. — Westm. 68: 176.
Geology and Mosaic Records, Higgins on. Chr. Obs. 32: 742.
— — Penn on. Ecl. R. 37: 37.
— and Natural History. (W. B. O. Peabody) No. Am. 61: 181.
— and Natural Religion. (E. Hitchcock) Am. Bib. Repos. 5: 113. — Quar. 56: 31. — Mo. R. 141: 330. — Ecl. R. 65: 23.
— and Palæontology. Pop. Sci. R. 2: 272. Same art. Ecl. M. 59: 343.
— and the Picturesque. Art J. 7: 275.
— and Protestantism. Dub. R. 44: 375.
— and Theology. (C. H. Hitchcock) Bib. Sac. 24: 363. — Chr. Obs. 59: 516.
— — Analogies between. (B. F. Hosford) Bib. Sac. 15: 300.
— — Hugh Miller's. Kitto, 22: 413.
— — Relations of. So. Q. 21: 48.
— and Zoölogy. For. Q. 25: 171.
— Animals and Plants in relation to Time. (St. G. Mivart) Contemp. 37: 99.
— Ansted's Practical. Month, 4: 199.
— Archaic Ages. (W. Downes) Belgra. 42: 413. Same art. Ecl. M. 95: 722.
— as revealed to Agriculture. (F. P. Lesley) Penn Mo. 12: 140.
— Atheisms of. Ecl. R. 107: 61. Same art. Ecl. M. 43: 545.
— Bakewell's. New York R. 5: 457. — Mo. R. 82: 164. 94: 657.
— Breislak's. Ed. R. 27: 144.
— Brown's. Am. Mo. R. 3: 46.
— Buckland's. Chr. R. 2: 552. — Quar. 29: 138. — Mus. 29: 77.
— Campbell's Circular Notes. Nature, 13: 481.
— Changes caused by the Deluge. (D. C. McLaren) Theo. & Lit. J. 12: 263.
— Chemical Study of. (D. Forbes) Pop. Sci. R. 7: 248.
— Conversations on. Mo. R. 117: 221. — (J. Tomlinson) Peop. J. 7: 103–354.
— Dana's Manual of. (E. J. Chapman) Canad. J. n. s. 8: 49. — (A. Gray) No. Am. 97: 372. — (J. Johnston) Meth. Q. 25: 378.
— Darwin's. (J. W. Judd) Nature, 15: 289.
— Daubrée's Experimental. (J. L. Smith) Am. J. Sci. 119: 386.
— De la Beche's. Am. Mo. R. 2: 19.
— Discussion of sundry Objections to. (J. B. Perry) Cong. Q. 12: 217.
— Doctrine of Uniformity in. (H. W. Crosskey) Mod. R. 1: 336.
— Dynamical. (T. S. Hunt) Am. J. Sci. 105: 264.
— Earth Sculpture. (A. Geikie) Nature, 9: 50, 89, 110.
— Engineering. (W. H. Penning) Ecl. Engin. 20: 473. 21: 40.
— Evolution of the Science, 1842. Chr. Rem. 3: 161.
— Facts and Inferences of. (G. W. Montgomery) Univ. Q. 2: 1.
— Few Words on. (M. Norris) Godey, 46: 19.
— Field, Penning's. Nature, 14: 471
— First Chapter of the Geological Period. (D. Forbes) Pop. Sci. R. 11: 349. Same art. Ecl. M. 80: 32.
— for Beginners. Ecl. R. 77: 558.
— Future of. Westm. 58: 67.
— Geikie's Story of a Boulder. Canad. J. n. s. 3: 493.
— Green's. Nature, 13: 505.
— Greenough's. Ed. R. 33: 80. — Ed. Mo. R. 4: 557. — Mo. R. 90: 376.
— Harvard School of. (N. S. Shaler) Am. Natural. 10: 29.
— Hayden's Essays on. (J. W. Webster) No. Am. 12: 134.
— Hints to Students in. (P. A. Brown) So. Lit. Mess. 1: 162, 300.

Geology, History of. Cong. M. 19: 352-565.
— Hitchcock's. (S. L. Dana) No. Am. 52: 103.
— Hitchcock's Religion of. (D. N. Lord) Theo. & Lit. J. 5: 353. — (R. P. Stebbins) Chr. Exam. 53: 51. — Ecl. R. 75: 216. Same art. Am. Ecl. 3: 576. — Ecl. R. 95: 468. — Kitto, 9: 281. — Prosp. R. 7: 458.
— Hudson River Age of the Taconic Schists. (J. D. Dana) Am. J. Sci. 117: 375. 118: 61.
— Human Period in. Chamb. J. 58: 593.
— Hunt's Essays on. (J. D. Dana) Am. J. Sci. 109: 102.
— Huttonian and Neptunian Systems of. (F. Jeffrey) Ed. R. 2: 337.
— Igneous Rocks and Volcanoes. (T. S. Hunt) Canad. J. n. s. 3: 201.
— Importance of Surveying in. (B. S. Lyman) Ecl. Engin. 11: 334.
— in 1851. Dub. Univ. 38: 639. Same art. Ecl. M. 25: 172.
Introduction to the Study of. Dub. Univ. 2: 167.
— Intrusive Rocks of Montreal. (T. S. Hunt) Canad. J. n. s. 5: 426.
— Ireland and Spain formerly connected by Land. St. James, 5: 409.
— Is the Science true? Am. Presb. R. 1: 83.
— Jukes's Manual of. Nature, 5: 170.
— Lecture on. (A. Geikie) Nature, 7: 164, 183.
— Lyell's Elements of. Ed. R. 69: 406.
— — Student's Edition. (J. B. Perry) Bib. Sac. 29: 479.
— Lyell's Principles of. (T. McK. Hughes) Nature, 5: 165, 466. — (Sir H. de la Beche) Quar. 48: 411. — (W. Whewell) Quar. 47: 103. 53: 406. — Quar. 89: 213. — Mo. R. 123: 38. 127: 352. — Mus. 18: 13, 107. — (H. B. Adams) No. Am. 107: 465.
— Mantell's Wonders of. (B. Silliman) Am. J. Sci. 39: 1.
— Middle Age of. (L. Agassiz) Atlan. 12: 212.
— Miller's Cruise of the Betsey. Fraser, 58: 292. Same art. Liv. Age, 59: 437.
— Miller's Footprints of the Creator. No. Brit. 12: 239. Same art. Liv. Age, 25: 145. — (Sir D. Brewster) No. Brit 12: 443. — (F. Close) Ex. H. Lec. 13: 239.
— Miller's Testimony of the Rocks. Am. Ch. Mo. 2: 229. — Canad. J. n. s. 2: 201. — Chr. Obs. 58: 14, 547. — Chr. R. 22: 449. — Brit. Q. 26: 255. Same art. Ecl. M. 42: 271. — Liv. Age, 54: 65. — Tait, n. s. 24: 261, 354.
— Modern Schools of. Quar. 125: 188.
— Murchison's Discoveries in. Ed. R. 112: 87.
— Murchison's Siluria. (Sir D. Brewster) No. Brit. 21: 505. — Quar. 64: 102. — (B. Silliman) Am. J. Sci. 68: 394. — (J. D. Whitney) Am. J. Sci. 69: 371.
— Museum of practical. (R. Hunt) St. James, 3: 3. — (Sir R. I. Murchison) Am. J. Sci. 72: 232. — Chamb. J. 26: 9. — Fraser, 43: 618. Same art. Ecl. M. 23: 478. — Am. J. Educ. 6: 239. — Penny M. 12: 319.
— New Museum of. Nature, 13: 227.
— not atheistical. Chr. Obs. 39: 210.
— Objections to modern. Chr. Obs. 39: 152, 199.
— Ocean, Geology of the Drift. Ecl. M. 50: 56, 163.
— of the Alps. (T. S. Hunt) Am. J. Sci. 103: 1.
— of Amazon River. (C. F. Hartt) Am. Natural. 8: 673.
— of America. (T. A. Conrad) Am. J. Sci. 35: 237. — Ed. R. 30: 374. — Westm. 38: 76. — Anal. M. 13: 322. — (T. S. Hunt) Am. J. Sci. 81: 392. — West. J. 13: 256. — (H. D. Rogers) J. Frankl. Inst. 63: 224, 319, 363.
— — Catlin's. (T. R. Jones) Nature, 2: 371.
— — Emmons on. Am. J. Sci. 69: 397.
— — Hayden's. Nature, 4: 24.
— — Marcou's. (J. D. Dana) Am. J. Sci. 76: 323.
— — Pioneers in. (G. W. Clinton) Hist. M. 19: 21.
— — Plan of Development in. (J. D. Dana) Am. J. Sci. 72: 335.
Geology of Andes of Ecuador. (J. Orton) Am. J. Sci. 97: 242.
— of Appalachians. (N. S. Shaler) Am. Natural. 5: 178.
— of the Arctic Regions. (C. E. de Rance) Nature, 11: 447-508.
— of Bosphorus. (G. Washburn) Am. J. Sci. 106: 186.
— of Brazil. (C. F. Hartt) Am. J. Sci. 111: 466.
— of the Burlington Limestone. (W. H. Niles and C. Wachsmuth) Am. J. Sci. 92: 95.
— of California. (J. D. Whitney) Am. J. Sci. 88: 256.
— — of San Francisco County. Pioneer, 1: 225.
— — Whitney's. (W. H. Brewer) Am. J. Sci. 91: 231, 351.
— of Canada, 1853-56. (S. Fleming) Canad. J. n. s. 1: 238. — Canad. J. n. s. 3: 320. 4: 265.
— — of Belleville. (E. J. Chapman) Canad. J. n. s. 5: 41.
— — of Ontario. (E. J. Chapman) Canad. J. n. s. 14: 580.
— — of S. W. Ontario. (T. S. Hunt) Am. J. Sci. 96: 355.
— — Physical. (C. Robb) Canad. J. n. s. 5: 497.
— — Quebec Group of Rocks. (Sir W. E. Logan) Canad. J. n. s. 6: 40.
— of China and Japan. (R. Pumpelly) Am. J. Sci. 91: 145. — (A. S. Bickmore) Am. J. Sci. 95: 209. — (Baron F. von Richthofen) Am. J. Sci. 100: 410.
— of Connecticut; Chloritic Formation of the New Haven Region. (J. D. Dana) Am. J. Sci. 111: 119.
— of Costa Rica. (W. M. Gabb) Am. J. Sci. 109: 198.
— of N. E. Dakota. (F. V. Hayden) Am. J. Sci. 93: 15.
— of the Deluge. Ed. R. 39: 196.
— of the Drift. Lond. Q. 13: 375.
— of England. Ed. R. 29: 311. Same art. Portfo. (Den.) 20: 91.
— — Cretaceous Rocks of. (P. B. Brodie) Recr. Sci. 2: 293.
— — Excursion to Cotswold Hills. (J. R. Leifchild) Recr. Sci. 2: 88.
— — Origin of our Scenery. (H. B. Woodward) Pop. Sci. R. 14: 57.
— — Rambles in Montgomeryshire. (J. R. Leifchild) Recr. Sci. 3: 185.
— — Scene in Isle of Wight. (S. J. Mackie) Recr. Sci. 1: 126.
— — Silurian, Cambrian, and Laurentian Systems. Brit. Q. 48: 125.
— — Silurian, Devonian, and Carboniferous Rocks in the London Era. (R. Etheridge) Pop. Sci. R. 18: 279.
— — Woodward's. Nature, 14: 556.
— of France, Scrope's. (C. Lyell) Quar. 36: 437.
— — Excursions of Geological Society for 1878. (E. D. Cope) Am. Natural. 12: 771.
— of Great Britain. Brit. Q. 14: 455.
— of the Green Mountains. (J. D. Dana) Am. J. Sci. 103: 179, 250.
— of the Gulf of Mexico. (E. W. Hilgard) Am. J. Sci. 102: 391. — (E. W. Hilgard) Am. Natural. 5: 514.
— of Henry Mts., Gilbert's Report. Am. J. Sci. 119: 17.
— of the Hudson's Bay Territories. (A. K. Isbister) Am. J. Sci. 71: 313.
— of Illinois, Upper. (C. U. Shepard) Am. J. Sci. 34: 134.
— of Indiana. Nature, 8: 228.
— of Iowa, Hall ana Whitney's Report on. Am. J. Sci. 77: 103.
— — Southwestern. (C. A. White) Am. J. Sci. 94: 23.
— of Jesso, Japan. Penn Mo. 7: 30.
— of Kansas. (F. V. Hayden) Am. J. Sci. 94: 32. — (G. C. Swallow) Am. J. Sci. 76: 182.
— — Carboniferous and Cretaceous Rocks. (F. B. Meek) Am. J. Sci. 89: 157.
— — Lower Cretaceous. (F. B. Meek and F. V. Hayden) Am. J. Sci. 77: 219.
— — Triassic. (F. B. Meek and F. V. Hayden) Am. J. Sci. 77: 31.

Geology of Kentucky, Owen on. J. Frankl. Inst. **66**: 138.
— of Lower Louisiana. (E. W. Hilgard) Am. J. Sci. **97**: 77.
— Reconnoissance of. (E. W. Hilgard) Am. J. Sci. **98**: 331.
— of Massachusetts. (C. T. Jackson) No. Am. **42**: 422. — (C. B. Adams) No. Am. **56**: 435. — (E. Hitchcock) Am. J. Sci. **1**: 106. **22**: 1. — (C. U. Shepard) Am. J. Sci. **36**: 363.
— of Michigan. (E. J. Chapman) Canad. J. n. s. **7**: 73.
— of the Mississippi Delta. (E. W. Hilgard) Am. J. Sci. **101**: 238, 356, 425.
— of Missouri. (H. King) West. J. **8**: 228.
— — Researches in. (M. M. Manghas) West. J. **9**: 382.
— — Survey of. (M. Tarver) West. J. **3**: 12, 76.
— of Narragansett Bay. (N. S. Shaler) Am. Natural. **6**: 518, 611, 751.
— of New England, Eastern. (T. S. Hunt) Am. J. Sci. **100**: 83.
— of New York. New York R. **4**: 71. **5**: 477. **8**: 103. — (G. E. Hayes) Am. J. Sci. **31**: 241. **35**: 86. — Am. J. Sci. **36**: 1. **39**: 95. **40**: 73. **42**: 227. **46**: 143. **48**: 296. **51**: 43. **53**: 57, 164.
— of Nova Scotia, Dawson's. Canad. J. n. s. **1**: 39.
— of the older Rocks. (Sir R. I. Murchison) Am. J. Sci. **83**: 1.
— of Oregon. (T. Condon) Overland, **3**: 355.
— of Oxford, Phillips's. Nature, **5**: 145.
— of Palestine. (A. Geikie) Nature, **1**: 509.
— of Pennsylvania; Ancient Sea. (A. R. Leeds) J. Frankl. Inst. **92**: 55, 133.
— — Foundation Stones. (A. R. Leeds) J. Frankl. Inst. **91**: 337, 412.
— — Survey of 1873. (J. P. Lesley) J. Frankl. Inst. **95**: 194.
— of Russia. Quar. **77**: 348.
— — Murchison's. Brit. Q. **6**: 289. — (Sir D. Brewster) No. Brit. **5**: 179. — Am. J. Sci. **53**: 153.
— of Santa Domingo. (W. M. Gabb) Am. J. Sci. **101**: 252.
— of Scotland. Ed. R. **38**: 413.
— — Changes in recent Times. No. Brit. **36**: 314. Same art. Ecl. M. **57**: 1.
— — Clydesdale and Arran. No. Brit. **32**: 273.
— — Geikie's Map of. Nature, **14**: 567.
— — Recent Discoveries in. No. Brit. **35**: 125.
— of Spanish Peninsula, Bibliog. of. Pract. M. **5**: 163.
— of Texas, Western. (W. P. Jenney) Am. J. Sci. **107**: 25.
— — and of Chihuahua, Mexico. (J. P. Kimball) Am. J. Sci. **98**: 378.
— of the United States; Brown Hematite Deposits of the Great Valley. (F. Prime, jr.) Am. J. Sci. **109**: 433.
— — Chart of. (F. H. Bradley) Am. J. Sci. **112**: 286.
— — Colorado Plateau Province as a Field for. (G. N. Gilbert) Am. J. Sci. **112**: 16, 85.
— — Country north of the Colorado. (J. W. Powell) Am. J. Sci. **105**: 456.
— — Cretaceous Strata of. (J. Hall) Am. J. Sci. **74**: 72.
— — Marcou's Geological Map. Am. J. Sci. **67**: 199. — (W. P. Blake) Am. J. Sci. **72**: 383.
— — of Eastern Margins of the Rocky Mountains. (F. V. Hayden) Am. J. Sci. **95**: 322.
— — of Eastern Uintah Mountains. (O. C. Marsh) Am. J. Sci. **111**: 191.
— — of the 40th Parallel, King's. (R. Pumpelly) Am. J. Sci. **117**: 296.
— — — Paleozoic Subdivisions in. (C. King) Am. J. Sci. **111**: 475.
— — of the Great Lakes. (J. S. Newberry) Am. Natural. **4**: 193.
— — of the Lake Superior Land District. (J. W. Foster and J. D. Whitney) Am. J. Sci. **67**: 11.
Geology of the United States, of Missouri and Red River Country, Featherstonhaugh's Report on, 1835. J. Frankl. Inst. **21**: 109, 184.
— — of Missouri and Yellowstone Rivers. (F. V. Hayden) Am. J. Sci. **81**: 229.
— — of North. States. (J. W. Webster) No. Am. **11**: 225.
— — of Southwest. (E. W. Hilgard) Am. J. Sci. **104**: 265.
— — of Western States. (J. Hall) Am. J Sci. **42**: 51.
— of Utah Mining Districts. (B. Silliman) Am. J. Sci. **103**: 195.
— of Vermont. (T. S. Hunt) Am. J. Sci. **96**: 222.
— — and Berkshire. (J. D. Dana) Am. J. Sci. **114**: 37, 257.
— — Western. (J. B. Perry) Am. J. Sci. **97**: 341.
— of Virginia, in the Blue Ridge. (W. M. Fontaine) Am J. Sci. **109**: 14, 93.
— — Great Conglomerate on New River. (W. M. Fontaine) Am. J. Sci. **107**: 459, 573.
— of Wisconsin, etc., Owen's. Am. J. Sci. **66**: 86.
— of Western Wyoming. (T. B. Comstock) Am. J. Sci. **106**: 426.
— Old Red Sandstone of Western Europe. (A. Geikie) Nature, **17**: 471.
— Opinions of Voltaire and Laplace on. (P. M. Duncan) Pop. Sci. R. **19**: 310.
— Past and future Work of. (J. Prestwich) Nature, **11**: 290, 315.
— Philosophy of modern. (G. Bugg) Chr. Obs. **28**: 367.
— Physical. (S. Haughton) Nature, **18**: 266.
— Physiographic and Dynamical. (R. Owen) J. Frankl. Inst. **92**: 270.
— Popular. (C. Kingsley) Pop. Sci. Mo. **1**: 613. — (J. Mitchinson) Contemp. **4**: 37.
— — and Artistic. (E. Forbes) Dub. Univ. **42**: 338.
— Post-Tertiary. (A. H. Green) Nature, **9**: 318, 339.
— Pre-Adamite World. So. Lit. Mess. **21**: 522.
— Present State of, 1851. Dub. Univ. **38**: 639.
— Principles of. Am. J. Sci. **21**: 1. — Mus. **20**: 597.
— Progress of modern. Lond. Q. **26**: 157. — Quar. **106**: 138.
— Puzzles of. Ecl. M. **42**: 25.
— Recent Advances in. (J. W. Foster) Am. Natural. **4**: 449.
— Recent Discoveries in. (R. Patterson) Am. Presb. R. **18**: 215. — Am. Ecl. **1**: 386.
— Recent Theories in. (F. Bowen) No. Am. **69**: 256
— Recent Works on, 1838. Ecl. R. **67**: 301.
— Religion of. (J. J. Dana) Bib. Sac. **10**: 505. — (C. H. Hitchcock) Bib. Sac. **17**: 673. — (J. S. Lee) Univ. Q. **8**: 329.
— Religious Aspect of. (A. P. Stanley) Good Words, **16**: 273.
— Scottish School of. (A. Geikie) Nature, **5**: 37, 52.
— Sedimentary Rocks. (T. S. Hunt) Canad. J. n. s. **2**: 355.
— Siluria. Hogg, **13**: 57.
— Silurian Beach. (L. Agassiz) Atlan. **11**: 460.
— Silurian System. (T. A. Conrad) Am. J. Sci. **38**: 86. — Ed. R. **73**: 1.
— Skepticism in. Ed. R. **147**: 354. Same art. Liv. Age, **137**: 707.
— Study of. (S. L. Metcalf) Knick. **3**: 225.
— Suggestions on. Cong. M. **20**: 765.
— Systematic, King's. (H. Adams) Nation, **28**: 73.
— Systems of. (T. C. Gray) No. Am. **8**: 396.
— Taconic System. (J. D. Dana) Am. Natural. **6**: 197.
— Three Climates of. (C. B. Warring) Penn Mo. **11**: 377, 470, 554.
— Three great Problems of. (S. H. Janes) Canad. Mo. **12**: 500.
— Town. (C. Kingsley) Good Words, **13**: 18–443.
— Treatise on, in Encyclopædia Brit. Chr. Rem. **4**: 233.
— Ure's System of. Mo. R. **118**: 591.
— Van Rensselaer's Lectures on. U. S. Lit. Gaz. **2**: 287.
— *versus* Development. Fraser, **42**: 355.

Geology, Volcanic. New York R. **3**: 20.
— Voyage of H. M. S. Beagle. Brit. Q. **5**: 358.
— Werner on Veins. (J. Playfair) Ed. R. **18**: 80.
— What is under the Plow. (J. E. Taylor) Belgra. **13**: 478.
See Earth; Creation.
Geomancy, Divination by. Colburn, **138**: 115.
Geometric Tracery. Art J. **3**: 86.
Geometrical Instincts. (T. Hill) Unita. R. **2**: 218.
Geometrical Puzzles. (F. R. J. Hervey) Once a Week, **16**: 64, 111.
Geometrical Teaching. Nature, **23**: 415.
Geometry. (K. von Raumer) Am. J. Educ. **8**: 155.
— Algebraic, System of. Westm. **3**: 280.
— Analytical. (A. B. Dod) Princ. **13**: 523.
— Ancient, Methods of. So. R. n. s. **10**: 40.
— and Algebra. (F. J. Grund) Am. Inst. of Instruc. **1830**: 183.
— and Biology. (T. Hill) Unita. R. **9**: 129.
— and the Calculus. So. R. **1**: 107.
— Axioms of. (J. P. N. Land) Mind, **3**: 551. — (H. Helmholtz) Mind, **1**: 301. **3**: 212.
— — Origin and Meaning of. (H. Helmholtz) Ecl. Engin. **15**: 501.
— Burchett's Practical Plane. Nature, **13**: 223.
— Descriptive, of one Plane. Math. Mo. **3**: 133.
— Elementary Practical. (J. M. Wilson) Nature, **4**: 387.
— Fundamental Definitions and Propositions of. (S. Newcomb) Nature, **21**: 293.
— Helmholtz on. (W. S. Jevons) Nature, **4**: 481.
— Hypotheses at the Bases of. (B. Riemann) Nature, **8**: 14, 36.
— Imaginary, and Truth of Axioms. (G. H. Lewes) Fortn. **22**: 192.
— Improvements needed in. So. R. n. s. **6**: 373.
— Leslie's Elements of. (J. Playfair) Ed. R. **20**: 79. — Ecl. R. **11**: 193. — Quar. **4**: 25.
— Morell's. Nature, **3**: 323.
— The new. Nature, **13**: 102.
— New Works on. Nature, **6**: 118.
— of Position applied to Surveying. (J. B. McMaster) Ecl. Engin. **18**: 9, 177.
— Pre-Euclidian. Nature, **3**: 483.
— Problems relating to Curves. (J. W. Martin) Canad. J. n. s. **5**: 331.
— Second Book in. (T. Hill) Math. Mo. **1**: 252, 283, 409. **2**: 102, 140, 320.
— Smith's Blanchet's Legendre. So. R. n. s. **12**: 95.
— Teaching and Study of. (A. T. Bledsoe) So. R. n. s. **1**: 286. — (Dr. Hirst) Nature, **5**: 401.
— Uses of. (T. Hill) Bib. Sac. **32**: 498.
— Walker's Elements of. (C. C. Felton) No. Am. **30**: 389.
— Watson's Descriptive. Nature, **11**: 265.
— without Axioms. (T. P. Thompson) Westm. **13**: 503. **20**: 424.
Georama, The. Lond. M. **20**: 501.
George I. of England. (W. M. Thackeray) Cornh. **2**: 1. Same art. Liv. Age, **66**: 323. Same art. Harper, **21**: 395.
— and Aphroessa Island. Once a Week, **15**: 38.
— Early Days of; Lady Cowper's Diary. Fraser, **69**: 566.
George II. (W. M. Thackeray) Cornh. **2**: 175. Same art. Liv. Age, **66**: 550. Same art. Harper, **21**: 525.
— Court of. (N. S. Dodge) Am. Whig R. **8**: 561.
— — Costume and Characters of. (A. Strickland) Colburn, **74**: 218.
— Era of. Quar. **128**: 110. Same art. Liv. Age, **104**: 579.
— his Queen, and Frederick, Prince of Wales. (H. B. Baker) Gent. M. n. s. **18**: 466.
— Last ten Years of. Mo. R. **98**: 1.
— Life and Times of. Blackw. **64**: 327. — So. Lit. Mess. **15**: 296. — Liv. Age, **11**: 393.
George II., Memoirs of Reign of, Hervey's. Quar. **82**: 501. Same art. Ecl. M. **14**: 173. — Ed. R. **88**: 488. — Ecl. R. **88**: 184. — Temp. Bar, **54**: 173. — Fraser, **37**: 665.
— Reign of. Blackw. **61**: 194. Same art. Ecl. M. **10**: 456. — Ed. R. **37**: 1.
— Times of. Blackw. **62**: 431. Same art. Liv. Age, **16**: 17.
— Walpole's Memoirs of. Colburn, **4**: 357.
George III. (W. M. Thackeray) Cornh. **2**: 257. Same art. Liv. Age, **67**: 67. Same art. Harper, **21**: 671. — Blackw. **6**: 574. **101**: 699.
— and Catholic Question. (H. Brougham) Ed. R. **46**: 163.
— and Fox. Quar. **105**: 463.
— and George IV., Public Characters of Reigns of. (H. Brougham) Ed. R. **68**: 191. **69**: 1. **70**: 90.
— — Reigns of. Mus. **18**: 385. **33**: 452, 577. — Mo. R. **147**: 366.
— and his Times. Art J. **15**: 209.
— and Pitt, Letters of. (J. W. Croker) Quar. **36**: 285.
— and the Regency, Memoirs of. Dub. Univ. **48**: 84.
— Anecdotes of. Anal. M. **15**: 497. — Chr. Mo. Spec. **2**: 632.
— Belsham's Reign of. Ed. R. **2**: 177.
— Buckingham's Memoirs of. New Q. **2**: 157. **4**: 287.
— Character of. Quar. **122**: 281. Same art. Liv. Age, **93**: 457. — Liv. Age, **92**: 480.
— Correspondence of, with Bishop Hurd. Bentley, **26**: 325, 510.
— Court of. So. R. n. s. **16**: 349.
— — and Cabinets of. Quar. **92**: 421. — Ecl. R. **102**: 72.
— Death of. Lond. M. **1**: 329.
— Earlier Years of the Reign of. Fraser, **45**: 485.
— Early Administrations of. (T. B. Macaulay) Ed. R. **80**: 526. — Ed. R. **126**: 1. Same art. Liv. Age, **94**: 771.
— Family of, with portraits. (K. M. Rowland) Harper, **61**: 511.
— First Decade of Reign of. Quar. **90**: 503. Same art. Liv. Age, **33**: 337.
— Insanity of. (H. Butterworth) Atlan. **37**: 534. — (I. Ray) Liv. Age, **46**: 515. Same art. Ecl. M. **37**: 172. — Liv. Age, **73**: 335.
— Knight's Pictorial History of Reign of. Ecl. R. **78**: 134. **84**: 205.
— Letters to Lord North. (C. C. Hazewell) No. Am. **105**: 357. — Liv. Age, **47**: 672.
— Life and Times of. Ecl. R. **125**: 1.
— Massey's History of. Ecl. R. **101**: 577.
— Men of Letters of Reign of. *See* Brougham's Lives.
— Mental Grandeur of his Reign. (A. Alison) So. Lit. Mess. **9**: 517.
— Observations on. Meth. M. **43**: 299.
— Opposition under. Canad. Mo. **5**: 265. — So. R. n. s. **15**: 349.
— Phillimore's Reign of. Ed. R. **118**: 523. — Ecl. R. **120**: 46.
— Private Correspondence of. Liv. Age, **23**: 350. **24**: 121.
— Rae's Reign of. (A. V. Dicey) Nation, **18**: 397.
— Recovery from Illness, 1788. (J. Humphreys) Colburn, **157**: 781.
— Reign of. Chr. Obs. **6**: 19–800. **7**: 161, 226, 440. **8**: 22.
— Rose's Memoirs of Times of. Chr. Obs. **60**: 132.
— Secret Service under. Liv. Age, **130**: 635.
— Social Era of. Blackw. **102**: 154. Same art. Liv. Age, **95**: 140.
— Statesmen of Time of, Brougham's. Mo. R. **162**: 441.
— Statue at Windsor. Penny M. **1**: 337.
— Times of. So. R. n. s. **18**: 275.
— Two Attempts to assassinate. All the Year, **17**: 113

George III., Walpole's Memoirs of Reign of. (J. W. Croker) Quar. **27**: 178. — (J. W. Croker) Quar. **77**: 253. Same art. Ecl. M. **7**: 493. — Dub. Univ. **25**: 227. — Tait, n. s. **12**: 117. Same art. Ecl. M. **4**: 415. — Blackw. **57**: 353. — Blackw. **58**: 713. Same art. Liv. Age, **8**: 121. — Ecl. R. **109**: 239. — Liv. Age, **60**: 613. **61**: 375.
George IV. (W. M. Thackeray) Cornh. **2**: 385. Same art. Liv. Age, **67**: 341. Same art. Harper, **21**: 823.
— and Queen Caroline. (H. Brougham) Ed. R. **67**: 1, 556. **68**: 191.
— and William IV.; Greville Journals. (E. L. Stanley) Fortn. **22**: 798. — Brit. Q. **61**: 150. — Ed. R. **140**: 515. Same art. Liv. Age, **124**: 3. — Liv. Age, **123**: 730. *See* Greville Memoirs.
— Character of. Westm. **14**: 103. — Mus. **18**: 385.
— Coronation of, 1821. Niles's Reg. **21**: 54. — (W. Abbot) Knick. **23**: 138. — (E. Herbert) Lond. M. **4**: 184. — Bentley, **4**: 65. — Blackw. **9**: 337. — Meth. M. **44**: 917. — Portfo.(Den.) **26**: 340.
— Croly's Life and Times of. Am. Q. **9**: 314. — So. R. **7**: 251. — Ecl. R. **52**: 477. — Mus. **42**: 349.
— Court of. Bentley, **45**: 479. — Ecl. M. **51**: 518.
— — Memoirs of. Dub. R. **46**: 252. — Ed. R. **110**: 60.
— — Secret History of. Colburn, **79**: 14–465. **80**: 161–432. **81**: 58–425.
— Death of. Fraser, **1**: 758.
— Diary of Times of. (J. W. Croker) Quar. **61**: 150.
— Fashion and Frivolity under. Temp. Bar, **63**: 197.
— Fitzgerald's Life of. Westm. **116**: 70. — (A. V. Dicey) Nation, **33**: 51.
— Loves of. (P. Fitzgerald) Belgra. **14**: 449.
— Obituary of. Ann. Reg. **6**: 269.
— Times of. Mo. R. **145**: 235.
— — Brougham's Review of. Fraser, **18**: 1.
— Visit to Scotland of, 1822. Blackw. **12**: 253, 268.
— Was he married to Mrs. Fitzherbert? Ecl. M. **38**: 111.
— When he was King. (P. Fitzgerald) Month, **39**: 512. **40**: 80–453. **41**: 1, 153.
— Wilkins's Drama of Statue of. Tait, **3**: 369.
Georges, The four. (W. M. Thackeray) Cornh. **2**: 1–385. Same art. Harper, **21**: 395–823.
— Era of. (J. W. Croker) Quar. **53**: 448.
— Thackeray's. Chamb. J. **26**: 353. Same art. Liv. Age, **52**: 205.
George, St., Patron Saint of England. Liv. Age, **77**: 579.
— a Poem. (F. Parke) Dub. Univ. **88**: 576.
— and the Dragon, Legend of. Chr. Rem. **45**: 316. — (Mrs. Bushby) Bentley, **63**: 488. Same art. Ecl. M. **71**: 823. — Colburn, **146**: 227. — House. Words, **14**: 258.
George, Enos, Bishop. Am. Meth. M. **12**: 5.
George, Ernest. Etchings of the Loire. (P. G. Hamerton) Portfo. **6**: 60.
George, Kara or Czerni, of Servia. Cornh. **32**: 213. Same art. Ecl. M. **85**: 461.
George's little Girl. (M. E. W. Sherwood) Atlan. **43**: 619.
George, Fort, History of. (B. F. DeCosta) Am. Bibliop. **3**: *passim* **9**: 36.
George, Lake. (S. G. W. Benjamin) Harper, **59**: 321.— (T. A. Richards) Harper, **7**: 161.— (H. James, jr.) Nation, **11**: 119, 135. — Putnam, **10**: 145.
— a Poem. (M. B. Morse) Cath. World, **32**: 272.
— and Lake Champlain. (J. Bonsall) Potter Am. Mo. **10**: 321.
— College Camp at. (R. R. Bowker) Scrib. **17**: 617.
George Bedillion, Knight. (R. H. Davis) Atlan. **19**: 155, 289.
George Bulcombe; a Novel. So. Lit. Mess. **3**: 49.
George Canterbury's Will. (Mrs. H. Wood) Tinsley, **4**: 193–489. **5**: 35–617. **6**: 65–458
George Eliot. (C. K. Paul) Harper, **62**: 912. — (E. Simcox) 19th Cent. **9**: 778. Same art. Liv. Age, **149**: 791. — Lond. Q. **57**: 154.— (E. Dowden) Contemp. **20**: 403. Same art. Ecl. M. **79**: 562. Same art. Liv. Age, **115**: 100.— (W. C. Brownell) Nation, **31**: 456. — Blackw. **129**: 255. Same art. Liv. Age, **148**: 664. Same art. Ecl. M. **96**: 433. — (G. B. Smith) St. Paul's, **12**: 592.— (F. Maguire, jr.) Internat. R. **7**: 17. — Liv. Age, **58**: 274. **148**: 318. — Ecl. M. **96**: 353. — (M. F. Sullivan) Dial (Ch.), **1**: 181. — (A. E. Johns) So. M. **14**: 65. — Tinsley, **3**: 565. — Victoria, **31**: 56.
— Adam Bede. Ed. R. **110**: 223. — Blackw. **85**: 490. — Westm. **71**: 486. — Dub. R. **47**: 33.
— — and recent Novels. Bent. Q. **1**: 433.
— and Carlyle. (J. Bryce) Nation, **32**: 201.
— and Comtism. Lond. Q. **47**: 446.
— and George H. Lewes. Galaxy, **7**: 801.
— and George Sand. Ecl. M. **88**: 111.
— and Hawthorne. No. Brit. **33**: 165.
— and her Novels. Ev. Sat. **10**: 186.
— Art of. Penn Mo. **10**: 579.
— as a Novelist. Westm. **110**: 105.— (S. B. Herrick) So. R. n. s. **3**: 332.
— as a Poet. (M. Browne) Contemp. **8**: 387. Same art. Ev. Sat. **6**: 79.—(G. A. Simcox) Ev. Sat. **16**: 667.
— Catholic View of. Month, **42**: 272.
— Critical Study of. (L. Stephen) Cornh. **43**: 152. Same art. Liv. Age, **148**: 731. Same art. Ecl. M. **96**: 443.
— Daniel Deronda. Ed. R. **144**: 442. — (H. James, jr.) Atlan. **38**: 684. — (E. P. Whipple) No. Am. **124**: 31. — (S. Colvin) Fortn. **26**: 601. — (A. V. Dicey) Nation, **23**: 230, 245.—Brit. Q. **64**: 472.—Ecl. M. **87**: 657. — (R. R. Bowker) Internat. R. **4**: 68. — (O. G. Garrison) Western, **3**: 603. — Potter Am. Mo. **8**: 75. — (J. Picciotto) Gent. M. n. s. **17**: 593. — Canad. Mo. **9**: 250, 343. **10**: 362. — (A. S. Richardson) Victoria, **28**: 227.
— — Deronda's Mother. Temp. Bar, **49**: 542. Same art. Liv. Age, **133**: 248. Same art. Ecl. M. **88**: 751.
— — Mordecai; a Protest against the Critics by a Jew. (J. Jacobs) Macmil. **36**: 101. Same art. Liv. Age, **134**: 112.
— Early Life of. Liv Age, **148**: 381.
— Felix Holt. Blackw. **100**: 94. — Ed. R. **124**: 435. Same art. Liv. Age, **91**: 432. — (A. G. Sedgwick) No. Am. **103**: 557. — (H. James, jr.) Nation, **3**: 127. — Westm. **86**: 200. — Contemp. **3**: 51. — Ecl. R. **124**: 34. — Chamb. J. **43**: 508.
— — and Romola. Chr. Rem. **52**: 445.
— First Romance of. (R. E. Francillon) Gent. M. n. s. **17**: 411.
— Genius of. Dub. R. **88**: 371. — (Mrs. S. B. Herrick) So. R. n. s. **13**: 205.
— Ideal Ethics of. Liv. Age, **142**: 123.
— in Derbyshire. Lond. Soc. **27**: 311, 439. **28**: 20.
— Later Manner of. Canad. Mo. **11**: 261.
— Legend of Jubal. Macmil. **22**: 1.
— Life and Writings of. (W. F. Rae) Internat. R. **10**: 447, 497.
— Middlemarch. Quar. **134**: 336. — Ed. R. **137**: 246. — (S. Colvin) Fortn. **19**: 142. — Blackw. **112**: 727. Same art. Liv. Age, **116**: 131. Same art. Ecl. M. **80**: 215. — (A. V. Dicey) Nation, **16**: 60, 76. — (T. S. Perry) No. Am. **116**: 432. — Brit. Q. **57**: 407.— Lond. Q. **40**: 99. — Canad. Mo. **3**: 549. — (H. G. Spaulding) O. & N. **7**: 352. — (W. H. Browne) So. M. **12**: 373.
— — and Daniel Deronda. (E. Dowden) Contemp. **29**: 348.
— — and Fleurange, Comparison between. (J. McCarthy) Cath. World, **17**: 775.

George Eliot. Mill on the Floss. Westm. **74**: 24. — Macmil. **3**: 441. — Blackw. **87**: 611. — Dub. Univ. **57**: 192.
— Moral Influence of. Contemp. **39**: 173. Same art. Liv. Age, **148**: 651.
— Novels. Quar. **108**: 469. — (J. Morley) Macmil. **14**: 272. Same art. Ecl. M. **67**: 488. — (H. James, jr.) Atlan. **18**: 479.—(I. M Luyster) Chr. Exam. **70**: 227. — (W. C. Wilkinson) Scrib. **8**: 685. — (H. H. Lancaster) No. Brit. **45**: 197. — Nat. R. **11**: 191. — Ho. & For. R. **3**: 522.
— Poems. (H. James, jr.) No. Am. **119**: 484.
— Religion of. Dub. R. **89**: 433.
— Religious Influence of. (J. E. Carpenter) Unita. R. **3**: 357.
— Romola. Blackw. **116**: 72. — Westm. **80**: 344. — Land We Love, **1**: 134.
— Silas Marner and Holmes's Elsie Venner. Macmil. **4**: 305.
— Spanish Gypsy. Ed. R. **128**: 525. — Westm. **90**: 183. — (H. James, jr.) No. Am. **107**: 620. — (H. James, jr.) Nation, **7**: 12. — (J. Morley) Macmil. **18**: 281. Same art. Ecl. M. **71**: 1276.— Blackw. **103**: 760. — Brit. Q. **48**: 503. — (J. Skelton) Fraser, **78**: 468. — St. James, **22**: 478. — St. Paul's, **2**: 583. — Lond. Q. **31**: 160. — (W. H. Browne) So. R. n. s. **4**: 383. — Ev. Sat. **6**: 1.
— Theophrastus Such. Ed. R. **150**: 557. — (G. Allen) Fortn. **32**: 144. — Westm. **112**: 185.—(G. E. Woodberry) Nation, **28**: 422.—Fraser, **100**: 103.—Canad. Mo. **16**: 333. — (R. W. Boodle) Unita. R. **12**: 292.
— Village Life according to. (T. E. Kebbel) Fraser, **103**: 263. Same art. Liv. Age, **148**: 608.
— Works of. (E. L. Wentworth) Nat. Q. **1**: 455. — (J. R. Haskins) Potter Am. Mo. **9**: 260, 334. — Brit. Q. **45**: 141.
George Karr pays his Debts. Lond. Soc. **18**: 327.
George Lovelace's Temptation. Belgra. **23**: 229.
George Sand. *See* Dudevant, A. L. A. D.
George Silverman's Explanation. (C. Dickens) All the Year, **19**: 180–396. Same art. Atlan. **21**: 118–277.
George Venn and the Ghost. Lond Soc. **8**: 560.
Georgel, Abbé. Ed. R. **30**: 425.
Georges-Weimer, Marguerite. (C. Hervey) Temp. Bar, **62**: 253.
Georgetown, Guiana, Congregational Church at. (J. Ketley) Cong. M. **23**: 1, 166, 835.
Georgetown College, D. C. (D.A.Casserly) Scrib. **20**: 665.
Georgia. De Bow, **10**: 65, 243, 375.
— and her Resources. De Bow, **8**: 39.
— Caruther's Historical Address. So. Q. **3**: 537.
— Centers of primitive Manufacture in. (C. C. Jones, jr.) M. Am. Hist. **5**: 346.
— Cherokee Controversy. (S. E. Sewell) Chr. Exam. **9**: 107. — Ann. Reg. **6**: 91.— So. R. **2**: 541. — Niles's Reg. **32**: 89, 108. **37**: 40. **40**: 244.
— Church's Historical Address. So. Q. **8**: 421.
— Duties and Destiny of. So. Q. **8**: 42.
— Early History of, with map. (S. G. Drake) N. E. Reg. **26**: 260.
— Governor's Message, 1817. Niles's Reg. **13**: 216.
— — 1818. Niles's Reg. **15**: 357.
— — 1819. Niles's Reg. **17**: 221.
— — 1820. Niles's Reg. **19**: 213.
— — 1821. Niles's Reg. **20**: 181.
— — 1822. Niles's Reg. **23**: 203.
— — 1823. Niles's Reg. **25**: 201.
— — 1825. Niles's Reg. **28**: 238, 315.
— — 1826. Niles's Reg. **29**: 200.
— — 1827. Niles's Reg. **33**: 220.
— — 1828. Niles's Reg. **35**: 221.
— — 1829. Niles's Reg. **37**: 205.
Georgia, Governor's Message, 1830. Niles's Reg. **40**: 27.
— — 1831. Niles's Reg. **41**: 313.
— — 1832. Niles's Reg. **43**: 206.
— — 1834. Niles's Reg. **47**: 205.
— Habersham's Expedition, 1782. Hist. M. **4**: 129.
— Historical Sketches of. Knick. **32**: 140, 339.
— Historical Society. So. Q. **3**: 40. — (W. B. Stevens) Am. Q. Reg. **12**: 344.
— — Collections of. Chr. Exam. **29**: 113.
— Illustrated. So. Q. **18**: 24.
— Journey to. (F. K. Butler) Bentley, **12**: 1, 113.
— Miss Kemble's. Liv. Age, **78**: 25.
— Legislature of, 1825. Niles's Reg. **28**: 271, 347.
— Life and Scenery in. Knick. **34**: 113.
— Mineral Resources of. De Bow, **24**: 58.
— Natural History in its Relation to. De Bow, **16**: 354.
— Pedagogue in. (H. Hodges) Putnam, **5**: 187.
— Pine Forests of. Hunt, **43**: 445.
— Public Works of. (A. Norton) No. Am. **23**: 211. — (J. Sparks) No. Am. **24**: 466.
— Scenes. So. Lit. Mess. **2**: 287. **6**: 572, 775. **10**: 260.
— Statistics of, 1869. Am. J. Educ. **18**: 311.
— Stevens's History of. So. Q. **13**: 470. — (C. W. Upham) No. Am. **67**: 291.
— Travels in. (E. King) Scrib. **8**: 385.
Georgia Plantation. (D. C. Barrow, jr.) Scrib. **20**: 830.
Georgia in Turkey. Cornh. **28**: 156. Same art. Liv. Age, **119**: 220. Same art. Ev. Sat. **15**: 210.
— and Caucasus, Klaproth's Travels in, 1807–8. (J. Foster) Ecl. R. **23**: 328.
See Transcaucasia.
Georgie's Wooer; a Tale. All the Year, **40**: 451–544. **41**: 20–93.
Georgie Lisle. (E. Lysaght) Dub. Univ. **83**: 16, 141, 266.
Gerald Fitzgerald. (C. Lever) Dub. Univ. **51**: 1–643. **52**: 3–651. **53**: 31–676. **54**: 102.
Geraldin; a Play. Am. Whig R. **13**: 312.
Geraldine; a Poem. Colburn, **11**: 42.
Geraldine; a Tale of Conscience. Dub. R. **6**: 480.
Geraldine Fitzmaurice. Fraser, **35**: 360.
Geraldine of Desmond. Colburn, **26**: 80.
Geraldine, Surrey's. *See* Fitzgerald, Lady E.
Geramb, Ferdinand. Pilgrimage to Jerusalem, 1831. Colburn, **52**: 351.
Gerando, Auguste de. (M. L. Putnam) Chr. Exam. **58**: 1, 165, 402.
Gerar and its Philistine Inhabitants. Kitto, **25**: 309.
Gerard, Balthazar. Bentley, **29**: 404.
Gerard, Jules, the Lion-Killer of Algeria. Colburn, **101**: 253. Same art. Liv. Age, **42**: 273.
— and Munchausen. Internat. M. **4**: 587.
— Sporting Exploits of. Ecl. M. **37**: 103.
Gerbet, l'Abbé. (C A. Sainte-Beuve)Cath.World, **3**: 308.
Gerhard, Paul. (J. G. Morris) Evang. R. **2**: 282.
Géricault, Théodore. Art J. **3**: 117.
Germs. (J. Tyndall) Nature, **13**: 252, 268. — (J. Tyndall) Am. Natural. **10**: 347.
— Tyndall on. Am. J. Sci. **111**: 305.
Germ Theory. (H. C. Bastian) Nature, **4**: 458. — Nature, **15**: 446. — Chamb. J. **53**: 145. **54**: 717.
— Atmospheric. Nature, **1**: 351.
— and Spontaneous Generation. Contemp. **29**: 901. Same art Sup. Pop. Sci. Mo. **1**: 109.
— in Disease. (H. C. Bastian) Sup. Pop. Sci. Mo. **2**: 310.
Germain, Lord George. Hist. M. **8**: 162.
Germain, Sophie. (I. Scott) Liv. Age, **67**: 378.
German in America. (S. Osgood) Chr. Exam. **51**: 350.
— in England. For. Q. **29**: 370.
— Life of a speculative. Blackw. **45**: 837.
German's Daughter; a Tale. So. Lit. R. **6**: 737.
Germans, Ancient, History of. For. Q. **7**: 145.
— and Celts. Ed. R. **108**: 166.

Germans and Gauls under the Romans. Dub. Univ. **77**: 601.
— and their Literature. Dem. R. **24**: 44.
— Emigration of, to America. (E. Everett) No. Am. **11**: 1. — (W. M. Reynolds) Evang. R. **13**: 1.
— French, and English. Brit. Q. **13**: 331.
— from a Roman Point of View. St. James, **27**: 742.
— in New York City. (C. D. Shanly) Atlan. **19**: 555.
— in Pennsylvania. (G. F. Baer) Mercersb. **23**: 248.
— in the United States. (F. K. Levan) Mercersb. **17**: 523. — (G. Schwab) Nation, **30**: 310. — (E. Spiess) Luth. Q. **5**: 355.
— Life of, 1859. (G. B. Russell) Mercersb. **11**: 536.
— State and Prospects of. (H. Bokum) Am. Inst. of Instruc. **1835**: 89.
— Trials of early. Hist. M. **4**: 100.
— in the West. (J. J. Lalor) Atlan. **32**: 459.
— Origin of. Mo. R. **165**: 151.
— Political Rights of. For. Q. **36**: 90.
— Primeval. Cath. World, **23**: 47.
German Almanacs for 1855. Bentley, **37**: 176. Same art. Ecl. M. **34**: 531.
— 1867. Bentley, **61**: 94.
— 1868. Bentley, **63**: 33.
German-American Romances. Blackw. **57**: 251, 331, 561.
German Amusements. Liv. Age, **71**: 28.
German Anthology. Dub. R. **19**: 312.
— 12th-13th Centuries. Ecl. R. **43**: 308.
German Astronomers. (N. Bowditch) No. Am. **10**: 260.
German Atheism and French Socialism. Hogg, **2**: 241, 264.
German Ballads. (M. von Bothmer) Dub. Univ. **83**: 522. — Dub. Univ. **18**: 19.
— Boyd's Book of. Dub. Univ. **31**: 305.
German Baths and Play-Houses. (F. M. Whitehurst) Belgra. **15**: 319.
German Biblical Criticism. New York R. **2**: 133.
German Boarding-School, Life in a. Fraser, **92**: 353. Same art. Liv. Age, **127**: 116.
German Boys and Men. (M. Pyne) Lippinc. **25**: 730.
German Brothers; a Tale. Dub. Univ. **11**: 646.
German Carbonarist, Biography of a. (J. D. Wallenstein) No. Am. **28**: 58.
German-Catholic Church. (H. Rogers) Ed. R. **83**: 100. — Prosp. R. **1**: 498. — Brit. Q. **3**: 149.
German-Catholic Movement. (J. Walker) Chr. Exam. **42**: 55.
German Church of the United States and Germany. (P. Schaff) Mercersb. **7**: 136.
German Cities, Lingerings in. (H. Bedford) Month, **38**: 18-506. **39**: 31.
German Comic Papers. (J. Duboc) Internat. R. **4**: 191.
German Comic Romances, Early. For. Q. **20**: 287.
German Constancy. Ecl. M. **76**: 115.
German Cotillon. (G. D. Budd) Galaxy, **4**: 145.
German Criminal Trials. Mus. **20**: 203.
German Dialect-Poets. (W.W. Crane) Appleton, **24**: 136.
German Drama. (J. Pollock) Contemp. **21**: 335. — Colburn, **4**: 145.
— and Early English. (W. J. Thoms) Colburn, **61**: 19.
German Dueling. Mus. **25**: 84.
German Epics and English Hexameters. Dub. Univ. **44**: 55.
German Epigrams. Lond. M. **9**: 237, 364, 599.
German Fatherland, What is? (W. Wells) Hours at Home, **3**: 469.
— Where is? Chamb. J. **15**: 305.
German Forest, Hunting in. (J. Whittle) Bentley, **27**: 404.
German Forest Village. Chamb. J. **57**: 248.
German Gastronomy. Chamb. J. **32**: 417.
German Genius and Taste. (F. Jeffrey) Ed. R. **42**: 409.
German Genius, Characteristics of. (J. Stirling) For. Q. **29**: 309. Same art. Am. Ecl. **4**: 416.
German Gibbet. Lond. M. **20**: 353.
German Governesses. Victoria, **28**: 430.
German Handicraftsmen. (B. S. Blyth) Once a Week, **11**: 202.
German Hartz. (J. M. Hoppin) Knick. **35**: 189.
German Headsman, Autobiography of. Blackw. **63**: 148.
German Imperial Bank. Bank. M. (N. Y.) **32**: 262.
German Inn in the 16th Century. Penny M. **14**: 495.
German Jubilee. Once a Week, **15**: 427.
German Ladies, Biographies of. (Miss Rigby) Quar. **73**: 142. Same art. Ecl. M. **1**: 305.
German Landlady (H. H. Jackson) Atlan. **26**: 441.
German Language. Ed. Mo. R. **4**; 164.—West. M. **1**: 305.
— Dictionary of Flügel and Sporschil. No. Am. **50**: 279.
— Grammar of, Noehden's. (T. D. Woolsey) New Eng. **1**: 141.
— — Westphal's. (J. Hadley) No. Am. **112**: 441.
— in Lutheran Institutions. (J. D. Severinghaus) Luth. Q. **3**: 228.
— Modern, Rückert's History of. (J. M. Hart) Nation, **22**: 103. **24**: 195.
— Study of. Chr. R. **1**: 263. **6**: 446.—Am. Mo. R. **3**: 508.
— — in America. (C. H. Brigham) Chr. Exam. **87**: 1.
— — in German Schools. (R. von Raumer) Am. J. Educ. **11**: 155, 400. **12**: 460.
— — Method of. (E. A. Walker) Univ. Q. **1**: 221.
— — Plea for. (J. W. Nevin) Evang. R. **15**: 515.
German Legion, Beamish's History of. Mo. R. **145**: 507.
German Legions, The King's. Blackw. **43**: 739.
German Literary Celebrities, Recollections of. Westm. **72**: 164.
German Literature. (T. Carlyle) Ed. R. **46**: 304. — (C. Beck) No. Am. **43** : 163. — (A. B. Chapin) Chr. Q. Spec. **7**: 13. — (G. Ripley) Chr. Exam. **11**: 373. — (C. C. Felton) Chr. Exam. **27** : 214. — Am. Bib. Repos. 2d s. **2**: 198. — Am. Q. **2**: 171. **3**: 150. **4**: 157. — Ed. R. **63**: 232. — Selec. Ed. R. **3**: 1. — For. Q. **16**: 1. **20**: 121. **23**: 117. **30**: 158. — Chr. R. **4**: 370. **5**: 533. **6**: 269. — So. Q. **11**: 90. — Dem. R. **24**: 44. — Ecl. Mus. **1**: 299. — Mo. R. **112**: 43. **114**: 261. **116**: 199. **119**: 81. — Brit. Q. **8**: 119. Same art. Ecl. M. **15**: 306. — Blackw. **45**: 247. **50**: 143. — Dial, **1**: 315. — (G. Fitzhugh) De Bow, **29**: 280. — Liv. Age, **55**: 381. — Chr. R. **6**: 269.
— Belles-Lettres, Recent, 1835. Quar. **53**: 215. — Mus. **26**: 539.
— Contemporary. Westm. **57**: 323, 677.
— from 1848 to 1852. New Q. **1**: 96.
— Glance at recent. Brit. Q. **20**: 86
— Hosmer's History of. (F. H. Hedge) Unita. R. **11**: 248, 576.
— Humorous and Satirical Writers. Ecl. R. **82**: 287, 446.
— in America, Early. (J. H. Dubbs) Mercersb. **25**: 371.
— Influence of English on. (J. B. Angell) No. Am. **84**: 311.
— Lady Novelists of. No. Brit. **7**: 368. Same art. Liv. Age, **14**: 577.
— Links in. Tinsley, **12**: 568. Same art. Liv. Age, **118**: 286.
— Mediæval; W. von Eschenbach. Nat. Q. **16**: 136.
— — *versus* Vaticanism. (K. Blind) Internat. R. **8**: 167.
— Menzel on. Blackw. **50**: 143. — Ed. R. **63**: 442. — Ecl. R. **65**: 396, 503, 614. **66**: 217, 443, 554. **73**: 510.
— of 14th and 15th Centuries. (T. Carlyle) For. Q. **8**: 347.
— Old Story Books. *See* German Story Books.
— Popular and traditionary. Colburn, **4**: 289.
— Present State of. Am. Mo. M. **8**: 1.
— Prussian Influence on. Brit. Q. **56**: 179.
— Recent, 1856. (E. J. Young) Chr. Exam. **61**: 197.
— Religious. For. Q. **21**: 247.

German Literature; School of Irony. Blackw. 38: 376.
— — of Tragedy. Blackw. 18: 286.
— Songs of the Liberation War, 1813. Tait, n. s. 7: 409.
— Bayard Taylor on. Penn Mo. 11: 441.
— Traits and Tendencies of. Blackw. 50: 43.
— Translations from. (G. P. Marsh) Am. Whig R. 2: 256. — (F. Cunningham) Chr. Exam. 38: 402. — Blackw. 3: 416.
— Zander's Lectures on. Dub. Univ. 1: 335.
See German Novelists; German Poets; German Prose-Writers.
German Love. Fraser, 55: 396.
German Love; a Tale. (M. Müller) Canad. Mo. 6: 100, 198.
German Love Songs. Liv. Age, 57: 305.
German Metaphysics. (F. H. Hedge) Chr. Exam. 14: 119. — (D. N. Lord) Theo. & Lit. J. 3: 122.
German Mystery. Bentley, 58: 518.
— A real. Temp. Bar, 3: 69.
German Mythology, Grimm's. For. Q. 21: 360.
German Naturalists and Physicians, Meeting at Innsbruck. (A. Geikie) Nature, 1: 22.
— — Association of. (A. Oppenheim) Nature, 13: 32, 56.
German Neology. (H. Bokum) Chr. Q. Spec. 6: 509.
German Novelists. Mo. R. 111: 136. 113: 157. — Mus. 10: 29. — Ecl. M. 80: 599.
German Novels. Ecl. R. 84: 465.
— and Novelists. (E. V. Blake) Nat. Q. 35: 83, 284. — (J. G. Rosengarten) Penn Mo. 2: 17.
German Ocean, Bed of. (J. E. Taylor) Belgra. 12: 113.
German Opera. Fraser, 24: 69. 26: 121.
German Pastor's Experiences, Dr. Buchsel's. Cong. 2: 229.
German Peace Jubilee, 1871. Fraser, 83: 724.
German Peace Festival in London, 1871. Good Words, 12: 489.
German Peasant Romance. Cornh. 32: 597.
German Periodicals. (W. Menzel) Am. Ecl. 2: 269.
German Philosophers, Early. (M. Schele de Vere) Chr. R. 24: 137.
— of the Soul. (R. H. Whitelock) Westm. 52: 111.
German Philosophy. Fraser, 15: 716. — Ecl. R. 66: 443.
— and Christian Theology. (R. Vaughan) Brit. Q. 2: 297.
— and Political Life. Lond. Q. 35: 287.
— and Schopenhauer's Pessimism. (A. Alexander) Princ. n. s. 1: 492.
— and Theology, Müller's. No. Brit. 12: 411.
— Modern. Bent. Q. 1: 413.
— Results of. Brit. Q. 7: 404.
— Sketch of. (H. B. Smith) Bib. Sac. 2: 260.
See Philosophy.
German Plays and Actors. For. Q. 32: 197.
German Playwrights. (T. Carlyle) For. R. 3: 94.
German Poetry. (K. Blind) Dark Blue, 3: 164. — (J. M. Mackie) No. Am. 58: 79. — (T. Carlyle) Ed. R. 53: 151. — Am. Q. 7: 436. 10: 194. — Selec. Ed. R. 1: 226. — Fraser, 4: 167, 540. 5: 280. — Irish Q. 8: 626. — Colburn, 113: 231. — Westm. 70: 293.
— Early. Brit. Q. 11: 371.
— Lyrical. Ed. R. 56: 37. — Tait, n. s. 11: 364. 13: 94.
— — Specimens of; (translated by J. H. Merivale) Colburn, 58: 126–328. 59: 118.
— Popular. (Mrs. Robinson) No. Am. 42: 265.
— — Specimens of. Tait, n. s. 5: 704.
— Survey of, Taylor's. Lond. M. 22: 188.
German Poets, Living Political. Ecl. M. 1: 275. 2: 64.
— Minor; Freiligrath. Nat. Q. 22: 341.
— Modern, Specimens of. Tait, n. s. 10: 131.
— Recent, 1848. Prosp. R. 4: 34.
German Polite Literature. Ecl. R. 66: 554.
German Political Opinions. Brit. & For. R. 10: 25.
German Political Squibs and Crotchets. For. Q. 35: 429.
German Popular Prophecies. Blackw. 67: 560. Same art. Liv. Age, 25: 529. Same art. Ecl. M. 20: 465.
German Preachers and Preaching in this Century. Lond. Q. 54: 303.
German Prince (Pückler Muskau), Tour of. For. Q. 9: 290. 17: 253. — Ed. R. 54: 384. — Fraser, 5: 533. — Am. Q. 12: 139. — Westm. 16: 225. — Mo. R. 126: 579. 127: 503. — Am. Mo. R. 3: 231.
German Professors. Cornh. 10: 342.
German Prose Classics. Blackw. 29: 9, 133.
German Prose Writers. (D. R. Jacques) Hunt, 19: 41. — (A. P. Peabody) No. Am. 67: 464. — (W. H. Furness) Chr. Exam. 44: 263. — Dub. R. 11: 134.
German Protestantentag, The twelfth. (J. R. Hanne) Mod. R. 1: 639.
German Protestantism. Brit. Q. 13: 432.
German Proverbs. Penny M. 14: 398.
German Pulpit. Mo. R. 121: 139.
German Quarrels and Unities. Fraser, 43: 137.
German Question, Bülow-Cummerow on. Fraser, 41: 90.
German Rationalism. (F. Cunningham) Chr. Exam. 10: 346. — (A. P. Peabody) Chr. Exam. 27: 221. — Chr. R. 5: 243. — Am. Ecl. 2: 545.
— in its early Indications. (O. T. Dobbin) Kitto, 1: 126.
— in recent Developments. (O. T. Dobbin) Kitto, 1: 257.
German Reformed Church. (E. V. Gerhart) Bib. Sac. 20: 1. — (G. B. Russell) Mercersb. 14: 232.
— and Calvinism. (T. G. Apple) Mercersb. 19: 450.
— Dogmatics of. (J. H. A. Ebrard) Mercersb. 9: 249. 10: 58.
— Faith, etc., of. (E. V. Gerhart) Mercersb. 14: 249.
— Growth and Mission of. (G. W. Williard) Mercersb. 5: 600.
— Introduction to Hist. of. (L. Meyer) Mercersb. 2: 203.
— Origin, Doctrines, etc. (H. Rust) Mercersb. 6: 487. 7: 20.
— Proposed Liturgy. (S. Fuller) Am. Church R. 11: 48.
— Relation to Calvinism and Lutheranism. (H. Heppe) Mercersb. 5: 181.
— Synod of, at Frederick. (P. Schaff) Mercersb. 11: 1.
— — General, 1869. (T. G. Apple) Mercersb. 17: 156.
— — — 1875. (T. G. Apple) Mercersb. 22: 435.
— — — 1878. (T. G. Apple) Mercersb. 25: 329.
— Theology of. (T. G. Apple) Ref. Q. 27: 624.
— Why Reformed? (J. H. Sykes) Mercersb. 19: 563.
German Requisitions. Belgra. 20: 535.
German Romance. (C. W. Hutson) So. R. n. s. 3: 75.
German Romances, Chivalrous. Dub. Univ. 2: 23.
German Romanticists; Wilhelm Hauff. Brit. Q. 14: 87. Same art. Ecl. M. 24: 145.
German Silver Wedding. (G. B. Stuart) Argosy, 32: 69.
German Singers and English Audiences. Colburn, 100: 312.
German Socialism. (W. Brown) Atlan. 44: 521. — No. Brit. 11: 406.
— in the 16th Century. All the Year, 44: 32.
German Socialists and the Reichstag, 1880. (J. W. Bell) Canad. Mo. 19: 37.
German Society, Recent Changes in. Temp. Bar, 10: 86.
German Soldier. Ecl. M. 60: 162.
German Spion, Views from. (Bret Harte) Belgra. 38: 412.
German Stage, Glance at. (H. S. Wilson) Gent. M. n. s. 14: 687.
German Story Books, Old. Brit. Q. 17: 397. Same art. Ecl. M. 29: 531. — Chamb. J. 24: 316
German Student's Tale. Bentley, 9: 516.
German Students at the Beginning of this Century. Temp. Bar, 36: 52.
— Character of. Dem. R. 10: 238. — Westm. 31: 159.
— Duels of. (J. Galt) Blackw. 16: 557. — (G. M. Towle) Hours at Home, 3: 369, 439. — Mus. 44: 173. — Tait, n. s. 8: 685.
German Student-Life. (J. Galt) Blackw. 17: 329. — (A. H. Baynes) Fraser, 104: 630. Same art. Liv. Age, 151: 749. — (W. Howitt) Ecl. M. 14: 386. — (C. C. Tiffany) Penn Mo. 1: 41–210.

German Student-Life and Travel. (E. A. Walker) University Q. **1**: 29.
— Howitt's. Dem. R. **10**: 238.—Ecl. R. **74**: 683.—(W. B. O. Peabody) No. Am. **56**: 300.—Mo. R. **156**: 371.—Howitt, **3**: 264, 280.
— Lights and Shadows of. Dub. Univ. **32**: 245, 421.
— Sketches of. (E. Lloyd) Colburn, **104**: 433.
German Tables d'Hôte. Temp. Bar, **18**: 196.
German Tales. Brit. Q. **6**: 189.
German Theology. (J. Hunt) Contemp. **18**: 559.—(G. W. Burnap) Chr. Exam. **32**: 319.—Westm. **44**: 407.—Mo. R. **114**: 322. **116**: 305. **117**: 447.
— and Philos., Influence of. (F. Tholuck) Bib. R. **3**: 95.
— Influence of Moral Philosophy on. (O. T. Dobbin) Kitto, **2**: 281.
— Reaction in, 1854. (E. J. Young) Chr. Exam. **58**: 317. **59**: 317.
German Tourists. Westm. **22**: 510.—Mo. R. **120**: 336.
German Tragedy, Modern. (R. P. Gillies) For. Q. **1**: 565.
German Translation of Pickwick Papers. Dub. R. **8**: 160.
German Tribes, Arnold's Settlements of. (W. F. Allen) No. Am. **123**: 151.
German Turnfest. (G. P. Upton) Lakeside, **2**: 239.
German Unity. Liv. Age, **24**: 145.
German Universities. *See* Germany, Universities of.
German Views of English Criticism. Am. Whig R. **6**: 497.
German Watering-Places. Quar. **50**: 308. Same art. Select J. **4**: [67. Same art. Mus. **24**: 575.
German Wit; Heinrich Heine. Westm. **65**: 1. Same art. Ecl. M. **37**: 316. Same art. Liv. Age, **48**: 513.
German Workman. Liv. Age, **34**: 457.
German Zollverein. Ed. R. **79**: 105.—(F. J. Grund) No. Am. **58**: 55.
— and French Colonial Duties. For. Q. **22**: 299.
and Hanse Towns. (J. L. Tellkampf) Hunt, **14**: 159, 227. **15**: 225.
— Principles of. Ed. R. **75**: 515.
Germania Orchestra, Old. (J. Bunting) Scrib. **11**: 98.
Germanic and Latin Races. (T. Appel) Mercersb. **19**: 5.
Germanic Confederation. Brit. Q. **38**: 223.—Brit. & For. R. **4**: 169.
— and Austria. Quar. **84**: 425.
— Formation of. (C. K. Adams) No. Am. **113**: 374.
Germanic Diet. Nat. R. **18**: 503.
Germanic Languages. *See* Teutonic Languages.
Germanic Mythology. (K. Blind) Contemp. **23**: 621. *See* Mythology.
Germanic Nations and Christianity. (A. Michelsen) Luth. Q. **8**: 501.
Germanic Races, Advent of, into Europe. (D. Wilson) Ed. New Philos. J. **58**: 33.
Germanic States. Quar. **83**: 451.
Germanicus; a Song. St. James, **28**: 497.
Germantown, Pa., Battle of. (A. C. Lambdin) Pennsyl. M. **1**: 368.
— Battle-Ground of. Godey, **29**: 241.
— Settlement of. (S. W. Pennypacker) Pennsyl. M. **4**: 1.
Germany. New Eng. M. **4**: 97.—Mo. R. **111**: 352. **119**: 575.
— American Family in. (J. R. Browne) Harper, **27**: 160, 306.
— and Austria, 1849. Quar. **84**: 185.
— — 1863. Ho. & For. R. **3**: 35.
— — Alliance of, 1879. (A. Laugel) Nation, **29**: 269. —(E. de Laveleye) Fortn. **32**: 785.
— — and Russia, 1879. (A. Laugel) Nation, **29**: 307.
— and Commercial Treaty of Berlin. Hunt, **11**: 491.
— and Denmark, 1864. Colburn, **130**: 493.
— and Egypt. (G. von Bunsen) 19th Cent. **2**: 167.
— and England, Early Intercourse between. Westm. **75**: 403.
Germany and France. Blackw. **117**: 765. Same art. Ecl. M. **85**: 196.
— — and England, 1870. Ed. R. **132**: 554. Same art. Liv. Age, **107**: 515.
— — and Prussia, 1870. Dark Blue, **1**: 97.
— — and Russia, 1853. No. Brit. **19**: 519.
— — as Military Powers. (F. J. Lippitt) O. & N. **7**: 491.—(A. v. Fircks) J. Statis. Soc. **38**: 112.
— — England and Russia. Liv. Age, **42**: 376.
— — French Designs. (K. Blind) Fortn. **15**: 53.
— — National Characteristics of. (C. G. Greene, jr.) Nat. Q. **22**: 270.
— and the Germans. Quar. **58**: 297.—Mo. R. **140**: 111.
— and Greece, and the Scandinavian Powers. Fraser, **49**: 718.
— and Holland. (M. de Beaufort) 19th Cent. **3**: 402.
— and Italy, Net Results of 1848. (W. R. Greg) No. Brit. **15**: 359. Same art. Liv. Age, **30**: 512.
— — and England, 1851. Brit. Q. **13**: 190.
— — Latest Books on, 1850. Fraser, **42**: 446.
— and the King of Prussia, Radowitz on. Quar. **88**: 172.
— and its Parliament, 1848. Blackw. **64**: 515.
— and Prussia. (G. R. Pauli) Fraser, **83**: 207.
— and the Revolution. Pamph. **15**: 497.
— and Russia. (W. Wells) Meth. Q. **30**: 510.
— — 1872. Dark Blue, **3**: 544.
— — and France, 1869. St. Paul's, **3**: 147.
— — Slade's Travels in, 1838–39. Mo. R. **152**: 311.
— and the War, 1859. Colburn, **116**: 253.
— Bohemia, and Hungary. Dub. Univ. **14**: 33.
— Book Trade of. Ecl. R. **65**: 614.—(H. Meidinger) Hunt, **9**: 399.
— Bureaucracy in. (F. von Schulte) Contemp. **37**: 432.
— Madame de Bury's. Ecl. R. **82**: 562.
— Charities of. (W. Wells) Scrib. **3**: 408.
— Church and Theology of, during 19th Century. Nat. R. **18**: 191.
— — Ecclesiastical Crisis in, 1854. (J. Mueller) Chr. Exam. **58**: 198.
— — Ecclesiastical Subjection in. (E. L. Godkin) Nation, **16**: 313.
— — Evangelical Church Diet. (P. Schaff) Mercersb. **9**: 1.
— — Dr. Nevin and the German Church. (D. N. Lord) Theo. & Lit. J. **5**: 636.
See German Reformed Church; Old Catholics: Roman Catholics; etc.
— Church and State in. (J. A. Reubelt) Chr. Q. **7**: 433. —(D. A. Wasson) Unita. R. **5**: 1.—Cath. World. **17**: 513.
— — — 1875. (N. C. Schaeffer) Mercersb. **22**: 341.
— — — New Relations of. (J. B. Paton) Fortn. **23**: 169.
— Church History of. (J. W. Alexander) Princ. **22**: 347.
— Cities of, and German Citizenship. Westm. **55**: 534. Same art. Liv. Age, **30**: 283.
— Coinage of. (G. Bradford) Nation, **22**: 294.
— Commerce with. (J. L. Tellkampf) Hunt, **14**: 227.
— Conflict of Faith and Infidelity in. (F. L. Nagler) Meth. Q. **41**: 128.
— Constitutional. Contemp. **20**: 839.
— Constitutional Prospects of. Ecl. M. **78**: 629.
— Conversion to Christianity. (G. Lechler) Mercersb. **25**: 352.—Chr. R. **10**: 544.
— Courts of. Brit. Q. **24**: 71.
— Crumbs from the Rhineland. (A. Gray) Lippinc. **10**: 9.
— Dwarf Cities of. (H. W. Brewer) Art J. **33**: 257.
— Dwight's Travels in. Am. Q. **6**: 189.—(J. D. Wallenstein) No. Am. **29**: 389.
— Eating in. (W. L. T. Price) So. M. **9**: 460.
— Ecclesiastical Press in, before the Reformation. (B. Murphy) Cath. World, **32**: 650.
— Economic Revolution in, 1879. (H. Tuttle) Nation, **29**: 91.

Germany, Effect of Receipt of French Indemnity, 1873. Bank. M. (L.) **33**: 789, 1065.
— Empire of, 1848. Ed. R. **88**: 238. Same art. Ecl. M. **15**: 22. — Ecl. M. **15**: 375.
— — 1851. Ed. R. **91**: 584. Same art. Ecl. M. **20**: 349. Same art. Liv. Age, **25**: 417.
— — Eagle of. Cornh. **15**: 612.
— — New, 1871. Ed. R. **133**: 459. — (M. Heilprin) Nation, **12**: 22. — (F. Schaller) So. M. **11**: 707. — (J. D. Severinghaus) Luth. Q. **1**: 413. — (H. v. Sybel) Fortn. **15**: 1. Same art. Ecl. M. **76**: 257. — Brit. Q. **44**: 503. Same art. Ecl. M. **68**: 1. — (H. Tuttle) Harper, **63**: 591. — Ecl. M. **76**: 243.
— — — and Panslavism. (F. H. O'Donnell) Dark Blue, **1**: 549.
— English Opinions on. For. Q. **34**: 148. Same art. Ecl. M. **3**: 399.
— Ethnology of. (H. H. Howorth) Anthrop. J. **7**: 211.
— — Latham and Grimm on. Nat. R. **4**: 106.
— Folk-Life in By-Ways of. (W. Wells) Scrib. **5**: 590.
— Fortresses of. Colburn, **105**: 1.
— Future of. Brit. Q. **40**: 491. Same art. Ecl. M. **63**: 482.
— Getting Home to England from. Argosy, **10**: 194.
— Getting Married in. Atlan. **47**: 36.
— Half-Culture in. (K. Hillebrand) Contemp. **38**: 199.
— Hawkins on. Mo. R. **146**: 352.
— Heine on. (H. H. Milman) Quar. **55**: 1. — Westm. **23**: 291.
— Hints on Residence in. Hogg, **13**: 103.
— History of. For. Q. **15**: 388.
— — Ancient. (S. V. Mays) Mercersb. **15**: 228. — Ecl. R. **106**: 159.
— — Annals for 1835. Blackw. **37**: 386.
— — Brunswick Revolution. For. Q. **7**: 184.
— — Civil and military. Mo. R. **84**: 347.
— — Chronicles of, Pertz's. For. R. **2**: 326.
— — Chronicles of Teutonic Knights. Ed. R. **108**: 197.
— — Court in the 18th Century. Chamb. J. **25**: 87.
— — from Congress of Rastadt to Battle of Jena. (S. Austin) Ed. R. **86**: 329. Same art. Liv. Age, **15**: 433. Same art. Ecl. M. **6**: 368.
— — from Huss to Luther, Lindner's. (W. F. Allen) No. Am. **123**: 165.
— — from 1760 to 1814. (S. Austin) Fraser, **51**: 196.
— — Gleanings from Archives of. Ed. R. **116**: 178.
— — Hanseatic League. For. Q. **7**: 130.
— — Lewis's. Canad. Mo. **6**: 569.
— — Liberation War in. For Q. **34**: 26. Same art. Ecl. M. **3**: 369.
— — Military, of the 16th Century. For. Q. **14**: 31.
— — Negotiations on Swedish Invasion, 1614–30. (B. Moses) New Eng. **33**: 421.
— — Peasant War in the 16th Century. Westm. **50**: 131. Same art. Ecl. M. **15**: 541.
— — Revolution of 1848. Blackw. **64**: 373. **66**: 206, 424. — (J. M. Mackie) Am. Whig R. **8**: 345. — Mass. Q. **2**: 137.
— — Romans in. So. Lit. Mess. **17**: 37.
— — since Peace of Frankfort to 1879. Ed. R. **150**: 301.
— — Vehse's German Courts. Ed. R. **104**: 399.
— — Venedey's. Colburn, **109**: 102.
— — War of Independence. Brit. & For. R. **14**: 411.
— — Wars in, Reminiscences of. For. Q. **34**: 265.
— Histories of, Recent. (F. Kapp) Nation, **31**: 424.
— Hodgskin's Travels in. Blackw. **6**: 536.
— Home Life in. Fraser, **91**: 40–774. **92**: 195, 616, 774. **93**: 100. Same art. Ecl. M. **84**: 478, 703. **85**: 92–472. **86**: 176, 349, 464. Same art. Liv. Age, **124**: 431, 629. **125**: 55–628. **126**: 112–613. — (H. von Holst) Nation, **24**: 101. — So. R. n. s. **15**: 362.
— — Brace's. Dem. R. **33**: 49. — Liv. Age, **39**: 656.
Germany, Home Life in, in the 15th Century. Liv. Age, **143**: 74–301.
— Imperial Federalism in. (F. von Holtzendorff) Internat. R. **5**: 82, 247.
— in 15th Century, Recent Works on. (A. Thijon) Dub. R. **89**: 106.
— in 16th Century. For. Q. **7**: 337. — Mus. **19**: 267.
— in 1799–1800. Liv. Age, **70**: 547.
— in 19th Century, Treitschke on. (W. F. Allen) Nation, **29**: 131.
— in 1814–15, Distress in. Chr. Obs. **13**: 122, 205. **14**: 191.
— in 1830. (J. Q Adams) Ann. Reg. **6**: 137.
— in 1831, Strang on. Mo. R. **140**: 549.
— in 1832. Tait, **1**: 689.
— in 1848. Blackw. **64**: 373.
— in 1849. No. Brit. **10**: 240.
— in 1868. Ed. R. **128**: 237.
— in 1870, during the Franco-Prussian War. Temp. Bar, **30**: 270, 400.
— in 1880. (F. Kapp) Nation, **31**: 217.
— Industry in, 1874. (F. Springmühl) Pract. M. **4**: 240.
— Influence of, on Civilization. For. Q. **24**: 56.
— Intimate Life of a Noble Family in. Atlan. **46**: 349, 496, 638.
— Jacobs's View of. Mo. R. **101**: 360.
— Jurisprudence of, in the Middle Ages. (M. Thevenin) No. Am. **121**: 210.
— — in 1834. Westm. **22**: 131.
— — in 1848. No. Brit. **10**: 130.
— Kulturkampf in, History of. Dub. R. **86**: 327. **87**: 360.
— Kyffhäuser, Legends of. (B. Taylor) Atlan. **21**: 614.
— Law in. No. Am. **119**: 490.
— Legislation in. Am. Law R. **10**: 270.
— Letters from. Dub. Univ. **22**: 336, 743. — For. R. **4**: 292. — Mus. **16**: 33.
— — 1799. (S. T. Coleridge) Colburn, **45**: 211–302.
— Letters on, 1818. Blackw. **3**: 24.
— Liberalism in, 1871, Prospects of. (K. Hillebrand) Fortn. **16**: 387.
— Liberty in. (L. A. Montefiore) 19th Cent. **4**: 222, 735. **5**: 264.
— Libraries and Librarians of. (G. F. Arnold) Lib. J. **5**: 131.
— Life in. Dub. Univ. **49**: 347. — Ecl. M. **41**: 38.
— — and in Poland. Hogg, **15**: 401.
— — before 1815. Cornh. **13**: 675.
— — Howitt on. Ecl. R. **77**: 327. — Tait, n. s. **10**: 32. — Mo. R. **160**: 61.
— — in a North German Château. (Countess von Lauenbrück) St. James, **18**: 76–461. **19**: 52-422. **20**: 27–446.
— — Literary. Chamb. J. **30**: 91. Same art. Liv. Age, **58**: 949.
— — Natural History of. Westm. **66**: 51. Same art. Liv. Age, **50**: 449.
— — Rural and domestic. So. Lit. Mess. **10**: 563.
— — Sketches of. Liv. Age, **13**: 241.
— Life and Literature in. (W. Wells) Meth. Q. **35**: 422.
— — and Manners in, Mayhew on. Chr. Obs **64**: 361.
— — and Society in, 1600–1800. Westm. **77**: 358.
— Living in. (F. Tiffany) O. & N. **5**: 718.
— — Cost of. Nation, **28**: 99.
— Love in. Fraser, **55**: 396. Same art. Liv. Age, **54**: 51.
— Manufactures of, and English Corn Laws. Mus. **35**: 505.
— Metaphysical Studies in. Selec. Ed. R. **3**: 226.
— Military Future of. (C. C. Chesney) Macmil. **32**: 471. Same art. Liv. Age, **127**: 811. Same art. Ecl. M. **85**: 652.
— Military Resources of, 1855. Colburn, **104**: 1–379.
— Military Spirit of, 1871. (J. K. Hosmer) Atlan. **27**: 433.
— Military System of. Tait, n. s. **18**: 1.

Germany, Mineral Waters of. Fraser, **44**: 149. Same art. Liv. Age, **32**: 257.
— Miners of. (R. A. Smith) Good Words, **12**: 137.
— Minor States of. Colburn, **141**: 370.
— Month's Holiday in. (A. Harrison) Lippinc. **2**: 175.
— Music and Manners in, Chorley's. Tait, n. s. **8**: 506.
— National Assembly of. Bentley, **24**: 329.
— Naval Power of, Growth of. Ed. R. **144**: 1.
— Neale's Travels in. Mo. R. **88**: 337.
— New Hyperion. (E. Strahan) Lippinc. **12**: 9–625. **13**: 9–649. **14**: 9–649.
— New Year's Eve in. Sharpe, **25**: 141.
— Newspapers in. (O. L. Misch) Lakeside, **9**: 207. — Cornh. **7**: 748. — N. Ecl. **7**: 302. — For. Q. **33**: 201. Same art. Ecl. M. **3**: 167.
— Nihilism and Pessimism in. (C. Waldstein) 19th Cent. **3**: 1120. Same art. Sup. Pop. Sci. Mo. **3**: 248.
— North, Account of. Lond. M. **14**: 501.
— — and South, contrasted. (W. H. Riehl) Cornh. **9**: 566.
— — Notes from. Lond. M. **13**: 336, 407.—Fraser, **11**: 507.
— Paparchy and Nationality. Brit. Q. **61**: 1.
— Parliaments of, Chat about. (W. Wells) Scrib. **9**: 652.
— Parliamentary Leaders of. (H. Tuttle) Gent. M. n. s. **14**: 300.
— past and future. Fraser, **51**: 331.
— — and present. Ed. R. **152**: 503.
— Patriotic Songs of. Quar. **129**: 485.
— Peasants of North. (M. Porter) Penn Mo. **10**: 126.
— Peasant Customs of South. Ev. Sat. **17**: 432.
— Peasant Life in. Westm. **66**: 51.
— Peasant Proverbs of Northern. Chamb. J. **24**: 170.
— Penal Jurisprudence in. (N.W. Senior) Ed. R. **82**: 318.
— Periodical Literature in. Lond. M. **17**: 1.
— Political Prisoner in Revolution of 1848. House. Words, **14**: 75–205.
— Political Rights of People of. For. Q. **36**: 168.
— Politics in. (H. Tuttle) Fortn. **27**: 676.
— — in 1849. Dub. R. **26**: 481. — Ed. R. **89**: 537. Same art. Liv. Age, **21**: 577.
— — in 1850; Menace of War. Ed. R. **93**: 186.
— — in 1863; Struggle for Federative Reform. Fraser, **68**: 549.
— — in 1864; Projected Reforms. Brit. Q. **40**: 491. Same art. Ecl. M. **63**: 482.
— — in 1866. Colburn, **137**: 322.
— — — New Germany. (E. Dicey) Macmil. **14**: 481. Same art. Ev. Sat. **2**: 484. — Ed. R. **128**: 237. Same art. Ecl. M. **72**: 539.
— — in 1867. (F. Kapp) Nation, **4**: 92.
— — in 1870; Reconstruction of Germany. (W. C. Cartwright) Fraser, **74**: 366. Same art. Ecl. M. **67**: 668. Same art. Appleton, **22**: 118. — No. Brit. **50**: 253. — Westm. **97**: 324.
— — — Stein on. Westm. **111**: 329.
— — in 1879. (H. Tuttle) Fortn. **32**: 329.
— — — Reaction in. (H. Tuttle) Nation, **28**: 381.
— Popular Lectures in. (S. Powers) Lippinc. **7**: 581. — Broadw. **8**: 481.
— Press in, and the Government. Month, **24**: 410.
— Protestant Pulpit in. (A. Schwartz) Contemp. **24**: 397.
— Protestant Union in. (J. Gibb) Contemp. **12**: 413.
— Protestantism in. (T. Moore) Ed. R. **54**: 238. — Brit. Q. **13**: 432. — Dub. R. **19**: 401. — No. Brit. **20**: 423. — Prosp. R. **1**: 263.
— — in 1847. Prosp. R. **3**: 254.
— — in 1855. Brit. Q. **23**: 412.
— — in 1877. Cong. **6**: 321, 467.
— Recollections of. Fraser, **21**: 53.
— Religion in. (F. A. Tholuck) Bib. Sac. **4**: 236. — (C. Hodge) Princ. **18**: 514. — Ecl. R. **66**: 217. — Spirit Pilg. **1**: 96. **3**: 57. — (G. R. Noyes) Chr. Exam. **19**: 41. — Am. Meth. M. **12**: 312. — Theo. R. **2**: 218.
Germany, Religion in, and Theological Scholarship. (C. R. Gregory) Unita. R. **10**: 73.
— — History and present State of, 1857. Lond. Q. **9**: 390,
— — in 1830. Cong. M. **13**: 337.
— — Reawakening of Christian Life in. No. Brit. **16**: 279.
— Religious and Political State of, 1848. (J. Weiss) Chr. Exam. **43**: 394.
— Religious Condition of, 1879. (F. von Schulte) Contemp. **35**: 773.
— Religious Life in. Chr. Obs. **70**: 570.
— Religious Movement in, 1846. (H. Rogers) Ed. R. **83**: 100. — Fraser, **33**: 694.
— — 1870–72. Ed. R. **137**: 529. — Ecl. M. **77**: 111. — (J. M. Capes) Contemp. **18**: 376. Same art. Ecl. M. **77**: 694.
— Religious Opinion in. (G. S. Hall) Nation, **30**: 346.
— Religious Parties in. Lond. M. **3**: 299.
— Religious Persecution in. Brit. & For. R. **7**: 457.
— Religious Prospects of, 1856. (E. J. Young) Chr. Exam. **60**: 30.
— Religious Worship in. (C. S. Park) Bib. Sac. **14**: 784.
— Reminiscences of, 1813. Blackw. **48**: 746. — Mus. **41**: 217.
— Rhine and the Danube. Once a Week, **28**: 315.
— Semple's Tour in. Ed. R. **22**: 434.
— Mrs. Shelley's Rambles in. Tait, n. s. **11**: 729.
— Short Time in. (W. Maynard) Once a Week, **17**: 590, 645.
— Sketches of Travel in. (J. S. Blackie) Dark Blue, **2**: 91, 193, 320.
— Social Democracy in. (J. Huber) Internat. R. **5**: 793. — (J. F. Smith) Theo. R. **16**: 44. — (W. Brown) Nation, **29**: 221.
— Social Life in. Mo. R. **151**: 413.
— — Changes of. (S. Austin) Ed. R. **77**: 138. Same art. Ecl. Mus. **2**: 146.
— Socialism in. *See* German Socialism.
— Society in. Quar. **23**: 434.
— — forty Years since. (Lady Duff-Gordon) Macmil. **36**: 410. Same art. Liv. Age, **135**: 53. Same art. Ecl. M. **89**: 740.
— Sources of Discontent in. (K. Hillebrand) Contemp. **38**: 40. Same art. Liv. Age, **146**: 497.
— Southern. For. Q. **1**: 435.
— — Frontiers of. Month, **5**: 66.
— — Notes in, 1866. Fraser, **76**: 238.
— — Pleasant Customs in. All the Year, **32**: 540.
— — Sights in. (A. Paynter) Howitt, **1**: 149–359. **2**: 53, 154, 173.
— — Village Life in. (H. T. Finck) Nation, **29**: 324.
— Southwestern, 1870. (M. Heilprin) Nation, **11**: 85.
— Spas of. (B. Murphy) Galaxy, **22**: 200. — Tait, n. s. **4**: 598.
— — Gambling. (J. H. Browne) Harper, **45**: 1.
— Madame de Staël on. (Sir J. Mackintosh) Ed. R. **22**: 198.—(R. Heber) Quar. **10**: 355.—Ecl. R. **19**: 1.
— Statistics of, 1869. Am. J. Educ. **18**: 553.
— Strength and Weakness of, 1860. Westm. **74**: 134.
— Summer Excursion in. Chamb. J. **9**: 97, 225, 281. **10**: 57, 92, 136.
— Summer in. Tait, n. s. **4**: 589.
— Teutoburger Forest. (B. Taylor) Atlan. **23**: 40.
— Theological Journals of. Bib. Sac. **34**: 767.
— Tour in. Ed. R. **41**: 78. — Quar. **31**: 174. — Blackw. **6**: 535. — Mus. **5**: 316. — Temp. Bar, **18**: 259.
— Travels in. Broadw. **8**: 312.
— Ultra-Liberal Press of. For. Q. **10**: 150.
— United Republics of. Dem. R. **31**: 44.
— Unity of. (D. T. Strauss) O. & N. **2**: 604. — Ev. Sat. **9**: 610.
— — Bismarck and. (D. Ker) Nat. Q. **39**: 30.
— — German View of. (K. Blind) Nat. Q. **24**: 326.

Germany, Universities of. (F. Bôcher) Atlan. **7**: 257. — (W. C. Perry) Macmil. **37**: 148. Same art. Ecl. M. **90**: 544. Same art. Sup. Pop. Sci. Mo. **2**: 244. — (K. von Raumer) Am. J. Educ. **6**: 9. **7**: 52. — (R. Baird) Am. Q. **10**: 341. **11**: 128. — (G. H. Bode) No. Am. **27**: 317. — (F. C. von Savigny) Lit. & Theo. R. **2**: 635. — (J. L. Kingsley) Chr. Q. Spec. **1**: 634. — Westm. **24**: 102. — U. S. Lit. Gaz. **4**: 102. — Select J. **4**: 71. — Ed. R. **59**: 211. — (H. Wimmer) Bib. Sac. **7**: 360. — Dub. Univ. **46**: 82. Same art. Ecl. M. **36**: 599. Same art. Liv. Age, **46**: 476. — Evang. R. **9**: 129. — Univ. Q. **35**: 348.

— — Academic Liberty in. (H. Helmholtz) Nature, **18**: 50, 78.

— — American Student in. (N. Porter) Mercersb. **12**: 97. — (N. Porter) New Eng. **15**: 574.

— — and others. (E. P. Evans) Nation, **7**: 212.

— — Decline of. (A. T. S. Goodrick) Macmil. **142**: 180. Same art. Ecl. M. **95**: 319. — (G. S. Hall) Nation, **31**: 302.

— — Getting a D. D. in. Nation, **20**: 343.

— — Hart on. (C. Carroll) Nation, **19**: 400.

— — How they work at. (S. Powers) Nation, **2**: 695.

— — Library Management in. (E.W. Hall) Lib. J. **2**: 75.

— — Life in. (J. M. Hart) Putnam, **12**: 496. — Broadw. **5**: 114.

— — Student Societies in. Am. J. Educ. **7**: 160.

— University Education in. Liv. Age, **104**: 3.

— University Town in. Putnam, **8**: 70.

— Vacation Ramble in. (H. Bedford) Month, **22**: 410. **23**: 36–409. **24**: 17–147.

— Village Life in. Hogg, **7**: 17–197. **9**: 298, 408.

— Wayside Pictures through. Bentley, **24**: 128–568. **25**: 57–624. **26**: 35–145.

— Weber's. Blackw. **48**: 119.

— Workingman of. Penn Mo. **1**: 380.

— Young. Fraser, **49**: 81.

See Black Forest; Prussia; Rhine; etc.

Germelshausen; a Tale. (F. Gerstaecker) Month, **12**: 75, 188. Same art. Harper, **53**: 529.

Germination and Vegetation, Influence of organic and inorganic Bodies upon. (M. C. Lea) Am. J. Sci. **93**: 197.

Gérome, Jean Léon. (R. Ménard) Portfo. **6**: 82. — Art J. **29**: 26. **30**: 279. — Galaxy, **1**: 681.

— In a Caravan with. Lippinc. **13**: 279, 532.

Gerontius, Dream of. (J. H. Newman) Month, **2**: 415, 532.

Geronymo, the Moorish Martyr. (A. M. H. Watts) Once a Week, **11**: 425.

Gerry, Elbridge, Life of. (E. Everett) No. Am. **28**: 37. — Am. Q. **3**: 469.

Gerrymander. Am. Law R. **6**: 283.

— History of the. Am. Hist. Rec. **1**: 504. **2**: 69.

Gersau, Switzerland; a Liliputian Republic. (A. Gautier) Liv. Age, **107**: 579.

Gerson, John. Am. Presb. R. **7**: 242.

Gerstaecker, Friedrich, with portrait. Appleton, **8**: 180.

— Autobiography of. So. M. **8**: 166.

Gertru, or the Maid of Charleston. So. Lit. Mess. **13**: 52.

Gertrude, St., Thoughts on. (A. de Vere) Month, **3**: 221. Same art. Cath. World, **2**: 405.

Gertrude; a Novel. So. Lit. Mess. **10**: 513. **11**: 178.

Gertrude Bohun. Fraser, **41**: 307.

Gertrude de Chanzane. (E. de Pressensé) Dub. Univ. **86**: 21, 202.

Gertrude Erle. (Mrs. A. Fraser) Tinsley, **17**: 319.

Gertrude Hoffman; a Tale. So. Lit. Mess. **6**: 417.

Gerty's Necklace. (F. Locker) Blackw. **110**: 738.

Gesang Verein, Reminiscences of. Once a Week, **13**: 288.

Gesenius, F. H. W., and Nordheimer. (E. Robinson) Bib. Sac. **1843**: 361.

Gesenius, F. H. W. Doctrine of the Accents and Makkeph. (J. T. M. Falkenau) Bib. Sac. **7**: 650.

Gesner, Conrad, Life of. Fraser, **47**: 48. Same art. Ecl. M. **28**: 366.

— and his Works. Anal. M. **13**: 459. **14**: 8.

Gesner, John M. (K. von Raumer) Am. J. Educ. **5**: 741.

Gesta Romanorum. Fraser, **40**: 167. Same art. Ecl. M. **18**: 526. Same art. Liv. Age, **23**: 407. — O. & N. **6**: 531, 713.

Gestation, Unusual Modes of. (J. Wyman) Am. J. Sci. **77**: 5.

Gesticulation. Tinsley, **10**: 656.

— Italian. Dub. R. **3**: 1.

Gesture, Philosophy of. Portfo. (Den.) **10**: 621. **11**: 38.

Gestures, Oriental. Once a Week, **22**: 301.

Gesture Language. Chamb. J. **42**: 678. — Intel. Obs. **7**: 451.

— of South Italy. Chamb. J. **48**: 209. Same art. Ev. Sat. **10**: 407.

Gethsemane, Agony of. (L. Mayer) Am. Bib. Repos. **5**: 294.

Getting on. (W. Chambers) Chamb. J. **53**: 353.

— in the World. (M. Harland) Godey, **82**: 135–419.

— in the World. Temp. Bar, **44**: 474.

Gettysburg, Battle of. (E. P. Alexander) So. Hist. Pap. **4**: 235. — (R. H. Anderson) So. Hist. Pap. **3**: 49. — (R. I. Ewell) So. M. **12**: 683. — (W. S. Hancock) Galaxy, **22**: 821. — (A. P. Hill) So. Hist. Pap. **2**: 222. — (O. O. Howard) Atlan. **38**: 48. — Blackw. **94**: 365. Same art. Liv. Age, **79**: 291. — (R. E. Lee) So. M. **11**: 205. — (J. Longstreet) So. M. **14**: supp. 49. — (R. E. Rodes) So. Hist. Pap. **2**: 135. — (J. B. Robertson, W. W. White, H. L. Benning, and J. B. Kershaw) So. Hist. Pap. **4**: 161. — Land We Love, **2**: 39. — So. R. n. s. **5**: 419. — (C. M. Wilcox) So. Hist. Pap. **6**: 97. **7**: 280. — (W. C. Oates) So. Hist. Pap. **6**: 172. — (L. McLaws) So. Hist. Pap. **7**: 64.

— — and Gen. Meade. (C. Devens) Hist. M. **22**: 16.

— — Bates on. (W. Allan) So. Hist. Pap. **1**: 365.

— — Causes of Lee's Defeat. (J. A. Early, A. L. Long, F. Lee, W. Allan, and W. H. Taylor) So. Hist. Pap. **4**: 49. — (E. P. Alexander, C. M. Wilcox, A. L. Long, and W. H. Taylor) So. Hist. Pap. **4**: 97. — (J. B. Hood and H. Heth) So. Hist. Pap. **4**: 145. — (J. A. Early) So. Hist. Pap. **4**: 241. — (J. H. Lane and J. B. Walton) So. Hist. Pap. **5**: 38. — (L. P. d'Orleans and I. Sheibert) So. Hist. Pap. **5**: 88.

— — Confederate Reports. So. Hist. Pap. **8**: 41–515.

— — Episode of. Cath. World, **33**: 449.

— — Field of. (J. T. Trowbridge) Atlan. **16**: 616.

— — — Later Rambles over. (M. Jacobs) U. S. Serv. M. **1**: 66, 158.

— — Four Days at. (J. Y. Foster) Harper, **28**: 381.

— — Garnett's Brigade at. (C. S. Peyton) So. Hist. Pap. **3**: 215.

— — Heth's Report. So. Hist. Pap. **6**: 258.

— — How it was lost. So. R. n. s. **23**: 423.

— — Johnston's Report. So. Hist. Pap. **6**: 254.

— — Lee at. (J. D. Imboden) Galaxy, **11**: 507.

— — Lee's Strength and Losses at. (W. Allan) So. Hist. Pap. **4**: 34.

— — Letter on. (E. P. Alexander) So Hist. Pap. **5**: 201.

— — Notes on. (W. Swinton) Hours at Home, **3**: 88.

— — Operations at. (F. Lee) So. Hist. Pap. **5**: 162.

— — — after. (J. E. B. Stuart) So. Hist. Pap. **2**: 66.

— — Relative Numbers at. (Count de Paris) So. Hist. Pap. **6**: 10. — (J. A. Early) So. Hist. Pap. **6**: 12.

— — Reply to Longstreet's second Paper. (J. A. Early) So. Hist. Pap. **5**: 270.

— — Report on. (W. N. Pendleton) So. Hist. Pap. **5**: 194.

Gettysburg, Battle of, Secret History of. (E. A. Palfrey) So. Hist. Pap. 8: 521.
— — G. H. Steuart's Brigade at. So. Hist. Pap. 2: 105. — (R. H. McKim) So. Hist. Pap. 5: 291.
— — Story of. (W. Baird) So. M. 12: 654.
— — Strength of both Armies at. (L. P. d'Orleans) So. Hist. Pap. 5: 204. — (W. H. Taylor) So. Hist. Pap. 5: 239.
— Campaign of. (R. E. Lee) So. Hist. Pap. 2: 33.
— — and Battle. (J. Longstreet) So. Hist. Pap. 5: 54, 258.
— — Pleasanton's Report. Hist. M. 17: 36.
— — Report on. (J. A. Early) So. M. 11: 311, 385.
— College Hospital in. Land We Love, 2: 290.
— National Cemetery of. (J. P. Thompson) Hours at Home, 2: 181.
— Pennsylvania College. (M. L. Stoever) Evang. R. 2: 539. 16: 103.
— Theological Seminary. (M. L. Stoever) Evang. R. 5: 413, 515.
— — History of. (J. G. Morris) Luth. Q. 6: 525.
— — Necrology of. (R. Weiser) Luth. Q. 7: 43.
Gévaudan, Wild Beast of. House. Words, 18: 544. — Ev. Sat. 3: 820. — (J. Grant) Argosy, 4: 54.
Geysers, Action of. Westm. 67: 207.
— and how they are explained. (J. LeConte) Pop. Sci. Mo. 12: 407.
— of California. (H. B. Auchincloss) Contin. Mo. 6: 280. — (B. P. Avery) Scrib. 6: 641. — (G. L. Goodale) Am. Natural. 1: 337. — (J. F. Manning) Lippinc. 6: 633. — Potter Am. Mo. 12: 60.
— of Iceland. St. James, 5: 334.
— — Visit to. Ev. Sat. 5: 487.
— of New Zealand. (J. Martin) Pop. Sci. R. 18: 366.
— — Visit to. (C. Bunbury) Fraser, 99: 761. Same art. Liv. Age, 141: 812. Same art. Pop. Sci. Mo. 15: 356.
— of Yellowstone and Firehole Rivers. (F. V. Hayden) Am. J. Sci. 103: 105, 161. — (A. Geikie) Macmil. 44: 421. Same art. Appleton, 26: 538.
Gheel, At. (M. G. Brodie) Good Words, 18: 493.
— City of the Simple. (H. Campbell) Lippinc. 24: 698.
— Insane Colony at. (Dr. Isaacs) Cath. World, 7: 824. — All the Year, 20: 277. — Knick. 55: 267. — Once a Week, 20: 167. — St. Paul's, 4: 79.
— Village of. Chamb. J. 29: 273.
Ghent. House. Words, 14: 20.
— Ancient Beguinage of. (A. Nampon) Cath. World, 1: 514. — Lond. Soc. 27: 220. — Lippinc. 8: 310.
— Economic Experiment in. (J.G. Fitch) Macmil. 29: 429.
— Treaty of. Niles's Reg. 22: 198–327. 23: 7, 22, 246.
Ghetto of Rome. Fraser, 42: 651. Same art. Internat. M. 2: 393. — Bentley, 64: 486.
— Story of. Bentley, 44: 79.
Ghika, Helen, Princess Dora d'Istria. *See* Koltzoff-Massalsky, H. G.
Ghilzies, Residence among, 1839–40. (Maj. Lynch) Dub. Univ. 24: 326–686.
Ghincoteague Island, Va. (H. Pyle) Scrib. 13: 737.
Ghirlandaja, Il; a Legend of Florence. Fraser, 30: 190.
Ghost, The; a Tale. Putnam, 7: 20.
— and Bone-Setter. Dub. Univ. 11: 50.
— as a modern Convenience. (M. Hosmer) Lippinc. 6: 54.
— at Laburnam Villa. Belgra. 12: 213.
— at Mansfield. (A. S. Deas) So. M. 11: 666.
— at the Rath; a Story. All the Year, 15: 329. Same art. Ecl. M. 67: 110.
— I met on Waterloo Bridge. Once a Week, 13: 301.
— in the Cap'n Brown House. (H. B. Stowe) Atlan. 26: 654.
— in the Green Park. (D. Cook) Once a Week, 9: 309.
— in the Library of Winterbury Cathedral. Cath. World, 1: 679.
Ghost, The, in the Snow. Once a Week, 30: 127–238.
— in a State Room. Galaxy, 6: 172.
— of Aldrum Hall. Argosy, 30: 434.
— of Art. House. Words, 1: 385.
— of Barbarossa. (G. A. Sala) Belgra. 27: 453.
— of Botathen. All the Year, 17: 501.
— of Gashleigh Court. (G. A. Sala) Temp. Bar, 9: 522.
— of Hamlet, Character of. Fraser, 32: 350.
— of the late Mr. James Barber. (W. H. Wills) House. Words, 1: 87.
— of the Lime-Kiln; a Tale. Cath. World, 12: 838.
— of little Jacques. (A. M. Hoyt) Atlan. 11: 213. Same art. Sharpe, 40: 198.
— of a Love Story. House. Words, 8: 559.
— of Lyntwold Hall. Victoria, 15: 503.
— of Mont-Fleuri. Chamb. J. 39: 327.
— of Morcar's Tower. Blackw. 126: 60. Same art. Liv. Age, 142: 349.
— of the Oratory; a Poem. Blackw. 18: 433.
— of Pit Pond. House. Words, 10: 170.
— of Rummelsberg. (J. L. Ver Mehr) Overland, 10: 16.
— of St. Peter's. (D. Costello) Bentley, 45: 11.
— of a Story. (A. H. Forrester) Bentley, 21: 458.
— of Ten Broek Van der Heyden. Lippinc. 6: 345.
— of the Wesley Family. All the Year, 28: 198.
— on the River; a Tale. St. James, 15: 456.
— or Grizzly? Lond. Soc. 21: 511.
— Scientific Observation on. (J.A. Wilson) Belgra. 36: 45.
— that appeared to Mrs. Wharton. House. Words, 2: 139.
— with the Golden Casket. Lond. M. 4: 129.
— who made himself useful. (E. Spencer) Scrib. 5: 571.
Ghost's Adventure; a Story. Western, 6: 81, 165.
Ghost's Summons. (A. Buisson) Belgra. 4: 359.
Ghosts. (I. T. Hopkins) Scrib. 13: 342. — (E. W. Nall) So. M. 9: 601. — Lond. M. 9: 253.
— and Apparitions, Anecdotes of. (J. Hogg) Fraser, 11: 103.
— and Fairies, Gossip about. Dub. Univ. 62: 691.
— and Ghost Seeing. (F. W. Clarke) O. & N. 6: 284.
— and Ghost Seers. (Dr. Sam. Brown) No. Brit. 9: 393. Same art. Ecl. M. 15: 348. Same art. Liv. Age, 18: 490. — New Eng. M. 4: 386.
— — German. Dub. Univ. 17: 33, 217.
— and Ghost Stories. Dub. Univ. 72: 394.
— and Goblins, Notes on. Cornh. 27: 451. Same art. Ecl. M. 80: 730. Same art. Liv. Age, 117: 627. Same art. Ev. Sat. 14: 452.
— and Sorceresses in India. Chamb. J. 20: 185.
— Books concerning. (A. Smith) Bentley, 25: 91.
— Crowe's Night-Side of Nature. So. Lit. Mess. 17: 1.
— Do they appear? (C. E. Gast) Mercersb. 19: 294.
— Eatable. All the Year, 10: 181.
— everywhere. Chamb. J. 41: 401.
— Fact or Fancy? (G. C. Swayne) Once a Week, 15: 554.
— Haunted and Haunters. (Sir E. B. Lytton) Harper, 22: 365.
— Impersonation of. Lond. M. 9: 368, 461. 10: 65.
— in Australia. Chamb. J. 39: 363.
— in Court. All the Year, 15: 428.
— inconsistent with Reason. New Eng. M. 2: 8.
— Invisible. House. Words, 16: 157.
— Latest Thing in. Once a Week, 6: 99.
— Modern. Bentley, 43: 32.
— — Experience with. Potter Am. Mo. 17: 542.
— Natural. All the Year, 22: 305.
— New Discoveries in. Internat. M. 5: 387.
— of Darkdene. (H. S. Wilson) St. James, 41: 627.
— of the Day. Dub. Univ. 62: 337. Same art. Ecl. M. 61: 61.
— of Glenlussa. Belgra. 9: 121.
— of our old Cemetery. Mo. Rel. M. 32: 85.

Ghosts of the Old and New School. Nat. R. **7**: 1. Same art. Ecl. M. **45**: 362, 539. Same art. Liv. Age, **58**: 483. Same art. Ev. Sat. **6**: 653.
— of the Season. (T. H. S. Escott) Belgra. **9**: 456.
— on the Stage at Hoxton. Temp. Bar, **8**: 503.
— Patient. (W. B. Adams) Once a Week, **9**: 361.
— Plea for Old Bogey. Sharpe, **37**: 217.
— present and past. (F. J. S. Edgcombe) Fraser, **80**: 649.
— Real, and Second Sight. Blackw. **61**: 541. Same art. Liv. Age, **13**: 529.
— Remarks on. Portfo.(Den.) **15**: 131.
— that I see; a Tale. Sharpe, **51**: 169, 241, 289.
— Three. (R. Terry) Galaxy, **12**: 195.
— Trade in. Tinsley, **27**: 67.
Ghosts' Debate; a Tale. Eng. Dom. M. **8**: 214.
Ghost Chamber, Night in a. Belgra. **19**: 377.
Ghost Club, The. Eng. Dom. M. **12**: 153.
Ghost Dead-Bell; a Story. Dub. Univ. **59**: 473. Same art. Ecl. M. **56**: 210.
Ghost Gossips. Bentley, **9**: 462, 622.
Ghost Illusion, Prof. Pepper's. J. Frankl. Inst. **77**: 418.
Ghost Lover. Chamb. J. **23**: 225, 245.
Ghost Play. Chamb. J. **27**: 303.
Ghost Raiser. House. Words, **5**: 83.
Ghost Riders. (C. F. Hoffmann) Bentley, **4**: 471.
Ghost Seeing. (F. H. Hedge) No. Am. **133**: 286.
Ghost Seer of Prevorst. For. Q. **22**: 265.
Ghost Story. (D. M. Craik) Liv. Age, **45**: 275. — (W. T. Greene) Colburn, **162**: 522. — House. Words, **11**: 170 — Sharpe, **40**: 254. (A. E. Wetherald) Canad. Mo. **19**: 499. — Tait, **3**: 79.
— An authentic. Dub. Univ. **82**: 609.
— A Hampshire. Gent. M. n. s. **9**: 547, 666.
— My Grandfather's. Belgra. **17**: 113.
— of Normandy. Internat. M. **4**: 512.
— of the Revolution. (W. Seton) Cath. World, **14**: 261.
— Pyrenean. (A. B. Le Geyt) Victoria, **9**: 297.
— True. Sharpe, **12**: 245.
— What it did. Belgra. **13**: 466.
Ghost Stories. (G. W. Peck) Am. Whig R. **8**: 411, 529, 627. — Blackw. **20**: 192. — Mus. **4**: 225. — All the Year, **25**: 77. — Atlan. **43**: 286.
— of Chapelizod. Dub. Univ. **37**: 85, 427. Same art. Harper, **2**: 499.
— Russian. Ecl. M. **79**: 463. — Ev. Sat. **13**: 191.
— Scenes for. (J. Hatton) Colburn, **166**: 240.
— unveiled. Chamb. J. **55**: 602. **56**: 167. **58**: 171, 277.
Ghost Talk. All the Year, **19**: 159.
Ghostcraft, Chapters on. Dub. Univ. **19**: 1.
Ghostly Business. Ecl. M. **59**: 306.
Ghostly Drummer of Tedworth. All the Year, **26**: 462.
Ghostly Night at Ballyslaughter; a Tale. (J. Sheehan) Temp. Bar, **31**: 227.
Ghostly Quarters. All the Year, **5**: 427.
Ghostly Rental. (H. James, jr.) Scrib. **12**: 664.
Ghostly Warning. (E. C. Gale) Lippinc. **18**: 760.
Ghoul, The. Belgra. **33**: 342.
Ghouls and Vampires. Ev. Sat. **11**: 30.
Ghuznee, Fall of. (J. Cave-Brown) Good Words, **13**: 629.
— Siege of. Cornh. **41**: 201.
Giacomo da Valencia; or the Student of Bologna. Blackw. **62**: 359.
Giannetto. (M. E. Majendie) Blackw. **117**: 1, 145. Same art. Liv. Age, **125**: 534–793. **126**: 35.
Gianni, Lapo. Early Italian Poet. Lond. M. **8**: 643.
Giannone. (W. W. Story) Blackw. **92**: 738.
Giant, Irish; O'Donoghue of the Glenns. Tait, **1**: 665.
— Wilmington. Once a Week, **30**: 209.
Giant Yéous. (Geo. Sand) O. & N. **8**: 645.
Giant's Sword; a Poem. (C. H. Waring) Belgra. **3**: 32.
Giants. Nat. M. **9**: 438. — Lakeside, **3**: 363. — Once a Week, **29**: 500. — (A. Wilson) Gent. M. n. s. **19**: 335. — Tinsley, **7**: 517.
— Adventures with. Chamb. J. **19**: 346. Same art. Liv. Age, **38**: 149.
— Ancient and modern. Dub. Univ. **66**: 193.
— and Dwarfs. (W. A. Seaver) Harper, **39**: 202. — Fraser, **54**: 140, 286.
— — among Animals. Temp. Bar, **1**: 533. **3**: 363.
— — St. Hilaire on. Ed. New Philos. J. **15**: 142.
— — and Fairies. Galaxy, **1**: 26.
— and Sons of God; Gen. vi. 1–5. Kitto, **40**: 123.
— Ogres, and Cyclops. (L. Hunt) Colburn, **43**: 170.
— their own Killers. All the Year, **3**: 477.
Giants' Causeway, Architect's Acct. of. Ecl. Engin. **3**: 266.
— Visit to. (W. Howitt) Howitt, **3**: 153.—Broadw. **2**: 510.
Giant Cities of Bashan. (L. J. Fletcher) Univ. Q. **33**: 67. — Hours at Home, **2**: 284.
Giant Despair. (R. Buchanan) Gent. M. n. s. **13**: 301.
Gibbes, Mary Anna. (Mrs. E. F. Ellet) Godey, **59**: 224.
Gibbon, Edward. (W. D. Howells) Atlan. **41**: 99. — (H. Rogers) Liv. Age, **53**: 449. — Nat. R. **2**: 1. — N. E. Reg. **29**: 233. — Chr. R. **13**: 34. — Dem. R. **20**: 521.
— and his Biographers. Dub. R. **24**: 381.
— and his Protestant Editors. Dub. R. **8**: 189.
— and Voltaire. (A. D. Vandam) Tinsley, **19**: 11. — Colburn, **58**: 558. — Hogg, **5**: 211.
— Autobiography. Blackw. **130**: 229.—St. Paul's, **3**: 570.
— Guizot's Edition of. (H. H. Milman) Quar. **50**: 273. Same art. Mus. **24**: 526.
— Inedited Letter of. Fraser, **43**: 291. Same art. Liv. Age, **29**: 178. Same art. Internat. M. **3**: 126.
— Infidelity of. (L. Withington) Lit. & Theo. R. **2**: 38.
— Life and Writings of. Fraser, **46**: 438. Same art. Ecl. M. **27**: 392. Same art. Liv. Age, **35**: 417.
— Literary Culture of. Am. J. Educ. **28**: 577.
— Love Passage of. Cornh. **44**: 152. Same art. Ecl. M. **97**: 453.
— Loves of. (P. Fitzgerald) Belgra. **12**: 223.
— Memoirs of. Ecl. M. **68**: 496.
— Milman's Edition of. Quar. **62**: 360.
— Milman's Life of. Ecl. R. **70**: 142.
— Miscellaneous Works. (T. D. Whitaker) Quar. **12**: 369. — Ecl. R. **23**: 1, 180. — Portfo.(Den.) **23**: 361.
— on Number of Early Christians. (J. Murdock) Am. Church R. **7**: 351.
— Views of the Church examined. (E. E. Higbee) Mercersb. **16**: 93.
— Was he an Infidel? (J. M. Macdonald) Bib. Sac. **25**: 536.
— Works of. Quar. **12**: 368. — Anal. M. **6**: 89.
Gibbons, Archbp., and Dr. Stearns. Am. Cath. Q. **5**: 84.
Gibbons, Grinling. Chamb. J. **47**: 330.
— Carvings of. Art J. **8**: 85.
Gibbs, Josiah W., Discourse on. (G. P. Fisher) New Eng. **19**: 605.
Gibbs, W. A. Battle of the Standard. (B. M. Ranking) Dub. Univ. **90**: 757.
Gibeah; Lesson for the Times. Bost. R. **1**: 505.
Gibraltar. (G. M. Towle) Harper, **55**: 76.—All the Year, **24**: 564. — (A. Griffiths) Art J. **33**: 341. — Bentley, **30**: 411. — Chr. Mo. Spec. **4**: 72. — House. Words, **19**: 42. — Lond. Q. **22**: 337. — Penny M. **3**: 19. — Sharpe, **47**: 251. Same art. Ecl. M. **71**: 1113.
— and Spain. Brit. Q. **36**: 321. Same art. Ecl. M. **58**: 108.
— Bartlett's. Chamb. J. **15**: 43.
— Description and History of. Westm. **78**: 370.
— Fortress or Colony? (T. H. S. Escott) Macmil. **36**: 472.
— Legend of. Blackw. **70**: 522. Same art. Liv. Age, **31**: 506.
— Letters from. Dub. Univ. **16**: 625.
— Mediterranean Stairs. Colburn, **87**: 47.

Gibraltar, Reminiscences of. Colburn, **169**: 339, 519.
— St. Michael's Cave. Once a Week, **12**: 555.
— Scamper over Tarec's Mount. St. James, **28**: 541.
— Town and Fortifications of. Nat. M. **12**: 404.
— Urquhart's Pillars of Hercules. (R. Ford) Quar. **86**: 415.
Gibraltar Current. (W. B. Carpenter) Nature, **4**: 468.
Gibson, John, Sculptor, with portrait. Art J. **1**: 139. — with portrait (E. Walford) Once a Week, **14**: 218. — Ev. Sat. **1**: 230. — Cornh. **17**: 540.
— Anecdote of. St. James, **29**: 310.
— Designs of. Art J. **5**: 63.
— Life of. Ed. R. **131**: 392. — Nation, **10**: 273.
— Recollections of. Ev. Sat. **5**: 686.
— Tinted Venus. Cornh. **6**: 279.
— Works of. Art J. **13**: 204.
Gibson, J. B., Chief Justice, Sketch of. (J. Clark) Mercersb. **8**: 94.
Gibson, John Ward, Narrative of. Liv. Age, **22**: 241.
Gibson, Wm., Poems of. Dem. R. **42**: 307.
Giddings, Joshua R. Republic, **4**: 322.
Giddings, Salmon. (J. C. Roy) New Eng. **33**: 513.
Gideon Brown; a Story of the Covenant. All the Year, **23**: 372, 396.
Giersfeld and Bourtanger Moor. (F. Schaller) So. M. **13**: 1.
Giesecke, Sir Charles Lewis. Dub. Univ. **3**: 161, 296. **7**: 494.
Gieseler, J. C. L. (Dr. Redepenning) Kitto, **16**: 365.
Giffard Injector, Theory of. Ecl. Engin. **10**: 182.
Gifford, R. S., and his Paintings. Art J. **29**: 310.
Gifford, William. Bentley, **40**: 104. Same art. Ecl. M. **39**: 115. Same art. Liv. Age, **50**: 507.
— Life of. Mus. **12**: 429, 544.
Gift of Ægir; a Danish Romance. (A. Oehlenschlager) St. James, **15**: 489.
Gifts, The. (W. Pickersgill) Colburn, **112**: 74–175.
Gifts, The; an Arab Paraphrase. (R. W. Buchanan) St. James, **5**: 161.
Gifts. Dial, **4**: 93.
— Gossip about. All the Year, **37**: 9.
Gift Books and Annuals, 1852. So. Q. **21**: 176.
Gift Horses. Chamb. J. **40**: 412.
Gigi's; a Roman Art School. (M. B. Wright) Lippinc. **27**: 1.
Gil Blas and Don Quixote. (C. H. Drew) Penn Mo. **3**: 555.
— and Archbp. of Granada. (F. Jacox) Colburn, **132**: 405.
— Llorente's Observations on. Mo. R. **102**: 535.
— Who wrote? (A. H. Everett) No. Am. **25**: 278. — (H. Van Laun) Gent. M. n. s. **26**: 213. — Blackw. **55**: 698. — Anal. M. **2**: 165.
Gil Garay. (J. W. Palmer) Galaxy, **2**: 365.
Gilbart, James William, with portrait. Hunt, **19**: 68. — with portrait, Bank. M. (L.) **2**: 7. **23**: 652. — Bank. M. (N. Y.) **14**: 851.
Gilbert, Eliphalet W. (B. J. Wallace) Am. Presb. R. **2**: 353.
Gilbert, Sir Humphrey, Last Letters of. (S. G. Drake) N. E. Reg. **13**: 197.
— Plea for a London Academy. Arch. **21**: 506.
Gilbert, Sir John. (J. B. Atkinson) Portfo. **2**: 49. — with portrait, Ev. Sat. **11**: 436.
— Technical Notes on. (P. G. Hamerton) Portfo. **7**: 13.
Gilbert, Mrs. Ann Taylor, of Ongar, Autobiography of. (A. V. Dicey) Nation, **20**: 332.
Gilbert, N. J. L., Malfilâtre, and Chénier. Once a Week, **15**: 370.
Gilbert, Sir Walter, and Indian Army. Bentley, **33**: 627.
Gilbert, William. (H. A. Page) Contemp. **12**: 437.
— Hurricane. Retros. **10**: 160.
Gilbert, William Schwenck. (P. Wrey) Lond. Soc. **27**: 13. — (K. Field) Scrib. **18**: 751.
Gilbert, William Schwenck, as a Dramatist. (W. D. Adams) Belgra. **45**: 438. — (W. Archer) St. James, **49**: 287.
— The Bab Ballads. Chamb. J. **46**: 539.
— Wicked World. Dark Blue, **4**: 707. — Once a Week, **28**: 117.
Gilbert Genealogy. (J. W. Thornton) N. E. Reg. **4**: 223, 339.
Gilbert Gurney. (T. Hook) Colburn, **41**: 273. **44**: 153.
Gilbert Rugge. Fraser, **69**: 551, 670. **70**: 20–165. **71**: 43–702. **72**: 36–761. **73**: 27.
Gilbert Singleby. Bentley, **59**: 146.
Gilds. *See* Guilds.
Gildas, Historical Passage in. (S. Pegge) Arch. **5**: 272.
Gilded Youth. (T. H. S. Escott) Belgra. **24**: 283.
Gilder, Richard W. The New Day; a Poem. (B. Taylor) Internat. R. **3**: 410.
Gilding. J. Frankl. Inst. **4**: 268, 339, 388. **5**: 33–234.
— Silvering, and Tinning. J. Frankl. Inst. **1**: 246, 306. **2**: 60.
— Thread and Fiber. Art J. **8**: 337.
Gile, Samuel, Biography of. Am. Q. Reg. **10**: 217.
Gilead, Land of, Oliphant's. (W. P. Garrison) Nation, **32**: 336.
Giles Chawbacon. Bentley, **10**: 609.
Giles, Ernest; his Travels across the Australian Desert. (F. A. Edwards) Gent. M. n. s. **21**: 190.
Gilfillan, George. (L. Cross) Colburn, **163**: 441. — Ecl. M. **13**: 276. — Liv. Age, **61**: 579. — Colburn, **96**: 265. Same art. Liv. Age, **35**: 534.
— Bards of the Bible. Ecl. R. **93**: 718. — New Eng. **9**: 198. — Kitto, **7**: 419. — (M. Stuart) No. Am. **73**: 238.
— Gallery of Literary Portraits. (T. De Quincey) Tait, n. s. **12**: 724, 756. — Ecl. R. **91**: 174. — Ecl. M. **20**: 124. — Dub. Univ. **27**: 652. — (R. H. Bacon) Am. Whig R. **5**: 386. — Brit. Q. **11**: 111. Same art. Ecl. M. **20**: 124.
Gilfillan, Robert, Songs and Poems of. Ecl. R. **94**: 567.
Gill, Edmund, Works of. Art J. **26**: 41.
Gill, John, Theology of. (D. T. Fisk) Bib. Sac. **14**: 343.
Gill, Michael Henry. Irish Mo. **7**: 223.
Gill, Thomas H., an unknown Hymn-Writer. (F. M. Bird) Hours at Home, **6**: 374.
Gill Genealogy. N. E. Reg. **33**: 339.
Gillam, Elizabeth. (Mrs. E. F. Ellet) Godey, **54**: 339.
Gillet, Helen, Story of. Colburn, **40**: 51.
Gillett, Ezra H., Plagiarism of. (C. E. Grinnell) No. Am. **101**: 213.
Gillies, John. History of the World. Ed. R. **11**: 40.
Gillies, Robert P. German Stories. Blackw. **20**: 844.
— Memoirs of a literary Veteran. Dub. Univ. **37**: 590. — Ecl. R. **96**: 175.
Gillmore, Parker. Hunter's Adventures in the West. Chamb. J. **48**: 98.
Gillmore, Gen. Quincy A., with portrait. Ecl. Engin. **7**: 1.
Gillott, Joseph, and Steel-Pen Trade. Pract. M. **1**: 322.
Gillotype Engraving Process. J. Frankl. Inst. **110**: 136.
Gillray, James. (G. A. Sala) Belgra. **23**: 166.
— Caricatures of. Retros. **17**: 255. Same art. Ecl. M. **30**: 129.
Gilman, Daniel Coit, with portrait. Ecl. M. **85**: 119.
Gilman, John Taylor. Ann. Reg. **4**: 182.
Gilman, Samuel, Sermons of. Chr. Disc. **4**: 33.
Gilmer, Thomas W., Address of. So. Lit. Mess. **3**: 97.
Gilmour's Ward; a Story. Eng. Dom. M. **1**: 1–174.
Gilpin, Bernard, Life of. Chr. Obs. **8**: 210–409.
Gilpin, Charles, with portrait. Peop. J. **8**: 301.
Gilpin, Henry D., with portrait. Dem. R. **8**: 512.
Gilpin, Joshua Rowley. Chr. Obs. **10**: 605, 669.
Gilpin, William, Church and School of. Penny M. **4**: 92.
Gilson, Helen L. (P. M. Clapp) O. & N. **5**: 457, 560.

Gilt and Gingerbread; or Tom Fool's Day in the City. Fraser, 50: 618.
Gimmal Ring, Remarks on a. (R. Smith) Arch. 14: 7.
Ginevra; a Story. (C. Owen) Galaxy, 13: 256.
Ginevra da Siena. (W. W. Story) Blackw. 99: 673. Same art. Liv. Age, 90: 3.
Ginger, Cultivation of. Penny M. 9: 247.
Ginx's Baby. (E. G. Martin) Nation, 12: 203.
Gioberti, Vincenzo. (J. B. Torricelli) Chr. Exam. 71: 237. — Dub. Univ. 50: 460. — No. Brit. 11: 369. — Brownson, 7: 409. — Prosp. R. 3: 423.
— Philosophy of. Brownson, 21: 129, 293.
Giorgione. *See* Barbarelli, G.
Giotto and Cimabue. (W. de B. Fryer) Penn Mo. 12: 574, 654.
— Gospel of Labor. (S. Colvin) Macmil. 35: 448.
Gipsy, The, and the Dupe. Fraser, 22: 577.
— of Debretzin. Portfo.(Den.) 33: 488.
— of Sardis. Colburn, 44: 299. 45: 10.
Gipsies. Blackw. 99: 565. — Chamb. J. 36: 265. 57: 737. — (F. Bowen) No. Am. 55: 72. — Am. J. Sci. 24: 342. — Mo. R. 84: 412. — Anal. M. 10: 492. — Dem. R. 11: 58. — (J. O. Noyes) Knick. 51: 551. 52: 10. — Sharpe, 7: 169. — Univ. Q. 16: 393. — Chr. Obs. 8: 769. 9: 278.
— Adventures of. Blackw. 7: 48–374.
— At the Court of the King of. All the Year, 6: 69.
— at Rome. Penny M. 14: 297.
— Attila and Zend-Cali. (J. O. Noyes) Nat. M. 13: 441.
— Border. Once a Week, 6: 431.
— Christmas Gathering. (W. R. S. Ralston) Good Words, 9: 96.
— Customs and Habits of, Hoyland on. Ecl. R. 26: 579.
— Gitanos and their Ways. (J. O. Noyes) Nat. M. 13: 497.
— Glimpses of. All the Year, 21: 536.
— History of. All the Year 15: 224. — Ecl. R. 123: 128.
— — and Character of. Nat. Q. 28: 162.
— Hungarian. Nat. M. 4: 305. — Sharpe, 18: 377.
— in Egypt. (A. von Kremer) Anthrop. R. 2: 262.
— in England. (V. S. Morwood) Victoria, 9: 291–499. 10: 40. 12: 202–414. 14: 71. — Meth. M. 51: 242. — Quar. 101: 468.
— in Europe. (J. O. Noyes) Nat. M. 13: 104, 344. — Penny M. 7: 17, 114.
— Language and Customs of. Dub. Univ. 70: 38.
— of Art. (H. Murger) Sharpe, 48: 316. 49: 217. Same art. Knick. 41: 12–419. 42: 19–596. 43: 20–485.
— of the Danube. Chamb. J. 25: 273. Same art. Liv. Age, 49: 731.
— of Fife, Anecdotes of. Blackw. 2: 282, 523. 3: 14, 393.
— of Hesse-Darmstadt. Blackw. 2: 407.
— of Scotland. (Sir W. Scott) Blackw. 1: 43, 154, 615. — Sharpe, 13: 321.
— of Spain. Ed. R. 74: 24. Same art. Am. Ecl. 3: 102. — Dub. Univ. 21: 248. — Brit. & For. R. 13: 367. — Blackw. 50: 352. — U. S. Cath. M. 2: 257.
— — Borrow's. Mus. 43: 321. 44: 476. — Ed. R. 74: 45. — Mo. R. 155: 107. — U. S. Cath. M. 2: 257.
— — — and Bible in Spain. Dub. Univ. 21: 248.
— of Switzerland. Nat. M. 11: 152.
— Origin of. Hogg, 4: 183. — Pop. Sci. Mo. 16: 540.
— — and Character of. So. R. n. s. 13: 85.
— — and Destiny of. Dub. Univ. 76: 315.
— — and History of. Temp. Bar, 47: 65.
— — and Wanderings of. (A. Clarke) Ed. R. 148: 117. Same art. Liv. Age, 138: 515.
— — Charnock's. Anthrop. R. 4: 89.
— Ottoman. Chamb. J. 55: 225.
— Petty Romany. (J. Lucas) 19th Cent. 8: 578.
— Russian. (C. G. Leland) Macmil. 41: 43, 117. Same art. Appleton, 23: 156.
Gipsies, Simson's History of. (C. S. Wyman) Nation, 3: 107. — Cath. World, 3: 702. — Bentley, 59: 164. Same art. Ecl. M. 66: 539. — Bentley, 63: 411. Same art. Ecl. M. 70: 743.
— Transformation of. Once a Week, 11: 498.
— Wallachian. House. Words, 8: 139.
See Bohemians; Zigeuner.
Gipsy Ball. Ev. Sat. 13: 691.
Gipsy Concert at Moscow. All the Year, 11: 156.
Gipsy Dialect, Smart on. (F. Hall) Nation, 20: 116.
Gipsy Journal. (S. Tytler) Good Words, 9: 701, 745.
Gipsy Lady; a Tale. Bentley, 64: 150, 269, 409.
Gipsy Language. (W. Marsden and J. Bryant) Arch. 7: 382, 387.
Gipsy Life in Europe. (W. Wells) Hours at Home, 2: 146.
Gipsy King. House. Words, 19: 89.
Giraffe, The. Hogg, 6: 129. — Penny M. 1: 187, 308.
— Horns of. (T. S. Cobbold) Intel. Obs. 2: 12.
Giraffes at the Zoölogical Gardens. Penny M. 5: 233.
Giraldo, the Hermit. Hogg, 7: 72–152.
Giraldus Cambrensis. Ed. R. 8: 399. — Dub. Univ. 35: 1, 192, 383.
— and his Adversaries. Dub. R. 28: 141.
— Life of. (T. R. Lounsbury) New Eng. 37: 717. 38: 50. 39: 70.
Girard, Jacques. Trials of a French Journalist. Cornh. 32: 691.
Girard, Stephen. Bank. M. (N. Y.) 2: 17. — Godey, 34: 273. — Hogg, 7: 206. — House. Words, 17: 618. Same art. Liv. Age, 58: 237.
— and Girard College. (J. Parton) No. Am. 100: 70.
— Biography of. (J. H. Lanman) Hunt, 4: 359. — Ann. Reg. 7: [387. — New Eng. M. 2: 149. 3: 59.
— Will of. Niles's Reg. 41: 347, 368, 390. 45: 123. — U. S. Cath. M. 3: 493.
— — and Webster's Plea. (H. Humphrey) New Eng. 3: 89.
Girard College. (W. B. Reed) No. Am. 51: 23. — (E. C. Wines) Am. Inst. of Instruc. 1842: 85. — New York R. 6: 369. — Am. Q. 13: 143. — Meth. Q. 1: 165. — Brownson, 6: 162. — Niles's Reg. 44: 349. — (T. U. Walter) J. Frankl. Inst. 25: 354.
— and its Founder. Am. J. Educ. 27: 593. — Nat. Q. 8: 81.
— Laying of Corner-Stone. (N. Biddle) J. Frankl. Inst. 16: 150, 228.
— Report, 1838–39. (T. U. Walter) J. Frankl. Inst. 26: 27. 27: 167.
Girardet, Edward Henry, Obituary of. Art J. 32: 208.
Girardin, Delphine Gay de. Lond. Soc. 21: 519. Same art. Ecl. M. 79: 220. — Ev. Sat. 12: 685. — Irish Q. 8: 807. — For. Q. 32: 470. Same art. Liv. Age, 1: 545.
— Lady Tartuffe. Blackw. 73: 430.
— Novels of. St. James, 46: 37.
— School for Journalists. For. Q. 25: 113.
Girardin, Emile de. (A. Rhodes) Galaxy, 18: 742. — (V. Vaughan) Galaxy, 6: 678. — (W. Welles) Hours at Home, 8: 389. — Irish Q. 8: 807. — Dem. R. 25: 497. — Blackw. 56: 237.
— Cours de Littérature. Dub. Univ. 23: 589.
Girardin, St. Marc. Colburn, 105: 229. Same art. Ecl. M. 36: 1093.
Girders and Trusses, Depth of straight. (E. Alder) Ecl. Engin. 16: 42.
— and Draw Spans, Continuous. (A. J. Du Bois) J. Frankl. Inst. 102: 17, 105.
— and Suspension Chains, Combining. (P. W. Barlow) J. Frankl. Inst. 65: 301, 361.
— Comparative Strength of trussed and plain. (J. McClure and E. Morris) J. Frankl. Inst. 33: 361.
— Compound or trussed Cast-Iron Beams, or. (W. Fairbairn) J. Frankl. Inst. 58: 227, 300.

Girders, Construction of Wrought-Iron Lattice. (T. Cargill) J. Frankl. Inst. **76**: 1–375. **77**: 11, 73.
— Continuous. (C. Bender) Ecl. Engin. **15**: 289, 563. — (M. Merriman) Ecl. Engin. **15**: 461. — (J. D. Crehore) Ecl. Engin. **16**: 323. — (M. S. Hudgins) Ecl. Engin. **19**: 553. — (F. E. Kidder) Ecl. Engin. **25**: 49.
— Economic Angles in parallel Open-Work. J. Frankl. Inst. **73**: 297. **74**: 21, 81.
— Economic Construction of. J. Frankl. Inst. **74**: 82–153.
— Effect of Impact on Wrought-Iron. (W. Fairbairn) J. Frankl. Inst. **79**: 16.
— Lattice. J. Frankl. Inst. **72**: 15.
— Loads on. Ecl. Engin. **7**: 30. — (E. S. Gould) Ecl. Engin. **7**: 301.
— Minimum Material in a trussed. (W. Bouton) J. Frankl. Inst. **80**: 73.
— Moments and Reactions of. (M. Merriman) J. Frankl. Inst. **99**: 206, 255.
— Railroad, Dynamical Deflection and Strain of. (H. Cox) J. Frankl. Inst. **47**: 73, 145.
— Riveted Plate. (T. Cooper) Ecl. Engin. **17**: 209.
— Strength of Cast-Iron. J. Frankl. Inst. **41**: 192. — (J. G. Lynde) J. Frankl. Inst. **69**: 261.
— Trussed. (D. Wood) J. Frankl. Inst. **78**: 230, 306, 375. **79**: 97, 308. **80**: 1. — (S. W. Robinson) J. Frankl. Inst. **79**: 164.
— Use of rolled. Ecl. Engin. **12**: 234.
— Vibratory Action on Strain of. (W. Fairbairn) J. Frankl. Inst. **77**: 301.
Girder Work, Uniform Stress in. (C. Reilly) J. Frankl. Inst. **80**: 83.
Girl and Grandfather. Temp. Bar, **60**: 470.
— at Rudder Grange. (F. R. Stockton) Scrib. **10**: 285.
— from the Lake; a Story. (R. Mulholland) Irish Mo. **9**: 395–627.
— from the Workhouse. All the Year, **8**: 132.
— of the Period. Once a Week, **28**: 234.
Girls. (E. O. Smith) Potter Am. Mo. **14**: 365.
— American, Health of. (T.W. Higginson) Atlan. **9**: 722.
— Beautiful. All the Year, **14**: 60.
— Education of. *See* Women, Education of.
— English. All the Year, **39**: 557.—Good Words, **2**: 533.
— — Special Work of. (I. Reaney) Cong. **7**: 156–288.
— Go-ahead. Belgra. **17**: 347.
— Nice. (W. Sawyer) Belgra. **5**: 63.
— of the Period, Two. Macmil. **19**: 323.
— Plea for. (J. J. Talbot) Penn Mo. **8**: 902.
— reared in English Workhouses. Month, **1**: 136.
— rescued from the Workhouse. (I. de Liefde) Good Words, **7**: 692.
— What they can do. Chamb. J. **58**: 161.
— What shall we do with our? Irish Mo. **6**: 501.
— Young Working. (Mrs. C. Marten) Irish Mo. **7**: 469.
See Industrial Schools.
Girls' Brothers. Temp. Bar, **27**: 169.
Girls' Sketching-Camp. (O. T. Miller) Harper, **63**: 522.
Girlhood, Ideal, in modern Romance. (H. Giles) Chr. Exam. **64**: 365.
Girolamo, detto il Fiorentino; a Poem. (W. W. Story) Atlan. **39**: 554.
Girondists. (T. A. Bent) Potter Am. Mo. **6**: 422.
— Lamartine's History of. (C. W. Upham) No. Am. **66**: 288. — (K. Armstrong) Am. Whig R. **7**: 358. — Ed. R. **87**: 1. Same art. Liv. Age, **16**: 289. Same art. Ecl. M. **13**: 219. — Fraser **36**: 253. — So. Q. **16**: 53. — Liv. Age, **18**: 577. — Ecl. R. **87**: 291, 486. — Dem. R. **34**: 419.
See France, Revolution.
Girton College. (M. B. Edwards) Fraser, **91**: 561. Same art. Ecl. M. **85**: 112. — (E. Shirreff) Fortn. **20**: 87. — (E. Minturn) Nation, **22**: 58.
— and Newnham College. Good Words, **22**: 319.
Girton College and Smith College. Nation, **22**: 112.
Gisborne, Thomas. Essays. Ecl. R. **37**: 217.
— Poems and Sermons. Chr. Obs. **3**: 34, 220, 298. **8**: 657.
Gislain, Edward. (W. C. Robinson) Month, **25**: 265.
Gisquet, M. Memoirs. Dub. Univ. **21**: 568. — Ecl. Mus. **2**: 334. — Fraser, **23**: 584.
Giulietta. (W. W. Story) Blackw. **96**: 241.
Giulio; a Tale. Colburn, **13**: 119.
Giulio Romano. (C. Van Vinkbooms) Lond. M. **4**: 418.
Giuseppe; a Corsican Story. Month, **7**: 414, 495.
Giuseppe Recca. Fraser, **19**: 80.
Giusti, Giuseppe. Cornh. **8**: 466. — (F. E. Trollope) Belgra. **41**: 89.
— and his Times. No. Brit. **41**: 437. Same art. Ecl. M. **64**: 367.
— Life, Letters, and Poems of. Chr. Rem. **43**: 257. — Brit. Q. **17**: 54. Same art. Liv. Age, **37**: 195.
— Satires. (W. D. Howells) No. Am. **115**: 31.
Give me some Work; a Tale. Colburn, **161**: 13, 150.
Given unsought. Lond. Soc. **25**: 524.
Giving, Munificence in. Am. Church R. **24**: 96.
— Systematic. Chr. Obs. **62**: 269.
See Beneficence; Benevolence.
Glacial Action about Penobscot Bay. (J. De Laski) Am. J. Sci. **87**: 335.
— in N. E. Anatolia. (W. G. Palgrave) Nature, **6**: 536.
— on the Green Mountain Summits. (E. Hungerford) Am. J. Sci. **95**: 1.
— on Mount Katahdin. (J. De Laski) Am. J. Sci. **103**: 27.
Glacial and Champlain Eras in New England. (J. D. Dana) Am. J. Sci. **105**: 198.
Glacial Drift, Andrews on. (E. W. Hilgard) Am. J. Sci. **93**: 241.
— beneath the Bed of Lake Michigan. (E. Andrews) Am. J. Sci. **93**: 75.
— in Canada, etc. (H. Y. Hind) Canad. J. n. s. **9**: 253.
— of North London. (H. Walker) Nature, **8**: 287.
— Superposition of, upon residuary Clays. (W. J. McGee) Am. J. Sci. **118**: 301.
Glacial Epoch, Effect on the Distribution of Insects in North America. (A. R. Grote) Am. J. Sci. **110**: 335.
— The Last, Drayson's. Nature, **8**: 301.
Glacial Features of Green Bay. (N. H. Winchell) Am. J. Sci. **112**: 15.
Glacial Formations at Glen Roy, Scotland. (L. Agassiz) Atlan. **13**: 723.
Glacial Marks on the Pacific and Atlantic Coasts compared. (A. S. Packard, jr.) Am. Natural. **11**: 674.
Glacial Motion, Theory of. (A. R. Wallace) Nature, **3**: 309.
Glacial Origin of certain Lakes. (A. C. Ramsay) Am. J. Sci. **85**: 324.
Glacial Period. (L. Agassiz) Atlan. **13**: 224. — All the Year, **36**: 113. — Sharpe, **48**: 307.
— Cause and Influence of. (D. Trowbridge) Nat. Q. **28**: 307.
— in America. (L. Agassiz) Atlan. **14**: 86.
— in Eastern North America. (G. F. Wright) Am. J. Sci. **121**: 120.
— in Northeast Anatolia. Nature, **5**: 444.
— Man and. (T. Belt) Pop. Sci. Mo. **12**: 61.
See Ice Age.
Glacial Phenomena. No. Brit. **31**: 89. Same art. Ecl. M. **48**: 344.
— in Maine. (L. Agassiz) Atlan. **19**: 211, 281.
— in the Vicinity of New York City. (R. P. Stevens) Am. J. Sci. **114**: 88.
— in Yellowstone Park. (W. H. Holmes) Am. Natural. **15**: 203.
— of the Maumee Valley. (G. K. Gilbert) Am. J. Sci. **101**: 339.
— Recurrence of. (A. C. Ramsay) Nature, **5**: 64.

Glacial Theory. (L. Agassiz) Ed. New Philos. J. 33: 217. 35: 1. — Chamb. J. 14: 147. — (J. D. Forbes) Am. J. Sci. 46: 172. — (M. Desor) Am. J. Sci. 53: 313. — Ed. R. 75: 49. Same art. Am. Ecl. 4: 1. — Ecl. Mus. 1: 383. — (R. Chambers) Ecl. M. 21: 485.
— of Count Rumford. (Lord Brougham) Ed. R. 4: 415.
— of Professor Agassiz. Am. J. Sci. 42: 346.
Glacial Theories. (G. L. Vose) No. Am. 96: 1. — Quar. 114: 76.
Glacier and the Shore. Chamb. J. 49: 69. Same art. Ecl. M. 78: 625.
— Greenland. (I. I. Hayes) Harper, 44: 204.
— The Tchingel. Chamb. J. 6: 93.
Glaciers. (Sir D. Brewster) No. Brit. 31: 90. — Brit. Q. 32: 341. — Chamb. J. 51: 23. Same art. Ecl. M. 82: 365. — Dub. R. 49: 40. — Hogg, 1: 62. — Knick. 63: 43. — (J. D. Forbes) Good Words, 3: 342, 404.
— Active, in United States. (C. King) Atlan. 27: 371.
— Agency of, in the Erosion of Valleys. (W. H. Niles) Am. J. Sci. 116: 366.
— Ancient, in Auvergne. (W. S. Symonds) Nature, 14: 179.
— — of Rocky Mountains. (A. Geikie) Am. Natural. 15: 1.
— — of the Sierra Nevada. (J. LeConte) Am. J. Sci. 110: 126.
— — Welsh. (H. Pearce) Dub. Univ. 84: 192.
— and Glacial Action in California. (J. Muir) Overland, 12: 393, 489. 13: 67-530. 14: 64.
— and Glacier Theories. Nat. R. 9: 1.—Westm. 67: 418.
— and Guides. Once a Week, 2: 509.
— and Ice. (W. F. Barrett) Pop. Sci. R. 5: 41.
— and Icebergs of Scotland, Ancient. No. Brit. 39: 286. Same art. Ecl. M. 62: 277.
— and their Phenomena. (D. Trowbridge) Nat. Q. 28: 35.
— Damming of Streams during Melting of. (J. D. Dana) Am. J. Sci. 111: 178.
— Descent of. (H. Moseley) J. Frankl. Inst. 61: 211.
— — Moseley on. (J. LeConte) Am. J. Sci. 70: 335.
— External Appearance of. (L. Agassiz) Atlan. 13: 56.
— Forbes on. Mo. R. 162: 11.
— — and his Biographers. (J. Tyndall) Contemp. 22: 484. Same art. Pop. Sci. Mo. 3: 746.
— Formation of. (L. Agassiz) Atlan. 12: 568.
— Garden of. Liv. Age, 14: 373.
— Geikie on. O. & N. 10: 506.
— Hassler Glacier in Straits of Magellan. (E. C. Agassiz) Atlan. 30: 472.
— in Central France. (J. D. Hooker) Nature, 13: 31.
— in Mohawk Valley. (J. D. Dana) Am. J. Sci. 85: 243.
— in White Mountains. (A. S. Packard, jr.) Am. Natural. 1: 260.—(G. L. Vose) Am. Natural. 2: 281.—(L. Agassiz) Am. Natural. 4: 550. — (A. S. Packard, jr.) Am. J. Sci. 93: 42.
— Internal Structure and Progression of. (L. Agassiz) Atlan. 12: 751.
— Leading Phenomena of. (J. D. Forbes) Ed. New Philos. J. 35: 221. 36: 217.
— Motion of. (J. Aitken) Nature, 7: 287.
— — Cause of. (J. L. Thompson) Canad. J. n. s. 12: 412.
— — Moseley on. (W. Mathews) Am. J. Sci. 103: 99.
— Night among. Chamb. J. 40: 257. 42: 174.
— of Alaska. (W. P. Blake) Am. J. Sci. 94: 96.
— of the Alps. (J. de Charpentier) Ed. New Philos. J. 33: 104. — (C. Dewey) Chr. R. 28: 296. — (J. D. Forbes) Ed. New Philos. J. 33: 338. 34: 1, 133.— (J. F. Hugi) Ed. New Philos. J. 10: 332. 11: 74.— Ed. R. 80: 135. 113: 221. — Dub. Univ. 48: 549. — Fraser, 62: 793. — (G. Molloy) Irish Mo. 5: 541. — Penny M. 13: 15.
— — Chamonix. (C. Martins) Ed. New Philos. J. 43: 54.
— — Destruction of Val de Bagne, 1818. Blackw. 4: 87.
Glaciers of the Alps, Downward Progress of. (E. Collomb) Ed. New Philos. J. 47: 104.
— — Ramsay's. (E. J. Chapman) Canad. J. n. s. 5: 51.
— — Tyndall's. Liv. Age, 66: 619. 67: 280.
— of Brazil. (A. R. Wallace) Nature, 2: 510.
— of California, Living. (J. Muir) Harper, 51: 769.
— of Connecticut River Valley. (J. D. Dana) Am. J. Sci. 102: 233.
— of Great Britain. (G. P. Bevan) Once a Week, 1: 227.
— of New England. (J. D. Dana) Am. J. Sci. 102: 324.
— of Norway. Dub. Univ. 43: 509. — No. Brit. 21: 201. Same art. Liv. Age, 43: 147. — Hogg, 11: 147.— (H. M. Baird) Pop. Sci. Mo. 7: 458.
— — Forbes's. Fraser, 49: 426.
— of the Sierras. (J. LeConte) Am. J. Sci. 105: 325.
— of Virginia. (R. P. Stevens) Am. J. Sci. 106: 371.
— on Mts. of Pacific Slope. (C. King) Am. J. Sci. 101: 157.
— Polar. (C. C. Merriman) Pop. Sci. Mo. 8: 702. 9: 178.
— Recent and extinct. (W. S. Symonds) Pop. Sci. R. 15: 169.
— Retreat of European. (C. Dufour) Pop. Sci. R. 20: 317.
— Science on. Sharpe, 9: 236.
— Striæ on Mount Monadnock. (G. A. Wheelock) Am. Natural. 7: 466.
— Veined Structure of. (E. Whymper) Nature, 1: 266.
— Week among. (H. A. Grant) Am. J. Sci. 46: 281. — Ecl. M. 3: 109.
Glacier Meadows of the Sierra. (J. Muir) Scrib. 17: 478.
Gladiator of Ravenna, Halm's. Fraser, 55: 329.
Gladiatorial Games, Christianity in Suppression of. (J. Eastwood) Univ. Q. 35: 284.
Gladness, Grave of. (J. B. Brown) Cong. 1: 530.
— of Nature. (G. I. Cowan) Peop. J. 5: 289.
Gladstone, William Ewart. Liv. Age, 12: 126. — (F. Arnold) Lond. Soc. 15: 97.—(A. T. Innes) Contemp. 15: 630. — (J. McCarthy) New Ecl. 4: 257. — (N. Sheppard) Lakeside, 1: 274. — (G. M. Towle) Putnam, 13: 287. — Blackw. 97: 240, 261. — with portrait (A. Young) Appleton, 7: 141. — Dub. Univ. 81: 281. — Ev. Sat. 7: 243. — Ecl. M. 28: 498. 35: 256. 95: 246.— with portrait, Ecl. M. 66: 254. — Internat. R. 5: 588. — Nat. R. 11: 219. — (H. Dunckley) Fortn. 33: 26. — Liv. Age, 144: 387.— (C. H. Hill) Internat. R. 8: 337. — Scrib. 21: 125.
— Administration of, 1868–73. Brit. Q. 58: 189.— Westm. 91: 360. 99: 208. 102: 299.
— — Men of. Gent. M. n. s. 12: 205.
— Ancestors of. (J. Veitch) Fraser, 101: 805.
— and the Anglican Establishment. Cong. 4: 449.
— and the Bulgarian Horrors. (E. Gaisford) St. James, 39: 100.
— and Cabinet in Council, 1870. Ev. Sat. 9: 451, 456.
— and his Chapter of Autobiography. Macmil. 19: 273.
— and the Heroic Ages. Nat. Q. 20: 141.
— and the Irish Farmers. (J. G. McGee) Cath. World, 11: 242.
— and the Nation, 1880. Brit. Q. 71: 171.
— and our Empire. (E. Dicey) 19th Cent. 2: 292.
— Apology. Quar. 126: 121. — St. James, 23: 433.
— as a Man of Letters. Fraser, 100: 657. Same art. Appleton, 23: 40.
— at Edinburgh, 1860. Ecl. R. 112: 48.
— Character of. Canad. Mo. 10: 452.
— Church Principles. Ecl. R. 73: 369.
— Durham Letter of. Month, 22: 257.
— Eleventh Budget. Blackw. 129: 640.
— Ethics of Gladstonianism. Blackw. 130: 634.
— Fall of Government of, 1874. Dub. R. 74: 450.— Brit. Q. 59: 470. — Cong. 4: 65. — Month, 18: 411.
— Financial Statements of, 1860–63. Brit. Q. 39: 291.
— Gleanings of past Years. Internat. R. 7: 98.
— in the Canvass of 1879. Nation, 30: 7.

Gladstone, William Ewart, in Scotland, 1869, Speeches of. Quar. **149**: 251.
— — 1880. Fraser, **101**: 103.
— Juventus Mundi. Chr. Obs. **69**: 755. — Ev. Sat. **8**: 289. — (W. F. Allen) Nation, **9**: 254.
— Latest Discovery of. Month, **25**: 137.
— Ministerial Embarrassments of, 1881. Quar. **151**: 535.
— Ministry of, in 1881. Gent. M. n. s. **25**: 725.
— New financial Policy of. Macmil. **14**: 130.
— on Church and State. (T. B. Macaulay) Ed. R. **69**: 231. — Quar. **65**: 97.
— on Strauss and modern Thought. (C. Beard) Theo. R. **10**: 253.
— on Vaticanism. Dub. R. **76**: 170–516. — (T. B. Parkinson) Month, **22**: 478. **23**: 67, 161.
— — External Aspects of the Controversy. Month, **23**: 1.
— — Has Father Newman confuted? (W. Nevin) Macmil. **31**: 420.
— Oratory of. Fraser, **34**: 653.
— Pilgrimage of. Blackw. **127**: 124.
— Poem by, on Death of an Infant. Good Words, **12**: 365.
— Policy of, and the new Equilibrium. (R. A. Earle) Fortn. **30**: 568.
— Political Portrait of. St. James, **24**: 393.
— Political Sketch of. Hogg, **10**: 83.
— Religious Inconsistencies of. Westm. **99**: 367.
— Retirement from the Liberal Leadership, 1875. Brit. Q. **61**: 478. — (J. Bryce) Nation, **20**: 109.
— Return to Office, 1880. Am. Cath. Q. **5**: 533.
— Smith's Life of. (A. G. Sedgwick) Nation, **30**: 309.
— Statesmanship of. Brit. Q. **50**: 175.
— Stump Ministry of; its first Session. Blackw. **128**: 515.
— Two Studies of. Contemp. **36**: 398.
— Unpopularity of, 1871. (E. L. Godkin) Nation, **13**: 190.
Gladstone Family, Fortunes of. Lond. Soc. **37**: 385.
Gladys the Lost; a Poem. (M. Collins) Temp. Bar, **5**: 511.
Glamis, Mystery of. All the Year, **46**: 229.
Glammis Castle, Visit to. (W. Howitt) Howitt, **2**: 121.
Glamorgan, Descent of Lordship of. Antiquary, **2**: 102.
Glamour; a Tale. (Countess von Bothmer) Belgra. **8**: 357, 545.
Glanvil, Joseph, Pyrrhonism of. Retros. **17**: 105.
Glapthorne, Henry, Plays of. Retros. **10**: 122.
Glarus, Glimpse of. (G. C. Swayne) Once a Week, **17**: 563.
Glasgow. (W. C. Taylor) Bentley, **8**: 558. — Penny M. **4**: 377, 425.
— Ancient. (E. Walford) Gent. M. n. s. **9**: 525.
— Bank of, Failure of, 1878. Bank. M. (N. Y.) **33**: 331, 389. — Bank. M. (L.) **38**: 917. — Brit. Q. **70**: 157. — Fortn. **30**: 882.
— Bank Frauds in. (W. Chambers) Chamb. J. **55**: 769.
— Broomielaw Bridge. Penny M. **6**: 373.
— Christmas Week at. Fraser, **55**: 204.
— City Bank of. Bank. M. (N. Y.) **34**: 606.
— Clubs of. Bentley, **38**: 566. Same art. Ecl. M. **37**: 253. — Chamb. J. **24**: 406.
— College Life at. Fraser, **53**: 505.
— Dinner in. Blackw. **14**: 459.
— down the Water. Fraser, **54**: 501. Same art. Liv. Age, **52**: 16.
— Drainage System of. Ecl. Engin. **19**: 112.
— Geological Exhibition in. (J. Mayer) Nature, **7**: 128.
— in the 18th Century. (W. Chambers) Chamb. J. **15**: 166–347. Same art. Ecl. M. **23**: 163, 353, 451.
— in 1851. Dub. Univ. **38**: 628. Same art. Ecl. M. **25**: 85.
— Industrial. Chamb. J. **14**: 83, 99, 121.
— past, present, and future. Tait, n. s. **14**: 104.
— Rambles around. Blackw. **83**: 467.
— Residence in. U. S. Lit. Gaz. **2**: 222.
— Royal Exchange. Penny M. **6**: 361.
— Science Lectures in. (J. Mayer) Nature, **11**: 233.
— Social Habits at, in last Century. Penny M. **4**: 439.
Glasgow, Social Science in, 1860. Tait, n. s. **27**: 537.
— Trongate and Buchanan Street. (G. A. Sala) Temp. Bar, **16**: 338.
— — to Argyle Street. (G. A. Sala) Temp. Bar, **16**: 489.
— University of. Quar. **14**: 162.
— — Library of. (R. B. Spears) Lib. J. **2**: 176.
— — — Management of. Blackw. **2**: 421.
— — Physical Science in. (J. T. Bottomley) Nature, **6**: 29.
— — Rectorship of. Blackw. **13**: 93.
— Visit to. All the Year, **26**: 277.
— — in May, 1852. Art J. **4**: 201.
— Vital Statistics of. (R. Cowan) J. Statis. Soc. **3**: 257.
Glass, Capt. George. Chamb. J. **55**: 56.
Glass, Francis. Washingtonii Vita. So. Lit. Mess. **2**: 52. — (J. L. Kingsley) No. Am. **43**: 28. **44**: 270. — Knick. **8**: 473.
Glass. All the Year, **27**: 201. — Chamb. J. **3**: 231. **41**: 841. — Ev. Sat. **9**: 254.
— Action of Sunlight on. (T. Gaffield) Am. J. Sci. **94**: 244, 316.
— American. Niles's Reg. **16**: 308.
— Ancient. Art J. **24**: 3. — Antiquary, **4**: 75, 152, 199.
— Art Work in. Dub. Univ. **95**: 72.
— as a Material for Construction. Am. Arch. **7**: 286.
— Bending, Blowing, and Cutting of. (M. Faraday) J. Frankl. Inst. **6**: 92–361.
— Berkshire Crystal. (H. Brown) Hours at Home, **11**: 524.
— Colored, Making of. Ev. Sat. **9**: 126.
— Crystalline, Nature of. (C. M. Wetherill) Am. J. Sci. **91**: 16.
— Decomposed, Crystallization and Polarization of. (Sir D. Brewster) J. Frankl. Inst. **72**: 306.
— Early Christian. (A. W. Franks) F. Arts Q. **2**: 378. — Kitto, **34**: 253.
— Flint-Glass Factory. Penny M. **10**: 81.
— for decorative Purposes, Manufacture of. (H. J. Powell) Am. Arch. **10**: 19.
— Harcourt's Researches on. Nature, **4**: 351.
— Hardened or tempered. Pract. M. **5**: 135. — Ecl. Engin. **14**: 511.
— Historical Account of. Penny M. **3**: 178.
— in all Ages. (C. Montague) Potter Am. Mo. **14**: 33.
— Manufacture of. (H. N. Finn) Am. J. Sci. **16**: 112. — Carey's Mus. **6**: 119. — (D. Jarvis) Hunt, **27**: 383–749. **28**: 119, 379, 513. — (F. Pellatt) J. Frankl. Inst. **42**: 271. — (W. Chaffers) Art J. **18**: 25–278. — Chamb. J. **52**: 478. — Sharpe, **4**: 148, 170, 188
— — Ancient and mediæval. Cornh. **16**: 580.
— — and Porcelain Manufactures by ancient Egyptians. Ed. New Philos. J. **25**: 101. — Liv. Age, **5**: 527.
— — Curiosities of. Chamb. J. **11**: 309. — Ecl. R. **90**: 289.
— — in Bohemia. (M. L. P. Debette) J. Frankl. Inst. **39**: 109, 183, 273.
— — in India. J. Frankl. Inst. **5**: 391.
— — of Crown and Sheet. J. Frankl. Inst. **62**: 205, 275.
— — of Filigree, Flint, and Crown. (G. Bontems) J. Frankl. Inst. **41**: 268, 346, 408. **42**: 342.
— — of polished Sheet. (R. Pilkington) J. Frankl. Inst. **80**: 126.
— of Bohemia. Internat. M. **4**: 291.
— Optical Constants of. (C. S. Hastings) Am. J. Sci. **115**: 269.
— Origin and History of. J. Frankl. Inst. **5**: 103.
— Painted, in Household Decoration. (C. A. Cole) Harper, **59**: 655.
— — in House of Lords. Dub. Univ. **29**: 131.
— Plate. Chamb. J. **58**: 807. — Peop. J. **11**: 173. — House. Words, **2**: 433. Same art. Ecl. M. **22**: 552.
— — Machinery for Manufacture of. (G. H. Daglish) J. Frankl. Inst. **78**: 397.

Glass, Prince Rupert's Drops. (W. Leighton, jr.) Pop. Sci. Mo. 8: 315.
— Refractive and dispersive Powers of. For. Q. 1: 424.
— Silvering and Gilding of. (J. Liebig) J. Frankl. Inst. 62: 318.
— — Art of. Chamb. J. 15: 63.
— — Process for. J. Frankl. Inst. 44: 248.
— Soluble. (J. N. von Fuchs) J. Frankl. Inst. 64: 121, 194, 265. — (C. A. Joy) Ecl. Engin. 3: 496.
— — Production of. Pract. M. 7: 336.
— Stained. (C. S. Wayne) Potter Am. Mo. 8: 331. — Art J. 11: 38. — (A. H. Miller) Art. J. 33: 69. — Chamb. J. 56: 519.
— Strength of various Kinds of. J. Frankl. Inst. 69: 311.
— Toughened. (P. F. Nursey) Pop. Sci. R. 14: 225. Same art. Ecl. M. 85: 457. Same art. Pop. Sci. Mo. 7: 554. Same art. Liv. Age, 130: 185. — Ecl. Engin. 13: 416.
— — French Experiments on. Pract. M. 5: 294.
— — Manufacture of. J. Frankl. Inst. 102: 371. 103: 45. — Pract. M. 6: 292.
— — Roger de la Bastie's. Pract. M. 5: 340.
— Venetian. Antiquary, 4: 75.
— — Ancient and modern. Cornh. 19: 459.
— — and Enamel Mosaics. Ev. Sat. 7: 601.
— — Modern. Art J. 18: 257.
— — Revival of. Art J. 32: 58.
Glass-Blowing, Art of. (M. Lafonde) J. Frankl. Inst. 15: 254, 327.
— as a Fine Art. (L. Abbott) Harper, 42: 337.
— for little Folks. (L. E. Chollet) Harper, 38: 742.
Glass-Collectors, Hints to. (A. Nesbit) Art J. 33: 337.
Glass-Factory, Day at a. Penny M. 13: 249.
Glass Globes and Cylinders, Resistance of. (Fairbairn and Tate) J. Frankl. Inst. 69: 63.
Glass Hatchet; a Story. Victoria, 12: 334.
Glass Houses, Moral. St. Paul's, 1: 220.
Glass-Painting. (L. C. Boistiniere) U. S. Cath. M. 4: 516. — Art J. 21: 231. — J. Frankl. Inst. 42: 276, 429.
— Ancient. (R. Masters) Arch. 8: 321.
— Art of. Godey, 54: 491. 55: 11, 107.
— in England. (N. D. Levett) Dub. Univ. 95: 361.
— Modern. Ed. R. 125: 154.
— Styles and Art of. Chr. Rem. 15: 1.
— Treatise on. Tait, n. s. 13: 127.
Glass-Rope Hyalonema. (W. Thomson) Intel. Obs. 11: 81.
Glass-Staining. (Prof. Schubarth) J. Frankl. Inst. 41: 181.
Glass Threads, Imperfect Elasticity of. (W. H. Goode) J. Frankl. Inst. 28: 367.
Glass Ware, How to take Care of. Pract. M. 5: 269.
Glass Wares, Imported. Niles's Reg. 16: 403.
Glass Windows, Did the Jews use? Kitto, 21: 59.
Glass Work. (A. A. Du Bois) Potter Am. Mo. 17: 241.
Glass-Works, Falcon, London. Hogg, 13: 15.
— of Murano. Am. Arch. 5: 127.
— Regenerating Gas Furnaces for. Pract. M. 6: 71.
Glassford, James. Lyrical Translations. Ed. R. 60: 353. 84: 102.
Glastonbury, British and English. (E. A. Freeman) Macmil. 42: 456.
— in Church History. Dub. R. 63: 86.
— Legend of, A. D. 62. Cath. World, 7: 517.
— Pilgrimage to. (E. Walford) Gent. M. n. s. 23: 616.
Glastonbury Abbey. (O. T. Hill) Dub. Univ. 66: 483, 631. 67: 24–643. 68: 321. 69: 87, 691. 70: 309. Same art. Cath. World, 2: 662. 3: 150. Same art. Liv. Age, 87: 577. — Am. J. Educ. 26: 273.
— Ancient Cup belonging to. (J. Milner) Arch. 11: 411.
Glastonbury Thorn, Old Diary of a Journey to. (G. Smith) Reliquary, 15: 45–201. 16: 19.
Glaucus. (E. Spencer) So. M. 13: 257.
Gleaner, Periodical Essays, edited by Nathan Drake. (J. Foster) Ecl. R. 16: 1141.
Gleichen Legend. (J. L. Ver Mehr) Overland, 8: 16, 110.
Gleig, George, Bishop. Blackw. 125: 306. Same art. Liv. Age, 141: 170.
— Sermons of, 1793–1803. Chr. Obs. 2: 480.
Gleig, George Robert, with portrait. Fraser, 10: 282.
— Chronicles of Waltham. Westm. 24: 124. 31: 444.
— Memoir of, with portrait. Colburn, 49: 220.
Glen, Alexander, Home of. Good Words, 15: 675.
Glenbervie, Lord. Translation of Forteguerri's Ricciardetto. Lond. M. 5: 429.
Glencairn; a Dramatic Story. (W. Chambers) Chamb. J. 52: 721, 738, 755.
Glen-Cluany, Through. (J. Leitch) St. James, 19: 309.
Glencoe; a Historical Ballad. (J. S. Blackie) Good Words, 9: 511.
Glencoe; a Poem. (W. Leighton) St. James, 25: 706.
Glencoe, Massacre of. Blackw. 86: 1.
— Twenty-six Hours at. Cornh. 23: 586. Same art. Ecl. M. 77: 97.
— Widow of. (W. E. Aytoun) Blackw. 62: 700.
Glendaloch, Hist. and Antiquities of. Dub. Univ. 78: 231.
Glendearg Cottage. (Miss Christmas) Bib. R. 3: 273.
Glendowr, Owen, History of. Retros. 13: 30.
— True Story of. (W. Sikes) Appleton, 18: 51.
Glenelg, Through. (J. Leitch) St. James, 19: 32.
Glen Fruin, Raid of. Fraser, 76: 783.
Glengariff. Penny M. 8: 25.
Glengoldy. (H. Hardy) So. M. 12: 234–413.
Glen Morrison, Through. (J. Leitch) St. James, 19: 445.
Glen Roy, Parallel Roads of. (J. Tyndall) Pop. Sci. R. 15: 375. — Pop. Sci. Mo. 10: 309.
— Up. Cornh. 36: 701.
Glenshiel, Through. (J. Leitch) St. James, 19: 158.
Glimmer's Picture Dream. (J. F. Bowman) Overland, 7: 399.
Glimmerings. Dial, 1: 379.
Glimpses and Mysteries. (A. H. Forrester) Bentley, 17: 357, 632. 18: 90–627.
— in the Mountains. Dub. Univ. 23: 409.
— of the Future. Blackw. 112: 282.
— of Ghost-Land. (L. H. Hooper) Lippinc. 12: 227.
— of the Gifted; a Legend of Venice. Fraser, 29: 418.
Globe, Equigraphic Projections of. (R. A. Proctor) Intel. Obs. 9: 429.
— Lenox. (B. F. De Costa) M. Am. Hist. 3: 529.
— Nancy. (B. F. De Costa) M. Am. Hist. 6: 183.
— of Euphrosynus Ulpius, 1542. Hist. M. 6: 203. — (B. F. De Costa) M. Am. Hist. 3: 17.
Globes, Use of, in Teaching. (A. Fleming) Am. Inst. of Instruc. 1841: 163.
Glorvina. (J. S. Knowles) Bentley, 1: 614. 2: 304.
Glory and Misfortune. (Mrs. Bushby) Colburn, 141: 49, 196.
— Chapter on. New Eng. M. 7: 199.
— National. Blackw. 116: 723. Same art. Liv. Age, 124: 215.
— of God, Hope of. (R. Candlish) Good Words, 22: 251.
Gloucester, Robert, Duke of, Seal belonging to. (J. Milles) Arch. 7: 69.
— Coin of. (J. Colebrooke) Arch. 4: 132.
Gloucester, Duchess of. Liv. Age, 54: 380.
Gloucester and Cirencester. (L. S. Costello) Bentley, 20: 390.
— Bishops of. (G. Burgess) Am. Church R. 19: 376.
— Cathedral of. All the Year, 33: 541. — Penny M. 14: 153.
— — Picture of Last Judgment in. (G. Scharf) Arch. 36: 370.
— Corpse of one of the Abbots of. (J. Cooke) Arch. 9: 10.
— Visit to. All the Year, 2: 51.

Gloucester, Mass. (S. G. W. Benjamin) Harper, **51**: 465. — (G. H. Proctor) Lippinc. **1**: 497.
Gloucestershire, Achievements of, Samuel Lysons on. Colburn, **123**: 111.
— Chain of ancient Fortresses in. (T. J. L. Baker) Arch. **19**: 161.
Gloves. All the Year, **9**: 425. — Ev. Sat. **11**: 238.
— Chapter on. Chamb. J. **26**: 392.
— Hand's-Breadth about. Hogg, **7**: 239.
— History of. All the Year, **43**: 329. — Chamb. J. **34**: 398.
— Manufacture of. Penny M. **12**: 94, 101.
Glover, John. Art J. **2**: 216.
Glover, Josse, Sketch of. N. E. Reg. **30**: 26.
Glover, Julia Betterton. (D. Cook) Gent. M. n. s. **24**: 437. — (T. I. Grinsted) Bentley, **41**: 210.
Glover, Richard. Political Memoirs. Ed. R. **22**: 475.
Glow-Worm, The. (P. M. Duncan) Pop. Sci. R. **18**: 225. — (E. Jesse) Once a Week, **3**: 578. — Hogg, **8**: 183.
— Light-emitting Apparatus of. (H. Fripp) Pop. Sci. R. **5**: 314.
Glück, Christopher W., and Haydn. (H. R. Haweis) Contemp. **7**: 535. **8**: 221.
— and his Music. Temp. Bar, **26**: 29.
— in Paris. (Mrs. E. F. Ellet) Godey, **23**: 50. — Dem. R. **19**: 106.
— Iphigenia in Taurus. (J. Hullah) Fortn. **5**: 212.
Glucose and Grape Sugar. (W. H. Wiley) Pop. Sci. Mo. **19**: 251.
Glue, Marine. Penny M. **14**: 330.
— — Jeffery's. J. Frankl. Inst. **36**: 197. **37**: 417. **38**: 432. **40**: 276.
Glutton, The. Penny M. **6**: 17.
— Confessions of an English. Blackw. **13**: 86.
— Passages in the Life of a. Dem. R. **32**: 11.
Glycerine and oily Acids, Constitution of. (J. C. Booth) J. Frankl. Inst. **45**: 365.
— Economical Applications of. (H. Wurtz) Am. J. Sci. **76**: 195.
— Use and Abuse of. (C. A. Joy) Ecl. Engin. **2**: 582.
Glyn, Isabella. Ev. Sat. **10**: 67.
Gneisenau, Count N. von. Bentley, **57**: 149. Same art. Ecl. M. **64**: 510.
Gnome, The. (R. Buchanan) Gent. M. n. s. **14**: 52.
Gnostics, The, and their Remains. Chr. Rem. **50**: 459.
— Philosophy of. (G. B. Cheever) Am. Bib. Repos. 2d s. **3**: 353. **6**: 253.
Gnostic Heresies of 1st and 2d Cent. Chr. Obs. **75**: 438.
Gnostic Testimonies to New Testament, De Groot on. (H. M. Harmon) Meth. Q. **30**: 485.
Gnosticism. (E. Harwood) Am. Church R. **10**: 259. — (J. H. Allen) Unita. R. **10**: 543. — (E. H. Sears) Mo. Rel. M. **41**: 101. — Art J. **17**: 41. — Dub. R. **76**: 56. — Meth. M. **53**: 325.
— Analysis of. (P. Schaff) Mercersb. **10**: 520.
— History of. (T. Parker) Chr. Exam. **24**: 112. — For. Q. **5**: 569. — Ecl. R. **54**: 373.
— outlined. (J. C. C. Clarke) Bapt. Q. **1**: 35.
Gnu, The. Penny M. **6**: 433.
Goal of Spring; a Poem. (J. F. Colman) Atlan. **3** o.
Goat, Angora. (J. Hayes) Overland, **5**: 416.
— Asiatic. De Bow, **24**: 191.
— Shawl, in Europe and Australia. Penny M. **7**: 266.
Goats, Milch. Eng. Dom. M. **3**: 119.
Goatherd of Lorraine. Eng. Dom. M. **15**: 184-296. **16**: 19-74. — Liv. Age, **42**: 260.
Goatsuckers, North American. (D. Scott) Am. Natural. **7**: 669.
Gobelin Tapestry Manufactory. Once a Week, **14**: 471.
Gobemouchian Ideal of Government. (W. H. Browne) So. R. n. s. **4**: 189.
Gobi, Desert of. Colburn, **133**: 218.
Gobineau, Comte de. Les Pléiades. (R. Lytton) Fortn. **22**: 293.
Goblet, The; a Poem. (A. Brackett) Scrib. **16**: 659.
Goblin of the Ice. (I. I. Hayes) Scrib. **1**: 246.
Goblins. Blackw. **14**: 639. — House. Words, **9**: 170, 409.
Goblin Miner at Fiery Creek. (W. T. Greene) Colburn, **160**: 442.
Goby, The Long-Jawed. (W. N. Lockington) Am. Natural. **11**: 474.
Goby-Hunting. (P. H. Gosse) Good Words, **2**: 384.
God, a moral Governor. (E. Pond) Theo. & Lit. J. **10**: 624.
— Administration of, Confidence in. (R. W. Landes) Am. Bib. Repos. 3d s. **3**: 347.
— Agency and Government of. (L. Woods) Am. Bib. Repos. 2d s. **11**: 123. **12**: 410.
— — Dr. Emmons's Theory. (A. Bullard) Am. Bib. Repos. 2d s. **10**: 352.
— — in material Phenomena. (J. Cummings) Meth. Q. **11**: 9.
— — in the material Universe. Chr. Exam. **18**: 314.
— — in the Production of Matter. (G. J. Chase) Bib. Sac. **5**: 342.
— and Creation. (J. P. Lacroix) Chr. Q. **8**: 202.
— and Man, United Agencies of. Mercersb. **4**: 145.
— and Nature. (H. Goodwin) 19th Century, **7**: 503. Same art. Pop. Sci. Mo. **17**: 27. — (J. Martineau) Nat. R. **11**: 482. — (O. A. Brownson) Cath. World, **12**: 694.
— — and Man. (T. Appel) Ref. Q. **27**: 263.
— — Ulrici on. (B. P. Bowne) New Eng. **33**: 623.
— and the physical Forces. (S. D. Hillman) Meth. Q. **39**: 642.
— and Revelation. (S. Tyler) Princ. **34**: 1.
— Anger of, compatible with his Love. (I. M. Atwood) Univ. Q. **34**: 221.
— Arrangements of. (L. P. Hickok) Am. Presb. R. **6**: 177.
— Attributes of. Meth. M. **28**: 20.
— — Drew on. Ecl. R. **39**: 289.
— — exhibited in Grecian Poetry. (Tayler Lewis) Am. Bib. Repos. 2d s. **10**: 81.
— — Macculloch on. Ecl. R. **67**: 37.
— Being of. (E. P. Peabody) Chr. Exam. **65**: 239. — (M. P. Squier) Am. Presb. R. **15**: 357.
— — and Sovereignty of. (J. Nicols) Am. Meth. M. **17**: 73.
— — Arguments for. Ecl. R. **123**: 423.
— — demonstrated. (G. F. Cox) Am. Meth. M. **20**: 134.
— Being acquainted with. (N. Macleod) Good Words, **14**: 581.
— Belief in. (C. C. Everett) Unita. R. **15**: 550.
— — Truths consequent upon. (A. B. Muzzey) Unita. R. **11**: 401.
— Blessing of his Presence. (A. Watson) Good Words, **22**: 33.
— Chinese Word for. (E. W. Lyle) Am. Church R. **7**: 32. — Bib. Sac. **35**: 732. — Kitto, **13**: 411.
— Christian Doctrine of. (E. V. Gerhart) Bib. Sac. **37**: 686.
— Christian Idea of. (G. Matheson) Brit. Q. **71**: 127.
— Concept of, as the Ground of Progress. (G. T. Ladd) Bib. Sac. **35**: 619.
— — Difficulties of. (G. T. Ladd) Bib. Sac. **34**: 593.
— — History and. (G. T. Ladd) Bib. Sac. **37**: 593.
— — Origin of. (G. T. Ladd) Bib. Sac. **34**: 1.
— — Plato's. (S. J. Douglass) New Eng. **28**: 539.
— Conceptions of. (K. Cook) Dub. Univ. **90**: 308.
— — Are they reliable? Chr. R. **25**: 539.
— Decrees of. (D. T. Fiske) Bib. Sac. **19**: 400.
— The Divine Man. Mo. Rel. M. **21**: 249, 347.
— Doctrine concerning. (S. D. Simonds) Meth. Q. **25**: 412.
— Duty, and Immortality. (F. W. Newman) Theo R. **16**: 1. — (T. G. Grey) Theo. R. **16**: 208.
— Eternal Purposes of, consistent with Man's free Agency. (J. W. Ward) Bib. Sac. **4**: 77.

God, Eternity of; a Poem from the German. Mass. Q. 2: 183.
— Ethical Nature of. (Dr. Dorner) Bib. Sac. 36: 212.
— Existence of. (D. P. Noyes) Bib. Sac. 13: 388. — (J. Ming) Am. Cath. Q. 6: 92, 229, 643. — Chr. Mo. Spec. 1: 414, 586.—(L. P. Hickok) Am. Bib. Repos. 2d s. 5: 273. 6: 350. — Quar. 16: 39. — Brownson, 9: 141.
— — and natural Attributes of. (G. I. Chace) Bib. Sac. 7: 326.
— — argued from final Causes. (M. Valentine) Luth. Q. 1: 165.
— — Arguments for. Bib. R. 3: 330.
— — Brown and Sumner on. Chr. Obs. 16: 101, 175.
— — Gillespie's Necessary. Ecl. R. 82: 720.
— — known to Reason. (M. Gavin) Month, 32: 153.
— — Nature of the Argument for. (E. Hutchinson) Chr. R. 22: 325.
— — Proof of. (J. Alden) Am. Bib. Repos. 9: 421.
— — — from Nature. (M. Hopkins) Am. Q. Obs. 1: 299.
— — Proofs of. (J. S. Maginnis) Bib. Sac. 8: 699.
— False Notions respecting. (R. W. Dickenson) Lit. & Theo. R. 6: 49.
— Fatherhood of. (C. C. Everett) O. & N. 1: 52. — (H. L. Mansel) Good Words, 8: 131. — (J. Tulloch) Good Words, 13: 198. — Ecl. R. 123: 148. — Theo. R. 2: 551.
— Felicity of. (L. Withington) Am. Presb. R. 19: 518.
— Forbearance of, an Occasion of Sinning. Chr. Mo. Spec. 8: 382.
— Foreknowledge of. Am. Meth. M. 21: 39. — Meth. M. 39: 410.
— — Bromley on. Meth. M. 43: 345.
— Forgiveness of. Conditions of. (F. Jenks) Chr. Exam. 3: 379.
— Freedom of. Mo. Rel. M. 24: 257.
— Glory of, in concealing. (E.C.Butler) Unita.R.14: 359.
— Goodness of, Equity of. Bost. R. 4: 525.
— — Is God good? (E. S. Phelps) Atlan. 48: 532.
— Government of. (P. Bergstresser) Evang. R. 21: 377.
— — and Grace, Williams on. Ecl. R. 19: 28, 329.
— — and Man. (G. W. Logan) Chr. Q. 7: 227.
— — Bledsoe's Theodicy. (D. Curry) Meth. Q. 14: 263. — So. R. n. s. 9: 166, 437.
— — Checks and Counterchecks of. (J. H. Fyfe) Good Words, 2: 589.
— — General Principles of. Kitto, 40: 385.
— — Illustrations of. (D. Grosvenor) Chr. Q. Spec. 8: 80.
— — McCosh on. (T. S. King) Univ. Q. 8: 402. — Brit. Q. 11: 500. — Dub. Univ. 36: 470. — Meth. Q. 12: 458. — (A. T. Bledsoe) Meth. Q. 34: 458. — No. Brit. 13: 509. — Hogg, 14: 77.
— — Mercy in. (O. A. Skinner) Univ. Q. 13: 243.
— — Method of. (R. E. Pattison) Chr. R. 17: 183. — Kitto, 14: 349.
— — Principles of. Kitto, 40: 385.
— — Smith on. Ecl. R. 28: 336, 539.
— Grace of. (M. Goodrich) Univ. Q. 15: 221.
— Gratitude to. Chr. Mo. Spec. 1: 557.
— Hebrew Ideas of. (W. R. Alger) Chr. Exam. 45: 27.
— Holiness of. (S. Lavington) Cong. M. 19: 603.
— Idea of. (C. A. Bartol) Radical, 3: 273. — (A. M. Fairbairn) Contemp. 18: 416. — (R. W. Dickenson) Lit. & Theo. R. 2: 541. — So. R. n. s. 15: 253. 16: 249.
— — and the Bible. (T. G. Apple) Mercersb. 21: 473.
— — and Human Knowledge. (T. G. Apple) Mercersb. 21: 463.
— — and the Truths of Christianity. (T. S. King) Univ. Q. 5: 407.
— — as a Law of religious Development. (J. Miley) Meth. Q. 25: 5.
— — Man's innate. (F. Bowen) Bib. Sac. 33: 740.
God, Image of. (R. Eddy) Univ. Q. 22: 55.
— in History. (J. Cumming) Ex. H. Lec. 4: 35.
— — and in Science. (L. H. Steiner) Mercersb. 14: 133.
— — Bunsen's. (C. H. Dall) Chr. Exam. 85: 24.
— in Humanity. (J. Martineau) O. & N. 6: 401, 518.
— in the Indo-European Mythology. (J. Darmesteter) Contemp. 36: 274. Same art. Liv. Age, 143: 222.
— in Nature. (J. Martineau) O. & N. 6: 54, 156. — (J. Martineau) Theo. R. 9: 373. — (A. M. Mayer) Evang. R. 17: 123. — (J. Few Smith) Evang. R. 11: 83. — (T. Abbott) Univ. Q. 25: 426.
— — Revelation of. (H. Carleton) Theo. & Lit. J. 10: 450.
— — Special Interpositions of. (E. Hitchcock) Bib. Sac. 11: 776.
— in Psychology. (J. P. Lacroix) Chr. Q. 6: 75.
— in Science. (J. Cumming) Ex. H. Lec. 6: 199.
— in the World. (A. Winchell) Meth. Q. 36: 511.
— Incomprehensibility of. (J. R. Keiser) Evang. R. 8: 153.
— Indifference to common Goodness of. (W. H. Furness) Chr. Exam. 1: 433.
— Indiscriminate Proposals of Mercy of. (R. L. Dabney) Princ. n. s. 2: 33.
— Indwelling. (J. W. Chadwick) Radical, 5: 357.
— Infinity of. (S. Cobb) Univ. Q. 22: 28.
— — developed by the Incarnation of Christ. (E. G. Sears) Chr. R. 14: 23.
— Inspiration from, true Doctrine of. (E. T. Fitch) Bib. Sac. 12: 217.
— Is He cognizable by Reason? (A. Winchell) Meth. Q. 32: 442.
— Is He unknowable? (J. B. Dalgairns) Contemp. 20: 616.
— is Love. (E. Pond) Theo. & Lit. J. 12: 571.
— Justice of. (E. Pond) Am. Bib. Repos. 3d. s. 4: 586. — Chr. Disc. 5: 188. — (F. Schleiermacher) Mo. Rel. M. 41: 157.
— — as a Theme for the Preacher. (A. H. Coolidge) New Eng. 21: 74.
— Kingdom of. (J. Drummond) Theo. R. 4: 318.
— Knowledge of. (F. Bayma) Cath. World, 22: 656, 841. — (N. Macleod) Good Words, 15: 245. — (Mrs. Montgomery) Cath. World, 23: 128–565. — Bost. Q. 4: 308. — (L. H. Atwater) Princ. 32: 648.
— — Can He be known? (C. Hodge) Princ. 36: 122.
— — from Nature and Revelation. Danv. Q. 1: 140.
— — Gratry on. Brownson, 12: 1, 281.
— — Philosophy and. (W. D. Wilson) Am. Church R. 13: 1.
— — Validity of our. (O. Dewey) O. & N. 2: 199.
— Known and Unknown in the Nature of. (O. Dewey) Unita. R. 1: 201.
— known only by Faith. (G. Duffield) Theo. & Lit. J. 5: 79.
— Law and Justice of. (O. D. Miller) Univ. Q. 6: 160.
— Living on. (L. Withington) Lit. & Theo. R. 3: 98.
— Love of. (H. Ballou) Univ. Q. 3: 246.
— Man's Dependence on. Chr. Mo. Spec. 1: 227.
— Man's Enmity to. (J. W. Thompson) Chr. Exam. 42: 181.
— manifested in Christ. (J. W. Nevin) Mercersb. 15: 549.
— Mercy of, Despair of. Chr. Mo. Spec. 2: 620.
— Mercies of. Chr. Q. Spec. 9: 134.
— Moral Attributes of. (G. I. Chace) Bib. Sac. 7: 686.
— Moral Government of. (S. D. Cochrane) Bib. Sac. 11: 254. — (B. N. Martin) New Eng. 6: 249.
— — and Man's Freedom. (B. F. Cocker) Princ. n. s. 3: 54.
— — N. W. Taylor on. (B. N. Martin) New Eng. 17: 903. — (L. H. Atwater) Princ. 31: 489.
— Name of the Lord. (J. M. Johnson) Am. Presb. R. 15: 465.
— — and Idea of. (J. W. Howe) Chr. Exam. 78: 198.

God, Name of, Doctrine of. (J. B. Walker) Cong. R. **10**: 343.
— — The Name Jehovah. Am. Presb. R. **6**: 86.
— — — considered as a memorial Name. (A. McWhorter) Bib. Sac. **14**: 98.
— — — McWhorter on. (G. R. Noyes) Chr. Exam. **62**: 295.
— — Shaddai. Bib. R. **5**: 301.
— — Theology of the lost Word. (J. F. Garrison) Am. Church R. **27**: 528.
— Names of, in Hebrew Scriptures. (E. Lord) Am. Presb. R. **16**: 268.
— — and Titles of. (W. M. Thomson) Bib. Sac. **31**: 136.
— National Conceptions of. Westm. **60**: 289.
— Nature of. Kitto, **28**: 141, 351.
— — Melancthon on. (J. A. Seiss) Evang. R. **12**: 11. *See* Anthropomorphism.
— Necessary Existence of. Kitto, **14**: 332.
— Obligation to worship. Brownson, **2**: 137.
— of Humanity. (O. B. Frothingham) Radical, **10**: 241.
— of Israel. (D. Brown) Radical, **3**: 79.
— — a History. (J. Jacobs) 19th Cent. **6**: 481. Same art. Liv. Age, **143**: 166.
— of the Living. (J. C. Parsons) Unita. R. **11**: 20.
— Omnipresence of. Am. Meth. M. **13**: 45.
— Oneness of, in Revelation and Nature. (A. Phelps) Bib. Sac. **16**: 836.
— Only-Begotten of, in John i. 18. (J. Drummond) Theo. R. **8**: 468.
— or Force? (O. Cone) Univ. Q. **36**: 424.
— Personal. (H. C. DeLong) Mo. Rel. M. **47**: 513.
— — Evidences suggestive of a. (G. E. Watson) Univ. Q. **35**: 428.
— Personality of. (J. B. Dalgairns) Contemp. **24**: 321. —(H. Lotze) New Eng. **40**: 173. —(W. T. Harris) No. Am. **131**: 241. —(G. H. Emerson) Univ. Q. **14**: 311. —(C. Henry) Radical, **7**: 230. —Mo. Rel. M. **36**: 26.
— Power of, seen in the Phenomena of Life. (A. Potter) Peop. J. **5**: 301.
— Prayer to, and Immutability of. (H. Jones) Chr. Mo. Spec. **9**: 565.
— Prescience of, and Providence. (Q. Whitney) Univ. Q. **34**: 322.
— Presence of. (S. E. Coues) Chr. Exam. **24**: 171.
— — in Nature and the Soul. Dial, **1**: 58.
— — Sense of. Liv. Age, **24**: 139.
— Providence of. (B. W. Dwight) Bib. Sac. **21**: 584. —(E. H. Sears) Chr. Exam. **68**: 21.
— — and physical Laws. (E. A. Park) Bib. Sac. **12**: 179.
— Providential and perceptive Will of. Chr. Mo. Spec. **1**: 337, 445.
— Providential Government of. (G. J. Baird) Princ. **30**: 319.
— Purpose of, in the Reconciliation of All. (H. Ballou, 2d) Univ. Q. **3**: 79.
— Revelations of. (S. Crane) Univ. Q. **37**: 55.
— Search for. (S. Johnson) Radical, **7**: 257.
— Self-Existence of. (C. B. Rice) Cong. R. **8**: 222.
— Son of; Meaning of the Phrase. Gen. Repos. **2**: 241. **3**: 46, 233.
— Sovereignty of. (L. A. Fox) Luth. Q. **10**: 484. —(T. Lewis) Mercersb. **12**: 410. —(J. W. Twiss) Univ. Q. **16**: 86.
— — Analogies to illustrate. (W. S. Tyler) Cong. M. **21**: 601, 686, 757.
— — and Use of Means. Danv. Q. **1**: 164.
— — in the Gospel. (C. Chase) Am. Church R. **12**: 424.
— — in Salvation of Sinners. Chr. Mo. Spec. **1**: 115.
— — Payne on. Bib. R. **4**: 322. —Cong. M. **20**: 309.
— Space a Proof of Existence of. Am. Meth. M. **9**: 3.
— Suffering of. (R. G. Vermilye) Bost. R. **5**: 1.
God, Supreme, in the Indo-European Mythology. (J. Darmesteter) Contemp. **36**: 274.
— the Supreme Disposer and Moral Governor. (E. Pond) Bib. Sac. **21**: 838.
— Symbolic Conceptions of. (C. P. Cranch) Unita. R. **9**: 241.
— Trusting in. Chr. Obs. **11**: 631.
— Truth of. (E. P. Marvin) Cong. R. **8**: 105.
— the ultimate End of all Things. Princ. **4**: 94.
— Unchangeableness of. (I. A. Dorner) Bib. Sac. **36**: 27, 210.
— Unity of, in Heathendom. (J. Rickaby) Month, **17**: 58. —Irish Mo **5**: 315.
— Universality of the Providence of. Kitto, **6**: 422.
— the Unknowable. Chr. Obs. **77**: 848.
— — and the Knowable. (J. P. Hopps) Theo. R. **12**: 218.
— Unveiling of. (C. T. Canfield) Unita. R. **14**: 60.
— Veracity and Rectitude of. Chr. Mo. Spec. **1**: 283.
— Ways of; Element of Time in interpreting. Princ. **42**: 87.
— — the Abyss of Darkness. So. R. n. s. **10**: 14.
— Will of. (G. Bush) Meth. Q. **19**: 288.
— — done on Earth. (N. Macleod) Good Words, **13**: 624.
— with Man. (J. May) O. & N. **4**: 665.
— without Passions. (J. Woodbridge) Lit. & Theo. R. **1**: 42.
— Word of. (N. L. Frothingham) Chr. Exam. **54**: 277.
— — Limitations of. (T. Vickers) Radical, **7**: 201.
— Works of. (A. Norton) Chr. Exam. **1**: 420. —Chr. Mo. Spec. **4**: 337.
— Yahveh and the other Gods. (A. Kuenen) Theo. R. **13**: 329.
God is our Aid; a Christmas Tale. Cath. World, **14**: 364.
God of the Poor; a Poem. (W. Morris) Fortn. **10**: 139.
God save the Queen, Who wrote? Chamb. J. **44**: 775.
God's Acre. (B. Murphy) Cath. World, **16**: 266.
Godlike Love. (R. Buchanan) Gent. M. n. s. **13**: 430.
Gods of Old; a Poem. (W. Wallace) Am. Whig R. **2**: 27.
Gods, Underground. (W. Stigand) Belgra. **8**: 483.
Godard, Grand. All the Year, **5**: 126.
Goddesses of Liberty in French Revolution. Colburn, **143**: 74. Same art. Ecl. M. **71**: 1258.
Goderich, Lord, and Wellington Administrations. Westm. **116**: 293.
Godfather, The. Godey, **21**: 203.
Godfather's Picture-Book. (H. C. Andersen) Ev. Sat. **6**: 695.
Godfrey, Sir E. Bentley, **41**: 296.
Godfrey Family; or Questions of the Day. (M. A. Stav) Cath. World, **4**: 30–750. **5**: 34.
Godfrey's White Queen. Blackw. **126**: 129, 313. Same art. Liv. Age, **143**: 152, 205.
Godiva, Lady, at Home. (M. D. Conway) Harper, **33**: 625.
Godkin, Edward L. (E. Benson) Galaxy, **7**: 869.
Godliness, Mystery of. (E. Henderson) Am. Bib. Repos. **2**: 1.
Godman, John D. (Dr. Lindsley) No. Am. **40**: 87.
Godolphin, Mrs., Evelyn's Life of. Quar. **81**: 351. —Chr. Obs. **47**: 680. —Belgra. **30**: 216. —(C. C. Smith) Chr. Exam. **43**: 344. Same art. Liv. Age, **15**: 398. —Liv. Age, **14**: 181.
Godoy, Manuel de. Westm. **25**: 28. —Mo. R. **139**: 325.
Godsey, Susan C., Remarkable Case of Sleeping. Ev. Sat. **9**: 731.
Godwin and Harold, Earls. No. Brit. **52**: 28.
Godwin, George, with portrait. Colburn, **167**: 182.
Godwin, Parke. (E. Benson) Galaxy, **7**: 230.
Godwin, William. (A. V. Dicey) Nation, **22**: 278. —(E. Quincy) No. Am. **123**: 221. —(L. Stephen) Fortn. **26**: 444. —with portrait, Fraser, **10**: 463. —(G. F. Deane) Am. Whig R. **8**: 259. —Lond. M. **2**: 163.

Godwin, William, and Shelley. (Sir L. Stephen) Cornh. 39: 281. Same art. Appleton, 21: 344. Same art. Liv. Age, 141: 67.
— and Mary Wollstonecraft. (S. R. T. Mayer) St. James, 38: 79.
— Character and Works of. (H. T. Tuckerman) So. Lit. Mess. 16: 129.
— Cloudesley. Blackw. 27: 711.
— Fleetwood. (Sir W. Scott) Ed. R. 6: 182.
— Fragment of a Romance. Colburn, 37: 32.
— Friends and Contemporaries of. Temp. Bar, 46: 325. Same art. Ecl. M. 86: 599.
— Letters from Coleridge to. Macmil. 9: 524.
— Life and Character of. Westm. 106: 365.
— — and Writings of. Temp. Bar, 46: 325.
— Mandeville. (W. Phillips) No. Am. 7: 92. — Quar. 18: 176. — Blackw. 2: 268, 402.
— Notes on. (T. De Quincey) Tait, n. s. 12: 724.
— Novels. Fraser, 2: 38.
— Thoughts on Man. Chr. Exam. 11: 263. — Mo. R. 124: 515. — Fraser, 3: 569.
— Transfusion; a Novel. Mo. R. 137: 240.
— Writings and Opinions of. (G. B. Smith) St. James, 41: 391, 497.
Godwyn's Ordeal. (Mrs. J. K. Spender) Eng. Dom. M. 24: 1–281. 25: 20–291.
Goel, The. (J. Fenton) Theo. R. 15: 495.
Goelet, Capt. Francis, Journal of, 1746–50. N. E. Reg. 24: 50.
Goergey, A., and Hungary. Ecl. R. 97: 1. — New Q. 1: 329.
Goerres, John J. Cath. World, 6: 497. — Dub. R. 6: 31.
Goethe, Elizabeth, Mother of the Poet. Appleton, 7: 692. — (J. W. Scherer) Fraser, 90: 399. — (A. S. Gibbs) Lippinc. 24: 547.
— Letters of. (Mrs. E. Clarke) Fraser, 104: 515. Same art. Liv. Age, 151: 246.
Goethe, Johann Wolfgang von, with portrait. (T. Carlyle) Fraser, 5: 206. — (E. Everett) No. Am. 4: 217. — (G. Bancroft) No. Am. 19: 303. — (C. C. Felton) Chr. Exam. 8: 187. — (L. Woods, jr.) Lit. & Theo. R. 2: 282. — (T. Carlyle) For. Q. 10: 1. 12: 81. 14: 131. 16: 328. — Brit. & For. R. 14: 78. — Blackw. 16: 369. 46: 476, 597. 47: 31, 607. 56: 54, 417. 57: 165. — Dem. R. 10: 581. 19: 443. 20: 14. 24: 66. — Westm. 1: 370. — Ed. R. 26: 304. 28: 83. — (A. E. Kroeger) Radical, 2: 273, 332. — U. S. Lit. Gaz. 2: 81. — So. Q. 11: 441. — For. R. 2: 1. — Blackw. 112: 675. Same art. Ecl. M. 80: 172. Same art. Liv. Age, 116: 3. — Dial, 2: 1. — Ecl. R. 104: 447. — Ev. Sat. 14: 1. — Ed. R. 106: 194. Same art. Liv. Age, 54: 769. — Liv. Age, 61: 181. Tait, 1: 314.
— and Bettina. (C. White) Nat. Q. 41: 74.
— — Few Words for Bettina. Blackw. 58: 357.
— and Dumas. (H. James, jr.) Nation, 17: 292.
— and Eckermann. (A. M. Machar) Canad. Mo. 16: 230, 386. — Dub. Univ. 37: 732.
— and Fredrika Brion. Once a Week, 11: 358.
— and Germans. Blackw. 45: 247.
— and German Fiction. (F. G. Fairfield) J. Spec. Philos. 9: 303.
— and his Contemporaries. Westm. 24: 197. — Dub. Univ. 8: 350.
— and his Critics. Fraser, 36: 481.
— and F. Mendelssohn-Bartholdy. Bentley, 49: 68. — Ev. Sat. 9: 247. 17: 365. — Temp. Bar, 42: 165.
— and J. S. Mill, contrasted. Westm. 102: 38.
— and Minna Herzlieb. (A. Hamilton) Contemp. 27: 199. Same art. Liv. Age, 128: 554.
— and Religion. (J. F. Smith) Theo. R. 6: 76.
— and Schiller. Land We Love, 5: 170.
Goethe, Johann Wolfgang von, and Schiller, Characteristics of. Dub. Univ. 87: 684.
— — Dwight's. (G. S. Hillard) No. Am. 48: 505. — (G. Bancroft) Chr. Exam. 26: 360.
— — Friendship of. (W. H. Wynn) New Eng. 32: 718.
— — Poems. Bost. Q. 2: 187.
— — Weimar under. (H. S. Wilson) Contemp. 29: 271. Same art. Liv. Age, 132: 550.
— and Shakspere, Female Characters of. No. Brit. 8: 265. Same art. Ecl. M. 14: 1. — (D. Masson) Brit. Q. 16: 512. Same art. Liv. Age, 36: 605.
— and Suleika. Western, 1: 621.
— and Washington. (C. A. Bartol) Chr. Exam. 60: 317.
— and Werther. Liv. Age, 43: 334. — Nat. R. 1: 197.
— Aphorisms of. Am. Mo. 7: 448.
— as a Man of Science. Westm. 58: 479. Same art. Ecl. M. 27: 460.
— Ausgewählte Prosa, Hart's. Dub. Univ. 89: 147.
— Autobiographical Sketches. Lond. M. 7: 68.
— Caro's Philosophy of. (E. Dowden) Contemp. 6: 49, 442. Same art. Ecl. M. 69: 693.
— Character and moral Influence of. Ed. R. 106: 194.
— Characteristics of. Nat. R. 2: 241. Same art. Liv. Age, 50: 1.
— — Mrs. Austin's. Ed. R. 57: 371. — Mo. R. 131: 307. — Mus. 23: 500.
— Conversations with. Colburn, 91: 256. — Bost. Q. 3: 20. — Westm. 50: 555. Same art. Ecl. M. 16: 460. — For. Q. 18: 1.
— — with Eckermann. Dub. Univ. 37: 732.
— — with Müller. Radical, 8: 111–403.
— Cornelia, the Sister of. (P. F. André) Victoria, 6: 97.
— Correspondence with a Child. Dial, 2: 313. — Tait, n. s. 9: 157. — Mo. R. 144: 386.
— Correspondence with the Duke of Saxe Weimar. Nat. R. 18: 1.
— Death of. Colburn, 34: 507.
— — Poem on. (T. Irwin) Dub. Univ. 50: 333.
— Dedication prefixed to his Poems. Lond. M. 9: 186.
— Dissertation on. (F. A. Rauch) Mercersb. 12: 329.
— Early Youth of. (F. Schaller) So. M. 14: 253.
— Edinburgh Review on. Blackw. 4: 211.
— Egmont. (D. P. Noyes) Am. Whig R. 1: 183.
— Elective Affinities. Walsh's R. 3: 51.
— Falk's Character of. Colburn, 38: 302.
— Faust. (R. P. Gillies) Blackw. 7: 236. — Canad. Mo. 9: 123. — (K. Rosenkranz) J. Spec. Philos. 9: 48, 225, 401. — Dub. Univ. 64: 537. Same art. Ecl. M. 64: 97. — For. Q. 25: 90. — Blackw. 7: 235. — Quar. 34: 136. — Westm. 25: 266. — Lond. M. 2: 125. — O. & N. 4: 471. — (J. S. Hittel) Pioneer, 3: 204. — So. Lit. J. 4: 264.
— — and the Devil. Fraser, 23: 269, 464.
— — and its English Critics. Lond. Q. 55: 118.
— — and Margaret. (K. Rosenkranz) J. Spec. Philos. 10: 37.
— — and minor Poems. Dub. Univ. 7: 278.
— — Anster's Translation. Ed. R. 62: 36. — Dub. Univ. 6: 97.
— — Blackie's Translation. St. James, 48: 98.
— — — and Syme's Translation. Fraser, 10: 88.
— — Brooks's Translation. (Mrs. C. R. Corson) New Eng. 22: 1. — (F. H. Hedge) Chr. Exam. 63: 1.
— — English Translations. Cornh. 26: 279. Same art. Liv. Age, 115: 412.
— — Facts and Fancies about. (H. S. Wilson) Mod. R. 1: 771. 2: 148.
— — for English Readers. (E. J. Hasell) St. Paul's, 11: 694. 12: 403.
— — Gower's. Lond. M. 16: 164.
— — Hayward's Translation. Fraser, 7: 532. — Ed. R 57: 107.

Goethe, Johann Wolfgang von. Faust in the German Puppet Shows. Fraser, **37**: 32.
— — Klingemann's. (R. P. Gillies) Blackw. **13**: 649.
— — Letters on. (H. C. Brockmeyer) J. Spec. Philos. **1**: 178. **2**: 114.
— — Martin's Translation. No. Brit. **44**: 95.
— — Poetical Translations. Blackw. **47**: 223.
— — Sacred Poetry of. Dub. R. **9**: 477.
— — Second Part of. (W. H. Goodyear) Lippinc. **19**: 223. — (K. Rosenkranz) J. Spec. Philos. **1**: 65. **11**: 113. — Dub. Univ. **2**: 361. **64**: 537. — For. Q. **12**: 81. — Fraser, **68**: 497.
— — set to Music. All the Year, **9**: 439.
— — Survey of. (J. L. Lincoln) Bapt. Q. **3**: 278.
— — Taylor's Translation. (J. R. Dennett) Nation, **12**: 201. — Broadw. **8**: 159.
— — Translations from. (J. A. Harris) Penn Mo. **12**: 765, 837.
— — Translations of. Westm. **25**: 366.
— Female Characters of. No. Brit. **8**: 265.
— Fragments by. Fraser, **6**: 383.
— Funeral of; a Poem, translated. (A. H. Everett) Dem. R. **11**: 471.
— Genius and Influence of. (H. Merivale) Ed. R. **92**: 188. Same art. Ecl. M. **21**: 98. Same art. Liv. Age, **26**: 365.
— — and Works of. Dub. Univ. **60**: 671. Same art. Ecl. M. **58**: 295.
— Goetz von Berlichingen. Blackw. **16**: 369.
— Gossip about, in Frankfort. Liv. Age, **143**: 440. Same art. Ecl. M. **94**: 190.
— Grimm on. (J. M. Hart) Nation, **25**: 199.
— Helena. (T. Carlyle) For. R. **1**: 429.
— — translated by T. Martin. Fraser, **57**: 63.
— Hermann and Dorothea. Fraser, **41**: 33.
— — translated. Dem. R. **23**: 261, 355, 450.
— House of, at Frankfort. (A. S. Gibbs) Scrib. **11**: 113.
— in his old Age. Liv. Age, **132**: 482.
— Influence on modern Thought. (J. A. Chase) Western, **7**: 509.
— Iphigenia; translated. Dub. Univ. **23**: 303. — Dem. R. **24**: 460. **25**: 68, 358.
— Lewes's Life and Works of. (J. B. Angell) Chr. R. **21**: 412. — Bentley, **39**: 96. — Chr. Obs. **74**: 247. — Brit. Q. **23**: 468. — Dem. R. **37**: 157. — Fraser, **52**: 639. Same art. Liv. Age, **48**: 148. Same art. Ecl. M. **37**: 200. — Liv. Age, **48**: 91. — Putnam, **7**: 192. — New Q. **5**: 11. — Westm. **65**: 273.
— Life and Writings of. (Mrs. L. Phelps) Am. Church R. **16**: 505.
— Maxims and Reflections from. Fraser, **93**: 338. Same art. Ecl. M. **86**: 745. Same art. Liv. Age, **129**: 117.
— Memoirs of. Colburn, **5**: 521. **10**: 473.
— Menzel's View of. Dial, **1**: 340.
— Moral Tendency of his Writings. So. Lit. Mess. **22**: 180.
— Mother of. *See* Goethe, Elizabeth.
— Native Place of. Dem. R. **35**: 132.
— Novelle; translated. (T. Carlyle) Fraser, **6**: 383.
— on Art and Antiquity. Lond. M. **1**: 523.
— on Hamlet. (H. S. Wilson) Lond. Soc. **28**: 308.
— Philosophy of. Ecl. M. **68**: 712.
— Poems and Ballads. (A. H. Clough) Fraser, **59**: 710. Same art. Ecl. M. **49**: 53. — Bentley, **45**: 401. — Blackw. **56**: 54, 417. — Lond. Q. **12**: 121.
— Posthumous Works. Select J. **3**: [16. — Dub. Univ. **2**: 361.
— Prometheus. Dub. Univ. **36**: 520.
— Recent Works on, 1881. (T. W. Higginson) Nation, **32**: 408.
— Recollections of. For. Q. **32**: 182.
— Relation of, to Christianity. Nat. M. **1**: 468.
— Religion of. (A. Schwartz) Macmil. **29**: 128.
Goethe, Johann Wolfgang von, E. Scherer on. Quar. **145**: 143. Same art. Liv. Age, **136**: 451.
— Scientific Biography of, Faiore's. (Sir D. Brewster) No. Brit. **38**: 107.
— Social Romances. (K. Rosenkranz) J. Spec. Philos. **2**: 120, 215. — J. Spec. Philos. **4**: 145, 268.
— Sorrows of Werther; translated. Western, **5**: 345.
— — French Criticism on. Lond. M. **1**: 49.
— — Originals of. (C. E. Meetkerke) Temp. Bar, **47**: 244. Same art. Liv. Age, **130**: 172.
— Story of the Snake. J. Spec. Philos. **5**: 219.
— The Tale; translated. (T. Carlyle) Fraser, **6**: 257.
— Tasso. Chamb. J. **16**: 87. — Fraser, **13**: 526. — Blackw. **58**: 87. — Mo. R. **114**: 182.
— — Scenes and Passages from. Colburn, **40**: 1.
— Theory of Colors. Ed. R. **72**: 99. — Quar. **10**: 427. — (J. Tyndall) Fortn. **33**: 471. — Pop. Sci. Mo. **17**: 215, 312.
— Visit to, in Weimar. Hours at Home, **1**: 145.
— Visit to the Home of. Colburn, **104**: 203. Same art. Liv. Age, **46**: 39.
— Weimar under Schiller and Goethe. (H. S. Wilson) Contemp. **29**: 271.
— Wilhelm Meister. (H. James, jr.) No. Am. **101**: 281. — Blackw. **15**: 619. — So. R. **3**: 353. — (F. Jeffrey) Ed. R. **42**: 409. — Lond. M. **10**: 189, 291. — (D. A. Wasson) Atlan. **16**: 273, 448. — So. Lit. Mess. **17**: 431.
— Words of Wisdom from. Blackw. **130**: 785.
— Works and Influence of. (E. I. Sears) Nat. Q. **5**: 227.
— Youth of. (Mrs. E. M. Mitchell) Western, **2**: 347. — Sharpe, **8**: 155, 237.
Göttingen in 1824. Putnam, **8**: 595.
— Letters from. U. S. Lit. Gaz. **5**: 135, 271.
— Trip of the "Dilettanti" to. Bentley, **29**: 293.
— University of. Chr. Mo. Spec. **8**: 412.
— — King and Professors. (O. Seidensticker) Penn Mo. **3**: 648.
— — Princeton Graduate at. (J. M. Hart) Am. J. Educ. **27**: 625.
Goffe and Whalley, the Regicides. Worc. M. **1**: 208. *See* Regicides.
Gog and Magog. (L. Hunt) Colburn, **48**: 178. — Art J. **8**: 351. — Ev. Sat. **3**: 729. — Theo. & Lit. J. **4**: 163.
— Query concerning. (J. Priestley) Theo. Repos. **6**: 203.
— Remarks on. (S. Weston) Arch. **18**: 263.
Gog, Magog, & Co. (L. Abbott) Harper, **46**: 681.
Gogol, Nikolai W., Russian Author. (C. E. Turner) Fraser, **96**: 357, 491. — Brit. Q. **47**: 327.
Go, Going, Gone. Fraser, **23**: 15.
Going about in the World. Lond. Soc. **36**: 204.
Going an Errand. Lippinc. **5**: 95.
Going for a Song. House. Words, **18**: 569.
Going, Gone. (J. P. Anthony) Pioneer, **3**: 24.
Going Home. Tinsley, **4**: 260.
Going in; a Tale. (C. W. Elliott) Galaxy, **1**: 693.
Going into Business; a Tale. All the Year, **13**: 378-428.
Going on. (A. K. H. Boyd) Fraser, **65**: 715. Same art. Ecl. M. **56**: 498.
Going out of Alessandro Pozzone. (R. Dowling) Belgra. **36**: 211.
Going out of Town. Colburn, **57**: 305.
Going South. (E. S. Phelps) Atlan. **37**: 25.
Going to the Bad. St. James, **26**: 289.
Going to the Cattle-Show. Lond. Soc. **6**: 520. Same art. Ecl. M. **64**: 382.
Going to the Dogs. Cornh. **8**: 358.
Going to the Shows. Bentley, **39**: 273. Same art. Liv. Age, **49**: 179.
Going with the Tide; a Poem. St. James, **17**: 384.
Goître and Crêtinism. Ecl. R. **104**: 278.
Gokah, Falls of. Bentley, **53**: 206.
Golconda, Picnic at. Once a Week, **28**: 12.

Golconda, Tombs of the Kings of. Once a Week, **30**: 698.
Gold. (A. E. Outerbridge) J. Frankl. Inst. **103**: 281, 368. — (R. J. Walker) Contin. Mo. **2**: 743. **3**: 279. — Colburn, **91**: 436. — House. Words, **4**: 77. — Once a Week, **21**: 515.
— Accumulation of. Bank. M. (N. Y.) **27**: 276.
— alloyed with Rhodium. Am. J. Sci. **11**: 298.
— an Incumbrance on Commerce. (H. Brougham) Ed. R. **2**: 101.
— and Bread, and Something more. Once a Week, **9**: 454.
— and Currency. Bank. M. (N. Y.) **8**: 525.
— and Dross; a Tale. Temp. Bar, **1**: 64.
— and Emigration. Fraser, **46**: 127.
— and the Exchanges. (F. Jourdan) Bank. M. (N. Y.) **16**: 105.
— and Gems, Treatment of. Internat. M. **5**: 524.
— and Glitter. (W. Duthie) Belgra. **10**: 461.
— and Gold Seekers. (H. M. Villiers) Ex. H. Lec. **8**: 139.
— and Paper. Bank. M. (N. Y.) **16**: 571.
— and Silver. Bank. M. (N. Y.) **13**: 191.
— — and Free Trade. Bank. M. (N. Y.) **14**: 329.
— — and Jewelry Manufactures. Pract. M. **4**: 386.
— — as Money. (A. W. Paine) Bank. M. (N. Y.) **31**: 289.
— — as Standards of Value. (L. Spooner) Radical R. **1**: 751.
— — compared. Hunt, **49**: 89.
— — Consumption of, in the Arts. Bank. M. (N. Y.) **17**: 169.
— — Earliest Uses of. Ed. New Philos. J. **13**: 136.
— — from Copper Pyrites. (M. F. Claudet) Pract. M. **1**: 47.
— — Future of. (C. F. McCoy) Bank. M. (N. Y.) **32**: 785.
— — in China. Dub. Univ. **2**: 42.
— — Mines of. (G. F. Holmes) De Bow, **21**: 30.
— — — in Mexico. (J. Sparks) No. Am. **21**: 439. — (N. Hale) No. Am. **14**: 431.
— — Mining of, in Russia. (T. W. Knox) Overland, **4**: 345.
— — Movements of. Bank. M. (N. Y.) **16**: 60.
— — Production of. Bank. M. (N. Y.) **7**: 127. **16**: 134. **18**: 409. **23**: 241. **27**: 161, 710.
— — — and Use of. (A. W. Paine) Bank. M. (N. Y.) **30**: 457.
— — produced in America, 1492–1848. West. J. **11**: 96.
— — — from 1492. De Bow, **17**: 131.
— — Relative Values of. Bank. M. (N. Y.) **9**: 475.
— — Scarcity of. (G. M. Weston) Bank. M. (N. Y.) **31**: 47.
— — sent from America to Europe, 1492–1848. Bank. M. (L.) **11**: 523. — (J. T. Danson) J. Statis. Soc. **14**: 11.
— — Statistics of increased Production of, 1852. Bank. M. (L.) **12**: 284.
— — Supply and relative Value of. Bank. M. (N. Y.) **7**: 183.
— — Uses of, in the Arts. Bank. M. (N. Y.) **9**: 665.
— — Value of, in different Places. (G. M. Weston) Bank. M. (N. Y.) **35**: 423.
— — Where do they go? Bank. M. (N. Y.) **11**: 303.
— Gold and Silver Bullion and Coins. Bank. M. (N. Y.) **17**: 383. **18**: 973.
— Gold and Silver Coins, Manual of. Hunt, **7**: 267.
— Gold and Silver Money of the West and of the East. Brit. Q. **41**: 444.
— Gold and Silver Placers of the United States and British America. Colburn, **142**: 612.
— and social Politics. (R. H. Patterson) Blackw. **94**: 499.
— and Trade. Bank. M. (N. Y.) **7**: 758.
— Artificial Crystals of. (A. H. Chester) Am. J. Sci. **116**: 29.
— as an Art Material. (P. L. Simmonds) Art J. **27**: 7, 37.
— as a Standard of Value. (M. Chevalier) Bank. M. (L.) **18**: 108.
Gold as the Standard of Value. Bank. M. (L.) **2**: 320.
— — at Hamburg. Bank. M. (L.) **16**: 757.
— Aureus; or, Vindication of a Sovereign. Bank. M. (L.) **21**: 681, 775, 838.
— Chemistry and Mineralogy of. (T. L. Phipson) Macmil. **8**: 469.
— City of. (R. H. Patterson) Blackw. **96**: 367.
— Contracts in, Law of. Bank. M. (N. Y.) **23**: 648.
— Controversy on, 1863. Bank. M. (L.) **23**: 729.
— Curious Facts relating to. Bank. M. (L.) **12**: 302. Same art. Bank. M. (N. Y.) **7**: 174.
— Daily Price of, in New York, 1862–63. Bank. M. (N. Y.) **18**: 578.
— — 1862–69. Bank. M. (N. Y.) **24**: 633.
— Depreciation of. (F. Bowen) No. Am. **76**: 507. — (W. S. Jevons) Bank. M. (N. Y.) **24**: 6. — (G. Walker) No. Am. **89**: 340. — Bank. M. (L.) **23**: 812, 837. — Bank. M. (N. Y.) **13**: 916. **15**: 276. — Westm. **81**: 88.
— — Chevalier on. (A. Walker) Hunt, **41**: 147. — Ed. R. **112**: 1. — Tait, n. s. **27**: 599.
— — Effect of Reduction in intrinsic Value of. Bank. M. (L.) **11**: 533.
— — Probable, 1857. Bank. M. (L.) **17**: 859, 955.
— — Results of. Cornh. **9**: 97.
— Discoveries of. Quar. **91**: 504.
— — in Australia and California. No. Brit. **21**: 531.
— — in California, Effect of. Blackw. **69**: 1. — Brit. Q. **17**: 546. — Nat. R. **17**: 447. — No. Brit. **42**: 300. — (E. A. Meredith) Canad. J. n. s. **1**: 430. — (G. Tucker) Hunt, **24**: 19.
— in the 19th Century. Bank. M. (N. Y.) **11**: 367.
— in South Africa. Bank. M. (L.) **28**: 1041.
— Diving for, 1849. (H. Degroot) Overland, **13**: 273.
— Divisibility of. (A. E. Outerbridge, jr.) Pop. Sci. Mo. **11**: 74. — Penny M. **7**: 402.
— Emigration and. Blackw. **74**: 117.
— Essay towards a Solution of the Question. (J. E. Cairnes) Fraser, **60**: 267.
— Export of. Bank. M. (N. Y.) **12**: 273. **33**: 749.
— Fixed Price of. Bank. M. (L.) **7**: 475, 608.
— Fluctuations in. Bank. M. (N. Y.) **30**: 281, 342, 430. **33**: 792.
— for commercial Nations. Bank. M. (N. Y.) **32**: 883.
— Free Trade in. Bank. M. (L.) **21**: 434.
— Future Value of. (P. Greg) Fraser, **59**: 730. Same art. Bank. M. (N. Y.) **14**: 114. — (E. de Laveleye) 19th Cent. **10**: 455.
— Great Gold Conspiracy, 1864. (J. Bonner) Harper, **40**: 746.
— Great Gold Flurry, 1869. (J. A. Peters) Putnam, **15**: 587. — Westm. **94**: 411. **95**: 589.
— History and Fluctuations of. (A. von Humboldt) Am. Ecl. **2**: 514.
— in all Ages. De Bow, **29**: 739.
— in ancient Times. Dub. Univ. **56**: 236.
— in Australia. (A. H. Guernsey) Harper, **6**: 16. — Ed. R. **117**: 82. — Colburn, **93**: 353. — Quar. **107**: 1.
— — as affecting industrial Progress. (H. S. Chapman) J. Statis. Soc. **26**: 424.
— — Digging for. Colburn, **96**: 76.
— — Discovery of. Bank. M. (L.) **11**: 565–691. **12**: 407.
— — — Local Effects of. J. Statis. Soc. **24**: 198.
— in California, 1849–50. (J. D. B. Stillman) Overland, **11**: 226–539. **12**: 40, 156, 250. — So. Q. **21**: 301.
— — First. Bank. M. (N. Y.) **36**: 313.
— — in deep Placers of the Yuba, Nevada Co. (B. Silliman) Am. J. Sci. **90**: 1.
— — in the Foot-Hills of the Sierra Nevada. (B. Silliman) Am. J. Sci. **95**: 92.
See California.

Gold in Great Britain. Art J. **22**: 200. — Colburn, **100**: 14, 355.
— in India. (E. B. Eastwick) Gent. M. n. s. **24**: 96.
— in its natural Sources. Lond. Q. **8**: 50. Same art. Ecl. M. **41**: 355.
— in Metallic Sulphides. (A. Ott) J. Frankl. Inst. **87**: 128.
— — in Nova Scotia. (O. C. Marsh) Am. J. Sci. **82**: 395.
— All the Year, **18**: 60. — Chamb. J. **38**: 319.
— in Scotland. Chamb. J. **18**: 60. — Hogg, **10**: 305.
— Influence of. Blackw. **76**: 576, 672.
— Influx of, 1879. Bank. M. (N. Y.) **34**: 249.
— — Effects upon Trade, 1852. Quar. **90**: 492.
— Is it appreciating? 1876. Bank. M. (N. Y.) **30**: 593.
— Language and. (A. H. Louis) O. & N. **7**: 407.
— Lectures on. Bank. M. (N. Y.) **7**: 353. — Chamb. J. **19**: 7.
— Mechanical and Chemical Treatment of. (J. D. Whelpley) Am. J. Sci. **87**: 401.
— Mineral History and Separation of. (W. Lewis) J. Frankl. Inst. **2**: 79, 168, 196.
— Mosaic. J. Frankl. Inst. **1**: 139.
— Natural and Civil History of. Blackw. **71**: 517.
— New Supplies of. Bank. M. (N. Y.) **8**: 315, 381.
— past, present, and future. New Q. **2**: 143.
— Philosopher's Stone. (W. E. Hagen) Am. Natural. **11**: 32.
— Plethora of, Decade of. Bank. M. (N. Y.) **14**: 921.
— Praise of. Tait, **1**: 325.
— Premium on, Advance in, 1874. Bank. M. (N. Y.) **29**: 657.
— — Government Interference with. (A. Walker) Lippinc. **5**: 336.
— Process for extracting. (Jackson and Ott) J. Frankl. Inst. **80**: 24.
— Prospective Value of. Bank. M. (N. Y.) **7**: 193.
— Purification of. (M. Boussingault) J. Frankl. Inst. **20**: 181.
— Question of, 1869. (J. B. Hodgskin) Nation, **9**: 284.
— — and Prices in Germany. (T. E. C. Leslie) Fortn. **18**: 554.
— Refining of. (L. A. Garnett) Hunt, **56**: 301.
— Relative Value of. De Bow, **18**: 376.
— Rise in Value of, 1878. Bank. M. (L.) **38**: 842.
— Supply of. (J. D. Whitney) No. Am. **75**: 277.
— — from California, 1849. Bank. M. (L.) **9**: 129.
— — — 1851. Bank. M. (L.) **11**: 692.
— — Effects of the Increase of. (G. F. Holmes) De Bow, **21**: 103. — (M. Tarver) West. J. **2**: 141. **4**: 1.
— — — on Currency. Bank. M. (L.) **11**: 361, 669.
— — — on Prices. Bank. M. (N. Y.) **29**: 696.
— — — Social and economical. (H. Fawcett) Macmil. **2**: 186.
— Value of. O. & N. **9**: 266.
— — Present and prospective. (A. B. Johnson) Hunt, **24**: 275.
— Working in. Fraser, **64**: 439.
See Specie.
Gold Bluffs, Auriferous Gravel Deposit of. (A. W. Chase) Am. J. Sci. **107**: 379.
Gold Chain Manufactory, Visit to. (J. R. Mills) Putnam, **2**: 46.
Gold Coast. Ed. R. **138**: 569.
— People of. (W. F. Daniell) Ed. New Philos. J. **52**: 289. **53**: 120, 333.
Gold Coast of California and Oregon. (S. Johnson) Overland, **2**: 534.
Gold Coins, Hatchett on. (Lord Brougham) Ed. R. **3**: 452.
— Report on, 1823. Niles's Reg. **23**: 391.
— Table of. Hunt, **1**: 448.
Cold Coinage. Ecl. Engin. **5**: 393.
— Abrasion of. Bank. M. (L.) **23**: 878.
— for Twenty-four Years. J. Statis. Soc. **35**: 376.
Gold Contracts. Bank. M. (N. Y.) **33**: 418.
Gold Currency, how diminished in Weight. Tait, n. s. **5**: 744.
Gold-Digger's Story; a Poem. (G. Fullerton) Temp. Bar, **28**: 349.
Gold-Digging in Australia. (J. Manning) Overland, **3**: 264.
— in the Time of Queen Elizabeth. (W. N. Sainsbury) Once a Week, **15**: 607.
Gold-Digging Mania. (T. De Quincey) Liv. Age, **36**: 597.
Gold-Diggings in Australia. Chamb. J. **19**: 39.
— in British Columbia. Chamb. J. **30**: 182, 197.
— in Otago, New Zealand. Colburn, **124**: 219.
Gold-Dredging on the Clutha. Chamb. J. **56**: 365.
Gold Egg; a Poem. (J. R. Lowell) Atlan. **15**: 528.
Gold Elsie. (E. John) Broadw. **8**: 327–488. **9**: 1–345.
Gold Fever, 1849. (H. T. Tuckerman) Godey, **38**: 205.
— at South Wales. Chamb. J. **31**: 289.
— in Australia. Chamb. J. **17**: 282.
Gold Districts. Am. Q. **11**: 66.
Gold Fields and Gold Miners. Bank. M. (N. Y.) **17**: 953. — Ed. R. **117**: 82.
— of California and Oregon. (W. P. Blake) Am. J. Sci. **70**: 72.
— of New Zealand. Blackw. **105**: 298.
— of Nova Scotia. (A. Gilman) Atlan. **13**: 576.
— of South Africa. Colburn, **143**: 489.
— with the Gilt off. Chamb. J. **34**: 343.
Gold-Finder; a Poem. Blackw. **71**: 607.
Gold Fish. Godey, **50**: 119.
— Death among. Recr. Sci. **1**: 51.
Gold-Gravel Ranges. (M. Thomson) Overland, **11**: 393.
Gold Hair; a Poem. (R. Browning) Atlan. **13**: 596.
Gold Herb, The. Once a Week, **19**: 334.
Gold-Hunting. House. Words, **13**: 448–472.
— in California. (E. G. Squier) Am. Whig R. **9**: 84.
— on Queen Charlotte's Island. (W. M. Turner) Overland, **14**: 167.
Gold Lake Fever. (T. W. Brotherton) So. M. **13**: 564, 641.
Gold Loan Contracts. Bank. M. (N. Y.) **33**: 938.
Gold Mania in U. S., 1848. (P. Godwin) Peop. J. **7**: 39, 57.
Gold Mine in England, Discovery of. Bank. M. (L.) **12**: 291, 677.
— near Fredericksburg, Va. (M. F. Maury) Am. J. Sci **32**: 325.
Gold Mines. No. Brit. **14**: 452.
— and Gold Laws. West. M. **2**: 617.
— and Prices in England. (T. E. C. Leslie) Fortn. **19**: 769.
— and Silver Mines, New. (R. H. Patterson) Brit. Q. **71**: 31.
— of Australia, Westgarth's. New Q. **6**: 409.
— of California. (G. Tucker) Hunt, **23**: 19.
— of Ethiopia. (S. Birch) Arch. **34**: 357.
— of Ireland. Penny M. **13**: 426.
— of Georgia. (W. Phillips) Am. J. Sci. **24**: 1.
— of Nevada. (J. D. Whitney) No. Am. **113**: 203.
— of North Carolina. (D. Olmsted) Am. J. Sci. **9**: 5. — (E. Mitchell) Am. J. Sci. **16**: 1. — (C. E. Rothe) Am. J. Sci. **13**: 201. — (F. L. Smith) Am. J. Sci. **32**: 103. — Am. Alma. **1841**: 211. — Hunt, **11**: 63.
— of Russia. (A. P. Molitor) Overland, **15**: 71. — Hunt, **12**: 347.
— of Scotland. Chamb. J. **11**: 358.
— of Siberia. Hunt, **12**: 554.
— — and California. Quar. **87**: 396. Same art. Liv. Age, **27**: 444.
— of Virginia. (B. Silliman) Am. J. Sci. **32**: 98.
— Southern. (J. Peck) Am. J. Sci. **23**: 1. — Niles's Reg. **40**: 205.
Gold-Mining. (T. Evans) Overland, **4**: 496.
— as an Investment. St. James, **48**: 428.

Gold-Mining; Curiosities of the Pay Streak. (P. Mulford) Lippinc. **7**: 475.
— in California. (W. V. Wells) Harper, **20**: 598. — Hunt, **27**: 445.
— in England. Chamb. J. **21**: 49.
— in Georgia. Harper, **59**: 506.
Gold-Mining District of Grass Valley, Cal. (B. Silliman) Am. J. Sci. **94**: 236.
Gold Movement in Congress, 1864. Bank. M. (N. Y.) **18**: 761.
Gold Note Currency. Bank. M. (N. Y.) **13**: 161.
Gold Nuggets and Gold Dust, Origin of. (A. Murray) Ecl. Engin. **3**: 249.
Gold Pen, History of. De Bow, **9**: 332.
Gold-Producing Apparatus, Tellier's. Pract. M. **4**: 245.
Gold Product. De Bow, **18**: 241. — Bank. M. (L.) **19**: 367.
— Effect of increased. Bank. M. (L.) **22**: 616, 685.
— in 1860. Bank. M. (L.) **20**: 749.
— of the Pacific. Bank. M. (N. Y.) **18**: 802.
— of the World. Bank. M. (N. Y.) **17**: 865. **18**: 1. — Westm. **81**: 88. Same art. Bank. M. (N. Y.) **18**: 865.
Gold Quartz, Treatment of. Ecl. Engin. **4**: 33.
Gold Question, Essay towards a Solution of. (J. E. Cairnes) Fraser, **61**: 38.
Gold Region, Hand of God in. New Eng. **8**: 80.
Gold Room in New York. (K. Cornwallis) So. M. **17**: 413, 535. — (K. Cornwallis) Internat. R. **2**: 173.
— — Last Field-Day in. Fraser, **81**: 107.
Gold Sands of Pacific Coast. (M. Thomson) Overland, **10**: 393.
Gold-Seekers of Sacramento. Hogg, **4**: 104, 124.
Gold-Worshipers. Chamb. J. **15**: 340.
Golden Age; a Poem. Blackw. **72**: 521.
— Heathen Views on, and the Bible. Princ. **42**: 360.
Golden Arrow; a Story. (W. L. Alden) Galaxy, **12**: 235.
Golden Bee; a Poem. (M. Bentham-Edwards) Good Words, **15**: 312.
Golden Bee; a Poem. All the Year, **3**: 108.
Golden Calf. (F. A. Cox) Kitto, **4**: 73.
Golden Dreams; a Christmas Story. (A. Fabre) Lippinc. **3**: 112.
Golden Fleece. (G. Hodder) Bentley, **24**: 323.
— Grillparzer's. Blackw. **24**: 155. — (N. L. Frothingham) No. Am. **16**: 283.
Golden Furrows; a Poem. (G. Turner) Belgra. **11**: 84.
Golden Gate; a Poem. (W. H. Rhodes) Pioneer, **3**: 299.
Golden Gate Park. (B. P. Avery) Overland, **12**: 573.
Golden Guillotine; a Tale. Dub. Univ. **41**: 22. Same art. Liv. Age, **36**: 361.
Golden Hind, Passengers of. (S. G. Drake) N. E. Reg. **1**: 126.
Golden Ingot. Knick. **52**: 176.
Golden Legend, as treated by various Writers. Dub. Univ. **39**: 547.
Golden Legends; a Poem. (R. H. Barham) Bentley, **3**: 494. **5**: 289. **6**: 88. **8**: 602. **13**: 95.
Golden Lion of Granpere. (A. Trollope) Harper, **44**: 420–881. **45**: 84–546.
Golden Mesh. Appleton, **21**: 402.
Golden Peninsula; a Vision. Fraser, **39**: 155.
Golden Pillar; a Fable. Chr. Obs. **5**: 221.
Golden Sorrow; a Novel. (Mrs. C. Hoey) Chamb. J. **49**: 1–326.
Golden Wedding; a Poem. (H. R. Hudson) Harper, **48**: 66.
— a Poem. (W. MacIlwaine) Dub. Univ. **88**: 272.
— of Longwood; a Poem. (J. G. Whittier) Atlan. **33**: 13
— Poems for. (R. H. Stoddard, G. H. Boker, and B. Taylor) Lippinc. **3**: 33.
Golden Words; a Poem. (A. A. Procter) Good Words, **4**: 74.
Goldie, Thomas, Rise and Downfall of. Hogg, **3**: 313.
Golding, Arthur, Ovid, and Turner. (C. Monkhouse) Art J. **32**: 329.
Golding, Richard. Art J. **19**: 6.
Goldoni, Carlo. (W. D. Howells) Atlan. **40**: 601. — Cornh. **14**: 726. Same art. Ecl. M. **68**: 202. — Temp. Bar, **57**: 220.
— and Life in Italy 125 Years since. St. Paul's, **4**: 482.
— and his Plays. Once a Week, **10**: 721.
— and his Theatrical Works. Anal. M. **7**: 265.
— Autobiography. Blackw. **130**: 516. Same art. Liv. Age, **151**: 259.
— Comedies. (J. Picciotto) Dub. Univ. **77**: 410.
Goldsmid, Sir Isaac L. Bank. M. (L.) **19**: 375, 449. **20**: 220.
Goldschmidt, Jenny Lind, at Exeter Hall, 1856. Art J. **8**: 28.
— Career of. Victoria, **31**: 340.
Goldsmith, Oliver. (Lord E. B. Lytton) Ed. R. **88**: 193. Same art. Liv. Age, **18**: 345. — (T. B. Macaulay) Harper, **14**: 633. — (T. B. Macaulay) Liv. Age, **53**: 513. — (G. M. Towle) Harper, **48**: 681. — (E. Townbridge) Sharpe, **48**: 260. — (G. M. Towle) Appleton, **11**: 459. — (E. T. Channing) No. Am. **45**: 91. — (H. T. Tuckerman) So. Lit. Mess. **6**: 267. — (R. Robbins) Chr. Q. Spec. **10**: 18. — Am. Whig R. **10**: 498. — No. Brit. **9**: 187. Same art. Ecl. M. **14**: 365. Same art. Liv. Age, **17**: 577. — Meth. Q. **9**: 351. — Am. Q. **21**: 460. — New York R. **1**: 280. — Mus. **6**: 1. **31**: 126. — Blackw. **67**: 137, 297. Same art. Ecl. M. **20**: 87, 184. — Dub. Univ. **7**: 30. — Fraser, **15**: 387. — Ecl. R. **65**: 114. **110**: 597. — Art J. **16**: 305, 326. — Bentley, **24**: 193. — Chamb. J. **9**: 343. — Penny M. **11**: 25. — Portfo.(Den.) **6**: 210.
— and his Biographers. Dub. Univ. **32**: 315. Same art. Liv. Age, **19**: 145. — (F. Laurence) Sharpe, **11**: 1. Same art. Liv. Age, **24**: 337.
— and Johnson. De Bow, **28**: 504.
— and La Bruyère. (W. C. Russell) Argosy, **5**: 263.
— Centenary of. (W. J. Fitzpatrick) Dub. Univ. **83**: 438.
— Deserted Village. Belgra. **30**: 98. — Portfo.(Den.) **12**: 315.
— — illustrated by Etching Club. Blackw. **51**: 122.
— — Visit to. Mo. Rel. M. **27**: 221.
— Early Haunts of. (J. J. Keily) Irish Mo. **7**: 194.
— Forster's Life of. Colburn, **83**: 98. — Quar. **95**: 394. Same art. Liv. Age, **43**: 531. Same art. Ecl. M. **34**: 1. — Brit. Q. **8**: 1.
— Fortune and Friends of. Nat. M. **9**: 209, 416.
— Grave of. Colburn, **124**: 426.
— in Boswell's Johnson. (W. N. Nelson) So. M. **8**: 140.
— Irving's Life of. (C. M. Kirkland) No. Am. **70**: 265. — Chr. Obs. **51**: 469.
— Life of. Portfo.(Den.) **27**: 473.
— — and Poetry of. Lond. M. **5**: 105.
— Macaulay on. Dub. R. **43**: 82.
— Personality of. (R. B. S Knowles) Dub. Univ. **88**: 352.
— Poetry of. Art J. **3**: 120. — (R H. Dana) No. Am. **8**: 309.
— Prior's Life of. (W. Empson) Ed. R. **65**: 204. — (E. T. Channing) No. Am. **45**: 91. — Mo. R. **142**: 163. — Colburn, **49**: 282. — Ecl. R. **65**: 114. **66**: 27. — Quar. **57**: 273. — Tait, n. s. **4**: 238. **5**: 163.
— Vicar of Wakefield. Blackw. **53**: 771. — (E. Everett) No. Am. **4**: 248.
Goldsmith's Work of M. Morel. Art J. **2**: 289.
Goldsmiths, Marks of. Art J. **7**: 269.
— Mediæval. Chamb. J. **48**: 374. Same art. Ecl. M. **77**: 488.
Goldsmith's Hall, London. Penny M. **3**: 17.
Goldstücker, Theodor Nature, **5**: 400.
Goldwell, Thomas, Bishop of St. Asaph. (T. F. Knox) Month, **26**: 53, 129.

Golf. Lond. Soc. **4**: 165. — Chamb. J. **39**: 29. — Fraser, **50**: 204.
— Game and the Player. Cornh. **15**: 490.
— Links of St. Mungo. Macmil. **8**: 404.
— New Game for Ladies. (W. W. Tulloch) Belgra. **8**: 78.
— Royal Game of. Chamb. J. **32**: 92. **54**: 705.
Golf Stories. Belgra. **32**: 346.
Golf Tournament. Chamb. J. **30**: 156. — Once a Week, **9**: 694.
Goliath; a Story. (D. Lowry) Potter Am. Mo. **14**: 213.
Golovin, Ivan. (J. J. Ryan) Putnam, **2**: 182.
Goltz, G. F. Christian Dogmatics. Bib. Sac. **31**: 378, 576.
Gomes, Joam B. Tragedy, the new Castro. Blackw. **23**: 601.
Goncourt, Edmond and Jules. (E. Reclus) Atlan. **41**: 180.
Gonda. (J. L. Ver Mehr) Overland, **13**: 452.
Gondola, The. Penny M. **3**: 159.
Gondomar, Count of, and the Spanish Marriage. Lond. Soc. **40**: 122.
Gonds and Bygas of the Eastern Sathpuras. Ev. Sat. **13**: 629.
Gone, Gone, Gone. (A. K. H. Boyd) Fraser, **64**: 296. Same art. Ecl. M. **54**: 384.
Gone to Jail. All the Year, **7**: 487.
Gongs, Chinese, Composition of. J. Frankl. Inst. **19**: 135.
— Manufacture of. (G. W. Yapp) Ecl. Engin. **17**: 206. — Pract. M. **7**: 148.
Gongora, Luis de, Life and Times of. Dub. R. **54**: 95.
Gonsalvo of Cordova. (J. P. C. de Florian) So. Lit. Mess. **21**: 212–729.
Gonzaga Family of Italy. (A. Tacchella) Atlan. **40**: 197.
Gooch, Sir Daniel. Colburn, **165**: 1390.
Good, John Mason. Book of Nature. U. S. Lit. Gaz. **5**: 407. — Mo. R. **111**: 70.
— Life of. Spirit Pilg. **3**: 196. — Mus. **15**: 359. — Ecl. R. **47**: 537. — Chr. Obs. **27**: 170, 193.
Good and Evil; an Essay. (F. Eberty) Macmil. **4**: 357, 456.
— — Triumph of the Good. (J. G. Adams) Univ. Q. **30**: 81. — Good Words, **21**: 265.
— for Evil. (J. F. Bouverie) Dub. Univ. **85**: 407.
— Way to do. (E. B. Hall) Chr. Exam. **21**: 306.
Good Caliph of Bagdad. All the Year, **3**: 32.
Good Cheer. (S. Menzies) Fraser, **104**: 762.
— Science of. St. James, **9**: 47, 195.
Good Deacon's Dream. (T. Tuttle) Potter Am. Mo. **17**: 303.
Good Fight, A. (C. Reade) Once a Week, **1**: 11–273.
Good for Nothing. (H. H. Boyesen) Scrib. **10**: 361. — (G. J. W. Melville) Fraser, **63**: 1–685. **64**: 18–690.
Good-for-Nothing, The. (E. Mayhew) Bentley, **4**: 94.
Good Hope, Cape of. Chr. Exam. **17**: 388. — (Sir J. Barrow) Quar. **22**: 203. — Quar. **25**: 453. — Bentley, **29**: 607. — Brit. & For. R. **4**: 343. — Mo. R. **103**: 296. — (H. W. Tyler) 19th Cent. **4**: 1121.
— and British Caffraria. Brit. Q. **24**: 381.
— and the Kafirs. Ed. R. **62**: 455. — Bentley, **30**: 241–587. **31**: 33. — House. Words, **3**: 30.
— and South Africa. Quar. **108**: 120.
— British Capture of, 1806. (C. Smith) Ed. New Philos. J. **11**: 97.
— British Government of. Colburn, **22**: 165.
— Climate at. (W. J. Black) Geog. M. **5**: 121.
— Emigration to. Blackw. **5**: 523. **6**: 78.
— The rebel Boers. Colburn, **85**: 74.
— Recollections of. Bentley, **29**: 549. — Sharpe, **18**: 313, 367.
— Sketches of. Bentley, **30**: 184. — Blackw. **71**: 289.
— Visit to Table Mt. (J. A. Maitland) St. James, **18**: 61. *See* Africa, South; Table Mountain.
Good Intentions. Colburn, **66**: 346.
Good Investment. (W. J. Flagg) Harper, **44**: 45–894. **45**: 95, 231.
Good-Looking People, Are we a? (R. Tomes) Putnam, **1**: 308.
Good Looks; historically considered. Cornh. **14**: 334. Same art. Ecl. M. **67**: 560.
Good Match. (A. E. T. Watson) Lond. Soc. **24**: 49.
Good Men, Sins of, why recorded in the Scriptures. (W. B. Sprague) Hours at Home, **1**: 223.
Good Morning's Work; a Story. Tinsley, **6**: 99.
Good Night; a Poem. (F. Greenwood) Cornh. **7**: 131.
Good old Cause, The. Dub. Univ. **2**: 241.
Good old Time, and our own. Cath. World, **8**: 380.
Good old Times. Colburn, **6**: 428.
Good old Times; 14th Century. Peop. J. **5**: 241, 257.
Good Sense and Eloquence. (G. F. Simmons) Chr. Exam. **25**: 255.
Good Sir Walter; a Family Portrait. Lond. M. **22**: 460.
Good Stories of Man and other Animals. (C. Reade) Belgra. **29**: 437. **30**: 1–385. **31**: 1–433. **32**: 53–453.
Good Taste. Ev. Sat. **9**: 195.
Good Templars. (A. J. H. Crespi) Colburn, **155**: 508. — Cong. **2**: 616. — Chamb. J. **54**: 167.
Good Time coming. (E. R. Tyler) New Eng. **5**: 388. — Dem. R. **26**: 151.
Good Wife; a Norwegian Story. Contin. Mo. **1**: 290.
Good Works. Cong. M. **1**: 148.
— Merit of. Cath. World, **7**: 125.
Goodale, Elaine and Dora, Two Infant Phenomenons. (J. Payn) Gent. M. n. s. **24**: 611.
Goodall, Fred. B. Art J. **2**: 213.
Good-bye, Sweetheart; a Novel. (R. Broughton) Temp. Bar, **32**: 433. **33**: 1–433. **34**: 1–431. **35**: 1–557. Same art. Appleton, **6**: 101–733.
Goode, F. Missionary Sermon. Chr. Obs. **39**: 722, 791.
Goode, W. Rule of Faith. Ecl. R. **76**: 361.
Goodell, Abner C. Address at Salem, 1875. N. E. Reg. **29**: 341.
Goodell, William, with portrait. Ecl. M. **56**: 114. — (I. Bird) Hours at Home, **5**: 377.
Goodenough, James Graham, Commodore. (J. Morseby) Macmil. **33**: 177. — Dub. Univ. **88**: 486. — Geog. M. **3**: 271. — (A. M. Symington) Good Words, **18**: 638. Same art. Liv. Age, **135**: 178.
Goodhue, Jonathan, Life of. Hunt, **21**: 40.
Goodier, Benjamin, Memoir of. (H. Ware, jr.) Chr. Exam. **2**: 329.
Goodman, Richard, Residence of. (W. Hall) Potter Am. Mo. **13**: 442.
Goodrich, Chauncey A. (T. D. Woolsey) New Eng. **18**: 328.
Goodrich, Samuel G. Liv. Age, **65**: 619. — U. S. Lit. Gaz. **7**: 736.
— Poems. Internat. M. **2**: 153.
Goodrich, William M., Organ-Builder. New Eng. M. **6**: 25.
Goodwin, Daniel, and his Descendants. Hist. M. **14**: 191.
Goodwin, Hersey B. (C. Palfrey) Chr. Exam. **21**: 273.
Goodwin, Harvey, Bishop of Carlisle. Cong. **5**: 239.
— Hulsean Lectures for 1855. Chr. Obs. **56**: 250, 374.
Goodwin, John. (D. A. Whedon) Meth. Q. **23**: 357. **29**: 485. — Cong. M. **5**: 533.
Goodwin, Robert M., Trial of, for Manslaughter. (H. Wheaton) No. Am. **11**: 114.
Goodwin, Thomas, Works of. Ecl. R. **123**: 472.
Goodwood. All the Year, **36**: 469.
— and Bognor. Temp. Bar, **6**: 236.
— as it was, and is. Once a Week, **13**: 213.
Goodwood Races, Trip to. (J. A. Dickson) Lippinc. **28**: 72
Goodyear, Charles. (J. Parton) No. Am. **101**: 65.
— Discourse on. (S. W. S. Dutton) New Eng. **18**: 774.
Gookin, Gen. Daniel, of Cambridge. N. E. Reg. **3**: 123. — (J. W. Thornton) N. E. Reg. **4**: 185.

Gookin, Gen. Daniel, of Cambridge. History of New England. (J. W. Thornton) N. E. Reg. **13**: 347.
Gookin, Daniel, of Sherborn. (J. W. Thornton) N. E. Reg. **4**: 79.
Gookin Genealogy. (J. W. Thornton) N. E. Reg. **1**: 345. **2**: 167. **4**: 79.
Goolbie; a Tale. (H. Chesen) St. James, **38**: 398.
Goold, Serjeant. Colburn, **10**: 121.
Goose, The. Chamb. J. **41**: 445.
— Barnacle. (G. N. Lawrence) Am. Natural. **5**: 10.
Goose Clubs. Broadw. **1**: 281.
Goose Girl; a Poem. (E. Keary) Ev. Sat. **8**: 479.
Goose Quills and Steel Pens. Tait, **3**: 280.
Gooseberries, in North of England. Penny M. **3**: 314.
— Wild. (A. Gray) Am. Natural. **10**: 270.
Goose Tree Myth. Pop. Sci. Mo. **4**: 565.
Gopher, Prairie. (E. Coues) Am. Natural. **9**: 147.
Gorbaczewski, John. Ed. R. **132**: 363.
Gordon, Alexander, Antiquary. (D. Wilson) Canad. J. n. s. **14**: 9. **15**: 122.
Gordon, Alexander, Trial and Execution of. Bentley, **64**: 469, 551.
Gordon, Lieut.-Col. C. G., Chinese Campaign under. Fraser, **79**: 135.
Gordon, Lady Duff, and her Works. (Mrs. C. E. Norton) Macmil. **20**: 457. — (E. C. Gray) Good Words, **16**: 637. Same art. Liv. Age, **103**: 71.
— Letters from Egypt. (H. James, jr.) Nation, **20**: 412.
— Short Memoir by her Daughter. Macmil. **30**: 530. Same art. Liv. Age, **123**: 338.
Gordon, Lady Jean. (W. Chambers) Chamb. J. **52**: 33. Same art. Ecl. M. **84**: 486.
Gordon, Sir James A., the last of Nelson's Captains. Macmil. **19**: 353. Same art. Ecl. M. **72**: 480.
Gordon, Sir J. Watson. Art J. **2**: 373.
Gordon, Patrick. Lond. Q. **14**: 494. — Blackw. **89**: 485.
— Career in Russia. Ecl. M. **26**: 145.
— Diary of. Ed. R. **104**: 24. — Quar. **90**: 314. — Fraser, **44**: 397.
Gordon, P. L., Personal Memoirs of. Mo. R. **122**: 489.
Gordon, Robt. Sermons. Ecl. R. **43**: 253. — Hogg, **11**: 509.
Gordon, William, Historian of American Revolution. Hist. M. **6**: 41.
Gordon and French Families. (C. Sotheran) Antiquary, **4**: 129.
Gordon Graham. (J. A. Crofts) Colburn, **158**: 342, 455.
Gordon of Brackley; Ancient Scottish Ballad. Lond. M. **9**: 355.
Gordon Riots. (W. Thornbury) Antiquary, **4**: 161–197. — Dub. R. **72**: 381. **73**: 50.
— and Newgate. All the Year, **27**: 421.
Gore, Catherine Frances, with portrait. Colburn, **49**: 434.
— Banker's Wife. Tait, n. s. **10**: 702.
— Fair of May Fair. Westm. **17**: 468. Same art. Select J. **1**: [118. — Tait, **1**: 389.
— Greville; or a Season in Paris. Tait, n. s. **8**: 186.
— Jerningham. Tait, n. s. **3**: 526.
— Pin Money. Westm. **15**: 433.
— Polish Tales. Tait, **3**: 234.
— Preferment. Tait, n. s. **7**: 41.
— Women as they are. (T. H. Lister) Ed. R. **51**: 444.
— Works of. Colburn, **95**: 157. Same art. Ecl. M. **27**: 527. Same art. Liv. Age, **34**: 545.
Gore, Francis, and Upper Canada. Fraser, **47**: 627.
Goredale. Penny M. **2**: 189.
Gore House. Colburn, **86**: 135. Same art. Ecl. M. **17**: 456. Same art. Liv. Age, **22**: 145.
Goree, an African Fairhaven. Lippinc. **18**: 414.
Gorgeana, Early Records of. N. E. Reg. **35**. 42.
Gorges, Sir Ferdinando, Defense on Charge of betraying the Earl of Essex. (J. Bruce) Arch. **33**: 241.
Gorges, Sir Ferdinando, and Popham, Colonial Schemes of. (J. W. Thornton) Cong. Q. **5**: 143.
Gorges, Ferdinando, jr., Plagiarism of. No. Am. **106**: 319.
Gorges Genealogy. (S. G. Drake) N. E. Reg. **15**: 18. — N. E. Reg. **29**: 44.
Gorgias in California. (M. Kellogg) Overland, **1**: 534.
Gorham, George C. Bentley, **27**: 612.
— *versus* Bishop of Exeter, 1850. Brit. Q. **11**: 411. — Ecl. R. **91**: 626. — Ed. R. **92**: 263.
— — Judgment in Case of. Dub. R. **28**: 233.
Gorhambury, From Gray's Inn to. Once a Week, **7**: 276.
Gorilla, The. (W. Hincks) Canad. J. n. s. **8**: 315. — (K. Prosper) Recr. Sci. **3**: 105. — (L. J. Sanford) Am. J. Sci. **83**: 48. — All the Year, **1**: 112. **5**: 237. — Ev. Sat. **4**: 68. — Good Words, **2**: 464.
— and other Apes. (R. A. Proctor) Gent. M. n. s. **19**: 413.
— as I found him. (W. W. Reade) Belgra. **3**: 230. Same art. Ecl. M. **69**: 498.
— and his Country. Colburn, **122**: 186. Same art. Ecl. M. **53**: 524.
— Brain of. (G. D. Thane) Nature, **15**: 142.
— Du Chaillu on. No. Brit. **35**: 219. — Temp. Bar. **3**: 482.
— Habits of. (W. W. Reade) Am. Natural. **1**: 177.
— Limbs of, Owen's. Anthrop. R. **1**: 149.
— our nearest Relative. All the Year, **1**: 112. Same art. Liv. Age, **62**: 57.
Gorillas and Cannibals. Chamb. J. **35**: 394.
Gorilla Country, Africa and the. Ecl. R. **113**: 578.
Gormandizing, Memorials of. (W. M. Thackeray) Fraser, **23**: 710.
Gormandizing School of Eloquence. Blackw. **14**: 73, 497.
Gornlay, Queen of Ireland. (C. Scott) Dub. Univ. **82**: 475.
Gort, Charles Vercker, Viscount, with portrait. Dub. Univ. **19**: 336.
Gortchakoff, Prince Alexander. (A. C. J. Gustafson) Atlan. **44**: 213. — (A. F. Hewit) Cath. World, **24**: 721. — (A. Laugel) Nation, **21**: 23. — with portrait, Ecl. M. **64**: 393. — with portrait, Ev. Sat. **10**: 41.
— and Bismarck. Blackw. **120**: 448. Same art. Ecl. M. **87**: 667. — Ed. R. **144**: 203.
Gorton, Samuel. (C. Deane) N. E. Reg. **4**: 201.
— Life of. (J. M. Mackie) Sparks's Am. Biog. **15**: 317.
Goshen, Journey through the Land of. (G. W. Samson) Chr. R. **14**: 141, 455. **15**: 214.
Goslar, Day's Wandering in. Once a Week, **17**: 598, 616.
Gosnold and Pring, 1602–3. (B. F. De Costa) N. E. Reg. **32**: 76.
Gospel, The. (S. E. Shepard) Chr. Q. **7**: 39.
— a Gift to the Imagination. (H. Bushnell) Hours at Home, **10**: 158.
— a new Creation. Chr. Disc. **4**: 225.—Chr. Exam. **1**: 257.
— a Remedy for Sin. (G. W. S.) Univ. Q. **20**: 298.
— a Sword. (H. R. Nye) Univ. Q. **25**: 195.
— a Witness to all Nations. (J. Richards) Theo. & Lit. J. **6**: 558.
— and the Age. Chr. Rem. **8**: 265.
— better than the Law to sustain Public Integrity. (J. M. Hoppin) New Eng. **38**: 537.
— for all the World. (J. G. Adams) Univ. Q. **37**: 342.
— the Friend to Liberty. (S. H. Cowles) Chr. Mo. Spec. **10**: 10.
— Glorying in. Chr. Disc. **5**: 250.
— Human Character exhibited in. Chr. Mo. Spec. **5**: 281.
— in Old Testament. (F. W. C. Umbreit) Evang. R. **1**: 39.
— Influence of, in liberalizing the Mind. (M. Hopkins) Am. Bib. Repos. **10**: 419.
— Intelligent Adherence to. (D. C. Haynes) Chr. R. **11**: 398.
— of the Age. Bib. R. **4**: 503.
— of the Kingdom. (H. W. Brown) Radical, **2**: 529.
— of Travelers. (A. P. Stanley) Good Words, **18**: 663.
— or Fiction. (D. Y. Heisler) Mercersb. **25**: 258.
— Preaching of. (B. Kurtz) Evang. R. **1**: 524.

Gospel, The; Relations to Civil Law. (P. Cooke) Princ. 15: 110.
— Why Mankind neglect. Chr. Mo. Spec. 6: 453.
Gospel History. (J. A. Alexander) Princ. 20: 592.
— Formation of. Month, 6: 289.
— Outlines of. Dub. R. 55: 421.
Gospel Narratives, Eclectic Use of. (J. A. Pictou) Mod. R. 2: 172.
Gosport Navy Yard, Abandonment of. (G. Welles) Galaxy, 10: 109.
Gossip. Tinsley, 11: 103.
— among the Infernals. Dub. Univ. 23: 245.
— and Gossiping. Fraser, 100: 90.
— Land of. (B. R. Parkes) Argosy. 1: 236.
— Literature of. St. James, 1: 110.
— of Gold Hill. (W. W. Macomber) Overland, 10: 209.
— of History. Cornh. 35: 325.
— on Rivers. (S. S. Cox) Knick. 37: 343.
— Royal and Noble. Cornh. 36: 185.
Gossips, Some recent. Dub. Univ. 81: 497.
Gossiping. New Eng. M. 6: 459.
Gossner, John E., the Scholar and Teacher. Good Words, 1: 177, 282.
Gosson, Stephen. Cong. 1: 592.
Gotama. *See* Buddha.
Goths. Hogg, 1: 90.
— and their Language. Danv. Q. 1: 134.
— at Ravenna. Brit. Q. 56: 297.
Gotha Almanac. Chamb. J. 13: 14.
Gotha Canal. (C. U. C. Burton) Nat. M. 10: 57.
Gotham, Drolleries of. Dub. Univ. 86: 488.
— Men of. Sharpe, 40: 147.
Gothenburg and Sweden, 1879. (A. M. Symington) Good Words, 21: 317.
— Licensing System of. Macmil. 28: 522. — (C. C. Andrews) Internat. R. 8: 402.
— Reformed Public Houses. (M. W. Moggridge) Macmil. 38: 467.
Gothic Architecture. *See* Architecture.
Gothic Art and Architecture. Brit. Q. 10: 46. 52: 451.
Gothic Language. *See* Mœso-Gothic.
Gothic Laws of Spain. Ed. R. 31: 94.
Gothic Ornaments of the Duomo, etc. of Pisa. (A. Taylor) Arch. 20: 537.
Gothic Revival. (G. Mansfield) Cath. World, 25: 639.
— Eastlake's. (R. Sturgis) Nation, 14: 275. — Dub. R. 70: 440.
See also Architecture.
Gottfried von Strassburg. Hymn to the Virgin. Cath. World, 13: 240.
Gottfried's Success. (R. Dana) Harper, 44: 575.
Gotthelf, J. Tales. Westm. 48: 202.
Göttingen. *See* Goettingen.
Gottschalk, Louis M., Diary of. (C. S. Holt) Dial (Ch.), 2: 141.
Gouf, F. de la Boullaye le, Travels of. Retros. 17: 78.
Gouges, Madame de. All the Year, 43: 305.
Gough, Lord, with portrait. Dub. Univ. 36: 192.
Gough, John B. Chamb. J. 5: 375. — So. Lit. Mess. 28: 177.
Goujon, Jehan. (E. F. S. Pattison) Portfo. 2: 22.
Gould, Benj. Apthorp. Uranometria Argentina. Am. J. Sci. 119: 376.
Gould, Hannah F. So. Lit. Mess. 2: 115. — New Eng. M. 4: 309.
— and Mrs. Sigourney. (O. W. B. Peabody) No. Am. 41: 430.
— Poems of. (F. W. P. Greenwood) Chr. Exam. 14: 320. — Am. Mo. R. 2: 75.
Gould, John, F. R. S., Obituary of. Nature, 23: 365.
Gould, John W., Obituary of. Knick. 13: 34.
Gould, Mary. (Mrs. E. F. Ellet) Godey, 39: 249.
Gould, S. Baring, with portrait. Appleton, 4: 673.
— Works of. Lond. Q. 40: 44.
Gounod, Charles François, with portrait. Appleton, 11: 394. — (A. Ogilvy) Once a Week, 17: 319. — Eng. Dom. M. 3: 456. — Galaxy, 7: 425.
— Gallia. (Mrs. R. Barker) Cath. World, 30: 71.
Gourgaud, Gen. Narrative of Campaign of 1815. (M. M. Scott) Blackw. 4: 220.
Gourgues, Dominique de. (M. P. Thompson) Cath. World, 21: 701.
Gourmands and Gormandizing. All the Year, 20: 270.
Gournay, M. de J., Demoiselle de. House. Words, 4: 534.
Gout, The. All the Year, 11: 583. — Chamb. J. 42: 463.
— and Stone, Causes of. Portfo. (Den.) 19: 32.
— Eau Médicinale in. Quar. 3: 368.
— Good Quality of. All the Year, 1: 102.
— Honor of. Retros. 11: 35.
— Praise of. Lond. M. 10: 91.
— Scudamore's Treatise on. Mo. R. 84: 293.
Gouty-Stem Tree. (J. R. Jackson) Student, 1: 401.
Governess; a Tale. So. Lit. Mess. 4: 93.
Governess System, Modern. Fraser, 30: 571.
Governesses. (M. Calverley) Good Words, 19: 390. — Peop. J. 5: 247.
— Health of. (H. Martineau) Once a Week, 3: 267.
— Home for. Victoria, 7: 64.
— Social Position of. Fraser, 37: 411.
Governesses' Benevolent Institution. St. James, 4: 501. — Peop. J. 5: 135.
Government. (E. Lucas) Month, 32: 198, 436. 33: 150. — Dub. Univ. 35: 682.
— Administrative Reform. Colburn, 107: 127.
— Allegiance to. Univ. Q. 19: 258.
— American Governments. (E. E. Hale) O. & N. 11: 517.
— and the Church. (M. F. Sullivan) Am. Cath. Q. 1: 353.
— and Class Legislation. (H. Crompton) Fortn. 20: 25.
— and Constitutional Law. (B. Tucker) So. Lit. Mess. 5: 587.
— and Currency. (H. Middleton) Hunt. 13: 311, 412.
— — Middleton's. So. Q. 18: 123.
— and Equality. (Earl of Desart) Dark Blue, 3: 127.
— and Legislation, Ancient and modern. De Bow, 29: 721.
— and Popular Education. (E. C. Wines) Bib. Sac. 8: 737.
— and Religion. (J. H. A. Bomberger) Mercersb. 3: 305. — So. R. n. s. 11: 371.
— as a Branch of Popular Education. (J. Story) Am. Inst. of Instruc. 1834: 234.
— Best. (F. H. Hedge) Chr. Exam. 72: 313.
— by a Liberty Boy. Dub. Univ. 35: 682.
— Calhoun's Disquisition on. So. Q. 23: 333.
— Calhoun's Theory of. (F. Bowen) No. Am. 76: 473.
— Ceremonial, Evolution of. (H. Spencer) Fortn. 29: 1-772.
— Some Checks and Balances in. (T. M. Cooley) Internat. R. 3: 317.
— Civil. (W. A. Grayson) So. Lit. Mess. 25: 321.
— — and the Bible. Am. Whig R. 12: 511.
— — Divine Origin and Supremacy of. Danv. Q. 4: 327.
— — Elements of. Dub. Univ. 11: 637.
— — Ethics of. (D. A. Gorton) Nat. Q. 37: 209.
— — Intrinsic End of. Dub. R. 53: 66.
— Conservative. Blackw. 37: 431.
— Cost of. Bank. M. (N. Y.) 1: 629.
— Dialogue on the best Form of. Chr. Rem. 46: 286.
— Divine. *See* God, Government of.
— Double. Dub. Univ. 51: 460.
— Duties of the State. Fraser, 85: 737.
— Excessive. (H. Robinson) Overland, 7: 433.
— Federal. (J. G. Palfrey) No. Am. 54: 212.
— — Freeman on. (T. Chase) No. Am. 101: 612.
— Forms of. Ed. R 136: 83.
— — Sir G. C. Lewis on. Ed. R. 118: 138.

Government from above and from below. (F. W. Newman) Fraser, 82: 121.
— Functions of. (T. D. Huxley) Fortn. 16: 525. — (H. Spencer) Fortn. 16: 627.
— Gobemouchian Ideal of. (W. H. Browne) So. R. n. s. 4: 189.
— Helps's Thoughts on. (Goldwin Smith) Canad. Mo. 1: 561. — (E. D. J. Wilson) Dark Blue, 2: 640.
— How to build a Nation. (J. P. Thompson) New Eng. 28: 19.
— Human, a Divine Institution. (B. Hart) New Eng. 3: 525.
— Hurlbut's Essays on. Dem. R. 17: 189.
— Influence of Climates upon. So. R. n. s. 9: 409.
— Laissez-faire. Fraser, 81: 72.
— Lecture on. (B. Tucker) So. Lit. Mess. 3: 208.
— Lieber on Civil Liberty and Self-. (T. D. Woolsey) New Eng. 14: 329. — So. Lit. Mess. 19: 713. — So. Q. 25: 300.
— Local, among different Nations. (Sir C. W. Dilke) J. Statis. Soc. 37: 313.
— — Cost of, in England. (P. G. Craigie) J. Statis. Soc. 40: 262.
— — in United States and abroad. (R. P. Porter) Princ. n. s. 4: 172.
— — Parish Law. Brit. Q. 48: 415.
— Local Self-, and Centralization. Ecl. R. 94: 354.
— Ministerial Responsibility. Westm. 66: 188.
— Monarchy and Democracy. Knick. 64: 338, 385.
— a moral Power. (T. Lewis) Am. Bib. Repos. 3d s. 3: 65, 214.
— Municipal. Dem. R. 24: 481.
— — City Clerks. Once a Week, 13: 107, 119.
— Ocane on. West. R. 1: 17.
— of our great Cities. (E. L. Godkin) Nation, 3: 312.
— of Dependencies, Lewis on. Blackw. 51: 213. — Ed. R. 83: 512. — Mo. R. 156: 168.
— Origin and Design of. (T. Paine) Carey's Mus. 1: 20, 99.
— — and Foundations of. Am. Whig R. 2: 327, 437. 3: 273. — Dem. R. 13: 129, 241, 353.
— — and Functions of. (J. P. Thompson) New Eng. 7: 530.
— Pacificators. Dub. Univ. 10: 217.
— Paternal. (S. Blackstone) St. Paul's, 12: 718.
— Philosophy of. Sharpe, 25: 303, 333. 26: 14-278.
— Progress of Personal Rule. (H. Duncley) 19th Cent. 4: 785.
— Popular. (O. A. Brownson) Dem. R. 12: 529. 29: 516.
— — Popular Knowledge necessary to. (J. C. Bruce) So. Lit. Mess. 19: 292.
— Popular Fallacies on Functions of. Westm. 107: 305.
— Premier and President. Fraser, 86: 391.
— Proper Functions of. Temp. Bar, 7: 419, 505.
— Reciprocal Duties of State and Subject. (J. A. Froude) Fraser, 81: 286.
— Relation of State and Municipal. (S. Bowles) Am. Soc. Sci. J. 9: 140.
— Religious Base of. (A. Hovey) Bapt. Q. 6: 42.
— Representative. (H. W. Warren) Am. Whig R. 7: 280.
— — Republican. (J. G. Jones) Victoria, 21: 385.
— Republican Form of, Advantages of. (H. Flanders) No. Am. 89: 99.
— Responsible. (V. B. Denslow) Internat. R. 4: 230.
— Right of, over Human Life. (E. R. Tyler) New Eng. 3: 562.
— Science in. (T. Gray) J. Spec. Philos. 10: 290.
— Science of. (S. G. Fisher) Am. Mo. M. 12: 201.
— — Retrogression in. (E. L. Godkin) No. Am. 110: 398.
— Self-, Progress of. (W. Dowe) Nat. Q. 36: 205.
— Source of, Authority of. Dub. R. 56: 279.
— Sphere and Duties of. (J. Chapman) Westm. 62: 473.
Government, Thoughts upon. (A. Helps) Macmil. 26: 27, 219, 457. Same art. Ecl. M. 79: 37, 296, 664. 80: 461.
— Tract on. (R. B. Rhett) So. Q. 25: 486.
— Three Experiments in. (J. F. Tuttle) Am. Bib. Repos. 3d s. 1: 1.
— True Functions of. (J. McKrum) De Bow, 4: 95.
— True Theory of. (A. P. Upshur) So. Lit. Mess. 22: 401.
— Yeaman's Study of. (J. N. Pomeroy) Nation, 12: 403. *See* Despotism; Liberty; Representative Government; State, The; etc.
Governments, Arbitrary, Policy and Fate of. Ed. R. 39: 281. — Selec. Ed. R. 4: 342. — Mus. 4: 385.
— Federative, Power and Stability of. Ox. Prize Ess. 4: 239.
— Rights of. Dub. R. 50: 397.
— Strong. St. James, 24: 410.
— Subversion of ancient. Quar. 45: 450.
Government Contracts. Am. Law R. 4: 1.
Government Loans. Am. Law R. 3: 218.
Governor Fox; a Tale. Liv. Age, 5: 227.
Governor's Island, N.Y., Garrison Life at. (W. H. Rideing) Scrib. 21: 593.
Governors and Legislators, Compensation of, 1821. Niles's Reg. 20: 55.
Governor, Steam-Engine, and Governor-Valve, Patent. Pract. M. 2: 160.
Governors, Engine. (J. Haug) J. Frankl. Inst. 107: 83. — (L. d'Auria) J. Frankl. Inst. 107: 185, 387. 109: 266.
— Isochronous. (A. K. Mansfield) J. Frankl. Inst. 102: 233.
Gow, Neil, with portrait. Hogg, 8: 289. — Liv. Age, 61: 707.
Gowans, Wm. (S. S. Purple) Am. Bibliop. 3: 5. 4: 127.
Gower, John. Retros. 16: 103.
— and his Works. Brit. Q. 27: 1. Same art. Liv. Age, 57: 163.
— Confessio Amantis. Fraser, 59: 571.
Gower, Scotland. (D. T. Evans) Colburn, 66: 362.
Gower, Lord Leveson, Poems and Translations. (W. Empson) Ed. R. 52: 231.
Gowrie, Earl of, Conspiracy of. (J. Bruce) Arch. 33: 143. — Nat. R. 3: 255. Same art. Liv. Age, 51: 321.
— Trial and Death of, 1584. (J. Bruce) Arch. 33: 143.
— — Documents relating to. (J. Bruce) Arch. 34: 190.
Goya, F. J. (P. G. Hamerton) Portfo. 10: 67-99.
Goza, Clockmaker's Salt-Works at. Penny M. 5: 326.
— Remains of the Giant's Tower at. (W. H. Smyth) Arch. 22: 294.
Gozlan, Leon, Writings of. Dub. Univ. 63: 673.
Gozon, Dieudonné de. (W. J. Walter) U. S. Cath. M. 3: 645.
Gozzi, Carlo, A Venetian of the 18th Century. (H. M. Benson) Lippinc. 20: 347.
— Turandot; a Dramatic Fable. Blackw. 33: 371.
Grab Collection, The great. Chamb. J. 23: 18.
Grabbe, C. Cinderella. Blackw. 41: 668.
Gracchi, The. (E. S. Creasy) Bentley, 31: 475. Same art. Ecl. M. 26: 229. — Westm. 18: 43.
Gracchus, Caius. So. Q. 20: 62.
Grace and Arminianism. (J. C. Rankin) Princ. 28: 38.
— — Princeton Review on. Meth. Q. 16: 257.
— and Nature. (D. Y. Heisler) Mercersb. 22: 297. — (J. W. Nevin) Mercersb. 19: 485.
— Doctrine of. Chr. Mo. Spec. 6: 289.
— Doctrines of. Chr. Mo. Spec. 1: 117.
— Father Mazella's Treatise on. (A. F. Hunt) Cath. World, 28: 131.
— Hogg on the Economy of. Cong. M. 10: 607.
— of God, Man's Dependence on. (S. R. Andrew) Chr. Q. Spec. 7: 76.

Grace on Drafts at Sight. (D. R. Jacques) Hunt, **19**: 399.
Grace at Meals. Chr. Obs. **2**: 469, 593. **16**: 142.
Grace before Meat. (C. Lamb) Lond. M. **4**: 469.
Grace Allen. All the Year, **26**: 98. — Ev. Sat. **11**: 502.
Grace Dawson. Appleton, **1**: 106.
Grace Dorrien. Tait, n. s. **23**: 37–340.
Grace Kennedy; a Tale. Dub. Univ. **36**: 337, 443, 556. Same art. Liv. Age, **27**: 119, 293, 541.
Grace Owen's Engagement. (R. E. Francillon) Blackw. **103**: 651. **104**: 44. Same art. Liv. Age, **98**: 44, 291.
Grace Selwode. (J. Goddard) Once a Week, **25**: 50–578.
Grace Seymour's Mission; a Tale. (K. O'Meara) Cath. World, **18**: 668, 806.
Graces, The; a Poem. Blackw. **33**: 527.
Gracian, Balthasar. (M. E. G. Duff) Fortn. **27**: 328.
Gradgrind, Mr., typically considered. (F. Jacox) Bentley, **60**: 613.
Graduates and Undergraduates. Colburn, **63**: 212–449. **64**: 17–491. **65**: 49–240.
— of New England and New York Colleges. *See* Colleges.
Græca Majora, Dalzel's. Ed. R. **2**: 211.
— Popkin's Dalzel's. (G. Bancroft) No. Am. **23**: 142.
Græfe, A. v., of Berlin. (W. H. Milburn) Harper, **47**: 595.
Graefenberg. Putnam, **9**: 244.
Graefrath, Hofrath of. Liv. Age, **49**: 371.
Graf de Tropp. Fraser, **27**: 195.
Graffiti, or Wall Scribblings. Liv. Age, **148**: 758.
Grafting, Consequences and Effects of. (M. T. Masters) Pop. Sci. R. **10**: 141.
Grafton, Joseph, Life of. Chr. R. **14**: 245.
Grafton, Mass., Council at, 1744. Cong. Q. **4**: 247.
— Ministers of. Am. Q. Reg. **10**: 57.
Graham, Andrew. Dub. Univ. **13**: 96.
Graham, Sir James. Westm. **41**: 319. — Blackw. **93**: 436. — Hogg, **5**: 225.
— on Coin and Currency. Westm. **41**: 319.
— Oratory of. Fraser, **33**: 136.
Graham, John, of Claverhouse, and the Covenanters. (J. T. Morse, jr.) Nat. Q. **10**: 259.
— and Lord Macaulay. Blackw. **88**: 155. Same art. Liv. Age, **66**: 656.
— Macaulay and Aytoun on. No. Brit. **13**: 1.
— Napier's Memorials of. Liv. Age, **63**: 290.
Graham, Marie. Three Months near Rome. Ed. R. **35**: 140. — Mo. R. **94**: 173. — Lond. M. **2**: 306.
Graham, Mary Jane. (S. R. Andrew) Chr.Q. Spec. **6**: 381.
Graham, Miss Stirling. (W. Chambers) Chamb. J. **55**: 65.
Graham, Thomas, Lord Lynedoch. Ed. R. **152**: 303. — (R. D. Osborn) Nation, **31**: 361.
Graham, Thomas, Master of the Mint. (J. Bryce) Macmil. **22**: 183. — (A. W. Williamson) Nature, **1**: 20.
— Memoir of. (J. P. Cooke, jr.) Am. J. Sci. **101**: 115.
Graham, Clan of, Ireland. (W. Scott) Dub. Univ. **1**: 325.
Graham's Island. Sharpe, **5**: 240.
Grahame, James. Blackw. **1**: 596.
— British Georgics. Chr. Obs. **5**: 437. **9**: 628. — (F. Jeffrey) Ed. R. **16**: 213. — (R. Southey) Quar. **3**: 456. — Ecl. R. **4**: 792. **12**: 769.
Grain, Harvesting and Storing of. Pract. M. **5**: 229, 276.
— Proclamation of Elizabeth on Scarcity of. (F. Douce) Arch. **14**: 27.
Grain and Flour Trade. De Bow, **4**: 159.
Grain-Binder Attachment to Harvesters. Pract. M. **2**: 209.
Grain Crop of 1855. Bank. M. (N. Y.) **10**: 169.
Grain Elevators, Cleaners, and Driers. (A. P. Boller) J. Frankl. Inst. **82**: 1, 73.
Grain Fields of Russia and America. (D. Ker) Nat. Q. **39**: 318.
Grain Market, Home and Foreign. (J. D. B. De Bow) De Bow, **1**: 33.
Grain Worms. Penny M. **2**: 301, 334.
Grained for Life. Ev. Sat. **11**: 586.
Grainger, Richard. (H. Martineau) Once a Week, **5**: 401.
Grammar. (G. Brown) Am. Inst. of Instruc. **1831**: 137.
— and Language. Lond. Q. **12**: 387.
— Bopp's Comparative. (L. and R. L. Tafel) Bib. Sac. **18**: 771.
— Comparative. (W. D. Whitney) No. Am. **111**: 199.
— Criticism and Logic, Smith's. Mo. R. **107**: 61.
— gone mad. Ev. Sat. **2**: 643.
— of Dionysius, the Thracian; translated. (T. Davidson) J. Spec. Philos. **8**: 326.
— of the New Testament Dialect. Chr. Obs. **48**: 182.
— Outlines of Universal. Mo. R. **83**: 84.
— Problem of. (H. M. Mason) Western, **2**: 352.
— Wilson's Essay on. Anal. M. **11**: 177.
See English Language; French Language; etc.
Grammar Schools. Pamph. **13**: 261. **16**: 337. **19**: 88.
— Endowed, of England. Am. J. Educ. **28**: 737.
— — Clerical Masterships of. Cong. **1**: 169.
— — of Ireland. Am. J. Educ. **15**: 721.
— English. (J. Sutherland) Gent. M. n. s. **1**: 155–438.
— — Smaller. Brit. Q. **38**: 51.
— Irish. (M. Arnold) Fortn. **36**: 137.
— Original, of New England. Am. J. Educ. **16**: 105.
Grammarless Tongue. (R. G. White) Galaxy, **7**: 267.
Gramme Machine. (M. F. O'Reilly) Pop. Sci. R. **12**: 265.
Grammont, Count de, with portrait. Ev. Sat. **9**: 487, 496.
— Memoirs; Bohn's Edition. Fraser, **34**: 603.
Grampians, Excursion into the. Nature, **10**: 90.
Grana Weal, Fragments from Hist. of. Dub. Univ. **3**: 194.
Granada. (A. Griffiths) Art J. **33**: 17, 49.—Bentley, **5**: 264.
— and the Alhambra. (G. B. Cheever) Knick. **19**: 120, 197, 329. — (S. P. Scott) Lippinc. **27**: 425.
— Irving's Conquest of. (W. H. Prescott) No. Am. **29**: 293. — Quar. **43**: 55. — Am. Mo. R. **5**: 190. — Mo. R. **119**: 430.
Granary of the West. (J. W. Scott) Hunt, **16**: 363.
Granby; a Novel. Mo. R. **109**: 97. — (Syd. Smith) Ed. R. **43**: 395.
Grand-Assize Cause. Ecl. M. **46**: 555.
Grand Duchess, The. (G. A. Sala) Belgra. **4**: 303.
Grand Jury. Chamb. J. **41**: 305. — All the Year, **5**: 574.
Grand Juries. Westm. **19**: 88.
— Functions of. West. Law J. **3**: 210.
Grand Jury Laws and County Public Works. Dub. Univ. **27**: 346.
Grand Manan Island. (E. Abbott) Harper, **56**: 541. — (B. F. De Costa) Hours at Home, **11**: 224.
Grand Pré, Nova Scotia; Scene of Evangeline. (G. Mackenzie) Canad. Mo. **16**: 337.
Grand Traverse Bay. (M. Thompson) Lippinc. **28**: 321.
Grand Trunk R. R. (M. B. Hewson) Canad. Mo. **8**: 276.
Grande Chartreuse. *See* Chartreuse, Grande.
Grands Jours d'Auvergne. Quar. **81**: 187. Same art. Liv. Age, **14**: 250. — Blackw. **63**: 47. Same art. Liv. Age, **16**: 309.
Grandfather and I. Chamb. J. **42**: 609.
Grandfather's Musings. Chamb. J. **42**: 193.
Grandfather's Story. (F. R. Thomas) Victoria, **28**: 16.
Grandfather's Story. House. Words, **6**: 593.
Grandfathers and Grandchildren. (J. Wilson) Blackw. **50**: 632.
Grandier, Urban; a French Record of 17th Century. St. Paul's, **3**: 326.
Grandissimes, The. (G. W. Cable) Scrib. **19**: 97–841. **20**: 24–812.
Grandmother, The. (H. C. Andersen) Temp. Bar, **32**: 370.
Grandmother Prentice. (P. Mulford) Overland, **12**: 449.
Grandmother's Apology; a Poem. (A. Tennyson) Once a Week, **1**: 41.
Grandmother's Story. (C. B. Conant) Overland, **5**: 475.
Grandmothers, Chapter on. Dub. Univ. **23**: 248.

Grandmothers, In Praise of. Macmil. **4**: 323.
— Plea for our. (B. Murphy) Cath. World, **23**: 421.
Grandson of Candide. (H. D. Traill) Dark Blue, **2**: 560.
Grange, Lady, Story of. Chamb. J. **5**: 145. — (W. Chambers) Chamb. J. **51**: 449.
— — New Light on. Blackw. **66**: 347. Same art. Liv. Age, **23**: 59.
Grange Garden. (H. Kingsley) St. James, **36**: 337-561. **37**: 61-561. **38**: 93-449.
Granges of the Patrons of Husbandry. (Mrs. P. Swalm) O. & N. **8**: 96.
— and Farmers' Clubs in America. Cornh. **28**: 556.
— and Free Trade. Republic, **1**: 513.
— and the Potter Law. Internat. R. **3**: 665.
Granger Movement in Western States. (C. F. Adams, jr.) No. Am. **120**: 394. — (W. C. Flagg) Am. Soc. Sci. J. **6**: 100. — Nation, **16**: 329. — (W. G. Sumner) Nation, **16**: 381. — (E. L. Godkin) Nation, **17**: 68, 156. **18**: 55. **19**: 36. — (M. Howland) Lippinc. **12**: 338.
— Agricultural Exposition of Corporate Law. Nation, **17**: 140.
— and the Railroads. (C F. Adams, jr.) Nation, **16**: 249. — (E. F. Adams) Nation, **19**: 121, 234. — (F. R. Leland) Nation, **20**: 189.
— — Potter Law. (E. L. Godkin) Nation, **19**: 231.
— — Rates of Transportation. Nation, **17**: 36.
— — Right to confiscate. (A G. Sedgwick) Nation, **19**: 199.
— — Watered-Stock Hallucination. (A. G. Sedgwick) Nation, **17**: 237. — (E. L. Godkin) Nation, **17**: 285.
— Collapse of. (E. L. Godkin) Nation, **22**: 57.
— Decisions of the Supreme Court. (D. A. Wells) Nation, **19**: 282. — (E. L. Godkin) Nation, **20**: 53. — Nation, **24**: 143.
— Granger Theory applied to. (E. L. Godkin) Nation, **27**: 37.
Grangerism and retrospective Legislation. (F. Wharton) Internat. R. **3**: 50.
Granier, Paul. Ev. Sat. **9**: 731.
Granite. (M. G. Watkins) Once a Week, **15**: 539.
— New Hampshire, and its Contact Phenomena. (G. W. Hawes) Am. J. Sci. **121**: 21.
— Sonorous, and Sand-Hills. Penny M. **12**: 135.
— Use of. (G. Wilkinson) J. Frankl. Inst. **70**: 265.
Granitic Rocks. (T. S. Hunt) Am. J. Sci. **101**: 82, 182. **103**: 115.
Granny Latham's Revenge; a Story. Cornh. **14**: 313.
Granny's Vagabond Acquaintance. Tinsley, **15**: 31.
Grant, Mrs. Anne, of Laggan. (W. Wilson) Am. Hist. Rec. **3**: 539. — (A. Norton) No. Am. **60**: 126. — No. Brit **1**: 99. — Liv. Age, **1**: 412. **2**: 550. — Ecl. M. **2**: 161. — Mus. **37**: 144. — Blackw. **3**: 187.
— and her Contemporaries. Fraser, **29**: 411.
— Letters from the Mountains. (J. Foster) Ecl. R. **6**: 1064.
— Memoirs of. (J. T. Gordon) No. Brit. **1**: 99. — (J. Foster) Ecl. R. **9**: 165. — Chr. Obs. **44**: 472, 550, 614. — Tait, n. s. **11**: 174. — Ecl. R. **80**: 173.
Grant, Asahel, and the Nestorians. (J. L. Dimon) New Eng. **11**: 440.
Grant, Baldric, the Polytechnist. Chamb. J. **6**: 155.
Grant, Charles, Memoir of. Chr. Obs. **24**: 69, 133.
— Prize Poem of. Chr. Obs. **4**: 225.
— Restoration of Learning; a Poem. Ecl. R. **1**: 378.
Grant, Francis, with portrait. Ecl. M. **66**: 771. — Am. Arch. **4**: 157.
Grant, Sir Hope. Blackw. **117**: 638.
Grant, James. Great Metropolis. Ecl. R. **65**: 558. — Fraser, **14**: 710. — (H. W. Longfellow) No. Am. **44**: 461. — So. Lit. Mess. **3**: 309.
— Paris and its People. Fraser, **28**: 702.
— Random Recollections. Ecl. R. **68**: 292.
Grant, L. K., Ninfa. Chr. Rem. **14**: 123.
Grant, Maria M., Novels of. (G. B. Smith) St. James, **40**: 165.
Grant, Robert. Bench and the Bar. Ecl. R. **66**: 627.
Grant, Robert Edmond. Nature, **10**: 355.
Grant, Thomas, Bishop of Southark. (M. Russell) Irish Mo. **7**: 89.
— Obituary of. (J. Virtue) Month, **13**: 24.
Grant, Ulysses S. (E. A. Duyckinck) Putnam, **11**: 114. — U. S. Serv. M. **1**: 561. — with portrait, Ev. Sat. **11**: 511. — Fraser, **79**: 602. — Hours at Home, **3**: 176.
— Administration of. (G. W. Julian) No. Am. **126**: 262. — Internat. R. **4**: 145.
— and his Cabinet, 1869. (E. I. Sears) Nat. Q. **18**: 359.
— and his Campaigns. (R. B. Irwin) U. S. Serv. M. **5**: 252.
— and Horace Greeley. Nat. Q. **25**: 105, 369.
— and Horatio Seymour, as Presidential Candidates. Once a Week, **19**: 211.
— and strong Government. (J. S. Black) No. Am. **130**: 417.
— and Washington. (G. B. Loring) O. & N. **5**: 337.
— as a Soldier and Civilian. — (D. H. Maury) So. Hist. Soc. **5**: 227.
— Badeau's Life of. (F. W. Palfrey) Nation, **32**: 461. — Appleton, **26**: 138.
— Civil and Military Administration of. (C. P. Kingsbury) Nat. Q. **35**: 213.
— Coming Administration of, 1869. Chr. Exam **86**: 30.
— Grantism *vs.* Cæsarism. (E. I. Sears) Nat. Q. **29**: 256.
— Indian Policy of. (S. G. Arnold) Meth. Q. **37**: 409.
— Intellectual Character of. (A. Badeau) Atlan. **23**: 625. — Dub. Univ. **81**: 177.
— Military Life of. (C. C. Chesney) Ed. R. **129**: 230.
— on the Battle-Field. (E. Lawrence) Harper, **39**: 210.
— on Finances. Penn Mo. **6**: 63.
— Political Career of. (W. P. Garrison and E. L. Godkin) Nation, **24**: 127.
— Political Education of, abroad. (E. L. Godkin) Nation, **30**: 130.
— Presidential Message, 1876. (L. Rosecrans) Cath. World, **22**: 707.
— Presidential Policy of. (H. Adams) No. Am. **111**: 29. **119**: 33.
— Recollections of. (W. F. G. Shanks) Harper, **31**: 68. **35**: 210.
— Rehabilitation of. (W. P. Garrison) Nation, **28**: 258.
— Revival of the Grant Boom. (E. L. Godkin) Nation, **29**: 236.
— Round the World with. Quar. **150**: 205.
— Speech at Des Moines, 1875. (L. Rosecrans) Cath. World, **22**: 433.
— Third Term for. (G. S. Boutwell) No. Am. **133**: 370. — Penn Mo. **11**: 318.
— — and the Machine. (H. White) Nation, **30**: 320.
— — Specific Argument against. (E. L. Godkin) Nation, **30**: 342.
— — What it would mean. (E. L. Godkin) Nation, **30**: 412.
See United States Politics, Election of 1880.
Grant, William James. Art J. **16**: 233.
Grant, W. J., Visit to Farm of. (R. Keeler and A. R. Waud) Ev. Sat. **11**: 525.
Grant Family Memorials. (J. W. Dean) N. E. Reg. **21**: 173.
Grant-Duff, M. E. Miscellanies. (G. Walker) Nation, **28**: 270.
Grant-Highlanders, Mutiny of. Chamb. J. **27**: 22. Same art. Liv. Age, **53**: 317.
Granvelle, Cardinal. (W. C. Robinson) Month, **36**: 472.
Granville, Dr. Augusto Bozzi, Autobiography of. Chamb. J. **52**: 26. — Lond. Q. **44**: 141.
Granville, G. L. G., Earl, Political Portrait of. St. James, **24**: 166.

Granville, John Carteret, Earl. Colburn, **129**: 39.
Granville de Vigne; a Novel. (L. de la Ramé) Colburn, **121**: 15–471. **122**: 100–463. **123**: 82–443. **124**: 74–472. **125**: 49–437. **126**: 93–453. **127**: 79–446. **128**: 79–239.
Grape, The, and the Star; a Poem. Dub. Univ. **63**: 338.
— from a Thorn; a Novel. (J. Payn) Cornh. **43**: 1–741. **44**: 1–741.
Grape Blight. Chamb. J. **19**: 124.
Grape Culture. (J. M. Merrick, jr.) No. Am. **100**: 522. **109**: 155. — Land We Love, **2**: 355. — (H. W. Ravenal) Land We Love, **4**: 208.
Grape Cure at Durkheim. Liv. Age, **75**: 475.
Grape Disease. (C. V. Riley) Am. Natural. **6**: 532, 622.
— The Phylloxera. (C. V. Riley) Pop. Sci. Mo. **5**: 1.
Grape Vines, Pruning and Training of. West. J. **10**: 256. — (H. W. Ravenal) Land We Love, **3**: 167.
Grapes, Wine, and Vinegar. Fraser, **93**: 613.
See Vine; Wine.
Grapes and Thorns; a Tale. (M. A. Tincker) Cath. World, **17**: 362–792. **18**: 10–772. **19**: 68–671.
Graphs, Glyphs, and Typos. Chamb. J. **43**: 85.
Graphics. (G. L. Vose) Ecl. Engin. **12**: 529.
Graphic Arts. So. R. n. s. **21**: 74.
Graphic Method in Experimental Sciences. (G. S. Hall) Nation, **29**: 238.
— of studying Physical Laws. (E. C. Pickering) J. Frankl. Inst. **91**: 272.
Graphical Statics, General Method in. (H. T. Eddy) Ecl. Engin **18**: 22–385.
— Internal Stress in. (H. T. Eddy) Ecl. Engin. **19**: 1–234.
— New Constructions in. (H. D. Eddy) Ecl. Engin. **16**: 1–481. **17**: 1, 97.
— New Method of. (A. J. Dubois) Ecl. Engin. **12**: 161–385.
Graphotype, The. Art J. **21**: 313. — (J. Carpenter) Once a Week, **16**: 181. — (H. Lawson) Pop. Sci. R. **5**: 207. — F. Arts Q. **4**: 231.
Graptolites. (W. Carruthers) Intel. Obs. **11**: 283, 365.
— Nicholson on. Nature, **5**: 418.
Grasmere, Recollections of. (T. De Quincey) Tait, n. s. **6**: 93, 569, 804.
Grasp of a withered Hand; an Irish Story. Lond. Soc. **38**: 407.
Grass. (J. Buckman) Pop. Sci. R. **1**: 186.
— of the Field. Once a Week, **9**: 160.
Grasses. (W. W. Bailey) Am. Natural. **5**: 616.
— and Wild Flowers. Galaxy, **5**: 690.
— Instructions on. Hogg, **7**: 259, 362.
Grass-Cloth of China. Chamb. J. **16**: 214.
Grasshoppers, Songs of. (S. H. Scudder) Am. Natural. **2**: 113.
Grasshopper Plague. (J. Sheehan) Temp. Bar, **24**: 370.
Grass Valley, Cal., Gold-Mining District of. (B. Silliman) Am. J. Sci. **94**: 236.
Gratitude. Temp. Bar, **8**: 37.
Gratry, Auguste J. S., Abbé. O. & N. **5**: 377.
— Souvenirs. Month, **21**: 483.
Grattan, Henry. Blackw. **46**: 392, 529. — Dub. Univ. **7**: 229. **87**: 225.
— Eloquence at the Bar. West. Law J. **3**: 241.
— Life and Speeches of. Portfo.(Den.) **29**: 275.
— — and Times of. Dub. Univ. **14**: 429. — Mo. R. **149**: 575. — Dub. R. **15**: 200.
— Miscellaneous Works of. Mo. R. **99**: 359.
— Speeches of. (J. Foster) Ecl. R. **17**: 204. — Ecl. R. **36**: 1. — Ed. R. **38**: 44. — Mo. R. **98**: 113. — Mus. **1**: 204.
Grattan, Thomas Colley. Dub. Univ. **42**: 658. — with portrait, Colburn, **32**: 77.
— Heiress of Bruges. Westm. **14**: 146.
— High-Ways and By-Ways. U. S. Lit. Gaz. **2**: 121. — Lond. M. **18**: 448.
Gratton, J., Quaker Preacher. (S. T. Hall) Reliquary, **1**: 21.
Grattoni, Severino, with portrait. Ev. Sat. **11**: 437.
Gratuities to Servants in England. All the Year, **6**: 200, 349. — Once a Week, **27**: 401. *See* Tips.
Graunt on the Bills of Mortality, 1665. Cong. M. **8**: 541.
Grave at Spitzbergen; a Poem. (C. F. Alexander) Dub. Univ. **52**: 744.
Grave by the Lake. (J. G. Whittier) Atlan. **15**: 561.
Graves, Ancient, of California. (P. Schumacher) Overland, **13**: 297.
— and Epitaphs. House. Words, **6**: 105.
— and Goblins. New Eng. M. **8**: 438.
— Noted. (E. Wilberforce) Once a Week, **7**: 302.
— Two. Fraser, **34**: 13.
Grave-Digger's Daughter, The; a Tale. Dub. Univ. **14**: 438.
Grave Mounds of Derbyshire. (L. Jewitt) Intel. Obs. **12**: 180–459.
Grave Robbing and Dissection. (T. S. Sozinsky) Penn Mo. **10**: 206.
Gravelotte revisited. Fraser, **88**: 418.
Gravelotte, Battle of, Winn's. Colburn, **148**: 204.
Graves, A. P. Songs of Killarney. (G. B. Smith) Fraser, **88**: 201. — (A. M. Williams) Cath. World, **32**: 735. — Once a Week, **29**: 226.
Graves, Dean, Writings of. Dub. Univ. **17**: 634.
Graves, Dr., Murder of. House. Words, **12**: 524.
Graves, Richard, Life and Writings of. Fraser, **24**: 76. — Chr. Obs. **41**: 106.
Graves, Robert J., with portrait. Dub. Univ. **19**: 260.
Gravesande, C. N. S. van 'S. Etchings. (P. G. Hamerton) Portfo. **4**: 135.
Graveyard in the Hills; a Poem. Dub. Univ. **50**: 78.
— Meditation in a. Temp. Bar, **13**: 552.
Graveyards. (G. Waterston) So. Lit. Mess. **9**: 652. — Knick. **7**: 373. — Dem. R. **14**: 410.
— Chadwick's Report on Interment in Towns, 1844. Mo. R. **163**: 324.
— Gatherings from. Westm. **37**: 201.
— Pestiferous Effects of. Westm. **40**: 149.
— Unlawful Disinterment in. (R. Goode) Quar. **42**: 1.
— Walker on London. Mo. R. **151**: 161.
See also Churchyards.
Graveyard Idyl. (H. A. Beers) Lippinc. **26**: 484.
Graveyard Mansion. Pioneer, **4**: 269.
Gravitation. (H. F. Walling) Am. J. Sci. **90**: 254.
— Denison's New Theory of. Mo. R. **163**: 355.
— Force of. (M. Faraday) J. Frankl. Inst. **70**: 25, 193.
— from Surface of Earth to Center. (J. W. Nystrom) J. Frankl. Inst. **52**: 205.
— Law of. (J. T. Duffield) Evang. R. **17**: 236. — (G. P. Young) Canad. J. n. s. **14**: 589.
— Vince on. Ed. R. **13**: 101. — Ecl. R. **6**: 663.
Gravity, Acceleration of, at Tokio, Japan. (T. C. Mendenhall) Am. J. Sci. **120**: 124.
— and Magnetic Inclination. (P. E. Chase) Am. J. Sci. **90**: 166.
— and Magnetism, Numerical Relations of. (P. E. Chase) Am. J. Sci. **89**: 312.
— Determination of the Force of, in Japan. (T. C. Mendenhall) Am. J. Sci. **121**: 99.
— Energy of. Ecl. Engin. **9**: 159.
— Influence of, on Magnetic Declination. (P. E. Chase) Am. J. Sci. **90**: 83.
— Specific. (R. Hare) J. Frankl. Inst. **1**: 42, 99, 157.
Gray, Asa. Pop. Sci. Mo. **1**: 491. — with portrait, Ecl. M. **94**: 250.
— and Scientific and Religious Beliefs. Presb. R. **1**: 586.
— Botany. So. Q. **15**: 444.
Gray, David. Cornh. **9**: 164.

Gray, David, Poems of. Dub. Univ. 88: 303. — Ed. R. 115: 567. — Chamb. J. 38: 75. — Liv. Age, 75: 88. — Ecl. R. 116: 19.
Gray, Elisha. (G. B. Prescott) Pop. Sci. Mo. 14: 523.
Gray, Francis C. Phi Beta Kappa Address, 1816. No. Am. 3: 289.
— Phi Beta Kappa Poem. No. Am. 52: 262.
Gray, Frederick T. Addresses. (E. Peabody) Chr. Exam. 54: 90.
— Sermon on Death of. (E. Peabody) Mo. Rel. M. 13: 219.
Gray, Mrs. James. Dub. Univ. 25: 327. Same art. Liv. Age, 5: 198. — with portrait, Dub. Univ. 29: 360. Same art. Ecl. M. 11: 47.
— Remains of. Dub. Univ. 25: 318, 397, 547. 26: 211, 393, 683. 27: 201.
Gray, John C. Phi Beta Kappa Oration. No. Am. 13: 478.
Gray, John Edward. Nature, 11: 368.
Gray, Bishop Robert, Life of. (C. K. Paul) Theo. R. 13: 70. — Westm. 106: 80. — Chr. Obs. 76: 7.
Gray, Stephen, a First Electrician. (B. W. Richardson) Gent. M. n. s. 27: 460.
Gray, Thomas. (E. Jesse) Bentley, 23: 133. — (T. S. Perry) Atlan. 46: 810. — Am. Whig R. 14: 30. — Blackw. 75: 242.
— and Literature of 18th Century. Temp. Bar, 3: 402.
— and his School. (Sir J. Stephen) Cornh. 40: 70. Same art. Liv. Age, 142: 259.
— and Wordsworth. Quar. 141: 104.
— Correspondence with W. Mason. Prosp. R. 10: 369. — Chr. Rem. 27: 413.
— Elegy in a Country Churchyard. (J. D. Howard) No. Am. 96: 312. — Art J. 6: 72.
— — Blackwood Strictures on. So. Lit. Mess. 20: 345.
— — Scene of. (E. Jesse) Tait, n. s. 14: 709.
— — Stoke Poges and. St. James, 21: 214.
— Footprints of. (R. de Peverll) Once a Week, 14: 630.
— Grave of. Chamb. J. 3: 410.
— Letter to Count Algarotti. Blackw. 4: 38.
— Letters of. All the Year, 35: 228.
— Life and Works of. Quar. 11: 304. 94: 1. Same art. Ecl. M. 31: 433. Same art. Liv. Age, 40: 579. — Fraser, 25: 541.
— Poems of; Mitford's Edition. Brit. & For. R. 6: 397. — Temp. Bar, 40: 176.
— Retrospective Criticism. (C. Redding) Colburn, 135: 432.
— Side-Light on his "Bard." (G. Allen) Gent. M. n. s. 23: 721.
— Tomb of. (Mrs. S. C. Hall) Nat. M. 7: 296.
— Works of. (Sir E. B. Lytton) Westm. 27: 1*.
Gray, Rev. Thomas. (F. Parkman) Chr. Exam. 43: 248.
— Sermons of. Chr. Disc. 4: 391
Gray, Thomas, Author of Railway System. (W. Howitt) Peop. J. 2: 58.
Gray, William, Biography of. Hunt, 2: 409.
Gray, William, Memoir of. Chr. Obs. 46: 129, 193.
Gray and Coytmore Family Genealogy. (W. S. Appleton) N. E. Reg. 34: 253.
Gray's Sketches from the Antique. Dub. Univ. 23: 663.
Gray, Me., Materials for History of. N. E. Reg. 10: 164.
Gray Champion. New Eng. M. 8: 20.
Gray Collection of Engravings at Harvard College. (R. Sturgis) Nation, 10: 30.
Gray Eyes. (E. W. Thompson) Lippinc. 11: 86.
Gray Jockey. (F. H. Ludlow) Harper, 32: 504.
Gray's Inn Road, Cup of Tea in. (J. G. Harwood) St. James, 40: 556.
Gray's Peak, Colorado, Ascent of. (E. T. Mallet, jr.) Scrib. 4: 576. — (R.W. Raymond) Overland, 5: 512.
Gray Woman; a Story. All the Year, 4: 300, 321, 347. Same art. Liv. Age, 68: 486, 561.
Grayling, The. (A. H. Baldwin) Once a Week, 16: 372.
Grayling, The, Haunts of. (M. Thompson) Lippinc. 28: 268.
— Michigan. (T. Norris) Scrib. 19: 17.
Grayrue Hall. (E. Spencer) So. M. 12: 1, 129.
Grayrigg Grange. House. Words, 15: 579.
Grayson, A. J., Life of. (Bret Harte) Overland, 4: 168.
Grayson Griffith; a Tale. So. Lit. Mess. 1: 605.
Great, The, en Déshabillé. Temp. Bar, 63: 353.
Great Air-Engine. (R. H. Davis) Atlan. 12: 701.
Great Ascidian. (W. W. Lord) So. M. 12: 556.
Great Ball and a great Bear. (B. White) Belgra. 4: 276.
Great Britain, Agricultural Statistics of. (J. Caird) J. Statis. Soc. 31: 127, 222. 32: 61.
— Agriculture of; Exhaustion of Soil. Quar. 134: 152.
— — Rural Economy. Ed. R. 103: 82.— Blackw. 77: 65. *See* Agriculture.
— Antiquities of, Primeval. (E. A. Freeman) No. Brit. 17: 459. *See* Archæology; Britain; England, Antiquities.
— Army of. (Sir J. Adye) 19th Cent. 6: 344. — Blackw. 35: 405. 60: 129. 101: 133–444. 109: 389. — Dub. Univ. 47: 489. — Fortn. 6: 435. — Tait, n. s. 24: 651. — Irish Q. 5: 590.
— — Administration of. Cornh. 19: 309. — Quar. 129: 244, 509. — St. Paul's, 3: 552. — Mo. R. 146: 266.
— — — and the Control Department. Macmil. 23: 161.
— — — and Government Policy. Quar. 131: 522.
— — and the Crown. Quar. 146: 232.
— — and its Officers. No. Brit. 12: 499.
— — and the Maneuvers of 1872. Temp. Bar, 37: 213.
— — and the People. Fraser, 38: 211, 635. 39: 298. — (J. Holms) 19th Cent. 3: 97, 355.
— — and War Office. (G. F. Crawford) Belgra. 11: 466.
— — as it is and as it should be. St. Paul's, 1: 600. — Tait, n. s. 2: 355.
— — Autumn Maneuvers. (G. R. Gleig) Fraser, 86: 533.
— — Barrack Accommodation. Dub. Univ. 51: 210.
— — The British Soldier. Colburn, 121: 127.
— — British Troops in the Service of France. Colburn, 103: 370.
— — Campaigns of 1793–94. Dub. Univ. 43: 115.
— — Career of the 52d Regiment. Chr. Rem. 54: 239.
— — Control in. (D. Lysons) Blackw. 116: 466.
— — Crime in. (P. Beaton) Good Words, 11: 595.
— — Clothing Depot. (S. L. Blanchard) Belgra. 20: 479. — Temp. Bar, 18: 251.
— — Cost of. (W. H. Sykes) J. Statis. Soc. 27: 1. — Cornh. 7: 310.
— — Cruel Punishments in. Cornh. 15: 499.
— — Defects in. Temp. Bar, 13: 292.
— — The Dragoons and their Horses. Temp. Bar, 13: 391. Same art. Ecl. M. 64: 563.
— — Education in. Fraser, 33: 719. — Good Words, 4: 391.
— — England and her Soldiers. Chamb. J. 31: 393.
— — Eng. and French Armaments. Dub. Univ. 56: 387.
— — English Troops in the East. Fraser, 73: 558. Same art. Ecl. M. 67: 19.
— — Enlisting in. (J. Greenwood) Hours at Home, 7: 480. — All the Year, 15: 306. — Cornh. 10: 207.
— — — Act on. Blackw. 108: 1.
— — — Limitation of. Blackw. 106: 279.
— — Esprit de Corps of. Chamb. J. 45: 801.
— — Estimates for. Dub. Univ. 59: 505. Same art. Ecl. M. 56: 267.
— — First Rank in. Chamb. J. 26: 257.
— — Flogging in. (A. Forbes) 19th Cent. 6: 604. — All the Year, 43: 272.
— — French Officer in. All the Year, 16: 6.
— — Froberg's Regiment. Colburn, 23: 525.
— — German View of. Fortn. 32: 611.
— — Grenadier Guards. Ed. R. 140: 462.

Great Britain, Army of, Health of. Ed. R. **108**: 136.— Nat. R. **17**: 323.—Westm. **71**: 52.
— — How to make it popular. St. Paul's, **7**: 366.
— — Improved Condition of. Hogg, **8**: 73.
— — in 1864, Strength of. No. Brit. **39**: 259.
— — in 1869. Ed. R. **133**: 207.
— — in 1876. (A. C. Sellar) Nation, **22**: 76.
— — in India. All the Year, **41**: 59, 129.
— — Interior Economy of a Regiment. (C. J. Stone) Belgra. **16**: 465.
— — Life in. Cornh. **7**: 441.—Dub. Univ. **34**: 26.
— — — in Royal Military Academy. Lond. Soc. **35**: 561.
— — — of the Rank and File. Chamb. J. **46**: 328.
— — Long and short Service. (Sir G. Wolseley) 19th Cent. **9**: 558.—(H. O. A. Foster) 19th Cent. **9**: 905.
— — "Militär-Wochenblatt" on. Macmil. **44**: 294.
— — Military Impotence of. (A. Kirchhammer) 19th Cent. **9**: 577.
— — Militia of. Irish Q. **5**: 349.
— — — Campaign with. Lond. Soc. **18**: 33.
— — Mobilization of. All the Year, **28**: 494. **40**: 295. —Blackw. **119**: 131. **120**: 509.—Colburn, **158**: 558.—Fraser, **93**: 261.
— — Mode of increasing the Regular. Ed. R. **9**: 171.
— — Moral Aspects of. Lond. Q. **23**: 356.
— — Mortality in. (W. A. Guy) Fraser, **57**: 487.
— — National Training to Arms. (Sir H. Havelock) Fortn. **25**: 430.
— — New Royal Warrants. Fraser, **85**: 261.
— — Organization of. Blackw. **105**: 152.—Westm. **95**: 485. **96**: 137.—Macmil. **22**: 401.
— — — Autumn Maneuvers and. Macmil. **25**: 71.
— — Our Defenses. (J. E. Cairnes) Fortn. **15**: 167.
— — Our future. Fraser, **92**: 1.
— — Our National Insurance. Macmil. **20**: 170.
— — past and present. Dub. Univ. **71**: 629.
— — Popular Names and singular Mottoes of British Regiments. Lond. Soc. **34**: 555.
— — Private Soldier as he is. St. Paul's, **2**: 92.
— — Promotion in. Colburn, **101**: 489.
— — — and Retirement. (A. D. Hayter) Fortn. **27**: 410. —Blackw. **120**: 601.
— — — by Purchase in. Colburn, **90**: 279. **104**: 83. —Dub. Univ. **50**: 489.—No. Brit. **23**: 521.— Quar. **124**: 525.—Temp. Bar, **11**: 197.
— — Raw Recruits in. Once a Week, **8**: 244.
— — Recruiting for. (Sir W. Crofton) Contemp. **27**: 460. —(F. H. Noott) Macmil. **11**: 81.—Once a Week, **16**: 696.
— — — Are good Recruits worth paying for? (W. T. M. Torrens) Gent. M. n. s. **15**: 450.
— — — Difficulty of. (C. H. Malan) Fortn. **5**: 406.— All the Year, **14**: 464.
— — — in 1875. Ed. R. **143**: 36.
— — Reform of. Ed. R. **153**: 184.—Blackw. **128**: 553. —(E. L. Godkin) Nation, **4**: 415.—(Sir C. Trevelyan) St. Paul's, **4**: 176.—Blackw. **119**: 103.— Cornh. **18**: 671. **19**: 309.—Ed. R. **101**: 537.— Macmil. **35**: 496.—Nat. R. **5**: 257.—New Q. **7**: 89.—St. Paul's, **4**: 95.—Temp. Bar, **1**: 103.
— — — and Parliament. St. Paul's, **2**: 451.
— — — Government Scheme of. Fraser, **83**: 469.
— — — Limited Enlistment. No. Brit. **9**: 509.
— — — Needed. Temp. Bar, **12**: 484.
— — — Political Consequences of. Fraser, **89**: 795.
— — Reformers of, Hints to. St. Paul's, **7**: 488.
— — Refutation of Aspersions on. Blackw. **35**: 405.
— — Regimental Distinctions, Traditions, and Anecdotes. (W. W. Knollys) Gent. M. n. s. **19**: 225.
— — Regimental System in. Fraser, **51**: 485.
— — Regulation of. (J. L. Seton) Colburn, **149**: 75-314.
Great Britain, Army of, Reorganization of. (G. R. Gleig) Fraser, **85**: 597.—(M. L. Meason) Dub. R. **89**: 86. —(C. E. Trevelyan) Good Words, **12**: 72.—(R. Williams) Internat. R. **6**: 518.—Fraser, **77**: 545.
— — Romance of the Ranks. (M. E. C. Walcott) Once a Week, **3**: 576.
— — Short Service and its Supporters. Blackw. **129**: 591.
— — Social Aspects of. (J. H. Fyfe) Good Words, **14**: 490.
— — Social, Moral, and Intellectual Condition of. Westm. **45**: 1.
— — Volunteer Establishment. Colburn, **119**: 379.— Once a Week, **3**: 81.
— — — and National Defense. Quar. **112**: 110.
— — — Crisis in. Broadw. **1**: 78.
— — Twenty-one Years of. (R. Lloyd-Lindsay) 19th Cent. **10**: 206.
— — Why is it unpopular? St. Paul's, **7**: 240.
See also below, Great Britain, Military System of.
— Art in. *See* Art in Great Britain.
— as a naval Power. (R. S. Robinson) 19th Cent. **7**: 389.
— Ayton's and Daniell's Voyage round. (J. Foster) Ecl. R. **27**: 330, 419.
— Cabinets and Statesmen of. No. Brit. **24**: 183.
— — Chronological Table of. Westm. **37**: 171.
— Christianity in, Early. Lond Q. **29**: 1.
— Churches in, Early. (J. D. Baldwin) Bib. Sac. **32**: 650. *See* Britain.
— Civil Service. (R. Wynford) Lippinc. **13**: 616.— Hunt, **60**: 210.—Lond. Q. **27**: 328. **36**: 366.
— — Statistics of. (W. Farr) J. Statis. Soc. **11**: 103.
See Civil Service.
— Climate of. (A. Buchan) Good Words, **6**: 458.— (Lord de Mauley) Gent. M. n. s. **18**: 452.—Intel. Obs. **11**: 113.
— Colonial Distinctions. Fraser, **90**: 316.
— Colonial Empire of. De Bow, **6**: 310.
— Colonial Governor, What is a? (E. D. J. Wilson) 19th Cent. **4**: 1053.
— Colonial Legislation. Ecl. R. **65**: 188, 356.—Gent. M. n. s. **24**: 59.
— Colonial Neglect and foreign Propitiation. Blackw. **46**: 752. Same art. Mus. **38**: 34.
— Colonial Office and South Africa. Ecl. R **86**: 728.
— Colonial Policy of. (P. S. Hamilton) St. James, **32**: 701.—Ed. R. **131**: 98.—(A. Mills) Contemp. **11**: 216.—Portfo.(Den.) **18**: 66.—St. James, **30**: 501.
— — Earl Grey on. Dub. Univ. **41**: 758.
— — in the Government of Colored Races. No. Brit. **44**: 388.
— Colonial Politics, 1848. (L. Sabine) No. Am. **67**: 1.
— Colonial Reform Party. Colburn, **88**: 211.
— Colonial Reforms, 1853. Ecl. R. **98**: 458.
— Colonial System of. Knick. **53**: 113.
— Colonial Trade. (J. H. Lanman) Hunt, **10**: 38.— Am. Whig R. **10**: 80.
— Colonial Undertaking. Blackw. **20**: 304.
— Colonies of. (J. A. Froude) Fraser, **81**: 1. **82**: 269. Same art. Liv. Age, **104**: 413.—Blackw. **23**: 891. **25**: 633. **27**: 223, 455. **29**: 186, 454. **30**: 774. **34**: 231, 611.—Brit. Q. **10**: 463.—Dub. Univ. **13**: 389. **64**: 483. **84**: 657.—(J. A. Froude) Princ. n. s. **1**: 885.—(A. Hamilton) J. Statis. Soc. **35**: 107.—(H. C. Richards) St. James, **44**: 276.—(E. D. J. Wilson) Dark Blue, **1**: 770.—Bentley, **32**: 487, 633.—Fraser, **6**: 437. **65**: 551. **68**: 454. **93**: 269.—(G. Baden-Powell) Fraser, **97**: 1.—No. Brit. **19**: 345. **36**: 535.—Quar. **114**: 125.—St. James, **40**: 693. **41**: 87.—Westm. **105**: 295.
— — Administration of. Ed. R. **98**: 62.
— — — Lord Grey's. Fraser, **47**: 485.
— — Aid from, in War Time. Westm. **113**: 1.

Great Britain, Colonies of, and Colonists. (W. H. G. Kingston) Colburn, **85**: 354.
— — and Emigration. Hogg, **2**: 51.
— — Church Government in. (W. H. Fremantle) Contemp. **1**: 311. **5**: 489. — (H. Cotterill) Contemp. **2**: 166. — (R. Gray) Contemp. **3**: 283.
— — Colonist's Thoughts about. Dub. Univ. **86**: 623.
— — Commercial Progress of. (E. T. Blakely) J. Statis. Soc. **28**: 34.
— — — 1827–46. (J. T. Danson) J. Statis. Soc. **11**: 349.
— — Confederation of. St. James, **41**: 191.
— — Constitutions for. Colburn, **86**: 335. **88**: 376.
— — — and Defenses of. No. Brit. **33**: 83.
— — Crisis in, 1831. Fraser, **3**: 125.
— — Custom-Houses in. (E. Langton) Fraser, **98**: 482.
— — Debate on. St. James, **30**: 389.
— — Dilke's Travels in. Ed. R. **129**: 455.
— — Dismemberment, or a united Empire? St. James, **30**: 279.
— — Discontent in. Blackw. **26**: 332.
— — Ecclesiastical State of. Quar. **75**: 201.
— — Emigrant Colonies. Tait, n. s. **1**: 401.
— — Emigration to. Victoria, **8**: 268. — Blackw. **52**: 206. — Mus. **37**: 201. — Fraser, **28**: 426.
— — Englishmen in their Dealing with Subject Races. Ev. Sat. **9**: 674.
— — Expenditure on. Westm. **24**: 1.
— — Expense of. Tait, n. s. **5**: 473.
— — Fate of. Fraser, **2**: 226.
— — Future of. Colburn, **148**: 246.
— — Greater and Lesser Britain. (Sir J. Vogel) 19th Cent. **1**: 809.
— — Home. Quar. **41**: 522.
— — How shall we retain? (Earl Grey) 19th Cent. **5**: 935.
— — How not to retain. (Lord Norton) 19th Cent. **6**: 170.
— — in the West. Fraser, **4**: 436.
— — in West Indies. Lond. Q. **17**: 540.
— — Letters on. (J. McQueen) Blackw. **23**: 891. **25**: 633. **27**: 223.
— — Martin's History of. Dub. Univ. **3**: 647. — Mo. R. **133**: 402. **135**: 250. **136**: 63. **137**: 166. **138**: 593.
— — Military Defense of. Ed. R. **115**: 104.
— — Misgovernment of. Blackw. **44**: 624.
— — Penal. *See* Penal Colonies.
— — Question of, 1870. (H. Merivale) Fortn. **13**: 152.
— — — Voice from the Colonies on. Fraser, **79**: 202.
— — the "Pariahs of the Empire." St. James, **34**: 305.
— — Parliaments in. Cornh. **18**: 484.
— — Political Relation to England. (J. Chapman) Westm. **58**: 398. — Westm. **93**: 1.
— — Press of. Colburn, **11**: 442.
— — Protection of. Ed. R. **84**: 236. Same art. Liv. Age, **10**: 585.
— — Reform in. Fraser, **41**: 366. — Ecl. R. **83**: 576. — Tait, **2**: 714.
— — Representative Government in. (A. Mills) 19th Cent. **8**: 237.
— — Roebuck on. Fraser, **39**: 624.
— — Goldwin Smith on. Dub. Univ. **59**: 259.
— — Shall we retain? Ed. R. **93**: 475.
— — Value of. Ed. R. **42**: 271. — Selec. Ed. R. **6**: 137. — (R. Lowe) Fortn. **28**: 618.
— Commerce of ancient. (J. Galt) Fraser, **4**: 403.
— — Exports, 1840–53. (R. Valpy) J Statis. Soc. **18**: 160.
— — Growing Preponderance of Imports over Exports. (S. Bourne) J. Statis Soc. **40**: 19, 645.
— — History of. Quar. **134**: 204.
— — in 1810. Quar. **3**: 50.
— — in 1820. Niles's Reg. **19**: 353.
— — in 1835. Colburn, **44**: 137.
— — in 1843. Hunt, **8**: 131.
Great Britain, Commerce of; New Markets for British Products. (G. Baden-Powell) 19th Cent. **10**: 43.
— — Progress of, 1855–75. (S. Bourne) J. Statis. Soc. **38**: 215.
— — — 1856–77. (W. Newmarch) J. Statis. Soc. **41**: 187.
— Commercial Decline of. Tinsley, **24**: 256.
— Commercial Power of. Westm. **4**: 337. — Mo. R. **107**: 239. — Quar. **30**: 368.
— Commercial Relations with France. Ed. R. **111**: 277.
— — with Poland. Brit. & For. R. **6**: 505.
— — with the United States. (H. Colman) Hunt, **6**: 458. — (G. S. Boutwell) Hunt, **7**: 72.
— Commercial Supremacy of. (A. J. Mundella) J. Statis. Soc. **41**: 87.
— Constitution of. (W. Bagehot) Fortn. **1**: 1, 313. **2**: 103, 595. **3**: 657. **4**: 257. **6**: 513, 807. **7**: 708. — (H. Brougham) Ed. R. **61**: 1. — Chr. Rem. **4**: 182.
— — and the Crown. Ed. R. **148**: 262. — Quar. **145**: 277. Same art. Liv. Age, **137**: 515.
— — Appeal for the old. Blackw. **33**: 358.
— — Creasy on. Am. Ch. Mo. **1**: 55. — Dub. Univ. **50**: 19. — New Q. **3**: 68.
— — Dangers of. Ed. R. **27**: 245. — Selec. Ed. R. **5**: 60.
— — Defense of. Pamph. **10**: 333.
— — D'Israeli's Vindication of. Westm. **31**: 533.
— — Euthanasy of. Tait, **4**: 40.
— — Fall of. Blackw. **32**: 55. — (T. P. Thompson) Westm. **17**: 514.
— — Freeman's Growth of. (A. V. Dicey) Nation, **15**: 169, 188.
— — History of. Ed. R. **150**: 1.
— — — Brodie's. (F. Jeffrey) Ed. R. **40**: 92.
— — — Erskine's. New Q. **10**: 288.
— — — Hallam's. (R. Southey) Quar. **37**: 194. — (T. B. Macaulay) Ed. R. **48**: 96. — Am. Q. **3**: 26. — Mo. R. **114**: 331. — Ecl. R. **49**: 92.
— — — May's. (C. C. Smith) No. Am. **97**: 216. — Dub. Univ. **58**: 542. — Ed. R. **115**: 211. — Liv. Age, **69**: 90.
— — — Stubbs's. (H. Adams) No. Am. **119**: 233. **123**: 161. — (A. V. Dicey) Nation, **20**: 152. **23**: 123. **28**: 233.
— — Letters on. Pamph. **12**: 143, 405.
— — Original Elements of. Lond. Q. **48**: 265.
— — Our Venetian. (F. Harrison) Fortn. **7**: 261.
— — Prospects of the new. Blackw. **32**: 343.
— — Reform in, 1854. (J. Chapman) Westm. **61**: 1.
— — — Proposed. Fraser, **88**: 600.
— — Earl Russell on. Ecl. R. **121**: 425.
— — since George III. Brit. Q. **38**: 29. **42**: 1. Same art. Ecl. M. **60**: 137.
— — Smith on. (Earl of Desart) Dark Blue, **3**: 256.
— — Structure and Theory of. Chr. Rem. **55**: 397.
— Convict System of. *See* Convicts.
— Court of, and St. James Palace. Dub. Univ. **79**: 581.
— Court of Queen Victoria. Contemp. **26**: 1.
— Dangers of, External. Blackw. **69**: 198.
— — Internal. Ed. Mo. R. **5**: 1. — Blackw. **69**: 257.
— Defense of. (J. A. St. John) Bentley, **23**: 89. — (G. Baden-Powell) Fraser, **98**: 1.
— — against herself. (E. Goadby) Macmil. **23**: 408.
— — Austrian View of. (Baron von Scholl) Macmil. **27**: 77.
— — Best Means of. Hogg, **9**: 261.
— — Harcourt on. (Major Knollys) Dark Blue, **3**: 43.
— — MSS. on. (S. Ayscough) Arch. **13**: 169.
— — Means of military. Macmil. **15**: 394.
— — Recollections of an old Volunteer. Colburn, **82**: 219.
— Defenses of. Macmil. **22**: 396. — No. Brit. **39**: 250.
— — Coast. No. Brit. **32**: 26.
— — Home. Macmil. **15**: 277.

Great Britain, Defenses of, Military. Westm. **74**: 465.
— — National. Ed. R. **98**: 405. — Fraser, **60**: 643. — Lond. Q. **15**: 553. — Once a Week, **24**: 121. — Quar. **130**: 1.
— — or a Standing Army. (J. E. Cairnes) Fortn. **15**: 167.
— — Proposed. Fraser, **62**: 218.
— — Second Line of. Once a Week, **3**: 544, 600.
— — the Silver Streak. (Adm. Lord Dunsany) 19th Cent. **9**: 737. Same art. Liv. Age, **149**: 753.
— Defenseless State of, Head's. Quar. **88**: 269. — Blackw. **68**: 736. Same art. Liv. Age, **28**: 145. — Dub. Univ. **37**: 116.
— Defensible Strength of. Fraser, **32**: 599, 697. Same art. Liv. Age, **8**: 139.
— Defensive Armament of. Ed. R. **96**: 194.
— Dependence of, on United States. Dem. R. **19**: 3.
— Diplomatic and Consular Services of. Macmil. **5**: 218. — Ed. R. **139**: 68. — Colburn, **37**: 418. — Cornh. **22**: 546. — Quar. **105**: 74.
— Early Mythology and Poetry of. Hogg, **12**: 273.
— Effacement of. (F. Harrison) Fortn. **15**: 145.
— Empire of. (W. Arthur) Hogg, **1**: 260. — Mo. R. **109**: 402. **131**: 98. — Quar. **43**: 262. — Blackw. **35**: 405.
— — and Humanity. (F. Harrison) Fortn. **33**: 288.
— — Cause of Overthrow at Work. Blackw. **59**: 692.
— — Future of. Westm. **94**: 47. Same art. Liv. Age, **106**: 387.
— — Imperial Confederation. (R. Fisher) Canad. Mo. **15**: 543. — (E. Jenkins) Contemp. **16**: 165. **17**: 60. — (J. Whitman) Canad. Mo. **15**: 319. — Fraser, **84**: 109, 249. — Westm. **111**: 299. **112**: 46, 313. — (W. J. Smith) Fraser, **84**: 384.
— — Imperial Policy of. (J. Lubbock) 19th Cent. **1**: 37. — Westm. **111**: 421.
— — Imperial Question. Fraser, **84**: 403.
— — in the East, Bjornstjerna on. Mo. R **153**: 324.
— — in India. (E. Peabody) Chr. Exam. **48**: 1.
— — Integration of. (E. Burritt) Canad. Mo. **12**: 124.
— — Integrity of. (Lord Blachford) 19th Cent. **2**: 355.
— — Mr. Lowe and Lord Blachford on. (J. Vogel) 19th Cent. **3**: 617.
— — McCulloch's. (S. Colwell) Princ. **13**: 416.
— — Moral and Political State of. Fraser, **3**: 223.
— — or no Empire? Fraser, **86**: 667.
— — Pebrer's Resources of. Ecl. R. **58**: 22.
— — Policy of Aggrandizement. (Goldwin Smith) Fortn. **28**: 303.
— — Prospects of. Dub. Univ. **13**: 1.
— — Rise of the modern. Quar. **146**: 331.
— Ethnology of. (T. H. Huxley) Contemp. **14**: 511.
— Financial Condition of, in 1816. (H. Adams) No. Am. **104**: 354.
— — in 1834. (R. M. Martin) Colburn, **39**: 288, 446. **40**: 61-334.
— — in 1878, Accumulation of Capital. (R. Giffen and W. Newmarch) Bank. M. (L) **38**: 187, 574. Same art. Statis. Soc. J. **41**: 1.
— — in 1880. Bank. M. (N. Y.) **34**: 538.
— Financial Depression in, 1876. (E. L. Godkin) Nation, **22**: 344.
— — and the Ten Per Cent, 1866. Fraser, **74**: 229. Same art Ecl. M. **67**: 465.
— Finances of. (Lord Hobart) Macmil. **11**: 253. — Blackw. **31**: 598. — Ed. R. **25**: 541. — Victoria, **3**: 385.
— — and of France. (G. Balfour) J. Statis. Soc. **29**: 323.
— — and Sinking Fund. Brit. & For. R. **12**: 95. — Pamph. **2**: 203.
— — Britannia's Head for Figures. All the Year, **11**: 557.
— — Budget of 1842. Ed. R. **75**: 187.
— — — of 1848. Blackw. **63**: 383.
— — — of 1859. (L. Levi) Fraser, **61**: 434.
Great Britain, Finances of; Budget of 1867, and the National Debt. (Lord Hobart). Fortn. **7**: 615.
— — Coinage of. (H. Goodwin) Contemp. **4**: 16.
— — Committee on, 1829. Quar. **41**: 492.
— — Currency. Irish Q. **6**: 148.
— — — Laws of. (J. W. Gilbart) J. Statis. Soc. **17**: 289.
— — Expenditures. Broadw. **4**: 209.
— — Funding System. Ed. R. **39**: 1.
— — Gladstone's Financial Statements, 1853-63. Ho. & For. R. **4**: 1.
— — History of, Doubleday's. No. Brit. **7**: 337.
— — in 1832. Blackw. **31**: 598.
— — in 1842-61. Chr. Rem. **45**: 328.
— — in 1854. (L. Faucher) Bank. M. (L.) **15**: 15.
— — Is she spending her Capital? (G. Walker) Bank. M. (N. Y.) **33**: 107.
— — Loans by Italian Merchants to, 13th and 14th Centuries. (E. A. Bond) Arch. **28**: 207.
— — — raised by Pitt, 1793-1801. (W. Newmarch) J. Statis. Soc. **18**: 104, 242.
— — Money Market in England. (G. Bradford) No. Am. **119**: 331.
— — of a reformed Parliament, 1832. Blackw. **29**: 968.
— — past and present. (J. E. T. Rogers) Contemp **34**: 281.
— — Perils of the System. Temp. Bar. **50**: 497.
— — Pitt and his Successors. Blackw. **34**: 179.
— — Progress of Expenditures, 1800-60. (L. Levi) J. Statis. Soc. **24**: 55.
— — Prospects in 1849. Ed. R. **89**: 518.
— — Public Accounts. (F. W. Rowsell) Contemp. **26**: 447.
— — Questions for reformed Parliament, 1868. (R. Giffen) Fortn. **8**: 711.
— — Reform in, 1848. Ecl. R. **89**: 273. — No. Brit. **9**: 269.
— — — in 1859. Ecl. R. **111**: 196.
— — Revenue of. Am. Q. Reg. **6**: 258.
— — Right Use of Surplus. (W. R. Greg) Contemp. **26**: 545.
— — Thirty Years' Expenses. Chamb. J. **41**: 134.
— — under the Grey Ministry. Blackw. **31**: 598.
— — Ways and Means of. Once a Week, **20**: 477, 497.
— — Wellington on. Blackw. **32**: 375.
— — Whig and Tory. Blackw. **46**: 494.
— Foreign Policy of. (W. R. Greg) 19th Cent. **4**: 393. — (Sir F. B. Head) Quar. **67**: 254. — Brit. & For. R. **11**: 631. — For. Q. **8**: 33, 391. — Ed. R. **13**: 186. **68**: 262. — Mus. **35**: 297. **40**: 161. — Liv. Age, **48**: 116, 444, 508. — Nat. R. **17**: 465. — No. Brit. **19**: 45. — Westm. **20**: 323. **61**: 190.
— — and Foreign Commerce. Blackw. **39**: 49, 145.
— — and Home Prospects, 1841. Fraser, **23**: 235.
— — Austrian Views of. Colburn, **94**: 253.
— — Lord Beaumont on. Quar. **85**: 225.
— — Cost of. Fraser, **100**: 564.
— — in the East and West. Mus. **41**: 311.
— — in Europe. Fraser, **63**: 135.
— — in 1806-7. Ed. R. **21**: 219.
— — in 1817. Ed. R. **28**: 106.
— — in 1836. Mo. R. **141**: 129.
— — in 1840. Ed. R. **71**: 545.
— — in 1857. Nat. R. **4**: 441.
— — in 1859. Liv. Age, **61**: 620.
— — in 1860-61. Dub. R. **49**: 416.
— — in 1864. Brit. Q. **40**: 382. — No. Brit. **40**: 507. — Quar. **115**: 481.
— — in 1875, in the Mediterranean. (J. C. Paget) St. James, **37**: 375.
— — in 1878. Canad. Mo. **14**: 740.
— — Palmerston and. No. Brit. **34**: 255.
— — Peace Agitators. Quar. **85**: 452.

Great Britain, Foreign Policy of; Politico-Commercial Policy, Lord Bateman on. Pract. M. 7: 278.
— — Principle and no-Principle in. Nat. R. 13: 241.
— — with France and Spain. Colburn, 42: 482.
— Foreign Relations of. Dub. Univ. 16: 591. 17: 501. — Ed. R. 124: 275. — Fraser, 100: 851.
— — and Irish Policy. (E. S. Beesly) Fortn. 35: 229.
— — Christianity in. (J. L. Davies) Contemp. 38: 221.
— — Continental Connections. For. Q. 19: 135.
— — in 1839. (H. Brougham) Ed. R. 68: 495.
— — in 1864. No. Brit. 39: 538. Same art. Ecl. M. 61: 234.
— — in 1867. (J. Morley) Fortn. 7: 621.
— — in 1877. (E. de Laveleye) Fortn. 28: 25.
— — — Plain View of. (S. Laing) Fortn. 29: 335.
— — Place among the Nations. Macmil. 23: 358. — St. Paul's, 1: 275. — Westm. 71: 535.
— — — Future. (W. R. Greg) Fraser, 71: 719.
— — Spanish and Venetian Diplomacy of, 1603–25. (S. R. Gairdner) Fortn. 3: 344.
— — War Panic of, 1870. St. James, 27: 270.
— — with the Continent. For. Q. 19: 135. — Liv. Age, 42: 376. — Quar. 53: 229.
— — — in 1840. Blackw. 49: 97.
— — — in 1841. Blackw. 50: 449. — Mus. 43: 474.
— — — in 1846. Fraser, 29: 112.
— — — in 1857. Westm. 68: 415.
— — — in 1870. Ed. R. 132: 554. Same art. Liv. Age, 107: 515.
— — with France. Mo. R. 128: 100. — Mus. 40: 228. — Nat. R. 7: 280.
— — — in 1821. Quar. 25: 534.
— — — in 1830. Blackw. 28: 699.
— — — in 1833. (T. P. Thompson) Westm. 13: 240.
— — — in 1848. Quar. 83: 250.
— — — in 1870. (C. C. Chesney) Fortn. 14: 581.
— — — under Napoleon III. (L. Blanc) Lakeside, 1: 37. — (L. Blanc) Lippinc. 2: 595.
— — with Italy. Brit. Q. 14: 488. — Dub. Univ. 40: 85. — Once a Week, 10: 556.
— — with Germany, Early. Westm. 75: 403.
— — with Portugal. (F. W. Chesson) St. James, 34: 492.
— — with Russia. (J. C. Hodgson) St. James, 45: 239.
— — — in the East. Quar. 138: 568. — (D. Ker) Nat. Q. 38: 23.
— — — in 1878. Dub. R. 82: 465.
— — — Resources of England and Russia. Month, 33: 224.
— — with Spain, 1525. Dub. Univ. 82: 753.
— — with Turkey. (R. Congreve) Fortn. 26: 517.
— — — 1856–76. (G. Washburn) Internat. R. 6: 659. 7: 306.
— — — and the War, 1877. (E. de Laveleye) Fortn. 29: 153.
See Eastern Question.
— — with United States. (H. Flanders) Lippinc. 4: 109.
— — — Antagonism between. (H. D. Jenkins) Overland, 4: 571. — (N. Sheppard) Lakeside, 9: 98.
— — — — Causes of. Fraser, 87: 293.
— — — Consequences of War between. So. Lit. Mess. 8: 444.
— — — Controversies between. De Bow, 20: 365.
— — — Hurrah for a War. Dem. R. 9: 411.
— — — in 1826. Niles's Reg. 31: 266.
— — — in 1828. (E. Everett) No. Am. 27: 479.
— — — in 1841. (J. G. Palfrey) No. Am. 53: 412.
— — — in 1842. (M. F. Maury) So. Lit. Mess. 8: 381.
— — — in 1860–70. Canad. Mo. 1: 453.
— — — in 1865. Dub. Univ. 66: 709.
— — — — Danger of War. (G. Smith) Macmil. 11: 417. Same art. Liv. Age, 85: 219.
Great Britain, Foreign Relations of, with the United States; Practical Annexation of the United States. Dem. R. 19: 1. 29: 302.
— — — Treaty of 1815. Colburn, 3: 266.
— Future of. (W. H. Daniels) Lakeside, 3: 442.
— — Croly on. Dub. Univ. 12: 611.
— — Economic. (E. L. Godkin) Nation, 27: 328.
— — Greg's Rocks ahead. (A. Arnold and C. G. Lyttleton) Contemp. 24: 627. — (M. E. G. Duff) Fortn. 22: 581. — (W. R. Greg) Fortn. 22: 817.
— — Political, Montalembert on. Quar. 98: 534. — Dub. R. 40: 441. — Colburn, 106: 266.
— — Present and. Mus. 39: 377.
— — Speculations on. Blackw. 79: 726. Same art. Liv. Age, 50: 289.
— Future Attitude of. Fraser, 71: 79. Same art. Ecl. M. 65: 167.
— Future Corn Supply of. (R. Wilkes) Canad. Mo. 18: 113.
— Geological Elevation of. (G. P. Bevan) Once a Week, 12: 13.
— Geological Depressions of. (G. P. Bevan) Once a Week, 14: 498.
— Gold Rocks of. Colburn, 100: 14.
— Government of, Administrative Economy of. (F. W. Rowsell) Contemp. 22: 808.
— — Administrative Reform in. Brit. Q. 22: 145.
— — and its Functions. Temp. Bar, 7: 419. 13: 81.
— — Cabinet and its Functions. Bank. M. (N.Y.) 1: 295.
— — — History of. Bank. M. (N. Y.) 1: 636.
— — Crown and the Army. Quar. 146: 232.
— — Distribution of Representation in. Westm. 97: 469.
— — Extension of Franchise. Contemp. 3: 435. — Ed. R. 123: 263.
— — Features of English Monarchy. Tait, n. s. 5: 747.
— — Fischel on. Colburn, 125: 111.
— — How is Work of Nation done? Macmil. 24: 410.
— — Millar's View of. (F. Jeffrey) Ed. R. 3: 154.
— — The Monarchy. Quar. 148: 1. Same art. Liv. Age, 142: 771.
— — Pay of Ministers of the Crown. (W. Farr) J. Statis. Soc. 20: 102.
— — Popular Liberty in. (J. H. Morris) Potter Am. Mo. 7: 336.
— — Reconstitution of. (J. M. Ludlow) Contemp. 16: 499.
— — Representative. (F. Guizot) Sharpe, 12: 135.
— — Republicanism in. Fraser, 83: 751. Same art. Ecl. M. 77: 202.
— — Revolutionary Tendency in. (Goldwin Smith) No. Am. 108: 221.
— — Revolution of 19th Century. (J. R. Seeley) Macmil. 22: 242, 347, 435. Same art. Ecl. M. 75: 470, 577. Same art. Liv. Age, 106: 579. 107: 67, 387.
— — Queen and a United Empire. St. James, 33: 309.
— — Reform in War Departments. Ed. R. 100: 534.
— — Representative Reform in. Ed. R. 106: 254.
— — Royal Prerogative. (H. Brougham) Ed. R. 52: 130.
— — Russell on. Mo. R. 97: 146.
— — Spirit of. Westm. 1: 146.
— Historical Manuscripts Commission. (J. Piggot, jr.) Fraser, 85: 696. Same art. Liv. Age, 114: 22.
— History of. (W. J. Walter) Rel. Cab. 1: 537.
— — Administrations of. Blackw. 71: 320.
— — Ancient. Ecl. R. 34: 322, 463.
— — Belsham's. Ed. R. 6: 421. — Ecl. R. 2: 641.
— — Danes and Norwegians in. Dub. R. 32: 184.
— — Origin of the Inhabitants of. (S. Greatheed) Arch. 16: 95.
— — Wade's Chronology of. Ecl. R. 71: 227.
See Britain; Britons; England.
— in 1748. Sharpe, 22: 43.

Great Britain in 1825. Ann. Reg. **1**: 207.
— in 1827. Ann. Reg. **2**: 307.
— in 1828. Ann. Reg. **3**: 153.
— in 1829. Colburn, **26**: 570. **28**: 183.
— in 1832. Blackw. **31**: 569.
— in 1833. For. Q. **12**: 334.
— Income Tax of, Contributions to. Colburn, **65**: 359.
— — Reform in. Blackw. **73**: 246.
See Income Tax.
— Industrial Condition of. Bank. M. (N. Y.) **33**: 673.
— Laws of, State of. Quar. **21**: 398.
— — Statute, History of. (W. Tayler) J. Statis. Soc. **17**: 143.
— Legal Reform in, Progress of. Ed. R. **111**: 189.
— Life in, Effects of Emigration on. No. Brit. **18**: 259.
— — Defects of. No. Brit. **47**: 497.
— — Domestic Manners. Fraser, **5**: 598, 690. **6**: 105, 250.
— — Improvements in Food, Clothing, and Lodging. Penny M. **5**: 507.
— — Occupations of the People. Penny M. **13**: 366.
— — Society in. West. M. **3**: 185.
— — State of the Rural Population. Colburn, **43**: 281.
— Maritime Supremacy of. Mus. **15**: 481.
— Middle Classes in. (S. H. Perkins) Chr. Exam. **48**: 266.
— Military Comparison of, with France. Temp. Bar, **32**: 54.
— Military Education in. Am. J. Educ. **14**: 523.
— Military Establishment of. Liv. Age, **17**: 547.
— Military Force of. Quar. **25**: 67.
— Military Panics in, and their Remedy. (C. C. Chesney) Macmil. **23**: 449.
— Military Policy of. Blackw. **20**: 214, 573.
— Military Position of. Fortn. **24**: 108.
— Military Power of, in 1854 and 1878. (Sir G. Wolseley) 19th Cent. **3**: 433. Same art. Liv. Age, **137**: 195.
— — 1878. (E. L. Godkin) Nation, **26**: 163.
— Military Requirements of. (G. I. Wolseley) Macmil. **23**: 524.
— Military Spirit of. Once a Week, **1**: 442.
— Military System of. Colburn, **153**: 406. — Tinsley, **5**: 459.
— — and the National Debt. Fraser, **92**: 364.
— — Can England bear the Cost of a great War? Fraser, **97**: 537.
— — Defects and Organization of. Westm. **69**: 530.
— Militia of. *See* Great Britain, Army of.
— Mining Industries of, 1856. (R. Hunt) J. Statis. Soc. **19**: 201, 311.
— National Debt of. Ed. Mo. R. **3**: 226. — Brit. & For. R. **12**: 95. — Ed. R. **3**: 468. **24**: 294. — Bank. M. (N. Y.) **1**: 556. **4**: 121. **16**: 81. — Chamb. J. **34**: 164. — Tait, n. s. **3**: 293.
— — and Stock Exchange. Blackw. **66**: 655.
— — and Taxation. Prosp. R. **4**: 239.
— — before the Revolution. St. Paul's, **4**: 84.
— — Debate on, 1853. Bank. M. (L.) **13**: 305.
— — Heathfield on. Blackw. **6**: 441.
— — Plans for paying. Chamb. J. **17**: 52.
— — — for reducing. Ed. R. **46**: 390. **47**: 59. — Pamph. **9**: 415. **15**: 577. **16**: 481. **17**: 45. **18**: 305. **20**: 499. **21**: 365. — Blackw. **6**: 441. **23**: 341.
— National Income of. Contemp. **8**: 86.
— Naval Defenses of. Blackw. **101**: 1, 199.
— Naval Power of. (G. Reynolds) Atlan. **12**: 94. — Ed. R. **147**: 495.
— — and Colonies. Sharpe, **38**: 143.
— — and Military. (F. B. Head) Bentley, **28**: 653.
— — and Policy of. (T. Brassey) Contemp. **27**: 791.
— Navy of. (H. Kingsley) Lond. Soc. **24**: 417. — Ed. R. **10**: 1. — (E. J. Reed) Macmil. **23**: 1. — (R. Willett) Arch. **11**: 154. — (C. Whitehead) Bentley, **22**: 513. — Blackw. **21**: 737. **55**: 462. **94**: 697.

Great Britain, Navy of. Blackw. **109**: 357. — Canad. Mo. **13**: 240. — Chamb. J. **21**: 217. — Cornh. **3**: 119. **4**: 715. — Ed. R. **118**: 166. — Fraser, **19**: 348. **91**: 608. — Liv. Age, **1**: 78. — Niles's Reg. **13**: 203. — Penny M. **8**: 70.
— — Admirals of. Cornh. **15**: 538.
— — as it was. Chamb. J. **54**: 161.
— — Blue Jackets and Marines of. Fraser, **92**: 131.
— — Chaplains and Religion in. Chr. Rem. **33**: 227. — (W. Dawson) Contemp. **12**: 92.
— — Complete List of. (W. Latham) Arch. **13**: 27.
— — Condition of, 1848. Fraser, **38**: 548.
— — — and Prospects of, 1865. Fraser, **71**: 61.
— — — and Defects of, 1874. Westm. **102**: 70. — Fraser, **94**: 403.
— — Cost of. Quar. **142**: 290.
— — Decay of. Blackw. **35**: 675.
— — Discipline in. Lond. Soc. **36**: 242. — Fraser, **95**: 269.
— — Dupin on. Mo. R. **86**: 502.
— — Early Account of. Arch. **12**: 217. — Mo. R. **130**: 240.
— — Education in. (J. G. Goodenough) Fraser, **83**: 606.
— — Efficiency of. Quar. **126**: 207.
— — Fleet of the future. Blackw. **95**: 267.
— — Flogging in. Ed. R. **47**: 403. *See* Flogging.
— — Future of. (R. Main) Fortn. **2**: 738.
— — History of. Penny M. **7**: 115-340.
— — — Brenton's. Colburn, **47**: 492.
— — — 1793-1802. Ecl. R. **36**: 512.
— — — 1812-59. Ecl. R. **110**: 420.
— — in Time of Elizabeth. (J. P. Collier) Arch. **33**: 191.
— — in Time of James I. (J. Brand) Arch. **15**: 53.
— — in 1824, Penrose on. Chr. Obs. **25**: 360, 441.
— — in 1865. (W. H. Sykes) J. Statis. Soc. **29**: 36.
— — in 1871. Ecl. Engin. **4**: 370.
— — Internal Economy of. Lond. Soc. **35**: 257.
— — Iron-clad. Chamb. J. **46**: 709, 729. — Cornh. **23**: 55. — Temp. Bar, **1**: 232.
— — Men and Manners in. Cornh. **14**: 462.
— — Mismanagement of. Quar. **129**: 392.
— — — Continued. Quar. **131**: 440.
— — Monitors in. Chamb. J. **49**: 170.
— — New Frigates in. Fraser, **95**: 158.
— — Naval Brigades. Lond. Soc. **36**: 417.
— — Nicolas on. Blackw. **62**: 82.
— — Notes on. Fraser, **92**: 674.
— — The One-legged Lieutenant. Bentley, **59**: 539. Same art. Ecl. M. **67**: 171.
— — Organization in. Ed. R. **113**: 282.
— — past and present. Brit. Q. **40**: 126.
— — Personnel of. (J. C. Paget) St. James, **36**: 349.
— — Progress of. Dub. Univ. **48**: 159.
— — Reconstruction of. Cornh. **4**: 715. **5**: 550. **23**: 55.
— — Reform in. Cornh. **3**: 90.
— — Reorganization of. Temp. Bar, **13**: 535.
— — Requirements of. Brit. Q. **60**: 368.
— — Screw Ships in. Chamb. J. **31**: 229.
— — Social History of. Cornh. **12**: 374.
— — Steam Warfare. Brit. Q. **30**: 56.
— — Training of Officers. Blackw. **96**: 20.
— — Training Ship. Lond. Soc. **6**: 336.
— Parliament of. *See* Parliament.
— Parliamentary Government in. (J. F. Stephen) Contemp. **23**: 1, 165. — Ed. R. **125**: 578.
— — and Representation. No. Brit. **28**: 437.
— — Earl Grey on. Ed. R. **108**: 271.
— — Origin of. (E. A. Freeman) Internat. R. **3**: 721.
— Ordnance Survey. Bent. Q. **2**: 335.
— Parties in. (G. M. Towle) Galaxy, **1**: 416.
— — Faction Fights of. Bent. Q. **1**: 343.
— — Liberal Party and its Leaders. (J. Chamberlain) Fortn. **20**: 287.
— — Struggles of. Dub. R. **44**: 336.

Great Britain, Parties in; Toryism and its Leaders. (J. McCarthy) Galaxy, **7**: 687.
— — Whig Party, Lord Holland's Memoirs of. Quar. **91**: 217. **94**: 384.
— Peerage of. (R. Wynford) Lippinc. **14**: 443.
— Policy of, Amicable and amiable in. Westm. **28**: 247.
— — Conservative, Future of. St. James, **24**: 22.
— — Past and Future of. Quar. **127**: 538.
— — General. Fraser, **30**: 491.
— Politics of, County. St. James, **22**: 33.
— — Critical Elections. Cornh. **18**: 601.
— — Electioneering in England. Once a Week, **19**: 90.
— — — Great Westminster Canvass. (M. D. Conway) Harper, **31**: 732.
— — in 1806. Ed. R. **8**: 90.
— — in 1807, Danger of Country. (F. Jeffrey) Ed. R. **10**: 1.
— — — Review of. Chr. Obs. **6**: 109.
— — in 1809. (F. Jeffrey) Ed. R. **15**: 451. — Quar. **2**: 443.
— — in 1811, Montgaillard's. Gen. Repos. **2**: 104.
— — in 1816; Distresses of the Country. Ed. R. **26**: 255.
— — in 1817; Popular Disaffection. Quar. **16**: 511.
— — in 1818. Ed. R **30**: 181.
— — — Edinburgh Review on. Blackw. **3**: 715.
— — in 1819, and Ireland in 1833. Dub. Univ. **1**: 436.
— — — State of the Country. (F. Jeffrey) Ed. R. **32**: 293.
— — in 1820–32; Radicals and Reformers. Tait, **3**: 198–599.
— — in 1820. (R. Southey) Quar. **22**: 492.
— — in 1825. Colburn, **16**: 491.
— — in 1826. Westm. **6**: 249. — Colburn, **23**: 180.
— — in 1827. Colburn, **22**: 193.
— — — The Ministry. Ed. R. **46**: 415.
— — in 1828; Emancipation Bill. Colburn, **25**: 300.
— — in 1829; Court and Cabinet. Blackw. **26**: 696.
— — — Internal Policy. Quar. **42**: 229.
— — — Progress of Reform. Colburn, **31**: 385–541.
— — — State of Country. (R. Southey) Quar. **39**: 475.
— — — What will follow Reform Bill? Colburn, **32**: 97.
— — in 1830–40. Mus. **38**: 237.
— — — Political Retrospect of. Westm. **37**: 394. Same art. Am. Ecl. **4**: 124.
— — in 1830–32. Brit. Q. **15**: 390.
— — in 1830. (J. Q. Adams) Ann. Reg. **5**: 419. — Mo. R. **121**: 492.
— — — The Election and the Ministry. (H. Brougham) Ed. R. **52**: 261.
— — — The Ministry and the Parties. (H. Brougham) Ed. R. **51**: 564.
— — — Moral and Political State of the Country. (J.W. Croker) Quar. **44**: 261.
— — — Political Anticipations. Blackw. **28**: 719.
— — — Reform Act. Prosp. R. **8**: 219.
— — — State of the Nation. Niles's Reg. **39**: 453.
— — — Whig Ministry. Ed. R. **95**: 517.
— — in 1831. (R. Rush) Ann. Reg. **6**: 235. — Mo. R. **123**: 424.
— — — Reform. Ecl. R. **53**: 446.
— — in 1832. Blackw. **31**: 425. — (J. Q. Adams) Ann. Reg. **8**: 196. — (R. Southey) Quar. **46**: 274. — Ed. R. **53**: 232. — (Lord Campbell) Fraser, **65**: 213.
— — — Progress of Misgovernment. (R. Southey) Quar. **46**: 544.
— — in 1832–48, Reform Question. (W. N. Molesworth) Fortn. **7**: 389.
— — in 1832, Irish Reform Bill. Tait, **1**: 503, 633, 768.
— — — Reform Bill of. Tait, **1**: 17–781. **2**: 496.
— — — — Results of. Ecl. R. **55**: 471.
— — — — Working of. Tait, **2**: 496.
— — — Reform Ministry and the People. Tait, **2**: 1.
— — — Scottish Reform Bill. Tait, **1**: 107–633.
— — in 1833. (J. W. Croker) Quar. **50**: 218. — Blackw. **33**: 115.
Great Britain, Politics of, in 1833; Reform Bill. Dub Univ. **1**: 1.
— — — — and Irish Election Laws. Dub. Univ. **12**: 110.
— — — — First Fruits of. Mo. R. **132**: 178.
— — — — Stages of the Revolution. Mus. **21**: 258, 278.
— — — Reform Ministry and Parliament. Quar. **50**: 218. — Dub. Univ. **2**: 465.
— — in 1834. Blackw. **35**: 883.
— — — Popular Reform Movement. Tait, **4**: 325.
— — — Scenes in the House of Lords. Colburn, **41**: 190.
— — in 1835. Blackw. **37**: 431. — Mo. R. **136**: 385.
— — — State and Tendency of. Brit. & For. R. **2**: 673.
— — — State of Parties. Ed. R. **61**: 242. — (H. Brougham) Ed. R. **62**: 185. — Westm. **30**: 1.
— — — Von Raumer's. (J. G. Palfrey) No. Am. **43**: 445. — For. Q. **17**: 209. — Ecl. R. **65**: 151. — So. Lit. Mess. **2**: 507. — Fraser, **13**: 631. — Ed. R. **63**: 198. — (J. W. Croker) Quar. **56**: 580.
— — in 1836; Parliamentary Session. (J. W. Croker) Quar. **57**: 230.
— — in 1837; Parties and the Ministry. (J. S. Mill) Westm. **28**: 1. — Ecl. R. **67**: 97. — Ed. R. **64**: 537. — (W. Empson) Ed. R. **65**: 265*.
— — in 1838; Review of National Position. Ecl. R. **68**: 692.
— — in 1839. Ecl. R. **69**: 714.
— — — Conduct of the Ministry. (J. W. Croker) Quar. **65**: 283.
— — — Household and the Ministry. (J. W. Croker) Quar. **64**: 232.
— — in 1840; Review of the Year. Fraser, **22**: 752.
— — — State of Parties. (Sir E. B. Lytton) Ed. R. **70**: 245. — (Lord Monteagle) Ed. R. **71**: 275, 493.
— — in 1841. Blackw. **49**: 406, 507. **50**: 1, 83, 228. — For. Q. **28**: 469.
— — — Budget and the Dissolution. (J. W. Croker) Quar. **68**: 239.
— — — Grounds and Objects of Budget. Ed. R. **73**: 502.
— — — Old and new Ministry. (J. W. Croker) Quar. **68**: 494.
— — in 1842. Blackw. **51**: 130, 141, 398. **52**: 143, 271. — Brit. & For. R. **14**: 191.
— — — State of Parties. Ed. R. **74**: 506. **76**: 241.
— — in 1843. Blackw. **53**: 1.
— — — Perils of the Nation. Mo. R. **161**: 350.
— — — Policy of Ministers. (J.W. Croker) Quar. **72**: 553.
— — — State of Parties. Ed. R. **78**: 517.
— — in 1844. Fraser, **30**: 119. — (A. Dunlop) No. Brit. **1**: 223.
— — — Legislation of the Year. Westm. **42**: 318.
— — — State of Parties. (Lord Monteagle) Ed. R. **80**: 474. — Chr. Rem. **7**: 667.
— — in 1845; Legislation of the Year. Westm. **45**: 345.
— — — Ministerial Policy. Fraser, **32**: 496. Same art. Liv. Age, **5**: 169.
— — — National Crisis. Ecl. R. **83**: 116.
— — — State of Country. (J. Moncrieff) No. Brit. **3**: 212.
— — in 1846. Fraser, **34**: 118.
— — — Cabinet Mysteries. Fraser, **33**: 121.
— — — Ministerial Measures. Blackw. **59**: 373.
— — — New Ministry. Brit. Q. **4**: 259.
— — in 1847, Crisis of. Ecl. R. **85**: 758.
— — — Late and present Administrations. Ecl. R. **86**: 1.
— — — Parliamentary Prospects. Quar. **81**: 541. — (W. Howitt) Howitt, **2**: 6, 111.
— — in 1848. Blackw. **64**: 261.
— — — Ministerial Measures. Quar. **82**: 261.
— — — State of Parties. Ed. R. **87**: 138.
— — in 1849. Blackw. **65**: 357.
— — — Political Anticipations. Westm. **51**: 93.
— — — State of the Nation. Westm. **52**: 81.
— — — — of Parties. No. Brit. **10**: 501.

Great Britain, Politics of, in 1850; Ministerial Measures. Blackw. **67**: 377.
— — in 1851. Blackw. **70**: 607.
— — — Reforms since 1800. Brit. Q. **14**: 114. Same art. Ecl. M. **24**: 186.
— — in 1852; Government and Elections. Fraser, **46**: 112.
— — — Fall of the Derby Ministry. Ed. R. **97**: 240.
— — — House of Commons. Quar. **95**: 1.
— — — Old and new Ministries. Quar. **90**: 567.
— — — State of Parties. No. Brit. **17**: 559. — Fraser, **45**: 225.
— — in 1853; Government and Country. Fraser, **47**: 235.
— — — New Cabinet. Liv. Age, **38**: 788.
— — — — Personnel of. Fraser, **47**: 332.
— — in 1854; England at War. Fraser, **49**: 369.
— — — Reform Bill and the War. Fraser, **49**: 487.
— — in 1855; Government, the Aristocracy, and the Country. Fraser, **51**: 354.
— — — Foreign Policy. Brit. Q. **21**: 182.
— — — Political Crisis. Fraser, **51**: 715.
— — — Sketches of Parliament. Sharpe, **31**: 123, 179.
— — — War Committee, the Ministry, and the Conference. Fraser, **51**: 476.
— — in 1856; Anti-Palmerston Confederacy. (C. Redding) Colburn, **109**: 417.
— — — Foreign Policy and the next Campaign. Nat. R. **2**: 213.
— — — Parliament and the Opposition. (C. Redding) Colburn, **108**: 158. **109**: 322.
— — — Secret of the Session. Colburn, **108**: 37.
— — in 1857. Fraser, **55**: 364.
— — — Elections. Fraser, **55**: 486.
— — — Recess of Parliament. Colburn, **109**: 243.
— — — The Session. Colburn, **110**: 489.
— — in 1858; New Ministry. Fraser, **57**: 511.
— — — State of Parties. No. Brit. **29**: 257.
— — in 1859–65; Parliamentary Proceedings. Brit. Q. **42**: 157.
— — in 1859. Bent. Q. **1**: 1, 343.
— — — Domestic and foreign. (D. Masson) Macmil. **1**: 1. — Fraser, **59**: 629.
— — — Elections and the War, 1857 and 1859. Fraser, **59**: 757.
— — — Foreign Policy. Dub. Univ. **54**: 166.
— — — New Administration. Fraser, **60**: 122.
— — — Reform Bill. No. Brit. **30**: 228. — Tait, n. s. **26**: 1, 121, 685.
— — — — The Borough Question, the Franchise. Brit. Q. **29**: 237, 531.
— — in 1860. Bent. Q. **2**: 303. — Dub. Univ. **55**: 634, 734.
— — — Reform Bill. Dub. Univ. **55**: 597.
— — — — and its Results. Nat. R. **10**: 421.
— — — Two Budgets. (W. A. Porter) Macmil. **2**: 416.
— — in 1862. Dub. Univ. **60**: 380.
— — — Conservative Reaction. Ho. & For. R. **1**: 26.
— — in 1864; House of Commons. Quar. **116**: 245.
— — — Party Prospects. Brit. Q. **39**: 201.
— — — Political Temper of the Nation. (B. Price) Fraser, **69**: 135.
— — in 1865. (C. Redding) Colburn, **133**: 487. — Dub. Univ. **66**: 112, 228, 351.
— — — The Elections. Quar. **118**: 280.
— — in 1866; last and present Ministries. Fraser, **74**: 243.
— — — New Parliament. Brit. Q. **43**: 187.
— — — New Reform Bill. Brit. Q. **44**: 182. **45**: 222. — Dub. Univ. **67**: 597. — (E. Dicey) Nation, **2**: 424.
— — — — and the Government. Fraser, **73**: 477.
— — — — and the Parties. No. Brit. **44**: 213.
— — — — Why we want a. Fraser, **74**: 545.
— — — Policy and Prospects of the Government. Fraser, **73**: 1.
— — — State of Parties. Ed. R. **125**: 269.
Great Britain, Politics of, in 1867; Catholic and Party. Dub. R. **60**: 382.
— — — Conservative Surrender. Quar. **123**: 533.
— — — Conservative Transformation. Fraser, **76**: 654.
— — — Ministerial Prospects. Fraser, **75**: 131.
— — — — and Reform. Fraser, **75**: 415.
— — — Radicals, New School of. Quar. **124**: 477.
— — — Parliament of 1867 and Sequel. Ed. R. **126**: 540.
— — — Reform Bill. (C. Redding) Colburn, **141**: 205. — St. Paul's, **1**: 8, 148. — Dub. Univ. **70**: 166.
— — — — and Revolution. Galaxy, **2**: 16.
— — — — and the State of Parties. Brit. Q. **46**: 180.
— — — — Aspects of. No. Brit. **47**: 205.
— — in 1868–74; Gladstone Administration. Brit. Q. **58**: 189.
— — in 1868. (L. Stephen) No. Am. **107**: 543. — Brit. Q. **48**: 240.
— — — The Elections. No. Brit. **49**: 484.
— — — — of 1868 and 1874. (J. B. Martin) J. Statis. Soc. **37**: 193.
— — — Old Parties and new Policy. (J. Morley) Fortn. **10**: 320.
— — — Parliament, Amenities of. St. James, **22**: 749.
— — — Party Prospects. No. Brit. **38**: 234.
— — — Politics of young England. Fraser, **77**: 71, 333.
— — in 1869; Political Survey. St. James, **23**: 865. **24**: 266.
— — — Repentance of Tory Party. No. Brit. **51**: 478.
— — in 1870; Home Policy. No. Brit. **52**: 182.
— — — Home Politics, Grant's. Fraser, **82**: 403.
— — in 1871; Liberal Triumvirate. (J. McCarthy) Galaxy, **7**: 35.
— — — Political and Ecclesiastical Situation. Lond. Q. **37**: 176.
— — — Position of. (H. Fawcett) Fortn. **16**: 544.
— — — The Session. Brit. Q. **54**: 485.
— — in 1872. Quar. **133**: 558. — Fraser, **85**: 1.
— — in 1874. Dub. Univ. **83**: 347.
— — — Fall of Gladstone. Dub. R. **74**: 450.
— — — Liberal Party. Quar. **136**: 251, 566.
— — — The new Parliament. Brit. Q. **59**: 470.
— — — Party Politics. (J. A. Froude) Fraser, **90**: 1.
— — — Radical Programme. Quar. **135**: 539.
— — — Tory Administration and its Whig Admirers. Brit. Q. **60**: 171.
— — — Turn of the Tide; what does it mean? Fraser, **89**: 269.
— — in 1875; Conservative Government. Quar. **139**: 550.
— — — Conservative Reaction. (F. Harrison) Fortn. **21**: 297.
— — — Liberal Programme, Next Page of. (J. Chamberlain) Fortn. **22**: 405.
— — in 1876–78; Parliamentary Debates. Quar. **147**: 264. — Ed. R. **149**: 244.
— — in 1876; Parliament and Public Moneys. Quar. **141**: 224.
— — in 1877; Political Agitation. (E. Gaisford) St. James, **40**: 332.
— — — Reform Bill, A new. (R. Lowe) Fortn. **28**: 437.
— — — — of the Future. (T. Hare) Fortn. **29**: 75.
— — in 1878; Home and Foreign Affairs. (J. Morley) Fortn. **30**: 150–902.
— — — Liberal Party and Foreign Politics. Quar. **144**: 555.
— — — Liberal Party Caucus. (E. L. Godkin) Nation, **27**: 141.
— — — Meeting of Parliament. Quar. **145**: 257.
— — in 1878–79; Parliamentary Debates. Ed. R. **150**: 281.
— — in 1879; Chances for a long Conservative Régime. (W. Bagehot) Fortn. **30**: 787.
— — — The Country and the Government. (W. E. Gladstone) 19th Cent. **6**: 201.

Great Britain, Politics of, in 1879; Government and its Critics. (E. D. J. Wilson) 19th Cent. **5**: 386.
— — — Her Majesty's next Ministers. (H. W. Lucy) Gent. M. n. s. **23**: 548.
— — — Home and Foreign Affairs. Fortn. **31**: 152–963. **32**: 155–913.
— — — Liberal Prospects. Nation, **28**: 280.
— — — Opposition Leaders. Nation, **29**: 171.
— — — State of public Business. Fraser, **100**: 276.
— — in 1880. Brit. Q. **71**: 437.
— — — Docility of an Imperial Parliament. (R. Lowe) 19th Cent. **7**: 557.
— — — The Election. Fraser, **101**: 421, 504, 571. **102**: 397, 417. — Blackw. **127**: 530. — Westm. **113**: 479.
— — — — and its Results. Brit. Q. **72**: 171.
— — — — Conservative Collapse. (J. Morley) Fortn. **33**: 607.
— — — — Conservative Defeat. Quar. **149**: 549.
— — — — Conservative View of. (T. E. Kebbel) 19th Cent. **7**: 905, 1057. — (A. Austin) Fortn. **33**: 834.
— — — — Cost of. (W. P. Courtney) Fortn. **35**: 467.
— — — — in the Counties. (W. E. Bear) Fortn. **33**: 720.
— — — — Lessons of. (W. Chamberlain) Internat. R. **8**: 666.
— — — — Liberal Majority. (J. R. Thursfield) Macmil. **42**: 69.
— — — — Nonconformist's View of. (J. G. Rogers) 19th Cent, **7**: 628.
— — — — Reign of Bunkum. Blackw. **127**: 666.
— — — Has Conservatism increased since the Reform Bill? (A. Frisby) Fortn. **36**: 718.
— — — Ministerial Progress. Blackw. **128**: 256.
— — — The new Ministry. Blackw. **127**: 788.
— — — — and its Work, 1880. Fraser, **102**: 135.
— — — Reform Bill. (H. Fawcett) 19th Cent. **7**: 443.
— — — Parties, and the Distribution of Seats. (W. A. Hunter) Fortn. **34**: 58.
— — — Reform of County Constituencies. (T. W. Fowle) Fortn. **34**: 458.
— — in 1881. Blackw. **129**: 412. — Fraser, **103**: 136, 411, 553. **104**: 132-800.
— — — Conservative Tactics. Fraser, **103**: 822.
— — — Next Leap in the Dark. (Earl Fortescue) 19th Cent. **9**: 517.
— — — Revolutionary Party. Quar. **151**: 285.
— — — State of Parties. (T. E. Kebbel) 19th Cent. **9**: 491.
— — Interference of the Crown in. (E. L. Godkin) Nation, **28**: 414.
— — On the English Hustings. (G. M. Towle) Lippinc. **6**: 389.
— — Parliamentary Candidates. Tait, **1**: 515, 651.
— — Policy, and Land Tenure in, L. Blanc's Criticism on. Westm. **88**: 381.
— — Reform Question from 1848 to 1866. (W. N. Molesworth) Fortn. **7**: 733.
— — Tory Leadership, after Beaconsfield. (J. Bryce) Nation, **32**: 366.
— Poor-Laws, etc. *See* Poor.
— Population of. Quar. **53**: 56. — (J. Strang) Canad. J. n. s. **7**: 129.
— — and Wealth of. Bank. M. (N. Y.) **4**: 218.
— — Births, Deaths, and Marriages. Lond. Q. **10**: 188. **27**: 38. **32**: 379.
— — Census of. *See* Census of Great Britain.
— — compared with France. (C. M. Willich) J. Statis. Soc. **21**: 297.
— — in 1822. Niles's Reg. **23**: 105.
— — in past Epochs. Westm. **61**: 323.
— — Movement of. (J. Angus) J. Statis. Soc. **17**: 117.
— — of English Cities, temp. Edw. III. (T. Amyot) Arch. **20**: 524.
— — past and present. St. James, **2**: 21.
Great Britain, Population of, Vital Statistics of. Ecl. R. **109**: 406. — All the Year, **15**: 582. — Quar. **145**: 94. Same art. Ecl. M. **90**: 385.
— Position and Prospects of. Am. Ecl. **1**: 479. — Blackw. **26**: 464. **55**: 103. — Ed. R. **36**: 374. **58**: 151. — Mus. **15**: 47, 454.
— Post-Office System of. Lond. Q. **5**: 158. Same art. Ecl. M. **36**: 1022.
— — Reform in, Results of. Ed. R. **120**: 58.
— Premiers of. Month, **4**: 221, 331. **5**: 28, 265, 487. **6**: 33–512. **7**: 222, 397, 503.
— Progress of. Quar. **32**: 160. — Westm. **40**: 425. — West. J. **6**: 236, 290. — Ecl. R. **98**: 521. — (C. Redding) Colburn, **141**: 430.
— Prosperity of. (H. Fawcett) Fortn. **15**: 40.
— Public Records of. Penny M. **10**: 308.
— — Calendars of State Papers. Month, **3**: 288, 346, 453.
— — National Archives. Lond. Q. **26**: 44.
— Public Registry in. Ed. R. **51**: 159.
— Religious Condition of. Lond. Q. **5**: 179.
— — British Churches and British People, Miall's. Prosp. R. **6**: 230.
— Religious Equality and Theories of Comprehension. Brit. Q. **69**: 92.
— Religious Statistics, 1851. Chr. Rem. **27**: 378.
— Resources of. Dub. R. **36**: 165. — (J. Yeats) J. Statis. Soc. **18**: 367. — (T. H. Farrer) Fortn. **29**: 384. — Quar. **12**: 398.
— — Chalmers on. Ecl. R. **8**: 575.
— Revolution in, Prophesied. Dem. R. **16**: 112. — (A. Pember) Lippinc. **5**: 279. — (G. M. Towle) Putnam, **11**: 197.
— Statistics of, 1869. Am. J. Educ. **18**: 567.
— — Land-Tax, 1636–1856. (F. Hendriks) J. Statis. Soc. **20**: 241.
— — Notes on. Penny M. **1**: 26–374. **2**: 111, 115.
— — State and Defects of. Ed. R. **61**: 154.
— Survey of, Cadastral. Ed. R. **118**: 378.
— — Domesday Book of 1873. (F. Purdy) J. Statis. Soc. **39**: 393.
— — Geological. (F. von Hauer) Ed. New Philos. J. **48**: 227.
— — Hydrogeological. (J. Lucas) Nature, **18**: 494.
— — Hydrological. (F. R. Conder) Fraser, **98**: 20.
— — of East Coast. (G. W. Manby) Colburn, **2**: 1–306.
— — Ordnance. Bent. Q. **2**: 335. — Penny M. **13**: 389, 402.
— — — State of, 1876. Geog. M. **3**: 192.
— Taxation in. Ed. R. **111**: 236. — Bank. M. (N. Y.) **16**: 728. — Colburn, **44**: 485. **46**: 493.
— — Local. Ed. R. **85**: 53.
— — Tait's Letter on Poor-Laws, Corn-Laws, etc. (E. Elliott) Tait, n. s. **4**: 56.
— Travels in, Colton's. West. M. **4**: 254.
— — Crumbs of Travel. (J. W. De Forest) Atlan. **38**: 696.
— — Baron d'Haussez's. Ed. R. **58**: 151. — Quar. **50**: 142.
— — Dupin's. Mo. R. **95**: 490.
— — Journal of. Portfo. (Den.) **16**: 209.
— — Stewart's Sketches of. (J. A. Alexander) Princ. **7**: 134.
See England; Scotland; Ireland; Wales.
Great Carrack, The, Capture of. (W. R. Drake) Arch. **33**: 209. — Chamb. J. **23**: 371. Same art. Liv. Age, **46**: 300.
Great Cat and Dog Question. House. Words, **1**: 172.
Great Circumbendibus. (G. A. Sala) Belgra. **6**: 559.
Great Cotwyn, Rotten Borough of. Victoria, **35**: 179.
Great Deadwood Mystery. (Bret Harte) Scrib. **17**: 177.
Great Doctor. (A. Cary) Atlan. **18**: 12, 174.
Great Dribbleton Cricket Match. Lond. Soc. **20**: 1.

Great Eastern, Steamship. (W. B. Adams) Once a Week, **1**: 205. — Chamb. J. **22**: 313. **26**: 56. **32**: 188. — Liv. Age, **45**: 763. — Quar. **98**: 433. Same art. Ecl. M. **38**: 289. Same art. Liv. Age, **49**: 675. — Tait, n. s. **25**: 679. Same art. Ecl. M. **46**: 249. — Liv. Age, **53**: 637. — Am. Alma. **1860**: 194.
— Details of. (C. H. Haswell) J. Frankl. Inst. **68**: 386.
— Equinoctial Trip on. All the Year, **6**: 204.
— Explosion on, 1859. J. Frankl. Inst. **68**: 277.
— Fortunes and Misfortunes of. Chamb. J. **41**: 167.
— Schooling of. (W. B. Adams) Once a Week, **1**: 248.
— Trials of. (E. J. Reed) Once a Week, **1**: 264.
Great Eastern Photographs. Temp. Bar, **18**: 424.
Great Expectations. (C. Dickens) All the Year, **4**: 169–553. **5**: 1–433.
Great Grandfathers, Customs of. All the Year, **20**: 281.
Great Grandmothers. Lond. Soc. **36**: 489.
Great Griefs as a Medicine to less. (F. Jacox) Bentley, **60**: 388.
Great Hoggarty Diamond. (W. M. Thackeray) Fraser, **24**: 324–717.
Great Lawsuit; Man *versus* Men; Woman *versus* Women, Dial, **4**: 1.
Great Liverpool, Loss of, Feb., 1846. Colburn, **76**: 493.
Great Malvern Priory, Refectory of. (G. Blose) Arch. **30**: 514.
Great Man, The. (A. P. Selby) Lakeside, **1**: 302.
— What is a? (T. Purnell) St. James, **4**: 39.
Great Men. (D. G. Ingraham) Radical, **4**: 34.
— Great Thoughts, and the Environment. (W. James) Atlan. **46**: 441.
— — Replies. (J. Fiske) Atlan. **47**: 75. — (Grant Allen) Atlan. **47**: 371.
— Influence of. (J. W. McLane) New Eng. **11**: 247.
— Mission of. So. R. n. s. **9**: 643.
— of America. So. Lit. Mess. **14**: 212.
— Personal Aspect of. (E. O. Haven) Lakeside, **4**: 340.
Great Order of the Cave. (F. C. Ewer) Pioneer, **3**: 193.
Great Orme's Head Mountain. Antiquary, **4**: 307.
Great People. Colburn, **48**: 319.
Great Prize. Lond. Soc. **6**: 200.
Great Revolution in Pitcairn. (S. L. Clemens) Atlan. **43**: 295.
Great Salt Lake. (A. S. Packard, jr.) Am. Natural. **10**: 675. — All the Year, **5**: 509. — Chamb. J. **19**: 362.
— Ancient Outlet of. (G. K. Gilbert) Am. J. Sci. **115**: 256. — (A. C. Peale) Am. J. Sci. **115**: 439.
— and the Mormons. Ecl. R. **96**: 669.
See Mormons.
Great Scar Limestone. Chamb. J. **30**: 293.
Great Staffordshire Tragedy. Tinsley, **6**: 231.
Great Strike at Errickdale. (M. L. Emery) Cath. World, **24**: 843.
Great Tey, Tenures, Customs, etc., of the Manor of. (T. Astle) Arch. **12**: 25.
Great Tragedian. Blackw. **64**: 345.
Great Unbenefited. (E. S. Lintott) St. James, **46**: 432.
Great Unknown. (F. Hardman) Blackw. **40**: 673.
— a Jest from the German. Blackw. **68**: 698.
Great Unloaded. Blackw. **125**: 345. Same art. Liv. Age, **141**: 181.
Great Western Jungle. Colburn, **51**: 58–338. **52**: 58. **53**: 31–325.
Great Yarmouth; Semi-Dutch Town. (E. Meteyard) Good Words, **12**: 381.
Greatness, Disadvantages of. (I. A. Safford) Western, **4**: 567.
— in Men. (F. L. Dingley) University Q. **4**: 55.
— Scholar's Ideal of. (J.W. Ward) University Q. **1**: 287.
— True. So. R. n. s. **19**: 205.
Greatrakes Family, Notes on. (S. Hayman) Reliquary, **4**: 81, 220. **5**: 94. **9**: 162.
Greatshakes, Valentine. Penny M. **10**: 421.
Greaves, James P. Dial, **3**: 247.
Grebes, Natural History of. Penny M. **6**: 212.
Greece. (T. D. Woolsey) New Eng. **5**: 1. — (E. Everett) No. Am. **17**: 398. — For. Q. **3**: 197. — Liv. Age, **1**: 76. — Quar. **124**: 199.
— Acarnania. (C. H. Brigham) No. Am. **97**: 180.
— Adventures of an English Officer in, 1826. Colburn, **17**: 172–201.
— — of a Foreigner in. Lond. M. **15**: 462. **16**: 40–531. **17**: 73.
— Ancient. (C. A. Bristed) Am. Whig R. **7**: 178, 286. — Hogg, **8**: 389.
— — Abbott's Hellenica. (L. Dyer) Nation, **30**: 476.
— — and modern. (T. D. Woolsey) Am. Bib. Repos. 2d s. **7**: 441.
— — — Felton's. (W. F. Allen) Nation, **4**: 185.
— — and Rome, Children's Plays in. Cornh. **20**: 285.
— — City Life in. (G. O. Trevelyan) Macmil. **13**: 407.
— — colonized from India, Pococke on. Ecl. R. **96**: 159.
— — Constitutional History of. Brit. Q. **1**: 413. — (H. S. Legaré) New York R. **7**: 1. — Ecl. M. **5**: 478.
— — Early Days of. (T. Chase) No. Am. **87**: 481.
— — Female Society in. (Sir D. K. Sandford) Quar. **22**: 163. — (J. Donaldson) Contemp. **32**: 647. **34**: 700. Same art. Liv. Age, **141**: 106, 153.
— — Field Sports of. Quar. **118**: 468.
— — Fortresses of. (W. Hamilton) Arch. **15**: 315.
— — Generals of. (W. Dowe) No. Am. **76**: 31.
— — History and Literature of. So. Lit. Mess. **14**: 129.
— — Kinship in. (J. F. McLellan) Fortn. **4**: 569, 682.
— — Monuments of. Art J. **3**: 130, 187, 228. — Internat. M. **5**: 4.
— — Philosophic Schools of. Nat. M. **1**: 16.
— — Philosophy and Religion of. Chr. R. **2**: 515.
— — Phœnicians in. (A. H. Sayce) Contemp. **34**: 60. Same art. Liv. Age, **140**: 175.
— — Politics of. (E. Everett) No. Am. **18**: 390. — U. S. Lit. Gaz. **1**: 17.
— — Private Life of. Quar. **79**: 335.
— — Progress in Government of. (G. H. Emerson) Univ. Q. **9**: 113.
— — Public Economy of. (A. Harkness) Bib. Sac. **15**: 179. *See* Athens.
— — Religion of. (J. T. Champlin) Chr. R. **10**: 530.
— — — and Laws of, Coulanges's. (J. N. Pomeroy) Nation, **18**: 204.
— — Science of. (G. L. Cuvier) Ed. New Philos. J. **8**: 344. **9**: 41.
— — Struggle of, for Union. (F. W. Newman) Fraser, **89**: 466. Same art. Liv. Age, **121**: 707.
— and Civilization. (G. Allen) Sup. Pop. Sci. Mo. **3**: 398.
— and England; a Poem. (E. W. Gosse) Temp. Bar, **50**: 104.
— and the Greek Kingdom. Ed. R. **103**: 386.
— and the Greek Question, 1850. Brit. Q. **12**: 111.
— — 1879. (J. Rae) Brit. Q. **70**: 177.
— and the Greeks. Lond. Q. **20**: 130. Same art. Ecl. M. **59**: 277. — (W. J. Stillman) Fortn. **34**: 556.
— — in 1858. Sharpe, **28**: 134.
— and Greek Museums. (J. Arbuckle) Scrib. **14**: 65.
— and her Claims, 1881. Blackw. **129**: 539.
— and Ionian Islands Mure's. Westm. **19**: 493. — Quar. **70**: 129. Same art. Am. Ecl. **4**: 433. — Mo. R. **157**: 371.
— and Italy, Sketches in. Bost. R. **3**: 477.
— and Rome, Domestic Life in. Mo. R. **132**: 520.
— and Russia. Westm. **1**: 453.
— — and Turkey. Fraser, **49**: 718.
— and the Treaty of Berlin. (W. E. Gladstone) 19th Cent. **5**: 1121.

Greece and Turkey. (J. Q. Adams) Ann. Reg. **2**: 393. **6**: 159. — Select J. **2**: [198. — Mo. R. **131**: 51. — (Syd. Smith) Ed. R. **1**: 281.
— — De Vere's. Ecl. R. **92**: 283. Same art. Internat. M. **1**: 255.
— — in 1881. (E. Lenormand) Contemp. **39**: 637.
— Anderson's Tour in. (E. Everett) No. Am. **34**: 1. — Spirit of Pilg. **4**: 311.
— Antiquities of. Lakeside, **9**: 254. — So. Q. **11**: 273.
— — Modern Writers on. (G. W. Leyburn) Internat. R. **2**: 317, 430.
— Archæology in, Progress of. (W. J. Stillman) Nation, **31**: 168.
— at the Congress of Berlin. (G. J. S. Lefevre) Fortn. **30**: 271.
— at the Time of Peloponnesian War. Fraser, **24**: 127.
— Attic Historians and Col. Mure. (E. A. Freeman) Nat. R. **6**: 69.
— Bankruptcy of. Blackw. **54**: 345. **55**: 785.
— Chateaubriand's Travels in, 1806-7. Ecl. R. **15**: 12.
— Claims of. (A. Arnold) Gent. M. n. s. **22**: 705.
— Cochrane's Wanderings in. Mo. R. **143**: 548.
— Commerce of. (F. Strong) Hunt, **7**: 109.
— Confederation of, Report on. Pamph. **22**: 551. **23**: 37.
— Constantinople, and Russia. St. James, **44**: 24.
— Constitution of Macedonia, Mitford's. Blackw. **5**: 443.
— Country Life in. Lond. Soc. **33**: 514.
— Crowe's Greek and the Turk. Liv. Age, **39**: 24.
— Dodwell's Tour through. Mo. R. **92**: 256, 337.
— Ecclesiastical Independence of. (H. M. Baird) Meth. Q. **17**: 594.
— Egypt and Holy Land, Clarke's Travels in. (R. Heber) Quar. **9**: 162. — (J. Foster) Ecl. R. **24**: 18, 292.
— Lord Elgin's Pursuits in. (J. Foster) Ecl. R. **15**: 355.
— Emigration to. Penny M. **2**: 239, 247.
— English Scholar in. Fraser, **58**: 285.
— Ethics of. (A. Neander) Bib. Sac. **10**: 476, 789.
— Excursions in. Month, **34**: 67.
— Fiedler's Tour through. For. Q. **26**: 337.
— First Philosophers of. For. Q. **30**: 61.
— From Rome to Athens. (C. D. Cobham) Good Words, **16**: 334, 407.
— Garston on, 1842. Mo. R. **158**: 219.
— Sir William Gell's. Ed. R. **38**: 314.
— George I., New King of. (H. J. Warner) Chr. Exam. **77**: 41.
— Giffard's Tour in. Quar. **59**: 217.
— Hartley's Researches in. Meth. M. **55**: 113.
— Hellas. (J. M. Hoppin) Putnam, **12**: 313.
— — and Civilization. (G. Allen) Gent. M. n. s. **21**: 156.
— Hellenic Factor in Eastern Problem. (W. E. Gladstone) Contemp. **29**: 1.
— Hellenic Nationality and the East. (K. Blind) Putnam, **14**: 562.
— Hellenic Studies. (C. T. Newton) Macmil. **40**: 424.
— Hill's Essays on the State of. Mo. R. **91**: 357.
— Histories of. Ecl. R. **53**: 435.
— History of. Am. Mo. R. **4**: 449.
— — Clavier's. Quar. **5**: 1.
— — Cox's. (F. Allen) No. Am. **119**: 208. — (C. Kenny) Theo. R. **12**: 424. — Brit. Q. **61**: 43. — Ed. R. **141**: 242.
— — Curtius's. (H. M. Baird) Meth. Q. **31**: 533. — (J. Hadley) Nation, **12**: 240. — (L. R. Packard) Nation, **19**: 333.
— — — and Grote's. Lond. Q. **28**: 1. — (L. R. Packard) New Eng **34**: 123.
— — during the Macedonian Period. (E. A. Freeman) No. Brit. **21**: 425.
— — Finlay's. (H. J. Warner) Chr. Exam. **72**: 403. — Ed. R. **148**: 232.
Greece, History of, Grote's. (E. A. Freeman) No. Brit. **25**: 141. — (N. E. Frothingham) Chr. Exam. **62**: 55. — (W.W. Goodwin) No. Am. **78**: 150. — (J. S. Mill) Ed. R. **84**: 343. — Ed. R. **91**: 118. **94**: 204. — (J. S. Mill) Ed. R. **98**: 425. — Ed. R. **105**: 305. — (G. H. Lewes) Westm. **46**: 381. — Blackw. **62**: 129. — (J. T. Champlin) Chr. R. **16**: 481. — (C. C. Felton) Chr. Exam. **48**: 292. — (G. H. Emerson) Univ. Q. **14**: 54. — Bentley, **39**: 533, 637. — Brit Q. **13**: 289. — Dub. Univ. **28**: 200. **35**: 753. **45**: 477. — Ecl. R. **84**: 257. **86**: 289. — Internat. M. **1**: 15. — New Q. **5**: 437. — Lond. Q. **7**: 51. — (J. C. Moffat) Princ. **29**: 50. — Putnam, **8**: 179. — Quar. **78**: 113. **86**: 384. **88**: 41. Same art. Liv. Age, **28**: 398. — Quar. **99**: 60. — Tait, n. s. **13**: 375.
— — History of Athenian Democracy. (W. A. Larned) New Eng. **18**: 651.
— — Insurrection of 1854. Colburn, **102**: 238.
— — Later. Brit. Q. **68**: 162.
— — Mitford's. Quar. **25**: 154. — (Lord Brougham) Ed. R. **12**: 478. — Mo. R. **92**: 1, 156. — Lond. M. **12**: 193.
— — Place of, in providential Order of the World. (W. E. Gladstone) Ecl. M. **66**: 137.
— — — Gladstone on. Month, **4**: 70.
— — Revolution of 1821-28. (A. H. Everett) No. Am. **27**: 254. — (E. Everett) No. Am. **29**: 138. — Am. Q. **3**: 190. **5**: 99. — Fraser, **7**: 191. — Blackw. **12**: 467. — with map, Blackw. **20**: 543, 716, 824. — (T. De Quincey) Blackw. **33**: 476. — Quar. **28**: 475. — Mo. R. **105**: 184. — Pamph. **21**: 167, 189. **22**: 199. **23**: 207. **24**: 415. — Mus. **3**: 500. **18**: 166, 221. — (G. W. Leyburn) So. M. **13**: 284. **14**: 385. — Blackw. **76**: 119. — Brit. Q. **66**: 434. Same art. Ecl. M. **58**: 377. — Chr. Rem. **48**: 231. — Portfo.(Den.) **31**: 147.
— — — Adventure during. Blackw. **52**: 668.
— — — and European Diplomacy. For. Q. **5**: 271. — Mus. **16**: 193.
— — — and Turkish Revolution. Dub. Univ. **8**: 196.
— — — Causes and Outbreak of. Month, **29**: 86-435.
— — — Finlay's History of. Ed. R. **117**: 570. Same art. Liv. Age, **138**: 771.
— — — Historical Sketch of. West. Mo. R. **2**: 446, 496.
— — Revolutions of 1862. (H.M.Baird) Meth. Q. **23**: 227.
— — — Fall of King Otho. Blackw. **94**: 586.
— — Thirlwall's. So. Q. **11**: 273. — Ecl. R. **69**: 98. — Ecl. R. **82**: 129. Same art. Ecl. M. **7**: 163. — Ed. R. **62**: 83.
— — under the Romans, Finlay's. Blackw. **56**: 524. — Fraser, **30**: 450.
— Holland's Travels in. Portfo.(Den.) **15**: 310.
— Hughes's Travels in. Colburn, **29**: 201-316.
— in 1801-6. Anal. M. **15**: 44.
— in 1821-22. Pamph. **23**: 97.
— in 1822, French and British Agents in. Niles's Reg. **23**: 49.
— in 1823. Niles's Reg. **25**: 298.
— in 1823-24. U. S. Lit. Gaz. **2**: 1, 41. — Mo. R. **104**: 280. **106**: 300.
— in 1825. U. S. Lit. Gaz. **4**: 204. — Ann. Reg. **1**: 263. — Mo. R. **109**. 10. — Mus. **8**: 289. — Ecl. R. **43**: 193.
— — Bulwer's. Lond. M. **14**: 1.
— — G. Pecchio's. Colburn, **14**: 291-409.
— in 1826. Ecl. R. **44**: 97.
— in 1827. Niles's Reg. **33**: 7, 45.
— in 1829. Ann. Reg. **3**: 403.
— in 1830. Mo. R. **122**: 375. — Niles's Reg. **38**: 159.
— in 1831. Mo. R. **124**: 92.
— in 1842, Condition of. (G. Sumner) Dem. R. **8**: 204. — Mus. **13**: 51.
— in 1843-44, Lord Nugent's. Quar. **78**: 297.
— in 1848, Political Condition and Prospects of. Mass. Q. **1**: 63.

Greece in 1862. Brit. Q. 37: 191.
— in 1879. (T. Davidson) Internat. R. 6: 597.
— — Question of, and England. (J. Rea) Brit. Q. 70: 177.
— — — Notes from Epirus. Blackw. 127: 110.
— in 1880. (A. Lowrey) Meth. Q. 40: 681.
— In Quarantine at Syra. Cornh. 13: 173.
— Independence of, Revival of. (Lord Stratford de Redcliffe) 19th Cent. 4: 377, 932.
— Islands and Shores of. (W. C. Prime) Harper, 17: 594.
— — Cruising about. Tait, n. s. 9: 402.
— Journal in. (C. F. F. Clinton) Bentley, 16: 191–337.
— Journey in, 1822. Lond. M. 23: 481.
— Leake's Researches in. Ed. R. 24: 353.—Quar. 11: 458.
— Legal Oratory of. Quar. 29: 313.
— Legends and early Hist of. (G. Grote) Westm. 39: 285.
— Letters from. So. Lit. Mess. 6: 763.
— — 1822. Niles's Reg. 23: 14.
— Life at Rhodes. Victoria, 4: 299. 5: 14.
— Litigation in. (B. L. Gildersleeve) So. M. 12: 395. 13: 272.
— Massacre at Scio. Mus. 23: 621.
— Massacre in, 1870. Blackw. 108: 240.
— Mediæval and modern. (E. A. Freeman) Nat. R. 18: 78.
— — and Trebizond, Finlay's. Fraser, 51: 291.
— Milnes's Tour in. Mo. R. 133: 1.
— Modern. (A. N. Arnold) Bapt. Q. 5: 20. — (E. H. Bunbury) Contemp. 1: 50. — (C. C. Felton) No. Am. 62: 429. — (E. M. Geldart) Mod. R. 2: 26. — (H. Sandwith) Brit. Q. 71: 53. — Westm. 20: 274. — Blackw. 43: 469, 620. 52: 120. 67: 526. 76: 403. — Quar. 23: 325. — Mo. R. 124: 460. — (A. L. Koeppen) De Bow, 13: 134, 217. — Ecl. R. 75: 627. — Fraser, 21: 649. 22: 81. — Chr. Obs. 72: 625. — So. Lit. Mess. 22: 90.
— — a Poem. (Mrs. F. Hemans) Portfo. (Den.) 25: 288.
— — and the Greeks. Westm. 79: 183.
— — and its Islands. Temp. Bar, 42: 238.
— — Civilization in. Blackw. 4: 513.
— — Customs of. (H. M. Baird) Putnam, 3: 135.
— — during the last thirty Years. No. Brit. 38: 134.
— — Final Deliverance of. (C. P. Castanis) Knick. 14: 295.
— — Finlay's History of. (J. P. Mahaffy) Contemp. 31: 728. Same art. Ecl. M. 90: 575.
— — Hist. of, 1833–54. (A. L. Koeppen) Mercersb. 6: 435.
— — Language and Literature of. No. Brit. 20: 135.
— — F. Lenormant on. Colburn, 136: 127.
— — Political and Intellectual Life in. (N. Kasasis) Contemp. 36: 164.
— — Popular Songs of. Colburn, 11: 139.
— — Popular Superstition of. Fraser, 11: 218.
— — Sketches of. Blackw. 43: 469, 620, 816.
— — Social Condition of. (S. G. W. Benjamin) No. Am. 97: 533.
— — Songs and Legends of. (Lady Verney) Contemp. 27: 96.
— — Webster's Speech on. Niles's Reg. 25: 342.
— Mure's Tour in. Ed. R. 75: 492. — Quar. 70: 129.
— Notes in. Month, 25: 16.
— Notes of Travel in. Dub. Univ. 39: 316, 518, 758.
— Orators of. Ed. R. 145: 333. — (T. De Quincey) Tait, n. s. 6: 374.
— Over Ilium and Ida. (W. J. Armstrong) Atlan. 33: 173.
— Panegyrical Oratory of. Quar. 27: 362.
— Peloponnesus in March. Contin. Mo. 2: 74.
— People and Kingdom of. (E. A. Freeman) Ed. R. 103: 386.
— Political Condition of, 1868. (L. R. Packard) Nation, 6: 33.
— — 1881. (W. J. Stillman) Nation, 33: 313.
— Position and Future of. (C. K. Tuckerman) Lippinc. 9: 679.
— Pouqueville's Travels in, 1798–1801. Ecl. R. 4: 756–943.
Greece, Prehistoric. (J. Pyne) Nat. Q. 31: 306.
— Prehistoric Archæology in. (G. Finlay) Am. J. Sci. 100: 251.
— Progress of. (R. C. Jebb) Macmil. 39: 419. Same art. Liv. Age, 141: 195. — Hunt, 57: 317.
— Question of, 1827. Am. Q. 1: 254. — Quar. 35: 221. — Westm. 6: 113. — Colburn, 23: 113.
— — in 1830. Quar. 43: 495.
— — — and Quarterly Review. Fraser, 2: 484.
— — in 1850. Ecl. R. 92: 230. — Brit. Q. 12: 111.
— Rambles and Studies in, Mahaffy's. (W. J. Stillman) Nation, 24: 238.
— Relations with America. Dem. R. 32: 119.
— Religion in, in 1830. Ecl. R. 54: 46.
— — in 1857. Westm. 67: 228.
— Resurrection of 1880. (E. L. Godkin) Nation, 31: 24.
— Rural Life and Scenery in. Month, 33: 448.
— Russian Policy in. For. Q. 16: 361.
— Scene and Adventure in, An old. Dub. Univ. 62: 423. Same art. Ecl. M. 61: 126.
— Senior's Journal in. Ed. R. 110: 518. Same art. Liv. Age, 64: 139. — Nat. R. 9: 316.
— Seven Sages of, and their Sayings. Ecl. M. 14: 85.
— Sketches in. Dub. R. 29: 1.
— Sketches of Travel in. (J. A. St. John) Tait, n. s. 16: 509–779. 17: 17–344.
— Social State of. (L. R. Packard) Nation, 8: 89.
— Spirit of Change in Southern Europe. (J. H. Skene) Colburn, 87: 34, 162.
— the spoilt Child of Europe. (R. W. Hanbury) 19th Cent. 6: 928.
— Statistics of. (D. Bikelas) J. Statis. Soc. 31: 265.
— Theism and Ethics of. (K. Cook) Dub. Univ. 92: 584, 641.
— Travels in. (A. L. Koeppen) Mercersb. 6: 258, 435, 531. 7: 1, 163. 8: 350. 9: 108, 402. 11: 149. 12: 1. — Am. Mo. M. 12: 178. — Broadw. 4: 383. — Quar. 126: 479.
— Visit to. (J. H. Browne) Blackw. 35: 56, 392.
— War Sketches in. Lond. M. 19: 553.
— Wars of, and their Causes. Cornh. 17: 462.
— Wyse's Excursion in the Peloponnesus. Ecl. M. 66: 177.
— Wyse's Journal in. Dub. Univ. 66: 693.
See Byzantine Empire; Hellenism.
Greeks, The. (J. Bowring) Howitt, 1: 248.
— Ancient, Social Life among. Cornh. 42: 601. Same art. Ecl. M. 96: 50. Same art. Appleton, 25: 28.
— — and modern. Meth. M. 56: 97.
— and Romans, Life of, Guhl and Koner's. Internat. R. 3: 99.
— — Private Life of. Quar. 79: 336. Same art. Ecl. M. 11: 112. Same art. Liv. Age, 13: 600.
— — Virtues and Manners of, compared with modern Nations. Ox. Prize Ess. 4: 185.
— and Turks, 1821. Niles's Reg. 20: 207. 22: 389.
— — 1822. Niles's Reg. 23: 111, 215.
— — 1825. Niles's Reg. 28: 219.
— — 1853. Quar. 94: 509.
— — Wayfaring Sketches among. Dub. Univ. 30: 241.
— Anthropology of. Anthrop. R. 6: 154.
— Dalzel's Lectures on. Ecl. R. 34: 121. — Quar. 26: 243
— Egypt and Pre-Homeric. (A. Lang) Fraser, 100: 171.
— Humanity of. (J. P. Mahaffy) Macmil. 33: 355.
— in Turkey, and England. Cornh. 18: 718.
— Ionian Origin of. (T. Chase) No. Am. 87: 481.
— Modern, Nationality of. (A. L. Koeppen) Mercersb. 9: 402.
— — Observ. on. (L. R. Packard) New Eng. 26: 656.
— — Tuckerman on. (L. R. Packard) Nation, 15: 429.
— Monotheism among. (O. Cone) Univ. Q. 30: 171. — (E. Zeller) Contemp. 4: 359.
— Religion of. (E. L. Magoon) Chr. R. 21: 425.

Greeks, The, Religion and Philosophy of. (A. C. Hendrick) Chr. R. **15**: 95.
— — illustrated by Greek Descriptions. (C. T. Newton) 19th Cent. **3**: 1033. **4**: 303.
— — De Quincey and. (S. A. Bean) Chr. Exam. **80**: 154.
— — Primitive. (T. Lewis) Am. Presb. R. **20**: 5.
Greek People, Character, Condition, and Prospects of. (J. S. Blackie) Westm. **62**: 345.
Greek Race, Political Condition and Prospects of. (H. M. Baird) Meth. Q. **22**: 22.
Greek Alphabet. Chr. Mo. Spec. **2**: 347.
— Sophocles on. (F. Bowen) No. Am. **67**: 257.
Greek and Albanian Costumes. Penny M. **5**: 179–220.
Greek and Roman Antiquities, Smith's Dictionary of. (C. C. Felton) No. Am. **70**: 424.
Greek Anthology. New York R. **5**: 49.
— Chrysanthema gathered from. (W. M. Hardinge) 19th Cent. **4**: 869. Same art. Liv. Age, **139**: 554.
— Bland's. Quar. **10**: 139. — Anal. M. **3**: 265.
— Merivale's. (H. A. Coleridge) Quar. **49**: 349.
— Translations from. Ed. R. **9**: 319. — (W. Hay) Blackw. **33**: 865. **34**: 115–961. **37**: 652. **38**: 142–642. **39**: 128–793. **40**: 274, 557. **41**: 238, 622.
Greek Article. (M. Stuart) Am. Bib. Repos. **4**: 277.
— Doctrine of. Quar. **2**: 174.
— — Middleton's. Ecl. R. **8**: 671, 767, 869.
— in the New Testament, Middleton on. Chr. Obs. **9**: 155–308.
— — Definitive, Sharpe on. Chr. Obs. **1**: 438. **2**: 363, 419.
Greek Authoresses. (Sir D. K. Sandford) Ed. R. **55**: 182.
Greek Authors, Ancient. So. Lit. Mess. **2**: 301.
Greek Banquets. (Sir D. K. Sandford) Ed. R. **56**: 350.
Greek Beauty and modern Art. (F. W. Cornish) Fortn. **20**: 326. Same art. Ecl. M. **81**: 612.
Greek Church. (E. Laurence) Harper, **45**: 405. — (J. M. Manning) Bib. Sac. **15**: 501. — Blackw. **79**: 304. — Chr. R. **26**: 202. — Chr. Rem. **18**: 114. — Am. Church R. **22**: 280. — (D. d'Istria) Am. Church R. **34**: 59. **35**: 85. — Dub. R. **23**: 406. — (J. T. Lamy) Dub. R. **87**: 22. — Ecl. R. **100**: 513. **107**: 301. — Nat. M. **7**: 448. — Nat. Q. **20**: 53. — (J. A. Keogh) Cath. World, **10**: 758.
— and Russian. Chr. R. **20**: 519. — Dub. R. **23**: 406.
— History of. So. R. n. s. **23**: 176. **24**: 124.
— in 1855. (F. W. Holland) Chr. Exam. **59**: 57.
— in London. (W. Gilbert) Good Words, **6**: 152.
— in its Relation to the Latin. (R. B. Welch) Meth. Q. **25**: 325, 510.
— in relation to the Protestant. (R. B. Welch) Meth. Q. **26**: 496. **27**: 369.
— in Russia, Pinkerton's State of. Chr. Obs. **13**: 378.
— — State of, 1814. Ecl. R. **20**: 429.
— Modern, Theology of. (A. N. Arnold) Bib. Sac. **21**: 816.
— Orthodox. (D. d'Istria) Internat. R. **1**: 528.
— Recent Apologies for. Lond. Q. **5**: 124.
— Stourdza on. (A. N. Arnold) Chr. R. **28**: 31.
— Union with. (G. W. Kitchin) Contemp. **6**: 186.
See Eastern Church; Russia, Church of.
Greek Civilization in the East. Quar. **149**: 125. Same art. Liv. Age, **144**: 515.
Greek Coins. (S. Weston; S. B. Howes) Arch. **16**: 9, 14.
Greek Comedy; Aristophanes. Fraser, **15**: 285. **18**: 127, 317. **19**: 639. **20**: 379. — (E. I. Sears) Nat. Q. **3**: 70.
— Meander. (E. I. Sears) Nat. Q. **16**: 1.
Greek Composition. (J. Hadley) No. Am. **111**: 211.
Greek Courts of Justice. Westm. **7**: 227. — Quar. **33**: 332.
Greek Culture, Influence of. (F. Wharton) Bib. Sac. **30**: 144.
Greek Democracy. Westm. **96**: 342.
Greek Dinners. (F. A. Paley) Fraser, **103**: 197. Same art. Liv. Age, **150**: 493. Same art. Appleton, **25**: 320.
Greek Drama. So. Lit. Mess. **2**: 552. — (J. Proudfit) Am. Bib. Repos. 2d s. **1**: 449. — Blackw. **30**: 350. — Penny M. **8**: 188–223.
— and Romantic Drama. Blackw. **59**: 54.
— Beauties of. So. Lit. Mess. **24**: 58.
— Musical and Religious Importance of. For. Q. **24**: 248.
Greek Dramatic Poets. Quar. **44**: 389. — (C. Minnigedore) So. Lit. Mess. **8**: 606, 793. **9**: 96. — Dub. Univ. **44**: 606. — Nat. M. **8**: 443.
— Spirit of. Colburn, **35**: 211.
Greek Elegy. (H. N. Coleridge) Quar. **48**: 69. **49**: 349.
— and Epitaph. Dub. Univ. **9**: 407.
Greek Epigrams; translated. Temp. Bar, **41**: 493.
Greek Epitaphs and Inscriptions. (H. C. Lea) Knick. **22**: 97.
Greek Fire. (E. C. Boynton) U. S. Serv. M. **1**: 50. — Chamb. J. **40**: 260.
— Ancient and modern History of. (B. W. Richardson) Pop. Sci. R. **3**: 164. Same art. Ecl. M. **61**: 332.
— and Gunpowder. Blackw. **59**: 749.
— of the Middle Ages. Mus. **2**: 1.
Greek Fool, The. Blackw. **116**: 286. Same art. Ecl. M. **83**: 597.
Greek Gardens. Chamb. J. **41**: 541. Same art. Ecl. M. **63**: 322.
Greek Girl. Blackw. **120**: 600.
Greek Humanists, Nature and Law. Westm. **113**: 385.
Greek Hymn. Cornh. **33**: 661.
Greek Hymns and Meters. Chr. Rem. **37**: 280.
Greek Idyls. (D. K. Sandford) Ed. R. **63**: 317.
Greek Imagination, Characteristics of. Dub. Univ. **62**: 687. Same art. Ecl. M. **61**: 247.
Greek Inscription from Athens. (D. Wray) Arch. **2**: 216.
Greek Inscriptions. (C. T. Newton) Contemp. **29**: 70.
Greek Interiors. Fraser, **32**: 253.
Greek Lady's Narrative. (H. Aïdé) Lond. Soc. **27**: 452.
Greek Language. (B. J. Wallace) Am. Presb. R. **1**: 259.
— Acquisition of. Knick. **8**: 249.
— and Dialects. (P. Buttman) Am. Bib. Repos. **1**: 692.
— and Hebrew, Affinities of. (J. Strong) Meth. Q. **25**: 430.
— and Sanscrit, Comparative Accentual System of. (W. H. Green) Princ. **27**: 680.
— at the Universities. Quar. **134**: 457.
— Conjunctions in. (J. W. Gibbs) Am. J. Sci. **37**: 112.
— Correlatives in. (J. W. Gibbs) Am. J. Sci. **34**: 337.
— Decline and Corruption of. Quar. **23**: 136.
— Grammar of, Buttmann's. (G. Bancroft) No. Am. **18**: 99. — Am. Mo. R. **4**: 480.
— — Jelf's. (W. W. Goodwin) No. Am. **95**: 317.
— — Kuhner's. (Prof. Harrison) Meth. Q. **4**: 627.
— in Palestine. (Prof. Hug) Am. Bib. Repos. **1**: 530.
— Modern. (J. E. Boise) Bib. Sac. **17**: 634. — Chr. Q. Spec. **9**: 283. — (S. G. Howe) Am. J. Educ. **2**: 193.
— — and its Poetry. (A. L. Koeppen) Mercersb. **12**: 5.
— of New Testament. (G. H. Whittemore) Bapt. Q. **8**: 58.
— — Stuart's Grammar of. U. S. Lit. Gaz. **2**: 72. — (N. L. Frothingham) Chr. Exam. **2**: 144. — (J. A. Alexander) Princ. **7**: 233.
— — Style of. (Prof. Planck) Am. Bib. Repos. **1**: 638.
— — Winer's Grammar of. (J. L. Kingsley) Chr. Mo. Spec. **7**: 425. — Bapt. Q. **3**: 241.
— — Words in, from Hebrew and Aramæan. (L. S. Potwin) Bib. Sac. **33**: 52.
— — — from the Latin. (L. S. Potwin) Bib. Sac. **32**: 703.
See also Bible, New Testament.
— Prepositions in, Harrison on. (J. A. Broadus) Chr. R. **24**: 78. — (J. C. Moffat) Princ. **30**: 661.
— — in compound Words. (Prof. Tittmann) Am. Bib. Repos. **3**: 45.

Greek Language, Pronunciation of. (E. S. Dixwell) No. Am. 80: 49. — (L. R. Packard) New Eng. 30: 24. — (N. P. Seymour) Cong. R. 11: 215. — For. Q. 13: 60. — (J. Brazer) No. Am. 9: 92. — (J. Pickering) No. Am. 10: 272. — So. Lit. Mess. 1: 421. — Anal. M. 14: 88.
— — Blackie on. Ecl. R. 100: 659.
— Shall we give up? (E. A. Freeman) Fortn. 31: 290.
— Study of. (R. Croke) Am. J. Educ. 28: 372. — (M. Stuart) Am. Bib. Repos. 2: 690. — West. R. 4: 225. — Blackw. 109: 182.
— — as a Means of Education. (J. B. Kieffer) Ref. Q. 28: 485.
— Teaching. (T. Dwight) Meth. Q. 26: 90.
— — Experiment in reading at Sight. (A. C. Merriam) Education, 1: 160.
— — Method of. (T. Lewis) Am. J. Educ. 1: 285, 480.
— Verbs in, and in Latin. (W. D. Whitney) Bib. Sac. 7: 654.
Greek Legends and early History. (G. Grote) Westm. 39: 285.
Greek Lexicography. (J. R. Fishlake) Quar. 51: 144. Same art. Am. Bib. Repos. 4: 556. — (G. Bancroft) No. Am. 24: 142. — (F. A. Adams) No. Am. 64: 373. — (T. D. Woolsey) Bib. Sac. 1: 613. — Quar. 22: 302. 75: 157. — Westm. 1: 383. 13: 86. 14: 311. — Meth. Q. 7: 240. — Chr. R. 10: 71. — (C. J. Bloomfield) Quar. 22: 302.
— and English. (J. R. Fishlake) Quar. 75: 293.
Greek Lexicon, Donnegan's. Am. Mo. R. 3: 37.
— Hincks's. Westm. 14: 311.
— Jones's, 1823. Ecl. R. 39: 114. — Westm. 1: 383.
— of New Testament, Robinson's. Chr. Exam. 22: 124. — Chr. R. 2: 136. — Ecl. R. 67: 269. — (M. Stuart) No. Am. 72: 261. — (H. J. Ripley) Chr. R. 16: 461. — (N. L. Frothingham) Chr. Exam. 3: 247.
— Pickering's. (S. H. Taylor) Bib. Sac. 4: 196. — (F. A. Adams) No. Am. 64: 373. — Chr. Exam. 42: 137.
— Schrevelius's. (S. Willard) U. S. Lit. Gaz. 5: 21. — (G. Bancroft) No. Am. 24: 142.
— Sophocles's. O. & N. 2: 731.
— Stephens's Thesaurus. (C. J. Blomfield) Quar. 22: 302. 24: 376.
Greek Literature. (T. De Quincey) Tait, n. s. 5: 763. — Am. Meth. M. 22: 271. — Blackw. 116: 365. — Bentley, 30: 502. — Ecl. R. 73: 51. Same art. Am. Ecl. 2: 39. — Dem. R. 35: 73, 162.
— and Language. (C. C. Felton) No. Am. 42: 94. — Knick. 2: 42. — New Eng. 9: 161. — Prosp. R. 6: 332.
— and Roman, Study of. (C. Siedhof) Bib. Sac. 5: 23.
— Bees in. (C. C. Felton) No. Am. 93: 137.
— History of. So. R. 6: 32, 385.
— in England. Am. J. Educ. 24: 433.
— in Scotland. Westm. 16: 90.
— Modern. (A. Negris) No. Am. 29: 340. — (T. A. L. V. I. Robinson) No. Am. 43: 337. — For. Q. 1: 238. — Mo. R. 114: 429. — Ecl. R. 102: 701. — (E. Wigglesworth) Chr. Exam. 6: 324.
— Müller's. Ecl. R. 73: 51. Same art. Am. Ecl. 2: 39.
— Müller and Donaldson's History of. (T. L. Peacock) Fraser, 59: 357. — Bent. Q. 2: 543.
— Mure's History of. Ed. R. 92: 398. — Brit. Q. 16: 418. — Ecl. R. 91: 737. 97: 663. — Nat. R. 6: 69. 7: 516. — Quar. 87: 434. — New Q. 2: 360. 6: 294. — Tait, n. s. 17: 388. — Westm. 68: 568.
— — and the Attic Historians. (E. A. Freeman) Nat. R. 6: 69.
— — Principal Classical Writers. Am. Q. Reg. 6: 255.
— Quarterly Review on. Westm. 3: 223. 4: 233.
— Study of. (G. B. Cheever) Am. Q. Reg. 4: 273. 5: 33, 218.
— Translations from. Blackw. 37: 652.

Greek Literature, Translations from, German and English. For. Q. 33: 248.
— Written, Origin of. (F. A. Paley) Fraser, 101: 324. Same art. Liv. Age, 145: 30.
Greek MS. on Papyrus. (T. Young) Arch. 19: 156.
Greek Marriage Festival. Penny M. 1: 70.
Greek Meters and English Scholarship. (J. S. Blackie) For. Q. 23: 241.
Greek Mind in Presence of Death. (P. Gardner) Contemp. 31: 144. Same art. Liv. Age, 136: 280. Same art. Sup. Pop. Sci. Mo. 2: 265.
Greek Monasteries of Mount Athos. (B. Murphy) Cath. World, 33: 163.
Greek Names in Shakspere. Cornh. 33: 203.
Greek Novels. Temp. Bar, 1: 407, 565. 2: 357.
Greek Odes. (C. Minnigedore) So. Lit. Mess. 13: 741. 14: 184.
Greek Orators. Ed. R. 36: 82. — (H. Nettleship) Macmil. 35: 40.
Greek Painters. (A. S. Murray) Contemp. 24: 468.
Greek Philosophy, Place of Socrates in. Westm. 114: 19.
— of Taste. *See* Æsthetics.
See also Philosophy.
Greek Physiognomists. Month, 8: 277, 470.
Greek Play at Harvard. *See* Sophocles, Œdipus.
Greek Poetry, No Love in. Internat. M. 2: 123.
— History of. (O. W. B. Peabody) No. Am. 50: 488.
— Lyrical. (H. N. Coleridge) Quar. 49: 349. — Westm. 98: 54. Same art. Liv. Age, 115: 195.
— Metrical Principles of. Ecl. R. 67: 395.
— Modern Lyrical. (E. N. Edmonds) Macmil. 44: 445. Same art. Liv. Age, 151: 482.
— Modern Popular. Knick. 18: 1.
— Pastoral. Dub. Univ. 10: 78.
— Popular. Westm. 2: 149.
— Romaic. Colburn, 38: 316.
Greek Poets. All the Year, 24: 232.
— and Poetry. Dem. R. 34: 164.
— Classical. Am. Mo. R. 1: 15.
— Gnomic. No. Brit. 49: 49.
— Idyllic. No. Brit. 48: 469.
— Lyric, Nine. (M. J. Walhouse) Gent. M. n. s. 18: 433.
— — Pindar. (E. I. Sears) Nat. Q. 32: 203.
— Minor. Fraser, 2: 53.
— Pastoral. Fraser, 12: 222, 394, 541. 13: 92, 600.
— Translations from. Chr. Rem. 52: 429.
Greek Press, Greswell's Early Parisian. Ecl. R. 58: 416. — Select J. 4: [1.
Greek Reader, Jacob's. (G. Bancroft) No. Am. 18: 280. — U. S. Lit. Gaz. 1: 33. — Am. Mo. R. 3: 158.
— Felton's. Chr. Exam. 29: 382.
Greek Remains in Africa. Blackw. 124: 340. Same art. Liv. Age, 139: 111.
Greek Rhythm and Meters. For. Q. 23: 241.
Greek Robbers. Chamb. J. 40: 171.
Greek Romance. St. Paul's, 4: 611.
Greek Romances. For. Q. 5: 108.
— Early. Blackw. 54: 109. 55: 33.
— Early Christian. (S. B. Gould) Contemp. 30: 858.
Greek Scene, An old. Dub. Univ. 62: 423.
Greek Slave, Powers's; a Poem. Internat. M. 2: 88.
Greek Song, A. Dub. Univ. 1: 126.
Greek Songs. Ecl. R. 43: 308.
— of Calabria. Cornh. 44: 725.
Greek Spirit in modern Literature. (R. St. J. Tyrwhitt) Contemp. 29: 552.
Greek Studies, Priority of. (Dr. Fisher) No. Am. 11: 209.
Greek Summer Scene, Ancient. Dub. Univ. 66: 94.
Greek Syntax, Farrar's. (W. W. Goodwin) No. Am. 107: 315.
— Goodwin's. (J. Hadley) No. Am. 102: 201.

Greek Thought and modern Problems. (G. S. Bower) Mod. R. **2**: 765.
— Early. Westm. **113**: 17.
Greek Tragedy. For. Q. **19**: 446. — Blackw. **1**: 39-593. — (T. De Quincey) Blackw. **47**: 145. — Ed. R. **47**: 418. — Month, **4**: 8, 292, 574. **5**: 385.
— Beauties of. Am. Mo. M. **1**: 129, 193.
— Choruses of. (H. W. Herbert) Dem. R. **10**: 25-598.
— Moral Element of. So. M. **17**: 225.
— Thoughts on. Am. Presb. R. **6**: 28.
Greek Tragic Drama. Lond. M. **7**: 625.
— Æschylus. (E. I. Sears) Nat. Q. **7**: 1.
— Sophocles. (E. R. Humphreys) Nat. Q. **2**: 129. — (E. I. Sears) Nat. Q. **13**: 137.
Greek Vases, Painted. Mo. R. **109**: 266.
Greek Waters, Cruise in. St. James, **47**: 39.
— Few Months in. (J. Milner) Once a Week, **16**: 132, 364.
Greek Wedding. Colburn, **23**: 86.
Greek Wisdom. Dub. Univ. **93**: 531. **94**: 71-443.
Greeley, Horace. (J. H. Browne) Harper, **46**: 734. — (G. E. Baker) Republic, **1**: 193. — (W. Chambers) Chamb. J. **50**: 49. — (M. D. Conway) Fraser, **86**: 474. — (J. C. Dent) Once a Week, **27**: 188. — with portrait, Ecl. M. **74**: 496. — with portrait, Ecl. M. **80**: 113. — Chamb. J. **23**: 212. — Nat. Q. **26**: 153. — Penn Mo. **4**: 50. — Putnam, **6**: 76. **11**: 638.
— and his white Hat. All the Year, **28**: 510.
— and P. T. Barnum contrasted. (W. H. Hurlbut) Chr. Exam. **58**: 245.
— as Candidate for Presidency. Mo. Rel. M. **47**: 598. — O. & N. **6**: 253.
— Death of. (E. L. Godkin) Nation, **15**: 362.
— Hints toward Reforms. So. Lit. Mess. **17**: 257.
— in 1872. (T. O. Howe) Republic, **2**: 41.
— Life and Times of, Ingersoll's. Lakeside, **9**: 506.
— Life of. (Sir R. de Camden) Potter Am. Mo. **4**: 417.
— Memoir of. Mo. Rel. M. **49**: 72, 117.
— Recollections of. (T. Weed) Galaxy, **15**: 372.
Green, Ashbell, Address of. Princ. **7**: 529.
— Life of. (J. W. Alexander) Princ. **21**: 563.
— Sermons of. Chr. Mo. Spec. **5**: 307.
Green, Duff, and Horne, Correspondence of. Niles's Reg. **37**: 103, 105, 125.
Green, Ezra. (G. H. Preble) N. E. Reg. **29**: 170.
Green, John, Will of, 1658. N. E. Reg. **5**: 248.
Green, John, and Public Library, Worcester, Mass. Am. J. Educ. **13**: 606.
Green, Martin. Meth. M. **26**: 3.
Green, Samuel. (J. S. Ropes) Cong. Q. **8**: 225.
Green, Thomas Hill, as a Critic. (R. Hodgson, jr.) Contemp. **38**: 898. — (Reply by T. H. Green) Contemp. **39**: 109. — (Answer by H. Spencer) Contemp. **39**: 305.
Green, Wm. Guide to Lakes of England. Blackw. **12**: 84.
Green Genealogy. (S. A. Green) N. E. Reg. **15**: 105.
Green Bay, Wisconsin, Early History of. (A. Grignon) Hist. M. **1**: 324.
— Fluctuations of Water-Level at. (C. Whittlesey) Am. J. Sci. **77**: 305.
— Glacial Features of. (N. H. Winchell) Am. J. Sci. **102**: 15.
Green-Beard and Slyboots. House. Words, **17**: 400.
Green Cloth; a Tale. Putnam, **9**: 530.
Green-Corn Dance of the Creek Indians. (J. H. Payne) Contin. Mo. **1**: 17.
Green Garments. Chamb. J. **13**: 25.
Green-Hand; a short Yarn. (G. Cupples) Blackw. **64**: 743. **65**: 314. **66**: 183-723. **67**: 76-701. **68**: 48, 291, 433.
Green Light. All the Year, **6**: 424.
Green Mantle. Lond. Soc. **8**: 385.
Green Mountains, Vt., Age of. (J. D. Dana) Am. J. Sci. **119**: 191.
— Geology of. (J. D. Dana) Am. J. Sci. **103**: 179, 250.
— Summits of, Glacial Action on. (E. Hungerford) Am. J. Sci. **95**: 1.
— Supposed Change of Level in. (W. K. Scott) Am. J. Sci. **88**: 243. *See also* Vermont.
Green Ring and the Gold Ring. House. Words, **9**: 272.
Green-Room. (E. Herbert) Lond. M. **5**: 236.
— Modern. (J. Knight) Belgra. **32**: 91.
Green Pastures and Piccadilly. (W. Black) Canad. Mo. **11**: 411, 457, 569. **12**: 1-612. **13**: 1. Same art. Liv. Age, **132**: 378-816. **133**: 43-766. **134**: 44-807. **135**: 39-752.
Green Tea; a Tale. All the Year, **22**: 501-572.
Green-Turtle Cay. Chamb. J. **44**: 303.
Greenaway, John. (W. B. Trask) N. E. Reg. **32**: 55.
Greenbacks. (H. Holt) Nation, **5**: 338.
— and the Banks. Bank. M. (N. Y.) **31**: 173.
— and Communism. (G. Walker) Bank. M. (N. Y.) **33**: 248.
— French. Chamb. J. **41**: 817.
— Future of. (H. White) Nation, **28**: 62.
— in Court. (S. G. Fisher) Bank. M. (N. Y.) **24**: 761.
— Redemption of. (J. K. Fisher) Bank. M. (N.Y.) **23**: 35. *See* Legal Tenders.
Greenback Currency. (E. G. Spaulding) Bank. M. (N.Y.) **30**: 438.
Greenback Issues, Powers of. Bank. M. (N. Y.) **30**: 671.
Greenback Party and its Friends, 1878. (H. White) Nation, **27**: 64.
Greenbackers. *See* National Party.
— of the 18th Century. (E. Stanwood) Nation, **27**: 126.
Greene, Mrs. Catharine. (Mrs. C. H. Halsey) Potter Am. Mo. **5**: 749.
Greene, David. (R. Anderson) Cong. Q. **8**: 325.
Greene, George W. Historical Studies. Chr. R. **15**: 255.
Greene, Gen. Nathaniel. (G. E. Ellis) No. Am. **106**: 689. — (R. H. Stoddard) Nat. M. **12**: 391. — (G. W. Greene) Pennsyl. M. **2**: 84.
— Anecdote of. Godey, **21**: 161.
— Bancroft on. Hist. M. **11**: 124. — (G. W. Greene) Hist. M. **12**: 78, 131.
— Life of. (W. F. Allen) Nation, **12**: 323, 450. — (G. W. Greene) Sparks's Am. Biog. **20**: 5. — (W. P. Mason) No. Am. **10**: 183. — (E. Brooks) No. Am. **15**: 416. — (M. Carey) Carey's Mus. **7**: 39, 210. — (G. E. Ellis) No. Am. **113**: 441.
— Memoir of, with portrait. (C. C. Coffin) N. E. Reg. **32**: 373. — West. R. **1**: 270.
— Oration on. (W. Hillhouse) Carey's Mus. **2**: 387.
— Papers of. Hist. M. **13**: 24, 160.
— Retreat from Carolina. (J. T. Headley) Am. Lit. M. **1**: 21.
— Southern Campaign, 1781. M. Am. Hist. **7**: 431.
— vindicated. (G. W. Greene) No. Am. **105**: 332.
Greene, Nath., of Boston, with portrait. Dem. R. **21**: 456.
— Tales from the German. (W. H. Prescott) No. Am. **46**: 156.
Greene, Robert. Temp. Bar, **16**: 551.
— Novels of. Dub. Univ. **47**: 197.
Greene Genealogy. (W. Phillips) N. E. Reg. **4**: 75.
Greenhouses, Domestic. Godey, **20**: 155.
Greenhow, Mrs.; a Poem. Temp. Bar, **30**: 529.
Greenland. (W. Pengelly) Pop. Sci. R. **10**: 267. — St. James, **25**: 658.
— Adventures of eight Sailors in. Meth. M. **29**: 123.
— Ancient and modern. Quar. **18**: 480.
— and Arctic Voyages. Mo. R. **88**: 62.
— and its Inhabitants. Cornh. **20**: 52.
— Colonization of. Penny M. **7**: 385.
— Crantz's History of. Mo. R. **93**: 259.

Greenland, Danish, Rink's. Dub. Univ. 90: 377. — Nature, 17: 57.
— Danish Races in. (Dr. Laing) No. Brit. 4: 77. Same art. Ecl. M. 7: 197. Same art. Liv. Age, 8: 1.
— Days and Nights in. (D. Walker) Good Words, 3: 69.
— Early Settlement of. Am. Church R. 21: 338.
— East, Notes on. (A. Pansch) Fraser, 85: 148. Same art. Ecl. M. 78: 459. Same art. Liv. Age, 112: 619.
— Egede's Description of. (J. Foster) Ecl. R. 30: 185.
— Esquimaux of, Traditions of. Chamb. J. 36: 216-365.
— Föhn of. (N. Hoffmeyer) Geog. M. 4: 225. — Nature, 16: 294.
— Glacier in. (I. I. Hayes) Harper, 44: 204.
— Graah's Expedition to, 1828. Mo. R. 144: 13.
— Historical Memorials of. Dub. R. 27: 35.
— The Land of Desolation. Chamb. J. 49: 390.
— Life in. — Pop. Sci. Mo. 8: 431. — Liv. Age, 102: 436. — Geog. M. 3: 206-291.
— Lost Colonies of. Westm. 27: 139*.
— Montgomery's Poem. Ecl. R. 30: 210.
— Old Norse Colonies of. (I. I. Hayes) Harper, 44: 65.
— Physical Geography of. (W. P. Alcott) Univ. Q. 2: 304. 3: 76.
— Researches in. (E. Whymper) Nature, 7: 8.
— Scoresby's Voyage to, 1822. Ecl. R. 38: 148.
— Statistics of. Geog. M. 3: 177.
Greenlanders, Manners of. Meth. M. 42: 133.
Greenland, N. H., Contributions to History of. N. E. Reg. 22: 451.
— Records of. N. E. Reg. 28: 251, 415. 29: 300.
Greenock, Dour Souters o'. (F. Brown) Peop. J. 7: 99.
Greenough, Horatio. Knick. 7: 343. — (G. H. Calvert) Putnam, 1: 317.
— Chanting Cherubs. (S. F. Cooper) Putnam, 15: 241.
— Statuary of. (G. S. Hillard) New Eng. M. 8: 41.
Greenough, Mrs. S. D. Treason at Home; a Novel. O. & N. 7: 349.
Greenough Genealogy. (J. H. Sheppard) N. E. Reg. 17: 167.
Green Sand. (P. B. Brodie) Recr. Sci. 3: 197.
Greenstead, Essex, Church at. Penny M. 13: 17.
Greenway Court, Residence of Sir Wm. Fairfax. Putnam, 9: 561.
Greenwell, Dora, Religious Writings of. (J. H. Ward) No. Am. 97: 387.
Greenwich, England. Penny M. 1: 97.
— Ancient Palace of. (Mrs. A. T. Thomson) Fraser, 35: 386.
— and Greenwich Men. (J. H. Reynolds) Bentley, 7: 279.
— Wet Easter at. St. Paul's, 10: 596.
Greenwich Fair. Bentley, 11: 511.
Greenwich Hospital. (E. Herbert) Lond. M. 4: 527. — Chamb. J. 42: 571. 46: 572. 49: 398. — Cornh. 12: 631.
— Painted Hall in. Penny M. 7: 1.
Greenwich Naval College. (Com. Usborne) St. James, 38: 21.
Greenwich Observatory. (J. Carpenter) Pop. Sci. R. 11: 267. — (G. Forbes) Good Words, 13: 792, 855. — Chamb. J. 3: 18. 42: 791. — Ed. R. 91: 299. Same art. Liv. Age, 25: 433. — House. Words, 1: 200-222. — Nature, 4: 103. — Penny M. 2: 308.
— Night at. Cornh. 7: 381.
Greenwich Park, Birthplace of Queen Elizabeth. St. James, 11: 491. Same art. Ecl. M. 64: 184.
Greenwich School forty Years ago, 1874. Fraser, 90: 246.
Greenwich Time. Blackw. 63: 354. Same art. Liv. Age, 17: 220. — Chamb. J. 44: 97. Same art. Ecl. M. 69: 84.
Greenwood, F. W. P. Essay on the Lord's Supper. Chr. Exam. 4: 79.
Greenwood, F. W. P., Frothingham's Sermon on. Chr. Exam. 35: 131.
— History of King's Chapel. Am. Mo. R. 3: 497.
— Life and Writings of. (J. H. Morison) Chr. Exam. 36: 227. — (E. S. Gannett) Chr. Exam. 41: 392.
— Sermons of. (F. Parkman) Chr. Exam. 19: 383. 29: 96. — (W. Ware) Chr. Exam. 30: 126, 271. — (H. Ware, jr.) Chr. Exam. 34: 84.
— Sketch of his Life. Mo. Rel. M. 4: 193.
Greenwood Cemetery. (J. G. Wilson) Hours at Home, 7: 359.
Greenwood Shrift; a Poem. (C. Bowles) Blackw. 42: 208.
Greg, Samuel, Sketch of. (H. A. Page) Good Words, 18: 588. Same art. Liv. Age, 135: 185.
Greg, Wm. R. Creed of Christendom. Ecl. R. 94: 410. — Brit. Q. 14: 178.
— Enigmas of Life. (A. V. Dicey) Nation, 16: 371, 386. — (J. Rickaby) Month, 20: 150. — Blackw. 113: 206. Same art. Liv. Age, 117: 53. — Victoria, 20: 439. — (W. H. Browne) So. M. 12: 626.
— Political Essays. (W. Smith) Contemp. 20: 211.
Gregariousness in Cattle and Men. (F. Galton) Macmil. 23: 353.
Gregg, Fort, Defense of. (J. H. Lane) So. Hist. Pap. 3: 19. 9: 102. – (N. Bartlett) So. Hist. Pap. 3: 82. — (C. M. Wilcox) So. Hist. Pap. 4: 18. 9: 168. — (N. H. Harris) So. Hist. Pap. 8: 475.
Gregory I., Pope. (G. F. Goddard) Contemp. 13: 422.
Gregory VII., Pope. (J. H. Perkins) No. Am 61: 20. — (Sir J. Stephen) Ed. R. 81: 143. Same art. Ecl. M. 5: 178. Same art. Liv. Age, 5: 417. — Dub. Univ. 20: 161, 299. — Ecl. R. 74: 288. — (H. M. Johnson) Meth. Q. 5: 504. — (R. Cardwell) Month, 23: 93, 347, 427. — (Count de Montalembert) Month, 24: 370, 502. 25: 104, 235, 379. — (J. Voigt) U. S. Cath. M. 2: 129. — Brownson, 24: 122, 203. — (J. W. De Forest) Galaxy, 14: 604. — (T. S. King) Univ. Q. 14: 285. — Chr. Rem. 1: 241. — Fraser, 74: 649. — New Dom. 20: 97.
— a Poem. (F. Parke) Dub. Univ. 89: 709.
— and his Age. U. S. Cath. M. 4: 513.
— and Henry IV Ecl. R. 95: 360.
— and Sylvester II. Dub. R. 6: 289.
— at Canossa, 8th Centenary of. Dub. R. 83: 107.
— Career of. (S. H. Stackpole) Bapt. Q. 9: 75.
— Dialogues of. (H. J. Coleridge) Month, 18: 321.
— Life of, Bowden's. Ecl. R. 74: 288.
— — Greisley's. Ecl. R. 56: 369.
— Pastoral of. (S. Pegge) Arch. 2: 68.
— Voigt's Character of. U. S. Cath. M. 7: 256.
Gregory XVI. U. S. Cath. M. 5: 445.
— and Pius VIII. Quar. 105: 92.
— Horæ Gregorianæ. Dub. Univ. 30: 224.
— Recollections of. Westm. 70: 85.
Gregory of Nazianzen. Westm. 56: 101. — Kitto, 9: 33. P. Schaff. — Princ. 39: 73.
— and Asceticism. Cong. M. 23: 510.
— Ullmann on. Chr. Obs. 51: 635.
Gregory, Patriarch, of Constantinople, Return of. (F. M. F. Skene) Good Words, 13: 452.
Gregory, Robert, Canon of St. Paul's. Cong. 5: 361.
Gregory, Sir W. H., Governor of Ceylon, with portrait. Dub. Univ. 88: 146.
Gregory Family. N. E. Reg. 23: 304.
Gregory Greedy, Life and Opinions of. Dub. Univ. 4: 328.
Gregory Hipkins the Unlucky. Blackw. 35: 981.
Gregory's Song. Hogg, 1: 24, 36.
Greig, John. Peop. J. 9: 107.
Greig, Sir Samuel, Memoir of. Dub. Univ. 44: 156.
Grellet, Stephen, the Quaker Evangelist. Lond. Q. 18: 156. — Chr. Obs. 62: 483. — Ecl. R. 118: 1. Same art. Liv. Age, 78: 291.

Grenoble. (C. W. Wood) Argosy, **21**: 47.
Grenville, Lord Geo. N. Portugal; a Poem. Quar. **7**: 151.
— Duke of Portland, and Percival. Month, **7**: 124.
Grenville, Sir R., and the Revenge. (R. Lendall) Geog. M. **5**: 233.
Grenvilles, The; Government by Families. (G. S. Venables) Macmil. **1**: 338. — Nat. R. **14**: 375.
Grenville Act. Fraser, **16**: 650. **17**: 521.
Grenville Papers. Ecl. R. **96**: 196. **97**: 210. — Fraser, **45**: 485.
— and Junius. (Sir D. Brewster) No. Brit. **19**: 475.
Gresham, Sir John. Lond. Soc. **2**: 385. **5**: 449.
Gresham, Sir Richard. Lond. Soc. **2**: 385.
Gresham, Sir Thomas, Burgon's Life of. Ecl. R. **71**: 537. — Mo. R. **150**: 259.
Gresham College. Nature, **11**: 2.
Gresley, Wm. Tales. Chr. Rem. **4**: 58, 661.
Gresset, Jean B. L., Writings of. Dub. Univ. **61**: 399.
Gretna. Eng. Dom. M. **15**: 218.
— Past and Present of. (R. Edgar) Good Words, **17**: 834.
Gretna Green. Belgra. **21**: 368. — House. Words, **5**: 198. Same art. Liv. Age, **33**: 560.
Gretti, Béowulf. (C. S. Smith) New Eng. **40**: 49.
Greuze, Jean-Baptiste. (S. Colvin) Portfo. **3**: 114. — (R. N. Wornum) Portfo. **8**: 85.
Grevavoe Elopement. Colburn, **123**: 172–434. **124**: 103, 231.
Grève, Place de. Chamb. J. **26**: 113.
Grewelthorpe Feud; a Story. Temp. Bar, **62**: 37.
Greville, C. C. F. Memoirs, 1818–37. (J. L. Patterson) Month, **24**: 181, 282. — (A. G. Stapleton) Macmil. **31**: 151, 203. — (E. L. Stanley) Fortn. **22**: 798. — Appleton, **13**: 113, 141. — Ed. R. **140**: 528. Same art. Liv. Age, **124**: 3. — Am. Law R **10**: 39. — Brit. Q. **61**: 150. — Canad. Mo. **7**: 226. — Chr. Obs. **75**: 122. — Penn Mo. **6**: 211. — Quar. **138**: 1. Same art. Liv. Age, **124**: 515. — Liv. Age, **123**: 730. — Fraser, **90**: 777. Same art. Ecl. M. **84**: 173. — New Q. **1**: 109. — Temp. Bar, **43**: 215, 499.
— and other Memoirs. Westm. **103**: 385.
— compared with Memoirs of Saint Simon. (M. Walsh) Cath. World, **21**: 266.
Gréville, H. Sketches of Russian Life. (W. R. S. Ralston) 19th Cent. **4**: 408.
Greville's Wife. Eng. Dom. M. **12**: 1–321. **13**: 1–129.
Grey, Earl. Dub. Univ. **4**: 291. — Liv. Age, **6**: 514.
— Administration of. Fraser, **11**: 113.—Colburn, **32**: 154.
— and Earl Spencer. (Lord J. Russell) Ed. R. **83**: 240.
— Colonial Administration. Fraser, **47**: 485.
— Correspondence on Reform Act, 1832. Fraser, **76**: 347.
— — with William IV. Ed. R. **125**: 517.
— Dinner to. Fraser, **10**: 480.
— Fall of. Blackw. **36**: 246. — Mus. **25**: 344.
— Ministry of. Tait, **3**: 71.
— Oratory of. Fraser, **33**: 466.
— Political Portrait of. St. James, **24**: 826.
Grey, Lady Jane. (H. W. Herbert) Godey, **42**: 97. — Am. Cath. Q. **1**: 680. — (D. Hume) Ecl. M. **19**: 558. — Colburn, **128**: 164. — Sharpe, **52**: 153. — Penny M. **2**: 55. — (C. White) Peop. J. **10**: 59.
— and her Times. Mus. **2**: 362.
— Life at Bradgate Park. Lond. M. **5**: 166.
Grey, The. (J. Lie) Liv. Age, **142**: 418.
Grey Cottage. (Mrs. Claxton) Argosy, **29**: 138.
Grey Friars, Letter of Filiation among. (C. Ord) Arch. **11**: 85.
Grey Mullet, The. Penny M. **11**: 369.
Grey Wolf and the Doctor; an Indian Sketch. (C. G. Leland) Temp. Bar, **45**: 185.
Grey Woman; a Tale. All the Year, **4**: 300, 321, 347.
Greyfriars, the Blue-Coat School. All the Year, **26**: 590.
Greyson, R. E. H., Correspondence of. Ecl. R. **106**: 271.
Greystone Hall. Ecl. M. **40**: 86. — Liv. Age, **51**: 685.
Greytown and adjacent Country. (S. P. Oliver) Nature, **4**: 206.
— Destruction of. Dem. R. **34**: 281.
Gridley, Maj.-Gen. Richard. Univ. Q. **33**: 314.
Grierson, Gen. Benjamin H. (G. M. McConnel) U. S. Serv. M. **5**: 424.
Griesbach, John J., Accuracy of. Gen. Repos. **1**: 89.
— Rothe's Memoir of. Colburn, **2**: 132.
Griffin, Bartholomew. (S. Lanier) Internat. R. **6**: 284.
Griffin, Clement, old Mathematician. Liv. Age, **17**: 589.
Griffin, Cyrus. (C. F. Taylor) Pennsyl. M. **3**: 317.
Griffin, Edward D. Convention Sermon. Chr. Mo. Spec. **10**: 541.
— Memoirs of, with portrait. (A. Nash) Am. Q. Reg. **13**: 365.
— Memoirs and Sermons. (J. Woodbridge) Lit. & Theo. R. **6**: 221. — Chr. R. **4**: 356. — (S. Miller) Princ. R. **11**: 404.
— Personal Reminiscences of. (S. H. Cox) Am. Presb. R. **6**: 587.
— Preaching of. (G. Shepard) Am. Bib. Repos. 3d s. **3**: 623.
— Remains of. (R. Palmer) Chr. Q. **3**: 651. — Am. Q. **10**: 475. — So. R. **8**: 326. — Blackw. **32**: 91. — (N. L. Frothingham) Chr. Exam. **11**: 270. — Am. Mo. R. **1**: 19. — Mus. **21**: 189. — (W. C. Bryant) No. Am. **34**: 119.
Griffin, Gerald. (H. Giles) Chr. Exam. **78**: 346. — Dub. Univ. **89**: 534.
— and Works. (J. G. McGee) Cath. World, **11**: 398, 667.
— Life of. Dub. Univ. **23**: 157. — Mo. R. **162**: 540. — Dub. R. **15**: 387. Same art. Ecl. M. **2**: 89.
— Works of. Dub. R. **16**: 281. — Brownson, **16**: 342.
Griffin, John, Memoir of. Cong. M. **17**: 501. **24**: 569. — Ecl. R. **73**: 155.
Griffin, Kirtland. (Z. Paddock) Nat. M. **12**: 532.
Griffin Genealogy. (G. Chandler) N. E. Reg. **13**: 108.
Griffin, La Salle's Ship, Construction and first Voyage of, 1679. Hunt, **7**: 252.
Griffins. House. Words, **15**: 427.
— in Switzerland. Colburn, **93**: 228–313.
Griffith, Charles. Port Philip. Dub. Univ. **25**: 173.
Griffith, Sir Richard, with portrait. Dub. Univ. **83**: 432. — (E. Hull) Nature, **18**: 627.
Griffith, Walter S. (H. H. McFarland) Cong. Q. **16**: 215.
Griffith Gaunt. (C. Reade) Argosy, **1**: 1–453. **2**: 1–409. Same art. Atlan. **16**: 641. **17**: 100–751. **18**: 94–606.
Griffith's Double; a Tale. (C. Hoey) All the Year, **35**: 217–567. **36**: 19, 500.
Griffiths, J. Travels. (M. Napier) Ed. R. **8**: 35.
Griffiths, Joseph, Memoir of. Cong. M. **1**: 337.
Griffone. (W. F. P. Napier) Bentley, **3**: 601. **4**: 74.
Grigg, John, with portrait. Hunt, **25**: 28. **49**: 249. — with portrait, De Bow, **13**: 201.
Grigg, Wm., with portrait. De Bow, **10**: 348.
Grigglebone Heir; a Poem. (C. Wilson) Dub. Univ. **45**: 219.
Grignon, Agricultural School at. Am. J. Educ. **21**: 564.
Grillparzer, Franz. Fraser, **46**: 213.
— Ancestress. (R. P. Gillies) Blackw. **6**: 247.
— Golden Fleece. (N. L. Frothingham) No. Am. **16**: 283. — (R. P. Gillies) Blackw. **24**: 155.
— King Ottakar. (R. P. Gillies) Blackw. **22**: 300.
— Sappho. (R. P. Gillies) Blackw. **21**: 404. — Mo. R. **94**: 253.
Grimaldi, Joseph. Bentley, **19**: 160. — Mo. R. **145**: 499.
— Genius of Pantomime. Temp. Bar, **55**: 94. Same art. Liv. Age, **140**: 497.
— Recollections of. Colburn, **50**: 375.
Grimes, James W. (A. S. Hill) No. Am. **123**: 186.

Grimke, Fred., on Free Institutions. (J. H. Perkins) No. Am. **69**: 440.
Grimke, Thos. S., Address of. Chr. Mo. Spec. **10**: 208.
— Discourses of. (C. C. Felton) Chr. Exam. **10**: 192.
— Letter on Public Affairs, 1829. Niles's Reg. **37**: 56.
— Sketch of. West. M. **2**: 613.
Grimm, Frederick Melchior, Baron. Colburn, **1**: 147.
— Correspondence. (J. H. Merivale) Quar. **9**: 89. **10**: 57. **11**: 399.
Grimm, Hermann. Invincible Powers. O. & N. **1**: 249.
Grimm, Jacob, Autobiography of. Ecl. M. **5**: 171.
— Correspondence of. (F. Jeffrey) Ed. R. **21**: 263. **23**: 292. — Quar. **9**: 89. **10**: 57. **11**: 399. — Anal. M. **2**: 359.
— Memoirs of. (W. Tudor) No. Am. **1**: 27, 196.
Grimm, Jacob and William. (G. J. Adler) No. Am. **100**: 390. — Chr. Exam. **77**: 232.
— German popular Stories. Lond. M. **7**: 91. — All the Year, **20**: 187.
Grimm's Ghost. Colburn, **4**: 63–398. **5**: 537. **7**: 38–365. **8**: 105–355. **10**: 111–369. **11**: 12–562.
Grimm's Law. (F. A. March) No. Am. **125**: 177. — (Lord Neaves) Blackw. **102**: 735. — (A. H. Sayce) Nature, **15**: 309.—(W. D. Whitney) Nation, **25**: 75.
Grimmelshausen, H. J. C. von. The adventurous Simplicissimus. (H. Tuttle) Gent. M. n. s. **17**: 41.
Grimston, Edward, Portrait of. Arch. **40**: 451.
— Will of. Arch. **45**: 124.
Grinding Wheel. Pract. M. **5**: 307.
Grindstone, How to use a. Pract. M. **3**: 173.
Grinfield, Thomas, Poems of. Ecl. R. **22**: 273.
Gringe Family. House. Words, **19**: 52.
Gringore, Pierre, Satires of. Retros. **17**: 198.
Grinnell Land, Who discovered? No. Am. **78**: 254.
Griper Greg. House. Words, **7**: 301.
Gripis-Spa, from the Elder Edda. Fraser, **89**: 227.
Griscom, John. Am. J. Educ. **8**: 325.
— Tour in Europe. (G. Ticknor) No. Am. **18**: 178.
Griselda. Chamb. J. **6**: 152.
Griselda; a Drama. Dub. Univ. **16**: 440.
Griselda, the Clerk's Tale; Remade from Chaucer. Blackw. **41**: 655.
Griselda; a Study at the Princess's Theater. (G. A. Sala) Belgra. **22**: 246.
Grisette, The. Putnam, **10**: 208.
Grisi, Giulia. (D. Cook) Once a Week, **5**: 218. — So. Lit. Mess. **7**: 242.
Grisquet, M., Prefect of Police, Memoirs of. Mo. R. **155**: 277.
Griswold, Alex. V, Bishop. (S. K. Lothrop) Chr. Exam. **39**: 248. — (S. W. S. Dutton) New Eng. **3**: 227.
Griswold, Chester A., So. Lit. Mess. **4**: 310.
Griswold, Rufus W. Knick. **36**: 162.
— Female Poets of America. (M. E. Montegut) Internat. M. **3**: 452.
Griswold, Fort, Groton, Conn., Massacre of. (C. B. Todd) M. Am. Hist. **7**: 161.
Grit. (E. P. Whipple) Atlan. **15**: 407.
Grizzly Papers. Overland, **6**: 92–563.
Groac'h, The. (E. Souvestre) So. M. **8**: 460.
Gröben Goblin. All the Year, **25**: 141.
Grondet, Madame. Liv. Age, **43**: 235.
Gronow, Capt. Rees H., last of the Dandies. (A. H. Guernsey) Harper, **25**: 745.
— Recollections of. Chamb. J. **38**: 182. **40**: 115.
— Reminiscences of. St. James, **5**: 393.
Grooves. (G. Stott) Belgra. **8**: 136.
Grosseteste, Robert. Meth. M. **58**: 345.
— Letters. Chr. Rem. **52**: 88. — Month, **39**: 591.
Grossi, Tommaso. I Lombardi alla prima Crocieta. For. R. 1: 238.
Grossi, Tommaso. Marco Visconti. For. Q **15**: 139. — Chr. Rem. **10**: 461.
Grosvenor Gallery. (A. D. Atkinson) Portfo. **8**: 97. — (S. Colvin) Fortn. **27**: 820. — (H. H. Statham) Macmil. **36**: 112. — (O. Wilde) Dub. Univ. **90**: 118. — Dub. Univ. **94**: 66. — Am. Arch. **6**: 29, 92.
Grote, George. (J. Davies) Contemp. **22**: 393. — (A. V. Dicey) Nation, **17**: 370. — (J. Owen) Theo. R. **10**: 503. — with portrait, (G. M. Towle) Appleton, **6**: 85. — with portrait, Ecl. M. **95**: 377. — with portrait, Ev. Sat. **9**: 442. — Chamb. J. **50**: 437. — Ed. R. **138**: 218. — Lond. Q. **42**: 393. — Quar. **135**: 98.
— as a Historian. (A. V. Dicey) Nation, **19**: 91.
— Death of. Ev. Sat. **11**: 42.
— Personal Life of. Chr. Obs. **73**: 633. — Westm. **100**: 129. Same art. Liv. Age, **118**: 451.
— Recollections of. (L. A. Tollemache) Macmil. **27**: 489. Same art. Ev. Sat. **14**: 509.
— Reminiscences of. (G. W. Greene) Atlan. **44**: 770.
Grote, Mrs. George. Eng. Dom. M. **16**: 120, 176. — Victoria, **32**: 379.
Grotesque in Things sorrowful. Lond. Soc. **1**: 425.
Grotesque Design, as exhibited in Art. Art J. **14**: 89.
Grotius, Hugo. (S. S. Hebberd) Univ. Q. **28**: 460.
— and his Times. (S. Osgood) Chr. Exam. **42**: 1.
— and the Source of International Law. Ed. R. **112**: 386.
— Anecdotes of. Meth. M. **48**: 249.
— Defense of. (F. H. Foster) Bib. Sac. **36**: 616.
— Life of. So. R. **1**: 457. — Mo. R. **112**: 337.
— on War and Peace, Whewell's. Fraser, **49**: 479.
Groton, Conn., Attack on, 1781. N. E. Reg. **10**: 127. *See also* Griswold, Fort.
Groton, Mass., Inscriptions at. N. E. Reg. **21**: 212.
— Materials for History of. N. E. Reg. **10**: 186, 243.
— Ministers of. Am. Q. Reg. **11**: 259.
— Petition, 1655. N. E. Reg. **14**: 48.
Grotta Ferrata. Art J. **7**: 199.
— Fair at. St. James, **44**: 416.
Grotto of Han. All the Year, **26**: 473.
Grottos and Groves. (C. Kingsley) Good Words, **12**: 323.
— Legends connected with. (W. F. Ainsworth) Colburn, **78**: 217.
— of the Nahr-El-Kelb. (J. Robertson) Good Words, **16**: 769.
Grouchy, Marshal. Anal. M. **13**: 473. **15**: 24.
Ground and lofty Tumbling. House. Words, **19**: 121.
Ground-Air, Hygienic Relations of. (M. von Pettenkoffer) Pop. Sci. Mo. **11**: 280.
Ground Swell; a Poem. Dub. Univ. **12**: 631.
Grouse. Quar. **118**: 1.
— American. Penny M. **10**: 186. — (C. E. Whitehead) Scrib. **14**: 417.
— of Europe. Penny M. **4**: 321, 329.
— Sand. All the Year, **10**: 78.
— What has become of them? Chamb. J. **29**: 86.
Grouse Drive. Chamb. J. **48**: 494.
Grouse Driving. Blackw. **113**: 328.
Grouse Hunting, Two Days of. Once a Week, **11**: 143.
Grouse Shooting. (A. Forbes) Gent. M. n. s. **13**: 305. — (J. Searle) Lippinc. **4**: 272. — Bentley, **4**: 271. — Broadw. **2**: 471.
— in Cantyre. (W. G. Starbuck) Temp. Bar, **18**: 56.
— in Galloway. (R. Somers, jr.) Lippinc. **14**: 483.
— in Scotland. Temp. Bar, **15**: 219. **18**: 56.
Groux, Charles C. A. de. Art J. **18**: 266.
Grove, W. R., with portrait. Appleton, **3**: 324.
Grove's Calendar of Nature. Dub. Univ. **34**: 217.
Groves, A. N. Indian Missions. Lond. Q **8**: 329.
Groves of Blarney Antiquary, **1**: 199.
Groweth down like a Toadstool; a Tale. (L. Broughton) St. James, **39**: 1–293. **40**: 81, 184.

Growing old. Cornh. 5: 495. — (D. M. Craik) Chamb. J. 28: 393. Same art. Liv. Age, 56: 321. — (A. K. H. Boyd) Fraser, 61: 787. — (A. K. H. Boyd) Fraser, 88: 262. Same art. Ecl. M. 50: 524.
— Art of not. (A. H. Currier) Bost. R. 6: 355.
— gracefully. (Mrs. C. M. Kirkland) Peop. J. 11: 211.
Growth. Univ. Q. 20: 393.
— a Necessity. (T. B Thayer) Univ. Q. 23: 101.
— and Progress. (A. R. Abbott) Univ. Q. 25: 261.
— Correlated. (W. W. Kinsley) Penn Mo. 7: 257.
Grubb, Thomas. Nature, 18: 570.
Grube, Adolph Edouard, Obituary of. Nature, 22: 435.
Grumbler, Thoughts of a. Am. Q. 22: 415. — (F. W. P. Greenwood) Chr. Exam. 23: 208.
Grumbling, Pleasures of. (A. B. Reach) Colburn, 74: 49.
Grün, Anastasius. Fraser, 46: 213. — Tait, n. s. 21: 257.
Grund, Francis J. The Americans. (C. Sumner) No. Am. 46: 106. — (S. Gilman) Chr. Exam. 24: 296.
Grundtvig, N. F. S. Ev. Sat. 13: 460.
Grundy, Felix, with portrait. Dem. R. 3: 161.
Grundy, Rev. T., Memoir of. Cong. M. 11: 281.
Grundy, Mrs. (E. Spencer) N. Ecl. 6: 335.
Gryll Grange. (T. L. Peacock) Fraser, 61: 447, 611, 757. 62: 47-705.
Guacho's Victim. Chamb. J. 48: 823.
Guaco or Snake-Plant. Chamb. J. 16: 343.
— Account of. (G. Bellamy) Meth. M. 44: 901.
— Virtues of. Meth. M. 41: 41.
Guadaloupe. Penny M. 12: 221.
Guadalupe, Cal., Fauna of. (S. Watson) Am. Natural. 10: 221.
Guadalupe, Our Lady of. Cath. World, 13: 189.
Gualberto's Victory; a Poem. Cath. World, 13: 96.
Guanajuato, In and under. (A. S. Evans) Overland, 4: 430.
Guano. (C. Colby) De Bow, 19: 219. — Chamb. J. 1: 135, 383. — House. Words, 6: 42. Same art. Liv. Age, 36: 199. — Chamb. J. 6: 333. Same art. Liv. Age, 12: 173. — (J. R. Blake) Land We Love, 2: 261. — Nat. M. 3: 553.
— and the Guano Trade. (E. R. Boyle) Hunt, 34: 430.
— Analysis of. (J. Davy) Ed. New Philos. J. 37: 313.
— Colombian. (C. Morfit) J. Frankl. Inst. 60: 325.
— Discovery of. Liv. Age, 1: 197.
— Experiments in Formation of. (J. Davy) Ed. New Philos. J. 38: 226.
— from Yorkshire Coast. Liv. Age, 3: 72.
— History and Uses of. De Bow, 16: 459.
— in the Cane-Field. De Bow, 17: 213.
— Peruvian, Early Hist. of. Ed. New Philos. J. 37: 409.
— Rock, from the Islands of the Caribbean Sea. (W. J. Taylor) Am. J. Sci. 74: 177.
— South American and African. (J. Davy) Ed. New Philos. J. 36: 290. Same art. Liv. Age, 1: 344.
— under the Microscope. Recr. Sci. 2: 63.
Guano Islands. Chamb. J. 35: 17.
— Phosphatic of the Pacific Ocean. (J. D. Hague) Am. J. Sci. 84: 224.
Guano Trade. Hunt, 11: 287, 381.
Guaranty and Suretyship. Hunt, 1: 418.
Guards' Ball. Lond. Soc. 4: 184.
Guard-Room Gossip. St. James, 25: 564.
Guardian Angel. (O. W. Holmes) Atlan. 19: 1-641. 20: 1-641.
Guardsmen, The three. Blackw. 57: 59.
Guarini, J. B., Homes and Haunts of. (T. A. Trollope) Belgra. 37: 190.
Guatemala. (C. Cushing) No. Am. 26: 127. — (E. Steele) Overland, 4: 252.
— Backwoods of. (F. L. Oswald) Lippinc. 25: 536.
— Brief Hist. of. (J. J. Peatfield) Overland, 14: 159, 215.
— Dunn on. Ecl. R. 49: 230.
Guatemala, Montgomery's Journey to, 1838. Mo. R. 152: 170.
— Sketch of. Colburn, 14: 578. 15: 63.
Guattari Atmospheric Telegraph. Nature, 2: 257.
Gubmuh. Lond. Soc. 25: 332.
Gude Conceit o' Oursel's. House. Words, 17: 260.
Gudin, Theodore, Obituary of. Art J. 32: 300.
Gudrun, Poem of. (F. Carter) New Eng. 34: 253.
Gudrun the Trusty. (H. Eckford) Penn Mo. 7: 93.
Guelph in Upper Canada, with plate. Fraser, 2: 456.
Guerero, Mexico, Coal and Iron Ore in. (N. S. Manross) Am. J. Sci. 89: 309.
Guerilla, The. Fraser, 36: 546, 719. 37: 224.
Guerilla Chief of Erlau. Sharpe, 18: 26.
Guérin, Eugénie de. (M. Arnold) Cornh. 7: 784. Same art. Liv. Age, 78: 66. — (G. Cerny) Cath. World, 3: 834. — (J. C. Colquhoun) Contemp. 4: 218. — (W. Forsyth) Ed. R. 120: 249. — (H. James, jr.) Nation, 1: 752. — Ecl. R. 123: 443. — Liv. Age, 80: 291. — Lond. Q. 26: 191. — Month, 5: 73, 319. — Nat. R. 12: 145. Same art. Liv. Age, 69: 3.
— and Maurice de. Cath. World, 1: 214. — Month, 1: 506. — (R. P. Dunn) Princ. 37: 544.
— — Home of. (M. A. Carey) Cath. World, 3: 411.
— Character of. (W. R. Alger) Mo. Rel. M. 36: 45.
— Journal and Letters. Chr. Rem. 47: 1. — Liv. Age, 75: 422. — (M. Trebutien) Victoria, 6: 289. — (H. James, jr.) Nation, 3: 206. — Liv. Age, 85: 141.
— Letters from Paris. (M. A. Carey) Cath. World, 3: 474.
— A Philistine's Opinion of. Victoria, 8: 162. Same art. Liv. Age, 92: 67.
Guérin, Maurice de. (M. Arnold) Fraser, 67: 47. — (H. James, jr.) Nation, 4: 187. — (V. Vaughan) Galaxy, 3: 790. — (A. Young) Cath. World, 4: 685.
— Character of (W. R. Alger) Mo. Rel. M. 36: 153.
— Journal of. (J. H. Senter) Chr. Exam. 82: 328.
— Journal, Letters, and Poems of. Chr. Rem. 47: 1.
Guernsey and Jersey, Ecclesiastical Affairs of. (H. Ellis) Arch. 31: 385.
— — Inglis on. Mo. R. 134: 126.
— and Sark. (G. E. Waring, jr.) Scrib. 10: 574.
— Duncan's History of. Mo. R. 156: 201.
— Educational Movement in. Victoria, 17: 271.
— in Midwinter. Tinsley, 2: 200.
— Out Marketing in. Temp. Bar, 20: 120.
— Reception of Queen Victoria at. (Mrs. White) Sharpe, 49: 145.
— State and Prospects of. Dub. Univ. 28: 624, 703.
— Visit to L'Ancresse. Once a Week, 11: 398.
See Channel Islands.
Guerrazzi, Francesco D. Autobiography. Ecl. R. 90: 22.
Guerre, Martin. All the Year, 18: 20.
— Case of. (E. Ashby) Lippinc. 9: 163. — Month, 14: 412.
— Imposture of. Tinsley, 10: 213.
Guerry, Abbé de, with portrait. Ev. Sat. 11: 55.
Guesclin, Bertrand du, and his Times. (W. H. Browne) So. R. n. s. 2: 284.
Guess; a Tale. All the Year, 18: 209.
Guest for the Night. House. Words, 6: 175.
Guest of Glenstrae; a Highland Story. (G. C. Munro) Peop. J. 4: 152.
Guest that won't go. (L. Blanchard) Colburn, 56: 518.
Guest's Confession. (H. James, jr.) Atlan. 30: 385, 566.
Guest's Story. House. Words, 6: 602.
Guests; a Poem. (C. Thaxter) Scrib. 14: 559.
Guette, Catherine de la, Sketch of. Once a Week, 14: 660, 688, 714. 15: 6.
Guggenbühl, Dr., and the Hospital of the Abenberg. Hogg, 2: 373.
Guiana, British. Chamb. J. 55: 233, 384
— — Alone in the Forest. Argosy, 5: 24.
— — and its Missionaries. Hogg, 1: 378.

Guiana, British, Dalton's History of. Colburn, **103**: 210. Same art. Liv. Age, **44**: 783. — Ecl. R. **101**: 708.
— — In the Wilds of. (M. Flint) Temp. Bar, **58**: 182.
— — Indian Picture-Writing in. (C. B. Brown) Anthrop. J. **2**: 254.
— — Naturalist's El Dorado. All the Year, **44**: 295.
— — Population of. (Earl Grey) J. Statis. Soc. **15**: 228.
— — Schomburgk on, 1840. Mo. R. **154**: 395.
— — Tribes of. (W. Harper) Anthrop. J. **6**: 324.
— Cayenne and French. Colburn, **137**: 1.
— Dutch. (W. G. Palgrave) Fortn. **24**: 801. **25**: 194, 536. Same art. Liv. Age, **128**: 154–726. **129**: 409.
— Natives of. (R. Schomburgk) Ed. New Philos. J. **41**: 361. — Penny M. **6**: 486.
Guicciardini, Francesco. Personal and Political Records. Quar. **131**: 416. Same art. Liv. Age, **111**: 579.
— Unpublished Writings of. Ed. R. **130**: 1.
Guiccioli, Countess. Galaxy, **8**: 558.
Guiche, Count de, Scenes in Life of. Fraser, **32**: 647.
Guides, Talk about. (M. S. Cummins) Atlan. **13**: 649.
Guide-Book, Early Roman. (J. Kempe) Gent. M. n. s. **27**: 597.
Guide-Books. Ed. R. **138**: 483.
— Old and new. Temp. Bar, **5**: 542.
Guido and Julius, Tholuck's. (F. W. Kremer) Mercersb. **8**: 198.
Guido the Witless. Lond. M. **2**: 369.
Guignet, Adrien. (P. G. Hamerton) Portfo. **5**: 142.
Guild of Literature and Art. Chamb. J. **15**: 321. Same art. Ecl. M. **23**: 401.
Guilds, Ancient, in England. (R. Cardwell) Month, **16**: 107. — (H. Pidgeon) Reliquary, **3**: 61.
— — and new Friendly and Trade Societies. (J. M. Ludlow) Fortn. **12**: 390. — (J. M. Ludlow) Contemp. **21**: 553, 737.
— Brentano's History of. (W. F. Allen) Nation, **11**: 354.
— English. (J. H. A. Bone) Atlan. **39**: 278. — Ed. R. **134**: 342.
— of the Church. Am. Ch. Mo. **3**: 334.
— of London. All the Year, **36**: 511, 532. — Fraser, **99**: 395. — Temp. Bar, **15**: 293. — Westm. **108**: 1.
See Companies.
Guild Clerk's Tale. House. Words, **2**: 437.
Guildhall, Riches at. Chamb. J. **24**: 355. Same art. Ecl. M. **37**: 423.
Guilford, Lord, North's Life of. (T. N. Talfourd) Retros. **2**: 238. — Dub. Univ. **10**: 185.
Guilford, Nathan. (W. T. Coggeshall) Am. J. Educ. **8**: 289.
Guilford, Ct., History of. (T. Ruggles) Hist. M. **15**: 225.
Guilford, Vt., Congregational Church at. (P. H. White) Cong. Q. **8**: 283.
Guillaume Dupuytren. Hogg, **1**: 265.
Guillotin, Dr. J. I. Chamb. J. **1**: 218.
— and the Sanson Family. All the Year, **36**: 6.
Guillotine, The. (J. W. Croker) Quar. **73**: 235. — Ev. Sat. **9**: 102, 286.
— Execution by. (J. A. Renshaw) Land We Love, **4**: 132.
— Revelations of. Colburn, **128**: 253.
Guillotined, How it feels to be. (L. Favour) Lakeside, **6**: 59.
Guilty and not guilty; a Novel. (M. S. Schwartz) St. James, **47**: 1–325. **48**: 42–434. **49**: 1–432.
Guilty or not guilty? All the Year, **6**: 344.
Guilty or not guilty? (S. B.-Gould) St. James, **17**: 484.
Guilty or not guilty? St. James, **19**: 453.
Guilty or not guilty? Sharpe, **26**: 373.
Guilty Thought; a Tale. Chamb. J. **32**: 151, 168.
Guimard, Marie Madeleine. Temp. Bar, **52**: 523.
Guinea, Fashions in. (Mrs. B. Hartley) Harper, **37**: 160.
— Indian Tribes of. Chamb. J. **46**: 173.
— Mission of. U. S. Cath. M. **7**: 135.
Guinea, Northern, Superstitions of. (J. L. Wilson) Princ. **27**: 600.
Guinea-Coast Smugglers. Chamb. J. **38**: 340.
Guinea Men. Chamb. J. **26**: 343.
Guinea Pigs. Chamb. J. **29**: 278.
Guinea Trade. (R. Postans) Bentley, **19**: 118.
Guinea Traders. Chamb. J. **20**: 269.
Guinea, the Coin, Origin of. Ev. Sat. **9**: 299.
Guineas an Incumbrance on Commerce. (H. Brougham) Ed. R. **2**: 101.
Guinea Box; a Story. (J. Payn) Cornh. **41**: 699. Same art. Liv. Age, **146**: 101.
Guion, Johanna Mary, Lady, Brooke's Life of. Ecl. R. **6**: 615.
Guipuzcoan Dances, Ancient. For. R. **2**: 334. **4**: 198.
Guiraud, Alexandre. Les Machabées. Lond. M. **6**: 341.
Guise, Henri, Duc de. Lond. Soc. **28**: 399.
— Assassination of. Ecl. M. **31**: 127.
Guise, Dukes and Cardinals of. Lond. Q. **1**: 442. Same art. Ecl. M. **31**: 508.
Guise, House of. Blackw. **68**: 1, 456. Same art. Ecl. M. **21**: 118. Same art. Liv. Age, **27**: 105.
Guise, Social Palace at. (E. Howland) Harper, **44**: 701.
Guitar, The. Penny M. **9**: 390, 394.
Guizot, François P. G. (Countess de Bury) No. Am. **87**: 184. — (A. Coquerel) O. & N. **11**: 46. — (A. Laugel) Nation, **19**: 248. — Lippinc. **7**: 110. — (J. Ward) Bentley, **23**: 435. — Brit. Q. **7**: 125. — Fraser, **27**: 145. — Blackw. **42**: 760. **56**: 786. — Ecl. M. **11**: 15. **83**: 606. — Liv. Age, **4**: 99. — Dub. Univ. **29**: 243, 265. — Ecl. Mus. **1**: 543. — (S. B. Treat) Am. Ecl. **2**: 231. — with portrait, Appleton, **11**: 769. — Ev. Sat. **17**: 440. — Lond. Q. **44**: 62. — with portrait. (D. Clarke) N. E. Reg. **29**: 129.
— and English Revolution. Fraser, **41**: 340.
— and the French Revolution, 1830. Colburn, **82**: 395.
— and Milton. Blackw. **43**: 303.
— and the Papacy. No. Brit. **36**: 139. Same art. Ecl. M. **55**: 504.
— and Right of Search. For. Q. **35**: 114.
— and the Spectator. Macmil. **23**: 347.
— at Val Richer. Fortn. **29**: 121.
— Character and Works of. (R. W. Lubienski) Overland, **13**: 410.
— Commission Historique, and English Record Commission. For. Q. **17**: 197.
— Essays and Lectures in History. (J. S. Mill) Ed. R. **82**: 381.
— Life of. Mo. R. **164**: 561. — Temp. Bar, **42**: 472. Same art. Liv. Age, **123**: 749.
— Meditations on Christianity. (M. Vilet) Cath. World, **7**: 338, 464. — (A. Stevens) Meth. Q. **25**: 485.
— Memoirs of his own Time. (J. Wilson) Fortn. **8**: 257. — Quar. **124**: 116. — Bentley, **43**: 501. — Bent. Q. **2**: 69. — Brit. Q. **28**: 149. — Chr. Obs. **59**: 221. — Colburn, **114**: 470. — Lond. Q. **12**: 335. Same art. Ecl. M. **48**: 334. — Ed. R. **108**: 408. — Fraser, **57**: 673. — No. Brit. **31**: 1.
— Ministry of Public Instruction. Quar. **84**: 238. — Am. J. Educ. **11**: 254, 357.
— on Democracy in France. Blackw. **48**: 522.
— on Modern History. For. Q. **16**: 407. — Ed R. **82**: 198. Same art. Ecl. M. **6**: 495.
— on Washington. (E Everett) No. Am. **51**: 69. — Dub. Univ. **17**: 295.
— on Washington and Monk. Liv. Age, **28**: 186.
— Personal and Political Life of. Quar. **94**: 122. Same art. Ecl. M. **32**: 1.
— Private Life of. (K. Hillebrand) Contemp. **39**: 478 Same art. Liv. Age, **149**: 104. — Appleton, **24**: 460 — (A. Laugel) Nation, **30**: 451, 471. **31**: 6.
— Sketch of. Chamb. J. **3**: 262.

Guizot, François P. G. Soirée at Monsieur Guizot's. Colburn, 60: 441.
Guizot, Mme. E. C. P., Life and Writings. Sharpe, 4: 153, 168, 185. Same art. Ecl. M. 12: 162.
Gully of Bluemansdyke. Lond. Soc. 40: supp. 23.
Gulf of Mexico and its Commerce. (M. Tarver) West. J. 7: 219.
— Basin of. (J. E. Hilgard) Am. J. Sci. 121: 288.
— Commercial Advantages of. (M. F. Maury) De Bow, 7: 510.
— Connection of, with Atlantic Ocean. De Bow, 20: 492.
— Later Tertiary Map of. (E. W. Hilgard) Am. J. Sci. 122: 58.
Gulf Service, Sketch of. Knick. 38: 112.
Gulf States and the Amazon. De Bow, 18: 364.
Gulf Stream. (A. D. Bache) Am. J. Sci. 80: 313.—(W. B. Carpenter) Good Words, 14: 17, 98.—(W. B. Carpenter) Nature, 2: 334.—(A. K. Johnston) Ed. New Philos. J. 73: 57.—(R. A. Proctor) Stud. & Intel. Obs. 1: 417.—(R. Russell) Ed. New Philos. J. 65: 70.—(W. C. Redfield) Am. J. Sci. 32: 349.—(M. Mohawk) Knick. 11: 415.—Chamb. J. 24: 228. Same art. Liv. Age, 47: 553.
— Agency of, in the Formation of Florida. (J. LeConte) Am. J. Sci. 73: 46.
— and Currents of the Sea. (M. F. Maury) So. Lit. Mess. 10: 393.—(M. F. Maury) Am. J. Sci. 47: 161.
— Anomalies in. (E. B. Hunt) Am. J. Sci. 77: 206.
— Currents of. Nav. M. 2: 243.
— Dredging of. (W. Huggins) Nature, 4: 87.
— Dredging Excursion in. (Mrs. E. C. Agassiz) Atlan. 24: 507, 571.
— Explorations of. (A. D. Bache) Am. J. Sci. 79: 199.
— Is it a Myth? St. Paul's, 4: 729. Same art. Ecl. M. 73: 544.
— New Theory of. (T. B. Maury) Harper, 41: 63.—Liv. Age, 6: 439.
— Observations on. Ed. Philos. J. 4: 76.
— The real. (I. I. Hayes) Galaxy, 13: 13.
— Recent Soundings in. (H. Mitchell) Am. J. Sci. 93: 69.
— Rocks and other Dredgings from. (S. P. Sharples) Am. J. Sci. 101: 168.
— Sources of. (J. E. Nagle) So. M. 11: 73.
Gulf Trade. (W. Phillips) De Bow, 12: 399.
Gulf-Weed. (M. P. Merrifield) Nature, 18: 708.
Gulf-Weed; a Poem. (H. H. Brownell) Ev. Sat. 11: 119.
Gull, Sir Wm. W. (F. Arnold) Lond. Soc. 31: 385.
Gulls. (W. J. Broderip) Fraser, 57: 585.
Gum, Sources and Uses of. Penny M. 13: 150.
Gum Arabic in the Soudan. Pract. M. 1: 291.
Gum Euphorbium. (J. Collins) Pract. M. 4: 107.
Gums and Resins of Commerce. (P. L. Simmonds) J. Frankl. Inst. 62: 122–388.
— — Vegetable. Art J. 10: 365.
Gumb, Daniel. Penny M. 5: 178.
Gummer's Fortune. (J. B. Hopkins) Once a Week, 26: 174–394.
Gun, Armstrong, and some Rivals. Lond. Soc. 1: 407.
— Explosion of, on the Thunderer. Ecl. Engin. 20: 355.
— An oval. Chamb. J. 22: 202.
— Palliser's big. All the Year, 13: 571.
— Whitworth. Ecl. Engin. 2: 506.
Guns, American. Internat. M. 5: 33.
— and Armor. (W. B. Adams) Once a Week, 6: 513.—(W. Dawson) Fraser, 87: 257.—Ecl. Engin. 16: 562. 25: 113.—Chamb. J. 53: 296.—(W. B. Adams) Once a Week, 3: 396.
— and Gunnery. New Q. 1: 238. 7: 248.
— and Projectiles. Intel. Obs. 5: 113.
— and Steel. (J. Whitworth) Pract. M. 3: 358.
— — Whitworth's. Pract. M. 4: 199.
Guns, Armstrong and Whitworth. Dub. Univ. 63: 544.
— Brass, in the Armory at Richmond. So. Lit. Mess. 21: 694.
— Bronze. Ecl. Engin. 3: 343.
— Construction of. (C. E. Dutton) J. Frankl. Inst. 93: 271, 333.—(C. E. Dutton) Pract. M. 3: 390.
— Great. Nature, 16: 25.
— Heavy, at Sea. Ecl. Engin. 8: 373.
— Report on large Wrought-Iron. (W. M. Crane) J. Frankl. Inst. 38: 326.
— Rifled. (W. J. Stillman) Atlan. 4: 444.
— Sporting Breech-Loader, and its Origin. (C. Waddy) Gent. M. n. s. 9: 429.
— Story of the. Chamb. 41: 299.
— — Sir E. Tennent's. Fraser, 69: 639, 773.
— Story of the big. All the Year, 11: 18.
— Story of the seven-inch. Ecl. Engin. 7: 495.
— Strong. All the Year, 3: 545.
— Trial of, at Woolwich. Ecl. Engin. 21: 349.
— *versus* Turrets. Ecl. Engin. 3: 135.
— Woolwich. Nature, 22: 293.
Gunboats and Iron-Clads, Revolution in the Construction of. (F. R. Conder) Dub. Univ. 92: 385.
— Spanish. Ecl. Engin. 2: 113.
Gun Carriage, Moncrieff's. Ecl. Engin. 15: 375.
Gun Carriages, Floating. Chamb. J. 48: 587.—(Sir W. G. Armstrong) Ecl. Engin. 1: 712.
— Rival. Ecl. Engin. 3: 487, 507.
Gun-Cotton. (T. T. S. Laidley) U. S. Serv. M. 1: 345.—Am. J. Sci. 53: 102–295.—Chamb. J. 42: 117.—J. Frankl. Inst. 42: 425. 43: 282.—Sharpe, 3: 199.
— and Gunpowder. (J. Scoffern) St. James, 10: 341.
— Application of. J. Frankl. Inst. 78: 141.
— as an explosive Agent. J. Frankl. Inst. 77: 37, 109.
— Chemical History and Application of. (Prof. Abel) J. Frankl. Inst. 79: 37, 133, 189.
— Explosion of, at Stowmarket. Nature, 4: 309.
— for Small-Arms. J. Frankl. Inst. 82: 239.
— History of. Ecl. Engin. 1: 434.
— How made. Ev. Sat. 4: 551.
— Improvements in. (S. J. Mackie) Ecl. Engin. 9: 260.—J. Frankl. Inst. 77: 35.
— War Department Report on. Ecl. Engin. 6: 479.
Gun-Cotton Water-Shells. Nature, 12: 314.
Gun Factory, Scott's, Visit to. (C. Waddy) Belgra. 18: 239.
Gungrog, Wales, Reminiscences connected with old Oak Paneling at. Colburn, 132: 328.
Gunilda, Coffin Plate and History of. (G. F. Beltz) Arch. 25: 398.
Gunn, Wm. Alphonsus. Sermons and Letters. (J. Foster) Ecl. R. 16: 1145.
Gunnar; a Norse Romance. (H. H. Boyesen) Atlan. 32: 13–681.
Gunnar and his sons, Story of. Fraser, 46: 644.
Gunnery, Greener on Science of, 1841. Mo. R. 156: 279.
— Hydraulic. Pract. M. 2: 144.
— Recent Experiments in. Nature, 21: 437.
— Long and straight Shots. Cornh. 1: 505.
— Theory and Practice of. Mus. 2: 530.
See Artillery; Ordnance.
Gunning. All the Year, 11: 585.
Gunning, The beautiful Misses, 1751. Cornh. 16: 418. Same art. Ev. Sat. 4: 578.
Gunning, Sophia, Lady Coventry. Lond. Soc. 5: 353.
Gunpowder. Chamb. J. 32: 197.—Ecl. Engin. 4: 604, 626.—(M. Faraday) J. Frankl. Inst. 43: 284.—House. Words, 4: 457.—Liv. Age, 4: 279.—Quar. 125: 106.
— and Alchemy. House. Words, 1: 135.
— and Detonating Matches. (A. Ure) J. Frankl. Inst. 11: 105, 202.
— and Greek Fire. Blackw. 59: 719.

Gunpowder and Gun-Cotton. (J. Scoffern) St. James, 10: 341. — Ecl. Engin. 3: 306.
— and its Effect on Civilization. Westm. 67: 392.
— and its Manufacture. New Q. 4: 151.
— and modern Artillery. Fraser, 82: 218.
— and modern Warfare. Dub. R. 85: 364.
— and other Explosives. (R. Wagner) Ecl. Engin. 7: 69.
— and Thermo-Chemical Theories. (M. Castan) Ecl. Engin. 12: 232.
— Early Use in English Army. (J. Hunter) Arch. 32: 379.
— Experiments on, 1843–44. (A. Mordecai) J. Frankl. Inst. 55: 300.
— Explosive Force of. (F. A. P. Barnard) Am. J. Sci. 86: 241.
— Extraordinary, 1865. J. Frankl. Inst. 79: 342.
— Improved Manufacture of. Ecl. Engin. 16: 305.
— Large and small Grain. (J. P. Morgan) Ecl. Engin. 16: 274.
— Laws for Dealers in. Hunt, 15: 92.
— Manufacture of. (J. G. Austin) Atlan. 26: 527. — Godey, 62: 493. — Lond. Soc. 4: 66 — Quar. 103: 218.
— — and Conveyance of. (A. H. Atteridge) Pop. Sci. R. 14: 40. Same art. Pop. Sci. Mo. 6: 717.
— — and Storage of. Westm. 94: 387.
— — during the Siege of Paris. Ecl. Engin. 6: 373.
— — of Pebble Powder. (J. P. Morgan) Ecl. Engin. 12: 452, 549.
— — Schultz's. (C. Waddy) Belgra. 18: 374.
— — without Water. Pract. M. 7: 372. — Ecl. Engin. 18: 437.
— Modern History of. Ecl. Engin. 21: 202.
— Patent Cotton. Ecl. Engin. 12: 305, 446.
— Pressure of. (W. E. Woodbridge) Am. J. Sci. 72: 153.
— Quickness in. (J. Shaw) J. Frankl. Inst. 4: 282.
— Recent Researches in. Ecl. Engin. 4: 299.
— Smokeless. Pop. Sci. Mo. 2: 61.
— Strength of American. J. Frankl. Inst. 4: 63, 127.
— Substitutes for. (F. A. Abel) J. Frankl. Inst. 82: 271. — (E. C. Boynton) U. S. Serv. M. 1: 611.
— Transport and Storage of. Chamb. J. 52: 200.
— White. (M. Pohl) J. Frankl. Inst. 72: 193, 281. 73: 200. — (J. Scoffern) Belgra. 8: 142. — Ev. Sat. 7: 538.
Gunpowder Plot. (J. Lancaster) Meth. M. 40: 752. — (A. C. Ewald) Gent. M. n. s. 27: 193. — Penny M. 8: 420.
— Discovery of. Arch. 12: 200*.
— Father Gerard's Narrative of. (J. G. McGee) Cath. World, 16: 176.
— Letters illustrative of. (J. Bruce) Arch. 28: 420.
— — of Winter and Lord Mounteagle. (D. Jardine) Arch. 29: 80, 96.
See Fawkes, Guy.
Gunshot Wounds. Chamb. J. 37: 287.
— Paré's Experiments in curing. Fraser, 51: 342.
Gunther, C. G., with portrait. Dem. R. 41: 156.
Gup-Travels in India. (Mrs. R. Church) Temp. Bar, 19: 75, 395. 20: 463. 21: 66–466.
Gurley, R. R. Colonization Mission of, to England. (A. Alexander) Princ. 14: 266.
Gurnall, W., Memoir of. Cong. M. 13: 281.
Gurnard Group of Fish. (D. C. Badham) Fraser, 46: 452.
Gurnel Duke's first Valentine. Lond. Soc. 15: 161, 241.
Gurney, A. Song of early Summer. New Q. 6: 82.
Gurney, Gen. Francis. Portfo.(Den.) 14: 230.
Gurney, Grisell, Memoir of. N. E. Reg. 22: 43.
Gurney, Joseph John, Memoir of, with portrait. Howitt, 1: 86. — Ecl. R. 100: 299. Same art. Ecl. M. 33: 367. — Chr. Obs. 55: 305. — Liv. Age, 42: 227. — Chr. Obs. 47: 119, 185. Same art. Liv. Age, 13: 193.
Gurney Family of Norwich. Lond. Soc. 10: 254.
Gurney, or two Fortunes. (D. Costello) Bentley, 46: 98–580. 47: 161–599. 48: 71, 207, 272.
Gurney Papers. (T. Hook) Colburn, 49: 9–457. 50: 1–443. 51: 1–433. 52: 1–433. 53: 1. 54: 1–289.
Gurowski, Count. (R. Carter) Atlan. 18: 625.
Gurtha; a Tale. Chamb. J. 44: 129–197.
Gustavus Adolphus. (J. W. Calcraft) Dub. Univ. 40: 48. — (B. Moses) New Eng. 33: 421. — (R. C. Trench) Hours at Home, 2: 110, 221. — Colburn, 126: 438. Same art. Liv. Age, 77: 342.
— and Wallenstein. (E. Lawrence) Harper, 42: 577.
— Gfrœrer's History of. Dub. R. 30: 69.
— Holling's Life of. Ecl. R. 68: 444.
Gustavus Adolphus Society. Kitto, 32: 19.
Gustavus III., of Sweden, and the Counter Revolution. Fraser, 78: 391.
— and the Illuminati. Chr. Obs. 74: 25.
Gustavus III. of Sweden; a Story. Dark Blue, 4: 127–511.
Gustavus IV., of Sweden, Last Years of Reign of. (R. Heber) Quar. 8: 302.
Gutenberg, J. (T. L. De Vinne) Scrib. 12: 73. — Ecl. M. 73: 114.
Gutenberg Jubilee in Germany. For. Q. 25: 446.
Guthrie, M., Ecclesiastical Portrait of. St. James, 26: 166.
Guthrie, Thomas. (J. B. Green) Unita. R. 4: 578. 5: 364. — Hogg, 3: 401. — with portrait, (J. Fraser) New Dom. 11: 223.
— Autobiography of. Canad. Mo. 11: 242. — Chr. Obs. 75: 573. — Cong. 3: 15. — Blackw. 115: 461. Same art. Ecl. M. 82: 740.
— Eloquence and Power of. Ecl. R. 109: 182. Same art. Ecl. M. 47: 51.
— Reminiscences of. Good Words, 14: 281.
Gutta Percha. (T. Oxley) Am. J. Sci. 55: 438. — (E. N. Kent) Am. J. Sci. 56: 246. — Liv. Age, 14: 402. — Hunt, 23: 241. — Chamb. J. 8: 39.
— and Caoutchouc, Decay of. (W. A. Miller) J. Frankl. Inst. 81: 128, 190.
— Manufacture of. West. J. 12: 85.
Gutters, Road. (W. H. Grant) J. Frankl. Inst. 84: 311, 377.
Gutzkow, Carl. (A. Ashbury) Lakeside, 4: 122.
Gutzlaff, Charles, Missionary to China. Hogg, 7: 302. — Internat. M. 1: 317.
Guy Deverell. (J. S. Le Fanu) Dub. Univ. 65: 36–661. 66: 67.
Guy Faux. (C. Lamb) Lond. M. 8: 477.
Guy Fawkes. (W. H. Ainsworth) Bentley, 7: 1–545. 8: 1–529. 9: 1–551. 10: 1–529.
Guy Neville's Ghost. (P. Greg) Blackw. 97: 342.
Guy Villiers. (L. de la Ramé) Bentley, 47: 630.
Guy's Cliff, Warwick. Penny M. 9: 443, 454.
Guy's Hospital, Statistics of Patients treated, 1854–61. (J. C. Steele) J. Statis. Soc. 24: 374.
Guy, Thos., Founder of Guy's Hospital. Penny M. 3: 286.
Guyaquil in 1833. Nav. M. 1: 227.
Guyon, Madame J. M. B. de la Mothe. Brit. Q. 17: 317 Same art. Ecl. M. 29: 429. Same art. Liv. Age, 37: 707. — Ecl. M. 75: 526. — Mo. Rel. M. 27: 158.
— and her religious Views. Chr. R. 3: 449.
— Life and Writings of. (D. Curry) Meth. Q. 8: 325. — (N. M. Williams) Chr. R. 16: 51. — (G. B. Cheever) Am. Bib. Repos. 3d s. 4: 608. — (S. Harris) New Eng. 6: 165. — (E. B. Hall) Chr. Exam. 43: 317. — Chr. Obs. 54: 829. 61: 509, 641. — Ecl. R. 102: 437.
Guyon, Gen. Richard D. Ecl. R. 103: 178.
Guyot, Arnold Henry. Earth and Man. So. Q. 19: 420.
Guzla. House. Words, 12: 545.
Guzman de Alfarache, the Spanish Rogue. Retros. 5: 189.
— and the Gusto Picaresco. Cornh. 35: 24.
Guzrab, Bhats and Charons of. Liv. Age, 72: 347.
Gwalior, or Gualior. Penny M. 13: 113.
Gweedore, Donegal. Dub. Univ. 41: 9.
Gwendoline's Harvest. (J. Payn) Chamb. J. 47: 1–278.

Gwyne, H. Poems. Mo. R. **105**: 251.
Gwynne, Nell. (Mrs. S. C. Hall) Internat. M. **3**: 9. — Tait, n. s. **22**: 282. Same art. Ecl. M. **35**: 419.
— and the Sayings of Charles II. Liv. Age, **34**: 397.
— and Lord Rochester's Poems. Ecl. M. **26**: 512. — Liv. Age, **34**: 28.
— as an Actress. Temp. Bar, **53**: 559.
— Letter of. Blackw. **3**: 547.
— Recollections of. Colburn, **54**: 87.
Gwynne, T. School for Dreamers. New Q. **2**: 241.
— Life and Death of Silas Barnstarke. New Q. **2**: 515.
Gyles, John, Minister of Henley. Cong. **7**: 214.
Gyles, Thomas. (J. A. Vinton) N. E. Reg. **21**: 352.
Gymnasium, German. (R. P. Keep) New Eng. **35**: 145. — (I. Loewenthal) Princ. **24**: 564.
— and English Public School. Meth. Q. **15**: 509.
— or a University. (C. V. Mays) Mercersb. **19**: 32.
Gymnastics. (T. W. Higginson) Atlan. **7**: 283. — (A. A. Livermore) No. Am. **81**: 51. — Am. Q. **3**: 126. — (J. Wilson) Blackw. **20**: 129. — Westm. **3**: 277. — Knick. **62**: 1. — Lond. M. **11**: 590.
— and Acrobatism. Chamb. J. **53**: 697.
— Age of. (F. L. Oswald) Pop. Sci. Mo. **13**: 129.
— for Schools. (J. J. Putnam) Am. Soc. Sci. J. **8**: 110.
Gymnastics, German, in London. (E. A. Bendall) Dark Blue, **3**: 79.
— Hygiene of. St. James, **21**: 172.
— Influence of, in Germany. Lond. M. **1**: 140.
— National Systems of Bodily Exercise. (A. Maclaren) Macmil. **7**: 277.
— New. (D. Lewis) Am. J. Educ. **11**: 531. **12**: 665.
— Old Greek Athletics. (J. P. Mahaffy) Macmil. **36**: 61.
See Athletics; Physical Education; Health.
Gynæceum of the Place Bleue; a Story. (E. Jerrold) Tinsley, **29**: 521.
Gypsies. *See* Gipsies.
Gypsum, Sources and Uses of. Penny M. **13**: 58.
Gyroscope. (J. G. Barnard) Am. J. Educ. **3**: 537. **4**: 529. **5**: 299. — (B. H. Rand) J. Frankl. Inst. **111**: 213. — (E. S. Snell) Am. J. Educ. **2**: 701. — (R. Stewart) J. Frankl. Inst. **65**: 122. — (E. G. Wood) Recr. Sci. **1**: 33.
— Applications of. Ecl. Engin. **12**: 360.
— Magneto-Electric. Nature, **21**: 593.
— Problem of. (J. Clark) J. Frankl. Inst. **80**: 21.
— Theory of. (C. J. Allen) J. Frankl. Inst. **61**: 394. **62**: 63. — (T. G. Ellis) Math. Mo. **3**: 209.

H

Haafner, M. I., Voyages of. Quar. **7**: 120.
Haarlem, Festival at, in honor of Coster. Lond. M. **8**: 272.
— Organ at. Penny M. **3**: 385.
Haarlem Lake, Draining of. (Prof. Downing) J. Frankl. Inst. **61**: 227. — (H. C. Bosscha) J. Frankl. Inst. **62**: 291, 361. **63**: 15.
Haas, F. H. de. Art J. **30**: 185.
Habakkuk, Prayer of, Chap. iii. (J. Strong) Meth. Q. **21**: 73.
Habberton, John. Helen's Babies. Chamb. J. **54**: 556.
Habeas Corpus. Ecl. R. **70**: 325.
— and Personal Liberty. Knick. **64**: 206, 289.
— New Act, 1858. Dub. R. **45**: 388.
— *versus* Martial Law. (J. Parker) No. Am. **93**: 471.
Haberfeld Treiben, in Upper Bavaria. Cornh. **16**: 667.
Haberzettel, M., Obituary of. Art J. **5**: 264.
Habington, Wm. (D. A. Casserly) Am. Cath. Q. **2**: 614.
— Castara. Retros. **12**: 274.
— Poems. (M. F. Egan) Cath. World, **32**: 132.
Habit. (H. L. Baugher) Evang. R. **7**: 190. — (J. B. Gough) Ex. H. Lec. **9**: 49.
— and Discipline, Review of Thoughts on. Chr. Obs. **44**: 435.
— and Intelligence, Murphy on. (G. Allen) Mind, **4**: 274.
— Law of. (J. Weiss) Radical, **7**: 12.
— Power of. Colburn, **6**: 326.
Habits. (J. Stretton) Argosy, **3**: 336.
— and Resolutions. Tait, n. s. **24**: 480.
— Physical, as related to the Will. (H. Calderwood) Princ. n. s. **6**: 145.
Habitations, Improper. Penny M. **11**: 397.
— of Man in all Ages. (M. Viollet-le-Duc) Am. Arch. **1**: 68–122.
Habitué's Note-Book, The. (C. Hervey) Colburn, **84**: 122–535. **85**: 125–502. **86**: 113–383. **87**: 373–490. **88**: 123–550. **89**: 129–381. **90**: 116–244.
Habrecht, Isaac. Tinsley, **20**: 160.
Hachette, Jeanne, the Maid of Beauvais. Eng. Dom. M. **10**: 209.
Hacienda, Description of a. (W. R. Turnbull) Overland, **7**: 514.
Hack, The Park. All the Year, **16**: 205.
Hack Horse that would n't go. (C. A. Bristed) Am. Whig R. **4**: 159.
Hacke, N. P., Memoir of. (G. B. Russell) Mercersb. **25**: 579.
Hackett, Horatio B. (H. S. Burrage) Bapt. Q. **10**: 403.
Hackett, James H., Souvenirs of. Galaxy, **14**: 550.
Hackett, Wm. H. Y., Memoir of, with portrait. (F. W. Hackett) N. E. Reg. **33**: 1.
Hackfall, Alum Springs at. Penny M. **4**: 133.
Hackländer, Friedrich Wilhelm. Moment of Fortune. Liv. Age, **58**: 767.
— Secret Agent. Blackw. **76**: 525.
— Tag und Nacht. Bentley, **47**: 251.
— Writings of. Sharpe, **26**: 97.
Hackney Theological Seminary. Am. Q. Reg. **12**: 67.
Hackney Coaches. Lond. M. **12**: 555.
— and Cabs of London. Chamb. J. **3**: 407.
Haconby, History of. Cornh. **40**: 707.
Had and would. All the Year, **22**: 255.
Had she but known. Lond. Soc. **29**: 514.
Had she but known; a Story. (T. Gift) Galaxy, **14**: 330.
Had we a celestial Visitant? (A. Shackleford) Lakeside, **7**: 483.
Haddo, Lord, 5th Earl of Aberdeen. Chr. Obs. **67**: 637.
Haddock, Charles Brickett, with portrait. Internat. M. **2**: 1.
Haddock, The, and John Doree. (A. H. Baldwin) Once a Week, **10**: 8.
Haddon Hall, Derbyshire. Antiquary, **3**: 85. — Penny M. **3**: 263.
— Chapel at. Reliquary, **12**: 1.
Haden, Seymour, Etchings of. (P. G. Hamerton) Scrib. **20**: 586.
Hades. (D. F. Brendle) Mercersb. **24**: 544. — (F. P. Cobbe) Fraser, **69**: 293.
— and Sheol. (E. T. Fitch) New Eng. **25**: 125.
— Fantasy of; a Poem. (G. Bloede) Western, **5**: 367.

Hades, Harpings upon. (C. A. Alexander) Knick. **42**: 465. Same art. Sharpe, **48**: 235.
— Heaven and Hell. Kitto, **10**: 35, 483. **11**: 56, 413.
— Jewish and Assyrian. (J. Fenton) Theo. R. **13**: 299.
Hadleigh, Summer Day at. (E. Walford) Once a Week, **15**: 331.
Hadleigh Castle. Ev. Sat. **2**: 307.
— Visit to. Once a Week, **15**: 166.
Hadley, James, Memorial of. (N. Porter) New Eng. **32**: 35.
Hadley, Mass., Attack on, in 1675. N. E. Reg. **28**: 379.
— Hopkins School at. (S. Judd) Am. J. Educ. **27**: 145.
— Ministers of. Am. Q. Reg. **10**: 270.
Hadrian's Villa. Am. Arch. **5**: 44.
Haeckel, Ernst, and Darwin. (T. H. Huxley) Pop. Sci. Mo. **6**: 592.
— and Virchow. (C. Elam) Contemp. **33**: 540.
— Evolution Theories. (G. W. Samson) Bapt. Q. **11**: 37.
— Gastræa Theory. (A. Agassiz) Am. Nat. **10**: 73.
Hafed, Prince of Persia, a new Evangelist. St. James, **38**: 615.
Háfiz, the Persian Poet. (Prof. Cowell) Macmil. **30**: 251. — (E. H. Palmer) Argosy, **3**: 110. — Fraser, **50**: 288. **63**: 228.
Hagada, Grünbaum on. (S. J. Barrows) Unita. R. **9**: 219.
Hagar and Ishmael. Nat. M. **9**: 236.
— Life of. (S. A. Brooke) Good Words, **21**: 388.
Hagar in our Wilderness, A. (J. E. Hood) Lakeside, **2**: 111.
Haggart, David. House. Words, **17**: 186.
Hagiocracy in Israel, Ewald on. (F. R. Conder) Theo. R. **12**: 70.
Hague, The. Penny M. **14**: 433.
— Court Ball at. (A. Rhodes) Scrib. **5**: 443.
— Idler in. Fraser, **61**: 238.
Hahn, Aug., on Interpretation. Am. Bib. Repos. **1**: 111.
Hahn-Hahn, Countess Ida. Internat. M. **4**: 17. — (J. J. Lalor) Cath. World. **31**: 308. — (M. H. Allies) Irish Mo. **9**: 246.
— Conversion of. Dub. R. **33**: 46.
— Letters of. For. Q. **30**: 381.
— Novels of. (L. P. Hale) O. & N. **4**: 481. — For. Q. **36**: 292. — Westm. **46**: 547.
— Writings of. Dub. Univ. **42**: 184. Same art. Ecl. M. **30**: 265. — (A. Hayward) Ed. R. **79**: 157.
Hahnemann, Samuel C. F., with portrait. Hogg, **7**: 225. — Liv. Age, **61**: 323.
— and Homœopathy. Ed. R. **50**: 504. *See* Homœopathy.
Haidinger, Wilhelm von. Nature, **3**: 450.
Hail and Hailstorms, Formation of. (M. de la Rive) Ed. New Philos. J. **21**: 280. — (M. de la Rive) J. Frankl. Inst. **25**: 201, 280.
— — in the Spray of the Yosemite Fall. (W. H. Brewer) Am. J. Sci. **110**: 161.
— Origin of. (F. Mohr) Canad. J. n. s. **8**: 35.
— Theory of. (J. P. Espy) J. Frankl. Inst. **21**: 240, 309. **22**: 100.
— — Objections to Espy's. (G. Hutchison) J. Frankl. Inst. **27**: 80.
Hailstones, Raindrops, and Snowflakes. (O. Reynolds) Nature, **17**: 207. Same art. Pop. Sci. Mo. **10**: 522.
Hail Storm at New York, 1st of July, 1853. (E. Loomis) Am. J. Sci. **117**: 35.
— of June 20, 1870. (H. C. Hovey) Am. J. Sci. **100**: 403.
Hail Storms, Phenomena and Causes of. (D. Olmsted) Am. J. Sci. **18**: 1. — **20**: 373. — (D. Olmsted) Ed. New Philos. J. **9**: 244. — Bentley, **49**: 536. Same art. Ecl. M. **53**: 359.
Hail Columbia! History of the Song. Nat. M. **9**: 88.
— Origin of. Hist. M. **5**: 280.
Haileybury School, Speech-Day at. Penn. Mo. **4**: 100.
Haines Genealogy. (A. M. Haines) N. E. Reg. **23**: 148, 430.
Hair, Human. (C. Waddy) Belgra. **16**: 498. — Eng. Dom. M. **2**: 48. **3**: 264–574. — Godey, **50**: 31–500. — House. Words, **9**: 61. Same art. Liv. Age, **41**: 42. — Irish. Q. **7**: 834. **9**: 282, 1021. — Ev. Sat. **14**: 520. — Quar. **92**: 305. Same art. Ecl. M. **29**: 207. Same art. Liv. Age, **37**: 429.
— and Beards. Temp. Bar, **3**: 247.
— — fashioned by Politics. (C. Mackay) Bentley, **7**: 300.
— and Hair-Dyeing. Ev. Sat. **3**: 432.
— and Head-Dresses, Fashions in. Fraser, **82**: 322. Same art. Ecl. M. **75**: 569. Same art. Liv. Age, **107**: 282.
— Artists in. Chamb. J. **44**: 657.
— Artists' Notes on. Art J. **9**: 194.
— as a Race-Character. (Pruner-Bey) Anthrop. R. **2**: 1.
— Capillary Freaks. (C. D. Shanly) Atlan. **19**: 66.
— Color of. (A. Dalzell) Liv. Age, **39**: 410.
— Coloring Matters in. (H. C. Sorby) Anthrop. J. **8**: **2**.
— Cosmetics for. (J. Scoffern) Belgra. **5**: 383.
— Dark, Prevalence in England. (J. Beddoe) Anthrop. R. **1**: 310.
— False. (F. Marshall) Bentley, **53**: 537. — Chamb. J. **36**: 65.
— Golden. Chamb. J. **42**: 408.
— Growth, Structure and Life of. (Dr. Bidder) Ed. New Philos. J. **31**: 165.
— Harvest of. Chamb. J. **30**: 119. Same art. Liv. Age, **59**: 355.
— How the Feelings affect. (D. H. Tuke) Pop. Sci. Mo. **2**: 158.
— How to promote, preserve, and keep luxuriant. Godey, **59**: 34–337.
— Long, Sermons against. N. E. Reg. **1**: 369.
— Long and short. All the Year, **22**: 137.
— Loss of. (G. Allen) Fortn. **31**: 778.
— Modes of dressing, among Roman Ladies. Blackw. **4**: 169.
— of Oceanic Races. (J. B. Davis) Anthrop. J. **2**: 95.
— Real and false. Chamb. J. **46**: 465.
— Red. Bentley, **29**: 532. Same art. Ecl. M. **23**: 314.
— Rowland on. New Q. **3**: 81.
— Trade in. Lond. Soc. **15**: 547. — Ev. Sat. **8**: 40.
— Treatment of. Dub. Univ. **81**: 394.
Hair-Brushing, Rotary. Chamb. J. **40**: 343.
Hair Chains. Atlan. **8**: 534.
Hair-Cutting in the East. (F. R. Feudge) Scrib. **8**: 714.
Hairdressers. Ev. Sat. **2**: 614.
Hairdressing. All the Year, **31**: 253.
— Fashions in. Ev. Sat. **11**: 359.
Hair-Dyeing. Ev. Sat. **1**: 675.
— Danger of. Ev. Sat. **10**: 83.
Hair Work. Eng. Dom. M. **12**: 283, 342.
— Art of ornamental. Godey, **58**: 123–551.
Hairbreadth 'Scapes; a Tale. Temp. Bar, **12**: 42.
Hake, Thomas G. Poems. (D. G. Rossetti) Fortn. **19**. 537. — Colburn, **148**: 454. **152**: 205.
Hake, The. (A. H. Baldwin) Once a Week, **11**: 320.
Hakem the Slave. Blackw. **58**: 560.
Hakem, Caliph, Divinity of the Druses. Ecl. M. **52**: 10.
Hakem-B'emr-Allah, Story of. Ecl. R. **112**: 419.
Hakluyt, Richard. (J. P. Collier) Arch. **33**: 283.
— Western Planting. (G. W. Greene) Nation, **25**: 229.
Hakluyt Society Publications. Brit. Q. **16**: 48.
Hakodadi. Chamb. J. **25**: 294.
Hakon Jarl; a Poem. (A. Oehlenschlager) St. James, **15**: 332.
Halcyon Days. (C. Chesebrough) Atlan. **14**: 675.
Haldane, Robert and J. A. (A. Geikie) New Eng. **19**: 269. — (W. Landels) Ex. H. Lec. **9**: 109. — (J. A. Alexander) Princ. **24**: 677. — Quar. **98**: 353. Same art. Ecl. M. **38**: 316. — Ecl. R. **96**: 341. Same art. Ecl. M. **27**: 306. — Chr. R. **18**: 283.

Haldeman, Samuel S. (C. H. Hart) Penn Mo. **12**: 584.
— on Latin Pronunciation. Brownson, **8**: 411.
Hale, David, Memoir and Writings of. (A. P. Peabody) Chr. Exam. **48**: 282. — Liv. Age, **20**: 373. — New Eng. **8**: 129.
Hale, Edward Everett. In his Name. (R. Metcalf) Unita. R. **1**: 346.
— Our new Crusade, Replies to Critics on. (E. E. Hale) O. & N. **11**: 389.
— Sermons. Unita. R. **12**: 546.
Hale, John, Memoir of. Am. Q. Reg. **10**: 247.
Hale, Sir Matthew. (D. Watson) Meth. M. **43**: 881. — with portrait, Am. Q. Reg. **10**: 113. — (S. R. Andrew) Chr. Q. Spec. **3**: 531. — Am. Mo. R. **2**: 384. — Ecl. R. **2**: 588. — Chr. Obs. **5**: 563, 589.
— Williams's Memoir of. Ecl. R. **62**: 185.
Hale, Capt. Nathan. (H. P. Johnston) Harper, **61**: 53. — Liv. Age, **76**: 430, 477. — Knick. **11**: 54. — Putnam, **7**: 476.
Hale, Sarah J. Godey, **41**: 326.
— Works of. Am. Mo. R. **4**: 239.
Hale, Thomas, of Newbury, Mass., English Origin of. (R. S. Hale) N. E. Reg. **35**: 367.
— Memoir of. (R. S. Hale) N. E. Reg. **31**: 83.
Haleakala, Crater of, Island of Maui. (W. D. Alexander) Am. J. Sci. **99**: 43.
Halen, Juan van. Am. Q. **8**: 409.
— Narrative of. Chamb. J. **6**: 82, 104.
Hales, John. (J. Tulloch) Contemp. **5**: 190.
— Falkland, Chillingworth; the earlier Latitudinarians. Nat. R. **17**: 1.
Half a Lifetime ago. House. Words, **12**: 229–276.
Half a Million of Money; a Tale. (A. B. Edward) All the Year, **13**: 289–601. **14**: 1–520.
Half an Hour in a Servant's Registry Office. Lond. Soc. **12**: 85.
Half and Half. (C. W. Stoddard) Overland, **10**: 86.
Half-Breed Races of Northwestern Canada. (A. P. Reid) Anthrop. J. **4**: 45.
Half-Brothers; a Tale. Dub. Univ. **52**: 586. Same art. Liv. Age, **60**: 12.
Half-Caste; an old Governess's Tale. Liv. Age, **31**: 554.
Half-Century Progress. Am. Church R. **4**: 60.
Half-Forgotten Claimant. (S. R. T. Mayer) St. James, **34**: 91.
Half-Holidays. Cornh. **9**: 555.
Half-Life and Half a Life. (E. H. Appleton) Atlan. **13**: 157.
Half out of the World. Month, **1**: 51.
Half the Penalty. (C. Hervey) Tinsley, **16**: 47.
Half-Tide Rock. Chamb. J. **56**: 669.
Half-Way. (G. Barrow) Atlan. **26**: 205, 347.
Half-Witted Guttorm. (K. Janson) Scrib. **17**: 866.
Halford, Sir Henry. Essays. (W. Ferguson) Quar. **49**: 175.
— Essays and Orations. Mo. R. **125**: 285.
Haliburton, Thomas Chandler. Bentley, **14**: 81. — Irish Q. **6**: 2, 17.
— The Attaché; or Sam Slick in England. Mo. R. **161**: 475. **165**: 558.
— The Clockmaker. Mo. R. **153**: 497.
— Hildreth, and the North American Review. Am. Church R. **4**: 523.
— Letter Bag of the Great Western. Mo. R. **151**: 306.
— Old Judge, or Life in a Colony. Fraser, **35**: 141, 308, 429. **36**: 76–576. — Hogg, **3**: 3, 29.
— Sam Slick's wise Saws. New Q. **2**: 391.
Haliout, The. All the Year, **14**: 142.
Halicarnassus, Discoveries at. Ed. R. **116**: 461.
— in the British Museum. Nat. R. **7**: 296. Same art. Ecl. M. **46**: 184, 323.
— Mausoleum of. (S. Colvin) Fortn. **15**: 472.
Haliens in America. Putnam, **9**: 1.
Halifax, George Savile, First Marquis of, and his Maxim "In medio tutissimus ibis." (A. C. Ewald) Temp. Bar, **53**: 211.
— Character of. (T. B. Macaulay) Liv. Age, **20**: 347.
Halifax, Nova Scotia. (J. Whitman) Canad. Mo. **15**: 421. — Penny M. **3**: 100.
— Massachusetts Soldiers at, in 1759. N. E. Reg. **28**: 413.
— Temperature at. (G. T. Kingston) Canad. J. n. s. **13**: 26.
Hall, A. Oakey. (C. F. Wingate) No. Am. **119**: 359. — with portrait, Ev. Sat. **11**: 404.
Hall, Capt. Basil, Autobiography of. Quar. **47**: 139.
— Fragments and Voyages. Mus. **19**: 175.
— Journal in Chili, Peru, and Mexico. Ed. R. **40**: 31. — Lond. M. **10**: 229.
— Letter from. Blackw. **41**: 31.
— Patchwork. Quar. **68**: 312. — Ed. R. **73**: 41.
— Schloss Hainfeld. Blackw. **40**: 842. **41**: 31. — Quar. **57**: 110. — So. Lit. J. **4**: 374.
— Sketches of Sea Life. (J. G. Lockhart) Quar. **45**: 145.
— Travels in America. (E. Everett) No. Am. **29**: 522. — Quar. **39**: 345. **41**: 417. — Westm. **11**: 416. — (H. S. Legaré) So. R. **4**: 321. — Mo. R. **117**: 503. — Mus. **16**: 233.
— Voyages. (J. Sparks) No. Am. **26**: 514. — (F. Jeffrey) Ed. R. **29**: 475. — U. S. Lit. Gaz. **1**: 209. — Mo. R. **125**: 59. **127**: 592. **134**: 133.
— — and Travels. Fraser, **8**: 593.
Hall, Capt. Charles F., among the Esquimaux. Temp. Bar, **16**: 144.
Hall, Edward Brooks, Memorial of. Chr. Exam. **80**: 385.
Hall, Lieut. Francis. Travels in America. (J. Gallison) No. Am. **9**: 135.
Hall, Frank, Works of. Art J. **28**: 9.
Hall, Gordon, Bardwell's Memoir of. Mo. R. **134**: 440.
— Letter of. Am. Q. Reg. **5**: 18.
— Recollections of. (E. Porter) Am. Q. Reg. **2**: 209, 220.
Hall, James, Writings of. Am. Mo. M. **5**: 9.
Hall, John, Memoir of. Cong. M. **22**: 413.
Hall, Joseph, Bishop. Chr. Obs. **8**: 609, 681, 745.
— Jones's Memoirs of. Cong. M. **9**: 130, 206. — Chr. Obs. **27**: 544, 610, 675. — Ecl. R. **48**: 362.
— Reminiscences of. Chr. Obs. **38**: 354–542.
— Wordsworth's Memoir of. Chr. Obs. **72**: 379.
Hall, Nathaniel, Sermon on Death of. (G. W. Briggs) Unita. R. **4**: 602.
Hall, Robert. (Dr. Hamilton) No. Brit. **4**: 54. — (J. Morgan) St. James, **37**: 600. — (H. Rogers) Liv. Age, **53**: 321. — Ecl. M. **31**: 273. — Nat. M. **2**: 131. — Meth. M. **54**: 327.
— and John Foster. (R. Vaughan) Brit. Q. **4**: 234.
— Character and Writings of. Ecl. M. **7**: 1. — Ecl. R. **79**: 169. — (A. P. Peabody) No. Am. **64**: 384. — (W. B. Sprague) Chr. Q. Spec. **3**: 202. — (G. Shepard) Am. Q. Obs. **3**: 67. — (F. Parkman) Chr. Exam. **10**: 64. — Meth. Q. **4**: 516. — Spirit Pilg. **1**: 437. — So. Q. **12**: 51. — (J. F. Clarke) Chr. Exam. **15**: 1. — Select J. **2**: 62. **3**: [43. — Mo. R. **131**: 360.
— Life and Works of. Ecl. R. **55**: 189, 397. — Chr. Obs. **33**: 95. — Tait, **2**: 773.
— Remarks on. Cong. M. **14**: 416.
— Sermons of. Chr. Obs. **43**: 291.
— Sketch of. Lond. M. **3**: 182.
— Sketches of Sermons by. Chr. Obs. **31**: 128–385.
— Works of. (J. J. Blunt) Quar. **48**: 100. — Ecl. R. **55**: 189, 397. — Cong. M. **16**: 609. — Am. Meth. M. **14**: 413.
Hall, Samuel Read. Am. J. Educ. **5**: 373.
Hall, Mrs. Samuel C. Godey, **45**: 134. — with portrait, Fraser, **13**: 718. — Dub. Univ. **16**: 146.
— Can Wrong be Right? Dub. Univ. **59**: 628.

Hall, Mrs. Samuel C. Lights and Shadows of Irish Life. Dub. Univ. **12**: 218.
— Memoir of. Colburn, **53**: 559.
— Tales of Woman's Trials. Dub. Univ. **7**: 205. — Mo. R. **136**: 244.
Hallam, Arthur H. (J. T. Fields) Atlan. **6**: 694.
— Remains of, in Verse and Prose. No. Brit. **14**: 486. Same art. Ecl. M. **22**: 461. Same art. Liv. Age, **28**: 556. — Liv. Age, **76**: 459. **79**: 218.
Hallam, Henry. Liv. Age, **60**: 707. **65**: 83.
— as a Historian (C. C. Smith) No. Am. **92**: 163.
— Middle Ages. So. Q. **27**: 46.
— Works of. Am. Bib. Repos. **11**: 247.—Dub. R. **40**: 392.
Hallberg-Broich. Bentley, **53**: 248.
Halle, City of, and its History. (E. C. Smyth) Hours at Home, **1**: 490.
Halleck, Fitz-Greene. (W. C. Bryant) Liv. Age, **100**: 515. — (E. A. Duyckinck) Putnam, **11**: 231. — (G. P. Lathrop) Atlan. **39**: 718. — (H. C. Alexander) Hours at Home, **6**: 367. — with portrait, Internat. M. **3**: 433. — with portrait, (J. G. Wilson) Potter Am. Mo. **4**: 217. — All the Year, **19**: 496. — Nat. M. **1**: 481. — New Eng. M. **1**: 153. — So. Lit. Mess. **8**: 242.
— and Abbie Flanner. (J. M. Kerr) Western, **5**: 466.
— Poems. Ecl. M. **72**: 248. — West. Lit. J. **1**: 122. — So. Lit. Mess. **2**: 326. — Am. Q. **21**: 399. — Knick. **26**: 553. — U. S. Lit. Mess. **6**: 8.
— Reminiscences of. (H. T. Tuckerman) Lippinc. **1**: 208. — (B. Taylor) No. Am. **125**: 60.
— Was he a Catholic? (L. T. Bennett) Putnam, **11**: 264.
Halleck, Gen. Henry Wager, Recollections of, in 1847–49. (S. H. Willey) Overland, **9**: 9.
Haller, Albrecht von. Nature, **17**: 223.
— Visit to. (J. J. Casanova) Colburn, **4**: 171–232.
Halley, James. Mus. **45**: 598. — Mo. R. **157**: 245.
Halley, Robert, Memoir of. Cong. **5**: 641.
Halley's Mount. Nature, **21**: 303.
Halliday, Andrew, with portrait. Once a Week, **26**: 388.
Hallock, Jeremiah, Memoir of. Chr. Mo. Spec. **10**: 529.
Hallock, Moses, Memoir of. Am. Q. Reg. **11**: 287.
Hallowed Ground: a Poem. (G. Pauline) Blackw. **45**: 595. — Dub. Univ. **17**: 526.
Halloween; or Christie's Fate. (M. G. Adams) Scrib. **3**: 26. *See* All Hallow Eve.
Hallow-Eve Spell. (G. C. Munro) Peop. J. **10**: 225.
Hallowell, Me., and its Library. (S. L. Boardman) N. E. Reg. **34**: 293.
Hallucination, Story of a. Galaxy, **23**: 218.
Hallucinations. (B. W. Richardson) Pop. Sci. R. **12**: 59. Same art. Ecl. M. **80**: 546. — Chamb. J. **49**: 324. — Once a Week, **6**: 262. — Ev. Sat. **12**: 631.
— and Illusions. Brit. Q. **36**: 387. Same art. Ecl. M. **58**: 41, 151.
— and Visions. Fraser, **60**: 625. Same art. Ecl. M. **49**: 83. Same art. Liv. Age, **64**: 119.
— of the Senses. (H. Maudsley) Fortn. **30**: 370. Same art. Pop. Sci. Mo. **13**: 698. Same art. Liv. Age, **139**: 259.
— Phantom Limbs. (S. W. Mitchell) Lippinc. **8**: 563.
Hallum, Bishop, Monumental Brass to. (R. Pearsall) Arch. **30**: 430.
Halm, Fred. Camoens; translated. Blackw. **48**: 220.
— Son of the Wilderness. So. Q. **21**: 426.
Halos. (S. D. W. Bloodgood) Am. J. Sci. **20**: 297. — (M. Griffith) Am. J. Sci. **38**: 22.
— Explanation of. Penny M. **14**: 431.
Halpine, Charles G. (F. J. O'Brien) Putnam, **4**: 213.
Hals, Franz, Unger's Etchings after. (W. B. Scott) Portfo. **5**: 167.
Halsewell, East Indiaman, Wreck of the. All the Year, **17**: 347.
Halswelle, K. Art J. **31**: 101.
Halt before Rome. (A. C. Swinburne) Fortn. **8**: 539.
Halves. (J. Payn) All the Year, **34**: 265–601. **35**: 1–193.
Halywell Priory, Warwickshire. (W. Hamper) Arch **19**: 75. — (N. Carlisle) Arch. **16**: 326.
Ham Family, Dover, N. H. N. E. Reg. **26**: 388.
Ham House in the Days of the Cabal. (Mrs. A. T. Thomson) Fraser, **34**: 392.
Hamann, Johann George. (J. M. Hoppin) Bib. Sac. **17**: 313. — (K. von Raumer) Am. J. Educ. **6**: 247.
Hamburg. Penny M. **8**: 97. **11**: 237.
— Alster Bassin. (G. A. Sala) Temp. Bar, **12**: 35.
— and the great Conflagration, with maps. (W. E. Hickson) Westm. **38**: 437.
— Commerce of. Hunt, **23**: 177.
— Christmas in. Harper, **18**: 359.
— Domestic Servants in. (G. A. Jackson) Once a Week, **1**: 159.
— during the War. Chamb. J. **47**: 813.
— English Reformed Church at. Cong. M. **16**: 129.
— French Occupation of, 1810. Once a Week, **24**: 263.
— Great Fire at. Penny M. **11**: 270.
— Letter from. Blackw. **11**: 67.
— Lloyds Transactions at. Colburn, **1**: 41.
— Rauhe Haus of. Chamb. J. **4**: 141.
— Semple's Tour, 1813. (J. Foster) Ecl. R. **19**: 170.
— Steam Trip to. Bentley, **1**: 509.
Hamburg Merchant in his Country House; translated. (T. P. Kettell) Hunt, **15**: 177.
Hamden Hill, Antiquities found at. (Sir R. C. Hoare) Arch. **21**: 39.
Hamel, the Obeah Man. Lond. M. **18**: 182.
Hamerton, Philip Gilbert. (H. N. Powers) O. & N. **8**: 196.
— and his Works. Internat. R. **3**: 775.
— as an Art Critic. (E. Benson) Atlan. **16**: 325.
— as an Artist. So. R. n. s. **21**: 74.
Hamilton, Alexander. (C. C. Hazewell) Atlan. **16**: 625. — (H. F. Jenks) Unita. R. **5**: 631. — (V. W. Kingsley) Nat. Q. **28**: 120. — (H. T. Tuckerman) No. Am. **86**: 368. — (C. F. Adams) No. Am. **53**: 71. — (F. L. Hawkes) New York R. **8**: 121. Same art. Liv. Age, **8**: 425. — Am. Q. **15**: 311. — Dem. R. **11**: 142. Chr. Exam. **29**: 243. — Walsh's R. **1**: 201. **2**: 1.
— and Jefferson. Liv. Age, **81**: 613.
— compared with Wm. Pitt. Portfo.(Den.) **16**: 9.
— Genius and Character of. (J. G. Baldwin) So. Lit. Mess. **22**: 371.
— Last Hours of. Hist. M. **6**: 176.
— Life and Genius of. (A. T. Bledsoe) So. R. n. s. **2**: 251.
— — and Works of. So. R. n. s. **6**: 1.
— Public Career of. (H. C. Lodge) No. Am. **123**: 113.
Hamilton, Andrew, of Pennsylvania. (J. F. Fisher) Hist. M. **14**: 49.
Hamilton, Lady Ann, Hour with. Bentley, **24**: 591.
Hamilton, Eliza M., Poems of. Dub. Univ. **12**: 237.
Hamilton, Mrs. Elizabeth. (T. Wyatt) Godey, **45**: 502. — Eng. Dom. M. **13**: 270.
— Cottagers of Glenburnie. (F. Jeffrey) Ed. R. **12**: 401.
— Essays of. Anal. M. **5**: 122. — Ecl. R. **20**: 17.
— Letters of. Chr. Obs. **5**: 694.
— Life of. Portfo.(Den.) **24**: 110.
— Memoirs of. Ecl. R. **27**: 497. — Chr. Disc. **2**: 122.
— Questions. (J. Walker) Chr. Exam **6**: 287.
Hamilton, Lady Emma. Blackw. **87**: 417.
Hamilton, Col. Henry, Narrative of, 1779 M. Am. Hist. **1**: 186.
Hamilton, James. Theo. Ecl. **7**: 177. — So. Lit. Mess. **26**: 53.
— Arnot's Life of. Lond. Q. **35**: 390.
— as a Theologian. Theo. Ecl. **6**: 117.
Hamilton, John C. Correspondence with W. B. Reed. Hist. M. **10**: supp. 177.

Hamilton, Luther. Nine Unitarian Lectures. Chr. Exam. **13**: 284.
Hamilton, Patrick, Lorimer's Life of. Chr. Obs. **57**: 736. Same art. Liv. Age, **56**: 257.
Hamilton, Philip, Duel and Death of. Hist. M. **12**: 193.
Hamilton, Richard W., Life of. Ecl. R. **91**: 455.
— Memoir of. Cong. **1**: 15.
— Nugæ Literariæ. Ecl. R. **75**: 91.
— Sermons of. Ecl. R. **58**: 430. **83**: 280.
Hamilton, Thomas. Cyril Thornton. So. R. **8**: 43. — Tait, **4**: 97.
— Death of. Blackw. **53**: 280.
— Translation of Antar. Mo. R. **94**: 277.
— Travels in America. *See* America.
Hamilton, Sir William. (S. C. Collins) Nat. Q. **30**: 33. — (H. James) Putnam, **2**: 470. — (F. L. Patton) Hours at Home, **10**: 251. — with portrait, Hogg, **8**: 401. — with portrait, Appleton, **2**: 466. — with portrait, Ecl. M. **43**: 278. — Blackw. **86**: 494. — Ecl. M. **29**: 98. — Cong. R. **11**: 185. — (S. Tyler) Princ. **31**: 635.
— and his Logical Reforms. (T. DeQuincey) Hogg, **9**: 273, 291. Same art. Ecl. M. **26**: 32, 523.
— and Mansel on Religious Thought. (J. R. Herrick) Bib. Sac. **26**: 442.
— and Mill, Philosophy of. (J. Haven) Bib. Sac. **25**: 501.
— and Dr. Thomas Reid. No. Brit. **10**: 144.
— Calderwood and Mill on Philosophy of. Dub. R. **57**: 474.
— Discussions. (G. J. Chace) Chr. R. **19**: 39. — So. Q. **24**: 289.
— Doctrines of. Westm. **78**: 83.
— Fragments of Philosophy. Ed. New Philos. J. **34**: 74.
— Jones's Critique of Philosophy of. (A. N. Littlejohn) Am. Church R. **17**: 601. — (J. Haven) Nation, **1**: 345.
— Lectures. Chr. R. **25**: 1. **26**: 466. — Ecl. R. **109**: 466. — No. Brit. **30**: 532. Same art. Ecl. M. **47**: 439.
— Life of. St. Paul's, **4**: 685. Same art. Ecl. M. **73**: 570. Same art. Liv. Age, **103**: 222.
— — and Metaphysics of. No. Brit. **27**: 418. Same art. Ecl. M. **43**: 264.
— Memoir of. No. Brit. **50**: 475.
— Metaphysics. (W. A. Larned) New Eng. **18**: 167. — (Dr. McCosh) Dub. Univ. **54**: 152.
— Mill's Examination of. (G. H. Emerson) Univ. Q. **23**: 79. — (O. B. Frothingham) Chr. Exam. **79**: 301. — (H. B. Smith) Am. Presb. R. **15**: 126. — (C. Wright) Nation, **1**: 278. — Ecl. R. **122**: 378. — Ed. R. **124**: 120. — Lond. Q. **25**: 410. — No. Brit. **43**: 1. — Westm. **85**: 1.
— on Perception. So. R. n. s. **13**: 463.
— Philosophy of. (J. Haven) Bib. Sac. **18**: 94. — Brit. Q. **16**: 479. Same art. Ecl. M. **28**: 70. — Meth. Q. **17**: 177. — (S. Tyler) Princ. **27**: 553. — Prosp. R. **9**: 340. — So. Lit. Mess. **29**: 1.
— Remains of. Meth. Q. **17**: 9.
— H. Spencer on. (T. S. Baynes) Contemp. **21**: 796.
— Veitch's Memoir of. Ed. R. **131**: 193. Same art. Liv. Age, **104**: 593. — Lond. Q. **33**: 1.
— Was he a Berkeleian? (J. H. Stirling) Fortn. **6**: 218.
Hamilton, Wm. G. Parliamentary Logic. (F. Jeffrey) Ed. R. **15**: 163.
Hamilton, Sir William Rowan. Am. J. Sci. **92**: 293. — with portrait, Dub. Univ. **19**: 94. — No. Brit. **45**: 37.
Hamiltons, The; an Australian Story. (H. M. Davidson) Chamb. J. **55**: 563–675.
Hamilton, Nev., Scenes in. (A. S. Evans) Overland, **2**: 273.
Hamilton College Library. (C. Huntington) Lib. J. **2**: 71.
Hamilton Literary and Theological Institution. (J. H. Raymond) Am. Q. Reg. **15**: 309.
Hamiltonian System of Instruction. Westm. **10**: 284. — Brit. Q. **2**: 143. Same art. Ecl. M. **6**: 229. — (Syd. Smith) Ed. R. **44**: 47. — Penn Mo. **6**: 636.
Hamlet. (E. F. Mosby) So. M. **9**: 348.
— Belleforest's. House. Words, **16**: 545.
— Byron and Shelley on Character of. Colburn, **29**: 327.
— Character of. (J. R. Lowell) No. Am. **106**: 629. — Blackw. **2**: 504. **24**: 585. **37**: 236. — Fraser, **14**: 1. — So. R. **3**: 380. — (G. Gilfillan) Ecl. M. **24**: 61. — New Eng. M. **5**: 458. — Anal. M. **5**: 68. — (H. N. Hudson) Am. Whig R. **7**: 94, 121.
— Difficulty about. Fraser, **99**: 394.
— a fat Man. (C. Edwards) Contin. Mo. **1**: 571.
— A Greek. Fraser, **102**: 511.
— Fechter's Rendition of. (K. Field) Atlan. **26**: 558. — (R. G. White) Nation, **10**: 118. — St. James, **2**: 371. — Ev. Sat. **9**: 274, 289. — O. & N. **3**: 359.
— Feigned Madness of. Blackw. **46**: 449.
— Ghost of. Fraser, **32**: 350.
— Life and Philosophy of. Sharpe, **19**: 233.
— Loneliness of. (E. Ferrier) Evang. R. **21**: 210.
— The lost. Colburn, **152**: 279.
— Maiming of. (A. C. Botkin) Lakeside, **9**: 444.
— Myth of. (E. Schuyler) Nation, **10**: 170.
— The new. Tinsley, **15**: 676.
— A Northern. (E. Rose) Fraser, **95**: 609.
— of Saxo Grammaticus. House. Words, **16**: 372.
— — and of Shakspere. Colburn, **152**: 279.
— Retzsch's Outlines of. For. Q. **2**: 697.
— Symptoms of a Mind diseased. (L. Blanchard) Colburn, **68**: 93.
— Theology of. (J. E. Rankin) Bost. R. **6**: 519.
— Voltaire on. St. Paul's, **9**: 173. Same art. Liv. Age, **111**: 791.
— the younger, Case of. (R. G. White) Galaxy, **9**: 535.
Hamlets of the Stage. (A. Sage) Atlan. **23**: 665. **24**: 188. *See also* Shakspere.
Hamley, E. B. Lady Lee's Widowhood. Liv. Age, **43**: 122.
Hamline, Leonidas L., with portrait. Meth. Q. **8**: 325.
— Life and Works of. (D. P. Kidder) Meth. Q. **41**: 1.
Hammer for light Forgings, Steam. (R. Peacock) J. Frankl. Inst. **73**: 325.
Hammers and Percussion. (A. Rigg) Pop. Sci. Mo. **9**: 11.
Hammerfest, Norway. All the Year, **12**: 232.
Hammersmith Ghost, Autobiography of. Fraser, **18**: 338.
Hammock, Pocket. Nature, **16**: 209.
Hammond, Benjamin, Descendants of. N. E. Reg. **30**: 28.
Hammond, Charles, with portrait. Am. J. Educ. **30**: 17.
Hammond, Jas. H. Eulogy on Calhoun. So. Q. **20**: 107.
Hammond, Col. M. C., Memoir of. De Bow, **24**: 338.
Hammond's Luck. Lond. Soc. **13**: 193.
Hammonds' Ugly Duckling. (J. Darrell) Argosy, **31**: 267.
Hampden, John. Nat. M. **3**: 97.
— and his Times. (T. B. Macaulay) Ed. R. **54**: 505. Same art. Select J. **1**: 1. — (R. Southey) Quar. **47**: 457. — Westm. **16**: 496. — Mus. **20**: 427. — Am. Q. **13**: 187. — Mo. R. **127**: 168. **129**: 439.
— Notes on. (Mrs. A. Tindal) Once a Week, **8**: 64.
— Nugent's Memorials of.—Colburn, **34**: 121.
Hampden, Renn Dickson, Bishop. Theo. R. **8**: 360.
— and Anglicanism. Dub. R. **69**: 66.
— and the See of Hereford. Chr. Rem. **15**: 213, 448. — Ecl. R. **87**: 221.
— Memorials of. Chr. Obs. **71**: 331.
Hampden Controversy. (R. S. Candlish) No. Brit. **8**: 534. — Fraser, **37**: 105. — (J. Williams) Am. Church R. **1**: 246.
Hampden House and Church. Penny M. **8**: 485.
Hampdens, The. (H. Martineau) Once a Week, **8**: 211–449.
Hampole, R. de. Account of his Stimulus Conscientio. (J. B. Yates) Arch. **19**: 314.

Hampshire, Eng., Church and Parish of Christ Church. Colburn, **1**: 143–422. — Penny M. **13**: 281.
— Domesday of. Fraser, **73**: 368.
— Legends of. All the Year, **31**: 445–542.
— Traditions of. All the Year, **32**: 60.
— Tropical Forests of. Nature, **15**: 229, 258, 279.
— Walk through. Temp. Bar, **15**: 391.
Hampshire County, Mass., Military Defense of, 1743. N. E. Reg. **13**: 21.
— Ministers of, to 1838. (B. B. Edwards) Am. Q. Reg. **10**: 379.
Hampstead and Highgate. St. James, **28**: 413.
— Summer Day at. (E. Walford) Once a Week, **11**: 169.
Hampstead Heath. (G. Hill) Sharpe, **31**: 200, 266. **32**: 30, 195. **33**: 101. — (H. King) Once a Week, **16**: 304. — (Mrs. C. A. White) Sharpe, **49**: 28. — House. Words, **4**: 15. — Lond. Soc. **37**: 477.
— Preservation of. All the Year, **17**: 198, 417.
Hampton, N. H., Burial Inscriptions at. N. E. Reg. **11**: 77.
Hampton, Va., Normal and Agricultural Institute at. (H. W. Ludlow) Harper, **47**: 672. — (M. F. Armstrong) Nation, **16**: 131.
Hampton Beach Rambles. (J. W. Chickering, jr.) Am. Natural **5**: 356.
Hampton Court. Penny M. **3**: 25. **10**: 377, 425.
— Few Hours at. (J. Eagles) Blackw. **48**: 764.
— Past and Present of. (Mrs. A. T. Thomson) Fraser, **34**: 172, 479.
— Pictures at. Lond. M. **7**: 616.
— Portraits from. (G. Scharf) Arch. **39**: 245. — Colburn, **17**: 272–316.
Hampton Roads, Battle of. So. Hist. Pap. **7**: 305.
Hananda, the Miracle Worker. Fraser, **86**: 244.
Hanbury, Benj., Historical Memoirs. Ecl. R. **70**: 335.
Hanbury, Daniel. Nature, **11**: 428.
Hanbury, Wm. A Churchman's Charity. Gent. M. n. s. **3**: 553.
Hancock, Albany. Nature, **9**: 43.
Hancock, John. (C. F. Adams) Pennsyl. M. **1**: 73.
— Biography of. (G. Mountfort) Hunt, **3**: 520.
— House of, at Boston. (A. Gilman) Atlan. **11**: 692.
— Letter of, 1775. N. E. Reg. **19**: 135.
— Letter to his Wife, 1777. N. E. Reg. **12**: 106.
— Reminiscences of. (W. H. Sumner) N. E. Reg. **8**: 187.
Hancock, Thomas. (A. Bradford) Hunt, **1**: 354.
Hancock, Winfield S. (M. W. Fuller) Dial (Ch.), **1**: 101.
— Civil Record of. So. R. n. s. **9**: 906.
— Nomination of. (E. L. Godkin) Nation, **31**: 4.
Hancock Genealogy. (W. H. Whitmore) N. E. Reg. **9**: 353.
Hancock Secret. (E. L. Linton) Ev. Sat. **11**: 598.
Hancock Co., Mass., proposed, 1775. N. E. Reg. **14**: 240.
Hancomb, Catherine, Strange Story of. (D. Butler) Once a Week, **7**: 442.
Hand, The Human. (H. Bronson) Chr. Q. Spec. **6**: 54. — (B. G. Wilder) Am. J. Sci. **94**: 44. — All the Year, **10**: 345. **35**: 124.
— Artificial Description of. J. Frankl. Inst. **40**: 57.
— Bell's Treatise on. Hogg, **1**: 129. — Mo. R. **132**: 424.
— Chiromancy. (A. Eubule-Evans) St. Paul's, **13**: 332.
— Left. All the Year, **23**: 609.
— phrenologically considered. Hogg, **2**: 253.
— Psychonomy of, Beamish's. Anthrop. R. **3**: 346.
— Right and Left. Penny M. **4**: 405.
— an unruly Member. (B. G. Wilder) Am. Natural. **1**: 414, 482, 631.
Hands. Blackw. **98**: 171. — Eng. Dom. M. **2**: 208. — Macmil. **12**: 72.
— and Gloves. Fraser, **36**: 290.
Hand and Soul. (D. G. Rossetti) Fortn. **14**: 692.
Hand in Hand; a Tale. (M. A. Tincker) Cath. World, **12**: 525.
Hand of Ethelberta; a Novel. (T. Hardy) Cornh. **32**: 1–733. **33**: 1–609.
Hand to Hand; a Tale. (R. H. Davis) Galaxy, **9**: 382.
Hand-Organs. Sharpe, **43**: 147.
— Nuisance of. Fraser, **56**: 719.
Hand-Shaking. All the Year, **23**: 466. — Dem. R. **34**: 346.
— Philosophy of. Tait, **1**: 212.
Handel, Geo. Frederick. (H. R. Haweis) Contemp. **10**: 503. **11**: 60. — (H. H. Stratham) Fortn. **33**: 53. — Tait, n. s. **24**: 403, 472. — House. Words, **15**: 588. — with portrait, Ecl. M. **41**: 138. — Brit. Q. **36**: 35. Same art. Liv. Age, **74**: 601. — Ecl. R. **105**: 616. — Penny M. **2**: 72. — Lond. Soc. **2**: 60.
— Genius of. St. James, **13**: 305.
— Haydn and Mozart. (S. A. Eliot) No. Am. **43**: 78.
— Messiah. (J. S. Dwight) Dem. R. **12**: 264. — (G. A. Macfarren) Am. Whig R. **9**: 135.
— — Autograph of. (J. Bennett) Macmil. **18**: 328. Same art. Ev. Sat. **6**: 289.
— Schœlcher's Life of. (G. F. Chorley) Ed. R. **106**: 227. Same art. Ecl. M. **42**: 433. — Fraser, **56**: 253.
Handel Festival. All the Year, **32**: 244.
Handel and Haydn Festival, 1871, Reminiscence of. Ev. Sat. **10**: 522.
Handerson, Worcester, Memoir of. Am. Q. Reg. **6**: 42.
Handkerchief. Cath. World, **15**: 849. — Ev. Sat. **12**: 73.
Handley Cross; or the Spa Hunt. Quar. **71**: 392. Same art. Ecl. Mus. **2**: 129.
Handsome; a Tale. Chamb. J. **49**: 769–827.
Handsome Housekeeper; a Story. (G. A. Sala) Belgra. **19**: 404.
Handsome John Gatsimer. (A. Cary) Harper, **40**: 848.
Handwriting. All the Year, **26**: 127. — Ev. Sat. **11**: 143. — Cath. World, **2**: 695.
— and Counterfeiting. Bank. M. (N. Y.) **34**: 22.
— as a Clew to Character. Ev. Sat. **11**: 378.
— A mere Question of. (F. Jacox) Colburn, **133**: 35.
— Peculiarities of. Appleton, **8**: 545.
— Thoughts on. (R. C. Sands) Knick. **12**: 318.
Handy Andy. (S. Lover) Bentley, **1**: 20–373. **5**: 89–479.
Hanging, Going to see a. Fraser, **22**: 150.
— in America. (E. C. Stedman) Putnam, **13**: 225.
— past and present. Tait, n. s. **10**: 233.
— Pleas against. Ev. Sat. **10**: 459.
— Revivals after. Chamb. J. **43**: 187.
— Story of One who was hanged. (J. McCormick) Overland, **2**: 518.
— Thoughts on. Tait, n. s. **8**: 314.
— Use of Chloroform in. (G. W. Peck) Am. Whig R. **8**: 283.
Hankinson, Thomas E., Works of Chr. Obs. **45**: 627.
Hanmer, Sir John. (H. Holbeach) St. Paul's, **10**: 386.
Hanmer, Sir Thomas, Life and Correspondence of. Mo. R. **146**: 427.
Hanna's Town, Destruction of, by Indians, 1782. Olden Time, **2**: 354.
Hannagan, Edward A., Portrait of. Dem. R. **18**: 403.
Hannah, J. (S. Gates) Meth. M. **26**: 193.
Hannah. (D. M. Craik) St. Paul's, **7**: 444–527. **8**: 33–580. **9**: 87–314. Same art. Liv. Age, **108**: 674, 737. **109**: 97–677. **110**: 91–654. **111**: 108–532.
Hannah Dawston's Child. (L. L. Pleasants) Atlan. **45**: 362.
Hannah Hervey. (T. Flint) Knick. **7**: 251.
Hannah Jane; a Poem. (D. R. Locke) Harper, **43**: 709.
Hannah Thurston. Contin. Mo. **5**: 456.
Hannay, James. Temp. Bar, **38**: 89. **49**: 234.
Hannibal. Blackw. **57**: 752.
— and Napoleon. So. Lit. Mess. **14**: 421. — Hogg, **8**: 327.
— Did he use Gunpowder? Fraser, **21**: 608.
— in Italy; a Poem. Temp. Bar, **12**: 393.
— Invasion of Italy. Westm. **14**: 42.
— on the Alps; a Poem. Temp. Bar, **12**: 231.

Hannibal, Passage of the Alps by. Ed. R. **43**: 163. — Ecl. R. **52**: 157.

— — a Poem. So. Lit. Mess. **23**: 137.

— Why he did not march on Rome. (F. G. Ireland) Penn Mo. **5**: 579.

Hanover. (E. Quincy) Nation, **3**: 92.

— and Netherlands, Importance of. For. R. **2**: 166.

— Commercial Treaty. Hunt, **5**: 177. **16**: 611. **19**: 411.

— Constitution of. For. Q. **20**: 378.

— Coup-d'Etat in. Brit. & For. R. **6**: 269. — Fraser, **52**: 443.

— Court of. (O. Meding) Contemp. **39**: 646. Same art. Liv. Age, **149**: 343.

— Ghost of a City. (R. Tomes) Putnam, **2**: 633.

— History of. Westm. **28**: 198.

— House of. Mo. R. **110**: 384.

— King of, and Stade Tolls. Ed. R. **74**: 359.

— Life in. (D. Costello) Bentley, **12**: 625. **13**: 26, 447.

— Village Life in. (W. Nordhoff) Pop. Sci. Mo. **16**: 467.

— Visit to. (H. Bedford) Month, **38**: 18.

Hanover, N. H., Dartmouth College. *See* Dartmouth College.

Hanover Sq. Rooms. (F. W. Fairholt) St. James, **2**: 283.

Hans Bendix; a Poem. Blackw. **10**: 264.

Hans Brenzel, the Smuggler. (W. H. G. Kingston) Bentley, **19**: 455.

Hans Ernst Mitterkamp; an Autobiography. Colburn, **113**: 45–470. **114**: 73–462. **115**: 212–464. **116**: 111–459. **117**: 203–467.

Hans Heiling's Rocks; from Körner. Blackw. **8**: 625.

Hans Memling's Love. Tinsley, **23**: 481, 586.

Hans Michel. Bentley, **25**: 21.

Hans Phaall; a Tale. (E. A. Poe) So. Lit. Mess. **1**: 565.

Hans Preller; a Legend of the Rhine Falls. (W. Alexis) Blackw. **128**: 176.

Hans Sachs and the Master Song. Cornh. **40**: 475.

Hans Schnaps' Spy-Glass; a Tale. (MM. Erckmann-Chatrian) Temp. Bar, **33**: 394. Same art. Ev. Sat. **11**: 454.

Hans Vogel; a Poetic Episode of the Franco-Prussian War. (R. Buchanan) Gent. M. n. s. **14**: 219.

Hanse Towns. Bank. M. (N. Y.) **30**: 99.

Hanseatic League, History of. For. Q. **7**: 130.

Hanseatic Merchants in London. Fraser, **47**: 699.

Hanserd Knollys Society, Works of. Ecl. R. **103**: 274.

Hansteen, Christopher. Nature, **8**: 349.

Hanway, Jonas, and first Umbrella. Ev. Sat. **11**: 151, 165.

Hanwell Lunatic Asylum. Chamb. J. **44**: 471. — Hogg, **8**: 129–361.

— Recollections of. Hogg, **9**: 8–237.

Hanworth. Fraser, **58**: 1–676. Same art. Liv. Age, **59**: 599–925. **60**: 105, 212.

Happiness. Blackw. **5**: 155. — (H. W. Hall) Unita. R. **14**: 505. — Irish Mo. **3**: 179. — Chr. Obs. **34**: 193.

— and Health. Chamb. J. **28**: 337.

— Best Means of promoting general. (J. Sewall, jr.) New Eng. **38**: 1.

— Connection between Piety and. Chr. R. **5**: 354.

— dependent on Ourselves. New Eng. M. **6**: 449.

— Dialogue on. (W. H. Mallock) 19th Cent. **6**: 425. Same art. Appleton, **22**: 355. — Liv. Age, **143**: 38.

— in different Gradations of Society. Anal. M. **16**: 151.

— Infidel's View of. (D. Y. Heisler) Mercersb. **20**: 12.

— the Object of God in Creation. Chr. R. **2**: 161.

— or Welfare? (F. Pollock) Mind, **2**: 269.

— Sources of. Mo. R. **131**: 85.

— the summum Bonum. (D. G. Thompson) Mind, **6**: 62.

— True, Sermon on. (D. Clapp) Mo. Rel. M. **2**: 313.

— Trust in God the Foundation of. Mo. Rel. M. **1**: 370.

Happy, Art of being. (A. H. Everett) No. Am. **27**: 115. — Am. Mo. R. **2**: 169. — (M. A. Fairman) Godey, **20**: 215. — (A. B. Johnson) Knick. **35**: 295.

Happy, though married. Chamb. J. **55**: 779.

Happy Dream; a Story. (S. Gibney) Tinsley, **29**: 566.

Happy Family. (J. McCarthy) Cath. World, **28**: 345.

Happy Hunting-Ground. (P. O. Sullivan) Harp[illegible] **61**: 324.

Happy Island. (E. E. Hale) Harper, **59**: 209.

Happy Jack. All the Year, **22**: 228.

Happy Land; a Poem. St. James, **40**: 499.

Happy Man, Passages in Life of. So. Lit. Mess. **7**: 836.

Hapsburg, Court of; a Poem. Fraser, **37**: 232.

— House of. All the Year, **31**: 126. — Month, **34**: 43. — Nat. Q. **8**: 128.

— — Episode in History of. (A. Hay) Belgra. **11**: 359. Same art. Ev. Sat. **9**: 366.

Hara-Kiri, Execution by, in Japan. (A. B. Mitford) Cornh. **20**: 549. Same art. Ecl. M. **74**: 89.

Haran and Serug, Assyria, Excursion to. Colburn, **162**: 62.

Harbaugh, Henry. (T. G. Apple) Mercersb. **15**: 165. — (C. G. Leland) Knick. **59**: 287.

— Poems of. (P. Schaff) Mercersb. **12**: 157.

Harbaugh's Harfe. (R. E. Thompson) Penn Mo. **1**: 281.

Harberton, Viscountess, with portrait. Victoria, **36**: 81.

Harbor of New York, Deposit of Silt in. (C. H. Haswell) J. Frankl. Inst. **65**: 161.

Harbor Defense. (J. G. Barnard) So. Lit. Mess. **11**: 25.

Harbors of North America. (D. Stevenson) Hunt, **2**: 309.

— Improvement of. (D. S. Howard) J. Frankl. Inst. **65**: 21.

— — New Method of, 1876. J. Frankl. Inst. **102**: 153. *See* Rivers and Harbors.

Harcourt's V'line Mango. (S. A. Shields) Lippinc. **28**: 84.

Hard and sharp Steeplechase; a Tale. Temp. Bar, **38**: 35.

Hard Road to travel. All the Year, **20**: 235.

Hard Struggle. (W. Marston) Liv. Age, **57**: 213.

Hard Swearing on a Church Steeple. (T. W. Lane) Putnam, **5**: 41.

Hard Times. (C. Dickens) House. Words, **9**: 141–597.

— and cheap Labor. (C. W. Elliott) Galaxy, **23**: 474.

— Causes and Cure of. (G. W. Burnap) Hunt, **8**: 493.

— Did Government cause? Penn Mo. **8**: 338.

Hard up. (F. J. O'Brien) Putnam, **4**: 50.

Hardcastle Crags. (R. M. Kettle) Colburn, **168**: 260.

Hardenberg, Friedrich von, called Novalis. Lond. Q. **17**: 325.

— and the Blue Flower. (H. H. Boyesen) Atlan. **36**: 689.

— Life and Writings of. Dub. R. **3**: 277.

— Memoirs of. Ed. R. **146**: 396.

— Writings of. Dub. Univ. **54**: 358. — (T. Carlyle) For. R. **4**: 97. — Westm. **13**: 170.

Hardin, Col. John. (M. T. Walworth) Hist. M. **15**: 233.

— Death at Buena Vista. (Gen. Guinnipp) Hist. M. **16**: 299.

Harding, Chester, Artist. (S. Bowles) Atlan. **19**: 484. — (O. Tiffany) Lippinc. **13**: 65.

Harding, James D. Art J. **16**: 39.

Harding, John. Arch. **1**: 87.

Hardinge, Lord Henry. (W. C. Taylor) Bentley, **23**: 1. — Bentley, **32**: 452. Same art. Ecl. M. **27**: 497.

Hardwick, Mass., Ministers of. Am. Q. Reg. **10**: 57.

Hardwick Hall. Antiquary, **3**: 217.

Hardwicke, Philip Yorke, Lord, Life and Times of. Blackw. **63**: 463. — Ecl. R. **87**: 744. — Westm. **49**: 348. Same art. Ecl. M. **15**: 1.

Hardwicke Reformatory School. Am. J. Educ. **3**: 789.

Hardy, Frederick D., Works of. Art J. **27**: 73.

Hardy, Gathorne, Polit. Portrait of. St. James, **24**: 678.

Hardy, Thomas. Pair of blue Eyes. (W. H. Browne) So. M. **13**: 365.

— Novels of. Brit. Q. **73**: 342.

Hardyng's Chronicle, Extracts from MS. Copy of. (H. Ellis) Arch. **16**: 139.

Hare, Augustus J. C. Memorials of a quiet Life. Chr. Obs. **72**: 902.

Hare Mrs. Augustus J. C. (C. K. Paul) Theo. R. **10**: 98.
Hare, Augustus Wm. Sermons. (J. J. Blunt) Quar. **59**: 33. — Chr. Obs. **38**: 452, 525.
— and J. C. Guesses at Truth. (J. Morley) Fortn. **7**: 116. — Blackw. **63**: 701.
Hare, Julius Charles. (J. H. Rigg) Meth. Q. **16**: 169, 329. — Quar. **97**: 1. Same art. Ecl. M. **36**: 895.
— and the English Review. Ecl. R. **89**: 657.
— Sermons of Faith. Prosp. R. **3**: 396.
Hare, Robert. Compound Blowpipe. Am. J. Sci. **2**: 281. **3**: 87.
— Notice of. Am. J. Sci. **76**: 100.
Hare Family. (E. L. Godkin) Nation, **16**: 287.
Hare, The, and the Rabbit. Penny M. **10**: 417.
— Does it chew the Cud? Kitto, **37**: 383.
— New Species of. (F. V. Hayden) Am. Natural. **3**: 113.
Harem, An African. Cornh. **23**: 726. Same art. Ecl. R. **77**: 165. Same art. Liv. Age, **110**: 181. — Ev. Sat. **11**: 143.
— of the Pasha of Widdin. Fraser, **18**: 679.
— of Saïd Pacha, Visit to. Once a Week, **7**: 387.
— Visit to. Chamb. J. **5**: 65.
— Visits to. Blackw. **15**: 199. **16**: 17. **18**: 657. — Mus. **4**: 481. **5**: 337. **8**: 193.
See Seraglio.
Harems of the East. Penny M. **7**: 484.
Harem Life. (E. De Leon) Harper, **46**: 364. — Appleton, **3**: 197, 226. — Bentley, **43**: 508. Same art. Liv. Age, **57**: 943. — Chamb. J. **43**: 365.
— Emeline Lott on. (J. G. Maline) Cath. World, **7**: 407.
Harford, J. S., Memoir of. Chr. Obs. **66**: 489.
Harkaway Sketches. (J. Mills) Bentley, **8**: 33, 337.
Harker and Blind. (J. T. McKay) Scrib. **4**: 302.
Harkness, Robert. Nature, **18**: 628.
Harlakenden Genealogy. N. E. Reg. **14**: 319. **15**: 327.
Harland, John. (J. Croston) Reliquary, **9**: 81.
— Reminiscences of. (T. Hunt) Reliquary, **14**: 28.
Harland, Marion, *pseud.* *See* Terhune, Mrs. M. V.
Harleian Dairy System. Mo. R. **121**: 56.
Harlem Plains, Battle of. (J. A. Stevens) M. Am. Hist. **4**: 351. **6**: 260.
Harlequin Fairy Morgana. All the Year, **12**: 40.
Harlequin, History of. Temp. Bar, **43**: 202.
Harlequinade, A. Chamb. J. **26**: 340.
Harley, John, the Veteran. Mo. R. **145**: 82.
Harley Patent. (Mrs. W. H. Palmer) Galaxy, **3**: 742.
Harley's Inheritance. (M. Northcott) Tinsley, **20**: 548.
Harlow, George Henry. (D. Cook) Once a Week, **6**: 94.
Harlow Genealogy. (T. P. Adams) N. E. Reg. **14**: 227.
Harmens, Jacob. *See* Arminius.
Harmless old Gentleman; a Tale. Putnam, **6**: 276.
Harmon, D. W. Travels in W. Caledonia. Quar. **26**: 409.
Harmonic and Basic Lines. (P. E. Chase) J. Frankl. Inst. **108**: 28.
Harmonies, Elementary Spectral. (P. E. Chase) J. Frankl. Inst. **104**: 288. **105**: 20.
Harmonists, The. (R. H. Davis) Atlan. **17**: 529.
— and George Rapp. (D. E. Nevin) Scrib. **17**: 703.
Harmonious Discords; a Dramatic Proverb. (H. St. Maur) Once a Week, **28**: 424.
Harmonious Effects. (M. L. Pool) Galaxy, **3**: 374.
Harmonograph, A new; Induction Balance. J. Frankl. Inst. **108**: 132.
Harmony, Demode's New System of. For. Q. **3**: 506.
— Haunts of. (A. Ogilvy) Once a Week, **16**: 265, 294.
— Imperfections of modern. (S. A. Pearce) Pop. Sci. Mo. **16**: 508.
— in Art. Art J. **17**: 65, 114.
— Physics and Physiology of. Westm. **104**: 432. Same art. Liv. Age, **130**: 195.
Harmony Night at our Histrionic Club. (H. Louther) Tinsley, **26**: 425.
Harms, Louis, of Hermannsburg. (M. L. Stoever) Evang. R. **17**: 285.
— and his Work. Good Words, **1**: 673-778.
— Schleiermacher, and De Wette. (Dr. Hagenbach) Meth. Q. **21**: 403.
Harnett, Cornelius, Seat of. (B. J. Lossing) Potter Am. Mo. **5**: 641.
Harneyhow's Hummock. (J. G. Austin) Lippinc. **3**: 608.
Harold the Dauntless, Poem of. Blackw. **1**: 76.
Harold II. and Earl Godwin. No. Brit. **52**: 28.
— Tomb of, Day at. Once a Week, **13**: 190.
Harold of Norway. Quar. **135**: 164.
Harold Rivers; a Tale. Chamb. J. **55**: 773-818.
Harold Skimpole. Bentley, **54**: 48.
Harold Vaughan's Wooing. (M. Henly) Colburn, **157**: 569.
Haroun-al-Raschid. Temp. Bar, **61**: 456. Same art. Ecl. M. **96**: 802. — Appleton, **25**: 346.
— and Saracenic Civilization. Putnam, **8**: 337.
— Modern. House. Words, **2**: 617.
— Story of. Colburn, **135**: 54.
Harper, Elizabeth. Godey, **45**: 45.
Harper, John, Life of. Potter Am. Mo. **4**: 480.
Harper, S. B. Bertrand. Fraser, **16**: 190.
Harper and Brothers, Publishing-House of. So. Lit. Mess. **5**: 629. — Liv. Age, **31**: 27.
Harper's Monthly and Weekly. Putnam, **9**: 293.
Harper's Weekly, an uncivil Journal. (J. G. Meline) Cath. World, **14**: 721.
Harper's Ferry and old Captain Brown. (W. E. Forster) Macmil. **1**: 306.
— Invasion of. (W. G. Day) So. M. **13**: 433. — Once a Week, **1**: 484.
— — Moral of, 1859. (L. Bacon) New Eng. **17**: 1066.
Harpocrates; a Poem. (B. Taylor) Atlan. **15**: 662.
Harpooner, Shipwreck of. Meth. M. **40**: 362.
Harpsichord, The. Chamb. J. **24**: 257.
Harriers, Day with the. St. James, **16**: 251.
Harrietta, or the rash Reply. Liv. Age, **30**: 300.
Harring, Harro, Sketch of. (A. H. Everett) Dem. R. **15**: 337, 462, 561.
Harrington, James, and his Oceana. Temp. Bar, **24**: 407.
Harrington, Jonathan, with portrait. (E. H. Goss) Potter Am. Mo. **5**: 513.
Harrington, William, Martyrdom of. (J. Morris) Month, **20**: 411.
Harrington Grange. (L. Sand) Sharpe, **34**: 180, 256, 312. **35**: 30, 88, 134.
Harris, C. Fiske, Library of. Am. Bibliop. **7**: 152.
Harris, Elizabeth, of Roxbury, Letters to, from England, 1654 and 1662. N. E. Reg. **5**: 307.
Harris, James, Earl of Malmesbury, Diaries and Corresp. of. (J. W. Croker) Quar. **74**: 508. **75**: 403.
Harris, Joel Chandler. Uncle Remus, etc. (T. F. Crane) Pop. Sci. Mo. **18**: 824.
Harris, John. Great Commission. Chr. R. **7**: 379. — (O. A. Brownson) Cath. World, **12**: 187.
— Man primeval. Ecl. R. **90**: 612.
— Pre-Adamite Earth. Ecl. R. **85**: 137. — (A. P. Peabody) No. Am. **70**: 391. — (D. W. Phillips) Chr. R. **14**: 402. — Brit. Q. **5**: 387. — So. Q. **21**: 48.
— Union. Ecl. R. **68**: 303.
Harris, Thomas Lake, and Community of Salem-on-Erie. Ev. Sat. **11**: 142.
— Spiritual Poems of. Temp. Bar, **27**: 454.
Harris, Thaddeus William. Horticultural Discourse. Am. Mo. R. **3**: 152.
Harris, William, Memoir of. Cong. M. **13**: 110, 165.
Harris, William T., with portrait. (H. Barnard) Am. J. Educ. **30**: 625.
Harrisburg, Pa. (J. W. Howe) O. & N. **2**: 62.
Harrisburg Presbytery, Fathers of. Am. Presb. R. **9**: 319.

Harrison, Gessner, Memorial of. So. R. n. s. **13**: 334.
Harrison, William, Strange Story of. Chamb. J. **48**: 174.
Harrison, Wm. H., with portrait. Portfo.(Den.) **13**: 305.
— and Governor Shelby. Niles's Reg. **14**: 185.
— Campaigns of. (B. J. Lossing) Harper, **27**: 145.
— Discourses on the Death of. Chr. Exam. **30**: 359.
— Historical Discourse of. (E. Everett) No. Am. **51**: 46.
— Life of. West. M. **3**: 82, 113, 222.
— Narrative of. West. Mo. R. **1**: 542.
Harrison, Wm. H. Notes and Reminiscences. Dub. Univ. **91**: 537, 698. **92**: 56–705.
Harroldstone Tower; a Tale. Colburn, **138**: 211, 313.
Harrow, Rambles round. (A. Rimmer) Belgra. **45**: 96–472.
Harrow School. Blackw. **94**: 457. **96**: 219.
— Football at. Lond. Soc. **5**: 246.
— Monitorial System of. Liv. Age, **41**: 367.
— Recollections of. (F. Trench) Temp. Bar, **28**: 467.
Harrowgate. (H. Curling) Bentley, **17**: 445.
Harry; a Story. (B. Webber) Tinsley, **26**: 60.
Harry; a Story. Lond. Soc. **40**: 605.
Harry Bolton's Curacy. Blackw. **69**: 180.
Harry Coverdale's Courtship. (F. E. Smedley) Sharpe, **18**: 1–340. **19**: 17–321. **20**: 1–321. **21**: 1–369. **22**: 35–365. **23**: 115.
Harry Heathcote of Gangoil. (A. Trollope) Liv. Age, **120**: 203–621.
Harry Lorrequer, Confessions of. (C. Lever) Dub. Univ. **9**: 145–402. **10**: 582, 737. **11**: 222, 753. **12**: 97–592. **13**: 133–677. **14**: 23–509. **15**: 21–159. **23**: 757.
Harry Martin's Wife. (G. B. Stuart) Argosy, **30**: 61. Same art. Liv. Age, **146**: 554.
Harry Richmond, Adventures of. (G. Meredith) Cornh. **22**: 257–641. **23**: 99–641. **24**: 102–604.
Harry Smith's Courtship. (Mrs. W. B. Hodgson) Peop. J. **4**: 209.
Harry Sumner's Revenge. Sharpe, **5**: 150. **8**: 214.
Hart, Charles, Obituary of. Art J. **32**: 171.
Hart, Emanuel B., with portrait. Dem. R. **40**: 520.
Hart, John S. Am. J. Educ. **5**: 91.
Hart, Luther. (N. Porter) Chr. Q. Spec. **6**: 476.
Hart, Nancy. (Mrs. E. F. Ellet) Godey, **37**: 201.
Harte, F. Bret. (N. Brooks) Scrib. **6**: 158. — Belgra. **45**: 232. — (E. S. Forman) O. & N. **4**: 712. — with portrait, Ev. Sat. **10**: 25, 42, 91. — (P. Godwin) Putnam, **16**: 109. — Chamb. J. **48**: 324. — Potter Am. Mo. **17**: 306. — Ecl. M. **76**: 752. — with portrait, Ecl. M. **80**: 371. — Ev. Sat. **15**: 358. — Temp. Bar, **39**: 257.
— London Spectator on. Ev. Sat. **10**: 486.
— Luck of Roaring Camp. Am. Bibliop. **3**: 54. — Blackw. **110**: 422.
— Poems of. (J. R. Dennett) Nation, **12**: 42. — Galaxy, **12**: 635.
— Writings of. (E. S. Nadal) No. Am. **124**: 81.
Hartebeest, Hunting the. (M. L. Meason) Broadw. **2**: 495.
Hartford, Conn. (C. H. Clark) Scrib. **13**: 1.
— Building in. Am. Arch. **1**: 339.
— Charter Oak at. *See* Charter Oak.
— Dutch House of Good Hope. N. E. Reg. **6**: 368.
— Female Seminary and its Founder. Am. J. Educ. **28**: 65.
— Grammar School at. Am. J. Educ. **28**: 185.
— High School at. (H. Barnard) Am. J. Educ. **22**: 339. **28**: 225.
— Hopkins Bequest at. Am. J. Educ. **28**: 185.
— in the olden Time, Stuart's. Knick. **42**: 259.
— New Capitol. Am. Arch. **5**: 17–206.
— Orphan Asylum Building. Am. Arch. **4**: 174.
— Records of. N. E. Reg. **12**: 173, 196, 331. **13**: 48–343. **20**: 234. **22**: 192. **23**: 42.
— Trinity College. (W. C. Brocklesby) Scrib. **11**: 601.
Hartford, Conn., Trinity College, New Buildings of. Am. Arch. **2**: 225.
Hartford Convention. (S. E. Baldwin) New Eng. **37**: 145. — (B. J. Lossing) Harper, **25**: 217. — (A. H. Everett) No. Am. **39**: 208. — Am. Q. **15**: 167. — New Eng. M. **6**: 181. — Niles's Reg. **26**: 219. **38**: 20. **39**: 434.
Hartford Wits. (F. Sheldon) Atlan. **15**: 187.
Hartington, S. C. Cavendish, Marquis of, Political Portrait of. St. James, **25**: 312.
Hartley, Col. Thomas, Life of. Portfo.(Den.) **34**: 109.
Hartley Colliery Calamity, 1862. (T. Sopwith) St. James, **3**: 401. *See also* Coal Mines.
Hartmann, E. von. Philosophy of the Unconscious. (L. Dumont) Pop. Sci. Mo. **2**: 152–311. — New Eng. **37**: 15.
Hartmann, Richard. Lond. Soc. **35**: 493.
Hartt, Charles F. Nature, **18**: 174. — (R. Rathbun) Pop. Sci. Mo. **13**: 231.
Hartwell House. (J. Wilkins) Once a Week, **14**: 304. — Hogg, **4**: 33.
— Smyth's Ædes Hartwellianæ. Colburn, **94**: 40.
— Visit to. Chamb. J. **22**: 133. Same art. Liv. Age, **43**: 19.
Hartwick Seminary, Hist. of. (W. Hull) Luth. Q. **8**: 592.
Hartz Mountains. (E. Everett) No. Am. **12**: 268. — (J. M. Hoppin) Knick. **35**: 189. — (H. Blackburn) Lond. Soc. **24**: 213. Same art. Harper, **47**: 67.
— In the Heart of. (M. Mitchell) Harper, **56**: 684.
— Mining in. St. James, **13**: 202.
— Reminiscences of. Canad. Mo. **8**: 425.
— Stroll in. Lond. Soc. **37**: 568.
— Village Ball in. (G. H. Putnam) Scrib. **4**: 755.
Harvard, John. Am. J. Educ. **5**: 523.
— and Harvard University. Potter Am. Mo. **4**: 172.
Harvard University. (H. E. Scudder) Scrib. **12**: 337. — (G Bancroft) No. Am. **33**: 216. — (J. Pickering) No. Am. **38**: 381. — (J. G. Palfrey) No. Am **52**: 338. — (A. P. Peabody) No. Am. **60**: 38. — (F. Bowen) No. Am. **68**: 503. — (G. E. Ellis) Chr. Exam. **45**: 342. — (B. B. Edwards) Am. Q. Reg. **3**: 263. — (A. Bradford) Am. Q. Reg. **9**: 329. — (E. S. Drone) Appleton, **11**: 807. — (J. G. Palfrey) Chr. Exam. **17**: 93. — U. S. Lit. Gaz. **1**: 108. — Spirit Pilg. **3**: 323, 359. **4**: 373. — Appleton, **3**: 253. — Am. J. Educ. **9**: 129. **27**: 129. — O. & N. **4**: 117.
— and Boston. Nature, **21**: 149.
— and Yale Universities. (G. M. Towle) Fortn. **8**: 398.
— Censures on, 1672. N. E. Reg. **35**: 121.
— Class-Day at. (M. A. Dodge) Atlan. **12**: 242. — Appleton, **10**: 113.
— Classical Studies in. (F. Bowen) No. Am. **54**: 35.
— Course of Study in. O. & N. **5**: 109. **6**: 108.
— Divinity School. (E. L. Godkin) Nation, **29**: 6–124. Mo. Rel. M. **38**: 161. — (J. Walker) Chr. Exam. **10**: 129. — (J. T. Austin) Chr. Exam. **10**: 136.
— — Future of. (W. C. Langdon) Atlan. **48**: 377.
— Eliot's History of. (F. Bowen) No. Am. **68**: 99, 503. — (J. L. Kingsley) New Eng. **7**: 140.
— Examinations for Women at. (C. F. Dunbar) Penn Mo. **9**: 284. — (C. J. Stillé) Penn Mo. **9**: 93. — (S. B. Wister) Penn Mo. **8**: 944. — Nation, **26**: 133, 183. — O. & N. **8**: 371.
— Experience with Elective Studies. Nation, **17**: 70.
— Graduates of. N. E. Reg. **4**: 175, 354.
— — from Salem. (J. P. Dabney) Am. Q. Reg. **15**: 185. — (J. P. Dabney) N. E. Reg. **5**: 47, 153.
— — Longevity of. (J. P. Dabney) Am. Q. Reg. **13**: 403. **14**: 377.
— — Loyalist. Am. Q. Reg. **14**: 167.
— — Memoirs of. (J. Farmer) N. E. Reg. **1**: 34.
— — Sibley's. (C. C. Smith) O. & N. **8**: 501.

Harvard University, Greek Professor in. No. Am. 1: 127.
— Gymnastic Exercises at. U. S. Lit. Gaz. 4: 115.
— Hedge on Reforms in. (T. D. Woolsey) New Eng. 25: 695.
— in the 17th Century. (G. E. Ellis) No. Am. 117: 141.
— in 1781. Hist. M. 1: 34.
— in 1786–87. (H. Adams) No. Am. 114: 110.
— Law School at. (C. Follen) No. Am. 36: 395.
— Letter to the President of, 1849. No. Am. 68: app.
— Library of. (C. A. Cutter) No. Am. 107: 568.
— — Catalogue of. (C. A. Cutter) No. Am. 108: 96.
— — Glance into Sumner Alcove. (K. V. Smith) Scrib. 17: 732.
— Medfield Contribution to. N. E. Reg. 10: 49.
— Medical College at. (J. Bigelow) No. Am. 4: 284.
— Memorial Biographies. (C. E. Norton) No. Am. 103: 498.
— Memorial Hall. (H. W. Bellows) Unita. R. 2: 477.
— — and Yale Memorial Building. (C. E. Norton) Nation, 5: 34.
— — Building of. N. E. Reg. 35: 360.
— Museum of Compar. Zoölogy. Am. J. Educ. 9: 613.
— Natural History Education at. Nature, 6: 394.
— New Liturgy in. (N. S. Richardson) Am. Church R. 11: 604.
— Observatory at. (J. Farrar) No. Am. 8: 205. — Nature, 15: 201.
— Old. Pioneer, 3: 300.
— Origin of Unitarianism in. Spirit Pilg. 2: 469.
— Patriotic Record of. (I. C. Ropes) Hours at Home, 2: 272.
— Peirce's History of. (C. C. Felton) Chr. Exam. 15: 311. — Am. Mo. R. 4: 301. — Mus. 43: 470. — Mo. R. 156: 92.
— Presidency of, 1868. (J. Fiske) Nation, 7: 547.
— Quincy's History of. (F. Parkman) Chr. Exam. 30: 56. — (J. L. Kingsley) Am. Bib. Repos. 2d s. 6: 177, 384. 7: 175. — (E. Pond) Am. Bib. Repos. 2d s. 7: 89, 253.
— Recent original scientific Work at. (J. R. W. Hitchcock) Pop. Sci. Mo. 17: 482.
— Recollections of. (T. Hughes and W. D. Rawlins) Ev. Sat. 10: 286, 466.
— Reform in. U. S. Lit. Gaz. 2: 209, 247, 281. 3: 12–205. — O. & N. 1: 74.
— Religion in. Radical, 3: 157.
— Religious and theological Interests of, 1845. Mo. Rel. M. 2: 289.
— Sectarianism of. (E. S. Gannett) Chr. Exam. 39: 261.
— Theological School of. Chr. Exam. 83: 220.
— Voluntary System at. Chr. Exam. 30: 140.
— Who was the first President of? (T. Farrar) N. E. Reg. 9: 269.
Harvard Lectureship at Cambridge, England. (C. E. Norton) Nation, 2: 457.
Harvest. (A. H. Baldwin) Fraser, 68: 307. — Cornh. 12: 358.
Harvest of Gold. Liv. Age, 33: 608.
Harvesting, Wet-Weather. Pract. M. 4: 257.
Harvest-Home; a Poem. (F. Tennyson) Fraser, 48: 632.
Harvest-Homes, Old. All the Year, 18: 164.
Harvey, Christopher. Cong. 4: 660.
Harvey, George, Historic Painter. Brit. Q. 4: 251.
Harvey, Joseph. Inquiry. (J. H. Linsley) Chr. Q. Spec. 3: 551.
Harvey, William. (T. H. Huxley) Fortn. 29: 167. Same art. Sup. Pop. Sci. Mo. 2: 385. — Art J. 18: 89. — Nature, 17: 417.
— and his Times. Month, 21: 466.
— and Vivisection. (J. H. Bridges) Fortn. 26: 1.
— on the Circulation of the Blood. Ed. R. 147: 25.
Harvey, William, Tercentenary of. Nature, 18: 145. — (B.W. Richardson) Gent. M. n. s. 20: 455.
Harvey Genealogy. (F. M. Hubbard) N. E. Reg. 12: 313.
Hasheesh. (C. Richet) Pop. Sci. Mo. 13: 482. — Chamb. J. 10: 341. — Nat. R. 6: 91. Same art. Ecl. M. 43: 305. Same art. Liv. Age, 56: 449.
— Amateur Assassin with. (W.L.Cowles) Belgra. 31: 353.
— and Opium. Dub. Univ. 95: 493.
— Apocalypse of. Putnam, 8: 625.
— Effects of. (M. S. de Luca) Intel. Obs. 2: 346.
— Experiences of. (S. Hibberd) Intel. Obs. 2: 435. Same art. Ecl. M. 59: 172.
— Vision of. (B. Taylor) Putnam, 3: 402.
Hasheesh Dream. (E. Phelps) Lakeside, 7: 141.
Hasheesh-Eater. Putnam, 8: 233.
— Confessions of a French. Once a Week, 18: 349.
Haslam, P. Meth. M. 28: 3.
Hasli-thal. (H. Bedford) Month, 26: 407.
Hassam Genealogy. N. E. Reg. 24: 414.
Hassler Scientific Expedition, 1871–72. O. & N. 6: 747.
Hastings, Lady Elizabeth, Sketch of. Meth. M. 28: 145.
Hastings, Frank A., Memoir of. Blackw. 58: 496.
Hastings, Lady Flora, Poems of. Ecl. R. 73: 572. — Tait, n. s. 8: 129.
Hastings, Selina, Countess. *See* Huntingdon.
Hastings, Walter, Descendants of. (L. N. H. Buckminster) N. E. Reg. 21: 350.
Hastings, Warren. (T. B. Macaulay) Ed. R. 74: 160. Same art. Am. Ecl. 3: 409. — Blackw. 34: 326. 49: 423, 638. — Dub. Univ. 18: 619, 693. — Anal. M. 13: 207. — (T. B. Macaulay) Mus. 44: 9. — Mus. 42: 197, 502. — Bentley, 10: 627. — Ecl. M. 34: 537.
— Chapter in Life of. Chr. Obs. 76: 569.
— Essay on the Effect of Moral Causes on the Prosperity of Nations. Fraser, 28: 667.
— Gleig's Memoirs of. Mo. R. 154: 165, 386.
— Life of. Penny M. 10: 387.
— — and Impeachment of. Liv. Age, 93: 67, 131.
Hastings Genealogy. (P. Stackhouse) N. E. Reg. 13: 134.
Hastings, Town of. (G. Hill) Sharpe, 30: 254, 301.
— and St. Leonards. Lond. Soc. 3: 128.
— Old. (M. B. Edwards) Good Words, 20: 319.
Hastings, Battle of. (G. B. Airy) Arch. 34: 231. — Blackw. 5: 259. Penny M. 10: 17.
— — Field of. (J. K. Hosmer) Nation, 13: 383.
Hastings, Castle of, and Chapel of Virgin Mary. Penny M. 3: 375.
Hasty Pudding; a Poem. (J. Barlow) Harper, 13: 145
Hats. (H. Jennings) Once a Week, 25: 321, 424. — Chamb. J. 32: 204. 36: 34. 56: 350.
— Æsthetics of Dress. Blackw. 57: 51.
— Manufacture of. (J. G. Austin) Atlan. 22: 428.
— Old. Chamb. J. 49: 580.
Hat Factory. Penny M. 10: 41.
Hatch Genealogy. (J. M. Hatch) N. E. Reg. 14: 197.
Hatfield, R. G., Death of. Am. Arch. 5: 65.
Hatfield, Mass., Ministers of. Am. Q. Reg. 10: 272.
— Bridge-Opening at, 1807. (J. Lyman) Hist. M. 12: 289.
Hatfield House. (H. James, jr.) Galaxy, 24: 351. — Antiquary, 4: 151, 201. — Quar. 141: 1.
Hathaway Strange. Lippinc. 7: 49, 147.
Hatherley, Lord. (W. P. Wood) Political Portrait of. St. James, 25: 763.
Hatherton, Lord. (C. Redding), Colburn, 128: 176.
Hatim Tai; an Arabian Tale. Colburn, 22: 341.
Hating. N. Ecl. 5: 524.
Hatters, Worshipful Company of. Chamb. J. 45: 721.
Hatton, Sir Christopher. Bentley, 21: 79.
Hatton, Joseph, with portrait. Colburn, 167: 187.
Hatton Family, Correspondence of. Ed. R. 150: 111. Same art. Liv. Age, 142: 515.
Hatton Garden Spoon. Liv. Age, 43: 559, 597.

Hauch, Carsten, and his latest Poem. No. Brit. **47**: 94.
Hauff, Wilhelm, German Romanticist. Brit. Q. **14**: 87. Same art. Ecl. M. **24**: 145.
— Works of. So. Q. **7**: 197.
Haug, Martin. (E. P. Evans) Unita. R. **7**: 378, 495.
Hauk, Minnie, with portrait. Victoria, **34**: 94.
Haunted and the Haunters. (E. B. Lord Lytton) Blackw. **86**: 224. Same art. Ecl. M. **48**: 389.
Haunted Bank of Hamburg. Chamb. J. **36**: 228.
Haunted Baronet; a Novel. (J. S. Le Fanu) Belgra. **12**: 69–453. **13**: 102.
Haunted Cask; a Tale. Chamb. J. **50**: 369.
Haunted Closet. (S. A. Weiss) Scrib. **3**: 708.
Haunted Enghenio. Blackw. **111**: 86. Same art. Ecl. M. **78**: 349.
Haunted Garden; a Tale. Temp. Bar, **24**: 257.
Haunted Grange. Dub. Univ. **2**: 693.
Haunted Hamlet; a Dramatic Sketch. (C. Osborne) Temp. Bar, **20**: 400.
Haunted Hilderton. All the Year, **15**: 498.
Haunted Hof; a Tale. Am. Mo. M. **3**: 169–386.
Haunted Hotel; a Mystery of Venice. (W. Collins) Belgra. **35**: 385. **36**: 107, 360. **37**: 110. Same art. Canad. Mo. **14**: 1–657.
Haunted House, Story of a. (Mrs. Romer) Bentley, **26**: 436. Same art. Liv. Age, **23**: 568.
Haunted House. (H. Parr) Liv. Age, **54**; 361, 419, 453.
Haunted House. All the Year, **2**: supp.
Haunted House. Knick. **59**: 38.
Haunted House. Lond. M. **6**: 63.
Haunted House. (G. Macdonald) Scrib. **7**: 272.
Haunted House at Willington. (W. Howitt) Howitt, **1**: 289.
— in Charnwood Forest. (W. Howitt) Howitt, **2**: 135.
— in Mexico. (W. Browne) Once a Week, **8**: 141.
— in Westminster. (J. S. Le Fanu) Belgra. **16**: 261.
— Narrative of. Dub. Univ. **60**: 476. Same art. Ecl. M. **58**: 54.
— near Hampstead. Bentley, **47**: 37.
Haunted Houses. (C. Mackay) Bentley, **7**: 161.
Haunted King and the loaded Dice. Putnam, **7**: 177.
Haunted Life; a Tale. Temp. Bar, **2**: 413.
Haunted Lighthouse. (C. S. Corfield) Belgra. **28**: 406.
Haunted Lives. (J. S. Le Fanu) Dub. Univ. **71**: 564, 669. **72**: 63–686.
Haunted Lodging-House. (Mrs. Abdy) Sharpe, **28**: 127.
Haunted London. All the Year, **1**: 20, 92.
Haunted Man. Chamb. J. **25**: 268.
Haunted Manor-House of Paddington. (C. Ollier) Bentley, **10**: 519.
Haunted Mine. (R. B. Peake) Bentley, **12**: 480.
Haunted Mines. (H. Stanton) Lakeside, **2**: 48.
Haunted Oven. (W. L. Blackley) St. James, **41**: 619.
Haunted People. Chamb. J. **9**: 385.
Haunted Precinct. All the Year, **42**: 153.
Haunted Race. Sharpe, **39**: 113.
Haunted Rock. (C. F. F. Woods) Belgra. **13**: 325.
— of Santa Barbara. (V. F. Russell) Overland, **11**: 425.
Haunted Shanty. (B. Taylor) Atlan. **8**: 57.
Haunted Ships, Legends of. Lond. M. **4**: 499.
Haunted Spring; a Poem. Mo. Rel. M. **4**: 500, 535.
Haunted Valley. (N. Brooks) Overland, **1**: 254.
Haunted Valley. (A. G. Bierce) Overland, **7**: 88.
Haunts of the Student; a Poem. (M. Junkin) So. Lit. Mess. **16**: 596.
Hauran, Egypt. Colburn, **120**: 253.
Hauser, Kaspar. (W. H. Browne) So. M. **14**: 394, 499. — Mus. **16**: 367. — Am. Mo. R. **3**: 225. — Chamb. J. **56**: 454. — Colburn, **120**: 484. — Ed. New Philos. J. **8**: 134. — Penny M. **3**: 47, 50, 58. **9**: 398, 406. — Liv. Age, **119**: 315. — Ecl. R. **58**: 58. — Howitt, **1**: 257, 273, 282. Same art. Ecl. M. **11**: 505.
— **Murder of. (J. H. Browne) Overland, 13: 425.**
Hauser, Kaspar, Sketch of. (A. Ogilvy) Once a Week, **16**: 575.
— Lord Stanhope on. Mo. R. **140**: 534.
— Who was? (G. N. Lieber) Atlan. **7**: 62.
Hausmann, Baron, at Home. Lakeside, **10**: 169.
Hausset, Mme. du. Lond. M. **11**: 434. — Westm. **5**: 249.
Hautcœur, Noble House of. Chamb. J. **19**: 105.
Hautefort, Mme. de, and Contemporaries. Nat. R. **3**: 317.
Haüy, René-Just. Am. J. Sci. **8**: 362.
Haüy, Valentin. (L. P. Brockett) Am. J. Educ. **3**: 477.
Havana. All the Year, **15**: 84–524. — Chamb. J. **48**: 49.
— Adventure in. Blackw. **9**: 305.
— American Boarding-House in. Once a Week, **5**: 569.
— Calle del Obispo. (G. A. Sala) Temp. Bar, **14**: 331.
— Commerce of. De Bow, **24**: 187.
— Commercial Formalities of. (C. Tyng) Hunt, **17**: 480.
— Glimpse of. (E. E. Ford) Galaxy, **17**: 662.
— Holy Week of 1869 in. (M. E. Tregent) Cath. World, **11**: 58, 212.
— How they live in. (R. G. White) Putnam, **1**: 185, 288. — Broadw. **7**: 186, 212.
— Letters from. Galaxy, **9**: 239, 346, 475.
— Madame Merlin's History of. So. Q. **7**: 153.
— Meteorology in. Nature, **8**: 294.
— Shops and Shopmen of. Hunt, **18**: 451.
— Sketches in. (H. P. Leland) Knick. **45**: 392, 488, 611.
— Street Scenes in. (F. H. Taylor) Harper, **58**: 682.
Havana Cigars. All the Year, **17**: 108.
Havana Cigaritos. All the Year, **16**: 272.
Havel River, Prussia. (A. Venner) Harper, **56**: 847.
Havelock, Sir Henry, with portrait. Ecl. M. **44**: 219, 242. — Brit. Q. **32**: 122. Same art. Ecl. M. **51**: 107. — Dub. Univ. **51**: 197. Same art. Ecl. M. **43**: 452. — Ecl. R. **107**: 371. **112**: 192. — Good Words, **1**: 369. — Nat. M. **12**: 509. — Tait, n. s. **25**: 185, 233. — Liv. Age, **65**: 801.
— in Afghanistan. (J. A. O'Shea) Tinsley, **26**: 260.
— Memoirs of. Chr. Obs. **60**: 521. — Tait, n. s. **27**: 292.
Havelok the Dane. House. Words, **17**: 543.
Haven, Alice B. Godey, **68**: 50.
Haven, Erastus O., with portrait. (D. C. Brooks) Lakeside, **3**: 325.
Haven, Nathaniel Appleton. (W. B. O. Peabody) No. Am. **27**: 154. — (H. Ware, jr.) Chr. Exam. **5**: 70.
Have n't Time; a Tale. Cath. World, **3**: 92.
Havergal, Frances Ridley. (P. Anton) Fraser, **102**: 479. — Lond. Q. **57**: 49.
Haverhill North Parish, History of. (D. Oliphant) Cong. Q. **8**: 333.
Having Law on one's Side. (F. Jacox) Bentley, **61**: 290.
Having too much and too little to do. Lond. Soc. **37**: supp. 55.
Hâvre de Grace. Penny M. **8**: 81.
— Conflagration of. (J. Sparks) No. Am. **5**: 157.
Hawaiian Islands. (T. M. Coan) Scrib. **2**: 561. — (F. Poe) De Bow, **24**: 347. — Appleton, **14**: 97, 129. — (S. Wilberforce) Quar. **112**: 219. Same art. Ecl. M. **57**: 317, 420. — De Bow, **13**: 457. — Putnam, **5**: 241.
— Among. (A. M. Manning) Overland, **4**: 214.
— and Captain Cook. Once a Week, **13**: 567.
— Anderson's. (A. P. Peabody) Bost. R. **5**: 244.
— Miss Bird's. Nature, **11**: 322.
— Civilization in. (G. B. Merrill) Overland, **1**: 69. — Broadw. **10**: 529.
— Cruise to. (J. T. Meagher) Lakeside, **5**: 261.
— Ellis's Tour through. Ecl. R. **43**: 456. — Chr. Obs. **26**: 291.
— Feast in. (J. T. Meagher) Overland, **2**: 434.
— in 1870. (W. Pepys) Colburn, **154**: 27.
— **Lady's Trip to.** (A. M. Manning) Overland, **3**: 84.
— **Lava Land.** (A. M. Manning) Overland, **3**: 489.

Hawaiian Islands, Life in. (Lieut. Bleecker) Putnam, **2**: 17.
— Missionary Interference at. Am. Presb. R. **14**: 227.
— Missionary Work in. (L. Bacon) New Eng. **31**: 494. — (T. M. Coan) Nation, **12**: 452.
— Jubilee of, 1870. Chr. Obs. **71**: 320.
— Peopling of. (T. M. Coan) Nation, **29**: 170.
— Reciprocity Treaty. Penn Mo. **6**: 425.
— Ride through Kauai. (J. T. Meagher) Lakeside, **4**: 293.
— Volcanic Disturbances of, 1868. (T. Coan) Am. J. Sci. **97**: 89.
— Volcanic Eruption at. (T. Coan) Am. J. Sci. **72**: 240.
— Volcanic Eruptions in, 1859. (M. Hopkins) Once a Week, **1**: 479. *See* Kilauea and Mauna Loa.
See Honolulu; Sandwich Islands.
Hawaii-Nei. (C. Nordhoff) Harper, **47**: 382, 544.
Hawaiian Divinity, Capt. Cook as a. (J. T. Meagher) Lakeside, **8**: 197.
Hawaiian Fun Beams. (E. Corwin) Overland, **9**: 314.
Hawaiians, a doomed People. Ecl. M. **61**: 250.
Hawarden Castle. Hogg, **4**: 117.
Haweis, H. Reginald, with portrait. (T. Hopkins) Dub. Univ. **90**: 396.
— Sermons of. Dub. Univ. **89**: 276.
Hawes, Joel, as a Preacher. (E. A. Lawrence) Cong. R. **10**: 541.
— Lectures to young Men. Chr. Mo. Spec. **10**: 474. — Spirit Pilg. **2**: 47.
— Tribute to the Pilgrims. (J. Leavitt) Chr. Q. Spec. **3**: 358. — Chr. Exam. **10**: 297.
Hawise; a Poem. (M. Collins) Dub. Univ. **62**: 189.
Hawk, Pigeon. (W. Wood) Am. Natural. **7**: 340.
— Red-Tailed. (W. Wood) Am. Natural. **3**: 393.
Hawks and modern Falconry. Cornh. **11**: 619.
— Nesting of. (E. Coues) Am. Natural. **8**: 596.
Hawker, Robert S., Life of. Dub. Univ. **87**: 611.
Hawkes, Mrs., Memoir of. (A. Alexander) Princ. **11**: 239.
Hawking. Tait, n. s. **8**: 805.
— at Loo. Colburn, **91**: 157.
— Historical Account of. Penny M. **3**: 391–475.
Hawkins, Dexter A., with portrait. Am. J. Educ. **31**: 129.
Hawkins, Sir John. Lond. Soc. **5**: 527. — (W. H. Smyth) Arch. **33**: 195.
Hawkins, Lætitia M. Anecdotes and Sketches. Lond. M. **7**: 261. — Portfo.(Den.) **30**: 209.
Hawks, Francis L. (E. A. Duyckinck) Putnam, **11**: 100. — (N. S. Richardson) Am. Church R. **19**: 1. — Am. Hist. Rec. **1**: 16.
Hawkshaw, Sir John, with portrait. Pract. M. **7**: 65.
Hawkstone; a Religious Novel. Dub. R. **19**: 129. — Brownson, **6**: 24.
Hawkwood, Sir John. All the Year, **35**: 80. — Bentley, **54**: 284.
Hawley, Gideon. Am. J. Educ. **11**: 94.
Hawley, Joseph. Memorial to Conn. General Assembly, 1725. N. E. Reg. **10**: 311.
Hawley, Gen. Joseph R., with portrait. Ecl. M. **87**: 762.
Haworth, Yorkshire, Hills about. Temp. Bar, **19**: 428.
— Visit to. Mo. Rel. M. **31**: 41.
— Winter Day at. Chamb. J. **45**: 124.
Haworth Churchyard, April, 1855. Fraser, **51**: 527.
Haworth's. (F. H. Burnett) Macmil. **38**: 417. **39**: 1–498. **40**: 14–459.
Hawthorn, The. (W. Hincks) Howitt, **1**: 301. — Penny M. **11**: 449.
Hawthorne, Alice. *See* Winner, Septimius.
Hawthorne, Julian. Autobiography. Dub. Univ. **96**: 53.
— Idolatry. Scrib. **9**: 385. — Ecl. M. **83**: 755.
— Writings of. (M. Collins) Dub. Univ. **90**: 236.

Hawthorne, Nathaniel. (C. W. Webber) Am. Whig R. **4**: 296. — (S. W. S. Dutton) New Eng. **5**: 56. — (A. P. Peabody) Chr. Exam. **25**: 182. — (H. W. Longfellow) No. Am. **45**: 59. — Dem. R. **16**: 376. — (W. H. Barnes) Meth. Q. **26**: 51. — (K. Cook) Belgra. **19**: 72. — (E. Dicey) Macmil. **19**: 241. — (C. Kendal) Sharpe, **41**: 29. — (G. P. Lathrop) Scrib. **11**: 799. — (J. V. O'Conor) Cath. World, **32**: 231. — (L. Stephen) Cornh. **26**: 717. — (R. H. Stoddard) Harper, **45**: 683. — (H. T. Tuckerman) Lippinc. **5**: 498. — (H. T. Tuckerman) Liv. Age, **81**: 518. — (H. T. Tuckerman) So. Lit. Mess. **17**: 344. — (E. P. Whipple) Atlan. **5**: 614. — with portrait, Appleton, **4**: 405. — Internat. M. **3**: 156. — Blackw. **94**: 610. Same art. Liv. Age, **80**: 15. — Colburn, **94**: 202. Same art. Liv. Age, **33**: 17. — Colburn, **98**: 202. Same art. Liv. Age, **38**: 154. Same art. Ecl. M. **29**: 481. — Cornh. **23**: 321, 444, 566. Same art. Liv. Age, **116**: 195. — Dub. Univ. **46**: 463. Same art. Ecl. M. **36**: 996. — Ev. Sat. **6**: 458. — Liv. Age, **65**: 707. — Nat. M. **2**: 17. — Nat. R. **11**: 453. Same art. Liv. Age, **68**: 217. — No. Brit. **49**: 173. Same art. Liv. Age, **99**: 67. — Once a Week, **18**: 563. — (W. B. Rands) St. Paul's, **8**: 151. Same art. Ecl. M. **77**: 174. — Tait, n. s. **22**: 33. **23**: 756.
— among his Friends. (G. H. Holden) Harper, **63**: 260.
— and Brook Farm. (M. D. Conway) Ev. Sat. **7**: 10.
— and George Eliot. No. Brit. **33**: 165.
— and Julian. (E. P. Peabody) Western, **1**: 352.
— and E. A. Poe. (E. Benson) Galaxy, **6**: 742.
— Blithedale Romance. (A. P. Peabody) No. Am. **76**: 227. — Brownson, **9**: 561. — Colburn, **95**: 334. — Liv. Age, **34**: 327. — New Q. **1**: 413. — Westm. **58**: 592.
— Character of. (G. W. Curtis) No. Am. **99**: 539.
— Day in the Haunts of. Overland, **4**: 516.
— English Note-Books. (J. R. Dennett) Nation, **11**: 59. — (G. S. Hillard) Atlan. **26**: 257.
— French and Italian Journals. (H. James, jr.) Nation, **14**: 172. — St. Paul's, **9**: 311.
— Genius of. (R. Collyer) Lakeside, **1**: 30. — (E. P. Peabody) Atlan. **22**: 359. — (A. Trollope) No. Am. **129**: 203.
— House of seven Gables. (A. P. Peabody) No. Am. **76**: 227. — Knick. **37**: 455.
— in Undress. Argosy, **13**: 109.
— Life and Writings of. Lond. Q. **37**: 48.
— Marble Faun. (Mrs. M. T. Gale) New Eng. **19**: 860. — (H. Reed) Western, **5**: 265. — (E. W. Robbins) New Eng. **18**: 441. — (W. L. Alden) Scrib. **2**: 493.
— Old Manse at Concord. (A. B. Harris) Appleton, **8**: 300.
— Passages from Note-Books of. Atlan. **17**: 1–725. **18**: 40–682. **20**: 15.
— Romance of Monte Beni. Westm. **73**: 624.
— Scarlet Letter. (A. W. Abbot) No. Am. **71**: 135. — Liv. Age, **25**: 203. — Brownson, **7**: 528. — Internat M. **1**: 102. — Ev. Sat. **11**: 390.
— Septimius Felton. (T. W. Higginson) Scrib. **5**: 100. — (G. P. Lathrop) Atlan. **30**: 452. — Ev. Sat. **11**: 630. **13**: 179.
— Supernatural in. (D. Libby) Overland, **2**. 138.
— Tales and Miscellanies contributed to the Democratic Review, viz.: —
— — Artist of the Beautiful. **14**: 605.
— — Buds and Bird Voices. **12**: 604.
— — Book of Autographs, **15**: 454.
— — Celestial Railroad. **12**: 515.
— — Chippings with a Chisel. **3**: 18.
— — Christmas Banquet. **14**: 78.
— — Dartmoor Prisoner. **18**: 31–457.
— — Egotism; or Bosom Serpent. **12**: 255.

Hawthorne, Nathaniel. Tales and Miscellanies contributed to the Democratic Review, viz: —
— — Fire Worship. **13**: 627.
— — Intelligence Office. **14**: 269.
— — New Adam and Eve. **12**: 146.
— — P.'s Correspondence. **16**: 337.
— — Procession of Life. **12**: 360.
— — Province House. **2**: 129, 360. **3**: 321. **5**: 11.
— — Roger Malvin's Burial. **13**: 186.
— — Select Party. **15**: 33.
— — Two Widows. **13**: 85.
— — Writings of Aubépine. **15**: 545.
— Transformation. Dub. Univ. **55**: 679.
— Visit to Frederika Bremer. Ev. Sat. **11**: 323.
— Writings of. (C. A. Cummings) Chr. Exam. **78**: 89. — (A. D. Mayo) Univ. Q. **8**: 272. — (A. C. Coxe) Am. Church R. **3**: 489. — So. R. n. s. **7**: 328.
Hawthorne, Mrs. Nathaniel, Tribute to. Ev. Sat. **10**: 287.
Hay, John. Scrib. **7**: 736.
— Pike County Ballads. Ecl. M. **77**: 485.
Hay, M. C. Hidden Perils. Canad. Mo. **10**: 179.
Hay Fever, Binz on. Nature, **10**: 26.
Hayden Geological Survey. Republic, **6**: 149.
Haydn, Francis Joseph. (J. S. Dwight) Dem. R. **14**: 17. — Eng. Dom. M. **3**: 152. — Godey, **45**: 337. — Tait, n. s. **25**: 719.
— and C. Glück. (H. R. Haweis) Contemp. **7**: 535. **8**: 221.
— and Mozart, Lives of. Ed. Mo. R. **1**: 321. — Quar. **18**: 73. — (S. A. Eliot) No. Am. **43**: 78.
— Apprenticeship of. Dem. R. **19**: 193, 298.
— First Lessons in Music and Love. (E. F. Ellet) Cath. World, **10**: 267. Same art. N. Ecl. **6**: 28.
— First Love of. Argosy, **12**: 75.
— Life of. West. R. **4**: 32.
— Struggle and Triumph of. (E. F. Ellet) Cath. World, **10**: 326.
— Two Periods in Life of. (E. F. Ellet) Godey, **29**: 213.
— Two Scenes in the Life of. Month, **22**: 90.
— Youth of; a Sketch. Dub. Univ. **40**: 179.
Haydock, Dr. Richard, the Sleeping Preacher. Chamb. J. **49**: 99.
Haydon, Benjamin Robert. (A. H. Guernsey) Harper, **53**: 651. — (E. E. Hale) No. Am. **78**: 535. — (E. V. Rippingille) Bentley, **20**: 212. — Blackw. **74**: 519. — Ecl. M **30**: 382. — Lond. Q. **46**: 400.
— and Leigh Hunt. (S. R. T. Mayer) St. James, **34**: 349.
— and Wilkie. Fraser, **36**: 53.
— Autobiography of. Fraser, **48**: 307.
— Character and Brain of. Zoist, **12**: 40.
— Correspondence and Table Talk; with a Memoir. Ed. R. **144**: 33.
— Death of. Liv. Age, **10**: 277.
— Life of. Art J. **5**: 187. — Chr. Rem. **26**: 323. — Ed. R. **98**: 518. Same art. Liv. Age, **40**: 3. — Liv. Age, **38**: 421. — New Q. **2**: 441.
— Paintings by. Blackw. **10**: 680.
— Picture of; Chairing the Members. Lond. M. **22**: 507.
— — Christ's Agony in the Garden. Lond. M. **3**: 537.
— — Christ's Entry into Jerusalem. Lond. M. **1**: 581.
— — Napoleon musing. Fraser, **50**: 154.
— Reform Banquet. Fraser, **9**: 792.
— Taylor's Life of. Ecl. R. **98**: 338. — Dub. Univ. **42**: 405. — Liv. Age, **38**: 550. — Quar. **93**: 558.
Hayes, Catherine, with portrait. Dub. Univ. **36**: 584.
Hayes, Rutherford B., Administration of. (E. L. Godkin) Nation, **32**: 144. — (T. Bacon) Atlan. **47**: 391.
— and the Republican Party, 1877. (E. L. Godkin) Nation, **25**: 264.
— Southern Policy of, 1877. Internat. R. **4**: 686.
— Two Years of Presidency of. (W. H. Allen) Atlan. **44**: 190.
Hayes Family. N. E. Reg. **27**: 79.

Hayley, William, Life and Writings of. (R. Southey) Quar. **31**: 263. — Blackw. **14**: 303. — Mo. R. **103**: 367. **105**: 1. — Lond. M. **10**: 502.
— Memoirs of. Colburn, **6**: 147. **8**: 147.
— Triumphs of Music. Ed. R. **6**: 56. — Ecl. R. **1**: 81.
Haym, R. Die romantische Schule. O. & N. **5**: 730.
Haymarket Theater. All the Year, **44**: 230.
Haynau, Gen. J. J., Outrage upon. Colburn, **90**: 241.
Hayne, Arthur P. (J. G. M. Ramsey) Land We Love, **2**: 391.
Hayne, Col. Isaac. Hist. M. **12**: 76. — So. R. **1**: 70.
Hayne, Paul H., with portrait. Ecl. M. **89**: 247.
— Legends and Lyrics. (M. J. Preston) So. M. **10**: 377.
— Poetry of. (S. Lanier) So. M. **16**: 40. — So. Lit. Mess. **21**: 122.
Hayne, Robert Y. Letter on the Tariff, 1828. Niles's Reg. **35**: 184, 199.
— Life and Speeches. So. Q. **8**: 496. — So. R. n. s. **8**: 275.
— Nullification Ordinance. Niles's Reg. **43**: 219.
— Nullification Proclamation. Niles's Reg. **43**: 308.
— Speech at Charleston, July 5, 1830. Niles's Reg. **38**: 376.
— — on the Tariff of 1832. Niles's Reg. **41**: 396.
— Speeches on Foot's Resolution. Niles's Reg. **37**: 415. **38**: 105.
Haynes, James. Conscience; or the Bridal Night. Lond. M. **3**: 436.
Haynes, Gov. John, Will of, 1646. N. E. Reg. **16**: 167.
Haynes, Lemuel. (J. J. Foot) Lit. & Theo. R. **4**: 429. — Am. Q. **9**: 324.
Haynes Family. (A. M. Haines) N. E. Reg. **32**: 310.
— Papers relating to. N. E. Reg. **24**: 422. **25**: 185.
Haynes Genealogy. (G. C. Haynes) N. E. Reg. **9**: 349.
Hays, Gen. Alexander. U. S. Serv. M. **2**: 266.
Hayti. (C. Cushing) No. Am. **12**: 112. **28**: 150. — Anal. M. **9**: 403. — Blackw. **4**: 130. — Niles's Reg. **25**: 50, 397. — All the Year, **2**: 444. **7**: 438. — Broadw. **3**: 305. — Chr. Obs. **7**: 641, 704, 772. **8**: 20, 81. — Ho. & For. R. **1**: 361.
— and the Dominican Republic. Am. Whig R. **14**: 144.
— and the Haytians. (W. H. Pierson) Putnam, **3**: 53. — Broadw. **7**: 454. — De Bow, **16**: 32.
— Candler on. Ecl. R. **76**: 104. — Mo. R. **158**: 531.
— Christophe, late Emperor of. Blackw. **10**: 545.
— Coronation of Faustin I., 1852. Ecl. M. **26**: 556.
— Emigration to. U. S. Lit. Gaz. **1**: 145. — Niles's Reg. **27**: 30.
— Franklin on State of, 1828. Ecl. R. **47**: 97.
— French Works on. Pamph. **13**: 165.
— Harvey's Sketches of. Mo. R. **114**: 365. — Ecl. R. **45**: 564.
— Has Freedom proved a Failure in? (M. Bird) Meth. Q. **22**: 561.
— History and Literature of. Niles's Reg. **19**: 197.
— in 1818. Niles's Reg. **14**: 263.
— in 1825. Ed. R. **41**: 497.
— in 1830. Mo. R. **122**: 160.
— Independence of. Niles's Reg. **22**: 391.
— Indian Race of. (J. A. Van Heusel) Am. J. Sci. **85**: 171.
— King of; from the German. Lond. M. **8**: 517.
— Life in. Knick. **18**: 300, 489. **19**: 34–453. **20**: 63–209.
— Negro Rule in. Nat. Q. **14**: 359.
— Past and present State of. Quar. **21**: 430.
— Proverbs of. (J. Bigelow) Harper, **51**: 130–583.
— Rainsford's Account of. Ed. R. **8**: 52. — Ecl. R. **3**: 405.
— Recent Revolutions in. For. Q. **33**: 239. Same art. Liv. Age, **2**: 65. Same art. Ecl. M. **3**: 125.
— Researches in, Ritter's. For. Q. **20**: 73. Same art Mus. **32**: 333.
— Settlement of. (J. Weiss) O. & N. **3**: 672.

Hayti, Statistics of. Niles's Reg. **28**: 403.
— Zoölogy of. (D. F. Weinland) Am. J. Sci. **76**: 210. *See* Santo Domingo.
Hayward, A. Essays. Fortn. **19**: 398.
Hayward, Charles, Biography of. (C. S. Wheeler) Chr. Exam. **27**: 114.
Haywood, William H., Portrait of. Dem. R. **18**: 243.
Hazael. (H. Ballou, 2d) Univ. Q. **10**: 158.
Hazara, Campaign in, 1668. Colburn, **145**: 224.
Hazard, R. G., Sketch of, with portrait. Appleton, **3**: 72.
— Writings of. (G. P. Fisher) No. Am. **109**: 367.
Hazard; a Tale. (C. Chesebrough) Galaxy, **6**: 465.
Haze and Dust. (J. Tyndall) Nature, **1**: 339.
Hazel, Uses of. Penny M. **13**: 131.
Hazeley Mill. (L. Crow) Once a Week, **15**: 85.
Hazen Family. (H. A. Hazen) N. E. Reg. **33**: 229.
Hazing in College. (C. F. Thwing) Scrib. **17**: 331.
Hazlewood School. Lond. M. **23**: 367.
Hazlitt, William. (G. F. Deane) Am. Whig R. **5**: 98. — Blackw. **17**: 361. — (L. Stephen) Cornh. **31**: 467. Same art. Liv. Age, **125**: 259. — (H. T. Tuckerman) Atlan. **25**: 664. — (L. Cross) Colburn, **166**: 284. — Bentley, **37**: 479. Same art. Ecl. M. **35**: 381.
— and Jeffrey. Blackw. **3**: 303.
— and his School. Anal. M. **12**: 201.
— and the Press. Am. Q. **20**: 265.
— as a Critic. (H. T. Tuckerman) So. Lit. Mess. **16**: 82. — Tait, n. s. **4**: 650.
— Characters of Shakspere. (F. Jeffrey) Ed. R. **28**: 472. — Quar. **18**: 485. — Mo. R. **92**: 153.
— Conversations of Northcote. Mo. R. **123**: 275.
— cross-questioned. Blackw. **3**: 550.
— in Switzerland; a Conversation. Fraser, **19**: 278.
— Lectures on Age of Elizabeth. Mo. R. **93**: 59.
— — on the Drama. Ed. R. **34**: 438.
— — on English Poetry. (R. H. Dana) No. Am. **8**: 276. — (J. Wilson) Blackw. **2**: 556, 679. **3**: 71. — Quar. **19**: 424.
— Liber Amoris. Temp. Bar, **61**: 330.
— Literary Remains. Ed. R. **64**: 395. — Dub. Univ. **8**: 406. — So. Lit. Mess. **2**: 667.
— Literature of the Age of Elizabeth. Lond. M. **1**: 185.
— Love Affair of, and Liber Amoris. (T. De Quincey) Tait, n. s. **5**: 361.
— Loves of. Belgra. **11**: 427.
— New Pygmalion. (D. Cook) Gent. M. n. s. **2**: 303.
— on public Characters. Ed. Mo. R. **3**: 297. — Quar. **22**: 158.
— Plain Speaker. Mo. R. **110**: 113. — Mus. **9**: 154.
— Political Essays. Mo. R. **93**: 250.
— Recollections of. Colburn, **29**: 469. — (F. G. Patmore) Liv. Age, **4**: 459.
— Round Table. Quar. **17**: 154.
— Spirit of the Age. Mo. R. **107**: 1. — Blackw. **17**: 361. — Lond. M. **12**: 182.
— Table Talk. (Sir F. Palgrave) Quar. **26**: 103. — Blackw. **12**: 157. — Mo. R. **101**: 55. — Lond. M. **3**: 545. **7**: 689. — Portfo.(Den.) **27**: 274.
— Writings of. Tait, n. s. **3**: 501, 713, 758.
— Winterslow. Am. Whig R. **14**: 138.
He heeded not. (G. MacDonald) Good Words, **4**: 226.
He is not far. (J. Weiss) J. Spec. Philos. **3**: 177.
He knew he was right. (A. Trollope) Ecl. M. **71**: 1421. **72**: 55–721. **73**: 61–728. Same art. Ev. Sat. **6**: 449–577.
He or She; a Tale. Temp. Bar, **21**: 129.
He, She, and It; a Tale. (E. Fawcett) Lippinc. **7**: 409. Same art. Broadw. **7**: 528.
He that will not when he may. (M. Oliphant) Macmil. **41**: 1–433. **42**: 1–436. **43**: 53. Same art. Liv. Age, **143**: 276–786. **144**: 13–787. **145**: 294. **146**: 212, 274.
He will come to-morrow. Blackw. **44**: 441.
He would be a Soldier! (R. M. Jepson) Lond. Soc. **29**: 246–526. **30**: 65.
Head, Francis B., and Colonial Office. Westm. **32**: 426.
— Canada. Dub. Univ. **13**: 501.
— Defenseless State of Great Britain. Quar. **88**: 269. — Blackw. **68**: 736. Same art. Liv. Age, **28**: 145.
— The Emigrant. Dub. R. **21**: 494. — Quar. **78**: 510. — Ed. R. **85**: 187. Same art. Liv. Age, **13**: 449. — So. Q. **13**: 187. — Liv. Age, **11**: 517.
— Journey across Pampas. (R. Southey) Quar. **35**: 114.
— Journeys in South America. U. S. Lit. Gaz. **6**: 14.
— Narrative. Quar. **63**: 457. — Ecl. R. **69**: 556.
— Works of. Westm. **29**: 461. — Am. Mo. M. **4**: 54.
Head, Sir George. Home Tours. (R. Southey) Quar. **59**: 314. — (J. W. Croker) Quar. **59**: 519. — Mo. R. **144**: 521.
— Forest Scenes in Canada. Westm. **12**: 103. — (R. Southey) Quar. **42**: 80.
Head, H. S., Sermons of. Ecl. R. **72**: 526.
Head, Hits on the. Once a Week, **25**: 475.
— of Bran; a Poem. (G. Meredith) Once a Week, **2**: 131.
— of the Church. (W. S. Tyler) Am. Bib. Repos. **11**: 344. **12**: 22.
— of Hercules; a Story. (J. M. Floyd) Galaxy, **23**: 52.
Heads of the People. Westm. **33**: 162.
Head-Dress, Female, in England. (J. A. Repton) Arch. **27**: 29.
— Ladies' Head-Gear. (F. W. Fairholt) St. James, **3**: 457.
Head-Dresses. Eng. Dom. M. **10**: 92. — Ev. Sat. **13**: 272, 533. — St. Paul's, **11**: 204, 319.
— and Hair, Fashions in. (J. A. Repton) Arch. **24**: 168. — Fraser, **82**: 322. Same art. Ecl. M. **75**: 569.
Headless Ghost. (H. W. Chetwynd) Tinsley, **27**: 424.
Headley, J. T. Cromwell. Dem. R. **23**: 333.
— Histories of. Meth. Q. **8**: 84.
— Letters from Italy. (H. T. Tuckerman) Dem. R. **17**: 203. — So. Q. **10**: 85.
— Napoleon and his Marshals. (W. B. O. Peabody) Chr. Exam. **42**: 174. — (W. T. Bacon) New Eng. **4**: 364. — (G. H. Colton) Am. Whig R. **3**: 537. **4**: 86.
— Sacred Mountains. (E. A. Poe) So. Lit. Mess. **16**: 606.
— Washington and his Generals. (G. H. Colton) Am. Whig R. **5**: 517, 638. — So. Lit. Mess. **13**: 316.
— Writings of. (E. O. Dunning) New Eng. **5**: 402. **6**: 482. — Meth. Q. **8**: 84.
Headsman, The; a Tale of Doom. Blackw. **27**: 190.
— of Strasburgh. (J. Pardoe) Ecl. M. **47**: 117.
Headsmen, Hereditary. All the Year, **8**: 37.
— of France. (E. About) Sharpe, **48**: 190. — Knick. **57**: 604.
Headstrong Phrenologist. (H. Mayhew) Bentley, **25**: 148.
Heady, Morrison, a blind Poet. (J. R. Anagnos) Unita. R. **15**: 425.
Healing by Royal Touch. (D. Cook) Once a Week, **15**: 219.
Healing Art, Varieties of. Chamb. J. **53**: 585.
— St. John Long's Discoveries in. Mo. R. **121**: 356.
Health. (L. H. Sigourney) So. Lit. Mess. **4**: 476. **7**: 123. — Chamb. J. **38**: 260. — Cornh. **3**: 332.
— and Beauty. Eng. Dom. M. **3**: 30–574. — Godey. **34**: 215.
— and Civilization. (F. Bacon) Am. Soc. Sci. J. **3**: 58.
— and Disease. New Eng. **9**: 223.
— — Geographical Distribution of. Hogg, **9**: 415.
— and Education. (E. S. Turner) Penn Mo. **10**: 194. — Temp. Bar, **4**: 47.
— — Kingsley on. Chamb. J. **51**: 571.
— and Heat. Ecl. M. **97**: 511.
— and Learning. (B. W. Richardson) Gent. M. n. s. **20**: 162. Same art. Sup. Pop. Sci. Mo. **2**: 398.

Health and Longevity, Thackrah on. Penny M. 1: 170. — Blackw. 23: 96. — (F. Jeffrey) Ed. R. 11: 195.
— and Morals, Effects of Trades on. (T. P. Jones) J. Frankl. Inst. 15: 78.
— — Public. Quar. 66: 115.
— and Recreation. (B. W. Richardson) Gent. M. n. s. 22: 330, 687.
— and Social Life of Young America. Am. Presb. R. 4: 658.
— at Home. (B. W. Richardson) Good Words, 21: 64-848. 22: 50, 753, 817. Same art. Appleton, 23: 311, 521. 24: 114, 376.
— Brigham on. (F. W. P. Greenwood) Chr. Exam. 14: 129. — Am. Mo. R. 4: 333. — Mo. R. 140: 397.
— By-Ways to. (W. W. Fenn) Tinsley, 18: 185. 19: 155.
— Characteristics of natural. Colburn, 5: 254.
— City of. (B. W. Richardson) Nature, 12: 523, 542. Same art. Ecl. Engin. 14: 31.
— Combe on. (D. Smith) Am. Meth. M. 22: 83.
— Committee on; what it can do. Chamb. J. 15: 135.
— Criterion of. Tait, n. s. 9: 61.
— Dress in relation to. (B. W. Richardson) Gent. M. n. s. 24: 469. Same art. Pop. Sci. Mo. 17: 182.
— Effect of Arts, Trades, etc., on. Meth. M. 56: 353.
— — of Railways on. Cornh. 6: 480.
— — of Trades on. J. Frankl. Inst. 11: 412.
— for Cities. (P. E. Church) Galaxy, 3: 837.
— Gospel of Hygiene. (J. V. O'Conor) Cath. World, 30: 232.
— Granville's Catechism of. Quar. 47: 394.
— Guardian of. Colburn, 1: 130-334.
— in France, Care of public. Ecl. R. 87: 440.
— in Japan. (E. S. Morse) Pop. Sci. Mo. 12: 280.
— in Town and Country. All the Year, 30: 388.
— Influence of Civilization on. (J. H. Bridges) Fortn. 12: 140. — For. Q. 1: 178.
— — of Dress, Exercise, and Sleep on. Lond. M. 23: 561.
— — of Employments on. (W. A. Guy) J. Statis. Soc. 6: 197, 283.
— — of Factory Life on. (A. G. Malcolm) J. Statis. Soc. 19: 170.
— — of the Imagination on. Colburn, 6: 53.
— — of Mechanical Employments on. So. Lit. Mess. 2: 241.
— — of Occupation on. Ed. New Philos. J. 57: 165. — Chamb. J. 26: 335. Same art. Liv. Age, 52: 255.
— — of Religion on. (J. Walker) Chr. Exam. 19: 302.
— Injury of popular Works on. (H. Bronson) Chr. Q. Spec. 8: 439.
— Insurance on. (G. W. Savage) Hunt, 19: 601.
— Laws of. (T. Bond) Pop. Sci. Mo. 10: 198. — So. Lit. J. 2: 453.
— Lay Sermon on. (J. Brown) Good Words, 2: 493.
— Light and Scenery as affecting. (A. Smith) Good Words, 2: 237.
— Little Health of Ladies. (F. P. Cobbe) Contemp. 31: 276. Same art. Liv. Age, 136: 302. Same art. Sup. Pop. Sci. Mo. 2: 355.
— Maintenance of. Cong. R. 9: 557.
— Mass. Board of, Report of, 1871. No. Am. 113: 214.
— — — 1874. No. Am. 119: 447.
— Moral and social Aspects of. (J. H. Bridges) Fortn. 28: 562. Same art. Ecl. M. 90: 129. Same art. Sup. Pop. Sci. Mo. 2: 141.
— Mussey on. Radical, 5: 76.
— National. (B. W. Richardson) Good Words, 17: 386-851. — Ecl. R. 98: 393.
— — Preservation of. (E. D. J. Wilson) Dark Blue, 2: 327.
— Neglect of the Conditions of. Chr. Rem. 40: 104.
— Neglected. Fraser, 50: 238.
Health of Americans and Europeans. (S. G. Young) Galaxy, 14: 630.
— of the Army. *See* Military Hygiene.
— of Body and Mind. (W. F. Wilkinson) Good Words, 7: 48, 114, 181.
— of different Races, Vital Statistics of. (E. Jarvis) Am. Soc. Sci. J. 7: 229.
— of Europe and America. Knick. 4: 272.
— of European Soldiers in India. (J. Bird) J. Statis. Soc. 26: 384.
— of Literary Men. (S. Forry) Meth. Q. 4: 605. — (W. Channing) No. Am. 8: 176.—Am. Q. Reg. 3: 1, 138.
— of London. Fraser, 36: 505. — Westm. 49: 224.
— of Ministers. Chr. Disc. 3: 138.
— of Seamen and Soldiers. (T. G. Balfour) J. Statis. Soc. 35: 1.
— of Soldiers in different Climates. (E. Balfour) J. Statis. Soc. 8: 193.
— — Means of maintaining. (E. Balfour) J. Statis. Soc. 11: 33.
— of Teachers and Pupils. (C. E. Beecher) Am. J. Educ. 2: 398.
— of Towns. Ecl. R. 77: 219.
— — Commission on. Chamb. J. 3: 41.
— — Improvements in. Chamb. J. 6: 91.
— Open Air and. (P. Niemeyer) Pop. Sci. Mo. 12: 216.
— Philosophy of good. (E. Spencer) Scrib. 2: 589.
— Preservation of. Lond. M. 19: 228.
— — in Schools. (W. Wood) Hesp. 3: 341.
— Public. (H. Sandwith) Fortn. 23: 254. — O. & N. 8: 228.
— — and Christian Duty. Cong. 3: 686.
— — as affected by the Seasons. (W. A. Guy) J. Statis. Soc. 6: 133.
— — Bill on. Fraser, 38: 444. — Hogg, 2: 105.
— — Conference of Boards of, 1874. Am. Soc. Sci. J. 7: 210.
— — in America. Nature, 6: 158.
— — in its Connection with Internal Improvements. De Bow, 26: 407.
— — Method of investigating. (F. G. P. Neison) J. Statis. Soc. 7: 40.
— — Noxious Occupations and. Hogg, 14: 405.
— — Responsibility of Government for. (D. A. Gorton) Nat. Q. 28: 1.
— — Science of. (W. Dowe) Nat. Q. 41: 119.
— — Standard of, for England. (E. H. Greenhow) J. Statis. Soc. 22: 253.
— Question of. Sharpe, 46: 65.
— Relation of Food to. Cornh. 4: 281. 7: 414.
— Respiration and. (J. Hutchinson) J. Statis. Soc. 7: 193.
— Sanitary Condition of Laboring Population. Tait, n. s. 9: 649.
— Sanitary Inquiries and Legislation, 1840. Tait, n. s. 8: 705.
— Science of. (C. Kingsley) Good Words, 14: 44. — Lond. Q. 50: 392.
— Student Life and. (E. Hitchcock) New Eng. 36: 405.
— through Education. (B. W. Richardson) Gent. M. n. s. 24: 288.
— Training in relation to. Cornh. 9: 219. 15: 92.
— Unhealthy Employments. (W. Jones) Colburn, 106: 166.
— United States National Board of. (G. E. Waring, jr.) Atlan. 44: 732. — Nation, 29: 123.
— Village Sanitary Work. (G. E. Waring, jr.) Scrib. 14: 176.
See Contagious Diseases; Diet; Dress; Ventilation; Physical Education; Women, Health of; etc.
Health Convention, 1838. (J. G. Palfrey) No. Am. 47: 381.

Health Laws and their Administration. (E. Harris) Am. Soc. Sci. J. 2: 176.
Health Resorts. (T. M. Coan) Harper, 58: 583.
Health-Seekers, Hints for; Sea or Mountain? (B. Yeo) Fortn. 28: 195. Same art. Ecl. M. 89: 469.
Healths, Drinking, Great Evil of. Retros. 12: 322.
Healthy Habitations. (W. Eassie) Ecl. Engin. 15: 436.
Healthy House, Bardwell's. Nature, 9: 60.
Heaping Coals of Fire. All the Year, 24: 532.
Heard, Jared M., Memorial of. (E H. Sears) Mo. Rel. M. 31: 273.
Hearing, Gough on. Ed. R. 2: 192.
— in Animals. (W. Houghton) Good Words, 5: 710.
— in Insects and Birds. (R. M. Lachlan) Nature, 15: 254, 292.
— in lower Animals. (W.W. Stoddart) Intel. Obs. 3: 398.
— Note-Deafness. Liv. Age, 137: 353.
— Preservation of. (S. Seyton) Harper, 60: 614.
— Sense of. (J. P. Pennefather) Dub. Univ. 85: 733. *See also* Deafness.
Hearne, Thomas. Blackw. 81: 537.
— Life of. Dub. Univ. 73: 331.
Hearnshaw, J. (R. Reece) Meth. M. 33: 249.
Hearses, Question of Ownership of. (N. Carlisle) Arch. 16: 279.
Heart and the Brain. (G. H. Lewes) Fortn. 1: 66. Same art. Cath. World, 1: 623.
— and Hearth; a Poem. (T. B. Read) Atlan. 19: 545.
— and the Key; a Tale. Bentley, 10: 377.
— and Sphygmograph. (A. H. Garrod) Nature, 9: 327.
— and State. Temp. Bar, 14: 540. Same art. Ecl. M. 65: 551.
— Effect of, on muscular Functions. (J. B. Hodgskin) Scrib. 4: 358.
— Enamel of. (J. D. Smith) Knick. 30: 145.
— Foul Air and Disease of. (C. Black) Pop. Sci. Mo. 2:183.
— Hardness of. Chr. Mo. Spec. 3: 617.
— Human. (I. Ashe) Pop. Sci. R. 1: 350. Same art. Ecl. M. 56: 306.
— — Laboring Force of. (S. Haughton) Nature, 1: 255. Same art. Ecl. Engin. 2: 229.
— The New. Chr. Mo. Spec. 6: 241.
— of John Middleton. (E. C. Gaskell) House. Words, 2: 325.
— of New England. (E. C. Stedman) Atlan. 29: 34.
— Purity of. Chr. Mo. Spec. 3: 225.
— Structure of; Errors attributed to Aristotle. (T. H. Huxley) Nature, 21: 1.
Heart's Problem. (C. Gibbon) Belgra. 45: 109–486.
Hearts; or, England a hundred Years ago. Colburn, 164: 33–421.
— and Hands. (S. Chilton) Overland, 15: 547. — (F. C. Fisher) Appleton, 12: 530–808.
— are Trumps. (Mrs. A. Fraser) Tinsley, 23: 38.
— Buried. All the Year, 27: 149.
— Burial of, Separate. Ev. Sat. 12: 132.
— Errant; a Story. Eng. Dom. M. 1: 161–356. 2: 19–246.
— in Mortmain. Prosp. R. 6: 494.
— of Oak. (C. W. Stoddard) Overland, 6: 352, 419, 507. 7: 61. — Knick. 38: 397, 515.
— — and Stone; a Poem. (H. Morford) Galaxy, 2: 23.
— of Oak Society. Chamb. J. 55: 155.
— *vs.* Diamonds. (C. Chester) Potter Am. Mo. 11: 97–441.
— win; or, Miss Rutherford's Fortune. Sharpe, 47: 1–190.
Heartbreak Cameo. (L. W. Champney) Galaxy, 23: 111.
Heartbreak Hill; a Poem. (C. Thaxter) Atlan. 31: 337.
Heart History of a heartless Woman. (S. P. King) Knick. 54: 174–577.
Heart Room and House Room. (F. Tiffany) O. & N. 2: 430.
Heart Sacrifice. (A. Beaufain) So. Lit. Mess. 23: 55.
Heart Struggle; a Tale. Temp. Bar, 4: 137, 195.
Hearth, The. Chamb. J. 35: 371.
— of the polished Stone Age. Nature, 3: 224. — (E. Perrault) Am. Natural. 5: 88.
— of Scrivelsby Court. (E. Carrington) Bentley, 5: 62.
Hearthrug Farces. (A. Muir) Lond. Soc. 39: 274, 458. 40: 1.
Heat. Am. J. Sci. 10: 79. — Chamb. J. 19: 36. — (H. Bedford) Irish Mo. 8: 24, 139. — Hogg, 3: 278.
— Absorption and Radiation of. (H. Debus) Pop. Sci. R. 3: 351, 498.
— and Electricity. Mo. R. 122: 535.
— and Health. Ecl. M. 97: 511.
— and Light. (S. Morey) Am. J. Sci. 2: 118.
— and Life. (F. Papillon) Pop. Sci. Mo. 2: 400.
— and Light, Chemical Sources of. (R. Bithell) Recr. Sci. 2: 280.
— and living Matter. (H. C. Bastian) Contemp. 24: 516.
— and Moisture, Leslie on. (J. Murray) Ed. R. 24: 339.
— and not Light a motive Power; or, Experiments with Radiometers. (H. A. Cunnington) Pop. Sci. R. 15: 128.
— and Steam. Ecl. Engin. 7: 432.
— and Vapor. (W. R. Johnson) Am. J. Sci. 21: 304.
— and Ventilation. Am. Arch. 3: 155, 164.
— and Water. Ecl. Engin. 11: 459.
— and Work. All the Year, 14: 29.
— Application in Arts, etc. (E. Péclet) J. Frankl. Inst. 8: 164.
— as a Mode of Locomotion. Ev. Sat. 11: 186.
— as a Mode of Motion. (J. Tyndall) Ed. R. 119: 1. Same art. Liv. Age, 80: 387. — Brit. Q. 38: 255. Same art. Ecl. M. 60: 55.
— — Tyndall on. (W. C. Wilson) Meth. Q. 25: 49.
— Cause of. (R. Hare) Am. J. Sci. 4: 142.
— Change of Color produced by. (E. J. Houston) J. Frankl. Inst. 92: 115.
— Chemical Affinity. (M. Faraday) J. Frankl. Inst. 70: 253.
— Combustion and Fuel. West. J. 8: 393.
— — of Coal Gas to produce. (J. Wallace) Ecl. Engin. 14: 417.
— Communicating, by Steam. (C. Potts) J. Frankl. Inst. 9: 395.
— Conduction of, in Gases. J. Frankl. Inst. 102: 302.
— Dependence of Life on. (W. B. Carpenter) Howitt, 1: 132, 159, 198.
— Detection of. (L. C. Cooley) J. Frankl. Inst. 96: 343. 97: 408.
— developed by Collision. (Prof. Tresca) Nature, 10: 400.
— Dissipation of Energy. (Lord Rayleigh) Ecl. Engin. 12: 519.
— Distribution of, in the Spectrum. (J. W. Draper) Am. J. Sci. 104: 161.
— — over the Earth. (P. E. Chase) Am. J. Sci. 94: 68. — (S. Forry) Am. J. Sci. 47: 18, 221. — (A. Humboldt) Ed. Philos. J. 3: 1, 256. 4: 23, 262. 5: 28.
— Dynamical Theory of. Ed. R. 119: 2. Same art. Ecl. M. 62: 129. — (W. A. Norton) Am. J. Sci. 105: 186. — No. Brit. 40: 40.
— — History of. (P. Poinier) Pop. Sci. Mo. 12: 206, 330.
— Early History of the Science of. (G. F. Rodwell) Ecl. Engin. 2: 207.
— Economic Production of. (J.W. McGauley) Intel. Obs. 2: 398.
— Effect of Compression on. Ed. R. 9: 19.
— evolved from Atmospheric Air. (J. Gorrie) Am. J. Sci. 60: 39, 214.
— Excessive, of Summer of 1825. Am. J. Sci. 10: 296.
— Expenditure of, in the Hot-Air Engine. (F. A. P. Barnard) Am. J. Sci. 66: 218, 351. 68: 161.
— Experiment in. Ev. Sat. 11: 583.
— Fourier on. For. Q. 8: 303.

Heat from different Kinds of Fuel. (M. Bull) J. Frankl. Inst. 1: 257, 360. 3: 47. 5: 273.
— given to a permanent Gas, Effects of. (M. J. Bourget) J. Frankl. Inst. 71: 173.
— in the Blast Furnace. Ecl. Engin. 3: 364.
— in Equilibrium, Mathematical Theory of. (S. Newcomb) Math. Mo. 2: 346.
— in its Relation to Construction. Ecl. Engin. 11: 413. — Am. Arch. 10: 7.
— in the Sun's Rays. (E. Foote) Am. J. Sci. 72: 377, 382.
— in Vacuo on Metals, Action of. (T. A. Edison) J. Frankl. Inst. 108: 333.
— Is Heat Motion? All the Year, 13: 534.
— Lardner on. Dub. Univ. 1: 563.
— Latent. (A. Beatty) West. J. 9: 232.
— — of Water. J. Frankl. Inst. 51: 189.
— Leslie on Nature and Propagation of, 1804. Ecl. R. 3: 181, 294.
— lost by Apparatus. (M. Bull) J. Frankl. Inst. 1: 281, 360. 3: 47. 5: 273.
— Maxwell on. (B. Stewart) Nature, 5: 319.
— Mechanical Action of. (W. J. M. Rankine) Am. J. Sci. 68: 64.
— Mechanical Equivalent of. J. Frankl. Inst. 71: 116. — (R. H. Thurston) J. Frankl. Inst. 97: 203. — (J. Violle) J. Frankl. Inst. 99: 357.
— Mechanical Theory of. (D. K. Clark) J. Frankl. Inst. 70: 163. — (A. R. Wolff) J. Frankl. Inst. 111: 34. — Ecl. Engin. 15: 276. 17: 158. — (A. R. Wolff) Ecl. Engin. 24: 11.
— — applied to the Steam Engine. (R. Clausius) Am. J. Sci. 72: 180, 364. 73: 25.
— — McCulloch on. J. Frankl. Inst. 102: 158.
— Melloni's Researches in Radiant. (J. Lovering) Am. Alma. 1850: 64.
— Molecular, of similar Compounds. (F. W. Clarke) Am. J. Sci. 108: 340.
— Morbid Effects of. (W. J. Youmans) Pop. Sci. Mo. 3: 497.
— Motion and Political Economy. Pop. Sci. Mo. 11: 329.
— Motion in. (M. T. Brigham) No. Am. 97: 402.
— Nature of, Leslie on. (Lord Brougham) Ed. R. 7: 63.
— New Theory of. (J. Abbott) Harper, 39: 322.
— New Theories and Facts of. Intel. Obs. 3: 367.
— of the Globe a constant Quantity. (F. Arago) Ed. New Philos. J. 16: 205.
— of the Interior of the Earth. (E. Hitchcock) No. Am. 28: 265. — Am. J. Sci. 15: 109. — For. Q. 8: 303.
— of the Seasons. Hunt, 6: 454.
— of Stars, measured. (T. A. Edison) Am. J. Sci. 117: 52.
— of the Sun. (P. M. Biklé) Luth. Q. 7: 71.
— — applied to industrial Purposes. Pract. M. 6: 174.
— Origin of Solar and Sidereal. (D. Kirkwood) Am. J. Sci. 115: 291.
— Physical Causes of principal Phenomena of. (J. Barton) J. Frankl. Inst. 24: 186.
— Principle of. (A. Beatty) West. J. 9: 303, 376.
— produced in the Body. (J. C. Draper) Am. J. Sci. 104: 445.
— Radiant. (J. Ericsson) Nature, 7: 273.
— — Action on Gaseous Matter. (J. Tyndall) J. Frankl. Inst. 111: 297. — (J. Tyndall) Pop. Sci. Mo. 19: 33.
— — Researches on. (J. Tyndall) J. Frankl. Inst. 77: 200.
— — Relations of, to Chemical Constitution, Color, and Texture. (J. Tyndall) Fortn. 4: 1. Same art. Liv. Age, 88: 801.
— — transmitted by Flames. (J. Ericsson) Ecl. Engin. 6: 113.
— — transmitted by incandescent spherical Bodies. (J. Ericsson) Ecl. Engin. 6: 451.
— — transmitted by inclined incandescent Radiators. (J. Ericsson) Ecl. Engin. 6: 225.
Heat, Radiant, Tyndall's Researches on. (W. F. Barrett) Nature, 7: 66.
— Radiation of. (B. F. Isherwood) J. Frankl. Inst. 105: 153. — (R. J. McClure) J. Frankl. Inst. 94: 351, 407.
— Recent Inquiries in. So. R. n. s. 7: 401.
— Count Rumford on. Ed. R. 4: 399.
— Solar. *See* Sun, Heat of.
— Thermal Energy. (J. Ericsson) Nature, 12: 517. 13: 114.
— — from the Sun. (J. Ericsson) Ecl. Engin. 14: 1-193.
— Theory of. (E. W. Morley) Bib. Sac. 24: 652.
— Transmission of. (M. Melloni) Am. J. Sci. 27: 228.
— Tyndall on. Blackw. 94: 679.
— Use of Flame Heat in Chemical Laboratory. (J. L. Smith) Am. J. Sci. 100: 341.
Heat Cure. Chamb. J. 58: 518.
Heat Engines, Limit of Efficiency of. (J. F. Klein) J. Frankl. Inst. 107: 145, 217, 289. — (W. A. Anthony) Pop. Sci. Mo. 17: 831.
Heat Motion, Means for converting into Work. (S. T. Preston) Nature, 17: 202.
Heat Spectra. (B. Stewart) Nature, 3: 276.
Heated Bodies, Law in Cooling of. (M. Bull) J. Frankl. Inst. 1: 360.
Heath, George, and his Poetry. (R. Buchanan) Good Words, 12: 171.
Heath, J. E. Lecture before Richmond Lyceum. So. Lit. Mess. 4: 705.
Heath, Robt. Clarastella. (H. Southern) Retros. 2: 227.
Heathen and the Old Testament. (C. A. Auberlen) Good Words, 4: 710.
— Character and Prospects of. Spirit Pilg. 2: 481.
— Difficulties of converting. (C. R. Jericho) Chr. Q. Spec. 10: 1. — Am. Q. Reg. 9: 69.
— Future State of. (E. Pond) Chr. R. 22: 31.
— inexcusable for their Idolatry. (J. K. Wight) Princ. 32: 427.
— Salvability of. (L. A. Gotwald) Luth. Q. 3: 411.
— Teaching of Science to. (R. Anderson) Am. Q. Obs. 2: 24. — (C. Hamlin) Lit. & Theo. R. 4: 518.
Heathen Chinee. (Bret Harte) Ev. Sat. 10: 404.
— in the South. (R. Keeler and A. R. Waud) Ev. Sat. 11: 117.
Heathen Nations, Primitive Traditions of. Fraser, 21: 507.
Heathen Religions, Comparative Theology of. (J. F. Clarke) Chr. Exam. 62: 183.
Heathen Worship, Elements of Truth in. (S. Hart) Am. Church R. 29: 223.
Heathendom and Revelation. (H. A. Braun) Cath. World, 33: 10.
Heathenism and Christianity. (E. Zeller) Contemp. 29: 1027. Same art. Sup. Pop. Sci. Mo. 1: 158. — Brownson, 9: 1.
— — Conflict of. (J. J. Keane) Am. Cath. Q. 5: 468.
— and Judaism, Döllinger on. Ho. & For. R. 1: 450.
— Christian Truth in. Bost. R. 4: 170.
— Downfall of. (H. H. Milman) Quar. 57: 29.
— Early History of. (J. C. Moffat) Princ. 37: 321.
— Nature and moral Influence of. (A. Tholuck) Am. Bib. Repos. 2: 80, 246.
— when Christ appeared. Dub. R. 61: 81, 441.
Heather, Amongst the. Cornh. 34: 465.
— a Native of the United States. (E. S. Rand, jr.) Am. J. Sci. 83: 22.
Heather-Bells. Once a Week; 11: 110.
Heatherly Hall; a Tale. St. James, 15: 180.
Heathland, Burning of. (R. M. Kettle) Colburn, 168: 589.
Heating and Ventilation. (A. C. Stimers) Ecl. Engin. 1: 313. — Am. Arch. 8: 231.
— by Radiation. (L. W. Leeds) J. Frankl. Inst. 108: 213.
Heating Agents, Gas and Electricity. (C. W. Siemens) Ecl. Engin. 24: 477.

Heats of Elastic Fluids. (M. V. Regnault) J. Frankl. Inst. 56: 26.
Heaven and the Universe. (J.P.Lange) Mercersb. 6: 136.
— Buddhist. (S. S. Hebberd) Western, 3: 383.
— Christian Idea of. (J.H. Phipps) Mo. Rel. M. 50: 397.
— Faber on the Locality of. (J. M. Macdonald) Princ. 27: 269.
— Figuier's Theory of. Ecl. M. 78: 723.
— Hades, and Hell. Kitto, 10: 35, 483. 11: 56, 413.
— Latest Glance at. (R. Collyer) Lakeside, 1: 265.
— Meditations on. Good Words, 1: 9-317.
— of Christianity. (T. A. Finley) Month, 35: 185.
— Real and ideal. (F. A. Gast) Mercersb. 17: 417.
— Recent Works on. Lond. Q. 21: 328.
— Recognition of Friends in. (F. W. P. Greenwood) Chr. Exam. 18: 222. — (T. Appel) Mercersb. 4: 92.
— under a local Aspect. (F. A. Gast) Mercersb. 18: 232.
— Will the Earth be? Bost. R. 6: 204.
Heavenly Citizenship. (W. Hull) Luth. Q. 5: 61.
Heavenly Symbol of Human Knowledge. (S. Hibberd) 2: 1.
Heavenly Vision. (S. Nott) Am. Q. Reg. 6: 263.
Heavens, The. (J. Richardson, jr.) Chr. Exam. 36: 194.
— Architecture of. Chr. R. 6: 595.—Ecl. R. 94: 47.
— — Nichol's. Mo. R. 144: 118.
— God's Glory in. (W. Leitch) Good Words, 1: 23-729.
— Mechanism of, Mrs. Somerville's. Quar. 47: 537. — Ed. R. 55: 1. — Me. R. 127: 133.
— Mysteries of. Colburn, 165: 1173. 166: 24, 167.
— Starry. (T. Appel) Mercersb. 20: 451.
— What fills the Star-Depths? (R. A. Proctor) Pop. Sci. R. 9: 271. Same art. Ecl. M. 75: 432.
Heavysege, C. Poetry of. (D. Clark) Canad. Mo. 10: 127. — (L. Murray) Canad. Mo. 10: 250. — (B. Taylor) Atlan. 16: 412.
Hebdomadary of Mr. Snooks, the Grocer. Colburn, 11: 436.
Hebe. (Miss Taylor) Lippinc. 19: 173.
Hebe's Jumbles. (A. R. Annan) Scrib. 4: 465.
Hebel, Johann Peter, German Poet. (H. Harbaugh) Hours at Home, 3: 553. — (B. Taylor) Atlan. 9: 430.
Heber, Reginald, Bishop, Hymns of. Blackw. 22: 617.
— Indian Journal. Quar. 37: 100. — (F. Jeffrey) Ed. R. 48: 312. — Am. Q. 4: 115.
— Life of. Fraser, 2: 121. — Ed. R. 52: 431. — (R. Robbins) Chr. Q. Spec. 3: 227. — Quar. 43: 366. — Mo. R. 122: 517. — Chr. Obs. 27: 1. 29: 569. 30: 453, 525, 589.
— Palestine and other Poems. Am. Q. 4: 271. — Ecl. R. 17: 128. — Chr. Rem. 2: 153. — Chr. Obs. 8: 725.
— Sermons of. (F.W. P. Greenwood) Chr. Exam. 7: 212. — So. R. 4: 241. — Chr. Obs. 15: 584. 30: 102.
— The Whippiad; a Satirical Poem. Blackw. 54: 100.
Hébert, Antoine A. E. (R. Ménard) Portfo. 6: 50.
Hebich, Samuel, Life of. Chr. Obs. 76: 139.
Hebraistics. Blackw. 50: 609.
Hebrew, Origin of the Name. (S. W. Barnum) Cong. Q. 6: 200.
Hebrew and Roman Learning, Genius of. (P. B. Spear) Bib. Sac. 11: 527.
Hebrew Article. (Profs. Stuart and Nordheimer) Am. Bib. Repos. 2d s. 6: 404.
Hebrew Concordance, Englishman's. Ecl. R. 82: 305.
— Fürst's. Ecl. R. 71: 533.
— Nordheimer's. Princ. 11: 305. — Lit. & Theo. R. 6: 571. — (T. Lewis) Am. Bib. Repos. 2d s. 7: 467.
Hebrew Criticism. (J. Nicholson) Kitto, 1: 160.
Hebrew Ethics in Evidence of Date of Hebrew Documents. (R. S. Poole) Contemp. 39: 629.
Hebrew Idyls. (M. J. Chapman) Fraser, 12: 642. 13: 121-440. 14: 18.
Hebrew Inscriptions in the Crimea. Chr. Obs. 69: 356.
Hebrew Ladies at their Toilet. (A. J. Schwartz) St. Paul's, 14: 286.
Hebrew Language. Ecl. R. 112: 439. — Ecl. M. 52: 51.
— Accents and Makkeph of, Gesenius's Doctrine of. (J. T. M. Falkenau) Bib. Sac. 7: 650.
— Affinity to Languages of Sandwich and Friendly Islands. Arch. 8: 81.
— and Greek, Affinity of. (J. Strong) Meth. Q. 25: 430.
— and Literature. (B. J. Wallace) Am. Presb. R. 9: 442. — (S. H. Turner) Am. Bib. Repos. 1: 491.
— Chrestomathy of, Stuart's. Princ. 1: 294.
— Forms in, Confusion of some. (E. Biley) Kitto, 38: 172.
— Grammar and Grammarians of. Ecl. R. 78: 597.
— — and Lexicography. (G. H. Whittemore) Bib. Sac. 29: 547.
— — Bush's. Am. Meth. M. 21: 461. — (J. A. Alexander) Princ. 7: 341.
— — — and Palfrey's. Chr. R. 1: 49.
— — Ewald's. (J. A. Alexander) Princ. 4: 568.
— — Gesenius's. Chr. Exam. 27: 277. — Chr. R. 4: 419.
— — — Extracts from. Cong. M. 15: 22-612.
— — Nordheimer's. (T. Lewis) Am. Bib. Repos. 5: 438. — (J. A. Alexander) Princ. 10: 196. — Meth. Q. 1: 485. — So. Q. 20: 390. — Chr. Q. Spec. 10: 587.
— — Seixas's. Chr. Exam. 15: 65. 18: 160.
— — Stuart's. (S. Willard) No. Am. 13: 473. — So. R. 5: 1. — Am. Mo. R. 1: 12. — Chr. Mo. Spec. 4: 196. — Spirit Pilg. 2: 260.
— — Willard's. (J. G. Palfrey) No. Am. 5: 63.
— Idiomatic Usages of Plural in. (W. L. Alexander) Kitto, 1: 279.
— Importance of, for studying Scripture. Cong. M. 25: 85.
— in the Time of Jerome. (F. Bosworth) Kitto, 3: 283.
— Lexicography of. (M. Stuart) Am. Bib. Repos. 8: 448. — (J. Nordheimer) Am. Bib. Repos. 11: 482.
— Lexicon of, Gesenius's. Chr. Exam. 1: 122.
— — Gibbs's. Am. Mo. R. 1: 12. — (J. A. Alexander) Princ. 4: 269.
— — Robinson's. (J. A. Alexander) Princ. 9: 88.
— — Roy's. (M. Stuart) No. Am. 46: 487. — Chr. R. 3: 124.
— — Winer's. (G. R. Noyes) Chr. Exam. 6: 347.
— Origin of. (C. A. Rassam) Bentley 64: 57, 230.
— Philology of. (F. Delitzsch) Am. Bib. Repos. 2d s. 10: 190.
— — and Lexicography of. (F. H. W. Gesenius) Am. Bib. Repos. 3: 1.
— — History of. (F. Barham) Fortn. 3: 566.
— — Sketch of. Cong. M. 11: 29.
— Sharp on Syntax and Pronunciation of. Chr. Obs. 3: 415, 525.
— Spirit and Characteristics of. (B. Maimon) Univ. Q. 36: 36.
— Study of. (B. B. Edwards) Am. Bib. Repos. 12: 113. — (M. Stuart) Am. Q. Reg. 1: 193. 7: 63. — (R. Martineau) Theo. R. 1: 574. — Kitto, 12: 138. — (F. A. Gast) Ref. Q. 28: 131.
— — in England. (F. Bosworth) Chr. R. 11: 485. 12: 109.
— — — Early. Kitto, 6: 1.
— — Wilson's Introduction to. Gen. Repos. 4: 249.
— Syntax of, Nordheimer's. (J. A. Alexander) Princ. 13: 250.
— Tenses of. Am. Bib. Repos. 11: 131. — (D. H. Wier) Kitto, 4: 308. 6: 484. — (J. G. Murphy) Kitto, 5: 194. 7: 216. — (S. Lee) Kitto, 6: 193. 7: 469. — (A. B. Rich) Bib. Sac. 31: 115. — Kitto, 13: 111.
— Translation from, Emotional Element in. (T. Lewis) Meth. Q. 22: 85. 23: 55, 382. 24: 57.
— Use of Negative Particles in. (C. M. Mead) Bib. Sac. 31: 487.
— Value of Study of, for a Minister. (E. J. Young) Unita. R. 11: 479.

Hebrew Language, Vowel Points in. Chr. Mo. Spec. 3: 236. — Gen. Repos. 4: 257.
— Words in, Orthography of. (J. W. Gibbs) Am. J. Sci. 24: 87.
Hebrew Legends. Chamb. J. 38: 212, 232.
Hebrew Literature. (R. Martineau) Theo. R. 16: 157. — Ecl. R. 85: 733. — Kitto, 10: 424.
— Characteristics of. (C. Morris) Unita. R. 12: 412.
— Etheridge on. Lond. Q. 7: 119.
— Recent. Kitto, 12: 307.
Hebrew MSS. in British Museum, Almanzi Collection. (W. Wright) Kitto, 37: 354.
— Inscriptions in Ancient Karaite. Chr. Obs. 69: 505.
Hebrew Monarchy, History of. Brit. Q. 8: 26.
Hebrew Music, Ancient. Dub. Univ. 41: 675. 42: 21. — Mo. R. 157: 474.
Hebrew Mythology. (H. C. Lea) Nation, 26: 12, 28.
Hebrew Poetry. (J. Albee) Chr. Exam. 64: 74. — Ecl. R. 115: 136. — (J. Reade) New Dom. 11: 193, 260. — (P. Schaff) Internat. R. 2: 187. — (G. H. A. von Ewald) Kitto, 1: 94, 295. — (R. Babcock) Chr. R. 12: 387. — New Eng. M. 1: 97. — Ecl. R. 115: 136. — Evang. R. 14: 390.
— Heilprin's Historical. (J. W. Chadwick) Nation, 29: 60. 31: 63.
— Lowth's Translations of. (G. B. Cheever) No. Am. 31: 337.
— Noyes's Translations of. (W. B. O. Peabody) No. Am. 35: 473. — (A. P. Peabody) No. Am. 63: 201. — (S. G. Bulfinch) Chr. Exam. 83: 175.
— of the Middle Ages. Kitto, 5: 373.
— Spirit of. Chr. Obs. 62: 337.
— Studies in. (B. B. Edwards) Bib. Sac. 5: 58.
Hebrew Princes. Mo. Rel. M. 24: 133, 237. 25: 80.
Hebrew Psalter. Ecl. R. 82: 678.
Hebrew Tales, Hurwitz's. Quar. 35: 86.
Hebrides, Among the. St. Paul's, 10: 52, 603.
— Around Mull. (M. S. Cummins) Atlan. 16: 11, 167.
— Colonsay and Oronsay. (W. W. Campbell) Harper, 47: 524.
— Day in. Dub. Univ. 32: 467.
— Gregory's History of. Tait, n. s. 3: 574.
— Long Island, or Outer. (J. Geikie) Good Words, 20: 18, 234, 523.
— Rambling in. (A. Smith) Temp. Bar, 4: 481.
— Romance of. (A. E. Barr) Harper, 61: 676.
— Rough Sketches from. Chamb. J. 53: 717, 785.
— Week in. Dub. Univ. 30: 576. — (W. Chambers) Chamb. J. 30: 49, 67.
Hebron, Ride from, to Petra. Bentley, 60: 140.
Hecker, Isaac T., and the Order of St. Paul. (O. B. Frothingham) Chr. Exam. 78: 1.
— Sermon of, 1869. (I. T. Hecker) Cath. World, 10: 289.
Heckewelder, John. Am. J. Sci. 31: 60.
Hecla, Mount. Penny M. 2: 495.
— Ascent of. (G. F. Rodwell) Nature, 18: 596. — Chamb. J. 44: 407.
— Description of. (S. B. Gould) Once a Week, 17: 657.
— Eruption of, in 1845. Dub. R. 25: 1.
— Lavas of. (G. F. Rodwell) Nature, 19: 280.
Hector and Andromache, Parting of. Penny M. 1: 306.
Hector Garret of Otter. Fraser, 58: 583, 706. Same art. Liv. Age. 60: 42, 149.
Hedding, Elijah. (S. W. Bush) No. Am. 82: 349. — (D. W. Clark) Meth. Q. 13: 9. — with portrait, Meth. Q. 8: 1.
— Life and Times of. (D. Curry) Meth. Q. 15: 589.
Hedge, Frederic H. Discourse. (G. S. Hillard) Chr. Exam. 17: 169.
Hedge-Popping. Chamb. J. 40: 286.
Hedged with Thorns. Eng. Dom. M. 14: 225-287. 15: 1-292. 16: 13.
Hedgehog, The. Chamb. J. 28: 41.
Hedgehogs of Brazil. (R. Rathbun) Am. J. Sci. 115: 82.
Hedonical Calculus of greatest possible Happiness. (F. Y. Edgeworth) Mind, 4: 394.
Hedonism and Ultimate Good. (T. H. Green) Mind, 2: 266. — (H. Sidgwick) Mind, 2: 27.
— and Utilitarianism. J. Spec. Philos. 10: 271.
Hedwige, Queen of Poland, History of. Dub. R. 55: 311. — Cath. World, 1: 145.
Hedwige, Saint. Cath. World, 26: 108.
Hedwige; a Tale. Colburn, 168: 595.
Heels. Ev. Sat. 11: 431.
Heeren, A. H. L. Historical Researches. Ed. R. 59: 87. — (T. Walker) No. Am. 28: 186. — Ecl. R. 68: 609. — So. Q. 3: 199. 5: 156.
— Polity and Commerce of Antiquity. For. Q. 5: 141.
— Rise and Progress of Political Theories. For. Q. 20: 340.
Hegel, George W. F. (T. C. Simon) Contemp. 13: 47, 398. — (A. Seth) Mind, 6: 513. — Nat. Q. 18: 108.
— Analysis of, J. E. Cabot's Article on. (A. C. Brackett) J. Spec. Philos. 5: 38.
— and his Critics. (G. S. Hall) J. Spec. Philos. 12: 93.
— and Pantheism. Am. Church R. 21: 382.
— and Schelling, G. H. Lewes on. (J. S. Henderson) Contemp. 20: 529.
— as a Politician. (J. S. Henderson) Fortn. 14: 262.
— as a Publicist. (K. Rosenkranz) J. Spec. Philos. 6: 258.
— Classic Art. J. Spec. Philos. 12: 145, 277.
— Dialectic Method of. (A. E. Kroeger) J. Spec. Philos. 6: 184.
— Encyclopædia of the Philosophical Sciences. (K. Rosenkranz) J. Spec. Philos. 5: 234.
— First Principle. J. Spec. Philos. 3: 344.
— Paul Janet on. (W. T. Harris) J. Spec. Philos. 1: 250.
— Life of. (J. W. Alexander) Princ. 20: 561. — Select J. 1: [46.
— Logic Question in his System. (Prof. Trendelenburg) J. Spec. Philos. 5: 349. 6: 82, 163, 350.
— on the Absolute Religion. J. Spec. Philos. 15: 9, 132.
— Phenomenology of Mind. J. Spec. Philos. 2: 94-229. 3: 166, 257. — (K. Rosenkranz) J. Spec. Philos. 6: 53.
— Philosophic Method of. (W. T. Harris) J. Spec. Philos. 8: 35.
— Philosophy of Art (C. Bénard) J. Spec. Philos. 1: 36-220. 3: 31-317.
— — of History. (K. Rosenkranz) J. Spec. Philos. 8: 1.
— — of Religion. (K. Rosenkranz) J. Spec. Philos. 7: (Oct.) 57.
— Psychology. (K. Rosenkranz) J. Spec. Philos. 7: 17.
— Relation with his Contemporaries. J. Spec. Philos. 11: 399.
— Romantic Art. J. Spec. Philos. 12: 403. 13: 113.
— Science of Absolute Spirit. (G. S. Hall) J. Spec. Philos. 7: (July) 44.
— of Rights, Morals, and Religion. J. Spec. Philos. 4: 38, 155.
— Secret of. (C. C. Everett) Chr. Exam. 80: 196.
— — Stirling's. (H. James) No. Am. 102: 264. — Anthrop. R. 4: 34. — Ecl. R. 121: 557.
— Symbolic Art. J. Spec. Philos. 11: 337. 12: 18.
— Trendelenburg as an Opponent of. (A. Vera) J. Spec. Philos. 7: 26.
Hegelian Assaults on the Four Gospels. (C. E. Stowe) Bib. Sac. 8: 503.
Hegelian Christianity. (J. W. Chadwick) O. & N. 3: 93.
Hegelian Contributions to English Philosophy. (T. M. Lindsay) Mind, 2: 476.
Hegelianism and Psychology. (R. B. Haldane) Mind, 3: 568.
Hegira, New. Am. Church R. 2: 264.
Heidelberg. Lond. Soc. 35: 394.
— and its Castle. (E. Roberts) Appleton, 20: 495.

Heidelberg at Fair Time. Once a Week, **4**: 128.
— Castle of. Penny M. **4**: 157.
— — and its great Tun. Penny M. **5**: 421.
— A German University Town. Argosy, **3**: 264, 390.
— Hints from. Hogg, **14**: 285, 393, 463.
— Illuminations at. Once a Week, **4**: 696.
— On the Terrace at. (W. H. Pollock) Macmil. **27**: 168.
— Tea-Party at. Chamb. J. **24**: 49.
Heidelberg Catechism. (J. W. Nevin) Mercersb. **4**: 155. —(P. Schaff) Am. Presb. R. **12**: 369.
— and the Bible. (H. J. Reutenik) Mercersb. **7**: 466.
— and Heidelberg Church System. (H. Harbaugh) Mercersb. **9**: 83.
— and Dr. Nevin. (J. W. Proudfit) Princ. **24**: 91.
— and Ursinus. (J. W. Nevin) Mercersb. **3**: 497.
— Dalton on. (F. K. Levan) Mercersb. **20**: 573.
— English Versions. (H. Parry) Mercersb. **13**: 71.
— Formation and Introduction of. (H. Harbaugh) Mercersb. **11**: 47.
— History and Genius of. (P. Schaff) Mercersb. **23**: 88.
— Literature of. (H. Harbaugh) Mercersb. **12**: 601.
Heidelberg University. Fraser, **20**: 171.
— Student Life in. (G. M. Towle) Hours at Home, **3**: 369, 439. — Lond. Soc. **26**: 434. — Dub. Univ. **27**: 173.
Heiden. Lond. Soc. **12**: 330.
Height and Weight. (E. Lankester) Nature, **2**: 230.
Heimskringla; Laing's Transl. Tait, n. s. **11**: 281, 369.
Heine, Heinrich. (M. Arnold) Cornh. **8**: 233. — (C. Grant) Contemp. **38**: 372. — (C. Beard) Theo. R. **13**: 174. — (A. Parker) Lippinc. **26**: 604. — (J. H. Browne) Appleton, **17**: 23. — (A. H. Japp) Brit. Q. **74**: 265. — (K. Hillard) Victoria, **22**: 501. — (K. Hillard) Lippinc. **10**: 187. — (J. K. Hosmer) Western, **4**: 667. — (W. H. Hurlbut) No. Am. **69**: 216. — Fraser, **26**: 733. **74**: 588. — (J. D. Lester) Fortn. **12**: 287. Same art. Liv. Age, **103**: 180. — Blackw. **122**: 74. — Cornh. **7**: 247. Same art. Liv. Age, **79**: 51. — Dub. Univ. **54**: 590. — Eng. Dom. M. **11**: 17, 83. — Ev. Sat. **8**: 417. — Putnam, **6**: 475. — Sharpe, **16**: 291, 362.
— and his Works. (E. I. Sears) Nat. Q. **13**: 56.
— Grave of. Ev. Sat. **16**: 128.
— Last Days of. (J. A. Harrison) So. M. **15**: 246. — Colburn, **117**: 363.
— Last Poems and Thoughts. (R. Lytton) Fortn. **13**: 257.
— Last Years of. Putnam, **8**: 517.
— Life and Works of. (H. G. Hewlett) Fraser, **94**: 600. — (E. B. Shuldham) Temp. Bar, **29**: 210.
— R. Lytton on. Ev. Sat. **9**: 211.
— on Religion and Politics. (L. A. Montefiore) Fortn. **28**: 325.
— Poem from the German of. (F. E. Weatherly) Dark Blue, **1**: 486.
— Poems of. No. Brit. **32**: 389.
— Prose Works of. (E. Spencer) So. M. **13**: 506.
— Translations from. (T. Martin) Blackw. **121**: 504. **122**: 501, 628. **123**: 81–599.
— Wit and Writings of. Westm. **65**: 1. Same art. Ecl. M. **37**: 316. Same art. Liv. Age, **48**: 513.
— Works and Times of. Tait, n. s. **18**: 618, 679. Same art. Ecl. M. **26**: 481.
— Writings of. Ed. R. **104**: 192.
Heinsii Poemata. Retros. **1**: 48.
Heintz, Wilhelm, Obituary of. Nature, **23**: 245.
Heir at Law; a Tale. Chamb. J. **22**: 81, 100, 121.
— of Crossley Hall. Sharpe, **25**: 46.
— of Hardington. House. Words, **18**: 412.
— of Mondolfo. (M. W. Shelley) Appleton, **17**: 12.
— of Roseton. (C. Bissell) Contin. Mo. **1**: 210.
— of the World; a Tale. (C. Chesebrough) Sharpe, **51**: 113. Same art. Knick. **50**: 13.
Heirs-Claimant, Celebrated English. Temp. Bar, **33**: 338. *See* Claimants.
— of the Bodley Estate. (H. E. Scudder) Appleton, **14**: 644–741.
— of Gauntry. *See* Gauntry.
— of Randolph Abbey. Dub. Univ. **39**: 98–733. **40**: 92. Same art. Internat. M. **5**: 375, 477.
Heiress; a Tale. (A. Strickland) Chamb. J. **1**: 21.
— and her Friends; a Tale. Blackw. **51**: 64.
— in Jeopardy. Lond. M. **8**: 43.
— of Avening Abbey. Bentley, **59**: 382.
— of Ballybrena; a Yachtsman's Tale. Bentley, **60**: 111.
— of Elkington. Lond. Soc. **3**: 343, 431.
— of Moato; a Tale. Temp. Bar, **19**: 493.
— of Red Dog. (Bret Harte) Belgra. **37**: 321.
— of Warlow Castle. Lond. Soc. **39**: 417.
Heiresses. Bentley, **43**: 231, 365.
Heirlooms. Chamb. J. **42**: 801.
Held asunder. Lond. Soc. **7**: 560.
Helderberg Mts., N. Y. (V. Colvin) Harper, **39**: 652.
Helen. (A. Leslie) Tinsley, **19**: 669.
Helen at the Loom. (G. P. Lathrop) Atlan. **32**: 698.
Helen and Cassandra; a Poem. (A. B. Richards) Once a Week, **14**: 454.
Helen Churchill's Lover. Belgra. **40**: 96.
Helen Crocket; a Tale. (J. Hogg) Fraser, **14**: 430.
Helen Gordon; a Story. (S. Symonds) Peop. J. **10**: 348.
Helen Lee. (W. Seton) Cath. World, **27**: 405, 454.
Helen Lyndsey. (Mrs. S.C. Hall) Sharpe, **17**: 27. **18**: 68.
Helen of Troy. (G. A. Sala) Belgra. **16**: 39. — Cornh. **31**: 444.
Helen's Dower. Eng. Dom. M. **4**: 18–288. **5**: 1–289. **6**: 1–118.
Helena, Empress, Country and Religion of. Kitto, **23**: 96.
Helena, Lady Harrogate; a Novel. (J. B. Harwood) Chamb. J. **55**: 1–547.
Helena Mathewson. House. Words, **16**: 12. Same art. Liv. Age, **54**: 599.
Helena's Troubles; a Tale. Sharpe, **52**: 145.
Heliand; a Religious Poem of the 9th Century. (J. Gibb) Fraser, **102**: 658. Same art. Liv. Age, **147**: 679.
— and Ancient Teutonic Rhythmic Gospel Harmony. For. Q. **7**: 371.
Helices and Helicoidal Surfaces. (J. M. Richardson) J. Frankl. Inst. **63**: 231.
Helicoidal Surface of a Screw Propeller. (J. H. Warner) J. Frankl. Inst. **63**: 153.
Helicon in hot Weather. (G. H. Colton) Am. Whig R. **2**: 310.
Heligoland, Island of. (A. Brassey) Macmil. **37**: 171. Same art. Liv. Age, **136**: 58. — (M. Mitchell) Harper, **57**: 68. — (W. F. Rae) Good Words, **14**: 311. — Bentley, **53**: 580. — Fraser, **37**: 543. — (Mrs. P. Sinnett) Peop. J. **4**: 3. — House. Words, **12**: 145. Same art. Liv. Age, **47**: 203.
— a Liliput Province. (W. W. Reade) Atlan. **20**: 247.
— Visit to. (Mrs. Forrester) Gent. M. n. s. **9**: 196.
Heliodorus. Ethiopics. (J. D. Lester) Fortn. **10**: 510. — Blackw. **53**: 109.
— Romances of. Dub. Univ. **80**: 603.
Heliography. (J. Carbutt) J. Frankl. Inst. **108**: 249. — Art J. **22**: 325, 357. — Penny M. **8**: 186.
— and Signaling. (A. S. Wynne) Ecl. Engin. **23**: 479.
Heliopolis, Temple of. (W. J. Shaw) Overland, **14**: 439.
Heliostatic Star-Disks, Phenomena developed by. (G. W. R. Pigott) Nature, **24**: 514.
Heliotrope in Geodetic Surveys, Use of. (L. M. Haupt) J. Frankl. Inst. **106**: 416.
Heliotype Process. (L. T. Cragin) O. & N. **8**: 376. — (W. H. Harrison) Nature, **4**: 85.
— or Photochemic Printing. St. James, **28**: 611.
Hell. Ecl. R. **124**: 509.

Hell and the Divine Veracity. (L. A. Tollemache) Fortn. 28: 843.
— and Science. (J. Bayma) Cath. World, 27: 321.
— Belief in. Pop. Sci. Mo. 12: 627.
— Descent of Christ into. *See* Jesus Christ.
— the Hebrew Sheol. (S. Wieting) Meth. Q. 16: 281.
— Japanese and Watts's. Theo. R. 11: 247.
— New View of. Mo. Rel. M. 47: 291.
— Dr. Pusey on. Month, 43: 550.
See Eternal Punishment; Future Punishment; Hades.
Hell-Gate, East River, N.Y. Potter Am. Mo. 5: 875, 894.
— Unbarring of. (J. E. Richardson) Scrib. 3: 33.
Hellas; a Poem. (E. B. Lytton) St. James, 1: 23.
Hellenes, Romans, and Israelites. Chr. R. 16: 96.
Hellenic Kingdom and Greek Nation, Finlay on. Mo. R. 141: 530.
Hellenic Thought and Modern Problems. (G. S. Bower) Mod. R. 2: 765.
Hellenism, Old and new. (H. T. Tuckerman) So. R. n. s. 8: 337. Same art. Liv. Age, 108: 259.
— Strauss and. Nat. R. 4: 181.
Hellenist, The Word, in Acts xi. 20. Kitto, 19: 111.
Helme, B. H., Sketch of. Land We Love, 3: 163.
Helmet, The. (B. Thomas) Victoria, 33: 420–467. 34: 1, 114. 35: 33.
— Bronze, found at Ribchester. (S. Weston) Arch. 13: 223.
Helmholtz, Hermann L. F. (J. C. Maxwell) Nature, 15: 389. Same art. Pop. Sci. Mo. 5: 231.
Helminths, Growth and Migrations of. (M. Cornu) Nature, 7: 265.
Helmsley Hall. Liv. Age, 8: 565.
Heloise. Fraser, 67: 29.
Helper, Hinton Rowan. Nojoque. (A. T. Bledsoe) So. R. n. s. 2: 485.
Helps, Arthur. (A. V. Dicey) Nation, 14: 323. — (H. Holbeach) Contemp. 14: 429. Same art. Liv. Age, 106: 305. — (J. Hullah) Macmil. 31: 550. Same art. Ecl. M. 85: 76. — Bentley, 38: 462. Same art. Ecl. M. 37: 50. Same art. Liv. Age, 48: 257. — Broadw. 6: 94. — Colburn, 156: 460. — O. & N. 2: 620.
— as an Essayist. (C. Kingsley) Macmil. 25 : 200. Same art. Canad. Mo. 1: 171. Same art. Ev. Sat. 12: 87. Same art. Liv. Age, 112: 422.
— Essays. Blackw. 70: 379. Same art. Ecl. M. 26: 502. — Chamb. J. 17: 84.
— Oulita, the Serf. (A. K. H. Boyd) Fraser, 57: 528.
— Style of. Good Words, 16: 247.
— Works of. Colburn, 94: 401. — No. Brit. 18: 471.
Helsingland, and its Superstitions. Antiquary, 4: 314.
Helston Furry-Day. Belgra. 14: 409.
Helter-Skelter Papers. Contin. Mo. 2: 175.
Helvetic and Rhætian Confederacies. Portfo. (Den.) 14: 556.
Helvetic Society of Natural Sciences. Nature, 7: 8.
Hemans, Mrs. Felicia Dorothea. (S. C. Hall) Art J. 18: 205. — (H. B. Baker) Argosy, 28: 189. — (G. Gilfillan) Tait, n. s. 14: 359. Same art. Ecl. M. 11: 420. Same art. Liv. Age, 14: 126. — Blackw. 64: 641. Same art. Ecl. M. 16: 272. Same art. Liv. Age, 20: 241. — So. Lit. Mess. 2: 611, 722. — Chr. R. 2: 356. — Am. Q. 1: 153. 21: 257. — Dub. Univ. 10: 123. — Ecl. M. 29: 327. — Eng. Dom. M. 26: 104. — Godey, 54: 420. — Hours at Home, 4: 25.
— and the Picturesque School. Fraser, 21: 127.
— and her Writings. (L. E. Landon) Colburn, 44: 425.
— Chorley's Memorials of. Mo. R. 141: 179.
— Genius and Character of. Am. Mo. M. 9: 228.
— Hymns for Childhood. Dub. Univ. 3: 203.
— Life and Works of. Chr. Obs. 40: 355. — Dub. R. 2: 245. — West. M. 4: 159.
Hemans, Mrs. Felicia Dorothea. Modern Greece; a Poem. Portfo. (Den.) 25: 288.
— Palace of Maremma. Colburn, 41: 17.
— Patriotic Lays of Italy. Colburn, 40: 444.
— Poetry of. (G. Bancroft) No. Am. 24: 443. — (A. Norton) Chr. Exam. 6: 35. 19: 328. — Chr. Exam. 27: 370. — New York R. 1: 199. — No. Am. 44: 265. — (F. Jeffrey) Ed. R. 50: 32. — So. Lit. Mess. 7: 380. — (L. J. Park) Chr. Exam. 3: 403. — Ed. Mo. R. 3: 373. — Quar. 24: 130. — Mo. R. 102: 177, 425. — U. S. Lit. Gaz. 5: 401.
— — Religious Character of. Chr. R. 5: 23. — Godey, 21: 165.
— Remains of. Ecl. R. 64: 31.
— Songs for Evening Music. Colburn, 40: 290.
— Stanzas on the Death of, with portrait. (L. E. Landon) Colburn, 44: 286.
— Thoughts during Sickness. Colburn, 43: 328.
Heminburgh, Sir Walter de, Chronicle of. Ecl. R. 96: 334.
Hemling, Hans, Triptych of. Month, 5: 530.
Hemlock Hollow. (H. Roosevelt) Lakeside, 4: 206.
Hemlocks, The; a Poem. Cath. World, 12: 643.
Hemp, Cultivation of. Penny M. 2: 319. — (J. T. Cleveland) West. J. 1: 439
— — and Preparation of. (E. F. Pittman) West. J. 5: 185, 220.
— History and Uses of. (R. Deakin) Recr. Sci. 1: 293. — (M. Tarver) West. J. 1: 500.
— Western. Hunt, 9: 98.
Hemp and Flax Machine. Niles's Reg. 22: 77.
Hemp-growing Region of the U. S. De Bow, 24: 56.
Hemphill, Freida. Irish Q. 7: 385.
Hempstead, Stephen, Life of. Ill. M. 2: 122.
Henchmen. (E. L. Godkin) Nation, 30: 399.
Hens, Inscrutable Ways of. (E. L. Bangs) Potter Am. Mo. 11: 22.
Hen Fever. *See* Poultry Mania.
Hende, William. Voyages and Travels. Ed. R. 32: 111.
Henderson, Alexander. (J. W. Alexander) Princ. 12: 481. — Blackw. 16: 1.
Henderson, James, and James Hinton. (C. J. Vaughan) Good Words, 19: 784.
Henderson and Nashville Railroad. West. J. 8: 17.
Hendrik, Hans, Arctic Traveler. Geog. M. 5: 28, 57. — Liv. Age, 139: 570. — (A. H. Markham) Good Words, 21: 88, 269.
Hendrik's Prophecy; a Poem. Putnam, 8: 459.
Hengist and Horsa. (T. Wright) Colburn, 80: 208.
Hengstenberg and German Protestantism. (A. J. Schem) Meth. Q. 22: 108.
Henley, John, Oratory of. Retros. 14: 206. — Mus. 10: 500.
Henley, Robert, Political Portrait of. St. James, 25: 763.
Hennebon; a Poem. (W. Black) St. James, 17: 170.
Hennepin, Louis, Father. Travels in America. Dem. R. 5: 190, 381. — (J. H. Perkins) No. Am. 48: 70. 49: 258. — (W. F. Poole) Dial (Ch.), 1: 253.
— never in Albany. Hist. M. 10: 268.
Henotheism. (M. Müller) Contemp. 33: 707.
Henrie, Captain Dan. Adventure with the Wolves. Dem. R. 24: 33.
Henrietta and Vulcan. (D. M. Colton) Contin. Mo. 3: 421.
Henrietta Maria, Queen of Charles I. (P. Bayne) Contemp. 29: 370. Same art. Liv. Age, 132: 603. — (A. Laugel) Nation, 26: 110. — (A. King) Argosy, 16: 351. — Sharpe, 1: 58, 66. — Liv. Age, 54: 285. — (T. Wright) Arch. 32: 25. — (F. P. Cobbe) St. James, 43: 606.
Henriette d'Angleterre, Madame. Cornh. 25: 290.
Henry I., Remains of, in Reading Abbey. (R. Nares) Arch. 18: 272.

Henry II.; a Historical Drama. Dub. Univ. **23**: 19. — Mo. R. **162**: 145.
— and Adrian IV. U. S. Cath. M. **4**: 657.
— Midnight Ride with. Fraser, **80**: 58.
Henry III., Letters illustrative of the Reign of. Chr. Rem. **52**: 88.
Henry IV., and Philip III. Ed. R. **154**: 224.
— Examination of his Tomb. (I. H. Spry) Arch. **26**: 440.
Henry V., Castle of, at Rouen. (E. Turner) Arch. **7**: 232.
— Memoirs of. Ecl. R. **69**: 193.
— Towle's Hist. of. (C. C. Hazewell) No. Am. **103**: 595.
— Tyler's Memoirs of. Dub. R. **7**: 356. — Mo. R. **146**: 568. — Ecl. R. **69**: 193.
— Youth of. (A. C. Ewald) Cornh. **43**: 430. Same art. Liv. Age, **149**: 501.
Henry VI., Entertainment of, at Bury St. Edmund's. (C. Ord) Arch. **15**: 65.
— Proceedings of the Court and Nobility in 1454. (Sir F. Madden) Arch. **29**: 305.
— Three Petitions to. (S. Lysons) Arch. **16**: 3.
— Verses by. Lond. M. **9**: 638.
Henry VII.. Bacon's History of. Fraser, **59**: 697.
— Letters and Papers of his Reign. Chr. Rem. **51**: 275.
— Marriage of his Daughter Mary. Arch. **18**: 33.
— Memorials of. Ed. R. **121**: 201. — No. Brit. **31**: 287. Same art. Liv. Age, **64**: 67.
Henry VIII. All the Year, **20**: 498.
— Age of Morton, Wolsey, and More. Dub. R. **40**: 1.
— and Anne Boleyn. (J. A. Froude) Fraser, **55**: 723. — Ecl. M. **52**: 131.
— and Catherine of Aragon. Month, **37**: 146.
— — Proposed Monument to. (W. Illingworth) Arch. **16**: 80.
— and Francis I., Interview of. (J. Caley) Arch. **21**: 175.
— — — Picture of. (J. Ayloffe) Arch. **3**: 185.
— and the Reformation. (J. W. Santee) Mercersb. **16**: 355.
— Audin's History of. Dub. R. **24**: 427.
— Character and Conduct of. Chr. Rem. **42**: 346.
— Court of. Mo. R. **110**: 195.
— Divorce Question, and Dissolution of Monasteries. Chr. Rem. **38**: 46.
— Entry into Lincoln, 1541. (F. Madden) Arch. **23**: 334.
— Foreign Policy of. Ecl. M. **67**: 744.
— Froude's Apology for. Dub. R. **41**: 307. — (R. H. Parkinson) Internat. R. **10**: 116. — Westm. **70**: 275. *See* England, History of, Froude's.
— Giustinian's Court of. Brit. Q. **21**: 442. — (J. A. Froude) Fraser, **51**: 441. — Liv. Age, **44**: 301.
— History of. Mo. R. **112**: 1.
— Holbein's Portraits of his Queens. (J. G. Nichols and G. Scharf) Arch. **40**: 71.
— Letter and Indenture of. (F. Stone) Arch. **16**: 181.
— Life of. Ecl. R. **66**: 250.
— Love Letters to Anne Boleyn. Pamph. **21**: 325. **22**: 113.
— Old Writers on the Life of. Chr. Rem. **49**: 124.
— Picture of, in Windsor Castle. (J. Topham) Arch. **6**: 179.
— Privy Purse Expenses. Lond. M. **19**: 92.
— Regulations of his Household. (O. S. Brereton) Arch. **3**: 154.
— Reign of. Liv. Age, **77**: 545. — Ecl. M. **45**: 46.
— Social Condition of England under. Westm. **95**: 92.
— Songs and Ballads by. (W. Chappell) Arch. **41**: 371.
— State MS. of Reign of. (J. P. Collier) Arch. **36**: 14.
— State Papers, and Divorce Case. Chr. Rem. **55**: 239.
— — of the Reign of. Fraser, **77**: 466. — Quar. **143**: 1.
— Suit of Armor for. (S. R. Meyrick) Arch. **22**: 106.
— Turner's History of the Reign of. Lond. M. **17**: 215.
— Treason under. Ev. Sat. **9**: 39.
— Tytler's Life of. Ecl. R. **66**: 250.
— Wardrobe Account of. (J. Caley) Arch. **9**: 243.
Henry III., of France. Tait, n. s. **26**: 145. Same art. Ecl. M. **47**: 65.
Henry IV., of France. Bentley, **3**: 511. — Fraser, **35**: 553. — Penny M. **8**: 467. — Tait, n. s. **27**: 167.
— and his Plan for a perpetual Peace. (S. R. Van Campen) Ecl. M. **82**: 483.
— and la belle Gabrielle. Temp. Bar, **48**: 461. Same art. Ecl. M. **88**: 221. Same art. Liv. Age, **126**: 796.
— and the Princess of Condé. Cornh. **20**: 292. Same art. Liv. Age, **103**: 33.
— Chambrier's Grand Design of. Ed. R. **6**: 162.
— Days of. Temp. Bar, **44**: 454.
— Letters of. For. Q. **29**: 38.
— Life of. Blackw. **62**: 371. — Mus. **6**: 202. — Mo. R. **104**: 309.
— Poirson's History of. Dub. R. **44**: 1.
— Works and Life of. Quar. **148**: 501. Same art. Liv. Age, **143**: 451.
Henry V., of France. Month, **15**: 120.
Henry VI., Emperor of Germany. (A. E. Kroeger) Western, **4**: 426.
Henry, Prince of Portugal, the Navigator. Ed. R. **128**: 200. — Geog. M. **4**: 157.
Henry, Prince of Wales. (J. Grant) Tinsley, **19**: 608.
— Wardrobe Account of. (W. Bray) Arch. **11**: 88.
Henry, A. and S., & Co., Commercial House of. Hunt, **19**: 63. — Lond. Soc. **38**: 446.
Henry, Alexander. Hunt, **34**: 36.
Henry, Caleb S. (G. W. Greene) No. Am. **94**: 525.
— Dr. Oldham at Greystones. (R. T. S. Lowell) Am. Church R. **13**: 211.
Henry, Charles Napier. Art J. **33**: 225.
Henry, Joseph. (S. Newcomb) Nation, **26**: 320. — with portrait, Ecl. M. **84**: 376. — Am. J. Sci. **115**: 462. — (A. M. Mayer) J. Frankl. Inst. **110**: 257. — Nature, **18**: 143. — Pop. Sci. Mo. **2**: 741.
— and Faraday. (A. M. Mayer) Pop. Sci. Mo. **18**: 76.
— Death of. Pop. Sci. Mo. **13**: 365.
Henry, Matthew. Spirit Pilg. **3**: 237. — (W. B. Sprague) Lit. & Theo. R. **1**: 280. — Am. Meth. M. **17**: 1.
— and Philip, Sketches of. Cong. M. **7**: 225, 282.
— as a Commentator. (W. L. Alexander) Kitto, **2**: 222.
Henry, Patrick. (W. W. Henry) Potter Am. Mo. **7**: 8. — (W. W. Henry) Pennsyl. M. **1**: 78. — (W. B. Sprague) Evang. R. **20**: 611. — Portfo.(Den.) **16**: 460.
— and the Com. of Safety. So. Lit. Mess. **25**: 350. **26**: 27.
— and Thomas Jefferson. Hist. M. **12**: 90.
— and the Revolution. (V. W. Kingsley) Nat. Q. **27**: 135.
— Character of. (W. W. Henry) Hist. M. **12**: 368. **22**: 272, 346.
— Historic Doubts concerning. (E. A. Pollard) Galaxy, **10**: 327.
— Life of. Meth. Q. **1**: 122. — (A. H. Everett) Sparks's Am. Biog. **11**: 209. — (J. Sparks) No. Am. **6**: 293. — (E. L. Magoon) So. Lit. Mess. **13**: 505 — Anal. M. **6**: 376. **10**: 441.
— Reminiscences of. (A. Alexander) Liv. Age, **26**: 205. — So. Lit. Mess. **16**: 366.
— Sketch of. Lond. M. **5**: 413, 564.
Henry, Philip. Meth. M. **35**: 481.
— and Matthew, on Baptism. Chr. Obs. **46**: 577, 595.
Henry, Samuel, Biography of. Hunt, **2**: 183.
Henry, Thomas C., Memoir of. Cong. M. **11**: 113.
Henry, Dr. Walter. Recollections of a Staff Surgeon. Quar. **67**: 453.
Henry, W. S. Campaign Sketches. So. Q. **18**: 427.
Henry Clay, Steamboat, Burning of, 1852. Knick. **40**: 342.
Henry Mountains, Geology of. Nature, **21**: 177.
Henry Norman and Mary Neville. (J. C. McCabe) So. Lit. Mess. **7**: 579.

Henryson, Robert, Poems of. St. James, **24**: 60. — No. Brit. **44**: 154.
Henshaw, Fred. Henry, with portrait. Colburn, **166**: 274.
Henshaw, J. P. K., Bishop, Life and Character of. (T. Atkinson) Am. Church R. **5**: 397.
Henshaw, Joshua. (A. H. Hoyt) N. E. Reg. **22**: 105.
Henslow, John Stephens. (E. L. Youmans) Pop. Sci. Mo. **3**: 159.
Hentzner, Paul. Travels. (H. Southern) Retros. **1**: 16.
Henwood, William Jory. (G. T. Bettany) Nature, **12**: 293.
Hepburn, Sir John. Sharpe, **15**: 266.
Hephæstion, Gaisford's. Ed. R. **17**: 381.
Hephzibah Guiness. (S.W. Mitchell) Lippinc. **21**: 425–738.
Heptarchy, Tale of the. Fraser, **18**: 179.
Her Chance; a Tale. (S. W. Kellogg) Lippinc. **11**: 317.
Her dearest Foe; a Novel. (A. F. Hector) Temp. Bar, **44**: 252–539. **45**: 115–541. **46**: 117–545. **47**: 119–555. Same art. Ecl. M. **85**: 129–694. **86**: 56–704. **87**: 43–462. Same art. Liv. Age, **126**: 808. **127**: 36–672. **128**: 35–652.
Her Face. House. Words, **18**: 258.
Her Father's Daughter; a Tale. Chamb. J. **56**: 585, 602.
Her first Appearance. House. Words, **19**: 29.
Her first Appearance; a Story. Temp. Bar, **57**: 36.
Her first Appearance. (D. Cook) Belgra. **26**: 243.
Her George. (C. M. A. Winslow) Lakeside, **4**: 113.
Her Grace, the Drummer's Daughter. (C. Chesebrough) Atlan. **2**: 532, 656.
Her imperial Guest. (J. Payn) Harper, **52**: 48.
Her last Appearance. (D. Cook) Liv. Age, **100**: 289.
Her Master; a Tale. (Mrs. C. Reade) Belgra. **21**: 464. **22**: 69.
Her Oath; a Story. (P. B. Marston) Galaxy, **24**: 603.
Her Secret. Broadw. **6**: 462, 500. **7**: 1–549.
Her Sphere; a Poem. (E. A. Allen) Scrib. **4**: 218.
Her Story. (H. P. Spofford) Lippinc. **10**: 678.
Her winning Ways. Colburn, **143**: 267–631. **144**: 75–645. **145**: 74–692. **147**: 439, 575. **148**: 175–598. **149**: 94–711.
Herakles and Hulas; a Poem. (F. B. J. Money) St. James, **38**: 610.
Herald, With an old. All the Year, **31**: 440.
Heralds and Coats of Arms. All the Year, **41**: 488.
— Half-Hours with. Eng. Dom. M. **8**: 156–335. **9**: 17–87.
Heralds' College and Visitations. N. E. Reg. **2**: 342.
— as a Source of Revenue. Macmil. **42**: 346.
Heraldic Arms of England. Penny M. **4**: 148.
Heraldic Devices of Richard II. and his Queen. (J. G. Nichols) Arch. **29**: 32.
Heraldic Reform. St. James, **16**: 442.
Heraldry. N. E. Reg. **1**: 225.
— and Pedigree. Westm. **60**: 85. Same art. Liv. Age, **39**: 3.
— Blazonry and Mottoes in 19th Cent. Tait, n. s. **9**: 227.
— Burke's General Armory. Mo. R. **161**: 16.
— Curiosities of. Ecl. R. **82**: 175.
— English. Art J. **19**: 252.
— in America. (W. H. Whitmore) Galaxy, **2**: 184. — (W. H. Whitmore) N. E. Reg. **12**: 289. **13**: 165.
— in New England. (W. H. Whitmore) N. E. Reg. **18**: 268. —(W. H. Whitmore) No. Am. **100**: 186.
— Manuals of. Ed. R. **121**: 328.
— may have Meaning. Art J. **8**: 279.
— Odd Coats of Arms. All the Year, **12**; 115.
— Old Notions on. Retros. **17**: 119.
— of Fish, Moule on. Mo. R. **158**: 332.
— Origin and Influence of. Nat. Q. **16**: 160.
— past and present. St. James, **13**: 92.
— Reform in. Dub. Univ. **78**: 679.
— Religious Aspect of. (R. Seton) Cath. World, **32**: 757.
— Royal Armory of England. Art J. **19**: 113, 149, 221. **20**: 21–269.
Heraldry, Science of. (F. R. Conder) Dub. Univ. **90**: 431.
— Scrope and Grosvenor Roll. Quar. **56**: 1.
— Some Uses of. (R. Seton) Cath. World, **32**: 524.
— Surnames and Arms. Cornh. **6**: 82.
— What is? (W. Partridge) Art J. **6**: 3–133.
See Blazon.
Herat and Afghanistan. Blackw. **95**: 462.
— and the Persian War. Westm. **67**: 173.
— to Ourenbourg, Journey from. Blackw. **51**: 691.
Heraud, Edith, and Laura Bateman, Comparison of. Victoria, **3**: 167.
Herbs and Herbalists, Spanish. Temp. Bar, **45**: 487.
— and Signatures. Chamb. J. **48**: 743.
— Superstitions in. Chamb. J. **33**: 201.
— Truth about. Chamb. J. **31**: 36.
Herbal, Henry's American. Anal. M. **7**: 248.
Herbaria, National. (W. T. T. Dyer) Nature, **7**: 243.
Herbarium Cases. (C. C. Parry) Am. Natural. **8**: 471.
Herbart, John Fred., and Education. Am. J. Educ. **28**: 45.
Herbert, Lord Edward, of Cherbury. (J. Hunt) Contemp. **6**: 468. Same art. Theo. Ecl. **6**: 564. — Blackw. **129**: 528. Same art. Liv. Age, **149**: 3.— (J. A. Picton) Mod. R. **2**: 623.
— Life of. Retros. **7**: 317.
Herbert, Geo. (A. N. Littlejohn) Am. Church R. **7**: 290. — Bost. R. **3**: 236. — Knick. **42**: 145. — Dub. Univ. **8**: 572. — Sharpe, **47**: 88. — Temp. Bar, **2**: 475.
— and contemporary Religious Poets. Brit. Q. **19**: 377. Same art. Liv. Age, **41**: 291. Same art. Ecl. M. **32**: 199.
— and his Times. Liv. Age, **74**: 339.
— and Keble. Brit. Q. **46**: 97. Same art. Liv. Age, **94**: 195.
— as a Lover of Nature. St. Paul's, **13**: 514.
— Life and Character of. Chr. Obs. **10**: 469, 533.
— — Times, and Poems of. Chr. Rem. **44**: 103.
— Memoir of. Cong. **4**: 214.
— Poems of. Art J. **8**: 76. — Retros. **3**: 215.
— The Temple. Cong. M. **6**: 153.
Herbert, Henry W. Internat. M. **3**: 289.
Herbert, Sidney, first Baron Herbert of Lea. Fraser, **65**: 198.
— Memorial of. All the Year, **6**: 102. — St. James, **3**: 213.
Herbert, Sir Thomas, Travels of. Retros. **18**: 332.
Herbert, Thomas Martin. (J. Matheson) Cong. **7**: 33.
Herbert, Wm. Attila, King of the Huns. Ed. R. **66**: 261. — Mo. R. **145**: 392.
— Miscellaneous Poetry. (Sir W. Scott) Ed. R. **9**: 211.
Herberts of Elfdale. (C. Crowe) Once a Week, **3**: 449–505.
Herbert Freer's Perplexities. Lond. Soc. **4**: 491. Same art. Ecl. M. **61**: 174.
Herbert Lacy; a Novel. Lond. M. **21**: 238.
Herbert Newton. (E. E. Darley) Godey, **23**: 56.
Herbert Orton; a Novel. (J. R. Musick) Potter Am. Mo. **10**: 261–422. **11**: 17–361.
Herborizing, Hints on. (A. H. Curtiss) Am. Natural. **6**: 257.
Herculaneum and Pompeii. (R. Freebairn) Meth. M. **34**: 273.
— Can it be excavated? (R. A. McLeod) Atlan. **40**: 641.
— Destruction of. Cornh. **17**: 286.
— Half-Hour at. (W. D. Howells) Nation, **2**: 429.
— How destroyed. (E. Beulé) Pop. Sci. Mo. **2**: 232.
— Manuscripts from. (E. Everett) No. Am. **14**: 296.
— Papyrus discovered at. (H. G. Bennett) Arch. **15**: 114.
— Papyri of. Ed. R. **116**: 318.
— Ruins of. (T. Young) Quar. **3**: 1. — Ed. R. **16**: 368.
Hercules. Blackw. **115**: 545.
Hercules Adamant. (C. Reade) Dark Blue, **4**: 79.

Herder, Johann Gottfried. (G. Bancroft) No. Am. **20**: 138. — (K. Hillebrand) No. Am. **115**: 104, 235. **116**: 389. — (K. von Raumer) Am. J. Educ. **6**: 195. — (J. H. W. Stuckenberg) Evang. R. **13**: 472. — Lond. M. **7**: 373. — Dub. R. **14**: 505. — Liv. Age, **54**: 119.
— as Theologian. (J. F. Smith) Theo. R. **9**: 179, 437.
— Letters on Study of Divinity. Chr. Disc. **2**: 233, 417. **3**: 1, 81, 171.
— Marsh's Life and Translation of. Chr. Exam. **18**: 167.
— Opinions and Services of. (G. Ripley) Chr. Exam. **19**: 172.
— Works of. For. Q. **37**: 281. — (F. Carter) Nation, **26**: 360.
Herdsman, The. (P. McTeague) Bentley, **7**: 235.
— of La Camargue. St. James, **3**: 445. **4**: 190. Same art. Liv. Age, **74**: 32, 124.
Here and there. Fraser, **22**: 43.
Hereafter. (A. H. Baldwin) Fraser, **69**: 418.
Hereditaries, Wisdom of the. Ecl. R. **90**: 626.
Hereditary Ability. (W. H. Whitmore) N. E. Reg. **23**: 285.
Hereditary Foes; a Tale. (K. P. Osgood) Scrib. **9**: 360.
Hereditary Genius, Galton on. (O. A. Brownson) Cath. World, **11**: 721. — Fraser, **82**: 251.
Hereditary Judges of England. (F. Galton) Macmil. **19**: 424.
Hereditary Honors; a Tale. Colburn, **34**: 433.
Hereditary Improvement. (F. Galton) Fraser, **87**: 116. Same art. Ecl. M. **80**: 296.
Hereditary Influence, Animal and Human. Westm. **66**: 135. Same art. Ecl. M. **39**: 1. Same art. Liv. Age, **51**: 1.
Hereditary Misfortune in Families. (J. W. Calcraft) Dub. Univ. **41**: 236. Same art. Ecl. M. **28**: 533.
Hereditary Rank. Ox. Prize Ess. **2**: 209.
Hereditary Rulers. (Marquis of Blandford) 19th Cent. **10**: 217.
Hereditary Talent. Chamb. J. **47**: 118.
— and Character. (F. Galton) Macmil. **12**: 157, 318.
Hereditary Traits. Cornh. **37**: 411. Same art. Sup. Pop. Sci. Mo. **3**: 26.
Hereditary Transmission of Habits. (W. B. Carpenter) Contemp. **21**: 295, 779, 867. Same art. Pop. Sci. Mo. **3**: 303. Same art. Liv. Age, **116**: 451. **117**: 240. — (G. G. Francis) Anthrop. J. **2**: 3.
Heredity. (G. Iles) Pop. Sci. Mo. **14**: 356. — (C. Wright) Nation, **20**: 405.
— and Education. (G. Batchelor) Unita. R. **14**: 37.
— Haeckel's New Theory of. (E. R. Lankester) Nature, **14**: 235.
— in Nervous Diseases. (E. Dupuy) Pop. Sci. Mo. **11**: 332.
— in Twins. (F. Galton) Anthrop. J. **5**: 324.
— Law of Likeness. (A. Wilson) Gent. M. n. s. **20**: 44.
— Laws of, Physical and moral. Brit. Q. **29**: 1. Same art. Liv. Age, **62**: 140.
— Mental. (D. Wilson) Canad. Mo. **9**: 397.
— Moral, Law of. (S. Meredith) Good Words, **18**: 601.
— Phenomena of. (F. Papillon) Pop. Sci. Mo. **4**: 55–170.
— Ribot on. (W. S. Jevons) Nature, **11**: 503.
— Theory of. (F. Galton) Anthrop. J. **5**: 329. — Contemp. **27**: 80.
— Typical Laws of. (F. Galton) Nature, **15**: 492–532.
Hereford. (L. S. Costello) Bentley, **17**: 605.
— Bishops of, Episcopal Rings of. (J. Merewether) Arch. **31**: 249.
— Cathedral of. Penny M. **14**: 1.
— — Merewether on Condition of, 1842. Mo. R. **161**: 162.
— See and Cathedral of. Antiquary, **4**: 209–293.
Herefordshire; Annals of a Border County. Fraser, **83**: 84.
— History of. Quar. **148**: 143.
Heremore-Brandon; a Tale. (S. G. Brownson) Cath. World, **8**: 522, 663, 784. **9**: 63, 188.
Hereot, Antoine, early French Poet. Lond. M. **5**: 37.
Heresy. Chamb. J. **44**: 724.
— and Heretics. Penn Mo. **3**: 612.
— Is it possible? (T. M. Clark) Am. Church R. **3**: 578.
— Progress in. (E. W. Reynolds) Univ. Q. **20**: 163.
— A Trial for, in 1620 (J. G. MacLeod) Month, **30**: 327. **31**: 78.
— What is a Heretic? (L. M. Dorman) New Eng. **23**: 324.
Heresies, how regarded by the early Church. (J. W. Nevin) Mercersb. **4**: 429.
— Newly found Treatise against all. Dub. R. **33**: 365.
— of the Working Classes. Westm. **77**: 60.
Heretic, The; a Tale from the Russian. Blackw. **55**: 133.
Heretics, Early. (J. H. Allen) Mod. R. **2**: 688. — Ecl. R. **85**: 576.
Hereward, the Saxon, Last Adventures of. (T. Wright) Colburn, **74**: 402.
Hergest, Red Book of. St. Paul's, **3**: 308.
Hering, George Edwards, Obituary of. Art J. **32**: 83.
Heriot, George. Dub. Univ. **28**: 68. Same art. Ecl. M. **9**: 65. — Penny M. **8**: 100. — Lond. Soc. **6**: 167.
— and his Hospital. Chamb. J. **4**: 218.
— Sketch of. Hogg, **11**: 9.
Heritage, Physical and moral. Brit. Q. **29**: 1. Same art. Liv. Age, **62**: 140.
Herkomer, Hubert, Works of. (J. Dafforne) Art J. **32**: 109.
Hermann, Père. (B. Murphy) Cath. World, **16**: 808.
Hermanstadt to Bucharest, Journey from. (C. R. O'Donnell) Fraser, **2**: 16.
Hermas, Shepherd of. Dub. R. **51**: 133.
Hermes Scythicus, Jamieson's. (T. Young) Quar. **14**: 96.
Hermes Trismegistus. (A. B. Alcott) Radical, **6**: 487. — (G. Masson) Kitto, **38**: 22.
Hermeneutics and Homiletics, Relative Value of, to the Preacher. (S. M. Vail) Meth. Q. **26**: 38, 371.
— Fairbairn's Manual of. Evang. R. **10**: 301.
— Origen's. (O. Cone) Univ. Q. **31**: 209.
— Sacred. (J. W. Nevin) Mercersb. **25**: 5.
— — Davidson's. Cong. M. **26**: 581.
— Seiler's. Cong. M. **18**: 359.
Hermesian Doctrine. Dub. R. **8**: 117. — Chr. Rem. **9**: 54.
Hermetic Philosophy. Ecl. R. **105**: 201.
Hermia; a Tale. (S. R. T. Mayer) St. James, **35**: 433.
Hermione. Tinsley, **1**: 689. **2**: 50.
Hermione, Story of the. Chamb. J. **39**: 45.
Hermippus Redivivus. (S. B. Gould) Once a Week, **17**: 143.
Hermit, The; a Tale of East Rock, New Haven, Conn. So. Lit. Mess. **9**: 246.
— Hymns of a. Mus. **38**: 232, 300, 480.
— of Bath. (A. Elder) Bentley, **14**: 344.
— of St. Paul's. (R. Postans) Bentley, **33**: 586.
— of Utica. (A. B. Johnson) Knick. **35**: 203.
— wanted. Chamb. J. **45**: 590.
Hermit's Year; a Tale. (C. Clarke) Temp. Bar, **20**: 473.
Hermits and Anchoritism. Hogg, **1**: 33.
— Ancient. (F. Parke) Dub. Univ. **82**: 469.
— and Recluses of the Middle Ages. (E. T. Cutts) Art J. **12**: 17. **13**: 97.
— Chapter on. Chamb. J. **50**: 445.
— Saints of the Desert. (P. Schaff) Meth. Q. **24**: 29. *See* Bigg, John.
Hermit Bob; a Tale. All the Year, **14**: 233.
Hermit Crabs; how they get Possession of their Shells. (A. Agassiz) Pop. Sci. R. **15**: 183.
Hermit Island. House. Words, **7**: 88.
Hermit Mouse; a Poem. Dub. Univ. **11**: 69.
Hermon, Mount, and its Neighborhood. (C. H. Brigham) Mo. Rel. M. **13**: 181.
— Excursion to Summit of. (J. L. Porter) Bib. Sac. **11**: 41.

Herndon, Wm. L., and the Amazon. (P. Godwin) Putnam, 3: 272.
Herne the Hunter. (F. Parke) Dub. Univ. 84: 487.
Herne Bay in Winter. Sharpe, 29: 66.
Herne's Oak, Windsor. Penny M. 11: 156.
Hernia, Munroe on. (Dr. Reeve) Ed. R. 3: 136.
— Radical Cure of. (H. Chase) J Frankl. Inst. 25: 95.
Hero. (G. M. Craik) Hours at Home, 10: 197–522. 11: 16–501.
Hero and Leander. Fraser, 56: 480. — Knick. 32: 197. Blackw. 41: 267.
— Notes on the Story of. Lond. Soc. 6: 560.
Hero's Reward. (L. de L. Ramé) Belgra. 39: 42.
Hero and Maiden; a Poem. (E. Bradley) Hogg, 15: 358.
— and Valet. Bentley, 47: 621.
— in spite of Himself. Irish Mo. 2: 308.
— or Heroine. (A. M. King) Cath. World, 10: 232–497.
Hero Harold. (M. B. Smedley) Good Words, 9: 160, 256.
Heroes. (W. Arthur) Ex. H. Lec. 6: 289. — Tinsley, 1: 421.
— Ancient and modern. (J. W. Calcraft) Dub. Univ. 40: 34, 407. 41: 147, 418. 42: 135. Same art. Ecl. M. 27: 106, 481.
— and Hero Worship, Carlyle on. Tait, n. s. 8: 379. — Mus. 43: 375.
— — and the Heroic in History. Chr. Rem. 6: 121, 451.
— and Heroism. Knick. 45: 551.
— and Valets. Cornh. 35: 46.
— God's, and the World's. (J. H. Gurney) Ex. H. Lec. 10: 327.
— of an Hour. Sharpe, 25: 238.
— Popular. Chamb. J. 40: 264.
— Spiritual. Meth. Q. 9: 217.
Hero Worship. (C. J. Lever) Blackw. 97: 696. — Chamb. J. 12: 129.
— Domestic. Colburn, 119: 475.
— Effects of. Hogg, 8: 143.
— in the Streets. Once a Week, 18: 204.
— of recent Historians. Ecl. R. 110: 105.
— Rise of. (G. L. Gomme) Colburn, 158: 551
Herod the Great. Bost. R. 4: 15.
— When was he made King of Judea? (W. S. Hooper) Meth. Q. 39: 546.
Herods, Five. (F. Trench) Chr. Obs. 65: 299.
Herodias; a Poem. (F. H. Doyle) Temp. Bar, 2: 50.
Herodotus. No. Brit. 20: 389.
— and Commentators. (E. A. Freeman) Nat. R. 15: 282.
— Illustrations of. Blackw. 78: 685.
— Larcher on. Ecl. R. 50: 32.
— Niebuhr's Geography of. Westm. 13: 335.
— Oxford Editions of. Quar. 2: 343.
— Philosophy of. (T. De Quincey) Blackw. 51: 1.
— Rawlinson's. (G. H. Emerson) Univ. Q. 18: 77. — Blackw. 85: 195. — Brit. Q. 28: 446. — Dub. R. 49: 348. — Ed. R. 111: 32. — (J. C. Moffat) Princ. 33: 261.
— Taylor's. Westm. 11: 181. — Ecl. R. 50: 23.
— Theology of. (R. B. Richardson) New Eng. 38: 549.
— Wheeler's Geography of. Ecl. R. 101: 556.
Heroic Ages and Mr. Gladstone. Nat. Q. 20: 141.
— of the North. For. Q. 35: 74.
Heroic Elegies. Dub. Univ. 2: 202.
Heroine; a Story. (E. O'Hara) Peop. J. 10: 79.
— and Mock-Hero in the Days of the Fronde. Fraser, 28: 485, 526.
— of Ostend. Fraser, 29: 439.
— of To-Day. (T. S. Arthur) Sharpe, 50: 271.
— of To-Day. Contin. Mo. 3: 543.
Heroines in modern Novels. Cornh. 11: 630.
Heroine Worship. Bentley, 39: 630.
Heroism. (C. Kingsley) Cornh. 27: 29. Same art. Ev. Sat. 14: 190. Same art. Liv. Age, 116: 347.
Heroism of La Petite Marie; a Story. (B. L. Macdonell) Canad. Mo. 18: 309.
Heron, Sir Hugh, Story of. Lond. M. 8: 285.
Herons. All the Year, 10: 114, 136.
— and Bitterns. (E. Jesse) Once a Week, 14: 322.
— Night. (S. Lockwood) Am. Natural. 12: 27.
Ερωτάω and Αἰτέω, Signification of. (E. Abbot) No. Am. 114: 171.
Herpetology, Holbrook's North American. (D. H. Storer) No. Am. 49: 145.
— Schreiber's European. Nature, 11: 271.
See Serpents; Reptiles.
Herr Budingen's Life Dream. Tinsley, 18: 388.
Herrera, Fernando de, el Divino. Tait, 3: 33.
Herrick, Edward C. (T. A. Thacher) New Eng. 21: 820.
Herrick, Robert. (F. T. Palgrave) Macmil. 35: 475. Same art. Liv. Age, 133: 349. — Cornh. 32: 176. Same art. Liv. Age, 127: 285. — Ev. Sat. 8: 378. — House. Words, 16: 322.
— and his Vicarage. Fraser, 47: 103.
— Life and Poems of. (F. M. Hubbard) No. Am. 84: 484.
— Poems of. Retros. 5: 156. — Quar. 4: 165. — Temp. Bar, 1: 166.
Herries, John Charles, Public Life of. Ed. R. 153: 390.
Herring, The. (W. N. Maccartney) Intel. Obs. 5: 368, — Chamb. J. 19: 324. — (T. H. Huxley) Nature, 23: 607. Same art. Pop. Sci. Mo. 19: 433. — Penny M. 6: 45, 51.
— Movements of. Nature, 11: 151.
— Natural History of. Chamb. J. 40: 29. — Nature, 14: 352.
— the poor Man's Fish. Gent. M. n. s. 2: 84.
Herrings, Among the. Chamb. J. 28: 225.
— and Herring-Fishing. (H. Lawson) Pop. Sci. R. 3: 304.
— and English Herring Fisheries. Westm. 82: 377.
Herring Fishery. All the Year, 10: 65. — Penny M. 2: 54.
— of Holland. Ed. New Philos. J. 65: 50.
— of Lochfyne. (J. G. Bertram) Macmil. 10: 341. — Once a Week, 20: 37.
— Scotch. Ev. Sat. 10: 573.
— with the Herring Fleet. (W. Senior) Gent. M. n. s. 13: 702.
Herring-Fishing. Chamb. J. 6: 143.
Herring Harvest. Chamb. J. 26: 23. — Cornh. 4: 440.
Herschel, Caroline. (E. S. Holden) Nation, 22: 281. — (I. Scott) Once a Week, 3: 318. Same art. Liv. Age, 67: 378. — (T. W. Webb) Nature, 13: 361. — (E. A. Youmans) Pop. Sci. Mo. 8: 736. 9: 58. — So. R. n. s. 20: 324. — Temp. Bar, 46: 237. Same art. Ecl. M. 86: 459. Same art. Liv. Age, 128: 816. — Victoria, 17: 264. 27: 125.
Herschel, Sir John F. W., with portrait. Appleton, 6: 141. — with portrait, Hogg, 8: 145. Same art. Ecl. M. 26: 492. — with portrait, Ev. Sat. 10: 593. — Ecl. M. 77: 497. — Liv. Age, 61: 515. — Nature, 4: 69.
— as a Theorist in Astronomy. St. Paul's, 8: 326.
— Complete Catalogue of Writings of. Math. Mo. 3: 220.
— Observations at Cape of Good Hope. No. Brit. 8: 491. Same art. Liv. Age, 16: 577. — Am. J. Sci. 55: 86. — Quar. 85: 1. — Ed. R. 88: 104.
— Outlines of Astronomy. (B. A. Gould, jr.) Chr. Exam. 47: 268. — Ed. R. 58: 164. — Ecl. R. 90: 576.
— Study of Natural Philosophy. Quar. 45: 374.
Herschel, Sir William. Liv. Age, 2: 125. — Niles's Reg. 23: 154. — For. Q. 31: 438. — Ecl. Mus. 2: 556. — Chamb. J. 1: 391.
— and Caroline. Quar. 141: 323. Same art. Liv. Age, 129: 643.
— and his Discoveries. (D. Trowbridge) Nat. Q. 25: 231.

Herschel, Sir William, as a Music Master. (E. Polko) Temp. Bar, **32**: 421. Same art. Ecl. M. **77**: 211.
— Holden's Life of. (J. R. Hind) Nature, **23**: 429, 453.
— Laplace, and James Watt. Chr. Rem. **35**: 38.
— Memoir of. (Baron Fourier) Ed. New Philos. J. **4**: 1. — Ed. Philos. J. **8**: 209.
— on the new Planets. (H. Brougham) Ed. R. **1**: 426.
Herschels, Story of. (W. Chambers) Chamb. J. **53**: 209.
— and the Star Depths. Cornh. **24**: 48. Same art. Ecl. M. **77**: 426. Same art. Liv. Age, **110**: 323.
Herstmonceaux Castle. *See* Hurstmonceaux.
Hertford, Marquises of. (R. Wynford) Lippinc. **13**: 191.
Hertzen, Alexander; Russian Revolutionist. (W. R. S. Ralston) Temp. Bar, **29**: 44.
Hervé Riel; a Poem. (R. Browning) Cornh. **23**: 257. Same art. Ecl. M. **76**: 546.
Herver Court. (A. Arnold) Once a Week, **16**: 289–589.
Hervey, Lord Arthur, Bishop of Bath and Wells. Cong. **5**: 626.
Hervey, James. Cong. M. **5**: 421.
— Letters. (J. Foster) Ecl. R. **14**: 1020.
Hervey, John, Lord. Temp. Bar, **54**: 173.
— Memoirs of the Reign of George II. Quar. **82**: 501. Same art. Liv. Age, **17**: 337. — Ed. R. **88**: 488. — Ecl. R. **88**: 184. — Fraser, **37**: 665.
Herwegh, George. Poems. For. Q. **31**: 58.
Herz, Henrietta. Penn Mo. **2**: 550.
Herzegovina and Austria. Brit. Q. **68**: 393.
— Insurgents of, Lady's Visit to, 1876. Cornh. **34**: 60. Same art. Liv. Age, **130**: 436. — Ecl. M. **87**: 328.
— Question of. Internat. R. **3**: 1.
Herzog's Encyclopedia. (C. P. Krauth) Evang. R. **7**: 580.
Hesiod. (J. A. Symonds) Fortn. **23**: 348. — Dub. Univ. **93**: 97, 153.
— Elton's Translation of. Blackw. **32**: 165, 505, 807. — Ed. R. **15**: 109.
— Life and Writings of. (H. H. Milman) Quar. **47**: 1.
Hesiodic Legends. Chr. Rem. **17**: 265.
Hesperus, Hymn to. (D. M. Moir) Blackw. **25**: 162.
Hess, Heinrich Maria. Art J. **17**: 97. — Hours at Home, **1**: 517.
Hesse, Charles, Prince of, Autobiography of. Ed. R. **123**: 483. Same art. Liv. Age, **90**: 195.
Hesse, Customs of the Reformed Church of. (E. W. Reinecke) Mercersb. **17**: 635.
— Our Country House in. All the Year, **40**: 272.
Hessians of the American Revolution. (C. Goepp) Nation, **1**: 721. — Hist. M. **10**: 7.
— — in Philadelphia. Pennsyl. M. **1**: 40.
Hessian Church in 16th Century. (H. Heppe) Mercersb. **5**: 199.
Hessian Fly and its Parasites. (E. C. Herrick) Am. J. Sci. **41**: 153.
Hester Benfield. Blackw. **81**: 339.
Hester Somerset; a Novel. (N. Michell) Colburn, **88**: 50–504. **89**: 86–462. **90**: 52–449. **91**: 207–333. **92**: 86–466. **93**: 66–478. **94**: 167–423. **95**: 89–306.
Hester's History; a Story. All the Year, **20**: 265–577.
Hetch-Hetchy Valley. (J. Muir) Overland, **11**: 42.
Heterogenesis, Practical Notes on. (W. H. Dallinger) Pop. Sci. R. **15**: 338.
Heteropathy, Aversion, Sympathy. (F. P. Cobbe) Theo. R. **11**: 1.
Heterophemy. (R. G. White) Galaxy, **20**: 691.
Hetty. (H. Kingsley) Once a Week, **20**: 111–387. Same art. Ev. Sat. **7**: 381–498.
Heubner, Heinrich L. Bib. R. **6**: 317.
Heugh, Hugh. Ecl. R. **84**: 697. **92**: 309.
— Life of. Kitto, **6**: 410. — No. Brit. **14**: 68.
— — McGill's. Hogg, **6**: 25.
Heung Noo in their Relations with China. Anthrop. J. **3**: 401. — (A. Wylie) Anthrop. J. **5**: 41.
Hever Castle. Antiquary, **3**: 121.
— and Village. Penny M. **7**: 284.
Hewit, Dr. H. S., Tribute to. Brownson, **22**: 545.
Hewitson, William C. Nature, **18**: 196.
Hewlett, J. T., Sketch of. Colburn, **79**: 399.
Hewley, Sir J., and Lady, Memoir of. Cong. M. **22**: 545.
Hewley, Lady, Charities of, Controversy on. Cong. M. **12**: 607. **15**: 72. **17**: 484, 744. **19**: 205. **25**: 934. **26**: 26–566.
Hexameter Verse. (A. H. Clough) Putnam, **2**: 138.
— English. (C. C. Felton) No. Am. **55**: 121. — Fraser, **36**: 665. Same art. Liv. Age, **16**: 172. — Fraser, **39**: 342. **42**: 62. — Blackw. **60**: 19, 327, 477. — Ed. R. **35**: 422. — Chr. Rem. **51**: 190. — Macmil. **5**: 487. — No. Brit. **19**: 129. — Tait, n. s. **21**: 219. *See also* Longfellow, H., Evangeline.
— and German Epics. Dub. Univ. **44**: 55.
— Recent. (S. H. Needles) Penn Mo. **9**: 145.
Hexham, Northumberland. Penny M. **9**: 452.
Hey, Wm., Pearson's Life of. Chr. Obs. **22**: 504.
Heylin, P. Voyage to France. (E. Taylor) Retros. **3**: 22.
Heyne, Christian Gottlob. Am. J. Educ. **28**: 867. — Liv. Age, **65**: 93. — Sharpe, **31**: 6, 64.
— Life of. (E. Everett) No. Am. **2**: 201. — (T. Carlyle) For. R. **2**: 437. — Liv. Age, **28**: 577.
Heyse, Paul. Novellen. Westm. **70**: 502.
Heywood, Charles. Nat. M. **3**: 337.
Heywood, John, Dramatic Works of. Cornh. **30**: 676.
Heywood, John H. (H. H. Barber) Unita. R. **11**: 435.
Heywood, Oliver, Catalogue of his Library. Cong. M. **17**: 337.
— Memoir of. Cong. M. **12**: 513.
— Puritan Relatives of. Cong. M. **19**: 69.
Heywood, Thomas, Plays of. Retros. **11**: 123.
Hezekiah, King. Chr. Obs. **70**: 832.
Hialmar Jarl; a Poem. (W. W. Young) Putnam, **15**: 242.
Hiawatha, New Legends of. Once a Week, **21**: 315.
Hibernation of Animals. (I. Lea) Am. J. Sci. **9**: 75. — (S. Woodruff) Am. J. Sci. **24**: 363. — Penny. M. **3**: 499.
Hibernian Ballads, Scraps of. Dub. Univ. **13**: 752.
Hibernian Nights' Entertainment. Dub. Univ. **5**: 58–705. **6**: 50–641. **7**: 97–579.
Hibernian Society's Report, 1807. (J. Foster) Ecl. R. **6**: 1096.
Hibernicisms in Philosophy. (Duke of Argyll) Contemp **19**: 145. Same art. Canad. Mo. **1**: 164.
Hick, S., Everett's Life of. Meth. M. **57**: 521.
Hickett's Hollow. (L. R. Fairfax) Scrib. **20**: 758.
Hickey, Wm. [Martin Doyle], with portrait. Dub. Univ. **15**: 374.
Hickok, L. P., Philosophy of. (J. H. Seelye) Bib. Sac. **16**: 253.
Hicks, Elias, and the Hicksite Quakers. (G. W. Burnap) Chr. Exam. **51**: 321.
Hicks, George E. Art J. **24**: 97.
Hicks, Thomas, and his Paintings. Art J. **30**: 166.
Hicks-Beach, Sir Michael. Dub. Univ. **85**: 654.
Hid in a Turf-Rick. (T. P. Battersby) Lond. Soc. **36**: 337.
Hidden, Samuel. Am. Q. Reg. **10**: 66.
Hidden Box; a Tale of the Covenanters. Chamb. J. **54**: 769.
Hidden Treasure. (F. C. Fisher) Appleton, **20**: 299, 397.
Hieroglyphs, Essay on. (G. Ebers) Penn Mo. **2**: 360.
Hieroglyphical Alphabet, Champollion on. Quar. **28**: 188. — Ecl. R. **40**: 330. **45**: 124.
Hieroglyphics, Egyptian. (E. Everett) No. Am. **32**: 95. — (A. B. Chapin) Chr. Q. Spec. **9**: 29. — Am. Q. **1**: 438. **9**: 339. — For. Q. **4**: 438. **25**: 1. **28**: 263. — Fraser. **9**: 629. — Westm. **4**: 40. — Blackw. **24**: 313. **44**: 105. — Ed. R. **45**: 95, 528. **57**: 461. **64**: 82. — Spirit Pilg. **4**: 98, 197. — Mo. R. **104**: 507. **107**: 175. **119**: 550. **165**: 95.

Hieroglyphics, Egyptian. (F. Arago) Ed. New Philos. J. **19**: 39. — Brit. Q. **12**: 79. Same art. Ecl. M. **21**: 352. — Chamb. J. **28**: 83. — Meth. M. **53**: 28. — (C. W. Wall) Dub. Univ. **9**: 61, 234.
— — Young and Champollion's Method of interpreting. (R. S. Poole) Arch. **39**: 471.
— — Demotic Grammar of. (W. H. Green) Princ. **27**: 649.
— of Easter Island. (J. P. Harrison) Anthrop. J. **3**: 370.
— Papyrus Prisse. O. & N. **3**: 559.
— Sharpe's Vocabulary of. Mo. R. **144**: 530.
— Wilkinson on. Fraser, **2**: 329.
Hieroglyphic and Cuneiform Interpretation. Quar. **147**: 430.
Hieroglyphic Inscriptions. (S. Birch) Arch. **35**: 116.
Hieroglyphic Literature. Ecl. R. **38**: 481.
Hieroglyphic Tablets in Easter Island. (J. P. Harrison) Nature, **10**: 399.
Hieronymians. (K. von Raumer) Am. J. Educ. **4**: 622.
Hieronymus Pop and the Baby; a Story. (S. Bonner) Harper, **61**: 20.
Hiffernan, Paul. Irish Q. **6**: 487.
Higgins, Matthew James. Cornh. **18**: 507.
Higginson, Francis. (J. B. Felt) N. E. Reg. **6**: 105.
Higginson, John, Elegy on. (N. Noyes) N. E. Reg. **7**: 237.
Higginson, Nathaniel. (J. Farmer) N. E. Reg. **1**: 34.
Higginson, Thomas W., with portrait. Ecl. M. **88**: 631.
— Malbone. Ev. Sat. **8**: 529.
High-Church Literature for the People. Lond. Q. **18**: 124.
High-Church Revival. (J. A. Froude) Good Words, **22**: 18–466.
High-Church Theory, Position of, 1847. Dub. R. **23**: 497.
High Cross, by Bonn. Dub. Univ. **13**: 537.
High-heeled Shoe. (A. Griffith) Potter Am. Mo. **16**: 121.
High Horse, Riding the. Temp. Bar, **15**: 348.
High Life in the last Century. Blackw. **55**: 164.
High Peak, Derbyshire, England, Archæology of. (W. Bennett) Reliquary, **1**: 94.
High School, Public. Am. J. Educ. **3**: 185.
— Supervision of, English View of. (S. S. Laurie) Education, **1**: 247.
See Boston; Chicago; Cincinnati; Hartford; etc.
High-School Policy of Massachusetts. (W. Barrows) New Eng. **16**: 854.
High-School System in Ontario. Canad. Mo. **3**: 35.
High Steeple of St. Chrysostom's. (E. W. Olney) Appleton, **20**: 501.
High Tide of December. (R. H. Davis) Atlan. **17**: 47. Same art. Sharpe, **52**: 281.
High Tide on the Coast of Lincolnshire. (J. Ingelow) Liv. Age, **79**: 575.
High Treason. *See* Treason.
Highbury Barn, Something about. Tinsley, **26**: 74.
Highbury College, England. Am. Q. Reg. **9**: 130.
Higher than the Church. (W. von Hillern) Tinsley, **20**: 425.
Higher Law. Dem. R. **27**: 508. — New Eng. **8**: 378. — Brownson, **8**: 81.
— Doctrine of. (J. Day) New Eng. **11**: 161.
Highest House in Wathendale. House. Words, **3**: 389.
High-flown Sentiment. Chamb. J. **45**: 568.
Highgate and Hampstead. St. James, **28**: 413.
— Memories of. Lond. Soc. **35**: 308.
Highgate Church. Penny M. **1**: 81.
Highlands after the Rebellion of '45. Blackw. **2**: 155.
— and the Clans, Browne's History of. Mo. R. **138**: 358.
— and Hebrides; Glimpses from Oban. Macmil. **6**: 421.
— Clans of. Ecl. R. **92**: 458.
— Destitution in. Blackw. **62**: 630.
— — and Irish Emigration. Quar. **90**: 163.
— Folk Lore of. Dub. Univ. **69**: 182.
— Gate of. Lond. Soc. **40**: 30.
— In. (A. K. H. Boyd) Fraser, **82**: 609.
Highlands, In the Heart of. Cornh. **43**: 90.
— Month in. Dub. Univ. **26**: 463.
— Notes of a Trip in. Chamb. J. **41**: 654.
— of Aberdeenshire. Chamb. J. **22**: 161.
— Plants on Summits of. (H. Macmillan) Macmil. **8**: 311.
— Puritanism in. Quar. **89**: 307.
— Sunday in. (J. C. Lees) Good Words, **22**: 235.
— Three Days' Walk in. Lond. M. **15**: 542.
— Through. Broadw. **3**: 84.
— Tour in. Mo. R. **93**: 390.
— Up. Once a Week, **17**: 477.
— Wandering Characters in. Once a Week, **21**: 215.
— West. No. Brit. **39**: 134.
— — Story-Hunting in. (C. Bede) Belgra. **31**: 275.
— Wild Sports and Natural History of. Blackw. **60**: 389. — Chamb. J. **6**: 220.
— Word on. (W. Chambers) Chamb. J. **10**: 193.
Highland Census, Recollections of. Chamb. J. **58**: 75.
Highland Character. Fraser, **3**: 489.
Highland Chief, one hundred Years ago. Dub. Univ. **30**: 327. Same art. Liv. Age, **15**: 145.
Highland Flora; a Poem. Good Words, **3**: 389.
Highland Hut, At a. (J. S. S. Glennie) Fraser, **90**: 518.
Highland Keeper. Chamb. J. **55**: 105.
Highland Parish in last Century. Chamb. J. **53**: 337.
— Reminiscences of. (N. Macleod) Good Words, **4**: 71–833.
Highland Pipers. Chamb. J. **2**: 86.
Highland Rambles, Lauder's. Dub. Univ. **9**: 651.
Highland Regiments, Stewart's Sketches of. Blackw. **11**: 387.
Highland Roads and Canals. Chamb. J. **40**: 197.
Highland Sergeant. Fraser, **16**: 294.
Highland Society, Transactions of. Ed. R. **4**: 63.
Highland Sport. Quar. **77**: 69. Same art. Liv. Age, **8**: 297.
Highland Story-Telling. Chamb. J. **34**: 407.
Highland Student. (J. C. Shairp) Good Words, **8**: 663.
Highlander of the last Age. Chamb. J. **8**: 241.
Highlanders at Home and abroad. Good Words, **1**: 468.
— at Well of Cawnpore; a Poem. Dub. Univ. **51**: 209.
— Celtic Manners of. Mo. R. **124**: 345.
— of France. (H. S. Fagan) Good Words, **8**: 97.
— of Scotland. Dub. Univ. **9**: 710.
— Origin and History of, Skene's. Ed. R. **66**: 416. — Mo. R. **142**: 498.
— Superstitions of, Mrs. Grant on. (F. Jeffrey) Ed. R. **18**: 480. — (J. Foster) Ecl. R. **15**: 160.
Highways and By-Ways. Ed. R. **38**: 454. — Lond. M. **11**: 189.
— Famous, of the World. (F. M. Colby) Potter Am. Mo. **12**: 1.
— History of. Ed. R. **119**: 340.
— National. (S. G. Fisher) Nation, **1**: 424, 616. **2**: 8.
— of England. (Viscount Midleton) 19th Cent. **10**: 555.
Highwaymen. (D. Cook) Once a Week, **11**: 666.
— Ancient and modern. Dub. Univ. **66**: 146.
— Anecdotes of. Fraser, **31**: 612.
— Hints for a History of. Fraser, **9**: 279.
— Irish. Putnam, **10**: 253.
— Lives and Exploits of. Dub. R. **4**: 335.
— String of. All the Year, **17**: 512.
Hilary; a Poem. (L. Larcom) Atlan. **12**: 159.
Hilary St. Ives. (W. H. Ainsworth) Colburn, **144**: 123–611. **145**: 1–707.
Hilda d'Ehrenburg. Fraser, **41**: 435.
Hilda's little Hood. (H. H. Boyesen) Scrib. **11**: 417.
Hildebrand. *See* Gregory VII., Pope.
Hildebrand, *pseud.* *See* Van Beets.
Hildegard. (D. Macleod) Knick. **40**: 245.
Hildesheim Treasure. (F. Lenormant) Pract. M. **1**: 59
— Visit to. (H. Bedford) Month, **38**: 189.

Hildreth, Samuel T. (C. S. Wheeler) Chr. Exam. **27:** 122.
Hildreth Genealogy. (R. Hildreth) N. E. Reg. **11:** 7.
Hilgenfeld's Introduction to New Testament. (P. H. Wicksteed) Theo. R. **12:** 515. **13:** 1.
Hill, Alonzo, Sermon on. (J. Allen) Mo. Rel. M. **46:** 41.
Hill, Gen. Ambrose P., Sketch of. Land We Love, **2:** 287.
Hill, Benson Earle. Recollections of an Artillery Officer. Mo. R. **141:** 45.
Hill, David Octavus. Art J. **2:** 309. **21:** 317.
Hill, Sir John, Actor and Quack. House. Words, **18:** 44. — Temp. Bar, **35:** 261.
Hill, Matthew Davenport, Memoir of. (A. G. Sedgwick) Nation, **28:** 421.
Hill, Sir Richard, Sidney's Life of. Ecl. R. **71:** 58. — Chr. Obs. **39:** 548.
Hill, Roger, Letters by and to, 1690 and 1699. N. E. Reg. **5:** 367.
Hill, Sir Rowland, and cheap Postage. Lond. Q. **56:** 22. Same art. Liv. Age, **149:** 515. — (R. D. Osborn) Nation, **32:** 138. — Ecl. R. **79:** 459. — West. M. **4:** 115.
— Life of. Dub. Univ. **26:** 47. — No. Brit. **3:** 290. — Sharpe, **1:** 137. — Tait, n. s. **12:** 380.
Hill, Rev. Rowland. (J. M. Freeman) Meth. Q. **23:** 250. — (H. Martineau) Liv. Age, **70:** 22. — Mus. **26:** 410. — Chr. Mo. Spec. **10:** 516. — Nat. M. **4:** 437. — Chr. Obs. **34:** 561.
Hill, Thomas, Author of the Mirror of Fashion, with portrait. Bentley, **9:** 87. — with portrait, Fraser, **10:** 172.
— Gossip about. Colburn, **80:** 137.
Hill, William, Life and Times of. Am. Presb. R. **2:** 41.
Hill Genealogy. (U. Parsons) N. E. Reg. **12:** 139, 258.
Hill, Up the. Cath. World, **25:** 45, 236.
Hill Farm. (R. J. King) Fraser, **76:** 42.
Hill Hall, Essex. Penny M. **14:** 277.
Hill Tribes of N. Aracan. (R. F. St. A. St. John) Anthrop. J. **2:** 233.
Hillern, Wilhelmine von. Lippinc. **11:** 115.
Hilles, Richard, Commonplace Book of. (J. A. Froude) Fraser, **58:** 127. Same art. Liv. Age, **58:** 963.
Hillhouse, Augustus L. (L. Bacon) New Eng. **18:** 557.
Hillhouse, James. Am. J. Educ. **6:** 325.
Hillhouse, James A. So. Lit. Mess. **7:** 329.
— Dramas and Discourses of. Chr. Exam. **27:** 285. — (J. G. Palfrey) No. Am. **50:** 231.
— Hadad. (F. W. P. Greenwood) No. Am. **22:** 13. — (H. Ware, jr.) Chr. Exam. **2:** 301. — U. S. Lit. Gaz. **2:** 96.
— Judgment. Chr. Disc. **3:** 209. — Chr. Mo. Spec. **3:** 466.
— Life and Character of. (L. Bacon) Chr. Q. Spec. **5:** 238.
— — and Works of. (H. T. Tuckerman) New Eng. **16:** 705.
— Percy's Masque. (W. C. Bryant) No. Am. **11:** 384.
Hillingford, Robert A. Art J. **23:** 213.
Hilloa, our Fancy. Dub. Univ. **3:** 25.
Hills, Joseph, Will of, 1687. N. E. Reg. **8:** 311.
Hills, Richard, Will of, 1639. N. E. Reg. **2:** 218.
Hillsborough, N. C., Historical Sketch of. (H. E. Colton) So. Lit. Mess. **23:** 161.
Hillyars and Burtons. (H. Kingsley) Macmil. **9:** 1–449. **10:** 17–442. **11:** 40–435.
Hilton, William, Descendants of. (J. T. Hassam) N. E. Reg. **31:** 179.
Himalaya Mountains. (C. F. G. Cumming) Good Words, **11:** 133. — (C. R. Markham) Geog. M. **4:** 113, 173. — (Baron von Richthofen) Geog. M. **5:** 183. — (A. Wilson) Blackw. **116:** 127–703. **117:** 69–600. Same art. Liv. Age, **125:** 172–803. **126:** 283. — Dub. Univ. **43:** 670. — Quar. **17:** 403. **22:** 415. **24:** 102. — Westm. **37:** 294. — Mo. R. **95:** 225, 409.
Himalaya Mountains; Ascent of Mt. Tonglo. (G. E. Bulger) Stud. & Intel. Obs. **4:** 350.
— Bear Hunt in. Temp. Bar, **19:** 229.
— Climate and Vegetation of. (T. Thomson) Ed. New Philos. J. **52:** 309.
— Convalescent Establishment in. Penny M. **3:** 14.
— Englishwoman among. (A. H. Guernsey) Harper, **53:** 839.
— Fraser on. Ecl. R. **33:** 68.
— Gerard's Account of Koonawur in. Mo. R. **156:** 403.
— Heights of Peaks of. (Hodgson and Herbert) Ed. Philos. J. **9:** 312. — (W. Lloyd) Ed. Philos. J. **10:** 18.
— Dr. Hooker's Journals in. Ed. R. **103:** 55. Same art. Liv. Age, **51:** 129. — (A. H. Guernsey) Harper, **9:** 604. — Liv. Age, **41:** 162.
— Hunting in. (O. Tiffany) No. Am. **92:** 239.
— Lloyd's Tours in. Tait, n. s. **7:** 227. — Mo. R. **151:** 421.
— Mountaineering in. Blackw. **119:** 429.
— Niti Pass. Penny M. **8:** 267.
— Passage of. (Sir J. Barrow) Quar. **22:** 415.
— Road Construction in. (J. Brown) Ecl. Engin. **10:** 500.
— Scientific Notes in. (A. Schuster) Nature, **13:** 393.
— Sketches of. Chamb. J. **56:** 85.
— Thomson's Western. Colburn, **96:** 151.
— Travels in, and Description of. Brit. Q. **39:** 120. Same art. Ecl. M. **61:** 273.
— Trip in. Liv. Age, **66:** 244.
— Wanderings in. Chamb. J. **52:** 663.
— White's Views and Tours among. Tait, n. s. **5:** 115.
Himalayan Provinces, Travels in. (Sir J. Barrow) Quar. **61:** 96.
Hinba, Visit to. Cornh. **41:** 171.
Hinchbrook. (J. C. Jeaffreson) Fraser, **51:** 224–653. **52:** 67–412.
Hinchcliff. Tinsley, **9:** 534.
Hinchingbroke Hall. Antiquary, **3:** 169.
Hinckley, Thomas. Verses on Death of his Wife. N. E. Reg. **1:** 92.
Hinckley Genealogy. (G. W. Messinger) N. E. Reg. **13:** 208.
Hincks, Sir Francis, with portrait. Dub. Univ. **88:** 534.
— Case of. Bank. M. (N. Y.) **34:** 341, 431.
Hincks, John, Sermons of. Chr. Exam. **12:** 344.
Hindoos. *See* Hindus.
Hindostan. Brit. & For. R. **2:** 186. — Mo. R. **95:** 17.
— Bacon's. Ecl. R. **65:** 447. — Tait, n. s. **4:** 397.
— Chatfield's Historical Review of. (J. Foster) Ecl. R. **10:** 1073.
— Daniell's Oriental Scenery. (J. Foster) Ecl. R. **2:** 472.
— Hours in. Bentley, **9:** 567. **10:** 121–247. **11:** 56–589. **12:** 178–188. **13:** 36–472.
— in 1839. Mo. R. **150:** 26.
— Marriage in. (J. W. Palmer) Atlan. **29:** 286.
— Modern History of. (A. Murray) Ed. R. **5:** 288.
— Mogul Dynasty in. Penny M. **8:** 237–398.
— My Heathen at Home. (J. W. Palmer) Atlan. **18:** 728.
— Newspapers of. Internat. M. **3:** 24.
— Religion of. Theo. Repos. **6:** 408. — Colburn, **96:** 222.
— Scenes and Characteristics of. (Sir J. Barrow) Quar. **55:** 174.
— Tour through. Mo. R. **104:** 165.
— Travels in. Mo. R. **154:** 418.
— Voyaging in. Fraser, **19:** 359. **20:** 42.
Hinds, Samuel. Three Temples of the One God. Chr. Obs. **50:** 35.
Hindus, The. (J. T. Dickinson) Chr. Exam. **64:** 173.
— Algebra and Arithmetic of. Ed. R. **21:** 365. **29:** 141.
— Ancient Civilization of. (E. I. Sears) Nat. Q. **3:** 1.
— Eight Years among. (W. McMillan) Evang. R. **21:** 443.
— Folk Lore of. Dub. Univ. **71:** 455.
— Geometry, Drawing, and Color among. Ecl. Engin. **12:** 256.

Hindus, The, Laws and Customs of. (J. D. Whelpley) Am. Whig R. 1: 290.
— — of Menu. (J. D. Whelpley) Am. Whig R. 1: 510.
— Marriage among. Anal. M. 14: 124.
— Memoirs of four Christian. (J. Foster) Ecl. R. 25: 91.
— Mysteries of Kanoba, or the Mesmeric Waren. Dub. Univ. 35: 17, 447.
— Mythology of. Mo. R. 128: 175.
— New Religion wanted for. (R. H. Elliot) Fraser, 84: 709. Same art. Liv. Age, 112: 360.
— Old and new Times for. Once a Week, 9: 8.
— Origin of. (A. L. Koeppen) Mercersb. 10: 296.
— Philosophy of the ancient. Mass. Q. 1: 401. — (T. Parsons) No. Am. 9: 3[illegible].
— Practical Religion of. (A. D. Rowe) Luth. Q. 10: 432.
— Religion and Character of. Ed. R. 29: 377.
— Sacred Books of. (J. B. Feuling) Chr. Exam. 85: 311. — (D. Wilson) No. Brit. 1: 366.
— Theater of. Mo. R. 136: 104.
— Theory of Demoniacal Possession among. Dub. Univ. 31: 315. 37: 52.
— Vindication of. Chr. Obs. 7: 104. — Ecl. R. 7: 252.
— Ward and Dubois on. Ecl. R. 31: 562.
— Waren; or Oracular Afflatus of. Dub. Univ. 33: 307. 34: 647.
— Wilson's Theater of. Ecl. R. 48: 328.
Hindu Astronomy, History of. Westm. 2: 274.
Hindu-Chinese Nations. Ed. R. 43: 373.
Hindu Chronology. Mo. R. 105: 10.
Hindu Civil Servants. All the Year, 22: 372.
Hindu Civilization. (M. F. Morris) Nat. Q. 8: 211.
Hindu Customs. Chamb. J. 54: 88.
— Loss of Caste. Ev. Sat. 10: 566.
Hindu Doctrine of Immortality. (J. D. Whelpley) Am. Whig R. 2: 267.
Hindu Drama. (E. Everett) No. Am. 26: 111. — Blackw. 34: 715. 35: 122. — Westm. 54: 1. — Ed. R. 22: 400. — Quar. 45: 39. — (Mrs. Postans) Sharpe, 11: 212.
— History and Character of. Westm. 67: 364.
Hindu Eclecticism. (R. C. Bose) Meth. Q. 41: 605.
Hindu Emigrants. Chamb. J. 28: 389. Same art. Liv. Age, 56: 431.
Hindu English, Specimens of. Chamb. J. 55: 174. *See* Indo-Anglian.
Hindu Epic Poetry, the Mahâbhârata. Westm. 89: 380.
Hindu Fairy Legends. Ecl. M. 72: 137.
Hindu Festival of the Pongol. Cornh. 17: 349.
Hindu Funeral. Chamb. J. 16: 157.
Hindu Gods. Hogg, 5: 372.
Hindu Horoscopes. (A. Allardyce) Good Words, 18: 312.
Hindu Households. (W. Knighton) Fortn. 35: 767. Same art. Liv. Age, 150: 227.
Hindu Idolatry and Christianity. (J. Foster) Ecl. R. 7: 252.
Hindu Infanticide. Quar. 6: 210. — Anal. M. 6: 439. — (J. Foster) Ecl. R. 15: 331.
Hindu Law. Mo. R. 109: 63.
Hindu Legend. All the Year, 23: 79.
Hindu Literature. (F. Hall) Nation, 26: 344.
Hindu Mathematics, Early. (E. S. Holden) Pop. Sci. Mo. 3: 334.
Hindu Medical Missions. Brit. Q. 6: 356.
Hindu Medicine. (W. Gilbert) Good Words, 19: 449.
Hindu Mendicants. Chamb. J. 53: 311.
Hindu Mythology and its Influence. Nat. Q. 20: 1.
— Dowson's Guide to. Nation, 29: 295.
Hindu Pantheon. Ed. R. 17: 311. — Hogg, 5: 347.
Hindu Philosophical Systems. Chr. Obs. 64: 543.
Hindu Philosophy. (W. R. Alger) No. Am. 86: 435. — (D. C. Scudder) Bib. Sac. 18: 535, 673.
Hindu Philosophy and the Bhagavad-Gita. (O. D. Miller) Univ. Q. 26: 389.
— Origin and Sequence of the various Systems. Westm. 78: 464.
Hindu Prejudices. (L. E. Rees) St. James, 14: 377.
Hindu Prince and Skeptic, Meditations of. Cornh. 36: 357.
Hindu Religion, Heterodoxies of. Westm. 78: 457.
Hindu Religious Sects, Tenets of. Chr. Obs. 19: 807.
Hindu Society and English Rule. Westm. 108: 289.
Hindu Theism. Anal. M. 15: 129.
— The new. (R. H. Elliot) Fraser, 85: 360.
Hindu Theology as taught by Rammohun Roy. No. Am. 6: 386.
Hindu Widows. Lond. M. 19: 541.
— Burning of. Blackw. 23: 161. — Quar. 89: 257. Same art. Liv. Age, 31: 356. — Mus. 12: 409.
Hindu Women, Rights of. Lond. Q. 56: 393.
Hinduism, Buddhism, and Islam. Nature, 17: 239.
— and Christianity. Ecl. R. 105: 515. — Liv. Age, 57: 359.
— Hardwick and Williams on. Chr. Obs. 58: 334.
— Inspired Writings of. Westm. 81: 144.
— Sacred Traditions of. (E. Burgess) Bib. Sac. 15: 844.
Hingham, Mass., First Settlers of. N. E. Reg. 2: 250.
— — from Norfolk County, England. N. E. Reg. 15: 25.
— Ministers of. Am. Q. Reg. 8: 152.
— Witchcraft at. N. E. Reg. 5: 263.
Hinton, James. (J. F. Payne) Mind, 1: 247.
— and his father. (G. Peard) Contemp. 32: 259. Same art. Sup. Pop. Sci. Mo. 3: 182.
— and his Philosophy. (C. R. Upton) Theo. R. 15: 572.
— as a religious Thinker. (H. H. Ellis) Mod. R. 2: 661.
— Pantheism of. (W. H. Gillespie) Kitto, 38: 90.
Hinton, Rev. James, Memoir of. Cong. M. 10: 146.
Hints. (L. Hough) Once a Week, 17: 265.
— from high Places. Dub. Univ. 1: 694. 2: 265. 3: 52. 4: 15. 9: 616.
— from Hygea. Fraser, 41: 295.
— of Nature. Chamb. J. 28: 33.
— of Spring; a Poem. Temp. Bar, 14: 249.
Hipparchus and Ptolemy, Discoveries of. (D. Trowbridge) Nat. Q. 17: 134.
Hippo, Visit to the See of St. Augustine. Good Words, 21: 669.
Hippocrates, Notes on. Colburn, 111: 406.
Hippolytus, St., and his Age, Bunsen's. (A. Hovey) Chr. R. 18: 425. — Am. Presb. R. 2: 450. — Chr. Rem. 25: 213. — Ecl. R. 97: 385. 100: 690. — (D. N. Lord) Theo. & Lit. J. 6: 353. — (A. P. Peabody) No. Am. 78: 1. — Ed. R. 97: 1. — Kitto, 10: 461. — No. Brit. 19: 85. — Prosp. R. 9: 118.
— and the Church of Rome, Wordsworth on. Chr. Obs. 53: 758.
— to Artemis. Fraser, 79: 39.
— Writings of. Chr. Obs. 69: 119.
Hippophagy and Onophagy. Temp. Bar, 19: 31.
Hippophagy, Mr., Spavinger's Speech on. (J. Greenwood) Lond. Soc. 13: 466.
Hippopotamus, The. Chamb. J. 14: 166.
— and her Baby. (F. Buckland) Pop. Sci. Mo. 3: 85.
— Is it the Behemoth of Scripture? Penny M. 7: 209.
— Mode of killing. (Dr. Rüppell) Penny M. 1: 68.
Hippothanasia; or the Last of Tails. (W. Jerdan) Bentley, 1: 319.
Hirell. (J. Saunders) St. James, 22: 89–606. 23: 65–823. 24: 97.
Hiring a Servant. (T. S. Arthur) Godey, 24: 166.
His at last. Once a Week, 29: 319–559.
His Best; a Story. Atlan. 46: 624.
His Brother Philip. (F. Lewees) Lippinc. 27: 606.
His Brother's Keeper. Chamb. J. 58: 168, 184.

His Brother's Keeper; a Tale. Temp. Bar, 30: 413, 554. 31: 74-408.
His Christmas Rose. Lond. Soc. 40: supp. 77.
His Country Cousin. (C. S. Wayne) Potter Am. Mo. 15: 449. 16: 49.
His Double. Appleton, 16: 385, 499.
His Excellency, Old Ugly. (W. M. Baker) Lippinc. 21: 619.
His Father's Son; a Story. (E. Fawcett) Galaxy, 21: 685.
His great Deed; a Tale. (R. H. Davis) Lippinc. 22: 343.
His Honor's Daughter. (O.M.Ellsworth) Putnam, 16: 71.
His Inheritance. (A. Trafton) Scrib. 14: 432-808. 15: 57-790. 16: 80-384.
His Irish Cousins. (N. Robinson) Cath. World, 27: 794.
His little Serene Highness. (F. Reuter) Liv. Age, 116: 20-784.
His little Sweetheart. (A. Fraser) Tinsley, 26: 125.
His little Ways. All the Year, 23: 19.
His long-lost Brother. (A. de Fonblanque) Tinsley, 29: 192.
His new Birth. (J. C. Ver Planck) Lippinc. 24: 312.
His own Detective; a Tale. Temp. Bar, 30: 394.
His own Executor; a Novel. Chamb. J. 50: 417-537.
His Patagonian Wife. (J. C. Cremony) Overland, 6: 67.
His second Inheritance. (F. Talbot) Belgra. 27: 213-548. 28: 117, 258.
His two Loves. (B. Dunphy) Tinsley, 19: 234.
His two Wives. (M. C. Ames) Ev. Sat. 16: 309-421.
His Wife's nearest Relation. Lippinc. 25: 204.
His young Lordship. (D. M. Craik) Ev. Sat. 2: 488.
Hiss, The, and its History. Lippinc. 22: 781.
Hissar and Kulab. (N. Mayef) Geog. M. 3: 326.
— Expedition to. (P. Lerch) Geog. M. 2: 334.
Hissing. Chamb. J. 51: 214.
— in Theaters. All the Year, 28: 468.
Histology, Lesson in comparative. (C. S. Minot) Am. Natural. 12: 339.
— Rutherford's Practical. Nature, 12: 433.
Historians, Ancient and modern. Am. Bib. Repos. 3d s. 2: 338. — (T. B. Macaulay) Ed. R. 47: 331. Same art. Selec. Ed. R. 2: 380.
— Early Greek. Mo. R. 165: 307.
— French. Mo. R. 164: 273.
— Italian. Mo. R. 157: 408.
— Latin. Mo. R. 165: 478.
Historic Doubts relative to Archbishop Whately. Dub. Univ. 5: 528.
— relative to Napoleon. *See* Whately, R.
— relative to the Battle of Bunker Hill. (C. Hudson) Chr. Exam. 40: 247.
Historic Fancies, Smythe's. Fraser, 30: 310. Same art. Ecl. M. 2: 328. — Colburn, 71: 527.
Historic Houses of America. Appleton, 11: 65-784. 12: 1-705.
Historic Phrases. (H. S. Edwards) Macmil. 35: 48.
Historic Speculations. So. Lit. Mess. 6: 606.
Historic Spirit, Nature and Influence of. (W. G. T. Shedd) Bib. Sac. 11: 345.
Historic Tableaux. Dub. Univ. 23: 1.
Historical Art in England. (F. T. Palgrave) Fraser, 63: 773.
Historical Authenticity. So. Lit. Mess. 2: 132, 176.
Historical Class-Book, Sullivan's. Chr. Exam. 16: 68.
Historical Collections, Recent. (C. C. Smith) No. Am. 93: 266.
Historical Committee of the American Philosophical Society. Anal. M. 13: 243.
Historical Composition. (W. H. Prescott) No. Am. 29: 293. — (M. B. Hope) Princ. 12: 550. — Hogg, 6: 33.
— Principles of. Portfo.(Den.) 23: 339. 24: 40.
Historical Contrast; a Poem. Cornh. 9: 133.
Historical Credibility. Dub. Univ. 92: 164, 324.
Historical Documents, Use of. (E. A. Freeman) Fortn. 16: 321. Same art. Liv. Age, 111: 159.
Historical Drama, Pennie and Collier on. Fraser, 5: 670.
Historical Faith. Chr. Mo. Spec. 9: 404.
Historical Fiction. (H. James, jr.) Nation, 5: 126. — Dub. R. 45: 328. *See also* Historical Romance.
Historical Inquiry, Progress of, in France. (Sir F. Palgrave) Ed. R. 73: 84.
Historical Literature, State of British and Continental. For. Q. 25: 49.
Historical Method, Weak Side of. (A. V. Dicey) Nation, 24: 217.
Historical Manuscript Commission. Chamb. J. 52: 251. — (J. Piggot, jr.) Fraser, 85: 696. 88: 714. 91: 348. 97: 288.
Historical Mystery, An. Cornh. 8: 720.
Historical Personages illustrated in Kensington Museum. St. James, 5: 509. 6: 74.
Historical Portraits. Lond. M. 22: 63.
Historical Prediction. (L. A. Tollemache) Fortn. 9: 295.
Historical Proof, Taylor on. Mo. R. 115: 321.
Historical Publications in Italy. Brit. & For. R. 11: 591.
Historical Reading, Course of. (T. B. Thayer) Univ. Q. 7: 5, 113.
Historical Register, New England, History of. (A. H. Hoyt) N. E. Reg. 30: 184.
Historical Researches; Camden Society Publications. Fraser, 22: 445. 25: 50, 690.
Historical Revelations, Recent, 1858. Dub. Univ. 51: 530.
Historical Romance. Quar. 35: 518. — Fraser, 5: 6, 207. — (G. H. Lewes) Westm. 45: 34. — Blackw. 58: 341.
— in Italy. (G. W. Greene) No. Am. 46: 325.
— Picturesque Style of. Blackw. 33: 621.
Historical Science in France. Brit. & For. R. 16: 72.
Historical Sight-Seeing. (A. Strickland) Sharpe, 11: 103.
Historical Societies, Fireproof Buildings for. Hist. M. 6: 329.
— in the United States. Hist. M. 14: 97.
See names of States; also, English.
Historical Study at Oxford. (E. A. Freeman) Bent. Q. 1: 282.
Historical Studies. Am. Church R. 4: 9.
Historical Tableaux; Conquests. (W. Chambers) Chamb. J. 7: 49.
— — Serfdom. (W. Chambers) Chamb. J. 7: 209.
— — Tutelage. (W. Chambers) Chamb. J. 7: 81.
Historical Tale of the 16th Century. Fraser, 24: 25.
Historical Writing, Progress of English. Selec. Ed. R. 3: 33.
History. (G. H. Emerson) Univ. Q. 12: 344. — Am. Q. 5: 85. — Univ. Q. 1: 164. — (T. B. Macaulay) Ed. R. 47: 331. Same art. Selec. Ed. R. 2: 380. Same art. Mus. 13: 581. — (T. Carlyle) Fraser, 2: 413. 7: 585. — Ecl. R. 113: 166.
— Aim of. (J. C. Moffat) Princ. 29: 212.
— Ancient. (G. F. Yates) Am. Lit. M. 1: 365.
— — Manuals of. Ed. R. 132: 154.
— — McLennan's Studies in. (Sir J. Lubbock) Nature, 15: 133.
— — Niebuhr's. Fraser, 46: 672.
— — Rawlinson's Ancient Monarchies of the East. Brit. Q. 49: 349.
— — Rawlinson's Herodotus. Brit. Q. 28: 446.
— Ancient and modern. (C. Cushing) No. Am. 28: 312. — (C. A. Goodrich) Chr. Q. Spec. 3: 75.
— — Contrasts of. (F. W. Newman) Fraser, 90: 388, 570, 749. 91: 110. Same art. Ecl. M. 83: 666. 84: 227, 329, 457. Same art. Liv. Age, 123: 195, 617. 124: 151. Same art. Ev. Sat. 17: 403.
— and Art. Art J. 14: 87.
— — Varieties of. (A. Hayward) Ed. R. 124: 341. Same art. Liv. Age, 91: 451.
— and Casuistry. (F. D. Maurice) Macmil. 2: 505.
— and Fiction. Once a Week, 13: 106.

History and its scientific Pretensions. (W. T. Thornton) Macmil. 8: 25.
— and Geology. (G. Allen) Fraser, 101: 769. Same art. Ecl. M. 95: 228.
— and Physical Geography. (E. T. Vaughan) Contemp. 5: 29.
— and Polities. (J. R. Seeley) Macmil. 40: 289, 369, 449. Same art. Liv. Age, 142: 707. 143: 23–748. Same art. Ecl. M. 94: 175.
— and Religion. Nat. R. 4: 394. Same art. Ecl. M. 41: 158.
— and Science, God in. (L.H.Steiner) Mercersb. 14: 133.
— Art of writing. Brit. Q. 23: 297. — Chamb. J. 12: 145. — Liv. Age, 48: 243.
— Arts considered as Tidemarks of. Liv. Age, 128: 131.
— as expounded by the Supreme Court. Putnam, 9: 538.
— as a Science. Cornh. 3: 666. 4: 25.
— Buckle's Treatment of. (D. A. Wasson) Chr. Exam. 74: 61.
— by modern Frenchmen. Brit. Q. 14: 405.
— By-Ways of. Bentley, 39: 165. — Blackw. 62: 347.
— Canons of the Credibility of. Chr. Rem. 31: 27.
— Causes of. (W. B. Brown) New Eng. 22: 157.
— Christian Conception of. (E. E. Higbee) Mercersb. 16: 62.
— — Blunt's. Chr. Obs. 67: 175.
— Constitutional. (E. Brooks) No. Am. 29: 265.
— Cosmical Unity in. (A. Bierbower) Nat. Q. 29: 207.
— Curious Repetitions in. (G. A. Leakin) Hours at Home, 9: 509.
— Cycles of. (W. W. Andrews) Cong. R. 7: 521.
— Difficulty of verifying. Chamb. J. 56: 503.
— Dignity of. (J. R. Dennett) Nation, 4: 417.
— Epochs of. Penn Mo. 6: 218.
— Embroidery of. (G. E. Pond) Galaxy, 24: 71.
— False Views of. So. Q. 22: 23.
— Forces in. (F. A. Henry) Princ. n. s. 7: 1.
— French Schools of. For. Q. 8: 326.
— Gain of. (C. C. Everett) Unita. R. 2: 16.
— God in. (J. Cumming) Ex. H. Lec. 4: 35. — (J. Martineau) O. & N. 7: 269. — Hours at Home, 5: 225. — Brit. Q. 25: 494.
— Gossip of. Cornh. 35: 325. Same art. Liv. Age, 133: 178. Same art. Ecl. M. 88: 526.
— Grace's Outlines of. Brownson, 6: 277.
— Hints upon. Blackw. 47: 65, 273. — Fraser, 36: 588. Same art. Ecl. M. 13: 92.
— How it is sometimes written. (A. H. Wratislaw) Fraser, 92: 519. — Month, 14: 87.
— How Literature may illustrate. (D. Masson) Macmil. 24: 200.
— Humbugs of. Once a Week, 21: 30.
— illustrated by Caricature. Ecl. M. 15: 549.
— Impostures of. Portfo.(Den.) 15: 369.
— in Germany Heeren's Works. Ecl. R. 68: 609.
— in the Year 3000. Cath. World, 7: 130.
— its Demand and Supply. Dem. R. 27: 262.
— Key to, Miss Peabody's. (W. B. O. Peabody) No. Am. 39: 200.
— Knowledge of. (Z. G. Willson) Western, 1: 626.
— Law of National Development. (O. W. Wight) No. Am. 88: 387.
— Laws of. (J. Fiske) Fortn. 10: 277. — (J. Fiske) No. Am. 109: 197. — (F. H. Hedge) No. Am. 111: 311.
— Materials for. Mus. 22: 229.
— Modern. (W. O. Johnson) No. Am. 80: 73.
— — Arnold's Lectures on. Chr. Rem. 5: 542. — Fraser, 26: 631. 33: 596. — Blackw. 53: 141. — Am. Whig R. 10: 248. — (W. R. Greg) Ed. R. 76: 357. Same art. Ecl. Mus. 1: 435. — Mo. R. 159: 67.
— — Half-Year of. Lond. Q. 36: 187.
— — Study of. (A. P. Stanley) Ex. H. Lec. 9: 347.
History, Modern Art and Science of. Westm. 38: 337.
— Modern Study of. Ox. Prize Ess. 3: 271.
— Mysteries of. Blackw. 68: 335. Same art. Ecl. M. 21: 331. Same art. Liv. Age, 27: 145.
— New Lamps of. (W. Swinton) Galaxy, 10: 97.
— New School of. (J. R. G. Hassard) Cath. World, 14: 549.
— Notes by a Reader of. Fraser, 26: 553.
— of 16th and 17th Centuries, Raumer's. Quar. 54: 78. — Mo. R. 136: 548.
— of 18th Century, Schlosser's. Ecl. M. 10: 38. — Westm. 44: 79.
— of 19th Century, Gervinus on. Tait, n. s. 20: 384.
— of our own Times. Ecl. M. 9: 165.
— — McCarthy's. Quar. 151: 156. — Month, 41: 205. — (J. MacCarthy) Cath. World, 32: 491.
— — 1860–1870; an eventful Decade. (J. C. Holbrook) Cong. R. 11: 147.
— of the World foretold in Genesis. Kitto, 27: 313. Same art. Ecl. M. 54: 79.
— Our Place in, 1866. (J. Seelye) Bib. Sac. 23: 211.
— Partisanship in. (E. D. Sanborn) Bib. Sac. 16: 603.
— Patriarchal Theory of. Colburn, 159: 409.
— Pearls and Mock Pearls of. (A. Hayward) Quar. 109: 307. Same art. Liv. Age, 69: 643.
— Philosophy of. (F. Bowen) No. Am. 93: 519. — (C. S. Henry) Putnam, 11: 407. — (J. H. MacMahon) Dub. Univ. 85: 497. — (H. C. Murphy) No. Am. 39: 30. — Meth. Q. 2: 383. — Blackw. 56: 786. Same art. Ecl. M. 4: 177. — Mo. R. 83: 149. — Am. Presb. R. 3: 1. — Chr. R. 24: 528. — Cornh. 9: 292.
— — Attempted. (L. Stephen) Fortn. 33: 672. Same art. Liv. Age, 145: 579.
— — Buckle's. (S. Y. McMasters) Am. Church R. 17: 103. — (J. S. S. Glennie) Fraser, 87: 482.
— — Flint's. (J. Morley) Fortn. 22: 338.
— — Hegel's. (K. Rosenkranz) J. Spec. Philos. 6: 340. — Nat. R. 7: 99. Same art. Ecl. M. 45: 1.
— — Miller on. Ecl. R. 41: 139.
— — Natural. Westm. 103: 329.
— — Goldwin Smith on. No. Brit. 37: 1.
— — Theories of. (H. Giles) No. Am. 95: 163.
— — Vico's. (J. D. Howard) Nat. Q. 9: 245.
— Plain, Plea for. (J. Gerard) Month, 32: 1.
— Plan in. (E. A. Lawrence) Princ. 43: 555.
— Primeval. Prosp. R. 2: 243.
— — Researches in. Quar. 52: 264.
— Problem of. (E. A. Lawrence) Am. Presb. R. 19: 478.
— Progress of. Walsh's R. 3: 1.
— Reading of. (S. L. Graham) Princ. 19: 211.
— Recent Revelations in. Dub. Univ. 51: 530. Same art. Ecl. M. 44: 346.
— Recent Studies in. Lond. Q. 41: 117.
— Relations of, to practical Life. (S. Howell) Education, 1: 255.
— Religion in. (K. I. Nitzsch) Theo. Ecl. 1: 127.
— Religious Aspect of. (A. P. Stanley) Good Words, 12: 548.
— repeats itself. Chamb. J. 56: 173.
— Romance of English, Neele's. Lond. M. 19: 464.
— Sacred, Study of. (J. G. McGee) Cath. World, 14: 421. — Westm. 115: 138.
— Science, and Dogma. Dub. Univ. 93: 188.
— Science of. (S. L. Caldwell) Bapt. Q. 1: 102. — (J. A. Froude) Hours at Home, 2: 321. — (A. O. Wright) Cong. R. 9: 438. — For. Q. 32: 325. — Brownson, 7: 1. — (C. C. S. Farrar) De Bow, 5: 58–445. — Fraser, 65: 651.
— — Buckle and Draper on. (E. B. Freeland) Contin. Mo. 4: 529, 610. 5: 161.
— — Froude on. (J. Morley) Fortn. 8: 226.

History, Science of, in France. Brit. & For. R. **16**: 72. Same art. Ecl. M. **1**: 161.
— Scientific Treatment of. (J. M. Buchan) Canad. Mo. **13**: 366.
— Sifting of Evidence in. (G. H. Lewes) Cornh. **8**: 113.
— Sources of. (J. Gairdner) Contemp. **38**: 533. Same art. Liv. Age, **147**: 311.
— — The Sphinx; Discourse on the Impotence of. (J. Skelton) Fraser, **64**: 54.
— Study of. (F. Bowen) No. Am. **75**: 247. — (E. A. Freeman) Fortn. **35**: 319. Same art. Ecl. M. **96**: 577. — (G. Smith) Atlan. **25**: 44. — (T. Wemyss) Cong. M. **27**: 892. — (W. J. Fox) Peop. J. **1**: 144, 187. — (R. W. Hanford) Peop. J. **8**: 61.— New Dom. **9**: 198, 263.
— — Arnold on. So. Q. **10**: 128.
— — at Oxford. (E. A. Freeman) Bent. Q. **1**: 282.
— — in College. (B. Sears) Bib. Sac. **22**: 251.
— — Charles Kingsley on. Westm. **75**: 305.
— — Methods of Historical Investigation. (H. Worsley) Dub. R. **88**: 269.
— — Province and Methods of. Nat. R. **14**: 224.
— — Goldwin Smith on. Westm. **76**: 293.
— — True Method of. (A. Dean) University Q. **2**: 310.
— Teaching, Aphorisms on. (K. von Raumer) Am. J. Educ. **8**: 101.
— — Theory of. Chr. Rem. **9**: 317.
— Theories of. Ecl. R. **118**: 434. — Cornh. **6**: 401.
— Thoughts on. Fraser, **2**: 413.
— Truth of. Mo. R. **120**: 110.
— Unity of. (E. A. Freeman) Appleton, **8**: 178.
— Universal. (O. A. Brownson) Dem. R. **12**: 457, 569. — (J. W. Mann) Mercersb. **1**: 444, 539. **2**: 12.
— — the earliest Ages. Fraser, **10**: 210.
— — Glimpses of. (A. D. White) New Eng. **15**: 398.
— — Idea of. (I. Kant) Lond. M. **10**: 385.
— — Smith's. Brit. Q. **46**: 289. Same art. Ecl. M. **70**: 141, 341.
— — Von Rotteck's. Ecl. R. **76**: 121.
— Use of. Ox. Prize Ess. **1**: 125.
— — and Meaning of. Westm. **62**: 420.
— Uses of. (M. Tarver) West. J. **10**: 77.
— — to the Preacher. (J. S. Sewall) New Eng. **22**: 420.
— *via* Poetry. Chamb. J. **46**: 282, 294.
— Writing of. So. Lit. Mess. **3**: 156.
— — and Stuart Rule in England. (J. Rowley) Fraser, **99**: 42.
— — and Teaching of. (J. R. Seeley) Macmil. **40**: 289, 369, 449. Same art. Liv. Age, **142**: 707. **143**: 23–748.
— — for the People. Hogg, **2**: 400.
History of an Adventurer. So. Lit. Mess. **7**: 187.
— of a Bachelor; a Tale. Dub. Univ. **44**: 47.
— of a Cosmopolite. (D. McLeod) Putnam, **4**: 325.
— of a Household. (D. M. Craik) Sharpe, **9**: 129, 198. **10**: 42.
— of Mr. Miranda. (D. Costello) Bentley, **45**: 225–628.
— of Oakley Common. Tait, n. s. **17**: 336, 400, 631.
— of an Epitaph. (G. H. Jessop) Overland, **13**: 444.
— of a Radical. Colburn, **48**: 273–447. **49**: 33–361.
Histories, American Common-School. (M. Wilson) Am. Bib. Repos. 3d s. **1**: 517. — (Reply to the above) Am. Bib. Repos. 3d s. **1**: 764.
— Providential and prophetical. Ed. R. **50**: 287.
Histrionic Metempsychosis. (J. Winsor) Galaxy, **6**: 549.
Hitchcock, Samuel Johnson. Knick. **29**: 14.
Hitchcock, Saml. Austin. (C. M. Hyde) Cong. Q. **16**: 517.
Hitchcock, William, Prairie Scout. (G. W. Nichols) Harper, **34**: 273.
Hittites, a forgotten Race in Asia Minor. (A. H. Sayce) Fraser, **102**: 223. Same art. Liv. Age, **146**: 736.
Hoang-Ho River, Double Delta of. (S. Mossman) Geog. M. **5**: 92, 152.
Hoar, Samuel. Putnam, **8**: 645.
Hoar, Samuel, Character of. Mo. Rel. M. **17**: 6.
Hoare, Charles J., Sermons of. Chr. Obs. **22**: 223.
Hoare, R. C. Giraldus Cambrensis. Ed. R. **8**: 399.
Hoaxes. Chamb. J. **56**: 203.
— Celebrated. Chamb. J. **50**: 486.
— Scientific. (A. De Morgan) Macmil. **1**: 218.
Hoaxing, Art of, from the Italian. Blackw. **12**: 589. **13**: 222, 400. **14**: 43.
Hoaxing Histories. Fraser, **25**: 636. **26**: 134, 271, 566.
Hobart, Bp. J. H., and Reviewers. Chr. Mo. Spec. **9**: 79.
— Consecration Sermon. (L. Bacon) Chr. Mo. Spec. **10**: 142.
— Memoir and Sermons on. Chr. Obs. **31**: 356.
— Sermons of. Chr. Obs. **26**: 26, 617.
Hobart, Peter, Lines on Death of, 1678. (B. Thompson) N. E. Reg. **14**: 141.
Hobbes, Thomas. (J. Hunt) Contemp. **7**: 185. — Westm. **87**: 344.
— English Works of. Chr. Exam. **29**: 320.
— Life and Writings of. Brit. Q. **6**: 155.
— Summary of the Views of. Penn Mo. **2**: 606.
— Works of. Chr. Rem. **12**: 84.
Hobbs Genealogy. (G. Hobbs) N. E. Reg. **9**: 255.
Hobbies. (T. De W. Talmage) Hours at Home, **8**: 131. — Chamb. J. **57**: 443.
— and Hobby-Riders. Am. Bibliop. **4**: 540. — Cath. World, **23**: 413. — (T. F. Dwight) Overland, **7**: 259.
Hobby-Horses. All the Year, **14**: 163.
— Chapter on. Tait, n. s. **19**: 431.
Hobby-Riders. (Mrs. H. V. Reed) Lakeside, **2**: 187.
Hobhouse, Sir John Cam, with portrait. Fraser, **13**: 568. — Ed. R. **133**: 289. Same art. Liv. Age, **109**: 515. — Colburn, **145**: 479.
— Charges against Eustace. Lond. M. **1**: 532.
Hobson's Choice. (D. Cook) Once a Week, **15**: 169–393.
Hochelaga. (W. B. O. Peabody) No. Am. **64**: 237. — Blackw. **60**: 464. — Dem. R. **19**: 255. — Liv. Age, **11**: 379.
Hoche-Lazare, the Invader of Ireland. Bentley, **63**: 595.
Hodge, Charles. (F. L. Patton) Presb. R. **2**: 349.
— and New Eng. Theology. (E. Pond) Bib. Sac. **30**: 371.
— Lecture in Theolog. Sem., Nov. 7, 1828. Princ. **1**: 75.
— Life of. (T. Dwight) New Eng. **40**: 222. — (J. W. Chadwick) Nation, **31**: 381.
Hodge and his Masters, Jefferies's. Chamb. J. **57**: 630.
Hodgson, J. E. (Tom Taylor) Portfo. **2**: 17.
Hodgson, Francis. (G. E. Woodberry) Nation, **28**: 72.
— Poems of. Ecl. R. **10**: 947.
Hodgson, Shadworth, on Free-Will. (W. G. Ward) Dub. R. **87**: 268.
Hodson, Maj. Wm. S. R. Ed. R. **109**: 545.—(T. Hughes) Fraser, **59**: 127. Same art. Liv. Age, **61**: 292.
Hofer, Andreas. Colburn, **132**: 118, 246.
— Hist. of, and Transactions in the Tyrol. Quar. **17**: 347.
— Monument to. Penny M. **6**: 57.
Hoffman, A. H., of Fallersleben. Appleton, **11**: 654.
Hoffman, C. Colden, Fox's Memoir of. Chr. Obs. **68**: 48.
Hoffman, Charles Fenno. Poems. (D. J. M. Loop) So. Lit. Mess. **14**: 97.
Hoffman, E. T. A. Kreisler. (V. Lee) Fraser, **98**: 767.
— Works of. (Sir W. Scott) For. Q. **1**: 60. — Blackw. **16**: 55.
Hoffman, Sarah, Memoir of. Chr. Obs. **22**: 605.
— Tales of the Manor. Portfo.(Den.) **29**: 411.
Hofwyl, Fellenberg's Institution at. Am. J. Educ. **3**: 591.
— in 1820–23. (R. D. Owen) Am. J. Educ. **26**: 359.
— My Student Life at. (R. D. Owen) Atlan. **15**: 550.
— Visit to. Penny M. **2**: 389.
Hog, The. Penny M. **10**: 237.
Hogs, About. (D. Piatt) Lippinc. **5**: 439.
Hog Business of the West. De Bow, **12**: 67.

Hog-Hunting in the Deccan Jungle. (M. L. Meason) Broadw. **2**: 41.
Hogan, John, with portrait. Dub. Univ. **35**: 72. — Art J. **2**: 376. — Irish Mo. **2**: 383. — Irish Q. **8**: 493.
Hogarth, George. Musical History. (G. W. Peck) Am. Whig R. **7**: 533.
Hogarth, Jane, and her Lodger. (D. Cook) Once a Week, **4**: 10.
Hogarth, William. (S. Colvin) Portfo. **3**: 146. — (Mrs. S. C. Hall) Nat. M. **7**: 197. Same art. Internat. M. **3**: 149. — (M. Oliphant) Blackw. **106**: 140. Same art. Liv. Age, **102**: 707. — (H. P. Palmer) Tinsley, **28**: 433. — (G. A. Sala) Cornh. **1**: 177-716. **2**: 97-438. — Ecl. M. **68**: 440. — Ecl. R. **125**: 253. — Portfo.(Den.) **13**: 71.
— and his Pictures. (S. Brown) Ex. H. Lec. **15**: 321.
— and his Works. Penny M. **3**: 121-481. **4**: 12-209.
— and Landseer. Art J. **31**: 302, 325, 361.
— and Lichtenburg. For. Q. **16**: 279.
— as a Historian. (W. J. Morgan) St. James, **44**: 206.
— Bewick and Green. (H. Coleridge) Blackw. **30**: 655.
— Genius of. Anal. M. **5**: 150.
— Harlot's Progress. Lond. M. **2**: 279.
— Illustrations of. Mo. R. **82**: 145.
— in London Streets. (G. W. Thornbury) Art J. **11**: 1.
— Paintings of. (T. Gautier) Temp. Bar, **6**: 258.
— Rake's Progress. Lond. M. **2**: 388.
— Tomb of, at Chiswick. Art J. **3**: 148. — (C. A. Collins) Macmil. **1**: 489.
Hoge, James. (W. S. Plumer) Princ. **36**: 89.
Hogg, James. Ed. Mo. R. **5**: 662. — Anal. M. **11**: 414. — Mo. R. **128**: 82. — with portrait, Fraser, **5**: 97. — Fraser, **1**: 291. **20**: 414. — Portfo.(Den.) **26**: 191. — (S. C. Hall) Art J. **18**: 313. Same art. Ecl. M. **67**: 696. Same art. Liv. Age, **91**: 321.
— Altrive Tales. Fraser, **5**: 482.
— Birthplace of. Tait, n. s. **14**: 507.
— Dinner to. Fraser, **5**: 114.
— First Visit to Jerusalem. Westm. **24**: 31.
— Jacobite Relics of Scotland. Ed. R. **34**: 148.
— Lay Sermons. Fraser, **10**: 1.
— Letter to his Reviewer. Blackw. **8**: 67.
— Letters to. Blackw. **2**: 501, 654.
— Mador of the Moor. Ecl. R. **25**: 174.
— Memoirs and Tales. Mo. R. **128**: 82. — Blackw. **10**: 43. — Mus. **21**: 97.
— Mountain. Mo. R. **95**: 428.
— Pilgrims of the Sun. Anal. M. **6**: 36. — Ecl. R. **21**: 280.
— Poems of. Dub. Univ. **88**: 724.
— Queen Hynde. Mo. R. **106**: 368.
— Queen's Wake. (W. Tudor) No. Am. **2**: 103. — Anal. M. **3**: 104. — (F. Jeffrey) Ed. R. **24**: 157. — Portfo. (Den.) **14**: 497.
— Recollections of. Mus. **37**: 438.
— Reminiscences of. (J. Morrison) Tait, n. s. **10**: 569, 626.
— Shepherd's Calendar. Blackw. **5**: 75, 210. **15**: 655.
— Some Particulars relative to. Colburn, **46**: 194-446.
— Strange Secret. Blackw. **23**: 822.
— Tales. (F. Dexter) No. Am. **9**: 1. — Mo. R. **93**: 263. — Blackw. **7**: 148.
— Three Perils of Women. Blackw. **14**: 427.
— Visit to. Am. Mo. M. **3**: 85.
— Winter Evening Tales. Lond. M. **1**: 666.
— Works of. Ecl. R. **123**: 335.
Hogg, Robert. (W. H. Maxwell) Bentley, **3**: 182.
Hogg, Thomas, Memoir of. Chr. Obs. **23**: 1.
Hohenlohe, Prince, Miracles of. Cong. M. **6**: 240.
Hohenstauffens, Raumer's History of the. For. Q. **3**: 559.
Hohenzollerns, The. (W. A. Nichols) Cong. R. **11**: 389.
Hoisting Apparatus. Ecl. Engin. **2**: 25.
Hokeday, Memoir on. (S. Denne) Arch. **7**: 244.
Holbach, Baron. System of Nature. (J. Morley) Fortn. **28**: 258.
Holbeach, Henry. (H. Duthus) Contemp. **12**: 398.
Holbein, Hans. (G. Kinkel) F. Arts Q. **5**: 223. — Art J. **19**: 55. — Ed. R. **125**: 410. — Penny M. **8**: 436. — Portfo. **9**: 1. — Westm. **8**: 244.
— and his Time. (L. Hinchman) Western, **6**: 361, 473.
— and Sir Joshua Reynolds. Cornh. **1**: 322.
— at his Easel. (C. Pebody) Gent. M. n. s. **19**: 364.
— Contemporaries and Successors of. (J. G. Nichols and G. Scharf) Arch. **39**: 19.
— Dance of Death. (F. Douce) Canad. J. n. s. **4**: 211. — (R. G. White) Atlan. **3**: 265.
— in National Portrait Exhibition. (A. Woltmann) Fortn. **6**: 151.
— Madonna. (S. R. Koehler) O. & N. **5**: 491.
— New Materials about. Ev. Sat. **11**: 295.
— Pictures in the Earl of Radnor's Collection. (J. G. Nichols) Arch. **44**: 435.
— Portraits of the Royal Family of England. (J. G. Nichols) Arch. **40**: 71.
— Will of. (W. H. Black; A. W. Franks) Arch. **39**: 1, 272.
Holberg, Ludvig. No. Brit. **50**: 440. — (P. Toft) Fraser, **84**: 69.
— Peter Paars. Dub. Univ. **8**: 178.
Holborn Races. All the Year, **25**: 12.
Holbrook, Josiah. Am. J. Educ. **8**: 229.
Holcombe, Wm. H. Writings. (D. K. Whittaker) N. Ecl. **7**: 61.
Holcroft, Sir Thomas. (G. R. Corner) Arch. **38**: 389.
Holcroft, Thomas, Actor and Author. Eng. Dom. M. **16**: 133. — Temp. Bar, **54**: 469.
— Tales. Ed. R. **9**: 101.
— Travels of. (F. Jeffrey) Ed. R. **4**: 84.
Holden, Horace. Narrative of Shipwreck. (J. G. Palfrey) No. Am. **43**: 206.
Holden, Isaac, Woolcomber. Lond. Soc. **35**: 153.
Holden, Mass., Ministers of. Am. Q. Reg. **10**: 58.
Hole, Richard, Memoir of. Blackw. **5**: 65.
Holford, Margaret. Margaret of Anjou. Ecl. R. **24**: 73.
— Wallace. Ecl. R. **12**: 1103.
— Warbeck of Wolfstein. Mo. R. **94**: 235.
Holiday, B. Marriage of the Arts. Retros. **8**: 304.
Holiday in West of England. (S. F. Hopkins) Galaxy, **19**: 775.
— Peculiar. Liv. Age, **134**: 437.
— True Value of a. Potter Am. Mo. **15**: 386.
Holidays. (H. T. Tuckerman) No. Am. **84**: 334. — Dem. R. **34**: 56.
— and Recreation. Cornh. **16**: 315.
— Christmas. (W. Payne) Am. Church R. **6**: 512.
— for Children. Portfo.(Den.) **31**: 218. — (H. Bushnell) Am. J. Educ. **13**: 93.
— Hints for. (J. Wilson) Blackw. **20**: 1, 255, 397.
— History of. (G. C. McWhorter) Harper, **32**: 164, 358.
— National. Chr. Rem. **6**: 413.
— — Manners's Plea for. Chr. Obs. **43**: 170.
— Rhapsody for August. Cornh. **2**: 242.
— Summer. (R. W. Dale) Good Words, **8**: 547.
— Whither shall I go? (E. Gaisford) St. James, **38**: 635.
See Half-Holidays; Holy Days.
Holiday Notes. Dub. Univ. **76**: 389.
Holiday Ports. (P. Fitzgerald) Belgra. **24**: 251.
Holiday Reminiscence. Dub. Univ. **72**: 330.
Holiday Romance. (C. Dickens) All the Year, **19**: 156-396.
Holiday Sketch. St. James, **19**: 111.
Holiday Time, Close of, with Thoughts on Pulpits. (A. K. H. Boyd) Fraser, **68**: 648. Same art. Ecl. M. **61**: 55.
Holiday Travel-Books. Fraser, **100**: 397.

Holiday Trip to Gravesend and Rochester. Fraser, **31**: 534.
Holiness. (J. O. A. Clark) Meth. Q. **37**: 505. — (J. T. Peck) Meth. Q. **11**: 505.
— and Sin, Nature of. So. R. n. s. **9**: 848.
— Biblical Conception of. Lond. Q. **52**: 54.
— of Redeemed, legal not gracious. Am. Presb. R. **1**: 275.
Holkham Hall. Bentley, **5**: 524.
Holland, Catherine, Autobiography of. (Mrs. R. Barker) Cath. World, **29**: 153.
Holland, E. G. Reviews and Essays. Brownson, **7**: 135.
Holland, Sir Henry. Nature, **9**: 8.
— Medical Notes and Reflections. Quar. **65**: 315.
— Recollections of. Brit. Q. **55**: 461. Same art. Ecl. M. **78**: 641. —Chr. Obs. **72**: 866. —(A. Hayward) Quar. **132**: 157. Same art. Liv. Age, **112**: 643. — Canad. Mo. **1**: 282.
— Travels in Greece. (J. Foster) Ecl. R. **25**: 353. — Quar. **23**: 325. — Ed. R. **25**: 455.
Holland, Lord Henry R. V. (T. B. Macaulay) Ed. R. **73**: 560. Same art. Mus. **43**: 59. — Mus. **41**: 529.
— Foreign Reminiscences. Quar. **88**: 492. Same art. Liv. Age, **29**: 385. — Ed. R. **93**: 137. Same art. Liv. Age, **29**: 25. Same art. Ecl. M. **22**: 385. — Blackw. **69**: 234. — Ecl. R. **93**: 335. — Fraser, **43**: 220. — Liv. Age, **28**: 453. — Dem. R. **28**: 401. — So. Q. **20**: 133. — Internat. M. **2**: 465.
— House of, at Kensington. Quar. **135**: 405. Same art. Ecl. M. **82**: 129. Same art. Liv. Age, **119**: 515. — House. Words, **9**: 8, 38. Same art. Ecl. M. **32**: 222. — Penny M. **11**: 4. — Chamb. J. **50**: 817. Same art. Ev. Sat. **15**: 595. — Nation, **17**: 408.
— — and its Inhabitants. (Mrs. A. T. Thomson) Fraser, **35**: 148. Same art. Liv. Age, **13**: 245.
— — Romance of. (A. H. Guernsey) Galaxy, **18**: 333.
— Memoirs. Dub. R. **37**: 1. — Mo. R. **155**: 80.
Holland, James. Ev. Sat. **9**: 195.
Holland, John. (L. Jewitt) Reliquary, **15**: 145.
Holland, Josiah G. (M. Walsingham) Potter Am. Mo. **13**: 449. — (A. J. H. Duganne) Potter Am. Mo. **17**: 455. — Canad. Mo. **20**: 556.
— Writings of. (R. T. S. Lowell) No. Am. **95**: 81.
Holland, Samuel, and the State Quarries of North Wales. Pract. M. **3**: 81.
Holland. (H. Bedford) Month, **28**: 448. — (R. T. Pritchett) Good Words, **21**: 22-373. — (R. P. Spiers) Am. Arch. **10**: 88. — (J. H. Browne) Harper, **44**: 165, 349. — (M. Talbot) Harper, **24**: 446. — (C. W. Wood) Argosy, **23**: 44-448. **24**: 43-477. — Bentley, **26**: 360. — Dub. Univ. **21**: 224. — House. Words, **16**: 398-501. **17**: 93-526.
— Agricultural Colonies for Poor in. Good Words, **4**: 347.
— and Belgium. Dub. R. **5**: 463.
— — Affairs of. Colburn, **29**: 412.
— — Religious Condition of. (J. J. Tayler) Theo. R. **5**: 91.
— and Germany. (M. de Beaufort) 19th Cent. **3**: 402.
— and its People. Appleton, **25**: 55.
— and Netherlands. (N. Macleod) Good Words, **3**: 513.
— Arminians in. Meth. M. **36**: 23.
— Banking in. Bank. M. (L.) **17**: 573.
— Louis Bonaparte on Government of. Ecl. R. **32**: 67. — Mo. R. **94**: 225.
— Carr's Tour in, 1806. (J. Foster) Ecl. R. **6**: 953.
— Church of. (A. Réville) Chr. Exam. **70**: 91. **71**: 116.
— — Forms of. (J. Forsyth) Theo. & Lit. J. **11**: 478.
— Cities of the Zuyder Zee. (A. H. Guernsey) Appleton, **16**: 150, 246.
— Commerce of. Penny M. **8**: 372.
— — and Industry of. Tait, n. s. **13**: 661.
— — Rise and Fall of. Ed. R. **51**: 418.
— Court of, under Louis Bonaparte. Mo. R. **100**: 483.
— Davies's Hist. of, 10th-18th Centuries. Mo. R. **157**: 555.
Holland, Defenses of. (C. L. Graneisen) St. James, **37**: 401.
— Dikes and Canals of. Penny M. **13**: 43.
— Diplomacy of, and Indian Piracy. Ed. R. **96**: 54.
— Draining in. (G. E. Waring, jr.) Scrib. **9**: 714. **10**: 52.
— Dutch and their dead Cities. Blackw. **118**: 527. Same art. Ecl. M. **86**: 81. Same art. Liv. Age, **127**: 610.
— Dutch at Home. (A. Rhodes) Galaxy, **12**: 66. **14**: 583.
— Dutch Conquest of. (A. H. Guernsey) Galaxy, **22**: 220.
— Dutch Farming. (G. E. Waring, jr.) Scrib. **10**: 195.
— Dutchman at Home. Ecl. M. **76**: 747. **77**: 228.
— Fighting the Enemy in. Once a Week, **19**: 399-460.
— Grave Remonstrance with some English Travelers in. Argosy, **1**: 347.
— in 1672. (C. Bryant) Month, **25**: 484.
— Industry and Drainage of. Ed. R. **86**: 221. Same art. Liv. Age, **16**: 241.
— Inundations in. (J. De Liefde) Good Words, **2**: 632.
— — in 1825. Lond. M. **21**: 362.—Penny M. **10**: 437, 447.
— Land of Windmills and Steeples. Colburn, **166**: 409.
— Language and Literature of. For. Q. **4**: 36.
— Liberal Christianity in. (J. Fretwell) Unita. R. **5**: 197.
— Life in. Lond. Soc. **19**: 330, 538.
— Literature of, during the 19th Century. (A. Schwartz) Macmil. **33**: 155, 267.
— Living Poets of. Westm. **10**: 36.
— Motley's Rise of Dutch Republic. (F. W. Palfrey) No. Am. **83**: 182. — Evang. R. **8**: 143. — (J. Weiss) Chr. Exam. **61**: 99. — Liv. Age, **49**: 175. **57**: 1018. — No. Brit. **25**: 376. — Westm. **65**: 313. Same art. Liv. Age, **49**: 449.
— Motley's United. Blackw. **89**: 555. — Ed. R. **113**: 182. — (G. Ripley) Harper, **22**: 639. *See* **Netherlands.**
— My Tour in. Cornh. **6**: 616.
— Negotiations with, 1818. Niles's Reg. **14**: 89.
— Old Catholic Church of. O. & N. **6**: 627.
— Pauper Colonies of. Lond. M. **22**: 440.
— Pictures from. (R. T. Pritchett) Good Words, **22**: 678.
— Pictures in. (Lady Verney) Contemp. **30**: 264. Same art. Ecl. M. **89**: 308. Same art. Liv. Age, **134**: 689.
— Political Reformation in. No. Brit. **23**: 422.
— Protestantism in, 1877. Cong. **6**: 176.
— Prussian Campaign in, 1787. Ed. R. **142**: 521. Same art. Liv. Age, **128**: 259.
— Religion and Education in, 1831. Ecl. R. **64**: 169-481.
— Religious Condition of. (J. W. Alexander) Princ. **5**: 19.
— Republic of. (W. P. Riddell) De Bow, **12**: 280.
— Rural Industry and Drainage in. Ed. R. **86**: 419.
— Scenes in. Knick. **18**: 237.
— Scotchman in. Cornh. **8**: 539.
— Sketches of. (A. Paynter) Peop. J. **2**: 190, 278, 339.
— South. Mo. R. **126**: 69.
— Ten Hours in. (P. Mulford) Overland, **11**: 412.
— Theology in. Fraser, **67**: 358.
— — Current. (P. H. Wicksteed) Theo. R. **11**: 264.
— — Modern. (J. F. Hurst) Meth. Q. **31**: 250. — (P. H. Wicksteed) Unita. R. **4**: 217. **5**: 215.
— — past and present. Theo. R. **1**: 255.
— — Roman Catholic mystic. Chr. Rem. **25**: 328.
See Netherlands.
Holland House. *See* Holland, Lord H. R. V., House of.
Holley, Horace, Memoir of. (E. Everett) No. Am. **27**: 403. — West. Mo. R. **2**: 212.
Hollinshead, John, with portrait. Once a Week, **27**: 166.
Hollis, Thomas. N. E. Reg. **2**: 265.
— Memoir of. (J. Walker) Chr. Exam. **7**: 64. — Spirit Pilg. **2**: 581.
Hollis, N. H. (S. T. Worcester) N. E. Reg. **27**: 377.
— in the Revolution. N. E. Reg. **28**: 52, 146, 216. **30**: 288. **31**: 23, 169.
— Ministers' Association. (A. W. Burnham) Cong. Q. **10**: 186.

Holly, The. Penny M. **8**: 4.
— and Ivy. Dub. Univ. **46**: 635.
— Chapter on. (J. R. Jackson) Once a Week, **16**: 19.
Holly Cottage. Fraser, **34**: 198. Same art. Liv. Age, **10**: 491.
Holly-Tree, The. (B. L. Green) Hogg, **5**: 172.
Holly-Tree Inn. (C. Dickens and others) House. Words, **12**: supp.
Holly Wreaths and Rose Chains. (L. de la Ramé) Bentley, **46**: 623.
Holman, Lieut. James, the blind Traveler, with portrait. Peop. J. **4**: 213.
— Voyage round the World. Fraser, **11**: 653. — Mo. R. **134**: 23. **136**: 169. **137**: 26. **138**: 507.
Holmby House; a Novel. (G. J. W. Melville) Fraser, **59**: 1–679. **60**: 24–685. **61**: 64, 204, 338. Same art. Liv. Age, **61**: 9, 93, 229. **62**: 172–344. **63**: 148–658. **64**: 94–735.
Holmes, Abiel. American Annals. (J. Sparks) No. Am. **29**: 428. — (R. Southey) Quar. **2**: 309.
— Obituary Notice of. Am. Alma. **1836**: 316.
Holmes, David. Letter on Unitarianism. Chr. Disc. **5**: 54.
Holmes, Mrs. D. Poems. Dub. Univ. **23**: 343.
Holmes, Oliver Wendell. (K. Cook) Belgra. **20**: 222. — with portrait, Ev. Sat. **11**: 624, 642. — (F. H. Underwood) Scrib. **18**: 117. — with portrait, Appleton, **12**: 545. — (R. Palmer) Internat. R. **8**: 501. — with portrait, Ecl. M. **80**: 632. — Bost. R. **2**: 583. — Ev. Sat. **14**: 466. — Irish Q. **5**: 193. — Nat. M. **3**: 502.
— and his Writings. Dub. Univ. **84**: 376.
— as a Humorist. Brit. Q. **52**: 324.
— Astræa. Knick. **37**: 142.
— Autocrat of the Breakfast Table. Chamb. J. **31**: 59. — Liv. Age, **60**: 630.
— Breakfast to, 1880. Atlan. **45**: supp.
— Britain and America. Canad. J. n. s. **3**: 365.
— Elsie Venner. Bost. R. **1**: 384. — Dub. Univ. **59**: 401. — Nat. R. **13**: 359. Same art. Liv. Age, **71**: 435.
— — and Silas Marner. (J. M. Ludlow) Macmil. **4**: 305.
— Guardian Angel. Ev. Sat. **4**: 728.
— Poems of. (J. G. Palfrey) No. Am. **44**: 275. — (J. G. Whittier) Knick. **26**: 570. — Liv. Age, **20**: 516. — Knick. **61**: 189.
— Prize Dissertations. (E. Hale) No. Am. **47**: 161.
— Urania. (F. Bowen) No. Am. **64**: 208.
— Verses on. (G. H. Clark) Knick. **47**: 336.
— Writings of. Colburn, **99**: 77. Same art. Liv. Age, **39**: 100. Same art. Ecl. M. **30**: 532. — So. R. n. s. **13**: 26.
Holmes, Robert, with portrait. Dub. Univ. **31**: 122.
Holmfirth Flood, Visit to the Scene of. Chamb. J. **17**: 353.
Holst, Theodore Maria von, the Painter. Peop. J. **3**: 101.
Holstein and Schleswig Question. Fraser, **38**: 49. *See* Denmark.
Holt, John S. (C. W. Hutson) N. Ecl. **6**: 88.
Holt, Joseph. Dub. Univ. **12**: 72. — Mo. R. **145**: 325.
Holt, Joseph, of Wilton, N. H. Journal in 1758. N. E. Reg. **10**: 307.
Holton, Samuel, Biography of. Am. Q. Reg. **13**: 79.
Holwood Hill, Recent Discoveries at. (A. J. Kempe) Arch. **22**: 336.
Holy Alliance. (E. Robinson) No. Am. **17**: 340. — For. Q. **8**: 49, 427. — Ed. R. **38**: 241. **39**: 467. **40**: 414. — Niles's Reg. **20**: 313. **24**: 365.
— and Edinburgh Review. Blackw. **15**: 317.
— Declaration of England against. Pamph. **18**: 1.
— Designs of. Selec. Ed. R. **4**: 355.
— Moore's Fables for. Blackw. **13**: 574. — Westm. **1**: 18.
— The New, 1864 Ecl. R. **120**: 328.
Holy Cave of Manresa. (M. P. Thompson) Cath. World, **26**: 821.
Holy Days, National, and the Catholic Church. Dub. R. **14**: 481. *See* Festival Days; Holidays.
Holy Fair. St. James, **24**: 742.
Holy Ghost, Scriptural Usage of the Phrase. (W. R. French) Univ. Q. **30**: 289. *See* Holy Spirit.
Holy Grail, The. (E. Spencer) Hours at Home, **14**: 489. — Cath. World, **8**: 137. — Ev. Sat. **10**: 418.
— Legend of. Tinsley, **6**: 106. Same art. Ecl. M. **74**: 432.
— Myths of, and the German Grail-Saga. Once a Week, **24**: 145, 190.
— Sangreal. (G. MacDonald) Good Words, **4**: 454.
Holy Homes. (E. Meteyard) Sharpe, **23**: 1. **26**: 193.
Holy Ireland; a Story. (G. Griffin) Irish Mo. **6**: 573, 611.
Holy Isle, Legend of the. St. James, **29**: 601.
Holy Land. *See* Palestine.
Holy Orders, How to enter. (H. Hayman) St. James, **38**: 189.
— Indelibility of. Ed. R. **89**: 148.
Holy Places. Quar. **93**: 432. Same art. Ecl. M. **30**: 494.
Holy Roman Empire, Bryce's. No. Brit. **42**: 183. — Penn Mo. **8**: 785.
— Influence of a historical Idea. Macmil. **11**: 155.
Holy Rood, Poem of. (J. M. Kemble) Arch. **30**: 31.
Holy Sepulcher. (W. H. Dixon) Gent. M. n. s. **18**: 334.
— Church of. (W. H. Bartlett) Sharpe, **6**: 81.
— Genuineness of. (T. Lewin) Arch. **41**: 116.
— True Site of. (L. J. Fletcher) Univ. Q. **31**: 438.
Holy Spirit, The. (W. R. French) Univ. Q. **19**: 266. — Am. Presb. R. **10**: 410.
— and the Church. Danv. Q. **2**: 472.
— and an efficient Ministry. Cong. M. **26**: 710.
— and Mediation of Christ. Cong. M. **14**: 412, 599, 721.
— and the natural World. (D. Gans) Mercersb. **13**: 265.
— Arthur's Tongue of Fire. Lond. Q. **6**: 383.
— Author of human Advancement. Theo. & Lit. J. **4**: 280.
— Bampton Lectures on. Lond. Q. **32**: 160.
— Baptism of. (W. Crosbie) Cong. **2**: 648. — (D. C. Eddy) Bapt. Q. **5**: 335.
— Blasphemy against. (G. W. Clark) Bapt. Q. **2**: 445. — (W. J. Clark) Princ. **18**: 376. — Cong. M. **11**: 142.
— Communion with. Chr. Q. Spec. **9**: 345.
— Dependence of the Church upon. (F. W. Conrad) Evang. R. **17**: 461.
— Doctrine of. (T. Hill) Chr. Exam. **52**: 384. — (G. R. Leavitt) Cong. Q. **11**: 392. — (S. Osgood) Chr. Exam. **81**: 217.
— Faber on. Ecl. R. **20**: 50.
— — and Hall on. Chr. Obs. **12**: 523.
— False Faith in regard to. (D. Gans) Mercersb. **14**: 67.
— Gift of. (J. Beaty, jr.) Chr. Q. **3**: 501.
— Hare's Mission of the Comforter. Bib. R. **3**: 41.
— in Conversion. (A. I. Hobbs) Chr. Q. **7**: 23.
— in Regeneration. (S. Williston) Am. Bib. Repos. 3d s. **1**: 493. — (L. P. Hickok) Chr. Q. Spec. **7**: 301. — (E. Lyman) Chr. Q. Spec. **7**: 591. — Chr. R. **11**: 510.
— in troublous Times. Bost. R. **1**: 338.
— Influence of. (D. N. Sheldon) Unita. R. **2**: 413. — Am. Bib. Repos. 3d s. **2**: 633.
— Liturgical Invocation of. Chr. Rem. **49**: 475.
— Methods of. (C. Cushing) Cong. Q. **10**: 17.
— New Testament Doctrine of. Danv. Q. **4**: 167. — (A. S. Chesebrough) New Eng. **37**: 462.
— Office and Mission of. (A. G. Pease) Mercersb. **23**: 430, 558.
— — Simeon on. Chr. Obs. **32**: 40, 205.
— — Stowell on. Brit. Q. **10**: 357.
— Operation of. Quar. **31**: 111.
— Personality of. (W. C. Child) Chr. R. **17**: 515. — Bost. R. **3**: 437.
— — and Divinity of. (D. Gans) Mercersb. **14**: 464.
— Presence in the Word. (J. G. Warren) Chr. R. **17**: 213

Holy Spirit, The, Procession of. Am. Church R. **21**: 244.
— Promise of. (E. E. Mason) Am. Bib. Repos. 3d s. **4**: 67.
— Romanist Doctrine of. Lond. Q. **40**: 162.
— Sin against. (J. Bate) Meth. Q. **18**: 290. — (H. N. Burton) Bost. R. **5**: 371.
— Thoughts on, Hewlett's. Bib. R. **2**: 387.
— Union of, with Church. (T. W. Jenkyn) Bib. R. **3**: 28.
— Unity of. (C. A. Bartol) Chr. Exam. **78**: 26.
— Use and Meaning of the Phrase. (H. Ware) Chr. Disc. **1**: 260.
— Witness of. (M. L. Stoever) Evang. R. **10**: 296. — Chr. Mo. Spec. **10**: 65. — Am. Meth. M. **19**: 457.
— — J. Wesley on. Am. Meth. M. **18**: 241.
— Work of. (W. C. Child) Chr. R. **19**: 408. — Bib. R. **2**: 401. **6**: 577. — Spirit Pilg. **2**: 595. — Cong. M. **10**: 350, 418, 470.
Holy Thursday at Court of Austria. (W. I. Kip) Overland, **2**: 164.
Holy Week. U. S. Cath. M. **7**: 200.
— at Rome. (J. J. Jarves) Harper, **9**: 20, 158, 317. — (N. Wiseman) U. S. Cath. M. **2**: 46–235.
— in Rome; a Poem. (Com.Gibson) Cath.World, **29**: 284.
— Office of. Dub. R. **24**: 1.
— Wiseman on Ceremonies of. Mo. R. **149**: 375.
Holyoake, Geo. J., and Atheism. Tait, n. s. **22**: 700.
Holyoke, Dr. Edmund Augustus. Am. Q. Reg. **13**: 79.
Holyrood, Bothwell's Attempt on. Blackw. **2**: 30.
Holyrood House. Penny M. **1**: 188.
Holyrood Palace. (B. H. Young) Land We Love, **4**: 30.
Homburg and Gambling Spas. Lond. Soc. **2**: 492.
— and Wiesbaden, Gambling Sketches from. Lond. Soc. **9**: 491. Same art. Ecl. M. **67**: 147.
— Day at. All the Year, **44**: 352.
— Gambling at. Cornh. **12**: 221. — (E. G. Buffum) Galaxy, **3**: 493. — All the Year, **2**: 517. — (J. Kirkland) Putnam, **12**: 129.
— in November, 1871. (J. Hutton) Belgra. **19**: 55.
— Tale of. Chamb. J. **51**: 657. **55**: 393.
— To, and back for a Shilling. Ecl. M. **65**: 442.
— Week in the Bergstrasse. Lippinc. **8**: 354.
Home, Daniel D., the Spiritual Medium. All the Year, **9**: 133. — Cornh. **2**: 211. — Chamb. J. **31**: 243. — Galaxy, **19**: 86. — No. Brit. **39**: 174. Same art. Ecl. M. **60**: 173, 291.
Home, Henry. *See* Kames, Lord.
Home, John, Author of Douglas. Colburn, **57**: 289. **58**: 164. — Dub. Univ. **71**: 657. Same art. Liv. Age, **98**: 165.
— Life and Works. (Sir W. Scott) Quar. **36**: 167.
Home. (J. F. W. Ware) Mo. Rel. M. **27**: 93. — (T. Westwood) Fraser, **51**: 289.
— a Poem. (D. Greenwell) Cornh. **8**: 357.
— Æsthetics of. Nat. Q. **30**: 155.
— and the Age. Mo. Rel. M. **23**: 1.
— and its Economies. (J. Ruskin) Contemp. **21**: 927.
— and Politics. (L. M. Child) Hogg, **3**: 34.
— Anglo-Saxon. Ecl. R. **117**: 72.
— At, and Homeless. St. James, **22**: 689.
— An Englishman's. Dub. Univ. **5**: 267.
— Healthy Discipline of. (T. H. Yeoman) Peop. J. **7**: 204–259.
— Institution and Constitution of. (J. F. W. Ware) Mo. Rel. M. **27**: 205.
— made attractive. (G. Fitzhugh) De Bow, **28**: 624
— made unhealthy. (H. Martineau) Harper, **1**: 601.
— New England. (J. F. W. Ware) Mo. Rel. M. **26**: 341.
— of the hundred blind Men. House. Words, **4**: 195. Same art. Liv. Age, **32**: 161.
— of the Past. (F. Talbot) Belgra. **25**: 122.
— of the present Day. Belgra. **24**: 226.
— of the two Widows. (O. F. Adams) Lippinc. **23**: 597.
— of Woodruffe the Gardener. House. Words, **1**: 518–569.
Home or Hospital. (H. Martineau) Once a Week, **1**: 419.
— Restraints of. (C. J. Vaughan) Good Words, **8**: 310.
— without Hands. Belgra. **34**: 221.
Home, sweet Home. Tinsley, **9**: 142–642. **10**: 38–649. **11**: 49–632. **12**: 36–518. — Sharpe, **29**: 92–236.
Homes, Artistic. Temp. Bar, **43**: 673. Same art. Ecl. M. **84**: 758. — (H.Cox) Potter Am. Mo. **17**: 142, 257.
— Associated, for the Middle Classes. (M. Gillies) Howitt, **1**: 171, 270. **2**: 39.
— Attractive. (M. H. Ford) Potter Am. Mo. **16**: 53.
— Democratic. (J. R. Dennett) Nation, **6**: 128.
— English Workingmen's. (C. Barnard) Scrib. **13**: 348.
— for the People. (H. H. Barber) Unita. R. **6**: 370. — (C. E. Illsley) Western, **4**: 448, 527.
— Hand-made. (H. Reid) St. James, **47**: 284.
— of America. Art J. **29**: 260. **30**: 20–295.
— of the London Poor. Chamb. J. **53**: 230.
— of other Days in England. Chamb. J. **49**: 358.
— Organized. (W. F. Channing) Pop. Sci. Mo. **9**: 733.
— Planning and Adornment of. (C. E. Illsley) Western, **3**: 215, 255.
Home Colonies in Belgium and France. For. Q. **13**: 132.
Home Comforts and Amusements. (E. C. Guild) Unita. R. **8**: 526.
Home Decoration and Holiday Gifts. (M. Ford) Potter Am. Mo. **15**: 459.
Home Education, Taylor on. Westm. **34**: 496. — Ecl. R. **67**: 653.
Home Evangelization. (A. S. Chesebrough) Cong. Q. **8**: 160. — (H. L. Baugher) Evang. R. **3**: 301.
— in Connecticut. (L. W. Bacon) New Eng. **18**: 998.
Home Feeling. (H. Harbaugh) Hours at Home, **1**: 409. **2**: 56.
Home Harvest. (J. C. Miller) Ex. H. Lec. **11**: 283.
Home Influences. (J. F. W. Ware) Mo. Rel. M. **27**: 341.
Home Intercourse. (J. F. W. Ware) Mo. Rel. M. **27**: 290.
Home League. (C. C. Haven) Hunt, **8**: 64. — Dem. R. **9**: 539.
Home Life. Westm. **103**: 173.
— Brown on. Ecl. R. **124**: 47.
— during Election Time. (E. Crump) Tinsley, **27**: 48.
— Ware on. Mo. Rel. M. **31**: 10.
Home Missionary Society. Chr. Q. Spec. **3**: 513.
Home Missionaries of New England, First. (J. H. Means) Cong. Q. **10**: 167.
Home Missions. Princ. **4**: 72. — Theo. R. **1**: 136, 293.
— Address on. (T. Stratten) Cong. M. **24**: 813.
— and Christian Colleges, Mutual Relations of. (J. E. Roy) Cong. Q. **19**: 29.
— Appeal and Plan for. Cong. M. **22**: 677. **23**: 39, 177.
— Co-operation in. New Eng. **17**: 1016.
— 50 Years of, in Illinois. (J. E. Roy) New Eng. **35**: 561.
— in early Times. (J. S. Clark) Cong. Q. **1**: 53.
— in England. Lond. Q. **24**: 27.
— Lutheran. (M. Officer) Evang. R. **17**: 257. — (J. C. Kauffman) Luth. Q. **6**: 415.
— — in the U. S. (D. M. Henkel) Evang. R **21**: 377.
— of the Episcopal Church. Am. Church R. **22**: 83. — (J. H. Egar) Am. Church R. **12**: 398.
— Scottish. No. Brit. **30**: 202.
— What they have done for Illinois. (J. E. Roy) Cong. R. **9**: 401.
See Evangelization.
Home Rule. Westm. **100**: 362.
— Common Sense of. (J. McCarthy) 19th Cent. **7**: 406. — (D. J. Wilson and J. McCarthy) 19th Cent. **7**: 567.
— Fallacies concerning. (J.O'C. Power) Fortn. **32**: 224.
— from a Saxon Standpoint. (J. Spalding) Colburn, **154**: 432.
— in Ireland. (W. O'C. Morris) Fortn. **17**: 16.
— Ireland's Experiences of. Fraser, **85**: 206.
— in several Countries. (Sir G.Campbell) Fortn. **33**: 644.

Home Rule, Suggestion as to. 19th Cent. **6**: 89.
Home-Rule Candidates; a Tale. (N. Robinson) Cath. World, **26**: 669, 742. **27**. 16, 210.
Home-Rule Experiment in Ceylon. (W. Digby) Fortn. **24**: 241.
Homesick; a Poem. (E. Letherbrow) Cornh. **7**: 601.
Home Side of a Scientific Mind. Dub. Univ. **91**: 105-454.
Homesickness. Penny M. **9**: 447. — Ev. Sat. **1**: 179.
Homespun Songs. (R.G. Haliburton) Blackw. **113**: 610.
Home Trade preferable to Foreign. (C. C. Haven) Hunt, **8**: 343.
Home Travel; Devonshire. (J. Dennis) Fortn. **5**: 587.
— Westmoreland and Cumberland. (J. Dennis) Fortn. **6**: 445.
Homeless Gentlemen, Our. Chamb. J. **33**: 140.
Homely Heroine; a Tale. Chamb. J. **51**: 65. Same art. Liv. Age, **121**: 282.
Homely Man. (C. A. Washburn) Pioneer, **4**: 291.
Homer. (A. S. Packard) No. Am. **37**: 340. — Fraser, **32**: 572. — Blackw. **42**: 734. — Quar. **101**: 80. — (R. D. Windes) So. M. **12**: 50. — Mo. R. **148**: 317.
— Achilles's Reply to Envoys of Agamemnon. (W. E. Gladstone) Contemp. **23**: 841. Same art. Ecl. M. **83**: 46. Same art. Liv. Age, **121**: 687.
— a Favorite of Time. (J. G. Herder) Blackw. **42**: 702.
— Age of. (J. P. Mahaffy) Macmil. **38**: 405. **39**: 314, 524. — (F. A. Paley) Macmil. **39**: 411.
— Ambrosian Codex of. Lond. M. **3**: 273.
— and Epic Poetry. Knick. **8**: 14.
— and Homeridæ. (T. De Quincey) Blackw. **50**: 411-747.
— and Old Testament. (J. B. Hague) Bapt. Q. **6**: 443.
— and recent Critics. (A. Lang) Fortn. **23**: 575.
— and Troy. (T. B. Browne) Contemp. **12**: 481.
— Andromache; Daughters of Priam. Blackw. **117**: 305.
— Antiquity of the Homeric Poems. (H. Hayman) Contemp. **12**: 50.
— as a Study. (R. W. Bailey) So. Lit. Mess. **23**: 109.
— Bas Relief of Apotheosis of. Lond. M. **3**: 81.
— Batrachomyomachia; translated. (F. T. Price) Blackw. **43**: 202. Another translation, Blackw. **43**: 631. — Lond. M. **4**: 269, 388.
— Bryant's Translation. (E. I. Sears) Nat. Q. **25**: 118. — (W. C. Wilkinson) Hours at Home, **11**: 485.
— Character of Achilles. Westm. **102**: 327.
— Contradictions in. Brit. & For. R. **9**: 662.
— Critics and Translators of. No. Brit. **36**: 345.
— Dante and Michael Angelo. Blackw. **57**: 1.
— Derby and Arnold on. (L. R. Packard) New Eng. **25**: 47.
— Epithets of Movement in. (W. E. Gladstone) 19th Cent. **5**: 463.
— Geddes on the Homeric Problem. (E. A. Freeman) Contemp. **34**: 442.
— Gladstone's Juventus Mundi. Macmil. **21**: 28. — No. Brit. **51**: 1.
— Gladstone's Studies in. (E.A.Freeman) Nat.R. **7**: 40.— Bent. Q. **1**: 33. — Blackw. **84**: 126. — Colburn, **114**: 300. — Ecl. R. **109**: 449. — Ed. R. **108**: 502. — No. Brit. **29**: 25. — So. R. n. s. **21**: 160. — (B. Zincke) Fraser, **59**: 50, 192.
— Heyne's. (W. Maginn) Ed. R. **2**: 308.
— Historic Credibility of. (G. W. Cox) Fortn. **7**: 567.
— — Gladstone on. (G. W. Cox) Fortn. **12**: 241.
— Historical Value of the Iliad and Odyssey. Chr. Rem. **36**: 331.
— Hymn to Aphrodite. Blackw. **51**: 579.
— — to Hermes; translated. (E. Kenealy) Dub. Univ. **29**: 296.
— — to Pan; translated. Lond. M. **5**: 161.
— Hymns of; translated. Blackw. **31**: 319, 742. **32**: 33. **51**: 579. **52**: 139, 154.
Homer. The Iliad. (C. C. Harris) University Q. **4**: 209. — Blackw. **50**: 618. — Westm. **43**: 331. — (Translated by J. A. Martling) Western, **1**: 617-746. **2**: 20-212.
— — Brandreth's Translation. Chr. Rem. **12**: 398.
— — Bryant's Translation. (T. W. Higginson) Radical, **7**: 425. — (C. T. Lewis) No. Am. **112**: 328. — (J. B. Thayer) O. & N. **2**: 259. — (M. W. Hazeltine) Cath. World: **15**: 381. — Putnam, **15**: 366.
— — Characters of. Am. Mo. M. **6**: 161, 310.
— — Derby's Translation. (J. R. Lowell) No. Am. **101**: 303. — (F. A. Rudd) Cath. World, **8**: 740. — Blackw. **97**: 439. — Dub. Univ. **65**: 152. — Ed. R. **121**: 136. Same art. Ecl. M. **64**: 401. — Ecl. R. **121**: 89. — Nat. Q. **11**: 205. — Quar. **117**: 93.
— — — and Bryant's. So. R. n. s. **8**: 39.
— — English and German Versions. Chr. Rem. **51**: 190.
— — Felton's. Am. Mo. R. **4**: 93. — Am. Q. **14**: 143.
— — in English Ballad-Meter. Tinsley, **7**: 597.
— — in English Hexameters; Book I. (J. F. W. Herschel) Cornh. **5**: 590.
— — — Book I. Blackw. **59**: 610.
— — — Book XXIV. Blackw. **59**: 259.
— — — Dart's. (W. Whewell) Macmil. **5**: 487.
— — in English Trochaics; Book XXII. (W. E. Aytoun) Blackw. **45**: 634.
— — Legal Merits of. Blackw. **48**: 355.
— — Munford's. (C. C. Felton) No. Am. **63**: 149. — (C. A. Bristed) Am. Whig R. **4**: 350. — (N. L. Frothingham) Chr. Exam. **41**: 205. — So. Q. **10**: 1.
— — New Hexameter Translation of. (W. Whewell) Macmil. **6**: 297.
— — Penn's. Mus. **1**: 374.
— — Poetical Merit of. Am. Q. Reg. **9**: 235.
— — Structure of. (H. W. Lucas) Month, **35**: 22, 382.
— — Translations. Fraser, **78**: 518. — Lond. Q. **43**: 363.
— — Williams's Translation. Ecl. R. **4**: 1007.
— Iris of, and Bow of Genesis. (W. E. Gladstone) Contemp. **32**: 140.
— Lachmann's Essays on. Quar. **81**: 381.
— Men and Women of. (E. I. Sears) Nat. Q. **4**: 1.
— Mineralogy of. Portfo.(Den.) **11**: 409.
— Morality of. (D. A. Wasson) No. Am. **107**: 501.
— Mythology of. (W. E. Gladstone) 19th Cent. **6**: 746.
— — and Religion of; a Reply to Mr. Gladstone. (G. W. Cox) Fraser, **100**: 798.
— Odyssey. Quar. **147**: 533.
— — Authorship of. (F. W. Newman) Fraser, **88**: 575.
— — Bryant's. (J. B. Thayer) O. & N. **6**: 339.
— — Du Cane's. Blackw. **129**: 368.
— — Hayman's. Brit. Q. **58**: 414.
— — New Version of. Ed. R. **51**: 463.
— — Text of. Chr. Rem. **52**: 47.
— — Translations of. Blackw. **91**: 345.
— — — Worsley's. Ed. R. **117**: 353.
— Ossian, Chaucer. (H. D. Thoreau) Dial, **4**: 290.
— Parting of Hector and Andromache. (G. Smith) Canad. Mo. **4**: 109.
— Penelope and other Women of. Cornh. **32**: 52.
— Philosophy of. Am. Ecl. **2**: 146.
— Place of, in History. (W. E. Gladstone) Contemp. **24**: 1, 175. Same art. Liv. Age, **122**: 361, 742. Same art. Ecl. M. **83**: 129, 471.
— Plains of Troy. Quar. **66**: 355.
— Poems of. So. R. n. s. **23**: 69. — Am. Q. **2**: 307. — (S. North) New Eng. **3**: 216. — Westm. **46**: 381. — Quar. **43**: 121. — So. Lit. Mess. **13**: 698.
— — Age of. (H. W. Lucas) Month, **36**: 249, 359.
— — Authorship of. Ed. R. **133**: 358.
— — Characteristics of. (J. Cooper) Bib. Sac. **34**: 546.
— — Dialogue on. Lond. M. **4**: 481.
— — Origin of. (H. H. Milman) Quar. **44**: 121.

Homer, Poems of, Origin and Character of. (G. W. Cox) Fortn. 9: 419.
— — Problem of. (J. S. Blackie and W. D. Geddes) Contemp. 38: 281, 518.
— Pope's MS. Notes on Tickell's. (J. Conington) Fraser, 62: 260.
— Priam and Hecuba, Translation from. Macmil. 2: 383.
— Prize Dissertation on. Blackw. 14: 343.
— Purer religious Ideas of, Origin of. (F. Koester) Am. Presb. R. 14: 56.
— Reading of, in School. (J. G. R. McElroy) Penn Mo. 8: 762.
— Ruskin on ancient and modern Poets. Fraser, 53: 648.
— Dr. Schliemann on. (W. H. Mason) Macmil. 34: 448.
— Shield of Achilles. (W. E. Gladstone) Contemp. 23: 329. Same art. Ecl. M. 82: 402. Same art. Liv. Age, 121: 110. Same art. Canad. Mo. 5: 249.
— Site of Homeric Troy. (H. Schliemann) Arch. 45: 29.
— Slicing of Hector. (W. E. Gladstone) 19th Cent. 4: 752.
— Sotheby's. Blackw. 29: 668, 829. 30: 93, 847. 31: 145. 35: 1, 153. — Mo. R. 122: 222. — (D. K. Sandford) Ed. R. 51: 463.
— Study of. (J. R. Boise) Bib. Sac. 4: 323.
— Theology of. Ecl. M. 44: 399.
— Translation of. (J. H. Allen) Chr. Exam. 74: 337. — Fraser, 65: 769. — (H. Southern) Retros. 3: 167. — Westm. 77: 150.
— — Arnold on. Fraser, 63: 703. — (C. C. Felton) No. Am. 94: 108.
— — Newman on. (C. C. Felton) No. Am. 94: 541.
— Translators of. (H. M. Baird) Meth. Q. 32: 357, 619. — (J. S. Blackie) Macmil. 4: 268. — Brit. Q. 41: 290. — Dub. Univ. 59: 643. 60: 28. — Nat. R. 11: 283. Same art. Liv. Age, 67: 797. — Lond. Q. 9: 334. Same art. Ecl. M. 43: 342. — (C. A. Bristed) Am. Whig R. 4: 350.
— Trojan War. Blackw. 45: 366.
— Williams's. (W. Mure) Ed. R. 77: 44.
— Prof. Wilson on. Blackw. 82: 177. Same art. Ecl. M. 42: 238.
— Women of. (H. G. Spaulding) Chr. Exam. 68: 1. — (J. W. Stearns) No. Am. 91: 301.
— Words for Soul in. (C. F. Keary) Mind, 6: 471.
— Writings of. Penny M. 7: 133, 141.
Homer, William Bradford. (E. Holt) Am. Bib. Repos. 2d s. 8: 177. — (W. P. Lunt) Chr. Exam. 33: 111. — Chr. R. 7: 364.
Homer, Winslow, and his Paintings. Art J. 30: 225.
Homer, N. Y., Congregational Church in. (J. C. Holbrook) Cong. Q. 9: 246.
Homeric Age. (J. L. Lincoln) Bapt. Q. 4: 317.
— Life in. Temp. Bar, 60: 37. Same art. Liv. Age, 147: 180.
Homeric Ballads; translated. (W. Maginn) Fraser, 17: 1–506. 18: 71–489. 22: 383. 25: 521. 26: 61, 439.
Homeric Characters, in and out of Homer. Quar. 102: 204.
Homeric Controversy. Quar. 87: 235.
Homeric Life. Fraser, 44: 76.
Homeric Problems, New Solutions of. (H. W. Lucas) Month, 35: 22, 382. 36: 249.
Homeric Question. (T. Chase) No. Am. 71: 387. — (W. A. Stevens) Bib. Sac. 28: 627. — (W. S. Tyler) Bib. Sac. 14: 681. — Quar. 125: 440.
— New Theory of. (W. D. Geddes) Contemp. 26: 234.
— New View of. (A. S. Murray) Contemp. 23: 218.
Homeric Studies. (M. Heilprin) Nation, 9: 416.
Homerology. (W. E. Gladstone) Contemp. 27: 632, 803. 28: 282.
Homerton Academy. Cong. M. 8: 133, 187.
— Recollections of. (R. Halley) Cong. 3: 257.
Homestead, Memories of the; a Poem. Mo. Rel. M. 7: 295.
Homestead Bill. (R. J. Walker) Contin. Mo. 2: 627.
Homestead Exemption Act of N. H. Hunt, 25: 197.
Homicidal Monomania. Liv. Age, 36: 87.
Homicide. Chamb. J. 42: 582. — (C. C. Carroll) West. Law J. 4: 289.
— in Self-Defense. (S. D. Thompson) Am. Law R. 14: 545.
— Law of. (J. Parker) No. Am. 72: 178.
— Memoirs of a. Fraser, 13: 428.
Homiletics. (C. F. Schaeffer) Evang. R. 5: 301. — Evang. R. 7: 181. — (C. P. Krauth) Evang. R. 9: 338.
— and Hermeneutics, Relative Value of, to the Preacher. (S. M. Vail) Meth. Q. 26: 38, 371.
— and Pulpit Eloquence. Meth. Q. 1: 283.
— Distinctive Nature of, and Reasons for Cultivation. (W. G. T. Shedd) Am. Presb. R. 14: 384.
— Evangelical. Meth. Q. 7: 63.
— Kidder's. (F. G. Hibbard) Meth. Q. 24: 641.
— Porter's, English Edition of. (G. Payne) Cong. M. 19: 739.
Homilies, English Metrical. Dub. Univ. 60: 305.
Homines apud Inferos. So. Lit. Mess. 6: 55.
Homme qui crie, L'. (F. A. Dixon) Canad. Mo. 15: 92.
Homœopathic Miracle. Tait, n. s. 19: 665. Same art. Liv. Age, 35: 554.
Homœopathist, Confessions of a. Tait, n. s. 13: 185.
Homœopathy. (Sir B. C. Brodie) Fraser, 64: 337. Same art. Liv. Age, 71: 157. — Quar. 71: 46. — Knick. 4: 177. — Ed. R. 50: 504. — Select J. 3: [68. — Chr. Exam. 32: 245. — Penny M. 3: 115. — (K. Thaler) Tait, n. s. 18: 732. Same art. Liv. Age, 32: 517. — Mo. R. 139: 526. 158: 226.
— and Allopathy. (E. L. Godkin) Nation, 5: 335, 439.
— and Animal Magnetism. Mo. R. 146: 471.
— and Orthodoxy. Putnam, 2: 639.
— examined. So. Q. 28: 177.
— Hahnemann on. (D. K. Sandford) Ed. R. 50: 504. — Ecl. R. 95: 16. Same art. Liv. Age, 33: 105.
— Principles, Theory, and Practice of. Tait, n. s. 13: 391.
Homoplasy and Mimicry. (A. W. Bennett) Nature, 5: 12.
Honduras, Gulf of, Islands in. Dem. R. 31: 544.
Hone, Wm. Antiquary, 2: 295. — Once a Week, 25: 290.
— Verses to. (C. Lamb) Lond. M. 12: 16.
Honest Farmer. (J. Payn) Belgra. 39: 457.
Honest Farmer; a Poem. Fraser, 96: 748.
Honest John Vane. (J. W. DeForest) Atlan. 32: 66–574.
Honest Miller; a Poem. Mo. Rel. M. 20: 40.
Honest Penny; a Story. Chamb. J. 16: 233, 250.
Honesty. Lond. M. 7: 151.
— Common, as an indispensable Part of the Christian Religion. Ev. Sat. 11: 258.
— National. (L. E. Chittenden) Putnam, 11: 625.
— Nature and Uses of. Penny M. 9: 31.
Honey, Wild. Chamb. J. 36: 408.
Honeymoon, The. (S. L. Blanchard) Belgra. 8: 426.
— Occultation of. (L. Stockton) Lippinc. 27: 74.
Honeymooning. Tinsley, 26: 395.
Hong-Kong, China. Penny M. 11: 500. — Mus. 42: 360.
— Canton, and Macao. Cornh. 37: 278. Same art. Liv. Age, 137: 51.
— With Opium to. All the Year, 15: 537.
Honolulu, Feast of Lanterns in. (Lieut. Bleecker) Putnam, 1: 558.
Honolulu Newspaper. Chamb. J. 23: 34. Same art. Ecl. M. 34: 488. Same art. Liv. Age, 44: 549.
Honolulu Society. Overland, 1: 561.
Honor among Thieves. Chamb. J. 19: 373.
— Law of. (E. A. Freeman) Fortn. 26: 731. — Fraser, 71: 316.
— Sense of. Ox. Prize Ess. 2: 167.
Honors divided. (M. Farrow) Tinsley, 16: 57–637. 17: 1–643.
Hon. Alice Brand's Correspondence. Tinsley, 1: 110–749.

Honorable Gentlemen; a Tale. Bentley, **62**: 205, 302.
Honoria. Tinsley, **14**: 432.
Honorius, Pope. (T. B. Parkinson) Month, **38**: 69.
— Orthodoxy of. Dub. R. **64**: 173.
— Renouf on. Dub. R. **63**: 200. **66**: 372. — (F. Bottalla) Dub. R. **69**: 361. **71**: 85. **72**: 137.
Hood, Thomas, with cuts. (F. Burditt) Westm. **29**: 119. — (C. C. Clarke) Gent. M. n. s. **8**: 659. — (T. H S. Escott) Belgra. **32**: 337. — (J. B. Fox) Chr. Exam. **69**: 415. — (H. Giles) Atlan. **6**: 513. — (G. Gilfillan) Tait, n. s. **14**: 69. Same art. Ecl. M. **10**: 496. Same art. Liv. Age, **12**: 540. — (S. C. Hall) Art J. **17**: 185. Same art. Ecl. M. **65**: 218. — (G. Massey) Hogg, **13**: 320. Same art. Ecl. M. **35**: 169. Same art. Nat. M. **7**: 133. — (D. Masson) Macmil. **2**: 315. — (S. R. T. Mayer) Victoria, **8**: 385–481. — (E. C. Stedman) Scrib. **7**: 463. — with portrait, Once a Week, **27**: 100. — Dub. Univ. **81**: 99. — St. James, **20**: 455. — Hogg, **2**: 209. — Liv. Age, **5**: 310. **6**: 64, 116. **42**: 409. **61**: 3. **114**: 225. — Lond. Q. **21**: 90. — So. Lit. Mess. **18**: 600. — (H. W. Lucy) Gent. M. n. s. **14**: 77.
— Bridge of Sighs. Liv. Age, **1**: 198.
— Charge of Plagiarism against. (G. T. Lowth) Temp. Bar, **36**: 273.
— Comic Annual, 1839. Mo. R. **148**: 359.
— — 1842. Mo. R. **156**: 600.
— Elm-Tree. Colburn, **66**: 1.
— Etching moralized. Colburn, **67**: 1.
— The Forge. Colburn, **68**: 289.
— Genius of. (F. W. Shelton) Am. Whig R. **3**: 481. — (F. W. Shelton) Knick. **36**: 131.
— Gossip about. Colburn, **82**: 337.
— Haunted Horse. Liv. Age, **2**: 472.
— Hood's Own. Tait, n. s. **13**: 738.
— Last Laugh with. Chamb. J. **34**: 92. Same art. Liv. Age, **66**: 783.
— Letters of. All the Year, **35**: 279.
— Life and Writings of. Quar. **114**: 332. Same art. Liv. Age, **79**: 361. — (J. Fraser) Westm. **95**: 337. Same art. Liv. Age, **109**: 451.
— Memorial to. Nat. M. **5**: 397.
— Memorials of. Brit. Q. **46**: 323. — Dub. R. **49**: 300. — Liv. Age, **66**: 380
— More Hullabaloo. Colburn, **66**: 145.
— National Tales. Mo. R. **112**: 431. — Lond. M. **17**: 454.
— Poetry of. Chamb. J. **22**: 103. — Chr. Obs. **63**: 677. — Chr. Rem. **11**: 316. — Dub. R. **20**: 386. — Ed. R. **83**: 375. — Knick. **30**: 349. — Westm. **31**: 119. — Dub. Univ. **27**: 563. Same art. with portrait, Ecl. M. **8**: 289. — Mo. R. **114**: 253. — Ecl. R. **83**: 285.
— Recollections of. Brit. Q. **46**: 323. Same art. Ecl. M. **70**: 96, 198. Same art. Liv. Age, **95**: 323.
— Rhymes for the Times. Colburn, **59**: 528. **60**: 83–392.
— Sad Side of the Humorist's Life. Ecl. R. **114**: 659. Same art. Liv. Age, **72**: 220.
— Tale of a Trumpet. Colburn, **62**: 120. **63**: 157.
— Tylney Hall. Tait, n. s. **1**: 751. — Mo. R. **135**: 555.
— Up the Rhine. Mo. R. **151**: 109.
— Whims and Oddities. Blackw. **21**: 45. — Mus. **10**: 298. — Lond. M. **16**: 496. **19**: 537.
— Works of. Liv. Age, **76**: 126.
Hood, Mount, and the Sierra Sandia, Ascents of. Bentley, **62**: 368. Same art. Ecl. M. **70**: 368.
— First Ascent of. Liv. Age, **43**: 321.
Hoodlum Band; a Condensed Novel. (Bret Harte) Temp. Bar, **52**: 87. Same art. Godey, **96**: 33.
Hooft, Pieter C., the Dutch Milton. Cornh. **35**: 596. — Fraser, **49**: 349.
Hook, James. Percy Mallory. Portfo.(Den.) **32**: 121.
Hook, James Clarke. (F. G. Stephens) Portfo. **2**: 181.
Hook, Theodore Edward. (H. B. Baker) Belgra. **34**: 193. — (S. C. Hall) Art J. **17**: 105. — (Mr. and Mrs. S. C. Hall) Atlan. **15**: 477. — Bentley, **10**: 320. — with portrait, Colburn, **63**: 137. Same art. Ecl. M. **16**: 399. — with portrait, Fraser, **9**: 436. **24**: 518. — Quar. **72**: 29. — Dub. Univ. **33**: 81. — Westm. **28**: 169. — Liv. Age, **35**: 469. — Chamb. J. **5**: 91. — Ecl. M **27**: 258.
— Anecdotes of. Mus. **43**: 356. **44**: 93.
— Barham's Life of. Colburn, **85**: 66.
— Gossip about. Colburn, **80**: 461.
— Maxwell. Westm. **15**: 155.
— Peregrine Bunce. (J. G. Lockhart) Quar. **72**: 53.
— Sayings and Doings. Blackw. **15**: 334. **17**: 221. — Lond. M. **11**: 379. **21**: 381.
Hook, Walter Farquhar, Dean of Chichester. Cong. **4**: 321.
— Call to Union answered. Fraser, **19**: 1.
— Life and Letters. Quar. **148**: 33.
— Sermons. Ecl. R. **76**: 502.
Hooke, Robert. Ed. R. **152**: 1.
Hooker, Herman, with portrait. Internat. M. **5**: 442.
Hooker, Sir Joseph Dalton. (A. Gray) Nature, **16**: 537. — with portrait, Pract. M. **7**: 225. — with portrait, Pop. Sci. Mo. **4**: 237.
Hooker, Richard. (A. P. Stanley) Good Words, **14**: 26. — (E. P. Whipple) Atlan. **22**: 674. — Ecl. R. **116**: 277. — No. Brit. **26**: 463. Same art. Liv. Age, **56**: 328. — Sharpe, **13**: 282.
— Ecclesiastical Polity. Cong. M. **13**: 645.
— Quaintness of. Atlan. **37**: 727.
— Visit to Parish of. Chr. Obs. **20**: 615.
Hooker, Saml., Biog. of. (J. Farmer) Am. Q. Reg. **9**: 230.
Hooker, Sir Wm. Jackson. (A. Gray) Am. J. Sci. **91**: 1.
Hoole, Charles. Am. J. Educ. **17**: 191.
Hoops and Farthingales. Godey, **62**: 109.
Hoop-Skirts; Female Cooperage. Putnam, **10**: 123.
Hooper, John, Memoir of. Cong. M. **9**: 113.
Hooper, Lucy, Poetical Remains of. Dem. R. **11**: 90.
Hooper, Robert. (J H. Sheppard) N. E. Reg. **22**: 283.
Hooper, Stephen. (S. L. Knapp) Bost. Mo. **1**: 135.
Hooper, William. Letters. Hist. M. **14**: 87.
Hoopoe, The. Penny M. **5**: 33.
Hoosac Tunnel. (R. Connor) Nation, **21**: 114. — (W. Gladden) Scrib. **1**: 143. — Nature, **9**: 170. — J. Frankl. Inst. **91**: 145.
— Ventilation of. (T. Doane) Ecl. Engin. **16**: 359.
Hooton, Charles. Poems. Colburn, **75**: 285, 402. **76**: 141, 359, 480. **77**: 29–482.
— Sketch of. Colburn, **79**: 397.
Hops. (J. R. Jackson) Good Words, **13**: 645. — Chamb. J. **40**: 333. — House. Words, **6**: 109.
— Among. (A. W. Drayson) St. James, **10**: 432.
— and Beer. All the Year, **36**: 180.
— Cultivation of. (L. J. Jennings) Once a Week, **7**: 109. — Penny M. **4**: 452. — Ed. R. **116**: 491.
— of Surrey. (L. Crow) Once a Week, **17**: 370.
Hop Garden; a Kentish Sketch. Dub. Univ. **42**: 173.
Hop Gardens, English. All the Year, **22**: 102.
— of Kent. (A. H. Japp) Good Words, **20**: 788.
Hop-Pickers, Three Weeks with. Fraser, **96**: 635. Same art. Liv. Age, **135**: 789.
Hop-Picking. (M. Deane) Lippinc. **16**: 630.
Hop-Raising in Kent. (I. Kentish) Once a Week, **5**: 492.
Hop Trade in New England Hunt, **14**: 395.
Hope, James, Memoir of. Chr. Obs. **42**: 780.
Hope, Thomas. Anastasius. (W. Gifford) Quar. **24**: 511. — (P. Q. Keegan) Colburn, **160**: 674. — Blackw. **10**: 200, 312. — Lond. M. **1**: 76 — Portfo.(Den.) **23**: 433. — (E. Everett) No. Am. **11**: 271. — (Syd. Smith) Ed. R. **35**: 92. — Ed. Mo. R. **4**: 423. — Mo. R. **91**: 1, 131.
— Origin and Prospects of Man. Mo. R. **125**: 390.
Hope Rashleigh; a Tale. All the Year, **14**: 65.

Hope Scott, J. R., Newman's Memorial to. (J. H. Coleridge) Month, **19**: 274.
Hope. Argosy, **11**: 429. — Chr. Obs. **12**: 78.
Hope deferred at Sea. All the Year, **23**: 446.
Hope for our Country. (C. P. Sheldon) Chr. R. **18**: 372.
Hopes and Fears; a Novel. (C. Yonge) Liv. Age, **64**: 77–467. **65**: 140, 412, 671. **66**: 31, 301. **67**: 644, 707, 772. **68**: 3–259.
Hopeful Tackett. (R. Wolcott) Contin. Mo. **2**: 262.
Hopeless Attachment. (T. M. Osborne) O. & N. **8**: 169.
Hôpital, Michel de l'. *See* L'Hôpital.
Hopkins, Albert. (J. Bascom) Bib. Sac. **32**: 350.
Hopkins, Edward, and the Hopkins Bequest. Am. J. Educ. **28**: 177.
Hopkins, Ezekiel, Bishop, Works of. Ecl. R. **13**: 97.
— — Pratt's Edition. Chr. Obs. **9**: 498.
Hopkins, George W., with portrait. Dem. R. **41**: 506.
Hopkins, John B., with portrait. Once a Week, **27**: 230.
Hopkins, John Henry, Bp. of Vt. Am. Church R. **25**: 260.
— Writings of. (A. Lamson) Chr. Exam. **20**: 342.
Hopkins, Johns. (C. H. Dall) Unita. R. **12**: 152.
Hopkins, Mark, with portrait. Ecl. M. **42**: 568. — with portrait, Ecl. M. **89**: 634. — Am. J. Educ. **11**: 219.
— Address at Mount Holyoke Seminary. (G. B. Emerson) Chr. Exam. **30**: 340.
— Lowell Lectures. (N. Porter) New Eng. **4**: 401. — (E. Peabody) Chr. Exam. **41**: 216. — (J. W. Alexander) Princ. **18**: 359.
Hopkins, Samuel. (L. Whiting) Cong. Q. **6**: 1. — Nat. M. **1**: 554.
— Character of. (J. H. Jones) University Q. **3**: 95.
— Park's Memoir of. (L. Bacon) New Eng. **10**: 448.
— Theology of. (E. Pond) Bib. Sac. **19**: 633.
— Works of. (E Beecher) Bib. Sac. **10**: 63.
Hopkins, Stephen. (B. F. DeCosta) N. E. Reg. **33**: 300.
Hopkins Genealogy. (S. Judd) N. E. Reg. **5**: 43.
Hopkinsianism and Presbyterian Church in America. (E. H. Gillett) Hist. M. **18**: 193.
— before Hopkins. Am. Presb. R. **20**: 110.
— Letter from Roger Sherman on. Am. Presb. R. **19**: 680.
— Sketch of. Chr. Exam. **33**: 169.
Hopkinson, Francis, with portrait. (C. R. Hildeburn) Pennsyl. M. **2**: 314.
Hopkinson, Joseph, Biog. of. (F. Wharton) Hunt, **7**: 397.
Hopkinton, Mass., Ecclesiastical Council at, Sept. 19, 1735. Cong. Q. **5**: 342.
— Records of. N. E. Reg. **14**: 155, 209.
Hopley, Mrs., Memoir of. Cong. M. **14**: 325.
Hopper, C. Meth. M. **25**: 395.
Hoppner, John, and Sir Thomas Lawrence. Chamb. J. **35**: 327. Same art. Liv. Age, **71**: 35.
Horace. (M. Seton) Colburn, **165**: 813, 1369. — (G. Watson) So. M. **9**: 57. — (J. Etheredge) Peop. J. **10**: 270. — Lond. Soc. **17**: 183.
— and Catullus. Temp. Bar, **15**: 588.
— — Love Songs of. (R.W. Buchanan) St. James, **9**: 343.
— and his Translators. Brit. Q. **51**: 37. — (J. Hannay) Quar. **104**: 325. Same art. Ecl. M. **46**: 301.
— and his Works. Brit. Q. **18**: 202.
— and Juvenal. (J. W. Ball) Land We Love, **3**: 462.
— — as Satirists. Knick. **33**: 485. **34**: 37.
— and Tasso. Ed. R. **92**: 533. Same art. Liv. Age, **27**: 385. Same art. Ecl. M. **22**: 170.
— and Virgil, Translators of. (D. Casserly) Cath. World, **25**: 721. **26**: 309, 732. **27**: 35.
— Art of Conduct. Cornh. **34**: 23.
— Burns, and Béranger. Cornh. **17**: 150. Same art. Liv. Age, **97**: 3.
— Conington's Translation. Nat. R. **17**: 26. — Liv. Age, **77**: 362.
— Failure of the Translators of. Blackw. **13**: 542.
Horace, Life and Writings of. (H. H. Milman) Quar. **62**: 287. Same art. Mus. **35**: 30.
— Lincoln's. Chr. R. **16**: 408.
— Love Songs of. (W. E. Aytoun) Dub. Univ. **34**: 221.
— Lyrics of. Blackw. **116**: 498. **118**: 112, 336.
— Lytton's Translation. Quar. **127**: 478. — (B. L. Gildersleeve) N. Ecl. **6**: 471.
— Martin's Translations. Ed. R. **133**: 530. — Fraser, **61**: 675. — Nat. R. **11**: 93. Same art. Liv. Age, **67**: 323.
— New Translations of. Fraser, **42**: 672.
— Ode I., Lib. I., translated. Fraser, **40**: 317.
— Odes of. Fraser, **13**: 739. **14**: 87–739. — Prosp. R. **9**: 272.
— — and Epodes of, Sewell's. Ed. R. **93**: 91.
— — and recent Translators. Lond. Q. **42**: 1.
— — Newman's Translation. Colburn, **98**: 339. — Ecl. R. **97**: 695.
— — Thornton's Translation. (J. H. McDaniels) Nation, **27**: 166.
— — translated. Dub. Univ. **23**: 528.
— Penn's Moral Odes of. Mo. R. **82**: 357.
— Poet of Middle-aged Men. Fraser, **74**: 309.
— Rambling Remarks on. Fraser, **31**: 39, 253, 561.
— Satires of. (S. Hart) Am. Church R. **30**: 435.
— Satire I., Lib. I., transl. by T. Martin. Fraser, **75**: 496.
— Satire IX., transl. by T. Martin. Fraser, **78**: 214.
— Sewell's. Dub. Univ. **37**: 241. — Ed. R. **94**: 47.
— Translations from. (W. C. Bryant) No. Am. **5**: 334. — Dub. Univ. **1**: 433, 653. — Gen. Repos. **1**: 129.
— Translations of. Blackw. **94**: 184.
— — Recent, 1868. Chr. Rem. **56**: 19.
— Two Philosophies of. Cornh. **32**: 64.
— Vernal Odes of. (W. M. Nevin) Mercersb. **3**: 144.
— Way's Translation. Dub. Univ. **88**: 494.
— without his Toga; Poetical Epistles. (E. Heron) Temp. Bar, **38**: 431. **39**: 34, 196. **41**: 43, 194.
— Works and Times of. Chr. Rem. **18**: 267.
— Wrangham's Translations. Ecl. R. **34**: 502. — Blackw. **7**: 369. — Lond. M. **5**: 277.
Horace; a Novel. (M. Seton) Colburn, **164**: 65–687. **165**: 813–1369. **166**: 90.
Horace at Cambridge; a Poem. (A. D. Hammond) Dub. Univ. **85**: 479.
Horace Carew; a Tale. Sharpe, **45**: 295. **46**: 12–247.
Horace Draper; a Tale. (J. T. W. Bacot) Colburn, **158**: 181–699. **159**: 101–444.
Horace Saltoun; a Novel. Cornh. **3**: 229, 299, 433.
Horæ Academicæ. Dub. Univ. **2**: 211.
Horæ Apocalypticæ, Elliott's. Chr. Obs. **65**: 184.
Horæ Cantabrigienses. Blackw. **3**: 548. **4**: 63. **6**: 47. **7**: 292. **8**: 123, 373. **10**: 552. **15**: 42.
Horæ Catnachianæ. Fraser, **19**: 407.
Horæ Danicæ. (R. P. Gillies) Blackw. **7**: 73. **8**: 290, 646. **9**: 43.
Horæ Dramaticæ. (T. L. Peacock) Fraser, **56**: 482.
Horæ Evangelicæ, Birk's. Chr. Obs. **53**: 450.
Horæ Gallicæ. Fraser, **1**: 79.
Horæ Germanicæ. (R. P. Gillies) Blackw. **6**: 121–525. **7**: 235–545. **8**: 45, 384, 543. **9**: 481. **11**: 38. **12**: 218. **13**: 3, 649. **14**: 377 **16**: 194, 312, 369. **17**: 299, 417, 673. **19**: 404. **21**: 214, 464. **22** 300. **24**: 155.
Horæ Gregorianæ. Dub. Univ. **30**: 224.
Horæ Hispanicæ. (R. P. Gillies) Blackw. **6**: 481. **7**: 259. **8**: 360.
Horæ Italicæ. (R. P. Gillies) Blackw. **18**: 545. **19**: 173. **20**: 164. **21**: 727. **22**: 571.
Horæ Lutetianæ. Fraser, **12**: 551.
Horæ Nicotiana. (R. P. Gillies) **5**: 47, 205.
Horæ Offleanæ. Bentley, **9**: 272, 413.
Horæ Sinicæ. (D. M. Moir) Fraser, **11**: 542. **17**: 259.

Horaks, Tent-Life with. (G. Kennan) Putnam, 13: 18.
Horatian Lyrics. Blackw. 112: 484. 115: 299.
Horburg, the Swedish Painter; translated. (G.P. Marsh) Am. Ecl. 1: 313.
Horites, The. (J. Campbell) Canad. J. n. s. 13: 510.
Hormuz, Island of. (A. W. Stiffe) Geog. M. 1: 12.
Horn, Count van. Chamb. J. 7: 169.
Horn, Rauhen-Haus at. Am. J. Educ. 3: 603.
Horn and Tortoise-Shell. (A. Aikin) J. Frankl. Inst. 30: 256.
Horn, The, as a Charter of Conveyance. (S. Pegge) Arch. 3: 1.
Horns belonging to different Families, etc. (S. Pegge) Arch. 3: 13.
— given by Henry I. to Carlisle Cathedral. (W. Cole) Arch. 5: 340.
— Vision of. (C. Lamb) Lond. M. 11: 29.
Hornby Castle. Lond. Soc. 37: 168.
Horne, Bp. George, Life of. (N. E. Cornwall) Am. Church R. 1: 591. — (H. J. Rose) Contemp. 4: 525.
Horne, Richard Henry. Cosmo de' Medici. Dub. Univ. 86: 504. — Mo. R. 143: 133.
— Criticisms on Contemporaries. Tinsley, 7: 626.
— New Spirit of the Age. Westm. 41: 357. — Dem. R. 15: 49. — So. Q. 7: 312. 15: 41. — So. Lit. Mess. 11: 55.
— Poetry of. (W. W. Tullock) St. James, 38: 370.
Horne, Thomas H. Introduction to the Scriptures. (C. W. Upham) No. Am. 17: 130.
— — Davidson's Edition. Chr. Obs. 57: 302, 382.
Horne, William. Fraser, 33: 7.
Horneman, Fred. Travels from Cairo to Mourzouk. (H. Brougham) Ed. R. 1: 130.
Horner, Francis. (F. Bowen) No. Am. 78: 174. — (J. L. Lincoln) Chr. R. 19: 361.
— Correspondence of. Liv. Age, 41: 159.
— Memoir of. Ecl. R. 77: 506. — Mo. R. 160: 531.
— Memoirs and Correspondence. (Lord Monteagle) Ed. R. 78: 261. — Quar. 72: 108. — Tait, n. s. 10: 296. — Blackw. 1: 1. — Ecl. Mus. 3: 536.
Horner, Leonard. Macmil. 10: 319.
Hornet of New South Wales, Instinct of. (J. McGarvie) J. Frankl. Inst. 6: 184.
Hornet, Ship, Shipping-List of the, 1813. N. E. Reg. 28: 392.
Hornswoggled, a Western Plant. Lond. Soc. 39: 265.
Horologium, Roman, found in Italy. (R. Gough) Arch. 10: 172.
Horologia of Ancients. (B. Bell; R. Gale) Arch. 6: 133.
Horology. All the Year, 21: 487. Same art. Ev. Sat. 7: 625. — Chamb. J. 41: 807.
— Curiosities in Horological Reckoning. (W. F. Mappin) Internat. R. 11: 179.
Horrocks, Jeremiah, the Astronomer. Ed. R. 152: 1. — Argosy, 18: 379. — Nature, 8: 117, 137. Same art. Liv. Age, 118: 179. — Dub. Univ. 83: 709.
— Memorial to. Nature, 11: 31.
— Memoirs of, Whatton's. Pract. M. 5: 159.
Horror; a true Tale. Blackw. 89: 64.
Horror in the House. Chamb. J. 34: 177, 198.
Horse, The. De Bow, 18: 619.
— Action of. (A. H. Garrod) Nature, 10: 39.
— Age of, Judging. Penny M. 1: 147.
— Anatomy of, Steele's. Nature, 15: 310.
— and Man. (A. A. Knox) Once a Week, 1: 114.
— and Owner. (J. G. Wood) Good Words, 22: 426, 635.
— and his Rider. Fraser, 63: 114.
— Clarendon on. Dub. Univ. 21: 186.
— Eclipse, The Racer. All the Year, 19: 223.
— Equine History. (J. J. Nicholls) Victoria, 28: 305.
— Foot of, Miles on. Quar. 78: 49. Same art. Liv. Age, 10: 305.
Horse, The, Fossil, from the Tertiary of Nebraska. (O. C. Marsh) Am. J. Sci. 96: 374.
— Sir Francis Head on. Chamb. J. 35: 19.
— How he is cheated and abused. (E. I. Sears) Nat. Q. 27: 346.
— in Geology. Pop. Sci. Mo. 16: 258.
— in the Malayan Archipelago. Penny M. 7: 312.
— in modern Society. (E. L. Godkin) Nation, 15: 277.
— in Motion. (T. A. Dodge) Dial (Ch.), 2: 288.
— Locomotion of. Pop. Sci. Mo. 6: 129.
— Necessary Food for. (M. Bixio) Ecl. Engin. 19: 245.
— Question of Ribs in. (T. M. Müller) Pop. Sci. Mo. 7: 214.
— Rarey's Method of taming. Chamb. J. 29: 261.
— Saddle-. (G. E. Waring, jr.) Scrib. 15: 84.
— Something about. (T. B. Thorpe) Harper, 13: 751.
— Thoroughbred. (G. E. Waring, jr.) Scrib, 15: 157.
— — English and Arabian. (W. S. Blunt) 19th Cent. 8: 411.
— Tractive Power of. (E. Morris) J. Frankl. Inst. 28: 79.
— Wild, Species of. Penny M. 14: 414.
Horses. (C. J. Lever) Blackw. 98: 679. — Chamb. J. 42: 502.
— American, Anecdotes of. Penny M. 9: 19.
— and Horse-Copers. (A. Wynter) Once a Week, 11: 453.
— and Horse-Dealing. Tinsley, 8: 277.
— and Horsiness. Temp. Bar, 14: 443.
— and Riding, Nevile on. (G. E. Waring, jr.) Nation, 26: 420.
— and their Feet. (Sir G. W. Cox) Fraser, 102: 784. Same art. Pop. Sci. Mo. 18: 468.
— and Treatment of. (M Chambers) Chamb. J. 52: 289.
— Anecdotes of. Bentley, 31: 225. Same art. Ecl. M. 26: 20. Same art. Liv. Age, 33: 249.
— Arabian. (Abd-el Kader) House. Words, 7: 190. — (R. D. Upton) Fraser, 94: 375. — Chamb. J. 41: 84. Same art. Ecl. M. 62: 291.
— Bits and Bearing-Reins. Blackw. 117: 742.
— Bitting of. Penny M. 5: 159.
— Breeding of. Ed. R. 138: 426.
— Breeds and Races of. All the Year, 11: 319.
— British. Penny M. 10: 225.
— Classes and Breeds of. (D. Low) Ed. New Philos. J. 40: 179.
— English. Ed. R. 120: 114.
— — and Eastern. (Sir F. H. Doyle) Fortn. 35: 572, 704.
— English Thoroughbreds and their Victories. Once a Week, 17: 275.
— in the East, and Treatment. Penny M. 11: 447, 454.
— Introduction into N. Am. Colonies. Hist. M. 5: 353.
— Ladies' Hacks and Hunters. Tinsley, 1: 470.
— Performing. Chamb. J. 35: 300.
— Polydactyle. (O. C. Marsh) Am. J. Sci. 117: 499.
— Real. All the Year, 26: 510.
— Roman and Neapolitan. Penny M. 14: 374.
— Smith on. Mo. R. 155: 378.
— Something about. Scrib. 14: 195.
— Thoroughbred. (H. Comstock) Internat. R. 7: 197.
— — at School. All the Year, 43: 442.
— Vital Statistics of Cavalry. (T. G. Balfour) J. Statis. Soc. 43: 251.
— Wild, and Kangaroos. Gent. M. n. s. 26: 440.
Horse Armor. *See* Armor.
Horse-Breaking in the Bush. Chamb. J. 58: 426.
— in the 19th Century. Macmil. 3: 131.
Horse-Car Manners. Ev. Sat. 10: 523, 595.
Horse-Dealer; a Tale of Denmark. (C. Winther) Blackw. 64. 232.
Horse-Dealing, Extraordinary. All the Year, 19: 252.
— Screws. Colburn, 62: 453.

Horseflesh as Food. (P. Blot) Galaxy, 3: 280. — Blackw. 103: 547. — Ev. Sat. 5: 681. 11: 487. — House. Words, 13: 313. — Temp. Bar, 19: 31. *See* Hippophagy.
Horse Food. Penny M. 5: 94.
Horse-Growers, Our great. (C. W. Elliott) Galaxy, 7: 413.
Horse-Guards, Tape at the. All the Year, 6: 568.
Horse-Keeping and Horse-Dealing. Cornh. 3: 614.
Horsemanship. (F. Rogers) U. S. Serv. M. 1: 263. — New Eng. M. 9: 160. — Blackw. 105: 106. — Mo. R. 149: 201.
— Hints to Ladies on. Godey, 37: 45-361. 64: 246.
— Riding, Remarks about. Godey, 66: 252.
— Saddling and Bitting. Fraser, 79: 808.
See Equestrians.
Horse Nails by Machinery. Pract. M. 1: 12.
Horse Pictures, Pair of. All the Year, 19: 270.
Horse-Power, Nominal. (J. M. Gray) Ecl. Engin. 7: 96.
— of Steam Engines. (E. Brown) J. Frankl. Inst. 91: 187.
— of Steam Boilers. J. Frankl. Inst. 91: 187. 92: 91. 94: 91, 377. 96: 396.
Horse Question. (W. Chambers) Chamb. J. 50: 673.
Horse-Racing. (C. J. Apperley) Quar. 49: 381. — (E. L. Godkin) Nation, 3: 293. — All the Year, 37: 14, 152. — St. Paul's, 2: 34.
— Among the Tipsters. All the Year, 28: 156.
— and Gambling. (L. H. Curzon) Contemp. 30: 376.
— and Training Stables. All the Year, 24: 509, 540, 611.
— at Ballyskelter. All the Year, 24: 465.
— Bets on. Chamb. J. 38: 45.
— Betting on. Chamb. J. 45: 449. — (R. A. Proctor) Sup. Pop. Sci. Mo. 4: 83.
— — Bookmakers for. Chamb. J. 45: 177. — All the Year, 20: 13.
— The English Turf. Broadw. 3: 75. — Fraser, 68: 806.
— Frauds in. (J. T. Morse, jr.) Am. Law R. 12: 430.
— Grand Prize of Paris. (E. Dicey) Macmil. 8: 324.
— in France. Chamb. J. 52: 91. — (L. Lejeune) Lippinc. 26: 321, 452.
— in India. All the Year, 15: 247. Same art. Ev. Sat. 1: 405.
— Modern. Ed. R. 151: 411.
— Over the Hills to the Races. (J. C. Brenan) Sharpe, 45: 260.
— Present Condition and Prospects of. St. Paul's, 1: 60.
— Royal Family as Racers. All the Year, 36: 154.
— Running Turf in America. (H. Busbey) Harper, 41: 91, 245.
— Turf Ethics in 1868. Broadw. 1: 375.
See Derby, etc.
Horse-Railroads, American. All the Year, 5: 40. *See* Tramways.
Horseshoes. Art J. 21: 352. — Chamb. J. 43: 159. 46: 73. — Penny M. 8: 21.
— Antiquity of. (J. Milles) Arch. 3: 35.
— Chapter on. Ev. Sat. 7: 219.
— History and Antiquity of. (L. Jewitt) Stud. & Intel. Obs. 4: 411.
— India-Rubber. Pract. M. 4: 431.
— on Church Doors. Belgra. 4: 32.
Horse-Shoeing. Liv. Age, 21: 411.
— among the Ancients. (S. Pegge) Arch. 3: 39.
Horse Show at Islington. Belgra. 18: 63.
Horse Shows. Once a Week, 13: 133.
Horse Taming. (T. B. Thorpe) Harper, 22: 615. — Brit. Q. 28: 547. Same art. Ecl. M. 46: 80. — House. Words, 18: 82, 428.
— and Mr. Rarey. (G. J. W. Melville) Fraser, 58: 570. Chamb. J. 29: 261. Same art. Liv. Age, 57: 694.
Horse Trappings found at Westhall. (H. Harrod) Arch. 36: 454.
Horse-Wedding in Wales. (A. Beale) Temp. Bar, 34: 406.
Horsley, Samuel. Controversy with Dr. Priestley. Gen. Repos. 1: 26, 229. 2: 7, 257. 3: 13, 250. — (J. W. Daniel) Good Words, 15: 825.
— Sermons. Quar. 3: 398. 9: 30. — Ed. R. 17: 455. — Mo. R. 84: 82. — Anal. M. 4: 268. — Chr. Obs. 9: 557, 618.
Horsman, Edward, Speeches of. Chr. Obs. 50: 174.
Hortense, Princess, in Retirement. Colburn, 19: 341.
Hortense, Queen. Bentley, 56: 24. Same art. Ecl. M. 63: 80. — Colburn, 123: 358. Same art. Ecl. M. 55: 87. Same art. Liv. Age, 71: 584. — Liv. Age, 72: 329, 725. — For. Q. 21: 284.
— and Napoleon III. Bentley, 58: 101. Same art. Ecl. M. 65: 330.
Hortensius, Orator. (E. G. Parker) Chr. Exam. 64: 325.
Horticultural School for Women. O. & N. 3: 117.
Horticultural Society, Royal. (N. A. Lindsay) St. James, 37: 523.
Horticulture. (C. Barnard) O. & N. 5: 650, 772. 6: 243, 499. — (L. H. Sigourney) Godey, 21: 179. — Am. Q. 21: 364. — Ed. R. 34: 357.
— Address on. (Z. C. Lee) So. Lit. Mess. 5: 758.
— for the South. De Bow, 20: 214.
— in New England. (J. C. Gray) No. Am. 47: 423.
— Lindley's Theory of. Ecl. R. 73: 276.
— Possibilities of. (S. B. Parsons) Harper, 62: 515.
— Rise and Progress of. Quar. 24: 400.
— Scientific. Nature, 18: 562.
See Gardening.
Hosack, David. (J. W. Francis) Hist. M. 4: 161
Hosea Biglow's Speech in March Meeting; a Poem. (J. R. Lowell) Atlan. 17: 636.
Hosein, Death of. Good Words, 17: 695.
Hosford, Benjamin Franklin. Cong. R. 7: 390.
Hosiery, Statistics of. J. Frankl. Inst. 39: 359.
Hosmer, Geo. W. (H. W. Bellows) Unita. R. 16: 154.
Hosmer, Harriet. (L. M. Child) Liv. Age, 56: 697. — with portrait, Ecl. M. 77: 245. — Victoria, 32: 380.
Hospes Civitatis. (R. H. Stoddard) Scrib. 12: 584.
Hospice for the Dying. Irish Mo. 8: 200.
Hospices of Paris. (W. Burnet) Good Words, 15: 858.
Hospital at Ratcliffe, Mrs. Heckford's. (H. A. Page) Good Words, 15: 307.
— before Metz. (F. Lees) Good Words, 14: 322.
— Bethlehem. House. Words, 16: 121.
— Bournemouth Sanatorium. Victoria, 8: 426.
— Day with Out-Patients. (T. Fox) Good Words, 7: 232.
— for Children. (D. M. Craik) Macmil. 6: 252.
— — Visit to. Fraser, 49: 62.
— for Incurables at Putney. Cornh. 17: 735.
— for Infant Crétins. Chamb. J. 9: 296. Same art. Liv. Age, 18: 174.
— Founding a. Am. Church R. 33: 167.
— Great Northern. (E. L. Linton) Good Words, 12: 794.
— in Paris, Life in. Hogg, 13: 284.
— Inner Life of. Cornh. 5: 462.
— London, Day in. All the Year, 29: 437. — House. Words, 2: 457.
— — Night in. (E. L. Linton) Belgra. 39: 31.
— of St. Thomas. Nature, 3: 201, 503. — Ev. Sat. 11: 80.
— Royal, at Kilmainham. Dub. Univ. 7: 222.
— St. Katharine's. Fraser, 75: 65.
— Visitor's Hour. All the Year, 43: 350.
Hospitals. (S. A. Rabourg) Cath. World, 8: 42.
— and Homes for Convalescents. (F. Arnold) Good Words, 15: 659.
— and the Poor. Fraser, 93: 715.
— Benefits of. (W. A. Guy) J. Statis. Soc. 19: 12.
— Charity. Victoria, 5: 429.

Hospitals, Construction of. (T. B. Curtis) No. Am. **123**: 233. — Nature, **1**: 277.
— — New French System of. Am. Arch. **10**: 62.
— Convalescent. All the Year, **44**: 325.
— Cottage. Month, **9**: 209. — (H. C. Burdett) Am. Arch. **8**: 305.
— for Children, English. Cornh. **19**: 235.
— for the Sick, Origin of. Blackw. **1**: 130.
— Free, System of. (W. Chambers) Chamb. J. **56**: 481.
— History of. House. Words, **12**: 457. Same art. Liv. Age, **48**: 325.
— How to make them more useful. (W. F. Clarke) Contemp. **35**: 91.
— Indian Barracks and. Fraser, **69**: 691.
— Military, a Century ago. Fraser, **51**: 399.
— Florence Nightingale's Notes on. (C. A. Cummings) Chr. Exam. **77**: 286.
— Nurses and Doctors in. (W. Moxon) Contemp. **37**: 872.
— of Edinburgh and the Hospital System. Hogg, **12**: 44.
— of London. Dub. Univ. **77**: 584. — Chamb. J. **50**: 422. — Fraser, **90**: 179, 670. — (W. Gilbert) Contemp. **31**: 770.
— of Paris. Cath. World, **18**: 124.
— Pre-Christian. Westm. **108**: 426. Same art. Liv. Age, **135**: 451.
— Provincial, Defects of. Cornh. **12**: 555.
— Relation to Pauperism. (W. G. Wylie) Pop. Sci. Mo. **9**: 738.
— Rich, and poor Homes. (W. T. M. Torrens) Gent. M. n. s. **15**: 292.
— State, Condition of. (E. Hart) Fortn. **3**: 217.
— Tent. (J. F. Jenkins) Am. Soc. Sci. J. **7**: 270.
— Torts of. (E. B. Callender) Am. Law R. **15**: 640.
— Use and Abuse of. (W. F. Clark) Macmil. **25**: 448. **28**: 341.
— Ventilation of. Fraser, **92**: 577.
— Village. (A. Wynter) Good Words, **7**: 348.
See Guy's Hospital.
Hospital Administration, Honorary Element in. (R. B. Rawlings) Fraser, **104**: 57.
Hospital Life. Chamb. J. **29**: 297.
— in New York. (W. H. Rideing) Harper, **57**: 171.
Hospital Mistletoe. (J. Hatton) Belgra. **13**: 289.
Hospital Nurse. Fraser, **51**: 96.
Hospital Nurses, as they are and ought to be. Fraser, **37**: 539.
Hospital Nursing. (H. C. Burdett) Fraser, **102**: 112.
— Volunteer. (E. Garrett) Macmil. **15**: 494.
Hospital Out-Patients. All the Year, **46**: 223.
Hospital Outlines; Poems. (W. E. Henley) Cornh. **32**: 120.
Hospital Reform. (H. C. Burdett) Fraser, **103**: 501.
Hospital Reminiscences in Germany. (R. S. Dewey) Nation, **12**: 415.
Hospital Sketches. All the Year, **44**: 516.
Hospital Student. House. Words, **15**: 536.
Hospital Training School, St. Thomas's. (F. Nightingale) Good Words, **9**: 360.
Hospital Transport in War. (B. Hill) Contemp. **16**: 660.
Hospital Visiting. Chamb. J. **46**: 513.
Hospitality. (M. B. Carret) Unita. R. **5**: 528. — All the Year, **12**: 91. Macmil. **23**: 242.
— Fashionable. Dub. Univ. **75**: 703.
— Modern. (Mrs. P. W. B. Carothers) Godey, **47**: 120.
Hostages to Fortune; a Novel. (M. E. Braddon) Belgra. **25**: 5–437. **26**: 5–437. **27**: 5–437. **28**: 86.
Hostelry of thirteen hung Men. Bentley, **63**: 606.
Hostess of the Raven. All the Year, **34**: 234, 256.
— A very charming. (J. B. Hopkins) Belgra. **9**: 58.
Hot Cross Buns. (J. Goddard) Once a Week, **16**: 468.
Hot Springs in the Pyrenees. (A. S. Herschel) Intel. Obs. **8**: 439. *See* Geysers.
Hot-Water Cure. Colburn, **66**: 439.
Hotel of the Future. (M. A. Dodge) Scrib. **11**: 108.
— The great American. (R. Keeler) Lippinc. **10**: 295.
— Western, Forty Days in a. (J. M. Mackie) Putnam, **4**: 622.
Hotel Chaos at Metz, 1870. All the Year, **24**: 582.
Hôtel des Invalides. (N. S. Dodge) Lakeside, **8**: 115. — Penny M. **13**: 265.
Hotels. (G. de M. Soares) Tinsley, **28**: 447. — Chamb. J. **39**: 345. — No. Brit. **24**: 505.
— American. Putnam, **15**: 23.
— and Food in America. Temp. Bar, **2**: 345.
— Big. Chamb. J. **42**: 759.
— English. Ev. Sat. **5**: 691.
— — and Foreign. Chamb. J. **8**: 153.
— Grand, Philosophy of. (G. A. Sala) Belgra. **20**: 137.
— Large, Question of. Chamb. J. **21**: 152.
— Mammoth, Hints on. Temp. Bar, **9**: 198.
— Modern. (Mrs. A. M. Plunkett) Scrib. **6**: 486.
— Reform in. Chamb. J. **42**: 481.
— San Francisco. (W. M. Laffan) Overland, **5**: 176.
— Six European. (W. Sikes) Appleton, **16**: 14.
Hotel Bills, Batch of. Lond. Soc. **39**: supp. 28.
— Pleasures of. Macmil. **23**: 159.
Hotel Life, English. Ev. Sat. **13**: 318.
Hottentot, Skeleton of. (J. Wyman) Anthrop. R. **3**: 330.
Hottentot Race. (M. J. A. R. Smit) Pop. Sci. R. **20**: 147. — Penny M. **2**: 69.
— and Caffres. Westm. **26**: 93. Same art. Mus. **31**: 234.
Houdin, Robert, Conjurer. (O. Logan) Harper, **55**: 817.
— Confidences d'un Prestidigitateur. Bentley, **45**: 412.
— Life of. Westm. **72**: 91.
— Memoirs of. So. Lit. Mess. **29**: 401.
Houet, Madame, Sketch of. Once a Week, **6**: 524.
Hough, John, Bishop, Wilmot's Life of. (J. Foster) Ecl. R. **15**: 526.
Houghton, Douglass, Memoir of. Am. J. Sci. **55**: 217.
Houghton, John. House. Words, **14**: 453.
Houghton, R. M., Lord. *See* Milnes, R. M.
Hougoumont. Penny M. **4**: 229.
Hounds and Horses at Rome. Blackw. **62**: 485.
Hounslow Heath, Highwaymen of. All the Year, **21**: 39.
Hour before Dawn. (M. F. Curtis) Atlan. **2**: 778.
— in Janet Rye's Life; a Tale. Sharpe, **40**: 1.
— of Prayer. Fraser, **51**: 592.
— of Rain. Lippinc. **21**: 491.
Hour-Glasses and Water-Clocks. All the Year, **30**: 591.
Hour Rule in House of Representatives. (T. R. Lounsbury) Nation, **2**: 696.
Hours in a Country Library. Sharpe, **50**: 80.
— of the Day, Use of. Belgra. **24**: 290.
— of Solitude; a Poem. Dub. Univ. **12**: 695.
— on Loch Etive. (J. C. Shairp) Good Words, **14**: 151.
Housatonic, U. S. Ship, Wreck of. Once a Week, **25**: 151.
House across the Street; a Tale. All the Year, **40**: 371, 397. Same art. Liv. Age, **137**: 691.
House and Home. Once a Week, **30**: 468.
House and its three Tenants. Dub. Univ. **32**: 76, 161.
House, Anecdote about an old. Fraser, **33**: 434.
House, Blaswick. Bentley, **48**: 371, 479, 595. **49**: 196–623.
House by the Churchyard. (J. S. Le Fanu) Dub. Univ. **58**: 387, 515, 643. **59**: 5–655. **60**: 38–660. **61**: 151.
House divided against itself; a Tale. Dub. Univ. **56**: 586, 688. **57**: 15.
House dug out of Bog at Drumkelin. (W. Mudge) Arch **26**: 361.
— Englishman's new. All the Year, **39**: 5.
House in the Jungle; a Tale. Chamb. J. **55**: 425–470.
House in Piccadilly. Lond. Soc. **1**: 127–435.
House in St. John's Wood. St. James, **28**: 225.
House in the Terrain. Bentley, **16**: 425.

House of Cards. Tinsley, **2**: 165–642. **3**: 47–682. **4**: 72. Same art. Liv. Age, **98**: 548–812. **99**: 33–602. **100**: 17–559.
House of Charity, Soho Square, London. (G. A. Sala) Temp. Bar, **20**: 35.
House of Commons. (J. Morley) Fortn. **32**: 186. — Chamb. J. **56**: 301. — (W. H. Rideing) Lippinc. **27**: 453. — Ecl. M. **28**: 336. **30**: 232. — Quar. **95**: 1. Same art. Ecl. M. **33**: 174.
— Afternoon Glance at. Chamb. J. **30**: 154.
— Business of. (E. H. K. Hugessen) Macmil. **38**: 289. — Ed. R. **133**: 57.
— Dining Arrangements of. Pract. M. **1**: 351.
— Exclusion of Clergy from. (J. E. T. Rogers) Fraser, **75**: 769.
— Field Night in. (F. Wayland) Atlan. **8**: 663.
— from the Ladies' Gallery. Cornh. **8**: 429.
— Future of. (O. Hill) Fortn. **28**: 631.
— High Pressure at. All the Year, **40**: 128.
— History of. Quar. **77**: 192. — Westm. **22**: 163. — U. S. Lit. Gaz. **2**: 109. — Brit. Q. **1**: 472. — Ecl. R. **78**: 444. **80**: 650.
— Ill-Manners in. Temp. Bar, **5**: 464.
— In the Gallery of. Chamb. J. **45**: 737.
— Inside the. Blackw. **121**: 25.
— Large Number in. Westm. **27**: 209. Same art. Ecl. M. **88**: 468.
— List of Members, 1806–7. Chr. Obs. **5**: app.
— — 1818, 1820. Chr. Obs. **17**: 849. **19**: 869.
— My Night in. Chamb. J. **27**: 97.
— New House for. Art J. **4**: 64. — (H.W. Lucy) Fraser, **103**: 325. — Westm. **22**: 163.
— Personalities of. Colburn, **162**: 419, 516, 675. **163**: 53–637. **164**: 25–572.
— Personnel and Oratory of. (T. H. S. Escott) Fraser, **90**: 504.
— Procedure in, Reform of. Gent. M. n. s. **27**: 107.
— Public Business in. (H. C. Raikes) 19th Cent. **6**: 769.
— Random Recollections of. Mo. R. **138**: 487.
— Religious Instinct of. Westm. **114**: 437.
— Sketches in. Lond. Soc. **16**: 112–367.
— Speaker of. Chamb. J. **55**: 580.
— — Qualifications for. Blackw. **3**: 141.
— Strangers in. Blackw. **108**: 478.
— Townsend's History of. Mo. R. **161**: 207.
— Ventilation of. Chamb. J. **48**: 241.
House of Correction, An American. (E. P. Edwards) St. Paul's, **13**: 419.
House of Entertainment. (H. E. Scudder) Atlan. **42**: 305, 438.
House of Fernberg. (Mrs. E. F. Ellet) Godey, **25**: 258.
House of Lords. (H. Fawcett) Fortn. **16**: 491. — Fraser, **95**: 173. Same art. Liv. Age, **132**: 797. — (F. W. Rowsell) Stud. & Intel. Obs. **1**: 93. — (A. C. Sellar) Nation, **22**: 274. — Ed. R. **60**: 24. — Westm. **24**: 47. — Lond. Soc. **17**: 76, 129. — (S. F. Page) Macmil. **25**: 493. — (J. E. T. Rogers) No. Am. **131**: 44.
— American in. (F. Wayland, jr.) Atlan. **12**: 137.
— and House of Commons. Mus. **20**: 197, 370.
— and its Leaders. (G. M. Towle) Hours at Home, **10**: 432. — St. James, **25**: 449.
— before Committee and after, 1869. St. James, **24**: 603.
— Business of. (Lord Zouche) 19th Cent. **5**: 612.
— Decay and Condition of, 1878. Westm. **110**: 1.
— Defense of. Month, **43**: 277.
— Forty Years of. (F. Bowen-Graves) Fortn. **19**: 89, 231.
— Functions of. (F. W. Newman) Fraser, **75**: 785.
— in 1509. St. James, **34**: 25, 177.
— in 1511. St. James, **34**: 248.
— in 1514–15. St. James, **34**: 338.
— Night with. Ecl. M. **33**: 363.
— Pillars of the State. Blackw. **128**: 271.
House of Lords, Position and Practice of. (Lord Houghton) Fortn. **17**: 1. — (Lord Houghton) Canad. Mo. **1**: 270.
— Question of. (J. B. Kinnear) Fortn. **12**: 270.
— Random Recollections of, 1830–36. Mo. R. **140**: 22.
— Reform of. Ed. R. **64**: 232.
— Ups and Downs in. Cornh. **3**: 534.
— Use of. Dub. Univ. **6**: 71.
— What is the? Nat. R. **11**: 110.
House of McVicker. (M. L. Thompson) Atlan. **44**: 453.
House of one's own. Chamb. J. **39**: 337.
House of Pennypacker & Son. (J. W. Watson) Lippinc. **6**: 293.
House of Representatives, Rules and Customs of. (J. D. Cox) Nation, **26**: 225, 239.
House of seven Chimneys. (W. H. Ainsworth) Bentley, **56**: 441, 551. **57**: 1–551. **58**: 1, 189, 315.
House of the Sun. (C. W. Stoddard) Overland, **9**: 454.
House of Uncommons, Inquiry into the System of Blockheads, etc. Fraser, **22**: 695.
House of Yorke; a Tale. (M. A. Tincker) Cath. World, **13**: 15–746. **14**: 16–738. **15**: 18, 150, 295.
House on the Hill. (W. C. Bartlett) Overland, **10**: 259.
House opposite; a Story. (M. L. Pool) Galaxy, **3**: 212.
House that Jack built. (C. W. Stoddard) Overland, **10**: 555.
House that Jack built. (L. S. Houghton) Potter Am. Mo. **16**: 153.
House that Jack built. (M. A. Tincker) Cath. World, **16**: 212, 336, 507.
— Jewish Origin of the Story. Cong. M. **14**: 28.
House that Susan built. (S.W. Kellogg) Lippinc. **17**: 441.
House to let. (C. Dickens and others) House. Words, **18**: supp.
Houses and Homes. (W.T. Gairdner) Good Words, **3**: 411.
— and Households, Old English. Brit. Q. **14**: 369.
— and Modes of Living 500 Years ago. All the Year, **4**: 53.
— and their Memories. Once a Week, **24**: 361.
— Architecture of. Ecl. Engin. **25**: 133. — (J. J. Stevenson) Am. Arch. **8**: 15.
— Construction of. Tait, n. s. **27**: 428. — (J. Burroughs) Scrib. **11**: 333.
— — Health and Comfort in. (J. W. Hayward) Pop. Sci. Mo. **4**: 69.
— — Improper. (W. Chambers) Chamb. J. **56**: 49.
— — Improvements in. Ecl. Engin. **15**: 172.
— — in America. Putnam, **10**: 107.
— — Mistakes in. Am. Arch. **5**: 111.
— — Technical Education in. Nature, **5**: 157.
— Country, Hints for Builders of. (C. Vaux) Harper. **11**: 763.
— Damp. Ecl. Engin. **17**: 57.
— Decoration of. Cornh. **42**: 61.
— — Hints on. (W. Morris) Am. Arch. **8**: 15.
— — Taste in. Penny M. **5**: 482.
See Decoration.
— Drainage of. (F. C. Cotton) Ecl. Engin. **16**: 113. — (T. M. Reade) Ecl. Engin. **16**: 232.
— English, in the Middle Ages. House. Words, **4**: 121.
— — of the olden Time. Chamb. J. **18**: 381.
— Furnishing. (J. B. Atkinson) Good Words, **21**: 452.
— Healthy. (W. Eassie) Ecl. Engin. **15**: 436.
— House Accommodation of England and Wales. (R. H. I. Palgrave) J. Statis. Soc. **32**: 411.
— How I built myself a House. Chamb. J. **42**: 161.
— How to make and live in. Blackw. **59**: 759. **60**: 349. **61**: 727.
— in different Countries. Chamb. J. **38**: 84
— in Flats, Parisian. Ecl. Engin. **14**: 209.
— moving, in America. Penny M. **6**: 67. **11**: 284.
— Moving Brick. (C. S. Close) J. Frankl. Inst. **100**: 178.
— of the Poor in Towns. Cornh. **30**: 74.

Houses of Refuge, England. (J. C. Parkinson) Temp. Bar, **17**: 32.
— of Workingmen. Tait, n. s. **27**: 594.
— Old. Am. Mo. M. **10**: 336. — Cornh. **13**: 611.
— Our. Galaxy, **1**: 196.
— Painting. Am. Arch. **10**: 194.
— Physiognomy of. Chamb. J. **53**: 331.
— Relation of Air to. (M. von Pettenkoffer) Pop. Sci. Mo. **11**: 196.
— Suburban. St. Paul's, **7**: 516.
— Timber, Old English. Penny M. **13**: 89.
— Varieties of. Chamb. J. **10**: 226.
— Walls of. Once a Week, **20**: 4.
— Warming and ventilating. (C. Sylvester) J. Frankl. Inst. **7**: 311, 379. *See* Air; Ventilation; etc.
— Wholesome, Liddle's. Pract. M. **1**: 153.
— Wooden, Building of. Penny M. **6**: 437.
See Dwellings.
Housebreaking, Science of. Cornh. **7**: 79.
House Fly, Proboscis of. (G. Macloskie) Am. Natural. **14**: 153. *See* Fly.
Household and the Ministry, 1839. Quar. **64**: 232.
Household of Sir T. More. (A. Manning) Sharpe, **13**: 99. **14**: 157. Same art. Harper, **2**: 616, 818. **3**: 42–757.
Households and Homes. Eng. Dom. M. **15**: 75–299.
Household Art. (E. Balfour) Good Words, **20**: 658. Same art. Appleton, **22**: 556. *See* Art.
Household Book of Edward Stafford, Duke of Buckingham. (J. Gage) Arch. **25**: 311.
— of James V. of Scotland. (H. Ellis) Arch. **22**: 1.
— of a Lady in 17th Century. (J. Webb) Arch. **37**: 189.
— of the Lestranges of Hunstanton. (D Gurney) Arch. **25**: 411.
— of Thomas Cony. (E. Turnor) Arch. **11**: 22.
Household Consecration. (W. Warren) Cong. R. **9**: 475.
Household Dangers, Some common. Chamb. J. **56**: 753.
Household Duties. (P. Landriot) Cath. World, **7**: 700.
Household Economy, School Lessons in. (Mrs. W. Shaen) Good Words, **12**: 771.
Household Education, Miss Martineau's. (F. A. Farley) Chr. Exam. **46**: 443.
Household Ornaments, Old. All the Year, **25**: 416.
Household Scenery. Liv. Age, **35**: 305.
Household Servants. Fraser, **8**: 701.
Household Skeletons. (L. Kip) Putnam, **5**: 384.
Household Taste. Penn Mo. **3**: 667. — (E. E. Salisbury) New Eng. **36**: 310.
— Eastlake's. (P. W. Clayden) Fortn. **11**: 375.
Householders in Danger from Populace. Westm. **16**: 217.
House-Hunting. (E. A. Helps) Good Words, **10**: 764. — All the Year, **16**: 84. — St. Paul's, **6**: 592.
— Experiences in France. Dub. Univ **60**: 93.
Housekeepers, Hints to. Eng. Dom. M. **12**: 278. **13**: 30–343.
— Troubles and Adventures of. Chamb. J. **20**: 89.
Housekeeping. Cornh. **29**: 69 Same art. Ev. Sat. **16**: 121.
— Co-operative. (R. Fisher) 19th Cent. **2**: 283. — (E. M. King) Contemp. **23**: 66. — (Z. F. Pierce) Atlan. **22**: 513, 682. **23**: 29, 161, 286.
— English and American. Ev. Sat. **7**: 107.
— Future of. (J. V. Seart) Atlan. **48**: 331.
— Hints on. Cath. World, **10**: 610.
— How Housekeepers can save the most Time. (M. Blake) Scrib. **15**: 554-858.
— Ingenious Aids to. Lond. Soc. **14**: 414.
— Middle-Class. Tinsley, **1**: 734.
— Model. Land We Love, **5**: 52.
— Old English, 1685-1761. Lond. Soc. **8**: 226.
— The Order of a Nobleman's Household. (Sir J. Banks) Arch. **13**: 315.
House-Marks of Ditmarshers and Angeln. (B. Williams) Arch. **37**: 371.
Housewives, Fine Ladies and good. Once a Week, **20**: 30.
— Hint to. (C. Strange) Once a Week, **5**: 663.
— Mountain, of Virginia. So. Lit. Mess. **1**: 472.
Housman, Robert. (A. Alexander) Princ. **18**: 400.
— Life of. Chr. Obs. **41**: 221.
Houssaye, Arsene. Sketches and Essays. Blackw. **69**: 716.
— Men and Women of the 18th Century. So. Q. **22**: 63.
Houston, John Alexander. Art J. **21**: 69.
Houston, Sam. (W. H. Rhodes) Pioneer, **4**: 162. — Niles's Reg. **35**: 139. **36**: 171, 179.
— and his Republic. Am. Whig R. **5**: 566.
— Assault on Mr. Stanberry. Ann. Reg. **7**: 117. — Niles's Reg. **42**: 128, 259.
— Fraud imputed to. Niles's Reg. **42**: 376.
— Portrait of. Dem. R. **20**: 99.
Houston, Mrs. Hesperos. Liv. Age, **25**: 84.
Houvald, E. von. The Light-Tower. (R. P. Gillies) Blackw. **13**: 3.
Houx, Jean le, Poetry of. Fraser, **21**: 51.
Hovey, Charles Edward. Am. J. Educ. **8**: 94.
How Family Genealogy. N. E. Reg. **4**: 63.
How Algy won the Bet. Lond. Soc. **14**: 1.
How Bella kept Faith with her Lover. Eng. Dom. M. **11**: 23.
How Bill was mistaken. (J. W. Gally) Overland, **13**: 357.
How Brooke became a Fellow-Craftsman. Lond. Soc. **40**: 507.
How Captain Ascott floored the Ghost. (W. W. Harney) Atlan. **40**: 207.
How Charlie Blake went in for the Heiress. Lond. Soc. **5**: 385.
How Croquet first came to Holcroft. Lond. Soc. **2**: 289.
How Frank Thornton was cured. (C. Lever) Blackw. **104**: 186.
How George Howard was cured. (J. McCarthy) Cath. World, **18**: 49.
How Ham was cured. (J. Woodville) Lippinc. **15**: 492.
How he married her. Tinsley, **11**: 108.
How he was cured. (W. C. Russell) Temp. Bar, **45**: 500.
How he won her. (L. Broughton) St. James, **38**: 601.
How I became an Egyptian. Dub. Univ. **46**: 610.
How I became a Pagan. (C. A. Halbert) Lippinc. **5**: 443.
How I became a Yeoman. Blackw. **60**: 358.
How I came to be married. Putnam, **6**: 572.
How I came to be a Manager. (F. Talbot) Belgra. **28**: 567.
How I came to be a Sloven. Blackw. **62**: 658.
How I came to like Diamonds. Putnam, **6**: 40.
How I caught my first Salmon. Blackw. **121**: 728.
How I caught my first Trout. (J. H. Keene) Belgra. **39**: supp. 66.
How I courted Lulu. Putnam, **7**: 347.
How I discounted my Bill. All the Year, **13**: 557.
How I fell among Thieves. Blackw. **127**: 100.
How I fought my first Duel. Belgra. **29**: 68.
How I gained a Wife and fell into a Fortune. Lond. Soc. **2**: 414, 543.
How I got cured of Consumption. (W. J. Tate) Dub. Univ. **76**: 200.
How I got my Cork Legs. St. James, **12**: 222.
How I got the Pirate's Treasure. (J. J. Robbins) Overland, **7**: 183.
How I got rich against my Will. Lakeside, **2**: 333.
How I heard my own Will read. Belgra. **1**: 469.
How I killed a Cariboo. Fraser, **58**: 470.
How I live, and with whom. Putnam, **3**: 320.
How I lost the County. (F. Talbot) Belgra. **22**: 220.
How I lost my Uncle's Property. St. James, **11**: 212.
How I married to escape being hanged. Dub. Univ **40**: 676.

How I met my Fate. (W. A. Thompson) Lippinc. **5**: 507.
How I quitted Naples. Cornh. **2**: 192.
How I sailed the Flying Scud. (G. Mackenzie) Canad. Mo. **10**: 516.
How I set about paying my Debts. Lond. Soc. **11**: 385.
How I shot my first Snipe. Belgra. **27**: 533.
How I spent my Holiday in Town. (W. W. Fenn) Lond. Soc. **36**: 357.
How I stood for the Dreepdaily Burghs. Blackw. **62**: 259.
How I stood for the Hallamshire Boroughs. Lond. Soc. **14**: 398.
How I was rusticated from Cambridge. Temp. Bar, **35**: 112. Same art. Canad. Mo. **1**: 471.
How I was tracked by Trappers. (L. de la Ramé) Bentley, **49**: 521.
How I went to the Bar, and after. Lond. Soc. **17**: 497.
How I went to Court. (G. A. Sala) Belgra. **23**: 294.
How I went to the Levee. Macmil. **34**: 254. Same art. Liv. Age, **130**: 490.
How I went to Sea. House. Words, **6**: 49.
How I won Polly and a Postmastership. (T. Hood) Belgra. **1**: 324.
How I won a Wife. (F. Reuter) Liv. Age, **128**: 17.
How I wronged my Friend. Belgra. **3**: 49.
How I wrote a Novel. (M. C. Hay) Belgra. **28**: 360.
How it happened. (C. Perry) Lakeside, **9**: 288.
How it happened. (E. Campbell) Canad. Mo. **16**: 396.
How it happened. (N. Rosaro) Liv. Age, **132**: 560.
How it happened; a Tale. All the Year, **25**: 67.
How Jack Breeze missed being a Pasha. (H. George) Overland, **6**: 164.
How Jack Harris became an Æsthetic. (J. H. McCarthy) Belgra. **41**: 61.
How Jack Hastings sold his Mine. (Mrs. F. F. Victor) Lakeside, **5**: 204.
How John was drilled. Blackw. **114**: 265.
How Kate discovered America. Lond. Soc. **9**: 393.
How Kendrick married Juliet Eustis. (F. E. Wadleigh) Argosy, **32**: 280.
How Lady Louisa Moor amused herself. (Miss Taylor) Lippinc. **15**: 571.
How Lida disposed of her Lovers. (M. McConnell) Lakeside, **6**: 354.
How Lisa loved the King. (Geo. Eliot) Blackw. **105**: 513. Same art. N. Ecl. **5**: 30. Same art. Liv. Age, **101**: 635.
How Love lived in Flowers. (W. T. Greene) Colburn, **161**: 185.
How Meo Varalla won his first Love. Temp. Bar, **33**: 470.
How Mother did it. (J. R. Hadermann) Lippinc. **8**: 335.
How Mr. Biffles was garroted. Putnam, **9**: 414.
How Mr. Blewstring got chiseled out of fifty Pounds. Temp. Bar, **25**: 40.
How Mr. Frye would have preached it. (E. E. Hale) Atlan. **19**: 198.
How Mr. Penlake exercised a Proctor. (C. Reade) Belgra. **22**: 420.
How Mr. Storm met his Destiny. (H. H. Boyesen) Scrib. **13**: 547.
How Mr. Winter won and lost his Seat for Goldborough. Lond. Soc. **17**: 531.
How my Debts were paid. Belgra. **2**: 182.
How my Eyes were opened. Liv. Age, **58**: 998.
How one Woman kept her Husband. (Saxe Holm) Scrib. **3**: 467.
How our Polly was won; a Sketch. Dub. Univ. **89**: 741.
How Roessels Gulch panned out. (M. McConnell) Lakeside, **10**: 17.
How Robinson lost his Fellowship. Chamb. J. **48**: 273, 299.
How Russians meet Death. (I. Tourgénieff) Temp. Bar, **48**: 496. Same art. Liv. Age, **132**: 175.
How Santa Claus came to Simpson's Bar. (Bret Harte) Atlan. **29**: 349.
How Sharp Snaffles got his Capital and his Wife. (W. G. Simms) Harper, **41**: 667.
How she found out. (R. T. Cooke) Galaxy, **20**: 497.
How she kept her Vow. (S. G. W. Benjamin) Lippinc. **26**: 594.
How Sir Courtney de Vere was Water-bewitched. (W. Jones) Colburn, **144**: 300.
How Snooks got out of it. Lond. Soc. **38**: 145.
How Steenwykerwold was saved. (P. T. Hogan) Cath. World, **26**: 547.
How that Cup slipped. Harper, **59**: 589.
How the Balance came out at all. (C. Clarke) Temp. Bar, **19**: 120.
How the Bank came to Grief. All the Year, **13**: 102–485.
How the C. Family got their Estate. (E. Townbridge) Sharpe, **52**: 209.
How the Captain came in. (R. C. Myers) Potter Am. Mo. **17**: 69.
How the Course of true Love really did run smooth. Lond. Soc. **17**: 114.
How the first Cutter was swamped, etc. Sharpe, **50**: 131.
How the "Gadfly" failed. Belgra **17**: 54.
How the Howe Family rose and fell. (A. Clyde) Sharpe, **44**: 131.
How the New York and London Petroleum Company was floated. Dub. Univ. **81**: 321.
How the old Horse won the Bet. (O. W. Holmes) Atlan. **38**: 44.
How the old Love fared. House. Words, **15**: 607.
How the Prussians invaded Brighton. Lond. Soc. **19**: 453.
How the Rev. Mr. Chasuble made a Sensation. (E. Chamberlin) Lakeside, **3**: 450.
How the Ship came in. (R. Grahame) Galaxy, **14**: 448.
How the Spirits tormented me. (R. Frothingham) Galaxy, **4**: 994.
How the Storm came; a Poem. Scrib. **2**: 605.
How the Uhlans took Mousseux-les-Caves. Cornh. **22**: 566.
How the Widow crossed the Line. (R. H. Davis) Lippinc. **18**: 717.
How the Wrong was done, etc. (V. F. Townsend) Sharpe, **41**: 134.
How to get married. Belgra. **6**: 531.
How to grow young again. (J. Saunders) Peop. J. **6**: 331.
How to sell a Clock. Peop. J. **8**: 259.
How Uncle Gabe saved the Levee. (W. L. Murfree) Scrib. **16**: 848.
How Violet got a Beau. Lond. Soc. **14**: 229.
How we celebrated Scott's Centenary. Lond. Soc. **20**: 275.
How we floated the Bank. All the Year, **12**: 493.
How we got away from Naples. Fraser, **100**: 673. Same art. Liv. Age, **144**: 73.
How we got married. Lond. Soc. **38**: supp. 17.
How we live now. (A. Thomas) Eng. Dom. M. **25**: 9–298. **26**: 74–234.
How we lost a Treasure. Lond. Soc. **39**: 28.
How we lost our Minister. House. Words, **14**: 236.
How we met. (Miss Taylor) Lippinc. **13**: 197.
How we stood for Muddleton. (R. B. Wormald) St. James, **13**: 320.
How we took a Farm, and the Results. (R. D. Gibney) Temp. Bar, **28**: 489.
Howard, Bezaleel. (W. B. O. Peabody) Chr. Exam. **22**: 157.
Howard, Geo. W. F., Earl of Carlisle. *See* Carlisle.
Howard, H., Earl of Northampton. *See* Northampton.
Howard, Henry, Earl of Surrey. *See* Surrey.

Howard, John, the Philanthropist. (S. Osgood) Mo. Rel. M. **6**: 193, 241. — (Lady Pollock) Temp. Bar, **48**: 252. — Ecl. R. **90**: 541. — Nat. M. **4**: 69. — Penny M. **7**: 212. — Sharpe, **10**: 248.
— as a Statist. (W. A. Guy) J. Statis. Soc. **36**: 1.
— Brown's Memoir of. Ecl. R. **39**: 414.
— Dixon's Life of. Blackw. **67**: 50. Same art. Ecl. M. **19**: 338. — Liv. Age, **23**: 171.
— Life of. New Eng. M. **5**: 332. — Ed. Mo. R. **1**: 95. — (R. Robbins) Chr. Q. Spec. **3**: 393. — Am. Mo. R. **4**: 255. — Mo. R. **105**: 422.
— Memoirs of. Chr. Obs. **24**: 363, 423. **50**: 400.
— True Place of, in History. (W. A. Guy) J. Statis. Soc. **38**: 430.
Howard, John Eager, with portrait. (E. Read) M. Am. Hist. **7**: 276.
Howard, Leonard, Letters of. Retros. **15**: 1.
Howard, Maj.-Gen. Oliver O. Hours at Home, **1**: 565.
— and Freedmen's Bureau. (E. Spencer) So. M. **13**: 633.
Howard, Philip, Earl of Arundel, and his Wife. Liv. Age, **54**: 741.
— Life of. Dub. R. **43**: 273.
— Writings of. Lond. M. **8**: 605.
Howard, Gen. T. A., with portrait. Dem. R. **20**: 233.
Howard, Lord William. A Border Chieftain's Tower. Colburn, **108**: 357.
Howard's Son; a Tale. All the Year, **18**: 258, 282.
Howards of Maryland. (E. Read) M. Am. Hist. **3**: 239.
Howden Church, Yorkshire. Penny M **5**: 132.
Howe, Elias, jr., and the Sewing-Machine, with portrait. Pract. M. **5**: 321.
Howe, John. Chr. R. **4**: 518. — Ecl. R. **118**: 512. — Lond. Q. **21**: 355. — Meth. M. **36**: 321. — with portrait, Cong. M. **16**: 1.
— and his Contemporaries. Am. Presb. R. **4**: 1.
— and Times of the Puritans. (R. Machray) Ex. H. Lec. **18**: 247.
— Blessedness of the Righteous opened. (L. Withington) Cong. R. **7**: 559.
— Life and Works of. Chr. R. **4**: 518. — Mus. **11**: 289. — Ecl. R. **88**: 385.
— Rogers's Life of. Cong. M. **19**: 693. — Ecl. R. **63**: 353.
— Works of. (S. Miller) Princ. **3**: 177. — Lit. & Theo. R. **4**: 538. — (J. Brazer) Chr. Exam. **20**: 191.
Howe, Joseph. (G. M. Grant) Canad. Mo. **7**: 377, 497. **8**: 20, 115.
— Sketch of. (M. J. Griffin) St. James, **32**: 485.
Howe, Julia Ward. Passion Flowers. (H. T. Tuckerman) So. Q. **26**: 180. — Knick. **43**: 353.
Howe, N. Century Sermon. (W. Tudor) No. Am. **4**: 93.
Howe, Gen. R., and Gen. C. Gadsen, Duel between, 1777. Hist. M. **4**: 265.
Howe, Richard, Earl, Admiral. (R. Southey) Quar. **62**: 1.
— Barrow's Life of. Ed. R. **67**: 320. — Dub. Univ. **17**: 693. — Mo. R. **145**: 193. — Ecl. R. **67**: 178.
Howe, Samuel, Life and Character of. (E. B. Hall) Chr. Exam. **5**: 185.
Howe, Dr. Samuel G. Ev. Sat. **10**: 546. — Am. J. Educ. **11**: 389.
— Tribute to. (H. H. Barber) Unita. R. **5**: 191. — (O. W. Holmes) Atlan. **37**: 464.
Howe, Sen. T. O. Attack on the Administration. (E. L. Godkin) Nation, **26**: 222.
Howe's Cave, Schoharie Co., N. Y. Contin. Mo. **1**: 422. — Sharpe, **14**: 88.
— Visit to. (S. North) Knick. **37**: 211. Same art. Liv. Age, **31**: 276, 480.
Howe's Masquerade. (N. Hawthorne) Hesp. **1**: 234.
Howel, J., Welsh Poet. (S. Wilson) Victoria, **10**: 490.
Howells, William Dean, with portrait. Ecl. M. **88**: 376.
— Dr. Breen's Practice. (H. A. Huntington) Dial (Ch.), **2**: 214.
Howells, William Dean. Counterfeit Presentment. Penn Mo. **9**: 400.
— Fearful Responsibility. (F. F. Browne) Dial (Ch.), **2**: 85.
— Foregone Conclusion. (H. James, jr.) No. Am. **120**: 207.
— Novels. (Mrs. S. Orr) Contemp. **37**: 741. — Liv. Age, **145**: 599. — (W. C. Brownell) Nation, **31**: 49.
— Undiscovered Country. (B. Adams) Internat. R. **9**: 149. — (C. P. Wooley) Dial (Ch.), **1**: 52.
Howitt, Mary. Godey, **45**: 320.
— Early Poems of. Ecl. R. **85**: 283.
Howitt, Richard. Reliquary, **10**: 209. **11**: 17–141.
Howitt, William. (M. P. Lowe) Unita. R. **11**: 560. — Dub. Univ. **55**: 469.
— and Mary. Knick. **39**: 514. — Liv. Age, **135**: 504.
— Book of the Seasons. Westm. **14**: 456.
— German Experiences. Ecl. R. **80**: 556.
— Homes and Haunts of British Poets. Am. Whig R. **6**: 516. — Fraser, **35**: 210. — Liv. Age, **13**: 152.
— Pantika. Tait, n. s. **2**: 290.
— Rural Life in England. Ecl. R. **68**: 410.
— Student's Life in Germany. Chr. Exam. **32**: 71. — (W. B. O. Peabody) No. Am. **56**: 330. — Ecl. R. **77**: 327. — Dem. R. **10**: 238.
— Visits to remarkable Places. Chr. Exam. **30**: 174. — Fraser, **23**: 725. — Ecl. R. **71**: 551. **75**: 193. — Mo. R. **151**: 232. **157**: 113.
Howland, John, Stone's Life of. (C. T. Brooks) Chr. Exam. **62**: 200.
— and Providence Schools. Am. J. Educ. **27**: 713.
Howland Will Case. Am. Law R. **4**: 625.
Howleys, Last of the. Ecl. M. **34**: 125.
Howling Dervishes. Chamb. J. **25**: 233. Same art. Ecl. M. **38**: 362.
Howqua, the Senior Hong Merchant. Hunt, **10**: 459.
Hoxton Academy and Chapel. Cong. M. **8**: 524, 581.
Hoyle, Charles. Exodus; a Poem. Ed. R. **11**: 362.
Hoyt, Ralph, Poems of. So. Q. **16**: 224.
— Sketches of Life and Landscape. (E. E. Beardsley) Am. Church R. **1**: 274.
Hrolf Krake. (S. B. Gould) Once a Week, **10**: 585.
Hu Hirwan's Ghost. (S. Williams) Overland, **2**: 83.
Hubbard, Henry, with portrait. Dem. R. **9**: 182.
Huber, Francis, Life and Writings of. (A. P. De Candolle) Am. J. Sci. **23**: 117. — For. Q. **10**: 561. — Select J. **2**: [121. — (Mrs. S. B. Herrick) Pop. Sci. Mo. **6**: 486. — (A. P. De Candolle) Ed. New Philos. J. **14**: 283.
Huber, V. A., Life of. (W. M. Griswold) Nation, **32**: 445.
Hübner's Ramble round the World. Quar. **143**: 238. — Liv. Age, **132**: 771.
Hudibras, Imitations of. Retros. **3**: 317.
— Selections from. (S. Butler) Penny M. **13**: 9–484. **14**: 20–273.
Hudson, George, the Railroad King. Ev. Sat. **12**: 74. — Fraser, **36**: 215. — Hunt, **29**: 36.
— and English Railways. Bank. M. (L.) **11**: 746.
— Career of. Tait, n. s. **16**: 319.
Hudson, Henry, the Navigator. (G. M. Asher) Macmil. **14**: 459. Same art. Liv. Age, **94**: 397. — Liv. Age, **69**: 70. — (J. R. Dennett) Nation, **2**: 740.
— Fate of. Ill. M. **2**: 41.
— Life of. (H. R. Cleveland) Sparks's Am. Biog. **10**: 187.
Hudson, Henry N. *See* Shakspere.
Hudson and Mohawk Railroad. (S. D. W. Bloodgood) Am. J. Sci. **21**: 141.
Hudson River and its early Names. (S. F. Cooper) M. Am. Hist. **4**: 401.
— Country Home on. (J. M. Winchell) Galaxy, **24**: 84.
— from the Wilderness to the Sea. Art J. **12**: 5–365. **13**: 21–361.

Hudson River; illustrated. (T. A. Richards) Knick. **54**: 225, 353. **55**: 1, 129. — (J. Burroughs) Scrib. **20**: 481.
— Romance of. (B. J. Lossing) Harper, **52**: 633, 822. **53**: 32.
— Running the Rapids of the Upper. (C. H. Farnham) Scrib. **21**: 857.
— Scenes and Stories of. Am. Mo. M. **7**: 80, 401. **8**: 14, 105.
— Up the. (J. W. Hengiston) Colburn, **97**: 499.
— Who discovered? (B. F. De Costa) Galaxy, **8**: 129.
— Winter Sunrise on. (C. T. Brooks) O. & N. **7**: 700.
Hudson River Railroad. (J. B. Jervis) Hunt, **22**: 278.
Hudson's Bay. Blackw. **63**: 369. Same art. Ecl. M. **14**: 19. — Mo. R. **87**: 66. — Once a Week, **20**: 541.
— and its Furs. Chamb. J. **33**: 293.
Hudson's Bay Company. (W. Forsyth) Good Words, **10**: 358, 394. — (H. M. Robinson) Harper, **59**: 18. — Chamb. J. **10**: 242. — Dem. R. **12**: 345. — Dub. Univ. **51**: 430. — House. Words, **8**: 449, 471. — Liv. Age, **53**: 156. **56**: 120. — No. Brit. **50**: 159. — Westm. **88**: 85. Same art. Liv. Age, **94**: 323.
— Arctic Expedition of. Liv. Age, **15**: 568.
— Career of. (J. Bryce) Canad. Mo. **5**: 273.
— Discoveries of. (Sir J. Barrow) Quar. **73**: 113.
— History and Dissolution of. Cornh. **22**: 159.
— Life in Fort of. Chamb. J. **56**: 705.
Hudson's Bay Service, Life in. Liv. Age, **18**: 1.
Hudson's Bay Territory. Ed. R. **109**: 122. — Liv. Age, **23**: 583.
— Dog-Sledges in, A Day with. (H. M. Robinson) Lippinc. **23**: 265.
— Geology of. (A. K. Isbister) Am. J. Sci. **71**: 313. *See* Rupert's Land.
Huegel, Baron Charles. Nature, **2**: 356.
Huel Rose; a Tale. Blackw. **24**: 737.
Huet, Peter Daniel, Bishop, Life of. Quar. **4**: 103. — Chr. Obs. **11**: 33. — Ecl. R. **11**: 481.
— Life and Opinions of. Quar. **97**: 291.
Huggins, John. Autobiography. Lond. M. **3**: 375.
Hugh, St., Bishop of Lincoln. (G. G. Perry) Contemp. **13**: 381. — (J. A. Froude) Fraser, **81**: 220. Same art. Liv. Age, **104**: 685.
— Credibility of the Story of. Chamb. J. **15**: 111.
— Protestant Life of. (T. E. Bridgett) Dub. R. **86**: 355.
— Story of. (J. Walton) Month, **17**: 398. **18**: 122.
Hugh Granger's Wooings; a Story. (E. Read) Galaxy, **17**: 789. **18**: 75, 210.
Hugh Hamilton's Wife; a Tale. Sharpe, **41**: 34.
Hugh Melton. (K. King) Belgra. **26**: 261–545. **27**: 117.
Hugh Oatcake. Colburn, **89**: 164.
Hugh's Vendetta. (F. C. Fisher) Appleton, **9**: 1–101.
Hughes, Arthur. (W. M. Rossetti) Portfo. **1**: 113.
Hughes, George. Cong. **2**: 464.
Hughes, Abp. John. Brownson, **23**: 78. — Knick. **63**: 434.
— and N.Y. Riots. (A. C. Coxe) Am. Church R. **15**: 435.
Hughes, Joseph. Ecl. R. **62**: 31. — Cong. **18**: 329, 393.
Hughes, Thomas, with portrait. Appleton, **9**: 144. — with portrait, Ev. Sat. **9**: 609 — with portrait, Ecl. M. **95**: 759.
— Tom Brown's School Days at Rugby. Brownson, **17**: 462. — Chr. Obs. **58**: 491. — Dub. Univ. **50**: 653. — Ecl. R. **107**: 422. — Ed. R. **107**: 172. — New Q. **6**: 389.
Hugo, Victor. (W. H. Browne) N. Ecl. **4**: 204. — (K. Cook) Lond. Soc. **22**: 501. Same art. Ecl. M. **80**: 324. — (C. A. Cummings) Chr. Exam. **76**: 301. — (E. F. Morley) Western, **4**: 323. — (F. W. H. Myers) 19th Cent. **5**: 773, 955. — (T. S. Perry) Atlan. **36**: 167. — (A. Laugel) Internat. R. **11**: 283, 391. — (S. Smiles) Howitt, **3**: 368. — (C. Redding) Colburn, **138**: 81.
Hugo, Victor. (E. F. Wheeler) Potter Am. Mo. **16**: 529. — Appleton, **1**: 11. — Argosy, **20**: 185. — Blackw. **100**: 744. — Blackw. **122**: 157. Same art. Ecl. M. **89**: 399. — Brit. Q. **67**: 340. — Chamb. J. **40**: 185. — Colburn, **168**: 356. — Ev. Sat. **2**: 303. — with portrait, Ev. Sat. **9**: 625. — with portrait, Peop. J. **8**: 275. — Fraser, **67**: 372. — Temp. Bar, **9**: 576. **50**: 367. **59**: 251. Same art. Liv. Age, **146**: 241. — Westm. **31**: 389. — Fraser, **26**: 740. — Fraser, **33**: 515. Same art. Ecl. M. **8**: 508.
— and the Constables. (C. Hugo) Putnam, **14**: 29.
— and his Writings. Westm. **63**: 424.
— and Romanticism. Temp. Bar, **42**: 317.
— and Sainte-Beuve. Nat. Q. **20**: 32.
— L'Âne. (A. Laugel) Nation, **31**: 407.
— L'Année terrible. (C. A. Bristed) Nation, **14**: 393. — (S. Colvin) Macmil. **26**: 326. — (A. C. Swinburne) Fortn. **18**: 243. Same art. Ev. Sat. **13**: 396. — Dark Blue, **4**: 26. — Lond. Soc. **24**: 139. — St. Paul's, **12**: 431.
— as a Dramatist. (J. B. Mathews) Scrib. **22**: 688.
— as a Novelist. (W. H. Browne) So. R. n. s. **1**: 453.
— at the Age of thirty-two. Tait, n. s. **1**: 310.
— at Home. (L. H. Hooper) Lippinc. **22**: 639. — (S. P. Oliver) Gent. M. n. s. **4**: 713. — Ev. Sat. **7**: 165, 217. — Once a Week, **19**: 563.
— Career of. Once a Week, **20**: 1.
— Les Contemplations. Colburn, **108**: 213.
— Development of Genius of. (A. Laugel) Nation, **32**: 7, 41.
— Dramas. (C. Barrère) Macmil. **30**: 281. — (F. K. Butler) No. Am. **43**: 133. — Am. Q. **19**: 167. — Westm. **34**: 287. — Select J. **3**: [57. — For. Q. **6**: 455. **8**: 196. **17**: 417. **31**: 193. — Dem. R. **13**: 378.
— Dramatist, Novelist, Poet. (K. Hillard) Lippinc. **9**: 188.
— Les Enfants. Dub. Univ. **60**: 430.
— Evening at the House of. (L. H. Hooper) Appleton, **12**: 204. — (G. C. Fisher) Galaxy, **24**: 200. — Tait, n. s. **15**: 234.
— Genius and Writings of. (A. R. Spofford) No. Am. **81**: 324.
— Hernani. Am Mo. M. **9**: 41.
— — First Performance of. Ev. Sat. **11**: 151.
— Histoire d'un Crime. (A. V. Dicey) Nation, **25**: 382, **26**: 389.
— Home of. (G. Cluseret) Galaxy, **1**: 133.
— Hunchback of Notre Dame. Fraser, **12**: 89.
— in Exile. (T. L. L. Teeling) Irish Mo. **8**: 191.
— Last Days of a Condemned. Mo. R. **152**: 252.
— Latest Poems. (G. H. Lewes) Fortn. **3**: 181.
— Legend of the Ages. (J. M. Ludlow) Macmil. **1**: 131. — Dub. Univ. **55**: 221, 320. Same art. Ecl. M. **49**: 509. **50**: 65.
— Letters on the Rhine. Quar. **71**: 315. — Fraser, **27**: 411.
— Life and Writings of. Westm. **80**: 483.
— Literature of. Ecl. M. **57**: 489.
— Lucrezia Borgia. Am. Mo. M. **8**: 163.
— Lyrics of. (Countess de Bury) No. Am. **83**: 476. — Fraser, **32**: 358. Same art. with portrait, Ecl. M. **24**: 433.
— Man who laughs. (J. Burroughs) Nation, **9**: 509. — (A. C. Swinburne) Fortn. **12**: 73. Same art. Ev. Sat. **8**: 129. — Fraser, **80**: 798. — Macmil. **20**: 163. — St. Paul's, **4**: 466.
— Memoirs of. Colburn, **128**: 474.
— Les Misérables. (Mrs. C. R. Corson) New Eng. **23**: 454. — Blackw. **92**: 172. — Bost. R. **3**: 52. — Brit. Q. **37**: 121. — Cornh. **6**: 704. — Ecl. M. **58**: 195. — Ecl. R. **116**: 451. — Ed. R. **117**: 208. — Ho. & For. R. **1**: 392. — Quar. **112**: 271. — St. James, **4**: 217. — Temp. Bar, **6**: 572. — Westm. **79**: 77.

Hugo, Victor, New Volumes by, 1881. (G. Saintsbury) Fortn. 36: 40.
— Ninety-three. (H. James, jr.) Nation, 18: 238. — (J. Morley) Fortn. 21: 359. Same art. Ecl. M. 82: 624. — Blackw. 115: 750.
— Les Orientales. Lond. M. 23: 240.
— Le Pape. (A. Laugel) Nation, 26: 415.
— Poems and Novels. For. Q. 4: 205.
— Poetry of. (E. Dowden) Contemp. 22: 175. — Brit. Q. 32: 71.
— Religions and Religion. (A. C. Swinburne) Fortn. 33: 761.
— Romances. (L. Stephen) Cornh. 30: 179. Same art. Ecl. M. 83: 432. Same art. Ev. Sat. 17: 311.
— To; a Poem. (A. Tennyson) 19th Cent. 1: 547. Same art. Liv. Age, 134: 66.
— Toilers of the Sea. Ecl. R. 123: 386. — Ev. Sat. 1: 500. — Fortn. 5: 30. — Fraser, 73: 735. — Ecl. M. 67: 77.
— Two Visits to. (H. H. Boyesen) Scrib. 19: 184.
— Writings of. Mo. R. 149: 167.
Hugo, Madame Victor. St. James, 23: 189.
Hugo the Bastard. (R. Buchanan) Temp. Bar, 18: 395.
Hugo van Geest; a Tale of the Netherlands. Hours at Home, 4: 58.
Huguenot, Little. House. Words, 17: 80.
— Origin of the Word. (J. W. Calcraft) Dub. Univ. 40: 203. Same art. Ecl. M. 27: 184.
— Story of a. Ecl. R. 124: 447.
Huguenots. (J. H. Chapin) Univ. Q. 26: 328, 451. — (G. P. Disosway) Meth. Q. 4: 383. — Ecl. M. 16: 21. — (E. Lawrence) Harper, 41: 801. — (W. H. Ryder) Univ. Q. 15: 55. — Am. Presb. R. 5: 177. — Blackw. 74: 1. — Dub. Univ. 44: 98. — N. E. Reg. 1: 332. — Prosp. R. 9: 72.
— and Queen Elizabeth. (A. Laugel) Nation, 29: 110, 140.
— Annals of. Ed. R. 124: 86. Same art. Liv. Age, 90: 523.
— at the Galleys. Quar. 120: 39. Same art. Ecl. M. 67: 600. Same art. Liv. Age, 90: 643.
— Browning's History of, 1598–1838. Mo. R. 149: 446.
— Coligny. Brit. Q. 61: 297.
— Early. So. Lit. Mess. 7: 335.
— History of. Chr. Rem. 55: 345. — Liv. Age, 20: 145.
— — Weiss's. Ed. R. 99: 454. Same art. Ecl. M. 32: 433. Same art. Liv. Age, 41: 483. — Ecl. R. 99: 655. — Blackw. 74: 1. Same art. Liv. Age, 38: 451.
— in America. (G. P. Disosway) Contin. Mo. 1: 151, 298, 461. — Chr. Obs. 44: 463. — Knick. 53. 234.
— — and in France. (L. J. Hall) Chr. Exam. 36: 74.
— in the Calaisis. All the Year, 45: 303, 379.
— in England. (H. James, jr.) Nation, 6: 32.
— in Germany. (F. Kapp) Nation, 15: 88.
— Last of. (G. P. Disosway) Meth. Q. 17: 247.
— Modern. (J. M. Bruce) Lippinc. 17: 694.
— of Geneva. Colburn, 128: 111.
— of New Rochelle. (G. P. Disosway) Contin. Mo. 3: 1.
— of New York City. (G. P. Disosway) Contin. Mo. 2: 193.
— of Staten Island. (G. P. Disosway) Contin. Mo. 1: 683.
— of Virginia. (G. P. Disosway) Contin. Mo. 3: 348.
— Persecution of, under Louis XV. (D. N. Lord) Theo. & Lit. J. 6: 640.
— Peyrat's History of. Chr. Obs. 54: 29.
— Rise of, Baird's. (E. B. Otheman) Meth. Q. 41: 108. — Liv. Age, 149: 451.
— Smiles's. Dub. Univ. 89: 279.
— Stories of. Nat. M. 4: 345.
— Sufferings of. Meth. M. 28: 437.
— Tale of. So. Lit. Mess. 4: 734.
Huguenots, Traits and Stories of. (E. C. Gaskell) House. Words, 8: 348. Same art. Liv. Age, 40: 185. Same art. Ecl. M. 31: 373.
— Wycliffe and. Blackw. 88: 231.
Huguenot Captain. Blackw. 38: 790. 39: 17. Same art. Mus. 28: 281, 351.
Huguenot Family. (C. M. Sedgwick) Godey, 25: 144, 189.
— Story of a. (S. Smiles) Good Words, 18: 99, 265.
Huguenot Maiden. (J. E. Jackson) Fraser, 61: 433.
Huitramannaland, Position of. Hist. M. 9: 364.
Huldah the Help. (E. Eggleston) Scrib. 1: 189.
Hulee, Travels of a Philosopher in the famous Empire of. Fraser, 83: 703.
Hulks, on Board the. Chamb. J. 41: 419.
Hull, Hezekiah, Obituary of. (D. L. Ogden) Chr. Mo. Spec. 7: 556.
Hull, Capt. Isaac, Biography of. Anal. M. 1: 226.
— Court of Inquiry. Niles's Reg. 23: 187, 227.
Hull, Robert, Life of. Select J. 3: [43.
Hull, William, Conduct at Detroit in 1812. (S. C. Clarke) N. E. Reg. 9: 41. — (W. H. Sumner) N. E. Reg. 11: 13, 167.
— Life and Services of. So. Lit. Mess. 14: 319.
— Residence of. (B. J. Lossing) Potter Am. Mo. 5: 561.
Hull, England, Description of. Penny M. 3: 353.
— Frost's History of. Retros. 15: 194.
Hull, Mass., Burial Inscriptions at. N. E. Reg. 12: 207.
— Records of. N. E. Reg. 27: 360. 31: 76.
Hullah, John, with portrait. Dub. Univ. 95: 323.
Hulls, Jonathan, Inventor of the Steamboat. Chamb. J. 52: 341.
Human Ability and Divine Grace. Chr. Disc. 5: 256.
Human Automatism, Doctrine of. (W. B. Carpenter) Contemp. 25: 397, 940.
Human Body, Structure and Functions of. (A. J. H. Crespi) Colburn, 160: 566.
— and its Connection with Man, Wilkinson's. Ecl. R. 95: 422.
Human Bodies, Unlawful Disinterment of. (R. Gooch) Quar. 42: 1.
Human Bones found filled with Lead. (J. Worth) Arch. 4: 69.
Human Caloric, Marvels of. Ecl. M. 48: 71.
Human Character, Æsthetics of. (J. Sully) Fortn. 15: 505.
— Curious Researches into. Chamb. J. 55: 181.
— Future of. Ev. Sat. 4: 619.
— Science of. (W. H. Mallock) Contemp. 40: 934.
Human Countenance, Expression of Emotions in. (H. Calderwood) Internat. R. 6: 195.
Human Curiosities. Chamb. J. 56: 262.
Human Destiny in America. (R. W. Haskins) Knick. 30: 399.
— New Hypothesis of. (W. Bridges) Howitt, 1: 162.
Human Depravity, Restraint upon. Chr. Mo. Spec. 4: 172. *See* Conflict of Ages.
Human Entomology. Hogg, 9: 158.
Human Evolution, Problem in. (G. Allen) Fortn. 31: 778.
Human Excellence, Three Ideals of. (F. D. Conder) Dub. Univ. 93: 257.
Human Faculties, Culture of. (E. Beecher) Chr. Mo. Spec. 8: 388.
Human Figure, The Beautiful in. Art J. 6: 150.
Human Footprints in Limestone. (D. D. Owen) Am. J. Sci. 43: 14.
Human Form Divine. Eng. Dom. M. 2: 16–336.
Human Frailty, Origin and Purpose of. (M. H. Doolittle) Radical, 3: 468.
Human Government a Divine Institution. (J. P. Thompson) New Eng. 3: 525.
Human History, Divine Footsteps in. Chr. Obs. 62: 750.
Human Improvement. Chr. R. 2: 102.

Human Influence, Sphere of. (T. Hill) Chr. Exam. **45**: 424.
Human Instrumentality in God's Work. (M. Valentine) Luth. Q. **11**: 418.
Human Intellect. *See* Intellect.
Human Jaw from the Cave of La Naulette. (C. C. Blake) Anthrop. R. **5**: 294.
— from Suffolk. (R. H. Collyer) Anthrop. R. **5**: 221.
Human Justice, or Government a moral Power. (T. Lewis) Am. Bib. Repos. 3d s. **3**: 65.
Human Knowledge. *See* Knowledge.
Human Life and Practical Ethics, De Wette's. Chr. R. **7**: 600.
— Duration of. Dub. Univ. **66**: 53.
— Picture of, from Greek of Cebes. Mo. Rel. M. **9**: 13.
— Plea for. All the Year, **2**: 506.
— Right of Government over. (E. R. Tyler) New Eng. **3**: 562.
Human Nature. (C. P. Krauth) Evang. R. **9**: 522. — So. R. n. s. **8**: 1.
— as Authority in religious Doctrines. (G. H. Emerson) Univ. Q. **18**: 29.
— Is it religious? (E. V. Gerhart) Ref. Q. **26**: 377.
— Mystical Phenomena of. (S. Osgood) O. & N. **7**: 602.
— our Knowledge of it. (C. P. Krauth) Evang. R. **9**: 522.
— Philosophy of. (W. Phillips) No. Am. **45**: 460.
— Physiological Aspects of. So. R. n. s. **15**: 312.
— Problems in. Ecl. R. **119**: 277. — Ecl. M. **62**: 156. Same art. Liv. Age, **81**: 170.
— Study of. (H. W. Bucher) Pop. Sci. Mo. **1**: 327.
Human Occupations compared. Knick. **12**: 433, 475.
Human Perfectibility. Fraser, **1**: 147.
Human Progress. Westm. **52**: 1. Same art. Ecl. M. **19**: 1.
— Law of. (W. W. Lord) Princ. **18**: 1.
— Survey of. Chamb. J. **36**: 200.
— Theory of. Brit. Q. **14**: 1. — Kitto, **7**: 126. — Ecl. R. **93**: 389.
Human Race. (I. C. Knowlton) Univ. Q. **20**: 347.
— Common Origin of. (W. Brock) Ex. H. Lec. **4**: 105.
— Destiny of. (A. A. Miner) Univ. Q. **4**: 181.
— Development of, Geiger on. (G. Allen) Mind, **6**: 278.
— Diversity of Species in. (C. Hodge) Princ. **34**: 435.
— Plurality of, Pouchet's. Anthrop R. **3**: 120.
— Statistics of. (D. Wight) Cong. Q. **6**: 197.
— Unity of. (H. Bronson) Chr. Q. Spec. **3**: 56. — (W. N. Barber) Univ. Q. **12**: 290. — (A. de Quatrefages) Theo. Ecl. **3**: 49. — (F. D. Stem) Mercersb. **3**: 129. — (R. Turnbull) Chr. R. **17**: 68.
— — Agassiz on. Princ. **41**: 5.
— — disproved by the Hebrew Bible. (S. A. Cartwright) De Bow, **29**: 129.
— — Testimony of Geology to. Nat. R. **10**: 279. Same art. Ecl. M. **51**: 1.
— When did it begin? (W. W. Kinsley) Penn Mo. **10**: 677, 736. — (W. W. Kinsley) Lakeside, **7**: 196.
See Man.
Human Remains found in County Down. (Countess of Moira) Arch. **7**: 90.
— from the Holy Land. (C. C. Blake) Anthrop. J. **2**: 53.
— from Iceland. (R. F. Burton) Anthrop. J. **2**: 342.
— from Moulin-Quignon. (A. Tylor) Anthrop. R. **1**: 166.
— from Palmyra. (C. C. Blake) Anthrop. J. **1**: 312.
— from the Rock Tombs in Malta. (J. Thurman) Arch. **40**: 489.
Human Rights and modern Philosophy. Am. Whig R. **2**: 327, 437.
— Hurlbut's Essays on. So. Q. **14**: 131.
— *versus* Divine Rights. Dem. R. **24**: 291.
Human Sacrifice, A. Cornh. **34**: 316. Same art. Liv. Age, **131**: 35.
Human Sacrifices. Once a Week, **30**: 42.
— among the Romans. (H. G. Liddell) Arch. **40**: 242.
Human Skin. (I. Ashe) Ecl. M. **59**: 317.
Human Species, and its Races. (H. Schaafhausen) Anthrop. R. **7**: 366.
— Growth of. Hogg, **12**: 62.
— Quatrefages on. (W. L. Distant) Nature, **20**: 429. — (C. M. O'Leary) Cath. World, **31**: 212.
Human Vegetation. (H. Macmillan) Macmil. **6**: 459. Same art. Ecl. M. **57**: 556. Same art. Liv. Age, **76**: 160.
Humane Society, Mass. (R. B. Forbes) Hunt, **19**: 627.
Humanists, The. Brownson, **16**: 38.
— Italian, and the Popes. Ed. R. **136**: 114.
Humanitarian Effort, Relation of Christianity to. (L. P. Brockett) Meth. Q. **18**: 452.
Humanitarianism. (E. L. Godkin) Nation, **6**: 68.
Humanity and Christianity. (J. W. Nevin) Mercersb. **20**: 469.
— Bodichon on. Anthrop. R. **3**: 287.
— Destiny of. (Lady Wilde) Dub. Univ. **89**: 627.
— Development of. Bost. Q. **2**: 449.
— Doctrine of. (L. P. Leroux) Fortn. **17**: 324.
— Future of, on Earth. (E. D. Morris) Presb. R. **1**: 319.
— Idea of, Consummation of. (T. Lewis) Am. Bib. Repos. 3d s. **3**: 731.
— Laurent's History of. Penn Mo. **6**: 362.
— Leroux on. Bost. Q. **5**: 257.
— Normal. (S. H. Giesy) Mercersb. **14**: 528.
— progressing to Perfection. (L. P. Hickok) Am. Presb. R. **17**: 532.
— Religion of. (O. B. Frothingham) Radical, **10**: 241, 321, 401.
Humber Tunnel. Ecl. Engin. **9**: 360.
Humbleys; or the New-Comers. Hogg, **6**: 312, 328.
Humboldt, Alexander von. (L. Agassiz) Liv. Age. **61**: 643. **103**: 47. — (J. W. Foster) Lakeside, **2**: 39. — (J. H. Friswell) Recr. Sci. **1**: 15, 55. — (H. Stevens) Am. J. Sci. **99**: 1. — (H. T. Tuckerman) Godey, **41**: 133. — with portrait, Ecl. M. **48**: 33. — Am. Presb. R. **8**: 240. — Bentley, **45**: 620. — Blackw. **58**: 541. — Ecl. M. **15**: 133. — Nature, **8**: 238. — Univ. Q. **17**: 23.
— American Researches. (J. Leslie) Ed. R. **16**: 223. — Ed. R. **19**: 164. — (J. Leslie) Ed. R. **24**: 133. — Quar. **15**: 440.
— and William. (D. H. Montgomery) Radical, **6**: 405.
— as a representative Man. (R. Harris) University Q. **2**: 46.
— Asiatic Discoveries. Dub. Univ. **1**: 549.
— Aspects of Nature. No. Brit. **12**: 121. Same art. Liv. Age, **23**: 587. Same art. Ecl. M. **19**: 374.
— Astronomical Labors. Ed. R. **27**: 99.
— at the Court of Berlin. (R. M. Milnes) Fraser, **62**: 592. Same art. Liv. Age, **67**: 753.
— at Home. (B. Taylor) Ecl. M. **40**: 388.
— Biographical Tableaux of. Sharpe, **23**: 58–234. Same art. Ecl. M. **37**: 473. **38**: 87, 206.
— Career of. Good Words, **1**: 209.
— Correspondence with Varnhagen von Ense. Ed. R. **112**: 213. Same art. Liv. Age, **66**: 426. — Ecl. M. **51**: 230.
— Cosmos. (Sir D. Brewster) No. Brit. **4**: 202. — (D. C. Gilman) New Eng. **18**: 277. — (Sir J. F. W. Herschel) Ed. R. **87**: 17. Same art. Liv. Age, **16**: 385. — Brit. Q. **3**: 320. — Liv. Age, **12**: 327. — (J. Lovering) Chr. Exam. **48**: 53. — Quar **77**: 154. Same art. Ecl. M. **7**: 353. — Fraser, **37**: 208 — (C. G. Forshey) De Bow, **9**: 150, 271. — (A. W. Ely) De Bow, **12**: 370. — (S. D. Hillman) Meth. Q. **20**: 414 — (Sir H. Holland) Ed. R. **94**: 49. — Am. Whig R. **3**: 598. — Ecl. R. **95**: 215, 720. Same art. Ecl. M. **26**: 433. — Ecl. R. **108**: 427. — (S. Tyler) Princ. **24**: 382. — Tait, n. s. **13**: 123.

Humboldt, Alexander von. Cosmos and Sidereal Astronomy. Quar. **94**: 49.
— Cuba. Mus. **14**: 444.
— Eulogy on. (L. Agassiz) Am. J. Sci. **78**: 96.
— Geological Investigations. (F. Hermann) Ed. New Philos. J. **32**: 205.
— An Hour with. Liv. Age, **15**: 151. — (B. Taylor) Liv. Age, **52**: 400.
— In Memoriam. Fraser, **60**: 15.
— in Politics. (K. Blind) Internat. R. **9**: 634.
— Letters of. Ecl. R. **112**: 139. — Liv. Age, **65**: 437.
— Obituary Notice of. Am. J. Sci. **78**: 164.
— Personal Narrative. (Sir J. Barrow) Quar. **14**: 368. **18**: 135. **21**: 320. **25**: 365. — Ed. R. **16**: 223. **25**: 86. — Mo. R. **88**: 234. **90**: 14. **100**: 264. **104**: 225. — Dub. Univ. **1**: 107. — Ed. Mo. R. **4**: 262. — Anal. M. **13**: 501. — (J. Leslie) Ed. R. **25**: 86.
— Pilgrimage to Grave of. (C. Burgin) Lippinc. **2**: 59.
— Sketch of, with portrait. Hogg, **1**: 273.
— Tableau Physique. Ed. R. **16**: 223.
— Travels of. Ecl. R. **44**: 288, 522.
— — in Ural and Altai Mountains. For. Q. **20**: 402.
— Visit to. Liv. Age, **24**: 450.
— Works of. (E. Everett) No. Am. **16**: 1.
Humboldt, William von. Quar. **124**: 504. — Liv. Age, **17**: 542.
— as a Comparative Philologist. (G. J. Adler) Nat. Q. **11**: 228.
— Letter to a female Friend. Liv. Age, **24**: 43.
— Works of. For. Q. **28**: 334.
Humboldt Valley. (W. W. Bailey) Am. Natural. **4**: 27.
Humbug. Once a Week, **24**: 570.
— Essay on. Fraser, **52**: 30.
— March of. Fraser, **4**: 85.
— Philosophy of. Bentley, **6**: 599.
— Proposals for a Dictionary of. Colburn, **67**: 190.
Humbugiana. (D. McCauley) De Bow, **1**: 444. — Hogg, **13**: 224.
Humbugs in New York. So. Lit. Mess. **5**: 380.
Hume, David. (M. Oliphant) Blackw. **105**: 665. Same art. Liv. Age, **102**: 29. — Quar. **149**: 287. — (J. Hunt) Am. Presb. R. **18**: 544. — (J. Hunt) Contemp. **11**: 79.
— Alleged Plagiarisms from Thomas Aquinas. Blackw. **3**: 653.
— and his Influence on History. (E. Lake) Quar. **73**: 536. Same art. Liv. Age, **1**: 161.
— and Huxley. (W. Mountford) Mo. Rel. M. **46**: 396.
— and Kant; Philosophy of Causality. (J. H. Stirling) Princ. n. s. **3**: 178.
— and the Skeptical Philosophy. Ecl. R. **84**: 317.
— Argument against Miracles. Blackw. **46**: 91.
— Burton's Memoirs of. (E. Lake) Quar. **78**: 75. Same art. Liv. Age, **10**: 249.
— Character of. Anal. M. **1**: 377.
— History of England. Ed. R. **40**: 92. — (F. Bowen) No. Am. **69**: 537.
— Huxley's Life of. (G. C. Robertson) Mind, **4**: 270. — — (J. Veitch) Nature, **19**: 453.
— Kant's Reply to. (J. Watson) J. Spec. Philos. **10**: 113.
— Letter of Dr. Horne to Adam Smith on. Meth. M. **28**: 67.
— Letters of. Mus. **44**: 441. — Mo. R. **157**: 107.
— Life and Correspondence of. (J. Moncrieff) No. Brit. **7**: 539. — (W. Empson) Ed. R. **85**: 1. Same art. Liv. Age, **12**: 499. — Dub. Univ. **27**: 356, 576. Same art. Ecl. M. **8**: 80, 258. — Westm. **46**: 144. — Chr. Rem. **13**: 62. — Tait, n. s. **13**: 137, 205.
— Martin, and Canning. Blackw. **11**: 230.
— Philosophical Works. (J. Walker) Chr. Exam. **57**: 421. — Brownson, **12**: 445. — So. R. n. s. **11**: 92, 309.
— Philosophy of. (W. C. Taylor) Bentley, **19**: 494. — Brownson, **23**: 482. — Chr. R. **20**: 219.
Hume, David, Philosophy of, Huxley's Exposition of. (N. Porter) Princ. n. s. **4**: 421.
— Private Correspondence of. Ed. Mo. R. **5**: 127. — Mo. R. **97**: 347.
— Ritchie's Life of. Chr. Obs. **7**: 646. — (J. Foster) Ecl. R. **7**: 1.
— Voltaire and Rousseau. (J. Murdock) New Eng. **1**: 169.
Hume, Joseph, Life of. Dem. R. **35**: 291. — Peop. J. **4**: 37. — Liv. Age, **45**: 83.
Hume, Mary C. Poems. Ecl. M. **58**: 343.
Humility. Chr. Mo. Spec. **1**: 63. — Dub. Univ. **93**: 222.
— the Basis of moral Greatness. (F. A. Rauch) Mercersb. **13**: 611.
Humite of Monte Somma. (A. Scacchi) Am. J. Sci. **64**: 175.
Humming-Bird of the California Water-Falls. (J. Muir) Scrib. **15**: 545.
Humming-Birds. (J. H. Partridge) Pop. Sci. Mo. **5**: 277. — (A. R. Wallace) Fortn. **28**: 773. Same art. Liv. Age, **136**: 3. — Appleton, **1**: 487. — (S. A. Hubbard) Harper, **63**: 25. — (J. V. Cheney) Scrib. **22**: 760. — Fraser, **65**: 457. Same art. Ecl. M. **56**: 253. — Knick. **62**: 317. — Sharpe, **41**: 121. — Penny M. **4**: 135.
— Origin of. Dub. Univ. **23**: 534.
— Something about. (M. Russell) Hours at Home, **9**: 536.
Humming-Bird Hawk-Moth. (Mrs. Ward) Intel. Obs. **9**: 39.
Humor. (H. T. Tuckerman) Godey, **39**: 7. — Cornh. **33**: 318. Same art. Ecl. M. **86**: 577. Same art. Liv. Age, **129**: 234.
— American. (S. S. Cox) Harper, **50**: 690, 847. — Brit. Q. **52**: 324. Same art. Ecl. M. **76**: 1. — Cornh. **13**: 28. — No. Brit. **33**: 461. — Ecl. M. **33**: 137. **35**: 267. — All the Year. **6**: 190. — Bentley, **27**: 137, 415, 504.
— — Slicks, Downings, and Crocketts. Westm. **32**: 137.
— — Traits of. Irish Q. **2**: 171.
See also Humor, Yankee.
— among Monarchs. Temp. Bar, **36**: 489.
— and its Sphere. (E. H. Gillette) Hours at Home, **5**: 145.
— and Wit. (S. Cox) Victoria, **23**: 123.
— Boston Wit and. (W. Mitchell) Lippinc. **1**: 552.
— Facetiæ. No. Brit. **46**: 381.
— Feminine. Victoria, **17**: 368.
— German, Specimens of. Bentley, **57**: 310.
— Legislative. (S. S. Cox) Harper, **51**: 713. **52**: 119, 271.
— Modern Puritan. Cong. **1**: 280.
— of various Nations. (F. P. Cobbe) Victoria, **1**: 193.
— Rustic. (C. A. H. Crosse) Once a Week, **12**: 459.
— Scottish. No. Brit. **35**: 480. — Once a Week, **24**: 546.
— Sense of. Ev. Sat. **11**: 239.
— Waifs from Field, Camp, and Garrison. (J. F. Fitts) Lippinc. **6**: 303.
— Yankee. Quar. **122**: 212. Same art. Liv. Age, **92**: 673. — (G. Massey) Ev. Sat. **3**: 330.
See Absurdity; Comic; Jesters; Jokes; Wit and Humor.
Humors of the North. Fraser, **15**: 20–591. **19**: 50. **22**: 658.
Humorist, The. Colburn, **49**: 78.
— Character of. (W. H. Pater) Fortn. **29**: 466. Same art. Liv. Age, **139**: 533.
Humorist's Life, Sad Side of. Ecl. R. **114**: 659. Same art. Liv. Age, **72**: 220.
Humorists, American. Cornh. **13**: 28. — (A. G. Sedgwick) No. Am. **102**: 586.
— Dickens and Thackeray. Ecl. M. **16**: 370. Same art. Liv. Age, **21**: 224.
— English, of 18th Century. Prosp. R. **9**: 468.
— Modern, 1860. Dub. R. **48**: 107.
— Recent; Aytoun, Peacock, Prout. No. Brit. **45**: 75. Same art. Liv. Age, **91**: 131.

Humorists, Thackeray's English. Colburn, **98**: 262. — Internat. M. **4**: 24.
Humorous Man. Lond. M. **3**: 505.
Humphrey, David, History of the Propagation Society. Am. Church R **4**: 433, 622. **5**: 108–615.
Humphrey Grainger's Losses; a Tale. Temp. Bar, **9**: 39.
Humphrey, Heman. Nat. M. **2**: 113.
— Letter of. Lit. & Theo. R. **1**: 31.
— Pastoral Sermon. Chr. Mo. Spec. **8**: 428.
Humphreys, Gen. Benjamin G. N. Ecl. **5**: 179.
Humphreys, Charles. (A. A. Humphreys) Pennsyl. M. **1**: 83.
Humphreys, Col. David. Embassy to Algiers, 1793. Hist. M. **4**: 262, 296, 359.
— Monument to. Chr. Mo. Spec. **2**: 367.
— on Agriculture. (W. Tudor) No. Am. **4**: 98.
— Poems of. Carey's Mus. **1**: 230. **3**: 273.
Humphreys, J., Memoir of. Cong. M. **22**: 1.
Hunchback, The. (A. Sullivan) Putnam, **2**: 79.
Hunchback; a Pennsylvania Story. So. Lit. Mess. **7**: 745. **8**: 330, 677.
Hunchback of Strasburg. Chamb. J. **17**: 387. Same art. Ecl. M. **27**: 100. Same art. Liv. Age, **34**: 168.
Hunchback Cashier. Colburn, **156**: 189–548. **157**: 107.
Hundred Years ago [1781]. (W. Dennehy) Cath. World, **33**: 736.
Hunebedden in Drenthe. (D. Lubach) Anthrop. J. **6**: 158.
Hung and unhung. (R. Wilson) Lippinc. **14**: 705.
Hungarian Address, 1866. (M. Heilprin) Nation, **2**: 327.
Hungarian Books. Fraser, **41**: 477.
Hungarian Crown, Adventures of. Once a Week, **17**: 57.
Hungarian Dervish. All the Year, **13**: 66.
Hungarian Military Sketches. Blackw. **69**: 89.
Hungarian Nation. Brownson, **8**: 492.
Hungarian Political Romance. Ecl. R. **91**: 408.
Hungarian Popular Songs. (C. G. Leland) Internat. M. **5**: 332.
Hungarian Sketches, Jokai's. Fraser, **51**: 192.
Hungarian Tale. All the Year, **19**: 487.—Lond. M. **23**: 78.
Hungarian Traveler in England. For. Q. **20**: 179.
Hungarian Types and Austrian Pictures. (E. King) Lippinc. **23**: 137, 277.
Hungarians, The. Chamb. J. **12**: 6. — Hogg, **4**: 83.
— Among. Argosy, **32**: 265.
Hungary. (J. O. Noyes) Nat. M. **10**: 8. **12**: 205. — Am. Whig R. **14**: 127. — Fraser, **65**: 698. — Prosp. R. **5**: 369.
— along the Danube. Temp. Bar, **6**: 61, 244, 348.
— and Austria, 1849 Brownson, **9**: 195. — Ed. R. **90**: 230. Same art. Liv. Age. **22**: 433. — Blackw. **65**: 614, 697. Same art. Liv. Age, **21**: 548. **22**: 103. — Westm. **51**: 419. — Ecl. R. **90**: 364.
— — in 1861. Fraser, **64**: 517. — (B. Price) Fraser, **65**: 384. — Colburn, **122**: 492. — Dub. R. **50**: 349.
— and British Policy. Brit. Q. **11**: 230. Same art. Liv. Age, **25**: 337.
— and Croatia. (E. Fitzmaurice) Macmil. **36**: 34.
— and England. Ecl. R. **91**: 49.
— and her Institutions in 1839–40, Pardoe on. Mo. R. **153**: 457.
— and the Hungarians. Hogg, **2**: 168.
— — in 1849. Ecl. M. **22**: 43.
— and Kossuth. (J. H. Perry) Meth. Q. **12**: 262. — Ecl. R. **100**: 363. — Brit. Q. **14**: 544.
— and the Lower Danube. (E. Hull) Dub. Univ. **83**: 257.
— and Roumania since 1848. (K. Blind) No. Am. **109**: 176.
— and Slavonic Movement. (J. M. Mackie) Am. Whig R. **8**: 611.
— and Transylvania, Commerce of. (G. F. S. de Cassali) Hunt, **21**: 191.
— — Abuses in. For. R. **5**: 223.
Hungary and Transylvania, Paget's. Dub. R. **8**: 89. — Mo. R. **151**: 141.
— Austria and the Government of. Westm. **73**: 457.
— Austrian. Cath. World, **32**: 33.
— Bif-steck à l'Anglaise. Temp. Bar, **59**: 179.
— Bright's Travels in. Ed. R. **31**: 214.
— British Blue-Book on, 1852. Tait, n. s. **19**: 37.
— City of Füred. Temp. Bar, **59**: 385.
— Constitutional Crisis in. No. Brit. **52**: 493.
— Coronation of Francis Joseph, 1867. Cornh. **16**: 212.
— Country Life in, before the Elections. (A. J. Patterson) Fortn. **5**: 705.
— Day at Adelsberg. (F. P. Cobbe) Victoria, **2**: 202.
— Election in. (A. J. Patterson) Fortn. **6**: 129.
— Electoral Laws of. (A. J. Patterson) Fortn. **5**: 1.
— German Books on. Ed. R. **91**: 496.
— Gerando and the Struggle in. (M. L. Putnam) Chr. Exam. **58**: 1, 165, 402.
— Glimpses of Magyar Land. (E. Dicey) Macmil. **13**: 376.
— Goth and Hun, 1848. Tait, n. s. **18**: 495.
— History of. House. Words, **4**: 249, 281.
— in 1849. (L. Pardoe) Sharpe, **10**: 91. — Brit. Q. **10**: 548.
— in 1851. (C. L. Brace) Bentley, **31**: 516, 652. — Irish Q. **2**: 563.
— in 1852. De Bow, **13**: 433.
— in 1855. Ecl. R. **102**: 479.
— in 1878. (M. Heilprin) Nation, **27**: 394. — (A. Laugel) Nation, **27**: 252.
— Life in. (J. O. Noyes) Nat. M. **9**: 305.
— — and Literature in. Brit. Q. **11**: 514.
— — Romance of. Ecl. R. **91**: 408.
— Literature of. Mo. R. **113**: 132.
— — and Prospects of. Nat. Q. **14**: 108.
— Magyar Rural Life. (J. D. Fenton) Victoria, **7**: 320.
— Marmont's Tour in. Blackw. **42**: 405.
— Mineral Wealth of, 1871. Pract. M. **1**: 449.
— Mines and Mining of. Pract. M. **2**: 234. **3**: 98.
— National Manners in. Penny M. **7**: 199.
— Non-Intervention in. Brit. Q. **15**: 253.
— Pardoe's City of the Magyar. Tait, n. s. **8**: 60.
— past and present. (J. McClenahan) Nat. Q. **1**: 316.
— Peasant Life in. (R. K. Tertzky) Howitt, **1**: 50. **2**: 22, 34. — Nat. R. **9**: 31. Same art. Ecl. M. **48**: 24. — (R. K. Tertzky) Peop. J. **6**: 37.
— Political Relations of, 1842. Dub. Univ. **19**: 781.
— Presburg and Pesth. Temp. Bar, **55**: 339.
— Present State of. Hogg, **7**: 373, 392.
— Protestantism in. (D. D. Demarest) Princ. **28**: 208.
— Pulszky's Tales and Traditions of. Ed. R. **94**: 127. — Ecl. R. **94**: 18.
— Question of, 1849. Fraser, **39**: 687.
— Races and Resources of. Lond Q. **48**: 67.
— Religious Oppression in. (C. L. Brace) No. Am. **87**: 343.
— Revolt and War in, 1848–49. Tait, n. s. **15**: 732. **16**: 483, 601. **17**: 510. — Brownson, **8**: 29, 164. — (C. C. Felton) No. Am. **75**: 424. — Ed. R. **97**: 119. — Brit. Q. **13**: 1. — Dem. R. **31**: 505. — Ecl. R. **91**: 750. **92**: 641.
— — and Arthur Görgey. Ecl. R. **97**: 1.
— — and Kossuth. Ecl. R. **94**: 748.
— — Campaigns in, 1848 and 1849. Quar. **92**: 354.
— — Captive of Peterwaradein. Sharpe, **13**: 176.
— — History of. Fraser, **44**: 488, 695. **45**: 94–687.
— — Narrative of. Bentley, **28**: 194.
— — What next? Brit. Q. **10**: 548.
— Russians in, 1849. Fraser, **40**: 219.
— Statistics of. J. Statis. Soc. **39**: 734.
— Tokay Districts of. Penny M. **13**: 478.
— Unitarianism in. (H. H. Barber) Unita. R. **12**: 427.
— Von Beck's Personal Adventures in. Liv. Age, **28**: 77.

Hungary, War of the Races in, 1849. (F. Bowen) No. Am. **70**: 78. **72**: 205. — (Mrs. M. L. Putnam) Chr. Exam. **48**: 44.
— Works on. So. Lit. Mess. **16**: 500. **17**: 505.
— Year in. Colburn, **17**: 442.
See Magyars.
Hunger and Thirst, Phenomena of. Blackw. **83**: 1. Same art. Ecl. M. **43**: 486. Same art. Liv. Age, **56**: 416.
Hungerford, Agnes, Inventory of her Goods, 1523. (J. G. Nichols and J. E. Jackson) Arch. **38**: 353.
Hungerford Market. Penny M. **1**: 169.
Hungry Heart. (J. W. De Forest) Lippinc. **6**: 189.
Hunt, Alfred W., Technical Notes on. (P. G. Hamerton) Portfo. **7**: 155.
Hunt, F. K. Fourth Estate. No. Brit. **13**: 86.
Hunt, Henry, Will of, 1662. N. E. Reg. **9**: 33.
Hunt, John, Missionary among the Cannibals. Mo. Rel. M. **25**: 145.
Hunt, Leigh. (W. H. Barnes) Meth. Q. **20**: 245. — (G. Gilfillan) Tait, n. s. **13**: 655. Same art. Liv. Age, **11**: 368. — Am. Whig R. **4**: 17. — with portrait, Ecl. M. **9**: 384. — Anal. M. **4**: 73. — with portrait, Fraser, **9**: 643. — (J. Savage) Dem. R. **27**: 426. — (C. N. Gregory) Western, **7**: 365. — (S. C. Hall) Art J. **17**: 317. Same art. Ecl. M. **66**: 17. — (G. M. Towle) No. Am. **97**: 155. — (H. T. Tuckerman) So. Lit. Mess. **7**: 473. — with portrait, (M. Howitt) Peop. J. **1**: 268. — Bentley, **38**: 96. Same art. Ecl. M. **36**: 701. — Blackw. **2**: 38. — Broadw. **4**: 307. — Cornh. **1**: 85. Same art. Liv. Age, **64**: 421. — Liv. Age, **63**: 213. — No. Brit. **33**: 356. Same art. Liv. Age, **68**. 29.
— and his Family. Appleton, **22**: 135.
— and Lord Brougham. (S. R. T. Mayer) Temp. Bar, **47**: 221. Same art. Ecl. M. **87**: 164. Same art. Liv. Age, **130**: 239.
— and B. R. Haydon. (S. R. T. Mayer) St. James, **34**: 349.
— and Charles Ollier. (S. R. T. Mayer) St. James, **35**: 387.
— and Southwood Smith. (S. R. T. Mayer) St. James, **35**: 76.
— Art of Love. Blackw. **12**: 775.
— as a Poet. (A. T. Kent) Fortn. **36**: 224. — Ecl. M. **97**: 550.
— Autobiography. No. Brit. **14**: 143. — Chamb. J. **14**: 19. Same art. Ecl. M. **21**: 247. — Dub. Univ. **36**: 268. — Am. Whig R. **13**: 34. — Ecl. R. **92**: 409. — Internat. M. **1**: 35, 130. — Sharpe, **12**: 121. — Tait, n. s. **17**: 563.
— Bacchus in Tuscany. Blackw. **18**: 155.
— Book for a Corner. Hogg, **3**: 108.
— Correspondence. Chamb. J. **37**: 266.
— Descent of Liberty. Anal. M. **6**: 113.
— Feast of the Poets. Anal. M. **4**: 243.
— Foliage; Poems. Portfo.(Den.) **21**: 394. — Blackw. **6**: 70. — Quar. **18**: 324. — Ecl. R. **28**: 484.
— Gossip about. Colburn, **81**: 84.
— Hero and Leander, and Bacchus and Ariadne. Lond. M. **2**: 45.
— Imagination and Fancy. Brit. Q. **1**: 563. — Ecl. M. **5**: 500. — Dub. Univ. **25**: 649.
— Legend of Florence. Blackw. **47**: 303.
— Letters to. Blackw. **2**: 414. **3**: 196.
— Literary Life of. All the Year, **7**: 115. Same art. Liv. Age, **73**: 585.
— Literary Pocket-Book. Blackw. **6**: 235. **10**: 574.
— Men, Women, and Books. Dub. Univ. **30**: 386. — Liv. Age, **14**: 188.
— on the Italian Poets. For. Q. **36**: 333.
— on the Pension List. (G. Gilfillan) Tait, n. s. **14**: 522. Same art. Ecl. M. **12**: 118.
— Personal Reminiscences of. Ev. Sat. **9**: 50.
Hunt, Leigh, Poems of. So. Lit. Mess. **10**: 619. — Colburn, **37**: 297. — Liv. Age, **66**: 125. — Tait, **2**: 630. — Macmil. **6**: 238.
— Reminiscences of. Dub. Univ. **58**: 610.
— Round Table. Anal. M. **7**: 278.
— Sketches. (G. W. Peck) Am. Whig R. **6**: 300.
— Songs and Chorus of the Flowers. Colburn, **47**: 17.
— Story of Rimini. Blackw. **2**: 194. — (W. Tudor) No. Am. **3**: 272. — Quar. **14**: 473. — (W. Hazlitt) Ed. R. **26**: 476.
— Stories of Italian Poets. Liv. Age, **8**: 481.
— The Town. Dub. Univ. **32**: 669.
— Ultra Crepidasius. Blackw. **15**: 86.
— Wallace and Fawdon. Colburn, **89**: 269.
— Wit and Humor. Liv. Age, **12**: 97. — Westm. **48**: 24. Same art. Liv. Age, **15**: 344. — Ecl. M. **12**: 456. — Dub. Univ. **29**: 74. — Fraser, **34**: 735.
— Works of. Liv. Age, **1**: 342.
Hunt, Memucan, with portrait. De Bow, **13**: 416.
Hunt, Robert. Panthea. Hogg, **4**: 307.
— Poetry of Science. No. Brit. **13**: 117. Same art. Ecl. M. **20**: 289. — Ecl. R. **90**: 36. — Fraser, **39**: 378.
Hunt, Thomas Sterry. Pop. Sci. Mo. **8**: 486.
— Address of. (J. D. Dana) Nature, **5**: 329.
Hunt, Washington, with portrait. Am. Whig R. **9**: 522.
Hunt, Wm. Henry, Water-Color Painter. Fraser, **72**: 525.
Hunt, Wm. Holman. (F. G. Stephens) Portfo. **2**: 33. — with portrait, Appleton, **11**: 656. — with portrait, Ecl. M. **85**: 632.
— Finding of Christ in the Temple. (F. T. Palgrave) Fraser, **61**: 643. — Macmil. **2**: 34.
— Isabel. (B. Cracroft) Fortn. **9**: 648.
— The Shadow of Death. Cong. **3**: 29.
— Technical Note on. (P. G. Hamerton) Portfo. **6**: 45.
Hunt, William Morris, with portrait. (M. R. Oakey) Harper, **61**: 161 — (S. W. Whitman) Internat. R. **8**: 389. — Lippinc. **11**: 111.
— and his Paintings. Art J. **30**: 116.
— Exhibition of his Pictures. Am. Arch. **6**: 173.
— Influence of, on Painting. (S. G. W. Benjamin) Am. Arch. **7**: 59.
— Records of. (H. C. Angell) Atlan. **45**: 559, 630, 753. **46**: 75.
— Talks on Art. (J. F. Weir) New Eng. **37**: 160. — Portfo. **9**: 79.
— Teaching of. (F. D. Millet) Atlan. **46**: 189.
Hunt for a Publisher. (Mrs. Bushby) Colburn, **143**: 683. **144**: 44.
— for Smugglers. (P. Mulford) Atlan. **31**: 202.
— with Yankton Sioux. (T. E. Leeds) Galaxy, **16**: 552.
Hunted down. (C. Dickens) All the Year, **3**: 397, 422.
Hunter, John, Memoir of. Ecl. R. **25**: 372.
— Life and Genius of. Dub. R. **2**: 277.
— Sketch of. So. Lit. Mess. **13**: 312.
Hunter, Mrs. John, Poems of. (F. Jeffrey) Ed. R. **1**: 421.
Hnnter, R. M T., Correspondence with. Dem. R. **29**: 77.
Hunter, Wm. Travels. (Lord Brougham) Ed. R. **4**: 207.
Hunter's School of Arts and Industrial School at Madras. Art J. **5**: 280, 310.
Hunterian Museum. House. Words, **2**: 277. — Once a Week, **3**: 623.
Hunter's Wife; a Tale. Chamb. J. **15**: 403.
Hunters, Ancient. Am. Mo. M. **7**: 245.
— Mighty. Chamb. J. **45**: 107.
Hunting. Chamb. J. **49**: 587. — Gent. M. n. s. **2**: 57. — Lond. M. **7**: 245. — So. Lit. Mess. **17**: 45.
— a Dragon. (E. Spencer) So. M. **9**: 163.
— Ancient, of Great Britain. (S. Pegge) Arch. **10**: 156.
— and Hunters. Fraser, **62**: 613.
— Artifices employed by rude Nations in. Penny M. **14**: 206, 218.
— Beckford's Thoughts on. Retros. **13**: 230.

Hunting; The Chase in Africa. (Gen. Daumas) Sharpe, **17**: 361.
— Chassaing's Chasses au Lion. Bentley, **58**: 145.
— Clergymen addicted to. Cornh. **20**: 172.
— Coursing in England. Broadw. **2**: 1.
— Expedients in. Chamb. J. **41**: 270.
— in Cashmere. (J. F. Elten) Putnam, **13**: 436.
— in England. Eng. Dom. M **11**: 210, 272.
— in the Field. (A. Trollope) Good Words, **20**: 99.
— in France. (L. Lejeune) Lippinc. **21**: 192. — (W. P. Lennox) Once a Week, **16**: 44.
— in the Himalaya. Liv. Age, **66**: 626.
— Literature and Philosophy of. Ecl. R. **99**: 718.
— in the Midlands. Lond. Soc. **21**: 34.
— Meet in the Campagna. (T. A. Trollope) Lippinc. **13**: 573.
— of Badlewe; a Dramatic Tale. Portfo.(Den.) **24**: 74.
— Torch-Hunt in Tennessee. Putnam, **10**: 231.
— under the Cypress. (R. Wilson) Lippinc. **14**: 94.
— Wild Deer. (T. Carlisle) St. James, **33**: 426.
— with the Nizam's Cheetahs. (D. Sassoon) St. James, **43**: 904.
See Trapping; Wild Sports. *Also names of different animals, as* Bison; Eland; Elephant, etc.
Hunting Tour in 1864–65. St. James, **12**: 467. **13**: 37.
Hunting Tours, Apperley's. Mo. R. **136**: 359.
Huntingdon, Selina, Countess of, Life and Times of. Chr. Exam. **29**: 274. — Liv. Age, **55**: 283. — Mo. R. **150**: 373. — Ecl. R. **70**: 609. Same art. Mus. **38**: 167.—Chr. Obs. **57**: 691.
Huntington, Daniel. (H. T. Tuckerman) Putnam, **11**: 374. — Godey, **33**: 68.
Huntington, Frederick D. Sermons. (S. W. S. Dutton) New Eng. **14**: 429. — (W. I. Budington) New Eng. **18**: 190.
— Withdrawal from Monthly Religious Magazine. Mo. Rel. M. **20**: 361.
Huntington, Jedediah V. Alban. Am. Whig R. **14**: 488.
— Lady Alice. (A. P. Peabody) No. Am. **70**: 225. — Liv. Age, **21**: 409. — (S. H. Turner) Am. Church R. **2**: 505. — So. Lit. Mess. **15**: 529.
Huntington, Joshua, Memoir of. Chr. Mo. Spec. **1**: 449.
Huntington, Leverett, Memoir of. Chr. Mo. Spec. **2**: 293.
Huntington, Samuel. (A. H. Clapp) Cong. Q. **6**: 317.
Huntington, Mrs. Susan. Chr. Mo. Spec. **8**: 309.
Huntington, Thomas. (F. S. Pease) N. E. Reg. **10**: 283.
Huntington, Wm., Life and Works of. (R. Southey) Quar. **24**: 462.
Huntington Genealogy. (F. S. Pease) N. E. Reg. **1**: 343. — (J. Huntington) N. E. Reg. **5**: 163. — (S. H. Conger) N. E. Reg. **8**: 186.
Huntington Peerage. Ed. Mo. R. **4**: 191.
Hunyadi, Count, Hero of Hungary. Dub. Univ. **57**: 39. Same art. Ecl. M. **52**: 382.
Hurculanensia. Ed. R. **16**: 368.
Hurd, Nathaniel, with portrait. New. Eng. M. **3**: 1.
Hurd, Bp. Rich., and Contemporaries. No. Brit. **34**: 375.
— Correspondence with George III. Bentley, **26**: 325, 510.
— Life and Writings of. Liv. Age, **66**: 711. — Chr. Obs. **61**: 260. — Chr. Rem. **40**: 262.
Hurdis, John, Poems of. Retros. **1**: 57.
Hurdwaar, India. Hogg, **2**: 356.
— Holy Fair of. Cornh. **12**: 609.
Hurlbut, Martin L., Memoir of. (S. A. H.) Chr. Exam. **35**: 41.
Hurlbut, William Henry. (E. Benson) Galaxy, **7**: 30.
Hurley House, Berks. Penny M. **7**: 60.
Hurlingham Park. All the Year, **43**: 179. — Broadw. **5**: 81.
Huron Indians and their Head-Form. (D. Wilson) Canad. J. n. s. **13**: 113.
— — Wilson on. Nature, **6**: 264.
Huron Indians, Conversion of. (A. J. Thébaud) Month, **40**: 379. **41**: 60. **42**: 379. **43**: 337. — Chr. Rem. **55**: 277.
— Language of. Hist. M. **2**: 197.
— Last of. (W. H. Withrow) Canad. Mo. **2**: 409.
Huron, Lake, Botany of. (J. Gibson and J. Macoun) Canad. J. n. s. **14**: 467.
Hurricane. (D. T. Ansted) Pop. Sci. R. **7**: 10.
— at Antigua. *See* Antigua.
— at Shelbyville, Tenn., 1830. (J. H. Kain) Am. J. Sci. **31**: 252.
— in New England, Sept. 1815. (N. Darling) Am. J. Sci. **42**: 243.
— of 8th of April, 1838. (J. Floyd) Am. J. Sci. **36**: 71.
— of Sept. 1853, in the Atlantic. (W. C. Redfield) Am. J. Sci. **68**: 1, 176.
— of May, 1862, in England. (E. J. Lowe) Intel. Obs. **1**: 439.
— Ride in a, through the Sugar Canes. (R. Hardy) Fraser, **41**: 292. Same art. Liv. Age, **25**: 127.
— Typhoon, and Tornado. (D. T. Ansted) Pop. Sci. R. **7**: 10. Same art. Ecl. M. **70**: 283. Same art. Ev. Sat. **5**: 216.
Hurricanes. All the Year, **23**: 437. — Chamb. J. **42**: 519. — (W. C. Redfield) Nav. M. **1**: 302.
— and Storms of the United States and West Indies. (W. C. Redfield) Am. J. Sci. **25**: 114. **51**: 1–333.
— Courses of. Am. J. Sci. **35**: 201.
See Cyclones.
Hurry and Leisure, Concerning. (A. K. H. Boyd) Fraser, **60**: 145. Same art. Ecl. M. **48**: 469. Same art. Liv. Age, **66**: 787.
Hurst Castle, Day at. Blackw. **15**: 35.
Hurstmonceaux Castle. Dub. Univ. **78**: 220. — Penny M. **14**: 217.
— a Poem. St. James, **35**: 100.
Hurston Hall; a Tale. Cath. World, **10**: 449.
Hurter, Frederick, Historian. (J. Martinof) Cath. World, **3**: 115.
Husband and Wife, Rights and Liabilities of. Ed. R. **105**: 181. Same art. Ecl. M. **40**: 486.
Husband and Wife; a Tale. Chamb. J. **32**: 327, 340.
Husband, Wife, Child. (A. P. Putnam) Mo. Rel. M. **47**: 62.
Husband's Complaint. Lond. M. **22**: 43.
Husband's Friend; a Tale. Putnam, **10**: 334.
Husband Lover. Dub. Univ. **20**: 556, 717.
Husbands and Wives, Young. Temp. Bar, **26**: 498.
— Apology for. Chamb. J. **18**: 385.
Husbandry, Ancient Roman. Ecl. R. **106**: 453.
— System of, for the South. (H. W. Ravenel) De Bow, **28**: 106.
Husbandry Implements, Improved. De Bow, **6**: 131.
See Agriculture.
Hush! (Mrs. Gore) Bentley, **14**: 65.
Hushed up. (A. de Fonblanque) Lond. Soc. **33**: 273.
Huskisson, William. Complete Letter-Writer. Blackw. **24**: 107.
— Death of, and approaching Parliament. Fraser, **2**: 251.
— Speech on Free Trade. Blackw. **19**: 474.
— — on Shipping Interest. Blackw. **22**: 1, 135.
Husks. (M. V. Terhune) Godey, **66**: 29–546. **67**: 52, 159.
Husks that the Swine did eat. (S. H. Cox) Am. Bib. Repos. 2d s. **3**: 112.
Huss, John. (A. H. Wratislaw) Kitto, **40**: 97, 329.
— and his Writings. Am. Presb. R. **5**: 228.
— and the Hussites. U. S. Cath. M. **4**: 409.
— and the Ultramontanes. (A. H. Wratislaw) Contemp. **19**: 238. Same art. Liv. Age, **112**: 427.
— Attempt to canonize. Month, **15**: 425. — (W. F. Stevenson) Good Words, **4**: 339.
— Life and Letters of. (H. W. Torrey) No. Am. **65**: 265.

Huss, John, Life and Times of. (J. L. Jewett) Meth. Q. 3: 220. — (J. J. Smyth) Evang. R. 18: 473.
— Precursors of, in Bohemia. (A. H. Wratislaw) Contemp. 13: 196.
— Publication of his Works in Bohemian. (A. H. Wratislaw) Kitto, 40: 97, 329. — (A. H. Wratislaw) Contemp. 10: 530.
— Sermons of. (E. H. Gillett) New Eng. 23: 610.
— Story of. (H. Rogers) Good Words, 7: 21. Same art. Liv. Age, 88: 341.
— Trial and Execution of. (E.H.Gillett) Harper, 17: 637.
Huss Festival at Prague. (W. R. S. Ralston) Good Words, 10: 839.
Hussar, Origin of the Word. Ev. Sat. 11: 415.
Hut, The. (H. J. Brent) Knick. 49: 1–598. 50: 62–372.
Hutcheson, Francis, Sketch of. Bank. M. (N. Y.) 31: 427.
Hutchings, Wm. (J. Williamson) Am. Hist. Rec. 3: 241.
Hutchinson, Anne. (E. Lawrence) Hist. M. 11: 151.
— Life of. (G. E. Ellis) Sparks's Am. Biog. 16: 169.
Hutchinson, Col. John, Life of. (F. Jeffrey) Ed. R. 13: 1. — Ecl. R. 5: 16. — Internat. M. 4: 239.
Hutchinson, Lucy. (J. Hutton) Belgra. 32: 95.
Hutchinson, Thomas, with portrait. N. E. Reg. 1: 297.
Hutchinson Family of Musicians, with cut. (M. Howitt) Peop. J. 1: 225.
— in Grasmere. (H. Martineau) Peop. J. 2: 1.
Hutchinson Genealogy. (J. L. Chester) N. E. Reg. 22: 236. — (W. H. Whitmore) N. E. Reg. 19: 13. — N. E. Reg 20: 355. 27: 81.
Huth, Nicolas's History of Earldom of. Mo. R. 158: 31.
Hutten, Ulrich von. (J. Parkman) Chr. Exam. 75: 339.— Ecl. R. 108: 54. Same art. Ecl. M. 45: 89. — Ecl. R. 118: 191. — Nat. M. 13: 243.
— and his Times. Fraser, 40: 207.
— as a Satirist. Cornh. 16: 613.
— Life and Writings of. Lond. Q. 28: 65.
— Strauss's Life and Times of. Chr. Obs. 74: 892. — Colburn, 112: 204. — Nat. R. 6: 280.
Hutton, Charles, Life and Writings of. Portfo. (Den.) 30: 265.
— Mathematical Tracts. Ed. R. 22: 88. — Quar. 9: 400.
Hutton, James, Moravian Missionary. Tait, n. s. 24: 367.
— and James Henderson. (C. J. Vaughan) Good Words, 19: 784.
Hutton, Richard H., as Critic and Theologian. (S. D. Collet) Contemp. 16: 634.
Hutton, Samuel. Reliquary, 11: 215.
Hutton, Wm., Life of. Ecl. R. 26: 440. — Mo. R. 82: 202.—Dem. R. 14: 498.—Penny M. 5: 445–499.
Huxley, Thomas Henry. (E. Haeckel) Nature, 9: 257. — (E. Haeckel) Pop. Sci. Mo. 4: 739. — (B. G. Wilder) Nation, 11: 407. — with portrait, Ecl. M. 73: 243. — with portrait, Once a Week, 27: 188.
— Address at the Harvey Tricentenary. Pop. Sci. Mo. 13: 396.
— Agnosticism in his Life of Hume. (J. McCosh) Pop. Sci. Mo. 15: 478.
— American Lectures of. (E. R. Lankester) Pop. Sci. Mo. 11: 709.
— and Evolution. (A. Winchell) Meth. Q. 37: 289.
— and Hume. (W. Mountford) Mo. Rel. M. 46: 396.
— Critiques and Addresses. (W. H. Browne) So. M. 13: 372.
— Exposition of Hume's Philosophy. (N. Porter) Princ. n. s. 4: 421.
— Hypothesis of. (Lord Blachford) Contemp. 26: 614.
— in New York. (J. W. Dawson) Internat. R. 4: 34.
— Lay Sermons. (S. C. Bartlett) Cong. R. 11: 270. — Nature, 3: 22.
— Lectures of. (E. L. Godkin) Nation, 23: 192.
— Writings of. (D. R. Goodwin) Am. Presb. R. 20: 302. — (C. S. Minot) Internat. R. 11: 527.
Huxleyism. (W. T. Thornton) Contemp. 20: 666.
Huysman, Cornelius. Art J. 3: 79.
Hyas the Athenian. Fraser, 38: 16. Same art. Liv. Age, 18: 203.
Hyacinth; a Story. Temp. Bar, 36: 69.
Hyacinth, The. (W. Hincks) Howitt, 1: 245.
Hyacinthe, Father. *See* Loyson, C.
Hyacinthine Locks. (J. E. Tennent) St. James, 3: 439.
Hyæna, The. House. Words, 6: 373.
Hyæna-Den, near Wells, England. (W. Boyd) Canad. J. n. s. 7: 377.
Hyatt, John. Sermons. (J. Foster) Ecl. R. 14: 640.
Hybrid Races of Animals and Men. De Bow, 19: 535.
Hybridity in Animals. (S. G. Morton) Am. J. Sci. 53: 39, 303.
— Phenomena of. Anthrop. R. 2: 164.
Hybridizing. West. J. 11: 337.
Hyde, Alvan, with portrait. Am. Q. Reg. 8: 1. —(C. Yale) Lit. & Theo. R. 5: 544.
Hyde Park, past and present. Peop. J. 11: 176.
— Summer Day in. Once a Week, 13: 113.
— Walk in. Temp. Bar, 49: 222.
Hyde Park Preachings. All the Year, 5: 117.
Hyder Ali; Indian Prince. Penny M. 8: 409. — Mo. R. 159: 364.
Hyder Saibe; an Indian Tale. Colburn, 41: 476.
Hyderabad, Visit to. Once a Week, 27: 386.
Hydra, Island of. Penny M. 3: 322.
Hydra Tuba. (A. Ramsay) Recr. Sci. 2: 54.
Hydræ, Ancient and modern. (R. Denkin) Recr. Sci. 3: 3.
Hydraulic Brake, Henderson's. Pract M. 5: 298.
Hydraulic Bucket Engine. (P. Westmacott) Ecl. Engin. 4: 80.
Hydraulic Buffers. (H. Clerk) Ecl. Engin. 1: 984. 2: 168.
Hydraulic Contrivances of India. Ecl. Engin. 11: 228.
Hydraulic Double Float. (H. L. Abbot) Ecl. Engin. 13: 330.
Hydraulic Engines, High-Pressure. (A. Rigg) Ecl. Engin. 9: 346.
Hydraulic Experiments at Roorkee. (A. Cunningham) Ecl. Engin. 14: 542. — Ecl. Engin. 25: 209.
Hydraulic Forging. (J. O. Butler) Ecl. Engin. 15: 553. — Pract. M. 6: 340.
Hydraulic Gunnery. Ecl. Engin. 9: 374.
Hydraulic Joints. Ecl. Engin. 2: 202.
Hydraulic Machine Tools. Pract. M. 3: 130.
Hydraulic Modules. Ecl. Engin. 12: 40.
Hydraulic Motor. Pract. M. 5: 234.
Hydraulic Power, Accumulated. Ecl. Engin. 1: 778, 924.
Hydraulic Presses, Cylinders for. Ecl. Engin. 3: 67.
Hydraulic Ram, Montgolfier. (W. Jones) J. Frankl. Inst. 106: 186.
— Notes on. J. Frankl. Inst. 43: 133, 404.
— Report on Birkinbine's. J. Frankl. Inst. 50: 353.
— — on Gatchell's, 1853. J. Frankl. Inst. 55: 428.
Hydraulic Valves. Ecl. Engin. 11: 410.
Hydraulic Works at Algiers, 1840. (M. Poriel) J. Frankl. Inst. 29: 177.
Hydraulics as a Branch of Engineering. (G. Rennie) J. Frankl. Inst. 19: 56, 125.
— as an exact Science. (H. Heineman) Ecl. Engin. 6: 198.
— Experiments in. Ecl. Engin. 14: 310.
— New Principles of. (L. d'Auria) J. Frankl. Inst. 105: 73.
— of great Rivers. Ecl. Engin. 11: 210. *See* Rivers.
— Our Knowledge of. Ecl. Engin. 10: 408.
— Solution of a Problem in. (C. Herschell) J. Frankl. Inst. 92: 105, 181.
Hydric Sulphide, New Mode of manipulating. (J. P. Cooke, jr.) Am. J. Sci. 113: 427.
Hydrocephalus, Yeats on, 1815. Ecl. R. 22: 250.
Hydro-Dynamometer. (M. de Perrodil) Ecl. Engin. 17: 481.

Hydrogen. (A. Oppenheim) J. Frankl. Inst. **100**: 426. **101**: 64, 117, 209.
— and Air, Liquefaction and Solidification of. (W. N. Hartley) Pop. Sci. R. **17**: 155.
— and its Substitutes for the Lime-Light. J. Frankl. Inst. **103**: 209.
— Liquefaction of. (M. L. Cailletet) J. Frankl. Inst. **105**: 128. — (R. Pictet) J. Frankl. Inst. **105**: 191.
— — and Solidification of. (R. Pictet) J. Frankl. Inst. **106**: 334.
— Peroxide of. (A. Oppenheim) J. Frankl. Inst. **101**: 212, 262.
— Relation to Palladium. (T. Graham) J. Frankl. Inst. **87**: 256.
— Relations to Water. (T. S. Hunt) Am. J. Sci. **67**: 194.
Hydrogen Flame, Phenomena with. (W. F. Barrett) Nature, **5**: 482.
Hydrogen Gas. Niles's Reg. **20**: 412.
Hydrogenium. (R. Hunt) Pop. Sci. R. **8**: 233.
Hydro-Geological Surveys. (B. Latham) Ecl. Engin. **16**: 84.
Hydrographic Office at Washington. (L. Bagger) Appleton, **13**: 592.
Hydrography. Pop. Sci. Mo. **8**: 513.
— Advances in, 1857. Chr. Rem. **34**: 213.
— Smyth's Mediterranean. Fraser, **49**: 674.
Hydroids. (Mrs. S. B. Herrick) Pop. Sci. Mo. **8**: 17.
— of the Gulf Stream. Nature, **18**: 326.
Hydro-Incubation. Nature, **18**: 542.
Hydrometers. (R. Hare) Am. J. Sci. **11**: 115.
— Valuation of Solutions by Means of. (C. R. A. Wright) Pract. M. **1**: 239.
Hydronamic Formulæ. Ecl. Engin. **9**: 318.
Hydropathy, or the Water Cure. (E. Tyler) New Eng. **5**: 149. — (W. P. Atkinson) Chr. Exam. **45**: 33. — Liv. Age, **3**: 19. — Mo. R. **158**: 238. — Tait, n. s. **9**: 379.
— Gully on. Tait, n. s. **13**: 742.
— in France and Italy. St. James, **35**: 517.
— Life in a Tub. Irish Q. **8**: 589.
— My Escape from. Lond. Soc. **11**: 481.
Hydrophobia. (H. W. Acland) Contemp. **31**: 378. Same art. Sup. Pop. Sci. Mo. **2**: 338. — (J. Scoffern) St. James, **11**: 165. — Nature, **17**: 117, 139. — Chamb. J. **10**: 81. — Westm. **2**: 324. — Niles's Reg. **16**: 363. — Mo. R. **122**: 449. — Carey's Mus. **1**: 128. **8**: 68, 100. — Liv. Age, **20**: 463.
— and its Phenomena. Blackw. **90**: 222. Same art. Ecl. M. **54**: 317.
— and Rabies. (Sir T. Watson) 19th Cent. **2**: 717. Same art. Sup. Pop. Sci. Mo. **2**: 218. Same art. Liv. Age, **136**: 220.
— Dogs and their Madness. Ev. Sat. **17**: 45, 99.
— Facts relating to. (B. Silliman) Am. J. Sci. **23**: 143.
— Remedies for. All the Year, **29**: 17.
— Superstitions of. (C. P. Russell) Pop. Sci. Mo. **6**: 174.
Hydrostatic Bed for Invalids. (Dr. Arnott) Penny M. **1**: 214.
Hydrostatic Trough. (D. Wood) J. Frankl. Inst. **77**: 289.
Hydrozoa, New Order of. (G. J. Allman) Nature, **10**: 251.
Hyene, M. de, Duel of. Liv. Age, **58**: 115.
Hyères. Dub. Univ. **81**: 25, 261.
— Wintering in. (J. A. Wilson) Belgra. **41**: 41.
Hygeia, the City of Health. Chamb. J. **54**: 33.
Hygiene and Parkes's Museum. (G. V. Poore) Good Words, **20**: 553.
— and Public Health. Am. Arch. **6**: 115, 130, 163.
— — Buck on. (B. G. Wilder) Nation, **29**: 260.
— Doctoring begins at Home. Liv. Age, **46**: 777.
— Domestic. (D. A. Gorton) Nat. Q. **29**: 316.
Hygiene, Dunglison's Elements of. Mo. R. **140**: 65.
— Gospel of. (J. V. O'Conor) Cath. World, **30**: 232.
— in higher Education of Women. (A. H. Bennett) Pop. Sci. Mo. **16**: 519.
— Literature of. (F. Bacon) Nation, **8**: 392.
— Modern and Mediæval. Lond. Q. **1**: 131.
— of Air and Water. Nature, **7**: 318.
— of the Seasons. (A. Donné) Canad. Mo. **4**: 153.
— of Water. Nat. Q. **40**: 67.
See Military Hygiene.
Hygienic Change of Air. Chamb. J. **18**: 6.
Hygienic Precepts. All the Year, **36**: 224.
Hygrometer, The. Penny M. **10**: 246.
— Condensing. Nature, **17**: 14.
Hygrometric Observations, On. (J. P. Espy) J. Frankl. Inst. **11**: 221, 361. **17**: 81.
Hylas. (H. Hayman) Contemp. **7**: 277.
Hylas; a Poem. (J. Mew) Belgra. **13**: 35.
Hylas; a Poem. Dub. Univ. **1**: 42.
Hymenoptera; Our six-footed Rivals. Pop. Sci. Mo. **12**: 196. 349.
Hymn, Anglo-German. (W. C. Dessler) Mercersb. **11**: 422. — (F. Hartman) Mercersb. **11**: 424.
— Anglo-Latin. (St. Bernard) Mercersb. **11**: 304. — (St. Bonaventura) Mercersb. **11**: 305.
— Cœlestis Urbs Jerusalem. (C. Kent) Month, **23**: 447.
— of Cleanthes. Broadw. **8**: 368.
— of the Cross. (St. Bonaventura) Mercersb. **10**: 480.
— of the Dunkers. (J. G. Whittier) Atlan. **39**: 529.
— of Prudentius. (R. Ornsby) Month, **18**: 377.
— of St. Teresa. (D. F. McCarthy) Month, **18**: 235.
— to Apollo. (J. Mew) Once a Week, **16**: 407.
— What is a? Ecl. R. **123**: 62.
Hymns. (W. O. White) Unita. R. **3**: 275. — Am. Meth. M. **14**: 72. — Ecl. R. **117**: 241. — Prosp. R. **3**: 70.
— Alteration of. (C. H. Brigham) Chr. Exam. **72**: 352. — Cong. **4**: 59.
— and Hymnals, Mediæval and modern. Chr. Rem. **46**: 105.
— and Hymn Books. (J. C. Jones) Theo. R. **11**: 295. — Chr. Rem. **18**: 302. — Lond. Q. **16**: 189.
— and Hymn-Singing. (W. C. Wood) Cong. Q. **16**: 588. — Chr. Obs. **74**: 99, 196.
— and Hymn Tunes for Congregational Worship. Fraser, **62**: 299.
— and Hymn-Writers. Liv. Age, **57**: 981. — Chr. Obs. **61**: 588.
— — German. (C. B. Pearson) Contemp. **5**: 471.
— and Psalms. (C. K. Whipple) Radical, **2**: 12, 76.
— and Songs of the Church, Wither's. Liv. Age, **52**: 440.
— Anglo-German. (P. Gerhardt) Mercersb. **11**: 415.
— Beard's Collection of. (H. Ware, jr.) Chr. Exam. **24**: 90.
— Biography of certain. (W. F. Stevenson) Good Words, **3**: 641. Same art. Liv. Age, **76**: 609.
— by a Hermit. (J. Sterling) Blackw. **47**: 80–526.
— Christian Psalmist. Lit. & Theo. R. **4**: 59.
— Church Hymnal. (J. G. Freese) Am. Church R. **32**: 376.
— Early Christian Songs. No. Brit. **27**: 194. Same art. Liv. Age, **54**: 724. Same art. Ecl. M. **42**: 475.
— Evangelical Hymnal. (E. W. Gilman) New Eng. **40**: 257.
— for Children. Chr. Rem. **3**: 435.
— for Public Worship. Chr. Rem. **5** : 39. — (E. Peabody) Chr. Exam. **47**: 204.
— from Compilers' Hands. (R. T. S. Lowell) Am. Church R. **14**: 34.
— from the German. (J. H. Good) Mercersb. **1**: 508.
— — Miss Cox's. Dub. R. **12**: 279.
— Irish Church Hymnal. Dub. Univ. **84**: 641.
— Lyra Innocentium. Prosp. R. **2**: 521.

Hymns, Makers and Menders of. Am. Presb. R. 6: 605.
— Mediæval. (O. T. Hill) Dub. Univ. 68: 497. Same art. Cath. World, 4: 804. — Bost. R. 3: 361.
— Methodist. (J. Floy) Meth. Q. 4: 165. 8: 602. 9: 662. — Am. Meth. M. 14: 178.
— — and C. Wesley. (J. G. Hale) Bost. R. 5: 296.
— — Revised. Meth. Q. 39: 522.
— Nature and Offices of. (F. D. Huntington) Mo. Rel. M. 11: 268.
— Negro. (T. W. Higginson) Atlan. 19: 685.
— Nonconformist Poetry. Bib. R. 4: 372.
— of the Church. (H. Harbaugh) Am. Presb. R. 14: 266.
— of the English Nonconformists. (I. A. Bird) Liv. Age, 97: 387.
— of the Populace. Blackw. 101: 300. Same art. Liv. Age, 93: 3.
— of Primitive Church. (A. Lamson) Chr. Exam. 38: 1.
— of the Reformation. Liv. Age, 89: 742.
— Origin of. (A. P. Putnam) Unita. R. 1: 224.
— Sentimentalism in. (F. M. Bird) Am. Church R. 30: 216.
— to the Gods. (A. Pike) Blackw. 45: 819.
— to the Virgin, Early English. Month, 18: 471.
— Text of. (F. M. Bird) Nation, 3: 117.
— Tinkering of. (C. C. Nott) Nation, 3: 65.
— Unreality in. Am. Church R. 26: 367.
— Village. (R. Robbins) Chr. Mo. Spec. 7: 34.
— West Boston Society's Collection. (A Norton) Chr. Exam. 1: 41.
— Willard's Regular. Chr. Exam. 1: 224.
— Wither's Hallelujah. Liv. Age, 58: 316.
See also Psalmody.
Hymn Book, Congregational. Cong. M. 20: 711, 787.
— Methodist. Am. Meth. M. 12: 143. — Meth. Q. 30: 433. — (J. M. Buckley) Meth. Q. 36: 309. — Meth. M. 54: 822.
— — New. Lond. Q. 45: 356. — Meth. Q. 31: 522.
— of Ministerium of Pennsylvania. (A. J. Weddel) Evang R. 17: 210.
Hymn Books. Chr. Disc. 3: 360. — (F. W. P. Greenwood) Chr. Exam. 13: 163. — (E. Peabody) Chr. Exam. 41: 422.
— Church. Contemp. 1: 434.
— English Lutheran. (W. M. Reynolds) Evang. R. 11: 175, 401.
— New. (N. L. Frothingham) Chr. Exam. 40: 29.
Hymn-Singing. (J. S. Curwen, jr.) Cong. 3: 209.
Hymn Tunes and Graveyards. Am. Mo. M. 8: 530.
— Old and new. (J. S. Curwen, jr.) Cong. 4: 415, 478.
Hymnal, Church. (J. G. Freese) Am. Church R. 32: 376.
— What it should be. (C. C. Nott) Nation, 3: 155.
Hymnody, Ancient. (J. Challen) Chr. Q. 1: 477.
— Latin. (J. Anketell) Am. Church R. 28: 10–499.
— of Episcopal Church. (J. S. Kidney) Am. Church R. 18: 193.
Hymnography, Greek, Examples of. Chr. Rem. 55: 323.
Hymnology. (A. Phelps) Bib. Sac. 16: 186. 17: 134. — (W. M. Reynolds) Evang R. 7: 422. — (B. J. Wallace) Am. Presb. R. 6: 488. — Ecl. R. 102: 535. — Quar. 111: 318. Same art. Liv. Age, 73: 451. — Liv. Age, 50: 129. — (H. A. Hill) Bib. Sac. 24: 318.
— Æthiopic. (Transl. by J. M. Rodwell) Kitto, 36: 321.
— Ancient. (P. Schaff) Hours at Home, 3: 259.
— and Psalmody. Ecl. R. 61: 399.
— Biblical and Classical. Chr. R. 21: 283.
— Brief History of. (J. Anketell) Am. Church R. 31: 443.
— Catholic. Dub. R. 26: 300.
— Church Song. Cath. World, 20: 404.
— Early Reformed. (J. H. Dubbs) Ref. Q. 27: 504.
Hymnology, Eccentricities of; Early Moravian Hymn Books. Kitto, 33: 249.
— English. (W. M. Reynolds) Evang. R. 7: 422, 563. 8: 237. — (R. P. Dunn) Princ. 30: 52.
— — History and Prospects of. (J. M. Neale) Chr. Rem. 18: 302. Same art. Liv. Age, 25: 241.
— — Old. Chr. Obs. 40: 524, 587.
— — since the Reformation. (E. T. Palgrave) Good Words, 10: supp. 44. Same art. Liv. Age, 101: 195.
— English Lutheran. (W. M. Reynolds) Evang. R. 11: 175, 401.
— Freaks of. Galaxy, 24: 662.
— German. (C. T. Brooks) Chr. Exam. 69: 234, 402. — (C. B. Pearson) Contemp. 5: 471. — (W. M. Reynolds) Evang. R. 1: 308, 590. — (P. Schaff) Mercersb. 12: 228. — Dub. Univ. 52: 617. Same art. Ecl. M. 46: 211. Same art. Liv. Age, 60: 67. — Liv. Age, 47: 349. — (J. W. Alexander) Princ. 22: 574.
— — and English. Chr. Obs. 59: 704, 834.
— — Miss Cox's. Dub. R. 12: 279.
— — Deutsches Gesangbuch and the Church. (E. V. Gerhart) Mercersb. 12: 165.
— — New German Hymn Book, 1850. Evang. R. 1: 590.
— — Two Centuries of. (W. F. Stevenson) Good Words, 4: 539.
— — Winkworth's Lyra Germanica. Evang. R. 8: 591.
— History of. (J. W. Nevin) Mercersb. 8: 549.
— Methodist. (F. M. Bird) Bib. Sac. 21: 127, 284.
— of the Abyssinian Church. (J. M. Rodwell) Kitto, 38: 388.
— of the Church of England. Chr. Rem. 7: 85.
— Plymouth Collection. (L. W. Bacon) New Eng. 14: 92.
— Sabbath Hymn Book. (J. Floy) Meth. Q. 21: 49. — (J. S. Ropes) New Eng. 17: 35.
— Unchurchly. (E. V. Gerhart) Mercersb. 12: 141.
— Voice of Christian Song. Tait, n. s. 25: 431.
— Wesleyan. Lond. Q. 56: 436.
Hypæthral Question. Am. Arch. 5: 194, 202. 6: 3–199.
Hypæthral Temple, Restoration of. Am. Arch. 5: 11, 22.
Hypatia; a Novel. (C. Kingsley) Fraser, 45: 1–700. 46: 31–687. 47: 62–417.
Hypatia; a Poem. (E. C. Stedman) Scrib. 5: 746.
Hypatia of Alexandria. (M. Lloyd) Potter Am. Mo. 10: 116. — Colburn, 127: 153. — Mo. Rel. M. 6: 555. 7: 31.
Hyperbola and Ellipse, Properties of Curvature in. (C. Wright) Math. Mo. 2: 198.
Hyperbole, Social. Blackw. 100: 672.
Hyperbolic Wheels. (L. G. Franck) Ecl. Engin. 13: 536.
Hyperides, New Fragments of. (Schaefer) Meth. Q. 13: 58.
Hypnotics. (A. F. Hewit) Cath. World, 8: 289.
Hypnotism. (G. J. Romanes) Nature, 18: 492. Same art. Pop. Sci. Mo. 3: 573. — (G. J. Romanes) 19th Cent. 8: 474. Same art. Liv. Age, 147: 241. Same art. Pop. Sci. Mo. 18: 108. Same art. Ecl. M. 95: 621. — (L. H. Steiner) Mercersb. 13: 245.
— Artificial. (R. Heidenhain) Pop. Sci. Mo. 18: 362.
— in Animals. (J. Czermak) Pop. Sci. Mo. 3: 618. 4: 75. — (F. C. Clarke) Pop. Sci. Mo. 9: 211.
— Recent Researches on. (G. S. Hall) Mind, 6: 98.
— Studies on. (G. S. Hall) Nation, 30: 323.
Hypochondria, Hints on. Colburn, 41: 212.
Hypochondriac, The. Colburn, 57: 193.
— Cure of a. (Mrs. Seba Smith) Godey, 20: 55.
— Memoirs of. Lond. M. 6: 249, 352.
Hypochondriacs. Colburn, 5: 470.
Hypochondriasis and Hysteria. For. Q. 12: 110. Same art. Mus. 23: 349.
Hypocrisy. Colburn, 11: 301.

Hypothesis, Place of, in Reasoning. (G. Hall) New Eng. 14: 481.
— Use of. (W. S. Jevons) Fortn. 20: 778. — (J. Venn) Mind, 3: 43.
Hyrax of Syria. (C. H. Middleton) Intel. Obs. 4: 134. — Penny M. 4: 353.
Hyrcanian Sea, Note on. (H. Wood) Nature, 12: 51.
Hyssop of Scripture. (J. F. Royle) Kitto, 4: 257.
Hysteria and Demonism. (C. Richel) Pop. Sci. Mo. 17: 86, 376.
— and Devotion. All the Year, 2: 31.
— on Parnassus. (T. H. S. Escott) Belgra. 26: 485.
Hysterics. (R. Ludlam) Lakeside, 7: 358.
Hythe. All the Year, 37: 35.

I

I and my Chimney. Putnam, 7: 269.
I do not love you; a Story. Cornh. 27: 330.
I dream of thee; a Poem. (R. Scott) Dub. Univ. 86: 532.
I Fiorelli Italiani. Dub. Univ. 7: 24–650. 11: 601.
I never liked Lewis. (B. Jerrold) Lond. Soc. 18: 464.
I owe you Nothing, Sir. Fraser, 36: 36.
I publish the Banns of Marriage. (J. Doran) Liv. Age, 64: 623.
I remember. (P. J. Bailey) Lond. Soc. 4: 222.
Iago, Acting of. (R. G. White) Atlan. 48: 203.
— and motiveless Malignity. (F. Jacox) Colburn, 136: 165.
— A stage. Cornh. 33: 91.
Iambic Verse, Trisyllabic Feet in. (W. C. Bryant) No. Am. 9: 426.
Ianthe's Wedding. (R. Jocelyn) St. James, 49: 40.
Iatronicus. (E. Spencer) N. Ecl. 7: 135.
Ibernium, Identification of the Site of. (C. Warne) Arch. 39: 85.
Ibex, The. Penny M. 5: 156.
Ibex-Hunting. Chamb. J. 50: 685.
Ibis-Shooting in Louisiana. Chamb. J. 20: 6.
Ibn Batuta, Travels of. (B. Taylor) Contin. Mo. 1: 273. — House. Words, 11: 61.
Ibn Zafer, Solwân. Ecl. R. 97: 73.
Ibrahim Pasha, with portrait. Peop. J. 1: 337.
— in Syria, 1831. (W. F. Ainsworth) Colburn, 77: 348.
Ibsen, Henrick, the Norwegian Satirist. (E. W. Gosse) Fortn. 19: 74. Same art. Ev. Sat. 14: 133. – (W. Archer) St. James, 48: 27, 104.
Icarus; a Poem. (B. Taylor) Atlan. 6: 457.
Ice. All the Year, 20: 180. — Ev. Sat. 11: 347. — De Bow, 19: 709. — House. Words, 3: 481.
— American, How it first went to England. Ev. Sat. 10: 445.
— Anchor, Notes on. (T. C. Keefer) Canad. J. n. s. 7: 173.
— and Ice-Houses. Carey's Mus. 12: 175.
— Arctic, Dall's Observations on. (N. H. Winchell) Am. J. Sci. 121: 358.
— Artificial. Chamb. J. 8: 52. — Nat. M. 13: 414. — Pract. M. 7: 271. *See* Ice-Making.
— at high Temperatures. (T. Carnelley) Am. J. Sci. 121: 385. — (T. Carnelley) Pop. Sci. R. 20: 128.
— Causes of Holes that occur in. (J. Ferguson) J. Frankl. Inst. 29: 278.
— Commercial History of. (F. H. Forbes) Scrib. 10: 462.
— Contraction and Expansion of. (J. H. Dumble) Canad. J. n. s. 5: 418.
— Cutting, on Lake Huron. (M. Coldwell) Canad. Mo. 7: 135.
— Expansive Power of. Am. J. Sci. 9: 136.
— Dissolution of Field. (C. Whittlesey) Am. J. Sci. 79: 111.
— Formation of. (B. Silliman) Am. J. Sci. 3: 179
— — of Bottom. (E. Edlund) Intel. Obs. 6: 405.
Ice, Ground. Penny M. 11: 311.
— in Kennebec River. (F. Gardiner) Am. J. Sci. 90: 20.
— Magic Palace of, in Russia. (S. F. Cooper) Putnam, 15: 160.
— Making, and Ice-Machines. (W. N. Hartley) Pop. Sci. R. 16: 270. — (W. F. Rae) Good Words, 20: 194. — (W. N. Hartley) Pop. Sci. R. 16: 270. Same art. Sup. Pop. Sci. Mo. 1: 373. — Chamb. J. 30: 4. 57: 439. — Pract. M. 7: 262.
— — by Steam. (J. Phin) Putnam, 16: 226.
— — in Bengal. Penny M. 6: 197.
— — in the Tropics. (T. A. Wise) Nature, 5: 189.
— — Machines for. J. Frankl. Inst. 76: 104. 78: 109, 176. 101: 266, 347, 413. 102: 49, 135. 107: 73. — Ecl. Engin. 1: 911.
— — — Pictet's. Nature, 13: 432.
— — Theory of. (M. Ledoux) Ecl. Engin. 21: 89, 177, 314.
— Mechanical Properties of. (W. Matthews, jr.) Nature, 1: 534.
— Melting and Regelation of. (J. T. Bottomley) Nature, 5: 185. — (J. Aitken) Nature, 6: 396.
— of our Northern Lakes, Sudden Disappearance of. (J. G. Totten) Am. J. Sci. 78: 359.
— on Inland Waters, Solution of. (B. F. Harrison) Am. J. Sci. 85: 49.
— Phenomena of. (J. H. Dumble) Canad. J. n. s. 3: 414. — (J. H. Dumble) J. Frankl. Inst. 67: 50.
— — in the Lake District. (J. C. Ward) Nature, 11: 309.
— Physics of. (E. Lewis, jr.) Pop. Sci. Mo. 5: 399.
— Polar. (H. N. Moseley) Nature, 20: 573.
— — and Tropical. Sharpe, 30: 233.
— Preservation of. (H. Meidinger) J. Frankl. Inst. 102: 136. — Ev. Sat. 11: 91.
— Rifts of, in the Rocks of Mt. McClellan, Col. (E. L. Berthoud) Am. J. Sci. 111: 108.
— Subterranean. Fraser, 71: 784.
— under low Pressures, Experiments on. (T. Carnelley) Nature, 23: 340.
— Wenham Lake. Fraser, 47: 110.
Ice Age. (L. Agassiz) Am. Ecl. 3: 307, 512. 4: 1. — (J. A. W. Oliver) Tinsley, 29: 436. — (H. W. Crosskey) Theo. R. 11: 348. — (C. E. Dutton) Penn Mo. 6: 286. — (L. P. Gratacap) Pop. Sci. Mo. 12: 319. 14: 90. — (H. B. Norton) Pop. Sci. Mo. 15: 833.
— Causes of Cold in. (J. S. Newberry) Pop. Sci. Mo. 9: 280.
— Climate and Time. (R. Hunt) Pop. Sci. R. 14: 234.
— Evidences of. (H. Woodward) Pop. Sci. R. 16: 105. Same art. Ecl. M. 89: 104.
— Geikie's. Pop. Sci. Mo. 4: 641.
— Glacial Epochs. Quar. 148: 223.
— in Switzerland. (A. Geikie) Nature, 2: 310.
See Glacial Theory; Glaciers.
Ice Amusements. Penny M. 8: 468.
Ice Boat, Construction of. (A. C. Jones) J. Frankl. Inst. 63: 85, 279.

Ice Boat, Description of, 1856. (H. Howson) J. Frankl. Inst. **62**: 283.
— How to build. (C. H. Farnham) Scrib. **22**: 658.
— Possible Velocity of. (Z. B. Tower) Ecl. Engin. **21**: 514.
Ice-Boat Problem. (Z. B. Tower) Ecl. Engin. **22**: 83.
Ice-Boating in Canada. Chamb. J. **57**: 668.
— on the Hudson. (C. H. Farnham) Scrib. **22**: 528. — Ev. Sat. **10**: 199.
Ice-Breaker, Townsend's. Hunt, **5**: 444.
Ice Cave in Russia. Hogg, **6**: 176.
Ice Caves. Chamb. J. **12**: 169.
— Nature's. Liv. Age, **23**: 253.
— of the Alps. Mus. **2**: 399.
— of Annecy. (C. F. Browne) Good Words, **7**: 740.
— of Washington Territory. (R. W. Raymond) Overland, **3**: 421.
Ice Cavern in the Justisthal. (H. King) Once a Week, **11**: 639.
Ice Culture. Chamb. J. **41**: 99. Same art. Ecl. M. **62**: 17.
Ice Drift and Currents of North Atlantic. (W. C. Redfield) Am. J. Sci. **48**: 373.
Ice Harvest, American. Chamb. J. **52**: 36.
Ice Hero, Hans Hendrik. (A. H. Markham) Good Words, **21**: 88, 269.
Ice Houses, Chinese. Godey, **50**: 242.
Ice Mountain in Hampshire County, Va. (C. B. Hayden) Am. J. Sci. **45**: 78.
Ice Rinks. Am. Arch. **1**: 205.
Ice Sheet, Thickness at any Latitude. (W. J. McGee) Am. J. Sci. **122**: 264.
Ice Storm, An. Once a Week, **8**: 349.
Ice Trade. Chamb. J. **41**: 99. — Hunt, **33**: 169.
— American. Chamb. J. **11**: 93.
— of United States. Hunt, **11**: 377. — (N. J. Wyeth) Am. Alma. **1849**: 175. Same art. Bank. M. (N. Y.) **3**: 406.
Iced Water. Cornh. **7**: 545.
Icebergs. Ecl. R. **114**: 595.
— After, with a Painter, Noble's. Ecl. M. **55**: 94. — Liv. Age, **71**: 472.
— and Boulders. (J. Rae) Canad. J. n. s. **4**: 180.
— and Floating Islets. Hogg, **4**: 374.
— Observations on. (T. A. Latta) Ed. Philos. J. **3**: 237.
Iceberg Theory of Drift. (P. Dobson) Am. J. Sci. **46**: 169.
Iceland. (Syd. Smith) Ed. R. **3**: 334. — (A. Trollope) Fortn. **30**: 175. — (Sir D. Wedderburn) 19th Cent. **8**: 218. — Chamb. J. **52**: 741. — Dub. Univ. **84**: 349. — Ecl. R. **115**: 114.
— Age of Igneous Rocks of. (J. Geikie) Nature, **24**: 605.
— and its Phenomena. Lond. Q. **19**: 121. Same art. Ecl. M. **58**: 14.
— and Faroe Island, Visit to. (R. Chambers) Chamb. J. **24**: 129–282.
— and its Geysers. St. James, **5**: 334.
— and the Icelanders. Chr. Rem. **24**: 255. — New Eng. M. **1**: 311.
— and its Explorers. Ed. R. **143**: 222.
— and its physical Curiosities. Brit. Q. **33**: 325. Same art. Ecl. M. **53**: 216, 388. Same art. Liv. Age, **69**: 421.
— and Spitzbergen, Yacht Voyage to, Lord Dufferin's. Quar. **102**: 438. — Lond. Q. **9**: 174. Same art. Ecl. M. **43**: 33.
— Annals of. (W. Fiske) Nation, **30**: 63.
— Barrow's Visit to. Quar. **54**: 355. — Mo. R. **136**: 533.
— Boiling Springs of. Westm. **67**: 198. Same art. Ecl. M. **41**: 114.
— Burton's Ultima Thule. Nature, **12**: 509.
— Californian in. (J. R. Browne) Harper, **26**: 145–448.
— Cataract at Fossvöllum. Penny M. **7**: 449.
— Caverns and Banditti in. Penny M. **7**: 409.
Iceland, Celebration in, 1874. (C. W. Field) St. James, **34**: 559.
— Change of Faith in. Quar. **111**: 115.
— Early Bishops of. Chr. Rem. **56**: 311.
— Eruption of Mt. Hecla in 1845. Dub. R. **25**: 1.
— Eruptive Phenomena of. (J. Tyndall) J. Frankl. Inst. **56**: 402.
— Flora of. (W. L. Lindsay) Ed. New Philos. J. **71**: 64.
— Forbes on. Dub. R. **50**: 1. — Ecl. R. **113**: 527. — Ed. R. **113**: 532.
— Geysers of. Penny M. **2**: 473.
— Henderson's. (O. W. B. Peabody) No. Am. **35**: 75. — Quar. **19**: 291. — Anal. M. **14**: 456. — Spirit Pilg. **4**: 212. — (J. Foster) Ecl. R. **28**: 21, 174, 253. — Cong. M. **1**: 369, 431.
— Hooker's. (J. Foster) Ecl. R. **15**: 562.
— Impressions of. (J. Bryce) Cornh. **29**: 553. Same art. Liv. Age, **121**: 750. Same art. Ecl. M. **83**: 33. Same art. Ev. Sat. **16**: 652.
— In. (E. J. Oswald) Good Words, **17**: 472, 543, 632.
— in the Year 1000. Fraser, **46**: 643.
— in the Year 1100. Ed. R. **114**: 425.
— Journey into. (S. B. Gould) Good Words, **8**: 87.
— King of. Colburn, **126**: 118. Same art. Ecl. M. **57**: 340.
— Legendary Lore of. Westm. **86**: 122.
— Literary Societies of. For. Q. **9**: 41.
— Mackenzie's Travels in. Ed. R. **19**: 416. — (R. Southey) Quar. **7**: 43.
— Millenary of. Nature, **10**: 279.
— Modern; Autobiography of Jòn Jònsonn. Fraser, **95**: 1. Same art Liv. Age, **132**: 407.
— Moors of. (D. Ker) Appleton, **19**: 38.
— Notes from. (G. F. Rodwell) Nature, **20**: 532.
— Old; the Burnt Njal. Brit. Q. **34**: 323. Same art. Ecl. M. **55**: 11, 167.
— Ida Pfeiffer's Visit to. Dub. R. **33**: 336.
— Physico-Geographical Sketch of. Westm. **52**: 264.
— Sulphur in. Dub. Univ. **84**: 397.
— Summer in. Chamb. J. **46**: 27.
— To. (Mrs. Blackburn) Good Words, **20**: 429–622.
— Vatna Jokull, On the. (W. L. Watts) Fraser, **90**: 693. Same art. Liv. Age, **124**: 175.
— Visit to, 1857. (J. W. Bushby) Colburn, **112**: 429. **113**: 118–344.
— Vital Statistics of. (P. A. Schleisner) J. Statis. Soc. **14**: 1.
— Volcanoes of. Nature, **16**: 105.
— What I saw in. Ecl. M. **55**: 518.
Icelanders. Penny M. **2**: 442, 452.
Icelandic Dictionary, Cleasby and Vigfusson's. (J. Bryce) Nation, **18**: 399. — Ed. R. **140**: 228.
Icelandic Legends. Dub. Univ. **64**: 65.
Icelandic Letter; a Tale. So. Lit. Mess. **9**: 673, 721.
Icelandic Literature. Nat. Q. **21**: 256. **28**: 61.
— Ancient. Am. Church R. **24**: 274.
— Egill's Saga; translated. (E. Burritt) Am. Ecl. **1**: 488. — Cornh. **40**: 21.
— Frithiof the Bold; translated. (W. Morris) Dark Blue, **1**: 42, 176.
— Historical; translated. (G. P. Marsh) Am. Ecl. **1**: 446. **2**: 131.
Icelandic Lore and Scenery. Dub. Univ. **62**: 469. Same art. Ecl. M. **61**: 97.
Icelandic Religious Song. Dub. Univ. **77**: 354.
Icelandic Sagas. (Earl Dufferin) Canad. Mo. **1**: 550. — Lond. Q. **36**: 35.
— and Scenes. Dub. Univ. **62**: 459.
Ichabod; a Poem. Colburn, **169**: 148.
Ichabod; a Story. Dub. Univ. **94**: 257–660.
Ichaboe, the Guano Island. Chamb. J. **43**: 493.
Ichneumon, The. (W. Tudor) No. Am. **2**: 379. — Hogg, **2**: 108. — Penny M. **2**: 503.

Ichneumon, The, a Pet in India. Chamb. J. 16: 223.
Ichneumon Flies and their Larvæ. Once a Week, 6: 494.
Ichthyology. *See* Fishes.
Ichthyosaurus, Complete Specimen of. Ev. Sat. 10: 407.
Icon Basilike. *See* Eikon.
Iconium, Account of. Cong. M. 16: 399.
Iconoclast of Sensibility. (T. G. Appleton) O. & N. 7: 691.
Icononzo, Natural Bridges of. Penny M. 2: 364.
Ida Conway; a Tale. Fraser, 62: 285–735. 63: 70–730. 64: 71, 219.
Idaho and Montana, Travels in. (W. Barrows) Bost. R. 5: 118, 269.
— Rough Times in. (C. H. Miller) Overland, 5: 280.
— Statistics of, 1869. Am. J. Educ. 18: 492.
Idalia. (L. de la Ramé) Colburn, 133: 310–450. 134: 63–445. 135: 75–453. 136: 69–457. 137: 63–447. 138: 97–446. 139: 113, 189.
Idas; an Extravaganza. Blackw. 117: 32.
Idea within and without itself. (A. Vera) J. Spec. Philos. 8: 289. — (T. Gray) J. Spec. Philos. 9: 138.
Ideas. (A. Vera) J. Spec. Philos. 8: 107. — Fraser, 103: 117.
— as Essence and Force. (A. Vera) J. Spec. Philos. 8: 228.
— Association of. (W. James) Pop. Sci. Mo. 16: 577.
— English Doctrine of. (C. S. Peirce) Nation, 9: 461.
— Natural Hist. of. (W. F. Ainsworth) Colburn, 167: 406.
— Old Quarrel about. Cath. World, 5: 145.
— Origin of. (W. S. Hill) Am. Cath. Q. 1: 436.
— — Degerando on. (M. Napier) Ed. R. 5: 318.
— Platonic Doctrine of. Cornh. 12: 452. — (C. W. Guernsey) New Eng. 34: 705.
— Progress of. Chr. Q. 8: 364.
Ideals. (E. E. Hale) Harper, 54: 575.
— of Every-Day Life. Dial, 1: 307, 446.
— Three extreme. Quar. 144: 380.
Ideal Characters. (E. Burritt) Canad. Mo. 15: 145.
Ideal Houses; an Essay. Cornh. 1: 475.
Ideal Knowledge. Cornh. 6: 64.
Ideal Love. Colburn, 73: 265.
Idealism and Berkeley. (O. A. Brownson) Brownson, 1: 29. — Blackw. 51: 812. 53: 762.
— and Realism. (H. Lotze) J. Spec. Philos. 6: 4.
— Berkeley's. No. Brit. 34: 452.
— Critical, in France. (P. Janet) Contemp. 36: 212.
— Ferrier's Demonstrative. (L. H. Atwater) Princ. 29: 258.
— in Life. (W. D. Le Sueur) Canad. Mo. 13: 414.
— Introduction to. (F. W. J. Schelling) J. Spec. Philos. 1: 159.
— Kant's Refutation of. (H. Sidgwick and E. Caird) Mind, 5: 111.
— Materialism, or Dualism? (F. Bowen) Princ. n. s. 1: 423.
— of Berkeley and Collier. No. Brit. 53: 368.
Idealist, Dreamings of. Lond. M. 22: 122.
Idealists, The; a Socratic Dialogue. (J. D. Whelpley) Am. Whig R. 3: 258.
Ideality *versus* Reality. (J. B. Marshall) Hesp. 1: 300.
Identification; a Tale. Dub. Univ. 52: 80.
Identity, Cherished. St. James, 26: 638.
— Condillac and. (L. Adams) New Eng. 35: 440.
— Necessary Truths and. (L. Adams) New Eng. 35: 733.
— of Man after Death. (A. Coquerel) Mo. Rel. M. 9: 158.
— of Persons. Penny M. 11: 101.
— Question of. (F. P. Powers) Lakeside, 6: 155.
Identities, Personal. Blackw. 94: 733.
Ideville, Henri de. Diplomatic Journal in Italy. Quar. 133: 487. Same art. Liv. Age, 115: 771.
Idiocy. (H. G. Atkinson) Zoist, 2: 163.
— and Blindness. (W. H. Hurlbut) Chr. Exam. 44: 448.
— and Insanity in Denmark. (J. R. Hubertz) J. Statis. Soc. 16: 244.
Idiocy, Causes and Prevention of. (C. Sumner) Mass. Q. 1: 308, 509.
— in Massachusetts. So. Lit. Mess. 15: 367.
— Treatment of. No. Brit. 49: 73.
Idiomatic Iterations. Belgra. 24: 157.
Idiot; a Russian Tale. (I. Tourgénieff) Temp. Bar, 29: 249.
Idiots. (W. H. Wills) House. Words, 7: 313. 9: 197. Same art. Liv. Age, 38: 218. — Dem. R. 21: 227.
— Asylums for. Ed. R. 122: 37. Same art. Liv. Age, 86: 385.
— and Imbeciles, Management of. No. Brit. 39: 120. Same art. Ecl. M. 60: 187.
— Education of. Appleton, 3: 182. — So. Lit. Mess. 15: 65. — Chamb. J. 8: 169. Same art. Liv. Age, 15: 423. — Chamb. J. 8: 262. Same art. Liv. Age, 16: 79.
— — at Bicêtre. Chamb. J. 7: 20, 71, 105. — Westm. 49: 70. Same art. Ecl. M. 14: 219. Same art. Liv. Age, 13: 369.
— Election of. Once a Week, 19: 128.
— Favored. Chamb. J. 35: 302.
— Happy. All the Year, 11: 564.
— Influence of Music on. Chamb. J. 26: 377. Same art. Liv. Age, 52: 310.
— Institution for, in Berlin. (E. H. Clarke) Chr. Exam. 51: 360.
— Institutions for. (L. P. Brockett) Nat. M. 9: 289.
— Instruction of. (L. P. Brockett) Am. J. Educ. 1: 593.
— Schools for, in France. (N. S. Dodge) Lakeside, 7: 455.
— Treatment of, in France. (S. I. Lesley) O. & N. 4: 502.
— — and Training of. (E. Seguin) Am. J. Educ. 2: 145.
— What has been done for. (L. P. Brockett) Atlan. 1: 410.
Idiot Asylum at Syracuse, N. Y. Am. J. Educ. 4: 417.
Idiot Boy's Sunbeam. (C. M. McLachlan) Hogg, 2: 163.
Idiot Colony at Chaterham. (W. Gilbert) Good Words, 13: 271.
Idle Lake, The. All the Year, 27: 180.
Idleness, Philosophy of. (A. H. Forrester) Bentley, 12: 79.
— Plea for. Putnam, 10: 360.
— Praise of. Once a Week, 18: 93.
Idler, Passages in the Life of an. Fraser, 2: 582. 3: 305. 4: 143. 6: 689.
Idlers. Chamb. J. 53: 449.
— Apology for. Cornh. 36: 80. Same art. Ecl. M. 89: 289. Same art. Liv. Age, 134: 433.
Idlewild. *See* Willis, N. P.
Idling away Existence. (W. Chambers) Chamb. J. 55: 721.
Idol of an Hour; a Story. (M. Collins) Tinsley, 27: 33.
Idols. Ev. Sat. 5: 622.
— of Moab. Cong. 2: 410.
— Worship of. Cong. M. 1: 22.
Idolatry. (J. V. Blake) Radical, 8: 396. — U. S. Cath. M. 4: 273.
— and Fetich-Worship. (H. Spencer) Pop. Sci. Mo. 8: 158.
— better than Atheism. Univ. Q. 19: 283.
— Heathen inexcusable for. (J. K. Wight) Princ. 32: 427.
— in India, British Patronage of. Cong. M. 20: 341. 22: 418. — Ecl. R. 66: 233.
— in modern Society. Cornh. 19: 689.
— Modern. Ecl. R. 125: 424.
— of Ceylon, Hardy on British Government and. Mo. R. 154: 369.
— Swan's Poem on. Ecl. R. 45: 439.
See Worship.
Idumea, and its present Inhabitants. Am. Bib. Repos 3: 247, 393.
Idyl of the Plague; a Poem. St. James, 47: 367.
Idyl of Red Gulch. (Bret Harte) Overland, 3: 569.
Idyl of the White Ranche; a California Sketch. (I. D. Hardy) Tinsley, 28: 135.

If, Logic of. (G. C. Robertson) Mind, 2: 264.
If I were a Voice. (C. Mackay) Internat. M. 1: 17.
Iffley Church. Penny M. 14: 332.
Ightham, Mote in. (E. Walford) Once a Week, 14: 399, 445.
Ignatieff, Gen. Dub. R. 81: 69.
Ignatius of Theophorus. Chr. Obs. 2: 65-581.
Ignatius, St. Am. Church R. 21: 563.
— and Christ's Person. (E. E. Higbee) Mercersb. 4: 497.
— and his Times. (J. Forsyth) Princ. 21: 378.
— Claim to Inspiration. Chr. Obs. 40: 392, 476, 596.
— Cureton's Corpus Ignatianum. Chr. Obs. 49: 681.
— Cureton's Vindicæ Ignatianæ. Bib. R. 1: 443.
— Epistles of. (J. B. Lightfoot) Contemp. 25: 337. — (J. Murdock) New Eng. 7: 501. — New York R. 1: 367. — Kitto, 5: 339. — Brit. Q. 24: 422. — Dub. R. 44: 412. 73: 349. — Ed. R. 90: 155. — Quar. 88: 69. — (C. F. Thwing) Meth. Q. 40: 31.
— — Literary History of. Bib. R. 1: 15.
— — Syriac Version of. (C. F. Cruse) Am. Church R. 1: 566. — (J. Murdock) Am. Church R. 2: 194. — Bib. R. 1: 98.
— Life and Writings of. Chr. Mo. Spec. 5: 393.
— Meditations of. Brownson, 19: 360.
— Testimony of, to Christianity. Brit. Q. 63: 341.
Ignatius, Father, Ecclesiastical Portrait of. St. James, 25: 727.
"Ignatius, Father," a religious Impostor. Temp. Bar, 15: 139.
Ignatius Loyola. *See* Loyola.
Ignis Fatuus, Observations on. (L. Blesson) J. Frankl. Inst. 15: 408. — (J. Mitchell) J. Frankl. Inst. 8: 73.
Ignoble Conduct of a Nobleman. House. Words, 8: 477.
Ignorance, Chapter on. Knick. 7: 50.
— Duties of. Cornh. 39: 455. Same art. Liv. Age, 141: 244.
— Foster on Popular. Ecl. R. 32: 205.
— Guide to. Tinsley, 27: 259.
— of Man. Nat. R. 14: 507. Same art. Ecl. M. 57: 305.
Ignorant Folk. All the Year, 47: 302.
Iguanodon, Fossil. Penny M. 2: 27.
Ileen-ny-shiefre. (E. Townbridge) Sharpe, 52: 308.
Ilenovar; a Poem. (W. G. Simms) So. Lit. J. 4: 314.
Ilfracombe. Lond. Soc. 12: 25.
Ilg, Albert. Dream of Poliphilus. Ev. Sat. 13: 542.
Iliad. *See* Homer.
Iliad of Sandy Bar. (Bret Harte) Overland, 5: 479.
Ilka on the Hill-Top. (H. H. Boyesen) Scrib. 19: 120.
Ilkley, England. (M. D. Conway) Harper, 48: 642, 819.
Ill-Conducting Conductor. (F. Talbot) Belgra. 29: 243.
Ill-Humorist; or our Recantation. Colburn, 71: 1.
Ill-Will; an Acting Charade. (F. Marryat) Colburn, 50: 92.
Illegitimacy, Statistics of. (W. G. Lumley) J. Statis. Soc. 25: 219.
— — in London. (W. Acton) J. Statis. Soc. 22: 491.
Illinois. (J. M. Higbee) No. Am. 51: 92. — (S. C. Clarke) Atlan. 7: 579.
— and Missouri. (E. Hollister) Chr. Mo. Spec. 5: 20.
— and her Resources. Hunt, 5: 427.
— and the West. (J. W. Thompson) Chr. Exam. 26: 17.
— Birkbeck's Letters from. (W. T. Spooner) No. Am. 8: 347. — Ed. Mo. R. 1: 1. — Ed. R. 30: 120. — Quar. 19: 54.
— Coal Measures of. (R. P. Stevens) Am J. Sci. 76: 72.
— Conquest of. (B. B. Minor) De Bow, 4: 366, 450.
— Constitution of. Niles's Reg. 15: 93.
— — 1870. (L. D. Ingersoll) Lakeside, 4: 277.
— Description of. (Mrs. C. M. Kirkland) Contin. Mo. 3: 513.
— Early American Settlements in. (J. M. Peck) West. M. 1: 73.
Illinois in Spring-Time. (C. M. Kirkland) Atlan. 2: 475.
— Internal Navigation of. (Ed. Coles) Ill. M. 1: 19.
— Irish Settlements in. (W. J. Onahan) Cath. World, 33: 157.
— Life in. Once a Week, 4: 399.
— Military Bounty Lands in. West. M. 5: 334.
— Notes on. West. M. 1: 185.
— — in 1830. Ill. M. 1: 55-542. 2: 8-488.
— State Teachers' Association. Am. J. Educ. 16: 149.
— Statistical View of. (J. L. Peyton) De Bow, 19: 247, 405.
— Statistics of, 1869. Am. J. Educ. 18: 316.
— Travelers' Directory for. (S. M. Bowman) Meth. Q. 3: 402.
— Vegetation of. (G. H. Perkins) Am. Natural. 9: 385.
— What Home Missions have done for. (J. E. Roy) Cong. R. 9: 401.
Illinois College, History of. Am. J. Educ. 1: 225.
Illness, Pleasures of. All the Year, 14: 560.
Illouscha; a Shadow of Russian Life. (Smirnov) Temp. Bar, 61: 58.
Illuminati, Secret Order of. Dub. Univ. 81: 67.
Illuminated Books. Internat. M. 1: 69.
Illuminated Latin Psalter. (E. A. Bond) F. Arts Q. 1: 77.
Illuminated Manuscripts. Chamb. J. 41: 294.
— of the Middle Ages. Brit. Q. 9: 70. Same art. Liv. Age, 21: 585.
Illuminating Manuscripts, Art of. Penny M. 8: 28-148.
Illumination in a Missal. (F. Douce) Arch. 12: 200.
— Missal Painting. Dub. Univ. 68: 363. Same art. Cath. World, 4: 303.
Illumination and the Electric Light. (F. R. Conder) Dub. Univ. 93: 129.
— and Water Supply of London. (F. R. Conder) Fraser, 94: 45.
— Artificial. (E. Frankland) J. Frankl. Inst. 78: 30.
— Influence on Air of. (A. Ott) J. Frankl. Inst. 86: 266.
— with Mineral Oils. (J. C. Booth and T. H. Garrett) J. Frankl. Inst. 73: 373.
Illusions. Irish Q. 7: 860. — Irish Mo. 4: 441.
— and Hallucinations. Brit. Q. 36: 387. Same art. Ecl. M. 58: 41, 151.
— Historical. (J. Reade) New Dom. 13: 337.
— Philosophical and other. Brit. Q. 42: 79.
— Sully on. (J. Burns-Gibson) Mind, 6: 413. — (G. J. Romanes) Nature, 24: 185.
Illustrated Books. Lond. Q. 11: 474. — Quar. 74: 168. — St. James, 9: 23. — Am. Bibliop. 3: 169, 322, 378. 4: 70. — Dub. Univ. 37: 537.
— Children's. (W. M. Thackeray) Fraser, 33: 495.
Illustration, Art of, Phases of. (W. Meynell) Art J. 33: 85.
— in Literature. Blackw. 110: 754. Same art. Liv. Age, 112: 67. — Westm. 51: 92.
— Power of. Chr. R. 9: 357.
Illustrations of Irish Pride. (Mrs. S. C. Hall) Colburn, 46: 352.
Illustrative Imagery. (H. Bacon) Univ. Q. 2: 175.
Illustrious Dr. Mathéus; a Tale. (MM. Erckmann-Chatrian) Temp. Bar, 32: 205-491. 33: 36, 205.
Illyria. (C. F. F. Clinton) Bentley, 15: 612. 16: 46.
— and its Emperors. Brit. Q. 64: 1. Same art. Liv. Age, 131: 67.
— Sketches of. (G. R. Gleig) Colburn, 56: 234. 57: 17.
Illyrians, past and present. Fraser, 93: 170.
Illyrian Literature. (G. F. Comfort) Meth. Q. 23: 74.
Illyrian Poetry. Mo. R. 114: 375. — For. Q. 2: 662.
Ilted Smith; a Story of the Middle Classes. Tait, n. s. 21: 38-712.
Image of the Norman Knight. Fraser, 34: 42.

Images, Generic, and Automatic Representation, Galton on. (G. C. Robertson) Mind, **4**: 551. — 19th Cent. **6**: 157. Same art. Pop. Sci. Mo. **15**: 532.
— in Churches, Use of. U. S. Cath. M. **4**: 491.
— Veneration of. Brownson, **7**: 39.
Image Worship in the Church, Early. Chr. Obs. **77**: 30.
— History of. Ecl. R. **86**: 720.
Imagery, Mental, Galton on Statistics of. (A. Bain) Mind, **5**: 564.
Imaginary Conversation, An. (F. B. Perkins) Putnam, **13**: 358.
Imaginary Conversations. (W. S. Landor) Fraser, **52**: 560. **53**: 443.
Imaginary Quantities, Buëe on. (H. Brougham) Ed. R. **12**: 306.
— Geometrical Interpretation of. (M. Argand) Ecl. Engin. **24**: 16–313.
— Woodhouse on. (H. Brougham) Ed. R. **1**: 407.
Imagination. (O. A. Brownson) Dem. R. **12**: 48. — (E. Coues) Pop. Sci. Mo. **11**: 455. — So. Lit. Mess. **21**: 226.
— and Fact. Am. Whig R. **14**: 392.
— and Fancy, Hunt's. Dub. Univ. **25**: 649. Same art. Ecl. M. **5**: 500.
— and Language. (M. C. Putnam) Putnam, **11**: 301.
— as a national Characteristic. St. Paul's, **4**: 61.
— as the plastic Principle of Nature, Frohschammer on. (D. W. Simon) Mind, **2**: 398.
— Cultivation of. (G. J. Goschen) Liv. Age, **141**: 620. — Dem. R. **22**: 33.
— Force of. (G. B. Griffith) Potter Am. Mo. **15**: 201.
— Functions and Culture of. Brit. Q. **46**: 45. Same art. Ecl. M. **69**: 257.
— in the Preacher. New Eng. **3**: 548.
— in Science, Tyndall on. Stud. & Intel. Obs. **5**: 423.
— Influence of, on Health. Colburn, **6**: 53.
— Influence of Natural Scenery on. (H. P. Haynes) Godey, **47**: 149, 224.
— Nature and Value of. (H. L. Baugher) Evang. R. **11**: 503.
— Observation and. (J. H. Browne) Appleton, **18**: 511.
— Ode to. (C. E. Havens) Pioneer, **3**: 353.
— Phenomena of. (Lord Houghton) Fortn. **31**: 62. — Appleton, **21**: 159.
— — of diseased. Lond. M. **1**: 250.
— Pleasures of. (Mrs. J. G. Brooks) Hogg, **9**: 21.
— Practical Uses of. (T. C. Finlayson) Cong. **7**: 385.
— Training of. (E. Davies) Contemp. **12**: 25. Same art. Liv. Age, **103**: 131.
— Use and Abuse of. (J. McCosh) Ex. H. Lec. **12**: 377.
— — — in Philosophy. Chr. R. **10**: 511.
— — in Science. (M. M. P. Muir) Colburn, **166**: 614.
— Vagaries of. Chamb. J. **16**: 220. Same art. Internat. M. **4**: 638.
— Writers on. Colburn, **6**: 259.
Imaginative Literature. No. Brit. **33**: 165. Same art. Ecl. M. **51**: 237.
Imbecile and Idiotic, Education of. No. Brit. **39**: 120. Same art. Ecl. M. **60**: 187.
— Improved Treatment of. (W. Chambers) Chamb. J. **51**: 553.
See Idiots.
Imitation and Plagiarism. Cong. M. **6**: 245.
Imitation Monk; a Poem. So. R. n. s. **10**: 461.
Imitation of Jesus Christ. *See* Kempis, Thomas à.
Imitations, Literary. Putnam, **8**: 113.
Immaculate Conception. (G. W. Samson) Chr. R. **22**: 380.
— Dogma of. (H. B. Smith) Meth. Q. **15**: 275.
— Laborde on. Chr. Obs. **55**: 316.
— Little Office of. (E. Waterton) Month, **33**: 96.
Immaturity; Discourse on Veal. (A. K. H. Boyd) Fraser, **64**: 199. Same art. Ecl. M. **54**: 193. Same art. Liv. Age, **70**: 643.
Immeritus Redivivus; a Romanesque. Sharpe, **17**: 1–160.
Immermann, Karl. New Münchausen. For. Q. **31**: 1.
Immigrant, The. (J. Sill) Godey, **25**: 180, 217.
— in Canada. (T. White) Canad. Mo. **2**: 2.
Immigrant's Progress. (W. H. Rideing) Scrib. **14**: 577.
Immigrants, Protection to. Republic, **1**: 577.
Immigration. (F. Kapp) Am. Soc. Sci. J. **2**: 1. — (T. White) Canad. Mo. **1**: 193. — Bank. M. (N. Y.) **30**: 173. — De Bow, **18**: 699.
— Evils and Dangers of. (W. Barrows) New Eng. **13**: 262.
— Juvenile Pauper. Canad. Mo. **12**: 292.
— Labor, and Prices. (H. Clarke) Bank. M. (L.) **13**: 731.
— Philosophy of. (W. Brown) Canad. Mo. **15**: 696. — (J. G. McGee) Cath. World, **9**: 399.
— to the United States. (E. Jarvis) Atlan. **29**: 454. — (W. J. Mann) Mercersb. **2**: 620. — (A. H. Everett) No. Am. **40**: 457. — (O. C. Gardiner) Am. Whig R. **6**: 455, 633. **7**: 419. — Niles's Reg. **14**: 380. **18**: 157. — De Bow, **5**: 243. **21**: 574.
— — German. (E. Everett) No. Am. **11**: 1.
— — in 1790–1852. (L. Schade) Hunt, **33**: 509.
See Emigration.
Immorality in Authorship. (R. Buchanan) Fortn. **6**: 289.
Immortal or Mortal? (S. M. Shute) Bapt. Q. **10**: 205.
Immortal Life. (J. Walcott) Overland, **8**: 190.
Immortals by Accident. Dub. Univ. **59**: 582.
Immortality. (W. Bement) New Eng. **11**: 362. — (E. Buckingham) Mo. Rel. M. **47**: 330. — (S. W. McDaniel) Mo. Rel. M. **48**: 193. — (F. P. Cobbe) Theo. R. **9**: 506. **10**: 438. — (D. Y. Heisler) Mercersb. **20**: 17. — (W. H. Hill) Am. Cath. Q. **2**: 123. — (C. C. Everett) O. & N. **4**: 313. — (E. Finley) Radical, **7**: 385. — (W. H. Furness) Unita. R. **9**: 549. — (E. Garbett) Chr. Obs. **77**: 673, 768, 840. — (F. A. Henry) Am. Church R. **28**: 410. — (T. W. Higginson) Radical, **5**: 385. — (H. K. Jones) J. Spec. Philos. **9**: 27. — (G. S. Morris) Bib. Sac. **33**: 695. — (A. B. Muzzey) Unita. R. **5**: 605. — (E. Payson) Scrib. **14**: 187. — (G. Smith) Canad. Mo. **9**: 408. — J. Spec. Philos. **4**: 97. — Brit. Q. **56**: 338. Same art. Liv. Age, **115**: 515. — Cong. M. **3**: 18, 132. **28**: 36. — Am. Bib. Repos. **10**: 411. — (J. Tuckerman) Chr. Exam. **3**: 365. — Dem. R. **22**: 59, 124, 225. — Danv. Q. **1**: 115. **2**: 282. — Univ. Q. **16**: 382.
— and Annihilation. Bost. R. **1**: 445.
— and Astronomy. (T. B. Thayer) Univ. Q. **10**: 5.
— and Christianity. (T. W. Fowle) Contemp. **19**: 719.
— and Evolution. (S. S. Hebberd) Univ. Q. **34**: 22. — (J. E. Wells) Canad. Mo. **10**: 291.
— and Immateriality. Fraser, **13**: 694.
— and modern Thought. (J. Owen) Theo. R. **7**: 410.
— and Mortality. (T. W. Fowle) Contemp. **19**: 673.
— and Religion. Theo. R. **12**: 488.
— and Science. (J. W Chadwick) Unita. R. **4**: 554. — (T. W. Fowle) Contemp. **19**: 461. Same art. Ecl. M. **78**: 535. Same art. Pop. Sci. Mo. **1**: 26.
— Argument from Analogy. (I. C. Knowlton) Univ. Q. **20**: 237.
— Arguments for. (E. Buckingham) Chr. Exam. **40**: 349.
— — from Nature and from Scripture. (T. M. Post) New Eng. **14**: 115, 161.
— as indicated by Science. (A. B. Blackwell) Unita. R. **7**: 514.
— Belief in. (A. M. Fairbairn) Contemp. **20**: 27, 371. Same art. Liv. Age, **114**: 67, 707.
— — Ancient Hebrew. (S. Tuska) Bib. Sac. **17**: 787.
— Christ and the Doctrine of. (G. Matheson) Princ. n. s. **4**: 144.

Immortality; Does Psyche fly out of the Window? (S. B. Goodenow) New Eng. 40: 643.
— Eternal Punishment and. Kitto, 36: 433.
— Hindu Doctrine of. (J. D. Whelpley) Am. Whig R. 2: 267.
— Hinton's Doctrines of. Ecl. R. 90: 338.
— Hints of, in moral Nature of Man. (Z. H. Howe) Univ. Q. 19: 148.
— Idea of. (C. O. Whitman) Radical, 9: 53.
— Implicit Promise of; a Poem. Macmil. 23: 66.
— in Light of Science. (W. J. Potter) Radical, 8: 313.
— Indestructibility of Force an Argument for. (E. C. Bolles) Univ. Q. 23: 213.
— Life and Death; the Sanctions of the Law of Love. Lond. Q. 51: 265.
— Moral Argument for. (E. Thomson) Meth. Q. 20: 5.
— Natural. (T. Munnell) Chr. Q. 6: 29.
— Natural Evidences of. (E. G. Smith) Chr. Q. Spec. 8: 556. — (T. M. Post) Am. Bib. Repos. 2d s. 12: 294.
— New Phases of the Argument for. (C. A. Stork) Luth. Q. 2: 100.
— New Testament Views of, Alger on. Mo. Rel. M. 31: 69.
— of good Deeds. Bost. R. 1: 579.
— of the moral Powers. (C. Follen) Chr. Exam. 8: 265.
— Perowne on. Chr. Obs. 69: 416.
— Philosophical Argument for. Cong. M. 2: 30, 77.
— Physical Speculations on. (C. Beard) Theo. R. 12: 406.
— Plato's Views on. (T. S. King) Univ. Q. 4: 73. — (S. Ellis) Univ. Q. 37: 389.
— — and Paul's. (W. K. Pendleton) Chr. Q. 6: 373.
— Practical Aspects of. Theo. R. 7: 200.
— Proof of. (T. S. Lathrop) Univ. Q. 31: 410.
— Proofs of. (C. F. Goeschel) J. Spec. Philos. 11: 65, 177, 372. — J. Spec. Philos. 7: (July) 89.
— Rational Grounds for. (L. Curtis) New Eng. 36: 647.
— Thoughts on. (I. Dolman) Radical, 9: 205. — Knick. 22: 395.
Imogen, in Shakspere and in Sculpture. Fraser, 70: 506. Same art. Ecl. M. 63: 472.
Imogen in Wales; a Poem. (T. Irwin) Dub. Univ. 56: 480.
Impartiality. Irish Mo. 5: 266.
Impeachment. Chamb. J. 45: 213.
— of Andrew Johnson. *See* Johnson, Andrew.
Imperfections of Others. (R.W. Dale) Good Words, 8: 454.
Imperial Administration. (Earl of Carnarvon) Fortn. 30: 751.
Imperial Federation. (J. Vogel) Canad. Mo. 12: 232.
Imperial Hospitalities. Chamb. J. 34: 33.
Imperial Life, Curiosities of; Autobiography of Catherine II. Nat. R. 8: 32. Same art. Ecl. M. 46: 494.
Imperial Pardon, An. Belgra. 37: 170.
Imperial Review, An. (J. A. O'Shea) Tinsley, 26: 526.
Imperialism. (R. Lowe) Fortn. 30: 453. — Fraser, 55: 493. Same art. Liv. Age, 54: 1. — Tait, n. s. 23: 321.
— and Constitutionalism in Rome, France, and England. Chr. Rem. 32: 265.
— and Socialism. (F. Seebohm) 19th Cent. 7: 726.
— End of French. (E. L. Godkin) Nation, 28: 431.
— in America. Galaxy, 8: 656.
Imperium et Libertas. Westm. 113: 91.
Impertinent Curiosity, or curious Impertinence. Lond. M. 17: 25.
Implements in Drift, New Jersey. (C. C. Abbott) Am. Natural. 7: 204.
Impoliteness as a national Institution. (C. A. Bristed) Galaxy, 15: 181.
Imports in Massachusetts, Petitions against, 1668. N. E. Reg. 9: 81.
— of New York. Hunt, 14: 274.
— of Sugars, Molasses, etc., 1790–1844. Hunt, 14: 291.
— of United States from 1833 to 1842. Hunt, 8: 173.
— — 1845. Hunt, 14: 574.
Impossibilities. Colburn, 45: 475.
Impossible Story. An. (B. Taylor) Scrib. 16: 131.
Impost; a stupendous Deception. (S. Beaman) Dem. R. 27: 439.
Imposts and Burdens. (A. Strayler) Belgra. 13: 429.
— Chaptal on. Anal. M. 15: 321, 400.
Impostors. All the Year, 19: 615.
— Eminent. St. James, 7: 265.
— Some noted. Dub. Univ. 82: 14.
— Two, of the 18th Century. Cornh. 39: 568.
Imposture and Credulity. Dub. Univ. 67: 218. Same art. Ecl. M. 71: 834, 994.
Impostures. Blackw. 51: 51. — Mus. 44: 346.
— Extraordinary. Chamb. J. 19: 37. — (R. Lewin) Lippinc. 5: 217.
— Literary. (D. Fosdick) Am. Bib. R. 11: 39.
Impresario, The enterprising. Once a Week, 16: 521–743.
Impressions et Souvenirs. (A. L. A. Dudevant) Dub. Univ. 87: 70.
Impressions on Alluvial Clay in Hadley, Mass. (C. H. Hitchcock) Am. J. Sci. 69: 391.
Impressment of Seamen. Pamph. 24: 383, 463. — Ed. R. 41: 154. — (T. P. Thompson) Westm. 20: 489. — Blackw. 20: 745. — Pamph. 14: 381. 23: 225. — Tait, 4: 374.
Imprisonment and Transportation. Blackw. 55: 533.
— for Debt. *See* Debt.
Imprisonments, Short, Results of. Nat. R. 8: 64.
Improvement, Duty of continual. (A. Norton) Chr. Exam. 2: 412.
— of Time, Foster on. (D. E. Snow) Bost. R. 5: 51.
Improvements, Modern. Am. Whig R. 8: 581.
— of my Time. Chamb. J. 32: 129.
Improvisatore and the Heeler. (F. W. Loring) O. & N. 2: 670.
Improvisatrice, The. Ecl. M. 45: 217.
Improvvisatori. Penny M. 8: 145.
Impudence, Modern. (H T. Tuckerman) Chr. Exam. 65: 419.
Imputation, Doctrine of. (R. W. Landis) Danv. Q. 1: 390, 553. 2: 58, 248, 514. — (N. W. Taylor) Chr. Q. Spec. 3: 297, 497. — (C. Hodge) Princ. 2: 425. — Princ. 11: 553. — So. Q. 4: 255. — Am. Presb. R. 3: 89.
— Forensic. Kitto, 40: 160.
— Rationale of. (E. Cutler) Cong. R. 7: 1.
In the Abbot's Seat; a Story. Argosy, 29: 466.
In the Apple Orchard; a Tale. (Mrs. Forrester) Temp. Bar, 23: 335.
In Aunt Mely's Cabin. (S. Bonner) Lippinc. 21: 245.
In the back Street. (I. G. Meredith) Galaxy, 15: 115.
In the Barn; a Poem. (B. F. Taylor) Scrib. 8: 580.
In a Box. Galaxy, 8: 536.
In the Brook. (S. C. Woolsey) Scrib. 3: 567.
In the Camp. (R. W. Buchanan) St. James, 6: 422.
In Captivity; a Poem. (C. D. Cameron) Cornh. 13: 639.
In a Cellar. (H. E. Prescott) Atlan. 3: 151.
In Charge of Treasure. Chamb. J. 42: 410.
In Clover. (G. W. Thornbury) Lond. Soc. 18: 239.
In the Cloister Gallery. Broadw. 8: 210.
In a Corner of Bohemia. (M. Collins) Tinsley, 24: 565. 25: 74, 165.
In the Cradle of the Deep. (C. W. Stoddard) Lippinc. 11: 310.
In Danger. Chamb. J. 51: 145–261.
In the Dark. (T. Gift) Galaxy, 17: 671.
In the Dark. (K. P. Osgood) Lippinc. 10: 549.
In the Dead of Night. Argosy, 17: 1–401. 18: 1–401.
In Doubt. (T. A. Harcourt) Overland, 13: 280.
In the Dusk at Düsseldorf. Lond. Soc. 33: 472.
In the Enemy's Lines. (J. F. Fitts) Galaxy, 4: 700.
In Exile; a Poem. (C. H. Miller) Lakeside, 9: 360.

In Exile; a Story. (M. H. Foote) Atlan. 48: 184.
In Extremis; a Poem. (E. Renaud) Putnam, 15: 445.
In Extremis; a Poem. Broadw. 6: 187.
In the Family. Tinsley, 5: 81.
In 15. Colburn, 153: 532.
In the Five-Acre Field. (K. Roche) Irish Mo. 5: 723.
In the Garden; a Poem. (H. McE. Kimball) Scrib. 4: 168.
In the Garden. (M. Oliphant) Blackw. 94: 244.
In the Garden. (W. W. Story) Blackw. 96: 447.
In the Gloaming (Mrs. J. H. Riddell) Temp. Bar, 22: 180.
In the Gold Avenue. (V. W. Johnson) Harper, 52: 75.
In a Gondola; a Poem. (A. Paracelsus) Cornh. 14: 564.
In the gray Goth. (E. S. Phelps) Atlan. 20: 559.
In great Waters. Belgra. 15: 229.
In the Greenwood. Cath. World, 11: 589.
In the green Woods. (C. Owen) Canad. Mo. 11: 269.
In the Heart of the Earth. Lond. Soc. 16: 50.
In the Heart of a Hill. (J. Payn) Harper, 44: 123.
In the Himalayas; a Story. Canad. Mo. 18: 126.
In Honor bound. (C. Chesebrough) Harper, 48: 717.
In the House of a Friend. (Mrs. Notley) Eng. Dom. M. 20: 1–284. 21: 1–287. 22: 10–293. 23: 12–295.
In the House of Mæcenas; an imaginary Conversation. (G. S. Smythe) Temp. Bar, 34: 186.
In the Interests of Science. (R. H. D. Barham) Temp. Bar, 40: 186.
In Jeopardy. All the Year, 15: 65.
In the Land of the Eisteddfod. Cornh. 8: 478.
In Life and in Death. (A. L. Walker) Blackw. 105: 183.
In the Lion's Den. Bentley, 57: 363. Same art. Ecl. M. 64: 748.
In Loco Parentis. Temp. Bar, 2: 557.
In Lodgings at Knightsbridge. Temp. Bar, 16: 272–567. Same art. Liv. Age, 88: 823, 903.
In Love with a Shadow. (T. A. Janvier) Lippinc. 6: 518.
In the Midnight. (Lady Wilde) Dub. Univ. 89: 44.
In the Mist; a Story. (M. E. Penn) Argosy, 32: 306.
In a Month. (A. Brewster) Lippinc. 2: 167.
In my Mind's Eye, Horatio! Belgra. 9: 511.
In my Study Chair. Blackw. 118: 273. 119: 21. Same art. Ecl. M. 85: 641.
In my Youth. Temp. Bar, 5: 391.
In November; a Poem. (C. Gibbon) Temp. Bar, 6: 558.
In a Nutshell. (F. E. Wadleigh) Potter Am. Mo. 13: 33, 105, 185.
In Occupation. Chamb. J. 43: 337, 361.
In the Orangery. Lond. Soc. 33: 130.
In the Organ-Room. Tinsley, 7: 390.
In Paradise. Galaxy, 14: 248.
In Pastures green. (C. Gibbon) Gent. M. n. s. 17: 129.
In Peril, Alongside. Sharpe, 47: 143.
In Pursuit; a Story. St. James, 10: 179.
In queer Company. Belgra. 22: 339.
In Quest. (J. C. Freund) Dark Blue, 3: 732.
In Quest of a Nest. (T. Carlisle) St. James, 37: 257.
In Request rather. Belgra. 8: 41.
In Richmond Park. Fraser, 54: 511.
In Richmond Park; a Poem. (Earl of Southesk) Gent. M. n. s. 17: 31.
In the Ring. All the Year, 13: 18. Same art. Liv. Age, 84: 417.
In the Rue Froide. Liv. Age, 123: 529, 694.
In Search for a Soul. (A. Gray) Lippinc. 27: 463.
In Search of the Picturesque. (C. F. Woolson) Harper, 45: 161.
In Search of a Place. Knick. 42: 441.
In Search of a Tea-Cup. Temp. Bar, 36: 216.
In September: a Poem. (A. Paracelsus) Dark Blue, 2: 64.
In the Shadow of Death. (J. Poole) Canad. Mo. 18: 420.
In the Shadow of the Scaffold; a Story. (J. A. O'Shea) Tinsley, 29: 222.
In the Sierras. (L. H. Foote) Overland, 7: 324.
In Sight of the Mountains. (H. N. Duff) St. James, 39: 715.
In Sir Rupert's Room. Ev. Sat. 11: 634.
In Snow. Fraser, 99: 134.
In a Stereoscope. (L. Walter) Sharpe, 40: 83.
In a Studio. (W. W. Story) Blackw. 117: 481, 713. 118: 301, 674. 120. 21. Same art. Liv. Age, 126: 241–412. 127: 88. 128: 112, 215.
In the Sunshine. (T. Storm) Canad. Mo. 1: 152.
In Sutton Woods; a Poem. (A. Austin) Temp. Bar, 3: 46.
In the Temple Gardens. Temp. Bar, 2: 276.
In that State of Life. All the Year, 24: 18–481.
In this World; a Novel. (M. Collins) Dub. Univ. 91: 80–680. 92: 33–569.
In a Transport. (C. W. Stoddard) Overland, 11: 272.
In a Trumpet. (I. F. Hopkins) Scrib. 9: 244.
In Trust. (J. Ingelow) Fraser, 103: 145–711. 104: 1–683. Same art. Liv. Age, 150: 332–790. 151: 19–217.
In the Tunnel. (Bret Harte) Overland, 2: 284.
In the Twilight. (D. M. Craik) Good Words, 4: 599.
In the Valley of Shadows. (H. E. Warner) Scrib. 2: 650.
In War-Time; a Poem. (J. G. Whittier) Atlan. 10: 235.
In the West. Fraser, 64: 123.
In the whole wide World; a Story. (L. C. Moulton) Galaxy, 14: 238.
In the Woods; a Poem. (G. Meredith) Fortn. 14: 179.
In the wrong Place. Dub Univ. 95: 29.
In Xto. (J. L. Ver Mehr) Overland, 4: 238.
Inability, Doctrine of, Modern Explanations of. (L. H. Atwater) Princ. 26: 217.
Inanimate Objects, Against. Chamb. J. 43: 657.
Inca and his Bride. Blackw. 63: 750.
Incas, History, Laws, Customs, and Language of the. Westm. 90: 118. Same art. Ecl. M. 71: 1293, 1490.
— Last of. Bost. Mo. 1: 458.
Incapables. (J. F. Watkins) Overland, 2: 524.
Incapacities, Four, Some Consequences of. (C. S. Peirce) J. Spec. Philos. 2: 140, 193.
Incarnation, The. *See* Jesus Christ, Incarnation of.
Incendiarism; its Cause and Cure. Fraser, 30: 243.
Incendiary, The; Attorney's Reminiscences. Chamb. J. 17: 355. Same art. Ecl. M. 26: 538.
Incest, Levitical Law of. (J. Sturtevant) Am. Bib. Repos. 2d s. 8: 423.
Inch, Ancient Standard of the British. (J. Taylor; H. Hennessy; J. Yates) J. Frankl. Inst. 72: 298–348.
— Sacred Character of the British. (W. P. Garrison) Nation, 3: 16.
Inchbald, Elizabeth. Temp. Bar, 1: 483. 55: 460.
— Memoirs of. (J. Boaden) Tait, 3: 753. — (F. A. Durivage) No. Am. 37: 445. — Mo. R. 131: 476. — Fraser, 8: 536. — Eng. Dom. M. 26: 244, 294.
Inchiquin the Jesuit's Letters. Quar. 10: 494. — Portfo. (Den.) 5: 300, 385. 13: 123. 14: 150, 254.
Incidents of real Life. Fraser, 34: 42.
Incledon, Charles Benjamin, Actor, Recollections of. Colburn, 53: 216.
Inclined Plane, Motion on an. (T. Sherwin) Math. Mo. 3: 206.
— of J. Renwick. J. Frankl. Inst. 2: 257, 321.
Inclined Planes. J. Frankl. Inst. 7: 426. 9: 49, 54, 248.
— for Mountain Roads. (E. M. Rogers) Ecl. Engin. 24: 56.
Inclosure Commission of England. (J. W. Tottie) J. Statis. Soc. 25: 297.
Incombustible Men. Chamb. J. 12: 45.
Income, Definitions of the Word. (J. E. T. Rogers) J Statis. Soc. 28: 242.
Incomes, Small; how to better them. St. James, 35: 211.
Income Tax. (H. C. Kingsley) New Eng. 37: 543. — Fraser, 47: 157. — Bank. M. (L.) 22: 785. 23: 8, 68.
— and Congress. (G. Marsland) Bank. M. (N. Y.) 32: 678.

Income Tax and new Tariff. Dub. Univ. 20: 364.
— and Property Tax. (W. Farr) J. Statis. Soc. 16: 1. — Ed. R. 57: 143.
— — Reconstruction of. (L. Levi) J. Statis. Soc. 37: 155.
— and Silver Agitators. (E. L. Godkin) Nation, 26: 163.
— Communism of a discriminating. (D. A. Wells) No. Am. 130: 236.
— History of. Bank. M. (N. Y.) 20: 870.
— how it should be collected. (E. L. Godkin) Nation, 9: 452.
— How may it be supplanted? Fraser, 69: 507.
— How to abolish. (L. Bradley) Contemp. 38: 101.
— in Great Britain. Bank. M. (L.) 34: 373. — Ed. R. 97: 530.
— — and the Plans for its Reform. Fraser, 65: 403. — Westm. 77: 97.
— — in 1845. Tait, n. s. 12: 134, 270.
— — in 1857. Tait, n. s. 24: 2, 65.
— in the United States and England. (E. L. Godkin) Nation, 26: 287.
— Principles of. (James Booth) J. Statis. Soc. 23: 455.
— Renewal of. Blackw. 68: 611.
— Suggestions on. (J. R. McCulloch) Bank. M. (N. Y.) 16: 279.
— Undiscriminating. (W. L. Sargant) J. Statis. Soc. 25: 339.
— — Objections to. (W. L. Sargant) J. Statis. Soc. 24: 213.
— why not applied to Ireland. Dub. R. 13: 155.
— Word or two about. Fraser, 47: 157.
Income-Tax Grievances. Dub. Univ. 57: 460.
Incompatible. (A. W. H. Howard) Lippinc. 4: 614.
Incompatibility of Temper. (A. B. Haven) Godey, 64: 50–474.
Inconsideration, On. Chr. Obs. 38: 73.
Inconsistency. Cornh. 4: 58.
Inconsolable Society, Some Account of the. (L. Blanchard) Colburn, 50: 400.
Incubation, Artificial, Bucknell on, 1839. Mo. R. 150: 450.
Incumbent of Bagshot. Belgra. 10: 185.
Incumbered Estates Court. All the Year, 5: 569, 593. — Dub. Univ. 36: 311.
Incorporation. Dem. R. 9: 105.
Incurables. Chamb. J. 51: 389.
Incurable Hospital at Putney. Cornh. 17: 735.
Indecent Publications. (E. I. Sears) Nat. Q. 14: 150.
Independence. Irish Mo. 5: 136.
— American. (I. N. Danforth) So. Lit. Mess. 13: 502.
— Celebration of our national. Chr. Mo. Spec. 6: 306.
— of Mind. Chr. Obs. 14: 155.
— of Thought. (E. P. Ely) Princ. 5: 358.
— Thoughts on. West. J. 7: 340.
Independence, Mo. (W. Gilpin) West. J. 11: 31.
Independent Ku-Klux, An; a Story. (J. W. De Forest) Galaxy, 13: 480.
Independent Ministers in England, List of. Cong. M. 14: 804. 15: 192.
Independent Opinion, An. (J. Payn) Belgra. 38: 434.
Independent Voter's Place in Politics. (C. C. Nott) Nation, 20: 308.
Independents, The, Hanbury's Memorials of. Cong. M. 25: 547, 617. — Ecl. R. 75: 288.
— Present Position of, in British Empire. Cong. M. 25: 923.
Independency, Fletcher's History of. Bib. R. 6: 519.
— in Scotland. Cong. M. 2: 23–781. 4: 22.
Index, Making an. Lond. Soc. 35: 470.
— of Papers on Mathematical and Physical Science. (E. B. Hunt) Am. J. Sci. 70: 341.
Index to Periodical Literature, Poole's. (W. S. Biscoe) Lib. J. 1: 279. — (W. F. Poole) Lib. J. 4: 159. — Lib. J. 1: 116. — (F. F. Browne) Dial (Ch.), 2: 267.
— — Committee's Reports. Lib. J. 1: 181–365. 2: 16.
— — Committee's 6th Report. Lib. J. 3: 57.
— — Continuation of. (J. B. Bailey) Lib. J. 4: 187.
— — Discussion at London Conference. Lib. J. 2: 266.
— — in England. (R. Harrison) Lib. J. 3: 59, 119, 189. — (H. O. Coxe) Lib. J. 3: 59, 155.
— — Plan of. (W. F. Poole) Lib. J. 3: 109.
— — Report at Oxford Conference. Lib. J. 3: 299.
— — Report on, 1881. (W. F. Poole) Lib. J. 6: 132.
— — Symposium on. (S. B. Noyes) Lib. J. 3: 141. (J. Winsor) 143. (F. B. Perkins) 143. (J. L. Whitney) 144. (J. Schwartz) 145. (W. I. Fletcher) 147. (C. A. Cutter) 148. (W. F. Poole) 178.
— to Subjects, Universal. (J. A. Cross) Lib. J. 2: 191.
Index Expurgatorius. Dub. Univ. 10: 725. — Brit. Q. 14: 133. — Nat. R. 15: 48.
Index Librorum Prohibitorum. Brit. Q. 14: 133.
Index Rerum. *See* Commonplace-Book.
Indexes, Allibone's Excerpts on Need of. Lib. J. 4: 451.
— Blank-Book. (M. Dewey) Lib. J. 5: 318.
— Libraries, and Cyclopædias. (A. Hunter) St. Paul's, 12: 464.
— Subject, to Transactions of learned Societies. (R. Garnett) Lib. J. 4: 111.
— to Books. Hist. M. 10: 71.
— to Periodicals. Lib. J. 1: 359.
Index Society. Lib. J. 3: 24–370. 4: 54.
— and its Field. (H. B. Wheatley) Lib. J. 3: 105.
Indexing, Co-operative. Lib. J. 1: 113, 226.
— An Evitandum in. (B. R. Wheatley) Lib. J. 2: 178.
— Rules of the Index Society for. (H. B. Wheatley) Lib. J. 3: 228.
— Some Points of. (W. I. Fletcher) Lib. J. 4: 243.
India. (C. Redding) Colburn, 111: 243. — (E. Thomson) Meth. Q. 27: 165. — Blackw. 38: 803. — Am. Q. 18: 20. — (J. C. Lowrie) Princ. 10: 219. — Ed. R. 15: 327. 16: 128. — Select J. 1: [50. — Mo. R. 122: 191.
— Aborigines of. (D. C. Scudder) Bib. Sac. 17: 709.
— — of East. (J. Briggs) Ed. New Philos. J. 51: 331.
— Administration of Justice in. (J. H. Nelson) Fortn. 34: 300.
— Adventures in. (E. Townbridge) Sharpe, 32: 12. — Dub. Univ. 61: 564.
— Agriculture in. Blackw. 113: 147.
— Alexander's Travels to India and England. Lond. M. 18: 212.
— Alps of. (M. Ellis) Good Words, 8: 550. — Fraser, 93: 652.
— Ancient. Chr. R. 24: 458. — Nat. R. 4: 334.
— — and Mediæval. (F. P. Cobbe) Fraser, 81: 343. Same art. Ecl. M. 74: 563.
— — Arrian on. Penny M. 1: 354.
— — Connection with, in past Times. Chamb. J. 8: 81.
— — Geography of. (F. M. Müller) Nature, 4: 381.
— — Literature of. (J. Foster) Ecl. R. 10: 843.
— — Philosophy in. Lond. Q. 47: 81.
— — Relations with Greece and Rome. (W. H. Green) Princ. 38: 394.
— — Spier's Life in. New Q. 6: 48.
— and British Colonial Empire, 1880. (W. T. Thornton) Westm. 113: 181, 504. 114: 193, 489. 115: 239, 527. 116: 119, 479.
— and China. Knick. 4: 109.
— — Communication between. Colburn, 151: 302.
— and England. Fraser, 8: 593.
— and Europe, 1865. Colburn, 134: 127.
— and the Hindus. De Bow, 10: 269.
— and its Palaces. Potter Am. Mo. 4: 295. 5: 699.
— and Lancashire. (R R. Jackson) Fortn. 25: 877.

India and her Neighbors, Andrew's. Colburn, **163**: 470.
— and Russia. Quar. **147**: 229.
— and Silver Coinage in U. S. Bank. M. (N. Y) **34**: 198.
— Anglo-Indian Life. Mo. R. **145**: 174.
— Anglo-Indian Photographs. Belgra. **32**: supp. 79. — Blackw. **121**: 541. Same art. Liv. Age, **133**: 565.
— Annexation of Mysore. (J. Morley) Fortn. **6**: 257.
— Anomalies in. (U. R. Burke) Dub. Univ. **90**: 257–654.
— Archæological Survey of. Geog. M. **1**: 200.
— Army of. (G. R. Gleig) Ed. R. **97**: 183. — (M. L. Meason) Fraser, **93**: 614. — (M. L. Meason) Macmil. **39**: 158. — Blackw. **21**: 563. — All the Year, **41**: 59, 129. — Fraser, **56**: 164. **73**: 466. — No. Brit. **29**: 211. — (G. I. Wolseley) No. Am. **127**: 132.
— — Defects in. Mo. R. **112**: 274.
— — Indian Troops in Europe. (J. L. Vaughan) Contemp. **32**: 665.
— — Origin and State of. Quar. **18**: 385. — Blackw. **21**: 563.
— — Sanitary State of. Quar. **116**: 413. — (J. Bird) J. Statis. Soc. **26**: 384. — J. Statis. Soc. **3**: 113. **4**: 137.
— — Vital Statistics of. (W. H. Sykes) J. Statis. Soc. **10**: 100. **14**: 109.
— Arts and Manufactures of. (J. F. Boyle) Am. J. Sci. **64**: 160. — Chamb. J. **20**: 45.
— Arts in. Art J. **3**: 149.—(J. J. Young) Lippinc. **26**: 532.
— Astronomy of. Ed. R. **10**: 455.
— Ball's Jungle Life in. Nature, **21**: 373.
— Banking and Currency in, 1860. Bank. M. (L.) **20**: 201.
— Banking Institutions of, 1847. Bank. M. (L.) **6**: 333. **7**: 9–536.
— Barracks and Hospitals in. Fraser, **69**: 691.
— Barthelemy's Voyage to. Ed. R. **15**: 363.
— Bevan's Thirty Years in, 1808–38. Mo. R. **149**: 192.
— Bible in. (J. Makepeace) Ex. H. Lec. **19**: 399.
— — in South. Lond. Q. **17**: 182.
— Bleeding to Death of, by the English. (H. M. Hyndman) 19th Cent. **8**: 157.
— Books on, 1839. Chr. Obs. **40**: 225, 303.
— — Recent, 1857. Dub. Univ. **50**: 468.
— British. (W. Arthur) Ex. H. Lec. **2**: 1. — (D. M. Balfour) Univ. Q. **28**: 40.—(C. C. Hazewell) Atlan. **1**: 85. — (Col. Pelly) Fortn. **2**: 31. — (J. W. Wiley) Nat. M. **10**: 227, 315, 425. — Ecl. M. **16**: 251. — Ecl. R. **71**: 304. — So. Q. **3**: 199. — (T. B. Macaulay) Ed. R. **70**: 157. — (E. Peabody) Chr. Exam. **48**: 1. — Chr. R. **25**: 53. — Dub. Univ. **32**: 607. — New Q. **1**: 343. **2**: 39, 347.
— — Administration of Justice in. Ed. R. **73**: 425. — Nat. R. **18**: 136. — New Q. **6**: 240. **8**: 543. — For. Q. **13**: 406.
— — and China. Hunt, **8**: 249.
— — and Christianity, 1840. Mo. R. **152**: 240.
— — Colonization and Commerce of. Westm. **11**: 326.
— — from a French View. Once a Week, **8**: 403.
— — Government of. Westm. **19**: 107. **57**: 358. — Brit. & For. R. **11**: 151. — (W. Adam) De Bow, **9**: 1, 129, 276. — Pamph. **24**: 287. — Ed. R. **53**: 438. **76**: 171. **84**: 452. — Ecl. M. **12**: 326. — Brit. Q. **17**: 481. — Colburn, **153**: 500. — (C. Walker) Fraser, **81**: 248. **82**: 458. — (W. W. Hunter) Cornh. **41**: 21, 152. — New Q. **2**: 175. — Quar. **92**: 46.
— — — and the House of Commons. Brit. Q. **28**: 199.
— — — and Interests of Great Britain. Westm. **57**: 357.
— — — concerning John's Indian Affairs. (R. H. Elliot) Fraser, **84**: 214, 492. **85**: 193.
— — — Functions of. **88**: 207.
— — — Future. Ecl. R. **107**: 443.
— — — how to treat India. Fraser, **99**: 107.
— — — how it is governed, 1852. Fraser, **46**: 713.
— — — in 1853. Ecl. R. **98**: 100.
— — — — New Bill for. No. Brit. **19**: 552.
India, British, Government of, in 1858. New Q. **7**: 73.
— — — — Letter on the proposed Council of Eight, 1858. Fraser, **57**: 371.
— — — in 1869–70. Administration of Berar. Ed. R. **137**: 225.
— — — in 1876. Westm. **106**: 309.
— — — in 1879. Dub. R. **84**: 454.
— — — — Simple Way out of the Difficulty. (R. Lowe) Fortn. **32**: 24.
— — — Liabilities and Resources of. Westm. **72**: 112.
— — — Principles of. Nat. R. **6**: 1.
— — — under Lord Auckland and Lord Ellenborough. Bentley, **30**: 628.
— — — under three Administrations, 1844–62. Brit. Q. **48**: 350.
— — Government of Ava. Cornh. **40**: 213.
— — Grievances of. Dark Blue, **3**: 325.
— — Her Majesty's Vassals in. (F. Goldie) Month, **23**: 314.
— — History of. Ecl. R. **82**: 1. — Westm. **69**: 180.
— — — Martin's. Ecl. R. **71**: 219.
— — — Mill's. Ecl. R. **31**: 97, 218. — Ed. R. **31**: 1. — Mo. R. **95**: 337. **96**: 154.
— — — Thornton's. (W. Robertson) No. Brit. **2**: 324.— Chr. Obs. **57**: 662, 753. — Mo. R. **156**: 239.
— — — Wilson's. For. Q. **35**: 34.
— — in 1825. Blackw. **17**: 574, 701. **18**: 183, 303, 401. — Mo. R. **129**: 1.
— — in 1838. Mo. R. **151**: 77.
— — in 1840, Condition of. Ecl. R. **71**: 304. — Ed. R. **71**: 327. — Mus. **40**: 145.
— — in 1844. Fraser, **30**: 743.
— — in 1853. New Q. **2**: 475. **3**: 28.
— — Indian Heroes and Indian Reform. New Q. **8**: 22.
— — Industrial Resources of. Quar. **113**: 289.
— — Invasion of. Blackw. **22**: 267. — Mus. **16**: 80.
— — Law and Constitution of. Westm. **17**: 75.
— — Peasants of. House. Words, **4**: 389.
— — Policy of, and Governor-General. For. Q. **37**: 212.
— — Political History of. Blackw. **20**: 689.
— — Political Prospects in. For. Q. **36**: 486.
— — Shops and Shopping in. (E. Roberts) Hunt, **25**: 314.
— — Sketches of. Mus. **2**: 128.
— — Society in. Mus. **23**: 260.
See Canning; Dalhousie; Lawrence; etc.
— British Conquests in, St. John's History of. Ecl. R. **96**: 595.
— British Empire in. (Sir H. B. Edwardes) Ex. H. Lec. **16**: 1. — (L. J. Trotter) Contemp. **15**: 113.
— — Course of. Dem. R. **40**: 177.
— — Garcin de Tassy on. (J. von Döllinger) Contemp. **35**: 385.
— — Stability of. (S. J. Owen) Contemp. **31**: 494.
— British Officer arraigned for preaching in, 1857. Liv. Age, **55**: 555.
— British Policy in. Westm. **84**: 185.
— British Power in. Dem. R. **40**: 401. — For. Q. **36**: 261.
— — Huber on Rise and Progress of. Ecl. R. **68**: 125.
— British Rule in. Dub. Univ. **43**: 493. — Lond. Q. **1**: 233. — Quar. **104**: 224. — St. Paul's, **2**: 347.
— — Benefits of. Westm. **78**: 112.
— — Character of. Westm. **90**: 1.
— — Failure of. (R. D. Osborn) Nation, **29**: 155, 204.
— Building and Materials in. Ecl. Engin. **19**: 240.
— Building Arts in. (Gen. Maclagan) Ecl. Engin. **25**: 118.
— Bundelkund Province. Tait, n. s. **14**: 682.
— Burmese Empire. Am. Q. **7**: 136.
— Burmese War. (R. Southey) Quar. **35**: 481. — Mo. R. **112**: 195. — Mus. **10**: 353. **11**: 97.
— — Week of Camp Life in. Fraser, **87**: 693. Same art. Ecl. M. **81**: 171. Same art. Ev. Sat. **15**: 45.
— Campaign against Hindu Fanatics, 1863. Cornh. **9**: 357.

India, Canning's Administration of. Ed. R. 117: 444. — No. Brit. 37: 222.
— Mary Carpenter's Work in. (H. W. Holland) Chr. Exam. 85: 179.
— Castes and Clans in. (A. C. Lyall) Fortn. 27: 97.
— — and Creeds of. Blackw. 85: 308.
— — and Occupations of. (J. D. Whelpley) Am. Whig R. 1: 394.
— — and Tribes of. Penny M. 12: 9–429.
— Catholicism in. Dub. R. 26: 179.
— Caunter's Scenes in, 1836 Mo. R. 138: 344.
— Central Provinces of. Ed. R. 135: 196.
— — Forest Life in. Chamb. J. 49: 214.
— — Highlands of, Forsyth's. (M. T. Sale) Nature, 6: 99.
— — Malcolm on, 1824. Ecl. R. 40: 115.
— Character of the People of. Anal. M. 15: 89. 16: 288.
— Child Life in. (J. W. Palmer) Atlan. 1: 625.
— Christian Conversions in. Bent. Q. 1: 183.
— Christianity in. (H. Beveridge) Theo. R. 6: 465. — (J. B. Heard) Dub. Univ. 53: 515, 643. — (E. Hoole) Am. Meth. M. 14: 361. — Blackw. 85: 462. — Chr. Obs. 7: 257. 12: 127–545. — Chr. Disc. 5: 295. — (J. Tuckerman) Chr. Exam. 1: 301. — Mo. R. 105: 94. — Liv. Age, 3: 420. — Contemp. 1: 123. — Dub. Univ. 52: 643. — Ecl. R. 7: 154, 336, 440. 8: 627. — Fraser, 96: 306. — (A. Duff) Ex. H. Lec. 6: 77. — Kitto, 8: 203. — Lond. Q. 10: 1. — Meth. M. 35: 543. 36: 460, 848. — No. Brit. 13: 583. — (I Loewenthal) Princ. 27: 283.
— — Can India be Christianized? Fraser, 96: 762.
— — Cunningham on, 1808. (J. Foster) Ecl. R. 8: 1115.
— — Dubois on, 1823. Ecl. R. 38: 289, 438. — Meth. M. 46: 673.
— — — Reply to. Ecl. R. 40: 61.
— — Duty of Great Britain to Christianize. Chr. Obs. 11: 261, 353.
— — Cunningham on. Chr. Obs. 7: 248.
— — Hough on. Chr. Obs. 61: 418.
— — Our Religious Policy in. (A.C.Lyall) Fortn. 17: 387.
— — Works on. Chr. Obs. 48: 534.
See below, India, Missions in.
— A Christmas in. Fraser, 89: 150. Same art. Liv. Age, 120: 757.
— Church in. (J. J. Blunt) Quar. 35: 446.
— — Ancient. Chr. Exam. 2: 149, 313.
— — Disestablishment and Disendowment in. Cong. 3: 646.
— Episcopate in, and Church Missionary Society. Chr. Rem. 36: 64.
— — Heber on. Quar. 35: 445.
— — in 1865. Chr. Obs. 65: 433.
— Civil Service in. (A. J. Balfour) Fortn. 28: 244. — (G. Chesney) 19th Cent. 5: 1038. — (L. Playfair) Fortn. 28: 115. — (W. B. Scoones) Macmil. 30: 365. — Tinsley, 29: 230. — Blackw. 79: 456. 89: 115, 261. — Fraser, 74: 427. 88: 433, 552. 89: 293.
— — and its Examinations. Lond. Q. 30: 153. — (L. Griffin) Fortn. 23: 522.
— — and Public Schools. (H. Mann) J. Statis. Soc. 28: 150.
— — as a Profession. Macmil. 4: 257.
— — Prospects of. Fraser, 54: 270.
— Civilizing, Buchanan's Memoir on. Chr. Obs. 5: 308.
— Classical Studies in. (M. Müller) Contemp. 18: 141.
— Climate and Government of. Cornh. 6: 241.
— Cockburn's Prize Dissertation on. Ed. R. 6: 462.
— Colonization in. No. Brit. 30: 441.
— Commerce of. Dub. Univ. 52: 142. — Ed. R. 10: 334. — (T. P. Thompson) Westm. 14: 93.
— — and Government of. Quar. 9: 218.—Ecl. R. 17: 453.
— — European, Macpherson's. Quar. 8: 114.
— — External. (W. H. Sykes) J. Statis. Soc. 19: 107.
India, Commerce of, Freedom of, and Settlement in India. Ed. R. 48: 336.
— — Mediterranean. (R. Park) Hunt, 6: 201.
— Commercial Wrongs and Claims of. Ed. R. 72: 340.
— Conjurer of. All the Year, 13: 57.
— Conquest of Scinde. Ed. R. 79: 476.
— Conversion of. Bent. Q. 1: 183.
— Cotton Culture in. Ed. R. 115: 478. — Dub. Univ. 49: 678.
— Cotton Supply of. Ecl. R. 95: 391. 96: 129.
— Craufurd's Researches in. Mo. R. 91: 383.
— Currency of. (G. M. Weston) Bank. M. (N. Y.) 33: 853. — Bank. M. (N. Y.) 33: 505.
— — and Exchange with. (I. T. Smith) Westm. 115: 506. — (J. B. Robertson) Westm. 114: 459.
— — Losses from the single Standard. Bank. M. (N. Y.) 33: 425.
— Customs of, Some bad old. All the Year, 35: 269, 295.
— Daily Mail-Route to. Colburn, 142: 505.
— Dalhousie's Administration in. Blackw. 80: 233. — Ed. R. 117: 1. — New Q. 5: 470. 6: 103. — Fraser, 52: 123.
— Dangers in. Macmil. 15: 412.
— Dangerous Glory of. (F. W. Newman) Fraser, 90: 448.
— Daniell's Oriental Scenery. (J. Foster) Ecl. R. 24: 472.
— Davidson's Travels in. Blackw. 55: 321.
— Dawk Traveling in. Penny M. 12: 156.
— Detective in. Chamb. J. 25: 49.
— Defense of. (A. Fraser) Fraser, 75: 557.
— My Indian Diary. Colburn, 67: 99–481. 68: 81–480.
— Dilemma in, July, 1880. (H. Grey) Contemp. 38: 25.
— Domestic Life in. Mo. R. 132: 1. — Belgra. 28: 100, 535.
— Drama in; Cymbeline in a Hindu Playhouse. (H. Littledale) Macmil. 42: 65. — Liv. Age, 145: 695.
— Duties of England to. Fraser, 64: 674.
— Early Traveling Experiences in. (F. Hall) Lippinc. 15: 338.
— East India Company. *See* East India Company.
— Eastern, Martin on. Mo. R. 145: 469. 146: 508.
— Eastern Peninsula of. Ed. R. 22: 331.
— Economic Position of. (A. J. Wilson) Fraser, 94: 457.
— Education in. Westm. 48: 553. — Ecl. R. 70: 393.— Chamb. J. 30: 131.
— — and Society in. Temp. Bar, 11: 295.
— — Blackey at School. Fraser, 55: 679.
— — Female. (M. Cursetjee) Victoria, 11: 185.
— — Government. Chr. Obs. 69: 337, 501.
— — in 1838, Trevelyan on. Ecl. R. 70: 393.
— — National. (W. T. Thornton) Cornh. 23: 282.
— — New Measure for. Lond. Q. 3: 159.
— Educational Institutions of East India Company (W. H. Sykes) J. Statis. Soc. 8: 103, 236.
— Educational Wants of. Chr. Obs. 60: 494, 574.
— Ellenborough's Administration. (A. J. Arbuthnot) Contemp. 24: 374. — Brit. Q. 60: 68. — Ed. R. 141: 31.
— Ellenborough's Policy in. For. Q. 34: 479.
— Emigration to. Chamb. J. 43: 394.
— Employment of Capital in. (U. R. Burke) Dub. Univ. 91: 93.
— Engineers in. Fraser, 98: 559. — Ecl. Engin. 21: 285.
— Engineering in. Ecl. Engin. 6: 47. 9: 501.
— Engineering Works in. Ecl. Engin. 16: 177.
— England's Position in, 1873. (J. Routledge) Macmil. 27: 529.
— — 1875. Westm. 103: 346.
— English in. (T. W. Knox) Harper, 58: 568. — (W. D. Whitney) New Eng. 16: 100. — Bentley, 42: 331. — Chamb. J. 7: 118. — Dub. Univ. 83: 611. — Once a Week, 6: 484. — For. Q. 6: 148. — Westm. 4: 261.
— Englishwomen in. (M. Townsend) Victoria, 1: 69.
— Entomology of. (R. McLachlan) Nature, 21: 173.

India, Epic Poetry of. Ho. & For. R. 4: 512.—Westm. 50: 34.
— European in. Chamb. J. 52: 371.
— European Adventurers in. Ed. R. 134: 361. Same art. Liv. Age, 111: 515.
— European Writers on. (J. Avery) New Eng. 35: 431.
— Evidence Act for. (H. S. Maine) Fortn. 19: 51.
— Exchange Difficulty with. Westm. 114: 173.
— Expectations of. (W. Harris) Fraser, 93: 442.
— Fall of the Sikh Empire. No. Brit. 11: 618.
— Famine in. (G. W. Forest) Good Words, 18: 778.—All the Year, 6: 519.—Argosy, 2: 469.
— — and Debt in. (W. G. Pedder) 19th Cent. 2: 177.
— — and the Press. (A. Colvin) Fortn. 21: 484.
— — Experiences of. Cornh. 36: 473. Same art. Ecl. M. 89: 746.
— — in 1866. No. Brit. 46: 242. Same art. Ecl. M. 68: 746. 69: 69.
— — in 1868–69. Ev. Sat. 10: 418.
— — in 1874. Fraser, 90: 293.
— — in 1876–77. Geog. M. 4: 286.—(A. C. Sellar) Nation, 25: 209.—(R. D. Osborn) Nation, 29: 204.—(R. D. Osborn) Contemp. 37: 227.
— — — Commission on. Nature, 22: 553.—Blackw. 128: 726.
— — Orissa. (H. S. Fagan) Contemp. 4: 73.
— — Prevention of. Fraser, 75: 358.
— Famines in. (G. Chesney) 19th Cent. 2: 603.—Ed. R. 146: 68.—(H. P. Malet) Geog. M. 2: 73, 136.—Lond. Q. 49: 297.—Westm. 109: 139.
— — and Floods in. Macmil. 37: 236.
— — Browne on. Dub. Univ. 89: 787.
— Ferrier's Travels in. Ed. R. 105: 266.
— Festival of the Pongol. Cornh. 17: 349.
— Financial Difficulties of. (J. Dacosta) Westm. 107: 196.
— Finances of. Fraser, 60: 534. 82: 31. 101: 24.
— — and Bimetallism. (J. B. Robertson) Westm. 115: 200.
— — and Trade of. Bank. M. (N. Y.) 31: 449.
— — Bankruptcy in. (H. M. Hyndman) 19th Cent. 4: 585. 5: 443.
— — Budgets of, Deficits in. Fraser, 99: 667.
— — in 1853. (J. Chapman) Westm. 60: 177.
— — in 1855. Bank. M. (L.) 15: 549.
— — in 1856. Bank. M. (L.) 16: 472.
— — in 1859. Bank. M. (L.) 19: 145.—Brit. Q. 30: 465.—(W. H. Sykes) J. Statis. Soc. 22: 455.
— — in 1871, Deficit in. Fraser, 83: 14.
— — in 1873, and House of Commons. (L. Griffin) Fortn. 20: 488.
— — in 1876. (Sir G. Campbell) Fortn. 25: 514.
— — in 1879. Bank. M. (N. Y.) 34: 33.—(G. Chesney) 19th Cent. 5: 97.—(G. Chesney) Fortn. 31: 842.—(H. Fawcett) 19th Cent. 5: 193.—Blackw. 128: 124.
— — in 1880. (R. Strachey) 19th Cent. 7: 1078.—(S. Laing) 19th Cent. 7: 1065.—(R. Osborn) Contemp. 38: 270.
— — New Departure in. (H. Fawcett) 19th Cent. 6: 639.
— — Proposed Loans, 1879. (H. Fawcett) 19th Cent. 5: 872.
— — Revenue System of. Ed. R. 55: 79.
— — Solvency and Resources of. Fraser, 98: 778.
— — Statistics of Revenue and Taxation in. (F. Hendriks) J. Statis. Soc. 21: 223.
— First Glimpse of. (E. Townbridge) Sharpe, 31: 242.
— Food in. Chamb. J. 51: 323.
— — Has India Food for its People? (H. J. S. Cotton) Fortn. 28: 863.
— for the Indians. St. James, 22: 145.
— Forbes's Oriental Memoirs, 1768–85. (J. Foster) Ecl. R. 20: 405, 440, 631.
— French in. Ed. R. 127: 537.
India, French Writers on. Colburn, 112: 60.
— Frontier of Northwestern. Brit. Q. 67: 385.—Cornh. 20: 539.—Geog. M. 5: 4.
— — Defenders of our. Cornh. 20: 539. Same art. Ecl. M. 74: 147.
— — Pass of Alexander from Central Asia to. Colburn, 153: 317.
— — Scientific. (Sir H. Norman) Fortn. 31: 1. Same art. Liv. Age, 140: 435.
— Frontier Policy. Blackw. 122: 220.
— Frontier Wars of. No. Brit. 16: 230.
— Further, and S. W. China. (H. Yule) Geog. M. 2: 97.
— Future of. (E. Perry) 19th Cent. 4: 1083.—(H. Taylor) Contemp. 39: 464.
— Gang-Robbers of. (L. Ritchie) Chamb. J. 14: 321, 344.
— Gangetic Provinces of. Blackw. 76: 133.
— Geographical Configuration of. (H. and R. de Schlagintweit) Am. J. Sci. 84: 101.
— Geology of. Nature, 20: 191.
— — and Ethnology of. Ed. R. 141: 330.
— Goddard's March across. Bentley, 52: 378, 516.
— Gold in. (E. B. Eastwick) Gent. M. n. s. 24: 96.
— Gond and Byga People. Cornh. 26: 595.
— Graham's Residence in. Quar. 8: 406.
— Grass Widowers in. Chamb. J. 35: 145.
— Great-Shoe Question. All the Year, 7: 381.
— Handicrafts in. Chamb. J. 15: 342. Same art. Liv. Age, 30: 141.
— Health, Industry, and Education in. O. & N. 10: 517.
— Bishop Heber's Journal in. Am. Q. 4: 115.—Quar. 37: 100.—(F. Jeffrey) Ed. R. 48: 312.—Mus. 12: 490, 588.—Ecl. R. 47: 289, 406.
— Heroes of. Westm. 70: 350. Same art. Ecl. M. 46: 20.
— Hervey's Ten Years in. Fraser, 42: 479.
— Hill Regions of, English Stations in. J. Statis. Soc. 44: 528.
— Hill Scandals. (S. L. Blanchard) Belgra. 1: 166.
— Hill Tribes in. No. Brit. 38: 362.—Dub. Univ. 93: 143.
— History of, Allen's. (W. Barrows) New Eng. 15: 39.
— — Ancient and recent. Chr. Obs. 67: 389.
— — Elliot's and Wheeler's. No. Am. 106: 340.
— — Elphinstone's. Quar. 68: 377.—Mo. R. 155: 33.
— — — and Wilson's. Dub. Univ. 25: 631.
— — Erskine's. New Q. 3: 467.
— — Taylor's Popular. Ecl. R. 77: 425.
See India, British, History of.
— Hodson of Hodson's Horse. (T. Hughes) Fraser, 59: 127.
— Hoffmeister's Letters from. Westm. 48: 181.
— Holy Day at Hurdevar. Cornh. 12: 609.
— Housekeeping in. All the Year, 8: 491.
— How to see. All the Year, 25: 420.
— Hügel's Travels in Kashmir and Punjab. No. Brit. 2: 444.
— Human Sacrifice in. All the Year, 35: 272, 297.—Blackw. 52: 177.
— — and Infanticide in. Ed. R. 119: 389.
— Hunter on. (W. D. Whitney) No. Am. 108: 655.
— Hunting Adventures in. (G. Cumming) Scrib. 3: 305.
— Impoverishment of, not proven. (J. Morley) Fortn. 30: 867.
— in 1825. Blackw. 17: 574, 701. 18: 183, 303, 401.
— in 1835. Mo. R. 136: 516.
— in 1838. Mo. R. 148: 1.
— in 1839. Quar. 63: 369.
— in 1856. (N. Allen) No. Am. 82: 404.—Tait, n. s. 23: 311.
— in 1858. Tait, n. s. 25: 371.—Brit. Q. 27: 202.—(I. Loewenthal) Princ. 30: 452.—Ed. R. 107: 1.
— in 1860. No. Brit. 34: 1.
— in 1863. Fraser, 68: 1.

India in 1880, Temple's. Quar. **152**: 50.
— in cold Weather. Chamb. J. **58**: 686.
— in hot Weather. Chamb. J. **58**: 828.
— in the Rains. Chamb. J. **58**: 790.
— Influence of, on English Opinion. (A. V. Dicey) Nation, **22**: 82.
— Intemperance in. (L. Ritchie) Chamb. J. **6**: 69.
— Invasions of, from Central Asia. Month, **35**: 593.
— Iron-making Districts of. Ecl. Engin. **4**: 43.
— Irrigation in. *See* Irrigation.
— Islands of, History and Languages of. Ed. R. **23**: 151.
— — Trade of. Ed. R. **29**: 35.
— Island-Temples of. (J. M. Church) Potter Am. Mo. **10**: 275.
— Jacquemont's Letters from. (T. P. Thompson) Westm. **22**: 304. **46**: 270. — For. Q. **12**: 107. — Mo. R. **135**: 350.
— Jesuit Missions in. Dub. R. **32**: 386.
— Journal in. Sharpe, **32**: 174.
— — of Embassy to Asia, 1827. Quar. **41**: 27. — Westm. **12**: 332. — Mus. **15**: 260.
— Journey from Marseilles to. Temp. Bar, **25**: 389.
— — to Bombay. Tait, n. s. **8**: 235.
— Judges of, British and native. Ed. R. **130**: 539.
— Kaye and Marshman on. Dub. Univ. **54**: 334.
— Kaye's Lives of Officers in. Fraser, **76**: 587. — Dub. Univ. **70**: 466. — Lond. Q. **30**: 60.
— Laing's England's Mission in the East. Fraser, **67**: 528.
— Lord Lake's Campaign in, 1804. All the Year, **28**: 422.
— Land in. Blackw. **95**: 597. — (L. J. Trotter) Brit. Q. **74**: 109.
— — Sale of waste, and Redemption of Land Tax. Fraser, **67**: 1.
— Land Revenue of. Fraser, **70**: 37.
— — and the Village System. Colburn, **111**: 379.
— Land Tenure in. New Q. **6**: 361. — Westm. **89**: 197.
— — Agrarian Distress and Discontent. Quar. **147**: 376.
— Land of the Veda. (Mrs. S. B. Herrick) So. R. n. s. **13**: 49. — (J. W. Waugh) Meth. Q. **33**: 230.
— Languages of, and Roman Alphabet. Liv. Age, **64**: 286.
— Lord Lauderdale on Affairs of, 1809. Ed. R. **15**: 235.
— Law in, and for. Westm. **77**: 1.
— Laws of. Lond. Q. **50**: 24.
— Sir Geo. Lawrence's 43 Years in. Chamb. J. **51**: 485.
— Lord Lawrence's Administration in. Ed. R. **131**: 305. — Brit. Q. **56**: 487. — No. Brit. **32**: 345.
— Leaf-wearing Tribe of. (M. J. Walhouse) Anthrop. J. **4**: 369.
— Letters from, Eden's. Temp. Bar, **29**: 458. **30**: 28–515. **31**: 349.
— Letters on. (G. A. Trevelyan) Macmil. **8**: 80–421. **9**: 16–482. **10**: 1
— Life in. Fraser, **79**: 341, 585, 721. **80**: 67, 326, 704. **81**: 456. — Ecl. M. **14**: 263.
— — in Cantonment. Chamb. J. **22**: 413.
— — Tales of. Colburn, **20**: 771.
— Literature of. Knick. **61**: 477. — No. Brit. **25**: 207.
— — Flowers of Anglo-Indian. (H. T. White) St. James, **42**: 337. Same art. Liv. Age, **137**: 438. *See* Rig-Veda; Sanscrit.
— Little Games in. Lond. Soc. **32**: 218.
— Little War with the Naikras, 1868. Cornh. **18**: 626.
— Loafers in. All the Year, **22**: 178.
— Looshai Country and Annexation. (W. F. B. Laurie) Dark Blue, **3**: 187.
— Lord Lytton's Administration in. (R. D. Osborn) Contemp. **36**: 553.
— Madras Disturbance, 1810. Quar. **5**: 138.
— Magistrate's Life in. Lond. Soc. **9**: 145, 257.
— — Recollections of. Colburn, **162**: 503–641. **163**: 23–160. **164**: 51–625. **165**: 744–1394. **166**: 110–434.
India, Malcolm's. Ed. R. **20**: 38. — (F. Jeffrey) Ed. R. **40**: 279. — Quar. **29**: 382. — Mo. R. **103**: 1, 113. **111**: 167.
— Manners and Customs of. (T. Parsons) No. Am. **9**: 36. — Chr. Mo. Spec. **1**: 362.
— March in. Fraser, **12**: 664.
— Massie on Continental. Mo. R. **151**: 169.
— Lord Mayo's Administration in. Ed. R. **143**: 387.
— — and the Umballa Durbar. Blackw. **107**: 61.
— — Assassination of. (R. H. Elliot) Fraser, **85**: 395.
— Measurement of Meridian in. Ed. R. **87**: 392.
— Memoirs of Mohammed Baber. Westm. **8**: 475. — (F. Jeffrey) Ed. R. **46**: 39. — Mo. R. **112**: 254.
— Meteorology of, Blanford's. Nature, **11**: 145.
— — of the Famine. (A. Buchan) Nature, **16**: 425.
— Migratory Tribes of Central. (E. Balfour) Ed. New Philos. J. **35**: 29.
— Military Indophobia. Once a Week, **22**: 72.
— Military Revolt in. Nat. R. **5**: 440.
— Military Situation in, 1865. Fraser, **72**: 710. Same art. Ecl. M. **66**: 318.
— Mineral Resources of. (W. T. Blanford) Ecl. Engin. **9**: 270.
— Ministerial Misrepresentations of. (R. D. Mangles) Ed. R. **77**: 261.
— Lord Minto in. Ed. R. **151**: 228.
— Missionary Health-Officer in. (F. Nightingale) Good Words, **20**: 492, 565, 635.
— Missionary Impediments in. Chr. Obs. **45**: 65.
— Missionary Sketches in North. Chr. Obs. **58**: 843.
— Missionary Stations in South Chr. Obs. **47**: 385.
— Missionary Work in. (R D. Osborn) Theo. R **4**: 65.
— Missions in. (D. O. Allen) New Eng. **19**: 365. — Meth. Q. **29**: 30. — (Syd. Smith) Ed. R. **12**: 151. — Quar. **138**: 345. Same art. Liv. Age, **125**: 515. Blackw. **105**: 94. — Ecl. M. **72**: 401. — (W. F. Stevenson) Good Words, **20**: 48–818. — Chr. Obs. **55**: 597, 721. **73**: 54.
— — and Hindu Philosophy. Kitto, **28**: 324.
— — and Wm. Taylor. (J. T. Gracey) Meth. Q. **37**: 251.
— — Are they a Failure? (J. E. Scott) Meth. Q. **41**: 424.
— — Baptist. Ecl. R. **42**: 482.
— — Claims of. Chr. Obs. **67**: 457.
— — Deputation of A. B. C. F. M. to. Am. Presb. R. **5**: 266.
— — Duff's Educational Work in. (G. Smith) Good Words, **19**: 307.
— — German. Colburn, **103**: 433.
— — in 1808. (J. Foster) Ecl. R. **7**: 441.
— — Letters from first Missionaries. Chr. Obs. **9**: 329–733. **10**: 1, 65.
— — Martyn and Groves. Lond. Q. **8**: 329.
— — Methodist. (J. E. Scott) Meth. Q. **36**: 79. — Meth. M. **46**: 451.
— — Native Ministry in. Lond. Q. **30**: 1.
— — of Lutheran Church. (A. D. Rowe) Luth. Q. **9**: 362.
— — Pearson on. (J. Foster) Ecl. R. **11**: 124.
— — Protestant. (B. H. Badley) Meth. Q. **36**: 678. — (J. G. McGee) Cath. World, **15**: 690.
— — Unitarian. (C. H. A. Dall) Unita. R. **4**: 611. — (M. P. Lowe) Unita. R. **11**: 443. — Chr. Exam. **63**: 36.
— — Waring on, 1807. Chr. Obs. **7**: 45, 123, 396.
— — Wilberforce on, 1813. (J. Foster) Ecl. R. **19**: 526.
— Mistaken Ideas of. Chamb. J. **53**: 423.
— Modern. Bentley, **31**: 465.
— — Maurice's. (A. Hamilton) Ed. R. **5**: 288.
— — Wylie's. Ecl. R. **77**: 538.
— Mohammedan Revival in. Cornh. **24**: 121. Same art. Ecl. M. **77**: 660.
— Monsoon in. Chamb. J. **53**: 749.
— Mornington's Administration in. Prosp. R. **3**: 320.

India, Mountains of. (T. W. Saunders) Nature, **21**: 96.
— Mundy's Sketches. Penny M. **1**: 135.
— Mutiny in, 1857–58. Quar. **102**: 534. **103**: 253. — Westm. **112**: 358. — Ed. R. **106**: 544. **124**: 299. **133**: 90. — (J. H. Jones) New Eng. **17**: 357. — (E. I. Sears) No. Am. **86**: 487. — Blackw. **82**: 372–643. **83**: 94–719. **84**: 24–700. **88**: 172. **89**: 501. **115**: 102 — (G. S. Jones) Cornh. **11**: 88. — Chr. Exam. **64**: 107. — Chr. Obs. **58**: 86, 322. **59**: 50. — Colburn, **111**: 66. — Chr. Rem. **35**: 362. — Cornh. **7**: 42. — Dub. Univ. **50**: 236–742. **73**: 666. — Ecl. R. **106**: 524. **108**: 332. — Fraser, **57**: 544. **58**: 245, 730. — Tait, n. s. **24**: 502–697. — Liv. Age, **54**: 684. **55**: 186, 437. — Lond. Q. **9**: 208. Same art. Ecl. M. **43**: 59. — Nat. M. **12**: 145. — New Q. **6**: 463. — No. Brit. **27**: 254. Same art. Ecl. M. **42**: 449. — (J. C. Lowrie) Princ. **30**: 27. — (Sir R. de Camden) Potter Am. Mo. **4**: 57.
— — Anglo-Indian View of. Fraser, **57**: 269, 473.
— — Causes of. Bentley, **43**: 60.
— — — and Consequences of. (Mrs. S. B. Herrick) So. R. n. s. **13**: 410.
— — Crisis of. Lond. Q. **9**: 530. — Dub. Univ. **65**: 56.
— — Extent of. Fraser, **57**: 358.
— — Horrors of. Tait, n. s. **25**: 126, 186.
— — How we escaped from Delhi. (C. J. Le Bas) Fraser, **57**: 184.
— — India in Mourning. Fraser, **56**: 737.
— — Kaye's History of. Fraser, **70**: 757. **83**: 232. — Chr. Obs. **76**: 411.
— — Last Picture of. Chamb. J. **33**: 302. Same art. Liv. Age, **65**: 737.
— — Life during, Aspects of. Good Words, **1**: 250–394.
— — Malleson's History of. (F. Hall) Nation, **28**: 218.
— — Men of. Fraser, **57**: 686.
— — My Escape from Futtehghur. (G. S. Jones) Cornh. **11**: 88.
— — Noble Deed in. Chamb. J. **56**: 758.
— — Perils in. House. Words, **19**: 174.
— — Recollection of, 1857–58. Liv. Age, **137**: 311.
— — Ride for Life in. Blackw. **123**: 182. Same art. Ecl. M. **90**: 441.
— — Russell's Diary in. Tait, n. s. **27**: 152.
— — Two Marches in. Dub. Univ. **62**: 350.
— — Village System and. Fraser, **58**: 609.
See Lucknow.
— Mutinies in. Fraser, **56**: 238, 627.
— Myths of. Ecl. M. **71**: 1304.
— Narrow-Gauge Railways in. Ecl. Engin. **7**: 493.
— Nations of, and their Manners. Ed. R. **98**: 33.
— Natives of. (Lord Northbrook) Fraser, **102**: 721.
— Native Armies of. (Lt. Gen. Sir J. Adye) 19th Cent. **7**: 685.
— Native Industry of. Chamb. J. **37**: 333.
— Native Life in. (M. Bennet) Dub. Univ. **81**: 601. — Mo. R. **127**: 233. — Mus. **21**: 38.
— Native Press in. Am. Q. **5**: 203.
— Native Prince of, and his British Ally. (J. Hutton) St. James, **30**: 470.
— — in London. Good Words, **12**: 421.
— Native Princes of. Ed. R. **144**: 169. — Portfo. **7**: 38, 137.
— — and East India Company. Brit. & For. R. **8**: 154.
— — and Proclamation of British Empire. Quar. **145**: 418.
— — British Treatment of. Westm. **79**: 115.
— — Despotism of. (C. E. Norton) No. Am. **88**: 289.
— — Legal and Political Relations to England. Westm. **69**: 453.
— — protected. (Sir D. Wedderburn) 19th Cent. **4**: 151.
— Navy of, History of. Ed. R. **148**: 343.
— — Survey of. For. Q. **35**: 454.
India, New Constitution for, 1881. (R. H. Elliot) Fraser, **103**: 166.
— News from; a Poem. Dub. Univ. **50**: 292.
— Newspaper of. Temp. Bar, **6**: 502.
— Night of Adventure in. (F. Hall) Lippinc. **16**: 748.
— Night Mail-Train in. Fraser, **54**: 680. Same art. Liv. Age, **52**: 404.
— Non-Regulation Provinces of. Fraser, **65**: 285.
— Lord Northbrook and Lord Lytton, 1880. Brit. Q. **72**: 442.
— Northern; a Poem. Dub. Univ. **33**: 523.
— — Abode of Snow in. Blackw. **117**: 69–508. **118**: 60. Same art. Liv. Age, **125**: 172–803. **126**: 283.
— — Canals of. (G. C. S. Moncrieff) Good Words, **8**: 807.
— — Conolly's Journey to. Ed. R. **60**: 54.
— — Days in. (N. Macleod) Good Words, **11**: 16–426.
— — Tribes of. (T. Farquhar) Good Words, **13**: 495.
— Notes of an Indian Journey. (M. E. G. Duff) Contemp. **25**: 894. **26**: 44–785.
— Notes on. (J. Routledge) Macmil. **32**: 223, 374, 457. — Dub. Univ. **51**: 320. — Chamb. J. **48**: 820.
— Notes on the Affairs of, 1850. Dub. Univ. **34**: 592, 700.
— Notes on the Way in. (J. Caird) 19th Cent. **6**: 119–705.
— Note-Book in, Stray Leaves from. St. James, **19**: 296. **20**: 166.
— Opium Revenue of. Fraser, **66**: 399.
— Oude, English Usurpation of. For. Q. **23**: 93.
— — Right of Occupancy in. Fraser, **72**: 77.
— Overland Journey to. Mo. R. **123**: 226. — Blackw. **57**: 204.
— — Conolly's. (Sir J. Barrow) Quar. **52**: 38.
— Paganism in, Decline of. (J. B. Heard) Dub. Univ. **53**: 131.
— Pageant in. Chamb. J. **25**: 385.
— Pamphlets on. Chr. Exam. **1**: 239.
— Pantheism in. Lond. Q. **47**: 309.
— Paper Materials from. Pract. M. **7**: 266.
— Past and Present of. Chamb. J. **27**: 355.
— Past and Future of. (I. Loewenthal) Princ. **26**: 593.
— Peasants of. Westm. **110**: 135.
— Penal Code for. Westm. **29**: 393.
— People of. (F. Nightingale) 19th Cent. **4**: 193.
— — and Administration of. Westm. **109**: 355.
— — and Governments. (J McGreggor) Ecl. M. **30**: 219.
— Peoples of. (G. M. Towle) Appleton, **15**: 737, 769, 801.
— Periodical Literature in. Dark Blue, **4**: 63. — Bentley, **1**: 534. — Am. Q. Reg. **7**: 40.
— Physical Features and Inhabitants of. Lond. Q. **9**: 208. Same art. Ecl. M. **43**: 74.
— Pictures of. Chamb. J. **44**: 45.
— Pilgrim in. Bentley, **28**: 520.
— Plagues of. Chamb. J. **37**: 145.
— Police of. Once a Week, **29**: 475.
— Police Court in. Once a Week, **30**: 631.
— Political and social. (M. E. G. Duff) Contemp. **26**: 857.
— Political Agents in. No. Brit. **7**: 420.
— Political History of, Malcolm's. Ecl. R. **13**: 473.
— Poor of. (C. Grant) 19th Cent. **2**: 868.
— Poor Whites of. (A. Arbuthnot) Macmil. **30**: 554.
— Popular Poetry of. Nat. M. **8**: 39.
— Portraits of my Helps in. Lond. Soc. **39**: 53.
— Portuguese in. (S. G. W. Benjamin) New Eng. **24**: 461.
— Prices of Food in. (W. H. Sykes) J. Statis. Soc. **10**: 289.
— Prince of Wales in. Appleton, **18**: 1. — Lond. Q. **45**: 422.
— Prison in, Ten Years in. All the Year, **23**: 544.
— Proffered Salvation of England, 1847. (W. Howitt) Howitt, **2**: 228, 274, 329.
— Progress of. Ed. R. **119**: 95.
— — Facts of. (M. Williams) Contemp. **32**: 29, 417.
— — Social and religious. Lond. Q. **31**: 349.

India, Public Affairs of. (C. Redding) Colburn, 111: 116.
— Public Works in. (W. H. Sykes) J. Statis. Soc. 21: 121. — Bank. M. (N. Y.) 31: 684. — Brit. Q. 65: 391. — Ecl. Engin. 10: 412. — No. Brit. 50: 226. — Westm. 102: 439. — Fraser, 66: 77. *See above*, India, Engineering in.
— The Punjab. Ed. R. 89: 184.
— — Administration of, 1859. Brit. Q. 29: 433. — New Q. 3: 429.
— — War of. Quar. 78: 175.
— — Year on, Edwardes's. Dub. Univ. 37: 411.
— Question of. Blackw. 33: 776.
— — Progress of. Fraser, 47: 473.
— — What is the Indian Question? Fraser, 48: 234. 50: 454.
— Races of, Elliot's. Nature, 2: 43.
— Railway to. (V. L. Cameron) Ecl. Engin. 25: 410.
— — Best Route for. (B. Houghton) Ecl. Engin. 23: 97.
— — Fiction and Fact. (W. S. Blunt) Fortn. 32: 702.
— — Russian Ideas upon. Colburn, 152: 183.
— — Suez and Euphrates Routes to. Quar. 102: 354.
— Railways in. All the Year, 10: 564. 11: 31. — Bentley, 62: 499. — Cornh. 20: 68. — Ecl. Engin. 2: 126. 3: 510. — Ed. R. 149: 104. — For. Q. 35: 382. 36: 306. — Hunt, 61: 159. — No. Brit. 49: 313. — Pract. M. 2: 177. — Quar. 125: 48. — Westm. 92: 1. — Fraser, 37: 414.
— Railway Traveling in. All the Year, 36: 219.
— Rainfall in. Nature, 17: 273.
— — and Sun-Spots. Nature, 16: 171.
— — in South. (J. A. Broun) Nature, 16: 333.
— Rambles in the Tropics. (F. R. Feudge) Lippinc. 197: 302.
— Religion in. Cong. M. 11: 39, 90. — Meth. M. 30: 351. — Bib. R. 5: 449.
— Religion of a Province in. (A. C. Lyall) Fortn. 17: 121. Same art. Liv. Age, 112: 673.
— Religions of. Blackw. 82: 743.
— — and China. Theo. & Lit. J. 11: 134. — (C. W. Clapp) New Eng. 39: 487.
— — and Government of. Ecl. R. 109: 125.
— — Johnson's. O. & N. 6: 731.
— Religious Fairs in. (W. Knighton) 19th Cent. 9: 838.
— Religious Future of. (W. H. Fremantle) Contemp. 15: 67.
— Religious Revival in. Cong. 3: 733.
— Religious Situation in. (A. C. Lyall) Fortn. 18: 151.
— Religious State of, 1852. (H. R. Hoisington) Bib. Sac. 9: 237.
— Religious Tendencies of. Dub. R. 65: 261.
— Religious Thought in, Progress of. (M. Williams) Contemp. 33: 242. 34: 19. 35: 843.
— Reminiscences of. (J. C. Watt) So. M. 15: 592. — Bentley, 43: 475. — Victoria, 2: 533. 3: 427, 552. 4: 170. 5: 465.
— Reminiscences of an Officer in. Chamb. J. 57: 569, 583.
— Resources of. Westm. 79: 396.
— — Royle on. Tait, n. s. 8: 199. — Mo. R. 153: 333.
— Revenues of. Quar. 130: 93.
— Rickard on. Ecl. R. 48: 260.
— Rivers of. Penny M. 3: 399.
— Robbers in. Chamb. J. 58: 309.
— Rock-cut Temples in. Ed. R. 122: 371.
— — Fergusson's. Liv. Age, 81: 89.
— — of Elephanta in Bombay. Potter Am. Mo. 6: 137.
— Roof of the World. Blackw. 128: 462. Same art. Appleton, 24: 503. Same art. Ecl. M. 95: 664.
— Rousselet's. Scrib. 11: 65. — Westm. 105: 386. Same art. Liv. Age, 129: 451.
— Route to. (E. Dicey) 19th Cent. 1: 665.
— — Allen's New. Ecl. R. 102: 454.
India, Route to, by Euphrates Valley. (W. B. Keer) Fraser, 90: 424. — Ecl. R. 105: 320. — Pract. M. 1: 177. — (W. P. Andrew) Ecl. Engin. 22: 474.
— — Constantinople and. (H. M. Havelock) Fortn. 27: 119.
— — Herat and. Westm. 67: 173.
— — Isthmian. Nature, 1: 110.
— — through Egypt. (J. Foster) Ecl. R. 30: 1.
— Routes to, Proposed. (J. P. Thompson) No. Am. 83: 133.
— Russia on the Way to. Nat. Q. 4: 105. — (G. Chesney) 19th Cent. 3: 605. Same art. Liv. Age, 137: 259.
— The Ryot. Chamb. J. 29: 132.
— Sir Salar Jung and the Berars. (G. A. Henty) Tinsley, 18: 617.
— Sanchi Tope at Bhopaul. Potter Am. Mo. 6: 300.
— Santal Rebellion of 1855. Cornh. 18: 231.
— Savage Life in. (W. Knighton) Contemp. 39: 403.
— Scenery of a Stream in. Fraser, 92: 785.
— Scenes and Characteristics of. Ecl. R. 62: 414.
— — in the Mofussil. Select J. 1: 293. 2: 76, 188.
— Scotch. Princ. 17: 61.
— Scraps from. (J. Hutton) Tinsley, 19: 428.
— Self-Government in. Brit. Q. 38: 421.
— Seven Years of an Officer's Life in. Bentley, 42: 379, 530, 581.
— Servants in. All the Year, 9: 416. — Chamb. J. 33: 366.
— Service in. Ecl. M. 71: 1019.
— Siege of Bhurtpore. Blackw. 23: 445, 914.
— Silver Question in. (G. M. Weston) Bank. M. (N. Y.) 34: 198, 293.
— Six Months in. Fraser, 53: 92, 198.
— Sketches from the Ganges. Colburn, 29: 217, 549.
— Sketches in. Dub. Univ. 90: 747.
— Sketches of. (F. Jeffrey) Ed. R. 41: 31. — Colburn, 11: 56. 13: 29. — (J. Foster) Ecl. R. 25: 337. — Lippinc. 17: 37-409.
— Skinner's Adventures in. Select J. 1: [7. — Mo. R. 141: 309.
— Slavery in, 1840. Mo. R. 152: 419, 523.
— Sleeman's Recollections of an Indian Official. For. Q. 34: 369.
— Social and Political Aspects of. (A. Phillips) Internat. R. 2: 454.
— Social Scandals in. Cornh. 14: 422.
— Society in. Bentley, 31: 242. — Mo. R. 133: 186. — Colburn, 22: 224. 23: 336. — Ed. R. 48: 32. — Once a Week, 28: 563.
— — Exaggerations as to. Temp. Bar, 11: 409.
— — Progress of. Tait, n. s. 4: 765.
— Some Suggestions for. (S. A. Ali) 19th Cent. 7: 963.
— Something to be done in. All the Year, 10: 103.
— Southern Sketches from. Fraser, 90: 64.
— Sporting in. Bentley, 63: 527. — Chamb. J. 2: 97, 299.
— — Shakspear's Wild Sports of. Liv. Age, 66: 155.
— — Sketches of. Colburn, 25: 409. 26: 231.
— — Tennant's Recreations in. Ed. R. 4: 303.
— Statesmen of. Ed. R. 102: 147.
— Steam Communication with. Penny M. 11: 225, 235. — Ed. R. 60: 445. 147: 104. — Tait, n. s. 5: 571. 6: 293. *See* India, Railway to.
— Subjugation of, to England, Providential Design in. Chr. Obs. 7: 568, 639, 702. 8: 83, 220.
— Subsidiary System in. (J. Hutton) Contemp. 6: 172.
— Superstition in. (C. H. A. Dall) Unita. R. 9: 452.
— Suppression of Public Discussion in. Pamph. 24: 33.
— Surveys in. (F. C. Danvers) Ecl. Engin. 17: 547. — Geog. M. 3: 330.
— — Marine. Geog. M. 1: 133.
— — — in 1874-76. Geog. M. 4: 99.
— — Statistical. Geog. M. 3: 240.

India, Surveys in, Topographical. Once a Week, **20:** 343.
— — Trigonometrical. Ecl. Engin. **3:** 299. **13:** 367. — Nature, **12:** 72.
— Sutlej, Campaign of. Blackw. **59:** 625. — No. Brit. **5:** 246.
— Tartar Conquests in. Ecl. R. **100:** 528.
— Taxation in. Quar. **149:** 486. — (S. Chunder-Dutt) Fraser, **94:** 302. — Westm. **94:** 25.
— Taxation of Englishmen in. Ed. R. **47:** 134.
— Telegraph to. Hunt, **49:** 281.
— Tennant's Effects of British Government on. (J. Foster) Ecl. R. **11:** 247.
— Textile Fabrics of. Once a Week, **16:** 325. Same art. Liv. Age, **93:** 712.
— Textile Products compared with Russian. Ed. R. **102:** 40.
— — and Costumes. Ed. R. **126:** 125.
— Theism in. Dub. R. **66:** 313. — (S. D. Collet) Contemp. **13:** 230. Same art. Liv. Age, **104:** 771.
— — New Theistic Movement in. (H. H. Barber) Unita. R. **12:** 323.
— Three Months' March in, 1833. Mo. R. **154:** 36.
— Tod's Annals and Antiquities of Rajasthan. (T. P. Thompson) Westm. **15:** 143. Same art. Select J. **1:** [97. — Am. Q. **10:** 356. — Quar. **48:** 1. — Mo. R. **120:** 393.
— Torture in. Ed. R. **103:** 153. — Liv. Age, **48:** 109.
— Tour through Spiti. Chr. Rem. **49:** 357.
— Trade of. *See* India, Commerce of.
— Trades-Unionism in. (W. Traut) Fortn. **32:** 261.
— Travels in. (Mrs. R. Church) Temp. Bar, **19:** 75, 395. **20:** 463. **21:** 66–466. — Colburn, **157:** 211–458.
— — Sketches of. (J. W. Massie) Tait, n. s. **7:** 335.
— — 27 Years of. Tait, n. s. **24:** 100–737. **25:** 24–525.
— Traveling in. Dub. Univ. **26:** 563.
— Tree and Serpent Worship in, Fergusson's. Anthrop. R. **7:** 217.
— Trevelyan on. Lond. Q. **23:** 169.
— Uncovenanted Service. Fraser, **103:** 461.
— Universities in. Dub. Univ. **87:** 494.
— An unhappy Valley. Bentley, **63:** 62.
— Up among the Pandies. Bentley, **44:** 448. **45:** 33–611.
— Up-Country Fair in Behar. Bentley, **60:** 514.
— Upper, Davidson's Travels in. Mo. R. **162:** 459.
— Lord Valentia's Travels to, 1802–6. (J. Foster) Ecl. R. **10:** 689, 811, 915.
— Value of, to England. (G. Chesney) 19th Cent. **3:** 227. Quar. **120:** 198.
— Vellore Massacre, 1806. Colburn, **111:** 489.
— Vernacular Press in. (R. Lethbridge) Contemp. **37:** 459.
— Views in. (Capt. Lyon) Pop. Sci. Mo. **2:** 614.
— Von Orlich's Travels in. Ecl. R. **82:** 272.
— Voyage Home from. Lond. Soc. **39:** supp. 89.
— Voyage to Calcutta. Portfo.(Den.) **30:** 139.
— Wahabeeism in. Westm. **97:** 359.
— Wanderings in. House. Words, **16:** 457–505. **17:** 12–254.
— War in, 1839. Tait, n. s. **6:** 518.
— in 1851. Westm. **55:** 49.
— Warfare in, Romance of. No. Brit. **12:** 193.
— Water in, Storage and Distribution of. (G. Gordon) Ecl. Engin. **6:** 422. **10:** 176, 212.
— Water Arrival in. (F. Nightingale) Good Words, **19:** 493.
— Wealth of, Development of. (T. Hare) Macmil. **3:** 417.
— Wellesley's Administration. (H. Brougham) Ed. R. **63:** 537. — Ed. R. **148:** 1.
— Wellesley's Dispatches from. (H. Brougham) Ed. R. **66:** 151.
— West Coast of, Along. Fraser, **91:** 616.
India, Western, Random Sketches of. Tait, n. s. **6:** 28.
— Why keep? (Grant Allen) Contemp. **38:** 544.
— Widow-Burning in. Blackw. **23:** 161. — (J. Foster) Ecl. R. **25:** 427. — Quar. **89:** 258. Same art. Ecl. M. **25:** 45.
— Wilberforce on moral and religious Instruction in. Pamph. **3:** 43.
— Wilks's Southern Sketches of. Quar. **6:** 103. **18:** 47.
— Witch-Murders in. Cornh. **16:** 409.
— Women of. Lond. Q. **16:** 145. Same art. Ecl. M. **53:** 241. — Brit. Q. **63:** 77.
— Work in. Good Words, **12:** 811.
— Wrongs of, Past. Chr. Obs. **67:** 294.
— Year in. Dub. Univ. **53:** 47.
— Yesterday and To-Day in. All the Year, **10:** 184.
See Assam; Bengal; Cashmere; *and other names of sections of the country. Also,* Hindostan; Mahrattas; East India Company; Ganges; etc.
India House, New, London. Cornh. **16:** 356. *See* East India Company.
India Institute, Proposed. Fraser, **91:** 493.
India Museum, Whitehall. All the Year, **22:** 209. — Once a Week, **17:** 246.
India-Rubber. House. Words, **7:** 29. — Penny M. **1:** 242.
— History and Properties of. (C. Davis) J. Frankl. Inst. **9:** 123.
— Litigation on. Hunt, **34:** 319.
— Manufacture of. (A. Ure) J. Frankl. Inst. **29:** 250. — All the Year, **7:** 141. — Once a Week, **9:** 51.
— Uses of, in the Arts, 1854. Art J. **6:** 341.
— Visit to Macintosh's Factory. Liv. Age, **25:** 279.
— Vulcanized. Chamb. J. **8:** 5. Same art. Liv. Age, **14:** 397.
India-Rubber Industries. (T. Bolas) Pop. Sci. Mo. **17:** 802.
India-Rubber Shoes, Manufacture of. Chamb. J. **28:** 165.
— for Horses. Pract. M. **4:** 431.
India-Rubber Tires *versus* Iron. Ecl. Engin. **5:** 402.
India-Rubber Trees in Brazil. Geog. M. **4:** 152, 182, 211.
India-Rubber Web, Manufacture of. (F. Peale) J. Frankl. Inst. **23:** 109.
See Caoutchouc; Gutta-Percha.
Indian Archipelago. (T. Dalton) Hunt, **42:** 183. — All the Year, **19:** 513. — Quar. **11:** 483. **28:** 111. — Ecl. R. **105:** 269. — Am. J. Sci. **56:** 157. — New Q. **2:** 267. — Dub. Univ. **41:** 315.
— and the Inhabitants. Ed. New Philos. J. **44:** 348.
— Bickmore's. (W. P. Garrison) Nation, **8:** 298. — Chamb. J. **46:** 188.
— Borneo, etc., Heath's. Ecl. R. **83:** 552. **88:** 671.
— Coal-Fields of. Am. J. Sci. **73:** 157.
— Commercial Relations of. Fraser, **34:** 379.
— Crawfurd's History of. Ecl. R. **34:** 228.
— Dutch and English in. Tait, n. s. **16:** 1.
— Piracy in. Ed. R. **88:** 63. Same art. Liv. Age, **18:** 308.
— St. John's History of. Ecl. R. **97:** 677.
— Straits Settlements. (W. A. Gliddon) De Bow, **12:** 362, 465.
— Trade and Piracy of. (W. A. Gliddon) Hunt, **24:** 562. **25:** 49.
— Tribes of. (N. W. Beckwith) Canad. Mo. **10:** 406.
Indian Impudence. (C. G. Leland) Temp. Bar, **48:** 189.
Indian Magistrate, Recollections of. Colburn, **164:** 51–625.
Indian Ocean, Countries and Languages of. For. Q. **14:** 369.
Indian, The old. (C. Lanman) So. Lit. Mess. **7:** 199.
— The Red. Fraser, **29:** 655.
Indian's Tale, An. Lond. M. **10:** 139.
Indians of America. (L. Cass) No. Am. **22:** 53. **26:** 357. — (J. Sparks) No. Am. **19:** 463. — (L. Bliss) No. Am. **44:** 301. — No. Am. **47:** 134. — (J. H. Perkins) No. Am. **49:** 277.

Indians of America. (P. Lindsley) Am. Bib. Repos. 2d s. 7: 1. — (G. Copway) Am. Whig R. 9: 631. — (R. M. Caufland) Carey's Mus. 5: 17. — Am. Q. 3: 395. — Mus. 5: 20. — So. Lit. Mess. 6: 191, 333. — U. S. Lit. Gaz. 1: 292. — De Bow, 5: 272. 6: 100. — Brownson, 8: 118. — Mo. R. 107: 25. 143: 279. 147: 349. — Niles's Reg. 15: 185, 420. 50: 61. — Quar. 31: 76. —(Sir T. B. Head) Quar. 65: 384. — Chr. R. 1: 369. — (A. Alexander) Princ. 10: 513. — (J. S. Brisbin) Potter Am. Mo. 14: 291. — (A. H. Hill, jr.) Potter Am. Mo. 15: 142. — (B. J. Lossing) Harper, 40: 793. — (J. Loughborough) West. J. 1: 598. — Chr. Obs. 22: 54, 81. — Colburn, 52: 119–350. — Ecl. R. 50: 116. 67: 704. — Galaxy, 19: 76. — Liv. Age, 139: 434. — Penny M. 4: 38, 53. — So. Q. 24: 59.

— Adventures among. Lond. M. 20: 548.

— Affairs of. Niles's Reg. 16: 405. 32: 318. — (A. Alexander) Princ. 10: 513. — Dem. R. 18: 333. — Dub. Univ. 34: 593, 700.

— American Autochthon. (C. C. Abbott) Am. Natural. 10: 329.

— and the Army. (J. D. Cox) Nation, 30: 291.

— and Aztecs, Arts among. (T. Ewbank) Internat. M. 4: 307.

— and their Champions. (F. Gilbert) Dial (Ch.), 2: 12.

— and the Puritans. Am. Church R. 3: 208, 559.

— — Did Pilgrims wrong? (J. S. Clark) Cong. Q. 1: 129.

— and the Trappers. Colburn, 85: 437.

— Anecdotes of. Colburn, 11: 276.

— Antiquity of. (C. C. Abbott) Am. Natural. 10: 65.

— Antiquities of. *See* American Antiquities.

— Aptitude of, for Agriculture. (J. Heywood) J. Statis. Soc. 33: 456.

— Apache-Shooting, Camp Grant Massacre, 1871. Ev. Sat. 11: 171, 339

— Arizona Chiefs. (J. C. Cremony) Overland, 8: 201.

— Bibliography of, Field's. (J. Anderson) Nation, 17: 341.

— Biography of. (B. B. Thatcher) No. Am. 33: 407. 34: 429. — (W. B. O. Peabody) No. Am. 36: 472. — Am. Mo. R. 2: 66. 3: 63. — (W. J. Snelling) Chr. Exam. 13: 386. — Dem. R. 12: 401. — Spirit Pilg. 6: 41.

— Bouquet's Exped. (J. T. Headley) Harper, 23: 577.

— Brush with. Once a Week, 30: 736, 762.

— Captivity among, Hunter's. Lond. M. 15: 317. — Mo. R. 102: 243, 368.

— Catlin's. Ed. R. 74: 415. — (H. R. Schoolcraft) No. Am. 54: 283. — (H. R. Schoolcraft) Lit. & Theo. R. 2: 96. — Quar. 65: 209. — Westm. 37: 122. — New York R. 10: 419. — So. Lit. Mess. 11: 202. — Dub. Univ. 19: 371. — Mo. R. 156: 318. — Mus. 43: 495. 44: 46. — Tait, n. s. 8: 792. 9: 106.

— Character of. So. Lit. J. 1: 101. 2: 13. — Anal. M. 3: 145.

— Characteristics of. (S. G. Morton) Ed. New Philos. J. 38: 141.

— Chiefs of Six Nations in Boston, 1777. Hist. M. 3: 102.

— Children among. (H. W. Elliott) Harper, 57: 829.

— Christian. Niles's Reg. 24: 380.

— Citizenship of. (F. A. Walker) Internat. R. 1: 305. — Ev. Sat. 11: 627.

— Civilization of. (J. Gibbon) Penn Mo. 5: 300. — Ed. R. 8: 442. — Niles's Reg. 17: 345. 22: 231. 26: 91. 30: 22, 273. — (C. C. Andrews) No. Am. 90: 57. — Nation, 28: 31.

— — Hammerer's Plan for, 1765. N. E. Reg. 11: 292.

— Clay's Speech on. Niles's Reg. 48: 84.

— Condition of. (V. Colger) Putnam, 14: 367, 474. — Ecl. R. 52: 77.

— — in 1860. Westm. 74: 333.

Indians, Conflicts and Adventures with. West. R. 1: 46–353. 2: 120–369. 3: 362. 4: 235, 305.

— Cooper's. (J. E. Cooke) Appleton, 12: 264.

— Cranial Type of. (D. Wilson) Canad. J. n. s. 2: 406.

— — Prevailing. (D. Wilson) Ed. New Philos. J. 64: 1.

— Customs of. (T. Parkman) No. Am. 101: 28.

— — Curious. (W. J. Hoffman) Am. Natural. 13: 6.

— Depopulation of. Anal. M. 7: 318.

— Education of. (A. C. Brackett) Harper, 61: 627.

— — at Hampton and Carlyle. (H. W. Ludlow) Harper, 62: 659.

— Eloquence of. (W. Tracy) Appleton, 6: 543. — (C. Atwater) M. Am. Hist. 5: 211.

— Escape from. (S. Hyacinth) Overland, 2: 463.

— Ethnography of Tribes on Northwest Coast. (J. Scouler) Ed. New Philos. J. 41. 168.

— Ethnologic Studies among. (M. M. Meline) Cath. World, 33: 255.

— Ethnology of America. (G. A. Mabile) Am. J. Educ. 17: 425. — Dem. R. 11: 603. 28: 429. — (E. G. Squier) Am. Whig R. 9: 385.

— — of N. W. America. (A. H. Sayce) Nature, 18: 165.

— Expedition of Pennsylvania Frontiersmen against, in 1782. Hist. M. 21: 207.

— Extermination or Civilization of. Republic, 2: 308.

— Extinct Tribes of. Hist. M. 7: 175.

— Folk-Lore of. Ecl. M. 71: 1460.

— Future of. St. James, 47: 280.

— Genius of, Instances of. Portfo. (Den.) 16: 319.

— Geographical Distribution of. (L. H. Morgan) No. Am. 110: 33.

— Harmer's Expedition against, 1790. West. R. 2: 179.

— Heckewelder's History of. West. R. 1: 65. — Portfo. (Den.) 22: 248.

— History of. (C. C. Felton and J. Sparks) No. Am. 47: 134. — (N. Hale) No. Am 9: 155.

— — Scrap of. (J. R. Brodhead) Hist. M. 17: 38.

— Homes of. Galaxy, 21: 513.

— Hostilities with, 1867. (G. E. Pond) Nation, 4: 51.

— — in 1877; the Nez Percés. (G. Mallery) Nation, 25: 20, 69.

— — in 1878; Bannock War. (G. Mallery) Nation, 27: 51.

— Howard's Treaties with. O. & N. 6: 620.

— Hybridity and Absorption of. (D. Wilson) Canad. J. n. s. 14: 432.

— Identity of Andastes, Minquos, Susquehannas, and Conestogues. Hist. M. 2: 294.

— Idolatry of. (D. G. Brinton) Hist. M. 9: 298.

— Indian's Views of Affairs of. No. Am. 128: 412. Same art. Canad. Mo. 15: 615.

— Indios Bravos of British Honduras. Liv. Age, 34: 513.

— Ingenuity of; the Tepiti. (T. Ewbank) Hist. M. 11: 145. — J. Frankl. Inst. 81: 124.

— Intercourse with. Ill. M. 1: 352–509.

— Irving's Sketches of American, 1833. Mo. R. 138: 74.

— Mrs. Jackson's Century of Dishonor. (J. D. Cox) Nation, 32: 152.

— Kane's Wanderings among. Liv. Age, 61: 289.

— Knowledge of, essential to their Safety. Ecl. R. 80: 224.

— Languages of. (L. Cass) No. Am. 26: 377. — (H. R. Schoolcraft) No. Am. 45: 34. —(E. Jones) Am. Q. 3: 391. —(J. Pickering) No. Am. 9: 179. — Anal. M. 13: 250. — U. S. Lit. Gaz. 4: 262. 6: 40. — Carey's Mus. 5: 22, 142. — (E. Nason) N. E. Reg. 20: 309. — (E. Jacker) Am. Cath. Q. 2: 304.

— — Adjectives of Color in. (A. S. Gatschet) Am. Natural. 13: 475.

— — Lord's Prayer in Mikasuke. Hist. M. 10: 288.

— — of Norumbega. (J. H. Trumbull) Hist. M. 17: 239.

— — of Oregon Territory. (R. G. Latham) Ed. New Philos. J. 39: 157.

Indians, Languages of, of Pacific States. (A. S. Gatschet) M. Am. Hist. 1: 145.
— — of Santa Cruz, Vocab. of. Hist. M. 7: 220. 9: 147.
— — Specimen of Montagnais. Hist. M. 7: 268.
— — Vocabulary of. Am. Hist. Rec. 1: 308.
— — — of the Kah-we-yah and Kah-so-wah. (J. H. Riley) Hist. M. 13: 238.
See Huron; Iroquois; Mohawk; *and other names of tribes.*
— La Salle's Account of. M. Am. Hist. 2: 238.
— Laws for. (S. Martin) Penn Mo. 11: 808.
— Legal Position of. (G. F. Canfield) Am. Law R. 15: 21.
— Life of, Glimpses of. Appleton, 4: 117–685.
— McKenney's. (A. P. Peabody) No. Am. 63: 481. — For. Q. 37: 479. Same art. Liv. Age, 10: 461. Same art. Ecl. M. 9: 1. — Chamb. J. 7: 26.
— President Madison's Talk with. Niles's Reg. 28: 175.
— Management of. Nat. Q. 40: 27.
— Manners and Customs of. (E. Palmer) Am. Natural. 12: 308. — West. Mo. R. 1: 139–325. — (W. Wells) West. R. 2: 45, 110, 160.
— Massacre of the Conestogoe by the Paxton Boys. Hist. M. 9: 203.
— Massacres by, in Massachusetts, 1703–46. (L. M. Bottwood) N. E. Reg. 9: 161.
— Means of Subsistence of. (L. H. Morgan) No. Am. 109: 391.
— Mismanagement of. (J. G. Shea) Am. Cath. Q. 6: 520.
— Mission to, by Friends of Pennsylvania, 1773. Hist. M. 17: 103.
— — Zeisberger's. (R. E. Thompson) Penn Mo. 2: 97, 188.
— Missions to. O. & N. 7: 119.
— — and Schools for. Am. J. Educ. 27: 17.
— — Catholic. (P. J. De Smet) U. S. Cath. M. 2: 113, 288. — (A. Thébaud) Month, 30: 145. 31: 27. 33: 480. 35: 352. 36: 168, 524. 37: 228. 38: 551. 39: 531. 40: 379. 41: 60. 42: 379. 43: 337.
— — — in Michigan and Wisconsin. (E. Jacker) Am. Cath. Q. 1: 404.
— — Moravian. Am. Hist. Rec. 1: 11.
— — Shecomeko. Am. Hist. Rec. 3: 60.
— Mythology of. (J. Anderson) Nation, 7: 72. — (J. Fiske) No. Am. 107: 636.
— — Legend of Chata-Muskokee Tribes. (D. G. Brinton) Hist. M. 17: 128.
— — of Dakotas. (J. Anderson) Nation, 11: 61.
— Natural History of. (S. Forry) Am. Bib. Repos. 2d s. 10: 29.
— New Negotiations with. Hunt, 53: 299.
— Nights in an Indian Lodge. Am. Mo. M. 5: 62, 146.
— Numeral Systems of. Hist. M. 9: 249.
— of Arizona, New Mexico, etc. (E. Palmer) Am. Natural. 11: 735.
— of Brit. America. (J. H. Lefroy) Am. J. Sci. 66: 189.
— — and the Esquimaux. Cath. World, 3: 557.
— — and N. W. Coast. (A. C. Anderson) Hist. M. 7: 73.
— of California. (E. E. Chever) Am. Natural. 4: 129. — (S. Powers) Overland, 8: 325, 425, 530. 9: 155, 305, 498. 10: 322, 535. 11: 105. 12: 21, 412, 530. 13: 542. 14: 297. — Colburn, 100: 179.
— — Gallinoméros. (S. Powers) Lakeside, 7: 352, 448.
— of Canada. (S. W. McDaniel) O. & N. 2: 377.
— of Connecticut. (L. Ray) New Eng. 1: 312.
— — of Housatonic Valley. (E. W. B. Canning) M. Am. Hist. 2: 734.
— of Long Island. Knick. 32: 237.
— of Maine, Bashaba and the Tarratines. (J E. Godfrey) Hist. M. 13: 98.
— of New England. (L. Sabine) Chr. Exam. 52: 96.
— — Memoir of. Bost. Mo. 1: 449, 525, 609.
— — Number in 1726. N. E. Reg. 20: 7.
Indians of North Carolina. (F. Kidder) Hist. M. 1: 161.
— of Oregon. (F. F. Victor) Overland, 7: 344, 425.
— of the Pacific Coast. (J. D. Edgar) Canad. Mo. 6: 93. — (J. L. Diman) No. Am. 121: 442. — (B. J. Lossing) Potter Am. Mo. 8: 36.
— — Bancroft's. Ed. R. 144: 283. Same art. Liv. Age, 131: 451. — (J. Anderson) Nation, 21: 182, 199, 421. — Overland, 13: 551. 14: 482, 580. 15: 108, 590. — (F. Parkman) No. Am. 120: 34. — So. R. n. s. 20: 63. — Westm. 103: 416.
— of Red River of the North. (P. Kane) Canad. J. n. s. 1: 128.
— of Soreto. (A. Raimondy) Anthrop. R. 1: 33.
— of South America. (J. Sparks) No. Am. 19: 198.
— of Stadacona and Hochelaga. Hist. M. 9: 144.
— of To-Day. Chamb. J. 49: 721.
— of United States. Bost. R. 2: 517. — De Bow, 17: 68.
— — Past, Present, and Future of. De Bow, 16: 143.
— of the Upper Missouri, De Smet's. Month, 5: 322.
— of Vermont, Relics of. (G. H. Perkins) Am. Natural. 5: 12.
— of Ysleta. (G. Butler) Cath. World, 17: 422.
— Origin of. (G. S. Jones) Penn Mo. 5: 358. — (A. Alexander) Princ. 13: 54. — (N. Hale) No. Am. 9: 356. — Dem. R. 11: 603. — (F. Smith) De Bow, 3: 565. — (B. S. Barton) Portfo.(Den.) 7: 507. — Portfo.(Den.) 13: 231, 519. 14: 7. 15: 458. 16: 1. — Bost. Mo. 1: 419. — U. S. Cath. M. 5: 588.
— Outbreaks of. (A. A. Woodhull) Nation, 19: 85.
— Past and Present of. Am. Whig R. 1: 502.
— Penhallow Papers on. N. E. Reg. 32: 21.
— Plants used by. (E. Palmer) Am. Natural. 12: 593, 646.
— Poetry of. (J. S. Brisbin) Harper, 57: 104.
— Quaker Labors in behalf of. Ecl. R. 81: 685.
— Question of. (E. Coues) Penn Mo. 10: 180. — (J. D. Cox) Internat. R. 6: 617. — (F. H. Head) Overland, 4: 105. — (N. A. Miles) No. Am. 128: 304. — (S. E. Sewall) Chr. Exam. 9: 107. — (F. A. Walker) No. Am. 116: 329. — (F. A. Walker) Penn Mo. 5: 828. — Nation, 10: 389. — (E. Butler) Cath. World, 26: 195.
— — and the Church. (J. M. Linn) Presb. R. 1: 677.
— — in 1857. (S. P. Riggs) New Eng. 15: 250.
— — in 1867. (A. L. Riggs) Nation, 5: 356.
— — in 1868. (E. L. Godkin) Nation, 7: 544.
— — in 1871, in Arizona. Ev. Sat. 11: 342.
— — in 1872. (J. N. Trask) O. & N. 8: 232.
— — in 1876. (L. H. Morgan) Nation, 23: 40.
— — — Custer Tragedy. (E. L. Godkin) Nation, 23: 21.
— — in 1878. (L. H. Morgan) Nation, 27: 332.
— — — Otis on. (G. Mallery) Nation, 27: 13.
— — in 1881. (C. Schurz) No. Am. 133: 1.
— — — Schurz on. (G. F. Canfield) Nation, 32: 457.
— Religion of. (J. Pickering) No. Am. 11: 103. — Anal. M. 16: 34. — So. R. 2: 305.
— Removal of. (L. Cass) No. Am. 30: 62. — (J. Evarts) No. Am. 31: 396. — Dem. R. 14: 169. — So. R. 2: 541. — Niles's Reg. 27: 363.
— Rights of. West. R. 4: 293.
— — to the Soil. Fraser, 29: 671.
— Schools for. Niles's Reg. 16: supp. 91.
— Schoolcraft on. (F. Bowen) No. Am. 77: 245. — Canad. J. n. s. 3: 437.
— Secret Societies of. (D. J. Macgowan) Hist. M. 10: 139.
— Sepulchral Pits in Canada. (E. W. Bawtree) Ed. New Philos. J. 45: 86.
— Shell Money of. (R. E. C. Stearns) Overland, 11: 335.
— Siege of Fort Atkinson. Harper, 15: 638.
— Sign Language of. (I. J. Cooper) West. J. 7: 430. — (F. W. Prewitt) West. J. 5: 176. — Chr. Obs. 24: 615. — Hist. M. 10: 86.

Indians, Sketches of. (C. G. Leland) Temp. Bar, **45**: 185. **46**: 201. **47**: 77.
— Slavery among. So. Lit. Mess. **28**: 333.
— Social Life among. (W. H. Dall) Am. Natural. **12**: 1.
— Southern, Jones's. (W. H. Browne) So. M. **13**: 237.
— Speech and Mental Capacity of. (E. Jacker) Am. Cath. Q. **3**: 255.
— Stories of. All the Year, **23**: 156–394.
— Sullivan's Expedition against the Five Nations. (N. Davis) Hist. M. **13**: 198.
— Superstitions of. (F. Parkman) No. Am. **103**: 1.— De Bow, **16**: 128.
— — Belief in inferior Spirits. (J. A. Van Henvel) Am. Presb. R. **12**: 111.
— Tales of. Portfo.(Den.) **19**: 227, 304.
— Theology of. Nat. Q. **7**: 22.
— Trade with. Niles's Reg. **18**: 140. **22**: 249.
— Treatment of. (L. Cass) No. Am. **24**: 365.—(E. Howland) Harper, **56**: 768.—Cornh. **20**: 313.—(L. E. Dudley) Scrib. **10**: 484.
— — Systems of Canada and United States. (G. Mallery) Nation, **25**: 147.
— Tribes east of the Mississippi. Olden Time, **1**: 386.
— — of 35th Parallel. (J. W. Palmer) Harper, **17**: 448.
— United States Policy with. (R. J. Hinton) Nation, **2**: 102, 134.—(R. Patterson) Overland, **11**: 201.—(T. S. Williamson) Am. Presb. R. **13**: 587.—No. Am. **99**: 449.—Bost. Q. **2**: 229.—Dem. R. **14**: 169.—(H. H. Jackson) Scrib. **19**: 775.
— — and Religious Liberty. (P. Girard) Cath. World. **26**: 90.
— — President Grant's. (S. G. Arnold) Meth. Q. **37**: 409.—(C. Lowe) O. & N. **3**: 497.
— — Proposed. (H. F. Bond) Unita. R. **7**: 639.
— — Transfer of the Indian Bureau. (A. G. Sedgwick) Nation, **28**: 7.—(J. N. Pomeroy) Nation, **13**: 100.
— Uprising of, in Minnesota in 1862. St. James, **6**: 231.
— Villages of. Penny M. **13**: 109.—(W. G. Simms) So. Lit. J. **3**: 343.
— Virtues of. (H. M. Robinson) Potter Am. Mo. **8**: 272.
— Voice from. Dub. Univ. **93**: 549.
— Wanderings among. (P. Kane) Canad. J. n. s. **4**: 186.—No. Brit. **31**: 72.
— War with, Lord Dunmore's. Olden Time, **2**: 8, 37.
— — of 1675, Letter and Diary of Noah Wright. (S. W. Williams) N. E. Reg. **2**: 207.
— — of 1776. (D. L. Swain) Hist. M. **12**: 273.
— Wars with, in New England. (S. G. Drake) N. E. Reg. **12**: 1, 161. **15**: 33, 149, 257.
— — Papers on. N. E. Reg. **3**: 23, 163. **8**: 239.
— War Paint and Medicine-Bags. All the Year, **2**: 421.
— west of the Mississippi. (E. Robinson) Am. Bib. Repos. **5**: 241.
— What to do with. (G. Reynolds) Unita. R. **8**: 139.—Cath. World, **6**: 403.
See also names of tribes, as Chippeway; Dakota; Delaware; etc.
Indian Axes from West Virginia. (C. C. Abbott) Nature, **12**: 478.
Indian Battle Rock, Story of. (A. W. Chase) Overland, **14**: 179.
Indian Bible, Eliot's. Am. Bibliop. **2**: 6, 60.
Indian Captives; a Tale. (H. King) So. Lit. Mess. **3**: 22.
Indian Captives in 1688 and 1694. N. E. Reg. **18**: 165, 166.
Indian Children put to Service, 1676. N. E. Reg. **8**: 271.
Indian Churches on Nantucket. (S. D. Hosmer) Cong. Q. **7**: 31.
Indian Corn. (J. B. D. De Bow) De Bow, **1**: 465.—Hogg, **9**: 311.
— Composition of. (W. O. Atwater) Am. J. Sci. **98**: 352.
— Fame of. De Bow, **4**: 237.
Indian Corn for Food, Elihu Burritt's Receipts for. Chr. Obs. **46**: 539.
— in Milk. (W. G. Simms) Godey, **34**: 62–249.
— Insects destructive of. (C. Taylor) Harper, **23**: 316.
Indian Council, The Black Robe at. (P. J. De Smet) Month, **10**: 278.
— Grand, at Okmulgee. (A. M. Williams) Lippinc. **24**: 371.
— Last, on the Genesee. (D. Gray) Scrib. **14**: 338.
Indian Country, Letters from. Knick. **20**: 1.
— Passports through. Niles's Reg. **34**: 110.
Indian Eloquence. Knick. **7**: 385.
Indian Feats of Legerdemain. So. Lit. Mess. **1**: 657.
Indian Graves in Chester County, Pennsylvania. (E. A. Barber) Am. Natural. **13**: 294.
Indian Lands in Georgia. Niles's Reg. **26**: 139, 275.
Indian Legend, An. Canad. Mo. **13**: 201.
Indian Legends. (W. Elder) No. Am. **112**: 1.
Indian Meal. Fraser, **39**: 561. Same art. Liv. Age, **22**: 265.
Indian Method of making Fire. J. Frankl. Inst. **75**: 111.
Indian Myths. (D. G. Brinton) Hist. M. **12**: 3.
Indian Names. Olden Time, **1**: 325.
— Beauty of. So. Lit. Mess. **7**: 477.
— in Virginia. (J. H. Trumbull) Hist. M. **17**: 47.
— of American States. Chamb. J. **55**: 663.
— of the Months. (S. Judd) N. E. Reg. **10**: 166.
— on the Androscoggin. Hist. M. **8**: 237.
Indian Narrative, Tanner's. Am. Q. **8**: 108.
Indian Netsinkers. (C. Rau) Am. Natural. **7**: 139.
Indian Picture-Writing. Fraser, **65**: 332.
Indian Pipestone, Trip to the Quarry. (C. A. White) Am. Natural. **2**: 644.
Indian Pottery of Brazil. (C. F. Hartt) Am. Natural. **5**: 259.
— of the Salt-Springs, Ill. (G. E. Sellers) Pop. Sci. Mo. **11**: 573.
Indian Relics near Brockville. Canad. J. n. s. **1**: 329.
Indian Remains in Canada. (D. Wilson) Canad. J. n. s. **1**: 511.
Indian Reservation, Visit to an. Once a Week, **9**: 176.
Indian Reservations, Factory System for. (L. H. Morgan) Nation, **23**: 58.
Indian Sachems and Queen Anne. Am. Hist. Rec. **3**: 462.
Indian Scepter, Ancient. (C. C. Abbott) Am. Natural. **10**: 673.
Indian Shell-Heaps in Maine. (J. Wyman) Am. Natural. **1**: 561.
Indian Sports. Mus. **26**: 640.
Indian Stone Implements. (J. J. H. Gregory) Am. Natural. **4**: 483.
Indian Stone Tubes and Tobacco-Pipes. (C. C. Abbott) Nature, **14**: 154.
Indian Summer. Dem. R. **3**: 153.—Am. J. Sci. **27**: 140.—(L. Foot) Am. J. Sci. **30**: 8.—(J. E. Willet) Am. J. Sci. **94**: 340.
— Poetry and Philosophy of. (T. B. Maury) Harper, **48**: 89.
Indian Tale, An. Godey, **56**: 45.
Indian Tales and Legends, Schoolcraft's. (H. Whiting) No. Am. **49**: 354.
Indian Territory. (T. R. Jenness) Atlan. **43**: 444.—(M. W. Reynolds) Lakeside, **4**: 260.
Indian Tradition of the Creation of Nantucket Island. U. S. Lit. Gaz. **4**: 357.
— The Man made of Ashes. U. S. Lit. Gaz. **5**: 204.
Indian Traditions. (D. Zeisberger) Olden Time, **1**: 271.
Indian Treaty, 1752. N. E. Reg. **20**: 32.
— at Fort Stanwix, 1768. Olden Time, **1**: 399.
— — 1784. Olden Time, **2**: 404.
Indian Treaty Scene. Am. Mo. M. **7**: 465.

Indian Trust Bonds, Opinion of J. Cleaveland on. Bank. M. (N. Y.) **15**: 883.
Indian Workshop for Arrow Heads. (B. P. Avery) Overland, **11**: 489.
Indiana. Chr. Mo. Spec. **1**: 401, 463. — De Bow, **1**: 512.
— Archæological Explorations in. (F. W. Putnam) Am. Natural. **9**: 410.
— Capitol Bill. Am. Arch. **2**: 98.
— Central, Pioneer Settlers of. (J. Coburn) Hist. M. **22**: 201.
— a Century ago. (A. A. Graham) Potter Am. Mo. **12**: 161, 289.
— Coal Measures of. (E. T. Cox) Am. Natural. **5**: 547.
— Constitution of. Niles's Reg. **13**: 85.
— Geology and Mineralogy of. (W. B. Stilson) Am. J. Sci. **1**: 131.
— Hoosiers at Home. (M. Dean) Lippinc. **23**: 441.
— Public Debt of. Bank. M. (N. Y.) **3**: 164.
— Resources and Prospects of. De Bow, **7**: 246.
— State Debts of. (T. P. Kettell) Hunt, **21**: 147.
— State Teachers' Association. Am. J. Educ. **16**: 765.
— Statistics of, 1869. Am. J. Educ. **18**: 324.
Indiana Bond Fraud, 1861. Bank. M. (N. Y.) **17**: 77.
Indictments. Chamb. J. **29**: 36.
Indicator Diagrams, Steam. J. Frankl. Inst. **51**: 91–220. **52**: 285, 348. — (G. H. Babcock) J. Frankl. Inst. **88**: 193. *See* Steam.
Indies, Raynal's History of. (J. Morley) Fortn. **28**: 705.
Indigestion. (T. E. Clark) Galaxy, **6**: 694. — Ecl. R. **45**: 97, 265, 405.
— and Insanity. Ecl. R. **48**: 310.
— as a Cause of Nervous Depression. (T. C. Brunton) Pop. Sci. Mo. **18**: 226, 374.
— Phillips on. Mo. R. **103**: 167.
Indigo. House. Words, **17**: 436. — (J. C. Booth) J. Frankl. Inst. **31**: 161, 224, 296.
— All about. (T. Smith) Good Words, **3**: 43.
— and Indigo Trade. Hunt, **13**: 227.
— and its artificial Production. (H. E. Roscoe) Nature, **24**: 227. — (H. E. Roscoe) J. Frankl. Inst. **112**: 295.
— A blue Mutiny, 1861. Fraser, **63**: 98.
— Manner of manufacturing. (C. H. Weston) J. Frankl. Inst. **8**: 233, 311.
— Manufacture of, in United States. (W. Partridge) Am. J. Sci. **18**: 237. — J. Frankl. Inst. **10**: 193.
Indigo Planters and Plantations. Penny M. **12**: 178.
Indigo-Planting in Bengal. Fraser, **65**: 610. — Brit. Q. **37**: 245.
Indiscretion in the Life of an Heiress. (T. H. Hardy) Liv. Age, **139**: 11, 76.
Indiscriminate Acquaintances. Chamb. J. **53**: 680, 692.
Individual, The, and the Crowd. Fraser, **63**: 593.
Individualism. (C. S. Albert) Luth. Q. **7**: 447. — (H. H. Weld) Am. Church R. **29**: 186. — (W. Kirkus) Am. Church R. **34**: 221.
— Growth of. (E. McPherson) Evang. R. **8**: 533.
— in German Churches. (I. E. Graeff) Mercersb. **20**: 302.
— Principle of. Chr. R. **13**: 519.
— Theory of Political. (G. F. Holmes) De Bow, **22**: 133.
Individuality. (H. Blackburn) Victoria, **22**: 61. — (T. Pearson) Ex. H. Lec. **16**: 87. — (M. F. Taylor) So. M. **11**: 572. — (N. N. Withington) Radical, **2**: 705.
— and associated Character. (T. F. Risk) West. J. **5**: 157.
— Sermon on. (S. A. Brooke) Mo. Rel. M. **43**: 425.
Indo-Anglian Poet, An. (J. Payn) Gent. M. n. s. **24**: 370. Same art. Liv. Age, **145**: 49.
Indo-China, Mouhot's Travels in. Colburn, **133**: 253.
Indo-Chinese and Oceanic Races. (A. H. Keane) Nature, **23**: 199–271.
Indo-English Correspondence. Chamb. J. **47**: 551.
Indo-European Languages. (B. W. Dwight) Bib. Sac. **14**: 753. **15**: 97. **16**: 673. **17**: 266, 817. — Quar. **50**: 169.
— Coptic Element in. (J. Campbell) Canad. J. n. s. **13**: 282, 403.
— Groups and Characteristics. (R. G. Latham) Ed. New Philos. J. **47**: 293.
Indo-Europeans. *See* Aryans.
Indo-Germanic Natural Religion. (M. Besser) Bib. Sac. **34**: 167.
Indo-Mediterranean Railway. (V. L. Cameron) Macmil. **40**: 414.
Indo-Syrian Church. (J. Forsyth) Theo. & Lit. J. **12**: 420.
Induction and Deduction in Natural Science. (J. von Liebig) Cornh. **12**: 296.
— Basis of. (J. Lachelier) J. Spec. Philos. **10**: 307, 337. **11**: 1.
— Nature and Validity of. (H. N. Day) Am. Presb. R. **15**: 50.
— Philosophy of. (C. K. True) Meth. Q. **14**: 431.
Induction, Electrical, Phenomena of. (E. J. Houston) J. Frankl. Inst. **101**: 59.
Induction Apparatus, Ritchie's Rhumkorff's. J. Frankl. Inst. **70**: 64.
Induction-Currents Balance. (D. E. Hughes) Nature, **20**: 77.
Induction Tube of W. Siemens. (B. C. Brodie) Nature, **9**: 308.
Inductive Inference, Philosophy of. (W. S. Jevons) Fortn. **20**: 457.
Inductive Method in Theology. (J. G. Roberts) New Eng. **40**: 741.
Inductive Philosophy, Powell on the Spirit of. Chr. Obs. **55**: 522. — Theo. & Lit. J. **8**: 593.
Inductive Reasoning, Ground of Confidence in. (G. F. Wright) New Eng. **30**: 601.
Inductive Sciences, American Discoveries in. (R. J. Walker) Contin. Mo. **6**: 22.
— History of. Ed. R. **66**: 58.
— Whewell's. (Sir J. F. W. Herschel) Quar. **68**: 177. Same art. Am. Ecl. **2**: 333, 409.
— Whewell's Philosophy of. Ecl. R. **73**: 625.
Inductive System of Philosophy. Chr. R. **5**: 194. — Mass. Q. **1**: 168. — Ed. R. **74**: 140. — Quar. **45**: 374. — (J. D. Whelpley) Am. J. Sci. **55**: 33.
Indulgence of 1672. (J. B. Marsh) Cong. **1**: 460.
Indulgences. (J. O'F. Pope) Month, **42**: 394.
— Infallible. All the Year, **23**: 366.
Indus, Burnes's Voyage on the. Mo. R. **134**: 450.
— Trade and Navigation of. Mo. R. **144**: 106.
— Up the. Chamb. J. **17**: 81.
Industrial Affairs, Rectifications in. (W. R. Greg) Fortn. **30**: 200.
Industrial Arbitration and Conciliation. (J. D. Weeks) Am. J. Soc. Sci. **10**: 194.
Industrial Art. Pract. M. **6**: 103.
— Austrian. (B. Wirth) Art J. **33**: 268.
— Education in. (W. Smith) Penn Mo. **6**: 492. — (J. J. Talbot) Penn Mo. **10**: 745.
— — in the United States. (E. S. Drone) Internat. R. **2**: 636.
— Rustic Theory of. Ecl. Engin. **17**: 121.
— State of. (C. L. Eastlake) Ecl. Engin. **17**: 29.
— Study of. (J. Ruskin) Pract. M. **2**: 378.
Industrial Classes, Distribution of. (G. Tucker) Hunt, **9**: 47.
— of Europe. Brit. Q. **23**: 387.
Industrial College, Prince Albert's. (Sir D. Brewster) No. Brit. **17**: 520.
Industrial Competition, International. (J. Wharton) Am. Soc. Sci. J. **4**: 49. — Penn Mo. **1**: 476. **2**: 28.
Industrial Co-operation. (F. Harrison) Fortn. **3**: 477.

Industrial Correspondence from Paris, 1874. (F. Moigno) Pract. M. 4: 317. 5: 31.
— from Vienna, 1874. (E. Leonhardt) Pract. M. 4: 320.
Industrial Crisis, Character of, 1877. (P. Girard) Cath. World, 26: 122.
Industrial Depression, Causes of. (E. L. Godkin) Nation, 27: 206. — Bank. M. (N. Y.) 33: 19.
Industrial Education. (J. Hayes) Overland, 12: 338. — (J. S. Clarke) J. Frankl. Inst. 112: 218. — Brit. Q. 16: 133. — No. Brit. 24: 1. — (S. P. Thompson) Contemp. 38: 472. Same art. Pop. Sci. Mo. 18: 26, 202. — Dub. Univ. 42: 295. — Penn Mo. 6: 414. — Unita. R. 1: 263. 2: 191.
Industrial Exchanges, Barhydt's. So. R. 15: 460.
Industrial Exhibitions. All the Year, 12: 535. 24: 320.
— on a small Scale. Chamb. J. 41: 506.
Industrial Growth. (D. A. Wells) Bank. M. (N. Y.) 29: 953.
Industrial History of Nations. Brit. Q. 4: 179.
— of the United States. (A. S. Bolles) Penn Mo. 10: 307.
Industrial Migrations. Chamb. J. 57: 791.
Industrial Pathology. Chamb. J. 22: 355.
Industrial Reconstruction. (E. Atkinson) Internat. R. 5: 530.
Industrial Reform. Dem. R. 23: 513.
Industrial Relationships. Dub. Univ. 94: 1.
Industrial Scholarships, Whitworth's. Pract. M. 3: 322.
Industrial School, Annals of an. (Dr. Goodwin) Macmil. 2: 13.
Industrial Schools. (W. B. McMurrich) Canad. Mo. 2: 424. — Peop. J. 2: 192, 213, 262. 3: 86. — (J. Williams) O. & N. 7: 624. — De Bow, 18: 265.
— and Home Office. (E. L. Stanley) 19th Cent. 10: 913.
— for Girls, Lancaster, Mass. Am. J. Educ. 16: 652.
— for poor Children. Fraser, 40: 437.
— Italian. Victoria, 11: 481.
— Plan of. (W. Petty) Am. J. Educ. 22: 199.
— — London, 1647. (W. Petty) Am. J. Educ. 11: 197.
Industrial Science, Neglect of. Westm. 52: 81.
— Syme on. Dub. Univ. 89: 403.
Industrial Stories. Chamb. J. 50: 108.
Industrial Training, The French on. Chamb. J. 16: 79.
Industrial University, Proposed. (R. St. J. Tyrwhitt) Contemp. 30: 414.
Industry, Aids and Obstructions to. Victoria, 4: 1.
— and Agriculture. Penn Mo. 7: 61.
— and Civilization, Diversified. (D. H. Mason) Lakeside, 11: 75.
— and Idleness. (T. S. Arthur) Godey, 24: 1.
— and its Reward in Great Britain and Ireland. Westm. 37: 216.
— and Skill of France and England compared. Ed. R. 32: 340.
— Application of Science to. Ecl. Engin. 4: 38.
— Domestic. (J. H. Lanman) Hunt, 2: 353.
— English. (R. Southey) Quar. 34: 45.
— in United States. Anal. M. 14: 84.
— Instincts of. (S. Martin) Ex. H. Lec. 6: 425.
— Migration of Centers of Industrial Energy. (L. Courtney) Fortn. 30: 801. Same art. Liv. Age, 140: 323.
— Native. All the Year, 32: 436.
— New Principle of. (G. J. Holyoake) 19th Cent. 4: 494.
— of Nations, Eisdell on. Ecl. R. 70: 346.
— of the People. Blackw. 68: 106.
— Organization of unremunerative. (E. Simcox) Fraser, 98: 609. Same art. Sup. Pop. Sci. Mo. 4: 156.
— Partnerships of. St. James, 22: 719.
— Products of. (G. Tucker) Hunt, 9: 136, 220.
— Progress of Human. Ecl. Mus. 1: 289.
— Revolutions in. (W. H. Perkin) Lond. Soc. 37: 231.
— Rights of. Mo. R. 127: 1.
Industry, Three Triumphs of. (M. Schele de Vere) Lippinc. 6: 500.
— Two Decades of. (M. G. Mulhall) Contemp. 40: 818.
Industries, English National. Nature, 6: 97.
— Influence of, on the United States. (J. L. Stevens) Internat. R. 11: 580.
Inebriates, Classified and Clarified. (J. W. Palmer) Atlan. 23: 477.
Inebriate Asylum, Binghamton, N. Y. (J. W. Palmer) Atlan. 24: 109. — (H. T. Tuckerman) No. Am. 94: 387. — Putnam, 14: 17.
Inebriate Asylums. (D. Dalrymple) Macmil. 26: 110. — (J. Parton) Atlan. 22: 385.
Inedited Fragment, An. Fraser, 51: 45.
Inelegant Extracts. All the Year, 26: 175.
Inertia. (A. M. Mayer) J. Frankl. Inst. 86: 45. — J. Frankl. Inst. 13: 5.
— and Gravitation. (J. D. Whelpley) Ecl. Engin. 5: 496, 605.
— and Momentum. (J. D. Whelpley) Ecl. Engin. 6: 81.
— Formulæ for. (J. W. Davis) Ecl. Engin. 21: 17.
— Moment of. (R. Briggs and L. D'Auria) J. Frankl. Inst. 108: 73.
— Motion, and Force. (J. C. Trautwine) J. Frankl. Inst. 74: 109, 194.
— of Surfaces, Moment of. (D. Wood) J. Frankl. Inst. 81: 91.
Inevitable Baby. St. James, 23: 113.
Inez de Castro of Portugal. (R. Davey) Galaxy, 24: 305.
Inez, Sor Juana de la Cruz. Cath. World, 13: 47
Infallibility and Religious Truth. (J. B. Dalgairns) Contemp. 18: 1.
— Catholic and Protestant Claims to. (J. Martineau) Westm. 25: 425.
— Extent of the Church's. Dub. R. 56: 41. — (M. Gavin) Month, 43: 109.
— Papal. (H. J. Coleridge) Month, 12: 612. — (F. H. Hedge) Mo. Rel. M. 44: 289. — (A. F. Hewit) Cath. World, 13: 577. — Brownson, 22: 322. 24: 105. — Am. Church R. 22: 105. — Dub. R. 57: 121. 83: 153, 463. — (Prof. Reinkens) Mercersb. 20: 117.
— — and Civil Allegiance. (H. Lincoln) Bapt. Q. 9: 204.
— — and Gallicanism. (J. A. Dorner) Contemp. 17: 591.
— — and the German Bishops. (By a Catholic Priest) Mercersb. 20: 213.
— — Difficulties of. Month, 13: 115.
— — Dogma of. (B. A. Hinsdale) Chr. Q. 2: 392. — (C. Z. Weiser) Mercersb. 21: 181.
— — Fables about. (M. Gavin) Month, 43: 179.
— — Galileo and. (E. Lawrence) Harper, 49: 417.
— — Latin Text of the Decree, 1870. Mercersb. 20: 191.
— — — and Translation. (J. A. Brown) Luth. Q. 1: 585.
— — L. Maimbourg on. (E. H. Baverstock) Contemp. 25: 663.
— — Necessity of. (D. Gans) Am. Cath. Q. 5: 67.
— — Popular Objections to. Cath. World, 14: 597.
— — Refuted. (J. C. Wightman) Bapt. Q. 8: 37.
— — Reply to Archbishop of Munich. (I. von Döllinger) Mercersb. 20: 199.
— — The True and the False. Mercersb. 22: 313.
— Protestant. (J. A. Brown) Luth. Q. 2: 161.
Infallible Church, or Book. (D. Walk) Chr. Q. 1: 38.
Infallible; a Story. Chamb. J. 53: 394. Same art. Liv. Age, 130: 276.
Infancy, Notes on. (F. H. Champneys) Mind, 6: 104.
— Perez on. (R. Flint) Mind, 3: 546. — (J. Sully) Mind, 5: 385. 6: 281.
— Sanitary Aspects of. Ecl. R. 133: 537.
Infant, Biographical Sketch of an. (C. Darwin) Mind, 2: 285. Same art. Sup. Pop. Sci. Mo. 1: 345.
Infants, Character of. (E. Pond) Bib. Sac. 9: 746.

Infants, Church Membership of. (S. F. Smith) Chr. R. **9**: 445, 481. — (C. Hodge) Princ. **30**: 347.
— — Logic of. (B. H. Nadal) Meth. Q. **31**: 48.
— Church Relation of. (F. G. Hibbard) Meth. Q. **20**: 297.
— Communion of. Chr. R. **13**: 334.
— Custody of, in Divorce Cases. Brit. & For. R. **7**: 269. — Fraser, **19**: 205.
— Damnation of, Dr. Beecher on. (F. Jenks) Chr. Exam. **4**: 431. **5**: 229, 310.
— Limbo of. St. James, **1**: 373.
— Moral Condition of. (C. Brooks) Meth. Q. **24**: 552. — (F. G. Hibbard) Meth. Q. **19**: 632.
— Mortality of. Temp. Bar, **8**: 513.
— Parental and Infantile Culture. (E. Seguin) Pop. Sci. Mo. **10**: 37.
— Reflection on. (G. A. Sala) Temp. Bar, **6**: 492.
— Salvation of. (N. S. Strassburger) Mercersb. **12**: 385. — (A. Tobey) Bib. Sac. **18**: 383. — (H. C. Townley) Chr. R. **28**: 416. — Am. Church R. **26**: 519. — Ecl. R. **36**: 216.
— — Relation of Atonement to. Bost. R. **4**: 321.
— — Suffering and. So. R. n. s. **9**: 1, 249. **16**: 67. *See* Children.
Infant Baptism. *See* Baptism.
Infant Labor. (Lord Ashley) Quar. **67**: 171.
Infant Schools. Chr. Rem. **4**: 362. — (J. Simpson) Peop. J. **5**: 87, 129.
— Management of. (M. M. Carll) Am. Inst. of Instruc. **1834**: 99.
— Wilderspin on. Penny M. **1**: 210.
Infant School System of Education. (W. Russell) Am. Inst. of Instruc. **1830**: 97.
Infanticide. Dub. R. **45**: 54.
— amongst Poor of England. (E. Dicey) Nation, **1**: 270.
— in China. (H. J. Coleridge) Month, **36**: 309.
— in India. Ed. R. **119**: 389.
— — Moor on. Ecl. R. **15**: 331.
— — Suppression of. Fraser, **49**: 288.
— in the Sandwich Islands. Meth. M. **49**: 306.
— Punishment of. (C. A. Fyffe) 19th Cent. **1**: 583.
Infatuation; a Tale of the Times. Godey, **22**: 150.
Infection and Putrefaction, Relation of the Atmosphere to. Pop. Sci. Mo. **8**: 686.
— Spread of. Chamb. J. **52**: 732.
Inference, Intuition and. (D. G. Thompson) Mind, **3**: 339, 468.
Infernal Divinities, Ancient and modern. (E. I. Sears) Nat. Q. **18**: 1.
Infernal Machines. Appleton, **23**: 560.
Infernal Marriage. (B. Disraeli) Colburn, **41**: 293. **42**: 144.
Infernal Spirits, Scripture Doctrine of. (E. White) Cong. **1**: 585, 661.
Inferno of Dante and St. Patrick's Purgatory. (F. Vinton) Bib. Sac. **30**: 275. *See* Dante.
Infidels, Credulity of. Meth. M. **28**: 495.
— Prosecution of. Westm. **2**: 1. — Chr. Disc. **3**: 202. — (F. Parkman) Chr. Exam. **16**: 91.
— Right of, to testify as Witnesses. Chr. R. **1**: 479. — (J. A. Bolles) Chr. Exam. **25**: 157. — (W. M. Holland) Chr. Q. Spec. **1**: 438.
Infidel Philosophy, Modern. (H. Stowell) Ex. H. Lec. **4**: 133.
Infidel Publications. (G. E. Ellis) Chr. Exam. **17**: 332.
Infidelity. (W. C. Fowler) Chr. Q. Spec. **5**: 469. — Chr. R. **2**: 271. — (F. M. Holland) Radical, **2**: 732. — (I. C. Knowlton) Univ. Q. **30**: 64.
— a Sign of the Times. Theo. & Lit. J. **5**: 275.
— and Christianity, Conflict of. (J. T. Tucker) Cong. Q. **20**: 309.
— and Faith in Germany. (F. L. Nagler) Meth. Q. **41**: 128.
Infidelity and the Restoration of Belief. Westm. **58**: 173.
— and Superstition. Chr. R. **3**: 134.
— — Riddle's Natural History of. Chr. Obs. **53**: 400.
— Aspects, Causes, and Agencies of. (R. W. Dickinson) Theo. & Lit. J. **6**: 620.
— Causes of. Chr. Obs. **19**: 800. — Ecl. R. **98**: 432.
— Christlieb on. So. R. n. s. **16**: 1.
— Course of. Chr. Obs. **64**: 1.
— Dangers of. Chr. Disc. **3**: 332.
— Demands of, satisfied by Christianity. (S. Harris) Bib. Sac. **13**: 272.
— Errors in Reasoning of. (S. Harris) New Eng. **12**: 341.
— Essence and End of. Chr. R. **20**: 548.
— Foundations of. Mercersb. **16**: 435.
— in France, Modern. Liv. Age, **36**: 439. — Chr. Obs. **53**: 46.
— in the United States. Spirit Pilg. **6**: 204.
— Irving on. Cong. M. **9**: 307.
— Marvelousness of. (M. C. Taylor) Good Words, **13**: 235.
— Masquerade of. (W. W. Lord) Am. Church R. **6**: 398.
— Modern, Archbishop of Canterbury on. Colburn, **167**: 561.
— — Characteristics of. Chr. Exam. **17**: 23. — Chr. R. **6**: 191.
— — Forms of. Am. Ch. Mo. **1**: 335, 446.
— Nelson on. (A. D. Eddy) Am. Bib. Repos. **10**: 89.
— The new, 1853. (N. Porter) New Eng. **11**: 277.
— of the 19th Century. No. Brit. **15**: 35.
— of the Times. Chr. Obs. **22**: 92.
— or Atheism. (A. F. Hewit) Cath. World, **16**: 221.
— Pearson on. Chr. R. **19**: 258. — Ecl. R. **98**: 740. — (A. Gosman) Princ. **26**: 349.
— Popular, Hooker's. New York R. **2**: 483.
— — in London. Kitto, **34**: 320. Same art. Theo. Ecl. **2**: 277.
— portrayed. Am. Meth. M. **19**: 86.
— Principles of. (D. Y. Heisler) Mercersb. **20**: 5.
— Progress of. (R. Southey) Quar. **28**: 493. — Month, **22**: 68.
— Reign of. (T. Dwight) Chr. Mo. Spec. **6**: 75.
— Self-Contradictions of. (A. N. Littlejohn) Am. Church R. **6**: 101.
— Thomson's Sermons on. Ecl. R. **37**: 551.
— Ultimate Grounds of. (W. D. Wilson) Am. Church R. **14**: 193.
— *versus* Christianity. (D. R. Goodwin) No. Am. **75**: 1.
— Weakness of. (I. S. Spencer) Hours at Home, **1**: 73.
— What constitutes? Spirit Pilg. **3**: 1, 447.
Infinite and Finite. (W. M. Bicknell) Unita. R. **6**: 499.
— in Philosophy. (T. Hill) Mo. Rel. M. **46**: 101.
— Perception of. (C. C. Clarke) Month, **42**: 93, 216.
— Philosophy of. No. Brit. **22**: 113. — Ecl. R. **114**: 431.
Infinity, Idea of, Physical and Metaphysical. (E. B. Hunt) Am. J. Sci. **75**: 1.
— Notes on. (R. A. Proctor) Gent. M. n. s. **24**: 415. Same art. Liv. Age, **145**: 451.
Infiorato of Genzano, The. Cath. World, **2**: 608.
Infirmaries, Metropolitan, for the Pauper Sick. (E. Hart) Fortn. **4**: 459.
Infirmity, Argument of. (R. Owen) Fraser, **76**: 531.
Inflation. *See* Currency; Inflation.
Inflexible, The Iron-clad. Nature, **16**: 201, 221. **17**: 137.
— and her Armament. (A. H. Atteridge) Pop. Sci. R. **15**: 60.
— Dangers and Warnings of. (Sir R. S. Robinson) 19th Cent. **3**: 278.
Influence. Chamb. J. **15**: 7.
— Methods of, Sermon on. (E. Peabody) Mo. Rel. M. **11**: 1.
— of Surroundings. Dub. Univ. **78**: 73.
— Sphere of Human. (T. Hill) Chr. Exam. **45**: 424.

Influences, Unrecognized. (I. F. Mayo) Good Words, **16**: 285.
Informer, The. (J. Nugent) Dem. R. **14**: 386.
Informer; a Tale. Dub. Univ. **56**: 187. Same art. Liv. Age, **66**: 673.
Infusoria as Parasites. (W. S. Kent) Pop. Sci. R. **19**: 293.
— Balbiani on Reproduction of. Intel. Obs. **1**: 463.
— Ciliate, Our Knowledge of. (G. J. Allman) Nature, **12**: 136, 155, 175.
— Experiments on the Formation of. (J. Wyman) Am. J. Sci. **84**: 79.
— Haeckel on. Nature, **9**: 247.
— History of, Pritchard's. (W. Hincks) Canad. J. n. s. **7**: 368.
— in Dust Showers and Blood-Rain. (C. G. Ehrenberg) Am. J. Sci. **61**: 372.
— Molecular Origin of. (J. H. Bennett) Pop. Sci. R. **8**: 51.
— Origin of. Intel. Obs. **2**: 320.
— Preservation of. (J. Bovell) Canad. J. n. s. **8**: 341.
— Pritchard's History of. (W. Hincks) Canad. J. n. s. **7**: 368.
Infusorial Circuit of Generations. (T. C. Hilgard) Am. J. Sci. **102**: 20, 88.
Infusorial Earth and its Uses. (W. H. Wahl) Pract. M. **7**: 49. — (W. H. Wahl) J. Frankl. Inst. **102**: 407.
Infusorial Life, Conditions of. Intel. Obs. **1**: 85.
— Developmental Hist. of. (J. Hogg) Intel. Obs. **10**: 356.
Ingelow, Jean. Tinsley, **3**: 385. — St. Paul's, **10**: 632. — (E. M. Converse) Hours at Home, **9**: 39. — with portrait, Appleton, **8**: 681. — Ecl. M. **82**: 503.
— Poems. (T. Bayne) St. James, **38**: 179. — Land We Love, **6**: 91. — Cath. World, **24**: 419. — Liv. Age, **80**: 181. — (F. L. Max) Canad. Mo. **17**: 13, 141.
— Story of Doom. (H. P. Spofford) Galaxy, **4**: 562.
Ingemann, Bernhard S. Chamb. J. **30**: 250.
— Masaniello; a Tragedy. (R. P. Gillies) Blackw. **9**: 43.
— Poetry. For. R. **2**: 67. — For. Q. **21**: 132.
Ingenious Wobbler. Lond. Soc. **7**: 289.
Ingenuity, Impromptu. Chamb. J. **57**: 699.
— Misapplied. Penny M. **14**: 306.
— Perverted. Chamb. J. **56**: 369. — All the Year, **7**: 534.
— Some Instances of. Am. Arch. **10**: 22.
Ingersoll, Charles Jared, with portrait. Dem. R. **6**: 339. **16**: 221.
— Discourse. (J. Sparks) No. Am. **18**: 157. **22**: 212.
Ingersoll, Jonathan, Obituary of. Chr. Mo. Spec. **5**: 111.
Ingersoll, Joseph R., with portrait. Am. Whig R. **8**: 101.
— Address. So. Lit. Mess. **4**: 165.
Ingersollism, Historic Glances at. (I. E. Graeff) Ref. Q. **27**: 602.
Ingham, S. D. Letter to the President, 1831. Niles's Reg. **40**: 411.
— Speech of. Niles's Reg. **40**: 319, 346, 374.
Ingleborough within. Chamb. J. **29**: 341.
Inglesby, William H. Masonic Address. So. Q. **3**: 244.
Ingleside Chit-Chat. Knick. **36**: 339. **37**: 120.
Ingleside Reminiscences. Knick. **36**: 520.
Inglis, Sir Robert. Fraser, **34**: 647. Same art. Liv. Age, **12**: 77.
Inglis, Sir Robert Harry, and Wilberforce. Chr. Obs. **65**: 515, 610.
— Speech on Catholic Question. Blackw. **24**: 811.
Ingoldsby, Thomas. *See* Barham, R. H.
Ingraham, Edward D., with portrait. Dem. R. **25**: 77.
Ingraham, J. H. Burton. So. Lit. Mess. **4**: 561.
— Captain Kyd. Hesp. **3**: 85.
— Lafitte, the Pirate. West. Lit. J. **1**: 262. — So. Lit. Mess. **2**: 593.
Ingratitude of the Republic. Harper, **61**: 118.
Ingres, Jean D. (T. F. Wedmore) Macmil. **24**: 52. — (T. F. Wedmore) Contemp. **5**: 458. — (G. C. Swayne) Once a Week, **16**: 221.
Inhabitants of a Country Town. (M. R. Mitford) Colburn, **39**: 152-278. **40**: 223. Same art. Select J. **3**: 101, 230.
Inhabitants, The; a Tale. Blackw. **15**: 659.
Inhabited Well. Blackw. **14**: 93.
Inheritance. (C. Darwin) Nature, **24**: 257. — (C. Darwin) Pop. Sci. Mo. **19**: 663.
Inheritance, The. (MM. Erckmann-Chatrian) Lakeside, **11**: 169.
Inheritance in France, Law of. (W. P. Garrison) Nation, **15**: 218.
Inheritor and Economist; a Poem. Dub. Univ. **33**: 638.
Inhumanity, Revival of. (F. Harrison) Fortn. **19**: 667.
Iniquities at Rome. Chr. Obs. **44**: 513, 577.
— of the Times. Chr. Obs. **22**: 393, 461, 537.
Injectors. (P. H. Rosenkranz) Ecl. Engin. **8**: 71.
Injin Joe; a Poem. Temp. Bar, **43**: 601.
Injustice, Borderland of. Chamb. J. **20**: 113.
Ink, Manufacture of. Chamb. J. **12**: 120.
— Natural. Ev. Sat. **10**: 463.
Inks, Gold and Silver, How to make. Pract. M. **5**: 275.
— Writing, Chemistry of. (J. Underwood) Bank. M. (N. Y.) **32**: 894, 962.
Inkerman, Battle of. Blackw. **117**: 451.—Ed. R. **141**: 522.
— and its Lessons. (J. C. Paget) St. James, **36**: 14.
— French Soldier at. Broadw. **6**: 82.
— Kinglake on. Chr. Obs. **75**: 420.
Inland Navigation. Niles's Reg. **13**: 125.
— English. (F. R. Conder) Fraser, **95**: 422.
— of New York. (H. S. Dexter) Hunt, **9**: 148.
— of Pennsylvania. Niles's Reg. **21**: 229.
Inland Sea, No. Africa. (H. H. Gorringe) Nation, **27**: 236.
Inland Seas, Physical Conditions of. (W. B. Carpenter) Contemp. **22**: 372.
Inland Transport. Ed. R. **56**: 99.
Inman, William, with portrait. Colburn, **168**: 177.
Inn of Wolfswald. (C. F. Hoffman) Bentley, **4**: 49.
— Very queer. Lond. Soc. **38**: 513.
Inns. (S. G. W. Benjamin) Appleton, **18**: 132. — (H. T. Tuckerman) Putnam, **1**: 612. — Chamb. J. **9**: 161. Same art. Liv. Age, **17**: 404. — Chamb. J. **41**: 145.
— Continental. Chamb. J. **6**: 189.
— Evenings at. Colburn, **114**: 294.
— Law of. Chamb. J. **46**: 89.
— Old and new. All the Year, **15**: 559.
— Thoughts on. Colburn, **74**: 305.
— Three strange old. Lond. Soc. **39**: 563.
Inns of Court. All the Year, **7**: 198. — Blackw. **79**: 61. — Chamb. J. **56**: 538. — Penny M. **4**: 249. — Mo. R. **140**: 167.
— and Barristers. Chamb. J. **38**: 78.
— and Chancery. Sharpe, **11**: 12. — Ecl. R. **1**: 412.
— The little. All the Year, **20**: 472.
Inner and Middle Temple, Arms of. (D. Barrington) Arch. **9**: 127.
Inner Life, Tides of. (F. P. Cobbe) Mod. R. **1**: 183.
Inner Mission of Germany. (P. Schaff) Mercersb. **9**: 26.
Innermost Room. (M. Oliphant) Blackw. **101**: 338.
Innes Tragedy. Chamb. J. **16**: 143.
Innesmurray, Island of. Once a Week, **9**: 195.
— Pilgrimage to. Irish Mo. **5**: 433.
Innocence and Crime. House. Words, **1**: 431.
— State of. Kitto, **16**: 56.
Innocent III., Pope. (T. H. Gill) Cong. **7**: 339. — New Dom. **20**: 387.
Innocent IV., Pope. (T. H. Gill) Cong. **7**: 667.
Innocent, Metropolitan of Moscow. (C. R. Hale) Am. Church R. **29**: 402.
Innocent; a Story. (M. Oliphant) Liv. Age, **117**: 172-790. **118**: 164-786.
Innocents, Chapter on. Fraser, **67**: 333.
Innocent Avenger. (P. Benjamin) So. Lit. Mess. **5**: 671.

Innovations and Novelties. Hogg, **7**: 193.
Innovators, Plea for. (J. R. Boise) Lakeside, **2**: 91.
Innuendo, Beauties of. Lond. M. **10**: 348.
Inquisition, The. Princ. **21**: 174. — (R. Southey) Quar. **6**: 313. — Mo. R. **91**: 396. — Chr. Mo. Spec. **10**: 191. — Niles's Reg. **21**: 329. — (P. Fredet) U. S. Cath. M. **2**: 449. — (J. G. Shea) Am. Cath. Q. **1**: 254. — Am. Church R. **26**: 552. — Dub. R. **60**: 53. — Liv. Age, **46**: 822. — Meth. M. **50**: 679.
— and Jesuits. (J. Watkins) Colburn, **2**: 301.
— Anecdotes of. Blackw. **1**: 250.
— Dominic and. (E. Lawrence) Harper, **42**: 730.
— History of. Dub. R. **28**: 421.
— — Lavallée's. Ecl. R. **11**: 209.
— — Rule's. (G. T. Fisher) Nation, **18**: 413. — Dub. Univ. **72**: 697. Same art. Ecl. M. **72**: 236.
— in England. (J. Skelton) Fraser, **63**: 385.
— in Italy. Meth. M. **39**: 695.
— Last Ash of. All the Year, **21**: 101.
— Letters on. (Count de Maistre) Rel. Cat. **1**: 23–274.
— Roman. Dub. R. **5**: 72. — Galaxy, **9**: 646. **10**: 356.
— Serafino de Carcel's Narrative, 1680. House. Words, **19**: 243.
— Spanish. Cong. **5**: 462. — Dub. Univ. **84**: 335. — Meth. M. **39**: 660.
— — and the Holy See. Dub. R. **61**: 163.
— — History of. West. Mo. R. **2**: 27.
— — — Llorente's. Chr. Obs. **27**: 152. — Ecl. R. **31**: 462. — Portfo.(Den.) **34**: 388.
— — Modern. Colburn, **10**: 522.
— unmasked. Ecl. R. **27**: 236, 347. — Portfo.(Den.) **25**: 310.
— Van Halen's Escape from. Colburn, **20**: 282.
— Venetian, Records of. Cornh. **23**: 41. Same art. Liv. Age, **108**: 351. Same art. Ecl. M. **76**: 286.
Inquisitiveness. Am. Mo. M. **11**: 276.
Insane, The. St. James, **27**: 383.
— Autobiography of. Liv. Age, **43**: 51.
— Catholic poor. Month, **19**: 401.
— Confinement of. Am. Law R. **3**: 193.
— Government Supervision of. (E. Van de Warker) Penn Mo. **10**: 254.
— Hist. of Ameliorations in Treatment of. Westm. **85**: 331.
— Humane Treatment of. Westm. **67**: 284.
— in the United States, Table of. Hunt, **8**: 290, 460.
— Inside Bedlam. Tinsley, **3**: 456.
— Legislation for. (D. H. Tuke) Contemp. **30**: 743.
— Maniacs and Madhouses of Paris. (L. H. Hooper) Lippinc. **21**: 761.
— Mortality of Lunatics. (W. Farr) J. Statis. Soc. **4**: 17.
— Poor, Duty of States towards. (J. B. Chapin) Am. Soc. Sci. J. **6**: 60.
— Punishability of. (W. A. Hammond) Internat. R. **11**: 440.
— Rooted Sorrows. (J. C. Browne) Gent. M. n. s. **6**: 456.
— Strange Letter of a Lunatic. (J. Hogg) Fraser, **2**: 526.
— Tame Lunatics. (W. H. Lewis) Belgra. **9**: 109.
— Treatment of. Quar. **74**: 224, 416. — (L. P. Brockett) Nat. M. **11**: 517. **12**: 25. — (E. I. Sears) Nat. Q. **7**: 207. — Belgra. **10**: 206, 467. — (W. A. Hammond) Internat. R. **8**: 225. — Tait, n. s. **6**: 746. — Westm. **18**: 129. **37**: 305. **43**: 86.
— — Conolly on. Ecl. R. **105**: 243. Same art. Ecl. M. **57**: 450. — New Q. **5**: 398.
— — in England. Temp. Bar, **5**: 528.
— — in Massachusetts. (S. G. Howe) No. Am. **56**: 171.
— — Moral. (E. Hopkins) Fraser, **95**: 444. Same art. Liv. Age, **133**: 425.
— — Non-Restraint in. Ed. R. **131**: 418.
Insane Asylum, Afternoon in a. (E. Faithfull) Victoria, **21**: 327.
— at Morningside. Hogg, **10**: 316. **11**: 78, 323.
Insane Asylum at Worcester. Chr. Exam. **26**: 248.
— Bethlehem. Liv. Age, **55**: 297.
— Bicêtre. Chamb. J. **7**: 20, 71, 105.
— Blackwell's Island. (W. H. Davenport) Harper, **32**: 273.
— Colney Hatch. Westm. **48**: 119.
— Eastern. Sharpe, **18**: 110.
— for Convicts. Cornh. **10**: 448.
— Hanwell. (H. Martineau) Tait, n. s. **1**: 305.
— in Palermo. House. Words, **2**: 151.
— near York, Tuke on. (Syd. Smith) Ed. R. **23**: 189.
— North Wales. Hogg, **5**: 249.
Insane Asylums. (A. Wynter) Quar. **101**: 353. Same art. Ecl. M. **41**: 492. — Westm. **43**: 162. **47**: 119. **49**: 70. — Ed. R. **28**: 432. — Liv. Age, **13**: 586. — Mo. R. **119**: 173. — (L. P. Brockett) Nat. M. **11**: 315. — Chamb. J. **58**: 385. — (E. M. Lawney) Penn Mo. **10**: 431. — (G. B. Massey) Penn Mo. **10**: 835. — (I. Ray) Penn Mo. **11**: 22. — Penny M. **10**: 22.
— American. (I. Ray) No. Am. **79**: 66.
— and Treatment of Insane. Tait, n. s. **6**: 746.
— Bedlams of Stamboul. (W. Goodell) Atlan. **28**: 527.
— Despotism in. (D. B. Eaton) No. Am. **132**: 263.
— English. Temp. Bar, **5**: 528. — (C. Reade) Ev. Sat. **9**: 123.
— — County. (F. Scott) Fortn. **32**: 114.
— — in 1815, Reports on. Ecl. R. **23**: 293.
— — in 1816. Pamph. **6**: 227.
— for the Poor. No. Brit. **3**: 387.
— French. Month, **8**: 148.
— — Iniquitous. Cornh. **19**: 699.
— Life in. Lond. Q. **3**: 457. — Ecl. M. **34**: 291.
— Management of. (L. C. Davis) Atlan. **21**: 588. **22**: 227. — (E. Van de Warker) Penn Mo. **8**: 618.
— Middle-Class. Month, **2**: 342.
See Gheel.
Insanity. (J. Scoffern) St. James, **13**: 373. — (A. Brigham) No. Am. **44**: 91. — (W. Rush) Knick. **7**: 33. — Ed. R. **2**: 160. — Quar. **24**: 169. **42**: 350. — Mo. R. **118**: 102. — Mus. **14**: 359 — Dem. R. **34**: 146. — Colburn, **57**: 364.
— among Slaves. (D. H. Hill) Land We Love, **1**: 349.
— and Crime. (W. A. Guy) J. Statis. Soc. **32**: 159. — (W. Hooker) New Eng. **14**: 32. — (D. M. Means) New Eng. **35**: 323. — Intel. Obs. **5**: 131. — Temp. Bar, **1**: 135
— and Eccentricity. (T. Mayo) Liv. Age, **70**: 216.
— and Idiocy in Denmark. (J. R. Hubertz) J. Statis. Soc. **16**: 244.
— and Indigestion. Ecl. R. **48**: 310.
— and Law. (H. Maudsley) Pop. Sci. Mo. **5**: 77.
— and Madhouses. (D. Uwins) Quar. **15**: 387. — Mus. **37**: 514.
— and modern Civilization. (H. P. Stearns) Scrib. **17**: 582.
— and modern Life. (D. H. Tuke) Macmil. **37**: 130. Same art. Pop. Sci. Mo. **12**: 432. Same art. Liv. Age, **136**: 178.
— and Phrenology. (C. C. Blake) Anthrop. R. **1**: 476.
— and Physical States. (D. A. Gorton) Nat. Q. **39**: 1.
— and Sex. (J. Thurnam) J. Statis. Soc. **7**: 310.
— and Usefulness. (H. Butterworth) Hours at Home, **6**: 414.
— Art of making Madmen. (Dr. Fossati) Zoist, **5**: 34.
— as a Defense in Criminal Cases. (D. B. Ogden) Am. Law R. **11**: 661. — (E. B. Hill) Am. Law R. **15**: 598, 717. — Fraser, **27**: 444. — (F. Bowen) No. Am. **60**: 1. — So. Lit. J. **1**: 148. — So. Lit. Mess. **10**: 667. — (I. Edwards) Am. Whig R. **8**: 269. — Dub. Univ. **21**: 626. — Westm. **39**: 457. — Brit. & For. R. **15**: 152. — Ecl. Mus. **2**: 230. — Blackw. **68**: 548. — (W. H. Hill) Am. Cath. Q. **5**: 137.

Insanity as a Defense in Murder Trials. Dub. R. **46**: 58.
— Broadmoor and our Criminal Lunatics. (D. H. Tuke) Macmil. **38**: 137. Same art. Liv. Age, **38**: 215.
— Burrows on. Ecl. R. **32**: 128.
— Causes of. (E. Jarvis) No. Am. **89**: 316.
— — and Treatment of. U. S. Cath. M. **7**: 196.
— Conolly on. Ecl. R. **53**: 149.
— Contagious Madness. Victoria, **13**: 429. — Ev. Sat. **11**: 31.
— Criminal. (G. J. Davey) Zoist, **1**: 253.
— Different Forms of. Zoist, **1**: 397.
— Disease, and Religion. Lond. Q. **8**: 145. Same art. Ecl. M. **41**: 145.
— Effects of unnoticed. Dub. Univ. **6**: 666.
— Extent of. (G. M. Beard) Dub. Univ. **79**: 689.
— First Beginnings of. Cornh. **5**: 481.
— Gooch on. (W. Fergusson) Quar. **41**: 162.
— Hastam, Arnold, and Others on. (T. Young) Quar. **2**: 155.
— Hereditary. (J. Ray) No. Am. **109**: 1.
— Hill on the Cure of. Ecl. R. **21**: 39.
— Humanity and. (M. Du Camp) Pop. Sci. Mo. **2**: 218.
— in Europe, Statistics of. For. Q. **20**: 39.
— in France. (J. Carne) Colburn, **50**: 15-455. **51**: 13. **53**: 60. — Colburn, **56**: 550.
— in Massachusetts. (S. G. Howe) No. Am. **56**: 171.— (R. C. Waterston) Chr. Exam. **33**: 338.
— — Statistics of. (I. Ray) No. Am. **82**: 78.
— in the United States. So. Lit. Mess. **10**: 178.
— Increase of. No. Brit. **50**: 123. — (J. M. Granville) 19th Cent. **5**: 523.
— Incubation of. Ecl. R. **114**: 184. Same art. Ecl. M. **54**: 225.
— Inquiries relative to. (D. Uwins) Quar. **24**: 169.
— Invariable Test of. Mo. Rel. M. **32**: 331.
— Juries, Judges, and. (H. Maudsley) Pop. Sci. Mo. **1**: 440.
— Law of. Am. Law R. **4**: 236.
— — Case of Nottidge *versus* Ripley. Fraser, **40**: 363.
— Legal Aspects of. Cornh. **5**: 220.
— Legal Tests of. Cornh. **12**: 426.
— Legislation on. No. Brit. **36**: 453.
— Medical Jurisprudence of. (A. L. Soule) No. Am. **79**: 327.
— — Ray on. Mo. R. **150**: 147.
— Mental Epidemics. Dub. R. **10**: 348.
— Metaphysics of. (J. M. Wilcox) Am. Cath. Q **3**: 43.
— Moral. (L. H. Atwater) Princ. **29**: 345.
— — and Legal. Fraser, **51**: 245. Same art. Ecl. M. **35**: 116.
— — Ray on. (H. F. Buswell) Nation, **12**: 322.
— Munro on. Zoist, **9**: 32.
— Nature of. (T. L. Wright) Dem. R. **27**: 447.
— Pathology of. (G. J. Davey) Zoist, **1**: 111.
— Phenomena of. Pamph. **15**: 99.
— Philosophy of. Fraser, **25**: 553.
— Ray on. (H. F. Buswell) Nation, **16**: 272.
— Recollections of a restored Lunatic. (S. W. Newell) Scrib. **6**: 354.
— Reid on. Anal. M. **10**: 61. — Ecl. R. **24**: 183.
— relieved by Musical Exercises. Ecl. R. **85**: 206.
— Scottish Lunacy Commission. No. Brit. **27**: 106.
— Shakspere's Delineations of. (J. R. Dennett) Nation, **2**: 758.
— Society *versus*. (W. A. Hammond) Putnam, **16**: 326.
— Spurzheim on. Mo. R. **88**: 186.
— Statistics of. Penny M. **6**: 351.
— — in London, 1840. J. Statis. Soc. **3**: 143.
— — of Bethlem Hospital, 1843. Mo. R. **162**: 395.
— — of Insane Poor of Great Britain. J. Statis. Soc. **30**: 158, 336.
Insanity, Tendency of misdirected Education to. (E. Jarvis) Am. J. Educ. **4**: 591.
— Treatment of. (C. D. Robinson) Scrib. **12**: 634.
— under English Law. (W. Gilbert) Good Words, **8**: 116.
— Various Forms of. (G. M. Beard) Putnam, **12**: 513.
— Who is sane? (E. P. Rowsell) Colburn, **114**: 189.
— Winslow's Lettsomian Lectures on. Chr. Obs. **56**: 229.
— Wood and Burnett on. Zoist, **10**: 103.
Inscription at Ancyra. (W. M. W. Call) Fortn. **6**: 200.
— Bilingual, from a Vase at Venice. (T. J. Pettigrew) Arch. **31**: 275.
— on ancient Pillar from Alexandria. (G. Costard) Arch. **7**: 1.
— on an Olla in Fitzwilliam Museum, Cambridge. (H. C. Cooke) Arch. **43**: 56.
— on Rock in North America. (M. Lort and C. Vallancey) Arch. **8**: 290, 302.
Inscriptions, Ancient and Bible. (B. J. Wallace) Am. Presb. R. **9**: 623.
— — Deciphering of. Fraser, **67**: 121.
— — One Primeval Language. Liv. Age, **36**: 82.
— Babylonian and Assyrian. (W. F. Ainsworth) Colburn, **78**: 441.
— Brazilian Rock. (C. F. Hartt) Am. Natural. **5**: 139.
— Christian and Jewish. Ed. R. **120**: 217.
— Greek Christian. (G. T. Stokes) Contemp. **37**: 977.
— in Ancient Gaul, Christian. Chr. Obs. **71**: 421. — Brit. Q. **61**: 125. — (W. G. Humphry) Contemp. **3**: 410.
— Latin. Quar. **78**: 61.
— Latin Christian (G. T. Stokes) Contemp. **39**: 91.
— Moabite. (A. L. Rawson) Nation, **19**: 397.
— on Leaves of Lead, in the British Museum. (W. de G. Birch) Arch. **44**: 123.
— Pagan, and Christian Cemeteries. Month, **14**: 20.
— Persian and Assyrian. Quar. **79**: 413.
Insect, Life of an. Chamb. J. **13**: 92.
Insects. (W. M. Williams) Potter Am. Mo. **17**: 526. — Liv. Age, **50**: 303. — Mus. **21**: 212. — Mo. R. **128**: 317. — Sharpe, **6**: 220. **7**: 195. **9**: 133. **10**: 149, 271. — West. M. **1**: 97, 275.
— Acute Senses of. (W. M. Williams) Belgra. **44**: 75. Same art. Pop. Sci. Mo. **19**: 43.
— Ancestry of. (Sir J. Lubbock) Nature, **8**: 249.
— and Flowers. (A. W. Bennett) Pop. Sci. R. **14**: 113.
— and Plants, Relations between. (J. Lubbock) Fortn. **27**: 478. Same art. Liv. Age, **133**: 278.
— and their Allies. (A. S. Packard, jr.) Am. Natural. **1**: 73.
— Appetite of. Once a Week, **4**: 300.
— at Home, Wood's. Nature, **5**: 65.
— at the Zoo. Chamb. J. **58**: 644.
— Australian, Recollections of. Colburn, **162**: 195.
— Bristle-Tails and Spring-Tails. (A. S. Packard, jr.) Am. Natural. **5**: 91.
— British. Mo. R. **120**: 407.
— — Staveley's. (A. R. Wallace) Nature, **4**: 22.
— Center of Gravity in. (F. Plateau) Nature, **5**: 297.
— Civilization among. Ev. Sat. **15**: 641.—Ecl. M. **82**: 86.
— Conservatism in. Ecl. M. **96**: 267.
— Cucuio, or Fire Beetle. (G. A. Perkins) Am. Natural. **2**: 422.
— Devonian, Relation to existing Types. (S. H. Scudder) Am. J. Sci. **121**: 111.
— Diptera of the Amberfauna. (H. Loew) Am. J. Sci. **87**: 305.
— Distribution of Plants by. (F. B. White) Am. Natural. **7**: 268.
— Edible. Chamb. J. **41**: 254. Same art. Ecl. M. **63**: 197.
— Effect of the Glacial Epoch on the Distribution of. (A. R. Grote) Am. J. Sci. **110**: 335.
— Eggs of, Structure and Beauty of. (J. Hogg) Intel. Obs. **12**: 321.

Insects, Embryogeny of, Discoveries in. (H. Fripp) Pop. Sci. R. **6**: 119.
— Enemies of Books. Scient. Am. supp. **6**: 2200, 2282. — (H. A. Hagen) Lib. J. **4**: 251.
— Enemies we import. (S. Lockwood) Pop. Sci. Mo. **1**: 620.
— English, Natural History of. Retros. **15**: 230.
— Evolution of. (A. Wilson) Gent. M. n. s. **26**: 577.
— Experiments in killing, with Pyrethreum roseum. (W. L. Carpenter) Am. Nat. **13**: 176.
— Farmer's Friends and Foes. Quar. **124**: 445.
— Feet of. (L. L. Clarke) Intel. Obs. **2**: 393
— Fertilizations of Flowers by. (W. J. Beal) Am. Natural. **1**: 254, 403. — (A. W. Bennett) Am. Natural. **7**: 680.
— Field and Forest. (E. A. Samuels) Scrib. **18**: 496.
— Fossil. (S. H. Scudder) Am. Natural. **6**: 665.
— found in Mrs. Coate's Bath. (J. G. Wood) Dark Blue, **1**: 693.
— Generation of. Chamb. J. **25**: 309. Same art. Liv. Age, **50**: 83.
— Geological Antiquity of. (J. E. Taylor) Pop. Sci. R. **17**: 36.
— Habits of. (W. B. O. Peabody) No. Am. **35**: 195. — So. Lit. J. **2**: 409. — (M. Schele de Vere) Scrib. **3**: 54.
— Highland. (E. C. Rye) Intel. Obs. **10**: 124.
— History of. Ed. R. **37**: 122. — Mo. R. **121**: 370. — Mus. **1**: 261.
— Homes of. Chamb. J. **41**: 407.
— Household Pests. (C. Taylor) Harper, **22**: 30.
— in Disguise. (T. W. Wood) Stud. & Intel. Obs. **2**: 81.
— inhabiting Salt Water. (A. S. Packard, jr.) Am. J. Sci. **101**: 100.
— Injurious. (H. Shimer) Am. Natural. **3**: 91. — (A. S. Packard, jr.) Am. Natural. **7**: 524.
— injurious to the Elm. (H. N. Humphreys) Intel. Obs. **2**: 28. — (S. Hibberd) Intel. Obs. **2**: 191.
— injurious to the Turnip Crops. (W. Houghton) Pop. Sci. R. **5**: 1.
— Instinct in. (G. Pouchet) Pop. Sci. Mo. **3**: 12–149.
— Language of. Penn Mo. **9**: 296.
— Life and Intelligence of. Tait, n. s. **12**: 400.
— Locomotion of. (C. A. Burgin) Lippinc. **8**: 299. — Broadw. **8**: 322.
— mentioned in Plays of Shakspere, Natural History of. Mo. R. **146**: 599.
— Metamorphosis of. (P. M. Duncan) Nature, **7**: 30, 50. — (A. R. Wallace) Nature, **2**: 329. — Chamb. J. **57**: 155.
— Michelet's L'Insecte. Colburn, **112**: 127.
— Mimicry in the Colors of. (H. A. Hagen) Nature, **7**: 113. Same art. Am. Natural. **6**: 388.
— Mold as a Destroyer of. (C. G. Siewers) Am. Natural. **13**: 681.
— Muscular Strength of. Chamb. J. **50**: 222.
— Nature's Limiting of. (A. S. Packard, jr.) Am. Natural. **8**: 270.
— Neuter. (P. Wolf) Pop. Sci. Mo. **15**: 470.
— A notable Congress. (C. Taylor) Harper, **25**: 732.
— Obnoxious, Destruction of, by Fungoid Growths. (A. N. Prentiss) Am. Natural. **14**: 575, 630.
— of Commerce. Ecl. M. **33**: 322.
— of England. Retros. **15**: 230.
— of the Months. (H. G. Adams) Hogg, **9**: 65–299.
— of Natal. (Dr. Mann) Stud. & Intel. Obs. **4**: 130.
— Origin and Metamorphoses of. (Sir J. Lubbock) Nature, **7**: 446, 487. **8**: 31–207.
— — Lubbock on. Nature, **5**: 27.
— — Wallace on. Nature, **5**: 350.
— Our little Friends. All the Year, **11**: 562.
— Parasitic. (A. S. Packard, jr.) Am. Natural. **4**: 82.
Insects, Phosphorescent, Metamorphoses of. (Mrs. V. O. King) Am. Natural. **12**: 354.
— Sense-Organs of. (A. S. Packard, jr.) Am. Natural. **11**: 418.
— Sensibility and Intelligence of. Blackw. **43**: 589.
— Smallest known. (J. D. Cox) Am. Natural. **12**: 445.
— Some noxious. (J. G. Wood) Good Words, **21**: 414, 448.
— Spiracles in. (A. S. Packard, jr.) Am. Natural. **8**: 531.
— Strange Wanderers. (M. Schele de Vere) Hours at Home, **11**: 8.
— Tenacity of Life in. Chamb. J. **17**: 121.
— Transformations of. Mo. R. **123**: 16.
— under the Bark. (J. G. Wood) Dark Blue, **1**: 294.
— Unwelcome Guests of. (B. G. Wilder) Harper, **37**: 467.
— Use of the Antennæ in. (L. Trouvelot) Am. Natural. **11**: 193.
— used as Food. Penny M. **14**: 191.
— Variety in, Swinton on. Nature, **22**: 579.
— Vision and Sleep of. (R. Hill) Intel. Obs. **1**: 102.
— Warfare of. Once a Week, **6**: 373.
— Wings of. Chamb. J. **17**: 309.
— — Nature's Painting. (T. W. Wood) Recr. Sci. **2**: 33.
Insect Architecture. Ecl. R. **52**: 37. Same art. Mus. **16**: 515.
Insect Foes. Nature, **15**: 84. **16**: 104.
Insect Larva, Microscopic Anatomy of. (E. R. Lankester) Pop. Sci. R. **4**: 605.
Insect Life, Effect of high Temperature on. (E. C. Rye) Stud. & Intel. Obs. **2**: 180.
— Episodes of. Fraser, **43**: 381, 663. **44**: 290. Same art. Liv. Age, **30**: 153, 213. **31**: 209. — Ecl. R. **91**: 306. Same art. Liv. Age, **26**: 261. — Hogg, **2**: 342. — Tait, n. s. **16**: 62.
— in Winter. (S. F. Cooper) Putnam, **15**: 424. — Broadw. **7**: 570.
Insect Miscellanies. Mus. **20**: 247. — Mo. R. **126**: 309.
Insect Powder. (W. Saunders) Am. Natural. **13**: 572.
Insect World. De Bow, **25**: 430.
Insecticides. Pract. M. **1**: 399.
Insectivorous Plants. (F. Darwin) Nature, **17**: 222. — (A. Gray) Nation, **18**: 216, 232. — (S. B. Herrick) Scrib. **13**: 804. — (E. Hopkins) Contemp. **35**: 37.
— Darwin's. (A. W. Bennett) Nature, **12**: 206, 228. — (A. Gray) Nation, **22**: 12, 30.
Inside a Stage Coach; a Tale. (Miss Saunders) Cath. World, **6**: 412.
Inside Passenger. Sharpe, **29**: 57.
Insignificant, Importance of the. Chamb. J. **10**: 86.
Insincerity, Fatal Effects of. So. Lit. Mess. **9**: 606.
Insolvency amongst Merchants. (L. McKnight) De Bow, **16**: 311.
— and Bankruptcy. (C. H. Carroll) Hunt, **60**: 193.
— and the National Wealth. Bank. M. (N. Y.) **32**: 85.
— Financial Losses by. Bank. M. (N. Y.) **31**: 94.
— Laws of Russia on. (C. Clark) Hunt, **6**: 419.
— Legislation upon. Canad. Mo. **2**: 419.
— Morality of. Hunt, **8**: 294.
— Preferences in. Hunt, **7**: 352.
Inspiration. (J. May) Radical, **3**: 692. — (C. F. Schaeffer) Evang. R. **15**: 293. — (D. Gans) Mercersb. **15**: 367. — (F. H. Hedge, E. A. Washburn, C. Giles, J. P. Newman, J. Gibbons, and J. Fiske) No. Am. **127**: 304. — (J. Lillie) Chr. Q. **6**: 42. — (J. Priestley) Theo. Repos. **4**: 17, 364. — Kitto, **5**: 437. **7**: 315. — (F. A. D. Tholuck) Kitto, **13**: 331. **31**: 353. — (R. A. Redford) Brit. Q. **72**: 99. Same art. Luth. Q. **10**: 592. — (J. Torrey) Bib. Sac. **15**: 314. — (G. Hill) Univ. Q. **25**: 302. — (F. T. Washburn) Mo. Rel. M. **49**: 215. — (W. E. Manley) Univ. Q. **10**: 51. — No. Brit. **27**: 215. — (A. A. Hodge and B. B. Warfield) Presb. R. **2**: 225. — (C. Hodge) Princ. **29**: 660. — Theo. Repos. **2**: 295.

Inspiration and Historic Element in Scriptures. (J. Bascom) Am. Presb. R. **19**: 90.
— and Naturalism. Brit. Q. **14**: 178.
— and Revelation. (E. P. Barrows) Bib. Sac. **24**: 593. **29**: 427, 640. **30**: 305. — (M. J. De Long) Univ. Q. **36**: 186. — (J. May) Radical, **5**: 107. — Kitto, **37**: 167.
— — Morell on. (C. Hodge) Princ. **41**: 489.
— Catholic Doctrine of. (A. F. Hewit) Cath. World, **33**: 523.
— Church of England on. Brit. Q. **39**: 415.
— Critical Theories of. (C. A. Briggs) Presb. R. **2**: 550.
— T. F. Curtis on. (H. G. Spaulding) Chr. Exam. **83**: 294.
— Discrepancy not incompatible with. Kitto, **13**: 71.
— Doctrine of. (B. Grant) Bib. R. **6**: 289. — Brit. Q. **14**: 189. Same art. Ecl. M. **41**: 335.
— — and Theory of. (J. H. Allen) Chr. Exam. **77**: 265.
— Extent of. (E. P. Gould) Bib. Sac. **35**: 326.
— Henderson on. Cong. M. **21**: 107. — Ecl. R. **65**: 97.
— Internal Evidences of. (T. Raffles) Ex. H. Lec. **4**: 285.
— Lee on. (E. Pond) Bib. Sac. **15**: 29. — Am. Ch. Mo. **1**: 44, 188.
— Limitation of. Kitto, **38**: 104.
— Nature and Extent of. Chr. Exam. **8**: 362. — Kitto, **34**: 257.
— — and Proof of. Am. Church. R. **26**: 452, 481.
— of the Apostles. (J. Priestley) Theo. Repos. **4**: 189. — (Dr. Steudel) Chr. R. **26**: 69, 215. **27**: 67.
— of the Bible. (A. P. Peabody) Chr. Exam. **32**: 204. — (L. Woods) Chr. R. **9**: 1. — (M. Stone) Chr. R. **12**: 219. — (E. H. Sears) Chr. Exam. **35**: 340. — Spirit Pilg. **1**: 402, 474, 624. **2**: 9–289. **3**: 369, 420. — (E. Turner) Univ. Q. **6**: 382. — (J. S. Lee) Univ. Q. **5**: 343. — Kitto, **5**: 437. — (I. M. Atwood) Univ. Q. **22**: 285. — (H. W. Bellows) O. & N. **1**: 207. — (J. Bennett) Cong. M. **21**: 24, 82. — (D. Curry) Meth. Q. **18**: 256. — (D. Gans) Mercersb. **15**: 367. — (G. Haven) Meth. Q. **27**: 325. **28**: 5, 165. — (G. Hill) Univ. Q. **25**: 302. — New Eng. **36**: 694. — (A. H. Kremer) Ref. Q. **26**: 562. — (J. Pye Smith) Cong. M. **20**: 694. — (Dr. Tholuck) Kitto, **31**: 353. — (W. Walford) Cong. M. **21**: 39. — (C. K. Whipple) Radical, **5**: 54. — (J. Williams) Am. Church R. **9**: 1. Same art. Kitto, **17**: 371. — Bost. R. **3**: 190. **4**: 429. — Chr. Obs. **70**: 81. — Chr. Rem. **44**: 333. — Kitto, **36**: 274. — Theo. & Lit. J. **9**: 609. **10**: 1–529. — Westm. **66**: 206.
— — and Infallibility. Brownson, **5**: 198, 273. — Kitto, **14**: 141.
— — Aphorisms on. (L. Bacon) New Eng. **37**: 10.
— — Curtis on. (L. Moss) Bapt. Q. **2**: 83.
— — Dyer on. (H. M. Dexter) New Eng. **7**: 515.
— — Dynamical Theory of. Chr. Rem. **31**: 1.
— — Extracts on. Kitto, **34**: 257.
— — Gaussen on. (G. W. Burnap) Chr. Exam. **32**: 319. — Mo. R. **158**: 1. — Ecl. R. **75**: 365.
— — Tayler Lewis on Divine Human, in Scriptures. (B. N. Martin) New Eng. **18**: 125.
— — Partial. Chr. Obs. **68**: 485.
— — Plenary. (J. Hascall) Am. Meth. M. **20**: 156. — (A. H. Kremer) Ref. Q. **26**: 562. — Meth. Q. **5**: 594. — (T. Lewis) Meth. Q. **30**: 110. — Chr. Obs. **70**: 384.
— — Rothe on. (E. Janes) New Eng. **30**: 694. **31**: 272, 423.
— — Theories of. Am. Presb. R. **13**: 312.
— — — Current. Lond. Q. **10**: 285. Same art. Ecl. M. **49**: 295.
— — Verbal. (E. P. Barrows) Bib. Sac. **29**: 427. — (W. R. C. Rogers) Kitto, **35**: 184.
— of the Evangelists. Kitto, **23**: 117.
— of Moses. (J. Priestley) Theo. Repos. **4**: 27, 123.
Inspiration of the Prophets. (O. Cone) Univ. Q. **36**: 115.
— Physiology of. (D. A. Gorton) Nat. Q. **36**: 310.
— Problem of. (C. W. Clapp) New Eng. **19**: 809.
— Queries concerning. Theo. Repos. **1**: 453.
— Theory of, from Scripture. Kitto, **37**: 322.
— Theories of. (Dr. Walker) Evang. R. **3**: 492.
— — Recent. No. Brit. **18**: 138.
— — Subjective. (C. Elliott) Princ. n. s. **8**: 192.
— Thornwell on. Chr. R. **22**: 403.
— under a mediating View. (H. M. Whitney) Cong. R. **10**: 453.
— Walworth's Gentle Skeptic. Brownson, **20**: 312.
— What is? Chr. Obs. **61**: 253.
— Woods on. (A. Alexander) Princ. **3**: 3. — Ecl. R. **56**: 156.
Inspired Lobbyist. (J. W. De Forest) Atlan. **30**: 676.
Installation of Pastors. (H. E. Barnes) Cong. Q. **20**: 604.
— Relation of, to the Pastorate. (S. C. Bartlett) Cong. Q. **10**: 340.
Instinct. (J. Bascom) Bib. Sac. **28**: 654. — (S. Hibberd) Intel. Obs. **3**: 436. — (E. Jesse) Once a Week, **4**: 321. — Westm. **48**: 352. Same art. Liv. Age, **16**: 345. — Liv. Age, **17**: 595. — (L. A. Jones) Atlan. **5**: 513. — (G. H. Lewes) Nature, **7**: 437. — (D. A. Spaulding) Nature, **6**: 485. — (Duke of Argyll) Contemp. **38**: 699.
— and Acquisition. (D. A. Spaulding) Nature, **12**: 507. Same art. Pop. Sci. Mo. **8**: 310. — (G. J. Romanes) Nature, **12**: 553. Same art. Pop. Sci. Mo. **8**: 449.
— and Intellect. (G. Harris) Anthrop. J. **3**: 73. — (F. Bowen) No. Am. **63**: 91. — Knick. **22**: 404, 507.
— and Intelligence. (W. K. Brooks) Pop. Sci. Mo. **11**: 585. — (J. LeConte) Pop. Sci. Mo. **7**: 653. — (E. O. Haven) Lakeside, **7**: 231. — (M. Condereau) Anthrop. R. **6**: 399. — Ecl. R. **98**: 649. Same art. Ecl. M. **31**: 180. — West. M. **4**: 333.
See also Intellect; Intelligence.
— and Mind. (W. Sutton) Mo. **33**: 281, 391. — (Duke of Argyll) Contemp. **26**: 352. Same art. Ecl. M. **85**: 342. Same art. Liv. Age, **126**: 730.
— and Reason. (F. C. Clark) Am. Natural. **13**: 96. — (C. S. Henry) Hours at Home, **10**: 406. — (St. G. Mivart) Contemp. **25**: 763. Same art. Liv. Age, **125**: 387. — Zoist, **2**: 143.
— — distinguished. Chr. Obs. **50**: 79.
— — Jarrold on. Ecl. R. **66**: 402.
— — Smee on. Chamb. J. **14**: 276.
— and Training. Broadw. **5**: 466.
— Anecdote of. Belgra. **41**: 314. Same art. Ecl. M. **95**: 116.
— Brute Reason. (J. Le M. Bishop) Mind, **5**: 402, 575.
— Chadbourne on. (L. H. Morgan) Nation, **14**: 291. — (N. S. Shaler) No. Am. **115**: 225.
— Couch on. Chamb. J. **9**: 6.
— Curiosities of. Dub. Univ. **46**: 28. Same art. Ecl. M. **36**: 918.
— Demoralized. (M. Benton) Putnam, **11**: 521. — Liv. Age, **116**: 504.
— How Animals get Home. (E. Ingersoll) Scrib. **19**: 90.
— Kemp on. Dub. R. **38**: 113.
— Nature of. (S. Fish) Am. Bib. Repos. **11**: 74.
— Observations on young Animals. (D. A. Spalding) Macmil. **27**: 282. Same art. Ecl. M. **80**: 424. Same art. Liv. Age, **116**: 553.
— of the Hornet of New South Wales. (J. McGarvie) J. Frankl. Inst. **6**: 184.
— Perception and, in the lower Animals. Nature, **7**: 377, 409.
— — and Reasoning Power of Animals. (Dr. Paladilhe) Nature, **8**: 284.
— Question of. Nature, **8**: 77.
— Reason and Imagination. (C. W. Eimi) Dem. R. **15**: 408.

Instinct, Survival of. (E. Lewis, jr.) Pop. Sci. Mo. **4**: 88.
— Vagaries of. Dub. Univ. **81**: 90
— What is? Ecl. M. **60**: 374.
Instincts. (E. Jesse) Once a Week, **8**. 473.
— of Birds. (J. Blackwall) J. Frankl. Inst. **16**: 354. **17**: 68, 139.
— of certain Fishes in the Tropics. St. James, **3**: 349.
— Origin of certain. (C. Darwin) Nature, **7**: 417.
Instinctive Action, Definition of. (J. Sully) Mind, **6**: 114.
Institutions. All the Year, **25**: 391.
— and Men at Home and abroad. (S. Osgood) Mo. Rel. M. **45**: 570.
— Christian. (J. H. Morison) Mo. Rel. M. **49**: 201.
— Maine's Early History of. (A. V. Dicey) Nation, **20**: 225. — (T. E. C. Leslie) Fortn. **23**: 305.
Instruction, Division of Labor in. (T. Cushing, jr.) Am. Inst. of Instruc. **1839**: 19.
— Elementary Methods of. (J. H. Pestalozzi) Am. J. Educ. **7**: 673.
— General Methods of. (T. Morrison) Am. J. Educ. **9**: 294.
— Hamiltonian System of. (Syd. Smith) Ed. R. **44**: 47. — Westm. **10**: 284. — Brit. Q. **2** : 143. Same art. Ecl. M. **6**: 229.
— in Schools and Colleges. So. Q. **22**: 460.
— Inductive System of. U. S. Lit. Gaz. **3**: 241.
— Jacotot's System of. *See* Education.
— Popular Elementary. For. Q. **20**: 254.
— Subjects and Means of, Aphorisms. Am. J. Educ. **10**: 141.
Insulating Stand. (M. E. Mascart) Nature, **18**: 44.
Insult and Injury. Once a Week, **18**: 260.
Insults. (A. G. Sedgwick) Nation, **9**: 148.
Insurance, Accident. Victoria, **5**: 359.
— against Railway Accidents. Chamb. J. **14**: 227.
— and Assurance. All the Year, **13**: 437.
— Deposit. Bank. M. (L.) **3**: 330.
— Fidelity. (D. P. Bailey, jr.) Bank. M. (N. Y.) **32**: 590. — Bank. M. (N. Y.) **34**: 419.
— Fire. Penny M. **8**: 2.
— — and Fires. Quar. **96**: 1.
— — Historical and Statistical Account of. (C. Walford) J. Statis. Soc. **40**: 347.
— — Hist. and Law of. (W. W. Campbell) Hunt, **2**: 239.
— — New York Law of. Bank. M. (N. Y.) **17**: 57.
— — New York Report on, 1861. Bank. M. (N. Y.) **17**: 49.
— — Origin and Nature of. (G. W. Savage) Hunt, **4**: 159, 238.
— — Past and Present of. (J. Pyne) Nat. Q. **35**: 135.
— — Progress of, in Great Britain. (S. Brown) J. Statis. Soc. **20**: 135.
— Fraud on Underwriters. (J. Bergen) Hunt, **2**: 288.
— Frauds with Policies of. Bank. M. (L.) **3**: 261.
— General Expenditure Assurance Company. Victoria, **31**: 457.
— Good, bad, and indifferent. (E. I. Sears) Nat. Q. **14**: 385.
— Guarantee. Bank. M. (N. Y.) **5**: 89. — Bank. M. (L.) **10**: 293.
— Historical Notes on. Antiquary, **2**: 209.
— Life. Ecl. R. **109**: 37. — (Sir J. Barrow) Quar. **64**: 284. — (S. Raleigh) No. Brit. **12**: 1. Same art. Ecl. M. **19**: 326. — Ed. R. **45**: 482. — Westm. **9**: 384. — Quar. **35**: 1, 609. **64**: 157. — Bank. M. **1**: 704. **3**: 46, 398. — (E. W. Stoughton) Hunt, **2**: 222. — (F. Bowen) No. Am. **97**: 301. — (S. Newcomb) Internat. R. **2**: 353. — Dub. Univ. **35**: 182. **83**: 385. — (S. Homans) Am. Soc. Sci. J. **2**: 159. — De Bow, **21**: 299. — (J. B. Collins) Hunt, **26**: 196. **63**: 119. — (J. H. Van Amringe) Galaxy, **15**: 249, 396, 527. **23**: 686, 803. — New Q. **1**: 246. — Once a Week, **28**: 339. — Tait, n. s. **15**: 191–414. **16**: 326.
Insurance, Life, Advantages of. (Rev. Dr. Cook) Bank. M. (N. Y.) **4**: 370.
— — and Annuities. (M. A. Quetelet) Bank. M. (N. Y.) **5**: 541. — (J. F. Entz) Hunt, **16**: 48, 445.
— — and Banking. (J. S. Homans) Bank. M. (N. Y.) **30**: 49.
— — and Savings Banks. (A. B. Johnson) Hunt, **25**: 670.
— — and Sociology. Lakeside, **9**: 168.
— — Annals and Anecdotes of. Quar. **106**: 58. — Hogg, **10**: 168.
— — and vital Statistics. (W. Hardwicke) Pop. Sci. R. **6**: 271. Same art. Ecl. M. **69**: 298.
— — as an Investment. Bank. M. (N. Y.) **23**: 782. — Bank. M. (L.) **16**: 273.
— — at the South. (J. Nott) De Bow, **3**: 358.
— — Burt on. Bank. M. (N. Y.) **5**: 291.
— — Cases in. Bank. M. (N. Y.) **4**: 63.
— — Climate and Longevity. (J. M. Smith) Hunt, **74**: 319.
— — Companies for. Quar. **128**: 18.
— — Condition of, 1871. (J. B. Hodgskin) Nation, **12**: 54, 105.
— — dangerous. Bank. M. (L.) **12**: 443, 499.
— — Decisions in English Courts. Bank M. (N. Y.) **2**: 721.
— — Does it insure? (T. M. Coan) Harper, **62**: 273. — (Reply by S. H. Tyng, jr.) Harper, **62**: 754.
— — Exposition of. (J. Wilcox) Scrib. **13**: 646.
— — Failures of Companies. (S. Newcomb) Nation, **24**: 157.
— — — Causes of. Westm. **92**: 532.
— — for Laborers. (J. Y. Stratton) Victoria, **20**: 148.
— — for the Poor. (E. Wright) Am. Soc. Sci. J. **8**: 147.
— — History and Romance of. Tait, n. s. **20**: 456.
— — in France. Bank. M. (N. Y.) **16**: 214. — Bank. M. (N. Y.) **20**: 276.
— — in the United States (S. Homans) Bank. M. (N. Y.) **24**: 447. — (T. R. Smith) Hunt, **8**: 109, 237.
— — Institutions for. Lond. Q. **13**: 134.
— — — New. Colburn, **105**: 25.
— — Law of. Bank. M. (N. Y.) **13**: 461.
— — — Proposed Alteration in. Bank. M (L.) **10**: 181.
— — Methods of. (S. Homans) No. Am. **124**: 254.
— — Modern Basis of. (T. Wehle) Pop. Sci. Mo. **19**: 625.
— — Mortality of Baltimore, with reference to. (C. F. McCay) Fraser, **22**: 35.
— — Mutual. Hunt, **11**: 340. — (D. R. Jaques) Hunt, **16**: 152.
— — Mutual Advantage of. Bank. M. (N. Y.) **9**: 619.
— — National Bureau of. (J. B. Hodgskin) Nation, **6**: 306.
— — Necessity of Legislation on. Dub. R **8**: 49.
— — Nether Side of. (J. Wilcox) Scrib. **14**: 382.
— — Origin and History of. (T. Wehle) Pop. Sci. Mo. **19**: 482.
— — Policies of, Valuation of. (C. F. McKay) Hunt, **42**: 435, 558. **43**: 43–692. **44**: 58, 184.
— — Practical Business of. (T. Wehle) Pop. Sci. Mo. **19**: 732.
— — Premiums of. (C. F. McCay) Hunt, **18**: 49.
— — — and Policies of. Bank. M. (N. Y.) **4**: 138.
— — Principles of. Dub. Univ. **40**: 614. — (H. G. Tuckett) Bank. M. (N. Y.) **5**: 181. — Bank. M. (N. Y.) **10**: 119. **11**: 833. **13**: 810. **20**: 132.
— — Regulation of. (E. Wright) Hunt, **27**: 541.
— — Romance of. (C. Nordhoff) Harper, **19**: 661.
— — Surrender of Policies of. Bank. M. (L.) **11**: 646.
— — The; a Tale. Dub. Univ. **35**: 182.
— — Value of Annuities. Dub. R. **11**: 104.
— — What is wrong in? (C. T. Lewis) Internat. R. **4**: 312.

Insurance, Life, Wrecking of Companies. (J. Wilcox) Internat. R. 9: 83.
— Life and Health. Ecl. R. 111: 568.
— Marine. (Z. Cook, jr.) Hunt, 8: 169 — (J. D. B. De Bow) De Bow, 2: 1. — (E. W. Stoughton) Hunt, 1: 496. — (J. Balch) Hunt, 1: 491.— (W. Barnes) Hunt, 53: 102. — Hunt, 53: 271–426. 54: 52–188. — Penny M. 12: 15.
— — General Average. Ho. & For. R. 1: 335.
— — in England, 1833. Tait, 2: 323.
— — Profits of. (J. Balch) Hunt, 4: 444. — (Z. Cook, jr.) Hunt, 5: 63.
— — Progress of, in England. (E. S. Roscoe) Fraser, 96: 707.
— — Report on. Bank. M. (N. Y.) 17: 64.
— — Warrantees on Policies. (E. W. Stoughton) Hunt, 2: 26.
— Mutual, and individual Liability. (D. R. Jacques) Hunt, 13: 512.
— National. (W. L. Blackley) 19th Cent. 4: 834.
— — Bismarck's Scheme of. (W. L. Blackley) Contemp. 39: 610.
— — Compulsory. (W. W. Edwards) 19th Cent. 6: 893.
— — Few more Words on. (Earl of Carnarvon) 19th Cent. 8: 384.
— — House of Lords and. (W. L. Blackley) 19th Cent. 8: 107.
— Phillips on. (Judge Story) No. Am. 20: 47.
— State Aid and Control in. (H. S. Tremenheere) 19th Cent. 8: 275. — (H. S. Tremenheere) Fortn. 36: 701.
— Tale of. Chamb. J. 55: 280.
— Theory and Practice of. Hogg, 8: 161, 241. 9: 65–299.
— Theory of Probabilities. (S. Newcomb) Math. Mo. 3: 343.
Insurance Company, Dissenters', 1839. Ecl. R. 69: 520.
Insurance Companies in United States, 1869. Bank. M. (N. Y.) 22: 474.
— Profit and Loss of. Tait, n. s. 23: 502–745.
— Quackery of. (E. I. Sears) Nat. Q. 5: 359.
Insurance Decisions. Bank. M. (N. Y.) 20: 390.
Insurance Investments. (A. Page) Fortn. 32: 732.
Insurance Offices, British, 1850. Tait, n. s. 17: 455–645.
Insurance Policies, Waiver and Estoppel in. (H. G. Wood) Am. Law R. 15: 763.
Insurance Quackery and its Organs. (E. I. Sears) Nat. Q. 6: 317.
Insurance Society for Congregational Ministers. Cong. M. 17: 763.
Insurers, Attempt to defraud. Hunt, 4: 180.
— Liability to pay Contributions. (Z. Cook, jr.) Hunt, 4: 440.
Insurrection in Jamaica, 1865. Nation, 1: 678.
— in Tupac Amaru. (C. Cushing) No. Am. 20: 283.
Insurrectionists, Rights of. (J. Parker) No. Am. 94: 196.
Integrating Machine. (J. Thomson) Ecl. Engin. 15: 301.
Integration, Method of. (J. F. Encke) Math. Mo. 2: 276.
Intellect, Human. (A. Schopenhauer) J. Spec. Philos. 8: 243, 316. — Ecl. M. 73: 322.
— — and Cruelty. (G. Stott) Belgra. 9: 127.
— — and Evolution. (St. G. Mivart) Brit. Q. 74: 298.
— — and Feelings, Theology of. Ecl. R. 121: 205, 293.
— — and Instinct. (G. Harris) Anthrop. J. 3: 73.
— — Development of. (T. H. Shreve) West. Lit. J. 1: 192.
— — Differences of French and English. Victoria, 8: 416.
— — Education of. (A. T. Bledsoe) So. R. n. s. 2: 315.
— — in Music. (C. H. Brittan) Western, 5: 174.
— — Legacies of. (W. Jerdan) Bentley, 5: 632.
— — Mackay's Progress of. (D. R. Goodwin) No. Am. 75: 1. — Brit. Q. 12: 443. — Chr. Obs. 55: 614. — Westm. 54: 353.
Intellect, Human, Porter on. (J. Bascom) Bib. Sac. 27: 68. — (O. A. Brownson) Cath. World, 8: 671, 767. — (G. P. Fisher) No. Am. 108: 280. — (B. N. Martin) New Eng. 28: 114. — (C. S. Peirce) Nation, 8: 211.
— — Sanctified. Hogg, 2: 65.
— — Senses and, Bain on. Fraser, 53: 212.
— — Subaltern Rank of. (J. S. Kieffer) Ref. Q. 28: 458.
— — Town and Country as Producers of. Pop. Sci. Mo. 1: 600.
— — viewed physiologically. (A. Bain) Fortn. 3: 735.
— of Animals. Lond. Soc. 15: 43. — Nature, 19: 496, 519. 20: 21. — (G. J. Romanes) Nature, 20: 122.
— — and Human. (W. James) J. Spec. Philos. 12: 236.
Intellectual Action, Influence of, on Civilization. (H. R. Cleveland) Am. Inst. of Instruc. 1835: 143.
Intellectual and Moral Culture. (J. W. Thompson) Chr. Exam. 38: 57. — (E. Bartlett) Am. Inst. of Instruc. 1838: 31.
Intellectual and Moral Powers, Connection between. Chr. Obs. 13: 133.
Intellectual Centers. (B. Murphy) Cath. World, 15: 721.
Intellectual Conception. (J. Ruskin) Contemp. 17: 424.
Intellectual Dependence of Man on God. (W. B. Hackett) Lit. & Theo. R. 1: 584.
Intellectual Development of Europe, Draper's. Am. Presb. R. 12: 615. — Anthrop. R. 3: 29. — Westm. R. 83: 94. *See* Europe.
Intellectual Differences in the Human Race. (H. Lindsley) So. Lit. Mess. 5: 616.
Intellectual Diffidence. Chr. Obs. 9: 414.
Intellectual Education in Harmony with Moral and Physical. (J. Bates) Am. Inst. of Instruc. 1840: 1.
Intellectual Endowments. (Sir E. Brydges) Fraser, 8: 291.
Intellectual Faculties, according to Phrenology. (A. Bain) Fraser, 63: 715.
— Development of. (J. G. Carter) Am. Inst. of Instruc. 1830: 53.
Intellectual Improvement, Influence of moral on. (H. B. Hooker) Am. Inst. of Instruc. 1846: 39.
Intellectual Life. (W. D. Le Sueur) Canad. Mo. 7: 321.
— Drawbacks of. Liv. Age, 138: 701.
Intellectual Men, Infelicities of. Dem. R. 19: 378, 465.
Intellectual Operations and Organic Action. Quar. 45: 341.
Intellectual Outlook of the Age. (I. T. Hecker) Cath. World, 31: 145.
Intellectual Philosophy. (D. Barlow) Chr. Exam. 14: 291. — Mo. R. 118: 446. — Knick. 7: 553. — West. M. 4: 127.
— Adaptation of, to Instruction. (A. R. Baker) Am. Inst. of Instruc. 1833: 261.
— History of. (A. H. Everett) No. Am. 29: 67.
— Morell's. Tait, n. s. 14: 697.
— Young's Lectures on. Ecl. R. 66: 272. — Ed. R. 61: 52.
Intellectual Powers, Abercrombie on. (L. Leonard) No. Am. 36: 488.
Intellectual Self-Culture. West. J. 10: 435. 11: 60–297.
Intellectual Solace. (T. H. S. Escott) Belgra. 7: 587.
Intellectual Tendencies and Training. (D. Tucker) Canad. Mo. 19: 161.
— in America, Certain. (J. C. Adams) Univ. Q. 36: 371.
Intellectual Wild Oats. Fraser, 89: 602.
Intelligence and Scholarship, Relations of. (H. S. Huntington) Univ. Q. 4: 181.
— Evolution of. Nat. Q. 25: 209.
— of the People. Dem. R. 8: 36.
— Popularization of. (E. Franklin) Mercersb. 8: 441.
— Relation of, to Instinct. (M. Condereau) Anthrop. R. 6: 399.
— — to the Piety and Efficiency of the Church. (T. F. R. Mercein) Meth. Q. 13: 123.

Intelligence requisite to the Prosperity of a Nation. (E. H. Chapin) So. Lit. Mess. 5: 725.
— Taine on. (W. James) Nation, 15: 139. — (J. S. Mill) Fortn. 14: 121. — (G. C. Robertson) Nature, 4: 64. — Chr. Obs. 71: 891.
Intelligence Office. (N. Hawthorne) Dem. R. 14: 269.
Intemperance. (Sir W. Lawson) 19th Cent. 5: 405. — (F. Peek) Contemp. 29: 28. — U. S. Lit. Gaz. 4: 331. — Chr. Disc. 1: 55. 4: 235. — Princ. 13: 267, 471. — Meth. Q. 2: 91. — (H. Ware, jr.) Chr. Disc. 5: 446. — Chr. Exam. 5: 209. — (J. Ware) Chr. Exam. 9: 236. — (H. Ware) Chr. Exam. 12: 243. — (T. B. Fox) Chr. Exam. 14: 24. — (A. Dutton) Chr. Mo. Spec. 9: 587, 645.
— Address on. (T. Flint) West. Mo. R. 2: 79.
— Analogy of Slavery and, before the Law. (H. M. Whitney) New Eng. 39: 374.
— and Intolerance. Blackw. 102: 208.
— and Licensing Laws. Ed. R. 150: 133.
— and Poverty. (R. Quiddam) St. James, 39: 206.
— Birmingham Plan of regulating. (R. Lowe) Fortn. 27: 1.
— Bradford's Address. Chr. Exam. 3: 291.
— British Beer-Shop. (J. W. De Forest) Atlan. 38: 699.
— Causes and Cures of. Nat. R. 10: 107.
— Church of England's Duty. Chr. Obs. 73: 775.
— Drink Problem. (F. L. Oswald) Internat. R. 9: 670.
— Drunkenness, Abstinence, Restraint. Ed. R. 137: 398.
— Early Methodists on. Hist. M. 10: 314.
— Effect on National Prosperity and Wages. (T. P. Whittaker) Macmil. 33: 147.
— Effects of Legislative Restrictions on. Penny M. 4: 231.
— — on the Brain. Good Words, 7: 395.
— — on Character. (G. M. Fothergill) Pop. Sci. Mo. 14: 379.
— Experiences of a Dipsomaniac. Tinsley, 3: 321.
— Habitual Drunkenness. (J. C. Bucknill) Contemp. 29. 431.
— Laws respecting. Chr. Disc. 2: 207.
— Legal Regulation of. (A. Arnold) Fortn. 19: 478.
— Municipal Public Houses. (J. Chamberlain) Fortn. 27: 147.
— National Vice of England. (R. G. White) Atl. 46: 544.
— of ancient Literature. Am. Mo. M. 7: 259, 597.
— Over-Stimulation in Women. (F. H. Daly) Gent. M. n. s. 22: 111.
— Palfrey's Discourse. U. S. Lit. Gaz. 6: 184.
— Physiology of. Internat. M. 3: 98.
— Place and Power of Abstinence. (J. Miller) Ex. H. Lec. 12: 291.
— Political Economy of. (J. A. Bolles) Am. Q. Obs. 3: 5.
— Regulation of. (J. Chamberlain) Fortn. 25: 631.
— Sullivan and Ware on. Am. Mo. R. 2: 45.
— Swedish Laws on. Hogg, 3: 416. — (J. Chamberlain) Fortn. 26: 691.
— Vice of. (H. H. W. Hibshman) Ref. Q. 27: 476.
— A Woman's Question. Victoria, 13: 41.
See Alcoholism; Liquor; etc.
Intemperate, The. So. Lit. Mess. 6: 274.
— Plea for. Meth. Q. 2: 91.
— Rest for. Month, 9: 533.
— Retreat for. Chr. Disc. 5: 121.
Intensity, Gospel of. (H. Quilter) Macmil. 42: 391. 43: 80.
Intercepted Letters; a Tale of the Bivouac. Blackw. 63: 340. Same art. Liv. Age, 17: 211.
Intercession; a Poem. (A. C. Swinburne) Fortn. 12: 509.
Interchange of Commodities. (W. Hincks) Canad. J. n. s. 7: 180.
Intercollegiate Emulation. (W. D. Whitney) Nation, 16: 130.
Intercolonial Railway. Canad. Mo. 11: 105.
Intercommunication, Results of Celerity of. (H. L. Wayland) New Eng. 16: 790.
Intercourse, Facilities of. Mo. R. 111: 225.
— Means of, seventy Years ago. Penny M. 9: 43.
Interest among the Romans. Bank. M. (N. Y.) 30: 717.
— and cheap Currency. (C. H. Carroll) Hunt, 38: 35.
— at one per cent. (B. Price) Contemp. 29: 778. Same art. Sup. Pop. Sci. Mo. 1: 75.
— Computation of. (C. C. Gordon) Hunt, 5: 540. — (W. Palmer) Hunt, 6: 46. — (R. M. Bartlett) Bank. M. (N. Y.) 7: 929.
— — Law for. Hunt, 27: 169.
— — New Method of. (G. R. Perkins) Am. J. Sci. 47: 51.
— — Short Method of. (H. B. Auchincloss) Hunt, 36: 196.
— Exchange and Stock-Jobbing. (D. McCauley) De Bow, 1: 369.
— History and Future of. (T. E. C. Leslie) Fortn. 36: 640.
— Laws of Missouri on. (M. Tarver) West. J. 12: 229.
— of a Shilling; a Tale. Chamb. J. 43: 824.
— on Deposits, Payment of. (W. H. Whitmore) Nation, 17: 269.
— — Views on. Bank. M. (N. Y.) 31: 339.
— on Money. (D. Fosdick) Hunt, 22: 272, 492. 23: 52, 508. — Dub. R. 73: 323. — West. J. 5: 288.
— Pure. (A. Delmar) Nation. 1: 82.
— Rate of. (W. S. Hodge) Bank. M. (N. Y.) 13: 271, 337. — (R. H. Patterson) Blackw. 97: 589, 706. — Hunt, 2: 379. — Pamph. 8: 531. — Blackw. 98: 73. *See also* Usury.
— — Fluctuations in. (G. Marsland) Bank. M. (N. Y.) 32: 431.
— — — in Banks of England, France, and Germany. Bank. M. (L.) 38: 161, 285, 369.
— — Future. Bank. M. (N. Y.) 7: 319. 33: 665, 925.
— — Principles of. (R. Baxter) J. Statis. Soc. 39: 277.
— — Prospective, in U. S. (D. A. Wells) Nation, 12: 287.
— — What fixes? Hunt, 54: 423. — (E. Atkinson) Internat. R. 11: 22.
— Theory of. Am. Q. 22: 177.
Interiors in New York. Art J. 29: 329, 361. 31: 46, 141.
Interior Decoration, Studies in. Am. Arch. 2: 59–204.
Interior Department, U. S., 1869. Am. J. Educ. 18: 169.
Interior or hidden Life. Dial, 4: 373.
Interlinear Translations; Hamiltonian System. Penn Mo. 6: 636.
Intermarriage among Royal Families. Cornh. 7: 374.
— Bugbear of. (E. L. Godkin) Nation, 5: 481.
See Cousins; Marriage.
Intermediate Place. (E. Pond) Am. Bib. Repos. 2d s. 5: 464.
Intermediate State. (J. M. Baltzly) Luth. Q. 1: 268. — (W. R. Bagnall) Meth. Q. 12: 240. — (G. W. Clarke) Chr. R. 27: 239. — (C. J. Ehrehart) Evang. R. 20: 161. — (E T. Fitch) New Eng. 25: 125. — (J. H. P. Frost) Mercersb. 17: 20. — (J. P. Smeltzer) Luth. Q. 3: 267. — Am. Presb. R. 10: 241. — Chr. R. 20: 381. — Bost. R. 4: 66. — Kitto, 37: 92.
— Blakeman on. Theo. & Lit. J. 8: 527.
— Is it probationary? (J. E. Roy) New Eng. 29: 400.
— Scripture on. Kitto, 37: 92.
— — Luke xvi. 19–31. Chr. Obs. 15: 763.
Interment. *See* Burial.
Intermezzo. (H. P. Spofford) Atlan. 45: 32.
Internal Commerce of the West. (J. R. Williams) Hunt, 19: 19.
Internal Duties, Laws to abolish. Niles's Reg. 13: 316.
Internal Improvements. (H. Whiting) No. Am. 24: 1. — (J. M. Higbee) No. Am. 51: 130. — (C. F. Adams) No. Am. 51: 331. — (J. E. Bloomfield) Hunt, 13: 259. — (J. D. B. De Bow) De Bow, 2: 86. — (J. J. Albert) De Bow, 12: 402. — Am. Q. 8: 282. — New York R. 6: 301. — So. R. 2: 470.

Internal Improvements. Am. Whig R. **5**: 544. **6**: 111. — So. Q. **9**: 243. — So. Lit. Mess. **11**: 83, 188. — Dem. R. **18**: 295. **21**: 189. **22**: 483. — Ann. Reg. **5**: 191. **6**: 68. **7**: 159. — Niles's Reg. **13**: 283. **15**: 135, supp. 38. **31**: 114. **38**: 271–405. **39**: 243, 253. **40**: 146, 151, 225. **44**: 153. — De Bow, **14**: 78. — (L. Sherwood) De Bow, **19**: 81.
— at the West. (M. Tarver) De Bow, **7**: 403.
— Barbour's Speech on. Niles's Reg. **25**: 393.
— Clay's Speeches on. Niles's Reg. **15**: 140. **27**: 357.
— Effect of, on the Growth of Cities. (J. E. Bloomfield) Hunt, **13**: 259. — (J. A. Wright) Hunt, **16**: 263.
— in New York. (A. C. Flagg) Hunt, **24**: 35, 156, 447. **25**: 281–694.
— in North Carolina. (J. Sparks) No. Am. **12**: 16.
— in South Carolina. (J. L. Sullivan) No. Am. **13**: 143.
— Jefferson's Letter on. Niles's Reg. **37**: 79.
— Madison on. Niles's Reg. **21**: 145.
— Munroe on. Niles's Reg. **22**: 362, 391.
— Pennsylvania Convention, 1825. Niles's Reg. **29**: 59.
— Pennsylvania Report, 1828. Niles's Reg. **34**: 38.
— Power of Congress over. Dem. R. **28**: 148.
— — of the Government on. So. Q. **27**: 87.
— Report on, 1825. Niles's Reg. **28**: 89, 110, 191.
— — 1831. Niles's Reg. **40**: 207.
See also Roads and Canals.
Internal Intercourse in British Islands. Fraser, **10**: 294.
Internal Policy. (R. Southey) Quar. **42**: 228.
Internal Revenue; how to raise it. (W. I. Paulding) Putnam, **11**: 223.
— Law of 1864. Bank. M. (N. Y.) **19**: 609.
— Wells's Report on. Bank. M. (N. Y.) **23**: 857.
Internal-Revenue Amendment Bill. (J. Kirkland) Nation, **27**: 40.
Internal Trade of United States. (J. W. Scott) Hunt, **8**: 321, 447. **9**: 31.
— on the Mississippi River and New York Canals. (J. W. Scott) Hunt, **24**: 159.
Internal Transportation. Dem. R. **27**: 147.
International Affair. (F. H. Ludlow) Harper, **32**: 173, 313.
International Arbitration. *See* Arbitration.
International Working-Men's Association. (E. S. Beesly) Fortn. **14**: 517. — (J. Mazzini) Contemp. **20**: 155, 567. — (O. A. Brownson) Cath. World, **14**: 694. — (C. F. Dunbar) O. & N. **5**: 311. — Broadw. **8**: 451. — Dub. R. **69**: 447. — Ev. Sat. **11**: 626. — Fraser, **92**: 72, 181, 300. — Lippinc. **8**: 466. — Quar. **131**: 549.
— and Manchester School. (Lord Hobart) Fortn. **17**: 191.
— History of. (E. L. Godkin) Nation, **14**: 12. — (G. Howell) 19th Cent. **4**: 19.
International Carrying-Trade. (F. H. Morse) Internat. R. **6**: 532.
International Christianity. (J. L. Davies) Contemp. **38**: 221.
International Coinage. *See* Coinage, International.
International Communication by Language. (P. G. Hamerton) Internat. R. **1**: 721.
International Copyright. *See* Copyright.
International Courts, Private. Am. Law R. **6**: 393.
International Courtesy; Mr. Bancroft's Oration. Nat. Q. **12**: 250.
International Courtesies in Time of War. (W. L. Duff) Dark Blue, **2**: 237.
International Episode; a Tale. (H. James, jr.) Cornh. **38**: 687. **39**: 61.
International Exchanges. (F. Bowen) No. Am. **73**: 90.
International Exhibitions. (T. C. Archer) Penn Mo. **7**: 343.
International Industrial Competition. (J. Wharton) Penn Mo. **1**: 476. **2**: 28.
International Law. (J. E. Cairnes) Fortn. **2**: 641. — (T. E. C. Leslie) Fortn. **10**: 90. — (J. N. Pomeroy) Nation, **13**: 339. — (N. W. Senior) Ed. R. **77**: 303. — Ed. R. **112**: 386. **115**: 258. — (A. H. Everett) No. Am. **44**: 16. — (W. B. Lawrence) No. Am. **60**: 310. — Westm. **47**: 349. — Brit. & For. R. **9**: 144. — Dem. R. **21**: 23. — Mus. **37**: 289. — Hunt, **12**: 255. — So. M. **16**: 289.
— Association for Reform of. (J. B. Miles) Internat. R. **2**: 32.
— Bluntschli's. Am. Law R. **3**: 397.
— Code of. (D. D. Field) Am. Soc. Sci. J. **2**: 188.
— — Feasibility of. (E. Washburn) Internat. R. **4**: 537.
— — Private. Am. Law R. **2**: 599.
— Codification of. Am. Law R. **9**: 181.
— Commentaries on. Ed. R. **144**: 352.
— Conference on, at Oxford. Colburn, **167**: 513.
— Conferences at the Hague, 1875. (E. L. Godkin) Nation, **21**: 241.
— Grotius on War and Peace. Fraser, **49**: 479. — Knick. **62**: 150.
— Hautefeuille on some Questions of. (T. D. Woolsey) New Eng. **21**: 140.
— Importance of. So. Q. **28**: 1.
— Makers and Breakers of. (J. C. Paget) St. James, **36**: 611.
— Prescription in. (J. N. Pomeroy) Nation, **11**: 253.
— Proposed Changes in, 1875. (R. H. Dana, jr.) Nation, **20**: 167. — (W. E. Hall) Contemp. **26**: 735.
— Progress of. (J. B. Angell) Am. Soc. Sci. J. **8**: 40.
— Provisions of, concerning War. (J. Parker) No. Am. **95**: 1.
— Reaction in 1875. (A. G. Sedgwick) Nation, **20**: 309.
— Recent Aspects of, 1856. (T. D. Woolsey) New Eng. **14**: 560.
— Recent Developments in, 1870. (J. N. Pomeroy) Nation, **11**: 398. — (J. T. Morse, jr.) No. Am. **103**: 466.
— Relations of separate States to General Justice. (T. D. Woolsey) New Eng. **23**: 133.
— Some Points of. Am. Law R. **7**: 21.
— Study of. Chr. R. **26**: 128.
— Study in the Reform of. (G. F. Magoun) New Eng. **33**: 51.
— Trent and San Jacinto. Hunt, **46**: 1.
— The Virginius. (J. N. Pomeroy) Nation, **17**: 332, 348.
— What is the Use of? (E. L. Godkin) Nation, **8**: 368.
— Wheaton on. (J. T. Morse, jr.) No. Am. **103**: 626. — (W. B. Lawrence) No. Am. **104**: 309.
— Woolsey on. (H. W. Torrey) No. Am. **100**: 253.
International Literary Congress, 1878, Characteristics of. (W. D Bishop) Nation, **27**: 52.
International Monetary Conference. (H. White) Nation, **26**: 398.
International Morality. (Marquis of Ripon) Month, **35**: 157.
International Policy. (E. L. Stanley) Fortn. **5**: 636.
— Comte on. (W. H. Fremantle) Contemp. **3**: 477.
International Prejudices. Cornh. **34**: 45. Same art. Ecl. M. **87**: 318.
International Relations. (Lord Stratford de Redcliffe) 19th Cent. **2**: 471.
International Rights of Peace and War. (J. D. B. De Bow) De Bow, **1**: 190.
Interoceanic Communication, American. (J. E. Nourse) J. Frankl. Inst. **92**: 97–377. **93**: 305. **95**: 89. — De Bow, **19**: 493.
Interoceanic Ship Canal, American. Am. Whig R. **12**: 441. — Ecl. R. **91**: 711. — (H. H. Gorringe) Nation, **29**: 71. — (T. W. Osborn) Internat. R. **7**: 481. — Nature, **20**: 59. — (F. De Lesseps) No. Am. **130**: 1. — Ecl. Engin. **21**: 121.
— and F. De Lesseps. (D. Ammen) No. Am. **130**: 130.

Interoceanic Ship Canal and Monroe Doctrine. No. Am. **130**: 499.
— Route for. (C. De Fourcy) Pop. Sci. Mo. **16**: 380. *See* Atlantic Ocean and Pacific; Atrato; Darien; Nicaragua; Tehuantepec.
Interoceanic Ship-Railway. (J. B. Eads) No. Am. **132**: 223.
— Tehuantepec and. (J. A. Dillon) Harper, **63**: 905.
Interpolation, Formulæ for. (W. Ferrel) Math. Mo. **3**: 377.
Interpretation, Biblical. Chr. R. **5**: 211, 321. — (A. Alexander) Princ. **17**: 409.
— Diversity of. (J. A. Clark) Chr. R. **22**: 196.
— History of. (H. Rood) Chr. Mo. Spec. **8**: 169.
— Modern German Writers on. (A. Alexander) Princ. **5**: 9.
— Principles of. Chr. Mo. Spec. **2**: 9.
— Schools and Systems of. Princ. **27**: 226.
— Strauss's Mythical. Chr. R. **10**: 411.
Interpreter, The. (G. J. W. Melville) Fraser, **55**: 1–663. **56**: 47–675. Same art. Liv. Age, **52**: 689, 791. **53**: 738, 781. **54**: 19, 227, 475. **55**: 36–745. **56**: 473.
Interrogatives, English. (J. W. Gibbs) Am. Q. Reg. **5**: 170.
Interstate Extradition. Nat. Q. **40**: 128.
Intervention. Liv. Age, **14**: 284.
— British, in foreign Struggles. No. Brit. **38**: 490.
— Historical Review of. Dem. R. **30**: 52.
— International. Liv. Age, **32**: 37.
— Material and moral. (Lord Hobart) Macmil. **11**: 114.
— Monroe Doctrine on. (J. C. Welling) No. Am. **82**: 478.
— of the United States. Dem. R. **30**: 401, 554.
Interviewing. (J. R. Dennett) Nation, **8**: 66.
— Extraordinary. All the Year, **40**: 305.
Intolerance. (J. P. Quincy) Unita. R. **13**: 546. — Peop. J. **9**: 96.
— among the Ancients. Westm. **24**: 135.
— Clarke's History of. Ecl. R. **33**: 79. **37**: 450.
— Mallock's Plea for. (J. S. Sewall) New Eng. **38**: 339.
— Religious, in Massachusetts. (B. F. Bronson) Bapt. Q. **6**: 147, 280.
— — Principle of. Lond. Q. **4**: 377.
— Thoughts on. Meth. M. **35**: 657.
— Wyvill on. Quar. **2**: 301.
Intonation, Just. Nature, **15**: 159. *See* Music.
Intoxicating Liquors, History of. Dub. Univ. **14**: 586. *See* Liquors.
Intoxication, Arts of. (W. I. Gill) Meth. Q. **31**: 414.
Intra-Mercurial Observations. Nature, **14**: 534.
Intra-Mercurial Planet Question. Nature, **20**: 597.
Introspection, Illusions of. (J. Sully) Mind, **6**: 1.
Introversion; or Magical Readings of the Inner Man. (W. Cutter) Godey, **21**: 10.
Intuition and Induction. (J. Fenton) Colburn, **159**: 215.
— and Inference. (D. G. Thompson) Mind, **3**: 339, 468.
— Moral, *versus* Utilitarianism. (B. P. Bowne) New Eng. **32**: 217.
— Tendency of Thought to. (G. N. Abbott) Mercersb. **24**: 273.
Intuitions, Dynamical Theory of. (N. Smyth) New Eng. **37**: 353.
— McCosh on. (J. Dempster) Meth. Q. **21**: 267. — (C. Wright) Nation, **1**: 627. — Dub. Univ. **56**: 80.
— Relation of, to Thought and Theology. (J. Bascom) Am. Presb. R. **15**: 272.
Intuitional and Speaking Exercises. Am. J. Educ. **12**: 411.
Intuitional Religion. (J. Chaplin) Bapt. Q. **1**: 400.
Intuitional Teaching. Am. J. Educ. **31**: 177.
Intuitionalism and the Limits of Religious Thought. No. Brit. **30**: 137. Same art. Ecl. M. **47**: 312.
— Sidgwick on. (H. Calderwood) Mind, **1**: 197.
Intuitive Ideas. (J. Bascom) Bib. Sac. **23**: 1.
Intuitive Morals. Chr. Obs. **56**: 477.
Inundation, Middle Level, 1863. J. Frankl. Inst. **75**: 240.
— of Pesth. Fraser, **38**: 395, 503, 642.
Inundations of the Theiss. (G. Pollok) Nation, **28**: 244.
Inutilities, On the Usefulness of. Colburn, **64**: 235.
Invalid, Essays by an. Dub. Univ. **23**: 573. Same art. Ecl. M. **2**: 414.
— Privileges of. Chr. Mo. Spec. **9**: 632.
Invalid's Dinner Table. Once a Week, **13**: 176.
Invalids and Invalidism. Tait, n. s. **11**: 131.
— Winter Resorts for. All the Year, **33**: 270.
Invalid Dinner Tables. Chamb. J. **45**: 429.
Invalidism. (C. H. Butterworth) Victoria, **17**: 129.
— Ordered South. (R. L. Stevenson) Macmil. **30**: 68.
Invasion, The; a Tale. Cath. World, **8**: 18–746.
Invention and Patent Laws, Philosophy of. Fraser, **67**: 504.
— Future of. (W. H. Babcock) Atlan. **44**: 137.
— in France. All the Year, **39**: 197.
— Misdirected Effort in. (W. A. Ayres) Ecl. Engin. **17**: 509.
— Pioneers of. Dub. Univ. **66**: 296.
Inventions, Accidental. (J. Coryton) Macmil. **4**: 75.
— Age of Discovery. (M. Tarver) West. J. **3**: 141.
— American. (W. Chambers) Chamb. J. **23**: 228.
— and Discoveries, Opposition to. (S. Martin) Ex. H. Lec. **10**: 463.
— and Manufactures of United States. Hunt, **10**: 557.
— Anticipated. All the Year, **24**: 12. Same art. Liv. Age, **106**: 122.
— History of. J. Frankl. Inst. **39**: 278.
— — Beckmann's. Portfo. (Den.) **34**: 153, 190. — Quar. **14**: 405.
— Crude and curious. (E. H. Knight) Atlan. **39**: 517, 645. **40**: 22–689. **41**: 19–426.
— Influence on Credulity. (J. T. Trowbridge) Nation, **27**: 396.
— Minor. Sharpe, **22**: 217.
— Modern. Chamb. J. **34**: 306. Same art. Ecl. M. **52**: 193.
— of the Century. (P. E. Chase) J. Frankl. Inst. **103**: 274.
— Progress of Mechanical. Ed. R. **89**: 47. Same art. Ecl. M. **16**: 322.
— Protection for. Nature, **11**: 141, 191.
— What are we going to make? (E. Wright) Atlan. **2**: 90.
— Where are we to stop? Tait, n. s. **22**: 343.
— Marquis of Worcester's Century of. Chamb. J. **55**: 277. — J. Frankl. Inst. **3**: 313, 374. — Liv. Age, **38**: 283. — Quar. **32**: 397.
Inventor, Money Value of an. (W. B. Adams) Once a Week, **3**: 457.
— The Poor. All the Year, **33**: 485.
Inventor's Revenge; a Tale. Chamb. J. **46**: 739.
Inventors and Inventions. (E. Lawrence) Harper, **44**: 853. — All the Year, **2**: 353. Same art. Ecl. M. **52**: 193.
— Disappointments of. Penny M. **1**: 19.
— Rights of. Liv. Age, **28**: 95.
Inventory of Goods, 1523. (J. G. Nichols and J. E. Jackson) Arch. **38**: 353.
— — 1577. (F. W. Fairholt) Arch. **40**: 311.
Inverawe and Ticonderoga. (A. P. Stanley) Fraser, **102**: 501. Same art. Ecl. M. **95**: 740. Same art. Liv. Age, **147**: 350.
Inverness Character Fair. (A. Forbes) Gent. M. n. s. **12**: 317.
Inverquoich, Village of. (John Bull, jr.) Macmil. **7**: 447.
Invertebrate Animals, Huxley's Anatomy of. Nature, **16**: 517.
— Nature of Brain of. (H. C. Bastian) Pop. Sci. Mo. **9**: 712.
Invertebrate Palæontology in United States in 1879. (C. A. White) Am. Natural. **14**: 250.
Investiture, Ancient Symbol of. (R. Riddell) Arch. **11**: 45.
Investments. Chamb. J. **18**: 267. **51**: 637.

Investments for the Working Classes. (W. R. Greg) Ed. R. **95**: 405.
— How to invest safely. (F. R. Conder) Fraser, **97**: 114.
— Speculative. Blackw. **120**: 293.
Invisible, Perception of. (G. F. Rodwell) Macmil. **30**: 342. Same art. Ev. Sat. **17**: 259.
Invisible Eye; a Tale. (MM. Erckmann-Chatrian) Temp. Bar, **31**: 47.
Invited and Declining. (E. Yates) Temp. Bar, **4**: 326.
Invocation. (W. A. Kendall) Overland, **12**: 411.
Involuntary Excursion. All the Year, **44**: 155.
Involution and Evolution. (W. H. Butterfield) Western, **5**: 190.
— before Evolution. (M. H. Slosson) Chr. Q. **8**: 331.
Inward and the Outward. (F.A.Henry) New Eng. **36**: 24.
Inward Light of Quakerism. Am. Presb. R. **9**: 411.
Io, the Maiden who was in Love. Dub. Univ. **90**: 222.
Io Shell and its Habits. (J.Lewis) Am. Natural. **10**: 321.
Iodide, Ammonio-Argentic. (M. C. Lea) Am. J. Sci. **115**: 379.
Iodine. (E. Mylius) J. Frankl. Inst. **103**: 68.
— Sir H. Davy on. Ed. R. **23**: 486.
— Discovery and Uses of. Penny M. **7**: 479.
Iona. (G. D. Campbell) Good Words, **10**: 535, 614, 708. — F. Arts.Q. **4**: 418. — Month, **15**: 144. — Penny M. **1**: 324.
— and Staffa. Sharpe, **49**: 208.
— as it was and is. Hogg, **6**: 140.
Ionian Anthology. Mo. R. **134**: 37.
Ionian Islands. Colburn, **128**: 91. — Westm. **38**: 413. — Mo. R. **83**: 225. **102**: 138. — Quar. **29**: 86. — (A. U. Arnold) Chr. R. **14**: 625.
— Administration of. Quar. **91**: 315.
— and Malta, Davy on. Mo. R. **159**: 232.
— and their Government. Fraser, **46**: 593.
— Antiquarian Researches in. (J. Lee) Arch. **33**: 36.
— Holland's Travels in. (J. Foster) Ecl. R. **25**: 353.
— in 1848. Colburn, **85**: 416.
— in 1849. Colburn, **86**: 105.
— Jervis's History of. Ed. R. **97**: 41. — Colburn, **127**: 457.
— Napier on. Westm. **30**: 295.
— Physical Geography of. (D. T. Ansted) Pop. Sci. R. **2**: 458. **3**: 44.
Ionians, Primitive History of. (J. Campbell) Canad. J. n. s. **14**: 395, 559.
Ionian Name, Early History of. (E. von Curtius) Internat. R. **3**: 499.
Iowa, State of. De Bow, **15**: 509.
— Climate of. (T. S. Parvin) Am. J. Sci. **73**: 360.
— Coal-Measures of. (C. A. White) Am. J. Sci. **95**: 331.
— Drift Formations in Northeastern. (W. J. McGee) Am. J. Sci. **115**: 339.
— Drift Phenomena of Southwestern. (C. A. White) Am. J. Sci. **93**: 301.
— Growth of. (F. B. Perkins) O. & N. **7**: 631.
— Lakes of. (C. A. White) Am. Natural. **2**: 143.
— Missionary Excursion in. (A. Ravoux) U. S. Cath. M. **7**: 19–84.
— Resources of. (M. Tarver) West. J. **2**: 375.
— State Bank of. Bank. M. (N. Y.) **12**: 945.
— State Teachers' Association of. Am. J. Educ. **16**: 745.
— Statistics of, 1869. Am. J. Educ. **18**: 330.
— University of, Didactics in. (S. N. Fellows) Education, **1**: 393.
— — Library of. (A. N. Currier) Lib. J. **2**: 73.
— — Scientific Instruction at. Nature, **2**: 382.
Iowa College. (G. F. Magoun) New Eng. **32**: 438. — (G. F. Magoun) O. & N. **4**: 759.
Iphigenia at Tauris; translated from Goethe. So. Lit. Mess. **10**: 2, 65.
Iphis; a Masque. (M Collins) Dub. Univ. **68**: 191.
Iphis and Anaxarette; a Poem. (M. C. F. Münster) Once a Week, **4**: 98.
Ipsie. (H. A. Berton) O. & N. **8**: 35.
Ipswich, Mass., Early Families of. N. E. Reg. **2**: 174.
— Female Seminary. Am. Q. Reg. **11**: 368.
— Grammar School. (A. Hammett) N. E. Reg. **6**: 64, 159.
— Materials for History of. N. E. Reg. **7**: 77.
— Physicians of. (A. Hammett) N. E. Reg. **4**: 11.
— Subscription for Gen. Daniel Denison, 1648. N. E. Reg. **2**: 50.
— Week at. All the Year, **1**: 533.
Iran and Turan. (J. W. Jackson) Anthrop. R. **6**: 121, 286.
Ireland, William Henry. Cornh. **39**: 577.
— Literary Impostures of. Sharpe, **8**: 139. Same art. Ecl. M. **16**: 416.
— Shakspere Forgeries. All the Year, **26**: 205. — Fraser, **62**: 167. Same art. Liv. Age, **66**: 643. — Ev. Sat. **11**: 319.
Ireland. (E. A. Grattan) No. Am. **51**: 187. — (W. Sampson) No. Am. **24**: 321. — (J. P. Thompson) New Eng. **6**: 457. — (T. P. Thompson) Westm. **18**: 500. — (D. M. Balfour) Hunt, **18**: 579. — Am. Lit. M. **1**: 77, 145. — Ed. R. **57**: 248. — Brit. & For. R. **6**: 338. — Mus. **1**: 289. — Blackw. **15**: 269. **33**: 66–563. **36**: 747. **37**: 210. — Fraser, **41**: 250. **70**: 663. **74**: 1. — (R. Bickersteth) Ex. H. Lec. **2**: 225. — (W. Sewell) Quar. **76**: 247. — Brownson, **17**: 446. — Dub. Univ. **2**: 433. — Nat. R. **18**: 403. — Quar. **83**: 584.
— Act of Union with, compared with that with Scotland. (A. V. Dicey) Fortn. **36**: 168.
— Adventure in. Chamb. J. **52**: 540.
— Adventures in North of. Blackw. **40**: 459.
— Affairs of. English Notions of. Dub. Univ. **22**: 120.
— Agricultural and Commercial Condition of, 1849. Dub. Univ. **34**: 371.
— Agricultural Education in. Am. J. Educ. **8**: 567.
— Agricultural Improvement in, 1841. Dub. R. **10**: 489.
— Agricultural Statistics of, 1847. Bank. M. (L.) **8**: 583.
— — 1848. Bank. M. (L.) **9**: 579.
— Agriculture of. Dub. Univ. **83**: 641.
— — and waste Lands in. Brit. & For. R. **9**: 619.
— — Baldwin on. Nature, **10**: 203.
— All-Hallow Eve in. Colburn, **4**: 254.
— Ancient, O'Curry's. (J. G. McGee) Cath. World, **20**: 506.
— Ancient Life in. Dub. Univ. **62**: 194.
— and Absenteeism. Dub. R. **2**: 199. — Westm. **8**: 70. — (T. P. Thompson) Westm. **10**: 237. **19**: 516. — Westm. **23**: 411. — Quar. **33**: 455. — Ed. R. **43**: 54. — (H. L. Japhson) 19th Cent. **7**: 871. — Dub. Univ. **35**: 277.
— and England. (J. Morley) Fortn. **35**: 407. — Colburn, **10**: 481. — (G. A. Brodrick) Macmil. **24**: 32.
— — Federal Union between, 1841. Mo. R. **165**: 441. — Am. Ecl. **2**: 25.
— — in 1880. Fraser, **101**: 73.
— — in 1881, and the Gladstone Government. (H. O. Arnold-Foster) No. Am. **133**: 560.
— and France, Trade between. Dub. Univ. **57**: 208.
— and her Calumniators. Dub. R. **2**: 409.
— and her Need. Dark Blue, **2**: 665.
— and her Queen. Once a Week, **5**: 343.
— and her Rulers. Dub. Univ. **18**: 631. **22**: 612.
— — 1829–42. Tait, n. s. **11**: 743.
— — 1829–44. Dub. R. **17**: 1. — Mo. R. **162**: 365.
— and the Holy Alliance. Dem. R. **31**: 1.
— and the Irish. U. S. Cath. M. **4**: 205. — Fraser, **9**: 586, 654.
— — O'Connell's. Dub. Univ. **21**: 352, 459.
— and Irishmen. Dem. R. **35**: 42.
— and Italy. (W. C. Taylor) Bentley, **24**: 303.

Ireland and Daniel O'Connell. Dub. R. **78**: 472.
— and the Quarterly Review. Dub. Univ. **26**: 242.
— and the Repeal Question. Fraser, **9**: 253.
— and Scotland. (J. Godkin) Fortn. **9**: 319.
— and Spain once connected by Land. St. James, **5**: 409.
— and Union of Trades. Fraser, **4**: 626.
— Angler in, 1833. Mo. R. **135**: 560.
— Antiquities of. (T. Pownall) Arch. **3**: 355. **7**: 164. — Dub. R. **50**: 122. — Dub. Univ. **3**: 316. **35**: 300. **57**: 339. — Fraser, **49**: 112.
— — Towers and Temples. (J. Godkin) Fortn. **9**: 106.
— Apocryphal. Dub. Univ. **23**: 143.
— Appellate Court for. Dub. Univ. **83**: 496.
— Art and Artists in. Irish Q. **1**: 106. — Colburn, **7**: 385.
— as it was, is, and ought to be, Martin's. Dub. Univ. **3**: 583.
— as a Military Nation. Tait, **4**: 212.
— Atrocities in, An American Statesman on. Blackw. **127**: 271.
— Autumnal Night's Dream in. Blackw. **22**: 685.
— Banking in, Gilbart's History of. Mo. R. **140**: 384.
— Bar of. Colburn, **98**: 407.
— — as it was and is. Dub. Univ. **1**: 45.
— — Curran's Sketches of. Dub. Univ. **46**: 348. Same art. Ecl. M. **36**: 879.
— — Recollections of. Chamb. J. **55**: 200.
— — Sketches of. Colburn, **5**: 97–481. **6**: 1. **7**: 124–481. **8**: 1–393. **10**: 121. **14**: 393–497. **17**: 1. **19**: 105. **20**: 165–401. **23**: 17. **25**: 128–217. — Mus. **2**: 180.
— Barlow's. Mo. R. **82**: 52.
— Barrington's Memoirs. Blackw. **34**: 573. **35**: 204, 386. — Colburn, **29**: 189. **38**: 12. — Dub. Univ. **2**: 509.
— Barrow's Tour round, 1835. Mo. R. **140**: 421.
— before Christianity. Cath. World, **2**: 541.
— Beggars in. (N. W. Senior) Ed. R. **77**: 391. — Tait, n. s. **6**: 476. — Penny M. **6**: 477. — (L. Murray) Canad. Mo. **16**: 51. — Mo. R. **145**: 211.
— Bench of. Dub. Univ. **1**: 118.
— Bird's Nests in. Month, **5**: 551.
— Bogs of. (R. H. Horne) Peop. J. **6**: 134.
— Botany of. Dub. Univ. **8**: 223.
— Boycotted. (W. B. Jones) Contemp. **39**: 856. — (Reply by J. O'Leary) Contemp. **40**: 127. — (Answer by W. B. Jones) Contemp. **40**: 246. — (The answer examined by J. O'Leary) Contemp. **40**: 479.
— Boycotting in. Ecl. M. **97**: 209.
— Bridal Customs in. Colburn, **5**: 185.
— British Interests in. Blackw. **127**: 256.
— E. Burke on Affairs of. (A. V. Dicey) Nation, **33**: 135.
— Cain Patraic. (W. Dennehy) Cath. World, **30**: 785.
— Capabilities of. Dub. Univ. **9**: 46.
— Carr's Stranger in. Ed. R. **10**: 40. — (J. Foster) Ecl. R. **4**: 869, 976.
— Catholic. Fraser, **84**: 776.
— — in A. D. 600. Dub. R. **20**: 461.
— Catholics of. Ed. R. **31**: 246. — Blackw. **17**: 255.
— — and the Bible. Blackw. **16**: 491.
— — and Mr. Croly. Fraser, **10**: 711.
— — and the New Reformation. Blackw. **26**: 84. — Quar. **91**: 37. — Ecl. R. **94**: 657.
— — Letters of a Catholic Clergyman in, to a Friend in Rome. Blackw. **31**: 19.
— — Parnell's Apology for. (Syd. Smith) Ed. R. **10**: 299.
— — Penal Laws against. (Syd. Smith) Ed. R. **13**: 77. — Pamph. **20**: 185, 431. **21**: 97.
— Catholic Church in. Dub. Univ. **4**: 312. **7**: 75. — (W. Sewell) Quar. **67**: 117. — Dub. R. **10**: 184, 518. **11**: 196.
— — and British Liberalism. (M. Arnold) Fortn. **30**: 26.
— — Question of. Blackw. **24**: 409. **27**: 173. — (R. Southey) Quar. **38**: 535. — Brit. & For. R. **3**: 262.
Ireland, Catholic Church in, Sydney Smith on. Liv. Age, **5**: 352.
— — Statistics of. Dub. Univ. **11**: 510.
— — Ultramontane Policy in. Dub. Univ. **84**: 117. — Gent. M. n. s. **15**: 172.
— Catholic Clergy of. (T. H. Lister) Ed. R. **60**: 483 — (W. Sewell) Quar. **67**: 541.
— — and Elections. Blackw. **20**: 505.
— — Education of. Dub. Univ. **84**: 562.
— — Payment of. Ed. R. **74**: 474.
— Catholic Education in, and English Tories. (P. Gerard) Cath. World, **27**: 829.
— Catholic Emancipation in. (H. Bellingham) Cath. World, **30**: 104.
— Catholic Laity in. Fraser, **86**: 491.
— Catholic Rule in 1641–48. Ed. R. **151**: 437.
— Celt of, and of Wales. Cornh. **36**: 661.
— Celtic MSS. and their Contents. Dub. Univ. **70**: 399.
— Census of. Dub. Univ. **23**: 521.
— — Historic Notes on. Dub. Univ. **38**: 552.
— — in 1841. (Capt. Larcom) J. Statis. Soc. **6**: 323.
— — in 1851. Irish Q. **6**: 814.
— — in 1861. Fraser, **64**: 300. — Dub. Univ. **58**: 377.
— — in 1871. Fraser, **93**: 458.
— Chancery Amendment in. Dub. Univ. **50**: 569.
— Chief Justices of. (O. J. Burke) Dub. Univ. **89**: 481, 579. **90**: 622.
— Christianity in, Introduction of. Dub. Univ. **76**: 321, 437.
— Church of. (C. G. Greene, jr.) Nat. Q. **19**: 155. — (A. Trollope) Fortn. **2**: 82. — Brit. Q. **41**: 259. — St. Paul's, **1**: 206, 675. — Dub. R. **14**: 178. — Dub. Univ. **26**: 346, 379, 713. **82**: 498. — Ed. R. **123**: 454. — Fraser, **11**: 491. **70**: 1.
— — Ancient. (J. D. Baldwin) Bib. Sac. **32**: 650. — (M. W. Bondy) Cath. World, **11**: 472. — (F. H. O'Donnell) Month, **30**: 34. — (W. Dowe) Cath. World, **29**: 412. — (E. Pond) Bib. Sac. **28**: 21. — Cath. World, **7**: 764. **8**: 340. — Dub. R. **65**: 1. — Dub. Univ. **17**: 405. **77**: 450. — Fortn. **4**: 16. Same art. Theo. Ecl. **4**: 189. — Quar. **119**: 472. — (J. E. McGee) Cath. World, **5**: 828.
— — — Celtic. Ecl. R. **83**: 295.
— — — Moran's. (J. G. McGee) Cath. World, **7**: 356.
— — — Usages of. Chr. Rem. **48**: 1.
— — Abolition Bill. Dub. Univ. **6**: 125.
— — Address to Protestants of. Dub. Univ. **4**: 219.
— — and the Appropriation Clause. Dub. Univ. **7**: 471.
— — and the Land Question. Fraser, **76**: 221.
— — and Fenianism. (J. Godkin) Fortn. **9**: 191.
— — and the Irish Difficulty. Chr. Obs. **68**: 849, 932.
— — and Irish Methodism, 1849. Ecl. R. **91**: 63.
— — and the Land. (W. Hamilton) Princ. **40**: 398.
— — Commission on, and Coronation Oath. Dub. Univ **4**: 121.
— — Convocation of. Dub. Univ. **59**: 148.
— — Disestablishment of. (W. M. Brady) Contemp. **12**: 1. — (J. Godkin) Fortn. **2**: 280. — (J. McCarthy) Galaxy, **8**: 399. — (C. P. Reichel) Contemp. **15**: 180. — (W. G. Todd) Month, **12**: 421. — Chr. Rem. **56**: 110. — Dub. R. **63**: 72. — Westm. **86**: 281. — Fraser, **86**: 135.
— — — Act of 1869. (J. G. McGee) Cath. World, **9**: 239. — No. Brit. **50**: 568.
— — — before Parliament. Dub. Univ **62**: 229.
— — — Bill for. Fraser, **80**: 257.
— — — Effects of. Lond. Q. **52**: 24.
— — — Four Years' Experience of. Chr. Obs. **75**: 25, 113, 215.
— — — Results of. Brit. Q. **56**: 195.
— — Efforts for Education in. Ed. R. **43**: 197. — Selec. Ed. R. **3**: 469.

Ireland, Church of, Established. Colburn, **142**: 694. — Irish Q. **7**: 243. — Cong. **1**: 607. — Dub. R. **51**: 308. — (W. M. Brady) Contemp. **9**: 1, 432. — (G. Ensor) Tait, n. s. **3**: 222. — (W. C. Magee) Contemp. **7**: 429. — (F. D. Maurice) Contemp. **7**: 54, 586. — (J. M. Ludlow) Contemp. **9**: 558. — Blackw. **25**: 616. — Brit. Q. **49**: 459. — Colburn, **32**: 65. — Dub. R. **56**: 107. — Dub. Univ. **2**: 403. — Ho. & For. R. **3**: 436. — Irish Q. **6**: 600. — Nat. R. **16**: 269. — No. Brit. **45**: 344.
— — Exactions of. Cong. M. **18**: 739.
— — General Synod of. Chr. Obs. **71**: 533.
— — Hist. of. Dub. R. **51**: 379. — Dub. Univ. **68**: 231.
— — — from 11th to 17th Century. Dub. Univ. **77**: 211.
— — — Mant's. Dub. Univ. **15**: 243, 427.
— — in the 16th Century. Fraser, **78**: 675.
— — in the Time of Queen Elizabeth. (W. M. Brady) Fraser, **76**: 426. — Ed. R. **129**: 419.
— — in 1825. Quar. **31**: 492.
— — in 1835. (T. H. Lister) Ed. R. **61**: 490.
— — Incipient Plunder of. Blackw. **33**: 651.
— — Letter to the King. Blackw. **33**: 723.
— — The Ministry and. Fraser, **79**: 113.
— — Baptist Noel on. Ecl. R. **82**: 312.
— — Politics and History of. (J. C. MacDonnell) Contemp. **3**: 392.
— — Position and Claims of. Dub. Univ. **61**: 619.
— — Proselytizing of R. Catholics by. Chr. Rem. **5**: 640.
— — Pulpit Jurisdiction of. Dub. Univ. **9**: 501.
— — Question of. Westm. **31**: 228. — Blackw. **33**: 651, 723. — Pamph. **9**: 350. — Dub. Univ. **5**: 493. — (R. Southey) Quar. **38**: 535. — Brit. Q. **47**: 487. — Colburn, **144**: 567. — St. Paul's, **4**: 285.
— — — in 1868. Dub. Univ. **72**: 473.
— — — Parliamentary Doings on. Dub. Univ. **4**: 473.
— — Reconstruction of. Lond. Q. **33**: 397. — Chr. Obs. **70**: 331, 886. — Fraser, **77**: 19. — Quar. **127**: 493.
— — Reform of, 1833. Tait, **2**: 825. **3**: 131–671. — Dub. Univ. **28**: 366.
— — Reformers and Foes of. Dub. Univ. **63**: 363.
— — the Source of Social Disaffection. Ecl. R. **84**: 239.
— — State Provision for Clergy of, 1844. Dub. R. **16**: 186.
— — Temporal Power of. Westm. **89**: 65.
— — Troubles from, 1833. Tait, **2**: 388.
— Church and State in, Noel on. (J. Moncrieff) No. Brit. **4**: 255. — Brit. Q. **2**: 543.
— Churches of, Godkin on. (T. D. McGee) Cath. World, **7**: 200.
— — Miall's Policy in. Irish Q. **6**: 864.
— — Restitution of. (R. F. Farrell) Cath. World, **33**: 577.
— Church Education in. Dub. Univ. **15**: 556.
— Church History of. Chr. Rem. **50**: 311. — Dub. R. **51**: 379. — Irish Q. **2**: 196.
— Church Property of. Month, **8**: 46.
— Church System of. Westm. **89**: 442.
— Church Temporalities in. Fraser, **73**: 16.
— Civil Affairs of, 1826. Ed. R. **43**: 461.
— Civil Service in. Irish Q. **6**: 416.
— Civil Wars in. Mo. R. **127**: 202.
— — Taylor's. Fraser, **8**: 385.
— Civilization in. (T. Moore) Tait, n. s. **2**: 349.
— — Heathen and Mediæval. Meth. Q. **13**: 404.
— Clarendon's Administration in, 1847–52. Ed. R. **93**: 208. — Dub. Univ. **37**: 136.
— Clarendon's Defense of Affair at Dolly's Brae. Quar. **86**: 480.
— Clergy of, Education of. Dub. Univ. **52**: 358.
— — Meetings for. Blackw. **39**: 156.
— — State of. Dub. Univ. **10**: 727.
— Clerical Life in. Dub. Univ. **49**: 300.
— — Craig's. Colburn, **156**: 337.
Ireland, Climate of. Nature, **1**: 630.
— Coast of, Round. (G. P. Bevan) Once a Week, **10**: 49–245.
— Cockney's Journey to. Lond. M. **17**: 289.
— Coercion Bill, 1833. Blackw. **35**: 434. — Tait, **2**: 837. **3**: 401, 545, 548.
— Colloquies on recent Measures, 1829. Blackw. **25**: 752.
— Colonization of. Dub. Univ. **75**: 618.
— — Plan of. Liv. Age, **13**: 305, 405.
— Colonization from. No. Brit. **8**: 421.
— Conciliation of. (J. Morley) Fortn. **36**: 1.
— Conquest of, by the Anglo-Normans. Fraser, **13**: 269. — (E. Lawrence) Harper, **43**: 724.
— Conservatives of; what are they about? Dub. Univ. **11**: 746.
— Convent Life in. Fraser, **80**: 431.
— Conversion and Persecution in. Dub. Univ. **40**: 244.
— Convict System of. Cornh. **3**: 409.
— Cotton's Voyage to. Blackw. **6**: 284.
— Country Festivals in, 1800. Dub. Univ. **62**: 581.
— Crime in. Belgra. **22**: 49. — Dub. Univ. **14**: 251.
— — Government Dealing with. Quar. **128**: 560.
— — Lord Roden's Committee on. Ed. R. **70**: 503.
— Cromwell's Invasion of. Dub. R. **71**: 49. — Irish Mo. **3**: 158–446.
— Cromwellian Settlement of. (H. S. Fagan) Fortn. **5**: 758. — (E. L. Godkin) Nation, **11**: 240. — Dub. R. **58**: 107. **59**: 433. — Ed. R. **122**: 518. — Lond. Q. **36**: 409. — Month, **3**: 394.
— — Prendergast on. Chr. Obs. **70**: 904. — Fraser, **75**: 33.
— Curates of. Colburn, **39**: 65.
— Curran on, 1818. Mo. R. **87**: 250.
— Dancing in, 1800. Dub. Univ. **62**: 429.
— Danes and Norwegians in. Irish Q. **2**: 817. — Dub. Univ. **70**: 1. Same art. Cath. World, **5**: 768.
— Darbyism and Lay-Preaching in. Ecl. R. **120**: 315.
— Day or two in. So. Lit. Mess. **18**: 273.
— Depopulation of. Dub. R. **13**: 512.
— The Devil in. Lond. M. **9**: 453.
— Difficulty of, 1849. Westm. **50**: 436.
— Disturbances in. Pamph. **24**: 97.
— — in 1833. Fraser, **7**: 232, 458.
— — Local, 1830–34. Dub. R. **1**: 28.
— Dominican Schools in Ancient. Dub. R. **19**: 145.
— Dublin Exhibition, 1853. (W. Chambers) Chamb. J. **19**: 369, 409.
— — in 1865. (F. P. Cobbe) Fraser, **72**: 403.
— Dufferin's Inquiry into State of. Dub. Univ. **68**: 116.
— Early Buildings in. Dub. Univ. **71**: 106, 328.
— Early Hist. of, Romantic Stories from. Howitt, **2**: 301.
— Early Industrial Arts of. (M. Havesty) Cath. World, **3**: 549, 780.
— Early Institutions of. Dub. Univ. **86**: 129.
— Early Manuscripts of. Hogg, **4**: 294.
— Early Scholars of. (H. Harrisse) No. Am. **94**: 125.
— Economic Case of. Dub. Univ. **31**: 408.
— Education in, Intermediate. Irish Mo. **6**: 107.
— — — Working of the Act, 1880. (P. O'Reilly) Month, **39**: 193.
— — National Schools. (H. Bellingham) Month, **40**: 187.
— Emancipation in; what has it done? Colburn, **26**: 497.
— — and Repeal. Irish Mo. **3**: 515.
— Emigration to. Chamb. J. **19**: 308.
— Emigration from. (H. Giles) Chr. Exam. **52**: 361. — (T. E. C. Leslie) Fortn. **8**: 38.
— — and Tenant Right. Ho. & For. R. **4**: 339.
— — to England. Chamb. J. **10**: 261.
— Endowed Grammar Schools of. Am. J. Educ. **15**: 721. — Irish Q. **4**: 473.
— England's Policy towards. (R. Vaughan) Brit. Q. **1**: 582. Same art. Liv. Age, **5**: 347. — Dub. Univ. **25**: 505.

Ireland, England's Treatment of. Brit. Q. **44**: 1.
— English in, Froude's. Ed. R. **137**: 122. — (J. E. Cairnes) Fortn. **22**: 171. — (J. E. Cairnes) Canad. Mo. **6**: 270. — (A. V. Dicey) Nation, **16**: 355. **19**: 59, 75. — (W. E. H. Lecky) Macmil. **27**: 246. **30**: 166. Same art. Liv. Age, **116**: 387. — Brit. Q. **57**: 481. — Chr. Obs. **73**: 182. **74**: 407. — Dub. R. **72**: 421. — Dub. Univ. **81**: 79. — Ed. R. **139**: 468. — Internat. R. **2**: 117. — Quar. **134**: 169.
— English Mismanagement in. (J. S. Mill) Liv. Age, **96**: 771.
— English Notions of. Dub. Univ. **22**: 120. Same art. Ecl. Mus. **3**: 46.
— English Oppression of. (E. I. Sears) No. Am. **86**: 120.
— English Rule in. (E. I. Sears) Nat. Q. **12**: 358. — (J. L. Spalding) Cath. World, **24**: 799. — Dub. Univ. **76**: 83.
— English System in. Dem. R. **30**: 97.
— English Theories and Irish Facts. Dub. Univ. **6**: 683.
— English Tourists in. Dub. R. **3**: 401.
— Epidemic Disease in. Dub. R. **41**: 76.
— Epidemic Fever in, 1817-19. Ecl. R. **41**: 254, 537.
— Epidemics of the Famine in. Dub. Univ. **40**: 653.
— Episcopal Charges in. Chr. Obs. **43**: 614, 694.
— Estate in, Description of an. Dub. Univ. **80**: 516.
— Ethnology of. (R. G. Latham) Dub. Univ. **50**: 396. **51**: 90, 293. **54**: 185.
— Evils of. Blackw. **40**: 495, 812.
— — and their Remedies. For. Q. **37**: 105. — Ed. R. **49**: 300. — Dub. Univ. **26**: 61. — Quar. **38**: 53.
— Excursion in. (H. S. Fagan) Belgra. **21**: 87.
— — in 1849. So. Lit. Mess. **16**: 89.
— Faction in, and English Parties. Fraser, **99**: 159.
— Factions, Parsons, and Landlords in. Dub. R. **27**: 468.
— Familiar Epistles from. Fraser, **40**: 459, 554. **42**: 319. **46**: 151. **47**: 297. **53**: 38.
— Famine in, 1847. (W. Howitt) Howitt, **1**: 181. — (Mrs. Hoare) Howitt, **1**: 233. — Dem. R. **20**: 424. — Brit. Q. **5**: 504. — (O. C. Gardiner) Am. Whig R. **6**: 455, 633. **7**: 419. — Ed. R. **87**: 229. — Quar. **82**: 261. — Dub. Univ. **29**: 501. — Fraser, **35**: 491.
— — Tale of, Carleton's. Ecl. R. **85**: 495.
— — Three Days of the Famine at Schull. (R. C. Trench) Fraser, **36**: 1.
— Famines in. (W. Dennehy) Cath. World, **31**: 669.
— Farmer's Sunday Morning in. Month, **5**: 628.
— Federal Movement in. Fraser, **82**: 754.
— Federalism and Home Rule. (E. A. Freeman) Fortn. **22**: 204.
— — Butt on. Ed. R. **133**: 501.
— Fenians and Fenian Literature, Ancient. Cornh. **13**: 121. Same art. Ecl. M. **66**: 361. — (L. C. Seelye) Scrib. **1**: 517.
— Fifty Years' Residence in. (J. Hamilton) Macmil. **24**: 144, 225. **25**: 66, 339. Same art. Ecl. M. **77**: 367.
— Financial Grievance of. Ed. R. **142**: 307.
— Fisheries of. Dub. R. **3**: 133. **11**: 356. **24**: 98. **37**: 287. — Dub. Univ. **31**: 771. — Irish Q. **6**: 183, 400. — Quar. **72**: 473.
— — Salmon. Quar. **91**: 352.
— Fishing Village in. (J. L. Clonel) Harper, **60**: 682.
— Five Years in. Blackw. **51**: 474.
— Folk Lore of. *See* Folk Lore.
— for the British. (J. C. Morison) Fortn. **9**: 89.
— for the Irish. Tinsley, **1**: 607. Same art. N. Ecl. **1**: 195. — Liv. Age, **95**: 771.
— for Tourists. (M. E. Braddon) Belgra. **24**: 76, 177.
— Forbes's Travels in, 1852. New Q. **2**: 373.
— Forests of. Dub. Univ. **9**: 666.
— Fortnight in, in Lent, 1863. (A. V. Kirwan) Fraser, **67**: 670.
Ireland, Fortnight in Kerry. Fraser, **81**: 513. Same art. Ecl. M. **75**: 15.
— Franchise in, 1880. (C. Dawson) Fortn. **33**: 281.
— Francis's Speech on the War of 1805. Ed. R. **7**: 478.
— French in, 1798. All the Year, **18**: 34.
— French Tourist in. Dub. Univ. **73**: 78.
— French Views of. Dub. Univ. **58**: 269.
— from 1645 to 1649. For. Q. **34**: 2.
— from 1800 to 1880. (C. G. O'Brien) 19th Cent. **9**: 397.
— from 1840 to 1880. (W. B. Jones) Macmil. **41**: 505.
— from Swift to O'Connell. (G. L. Phillips) No. Am. **116**: 44.
— Mrs. Fry's Account of. Mo. R. **115**: 22.
— Gamble's View of, 1813. Ecl. R. **18**: 229.
— Geology of, Hull's. Nature, **18**: 354.
— George IV.'s Visit to. Blackw. **10**: 224, 319, 447.
— Giraldus Cambrensis on. Dub. R. **28**: 141. — Dub. Univ. **35**: 1, 192, 383.
— Glance at, 1867. Bentley, **61**: 246.
— Glimpse of. (G. Butler) Cath. World, **19**: 408, 526. — (A. F. Hewit) Cath. World, **9**: 738.
— Gold Mines of. Penny M. **13**: 426.
— Gossip about. All the Year, **20**: 465.
— Government of. Blackw. **20**: 527.
— — and the Conciliatory System. Fraser, **14**: 257.
— — how governed in 16th Century. (J. A. Froude) Fraser, **71**: 312. Same art. Liv. Age, **84**: 611.
— — How should it be governed? Blackw. **25**: 40.
— — How is it to be governed? Dub. Univ. **4**: 353.
— — Whig. Dub. Univ. **1**: 456.
— Grant's Impressions of. Tait, n. s. **11**: 766.
— Grattan's Speeches on. Portfo.(Den.) **29**: 275.
— Grievances of; Debates, 1843. Dub. Univ. **22**: 177.
— — Greatest. Howitt, **3**: 8.
— — Group of. Bentley, **62**: 281.
— — Morison on. (J. Morley) Fortn. **10**: 234.
— — What does she want? St. Paul's, **5**: 286.
— Half a Day in. Bentley, **33**: 669.
— Hall's Scenes, etc., in. Mo. R. **153**: 551. **162**: 171.
— Harvest Homes in. Dub. Univ. **62**: 679.
— Head's Fortnight in. Dub. R. **34**: 1. — Dub. Univ. **40**: 735. — Irish Q. **2**: 829. — New Q. **2**: 60. — Tait, n. s. **2**: 28.
— History of, Ancient Notices of. Dub. Univ. **75**: 591.
— — and Antiquities of. Dub. R. **23**: 469.
— — and Irish Character. Fraser, **64**: 644.
— — and Grievances of. Ecl. R. **79**: 601.
— — Annals of, by the Four Masters. Dub. R. **24**: 164. — Dub. Univ. **31**: 359, 571. — Lond. Q. **20**: 54. — Quar. **93**: 1.
— — Athlone and Aughrim, 1692. Cath. World, **5**: 119.
— — By-Ways of. Dub. Univ. **10**: 205-704. **11**: 87, 510, 629. **12**: 183-686. **13**: 69, 206, 322.
— — Chapter of. (J. Dyer) Penn Mo. **2**: 533. — Dub. Univ. **46**: 719. **47**: 55.
— — Chronicle of. St. James, **26**: 433. — Dub. Univ. **70**: 352.
— — Early Notes on. Month, **8**: 570.
— — Gordon's. (M. Napier) Ed. R. **10**: 116. — Ecl. R. **4**: 1022.
— — Henderson on. Mo R **86**: 388.
— — Insurrection of 1803. Dub. Univ. **1**: 541. Same art. Mus. **31**: 111. — Fraser, **14**: 546.
— — Insurrections and Anathemas. Dub. Univ. **13**: 69
— — Legendary. Dub. Univ. **75**: 462.
— — Materials for. Dub. R. **18**: 205. — Dub. Univ. **58**: 661.
— — Milesian Conquest of. Dub. Univ. **89**: 673. — (W. Chambers) Chamb. J. **7**: 49.
— — Military. Dub. R. **19**: 281.
— — Moore's. Westm. **23**: 169. — Dub. Univ. **5**: 613.

Ireland, History of, O'Driscol's. (F. Jeffrey) Ed. R. 46: 433. — Mo. R. 11[illegible]: 527. — Ecl. R. 47: 1.

— — Original Population of. Mus. 1: 409.

— — Plowden's. Ed. R. 5: 152.

— — Rebellion of 1641. Arch. 1: 96, 100. — Dub. R. 21: 65.

— — — and 1690. Chr. Rem. 4: 24.

— — Rebellion of 1798. (T. De Quincey) Tait, n. s. 1: 196, 263. — Mo. R. 116: 57. Same art. Mus. 13: 351. — Cath. World, 3: 122.

— — — Letter on Cruelty of Rebels. Meth. M. 22: 20.

— — Rebellion of 1848. Blackw. 64: 475. — Tait, n. s. 15: 560.

— — Records of. Irish Q. 1: 588.

— — Savage's Revolutionary. Dem. R. 38: 551.

— — 700 Years ago. (W. Allingham) Fraser, 82: 135.

— — Smiles's. Ecl. R. 80: 205.

— — Theiner's Materials of. Dub. R. 56: 372.

— — Wars in, Lord Castlehaven's Memoirs of. (W. Walsh) Cath. World, 22: 78.

— Hoare. Owenson, and Dudley on. Chr. Obs. 7: 182–319.

— Home Rule for. (J. G. McGee) Cath. World, 19: 54. — (W. O'C. Morris) Fortn. 17: 16. — Dub. Univ. 82: 257, 507. — Fraser, 84: 1. — Lond. Q. 42: 314.

— — Agitation on. Dub. Univ. 83: 466.

— — Conference on. Fraser, 89: 1.

— — Debate of 1874. Dub. Univ. 84: 244.

— — Experiences of. Fraser, 85: 206.

— — Fallacies in. (J. O'C. Power) Fortn. 32: 224.

— — from a Saxon Standpoint. (J. Spalding) Colburn, 154: 432.

— — in the 18th Century. Quar. 136: 498.

— — in 1878. (E. L. Godkin) Nation, 27: 313.

— — in 1880. (A. Frisby) Contemp. 38: 786.

— — Movement for. (A. M. Sullivan) Cath. World, 23: 500, 623.

— Home-Rulers in. Galaxy, 21: 164.

— — at Home. (R. Bagwell) Dub. Univ. 91: 207.

— — in Parliament. (R. Bagwell) Dub. Univ. 90: 364.

— How is the Law to be enforced in? (A. V. Dicey) Fortn. 36: 539.

— How Strafford governed, 1632–41. Irish Mo. 4: 205–506.

— Human Remains found in. (R. Pococke) Arch. 2: 32.

— Hunting in Ancient. Bentley, 44: 502.

— Ignorance and Apathy of. Chr. Obs. 38: 363.

— Illustrations of the State of. Ed. R. 58: 86.

— Improvement in Eng. Notions of. Dub. Univ. 35: 502.

— Improvement of. Ecl. R. 90: 759.

— in the Reign of Elizabeth. Dub. Univ. 32: 587.

— — of James I. Dub. R. 72: 1.

— in 1779. (W. Dennehy) Cath. World, 30: 36.

— in 1782. (W. Dennehy) Cath. World, 30: 240.

— in 1787. Chamb. J. 8: 158. — Dub. Univ. 21: 728. 22: 655. 27: 543.

— — MacGlashan on. Howitt, 2: 203.

— in 1790. Chamb. J. 43: 584.

— in 19th, and Scotland in 16th, Cent. Tait, 2: 83, 685.

— in 1808. (T. R. Matthews) Ed. R. 12: 336.

— — Newenham on. Ed. R. 14: 151.

— in 1813. Ed. R. 21: 340.

— in 1815 and in 1861. (S. C. Hall) St. James, 2: 235.

— in 1817. Ed. R. 29: 114.

— in 1818, Curwen on. Ecl. R. 29: 43.

— in 1820. Blackw. 7: 637. 8: 190.

— in 1822. Blackw. 12: 153. — Ed. R. 37: 60. — Mo. R. 100: 43.

— — Steven on. Ecl. R. 35: 159.

— in 1823. Blackw. 14: 534. 15: 1, 269.

— — O'Driscol on. Ecl. R. 37: 193.

— in 1824. Blackw. 13: 362. 15: 269.

— in 1825. Ed. R. 41: 357. — Lond. M. 12: 379.

— in 1826. Westm. 7: 1.

Ireland in 1827. Blackw. 22: 18.

— in 1828. Blackw. 24: 453, 550, 752. 25: 72, 193, 401. — Lond. M. 22: 318.

— in 1829. Blackw. 25: 401.

— in 1830. Colburn, 29: 580. — (Lady S. O. Morgan) Colburn, 28: 105.

— in 1831. Quar. 46: 410. — Blackw. 29: 467.

— — and the Reform Bill. Blackw. 30: 52.

— — Political Aspect of. Colburn, 31: 242.

— in 1833, and England in 1819. Dub. Univ. 1: 436.

— — Last Petition of the Irish People. Colburn, 37: 265.

— — Parliamentary Report on State of. Tait, 3: 1.

— — Repeal Question. Dub. Univ. 3: 713.

— in 1834. Fraser, 11: 193, 342. Same art. Mus. 26: 142.

— — Inglis's. Dub. Univ. 5: 1. — Mo. R. 135: 506.

— in 1835, Kennedy on. Mo. R. 138: 119.

— in 1836. Ecl. R. 64: 353. — (W. Sewell) Quar. 56: 219. — Fraser, 13: 181. — Dub. R. 1: 281.

— — Pacata Hibernia. Dub. R. 1: 474.

— in 1837. Blackw. 42: 429. — Dub. R. 3: 15.

— in 1838, Rambles in. Mo. R. 149: 125.

— — Tranquillity in. Blackw. 44: 795.

— in 1840, Registration Bill. Blackw. 48: 135.

— in 1842, Recent Pamphlets on. Dub. Univ. 19: 137.

— in 1843. Dub. R. 15: 148, 317.

— in 1844. (N. W. Senior) Ed. R. 79: 189.

— in 1845. Quar. 76: 247.

— in 1846. Quar. 79: 238. — Blackw. 59: 572. — (J. Moncrieff) No. Brit. 6: 509. — Prosp. R. 3: 1.

— in 1847. (W. Howitt) Howitt, 1: 90. — (J. Moncrieff) No. Brit. 6: 509. — Quar. 82: 266. — (W. Lovett) Howitt, 1: 220. 2: 339.

— — Measures for. Dub. R. 22: 230.
See above, Ireland, Famine in, 1847.

— — Lord Roden's Letter on. (R. H. Horne) Howitt, 1: 48.

— — State of. Quar. 79: 238.

— in 1848. Quar. 83: 584. — Blackw. 64: 480. — (H. Giles) Chr. Exam. 45: 111. — (A. Nicholson) Howitt, 3: 111, 335. — Dub. Univ. 32: 228.

— — Commissions in. Dub. Univ. 31: 389.

— — Crisis in. (Sir C. E. Trevelyan) Ed. R. 87: 229.

— — Miseries of, and their Remedies. Blackw. 64: 658. — (J. P. Thompson) New Eng. 6: 263.

— — State Prosecutions, 1848. Dub. Univ. 31: 785.

— in 1849, Point of Hope in. Chr. Obs. 49: app.

— — Relief of Distress in. Ed. R. 89: 221.

— in 1850. (T. E. C. Leslie) Macmil. 15: 314.

— — Impediments to Prosperity. Dub. R. 28: 399.

— in 1851. Dub. Univ. 37: 285. 38: 107. — Irish Q. 1: 579.

— in 1852. (A. M. Hall) Sharpe, 16: 248, 309. — Dub. Univ. 40: 369.

— in 1853. Westm. 59: 35.

— in 1856. Quar. 102: 59.

— in 1859. New Q. 8: 91. — Dub. Univ. 53: 212.

— in 1860. Dub. Univ. 56: 131. — Brit. Q. 32: 271.

— in 1861. Dub. Univ. 58: 503.

— in 1862. Dub. Univ. 61: 238.

— — Mulgrave's Speech on State of. (T. Hamilton) Ed. R. 66: 450.

— in 1864. Dub. Univ. 64: 110. — Fraser, 70: 663. Same art, Ecl. M. 64: 310.

— in 1865. Dub. Univ. 65: 363

— in 1867. Dub. Univ. 69: 231. — Fraser, 76: 117. — Fortn. 4: 284. — Dub. R. 60: 482. — No. Brit. 48: 243.

— in 1868. Dub. Univ. 72: 112. — (T. E. C. Leslie) Fortn. 9: 131. — Quar. 125: 254.

— in 1869. Quar. 127: 270.

— — and the new Ministry. Dub. R. 64: 203.

— — Situation in. (E. L. Godkin) Nation, 9: 557.

— in 1870. So. R. n. s. 8: 187.

— in 1872. Dub. Univ. 81: 631, 689.

Ireland in 1873. (Goldwin Smith) Contemp. **21**: 503. Same art. Canad. Mo. **3**: 116.
— — Address in Answer to Father Burke. (J. A. Froude) Fraser, **87**: 1.
— in 1874, Visit to. (W. M. Wyse) Cath. World, **21**: 765.
— in 1877. (C. H. Woodman) Appleton, **19**: 326.
— in 1878. (J. W. Kavanagh) Cath. World, **26**: 721.
— in 1879. (E. S. Robertson) Contemp. **36**: 451.
— — Demands of. (H. F. Neville) Dub. R. **85**: 137.
— in 1880. Ed. R. **151**: 99. — (N. Hancock) Fortn. **33**: 1. — (J. A. Froude) 19th Cent. **8**: 341. — (J. McCarthy, C. O'Brien, and Lord Lifford) 19th Cent. **8**: 861. — (H. Innes) Dub. Univ. **95**: 77, 236. — Chamb. J. **57**: 705. — Dub. Univ. **95**: 670.
— — Distress in. Month, **40**: 411. — Dub. R. **86**: 464.
— — and its Origin. Blackw. **128**: 244.
— — Forgotten Aspects of Irish Question. (M. MacColl) Contemp. **37**: 300. Same art. Appleton, **23**: 363.
— — Irish Party in House of Commons. Nation, **30**: 56.
— — Parnell's Mission to America. (E. L. Godkin) Nation, **30**: 23.
— — Poverty and National Distress in. (H. Bellingham) Cath. World, **30**: 610.
— in 1881. (M. MacColl, J. A. Farrer, and Lord Monteagle) Contemp. **39**: 129. — (F. Seebohm, E. D. J. Wilson, and Lord De Vesci) 19th Cent. **9**: 19. — (J. A. Farrar and S. C. Buxton) Contemp. **39**: 249, 288. — (J. H. Tuke, Lord Monteagle, and H. A. Blake) 19th Cent. **9**: 358. — (L. Courtney) Internat. R. **10**: 72, 243. — (W. M. Barbour) New Eng. **40**: 214. — Ed. R. **153**: 274.—Am. Cath. Q. **6**: 316.—St. James, **49**: 301. — (J. P. Ryan) Cath. World, **33**: 836.
— — and the Government. Blackw. **129**: 238.
— — English Panic in regard to. (J. Murdoch) Penn Mo. **12**: 192.
— — Last Chapter of Irish History. (G. C. Brodrick) Fraser, **103**: 100.
— — Parnell's Arrest. (G. D Wolff) Am. Cath. Q. **6**: 746.
— — Truth about. Quar. **151**: 242.
— Independence of. Dem. R. **42**: 271. —Westm. **89**: 344.
— Industrial Condition of. (J. N. Murphy) Dub. Univ. **75**: 445. — (T. Quigley) Am. Cath. Q. **4**: 67.
— — in 1853. Dub. Univ. **42**: 753.
— Industrial Exhibition of, 1853. Dub. Univ. **44**: 283.
— Industrial Museum of. Dub. Univ. **42**: 230.
— Industrial Resources of. Dub. R. **17**: 133. — Dub. Univ. **24**: 175.—(G. P. Bevan) J. Statis. Soc. **44**: 675.
— Industry and Benefactors of. Dub. Univ. **33**: 118.
— Injured. Blackw. **56**: 701.
— Insanity of Party in. Dub. Univ. **7**: 378.
— Intercepted Letters from. Blackw. **31**: 19.
— An Irish Utopia. (A. Church) Contemp. **16**: 71.
— Irish Writers on. Lond. M. **15**: 519.
— Is it irreconcilable? 1870. Dub. R. **66**: 451.
— Island of Saints, Rodenberg's. Cath. World, **14**: 335. — Colburn, **120**: 121.
— Jacobins of. (J. W. Flanegan) 19th Cent. **10**: 785.
— Jacobite Wars of. Dub. Univ. **67**: 699.
— Judicial and Criminal Statistics of. Dub. Univ. **79**: 101.
— Judicial Establishment of. (M. Savage) Fortn. **4**: 129.
— Judges of. (G. Fottrell) Fortn. **23**: 408.
— Justice for, Cheap. Dub. Univ. **37**: 638.
— Justice in, 1837. Tait, n. s. **4**: 781.
— Justice to, 1836. Blackw. **40**: 812. **42**: 828. — Fraser, **13**: 719. **14**: 45.
— — 1881. Dub. R. **88**: 165.
— Kinahan's Geology of. Nature, **19**: 382.
— Kohl on, 1843. Mo. R. **163**:
— Laboring Classes of, Measures for employing, 1839. Dub. R. **6**: 466.
— Land in, Agitation on, 1879. 19th Cent. **6**: 953. — (E. L. Godkin) Nation, **29**: 358.

Ireland, Land in, Agrarian Outrages in 1847. No. Brit. **7**: 505.
— — Bill of 1869–70, Gladstone's. (H. D. Hutton) Fortn. **13**: 377. — (W. O'C. Morris) Fortn. **13**: 487. — Dub. R. **67**: 178. — St. James, **25**: 721. — St. Paul's, **5**: 620. — Fraser, **85**: 296.
— — — Bright Clauses in. (W. T. Thornton) Fortn. **31**: 608.
— — — Working of, 1873. Fraser, **89**: 537.
— — Bill of 1881. (A. G. Rickey and Sir G. Campbell) Fortn. **35**: 543. — (Duke of Argyll) 19th Cent. **9**: 880. — (W. B. Jones) Macmil. **44**: 126. — (M. F. Sullivan) Am. Cath. Q. **6**: 508. — Dub. R. **89**: 220. — (Earl of Derby) 19th Cent. **10**: 473. — Blackw. **129**: 803. **130**: 405.
— — — and the Duke of Argyll. (G. S. Lefevre) 19th Cent. **9**: 1044.
— — — and English Land Question. Westm. **116**: 273.
— — — Emigration and Waste-Land Clauses. (C. O'Brien) Fortn. **35**: 757.
— — — Irish Conservative's View. (A. Traill) Fortn. **35**: 741.
— — Commission on. Dub. Univ. **25**: 471, 618.
— — Confiscation and Compensation. (E. D. J. Wilson) 19th Cent. **10**: 107.
— — Home Rule Policy on, 1874. Dub. Univ. **84**: 104.
— — How the System breeds Disaffection. Fraser, **77**: 259.
— — How to nationalize. (A. R. Wallace) Contemp. **38**: 716.
— — Land League and its Work. (T. P. O'Connor) Contemp. **38**: 981. Same art. Ecl. M. **96**: 243. — Irish Q. **1**: 25, 246. **4**: 103.
— — Legislation on. (Sir G. Campbell) Fortn. **35**: 18.
— — Owners of, 1881. (T. K. Brown) Penn Mo. **12**: 367, 416.
— — Question of, in 1848. Dub. R. **25**: 284.
— — — in 1851. Chamb. J. **16**: 88. — Irish Q. **1**: 97–716. **9**: 584.
— — — in 1853. Dub. Univ. **41**: 122.
— — — in 1864. (J. Godkin) Fortn. **1**: 385.
— — — in 1865. Dub. R. **57**: 453.
— — — in 1868. Lond. Q. **30**: 351.
— — — in 1869. Ed. R. **131**: 256. — Westm. **93**: 89, 408. — Brit. Q. **51**: 1. — Fraser, **81**: 121. — (E. Strachey and J. Hamilton) Macmil. **21**: 170, 279. — (E. L. Godkin) Nation, **9**: 266. — Mo. **12**: 86.
— — — in 1873. Dub. Univ. **83**: 513.
— — — in 1875. (H. de F. Montgomery) Macmil. **32**: 33.
— — — in 1876. (W. B. Jones) Fraser, **94**: 250.
— — — in 1880. (T. E. C. Leslie) Fraser, **102**: 828. — (T. E. C. Leslie) Appleton, **25**: 135. — (L. M. Moffatt) Canad. Mo. **18**: 654. — (P. J. Flattely) Cath. World, **31**: 433. — (H. C. Adams) New Eng. **40**: 68. — (J. McCarthy) Internat. R. **10**: 261. — (C. S. Parnell) No. Am. **130**: 388. — (P. Fitzgerald) 19th Cent. **7**: 493. — (M. Arnold) 19th Cent. **9**: 709, 1026. — (J. C. McCoan) Fraser, **101**: 378.
— — — in 1881. Brit. Q. **73**: 418. — Westm. **115**: 104. — Quar. **151**: 535. —(J. Curran) Canad. Mo **17**: 178.
— — — Literature of, 1869. No. Brit. **51**: 173.
— — — J. S. Mill on. (E. L. Godkin) Nation, **6**: 205.
— — — Pacification of, 1868. Dub. Univ. **71**: 713.
— — Reform in. (J. C. McCoan) Fraser, **101**: 378. — Brit. Q. **72**: 123.
— — Rents, Improvements and Landlords. (M. O'Brien) Fortn. **34**: 409.
— — Tenure of. Brit. Q. **51**: 1. — No. Brit. **51**: 435. — (M. Longfield) Fortn. **34**: 137. — Westm. **93**: 89. — Ecl. R. **82**: 99. — Dub. R. **24**: 349. — (M. F. Sullivan) Am. Cath. Q. **6**: 51. — Tait, n. s. **23**: 221. — Ho. & For. R. **2**: 346.

Ireland, Land in, Tenure of, Lord Dufferin on. Dub. Univ. **70**: 112.
— — — English Tenures. (F. Seebohm) Fortn. **12**: 626.
— — — History of. (J. G. McGee) Cath. World, **10**: 641. *See* Ireland, Tenant Right in.
— Landlords in. Dub. Univ. **28**: 443. **30**: 481.
— — and Mr. Froude. (P. Fitzgerald) 19th Cent. **3**: 1087.
— — and Repealers. Dub. Univ. **21**: 156.
— — and Tenants. Blackw. **55**: 638.
— — — in 1852. Dub. Univ. **39**: 133.
— — — in 1869. Dub. R. **65**: 443. **66**: 165.
— — — in 1880. Ed. R. **154**: 274.
— Law and Lawyers of. (R. S. Mackenzie) Nat. Q. **13**: 348.
— — of Tithes in. Dub. Univ. **5**: 79.
— Law Courts and Lord Brougham. Dub. Univ. **33**: 478.
— Laws of, Ancient. (J. G. McGee) Cath. World, **13**: 635. — Dub. Univ. **67**: 3. **75**: 161. — Cath. World, **2**: 129. **30**: 785. — (D. Fitzgerald) Fraser, **97**: 458.
— — Brehon. Dub. R. **68**: 385.
— Lecky on. (E. L. Godkin) Nation, **14**: 122.
— Legislation for. (Lord Sherbrooke) 19th Cent. **8**: 677.
— Letter on, 1813. Chr. Obs. **12**: 356.
— Letters from. (J. Carne) Colburn, **51**: 160, 449. **52**: 100, 315. **54**: 14. **55**: 33, 404. **56**: 121. **57**: 230. **58**: 224.
— Liberal Interest in. Dub. Univ. **12**: 249.
— Liberal Party in. Dub. R. **52**: 279.
— Liberty in. Brownson, **6**: 58.
— Life in. St. Paul's, **6**: 200.
— — Anecdotes of. (B. Murphy) So. M. **14**: 243.
— — Novels descriptive of. Ed. R. **52**: 410.
— — Old. Dub. Univ. **52**: 438. **77**: 361.
— — Realities of, Trench's. Quar. **126**: 61. Same art. Liv. Age, **100**: 579. — Ed. R. **129**: 102. — Fraser, **79**: 80. — Chr. Obs. **69**: 433.
— — Sketches of. Quar. **81**: 417. — Once a Week, **27**: 423–547. **28**: 60–452.
— Little. Good Words, **20**: 857.
— Loan Fund of. Chamb. J. **34**: 219.
— Locke on Recovery of. Ecl. R. **102**: 38.
— Lone Woman in. (Mrs. J. G. Cloud) Harper, **47**: 863.
— Lord Chancellors of, 1187–1870. (O. J. Burke) Dub. Univ. **75**: 646. **76**: 54–635. **77**: 31–662. **78**: 61–635. **79**: 28–613. **80**: 38–665. **81**: 35.
— — Lives of. Ed. R. **134**: 44. — Quar. **130**: 164. Same art. Liv. Age, **108**: 643.
— — — O'Flanagan's. (J. G. McGee) Cath. World, **13**: 228.
— Lord-Lieutenant of. What is Use of? Fraser, **12**: 475.
— Lords-Lieutenant of. (S. O. Morgan) Colburn, **25**: 105.
— Macaulay's Treatment of. Dub. R. **40**: 156.
— Mackenzie's Travels in. Walsh's R. **4**: 284.
— Madden's Revelations of. Dub. Univ. **31**: 1, 382.
— Madden's United Irishmen. Dub. Univ. **20**: 485. **22**: 685. **28**: 536.—Ecl. R. **76**: 400. — Tait, n. s. **9**: 578.
— Manufactures of. Peop. J. **7**: 271.
— — in 1852. Irish Q. **3**: 785.
— — Revival of. (M. F. Sullivan) Am. Cath. Q. **6**: 668.
— Martin's Ireland before and after the Union. Tait, n. s. **15**: 413.
— Martyrs of, O'Reilly's Memorials of. (J. G. Shea) Cath. World, **8**: 838.
— Medical Charities of. Brit. & For. R. **8**: 557. — Dub. Univ. **20**: 88.
— Members of Parliament from, in 1852. Dub. Univ. **39**: 769.
— Memorandums in, 1852. Lond. Q. **1**: 68.
— Military Trials in. Dub. Univ. **68**: 107. Same art. Ecl. M. **67**: 437
— Misery of, Causes of. Ed. R **41**: 356. Same art. Selec. Ed. R. **6**: 334.
Ireland, Miseries and Beauties of, 1838. Dub. R. **4**: 407.
— Misgovernment of. Brit. & For. R. **4**: 517.
— Missions to, in the early Ages. (R. Anderson) Bib. Sac. **25**: 346.
— Modern Usages of, classically illustrated. Dub. Univ. **10**: 449.
— Moral State of, in 1833. Dub. Univ. **1**: 349.
— Mount Mettray and the Blackwater. (J. Ryan) Cath. World, **30**: 389.
— Municipal Corporation Bill. Blackw. **41**: 813.
— Municipal Government. Westm. **48**: 82.
— Municipal Reform. Dub. Univ. **15**: 599.
— Music of, Ancient. Dub. Univ. **17**: 1. **90**: 754.
— — — Petrie's. Fraser, **58**: 111.
— My Expedition to. (G. Montagu) Dub. Univ. **44**: 310.
— Names of Places in. (W. Allingham) Fraser, **79**: 780.
— National Library for. Dub. Univ. **29**: 80.
— National Manuscripts of, Fac-Similes of. (C. A. Cole) Cath. World, **20**: 102, 213.
— Native and Saxon, O'Connell's Memoir of. Mo. R. **160**: 480.
— Natural History in, Progress of. Dub. Univ. **10**: 87.
— Needs of, and their Remedies. (H. M. Hyndman) Fortn. **33**: 208.
— New. Month, **8**: 154.
— New Nostrum for. Blackw. **129**: 655.
— New Year's Eve in. Ev. Sat. **9**: 98.
— Nooks and Corners of. St. James, **42**: 307.
— North of, Peep at. (G. W. Beers) Lippinc. **27**: 321. — Once a Week, **27**: 95.
— of the Irish. (M. C. O'C. Morris) Contemp. **21**: 252.
— Ogham Pillar Stones in. (H. M. Westropp) Anthrop. J. **2**: 201.
— Old. Belgra. **25**: 126.
— — and young. Dub. Univ. **21**: 65.
— Orange and Ribbon in. All the Year, **15**: 513.
— Orange Conspiracy, 1835. Tait, n. s. **2**: 569.
— Orange Lodges in. Blackw. **39**: 209. — Quar. **86**: 228.
— Orangeism in, History and Character of. (E. I. Sears) Nat. Q. **18**: 79.
— Orangemen of. Dub. Univ. **35**: 254. *See also* Orange.
— Ordnance Memoir on, 1844. Dub. R. **16**: 501. — Dub. Univ. **23**: 494.
— Orators of, Curran. Lond. Q. **8**: 473.
— Our Watering-Place in. Bentley, **63**: 503.
— Paddiana. Quar. **81**: 417.
— Pagan State of. Dub. Univ. **76**: 139.
— Parliament of. (W. M. Brady) Contemp. **10**: 263, 357.
— — Last Days of. (S. W. Young) Canad. Mo. **16**: 10.
— Parties in, Orange and Green. Penn Mo. **2**: 464.
— Past and Future of. Dub. Univ. **81**: 531.
— Peasant Proprietorship in. (M. O'Brien) Fortn. **34**: 579. — (J. H. Tuke) 19th Cent. **8**: 182. — (E. L. Godkin) Nation, **31**: 163. — Month, **40**: 442.
— Peasantry of. Quar. **68**: 337. — Anal. M. **5**: 265. — Select J. **2**: [48. — Dub. Univ. **2**: 509. — Am. Q. Reg. **5**: 207. — So. R. n. s. **15**: 117. — Tait, **1**: 151.
— — Education of. Blackw. **15**: 495.
— — Mrs. Hall's Stories of. Dub. Univ. **14**: 477.
— — Sketches of. Quar. **68**: 336. — Mus. **44**: 153.
— — Traits of. Ed. R. **96**: 384.
— Peat-Fuel of. Penny M. **13**: 414.
— Peerage of. Once a Week, **13**: 369.
— Penal Laws of. Dub. Univ. **10**: 205, 339.
— Perraud on. Ho. & For. R. **1**: 289.
— Pictures of. (J. H Browne) Harper, **42**: 496. — Tait, n. s. **3**: 141.
— Picturesque and romantic, 1838. Tait, n. s. **4**: 684.
— Pilgrimages in, 1850. House. Words, **2**: 29.
— Miss Plumptre's Residence in. Quar. **16**: 337.

Ireland, Plymouth Brethren and Lay Preaching in. Lond. Q. **27**: 1.
— Policy for. Fraser, **88**: 273.
— Policy in, English. Fraser, **87**: 778.
— — Gladstone's, 1869. Dub. R. **64**: 452.
— — in 18th Century. (J. Morley) Fortn. **17**: 196.
— — Last Instalment of, 1870. — (J. L. Whittle) Fraser, **83**: 273.
— — of the Disraeli Administration, and its Results, 1868. (W. O'C. Morris) Fraser, **78**: 143.
— — of the Whigs. Brit. & For. R. **10**: 246.
— — Peel's. Dub. Univ. **26**: 253.
— — wanted. Dub. R. **56**: 423. **58**: 485.
— Politics in; an Election in the Forties. (W. Carleton) Dub. Univ. **30**: 176, 287.
— — in 1822–23. Blackw. **14**: 534. **15**: 1.
— — in 1829. Blackw. **26**: 934.
— — in 1831; Elections. Colburn, **32**: 1.
— — in 1832; Reform Bill. Tait, **1**: 503, 633, 768.
— — in 1833. Dub. Univ. **2**: 602.
— — in 1838. Dub. R. **5**: 116.
— — in 1847; Relief Measures. Fraser, **35**: 370. — Dub. Univ. **29**: 656.
— — in 1848. Blackw. **63**: 113.
— — in 1849; Spirit of recent Legislation. Dub. R. **27**: 345.
— — in 1850. Dub. R. **29**: 96.
— — in 1868; Case of, before Parliament. Dub. R. **62**: 498.
— — — Debates on. St. James, **22**: 365.
— — in 1869. (E. L. Godkin) Nation, **8**: 390.
— — in 1870; the Irish Caldron. Quar. **128**: 251.
— — in 1871, in Parliament. Brit. Q. **54**: 485.
— — in 1873; at Election Time. Fraser, **88**: 158.
— — in 1874; the Elections. Fraser, **89**: 389. **92**: 233.
— — in 1879. (T. Quigley) Am. Cath. Q. **4**: 415. — (E. D. J. Wilson) 19th Cent. **6**: 1068.
— — Irish Churchman's View of. (J. J. Murphy) Contemp. **10**: 53.
— — Irish Proceedings. Colburn, **23**: 289–385.
— — Old Election Days. Cornh. **12**: 165.
— Poor of. Pamph. **29**: 457. — Quar. **46**: 390.
— — Condition of, 1828. Lond. M. **20**: 177.
— — — in 1835. Ecl. R. **63**: 144.
— — Perils of. Dub. Univ. **1**: 73. Same art. Mus. **23**: 49.
— — Self-supporting Institutions for. Penny M. **8**: 171.
— — State of. Dub. Univ. **7**: 349.
— Poor Laws of. Brit. & For. R. **4**: 1. — No. Brit. **12**: 21. — (W. Empson) Ed. R. **59**: 227. — (N. W. Senior) Ed. R. **84**: 267. — Blackw. **27**: 748. **33**: 811. — Mo. R. **121**: 309. — Dub. Univ. **31**: 537. **35**: 137. **57**: 709. **58**: 60. — Irish Q. **1**: 700. **7**: 88.
— — and the Times, 1846. Dub. Univ. **33**: 221, 401.
— — Bill of 1836. Dub. R. **2**: 51.
— — Bill of 1849. Dub. Univ. **10**: 69.
— — Peel on Confiscation. Dub. Univ. **33**: 508. *See also* Poor Laws.
— Popery in. *See* Ireland, Catholic Church in.
— Popular Superstitions of. Dub. Univ. **33**: 541, 707.
— Pothien-Still-Wake. Colburn, **5**: 442.
— Poverty in. Quar. **55**: 50.
— — and National Distress. (H. Bellingham) Cath. World, **30**: 610.
— — Romance of. Chamb. J. **8**: 171.
— Presbyterians in. (J. Godkin) Fortn. **3**: 89.
— Presbyterian Church in. (C. Porter) Dub. Univ. **84**: 205. — (J. A. Alexander) Princ. **31**: 717.
— — Endowed. Ecl. R. **83**: 385.
— — in 1830. Cong. M. **14**: 1.
— Press of. (T. F. O'Donnell) Gent. M. n. s. **10**: 223.
— — National. (P. H. Bagenal) Temp Bar, **60**: 326.
— Priests in. Fraser, **7**: 251.
Ireland, Priests in, in Politics. Fraser, **81**: 491. — Dub. R. **71**: 103, 257. **72**: 119. — Fraser, **81**: 44. — Westm. **68**: 340.
— — Provision for. Cong. M. **27**: 1.
— — Sketches of. Colburn, **23**: 259–515.
— Prison System of. (A. G. Sedgwick) Nation, **1**: 659.
— Prisons of. Dub. Univ. **85**: 641.
— Proprietorship in. Dub. Univ. **32**: 356.
— Proselytism in. Irish Q. **8**: 144, 709, 1345.
— Prosperity in, Statistics of. Dub. Univ. **52**: 712.
— Protestants of. Fraser, **15**: 49.
— — Dialogue between Head and Heart. Dub. Univ. **2**: 586.
— — Duties of. Dub. Univ. **26**: 114, 601.
— — Emigration of. Dub. Univ. **1**: 471. **4**: 1.
— — Lord Mulgrave and. Dub. R. **4**: 246.
— — Peel's Policy toward. Dub. Univ. **26**: 253.
— Protestant Affairs of, 1832. Blackw. **31**: 77.
— Protestant Assoc. and Catholics in. Dub. R. **1**: 499.
— Protestant Clergy of. Blackw. **43**: 805.
— Protestant Deputation from. Blackw. **37**: 210.
— Protestant Missions in. (H. Bellingham) Month, **37**: 258.
— Protestant Movements in, 1834. Dub. Univ. **4**: 333.
— — in 1837. Dub. Univ. **9**: 1.
— Protestant Proselytism in. (H. Bellingham) Cath. World, **32**: 621.
— Protestantism in. Ecl. R. **85**: 322.
— Provision Trade of, 1866. Fraser, **74**: 674.
— Quakerism in. (R. Bagwell) Temp. Bar, **61**: 384.
— Queen's Colleges in. Dub. R. **72**: 77. — Dub. Univ. **39**: 707. — Am. J. Educ. **9**: 579. — Lond. Q. **3**: 373.
— Queen's County. Dub. Univ. **44**: 256–649.
— Question of. (M. H. Seymour) Contemp. **5**: 502.
— — by a Continental Observer. Contemp. **40**: 756.
— Question of Questions. (W. Howitt) Peop. J. **1**: 251.
— Race Question in. (J. W. Jackson) Anthrop. R. **7**: 54.
— Railroads in. (Sir F. B. Head) Quar. **63**: 1. Same art. Mus. **35**: 451. — Dub. Univ. **13**: 376. **19**: 124. — (R. Hudson) Gent. M. n. s. **2**: 413.
— — and Canals in. Brit. & For. R. **8**: 245.
— — Commission on. Ed. R. **69**: 156.
— — Extension of. Dub. Univ. **82**: 129.
— — in 1836. Dub. R. **1**: 221.
— — in 1838. J. Statis. Soc. **1**: 257.
— — in 1839. Dub. R. **6**: 207.
— Rambles in. St. James, **47**: 266. **48**: 55.
— Recent Pamphlets on. Dub. Univ. **18**: 765. **19**: 137.
— Recollections of. Dub. Univ. **84**: 253.
— Records of. Dub. Univ. **29**: 312. — Dub. R. **52**: 318.
— Redistribution of Seats in. Fraser, **90**: 122.
— Regium Donum in. Ecl. R. **80**: 1.
— Religious History of, Godkin's. Dub. Univ. **82**: 251.
— Religious Revival in, 1860. Univ. Q. **19**: 5.
— Religious State of, Report of Hibernian Society on, 1807. (J. Foster) Ecl. R. **6**: 1096.
— Religious Struggle in. (H. Bellingham) Cath. World, **30**: 720. — (J. MacCarthy) Cath. World, **31**: 83.
— Religious Superstitions of. (Mrs. C. A. White) Sharpe, **35**: 243.
— Repeal Agitation in. (J. W. Croker) Quar. **75**: 222. — (E. A. Grattan) No. Am. **51**: 187. — Dem. R. **13**: 115. — Ed. R. **79**: 98. — Quar. **46**: 410. **72**: 300. **75**: 119. **76**: 133. — Brit. & For. R. **15**: 406. **16**: 616. — Brownson, **2**: 398. — Westm. **40**: 50. — Blackw. **34**: 573. **35**: 204, 386. **38**: 715. **54**: 264, 679. **55**: 518. — Dub. Univ. **21**: 759. **22**: 106, 240. **23**: 119, 394. **24**: 431. — Fraser, **3**: 1. **9**: 253. — Am. Ecl. **2**: 25. — Ecl. Mus. **3**: 369. — Ecl. M. **3**: 415. — Pamph. **6**: 421.
— Representatives of. Dub. Univ. **29**: 386.
— a Reproach to England. Blackw. **128**: 775.

Ireland, Resources and Commerce of. (E. Williams) Hunt, **7**: 160. — Dub. Univ. **2**: 433, 665. — Brit. Q. **2**: 353.
— Retribution due to. Dub. R. **5**: 496.
— Revolution in, The true. (J. E. McGee) Cath. World, **25**: 551.
— Revolutions in, Political and natural. Ed. New Philos. J. **25**: 324.
— Rinuccini's Nunciature in. Dub. R. **16**: 519.
— Rise and Fall of Irish Nation. Tait, **3**: 711.
— Rivers of. Dub. Univ. **26**: 315, 430. **27**: 31, 280, 427. **28**: 25, 399, 601. **29**: 175, 341, 764. **30**: 717. **31**: 626, 697. **34**: 665. **38**: 233. **42**: 208, 323, 391. **45**: 707. **46**: 621, 685.
— — Spenser on. (P. W. Joyce) Fraser, **97**: 315.
— Roman Intercourse with. Anthrop. R. **4**: 180, 366.
— Round Towers of. (T. Harmer) Arch. **9**: 268. — Dub. R. **19**: 1. — Dub. Univ. **3**: 375. **25**: 379. **77**: 560. — (T. Moore) Ed. R. **59**: 143. — Quar. **76**: 354. — Irish Mo. **7**: 533.
— Royal Constabulary of. Tinsley, **4**: 525.
— Run around. St. Paul's, **7**: 131.
— Rural Affairs of. Mo. R. **120**: 359.
— Rural Life in. Dub. Univ. **75**: 234.
— Scenes in. (J. L. Spalding) Cath. World, **24**: 384, 591. — (Mrs. C. Lilly) Cath. World, **28**: 261, 530. **29**: 202. — Am. Mo. M. **8**: 113.
— Scenery of. Art J. **5**: 198.
— — and other Things Irish. Blackw. **31**: 379.
— — and Society of. Dub. Univ. **8**: 112, 315.
— Schoolmaster and Priest in. Fraser, **87**: 385.
— Science and Art in. Nature, **13**: 309, 349, 370.
— Seditious Literature of. Dub. Univ. **31**: 159.
— Senior's Journals in. Ed. R. **128**: 324. — Dub. R. **64**: 1.
— Serpents, Absence of, from. (S. Pegge) Arch. **5**: 160.
— Shadow Land of. St. James, **10**: 320.
— Shamrockiana. Cornh. **20**: 666. **21**: 48, 167, 299.
— Simplicius on. Blackw. **7**: 637.
— Sins and Hopes of. Fraser, **41**: 721.
— Sketches in. Tait, n. s. **6**: 475, 685. **7**: 606. — (G. B. Whannel) Tait, n. s. **12**: 418, 497, 554. — Peop. J. **4**: 199, 256, 319.
— — on Highways in. (Mrs. S. C. Hall) Colburn, **42**: 190, 432. **43**: 17, 207. **44**: 81, 216. **45**: 182. — Blackw. **25**: 466, 565, 771. **26**: 72, 201. Same art. Mus. **14**: 530. **15**: 181, 233.
— Small Farmers of. (S. O'Grady) Fortn. **33**: 568. — Liv. Age, **145**: 407.
— Goldwin Smith on. Brit. Q. **35**: 87.
— Social Condition of. Dub. Univ. **27**: 633. — Chr. Rem. **8**: 456.
— — Gamble on. (J. Foster) Ed. R. **18**: 229.
— Social Disorganization in. Dub. Univ. **27**: 121.
— Social Life in, Ancient. Dub. Univ. **81**: 121, 241.
— Social, Political, Religious. Dub. Univ. **14**: 107, 210. — Ed. R. **119**: 279.
— Social Progress of. Ed. R. **106**: 99.
— Social Science and sunny Scenes in. Bentley, **51**: 162.
— Social State of. (W. B. Jones) Macmil. **42**: 227.
— Society in. Dub. Univ. **8**: 658.
— — and Manners in the North of. Anal. M. **14**: 354.
— — in the last Century. (E. Wilson) Lippinc. **20**: 183.
— Soldier's Life in. Lond. M. **17**: 191.
— South of. Colburn, **129**: 174, 309.
— — Lady Chatterton's Rambles in. Dub. Univ. **14**: 97.
— — Legends and Traditions. Blackw. **18**: 55.
— — Letters from, 1881. Irish Mo. **9**: 430, 480.
— Southwest Coast of. Bentley, **30**: 204.
— Sporting in. Dub. R. **10**: 382.
— Sportsman in. Dub. Univ. **16**: 23.
— State Labor in. Brit. & For. R. **7**: 128.
Ireland, State Papers of, 1509–73. Dub. Univ. **56**: 435.
— State Trials in. Ecl. M. **1**: 391, 452. **2**: 72, 226.
— — in 1844. Dub. R. **16**: 373. **17**: 198.
— — in 1848. Dub. Univ. **25**: 11. **32**: 599. — No. Brit. **9**: 541.
— Statistical and Political, Wakefield on. Ecl. R **17**: 229.
— Statistical Survey of. Dub. Univ. **6**: 313.
— Statistics of, 1855. Dub. Univ. **45**: 243.
— — Mason's. Quar. **13**: 76.
— Sufferings of. (W. N. Pendleton) So. R. n. s. **2**: 3. — Fraser, **83**: 378.
— — and their Remedy. (H. Snow) Mo. Rel. M. **4**: 543. — Blackw. **64**: 658.
— — Relief of, 1849. Ed. R. **89**: 221.
— Sugar Culture in. (J. Sproule) Dub. Univ. **83**: 129.
— Sullivan's New. (E. L. Godkin) Nation, **26**: 29.
— Survey of, 1655. Irish Q. **2**: 217.
— Survival of. (M. F. Sullivan) Am. Cath. Q. **3**: 104.
— Tales of. Mo. R. **135**: 75.
— Taxation in. Irish Q. **3**: 883. **9**: 1114.
— — Why exempted from Income Tax. Dub. R. **13**: 155.
— Temperance Movement in, 1840. Dub. R. **8**: 448.
— Tenant Compensation in, 1866. Ed. R. **125**: 187.
— Tenant Right in. Dub. Univ. **53**: 242.
— — in 1851. Dub. Univ. **37**: 159.
— — in 1854. Fraser, **49**: 234.
— — in 1866. Westm. **86**: 1.
— — in 1879. Fraser, **100**: 351.
— Terrorism in, 1877. Dub. Univ. **89**: 390.
— Thuggee in, 1862. All the Year, **7**: 374.
— Tithes in, 1832. Tait, **1**: 94.
— — the Cause of Discontent, 1834. Tait, **4**: 119, 386.
— — Question of, 1836. Ed. R. **63**: 156 — Niles's Reg. **37**: 61.
— Topography of. Dub. Univ. **37**: 327.
— Tour in. All the Year, **1**: 210.
— — An old. (W. Walsh) Cath. World, **21**: 497.
— — in Connaught. Fraser, **20**: 728.
— Tours, in 1848–49. Quar. **85**: 491.
— Townsend's Tour through. Blackw. **11**: 291.
— Tracts on, 1822. Mo. R. **98**: 57.
— Traveling in. Chamb. J. **14**: 157.
— — Progress of. Dub. Univ. **41**: 472.
— — Reminiscences of. Blackw. **19**: 267.
— Turn through Gaelic, 1872. (J. F. Campbell) Fraser, **88**: 50.
— Twaddling Tourists of. Dub. Univ. **24**: 504, 740.
— Two ancient Works of Art in. (Miss Stokes) Arch. **43**: 131.
— Two Aspects of. House. Words, **4**: 6, 27.
— Two Tourists in. Fraser, **80**: 178.
— — Third Tourist in. Fraser, **80**: 575.
— Ulster and its People. Fraser, **94**: 219. Same art. Liv. Age, **131**: 159.
— under Lord Clarendon, 1847–52. Dub. Univ. **39**: 237, 373.
— under Lord Mulgrave. Brit. & For. R. **4**: 517. — Dub. Univ. **9**: 577. — Ed. R. **66**: 220.
— under Lord Normanby, 1838. Dub. Univ. **13**: 520.
— under ordinary Law. Blackw. **129**: 269.
— under the Triple Alliance, 1839. Blackw. **45**: 212, 341.
— under the Whigs. Ecl. R. **88**: 613.
— Union in, Experiences of. Dub. Univ. **33**: 774.
— — Repeal of. Colburn, **83**: 347.
— Universities in. Irish Q. **1**: 222.
— — and English Universities. Dub. R. **1**: 68.
— — Attempts at Legislation on. Fraser, **87**: 514.
— — Bill of 1873. Cong. **2**: 247. — Dub. R. **72**: 448.
— — Bill of 1879. Quar. **148**: 289.
— — Proposed Roman Catholic University. Fraser, **84**: 481. — (J. L. Whittle) Fraser, **77**: 433.

Ireland, Universities in, Question of. (H. D. Hutton) Fortn. 16: 748. — (E. D. J. Wilson) 19th Cent. 6: 322. — Fraser, 85: 55. — Nation, 29: 108.
— — Reform in. Dub. Univ. 80: 455.
— University Education in. Contemp. 2: 435. — (J. E. Cairnes) Theo. R. 3: 116. — Ed. R. 135: 166. — Brit. Q. 70: 463. — Ho. & For. R. 2: 32.
— — and the Ministerial Crisis, 1873. Westm. 99: 529. — Quar. 134: 255.
— — Secularization of. Fraser, 81: 408.
— Viceroys of. Dub. Univ. 53: 361. — Dub. R. 58: 36.
— — Gilbert's History of. Dub. Univ. 66: 466.
— Viceroyalty in. Irish Q. 1: 134.
— vindicated, Carey's. Anal. M. 13: 417.
— Volcanoes in. (D. T. Ansted) Intel. Obs. 6: 174.
— Wakefield's. (Sir J. Mackintosh) Ed. R. 20: 346.
— — Misrepresentations of. Colburn, 2: 101.
— Wanderings in North of. Dub. Univ. 56: 259-678.
— Wants of. (A. Arnold) Gent. M. n. s. 23: 683.
— — in 1841. Dub. R. 10: 218.
— Waste Lands in. Dub. R. 39: 290.
— — Clearances and Improvements of. Westm. 50: 163.
— Watering Places of. Broadw. 1: 196.
— Weddings and Wakes in. Dub. Univ. 88: 292.
— West of, Excursions in. Tait, n. s. 10: 654.
— — Letters from. Tait, n. s. 13: 651, 792.
— — — 1865. Month, 2: 557.
— — Rambles in. Dub. Univ. 41: 79, 492.
— — Wanderings in. Tait, n. s. 2: 726.
— What Bianconi did for. (S. Smiles) Good Words, 15: 23, 114.
— What is to be done for? Fraser, 27: 235.
— What Nature has done for. Chamb. J. 6: 261.
— What shall we do for? Quar. 124: 255.
— What will become of? Blackw. 21: 61.
— Why is it as it is? Blackw. 22: 237. — (W. B. Jones) Macmil. 43: 125.
— Why it has been misgoverned. Internat. R. 11: 185.
— Wicklow Country. (H. S. Fagan) Contemp. 5: 362.
— Wild. (B. Dombavand) Lippinc. 7: 345, 502, 599. 8: 135-343.
— Wiseman's Tour in, 1858. Dub. R. 46: 499.
— Wits and Worthies of. Dub. Univ. 81: 697.
— Woes and Wants of. Dub. Univ. 75: 568.
— Women of. Dub. Univ. 13: 591. — Hogg, 4: 344.
— Works on. Blackw. 15: 544.
— Wrongs of, and English Remedies. St. James, 22: 246.
— — Economic. (R. E. Thompson) Penn Mo. 5: 713.
— — Proposed Remedies of. (J. H. Stack) Fortn. 8: 621.
— Yeomanry of. Tait, 1: 437.
— Young. (P. J. Smyth) Fortn. 34: 696.
— — and the Ireland of To-Day. (J. MacCarthy) Cath. World, 33: 39.
— — and John Mitchell. Gent. M. n. s. 14: 593
— — and O'Connell. Month, 41: 123.
— — The Felon's Track. Dem. R. 26: 133.
— — Poetry of. No. Brit. 35: 415.
See Killarney, *and other local names.*
Ireland's Mission. (W. M. Brady) Cath. World, 11: 193.
Ireland's Worthies; a Poem. Dub. Univ. 87: 532.
Irish, The Ancient. (D. Fitzgerald) Fraser, 92: 97.
— Anderson's Historical Sketches of. Ecl. R. 48: 343.
— at Home and abroad. Ed. R. 127: 502.
— Character of. (M. C. O'C. Morris) Contemp. 20: 104. — Dub. Univ. 20: 422.
— — Sketches of. Ecl. R. 53: 520.
— Characteristics of. (N. F. Davin) Dark Blue, 1: 732. — Lond. Soc. 39: 123. — Chr. Rem. 26: 431. Same art. Liv. Age, 41: 3.
— Customs and Superstitions of. Anal. M. 3: 456.
— Dewar on. Ecl. R. 16: 1195.
— Food of. (W. R. Wilde) Dub. Univ. 43: 127, 317.
Irish, The, in England. (J. O'C. Power) Fortn. 33: 410.
— in the U. S. (J. A. Froude) No. Am. 129: 519. — (E. A. Grattan) No. Am. 52: 191. — (Mrs. J. Sadlier) Cath. World, 6: 765. — All the Year, 21: 510. — Brownson, 12: 538. — Colburn, 125: 71. — Dub. R. 3: 452.
— — and Scotch. (D. E. Nevin) Mercersb. 3: 239.
— — Colonies of. (S. Byrne) Cath. World, 32: 346.
— — — in Illinois. (W. J. Onahan) Cath. World, 33: 157.
— — Maguire's. (J. Morley) Fortn. 9: 220. — Chr. Obs. 68: 561.
— in England. Dub. R. 41: 470.
— in Spain. Dub. Univ. 48: 281.
— Native. Lond. M. 22: 236.
— on Continent in early Middle Ages. Chr. Rem. 43: 467.
— Sketches of. Fraser, 4: 100.
— Stories about Paddy. Tait, 3: 54.
— Thebaud on the Irish Race. Brownson, 22: 488.
— Writers on. Dub. Univ. 1: 31. Same art. Mus. 23: 35.
Irish Academy Museum. Chamb. J. 29: 163.
Irish Acquaintance, Conversations with. Chamb. J. 13: 91-251. 14: 251-396.
Irish Adventurer; a Sketch. Dub. Univ. 77: 264.
Irish Agent, With an. All the Year, 41: 344.
Irish All-Souls Night. (C. Clive) St. James, 1: 40.
Irish and Highland Fictions, Identity of. Dub. Univ. 72: 585.
Irish Archæological Publications. Dub. Univ. 52: 629.
Irish Archæological Society. Dub. Univ. 17: 647.
Irish Archæology. (A. Clive) Dub. Univ. 88: 641.
Irish Army List of James II. Dub. R. 49: 190.
Irish Art. Dub. Univ. 52: 197.
— Ancient. (L. Jewitt) Art J. 28: 133, 177. 29: 174-366.
— at the Royal Academy. Dub. Univ. 84: 225.
Irish Assizes, Notable. All the Year, 19: 595.
Irish Ballads. Dub. Univ. 30: 127. 61: 442. — Dub. R. 19: 373. — Blackw. 84: 462. — Liv. Age, 47: 798.
— Modern Street. (A. M. Williams) Nation, 6: 135. — Liv. Age, 112: 308.
— Popular. Bentley, 14: 549.
Irish Ballad-Singers. Liv. Age, 32: 481.
Irish Bards, Four. Dub. Univ. 50: 143.
Irish Bardic Poetry. (A. M. Williams) Cath. World, 31: 791.
Irish Biography, Webb's. (E. L. Godkin) Nation, 27: 58.
Irish Book, Word about. Fraser, 2: 312.
Irish Books and Manuscripts, Old. (W. Dowe) Nat. Q. 36: 332.
Irish Brigade in the Service of France, 1698-1791. Fraser, 86: 732. Same art. Liv. Age, 116: 216. — Dub. R. 73: 145. — (J. G. McGee) Cath. World, 12: 313.
Irish Bulls. Chamb. J. 56: 702. — Chamb. J. 43: 539. Same art. Ev. Sat. 2: 273.
— Edgeworth's Essay on. (Syd. Smith) Ed. R. 2: 398.
Irish Chartered Schools, Abuses of. Ed. Mo. R. 1: 295.
Irish Chieftains. Dub. Univ. 81: 158.
— Home Life of. Dub. Univ. 53: 460.
— Inauguration of. Dub. Univ. 56: 529.
— "They were a great people, sir." (W. F. Butler) Contemp. 40: 93.
Irish Children's first Communion; a Poem. (M. Russell) Irish Mo. 5: 192, 254, 337.
Irish Cloak. Penny M. 11: 401-497.
Irish College at Paris. (R. F. Farrell) Cath. World, 33: 404.
Irish Constabulary, Royal. Chamb. J. 44: 667.
Irish Constituency. Dub. Univ. 5: 369.
Irish Convict Prisons at Smithfield. (M. Carpenter) Once a Week, 6: 11, 176, 664.
Irish Convicts' Progress. All the Year, 8: 31.
Irish Corporation Reform Bill. Dub. Univ. 7: 412.

Irish Cottagers. Mo. R. **122**: 505.
Irish Countess, Secret History of an. Dub. Univ. **12**: 503.
Irish Country Dance, Visit to an. Once a Week, **27**: 213.
Irish Court; a Tale. Belgra. **20**: 46.
Irish Courts of Quarter Sessions. Ed. R. **52**: 478.
Irish Courting, Old-fashioned. Liv. Age, **15**: 462.
Irish Discontent, past and present. Dub. Univ. **79**: 343.
Irish Doctor, Experiences of an. Chamb. J. **56**: 588.
Irish Domesday Book. (W. O'C. Morris) Fortn. **26**: 364.
Irish Donation to New England, 1676. (C. Deane) N. E. Reg. **2**: 245, 398.
Irish Election in Time of the Forties. Dub. Univ. **30**: 176, 287.
Irish Eloquence. Mo. R. **90**: 337.
— and Curran. (G Croly) Ex. H. Lec. **8**: 187.
Irish Emigrant Society. Niles's Reg. **14**: 211.
Irish Evidence, McCulloch's. Blackw. **19**: 55.
Irish Fair, Run through an. Once a Week, **27**: 251.
Irish Fairy Lore and Demonology. Dub. Univ. **64**: 640. **64**: 203, 243. — Quar. **32**: 197.
Irish Farmer's Sunday Morning; a Poem. (M. Russell) Irish Mo. **7**: 96.
Irish Female Writers. Dub. Univ. **3**: 431.
Irish Folk-Books of the last Century. Dub. Univ. **67**: 532. Same art. Cath. World. **3**: 679.
Irish Folk-Lore, Beasts, Birds, and Insects in. (L. McClintock) Belgra. **40**: 87. Same art. Ecl. M. **94**: 78.
Irish Fools, Sketches of. (T. C. Grattan) Colburn, **40**: 9.
Irish Forty-Shilling Freeholders. Blackw. **22**: 53. — (T. P. Thompson) Westm. **10**: 525.
Irish Garland. Blackw. **33**: 87.
Irish Garrison Tale. Dub. Univ. **38**: 49.
Irish Girl; a Tale. (C. M. Sedgwick) Dem. R. **10**: 129.
Irish Grievance Debates. Dub. Univ. **22**: 177.
Irish Heart, An. (T. W. Higginson) Scrib. **17**: 217.
Irish Hedge-Poets. (N. Williams) Cath. World, **26**: 406.
Irish Hedge-School. Dub. Univ. **60**: 600.
Irish Heiress; a Miniature Comedy. (R. Mulholland) Irish Mo. **9**: 236, 289.
Irish Highwayman. All the Year, **29**: 133.
Irish Historical Literature. Irish Q. **1**: 192, 409.
Irish Humor and Pathos. Westm. **32**: 405.
Irish Idiosyncrasies. Argosy, **20**: 137.
Irish Idyll. Belgra. **38**: 199.
Irish Ignis Fatuus. (E. D. J. Wilson) 19th Cent. **6**: 322.
Irish Iliad, An. Tinsley, **27**: 517.
Irish Laborers. Westm **22**: 65.
Irish Language. Portfo.(Den.) **12**: 409, 480. **13**: 333, 528.
— Ancient. Dub. Univ. **3**: 535.
— — Alphabet of. (C. Vallancey) Arch. **7**: 276.
— and Literature. Dub. R. **16**: 463.
— Dictionary of, Vallancey's Prospectus of an. Ed. R. **2**: 116.
Irish Law Students, Calamities of. Lond. M. **14**: 553.
Irish Lawyers and Statesmen of a bygone Generation. Macmil. **11**: 190.
— and Witnesses. Liv. Age, **34**: 589.
Irish League. Dub. Univ. **32**: 115.
Irish Legends. All the Year, **42**: 473, 583.
— of the 1st Century. Dub. Univ. **72**: 243.
Irish Linen Manufacture. Dub. Univ. **85**: 624.
Irish Literature. Irish Q. **4**: 241. — No. Brit. **24**: 117.
— Ancient. Lond. Q. **34**: 94.
— Ancient Historical. Dub. R. **50**: 475.
— Curiosities of. Dub. Univ. **9**: 341, 546.
— Historical Sketch of. Dub. Univ. **78**: 1.
— Miscellany of the Celtic Society. Dub. R. **31**: 53.
— Past and Present of, 1837. Dub. Univ. **9**: 365.
Irish Lyrics. Lond. Q. **10**: 343.
Irish Magic, Ancient. Dub. Univ. **63**: 148, 424.
Irish Mail, Her Majesty's. All the Year, **1**: 283.
Irish Mandarin. (J. B. O'Meara) Bentley, **12**: 600.
Irish Martyrs, and English. Month, **9**: 455.
Irish Metropolitan Conservative Society. Dub. Univ. **8**: 738.
Irish Melodies, Moore's. Westm. **3**: 115. — Mo. R. **87**: 419. — Blackw. **11**: 62.
— Mulligan's. Blackw. **10**: 613.
Irish Minstrelsy. Colburn, **117**: 30, 181. — Dub. Univ. **3**: 465. — Mo. R. **129**: 69. — (T. C. Croker) Fraser, **1**: 191, 314, 580. **2**: 41. **8**: 127.
— Hardiman's. Fraser, **15**: 555.—Dub. Univ. **4**: 152–514.
Irish Mule-Driver; a Poem. (S. Lover) Once a Week, **16**: 93.
Irish Mystery, An. Lond. Soc. **37**: supp. 90.
Irish Names, and their Metamorphoses. (G. Shee) Month, **43**: 327.
— Old. Dub. Univ. **74**: 324.
Irish National Song. Fraser, **3**: 537.
Irish National Tales. Westm. **9**: 422.
Irish Nationalism, Basis of. (R. Bagwell) Dub. Univ. **90**: 93.
Irish Nationality. Fraser, **85**: 525.
Irish Novels. Ed. R. **43**: 356.
— and Novelists. Dub. R. **4**: 495.
Irish Novelists; Didactic. Dub. Univ. **26**: 737.
Irish Orators; Curran. Lond. Q. **8**: 473. Same art. Ecl. M. **42**: 40.
Irish Oratory. Ed. R. **25**: 389.
— and Catholic Emancipation. Pamph. **10**: 141.
Irish Oyster-Eater's Account of himself. Blackw. **45**: 47–761.
Irish Poets. Irish Q. **5**: 697. — (C. C. Leeds) Dem. R. **29**: 258–522.
— and Poetry. Am. Whig R. **12**: 77, 141.—Bib. R. **3**: 61.
— Recent minor. (C. P. Mulvany) Canad. Mo. **16**: 130.
Irish Poetry. Irish Q. **7**: 313. **8**: 1325.
— Classical Verse. (T. H. L. Leary) Dark Blue, **1**: 791.
— Jacobite and later Celtic. (A. M. Williams) Cath. World, **33**: 626.
— Recent, 1865. Dub. R. **56**: 302.
Irish Points for English Meditation. Month, **7**: 481.
Irish Political Novels. Dub. Univ. **14**: 333.
Irish Poplin Trade. (C. Drew) Pract. M. **3**: 52. — Belgra. **15**: 307.
Irish Popular Songs. Dub. Univ. **14**: 91. — Mus. **36**: 225. — Blackw. **13**: 209. **17**: 318. — Tait, n. s. **6**: 287. — Dub. R. **22**: 317.
— Croker on. Mo. R. **148**: 560.
Irish Popular Superstitions. Dub. Univ. **35**: 82.
Irish Poverty. Quar. **55**: 50.
Irish Presbyterian Assembly. Ecl. R. **84**: 585.
Irish Pride. (E. Noble) Colburn, **159**: 165–634. **160**: 63–657. **161**: 65, 194.
Irish Priest. Tait, n. s. **14**: 425.
Irish Priests and English Landlords. Blackw. **39**: 689.
Irish Protestant, Letters from an. Dub. Univ. **8**: 367.
Irish Radicals and Irish Ideas. Fortn. **36**: 267.
Irish Reapers. (O'Hara Family) Tait, n. s. **5**: 271.
Irish Reformers, Early. Dub. Univ. **1**: 343.
Irish Rebels, and the Power of Great Britain. Fraser, **16**: 105.
Irish Republicans, and Gen. Washington. Hist. M. **15**: 201.
Irish Records. Dub. Univ. **29**: 314.
Irish Sketch, An. Chamb. J. **6**: 177.
Irish Sketch Book, Thackeray's. Dub. Univ. **21**: 647. — Fraser, **27**: 678.
Irish Songs. Bentley, **14**: 307. — Liv. Age, **35**: 484.
Irish Star Chamber. (R. Bagwell) Dub. Univ. **89**: 222.
Irish Story, An. Dub. Univ. **75**: 607.
Irish Story; a Poem. Dub. Univ. **86**: 354.
Irish Storyists; Lover and Carleton. Dub. Univ. **4**: 298.
Irish Street Songs. All the Year, **23**: 615.

Irish Superstitions. (P. McTeague Bentley, 9: 188. — Dub. Univ. 33: 541, 707.
Irish Surgeons, Great. (E. D. Mapother) Irish Mo. 6: 12–221.
Irish Tale, An. Dub. Univ. 37: 519, 602, 703.
Irish Tales. Blackw. 39: 689.
Irish Theatricals. Dub. Univ. 35: 117, 362.
Irish Tourists. Fraser, 15: 765. — Dub. Univ. 35: 1–383.
Irish Traits. Chamb. J. 55: 494, 588. 56: 253.
Irish Trinitarians, Lopez on. Dub. R. 67: 299.
Irish Tutorship, My. Fraser, 20: 667. 21: 33, 274.
Irish Union. Blackw. 34: 573. 35: 204, 386.
Irish Volunteers. (F. R. Killough) Cath. World, 10: 276.
Irish Vote and English Parties, 1879. Nation, 29: 8.
Irish Wake, Humors of an. Dub. Univ. 60: 145.
Irish Wedding; a Sketch. Dub. Univ. 60: 359.
Irish Wheat and Tares. Bentley, 63: 162.
Irish Widow; a Tale. Chamb. J. 55: 746, 761.
Irish Yeoman. Blackw. 23: 735, 875.
Irishman in Canada, Davin's. Canad. Mo. 12: 660.
Irishmen. Blackw. 14: 534.
Irishwomen, Illustrious. Dub. Univ. 90: 636.
Irenæus, St., of Lyons. (C. J. H. Ropes) Bib. Sac. 34: 284.
— and early Christianity. (J. Quarry) Brit. Q. 70: 96, 311.
— and Gnosticism. Dub. R. 76: 56.
— and Infant Baptism. (W. R. Powers) Am. Presb. R. 16: 239.
— Champion of Truth and Peace. (J. Tulloch) Good Words, 2: 388.
— Life of. Chr. Obs. 4: 1, 65, 129.
— Testimony to early Christianity. (J. Quarry) Brit. Q. 70: 96.
— Witness of, to Catholic Doctrine. Dub. R. 79: 117.
— Works of. Chr. Rem. 35: 402. — Ecl. R. 100: 257. — Chr. Obs. 68: 262.
Irene; a Tale. Lippinc. 6: 376, 491, 625. 7: 68, 203.
Irené; a Poem. Cornh. 5: 478.
Irene the Missionary. Atlan. 43: 426–759. 44: 64–598.
Irenics and Polemics. (J. F. Clarke) Chr. Exam. 57: 163.
Irétaba, a Mohave Chief. (C. G. Leland) Temp. Bar, 48: 330.
Irido-Platinum. Nature, 20: 341.
Iris; a Poem. (B. Taylor) Atlan. 29: 655.
Iris of Homer and Bow of Genesis. (W. E. Gladstone) Contemp. 32: 140.
Iron. Am. Q. 9: 352.
— Ancient Family of. (H. Wright) Once a Week, 15: 438, 459.
— and Carbon, Compounds of. (A. Gurlt) J. Frankl. Inst. 62: 335, 396.
— — Limits of Combination of. Pract. M. 5: 183.
— and Civilization. (A. S. Hewitt) Pop. Sci. Mo. 1: 339.
— and Coal. (J. Western) Lakeside, 3: 197.
— — as Factors of Wealth. Bank. M. (N. Y.) 32: 17.
— — Trade of Pennsylvania in, Statistics of, 1846. J. Frankl. Inst. 42: 124.
— and Ironworkers. (J. C. Tildesley) Gent. M. n. s. 6: 263.
— and the Smith. Ecl. Engin. 12: 142.
— and Steel. (R. Hunt) Pop. Sci. R. 1: 61. — (W. M. Williams) Nature, 2: 322, 363. 3: 211–410. 4: 226. — Ecl. Engin. 5: 609. — Quar. 120: 64.
— — Action of Acids on. (W. H. Johnson) Ecl. Engin. 10: 511.
— — — of Hydrogen and Acids on. (W. H. Johnson) Nature, 11: 393. Same art. Ecl. Engin. 12: 502. — (J. Parry) Ecl. Engin. 25: 162.
— — — of certain Solutions on. Pract. M. 5: 268.
— — at high Temperatures, Strength of. (C. R. Roelker) J. Frankl. Inst. 112: 241.
Iron and Steel at low Temperatures. (J. J. Webster) Ecl. Engin. 23: 298.
— — Carbon and Silicon in. Ecl. Engin. 5: 70.
— — Chromium and Aluminium in. (A. A. Blair) Am. J. Sci. 113: 421.
— — Coating with Copper. Pract. M. 5: 230.
— — Corrosion of, prevented. (F. S. Barff) Ecl. Engin. 18: 350.
— — a costly Fallacy. (W. M. Williams) Ecl. Engin. 3: 517.
— — Direct Process in Production of. (C. M. Du Puy) J. Frankl. Inst. 104: 377. 106: 404. — (C. M. Du Puy) Ecl. Engin. 11: 346. — (T. S. Blair) Pract. M. 5: 324. Same art. Ecl. Engin. 13: 313. — Ecl. Engin. 3: 232, 355. 9: 112. 25: 292. — (C. W. Siemens) Nature, 16: 467. — (C. W. Siemens) Ecl. Engin. 18: 40. — Pract. M. 1: 351. 7: 245.
— — Fuel and Process employed in the Production of. Pract. M. 7: 85.
— — in 1876. Ecl. Engin. 16: 31.
— — Hardening of. (R. Akerman) Ecl. Engin. 22: 485.
— — Influence of intense Cold on. Ecl. Engin. 4: 487.
— — Malleable, Manufacture without Fuel. (H. Bessemer) J. Frankl. Inst. 62: 267, 285. 68: 390. 69: 193.
— — Manufacture of. (T. Gill) J. Frankl. Inst. 1: 47–224. — Mo. R. 131: 158.
— — — Improvements in. (R. Akerman) Ecl. Engin. 19: 459. — (A. Laugel) J. Frankl. Inst. 58: 117. — (C. W. Siemens) Pract. M. 1: 305.
— — — in America. Ecl. Engin. 12: 300.
— — — in India, 1828. (F. Buchanan) J. Frankl. Inst. 5: 394. 7: 7.
— — Physical Changes in. Ecl. Engin. 21: 511.
— — Production of. Pract. M. 7: 346.
— — — in America. J. Frankl. Inst. 108: 194.
— — Soldering. Pract. M. 4: 22.
— — Strength of. Ecl. Engin. 3: 172.
— — Working. (C. Varley) J. Frankl. Inst. 14: 110–273.
— — Wrought, Tensile Strength of. (D. Kirkaldy) J. Frankl. Inst. 75: 310, 397. 76: 116.
— and Steel Armor Plates. Ecl. Engin. 21: 28.
— and Steel Constructions, Strength of. (J. J. Weyrauch) Ecl. Engin. 16: 442, 512.
— and Steel Industries. (D. Forbes) Ecl. Engin. 8: 132, 310.
— — of foreign Countries. (D. Forbes) Ecl. Engin. 5: 133, 234.
— — Progress of. (D. Forbes) Ecl. Engin. 9: 417. 11: 168, 537.
— and Steel Institute. (J. Mayer) Nature, 2: 394. 3: 470. 4: 361. 5: 417. 6: 326. 10: 377. 12: 28, 432.
— — Annual Meeting, 1873, Address at. (I. L. Bell) Ecl. Engin. 9: 34.
— — — at Barrow-in-Furness, 1874. Pract. M. 4: 262.
— — — — Address at. (I. L. Bell) Ecl. Engin. 11: 39.
— — — 1875, Address at. (W. Menelaus) Ecl. Engin. 13: 56.
— — — 1879, Address at. (E. Williams) Ecl. Engin. 21: 63.
— and Wages, Future of. (A. S. Hewitt) Ecl. Engin. 12: 3.
— Anthracite. J. Frankl. Inst. 30: 405.
— as a constructive Material. (C. H. Driver) Ecl. Engin. 13: 371. — Ecl. Engin. 3: 180. 4: 279. 16: 470. 19: 254. — Westm. 51: 104.
— — for Railroad Structures. J. Frankl. Inst. 49: 289, 361. 50: 361.
— Bessemer Process. Chamb. J. 26: 311. 27: 361.
— — complete. Ecl. Engin. 14: 538.
— — Generation of Heat in. (R. Akerman) Ecl. Engin. 7: 530.

Iron, Bessemer Process, Researches in. (W. M. Williams) Ecl. Engin. **14**: 333.
— — Spectrum of the Flame. (H. Wedding) Ecl. Engin. **2**: 449. — (J. M. Silliman) Am. J. Sci. **100**: 297.
— — under Pressure. Ecl. Engin. **2**: 225.
— Blast Furnace for smelting. (J. L. Smith) Am. J. Sci. **51**: 172. **52**: 95. — (S. S. Haldeman) Am. J. Sci. **56**: 74. — (M. L. Gruner) Ecl. Engin. **8**: 354, 450, 548. — (J. L. Smith) J. Frankl. Inst. **42**: 197, 261.
— — and Cupola. (A. Laird) Ecl. Engin. **9**: 256.
— — Charcoal. (G. Fraser) Ecl. Engin. **7**: 126.
— — Chemical Changes in. (C. R. A. Wright) Ecl. Engin. **12**: 461.
— — Closed Hearth. Ecl. Engin. **12**: 415.
— — Economy of. Ecl. Engin. **1**: 698. **3**: 83. — (T. M. Drown) Ecl. Engin. **6**: 230.
— — Schinz. Ecl. Engin. **2**: 28.
— — Tuyères for. (F. Buttgenbach) Ecl. Engin. **8**: 486.
— Breaking Weight of. J. Frankl. Inst. **71**: 34.
— — of Rolled, Experiments on. (F. A. Paget) J. Frankl. Inst. **77**: 368.
— Casson-Dormoy Puddling-Furnace. (E. F. Smith) Ecl. Engin. **15**: 51. — Pract. M. **5**: 262.
— Cast, Composition of. (M. E. Fremy) J. Frankl. Inst. **72**: 33, 259, 342.
— — Dilatation of, and Phenomena of Crane Ladle. (R. Mallet) J. Frankl. Inst. **99**: 156.
— — Durability of. (G. J. C. Dawson) Ecl. Engin. **5**: 316.
— — — in Sea Water. (E. B. Webb) J. Frankl. Inst. **74**: 327.
— — for Engineering Purposes. (J. S. Brodie) Ecl. Engin. **22**: 17.
— — Fracture of. Ecl. Engin. **22**: 507.
— — Malleable. (A. Ott) Ecl. Engin. **2**: 122, 381.
— — Manufacture of, Roberts. Pract. M. **4**: 353.
— — Method of refining. (Sir F. C. Knowles) Ecl. Engin. **10**: 113.
— — Methods of treating in the Foundry. (L. Colburn) J. Frankl. Inst. **80**: 41.
— — Mixing of. (T. D. Wilson) Ecl. Engin. **15**: 40.
— — Porosity of. Ecl. Engin. **6**: 134.
— — Treatment of melted. (R. Mushet) J. Frankl. Inst. **83**: 32.
— Casting under Compression. Pract. M. **2**: 158.
— Changes in internal Structure of. (C. Hood) J. Frankl. Inst. **35**: 118.
— Chemical Changes in Manufacture of. (F. C. Colvert) J. Frankl. Inst. **64**: 339.
— Chemistry of. (F. A. Abel) J. Frankl. Inst. **63**: 58.
— Chronic Decomposition of. (E. F. Smith) Am. J. Sci. **115**: 198.
— Cleveland and the World's Trade. Ecl. Engin. **13**: 28.
— Coating with Zinc, Copper, etc. (F. Pellatt) J. Frankl. Inst. **39**: 407. **40**: 66.
— Corrosion of. Ecl. Engin. **4**: 517. **25**: 75.
— — in Boilers. (B. F. Isherwood) J. Frankl. Inst. **108**: 80.
— — in Railway Bridges. (W. Kent) Pract. M. **5**: 265. — (W Kent) J. Frankl. Inst. **99**: 437.
— — in Ship-Plates. Ecl. Engin. **2**: 476.
— — Prevention of. (Prof. Barff) Ecl. Engin. **16**: 300. **20**: 438.
— Corrugated, Strength of. (J. E. Hart) Ecl. Engin. **1**: 129, 202.
— Crisis in, and its Lesson, 1880. Ecl. Engin. **23**: 236.
— Dephosphorization of. (R. Pink) Ecl. Engin. **23**: 214, 497. — (F. Gautier) J. Frankl. Inst. **109**: 83. **110**: 34, 87.
— — Basic Process of. (J. Reese) J. Frankl. Inst. **111**: 137.

Iron, Dephosphorization of, Basic Process of, Bessemer Plant adapted to. (A. L. Holley) J. Frankl. Inst. **111**: 25. — (A. L. Holley) Ecl. Engin. **24**: 37.
— Deterioration of, in Marine Steam Boilers. (J. A. Tobin) Ecl. Engin. **23**: 355.
— Early Uses of. (S. J. V. Day) Ecl. Engin. **9**: 230. **11**: 481.
— Effects of Cold on. Ecl. Engin. **1**: 532.
— — of Magnetization on. (A. M. Mayer) Am. J. Sci. **106**: 81.
— — of Strain on. (C. Huston) J. Frankl. Inst. **107**: 41.
— Electro-Deposition of. Pract. M. **6**: 31.
— Experiments on, McIntyre. (W. R. Johnson) J. Frankl. Inst. **27**: 1.
— Facts about. Intel. Obs. **5**: 419.
— Forging, Hints on. Ecl. Engin. **8**: 448. **9**: 32.
— Founding. Ecl. Engin. **1**: 705. — J. Frankl. Inst. **36**: 56–246.
— Fuchs's Method for the Determination of. (J. R. Brant) Am. J. Sci. **68**: 227.
— Fuel required to make a Ton of. Ecl. Engin. **7**: 315.
— Furnace Boilers. Ecl. Engin. **2**: 162.
— Geological Relations of. Ecl. Engin. **2**: 17.
— History of Decarburizing. Ecl. Engin. **1**: 193–709.
— Impurities in. (T. Rowan) Ecl. Engin. **1**: 551.
— in Dolerytes from New Hampshire. (G. W. Hawes) Am. J. Sci. **113**: 33.
— in the United States. (J. H. Lanman) Hunt, **6**: 511. — Hunt, **58**: 261.
— — Industry of, 1855. (Prof. Wilson) J. Frankl. Inst. **59**: 201.
— — Supply and Manufacture of. (J. S. Newberry) Internat. R. **1**: 754.
— Inoxidation of. (L. M. Stoffel) Ecl. Engin **21**: 13.
— Italian. All the Year, **12**: 391.
— Machine for bending and straightening. Pract. M. **6**: 92.
— Magnetic Strains in. (A. S. Kimball) Am. J. Sci. **118**: 99.
— Malleable, Bessemer's Improvements in making. J. Frankl. Inst. **63**: 133.
— — Manufacture of. (R. W. Davenport) Am. J. Sci. **104**: 270.
— — Transverse Strength of. (P. Barlow) J. Frankl. Inst. **20**: 58–264.
— Manufacture of. (A. Aikin) J. Frankl. Inst. **2**: 74. — (A. W. Humphreys) Ecl. Engin. **4**: 145. — Hunt, **28**: 764 — Niles's Reg. **38**: 349. — Quar. **109**: 105. Same art. Liv. Age, **69**: 609.
— — American. (R. W. Raymond) Atlan. **40**: 525. — Ecl. Engin. **15**: 274.
— — — Anthracite. (H. Fairbairn) J. Frankl. Inst. **47**: 393.
— — — in the West. O. & N. **6**: 488.
— — — Statistics of. Ecl. Engin. **3**: 467.
— — Direct Process. (C. M. Du Puy) J. Frankl. Inst. **112**: 1.
— — from Pig to Puddled Bar. Ecl. Engin **7**: 149.
— — Gilchrist's Process. Ecl. Engin. **25**: 61.
— — Henderson's Process. Ecl. Engin. **4**: 82.
— — Improvements in. (J. D. M. Stirling) J. Frankl. Inst. **56**: 36, 93.
— — in Great Britain, 1846. J. Frankl. Inst. **43**: 210.
— — — in 1870. (R. H. Thurston) J. Frankl. Inst. **91**: 29–320.
— — — Wilkie's. Liv. Age. **54**: 298.
— — in New South Wales. (H. L. Damsel) J. Frankl. Inst. **49**: 339.
— — in Pennsylvania. Hunt, **25**: 298. — (C. E. Smith) Hunt, **25**: 574, 656. — J. Frankl. Inst. **51**: 69.
— — in Russia. Ecl. Engin. **16**: 218.

Iron, Manufacture of, in Scotland. No. Brit. **4**: 126.
— — in South Wales. Westm. **50**: 76.
— — Novelty Works, N.Y. (J. Abbott) Harper, **2**: 721.
— — Processes and Products of. (C. W. Siemens) Ecl. Engin. **17**: 75.
— — with Coke and Gas. Ecl. Engin. **9**: 312.
See Iron and Steel.
— Metallurgy of. (R. Mallet) Ecl. Engin. **6**: 116. — Ecl. Engin. **8**: 243.
— Molecular Changes in. (R. H. Thurston) Ecl. Engin. **9**: 169, 237.
— — produced by Variations of Temperature. (R. H. Thurston) J. Frankl. Inst. **96**: 187, 269.
— Native, from Liberia, Africa. (A. A. Hayes) Am. J. Sci. **71**: 153.
— Notes on. (T. Morris) Ecl. Engin. **10**: 200.
— Octahedral Oligist. (T. S. Hunt) Am. J. Sci. **63**: 370.
— of the Pharaohs. (C. W. Vincent) Ecl. Engin. **9**: 103.
— Overstrain of. (R. H. Thurston) Ecl. Engin. **19**: 534.
— Oxalate of. (H. Croft) Canad. J. n. s. **6**: 18.
— Oxidation of. (F. G. Calvert) Ecl. Engin. **8**: 127. — Pract. M. **7**: 117.
— — Experiments in. (F. C. Calvert) Pract. M. **1**: 46.
— — Preservation from. Ecl. Engin. **23**: 255. — J. Frankl. Inst. **34**: 206, 279.
— Oxides of. (F. Kuhlmann) J. Frankl. Inst. **69**: 381.
— Pennsylvania Memorial on. So. Q. **22**: 1.
— Phosphorus in. Ecl. Engin. **18**: 64.
— — and Sulphur in, Removal of. (J. Hargreaves) Ecl. Engin. **3**: 588. — (G. J. Snelus) Ecl. Engin. **21**: 116.
— Pig, Manufacture of. Ecl. Engin. **1**: 140, 323.
— — Production of, in U. S., 1872-73. Ecl.Engin. **11**: 369.
— — Silicon in. (E. H. Morton) Ecl. Engin. **12**: 180.
— — Trade of Scotland in. (J. S. Jeans) Pract. M. **1**: 241.
— Preservation and Purity of. Ecl. Engin. **3**: 527.
— — from Rust. Chamb. J. **55**: 541.
— Produce of the World, Statistics of. Pract. M. **4**: 138.
— Production of. (W. H. Merritt) Canad. Mo. **16**: 32.
— — Statistics and Geography of. De Bow, **21**: 578. — (A. S. Hewit) De Bow, **22**: 44.
— Proto-Carbonate of, in Coal Measures. (W. B. Rogers) Am. J. Sci. **71**: 339.
— Puddling. (R. Lester) Ecl. Engin. **3**: 132. — Ecl. Engin. **21**: 520.
— Puddling and Fuel-saving. Ecl. Engin. **12**: 362.
— — Furnaces for. Ecl. Engin. **3**: 40.
— — or Refining. (G. A. Scherpf) Hunt, **19**: 447.
— — past and present. (P. Roberts) J. Frankl. Inst. **110**: 49.
— Railroad, Duty on. (M. Tarver) West. J. **12**: 77.
— — Manufacture of, in the U. S. Hunt, **16**: 97, 530.
— Resistance of, to Projectiles, Properties of. (W. Fairbairn) J. Frankl. Inst. **74**: 261, 319.
— — to Strain. Ecl. Engin. **9**: 113.
— Russia Sheet, Manufacture of. Ecl. Engin. **25**: 473.
— Silica and Titanium in. (T. M. Drown and P. W. Shimer) J. Frankl. Inst. **111**: 18.
— Smelting, Chemical Phenomena of. (I. L. Bell) Ecl. Engin. **6**: 407.
— — Past and Present of. (S. J. T. Day) Ecl. Engin. **9**: 494.
— Spongy. Ecl. Engin. **13**: 301.
— Strength of. (D. Mushet) J. Frankl. Inst. **35**: 134.
— — Laws of. J. Frankl. Inst **63**: 196.
— — Safe Load and ultimate. (Z. Colburn) J. Frankl. Inst. **76**: 195, 312.
— Technology of. Ecl. Engin. **14**: 460.
— — Recent Developments in. Ecl. Engin. **12**: 439.
— Testing, by Electro-Magnetism. (A. Herring) Ecl. Engin. **20**: 405.
— Texture of, Researches on. (M. Janoyer) J. Frankl. Inst. **98**: 134, 212.
Iron, Theory of the hot Blast. (I. L. Bell) Ecl. Engin. **6**: 545, 631.
— Uses and Manufacture of. Ed. R. **116**: 204.
— Warner Process. Ecl. Engin. **12**: 33.
— Welding. (R. Howson) Ecl. Engin. **15**: 525. — Ecl. Engin. **16**: 325. — (R. Howson) Ecl. Engin. **17**: 10.
— Working of Blast Furnaces with raw Coal. Ecl. Engin. **9**: 24.
— Wrought, Crystalline Fracture of. (M. A. Malberg) J. Frankl. Inst. **42**: 119, 185. — (R. Mallet) J. Frankl. Inst. **67**: 392. **68**: 154.
Iron Abutments. Ecl. Engin. **5**: 34.
Iron Age. Chamb. J. **41**: 535.
— Latest Promise of. Liv. Age, **52**: 173.
Iron Bars, Effects of Magnetization on. (A. M. Mayer) Am. J. Sci. **105**: 170.
Iron Beams, Forged, Experiments upon. Ecl. Engin. **2**: 561.
Iron Casket; a Tale of the Travaux Forcés. Belgra. **1**: 111, 238, 361.
Iron Castings, Hardness of. (R. Tyler) J. Frankl. Inst. **17**: 150.
— Ornamental. Art J. **10**: 220. **32**: 117.
— Real Reasons why they are accurate Copies of Mold. (R. Mallet) J. Frankl. Inst. **98**: 340.
Ironclads and Guns of the Future. (W. N. Hutchinson) Macmil. **42**: 280.
— and heavy Ordnance. (A. L. Holley) Atlan. **11**: 85.
— and Torpedoes. Blackw. **123**: 153.
— Dangers and Warnings of the Inflexible. (Sir R. S. Robinson) 19th Cent. **3**: 278.
— English. Chamb. J. **54**: 759. — Gent. M. n. s. **4**: 653. — Ecl. Engin. **8**: 443. — Cornh. **3**: 192. **4**: 715. **5**: 550. **23**: 55. — Temp. Bar, **1**: 232.
— Engines for. Pract. M. **4**: 50.
— for Coast Defense. Cornh. **2**: 493.
— Loss of the Captain. All the Year, **24**: 493.
— Merrimac and Monitor. Quar. **111**: 562.
— of Russia, Circular. (Adm. Popoff) Ecl. Engin. **12**: 492. — Ecl. Engin. **14**: 243. *See* Popoffkas.
— Peep into the inner Life of. Lond. Soc. **33**: 407.
— Question of. Ecl. Engin. **10**: 74.
— Turret. Chamb. J. **44**: 536. *See* Ships.
Iron-clad Field Artillery. (C. B. Brackenbury) 19th Cent. **4**: 40.
Iron-clad Forts. Cornh. **17**: 189.
Iron Cross, Decoration of. Ev. Sat. **9**: 612.
Iron Electrotype. Ecl. Engin. **6**: 14.
Iron Furnaces, Location of. (H. Fairbairn) J. Frankl. Inst. **48**: 393.
— of Malabar, and their Produce. Pract. M. **3**: 105.
Iron Gate; a Legend of Alderley. Blackw. **45**: 271.
Iron Horse; a Poem. (D. March) Knick. **14**: 413.
Iron Industry and Coal Supply. (I. L. Bell) Ecl. Engin. **10**: 401.
Iron Implements found in ancient Mine in North Carolina. (F. W. Simonds) Am. Natural. **15**: 7.
Iron Manufacture in Scotland. No. Brit. **4**: 126.
Iron Mask. (J. G. Meline) Cath. World, **10**: 754. **11**: 87. — Ed. R. **138**: 301. — Ecl. M. **80**: 747.
— Guess at. Ecl. M. **82**: 243.
— Man in. Cornh. **21**: 333. Same art. Ecl. M. **74**: 599. — (A. Blackwell) Once a Week, **3**: 242. Same art. Liv. Age, **67**: 230. — (E. Lawrence) Harper, **43**: 98. — Ev. Sat. **9**: 251. — (M. Topin) Cornh. **21**: 333. — Ed. R. **30**: 357. — Quar. **34**: 19. — So. Lit. Mess. **13**: 173. — Mo. R. **109**: 106. — N. Ecl. **6**: 376.
— — Is the Mystery solved? (J. F. Meline) Hours at Home, **10**: 553.
— New Guess at. Ev. Sat. **15**: 685.
— Story of. Ed. R. **138**: 301. Same art. Liv. Age, **119**: 579.
Iron Masks, Men in. Temp. Bar, **35**: 172.
Iron Masters' Trade Union. (F. Harrison) Fortn. **1**: 96.

Iron Mines and Works of the United States. (I. L. Bell) Ecl. Engin. 13: 35.
— of Antrim. (R. A. Watson) Dub. Univ. 83: 1.
Iron Monk. (A. LaForge) Overland, 11: 310.
Iron Monk; a Tale. Eng. Dom. M. 18: 98.
Iron Mountains of Missouri. (L. Feuchtwanger) Hunt, 16: 95.—(L. Grosvenor) Putnam, 3: 296.—(H. Cobb) West. J. 14: 124.
Iron Ore in Guerero, Mexico. (N. S. Manross) Am. J. Sci. 89: 309.
— Magnetic, of N. J. (J. C. Smock) Ecl. Engin. 13: 217.
— — Searching for, with Magnetic Needle. (J. C. Smock) Ecl. Engin. 16: 262.
— of Samakoff, Properties of. (W. Fairbairn) J. Frankl. Inst. 40: 190.
Iron Ores and Anthracites, Analysis of. (W. R. Johnson) J. Frankl. Inst. 28: 73, 289.
— Geol. Relations of. (W. W. Smyth) Ecl. Engin. 13: 83.
— in Azoic System. (J. S. Whitney) Am. J. Sci. 72: 38.
— of Marquette, Mich. (J. P. Kimball) Am. J. Sci. 89: 290.
— of Sweden. (C. Smith) Ecl. Engin. 13: 159.
— Reduction of. (W. W. Mather) Am. J. Sci. 24: 213.
Iron Pillars, Experiments with. (J. D. Crehore) Ecl. Engin. 19: 360.
Iron-Puddlers and Iron-Smelters. Fraser, 90: 55.
Iron Pyrites, Analysis of Magnetic. (M. H. Boye) Am. J. Sci. 63: 219.
— Sources and Uses of. (J. A. Phillips) Pop. Sci. R. 18: 114.
Iron Rails, Manufacture and Endurance of. (W. E. C. Coxe) Ecl. Engin. 15: 332.
— and Steel Rails, Manufacture of. (J. B. Pearse) Ecl. Engin. 11: 341.
— Test of. Ecl. Engin. 4: 137.
— Wear of. (W. E. C. Coxe) J. Frankl. Inst. 108: 125.
Iron Ring. St. James, 25: 626.
Iron Ring. Harper, 1: 808.
Iron Safe; a Poem (G. C. Swayne) Once a Week, 16: 734.
Iron Shields and Forts. Cornh. 17: 189.
Iron Ships and Bridges. (J. W. McGauley) Intel. Obs. 10: 257.
— and Shipbuilding. Ecl. Engin. 2: 357.
— Durability of. (Sir W. Fairbairn) Ecl. Engin. 9: 146.
Iron Shroud. (W. Mudford) Liv. Age, 59: 101.
Ironsides, Old. (J. F. Cooper) Putnam, 1: 473, 593.
Iron-Sponge Manufacture, Blair's. Ecl. Eng n. 11: 363.
Iron Steed. (P. K. Kilbourn) So. Lit. Mess. 10: 671.
Iron Structures, Preservation of. Ecl. Engin. 11: 50.
— Stability of. (W. M. Williams) Ecl. Engin. 10: 336.
Iron Surfaces, Preservation of. Ecl. Engin. 6: 245. 23: 145.
Iron Trade. (E. A. J. Merchant) Hunt, 12: 224.
— American, 1878. Ecl. Engin. 20: 215.
— and, Mineral Trades in the North of England. (T. Fenwick) Pract. M. 1: 208.
— British. Ecl. Engin. 17: 367.
— Cleaveland, and John Vaughan. Pract. M. 2: 241.
— of Europe and the U. S. (C. C. Childs) Hunt, 16: 574.
— of Pennsylvania, 1844–46. Hunt, 16: 201.
— of Sweden and Norway. Hunt, 6: 425.
— of the United States. (M. Tarver) West. J. 5: 143.
— of the World, Scrivenor's History of. Mo. R. 156: 183.
— Romance of. Once a Week, 13: 240.
— Statistics of. (H. Clarke) J. Frankl. Inst. 29: 211.
— Technical Education for. (J. Jones) Pract. M. 6: 323.
Iron Trade Association, British, Address before. (G. T. Clark) Ecl. Engin. 14: 427.
Iron Tubes, Strength of. Ecl. Engin. 5: 481.
Iron War Ships. All the Year, 6: 104.
— and heavy Ordnance. Temp. Bar, 5: 183.
See also Ironclads.
Iron Welcome; a Story. All the Year, 47: 154.
Ironwork, Ancient and modern. Am. Arch. 2: 181.
— Art. (M. Mauris) Art J. 31: 202, 228.
— Art of painting. Pract. M. 5: 9.
— Notes on. (G. Smith) Ecl. Engin. 22: 200.—(G. Smith) Am. Arch. 7: 6.
— Ornamental. (P. E. Chase) J. Frankl. Inst. 103: 355.
— Practical. Ecl. Engin. 11: 416.
Iron Workers, English. (A. Wynter) Once a Week, 10: 142.
Iron Works, Derbyshire, Day at. Penny M. 13: 73.
— Glasgow, Port Washington, Ohio. Pract. M. 4: 308.
— in New England. (J. Leonard) N. E. Reg. 11: 289.
— Low Moor. Lond. Soc. 36: 343.
— Millwall. Once a Week, 12: 566.
— Salisbury, Conn. (C. U. Shepard) Am. J. Sci. 19: 311.
— Use of heated Air in. (P. A. Dufrenoy) J. Frankl. Inst. 19: 122–415.
— Yorkshire. Chamb. J. 44: 220.
Irony, German School of. Blackw. 38: 376.
— Notes on. Chr. Obs. 69: 285.
— of Life. Blackw. 122: 411.
— Use of. Bib. Sac. 25: 537.
Iroquois Indians. (T. Cross) Canad. Mo. 5: 402.—(H. Whiting) No. Am. 64: 292.—Am. Whig R. 5: 177, 242, 447.
— and Delawares, Notes on. Pennsyl. M. 1: 163, 319. 2: 407.
— Champlain on. (S. Luckey) Nat. M. 12: 36.
— Conquests of. (E. Everett) No. Am. 51: 57.
— Father LeMoine on. (S. Luckey) Nat. M. 11: 407, 508.
— League of. (S. Luckey) Nat. M. 12: 317.
— — Morgan's. (J. Gibbon) Penn Mo. 5: 300.
— Letters on. Olden Time, 2: 67, 117, 289.
— Schoolcraft on. (H. Whiting) No. Am. 64: 292.
Iroquois Bourbon. So Q. 24: 141. *See* Williams, Eleazer.
Iroquois Vocabulary. Hist. M. 10: 114.
Iroquois, The; a Poem. (C. Sangster) Canad. Mo. 4: 211.
Irrigation, Denton on. Mo. R. 158: 104.
— in California. (F. Carpenter) Ecl. Engin. 16: 79.
— in Ceylon. (R. Abbay) Nature, 16: 509. Same art. Liv. Age, 135: 489. Same art. Ecl. Engin. 18: 52. —(H. Byrne) Ecl. Engin. 23: 197.
— in the East. Penny M. 10: 180.
— in India. (C. E. Norton) No. Am. 77: 439.—Blackw. 73: 207.
— — and Cotton Culture. Ecl. R. 106: 104.
— — Controversy on. (U. R. Burke) Dub. Univ. 91: 201.
— — in Northern. Ecl. Engin. 8: 367.
— — in Southern. (C. R. Markham) Geog. M. 1: 329, 364. 4: 279, 307.—Ecl. Engin. 18: 158.
— in Lombardy. Blackw. 73: 447.
— of the Plains. (E. L. Greene) Am. Natural. 6: 76.
— of Valley of Chimbote, Peru. (S. McElroy) J. Frankl. Inst. 81: 145.
— Practical Notes on. Pract. M. 3: 448. 5: 197.
— Theory of. (F. C. Danvers) Ecl. Engin. 12: 435.
— — and Practice of. Ecl. R. 106: 409.
Irrigation Canals kept clear of Silt. Ecl. Engin. 22: 26.
Irrigation Works in India. (J. Dacosta) Contemp. 27: 549.—Ecl. Engin. 11: 76.—(W. T. Thornton) Ecl. Engin. 15: 113.—Ecl. Engin. 17: 140.
— in Ceylon. (W. Phillpotts) Ecl. Engin. 11: 303.
Irrawaddy, Thousand Miles up the. Once a Week, 25: 217, 233.
Irritable Man, Autobiography of an. So Lit. Mess. 6: 522.
Irvine, Matthew. (J. B. Linn) Pennsyl. M. 5: 418.
Irvine, William, Papers of. Pennsyl. M. 5: 259.
Irving, Edward. (W. W. Andrews) New Eng. 22: 363, 778.—(D. Curry) Meth. Q. 23: 5.—(A. H. Guernsey) No. Am. 95: 293.—(W. Laudels) Ex. H. Lec. 19: 37.—(M. Oliphant) Cornh. 6: 271.—(C. K. Paul) Theo. R. 3: 89.—(R. Story) Macmil. 6: 71.—Ecl. M. 14: 503.—Meth. Q. 9: 109.

Irving, Edward. Dem. R. **14**: 496. — Blackw. **84**: 567. Same art. Liv. Age, **59**: 798. — Blackw. **91**: 737. — Bost. R. **3**: 172. — Colburn, **10**: 187. — Ecl. R. **100**: 1. **115**: 473. Same art. Ecl. M. **32**: 530. Same art. Liv. Age, **42**: 349. — Fraser, **67**: 62. — Lond. Q. **19**: 165. — No. Brit. **37**: 94. Same art. Liv. Age, **74**: 554. — Tait, n. s. **22**: 8. Same art. Ecl. M. **34**: 249.
— and his Adversaries. Fraser, **3**: 423.
— Chalmers, and A. J. Scott. Nat. R. **15**: 350.
— Death of. (T. Carlyle) Fraser, **11**: 99.
— Heaven and Hell of. Blackw. **14**: 346.
— Life of. Chr. Rem. **44**: 291. — (H. Lincoln) Chr. R. **28**: 234. — (T. S. Childs) Princ. **35**: 207.
— — Mrs. Oliphant's. Ed. R. **116**: 426. — Chr. Obs. **63**: 325, 511.
— Missionary Orations of. Cong. M. **8**: 202.
— Orations of. Blackw. **14**: 145, 192. Same art. Mus. **3**: 364. — Westm. **1**: 27. — (A. Lamson) Chr. Exam. **2**: 468. — Chr. Mo. Spec. **6**: 150, 199. **10**: 318. — Chr. Obs. **23**: 490, 557. — Lond. M. **8**: 186. — Portfo.(Den.) **31**: 5.
— Recollections of. (F. Saunders) Liv. Age, **29**: 211.
— Sketch of. Lond. M. **22**: 46.
— Sermon on the last Days. Chr. Obs. **29**: 503, 558.
— — on these evil Times. Ecl. R. **49**: 1.
— Trial of. Niles's Reg. **44**: 228.
— Writings of. Chr. Rem. **53**: 37. Same art. Liv. Age, **92**: 451.
See Irvingism.
Irving, Henry, the Actor. (L. F. Austin) Victoria, **22**: 169. — Victoria, **28**: 441. — with portrait (A. Lewis) Dub. Univ. **90**: 284. — Temp. Bar, **38**: 393. **39**: 547.
— and Signor Salvini. Gent. M. n. s. **14**: 609.
— as Mathias. Once a Week, **26**: 57.
— Hamlet of. Temp. Bar, **55**: 398.
— — and the Critics. Macmil. **31**: 236.
Irving, John B. Day on Cooper River. So. Q. **3**: 256.
Irving, Washington. (A. H. Everett) No. Am. **28**: 103. — (C. D. Warner) Atlan. **45**: 396. — (P. H. Mayer) Dem. R. **21**: 488. — with portrait, Dem. R. **9**: 573. — with portrait, Fraser, **4**: 435. — Blackw. **6**: 556. — (F. Jeffrey) Ed. R. **37**: 337. Same art. Selec. Ed. R. **2**: 472. — So. Lit. Mess. **8**: 725. — Ecl. M. **15**: 412. — (P. M. Irving) Cornh. **6**: 274. — (G. P. Lathrop) Scrib. **11**: 799. — (D. G. Mitchell) Atlan. **13**: 694. — (C. Redding) Colburn, **118**: 213. — (W. Townsend) Canad. Mo. **15**: 20. — (J. Wynne) Harper, **24**: 349. — Bentley, **19**: 622. — Colburn, **6**: 193. **8**: 193. Same art. Ecl. M. **29**: 155. Same art. Liv. Age, **37**: 646. — Cornh. **1**: 129. — (J. L. W. Page) St. James, **46**: 307. — Ecl. M. **64**: 497. — Irish Q. **8**: 915. — Portfo.(Den.) **25**: 131.
— Adventures of Captain Bonneville. Mo. R. **143**: 279.
— Alhambra. (A. H. Everett) No. Am. **35**: 265. — Westm. **17**: 132. — Am. Mo. **2**: 177.
— and his Friends. Ecl. M. **78**: 119.
— Astoria. So. Q. **8**: 191. — (E. Everett) No. Am. **44**: 200. — Am. Q. **21**: 60. — Westm. **26**: 318. — So. Lit. Mess. **3**: 59. — Mo. R. **141**: 487.
— at Sunnyside. Colburn, **131**: 297. — (H. J. Duncan) Canad. Mo. **15**: 717. — (T. A. Richards) Harper, **14**: 1.
— — in 1858. (J. E. Cooke) Hours at Home, **1**: 507.
— — Morning with. (J. E. Cooke) So. M. **12**: 710.
— Bracebridge Hall. (F. Jeffrey) Ed. R. **37**: 337. Same art. Mus. **2**: 276. — (E. Everett) No. Am. **15**: 204. — Blackw. **11**: 688. — Colburn, **5**: 65. — Ecl. R. **37**: 233. — Lond. M. **6**: 436. — Portfo.(Den.) **29**: 156.
— Bryant on. Liv. Age, **65**: 298.
Irving, Washington. Conquest of Grenada. (W. H. Prescott) No. Am. **29**: 293. — Am. Mo. **5**: 190. — Quar. **43**: 55. — Mo. R. **119**: 430. — Lond. M. **23**: 529.
— Crayon Miscellany. So. Lit. Mess. **1**: 646. — So. Lit. J. **1**: 8. — Westm. **3**: 329.
— Day with. (C. Lanman) Once a Week, **2**: 5.
— Genius of. (G. W. Greene) No. Am. **86**: 330.
— — and Writings of. (J. B. Cobb) Am. Whig R. **12**: 602.
— History of New York. Blackw. **7**: 360. — Mo. R. **94**: 67.
— Irvingiana. Liv. Age, **69**: 809.
— Letters of. Liv. Age, **80**: 38.
— Life and Letters of. (H. T. Tuckerman) Chr. Exam. **73**: 271. — Colburn, **127**: 165. **129**: 49. — Ecl. M. **59**: 383. — Liv. Age, **74**: 579. — Quar. **114**: 151. Same art. Liv. Age, **78**: 457.
— Memoir of. Portfo.(Den.) **33**: 436.
— Memorial of. (L. G. Clark) Knick. **55**: 113.
— Miscellanies. Fraser, **12**: 409.
— Recollections of. (G. P. Putnam) Atlan. **6**: 601. — (L. G. Clark) Lippinc. **3**: 552. — Contin. Mo. **1**: 689.
— Sketch Book. (R. H. Dana) No. Am. **9**: 322. — Ed. Mo. R. **4**: 303. — (F. Jeffrey) Ed. R. **34**: 160. — Quar. **25**: 50. — Mo. R. **93**: 198. — Lond. M. **10**: 401. — West. R. **2**: 244.
— Spanish Papers, etc. (J. R. Dennett) Nation, **3**: 265.
— Tales of a Traveler. Ecl. R. **42**: 65. — Blackw. **16**: 291. — Westm. **2**: 334. — Quar. **31**: 471. — U. S. Lit. Gaz. **1**: 177. — Mus. **6**: 83.
— Tour of the Prairies. (E. Everett) No. Am. **41**: 1. — Dub. Univ. **5**: 555. — Mo. R. **136**: 467.
— Visit to. Liv. Age, **63**: 822.
— Why he was never married. Ecl. M. **56**: 135.
— Willis at Sunnyside. Liv. Age, **54**: 699. **55**: 241.
— Wolfert's Roost. Colburn, **104**: 297. — (A. Stevens) Nat. M. **6**: 385. — Dub. Univ. **45**: 369. Same art. Ecl. M. **34**: 546.
— Works of. (R. Allyn) Meth. Q. **16**: 537. — Chr. R. **15**: 203. — So. Q. **8**: 69. — Colburn, **97**: 424.
Irving, Gen. William. Olden Time, **2**: 478, 532.
Irvingism and the Apostolate. (J. Williams) Am. Church R. **7**: 537.
— Baxter's Narrative of Facts. Cong. M. **16**: 159.
Irvingite Unknown Tongues. Cong. M. **15**: 35.
Irwin, Henry, School Sermon of. Dub. Univ. **11**: 624.
Irwin, Thomas. (M. Russell) Irish Mo. **5**: 757. **6**: 80.
— Poems. Dub. Univ. **68**: 464. — Irish Q. **6**: 301
Is Anything lost? (F. A. Doughty) Atlan. **47**: 262.
Is he Popenjoy? a Tale. (A. Trollope) All the Year, **39**: 217–553. **40**: 1–529. **41**: 1, 38.
Is he a Spy? Temp. Bar, **19**: 405.
Is Seeing Believing? (O. S. Adams) O. & N. **8**: 459.
Is she an Heiress? (P. Fitzgerald) Belgra. **43**: supp. 78.
Isaac and his Sons. (J. W. Thompson) Mo. Rel. M. **8**: 531. **9**: 49.
— Oblation of, figurative of Christ's Death. Theo. Repos. **6**: 60.
— on Mt. Moriah, a Type of Christ? (T. T. Titus) Evang R. **19**: 447.
Isaac Cheek, the Man of Wax. Blackw. **40**: 49, 340.
Isabel; or the Peatship of Breda. (J. L. Ver Mehr) Overland, **14**: 152.
Isabel Hastings; a Story. (C. R. Crespi) Colburn, **160**: 688.
Isabell Carr; a Scottish Story. (M. Oliphant) St. James, **2**: 271, 399. Same art. Liv. Age, **71**: 339, 574.
Isabella, Queen of Edward II., Last Days of. (E. A. Bond) Arch. **35**: 453.
— Mission to Court of France. (J. Hunter) Arch. **36**: 242.
Isabella I., Queen of Spain, Life of. (P. Forsyth) Godey, **51**: 17–506. — Nat. M. **6**: 481. **7**: 37.

Isabella II., ex-Queen of Spain. (J. S. C. Abbott) Harper, **38**: 347. — Fraser, **50**: 249. — St. Paul's, **3**: 277.
Isabella Czartoryski, Princess. Colburn, **45**: 493.
Isaiah. (A. G. Laurie) Univ. Q. **14**: 261.
Isaiah; Ascensio Isaiæ. (G. H. Schodde) Luth. Q. **8**: 513.
— his Vision of the Cross. (M. S. Terry) Meth. Q. **40**: 45.
— Old Age of. (E. H. Plumptre) Good Words, **5**: 857. Same art. Ecl. M. **64**: 59. Same art. Liv. Age, **84**: 369.
See Bible, Isaiah.
Isandúla, Battle of. (R. Buchanan) Contemp. **35**: 153.
Isaure, Clemence. (W. Besant) Temp. Bar, **60**: 165.
Isbel; a Story. Victoria, **36**: 483.
Ischia, Italy. (M. P. Thompson) Cath. World, **12**: 471. — Penny M. **3**: 241.
— Legend of. Lond. M. **3**: 141.
— Spring Visit to. Chamb. J. **56**: 193.
— Summer Days in. (L. Courtenay) Once a Week, **2**: 612.
— Trip to. (B. Taylor) Atlan. **22**: 155.
— Visit to. Once a Week, **13**: 67.
Isella, At. (H. James, jr.) Galaxy, **12**: 241.
Isham, Chester, Biog. of. (L. Bacon) Chr. Mo. Spec. **7**: 611.
— Sermons of. Chr. Mo. Spec. **7**: 623. **8**: 176.
Isham's Wife. (C. Chesebrough) Knick. **46**: 1.
Ishmael, Prophecies concerning. Am. Meth. M. **20**: 316.
Ishmael in London. St. James, **24**: 15.
Ishmaelite, From the Note-Book of an. (J. Dyer) Penn Mo. **7**: 807–945. **9**: 203.
Isidor Henselt's Pupil. (A. Stewart) Victoria, **26**: 516.
Isinglass of India, Royle on. Mo. R. **157**: 401.
Isis, Evening by the. Chamb. J. **16**: 119.
Islam. *See* Mohammedanism.
Island in the River. House. Words, **3**: 315–363.
Island Isolation; a Poem. (R. Howitt) Hogg, **9**: 313.
Island Life and Continental. (J. W. Dawson) Princ. n. s. **8**: 1.
— Wallace's. (G. Allen) Fortn. **34**: 773. Same art. Ecl. M. **96**: 254. — Westm. **116**: 41. — (A. Geikie) Nature, **23**: 357, 391. — Chamb. J. **58**: 369.
Island Princess. (T. Gift) All the Year, **41**: 117–261.
Islande Apocryphe. Dub. Univ. **23**: 143.
Islands, Imaginary. Lond. Soc. **1**: 80, 150.
— Water-Supply of. (F. C. Hill) Pop. Sci. Mo. **6**: 440.
Islay, Island of. Chamb. J. **18**: 110.
Isle Douteuse. (L. W. Champney) Appleton, **18**: 451.
Isle of France; Ramble among the Haunts of Paul and Virginia. Colburn, **69**: 478.
Isle of the Puritans. (J. W. De Forest) Harper, **14**: 512. **31**: 561.
Isle Royale; a Poem. (R. P. Nevin) Mercersb. **2**: 199.
Isles of the Amazons; a Poem. (J. Miller) Gent. M. n. s. **9**: 241–617. **10**: 1. Same art. Overland, **9**: 201–489. **10**: 9.
— of the Sea, Story of. (H. B. Tristram) Good Words, **18**: 67–706.
Isles of Shoals, N. H. (J. W. Chadwick) Harper, **49**: 663. — (C. Thaxter) Atlan. **24**: 177. **25**: 16, 204, 579.
— in 1653. (C. W. Tuttle) N. E. Reg. **25**: 162.
— Something about. (E. R. Church) Lippinc. **8**: 191.
Islesmen of the West; a Poem. Dub. Univ. **44**: 604.
Islington, London. All the Year, **28**: 61, 181.
Islington-super-Mare. All the Year, **41**: 252.
Islington Market, London, 1847. (W. Howitt) Howitt, **1**: 72.
Ismael Er-Raschydi. Hogg, **6**: 341, 364.
Ismail, Siege of. (G. Fitzhugh) De Bow, **29**: 293.
Ismail Pasha, Khedive of Egypt. (E. De Leon) Harper, **39**: 739. — with portrait, Pract. M. **6**: 33. — with portrait, Ev. Sat. **9**: 67, 336.
Ismailia, Baker's. (T. Hughes) Macmil. **31**: 99. Same art. Liv. Age, **124**: 228. Same art. Ecl. M. **84**: 164. — Lond. Q. **43**: 329. — Nature, **11**: 24. — Penn Mo. **6**: 436. — (C. I. Barnard) Nation, **25**: 59.
Ismay, Thomas Henry, with portrait. Colburn, **167**: 304.
Ismenia; or the Voice of Conscience. (F. Caballero) Victoria, **18**: 1.
Isms of 1840. (W. P. Garrison) Harper, **60**: 182.
Isobel, Ballad of. (J. Payne) Colburn, **165**: 1125.
Isocrates. (R. D. C. Robbins) Bib. Sac. **35**: 401, 593.
Isola; a Tale of the East. Tinsley, **29**: 429.
Isomorphism. Nature, **19**: 387.
Isoperimetrical Problems, Woodhouse's, 1810. Ecl. R. **14**: 584.
Isothermal Lines. (A. Humboldt) Ed. Philos. J. **3**: 1, 256. **4**: 23, 262. **5**: 28.
— Distribution of. (H. Hennessy) Am. J. Sci. **77**: 328.
Israel, Hannah Erwin. (Mrs. E. F. Ellet) Godey, **36**: 145. **59**: 225.
Israel, Aliens in. (J. K. Bennet) Bib. Sac. **13**: 564.
— and the second great Monarchy. (R. Hill) Evang. R. **11**: 369.
— and Sinai. Danv. Q. **2**: 496.
— The God of; a History. (J. Jacobs) 19th Cent. **6**: 481.
— Hope of. Meth. Q. **2**: 192.
— in Egypt. (B. W. Savile) Kitto, **34**: 1. **35**: 273. — Danv. Q. **2**: 445. — (J. Cumming) Ex. H. Lec. **19**: 319.
— — Exodus of. (E. Robinson) Am. Bib. Repos. **2**: 743. — (S. C. Bartlett) No. Am. **131**: 26.
— — — Borrowing from the Egyptians. (B. Kurtz) Evang. R. **16**: 136. — Danv. Q. **4**: 362.
— in the Wilderness. Danv. Q. **3**: 453.
— Place of, in History. (P. H. Wicksteed) Mod. R. **2**: 548.
— Right of, to Canaan. Bost. R. **1**: 472.
Israel Potter. (H. Melville) Putnam, **4**: 66–592. **5**: 63–288.
Israel Quarrell against Fortune. Knick. **51**: 262.
Israelite's Daughter. (M. S. Whitaker) So. Lit. J. **3**: 442.
Israfil; a Poem. (F. L. Mace) Harper, **54**: 809.
Issue Rolls, 1216–1625. Mo. R. **139**: 252. **140**: 315. **143**: 202.
Issy, Fort of, Twenty Days in. Once a Week, **25**: 463.
Istria, Seaboard of. (R. F. Burton) Anthrop. J. **7**: 341.
It; a Story. (B. Webber) Tinsley, **26**: 256.
It's all for the best; a Tale. Blackw. **59**: 231, 319.
It's Hame and it's Hame; a Song. (A. Cunningham) Lond. M. **6**: 220.
It is possible! (H. Zschokke) Hogg, **2**: 317.
It might have been. (C. H. Washburn) Pioneer, **4**: 75.
It might have been; a Poem. Putnam, **6**: 588.
Italia rediviva; a Poem. (W. Stigant) Temp. Bar, **1**: 175.
Italians, Afternoon with. Dub. Univ. **55**: 741.
— Ancient, Micali on. (G. W. Greene) No. Am. **48**: 1.
— — Science and Wisdom of. For. R. **5**: 380.
— Habits, Dress, Food, etc., of. Mus. **2**: 458.
— in New York. (C. Adams) Harper, **62**: 676.
— Poetry and Romance of. (W. H. Prescott) No. Am. **33**: 29.
— Wandering. Penny M. **2**: 42, 61.
Italian Academies and Universities. All the Year, **18**: 511.
Italian Antiquaries and Antichita. Blackw. **59**: 543, 765.
Italian Art and Literature before Giotto and Dante. (E. Fusco) Macmil. **33**: 228. **34**: 241.
Italian Art of Hoaxing. Blackw. **12**: 589. **13**: 222, 400. **14**: 43.
Italian Authoresses. (I. B. Torricelli) O. & N. **2**: 99.
Italian Bride. So. Lit. Mess. **23**: 145.
Italian Caffe and Conversazione. Chamb. J. **26**: 321.
Italian Classics, Anti-Papal Spirit of. Ed. R. **55**: 531.
Italian Clergy and the Pope. Nat. R. **14**: 68. Same art. Ecl. M. **55**: 289.
Italian Comedy. Am. Q. **7**: 305. — For. Q. **2**: 60. — For. R. **3**: 190. **4**: 408.
Italian Dialects; Handful of Patois Books. Fraser, **50**: 316, 521.
— Poetry of North Italy. Cornh. **30**: 703.

Italian Drama. Colburn, **53**: 337. **54**: 409.
— Early. (G. E. Mackay) Gent. M. n. s. **20**: 478.
Italian Epic Poetry. Mo. R. **143**: 526.
Italian Exile in America. So. Lit. Mess. **8**: 741.
Italian Families, Litta's Celebrated. For. Q. **28**: 362.
Italian Fiction, Realistic. (F. E. Trollope) Fortn. **36**: 459.
Italian Gentleman. Colburn, **38**: 56.
— Life, Travels, and Adventures of. Lond. M. **13**: 145, 293. **14**: 61, 469.
Italian Guides and Tourists. Dub. R. **6**: 1.
Italian Historians. Mo. R. **157**: 408.
Italian Hospitals in 1866. (M. Montemerli) Good Words, **9**: 296–558.
Italian Household Sketches. Once a Week, **5**: 192.
Italian Humorous Poetry. Colburn, **34**: 58–249.
Italian Improvvisatori. Colburn, **11**: 193.
Italian Intervention, 1848. Quar. **84**: 222.
Italian Language and Dialects. (H. W. Longfellow) No. Am. **35**: 283.
— and Dictionaries. No. Brit. **14**: 202.
— Origin of. (G. P. Marsh) No. Am. **105**: 1. — (W. W. Story) No. Am. **126**: 97.
— Pepoli on. Mo. R. **149**: 36.
Italian Letters. De Bow, **16**: 62.
Italian Letter-Writers. Penny M. **2**: 436.
Italian Libraries. (J. W. Mario) Nation, **6**: 287.
Italian Literary Life in the 18th Century. (V. Lee) Fraser, **97**: 779. **98**: 33.
Italian Literature. (J. Marsh) No. Am. **15**: 94. — Anal. M. **14**: 413. **15**: 147. — Mo. R. **108**: 352. **114**: 26. — For. Q. **17**: 428. — Blackw. **11**: 547. — Lond. M. **14**: 385.
— Augustan Age of. (J. Sparks) No. Am. **4**: 309.
— Debt of English to. (J. A. Symonds) Fortn. **23**: 371. Same art. Liv. Age, **125**: 131. — (J. M. Stuart) Fraser, **60**: 697.
— Decline of; Tuscan Age. Blackw. **10**: 328.
— History of. Quar. **11**: 1.
— — Guidici's. Fraser, **57**: 426. Same art. Ecl. M. **44**: 331.
— in the 14th Century. Dub. Univ. **46**: 288.
— in the 15th Century. Ed. R. **136**: 114.
— Modern. (H. R. Cheever) Nat. Q. **4**: 76.
— Notes on. Lond. M. **14**: 18.
— of the Revival. Brit. Q. **22**: 317.
— of the 18th Century. For. Q. **2**: 621.
— of the 19th Century. (G. W. Greene) No. Am. **50**: 301. — Westm. **28**: 132.
— Recent. Temp. Bar, **16**: 289. Same art. Ecl. M. **66**: 436.
— Sismondi on. Ecl. R. **41**: 193, 314.
— State of. Lond. M. **13**: 36.
— Tables of. For. Q. **29**: 535.
Italian MS. of 17th Cent. (G. F. Rodwell) Nature, **2**: 370.
Italian Merchant. (J. W. von Goethe) Fraser, **3**: 704.
Italian Merchants' Loans to King of England, 13th and 14th Centuries. (E. A. Bond) Arch. **28**: 207.
Italian Music. Am. Q. **1**: 371.
— and Lyrical Drama. For. R. **2**: 21.
Italian Musical Life in the 18th Century. (V. Lee) Fraser, **98**: 339, 423, 566.
Italian Nationality. U. S. Cath. M. **6**: 457, 513.
Italian Nightmares. All the Year, **7**: 261.
Italian Nobility, and French. Dub. Univ. **54**: 720.
Italian Novelle, Some. All the Year, **23**: 276, 301.
Italian Novels. For. Q. **17**: 472. **21**: 414. — Ed. R. **42**: 174.
— Early. (J. Mew) Gent. M. n. s. **18**: 734.
Italian Novelists. Westm. **7**: 115. — Mo. R. **116**: 226. — Mus. **6**: 425.
— and Novel-Writing. (L. Villari) Macmil. **38**: 20.
Italian Opera. *See* Opera.
Italian Painting and Painters, Modern. (J. J. Jarves) Art J. **32**: 261. — Appleton, **24**: 371.
Italian Peasant. All the Year, **24**: 438.
Italian Peasant Play. All the Year, **26**: 326, 345.
Italian Peasantry, Stories of. All the Year, **25**: 342.
Italian Philological Clubs. Nation, **20**: 239.
Italian Picture Book, Lewald's. Westm. **49**: 219.
Italian Poetry. Ed. R. **5**: 45. — (E. Lawrence) Harper, **56**: 816.
— and Patriotism. Fraser, **67**: 383. **68**: 603.
— Ariosto. (E. I. Sears) Nat. Q. **10**: 207.
— Growth of early. Nat. R. **15**: 60.
— Lyric. Am. Q. **16**: 42. — U. S. Lit. Gaz. **2**: 136–427.
— Narrative. (W. H. Prescott) No. Am. **19**: 337. **21**: 189.
— — and Romantic. (U. Foscolo) Quar. **21**: 486.
— — — Rauhe's. Ed. R. **71**: 371.
— Popular. (T. F. Crane) Internat. R. **9**: 155.
— Romantic. (A. Gallenga) No. Am. **47**: 206. — For. Q. **6**: 349. **15**: 48. — Fraser, **3**: 598.
Italian Poets. (E. Lawrence) Harper, **56**: 816. — Mo. R. **124**: 295. **127**: 105. — Dub. Univ. **25**: 424, 582. **26**: 80, 186, 581.
— Contemporary. Quar. **144**: 446. — Cornh. **8**: 308, 466. **10**: 683.
— Homes and Haunts of. (F. E. Trollope) Belgra. **40**: 157. **41**: 89. **42**: 60.
— Hunt's. For. Q. **36**: 333.
— of the 18th Century. So. Lit. Mess. **2**: 44, 122, 205. — So. Lit. J. **1**: 403.
— Modern. For. Q. **22**: 33. — Brit. &. For. R. **12**: 257. — Westm. **72**: 427. Same art. Ecl. M. **49**: 145. — (W. D. Howells) No. Am. **103**: 313. **104**: 317. — (F. Hueffer) Fortn. **35**: 488.
— Sismondi's. Ed. R. **25**: 31.
Italian Political Poems, Recent. For. Q. **36**: 179.
Italian Portraits. Blackw. **97**: 49.
Italian Pulpit Eloquence. For. Q. **10**: 335. Same art. Select J. **1**: 161. — Mo. R. **116**: 89.
Italian Salon of the 16th Century. (B. Murphy) So. M. **17**: 581.
Italian Scenery and Manners. Fraser, **7**: 318. **8**: 177.
Italian Singers, Dancers, and Fiddlers. Tait, **4**: 290.
Italian Sonnets, A few. Tait, n. s. **21**: 571.
— Specimens of. Lond. M. **8**: 652. **9**: 33–612. **10**: 55.
Italian Stage. (R. Davey) Lippinc. **15**: 90.
Italian Tales. Westm. **1**: 271.
Italian Theater. Fraser, **26**: 236.
Italian Tragedy. Am. Q. **15**: 351. — For. Q. **1**: 135. — Quar. **24**: 72. — Mo. R. **94**: 526. — Lond. M. **2**: 284.
Italian Volunteers. Chamb. J. **34**: 321.
Italian Writers on Languages. Mo. R. **116**: 366.
Italy. (E. Everett) No. Am. **12**: 198. — (H. T. Tuckerman) No. Am. **40**: 417. — (H. T. Tuckerman) Dem. R. **17**: 203. — (A. Pannizzi) No. Brit. **6**: 170. — For. Q. **22**: 325. — Brit. & For. R. **2**: 591. — Ed. R. **40**: 207. — Blackw. **45**: 62. — Mo. R. **115**: 256. **116**: 249. — (C. Buxton) Ex. H. Lec. **7**: 43. — (W. P. Merras) Lippinc. **7**: 266. — (J. H. Morison) Unita. R. **7**: 157. — (W. J. Stillman) Fortn. **32**: 829. — (W. Williams) Hours at Home, **3**: 31. — All the Year, **7**: 564. — Nat. R. **3**: 410. — Quar. **109**: 133.
— a Poem. Blackw. **11**: 280.
— an Allegory. Dub. Univ. **34**: 168.
— Ancient. Mus. **10**: 385.
— — Cities of. Lond. M. **9**: 122. **10**: 409, 517.
— — Landscape of. Blackw. **93**: 613. Same art. Ecl. M. **59**: 378. — (H. J. Warner) Nation, **3**: 490.
— and the Bourbons. Chr. Obs. **68**: 431.
— and the Christian Alliance. Brownson, **12**: 355.
— and England. Once a Week, **10**: 556.
— — English Sympathy with Italy. Month, **6**: 76.
— and Europe. For. Q. **14**: 298.
— and France, 1862. Brit. Q. **36**: 103. — Blackw. **92**: 503. Same art. Ecl. M. **57**: 529.
— — Pedestrian Tour through. Mo. R. **133**: 115.

Italy and France, Religious Condition of. (R. Burgess) Ex. H. Lec. **20**: 205.
— and Germany, Net Results of 1848 in. No. Brit. **15**: 359. Same art. Liv. Age, **30**: 512.
— and Great Britain, 1852. Dub. Univ. **40**: 85.
— and Greece, Sketches in. Bost. R. **3**: 477.
— and her foremost Men. Sharpe, **14**: 193. **15**: 340.
— and her Invaders, 376–476. Ed. R. **152**: 194.
— and Ireland, with portrait of Pius IX. (Dr. Taylor) Bentley, **24**: 303.
— and the Italians. Ed. R. **72**: 159. — Blackw. **25**: 94–705. **26**: 177. — For. Q. **16**: 245. — West. M. **3**: 358. — Mo. R. **153**: 55. **155**: 447.
— and Italian Nationality, 1860. Brit. Q. **31**: 493. Same art. Ecl. M. **50**: 236.
— and the Italian Questions. Dub. Univ. **33**: 204.
— and its Rulers. (W. McCall) Ex. H. Lec. **18**: 161.
— and Leo XIII., 1878. Dub. R. **82**: 473.
— and Napoleon III., 1859. Liv. Age, **61**: 47.
— and Napoleonism. No. Brit. **31**: 243.
— and the Papacy, Relations between. (J. Mazzini) Westm. **88**: 226.
— and the Papal States, 1856. Dub. R. **41**: 171.
— and Pius IX. (L. Monti) Scrib. **16**: 357. — (G. E. Ellis) Chr. Exam. **44**: 236. — with portrait, (G. F. S. de Casali) Am. Whig R. **6**: 529. — Dem. R. **22**: 301. — Am. Lit. M. **2**: 185. — Brownson, **5**: 117.
— and the Pope. (B. J. Keiley) Cath. World, **28**: 461. — (A. Saffi) Fortn. **7**: 436. — Fortn. **6**: 802.
— — and the Jesuits, 1847. Prosp. R. **3**: 423.
— and Rhineland, Fragments of. Blackw. **59**: 249.
— and the temporal Power. Month, **13**: 613.
— — White on. Mo. R. **156**: 456.
— and the Republic. (J. Mazzini) Fortn. **15**: 289. Same art. Ecl. M. **76**: 513.
— and Rome, 1861. (C. Redding) Colburn, **123**: 318.
— — in 1871. (J. W. Probyn) Fortn. **15**: 595.
— and Sicily, Travels in. For. Q. **2**: 275.
— and Switzerland, 1849. Blackw. **63**: 98.
— — Excursion Trip to. Temp. Bar, **12**: 584.
— and Ultramontanism. Dub. Univ. **57**: 742.
— Anglo-French Mediation in, 1848. Ecl. R. **90**: 517.
— Aristocracy of. For. Q. **28**: 362.
— Art and Nature in. Quar. **91**: 1. Same art. Ecl. M. **27**: 57.
— as it is, Nicolai's. For. Q. **16**: 165.
— — Laveleye's, 1880. Ed. R. **153**: 164.
— at the Time of the Renaissance, J. A. Symonds on. Quar. **145**: 1.
— at Work. Dub. Univ. **74**: 273.
— Austrian. Bent. Q. **1**: 301.
— Austrian Government of. Blackw. **36**: 530.
— Austrian Interventions in. Westm. **72**: 215.
— Austrian Oppression in. Westm. **86**: 147.
— Austrian Rule in. Chr. Rem. **43**: 257.
— Austrians in, 1848–49. Colburn, **97**: 169.
— Autumn Wanderings in. Cornh. **43**: 305.
— Beggars in. Once a Week, **4**: 23.
— Bell's Observations in. U. S. Lit. Gaz. **6**: 23.
— Blessington's Idler in. Colburn, **55**: 418. — Mo. R. **148**: 485. **154**: 98.
— Blunt's Vestiges of Manners in. Mo. R. **101**: 146.
— Bonapartism in. Westm. **72**: 526. Same art. Ecl. M. **49**: 214, 341.
— Brigandage in. (W. Chambers) Chamb. J. **54**: 4–727. — All the Year, **9**: 304.
— Brigands in. Blackw. **93**: 576.
— Broughton's Visits to. Dub. R. **46**: 135.
— Butler's Year of Consolation in. Ed. R. **86**: 176. — Quar. **81**: 440. Same art. Liv. Age, **15**: 481. — Westm. **47**: 399. — Tait, n. s. **14**: 413. — Liv. Age, **13**: 470.
Italy, Campaign in, 1859. Bent. Q. **1**: 629.
— Catholic Efforts in. Month, **22**: 1.
— Catholicism in. (L. Mariotti) Chr. Exam **25**: 273.
— Charitable Institutions of. Dub. R. **14**: 97. **15**: 29.
— Christmas in. (A. Gallenga) Colburn, **88**: 15.
— Church and State in. (D. Paul) Cath. World, **28**: 419. — (C. Pozzoni) Nat. Q. **38**: 108. — (J. W. Probyn) Fortn. **16**: 655. Same art. Ecl. M. **78**: 129. Same art. Liv. Age, **112**: 195. — (J. M. Stuart) Contemp. **30**: 86. Same art. Ecl. M. **89**: 129.
— Church Reform in, and Canon Wordsworth. (W. C. Langdon) Am. Church R. **16**: 261.
— Church Reformation in. Ed. R. **114**: 233.
— Church Spoliation in. Month, **22**: 463.
— Civil Marriage Bill in. (D. Paul) Cath. World, **29**: 715.
— Climates of, Hints for Tourists and Invalids on. (F. Booth) Nation, **2**: 330.
— Cobbett's Tour in. Westm. **14**: 174.
— Commerce and Industry of. Hunt, **15**: 19.
— — in the Middle Ages. (Mgr. R. Seton) Cath. World, **23**: 79.
— Conder's. Westm. **15**: 335. — Ecl. R. **62**: 221.
— Confiscation Laws of. (J. G. Lynch) Cath. World, **18**: 30.
— Cooper's Gleanings in. Hesp. **1**: 250, 305.
— Copyright in. For. Q. **26**: 289.
— Country Life in. Cornh. **44**: 604, 684. Same art. Liv. Age, **151**: 736.
— Country Residence in. Sharpe, **18**: 102.
— Cradle and Grave of the Arts. Blackw. **83**: 603. Same art. Ecl. M. **44**: 371.
— Dal Pozzo's Happiness of. Westm. **21**: 118.
— Dickens's Pictures from. Dub. R. **21**: 184.
— Diplomacy in, 1866. Dub. R. **74**: 267.
— Dramas in. Blackw. **53**: 551.
— Earthquakes in Southern. (J. P. Lacaita) Am. J. Sci. **78**: 210.
— Emigration from. (C. Negri) Geog. M. **1**: 218.
— English in. Westm. **6**: 325.
— English Statesmen on, 1851. Brit. Q. **14**: 488.
— Essays on Scenes in. (G. Ticknor) No. Am. **18**: 192.
— The Etruscans. (A. S. Murray) Contemp **26**: 716.
— Eustace's Tour in, 1813. Ed. R. **21**: 378. — Quar. **10**: 222. — Ecl. R. **20**: 465, 541.
— Excursion to Tivoli. (C. U. C. Burton) Nat. M. **10**: 209.
— Fanny Kemble and Lear in. Quar. **81**: 440.
— Farewell to. (A. Gallenga) Peop. J. **3**: 191.
— Lord Faucouberg's Embassy to, 1669. (Sir H. Ellis) Arch. **37**: 158.
— Finances of. Month, **21**: 382.
— First Impressions of. (N. Hawthorne) Good Words, **12**: 12–830.
— Following the Tiber. Lippinc. **15**: 30, 137.
— for the Italians. Ecl. M. **47**: 367.
— Forsyth's Remarks on. Ed. R. **22**: 376. — (J. Foster) Ecl. R. **18**: 533.
— Foreign Affairs of, 1859. Quar. **105**: 527. Same art. Liv. Age, **62**: 9.
— France, and Austria. Ed. R. **109**: 558.
— Franco-Italian Convention, September, 1864. Dub. R. **56**: 251.
— French Diplomatist in. Quar. **133**: 487.
— French Views of. Dub. Univ. **53**: 750.
— From Ancona to Rome. St. James, **16**: 413.
— From Rome to Narni. Tinsley, **3**: 72–518.
— Future of. Bentley, **57**: 23. Same art. Ecl. M. **64**: 626. — Colburn, **117**: 118. — (G. M. Towle) Hours at Home, **4**: 193. — Nat. R. **9**: 229.
— Galleries of, Studies in. Art J. **13**: 119.
— Garibaldi and Cavour. Cornh. **2**: 591.
— Germany, and England, 1851. Brit. Q. **13**: 190.

Italy, Headley's Letters from. U. S. Cath. M. 4: 773.
— Hills of, Rambles among. Hours at Home, 2: 399. 3: 323. 4: 41. 5: 36.
— Hillard's Six Months in. Fraser, 51: 205. — Chr. Exam. 55: 375. — Dub. R. 44: 290. — Brownson, 11: 107. — No. Am. 77: 422. — So. Lit. Mess. 20: 25.
— Historians of. (A. Gallenga) No. Am. 48: 325.
— Hist. Romance in. (G. W. Greene) No. Am. 46: 325.
— History of, Antiquarians and Critics of. Retros. 14: 136.
— — before the Roman Domination. Mo. R. 106: 500.
— — Botta's. For. Q. 1: 253. — Mo. R. 110: 496. — West. Mo. R. 3: 145.
— — Butt's. Dub. Univ. 56: 559.
— — Characteristics of. Ecl. R. 99: 447.
— — Contributions to. Month, 18: 242.
— — Farina's. Westm. 49: 512.
— — from 1440 to 1630. (F. Bowen) No. Am. 74: 371.
— — Insurrections in, and Mr. Mazzini. Dub. R. 18: 230.
— — Mediæval. No. Brit. 8: 161.
— — Modern. For. Q. 17: 60. — Westm. 11: 127. — Blackw. 16: 262. 61: 162.
— — — Wrightson's. Chr. Obs. 56: 333. — Colburn, 116: 117. — New Q. 4: 258.
— — Napoleon's Campaign, 1796–97. Temp. Bar, 35: 68.
— — Perceval's. Mo. R. 107: 113.
— — Piedmont in 1849 and 1859. Fraser, 60: 498.
— — Piedmontese at Rome. Month, 21: 129.
— — relative to the Italian People. Westm. 51: 224.
— — Revolution of 1848–49. (A. W. Little) No. Am. 93: 301. — Blackw. 70: 431. — No. Brit. 14: 319. — Ecl. R. 92: 147. 93: 204. — (H. M. Field) New Eng. 7: 72. — Quar. 83: 227. 84: 119, 269, 501. — Ed. R. 93: 33. 94: 17, 254. — Tait, n. s. 16: 185. 17: 408. — Victoria, 11: 97.
— — — Campaign in, of the Roman Republicans. Dem. R. 31: 193, 305.
— — — Defeat of. Ed. R. 93: 498. Same art. Liv. Age, 29: 445.
— — — Macfarland's. Ecl. R. 89: 629.
— — — Sketches of. Colburn, 104: 95–490.
— — Revolution of 1857. (H. T. Tuckerman) No. Am. 92: 15.
— — — Cause and Character of. Dub. R. 48: 150.
— — Revolution of 1867, and the Pope. (J. H. Newman) Cath. World, 4: 577. — Dub. R. 68: 1.
— — — and Rome. Dub. R. 62: 210. — Month, 24: 463.
— — — Campaign in. Colburn, 140: 127.
— — — Garibaldi's last Campaign. Cornh. 17: 111.
— — — How New Italy became a Nation. (C. Pozzoni) Internat. R. 3: 642.
— — Thirteen Years of Freedom in, 1861–74. (A. Gubernatis) Internat. R. 1: 479.
— — War of 1859. (C. C. Hazewell) Atlan. 4: 244. — (E. F. Hall) New Eng. 17: 708. — (G. P. Marsh) Chr. Exam. 67: 260. — Quar. 105: 527. — Tait, n. s. 26: 250–494.
— — — and Germany. Colburn, 116: 253.
— — — Battle-Fields of. Fraser, 61: 168.
— — — Campaign in. (E. Dicey) Macmil. 14: 241. — Bent. Q. 1: 629. — Colburn, 116: 238. — Ed. R. 110: 454.
— — — Campaigns of 1859, 1866, and 1870–71. Fraser, 84: 251.
— — — Crisis of Freedom in. (F. Lushington) Macmil 1: 55.
— — — Italy resurgent and Britain looking on. (T. Hughes) Macmil. 1: 494.
— — — Literature of. (Countess de Bury) No. Am. 90: 223.
— — — Peace of Villa Franca. Ecl. R. 110: 155.
— — — Seat of War. Knick. 54: 28.
Italy, History of; War of 1859, Track of. All the Year, 1: 293.
— — War with Austria, 1866. Westm. 87: 274.
— Hoare's Tour in. Mo. R. 93: 273.
— Hodgkin's Invaders of. (W. F. Allen) Nation, 32: 29.
— Hoffstetter's Journal in. Westm. 55: 215.
— Holiday Customs in. (E. M. Clerke) Cornh. 43: 193. Same art. Liv. Age, 150: 359.
— Impressions of. So. Lit. Mess. 20: 503. 25: 353.
— in the Middle Ages. (A. Gallenga) No. Am. 50: 43. — No. Brit. 8: 161. Same art. Ecl. M. 13: 100.
— in the 19th Century, Whiteside on. Chr. Obs. 51: 670. — Dub. R. 26: 1. — Quar. 83: 552. — Prosp. R. 5: 86.
— in 1812–13, Chateauvieux on. Ecl. R. 30: 581.
— in 1818–19, Reflections on. Lond. M. 1: 3.
— in 1831. Colburn, 31: 417.
— in 1840, State of the Arts in. (C. H. Wilson) Ed New Philos. J. 30: 90.
— in 1846. (G. F. S. de Casali) Am. Whig R. 5: 357.
— — Works on Condition of. Chr. Obs. 46: 416.
— in 1847, Papal States. Ed. R. 86: 494. Same art. Liv. Age, 15: 415.
— — Hopes of. (G. W. Greene) No. Am. 66: 1.
— in 1848. Bentley, 46: 69. — Irish Q. 2: 563. — (A. Gallenga) Colburn, 79: 249. 81: 253.
— — Gallenga on. Chr. Obs. 48: 558. — Brit. Q. 7: 464.
— in 1848–71. (E. Gryzanowski) No. Am. 113: 274.
— in 1850, and English Statesmanship. Brit. Q. 14: 488.
— — and Germany and England. Brit. Q. 13: 190.
— in 1854. (E. Peabody) No. Am. 78: 449.
— in 1856. Liv. Age, 50: 58.
— in 1859. Ecl. R. 109: 535.
— — Prospects of. Brit. Q. 30: 227.
— in 1860. Chr. Obs. 61: 112.
— — Affairs of Northern. Tait, n. s. 27: 190.
— — and France. Colburn, 118: 363.
— — Condition and Prospects of. (H. T. Tuckerman) Putnam, 14: 456.
— — Friends and Foes of. Colburn, 120: 1.
— — Glance at. Victoria, 3: 411–537. 4: 63–257.
— — Scenes in. (W. Arthur) Good Words, 1: 537.
— — Situation in. Cornh. 2: 487.
— in 1862, Condition and Prospects of. (A. Saffi) Macmil. 8: 224.
— — Political and Ecclesiastical. Chr. Rem. 43: 257.
— in 1864–66, La Marmora on. Month, 19: 381.
— in 1864. No. Brit. 42: 459.
— — Wylie on. Chr. Obs. 66: 448, 633.
— in 1865, Prospects of. Quar. 118: 371.
— — What Annexation has done for. Nat. R. 18: 19.
— — within and without. Brit. Q. 41. 220.
— in 1866, Church, State, and Society in. Chr. Rem. 53: 137.
— — Questions of the Day in. (L. M. Hogg) Contemp. 1: 642.
— in 1867. (H. T. Tuckerman) Putnam, 11: 105. — No. Brit. 47: 463.
— in 1868. Cath. World, 6: 814.
— — New Member of the European Family. St. Paul's, 1: 402.
— in 1878, Outlook in. (I. T. Hecker) Cath. World, 26: 1.
— in 1879, Political Prospects of. (T. A. Trollope) Brit. Q. 70: 418.
— in Transition, 1861. Lond. Q. 15: 285. Same art. Ecl. M. 52: 49.
— Independence and Unity of, 1859. Westm. 71: 444.
— Influence of France upon. (T. A. Trollope) St. James, 1: 413.
— Insurrections and Insurgents of Dub. Univ. 27: 304, 409.
— Intervention in. Quar. 84: 222.
— — in 1848. Ecl. R. 88: 517.

Italy; L'Italie est-elle la Terre des Morts? Fraser, **64**: 612.
— Journal in. Lond. M. **16**: 1, 147.
— Journey to Rome. (J. F. Meline) Galaxy, **11**: 708.
— Kings and Popes of. Ed. R. **93**: 171.
— Kingdom of. (W. Forsyth) Ed. R. **113**: 253. Same art. Ecl. M. **53**: 145.
— — in 1815 and 1865. Lond. Q. **24**: 446.
— — Progress of. Ed. R. **142**: 472.
— Lakes of. (R. A. McLeod) Lippinc. **21**: 393.
— — Pedestrian's Route to. (A. Cust) Fraser, **99**: 680.
— Land in, Reclamation of. Pract. M. **1**: 319.
— Letter from. Mus. **41**: 554.
— Letter from an Artist in, 1575. Lond. M. **18**: 361.
— Letters from. Blackw. **12**: 429–726. **13**: 276, 433, 698. — Dub. Univ. **20**: 155–694. — (H. Alford) Good Words, **5**: 243-937. — Dub. Univ. **19**: 46–525. — Dial, **1**: 387.
— Liberty in, Martyrs of. (J. Mazzini) Peop. J. **1**: 121, 293.
— Life in. Chamb. J. **26**: 1.
— — and Morals in. (J. J. Jarves) Harper, **10**: 320.
— — Confessions of an Italian Innkeeper. Colburn, **72**: 116.
— — Country. (A. Gallenga) Colburn, **74**: 32.
— — Cruelty of domestic. St. James, **35**: 167.
— — Peep into an Italian Interior. Chamb. J. **19**: 241. **20**: 41-409.
— — Pictures of. (A. J. C. Hare) Good Words, **14**: 42–847.
— — Scenes of. Bentley, **20**: 297.
— — Three Days in an Italian Home. Chamb. J. **23**: 65, 84.
— Living in. (K. K. C. Walker) Nation, **5**: 14.
— Macfarlane's Glance at. Colburn, **85**: 496.
— Malady called Pellagra in. Ed. R. **153**: 448.
— Manufactures and Resources of. Pract M. **7**: 207.
— Maremma and Pontine Marshes. Penny M. **12**: 374.
— Mariotti on Hist. and Literature of. Mo. R. **155**: 236.
— Mazzini on Royalty and Republicanism in. Internat. M. **2**: 265.
— Mazzini's Influence on. Contemp. **15**: 383.
— Miller's Travels in. Ed. R. **29**: 191.
— Minor Travels in. (W. D. Howells) Atlan. **20**: 337.
— Modern. Colburn, **131**: 379. — Dub. Univ. **53**: 270.
— Monasteries in, Suppression of. Dub. R. **65**: 76.
— Monnier's. Blackw. **89**: 403.
— Lady Morgan's. Quar. **25**: 529. — Mo. R. **96**: 225. — Portfo.(Den.) **26**: 228.
— Murdoch's Family Tour in. Tait, n. s. **13**: 451.
— Nationality of. Brit. Q: **31**: 492.
— Newspapers in. (A. de Gubernatis) Internat. R. **3**: 764. — (J. W. Mario) Nation, **6**: 129.
— Nicolai's Travels in. For. Q. **16**: 165.
— North. All the Year, **1**: 461. — Fraser, **27**: 643.
— — and the Tyrol. For. Q. **12**: 142.
— — Folk of. (A. Paynter) Howitt, **2**: 309, 371, 390.
— — Glimpse of. (J. Kavanagh) Month, **1**: 112.
— — Notes on. (N. Colgan) Irish Mo. **6**: 253, 544.
— Ramble to. (N. Macleod) Good Words, **3**: 449.
— — Scenery in. (A. Alison) Blackw. **2**: 544.
— — Springtime in. Colburn, **159**: 72–433.
— Notes and Notions from. Blackw. **97**: 659. Same art. Ecl. M. **65**: 257.
— Observatories of. (G. Rayet) Pop. Sci. Mo **11**: 538.
— of the 19th Century, Whiteside on. Quar. **83**: 552.
— of To-Day, 1869. (E. Dicey) Macmil. **20**: 114. Same art. Ev. Sat. **7**: 788.
— Our own Correspondent in. (M. B. Honan) Colburn, **95**: 284.
— Paper Money in, Inconvertible. (G. Walker) Nation, **22**: 190.
Italy, Parliamentary Government in, 1878. (K. Hillebrand) Nation, **28**: 9.
— past and present. (T. Prendergast) Nat. Q. **1**: 201.
— Peale's Notes on. Am. Q. **9**: 512.
— Peasant in. Fraser, **91**: 704. Same art. Ecl. M. **85**: 278. Same art. Liv. Age, **126**: 177.
— Philosophic Movement in. (L. Ferri) Princ. n. s. **4**: 253.
— Poetical and Devotional Superstition of. Mus. **15**: 299.
— Policy of, 1865. Temp. Bar, **13**: 192.
— — 1866. (W. C. Cartwright) Fortn. **5**: 641.
— — 1880, Home and Foreign. (A. Gallenga) Fortn. **36**: 27. Same art. Liv. Age, **150**: 387.
— Political Condition of, 1825. Ann. Reg. **1**: 249.
— Political Economists of, Pecchio on. For. R. **4**: 201.
— Political Future of. (D. Paul) Cath. World, **29**: 555.
— Political Life in, Eighteen Months of, 1849. (A. Gallenga) Colburn, **87**: 386.
— — Gallenga's. (W. H. Prescott) No. Am. **54**: 339.
— Politics of. (E. Gryzanowski) Nation, **10**: 39, 56. — For. R. **3**: 126.
— — in 1847. (A. Gallenga) Colburn, **81**: 240.
— — in 1859. Dub. Univ. **53**: 221.
— — in 1864. Dub. Univ. **64**: 628.
— — in 1867, Affairs of. Dub. R. **60**: 192. — (E. L. Godkin) Nation, **5**: 527.
— — in 1870, Crisis in. (E. Gryzanowski) Nation, **11**: 418.
— — in 1876, Questions in. Brit. Q. **63**: 160.
— — in 1878, New King of, and the new Pope. (A. de Gubernatis) Internat. R. **5**: 303.
— — in 1879. (E. de Laveleye) Fortn. **31**: 531. — (D. Paul) Cath. World, **30**: 275. — (I. T. Hecker) Cath. World, **29**: 679.
— — — Prospects of. (T. A. Trollope) Brit. Q. **70**: 418.
— — Liberal Party and Providence. (H. J. Anderson) Cath. World, **15**: 270.
— — Modern Italian Freedom. For. Q. **12**: 302.
— — Regionalism *versus* Political Unity in. (D. Paul) Cath. World, **27**: 27.
— — Spirit of Change in Southern Europe. (J. H. Skene) Colburn, **86**: 288–445.
— — State of Parties, 1848–57. Westm. **67**: 98.
— Prisons of, French Nobleman in. Month, **4**: 613.
— Protestant Movement in, 1860. Liv. Age, **66**: 158. — Quar. **114**: 480. — Cong. **5**: 489.
— Protestantism in. (C. K. True) Meth. Q. **6**: 485. — (W. Gladden) Scrib. **21**: 681. — No. Brit. **20**: 37.
— Pulpit in. (C. H. Brigham) Chr. Exam. **62**: 92.
— The Quadrilateral. Cornh. **5**: 93.
— Question of. (E. Gryzanowski) Nation, **10**: 402, 417. **11**: 5.
— — Arnold on. Dub. Univ. **54**: 470.
— — in 1848. Tait, n. s. **15**: 276, 349, 688.
— — in 1853. Dub. R. **34**: 203.
— — in 1856. Dub. Univ. **48**: 364, 505.
— — in 1858. Dub. Univ. **51**: 157. — No. Brit. **31**: 530.
— — in 1859. Colburn, **115**: 237. — Dub. Univ. **54**: 56–470. — Westm. **71**: 444. Same art. Liv. Age, **61**: 657. — Liv. Age, **62**: 505, 693. — New Q. **8**: 250.
— — in 1862. Dub. Univ. **59**: 716.
— — in 1865. (A. Laugel) Nation, **1**: 782.
— — True Difficulties of. Nat. R. **8**: 488. Same art. Ecl. M. **47**: 166.
— Railways in. (C. E. Lester) Hunt, **17**: 250.
— Rain Storm in. (M. C. Clarke) Atlan. **18**: 344.
— Rambles in. Anal. M. **12**: 1.
— — in 1816-17. West. R. **4**. 193, 342.
— Raumer on. For. Q. **25**: 352.
— Recent Tourists in, 1848 Dub. Univ. **32**: 405.
— Recollections of. Lond. M. **9**: 21.
— — of a Voyage to. Portfo.(Den.) **28**: 207.
— Regeneration of. (E. A. Washburne) U. S. Serv. M **1**: 583. **2**: 48. — Dub. Univ. **56**: 288.

Italy, Religion in. (L. M. Hogg) Good Words, 12: 753.
— — in 1831. For. Q. 10: 335. Same art. Select J. 1: 161.
— — in 1836. Dub. R. 1: 460.
— — in 1853. Westm. 60: 311.
— — in 1864. Theo. R. 1: 198.
— Religion, Love, and Marriage in. Chamb. J. 27: 145.
— Religious Condition of. Chr. Obs. 72: 407, 488.
— Religious Reform Movement in. (C. M. Butler) Theo. Ecl. 5: 143. — (W. C. Langdon) Am. Church R. 15: 235. 18: 242. 19: 548. — (H. C. Lea) No. Am. 107: 51.
— Religious Revivals in Mediæval. Cornh. 31: 54. Same art. Liv. Age, 124: 741.
— Religious Side of Italian Question. (J. Mazzini) Atlan. 20: 108. — (J. Mazzini) Westm. 88: 226. Same art. Ecl. M. 69: 513.
— Republican Movement in. (E. Castelar) Fortn. 18: 166. — (J. Mazzini) Fortn. 15: 289. — Dem. R. 31: 193.
— Republics of Middle Ages. Am. Q. 12: 442. — Quar. 7: 357. — Mo. R. 91: 484. 92: 481.
— — Sismondi's History of. Ecl. R. 37: 1.
— Right and Wrong in. (E. Gryzanowski) Nation, 9: 48.
— Roman Question, 1865. Dub. R. 57: 227.
— — 1868. Liv. Age, 96: 425.
— — 1871. Dub. R. 69: 421.
— Roman State from 1800 to 1850. Dub. R. 52: 503.
— Rome and Sardinia, 1855. Dub. R. 39: 164.
— Saracens in. Westm. 110: 57.
— Scenery of. U. S. Cath. M. 4: 57.
— — Volcanic Character of. Art J. 21: 65.
— Scientific Academies in, and the Papacy. Dub. R. 3: 150.
— Secret Societies of modern. Dem. R. 9: 260.
— seen through French Spectacles. Dub. Univ. 53: 750. Same art. Ecl. M. 47: 515.
— Sforzosi's History of. Mo. R. 147: 256.
— Mrs. Shelley's Rambles in. Tait, n. s. 11: 729.
— Sketch in, 1855. Colburn, 108: 485. 109: 88.
— Sketches in. (Lady M. W. Montagu) Tait, n. s. 4: 151. — (G. R. Gleig) Colburn, 56: 234. 57: 17. — Lond. M. 4: 31, 495, 644. 5: 60, 271. — Canad. Mo. 2: 225. — Once a Week, 9: 109, 165.
— — in 1841. Blackw. 50: 571, 722.
— — in 1842. Blackw. 52: 159, 485, 654.
— — in 1845. Blackw. 58: 617.
— Sketches of. Dem. R. 42: 40–292.
— — in Prose and Verse. Colburn, 4: 267–568.
— — of Travel in. (J. A. St. John) Tait, n. s. 16: 509–779.
— Social Equality in. (E. Gryzanowski) Nation, 9: 267.
— Society in. U. S. Cath. M. 6: 401.
— — during the last Days of Roman Republic. (J. A. Froude) Fraser, 94: 150. Same art. Ecl. M. 87: 425.
— Solfaterra and Solfatara of. Penny M. 12: 362.
— Southern, Craven's Tour in. Ed. R. 36: 153.
— — Dialects and Literature of. For. Q. 5: 158.
— — Easter Holidays in. Penny M. 4: 155, 175.
— — Summer in. (E. L. Linton) Gent. M. n. s. 20: 27.
— Spring in Rome and Southern. Colburn, 143: 664. 144: 86–586.
— Spring Wanderings in. (J. A. Symonds) Liv. Age, 149: 812.
— States of, 1827. Mo. R. 118: 57.
— — and Rulers in last Half of the 15th Century. Fraser, 64: 170.
— — Political Condition of. Ed. R. 55: 362. — Mus. 14: 351.
— Statistical Progress of. (S. Brown) J. Statis. Soc. 29: 197.
— Taine's. (H. James, jr.) Nation, 6: 373.
— Theological Literature and Education of. (A. Tholuck) Am. Bib. Repos. 1: 177.
Italy, Things new and old in. (M. G. Grey) Mod. R. 1: 714.
— Tour in. Temp. Bar, 21: 251, 404. — All the Year, 1: 253.
— Tours and Tourists in. Quar. 103: 346.
— Travel in. Dub. Univ. 78: 710. — Lond. M. 4: 140.
— — and Travelers in. (Mrs. Austin) Bentley, 20: 244.
— Mrs. Trollope's Visit to. Tait, n. s. 9: 726. — Mo. R. 159: 328.
— Tuckerman's Sketch-Book in. U. S. Cath. M. 7: 617.
— Unification of, and Count Cavour. (O. M. Spencer) Harper, 43: 329.
— — Hindrances to, 1860. Westm. 74: 386.
— United. (J. Picciotto) Dub. Univ. 78: 241.
— Unity of. (A. F. Hewit) Cath. World, 12: 844. — (H. J. Warner) Chr. Exam. 83: 187. — (O. A. Brownson) Cath. World, 13: 289.
— — and the National Movement in Europe, 1861. (J. S. Barker) Macmil. 3: 71.
— — Benefits of. (M. P. Thompson) Cath. World, 16: 792.
— — Growth of. Nat. R. 12: 189.
— University System of. (A. de Gubernatis) Internat. R. 2: 44.
— Upper, Extinct Kingdom of. Colburn, 84: 128.
— Vagrant Children of. Chamb. J. 54: 614.
— Valetudinarian in. Bentley, 32: 319.
— Vintage of. Penny M. 12: 29.
— Visit to, 1862. (W. Chambers) Chamb. J. 38: 17–263.
— Wanderings in. (B. Murphy) Galaxy, 15: 85, 388, 549. 16: 113, 380.
— — of a Painter in. Bentley, 10: 595.
— — through. (C. T. Ramage) Colburn, 136: 202–439. 137: 47–429. 138: 50–464. 139: 244. 140: 96. 141: 110–459. 142: 65.
— Where is? Brownson. 11: 219.
— Whyte's Pilgrim's Reliquary. Blackw. 59: 249.
— Wine Districts of. Penny M. 13: 462.
— Winter in, Carus's. Colburn, 114: 357.
— With Horace in. (H. D. Jenkins) Overland, 6: 9, 201.
— Women of. Lond. M. 16: 204.
— — Condition of. (E. Gryzanowski) Nation, 9: 456, 480.
— — Madame Pepoli's. For. Q. 28: 91. Same art. Am. Ecl. 3: 57.
— — Some famous. Victoria, 31: 236.
— — Treatment of. St. James, 35: 281.
— — Trollope's Decade of. Tait, n. s. 26: 431.
— Working-Classes in. O. & N. 6: 230.
— Wrongs and Desperation of. Liv. Age, 39: 230.
— Young, Cochrane on. Quar. 87: 533.
Ithaca, Ancient Capitol of. Nature, 18: 590.
— Gell's Antiquities of. Ecl. R. 9: 61, 120.
Itinerancy. (A. C. Barry) Univ. Q. 17: 348.
— Methodist. (J. T. Crane) Meth. Q. 26: 73, 206.
Ittenbach, Franz. Art J. 17: 136.
Iturea. (J. L. Porter) Bib. Sac. 13: 802.
Iuka, Battle of. (D. W. Maury) So. M. 11: 598.
Ivan; a Russian Tale. (T. Gaspey) Peop. J. 6: 1–127.
Ivan the Terrible. St. James, 22: 449.
Ivan VI., Czar of Russia. Penny M. 5: 370.
Ives, Eli, Discourse on. (S. W. S. Dutton) New Eng. 19: 930.
Ives, Levi Silliman, Bp. of N. Carolina. (N. S. Richardson) Am. Church R. 6: 58. — (J. Irwin) Am. Church R. 7: 233.
— Sermons. Princ. 17: 491.
Ives, Moses Brown. Am. J. Educ. 5: 311.
Ivo de Talboy's Picnic. (M. Collins) Belgra. 7: 353.
Ivor Bach. (C. H. Williams) Once a Week, 12: 502.

Ivory and its Applications. Chamb. J. **17**: 57. — Nat. M. **1**: 155.
— and its Imitations. (E. T. Landor) Galaxy, **24**: 792.
— Art in. Once a Week, **3**: 161.
— Box of carved, of the 6th Century. (A. Nesbitt and R. Ganucci) Arch. **44**: 321.
— Origin, Nature, and Uses of. Penny M. **8**: 230.
Ivories. (A. Nesbitt) Art J. **33**: 55, 81.
— Ancient and Mediæval. Ev. Sat. **14**: 126.
— Collections of, and their Prices. Cornh. **16**: 574.
Ivory-Carving in Dieppe. Once a Week, **7**: 415.
Ivory-Carvings, Antique. Art J. **7**: 276.
Ivory Gates; or the Shadow Lady. (C. F. Guernsey) Godey, **96**: 40–489. **97**: 50–492. **98**: 67–237.
Ivory Mine; a Tale. Internat. M. **1**: 117, 156, 210.
Ivory Paper, Preparation of. (S. Einsle) J. Frankl. Inst. **2**: 50.
Ivry, Battle of. Penny M. **2**: 147.
Ivy, The. (B. Barton) Lond. M. **1**: 62.
— Symbolism of. (C. G. Leland) Contin. Mo. **3**: 47.
Ixion in Heaven; a Sketch. Colburn, **35**: 514. **37**: 175.
Ixotle. (A. J. Grayson) Overland, **5**: 258.
Izard, Ralph, Correspondence of. Dem. R. **19**: 40.
Izdubar, The Poem of. Cath. World, **20**: 138.

J

Jabbering. (J. Nichol) Good Words, **22**: 837.
Jabez Oliphant. Fraser, **79**: 188–794. **80**: 129–738. **81**: 255, 388.
Jaca-Tree. Penny M. **3**: 433.
Jack, a Mendicant. (C. L. Pirkis) Belgra. **45**: supp. 56.
Jack among the Lawyers. Fraser, **18**: 270.
Jack and the Bean-Stalk. (A. I. Thackeray) Cornh. **28**: 311, 431. Same art. Liv. Age, **119**: 207–414. Same art. Ecl. M. **81**: 651. **82**: 221. Same art. Ev. Sat. **15**: 344, 457.
— Religious Aspect of the Myth. Once a Week, **18**: 192.
Jack and Mrs. Brown. (Miss Taylor) Lippinc. **21**: 57–350.
Jack the Giant-Killer. (A. I. Thackeray) Cornh. **16**: 589, 739. **17**: 1. Same art. Liv. Age, **95**: 540, **96**: 107, 266. Same art. Ev. Sat. **4**: 673, 804. **5**: 150.
Jack the Post. Temp. Bar, **36**: 88.
Jack's Aunt's flat Candlestick. Temp. Bar, **30**: 509.
Jack's Sister. Once a Week, **30**: 1–749.
Jack's Wife; a Story. Lond. Soc. **40**: supp. 65.
Jack Dessart; a Story. (B. Nash) Lakeside, **6**: 307.
Jack Downing's Letters. *See* Smith, Seba.
Jack Doyle's Daughter. (R. E. Francillon) All the Year, **47**: 1.
Jack Haviland; a Tale. Chamb. J. **46**: 363.
Jack Hazlitt; a Tale. Irish Mo. **2**: 22–472.
Jack Hinton, the Guardsman. (C. Lever) Dub. Univ. **19**: 293–691. **20**: 1–635. Same art. Mus. **44**: 409. **45**: 507, 836.
Jack Horner's Pie. All the Year, **37**: 347.
Jack Laybourne's Inheritance. Argosy, **30**: 271.
Jack Layford's Friend; a Christmas Story. Belgra. **10**: 226.
Jack Lofty. Bentley, **53**: 180.
Jack Maynard's Call. (T. M. Osborne) O. & N. **6**: 48.
Jack Moonlight. Blackw. **65**: 606.
Jack Moriarty and his Contemporaries. Fraser, **27**: 41–427. **28**: 30, 228.
Jack Myers. (P. Mulford) Overland, **15**: 380.
Jack of All Trades. (C. Reade) Harper, **16**: 109–481.
Jack o'Lantern. (W. Besant and J. Rice) Once a Week, **27**: supp.
Jack Osborne's Wooing; a Tale. Bentley, **63**: 315.
Jack Pugh's Legacy. (F. Talbot) Belgra. **18**: 517. **19**: 84.
Jack Purcel and the Crows. (Mrs. S. C. Hall) Godey, **23**: 37.
Jack Quartermain's Vision. Chamb. J. **57**: 152, 167, 186.
Jack Ricketts and the Widow. Blackw. **41**: 510.
Jack Rogers and his Tutor. Bentley, **59**: 249.
Jack Sepoy. Fraser, **54**: 359.
Jack Sheppard. (W. H. Ainsworth) Bentley, **5**: 1–563. **6**: 1–543. **7**: 92, 137. Same art. Mus. **35**: 407, 513. **36**: 133–530. **37**: 131, 361, 481.
Jack Stuart's Bet on the Derby. Blackw. **54**: 67.
Jackal, The. Penny M. **11**: 288.
Jackdaw and the Raven. (E. Jesse) Once a Week, **16**: 540.
Jackson, Andrew. (B. J. Lossing) Harper, **10**: 145. — with portrait, Dem. R. **10**: 80. — Blackw. **91**: 643. **100**: 623. — Colburn, **43**: 231.
— Address to the Army, 1821. Niles's Reg. **21**: 52.
— Administration of. (E. Everett) Ann. Reg. **6**: 9. — (A. H. Everett) Ann. Reg. **7**: 1. **8**: 1.
— and Henry Clay. So. Lit. Mess. **19**: 521, 585.
— and Calhoun; Correspondence on the Seminole War. Niles's Reg. **39**: 447. **40**: 11, 37.
— and his Cabinet, 1830. Niles's Reg. **40**: 143–201. *See also* Cabinet Resignations.
— and Scott, Correspondence between. Niles's Reg. **14**: 121.
— and the United States. For. R. **4**: 445.
— Anecdotes of. (A. Kendall) Dem. R. **11**: 272.
— Assault on Mr. Randolph. Niles's Reg. **44**: 170.
— at Nashville, 1825. Niles's Reg. **28**: 185.
— at New Orleans. Am. Q. **9**: 218. — Dem. R. **8**: 379. — (B. J. Lossing) Potter Am. Mo. **5**: 802.
— — Walker on. Dem. R. **37**: 201.
— Autograph Letter of. Dem. R. **17**: 15.
— Duel with Dickerson. (A. Koesis) Land We Love, **4**: 135.
— Fine of. (A. Kendall) Dem. R. **12**: 58.
— Hermitage of. (B. J. Lossing) Potter Am. Mo. **5**: 721.
— in Florida. Niles's Reg. **14**: 50, 90, 398. **21**: 171. *See also* Seminole War.
— Inauguration of. (E. Everett) Ann. Reg. **5**: 1. — Niles's Reg. **36**: 28. **44**: 21.
— Lawrence's Attempt to assassinate. Niles's Reg. **47**: 390, 418. **48**: 119.
— Letter in Reply to the Charge of being a Military Man. Niles's Reg. **28**: 20, 102.
— — on the Tariff, 1824. Niles's Reg. **26**: 245.
— Life of. West. R. **1**: 1, 87. — (Sir R. de Camden) Potter Am. Mo. **5**: 817.
— Memorial of, 1820. Niles's Reg. **18**: 329.
— Message, 1829. Niles's Reg. **37**: 247. — Ann. Reg. **5**: [1.
— — 1830. Niles's Reg. **39**: 253. — Ann. Reg. **6**: [47.
— — 1831. Niles's Reg. **40**: 276. — Ann. Reg. **7**: [45.
— — 1832. Niles's Reg. **43**: 243. — Ann. Reg. **8**: [80.
— — 1833. Niles's Reg. **45**: 231.
— — 1834. Niles's Reg. **47**: 224.
— — 1835. Niles's Reg. **49**: 248.
— — on the Maysville Road. Ann. Reg. **5**: [22.

Jackson, Andrew, Mrs. Barrey's Letter to. Niles's Reg. **38**: 219.
— Nullification Proclamation. Niles's Reg. **43**: 260, 339. — Ann. Reg. **8**: [96.
— Origin of Term "Old Hickory." Hist. M. **10**: 55.
— Parton's Life of. (W. J. Grayson) De Bow, **29**: 342.
— Presidency of, Reminiscences of. Republic, **6**: 289.
— Protest, 1834. Niles's Reg. **46**: 138.
— — Calhoun's Speech on. Niles's Reg. **46**: 213.
— — Forsyth's Speech on. Niles's Reg. **46**: 249.
— Reminiscences of. Contin. Mo. **2**: 318.
— Sketch of, with portrait. Ecl. M. **53**: 275.
— Trial of, in New Orleans. Am. Hist. Rec. **2**: 97.
— Veto of the Bank Bill. Niles's Reg. **42**: 365. — Ann. Reg. **7**: [60.
— — of the Land Bill. Niles's Reg. **45**: 285.
— — of the Lighthouse Bill. Niles's Reg. **43**: 307. — Ann. Reg. 8: 95.
— vindicated from Charges, 1827. Niles's Reg. **32**: 251.
— Von Holst's Administration of. (H. Adams) No. Am. **120**: 179.
— Washington, and Buchanan. Nat. R. **12**: 499.
Jackson, Charles T., with portrait. Pop Sci. Mo. **19**: 404.
Jackson, E. (G. Morely) Meth. M. **30**: 145.
Jackson, Sir George, Diaries and Letters of. Temp. Bar, **38**: 354.
Jackson, Helen Hunt, Writings of. Canad. Mo. **14**: 124.
Jackson, Henry R., Poetry of. (J. A. Turner) So. Lit. Mess. **18**: 179.
— Tallulah, and other Poems. So. Q. **19**: 257.
Jackson, Dr. James, Memoir of. Chr. R. **1**: 502.
Jackson, James, jr. (A. Norton) Chr. Exam. **19**: 83.
Jackson, John, amongst the Slaveholders of Santa Cruz. Mo. Rel. M. **23**: 113, 177.
— Memoirs of. Mo. Rel. M. **20**: 21–351.
Jackson, John, Bishop of London. Cong. **2**: 683.
Jackson, Patrick Tracy, with portrait. (J. A. Lowell) Hunt, **18**: 355.
Jackson, Thomas, Memoir of. Cong. M. **20**: 676.
Jackson, Thos., Autobiography of. Lond. Q. **41**: 307.
Jackson, Gen. Thomas J. [*Stonewall*]. (J. A. Early) So. M. **12**: 537. — (H. R. Jackson) Land We Love, **5**: 291. — (W. H. Kemper and M. D. Hoge) So. M. **17**: 699. — Scrib. **18** : 220. — Am. Hist. Rec. **2**: 493. — Broadw. **10**: 445.
— a Historical Study. (E. A. Pollard) Putnam, **12**: 733.
— Anecdote of. So. Hist. Pap. **9**: 424.
— at Fredericksburg. (J. A. Early) Hist. M. **18**: 32.
— Campaign in Shenandoah Valley. (F. W. Palfrey) Nation, **31**: 81. — So. Hist. Pap. **7**: 1.
— Death of. (H. K. Douglas) So. M. **14**: 370.
— Dispatches of. Land We Love, **1**: 114.
— in Lexington, Va. So. Hist. Pap. **9**: 41.
— Life of. Chr. Obs. **65**: 120.
— Sketch of. Land We Love, **1**: 73.
— Sketches of. (R. L. Dabney) Land We Love, **1**: 310.
— Unveiling Statue of. So Hist. Pap. **9**: 212.
— Wounding of. Land We Love, **1**: 179. — So. Hist. Pap. **6**: 230, 261.
Jackson, Maj. William. Am. Hist. Rec. **3**: 193. — (C. W. Littell) Pennsyl. M. **2**: 353.
Jackson, William, the Naturalist. Chamb. J. **12**: 165.
Jackson, Captain. (C. Lamb) Lond. M. **10**: 481.
Jackson of Exeter; a Psychological Memoir. Colburn, **35**: 256.
Jackson of Paul's. (H. Kingsley) Dark Blue, **1**: 302, 456.
Jackson, Mississippi. De Bow, **26**: 466.
Jacksonville, Ill. (A. A. Graham) Potter Am. Mo. **11**: 241.
Jacob. (J. F. Mackarness) Good Words, **10**: 402.
— and Esau. (F. B. Hornbrooke) Unita. R. **13**: 253.
— Death of; a Poem. (W. Alexander) Dub. Univ. **50**: 1.
— Dream of. Chr. Obs. **60**: 801.
Jacob, Flight of. Theo. R. **2**: 297.
— Wrestling of. (J. O. Skinner) Univ. Q. **32**: 160, 410.
Jacob of Edessa, Two Epistles of. Kitto, **38**: 430.
Jacobi, F. H. (W. C. Sawyer) Meth. Q. **40**: 486.
— and the Philosophy of Faith. (R. H. Worthington) J. Spec. Philos. **12**: 393.
Jacobins and Jesuits. For. R. **1**: 84.
Jacobinism, Gallicanism, and Jansenism. Dub. R. **37**: 98.
Jacobites, The. (A. C. Fraser) No. Brit. **5**: 329. Same art. Liv. Age, **10**: 537.
Jacobite Ladies of Murrays Hall. Cornh. **19**: 568.
Jacobite Memoirs. Westm. **21**: 78.
Jacobite Relics of Scotland, Hogg's. Ed. R. **34**: 148.
Jacobs, Mrs. Bela, Memoir of. Chr. R. **2**: 376.
Jacoby, Johann. (H. von Holst) Nation, **24**: 262.
Jacopo and the Goslings. (T. Hood) Lond. Soc. **18**: 539.
Jacotot, Jean Joseph. (R. H. Quick) Am. J. Educ. **26**: 545.
Jacquard, Joseph M., the Silk-Weaver of Lyons. Sharpe, **2**: 228. Same art. Liv. Age, **11**: 205.
Jacquard Loom. Penny M. **2**: 13.
— its Capabilities as an Engine of Art. Art J. **2**: 189.
Jacque, Charles. (R. Ménard) Portfo. **6**: 130.
Jacquemart, Jules. (F. Wedmore) 19th Cent. **9**: 681.
— Etchings from Pictures. (P. G. Hamerton) Portfo. **4**: 10.
Jacquemont, Victor. Liv. Age, **96**: 565. — Chamb. J. **57**: 103.
— Letters of. Ed. R. **130**: 56. — (Sir J. Barrow) Quar. **53**: 19.
Jacques; an Episode of '93. (D. C. Murray) Chamb. J. **58**: 744, 755.
Jacques in the Forest; a Sketch. Cornh. **13**: 307.
Jacques Bonhomme. Bentley, **20**: 55.
Jade and Kindred Stones. (F. W. Rudler) Pop. Sci. R. **18**: 337. — (L. Blondel) Smith's Rpt. **1876**: 402.
Jael. (T. A. Harcourt) Overland, **14**: 183.
Jaenicke, J., Memoir of. Cong. M. **11**: 393.
Jaffa. (N. Macleod) Good Words, **6**: 286.
Jago, Richard, Life and Writings of. Lond. M. **6**: 419.
Jaguar, Home of the. (F. L. Oswald) Lippinc. **21**: 440.
Jaguar Hunt. (J. T. Trowbridge) Atlan. **15**: 742.
Jahankueir, Emperor, Autobiography of. Quar. **51**: 96.
Jails and Almshouses, County. (C. L. Brace) Nation, **22**: 199.
— Austrian, Taste of. House. Words, **4**: 368.
Jail-Bird, Reflections of a. New Eng. M. **7**: 366.
Jail-Birds. Chamb. J. **44**: 384. **48**: 721.
Jainism. (M. Williams) Contemp. **36**: 644.
Jalisco, Lake Regions of, Rambles in. (F. L. Oswald) Lippinc. **24**: 281.
Jamaica, Island of. (M. O'C. Morris) Temp. Bar, **16**: 209. Same art. Ecl. M. **66**: 284. — (C. C. Starbuck) Contin. Mo. **4**: 284, 433. **5**: 461. — (G. Turner) Geog. M. **1**: 153–375. **2**: 78. — All the Year, **15**: 173. — Brit. Q. **32**: 99. — (J. Foster) Ecl. R. **9**: 324. — Ecl. R. **122**: 235. — Mo. R. **110**: 307.
— Agricultural and Commercial Association of. (J. M. Ludlow) Good Words, **7**: 672.
— Blue Mountains of. Blackw. **4**: 654. — (J. A. Wilson) Belgra. **39**: 245.
— Cast away in. (W. G. Sewall) Harper, **22**: 166.
— Day in Woods of. (P. H. Gosse) Good Words, **3**: 235.
— Emancipation in. (C. C. Starbuck) Contin. Mo. **4**: 1. — (C. S. Renshaw) New Eng. **6**: 557.
— Epicure in. (J. A. Wilson) Belgra. **44**: 285.
— in 1750. Once a Week, **30**: 712.
— in 1808–10. Quar. **6**: 147.
— in 1823, Williams's Tour in. Lond. M. **14**: 543.
— in 1841, Week in. Sharpe, **15**: 243.
— in 1850. Dem. R. **27**: 481.
— — Bigelow's. Liv. Age, **29**: 426.
— in 1853, Distress in. Westm. **59**: 327.

Jamaica, Island of, in 1854. (J. Linen) Knick. 43: 374.
— in 1866. Dub. R. 59: 362.
— in 1872. Quar. 139: 40.
— Insurrection in, 1865. (G. G. Hubbard) New Eng. 26: 53. — (B. P. Hunt) Liv. Age, 87: 521. — (G. Reynolds) Atlan. 17: 480. — Fraser, 73: 161. — Ecl. R. 122: 359. — Nation, 1: 678.
— — Report of Royal Commission on. Brit. Q. 44: 452.
— Letters from. (W. C. Bryant) Liv. Age, 24: 565, 593. 25: 125-412. 26: 251.
— Lewis's Journal of Residence in. Mo. R. 133: 498.
— Life in the Mountains of. Chamb. J. 43: 520.
— Madness of Slaveholders in. Tait, 2: 203, 246.
— Maroons of. (T. W. Higginson) Atlan. 5: 213. — Ev. Sat. 1: 50.
— Massacre in, 1865. (M. D. Conway) Radical, 2: 193, 507. — (R. A. Johnson) Hours at Home. 2: 537.
— Lord Metcalf's Government of. Blackw. 60: 662.
— Missions in. Cong. M. 25: 596, 753, 854.
— — Baptist. Cong. M. 26: 197.
— My Holiday in. Chamb. J. 57: 708-755. Same art. Liv. Age, 147: 749, 818. 148: 41.
— Naturalist in, Gosse's. Fraser, 45: 379. Same art. Liv. Age, 33: 396.
— Negro Life in. (G. O. Seilhamer) Harper, 44: 553.
— of To-Day. St. James, 15: 59, 188.
— Old Times in. Once a Week, 14: 581.
— Past and Present of. (G. W. Perkins) New Eng. 2: 560. — Tait, n. s. 10: 745. — Mo. R. 162: 432.
— Question of. Blackw. 46: 75. — Fraser, 73: 277. — Ed. R. 69: 527.
— Recollections of. Nat. M. 4: 240.
— Religion in. (J. Hodson) Cath. World, 26: 69.
— Religious State of. (C. S. Renshaw) New Eng. 4: 19.
— Revivals in. All the Year, 4: 521.
— Scenes and Customs in. Dub. Univ. 57: 675.
— Slave Insurrection in. Tait, 1: 81, 124, 241. — Ecl. R. 55: 244, 544.
— Stewart's View of. Mo. R. 102: 43.
— Sugar Culture and Slavery in, 1866. Westm. 88: 189.
— Sugar Farm in. Penny M. 5: 348.
— Taxation in. (R. A. Johnson) Nation, 1: 71.
— Underhill on. Ecl. R. 115: 245.
— Visit to. (J. A. Wilson) Belgra. 35: 415.
— Voyage to. Dial, 4: 116, 227.
James, the Apostle; Alleged Disagreement with Paul. (E. P. Barrows) Bib. Sac. 9: 761.
— and John, Lives of. Chr. Obs. 1: 345.
— and Paul compared. (L. W. Heydenreich) Evang. R. 14: 382.
James the Son of Alphæus, and James the Brother of the Lord, are they identical? (J. I. Mombert) Princ. 37: 1.
James the Less, Disciple of our Lord. Lond. Q. 13: 285.
James I., of England. House. Words, 13: 37. Same art. Liv. Age, 48: 785.
— Aikin's Memoirs of the Court of. Ecl. R. 36: 97. — Mo. R. 97: 225.
— and Charles I. (P. Bayne) Contemp. 24: 696, 904. Same art. Liv. Age, 123: 387, 549.
— and Lord Digby; a Reply to Mr. Spedding. (S. R. Gardiner) Fraser. 83: 571.
— and his Historians. Quar. 139: 1. Same art. Liv. Age, 126: 64.
— Coronation of. Penny M. 7: 186.
— Correspondence of. Liv. Age, 70: 163.
— Court of, Goodman's. Ecl. R. 70: 91. — Mo. R. 149: 149.
— — in Venetian Dispatches. Quar. 102: 398.
— — Progresses of. Quar. 41: 54.
— — Weldon's. Retros. 7: 29.
— Court and Times of. (T. Birch) Colburn, 83: 309.
James I., Critical Estimates of. Quar. 139: 1.
— Dekker's Entertainment to. Retros. 11: 88.
— English Society under. Brit. Q. 7: 73.
— Gardiner's History of. Fraser, 69: 419.
— Grants of Monopolies made by. (S. R. Gardiner) Arch. 41: 219.
— Letter from. Blackw. 2: 628.
— Navy of. (J. Brand) Arch. 15: 53.
— Nichols's Progresses of. Retros. 15: 387.
— Pecuniary Distress of. Blackw. 2: 312.
— Poet King of Scotland. Fraser, 90: 378. Same art. Liv. Age, 123: 232.
— Warrant to send Jewels to Spain. (R. Lemon) Arch. 21: 148.
James II. and Mary of Modena. Dub. R. 22: 428.
— and the Protestant Bishops. Ecl. R. 87: 34.
— Fox's History of. Chr. Obs. 7: 660, 712, 792. 8: 41. — (F. Jeffrey) Ed. R. 12: 271. — (J. Foster) Ecl. R. 8: 800, 900. 10: 638.
— — Heywood's Vindication of. (Syd. Smith) Ed. R. 18: 325. — (J. Foster) Ecl. R. 14: 1041. *See* Fox, C. J.
— Irish Army List of. Dub. R. 49: 190.
— Life of. Ed. R. 26: 402.
— What the United States owe to. (J. G. Shea) Am. Cath. Q. 2: 226.
— Will, and Inventory of his Goods. Arch. 18: 223.
James IV., of Scotland, Marriage of. Select J. 3: 110.
— Sword, Dagger, and Ring of. (Sir C. G. Young) Arch. 33: 335.
James V., of Scotland, Household Book of. (H. Ellis) Arch. 22: 1.
— Passages from Life of. Sharpe, 10: 152, 287, 344.
James, Charles T., Portrait of. De Bow, 9: 577.
James, G. P. R. (P. Frank) Ecl. M. 22: 98. — Peop. J. 10: 183.
— Adrian. New Q. 1: 278.
— Arrah Neil. Ecl. R. 83: 99.
— Forest Days. Mo. R. 160: 422.
— John Marston Hall. Am. Mo. M. 3: 338.
— Morley Ernstein. Tait, n. s. 9: 513.
— Novels of. (E. P. Whipple) No. Am. 58: 267. — Dub. Univ. 19: 341. — Am. Q. 22: 252. — Liv. Age, 10: 49. — (F. D. Huntington) Chr. Exam. 42: 101. — So. Lit. Mess. 6: 300. 9: 503. — Am. Mo. R. 3: 268.
— Poems on America. Am. Whig R. 12: 402.
— Recollections of. Bentley, 49: 192. Same art. Liv. Age, 69: 159.
— Sir Theodore Broughton. Dub. Univ. 32: 98.
James, Henry, jr. Portrait of a Lady. (H. A. Huntington) Dial (Ch.), 2: 214.
— Roderick Hudson. (S. B. Wister) No. Am. 122: 420.
James, John. Am. Meth. M. 16: 361.
James, John Angell. (J. C. Miller) Ex. H. Lec. 20: 165. — Ecl. R. 111: 175. 114: 1. — Liv. Age, 71: 132. — No. Brit. 37: 249. — with portrait, Hogg, 1: 65.
— Christian Professor. Ecl. R. 66: 538.
— Life and Letters of. Chr. Rem. 42: 319. — Lond. Q. 17: 205.
— Memoir of. (R. W. Dale) Cong. 6: 449.
— Sermons of. (R. Robbins) Chr. Mo. Spec. 9: 428.
— Works of. (W. B. Sprague) Lit. & Theo. R. 1: 595.
James von Artevelde; a Historical Romance. Westm. 53: 217.
James's Island, S. C. Land We Love, 6: 212.
James River, Along the. (J. E. Cooke) Galaxy, 2: 175.
Jameson, Mrs. Anna. Art J. 12: 157. — Blackw. 125: 207. Same art. Appleton, 21: 267. — (H. Bedford) Irish Mo. 4: 425. — Argosy, 31: 448. — (M. Focer) Potter Am. Mo. 14: 284. — Eng. Dom. M. 26: 43. — Liv. Age, 65: 445.

Jameson, Mrs. Anna. Characteristics of Women. Blackw. **33**: 124, 391, 539. — Am. Mo. R. **3**: 478. — Ed. R. **60**: 180. — Mo. R. **128**: 601.
— Christian Art. Cath. World, **1**: 246.
— Commonplace Book. Colburn, **103**: 193. Same art. Liv. Age, **44**: 778. — Irish Q. **5**: 173. — Liv. Age, **44**: 95.
— Communion of Labor. Dub. R. **41**: 123.
— Diary of an Ennuyée. Mo. R. **109**: 414.
— History of Our Lord. Dub. R. **55**: 402.
— Legends of the Madonna. Ed. R. **97**: 230.
— — of the Monastic Orders. Blackw. **69**: 305.
— Loves of the Poets. Am. Mo. R. **3**: 384. — Mo. R. **120**: 17. — Blackw. **26**: 524.
— Memoirs of. Ed. R. **149**: 84. — Canad. Mo. **14**: 765. — Penn Mo. **10**: 313 — Liv. Age, **139**: 636. — (M. P. Lowe) Unita. R. **11**: 214.
— Poetry of Sacred and Legendary Art. (C. Kingsley) Fraser, **39**: 283. — Ed. R. **89**: 381. — Brit. Q. **10**: 208. — Blackw. **65**: 175. — Dub. R. **30**: 453.
— Winter Studies and Summer Rambles. Brit. & For. R. **8**: 134.
— Writings of. Colburn, **99**: 457. Same art. Ecl. M. **31**: 211. Same art. Liv. Age, **40**: 147.
Jameson, John, with portrait. (G. Gilfillan) Hogg, **7**: 353.
Jameson, R. S., Sonnets to. (H. Coleridge) Lond. M. **7**: 180.
Jamestown, Va., 250th Anniversary of the Settlement of. So. Lit. Mess. **24**: 434.
— List of Ships arrived at, 1607–24. N. E. Reg. **30**: 414.
Jámi, the Persian Poet. Fraser, **54**: 603.
Jamie McQueeston; a Story. Peop. J. **11**: 40, 96.
Jamieson, John, Author of Scottish Dictionary. Tait, n. s. **8**: 514.
Jamieson, Robert, Sketch of. (G. Gilfillan) Hogg, **1**: 81.
Jamison, David. (E. B. O'Callaghan) M. Am. Hist. **1**: 21.
Jamrach, Charles, Museum of. (R. Rowe) Good Words, **20**: 165.
Jamyn, Amadis, early French Poet. Lond. M. **9**: 251.
Jan Mayen, the Mountain Island. Chamb J. **28**: 211. Same art. Liv. Age, **55**: 494.
Jane Eyre's School. Belgra. **5**: 237.
Jane Hearne's Trial; a Story. All the Year, **45**: 228–274.
Jane Gurley's Story. (E. S. Phelps) Hours at Home, **2**: 406, 494. **3**: 19–538.
Jane Ibbotson's Warning. (M. Howitt) Ev. Sat. **2**: 686.
Jane Marshall's Golden Wedding; a Story. (M. Fall) Tinsley, **26**: 430.
Jane Ogilvie; an Irish Tale. Portfo.(Den.) **31**: 34.
Jane Shore. Colburn, **163**: 337.
Jane Sinclair. (W. Carleton) Dub. Univ. **8**: 335–705.
Jane's Vocation. (G. L. Emery) Cath. World, **25**: 525.
Janes, Edmund S., Portrait of. Meth. Q. **10**: 1.
Janet's Repentance. (Geo. Eliot) Blackw. **82**: 55–519. Same art. Liv. Age, **54**: 399, 655. **55**: 158, 422, 677.
Janet Mason's Troubles. Liv. Age, **129**: 659, 793. **130**: 99.
Janin, Jules. (E. About) Ev. Sat. **17**: 92. — (J. E. Cooke) So. M. **15**: 455. — with portrait, Appleton, **10**: 620. — Knick. **59**: 78.
— and the Paris Feuilletonistes. Internat. M. **4**: 19.
— as a Critic. (J. D. Osborne) Scrib. **11**: 823.
— how he became a Journalist. Temp. Bar, **45**: 71.
— last of the Bohemians. (A. Rhodes) Galaxy, **19**: 214.
Janissaries, Fall of the. Chamb. J. **8**: 307.
Janney, Samuel L., Poems of. So. Lit. Mess. **5**: 505.
Jánnina, Greek or Turkish? (G. A. Macmillan) Macmil. **40**: 90. Same art. Liv. Age, **141**: 757.
Jans von Steufle's Donkey. (Mrs. Brooks) Cath. World, **15**: 92.
Jansen, Kristofer. Sigmund Bresteson. (H. H. Boyesen) No. Am. **115**: 379.
Jansen, Stephen Theodore, Biography of. Hunt, **3**: 148.
Jansenism. No. Brit. **29**: 282.
— Gallicanism, and Jacobinism. Dub. R. **37**: 98.
— History and Merits of. (S. M. Schmucker) Am. Bib. Repos. 3d s. **3**: 689.
— Jervis on. Dub. R. **74**: 362.
— Neale's History of. Dub. R. **45**: 428.
— Rise and Sufferings of. Kitto, **7**: 34.
Jansenists, The. (J. Chaplin) Chr. R. **21**: 161.
— and Clement XI. (J. Murdock) Am. Church R. **10**: 551.
— and Quesnel. (J. W. Alexander) Princ. **28**: 132.
— Dutch, and Dr. Wordsworth. Month, **15**: 492.
— History of. (S. K. Kollock) Princ. **28**: 112.
Jansenist Bible Society. Chr. Obs. **46**: 282.
Jansenist Church of Holland. Ecl. R. **108**: 138.
Jansenist Schism in Holland. (C. von Akm) Cath. World, **18**: 686, 838.
Januarius, St., of Naples. (A. Dumas) Canad. Mo. **5**: 45. — (F. Parke) Dub. Univ. **89**: 25.
— Liquefaction of Blood of. (P. N. Lynch) Cath. World, **13**: 772. **14**: 32–526. — Month, **3**: 81.
January. (W. Howitt) Howitt, **1**: 9.
— Gossip about. (C. A. White) Peop. J. **9**: 1.
January Day. Fraser, **63**: 41. Same art. Liv. Age, **68**: 771.
Japan. Ed. R. **96**: 348. Same art. Ecl. M. **28**: 21. — Quar. **114**: 449. **137**: 189. — Blackw. **112**: 369. Same art. Ecl. M. **79**: 513. — Blackw. **115**: 696. — All the Year, **6**: 284. — Chamb. J. **51**: 87. **58**: 214. — Colburn, **95**: 95. — Fraser, **69**: 101. — House. Words, **3**: 160. — Liv. Age, **14**: 466. — Lond. Q. **42**: 83. — Macmil. **26**: 493. — (F. Vinton) Putnam, **1**: 241. — Republic, **1**: 123. — Tait, n. s. **25**: 732.
— Adventure in. (G. P. Briggs) Scrib. **2**: 513. — Lippinc. **19**: 284.
— Adventures in. Chamb. J. **18**: 74. Same art. Liv. Age, **35**: 284.
— Alcock's Narrative. (A. H. Guernsey) Harper, **27**: 721. **28**: 18, 167. — Ed. R. **117**: 517.
— American in. (A. W. Habersham) Harper, **18**: 223. — Dub. Univ. **80**: 658.
— Americans in. De Bow, **27**: 371. — Liv. Age, **23**: 145.
— and China in 1865. Ed. R. **122**: 175.
— and the China Seas. Godey, **54**: 107, 203.
— and England, Earliest Intercourse between. St. James, **15**: 635.
— — Intercourse between. Chamb. J. **7**: 375.
— and the Japanese. (M. A. Bruhmet) Potter Am. Mo. **13**: 241, 321. — (T. F. R. Mercein) Meth. Q. **13**: 282. — Bentley, **44**: 623. — Chamb. J. **36**: 153. — Ed. R. **113**: 37. — Knick. **64**: 249. — No. Brit. **31**: 424. Same art. Ecl. M. **50**: 184. — Sharpe, **44**: 81. — So. R. n. s. **16**: 32.
— and the Jesuits. Am. Presb. R. **1**: 452, 588.
— and Malaysia, Claims of, 1837. Ecl. R. **71**: 105.
— — Voyages to, 1837. Mo. R. **149**: 88.
— and Manilla, Lady's Visit to. Liv. Age, **79**: 231.
— and the outside World, 1852–54. Ref. Q. **26**: 48.
— — Intercourse between, 1860. (E. H. House) Atlan. **5**: 721. — (N. Hale) Chr. Exam. **69**: 101. — Liv. Age, **2**: 242.
— and Prussia. Ev. Sat. **10**. 503.
— and the United States. Dem. R. **30**: 319.
— — Japanese Experience of our Civil Service. (D. A. Wells) Nation, **15**: 212.
— — New Treaty between, 1858. Fraser, **58**: 650.
— Architecture in. (J. Conder) Ecl. Engin. **18**: 509.
— Art in. (Sir R. Alcock) Art J. **29**: 73, 134. **30**: 77, 233, 261. — (R. Sturgis) Nation, **7**: 16–215. — Art J. **24**: 293.

Japan, Art in, Decorative. Ecl. Engin. **3**: 313.
— Art Manufactures of. Pract. M. **7**: 364.
— Artisan of. Ecl. Engin. **21**: 75.
— Ascent of Fusi-Yama. Ecl. M. **55**: 220. — (C. Gordon-Cumming) Harper, **61**: 649.
— awakened. (N. Brooks) Scrib. **3**: 669.
— Miss Bird's. (S W. Williams) New Eng. **40**: 201.
— Count de Beauvoir in. (E. Howland) Lippinc. **13**: 405.
— Botany of. (A. Gray) Am. J. Sci. **78**: 187.
— Call on a Bonze. (W. E. Griffis) Lippinc. **13**: 725.
— Central. (E. R. Crooke) Geog. M. **3**: 286.
— Ceramic Art of. Dub. R. **78**: 374.
— Change and Progress in. Ecl. M. **76**: 742.
— Children in. Ev. Sat. **16**: 429. — Liv. Age, **134**: 312.
— Chinaman's Journal in. Liv. Age, **62**: 186.
— Christianity in. Nat. R. **10**: 446.
— — Hundred Years of. Quar. **130**: 534. Same art. Ecl. M. **77**: 1.
— Civilization in. Chamb. J. **49**: 740.
— Commerce with. Hunt, **1**: 208.
— — Opening of. (W. C. Bryant) Am. Hist. Rec. **3**: 148, 291. — Liv. Age, **42**: 189.
— — Prospective. De Bow, **9**: 444.
— Commercial Condition of, 1872. Pract. M. **3**: 393.
— Commercial Mission to. Ecl. R. **91**: 573. — Fraser, **34**: 696. — Liv. Age, **25**: 548.
— Costumes and Customs of. Ev. Sat. **9**: 157, 308, 317.
— Cruise in. Blackw. **84**: 635. **85**: 49–532.
— Currency of. (J. Newton) Intel. Obs. **12**: 13.
— A Daimio's Life. (W. E. Griffis) Lippinc. **16**: 199.
— Daughters of. (F. B. Harris) Potter Am. Mo. **10**: 349.
— Diary in. Chamb. J. **47**: 364, 380.
— Doeff's Recollections of. (Sir J. Barrow) Quar. **56**: 415.
— Dolmens in. (E. S. Morse) Pop. Sci. Mo. **16**: 593.
— Elgin's Mission to. Bentley, **47**: 136. — (A. H. Guernsey) Harper, **21**: 311. — Dub. R. **48**: 401. — Dub. Univ. **55**: 425. — Ed. R. **111**: 96. — Liv. Age, **59**: 893.
— Embassy to. Dub. Univ. **35**: 732.
— Empire of. De Bow, **13**: 541. — Penny M. **7**: 377, 396.
— — in 1859. Colburn, **115**: 1.
— — Randall's. Liv. Age, **30**: 126.
— Engineering Education in. Nature, **16**: 44.
— English Influence in. (Sir C. W. Dilke) Fortn. **26**: 424.
— Englishmen in. (J. Denis) St. James, **9**: 308.
— European Connection, Religion, and People. Chr. Rem. **24**: 447.
— Excursion in. Belgra. **12**: 318.
— Expeditions to. Sharpe, **15**: 332. Same art. Ecl. M. **26**: 420.
— Eyes and Ears in. (G. W. Bacon) Hours at Home, **6**: 155.
— Facts about. (G. Webster) Overland, **7**: 459.
— Family in, and in Rome. (K. Minra) New Eng. **37**: 670.
— Firemen in. All the Year, **39**: 400.
— First British Legation in. Colburn, **127**: 379.
— Five Years in. (D. B. Simmons) Galaxy, **5**: 606.
— Foreign Relations of. (Dr. Macgowan) Contin. Mo. **4**: 333. — Fraser, **51**: 145. — (E. W. Clark) Internat. R. **4**: 51. *See* Japan and Great Britain; Japan and the U. S.; etc.
— Fortune's Journey to. Colburn, **128**: 300. — Liv. Age, **77**: 186.
— Fox Myths of. (W. E. Griffin) Lippinc. **13**: 57.
— Gardeners of. (E. Jesse) Once a Week, **4**: 581.
— General Description of. Westm. **73**: 508.
— Geological Changes in. (A. S. Bickmore) Am. J. Sci. **95**: 209.
— Golownin's Captivity in. (N. Hale) No. Am. **10**: 33. — Quar. **22**: 107. — Mo. R. **91**: 39. — Portfo. (Den.) **20**: 208, 244. — Ecl. R. **28**: 379. **29**: 244.
Japan, Griffis's Mikado's Empire. (A. H. Guernsey) Harper, **53**: 496. — (R. Pumpelly) Nation, **23**: 316. — Brit. Q. **67**: 1.
— Hara-Kiri in. (A. B. Mitford) Cornh. **20**: 549.
— Consul Harris's Progress in, 1858. Liv. Age, **59**: 834. **60**: 567.
— Health Matters in. (E. S. Morse) Pop. Sci. Mo. **12**: 280.
— History of, Brief. (N. Brooks) Overland, **9**: 105.
— History, Traditions, and Religions of, Reed's. (W. E. Griffis) Nation, **32**: 281.
— Holiday in. (H. F. Abell) Belgra. **31**: 314.
— Holy Places of. (J. Harris) Overland, **1**: 240.
— Houses in. Am. Arch. **1**: 26.
— Illustrations of. Mo. R. **99**: 337.
— in 1852. Dub. R. **33**: 269.
— in 1858–60, Ch. de Chassiron on. Colburn, **125**: 200.
— in 1860. Brit. Q. **31**: 466.
— Industries of. All the Year, **36**: 87. — Pract. M. **7**: 102.
— Inside. (W. E. Griffis) Lippinc. **12**: 174.
— Interior of. Hogg, **13**: 182.
— Jaunts in. (W. H. Hallock) Scrib. **2**: 241.
— Kiyôto, the Sacred City of. (C. A. G. Bridge) Ecl. M. **90**: 288.
— Lady's Wanderings in. Appleton, **25**: 148.
— Learned Societies in. Nature, **24**: 538.
— Letters from. (J. B. Putnam) Putnam, **11**: 631, 758.
— Life in. Chamb. J. **46**: 405. — All the Year, **36**: 341.
— MacFarlane's Account of. Ecl. R. **96**: 468. — Liv. Age, **35**: 324.
— Manners and Customs in. Tait, n. s. **8**: 330. — Brit. Q. **29**: 483. — Dub. Univ. **18**: 1. Same art. Mus. **26**: 191. — (Sir J. Barrow) Quar. **52**: 293.
— — Revolution of. Blackw. **115**: 696. Same art. Liv. Age, **122**: 238.
— — Siebold on. Mo. R. **154**: 465.
— Marriage in. All the Year, **31**: 415.
— — in high Life. (W. E. Griffis) Lippinc. **15**: 176.
— Martyrs of. Fraser, **67**: 396. Same art. Ecl. M. **59**: 40.
— — Canonization of. (C. H. Brigham) Chr. Exam. **74**: 246.
— Martyrdom of an Empire. (E. H. House) Atlan. **47**: 610.
— Mediterranean of. (C. A. G. Bridge) Fortn. **24**: 205. Same art. Liv. Age, **126**: 676. — Blackw. **90**: 613.
— Meteorology of. Nature, **14**: 295. **22**: 344.
— Mineral Resources of. Ecl. Engin. **15**: 424.
— Mint of, 1874. Bank. M. (L.) **35**: 169.
— Mission Fields in. (W. F. Stevenson) Good Words, **20**: 48–818.
— Missions in. Sharpe, **12**: 84.
— — Jesuit Attempts at. Chr. R. **25**: 632.
— — Sketches of early. Month, **11**: 25, 170, 234.
— Mitford's Tales of Old. (R. Sturgis) Nation, **13**: 245.
— Modern. (Sir D. Wedderburn) Fortn. **29**: 417, 529. Same art. Liv. Age, **137**: 222, 345. — Month, **15**: 136.
— Month in a Japanese Farmhouse. Temp. Bar. **44**: 356. Same art. Ecl. M. **85**: 403. Same art. Liv. Age, **126**: 468.
— Moral and Political Revolution in. Blackw. **101**: 427.
— Music in. All the Year, **5**: 149.
— Mythical Zoölogy of. (W. E. Griffis) Overland, **13**: 139.
— Mythology of Ancient. Westm. **110**: 27.
— New Language for. (E. E. Hale) O. & N. **7**: 345.
— Notes on. (L. Oliphant) Canad. J. n. s. **5**: 86.
— Old and New. (Sir R. Alcock) Contemp. **38**: 827.
— Paper-Making in. Chamb. J. **48**: 693. Same art. Ecl. M. **78**: 240.
— Perry's Expedition to. (E. E. Hale) No. Am. **83**: 233. — (R. Tomes) Harper, **12**: 441, 733. — New Q. **5**: 376. — Canad. J. n. s. **1**: 523. — Bentley, **40**: 387. — Dem. R. **32**: 64.
— Persecution in, Recent. Month, **19**: 161.

Japan, Political Tragedies in. Blackw. **91**: 424.
— Prehistoric Man in. (E. S. Morse) Nature, **17**: 89.— Nature, **21**: 350.
— — Traces of. (E. S. Morse) Pop. Sci. Mo. **14**: 257.
— Present and Future of. (E. H. House) Harper, **46**: 858.
— Prisons in. (W. E. Griffis) Overland, **15**: 289.
— Progress and Reform in. Ed. R. **136**: 244.
— Railway Trip in. Chamb. J. **54**: 26.
— Railways in. Ecl. Engin. **3**: 125.
— Recent Changes in. (K. Mitsukuri) Internat. R. **10**: 477.
— Recent Travels in, 1880. Quar. **150**: 305. Same art. Liv. Age, **147**: 451.— Lond. Q. **55**: 333.— Chamb. J. **31**: 100.
— Sir E. Reed's History of. Nature, **22**: 610.
— Reform in. Ed. R. **136**: 244. Same art. Liv. Age, **114**: 670.
— Rein's Travels in. (W. E. Griffis) Nation, **33**: 317.
— Religion of. (D. B. Simmons) Hours at Home, **7**: 435. —(M. A. Bruhmet) Potter Am. Mo. **13**: 161.
— Revolution of 1868–71. (W. E. Griffis) No. Am. **120**: 281.
— — Romance of. Ecl. M. **83**: 309.
— revolutionized. Ed. R. **154**: 122.
— Ride through Yedo. (A. B. Mitford) Fortn. **13**: 505.
— Romance in. Nat. R. **12**: 340. Same art. Ecl. M. **53**: 299.
— Russian Embassy to. Quar. **6**: 357.
— School in. (J. C. Ballagh) Harper, **57**: 663
— Sensation Diplomacy in. Blackw. **93**: 397.
— Sketch-Book in. (E. H. Hall) Dark Blue, **1**: 765.
— Social Life in. House. Words, **19**: 237, 561.
— Society, Art, and Industry of. Pract. M. **1**: 38.
— Some Pictures from. (N. Brooks) Scrib. **11**: 177.
— Something about. (G. B. Bacon) Hours at Home, **5**: 557. **6**: 82.
— Spalding's. Liv. Age, **48**: 395.
— Strange Professions in. All the Year, **44**: 534.
— Summer Outing in. Lond. Soc. **36**: 56.
— Tales of Old. (A. B. Mitford) Fortn. **13**: 668. **14**: 138.— Once a Week, **24**: 417.
— Theater in. All the Year, **38**: 40.
— — Day in. (E. H. House) Atlan. **30**: 257. Same art. Cornh. **26**: 341.
— — Glimpse of. Ecl. M. **75**: 424.
— Theaters of. Appleton, **2**: 449, 481.— Eng. Dom. M. **17**: 186.— Galaxy, **21**: 75.
— Three Years' Residence in. (Sir R. Alcock) Temp. Bar, **8**: 280.
— Titsingh's Illustrations of. Ecl R. **35**: 324.
— Traveling in. Belgra. **36**: 57.
— Treaties with. Liv. Age, **48**: 661.
— Village of. All the Year, **37**: 203.
— Visit to. (C. F. Winslow) Liv. Age, **10**: 335.
— Wanderings in. (A. B. Mitford) Cornh. **25**: 196, 302. Same art. Ecl M. **78**: 399, 662. Same art. Ev. Sat. **13**: 13, 203, 367. Same art. Liv. Age, **112**: 692. **113**: 30.
— Watering-Place in. Belgra. **32**: 475.
— What we know about, 1851. Bentley, **31**: 545.
— Yedo or Yeddo, Capital of the Taikun. (E. H. Hall) Lippinc. **3**: 322.
— Yokohama Pidgin. Liv. Age, **142**: 496
Japan Ware of Pontypool. Art J. **24**: 23.
Japanese, The. (W. J. A. Bradford) Chr. Exam. **55**: 22. —(J. A. Chessar) Nature, **1**: 190.— St. James, **2**: 466.
— at Home. All the Year, **7**: 271.
— Dress and Hair of. Ev. Sat. **5**: 651.
— in Washington, 1871. Ev. Sat. **11**: 295.
— Pictures of. (L. Abbott) Harper, **39**: 305.
— Something about. (G. W. Bacon) Hours at Home, **6**: 82.
Japanese Alloys. (R. Pumpelly) Am. J. Sci. **92**: 43.
Japanese Ambassadors' Journey to London. Cornh. **7**: 603.
Japanese and Chinese Students in America. (C. F. Thwing) Scrib. **20**: 450.
Japanese Ballet. Potter Am. Mo. **15**: 96.
Japanese Children. Ev. Sat. **17**: 429.
Japanese Doctor and his Works. (E. H. House) Atlan. **28**: 678.
Japanese Fan; a Poem. Cornh. **34**: 379.
Japanese Fragments. (S. Osborn) Once a Week, **3**: 33–437.
Japanese Indemnity Fund. (D. C. Gilman) Overland, **10**: 184.
Japanese Interiors. (W. E. McArthur) Overland, **6**: 15.
Japanese Ladies, Costumes of. Ev. Sat. **9**: 157.
Japanese Lacquer Ware. Ecl. Engin. **14**: 364.
Japanese Laureates. Lond. Q. **56**: 307.
Japanese Laws; or the Legacy of Syeyas. (W. E. Grigsby) Luth. Q. **7**: 207.
Japanese Literature and Art. Art J. **23**: 160.
Japanese Love-Story. Lond. Soc. **31**: 138.
Japanese Lyric Drama. Cornh. **34**: 479.
Japanese Melodies, Some. (C. L. Kellogg) Scrib. **14**: 504.
Japanese Merchant's Home. (W. E. Griffis) Overland, **12**: 31.
Japanese Miniature Odes. Cornh. **36**: 72. Same art. Ecl. M. **89**: 362.
Japanese Ornament. Eng. Dom. M. **15**: 69, 122.
Japanese Poetry, Ancient. Westm. **94**: 321.
— Bouquet of Japanese Verses. (C. A. DeKay) Scrib. **9**: 329.
Japanese Romance. (Sir D. Wedderburn) Fortn. **31**: 273.
Japanese Seismology. (C. G. Rockwood, jr.) Am. J. Sci. **122**: 468.
Japanese Sermons. (A. B. Mitford) Cornh. **20**: 196, 356.
Japanese Statesman at Home. (E. H. House) Harper, **44**: 583.
Japanese Story. Cornh. **44**: 345.
Japanese Story of Creation. (S. Robjohns) St. James, **34**: 187.
Japanese Stories, Modern. Belgra. **37**: 183.
Japanese Wrecks on American Coast. (H. Davis) Overland, **9**: 353.
Japanese Wrestlers. Chamb. J. **54**: 669.
Japanning and Varnishing. (T. P. Jones) J. Frankl. Inst. **2**: 31–283. **4**: 130. **5**: 270.
Jar of Gold; a Poem. Temp. Bar, **23**: 366.
Jarcke, C. E. Political Essays. Dub. R. **30**: 371.
Jardin d'Acclimatation, Fate of. Fraser, **85**: 17.
Jardin des Plantes, History of. Blackw. **14**: 121, 577.
Jardine, Sir William. Nature, **11**: 74.
Jargonium, a Compound of Uranium. J. Frankl. Inst. **89**: 276.
Jarocho Life. (M. Reid) Galaxy, **5**: 681.
Jaroslaff, City of. (Baron Haxthausen) Bentley, **24**: 97.
Jarousseau, J., Pastor of the Desert. Dub. Univ. **79**: 527.
Jarratt, Devereux, Account of. Chr. Obs. **32**: 507.
Jarvis, Samuel F. (N. S. Richardson) Am. Church R. **4**: 188.
— Church Chronology. (J. L. Kingsley) New Eng. **5**: 215. **6**: 378.— (S. F. Jarvis) Am. Church R. **1**: 82.
— Church of the Redeemed. (A. H. Vinton) Am. Church R. **4**: 112.
— Discourse on the Indian Tribes. (J. Pickering) No. Am. **11**: 103.
— History of the Church. Chr. Exam. **38**: 412.— (Prof. Ogilby) Meth. Q. **5**: 269.
— Reply to Dr. Milnor. Brownson, **5**: 20.
Jarvis, William, Life of. (H. Cutts) N. E. Reg. **20**: 193.
Jasher, Book of. (H. M. Johnson) Meth. Q. **7**: 82.— Ecl. R. **76**: 630.— Fraser, **5**: 643.— Chr. Rem. **30**: 385.— Dub. R. **39**: 199.— Kitto, **15**: 229.— Chr. Obs. **34**: 17.

Jasher, Book of, Bibliographical Notes on. (R. H. Horne) Cong. M. **17**: 82.
— Donaldson on. Lond. Q. **5**: 455. — Westm. **63**: 517.
Jasmin; a Tale. (M. P. Thompson) Cath World, **28**: 591.
Jasmin, Jacques, the Barber Poet. (H. Wheaton) Am. Whig R. **7**: 397. — Westm. **52**: 39. Same art. Liv. Age, **24**: 97. Same art. Ecl. M. **18**: 510. — Eng. Dom. M. **8**: 283. — No. Brit. **47**: 302. — (H. Coppée) Putnam, **14**: 404. — (J. A. Harrison) So. M. **12**: 641. — (H. W. Preston) Atlan. **37**: 34, 157. — Broadw. **6**: 149.
— An Evening with. Chamb. J. **20**: 17. Same art. Ecl. M. **30**: 272. Same art. Liv. Age, **38**: 537.
Jason's Quest. (C. W. Stoddard) Lippinc. **12**: 182.
Jasper Deane. (J. Saunders) Good Words, **18**: 465–825.
Jasper Howes; a Tale (V. F. Townsend) Sharpe, **48**: 241.
Java. Blackw. **6**: 318.
Jātaka Tales, Davids's. (S. Beal) Nation, **32**: 261.
Jaubert, Madame C. Souvenirs. (H. S. Wilson) Fortn. **36**: 346. Same art. Ecl. M. **97**: 637. — (A. Laugel) Nation, **32**: 89. — Blackw. **130**: 70. — Lippinc. **27**: 498.
Java and its Dependencies. Quar. **6**: 487.
— and the Dutch Coffee Monopoly. No. Brit. **46**: 319.
— and the Javanese. So. R. n. s. **20**: 129.
— by an Anglo-Batavian. Fraser, **63**: 506. **64**: 379.
— Commerce of. Hunt, **11**: 328.
— Dutch in. (Sir D. Wedderburn) Fortn. **29**: 96. Same art. Liv. Age, **136**: 323.
— Excursion to Buitenzorg. Fraser, **50**: 111.
— Jaunt in. (G. J. Oliver) Harper, **15**: 324.
— Life in. Lond. Q. **23**: 97. Same art. Ecl. M. **64**: 24.
— Raffles's. Ed. R. **31**: 395. — Quar. **17**: 72. — Mo. R. **86**: 337. — (J. Foster) Ecl. R. **32**: 105.
— Recollections of. (Sir J. Bowring) Fortn. **3**: 431. Same art. Ecl. M. **66**: 410.
— Vital Statistics of. (W. H. Sykes) J. Statis. Soc. **11**: 60.
Javanese, Notes on. (A. H. Kiehl) Anthrop. J. **6**: 346.
Javelin of the Franks. (W. M. Wylie) Arch. **35**: 48.
Jay, John. (E. H. Gillett) Hours at Home, **3**: 161. — (W. Sargent) No. Am. **81**: 346.
— Life of. (O. W. B. Peabody) No. Am. **37**: 315. — (W. H. Y. Hackett) Am. Whig R. **2**: 59. — (F. L. Hawkes) New York R. **9**: 273. — (F. L. Hawkes) Liv. Age, **8**: 220. — Am. Mo. R. **4**: 35. — Ann. Reg. **4**: 215.
— — and Character of. (H. T. Tuckerman) Contin. Mo. **6**: 336. — West. M. **4**: 178, 211.
— Treaty with Great Britain. (F. C. Gray) No. Am. **17**: 142.
Jay, William. (D. Curry) Meth. Q. **15**: 229. — Chr. R. **20**: 351. — Liv. Age, **59**: 472. — Nat. M. **5**: 24.
— Autobiography. (W. A. Larned) New Eng. **13**: 145. — Chr. Obs. **55**: 387. — Ecl. R. **100**: 570. — Lond. Q. **17**: 205. — Tait, n. s. **21**: 692. — Theo. & Lit. J. **7**: 690.
— Christian contemplated. Cong. M. **9**: 585.
— Works of. Meth. Q. **5**: 335. — (A. Alexander) Princ. **5**: 369.
Jay, Long-crested. (E. Coues) Am. Natural. **5**: 770.
Jays and Nutcrackers. (W. J. Broderip) Fraser, **56**: 457.
Jealousy of Lovers. Temp. Bar, **25**: 514.
Jean-Ah Pouquelin. (G. W. Cable) Scrib. **10**: 91.
Jeanie Burns. Lost Children. Bentley, **32**: 143. Same art. Liv. Age, **34**: 566.
Jeanne; a Tale. (K. S. Macquoid) Temp. Bar, **44**: 341.
Jeanne d'Albret, Queen of Navarre. Tinsley, **5**: 689.
Jeanne Dupont. Liv. Age, **110**: 785.
Jeannest, Emile. Art J. **9**: 227.
Jeannette. (J. Stretton) Dub. Univ. **81**: 289, 425.
Jeannette. (C. F. Woolson) Scrib. **9**: 232.
Jebb, John, Bishop, and Alex. Knox, Correspondence. Dub. Univ. **4**: 241. — Mo. R. **134**: 142. — Ecl. R. **60**: 376.
— Forster's Life of. Ecl. R. **63**: 454. — Mo. R. **140**: 33.
— Sermons. Chr. Obs. **14**: 655. **15**: 356–555. **16**: 71. **17**: 305.
Jebb, R. C. Translations into Greek and Latin. (F. W. H. Myers) Fortn. **20**: 645.
Jed Smith's strange Adventure. Chamb. J. **44**: 523.
Jedburgh. Tait, n. s. **14**: 744.
Jedburgh Abbey. Penny M. **14**: 305.
Jeddo, Fortune's. Liv. Age, **77**: 186.
— Notes from. (C. H. Gunn) St. James, **8**: 113.
— Sights in. (B. Taylor) Scrib. **3**: 132.
— Visit to. (J. B. Putnam) Putnam, **12**: 103.
Jeejeebhoy, Sir Jamsetjee, a Parsee Merchant. (C. E. Norton) No. Am. **73**: 135. — Hunt, **27**: 694. — Ecl. M. **62**: 498.
Jefferson, Joseph. (J. B. Runnion) Lippinc. **4**: 167.
— as Rip Van Winkle. (L. C. Davis) Lippinc. **24**: 57. — (S. Johnson) Radical, **6**: 133. — with portrait, Ev. Sat. **10**: 153, 162. — (A. G. Sedgwick) Nation, **9**: 247. — Appleton, **19**: 146. — O. & N. **2**: 684. — (L. C. Davis) Atlan. **19**: 750.
Jefferson, Joseph Brown, Memoir of. Ecl. R. **45**: 208.
Jefferson, Thomas. (J. Q. Adams) O. & N. **7**: 135. — (W. Dorsheimer) Atlan. **2**: 706, 789. — (V. W. Kingsley) Nat. Q. **30**: 278. — (E. Quincy) Nation, **13**: 309. — (J. F. Rueling) Meth. Q. **19**: 59. — Am. J. Educ. **27**: 513. — Am. Whig R. **12**: 33, 182, 290. — De Bow, **24**: 508. — Knick. **52**: 359, 479. — Liv. Age, **74**: 132. — with portrait, (S. G. Drake) N. E. Reg. **11**: 193.
— and Adams, Death of. Niles's Reg. **30**: 329, 345, 368.
— — Eulogies on. Am. Q. **1**: 54.
— and Coleridge. Hist. M. **9**: 24.
— and Charles James Fox. Dem. R. **27**: 193.
— and A. Hamilton. Liv. Age, **81**: 613.
— and his Times. Nat. M. **13**: 20.
— as a Lover. (J. E. Cooke) Appleton, **12**: 230.
— as a Sore-Head. (J. Parton) Atlan. **30**: 273.
— by the Light of 1863. (J. Sheldon) Contin. Mo. **5**: 129.
— Character of. (T. Bulfinch) No. Am. **91**: 107.
— College Days of. (J. Parton) Atlan. **29**: 16.
— Correspondence of. Colburn, **29**: 269.
— Enmity to Judge Marshall. Am. Q. **7**: 123.
— Family of. (A. H. Guernsey) Harper, **43**: 366.
— Glance at. (H. Flanders) Lippinc. **2**: 261.
— Governor of Virginia. (J. Parton) Atlan. **30**: 174.
— Home of, at Monticello. (B. J. Lossing) Harper, **7**: 145.
— in Continental Congress. (J. Parton) Atlan. **29**: 676.
— in House of Burgesses. (J. Parton) Atlan. **29**: 395.
— in War of the Revolution. (J. Parton) Atlan. **29**: 517.
— Last Moments of. Niles's Reg. **31**: 197.
— Letter on Education. Niles's Reg. **14**: 173.
— — to S. Smith. N. Ecl. **7**: 252.
— Life of. Dem. R. **35**: 371.
— — and Character of. New York R. **1**: 5. — (A. Ritchie) No. Am. **30**: 511. — (A. H. Everett) No. Am. **39**: 238. **40**: 170. — So. R. **5**: 100. — So. Lit. Mess. **4**: 207. — (A. P. Upshur) So. Lit. Mess. **6**: 642. — Ed. R. **51**: 496. **66**: 156. — Selec. Ed. R. **2**: 366. — Ecl. R. **69**: 249. — Mus. **16**: 558. **32**: 289. — Mo. R. **121**: 277.
— Minister to France. (J. Parton) Atlan. **30**: 405.
— Notes on Virginia; Revised Proofs. (E. B. O'Callaghan) Hist. M. **13**: 96.
— on Nullification. Niles's Reg. **43**: supp. 37.
— on Tariff, 1785. Niles's Reg. **24**: 133.
— Opinions on Slavery. (A. D. White) Atlan. **9**: 29.
— Papers of. Knick. **6**: 394, 537. — So. Lit. Mess. **3**: 31, 304.

Jefferson, Thomas, Parton's Life of. (J. P. Quincy) O. & N. **9**: 749. — (E. Gale) Penn Mo. **5**: 612. — (F. Sheldon) Nation, **18**: 284. — (F. Sheldon) No. Am. **118**: 405.
— Pecuniary Embarrassments of. Niles's Reg. **30**: 35, 280, 390.
— Political Opinions of. (S. Fowler) No. Am. **101**: 313.
— Private Character of. (E. O. Dunning) New Eng. **19**: 648.
— Randolph's Domestic Life of. (W. Baird) So. M. **10**: 495.
— Randolph's Memoir of. Ecl. R. **51**: 64. **52**: 139. — Westm. **13**: 312. — Liv. Age, **70**: 515.
— a Reformer of Old Virginia. (J. Parton) Atlan. **30**: 32.
— Rives on. So. Lit. Mess. **13**: 574.
— a Student of Law. (J. Parton) Atlan. **29**: 179.
— Tucker's Life of. (H. Brougham) Ed. R. **66**: 156. — Ecl. R. **69**: 249.
— a Virginia Lawyer. (J. Parton) Atlan. **29**: 312.
— Waifs from Monticello. (G. W. Bagby) Lippinc. **4**: 205.
— Writer of Declaration. (J. E. Cooke) Harper, **53**: 211.
— Writings of. Dem. R. **36**: 17.
Jeffrey, Francis. (C. Pebody) Gent. M. n. s. **5**: 28. Same art. Liv. Age, **106**: 92. — Anal. M. **14**: 52. — No. Brit. **13**: 146. — Liv. Age, **24**: 599. **25**: 172. — Dem. R. **27**: 320. — Bentley, **32**: 127. — Nat. M. **1**: 218. — Sharpe, **11**: 193. — (F. Bowen) No. Am. **75**: 296. — Blackw. **72**: 269, 461.
— and the Edinburgh Review. Westm. **58**: 95. Same art. Ecl. M. **26**: 558.
— and Gifford *vs.* Shakspere and Milton. Knick. **22**: 270.
— and Dr. Phillpotts. Blackw. **13**: 51, 476.
— and Rectorship of Glasgow. Blackw. **13**: 93.
— as a Reviewer. Cornh. **38**: 221.
— compared with Hazlitt. Blackw. **3**: 303.
— Contributions to the Edinburgh Review. (J. Moncrieff) No. Brit. **1**: 252. Same art. Ecl. M. **3**: 542. Same art. Liv. Age, **3**: 529. — Ecl. R. **79**: 434. — Mo. R. **163**: 1. — Chr. Rem. **7**: 347.
— Letter to. Blackw. **3**: 75.
— — on the Westminster Review. Blackw. **15**: 144, 558.
— Life of, Cockburn's. (H. T. Tuckerman) Chr. Exam. **53**: 229. — Chamb. J. **17**: 277. — Chr. Obs. **52**: 555. — Dub. R. **32**: 464. — Dub. Univ. **39**: 625, 722. — Ecl. R. **95**: 606. — Fraser, **45**: 557. — Hogg, **9**: 200. — House. Words, **1**: 113. Same art. Harper, **1**: 66. — Irish Q. **2**: 249. — Liv. Age, **33**: 278, 365. — New Q. **1**: 231. — No. Brit. **17**: 283. — Quar. **91**: 105. Same art. Liv. Age, **34**: 337. — Quar. **148**: 255. — Tait, n. s. **19**: 376. Same art. Ecl. M. **20**: 269.
— Obituary of. (J. Moncrieff) No. Brit. **13**: 273.
— Sketch of. (J. Clark) Mercersb. **5**: 207.
— Theory of Beauty. Westm. **53**: 1.
Jeffreys, Sir George. Dub. Univ. **74**: 460.
— Woolrych's Life of. So. R. **7**: 459. — Mo. R. **114**: 73.
Jeffries Manuscripts, Seals on. N. E. Reg. **31**: 56.
Jehan Ghir, Mogul Emperor, Autobiography of. Colburn, **26**: 201.
Jehovah and Elohim in Genesis. (W. Aikman) Meth. Q. **37**: 610.
— Angel of. (C. Goodspeed) Bib. Sac. **36**: 593.
— The Name. (E. Ballentine) Am. Bib. Repos. **3**: 730. — (A. Tholuck) Am. Bib. Repos. **4**: 89. — (W. H. Green) Evang. R. **16**: 86.
— — as a memorial Name. (T. Tyler) Kitto, **35**: 206. **36**: 197.
— — Meaning of. (P. de Lagarde) Bib. Sac. **35**: 544.
— — Rendering of. Bib. R. **3**: 21.
Jehovah-Jireh. (W. Crowell) Chr. R. **22**: 492.
Jelinck, Carl. Nature, **15**: 85.
Jellachlich, Ban of Croatia. Colburn, **85**: 28. Same art. Ecl. M. **16**: 358.
Jellalabad, Journey to. Bentley, **36**: 379. Same art. Liv. Age, **43**: 470.
Jelly-Fishes. (J. A. Allen) Canad. Mo. **11**: 407. — (E. S. Morse) Am. Natural. **1**: 244. — (A. Wilson) Belgra. **42**: 207. Same art. Ecl. M. **95**: 450. — (J. G. Wood) Once a Week, **7**: 232. — Chamb. J. **17**: 87. — Nat. M. **1**: 540. — Hogg, **12**: 292.
— New Fresh-Water. (G. J. Allman and G. J Romanes) Nature, **22**: 177.
— Tubular. (J. W. Fewkes) Am. Natural. **14**: 617.
Jem Catherwood's Vision. (J. J. Robbins) Overland, **4**: 52.
Jem McGowan's Wish; a Tale. Cath. World, **1**: 56.
Jem Nash, the dull Boy. Fraser, **69**: 336. Same art. Liv. Age, **81**: 51.
Jemmy Blinker; a Poem. Blackw. **127**: 253. Same art. Ecl. M. **94**: 464.
Jemili, Cruise of. (F. Walpole) Bentley, **35**: 278–479.
Jena. Bentley, **54**: 616.
— Campaign of, 1806. Temp. Bar, **36**: 245.
— Field of. (G. C. Swayne) Once a Week, **6**: 413.
— Student Life at. Am. J. Educ. **26**: 769.
— University Life at. Am. J. Educ. **26**: 779.
Jenifer's Prayer. (O. Crane) Cath. World, **3**: 17–318.
Jenisei River. (A. E. Nordenskiöld) Nature, **13**: 95, 275, 312. **14**: 380. **15**: 123.
— Natural History of. Nature, **16**: 367.
Jenkin, Mrs. C. Cousin Stella. Chr. Rem. **38**: 305.
Jenkins, Edward. Ginx's Baby. O. & N. **2**: 615.
Jenks Genealogy. (W. Jenks) N. E. Reg. **9**: 201.
Jenner, Edward. (I. Scott) Once a Week, **3**: 483. Same art. Liv. Age, **68**: 162. — with portrait, Anal. M. **9**: 48. — Chamb. J. **3**: 281. Same art. Liv. Age, **5**: 539. — Penny M. **7**: 269.
— and Vaccination. Chamb. J. **5**: 317. Same art. Liv. Age, **10**: 234.
— Baron's Life of. Mo. R. **146**: 622.
— Life of, with portrait. Portfo.(Den.) **33**: 512.
Jenner Genealogy. (W. S. Appleton) N. E. Reg. **19**: 247.
Jennie Stevenson; a Tale. Colburn, **35**: 344.
Jennings, Eliza, Tomb of. Portfo.(Den.) **11**: 535.
Jenny Basket; an American Romance. Tait, n. s. **12**: 699, 765. **13**: 116–289.
Jenyns, Soame, Works of. (A. Lamson) Chr. Exam. **3**: 136. — (H. Southern) Retros. **2**: 291.
Jephthah and his Daughter. (J. O. Skinner) Univ. Q. **18**: 56.
Jephthah's Daughter. (G. A. Simcox) Cornh. **15**. 606.
— Lamentation for; a Poem. Chr. Obs. **19**: 588.
Jephthah's Offering. (J. H. Kurtz) Evang. R. **6**: 386.
Jephthah's Vow. (S. Comfort) Meth. Q. **15**: 558. — (M. S. Terry) Meth. Q. **33**: 266. — (X. Betts) Am. Bib. Repos. 2d s. **9**: 143. — Dub. Univ. **12**: 273. — (S. Warren) Bib. Sac. **24**: 238 — Evang. R. **13**: 28. — (S. Talbot) Chr. R. **27**: 377.
— Exegetical Remarks on. (J. Muenscher) Am Church R. **4**: 415.
Jephtha Leathers; or the Philosophy of Failure. So. Lit. Mess. **10**: 48.
Jerbeh's Tower of Skulls. Am. Arch, **9**: 141.
Jerboa, The. Penny M. **6**: 412.
Jerdan, William, with portrait. Fraser, **1**: 605.
— Autobiography. Chamb. J. **17**: 375. Same art. Liv. Age, **34**: 155. — Dub. Univ. **40**: 289. — Ecl. R. **96**: 175. — Liv. Age, **33**: 606. — New Q. **1**: 270, 369. — Tait, n. s. **19**: 380, 569, 756. **21**: 117.
— Literary Experiences of. Westm. **58**: 507.
Jeremiah compared with St. Paul. (J. S. Howson) Good Words, **9**: 617.
Jeremiah Lillyboy. Once a Week, **25**: 111–177.
Jeremy Train, his Drive; a Poem. Scrib. **1**: 1.

Jericho, Plain of. (C. H. Brigham) Mo. Rel. M. **14**: 324.
— Punishment of Rebuilder of. Kitto, **17**: 364.
Jericho Rooms. All the Year, **24**: 304.
Jericho Theater. All the Year, **25**: 111.
Jerks, Ancient and modern. Knick. **52**: 373.
Jerome, St. (H. G. Spaulding) O. & N. **4**: 301. — Dub. R. **62**: 395. — Princ. **36**: 364.
— and his Correspondence. (J. McSwiney) Month, **22**: 14, 305. **24**: 393. **25**: 26.
— and his Ecclesiastical Correspondents. Theo. R. **1**: 27.
— and his Times. (S. Osgood) Bib. Sac. **5**: 117.
— and St. Augustine. Cong. **4**: 227.
— Letters of. (W. C. Lake) Contemp. **5**: 265. Same art. Liv. Age, **94**: 225.
Jerome of Prague. Meth. M. **45**: 508.
Jerome Bonaparte, King of Westphalia, Early Life of. Colburn, **122**: 119.
Jerome Bonaparte, Prince. (E. L. Didier) Internat. R. **11**: 120.
Jerome Bongrand's Heresy; a Tale about Priests. Cornh. **39**: 303. Same art. Liv. Age, **141**: 420.
Jerome Paturot, and Novels in general. (W. M. Thackeray) Fraser, **28**: 349.
— in Search of a Republic. Westm. **50**: 237.
Jerram, Charles, Memoirs of. Chr. Obs. **55**: 695.
Jerrold, Douglas. (J. Hannay) Atlan. **1**: 1. — (G. S. Phillips) No. Am. **89**: 431. — with portrait, (J. F. Sinnett) Ecl. M. **11**: 443. — Ecl. M. **42**: 277. — House. Words, **19**: 217. — Brit. Q. **10**: 192. — Liv. Age, **53**: 313. **54**: 336. — Colburn, **110**: 407. Same art. Liv. Age, **54**: 754. — Liv. Age, **60**: 420. — Sharpe, **29**: 177. — (H. Bedford) Month, **12**: 534.
— and modern Literary Life. No. Brit. **30**: 337.
— Genius and Writings of. Ecl. R. **99**: 419. Same art. Ecl. M. **32**: 166.
— Letters of. (C. & M. C. Clarke) Gent. M. n. s. **17**: 350, 498, 589.
— Life of. New Q. **8**: 127.
— — and Remains of. Ed. R. **110**: 99.
— Man made of Money. Brit. Q. **10**: 192. — Tait, n. s. **16**: 290.
— Recollections of. Knick. **54**: 474.
— Writings of. Liv. Age, **44**: 117.
Jerry Jarvis's Wig. (R. H. Barham) Bentley, **13**: 496.
Jersey, Dowager Countess of. Belgra. **2**: 343.
Jersey, Island of. (G. E. Waring, jr.) Scrib. **10**: 401. — Belgra. **21**: 355. — St. Paul's, **9**: 270.
— Affairs in. Fraser, **92**: 111.
— Anglo-French in. Chamb. J. **18**: 332.
— Chronicles of, Hugo's. Colburn, **112**: 467.
— Inglis on. Mo. R. **134**: 126.
— Jottings in. (G. C. Swayne) Once a Week, **3**: 216.
— Night-Job in. Chamb. J. **24**: 254.
— Notes on. (R. Rowe) Good Words, **12**: 597.
— Relics of non-historic Times. (S. P. Oliver) Nature, **2**: 166.
— Sketches of. Tait, n. s. **24**: 339–646.
Jersey, South, Buried Wealth of. (E. B. Duffey) Lippinc. **24**: 502
Jersey City, Resources and Manuf. of. Hunt, **15**: 597.
Jersey Prison Ship. (John Vandyke) Hist. M. **10**: supp. 7.
— John Vandyke on. Hist. M. **7**: 147.
Jerusalem. (C. H. Brigham) No. Am. **86**: 191. — (A. N. Gilbert) Chr. Q. **1**: 523. — (T. W. Holland) Lippinc. **8**: 631. — (N. Macleod) Good Words, **6**: 525, 587, 665. — (W. C. Prime) Harper, **14**: 557. — (W. S. Tyler) Hours at Home, **5**: 25. — (C. D. Warner) Atlan. **38**: 143, 301, 418. — (B. B. Edwards) No. Am **53**: 191. — Blackw. **47**: 317. — Chr. Mo. Spec. **1**: 579. — Broadw. **8**: 178. — (H. Martineau) Peop. J. **4**: 105, 134, 165. — Mus. **38**: 309. — Once a Week, **25**: 529.
Jerusalem and the East, Six Months in. All the Year, **25**: 15–180.
— Archæological Researches in. Chr. Rem. **49**: 182.
— Assizes of. (A. Ten Brook) Contin. Mo. **4**: 501. — Retros. **13**: 87.
— at the Close of New Test. History. Chr. Obs. **65**: 53.
— Barclay's City of the Great King. Theo. & Lit. J. **10**: 670. — (B. J. Wallace) Am. Presb. R. **6**: 637.
— Bartlett's Jerusalem revisited. Tait, n. s. **22**: 58.
— Bishopric of. Bib. R. **1**: 61. — Chr. Obs. **53**: 843.
— — and Bishop Gobat. Chr. Rem. **36**: 171.
— Burton's Journey to. Dub. Univ. **14**: 59.
— Capture of. Penny M. **7**: 469.
— Christ's Entry into. (J. Jones) Theo. & Lit. J. **12**: 47, 379.
— Christian. (A. F. Hewit) Cath. World, **33**: 452–767.
— Church of. (E. Lawrence) Harper, **40**: 860.
— — Persecution of. (B. Smith) Univ. Q. **36**: 171.
— Church of the Holy Sepulcher. (J. Mills) Kitto, **38**: 137.
— — Procession in. Cath. World, **5**: 232.
— City of Peace. (F. P. Cobbe) Fraser, **67**: 719.
— Council of, A. D. 51. Am. Church R. **23**: 40.
— Destruction of. Meth. M. **44**: 906.
— — Christ's Prophecy of. Theo. & Lit. J. **6**: 558. **10**: 408. — Chr. Obs. **36**: 663, 712, 777.
— Discoveries at. (L. Abbott) Harper, **43**: 195.
— Environs of. (C. H. Brigham) Mo. Rel. M. **15**: 420. **16**: 91, 183.
— Episcopate at. Cong. M. **25**: 27.
— Explorations in. (F. W. Holland) O. & N. **4**: 88. — (J. P. Thompson) No. Am. **113**: 154. — Colburn, **130**: 379. — Ed. R. **137**: 1.
— Fall of. (A. C. Tait) Good Words, **10**: 188.
— — Milman's Poem on. Ecl. R. **32**: 87.
— Fire-Balls of. (W. Williams) Radical, **8**: 201.
— From Jaffa to. Once a Week, **15**: 399.
— Geographical, Topographical, and Historical. Chr. Rem. **18**: 418.
— Baron Geramb's Visit to, 1831. Colburn, **52**: 351.
— Good Friday at. Month, **4**: 346.
— The Holy Fire. Colburn, **20**: 507.
— Holy Week in. (W. Everett) Cath. World, **7**: 77.
— in B. C. 9. (F. Delitzsch) Ev. Sat. **6**: 193.
— in 1827. (Lady Montefiore) Sharpe, **16**: 240.
— June Day in. (F. De itzsch) Bib. Sac. **31**: 528.
— Literary Society in. Hogg, **7**: 218.
— of To-Day. Ecl. M. **62**: 306.
— Ordnance Survey of. (H. S. Burrage) Bapt. Q. **2**: 156.
— Our Consul at. (A. Rhodes) Galaxy, **14**: 437.
— Present Condition of, 1822. Am. Meth. M. **6**: 135.
— Protestant Missions at. U. S. Cath. M. **7**: 505.
— Recent Researches in. Theo. Ecl. **5**: 487.
— Recovery of, Wilson's. Colburn, **148**: 367. — (C. K. Paul) Theo. R. **8**: 407.
— Siege of, by Titus. Chr. Obs. **65**: 197, 269.
— Site of the Holy Sepulcher. Bib. R. **4**: 231. — (E. Robinson) Bib. Sac. **1843**: 154.
— — of Mount Sion and the Temple. Chr. Rem. **43**: 422.
— Subterranean. Chr. Obs. **58**: 821. Same art. Liv. Age, **60**: 3. — Sup. Pop. Sci. Mo. **1**: 379. — Chamb. J. **54**: 182.
— Temple of, Site of. Dub. Univ. **79**: 195. — (T. Lewin) Arch. **44**: 17.
— The Temple Mount at. Colburn, **121**: 197.
— — Dome of the Rock. Dub. Univ. **31**: 411.
— to the Dead Sea. Chamb. J. **49**: 161.
— Topography of. (J. Forbes) Bib. Sac. **27**: 191. — (E. Robinson) Bib. Sac. **3**: 413, 605. — (J. P. Thompson) Bib. Sac. **15**: 444. — (S. Wolcott) Bib. Sac. **24**: 116, 565
— — and Archæology of. Chr. Rem. **37**: 391.

Jerusalem, Visit to. (L. P. Hale) O. & N. 4: 419.—All the Year, 24: 588.
— Walks about. Cong. M. 27: 610.
— Water Supply of. Kitto, 33: 133.
— Williams's. Dub. Univ. 26: 266.
Jervis, John. *See* St. Vincent.
Jessamine; a Poem. (G. P. Lathrop) Scrib. 10: 657.
Jesse, Capt. Notes of a Half-Pay. Ecl. R. 75: 298.
Jesse, Wm. Sermons. (J. Foster) Ecl. R. 15: 413.
Jessie Armstrong, the Lily of Linndale. (Mrs. M. St. Leon Loud) Godey, 22: 50.
Jessie's Dream. (H. J. Goldsmith) St. James, 38: 1–643. 39: 80.
Jessie's Lawsuit. (C. W. Cowper) Canad. Mo. 2: 25.
Jessie Trim. (B. L. Farjeon) Tinsley, 14: 1–636. 15: 1–633.
Jesso, Geological Survey of. Penn Mo. 7: 30. *See* Japan.
Jests of dying Men. (J. W. Calcraft) Dub. Univ. 40: 212.
Jest-Book, Greek. Blackw. 116: 286.
— Newcastle. House. Words, 9: 249.
Jest-Books, Old. (J. O. Halliwell) Bentley, 20: 594.
Jesters and Court Fools. Fraser, 30: 365.
— Old English. Lond. M. 7: 515, 621. 8: 589. 9: 239, 297, 517. 10: 61, 285, 406.
Jesting in the good old Time. Contin. Mo. 3: 237.
Jesuit, The; a Drama. (T. W. Whitley) Dem. R. 26: 235, 346, 439.
— in India. Dub. R. 32: 386.
— Modern. Brit. Q. 8: 150.
Jesuits, The. (J. Adams) No. Am. 5: 26, 309. 6: 129, 465. 7: 112. 8: 200.—For. R. 3: 309.—(N. S. Richardson) Am. Church R. 1: 575.—Kitto, 8: 38.—Brownson, 4: 305.—So. Q. 9: 149.—Mo. R. 83: 267.—Pamph. 6: 99.—Chr. R. 8: 181.—(O. Le Watte) Bentley, 24: 91.—(J. A. Corcoran) Am. Cath. Q. 1: 51.—(E. de Pressensé) Am. Church R. 27: 408.—(J. Tulloch) Good Words, 18: 689, 738.—Am. Mo. M. 6: 144.—Dub. Univ. 89: 320.—Kitto, 8: 38.—Quar. 137: 283.—Rel. Cat. 1: 449.—U. S. Cath. M. 4: 557.
— and Bismarck. Cath. World, 16: 1.
— and Sebastian Joseph Carvalho. Month, 31: 86.
— and the Civil Power. Liv. Age, 145: 317.
— and Clement XIV. (H. H. Milman) Quar. 83: 70.
— and Court of Louis XV., Tale of. Liv. Age, 4: 353.
— and Germany. (W. Wells) Math. Q. 34: 448.
— and Literature. Fraser, 10: 310.
— and Marquis de Pombal. Am. Cath. Q. 2: 51.
— and Protestants in South India. Chr. Obs. 57: 371.
— and their Schools. (K. von Raumer) Am. J. Educ. 5: 213.—Am. J. Educ. 6: 615. 14: 455.
— as a Missionary Order. Liv. Age, 11: 276.
— at Rome, Seymour's Mornings among. Chr. Obs. 49: 632.—(R. Davidson) Princ. 22: 143.—Liv. Age, 23: 241.
— Brief Account of. Meth. M. 38: 426.—Chr. Obs. 14: 166.
— Calumnies against. Dub. R. 50: 329.
— Confessions of an ex-Jesuit. Colburn, 125: 353.
— Constitutions of, respecting Instruction. Am. J. Educ. 27: 165.
— Curiosities of the Crusade against. Dub. R. 41: 66.
— Doctrines of. Quar. 138: 57.
— Expulsion of, from Germany. Fraser, 87: 631. Same art. Ecl. M. 81: 129.—(N. C. Schaeffer) Mercersb. 22: 5.
— Fall of. (J. Forsyth) Princ. 17: 239.
— Fifteen Months with. Tinsley, 28: 377.
— Historian of; Steinmetz. Fraser, 39: 143.
— Historical Sketch of. Putnam, 8: 312.
— History of. Ecl. R. 26: 497, 548. 88: 556.—Dub. R. 36: 451.
Jesuits, The, History of, Early. Retros. 9: 370.
— in Asia and America. Chr. Obs. 45: 493.
— in Canada, Parkman's. Dub. R. 64: 70.
— in China. Colburn, 112: 379.
— in England. (J. M. Capes) Contemp. 21: 27.
— — History of. Chr. Obs. 63: 740.
— in France. (A. Pannizzi) No. Brit. 2: 589.—(L. W. E. Rauwenhoff) Mod. R. 1: 559.
— — Cayla on. Chr. Obs. 63: 931.
— — Early History of. (H. Reuchlin) Bib. Sac. 5: 576.
— — Decree against, 1880. (A. Laugel) Nation, 30: 399.—Dub. R. 87: 155.
— — — and the Republic. (E. de Pressensé) Internat. R. 9: 499.
— — in 1844. Dub. R. 16: 407.
— in Japan. Am. Presb. R. 1: 452, 588.
— in Naples, Re-establishment of. Lond. M. 9: 228.
— in North America. (J. R. G. Hassard) Cath. World, 6: 192.—(H. James, jr.) Nation, 4: 450.—Nat. Q. 15: 346.—Dem. R. 14: 518.—(W. B. O. Peabody) Chr. Exam. 42: 360.—Dub. R. 23: 89.—(R. C. Clarke) Cath. World, 18: 541.
— — Missions in Canada. (M. J. Griffin) Canad. Mo. 1: 344.
— — — in Maryland. (J. G. Shea) Cath. World, 12: 114.
— — Parkman's. Chr. Rem. 55: 277. Same art. Liv. Age, 98: 259.—(N. Hale) Chr. Exam. 84: 347.
— — Relations of Discoveries in Canada and the United States. (E. B. O'Callaghan) Internat. M. 3: 185.
— in Paraguay. Mo. Rel. M. 10: 420, 455.
— in Paris. (R. L. Nicholson) Cath. World, 17: 701.
— in White Russia. (A. G. Knight) Month, 33: 47.
— Influence of. Brownson, 3: 172.
— Italy, and the Pope. Prosp. R. 3: 423.
— Lessons from Lives of. (C. Vince) Ex. H. Lec. 16: 189.
— Loyola and. (E. Lawrence) Harper, 39: 697.—(J. M. Finotti) Nat. Q. 3: 31.—(S. K. Kollock) Princ. 26: 647.—(J. H. Perkins) No. Am. 59: 412. *See also* Loyola.
— Novitiate of. New Dom. 9: 129.
— Old Calumny refuted. Irish Mo. 3: 254.
— Origin of the Society. Theo. & Lit. J. 8: 50.
— Principles and Policy of. Chr. R. 8: 346.
— — and Spirit of. So. Q. 28: 14.
— Quarterly Review and. Month, 22. 365.
— Reminiscences of an ex-Jesuit. (J. G. Shea) Putnam, 2: 214–664.
— Rise and Fall of. Bentley, 24: 316.
— School-Boy Recollections of. Colburn, 26: 97–352.
— Secret Instructions of. (L. W. Bacon) New Eng. 28: 533.—All the Year, 5: 396.—(J. B. Parkinson) Month, 19: 96.
— Secret Plan of, Leone's. Colburn, 84: 279.
— Some Attacks on. (A. Weld) Month, 30: 350, 463.
— Spiritual Discipline of. Am. Presb. R. 6: 559.
— Suppression of, in the 18th Century. U. S. Cath. M. 7: 337, 407.
— Views and Anticipations of. Dub. Univ. 22: 564.
— Why they are expelled. (E. I. Sears) Nat. Q. 25: 245.
— Works on. Chr. Obs. 48: 379.
Jesuit Brahmins of Madura. (C. F. Muzzy) Am. Presb. R. 18: 676.
Jesuit College in Rome. Temp. Bar, 6: 387.
Jesuit Instruction, Dangers of. Brownson, 3: 62.
Jesuit Martyrs; Campion and Walpole. Ed. R. 148: 469. Same art. Liv. Age, 140: 67.
— of the Commune. (K. O'Meara) Cath. World, 19: 505.
Jesuit Style of Church Architecture. (H. W. Brewer) Month, 35: 322.
Jesuitism as it is, 1851. Brit. Q. 13: 497.
— History of. New Dom. 18: 161, 250, 329.
— in England. Fraser, 19: 667.

Jesuitism; Koenig's Moderner Jesuitismus. New Q. **2**: 129.
— Political Relations of. Lond. Q. **5**: 363.
Jesus Christ. (H. S. Lobingier) Chr. Q. **8**: 519. — (J. R. Parsons) Chr. Q. **8**: 356.
— a Literal Sacrifice. Chr. Disc. **4**: 332.
— Actions of, recorded in New Test. Dub. R. **31**: 387.
— Actions and Sufferings of. (T. Stringfield) Am. Meth. M. **17**: 263. **18**: 132.
— Advent of. Am. Presb. R. **9**: 595.
— — in the Fullness of Time. (J. J. Van Oosterzee) Am. Presb. R. **15**: 375.
— Affirmations of. (A. Réville) Unita. R. **6**: 315.
— Agony in the Garden. (J. Priestley) Theo. Repos. **3**: 376, 476. **6**: 302, 347.
— Ancient Philosophy in relation to. Chr. R. **18**: 1.
— and Adam, Biblical Analogy between. Chr. R. **13**: 565.
— and Antichrist. (W. J. Barbee) Chr. Q. **7**: 390, 485.
— and the Apostles, Language of. Liv. Age, **76**: 155.
— and the Bible. (T. Doggett) Am. Presb. R. **17**: 215.
— and Christendom, Plumptre's Lectures on. (W. Benham) Contemp. **6**: 283. — Chr. Obs. **68**: 272.
— and Christianity. (W. H. Corning) New Eng. **14**: 250. — Hogg, **11**: 209.
— — Originality of. Bost. Q. **1**: 129.
— and Civilization. N. Ecl. **4**: 216.
— and the Conscience. Ecl. R. **120**: 531.
— and Criminal Law. (E. Ballantine) Am. Presb. R. **15**: 537.
— and the Demoniacs. (W. Everett) Unita. R. **10**: 53.
— and the Gospels. (W. H. Furness) Mo. Rel. M. **47**: 342, 423.
— and his Spirit. (J. W. Nevin) Mercersb. **19**: 353.
— and Hillel. (F. Delitzsch) Luth. Q. **11**: 530.
— and Humanity, Goodwin on. (J. M. Hoppin) New Eng. **34**: 573. — Internat. R. **3**: 105.
— and Nature. Mo. Rel. M. **50**: 173.
— and our Century. (L. A. Lipscomb) Meth. Q. **41**: 655.
— and Plato. (W. C. Stiles) Univ. Q. **35**: 437.
— and the Resurrection. (J. W. Nevin) Mercersb. **13**: 169.
— and Socrates. Radical, **3**: 47.
— as bearing Sin, New Testament View. (W. H. Cobb) Bib. Sac. **32**: 475.
— as Man, and Head of Church. Theo. & Lit. J. **8**: 615.
— as an Observer of Nature. (S. Merrill) Bib. Sac. **29**: 510.
— as Prophet and Messiah. (H. G. Spaulding) Chr. Exam. **83**: 79.
— as portrayed in the Gospels. (L. H. Atwater) Princ. **38**: 631.
— as Revealer of God. (E. F. Burr) New Eng. **12**: 177.
— as a Teacher. (I. D. Williamson) Univ. Q. **18**: 113.
— Ascension of. (G. N. H. Peters) Evang. R. **21**: 85.
— — Theology of. Lond. Q. **16**: 447.
— asleep. (H. Bushnell) Good Words, **5**: 800.
— attested by Miracles. Am. Bib. Repos. 3d s. **3**: 423.
— Authority of, as a Religious Teacher. (J. Brazer) Chr. Exam. **32**: 137. — (C. A. Bartol) Chr. Exam. **55**: 313. — (E. G. Brooks) Univ. Q. **21**: 324. — (E. de Pressensé) Cong. **1**: 39.
— Baptism of. (A. Réville) Unita. R. **4**: 391.
— — Import and Method of. (J. G. Hale) Cong. Q. **13**: 404.
— Baumgarten's History of. Ecl. R. **110**: 553.
— Beecher's Life of. O. & N. **5**: 93.
— Belief in; its Relation to Miracles and Evolution. (J. L. Davies) Contemp. **34**: 629.
— Betrayal of. Kitto, **31**: 319. — Chr. Mo. Spec. **6**: 609.
— Birth and Infancy of. Kitto, **12**: 351. **13**: 420.
— — Gregory Nazianzen on. (H. S. Boyd) Meth. M. **55**: 848.
— — Miles on. (A. P. Peabody) Unita. R. **9**: 226.
Jesus Christ, Birth and Infancy of, Providential Time of. (J. G. Herder) Mo. Rel. M. **20**: 377. *See below*, Jesus Christ, Chronology.
— Birthplace of, and Chronology of his Infancy. (J. Horner) Meth. Q. **32**: 216.
— blessing little Children. Art J. **11**: 221.
— Blood of. (N. M. Mann) Radical, **3**: 366.
— Brethren of. (C. Cutler) Bib. Sac. **26**: 745. — (P. Schaff) Bib. Sac. **21**: 855.
— Channing on. Mo. Rel. M. **49**: 151.
— Character of. (W. H. Furness) Chr. Exam. **15**: 277. — (A. A. Livermore) Unita. R. **12**: 395. — Theo. Ecl. **4**: 137.
— — as Basis of Religion. (T. W. Fowle) Contemp. **17**: 569. Same art. Liv. Age, **110**: 491.
— — from the Apostles. Theo. Repos. **3**: 79.
— — Moral. (E. Peabody) Chr. Exam. **26**: 273. **39**: 236. — (P. Schaff) Mercersb. **13**: 321.
— — Originality of. (G. Matheson) Contemp. **33**: 758. Same art. Liv. Age, **139**: 544.
— — Practical View of. Chr. Obs. **8**: 689.
— — Schenkel on. (J. W. Chadwick) Chr. Exam. **82**: 186. — Cong. R. **7**: 290.
— — Scriptural. (M. H. Doolittle) Radical, **2**: 680.
— — Sinlessness of. (F. W. Kremer) Ref. Q. **26**: 258. — Lond. Q. **12**: 145.
— Childhood of. (E. de Pressensé) Hours at Home, **2**: 419. — (A. Saphir) Good Words, **3**: 581.
— Chinese History of. Hogg, **2**: 352.
— Christ Principle. (S. Ashton) Univ. Q. **31**: 17.
— Christianity of. (J. P. Hopps) Theo. R. **15**: 63.
— Christologic Problem in. (G. N. Abbott) Mercersb. **16**: 200.
— Christology. (J. F. Chaffee) Meth. Q. **24**: 478. — (R. Graham) Chr. Q. **1**: 219. — (J. A. Reubelt) Chr. Q. **4**: 260. — Ecl. R. **120**: 144, 531. **123**: 491. — (W. H. Green) Princ. **31**: 438.
— — Contribution to. (S. S. Schmucker) Evang. R. **4**: 83. **5**: 35.
— — Dorner's. Dial, **2**: 485. — (E. D. Yeomans) Princ. **32**: 101.
— — Hengstenberg's. Lit. & Theo. R. **4**: 71. — (G. R. Noyes) Chr. Exam. **16**: 321.
— — Liebner's. (J. W. Nevin) Mercersb. **3**: 55.
— — The new. (F. W. Newman) Fortn. **20**: 740.
— — of the New Testament. Mo. Rel. M. **24**: 403. — Dub. Univ. **94**: 641. **95**: 581.
— — of Swedenborg and Channing. (B. F. Barrett) Unita. R. **9**: 286.
— — Revival of. (H. B. Smith) Hours at Home, **6**: 247.
— — Schleiermacher's. (O. Cone) Univ. Q. **27**: 162.
— Christus Conditor. (D. M. Reeves) Bapt. Q. **6**: 220.
— Chronology of the Birth of. (T. D. Woolsey) Bib. Sac. **27**: 290. — (K. Wieseler) Bib. Sac. **3**: 166, 653. — Kitto, **14**: 382.
— — of the Life of. Kitto, **21**: 369. **22**: 103, 168. — (P. Schaff) Presb. R. **1**: 446.
— — — Benson's. Ecl. R. **34**: 336.
— — of the Ministry of. (S. Sharpe) Theo. R. **4**: 297.
— — of Passion Week. Kitto, **32**: 180.
— — — Date of his Death. (C. E. Caspari) Bib. Sac. **28**: 469. — Quar. **132**: 47.
— Chronology, Topography, and Archæology of the Life of. (J. P. Thompson) Kitto, **32**: 42.
— the Church, and the Bible. Dub. R. **41**: 317.
— Circumcision of. (W. Rupp) Mercersb. **19**: 142.
— Claim of, as Saviour. (W. J. Potter) Radical, **2**: 347.
— Coleridge's Life of. Dub. R. **80**: 325.
— Coming of. (E. G. Brooks) Univ. Q. **31**: 389. — (P. C. Sinding) Mercersb. **13**: 572. — Meth. Q. **2**: 352. — (M. Goodrich) Univ. Q. **7**: 233.

Jesus Christ, Creatorship of. (N. L. Frothingham) Chr. Exam. **63**: 183.
— Credibility of Testimony concerning himself. (G. P. Fisher) New Eng. **24**: 207.
— Crucifixion of. Theo. & Lit. J. **12**: 691.
— — Darkness at. (J. Ferguson) Meth. M. **27**: 163.
— — the Foundation of Christianity. (W. B. Brown) New Eng. **21**: 485.
— — on Thursday. (J. K. Aldrich) Bib. Sac. **27**: 401.
— Day in the Life of. (C. S. Locke) Mo. Rel. M. **46**: 534.
— Death of. (W. Hanna) Good Words, **8**: 497.
— — and Resurrection of, Harmony of Narratives. Cong. M. **14**: 20, 145, 213.
— — Historical Influence of. (D. W. Simon) Bib. Sac. **25**: 733.
— — Physical Cause of. (D. W. Clark) Meth. Q. **9**: 185. — (R. Curran) Meth. Q. **28**: 221. — Am. Church R. **24**: 231. — Ecl. R. **87**: 738.
— — — Stroude on. Bib. R. **3**: 340. — Dub. R. **22**: 25.
— — Relation to the Law. Chr. R. **24**: 622.
— — Supernatural. (E. Cutler) Cong. R. **8**: 1.
— Deem's Life of. (T. Appel) Mercersb. **21**: 332.
— Deity of. (Prof. Flatt) Princ. **1**: 1, 159.
— — Scriptural Evidence of. (D. B. Ford) Bib. Sac. **17**: 535.
— — Unitarian View of. (G. E. Ellis) Chr. Exam. **60**: 335.
— Descent into Hell. (D. F. Brindle) Mercersb. **24**: 564. — (H. Cowles) Bib. Sac. **32**: 401. — (J. I. Swander) Mercersb. **21**: 580. — (J. I. Mombert) Evang. R. **17**: 1. — (J. Münscher) Bib. Sac. **16**: 309. — (J. M. Titzel) Mercersb. **19**: 261. — Fraser, **1**: 341. — Kitto, **24**: 17. — Meth. M. **47**: 24. — (Z. S. Barstow) Bost. R. **5**: 501. — (N. L. Frothingham) Chr. Exam. **50**: 401.
— Design of the Life and Death of. (J. Priestley) Theo. Repos. **1**: 17–400.
— Did he know Greek? (K. Cook) Dub. Univ. **90**: 457.
— Discourse at Capernaum. (E. P. Barrows) Bib. Sac. **11**: 693.
— Discourses in the Fourth Gospel. (O. Cone) Univ. Q. **23**: 295.
— — Stier on. (H. I. Schmidt) Evang. R. **1**: 54.
— — Unity of. (F. Gardiner) Bib. Sac. **31**: 416.
— — with Nicodemus and Woman of Samaria. Theo. Repos. **6**: 372.
— Divine and Human in. (L. Schoeberlein) Mercersb. **20**: 583. — (E. A. Lawrence) Bib. Sac. **24**: 41. — (G. A. Lintner) Evang. R. **14**: 523. — (Dr. Robins) Bib. Sac. **31**: 615. — (W. Nast) Meth. Q. **20**: 441. — (H. M. Goodwin) New Eng. **18**: 851. — Am. Presb. R. **10**: 223. — (J. W. Nevin) Mercersb. **3**: 220. — (S. Talbot) Bapt. Q. **2**: 129.
— Divinity of. (S. R. Calthrop) Mo. Rel. M. **27**: 250. — (J. E. Carpenter) Theo. R. **6**: 49. — (J. S. Crumbaugh) Evang. R. **18**: 559. — (J. C. Kimball) Mo. Rel. M. **38**: 197. — (J. Dempster) Am. Meth. M. **17**: 361. — (P. N. Lynch) Am. Cath. Q. **1**: 100, 475. — (R. Weiser) Evang. R. **11**: 574. — (R. W. Dickinson) Lit. & Theo. R. **5**: 116. — Gen. Repos. **2**: 1. — (C. Stetson) Chr. Exam. **23**: 64. — Am. Meth. M. **18**: 453. — Bost. R. **4**: 258. — Chr. Rem. **55**: 135. — Kitto, **28**: 351. — Mo. Rel. M. **8**: 177, 224.
— — believed by the Fathers. Meth. M. **51**: 320.
— — the Corner-Stone of Christianity. Theo. & Lit. J. **9**: 526.
— — Courayer on. Quar. **6**: 391.
— — in the Form of God, not equal with. Theo. Repos. **2**: 141.
— — Liddon's Bampton Lectures on, 1866. Chr. Obs. **67**: 745. — Lond. Q. **29**: 489.
Jesus Christ, Divinity of, not a Doctrine of the Old Testament. (G. R. Noyes) Chr. Exam. **19**: 273. **20**: 207, 319.
— — Only-Begotten, On the Reading. (E. Abbot) Unita. R. **3**: 560.
— — Recent Works on, 1872. (H. F. Jenks) Mo. Rel. M. **47**: 151.
— Doctrines, Miracles, and Prophecies of. Kitto, **23**: 233.
— Does He save, and how? (W. W. Adams) Cong. Q. **15**: 427.
— Early Development of. Kitto, **27**: 1.
— Early History of. Kitto, **27**: 113.
— — March on. Ecl. R. **47**: 74.
— Ecce Deus. (E. T. Vaughan) Contemp. **6**: 200.
— Ecce Deus-Homo. So. R. n. s. **19**: 227.
— Ecce Homo, Seeley's. (P. Bayne) Fortn. **5**: 129 — (W. E. Gladstone) Good Words, **9**: 33, 80, 177. Same art. Liv. Age, **96**: 259–609. **97**: 40. Same art. N. Ecl. **1**: 344. **2**: 73. — (G. Howison) Radical, **2**: 402, 625, 689. — (O. B. Frothingham) Nation, **2**: 613. — (D. F. MacDonald) Am. Church R. **18**: 397. — (J. H. Newman) Cath. World, **3**: 618. — (E. T. Vaughan) Contemp. **2**: 40. — (C. E. Norton) No. Am. **103**: 302. — (A. P. Stanley) Macmil. **14**: 134. — Chr. Exam. **81**: 109. — Liv. Age, **93**: 803. — Chr. Rem. **52**: 130. — Fraser, **73**: 746. **74**: 29. — Dub. Univ. **68**: 75. — Dub. R. **61**: 441. **62**: 177. — Kitto, **37**: 334. — Chr. Obs. **66**: 498, 579, 681. — Liv. Age, **89**: 872. **97**: 752, 794. — Lond. Q. **27**: 72. Same art. Theo. Ecl. **4**: 334. — Month, **4**: 551. — Quar. **119**: 515. Same art. Liv. Age, **89**: 435. — Theo. R. **3**: 161.
— — and modern Skepticism. No. Brit. **44**: 124. Same art. Ecl. M. **67**: 1.
— — Christ as portrayed in. (L. H. Atwater) Princ. **38**: 631. — (S. R. Mason) Bapt. Q. **4**: 39.
— — Gladstone on. So. R. n. s. **8**: 206.
— — Two Views of. Kitto, **37**: 334.
— Ellicott's Lectures on Life of. Chr. Obs. **61**: 181.
— Emmanuel. (W. P. Tilden) Unita. R. **5**: 646.
— the End of the Creation. (C. P. Jennings) Am. Church R. **29**: 161.
— Eschatology of. (C. E. Stowe) Bib. Sac. **7**: 452.
— — and of St. Paul. Mo. Rel. M. **30**: 32, 91, 163.
— The Essential. (J. Weiss) Radical, **3**: 459.
— Ethics of. (F. R. Conder) Fraser, **90**: 741. — (J. L. Stoddard) Radical R. **1**: 661. — (V. H. Stanton) Contemp. **24**: 503.
— Ewald's History of. Kitto, **16**: 303. — Nat. R. **1**: 92.
— Exaltation and Second Coming. (A. C. Kendrick) Bapt. Q. **4**: 1.
— Example of. (I. Hovykaas) Mod. R. **2**: 441, 713.
— — as a Minister. Am. Bib. Repos. **7**: 97.
— Faith in. (J. Priestley) Theo. Repos. **3**: 239.
— Farrar's Christ in History. (R. B. Lowrie) Am. Church R. **32**: 213.
— Farrar's Life of. (C. K. Paul) Theo. R. **11**: 481. — Quar. **138**: 177. — Month, **22**: 98. — Chr. Obs. **74**: 726. — Canad. Mo. **19**: 73. — Internat. R. **1**: 855.
— Foundation of the Church. (C. Ullmann) Bib. R. **4**: 465.
— Founder of Aryan Christianity. Dub. Univ. **93**: 59.
— Four Difficulties solved in. (N. Macleod) Good Words, **3**: 385.
— Friendship of. (R. S. Candlish) Good Words, **19**: 357.
— Frothingham's Views of. (J. F. Clarke) Chr. Exam. **86**: 192.
— Fullness of. (J. O. Skinner) Univ. Q. **26**: 188. — (N. Van Alstine) Luth. Q. **8**: 582.
— Furness's History of. (J. F. Clarke) Chr. Exam. **49**: 239. — (A. P. Peabody) No. Am. **71**: 464. — (C. C. Everett) O. & N. **3**: 474.

Jesus Christ, Genealogy of. (K. Wieseler) Kitto, **3**: 197. —(G. M Clelland) Bib. Sac. **18**: 410. — Kitto, **27**: 336.—(J. Strong) Meth. Q. **12**: 593.—Kitto, **26**: 63.
— — Exegesis of Matt. i. 1. (C. C. Starbuck) Bib. Sac. **38**: 508.
— — Post-Exilian Portion of. (B. B. Warfield) Presb. R. **2**: 388.
— Genealogies of, Hervey on. Chr. Obs. **54**: 525.
— — in Matthew and Luke. Evang. R. **6**: 168. — So. R. n. s. **22**: 344.
— — — Patristic Views. (F. Gardiner) Bib. Sac. **29**: 593.
— Glorification of. (T. G. Apple) Ref. Q. **27**: 304.
— — Historical Necessity of. (P. S. Davis) Mercersb. **21**: 295.
— God-Man. (G. A. Lintner) Evang. R. **14**: 523.
— Gospel preached by. Kitto, **13**: 183.
— Hanna's Life of. No. Brit. **50**: 315. Same art. Ecl. M. **73**: 513, 705.
— Harmony of opposite Qualities in Character and Teachings of. (T. S. King) Univ. Q. **7**: 393.
— Hase's Life of. Mo. Rel. M. **23**: 387.
— Head of the Church. (J. Eastwood) Univ Q. **20**: 377. —(R. P. Stebbins) Chr. Exam. **55**: 202.
— The historic. (T. C. Porter) Mercersb. **22**: 181. — (S. H. Giesy) Mercersb. **17**: 485.
— History and Character of, Hennell on. Prosp. R. **1**: 19.
— Humanity of. (T. G. Apple) Mercersb. **14**: 352. — (J. O. Skinner) Univ. Q. **17**: 275.
— — and his Divinity. (J. C. Koller) Luth. Q. **6**: 321.
— — in its fallen Form. (J. H. A. Bomberger) Mercersb. **5**: 164.
— — True. Mo. Rel. M. **32**: 69. — (H. Crosby) Bapt. Q. **4**: 350.
— in Art. Blackw. **96**: 573. — Ed. R. **120**: 94.
— — Eggleston on. So. R. n. s. **21**: 237.
— — Mrs. Jameson and Lady Eastlake on. Lond. Q. **23**: 416. — F. Arts Q. **4**: 132.
— in the Book of Genesis. Am. Church R. **24**: 397.
— in History. (H. S. Dickson) Evang. R. **15**: 212. — (O. B. Frothingham) Radical, **4**: 81. — (G. W. Samson) Chr. R. **19**: 272. — New Eng. **6**: 513.
— — Messiah and. (J. H. Allen) Unita. R. **8**: 608.
— in Moses and the Prophets, Lord on. Theo. & Lit. J. **6**: 168.
— in the Old Testament. (J. M. Titzel) Mercersb. **16**: 55. — (D. B. Ford) Chr. R. **21**: 204.
— in the Temple when twelve Years old. Kitto, **19**: 284.
— Incarnation of. (W. Alexander) Good Words, **8**: 264. — (D. W. Clark) Meth. Q. **11**: 114. — (J. F. Reubelt) Bib. Sac. **27**: 1. **28**: 43. — (J. A. Reubelt) Mercersb. **10**: 563. — Chr. Exam. **82**: 355. — Chr. Rem. **17**: 301, 348. — Am. Church R. **22**: 61. — Cong. M. **16**: 171. — Kitto, **17**: 315.
— — and Atonement. (S. Anselm) Bib. Sac. **11**: 729. **12**: 52.
— — and Eucharist, Wilberforce on. Chr. Obs. **53**: 588.
— — and Miracles. (R. H. McKim) Am. Church R. **34**: 203.
— — and the System which stands on it. (R. S. Storrs, jr.) Am. Presb. R. **18**: 324.
— — and Transubstantiation. (F. H. Hedge) Unita. R. **4**: 545.
— — Bushnell on. Brownson, **8**: 137. — Mo. Rel. M. **6**: 183.
— — Doctrine of. (E. E. Higbee) Mercersb. **4**: 490. — (W. J. Potter) Radical, **3**: 673.
— — Morris on. Brownson, **9**: 287.
— — Müller on. Lond. Q. **36**: 462.
— — Neale on. Brownson, **7**: 136.
— — of the Word in. Theo. & Lit. J. **12**: 677.
— — Sadler on. Chr. Obs. **67**: 261.
Jesus Christ, Incarnation of, Swedenborg on. (B. F. Barrett) Mo. Rel. M. **34**: 104, 119.
— — Truth of. (W. H. Kimball) Univ. Q. **23**: 184.
— — Wilberforce on. (J. W. Nevin) Mercersb. **2**: 164. — Chr. Obs. **50**: 250.
— — Wilberforce's Theory of, and Pantheism. Am. Church R. **4**: 428.
— — Word made Flesh. (P. W. Ellsworth) New Eng. **24**: 705.
— Infancy of. (H. Harbaugh) Mercersb. **18**: 138.
— Influence of. (E. J. Young) Mo. Rel. M. **47**: 381.
— — Books on. (C. A. Stork) Luth. Q. **10**: 101.
— — an Evidence of Messiahship. Univ. Q. **8**: 156.
— Injuries done to; N. Adams's Sermon. (E. B. Hall) Chr. Exam. **30**: 345.
— Inscription on Cross of. (L. Moss) Evang. R. **19**: 306.
— Inspiration and Impeccability of. (J. Priestley) Theo. Repos. **4**: 433. — Theo. Repos. **6**: 209, 247.
— Intellectual Greatness of. (W. L. Chaffin) Unita. R. **13**: 106.
— Intercession of. (E. Fisher) Univ. Q. **14**: 113.
— The Ivory. (G. H. Colton) Am. Whig R. **2**: 12.
— Jesus and the Christ. (D. A. Wasson) O. & N. **3**: 564.
— John's Testimony concerning. Chr. Disc. **2**: 109.
— Josephus's Testimony to. Meth. M. **58**: 189.
— Joshua a Symbol of. Theo. & Lit. J. **4**: 159.
— Keim's History of. (S. Osgood) Chr. Exam. **86**: 315. — Bib. Sac. **26**: 373.
— Kingdom of. (H. L. Baugher) Evang. R. **21**: 250. — (J. W. Yeomans) Princ. **33**: 385.
— — and Spirit of the Age. (S. Harris) Bib. Sac. **30**: 287.
— — Characteristics of. (S. Harris) Bib. Sac. **28**: 523.
— — delineated by Whately. Cong. M. **25**: 475.
— — Divine Agency in its Administration. (S. Harris) Bib. Sac. **28**: 686.
— — Duration of. (D. Van Valkenburg) Am. Bib. Repos. 2d s. **2**: 439. — (H. Mills) Am. Bib. Repos. **3**: 748.
— — Growth of. (C. R. Moor) Univ. Q. **34**: 289.
— — — Characteristics of. (S. Harris) Bib. Sac. **29**: 459.
— — Human Agency in. (S. Harris) Bib. Sac. **29**: 114.
— — Maurice on. Ecl. R. **71**: 150.
— — Nature of. (N. Hewitt) Lit. & Theo. R. **5**: 193.
— — Progress of, and Civilization. (S. Harris) Bib. Sac. **29**: 602.
— — Self-proven to be from God. (S. Harris) Bib. Sac. **28**: 302.
— — Triumph of, Scriptural Doctrine of. (S. Harris) Bib. Sac. **30**: 77.
— Lange's Life of. Bib. R. **6**: 261, 482.
— Last Commission of. (T. S. King) Univ. Q. **12**: 239.
— Last Days of. (H. B. Hackett) Bib. Sac. **36**: 342, 471, 665. — (N. Porter) Chr. Q. Spec. **10**: 37.
— the Life. (J. T. Bixby) Mo. Rel. M. **49**: 124. — (C. C. Everett) O. & N. **1**: 602.
— the Life and the Light. Am. Church R. **22**: 571.
— the Life of the World. (I. E. Graeff) Mercersb. **14**: 602.
— Life in. Lond. Q. **48**: 322.
— Life of. (F. W. Farrar) Macmil. **31**: 463. — (E. T. Vaughan) Contemp. **2**: 412. — Quar. **120**: 389. Same art. Liv. Age, **91**: 707.
— — a Reality. (J. McCosh) Good Words, **5**: 961. Same art. Liv. Age, **84**: 81. — (A. F. Hewit) Cath. World, **32**: 842. **33**: 108, 175, 351.
— — and modern Criticism. (B. Weiss) Contemp. **33**: 339. — Fraser, **69**: 49.
— — and Work of. Westm. **86**: 58.
— — Caspari's Introduction to. Chr. Obs. **76**: 371.
— — Incidents of. Theo. Repos. **3**: 301.
— — its own Witness. (J. M. McCulloch) Ex. H. Lec. **14**: 101.
— — Modern Explanations of. (W. Kirkus) Kitto, **32**: 394.

Jesus Christ, Life of, Outlines of. Cong. **5**: 310–734. **7**: 280.
— — Rationalistic. Chr. Rem. **47**: 189.
— — Savage on. (J. H. Allen) Unita. R. **15**: 151.
— — Works on. (S. J. Andrews) Bib. Sac. **22**: 177. — (C. M. Mead) Bib. Sac. **22**: 207.
— Lives of. (J. Wright) Theo. R. **9**: 467.
— — Ebrard's and Lange's. Brit. Q. **40**: 226.
— — Recent. No. Brit. **50**: 315. Same art. Theo. Ecl. **6**: 461.
— Light of the World. (C. J. Vaughan) Good Words, **6**: 47–872.
— Light and Life of the World. (H. Ballou, 2d) Univ. Q. **11**: 83.
— Love of. (J. H. Morison) Unita. R. **2**: 62.
— Ludolph's Life of. (H. J. Coleridge) Month, **17**: 337.
— Manhood of. Chr. R. **12**: 475.
— Manliness of. (T. Hughes) Good Words, **18**: 414–851.
— Mediatorial Character of, His own Testimony to. (Dr. Walker) Evang. R. **10**: 506.
— Mediatorial Work of. Univ. Q. **20**: 382.
— the Messiah or Jesus the Impostor. (N. M. Wood) Bapt. Q. **2**: 332.
— Messiahship of, Seal of. (A. A. Miner) Univ. Q. **3**: 301. *See* Messiah.
— Ministerial Character of, Sumner on. Chr. Obs. **35**: 428.
— Ministering of, and Christian Ministering. (R. B. Thurston) Am. Presb. R. **14**: 515.
— Ministry of. (A. D. Mayo) Mo. Rel. M. **49**: 329.
— — only one Year. Theo. Repos. **2**: 41.
— — System and Order of. (E. E. Hale) Chr. Exam. **76**: 80.
— Miracles of. *See* Miracles.
— Miraculous Conception of. (J. Priestley) Theo. Repos. **4**: 245, 484. — Theo. Repos. **5**: 83–148.
— Miraculous Power of, His Testimony to. (Dr. Walker) Evang. R. **12**: 173.
— Mission of. (W. R. French) Univ. Q. **26**: 222. — Dub. R. **61**: 441. **62**: 177.
— — Wood's Lecture on. Chr. Exam. **30**: 260.
— Modern Theories concerning. (J. A. Dorner) Contemp. **1**: 473. Same art. Liv. Age, **89**: 666.
— Mythical and real. Dub. Univ. **72**: 483.
— Name of. (J. A. Picton) Mod. R. **1**: 73.
— Napoleon I. on. Mo. Rel. M. **41**: 426.
— Naturalism and. (B. J. Pinkerton) Chr. Q. **2**: 522.
— Nature of. (R. Collyer) Radical, **3**: 1. — (G. T. Flanders) Univ. Q. **37**: 398. — (W. H. Furness) Unita. R. **4**: 1. — (C. Palfrey) Unita. R. **9**: 166.
— — and Character of. (S. Crane) Univ. Q. **27**: 34.
— — Furness and Bushnell on. (C. A. Bartol) Chr. Exam. **66**: 112.
— — inferred from the Universe. (E. B. Hall) Chr. Exam. **44**: 344.
— — Views of. (N. S. Folsom and E. H. Sears) Mo. Rel. M. **46**: 1–451. **47**: 10.
— a Nazarene, Matt. ii. 23. Chr. Obs. **6**: 90. **8**: 412, 545.
— Neander's Life of. (J. H. Morison) Chr. Exam. **46**: 76. — (P. Schaff) Meth. Q. **8**: 248.
— New Birth of. (O. B. Frothingham) Radical, **2**: 321.
— New Creation in. (J. W. Nevin) Mercersb. **2**: 1.
— New Portraiture of. (E. H. Sears) Mo. Rel. M. **37**: 81, 161.
— Obedience of. (J. A. H. Tittmann) Am. Bib. Repos. **8**: 1.
— an Obstacle to the Soul. (J. L. Hatch) Radical, **3**: 239.
— of Apocrypha. (O. B. Frothingham) Chr. Exam. **53**: 21.
— of the Gentiles. (O. B. Frothingham) Chr. Exam. **52**: 1.
— of the Evangelists. (J. T. Bixby) Chr. Exam. **87**: 20. — (J. H. Morison) Mo. Rel. M. **48**: 289. — So. R. n. s. **12**: 159. — Princ. **42**: 586.
— — and of St. Paul. (N. L. Frothingham) Chr. Exam. **49**: 1.
Jesus Christ of the Evangelists, the fourfold Biography. Brit. Q. **35**: 108. Same art. Ecl. M. **56**: 203.
— of History. (O. S. Munsell) Meth. Q. **22**: 579. — Brit. Q. **21**: 455.
— — and Prophecy. (J. F. Rowe) Chr. Q. **4**: 235.
— of Humanity. (O. B. Frothingham) Radical, **10**: 321.
— of the Jews. (O. B. Frothingham) Chr. Exam. **51**: 161.
— Old Testament Prophecies concerning. (E. Fisher) Univ. Q. **6**: 129.
— on Earth. (H. J. Richardson) Cong. R. **8**: 452.
— the only Foundation. Chr. R. **9**: 157.
— our Redemption. (J. W. Thompson) Chr. Exam. **52**: 272.
— Passion of. (J. I. T. Coolidge) Mo. Rel. M. **15**: 301.
— — Krummacher and Stier on. Lond. Q. **9**: 483.
— Perfection of. (J. F. Clarke) O. & N. **1**: 60.
— Periods of Life and Ministry of. Kitto, **20**: 65. **21**: 437.
— Person of. (O. B. Frothingham) Chr. Exam. **51**: 161. — (D. Gans) Mercersb. **6**: 505. — (R. G. Keyes) New Eng. **34**: 459. — (H. Schmid) Mercersb. **1**: 272. — Liv. Age, **80**: 531, 579. — Theo. Repos. **3**: 58, 133.
— — and modern Thought. Am. Church R. **24**: 70.
— — Belsham on. Ecl. R. **17**: 153, 305.
— — Constitution of. (T. H. Skinner) Princ. **43**: 256.
— — Godet on. Lond. Q. **42**: 417.
— — Lutheran Doctrine of. (J. A. Brown) Luth. Q. **2**: 256.
— — Orthodox Doctrine of. (P. Schaff) Theo. Ecl. **4**: 309.
— — Polycarp on. (E. E. Higbee) Mercersb. **4**: 583.
— — Sartorius on. (J. W. Nevin) Mercersb. **1**: 146.
— — Smith on. Ecl. R. **31**: 540.
— Personal Reign of. Cong. M. **10**: 465, 529, 590.
— Personal Relation to the Human Race. (G. N. Abbott) J. Spec. Philos. **8**: 351.
— Personality of. (A. A. Livermore) Unita. R. **3**: 545. — (N. Worcester) Chr. Exam. **21**: 85.
— — and Mission of. (C. T. Brooks) No. Am. **99**: 275.
— Philochristus. (J. L. Davies) Contemp. **31**: 804.
— Plan of. (J. G. Herder) Evang. R. **5**: 337.
— Policy towards Ecclesiastical Rulers of his Day. Chr. Obs. **71**: 641.
— Portrait of, in Leonardo Da Vinci's Last Supper. Cong. **1**: 23. — Ev. Sat. **9**: 305.
— Portraits of. (M. A. Lloyd) Penn Mo. **4**: 41. — Quar. **123**: 490.
— — Antiquity of. Art J. **13**: 1-233.
— — Marshall's. (Mrs. E. S. Morgan) Western, **4**: 57.
— The practical. (A. W. Jackson) Unita. R. **11**: 371.
— Prayer in the Garden. (N. Vansant) Meth. Q. **24**: 216.
— Prayers of. Kitto, **28**: 85.
— — Why did he pray? (J. Few Smith) Evang. R. **14**: 169.
— Praying in the Name of. Theo. Repos. **2**: 159.
— the Preacher's Model. (A. D. Smith) Am. Bib. Repos. 2d s. **9**: 149. — (W. Hull) Evang. R. **17**: 113.
— Preaching of, Bennet on. Cong. M. **19**: 701.
— — Never Man spake like this Man. (H. Stowell) Ex. H. Lec. **7**: 149.
— Preaching to the Spirits in Prison. (J. B. Miles) Bib. Sac. **19**: 1. — (M. L. Stoever) Evang. R. **10**: 74. *See* Spirits in Prison.
— Pre-existence of. (A. R. Abbott) Univ. Q. **21**: 448. — (J. O. Skinner) Univ. Q. **19**: 41.
— — of human Soul of. (J. Benson) Meth. M. **23**: 22. — (H. L. Kendall) Bib. Sac. **32**: 421. — Meth. M. **42**: 422.
— prefigured by Isaac. Theo. Repos. **6**: 60.
— Preparation for the Introduction of. (W. H. Williams) Bapt. Q. **5**: 429. — Kitto, **38**: 350.
— — in Apochryphal Period. (A. S. Twombly) New Eng. **36**: 329.

Jesus Christ, Preparation for, World at the Advent of. (A. St. John Chambre) Univ. Q. **17**: 42.
— — Traces of, in Profane Literature. (I. S. Hartley) Am. Presb. R. **18**: 708.
— Presence of, with the Church. Cong. M. **23**: 533, 809. **27**: 883.
— — — with his Ministers. Cong. M. **22**: 564-787.
— Pressensé's Life of. Lond. Q. **27**: 163.
— Price's Sermons on. Theo. Repos. **6**: 225, 349.
— Priesthood of. (J. G. Adams) Univ. Q. **22**: 476.
— — Jos. Parker on. (R. W. Dale) Cong. **6**: 65.
— — — Sacerdotal Prayer of. (A.W.Tyler) Bib.Sac.**28**: 323.
— Prophecy of his Sufferings. (H. L. Baugher) Evang. R. **21**: 128.
— Prophetic Office of. (H. Harbaugh) Mercersb. **19**: 465.
— Propitiation for Man's Sins. (M. Goodrich) Univ. Q. **22**: 69.
— Psychology in the Life of. (O. S. Taylor) Bib. Sac. **27**: 209.
— Public Life of, Coleridge on. Dub. R. **77**: 173.
— a Reality and not a Romance. (J. McCosh) Good Words, **5**: 961.
— Reappearings of. (E. H. Sears) Mo. Rel. M. **41**: 281.
— Reasonableness of certain Words of. (A. K. H. Boyd) Good Words, **3**: 19.
— Recent Studies on. (W. H. Wynn) Luth. Q. **6**: 161.
— Rejection and Passion of. Kitto, **15**: 268.
— — by the Jews. (A. H. Hand) Princ. **39**: 128.
— Relation to Believers. (D. T. Fiske) Bib. Sac. **27**: 714.
— — to Joseph. Kitto, **19**: 273.
— Religion of. (A. C. George) Meth. Q. **35**: 596.
— Religious Life in Palestine when he appeared. (D. Brown) Good Words, **7**: 97.
— Renan's Historiens Critiques de. Kitto, **31**: 51.
— Renan's Life of. (C. T. Brooks) No. Am. **98**: 195. — (O. B. Frothingham) Chr. Exam. **75**: 313. — (R. H. Hutton) Victoria, **1**: 385. — (E. de Pressensé) Theo. Ecl. **1**: 199. — (H. B. Smith) Am. Presb. R. **13**: 136. — Blackw. **96**: 417. — Brit. Q. **38**: 271. — Dub. R. **54**: 386. — Chr. Obs. **63**: 780. **64**: 143. — Ecl. R. **118**: 268. — Ed. R. **119**: 574. — Kitto, **32**: 150, 344. — Knick. **63**: 247. — Liv. Age, **79**: 32. — Lond. Q. **21**: 457. **22**: 235. — Nat. R. **17**: 524. — No. Brit. **40**: 184. — Temp. Bar, **10**: 44. — Westm. **80**: 537.
— — Christmas Thoughts on. (F. D. Maurice) Macmil. **9**: 190.
— — and Strauss's. (P. Schaff) Contin. Mo. **6**: 651.
— — — and Schleiermacher. (J. P. Westervelt) Princ. **38**: 133.
— Representative Character of. (O. A. Burgess) Chr. Q. **5**: 104.
— the Resurrection and the Life. (W. H. Furness) Mo. Rel. M. **3**: 193.
— Resurrection of. (J. G. Adams) Univ. Q. **24**: 174. — (W. Alexander) Good Words, **8**: 532. — (A. A. Baker) Cong. R. **7**: 40. — (O. A. Burgess) Chr. Q. **8**: 210. — (A. W. Goodnow) Bapt. Q. **7**: 420. — (W. E. Krebs) Mercersb. **16**: 401. — (W. J. Potter) Radical, **2**: 558. — (P. Schaff) Princ. n. s. **5**: 411. — (B. F. Westcott) Contemp. **30**: 1070. — Bib. R. **5**: 497. — Kitto, **14**: 54. — Lond. Q. **38**: 175. — Theo. & Lit. J. **10**: 53, 283, 371.
— — Accounts of. (T. Tebbets) Mo. Rel. M. **19**: 73.
— — Gospel Narrative of. Bib. R. **6**: 433. — Dub. R. **79**: 299.
— — Paul a Witness for. (G.P.Fisher) Bib. Sac. **17**: 620.
— — Proof of. (J. Priestley) Theo. Repos. **1**: 300.
— — scientifically considered. (A.Blauvelt) Scrib.**7**: 687.
— — Vision Theory of. (W. Calkins) Am. Presb. R. **16**: 349, 509.
— Resurrection Body of. Kitto, **9**: 341.
Jesus Christ, Revelation of God in. (J. W. Nevin) Mercersb. **18**: 325.
— Risen Christ. (G. S. Weaver) Univ. Q. **21**: 172.
— — Forty Days after the Resurrection. (J. M. Titzel) Mercersb. **18**: 262.
— — — Works on. Lond. Q. **10**: 156.
— Sacrifice of. (E. C. Wines) Theo. & Lit. J. **10**: 203. — (S. S. Hebberd) Univ. Q. **37**: 313. — Theo. Repos. **1**: 173, 225.
— Sacrificial Nature of the Death of. Bib. R. **5**: 265.
— Satisfaction of. Bib. Sac. **36**: 105-441.
— Scenes from the Life and Travels of. (J. L. Porter) Good Words, **2**: 231-435.
— Scott's Life of. Cong. **3**: 658, 719.
— Sears's Heart of. (J. M. Atwood) Univ. Q. **29**: 429.
— Second Advent of. (G. D. Boardman) Bapt. Q. **9**: 35. — (D. Brown) Good Words, **8**: 599. — (J. A. Brown) Bib. Sac. **24**: 629. — (D. D. Buck) Theo. & Lit. J. **7**: 158. — (E. F. Hatfield) Am. Presb. R. **13**: 197, 411. **14**: 195. — (A. Alexander) Princ. **19**: 564. — (S. R. Smith) Univ. Q. **1**: 381. — (J. T. Smith) Cong. R. **7**: 195. — (J. M. Titzel) Mercersb. **22**: 87. — Theo. & Lit. J. **11**: 310. **12**: 1, 273, 588. — (J. A. Brown) Luth. Q. **4**: 321.
— — Alexander on. Theo. & Lit. J. **13**: 204.
— — Augsburg Confession on. (J. A. Brown) Luth. Q. **4**: 52.
— — Christ's Teachings on. (H. Cowles) Bib. Sac. **28**: 485.
— — Signs of. (J. Richards) Theo. & Lit. J. **6**: 558.
— — Time of. (A. Hovey) Bapt. Q. **11**: 416.
— — — Would it hasten the Conversion of the World? (L. Swain) New Eng. **15**: 274.
— Self-Revelation of. (T. G. Apple) Mercersb. **21**: 246.
— Sermon on the Mount. Meth. Q. **20**: 56.
— — Brewster on. Chr. Obs. **8**: 773.
— Silence of Scripture concerning. No. Brit. **32**: 68.
— Sinlessness of. (J. A. Dorner) Am. Presb. R. **12**: 42-406.
— — and his Miracles. (J. B. Mozley) Contemp. **7**: 481. Same art. Theo. Ecl. **5**: 560.
See above, Jesus Christ, Character of.
— Socrates and. (W. Everett) Unita. R. **2**: 108.
— Son of God. (R. B. Drummond) Theo. R. **3**: 467. — (W. S. Tyler) Bib. Sac. **22**: 621. — (M. J. S. De Long) Univ. Q. **37**: 87.
— Son of Man. (J. J. van Oosterzee) Princ. n. s. **2**: 115. — (W. S. Tyler) Bib. Sac. **22**: 51.
— Sonship of. (A. Raleigh) Good Words, **8**: 201. — (M. Raymond) Meth. Q. **33**: 562. — Chr. Mo. Spec. **2**: 224. — Princ. **1**: 429.
— — Eternal. Meth. M. **41**: 186. — Theo. R. **5**: 51.
— the Spirit. Brownson, **18**: 137.
— — Hitchcock on. (O. B. Frothingham) Chr. Exam. **73**: 313.
— Spirit that was in. (J. Weiss) Radical R. **1**: 535.
— Strauss's Life of. For. Q. **22**: 101. — (T. Parker) Chr. Exam. **28**: 273. — (G. E. Ellis) Chr. Exam. **41**: 313. — Brit. Q. **5**: 206. — (S. G. Bulfinch) Chr. Exam. **39**: 145. — Dub. Univ. **28**: 268. — (P. Bayne) Fortn. **4**: 317. — (A. P. Peabody) No. Am. **91**: 130. — (H. A. Sawtelle) Chr. R. **21**: 321. — Bib. R. **1**: 54. — Theo. R. **1**: 335. — Prosp. R. **2**: 479. — Westm. **82**: 186, 291.
— — and Controversy caused by it. (H. B. Hackett) Kitto, **33**: 378.
— — and Neander's. (D. N. Lord) Theo. & Lit. J. **1**: 256.
— — and Renan's. (D. Bowen) Radical, **2**: 105.
— — — and Ecce Homo. Ed. R. **124**: 450. Same art. Ecl. M. **68**: 265. Same art. Liv. Age, **91**: 494.
— — and Schleiermacher. (J. P. Westervelt) Princ. **38**: 116.

Jesus Christ, Strauss's Life of, Mythical Theory of. (G. P. Fisher) New Eng. **23**: 203.
— the sublime Radical. (H. W. Beecher) Radical, **1**: 297.
— Sufferings of. (S. W. S. Dutton) New Eng. **5**: 415. — Am. Bib. Repos. 3d s. **2**: 381, 660. — (N. Worcester) Chr. Exam. **16**: 202. — (J. Floy) Meth. Q. **6**: 227. — (R. Turnbull) Chr. R. **11**: 584. — Chr. R. **13**: 422. — Meth. Q. **1**: 212. — (E. Pond) Bib. Sac. **7**: 205. — (J. Hawkins) Luth. Q. **2**: 193. — (R. Pike) Mo. Rel. M. **9**: 111.
— — Doctrine of. (J. P. Boyce) Bapt. Q. **4**: 385.
— — Need of. (J. C. Kimball) Mo. Rel. M. **27**: 79.
— — Perfect through. Cong. M. **27**: 333.
— Sun of Righteousness; a Sermon. (A. T. Bledsoe) So. R. n. s. **19**: 164.
— Supernaturalism of, scientifically considered. (A. Blauvelt) Scrib. **9**: 410.
— Supremacy as a Lawgiver. Chr. R. **14**: 568.
— Sympathy of. Chr. Disc. **5**: 414.
— Teachings of. (H. Ballou) Univ. Q. **6**: 264.
— — Doctrinal Contents of. (E. P. Gould) Bapt. Q. **11**: 1.
— Temptations of. (E. C. Anderson) Bapt. Q. **4**: 159. — (F. Johnson) Bapt. Q. **7**: 187. — (N. Macleod) Good Words, **12**: 116–649. — (H. New) Theo. R. **16**: 322. — (A. S. Patton) Cong. R. **8**: 333. — (L. S. Potwin) Bib. Sac. **22**: 127. — Bost. R. **3**: 162. — Chr. Obs. **48**: 433, 505. — Cong. M. **28**: 346. — Kitto, **12**: 415. **27**: 241.
— — in Wilderness. (J. J. van Oosterzee) Am. Presb. R. **18**: 753. — (W. A. Stearns) Bib. Sac. **11**: 155.
— — — Mill on. Chr. Obs. **49**: 105.
— — Orthodox View of. (G. E. Ellis) Chr. Exam. **56**: 297, 445.
— — Scheffer on. Bost. R. **1**: 223.
— — Third Temptation. Bost. R. **3**: 287.
— Testimony of. (J. W. Nevin) Mercersb. **24**: 5.
— Testimony of Josephus to. (E. Robinson) Chr. Mo. Spec. **7**: 126.
— — of the Old Testament to. (J. Packard) Am. Bib. Repos. 3d s. **3**: 393.
— Theology taught by. Princ. **43**: 120.
— — Thompson's. (R. Metcalf) O. & N. **3**: 220.
— Transfiguration of. (G. Brückner) Kitto, **40**: 368. — (C. P. Krauth, jr.) Evang. R. **2**: 237. — (H. B. Hackett) Bapt. Q. **7**: 449. — (G. F. Simmons) Chr. Exam. **42**: 270. — Theo. & Lit. J. **11**: 427. — Theo. Repos. **2**: 122.
— Trial of. (E. W. Hooker) Cong. R. **11**: 549. — Chr. R. **5**: 33. — (A. T. Innes) Contemp. **30**: 393, 810. — (A. T. Innes) Sup. Pop. Sci. Mo. **1**: 460. **2**: 61. Same art. Liv. Age, **134**: 729. **135**: 259.
— — and Crucifixion of. (H. W. Burrage) Bost. R. **6**: 407.
— — for Treason. (B. F. Hall) Am. Church R. **30**: 78.
— — Judicial. (E. P. Rogers) Am. Presb. R. **20**: 587.
— the true Corner-Stone. (J. F. Clarke) Mo. Rel. M. **12**: 339.
— the true Ideal of Man. (S. H. Giesy) Mercersb. **14**: 548.
— Trustworthiness of. (M. C. Taylor) Good Words, **13**: 535.
— Twofold Life of. (J. T. Tucker) Bib. Sac. **17**: 95.
— Tyndall's "Of Christ alone without Sin." (J. B. Mozley) Contemp. **7**: 481.
— Uhlhorn's Modern Representations of the Life of. (H. D. Catlin) Chr. Exam. **85**: 136.
— Unitarian Views of. Chr. Exam. **81**: 301.
— very God and Man. (E. Washburn) Am. Meth. M. **20**: 335.
— Ware on the Character of. (E. Beecher) Chr. Mo. Spec. **8**: 199.
Jesus Christ, What think ye of? (F. Frothingham) Unita. R. **14**: 570.
— Witness of Paul to. Princ. **42**: 263.
— — of Scripture to. (E. P. Miller) Am. Church R. **31**: 14.
— witnessing as to his Miraculous Powers. (Dr. Walker) Evang. R. **12**: 173.
— Work of, with Souls. (J. G. Adams) Univ. Q. **25**: 413.
— the World's Judge. (N. L. Frothingham) Chr. Exam. **63**: 359.
— Worship of. (M. P. Hayden) Chr. Q. **4**: 395. — Cong. M. **23**: 459. **24**: 84, 247, 250.
— — historically considered. (J. M. Whiton) Cong. R. **10**: 246.
— Yahveh Christ. (R. R. Coon) Chr. R. **23**: 127.
Jet. Argosy, **12**: 113.
— Whitby. All the Year, **32**: 155. — (H. Curwen) Pract. M. **2**: 24.
Jet; her Face or her Fortune? a Novel. (A. Edwards) Temp. Bar, **52**: 265–547. **53**: 121, 271. Same art. Appleton, **19**: 212–504. **20**: 50.
Jettison of Goods carried on Deck. (W. Phillips) Hunt, **3**: 432.
Jetty; a Jale. (J. C. Brenan) Sharpe, **47**: 93.
Jeu d'Amour; a Tale. Canad. Mo. **3**: 15.
Jevons, W. Stanley, Sketch of. Pop. Sci. Mo. **11**: 745.
Jew, The; a Tale from the Russian. Blackw. **76**: 691. Same art. Ecl. M. **34**: 376.
— Ancient and modern. (L. Hood) New Eng. **37**: 674.
— and Beggarman; a Tale. Dub. Univ. **6**: 702.
— Gentile, Christian; a Tale. Dark Blue, **3**: 1–615.
— Letter to a Christian by a. Pamph. **16**: 279.
— of Magdeburg. (H. A. Miles) O. & N. **7**: 334.
— of York. Fraser, **14**: 298.
— Roman, of the 1st Century. Chr. Obs. **59**: 318.
— Young, of Tunis. House. Words, **1**: 118.
Jew's Legacy; a Tale of the Siege of Gibraltar. Blackw. **70**: 648.
Jews, The. (D. M. Craik) Macmil. **7**: 434. — Dem. R. **34**: 497. — Knick. **53**: 41.
— Acts of the Assembly of, 1806. Ecl. R. **6**: 735, 831.
— Agitation against, Jewish View of. (L. Wolf) 19th Cent. **9**: 338.
— — Recent Phases of. (H. Adler) 19th Cent. **10**: 813.
— and Cromwell. Ecl. M. **73**: 80.
— and the Gentiles. (H. J. Schmidt) Evang. R. **8**: 485. — Univ. Q. **18**: 189.
— and Judaism. (H. Adler) 19th Cent. **4**: 133. — (H. McNeile) Ex. H. Lec. **9**: 411.
— and their Persecution. (E. I. Sears) Nat. Q. **15**: 207.
— and the Talmud after the Time of Christ. (Dr. Michelson) Kitto, **33**: 321.
— and the Ten Tribes. Mo. R. **143**: 153.
— Antagonism to Christ. (R. L. Gerhart) Mercersb. **24**: 394.
— at Damascus, Salomons on Persecution of, 1840. Mo. R. **153**: 35.
— at K'ae-fung-foo. (W. H. Green) Princ. **24**: 240.
— Burial Rites of. Good Words, **11**: 562.
— Can they be Patriots? (H. Adler) 19th Cent. **3**: 637. Same art. Liv. Age, **137**: 374. — (G. Smith) 19th Cent. **3**: 875.
— Captivity and its Mementos. Nat. M. **7**: 306, 453.
— Characteristics of the Race. (C. H. Brigham) Unita. R. **5**: 156.
— Church of. (R. B. Drummond) Theo. R. **3**: 73. — (W. H. Ryder) Univ. Q. **15**: 301.
— — History of. Ecl. M. **59**: 21.
— — Typified Character of. (T. Appel) Mercersb. **8**: 615.
— Civil Code of. Liv. Age, **144**: 506. **145**: 114–819. **146**: 56.
— Civil Government of, Wines's. (L. G. Clark) Knick. **22**: 168.

Jews, The, Civilization of, Ancient. (G. Collins) Univ. Q. **30**: 133.
— Coinage of, History of. Ecl. M. **63**: 490.
— Commonwealth of. Spirit Pilg. **2**: 319. — Mo. R. **119**: 247. Same art. Mus. **15**: 157.
— — and the Christian Church. (W. Adams) Am. Church R. **13**: 361.
— — Jahn's. (C. E. Stowe) Princ. **1**: 307.
— — Newman's. (A. Gosman) Princ. **22**: 234.
— Condition and Belief of, at the Coming of Christ; translated. (J. Murdock) Am. Bib. Repos. 2d s. **2**: 174. — (J. W. H. Streckenberg) Evang. R. **16**: 61.
— Condition and Customs of. Mus. **32**: 50.
— Councils of, Wittius on. Princ. **1**: 252.
— Crimean, Ancient Tomb Inscriptions of. (S. Davidson) Theo. R. **5**: 463.
— Criminal Code of. Liv. Age, **143**: 498–756.
— Customs of. Fraser, **29**: 597. — Chr. Obs. **20**: 222.
— Dietary System of. (W. M. Rosenblatt) Galaxy, **18**: 670.
— Domestic Economy of. (H. T. Armfield) Good Words, **8**: 731.
— Drummond's Œdipus Judaicus. Colburn, **2**: 8–510.
— Elegiac Poetry of. Chr. Mo. Spec. **5**: 470.
— Ewald on Hagiocracy of. (F. R. Conder) Theo. R. **12**: 70.
— Exodus of. (A. H. Guernsey) Harper, **45**: 35. — Ecl. R. **121**: 176.
— — and the Greek Exodus. Fraser, **14**: 461.
— — Credibility of. Quar. **1**: 80.
— Festivals among. U. S. Cath. M. **5**: 153.
— Fine Arts among. (J. S. Memes) Kitto, **3**: 50.
— Future Destiny of. (M. Tucker) Chr. Mo. Spec. **8**: 57, 502. — Chr. Obs. **61**: 463, 525.
— History of. (J. A. Seiss) Evang. R. **3**: 255. — (E. Peabody) Chr. Exam. **9**: 290. — (E. Wigglesworth) Chr. Exam. **45**: 48. — (W. B. O. Peabody) No. Am. **32**: 234. — Meth. Q. **2**: 192. — Spirit Pilg. **3**: 480. — Prosp. R. **4**: 1.
— — Mrs. Adams's. Chr. Obs. **15**: 99.
— — and Literature of. (A. J. Canfield) Univ. Q. **31**: 54.
— — Apocryphal Period of. (A. S. Twombly) New Eng. **36**: 329.
— — Ewald's. (J. H. Allen) Chr. Exam. **55**: 161. — (J. H. Allen) Unita. R. **2**: 467. — (A. J. Canfield) Univ. Q. **31**: 54. — (C. E. Grinnell) No. Am. **119**: 249. — (W. Salmond) Meth. Q. **34**: 396. — (J. Williams) O. & N. **5**: 615. — Chr. Obs. **74**: 934. — Ed. R. **142**: 432. — O. & N. **5**: 366.
— — Foreign Element in. (G. Mooar) Bib. Sac. **27**: 614.
— — Dr. H. Graetz and St. Paul on. Lond. Q. **51**: 449.
— — Heroes of. Westm. **98**: 285.
— — Illustrations of, from Tacitus. Cong. M. **16**: 657. **17**: 8, 152.
— — Last Revolt of, A. D. 131. (E. Renan) Contemp. **35**: 595. Same art. Liv. Age, **142**: 368.
— — Milman's. Ecl. R. **52**: 50. **118**: 116.
— — — and Stanley's. Ed. R. **119**: 137.
— — Modern. (J. A. Alexander) Princ. **19**: 378.
— — Rothschild's. Chr. Obs. **71**: 81.
— — Short. Meth. M. **34**: 62.
— — since A. D. 70. Ecl. R. **104**: 67.
— — Social and political. Chr. Rem. **32**: 357.
— — War under Trajan and Hadrian. (H. Muenter) Kitto, **7**: 439. Same art. Bib. Sac. **1843**: 393.
— Home Life of. (H. Zimmern) Fraser, **103**: 482. Same art. Liv. Age, **149**: 414.
— in America. (G. Gottheill) No. Am. **126**: 293. **127**: 81.
— — Ostracism of. (N. Morais) No. Am. **133**: 265.
— in China. (C. H. Brigham) Unita. R. **3**: 135. — House. Words, **3**: 452. Same art. Internat. M. **4**: 264. — Mus. **9**: 470.
Jews, The, in Constantinople. Am. Mo. M. **2**: 95.
— in Cornwall, Are there? (M. Müller) Macmil. **15**: 484. Same art. Ecl. M. **69**: 47.
— in the East, Beaton's. Liv. Age, **63**: 18.
— in Egypt, Condition of. Liv. Age, **24**: 511.
— in England. (P. Magnus) Theo. R. **13**: 413.—Chamb. J. **42**: 532. — Once a Week, **7**: 190.
— — Admission of, to Parliament. Tait, n. s. **17**: 427.
— — Ancient State of. Lond. M. **1**: 503.
— — Civil Disabilities of. (T. B. Macaulay) Ed. R. **52**: 363. — Selec. Ed. R. **5**: 203. — For. Q. **11**: 441. — Quar. **8**: 282. **81**: 526. — (T. P. Thompson) Westm. **10**: 435. **19**: 215. — Mo. R. **122**: 106. — Blackw. **68**: 73. — Fraser, **1**: 541. **36**: 623, 738. — Ecl. R. **87**: 359.
— — Early History of. (H. Southern) Retros. **1**: 200. — Mus. **5**: 1.
— — Emancipation of. Ed. R. **86**: 138.
— — History of. Hogg, **9**: 380.
— — in the Eastern Provinces. (E. Gaisford) St. James, **39**: 288.
— — Origin of. (J. Caley) Arch. **8**: 389.
— — Persecution of. (A. C. Ewald) Gent. M. n. s. **27**: 411.
— in Europe. Ecl. M. **88**: 500.
— — during the Middle Ages. Chr. Obs. **62**: 1, 96, 174. — (J. H. Bridges) Liv. Age, **55**: 769.
— — on the Continent. Colburn, **119**: 53.
— — Question of, 1880. (Goldwin Smith) 19th Cent. **10**: 494. Same art. Ecl. M. **97**: 810. — (S. H. Kellogg) New Eng. **40**: 328.
— — Religious State of. Cong. M. **28**: 329.
— in Germany. Contemp. **39**: 31. Same art. Ecl. M. **96**: 344. — (C. Grant) Contemp. **39**: 365. — (E. Schuster) Fortn. **35**: 371.
— — Movement against, 1880. (F. W. Taussig) Nation, **30**: 468.
— — Number and Distribution of. (C. R. Weld) J. Statis. Soc. **9**: 77.
— — Persecution of. (M. Sulzberger) Penn Mo. **12**: 100. — (G. S. Hall) Nation, **30**: 74.
— — Prussian Anti-Semitic League. (T. D. Danion) Cath. World, **33**: 131.
— in Great Britain. Fraser, **49**: 304. — Liv. Age, **31**: 298.
— — Mill's. New Q. **2**: 493. — Liv. Age, **38**: 488.
— in Jerusalem. Hogg, **4**: 288.
— in London. (W. Gilbert) Good Words, **5**: 864, 920.
— in Maryland. Niles's Reg. **15**: supp. 9.
— in Palestine. (C. H. Brigham) No. Am. **95**: 331.
— in Paris. (W. Gilbert) Good Words, **8**: 458.
— in Poland. For. Q. **27**: 241. — Brit. & For. R. **5**: 402. — Am. Q. Reg. **4**: 109.
— in Rome. Liv Age, **59**: 958.
— — B. C. 76–A. D. 140. (C. H. Brigham) Unita. R. **7**: 261.
— — in Heathen Times. (R. Seton) Cath. World, **28**: 336.
— — in Christian Times. (R. Seton) Cath. World, **29**: 25.
— in Russia. Tait, n. s. **22**: 23. Same art. Ecl. M. **34**: 354. Same art. Liv. Age, **44**: 467.
— in Spain. Nat. Q. **25**: 305.
— — in the earlier Centuries. Chr. Rem. **42**: 381.
— in Spain and Portugal. Brit. & For. R. **13**: 459. — Ecl. R. **88**: 681.
— — Finn's History of. Mo. R. **154**: 357.
— in U. S., Letter to. (T. Bulfinch) Chr. Exam. **15**: 15.
— in Western Europe. (B. Cracroft) Westm. **79**: 428. Same art. Ecl. M. **59**: 389.
— Kuenen's Religion of. (R. P. Stebbins) Unita. R. **10**: 297, 353.
— Land Tenure of, Primitive. (J. Fenton) Theo. R. **14**: 504.
— Law among, Humane Features of. (H. M. Field) Bib. Sac. **10**: 340.

Jews, The, Laws of, Wines on. (E. Pond) Theo. & Lit. J. **6**: 223. — (J. W. Yeomans) Princ. **25**: 656.
— Learning among. (J. Woodward) Arch. **4**: 212.
— Literature of. (C. H. Brigham) Chr. Exam. **64**: 346.
— — and Language of. (E. Renan) Bapt. Q. **7**: 237.
— Liturgy of. Liv. Age, **131**: 56.
— Lost Ten Tribes. Am. Presb. R. **10**: 652. — Nat. M. **6**: 109, 214.
— — and some recent Theories. Chr. Obs. **77**: 695.
— — Karens a Remnant of. (F. Mason) Cong. M. **19**: 397.
— Masada and its Tragedy. Nat. M. **13**: 302, 393.
— McCaul's Sketches of. Mo. R. **146**: 313.
— Men and Times of, J. H. Allen's. (O. B. Frothingham) Chr. Exam. **70**: 362.
— Metaphysical Schools among. (G. Masson) Kitto, **35**: 60, 374.
— Mission among. (B. Pick) Luth. Q. **6**: 357.
— Mode of Living of. Chr. Mo. Spec. **1**: 125.
— Modern, Cultivation of. (C. H. Brigham) No. Am. **83**: 351.
— Modern Judaism and Christianity. Lond. Q. **32**: 463.
— Monarchism among, Delaunay's. Lond. Q. **44**: 440.
— Monarchy of. Mass. Q. **1**: 225.
— — History of. Chr. Obs. **48**: 488.
— — Newman's. No. Brit. **16**: 119. — (J. H. Adams) Univ. Q. **13**: 5.
— — Origin of. (G. H. Shodde) Luth. Q. **11**: 178.
— Monotheism among. (W. Sanday) Theo. R. **13**: 486.
— Morality of. Mo. R. **122**: 251.
— Mythology of, Goldziher's. (J. W. Chadwick) Unita. R. **8**: 278.
— of Abyssinia. Chr. Obs. **69**: 938.
— of the present Day. (A. Rosenberg) St. James, **38**: 305.
— Opinion of foreign. Chr. Disc. **4**: 413.
— Orthodox, Sabbath among. Galaxy, **14**: 379.
— Our Israelitish Brethren. (J. Parton) Atlan. **26**: 385.
— Palfrey on Scriptures and Antiquities of. (A. P. Peabody) Chr. Exam. **53**: 1. — Mo. R. **153**: 253.
— Patriarchs of the West. Chr. Rem. **42**: 50. Same art. Liv. Age, **70**: 529.
— Pellat's Memoir of. Ecl. R. **50**: 519.
— People and Monarchy of. Ecl. R. **91**: 315.
— Persecution of. Mus. **40**: 227, 291.
— Persecutors of. (E. Lawrence) Harper, **49**: 79.
— Political Future of. (D. Ker) Nat. Q. **41**: 135.
— Principality of the Captive. (W. F. Ainsworth) Colburn, **74**: 315.
— Prophecies concerning Israel after the Captivity. Lond. Q. **53**: 1.
— Prophecy as to. Bib. Sac. **4**: 337. — Ecl. R. **9**: 219.
— Proselytism of, before the War of Titus. (F. W. Newman) Fraser, **97**: 693.
— Quakers, Scotchmen. (C. Lamb) Lond. M. **4**: 152.
— Rabbis and their Literature. (Prof. Nordheimer) Am. Bib. Repos. 2d s. **6**: 154.
— Records of, Giles on. (M. Heilprin) Nation, **27**: 72.
— Reform Movement among. (M. Heilprin) Nation, **6**: 488.
— Reformed. Blackw. **106**: 533.
— Religion of. (F. A. Gast) Mercersb. **21**: 477.
— — Ceremonies of. Cornh. **13**: 221.
— — Evolution of. (F. Adler) Pop. Sci. Mo. **9**: 589.
— — God of Israel. (J. Jacobs) 19th Cent. **6**: 481. Same art. Liv. Age, **143**: 166.
— — State of. (E. S. Calman) Am. Bib. Repos. 2d s. **3**: 398. **4**: 176.
— Representative System of. (J. L. Saalschütz) Bib. Sac. **15**: 825.
— Restoration of. Theo. & Lit. J. **2**: 15, 240, 453. — (J. S. Foulk) Mercersb. **18**: 386. — (B. J. Wallace) Am. Presb. R. **6**: 46. — Appleton, **23**: 276. — (W. Scott) Am. Meth. M. **21**: 361. — Chr. Obs. **6**: 29.
Jews, The, Restoration of. Chr. Obs. **14**: 809. **38**: 518, 554, 665. — Cong. M. **18**: 89, 152, 217. — Nat. M. **4**: 521. — (A. M. Osbon) Meth. Q. **16**: 577. — (D. N. Lord) Theo. & Lit. J. **2**: 15, 240, 453.
— Sacrificial System of. (R. B. Girdlestone) Chr. Obs. **75**: 296–926.
— Schools of. (A. Calmet) Kitto, **3**: 87.
— — Origin and History of. (O. D. Miller) Univ. Q. **37**: 261.
— Sects among, a Warning against modern Tendencies. (J. L. L. Davies) Good Words, **6**: 412.
— Sippurim. Fraser, **66**: 789.
— Social and Sanitary Laws of. (G. S. Drew) Contemp. **2**: 514.
— Stanley's Jewish Church. (A. V. Dicey) Nation, **24**: 30. — (J. H. Ward) Nation, **2**: 677. — Blackw. **100**: 494. — Bost. R. **3**: 377. — Chr. Obs. **63**: 608. **77**: 8, 103. — Contemp. **1**: 615. — Ecl. R. **117**: 101. **123**: 171. — Fraser, **74**: 135. — Kitto, **31**: 257. — Nat. R. **16**: 362.
— State and Prospects of. (F. Adler) No. Am. **125**: 133. — (H. H. Milman) Quar. **63**: 166. — Hesp. **3**: 140. — Cong. M. **27**: 485. — Quar. **38**: 114. **69**: 151. — Mus. **35**: 426. — Fraser, **22**: 253. — West. Mo. R. **2**: 437.
— Theocracy of. No. Brit. **13**: 264. — Fraser, **13**: 579, 682.
— Wailing-Place of; a Poem. Cornh. **13**: 211.
— What are they coming to? (W. M. Rosenblatt) Galaxy, **13**: 47.
— What the Greeks thought of the Religion of. (Plutarch) Princ. **42**: 49.
— What the World owes to. (J. McCulloch) Good Words, **4**: 775.
— Worship among. (I. N. Tarbox) New Eng. **21**: 406.
See also Judaism.
Jewel in Bodleian Library, Oxford. (S. Pegge) Arch. **1**: 161.
Jewels belonging to Sir C. Mordaunt. (S. Pegge) Arch. **3**: 371.
— Famous. Art J. **25**: 102–189.
— Genealogy of. Godey, **64**: 127. — Sharpe, **34**: 86. **50**: 191.
— In the Jewel Garden. Chamb. J. **45**: 36. Same art. Ecl. M. **71**: 1367.
— Losses of. Chamb. J. **53**: 664, 832.
— pledged to Cardinal Beaufort. (J. Caley) Arch. **21**: 34.
— sent to Spain by Order of James I. (R. Lemon) Arch. **21**: 148.
Jewel Case; a Story. Once a Week, **4**: 630. Same art. Liv. Age, **70**: 167.
Jewel House, Memoir on. (Sir G. Talbot) Arch. **22**: 114.
Jewel Robbery, The great. Chamb. J. **46**: 468.
Jewelry, Ancient Italian. (T. A. Trollope) Lippinc. **16**: 240.
— Ancient. (W. Duthie) Intel. Obs. **11**: 1.
— — Discourse on. (A. Castellani) Art J. **21**: 129.
— — Revival of. (A. Castellani) Penn Mo. **7**: 757.
— and Goldsmith's Work, in Syria, etc. Art J. **20**: 151, 205.
— Etruscan. Once a Week, **8**: 218.
— Grotesque. Tinsley, **1**: 743.
— Modern, and Art. (W. Duthie) Intel. Obs. **10**: 7.
— Processes employed in. (T. Gill) J. Frankl. Inst. **6**: 17.
— Saxon. Arch. **4**: 47.
— Scottish. (T. C. Archer) Art J. **26**: 109.
— Sham. Chamb. J. **50**: 775.
Jewelry Factory, Rouvenat. Pract. M. **2**: 244.
Jewelry Manufactures. Pract. M. **4**: 386.
Jewell, John, Bp. of Salisbury. Chr. Obs. **5**: 265, 329.
Jewess of the Cave; a Poem. Blackw. **31**: 820.
Jewish and Catholic Poor. Month, **6**: 481.

Jewish and Christian Dispensations. Chr. Mo. Spec. **5**: 283.
— — historically considered. (W. D. Wilson) Am. Church R. **11**: 193.
Jewish and Heathen Authors, Gray's Connection between. Ecl. R. **31**: 133.
Jewish Bookstore in New York. (M. L. Marks) Harper, **57**: 765.
Jewish Element, Proof of Apostolicity. (J. G. Shea) Am. Cath. Q. **3**: 674.
Jewish Heroine; a Tale. Bentley, **31**: 89, 140. Same art. Internat. M. **5**: 345, 491.
Jewish Lady, Toilette of. Blackw. **23**: 295.
Jewish Mediæval Philosophy, Spinoza and. (W. R. Sorley) Mind, **5**: 362.
Jewish Rabbi in Rome; a Poem. Blackw. **128**: 579.
Jewish Scriptures; the Masora. (J. B. Courtenay) Brit. Q. **73**: 310.
Jewish Service for the Dead, at Berlin. Cong. M. **17**: 588, 660.
Jewish Shekels, The first. (H. N. Humphreys) Intel. Obs. **4**: 328, 442.
Jewish Synagogue. (S. Gilman) No. Am. **23**: 67. — Chr. Mo Spec. **2**: 460.
Jewish Temple, Ritual of. Cong. **2**: 654. **4**: 41–673.
— — Perpetuity of. (J. Priestley) Theo. Repos. **5**: 403. **6**: 1.
Jewish Theology of Middle Ages. (H. P. Smith) Presb. R. **2**: 720.
Jewry, Laura. Cup and the Lip; a Novel. Chamb. J. **16**: 94.
— Tide of Life. New Q. **1**: 393.
Jew's-Harp, The. Penny M. **7**: 363.
— Life of C. Eulenstein. (T. P. Thompson) Westm. **20**: 74. Same art. Select J. **4**: [17.
Jim Bludso, of the Prairie Belle. (J. Hay) Ev. Sat. **10**: 452.
Jim Smith; a Story. (W. L. Alden) Galaxy, **14**: 403.
Jingoism. (W. Chambers) Chamb. J. **58**: 241.
Jinny's three Balls. Chamb. J. **46**: 369, 395.
Jitsu-go-kiyo; Buddhist Maxims. Cornh. **34**: 177.
Jo. (P. Mulford) Overland, **7**: 405.
Jo Bowers. (J. P. Caldwell) Overland, **2**: 538.
Jo of Lahaina. (C. W. Stoddard) Overland, **5**: 20.
Joachim and the Joachimites. (G. F. Holmes) So. M. **15**: 517.
Joan of Arc. (O. Delepierre) St. James, **13**: 64. — Argosy, **10**: 141. — (Lord Mahon) Quar. **69**: 281. — (S. Osgood) Putnam, **3**: 33. — (T. De Quincey) Tait, n. s. **14**: 184, 585. — (J. F. Clarke) Chr. Exam. **45**: 1. — Blackw. **47**: 284. — Mo. R. **106**: 238. — Mus. **6**: 226. — (A. Tovell) Western, **7**: 444. — Dub. R. **60**: 118. — Dub. Univ. **89**: 417. — Ecl. R. **124**: 177. — Liv. Age, **47**: 372. — Nat. M. **7**: 209. — Once a Week, **13**: 162. — Penny M. **2**: 6. — Portfo.(Den.) **33**: 137. — Tait, n. s. **22**: 311. **25**: 361.
— an Ecstatic. (J. W. Jackson) Zoist, **13**: 257.
— Death of. Am. Mo. M. **7**: 218.
— Fortunes of. (H. W. Herbert) Am. Mo. M. **5**: 1–476. **6**: 81, 253, 401.
— History of. (C. W. Russell) So. R. n. s. **2**: 86.
— House of. (M. Raymond) Cath. World, **21**: 697.
— in the Castle of Beaurevoir. Temp. Bar, **21**: 380.
— Letter by. Lond. M. **2**: 637.
— Martyrdom of; a Poem. Blackw. **2**: 425.
— Parr's Life of. (A Trollope) Fortn. **6**: 632.
— Poems on. (G. A. Simcox) Cornh. **16**: 584. — Am. Mo. M. **1**: 169. — St. Paul's, **7**: 66.
— Predecessors and Contemporaries of. Colburn, **143**: 92.
— Trial of. (J. Parton) Harper, **63**: 91.
— Wallon's. (A. Laugel) Nation, **22**: 409.
Joan, Pope. (R. B. Peake) Bentley, **12**: 148. — Bentley, **29**: 513.
— Fable of. (J. C. Meline) Cath. World, **9**: 1.
Joanna of Castile. Month, **14**: 245. — (A. C. Ewald) Gent. M. n. s. **25**: 682.
— Captivity of. Liv. Age, **103**: 515.
Joanna, Queen of Naples, Life of. Ecl. R. **41**: 385. — Quar. **31**: 65. — Westm. **1**: 554. — Colburn, **124**: 297.
Joanna of Sicily, Life of. Am. Mo. M. **11**: 113, 261, 551. **12**: 339.
Joannina and Ali Pasha, Visit to, 1819. (T. Lyman) No. Am. **10**: 429.
Joanny; the Fairies. (E. Townbridge) Sharpe, **52**: 132.
Job and Egypt. (R. Baker) Cath. World, **25**: 764.
— and his Times, Wemyss on. Mo. R. **149**: 268.
— Time of. (W. R. French) Univ. Q. **27**: 269. *See* Bible, Job.
Job and the Bug. (C. Hickox) Lippinc. **7**: 457.
Job Pippins, the Man who "couldn't help it." Blackw. **39**: 370, 472, 740.
Job's Comforters. (J. Poole) Colburn, **48**: 219.
Jocelin de Brakelord, Chronicle of. Brit. & For. R. **15**: 54.
Joceline, Elizabeth. Mother's Legacy to her unborn Child, 1625. Blackw. **71**: 491.
Jocelyn, Henry. (W. Willis) N. E. Reg. **2**: 204. **11**: 31.
Jockeys and their Trade. Temp. Bar, **49**: 324.
Jodelle, Estienne, early French Poet. Lond. M. **6**: 60.
Joe's Courtship; a Tale. Putnam, **9**: 484.
Joe Hale's red Stockings. (Saxe Holm) Scrib. **15**: 333.
Joe Miller and his Men. All the Year, **16**: 366.
Joe Oldoak's Revenge. (Mrs. White) Howitt, **1**: 299.
Joe Wickham's Reckoning. Chamb. J. **53**: 360.
Jogues, Isaac. (R. H. Clarke) Cath. World, **16**: 105.
— Memoir of. (J. Gerard) Month, **20**: 306.
Johan and Eureka; a Canterbury Tale. Fraser, **93**: 367.
Johan Falsen. House. Words, **6**: 148.
John, The Christian Name. Cornh. **39**: 323.
John, the Apostle, and James, Lives of Chr. Obs. **1**: 345.
— and Christian History. Good Words, **9**: 145. Same art. Liv. Age, **97**: 259.
— and his Critics. Dub. Univ. **74**: 123.
— and his Gospel. (Z. S. Barstow) Cong. R. **8**: 329. *See* Bible.
— at Ephesus. Mo. Rel. M. **39**: 29.
— his Doctrine of Christian Sonship. Lond. Q. **53**: 440.
— Later School of. (J. B. Lightfoot) Contemp. **27**: 471.
— Life and Character of. (E. E. Salisbury) Am. Bib. Repos. 2d s. **3**: 299. — (P. Schaff) Mercersb. **2**: 585.
— Relation to Peter, James, and Paul. (T. W. Hopkins) Bapt. Q. **7**: 310.
— Testimony of, concerning our Lord. Chr. Disc. **2**: 109.
— Vision of. (N. Macleod) Good Words, **15**: 121.
— Writings of. (J. H. A. Ebrard) Bapt. Q. **9**: 467. — (E. H. Sears) Mo. Rel. M. **43**: 4, 402.
— — Ewald on. Nat. R. **17**: 125.
John the Baptist. (C. E. Park) Bib. Sac. **34**: 173.
— a Poem. (F. W. H. Myers) Macmil. **19**: 315.
— and Elijah. Kitto, **9**: 420. **38**: 371.
— before Herod. (H. R. Haweis) Good Words, **21**: 92.
— Faith of; Matt. xi. 2–6. (T. G. Apple) Mercersb. **25**: 629.
— Food of. Am. Presb. R. **1**: 419.
— Mission of. (W. Jevons) Theo. R. **6**: 148. — Theo. Repos. **4**: 50–463. **5**: 64, 243. **6**: 216.
— — and Character of. Kitto, **20**: 325.
— not Elijah. Theo. & Lit. J. **11**: 73, 224.
— Reynolds on. Cong. **4**: 152.
John of Jerusalem, St. (W.W. Andrews) So. Lit. Mess. **9**: 417, 529, 579.
John, King of England, and Pope Innocent III. (H. W. Lucas) Month, **35**: 516.

John, King of England, as a Protestant Reformer. Dub. R. **6**: 436.
— Cause of his Death. (S. Pegge) Arch. **4**: 29.
— Historic Doubts concerning. Ecl. R. **121**: 523.
— Lord Chancellors and Keepers of the Seal of. (E. Foss) Arch. **32**: 83.
— Movements of his Court. (T. D. Hardy) Arch. **22**: 124.
John, King of France, Portrait of. (E. T. d'Eyncourt) Arch. **38**: 196.
John the Terrible, Czar of Russia, and Queen Elizabeth. (N. C. de Bogouschefsky) Reliquary, **16**: 1.
John, King of Ethiopia. Liv. Age, **134**: 570. — (E. de Leon) Internat. R. **7**: 671.
John, Don, of Austria. Blackw. **63**: 70. — Colburn, **120**: 165. — Dub. R. **88**: 1.
— and Heretics of Flanders. Blackw. **56**: 36.
John of Barneveld, Motley's. (A. Falconer) Fraser, **90**: 223. — (R. H. Howard) Meth. Q. **35**: 533. — Brit. Q. **60**: 392. — Chr. Obs. **74**: 810.
John Damascene, St. Dub. R. **64**: 331.
John of Ephesus, Ecclesiastical History of. (B. H. Cowper) Kitto, **25**: 372.
— Syriac Church History. No. Brit. **31**: 56.
John Népomucène, St., Canonization of. Month, **19**: 409.
John the Presbyter; was he John the Evangelist? (Prof. Milligan) Kitto, **40**: 106.
John XII., Pope. Am. Church R. **26**: 64.
John; a Story. (M. Oliphant) Blackw. **106**: 580, 647. **107**: 40–725. **108**: 61. Same art. Liv. Age, **103**: 683. **104**: 14-608. **105**: 23–594. **106**: 78, 278.
John; a Story. (B. S. Scranton) Galaxy, **4**: 675.
John; a Tale of a Dog. (M. A. Tincker) Cath. World, **16**: 622.
John and Joan; a Poem. Blackw. **7**: 437.
John and Margaret. Overland, **9**: 550.
John Biggs. (J. T. Irving) Knick. **42**: 551. **43**: 1, 277. Same art. Sharpe, **50**: 50, 89.
John Brown; a Poem. (C. Bain) Temp. Bar, **56**: 76.
John Bull, Esq. Dem. R. **32**: 236.
— abroad. Bentley, **8**: 121.
— and Jonathan. (C. Mackay) Canad. J. n. s. **3**: 166.
— and Nongtongpaw. Fraser, **30**: 418.
— Castle of. Fraser, **20**: 152.
— the Compassionate. Am. Whig R. **7**: 249.
— Fragments of his History. (G. Moir) Blackw. **30**: 954. **32**: 313. **34**: 890. **36**: 289. **37**: 18. **41**: 511. **69**: 69, 164. **73**: 166.
— Friendly Epistle to. Blackw. **19**: 631.
— in his own Pastures. Knick. **38**: 125, 345.
— in Tartary. Bentley, **11**: 592.
John Caldigate. Blackw. **123**: 391–713.
John Calthorpe's Theft. (J. M. Cobban) Belgra. **45**: 310.
John Christopher. (J. Goddard) Colburn, **159**: 325.
John Day Valley, Geology of. (T. Condon) Overland, **6**: 393.
John Decastro. Blackw. **81**: 99.
John Dobert. (W. M. Fisher) Overland, **13**: 560.
John Eastman's Compensation. (E. B. Cobb) Harper, **42**: 693.
John Fry, Cabman. (F. E. Weatherby) Lond. Soc. **28**: 70.
John Gilpin and Mazeppa. Blackw. **5**: 434.
— as a Solar Hero. Fraser, **103**: 353.
John Gilpin's Steam-Carriage Excursion to Harrow; a Poem. Chr. Obs. **28**: 180.
John Haller's Niece. (R. Gray) Dub. Univ. **70**: 537, 620. **71**: 52–544.
John Harley's Marriage. Chamb. J. **58**: 104.
John Harris, the Slaver; a Tale. (K. S. Macquoid) Temp. Bar, **45**: 479.
John Heathburn's Title. (F. H. Ludlow) Harper, **28**: 341, 466.
John Henry; a Story. (S. Chase) Lippinc. **27**: 376.
John Jordan. (J. R. Gilmore) Atlan. **16**: 434.
John Lamar. (R. H. Davis) Atlan. **9**: 411.
John Law. (W. H. Ainsworth) Bentley, **54**: 441, 551. **55**: 1–551. **56**: 77, 189, 318.
John Marchmont's Legacy; a Novel. (M. E. Braddon) Temp. Bar, **7**: 5–455. **8**: 5–455. **9**: 5–455. **10**: 15, 272.
John o' Groat's House. Meth. M. **39**: 223.
John Poltriggan's Christmas Story. Chamb. J. **57**: 793, 809, 819.
John Pooledoune. (W. Jerdan) Bentley, **1**: 599.
John Reed's Thoughts. (B. Taylor) Atlan. **31**: 356.
John Richardson's Relatives; a Story. Irish Mo. **2**: 447, 530, 582. **3**: 96–658.
John Rickson's Trial. (A. Robbins) Overland, **9**: 114.
John Rintoul. Blackw. **73**: 329, 410. Same art. Liv. Age, **37**: 113, 403.
John Rose, the Gauger. Lond. M. **21**: 404.
John Ryland's Wife. (J. K. Medbury) Galaxy, **1**: 67.
John Saltram's Wife; a Tale. Chamb. J. **50**: 721, 739.
John Singer's Story. Chamb. J. **30**: 245.
John Skeeme the Promoter. All the Year, **18**: 342, 376.
John Smith's Shanty. (R. Jefferies) Fraser, **89**: 135.
John Thomas Whiffler. St. James, **27**: 657.
John Tregancy's Dream. Sharpe, **30**: 293.
John Twiller. (D. P. Starkey) Dub. Univ. **48**: 535, 661. **49**: 81–666. **50**: 27.
John Underhill; a Poem. (J. G. Whittier) Atlan. **32**: 668.
John Warkinson's Wife. (R. Collyer) Lakeside, **11**: 68, 133.
John Welch's Wife; a Story. Galaxy, **19**: 245.
John Wilde. (T. A. Harcourt) Overland, **15**: 368.
John Whopper, the Newsboy. (T. M. Clark) O. & N. **2**: 49–416.
John's Hero. Blackw. **120**: 43. Same art. Liv. Age, **130**: 473.
John's Wife. (C. M. Hawksford) Lond. Soc. **32**: 294, 402.
John's Wife; a Tale. Temp. Bar, **2**: 254.
Johnnie Menzies. (A. Cunningham) Fraser, **1**: 399.
Johnny Appleseed. (W. D. Haley) Harper, **43**: 830.
Johnny Ludlow Papers. Argosy, **29**: 26–345. **31**: 26, 107.
Johnny Reb at Play. (A. C. Redwood) Scrib. **17**: 33.
Johns, John, Bishop of Virginia. (J. Packard) Am. Church R. **28**: 358.
Johns Hopkins University. (E. L. Godkin) Nation, **20**: 166. — (S. B. Herrick) Scrib. **19**: 199. — (E. Spencer) So. M. **16**: 71. — Nature, **12**: 456.
Johnson, Andrew, with portrait. (I. Smucker) Potter Am. Mo. **5**: 733. — Blackw. **100**: 623.
— and Abraham Lincoln. (G. Welles) Galaxy, **13**: 521, 663. — Chr. Exam. **81**: 400.
— and Reconstruction. (C. Mackay) Fortn. **4**: 477. — (C. E. Norton) No. Am. **102**: 250.
— as a popular Orator. (J. R. Lowell) No. Am. **102**: 530
— Defense of. (M. D. Conway) Fortn. **5**: 98.
— Impeachment of. (E. L. Godkin) Nation, **3**: 310. **4**: 170, 175, 214. **6**: 184–404. — (W. F. Allen) Nation, **6**: 490. — (E. I. Sears) Nat. Q. **16**: 372. **17**: 144. — Am. J. Educ. **18**: 225.
— on Civil Rights. (T. G. Shearman) Nation, **2**: 422.
— Policy of, 1866. New Eng. **25**: 711. — Fraser, **75**: 243.
Johnson, Lady Arabella. (L. H. Sigourney) Godey, **25**: 143.
— a Heroine of Puritan Times. (Mrs. Martyn) Hours at Home, **2**: 44.
Johnson, Cave, with portrait. Dem. R. **17**: 241.
— Portrait of. Am. Whig R. **10**: 243.
Johnson, Chapman. So Lit. Mess. **15**: 674.
Johnson, Cost. Forlorn Hope. Dem. R. **12**: 204.
Johnson, Eastman. (J. F. Fitts) Galaxy, **6**: 111.
Johnson, Edward. Philosophic Nuts. Mo. R. **154**: 285. **155**: 123.

Johnson, Sir John. (G. Livermore) Hunt, **34**: 306. — Am. Hist. Rec. **3**: 340.
— Orderly Book, 1776-77. M. Am. Hist. **6**: 204, 283.
Johnson, Osgood. Am. Q. Reg. **10**: 151.
Johnson, Reverdy, with portrait. Ecl. M. **86**: 502.
— and Charles Francis Adams. Once a Week, **19**: 348.
Johnson, Richard M., Portrait of. Dem. R. **14**: 335.
— Eulogy on. (J. C. Mather) Dem. R. **28**: 376.
— Sword presented to. Niles's Reg. **14**: 200.
Johnson, Rossiter. Condensed Classics. Penn Mo. **8**: 150.
Johnson, Dr. Samuel. (S. A. Allibone) Evang. R. **17**: 502. — (T. B. Macaulay) Harper, **14**: 483. — (T. B. Macaulay) Ecl. M. **40**: 424. Same art. Liv. Age, **53**: 1. — Bentley, **27**: 397. — De Bow, **28**: 504. — (J. Dennis) Brit. Q. **70**: 347. Same art. Liv. Age, **144**: 259. — Liv. Age, **52**: 742. **60**: 353. — Nat. M. **1**: 393, 488. **2**: 9-488.
— and the Fleet Street Taverns. (P. Fitzgerald) Gent. M. n. s. **26**: 305.
— and Garrick. No. Am. **4**: 38.
— and Dr. Hookwell. Quar. **87**: 32. Same art. Liv. Age, **26**: 337.
— and his Wife, Macaulay on. Cornh. **42**: 573. Same art. Liv. Age, **147**: 627.
— and Hume. Blackw. **3**: 511.
— and Hannah More. Chamb. J. **15**: 380.
— and Mrs. Piozzi. (P. Fitzgerald) Belgra. **15**: 183.
— and Sir Joshua Reynolds. Month, **3**: 403.
— and Richard Savage. Chamb. J. **7**: 65.
— and Mrs. Thrale. St. James, **1**: 243.
— and Warburton. Blackw. **8**: 243.
— Anecdotes of. Dem. R. **11**: 165.
— as Christian and Critic. Ecl. R. **101**: 153. Same art. Ecl. M. **34**: 492. Same art. Liv. Age, **45**: 221.
— Biographers and Critics of. Westm. **111**: 1. — Same art. Appleton, **21**: 308.
— Boswell's Letters on. Chr. Obs. **59**: 9.
— Boswell's Life of, condensed by Alex. Main. (J. R. Dennett) Nation, **18**: 253.
— — Croker's Edition. (W. B. O. Peabody) No. Am. **34**: 91. — (T. B. Macaulay) Ed. R. **54**: 1. Same art. Mus. **19**: 676. — (J. P. Dabney) Chr. Exam. **14**: 154. — Quar. **46**: 1. — Westm. **15**: 375. — Mo. R. **125**: 452. — (T. Carlyle) Fraser, **5**: 253, 379.
— Contemporaries and Biographers of. Dub. R. **23**: 203.
— Death-Bed of. Spirit Pilg. **1**: 212.
— Dictionary of. (F. Lawrence) Sharpe, **10**: 221. *See* English Language.
— Early Life of. Quar. **103**: 279. Same art. Liv. Age, **57**: 593.
— from a Scottish View. All the Year, **23**: 561.
— Ghost of. All the Year, **1**: 92.
— House in Bolt Court. All the Year, **1**: 93, 251.
— Imaginary Conversation. Hogg, **14**: 89.
— Irene at Drury Lane. (D. Cook) Once a Week, **5**: 651.
— Last Days of. Chr. Obs. **32**: 1-813. — Ecl. M. **62**: 199.
— Life of. (F. Jeffrey) Ed. R. **7**: 436. — Mus. **6**: 97. — with portrait, Portfo.(Den.) **24**: 148.
— — and Times of. Nat. M. **3**: 18-295.
— — and Writings of. Lond. M. **8**: 57, 169. — Quar. **105**: 176. Same art. Liv. Age, **60**: 777.
— Lives of the Poets. (M. Arnold) Macmil. **38**: 153. Same art. Liv. Age, **138**: 86. Same art. Sup. Pop. Sci. Mo. **3**: 281. *See* Poets.
— Observations on. Meth. M. **43**: 660. — Am. Meth. M. **4**: 287.
— Religious Character of. Meth. M. **56**: 92.
— Religious Friends of. Chr. Obs. **31**: 1. **32**: 1.
— Religious Life of, Hewlett's. Quar. **87**: 59.
— — and Death of. Hogg, **5**: 200, 214. — Dub. Univ. **36**: 477.
— Religious Opinions of. Month, **38**: 418.
Johnson, Dr. Samuel, Reminiscences of. (E. Thompson) Cornh. **17**: 622.
— Sketch of. Colburn, **152**: 376, 432.
— Style of. Portfo.(Den.) **25**: 300. **26**: 32.
— Unpublished Episodes in the Life of. (L. Jewitt) Gent. M. n. s. **21**: 692.
— without Boswell. (W. Cyples) Contemp. **32**: 707. Same art. Liv. Age, **138**: 541.
— Works and Reviewers of. (S. A. Allibone) Evang. R. **15**: 141.
— Worship of. (A. V. Dicey) Nation, **27**: 318.
— Writings of. (L. Stephen) Cornh. **29**: 280. Same art. Ecl. M. **82**: 527. Same art. Liv. Age, **121**: 91. Same art. Ev. Sat. **16**: 349.
Johnson, Samuel, first President of Columbia College. (G. E. Ellis) No. Am. **118**: 451. — Am. J. Educ. **7**: 461. — (J. H. Ward) Nation, **18**: 109. — N. E. Reg. **27**: 42. — Chr. Obs. **32**: 763, 829. — Am. J. Educ. **27**: 449.
Johnson, Mrs. Susanna. Narrative of Captivity, Correction of Errors in. (J. Willard) N. E. Reg. **4**: 305.
Johnson, W.A.B., Jowett's Memoir of. Chr. Obs. **54**: 275.
Johnson, Walter Rogers. Am. J. Educ. **5**: 781.
Johnson, Sir William. (G. W. Greene) Nation, **1**: 624. — (C. McKnight) Lippinc. **23**: 731. — (C. C. Smith) No. Am. **101**: 249.
— and Johnson Hall. (B. J. Lossing) Potter Am. Mo. **4**: 2.
— Descendants of. N. E. Reg. **33**: 81, 333. — (G. W. Johnson) N. E. Reg. **34**: 60.
Johnson, William Martin, Poetry of. Dem. R. **1**: 293, 458.
Johnson Genealogy. (P. Thompson) N. E. Reg. **8**: 359.
Johonnot Genealogy. (A. Johonnot) N. E. Reg. **6**: 357. **7**: 141.
Johnston, Gen. Albert Sidney. (J. D. Cox) Nation, **27**: 197, 214. — So. R. n. s. **10**: 78. — (B. W. Duke) So. Hist. Pap. **6**: 133.
Johnston, Alexander Keith. Nature, **4**: 225.
Johnston, John, of Sault Ste. Marie. (W. Kingsford) Canad. Mo. **20**: 1.
Johnstone, Chevalier de; Escapes of a Jacobite. All the Year, **27**: 301.
Joint in the Harness. (M. Northcott) Belgra. **28**: 388.
Joint-Stock Banker. (D. Costello) Bentley, **39**: 346, 471, 551. **40**: 5-345.
See Banking, Joint-Stock.
Joint-Stock Companies. (L. Levi) J. Statis. Soc. **33**: 1. **34**: 1. — Mo. R. **112**: 247. — Ecl. R. **96**: 68.
— New, in England in 1873. Bank. M. (N.Y.) **28**: 706.
Joinville, Jean, Sire de. All the Year, **32**: 508. — Once a Week, **18**: 499.
— Johnes's Translations of. Ed. R. **13**: 469. — Ecl. R. **6**: 1071.
Jokes. All the Year, **16**: 180, 366.
— Cracking. Once a Week, **29**: 402.
— Forgotten. Cornh **34**: 595. Same art. Ecl. M, **88**: 106.
— Old and new. Once a Week, **19**: 446.
— Practical. Chamb. J. **45**: 552. — All the Year, **46**: 280.
— — Strange. All the Year, **32**: 473.
— Round of old. All the Year, **28**: 322.
— Thoughts on. Once a Week, **25**: 45.
Jokers, Royal and Imperial. Ev. Sat. **13**: 693.
Jolin, Philip, Last Days of. Chr. Obs. **30**: 1, 65.
Jollie, T. Cong. M. **16**: 346.
Jolly Burglars. House. Words, **2**: 196.
Jolly Father Joe; a Poem. Blackw. **53**: 255.
Jolly Hermitage; a Tale. Putnam, **9**: 48.
Joly, Marie. La Ferme aux Pommiers. Liv. Age, **55**: 371.
Jomini, Henri, Baron. Ev. Sat. **7**: 565. — Galaxy, **7**: 874. — (C. F. Cromie) Fortn. **34**: 635. Same art. Liv. Age, **147**: 643.

Jomini, Henri, Baron, Life of. (G. Allen) U. S. Serv. M. **2**: 351.
— Military Operations. (F. W. Palfrey) No. Am. **101**: 223.
Jonah. (T. K. Cheyne) Theo. R. **14**: 211. — (C. E. Stowe) Bib. Sac. **10**: 739.
— and Paul at Sea. Good Words, **1**: 140.
— Raleigh on. Ecl. R. **124**: 474.
— Sign of the Prophet. (G. W. Lane) Meth. Q. **5**: 382. *See* Bible.
Jonas Fisher; a Poem. Belgra. **29**: 250.
Jonas Grubb's Courtship. (J. Y. Akerman) Bentley, **11**: 171.
Jonathan; a Story. (C C. Fraser-Tytler) Ecl. M **84**: 449, 612, 686. **85**: 213–753. **86**: 103, 189, 365.
Jonathan, Saint. Dem. R. **35**: 99.
Jonathan, Ship, Voyage to New England, 1639. N. E. Reg. **32**: 407.
Jonathan Bull and Mary Bull. So. Lit. Mess. **1**: 242.
Jonathan Frock. (H. Zschokke) Peop. J. **6**: 141–183.
Jonathan Jolter's Journal; a Poem. New Eng. M. **7**: 378.
Jones, Abner, Memoir of. Chr. Exam. **32**: 133.
Jones, Agnes Elizabeth, Memorials of. (C. L. Brace) Nation, **14**: 308.
Jones, David. Revolutionary Sermon. Hist. M. **14**: 92.
Jones, Edward Burne, Painter. Am. Arch. **6**: 87. — (S. Colvin) Portfo. **1** : 17. — with portrait, Dub. Univ. **94**: 40.
— Recent Paintings by. (F. Wedmore) Temp. Bar, **53**: 334.
— Visit to Home of. (K. Hillard) Scrib. **4**: 748.
Jones, Ernest. (J. P. Hopps) Dub. Univ. **93**: 357.
Jones, Geo. Visit to Egypt and Jerusalem. Chr. R. **2**: 11.
Jones, Horatio. N. E. Reg. **1**: 62.
Jones, Inigo, and his Work on York Gate. (J. W. Archer) Once a Week, **8**: 251.
Jones, Capt. Jacob, Biography of. Anal. M. **2**: 75.
Jones, Gen. James, with portrait. De Bow, **11**: 542.
Jones, James A. Haverhill. Westm. **15**: 218.
Jones, Joel, Memorial of. Theo. & Lit. J. **13**: 56.
Jones, John Paul. (B. J. Lossing) Harper, **11**: 145. — (J. K. Laughton) Fraser, **97**: 501.
— and Denis Duval. (E. E. Hale) Atlan. **14**: 493.
— Life of. (J. T. Headley) Am. Whig R. **4**: 228. — Am. Q. **7**: 409. — Anal. M. **8**: 1. **11**: 227. — Westm. **12**: 466. — U. S. Lit. Gaz. **3**: 51. — Mo. R. **108**: 48. — Ecl. R. **45**: 341.
— righted. All the Year, **23**: 425.
— Sherburne's Life of. Dem. R. **30**: 153.
— Sketch of. Lond. M. **9**: 492.
Jones, John Winter. Inaugural Address at English Librarians' Conference, 1877. Lib. J. **2**: 99.
Jones, Joseph. Poems. Mo. R. **162**: 479.
Jones, Owen, Sketch of. Pract. M. **3**: 400. — with portrait, Pract. M. **7**: 257.
Jones, Richard R., a noted Linguist. Chamb. J. **7**: 347. — Victoria, **13**: 157.
Jones, Thomas, Captain of the Discovery. (E. D. Neill) Hist. M. **15**: 31.
Jones, Thomas P., Memoir of. Chr. Exam. **45**: 313.
Jones, Thomas Rymer, Obituary of. Nature, **23**: 174.
Jones, Walter R. (W. A. Jones) Hunt, **33**: 423.
Jones, Sir William. Penny M. **8**: 121.
— Character of. (T. Walker) Ill. M. **2**: 550.
— Life of. (F. Jeffrey) Ed. R. **5**: 329. — Chr. Obs. **3**: 615, 685. — Ecl. R. **1**: 256, 345. — Portfo.(Den.) **27**: 444.
— — and Poetry of. Lond. M. **4**: 626.
— Poems of. So. Lit. Mess. **15**: 724.
Jones, Wm. A., Writings of. Dem. R **30**: 396.
Jones Family, Ancestry of. (E. F. Jones) N. E. Reg. **6**: 279.
Jones Family of Bethlehem, Pa. (J. H. Dubbs) Pennsyl. M. **4**: 209.
Jones's Farm, Battle of. (C. M. Wilcox) So. M. **16**: supp. 67.
Jonesboro', Ga., Battle of. (P. Anderson) So. Hist. Pap. **4**: 193. — (H. D. Clayton) So. Hist. Pap. **5**: 127.
Jonghe, Gustave de. Art J. **18**: 301.
Jonnes, M. de. Adventures of an old Sailor. Colburn, **114**: 175.
Jonson, Ben. (E. O. Blackburne) Victoria, **24**: 151. — (C. C. Clarke) Gent. M. n. s. **6**: 631. — (E. P. Whipple) Atlan. **20**: 403. — Bentley, **40**: 157. — Chamb. J. **5**: 37. — Dub. Univ. **63**: 380. Same art. Liv. Age, **81**: 583. — Ev. Sat. **17**: 253. — No. Brit. **24**: 447. Same art. Ecl. M. **37**: 433. Same art. Liv. Age, **50**: 321. — Nat. R. **6**: 112. Same art. Ecl. M. **44**: 1. Same art. Liv. Age, **56**: 542. — So. Lit. Mess. **5**: 287.
— and William Drummond. Fraser, **25**: 377. — Mo. R. **159**: 158.
— and his Works. Brit. Q. **25**: 285. Same art. Liv. Age, **54**: 193.
— Life, Character, and Writings of. Temp. Bar, **42**: 35. Same art. Ecl. M. **83**: 412.
— Life and Works of. Bent. Q. **2**: 404. Same art. Liv. Age, **65**: 67.
— Morose. Bentley, **56**: 16.
— Quarrel with Shakspere. No. Brit. **52**: 394.
— Sketch of. Colburn, **51**: 39.
— Works of. (T. Serle) Retros. **1** : 181. — Blackw. **45**: 145. Same art. Mus. **37**: 317. — So. R. **6**: 91.
Jonson, Margaret, Mother of Ben Jonson. House. Words, **3**: 609.
Jòn Jònsonn's Saga. (G. R. F. Cole) Fraser, **95**: 1. Same art. Liv. Age, **132**: 407.
Jony, E. Sylla. Quar. **28**: 97.
Jordan, Mrs. Dorothy Bland, Actress. Bentley, **41**: 408. — Temp. Bar, **51**: 174.
Jordan, Robert. (W. H. Whitmore) N. E. Reg. **13**: 221.
Jordans of Grange, The. Fraser, **12**: 12.
Jordan, River, and Dead Sea. No. Brit. **11**: 494. — (H. Martineau) Peop. J. **4**: 185.
— — Lynch's Expedition. Theo. & Lit. J. **2**: 288. *See also* Dead Sea.
— and its Valley. (E. Robinson) Am. Bib. Repos. 2d s. **3**: 265.
— Boat Voyage down. Chamb. J. **11**: 377.
— East of, Merrill's. (G. C. Noyes) Dial (Ch.), **2**: 229.
— Fortnight's Ride east of. Bentley, **59**: 481, 575. **60**: 68.
— Great Crevasse of. (L. Coleman) Bib. Sac. **24**: 248.
— Sources of. (W. M. Thomson) Bib. Sac. **3**: 184.
— Valley of. (W. H. Ward) Nation, **25**: 140.
Jörgensen, Jörgen, King of Iceland. Colburn, **126**: 118. Same art. Ecl. M. **57**: 340.—House. Words, **14**: 528.
— Travels in France and Germany. Ed. R. **28**: 371.
Josaphat, St. Dub. R. **80**: 46.
José Maria, the Bandit of Ronda. (J. Sheehan) Temp. Bar, **29**: 539.
Joselyne Genealogy. (S. G. Drake) N. E. Reg. **14**: 15.
Joseph. (J. F. Mackarness) Good Words, **10**: 505. — (J. W. Thompson) Mo. Rel. M. **9**: 241.
— and Brethren. (S. A. Brooke) Good Words, **21**: 212.
— and his Life and Death. (S. A. Brooke) Good Words, **21**: 235.
— in Egypt. Chr. Obs. **66**: 459.
Joseph, St., Devotion to. Dub. R. **68**: 412.
Joseph, King of Italy, Memoirs of. Ed. R. **100**: 348. **102**: 305. Same art. Liv. Age, **47**: 598.
Joseph II., Emperor of Austria. (F. P. Cobbe) Tinsley, **21**: 311. — Colburn, **123** : 276. Same art. Liv. Age, **72**: 53.
— Anecdote of. Good Words, **1**: 701.

Joseph II., Emperor of Austria, Austrian Revolution under. Temp. Bar, **51**: 373.
— Letters of. Bentley, **31**: 340.
Joseph, Indian Chief, Pursuit of. (J. Gibbons) Am. Cath. Q. **4**: 317.
Joseph's Adventure. (D. C. Macdonald) Lippinc. **23**: 375.
Joseph and his Friend. (B. Taylor) Atlan. **25**: 30–642. **26**: 41–665.
Joseph's Coat; a Story. (D. C. Murray) Belgra. **43**: 257, 385. **44**: 1–385. **45**: 1–385.
Josephine, Empress, and Malmaison. (M. Howland) Lippinc. **13**: 152. — Harper, **3**: 222.
— Divorce of. (J. S. C. Abbott) Ecl. M. **25**: 109. — (J. S. C. Abbott) Liv. Age, **27**: 561. — Ecl. M. **31**: 245. **52**: 134.
— First Court of. Colburn, **90**: 61. Same art. Liv. Age, **27**: 181.
— Imperial Anecdotes. Liv. Age, **36**: 235.
— Memoirs of. Am. Q. **14**: 464. — Ecl. M. **10**: 532. — So. R. **6**: 307. — Mo. R. **117**: 402. **118**: 244. Same art. Mus. **14**: 159. **15**: 310.
Josephine de Montmorenci. (A. Trollope) Galaxy, **8**: 825.
Josephine; or Love and Empire. Colburn, **155**: 317–634.
Josephine's Troubles; a Tale. (P. Fitzgerald) Month, **26**: 71–458. **27**: 73–481. **28**: 79.
Josephus, Flavius. Colburn, **117**: 38.
— and the Bible. Kitto, **6**: 292.
— and Apion. (E. Pond) Meth. Q. **30**: 274.
— and St. Paul. Kitto, **13**: 166.
— — Friendship of. Internat. M. **2**: 494.
— Life and Writings of. (M. L. Stoever) Evang. R. **21**: 415. — Bib. R. **1**: 372.
— Restoration of his Chronology. Kitto, **5**: 60.
— Works of. Fraser, **25**: 115.
Joshua. (J. F. Mackarness) Good Words, **10**: 714.
— Life and Death of. (J. S. Howson) Good Words, **9**: 490.
Joshua Haggard's Daughter. (M. E. Braddon) Belgra. **28**: 149–437. **29**: 5–551. **30**: 10–482. **31**: 21, 163.
Joshua Marvel. (B. L. Farjeon) Tinsley, **6**: 481–674. **7**: 1–674. **8**: 1–657. **9**: 1–524.
Josiah Morse, Case of. All the Year, **26**: 427–476.
Josselyn Genealogy. (T. W. Harris) N. E. Reg. **2**: 306. **4**: 97. *See also* Joselyne.
Jottings by the Way. Dub. Univ. **88**: 397.
Joubert, Joseph. Brit. Q. **68**: 361. — (M. M. Maitland) Gent. M. n. s. **24**: 459. — (M. Arnold) Nat. R. **18**: 168. — Same art. Liv. Age, **80**: 462.
— Extracts from the Pensées. Dub. Univ. **89**: 250.
Joule, James Prescot, Copley Medalist of 1870. (J. Tyndall) Nature, **5**: 137. — with portrait, Pop. Sci. Mo. **5**: 103.
Jourdain, Monsieur. (F. Jacox) Bentley, **63**: 460.
Journal des Mines. Ed. R. **8**: 78. **9**: 67.
— of an Aide-de-Camp. Ecl. M. **67**: 705.
— of Ernest Ray. Mo. Rel. M. **31**: 438. **32**: 107–305.
— of Miss Patience Caerhydon. Eng. Dom. M. **4**: 1–208. **5**: 18–298. **6**: 18–290. **7**: 84–298.
— of Old Barnes, on a Trip to Paris. Bentley, **7**: 457, 627. **8**: 69, 195.
— of a poor Musician. (S. M. Warner) Putnam, **12**: 58, 154.
— of a Woman; a Tale. (O. Feuillet) Eng. Dom. M. **25**: 2–282. **26**: 1–58.
— that was never kept. Sharpe, **5**: 277. **6**: 8, 109.
Journals and Journal-Keepers. Liv. Age, **75**: 147. — Bentley, **34**: 397. Same art. Liv. Age, **39**: 541.
Journals, Class and Trade. Cong. **5**: 44.
— of the British Provinces, 1836. Colburn, **48**: 137.
Journalism. (A. F. Bridges) Potter Am. Mo. **12**: 460. — (A. G. Sedgwick) Nation, **10**: 54. — (E. L. Godkin) Nation, **21**: 104. — Am. Whig R. **4**: 281. — Dem. R. **10**: 52.
Journalism. Westm. **18**: 195. Same art. Mus. **22**: 450. — Cornh. **6**: 52. — Blackw. **125**: 69. Same art. Liv. Age, **140**: 222. — Lippinc. **27**: 175. — Nation, **8**: 127. — Danv. Q. **2**: 406.
— Agonies of. (S. Walker) Lakeside, **5**: 175.
— American. (E. Faithfull) Victoria, **21**: 289. — (E. H. Hall) St. James, **32**: 529. — (J. Lesperance) Lippinc. **8**: 174. — So. Q. **19**: 500.
— and Journalists. (F. B. Sanborn) Atlan. **34**: 55.
— Anonymous. (T. Hughes) Macmil. **5**: 157. — (J. B. Kinnear) Contemp. **5**: 324. Same art. Ecl. M. **69**: 363. — (J. Morley) Fortn. **8**: 287. — St. Paul's, **2**: 217.
— as a Profession. (G. F. Parsons) Overland, **2**: 25. — (J. Wilcox) Galaxy, **4**: 797.
— British. Lond. Q. **38**: 87.
— Business Side of. (E. L. Godkin) Nation, **11**: 254.
— Casuistry of. Cornh. **28**: 198.
— Chapter in the History of. Tinsley, **12**: 22.
— Curiosities of. Chamb. J. **58**: 123.
— Eatanswill. Ev. Sat. **10**: 506.
— English. Fraser, **34**: 631. Same art. Ecl. M. **10**: 121. Same art. Liv. Age, **12**: 261. — Mus. **15**: 1, 145. — Nation, **31**: 59–303.
— — before 1800. (D. Gardner) No. Am. **114**: 39.
— — in 1832 and 1864. (T. H. S. Escott) Belgra. **28**: 39.
— — in France. St. James, **7**: 230.
— — "Our London Correspondent." (T. W. Reid) Macmil. **42**: 18.
— in the Far West. (E. Dale) Canad. Mo. **11**: 188.
— in France. Quar. **65**: 422. Same art. Liv. Age, **10**: 67. — Brit. Q. **3**: 468. — For. Q. **36**: 70. — Colburn, **130**: 244. — Cornh. **27**: 703. **28**: 411, 715. **29**: 154, 535.
— — in 18th Century. Temp. Bar, **1**: 473.
— — Political. (C. J. Wallis) Dub. Univ. **89**: 289.
— in Germany. (J. L. Spalding) Cath. World, **23**: 289. — Mo. R. **165**: 185.
— in New York. Am. Whig R. **14**: 408.
— Jovial. All the Year, **23**: 514.
— Judicious in. (E. L. Godkin) Nation, **6**: 105.
— Lecture on. Blackw. **68**: 691.
— Letter to a young Journalist. Scrib. **4**: 757.
— London Press. Am. Whig R. **14**: 505.
— Modern. Tait, n. s. **19**: 353. Same art. Liv. Age, **34**: 244.
— Morals and Manners of. (R. G. White) Galaxy, **8**: 840. **9**: 102.
— Newest Thing in. Contemp. **30**: 678.
— Old and new. Once a Week, **29**: 424, 446.
— Parisian. (A. Laugel) Nation, **14**: 286. — Ev. Sat. **9**: 82, 654.
— Philosophy of. Chamb. J. **13**: 404.
— £. s. d. of. Gent. M. n. s. **13**: 713.
— Profession of. (E. L. Godkin) Nation, **17**: 37.
— Protestant. Brownson, **24**: 441.
— Provincial. Once a Week, **19**: 310. — St. Paul's, **3**: 61.
— Schools of. (W. Reid) Scrib. **4**: 194.
— Trade of. St. Paul's, **1**: 306.
— What a Newspaper should be. (D. G. Croly) Putnam, **11**: 328.
— Women in. (N. M. Hutchinson) Galaxy, **13**: 499.
Journaliste malgré lui. Macmil. **142**: 270.
Journalists and Magazine Writers. Blackw. **125**: 69. Same art. Liv. Age, **140**: 387.
— Parisian, of To-Day. Cornh. **28**: 715. Same art. Ecl. M. **82**: 195. Same art. Ev. Sat. **16**: 16.
— School for. For. Q. **25**: 62.
Journalistic London. (J. Hatton) Harper, **63**: 657, 839.
Journey due north. (G. A. Sala) House. Words, **14**: 265–565. **15**: 2–249.
— from Genoa to Rome. Fraser, **25**: 43.
— from Paris to Ostend. Fraser, **11**: 33.

Journey in early Summer. (H. L. Dolsen) Overland, 9: 58.
— round the World, Narrative of. (Sir G. Simpson) Colburn, 80: 219.
— to Starston. (M. C. Croz) Temp. Bar, 63: 383.
— to the Unknown. (J. Hawthorne) Appleton, 15: 9–399.
— with a Moral; a Poem. Temp. Bar, 57: 315.
Jousting. All the Year, 38: 443, 471.
Jouvenet, John. Art J. 3: 233.
Jovellanos, G. M. de, Life and Works of. For. Q. 5: 547. — For. R. 4: 73
Joy of Engele. (M. Howitt) Howitt, 1: 223.
Joys of Earth; a Poem. (D. Greenwell) Good Words, 2: 52.
Joyce, Robert Dwyer. (M. Russell) Irish Mo. 6: 55.
Joyce Dormer's Story. (J. Boncœur) Once a Week, 16: 1–259.
Joye, George, Memoir of. Dub. Univ. 1: 164.
Joyous Knights; or Fratri Gaudenti. (B. J. O'Reilly) Am. Cath. Q. 6: 19.
Juan, Don, of Braganza. Am. Mo. M. 10: 273.
Juan Fernandez, Island of. Ev. Sat. 9: 113.
— and Robinson Crusoe. (H. Sedley) Putnam, 11: 325. — (J. R. Browne) Putnam, 1: 275.
— Visit to. Ev. Sat. 2: 456.
Juan Moreda, the Slave Hunter. Fraser, 36: 282.
Juana la Loca, Spanish Princess. Ed. R. 131: 341.
Juana of Castile. *See* Joanna of Castile.
Juancho, the Bull-Fighter. Blackw. 62: 197.
Juanita. (J. Clifford) Overland, 8: 350.
Juanita. Atlan. 3: 16.
Juarez, Benito, President of Mexico. Bentley, 53: 254. Same art Ecl. M. 60: 369.
— Personal Recollections of. (G. Butler) Cath. World, 16: 280.
Jubilee Singers. (W. Chambers) Chamb. J. 55: 17.
Jubilee Year; or God in History. Am. Church R. 4: 329.
Jubilees and Centenary Festivals. Chamb. J. 52: 60.
Judaism, accredited by Christianity. Theo. Repos. 5: 289, 366. 6: 39, 49.
— after the Captivity. Lond. Q. 30: 178.
— and Christianity. Bost. R. 2: 175. — Chr. Rem. 12: 222.
— and Heathenism, Döllinger on. Ho. & For. R. 1: 450.
— and the Jews, McCaul's Sketches of. Mo. R. 146: 313.
— and Romanism. (J. Wilson) Ex. H. Lec. 2: 189.
— before the Christian Era. Ecl. R. 42: 153.
— Character and Power of. (M. N. Adams) Radical, 7: 361.
— Future of. (W. H. Fremantle) Contemp. 32: 773.
— Genius of. Am. Church R. 25: 435. — Mo. R. 131: 117.
— Harold's Modern. Mo. R. 84: 18.
— in America. (P. Girard) Cath. World, 25: 365.
— in the Legislature. Blackw. 62: 724.
— Modern. Kitto, 8: 172. — Ed. R. 117: 180. — (J. W. Alexander) Princ. 3: 134. — (J. M. Hoppin) New Eng. 29: 624. — Ecl. R. 106: 342. — Gent. M. n. s. 15: 436.
— — Allen on. Ecl. R. 25: 431.
— — and Grace Aguilar. Ecl. R. 107: 134.
— Relation to Christianity. (F. Doncot) Cath. World, 27: 351, 564.
— Recent Aspects of, 1853. (S. Osgood) Chr. Exam. 54: 1.
— Reformed. (F. Adler) No. Am. 125: 327.
See also Jews.
Judas. (G. C. Hurlbut) Overland, 12: 20.
Judas Iscariot and St. Peter. (H. R. Carpenter) Unita. R. 15: 258.
— Ballad of. St. Paul's, 10: 183.
— Character and Repentance of. Chr. Obs. 35: 329.
— Confession of. (J. A. Bolles) New Eng. M. 8: 462.
— Critics on. Chr. R. 20: 321.
— Death of. Kitto, 12: 160.
Judas Iscariot, Fate of. Theo. Repos. 1: 63, 292.
— History and Character of. Theo. Repos. 3: 33.
— Life and Character of. Spirit Pilg. 6: 215, 251, 427. — Chr. R. 5: 328.
— Note on John xiii. 27. Theo. & Lit. J. 7: 303.
— Sin, Repentance, and Death of. (J. O. Skinner) Univ. Q. 34: 419.
— Two Pleas for. O. & N. 1: 525.
— Was he present at the Lord's Supper? (J. Priestley) Theo. Repos. 1: 141.
— a Witness for Christ. Theo. Repos. 2: 175.
Judd, Chauncey, Abduction of. Hist. M. 3: 263.
Judd, Sylvester. Fraser, 76: 45. — (R. P. Cutler) Mo. Rel. M. 10: 125.
— Life and Character of. (E. E. Hale) Chr. Exam. 58: 63. — (G. W. Hosmer) Mo. Rel. M. 13: 16.
— Margaret. (S. Osgood) No. Am. 84: 535. — (W. B. O. Peabody) No. Am. 62: 102. — (F. D. Huntington) Chr. Exam. 39: 418. — So. Q. 9: 507.
— Philo. (A. P. Peabody) No. Am. 70: 433.
— Richard Edney. (A. W. Abbot) No. Am. 72: 493.
— Writings of. (J. H. Morison) No. Am. 80: 420.
Judea and its Neighbors. Chr. Rem. 32: 357.
— Hill-Country of. (C. H. Brigham) Mo. Rel. M. 15: 43.
— Scenes in. (W. Ware) Chr. Exam. 27: 88, 245. 28: 89, 224.
Judge, The Anglo-Saxon. (C. C. Nott) Nation, 13: 52.
Judge, The; a Drama of American Life. (Mrs. S. J. Hale) Godey, 42: 21–298.
Judge of Divorce. (M. de Cervantes) Temp. Bar, 56: 93.
Judges and Lawyers, American, Manners of. Hist. M. 21: 94.
— Anecdotes of. Retros. 10: 60.
— Atrocious, Campbell's Lives of. Dem. R. 37: 244.
— of England. (W. Forsyth) Quar. 119: 326. — Chamb. J. 47: 181. — Fraser, 70: 89. Same art. Ecl. M. 63: 172. — Lond. Soc. 20: 408. — Tait, n. s. 16: 163. *See* Chief Justices; Chancellors.
— — and Ireland. Dub. R. 45: 107.
— — Foss's. Dub. R. 44: 269.
— — — and Campbell's. Dub. R. 46: 438.
— of the olden Time. Chamb. J. 19: 189.
— U. S. and British, 1866, List of. Am. Law R. 1: 224.
Judge not. House. Words, 2: 431.
Judging by Appearances. Bentley, 7: 508, 616. 8: 75.
Judgment, The Last. (J. Floy) Am. Meth. M. 20: 167. — Chr. Obs. 18: 137.
— in Matt. xxv. 31–46, and Rev. xx. 4–15. Theo. & Lit. J. 7: 498.
Judgment of Paris. (B. Disraeli) Colburn, 42: 304.
Judgments, Collective. (A. C. Thomas) Univ. Q. 27: 222.
Judicature, New. (M. Cookson) Fortn. 25: 277.
Judicature Acts in English Law. (E. S. Roscoe) Fraser, 93: 130.
Judicial Combat. Hogg, 4: 62.
Judicial Encroachment. Dem. R. 26: 243. 27: 126.
Judicial Institutions of England and France. For. Q. 2: 109.
— of Europe. For. Q. 3: 433. — Anal. M. 15: 16. — Mo. R. 96: 486.
Judicial Murder. All the Year, 6: 405.
Judicial Ordeals. (H. C. Lea) No. Am. 89: 32.
Judicial Partisanship. (F. Wharton) Internat. R. 4: 663, 760.
Judicial Power, Limitations of. (E. Washburn) Am. Soc. Sci. J. 8: 140.
Judicial Puzzles. Chamb. J. 52: 12.
— Spencer Cowper's Case. Blackw. 90: 19. Same art. Ecl. M. 54: 69.
Judicial Reform in Scotland. Ed. R. 51: 114.
Judicial System, Proposed Federal, 1876. (C. C. Nott) Nation, 22: 93.

Judiciary; American Judges. (J. Brice) Macmil. 25: 422. — Lippinc. 5: 654.
— and the Bar. (C. C. Nott) Nation, 15: 276.
— Elective. Am. Law R. 8: 1. — West. Law J. 5: 127.
— Federal, and the Repudiators. (J. F. Hume) Nation, 28: 5.
— Independence of. (F. Bowen) No. Am. 57: 400. — Am. Whig R. 2: 474. — (J. M. Van Cott) Am. Whig R. 4: 520. — (E. L. Peirce) Dem. R. 23: 37. — Ed. R. 44: 397.
— Reform in. (E. L. Godkin) Nation, 13: 365.
— Reports on, 1831. Niles's Reg. 39: 412, 417.
Judith, Book of. Kitto, 17: 342.
— and its Geography. (B. H. Cowper) Kitto, 26: 421.
Judith; or the Opera Box. Blackw. 47: 621.
Judith Bensadai; a Tale. So. Lit. Mess. 5: 469.
Judson, Adoniram. (E. B. Hall) Chr. Exam. 56: 96. — (J. H. Morison) No. Am. 78: 21.
— and Newell, Embarkation of. (S. M. Worcester) Chr. R. 14: 421.
— and Theo. Parker. (N. M. Williams) Bib. Sac. 26: 290.
— Missionary Character of. Chr. R. 13: 259. 14: 421.
— Memoir of. Ecl. R. 98: 690.
— Wayland's Life of. Prosp. R. 10: 119. — Chr. R. 19: 127.
Judson, Mrs. Ann H., Memoir of. (F. Parkman) Chr. Exam. 6: 252.
Judson, Mrs. Emily C., with portrait. Hogg, 2: 409.
— Kendrick's Life of. Liv. Age, 69: 188.
— Writings of. (L. J. Hall) Chr. Exam. 42: 393.
Judson, Mrs. Sarah Boardman, Sketch of. Hogg, 2: 345.
Judson Family, as Missionaries. Chr. Obs. 47: 158.
Juggernaut. (A. H. Guernsey) Harper, 57: 222.
— and Hurdwar. Mus. 26: 513.
— Festival of, June, 1838. (W. Lacey) Cong. M. 22: 281.
— True Story of. Chamb. J. 50: 7. Same art. Ecl. M. 80: 354.
— Worship of. Meth. M. 35: 24.
Juggler of fifty Years ago. Bentley, 61: 57.
— Two Tricks of an Indian. (E. S. Robertson) Dub. Univ. 92: 86.
Jugglers in India. (N. S. Dodge) Lakeside, 8: 463. — (F. Swanwick) Once a Week, 4: 40.
Jugurtha and Abd-el-Kader. (E. Clive) Bentley, 20: 83.
Jukes, Joseph Beete. Nature, 5: 98.
Jukovsky, V. A. (C. E. Turner) Fraser, 96: 195.
Julamerk; a Tale of the Nestorians. Peop. J. 7: 225.
Julia Cytherea; a Legend, in Verse, of the Renaissance. (R. Buchanan) Contemp. 33: 272.
Julia Howard, Youth of. Fraser, 20: 460, 604.
Julian, Roman Emperor and Apostate. (B. L. Gildersleeve) So. R. n. s. 3: 181. — (E. Pond) Cong. R. 10: 40. — (C. G. Prowett) Fraser, 83: 432. Same art. Liv. Age, 110: 3. — Colburn, 129: 404. — (N. Bangs) Meth. Q. 9: 387.
— and the Apostasy of Rome. Chr. Obs. 63: 399.
— and Frederick William IV. Ed. R. 88: 94.
— and Polytheism, Naville's. Lond. Q. 49: 159.
— Letters. Brit. Q. 65: 1. Same art. Liv. Age, 132: 387.
Julian, George W., Desertion of the Republican Party by. (T. O. Howe) No. Am. 126: 381.
Juliana, Mother, Revelations of. (M. W. Tileston) Unita. R. 9: 158.
Juliet; a Novel. (Mrs. H. Lovett-Cameron) Canad. Mo. 10: 277, 378, 470. 11: 1-644.
Juliet; a Story. (Mrs. H. L. Cameron) Belgra. 29: 293, 447. 30: 103-411. 31: 105-484. 32: 105, 242.
Juliette; a Norman Story. (D. Casserly) Cath. World, 25: 667.
Julius Cæsar, Shakspere's. Blackw. 37: 747. *See also* Shakspere.
Jullien, Louis G. Putnam, 2: 423.
Jullien, Louis G., and Berlioz. (D. Cook) Belgra. 41: 285.
July. (W. Howitt) Howitt, 2: 1.
July 4th, History of. (E. A. Pollard) Lippinc. 10: 56.
Jumièges, Abbey of. Penny M. 9: 329.
Jumnah, Antiquities of the. Fraser, 56: 672.
Jummoo and Kashmir, Drew's. Nature, 12: 550.
Jumpers of Maine. (G. M. Beard) Pop. Sci. Mo. 18: 170.
Jumping Procession of Luxemburg. (J. Murphy) Appleton, 20: 431.
June. (W. Howitt) Howitt, 1: 317.
— Our Garland for. Dub. Univ. 37: 667.
— Wanderings in. (J. Clare) Lond. M. 6: 5.
June Chantry. (J. T. McKay) Scrib. 14: 833.
June Days. (H. D. Thoreau) Atlan. 41: 711.
June Love-Story. Lond. Soc. 37: supp. 1.
June Music; a Poem. (M. Collins) Temp. Bar, 17: 379.
June Reminiscences. Ecl. Mus. 2: 412.
Jung, Sir Salar. All the Year, 36: 421.
Jung Bahadur, Indian Statesman. (O. E. Wheeler) St. James, 46: 162. — Liv. Age, 33: 206.
— Oliphant's Journey with the Camp of. Colburn, 95: 471.
Jung-Stilling, Heinrich. (L. Murray) Canad. Mo. 9: 26. — (S. F. Smith) Chr. R. 9: 290. — For. Q. 21: 247.
— Childhood and Early Years of. Tait, n. s. 2: 311.
Jungermanniæ. (M. Plues) Pop. Sci. R. 2: 493.
Jungfrau, Night Ascent of the. Sharpe, 42: 71.
Jungle in Central America. Temp. Bar, 22: 458. 23: 66.
— Jaunts in. (J. W. Gryllis) Colburn, 81: 67-441.
— Lost in. All the Year, 6: 88.
— Night in. All the Year, 5: 444. — Chamb. J. 51: 263.
— Perils of. Potter Am. Mo. 10: 170.
Jungle Fowl, Natural History of. Penny M. 4: 184.
Jungle Recollections. Fraser, 44: 18. Same art. Liv. Age, 30: 460. Same art. Internat. M. 4: 110.
Juniata River, Scenery of. (T. A. Richards) Harper, 12: 433.
Junior Army and Navy Stores. Colburn, 169: 182.
Junius. Sharpe, 43: 180, 234.
— and his Time. (J. M. Hawkins) Fraser, 90: 325.
— Jacques's History of. Mo. R. 161: 400.
— and Macaulay. Cornh. 1: 257.
— and Sir Arthur Gordon. Temp. Bar, 39: 335.
— Authorship of. (Sir J. Mackintosh) Ed. R. 29: 94. — (G. B. Cheever) No. Am. 29: 315. — (D. L. Child) No. Am. 34: 316. — (J. W. Croker) Quar. 90: 91. Same art. Ecl. M. 25: 409. Same art. Liv. Age, 32: 385. — Westm. 96: 406. — (Sir D. Brewster) No. Brit. 10: 97. Same art. Ecl. M. 16: 160. — Am. Mo. R. 1: 33. — New Eng. M. 1: 54. — Blackw. 18: 164. Same art. Mus. 7: 473. — Blackw. 34: 209. — Mo. R. 82: 69. 87: 189. 107: 354. — Am. Whig R. 13: 484. 14: 35. — Liv. Age, 27: 567. — Internat. M. 1: 469. — Portfo. (Den.) 10: 141. — Ecl. M. 28: 174. Same art. Liv. Age, 35: 559.
— discovered, Griffin's. Canad. J. n. s. 1: 58.
— Evidence from Handwriting of. Quar. 130: 328. Same art. Liv. Age, 109: 643. — (C. C. Smith) O. & N. 5: 261.
— Sir Philip Francis, and Lord Mansfield in Dec., 1770. (H. Merivale) Fortn. 9: 250. *See* Francis, Sir Philip.
— identified. Liv. Age, 27: 281.
— Identity of. (W. Dowe) Dub. Univ. 40: 20. Same art. Liv. Age, 34: 385. — Dub. Univ. 40: 1. Same art. Ecl. M. 27: 20.
— Last Phase of the Controversy. (H. Merivale) Cornh. 23: 668.
— Letters of. (C. F. Adams) No. Am. 55: 419. — (Sir D. Brewster) No. Brit. 19: 489. — (A. H. Stephens) Internat. R. 4: 601. — (T. Weed) Galaxy, 15: 605.
— — under their comic Aspect. Bentley, 50: 611. Same art. Liv. Age, 72: 150.

Junius; Memoirs of a celebrated Character, 1742–57. (J. Foster) Ecl. R. 20: 278.
— More about. (A. Hayward) Fraser, 76: 794.
— redivivus. Once a Week, 24: 549.— Tait, 3: 347.
— Was he Lord Lyttelton? Liv. Age, 42: 223.
— Waterhouse's Essay on. So. R. 7: 486. — (H. Ware, jr.) Chr. Exam. 10: 256.
— Woodfall's. (J. Foster) Ecl. R. 17: 113, 432. Same art. Anal. M. 2: 1.
Juno and Phillis. (Mrs. Forrester) Temp. Bar, 23: 42.
Junot, Madame. Memoirs of Napoleon. Quar. 46: 313.
Jupiter, Planet. (T. W. Webb) Nature, 3: 430.
— and its Satellites. (M. Mitchell) Am. J. Sci. 101: 393. 105: 454. 115: 38. — Chamb. J. 44: 486.
— and Saturn, Remarks on. (J. Nasmyth) J. Frankl. Inst. 55: 396.
— and Venus, Conjunction of, July 21, 1859. (Mrs. M. Ward) Recr. Sci. 1: 222.
— Cloud Masses of. (R. A. Proctor) Pop. Sci. Mo. 11: 81.
— Comet Family of. Once a Week, 20: 563.
— Condition of. (J. Browning) Stud. & Intel. Obs. 5: 1.
— a Giant Planet. (R. A. Proctor) Cornh. 25: 539. Same art. Ecl. M. 79: 43. Same art. Liv. Age, 113: 624. Same art. Pop. Sci. Mo. 1: 286.
— in 1869–70. (T. W. Webb) Pop. Sci. R. 9: 127.
— in 1870–71. (T. W. Webb) Pop. Sci. R. 10: 276.
— in October and November, 1880. (W. F. Denning) Pop. Sci. R. 20: 1.
— — What is it doing? (H. J. Slack) Belgra. 40: 453. Same art. Pop. Sci. Mo. 16: 737. Same art. Ecl. M. 94: 433.
— Life in. Cornh. 31: 691. Same art. Ecl. M. 85: 166.
— a Miniature Sun. St. Paul's, 8: 19. Same art. Ecl. M. 76: 669.
— News from. (R. A. Proctor) Pop. Sci. R. 12: 348. Same art. Ecl. M. 81: 679. Same art. Pop. Sci. Mo. 4: 433.
— Observations of. (J. Birmingham) Dub. Univ. 76: 485. — (J. Birmingham) Good Words, 13: 574. — (A. M. Mayer) J. Frankl. Inst. 89: 136.
— Occultation of. (N. Hall) Ex. H. Lec. 14: 29.
— Perturbations of Vesta by. Math. Mo. 2: 217.
— Photograph of Spectrum of. (H. Draper) Am. J. Sci. 120: 118.
— Satellites of. (R. A. Proctor) Stud. & Intel. Obs. 2: 217.
— — Light of. (T. W. Webb) Nature, 4: 442.
— without his Satellites. (R. A. Proctor) Pop. Sci. R. 6: 248. Same art. Ecl. M. 71: 1116.
Jura, Chalets in the. (P. Skelton) Once a Week, 1: 244.
— Night on the Summit of. Cornh. 8: 317.
— Quiet Nook in. (J. Ruffini) Macmil. 5: 277.
— Narbey's. Colburn, 145: 346.
Jurassic Ammonites, Biological Relations of. (A. Hyatt) Am. J. Sci. 110: 344.
Jurassic Birds and their Allies. (O. C. Marsh) Am. J. Sci. 122: 337.
Jurassic Dinosaurs. (O. C. Marsh) Am. J. Sci. 121: 167–571.
Jurassic Mammals. (O. C. Marsh) Am. J. Sci. 120: 235.
Jurisdiction, Duponceau on. Bost. Mo. 1: 485.
— Question of, in the Virginia Legislature. Niles's Reg. 20: 118, 155.
Jurisprudence. Lond. Q. 19: 146.
— American. Portfo.(Den.) 14: 590.
— and Apologetics, Recent Changes in. (F. Wharton) Princ. n. s. 2: 149.
— Austin on. (J. S. Mill) Ed. R. 118: 439. — Tait, 2: 343. — Westm. 18: 237. 19: 329.
— Codification of the Law. Lond. Q. 24: 432.
Jurisprudence, Comparative. (W. M. Irvins) Pop. Sci. Mo. 17: 577.
— Criminal, Sampson on. Mo. R. 155: 517.
— Equity, in England and America, Story on. Mo. R. 161: 466.
— English School of. (F. Harrison) Fortn. 30: 475, 682. 31: 114.
— Foster's Elements of. Ecl. R. 100: 714.
— French, and D'Aguesseau. Nat. R. 8: 441.
— Heron's History of. Dub. Univ. 56: 95.
— History of. Dub. R. 48: 451.
— in England. Ed. R. 114: 456.
— — Modern Phases of. Westm. 82: 261. Same art. Ecl. M. 64: 175.
— Materials of. (J. V. Campbell) Am. Law R. 14: 257.
— Present System of. (J. H. Lanman) Am. Q. Obs. 2: 128.
— Progress of English. Westm. 68: 511.
— Relation to Baconian Philosophy. (F. A. March) New Eng. 6: 543.
— Sacred and Civil. Danv. Q. 2: 168.
— Schools of. Lond. Q. 40: 1.
Jurist, The American. (J. C. Park) No. Am. 29: 418.
Jury Trial. (W. Barnes) Macmil. 5: 412. — Blackw. 27: 736. — (J. A. Pomeroy) No. Am. 92: 297. — (I. T. Hoague) Am. Law R. 11: 24. — Temp. Bar, 7: 550. — Ecl. R. 90: 749. — (A. S. Bolles) Lippinc. 9: 335. — (W. L. Davis) Putnam, 15: 175. — (C. C. Nott) Nation, 16: 428. — (D. B. Read) Canad. Mo. 15: 217. — Dem. R. 6: 463. — Knick. 15: 478. — Dem. R. 36: 91. — Penn Mo. 4: 700. — St. Paul's, 7: 88. — West. R. 1: 101. —Westm. 97: 289.
— Abuses of. No. Brit. 8: 82.
— Adam on. Quar. 57: 324. — Mo. R. 142: 285.
— and the Tweed Verdict. (C. C. Nott) Nation, 17: 351.—(T. W. Knox) Scrib. 3: 609.
— Curiosities of. Chamb. J. 50: 785.
— History of. Ecl. R. 98: 174. — No. Am. 119: 219.
— — Forsyth's. Chr. Obs. 52: 331.
— in Civil Cases. Blackw. 27: 736. — Knick. 18: 247.
— in Commercial Cases. (W. H. De Forest) Hunt, 35: 302.
— in Scotland. Tait, n. s. 4: 351.
— in Texas. Blackw. 54: 777.
— no Boon to Catholics. Dub. R. 43: 471.
— Origin of. Niles's Reg. 13: 139.
— Thompson on charging the Jury. (A. G. Sedgwick) Nation, 32: 45.
Juries. Chamb. J. 45: 321. — Ev. Sat. 5: 724.
— and Advocates. Fraser, 46: 571.
— as they were and are. Chamb. J. 26: 355.
— Bentham on the Art of Packing. Quar. 27: 377.
— Discharge of, without Prisoner's Consent. West. Law J. 4: 97.
— English and Irish. All the Year, 7: 421.
— Grand, Laurie on. Westm. 19: 88.
— Rights and Powers of. Westm. 8: 431.
— Special, and M. Cotta. Westm. 1: 146.
— Verdicts of English and Scotch. (H. Graham) Victoria, 4: 418.
Jury System, British. Dub. Univ. 32: 717.
— — Faults in. Brit. Q. 52: 57.
— of the United States. (S. T. Wallis) So. M. 12: 506.
Jurymen, Duties of Witnesses and. House. Words, 2: 100. — Blackw. 13: 673. Same art. Mus. 3: 239.
Just a Dream. Tinsley, 7: 269.
Just as it happened. Lond. Soc. 5: 169.
Just for a Day. (I. D. Coolbrith) Overland, 6: 33.
Just going to do it. (T. S. Arthur) Hogg, 4: 275.
Just too late; a Story. Colburn, 163: 543.
Justice. Liv. Age, 143: 506.

Justice à la Française. (R. Quiddam) St. James, **37**: 89.
– abroad. (F. Marshall) Fortn. **22**: 133.
— Administration of. (C. C. Bonney) Lakeside, **8**: 343. — (A. R. Wallace) Contemp. **23**: 43.
— and Fraternity. So. Q. **15**: 356.
— Cheap. (H. Crompton) Contemp. **35**: 801.
— Curiosities of. Chamb. J. **33**: 157.
— Divine. (E. Pond) Am. Bib. Repos. 3d s. **4**: 586. — Chr. Disc. **5**: 188.
— Ministry of. Westm. **107**: 1.
— Miscarriage of. (F. Peek) Contemp. **32**: 100.
— Nature and Office of. (J. Gorton) Univ. Q. **33**: 34.
— Provincial Administration of. Westm. **4**: 315.
— What is it? (L. Withington) Bib. Sac. **28**: 235.
Justices of the Peace. Fraser, **87**: 160. — (S. L. Sewall) No. Am. **19**: 390.
Justifiable or Unjustifiable? a Tale. Sharpe, **42**: 123.
Justification. (L. Clark) Am. Meth. M. **14**: 13. — Mo. Rel. M. **5**: 398, 443. — Chr. Obs. **2**: 5, 269. **28**: 799. — (S. Buel) Am. Church R. **3**: 169. — (C. A. Stork) Luth. Q. **6**: 94.
— and Regeneration. Chr. Obs. **47**: 193, 257, 321.
— and Romanism. (R. Smith) Lit. & Theo. R. **4**: 236.
— and Sanctification. Cong. R. **7**: 321. — Cong. M. **27**: 414.
— Bennett on. Ecl. R. **72**: 312.
— by Faith. (G. B. Kidd) Cong. M. **25**: 18. — (R. W. Landis) Am. Bib. Repos. **11**: 453. — (D. Curry) Meth. Q. **4**: 5. **5**: 5. — (C. D. Pigeon) Lit. & Theo. R. **6**: 521. — (C. Hodge) Princ. **12**: 268, 561. — Lit. & Theo. R. **6**: 188, 330. — (O. B. Frothingham) Chr. Exam. **41**: 272. — Chr. Mo. Spec. **8**: 334. — (H. A. Miles) Mo. Rel. M. **2**: 123. — (A. S. Hale) Chr. Q. **8**: 407. — Chr. Obs. **43**: 65. — (J. A. Dorner) Am. Presb. R. **17**: 186. — Evang. R. **11**: 225.
— — and its first Preacher. (E. H. Plumptre) Good Words, **7**: 67.
— — and Lutheranism. (S. W. Harkey) Luth. Q. **3**: 561.
— — and by Works. (H. Ballou, 2d) Univ. Q. **9**: 182.
— — as taught in recent Years. Chr. Obs. **77**: 908.
— — the Reformation Doctrine. (G. Thomasius) Luth. Q. **10**: 198.
— by Imputation. (J. H. A. Bomberger) Mercersb. **5**: 152.
— by Works. Am. Bib. Repos. 3d s. **4**: 325.
— Doctrine of. Am. Presb. R. **3**: 353. — Bost. R. **2**: 229. — Chr. Obs. **62**: 582, 865. — Cong. M. **24**: 39. — Lond. Q. **29**: 179.
— — Catholic. (A. F. Hewit) Cath. World, **6**: 432.
— — Faber on Primitive. Chr. Obs. **38**: 51, 121, 257.
— — Ritschl's Critical History of. (G. F. Magoun) Cong. Q. **19**: 376, 546. **20**: 33.
— James on. Cong. M. **24**: 377.
— Marsh on. Chr. Obs. **14**: 502, 581.
— Moral Effects of free. So. R. n. s. **12**: 369.
— Newman on. Ecl. R. **71**: 631.
— O'Brien's Sermons on. Ecl. R. **59**: 345.
— Papal, Puseyite, and Primitive. (J. Dowling) Chr. R. **11**: 309.
— Paul and James on. Kitto, **21**: 277.
— philologically considered. Bib. R. **1**: 267.
— Romish and Anglican Teachings on. Am. Church R. **3**: 169.
— Sermon on. (B. Ochino) Chr. Obs. **34**: 84.
— Todd on. Chr. Obs. **19**: 857.
— through Christ and Baptism. (H. Martinson) Mercersb. **5**: 287.
Justin Martyr. (J. A. Brown) Evang. R. **6**: 151. — (A. Lamson) Chr. Exam. **7**: 141, 303. — (C. E. Stowe) Bib. Sac. **9**: 821. — Chr. Obs. **3**: 649, 717. — Meth. M. **32**: 3.
— and the Fourth Gospel. (J. Drummond) Theo. R. **12**: 471. **14**: 155.
— Engelhardt on. (J. Drummond) Theo. R. **16**: 365.
— Life and Writings of. Kitto, **5**: 253. — Chr. R. **15**: 353. — Ecl. R. **81**: 186.
— on the new Birth. (J. Drummond) Theo. R. **12**: 471.
— or the Orthodox Faith, A. D. 150–165. (H. Ballou, 2d) Univ. Q. **3**: 272.
— Tomb of. (D. Barrington) Arch. **5**: 143.
Justin Vitali's Client. Cornh. **33**: 444. Same art. Liv. Age, **129**: 535.
Justinian, Edicts of, Account of. Chr. Obs. **9**: 193.
— Institutes of, Sandars's Edition. Fraser, **51**: 105.
— Law Reform in Days of. (T. Hodgkin) Contemp. **39**: 708. Same art. Liv. Age, **149**: 672.
Justinian; a Poem. (R. Buchanan) Contemp. **37**: 48. Same art. Ecl. M. **94**: 305.
Jute. Pract. M. **7**: 88.
— Manufacture of. (W. Fleming) J. Frankl. Inst. **110**: 199.
Jute-Workers. All the Year, **38**: 106.
Jutland. Bentley, **51**: 199.
— Coast of. (H. C. Andersen) Bentley, **53**: 188.
— Up in. Bentley, **55**: 625.
Juvenal, Badham's Translation of. Quar. **11**: 377.
— Historical Judgments. (W. A. Packard) Presb. R. **1**: 34.
— Hodgson's Translation of. Ed. R. **12**: 50. — Ecl. R. **7**: 511.
— Horace and. (J. W. Ball) Land We Love, **3**: 462.
— in London; Poems. Temp. Bar, **40**: 49–320. **46**: 244.
— Lewis's Translation of. Westm. **100**: 66.
— on the Decadence of Rome. (F. Ryan) Nat. Q. **8**: 229.
— Satires of. (S. Hart) Am. Church R. **26**: 235.
— Specimens of a new Translation of. Quar. **8**: 60.
Juvenile and Female Labor. Ed. **79**: 130.
Juvenile Books. *See* Children, Books for.
Juvenile Crime and Destitution. Chamb. J. **12**: 281, 347.
Juvenile Crime, Prevention and Reform of. (B. K. Peirce) Meth. Q. **32**: 601.
Juvenile Criminals, Correction of. Ed. R. **101**: 383. — Westm. **60**: 137. — (D. B. Read) Canad. Mo. **18**: 548. — Good Words, **22**: 458.
— Treatment of. No. Brit. **10**: 1. — Ecl. M. **2**: 350.
Juvenile Delinquency. (J. H. Allen) No. Am. **79**: 406. — (W. C. Taylor) Bentley, **7**: 470. — Ecl. R. **91**: 200. **99**: 385. — Ed. R. **94**: 403. — (Mrs. Surr) 19th Cent. **9**: 649. — Irish Q. **5**: 773. — Prosp. R. **2**: 297. **10**: 69.
— and the Glasgow Plan of Cure. (A. K. McCallum) J. Statis. Soc. **18**: 356.
— Small Arabs of New York. (C. D. Shanly) Atlan. **23**: 279.
— Society in Danger from Children. Prosp. R. **9**: 165.
— Street Boys. Sharpe, **22**: 339.
See Reformatory Education.
Juvenile Delinquents. Chr. Obs. **54**: 193.
— Treatment of. Irish Q. **4**: 1.
Juvenile Depravity. Ecl. R. **91**: 200. — (R. C. Waterston) Chr. Exam. **52**: 391. — Sharpe, **9**: 223. — Hogg, **2**: 148–398. **3**: 40–330.
— Remedies of. Hogg, **4**: 300.
Juvenile Labor. (W. C. Taylor) Bentley, **8**: 355.
Juvenile Party. Cornh. **3**: 513.

UNIVERSITY OF WOLVERHAMPTON
LEARNING & INFORMATION SERVICES

NOT TO BE
REMOVED FROM
THE LIBRARY